Renovating Carbon

ORO Editions
Publishers of Architecture, Art, and Design
Gordon Goff: Publisher
www.oroeditions.com
info@oroeditions.com

Published by ORO Editions

Contributors: Erik L'Heureux (Ed.), Giovanni Cossu (Ed.), Nader Tehrani, Eric Höweler, Heng Chye Kiang, Ho Puay-peng, Lakshmi Menon, Wolfgang Kessling, Nirmal Kishnani, Chris Knapp, Joshua Comaroff, Lam Khee Poh

Book Design: Studio Vanessa Ban LLP
www.vanessaban.info

ORO managing editor: Kirby Anderson

10 9 8 7 6 5 4 3 2 1 First Edition

ISBN: 978-1-954081-44-4

Color Separations and Printing: ORO Group Ltd.
Printed in China

ORO Editions makes a continuous effort to minimize the overall carbon footprint of its publications. As part of this goal, ORO Editions, in association with Global ReLeaf, arranges to plant trees to replace those used in the manufacturing of the paper produced for its books. Global ReLeaf is an international campaign run by American Forests, one of the world's oldest nonprofit conservation organizations. Global ReLeaf is American Forests' education and action program that helps individuals, organizations, agencies, and corporations improve the local and global environment by planting and caring for trees.

Renovating Carbon

Prologue

Erik L'Heureux
Giovanni Cossu

"The climate crisis is also a crisis of culture, and thus of imagination"

— Amitav Ghosh, *The Great Derangement*

The climate crisis has prompted deep introspection in the processes of development, urbanization, and architecture, particularly regarding their complicity and dependency on fossil fuels. Architecture and the building sector contribute to almost 40% of global CO2 emissions. Building operations constitute 28%, while the remaining 12% are attributed to material usage.[1] Concrete, steel, and aluminum are responsible for almost half of global industrial CO2 emissions. Yet, as the climate catastrophe no longer remains an exclusive scientific concern, it urgently lies intertwined in the world's political, economic, and spatial cultures. This entanglement requires us to probe the link between architecture and climate, fundamentally based on the reciprocity of energy, built form, and architecture. Decarbonization, the process of phasing out fossil fuel use from architecture, is not only a performative question but also holds implications for culture, design practices, and modes of living. Reducing operational carbon (the carbon released to produce energy consumed for building operations) and embodied carbon (the carbon produced from construction processes and materials) is at the heart of this process, requiring significant and complex cultural change that impacts expectations of comfort and how buildings are inhabited. Educational institutions, especially schools of architecture, design, and the built environment, have an important task at hand in propelling this cultural shift through their communities. In order to move forward, this movement needs to be consciously integrated into pedagogies and present in learning environments to a perceptible degree.

Carbon Pasts and Futures

In the eighteenth century, with the advent of the Industrial Age, people began to fuel machinery with energy derived from the combustion of fossilized carbon such as coal, petroleum, and natural gas. Industrialization and its subsequent "fossilized carbon capitalism" allowed societies to reorganize themselves around the availability of seemingly limitless energy that signaled the start of a new phase in human history: the carbon economy.[2] The emergent energy-intensive ways of life led to an energy culturethat reinforces the myth of a dense energy supply.[3] When applied to the processes of urbanization, the term "carbon form" refers to architectural typologies and taxonomies of urban forms that are linked to the consumption of fossil fuels by transportation, construction, and food production networks.[4] With global building projected to double in the next two decades,the challenge of reducing the carbon expenditure and imagining a carbonless future is a design and cultural opportunity — one linking technology, building systems, and the formal and aesthetic foundations of how architecture is conceptualized.[5] The crisis of imagination can begin to be tackled by imagining futures not yet inhabited and delivering those futures now. Imagination is a fundamental design act deeply embedded in architectural culture. But it also requires political will, capital, and change in the entire building ecosystem to bring such visions to fruition.

Adaptive reuse — the process of extending the lifespan of existing buildings and reusing materials to capitalize on already expended carbon and other resources to create new environments — is a critical step in this direction. It is an architectural approach not to build more but rather to use already existing carbon forms intelligently and with restraint. That this method grew in prominence, coinciding with the global oil crisis in the 1970s, speaks to its ingenuity as an architectural response to the scarcity of natural resources. In today's climate crisis, adaptive reuse "perpetuates a continuum of growth and change," assuming greater responsibility for the carbon embedded in architecture.[6]

In Singapore, urban regulations and developmental pressures have constructed an ecosystem of short building lifespans. Tearing down and building anew constitute up to 40% of embodied carbon emissions. New buildings have been designed as cultural symbols for a forward-looking future, especially in urbanizing Asia.[7] Adaptive reuse, in this context, has been limited to historical buildings or largely viewed as financially unfeasible. But this developmental process is starting to be interrogated, and in many ways, adaptive reuse will be Asia's future.

The National University of Singapore (NUS) is a large, publicly funded, research-intensive university. Its campus is straddled with aging buildings constructed in the early 1970s. As the University has grown in population and size, its development ambitions have shifted to spotlight targets of carbon neutrality in a comprehensive ten-year plan of campus redevelopment.[8] This University development ethos has also received a strong impetus with the recently launched Singapore Green Plan 2030, a critical, goal-driven approach

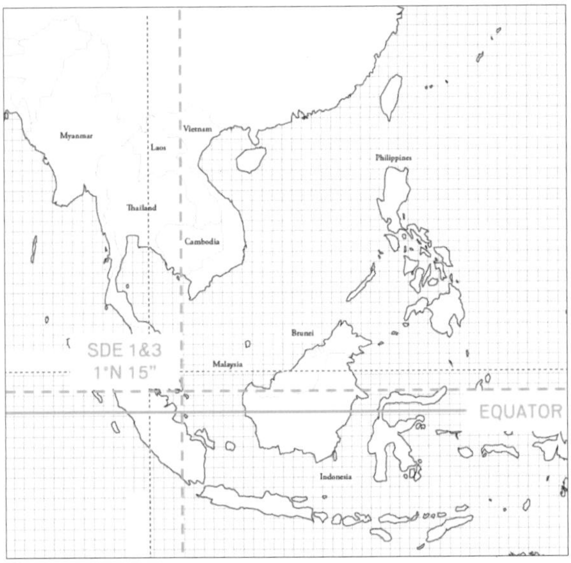

Fig 0.1 Map of South-east Asia, showing the location of Singapore (1°N 103°E) at the tip of the Malay Archipelago (left) and the location of the National University of Singapore campus in Singapore (right). *Courtesy: Erik L'Heureux.*

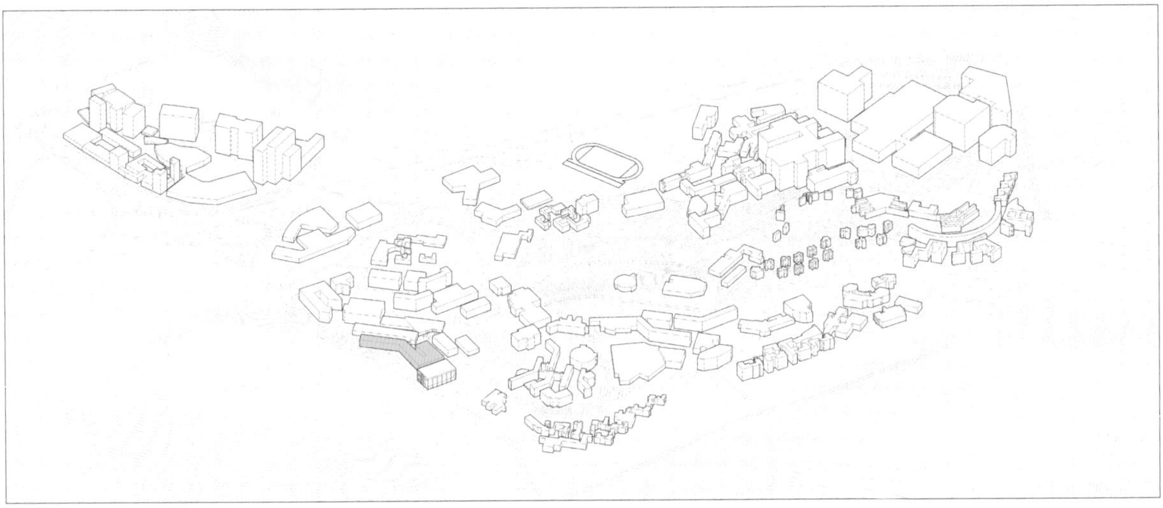

Fig 0.2 Site plan of the National University of Singapore campus, with the School of Design and Environment precincts in focus. *Courtesy: Special Projects, NUS School of Design and Environment.*

to sustainable development in Singapore that fast-tracks environmental, social, and governmental (ESG) measures that align with the United Nation's 2030 Sustainable Development Agenda.[9]

Within the NUS Campus, the College of Design and Engineering (CDE) is crafting architecture and sustainability leadership in Singapore by intertwining design education and research, advocating for sustainable design practices, innovating green policy, and transforming the campus with new and renovated buildings to serve as positive examples of sustainable, modern architecture in the tropics. This approach includes SDE 4 (completed January 2019), the first purpose-built net-zero-energy building in Singapore; the low-carbon, net-zero adaptive reuse of SDE 1 & 3 will be completed in 2022, with a proposed zero-carbon new building and an adaptive reuse of SDE 2 currently in the planning stages. These projects will provide more than 45,000 square meters of new and renovated studios, workshops, research centers, office spaces, and various public and social spaces. Most importantly, they are designed as pedagogical tools to influence a new generation of architects, engineers, landscape architects, and designers who will be

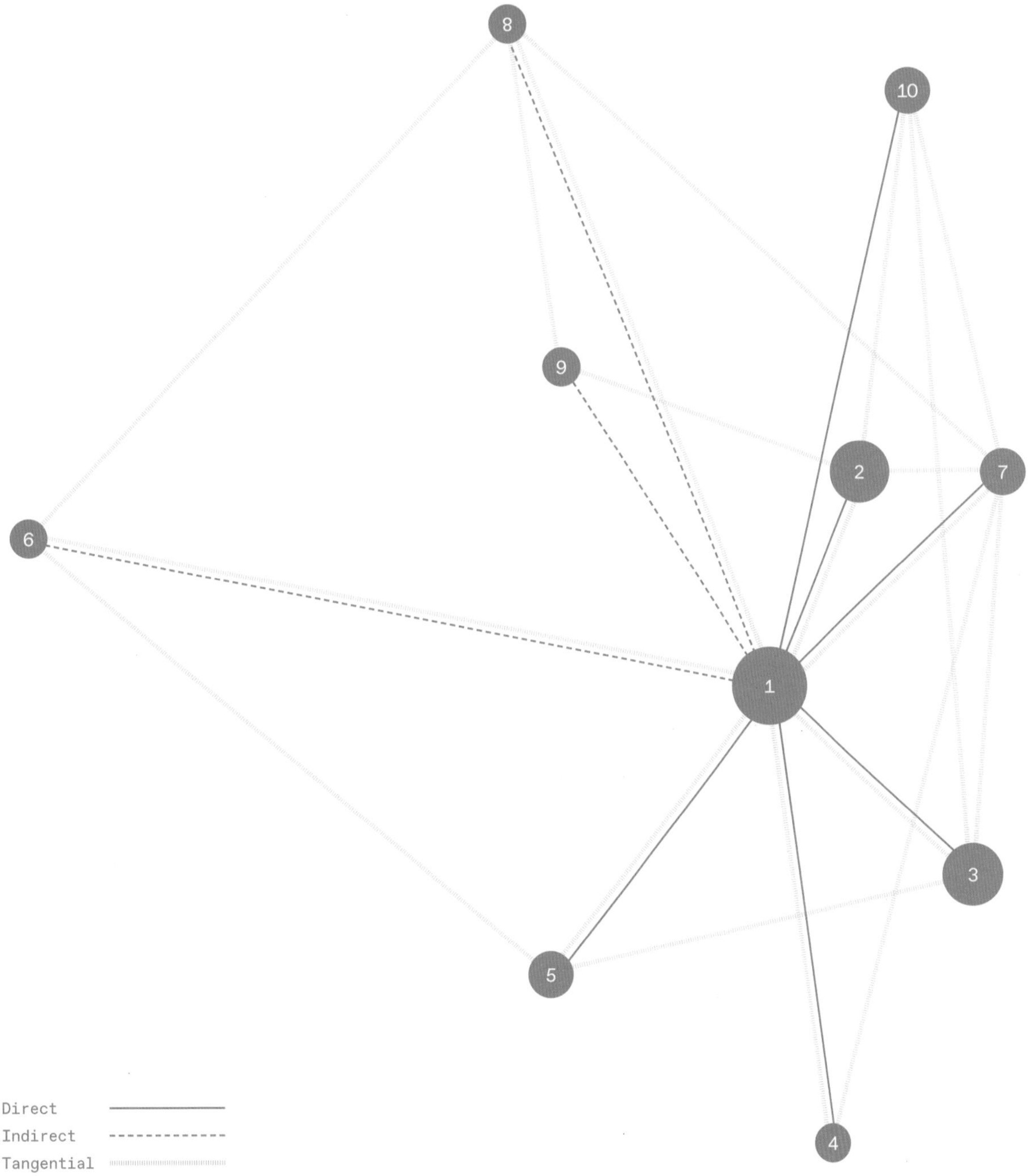

1	SDE 1 & 3	Carbon Transformations at the Equator	Erik L'Heureux
2	Architecture Schools + Pedagogy	Spatializing Schools of Thought	Nader Tehrani
3	Project Chronology	Two Different Approaches to Sustainability	Heng Chye Kiang
4	Spatial Experience	Carbon Dichotomies	Lakshmi Menon
5	Carbon Calculations	Evaluating the Hidden Carbon in SDE 1 & 3	Wolfgang Kessling
6	Systems Design Approach	A Problem of Problems	Nirmal Kishnani
7	Adaptive Futures	Manifesto for the Architecture School	Joshua Comaroff
8	Materiality	From Lifestyle to Life Cycle	Eric Höweler
9	Future Visions	Towards a Post-Anthropocene	Chris Knapp
10	Pedagogy	Spatializing Sustainability	Ho Puay-peng

Fig 0.3 Book features a constellation of conversations around the SDE 1 & 3 renovation.
Diagram by Ong Chan Hao.

committed to the critical transformation of the built environment and their surrounding culture. Together, these projects extend the school's history while leading design innovation into an era of rapid advancement in sustainability, architecture, and building technology.

The conversations presented in this book expand on themes from the renovation of SDE 1 & 3. The renovation's design utilizes the existing carbon form from the original 1976 structural frame to position itself as a tool to educate its students and the wider community around sustainability and carbon footprints. In the design process, in-house design architects, sustainability professionals, landscape architects, industrial designers, and energy engineers worked collectively to manifest *Research by Design* (R×D) efforts within the buildings' renovations.[10] The ethos of the school and its leadership asserted that every building is an opportunity for design research, oriented toward crafting sustainable architecture calibrated to the equatorial climate and the urban and natural systems within which it is situated. The texts within this book probe the themes of adaptive reuse, design agency, architectural ambitions, and decarbonization around the architecture of SDE 1 & 3. The conversations frames concerns around form, space, and order, as well as construction processes, material choices, building systems, and climate comfort as critical components impacting the campus, Singapore, and the larger ecosystem. The writing explores the SDE 1 & 3 renovation within the broader scope of how design functions within codependent networks, precinct-level systems, and sociopolitical relationships, widening the architectural imagination of adaptive reuse and low-carbon design that is tailored to the hot and wet climate of the equator.

It is this collective effort that constructs, shapes, and influences culture. Winston Churchill argued that the shape of the House of Commons Chamber was the essence of the British Parliament, asserting that "We shape our buildings, and afterwards, our buildings shape us." The buildings of SDE 1 & 3, along with the drawings, visualizations, studios, conversations, and institutional histories captured in this book, will serve as the basis for future design education: they will shape generations of architects from Singapore and beyond and set the pedagogical basis for those students who will live and breathe within its frame. Adaptive reuse will soon become the future of developing Asia, and even more so, the future of our warming world, and SDE 1 & 3 is just one part of this story as we confront the climate catastrophe with design imagination.

References

[1] World Green Building Council, "Bringing Embodied Carbon Upfront: Coordinated Action for the Building and Construction Sector to Tackle Embodied Carbon," Sept. 2019 https://www.worldgbc.org/sites/default/files/WorldGBC_Bringing_Embodied_Carbon_Upfront.pdf.

[2] Audrea Lim, "The Ideology of Fossil Fuels," *Dissent* 65, no. 2 (2018): 133-142.

[3] Mimi Sheller, "The Origins of Global Carbon Form," in *Log 47: Overcoming Carbon Form*, ed. Cynthia Davidson and Elisa Iturbe (New York: Anyone Corporation, 2019), 57-68.

[4] Elisa Iturbe, "Architecture and the Death of Carbon Modernity," in *Log 47: Overcoming Carbon Form*, ed. Cynthia Davidson and Elisa Iturbe (New York: Anyone Corporation, 2019), 11-24.

[5] UN Environment and International Energy Agency, "Towards a Zero-Emission, Efficient, and Resilient Buildings and Construction Sector: Global Status Report 2017," 2017, accessed Nov. 23, 2021, https://www.worldgbc.org/sites/default/files/UNEP%20188_GABC_en%20%28web%29.pdf.

[6] Liliane Wong, *Adaptive Reuse: Extending the Lives of Buildings* (Basel: Birkhäuser, 2016), 30.

[7] Mint Kang, "Tackling Embodied Carbon Is the Next Step of the Green Building Journey," *Eco-Business*, Jan. 7, 2020, https://www.eco-business.com/news/tackling-embodied-carbon-is-the-next-step-of-the-green-building-journey/.

[8] "Creating a Greener and More Sustainable Campus," *National University of Singapore News*, Mar. 25, 2021, https://news.nus.edu.sg/creating-a-greener-and more-sustainable-campus/.

[9] Ministry of Sustainability and the Environment, "Singapore Green Plan 2030: Our Global Commitment," Feb. 10, 2021, accessed Nov. 30, 2021, https://www.greenplan.gov.sg/

[10] Research by Design (RxD) is a mode of research that exploits design tools and methods in built projects to create applicable knowledge.

Terminology

The School of Design and Environment (SDE) was incorporated as part of the College of Design and Engineering in 2022. The references to SDE in this book reflect the School of Design and Environment designation from 2000-2022 and frame the time-frame when the majority of the design and construction of SDE 1 & 3 was completed. We have retained the SDE and School of Design and Environment nomenclature for consistency and historical accuracy.

Chapter 1
Spatializing Schools of Thought

Nader Tehrani

Introduction

The relationship between schools of thought and the spaces of learning within which they occur — their architecture — has a telling history, because it conjures up a theoretical predicament at the heart of an architectural debate that has persisted over the ages: that is, how form and content come into dialogue, whether in alignment, disjunction, or a difficult fit. Do pedagogies somehow emerge from the buildings within which they are housed, and can buildings set the stage for certain pedagogies?

Forms of buildings come to represent different things as meanings transform over time. A reference to the "White House" came to signify something completely different a few years ago, based on the extreme practices, philosophy, and actions of the administration of that time — an easy example, given the radical disparity as compared to the current presidency. And yet, the White House as a piece of architecture may not have significantly changed at all: not in its form, spaces, or materials.[1]

Of course, as architects, we like to think that what we design matters, and so nothing can be more disconcerting than the idea that what we do is arbitrary, imprecise, or uncontrollable, given the depth of specification we bring to its discipline. Notwithstanding, it is this disjunction between theories of production and the reception of works that, in great part, drives the schism between the world of ideas and objects. When Magritte wrote "*Ceci n'est pas une pipe*," we know it was not controversial as a proclamation; however, in the context of the image that floated above it, it became a scandalous meme of the very predicament we constantly confront as architects.[2] Of course, the linguistic analogy only goes so far. Architecture interacts with the human subject in a myriad of ways: through the senses, their cognition, and the advent of experience, among other things. As such, as architects, we like to think that what we design is not merely a reflection of the status quo, but in fact has the agency to impact and transform the world we live in, without which any attempt at giving theoretical body to what we do would be impotent.[3]

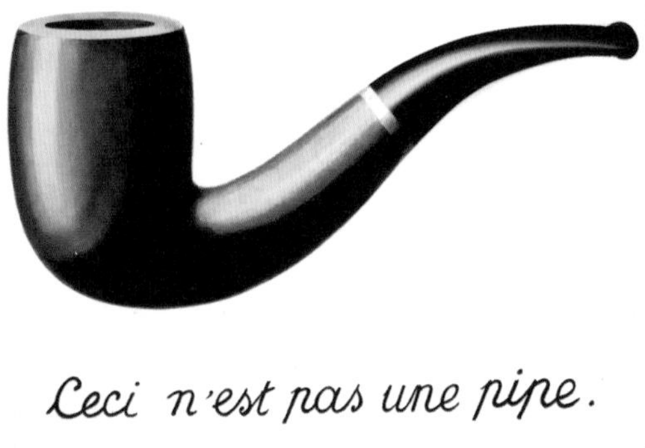

Fig 1.1 *Ceci n'est pas une pipe (The Betrayal of Images)* by Rene Magritte (1928-1929).

Courtesy: University of Alabama (distributed under fair use license)

What is interesting, then, is how the architecture of certain institutions becomes synonymous with a certain ethos despite the changes in administration and thinking. To this end, the underlying structures of organization, program, and materiality often produce conditions that make certain associations persist over time, such that an institutional memory arises that does not merely depend on the human protagonists driving the pedagogies within. The tension that is produced between the persistence of architectural form on the one hand, and the temporal discontinuity of the intellectual cultures that are housed within these forms on the other hand, is at the heart of this argument, and may be irreconcilable.

Fig 1.2 Bauhaus Building in Dessau by Walter Gropius. *Distributed under a CC-BY-SA-4.0 license.*

A Selective Pedagogical Autobiography

There are obvious examples to which architects commonly refer to help shape this argument, some of them canonical buildings such as Walter Gropius's Bauhaus, Paul Rudolph's Yale Art and Architecture Building, and Vilanova Artigas's Architecture and Urbanism College in the University of São Paulo. Each of them is a free-standing building and, in its own way, an embodiment of their author's intention to give spatiality to a pedagogical mission. While a thorough analysis of all three buildings is merited, I have instead arranged a series of other buildings, mostly renovations of existing buildings with which I have developed a more intimate relationship, balancing out disciplinary readings with the quotidian aspects of everyday inhabitation. Thus, a brief comparison between the Architectural Association (AA), the Harvard Graduate School of Design (GSD), The Cooper Union, and the Southern California Institute of Architecture (SCI-Arc) may help to frame these tensions as key protagonists within each institution — whether deans or directors — had worked within the spatial construct of their respective schools to amplify their cultures while also bringing in the critical pedagogical, cultural, and administrative changes of their time.[4]

Fig 1.3 Yale Art and Architecture Building by Paul Rudolph. *Distributed under a CC-BY-SA-3.0/GFDL license.*

Fig 1.4 Faculty of Architecture and Urbanism, University of São Paulo by Vilanova Artigas. *Distributed under a CC-BY-SA-3.0 license.*

The Architectural Association: The Global Domestic Interior

In 1971, the paired-up row houses on Bedford Square that gave space to the Architectural Association produced the intimacy of a space that substantiated its character as a gentleman's club. What Alvin Boyarsky inherited, as the school faced a critical historical challenge, was the choice to either stay independent and small or to become subsumed under the Imperial College as one of its many departments. For this reason, one might read a practical strategy into the reconceptualization of the AA, one that would make it fiscally solvent. In addition, any financial strategy needed to be aligned with an intellectual construct that could withstand the international competition of its time.[5]

Fig 1.5 The Architectural Association housed in the paired-up row houses on Bedford Square, London. *Distributed under a CC-BY-SA-4.0 license.*

From an architectural point of view, the row houses were not much to work with, notwithstanding the nobility of their address in the heart of London and the "elegance" of their interiors. For the most part, the spaces of the AA conformed to the typological layout of the row houses of Bedford Square: dignified, but not with the kind of spaces that afforded the volume of people that gathered for its lectures and openings. However, the programmatic arrangement of the AA also displayed its moments of architectural ingenuity, if only out of dire need. For instance, its auditorium, unable to fit within the striated constraints of a row house, had to cut perpendicularly across the grain of the party walls to traverse the width of two row houses to enable a larger public presence. The screen of the auditorium was displayed at 45 degrees fronting two distinct public seating spaces, perpendicular to each other, creating one focal point for the dual audiences: separated within two building structures but brought together through a visual point of convergence. Other spaces within the row houses were also adopted strategically to mediate between the practical realities of their limitations with the opportunities they offered as catalysts for change. Of them all, the bar sat at the core of the buildings on the second floor, above the lecture hall and gallery, next to the library. Needless to say, this was the space most known and talked about, as it gave rise to the debates of its time. Whether it was the alcohol or the mirrors of the bar that gave it the right ambience for informal discourse, intellectual friction and polemical challenges mattered less here than the fact that the row house, as a type, could gain the kind of flexibility and resilience to transform from a residential structure into an institution of international presence. The spatial and physical organization of the structures demonstrate that they do not require any customization of external form to fit the so-called function.

Beyond this, and behind this, it was Alvin Boyarsky's leadership that gave the AA the presence for which it is still known today, even though it has subsequently had three other leaders, each with their own merits. Faced with the impending danger of closure, Boyarsky realized that the AA required a completely different financial model and pedagogical strategy to address the diminutive nature of its physical infrastructure.

What Boyarsky also brought to the school was a consciousness that in order for a voice to exist, it would need to be heard, and the only way to do that from a diminutive row house was to amplify its message beyond architectural constraints: that is, through media and events that could gain a permanence long after his epoch and beyond the country's borders. The churning lecture hall and the revolving exhibition space were given a different presence through the added efforts of the AA's publications, which at that time exceeded the usual authority of a place of instruction; it served to instruct other faculties, not just students. Boyarsky himself built a curatorial rather than architectural practice; he understood that, as director, his ability to create discourse through pedagogical conversations outweighed the urgency of making buildings as such. In the protagonists he invited to teach at the AA, debate, friction, and discourse emerged, one that created the practices for which he is known: where would Koolhaas, Tschumi, and Hadid have gone were it not for their moment of trust and empowerment under Boyarsky? Alas, Boyarsky died in 1990, and with him passed an era that negotiated the challenges of leadership in the context of an architectural setting that was quite particular as a historic building; its adaptive reuse, tight as it was, was informed by the loosest of fits, and yet the character of the school persists even today with the expansion into more row houses, the introduction of dedicated studio spaces, and the transformation of the intellectual project in the era of digitization.

The Harvard Graduate School of Design: Pedagogy as Theater

Designed by John Andrews, the Gund Hall at the Harvard Graduate School of Design was completed in 1971. The idea behind the new project was to develop an open and flexible building where

Fig 1.6 The terraced morphology of the Gund Hall by John Andrews at the Harvard Graduate School of Design. *Photo by Eric Höweler.*

architecture, urban design, landscape architecture, and planning could share a space under one roof after a period of years of autonomy in different buildings. As such, Gund Hall could be said to be the manifestation of Josep Lluís Sert's pedagogical vision,[6] and one of the first to demonstrate a space for flexibility and interdisciplinarity.[7]

The terraced organization of the building is unmistakable in its morphological clarity; its stepped configuration is linked to a range of historical antecedents, and yet it is completely unprecedented as a space for work and collaboration.[8] Located in a single monumental hall capped by deep trusses, the "trays," as they are called, serve as studio platforms that are punctuated by a series of staircases that break the vast terraces into sectors and produce a redundancy of circulation that cannot merely be attributed to fire safety. Indeed, these stairs become the agent of social interaction (or avoidance, on occasion), as they offer a multitude of promenades up and down the building. The terracing of the building is launched by a mezzanine at the bottom that was originally conceived as a lounge. The ascending levels correspond to academic years, with the thesis year crowning the uppermost terrace. If the aesthetic of the building recalls factory spaces of industrial production, the terracing produces an effect that transforms a benign idea about production into the space of theater; that is, the terraces literally serve as theater seating looking from one level to another and creating, within the collective spirit of the civic space, a sense of individual "presence" as both the subject and object of voyeurism. If this interpretation seems overly panoptic, it is also obviously internalized in a myriad of ways by both professors and students alike. While certain students prefer a more contained and protected set of spaces "under" the terraces, others opt for the open theater of exposure. However, what dominates the space is the sense that the design process is a public activity, that architectural discourse is a collective project, and that somehow everyone, whether students or faculty, is subject to critical engagement; in effect, by analogy the entire building becomes one large "crit" space. As the agendas of each studio have the opportunity to merge and learn from each other, they also gain from the proximity and immediacy of friction, whereby differences play themselves out on the public stage of the terraces. In effect, this allows for many schools of thought under one umbrella.

From an administrative and intellectual perspective, the GSD succumbed to a radical detour from 1969 to 1980. With the controversial appointment of Maurice Kilbridge, a professor from Harvard's business school with a doctorate in mathematics, as its new dean, the new building gained a steward whose insight into design debates was limited. The temporal aspects of this turn of historical events are ironic, as the launching of a polemical building could not be matched with a leader who could absorb its spatial organization as part of a larger pedagogical plan. Instead, the very students and faculty appropriated its very order for the theater of dissent, resulting in the dean's ultimate demise.[9]

In 1980, with the hiring of Gerald McCue as dean and Henry Cobb as chair of the architecture faculty, the building finally gained a leadership that was deserving of its theatrical motivations. Cobb's launching speech, "Where I Stand," outlined a series of principles around which he would want the school to revolve architecture's commitment to the city, the coherence of a structural order to the program, the critical evaluation of rigor, a new openness that could draw in the necessary ideological friction to motivate varied forms of practices, and, finally, the presence of audacity: to risk, to fail, to challenge. As a practicing architect then in his mid-fifties, Cobb had already established himself as a reputable designer within a very successful partnership. Buildings such as the Hancock Tower and One Dallas Center, both built just years before his appointment, found ways to transform the mandates of corporate commissions toward more architecturally speculative ends, pushing building technologies to new uses, radicalizing the perceptual effects of commonplace materials, and teasing out invention out of the normative, even the banal. Still, by any measure of the academy, he would be seen as a safe and sound voice, not the one to take risks. For this reason, his ability to deliver the very tenets of his opening speech would be taken as a testament to his own audacity to transform the school almost instantly into a hotbed of debate. Not aiming to replicate the model of his practice within the academy, Cobb's curatorial strategy for newly invited faculty produced explosive reverberations within the school. With some embracing the new voices and others in complete resistance, what became clear was that he was able to convene a conversation that catalyzed debates of architectural history, the predicaments of form, and the speculative possibilities of translating ideas into spaces, rather than focusing on a centralization of power that might otherwise suffocate discourse. Notably, while Cobb's profile varied significantly from Boyarsky's, they shared the same intuitions when it came to the ability to build discourse through friction. Indeed, under Cobb, the spatial order of the GSD trays would be taken for the test ride of their life as a space of theatrical production.

The Foundation Building of the Cooper Union: The Sectional Metaphor

Meanwhile, at The Cooper Union, the Foundation Building designed by Fredrick A. Petersen, with subsequent renovations and additions by Petersen and architect Leopold Eidlitz, served as the platform for John Q. Hejduk as its dean. As an alumnus of the school, Hejduk was no stranger to the architecture program. After joining the (then still conjoined) School of Art and Architecture as a faculty member in 1964, he became its head a year later upon the departure of Dean Esmond Shaw. The renovation of the Foundation Building broke ground in 1971, the same year an exhibition titled "Education of an Architect: A Point of View" opened at the Museum of Modern Art. The temporal alignment between these two events is important; while Hejduk was designing the new layout of the Foundation Building, he was also focused on rethinking the architecture school's pedagogical program. Construction, which begn in 1971, took three years to complete. Shortly thereafter, the School of Art and Architecture broke off into separate divisions, establishing Hejduk as the first dean of the independent School of Architecture in 1975.

Originally conceived as a project for life safety, code, and modernization purposes, the renovation of the Foundation Building quickly transformed into a manifestation of — indeed, a manifesto for — Hejduk's pedagogical plans. The library was set at the building's base, as a foundation of knowledge; yet, somehow, the ethos of the school was rooted in the culture of craft, and the pedagogy required students to familiarize themselves with the tools of woodworking, casting, and welding, among other things. For this reason, the workshop on the fourth floor served as both the geographic and spiritual core of the building, sandwiched between the School of Architecture on the third floor and the School of Art on the fifth. In other words, the sectional diagram of the building was seen as a direct imprint of the ways in which Hejduk imagined the confluence of art and architecture in the context of "making."[10]

Of course, having inherited the building from Petersen and Eidlitz, Hejduk's mission was a challenging one, both structurally and from the perspective of the Landmarks Preservation Commission. He operated exclusively on the inte-

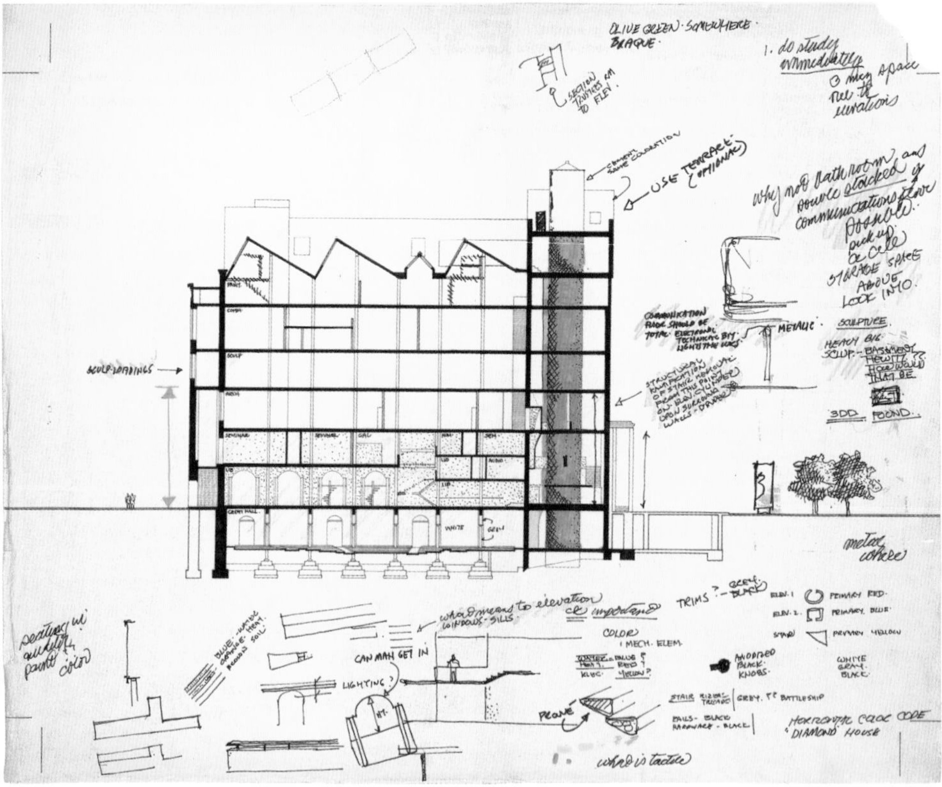

Fig 1.7 Sketches by John Hejduk (1971-1974). *Courtesy: The Irwin S. Chanin School of Architecture Archive, The Cooper Union.*

rior, but also found ways in which to contribute to the structural legacy of the building as a didactic strategy. The original building was constructed at a critical threshold in technological transformations, and thus the east side is built in a series of short spans with party walls while the west side is built as a long-span structure with an open plan, intended to serve as studios, workshops, and open spaces; the building is known for being one of the first to utilize rolled structural beams, at that time an inventive technology. In renovating the building, Hejduk effectively extended its structural narrative, translating his obsession with the Corbusian free plan by miniaturizing a nine-column grid (a riff on a pedagogical exercise of his own called the "Nine-Square Grid Problem") to fit into the plan of the Foundation Building's south-side lobby. The result is uncanny, because while completely normative at one level, its reduced scale defamiliarizes the idea of structure altogether. No longer there to serve as support per se, it creates a spatial cadence through which the core social activities of the schools could occur. Indeed, the nine-square grid falls directly in the critique spaces that were, and remain, the site of the school's main collective ritual; but its diminutive scale also helps to entangle the very activities it seeks to enable, as if to make the columns into figures in the spaces, participants in the activities.

Needless to say, as dean I now bring a personal reading that escapes historical distance to the spaces of The Cooper Union. I interpret its history and I inhabit the spaces within which certain events occurred while thinking about the relationship between the two. The platform that I inhabit in the Foundation Building, whether in the Great Hall, the Studio, or the Workshop, are all energized by vital mythologies; and so I benefit not only from the realities of its physical constraints but also from the narratives that its *mise-en-scène* has unleashed over time. Perhaps what is most relevant to this story is that the building embodies a certain urban character and culture that also escapes the particular pedagogies cast within it; predating Hejduk and surviving Vidler, the building continues to draw from the urban character of its context and be energized by the cultural vitality of the East Village.[11]

Architecture, too, can be seen as a *mise-en-scène* for the very events, functions, and programs that occur within it; and while traditional plays are scripted with overdetermination, other more experimental theaters, such as the *commedia dell'arte*, adopted improvisation as the basis for the interpretation of a sketch, much as we do in life as we play out our various roles in the context of the buildings we inhabit and the events we undergo.[12] Consider the decorum that is expected in a black-tie party in contrast to that of a rave: how we play out those roles is, in great part, also defined by the architecture that is its backdrop. In theater, everything on stage is meaningful, and whether it is an actor or a piece of furniture, its placement and role is to help advance a narrative. Thus, one can think of the architecture of the Architectural Association, the Harvard Graduate School of Design, and the Irwin S. Chanin School of Architecture as the *mise-en-scène* for the activities that are played out within them; whether they are an extension, a reflection, or a catalyst for the events that play out within them, these environments become somehow instrumental in the making of institutions.

SCI-Arc: Testing the Limits of Proportion

One school that has been through significant change in a short duration is the Southern California Institute of Architecture (SCI-Arc): first located in the medley of conjoined buildings in Santa Monica, then in a large industrial shed in Venice Beach, and subsequently in the long building it inhabits today, the former Santa Fe Freight Depot. While SCI-Arc has undergone significant historical and intellectual transformations in leadership, from Ray Kappe to Michael Rotondi and from Neil Denari to Eric Owen Moss and Hernán Díaz Alonso, the concept of the "college without walls" remains intact and is part of a shared legacy that is still practiced.[13] However, distinctly different from the Santa Monica campus on 1800 Berkeley Street, the Freight Depot building requires a linear promenade (approximately the length of the Empire State Building). The sheer extremity of its proportions and dimensions radicalizes the operations of the institution. Its 380-meter-long pin-up wall and its commuter system of skateboards and scooters over the length of the structure maintain the idea of a barrier-free environment. It is not a surprise that such a conceit of dimension and proportion might prompt a discussion between building typology, program, function, and their degree of correspondence. Invariably, it points to the challenge of claiming any sort of absolute determinism in relationships to questions of spatial organization.

SCI-Arc helps articulate that neither the most optimistic of architects nor the most positivist of clients can ensure the alignment between architectural form and human reception. Still, as vessels, buildings contain us; and as much as we are entrapped by them, we are also free to interpret them, use them, abuse them, and give them new functionalities that become part of their accrued cultural significance.

It is against this backdrop that NADAAA set out to design the Hinman Building at Georgia Tech, the Melbourne School of Design at the University of Melbourne, and the Daniels Faculty at the University of Toronto, three projects that we won at approximately the same time (circa 2008), when the economy was in the midst of a global fall. As architects, we naturally understood a great deal about design institutions in general, but more importantly, we came to understand the different cultures of these three schools and how their respective missions would create fundamentally different schools of thought. Thus, while the projects share a common program, they also maintain vastly different institutional perspectives. Our analytical task for each school was possibly the most important; if not to better understand the culture of each audience, then to compensate for the fact that the economic crisis dealt a near-fatal blow to all three projects. In other words, the common denominator that they all shared was a sense of critical choices: how to evaluate the indispensable and ensure that our architectural agendas were somehow couched in relation to the forces of integrated alibis.[14]

Fig 1.8 The high-bay splendor of the adaptive reuse of the Hinman Building by NADAAA.

Photo by Jonathan Hillyer.

The Hinman Building, Georgia Tech: Tectonic Inversion as a High-Bay Act

The Hinman Building is situated in the center of the Georgia Tech campus, next to the main library. The mission of the program was to expand the School of Architecture into a fourth building, slated for the masters and PhD programs. Concurrently, the entire center of campus was occupied by a parking lot, effectively giving primacy to vehicles over pedestrians. In tandem with the adaptive reuse of the Hinman Building, there was an initiative to transform the adjoining spaces into a series of quads for the central campus.

The Hinman Building was originally built in the 1930s by Paul M. Heffernan and designed for engineering research; its front entry was marked boldly with the sign "RESEARCH." Its most salient quality was a high-bay space that served as the space of construction and experimentation in the twentieth century. In the early parts of the commission, the pressures of space planning had the administration packing the high-bay with three stories of studio space, but after a sober recognition of the economic crisis, the program was revised to reduce student numbers and, in turn, to preserve the spatial splendor of the high-bay volume. Accordingly, in a nod to preservation, our proposal opened the high-bay space up to the main entry through various apertures that had been blocked for several decades, making it publicly accessible and open to view. Second, as a large open hall, it is celebrated as a potential

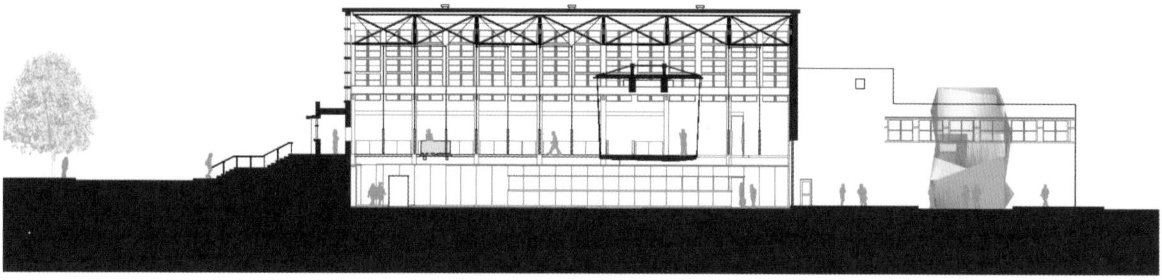

Fig 1.9 Reinterpreting the roof as a foundation. *Courtesy: NADAAA.*

public interior, and its flexibility allows it to serve as a platform for varied functions. Equally importantly, the space serves as a threshold to connect the main quad to a back "working court," where large-scale constructions can be fabricated outdoors. This required an approach that maintains the openness of the ground level, leaving it unencumbered by structures, static programs, and immobile elements. For this reason, we interpreted the building's characteristics in unorthodox ways, but always in a manner that enabled its reinvention and repurposing: in effect, we reinterpreted the roof as foundation and suspended all new interventions from the roof down so that they did not touch the ground. We repurposed the gantry crane to suspend a studio space to link the second and third level of the building by way of a programmed structure. We suspended a new spiral stair in the south wing to activate what had been the least accessible part of the building. We suspended a series of "guillotine" walls to connect the high-bay space with service spaces — galleries, crit spaces, and fab-labs — on the sides. Finally, we suspended the lighting on adjustable rods so it can be elevated for large-scale constructions and events that require uninterrupted height. By not touching the ground, the furnishings can be rolled around in varied configurations, and the space can serve a myriad of functions.

Beyond the design studio space within the high bay, the ancillary spaces to the north and south are reserved for an expanding series of research-based masters and PhD programs. Thus, students in computation, building technologies, material sciences, and sustainability may interact with students in the studio program in a more unmediated way, taking advantage of their spatial tangency to share intellectual agendas.

The flexibility of the high-bay space serves a heterogeneous agenda of events and rituals — some daily, others weekly, while others fall on a semester or annual basis — of drawing, collaborating, the construction of mock-ups, pop-up events, movies, Beaux-Arts balls, and graduations, as well as other less scripted events. They offer possibilities to drive the pedagogical agendas of the school as well as the emergence of a bottom-up studio culture.

Given that the majority of the project is an adaptive reuse, much of our work has gone into the assignment of characteristic features to respect the historic attributes of the building: for example, the high bay, the roof truss, and its gantry crane. This required the careful discernment of historic preservation tactics. The building's construction system (a hybrid of concrete, brick, steel, and wood) is unique, but also an exemplary experiment of its time. Given the heterogeneity of the existing palette, we restricted the use of materials within our own interventions, effectively grafting onto the existing elements to take on new functions, adaptability, and purpose. The tectonics of the existing building, in combination with the new interventions (if seen individually as exercises on their respective media), each take on a discursive role about the nature of preservation, renovation, and intervention — the three lenses through which we explored the project.

Returning to the main predicament, in what way does this project respond to the culture of the institution, and correspondingly, how does it imagine producing new cultural explorations?

Confronted with the preservation of a historic building, we saw this as an exercise in balancing a deep commitment to the heritage of the building while radically reinterpreting the protocols of its use. The seemingly benign tectonic inversion of using the roof as its foundation produces a paradigmatic shift in the building's ability to conform to varied circumstances. Thus, our response to the school's pedagogy was to imagine a consistent, yet changing, relationship between research and design, adopting the structure's flexibility to catalyze systemic reorganization over time.

Fig 1.10 The proposed atrium and surrounding corridors above insert an infrastructure of furniture for collaborative uses at the Melbourne School of Design.

Photo by Peter Bennetts.

Melbourne School of Design, Melbourne University: The Space of Pedagogy as Didactic Instrument

The Melbourne School of Design (MSD) was the result of an international competition whose main goal, in the words of Dean Tom Kvan, was to create a "design studio of the future" for a school that had no dedicated studio spaces, to create a "new academic environment" rooted in interdisciplinary work, to create "a living building" whose approach to sustainability would serve as a model of environmental stewardship, and to create a "pedagogical building" that would not only serve as an innovative space of learning, but also function as an exemplary didactic instrument. The mission of the building was thus effectively defined, and with it an effort to open up the school to its various programs in order to learn from each other, to collaborate, and to mix studio and research cultures. Located adjacent to the "Concrete Lawn," the main quad of the university, the building's strategic location was also to serve as the exemplary academic building for the campus. To this end, it was always imagined that the base of the building could host not only the design school but could also reach out to other academic disciplines, attracting their audiences for lectures, scholarship, exhibitions, and laboratories, and sharing its facilities with other departments.

Curiously, early pricing analysis exposed a tragic reality: while one of the main reasons for the new building was to create dedicated studio spaces, this was the one thing they could not afford within the allotted budget. As such, the organization of the building owes its composition, in great part, to our efforts to smuggle the studio space into the net-to-gross equation of its layout: effectively widening the corridors around the proposed atrium to insert an infrastructure of furniture for pin-up walls, model-making spaces, collaborative group tables, drafting desks, and seminar rooms. The budget for these furnishings is drawn from the existing FF&E (furniture, fixtures, and equipment) budget, but is then translated into the millwork scope. Accordingly, the architecture of the atrium eliminates the need for railings by cantilevering portions of these pieces of furniture and using a stainless steel mesh to "shrink-wrap" the furnishing to the slabs, creating a natural yet porous safety barrier. This alternative strategy is possibly the most critical aspect of this project; effectively, the strategy of "robbing Peter to pay Paul" enabled its core agenda. The atrium, populated by hot desks and informal areas, gives up to 75% of the students a workspace at any given time.

The irony of the new building is that, from a typological point of view, it is virtually identical to the building it replaced. However, understanding this, we also systemically analyzed the deficiencies of the former building in order to overcome them while also radicalizing its positive attributes. The previous building had an insular relationship to its context; the proposed building urbanized its connections by becoming porous on all sides and extending the university's main promenade through its base. The atrium of the old building was surrounded by solid walls, with little or no access into its court; in the new building, the atrium's edges are diaphanous, effectively making its court spatially open to programs on all sides. The corridors of the old building were wide purgatory spaces that were not well linked to classrooms or to the atrium;

in the new building, the furniture serves as a dynamic program in itself, deploying movable walls strategically and creating inglenooks for privacy while also offering flexible spaces for everyday interaction or special projects. The ground floor of the old building concealed its public programs; the new building exposes its library, auditoria, fabrication labs, and exhibit spaces, while lifting the atrium floor plate to the *piano nobile*, thus inviting the public to engage with its civic programs. The list of systemic change goes on, but in each scenario, we developed a critical dialogue with the liabilities of the old building while extending its culture, memory, and practices into a new facility. In effect, the ghost of the former building lives on in the new structure. Early on in the design process, we found the affinities between the old and proposed building so uncanny that we did, in fact, consider renovating the former building, but given the years of deferred maintenance and outmoded systems, this alternative was deemed the more expensive.

The MSD project also developed a series of architectural pieces — features, scenarios, rooms, and details — that rose to the occasion of the "pedagogical building." Here, we translated our lessons from Georgia Tech to a new context with other aims. For the atrium, we developed a structural system whose coffering serves as a deep two-way slab, spanning over twenty-two meters laterally. Fabricated from laminated veneer lumber (LVL) beams, the distortions of the coffering helps to block direct sunlight into the space while ensuring ample daylighting throughout working hours. More importantly, the depth of the roof provides the structure for a series of dedicated studio spaces that are suspended and stacked threefold in tension. Contrary to normative logic, the roof and suspended studios are conceived through a single self-similar tectonic system to establish a new integrative whole.[15] As a pedagogical strategy, the innate typological and tectonic differences between the roof structure and the suspended studio is challenged. Adopting the analogous tectonic logic of a classical palazzo, whereby the rustication at the base gives way to lighter orders as each floor stacks vertically, the roof coffers here contract incrementally with each floor, from massive members, to a bas-relief, and eventually to thin plywood sheets suspended in tension as the structure descends. This inverted tectonic organization is, of course, a reflection of its structural logic. Much like the Hinman Building, the suspended studio structure does not touch the *piano nobile*, precisely to enable the flexibility of public programs at its base.

The end grain on the bottom of the suspended structure produces a thin waffled ceiling that provides an open yet acoustically protected environment, patterned to absorb the necessary lighting, fire suppression, and sensor systems. Something that is as difficult to describe in words as it is to document in a photograph is the sense of levity produced by a massive monolith inexplicably suspended in space. Of course, the logic of the use of the atrium is its reason; the tectonic orders that descend from the roof are, in turn, an embodiment

Fig 1.11 The proposed building urbanizes its connections to its context, extending the main university promenade through its base. *Courtesy: NADAAA.*

of the structural performance of a suspended logic. Here, the pedagogical space is one and the same as the pedagogical instrument.

The MSD population is a large one; the cross-section of the MSD project is an index of the various cultures that it houses, from architecture to urbanism, planning to landscape, and real estate to construction, among other disciplines. The stacked organization of the atrium carefully orchestrates the formal assembly of varied infrastructures of furniture to strategically bring the varied disciplines into informal conversation, adopting happenstance and a serendipity of circulation to ensure the overlap and cross-pollination of diverse disciplinary groups.

In contrast, the suspended studio offers a respite from the merely rational: it belongs to the category of wonder, awe, and mystery — floating, as it were, within the open space of the atrium as an open signifier. It does not so much answer a question as it poses one: to what degree can pedagogy be specified and calculated, and how might that be upended by a formal, spatial, and phenomenal act that serves to manifest what a canonical lesson cannot?

Daniels Faculty of Architecture, Landscape, and Design, University of Toronto: Integration, Blending, and Negotiation of Disciplines

The Daniels Building at the University of Toronto is located at the center of Spadina Crescent, one of the few civic spaces in the city that deviate from the rigidity of the City of Toronto's grid. With the historic Knox College (built in 1875) anchoring its southern edge, the Crescent has been host to numerous programs over the decades: a theological school, military hospital, museum, and, laboratories for the research of insulin. As such, the building has already demonstrated its programmatic resilience in face of changes over time. When the University of Toronto considered this site for the new Daniels Faculty of Architecture, Landscape, and Design, it became clear that the cellular spaces of Knox College offered the ideal dimensions for classrooms, offices, conference areas, and spaces — effectively, these were spaces in need of acoustic and visual separation. Thus, beyond renovation and adaptive reuse, the commission entailed an expansion for all the open spaces required for studios, labs, and other spaces of congregation. With Knox College anchoring the southern portion of Spadina Crescent, the expansion to the north offered a few critical opportunities: giving Spadina Boulevard an iconic facade on its north side, urbanizing Spadina Crescent by making it accessible on the east-west axis, linking the university campus on the east to Hardbord Village neighborhood on its west, and providing much-needed flexible spaces for the Daniels Faculty of Architecture.

This also presented NADAAA with the opportunity to engage the faculty's three discipline streams of architecture, landscape architecture, and urban design to imagine a more engaged relationship between Spadina Crescent and the City of Toronto. As with our other design school projects, part of the design process involved a detailed understanding of how these three streams operated, and how we might incorporate their research into the organization of the building. For the latter, the GRIT Lab (Green Roof Innovation Testing Laboratory), the Construction Laboratory, and the Global Cities Institute all played an instrumental role in giving shape to key pedagogical spaces within the building. Each of them helped to form an important relationship with the city and landscape, informing our strategy for the building at large. To this end, the project can be seen as a delicate negotiation between architecture and landscape strategies; on the one hand, it adopts a generic volume to house the core of its special programs, while on the other, it

Fig 1.12 The roof produces a landscape that merges the structural, daylighting, and hydrological mandates of the building into one surface while capping the studio space.

Photo by Nic Lehoux.

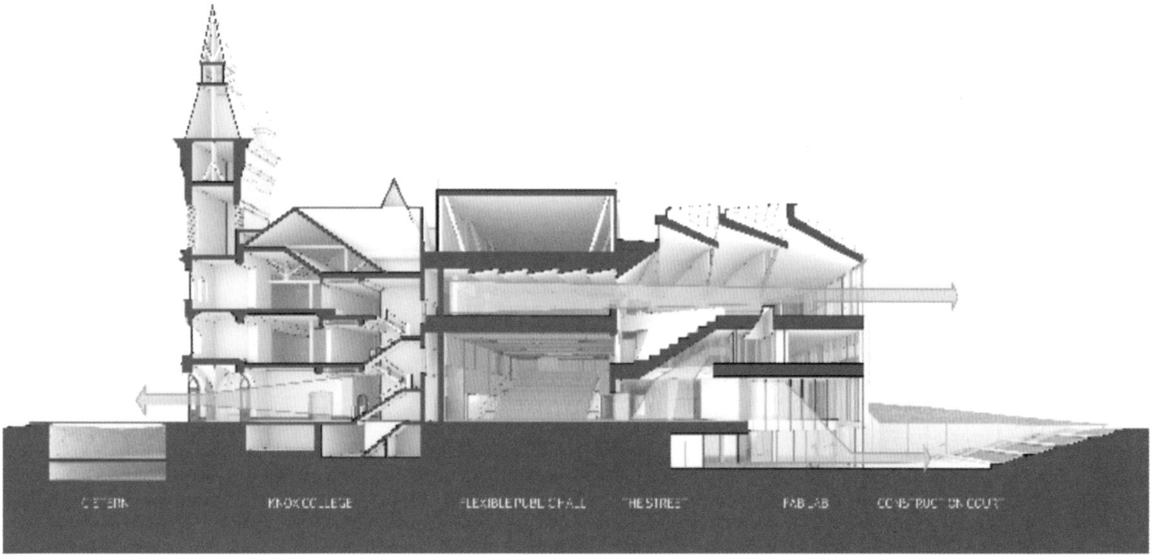

Fig 1.13 A new vertical promenade connects the inner pedestrian street with the top-floor studio space, drawing daylight deep into the dark core of the building. *Courtesy: NADAA.*

architecturalizes the landscape, sometimes tucking in additional programs and expansions in order to establish a more poignant relationship with the city and its urbanism.

By adopting the existing circulation logic of Knox College, the new addition extended the natural flow of its promenade into a tight loop, making for the most compact and economical of strategies. Despite the volumetric banality of the generic box, each floor slab within it is conceived as landscape; thus each slab is also deformed or sloped in order to establish dialogue with its context in strategic ways. On the street level, the gallery opens up onto a plaza on the east side, while the proposed Global Cities Institute reaches out toward the west to create a stoa in the direction of Hardbord Village; these two programs are reinforced by a new inner pedestrian street that forms a public conduit, effectively extending Russell Street through the building. On the north side, the lower level extends the fabrication lab into an outdoor court, where large-scale mock-ups can be built. The landscape in the north responds to this with volumetric adjustments that reinforce the symmetry of the site on axis with Spadina North, while accommodating the anomalies of the east and west. The second and third floor slabs are conjoined by the new vertical promenade that connects the inner street with the studio space on the top floor. This is the most important landscape within the building, as it visually connects the street with the undergraduate program on the second floor while physically connecting the same street with the third floor in a seamless fashion, drawing in natural light to the dark core of the building. To cap this off, the roof of the building produces a landscape that merges the structural, daylighting, and hydrological mandates of the building into one surface. This physical, spatial, and symbolic feature is one key gesture that brings together the various interdisciplinary forces to create an integrated strategy; this is the building's pedagogical moment. The roof also caps its most critical space, the studio. Aloft in the attic of the building, this open, flexible space serves as the building's most salient and iconic space, a public interior with a prospect over Spadina North.

The Formality of Specification and the Informality of Public Appropriation

At the heart of this discussion, there is perhaps an irreconcilable relationship between two views on the agency of architecture as a catalyst for intellectual and pedagogical consciousness. On the one hand, there is the Barthesian idea of *mise-en-scène*, whereby the architectural setting plays a scripted and therefore deterministic role in framing the actions, narratives, and scenarios that frame a school's presence. On the other hand, there is the counterpoint that sees the architectural setting as providing no more than an atmosphere, as if it were the musical score of a movie; meant to be stealthy and inconspicuous while blending into the very plot it sets. Here, the recessive role places architecture in the background, the victim of the human state of distraction. To be sure, were the music score of a thriller to be turned off, we would stop in our tracks, knowing that something irreducible is missing, that the tension and anxiety has been lost. In this sense, architecture is not exactly white noise, but more a catalytic agent and a protagonist. Its evidence comes in many forms: the trusses at the GSD that form the basis for the infamous "truss races," the Bunny Lounge at RISD that served as the basis for many unplanned encounters, and the AA bar which served the juice for the many debates for which it continues to be known. Beyond the formal pedagogies that frame the trajectories of these schools, there is the mortar of the informal cultures that are bred into the pores of its architecture; this is how architecture forms the culture of these settings. The architect's plight might be to anticipate the balance of formal and informal cultures and have the humility to know when the appropriation of the building is the result of unanticipated pedagogies; and the architect's satisfaction may lie in recognizing the success of having provided for the intelligence of its underlying infrastructure.

Postscript: Cooper Union, Resituated

As we revisit Cooper Union today, six years after my arrival, there is much to appreciate about the change in climate. To begin with, Cooper Union's longstanding mission of providing tuition-free education to its students is no longer in question, at least in principle. With recent commitments from the new administration, the debates of the past can now be confronted with the challenges of fiscal austerity, the mobilization of fundraising efforts, and the indispensability of aligning faculty research with funding potentials. The path to get to full scholarships is set at ten years, pending the necessary incremental yield that will continue to be part of the annual burden. While this has restored much faith in our administration, it has also helped to disentangle the relationship between "free education" (a tuition-free-based institution) and pedagogical content (the basis for academic freedom). In a prior generation these two ideas were mixed together, errantly but strategically, and used as a rhetorical device, one commonly cast into conversations to maintain ideological control over the culture of its pedagogies. To this end, an opening up of dialogue within the structure of our governance has also enabled the expansion of a curriculum in dire need of a wider lens. This includes the expansion of committees to include adjunct faculty and students, the opening of school governance to more members of the community (including alumni), launching specific initiatives that engage cultural and racial diversity, and making a broader commitment to discuss architecture's relationship to climate change. These are just some of the elements that have allowed multiple narratives to grow; not so much to make a school of thought, but to cultivate debates between schools of thought.

It is impossible to do justice to such a transformation at this juncture, if only because it is a work in progress and still in dire need of development, investment, and refinement. But the political structure that underlies this process remains important, and confronting it becomes increasingly imperative since doing so forms part of a set of changes that can be owned collectively. Developing that structure is the architecture on which we have been focused on for the past six years. If the political infrastructure of our inner governance has undergone a radical opening up, then the world around us has seen a very different evolution of political cultures at a national level, and certainly beyond — becoming ever more centralized, with executive power being adopted as de facto. If these cultures are viewed as two different worlds, there are obvious areas of separation, it is important to underscore how the national political milieu might impact the inner functioning of an institution, while recognizing that the administration of a college is always different than the governance of a school within it.[16]

The spaces that surround us continue to engage us, whether to delight, hinder, or serve us as pedagogical matter. The connection between the fiscal plan and the buildings that support the culture of the three schools (art, architecture, and engineering) is a critical part of the ten-year plan. On the one hand, due to the deferred maintenance of structures and spaces, a certain amount of building work will be central to enabling the infrastructure to support its pedagogies; on the other hand, if this work becomes part of an expense, it can only extend the ten-year plan if planned injudiciously. Curiously, setting some of the new work in motion has rekindled a new urgency to discuss matters of architecture in the context of restoration, preservation, and renovation. The school saw part of these challenges emerging in the first year of the new administration during the dialogue on gender-neutral bathrooms (with Cooper Union leading the national discussion).[17] However, it was with the insertion of new paper towel dispensers and toilet paper holders that the true nature of the debate became even more apparent; the specification of these fixtures could never have been deemed a design issue or the basis for protest and public outcry by the upper administration, which considered their selection to be a mere bureaucratic issue. This misperception also revealed a common, if unfortunate, eventuality that befalls all institutions: the fundamental separation of administrative cultures between those who govern and those who teach. It is a rare administration that recognizes that its own facilities are not merely part of a physical plant, but part of a cultural heritage and its pedagogical mission, right down to its toilet paper holders.

The notion of "characteristic features" and "reversibility" that are so central to preservation culture produced a head-on collision between the forces that saw the Foundation Building as a building of the nineteenth century and those who saw its more powerful voice emerging after the renovation of the 1970s under the direction of John Hejduk. Many narratives — and many ironies — underlie this discussion. For one, we are reminded that the initial project undertaken by Hejduk targeted code and life-safety issues within the Foundation Building but never deemed to rise to the occasion of a full renovation, nor reconceptualization of the structure, particularly on its southern end. However, the eventual transformations impacted the base of the building, where the structure engages the city, its urbanity, and the public realm: that Hejduk dared to challenge the historical structure is a testament to the idea that the fluid relationship between preservation, renovation, and adaptive reuse is much more dynamic than purists may want to admit. And in this light, buildings are thought of as living entities, with change being a central part of their lifetimes. If that were not poignant enough, the adoption of Le Corbusier's free plan as a model for the restructuring of the south end is also equally significant. The idea of the free plan reveals that since the structure is no longer stubbornly tied to loadbearing walls, then spatial demarcations (whether walls, panels, or movable partitions) can liberally move around columns. This is precisely what enables the types of figuration on display in the second and seventh floor lobbies, both classic tropes for the Corbusian handbook. What is interesting is that embedded in Le Corbusier's free plan is an ethic of dynamism, which in itself is a thesis that incapacitates the idea of stagnancy in the context of preservation: more directly, it allows for non-loadbearing walls to be moved as a rule and as a response to the programmatic needs of a building.

Naturally, the practical, theoretical, and emotional facets of this narrative are all being played out as I bring my deanship to a close; we shall see where the dust settles, but suffice it to say that as schools transform, so too administrations learn, change, and reveal new priorities over time. We have yet to see what awaits Cooper Union, but it will certainly extend beyond my oversight.

As the administration considers the transformations of the Foundation Building, we might also ask ourselves: what would Hejduk do if confronted with new programmatic opportunities and newfound constraints? Would he allow himself to undo his own renovation, and if so, adopting what design ethos? Would he still be shackled by the ethics of the free plan, or would he introduce other ingredients to offset the self-imposed heritage of restrictions he adopted from the modern movement?

To this end, my role has been controversial from both ends of the perspective: not completely embraced by those whose fidelity to the Hejduk renovation remains stubbornly steadfast, and equally not accepted by the very administration of which I am a part. Indeed, there is a legitimate narrative that would suggest that the limits of a dean's responsibilities are drawn within the borders of their school and its curriculum; but then there is another narrative that sees the real estate of the institution, its oversight of the facilities, its deferred maintenance, the preservation, renovation, and transformation of its spaces, and its programming as part of a dean's commitment and responsibility to the institution. In this version, a dean is not only an advisor but one who reveals pedagogical opportunities in the governance itself. More importantly, a dean's role as steward of an institution requires them to place their own design instincts on the back burner, if only to underscore the importance of serving as a good host (rather than author) for design. More than anything, these discussions have served as opportunities to create spaces of inclusion, bringing faculty, students, and scholars together to debate the relative agency of architecture in the transformation of intellectual cultures.

To this end, my engagement with the administration has revolved around a few key sites of opportunity for the campus and the School of Architecture specifically, all of which entail critical changes to its cultural potentials. At the base of 41 Cooper Square and the Foundation Building, we find the questions of how the buildings meet the street, how they are programmed, and to what degree they invite a broader public into Cooper Union. On the fourth floor, we have the question of how the historic workshop may enter the twenty-first century by expanding its infrastructure to include equipment that allows the intellectual environment of interdisciplinary "making" thrive; and on the third floor, in the School of Architecture, the question remains how the sacred space of the studio may provide an equitable space of research to each student in a fashion that reinforces collaborations.

Beyond the ethics that drive preservation and change, the Foundation Building is already confronted with a range of pressing urbanistic, programmatic, and user-based challenges. As a public building dedicated to civic discourse and debate, the infrastructure of the base of the building is significantly limited given the hundreds of the people it serves for the Great Hall events. Establishing a stronger urban rapport with Cooper Square, Astor Place, and Third and Fourth Avenues is a distinct opportunity, and it would require an open mind to craft strategies that transform a relatively insular building into something that serves a larger community.[18]

The current base of the Foundation Building is occupied by one of the most important of the public programs of the institution, its library. And yet, despite the transformational role that the Internet, online archives, and social media have had on access to information and data, Cooper Union has lagged behind when it comes to posing basic questions about the nature of research in the twenty-first century. Only very recently, Cooper Union launched a study in collaboration with Mary Burnham to analyze the base of the building and its potentials. How do we research differently in this day and age, and to what degree does the physical space of the library participate in that process? What programs may the library invite or tolerate? How will it share information? How will it become more public? And how can it cultivate a more inclusive presence in the neighborhood, if these guidelines are of relevance? To what degree can it absorb the city, as much as it gives back? These and many other questions are at stake.

The culture of digitization has also impacted another significant infrastructural program within the Foundation Building: the workshop. With the evolution of computation, digital manufacturing, and the computer-numerically-controlled (CNC) machinery that is germane to our time, the space of the traditional workshop stands to undertake fundamental transformations with the newly opened AACE Lab; this will also enable critical transformations in our pedagogies.

Finally, after many decades of neglect, the renovation of the studio space situated in the heart and soul of the architecture program has allowed for workspaces where students can develop an academic environment that they wish to foster. The challenges of this studio space define the very core of certain contradictions within the institution: the sacred nature of the studio space is also linked to an alleged philosophy of team-teaching that is supposed to bring competing and complementary points of view into conversation in space. Yet, no one to date has exposed that team-teaching is actually the result of the lack of dedicated real estate in the studio environment for the School of Architecture, resulting in the inability to give students and faculty ample space for individuated reviews and smaller-scale dialogue. For this reason, much of the School's pedagogies revolve around large-scale studio crits in the lobby, often with thirty students at any given time, and little time for individual, focused attention.

Due to the program's size, which is constrained by a delicate balance between its available real estate and the individual need for work space, the education of an architect at Cooper Union is more expensive than at most other schools. On top of the space needed for conventional drawings and model-making, the need for computing has added to the urgency of intelligently conceptualizing the studio of the future — especially given the Cooper Union doctrine of maintaining an agnostic view of media types and holding the digital, analogue, and physical in a delicate balance. If the instrumentality of certain media are the critical means through which certain ideas are accessed, then there are also certain ideas that withstand the influx of new media; centuries of architectural discipline have proven both claims. Thus, as we prepare for a space of production, we also know that what we are actually preparing is a place to rethink the discipline from within media.

Fig 1.14 Developing a space for architectural production while rethinking the discipline from within its media.

Courtesy: The Irwin S. Chanin School of Architecture Archive, The Cooper Union.

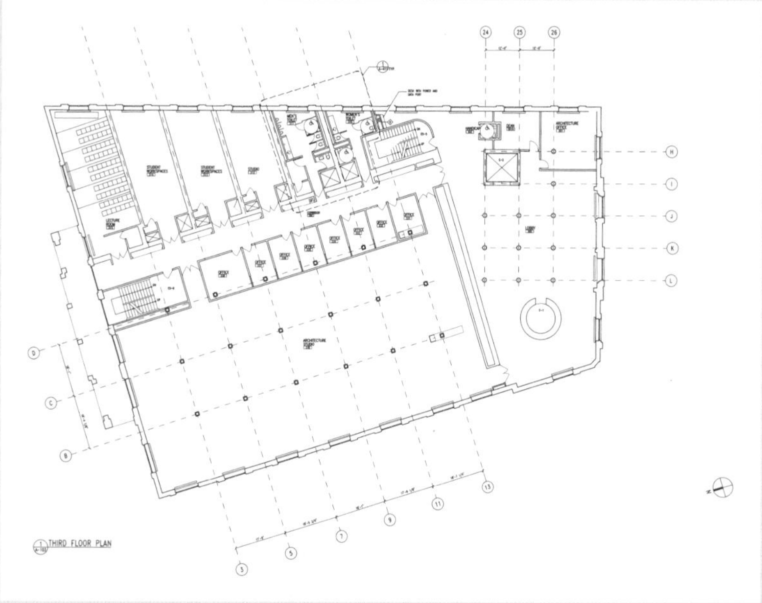

Fig 1.15 Floor plan of level three of the Foundation Building by Gruzen Samton LLP.

Courtesy: The Irwin S. Chanin School of Architecture Archive, The Cooper Union.

If constraints are usually seen as a liability, then the limitations at Cooper Union are being interpreted as an asset toward imagining the ways in which the studio space might become a more veritable intersection between the varied disciplines that fuel the intellectual imagination of the learning space. Design not through autonomy, but rather through its interaction with history, theory, building sciences, and the contingent impact of externalities, is driving us to bring isolated phenomena in the curriculum into conversation.[19] Within this context, we also realize that in order for the architect to bring something of consequence to the interdisciplinary table, he or she must be able to identify what the discipline's agency might be in the face of larger cultural and societal questions: that is, how the formal, spatial, and material aspects of the built environment impact the well-being of a people. For these reasons, while the coordination of first three foundational years are being amplified, the last two years are being consciously deregulated to encourage a wider reach toward collaborations with engineering and the arts, among other areas of work that may impact the fringes of the architectural discipline.

With desks that ascend and descend, back supports for chairs, storage for models, computers for in-studio rendering, screens for pin-ups, and seminar tables for collective events, the studio has evolved to better support student life.

Naturally, this last chapter brings into focus the relationship between architect as author and architect as administrator, client, advisor, or collaborator. And herein lies the most important lesson to date, revealing the critical relationships between pedagogies and space, the latent cultures that survive distinct administrations, and the processes and procedures of governance that produce critical relationships between means and ends. As an administrator, one has to confront many difficult aspects of principles, ethics, and compromises that situate the means and ends into a longer arc of relevance when viewed across a panorama of architecture schools, their schools of thought, and the institutions they have created.

References

[1] While each administration brings different schools of thought to the White House, this is a reference to the radical aberrations of the Trump presidency.

[2] Michel Foucault, *Ceci N'est Pas Une Pipe (This Is Not a Pipe)*, ed. James Harkness (Berkeley, CA: University of California Press, 1983), 19.

[3] Louis Althusser, *On the Reproduction of Capitalism: Ideology and Ideological State Apparatuses* (London: Verso Books, 2014). In his essay, Althusser distinguishes himself from Karl Marx, demonstrating the ways in which different ideological apparatuses (architecture being one of them) come to redefine culture from the bottom up. He therefore frees them from the subordinate status of being determined by the economic base.

[4] It is notable that except for the GSD, the other three precedents in focus here are transformations of existing buildings that help frame and contextualize the adaptive reuse of architecture schools presented by the NADAAA projects.

[5] Peter Cook, "Alvin Boyarsky (1928-1990)," *The Architectural Review*, Sept. 28, 2012, https://www.architectural-review.com/essays/reputations/alvin-boyarsky-1928-1990.

[6] "GSD to Start Construction Of Gund Hall," *The Harvard Crimson*, Nov. 3, 1969, https://www.thecrimson.com/article/1969/11/3/gsd-to-start-construction-of-gund/. Josep Lluís Sert is commonly credited as the disciplinary founder of "urban design."

[7] Eric Mumford, Hashim Sarkis, and Neyran Turan, *Josep Lluis Sert: The Architect of Urban Design*, 1953-1969 (New Haven: Yale University Press, 2008). But in the context of Gund Hall, the expansion of the other disciplines can be seen as an extension of the idea of specialization in other parallel streams.

[8] Of the examples, the GSD is the only new freestanding building, and yet its uncanny connection to the space of theater recalls Rossi's assertion that building typology is indifferent to function. The difficult but seamless transition from a theater-in-the-round to a series of residential units surrounding Piazza dell'Anfiteatro seems somehow fortuitous in hindsight. But it also far from inevitable, as it requires a leap of the imagination to project such a radically different narrative—and eventuality—onto a single structure. Though a new building, the GSD could have been the result of such a historical passage.

[9] "A New Dean for the GSD," *The Harvard Crimson*, Mar. 17, 1976, https://www.thecrimson.com/article/1976/3/17/a-new-dean-for-the-gsd/.

[10] Michael Blackwood, *John Hejduk: Builder of Worlds* (New York: Michael Blackwood Productions, 1992), https://vimeo.com/ondemand/hejduk.

[11] Anthony Vidler served as acting dean (2001) and dean (2002-2013) of the Irwin S. Chanin School of Architecture at the Cooper Union.

[12] Jorge Silvetti, "Representation and Creativity in Architecture: The Pregnant Moment," in *Representation and Architecture*, ed. O. Akin and E. G. Weinel (Silver Spring, MD: Information Dynamics, Inc., 1982), 159-184. In this article, Silvetti borrows Roland Barthes's semiotic device of *mise-en-scène* to recast it as "mise-en-architecture," attributing to architecture the voice and presence of a protagonist in a scene.

[13] Ray Kappe founded the Pomona department, served as the new school's first director, until 1987. Kappe was succeeded as director by Michael Rotondi, one of SCI-Arc's founding students. Neil Denari became director in 1997; Eric Owen Moss served as director from 2002-2015; Hernán Díaz Alonso was appointed Director and Chief Executive Officer effective Sept 1, 2015.

[14] No building is the result of a single line of reasoning. Most often, varied forces—urbanistic, typological, material, and sustainable practices, among other factors—come into conversation before being balanced out in a more synthetic way. Thus, the term "integrated alibi" refers to two qualities: first, that buildings are the result of integrated systems, and secondly, that those systems are far from truths. Rather, they are the result of a reasoning process that is often more narrative than scientific. An alibi is interesting because it can produce a narrative that proves why one is not guilty, or persuasively conceals the fact that one is; thus, the status of an alibi here is more of that of an excuse.

[15] "Self-similarity," *Wikipedia*, accessed Sept. 13, 2021, https://en.wikipedia.org/wiki/Self-similarity.

[16] I began this essay with a reference to national governance, connecting it to university-wide administration (i.e., the executive branch) before moving on to discussing the School of Architecture, which has its own internal governance but remains beholden to university-wide policies.

[17] See "Bathroom Confidential," Nov. 3, 2016, https://cooper.edu/about/news/bathroom-confidential.

[18] Nineteenth-century images of the Foundation Building show a thriving retail subdivision at its base, arguably at odds with the decorum of the architecture overhead. What types of productive heresies would its twenty-first century counterpart tolerate, or cultivate?

[19] It is important to note that, more than ever, architecture is being impacted by forces that have not been traditionally defined as part of its internal frame: biology, geography, and computation, among other intellectual branches.

Chapter 2
From Lifestyle to Life Cycle: And Other Readings of Carbon Form in Architecture

Eric Höweler

Of the various assessments and assignations of the contemporary moment, from postmodernism to planetarism, carbon form is emerging as one of the most impactful ways of describing a broad range of phenomena, including architecture and the built environment. Carbon form, the myriad manifestations of a material and economic paradigm, is all around us. Andreas Malm's writing on global warming and industrialization describes fossil capitalism and carbon modernity, mapping out the relationships between the use of fossil fuels and economic systems that define what we call modernity. Malm writes, "The fossil economy has the character of a totality, a distinguishable entity: a socio-ecological structure, on which a certain economic process and a certain form of energy are welded together."[1]

In her essay, "Overcoming Carbon Form," Elisa Iturbe enumerates the various manifestations of carbon form: "not only urban and architectural typologies but also the spaces and objects our everyday lives: fast food chains, roadside motels, a delivery truck full of bottled water idling on an asphalt street, the appliance section of a department store, military installations, the internet, Las Vegas, natural gas pipelines, the Indy 500."[2] Iturbe makes a compelling case for a reading of the predicament of the present as inextricably bound up in the logics of extraction, refinement, and combustion, one which renders all of architecture as complicit with carbon form. "In the totalizing framework of carbon modernity, architectural thought is constantly subsumed by the ideology of the fossil economy, making it impossible to decouple both the discipline and the practice of architecture from environmental collapse. Carbon form is everywhere, and the possibility of critical architecture is negated by its breadth."[3] What then, is architecture to do? What space is left for action? What space is left for practice?

Unlike the discourses of postmodernism and late capitalism, which were characterized by their immateriality, carbon form has a very tangible quality and offers some possibilities for architecture. Frederic Jameson's theories of postmodernism argue that everything falls under the rubric of consumer society, and architecture is the form of cultural production most closely tied to large amounts of capital.[4] This totalizing discourse is overwhelming, suffocating, and claustrophobic. If postmodernism was distinguished by its immateriality — it was the invisible and immaterial flows of capital that Jameson remarked upon — carbon form seems at least to provide a material analogue. Carbon as a thing. It is an element found in many forms and combinations and associated with material processes and products.

Focus

As carbon form comes into focus as the critical term for contemporary architecture and culture, its materiality seems to offer some means of engaging with it. Materiality in architecture seems to be experiencing a kind of resurgence.[5] Perhaps it is because of the profound irreality of our last year and a half of remote everything due to the COVID-19 pandemic. Perhaps because we are recognizing that it is matter and material practices that consume energy and determine our future climate crisis, materiality is our best hope for affecting different outcomes. As Antoine Picon writes in his book, *Materiality in Architecture*, "Architecture is a profoundly material practice." It is inescapably material in that it orders and reorders the world around organizing principles, schemas, and forms that are composed of materials that have been constructed, transported, fabricated, and harvested — in short, produced. A reading of architecture as a set of material flows profoundly recasts architecture as a sum of all the energy that produced it. Kiel Moe describes buildings as material in transit. The physical building that stands on the corner of Park Avenue and Fifty-Third street in New York is an "exquisite pile of technomass," an "object instance" otherwise known as the Seagram Building. Kiel Moe's analysis of that modernist icon in his book *Unless, The Seagram Building Construction Ecology*, reads the Seagram Building through the lenses of material ecologies, environmental load, and embodied energy.[6]

The title of the book contains a dire warning: "Unless architects begin to describe buildings as terrestrial events, processes and artifacts, architects will — to professional and collective peril — continue to operate outside the key environmental and political dynamics of this century."[7] Moe argues for an entirely new lens to assess architecture as a material, geological, and ecological artifact — essentially the substance of which it is made — and the embodied energy and labor that it represents.

Tracing materials back to their sources and understanding the processes entails the skills of a material scientist, a historian, a sociologist, and a detective. The investigation of the Seagram Building's material origins is what Moe refers to as a "terrestrial" reading. The making of a building shifts materials and "goods" from material sources to building sites, while transferring and accumulating environmental degradation and waste, what Moe calls "bads," to the sites of origin.

These impacts are what Moe calls "environmental loads," which he argues are being asymmetrically displaced from centers of power and wealth onto the peripheries where these materials come from. Only by understanding the expanded web of materials — their sources, waste factors, tailing, cutoffs, byproducts, and toxicological impacts — can we develop a true accounting of the real environmental footprint of architecture.

For Moe, "architects anachronistically still tend to focus on the design of buildings as objects, rather than the design of building as an active terrestrial monster of material, energy and social transformation."[8] How to change the habits of mind, of thinking of architecture as a finished product, rather than as a deeply material and social process? What agency does architecture have?

Moe's deep reading of the Seagram Building, pursuing "the details of details," suggests that architecture has tremendous agency and responsibility. Every choice we make and every material specified has extensive consequences beyond the building, in the world, and in communities. Each material choice is tied to a web of procurement and practices that stretches back to mines and forests, factories and families. Moe's stance toward material and construction ecologies is a demand that we rethink the very substance of architecture and its expanded footprint so we can understand its larger impact in a terrestrial world.

Reading

Every building embodies a material and energy paradigm of its time.[9] By carefully reading the built environment we can detect a set of assumptions, values, and concerns that have been concretized as built form. The clear monolithic glass of the Lever House, built in 1951, does little to reduce the heat gain through the curtain wall, relying on interior shades for solar control. Perhaps the discourse of clarity and transparency was part of the allure for Lever, a company built on selling cleaning products. Mies's slightly tinted bronze glass used on the Seagram Building in 1954 may have been an acknowledgment of the need to control solar heat gain, but was more likely a means of unifying the facade with a single tint. The high reflectivity of the glass of the John Hancock Tower in Boston, built in 1974, marks a moment where the energy performance of glass begins to be a factor in material selections. The visible light transmission through the Hancock's glass was significantly reduced by its reflective coating and green tint. The specification of glass from three different buildings, at three different times, reveals the energy paradigm and the intent of the architects at the moment they were selected.

Building form also signals attitudes about energy and environment. In 1916, the New York City Zoning Ordinance introduced setbacks zoning to control the bulk of buildings in the city to ensure that light and air would be available at street level. These regulations acknowledged the fact that daylight and ventilation are shared natural resources and architectural form should be regulated to ensure its equitable availability.[10] The sky exposure plane became a determinant of form in New York that has shaped buildings — and the New York skyline — since then.

Reading the skyline silhouettes of some of New York's towers reveals further energy embodiments. The Citicorp Center building, built in 1977 and conceived during the oil shock of the 1970s, features a south-facing sloped roof that was purportedly created to allow for solar panels. The solar panels were not installed, but the sloped gesture remains the distinctive feature of the tower. The generation of solar power by such a small area does little to offset the energy expenditures of a 1.3 million-square-foot tower in midtown Manhattan. Its distinctive *form* does speak to the discourse around energy and environment at that time. The built environment doesn't just consume energy, it embodies it and communicates it.

Renewable

Understanding the impacts of extraction-based building materials and their embodied energy has led to an intense focus on renewable materials for building. Timber has long been a fundamental building material across cultures. Compared to other building materials, such as steel and concrete, timber has a much lower embodied energy; it acts as a carbon sink, and it is a rapidly renewable resource.

It is important to think about timber — and all materials — as a set of processes and practices. Timber alone could be understood as having material properties based on species: grain character and orientation, structural properties, and carbon sequestration. But we know nothing of timber if we don't understand where it was harvested, what forestry practices produced it, how accessible or inaccessible it is, what labor will process it, and how it is configured, transported, and erected. These are the material and construction ecologies that define timber today.

In surveying current research in areas of renewable materials like timber, three areas seem especially promising: building typologies enabled by mass timber that address questions of density, the fabrication capacities of mass timber as a volumetric material, and the use of so-called "waste lumber" from diseased trees. Each area is illustrated by a design / research project that hints at possible alternative practices in carbon form.

The designs collected by the research project Timber City look to mass timber framing as a means to exceed the 5+1 type of residential construction, allowing for higher-density residential building types in middle-scale cities. This work assumes that mass timber framing can replace steel and concrete frame systems and still achieve combustibility ratings that allow for taller and denser construction. The application of mass timber in this application is as a replacement for higher-energy-intensity materials and structural systems, and contributes to a lower embodied energy for the buildings. The conceptualization of a high-density urbanism in a mid-rise city assumes that it produces urban land use patterns configured around pedestrian-focused public realms and served by public transportation. Density, enabled by material systems, incorporates transportation energy considerations. This approach combines the material and the territorial scales as well as embodied and operational energy thinking.

As part of our research into renewable and composite materials at Höweler + Yoon, we acknowledge the tremendous potential for engineered lumber to reconfigure wood into formats and configurations that surpass the traditional light wood framing dimensions and products that initially produced the ubiquitous balloon and platform frame. "Two-by" lumber produced from fast-growth species are limited by the dimensions of the source material, namely the size of the trunk. Engineered wood takes advantage of glues and composites, which reconfigure wood to improve yields and utilize components of varying qualities. However, the mass timber industry is primarily focused on cutting flat sheets and beams, relying on cutting sheets in planar configurations perpendicular to the surface. A multi-axis industrial robot has a far more three-dimensional work envelope, which allows it to cut volumetric elements, like blocks of stone.

Applying our research to the fabrication of large-format construction modules, we developed a stacked mass timber structure as a public art installation in Spokane. The project, called Stepwell, consists of seventy blocks of stacked

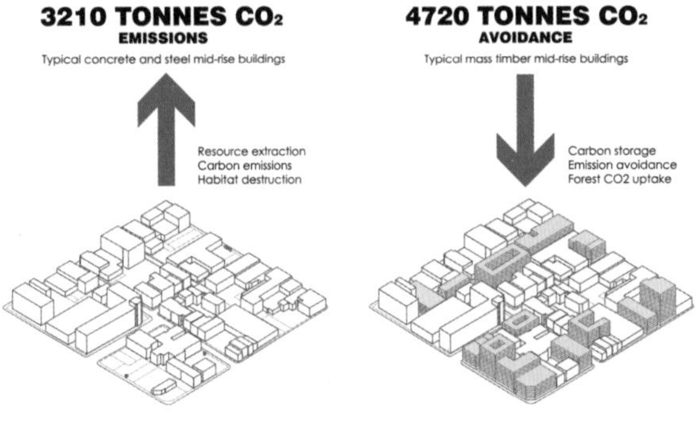

Fig 2.1 Timber City (ongoing) by Gray Organschi envisions a mass timber high-density housing typology for mid-scale cities, replacing steel and concrete frame systems.

Courtesy: Gray Organschi Architecture.

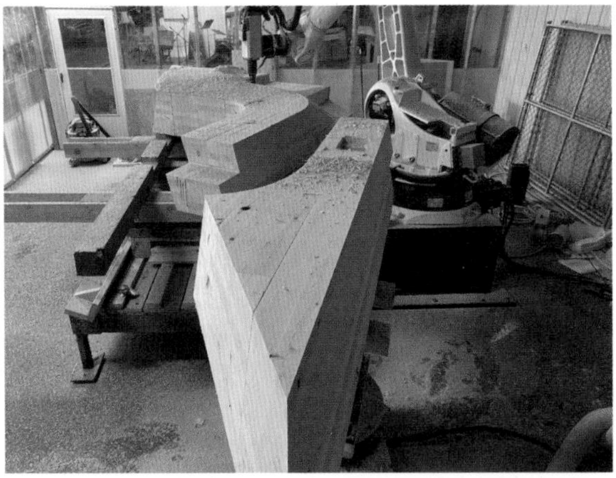

Fig 2.2 A multi-axis industrial robot sculpting volumetric mass-timber building components.

glue-laminated tiers of Alaskan yellow cedar. Components fabricated in the shop as volumetric blocks were transported to the site and erected in large pieces. Maximizing the size of blocks reduces the field labor and relies on the precision of a shop fabrication environment. Optimization involved making repeating blocks that stack to produce a certain "Stepwell" geometry, and erection sequences showed the process of assembling large volumetric parts to form the singular whole. Like all works of architecture, construction involves the assembling of discrete parts into a singular whole. How those parts fit together is key, as every joint is an interface of force, alignment, and expansion / contraction. Minimizing joints allows for more control and less field contingency.

For Stepwell, we opted to use glulam elements that are formed and milled to be assembled in a volumetric way. The volumetric use of mass timber to form the steps and walls of the Stepwell project suggests monolithic construction, more akin to masonry. Indeed, the conception of Stepwell as a cantilevered monolithic shell with a tension tie across the opening operates as a simple structural diagram of unit-to-unit transfer of loads.

The block shell structure of Stepwell presents an alternative to frame and skin applications. The majority of engineered wood construction consists of beams and panels, substitutions or replacements for columns, beams, and slabs. Stepwell is understood as a stereotomic volume that produces spatial and structural configurations that are analogous to vaults and shells rather than frames and skins. It proposes mass timber as a legible form as a means to communicate its embodiment of carbon form.

The final case study for alternative wood constructions takes as its point of departure the sourcing of wood, the capabilities of robotic fabrication, and the expressive potential for legible

Fig 2.3 Stepwell by Höweler + Yoon is a public art installation in Spokane, Washington, showcasing a stereotomic volume using stacked mass timber as spatial and structural configurations rather than as frames and skins.

Fig 2.4 Southeast view (above) and interior (left) of the Ashen Cabin at Ithaca, New York by HANNAH Design Office. The Ashen Cabin looks beyond conventional lumber sizing to incorporate irregular wood strips from diseased trees.

Photo by Andy Chen. Courtesy: HANNAH Design Office.

material and construction ecologies. The Ashen Cabin by HANNAH Design Office looks beyond conventional sourcing for lumber construction materials and finds potential in "waste wood" material. The cabin is constructed of robotically sawn irregular wood strips cut from diseased trees. The timber industry relies on healthy trees and regular lumber formats to achieve the standardization components that the construction industry assumes. Designers Leslie Lok and Sasa Zivkovic sought new uses for the ubiquitous diseased trees infested with emerald ash borer beetles. The use of 3D scanning and robotic sawing techniques allows for better utilization of the tree, including curved and branched sections. The slabbing of irregular wood panels produces a cladding material that is nonstandard, and the irregular components are applied to architectural applications where curvature is needed. The overhang around a projected window is achieved through a series of curved panels. Ashen Cabin finds its form from the source materials' original forms. The branching figure of the tree is still embedded in the expressive form of the house.

In procuring materials from sources outside of traditional "streams," HANNAH Design Office is able to insert new materials into building stock and unlock a natural resource that has been overlooked

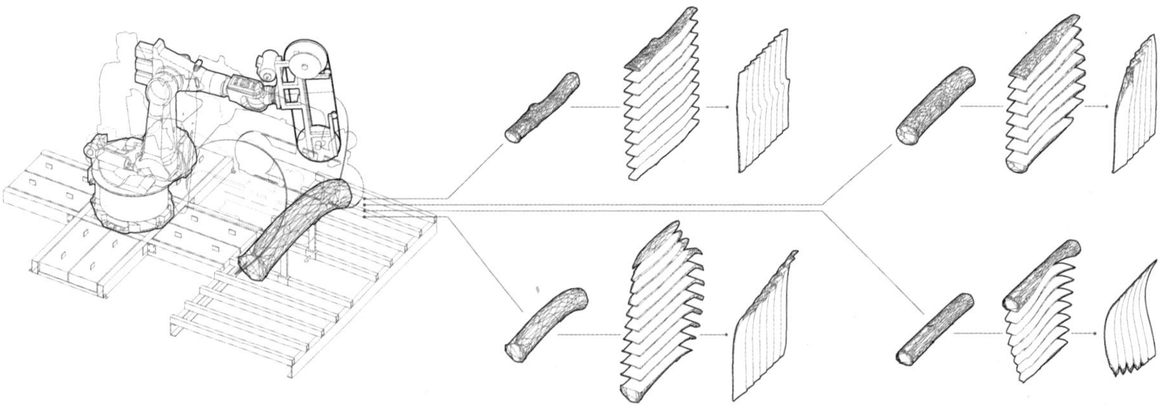

Fig 2.5 HANNAH Design Office employs 3D robotic saws to salvage irregular wood panels from curved and branched timber sections. This fabrication diagram shows robotic slicing of irregular wood geometries, tool paths, and corresponding surface conditions. *Courtesy: HANNAH Design Office.*

by the construction industry. The reordering of the design process that typically begins with straight and planar elements in order to accommodate curvature and the embrace of nonstandard building components points to a formal language that is inherent to the material and not imposed from outside. And the use of diseased lumber, which is the by-product of an ecosystem of invasive species and environmental degradation, allows the Ashen Cabin to serve as a kind of commentary on our connected and impacted planet.

These three sample cases seek to reveal new potentials for engineered and processed wood, not simply as a substitute for conventional construction components, but as alternatives that offer consequential impacts on land use and urban density, open up new reserves of undervalued raw materials, and, importantly, translate these new processes of procurement and production into legible structures. These forms of design research translate into specific formal outcomes: from the sculpted mass timber forms of Stepwell to the dendritic curvatures of the Ashen Cabin's articulations.

Dream

Looking back at the forces that produced the land-use aberration that is the American suburb, we might argue that government investment in the Highway and Defense Act promoted the single-family house as the ultimate goal of the American dream. As a standard set of components with just enough structural capacity to support a two-story house and a typical residential span, the light wood framing system was the primary material system that enabled the proliferation of fast and cheap construction that that dream was built out of. We might similarly argue that the American dream depicted in countless images of the single-family house was a lifestyle image. A powerful image of an alternative lifestyle that became a desire form — a form so powerful that it was sought out by the ascendant middle class. The consequences of the suburban land-use pattern and its impacts on the territory and on the planet continue to be felt as a consequence of a lifestyle.

In the discussion of carbon form, what do we mean when we say the word "form"? Is it a catch-all phase to denote matter? Is it analogous to carbon "stuff"? To carbon "things"? Or is the "form" in carbon form a specific manifestation of the carbon consumption and carbon lifestyle? Is there an inevitable link between style and form? Are lifestyles reliant on and expressive through carbon forms?

Life

While each age broadly embodies the energy paradigm of its time, and the built environment can be read as a materialization of the practices and priorities of its time, the specific architectural strategies for translating these attitudes into architectural form vary widely. Indeed, contemporary discourse around carbon form and the climate crisis has produced a broad array of responses that represent a range of priorities. Urban density and land use address questions of emissions related to transportation, which are bound up in aspirations about an ideal home, social mobility, and lifestyle. Life-cycle approaches to design focus on energy consumption by occupants for heating and cooling as well as operations. Embodied energy and construction ecology consider what materials and systems are being utilized and how much energy went into the making, transporting, and constructing of the building. Making these various issues legible is another important factor for design that seeks to change public opinions about energy and environment and enlist others to make more sustainable choices.

A comprehensive approach to addressing carbon form must engage in an array of these issues. No one approach will solve the problem, just as no one building will change the course of the impending climate emergency. What is needed is systemic change that affects building practices broadly, in ways that are easy for the nonexpert user, homeowner, and consumer to understand. To achieve real impact requires a combination of approaches: policy and regulation (energy codes, zoning controls), information campaigns (disseminating best practices), tools for design and implementation (simulation software), and accessible alternatives (choices in materials and systems). Design research that expands choices and disseminates information about best practices is essential to systemic change.

By learning from the power of lifestyle imagery — and its forms — and being conscious of the necessity of life-cycle considerations in planning, designers must bring the two terms into alignment and offer alternatives that incorporate a broad range of approaches, including embodied and operational understandings of energy ranging from the scale of the unit of construction to the territorial scale of procurement and production. The pairings of the terms "life cycle" and "lifestyle" offer some clues toward a possible way forward. The single building, no matter how "green," optimized, and certified, will not avert the climate crisis. The best hope for a green building is as a data point in the cumulative body of research and a road map for best practices for subsequent buildings. Each building is at once an embodiment of material and energy and a broadcast mechanism to communicate that embodiment. It is a component in a campaign to persuade others to change over from business-as-usual to alternative approaches to building and dwelling.

References

[1] Andreas Malm, *Fossil Capital: The Rise of Steam-Power and the Roots of Global Warming* (London: Verso Books, 2016), 12.

[2] Elisa Iturbe, "Architecture and the Death of Carbon Modernity," in *Log 47: Overcoming Carbon Form*, ed. Cynthia Davidson and Elisa Iturbe (New York: Anyone Corporation, 2019), 11-24.

[3] Iturbe, 24

[4] Fredric Jameson, "Postmodernism and Consumer Society," in *The Anti-Aesthetic: Essays on Postmodern Culture*, ed. Hal Foster (Port Townsend, WA: Bay Press, 1983), 111-125.

[5] Antoine Picon, *The Materiality of Architecture* (Minneapolis: University of Minnesota Press, 2021).

[6] Kiel Moe, *Unless: The Seagram Building Construction Ecology* (New York: Actar D, 2020).

[7] Moe, 28.

[8] Moe, 56.

[9] Barry Lord, *Art & Energy: How Culture Changes* (Washington, DC: American Alliance of Museums, 2014).

[10] Ironically, it was a massive office building in lower Manhattan that so grossly obscured the light and air of its neighbours that it triggered the 1916 Zoning Resolution. That building was the Equitable Building.

Chapter 3
Beyond Sustainability

Heng Chye Kiang
Ho Puay-peng
Lakshmi Menon

These three essays present the trajectory of SDE's transformation at different scales: the first from an urban / precinct lens, the second through an architectural / adaptive reuse standpoint, and the third via a granular, spatial narrative. These voices trace the history of the school, its infrastructural commitment to the educational and sociocultural landscape in Singapore, and its experiential and pedagogical effects on the community.

Two Different Approaches to Sustainability in SDE's Campus Rejuvenation by Heng Chye Kiang presents a holistic overview of the SDE 1 & 3 project, tracing its history, the chronology of campus transformation projects, and the significance of a multi-pronged (pedagogical, environmental, and symbolic) agenda. *Spatializing Sustainability: Housing a School of Architecture* by Ho Puay-peng illustrates the responsibilities and challenges, the symbolism, and the aspirations that surround the design of SDE 1 & 3. Finally, *Carbon Dichotomies* by Lakshmi Menon presents an insider's perspective of the SDE transformation: inhabiting the old, new, and the in-between environments.

Two Different Approaches to Sustainability in SDE's Campus Rejuvenation

Heng Chye Kiang

As a leading global center for the study and research of architecture and the built environment, the School of Design and Environment (SDE) at the National University of Singapore has been consistently engaged in research and education in architectural and environmental issues pertinent to Singapore, the Southeast Asian region, and the world in general since its founding more than six decades ago. From investigations into tropical, climate-responsive architecture and the symbols of nation building to greening the island-state and formulating responses to tackle the severe shortage in housing, SDE has always been at the forefront of addressing topical critical issues confronting Singapore's society. More recently, the school embarked on a concerted effort to renew its campus of three buildings to address changing pedagogical practices, increasing global concern for sustainability, and climate change.

Fig 3.1.1 SDE 1 courtyard before (top) and after (bottom) the renovation.

Photos by (top) Lakshmi Menon and (bottom) Ong Chan Hao.

A Little History

The School of Design and Environment began its history in 1958 as the Department of Architecture of the Singapore Polytechnic on Prince Edward Road. Its sister departments — the Department of Building and Estate Management and the Department of Building Science — were founded four years later. Together, they were transferred to the University of Singapore in 1969 and became the Faculty of Architecture, subsequently renamed the Faculty of Architecture and Building in 1972. After a stint of about six years at Lady Hill Road, it became the first faculty to move to its new home — the buildings now known as SDE 1, 2, and 3 — on the new Kent Ridge Campus in 1976. An minor renovation in the late 1980s added an extension to connect SDE 1 to SDE 3, thereby defining a central courtyard for the cluster of buildings. The faculty was ultimately renamed the School of Design and Environment (SDE) in 2000, a fitting change in view of a global shift in focus and the preoccupation of the faculty with the topical issues of design and environmental sustainability.

Also, important to note is that the school has grown significantly in size and in the number of programs offered since the late 1990s. During my tenure as dean of the SDE from 2007 to 2016, the growth in student population, shifts in pedagogical paradigms and technologies, the state of the academic buildings, and the concern for environmental sustainability created the necessary conditions for me to persuade the university in 2009 of the need to rejuvenate our built infrastructure. A plan for the addition of a new 8,500 m² wing (SDE 4) and the renovation of the three existing buildings was conditionally accepted by the university administration in the following year.

Naturally, the decision to design and build SDE 4 as a net-zero-energy building and, equally importantly, to design the building as a pedagogical tool that instructs and inspires our students by its design and operation was unanimously supported by all faculty members. SDE 4 will become an instrument as well as a subject for various types of building performance and technology-related research.

Fundraising was particularly difficult in the aftermath of the 2008 global financial crisis, and the university eventually undertook in 2013 to fund the entire rejuvenation programme, starting with SDE 4. The building, as a *tour de force* interpretation of contemporary tropical architecture, borrows vernacular principles and boasts design features that not only deliver user health and comfort in the tropical context, but are also meticulously programmed to be highly energy efficient. SDE 4 employs an innovative hybrid cooling system that effectively manages the building's energy consumption to supply 100% fresh precooled air, albeit with a higher usage temperature and humidity levels than in a conventional system. An elevated air speed (via ceiling fans) further augments the cooling. This feature reaped benefits during the COVID-19 pandemic, when air recirculation in enclosed indoor spaces became a health concern. Upon its completion in 2019, SDE 4 became the first building in Southeast Asia to be awarded the stringent Zero Energy Certification by the International Living Future Institute; 100% of SDE 4's energy needs (calculated on a net annual basis) is supplied by more than 1200 photovoltaic panels installed on its large overhanging roof. Following the success of this award-winning building, the National University of Singapore plans to use SDE 4 as a design blueprint to progressively upgrade and develop up to fifty net-zero-energy buildings by 2030.

Fig 3.1.2 SDE 4, the first purpose-built net-zero-energy building in Singapore, serves as a design prototype for the campus decarbonization plan. *Photo by Rory Gardiner.*

A Holistic Approach

Concurrent with the design and implementation of SDE 4, the plans for SDE 1, 2, and 3 were being developed; these, however, adopted a slightly different approach. As these were some of the earliest buildings erected on the University's campus, retaining and adapting them to satisfy evolving pedagogical needs and a new sustainability agenda became imperative. For SDE 1 & 3, long-desired spatial additions and alterations (such as an internal multistory shared central atrium and a formal canopied drop-off in SDE 3 leading to a green heart for the faculty building cluster) were implemented in addition to the features needed to fulfill current regulatory requirements and sustainability targets. Although the interior spaces were rationalized and redesigned, most of the existing buildings and their 1970s structural frames were retained. A low-energy hybrid cooling system has been deployed, with the result that the renovated building consumes very little energy. An attractive new champagne gold colored aluminum *brise-soleil* frame replaces the original ubiquitous grey louver system, blending with the adjacent similarly tinted perforated metal sunscreen at SDE 4.

There are several tangible and intangible merits to the conservation and reuse of the existing SDE 1 and SDE 3 buildings. These benefits range from environmental and economic to socio-cultural and emotional — the very constituent pillars of sustainability. To begin with, the reuse of SDE 1 & 3 has significant cost savings. As they are in good structural condition, the cost of renovating the buildings is substantially lower than that of demolition, site clearance, and reconstruction.

Even more important, perhaps, are the environmental benefits involved in the renovation and reuse of the existing building. The construction industry has long been a significant contributor to environmental damages such as high energy consumption, greenhouse gas emissions, solid waste generation, and resource depletion. Together, building and construction account for 39% of all carbon emissions globally, with operational emissions accounting for 28%.[1] Historically, building regulations have focused largely on reducing energy use (as opposed to emissions) from the operational stage because of its traditional dominance of life-cycle emissions. Much attention has been paid to strategies for the sustainable design of new buildings to mitigate the negative environmental impacts to achieve net-zero operational carbon worldwide. SDE 4, mentioned earlier, is a case in point.

Yet operational carbon emissions are only part of the story. The life cycle of a building is generally divided into the construction, operation, and demolition stages. Carbon emissions are released not only during operation but also during the other two stages, including the emissions associated with materials production and construction before the building is in operation, and the carbon emissions due to demolition and disposal which occur during the end-of-life stage. These emissions associated with materials and the construction process, commonly known as embodied carbon, have been primarily overlooked historically while accounting for around 11% of all global carbon emissions.[2] As buildings have become more operationally energy efficient with advanced design and technologies, the relative significance of tackling embodied carbon emissions is increasing.[3] Research suggests that demolition and equivalent new building construction will take decades to achieve the savings derived from the rehabilitation and reuse of existing buildings, in particular due to the negative environmental impacts of the construction process and the manufacturing and delivery of new materials.[4] Hence, it is necessary to promote renovation rather than demolition, which reduces reliance on carbon-intensive raw materials.

The School of Design and Environment is progressively expanding its sustainability targets from net-zero-energy buildings to integrated zero carbon developments. The innovative renovation of SDE 1 & 3, which retains its original structural frame, is a step in this direction. When structures are conserved and reused, energy and emissions are saved in two ways. First, not only is the embodied energy of the existing building saved, including the embodied energy of materials and construction; the amount of energy to process the construction materials and assemble the building is also saved. Second, the demolition energy for the existing building would also be saved, assuming that the original building has to be demolished for the new building to be constructed on its site.[5] By applying the building concept model from Advisory Council on Historic Preservation (1979),which measured the embodied energy of the existing building by assessing the building type and gross floor area, the embodied energy of SDE 3 alone is around 233,650 gigajoules (GJ).[6] This saved embodied energy is equivalent to about 50,700 tons of carbon dioxide, or approximately 228 km^2 of forests sequestering CO2 for a year. Apart from the saving of embodied energy and carbon emissions, conserving buildings rather than demolishing them can also significantly reduce the number of landfills. In 2019, construction and demolition debris contributed nearly 20% of the total waste generated in Singapore.[7] By 2030, Singapore aims to send about 30% less waste to Semakau Landfill in order to extend its lifespan beyond the estimated 2035.[8] The demolition of structures is estimated to account for 90% of total construction and demolition debris, while waste generated during construction accounts for less than 10%.[9] Renovating, instead of replacing, the original structures of SDE 1 & 3 is therefore beneficial for mitigating negative environmental impacts in terms of demolition waste.

Perhaps less quantifiable, but equally important, are the precious memories evoked by SDE 1 & 3. As one of the first buildings erected at the National University of Singapore, their conservation is not only about monetary savings and embodied energy, but also about retaining the spirit and identity of the School of Design and Environment. More than simply a tie to the past and to the generations of students who toiled in its studios, the very physical existence of SDE 3, for instance, is also an inspiration to current and future students when they realize that many of our nation's most eminent architects worked, like them, in these very same spaces.

In short, whereas the net-zero-energy SDE 4 is an excellent example of new architecture that fulfills the need for additional teaching spaces while simultaneously addressing issues of environmental sustainability, architectural pedagogy, and critical interpretation of tropical architecture, the renovation and reuse of SDE 1 & 3 is likewise an elegant answer to new pedagogical demands while holistically tackling the issue of sustainability in terms of environmental, economic, and social values.

The author acknowledges the research contribution of Xiang Xiaotong in the development of this essay.

References

[1] World Green Building Council, "Bringing Embodied Carbon Upfront: Coordinated Action for the Building and Construction Sector to Tackle Embodied Carbon," Sept. 2019, https://www.worldgbc.org/sites/default/files/WorldGBC_Bringing_Embodied_Carbon_Upfront.pdf.

[2] World Green Building Council, 07.

[3] Sheila Conejos, Craig Langston, and Jim Smith, "Designing for Better Building Adaptability: A Comparison of AdaptSTAR and ARP Models," *Habitat International* 41 (2014): 85–91, https://doi.org/10.1016/j.habitatint.2013.07.002.

[4] E. Eric Boschmann and Jessica N. Gabriel, "Urban Sustainability and the LEED Rating System: Case Studies on the Role of Regional Characteristics and Adaptive Reuse in Green Building in Denver and Boulder, Colorado," *The Geographical Journal* 179, no. 3 (Jan. 2013): 221–233, https://doi.org/10.1111/j.1475-4959.2012.00493.x.

[5] A. Duffy, A. Nerguti, C. E. Purcell, and P. Cox, *Understanding Carbon in the Historic Environment, Scoping Study, Final Report* (London: Historic England, 2019).

[6] United States Advisory Council on Historic Preservation, *Assessing the Energy Conservation Benefits of Historic Preservation: Methods and Examples* (Washington, DC: Government Print Office, 1979).

[7] National Environment Agency, "Waste Management: Waste Statistics and Overall Recycling," 2019, accessed Nov. 8, 2021, https://www.nea.gov.sg/our-services/waste-management/waste-statistics-and-overall-recycling.

[8] Audrey Tan, "Singapore Aims to Send One-Third Less Waste to Semakau Landfill by 2030: Amy Khor," *The Straits Times*, Aug. 30, 2019, https://www.straitstimes.com/singapore/environment/spore-aims-to-send-one-third-less-waste-to-semakau-landfill-by-2030-amy-khor.

[9] United States Environmental Protection Agency, "Sustainable Management of Construction and Demolition Materials," 2016, accessed Nov. 8, 2021, https://www.epa.gov/smm/sustainable-management-construction-and-demolition-materials.

Spatializing Sustainability: Housing a School of Architecture

Ho Puay-peng

Creating a building for a school of architecture that perfectly embodies the vision, priority, and values of that school has, historically, been a challenge. The identity of a school is usually synonymous with its architecture; a great example would be the Glasgow School of Art designed by Charles Rennie Mackintosh and constructed between 1897 – 1909. More contemporary examples abound, such as Rudolph Hall (Yale, Paul Rudolph, 1963), Gund Hall (Harvard, John Andrews, 1972), Milstein Hall (Cornell, OMA, 2011), Abedian School of Architecture Building (Bond, CRAB Studio, 2013), and the Melbourne School of Design (Melbourne, John Wardle Architects / NADAAA, 2014), to name just a few outstanding examples. It has often been said that the school of architecture building that the students occupy for the long duration of their degree serves an important educational role. All occupants, including students, faculty, and visitors, subconsciously imbibe the embodied values of the school through its architecture. The building can and should serve as a lived-in lab and facilitate many student learning opportunities. Most school of architecture buildings are architectural icons, defining their era's formal and stylistic breakthroughs. The spatial experience of the building should be innovative in order for students to learn from and emulate it.

The renovation of the buildings for the School of Design and Environment envisions a learning environment that supports sustainability during a period of climate emergency and engenders inclusivity and social cohesion in a predominantly virtual, post-pandemic era. These are values encapsulated in the broad definition of "design excellence." In redeveloping SDE 1 & 3, one of the earliest clusters of buildings on the Kent Ridge campus, the new design aims to preserve the memories carried on by decades of school alumni while also preserving the lineage of Singapore's post-independence modernist buildings and sustaining the identity of the extended SDE community. This adaptive reuse showcases the responsibility and power of design to leverage the built history of the campus in crafting learning spaces that will positively impact student lives and enable them to create better futures. From a conservation standpoint, the discourse around preserving built heritage through adaptive reuse has, in recent years, moved away from aesthetic / visual qualities to social and communal values; SDE's effort is an example of this shift. At the same time, the school has a responsibility to promote critical design interventions and solutions in light of the carbon challenges that we face today. Design excellence is, therefore, also a vision for action.

In Singapore, the "en-bloc" model of redevelopment (demolition and upgradation of older housing blocks for optimized land use) has lately been subject to concerns due to skyrocketing market prices.[1] Local groups have been calling for a re-evaluation of this model with the goal of preventing unnecessary demolition and subsequent social disruption. In addition, there have been growing conversations on conserving modernist structures for adaptive reuse, particularly ones that were part of the urban renewal drive in the 1970s and are therefore representative of the then-young nation's ability to develop cutting-edge design.[2] Internationally, we see a growing impetus for adaptive reuse, brought to the fore most recently with the awarding of the 2021 Pritzker Prize to the French architects Anne Lacaton and Jean-Philippe Vassal for their oeuvre of adaptive reuse projects. Recognizing the environmental costs of buildings from an energy and carbon emissions standpoint, Lacaton and Vassal develop ways of adapting existing spaces to meet new needs.[3] SDE anticipates similar positive trends in Southeast Asia and seeks to foster a pedagogical shift toward the development of critical thinking and design skills in these areas.

Since 2017, the Department of Architecture (DOA) has embarked on a journey of design excellence informed by research, integrating technological, social, and aesthetic concerns and knowledge into a livable and inspiring environment. As the department is home to many allied design disciplines — architecture, landscape architecture, planning, urban design, integrated sustainable design, and heritage conservation — our latest renovation strives to create an interdisciplinary heart for the school, one complete with experientially stimulating and environmentally responsible learning and working spaces.

Sustainability and Pedagogy

The decision to plan for a major renovation of SDE 1 & 3 instead of rebuilding was a significant move in championing sustainable development. The project successfully conserved the modernist architectural form and massing of the buildings while also preserving their embodied carbon. This decision is aligned with NUS's sustainability goal of reducing waste and minimizing our individual and organizational carbon footprints.

Sustainability as a strategy for design has been with us for decades now, and architecture schools around the world have researched, taught, and practiced sustainability for an equally long time. In this era of climate emergencies, sustainable design needs to become a cornerstone of design curricula. This is borne out of UNESCO's sustainable development goals (SDGs) in view of the worldwide cultural, community, and climate crisis. These goals endeavor to achieve an inclusive and peaceful environment with access to responsible sources of energy and water. They also promote well-being and quality education. At the same time, sustainability has permeated our department's curriculum and become a key objective of multidisciplinary degrees in environmental management, building performance, and diagnostics. The Master of Science in Integrated Sustainable Design (MSc ISD), the Master of Science in Environmental Management (MSc MEM), and the Master of Science in Building Performance and Sustainability (MSc BPS) programs address architecture and urban design as interrelated systems, a design strategy adopted in the renovation of SDE 1 & 3. Our newest addition, the Master of Arts in Architectural Conservation (MAArC), explores project conservation, adaptive reuse, and rethinking the carbon economy. Distinctively Asian, the program offers a contextual perspective on regional diversity, comprehensive knowledge development, and essential hands-on training for a range of careers in building conservation and the related fields.

Tropicality

Architecture must be rooted in the local context and express a place's specificity. Climate and local culture are key elements for design articulation. A building needs to respond to the local climate — also a learning point in our curriculum. Combatting the sun, harnessing the wind and rain, and capturing the light have guided the design of the SDE 1 & 3 building envelope and the interior. One example is the choice of folded horizontal louvers with varying gaps and angles that allow light and view to be part of the interior while blocking off the harsh afternoon sun. The louvers are also a reminder of a prominent element in the buildings' original facade. This attention to detail, one grounded in research and memory while addressing the climatic challenge, is an expression of design excellence.

Lush greenery is also a fundamental element of the tropics. SDE 1 & 3 are located within a typical tropical landscape with mature trees with large canopies. The buildings form one of the gateways into the central campus that leads to the departments of engineering, computing, the arts, and the social sciences, as well as the central library. By treating the gateway building as part of a landscape continuum and including a vibrant vertical garden, the renovation project locates itself firmly and proudly in the Singaporean context.

Openness and Transparency

The primary value of the school of architecture is to provide a platform for students and staff to explore design issues collaboratively and independently. An atmosphere of sharing and transparency is important for students, and this should be reflected in the architecture. Thus, the interior of the department's office is essentially an open space with large windows facing the courtyard, allowing the light and green of the landscape courtyard to filter through. This atrium is the totemic space of the Department of Architecture. It is easy to envision various activities happening here; its three-level flexible space allows for gatherings, events, and casual encounters. At times, it can be a solemn space for lectures; at others, a celebratory space for design reviews. It might be a working space at the beginning of the day and a reflective and communal space during the night. Moving away from the atrium, one enters the expansive studios. Again, openness and luminosity are the key guiding principles for these three levels of the design, which are now radically distinct from their former state. Here, in spaces that they can modify themselves, SDE students can collaborate and explore design ideas:

even ventilation can be visualized and spatialized in a studio that is fully open to the exterior.

The openness of these new studio spaces sustains every student's journey at the school; not only does it promote their well-being (and that of their tutors), but it also symbolically expresses inclusivity and sustainability. The ultimate objective is for the students to take ownership of their own education and learning pathways. We believe that the building that houses a school of architecture is both a pedagogical tool and a symbolic statement of the school's values. For the National University of Singapore, that means sustainability, wellness, and design excellence, and the newly renovated SDE 1 & 3 buildings are the physical manifestation of these values.

References

[1] Aradhana Aravindan, "Singapore's 'en-Bloc' Redevelopment Fever May Be Cooling," *Reuters*, Mar. 16, 2018, https://www.reuters.com/article/us-singapore-property-analysis-idUSKCN1GSORM.

[2] Singapore Heritage Society, *Too Young to Die: Giving New Lease of Life to Singapore's Modernist Icons* (Singapore: Singapore Heritage Society, 2018).

[3] Laura Raskin, "The Pritzker Prize Honors French Architects Lacaton & Vassal," *Architectural Record*, Mar. 16, 2021, https://www.architecturalrecord.com/articles/15036-the-pritzker-prize-honors-french-architects-lacaton-vassal.

A personal predilection for the ever-growing literature about the hot and humid climate led me to enroll at the School of Design and Environment (SDE) at the National University of Singapore (NUS) in 2015. My engagement with the school — first as a student, then as research staff, and later as a member of the Special Projects team — marked the onset of a critical period in the school's engagement with new (SDE 4) and upgraded (SDE 1, 2, & 3) campus infrastructure projects.[1] This essay recounts some individual and collective observations during this transitional period of inhabiting the old, new, and the in-between environments. The narrative focuses on my evolving experience with the campus buildings and offers an insider's perspective on the operation and use of spaces during the redevelopment process, one with serendipitous outcomes. Titled *Carbon Dichotomies*, this essay employs semantics to anchor larger discussions that are beyond the scope of the essay around the duality of design intents and its carbon outcomes.

Old-Fashioned with a Twist

One of my earliest visual recollections of the school, in late 2015, is a warm sense of familiarity with its postcolonial, modernist aesthetic — a leitmotif prevalent across the public institutions of the tropics. Fronting the NUS Kent Ridge Campus, the SDE 1 & 3 blocks exuded a heavy, authoritarian presence over the naturally undulating topography, ensuring a functional, seamless environment to study in. The verdant landscape with its immaculately pruned rain trees and tiger-grass-lined car parks defined a stark presence in the evergreen equatorial context.[2] A prominent yellow ocher stair core on the grey palette of the buildings offered an unusual zing to its appearance.

Past versus future: Upon entry, the buildings tended to infuse visitors with the weight of their history, and by extension the multitude of former lives that participated in their forty years of existence. Ad-hoc renovations to the buildings likewise spoke of the slow pace of the design profession, contrasting with the rapidly evolving ecosystem of design education.[3] The most striking quality of these buildings was their enforcement of levels and intermediary planes, primarily employed to navigate the steep topography of the site. The buildings encouraged a bodily preference for the horizontal over the vertical, while passively enabling hierarchy through the stacking of spatial programs. The users, students and faculty, were constantly on the move, increasingly engaged with screens and devices than with the buildings' physicality itself as they constantly adapted to keep up with the aspirations of a world-class institution.

Fish-Tank Environmentalism

The increasingly tech-based nature of design education demanded that students and faculty congregate in large studios, lecture halls, or computer labs. These high-occupancy spaces were tucked away deep into the floor plans, sealed from the outdoors. This seclusion was enabled by a blanket of artificial lighting and air conditioned down to 18 degrees (i.e., freezing cold for my tropically conditioned physiology). The internal layout strategically positioned faculty offices on the periphery overlooking student cohorts behind glass partitions informally known as the "fish tank" studios. The certainty of desk space and safe storage and the cultural fixation with temperate-like, air-conditioned spaces meant that students occupied these uncomfortable study environments despite all the aforementioned odds.

Teaching versus engaging: On a scholastic plane, we were being tutored by the best minds and spirited peer groups, building the knowledge and capacity to combat a rapidly warming and densifying built environment. This was in stark contrast to our spatial experiences inside the SDE buildings, which were disengaged from the passage of time and the alternating, daily cycles of rains and shine characteristic of the tropical rainforest climate in Singapore.

Standard versus adaptive: That said, there was a collective awareness that the buildings were outdated vessels for infrastructure systems, burdened with the glorious purpose of delivering user comfort. Central to this inquiry was the definition of comfort in the tropics, distinct from the temperate concept of comfort. We sat in drafty lecture theaters, listening to lessons on climate-responsive architecture, adaptive comfort models, and how to revive the agency of architecture to provide for occupant health and well-being.[4] The new lexicon mirrored the improved indoor comfort standards, particularly air-conditioning complemented by passive design features to minimize energy consumption.[5]

Building Systems and Human Data Points

Transitioning from student life into the research staff system improved my access to both student and staff spaces. The opportunity opened up a wider gambit of spaces and spatial experiences that offered insights into the complexity of institutional spaces and the effort involved in aligning building programs and systems with occupant behavior.

Without versus within: In line with NUS campus guidelines, entry into most indoor spaces are governed by access cards, without which user movement remains restricted to the outdoors. Apart from maintaining security, the cards streamline room occupancy and the energy use linked to air-conditioning, lighting, and usage of electrical outlets within spaces. The very act of inhabiting the spaces feeds into a larger repository of building systems use data, benefiting the many building science research projects in the school.[6] These experiences, situated within the same research ecosystem, validated the potential of evidence-based design and research by design inputs awaiting real-world manifestations.

From 2017 to 2019, the SDE campus was visibly transforming. With SDE 4 breaking ground on an adjacent site, and SDE 1 & 3 undergoing a scheduled relocation of occupants ahead of its renovation, the distinctions between the design school and the construction site began to blur. It was challenging and equally exciting to witness this transformation from its epicenter. On one hand, the inconvenience of construction next door, the internal displacement of staff and student facilities, and the economizing of indoor environmental quality dictated new modes of engaging with the environment. On the other hand, the optimism of the design and performative aspirations of the upcoming projects made it possible to overcome the difficult conditions.

In-Between Spaces

The limited availability of functional spaces required us to adapt to a hybrid work culture, including remote working on campus, much ahead of the pandemic. The absurdity of being uncommitted to a personal cubicle and the newness of space-sharing with peers was not without its benefits; however, it required unlearning conventional study and work habits.

Networked versus isolated: On a social level, it was inspiring to share work environments with the young students and members of the senior faculty, hypothetically dismantling the hierarchy embedded within academia. The hot-desking culturemeant minimalist work supplies contained within light backpacks; no more heavy desktop computers, less paper, and more digital outputs.[7] The relative lack of predictability in the coworking environment brought a sense of urgency to task and meeting schedules, and any decision-making was driven by this frugal engagement with the indoor environment. Given the limitations of indoor comfort, hot-desking spaces with views to the outside (and consequently better productivity and mental well-being) were highly sought after.

Visible versus invisible: It was evident that the opportunities of knowledge were no longer restricted to classrooms, libraries, or personal devices, but instead had expanded into these ephemeral, in-between spaces.

Exposed versus concealed: The unveiling of the existing building ducts and deep false ceilings on site revealed the entangled complexities of MVAC (Mechanical Ventilation and Air Conditioning) systems that work to keep buildings comfortably habitable. As these systems were progressively disabled, semi-outdoor, naturally ventilated spaces adjoining courtyards and corridors reclaimed prominence. When removed from the luxury of being indoors, one grows more attuned to the dynamics of the surrounding natural environment and the political act of sharing a space with others from different walks of life.

Onward and Upward

The opening of the net-zero-energy SDE 4 building in early 2019 set an important precedent for future developments on campus. It established a new sensorial quality to learning spaces through its tropical architecture and the innovative hybrid cooling system (HCS) that leverages adaptive comfort for energy savings. That the accrued design and research intelligence of the school is evidenced by SDE 4's creation is a matter of pride for the academic community.

As part of the Special Projects team, it was inspiring to witness the school's in-house expertise in design thinking, project management, and systems engineering come together to create and occupy a livable and sustainable environment. The experience colored my perceptions of design choices and their carbon / energy implications, giving me a better understanding of the reparative design approach in SDE 1 & 3 (detailed in Chapter 5) and its significance and relevance in the wider context. The period of transformation was marked by a value shift from an externalized, resource-consumptive linear model to one that is more humane, skin-felt, and experiential — in essence, a circular resource-regeneration model. As built environment professionals, having a world-class education is undeniably important for designing better buildings. However, understanding the complexities of our built environment and leveraging that experience to judiciously operate within superlative buildings is an equally critical and complex skill, more so now than ever in our post-pandemic, climate-apocalyptic contexts.

References

[1] The SDE Special Projects team is a multifaceted group of architects and energy and sustainability experts who offer in-house design expertise to oversee a portfolio of campus projects. The design team leads a process that emphasizes translational research wherein students and staff are consulted on SDE sustainability and design innovations.

[2] Situated one degree north of the equator, Singapore experiences a tropical rainforest climate (Köppen climate classification Af), with no true distinct seasons. The stable climate, with evenly spread rainfall and warmth, allows most rainforest trees to be evergreen, sometimes even eclipsing buildings. Rhett Butler, "Rainforest Structure and Character," *Mongabay.com*, Jul. 27, 2012, accessed Nov. 23, 2021, https://rainforests.mongabay.com/0201.htm.

[3] Diana Budds, "Rem Koolhaas: 'Architecture Has A Serious Problem Today,'" *Fast Company*, May 22, 2016, accessed Nov. 9, 2021, https://www.fastcompany.com/3060135/rem-koolhaas-architecture-has-a-serious-problem-today.

[4] "The adaptive model is based on the idea that outdoor climate influences indoor comfort because humans can adapt to different temperatures during different times of the year." Richard de Dear and G. S. Brager, "Towards an Adaptive Model of Thermal Comfort and Preference," *ASHRAE Transactions* 104, no. 1 (1998): 145-167, https://escholarship.org/uc/item/4qq2p9c6.

[5] "…[conventional] air conditioning accounts for about 60% of the energy consumption in non-residential buildings in Singapore." Gabriel Happle, Erik Wilhelm, Jimeno A. Fonseca, and Arno Schlueter, "Determining Air-Conditioning Usage Patterns in Singapore from Distributed, Portable Sensor," *Energy Procedia* 122 (2017): 313-318, https://doi.org/10.1016/j.egypro.2017.07.328.

[6] Prageeth Jayathissa, Matias Quintana, Mahmoud Abdelrahman, and Clayton Miller, "Humans-as-a-Sensor for Buildings—Intensive Longitudinal Indoor Comfort Models," *Buildings* 10, no. 10 (2020): 174.

[7] Gretchen Spreitzer, Peter Bacevice, and Lyndon Garrett, "Why People Thrive in Coworking Spaces," *Harvard Business Review*, Sept. 2015, https://hbr.org/2015/05/why-people-thrive-in-coworking-spaces.

Chapter 4
Carbon Transformations at the Equator

Erik L'Heureux

"I'd like to share a revelation that I've had during my time here. It came to me when I tried to classify your species, and I realized that you're not actually mammals. Every mammal on this planet instinctively develops a natural equilibrium with the surrounding environment, but you humans do not. You move to an area, and you multiply and multiply until every natural resource is consumed and the only way you can survive is to spread to another area. There is another organism on this planet that follows the same pattern. Do you know what it is? A virus. Human beings are a disease, a cancer of this planet. You're a plague, and we are the cure."

— Agent Smith, *The Matrix*
(dir. Lana and Lilly Wachowski), 1999

Fig 4.1 Film still of Hugo Weaving as Agent Smith from *The Matrix* (1999).

Courtesy: Warner Bros. Entertainment Inc.

Architecture as a Virus

In the 1999 cult science-fiction classic *The Matrix*, character Agent Smith reclassifies the human species based on their consumptive practices that have wreaked havoc on the ecosystems across the world. From Smith's AI vantage point, humans are not mammals but a virus, spreading their destructive practices globally. Humans have consumed resources at an increasingly unsustainable rate, coating the earth in human detritus, petroleum and its byproducts being the more durable remnants. COVID-19, assuming a zoonotic transfer occurred, is just one of the more visible and terrifying outcomes of this Anthropocene epoch and symbolic of the planetary imbalance that humans have created.

Architecture engages in virus-like activities: pulverizing limestone for cement, sucking up riverbeds for sand aggregate, excavating stone for paving, tearing down forests and jungles for lumber, and drawing up petroleum for gaskets, membranes, laminates, and waterproofing. Large holes are carved into the earth to expose aluminum and iron deposits, which are then scraped and scoured, shipped across oceans, formed by heat and pressure, and stacked, welded, and fastened by human and fossil fuel-powered machine labor. Carbon-based fuels, abstractly termed "energy," are also sucked from the earth's depths. The straws of drilling rigs and ocean platforms dot land and sea alike, pumping and slurping, refining and burning to shape the needs of buildings, cities, and urbanization — all virus-like processes. Carbon underpins this built infrastructure both operationally through its use and embodied in its structure: a landscape based on a hydrocarbon diet; and a resulting "carbon form."[1]

Externalities

Architecture makes violent acts on the earth legitimate and palatable by transforming raw material into building through the processes of design. Both conceptually and representationally, abstraction is at the core of the design process. Abstraction externalizes. It serves to compartmentalize and sanitize material until it is distinct from the ecosystem from which it is extracted. Architects use drawings, lines, vectors, codes, and symbols to separate and diminish materials' intersections with territory. For example, a line on a drawing sheet or a vector on the computer screen signifies a stone or steel hollow section in shape and dimension. The stone's shape and dimension take precedence over where it came from or the labor involved in its making. With contemporary Building Integrated Management (BIM), carbon can be calculated, but there is little room for input from the extraction site, the labor involved, or communities affected. Drawings dominate, abstracting and externalizing materials at the expense of the planet's health.

The history of abstraction can be traced to Brunelleschi and later Leon Battista Alberti, who advocated for a representational method relying on lines and geometry, thereby centering geometric and mathematical pursuits at the core of architecture.[2] Abstraction and geometrical concerns freed architecture from its material burden and shifted the discipline into the domain of mental imagination. Narratives, concepts, and visions are then the architect's primary mode of thinking, an intellectual pursuit of seduction and instruction separate from the physicality of material procurement, transformation, and fabrication.[3] By relying on lines and geometry architects censure, hide, and conceal ecological impacts by the very act of abstraction — removing that which gets in the way of the architectural vision. By censuring its more significant, ecosystem-wide impacts, abstraction works to fluidly transform material into building, building into architecture, and architecture into design culture, with each phase further shedding its relationship with pollution, environmental degradation, and affected communities.

The bifurcation between architecture and the builder only magnifies the distance between design and ecological impact, isolating the architect's agency. The effects on the planet's health are externalized when an architect specifies one form of concrete composition, steel type, or timber species for geometric, formal, structural, or aesthetic reasons. The architect is typically removed from the knowledge of where steel is being sourced from or what riverbed is providing the aggregate. In this way, the cancer of this planet is encouraged and enabled by the separation of architects from construction, fundamentally complicit in Agent Smith's allegation of viral spread.

The planet's ecosystem might not be totally lost if the domain shifts the conversation from the cultural concerns of abstraction to one that integrates the externalities of materials as a necessary part of the design process. Architects have the agency to recraft the discipline to different values resisting the "cancer of this planet." These new values would prioritize integration rather than externalization, an entanglement of geometry *and* carbon, form *and* material source, line *and* energy, space *and* performance.

Equatorial Models

The renovation of buildings SDE 1 & 3 at the School of Design and Environment (SDE) at National University of Singapore (NUS) offers an example of integrating design with operational and embodied carbon considerations at its core, internalizing carbon concerns rather than externalizing them.[4]

Creating buildings with less carbon impact informed many of the decisions embedded in the 22,000-square-meter renovation of the existing 1970s institutional buildings called SDE 1 & SDE 3 that house the Department of Architecture, the Department of Building, and the Department of Real Estate.[5]

As a case study, the transformation of SDE 1 & 3 provides neither a complete solution to the contemporary climate catastrophe nor a precise ready-made model of sustainability. Instead, the design represents a series of restorative values and techniques that balance material, energy, social, and pedagogical concerns with design, formal, and aesthetic ambitions advanced across the project's duration. Each design outcome strengthened the idea that the architecture is a pedagogical device that could make a value system advocating decarbonization visible.

Existing Carbon Artifacts

The design of SDE 1 & 3 leverages the scaffolding of the original master plan for the erstwhile University of Singapore by the Dutch urban planner Samuel Joshua van Embden. His bold vision of a networked campus traversed the hilly topography of Kent Ridge in southwest Singapore, with pathways and interconnected circulation circuits. In contrast to the quadrangles and landscaped courtyards of the original Bukit Timah campus, his design could be read as a spatial counter to the 1968 student riots that spread across university campuses in Europe and America. The Kent Ridge campus was organized as a tartan grid megastructure: a 4'-0" × 4'-0" planning grid with a secondary 2'-0" band for structural columns were applied regardless of the jungle-like setting or its hillside location.[6] Van Embden envisioned the modularity of this grid as a framework for the campus to grow and adapt in conjunction with evolving teaching frameworks and state educational ambitions.

Van Embden's architectural office, OD205, translated the master plan grid into three- and four-story buildings.[7] The buildings established the architectural vocabulary of the university campus and were characterized by the placement of

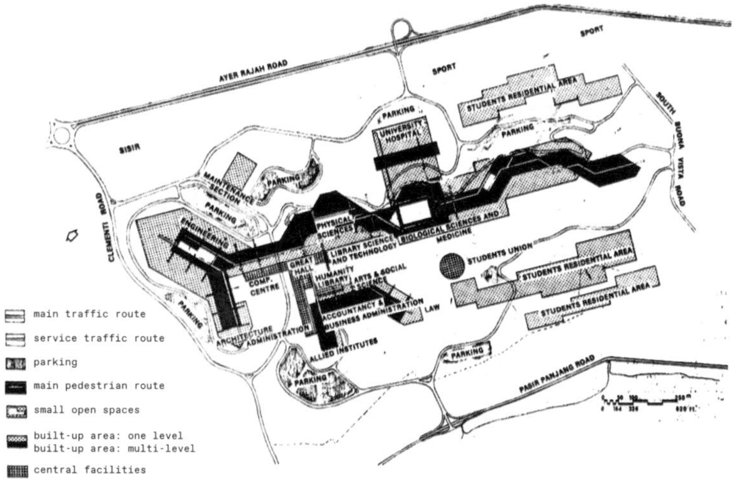

Fig 4.2 Scheme for the master plan from Singapore University on Kent Ridge Site (1970) by OD205. Model (top), zoning plan (left).

Courtesy: Center for Studies on Architecture, School of Design and Environment, NUS.

vertical circulation, with mechanical and technological systems on the exterior of the building, a manifestation of "served and servant spaces."[8] These choices were complemented by yellow ocher tiled ceilings, brown glazed paving brick, white mosaic exterior tiles, and anodized horizontal aluminum sunscreens. The screen's assemblage produced a heavy opaque eyebrow surrounding each floor plate, shielding the building from the sun's heat irrespective of orientation. A technological and engineering vision of a campus — a kit of parts — made the campus appear uniform and regular, communicating ideas of functionality, efficiency, and industrialization. This ethos was appropriate to a university cultivating students to enter the massively industrializing and internationalizing Singaporean economy at the time of the campus' construction.

SDE 1, SDE 2, and SDE 3 (then known as the Faculty of Architecture) were completed by 1977. Initially, all three buildings were naturally ventilated and open to the hot and humid tropical atmosphere. Air-conditioning was installed by 1983, powering visions of comfort for the campus body and ejecting students and faculty from the tropical context and thrusting them into a globalizing interior synthetic climate.

The renovation of SDE 1 & 3 began in 2015 and returned to the original design values of the master plan. The design extends the idea of durability — employing the buildings' free plan within the existing structural grid while recasting adaptability, design, and debate within the pedagogical spaces of the school. The pile foundations and embedded carbon in the structural frame, slab, and roof were artifacts to be repurposed and reworked alongside improving the spatial, atmospheric, and detail qualities of the interior and the envelope. By reusing existing carbon invested in the campus formation, the school could present an architectural vision of carefully conserving the university's resources.

The values of reuse and working with the existing materials are seemingly obvious; however, they run contrary to deeply embedded cultural expectations in Singapore, where new buildings represent a forward-looking nation-building narrative. New design and construction communicate a value system of apparent technological advancement and novel urbanization, values entrenched in the collective ambitions of national progress.

The existing buildings of SDE 1 & 3 were only thirty-nine years old when the redesign began. They occupied an ambiguous state: not sufficiently old enough to be considered historically important, not architecturally significant enough to be conserved outright. At the same time, the project scope was not equipped with the financial resources to construct new buildings, given that the new SDE 4 facility was under construction next door. Another set of values was needed to convince the university that decarbonization and careful attention to design, space, and detail would be valuable to the campus and pedagogically critical for the next generation of architectural students educated within its walls.

Although the existing concrete structure had architectural potential due to its generous scale, SDE 1 & 3's innards were highly problematic. The original buildings contained a four-story stack of deep floor plates; minor interior renovations from the 1980s through the 2000s sealed the envelope, replaced natural ventilation with ducted air-conditioning, and prioritized faculty offices over student spaces. Low acoustic ceilings, tightly partitioned rooms, and blocked access to view resulted in high CO_2 levels, poor ventilation, and a high buildup of volatile organic compounds from the glues and paint students use to make architectural representations. Moreover, the buildings lacked modern sprinkler systems, creating a high fire-risk interior environment for the design community.

Spatially, the floor slabs separated the student body into discrete levels, effectively severing the life of the school into a stack of stories. First-year students occupied the first floor of SDE 3, while the second floor accommodated second- and third-year students. Level 3 housed the Master of Architecture program, isolated from the floors below.[9] This spatial layering compartmentalized learning by seniority. A single dedicated public review space did not exist, and cross-year learning occurred only with significant effort, by traversing egress stairs between the levels and seeking out private reviews or discussions deep within the innards of the building.

By 1983, the studio environment prioritized thermal comfort as an implicit pedagogical symbol — separating sweat from intellectual toil, creating an escape from the tropical climate. This synthetic air environment symbolizes where work is to be done, framing student prospects of employment in white-collar, air-conditioned corporate spaces. Not only was air-conditioning a sign of escape from the equatorial climate, but through the tactile experience of air-conditioning, the student body received the symbolic message that their campus education was equivalent to one carried out in the temperate climates of Boston, San Francisco, or London. The design studios and faculty offices were corporate and generic, universalized spaces for architectural teaching and research simulating an environment that could be found anywhere in the Global North. Symbols throughout the floor plan and ceiling design included a 2' × 2' acoustic plenum ceiling, rows of moveable desks and chairs, and prolific air-conditioning to reinforce a design language in support of Singapore's nation-building narrative — a quest to continually transform the nation from a "third-world city to a first-world" efficiently air-conitioned metropolis.[10] The original buildings of SDE represented the first start of that transformational process for the students studying in its spaces.

Fig 4.3 Acoustic tile ceilings at 2.6 meters above the floor, fluorescent lighting, 2'×2' supply diffusers, and gridded return diffusers above raised vinyl floors and set behind metal bars constituted the interior environment. *Photo by Ong Chan Hao.*

Fig 4.4 On the exterior of the OD205 campus buildings, the perimeter slab overhangs became depositories for the collection of mechanical detritus. Air-conditioning compressors, refrigerant lines, cold water systems, and electrical trunking were all installed here after construction, effectively becoming the building's public face.

Photo by Ong Chan Hao.

Fig 4.5 The seventh-largest oil refinery globally, a visible expression of the carbon economy, is situated on Jurong Island and overlooks the Singapore Port at Pasir Panjang. The refinery is visible from the rooftop of SDE 1 & 3. *Photo by Darren Soh.*

The Renovation of the School of Design and Environment: The Integrated Equatorial Envelope

The renovation design of SDE 1 & 3 sought to resist the universal spaces of the school's original buildings. This resistance took significant time and design effort. The scope was initially limited to an interior scaled fit-out to replace the poorly conditioned air and update the life safety systems. The majority of the work fell under the university framework of "facility renewal (FR)," a term that means replacing air-conditioning, plumbing, fire suppression, electrical, and lighting systems to achieve code compliance. The renewal was fundamentally an engineering and system retrofit designed to deliver a universal temperate microclimate and safety, simulating the prevailing indoor environment of an architectural school in the Global North, just as the university had done in 1983, albeit with updated systems. The ability of the buildings (as works of architecture themselves) to be pedagogical tools was absent from this initial ambition. As the building frame was perceived to have a limited structural lifespan and therefore considered a depreciating asset, the budget would cap the scope to minor exterior upgrades. At the same time, to restrict the scale of the interior renovation, the design was to accommodate a floor-by-floor fit-out, retaining operations during the building process: in essence, a diminutive interior renovation of systems, partitions, and finishes.

However, there was also an aspirational belief at the school, under Heng Chye Kiang (Dean, 2007 – 2016), that the renovation represented a significant opportunity to transform the buildings to communicate contemporary pedagogical ideas of architecture to the student body. On the behest of Nirmal Kishnani (Vice Dean of Special Projects, 2015 – 2017) and Wong Yunn Chii (Head of Department, 2007 – 2017), I was asked to champion the work as the lead designer and establish a set of aspirations and a progressive architectural proposal that would rethink, challenge, and overcome the uninspired FR targets set by the university.[11] The buildings were conceived as pedagogical tools to influence how architecture is taught and debated; and structure the architecture so that students could learn from it. Following Tehrani's approach elaborated in Chapter 1, the design for SDE 1 & 3 was pedagogically founded on the importance of a public forum for exhibition and architectural debate, coupled with an equatorial envelope that engages with the tropical climate and latches the buildings to their climatic context. The design process began in April 2015, when a group of three Department of Architecture students and I established a set of eight principles that would drive the design from conception to completion:[12]

1. Introduce vertical social spaces to link the floor plates of the design studios. These volumes would center the community of the architecture program around the unique learning experiences of public reviews. Each studio space would be linked to a conjoined maker's and exhibition space so that display, debate, reviews, design, and fabrication could occur in public view across the length of the building.

2. Position a circulatory promenade at the building's front entrance that would immediately traverse an exhibition gallery for public display of architectural ideas. A large staircase would serve as a social center, seating, and interaction space to congregate, encouraging interpersonal dialogue. The staircase's proximity to review spaces and the exhibition gallery would publicize student drawings and models to the community circulating on its steps. Fixed gallery walls throughout the building was a counterstrategy to the previous, moveable and temporary pin-up boards that plagued the original SDE 3 configuration.

3. Strenghten the Department of Architecture's identity and clarity of entrance by a main front door at the urban ground level and a second portal at the higher campus level. Both entryways are designed with a significantly scaled social space to encourage interaction.

4. Utilize the existing concrete frame and its embedded carbon as durable and inspirational assets.

5. Increase the volumetric dimensions of the interior by strategic removal of partitions, ceiling assemblies, and plan clutter to allow for daylight to penetrate deep into the interior and make the complex section of the original building structure visible.

6. Remove air-conditioning and mechanical system symbols on the interior and exterior of the building. In terms of building performance, these removals are intended to reduce energy consumption, including reductions in lighting, plug, and the building systems load, while making the newly installed but highly minimized internal systems visible and accessible to the community as a pedagogical instrument.

7. Improve the air within by deploying a low operational carbon hybrid comfort system, an extension of the approach deployed at the net-zero-energy SDE 4 building, while reducing the embodied carbon of the system through fabric ducts. The design leverages the performative need for air volume for comfort while simultaneously expanding the generosity of the building section.

8. Screen the building from heat gain on the west by creating a deep veil, a *brise-soleil* that would be an integrated device and an aesthetic expression for the Department of Architecture, combining formal design and performance capabilities while camouflaging air intake and exhaust systems. The veil would unify the SDE micro-campus in coloration, filigree, and form to resist the individuated and unlinked architectural forms that predominated the campus expansion over the past two decades. The veil would establish a visual resonance with SDE 4, producing a delicate elevation serving as a background building linking to its neighbors.[13]

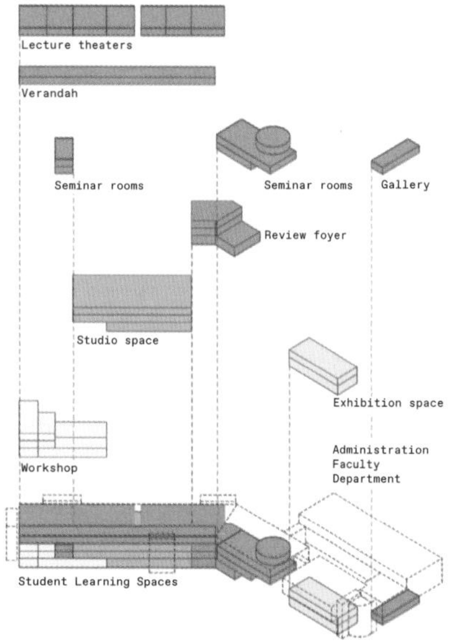

Fig 4.6 Overview of SDE 1 & 3 spatial and programmatic enhancements.

Courtesy: Special Projects, NUS School of Design and Environment

Subtracting Carbon

Subtraction rather than addition constitutes the majority of the design effort. Two openings were introduced to remove small sections of the original floor area.[14] Although the embodied carbon in the structure was viewed as an asset, significant spatial deficits needed rectification. The openings create a social commons that cuts through the building, linking the first floor to the third with a staircase and replacing the values of two-dimensional real estate with the qualitative values of the experience and munificence of volume. Volume is used operatively: to improve the experience of space, afford better air access, and facilitate interactions among the occupants.

On the interior, the antiquated air-conditioning system and low acoustic ceiling assemblies (containing plenums, ductwork, partitions, and obstructed clerestory windows) were removed. An ovoid subtraction links the first and second stories, bringing daylight and ventilation into the dark recesses of the floor plan, while a large atrium cuts through the center of the building providing linkages between each of the three stacked design studios.

The removals reveal substantial volumes that had previously been dedicated to air-conditioning systems. Removing the acoustic tile ceilings on the third story has exposed an expansive tiered underside of the fourth-story lecture theaters, creating a generous volume of 4.5 meters in height. Removals on the building's exterior include a dilapidated anodized aluminum screen, a yellow metal tile ceiling along the corridors, and a concrete air handling tower in the central courtyard. The removals not only erase old symbols of technology and refute a general symbolic ethos focused on engineering, but also return the experience of larger volumetric dimensions to the occupants, celebrating the structural frame and the systems snaking through the architecture as part of the design experience.

As a restorative design approach, architecture's role was recast from adding and developing to acts of removal and subtraction. This strategy shifted the architect's role to that of a subtractor, slicing, cutting, exposing, and making the embedded carbon into a visible cultural and design artifact, extending its lifespan and giving it new architectural qualities. In this sense, the design functions more as an archaeological excavation rather than the additive approaches that have primarily formed Singapore's contemporary architectural history.

Strategic Additions

A stair, a series of screens, and hybrid air provide significant spatial, performative, and experiential improvements. A sizeable sculptural staircase is introduced in the center of the student commons in SDE 3, linking all levels of the design studios and creating a mixing vessel of social exchange and personal interaction. The stair, constructed in concrete and clad in timber panels, ties into the existing structure, while the entryway exhibition gallery links the review spaces, design studios, and workshops. The social and educational functions of the school are arranged along a promenade of circulation, display, interaction, and debate as a *mise-en-scène*. Along its first flight, the stair tread depths are larger than standard code parameters to provide relaxed seating in front of the exhibition gallery.[15] As a social space, the stair ascends to a series of review and pin-up spaces linked to a coffee bar. The conflation of exhibition, debate, and social space is purposefully tight and compressed so that every being and occurrence in the school is displayed and accessible to all.

On the exterior, an aluminum and mild steel screen veil, 1.5 meters deep, encapsulates the western and northern elevations, operating to mitigate solar heat gain from the setting sun, reflecting daylight deep into the floor plate, and shed rainwater off the envelope. This deep veil, "a screen transformed into a thickened spatial envelop and enclosure merging optical sensorial and atmospheric qualities," is a concept I developed over years of design research.[16] It is structurally supported by light shelves that drive daylight through clerestory windows positioned along a grey inner window wall. Folded panels with inverted gables sit at the exterior of the deep veil and increase in height from the roof to the first story, enabling the dynamics of the light of the equatorial atmosphere to play out uniquely on every level and across the entirety of the western elevation. Stacked with varying folding angles, the overall effect recalls the stepped proportions of Louis Kahn's Phillips Exeter Academy Library, transformed into a delicate and porous filigree appropriate for the equator. The panels operate as components of the veil in various angles, to screen fire access panels, mechanical fresh air and exhaust ducts, and electrical conduits. The veil's horizontal members are stacked as a gradient, with each member rotated to optimize views from the inside outward and minimize glare while creating a shimmering effect across the envelope. The veil serves as a counter-symbol to the engineering signs manifest on the original campus. As an equatorial filter to climate and a porous interface to the atmosphere, concealing and disguising, the veil communicates an outward appearance of cohesion, formal clarity, and delicate integration.

Initially, the veil's design was intended as a recycled reconfiguration of the original anodized aluminum screen profiles of the 1970s building envelope. The design intent — to repurpose its embodied carbon — was correct, even though Singapore has not yet established a fully circular material economy. Like all material ecosystems, carbon was only one component of the decision-making process, and in this case, demands from the university regarding liability and guarantees of durability trumped the design aspirations. Timber was also explored as a carbon-negative material; however, the local building code currently prioritizes fireproof ratings, making it highly challenging to achieve compliance.

The design of the eastern elevation of SDE 3 called for building-integrated photovoltaics (BIPV) for energy needs and to camouflage the traces of various mechanical systems that covered the exterior of the building. Ultimately, however, the university's financial frameworks could not justify the cost of the BIPV, so the mechanical infrastructure that had accumulated over the building's history was left as found. A coat of grey paint constituted the architectural effort on the east elevation of SDE 3. Paint established a visible contrast between the values of integrated design along the west elevation and the building as a platform for mechanical detritus along the east, with the hopes that additional funding and value alignment will occur in the near future.

The veil on the west and north elevation is composed of aluminum and mild steel. With its high embodied carbon, aluminum appears contradictory to the aspiration of a low embodied carbon design. However, this material selection balanced the existing structural capabilities of the concrete frame; pile caps could not take the additional weight, so lightweight, durable, and easily assembled criteria guided the selection. The veil is configured around standard 25 × 25 mm aluminum hollow sections and 50 mm L-angles imported from China, assembled and coated in Singapore. Standardizing the materials for their repetitive panelized assemblage allows for factory-controlled precision and an expeditious on-site installation.

Gold painted mild steel railings circumventing the exterior circulation spaces of SDE 1 & 3 replaced the standard university polished stainless steel railings found across the campus. Fixing details were crafted to minimize potential areas for rust to secure a long-term durable and low-maintenance design. The anchor plate invokes the inverted gable of the elevation as a symbol while incorporating structural requirements in the smallest of details.

A mild steel screen crown surrounds a jungle-like courtyard in the heart of SDE 1, contrasting a naturalistic verdant and wild-looking landscape (that is, living carbon) with a delicate assemblage of vertical 50 mm flat metal bars (embodied carbon) overhead. The framed jungle sets up a dialogue between the aesthetics of an organized, patterned, filigree filter with the untamed, growing, and living carbon of the natural landscape. As the building blocks surround the courtyard, the noise levels are substantially reduced, and the sky is framed in a composed picture of sky, jungle, and architecture.[17]

The lightweight constitution of the golden screens creates a contrast between the existing heavy cast-concrete structural frame and the delicate assemblage of the new filter and veil. The material selection, color, and fixing details distinguish between old and new, heavy and light, and massive and arrayed elements. The horizontal light shelves cleave open at the gray-painted concrete columns, creating a gap between the two material systems allowing rainwater downpipes to slip between. The contrast between the metallic and reflective golden screen (new) and the gray-painted building mass (existing) establishes a color-coded dialogue of time read through the renovation. Gaps, exposed joint lines, and assembly details construct a language of delicacy and lightweight additions in contrast with the monolithic quality of the original concrete structure.

The veils of SDE 1 & 3 represent a model of intense design integration: the crucible of design aspiration, school values, Ministry of Education budgets, university ideals, and maintenance regimes. As Alejandro Zaera-Polo notes, "The building envelope forms the border, the frontier, the edge, the enclosure, and the joint: it is loaded with political content." Multiple forces and pressures coalesce around the veil: the complexities of the exterior equatorial climate; the inhospitable acoustic environment created by the adjacent road traffic; and the need to incorporate daylight, views, ventilation, ducted air intakes, sprinkler protection, fire access panels, structural parameters, cleaning cycles, and egress requirements. The veil navigates performative, functional, and code necessities while managing and organizing them into a series of experiential hierarchies that resonate with the campus, the climate, and the materials from which the veil is constructed.

On the interior, a hybrid comfort system

developed with Transsolar KlimaEngineering replaces air-conditioning to create a low-carbon, low-energy, high-quality, indoor-outdoor air environment. The hybrid air reduces humidity and operational temperature to 27° Celsius in a single-pass system without return air. The thermal air environment, its comfort amplified with elevated airspeed by ceiling fans, creates a high-quality indoor environment from 8 a.m. to 6 p.m. with CO2 levels equivalent to outdoor air. After hours, when students and faculty remain in the building, windows open across the envelope, fans accelerate, and the outdoor environment merges with the interior in a high-quality air medium that provides comfort within the tropical context.

SDE 1 & 3 are fully leaky buildings that use internal pressure to drive air through a series of thermal states: the cycle begins in a tempered office, where comfort demands are individually controlled; the air then leaks through a damper located above the door into the corridor, where it cools and spills into the stair core before pouring out the front entrance. As the air passes through each space, it changes its thermal and atmospheric constitution, transforming from cool to warm and retaining its high quality and low energy use along its path from a synthetic temperate to the natural tropical environment. Extended and modified from SDE 4, the hybrid air design adapts to the existing spatial realities of SDE 1 & 3.[18] This adaptation requires expert coordination between ducts, services, and the structural frame, as the preexisting slab heights compromised the required volumes above and below each fan. The design effort aimed to integrate and calibrate fans, light ducts, conduits, and electrical trunking to maximize air volume and ensure a robust airflow throughout the section. Fabric air supply ducts replaced metal ducts, and as a single pass system, the elimination of return ducts reduced approximately 50% of the material weight (and carbon) compared to conventional air-conditioning systems.

With an environmental push with Singapore's Green Plan 2030, the university embraced larger national ambitions and adopted net-zero energy as an essential goal for its campus. SDE 1 & 3 were initially designed with a super-low-energy approach to operational carbon. Further refinements, including increased efficiencies, maximizing a photovoltaic rooftop array, and initiating inhabitation changes, including powering down the building during semester breaks, afford SDE 1 & 3 to become net-zero-energy buildings from 2022 onward.[19]

With the operational carbon use of these two buildings designed to be net-zero, the critical narrative then folds to the embodied carbon budget. The operational carbon budget constitutes 85%, while the remaining 15% is embodied carbon found in the new materials added to the structural frame. In total, the design is estimated to contain less than one-fifth of the total carbon of an equivalent new building in Singapore.[20] These numbers assert that a careful and surgical reworking of Singapore's existing building landscape is possible — a rare occurrence in a city-state where demolition and building anew is the normative way of nation-building.

Because of the project's initially low design ambition, it afforded a space for the Special Projects team and I to operate as the primary designers, pushing for high-quality design where very few at the university saw its potential. This created the unique opportunity to have the school's in-house design experts directly shape and craft the school's environment from the macro scale to the detail scale. The design sets a structure for changes in architectural education; privileging doing less rather than more, removing rather than adding, and restoring architectural quality through volume and detail, integrating the equatorial context while advocating for environmental responsibility at all scales of the building.

Design Cultures

The design team put significant effort into constructing a culture of design as much as constructing a building out of materials. A 2016 studio, *Hot, Wet & Noisy, The Architecture of Our Own House* (see the Coda) engaged nine students to redesign the Department of Architecture. Their vision incorporated feedback from guest reviewers, teaching assistants, and lecturers probing and questioning the aspirations of the renovation.[21] Students from this studio then worked as part of the Special Projects team to synthesize and integrate various design and performance ambitions into the final design. Input, consultations, debates, and lectures with the community, student body, and faculty present a larger design ecosystem, using the buildings as a scaffolding for debates about the future of the department and the school.[22]

Future Ambitions

Material choices, fabrication sites, and energy sources are interdependent and intertwined with carbon. Research is required to count carbon and thoroughly understand the often opaque material streams of Southeast Asia. Which jungle is being cut to provide for the formwork? What river does the sand come from? What communities are being destroyed because of the material extractive processes that are nation-building Singapore?[23] For the design team to make decisions for the specifics of a building site, they require significant knowledge of the environments where steel and aluminum ore are excavated, where the materials to form concrete come from, and the full range of environmental impacts embodied in each material on sites far from Singapore. SDE 1 & 3 only lightly touched upon these concerns through the design process, though the design team is now forensically excavating the full material story to add to the overall carbon narrative described here. It will be for the faculty and students housed within the building to tackle this field of study head-on, to evaluate SDE 1 & 3, and interrogate the processes and decisions made.

The transformation of SDE 1 & 3 offers an encapsulation of value systems of design and a vector for architectural education in Singapore, outlining an ethos of subtracting rather than adding, conserving rather than demolishing, relying on natural ventilation rather than air-conditioning, and creating design quality rather than prioritizing quantity of real estate. The renovation has also set an example, a model, and a benchmark for net-zero-energy adaptive reuse. This will impact further transformations on the university campus in the decade to come.

The architecture of SDE 1 & 3 will also impact the next generation of architects taught within its frame, who will be exposed to the equator's climatic complexities and be taught to recognize the larger ecosystem of carbon embedded in the discipline. Repurposing their carbon inheritance will be central to that effort. SDE 1 & 3 offer a model that design is essential in communicating integrative values to students and the public, a value system based on internalizing carbon as part of the design process and embracing the campus's inherited carbon form as preferable to new construction. The two buildings will not solve the climate catastrophe, though the design approach claims that the first act of architectural decarbonization is to integrate and work carefully with what we have. As we remake our carbon legacy with care, thought, and collective commitment, we might be able to refute Agent Smith's claims by offering a necessary detour from the cancer of the planet, one building at a time.

Fig 4.7 The engagement with labor ecosystems in Singapore is almost invisible and plays out in the background of the building narrative.

Photo by Ong Chan Hao.

[1] Elisa Iturbe, "Architecture and the Death of Carbon Modernity," in *Log 47: Overcoming Carbon Form*, ed. Cynthia Davidson and Elisa Iturbe (New York: Anyone Corporation, 2019), 11-24.

[2] Alberti's treatise *De Pictura* (1435) is widely credited as the first scientific study on classical optics to establish "perspective" as a geometric instrument of architectural representation. Martin Kemp, *The Science of Art: Optical Themes in Western Art from Brunelleschi to Seurat* (New Haven: Yale University Press, 1992).

[3] Parametric design and digital fabrication attempts to maintain control of production by replacing the builder with robotic cutting, printing, and milling. This form of production commences only when materials are delivered to the workshop or factory, rather than controlling materials from their source.

[4] This essay describes the renovation of SDE 1 & 3 from 2015-2022. SDE 2 was put on hold in 2018 and commenced concept design in 2021. An image of SDE 4 can be found in chapter 3.1.

[5] The narrative of SDE 1 & 3 is messy and not linear. As the project extended over multiple years, the values that began the project evolved, budgets and university ambitions shifted, leadership changed, and project managers, consultants, and contractors circulated in and out of a long history. The collective values that crossed the entirety of the design process are visible, coherent, and transparent only with the completion of the buildings.

[6] Kevin Tan, ed., *Kent Ridge: An Untold Story* (Singapore: NUS Press, 2019), 259, https://doi.org/10.2307/j.ctvf3w2z1.258.

[7] OD205 (eponymously situated in Oude (Old) Delft, 205, the Netherlands) was an architects' collective consisting of S. J. van Embden, J. L. C. Choisy, Roorda van Eysinga, H. G. Smelt, and J. E. B. Wittermans. In 2016, the firm merged with a Rotterdam-based architecture studio to form the Defesche van den Putte (dvdp) architecture and urban design office. OD205, "De Geschiedenis van OD205 (The History of OD205)," accessed Oct. 16, 2021, https://www.od205.nl/geschiedenis/. Meng Ta Cheang served at OD205 and later became codirector of the School of Architecture, NUS, in 1984.

[8] In 1957, Louis Kahn elaborated this concept at the Royal Architectural Institute of Canada to provide meaningful form to the hierarchy of spaces. Louis Kahn and Alessandra Latour, *Writings, Lectures, Interviews* (New York, NY: Rizzoli International Publications, 1991).

[9] The spatial organization of student cohorts periodically changed but the isolation caused by the building's configuration remained constant.

[10] "Air conditioning was a most important invention for us, perhaps one of the signal inventions of history. It changed the nature of civilization by making development possible in the tropics. Without air conditioning you can work only in the cool early-morning hours or at dusk. The first thing I did upon becoming prime minister was to install air conditioners in buildings where the civil service worked. This was key to public efficiency." Kuan Yew Lee, "The East Asian Way—With Air Conditioning," *New Perspectives Quarterly* 26, no. 4 (2009): 111-120, https://doi.org/10.1111/j.1540-5842.2009.01120.x

[11] This ambition was further extended by the efforts of the administration under Lam Khee Poh (Dean, 2016-2022) and Ho Puay-peng (Head of Department, 2017-2022).

[12] Commencing in Apr. of 2015, the author and a small student team created the design concept, floor plans, elevations, sections, and foundational design principles. CPG Consultants was appointed as architect in Nov. of 2015 through the Office of Estate Development. The author continued advising the design direction as a faculty member until 2018, when he became Vice Dean of Special Projects. From 2018 to 2022, the Special Projects team provided design, details, integrated BIM models, and performance criteria working with the university-appointed consulting team.

[13] The development on the NUS campus jettisoned the cohesive principles of the van Emden plan by facilitating object-like buildings with distinct architectural vocabularies since 2000. The Mochtar Riady Building for the School of Business, with its glass curtain wall and symbolic trees; the Faculty of Engineering T-Lab, with its bulbus glass lobby; and the University Hall, with its inverted rotunda, represent an incongruous collection of varying design values.

[14] Subtraction to improve spatial quality works contrary to the university's effort to increase its real estate area holdings. In SDE 1 & 3, the quality of the space, not its quantum area, is the key to the design and key to representing the values for architectural education.

[15] The tread and riser dimensions borrow the same proportions as the Metropolitan Museum of Art exterior stair in New York City, creating a comfortable seating environment.

[16] Erik L'Heureux, *Deep Veils* (San Rafael, CA: ORO Applied Research + Design, 2014), 8.

[17] The courtyard's original manicured lawn has been replaced with a jungle.

[18] Wolfgang Kessling of Transsolar KlimaEngineering championed SDE 4's Hybrid comfort system. This system was adapted to SDE 1 & 3.

[19] Estimated targets subject to verification upon completion.

[20] The embodied energy for SDE 1 is estimated at +/-175 kg CO_2-eq/m^2 compared to 800–1000 kg CO_2-eq/m^2 for similar new construction in Singapore.

[21] "Hot, Wet & Noisy: The Architecture of Our Own House" in Semester II Academic Year 2015/2016 led by author (see Coda for more details).

[22] The design process included faculty members from the school, external consultants, and university representatives through a series of design charettes, workshops, and weekly project meetings over the seven-year time frame.

[23] A deeper understanding of Singapore's labor ecosystem is also critical to making informed material and design decisions. Labor concerns, which followed national regulations, hardly figured in this project, but the more significant downstream impacts on communities across South and East Asia were left opaque. Further research into labor and craftspeople building the campus could occur and positively impact all future building at NUS.

The Architecture of SDE 1 & 3

Fig 1 Exterior view of SDE 1

Fig. 2 Exterior view of SDE 1 on a cloudy day

15

Fig 3 Elevation of SDE 1 & 3

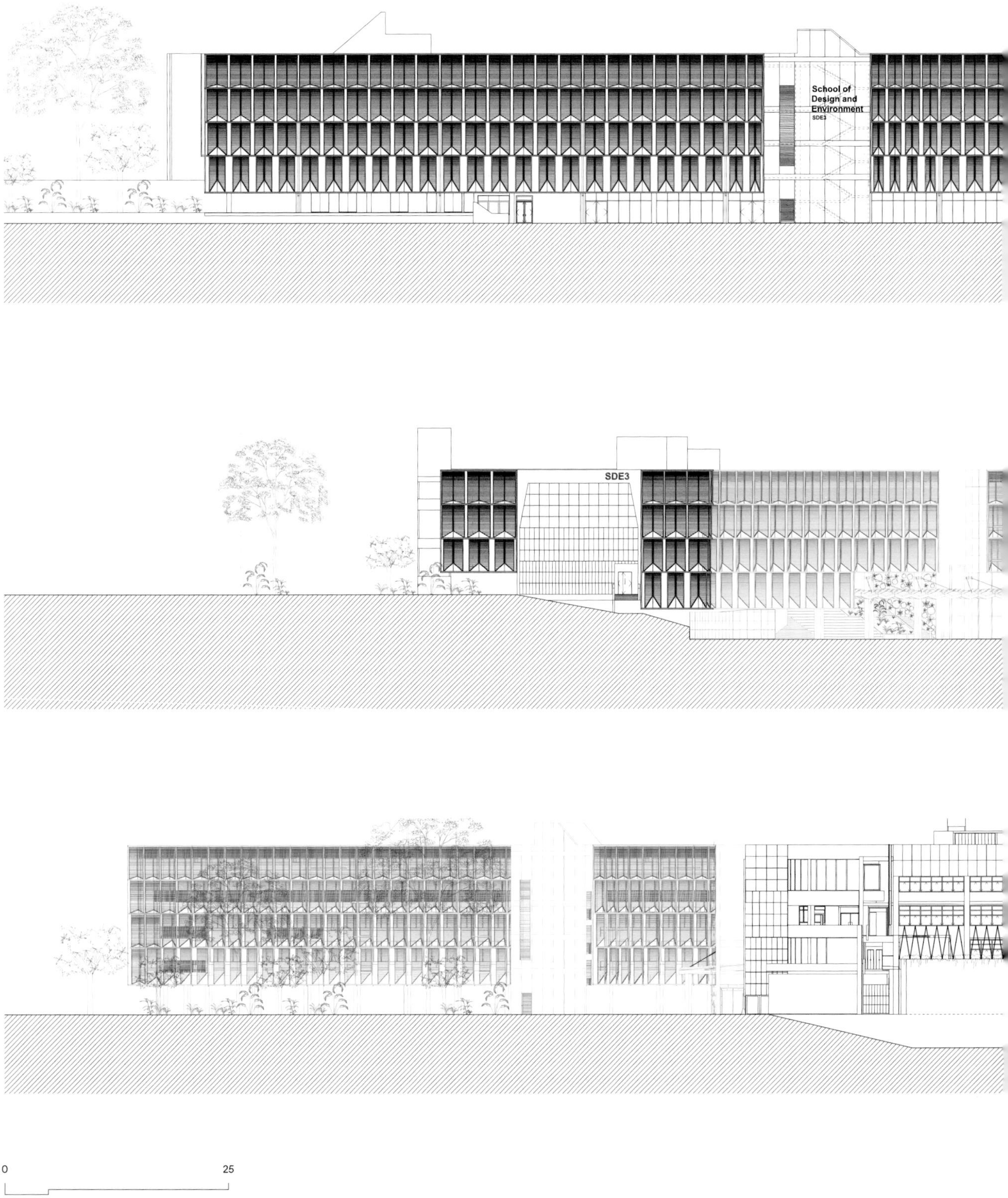

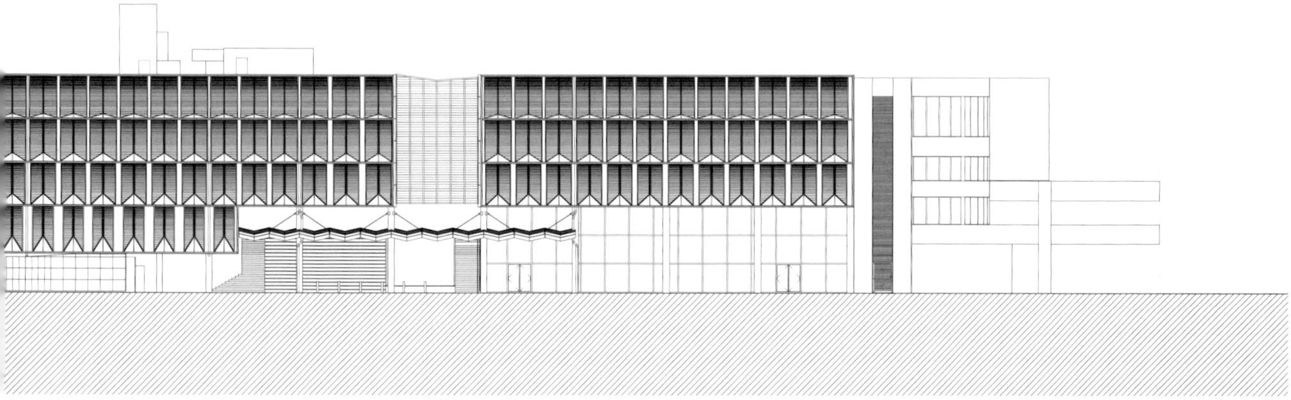

West elevation

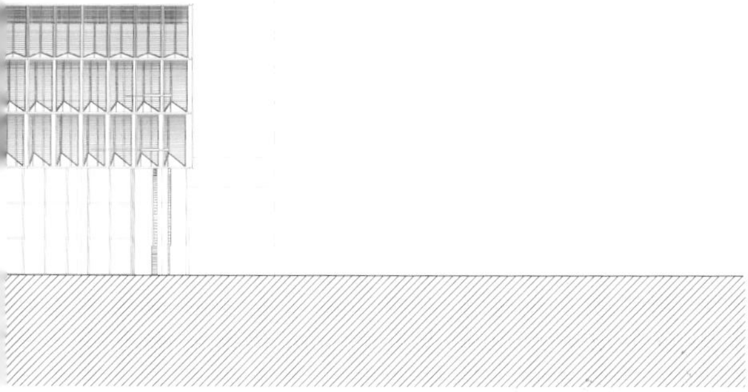

North elevation

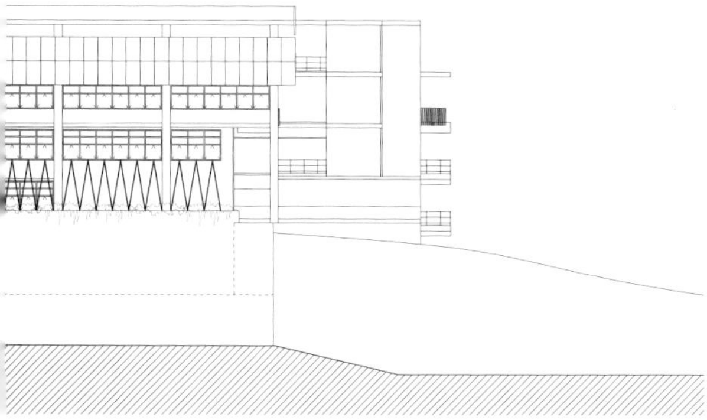

South elevation

Fig 4 Exterior view of SDE 1 from the southwest

Fig 5 Section and elevation of SDE 3 staircase

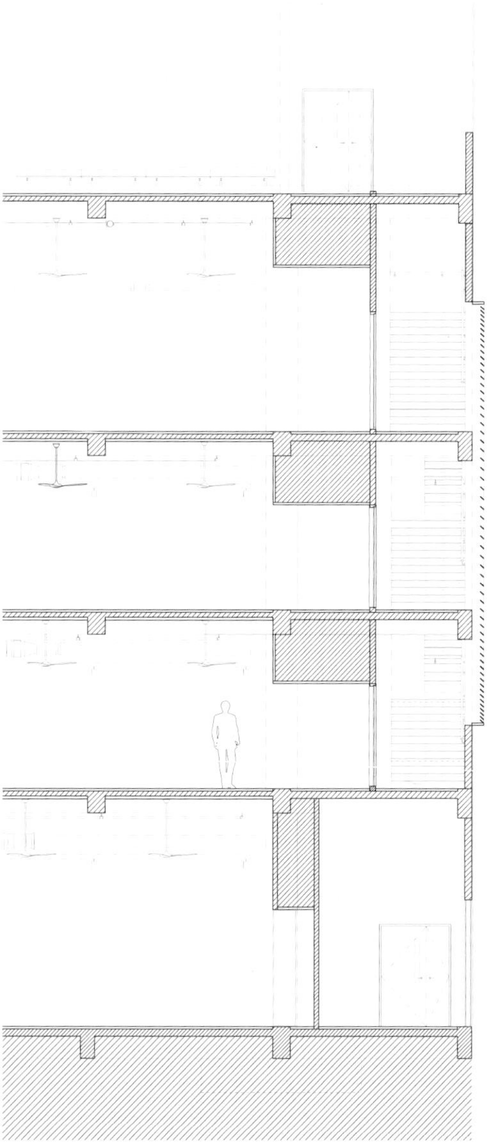

Staircase section

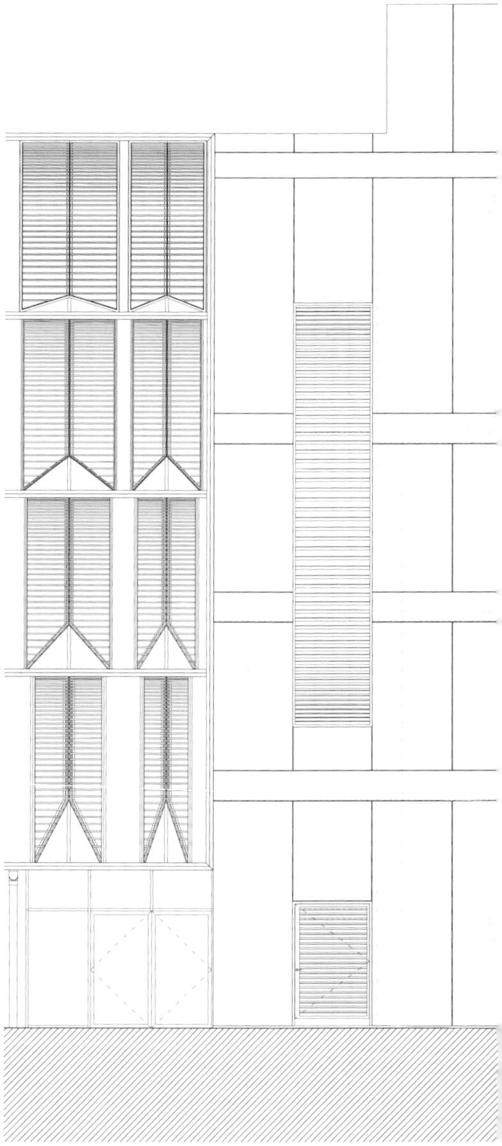

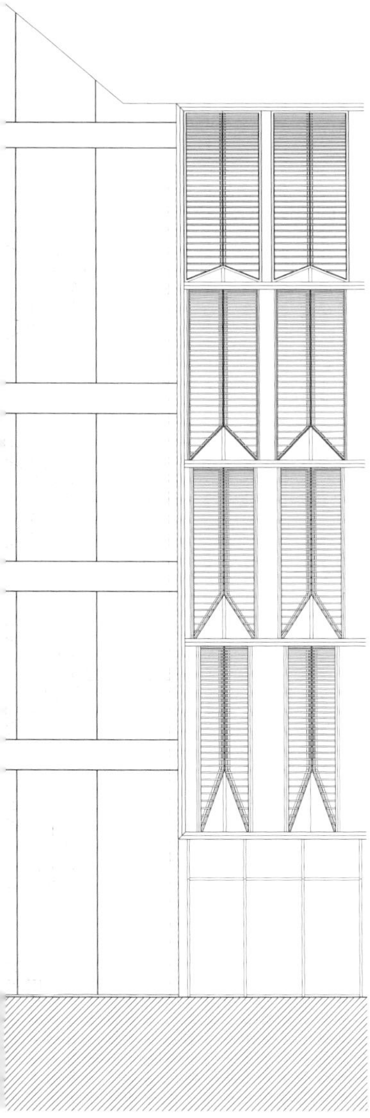

Staircase elevation facade

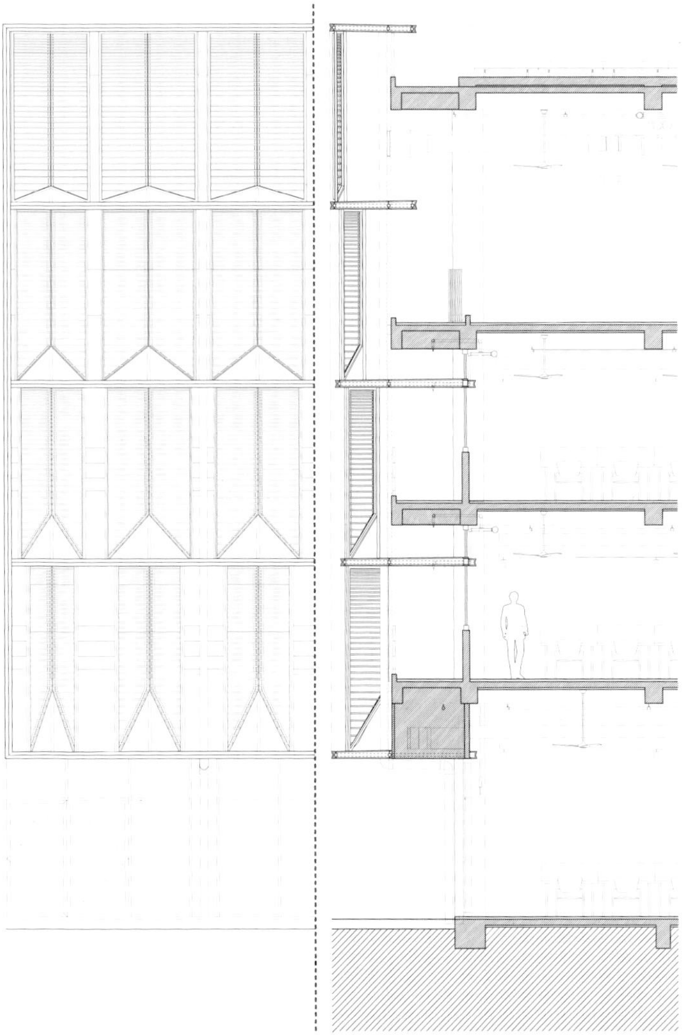

West envelope, part elevation & section

Fig 6 (left) Frontal detail of SDE 1 butterfly veil

Fig 7 (bottom) Oblique detail of SDE 1 butterfly veil

Fig 8 Interior view of SDE 1 & 3 canopy

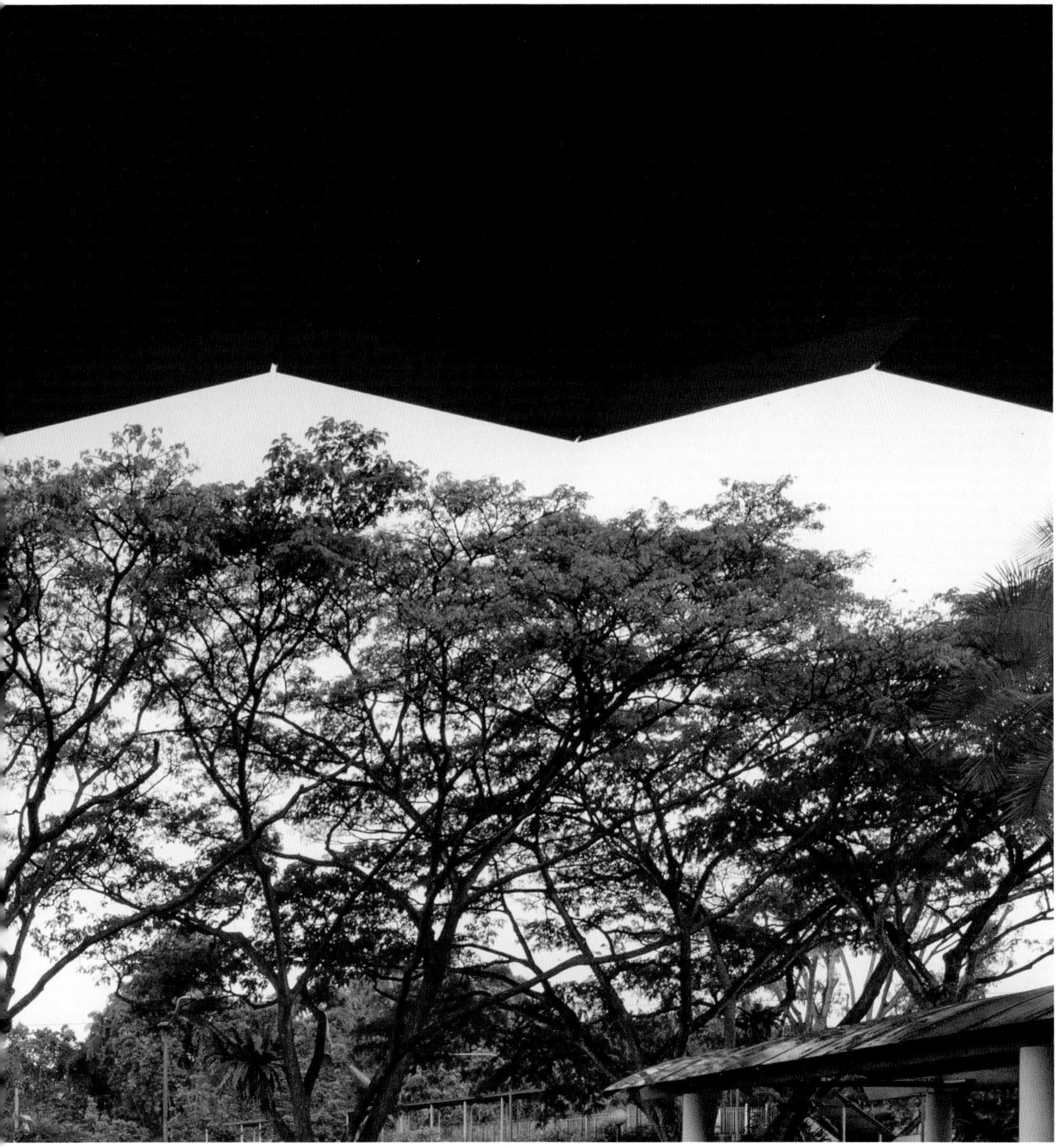

Fig 9 Detail view of butterfly veil from below

Fig 10 Detail of interface between veil and structure

Fig 11 Interior view of conference room

Fig 12 Detail section of butterfly veil

Fig 13 (right, top) Interior view of Department of Architecture Office

Fig 14 (right, bottom) Detail view of butterfly veil

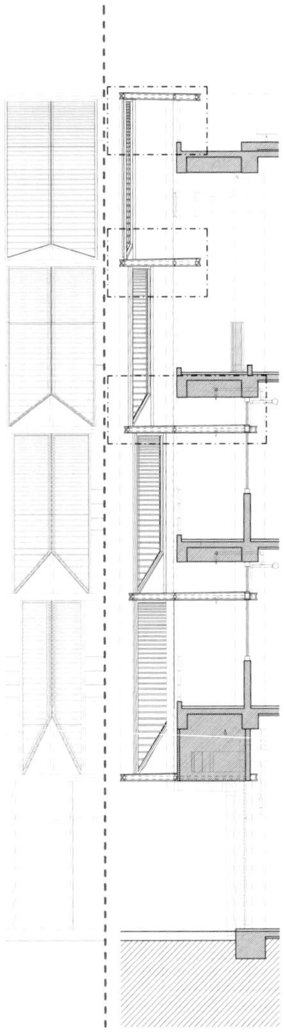

Butterfly veil, part elevation & section

0 2.5
0.5

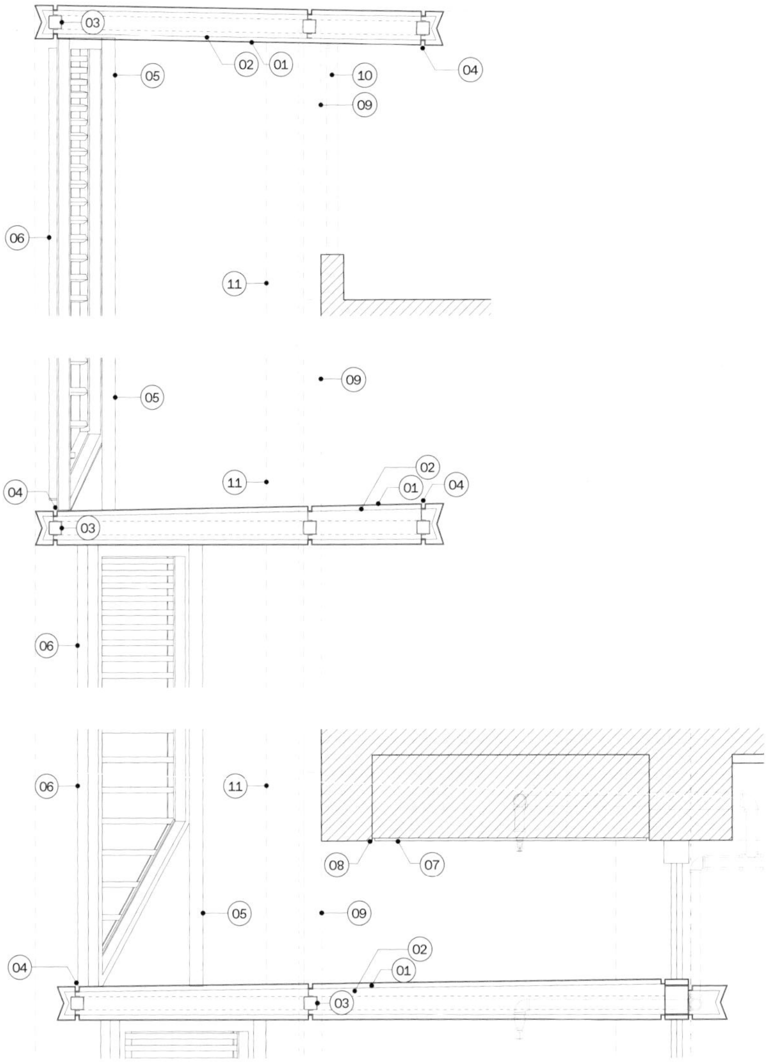

Butterfly veil blow-up detail

0 0.5
0.1

Legend

01	3mm aluminum cladding
02	20mm backer assembly
03	60×60mm aluminum RHS
04	20×15mm drip hole
05	60×60mm aluminum RHS
06	Aluminum louver screen
07	12mm gypsum board
08	12×12mm drip hole
09	100×60mm vertical steel
10	12×50mm aluminum railing
11	Rainwater drainpipe

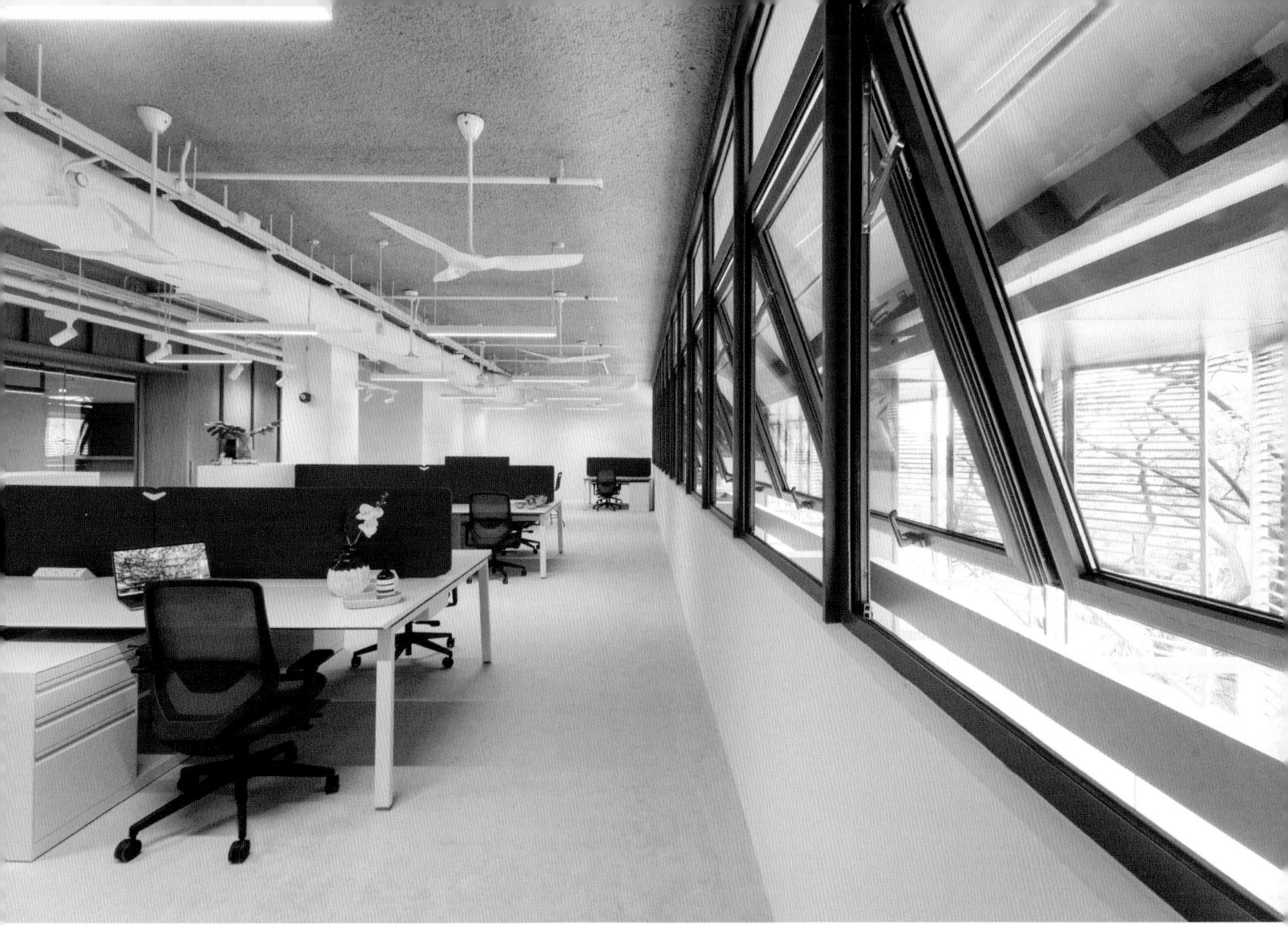

Fig 15 View of green wall at the grand staircase

Fig 16 Section across (top) SDE 1 jungle courtyard and (bottom) SDE 3 grand staircase

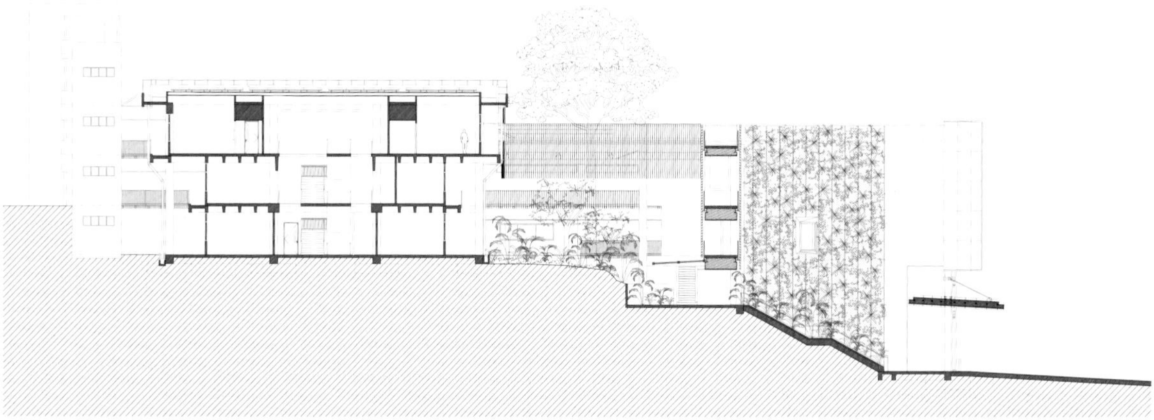

0 5
1

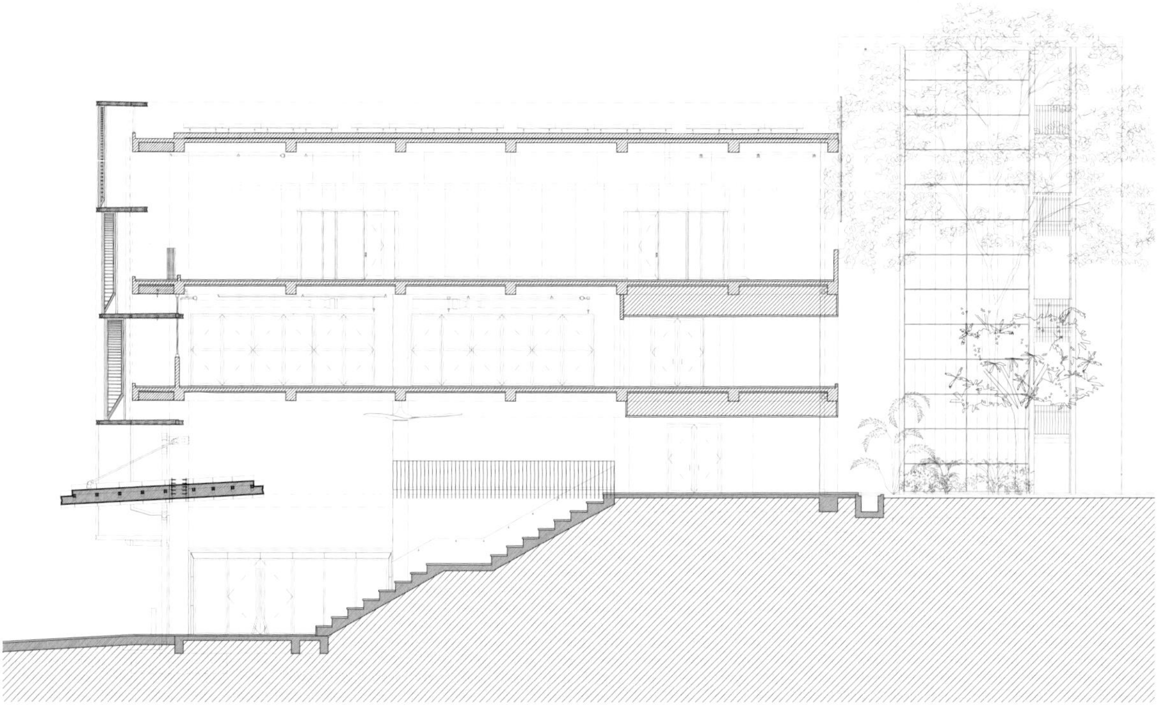

0 2.5
0.5

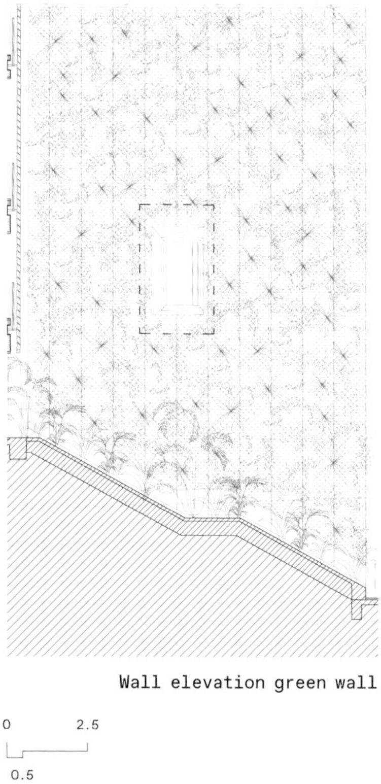

Fig 17 (top) Skyward view of view portal

Fig 18 (left) Elevation of green wall with portal

Fig 19 (top, left) Detail of elevation and plan of view portal

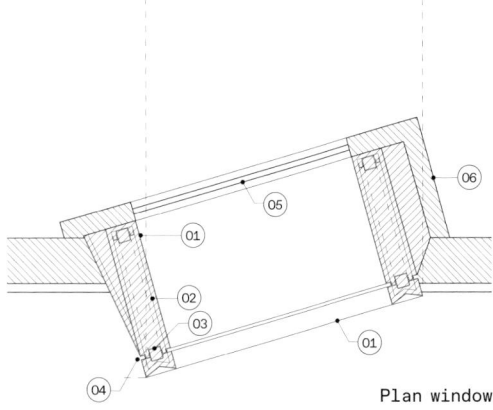

Fig 20 (top, right) Interior view of view portal

Legend

01 3mm aluminum panel
02 20mm backer assembly
03 60×60mm aluminum RHS
04 20×15mm drip hole
05 Glazing
06 Aluminum structure

0 0.5
0.1

Fig 21 (right) Exterior view of view portal

Fig 22 (top) View of SDE 1 jungle courtyard

Fig 23 (bottom) Section of SDE 1 across the jungle courtyard

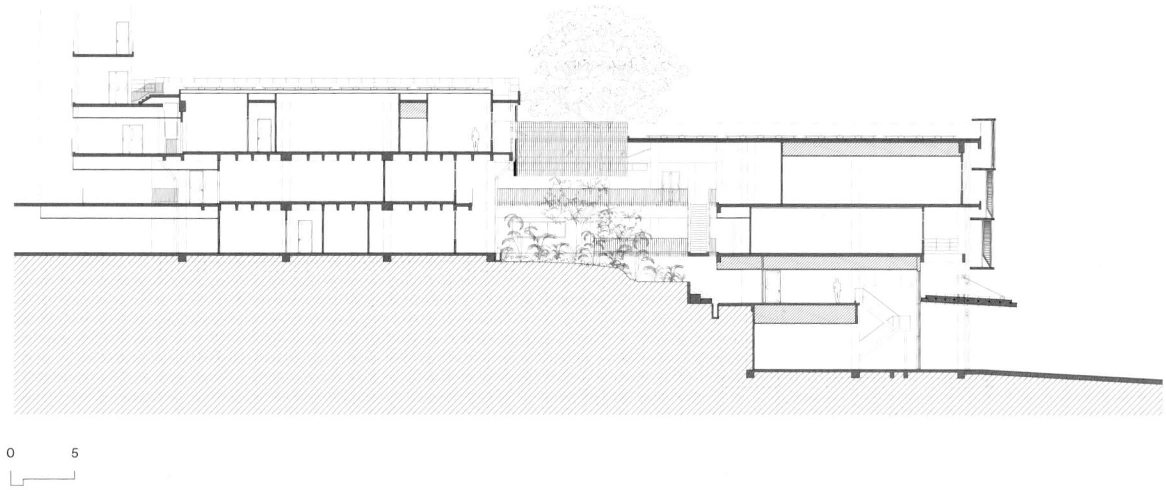

Fig 24 (top) View of courtyard verandah

Fig 25 (bottom) View of the jungle from verandah

Figs 26–36 Architectural details of SDE 1

Fig 37 (left) View of jungle courtyard after an evening shower

Fig 38 (right) Detail view of jungle and link bridge

Fig 39 Level 1 plan

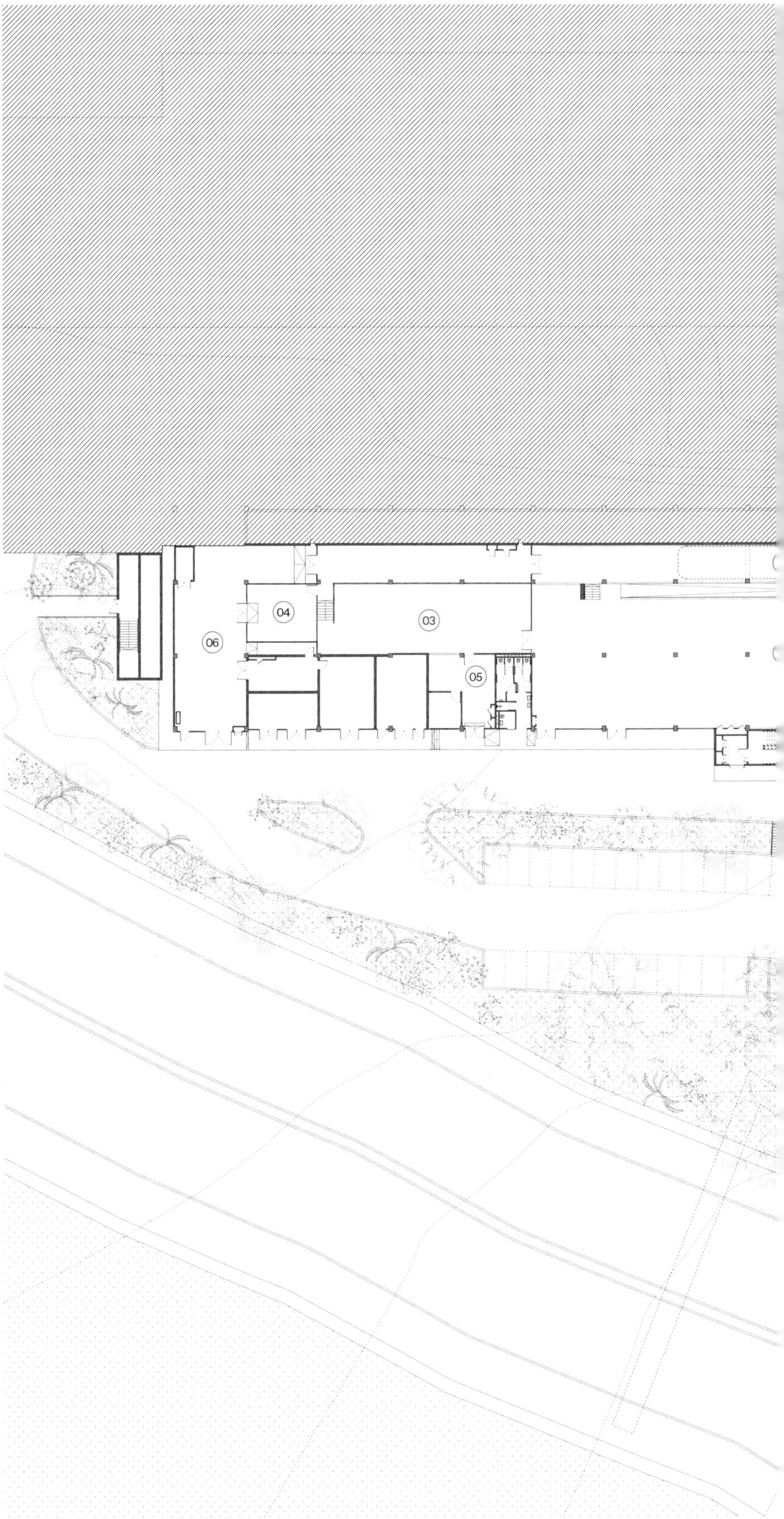

Legend

01 Studio space
02 Mezzanine level
03 Architecture workshop
04 Architecture assembly area
05 Architecture light making area
06 Wet / dry working area
07 Review foyer
08 Exhibition gallery
09 Entry foyer
10 Grand staircase
11 Grand hall

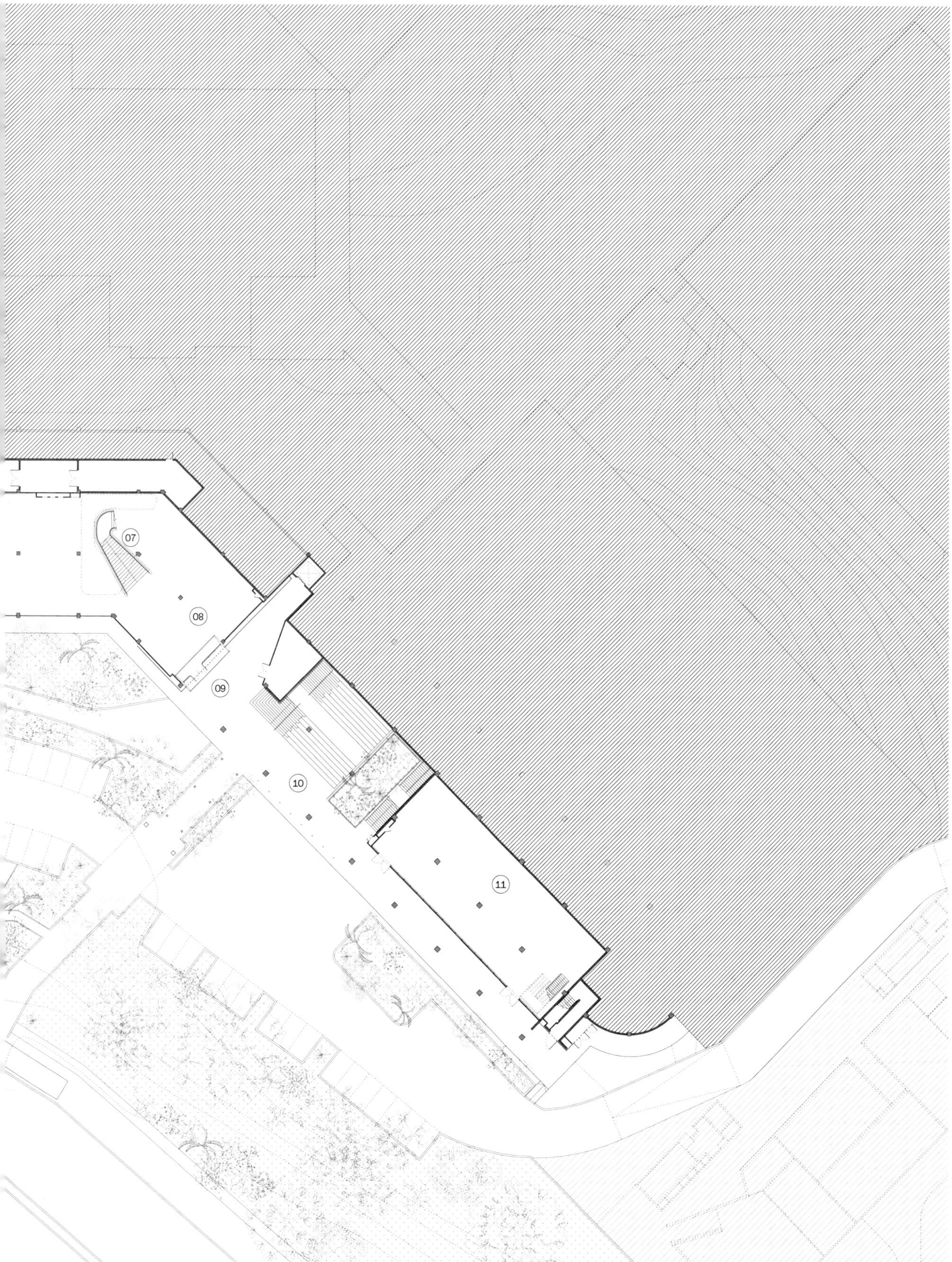
07
08
09
10
11

Fig 40 Level 2 plan

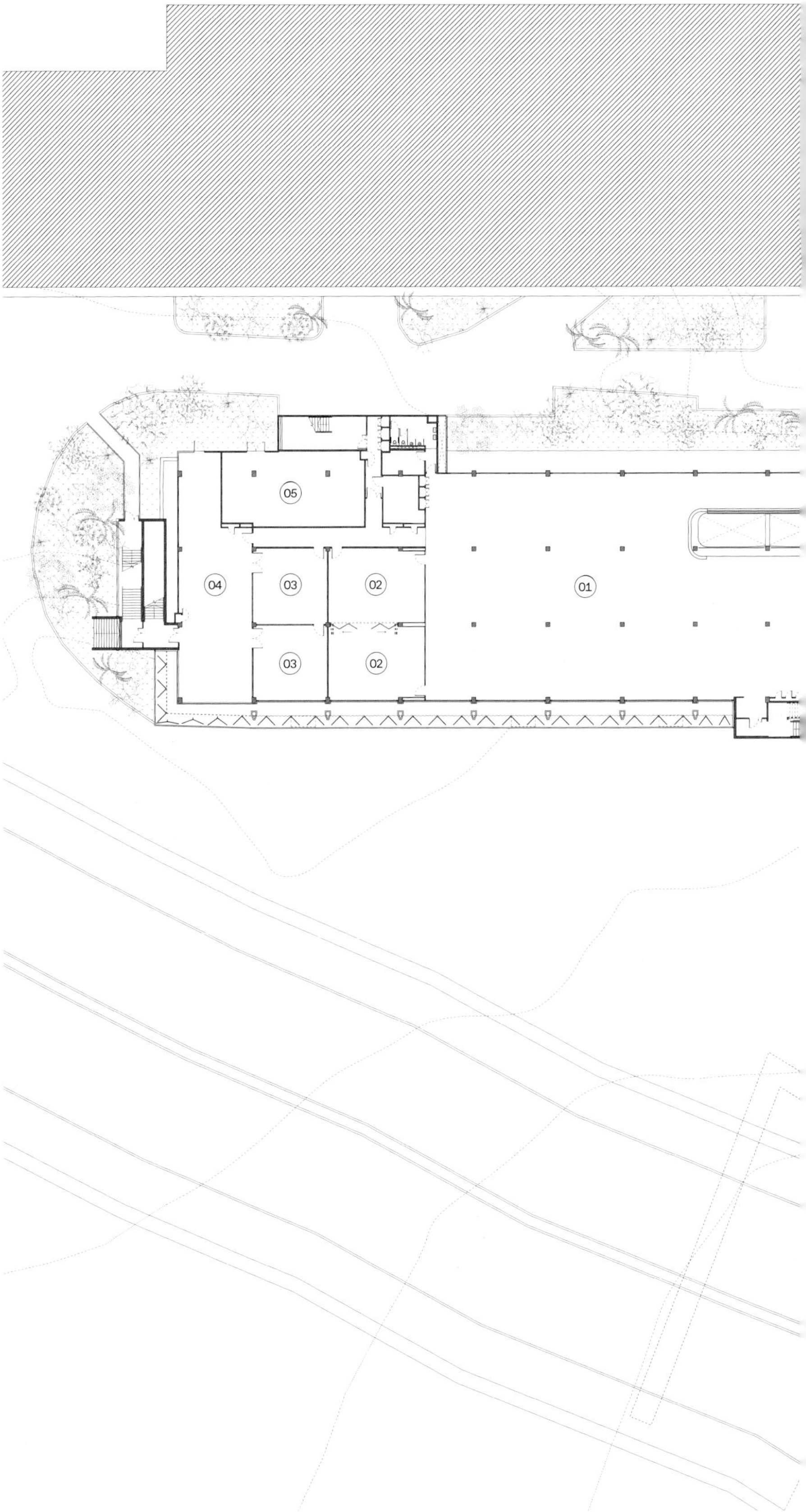

Legend

01 Studio space
02 Seminar room
03 Design maker workshop
04 Wet / dry working area
05 M & E room
06 Review foyer
07 Seminar room
08 Patio
09 Grand hall — mezzanine level
10 Staff lounge
11 Gallery

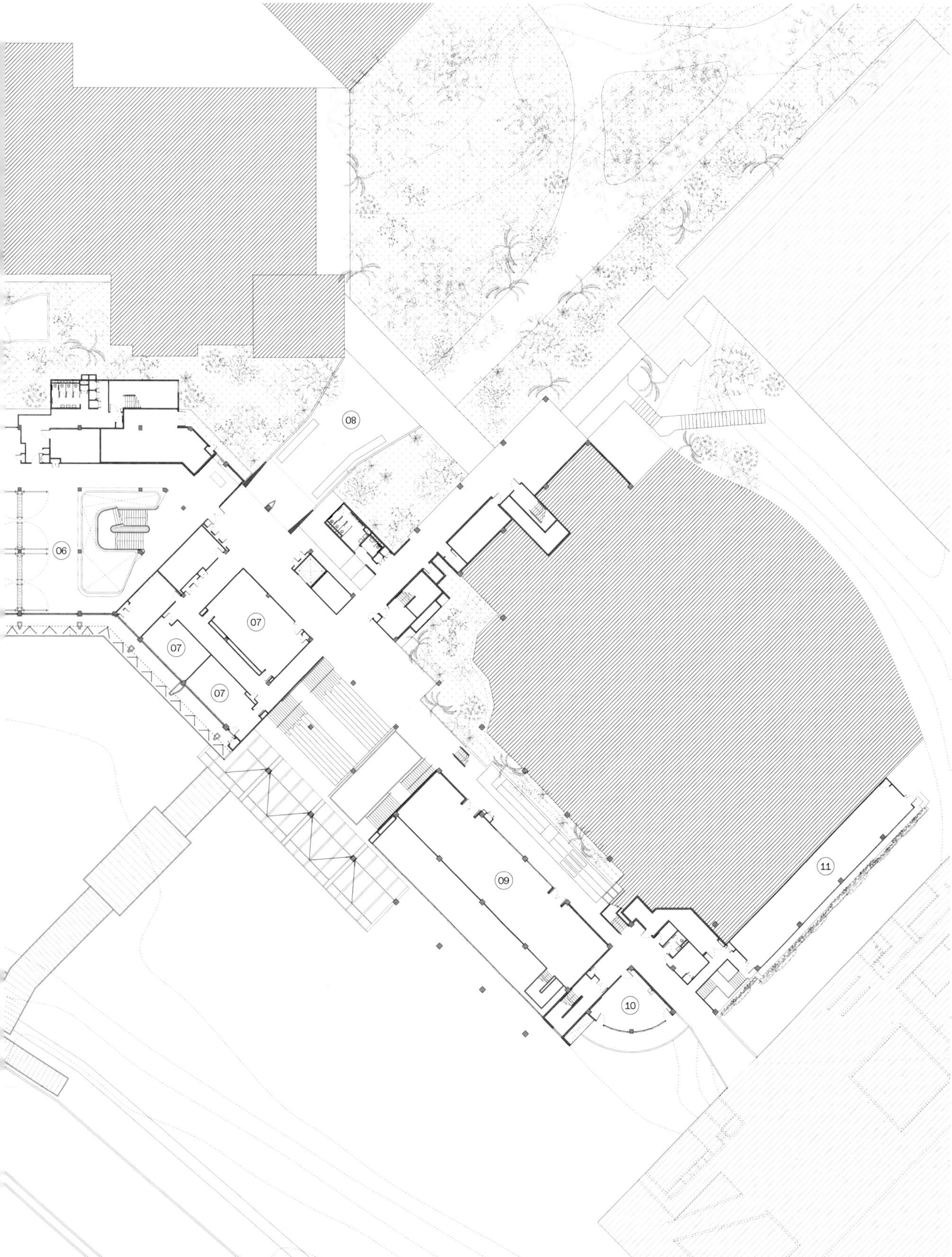
08
06
07
07
07
09
10
11

Fig 41 Level 3 plan

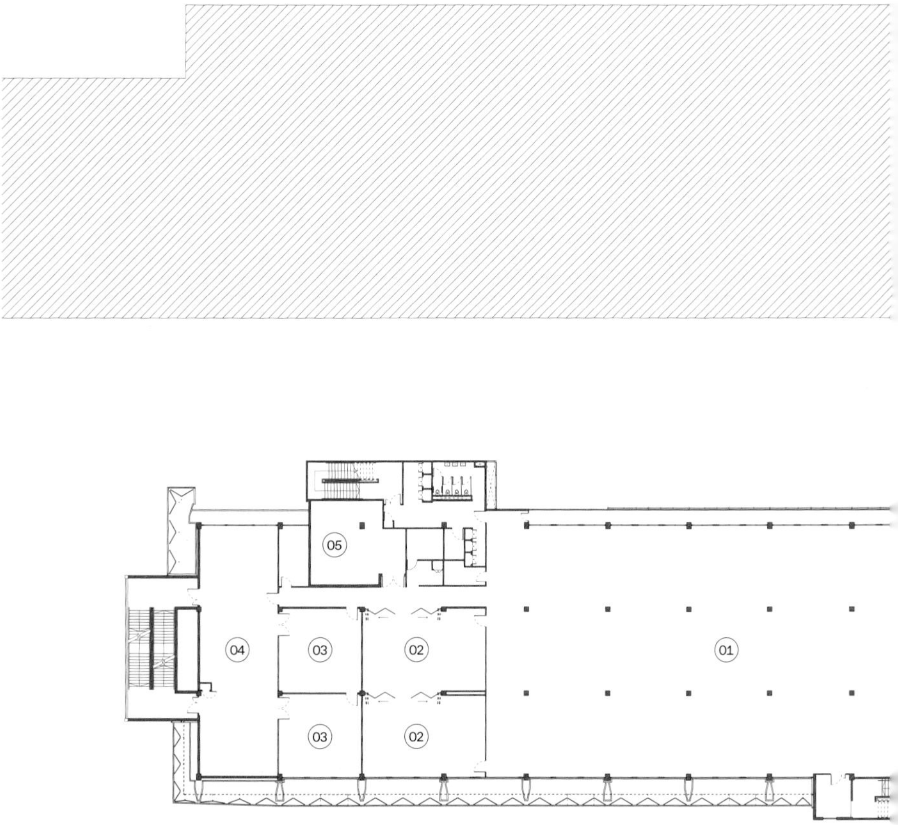

Legend

01 Studio space
02 Seminar room
03 Design maker workshop
04 Wet / dry working area
05 M & E room
06 Review foyer
07 PhD studio
08 Computer labs
09 Department of Architecture
10 Semi-outdoor public space
11 Office space
12 Department of Built Environment

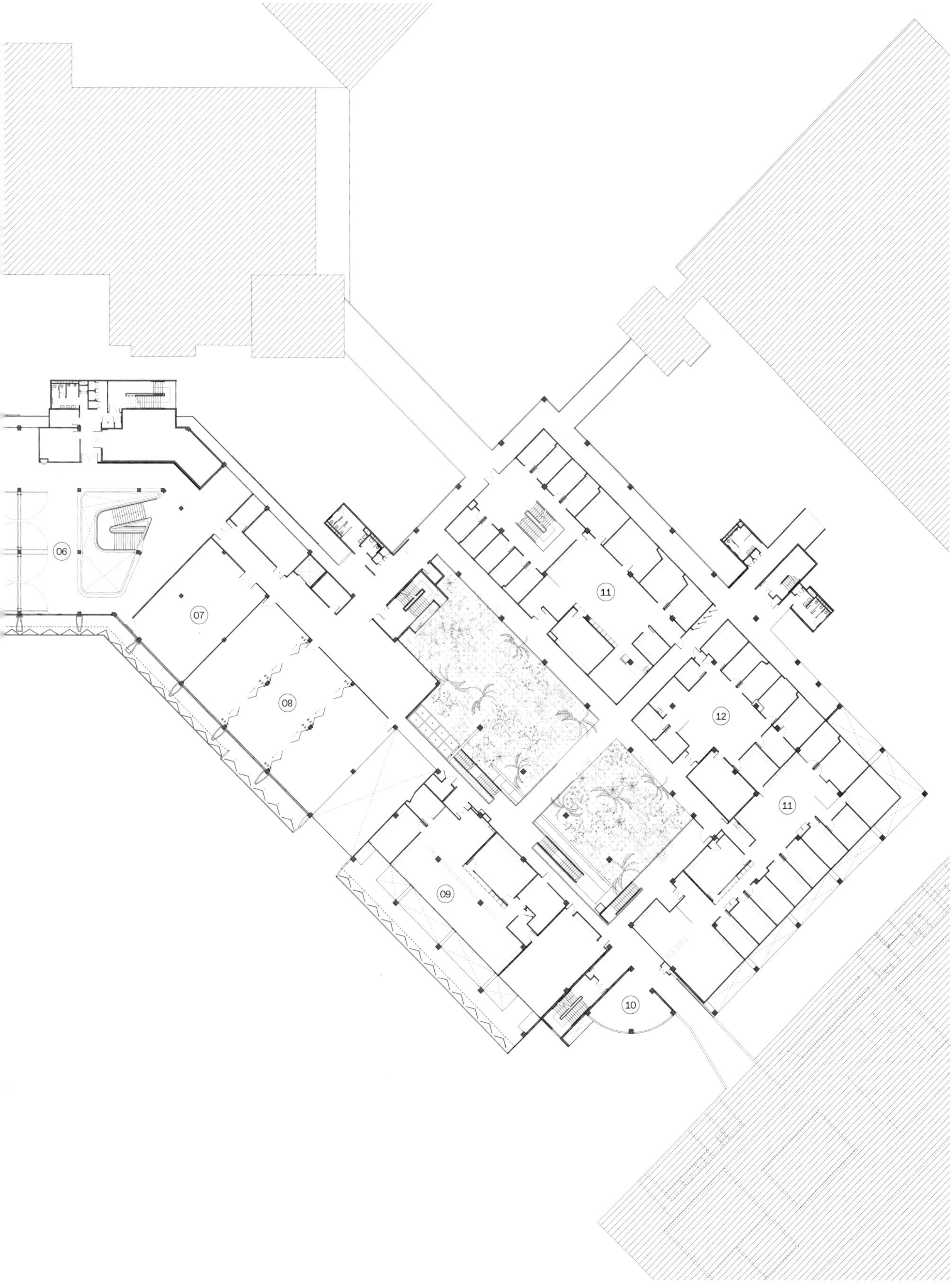
06
07
08
09
10
11
11
12

Fig 42 Level 4 plan

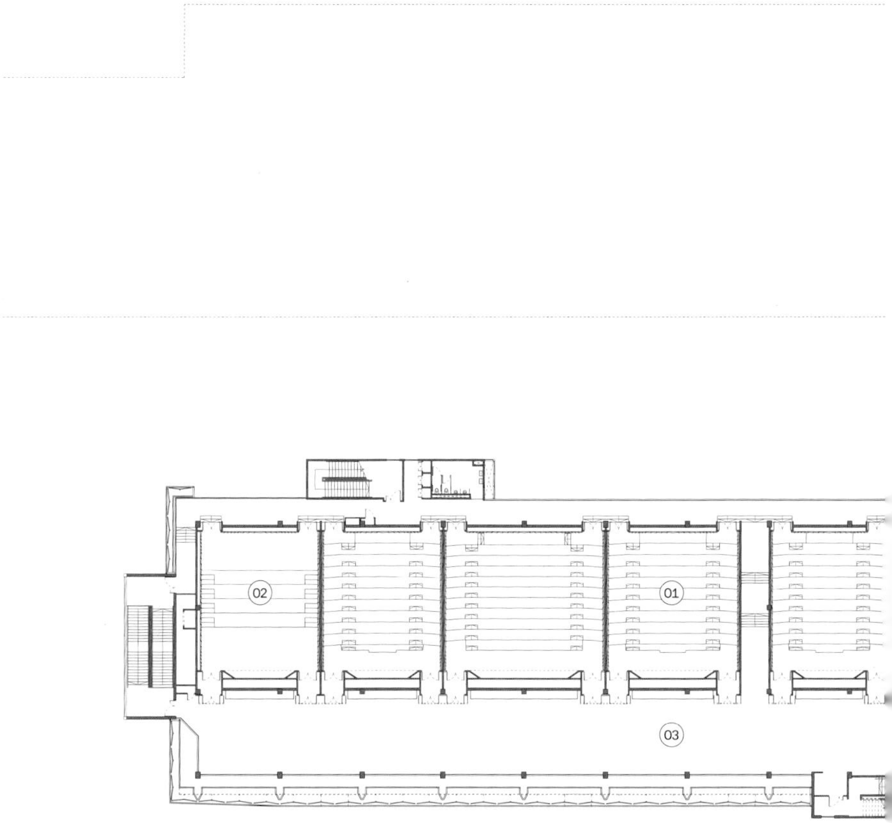

Legend

01 Design lecture theaters
02 Design forum
03 Verandah
04 Seminar room & research spaces
05 Barrel room
06 Co-Lab (collective lab)
07 Staff offices
08 Drum

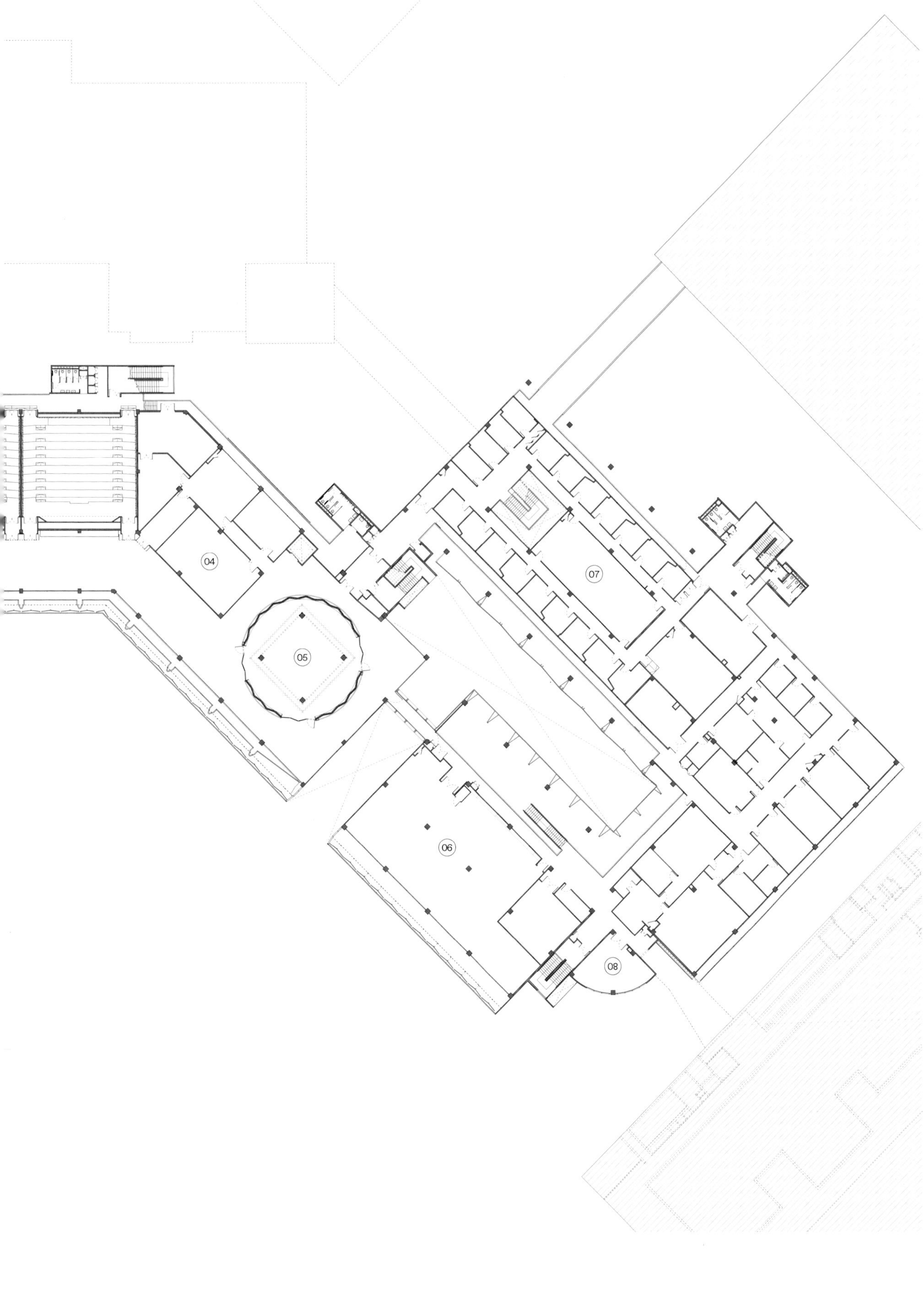
04
05
06
07
08

Fig 43 Section across SDE 3 (top) lecture theaters and (bottom) review foyer

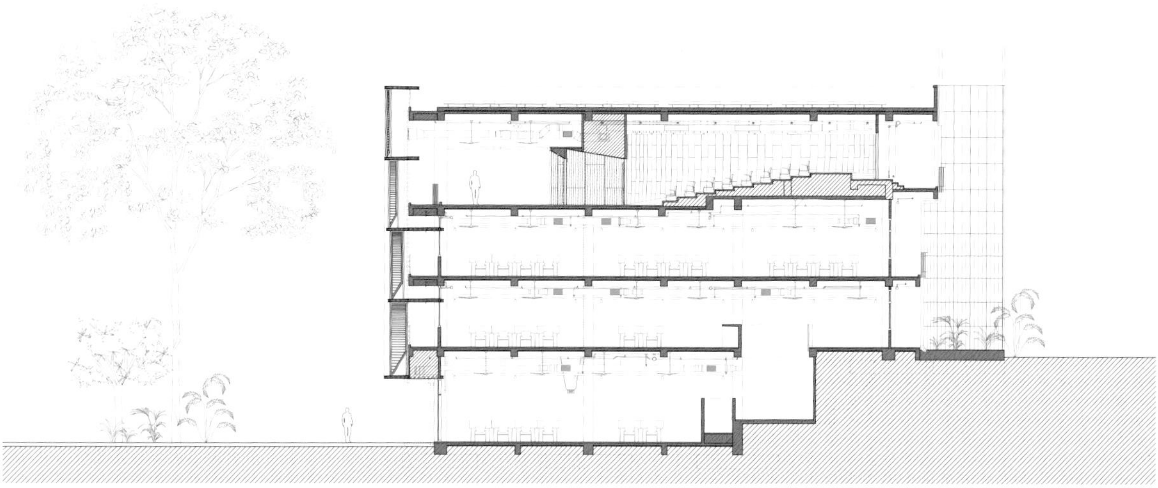

Section across lecture theaters

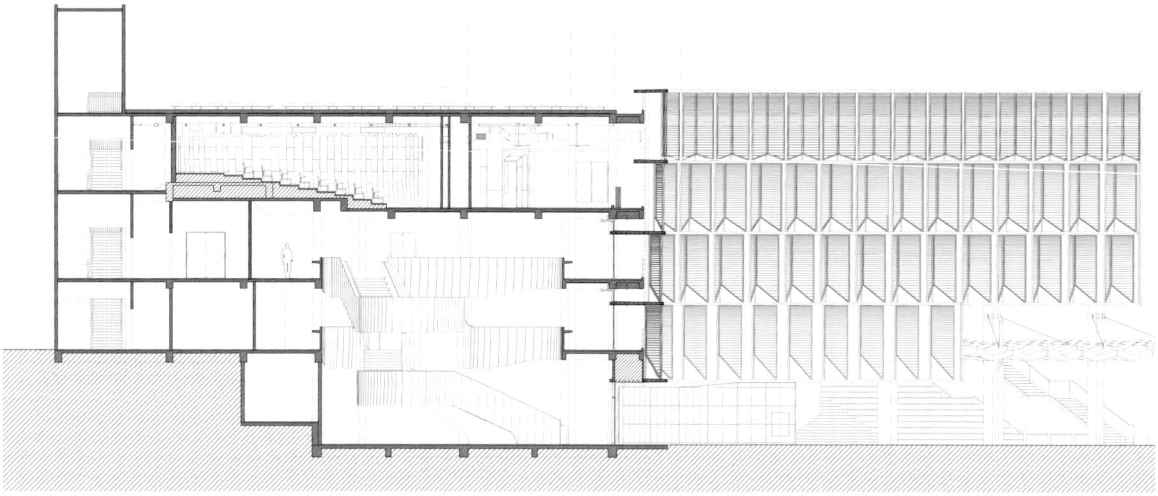

Section across review foyer

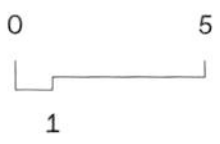

Fig 44 Exploded axonometric drawing of review foyer

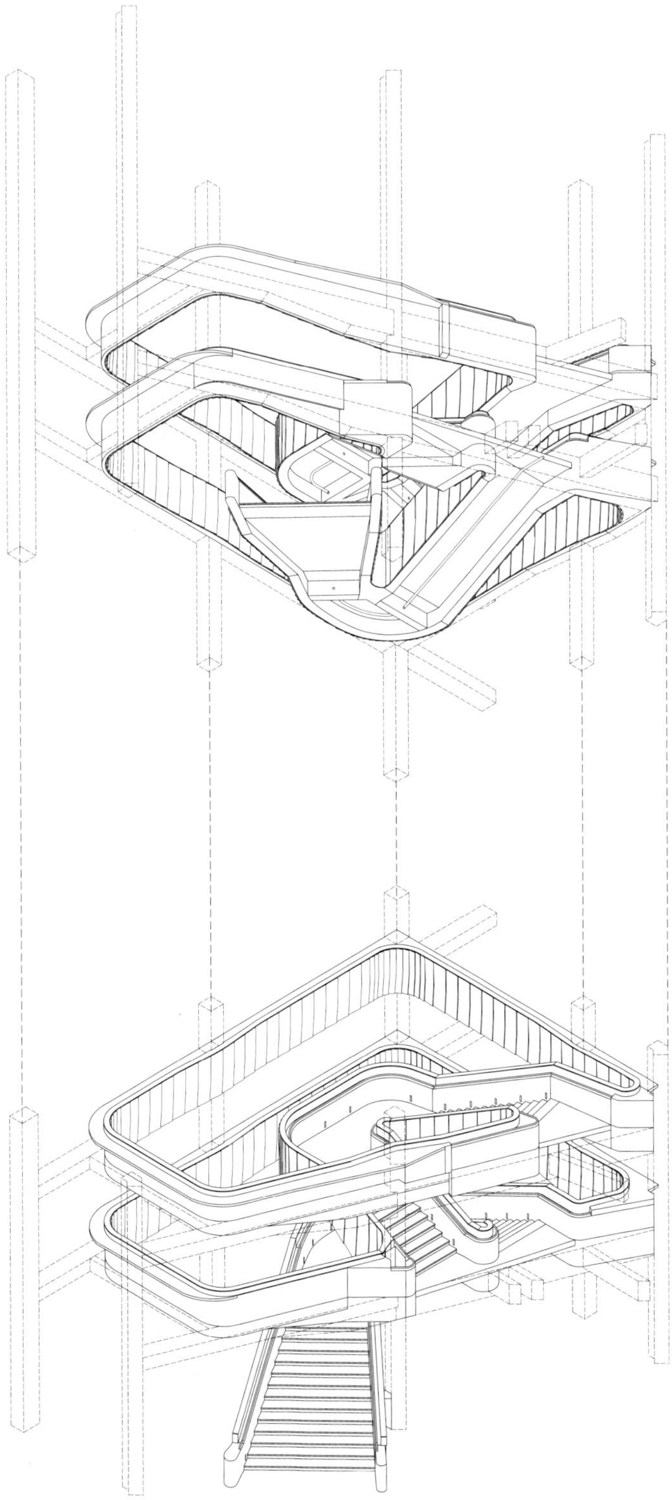

0 5

1

Fig 45 View of jungle verandah

Fig 46 (top) Detail of SDE 1 jungle courtyard

Fig 47 (right) View of jungle verandah

Fig. 48 Interior view of office space

Fig 49 Interior view of Department of Architecture office

Fig 50 (top) View of timber envelope around meeting rooms

Fig 51 (bottom) Detail view of timber panels

Fig 52 (right) Detail of timber panels in conference room

Fig 53 (top) Interior view of Department of Building office

Fig 54 (left) Interior view of meeting rooms

Fig 55 (right) View of office atrium

Fig. [illegible] West elevation of jungle courtyard

Figs 57–58 View of jungle courtyard in intense sun and rain

Fig 59 View of jungle courtyard in a heavy downpour

Fig 60 (top) Elevation of pleated veil

Fig 61 (bottom) View of pleated veil

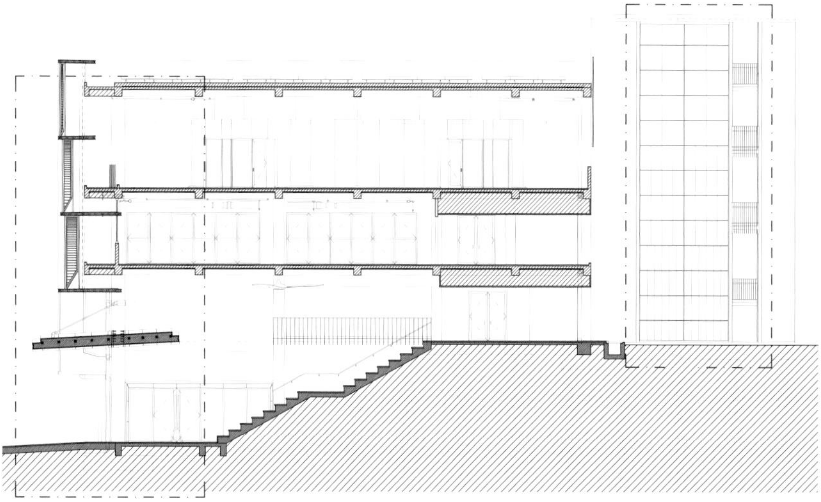

Cross section through grand staircase, barrel room and courtyard

0 2.5

0.5

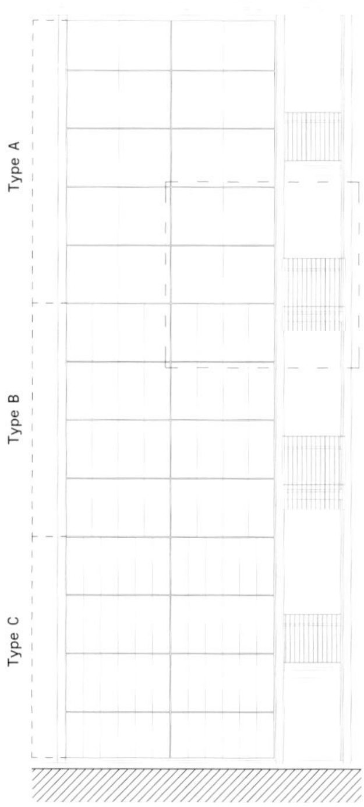

Elevation matrix of pleated veil types

0 2.5

0.5

Fig 62 Detail elevation of jungle staircase

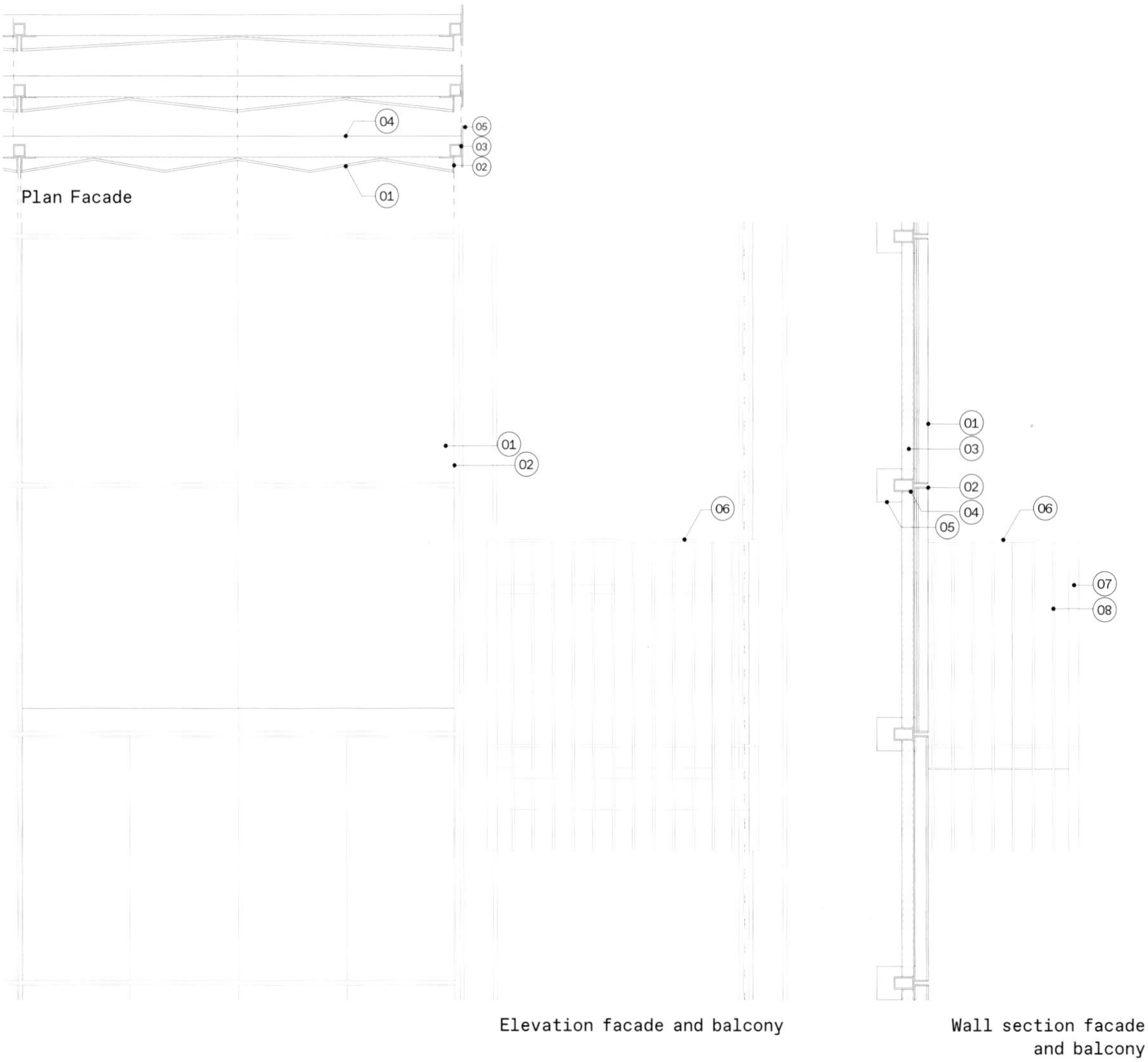

Legend

01	Expanded mesh
02	75×75×6mm sheet metal angle
03	60×60×5mm SHS
04	100×100×5mm SHS
05	200×200mm plate
06	50×12mm top rail flat bar
07	Main baluster 50×12mm flat bar
08	Intermediate baluster 25×12mm flat bar

0 0.5
0.1

Fig 63 Axonometric drawing of butterfly veils and solar performance

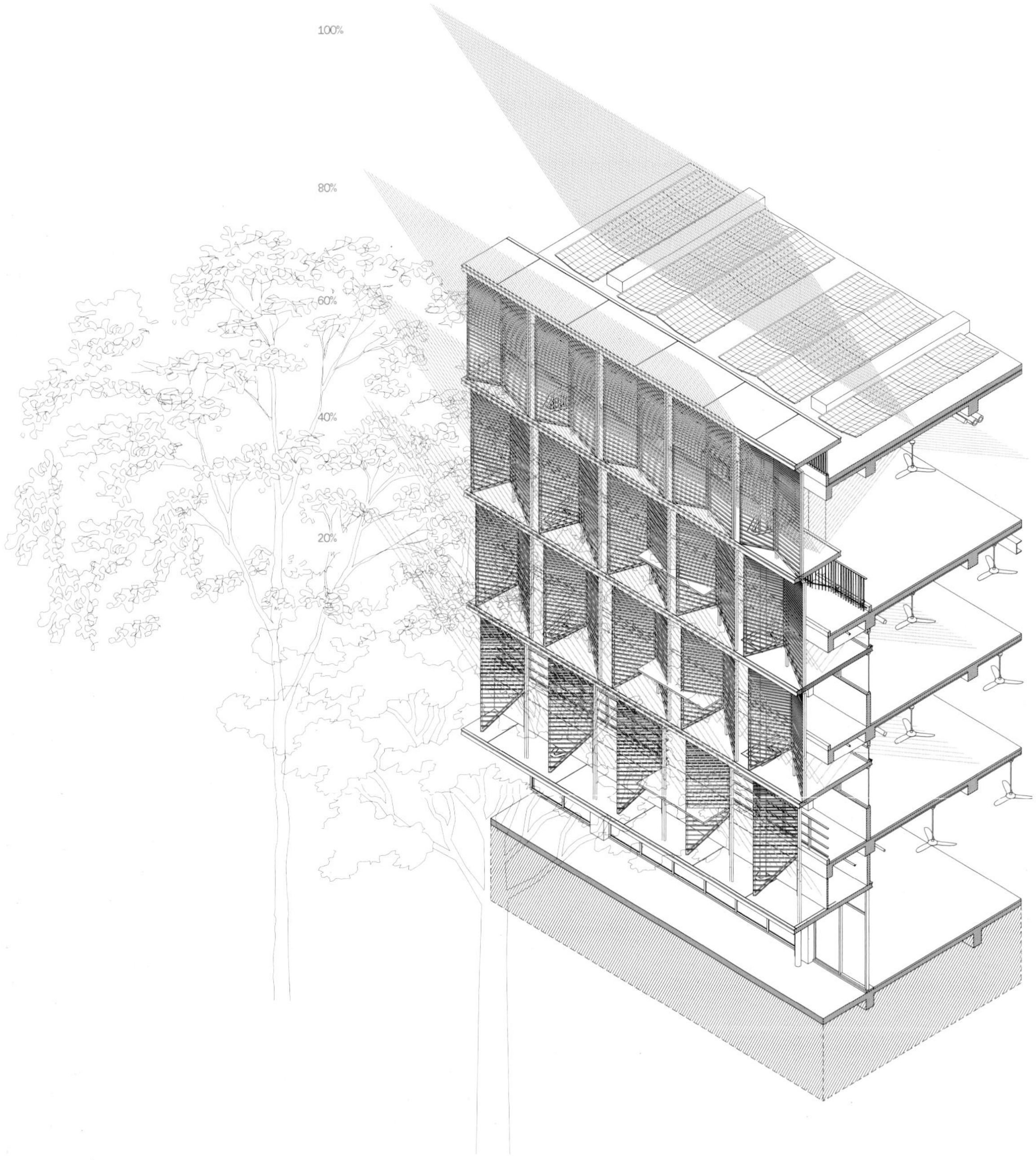

Legend

Sunlight

Fig 64 Detail of butterfly veil in the equatorial rain

Fig 65 Sectional axonometric drawing of SDE 3 with climatic performance

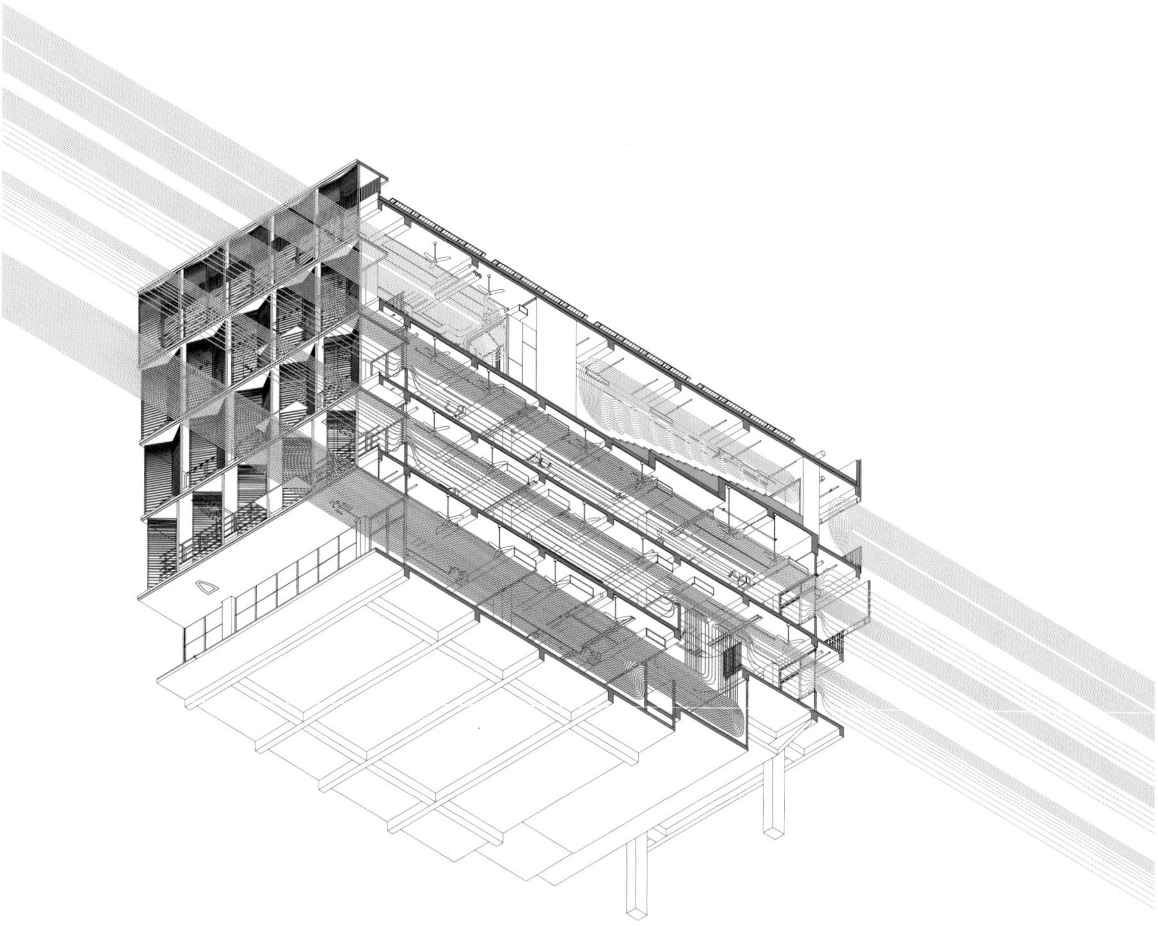

Legend

- Outside air
- Hybrid air
- Air conditioned

Fig 66 Sectional axonometric drawing of SDE 1 with climatic performance

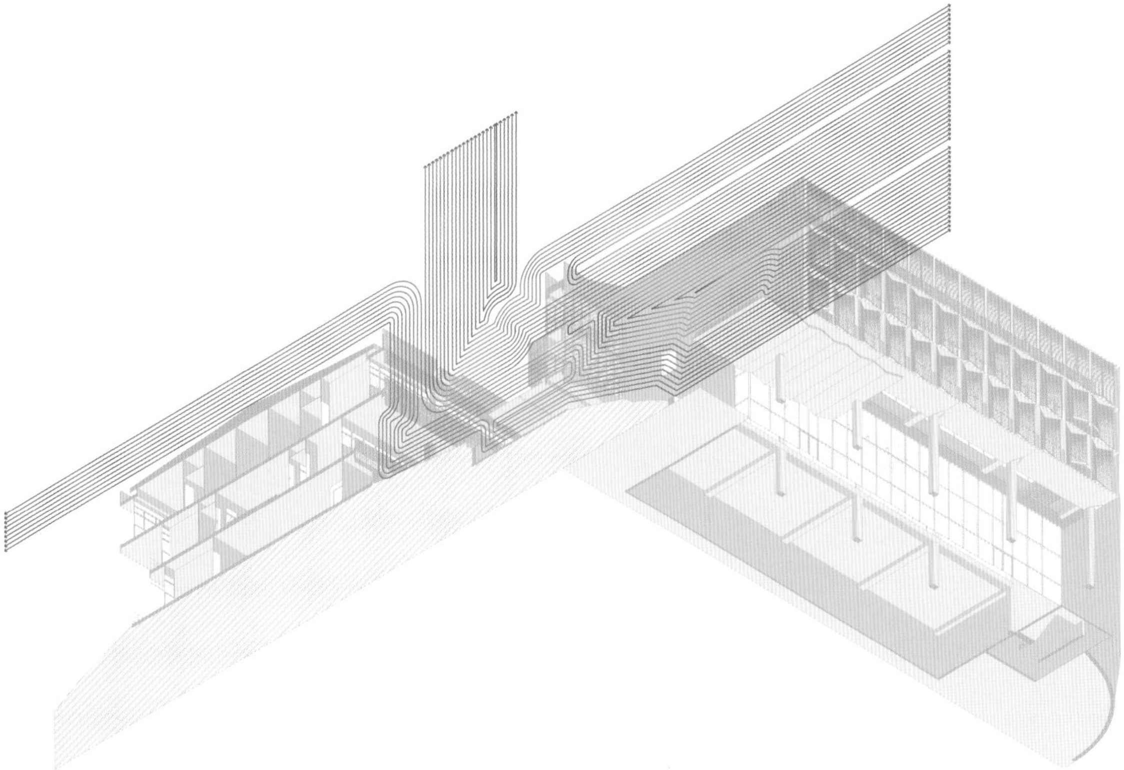

Fig 67 Exploded axonometric drawing of butterfly veil

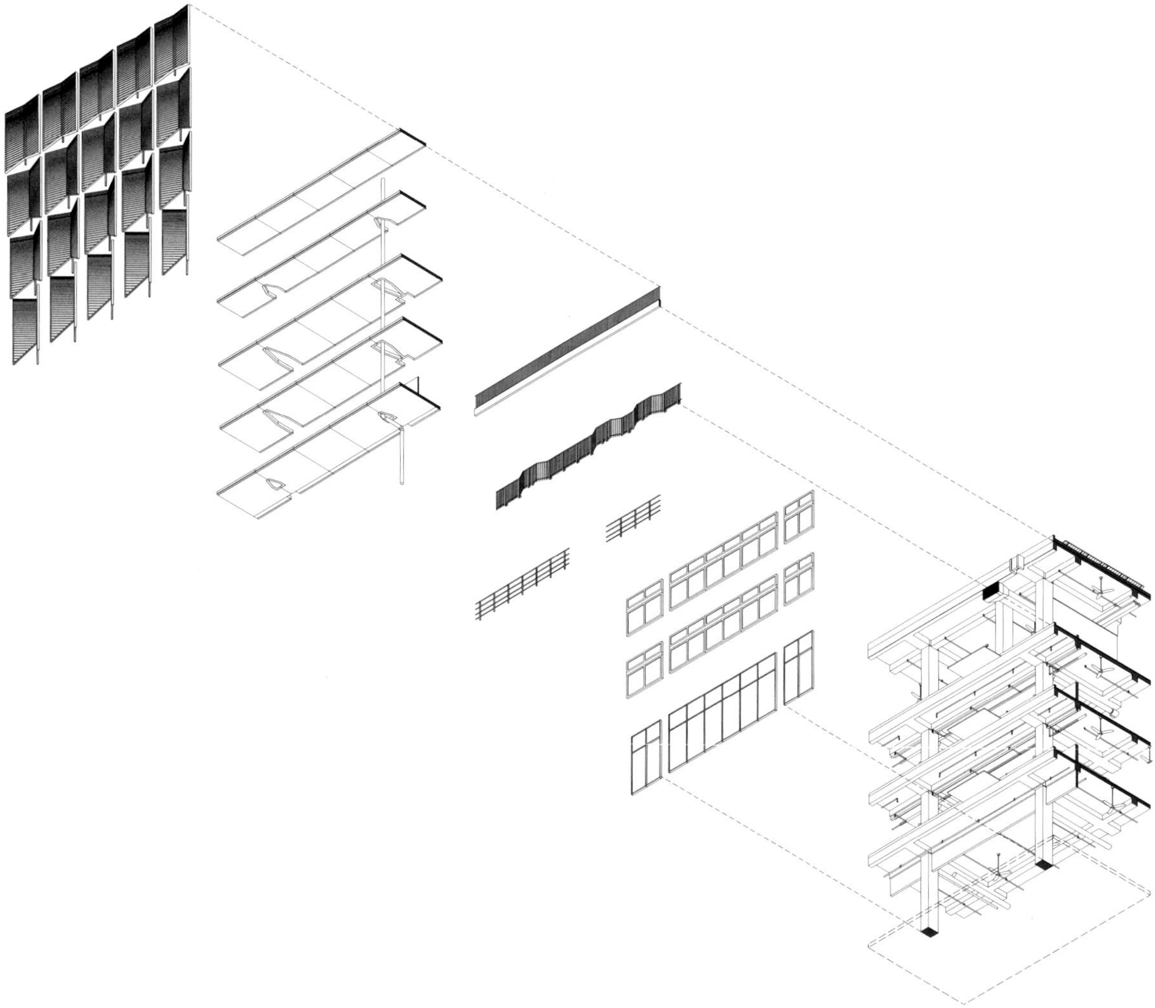

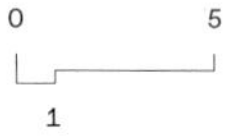

Fig 68 Section and detail sections of entrance canopy

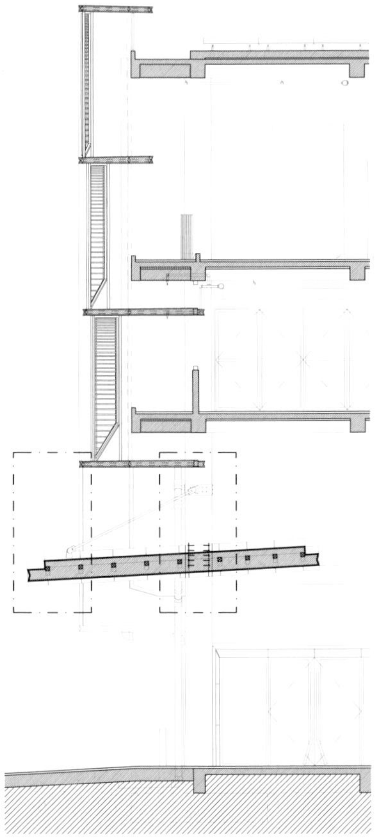

Wall section canopy

0 2.5
0.5

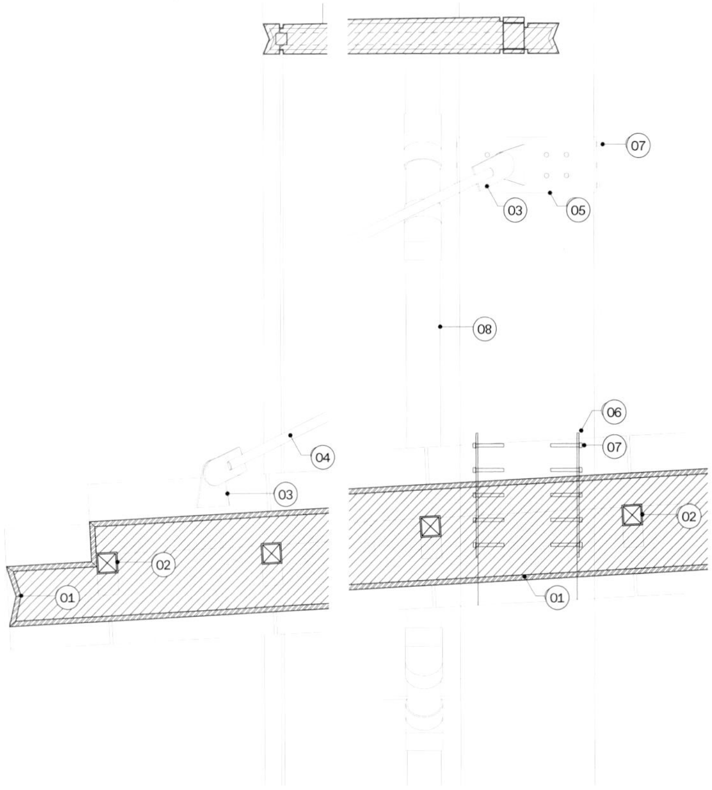

0 0.5
0.1

Wall section canopy blow-up

Legend

01	25mm aluminum panel with backer assembly
02	100×100mm aluminum RHS
03	Threaded rod anchor
04	Threaded rod
05	700×270mm plate
06	500×600mm plate
07	Multifix wedge anchor
08	Rainwater drainpipe

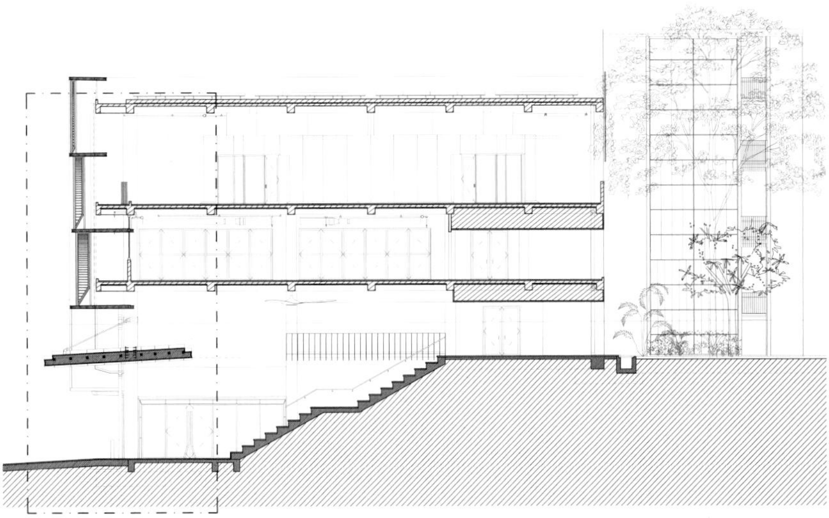

0 2.5
0.5

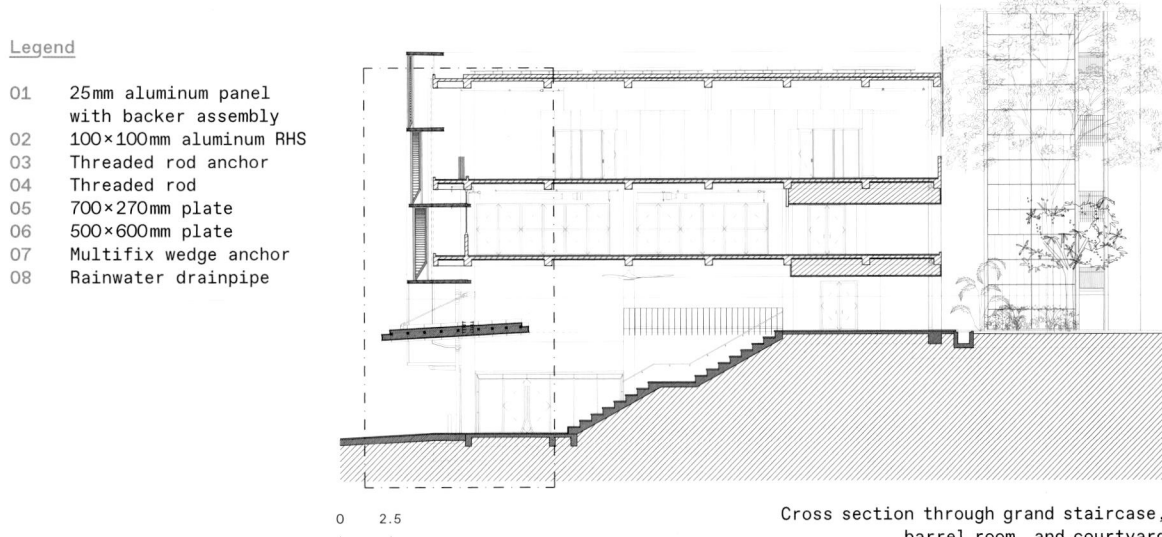

Cross section through grand staircase, barrel room, and courtyard

Fig 69 Night view of SDE 1

Fig 70 (right) View of SDE 1 verandah

Fig 71 (bottom) Night view of SDE 1 west elevation

Fig 72 View of jungle courtyard in the rain

Fig 1 West elevation of SDE 1: *Photo by Finbarr Fallon*

Painted in champagne gold, the deep envelope mirrors the intensity of the golden hue of the western setting sun.

Fig 2 West elevation of SDE 1: *Photo by Ong Chan Hao*

Patterned deep veils create an analogous relationship between vegetation and architecture.

Fig 3 West elevation
North elevation
South elevation

Elevations of SDE 1 & 3: the patterned deep veil elevation unifies the SDE buildings in coloration, filigree, and form.

Fig 4 Southwest elevation of SDE 1: *Photo by Ong Chan Hao*

A series of aluminum veils act as devices that modulate the equatorial climate from exterior to interior.

Fig 5 SDE 3 staircase section
SDE 3 staircase elevation facade
SDE 3 wall section details of west envelope

West elevation details: the deep veil is an integrated performance device that filters views, light, and air, while camouflaging air intake and exhaust systems on the elevation.

Fig 6 Detail of butterfly veil in contrast to the natural veil of the rain tree. *Photo by Ong Chan Hao*

Fig 7 Detail of the butterfly veil contrasts with the surrounding rain trees. *Photo by Ong Chan Hao*

Fig 8 Detail of SDE 1 canopy: *Photo by Ong Chan Hao*

The SDE 1 canopy as a mirror to the tree canopy.

Fig 9 The butterfly veil's horizontal sections rotate to create a gradient of color and lightness in response to sunlight. *Photo by Ong Chan Hao*

Fig 10 Interface detail at SDE 1: *Photo by Ong Chan Hao*

Lightweight aluminum deep veil anchorage details to the existing concrete structure.

Fig 11 Interior view of the department conference room: *Photo by Ong Chan Hao*

Awning windows, fire access, and pleated wall panels center the composition of the interior and exterior.

Fig 12 Section of west envelope
Envelope interface details

Detailed sections of the aluminum deep veil in conjunction with the existing structure.

Fig 13 Interior view of Department of Architecture office: *Photo by Ong Chan Hao*

The innovative hybrid cooling system combines the qualities of natural ventilation and tempered air, providing adaptive comfort and natural ventilation. The image alludes to the Paulo Mendes da Rocha House.

Fig 14 Drainpipe interface detail at SDE 1: *Photo by Ong Chan Hao*

The lightweight aluminum veil is delicately anchored to the existing structural frame, splaying to accommodate existing rainwater drainpipes.

Fig 15 Ground-level entry view of SDE 1: *Photo by Finbarr Fallon*

The entry staircase links the west entry with a jungle courtyard beyond.

Fig 16 SDE 1 section across jungle courtyard
SDE 3 section across the grand staircase

Section through the main staircase between SDE 1 & 3 ascending to the interior jungle courtyard.

Fig 17 Skyward view of vertical greenery: *Photo by Finbarr Fallon*

A champagne-gold portal peers out of the wild equatorial foliage.

Fig 18 Elevation details of vertical greenery:

Wall elevation with an angled portal nestled amidst the vertical greenery.

Fig 19 Angled portal:

Detail elevation and plan of the geometry of the torqued portal.

Fig 20 Interior view of the meeting room: *Photo by Ong Chan Hao*

Looking out into the entry staircase below.

Fig 21 Exterior view of the portal: *Photo by Ong Chan Hao*

Directing views to the social space below in an equatorial interpretation of the portal in Marcel Breuer's Whitney Museum.

Fig 22 North view of SDE 1 courtyard: *Photo by Ong Chan Hao*

A gold crown frames the jungle courtyard and equatorial sky at the center of SDE 1.

Fig 23 SDE 1 section of jungle courtyard.

Fig 24 Level 2 view of SDE 1 circulation spaces: *Photo by Finbarr Fallon*

Informal gathering terraces fronting the jungle courtyard, with windows to the grand hall and meeting rooms beyond.

Fig 25 Level 3 view of SDE 1 courtyard: *Photo by Finbarr Fallon*

A mild steel screen crown of vertical 50 mm flat metal bars outlines the jungle-looking landscape.

Figs 26–31 (left page) Clockwise from top left
Figs 32–36 (right page) Clockwise from top left
Photos by Finbarr Fallon & Ong Chan Hao

Design details of SDE 1 contrast with the heavy original concrete form, the light champagne-gold screens and portals creating a play of light and shadow.

Fig 37 West view of SDE 1 courtyard: *Photo by Ong Chan Hao*

The angled 50 mm vertical members and railings produce a dialogue of linear elements, sunshade, and rain screen with the verdant center.

Fig 38 West view of the jungle and beyond: *Photo by Ong Chan Hao*

The framed jungle sets up a dialogue between the aesthetics of an organized, patterned, filigree filter with the natural, living carbon of the landscape.

Fig 39 Floor plan of level 1
Fig 40 Floor plan of level 2
Fig 41 Floor plan of level 3
Fig 42 Floor plan of level 4

Floor plans illustrating the strategic subtractions and program additions to SDE 1 & 3.

Fig 43 SDE 3 section (north)—lecture theaters
SDE 3 section (south)—review foyer

The north section features subtractions between levels bringing daylight and ventilation deep into the recesses of the studio floors.The south section illustrates the newly inserted social staircase and lecture theater with the patterned deep veil elevation in the background.

Fig 44 Exploded axonometric of the staircase in SDE 3:

The social staircase straddles three tiers of large-span design studio spaces to encourage peer-to-peer social learning and public debates.

Fig 45 Level 4 view of SDE 1 corridors: *Photo by Finbarr Fallon*

The dialogue between building screen and vegetation occurs in the exterior covered circulation spaces and informal gathering terraces.

Fig 46 Detail of SDE 1 jungle courtyard: *Photo by Ong Chan Hao*

The golden crown around the courtyard hugs the jungle and accentuates the contrast of geometry and color.

Fig 47 View of courtyard: *Photo by Ong Chan Hao*

The jungle modulates the exterior climate, allowing the surrounding verandahs to become comfortable spaces for students and staff.

Fig 48 Interior view of office space: *Photo by Ong Chan Hao*

Diffused light pours in in the morning, illuminating the interior without the need for artificial light.

Fig 49 Interior view of Department of Architecture with meeting room at right with operable awning window wall for natural ventilation after hours, shown at left. A fabric duct hybrid cooling system increases the generosity of space while being a visual pedagogical tool. *Photo by Ong Chan Hao*

Fig 50 Exterior view of Department of Architecture meeting room clad in pleated teak laminate panels contrast with the spartan finishes of the surrounding spaces. *Photo by Ong Chan Hao*

Fig 51 Detail of timber panels: *Photo by Ong Chan Hao*

A window wall illuminates the timber panels, revealing the subtle kink that forms a pattern surrounding the conference room.

Fig 52 Detail of interior wall finishes: *Photo by Ong Chan Hao*

The pleated formal vocabulary links the exterior to the interior formally. The teak laminate samples a local material of Southeast Asia.

Fig 53 Interior view of Department of Building office: *Photo by Ong Chan Hao*

Pleated and screened walls demarcate waiting lobbies, workspaces, and meeting rooms.

Fig 54 Interior view of office meeting room where corridor, meeting room, and exterior jungle courtyard are linked visually. *Photo by Ong Chan Hao*

Fig 55 Level 4 view of SDE 1 atrium with exposed structural framing. *Photo by Finbarr Fallon*

Fig 56 West elevation of jungle courtyard: *Photo by Ong Chan Hao*

Operable windows on the elevation allow users to determine the amount of exterior air that enters their workspace.

Fig 57 Detail of jungle courtyard: *Photo by Ong Chan Hao*

The golden crown veil reflects the strong afternoon sunlight, softly illuminating the jungle and the banyan tree at the center.

Fig 58 Detail of jungle courtyard: *Photo by Ong Chan Hao*

A late afternoon rain washes away the heat, filling the courtyard with moisture and giving the light a hazy quality.

Fig 59 Detail of jungle courtyard: *Photo by Ong Chan Hao*

The downpour transforms the courtyard into a spectacle of jungle, veil, and rain.

Fig 60 SDE 3 section: staircase elevation.

Fig 61 South view of SDE 1: *Photo by Ong Chan Hao*

Elevations along the staircase extend a language of folded and pleated screens to the service cores.

Fig 62 SDE 3 staircase elevation details:

Mild steel railings and screens continue the language of filter, line, edge, mesh.

Fig 63 Axonometric of SDE 1:

Gradient modes of daylight filter into the spaces through the deep envelope with a rooftop photovoltaic array maximizing energy self-sufficiency.

Fig 64 West elevation of SDE 1: *Photo by Ong Chan Hao*

The butterfly veil and canopy of SDE 1 in a downpour.

Fig 65 Sectional worm's-eye axonometric of SDE 3:

The mixing of natural, air-conditioned, and hybrid-cooled modes of air in the renovated spaces.

Fig 66 Worm's-eye axonometric of SDE 1:

The renovation exfoliates the volume of the original structure with the dynamics of hot air amidst equatorial greenery.

Fig 67 Exploded worm's-eye axonometric of the deep veil:

The veiled elevation parasitically anchors onto the original structural frame.

Fig 68 Detailed sections of SDE entry canopy:

The entry canopy defines a single, direct entry from the urban ground level into the campus precincts.

Fig 69 Night view of SDE 1 grand hall: *Photo by Ong Chan Hao*

The architecture glows in the humid equatorial evening.

Fig 70 View of SDE 1 terrace: *Photo by Ong Chan Hao*

The terrace becomes a comfortable space for work at night, when the vehicular traffic slows down to a quiet drone.

Fig 71 View of west elevation: *Photo by Ong Chan Hao*

The veil transforms SDE 1 into a flowing filter at night.

Fig 72 SDE 1 level 4 view: *Photo by Erik L'Heureux*

The jungle courtyard in a monsoon storm.

Chapter 5
Calibrating the Carbon Problem

Wolfgang Kessling
Nirmal Kishnani

This section consists of two essays: *Evaluating the Hidden Carbon in SDE 1 & 3* by Wolfgang Kessling investigates the value of preserving embodied carbon through Life Cycle Analysis (LCA) undertaken over the multiple design scenarios of the SDE renovation. *A Problem of Problems* by Nirmal Kishnani speaks to recognizing design challenges and addressing them at their scales of complexity. These essays position the SDE renovation projects as important prototypes that belong to a larger systemic whole; their authors offer, respectively, quantitative and qualitative perspectives on the carbon conversation, while underlining the challenges that professionals need to work with in order to create positive change.

Evaluating the Hidden Carbon in SDE 1 & 3

Wolfgang Kessling

In the building sector, the carbon conversation has long been centered around expectations of thermal comfort and energy performance. Reducing carbon was linked to reducing operational energy or the carbon intensity of the energy supply. Though less understood, the extraction of natural resources for construction purposes and the production of building materials are also energy-intensive processes that release significant carbon emissions, among their other negative impacts.[1] Advancing the global agenda of decarbonizing the building sector is a major challenge. To reduce the burden on future generations, building projects today need to be on a pathway for zero-carbon operational energy and they must aggressively explore new design principles to reduce embodied carbon.

This pathway is explored with the SDE 1 & 3 building carbon story, which is discussed in the following essay. The first part explores the net-zero strategies for operational energy, while the second delves into the impact of avoiding carbon emissions by retaining the base buildings' embodied carbon. These different but complementary strategies are linked together through the carbon story of the project, thereby illustrating the vision for the reduction of the project's carbon footprint.

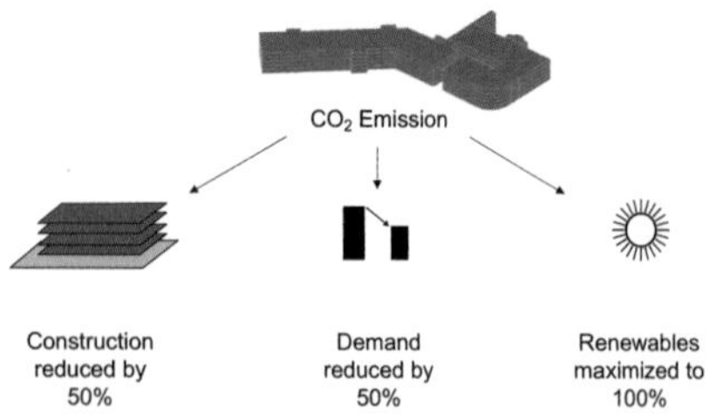

Fig 5.1.1 Original vision for reducing the carbon footprint of a tropical building. SDE 1 and SDE 3 apply a three-pronged approach to reduce CO2 emissions by addressing the construction process, energy consumption, and energy generation.

Part I: Creating Excellent Environmental Conditions for People

The goal of the renovation of the SDE 1 & 3 buildings was to create spaces of inspiring architectural quality while simultaneously designing a building that operates on a low-energy-demand basis. When SDE 1 & 3 were reviewed for refurbishment, the design team focused on the potential of the base buildings to create excellent environmental conditions for people through (i) daylight access and autonomy, (ii) thermal comfort, (iii) natural ventilation, and (iv) indoor air quality. The base buildings could deliver these qualities by reusing the building structures, upgrading the facades, and introducing innovations in designing for thermal comfort in the tropics.[2] By focusing on people's needs and the climatic and cultural context of the project, the quest to create these qualities through passive design and technical systems resulted in significantly reduced energy demand.

The Hidden Treasure

In the initial exploration of the existing base buildings, one of the most astonishing findings was the great hidden ceiling volumes. The structure for these two conjoined buildings was built in the late 1970s, when responsibility for building performance was shifted from architecture to HVAC systems. This resulted in the allocation of significant building height volumes within the suspended ceilings for the ductwork of cooling and ventilation systems, and some of these spaces were up to 1.8 m in height. All the floors had very low suspended ceilings, so the structure was not contributing to the building's performance and its spatial qualities, but it had the potential to. In order to take advantage of the existing structure and improve the spatial quality, the removal of the suspended ceilings was proposed. Such high ceilings in a new building would have been economically unfeasible.

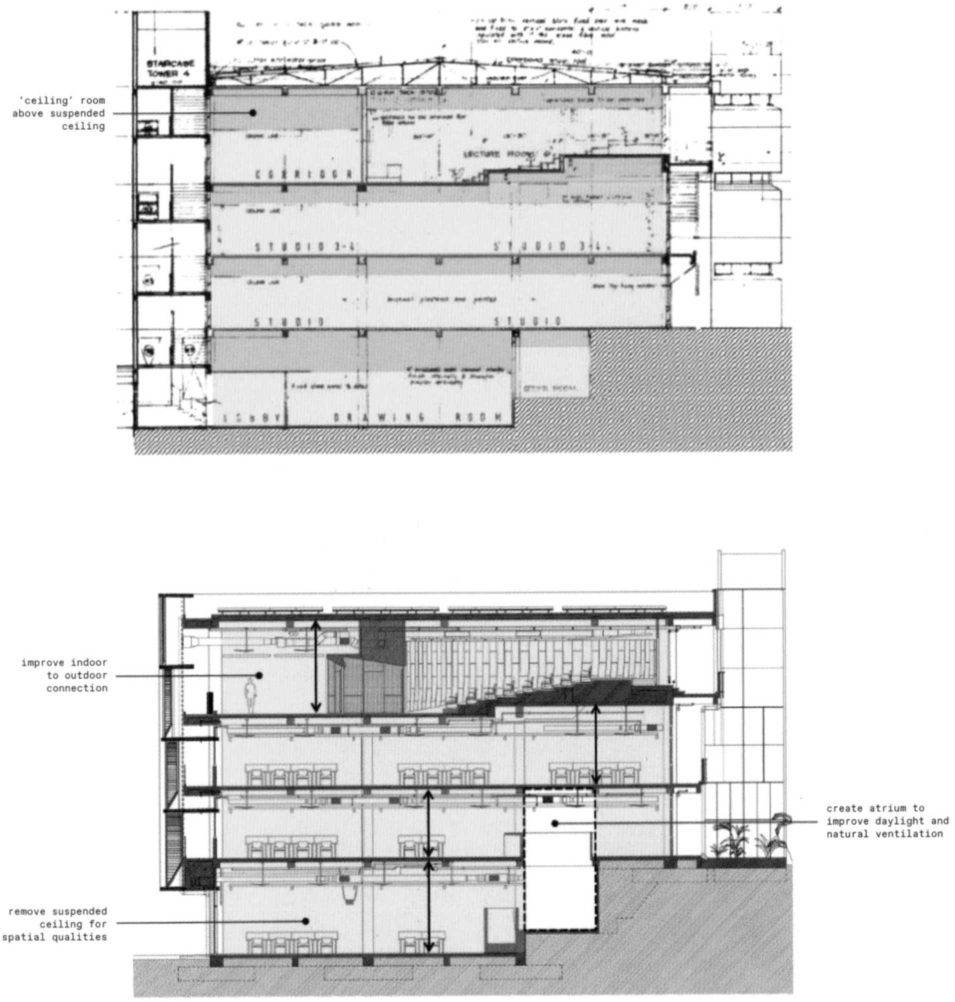

Fig 5.1.2 Indicative section with original suspended ceilings and compressed floor volumes before refurbishment (top). Proposed section showing changes improving daylight access and ceiling height (bottom).

Exploring Daylight Options

The original facade significantly limited the quality of daylight in the spaces. The existing brise-soleil completely shaded the transparent facade elements to protect the rooms from solar gains, but it also eliminated the possibility of using daylight in the buildings. The dark tones, high ceiling partitions, and suspended ceilings amplified this effect. It was recommended to refurbish all facades with high-selective sun-protective glazing to allow for daylight while simultaneously providing an efficient protection against solar radiation. The external shading is an essential part of the identity of the architectural ensemble. Therefore, many options for the reconfiguration of the external lamellas were studied, with the goal of reducing glare from the tropical skies while optimizing daylight and balancing solar gain. The potential of the combined effects for daylight turned out to be high, offering excellent daylit spaces and reducing the energy demand for artificial lighting.

Fig 5.1.3 Renderings with daylight impression before (top) and after inclusion of atrium and removal of suspended ceiling within the original structure (bottom).

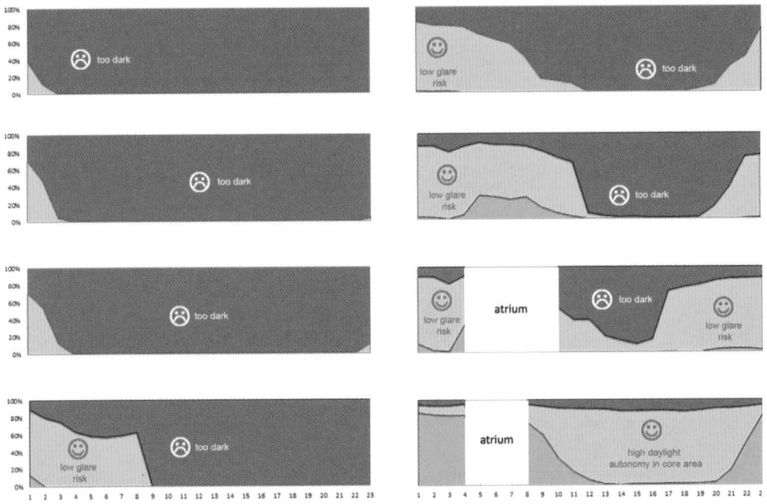

Fig 5.1.4 SDE 3 section indicating improvement in Useful Daylight Illuminance (UDI). Range: 300-2000 lux at 0.8 m FFL between 08:00-18:00 due to improvement of facade and inclusion of atrium.

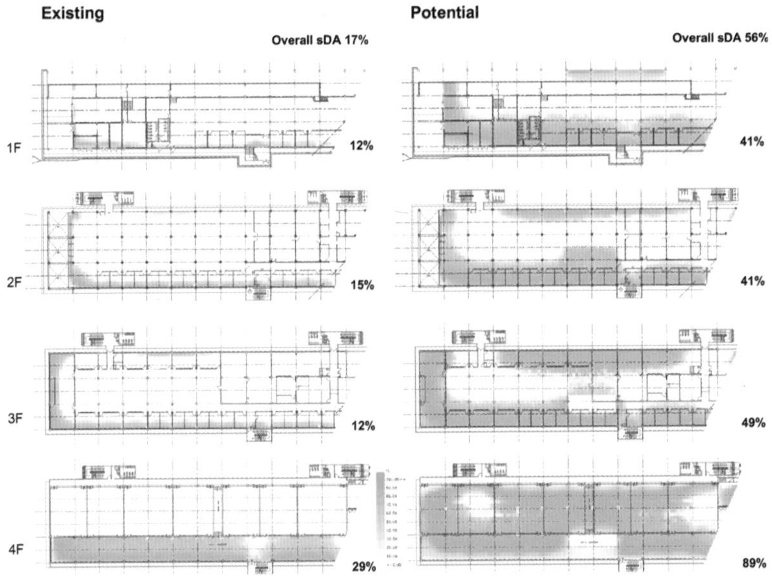

Fig 5.1.5 SDE 3 floor plans indicating improvement in Spatial Daylight Autonomy (sDA). Range: 300-2000 lux at 0.8 m FFL between 08:00-18:00 hours.

Numbers represent Spatial Daylight Autonomy, sDA range: 300-2000 Lux at 0.8m level, 8am to 6pm.

Improving the Indoor Environment with Hybrid Ventilation and Cooling Systems

Besides the lack of functionality for daylight performance, the facades were outdated in technical terms for solar gain control, U-values, air tightness, and operability for natural ventilation. Originally, the buildings were fully sealed and operated with air-conditioning and mechanical ventilation systems in almost all areas. When these systems were switched off after working hours, the buildings overheated and the indoor air quality became very poor for the students and faculty members who were still working in the studios.

To improve and optimize these environmental conditions, the design team studied innovative concepts to create a sequence of outdoor, transitional, and indoor spaces. The layout of thermal zones in the different program areas was organized as per their environmental requirements. Many areas were purposefully designed as outdoor areas, protected against wind and rain, but were also nicely daylit and provided with excellent natural ventilation. Major program areas now operate with a wider temperature and humidity range with hybrid cooling; that is, a combination of ceiling fans and mixed-mode mechanical and natural ventilation. Only where strictly required are indoor spaces fully air-conditioned.

The improvement of the indoor environment quality with hybrid ventilation and cooling systems had already been successfully explored in the SDE 4 building.[3] A hybrid cooling system delivers air temperature and humidity at higher set points than conventional air-conditioning systems. To offset this, the rooms are fitted with ceiling fans that increase air speed to improve the thermal sensation of the occupants.

As a single-pass system design with excellent air supply rates, there is no recirculating air; more fresh air is healthier for the building's occupants.[4] This means that there is no return air ducting, and the supplied air spills over into adjacent outdoor spaces, thereby enhancing the thermal comfort in these areas. Compared to conventionally cooled spaces, the slightly increased room temperatures result in smaller differences between indoor and outdoor spaces. This allows for a gentle switch from a tempered mechanical air supply to natural ventilation and significantly increases the value of designing facades and thermal zoning of tropical buildings for natural ventilation. Furthermore, there are significant implications for energy and carbon savings.

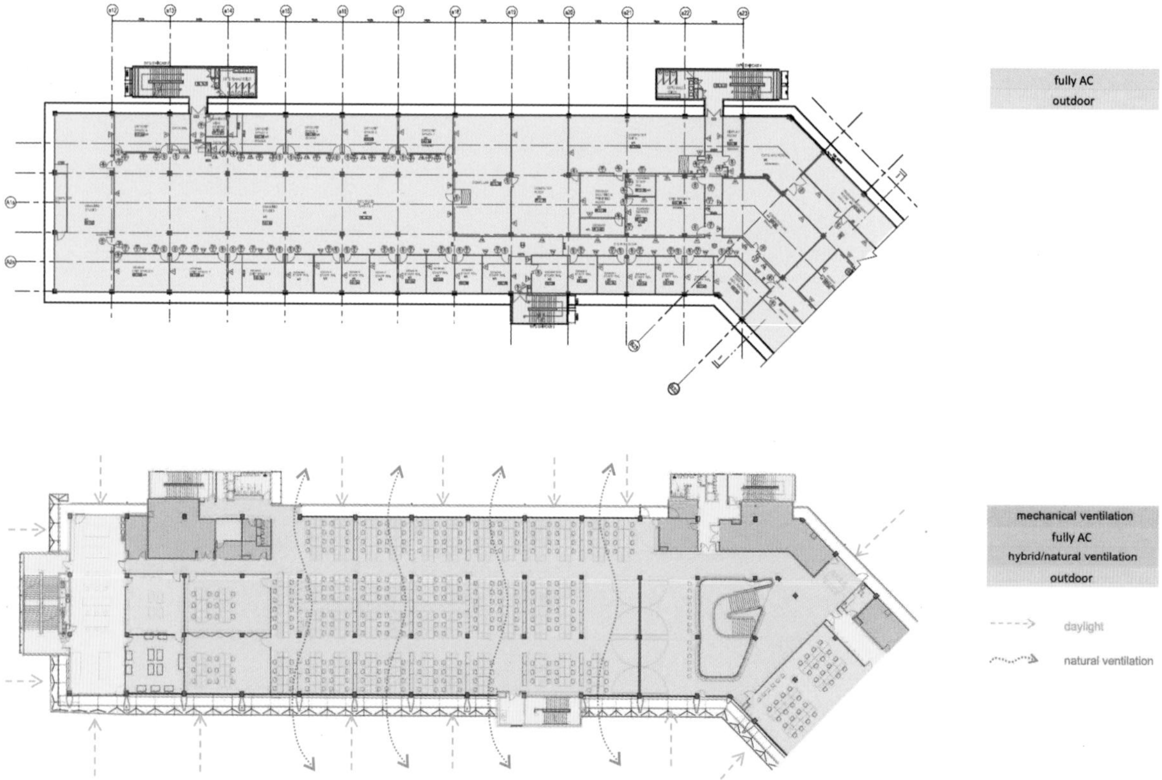

Fig 5.1.6 SDE 3 floor plans with original fully air-conditioned layout (top) and with improved thermal zoning with refurbished facade (bottom). Significant areas can be operated in hybrid ventilation mode: mechanical ventilation with supply of tempered air.

Low Energy by Design

The combined effects of the proposed interventions on energy demand are significant. The average energy use intensity (EUI) of the SDE 1 & 3 buildings across all program areas was estimated to be around 90 kWh/m²/yr (kilowatt-hour per square meter per year), significantly less than the 300 kWh/m²/yr average EUI for university buildings in Singapore.[5] Given the site constraints, about 50% of the total energy demand could be produced with an array of photovoltaic panels on the roof.[6]

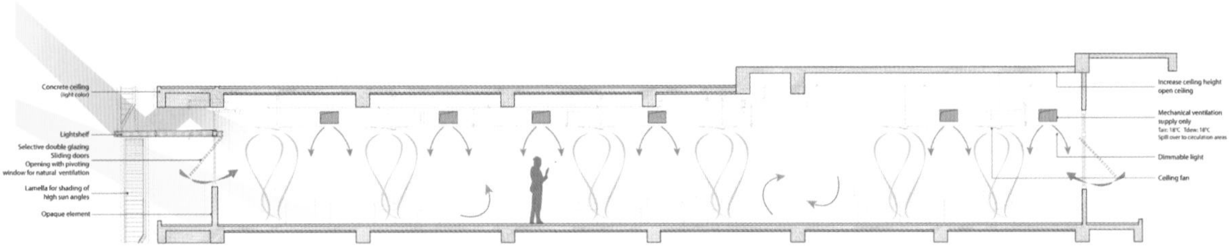

Fig 5.1.7 Typical section showcasing hybrid cooling concept elements such as the building facade working in conjunction with the MVAC system.

Part II: The Value of Embodied Carbon

As the base buildings were to be retained, the team estimated the embodied carbon in the original structures to put the emissions of operation and construction into perspective and complete the holistic carbon story.[7]

The production of buildings, from the extraction of natural resources to the construction, releases significant carbon emissions. To summarize the impact of the materials in the structures, the team performed a Life Cycle Assessment (LCA). This allowed us to estimate the "embodied carbon" of the buildings, a measure for their carbon intensity. The lower these emissions are, the lesser the carbon impact of the buildings is on the environment.

There are few studies on embodied carbon available for Singapore's building stock, and there is no available regional database on carbon emissions factors for building materials. The design team therefore adapted a methodology following the modular Life Cycle Models of the EN 15804 in a "cradle to gate" analysis. This included the three steps of production of building materials: raw material supply (A1), transport (A2), and manufacturing (A3). In the absence of a comprehensive source for regional emissions factors, emissions factors from the Inventory of Carbon and Energy (ICE) and the Oekobaudat (OKO) Sustainable Construction Information Portal were used.[8]
In addition, the emissions factors for cement and concrete were adapted from a LCA study on imported concrete for Singapore.[9] To estimate

the masses of the building materials, a 3D model of the main building structure and facade was used. The model was developed by the architects out of the historic plans and sections and updated to the status of refurbishment. For the estimation, the buildings were deconstructed into twelve major building elements for the base buildings, facades, and mechanical ventilation and air-conditioning (MVAC) systems. Each element was matched to the most appropriate material definition available in the databases, and the related emissions factors were assigned.

The limitations to this methodology include the following: The building model, particularly the original 1970s foundation elements, could be incomplete. The material compositions (for example, for the concrete and steel) are based on solely on conjectures and on-site observations. Available emissions factors haven't been developed for Singapore, nor are historic carbon factors for construction materials used in the seventies available. With the acknowledgement of the methodological limitations, the estimation of embodied carbon puts the reuse of the existing building structures into perspective vis-à-vis rebuilding the same structures at the same location. From this point of view, the value of reusing the base buildings lies in avoiding the environmental impacts that result from constructing a new building.[10]

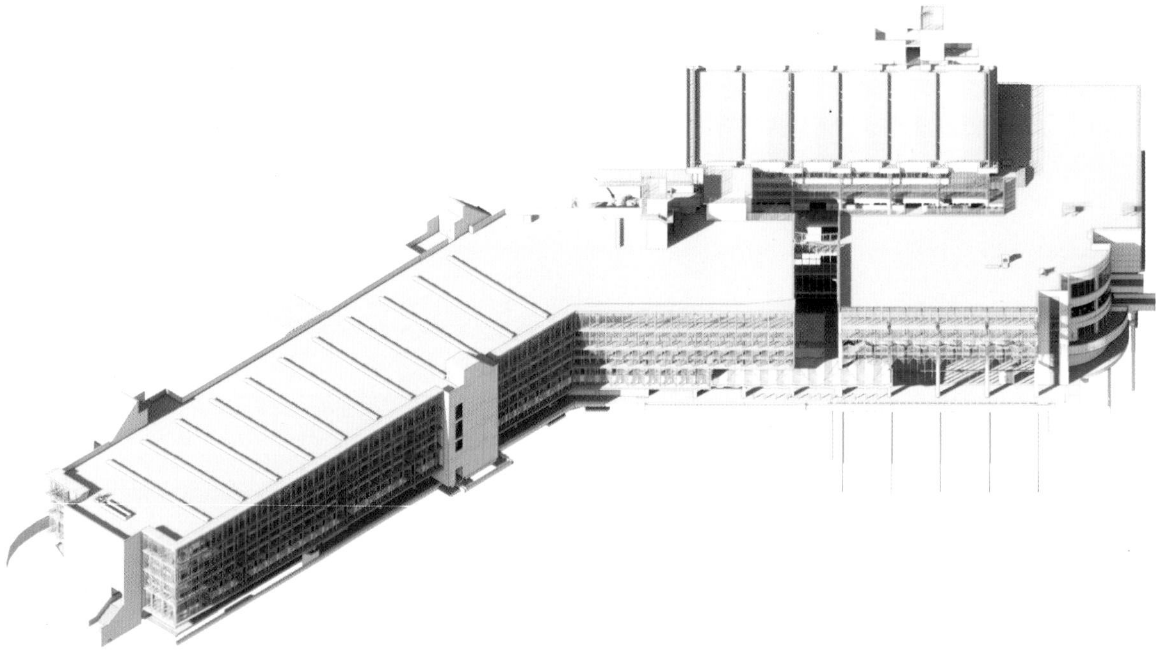

Fig 5.1.8 A 3D model of SDE 1 and SDE 3 was used for the Life Cycle Analysis (LCA) to estimate the masses of the main construction components to be retained and refurbished (top).

Fig 5.1.9 Detailed breakdown of the model by construction materials. Base building elements were retained (right).

No.	Construction Component Name	Construction Component Location	Material	Mass (tons)	Notes
01	Foundation	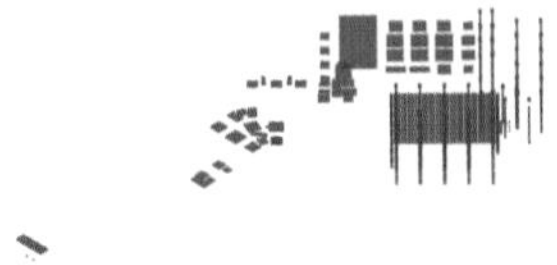	Concrete C30/37	5018	The estimated mass of the foundations was tripled as the 3D model only indicated foundations for 1/3 of the building.
02	Columns		Concrete with 4.5% reinforcing steel	2118	C30/37 concrete
03	Beams	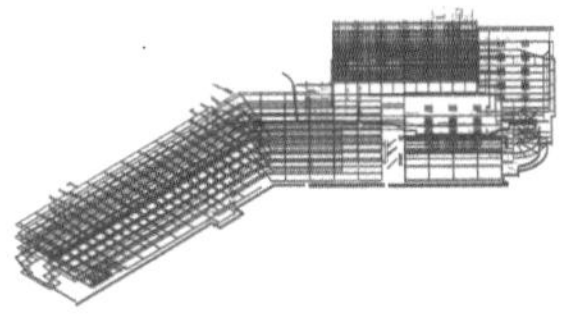	Concrete with 4% reinforcing steel	7218	
04	Walls	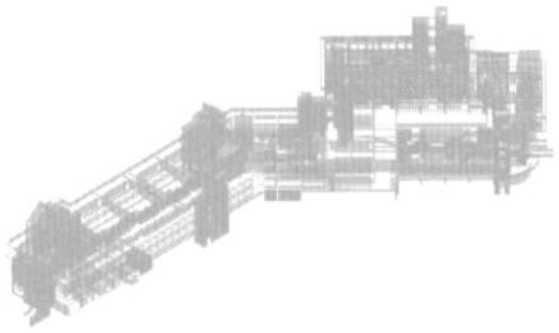	Concrete with 1% reinforcing steel	8067	
05	Floor		Concrete with 1% reinforcing steel	15200	
06	Stairs		Concrete with 1.5% reinforcing steel	1095	
07	Ceiling	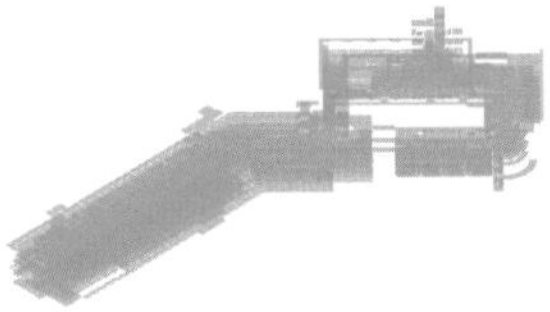	Plasterboard (false ceiling)	376	
08	Windows		Double glazing, aluminum frame	121	
09	Shading	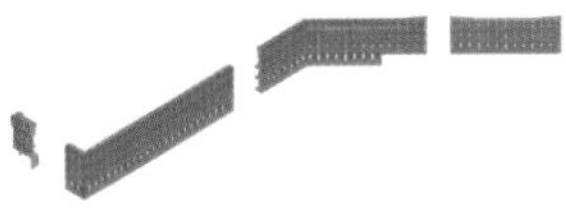	Aluminum, not recycled	53	The reuse of the existing shading material was considered as an option.

Five different scenarios were compared: (i) a totally new construction, rated with local concrete emissions factors; (ii) a totally new construction, rated with ICE emissions factors; (iii) a totally new construction, rated with Okobaudat emissions factors for 2019; (iv) the existing buildings (taking the refurbishment into account); and an optional scenario, (v), considering the reuse the aluminium for shading elements and a lean MEP (hybrid cooling) system.

Assuming a new building constructed at the site with the same size and functionality, the total specific embodied carbon emissions would be approximately in the range of 255 to 512 kg CO2-eq/m² (kilogram of carbon dioxide equivalent per square meter)of ground-floor area (GFA), which indicates a wide range of possible emissions.[11] The higher estimate is most likely the closest to the actual carbon emissions embodied in the existing structure. The lower estimate would represent a new construction made with greener material. The adaptive reuse of the base buildings and replacement of the elements in need of upgrade, such as the facades and the MVAC system, would reduce the carbon emissions. The so-called "recurring embodied carbon" would be approximately 95 kg CO2-eq/m² of GFA. This scenario most likely represents the best estimate for the refurbished base building. As an additional possibility, reusing the material of the shade systems and consequently implementing a lean hybrid cooling system would further reduce carbon emissions to approximately 60 kg CO2-eq/m² of GFA. The last option, pushing the limits to lower the embodied carbon, was not realized.

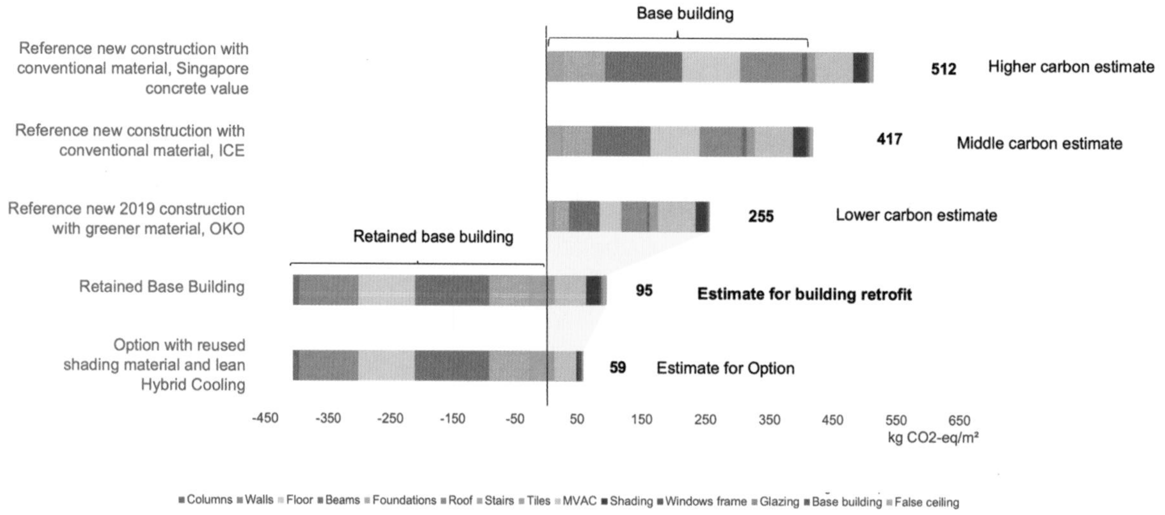

Fig 5.1.10 Estimation of embodied carbon.

The Carbon Story: Putting Carbon Emissions in Perspective

The net-zero design strategies for energy demand, energy generation, and retainment of embodied carbon tell the carbon story of the SDE 1 & 3 buildings from different perspectives that, in the end, merge into a holistic framework. Its final purpose is to be a tangible example of two things: a pathway to follow in order to lower carbon emissions and the establishment of accountable goals to be agreed upon with stakeholders.

The adaptive reuse and conservation of the base buildings gives value to past construction emissions. The retrofit emissions are estimated to be only 20% of what would hypothetically be emitted for a newly constructed building; these occur at the time of refurbishment. In the future, there will be operating emissions as the SDE 1 & 3 buildings host many generations of architects. Reducing the buildings' energy demand by 60% directly avoids those future carbon emissions. The savings will not only be related to the energy-efficient design, but also to the user's conscious operation. The shift of energy sources from fossil fuels to renewables contributes directly to the reduction of the emissions as well, but data on the use of the latter is limited.

While absolute carbon emissions remain abstract, when carbon emissions are outlined in per capita terms, the urgency of acting now — with every new building — becomes very clear. The sustainable world goal for the year 2030 is around 2.5 t CO2-eq/yr (tons of carbon dioxide equivalent per year) per capita.[12] The average per capita emissions of a Singaporean person in 2018 were about 8.4 t CO2-eq/yr. A part of this number is attributed to the construction and operation of buildings used for education and work. For a user of the SDE 1 & 3 buildings, the scenarios in this carbon story allocate per capita emissions of 1.7 t CO2-eq/yr (conventional new construction scenario) to 0.5 t CO2-eq/yr (adaptive reuse and hybrid cooling system scenario) to about 0.03 t CO2-eq/yr (all-renewable energy supply scenario).[13] The numbers highlight the relevance of restorative building practices and circular material economy models to transform the global and local building practices.

The SDE projects are earnestly exploring relevant options for low carbon / high comfort in buildings in the tropics. The university can be thought of as a living test bed where future professionals can experience firsthand how context-sensitive tropical design works and feels. It is our hope that they leave with the confidence and knowledge required to deliver it in practice.

The author acknowledges the support of Thomas Slater and Lucia Lara in the development of this essay.

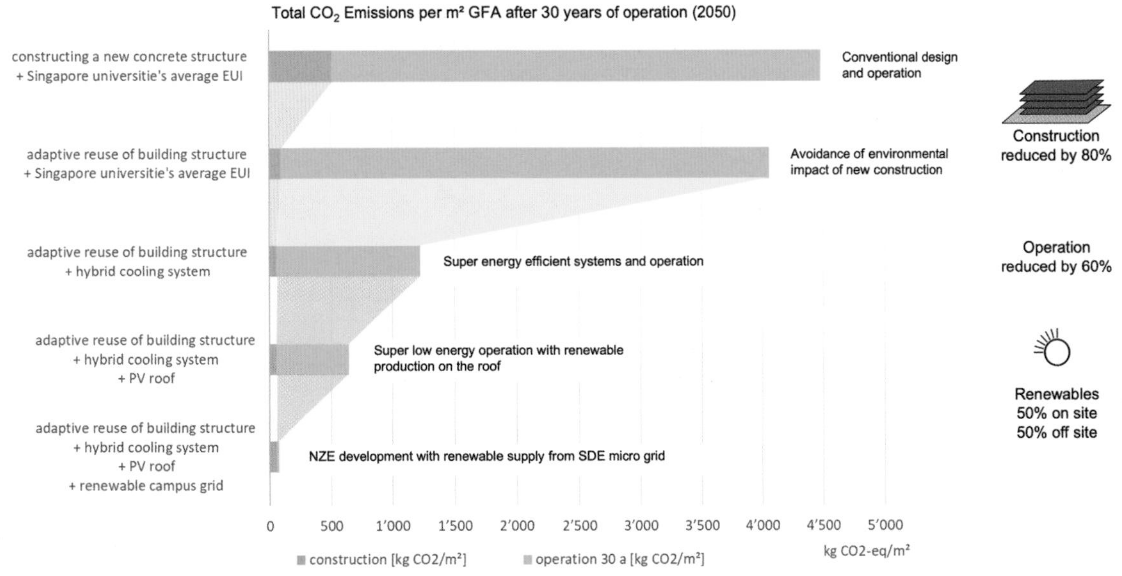

Fig 5.1.11 SDE 1 & 3's carbon story.

[1] Patrice Frey, L. Dunn, R. Cochran, K. Spataro, J. F. McLennan, R. DiNola, and B. Heider, "The Greenest Building: Quantifying the Environmental Value of Building Reuse," Preservation Green Lab/ National Trust for Historic Preservation, 2011, accessed Nov. 10, 2021, https://living-future.org/wp-content/uploads/2016/11/The_Greenest_Building.pdf.

[2] D. Kiehlman, R. Wang, and W. Kessling, "Narrative and Specifications of Climate and Energy Concept for SDE 3 Building (unpublished report)," Transsolar Energietechnik GmbH, 2015.

[3] W. Kessling, M. Engelhardt, and N. Kishnani, "Developing the Net Zero Energy Design," in *Cities, Buildings, People: Towards Regenerative Environments: Proceedings of the 32nd International Conference on Passive and Low Energy Architecture (PLEA)*, ed. Pablo La Roche and Marc Schiler, (Los Angeles: PLEA, 2016), accessed Nov. 10, 2021, https://transsolar.com/media/pages/publications/papers/plea-2016-developing-the-net-zero-energy-design-for-nus-sde4/6d634e712c-1613487274/plea2016_paper_net-zero-energy-design-for-sde4.pdf.

[4] N. Kishnani, "Beauty in Zero," in *FuturArc* 52 (Jan.-Feb. 2017): 18-25, https://www.bciasia.com/wp-content/uploads/2017/01/FA_EbookJanFeb17.pdf.

[5] Building and Construction Authority of Singapore, "Building Energy Benchmarking Report (2018)," accessed Nov. 10, 2021, https://www.bca.gov.sg/bess/benchmarking report/benchmarkingreport.aspx.

[6] Kiehlman et al., 05.

[7] J. Barot, V. Aguirre, L. Lara, and W. Kessling, "Assessment of Embodied Carbon for SDE 1 & 3 (unpublished report)," Transsolar Energietechnik GmbH, 2021. International Green Building Council, "Inventory of Carbon and Energy," Feb. 13, 2015, accessed Nov. 10, 2021, https://www.igbc.ie/resources/inventory-of-carbon-and-energy/.

[8] Federal Ministry of the Interior, Building, and Community, "ÖKOBAUDAT Database," accessed Nov. 10, 2021, https://www.oekobaudat.de/en.html.

[9] Aysegul Petek Gursel and Claudia P. Ostertag, "Impact of Singapore's Importers on Life-Cycle Assessment of Concrete," *Journal of Cleaner Production* 118 (2016): 140-150. https://doi.org/10.1016/j.jclepro.2016.01.051.

[10] Frey et al., 11.

[11] The quantity that describes, for a given mixture and amount of greenhouse gas, the amount of CO2 that would have the same global warming potential (GWP) when measured over a specified timescale
.

[12] United Nations Environment Programme, "Emissions Gap Report 2020: Executive Summary," 2020, https://wedocs.unep.org/bitstream/handle/20.500.11822/34438/EGR20ESE.pdf.

[13] Assumption: 12 square meters per person, 30 years of operation.

A Problem of Problems: Systems Thinking at the Drawing Board

Nirmal Kishnani

Author and activist Jane Jacobs once asked "(what) kind of problem the city is." In the 1970s, she argued, the city had been framed as the wrong problem type, which led to solutions that were, in effect, destroying urban life and character.[1] Each type had to be tackled with the appropriate "methods of analysis and discovery (and) strategies for thinking;" otherwise, a solution might mean nothing.[2] The problem types she alluded to were discussed at the time in the emerging field of complexity science.

This probing of process was challenging then and is more so now. Architects have come to see analytical methods, particularly in the sciences, as constraining, given that they are concerned mostly with the observable and measurable. This flies in the face of speculation and imagination, whose value cannot be easily quantified. Also, there isn't always the time in a live project to "analyze" and "discover"? And so the profession today isn't so much anti-science as it is likely to relegate science to downstream thinking, with firewalls between disciplines.

But let's unpack Jacobs's argument, using a simple design problem, and see where it takes us. The regulation of thermal exchange could be framed as any one of the three problem types: simple, complicated, and complex.

A simple problem is governed by laws of physical science, manifest as linear trajectories, and open to cause-effect analyses. A window doubles in size; the solar energy passing through the opening also doubles. The regulation of solar heat gain starts with precise information about sun angles and sky conditions, and moves on to optimize window-to-wall ratio, glass performance, etc.

Complicated problems adhere to the same rules of physics as simple ones, only with more variables. An air-conditioning system has mechanical parts, each with a coefficient of performance. This system must cope with multiple variables: solar heat gain, infiltration, and internal heat loads. This is harder to compute, but performance can still be predicted to a high degree of certainty since the exchange is compliant with the laws of thermodynamics. The goal is to balance the performance of parts, creating a whole within which the efficiency of one corresponds with another.

Typically, at the drawing board, thermal flows are framed as many simple and complicated problems (envelopes, cooling systems, lights, etc.) wherein each system is quantified and sized. The performance of the whole is assumed to be the sum of its parts. One plus one equals two, always.

The making of architecture, however, is neither a simple nor a complicated problem; it falls into the category of complex. Problems of complexity operate with more variables. Add to this the element of human behavior, and the whole can behave in unpredictable, nonlinear ways.

Let's say a building is fitted with vegetated walls and rooftop gardens, a common strategy for mitigating heat gain. This lowers the thermal flux through the envelope, reducing the work done by the building's cooling system. It might also affect the microclimate, i.e., by lowering ambient temperature, assuming the greenery is substantial. When this happens, the cooling system is affected by two feedback loops; one that reduces energy demand directly, and the other that, indirectly, creates a better microclimate, thereby decreasing the need for cooling. If both loops are concurrent, the system reaches a tipping point, a nonlinear drop in energy use.

Now let's situate this exchange within a larger system. Greenery on multiple buildings lowers outdoor temperatures and also, potentially, attracts birds and other fauna. Human well-being is shaped in two ways: greater thermal comfort and increased biophilic satisfaction. Each part, each subsystem, acts according to its own rules. Yet what emerges from their interaction is greater than the sum of these parts.

When the whole is greater than the sum of its

parts, we witness emergence. This can be a behavior, qualities, or attributes that result from the relation of parts that act autonomously but are amplified by feedback loops and tipping points. With emergence, one plus one is more (or less) than two, but we cannot be sure by how much. Action at one scale might also trigger a reaction at the next scale. A building affects a neighborhood, a neighborhood affects the city. Every object affects the wider system within which it is nested.

Most architects recognize the logic of this approach. We are taught to contextualize solutions. We seek something more than a mere assembly of parts. We use the term "system" to describe arrangements of elements that perform a function (say, a building envelope). There are, however, limits to how far we will go down this path. But first, let's backtrack to the word "system" to see how it is framed in complexity science.

A system, by definition, produces a unique characteristic that emerges from the interaction of its parts. Systems grow, self-organize, and self-repair.[3] They are imagined in one way, but can evolve into something altogether different. They have an organic and spontaneous order, wherein "the parts generate the whole ... while the whole organizes the parts."[4]

A complex living system, distinct from a simple or complicated one, is impossible to recreate. When an air conditioner breaks down, a technician repairs or replaces a component and puts it back together. When a complex system like a neighborhood is torn down, it loses its "system-ness." The people that take its place in newly constructed buildings will take time to forge relationships and become a new system.

To design with systems, we must visualize structure. This is the configuration of connections, the pathways and nodes that are bound by edge conditions. Structure is how parts of a system talk to each other, which ones are linked, which are not. Importantly, structure results in patterns of behavior. In the design of the SDE campus, for instance, there were questions on how occupants move from one block to another and how this structure of movement in turn creates a pattern of interactions between students and faculty.

Architects, in general, are only interested in spatial systems. These systems are ring-fenced, often within site and shell, which is as far as the brief and budget will let us maneuver. What is new, and forced on us by the sustainability imperative, is (a) the importance of nonspatial systems and (b) a widening of boundary conditions.

Energy, for instance, is a nonspatial system. The elements within an energy system are not bound by a need for proximity or juxtaposition. The electrical power from a solar panel flows through a building in a way that does not depend on the routing of cables. And since a nonspatial system does not affect form or spatial structure, architects will defer on energy, typically to engineers. This is a failure of imagination.

In SDE 4, energy was framed as a complex problem touching on multiple systems. The solar roof, for instance, extends past the building facade to reduce solar heat gain, which reduces the energy needed for cooling, which reduces the need for solar panels: a classic tipping point. The distribution of tempered air by the building's hybrid cooling system corresponds to a grid of ceiling fans and sensors that in turn relates to furniture layouts and the uncertainty of user behavior. The energy system is living and, in a sense, breathing in sync with the weather or the ebb and flow of occupants.

In the SDE campus there is also a reframing of the boundary. The courtyard in SDE 1, for instance, is as much about nonhuman visitors from a nearby biodiversity hotspot as it is about the needs of human occupants. There is interest in how decisions on SDE 1 & 3 have impacted a much bigger and nonspatial carbon system by conserving and adapting existing structures instead of constructing anew.

Mapping the multiplicity and scale of systemic layers forces a shift from object-making to pattern-shaping. Once we see that some systemic structures create good patterns and others create bad ones, it alters upstream design thinking.[5] We become interested in edge conditions between systems and scales. We set targets for exchanges and seek contiguity of flows between layers and elements; how, for instance, storm water moves through a building's systems into constructed landscapes, into natural ones.

In the design world, the label "sustainable" appears exhausted from misuse and overuse. A systems perspective can reboot the conversation and offer new signposts. The outcome we seek is more than the aggregated performance of parts. We are agreed on that. We must now agree that there is a need for integration, spatial, and nonspatial systems leading to new patterns that make a difference to the world we inhabit. To create these patterns, architects must reclaim the agency of form and see it as an act of creating newer and better systemic structures.

References

[1] Jane Jacobs, *The Death and Life of Great American Cities* (New York: Vintage, 1963), 428-448.

[2] Jacobs, 428.

[3] "Systems can change, adapt, respond to events, seek goals, mend injuries, and attend to their own survival in lifelike ways, although they may contain or consist of non-living things. Systems can be self-organizing, and often are self-repairing over at least some range of disruptions. They are resilient, and many of them are evolutionary. Out of one system other completely new, never-before imagined systems can arise." Donella H. Meadows, *Thinking in Systems: A Primer* (London: Earthscan, 2009), 2:12.

[4] Jeremy Lent, *The Patterning Instinct: A Cultural History of Humanity's Search for Meaning*, (Amherst, NY: Prometheus Books, 2017), 368.

[5] "Once we see the relationship between structure and behavior, we can begin to understand how systems work, what makes them produce poor results, and how to shift them into better behavior patterns. As our world continues to change rapidly and become more complex, systems thinking will help us manage, adapt, and see the wide range of choices we have before us. It is a way of thinking that gives us the freedom to identify root causes of problems and see new opportunities." Meadows, 2:12.

Chapter 6
Carbon Futures

Chris Knapp
Joshua Comaroff

This section consists of two essays: *Towards a Post-Anthropocene, Postmodern ~~Architecture~~* by Chris Knapp questions existing norms of architectural practice that continue to thrive in a largely modernist, westernized worldview in the era of climate change. *Manifesto for the Architecture School Building in a Time of Crisis, 2021* – by Joshua Comaroff is a playfully serious take on the responsibility of building for an apocalyptic future. Both essays explore issues about the ethos of architecture, its practice, and its engagement with a world outside of the design studio. Combined, these voices illustrate the need to unlearn the status quo and work toward a new normal of warming climates worldwide.

Towards a Post-Anthropocene, Postmodern ~~Architecture~~

Chris Knapp

"Architecture is the learned game, correct and magnificent, of forms assembled in the light."

—Le Corbusier, *Vers Une Architecture*

The framework of this essay is that of an educator and academic leading the implementation and delivery of climate-proactive curriculum at Australian schools of architecture and Australasian architecture programs. It might be an exercise in arranging deck chairs on the Titanic, given the dire outlook of the 2021 IPCC Report and the diminutive agency architects have in the USD $19 trillion per annum construction sector; yet one must be propelled by an optimism that we can recalibrate the Anthropocene.

One really cannot fault Le Corbusier or the contemporaries of his generation for embracing the technologies of the day to guide and infuse architecture with a new visual order. And similarly, it is hard to fault them for making what architecture appears to look like, and how it feels, matter more than anything else. For the moderns, the machine aesthetic broke with the traditions from the prior era and helped to define and forever transform (in the Western, and ultimately globalist, canon) the spatial, temporal, and material logics of the built environment that we still experience today. The architectural hero class of the early twentieth century did not invent the technologies that made this evolution practical—industrialized float glass, steel reinforcing, the elevator, electric lighting, and so on—yet they synthesized the prevailing conditions of the day into architectural form.

To live in the early twentieth century was to inhabit the earth in a manner ignorant of planetary limits, lacking even a basic appreciation for the totality of resources, for the impact of industrial production and consumption, or a comprehension of the systemic forces that shape global existence. It was a period of still-unbridled colonialism and conquest; a period of social and global upheaval evidenced by two world wars; of financial instability; and, importantly, apparently limitless material and energy reserves. One bears witness to this in the effortlessly disappearing window walls of the Villa Tugendhat and in the inch-thick uninsulated timber wall panels of Wright's Usonian dwellings. Energy, and the carbon from which it is generated, paled in significance to architecture's core Vitruvian mission to deliver robustness, practicality, and pleasure. These values had been serviced by architecture for millennia, and the Miesian generation was not one to challenge these classical ideals—aesthetics and function in particular—but rather one to package and rearange them into alignment with the avant-garde of their era. And so they did, and it spun out of control.

Fast-forward one hundred years ahead, and the naivete of the 1920s in climatic and sustainability terms could not be clearer. However, the continual actions and prevailing inability of present-day architects to genuinely check our carbonized existence appear grossly insufficient, if not suicidal, and willfully ignorant (ignorance of the worst kind). Our forebears did not have this awareness, and yet here we are: armed with more intelligence and capacity than at any other time in history, teetering on a knife's edge, and doing so very little about it. Reflecting upon the present, one can track the influence of the Modernists as their aesthetic ideals branched from central Europe to the Americas and beyond. Architecture schools and the generation of leaders who shaped the past two major generations of practitioners have delivered us into this significant tipping point of global proportions and implications for which we seem to lack the conviction to act meaningfully. How did we get here?

Take, for example, the buildings in which disciplinary training occurs at architecture schools. The Bauhaus in Dessau is the flagship of the Corbusian/Miesian paradigm outlined above, and the thinking and manner of this edifice was exported via Gropius to Boston. The irony is not lost on many who have studied architecture in what are really terrible buildings to occupy despite their manifestation of aesthetic sophistication. Yet this is an irony not often recognized at the outset of one's education, but only after a period of maturation and reflection. Think, dear reader, of the buildings you inhabited while gaining your professional education: were they warm in cold northern winters, or did they efficiently keep you cool despite the heat and humidity of summers without excessive mechanical conditioning? Did they minimize glare or offer a comfortable setting to endure tens of continuous hours fixed to a desk? More than likely, the answer is a resounding "no." Many of these buildings were designed by "great" architects: Paul Rudolph at Yale, John Andrews at Harvard, Mies van der Rohe at IIT; or they were designed by architects once removed from such heroes. These are the emblems of the thinking, values, and ideals of environmentally anachronistic practice.

The buildings that are the subject of this book offer an anecdote, or at the very least a counterpoint, to the twentieth-century paradigm. If the question is, "what should an architecture school look like in a post-carbon era?" then SDE 1 & 3 is one such answer. They are certainly buildings displaying an aesthetic, but this is driven first by climate and resource scarcity and secondarily by mannerism. The ideals represented in such a project are a significant shift from the aforementioned glass boxes and Brutalist enclaves where its designers were educated.

An academic or practitioner educated in the 1990s is today likely a senior academic, a member of an academic leadership team, or a director-level practitioner. This is the generation that took their influences from the lineage described above, but that now has the dubious and critical opportunity to redirect the entirety of global built-environment culture toward a post-carbon existence. This group studied between the 1980s to the early 2000s with some of the leading "paper architects," who wrote and drew so much yet built so little. If one learned about waste, it was the Loosian concern of misdirected craftsmanship. The foci were on postmodern philosophy, semiotics, more versions of aesthetic theory, and if fortunate, one had a seminar or two with a very well-meaning instructor whose worldview had been shaped by a Buckminster Fuller lecture, the Whole Earth Catalog, or direct experience with the 1970s energy crisis. Clearly the solution lies with the generation who are currently undertaking, or about to commence, the study of architecture.

An example of the well-meaning instructor is the late Donald Prowler, lecturer at the Princeton School of Architecture and the University of Pennsylvania (active 1976 – 2000). Prowler's subject, "Energy and Form," was delivered with a simple philosophy: a student should learn to crunch just enough of the quantifiable methods related to energy consumption using computer simulation such that when they designed with a pencil, their intuition could guide how much energy was embedded in the lines they drew. In one semester, this could be achieved for the heating and cooling loads that are the outcome of design strategies such as orientation, shading, insulation, and thermal mass. Without ever holding energy in one's hands, a kind of tacit appreciation for energy performance could be developed through Prowler's approach. Today, a similar example is Kiel Moe's research and teaching around energy analysis, an entirely comprehensive understanding of the resources invested in making a thing and its impact upon the geo- and biosphere, including the stewardship and responsibility for the impacts of their use. This perspective needs to be shared widely and urgently.

If Le Corbusier did demonstrate one valuable lesson for us to emulate today, it was how to break with the past by translating the present into something new. This was not only achieved through composition, but also through rhetoric. Every aspect of our discipline needs to change in order to decarbonize. It is not only a technical or technological issue; it is holistic, ideological, and it lies at the core of disciplinary norms. Could it not be that "architecture as we know it" must end?

SDE 1 & 3 foreshadows a post-carbon, post-Anthropocene, post-Architecture architecture. Let's now drive a stake through the past. Let's end Architecture and its obsession with meaning attached to idiosyncratic and artful indulgences. The making of a building can and should start with a carbon budget. The brief for a building should start with mapping its place in the biosphere and the systemic interdependencies it will impact. To practice with the skills and knowledge of this sort as a priority — with an intuition for how much carbon is captured in the thickness of the designer's pencil line — requires a divorce from the obsessions and fetishes of the past. The art of Architecture is a willful self-indulgence that we can no longer afford. The disengagement with context and with reality perpetuated by the Modernist project must end. As long as we see and hear the word "Architecture," we remain doomed. It is time for the end of Architecture.

Manifesto for the Architecture School Building in a Time of Crisis, 2021–

Joshua Comaroff

1. The new school of architecture must be taken as a microcosm of the climate emergency and the failure of the global capitalist order. Its building will thus serve both as evidence of this crisis and as a transmitter of new norms for the training and disciplinary expertise of the architect.

2. Heretofore, the equatorial climate will be imagined as one version of ecological crisis. It will be hot, damp, and continually present. (Post)colonial fantasies of dominating the tropical will be replaced by an earnest acknowledgment that our conditions represent a problematic future. This will come as a relief. We will no longer need to pretend. Jackets will be replaced by singlets. Hand-fans will come back into use. A new regime of self-presentation and body language will arise, as well as a tolerance for imperfect odors during pin-ups, reviews, and longer studio sessions.

3. The building, ideally, should leak. We can no longer afford to believe in imperviousness — in the separation of humans from weather. We are the weather. Now is the era of floods, of water in buildings. The new school must be porous and adapt to conditions of inundation. Ideally, water should enter studios through open windows or failed membranes. Pinned drawings should accumulate a history of small stains and damages. At the very least, rainfall should be wind-driven across corridors and courtyard floors. Utopia is not in architecture, but in footwear.

4. Thermal comfort shall be compromised. This is not a matter of adaptation — we will simply, all of us, be slightly too warm at all times. We will learn to appreciate the mercy of oscillating fans, breezes, and air conveyed by pressure differentials. We will remain aware of the climate; we will comment on it excessively. The isolation fantasies embodied in air-conditioning can no longer be supported. We will all be a bit damp and not so fresh. This "new" condition will connect us back to millions of years of human history.

5. The building shall not be an object. Rather, it must be an extension of spatial conditions, with only the loosest of formal coherences. Any sense of "composition" is to be strictly avoided. The building-as-object is a relic of triumphalism, of monuments. The new building must be, by contrast, a monument to managed failure. At the same time, object-building emerges from precisely the rule of commodity fetishism that has brought us to the brink of disaster. The collapse of the object will allow the building to absorb, evolve locally, be integrated and resolved in a rolling sequence of problems, opportunities, and compromises.

6. Veils shall be employed. These will serve as modesty cloths, to simply cover up those elements that we do not wish to be seen. This concealment will be only partial; we will all know what is behind the screen. Veils will allow our buildings dignity, without pretending to either moral perfection or coherence. Veils will leak. Rays of light and gaseous emissions will pass through. We will celebrate these, because they are evidence of our connectedness.

7. The building must be built upon the skeleton of an existing one. Our skill, going forward, is to know how to make do with relics and hand-me-downs. This shall once and for all abolish the dangerous fixation with new things. If we believe Aldo Rossi's assertion that the city is

a kind of cadaver, we must remake our world on these giant bones. This is how culture is created; no healthy civilization is based upon novelty. Consequently, the curriculum shall reorient itself away from Crusoe-esque notions of world-making, and focus on transformation as the architect's primary skill. Like the church builders of the Renaissance, no one will "create" a building; they will simply inherit one for a time and then die.

8. We will acknowledge that zero energy equals low efficiency. The fantasy that we can get everything and give up nothing is contrary to the fundamental laws of the physical universe. We will not pretend that low-emission buildings are simply clever versions of traditional ones, designed by smarter people who know better. Rather, we must recognize that new kinds of efficiency can emerge from buildings that fail conventional tests of spatial compactness and density. Rather, we will adopt a frankly "third world" intelligence in the use of precious resources. We will reduce latency and combine many functions in a common space. We will put up with the noise and lack of focus that this creates. The new school will return to our origins in markets, village commons, and the agora: a space of continual, side-by-side interaction and simultaneity. We will annoy each other, because this is the human condition and it is what nature wants.

9. The studio spaces will be dramatically reduced in size to represent the reduced standing of architecture as a profession. Our pedagogies will place value on refusal, diversion, and clever rejection of our clients' demands. The new expertise of the architect shall be in knowing how *not* to build. Students that achieve design objectives while doing the least shall be rewarded with high marks and honors. Intelligence arising from laziness or conservatism will be recognized for its own value.

10. In times of crisis, the architecture school shall continue to co-opt spaces from other buildings and faculties. This will be done as much as possible. Institutions, families, and other organizational social units will cease to be identified with specific buildings, but rather shall be acknowledged for the incontinent, associative things that they are. This practice is good for exchange, and also very helpful in destroying the fantasy of coherent objects and images in the practice of everyday life. Space sharing increases local density and potential local viral loading, such that we may share our germs and viruses and ideas with a broader community of colleagues. An added plus is the ability to outstation troublesome colleagues to far-flung, quasi-dilapidated buildings.[1]

11. Toilets shall be cleaned sporadically, incompletely, and according to no understandable schedule. Humanity sheds a lot of waste; we will learn to live with it.

12. There shall be landscapes, but not gardens. All flora within the boundary of the building will be planted in the ground. Landscape shall not be aestheticized, but will become matter-of-fact. It shall not indulge in nativist fantasies, nor will it attempt to get cute with curvilinear arrangements or excessively pruned specimens. Rather, any new green spaces shall honestly and casually represent the condition of the broader urban nature: mixed, heterogeneous, full of migrants and guests, unstable, and prone to change. It should also express its origin in disturbance — it is an environmental typology that arises from anthropogenic conditions, and it is in the process of finding new balances and accommodations and interactions. Maintenance shall be limited to once every six months to avoid excessive Singaporeanization.

13. There shall be no plants on the roof. Going forward into crisis, the architecture school building will not indulge in the image of reconciliation by abusively placing flora where it does not want to be: in tiny volumes of desiccated or expanded nonorganic planting materials. Plants on roofs and balconies indulge the concept that a building is "green" by *looking green*. There are no green buildings. All buildings are ecocidal, and the architect must weigh the consequences of their actions. Fantasies of innocence will be retired. If we are to be evil, we will acknowledge it. In future, all surfaces facing the sun should simply be painted white, or in light metallic tones, to increase albedo and reduce urban heat island effect.

14. There shall be no private spaces, nor privacy. Architects — and hence, students of design — must be forced to renounce any ideas of individualism, personal isolation, or exceptionalism with respect to relationships of reciprocity or mutual obligation with others.

Human social connectedness may be highly irritating, but it is (for better or worse) how we have survived to the point where we have ruined the planet. All architectural solutions must involve cooperation, and hence all spaces must emphasize collectivity. The majority of work shall be group work, and thus studio culture will reject the individual desk.

15. Once completed, the new architectural school building should be frozen for a minimum period of twenty-five years, with no substantial design changes. All additions and alterations must progressively decrease in scale, to be limited to touchpoints, posters, and nano-interventions. Each of the architect's mistakes must be lived with, endlessly reiterated and discussed and debated, as a "teachable moment."

16. All guests must bring their own snacks. Lunch will not be served.

Notes

[1] There should be no shock in this. All university departments have such colleagues. It is an established fact.

Epilogue

Lam Khee Poh

Building on the initiatives of the School of Design and Environment, the editors of this volume have engaged and solicited valuable contributions from colleagues across the globe who have dedicated their career to the pursuit of a sustainable future for present and future generations. The discourse is multidimensional, fascinating, and provocative. Particularly noteworthy is the consistent thread of critical thought that dissects, analyzes, and reconstitutes the constituent elements of our built environment's life cycle.

Climate change has been touted as a "super wicked problem,"and the carbon conundrum continues to confound even the smartest, most diehard proponents of innovative solutions.[1] Irrefutable statistics continue to remind us that the built environment sector is critical in making a significant impact on the reduction of total emissions. Yet on a global scale, we do not seem able even to level the curve, let alone bend it. Huge efforts to achieve reductions in some regions are more than offset by unbridled developments in others, where outmoded concepts and construction methods that adversely affect the carbon balance are still being deployed. We are still chasing our own tails.

There is good consensus that the current state of design and technology is not a barrier to these development goals. Even the often cited "excuse" of cost can be largely mitigated by economies of scale and creative design that effectively and efficiently integrate various building components and systems for total building performance.[2]

So what's holding us back? It seems to me that the sociopolitical will must be cultivated. The fallout of the climate crisis and its direct and indirect link to pandemics knows no boundaries, whether geopolitical, sociocultural, demographic, or economic. Everyone is susceptible, and the global connectedness of humanity reinforces that fact. The four "informal" laws of ecology are at play: 1, everything is connected to everything else; 2, everything must go somewhere; 3, nature knows best; and 4, there is no such thing as a free lunch.[3] In September 2015, 193 countries acknowledged these truths by officially adopting the United Nation's "Transforming Our World: The 2030 Agenda for Sustainable Development," which includes seventeen Sustainable Development Goals (SDGs). At least eight of those goals are inextricably related to the built environment.

Furthermore, the COVID-19 pandemic has starkly reminded us that we cannot continue to treat these goals, such as good health and well-being (SDG #3), or sustainable cities and communities (SDG #11) in a segregated manner if humanity and planet Earth are to survive.

Reports tracking progress in the Asia-Pacific region since 2016 have returned discouraging results on the meeting of interim goals. The interim assessment report posits that, on its current trajectory, the region may achieve less than 10% of the SDG targets while regressing on critical climate action goals.[4] Despite a brief dip in carbon dioxide emissions caused by the COVID-19 pandemic, the planet is still heading for a temperature rise of more than 3°C by 2100, far beyond the Paris Agreement targets.

However, for those of us in academia, it is noteworthy that quality education (SDG #4) is one that has seen encouraging gains and is generally progressing relative to the other goals. Although reports suggest that COVID-19 has wiped out twenty years of educational gains, we must persevere with the same conviction, spirit, and tenacity to evolve and meet the needs and challenges of the post-pandemic world.[5]

At SDE, we strive to accelerate capacity building at the intersection of design education, health and well-being, carbon economy, and climate resilience. Our urban and architectural design curricula are evolving to address the imminent recurrence of climate catastrophes and pandemics in the future. The remarkable academic building projects illustrated in this book each have a different genesis, but their design and construction processes, building systems, and attention to material selection demonstrate a keen consciousness of sustainable development. The SDE campus aims to deliver a "Well and Green" environment for the university community and to widen the visibility of new architectural possibilities in Asia. In particular, by coupling user comfort and wellness with the reduction of carbon emissions, SDE 1 & 3 demonstrate the possibilities of adaptive reuse projects in a hot and humid tropical climate.

With global building stock projected to double in the next two decades, the challenge of reducing the carbon expenditure offers a planning-design-construction opportunity.[6] It is time to rethink the creative aspects of technology and buildings systems as well as the culture and business model of the building industry. New pedagogical approaches must seek to address all facets of theory and practice as well as knowledge and experience. Beyond providing a necessary physical infrastructure for our students, these buildings serve as living laboratories for an immersive teaching and learning experience; at the same time, they open up research opportunities for faculty and students. This approach supports the school's ambition to inspire public acceptance of and appreciation for sustainable building prototypes by involving the campus community directly in the transition from a carbon culture to a culture of climate awareness.[7]

A critical shift from a technocentric model to a people-centric design paradigm is of paramount importance. Louis Sullivan said that "architecture is the crystallization of the thoughts and feelings of a civilization;" accordingly, our architecture should implicitly embody the physiological, psychological, sociological, and economic well-being of our people.

In this context, "walking the talk" reflects not only upon our academic and professional competencies, but also establishes our moral authority as role models who prepare future generations of design professionals, change makers in the building industry, and even policy makers who will one day lead our society's sustainable and resilient developments.

References

[1] "Carbon Conundrum: Can We Reduce Our Reliance on Carbon?" *Channel News Asia*, Mar. 31, 2020, https://www.channelnewsasia.com/watch/carbon-conundrum/carbon-conundrum-1481091.

[2] V. Hartkopf, V. Loftness, and P. Mill, "The Concept of Total Building Performance and Building Diagnostics," in *Building Performance: Function, Preservation, and Rehabilitation*, ed. G. Davis (West Conshohocken, PA: ASTM International, 1986), 5-22.

[3] Barry Commoner, *The Closing Circle: Nature, Man, and Technology* (New York: Knopf, 1980), 45.

[4] United Nations, "Asia and the Pacific SDG Progress Report 2021," Mar. 2021, https://www.unescap.org/sites/default/d8files/knowledge-products/ESCAP_Asia_and_the_Pacific_SDG_Progress_Report_2021.pdf#page=11.

[5] United Nations Department of Economic and Social Affairs: Sustainable Development, "Goals: 4. Ensure Inclusive and Equitable Quality Education and Promote Lifelong Learning Opportunities for All," accessed Nov. 1, 2021, https://sdgs.un.org/goals/goal4.

[6] UN Environment and International Energy Agency, "Towards a Zero-Emission, Efficient, and Resilient Buildings and Construction Sector: Global Status Report 2017," 2017, https://www.worldgbc.org/sites/default/files/UNEP%20188_GABC_en%20%28web%29.pdf.

[7] Lizzie Yarina, "Towards Climate Form," in *Log 47: Overcoming Carbon Form*, ed. Cynthia Davidson and Elisa Iturbe (New York: Anyone Corporation, 2019), 85.

Department of Architecture students were engaged in the ideational design process for SDE 1 & 3 through a master-level design studio. The studio-based design research focused on understanding and representing a set of architectural precedents from across the equator that provided an archive of passive performance techniques and a formal vocabulary that students could mine for their proposed transformations of the existing buildings. This research was coupled with climate concerns, from sun, daylight, and sound attenuation challenges to statutory regulations to real construction and budgetary challenges, all of which impacted the design outcomes by providing both a speculative and real project for students to engage with.

Studio Leader
Associate Professor
Erik L'Heureux

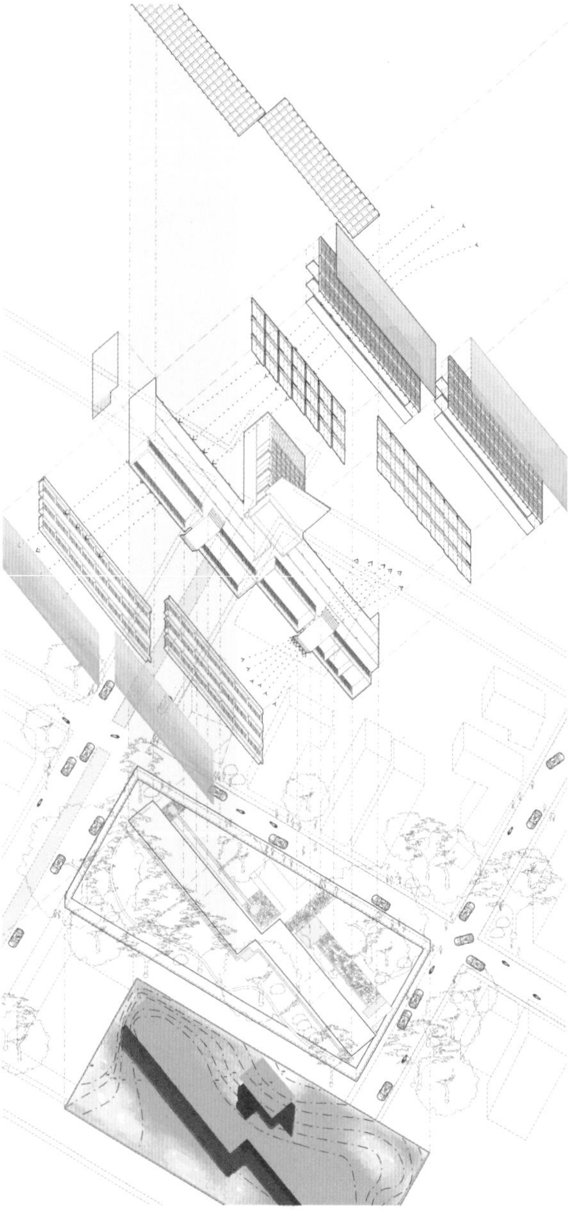

Golconde Dormitory, Puducherry, India,
by George Nakashima and Antonin Raymond.
Case study by Seow Yeong Chuan & Yamada Ayano.

Fig 1A (top) Model of the dormitory elevation.

Fig 2B (right) Exploded axonometric study of the Golconde Dormitory.

Faculty of Architecture and Urbanism (FAU), University of São Paulo, Brazil, by João Batista Vilanova Artigas and Carlos Cascaldi. Case study by Isabel Lye & Dora Paramita.

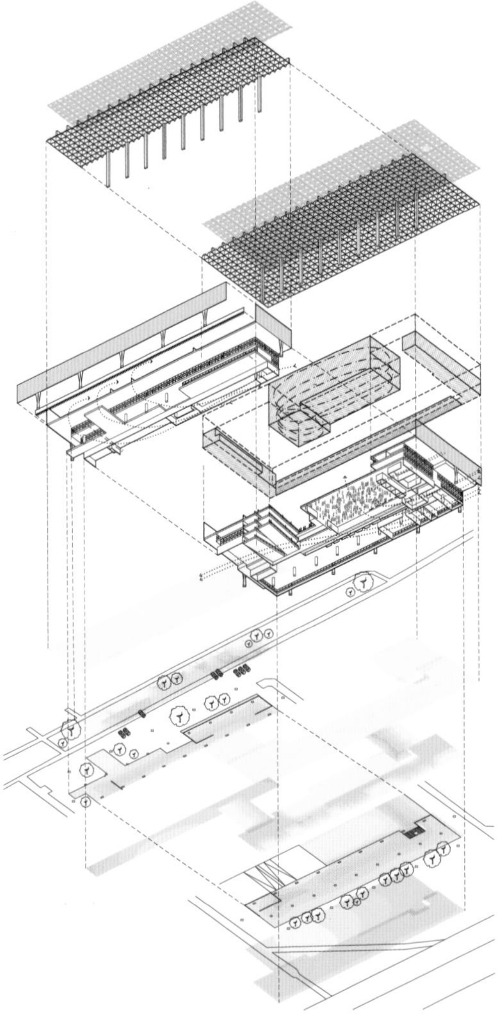

Fig 2A (top) Model of the FAU roof.

Fig 2B (bottom) Exploded axonometric study of the FAU building.

Former US Embassy, Accra, Ghana, by Harry Weese & Associates. Case study by Ng Yihui Mary Ann and Ng Sze Wee.

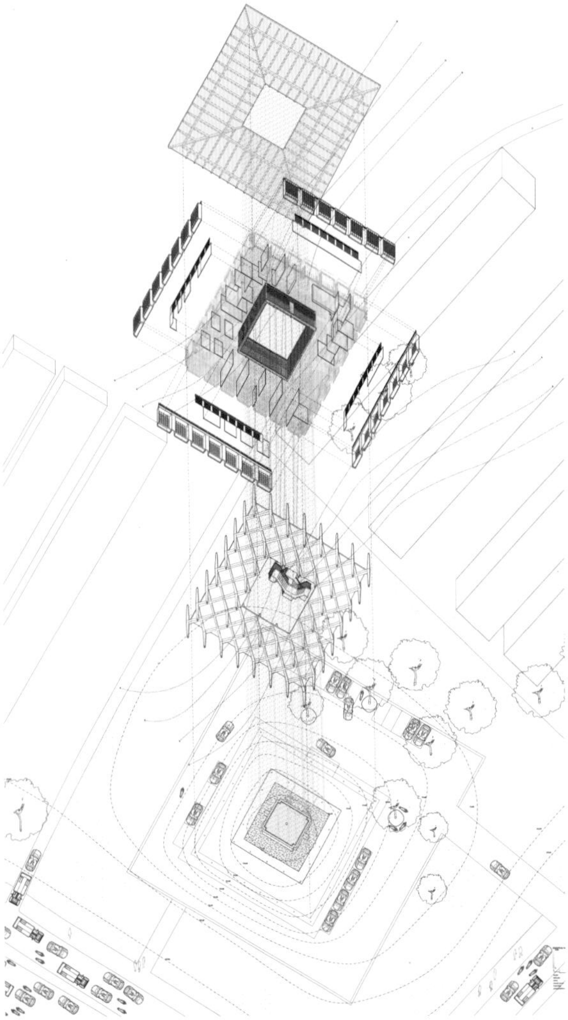

Fig 3A (top) Model of the Embassy corridors.

Fig 3B (bottom) Exploded axonometric study of the US Embassy building.

Kwame Nkrumah University of Science and Technology (KNUST) Library, Kumasi, Ghana, by James Cubitt and Partners. Case study by Chen Ronglyu, Tan Keng Chuan, and Woo Jie Kai.

Fig 4A (top left) Model photograph of the KNUST library elevation.

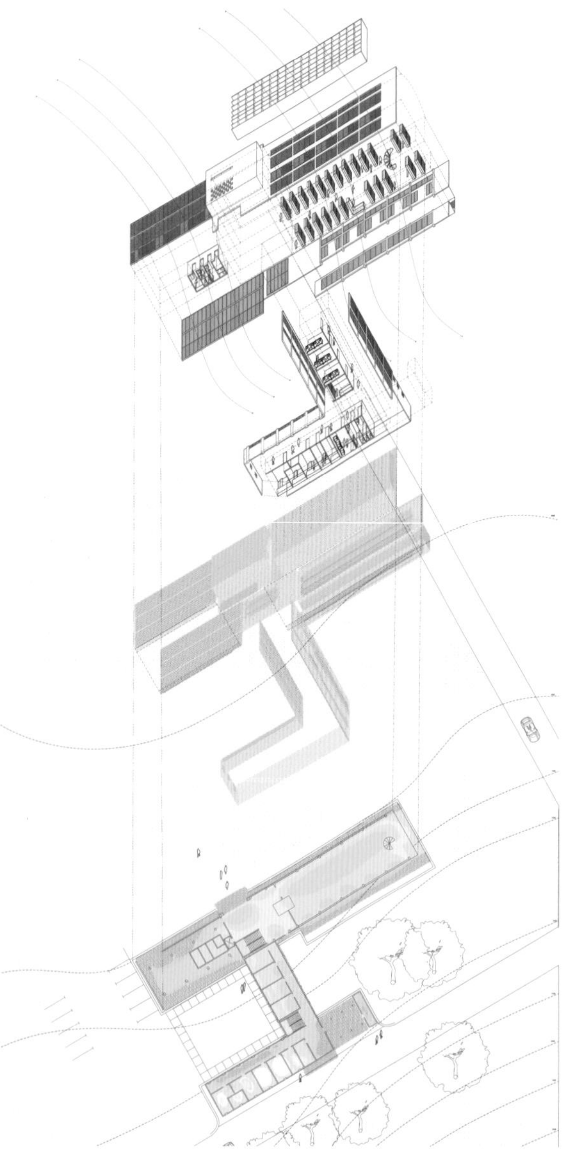

Fig 4B (bottom left) Exploded axonometric study of the KNUST library building.

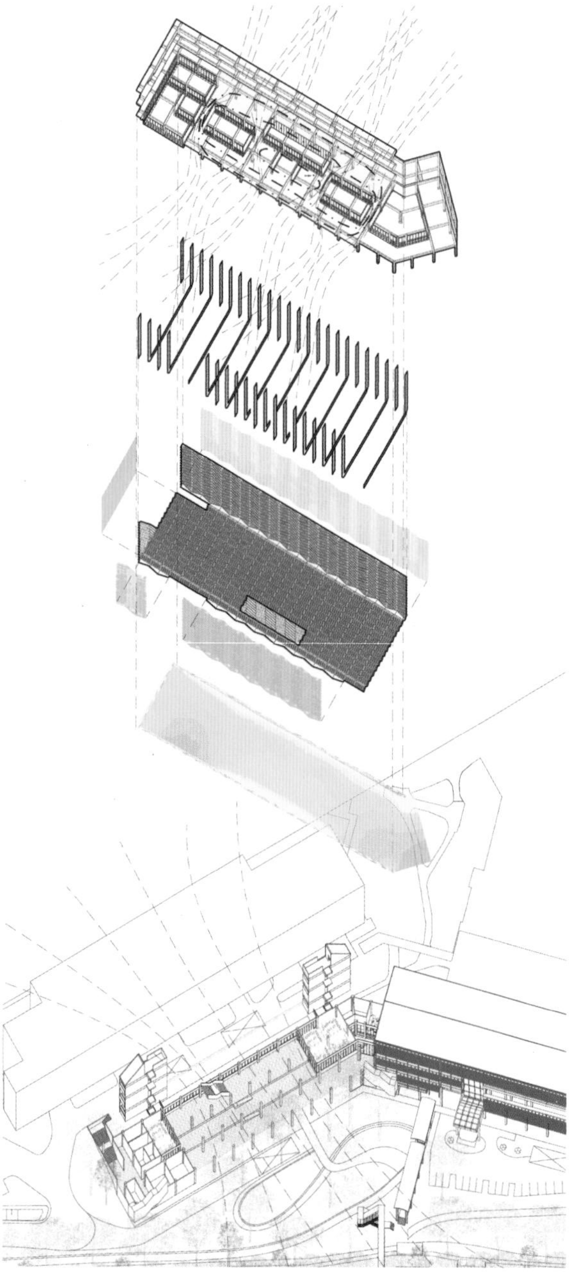

Fig 5 (below) SDE 3 redesign vision titled "Upper Lenticular" by Woo Jie Kai and Dore P. Tedjosiswojo.

Fig 6 Model and plan of SDE 3 redesign vision titled “Two” by Ng Yihui Mary Ann and Seow Yong Chuan.

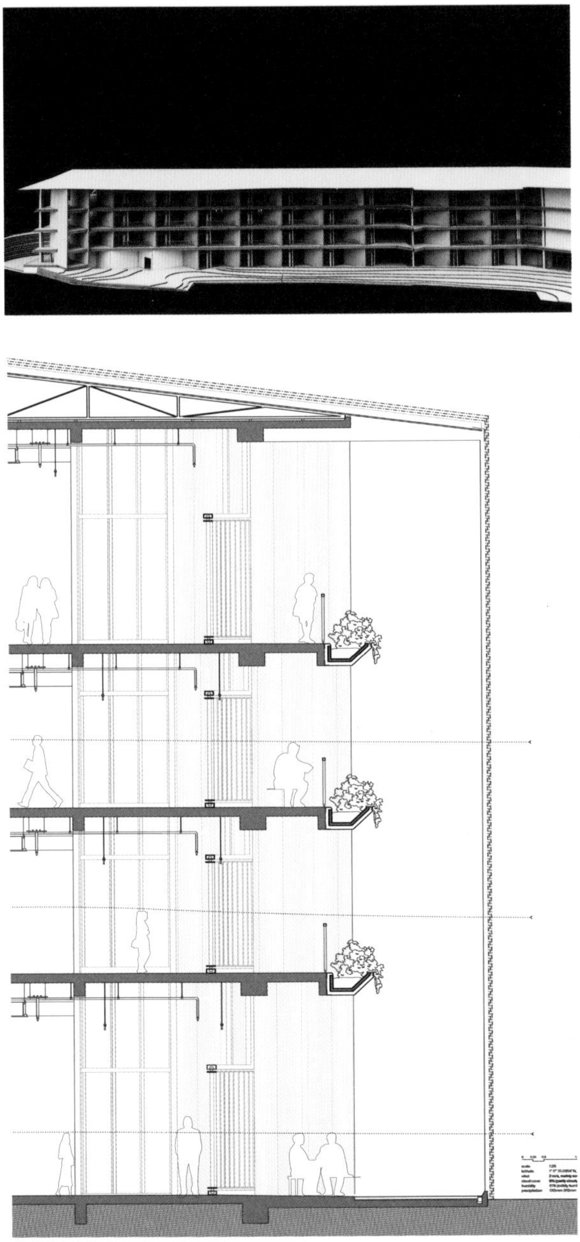

Fig 7 SDE 3 redesign vision titled “rear:front” by Ayano Yamada, Isabel Lye, and Ng Sze Wee.

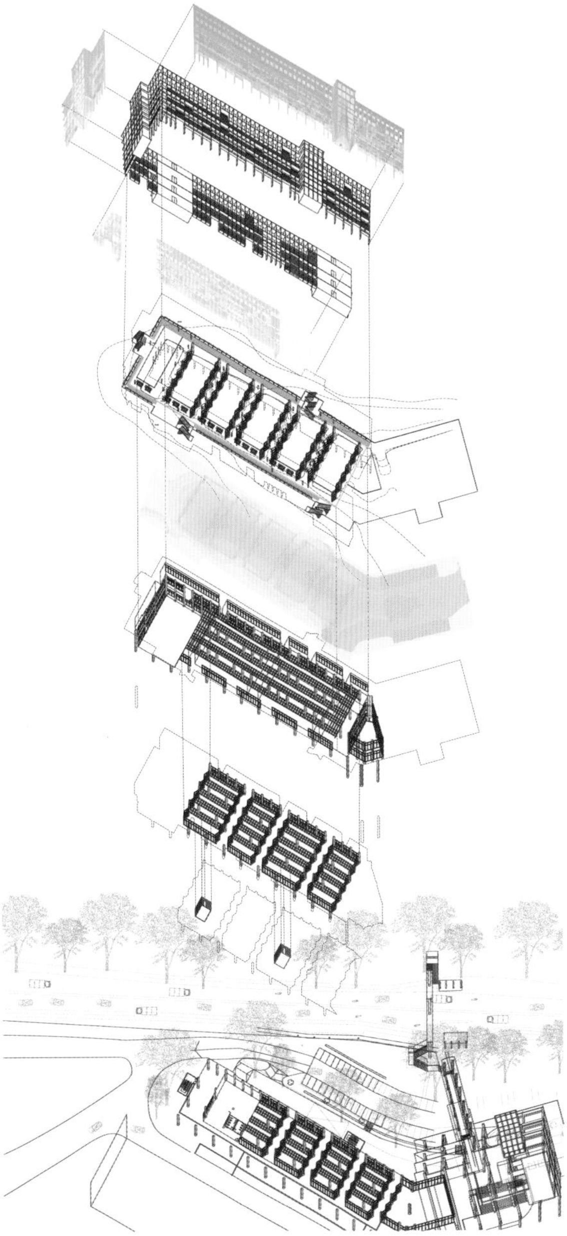

Fig 8 SDE 3 redesign vision titled “Concentrism” by Tan Kheng Chuan and Chen Ronglyu Cyril.

SDE 1 & 3 Design Detail Sketches

A curated selection of design sketches integral to the SDE 1 & 3 design process.

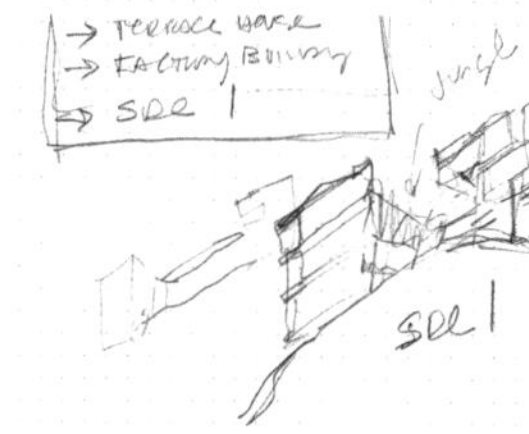

1

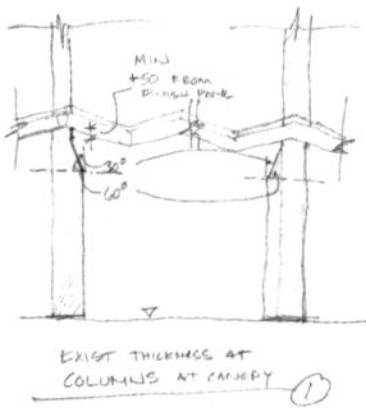

2

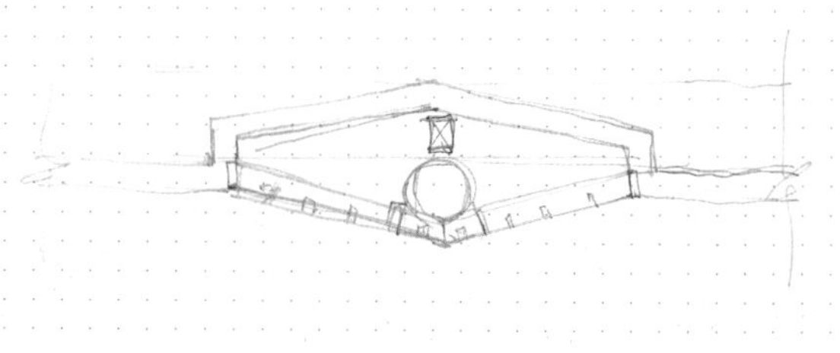

3

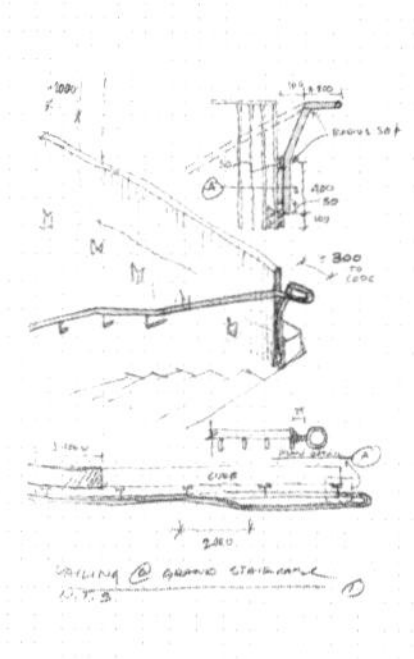

4

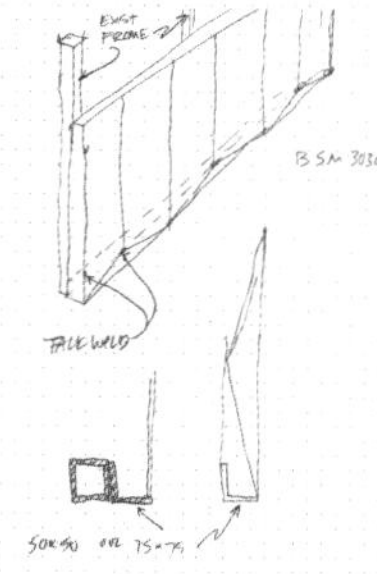

5

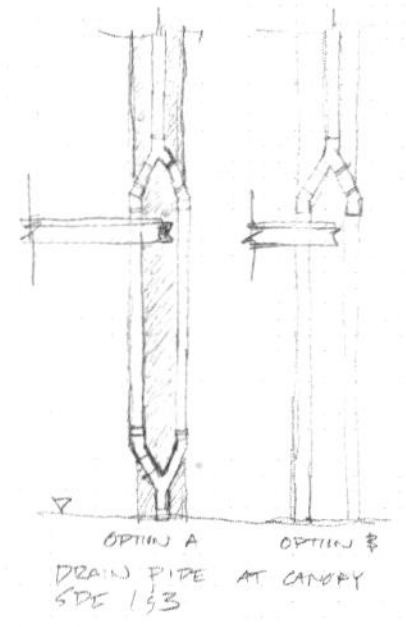

6

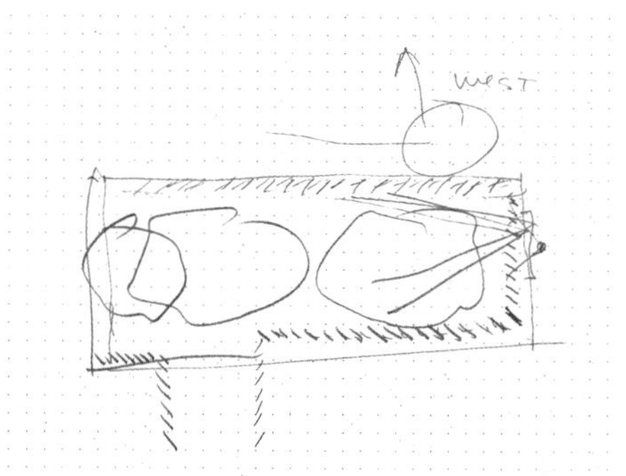

7

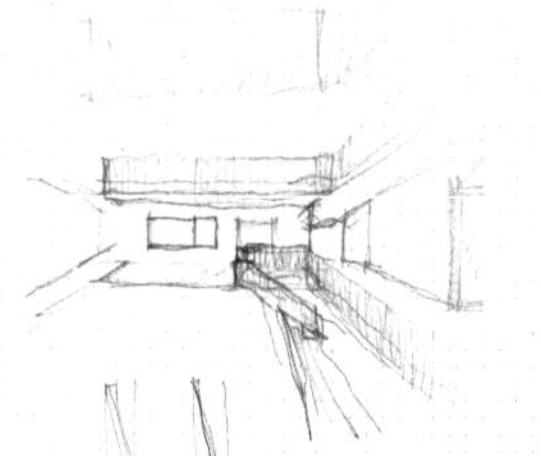

8

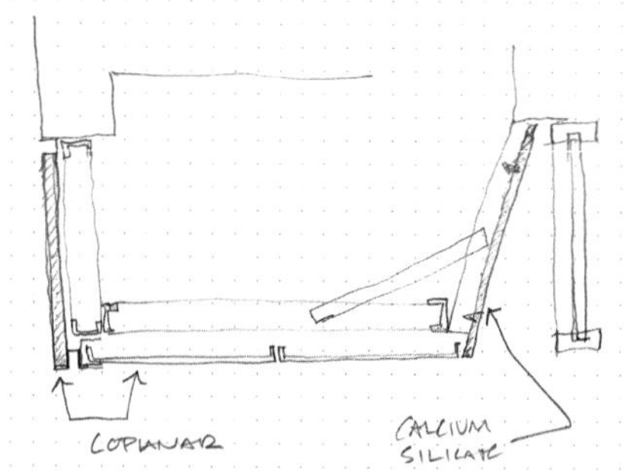

9

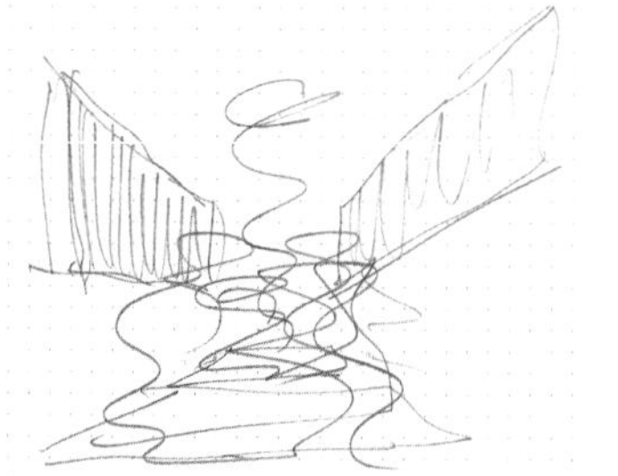

10

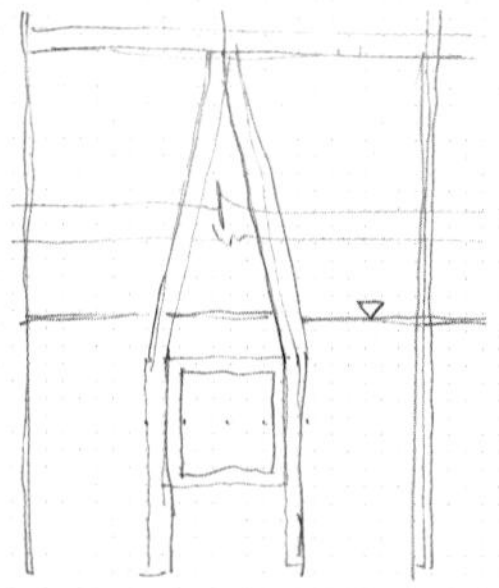

11

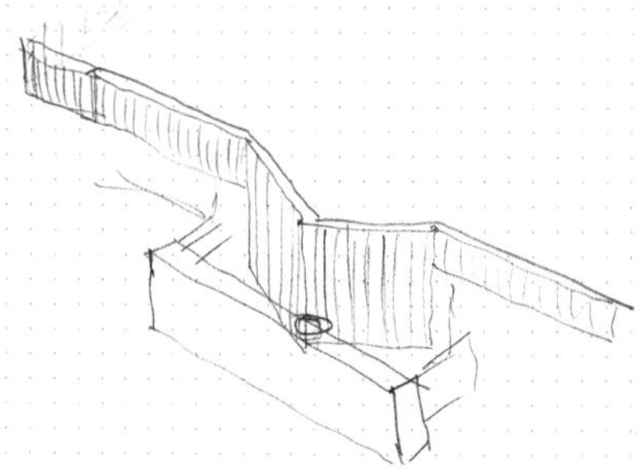

12

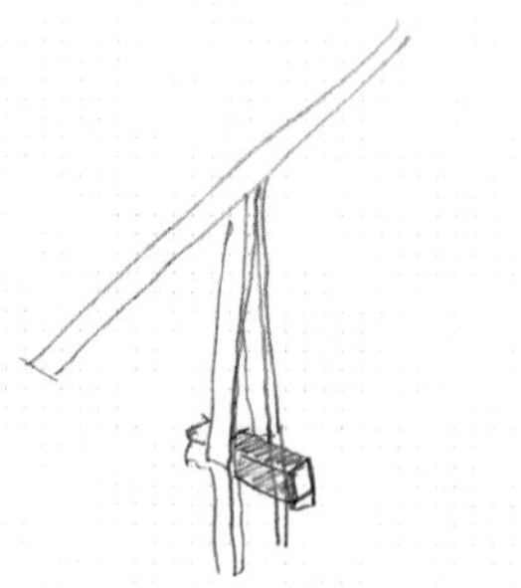

13

14

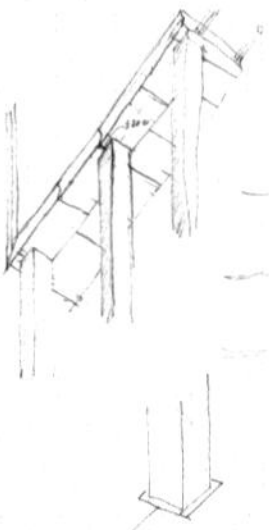

15

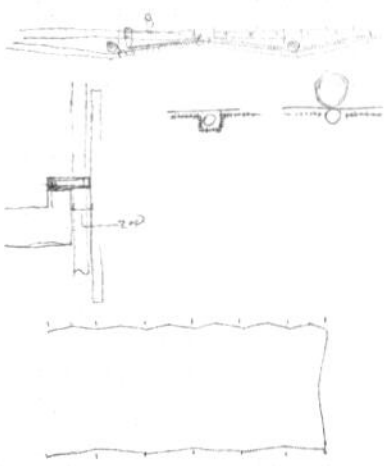

16

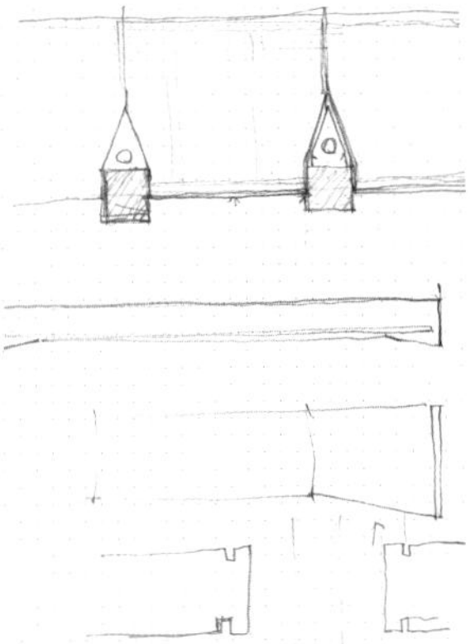

17

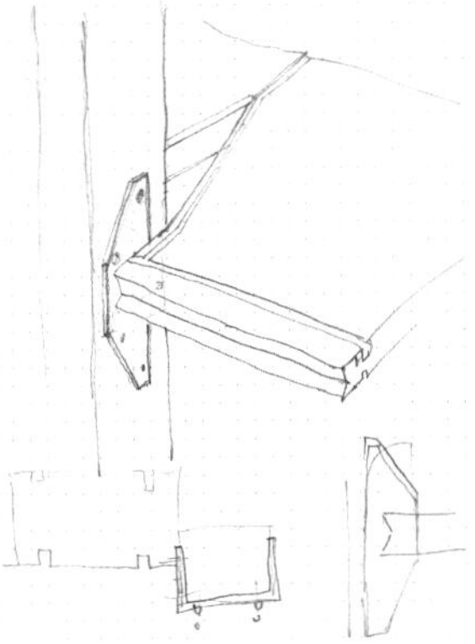

18

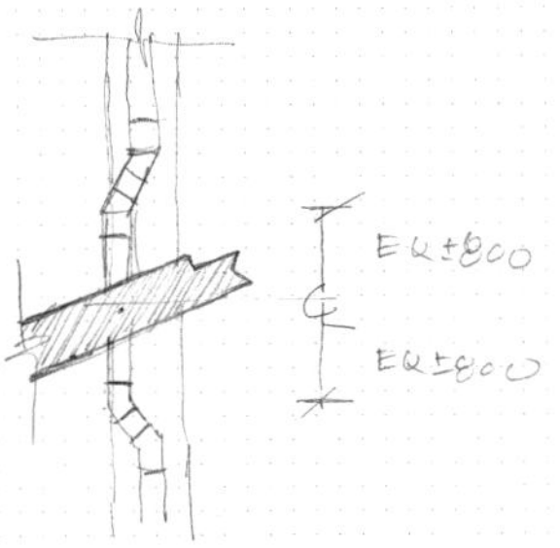

19

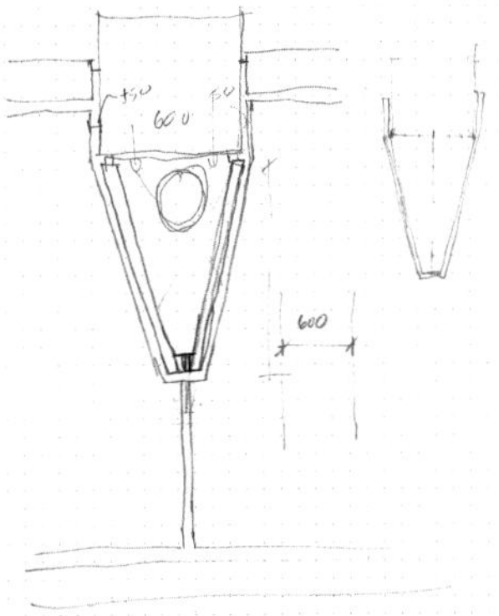

20

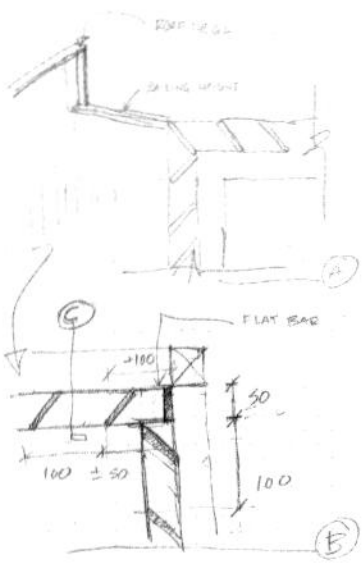

21

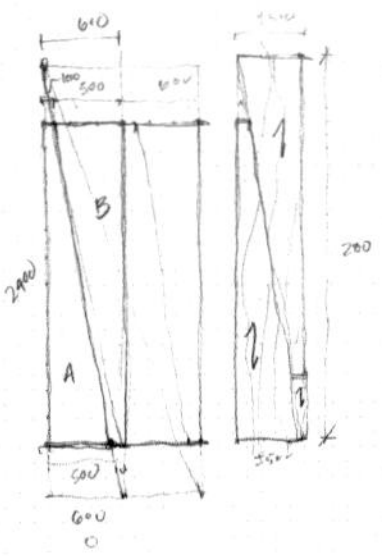

22

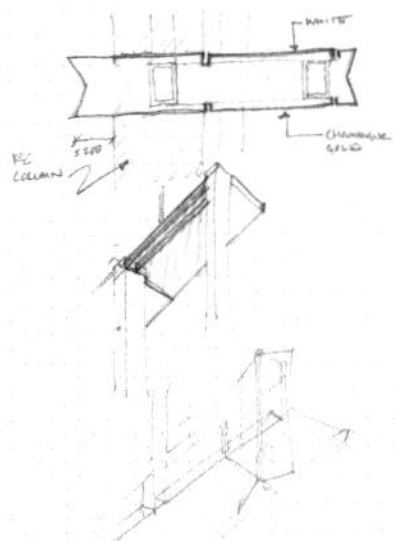

23

Fig 1 Sectional worms-eye view of SDE 1 jungle courtyard.

Fig 2 Entry canopy details interfacing existing structure.

Fig 3 Railing details integrating existing rainwater downpipes.

Fig 4 Railing details at jungle courtyard.

Fig 5 Detail of folded and pleated perforated metal mesh panels.

Fig 6 Detail of rainwater downpipes at canopy.

Fig 7 Detail of crown screen orientation at jungle courtyard.

Fig 8 Mild steel screen details surrounding the jungle courtyard.

Fig 9 Sectional detail of soffit and clerestory.

Fig 10 A framed jungle at SDE 1.

Fig 11 Detail of light shelves that cleave open at existing concrete columns.

Fig 12 Detail of perimeter screens splay to incorporate rainwater that downpipes.

Fig 13 Detail of railing support at link bridge.

Fig 14 Window detail on entry green wall.

Fig 15 Aluminum panel detail view from underside interfacing existing columns.

Fig 16 SDE 1 courtyard perimeter screen details in plan, folding to accommodate existing rainwater downpipes.

Fig 17 Detail of deep veil at existing columns.

Fig 18 Anchorage details of deep veil to existing columns.

Fig 19 Detail of rainwater downpipe and canopy.

Fig 20 Detail of aluminum interfacing existing columns and downpipes.

Fig 21 Corner details at jungle crown.

Fig 22 Details of interior folded timber panels and veneer sleeves.

Fig 23 Detail of aluminum panels and structural supports.

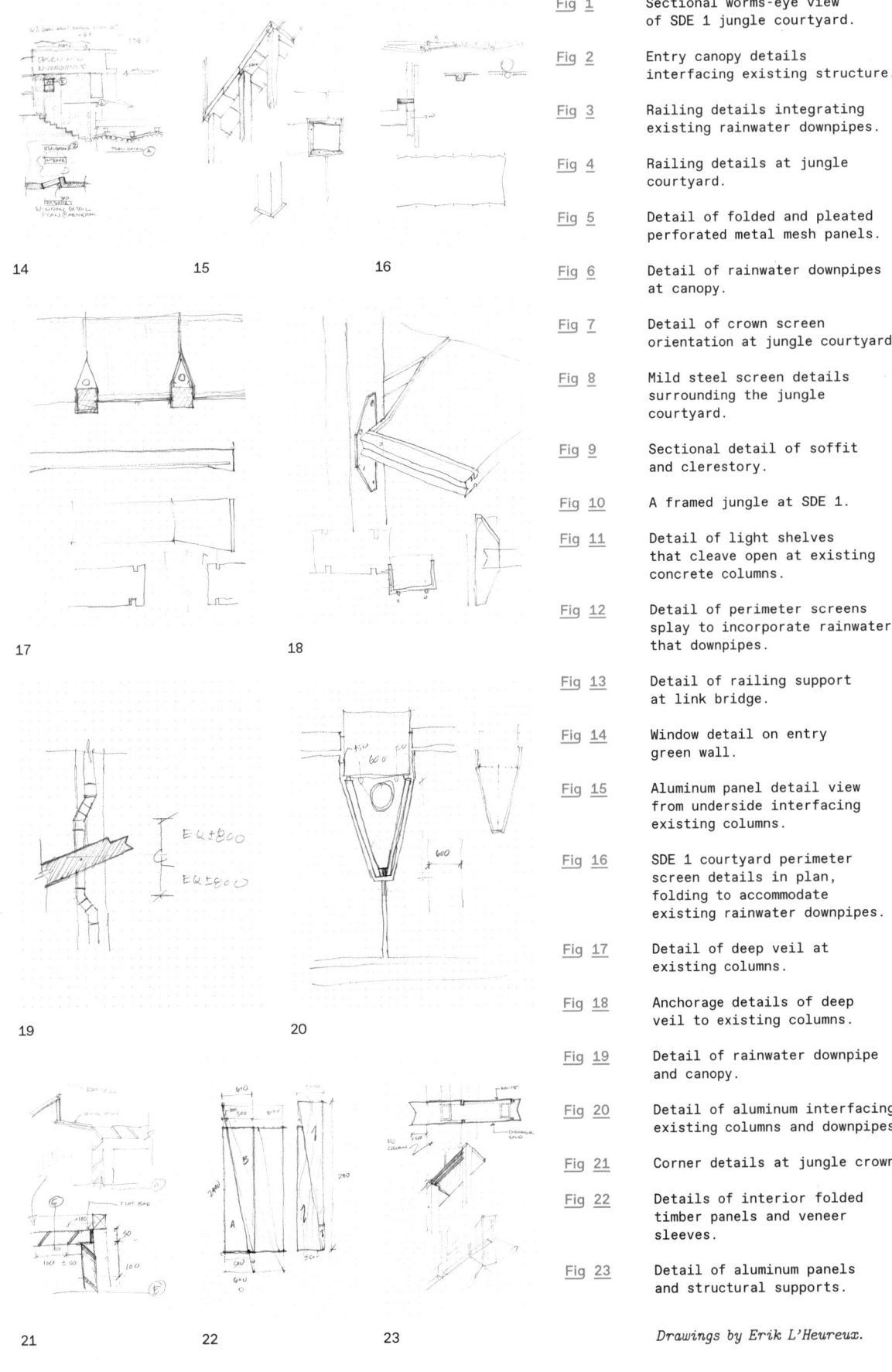

Drawings by Erik L'Heureux.

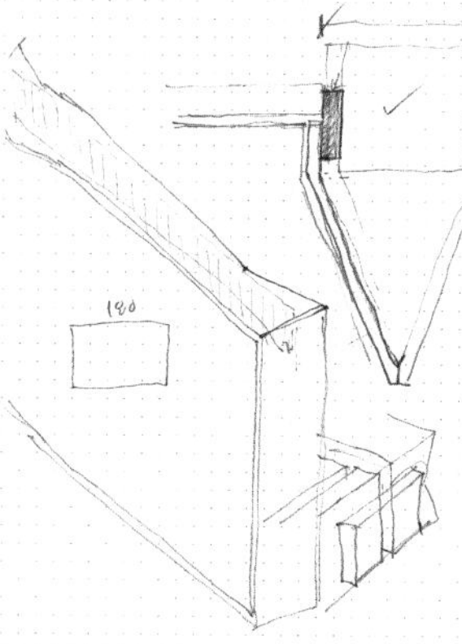

24

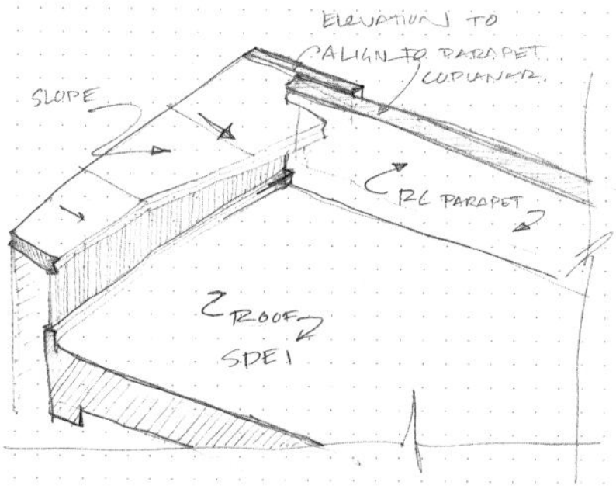

25

26

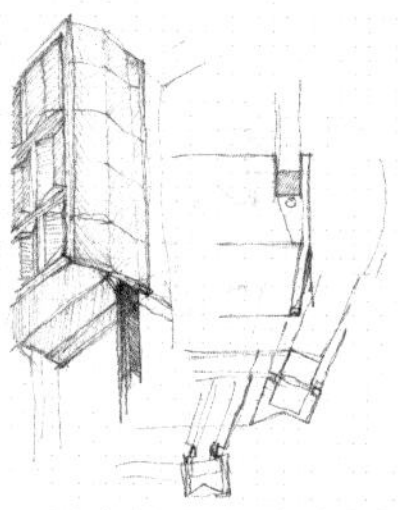

27

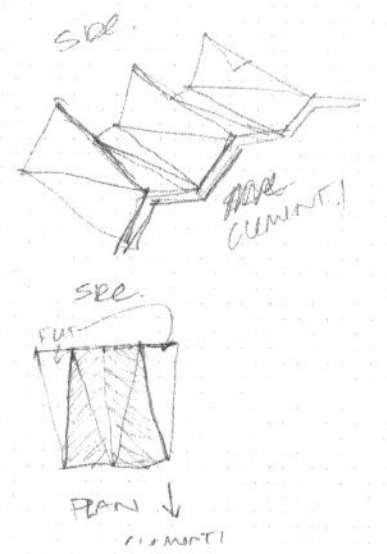

28

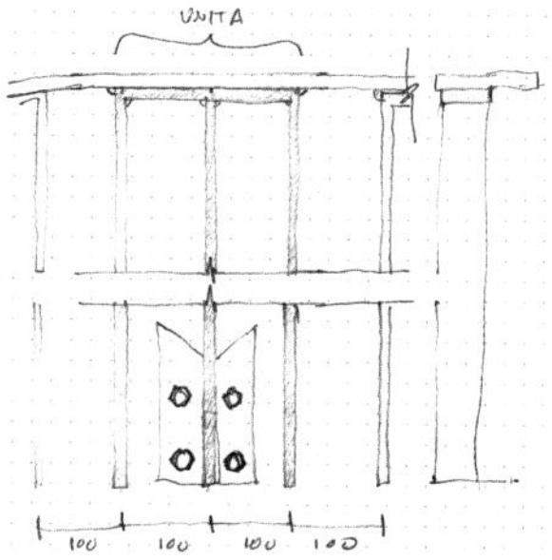

29

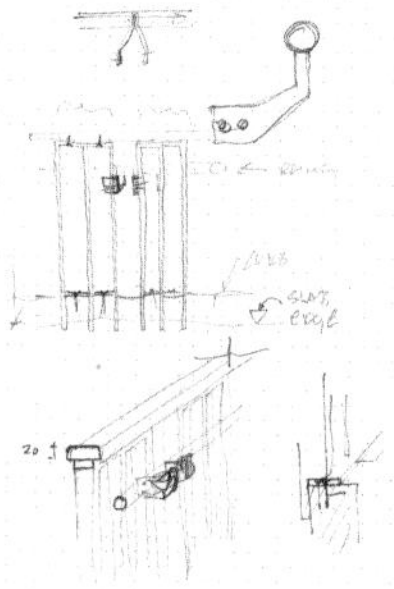

30

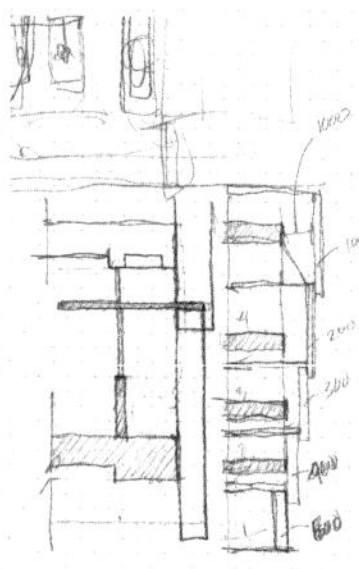

31

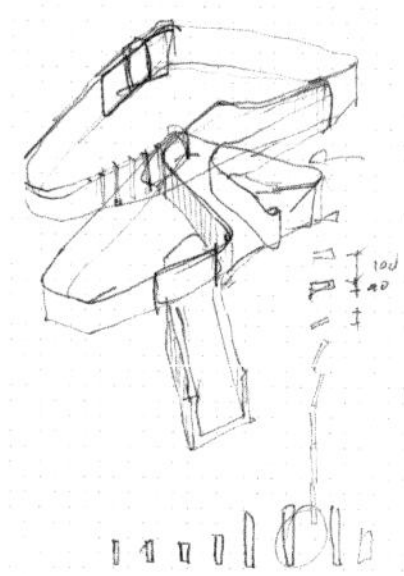

32

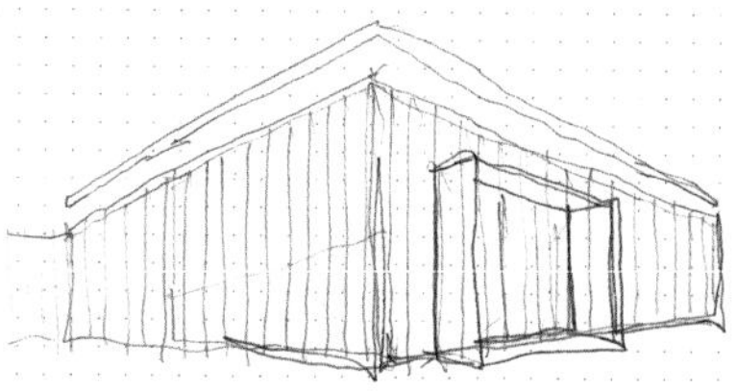

33

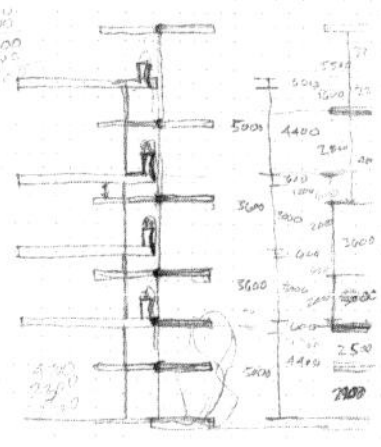

34

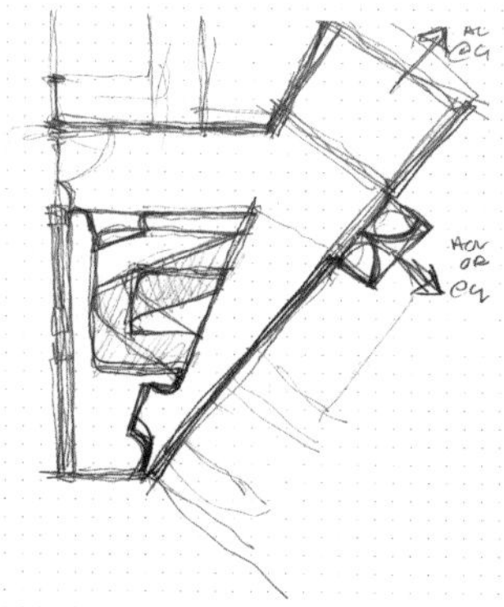

35

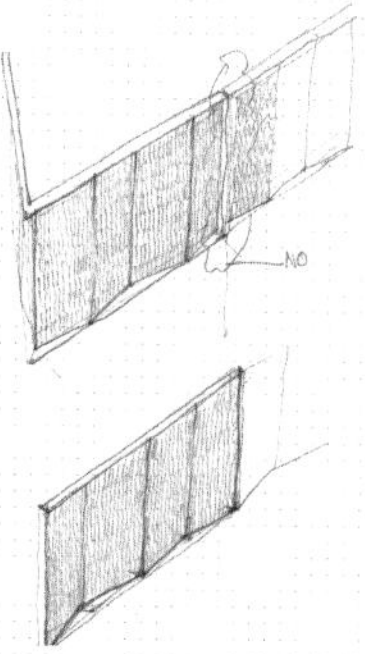

36

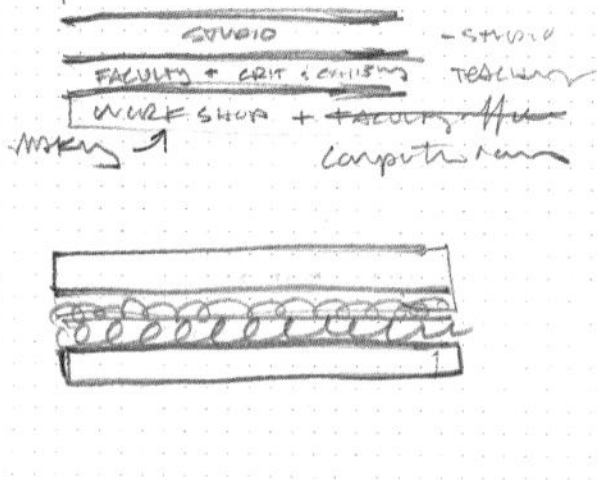

37

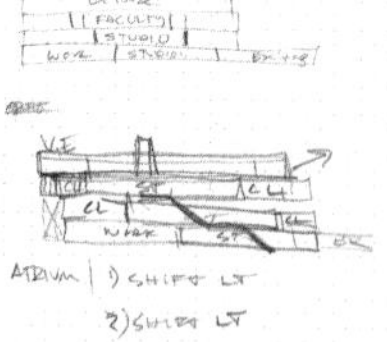

38

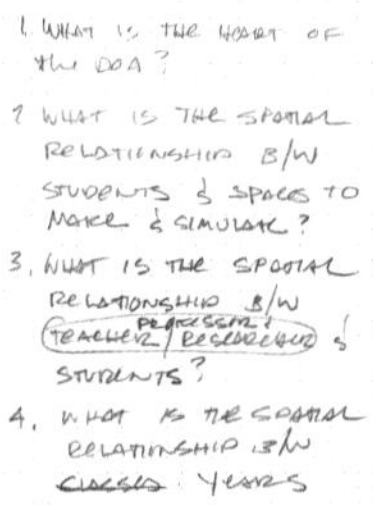

39

40

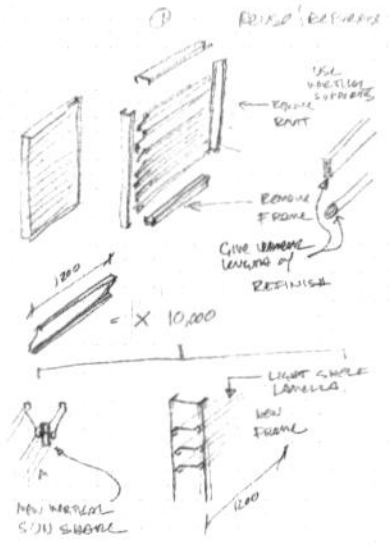

41

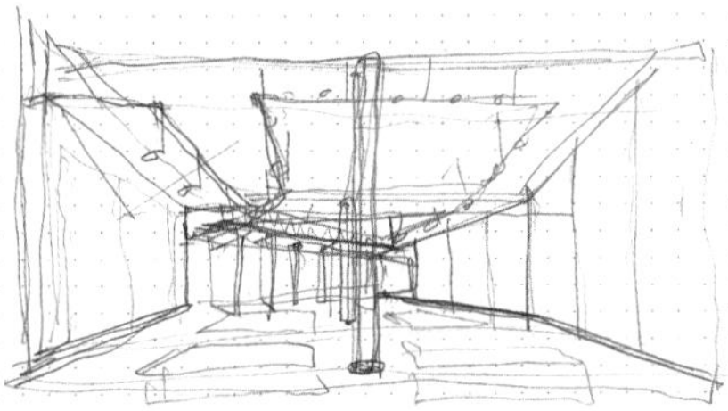

42

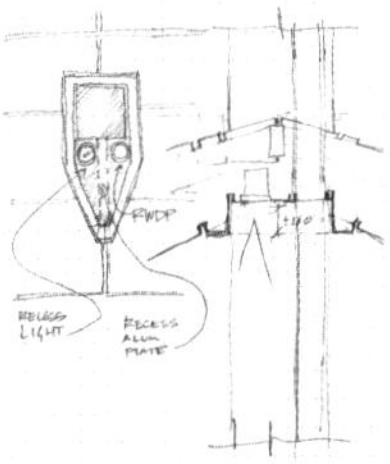

43

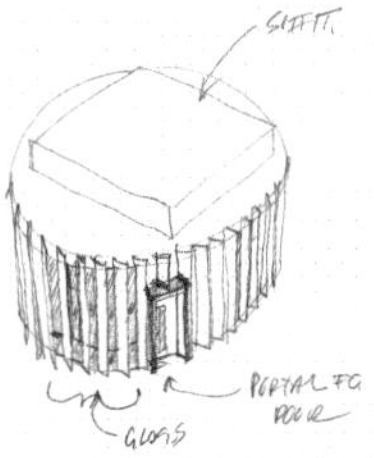

44

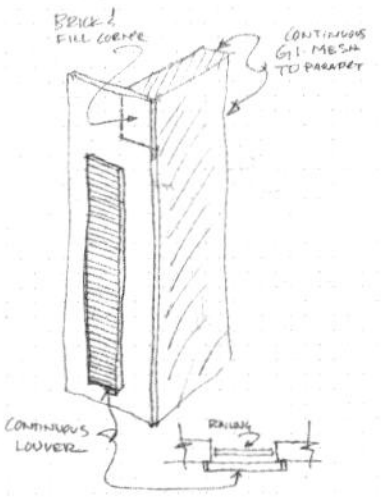

45

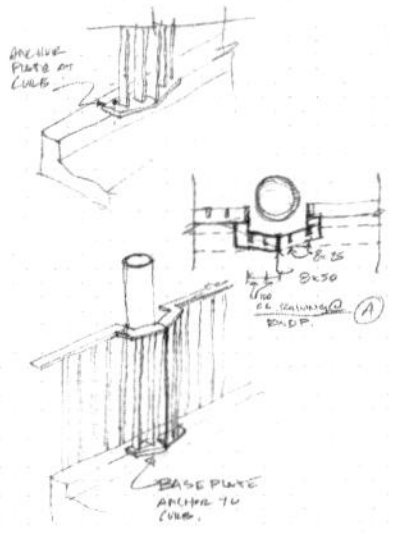

46

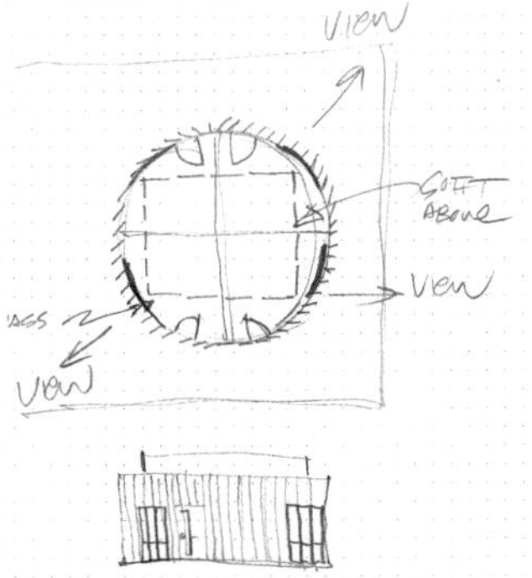

47

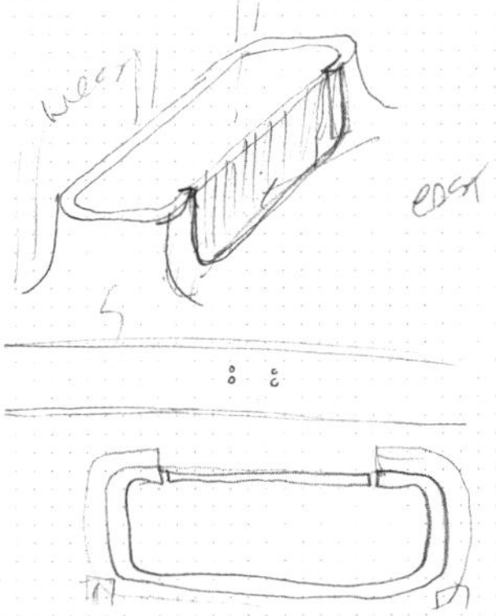

48

Fig 24 Detail of deep veil interfaces.

Fig 25 Detail of deep veil interfacing with existing parapet structure.

Fig 26 Concept sketch of the deep veil as parasitic addition.

Fig 27 Interface details of deep veil to existing building.

Fig 28 Concept sketch of entry canopy.

Fig 29 Anchorage details of railing and balustrade.

Fig 30 Handrail details.

Fig 31 Sectional detail of light shelves and overhanging deep veil.

Fig 32 Axonometric of continuous balustrade at social commons staircase.

Fig 33 Corner sketch of entry to exhibition gallery.

Fig 34 Detail sketch of light shelves and existing building dimensions.

Fig 35 Plan detail of social spaces surrounding review foyer.

Fig 36 Corner details of building metal mesh.

Fig 37 Sectional program redistribution.

Fig 38 Sketch for sectional reconfiguration.

Fig 39 Key questions reframing pedagogy through the renovation.

Fig 40 Deep veil elevation details.

Fig 41 Details of recycled configuration of original aluminum screen profiles.

Fig 42 Interior view of exhibition gallery and lighting.

Fig 43 Detail of lighting at canopy and existing columns.

Fig 44 Axonometric of level four barrel room.

Fig 45 Stair core louver details.

Fig 46 Rainwater drainpipes and railing junction details.

Fig 47 Plan details of barrel room.

Fig 48 Details of lightwells and floor interface.

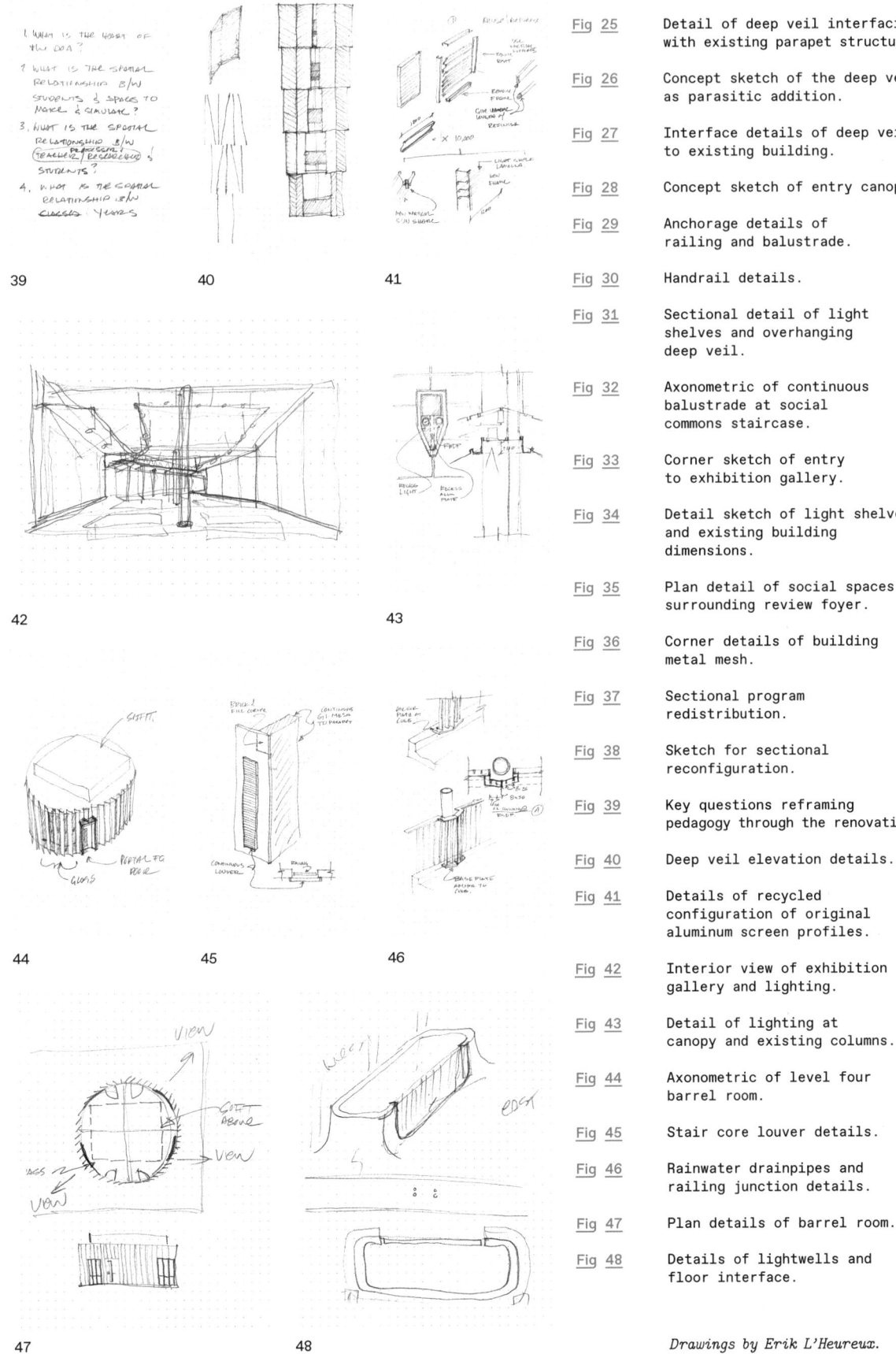

Drawings by Erik L'Heureux.

SDE 1 & 3 Archival Photos

1 est. 1980

2 est. 1980

3 est. 1980

4 est. 1989

5 est. 1980

6 est. 1985

Fig 1 West (entry) view of the SDE 3 fit-out renovations

Fig 2 West view of the Faculty of Architecture building prior to construction of frontal block of SDE 1

Fig 3 Southeast view of the access road to SDE 2 with the Faculty of Architecture building atop the hillock

Fig 4 Southwest view of SDE 3 fit-out renovations

Fig 5 South view of the Faculty of Architecture building with Faculty of Engineering buildings in the background

Fig 6 North view of the SDE 3 block of the Faculty of Architecture building

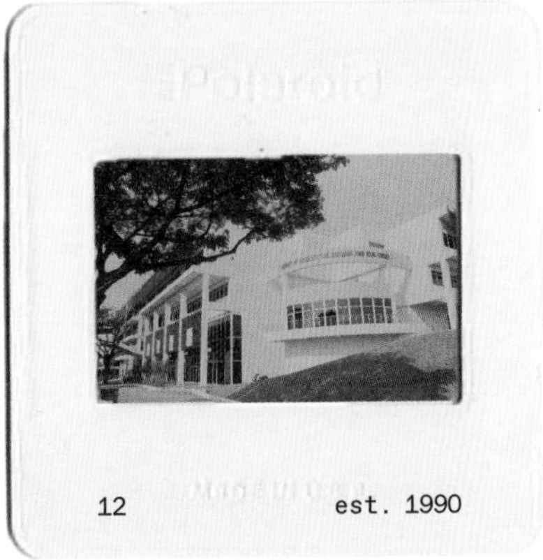

Fig 7 Students access the grand staircase from parking level

Fig 8 SDE 2 building with deep false ceiling

Fig 9 Excavation for the construction of frontal block of SDE 1

Fig 10 Northwest view of the SDE 1 & 3 blocks from Clementi Road

Fig 11 Construction of the vehicle drop-off entry canopy during the SDE 1 & 3 renovations

Fig 12 Southwest view of the renovated School of Design and Environment

All photos courtesy of Centre for Advanced Studies in Architecture, School of Design and Environment. Dates are approximate as the historical record is not clear.

Facts and Figures

Location:	Singapore	**Program:**	Exhibition galleries Review spaces 5 design studios 5 workshops 7 lecture theaters 4 laboratories 4 departments 13 seminar rooms 2 research centers 60 staff offices Social spaces
Climate:	Tropical, humid		
Size:	4 - 5 levels Gross Floor Area: 23,680 m^2 Site Area: 13,600 m^2		

SDE 1 & SDE 3 Resource Use:

On-site energy sourcing with rooftop photovoltaic panels.

Estimated annual energy demand:	1250 MWh/a
Estimated annual energy production:	1275 MWh/a
On-site energy sourcing (rooftop photovoltaic panels):	923 kWh/p
Energy intensity:	55 kWh/m^2/year

SDE 1 Post-occupancy Assessment:

Energy use intensity (EUI): — < 55 kWh/m^2/year

Value corrected for normal occupancy, assessment for a period 11 months of occupancy.

Rooftop photovoltaic capacity: — 422 kWh/p

Production is estimated to meet all energy consumption, making SDE 1 a net-zero-energy building with projected PV energy production 10-15% higher than its consumption.

Predicted photovoltaic energy production: — > 15% more than energy consumption

Predicted net-positive-energy performance to offset the embodied carbon emitted during construction.

Embodied energy: — > 175 kg CO2-eq /m^2 (low embodied carbon)

With its low embodied carbon footprint (in comparison to new constructions with embodied energy of 500-800 CO2-eq/m^2) and predicted net positive performance, SDE 1 is on track to be net-zero over its carbon lifecycle (embodied and operational).

SDE 1 Thermal Comfort:

Combination of natural ventilation, mechanical ventilation, air-conditioning, and a new hybrid cooling system supplying tempered air that is augmented by ceiling fans.

Passive: natural ventilation	25%
Active: air-conditioning	30%
Mechanical ventilation	5%
Hybrid: tempered air with ceiling fans	40%

Project Credits

School of Design and Environment
National University of Singapore

Lam Khee Poh	SDE Dean
Erik G. L'Heureux	Vice Dean (Special Projects) (2018-2022)
Heng Chye Kiang	Former SDE Dean (2007-2017)
Nirmal Kishnani	Former Vice Dean (Special Projects) (2013-2017)
Giovanni Cossu	Associate Director (Dean's Office)
Bertrand Lasternas	Associate Director (Dean's Office)

Erik G. L'Heureux, FAIA

Concept, Design, and Detail (2015–2022) with support by:

Amanda Mo
Anirudh Chandar
Astrid Mayadinta
Azizul Izwan B. Roslan
Epiphanie Barli Lie
Harsh Vardhan
Iven Peh
Joel Tay
Krista Yeong
Lakshmi Menon
Lee Lip Jiang
Ng Sze Wee
Ong Chan Hao
Reuben Lim
Stephanie Kui Hui Guat
Zeno Lee
Zuliandi Azli
Zulkarnain M. Zin

CPG Consultants Pte Ltd
Architects

E2000 Pte Ltd
Civil and Structural Engineers

WSP Consultancy Pte Ltd
Mechanical and Electrical Engineers

Transsolar Energietechnik GmbH
Climate Consultant (Concept Design)

IEN Consultants
Energy Consultant
(Schematic Design and Design Development)

CCW Associate Pte Ltd
Acoustics Consultant

SDE Special Projects, Yun Hye Hwang, with DP Green
Landscape Designers

SDE Special Projects
Interiors

Lian Soon Construction Pte Ltd
Contractors

Quants Associates
Quantity Surveyors

National University of Singapore
Developer

Office of Estate Development, University Campus Infrastructure
Project Manager

Special Thanks:
Florence Ling
David Cheong
Wong Yunn Chii

Erik G. L'Heureux, FAIA

Erik G. L'Heureux, FAIA, is a vice dean, the director of the Master of Architecture Programme, and a Dean's Chair Associate Professor at the School of Design and Environment, National University of Singapore, where he teaches the next generation of architects to be committed to the complexities and potentials of architecture located along the equator. Before arriving on the equator, he practiced architecture in New York City while teaching at the Irwin S. Chanin School of Architecture at The Cooper Union. His creative practice combines passive performance, pattern, and simplicity as a response toward the equatorial hot, wet climate and dense urban context manifesting through numerous buildings, including the design of SDE 1 & 3. The Wheelwright Prize from Harvard University has recognized his creative efforts, as well as several AIA New York and NY State Design Awards, SARA NY, National Design Awards, and INDE Design Awards. In addition to his design practice, his writing includes *Deep Veils* (ORO Editions, 2014); he was coeditor for *Drawing Climate* (Birkhäuser 2021), this publication, and numerous articles.

Giovanni Cossu

Giovanni Cossu is a sustainable development professional and associate director at the National University of Singapore. With experience in real estate and sustainability services, he is part of the senior management group at the School of Design and Environment where he oversees and manages a portfolio of campus redevelopment projects and corporate sustainability initiatives. This includes the design and construction of the first purpose-built net-zero-energy building in Singapore as well as the adaptive reuse of existing facilities aiming for net-zero carbon and net-zero water targets. He supports corporate sustainability development through industry partnerships and international collaborations resulting in programs such as the WELL Health and Safety Rating and the NUS WELL Portfolio. His work creates new opportunities of learning and real-world engagement for a wide community of students and industry professionals in Singapore and beyond.

Nader Tehrani is an Iranian-American designer and educator. In 2011, Tehrani and Katherine Faulkner co-founded NADAAA, a practice dedicated to the advancement of design innovation, interdisciplinary collaboration, and an intensive dialogue with the construction industry; later, Arthur Chang joined as a third partner. Tehrani is currently the dean of the Cooper Union's Irwin S. Chanin School of Architecture. Previously he was a professor of architecture at the MIT School of Architecture and Planning, where he served as head of the department from 2010 to 2014. In 1986, he founded Office dA with Rodolphe el-Khoury, and Mónica Ponce de León joined the firm in 1991.

Eric Höweler, AIA, LEED AP, is an architect, designer, and educator. Höweler is a co-founding principal and partner of Höweler + Yoon Architecture LLP, a research-driven studio of more than twenty designers. HYA has a reputation for work that is both technologically and formally innovative and deeply informed by human experience and a sensitivity to tectonics. He is currently an associate professor in architecture at the Harvard Graduate School of Design, where he teaches design studios and directs the Master of Architecture Thesis Program. Höweler's design work and research focuses on building technology integration and material systems. He is the coauthor of *Expanded Practice* (Princeton Architectural Press, 2009) and *Verify In Field: Projects and Conversations Höweler + Yoon* (Park Books, forthcoming 2021).

Heng Chye Kiang is the Provost's Chair Professor and immediate past dean of the School of Design and Environment at the National University of Singapore. Professor Heng teaches architecture, urban design, and planning, and has lectured at major universities in Europe and Asia. He has been appointed as a visiting professor to several universities in China, Korea, and Japan; currently, he is an honorary professor at CUHK. His research covers sustainable urban design, planning, and the history of Chinese cities. His books include *Singapore Chronicles: Urban Planning* (2018), *50 Years of Urban Planning in Singapore* (2016), *Re-Framing Urban Space* (2015), *On Asian Streets and Public Space* (2010), *A Digital Reconstruction of Tang Chang'an* (2006), and *Cities of Aristocrats and Bureaucrats* (1999).

Contributors

Ho Puay-peng holds the UNESCO Chair on Architectural Heritage Conservation and Management in Asia and is currently the head of the Department of Architecture at the School of Design and Environment, National University of Singapore. Following nearly thirty years of experience in academia, Professor Ho's main research interests are in architectural history and conservation practices, and how this knowledge can be translated into teaching and practice. Prior to joining the NUS in 2017, he was a professor of architecture and served as the director of the School of Architecture and the university dean of students at The Chinese University of Hong Kong. He has served as a conservation consultant, architect, and adviser to some 100 conservation projects in Hong Kong and Singapore since 2003, including PMQ, Haw Par Villa, Comix Homebase, Oil Street Art Space, Court of Final Appeal, and the new campus for the Chicago University Booth School. He is currently a member of the Senior Advisory Board of the Global Heritage Fund and a patron of the International Dunhuang Project of the British Library.

Lakshmi Menon is an Indian architect and former research associate at the School of Design and Environment. She is a registered architect with the Council of Architecture (India) and an IGBC accredited professional, having practiced as a junior architect in south India on projects ranging from small-scale residences to medium-scale industrial projects. She graduated from the National University of Singapore with a Master of Science degree in Integrated Sustainable Design (2017), expanding her interests in the technical and humanistic aspects of sustainability. She was the content writer of the JTC-funded publication *Weaving Webs* (2018) on hybrid buildings and the coauthor of academic papers and research proposals on equatorial architecture, urban greening, and systems thinking in Asian cities. She was a former columnist for *FuturArc Magazine*, writing on energy, sustainability, and urban policy.

Wolfgang Kessling is one of the directors of Transsolar Energietechnik GmbH, Munich, an international climate-engineering firm that approaches sustainability through innovative climate and energy concepts for buildings. Founded in 1992, the practice focuses on enhancing human comfort with minimum resource use. Kessling's experience with ventilation systems and energy-efficient buildings have led him to develop innovative solutions with architects and design teams in diverse climates around the world; over the years, his team has developed projects to improve outdoor comfort in urban settings. He has managed high-profile international projects of different scales and complexities, realizing sustainable designs celebrated for their architectural qualities as well as adaptive comfort projects focusing on practical and context-sensitive solutions. Kessling has been instrumental in spearheading the energy concepts of such prominent projects as the Cooled Conservatories at Gardens by the Bay, Singapore; the Zero Energy Office Building in Kuala Lumpur, Malaysia; and the Human Resources Headquarters at Novartis Basel, Switzerland.

Contributors

Nirmal Kishnani is a sustainability strategist, advising on projects and policies in Asia and scrutinizing the space between frontline theories and drawing-board pragmatism. As an author, educator, and advocate, he champions regenerative design tailored to the Asian context. His books *Greening Asia: Emerging Principles for Sustainable Architecture* (2012) and *Ecopuncture: Transforming Architecture and Urbanism in Asia* (2019) argue for upstream imagination over downstream mitigation and seek to reframe the role of the architect. As vice dean (2014 – 2017) at the School of Design and Environment, he steered the design process of the new net-zero-energy building. An educator since 2007, his innovative studio-based teaching integrated systems thinking with cross-disciplinary learning.

Chris Knapp is the head of the Abedian School of Architecture, Faculty of Society & Design, at Bond University. Prior to this, he was a lecturer in architecture at the University of Michigan. Knapp has worked in professional practice since 1999 in offices in the United States and Australia, and presently he is the director of the design and fabrication practice Studio Workshop. Knapp's research focuses on digital and computational design, computer-aided fabrication, construction systems, methodology, and craft. He has supervised and coordinated design theses, sits on several scientific committees, and has authored numerous publications including book chapters, journal articles, and peer-reviewed conference papers. His practice-based research has been exhibited in Kyoto, Los Angeles, Singapore, Wellington, Hobart, and several other Australian capital cities. He has served as treasurer of the Association of Architecture Schools of Australasia since 2014, and is an affiliate of the Australian Institute of Architects. Professor Knapp holds qualifications from Princeton University and the University of Michigan, and a PhD from RMIT's School of Architecture and Urban Design.

Contributors

Joshua Comaroff was born in Manchester, UK, and raised in Chicago. He studied literature and creative writing at Amherst College before joining the Master of Architecture and Master of Landscape Architecture programs at the Harvard University Graduate School of Design, where he worked as part of Rem Koolhaas's Harvard Project on the City. In 2009, he completed a PhD in cultural geography at the University of California Los Angeles (UCLA), writing about haunted landscapes and urban memory in Singapore. He has published writings about architecture, urbanism, and politics, with an Asian focus in *Public Culture*, *Cultural Geographies*, the *Journal of Architectural Education*, the *Journal of Southeast Asian Studies*, *CITY*, and elsewhere. He is a regular contributor to *Harvard Design Magazine*. Together with his partner, Ong Ker-Shing, Comaroff oversees Lekker Architects, a multidisciplinary design practice in Singapore. He works across a broad creative spectrum, with a special emphasis on design for the arts, for children, and for seniors. He is the recipient of Singapore's President's Design Award and Harvard's Wheelwright Travelling Fellowship. Together with Ong, he is the author of *Horror in Architecture*.

Lam Khee Poh is an educator, researcher, architect, and consultant who specializes in life cycle building information modeling and computational design support systems for total building performance analysis and building diagnostics. He is an emeritus professor of architecture at Carnegie Mellon University and is the currently appointed Provost's Chair Professor of Architecture and Building and dean of the School of Design and Environment, National University of Singapore. He is a licensed architect in the UK as well as an elected fellow of the Royal Institute of British Architects (FRIBA) for his significant contributions to architecture, the profession, and the community. He has completed many major funded research projects in Singapore and the US, and his findings are widely published. He is a member of the editorial boards of *Building Simulation* (Springer and Tsinghua University Press), and *Buildings* (MDPI AG, Switzerland). He is a member of the Singapore Future Economy Council Urban Systems Cluster Sub Committee, a director of the Centre for Liveable Cities Ltd., Singapore, and currently serves as an advisory board member of the City Developments Limited Singapore Sustainability Academy as well as a management board member of the Institute of Real Estate and Urban Studies at NUS.

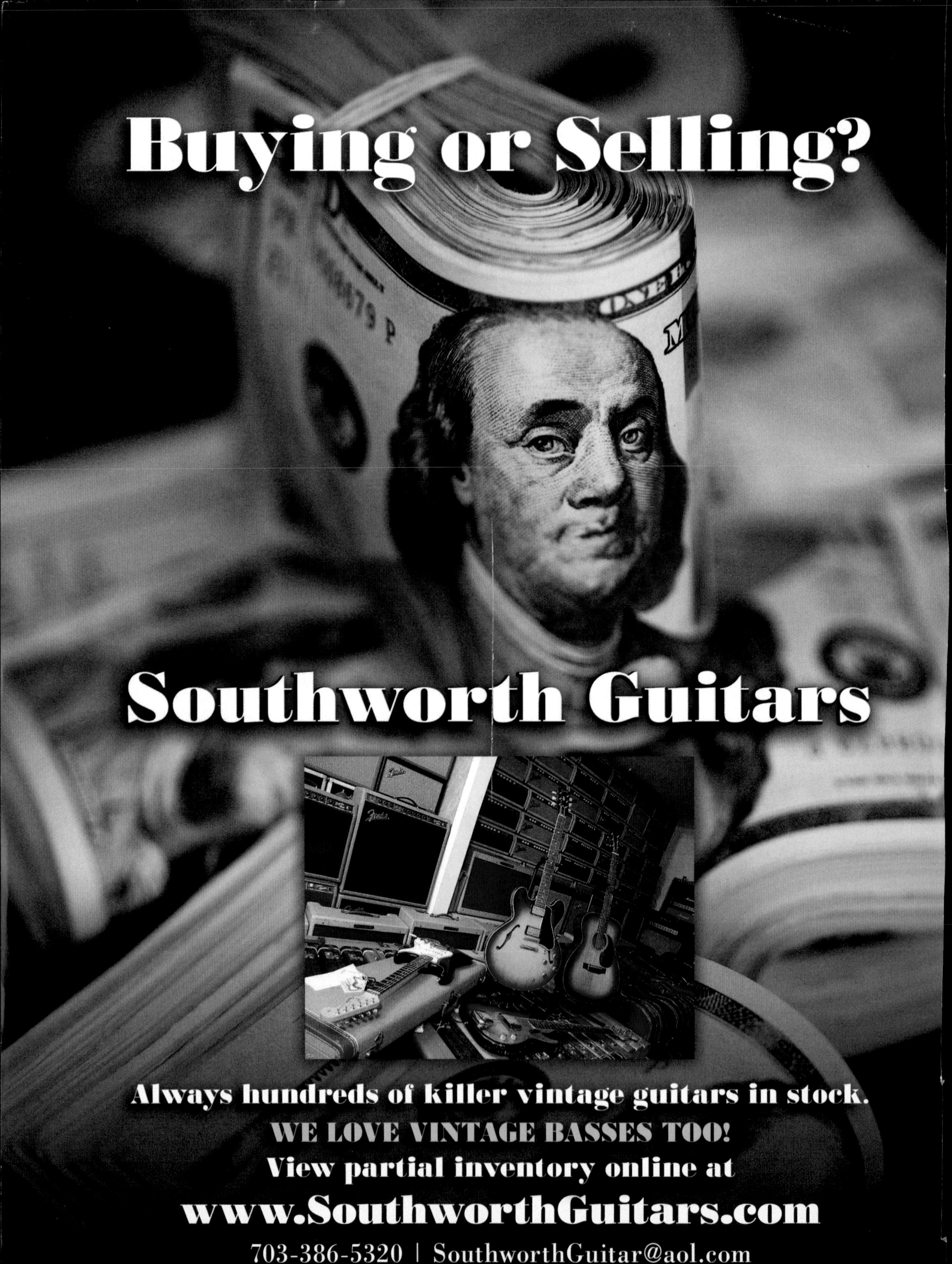
Buying or Selling?
Southworth Guitars
Always hundreds of killer vintage guitars in stock.
WE LOVE VINTAGE BASSES TOO!
View partial inventory online at
www.SouthworthGuitars.com
703-386-5320 | SouthworthGuitar@aol.com

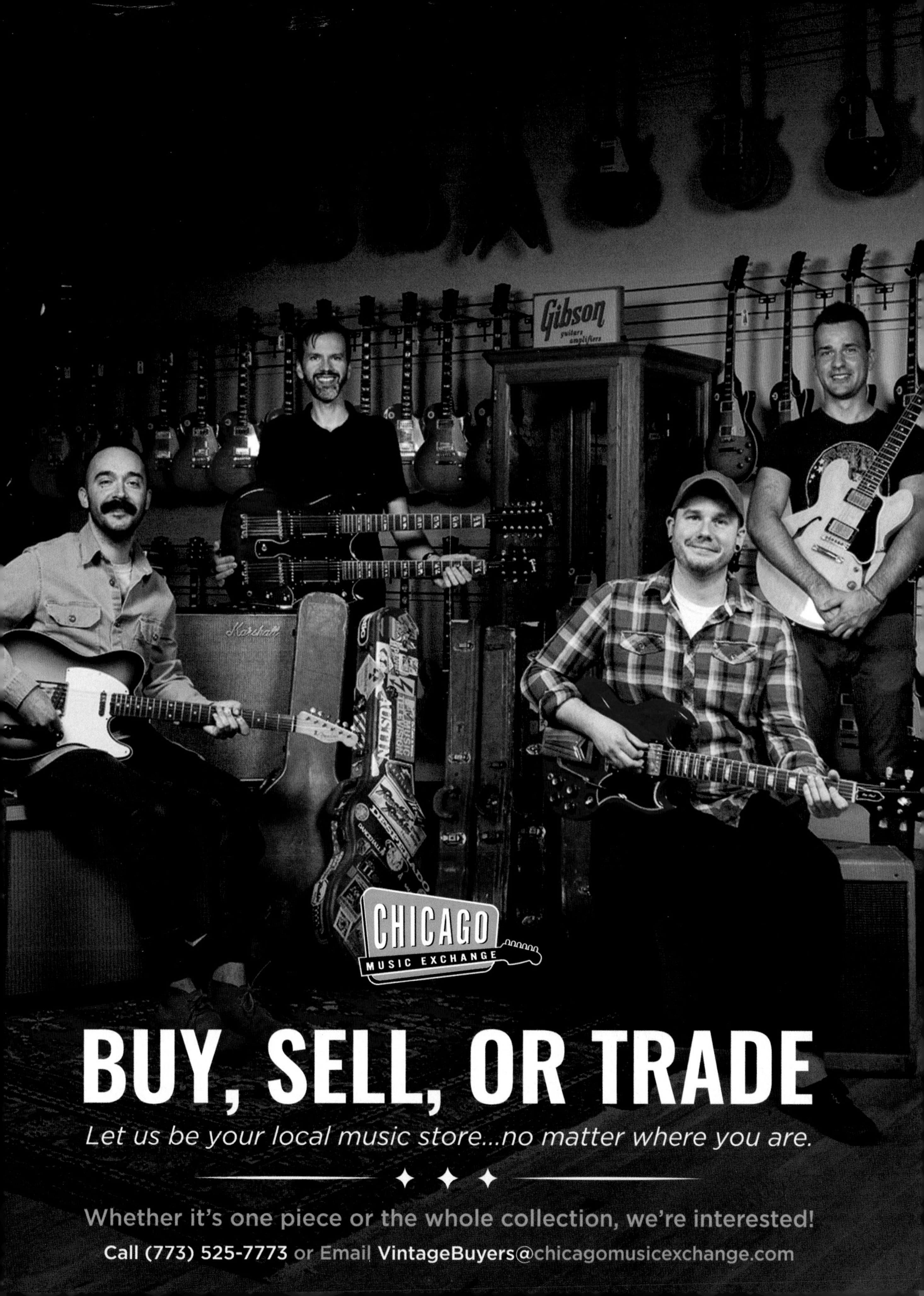
Gibson guitars amplifiers
Marshall
CHICAGO MUSIC EXCHANGE
BUY, SELL, OR TRADE
Let us be your local music store...no matter where you are.
Whether it's one piece or the whole collection, we're interested!
Call (773) 525-7773 or Email VintageBuyers@chicagomusicexchange.com

In loving memory of Jack Greenwood, 1990-2020

Alan Greenwood launched *Vintage Guitar* magazine in 1986 and in 1990 created *The Official Vintage Guitar Price Guide* (visit www.VintageGuitar.com to see everything *VG* now offers). His collection includes several vintage guitars, amps, effects, and ukuleles from the '20s to the '80s, as well as newer instruments. He lives in Bismarck, North Dakota.

Gil Hembree began collecting guitars in 1966 while working at Kitt's Music, in Washington, D.C. During his 30-year corporate career in Michigan he played in bands and continued to search for original-owner vintage guitars. In 2000, he became the co-author of *The Official Vintage Guitar Price Guide.* In '07, Hal Leonard released his biography of Ted McCarty: *Gibson Guitars: Ted McCarty's Golden Era: 1948-1966.* He and his wife, Jane, live in Austin, Texas.

The Official Vintage Guitar® magazine Price Guide

By Alan Greenwood and Gil Hembree

ISBN: 978-1-884883-44-6

Vintage Guitar, PO Box 7301, Bismarck, ND 58507, publishers of Vintage Guitar® magazine and Vintage Guitar® Online at www.VintageGuitar.com. Vintage Guitar is a registered trademark of Vintage Guitar, Inc.

Cover: 1968 Gibson Les Paul Special (left) courtesy of Dave Rogers. 1957 Gibson Les Paul Junior (middle) courtesy of Fretware. 1961 Gibson SG Special (right) courtesy of Dave Rogers. Photos property of *VG* Archive.
Back: 1957 Gibson Les Paul TV courtesy of Charlie Daughtry. 1958 Gibson Les Paul Special courtesy of Gary Dick. Photos property of *VG* Archive. Reverend Peyton: Tyler Zoller. Nick Perri: Derek Brad. Artie Leider: McKenzie River Music. Daniel Escauriza: Chicago Music Exchange. Howie Statland: Rivington Guitars.

Cover Design: Doug Yellow Bird/Vintage Guitar, Inc.

Printed in the United States of America

Vintage Guitar® magazine

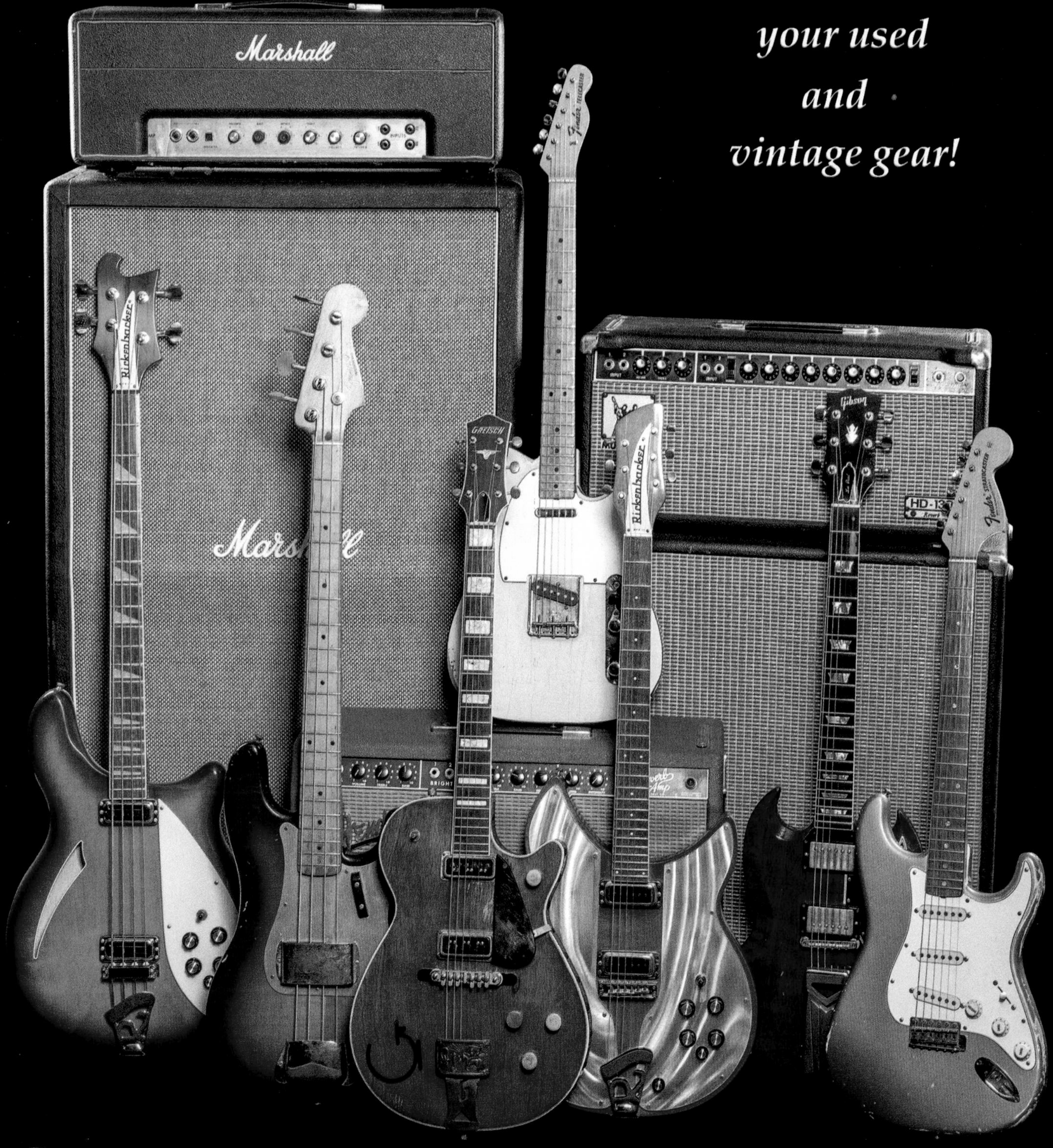

Marshall
Marshall
Gibson

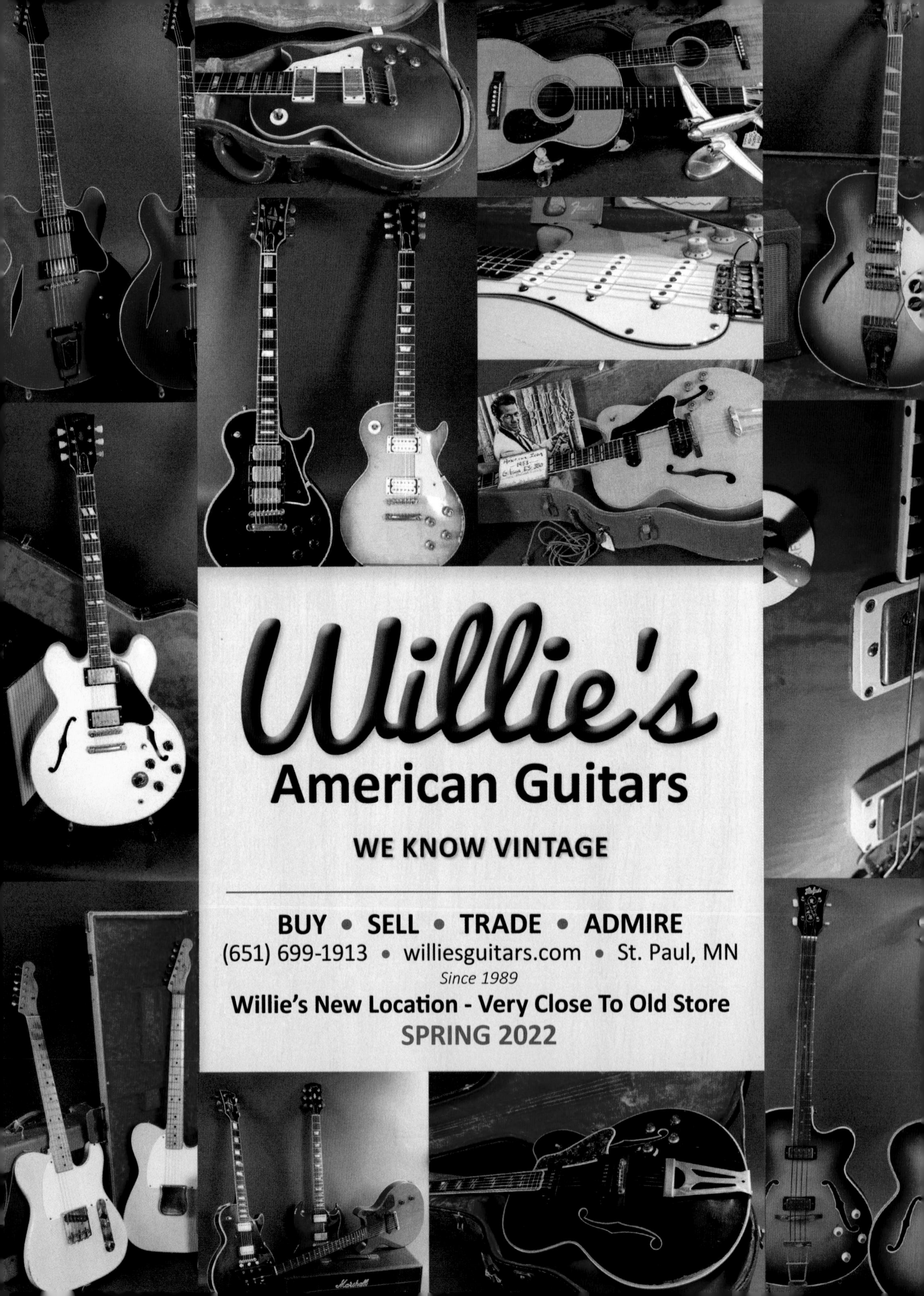
Willie's
American Guitars
WE KNOW VINTAGE
BUY • SELL • TRADE • ADMIRE
(651) 699-1913 • williesguitars.com • St. Paul, MN
Since 1989
Willie's New Location - Very Close To Old Store
SPRING 2022

VOX

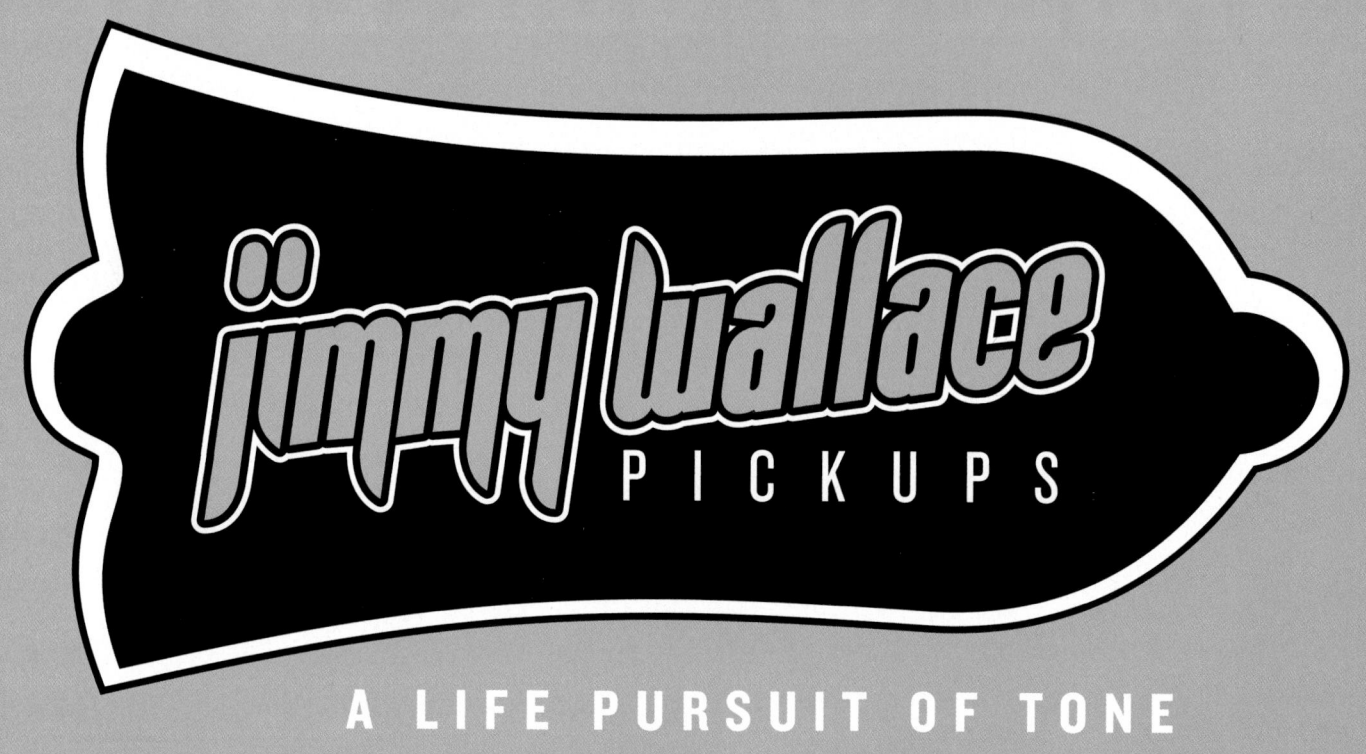

TABLE OF CONTENTS

Gary's
We Buy, Sell & Trade Fine Vintage Guitars
LASSIC GUITARS LLC
E PAY TOP $$$ FOR VINTAGE GUITARS AND BAS
513-891-0555 garysclssc@aol.com
erving Investors, Collectors and Professionals Worldwid
rysguitars.c

MAKE IT YOUR OWN
CUSTOMIZABLE • HUNDREDS OF OPTIONS • EASY INSTALLATION
FRALINPICKUPS.COM
Fralin PICKUPS
(804)-358-2699

AMIGO GUITAR SHOWS 2022 EVENTS
Co-sponsored by Vintage Guitar magazine
GUITARLINGTON
THE WORLD'S FINEST CONSUMER GUITAR EVENT!
BUY·SELL·TRADE
October 15 & 16, 2022
ARLINGTON CONVENTION CENTER
1200 Ballpark Way Arlington, TX
AMIGO NASHVILLE GUITAR SHOW
BUY·SELL·TRADE
March 26 & 27, 2022
WILLIAMSON COUNTY Ag EXPO PARK
Franklin, TN
AMIGO AGS GUITAR SHOWS LLC
Ruth Brinkmann
817-312-7659
ruthmbrinkmann@gmail.com
Dave Crocker
417-850-4751
davelcrocker@gmail.com
Larry Briggs
918-288-2222
amigoshows@stringswest.com
Facebook @ Amigo Guitar Shows
amigoguitarshows.com

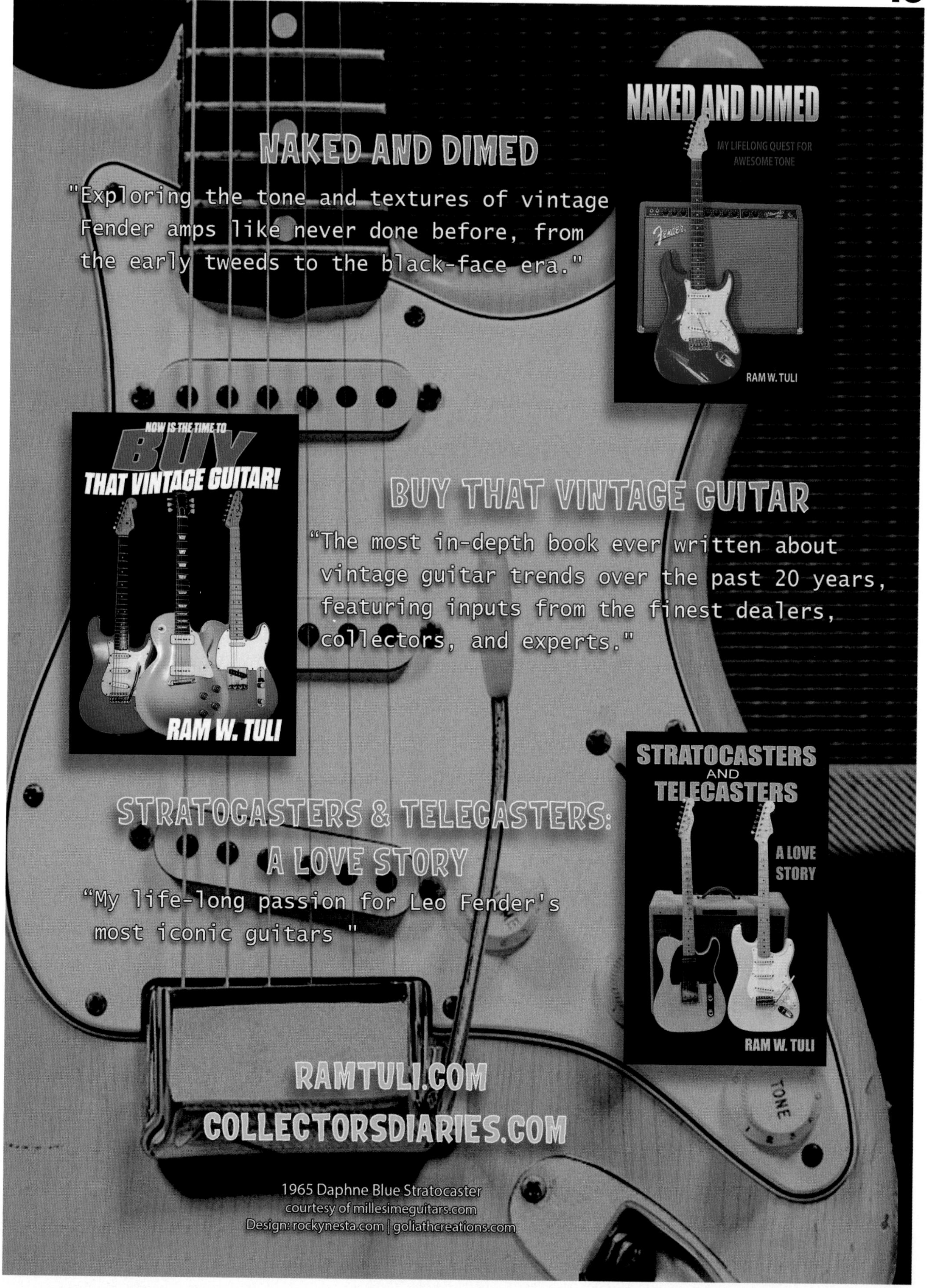
NAKED AND DIMED
"Exploring the tone and textures of vintage Fender amps like never done before, from the early tweeds to the black-face era."
NAKED AND DIMED
MY LIFELONG QUEST FOR AWESOME TONE
RAM W. TULI
NOW IS THE TIME TO
BUY
THAT VINTAGE GUITAR!
RAM W. TULI
BUY THAT VINTAGE GUITAR
"The most in-depth book ever written about vintage guitar trends over the past 20 years, featuring inputs from the finest dealers, collectors, and experts."
STRATOCASTERS & TELECASTERS: A LOVE STORY
"My life-long passion for Leo Fender's most iconic guitars "
STRATOCASTERS AND TELECASTERS
A LOVE STORY
RAM W. TULI
RAMTULI.COM
COLLECTORSDIARIES.COM
TONE
1965 Daphne Blue Stratocaster
courtesy of millesimeguitars.com
Design: rockynesta.com | goliathcreations.com

USING THE GUIDE

UNDERSTANDING THE VALUES

The values presented in *The Official Vintage Guitar Price Guide* are for excellent-condition, all-original instruments. Our definition of excellent condition allows for some wear, but the instrument should be well-maintained, with no significant blemishes, wear, repairs, or damage. All-original means the instrument has the parts and finish it had when it left the factory. Replacement parts and refinishes can greatly affect value, as can the appropriate case (or cover) in excellent condition. In many instances, a "wrong" case will not greatly affect value, but with the top-dollar collectibles, it can.

We use a range of excellent-condition values, as there is seldom agreement on a single price point for vintage and used instruments. A tighter range suggests there is a general consensus, while a wide range means the market isn't in strict agreement. A mint-condition instrument can be worth more than the values listed here, and anything in less-than-excellent condition will have a reduced value.

Repairs affect value differently. Some repair is necessary to keep an instrument in playable condition. The primary concern is the level of expertise displayed in the work and an amateurish repair will lower the value more than one that is obviously professional. A refinished guitar, regardless of the quality of the work, is generally worth 50% or less of the values shown in *The Guide*. A poorly executed neck repair or significant body repair can mean a 50% reduction in a guitar's value. A professional re-fret or minor, nearly invisible body repair will reduce a guitar's value by only 5%.

The values in the *The Guide* are for unfaded finishes. Slight color fade reduces value by only 5%, but heavy fading can reduce value by 25% to 50%.

FINDING THE INFORMATION

The table of contents shows the major sections and each is organized in alphabetical order by brand, then by model. In a few instances, there are separate sections for a company's most popular models, especially when there is a large variety of similar instruments. Examples include Fender's Stratocasters, Telecasters, Precision and Jazz basses, and Gibson's Les Pauls. The outer top corner of each page includes a dictionary-type index that tells the models or brands on that page. This provides a quick way to navigate each section.

The Guide has excellent brand histories and in most cases the guitar section has the most detailed information for each brand. When possible, *The Guide* lists each model's years of availability and any design changes that affect values.

More information on many of the brands covered in *The Guide* is available in the pages of *Vintage Guitar* magazine and on the "Features" section of our website, www.VintageGuitar.com.

The authors of *The Guide* appreciate your help, so if you find any errors or have additional information on certain brands or models, please drop us a line at Alan@VintageGuitar.com.

NEW RETAIL PRICING INFORMATION

The Guide continues to add information on individual luthiers and smaller shops. It's difficult to develop values on used instruments produced by these builders because much of their output is custom work, production is low, and/or they haven't been producing for a period of time sufficient to see their instruments enter the used/resale market. To give you an idea about their instruments, we've developed five grades of retail values for new instruments. These convey only the prices charged by the builder, and are not indicative of the quality of construction. *The Guide* applies this scale to all builders and manufacturers of new instruments.

The five retail-price grades are:
Budget - up to $250,
Intermediate - $251 to $1,000,
Professional - $1,001 to $3,000,
Premium - $3,001 to $10,000,
Presentation - more than $10,000.

The Guide uses the terms "production" and "custom" to differentiate between builders who do true custom work versus those who offer standard production models. "Production" means the company offers specific models, with no variations. "Custom" means they do only custom orders, and "production/custom" indicates they do both. Here's an example:

Jack Greenwood
1990-present. Premium grade, custom solidbody guitars built by luthier Jack Greenwood in Bismarck, North Dakota. He also builds effects.

This tells who the builder is, the type of instruments they build, where they build them, how long they've been operating under that brand, that they do only custom work, and that they ask between $3,000 and $10,000 for their guitars (premium-grade).We've applied the retail price grades and production and/or custom labels to most new-instrument manufacturers.

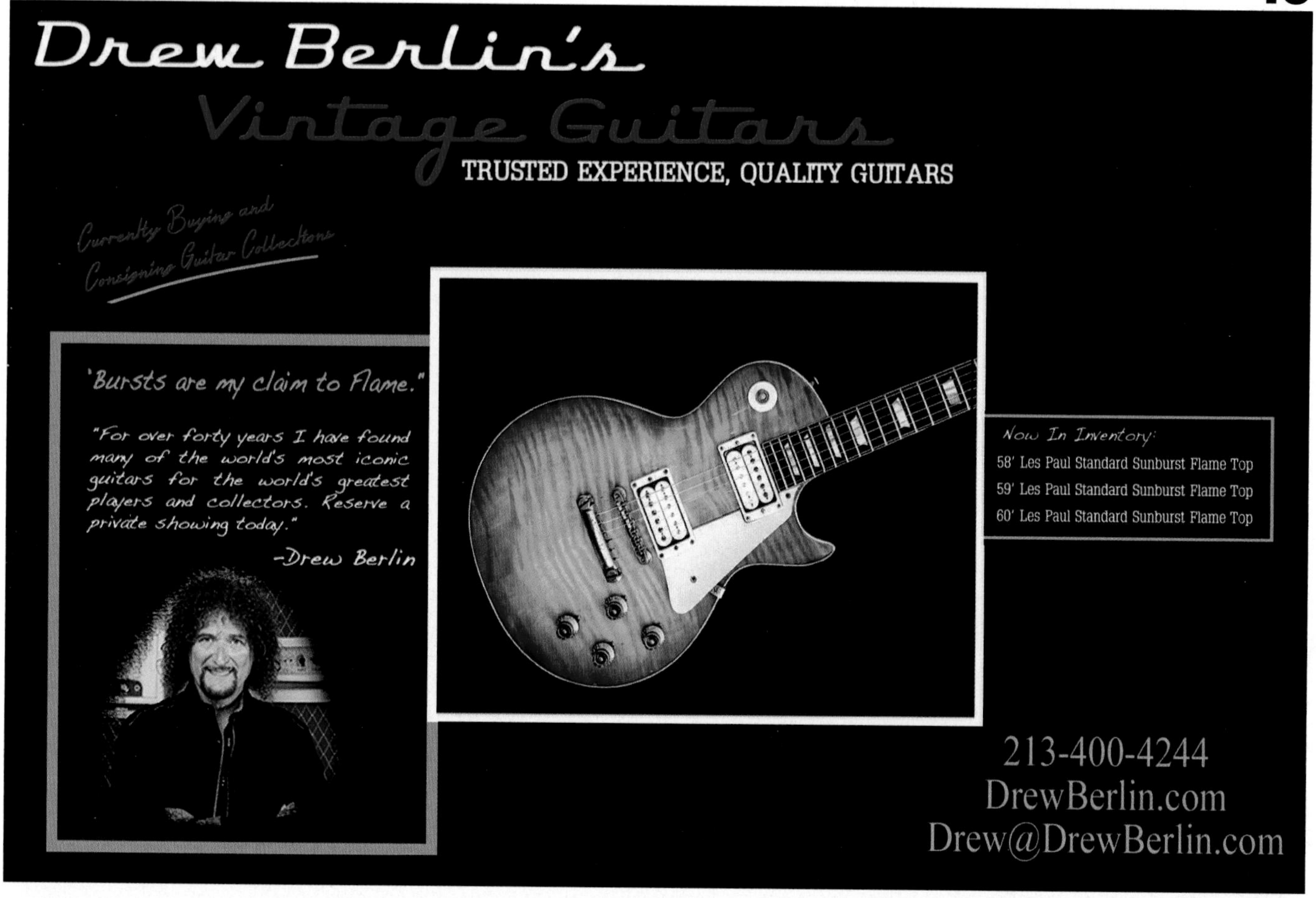
Drew Berlin's
Vintage Guitars
TRUSTED EXPERIENCE, QUALITY GUITARS
Currently Buying and Consigning Guitar Collections
"Bursts are my claim to Flame."
"For over forty years I have found many of the world's most iconic guitars for the world's greatest players and collectors. Reserve a private showing today."
-Drew Berlin
Now In Inventory:
58' Les Paul Standard Sunburst Flame Top
59' Les Paul Standard Sunburst Flame Top
60' Les Paul Standard Sunburst Flame Top
213-400-4244
DrewBerlin.com
Drew@DrewBerlin.com

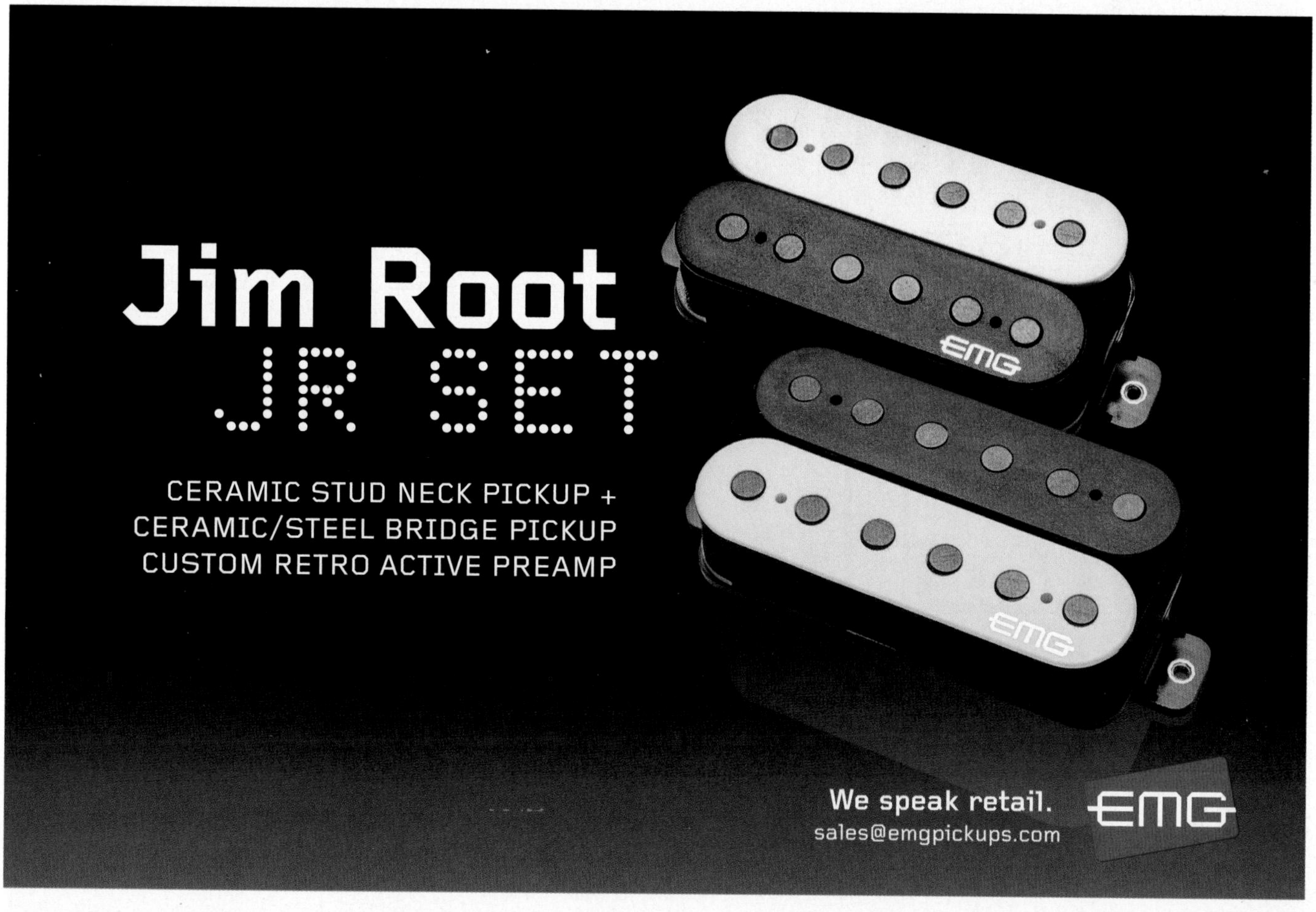
Jim Root
JR SET
CERAMIC STUD NECK PICKUP +
CERAMIC/STEEL BRIDGE PICKUP
CUSTOM RETRO ACTIVE PREAMP
EMG
EMG
We speak retail.
sales@emgpickups.com
EMG

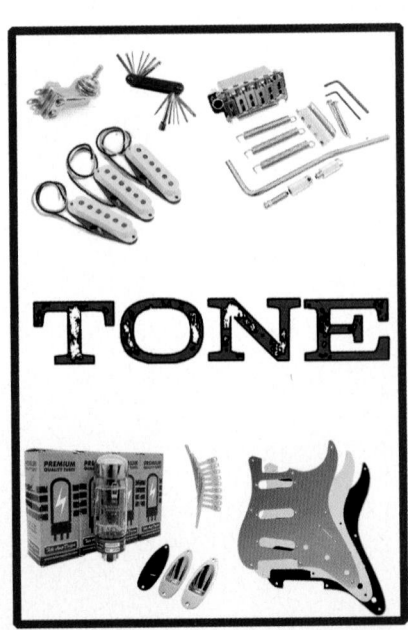

INTRODUCTION

Welcome to the 2022 edition of *The Official Vintage Guitar Price Guide*. If this is your first time with the book, please read "Using *The Guide*" on page 18. Regular buyers know we alternate sections for banjos and mandolins with those for ukuleles and steel guitars. We do this to maintain *The Guide*'s page count as the Guitars section continues to expand; this edition includes ukuleles and steel guitars.

42 INDEX

A perennial favorite, *Vintage Guitar*'s 42 Index tracks the cumulative value of a selection of models from the three largest companies of the "classic era" - 14 each from Fender, Gibson, and Martin. The Index line graph first appeared in the 2002 *Guide* and was comprised of 27 guitars/basses. In the 2003 and '04 *Guide*, we labelled it the "Guitar Collector's Index," with 27 members. In the '05 edition we expanded to 42 members and the "Guitar Collector's Index" became the "42 Guitar Index." One goal of the 42 Guitar Index was to have each of the three subgroups carry similar weight. For 1991, the Index shows a historical accumulative value for Fender at $50,875, Gibson at $51,100, and Martin at $51,750. The variance between them was a mere 1.7%. The Index excludes the most-valuable instruments for each brand, such as pre-war D-45s, Les Paul Standards (a.k.a. 'burst), early Explorers, and first-year Teles and Strats.

The Index rose 10.7% from 2021 to '22. The Fender segment increased 14.3%, Gibson increased 10.7%, and Martin increased 7.1%. The Fender group is entirely electric solidbody instruments, while the Martin group is 86% acoustics, and Gibson has a variety of electrics going from the student-level Les Paul Junior to the professional Super 400CES.

This year's Index shows highest individual values exceeding $30,000; Fenders exceeding that benchmark are the '52 Esquire, '53 Telecaster, and '56 Stratocaster; Gibsons are the '58 Les Paul Custom and '58 ES-335N; Martins are the '35 D-18, '44 D-28, '69 D-45, and '31 OM-28. Instruments under $10,000 are spread differently within the segments. Fender only has two below $10,000, Gibson and Martin each have seven.

We strive to ensure the Index provides a relevant reflection of the market, but it is intended only as a guide. The best way to annually evaluate your collection's value is to review *The Guide* page by page.

WHAT'S HOT?

There are many examples of instruments that increased in value by 20% or more in this year's *Guide*. Among guitars, the 1967-'70 Baldwin 706 and 706V are up 29% and 26%, respectively, and are selling at prices not seen since 2008. The '70s Chapman Stick (10- or 12-string) increased 22%. The production '05/'06 Charvel EVH Art Series in black/white, yellow/black and white/black/red increased 30% or more as a result of Edward Van Halen's passing. The '81-'86 Charvel San Dimas (serialized plate) increased by 30%. The '86-'89 made-in-Japan Charvel Series 1 (1A,1C,2,3,3A,3DR,3L,4,4A,5,5A,6,7, and 88LTD) are up 30%; this is the second year these guitars jumped 30%. Interestingly, Strats and Teles identified as MIJ have seen increased interest for the last several years. The Charvel Fusion Series - 1989-'91 Deluxe and '93-'96 Standard - followed the trend of the other MIJ Charvels by increasing 30%. MIJ ESP solidbodies from the '80s and early '90s are up 33%, thanks in part to being recognized as well-built guitars; the M-I Custom, M-I Deluxe, M-II, M-II Custom and M-II Deluxe are good examples.

The '66 Fender Electric XII with sunburst finish increased 22%. The Fender 25th Anniversary Strat is up 23% but only with original silver finish that is not flaking off. The 25th was the first model to return to the four-bolt neck and standard truss rod. The early-'79 version with flaking finish are worth 25% less than the '80, and actually decreased in value this year. Two 1992 Custom Shop Strats - the American Classic and American Classic Holoflake - both increased 26%. The 1994-3020 Dick Dale Custom Shop Strat is up 30%. The 1986-'99 '52 Telecaster, one of the early reissues, increased by 25%. Those made from

THE 42 INDEX

FROM FENDER
1952 blond Precision Bass
1952 blond Esquire
1953 blond Telecaster
1956 sunburst Stratocaster
1958 sunburst Jazzmaster
1958 blond Telecaster
1960 sunburst Stratocaster
1961 sunburst, stack knob, Jazz Bass
1962 sunburst, 3-knob, Jazz Bass
1963 sunburst Telecaster Custom
1963 sunburst Esquire Custom
1964 Lake Placid Blue Jaguar
1964 sunburst Precision Bass
1966 Candy Apple Red Stratocaster

FROM GIBSON
1952 sunburst ES-5
1952 Les Paul Model
1954 Les Paul Jr.
1958 sunburst EB-2 Bass
1958 Les Paul Custom
1958 natural ES-335
1958 Super 400CES
1959 Les Paul Jr.
1959 J-160E
1961 ES-355
1961 Les Paul SG
1964 sunburst Thunderbird II Bass
1965 EB-3 Bass
1969 sunburst Citation

FROM MARTIN
1931 OM-28
1936 00-28
1935 D-18
1944 scalloped-brace 000-28
1944 D-28
1950 D-28
1958 000-18
1959 D-18
1959 D-28E
1962 D-28
1967 GT-75
1968 000-18
1969 N-20
1969 D-45

'82 to '84 were already more valuable than '86-'99 models, so early ones did not experience a large increase.

The '91-'03 Gibson ES-135 with trapeze or stop tail increased 28%. The '59 ETG-150 tenor guitar is up 20%. Gibson's Heritage Model flat-top is up 28% for solid Brazilian rosewood ('65-'68 and laminated Indian rosewood ('68-'69), but the solid-Brazilian model is worth twice as much. The 2011 Gibson Hummingbird Custom Shop 12-string is up 31%. The Gibson Jumbo 35/J-35 from 1936 to '42 is up 30%. The Jumbo 55/J-55 from 1939-'43 is up 25%. These two classic Gibson models have recently seen

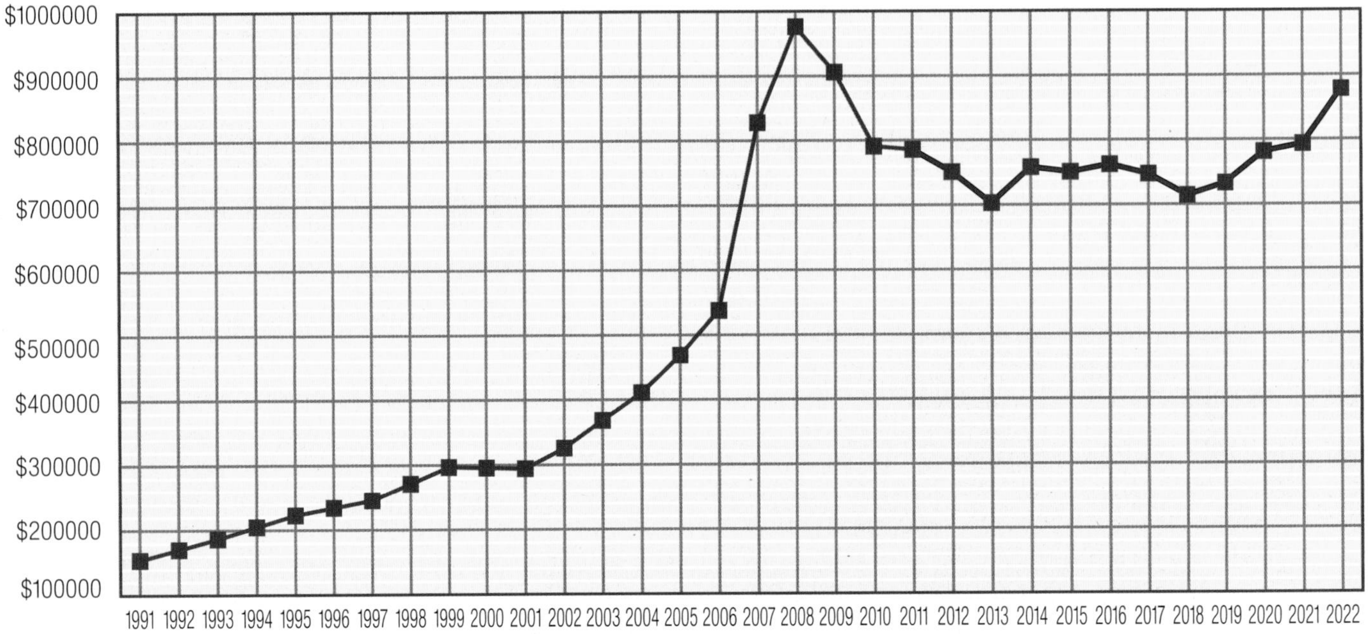

The 42 Guitar Index 1991 - 2022

GUITAR DEALER PARTICIPANTS

The information refined on these pages comes from several sources, including the input of many knowledgeable guitar dealers. Without the help of these individuals, it would be very hard for us to provide the information here and in each issue of *Vintage Guitar* magazine. We deeply appreciate the time and effort they provide.

Brian Goff
Bizarre Guitars

Garrett Tung
Boingosaurus Music

Dave Belzer
Burst Brothers

Walter Carter
Carter Vintage

Daniel Escauriza
Chicago Music Exchange

John Majdalani
Cream City Music

Dave Rogers
Dave's Guitar Shop

Drew Berlin
Drew Berlin's Vintage Guitars

Stan Werbin & S.J. "Frog"
Forgey
Elderly Instruments

Dewey Bowen
Freedom Guitar

Rick Hogue
Garrett Park Guitars

Gary Dick
Gary's Classic Guitars

Eric Newell
Gruhn Guitars

Richard Johnston
Gryphon Strings

Kennard Machol & Leonard Coulson
Intermountain Guitar & Banjo

Jim Singleton
Jim's Guitars

Kevin Borden
Kebo's BassWorks

Dave Hinson
Killer Vintage

Timm Kummer
Kummer's Vintage Instruments

Buzzy Levine
Lark Street Music

Larry Wexer
Laurence Wexer, Ltd.

Artie Leider
McKenzie River Music

Neal Shelton
Neals Music (California)

Lowell Levinger
Players Vintage Instruments

Howie Statland
Rivington Guitars

Eliot Michael
Rumble Seat Music

Sammy Ash
Sam Ash Music Stores

Eric Schoenberg
Schoenberg Guitars

Richard Gellis
Union Grove Music

Fred Oster
Vintage Instruments

Richard Friedman
We Buy Guitars

Nate Westgor
Willie's American Guitars

GAIN
TREBLE
MID
BASS
PRESENCE
MASTER
REVERB
MULTI-WATT
POWER
STANDBY
Boogie
California tweed

varying demand. The '70s Gibson J-45/J-45 Deluxe is up 24%, and trends are upending the old mores that '70s Gibsons were not worthy instruments. The '09 Gibson Les Paul '52 Tribute is up 20% but it should be in near-mint condition with all paperwork. The single-cut sunburst '54 Les Paul Junior increased 29% and the double-cut cherry version increased 27%. The 2016 Les Paul Limited Run Series Fort Knox model is up 21%. The '80s and '90s Gibson Les Paul Junior single-cut with a P-90 pickup is up 25%. The '79 Les Paul Standard with natural finish increase by 21%; models from this era vary in price depending on finish. All '60s Melody Makers - single- or two-pickup, are up 30%, as are '60s Epiphone Olympics, though they sell for slightly less. Also, the Melody Maker Joan Jett Signature with worn-white finish is up

A Charvel EVH Art Series and 1966 Fender Electric XII

DALLAS INTERNATIONAL
GUITAR FESTIVAL
2022
Guitar Festival
Dallas
44TH ANNUAL
DALLAS MARKET HALL
FRIDAY APRIL 29 – SUNDAY MAY 1
WWW.GUITARSHOW.COM

33%. The '83 Gibson Moderne Heritage Korina with natural finish is up 28%. The '85/'86 Q-200/Q-2000 and Q-300/Q-3000 increased 25%. Gibson Q-80 and Q-90 basses increased similarly. The '87-'91 US-1 with flame-maple top increased 20%.

Among other brands, the G&L Fallout is up 26% and both generations of the Invader are up 28%. The '02-'04 Godin Flat Five X is up 20%, while Guild's 1953/'54 X-100 and X-110 are up 32%, closing the gap with the Savoy X-150 that replaced them in the mid '50s. The '80s Hamer Steve Stevens models are up 30%. The '77-'80 Kramer 650-G Artist and 650-B Artist bass are both up 30%, and the Models 250, 350, and 450 guitars and basses have increased in value. Kramer's Baretta Series from the '80s are up 28% or more. Also, most of the Kramer Pacer Series from the '80s are up 25%. Kramers from this period had high-quality necks from Japan, and final assembly was in the U.S. In its '80s golden-age, Kramer was the largest-volume U.S.

Authors Gil Hembree and Alan Greenwood

RUMBLE RS SEAT MUSIC
An American Tradition
PREMIUM VINTAGE GUITARS
BUY. SELL. TRADE. TOP DOLLAR PAID.
TRANSONIC
1805 8TH AVE SOUTH, NASHVILLE, TN
615-915-2510

manufacturer. The '97-'04 Metropolitan models are up 22%. The '60s/'70s Ramirez 1A with Brazilian body and cedar top are up 29%.

The 1937 Martin 5-17 increased 23%, while the '91 D-16H is up 23%. Like the other listings in *The Guide*, the instrument must be in excellent original condition with original case. The '59 D-18E with two factory pickups is up 26%; considered an electric guitar, its ladder bracing makes its sound different from a D-18 when played acoustically. The D-28S from 1970-'94 increased by 20% or more.

Among basses, Fender's early-1964 Precision with spaghetti logo, green guard, and sunburst finish is up 31%. The late-'64 Precision, with newer logo and white guard, increased 31%. The '78-'79 Precision in various finishes is up 33%. The '97-'98 Precision Special made in Mexico with Precision and Jazz pickups increased 24%.

Gibson's '62-'65 EB-0F increased 22%, while the early-'65 EB-3 with wide-spaced Volume and Tone controls are up 28%. The later-'65 version (with narrow-spaced controls) runs about $1,400 less, but also saw a large increase. The '74-'82 Grabber and Grabber III are up 30%. The '71-'79 Les Paul Triumph/Recording bass is up 31%, and those with a white finish are worth more than natural. The Melody Maker bass from '67-'70, is up 23%.

For Hagstrom, the '67-'69 H-8 is up 38%; those in less-than-excellent condition would be considerably less. The '65-'73 Model 1B/F100B is up 36%.

In the Amps section, the 1964-'67 Fender blackface AA764 Vibro-Champ increased 33%. The 1960-'61 Gibson GA-30RV Invader in tweed (with reverb but no tremolo) increased by 30%. Tweed-covered Gibsons with reverb are the most-desirable models. The hard-to-find '56 GA-70 Country and Western is up 31%. The rare '56 GA-55 and GA-55V (vibrato) follow the pattern and are up 31%. The '63 Vox AC30/AC30 Twin Top combo with black covering increased by 31%. To fetch this price, the amp must be all-original (including handle) and in excellent cosmetic shape with virtually no tears or stains on the grille. Custom-color versions fetch more and increased 33%.

Just about everything on the pedalboard is up about 10-25%. With the effects market rebounding, staples such as vintage Big Muffs, Tube Screamers, Rats, and so on have been hard to find and have been selling for 20-30% more than in the past several years.

Vintage effects from the '90s are on the rise, especially among players who came of age at that time. Select Boss pedals are on the up. The '90s DOD FX series of pedals have appreciated in the last year - up to a 40% for some. Rockman Effects processors and headphone amps rapidly doubled and tripled in price last December.

Vintage, reissue, and even not-so-old pedals that have been modified by boutique pedal makers or engineers - Keeley and JHS in particular - have shot up in value, sometimes doubling in price.

Last but hardly least, Klon pedals took another huge leap. Gold-horsie Klon Centaurs are easily selling for larger sums, silver Klons are fetching big money, while gold non-horsie units somewhere between. In the Centaur's wake, the KTR is on the rise.

MORE INFORMATION

Much of the information in this book comes from *Vintage Guitar magazine*, which is offered in both print and digital formats; you can subscribe at www.VintageGuitar.com or find it on the newsstand. VintageGuitar.com has a vast trove of feature interviews, instrument histories and profile, gear and music reviews, and historical information on the brands and models covered in this book. You'll also find links to new exclusive lessons, *VG* podcasts, our online archives of *VG* back issues, the *VG* YouTube channel, and our free e-mail *VG Overdrive* newsletter. Find us on Facebook, Twitter, YouTube, and Instagram, where we talk guitars and offer prizes. We'd love to have you join us.

ACKNOWLEDGEMENTS

Wanda Huether, Editor of *The Guide*, keeps us on deadline and makes all this possible. Michael Dregni provided values, information, and photos for the effects section as did Randy Klimpert for the Ukuleles section. Doug Yellow Bird continues his fine work on the design and layout of the book. Larry Huether and Ward Meeker helped with editing and proofreading, James Jiskra, Johnny Zapp, and Mike Naughton handled the advertising and directory listings. We thank all of them for their usual fine work.

We use many sources to determine values, but the vintage instrument dealers who give their time and expertise to provide market information play an important role. Many provide info on brands and models, and they are acknowledged on page 26.

Once again, Heritage Auctions (HA.com) and Howie Statland at www.RivingtonGuitars.com graciously gave us access to their photo archives. Thanks to all the readers that submitted photos with a special shout-out to David Stone, Frank Manno, Tom Pfeifer, Greg Perrine, Matt Carleson, Michael J. Scanlon, and Tony Sheedy for sending pics of large portions of their collections.

Thank you,

Alan Greenwood, Gil Hembree, and Wanda Huether

UPDATES AND CORRECTIONS

If you spot errors in the information about brands and models, have information on a brand you'd like to see included, or produce instruments for sale and would like to be included in the next edition of *The Guide*, email Wanda at Library@VintageGuitar.com.

If a model is missing from *The Guide*, or if you spot something that needs to be clarified, please drop a line to Gil@VintageGuitar.com.

Marshall
Marshall

GUITARS

1966 Gretsch Chet Atkins Country Gentleman (6122); Frank Manno.

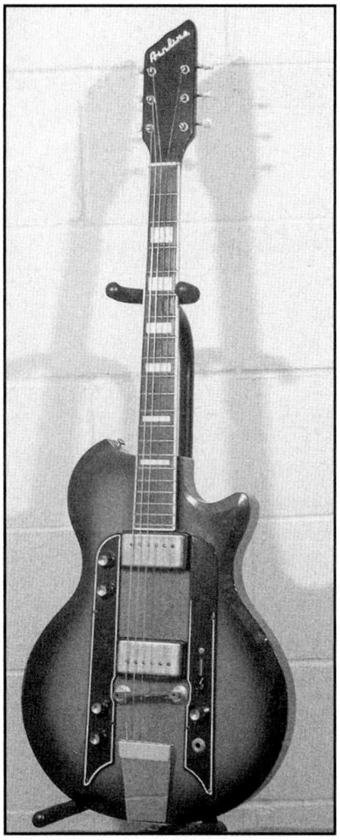

1960 Airline Town and Country
Tom Pfeifer

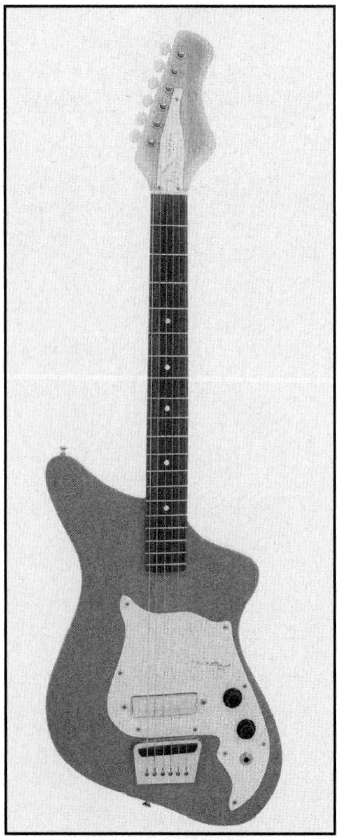

1960s Alamo Fiesta
Imaged by Heritage Auctions, HA.com

17th Street Guitars

2004-2009. Founded by Dave Levine and Colin Liebich. Professional grade, production/custom, solidbody guitars built by luthier John Carruthers in Venice, California.

A Fuller Sound

Luthier Warren Fuller began building professional and premium grade, custom nylon and steel-string flat-tops in '98 in Oakland, California.

Abel

Custom aircraft-grade aluminum body, wood neck, guitars built by twins Jim and Jeff Abel in Evanston, Wyoming. They offered the Abel Axe from '94-'96 and 2000-'01, and still do custom orders. They also made the Rogue Aluminator in the late '90s.

Axe

1994-1996. Offset double-cut aluminum body with dozens of holes in the body, wood neck, various colors by annodizing the aluminum body. Abel Axe logo on the headstock.

MODEL YEAR	FEATURES	EXC. COND. LOW	HIGH
1994-1996	Non-trem or trem	$575	$750

Abilene

Budget and intermediate grade, production, acoustic and electric guitars imported by Samick.

Abyss

See listing under Pederson Custom Guitars.

Acme

1960s. Imported inexpensive copy electric guitar models for the student market.

Acoustic

Ca. 1965-ca. 1987, 2001-2005, 2008-present. Mainly known for solidstate amps, the Acoustic Control Corp. of Los Angeles, California, did offer guitars and basses from around '69 to late '74. The brand has been revived on a new line of amps.

Black Widow

1969-1970, 1972-1974. Double-cut body, 2 pickups, and protective pad on back. The early version (AC500) had 22 frets, ebonite 'board and later one was 24 frets, rosewood 'board. Acoustic outsourced production, possibly to Japan, but final 200 or so guitars produced by Semie Moseley. The AC700 Black Widow 12-string was also available for '69-'70.

MODEL YEAR	FEATURES	EXC. COND. LOW	HIGH
1969-1970		$1,175	$1,550
1972-1974		$1,000	$1,325

Agile

1985-present. Budget grade, production, acoustic and electric guitars imported by Rondo Music of Union, New Jersey. They also offer mandolins.

Aims

Ca. 1972-ca. 1976. Aims (American International Music Sales, Inc.) instruments, distributed by Randall Instruments in the mid-'70s, were copies of classic American guitar and bass models. They also offered a line of Aims amps during the same time.

Airline

Ca. 1958-1968, 2004-present. Airline originally was a brand used by Montgomery Ward on acoustic, electric archtop and solidbody guitars and basses, amplifiers, steels, and possibly banjos and mandolins. Instruments manufactured by Kay, Harmony and Valco. In '04, the brand was revived on a line of imported intermediate grade, production, reissues from Eastwood guitars.

Acoustic Res-O-Glas Resonator

1964. Res-o-glas, coverplate with M-shaped holes, asymmetrical peghead.

MODEL YEAR	FEATURES	EXC. COND. LOW	HIGH
1964		$600	$775

Amp-In-Case Model

1960s. Double-cut, single pickup, short scale guitar with amplifier built into the case, Airline on grille.

MODEL YEAR	FEATURES	EXC. COND. LOW	HIGH
1960s		$500	$650

Archtop Acoustic

1950s-1960s. Various models.

MODEL YEAR	FEATURES	EXC. COND. LOW	HIGH
1950s-60s	Higher-end	$225	$300
1950s-60s	Lower-end	$100	$150

Electric Hollowbody

1950s-1960s. Various models.

MODEL YEAR	FEATURES	EXC. COND. LOW	HIGH
1950s	Kay Barney Kessel Artist copy	$700	$900
1960s	ES-175 copy	$375	$500
1960s	Harmony H-54 Rocket II copy	$375	$500
1960s	Harmony H-75 copy	$425	$550
1960s	Harmony H-76 Rocket III copy	$650	$850
1960s	Kay Barney Kessel Swingmaster copy	$550	$725
1960s	Kay Swingmaster copy	$325	$425
1960s	Kay Tuxedo copy	$575	$725
1960s	National Town & Country copy	$700	$900

Electric Res-O-Glas

1960s. Res-o-glas is a form of fiberglass. The bodies and sometimes the necks were made of this material.

MODEL YEAR	FEATURES	EXC. COND. LOW	HIGH
1960s	Model 7283 Jack White style	$1,700	$2,175
1960s	Model 7283, JB Hutto style	$1,700	$2,175
1960s	Other styles 1 pickup	$325	$425
1960s	Other styles, 2 pickups	$750	$975
1960s	Other styles, 3 pickups	$1,600	$2,075

Electric Res-O-Glas Resonator

1960s, 2010-present. Res-o-glas is a form of fiberglass. These models have resonator cones in the body.

MODEL YEAR	FEATURES	EXC. COND. LOW	HIGH
1960s		$675	$875
2010-2020	Folkstar	$525	$700

MODEL YEAR	FEATURES	EXC. COND. LOW	HIGH

Electric Solidbody (Standard Lower-End)

1950s-1960s. Various models.

1950s-60s		$150	$700

Electric Solidbody (Deluxe Higher-End)

1950s-1960s. Appointments may include multiple pickups, block inlays, additional logos, more binding.

1950s-60s		$600	$1,000

Flat-Top Acoustic

1950s-1960s. Various models.

1950s-60s	Higher-end, 14"-15" body	$250	$350
1950s-60s	Lower-end, 13" body	$100	$175

Alamo

1947-1982. Founded by Charles Eilenberg, Milton Fink, and Southern Music, San Antonio, Texas, and distributed by Bruno & Sons. Alamo started out making radios, phonographs, and instrument cases. In '49 they added amplifiers and lap steels. From '60 to '70, the company produced beginner-grade solidbody and hollow-core body electric Spanish guitars. The amps were all-tube until the '70s. Except for a few Valco-made examples, all instruments were built in San Antonio.

Electric Hollowbody

1950s-70s	Higher-end	$600	$1,000
1950s-70s	Lower-end	$150	$600

Electric Solidbody

1950s-70s	Higher-end	$600	$1,000
1950s-70s	Lower-end	$150	$600

Alamo Guitars

1999-2008. The Alamo brand was revived for a line of handcrafted, professional grade, production/custom, guitars by Alamo Music Products, which also offered Robin and Metropolitan brand guitars and Rio Grande pickups.

Tonemonger

2002-2005. Ash or African Fakimba offset double cut solidbody, 3 single coils, tremolo.

2002-2005		$600	$1,000

Alan Carruth

1970-present. Professional and premium grade, production/custom, classical and archtop guitars built by luthier Alan Carruth in Newport, New Hampshire. He started out building dulcimers and added guitars in '74. He also builds violins and harps.

Albanus

Ca. 1954-1977. Luthier Carl Albanus Johnson built around 75 high quality custom archtop guitars in Chicago, Illinois. He died in '77. He also built violins and at least two mandolins.

Alberico, Fabrizio

1998-present. Luthier Fabrizio Alberico builds his premium grade, custom, flat-top and classical guitars in Cheltenham, Ontario.

MODEL YEAR	FEATURES	EXC. COND. LOW	HIGH

Alden

2005-present. Budget and intermediate grade, production, acoustic and electric guitars, and basses designed by Alan Entwhistle and imported from China.

Alden (Chicago)

1960s. Chicago's Alden was a department store and mail-order house offering instruments from Chicago builders such as Harmony.

H-45 Stratotone

1960s. Alden's version of the H45 Stratotone Mars model, single plain cover pickup.

1960s		$375	$500

Alembic

1969-present. Premium and presentation grade, production/custom, guitars, baritones, and 12-strings built in Santa Rosa, California. They also build basses. Established in San Francisco by Ron and Susan Wickersham, Alembic started out as a studio working with the Grateful Dead and other bands on a variety of sound gear. By '70 they were building custom basses, later adding guitars and cabinets. By '73, standardized models were being offered.

California Special

1988-2009. Double-cut neck-thru solidbody, six-on-a-side tuners, various colors.

1988-2009		$1,850	$2,400

Distillate

1979-1991. Various wood options.

1979-1991		$2,100	$2,700

Little Darling

2006-present. Exotic woods offered, heart inlay at 12th fret, brass bird tailpiece.

2006-2020		$3,800	$5,000

Orion

1990-present. Offset double-cut glued neck solidbody, various colors.

1990-2016		$1,850	$2,400

Series I

1972-present. Neck-thru, double-cut solidbody, bookmatched koa, black walnut core, 3 pickups, optional body styles available, natural.

1970s-2013	12-string	$4,200	$5,500
1970s-2020	6-string	$4,200	$5,500

Alfieri Guitars

1990-present. Luthier Don Alfieri builds his premium and presentation grade, custom/production, acoustic and classical guitars in Long Island, New York.

Alhambra

1930s. The Alhambra brand was most likely used by a music studio (or distributor) on instruments made by others, including Regal-built resonator instruments.

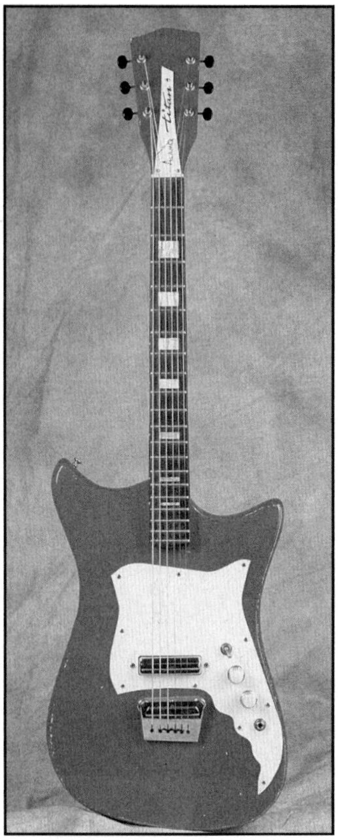

1964 Alamo Fiesta I

1964 Alden Chicago

Tom Pfeifer

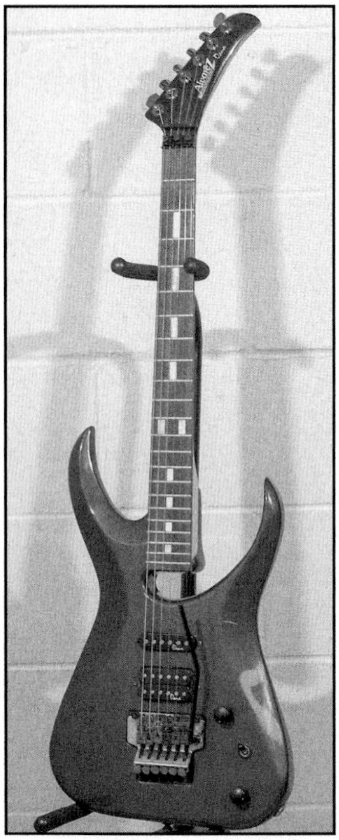

1992 Alvarez Dana Scoop
Tom Pfeifer

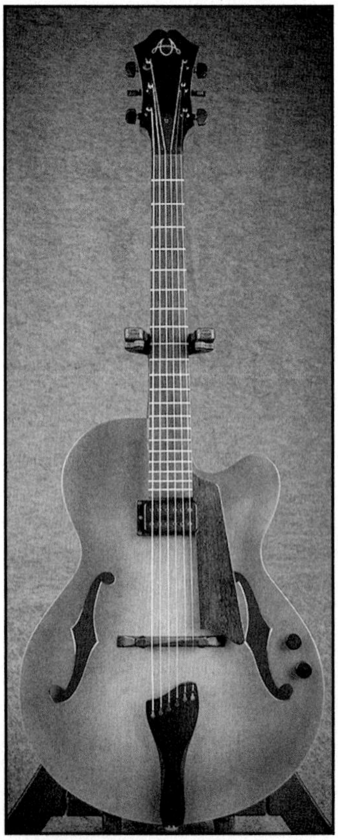

American Archtop Guitars
Dream American

MODEL YEAR	FEATURES	EXC. COND. LOW	HIGH

Allen Guitars

1982-present. Premium grade, production resonators, steel-string flat-tops, and mandolins built by Luthier Randy Allen, Colfax, California.

Alleva-Coppolo Basses and Guitars

1995-present. Professional and premium grade custom/production, solidbody electric basses and guitars built by luthier Jimmy Coppolo previously in Dallas, New York, Upland, California and now in Gadsden, Alabama.

Electric Solidbody

1995-2020. Various solidbody electric models, various options and materials.

1995-2020		$2,500	$5,000

Aloha

1935-1960s. Private branded by Aloha Publishing and Musical Instruments Company, Chicago, Illinois. Made by others. There was also the Aloha Manufacturing Company of Honolulu which made musical instruments from around 1911 to the late '20s.

Alosa

1947-1958. Luthier Alois Sandner built these acoustic archtop guitars in Germany.

Alpha

1970s-1980s. One of the brand names of guitars built in the Egmond plant in Holland. Sold by Martin for a while in the 1980s.

Alray

1967. Electrics and acoustics built by the Holman-Woodell guitar factory in Neodesha, Kansas, who also marketed similar models under the Holman brand.

Alternative Guitar and Amplifier Company

Intermediate grade, custom/production, solidbody electric guitars and basses made in Piru, California, by luthiers Mal Stich and Sal Gonzales and imported from Korea, beginning in 2006, under the Alternative Guitar and Amplifier Company, and Mal n' Sal brands.

AlumiSonic

2006-present. Luthier Ray Matter builds his production/custom, professional grade, aluminum/wood hybrid electric guitars in Bohemia and West Islip, New York.

Alvarez

1965-present. Intermediate and professional grade, production, acoustic guitars imported by St. Louis Music. They also offer lap steels, banjos and mandolins. Initially high-quality handmade guitars Yairi made by K. (Kazuo) Yairi were exclusively distributed, followed by lower-priced Alvarez line. In '90 the Westone brand used on electric guitars and basses was replaced with the Alvarez name; these Alvarez electrics were offered until '02. Many Alvarez electric models designed by luthier Dana Sutcliffe; several models designed by Dan Armstrong.

Alvarez Yairi

1966-present. Alvarez Yairi guitars are handcrafted and imported by St. Louis Music.

Alvarez, Juan

1952-2019. Professional and premium grade, production/custom, classical and flamenco guitars made in Madrid, Spain, originally by luthier Juan Alvarez Gil (died in 2001), then by son Juan Miguel Alvarez.

American Acoustech

1993-2001. Production steel string flat-tops made by Tom Lockwood (former Guild plant manager) and Dave Stutzman (of Stutzman's Guitar Center) as ESVL Inc. in Rochester, New York.

American Archtop Guitars

1995-present. Premium and presentation grade, custom 6- and 7-string archtops by luthier Dale Unger, in Stroudsburg, Pennsylvania.

American Conservatory (Lyon & Healy)

Late-1800s-early-1900s. Guitars, mandolins and harp guitars built by Chicago's Lyon & Healy and sold mainly through various catalog retailers. Mid-level instruments above the quality of Lyon & Healy's Lakeside brand, and generally under their Washburn brand. Generally of negligible value because repair cost often exceed their market value.

Acoustic

1920s	Spanish 6-string	$425	$550
1920s	Tenor 4-string	$425	$550

G2740 Monster Bass

Early/mid 1900s. Two 6-string neck (one fretless), acoustic flat-top harp guitar, spruce top, birch back and sides with rosewood stain, natural. Their catalog claimed it was "Indispensable to the up-to-date mandolin and guitar club."

1917		$2,700	$3,500

Style G Series Harp Guitar

Early 1900s. Two 6-string necks with standard tuners, 1 neck fretless, rosewood back and sides, spruce top, fancy rope colored wood inlay around soundhole, sides and down the back center seam.

1917	Natural	$2,700	$3,500

American Showster

1986-2004, 2010-2011. Established by Bill Meeker and David Haines, Bayville, New Jersey, building guitars shaped like classic car tailfins or motorcycle gas tanks. The Custom Series was made in the

MODEL YEAR	FEATURES	EXC. COND. LOW	HIGH

U.S.A., while the Standard Series (introduced in '97) was made in Czechoslovakia. They also made a bass. Bill Meeker started production again around 2010 until his death in late '11.

AS-57 Classic

1987-2004. American-made until 2000, body styled like a '57 Chevy tail fin, basswood body, bolt-on neck, 1 humbucker or 3 single-coils, various colors.

1987-1999	US-made	$3,300	$4,300
2000-2004	Import	$1,100	$1,500

The Biker/Tank

1987-1989. Alder body shaped like motorcycle gas tank, 3 single-coil or 2 humbucker pickups, maple neck, rosewood 'board.

1987-1989		$1,100	$1,450

Ampeg

1949-present. Founded in '49 by Everett Hull as the Ampeg Bassamp Company in New York and has built amplifiers throughout its history. In '62 the company added instruments with the introduction of their Baby Bass and from '63 to '65, they carried a line of guitars and basses built by Burns of London and imported from England. In '66 the company introduced its own line of basses. In '67, Ampeg was acquired by Unimusic, Inc. From '69-'71 contracted with Dan Armstrong to produce lucite "see-through" guitars and basses with replaceable slide-in pickup design. In '71 the company merged with Magnavox. Beginning around '72 until '75, Ampeg imported the Stud Series copy guitars from Japan. Ampeg shut down production in the spring of '80. MTI bought the company and started importing amps. In '86 St. Louis Music purchased the company. In '97 Ampeg introduced new and reissue American-made guitar and bass models. They discontinued the guitar line in '01, but offered the Dan Armstrong plexi guitar again starting in '05, adding wood-bodied versions in '08. They also offered a bass. In '05 LOUD Technologies acquired SLM and the Ampeg brand. In '18, the brand was sold to Yamaha.

AMG1

1999-2001. Dan Amstrong guitar features, but with mahogany body with quilted maple top, 2 P-90-style or humbucker-style pickups.

1999-2001	Humbuckers, gold hardware	$475	$625
1999-2001	Kent Armstrong pickups	$300	$400
1999-2001	P-90s, standard hardware	$300	$400

Dan Armstrong Lucite Guitar

1969-1971. Clear plexiglas solidbody, with interchangable pickups, Dan Armstrong reports that around 9,000 guitars were produced, introduced in '69, but primary production was in '70-'71, reissued in '98.

1969-1971	Clear	$1,950	$2,600
1969-1971	Smoke	$2,300	$3,000

Dan Armstrong Plexi Guitar

1998-2001, 2006-2011. Reissue of Lucite guitar, produced by pickup designer Kent Armstrong (son of Dan Armstrong), offered in smoked (ADAG2) or clear (ADAG1). Latest version is Japanese-made ADA6.

1998-2011	Clear or smoke	$625	$825

Heavy Stud (GE-150/GEH-150)

1973-1975. Import from Japan, single-cut body, weight added for sustain, single-coils or humbuckers (GEH).

1973-1975		$350	$450

Sonic Six (By Burns)

1964-1965. Solidbody, 2 pickups, tremolo, cherry finish, same as the Burns Nu-Sonic guitar.

1964-1965		$375	$500

Stud (GE-100/GET-100)

1973-1975. Import from Japan, double-cut, inexpensive materials, weight added for sustain, GET-100 included tremolo.

1973-1975		$350	$450

Super Stud (GE-500)

1973-1975. Double-cut, weight added for sustain, top-of-the-line in Stud Series.

1973-1975		$350	$450

Thinline (By Burns)

1963-1964. Semi-hollowbody, 2 f-holes, 2 pickups, double-cut, tremolo, import by Burns of London, same as the Burns TR2 guitar.

1963-1964		$500	$650

Wild Dog (By Burns)

1963-1964. Solidbody, 3 pickups, shorter scale, tremolo, sunburst finish, import by Burns of London, same as the Burns Split Sound.

1963-1964		$525	$675

Wild Dog De Luxe (By Burns)

1963-1964. Solidbody, 3 pickups, bound neck, tremolo, sunburst finish, import by Burns of London, same as the Burns Split Sonic guitar.

1963-1964		$550	$725

Anderberg

2002-present. Professional and premium grade, production/custom, electric guitars and basses built by luthier Michael Anderberg in Jacksonville, Florida.

Andersen Stringed Instruments

1978-present. Luthier Steve Andersen builds premium and presentation grade, production/custom flat-tops and archtops in Seattle, Washington. He also builds mandolins.

Andreas

1995-2004. Luthier Andreas Pichler built his aluminum-necked, solidbody guitars and basses in Dollach, Austria.

Andrew White Guitars

2000-present. Premium and presentation grade, custom, acoustic flat-top guitars built by luthier Andrew White in Morgantown, West Virginia. He also imports a production line of intermediate and professional grade, acoustic guitars from his factory in Korea.

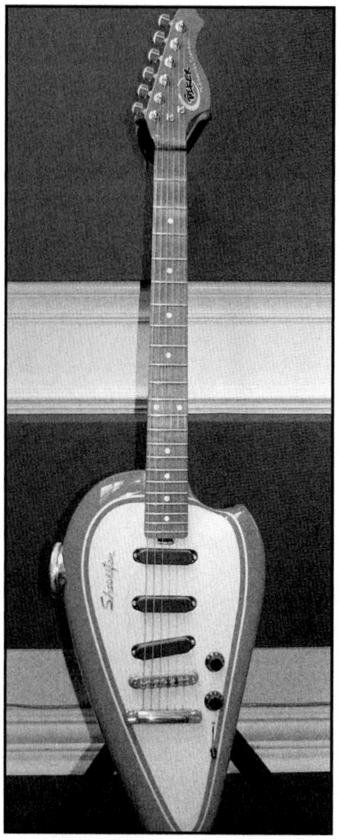

American Showster Biker

Billy White Jr.

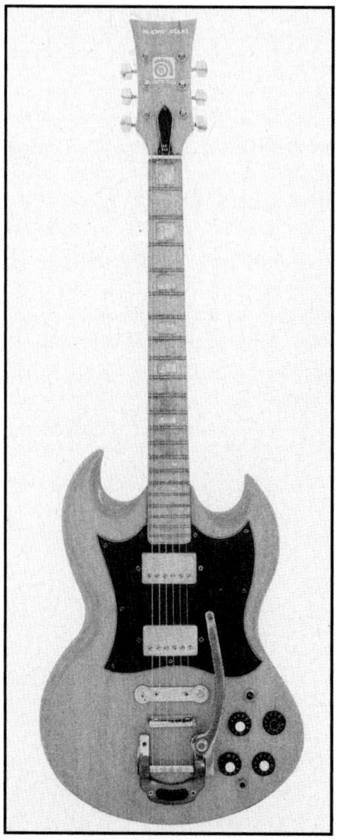

Ampeg Super Stud

Imaged by Heritage Auctions, HA.com

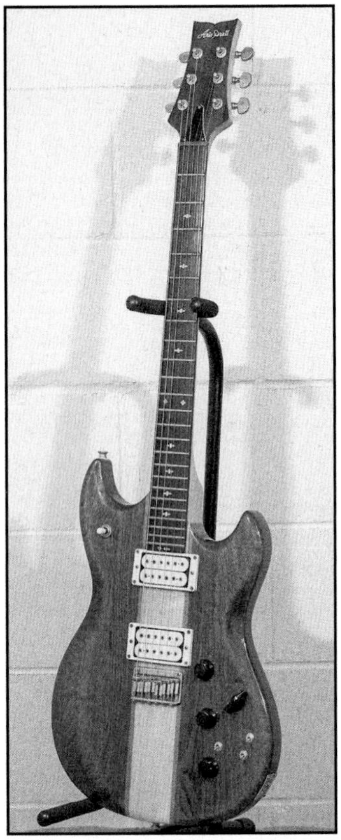

1980s Aria Pro II TS-600

Tom Pfeifer

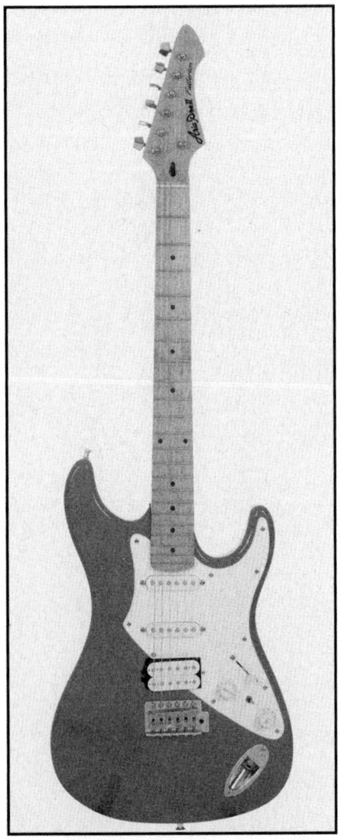

Aria Pro II Fullerton

Imaged by Heritage Auctions, HA.com

MODEL YEAR	FEATURES	EXC. COND. LOW	HIGH

Andy Powers Musical Instrument Co.

1996-2010. Luthier Andy Powers built his premium and presentation grade, custom, archtop, flat-top, and semi-hollow electric guitars in Oceanside, California. He also built ukes and mandolins.

Angelica

Ca. 1967-ca. 1990s. Entry-level guitars and basses imported from Japan.

Acoustic

1967-1972.$140$200

Electric Solidbody

1967-1972		$200	$300

Angus

1976-present. Professional and premium grade, custom-made steel and nylon string flat-tops built by Mark Angus in Laguna Beach, California.

Antares

1980s-1990s. Korean-made budget electric and acoustic guitars imported by Vega Music International of Brea, California.

Acoustic

1980s-90s	Various models	$75	$105

Double Neck 6/4

1990s. Cherry finish double-cut.

1990s		$425	$550

Solidbody

1980s-90s	Various models	$120	$170

Antique Acoustics

1970s-present. Luthier Rudolph Blazer builds production/custom flat-tops, 12 strings, and archtops in Tubingen, Germany.

Antonio Hermosa

2006-present. Imported budget grade, production, acoustic and acoustic/electric classical guitars from The Music Link.

Antonio Lorca

Intermediate and professional grade, production, classical guitars made in Valencia, Spain.

Apollo

Ca. 1967-1972. Entry-level guitars imported by St. Louis Music. They also offered basses and effects.

Electric

1967-1972 Japanese imports, various models

1967-1972		$200	$1,650

Applause

1976-present. Budget grade, production, acoustic and acoustic/electric guitars, basses, mandolins and ukes and previously solidbody electrics. Originally Kaman Music's entry-level Ovation-styled brand, it is now owned by Drum Workshop, Inc. The instruments were made in the U.S. until around '82, when production was moved to Korea. On the U.S.-made guitars, the back of the neck was molded Urelite, with a cast aluminum neck combining an I-beam neck reinforcement, fingerboard, and frets in one unit. The Korean models have traditional wood necks.

AA Models

1976-1990s. Acoustic, laminate top, plastic or composition body. Specs and features can vary on AA Models.

1976-1981	US-made	$135	$175
1980s-90s	Import	$70	$90

AE Models

1976-2000s. Acoustic/electric, laminate top, plastic or composition body. Specs and features can vary on AE Models.

1976-1981	US-made	$185	$240
1980-2000s	Import	$100	$130

Applegate

2001-present. Premium grade, production/custom, acoustic and classical guitars built by luthier Brian Applegate in Minneapolis, Minnesota.

APS Custom

2005-present. Luthier Andy Speake builds his production/custom, professional and premium grade, solidbody guitars in Victoria, British Columbia.

Arbor

1983-ca. 2013. Budget and intermediate grade, production, classical, acoustic, and solid and semi-hollow body electric guitars imported by Musicorp (MBT). They also offered basses.

Acoustic

1980s-2013	Various models	$75	$150

Electric

1980s-2013	Various models	$200	$300

Arch Kraft

1933-1934. Full-size acoustic archtop and flat-top guitars. Budget brand produced by the Kay Musical Instrument Company and sold through various distributors.

Aria Diamond

1960s. Brand name used by Aria in the '60s.

Electric

1960s. Various models and appointments in the '60s.

1960s		$385	$500

Aria/Aria Pro II

1956-present. Budget, intermediate and professional grade, production, electric, acoustic, acoustic/electric, and classical guitars. They also make basses, mandolins, and banjos. Aria was established in Japan in '56 and started production of instruments in '60 using the Arai, Aria, Aria Diamond, and Diamond brands. The brand was renamed Aria Pro II in '75. Aria Pro II was used mainly on electric guitars, with Aria used on others. Over the years, they have produced acoustics, banjos, mandolins, electrics, basses, amplifiers, and effects. Around

MODEL YEAR	FEATURES	EXC. COND. LOW	HIGH

'87 production of cheaper models moved to Korea, reserving Japanese manufacturing for more expensive models. Around '95 some models were made in U.S., though most contemporary guitars sold in U.S. are Korean. In '01, the Pro II part of the name was dropped altogether.

Early Arias don't have serial numbers or pot codes. Serial numbers began to be used in the mid '70s. At least for Aria guitars made by Matsumoku, the serial number contains the year of manufacture in the first one or two digits (Y##### or YY####). Thus, a guitar from 1979 might begin with 79####. One from 1981 might begin with 1#####. The scheme becomes less sure after 1987. Some Korean- made guitars use a serial number with year and week indicated in the first four digits (YYWW####). Thus 9628#### would be from the 28th week of 1996. However, this is not the case on all guitars, and some have serial numbers which are not date-coded.

Models have been consolidated by sector unless specifically noted.

Acoustic Solid Wood Top

1960s-present. Steel string models, various appointments, generally mid-level imports.

1960s-2020	$300	$550

Acoustic Veneer Wood Top

1960s-present. Steel string models, various appointments, generally entry-level imports.

1960s-2020	$160	$250

Classical Solid Wood Top

1960s-present. Various models, various appointments, generally mid-level imports.

1960s-2020	$200	$300

Classical Veneer Wood Top

1960s-present. Various models, various appointments, generally entry-level imports.

1960s-2020	$125	$175

Fullerton Series

1995-2000. Various models with different appointments and configurations based on the classic offset double-cut soldibody.

1995-2000	$300	$550

Herb Ellis (PE-175/FA-DLX)

1978-1987 (Model PE-175) and 1988-1993 (Model FA-DLX). Archtop hollowbody, ebony 'board, 2 humbuckers.

1978-1993	$550	$700

Solidbody

1960s-present. Various models, various appointments, generally mid-level imports.

1960s-2020	$450	$650

Titan Artist TA Series

1967-2012. Double cut, semi-hollow bodies, 2 pickups, various models.

1967-2012	$450	$650

Aristides

2010-present. Dutch engineer Aristides Poort developed the material (arium) used to build production/custom, premium grade, solidbody electric guitars in the Netherlands. They also build basses.

MODEL YEAR	FEATURES	EXC. COND. LOW	HIGH

ARK - New Era Guitars

2006-present. Luthier A. R. Klassen builds his professional and premium grade, production/custom, reproductions of vintage Larson Brothers instruments in Chesterton, Indiana.

Armstrong, Rob

Custom steel- and nylon-string flat-tops, 12 strings, and parlor guitars made in Coventry, U.K. by luthier Rob Armstrong, starting in 1971. He also builds mandolins and basses.

Arpeggio Korina

1995-present. Professional, premium and presentation grade, production/custom, korina wood solidbody guitars built by luthier Ron Kayfield in Pennsylvania.

Art & Lutherie

Budget and intermediate grade, production, steel- and nylon-string acoustic and acoustic/electric guitars. Founded by luthier Robert Godin, who also has the Norman, Godin, Seagull, and Patrick & Simon brands of instruments.

Artesano

Intermediate and professional grade, production, classical guitars built in Valencia, Spain, and distributed by Juan Orozco. Orozco also made higher-end classical Orozco Models 8, 10 and 15.

Artinger Custom Guitars

1997-present. Luthier Matt Artinger builds his professional and premium grade, production/custom, hollow, semi-hollow, and chambered solidbody guitars and basses in Emmaus, Pennsylvania.

Artur Lang

1949-1975. German luthier Artur Lang is best known for his archtops, but did build classicals early on. His was a small shop and much of his output was custom ordered. The instruments were mostly unbranded, but some have L.A. engraved on the headstock.

Asama

1970s-1980s. Some models of this Japanese line of solidbody guitars featured built-in effects. They also offered basses, effects, drum machines and other music products.

Ashborn

1848-1864. James Ashborn, of Wolcottville, Connecticut, operated one of the largest guitar making factories of the mid-1800s. Models were small parlor-sized instruments with ladder bracing and gut strings. Most of these guitars will need repair. Often of more interest as historical artifacts or museum pieces versus guitar collections.

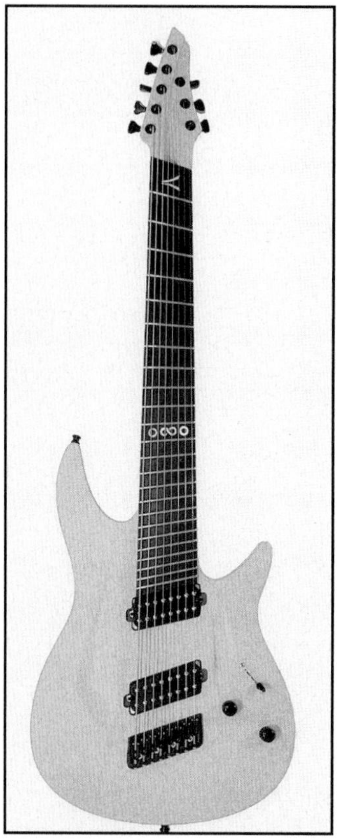

Aristides 080s

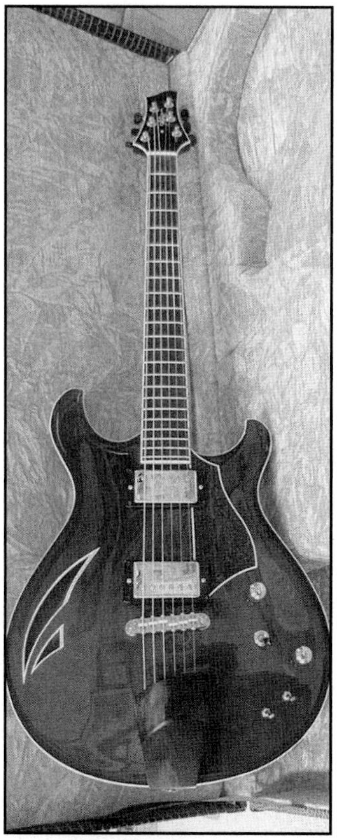

Artinger Semi-Hollow

Asher T Deluxe

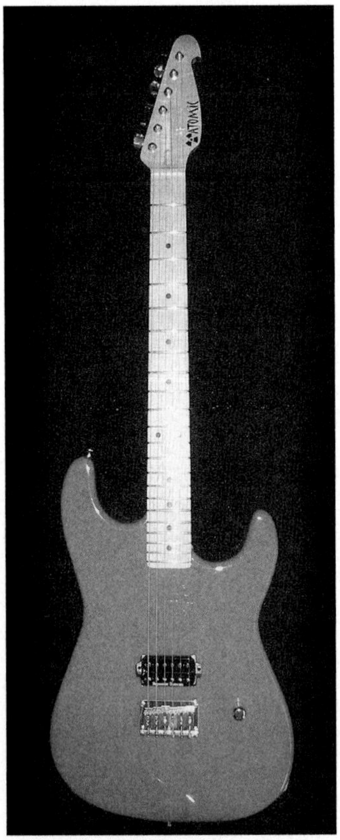

Atomic STD 1

MODEL YEAR	FEATURES	EXC. COND. LOW	HIGH

Model 2

1848-1864. Flat-top, plain appointments, no position markers on the neck, identified by Model number.

1855	Fully repaired	$425	$550

Model 5

1848-1864. Flat-top, higher appointments.

1855	Fully repaired	$1,050	$1,375

Asher

1982-present. Luthier Bill Asher builds his professional grade, production/custom, solidbody electric guitars in Venice, California. He also builds lap steels.

Ashland

Intermediate grade, production, acoustic and acoustic/electric guitars made by Korea's Crafter Guitars.

Astro

1963-1964. The Astro AS-51 was a 1 pickup kit guitar sold by Rickenbacker. German luthier Arthur Strohmer also built archtops bearing this name.

Asturias

Professional and premium grade, production, classical guitars built on Kyushu island, in Japan.

Atkin Guitars

1995-present. Luthier Alister Atkin builds his production/custom steel and nylon string flat-tops in Canterbury, U.K. He also builds mandolins.

Atlas

Archtop guitars, and possibly other types, built in East Germany and by Zero Sette in Italy.

Atomic

2006-present. Production/custom, intermediate and professional grade, solidbody electric guitars and basses built by luthiers Tim Mulqueeny and Harry Howard in Peoria, Arizona.

Audiovox

Ca. 1935-ca. 1950. Paul Tutmarc's Audiovox Manufacturing, of Seattle, Washington, was a pioneer in electric lap steels, basses, guitars and amps. Tutmarc was a talented Hawaiian steel guitarist and ran a music school and is credited with inventing the electric bass guitar in '35, which his company started selling in the late '30s.

Austin

1999-present. Budget and intermediate grade, production, acoustic, acoustic/electric, resonator, and electric guitars, basses, amps, mandolins, ukes and banjos imported by St. Louis Music.

Acoustic Flat-Top

1999-2020	Various models	$100	$130

Solidbody Electric

1999-2020	Various models	$150	$250

MODEL YEAR	FEATURES	EXC. COND. LOW	HIGH

Austin Hatchet

Mid-1970s-mid-1980s. Trademark of distributor Targ and Dinner, Chicago, Illinois.

Hatchet

1981. Travel guitar.

1981		$375	$500

Solidbody Electric

1970s-1980s. Various classic designs.

1970s-80s		$300	$400

Avalon

1920s. Instruments built by the Oscar Schmidt Co. and possibly others. Most likely a brand made for a distributor.

Avalon (Ireland)

2002-present. Luthiers Stevie Graham, Mark Lyttle, Ernie McMillan, Balazs Prohaszka and Robin Thompson build premium and presentation grade, production/custom, steel-string and classical, acoustic and electro-acoustic guitars in Northern Ireland. In '04-'05 their Silver series was imported from South Korea, and '05 the Gold series from Czech Republic.

Avante

1997-2007. Intermediate grade, production, imported sharp cutaway acoustic baritone guitars designed by Joe Veillette and Michael Tobias and offered by MusicYo. Originally higher priced instruments offered by Alvarez, there was the baritone, a 6-string and a bass.

AV-2 Baritone

1997-2007. Baritone guitar tuned B to B, solid spruce cutaway top, mahogany sides and back.

1997-2007		$250	$325

Avanti

1964-late 1960s. Italian-made guitar brand imported by European Crafts, of Los Angeles. Earlier models were plastic covered; later ones had paint finishes.

Electric Solidbody

1960s. Solidbody, 3 single-coils, dot markers.

1960s		$200	$300

Avar

Late-1960s. Import copy models from Japan, not unlike Teisco, for the U.S. student market.

Solidbody Electric

1969		$200	$300

Aztec

1970s. Japanese-made copy guitars imported into Germany by Hopf.

B.C. Rich

Ca. 1966/67-present. Budget, intermediate, and premium grade, production/custom, import and U.S.-made, electric and acoustic guitars. They also offer basses. Founded by Bernardo Chavez Rico in Los Angeles, California. As a boy he worked for his

MODEL YEAR	FEATURES	EXC. COND. LOW	HIGH

guitar-maker father Bernardo Mason Rico (Valencian Guitar Shop, Casa Rico, Bernardo's Guitar Shop), building first koa ukes and later, guitars, steel guitars and Martin 12-string conversions. He started using the BC Rich name ca. '66-'67 and made about 300 acoustics until '68, when first solidbody electric made using a Fender neck.

Rich's early models were based on Gibson and Fender designs. First production instruments were in '69 with 10 fancy Gibson EB-3 bass and 10 matching Les Paul copies, all carved out of single block of mahogany. Early guitars with Gibson humbuckers, then Guild humbuckers, and, from '74-'86, DiMarzio humbuckers. Around 150 BC Rich Eagles were imported from Japan in '76. Ca. '76 or '77 some bolt-neck guitars with parts made by Wayne Charvel were offered. Acoustic production ended in '82 (acoustics were again offered in '95).

For '83-'86 the BC Rich N.J. Series (N.J. Nagoya, Japan) was built by Masan Tarada. U.S. Production Series (U.S.-assembled Korean kits) in '84. From '86 on, the N.J. Series was made by Cort in Korea. Korean Rave and Platinum series begin around '86. In '87, Rich agrees to let Class Axe of New Jersey market the Korean Rave, Platinum and N.J. Series. Class Axe (with Neal Moser) introduces Virgin in '87 and in '88 Rave and Platinum names are licensed to Class Axe. In '89, Rico licensed the BC Rich name to Class Axe. Both imported and American-made BC Riches are offered during Class Axe management. In 2000, BC Rich became a division of Hanser Music Group.

During '90-'91, Rico begins making his upscale Mason Bernard guitars (approx. 225 made). In '94, Rico resumes making BC Rich guitars in California. He died in 1999.

First 340-360 U.S.-built guitars were numbered sequentially beginning in '72. Beginning in '74, serial numbers change to YYZZZ pattern (year plus consecutive production). As production increased in the late-'70s, the year number began getting ahead of itself. By '80 it was 2 years ahead; by '81 as much as 4 years ahead. No serial number codes on imports.

The American B.C. Rich company was first and foremost a custom shop, therefore surprising variants are possible for the models described below, especially in the early years of the company. Many of the first models were offered as either a Standard (also called Deluxe) model or as an upgrade called the Supreme model.

The Deluxe or Standard model has diamond markers, unbound rosewood fretboard, three-on-a-side tuners, generally solid mahogany body, some rare examples with maple body or other woods, some with runners or stringers of alternate exotic wood.

The Supreme model has specific options including cloud markers, fully bound ebony fretboard and three-on-a-side headstock, various woods including solid koa, maple, highly-figured maple (birdseye, quilted, curly), other exotic woods offered, most models with runners or stringers of alternating exotic wood, also available as single solid wood, mid-1980s with original Kahler tremolo unit option, custom colors and sunburst finishes generally on a custom order basis, certain custom colors are worth more than the values shown, early models circa '75-'82 had a Leo Quan Badass bridge option and those models are highly favored by collectors, early style control knobs had silver metal inserts and full electronics with Varitone and PreAmp and Grover Imperial bullseye tuners, the earliest models had red head mini-switches (later became silver-chrome switches). Technically speaking the Supreme model only applied to the Mockingbird, Eagle, Bich, and Wave.

The prime collector's market for B.C. Rich is the '72-'85 era. The Seagull, Eagle, Mockingbird, Bich, and Wave models are the true vintage models from that epoch.Pre-1985 BC Rich Standard Finishes were Natural, Gloss White, Black, Competition Red, Medium Blue, Metallic Red, and Cherry. Any other finish would be a Custom Color. Most custom colors started appearing in late 1978. Prior to '78, guitars had two tone transparent burst finishes, natural finishes and occasional one color paint schemes. Custom Color finishes are worth 10% more than standard finish colors.

Assassin

1986-1998, 2000-2010. Double-cut body, 2 humbuckers, maple thru-neck dot markers, various colors.

1986-1989	1st Rico era	$500	$650
1989-1993	Class Axe era, neck-thru	$500	$650
1994-1998	2nd Rico era USA, neck-thru	$450	$575
2000-2010	Includes QX & PX	$200	$260

B-28 Acoustic

Ca.1967-1982. Acoustic flat-top, hand-built, herringbone trim, pearl R headstock logo.

1967-1982		$1,350	$1,800

B-30 Acoustic

Ca.1967-1982. Acoustic flat-top.

1967-1982		$1,350	$1,800

B-38 Acoustic

Ca.1967-1982. Acoustic flat-top, herringbone trim.

1967-1982		$1,350	$1,800

B-41 Acoustic

1970s. Acoustic flat-top.

1970s		$1,450	$1,900

B-45 Acoustic

1970s. Hand-built, D-style acoustic flat-top.

1970s		$1,650	$2,200

Beast (U.S.A. Custom Shop)

1999-2015. Exaggerated four point cutaway body, flamed or quilted top.

1999-2015		$750	$1,000

Bich (U.S.A. Assembly)

1978-1998. Four-point sleek body, came in Standard top or Supreme with highly figured maple body and active EQ.

1978-1979	Standard/Deluxe	$1,850	$2,400
1978-1979	Supreme	$2,350	$3,100
1980-1985	Standard/Deluxe	$1,150	$1,500
1980-1985	Supreme	$2,050	$2,700

Avalon Pioneer 1-20

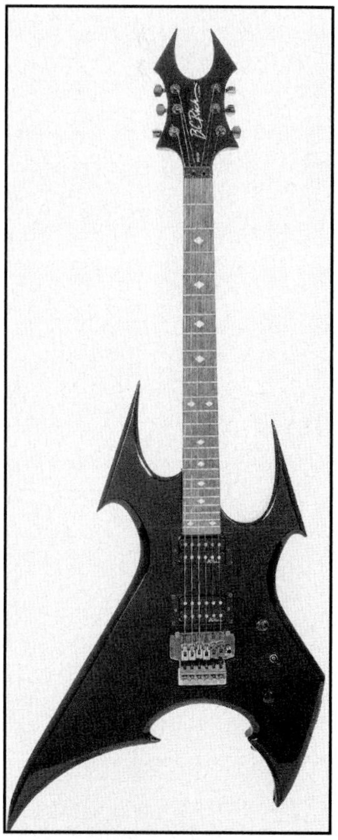

B.C. Rich Beast

Imaged by Heritage Auctions, HA.com

GUITARS

1982 B.C. Rich Bich

Erik Van Gansen

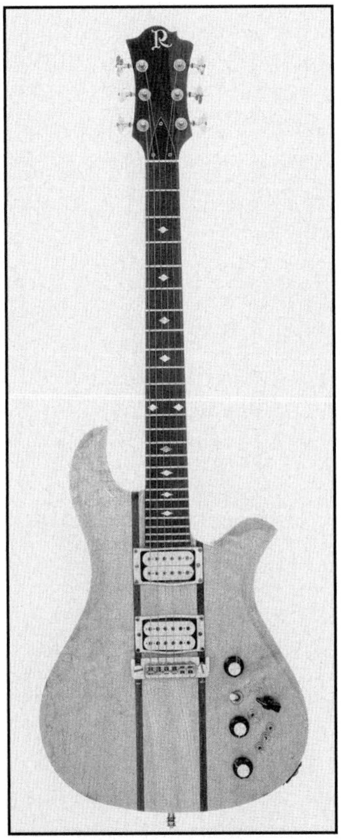

1978 B.C. Rich Eagle

Imaged by Heritage Auctions, HA.com

MODEL YEAR	FEATURES	EXC. COND. LOW	HIGH
1986-1988	Standard/Deluxe	$800	$1,025
1986-1988	Supreme	$1,675	$2,200
1989-1993	Class Axe era	$800	$1,025
1994-1998	2nd Rico era USA, bolt-on	$800	$1,025

Bich 10-String

1977-2015. U.S.-made, doubles on 4 low strings.

1977-1982	Highly flamed	$3,500	$4,500
1977-1982	Koa or koa/maple	$3,500	$4,500
1977-1982	Opaque finish	$3,000	$4,000
1985	Highly quilted	$3,200	$4,200
2005	Highly quilted	$2,900	$3,800

Black Hole

1988. Bolt neck, rosewood 'board, integrated pickup design, Floyd Rose.

1988		$175	$230

Body Art Collection

2003-2006. Imports, different graphics/different models issued each month from January '03 to March '04, 25th Anniversary model available into '06.

2003-2006	Various models	$150	$195

Bronze Series

2001-2007. Made in China. Includes 2 models; Mockingbird and Warlock.

2001-2007		$50	$65

Doubleneck Models

1980-1988. Doublenecks were sporadically made and specs (and values) may vary.

1980-1988	Bich	$4,500	$8,000
1980-1988	Eagle	$5,000	$9,000
1980-1988	Iron Bird	$4,000	$7,000
1980-1988	Mockingbird	$5,000	$9,000
1980-1988	Seagull	$5,500	$10,000

Eagle

1975-1982, 2000-2004. Made in USA, often called the Eagle model, but also called Eagle Deluxe or Eagle Standard, features include diamond inlays, unbound rosewood fretboard, 3-on-a-side tuners, generally solid mahogany body, some rare examples with maple body or other woods, some with runners or stringers of alternate exotic wood. (See additional notes in the Eagle Supreme listing.)

1975-1976	Custom Shop	$1,800	$2,400
1977-1982		$1,600	$2,100

Eagle Special (U.S.A.)

1977-1982. A variant of the Eagle with even more switches and electronic options, the extra options are not particularly considered an advantage in the BC Rich collector community, therefore an Eagle Special is worth less than the Standard or Eagle Supreme.

1977-1982		$1,500	$2,000

Eagle Supreme

1975-1982, 2000-2004. Made in USA, Eagle body style with specific options including cloud inlays, fully bound ebony fretboard, 3-on-a-side headstock, various woods including solid koa, maple, highly-figured maple (birdseye, quilted, curly), other exotic woods offered, most with runners or stringers of alternating exotic wood, also available as single solid wood, mid-'80s with original Kahler tremolo unit option, custom colors and sunburst finishes generally on a custom order basis, certain custom colors are worth more than the values shown, early models ca. '75-'82 had a Leo Quan Badass bridge option and those models are highly favored by collectors, early style control knobs with silver metal inserts, full electronics with Varitone and PreAmp and Grover Imperial bullseye tuners, the earliest models had red head mini-switches (later became silver-chrome switches).

MODEL YEAR	FEATURES	EXC. COND. LOW	HIGH
1975-1976	Custom Shop	$2,800	$3,700
1977		$2,800	$3,700
1978-1979		$2,600	$3,500
1980-1982		$2,550	$3,400
2000-2004		$1,600	$2,100

Eagle Supreme Condor

1983-1987. Less than 50 made, simplified electronics system based on customer's requests, features can include cloud inlays, fully bound ebony fretboard neck, bound 3-on-a-side headstock, bookmatched figured maple top over solid mahogany body with slight arch, no runners or stringers, basic electronics with master volume, master tone, and pickup switch, also commonly called Condor Supreme.

1983-1987		$1,125	$1,500

Elvira

2001. Elvira (the witch) photo on black Warlock body, came with Casecore coffin case.

2001		$350	$475

Exclusive EM I (Platinum Series)

1996-2004. Offset double-cut, bound top, 2 humbuckers.

1996-2004		$100	$150

Gunslinger

1987-1999. Inverted headstock, 1 (Gunslinger I) or 2 (Gunslinger II) humbuckers, recessed cutout behind Floyd Rose allows player to pull notes up 2 full steps.

1987-1989	Graphic designs	$575	$775
1987-1989	Standard finish	$550	$725
1989-1993	Class Axe era	$550	$725
1994-1999	2nd Rico era, bolt-on	$475	$625
1994-1999	2nd Rico era, neck-thru	$475	$625

Ironbird

1983-2004. Pointy body and headstock.

1983-1989		$825	$1,100
1989-1993	Class Axe era	$750	$1,000
1994-1998	2nd Rico era, bolt-on	$700	$925

Kerry King Wartribe 1 Warlock

2004-2015. Tribal Fire finish, 2 pickups.

2004-2015		$100	$150

Mockingbird

1976-present. Made in USA, often called the Mockingbird model, but also called the Mockingbird Standard or Mockingbird Deluxe, features include diamond inlays, unbound rosewood fretboard, 3-on-a-side tuners, generally solid mahogany body, some rare examples with maple body or other woods, some with runners or stringers of alternate exotic wood. In 2016 'Mk' added to name (Mk1, Mk3, Mk5, Mk7, Mk9, Mk11). (See additional notes in the Mockingbird Supreme listing.)

1976		$2,000	$2,700
1977-1978	Short horn	$1,950	$2,600
1979-1983	Long horn	$1,950	$2,600
1984		$1,800	$2,400

MODEL YEAR	FEATURES	EXC. COND. LOW	HIGH
1985		$1,675	$2,250
1986-1989	Last of 1st Rico era	$1,200	$1,600
1989-1993	Class Axe era	$1,200	$1,600
1994-1999	2nd Rico era, bolt-on	$1,125	$1,500
2000-2020	Custom Shop (COA)	$1,700	$2,200

Mockingbird Ice Acrylic

2004-2006. See-thru acrylic body.

2004-2006		$200	$300

Mockingbird Legacy

2019-present. Mahogany body, koa or quilted maple top, 2 humbucker pickups, Floyd Rose or STQ hardtail, various colors.

2019-2020		$750	$1,000

Mockingbird Supreme

1976-1989. Made in USA, Mockingbird body style with specific options including cloud inlays, fully bound ebony fretboard, 3-on-a-side headstock, various woods including solid koa, maple, highly-figured maple (birdseye, quilted, curly), other exotic woods offered, most with runners or stringers of alternating exotic wood, also available as single solid wood, mid-'80s with original Kahler tremolo unit option, custom colors and sunburst finishes generally on a custom order basis, certain custom colors are worth more than the values shown, early models ca. '76-'82 had a Leo Quan Badass bridge option and those models are highly favored by collectors, early style control knobs with silver metal inserts, full electronics with Varitone and PreAmp and Grover Imperial bullseye tuners, the earliest models had red head mini-switches (later became silver-chrome switches).

1976	Earlier short horn	$2,250	$3,000
1976-1978	Supreme short horn	$2,175	$2,900
1977-1978	Earlier short horn	$2,175	$2,900
1979	Later long horn	$1,900	$2,500
1980-1985		$1,900	$2,500
1986-1989		$1,800	$2,300
1989-1993	Class Axe era	$1,700	$2,200
1994-1999	2nd Rico era, bolt-on	$1,600	$2,100

Nighthawk

1978-ca.1982. Eagle-shaped body with bolt neck.

1978-1982		$550	$725

NJ Series/NJC Series

1983-2006. Earlier models made in Japan. Made in Korea '86 forward. All NJ models fall within the same price range. Models include; Assassin, Beast, Bich, Ironbird, Eagle, Mockingbird, Outlaw, ST III, Virgin, Warlock. C for Classic added in '06.

1983-1984	Early NJ Japan	$450	$600
1985-1986	Later Japan	$350	$450
1987-2006	Korea	$250	$325

Phoenix

1977-ca.1982. Mockingbird-shaped with bolt neck.

1977-1982		$550	$800

Platinum Series

1986-2006. Lower-priced import versions including Assassin, Beast, Bich, Ironbird, ST, Warlock.

1986-2006		$200	$300

Rave Series

1986-ca. 1990. Korean-made down-market versions of popular models.

1986-1990		$150	$250

Seagull

1972-1975. Single-cut solidbody, neck-thru, 2 humbuckers.

1972-1973	Earliest, 30 made	$2,400	$3,200
1973-1974		$2,100	$2,800
1975		$1,950	$2,600

Seagull II

1974-1977. Double-cut solidbody, neck-thru, 2 humbuckers. Transitional model in '75 between Seagull and Eagle, Seagull Jr. is used interchangable with Seagull II, the company made several variants during this period which some collectors consider to be Seagull Jr. while others consider to be Seagull II. The II/Jr. design finally was changed and called the Eagle.

1974	1st 50, Gibson pickups	$1,950	$2,600
1974	Moser, 16 made	$1,950	$2,600
1974	Other from '74	$1,950	$2,600
1976-1977		$1,800	$2,400

Seagull II/Seagull Jr.

1975-1977. Another transitional model starting in '75, the model name Seagull Jr. is used interchangable with Seagull II, the company made several variants during this period which some collectors consider to be Seagull Jr. while others consider to be Seagull II. The design finally was changed and called the Eagle.

1975-1977	II and Jr	$1,650	$2,200

Stealth I Series

1983-1989. Includes Standard (maple body, diamond inlays) and Series II (mahogany body, dot inlays), 2 pickups.

1983-1989	Series II	$1,275	$1,700
1983-1989	Standard	$1,275	$1,700

ST-III (U.S.A.)

1987-1998. Double-cut solidbody, hum/single/single or 2 humbucker pickups, Kahler tremolo.

1987-1989	Bolt-on	$550	$725
1987-1989	Neck-thru	$575	$750
1989-1993	Class Axe era	$550	$725
1994-1998	New Rico era, neck-thru & bolt-on	$550	$725

The Mag

2000. U.S. Handcrafted Series Mockingbird Acoustic Supreme, solid spruce top, quilt maple back and sides, pickup with preamp and EQ optional, dark sunburst.

2000		$450	$600

Warlock

1981-present. Made in USA, also called Warlock Standard, 4-point sleek body style with widow headstock. In 2016 'Mk' added to name (Mk1, Mk3, Mk5, Mk7, Mk9, Mk11).

1981-1989	Standard	$1,125	$1,500
1990-1999	2nd Rico era, bolt-on	$825	$1,100
1990-1999	2nd Rico era, neck-thru	$825	$1,100

Warlock Extreme

2019-present. Mahogany body, spalted maple and quilted maple top, 2 humbucker pickups, Floyd Rose, various colors.

2019-2020		$825	$1,075

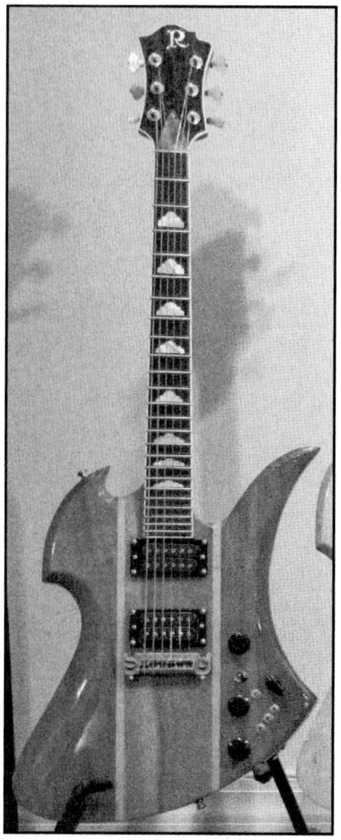

1977 B.C. Rich Mockingbird Supreme

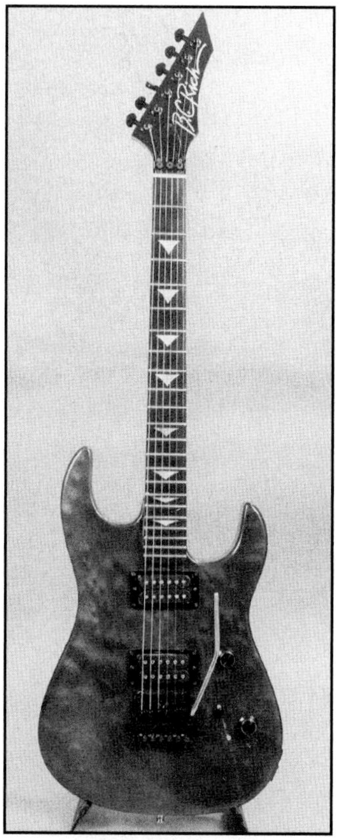

1986 B.C. Rich ST-III

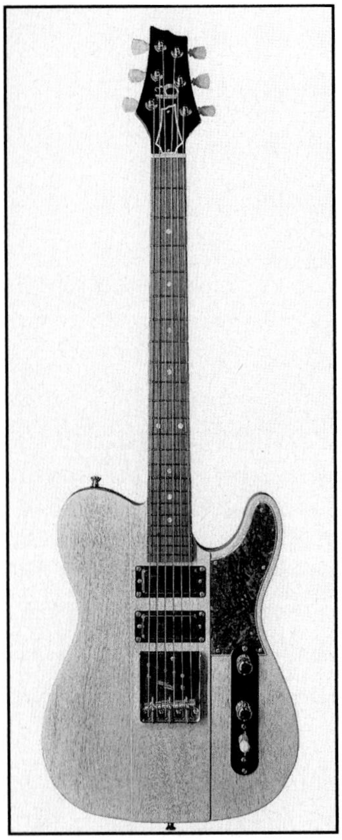

B3 Phoenix

Baden A-Style

MODEL YEAR	FEATURES	EXC. COND. LOW	HIGH

Warlock Ice Acrylic

2004-2006. See-thru acrylic body.

2004-2006		$225	$300

Wave

1983. U.S.-made, very limited production based upon the Wave bass.

1983		$1,800	$2,300

B.C. Rico

1978-1982. B.C. Rich's first Japan-made guitars were labeled B.C. Rico until they were sued for patent infringement on the Rico name. They made around 200 guitars and basses with the Rico headstock logo. After '82, B.C. Rich offered the NJ Series (Import) models.

Eagle

1978-1982. All mahogany, rosewood 'board, Dimarzio pickups, mother-of-pearl headstock logo.

1978-1982		$2,200	$2,800

Mockingbird

1978-1982. All mahogany, rosewood 'board, Dual DiMarzio humbuckers.

1978-198		$2,200	$2,800

RW-2A

1978-1982. Acoustic D-style, Brazilian rosewood laminate body, spruce top, herringbone trim, natural finish.

1978-1982		$525	$700

RW-7

1978-1982. D-style, spruce top, Brazilian rosewood back and sides, abalone markers, natural finish.

1978-1982		$525	$700

b3 Guitars

2004-present. Premium grade, custom/production, solid, chambered and hollow-body guitars built by luthier Gene Baker in Arroyo Grande, California. He previously made Baker U.S.A. guitars.

Babicz

2004-present. Started by luthier Jeff Babicz and Jeff Carano, who worked together at Steinberger, the company offers intermediate, professional, and premium grade, production/custom, acoustic and acoustic/electric guitars made in Poughkeepsie, New York, and overseas.

Bacon & Day

Established in 1921 by David Day and Paul Bacon, primarily known for fine quality tenor and plectrum banjos in the '20s and '30s. Purchased by Gretsch ca. '40.

Belmont

1950s. Gretsch era, 2 DeArmond pickups, natural.

1950s		$1,075	$1,400

Flat-Top

1930s-1940s. Large B&D headstock logo, fancy or plain appointments.

1930s	Fancy	$2,200	$2,900
1930s	Plain	$1,575	$2,100
1940s	Fancy	$1,800	$2,400
1940s	Plain	$1,400	$1,900

Ramona Archtop

1938-1940. Sunburst.

1938-1940		$600	$800

Senorita Archtop

1940. Lower-end, sunburst, mahogany back and sides.

1940		$1,575	$2,050

Silver Bell Style 1 Guitar Banjo (Bacon)

1920s. F-hole flange.

1920s		$2,800	$3,600

Style B Guitar Banjo (Bacon)

1920s. Banjo-resonator body with 6-string guitar neck.

1920s		$850	$1,100

Sultana I

1930s. Large 18 1/4" acoustic archtop, Sultana engraved on tailpiece, block markers, bound top and back, sunburst.

1938		$3,100	$4,100

Baden

Founded in 2006, by T.J. Baden, a former vice president of sales and marketing at Taylor guitars, initial production based on six models built in Vietnam, intermediate retail-price grade.

Baker U.S.A.

1997-present. Professional and premium grade, production/custom, solidbody electric guitars. Established by master builder Gene Baker after working at the Custom Shops of Gibson and Fender, Baker produced solid- and hollowbody guitars in Santa Maria, California. They also built basses. Baker also produced the Mean Gene brand of guitars from '88-'90. In September '03, the company was liquidated and the Baker U.S.A. name was sold to Ed Roman. Gene Baker currently builds b3 Guitars.

Baldwin

1965-1970. Founded in 1862, in Cincinnati, when reed organ and violin teacher Dwight Hamilton Baldwin opened a music store that eventually became one of the largest piano retailers in the Midwest. By 1965, the Baldwin Piano and Organ company was ready to buy into the guitar market but was outbid by CBS for Fender. Baldwin did procure Burns of London in September '65, and sold the guitars in the U.S. under the Baldwin name. Baldwin purchased Gretsch in '67. English production of Baldwin guitars ends in '70, after which Baldwin concentrates on the Gretsch brand.

Baby Bison (Model 560 by Mid-1966)

1966-1970. Double-cut solidbody, V headstock, 2 pickups, shorter scale, tremolo, black, red or white finishes.

1965-1966		$650	$850
1966-1970	Model 560	$600	$775

Bison (Model 511 by Mid-1966)

1965-1970. Double-cut solidbody, scroll headstock, 3 pickups, tremolo, black or white finishes.

1965-1966		$825	$1,075
1966-1970	Model 511	$775	$1,025

MODEL YEAR	FEATURES	EXC. COND. LOW	HIGH

Double Six (Model 525 by Mid-1966)

1965-1970. Offset double-cut solidbody, 12 strings, 3 pickups, green or red sunburst.

1965-1966		$1,075	$1,425
1966-1970	Model 525	$1,050	$1,400

G.B. 65

1965-1966. Baldwin's first acoustic/electric, single-cut D-style flat-top, dual bar pickups.

1965-1966		$500	$650

G.B. 66 De Luxe

1965-1966. Same as Standard with added density control on treble horn, golden sunburst.

1965-1966		$600	$775

G.B. 66 Standard

1965-1966. Thinline Electric archtop, dual Ultra-Sonic pickups, offset cutaways, red sunburst.

1965-1966		$500	$650

Jazz Split Sound/Split Sound (Model 503 Mid-1966)

1965-1970. Offset double-cut solidbody, scroll headstock, 3 pickups, tremolo, red sunburst or solid colors.

1965-1966		$650	$850
1966-1970	Model 503	$600	$775

Marvin (Model 524 by Mid-1966)

1965-1970. Offset double-cut solidbody, scroll headstock, 3 pickups, tremolo, white or brown finish.

1965-1966		$825	$1,075
1966-1970	Model 524	$775	$1,025

Model 706

1967-1970. Double-cut semi-hollowbody, scroll headstock, 2 pickups, 2 f-holes, no vibrato, red or golden sunburst.

1967-1970		$700	$900

Model 706 V

1967-1970. Model 706 with vibrato.

1967-1970		$725	$950

Model 712 R Electric XII

1967-1970. Double-cut semi-hollow body with regular neck, red or gold sunburst.

1967-1970		$450	$600

Model 712 T Electric XII

1967-1970. Model 712 with thin neck, red or gold sunburst.

1967-1970		$450	$600

Model 801 CP Electric Classical

1968-1970. Grand concert-sized classical with transducer based pickup system, natural pumpkin finish.

1968-1970		$450	$600

Nu-Sonic

1965-1966. Solidbody electric student model, 6-on-a-side tuners, black or cherry finish.

1965-1966		$500	$650

Vibraslim (Model 548 by Late-1966)

1965-1970. Double-cut semi-hollowbody, 2 pickups, vibrato, 2 f-holes, red or golden sunburst. Notable spec changes with Model 548 in '66.

1965-1966		$650	$850
1966-1970	Model 548	$600	$775

MODEL YEAR	FEATURES	EXC. COND. LOW	HIGH

Virginian (Model 550 by Mid-1966)

1965-1970. Single-cut flat-top, 2 pickups (1 on each side of soundhole), scroll headstock, tremolo, natural.

1965-1966		$825	$1,075
1966-1970	Model 550	$775	$1,025

Ballurio

Luthier Keith Ballurio builds his intermediate, professional, and premium grade, production/custom, solidbody and chambered guitars in Manassas, Virginia, starting in 2000.

Baltimore

2007-2008. Budget grade, production, solidbody electric guitars imported by The Music Link.

Bambu

1970s. Short-lived brand name on a line of guitars built by Japan's Chushin Gakki Co., which also built models for several other manufacturers.

Baranik Guitars

1995-present. Premium grade, production/custom steel-string flat-tops made in Tempe, Arizona by luthier Mike Baranik.

Barclay

1960s. Thinline acoustic/electric archtops, solidbody electric guitars and basses imported from Japan. Generally shorter scale beginner guitars.

Electric Solidbody

1960s. Various models and colors.

1960s		$175	$225

Barcus-Berry

Founded by John Berry and Les Barcus, in 1964, introducing the first piezo crystal transducer. Martin guitar/Barcus-Berry products were offered in the mid-'80s. They also offered a line of amps from around '76 to ca. '80.

Barrington

1988-1991. Imports offered by Barrington Guitar Werks, of Barrington, Illinois. Models included solidbody guitars and basses, archtop electrics, and acoustic flat-tops. Barrington Music Products is still in the music biz, offering LA saxophones and other products.

Acoustic/Electric

1988-1991. Acoustic/electric, flat-top single-cut with typical round soundhole, opaque white.

1988-1991		$155	$200

Solidbody

1988-ca 1991. Barrington's line of pointy headstock, double-cut solidbodies, black.

1988-1991		$155	$200

Bartell of California

1964-1969. Founded by Paul Barth (Magnatone) and Ted Peckles. Mosrite-inspired designs.

1967 Baldwin Model 706 V

Rivington Guitars

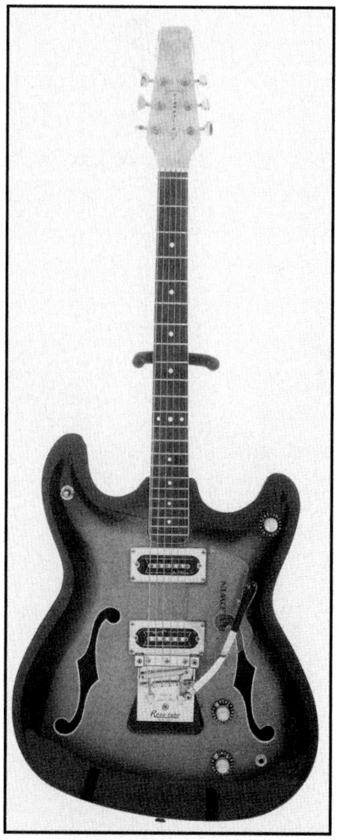

1965 Baldwin Vibrasilm

Imaged by Heritage Auctions, HA.com

Bazzolo Guitarworks

Bedell Wildfire

MODEL YEAR	FEATURES	EXC. COND. LOW	HIGH

Double Neck

1967		$1,900	$2,450

Electric 12

1967. Mosrite-style body.

1967		$1,075	$1,400

Barth

1950s-1960s. Paul Barth was involved with many guitar companies including National, Rickenbacker, Magnatone and others. He also built instruments under his own brand in California, including guitars, lap steels and amps. Most will have either a Barth logo on plastic plate, or decal.

Mark VIII

1959. Double-cut solidbody, 2 pickups, dot markers, Barth headstock logo.

1959		$2,100	$2,700

Bartolini

1960s. European-made (likely Italian) guitars made for the Bartolini Accordion Company. Similar to Gemelli guitars, so most likely from same manufacturer. Originally plastic covered, they switched to paint finishes by the mid '60s.

Solidbody

1960s		$425	$575

Bashkin Guitars

1998-present. Luthier Michael Bashkin builds his premium grade, custom, steel-string acoustics in Fort Collins, Colorado.

Basone Guitars

1999-present. Luthier Chris Basaraba builds his custom, professional grade, solid and hollowbody electric guitars and basses in Vancouver, British Columbia.

Bauer, George

1894-1911. Luthier George Bauer built guitars, mandolins, and banjos in Philadelphia, Pennsylvania. He also built instruments with Samuel S. Stewart (S.S. Stewart).

Baxendale

1974-present. Luthier Scott Baxendale builds his professional and premium grade, custom, steel-string acoustic and solidbody electric guitars in Athens, Georgia and previously in Colorado, Tennessee and Texas.

Bay State

Ca.1890-ca.1910. Bay State was a trademark for Boston's John C. Haynes & Co., and offered guitars and banjos.

Parlor Guitar

1900s. Small parlor size, mahogany body with salt & pepper binding.

1900s		$600	$775

Bazzolo Guitarworks

1983-present. Luthier Thomas Bazzolo began building his premium grade, production/custom, classical and flat-top guitars in Lebanon, Connecticut and since 2008 in Sullivan, Maine.

BC Kingston

1977-present. From 1977 to '96, luthier Brian Kingston built flat-top and semi-hollow acoustic guitars along with a few solidbodies. Presently he builds premium grade, production/custom, archtop jazz and semi-hollow guitars in Prince Edward Island, Canada.

Bear Creek Guitars

Luthier Bill Hardin worked for OMI Dobro and Santa Cruz Guitar before introducing his own line of professional and premium grade, custom-made Weissenborn-style guitars in 1995, made in Kula, Hawaii. He also builds ukes.

Beardsell Guitars

1996-present. Production/custom flat-tops, classical and electric solidbody guitars built by luthier Allan Beardsell in Toronto, Ontario.

Beaulieu

2006-present. Luthier Hugues Beaulieu builds his production/custom, professional and premium grade, flat-top, flamenco and classical guitars in Pont-Rouge, Quebec.

Beauregard

1992-present. Luthier Mario Beauregard builds his premium and presentation grade, production/custom, flat-top, archtop and jazz guitars in Montreal, Quebec.

Bedell Guitars

1964-present. Intermediate and premium grade, production/custom, flat-top guitars built in Spirit Lake, Iowa and imported from China, designed by luthier Tom Bedell, Dan Mills and Sophia Yang. They also offer Great Divide Guitars and in 2010 acquired Breedlove.

Behringer

1989-present. The German professional audio products company added budget, production, solidbody guitars in '03, sold in amp/guitar packages. They also offer effects and amps.

Beltona

1990-present. Production/custom metal body resonator guitars made in New Zealand by Steve Evans and Bill Johnson. Beltona was originally located in England. They also build mandolins and ukes.

MODEL YEAR	FEATURES	EXC. COND. LOW	HIGH

Beltone

1920s-1930s. Acoustic and resonator guitars made by others for New York City distributor Perlberg & Halpin. Martin did make a small number of instruments for Beltone, but most were student-grade models most likely made by one of the big Chicago builders. They also made mandolins.

Archtop

1920s-30s		$325	$425

Resonator Copy

1930s. Resonator copy but without a real resonator, rather just an aluminum plate on a wooden top, body mahogany plywood.

1938		$450	$600

Beltone (Import)

1950s-1960s. Japan's Teisco made a variety of brands for others, including the Beltone line of guitars, basses and amps. Carvin sold some of these models in the late 1960s. Italy's Welson guitars also marketed marble and glitter-finished guitars in the U.S. under this brand.

Electric Solidbody

1960s. Japan, 4 pickups.

1960s		$270	$350

Benedetto

1968-present. Premium and presentation grade, production/custom archtop and chambered solidbody guitars, built by luthier Robert Benedetto. He has also built a few violins and solidbodies. He was located in East Stroudsburg, Pennsylvania, up to '99; in Riverview, Florida, for '00-'06; and in Savanah, Georgia, since '07. He is especially known for refining the 7-string guitar. From '99 to '06 he licensed the names of his standard models to Fender (see Benedetto FMIC); during that period, Benedetto only made special order instruments. In '06, Howard Paul joined Benedetto as President of the company to begin manufacturing a broader line of more affordable professional instruments.

Benedetto (FMIC)

1999-2006. Premium and presentation, production/custom, acoustic and electric archtops. From '99 to '06, Bob Benedetto had an agreement with Fender (FMIC) to build Benedetto guitars under his guidance and supervision. The guitars were originally built in the FMIC Guild Custom Shop in Nashville, and later in Fender's Corona, California, facility.

Benedict

1988-present. Founded by Roger Benedict. Professional and premium grade, production/custom, solid and semi-hollow body guitars and basses built by luthier Bill Hager in Cedar, Minnesota.

Beneteau

1974-present. Custom, premium grade, classical, baritone and steel string acoustic guitars built first in Ottawa, Ontario, and since 1986 in St. Thomas, Ontario by luthier Marc Beneteau. He also builds ukuleles.

Bennett Music Labs

1998-present. Custom guitars built by luthier Bruce Bennett, who helped design the first Warrior line of instruments with J.D. Lewis. He also built amps and Brown Sound effects and also guitars for J. Backlund Designs.

Bently

Ca.1985-1998. Student and intermediate grade copy style acoustic and electric guitars imported by St. Louis Music Supply. Includes the Series 10 electrics and the Songwriter acoustics (which have a double reversed B crown logo on the headstock). St. Louis Music replaced the Bently line with the Austin brand.

Berkowitz Guitars

1995-present. Luthier David D. Berkowitz builds his premium grade, custom/production, steel string and baritone guitars and basses in Washington, D.C.

Bernie Rico Jr. Guitars

Professional and premium grade, production/custom, solidbody electrics guitars and basses built by luther Bernie Rico, Jr., the son of B.C. Rich founder, in Hesperia, California.

Bertoncini Stringed Instruments

Luthier Dave Bertoncini began building in 1995, premium grade, custom, flat-top guitars, in Olympia, Washington. He has also built solidbody electrics, archtops, mandolins and ukuleles.

Beyond The Trees

1976-present. Luthier Fred Carlson offers a variety of innovative designs for his professional and presentation grade, production/custom 6- and 12-string flat-tops in Santa Cruz, California. He also produces the Sympitar (a 6-string with added sympathetic strings) and the Dreadnautilus (a unique shaped headless acoustic).

Big Lou Guitar

Mid-2010-present. Located in Perris, California, owner Louis Carroll imports his intermediate grade, production, electric guitars from China.

Big Tex Guitars

Production/custom, professional grade, vintage-style replica guitars, started in 2000, built for owner Eric Danheim, by luthiers James Love, Mike Simon and Eddie Dale in Houston and Dripping Springs, Texas and Seattle, Washington.

Benedetto Benny
Imaged by Heritage Auctions, HA.com

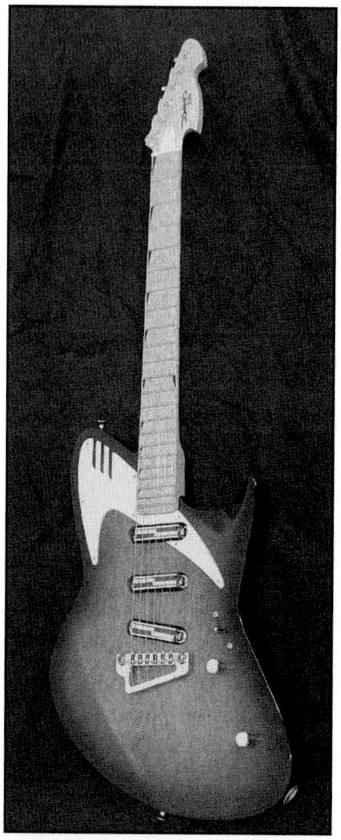

Bennett Music Labs JBD-800

GUITARS

1949 Bigsby

Imaged by Heritage Auctions, HA.com

Blade Texas Deluxe

Bigsby

Pedal steel guitars, hollow-chambered electric Spanish guitars, electric mandolins, doublenecks, replacement necks on acoustic guitars, hand vibratos, all handmade by Paul Arthur Bigsby, machinist and motorcycle enthusiast (designer of '30s Crocker motorcycles), in Downey, California. Initially built for special orders.

Bigsby was a pioneer in developing pedal steels. He designed a hand vibrato for Merle Travis. In '48, his neck-through hollow electrics (with Merle Travis) influenced Leo Fender, and Bigsby employed young Semie Moseley. In '56, he designed the Magnatone Mark series guitars and 1 Hawaiian lap steel. He built guitars up to '63.

He built less than 50 Spanish guitars, 6 mandolins, 70 to 150 pedal steels and 12 or so neck replacements. SN was stamped on the end of fingerboard: MMDDYY. In '65, the company was sold to Gibson president Ted McCarty who moved the tremolo/vibrato work to Kalamazoo. Bigsby died in '68. Fred Gretsch purchased the Bigsby company from Ted McCarty in '99 and sold it to Fender in 2019. A solidbody guitar and a pedal steel based upon the original Paul Bigsby designs were introduced January, 2002. These were modeled on the 1963 Bigsby catalog but look very similar to the typical Bigsby solidbodys made in the early '50s. Early Bigsby guitars command high value on the collectible market and values here assumes authentication by an industry expert.

Standard Models (Japan)

2007-2008. Various models made in Japan.

MODEL YEAR	FEATURES	EXC. COND. LOW	HIGH
2007	Model BY-48N	$1,000	$1,300
2007	Model BY-50	$1,000	$1,300
2007	Model BYS-48	$1,000	$1,300

Standard Solidbody (Spanish)

Late-1940s-1950s, 2002. Standard Guitar, solidbody, natural. Reissue offered in '02.

MODEL YEAR	FEATURES	EXC. COND. LOW	HIGH
1948		$185,000	$290,000
1949		$115,000	$280,000
1950-1956		$65,000	$250,000
2002	Reissue	$2,850	$3,700

Bil Mitchell Guitars

1979-present. Luthier Bil Mitchell builds his professional and premium grade, production/custom, flat-top and archtop guitars originally in Wall, New Jersey, and since '02 in Riegelsville, Pennsylvania.

Bill Foley Fine Instruments

2012-present. Luthiers Bill Foley, his son Sam, and Brad Lewis build professional and premium grade, custom electric guitars and basses in Columbus, Ohio.

Bilt Guitars

2010-present. Professional grade, production/custom, solidbody and semi-hollowbody electric guitars built in Des Moines, Iowa by luthiers Bill Henss and Tim Thelen.

Birdsong Guitars

2001-present. Luthiers Scott Beckwith and Jamie Hornbuckle build their professional grade, production/custom, solidbody guitars and basses in Wimberley, Texas.

Bischoff Guitars

1975-present. Professional and premium-grade, custom-made flat-tops built by luthier Gordy Bischoff in Eau Claire, Wisconsin.

Bishline

1985-present. Luthier Robert Bishline, of Tulsa, Oklahoma, mainly builds banjos, but did build flat-tops and resonators in the past, and still does occasionally.

Black Jack

1960s. Violin-body hollowbody electric guitars and basses, possibly others. Imported from Japan by unidentified distributor. Manufacturers unknown, but some may be Arai.

Blackbird

2006-present. Luthier Joe Luttwak builds his professional grade, production/custom, carbon fiber acoustic guitars in San Francisco, California. He also offers a uke.

Blackshear, Tom

1958-present. Premium and presentation grade, production, classical and flamenco guitars made by luthier Tom Blackshear in San Antonio, Texas.

Blade

1987-present. Intermediate and professional grade, production, solidbody guitars and basses from luthier Gary Levinson and his Levinson Music Products Ltd. located in Switzerland.

California Custom

1994-2010. California Standard with maple top and high-end appointments.

MODEL YEAR	FEATURES	EXC. COND. LOW	HIGH
1994-2010		$625	$850

California Deluxe/Deluxe

1994-1995. Standard with mahogany body and maple top.

MODEL YEAR	FEATURES	EXC. COND. LOW	HIGH
1994-1995		$475	$625

California Hybrid

1998-1999. Standard with piezo bridge pickup.

MODEL YEAR	FEATURES	EXC. COND. LOW	HIGH
1998-1999		$400	$550

California Standard

1994-2007. Offset double-cut, swamp ash body, bolt neck, 5-way switch.

MODEL YEAR	FEATURES	EXC. COND. LOW	HIGH
1994-2007		$300	$400

R 3

1988-1993. Offset double-cut maple solidbody, bolt maple neck, 3 single-coils or single/single/humbucker.

MODEL YEAR	FEATURES	EXC. COND. LOW	HIGH
1988-1993		$475	$625

R 4

1988-1993. R 3 with ash body and see-thru color finishes.

MODEL YEAR	FEATURES	EXC. COND. LOW	HIGH
1988-1992		$475	$625

MODEL YEAR	FEATURES	EXC. COND. LOW	HIGH

Texas Series

2003-present. Includes Standard (3 single-coils) and Deluxe (gold hardware, single/single/hum pickups).

2003-2010	Deluxe	$350	$475
2003-2010	Special	$325	$450
2003-2020	Standard	$325	$450

Blanchard Guitars

1994-present. Luthier Mark Blanchard builds premium grade, custom steel-string and classical guitars originally in Mammoth Lakes, California, and since May '03, in northwest Montana.

Blindworm Guitars

2008-present. Luthiers Andrew J. Scott and Steven Sells build premium and presentation grade, production/custom, acoustic, electric and electric-acoustic guitars, basses, mandolins, banjos and others in Colorado Springs, Colorado.

Blount

Professional and premium grade, production/custom, acoustic flat-top guitars built by luthier Kenneth H. Blount Jr. in Sebring, Florida. He started in 1985.

Blue Star

1984-present. Luthier Bruce Herron builds his production/custom guitars in Fennville, Michigan. He also builds mandolins, lap steels, dulcimers and ukes.

Bluebird

1920s-1930s. Private brand with Bluebird painted on headstock, built by the Oscar Schmidt Co. and possibly others. Most likely made for distributor.

13" Flat-Top

1930s		$125	$160

Bluebird Guitars

2011-present. Luthiers Rob Bluebird and Gian Maria Camponeschi build premium grade, custom, archtop and solidbody guitars in Rome, Italy. They build production resonator guitars in Bali, Indonesia. They also offer basses and ukuleles.

Blueridge

Early 1980s-present. Intermediate and professional grade, production, solid-top acoustic guitars distributed by Saga. In '00, the product line was redesigned with the input of luthier Greg Rich (Rich and Taylor guitars).

Bluesouth

1991-ca. 2006. Custom electric guitars built by luthier Ronnie Knight in Muscle Shoals, Alabama. He also built basses.

Boaz Elkayam Guitars

1985-present. Presentation grade, custom steel, nylon, and flamenco guitars made by luthier Boaz Elkayam in Chatsworth, California.

MODEL YEAR	FEATURES	EXC. COND. LOW	HIGH

Boedigheimer Instruments

2000-present. Luthier Brian Boedigheimer builds his professional and premium grade, production/custom, semi-hollowbody electric guitars in Red Wing, Minnesota.

Bohmann

1878-ca. 1926. Acoustic flat-top guitars, harp guitars, mandolins, banjos, violins made in Chicago Illinois, by Joseph Bohmann (born 1848, in Czechoslovakia). Bohmann's American Musical Industry founded 1878. Guitar body widths are 12", 13", 14", 15". He had 13 grades of guitars by 1900 (Standard, Concert, Grand Concert sizes). Early American use of plywood. Some painted wood finishes. Special amber-oil varnishes. Tuner bushings. Early ovalled fingerboards. Patented tuner plates and bridge design. Steel engraved label inside. Probably succeeded by son Joseph Frederick Bohmann.

Ca. 1896 12" body faux rosewood, 13", 14" and 15" body faux rosewood birch, 12", 13", 14" and 15" body sunburst maple, 12", 13", 14" and 15" body rosewood. By 1900 Styles 0, 1, 2 and 3 Standard, Concert and Grand Concert maple, Styles 1, 2, 3, 4, 5, 6, 7, 8, 9, 10, 11 and 12 in Standard, Concert, and Grand Concert rosewood.

14 3/4" Flat-Top

Solid spruce top, veneered Brazilian rosewood back and sides, wood marquetry around top and soundhole, natural. Each Bohmann should be valued on a case-by-case basis.

1896-1900	Brazilian	$900	$1,200
1896-1900	Other woods	$450	$600

Harp Guitar

1896-1899	All styles	$2,700	$3,500

Bolin

1978-present. Professional and premium grade, production/custom, solidbody guitars and basses built by luthier John Bolin in Boise, Idaho. Bolin is well-known for his custom work. His Cobra guitars are promoted and distributed by Sanderson Sales and Marketing as part of the Icons of America Series.

NS

1996-2011. Slot-headstock, bolt-on neck, single-cut solidbody, Seymour Duncan passive pickups or EMG active, from '96 to the fall of 2001 custom-built serial numbers to 0050 then from the fall of '01 to the present production model build starting with SN 0051.

1996-2001	Custom-built	$1,200	$2,500
2001-2011	Standard production	$675	$875

Bolt

1988-1991. Founded by luthier Wayne Bolt and Jim Dala Pallu in Schnecksville, Pennsylvania, Bolt's first work was CNC machined OEM necks and bodies made for Kramer and BC Rich. In '90, they started building solidbody Bolt guitars, many with airbrushed graphics. Only about 100 to 125 were built, around 40 with graphics.

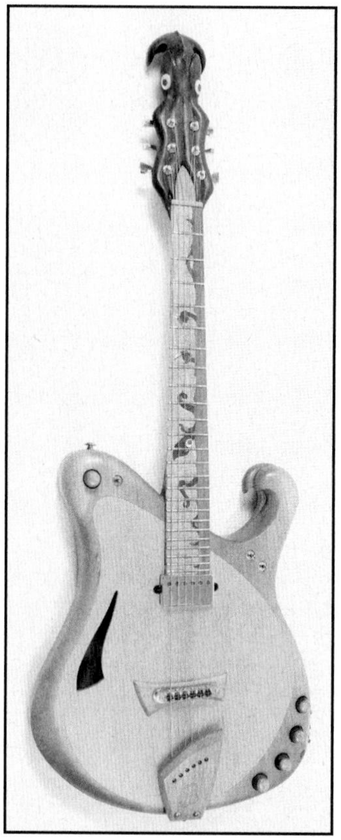

Blindworm The Mighty Kraken

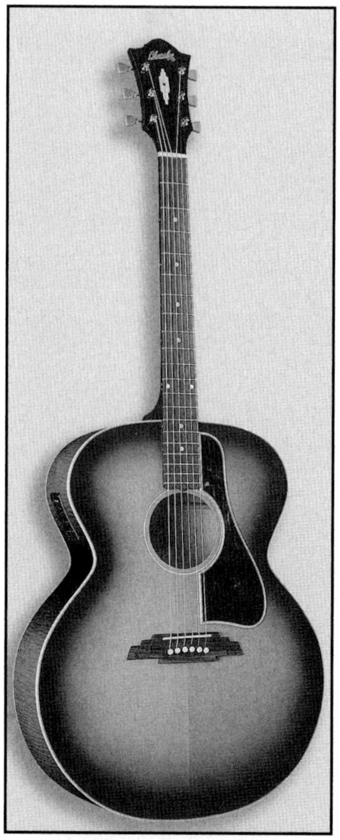

Blueridge BG-1500E

Bourgeois Country Boy

2015 Bourgeois JOM

Imaged by Heritage Auctions, HA.com

MODEL YEAR	FEATURES	EXC. COND. LOW	HIGH

Bond

1984-1985. Andrew Bond made around 1,400 Electraglide guitars in Scotland. Logo says 'Bond Guitars, London'.

ElectraGlide

1984-1985. Black carbon graphite 1-piece body and neck, double-cut, 3 single-coils (2 humbuckers were also supposedly available), digital LED controls that required a separate transformer.

1984-1985 With attachments $1,150 $1,500

Borges Guitars

2000-present. Luthier Julius Borges builds his premium grade, production/custom, acoustic guitars in Groton, Massachusetts.

Boucher

2005-present. Professional and premium grade, acoustic guitars built by luthier Robin Boucher in Quebec.

Boulder Creek Guitars

2007-present. Intermediate and professional grade, production, imported dreadnought, classical, and 12-string guitars, basses and ukes distributed by Morgan Hill Music of Morgan Hill, California.

Bourgeois

1993-1999, 2000-present. Luthier Dana Bourgeois builds his professional and premium grade, production/custom, acoustic and archtop guitars in Lewiston, Maine. Bourgeois co-founded Schoenberg guitars and built Schoenberg models from '86-'90. Bourgeois' 20th Anniversary model was issued in '97. Bourgeois Guitars, per se, went out of business at the end of '99. Patrick Theimer created Pantheon Guitars, which included 7 luthiers (including Bourgeois) working in an old 1840s textile mill in Lewiston, Maine and Bourgeois models continue to be made as part of the Pantheon organization.

A-500

Top-of-the-line acoustic cutaway archtop, natural.

1997 $3,800 $5,000

Blues

1996. D-style, all koa.

1996 $2,450 $3,150

Country Boy

1998-present. Pre-war D-style designed for Ricky Skaggs, Sitka spruce top, mahogany back and sides, Ricky Skaggs label, natural.

1998-2020 $2,250 $2,900

Country Boy Custom

1999-2016. Adirondack spruce top, figured mahogany back and sides.

1999-2016 $2,450 $3,150

Country Boy Deluxe

2003-2015. Country Boy with Adirondack spruce top, rosewood binding.

2003-2015 $2,450 $3,150

D - 20th Anniversary

1997. 20 made, bearclaw spruce top, rosewood back and sides, mother-of-pearl 'board, ornate abalone floral pattern inlay, abalone rosette and border, natural.

1997 $2,450 $3,150

D-150/Style 150

2002-present. Brazilian rosewood, premium Adirondack, abalone rosette. Called Style 150 in '20.

2002-2020 $4,500 $5,800

DBJC

Jumbo cutaway, Indian rosewood back and sides, redwood top, gloss finish.

2007 $2,675 $3,475

Georgia Dreadnought

2003. Mahogany, Adirondack.

2003 $1,800 $2,350

JOM

1993-2015. Jumbo Orchestra Model flat-top, 15 5/8". Model includes one with cedar top, mahogany back and sides, and one with spruce top, Brazilian rosewood back and sides.

1993	Brazilian rosewood	$4,500	$5,800
1993	Mahogany	$2,100	$2,700
1993-2015	Indian rosewood	$2,100	$2,700

JOMC/OMC

1995-2015. JOM (jumbo) cutaway.

1995-2011	OMC, figured mahogany	$3,000	$3,900
1995-2015	JOMC200, Indian rosewood	$2,500	$3,300

JR-A

1990s. Artisan Series, 15 5/8", spruce top, rosewood back and sides.

1990s $1,050 $1,375

LC-4 Archtop Limited Edition

2002. Limited edition of 12, signed and numbered, premium sitka and carved curly maple.

2002 $8,900 $11,600

Martin Simpson

1997-2003. Grand auditorium with unusual cutaway that removes one-half of the upper treble bout, Englemann spruce top, Indian rosewood back and sides, natural.

1997-2003 $2,050 $2,650

OM

1993-1999. Standard size OM, spruce top, rosewood back and sides.

1993-1999 $2,700 $3,475

OM Deluxe Artisan

2002. Indian rosewood, sitka.

2002 $1,750 $2,300

OM Soloist

1990s-present. Full-sized, soft cutaway flat-top, Adirondack spruce top, figured Brick Red Brazilian rosewood back and sides, natural.

1990-2020 $4,500 $5,800

Ricky Skaggs Signature

1998. D-style, rosewood sides and back, spruce top.

1998 $2,450 $3,150

MODEL YEAR	FEATURES	EXC. COND. LOW	HIGH

Slope D

1993-present. D-size, 16", spruce top, mahogany back and sides.

1993-2020		$2,800	$3,600

Vintage D

2000-present. Adirondack spruce (Eastern red spruce) top, optional rosewood back and sides.

2000-2020	Indian rosewood	$1,850	$2,450
2000s	Brazilian rosewood	$4,500	$5,800

Vintage OM

2005. Madagascar rosewood and Italian spruce top.

2005		$2,750	$3,550

Bown Guitars

Luthier Ralph Bown builds custom steel-string, nylon-string, baritone, and harp guitars, starting 1981, in Walmgate, U.K.

Bozo

1964-present. Bozo (pronounced Bo-zho) Podunavac learned instrument building in his Yugoslavian homeland and arrived in the United States in '59. In '64 he opened his own shop and has built a variety of high-end, handmade, acoustic instruments, many being one-of-a-kind. He has built around 570 guitars over the years. There were several thousand Japanese-made (K. Yairi shop) Bell Western models bearing his name made from '79-'80; most of these were sold in Europe. He currently builds premium and presentation grade, custom guitars in Port Charlotte, Florida.

Acoustic

1970s-1980s. US-made, 6- and 12-string, appointments vary.

1970s-80s		$1,500	$8,500

Bradford

Mid-1960s. Brand name used by the W.T. Grant Company, one of the old Five & Ten style retail stores similar to F.W. Woolworth and Kresge. Many of these guitars and basses were made in Japan by Guyatone.

Acoustic Flat-Top

1960s		$150	$200

Electric Solidbody

1960s	1 or 2 pickups	$150	$200
1960s	3 pickups	$200	$275
1960s	4 pickups	$260	$350

Bradley

1970s. Budget Japanese copy models imported by Veneman's Music Emporium.

Brawley Basses

Headquartered in Temecula, California, and designed by Keith Brawley, offering solidbody guitars and basses made in Korea.

Brazen

Starting in 2005, owner Steve Tsai, along with luthier Eddie Estrada, offered professional and premium grade, production, electric guitars. Steve also imports a line of intermediate grade guitars from China which are set up in the U.S.

MODEL YEAR	FEATURES	EXC. COND. LOW	HIGH

Breedlove

1990-present. Founded by Larry Breedlove and Steve Henderson. Intermediate, professional, premium, and presentation grade, production/custom, steel and nylon string flat-top built in Bend, Oregon and imported. They also build mandolins, basses, lapsteels and ukes. Several available custom options may add to the values listed here. They offered chambered electric guitars starting in 2008 but in January 2010, Breedlove discontinued all electric guitar production. Also in '10, they became part of Two Old Hippies.

Brentwood

1970s. Student models built by Kay for store or jobber.

K-100

1970s. 13" student flat-top, K-100 label inside back, K logo on 'guard.

1970s		$40	$55

Brian May Guitar Company

2006-present. Guitarist Brian May teamed up with Barry Moorhouse and Pete Malandrone to offer versions of his Red Special Guitar. They also offered a bass.

Brian May Special

2006-present. Mahogany solidbody, 3 pickups, various colors

2006-2020		$350	$475

Brian Moore

1992-present. Founded by Patrick Cummings, Brian Moore and Kevin Kalagher in Brewster, New York; they introduced their first guitars in '94. Initially expensive custom shop guitars with carbon-resin bodies with highly figured wood tops; later went to all wood bodies cut on CNC machines. The intermediate and professional grade, production, iGuitar/i2000series was introduced in 2000 and made in Korea, but set up in the U.S. Currently the premium grade, production/custom, Custom Shop Series guitars are handcrafted in La Grange, New York. They also build basses and electric mandolins.

C/DC/MC Series

1994-2011. Various models.

1994-2011		$800	$1,400

iGuitar Series

2000-present. Various models.

2000-2020		$625	$825

Brian Stone Classical Guitars

Luthier Brian Stone builds his classical guitars in Corvallis, Oregon.

Briggs

1999-present. Luthier Jack Briggs builds his professional and premium grade, production/custom, chambered and solidbody guitars in Raleigh, North Carolina.

Breedlove Pacific

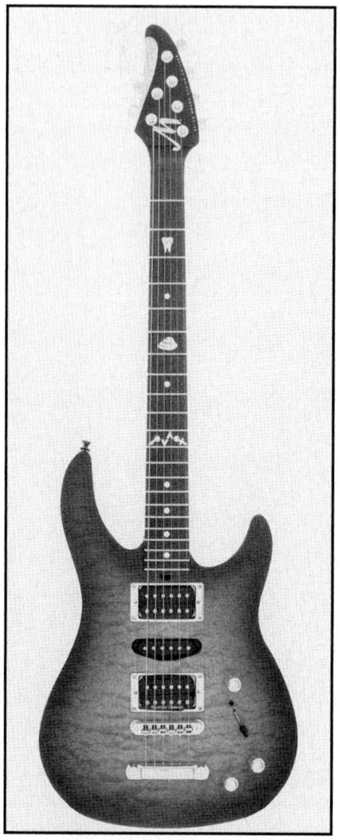

1999 Brian Moore C90

Imaged by Heritage Auctions, HA.com

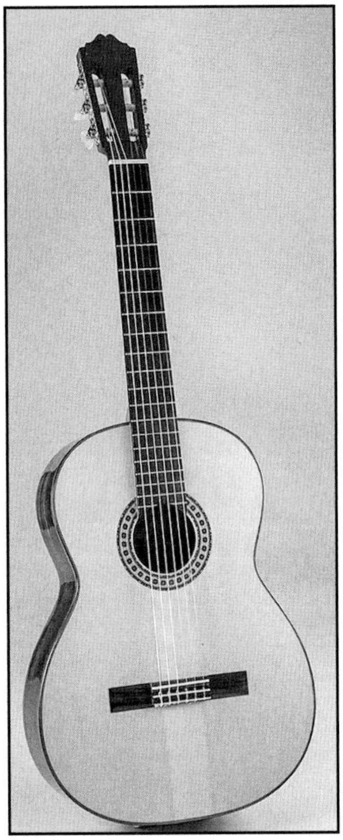

R. E. Bruné 30-S

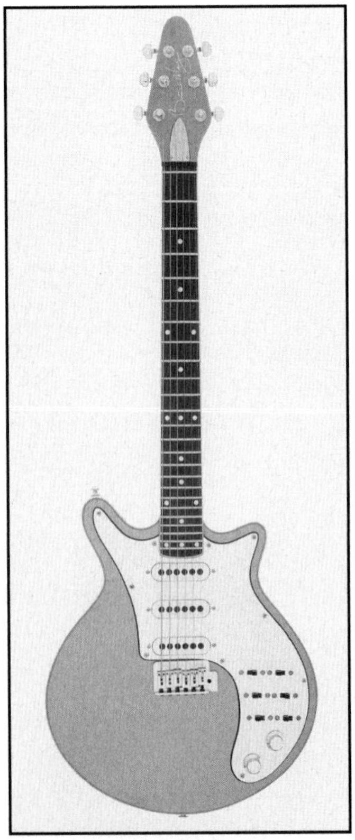

Burns Brian May Red Special
Imaged by Heritage Auctions, HA.com

MODEL YEAR	FEATURES	EXC. COND. LOW	HIGH

Broman

1930s. The Broman brand was most likely used by a music studio (or distributor) on instruments made by others, including Regal-built resonator instruments.

Bronson

Ca. 1934-early 1960s. George Bronson was a steel guitar instructor in the Detroit area and his instruments were made by other companies. They were mainly lap steels (usually sold with a matching amp), but some other types were also offered.

Honolulu Master Hawaiian

1938		$3,000	$3,900

Student Hawaiian

1930s	13" flat-top	$150	$200

Brook Guitars

1993-present. Simon Smidmore and Andy Petherick build their production/custom Brook steel-string, nylon-strings, and archtops in Dartmoor, U.K.

Brown's Guitar Factory

1982-present. Luthier John Brown builds professional and premium grade, production/custom, solidbody guitars, basses and lap steels in Inver Grove Heights, Minnesota.

Bruné, R. E.

1966-present. Luthier Richard Bruné builds his premium and presentation grade, custom, classical and flamenco guitars in Evanston, Illinois. He also offers his professional and premium grade Model 20 and Model 30, which are handmade in a leading guitar workshop in Japan. Bruné's "Guitars with Guts" column appeared for many years in *Vintage Guitar* magazine.

Bruno and Sons

Distributor Bruno and Sons marketed a variety of brands, including their own. Later became part of Kaman Music.

Harp Guitar

1924		$1,800	$2,300

Hollowbody Electric

1960s-1970s. Various imported models.

1960s		$145	$200

Parlor Guitar

1880-1920. Various woods used on back and sides.

1880-1920	Birch	$400	$525
1880-1920	Brazilian rosewood	$825	$1,100
1880-1920	Mahogany	$450	$575

Buddy Blaze

1985-present. Professional and premium grade, custom/production, solidbody electric guitars built by luthier Buddy Blaze from '85 to '87 in Arlington, Texas, and presently in Kailua Kona, Hawaii. He also designs intermediate grade models which are imported.

MODEL YEAR	FEATURES	EXC. COND. LOW	HIGH

Bunker

1961-present. Founder Dave Bunker built custom guitars and basses while performing in Las Vegas in the '60s and developed a number of innovations. Around '92 Bunker began PBC Guitar Technology with John Pearse and Paul Chernay in Coopersburg, Pennsylvania, building instruments under the PBC brand and, from '94-'96, for Ibanez' USA Custom Series. PBC closed in '97 and Bunker moved back to Washington State to start Bunker Guitar Technology and resumed production of several Bunker models. In early 2002, Bunker Guitars became part of Maple Valley Tone Woods of Port Angeles, Washington. Currently Bunker offers intermediate, professional, and premium grade, production/custom, guitars and basses built in Port Angeles. Most early Bunker guitars were pretty much custom-made in low quantities.

Burke

Ca. 1960-ca. 1966. 6- and 12- string electric guitars built by Glen Burke's Tuning Fork Guitar Company in Eugene and Grants Pass, Oregon and mostly sold in kit form. The guitars featured an aluminum neck-thru design with the body portion of the neck shaped being a rectangular box where the body wings are attached. Being kit guitars finishes, pickups, options and build quality will vary.

Burlesk Guitars

1994-present. Professional and premium grade, custom, solidbody electric guitars and basses, built by luthier James Burley in Alberta, Canada.

Burly Guitars

2007-present. Luthier Jeff Ayers builds his professional and premium grade, custom, solid and semi-hollowbody guitars in Land O' Lakes, Wisconsin. He plans on adding basses.

Burns

1960-1970, 1974-1983, 1992-present. Intermediate and professional grade, production, electric guitars built in the U.K. and Asia. They also build basses. Jim Burns began building guitars in the late-'50s and established Burns London Ltd in '60. Baldwin Organ (see Baldwin listing) purchased the company in '65 and offered the instruments until '70. The Burns name was revived in '91 by Barry Gibson as Burns London, with Jim Burns' involvement, offering reproductions of some of the classic Burns models of the '60s. Jim Burns passed away in August '98.

Baby Bison

1965. Double-cut solidbody, scroll headstock, 2 pickups, shorter scale, tremolo.

1965		$600	$800

Bison

1964-1965, 2003-present. Double-cut solidbody, 3 pickups, tremolo, black or white, scroll-headstock, replaced flat headstock Black Bison. Has been reissued with both types of headstocks.

1961-1962	Black, 4 pus, flat hs	$1,450	$1,950

MODEL YEAR	FEATURES	EXC. COND. LOW	HIGH
1962-1965	Black, 3 pus, scroll hs	$1,350	$1,750
1962-1965	White, 3 pus, scroll hs	$1,350	$1,750
2003-2020	Reissue	$400	$525

Brian May Signature Red Special

2001-2006. Replica of May's original Red Special but with added whammy bar. Korean-made.

2001-2006		$575	$750

Cobra

2004-present. Double-cut solid, 2 pickups.

2004-2020		$105	$135

Double Six

1964-1965, 2003-present. Solidbody 12-string, double-cut, 3 pickups, greenburst. Reissue made in Korea.

1964-1965		$1,250	$1,650
2003-2020		$200	$260

Flyte

1974-1977. Fighter jet-shaped solidbody, pointed headstock, 2 humbucking pickups, silver, has been reissued.

1974-1977		$600	$775

GB 66 Deluxe

1965. Like 66 Standard, but with bar pickups and add Density control.

1965		$700	$925

GB 66 Deluxe Standard

1965. Offset double-cut, f-holes, 2 Ultra-Sonic pickups.

1965		$650	$850

Jazz

1962-1965. Offset double-cut solid, shorter scale, 2 pickups.

1962-1965		$825	$1,075

Jazz Split Sound

1962-1965. Offset double-cut solid, 3 pickups, tremolo, red sunburst.

1962-1965		$1,000	$1,325

Marquee

2000-2020. Offset double-cut solid, 3 pickups, scroll headstock

2000-2020		$200	$260

Marvin

1964-1965. Offset double-cut solidbody, scroll headstock, 3 pickups, tremolo, white.

1964-1965		$1,400	$1,800

Nu-Sonic

1964-1965. Solidbody, 2 pickups, tremolo, white or cherry, has been reissued.

1964-1965		$725	$925

Sonic

1960-1964. Double shallow cut solid, 2 pickups, cherry.

1960-1964		$600	$775

Split Sonic

1962-1964. Solidbody, 3 pickups, bound neck, tremolo, red sunburst.

1962-1964		$850	$1,100

Steer

2000-2020. Semi-hollowbody, sound-hole, 2 pickups, non-cut and single-cut versions.

2000-2020		$300	$385

TR-2

1963-1964. Semi-hollow, 2 pickups, red sunburst.

1963-1964		$775	$1,000

Vibra Artist

1960-1962. Double-cut, mahogany, 3 pickups, 6 knobs.

1960-1962		$650	$850

Vibraslim

1964-1965. Double-cut, f-holes, 2 pickups, red sunburst.

1964-1965		$775	$1,000

Virginian

1964-1965. Burns of London model, later offered as Baldwin Virginian in '65.

1964-1965		$975	$1,275

Vista Sonic

1962-1964. Offset double-cut solid, 3 pickups, red sunburst.

1962-1964		$650	$850

Burnside

1987-1988. Budget solidbody guitars imported by Guild.

Solidbody Electric/Blade

1987-1988. Solidbody, fat pointy headstock.

1987-1988		$155	$200

Burns-Weill

1959. Jim Burns and Henry Weill teamed up to produce three solidbody electric and three solidbody bass models under this English brand. Models included the lower end Fenton, a small single-cutaway, 2 pickups and an elongated headstock and the bizarrely styled RP2G. Henry Weill continued to produce a slightly different RP line under the re-named Fenton-Weill brand.

Burny

1980s-1990s. Solidbody electric guitars from Fernandes and built in Japan, Korea or China.

Burrell

1984-2010. Luthier Leo Burrell built his professional grade, production/custom, acoustic, semi-hollow, and solidbody guitars and basses in Huntington, West Virginia. Leo retired in '10.

Burton Guitars

1980-present. Custom classical guitars built by luthier Cynthia Burton in Portland, Oregon.

Buscarino Guitars

1981-present. Luthier John Buscarino builds his premium and presentation grade, custom archtops and steel-string and nylon-string flat-tops in Franklin, North Carolina.

Byers, Gregory

1984-present. Premium grade, custom classical and Flamenco guitars built by luthier Gregory Byers in Willits, California.

1963 Burns Sonic
Imaged by Heritage Auctions, HA.com

1990 Burny RSG-140
Craig Brody

Byrd Super Avianti

Carvin Allan Holdsworth
Robbie Keene

MODEL YEAR	FEATURES	EXC. COND. LOW	HIGH

Byrd

1998-present. Custom/production, professional and premium grade, V-shaped electric guitars, built by luthiers James Byrd and Joe Riggio, in Seattle and several other cities in the state of Washington.

C. Fox

1997-2002. Luthier Charles Fox built his premium grade, production/custom flat-tops in Healdsburg, California. In '02 he closed C. Fox Guitars and moved to Portland, Oregon to build Charles Fox Guitars.

C.F. Mountain

1970s-early 1980s. Japanese copy acoustics made by Hayashi Musical Instrument Ltd with headstock logo that looks very much like that of a certain classic American guitar company.

Acoustic

1970s-80s		$55	$75

CA (Composite Acoustics)

1999-2010, 2011-present. Professional grade, production, carbon fiber composite guitars that were built in Lafayette, Louisiana. The company ceased production in February, '10. At the end of '10 CA was acquired by Peavey, which launched the new Meridian, Mississippi-based line in January, '11.

Califone

1966. Six and 12-string guitars and basses made by Murphy Music Industries (maker of the Murph guitars) for Rheem Califone-Roberts which manufactured tape recorders and related gear. Very few made.

Callaham

1989-present. Professional, production/custom, solidbody electric guitars built by luthier Bill Callaham in Winchester, Virginia. They also make tube amp heads.

Camelli

1960s. Line of solidbody electric guitars imported from Italy.

Solidbody Electric

1960s		$500	$650

Cameo

1960s-1970s. Japanese- and Korean-made electric and acoustic guitars. They also offered basses.

Electric

1960s-70s	Higher-end	$275	$360

Campbell American Guitars

2005-2015. Luthier Dean Campbell built his intermediate and professional grade, production/custom, solidbody guitars originally in Pawtucket, Rhode Island, then in Westwood, Massachusetts. From '02 to '05, he built guitars under the Greene & Campbell brand.

MODEL YEAR	FEATURES	EXC. COND. LOW	HIGH

Campellone

1978-present. Luthier Mark Campellone builds his premium grade, custom archtops in Greenville, Rhode Island. He also made electrics and basses in the '70s and '80s, switching to archtops around '90.

Deluxe

1990-present. 16" to 18" archtop, middle of the company product line, blond or sunburst.

1990-2020		$3,700	$4,800

Special

1994-present. 16" to 18" archtop, top of the company product line, carved spruce top, carved flamed maple back, flamed maple sides, blond or sunburst.

1994-2020		$4,400	$5,700

Standard

2000-present. 16" to 18" archtop, lower of the 3 model lines offered.

2000-2020		$2,800	$3,700

Canvas

2004-2012. Budget and intermediate grade, production, acoustic and electric guitars and basses imported from China by America Sejung Corp. until '11, then in South Korea.

Carbonaro

Luthier Robert Carbonaro began building in 1975, premium grade, production/custom, archtop and flattop guitars in Santa Fe, New Mexico. Relocated his shop to Mexico in 2016, then Vietnam in '19.

Carl Fischer

1920s. Most likely a brand made for a distributor. Instruments built by the Oscar Schmidt Co. and possibly others.

Carlos

Ca.1976-late 1980s. Imported copies of classic American acoustics distributed by Coast Wholesale Music.

Acoustic Flat-Top

1976-1980s	Various models	$50	$200

Carson Robison

1933-1938. Wards sold guitars endorsed by popular country artist Carson Robison. Built by Gibson, the guitars were the same as models sold under the Kalamazoo brand.

Model K

1933-1938. Flat top, ladder, K #926 same as Kalamzoo KG-11, K #1281/#1115 same as Kalamzoo K-14. Becomes the Recording King (Ward's main brand) Model K in '38.

1933-1935	K#926	$1,000	$1,300
1936-1938	K#1281/1115	$1,575	$2,100

Carvin

1946-present. Intermediate and professional grade, production/custom, acoustic and electric guitars and basses built in San Diego, California. They also offer amps and mandolins. Founded in Los Angeles by

MODEL YEAR	FEATURES	EXC. COND. LOW	HIGH

Hawaiian guitarist and recording artist Lowell C. Kiesel as the L.C. Kiesel Co. making pickups for guitars. Bakelite Kiesel-brand electric Hawaiian lap steels are introduced in early-'47. Small tube amps introduced ca. '47. By late-'49, the Carvin brand is introduced, combining parts of names of sons Carson and Gavin. Carvin acoustic and electric Spanish archtops are introduced in '54. Instruments are sold by mail-order only. Kiesel brand name revived by Carvin in '15 for use on their guitars.

2,000-4,000 guitars made prior to '70 with no serial number. First serial number appeared in '70, stamped on end of fingerboard, beginning with #5000. All are consecutive. Later SN on neck plates.

Approximate SN ranges include:

1970: First serial number #5000 to 10019 ('79).
'80-'83: 10768 to 15919.
'84-'87: 13666 to 25332.
'88-'90: 22731 to 25683.
'91-'94: 25359 to 42547.
'95-'99: 45879 to 81427.
'00-present: 56162 upward.

Acoustic/Electric AC/AE Series

1990s-2020	Various models	$350	$1,400

Solidbody B/C/D Series (Mid-Level)

1990s-2020	Various models	$350	$1,400

Solidbody Carved-Top (Higher-End)

2000s-2020	Various models	$800	$1,600

Casa Montalvo

1987-present. Intermediate and professional grade, production/custom flamenco and classical guitars made in Mexico for George Katechis of Berkeley Musical Instrument Exchange.

Casio

In 1987 Casio introduced a line of digital MIDI guitars imported from Japan, sporting plastic bodies and synthesizer features. They offered them for just a few years.

DG1

1980s. Squared plastic body.

1980s		$55	$85

DG10

1987-1989. Self-contained digital guitar.

1987-1989		$125	$165

DG20

1987-1989. Midi-capable digital guitar.

1987-1989		$165	$240

MG-500 Series MIDI Guitar

1987-1989. Cut-off teardrop (MG-500) or Strat-shaped (MG-510), basswood body, maple neck, rosewood 'board, 3 pickups.

1987-1989	500	$400	$575
1987-1989	510	$350	$475

PG-300

1988-1989. Similar to PG-380, but with less features.

1988-1989		$300	$400

PG-310

1988-1989. Similar to PG-380, but with less features.

1988-1989		$375	$500

MODEL YEAR	FEATURES	EXC. COND. LOW	HIGH

PG-380

1988-1989. Guitar synth, double-cut, over 80 built-in sounds, midi controller capable.

1988-1989		$500	$700

Casper Guitar Technologies

Professional grade, production/custom, solidbody electric guitars and basses built by luthier Stephen Casper in Leisure City, Florida, starting in 2009.

Cat's Eyes

1980s. Made by Tokai, Cat's Eyes headstock logo, see Tokai guitar listings.

Champion

Ca. 1894-1897. Chicago's Robert Maurer built this brand of instruments before switching to the Maurer brand name around 1897.

Champlin Guitars

2006-present. Professional and premium grade, custom, flat-top and archtop guitars, and mandolinettos, built by Devin Champlin in Bellingham, Washington.

Chandler

Intermediate and professional grade, production/custom, solidbody electric guitars built by luthiers Paul and Adrian Chandler in Chico, California. They also build basses, lap steels and pickups. Chandler started making pickguards and accessories in the '70s, adding electric guitars, basses, and effects in '84.

555 Model

1992-2000s. Sharp double-cut, 3 mini-humbuckers, TV Yellow.

1992-2000s		$550	$725

Austin Special

1991-1999. Resembles futuristic Danelectro, lipstick pickups, available in 5-string version.

1991-1999		$475	$625

Austin Special Baritone

1994-1999. Nicknamed Elvis, gold metalflake finish, mother-of-toilet-seat binding, tremolo, baritone.

1994-1999		$475	$625

LectraSlide

2000s. Single-cut, Rezo 'guard, 2 pickups.

2000s		$525	$675

Metro

1995-2000. Double-cut slab body, P-90 in neck position and humbucker in the bridge position.

1995-2000		$475	$625

Telepathic

1994-2000. Classic single-cut style, 3 models; Basic, Standard, Deluxe.

1994-2000	Basic	$400	$525
1994-2000	Deluxe 1122 Model	$475	$625
1994-2000	Standard	$450	$575

Casper CGT-20 Series Classic

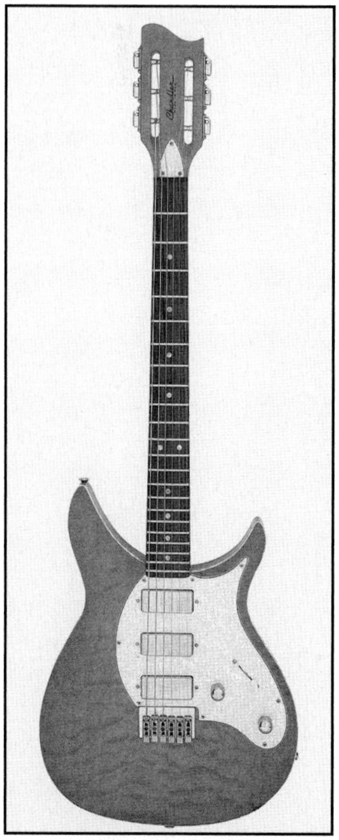

Chandler 555

Imaged by Heritage Auctions, HA.com

GUITARS

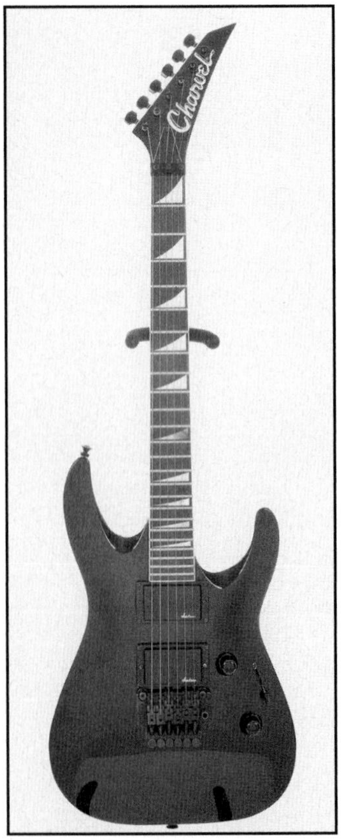

1990 Charvel 750XL Soloist
Imaged by Heritage Auctions, HA.com

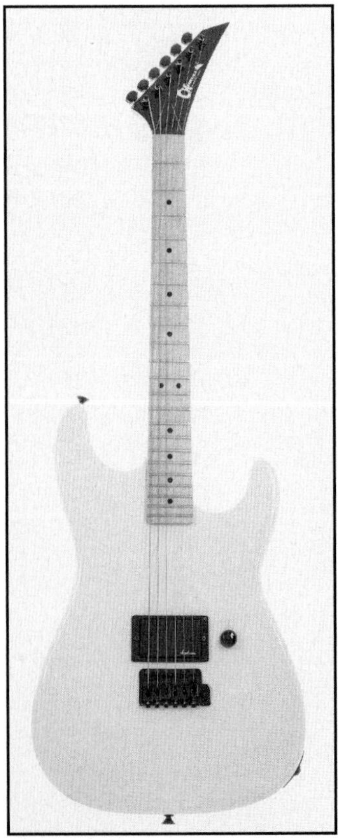

1987 Charvel Model 1
Imaged by Heritage Auctions, HA.com

MODEL YEAR	FEATURES	EXC. COND. LOW	HIGH

Chantus

Premium grade, production/custom, classical and flamenco guitars built in Austin, Texas, by luthier William King starting in '84. He also builds ukes.

Chapin

Professional and premium grade, production/custom, semi-hollow, solidbody, and acoustic electric guitars built by luthiers Bill Chapin and Fred Campbell in San Jose, California.

Chapman

1970-present. Made by Emmett Chapman, the Stick features 10 strings and is played by tapping both hands. The Grand Stick features 12 strings.

Stick

1970-present. Touch-tap hybrid electric instrument, 10 or 12 strings.

1970-2020	10- or 12-string	$1,700	$2,200

Char

1985-present. Premium grade, custom, classical and steel string acoustic guitars built in Portland, Oregon by luthier Kerry Char. He also builds harp-guitars and ukuleles.

Charis Acoustic

1996-present. Premium grade, custom/production, steel-string guitars built by luthier Bill Wise in Bay City, Michigan.

Charles Fox Guitars

1968-present. Luthier Charles Fox builds his premium and presentation grade, custom, steel and nylon string guitars in Portland, Oregon. He also produced GRD acoustic and electric guitars for '78-'82 and C. Fox acoustic guitars for '97-'02. He also operates The American School of Lutherie in Portland.

Charles Shifflett Acoustic Guitars

Premium grade, custom, classical, flamenco, resonator, and harp guitars, basses and banjos built by luthier Charles Shifflett, starting 1990, in High River, Alberta.

Charvel

1976 (1980)-present. Intermediate and professional grade, production, solidbody electric guitars. They also build basses. Founded by Wayne Charvel as Charvel Manufacturing in '76, making guitar parts in Asuza, California. Moved to San Dimas in '78. Also in '78 Grover Jackson bought out Charvel. In '79 or early '80 Charvel branded guitars are introduced. U.S.-made to '85, a combination of imports and U.S.-made post-'85. Charvel also manufactured the Jackson brand.

Charvel licensed its trademark to IMC (Hondo) in '85. IMC bought Charvel in '86 and moved the factory to Ontario, California. On October 25, 2002, Fender Musical Instruments Corp. (FMIC) took ownership of Jackson/Charvel Manufacturing Inc.

Pre-Pro (Pre-Production) Charvels began in November 1980 and ran until sometime in 1981. These are known as 'non-plated' indicating pre-production versus a production neck plate. Production serialized neck plates are considered to be San Dimas models which have a Charvel logo, serial number, and a PO Box San Dimas notation on the neck plate. These Serialized Plated Charvels came after Pre-Pros. Late '81 and '82 saw the early serialized guitars with 21-fret necks; these are more valuable. During '82 the 22-fret neck was introduced. The so-called Soft Strat-, Tele-, Flying V-, and Explorer-style headstocks are associated with the early San Dimas Charvel models. In late '82 the pointy headstock, called the Jackson style, was introduced. In '82 the Superstrat style with a neck plate was introduced. Superstrats with a Kahler tailpiece have a lower value than the Pre-Pro models (with Fender-style trem tailpiece).

Collectors of vintage Charvels look for the vintage Charvel 3-on-a-side logo. This is a defining feature and a cutoff point for valuations. Bogus builders are replicating early Charvels and attempting to sell them as originals so fakes can be a problem for Charvel collectors, so buyer beware.

Other electric guitar manufacturing info:
1986-1989 Japanese-made Models 1 through 8
1989-1991 Japanese-made 550 XL, 650 XL/Custom, 750 XL (XL=neck-thru)
1989-1992 Japanese-made Models 275, 375, 475, 575
1990-1991 Korean-made Charvette models
1992-1994 Korean-made Models 325, 425

Early Charvel serial numbers (provided by former Jackson/Charvel associate Tim Wilson):
The first 500 to 750 guitars had no serial number, just marked "Made In U.S.A." on their neckplates. Five digit serial numbers were then used until November '81 when 4-digit number adopted, starting with #1001.
1981: 1001-1095
1982: 1096-1724
1983: 1725-2938
1984: 2939-4261
1985: 4262-5303
1986: 5304-5491

Pre-Pro

November 1980-1981. Pre-Pros came in different configurations of body styles, pickups, and finishes. There are five basic Pre-Pro formats: the Standard Body, the Bound Body, the Graphic Body, the Flamed Top, and the Matching Headstock. It is possible to have a combination, such as a Bound Body and Matching Headstock. Line items are based on body style and can feature any one of four neck/headstock-styles used: the so-called Tele-headstock, Strat-headstock, Flying V headstock, and Explorer headstock. Finishes included white, black, red, metallic Lake Placid Blue,

MODEL YEAR	FEATURES	EXC. COND. LOW	HIGH

and special graphics. All original parts adds considerable value and it is often difficult to determine what is original on these models, so expertise is required. An original Fender brass trem tailpiece, for example, adds considerable value. The Pre-Pro models were prone to modification such as added Kahler and Floyd Rose trems. Price ranges are wide because this is a relatively new market without mature pricing.

1980-1981	Bound body	$2,700	$3,500
1980-1981	Flamed top, stained body	$3,500	$4,500
1980-1981	Graphic body	$3,000	$4,000
1980-1981	Matching headstock & body	$3,800	$5,000
1980-1981	Standard body	$2,300	$3,000

275 Deluxe Dinky

1989-1991. Made in Japan, offset double-cut solidbody, 1 single-coil and 1 humbucker in '89, 2 humbuckers after, tremolo.

1989-1991 $325 $425

325SL

1992-1994. Dot inlays.

1992-1994 $375 $500

325SLX

1992-1994. Surfcaster-like thinline acoustic/electric, dual cutaways, f-hole, on-board chorus, shark inlays, made in Korea.

1992-1994 $375 $500

375 Deluxe

1989-1991. Maple or rosewood 'board, dot inlays, single-single-humbucker.

1989-1991 $575 $750

475 Deluxe/Special

1989-1991. Introduced as Special, changed to Deluxe in '90, bound rosewood board, shark tooth inlays, 2 oval stacked humbuckers and 1 bridge humbucker. Was also offered as Deluxe Exotic with figured top and back.

1989-1991 $575 $750

525

1989-1994. Acoustic-electric, single-cut.

1989-1994 $325 $425

550XL

1987-1989. Neck-thru (XL), dot markers, 1 single-coil and 1 bridge humbucker.

1987-1989 $675 $875

625-C12

1993-2000. Acoustic-electric cutaway 12-string, spruce top.

1993-2000 $325 $425

625F/625ACEL

1993-1995. Acoustic-electric cutaway, figured maple top.

1993-1995 $365 $475

650XL/Custom

1989-1990. Introduced as neck-thru XL and discontinued as Custom, shark fin markers, 2 stacked oval humbuckers and 1 bridge humbucker, custom version of 550XL.

1989-1990 $700 $900

750XL Soloist

1989-1990. Shark fin markers, cutaway body, 2 humbuckers, large Charvel logo.

1989-1990 $750 $1,000

Avenger

1990-1991. Randy Rhoads-style batwing-shaped solidbody, 1 humbucker, 1 single-coil, tremolo, made in Japan.

1990-1991 $400 $525

Charvette

1989-1991. Charvette Series made in Korea, superstrat-style, model number series 100 through 300.

1990-1991 $300 $400

CX Series

1991-1994. Imported solidbodies, body-mounted or pickguard mounted pickups, standard or deluxe tremolo.

1991-1994 $200 $260

EVH Art Series

2004-2007. Offset double-cut solidbody, 1 humbucker, striped finish.

2004-2007	Black/white	$1,400	$4,200
2004-2007	White/black on red	$1,600	$4,400
2004-2007	Yellow/black	$1,400	$4,200

Fusion Deluxe

1989-1991. Double-cut solidbody, tremolo, 1 humbucker and 1 single-coil, made in Japan.

1989-1991 $675 $875

Fusion Standard/AS FX 1

1993-1996. Double-cut solidbody, tremolo, 1 regular and 2 mini humbuckers, made in Japan, also named AS FX1.

1993-1996 $650 $850

Model 1/1A/1C

1986-1988. Offset double-cut solidbody, bolt-on maple neck, dot inlays, 1 humbucker, tremolo, made in Japan. Model 1A has 3 single-coils. Model 1C has 1 humbucker and 2 single-coils.

1986-1988 $625 $825

Model 2

1986-1988. As Model 1, but with rosewood 'board.

1986-1988 $625 $825

Model 3/3A/3DR/3L

1986-1989. As Model 2, but with 1 humbucker, 2 single coils. Model 3A has 2 humbuckers. Model 3DR has 1 humbucker and 1 single-coil.

1986-1989 $625 $825

Model 4/4A

1986-1988. As Model 2, but with 1 regular humbucker and 2 stacked humbuckers (no pickguard), active electronics, dots in '86, shark-fin inlays after. Model 4A has 2 regular humbuckers and dot markers.

1986-1988 $775 $1,000

Model 5/5A

1986-1988. As Model 4A, but neck-thru, with JE1000TG active elctronics. Model 5A is single humbucker and single knob version, limited production, made in Japan.

1986-1988 $775 $1,000

Model 6

1986-1988. As HSS Model 4, but with shark's tooth inlays, standard or various custom finishes.

1986-1988 $875 $1,150

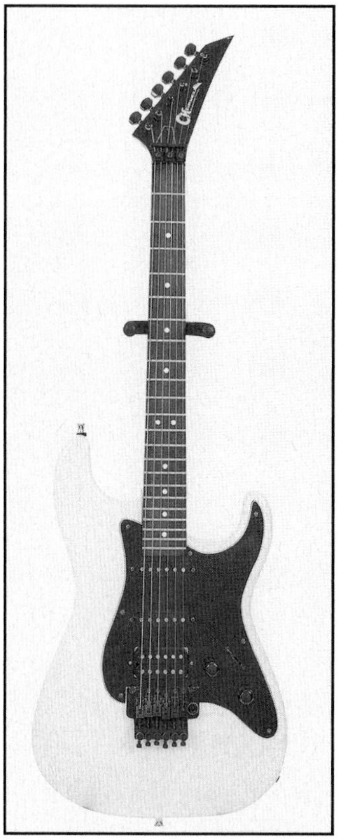

1986 Charvel Model 3

Imaged by Heritage Auctions, HA.com

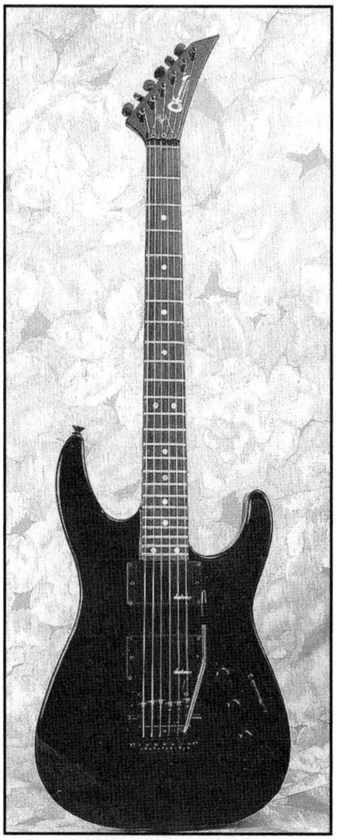

Charvel Model 5

Chris George

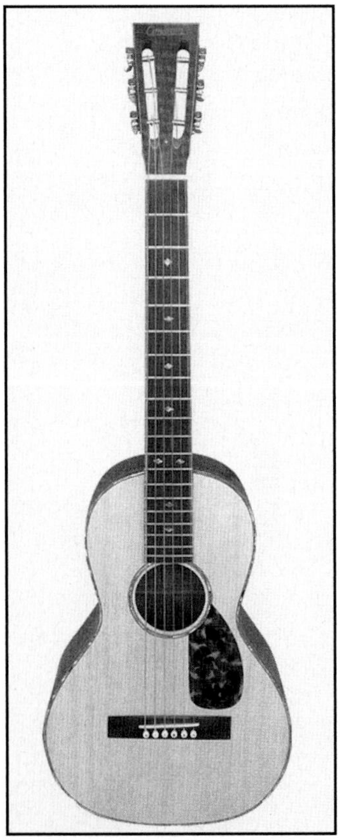

Cimarron Model P

MODEL YEAR	FEATURES	EXC. COND. LOW	HIGH

Model 7

1988-1989. Single-cut solidbody, bound top, reversed headstock, 2 single-coils, made in Japan.

1988-1989		$875	$1,150

Model 88 LTD

1988. Double-cut solidbody, 1 slanted humbucker, shark fin inlay, 1000 built, made in Japan.

1988		$875	$1,150

Predator

1989-1991. Offset double-cut, bridge humbucker, single-coil neck, bolt-on.

1989-1991		$475	$625

San Dimas Serialized Plated

1981-1986, 1995-1997. U.S.-made with San Dimas neck plate, bolt neck, rounded headstock early production, pointy headstock later, reissued in mid-'90s.

1981-1982	Soft headstock	$2,300	$3,000
1982-1986	Pointy headstock	$1,500	$2,000
1995-1997	Soft headstock	$650	$850

San Dimas LTD 25th Anniversary

2006. About 100 made, 25th Anniversary logo on neck plate with production number, highly figured top, high-end appointments.

2006		$1,200	$1,575

San Dimas Reissue (FMIC)

2004-present. USA Select series, alder body, bolt neck.

2004-2011	Custom Shop	$1,000	$1,300
2004-2020	Factory model	$725	$950

So-Cal Series

2008-2012. Offset double-cut solidbody.

2008-2012	Various options	$500	$1,025

ST Custom

1990-1991. Offset double-cut ash solidbody, 2 single-coils and 1 humbucker, rosewood 'board, tremolo, made in Japan.

1990-1991		$300	$400

ST Deluxe

1990-1991. Same as ST Custom but with maple 'board.

1990-1991		$300	$400

Standard

2002-2003. Typical offset double-cut Charvel body, 2 Seymour Duncan humbucker pickups, various opaque colors.

2002-2003		$295	$390

Star

1980-1981. The Star is considered by early-Charvel collectors to be Charvel's only original design with its unique four-point body.

1980-1981		$2,000	$2,600

Surfcaster

1991-1996. Offset double-cut, f-hole, various pickup options, bound body, tremolo, made in Japan.

1991-1996	1 single, 1 hum	$1,050	$1,350
1991-1996	2 singles, hardtail	$1,050	$1,350
1991-1996	2 singles, vibrato	$1,125	$1,475

Surfcaster 12

1991-1996. Made in Japan, 12-string version of Surfcaster, no tremolo.

1991-1996		$1,100	$1,425

Surfcaster Double Neck

1992. Very limited production, 6/12 double neck, Charvel logo on both necks, black.

1992		$1,800	$2,350

Surfcaster HT (Model SC1)

1996-2000. Made in Japan. Hard Tail (HT) non-tremolo version of Surfcaster, has single-coil and bridge humbucker.

1996-2000		$1,050	$1,350

Chiquita

1979-present. Intermediate grade, production guitars made by Erlewine Guitars in Austin, Texas (see that listing). There was also a mini amp available.

Travel Guitar

1979-present. Developed by Mark Erlewine and ZZ Top's Billy Gibbons, 27" overall length solidbody, 1 or 2 pickups, various colors.

1979-2020		$225	$475

Chris George

1966-present. Professional and premium grade, custom, archtop, acoustic, electric and resonator guitars built by luthier Chris George in Tattershall Lincolnshire, U.K.

Christopher Carrington

1988-present. Production/custom, premium grade, classical and flamenco acoustic guitars built by luthier Chris Carrington in Rockwall, Texas.

Chrysalis Guitars

1998-2015. Luthier Tim White built his premium grade, production/custom Chrysalis Guitar System, which included interchangeable components that can be quickly assembled into a full-size electric/acoustic guitar, in New Boston, New Hampshire. White introduced his new brand, Ridgewing, at January 2016 NAMM.

Cimar/Cimar by Ibanez

Early-1980s. Private brand of Hoshino Musical Instruments, Nagoya, Japan, who also branded Ibanez. Headstock with script Cimar logo or Cimar by Ibanez, copy models and Ibanez near-original models such as the star body.

Cimar

1982	Classical	$55	$75
1982	Double-cut solidbody	$165	$225
1982	Star body style	$165	$225

Cimarron

1978-present. Luthiers John Walsh and Clayton Walsh build their professional grade, production/custom, flat-top acoustic guitars in Ridgway, Colorado. Between '94 and '98 they also produced electric guitars.

Cipher

1960s. Solidbody electric guitars and basses imported from Japan by Inter-Mark. Generally strange-shaped bodies.

MODEL YEAR	FEATURES	EXC. COND. LOW	HIGH

Electric Solidbody

1960s. For any student-grade import, a guitar with any missing part, such as a missing control knob or trem arm, is worth much less.

1960s		$150	$250

Citron

1995-present. Luthier Harvey Citron builds his professional and premium grade, production/custom solidbody guitars and basses in Woodstock, New York. He also builds basses. In '75, Citron and Joe Veillette founded Veillette-Citron, which was known for handcrafted, neck-thru guitars and basses. That company closed in '83.

Clark

1985-present. Custom, professional grade, solidbody electric guitars and basses, built by luthier Ed Clark, first in Amityville, New York ('85-'90), then Medford ('91-'99) and presently Lake Ronkonkoma.

Clifford

Clifford was a brand manufactured by Kansas City, Missouri instrument wholesalers J.W. Jenkins & Sons. First introduced in 1895, the brand also offered mandolins.

Clovis

Mid-1960s. Private brand guitars, most likely made by Kay.

Electric Solidbody

Mid-1960s. Kay slab solidbody, 2 pickups.

1965		$285	$385

CMG Guitars

2012-present. Owner Chris Mitchell imports intermediate grade, acoustic and acoustic-electric guitars from China. He also offers professional grade, production/custom, electric guitars built by luthiers Russell Jones and James Horel in Statesboro, Georgia.

Cole

1890-1919. W.A. Cole, after leaving Fairbanks & Cole, started his own line in 1890. He died in 1909 but the company continued until 1919. He also made mandolins and banjos.

Parlor

1897. Small size, Brazilian rosewood sides and back, spruce top, ebony 'board, slotted headstock, dot markers.

1897		$675	$900

Coleman Guitars

1976-1983. Custom made presentation grade instruments made in Homosassa, Florida, by luthier Harry Coleman. No headstock logo, Coleman logo on inside center strip.

Collings

1986-present. Professional, premium, and presentation grade, production/custom, flat-top, archtop and electric guitars built in Austin, Texas. They also build mandolins and ukuleles. Bill Collings started with guitar repair and began custom building guitars around '73. In '80, he relocated his shop from Houston to Austin and started Collings Guitars in '86. In '06 they moved to a new plant in southwest Austin.

01

2005-present. Mother-of-pearl inlays, sitka spruce, mahogany neck, back & sides, ebony 'board and bridge, high gloss lacquer finish.

2005-2020		$2,400	$3,100

01A

2010-2017. As 0-1 with Adirondack spruce top.

2010-2017		$3,000	$3,900

01G

As 0-1 with German spruce top.

2009		$2,900	$3,850

01SB

Sitka spruce, mahogany.

2006-2015		$2,800	$3,700

02G

German spruce, sunburst.

1996		$3,000	$4,000

02H

Parlor, 12 frets.

2008		$2,500	$3,200

02SB

Parlor, 12 frets, 12-string.

2016		$3,000	$4,000

001G

German spruce.

2009		$2,900	$3,850

001MH

All mahogany body.

2010		$2,800	$3,700

002H

1999-present. Indian rosewood.

1999-2020		$2,500	$3,200

0041

2001. Premium Brazilian rosewood back and sides, Adirondack spruce top, abalone top purfling.

2001		$6,200	$8,000

0001 ICC

0001 with Indian rosewood back and sides.

2000s		$2,400	$3,100

0001 Series

1990s-present. 12-fret 000 size, Sitka spruce top (standard) or other top wood options, including mahogany, Adirondack, Honduran mahogany, etc.

1990s-2020	0001 Sitka	$2,400	$3,100
1990s-2020	0001A Adirondack	$3,000	$3,900
2006-2020	0001Mh Mahogany	$2,800	$3,700

0002H

1994-present. 15" 000-size, 12-fret, Indian rosewood back and sides, spruce top, slotted headstock. AAA Koa back and sides in '96.

1994-1995	Indian rosewood	$2,500	$3,200
1996	AAA Koa	$3,300	$4,100
2007-2020	Indian rosewood	$2,500	$3,200

Citron CF1

Collings 000-1

Collings AT-17

Collings CL Deluxe

MODEL YEAR	FEATURES	EXC. COND. LOW	HIGH

0002HAC

2009-present. With cutaway and herringbone trim.

2009-2020		$2,800	$3,700

00041

1999. Indian rosewood sides and back, Sitka spruce top, slotted headstock.

1999		$3,500	$4,600

290 Series

2004-present. Solid Honduran mahogany body, East Indian rosewood 'board, 2 P-90 style pickups, '50s style wiring, high gloss lacquer finish.

2004-2020	Deluxe	$1,650	$2,200

360 Baritone

2020-present. Solid ash body, doghair finish.

2020		$2,500	$3,200

360 LT

2015-present. Solidbody electric, level top (LT), mahogany, ash or alder body, rosewood 'board, high gloss nitro finish.

2015-2020		$2,450	$3,200

AT 16

2006-present. 16" archtop, limited numbers built, fully carved premium figured maple body and neck, carved solid spruce top, f-holes, high-end appointments, high gloss nitro finish.

2006-2020		$11,500	$15,000

AT 17

2008-present. 17" single-cut archtop, limited numbers built, S-holes, Adirondack or European spruce top, premium flamed maple back and sides, and premium appointments, sunburst or blonde. Options include scale length, pickup and bindings.

2008-2020		$10,500	$14,000

Baby Series

1997-present. Various 3/4 size models, Englemann (E) or German (G) spruce top, rosewood back and sides, Ivoroid with herringbone trim, tortoise 'guard, gloss nitro lacquer finish.

1997-2020	Various models	$2,400	$3,500

C10

1986-present. 000-size, mahogany back and sides, spruce top, sunburst or natural.

1986-2020		$2,400	$3,200

C10 Deluxe

1986-present. C10 with Indian rosewood back and sides (mahogany, flamed maple or koa optional), sunburst or natural.

1986-2020	Indian rosewood	$2,900	$3,800
1994-2000s	Flamed maple	$2,900	$3,800
1994-2000s	Koa	$2,900	$3,800
1994-2000s	Varnish	$2,900	$3,800
1994-2020	Mahogany	$2,900	$3,800

C100

1986-1994, 2019-present. Quadruple 0-size, mahogany back and sides, spruce top, natural, replaced by CJ Jumbo. Reintroduced '19 with Honduran mahogany back, sides and neck.

1986-1994		$2,900	$3,800
2019-2020		$2,900	$3,800

C100 Deluxe

1986-1994, 2019-present. C-100 with rosewood back and sides. Reintroduced in '19 with East Indian rosewood and Honduran mahogany.

1986-1994		$2,900	$3,800

CJ

1995-present. Quadruple 0-size, Sitka spruce top (standard), Indian rosewood back and sides, natural. Various other wood options available.

1995-2020	Sitka, Indian	$2,600	$3,400

CJ Koa ASB

2007. Adirondack spruce top, scalloped bracing ASB, flamed koa sides and back.

2007		$3,000	$4,000

CJ-35

2014-present. Sitka spruce top (standard), Honduran mahogany back, sides and neck, tigerstripe 'guard. Various other wood options available.

2014-2020	Sitka, mahogany	$2,650	$3,525

CJMh

2020-present. Sitka spruce top (standard), Honduran mahogany back, sides and neck, sunburst. Various other wood options available.

2020	Sitka, mahogany	$2,600	$3,475

CL Series (City Limits)

2004-present. City Limits Jazz series, fully carved flame maple top, solid Honduran mahogany body, East Indian rosewood 'board, high gloss lacquer finish.

2004-2020		$2,900	$3,800

Clarence White

1989-2000. Adirondack top, Brazilian rosewood back and sides (CW-28), or mahogany (CW-18), herringbone trim.

1989-2000	Brazilian CW-28	$6,200	$8,000
1993-2000	Mahogany CW-18	$3,000	$4,000

CW Indian A

2019-present. Collings Winfield (CW), named after the Walnut Valley Festival in Winfield, Kansas, modified version of standard dreadnought, Adirondack spruce top, East Indian rosewood back and sides, ivoroid binding with herringbone purfling.

2019-2020		$3,100	$4,100

D1 Gruhn

1989. Short run for Gruhn Guitars, Nashville, Gruhn script headstock logo, signed by Bill Collings, choice of Indian rosewood or curly maple back and sides, Engelman spruce top.

1989		$2,500	$3,300

D1 Series

1992-present. Dreadnought, Sitka spruce top (standard), mahogany back and sides. Various other wood options available.

1992-2018	D1A, Adirondack	$3,000	$3,900
1992-2018	D1H, Herringbone	$2,400	$3,100
1992-2020	D1, Standard specs	$2,400	$3,100
2010	D1VN, Vintage neck	$3,400	$4,500
2016-2020	D1AT, Adirondack, Torrefied	$3,700	$4,900

MODEL YEAR	FEATURES	EXC. COND. LOW	HIGH

D2 Series

1986-present. Dreadnought, Sitka spruce top (standard), Indian rosewood back and sides. Various other wood options available.

1986-1995	D2, Standard specs	$2,500	$3,200
1986-2020	D2H, Herringbone	$2,500	$3,200
1994	D2HV, Vintage neck	$2,500	$3,200
1994-2005	D2HB, Brazilian	$6,200	$8,100
2004-2010	D2HAV, Varnish	$3,500	$4,600
2004-2020	D2HA, Adirondack	$3,000	$4,000
2008	D2HGV, German spruce	$4,100	$5,400
2017-2020	D2HT, Traditional	$3,100	$4,100

D3 Series

1990-present. Dreadnought, Sitka spruce top (standard), Brazilian or Indian rosewood back and sides. Various other wood options available.

1990-1999	D3, Brazilian	$6,400	$8,300
2000-2020	D3, Indian	$2,700	$3,500
2004-2020	D3A, Adirondack	$3,800	$5,000

D42

2000s. Brazilian rosewood back and sides, fancy.

2000s		$6,400	$8,300

DS1/DS1A

2004-present. D-size, slope shoulders, 12 fret neck, slotted headstock, mahogany back and sides, A is Adirondack upgrade.

2004-2020		$3,000	$4,000

DS2H/DS2HA

1995-present. D-size, 12-fret, slotted headstock, Sitka spruce top, Indian rosewood back and sides, herringbone purfling. A is Adirondack upgrade.

1995-2020		$3,000	$4,000

DS41

1995-2007. Indian rosewood, fancy, abalone top trim, snowflake markers.

1995-2007		$3,500	$4,600

I-30

2017-present. Maple laminate top, f-holes, mahogany neck, 2 P-90 pickups.

2017-2020		$3,100	$4,100

I-35 Deluxe

2007-present. Premium flamed maple top (standard), mahogany body, gloss lacquer finish. Various other wood options available.

2007-2020	Various options	$3,800	$5,000

OM1 Series

1994-present. Orchestra model, Sitka spruce top (standard), mahogany back and sides, natural. Various other wood options available.

1994-2020	OM1, Standard specs	$2,400	$3,100
1994-2020	OM1A, Adirondack	$3,000	$3,900
2000-2016	OM1, Koa	$2,600	$3,400
2000-2016	OM1MH, Mahogany	$2,500	$3,200
2007-2016	OM1A Cutaway, Adirondack	$3,200	$4,200
2016-2020	OM1T, Traditional	$3,100	$4,100
2018-2020	OM1AT, Adirondack, Traditional	$4,400	$5,800
2020-2021	OM1 JL, Julian Lage	$3,550	$4,600

OM2 Series

1990-present. Sitka spruce top (standard), Indian rosewood back and sides. Various other wood options available.

1990-2020	OM2, Standard specs	$2,700	$3,500
1990-2020	OM2H, Herringbone	$2,900	$3,800
1998	OM2HAV, Varnish	$6,200	$8,000
2001	OM2H SSB, Brazilian	$6,200	$8,000
2003-2018	OM2HA, Adirondack, rosewood	$3,300	$4,300
2008	OM2H GSS, German spruce	$3,000	$4,000
2010	OM2HA Custom, Adirondack, mahogany	$3,300	$4,300
2018-2020	OM2HAT, Traditional, Adirondack	$4,100	$5,300

OM3 Series

1986-present. Sitka spruce top (standard), first Brazilian later Indian rosewood back and sides. Various other wood options available.

1986-1996	OM3HC Cutaway, Indian	$3,000	$4,000
1986-1999	OM3B, Brazilian	$6,300	$8,100
1994-2007	OM3HBA, Adirondack, Brazilian	$6,300	$8,100
2000-2020	OM3, Indian	$2,700	$3,500
2003	OM3, Figured maple	$2,700	$3,500
2004-2020	OM3A, Adirondack	$3,000	$4,000
2008-2020	OM3, Mahogany	$2,700	$3,500

OM41BrzGCut

2007. Brazilian rosewood sides and back, German spruce top, rounded cutaway.

2007		$6,200	$8,000

OM42B

Brazilian rosewood back and sides, Adirondack spruce top, fancy rosette and binding.

2000		$6,800	$9,000

OM42G

German spruce top.

1999		$3,500	$4,600

OMC2H

Adirondack top, Brazilian rosewood back and sides, herringbone trim.

2008		$6,200	$8,000

SJ

1986-present. Spruce top, quilted maple back and sides or Indian rosewood (earlier option), later mahogany.

1986-2020	Various options	$2,850	$3,800

Collings I-35

Collings SJ

Collings SoCo DLX

Conrad Acoustical Slimline 12-String

Imaged by Heritage Auctions, HA.com

MODEL YEAR	FEATURES	EXC. COND. LOW	HIGH

SJ41

1996		$6,200	$8,000

SoCo Deluxe

2007-present. Premium figured maple top over semi-hollow mahogany body, rosewood 'board, f-holes, various finish options.

2007-2020		$3,400	$4,400

Winfield

2004-2006. D-style, Adirondack spruce top, Brazilian or Indian rosewood back and sides, later mahogany.

2004	Indian	$3,000	$4,000
2005-2006	Brazilian	$6,200	$8,100
2006	Mahogany	$3,000	$4,000

Columbia

Late 1800s-early 1900s. The Columbia brand name was used on acoustic guitars by New York's James H. Buckbee Co. until c.1987 and afterwards by Galveston's Thomas Goggan and Brothers.

Comins

1992-present. Premium and presentation grade, custom archtops built by luthier Bill Comins in Willow Grove, Pennsylvania. He also builds mandolins and offers a combo amp built in collaboration with George Alessandro.

Commander

Late 1950s-early 1960s. Archtop acoustic guitars made by Harmony for the Alden catalog company.

Concertone

Ca. 1914-1930s. Concertone was a brand made by Chicago's Slingerland and distributed by Montgomery Ward. The brand was also used on other instruments such as ukuleles.

Conklin

1984-present. Intermediate, professional and premium grade, production/custom, 6-, 7-, 8-, and 12-string solid and hollowbody electrics, by luthier Bill Conklin. He also builds basses. Originally located in Lebanon, Missouri, in '88 the company moved to Springfield, Missouri. Conklin instruments are made in the U.S. and overseas.

Conn Guitars

Ca.1968-ca.1978. Student to mid-quality classical and acoustic guitars, some with bolt-on necks, also some electrics. Imported from Japan by band instrument manufacturer and distributor Conn/Continental Music Company, Elkhart, Indiana.

Acoustic

1968-1978. Various models.

1968-1978		$105	$180

Classical

1968-1978. Various student-level models.

1968-1978		$80	$135

Electric Solidbody

1970s. Various models.

1970-1978		$150	$210

MODEL YEAR	FEATURES	EXC. COND. LOW	HIGH

Connor, Stephan

1995-present. Luthier Stephan Connor builds his premium grade, custom nylon-string guitars in Waltham, Massachusetts.

Conrad Guitars

Ca. 1968-1978. Mid- to better-quality copies of glued-neck Martin and Gibson acoustics and bolt-neck Gibson and Fender solidbodies. They also offered basses, mandolins and banjos. Imported from Japan by David Wexler and Company, Chicago, Illinois.

Acoustic 12-String

1970s. Dreadnought size.

1970s		$130	$170

Acoustical Slimline (40080/40085)

1970s. Rosewood 'board, 2 or 3 DeArmond-style pickups, block markers, sunburst.

1970s		$360	$470

Acoustical Slimline 12-String (40100)

1970s. Rosewood 'board, 2 DeArmond-style pickups, dot markers, sunburst.

1970s		$360	$470

Bison (40035/40030/40065/40005)

1970s. 1 thru 4 pickups available, rosewood 'board with dot markers, six-on-side headstock.

1970s		$360	$470

Bumper (40223)

1970s. Clear Lucite solidbody.

1970s		$440	$575

Classical Student (40150)

1970s		$100	$135

De Luxe Folk Guitar

1970s. Resonator acoustic, mahogany back, sides and neck, Japanese import.

1970s		$200	$275

Master Size (40178)

1972-1977. Electric archtop, 2 pickups.

1972-1977		$335	$435

Resonator Acoustic

1970s. Flat-top with wood, metal resonator and 8 ports, round neck.

1970s		$400	$535

Violin-Shaped 12-String Electric (40176)

1970s. Scroll headstock, 2 pickups, 500/1 control panel, bass side dot markers, sunburst.

1970s		$400	$535

Violin-Shaped Electric (40175)

1970s. Scroll headstock, 2 pickups, 500/1 control panel, bass side dot markers, vibrato, sunburst.

1970s		$400	$535

White Styrene 1280

1970s. Solid maple body covered with white styrene, 2 pickups, tremolo, bass side dot markers, white.

1970s		$360	$475

Contessa

1960s. Acoustic, semi-hollow archtop, solidbody and bass guitars made in Italy by Zero Sette and imported by Hohner. They also made banjos.

Acoustic

MODEL YEAR	FEATURES	EXC. COND. LOW	HIGH
1960s		$80	$200

Electric Solidbody

1967. Various models.

MODEL YEAR	FEATURES	EXC. COND. LOW	HIGH
1960s		$230	$350

Contreras

See listing for Manuel Contreras and Manuel Contreras II.

Coral

1967-1969. In '66 MCA bought Danelectro and in '67 introduced the Coral brand of guitars, basses and amps.

Bellzouki 7021

1967. 12-string electric, modified teardrop shape with body points on treble and bass bouts, 2 pickups.

MODEL YEAR	FEATURES	EXC. COND. LOW	HIGH
1967		$1,125	$1,475

Combo/Vincent Bell Combo

1967-1969. Cutaway acoustic/electric,1 or 2 pickups.

MODEL YEAR	FEATURES	EXC. COND. LOW	HIGH
1967-1969	V1N6, 1 pu	$2,125	$2,775
1967-1969	V2N6, 2 pu	$2,450	$3,175

Firefly

1967-1969. Double-cut, f-holes, 2 pickups, with or without vibrato.

MODEL YEAR	FEATURES	EXC. COND. LOW	HIGH
1967-1969	2N, red	$675	$875
1967-1969	2N, sunburst	$675	$875
1967-1969	2V, vibrato, red	$975	$1,275
1967-1969	2V, vibrato, sunburst	$975	$1,275
1968-1969	F2N12, Electric XII, red	$975	$1,275
1968-1969	F2N12, Electric XII, sunburst	$975	$1,275

Hornet

1967-1969. Solidbody, 2 or 3 pickups, with or without vibrato, sunburst, black or red.

MODEL YEAR	FEATURES	EXC. COND. LOW	HIGH
1967-1969	2N, 2 pu, black or red	$950	$1,250
1967-1969	2N, 2 pu, sunburst	$825	$1,075
1967-1969	2V, 2 pu, vibrato, black or red	$1,050	$1,400
1967-1969	2V, 2 pu, vibrato, sunburst	$850	$1,150
1967-1969	3N, 3 pu, black or red	$1,050	$1,400
1967-1969	3N, 3 pu, sunburst	$950	$1,250
1967-1969	3V, 3 pu, vibrato, black or red	$1,125	$1,500
1967-1969	3V, 3 pu, vibrato, sunburst	$950	$1,250

Long Horn

1967-1969. Deep double-cut hollowbody, 2 lipstick tube pickups, 6 or 12-string, sunburst.

MODEL YEAR	FEATURES	EXC. COND. LOW	HIGH
1967-1969	L2N12, Electric XII	$1,150	$1,525
1967-1969	L2N6, 2 pu	$1,050	$1,400

Scorpion

1967-1969. Offset double-cut solidbody, 2 or 3 lipstick tube pickups, 12-string.

MODEL YEAR	FEATURES	EXC. COND. LOW	HIGH
1967-1969	2N12, 2 pu, black or red	$950	$1,275
1967-1969	2N12, 2 pu, sunburst	$825	$1,075
1967-1969	2V12, 2 pu, vibrato, black or red	$950	$1,275
1967-1969	2V12, 2 pu, vibrato, sunburst	$950	$1,275
1967-1969	3N12, 3 pu, black or red	$1,100	$1,475
1967-1969	3N12, 3 pu, sunburst	$950	$1,275
1967-1969	3V12, 3 pu, vibrato, black or red	$1,150	$1,525
1967-1969	3V12, 3 pu, vibrato, sunburst	$950	$1,275

Sitar

1967-1969. Six-string guitar with drone strings and 3 pickups (2 under the 6 strings, 1 under the drones), kind of a USA-shaped body.

MODEL YEAR	FEATURES	EXC. COND. LOW	HIGH
1967-1969	3S18, 18-string	$1,900	$2,500
1967-1969	3S19, 19-string	$2,000	$2,700
1967-1969	3S9, 9-string	$1,700	$2,250

Teardrop

1967-1969. Teardrop shaped hollowbody, 2 lipstick tube pickups.

MODEL YEAR	FEATURES	EXC. COND. LOW	HIGH
1968	T2N6	$1,625	$2,100

Córdoba

Line of classical guitars handmade in Portugal and imported by Guitar Salon International. By '13, U.S. production was added.

Classical

MODEL YEAR	FEATURES	EXC. COND. LOW	HIGH
2000s	Higher-end	$500	$1,800
2000s	Mid-level	$300	$500
2000s	Student-level	$175	$300

Cordova

1960s. Classical nylon string guitars imported by David Wexler of Chicago.

Grand Concert Model WC-026

1960s. Highest model offered by Cordova, 1-piece rosewood back, laminated rosewood sides, spruce top, natural.

MODEL YEAR	FEATURES	EXC. COND. LOW	HIGH
1960s		$225	$300

Corey James Custom Guitars

2005-present. Luthier Corey James Moilanen builds his professional and premium grade, production/custom solidbody guitars and basses in Howell, Michigan.

Coriani, Paolo

1984-present. Production/custom nylon-string guitars and hurdy-gurdys built by luthier Paolo Coriani in Modeila, Italy.

Cort

1973-present. North Brook, Illinois-based Cort offers budget, intermediate and professional grade, production/custom, acoustic and solidbody, semi-hollow, hollow body electric guitars and basses built in Korea.

Cort was the second significant Korean private-label (Hondo brand was the first) to come out of

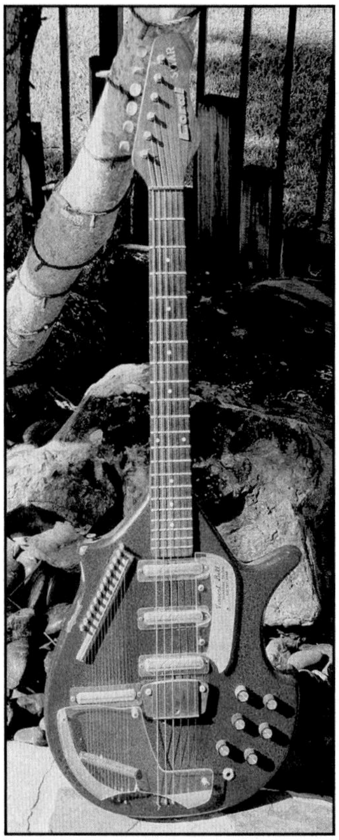

1968 Coral Sitar

Craig Brody

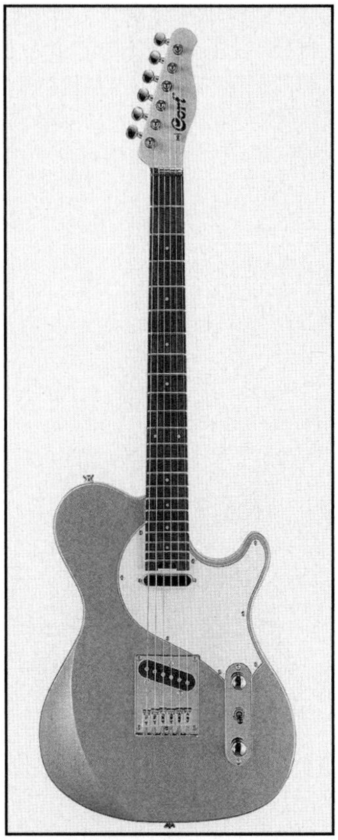

Cort Classic TC

CP Thornton Improv

CSR Serenata

MODEL YEAR	FEATURES	EXC. COND. LOW	HIGH

Korea. Jack Westheimer entered into an agreement with Korea's Cort to do Cort-brand, private-label, and Epiphone-brand guitars.

CP Thornton Guitars

1985-present. Luthier Chuck Thornton builds professional and premium grade, production/custom, semi-hollow and solidbody electric guitars in Sumner, Maine. Up to '96 he also built basses.

Crafter

1986-present. Crafter offers budget and intermediate grade, production, classical, acoustic, acoustic/electric, and electric guitars, basses and mandolins made in Korea. They also offer the Cruzer and Ashland brands of instruments. From '72 to '86 they made Sungeum classical guitars.

Cranium

Introduced 1996, professional grade, production/custom, hollow, semi-hollow, and solidbody electrics built by luthier Wayne O'Connor in Peterborough, Ontario.

Crescent Moon

Professional grade, production/custom, solidbody guitars and basses built by luthier Craig Muller in Baltimore, Maryland, starting 1999.

Creston

2004-present. Professional grade, custom, solidbody electric guitars and basses built by luthier Creston Lea in Burlington, Vermont.

Crestwood

1970s. Copies of the popular classical guitars, flat-tops, electric solidbodies and basses of the era, imported by La Playa Distributing Company of Detroit.

Acoustic 12-String

1970s		$175	$225

Electric

1970s. Various models include near copies of the 335 (Crestwood model 2043, 2045 and 2047), Les Paul Custom (2020), Strat (2073), Jazzmaster (2078), Tele (2082), and the SG Custom (2084).

1970s		$225	$475

Crimson Guitars

2005-present. Luthiers Benjamin Crowe and Aki Atrill build professional and premium grade, custom, solidbody guitars and basses in Somerset, U.K.

Cromwell

1935-1939. Budget model brand built by Gibson and distributed by mail-order businesses like Grossman, Continental, Richter & Phillips, and Gretsch & Brenner.

MODEL YEAR	FEATURES	EXC. COND. LOW	HIGH

Acoustic Archtop

1935-1939. Archtop acoustic, f-holes, pressed mahogany back and sides, carved and bound top, bound back, 'guard and 'board, no truss rod.

1935-1939	Various models	$650	$1,075
1935-1939	With '30s era pickup	$1,100	$1,400

Acoustic Flat-Top

1935-1939	G-2 (L-00)	$1,500	$1,900

GT-2 Tenor

1935-1939	1474" flat-top	$650	$1,075

GT-4 Tenor

1935-1939	16" archtop	$650	$1,075

Cromwell (Guild)

1963-1964. Guild imported these 2- or 3-pickup offset double cut solidbodies from Hagstrom. These were basically part of Hagstrom's Kent line with laminated bodies and birch necks. About 500 were imported into the U.S.

Solidbody

1963-1964		$900	$1,125

Crook Custom Guitars

1997-present. Professional grade, custom, solidbody electric guitars and basses built in Moundsville, West Virginia by luthier Bill Crook.

Crossley

2005-present. Professional grade, production/custom, solidbody and chambered electric guitars built in Melbourne, Victoria, Australia by luthier Peter Crossley.

Crown

1960s. Violin-shaped hollowbody electrics, solidbody electric guitars and basses, possibly others. Imported from Japan.

Acoustic Flat-Top

1960s. 6-string and 12-string.

1960s		$110	$150

Electric Archtop

1960s. Double pointed cutaways, 2 humbucking pickups, laminated top, full-depth body.

1960s		$350	$450

Electric Solidbody/Semi-Hollow

1960s. Student-level Japanese import.

1960s	Copy models	$250	$350
1960s	Standard models	$150	$200
1960s	Violin-shaped body	$250	$350

Crucianelli

Early 1960s. Italian guitars imported into the U.S. by Bennett Brothers of New York and Chicago around '63 to '64. Accordion builder Crucianelli also made Imperial, Elite, PANaramic, and Elli-Sound brand guitars.

Cruzer

Intermediate grade, production, solidbody electric guitars, basses, amps and effects made by Korea's Crafter Guitars.

MODEL YEAR	FEATURES	EXC. COND. LOW	HIGH

CSR

1996-present. Father and daughter luthiers Roger and Courtney Kitchens build their premium grade, production/custom, archtop guitars and basses in Byron, Georgia.

Cumpiano

1974-present. Professional and premium grade, custom steel-string and nylon-string guitars, and acoustic basses built by luthier William Cumpiano in Northampton, Massachusetts.

Curbow String Instruments

1994-2007. Premium grade, production/custom, solidbody guitars and basses built by luthier Doug Somervell in Morganton, Georgia. Founded by Greg Curbow who passed away in '05.

Custom

1980s. Line of solidbody guitars and basses introduced in the early '80s by Charles Lawing and Chris Lovell, owners of Strings & Things in Memphis, Tennessee.

Custom Kraft

Late-1950s-1968. A house brand of St. Louis Music Supply, instruments built by Valco and Kay. They also offered basses and amps.

Electric Solidbody

1950s-1960s. U.S.-made or import, entry-level, 1or 2 pickups.

1950s-60s	Import	$150	$225
1950s-60s	USA, Kay, 2 pickups	$425	$550

Sound Saturator

1960s	12-string	$350	$450

Super Zapp

1960s		$400	$500

Thin Twin Jimmy Reed (style)

Late-1950s-early-1960s. Single cut, 2 pickups, 4 knobs and toggle, dot markers.

1959	US-made	$575	$700

D.J. Hodson

1994-2007. Luthier David J.Hodson built his professional and premium grade, production/custom, acoustic guitars in Loughborough, Leicestershire, U.K. He also built ukes. He passed away in '07.

Daddy Mojo String Instruments Inc.

2005-present. Luthiers Lenny Piroth-Robert and Luca Tripaldi build their intermediate and professional grade, production/custom, solidbody electric, resonator and cigar box guitars in Montreal, Quebec.

Dagmar Custom Guitars

Luthier Pete Swanson builds custom, premium and presentation grade, acoustic and electric archtop guitars in Niagara, Ontario, starting in 2008.

MODEL YEAR	FEATURES	EXC. COND. LOW	HIGH

D'Agostino

1976-early 1990s. Acoustic and electric solidbody guitars and basses imported by PMS Music, founded in New York City by former Maestro executive Pat D'Agostino, his brother Steven D'Agostino, and Mike Confortti. First dreadnought acoustic guitars imported from Japan in '76. First solidbodies manufactured by the EKO custom shop beginning in '77. In '82 solidbody production moved to Japan. Beginning in '84, D'Agostinos were made in Korea. Overall, about 60% of guitars were Japanese, 40% Korean. They also had basses.

Acoustic Flat-Top

1976-1990. Early production in Japan, by mid-'80s, most production in Korea.

1976-1990		$150	$550

Electric Semi-Hollowbody

1981-early 1990s. Early production in Japan, later versions from Korea.

1981-1990		$150	$750

Electric Solidbody

1977-early 1990s. Early models made in Italy, later versions from Japan and Korea.

1981-1990		$150	$750

Daily Guitars

1976-present. Luthier David Daily builds his premium grade, production/custom classical guitars in Sparks, Nevada.

Daion

1978-1984. Mid- to higher-quality copies imported from Japan. Original designs introduced in the '80s. Only acoustics offered at first; in '81 they added acoustic/electric and solid and semi-hollow electrics. They also had basses.

Acoustic

1978-1985. Various flat-top models.

1978-1985	Higher-end	$400	$1,075
1978-1985	Lower-end	$150	$425

Electric

1978-1985. Various solid and semi-hollow body guitars.

1978-1985	Higher-end	$400	$1,075
1978-1985	Lower-end	$150	$425

Daisy Rock

2001-present. Budget and intermediate grade, production, full-scale and 3/4 scale, solidbody, semi-hollow, acoustic, and acoustic/electric guitars and basses. Founded by Tish Ciravolo as a Division of Schecter Guitars, the Daisy line is focused on female customers.

D'Ambrosio

2001-present. Luthier Otto D'Ambrosio builds his premium grade, custom/production, acoustic and electric archtop guitars in Providence, Rhode Island.

1966 Custom Kraft Lexington
Rivington Guitars

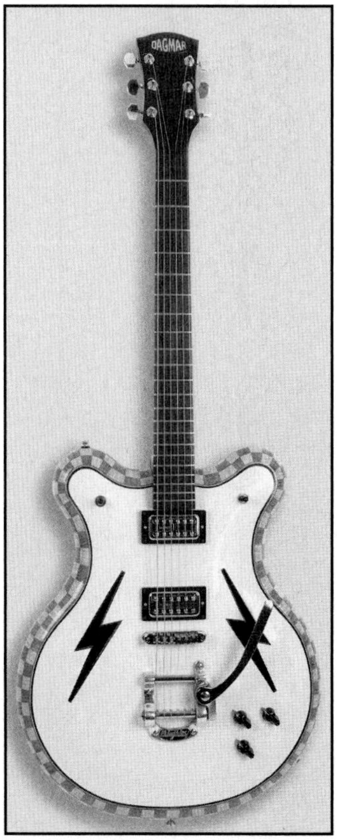

Dagmar Custom

1960s Danelectro Convertible

Tom Pfeifer

1967 Danelectro Dane-B

Rivington Guitars

Dan Armstrong

Dan Armstrong started playing jazz in Cleveland in the late-'50s. He moved to New York and also started doing repairs, eventually opening his own store on 48th Street in '65. By the late-'60s he was designing his Lucite guitars for Ampeg (see Ampeg for those listings). He moved to England in '71, where he developed his line of colored stomp boxes. He returned to the States in '75. Armstrong died in '04.

Wood Body

1973-1975. Sliding pickup, wood body, brown.

1973-1975		$1,450	$1,900

Wood Body AMG 100 (reissue)

Various wood body options, BLD (blond, swamp ash), CH (cherry, mahogany) and BK (black, alder).

2008-2009	BK	$325	$425
2008-2009	BLD	$525	$675
2008-2009	CH	$375	$500

Dan Armstrong Guitars

Introduced 2015, professional grade, production/custom, acrylic solidbody electrics based on the original Dan Armstrong models, built in Everett, Washington.

Dan Kellaway

1976-present. Production/custom, premium grade, classical and steel string guitars built by luthier Dan Kellaway in Singleton NSW, Australia. He also builds mandolins and lutes.

Danelectro

1946-1969, 1996-present. Founded in Red Bank, New Jersey, by Nathan I. (Nate or Nat) Daniel, an electronics enthusiast with amplifier experience. In 1933, Daniel built amps for Thor's Bargain Basement in New York. In '34 he was recruited by Epiphone's Herb Sunshine to build earliest Electar amps and pickup-making equipment. From '35 to '42, he operated Daniel Electric Laboratories in Manhattan, supplying Epiphone. He started Danelectro in '46 and made his first amps for Montgomery Ward in '47. Over the years, Danelectro made amplifiers, solidbody, semi-hollow and hollowbody electric guitars and basses, electric sitar, and the Bellzouki under the Danelectro, Silvertone, and Coral brands. In '48, began supplying Silvertone amps for Sears (various coverings), with his own brand (brown leatherette) distributed by Targ and Dinner as Danelectro and S.S. Maxwell. He developed an electronic vibrato in '48 on his Vibravox series amps. In '50 he developed a microphone with volume and tone controls and outboard Echo Box reverb unit. In the fall of '54, Danelectro replaced Harmony as provider of Silvertone solidbody guitars for Sears. Also in '54, the first Danelectro brand guitars appeared with tweed covering, bell headstock, and pickups under the pickguard. The Coke bottle headstock debuts as Silvertone Lightning Bolt in '54, and was used on Danelectros for '56 to '66. The company moved to Red Bank, New Jersey in '57, and in '58 relocated

MODEL YEAR | FEATURES | EXC. COND. LOW | HIGH

to Neptune, New Jersey. In '59, Harmony and Kay guitars replace all but 3 Danelectros in Sears catalog. In '66, MCA buys the company (Daniel remains with company), but by mid-'69, MCA halts production and closes the doors. Some leftover stock is sold to Dan Armstrong, who had a shop in New York at the time. Armstrong assembled several hundred Danelectro guitars as Dan Armstrong Modified with his own pickup design.

Rights to name acquired by Anthony Marc in late-'80s, who assembled a number of thinline hollowbody guitars, many with Longhorn shape, using Japanese-made bodies and original Danelectro necks and hardware. In '96, the Evets Corporation, of San Clemente, California, introduced a line of effects bearing the Danelectro brand. Amps and guitars, many of which were reissues of the earlier instruments, soon followed. In early 2003, Evets discontinued offering guitar and amps, but revived the guitar and bass line in '05.

MCA-Danelectro made guitars were called the Dane Series. Dane A model numbers start with an A (e.g. A2V), Dane B models start with a B (e.g. B3V), Dane C (e.g. C2N), and Dane D (e.g. D2N). The least expensive series was the A, going up to the most expensive D. All Dane Series instruments came with 1, 2 or 3 pickups and with hand vibrato options. The Dane Series were made from '67 to '69. MCA did carry over the Convertible, Guitarlin 4123, Long Horn Bass-4 and Bass-6 and Doubleneck 3923. MCA also offered the Bellzouki Double Pickup 7021. Each Dane Series includes an electric 12-string. Danelectro also built the Coral brand instruments (see Coral).

Baritone 6-String Reissue

1999-2003, 2008-present. Danelectro has offered several models with 6-string baritone tuning, often with various reissue-year designations, single- or double-cut, 2 or 3 pickups.

1999-2020	Various models	$375	$475

Bellzouki

1963-1969. 12-string electric. Teardrop-shaped body, 1 pickup, sunburst (7010) for '63-'66. Vincent Bell model (7020) with modified teardrop shape with 2 body points on both treble and bass bouts and 2 pickups for '63-'66. Same body as Coral Electric Sitar for '67-'69.

1963-1969	1 pu, teardrop body	$750	$975
1963-1969	2 pu, pointy body	$1,025	$1,325
1967-1969	2 pu, sitar body	$1,600	$2,100

Companion

1959-1960. Hollowbody double-cut, 2 pickups, concentric TV knobs.

1959-1960		$1,325	$1,725

Convertible

1959-1969. Acoustic/electric, double-cut, guitar was sold with or without the removable single pickup.

1959-1969	Acoustic, no pu, natural	$300	$400
1959-1969	Pickup installed, natural	$475	$625
1967-1969	Red, white, blue	$750	$975

Convertible Reissue

1999, 2000-2003. The Convertible Pro was offered '00-'03 with upgraded Gotoh tuners and metalflake and pearl finishes.

MODEL YEAR	FEATURES	EXC. COND. LOW	HIGH
1999-2003	Blond or green	$240	$315

Dane A Series

1967-1969. 1or 2 pickups, with or without vibrato (V), solid wood slab body, hard lacquer finish with 4 color options, 12-string also offered.

MODEL YEAR	FEATURES	EXC. COND. LOW	HIGH
1967-1969	1N12, Electric XII	$1,125	$1,475
1967-1969	2N12, Electric XII	$1,250	$1,625
1967-1969	N, 6-string, 1 pu	$825	$1,075
1967-1969	N, 6-string, 2 pu	$975	$1,275
1967-1969	V, 6-string, 1 pu	$975	$1,275
1967-1969	V, 6-string, 2 pu	$1,050	$1,375

Dane B Series

1967-1969. 2 or 3 pickups, with or without vibrato (V), semi-solid Durabody, 6 or 12 strings.

MODEL YEAR	FEATURES	EXC. COND. LOW	HIGH
1967-1969	12-string	$1,025	$1,350
1967-1969	6-string, 2 pu	$825	$1,075
1967-1969	6-string, 3 pu	$950	$1,250

Dane C Series

1967-1969. 2 or 3 pickups, with or without vibrato (V), semi-solid Durabody with 2-tone Gator finish, 6 or 12 strings.

MODEL YEAR	FEATURES	EXC. COND. LOW	HIGH
1967-1969	12-string	$1,475	$1,925
1967-1969	6-string	$1,250	$1,650

Dane D Series

1967-1969. 2 or 3 pickups, with or without vibrato (V), solid wood sculptured thinline body, 'floating adjustable pickguard-fingerguide', master volume with 4 switches, 6 or 12 strings.

MODEL YEAR	FEATURES	EXC. COND. LOW	HIGH
1967-1969	12-string	$1,200	$1,575
1967-1969	6-string, 2 pu	$950	$1,250
1967-1969	6-string, 3 pu	$1,075	$1,425

Danoblaster Series

2000-2003. Offset double-cuts, 3 pickups, built-in effects - distortion on the Hearsay, distortion, chorus, trem and echo on Innuendo. Also in 12-string and baritone.

MODEL YEAR	FEATURES	EXC. COND. LOW	HIGH
2000-2003		$115	$145

DC-3/DDC-3

1999-2003. Shorthorn double-cut, 3 pickups, seal-shaped pickguard, Coke bottle headstock, solid and sparkle finishes.

MODEL YEAR	FEATURES	EXC. COND. LOW	HIGH
1999-2003		$275	$350

DC-12/Electric XII

1999-2003. 12-string version of 59-DC.

MODEL YEAR	FEATURES	EXC. COND. LOW	HIGH
1999-2003		$325	$425

59-DC/'59 Dano (Standard Double Pickup Reissue)

1998-1999, 2007. Shorthorn double-cut, 2 pickups, seal-shaped pickguard, Coke bottle headstock, '07 version called '59 Dano.

MODEL YEAR	FEATURES	EXC. COND. LOW	HIGH
1998-1999		$240	$310

Deluxe Single Pickup

1959-1966. Double-cut, Coke bottle headstock, 1 pickup, 2 knobs.

MODEL YEAR	FEATURES	EXC. COND. LOW	HIGH
1959-1960	Walnut or white	$1,025	$1,350
1961-1966	Walnut, white, honey	$925	$1,200

Deluxe Double Pickup

1959-1966. As Single above, but with 2 pickups, and added master volume on later models.

MODEL YEAR	FEATURES	EXC. COND. LOW	HIGH
1959-1960	Walnut or white	$1,050	$1,400
1961-1966	Walnut, white, honey	$1,025	$1,325

Deluxe Triple Pickup

1959-1966. As Single above, but with 3 pickups, 3 knobs, and added master volume on later models.

MODEL YEAR	FEATURES	EXC. COND. LOW	HIGH
1959-1960	Walnut or white	$1,150	$1,500
1961-1966	Walnut, white, honey	$1,075	$1,400

Doubleneck (3923)

1958-1966. A shorthorn double-cut, bass and 6-string necks, 1 pickup on each neck, Coke bottle headstocks, white sunburst.

MODEL YEAR	FEATURES	EXC. COND. LOW	HIGH
1958-1966		$1,850	$2,450

Doubleneck Reissue

1999-2003. Baritone 6-string and standard 6-string double neck, shorthorn body style, or the 6-12 model with a 6-string and 12-string neck. Price includes $75 for a guitar case, but many sales do not seem to include a guitar case because of unusual body size.

MODEL YEAR	FEATURES	EXC. COND. LOW	HIGH
1999-2003		$460	$600

Electric Sitar

1968-1969. Traditional looking, oval-bodied sitar, no drone strings as on the Coral Sitar of the same period.

MODEL YEAR	FEATURES	EXC. COND. LOW	HIGH
1968-1969		$1,925	$2,500

Guitarlin (4123)

1958-1966. The Longhorn guitar, 2 huge cutaways, 31-fret neck, 2 pickups.

MODEL YEAR	FEATURES	EXC. COND. LOW	HIGH
1958-1960		$1,875	$2,450
1961-1966		$1,750	$2,300

Hand Vibrato Single Pickup (4011)

1958-1966. Short horn double-cut, 1 pickup, batwing headstock, simple design vibrato, black w/ white guard.

MODEL YEAR	FEATURES	EXC. COND. LOW	HIGH
1958-1966		$800	$1,025

Hand Vibrato Double Pickup (4021)

1958-1966. Same as Single Pickup, but with 2 pickups and larger pickguard.

MODEL YEAR	FEATURES	EXC. COND. LOW	HIGH
1958-1966		$900	$1,175

Hawk

1967-1969. Offered with 1 or 2 pickups, vibrato (V models) or non-vibrato (N models), 12-string model also offered.

MODEL YEAR	FEATURES	EXC. COND. LOW	HIGH
1967-1969	1N, 1 pu	$925	$1,200
1967-1969	1N12, Electric XII	$1,150	$1,500
1967-1969	1V, 1 pu	$1,025	$1,325
1967-1969	2N, 2 pu	$1,025	$1,325
1967-1969	2N12, Electric XII	$1,300	$1,700
1967-1969	2V, 2 pu	$1,125	$1,450

Hodad/Hodad 12-String

1999-2003. Unique double-cut with sharp horns, 6 or 12 strings, sparkle finish.

MODEL YEAR	FEATURES	EXC. COND. LOW	HIGH
1999-2003		$300	$400

Model C

1955. Single-cut, 1or 2 pickups, ginger colored vinyl cover.

MODEL YEAR	FEATURES	EXC. COND. LOW	HIGH
1955		$500	$650

1964 Danelectro 3923 Doubleneck
Izzy Miller

1964 Danelectro 4021
Craig Brody

1963 Danelectro Standard Double Pickup
Trey Rabinek

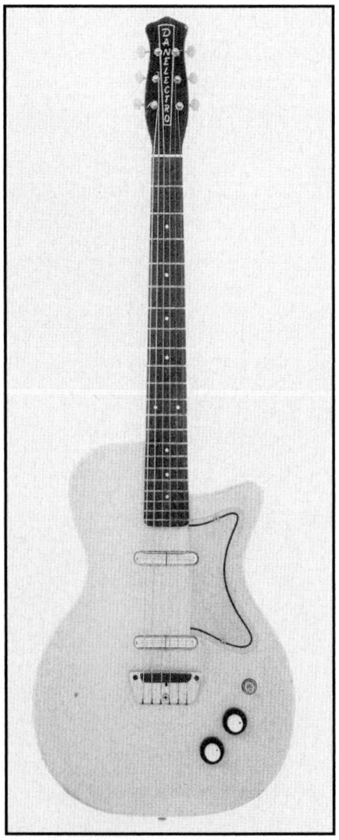

1957 Danelectro U2
Imaged by Heritage Auctions, HA.com

Pro 1

1963-1964. Odd-shaped double-cut electric with squared off corners, 1 pickup.

MODEL YEAR	FEATURES	EXC. COND. LOW	HIGH
1963-1964		$700	$900

Pro Reissue

2007. Based on '60s Pro 1, but with 2 pickups.

MODEL YEAR	FEATURES	EXC. COND. LOW	HIGH
2007		$230	$300

Slimline (SL) Series

1967-1969. Offset waist double-cut, 2 or 3 pickups, with or without vibrato, 6 or 12 string.

MODEL YEAR	FEATURES	EXC. COND. LOW	HIGH
1967-1969	12-string	$1,100	$1,425
1967-1969	6-string, 2 pu	$850	$1,100
1967-1969	6-string, 3 pu	$1,025	$1,325

Standard Single Pickup

1958-1966. Nicknamed the Shorthorn, double-cut, 1 pickup, 2 regular control knobs, kidney-shaped pickguard originally, seal-shaped 'guard by ca. 1960, Coke bottle headstock, in black or bronze.

MODEL YEAR	FEATURES	EXC. COND. LOW	HIGH
1958-1959	Kidney guard	$750	$975
1960-1966	Seal guard	$750	$975

Standard Double Pickup

1958-1966. As Single Pickup above but with 2 pickups and 2 stacked, concentric volume/tone controls, in black, bronze and later blond. The black, seal-shaped pickguard version of this guitar is often referred to as the Jimmy Page model because he used one. Reissued in 1998 as 59-DC.

MODEL YEAR	FEATURES	EXC. COND. LOW	HIGH
1958-1959	Kidney guard, black	$800	$1,050
1960-1966	Bronze	$775	$1,025
1960-1966	Jimmy Page, black	$1,150	$1,500
1961-1966	Blond	$925	$1,200

Standard Triple Pickup

1958. As Single Pickup above but with 3 pickups and 3 stacked, concentric pointer volume/tone controls, in white to bronze sunburst, very rare.

MODEL YEAR	FEATURES	EXC. COND. LOW	HIGH
1958		$1,025	$1,325

Tweed Models

1954-1955. First production models, single-cut, bell-shape headstock, 1 or 2 pickups, tweed vinyl cover.

MODEL YEAR	FEATURES	EXC. COND. LOW	HIGH
1954-1955	1 pu	$2,225	$2,925
1954-1955	2 pu	$2,425	$3,175

U-1

1955-1958. Single-cut, 1 pickup, 2 regular knobs, bell-shape headstock originally, switching to Coke bottle in late '55. The U Series featured Dano's new 'solid center' block construction.

MODEL YEAR	FEATURES	EXC. COND. LOW	HIGH
1955	Enamel, bell hdsk	$1,750	$2,300
1956-1957	Enamel, Coke hdsk	$1,600	$2,075
1956-1957	Ivory, Coke hdsk	$1,650	$2,150
1958	Enamel, Coke hdsk	$1,375	$1,800
1958	Ivory, Coke hdsk	$1,600	$2,100

U-1 '56 Reissue

1998-1999. Reissue of '56 U-1, various colors.

MODEL YEAR	FEATURES	EXC. COND. LOW	HIGH
1998-1999		$195	$250

U-2

1955-1958. As U-1, but with 2 pickups and 2 stacked concentric volume/tone controls.

MODEL YEAR	FEATURES	EXC. COND. LOW	HIGH
1955	Enamel, bell hdsk	$1,900	$2,475
1956-1957	Enamel, Coke hdsk	$1,725	$2,250
1956-1957	Ivory, Coke hdsk	$1,875	$2,450
1958	Enamel, Coke hdsk	$1,600	$2,100
1958	Ivory, Coke hdsk	$1,725	$2,250

U-2 '56 Reissue

1998-2003. Reissue of '56 U-2, various colors.

MODEL YEAR	FEATURES	EXC. COND. LOW	HIGH
1998-2003		$200	$260

U-3

1955-1958. As U-2, but with 3 pickups and 3 stacked concentric volume/tone controls.

MODEL YEAR	FEATURES	EXC. COND. LOW	HIGH
1958	Enamel, Coke hdsk	$1,750	$2,300

U-3 '56 Reissue

1999-2003. Reissue of '56 U-3, various colors.

MODEL YEAR	FEATURES	EXC. COND. LOW	HIGH
1999-2003		$250	$350

D'Angelico

John D'Angelico built his own line of archtop guitars, mandolins and violins from 1932 until his death in 1964. His instruments are some of the most sought-after by collectors. The binding on some D'Angelico guitars can become deteriorated and requires replacing. Replaced binding, even if excellent work, reduces the values shown by 20% or more.

D'Angelico (L-5 Snakehead)

1932-1935. D'Angelico's L-5-style with snakehead headstock, his first model, sunburst.

MODEL YEAR	FEATURES	EXC. COND. LOW	HIGH
1932-1935		$9,500	$12,200

Excel/Exel (Cutaway)

1947-1964. Cutaway, 17" width, 1- and 3-ply bound f-hole.

MODEL YEAR	FEATURES	EXC. COND. LOW	HIGH
1947-1949	Natural, original binding	$31,000	$40,000
1947-1949	Sunburst, original binding	$28,000	$36,000
1950-1959	Natural, original binding	$31,000	$40,000
1950-1959	Sunburst, original binding	$28,000	$36,000
1960-1964	Natural	$31,000	$40,000
1960-1964	Sunburst	$28,000	$36,000

Excel/Exel (Non-Cutaway)

1936-1949. Non-cut, 17" width, 1- and 3-ply bound f-hole, natural finishes were typically not offered in the '30s, non-cut Excels were generally not offered after '49 in deference to the Excel cutaway.

MODEL YEAR	FEATURES	EXC. COND. LOW	HIGH
1936-1939	Sunburst, straight f-hole	$15,000	$20,000
1938-1939	Sunburst, standard f-hole	$15,000	$20,000
1940-1949	Natural	$16,000	$21,000
1940-1949	Sunburst	$13,500	$17,500

New Yorker (Non-Cutaway)

1936-1949. Non-cut, 18" width, 5-ply-bound f-hole, New Yorker non-cut orders were overshadowed by the cut model orders starting in '47.

MODEL YEAR	FEATURES	EXC. COND. LOW	HIGH
1936-1939	Sunburst	$21,000	$27,000
1940-1949	Natural	$22,000	$29,000
1940-1949	Sunburst	$20,000	$26,000

MODEL YEAR	FEATURES	EXC. COND. LOW	HIGH

New Yorker Deluxe (Cutaway)

1947-1964. Cutaway, 18" width, 5-ply-bound f-hole, New Yorker non-cut orders were overshadowed by the cut model orders starting in '47.

1947-1949	Natural	$43,000	$56,000
1947-1949	Sunburst	$37,000	$49,000
1950-1959	Natural	$43,000	$56,000
1950-1959	Sunburst	$36,000	$48,000
1960-1964	Natural	$38,000	$50,000
1960-1964	Sunburst	$34,000	$44,000

New Yorker Special

1950-1964. Also called Excel New Yorker or Excel Cutaway New Yorker Cutaway, 17" width, New Yorker styling, not to be confused with D'Angelico Special (A and B style).

1950-1959	Natural	$28,000	$36,000
1950-1959	Sunburst	$25,000	$33,000
1960-1964	Natural	$25,000	$33,000
1960-1964	Sunburst	$22,000	$29,000

Special (Cutaway)

1950-1964. Generally Style A and B-type instruments made for musicians on a budget, plain specs with little ornamentation, not to be confused with New Yorker Special.

1950-1959	Sunburst	$9,500	$12,300
1960-1964	Sunburst	$8,500	$11,000

Special (Non-Cutaway)

1950-1964. Non-cut Special, not to be confused with New Yorker Special.

1950-1959	Sunburst	$5,800	$7,500
1960-1964	Sunburst	$5,000	$6,500

Style A

1936-1945. Archtop, 17" width, unbound f-holes, block 'board inlays, multi-pointed headstock, nickel-plated metal parts.

1936-1939	Sunburst	$10,000	$13,000
1940-1945	Sunburst	$9,000	$11,700

Style A-1

1936-1945. Unbound f-holes, 17" width, arched headstock, nickel-plated metal parts.

1936-1939	Sunburst	$10,000	$13,000
1940-1945	Sunburst	$9,000	$11,700

Style B

1933-1948. Archtop 17" wide, unbound F-holes, block 'board inlays, gold-plated parts.

1936-1939	Sunburst	$11,000	$14,500
1940-1948	Sunburst	$10,400	$13,500

Style B Special

1933-1948. D'Angelico described variations from standard features with a 'Special' designation, Vintage dealers may also describe these instruments as 'Special'.

1936-1939	Sunburst	$11,500	$15,000
1940-1948	Sunburst	$10,900	$14,100

D'Angelico (D'Angelico Guitars of America)

1988-present. Intermediate and professional grade, production/custom, archtop, flat-top, and solidbody guitars made in South Korea and imported by D'Angelico Guitars of America, of Colts Neck, New Jersey. From 1988 to '04, they were premium and presentation grade instruments built in Japan by luthier Hidesato Shino and Vestax. In '12, GTR announced they bought the brand name and are offering premium grade D'Angelicos built in the U.S.

D'Angelico (Lewis)

1994-2011. Luthier Michael Lewis built presentation grade, custom/production, D'Angelico replica guitars in Grass Valley, California, under an agreement with the GHS String Company, which owned the name in the U.S. He also builds guitars and mandolins under the Lewis name.

D'Angelico II

Mid-1990s. Archtops built in the U.S. and distributed by Archtop Enterprises of Merrick, New York. Mainly presentation grade copies of Excel and New Yorker models, but also made lower cost similar models.

Jazz Classic

1990s. Electric archtop, cutaway, carved spruce top, figured maple back and sides, single neck pickup, transparent cherry.

1990s		$2,200	$2,800

Daniel Friederich

1955-2015. Luthier Daniel Friederich built his custom/production, classical guitars in Paris, France.

D'Aquisto

1965-1995. James D'Aquisto apprenticed under D'Angelico until the latter's death, at age 59, in '64. He started making his own brand instruments in '65 and built archtop and flat-top acoustic guitars, solidbody and hollowbody electric guitars. He also designed guitars for Hagstrom and Fender. He died in '95, at age 59.

Avant Garde

1987-1994. 18" wide, non-traditional futuristic model, approximately 5 or 6 instruments were reportedly made, because of low production this pricing is for guidance only.

1990	Blond	$70,000	$90,000

Centura/Centura Deluxe

1993-1994. 17" wide, non-traditional art deco futuristic archtop, approximately 10 made, the last guitars made by this luthier, due to the low production this pricing is for guidance only.

1993-1994	Centura, sunburst	$85,000	$110,000
1993-1994	Deluxe, sunburst	$90,000	$120,000

Excel (Cutaway)

1965-1992. Archtop, 17" width, with modern thin-logo started in '81.

1965-1967	Blond	$31,000	$40,000
1965-1967	Sunburst	$29,000	$38,000
1968-1981	Blond	$31,000	$40,000
1968-1981	Sunburst	$29,000	$38,000
1982-1992	Blond	$33,000	$43,000
1982-1992	Sunburst	$31,000	$41,000

1937 D'Angelico Excel

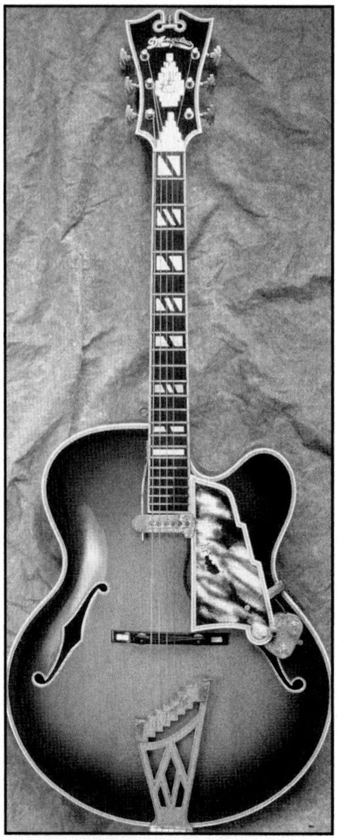

1961 D'Angelico New Yorker

Cartwright Thompson

1967 D'Aquisto New Yorker
Imaged by Heritage Auctions, HA.com

J. Thomas Davis

MODEL YEAR	FEATURES	EXC. COND. LOW	HIGH
Excel (Flat-Top)			
1970s-1980s. Flat-top, 16", flamed maple back and sides, Sitka spruce top, about 15 made, narrow Excel-style headstock, oval soundhole, D'Aquisto script logo on headstock.			
1970s-80s		$16,000	$21,000
Hollow Electric			
Early model with bar pickup, D'Aquisto headstock, '70s model with humbuckers.			
1960s-80s	Sunburst	$14,000	$18,000
Jazz Special			
1985	1st version	$14,000	$18,000
1988	2nd version	$19,000	$25,000
New Yorker Classic (Archtop)			
1986. Single-cut acoustic archtop with new modern design features such as large S-shaped soundholes.			
1986		$51,000	$66,000
New Yorker Classic (Solidbody)			
1980s. Only 2 were reported to be made, therefore this pricing is for guidance only.			
1980s		$16,000	$21,000
New Yorker Deluxe (Cutaway)			
1965-1992. Most are 18" wide.			
1965-1981	Blond	$38,000	$50,000
1965-1981	Sunburst	$34,000	$44,000
1982-1992	Blond	$40,000	$52,000
1982-1992	Sunburst	$37,000	$48,000
New Yorker Special (7-String)			
1980s. Limited production 7-string, single-cut.			
1980s		$29,000	$38,000
New Yorker Special (Cutaway)			
1966-1992. Most are 17" wide.			
1966-1992	Blond	$25,000	$33,000
1966-1992	Sunburst	$22,000	$29,000
Solo/Solo Deluxe			
1992-1993. 18" wide, non-traditional non-cut art deco model, only 2 reported made, because of low production this pricing is for guidance only.			
1992-1993	Blond	$90,000	$115,000

D'Aquisto (Aria)

May 2002-2013. Premium grade, production, D'Aquisto designs licensed to Aria of Japan by D'Aquisto Strings, Inc., Deer Park, New York.

MODEL YEAR	FEATURES	EXC. COND. LOW	HIGH
Various Models			
2002-2013		$1,500	$3,000

Dauphin

1970s-late 1990s. Classical and flamenco guitars imported from Spain and Japan by distributor George Dauphinais, located in Springfield, Illinois.

Dave King Acoustics

1980-present. Premium grade, custom/production, acoustic and resonator guitars built by luthier Dave King in Berkshire, U.K.

Dave Maize Acoustic Guitars

1991-present. Luthier Dave Maize builds his professional and premium grade, production/custom, flat-tops and basses in Cave Junction, Oregon.

David Rubio

1960s-2000. Luthier David Spink built his guitars, lutes, violins, violas, cellos and harpsichords first in New York, and after '67, in the U.K. While playing in Spain, he acquired the nickname Rubio, after his red beard. He died in '00.

David Thomas McNaught

1989-present. Professional, premium, and presentation grade, custom, solidbody guitars built by luthier David Thomas McNaught and finished by Dave Mansel in Locust, North Carolina. In '97, they added the production/custom DTM line of guitars.

Davis, J. Thomas

1975-present. Premium and presentation grade, custom, steel-string flat-tops, 12-strings, classicals, archtops, Irish citterns and flat-top Irish bouzoukis made by luthier J. Thomas Davis in Columbus, Ohio.

Davoli

See Wandre listing.

DBZ

2008-2012. Solidbody electric guitars from Dean B. Zelinsky, founder of Dean Guitars, and partners Jeff Diamant and Terry Martin. Dean left the partnership February, '12 and established Dean Zelinsky Private Label guitars.

de Jonge, Sergei

1972-present. Premium grade, production/custom classical and steel-string guitars built by luthier Sergei de Jonge originally in Oshawa, Ontario, and since '04 in Chelsea, Quebec.

De Paule Stringed Instruments

1969-1980, 1993-present. Custom steel-string, nylon-string, archtop, resonator, and Hawaiian guitars built by luthier C. Andrew De Paule in Eugene, Oregon.

Dean

1976-present. Intermediate, professional and premium grade, production/custom, solidbody, hollowbody, acoustic, acoustic/electric, and resonator guitars made in the U.S., Korea, the Czech Republic and China. They also offer basses, banjos, mandolins, and amps. Founded in Evanston, Illinois, by Dean Zelinsky. Original models were upscale versions of Gibson designs with glued necks, fancy tops, DiMarzio pickups and distinctive winged headstocks (V, Z and ML), with production beginning in '77. In '80 the factory was relocated to Chicago. Dean's American manufacturing ends in '86 when all production shifts to Korea. In '91 Zelinsky sold the company to Tropical Music in Miami, Florida. For '93-'94 there was again limited U.S. (California) production of the E'Lite, Cadillac and

MODEL YEAR	FEATURES	EXC. COND. LOW	HIGH

ML models under the supervision of Zelinsky and Cory Wadley. Korean versions were also produced. In '95, Elliott Rubinson's Armadillo Enterprises, of Clearwater, Florida, bought the Dean brand. In '97 and '98, Dean offered higher-end USA Custom Shop models. In '98, they reintroduced acoustics. From 2000 to '08, Zelinsky was once again involved in the company.

Dating American models: First 2 digits are year of manufacture. Imports have no date codes.

Baby ML

1982-1986, 2000-2014. Downsized version of ML model.

1982-1986	Import	$325	$425
1982-1986	US-made	$475	$625

Baby V

1982-1986, 2000-2014. Downsized version of the V model.

1982-1986	Import	$325	$425
1982-1986	US-made	$475	$625

Baby Z

1982-1986, 2000-2014. Downsized version of the Z model.

1982-1986	Import	$325	$425
1982-1986	US-made	$475	$625

Bel Aire

1983-1984. Solidbody, possibly the first production guitar with humbucker/single/single pickup layout, U.S.-made, an import model was introduced in '87.

1980s	Import	$325	$425
1983-1984	US-made	$475	$625

Budweiser Guitar

Ca.1987. Shaped like Bud logo.

1987		$175	$250

Cadillac (U.S.A.)

1979-1985. Single long treble horn on slab body.

1979-1985		$1,425	$1,850

Cadillac 1980

2006-2018. Block inlays, 2 humbuckers, gold hardware.

2006-2018		$350	$450

Cadillac Deluxe (U.S.A.)

1993-1994, 1996-1997. Made in U.S., single longhorn shape, various colors.

1993-1997		$1,000	$1,300

Cadillac Reissue (Import)

1992-1994. Single longhorn shape, 2 humbuckers, various colors.

1992-1994		$275	$350

Cadillac Select

2009-2017. Made in Korea, figured maple top, mahogany, pearl block inlays.

2009-2017		$325	$425

Cadillac Standard

1996-1997. Slab body version.

1996-1997		$1,250	$1,600

Del Sol

2008. Import, small double-cut thinline semi-hollow, ES-335 style body, rising sun fretboard markers.

2008		$290	$375

MODEL YEAR	FEATURES	EXC. COND. LOW	HIGH

Dime O Flame (ML)

2005-2018. ML-body, Dimebuckers, burning flames finish, Dime logo on headstock.

2005-2018		$325	$425

Eighty-Eight (Import)

1987-1990. Offset double-cut solidbody, import.

1987-1990		$175	$225

E'Lite

1978-1985, 1994-1996. Single-horn shape.

1978-1985		$950	$1,250
1994-1996		$875	$1,125

E'Lite Deluxe

1980s. Single-horn shape.

1980s		$1,150	$1,500

EVO XM

2004-present. Single-cut slab body, 2 humbuckers.

2004-2020		$100	$135

Golden E'Lite

1980. Single pointy treble cutaway, fork headstock, gold hardware, ebony 'board, sunburst.

1980		$1,150	$1,500

Hollywood Z (Import)

1985-1986. Bolt-neck Japanese copy of Baby Z, Explorer shape.

1985-1986		$125	$165

Jammer (Import)

1987-1989. Offset double-cut body, bolt-on neck, dot markers, six-on-a-side tuners, various colors offered.

1987-1989		$125	$165

Leslie West Standard

2008-2017. Flame maple top, mahogany body, rosewood 'board.

2008-2017		$350	$450

Mach I (Import)

1985-1986. Limited run from Korea, Mach V with six-on-a-side tunes, various colors.

1985-1986		$125	$165

Mach V (Import)

1985-1986. Pointed solidbody, 2 humbucking pickups, maple neck, ebony 'board, locking trem, various colors, limited run from Korea.

1985-1986		$125	$165

Mach VII (U.S.A.)

1985-1986. Mach I styling, made in America, offered in unusual finishes.

1985-1986		$1,000	$1,300

ML (ML Standard/U.S.A.)

1977-1986. There is a flame model and a standard model.

1977-1986	Burst flamed top	$1,950	$2,525
1977-1986	Burst plain top	$1,850	$2,425
1977-1986	Common opaque finish	$1,550	$2,000

ML (Import)

1983-1990. Korean-made.

1983-1990		$425	$550

Soltero SL

2007-2010. Made in Japan, single-cut solidbody, 2 pickups, flame maple top.

2007-2010		$1,400	$1,800

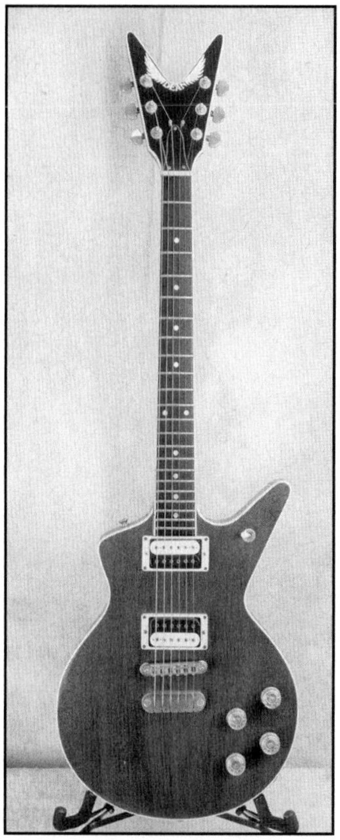

1980 Dean Golden E'Lite
Olivia's Vintage

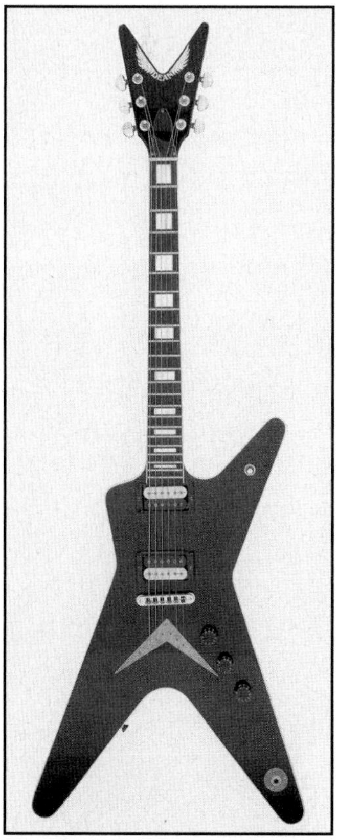

1981 Dean ML
Imaged by Heritage Auctions, HA.com

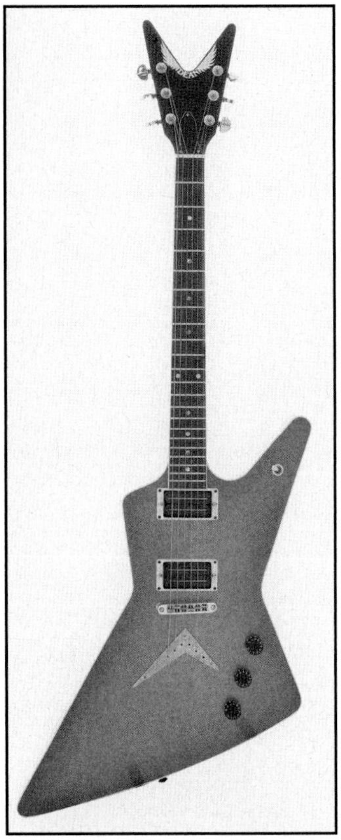

1979 Dean Z Standard

Imaged by Heritage Auctions, HA.com

200 DeArmond Starfire Special

USA Time Capsule Exotic V

2005-2014. Flying V style, solid mahogany body with exotic spalted and flamed maple top, Dean V neck profile (split V headstock).

MODEL YEAR	FEATURES	EXC. COND. LOW	HIGH
2005-2014		$1,900	$2,500

USA Time Capsule Z

2000-2014. Explorer style body, figured maple top.

MODEL YEAR	FEATURES	EXC. COND. LOW	HIGH
2000-2014		$1,900	$2,500

V Standard (U.S.A.)

1977-1986. V body, there is a standard and a flame model offered.

MODEL YEAR	FEATURES	EXC. COND. LOW	HIGH
1977-1981	Burst flamed top	$2,200	$2,900
1977-1981	Burst plain top	$1,900	$2,500
1977-1981	Common opaque finish	$1,600	$2,100
1982-1986	Burst flamed top	$1,850	$2,400
1982-1986	Burst plain top	$1,700	$2,200
1982-1986	Common opaque finish	$1,400	$1,800

Z Standard (U.S.A.)

1977-1986. Long treble cutaway solidbody, 2 humbuckers.

MODEL YEAR	FEATURES	EXC. COND. LOW	HIGH
1977-1983	Common finish	$1,300	$1,700
1977-1983	Rare finish	$1,700	$2,200

Z Autograph (Import)

1985-1987. The first Dean import from Korea, offset double-cut, bolt neck, dot markers, offered in several standard colors.

MODEL YEAR	FEATURES	EXC. COND. LOW	HIGH
1985-1987		$200	$260

Z Coupe/Z Deluxe (U.S.A. Custom Shop)

1997-1998. Mahogany body offered in several standard colors, Z Deluxe with Floyd Rose tremolo.

MODEL YEAR	FEATURES	EXC. COND. LOW	HIGH
1997-1998		$825	$1,025

Z Korina (U.S.A. Custom Shop)

1997-1998. Z Coupe with korina body, various standard colors.

MODEL YEAR	FEATURES	EXC. COND. LOW	HIGH
1997-1998		$950	$1,225

Z LTD (U.S.A. Custom Shop)

1997-1998. Z Coupe with bound neck and headstock, offered in several standard colors.

MODEL YEAR	FEATURES	EXC. COND. LOW	HIGH
1997-1998		$950	$1,225

Dean Markley

The string and pickup manufacturer offered a limited line of guitars and basses for a time in the '80s. They were introduced in '84.

Dean Zelinsky Private Label

2012-present. Premium grade, production/custom, hollow, semi-hollow and solidbody electric guitars built in Chicago, Illinois by luthier Dean Zelinsky, founder of Dean Guitars. He also imports a line of intermediate grade guitars from South Korea and Indonesia.

DeArmond Guitars

1999-2004. Solid, semi-hollow and hollow body guitars based on Guild models and imported from Korea by Fender. They also offered basses. The DeArmond brand was originally used on pickups, effects and amps built by Rowe Industries.

Electric

1999-2004. Various import models, some with USA electronic components.

MODEL YEAR	FEATURES	EXC. COND. LOW	HIGH
1999-2004	Jet Star (Polara style)	$350	$450
1999-2004	Various models	$225	$625

Dearstone

1993-2017. Luthier Ray Dearstone built his professional and premium grade, custom, archtop and acoustic/electric guitars in Blountville, Tennessee. He also built mandolin family instruments and violins.

Decar

1950s. A private brand sold by Decautur, Illinois music store, Decar headstock logo.

Stratotone H44 Model

1956. Private branded Stratotone with maple neck and fretboard instead of the standard neck/fretboard, 1 pickup and other Harmony H44 Stratotone attributes, bolt-on neck.

MODEL YEAR	FEATURES	EXC. COND. LOW	HIGH
1956		$450	$600

DeCava Guitars

1983-present. Professional and premium grade, production/custom, archtop and classical guitars built by luthier Jim DeCava first in Stratford, then Ansonia, Connecticut. He also builds ukes, banjos, and mandolins.

Decca

Mid-1960s. Acoustic, solid and hollow body guitars, basses and amps made in Japan by Teisco and imported by Decca Records, Decca headstock logo, student-level instruments.

Acoustic Flat-Top

1960s. Decca label on the inside back.

MODEL YEAR	FEATURES	EXC. COND. LOW	HIGH
1960s		$75	$175

Electric Solidbody

1960s. Teisco-made in Japan, 3 pickups, sunburst.

MODEL YEAR	FEATURES	EXC. COND. LOW	HIGH
1960s		$275	$350

Defil

Based out of Lubin, Poland, Defil made solid and semi-hollowbdy electric guitars at least from the 1970s to the '90s.

DeGennaro

2003-present. Premium grade, custom/production, acoustic, archtop, semi-hollow and solidbody guitars, basses and mandolins built by luthier William DeGennaro in Grand Rapids, Michigan.

Del Oro

1930s-1940s. Flat-top (including cowboy stencil models) and resonator guitars, built by Kay. At least the cowboy stencils were sold by Spiegel.

Small Acoustic

MODEL YEAR	FEATURES	EXC. COND. LOW	HIGH
1930s	13" to 14" body	$150	$225

MODEL YEAR	FEATURES	EXC. COND. LOW	HIGH

Del Pilar Guitars

1956-1986. Luthier William Del Pilar made his classical guitars in Brooklyn, New York.

Classical (Rosewood)

1950s-1980s. Brazilian rosewood back and sides, cedar top, quilt rosette, 9-ply top binding.

1960-1969		$2,000	$5,000

Del Vecchio

1902-present. Casa Del Vecchio builds a variety of Spanish instruments including acoustic and resonator guitars in São Paulo, Brazil.

Delaney Guitars

2004-present. Luthier Mike Delaney builds his professional grade, production/custom, chambered, solidbody, and semi-hollowbody electric guitars and basses in Atlanta, Georgia. Prior to 2008 he built in Florence, Montana.

Delgado

1928-present. Delgado began in Torreon, Coahuila, Mexico, then moved to Juarez in the '30s with a second location in Tijuana. In '48 they moved to California and opened a shop in Los Angeles. Since 2005, Manuel A. Delgado, a third generation luthier, builds his premium and presentation grade, production/custom, classical, flamenco and steel string acoustic guitars in Nashville, Tennessee. He also builds basses, mandolins, ukuleles and banjos.

Delirium Custom Guitars

Luthiers Patrick and Vincent Paul-Victor along with Gael Canonne build their professional and premium grade, production/custom, solidbody electric guitars in Paris and Toulouse, France.

Dell'Arte

1997-present. Production/custom Maccaferri-style guitars from John Kinnard and Alain Cola. In '96, luthier John Kinnard opened a small shop called Finegold Guitars and Mandolins. In '98 he met Alain Cola, a long time jazz guitarist who was selling Mexican-made copies of Selmer/Maccaferri guitars under the Dell'Arte brand. Cola wanted better workmanship for his guitars, and in October '98, Finegold and Dell'Arte merged. As of May '99 all production is in California.

Delta Guitars

2005-2010. Acoustic, acoustic/electric, and solidbody electric guitars from Musician's Wholesale America, Nashville, Tennessee.

Dennis Hill Guitars

Premium and presentation grade, production/custom, classical and flamenco guitars built by luthier Dennis Hill in Panama City, Florida. He has also built dulcimers, mandolins, and violins.

MODEL YEAR	FEATURES	EXC. COND. LOW	HIGH

Desmond Guitars

1991-present. Luthier Robert B. Desmond builds his premium grade, production/custom classical guitars in Orlando, Florida.

DeTemple

1995-present. Premium grade, production/custom, solidbody electric guitars and basses built by luthier Michael DeTemple in Sherman Oaks, California.

DeVoe Guitars

1975-present. Luthier Lester DeVoe builds his premium grade, production/custom flamenco and classical guitars in Nipomo, California.

Diamond

Ca. 1963-1964. Line of sparkle finish solidbody guitars made in Italy for the Diamond Accordion company.

Ranger

Ca. 1963-1964. Rangers came with 1, 2, 3, or 4 pickups, sparkle finish.

1960s		$500	$650

Dick, Edward Victor

1975-present. Luthier Edward Dick currently builds his premium grade, custom, classical guitars in Denver, Colorado (he lived in Peterborough and Ottawa, Ontario until '95). He also operates the Colorado School of Lutherie.

Dickerson

1937-1947. Founded by the Dickerson brothers in '37, primarily for electric lap steels and small amps. Instruments were also private branded for Cleveland's Oahu company, and for the Gourley brand. By '47, the company changed ownership and was renamed Magna Electronics (Magnatone).

Dillion

1996-present. Dillion, of Cary, North Carolina, offers intermediate grade, production, acoustic, acoustic/electric, hollow-body and solidbody guitars, basses and mandolins made in Korea and Vietnam.

Dillon

1975-2006. Professional and premium grade, custom, flat-tops and basses built by luthier John Dillon in Taos, New Mexico, and in Bloomsburg, Pennsylvania ('81-'01).

Dino's Guitars

Custom, professional grade, electric solidbody guitars built by a social co-op company founded by Alessio Casati and Andy Bagnasco, in Albisola, Italy. They also build effects.

2000 DeArmond X-155

DeTemple Spirit Series Stellacasta

DiPinto Orbital

Dobro D-10

Bernunzio Uptown Music

DiPinto

1995-present. Intermediate and professional grade, production retro-vibe guitars and basses from luthier Chris DiPinto of Philadelphia, Pennsylvania. Until late '99, all instruments built in the U.S., since then all built in Korea.

Ditson

1835-1937. Started in Boston by music publisher Oliver Ditson, by the end of the 1800s the company was one of the East Coast's largest music businesses, operating in several cities and was also involved in distribution and manufacturing of a variety of instruments, including guitars and ukes. From 1916-1930 Ditson guitars were made by Martin. The majority of Martin production was from '16 to '22 with over 500 units sold in '21. Ditson also established Lyon and Healy in Chicago and the John Church Company in Cincinnati.

Values for Ditson Models 111 and 1-45 would be equivalent to those for Martin models from that era with similar specs.

Concert Models

1916-1922. Similar in size to Martin size 0. Models include Style 1, Style 2 and Style 3.

MODEL YEAR	FEATURES	EXC. COND. LOW	HIGH
1916-1922	Style 1	$4,225	$5,525
1916-1922	Style 2	$4,950	$6,550
1916-1922	Style 3	$5,450	$7,150

Standard Models

1916-1922. Small body similar to Martin size 3, plain styling. Models include Style 1, Style 2 and Style 3.

MODEL YEAR	FEATURES	EXC. COND. LOW	HIGH
1916-1922	Style 1	$2,725	$3,625
1916-1922	Style 2	$3,250	$4,325
1916-1922	Style 3	$4,250	$5,650

D'Leco Guitars

1991-2003. Guitarist Maurice Johnson and luthier James W. Dale built premium grade, production/custom archtops in Oklahoma City, Oklahoma.

DM Darling Guitars

Beginning 2006 luthier Denis Merrill builds professional and premium grade, custom, acoustic, classical, resonator and solidbody guitars in Tacoma, Washington. From 1978 to '06 he built under his own name and Merrill Custom Shop. He also builds mandolin family instruments.

Dobro

1929-1942, ca. 1954-2019. Currently, professional and premium grade, production, wood and metal body resophonic guitars offered by Gibson.

Founded 1929 in Los Angeles by John Dopyera, Rudy Dopyera, Ed Dopyera and Vic Smith (Dobro stands for Dopyera Brothers). Made instruments sold under the Dobro, Regal, Norwood Chimes, Angelus, Rex, Broman, Montgomery Ward, Penetro, Bruno, Alhambra, More Harmony, Orpheum, and Magn-o-tone brands.

Dobro instruments have a single cone facing outward with a spider bridge structure and competed with National products. Generally, model names are numbers referring to list price and therefore materials and workmanship (e.g., a No. 65 cost $65). Because of this, the same model number may apply to various different instruments. However, model numbers are never identified on instruments!

In '30, the company name was changed to Dobro Corporation, Ltd. In '32, Louis Dopyera buys Ted Kleinmeyer's share of National. Louis, Rudy and Ed now hold controlling interest in National, but in '32 John Dopyera left Dobro to pursue idea of metal resophonic violin. In December of '34 Ed Dopyera joins National's board of directors (he's also still on Dobro board), and by March of '35 Dobro and National have merged to become the National Dobro Corporation. Dobro moves into National's larger factory but continues to maintain separate production, sales and distribution until relocation to Chicago is complete. Beginning in early-'36 National Dobro starts relocating its offices to Chicago. L.A. production of Dobros continues until '37, after which some guitars continue to be assembled from parts until '39, when the L.A. operations were closed down.

All resonator production ended in '42. Victor Smith, Al Frost and Louis Dopyera buy the company and change the name to the Valco Manufacturing Company. The Dobro name does not appear when production resumes after World War II.

In mid-'50s - some sources say as early as '54 - Rudy and Ed Dopyera began assembling wood-bodied Dobros from old parts using the name DB Original. In about '59, some 12-fret DB Originals were made for Standel, carrying both DB Original and Standel logos. In around '61, production was moved to Gardena, California, and Louis Dopyera and Valco transferred the Dobro name to Rudy and Ed, who produce the so-called Gardena Dobros. At this time, the modern Dobro logo appeared with a lyre that looks like 2 back-to-back '6s'. Dobro Original debuts ca. '62. In late-'64 the Dobro name was licensed to Ed's son Emil (Ed, Jr.) Dopyera. Ed, Jr. designs a more rounded Dobro (very similar to later Mosrites) and has falling out with Rudy over it.

In '66 Semi Moseley acquires the rights to the Dobro brand, building some in Gardena, and later moving to Bakersfield, California. Moseley introduced Ed, Jr's design plus a thinline double-cutaway Dobro. He also made MoBros during this time period. Moseley Dobros use either Dobro or National cones. In '67 Ed, Sr., Rudy and Gabriella Lazar start the Original Music Instrument Company (OMI) and produce Hound Dog brand Dobros. In '68 Moseley goes bankrupt and in '70 OMI obtains the rights to the Dobro brand and begins production of OMI Dobros. In '75 Gabriella's son and daughter, Ron Lazar and Dee Garland, take over OMI. Rudy Dupyera makes and sells Safari brand resonator mandolins. Ed, Sr. dies in '77 and Rudy in '78. In '84 OMI was sold to Chester and Betty Lizak. Both wood and metal-bodied Dobros

MODEL YEAR	FEATURES	EXC. COND. LOW	HIGH

produced in Huntington Beach, California. Chester Lizak died in '92. Gibson purchased Dobro in '93 and made Dobros in Nashville, Tennessee.

Dobros generally feature a serial number which, combined with historical information, provides a clue to dating. For prewar L.A. guitars, see approximation chart below adapted from "Gruhn's Guide to Vintage Guitars." No information exists on DB Originals.

Gardena Dobros had D prefix plus 3 digits beginning with 100 and going into the 500s (reportedly under 500 made). No information is available on Moseley Dobros.

OMI Dobros from '70-'79 have either D prefix for wood bodies or B prefix for metal bodies, plus 3 or 4 numbers for ranking, space, then a single digit for year (D XXXX Y or B XXX Y; e.g., D 172 8 would be wood body #172 from '78). For '80-'87 OMI Dobros, start with first number of year (decade) plus 3 or 4 ranking numbers, space, then year and either D for wood or B for metal bodies (8 XXXX YD or 8 XXX YB; e.g., 8 2006 5B would be metal body #2008 from '85). From '88-'92, at least, a letter and number indicate guitar style, plus 3 or 4 digits for ranking, letter for neck style, 2 digits for year, and letter for body style (AX XXXX NYYD or AX XXX NYYB).

L.A. Guitars (approx. number ranges, not actual production totals):

1929-30	900-2999
1930-31	3000-3999
1931-32	BXXX (Cyclops models only)
1932-33	5000-5599
1934-36	5700-7699
1937-42	8000-9999

Angelus

1933-1937. Wood body, round or square neck, 2-tone walnut finish, continues as Model 19 in Regal-made guitars.

1933-1937	Round neck	$1,150	$1,500
1933-1937	Square neck	$1,225	$1,600

Artist M-16

1934-1935. German silver alloy body, engraved.

1934-1935	H square neck	$3,350	$4,350
1934-1935	M round neck	$5,375	$6,975

Columbia D-12

1967-1968. Acoustic 12-string, typical Dobro resonator with spider style bridge, made during Dobro-Moseley era.

1967-1968		$750	$975

Cyclops 45

1932-1933. Bound walnut body, 1 screen hole.

1932-1933	Round neck	$2,475	$3,250
1932-1933	Square neck	$2,950	$3,850

D-40 Texarkana

1965-1967. Mosrite-era (identified by C or D prefix), traditional Dobro style cone and coverplate, dot inlays, Dobro logo on headstock, sunburst wood body. Red and blue finishes available.

1965-1967	Sunburst, square neck	$950	$1,225

D-40E Texarkana

1965-1967. D-40 electric with single pickup and 2 knobs.

1965-1967		$1,025	$1,325

D-100 The Californian

1965-1969. Dobro's version of Mosrite (thus nicknamed the "Mobro") thinline double-cut, resonator, 2 small metal ports, 2 pickups, 2 knobs, sunburst.

1965-1969		$1,425	$1,850

DM-33 California Girl/DM-33H

1996-2006. Chrome-plated bell brass body, biscuit bridge, spider resonator, rosewood 'board. Girl or Hawaiian-scene (H) engraving.

1996-2006		$1,300	$1,700

Dobjo

Dobro body, banjo neck, 5-string.

1989		$1,025	$1,325

Dobro/Regal Model 19

Ca.1934-1938. In the 1930s Dobro licensed Chicago's Regal Company to build Dobro-style guitars. The headstocks on these models can have a Dobro logo, Regal logo, or no logo at all. The 19 is a lower-end model, round holes in coverplate, square neck.

1934-1938		$1,150	$1,500

Dobro/Regal Model 46/47

1935-1942. Dobro/Regal 46, renamed 47 in '39, aluminum body, round neck, 14 frets, slotted headstock, silver finish. Degraded finish was a common problem with the Dobro/Regal 47.

1935-1938	46	$1,425	$1,850
1939-1942	47, original finish	$1,950	$2,550

Dobro/Regal Model 62/65

1935-1942. Renamed Model 65 in '39, nickel-plated brass body, Spanish dancer etching, round or square neck. Note: Dobro/Regal 65 should not be confused with Dobro Model 65 which discontinued earlier.

1935-1938	62, round neck	$2,350	$3,050
1935-1938	62, square neck	$2,350	$3,050
1939-1942	65, round neck	$2,350	$3,050
1939-1942	65, square neck	$2,350	$3,350

Dobro/Regal Tenor Model 27-1/2

1930. Tenor version of Model 27.

1930		$540	$700

Dobrolektric

1996-2005. Resonator guitar with single-coil neck pickup, single-cut.

1996-2005		$1,150	$1,500

DS-33/Steel 33

1995-2000. Steel body with light amber sunburst finish, resonator with coverplate, biscuit bridge.

1995-2000		$875	$1,150

DW-90C

2001-2006. Single sharp cutaway, wood body, metal resonator, f-hole upper bass bout.

2001-2006		$850	$1,125

E3 (C, M, W, B)

Late 1970s-1986. Double-cut solidbodies with necks and bodies of laminated select hardwoods (Cinnamon, Maple, Walnut) or plain Black (B) finish, 2 pickups.

1979-1986	C, M, W	$1,175	$1,525

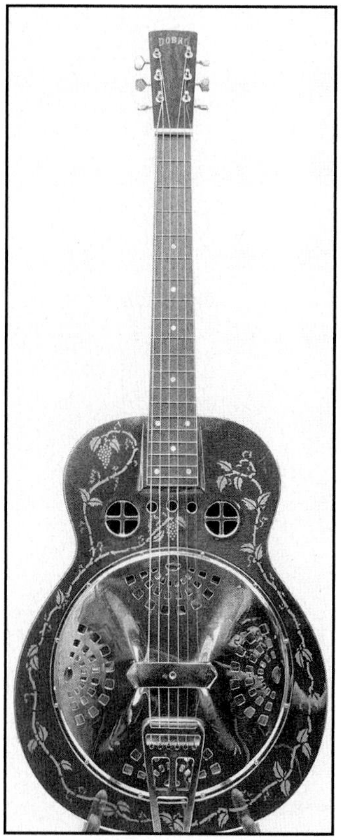

1937 Dobro Model 62

Bernunzio Uptown Music

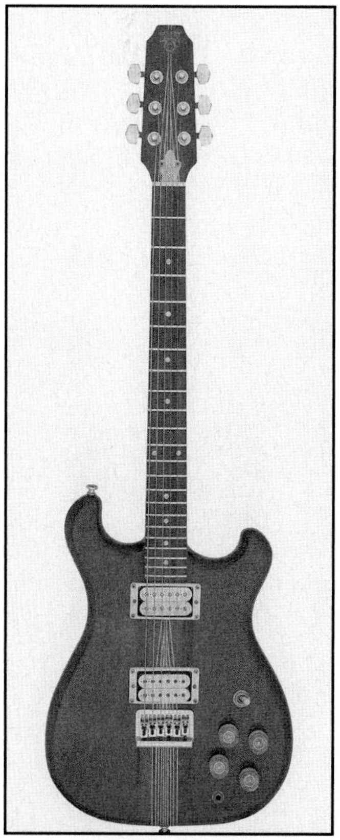

1986 Dobro E3 C

Imaged by Heritage Auctions, HA.com

GUITARS

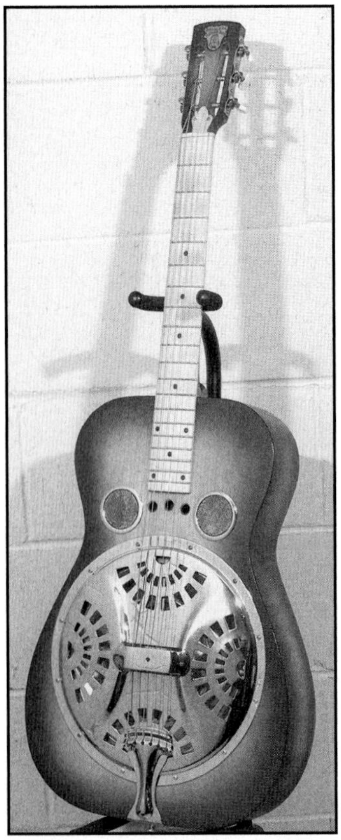

2003 Dobro Hound Dog
Tom Pfeifer

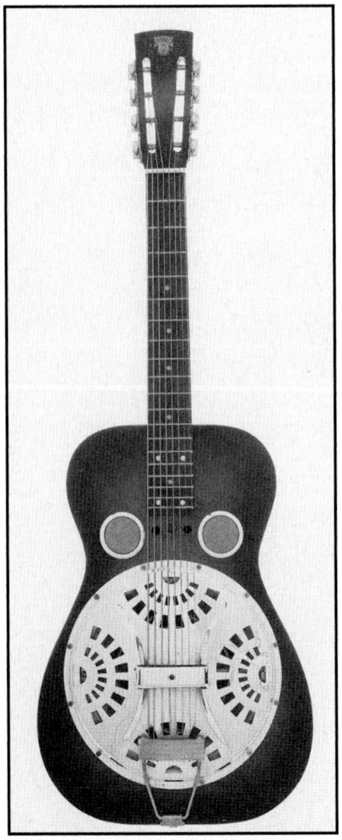

1973 Dobro Model 63
Imaged by Heritage Auctions, HA.com

MODEL YEAR	FEATURES	EXC. COND. LOW	HIGH

F-60/F-60 S
1986-2005. Round neck (60, discontinued '00) or square neck (60 S), f-holes, brown sunburst.

1986-2005		$1,150	$1,500

Gardena
1968. Electric Dobro body, 2 knobs, single-coil soap bar pickup.

1968		$750	$975

Hound Dog
2002-2019. Laminated wood, 10 1/2" spider-bridge resonator.

2002-2019		$350	$475

Hula Blues
1987-1999. Dark brown wood body (earlier models have much lighter finish), painted Hawaiian scenes, round neck.

1987-1999		$1,075	$1,400

Jerry Douglas
1995-2005. Mahogany body, square neck, limited run of 200 with signature, but also sold without signature.

1995-2005		$1,850	$2,450

Josh Graves
1995-2005. First 200 made were signed, single bound ample body, spider cone, nickel plated. Includes DW Josh Graves and Uncle Josh Limited models.

1995	Signed	$1,550	$2,050
1996-2005	Unsigned	$1,250	$1,650

Leader 14M/14H
1934-1935. Nickel plated brass body, segmented f-holes.

1934-1935	H square neck	$1,950	$2,550
1934-1935	M round neck	$1,650	$2,150

Model 25
1930-1935. Sunburst wood body, f-holes upper bout, large single metal cone, square neck.

1930-1935		$1,500	$1,950

Model 27 (OMI)
1976-1994. Wood body, square neck.

1976-1994		$1,200	$1,550

Model 27 Cyclops
1932-1933.

1932-1933	Round neck	$1,650	$2,150
1932-1933	Square neck	$1,750	$2,250

Model 27 Deluxe
1995-2005. 27 with figured maple top, nicer appointments.

1996-2005		$1,550	$2,025

Model 27/27G
1933-1937. Regal-made, wooden body.

1933-1937	Round neck	$1,350	$1,750
1933-1937	Square neck	$1,575	$2,050

Model 32
1939-1941. Regal-made, wooden body.

1939-1941		$1,800	$2,350

Model 33 (Duolian)
1972. Only made in '72, becomes Model 90 in '73.

1972		$925	$1,200

MODEL YEAR	FEATURES	EXC. COND. LOW	HIGH

Model 33 H
1973-1997 (OMI & Gibson). Same as 33 D, but with etched Hawaiian scenes, available as round or square neck.

1980s-90s	Round neck	$1,350	$1,750
1980s-90s	Square neck	$1,350	$1,750

Model 35 (32)
1935-1942. Metal body, called Model 32 (not to be confused with wood body 32) for '35-'38.

1935-1942		$2,000	$2,600

Model 36
1932-1937. Wood body with resonator, round or square neck.

1932-1937	Round neck	$1,200	$1,550
1932-1937	Square neck	$1,550	$2,000

Model 36/36 S
1970s-1997, 2002-2005. Chrome-plated brass body, round or square (S) neck, dot markers, engraved rose floral art.

1970s-2005		$1,425	$1,850

Model 37
1933-1937. Regal-made wood body, mahogany, bound body and 'board, round or square 12-fret neck.

1933-1937	Round neck	$1,425	$1,850
1933-1937	Square neck	$1,750	$2,250

Model 37 Tenor
1933-1937 (Regal). Tenor version of No. 37.

1933-1937		$875	$1,150

Model 45
1934-1939. Regal-made wood body, round or square neck.

1934-1939	Round neck	$1,750	$2,250
1934-1939	Square neck	$2,025	$2,625

Model 55/56 Standard
1929-1934. Model 55 Standard, renamed 56 Standard 1932-1934. Unbound wood body, metal resonator, bound neck, sunburst.

1929-1934	Round neck	$1,550	$2,025
1929-1934	Square neck	$1,875	$2,450

Model 60
1933-1936. Similar to Model 66/66B.

1933-1936	Round neck	$3,550	$4,650
1933-1936	Square neck	$4,450	$5,750

Model 60 Cyclops
1932-1933. Round neck, 12-fret model, black walnut finish.

1932-1933		$3,550	$4,650

Model 60/60 D (OMI)/60 DS
1970-1993. Wood body (laminated maple) with Dobro resonator cone, model 60 until '73 when renamed 60 D, and various 60 model features offered, post-'93 was Gibson-owned production.

1970-1993	Model 60 Series	$900	$1,200

Model 63
1973-1996. Wood body, 8-string, square neck.

1973-1996		$975	$1,275

Model 64
1980s-1995. Walnut body, tree-of-life inlay.

1982		$1,350	$1,750

MODEL YEAR	FEATURES	EXC. COND. LOW	HIGH

Model 65/66/66 B

1929-1933. Wood body with sandblasted ornamental design top and back, metal resonator, sunburst. Model 66 B has bound top.

1929-1931	Model 65	$2,200	$2,900
1932-1933	Model 66	$2,200	$2,900
1932-1933	Model 66 B	$2,200	$2,900

Model 66/66 S

1972-1995. Wood body with sandblasted ornamental design top and back, metal resonator, sunburst, round or square (S) neck.

1972-1995		$825	$1,075

Model 75/Lily of the Valley

1972-1997, 2002-2005. Chrome plated bell brass body resonator, round neck, Lily of the Valley engraving.

1972-1997		$1,625	$2,100

Model 85/86

1929-1934. Wood body, triple-bound, round or square neck, renamed 86 in '32.

1929-1934		$2,175	$2,825

Model 90 (Duolian) (OMI)

1972-1995. Chrome-plated, f-holes, etched Hawaiian scene.

1972-1995	Various models	$800	$1,500

Model 90 (Woodbody)/WB90 G/WB90 S

1980s-2005. Maple body with upper bout f-holes or sound holes, round neck, metal resonator with spider bridge, sunburst.

1984-2005		$975	$1,275

Model 125 De Luxe

1929-1934. Black walnut body, round or square neck, Dobro De Luxe engraved, triple-bound top, back and 'board, nickel-plated hardware, natural.

1929-1934	Round neck	$5,000	$6,500
1929-1934	Square neck	$9,150	$12,000

Professional 15M/15H

1934-1935. Engraved nickel body, round (M) or square (H) neck, solid peghead.

1934-1935	H square neck	$2,400	$3,125
1934-1935	M round neck	$2,100	$2,725

Dodge

1996-present. Luthier Rick Dodge builds his intermediate and professional grade, production, solidbody guitars with changeable electronic modules in Tallahassee, Florida. He also builds basses.

Doitsch

1930s. Acoustic guitars made by Harmony most likely for a music store or studio.

Domino

Ca. 1967-1968. Solidbody and hollowbody electric guitars and basses imported from Japan by Maurice Lipsky Music Co. of New York, New York, previously responsible for marketing the Orpheum brand. Models are primarily near-copies of EKO, Vox, and Fender designs, plus some originals. Models were made by Arai or Kawai. Earlier models may have been imported, but this is not yet documented.

MODEL YEAR	FEATURES	EXC. COND. LOW	HIGH

Electric

1967-1968. Various models include the Baron, Californian, Californian Rebel, Dawson, and the Spartan.

1967-1968		$250	$500

Dommenget

1978-1985, 1988-present. Luthier Boris Dommenget (pronounced dommen-jay) builds his premium grade, custom/production, solidbody, flat-top, and archtop guitars in Balje, Germany. From '78 to '85 he was located in Wiesbaden, and from '88-'01 in Hamburg. He and wife Fiona also make pickups.

Don Musser Guitars

Luthier Don Musser, in 1976, began building custom, classical and flat-top guitars in Silver City, New Mexico. He later moved his shop to Cotopaxi, Colorado.

Doolin Guitars

1997-present. Luthier Mike Doolin builds his premium grade, production/custom acoustics featuring his unique double-cut in Portland, Oregon.

Dorado

Ca. 1972-1973. Six- and 12-string acoustic guitars, solidbody electrics and basses. Brand used briefly by Baldwin/Gretsch on line of Japanese imports.

Acoustic Flat-Top/Acoustic Dobro

1972-1973. Includes folk D, jumbo Western, and grand concert styles (with laminated rosewood back and sides), and Dobro-style.

1972-1973	Higher-end models	$225	$350
1972-1973	Lower-end models	$125	$165
1972-1973	Mid-level models	$160	$350

Solidbody Electric

1972-1973. Includes Model 5985, a double-cut with 2 P-90-style pickups.

1972-1973		$225	$350

Douglas Ching

Luthier Douglas J. Ching builds his premium grade, production/custom, classical, acoustic, and harp guitars currently in Chester, Virginia, and previously in Hawaii ('76-'89) and Michigan ('90-'93). He also builds ukes, lutes and violins.

D'Pergo Custom Guitars

2002-present. Professional, premium, and presentation grade, production/custom, solidbody guitars built in Windham, New Hampshire. Every component of the guitars is built by D'Pergo.

Dragge Guitars

1982-2010. Luthier Peter Dragge builds his custom, steel-string and nylon-string guitars in Ojai, California.

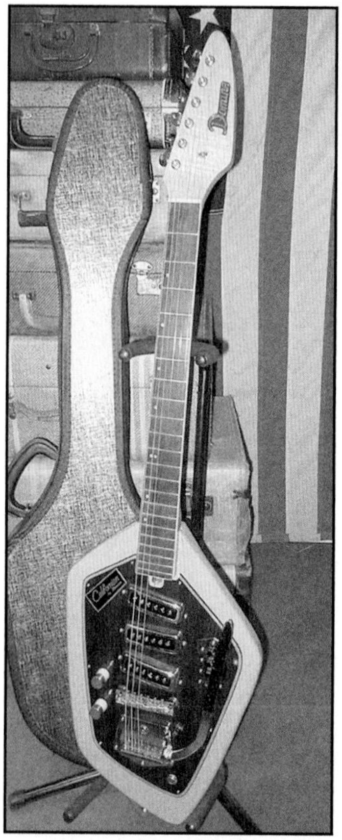

1965 Domino Californian

Rivington Guitars

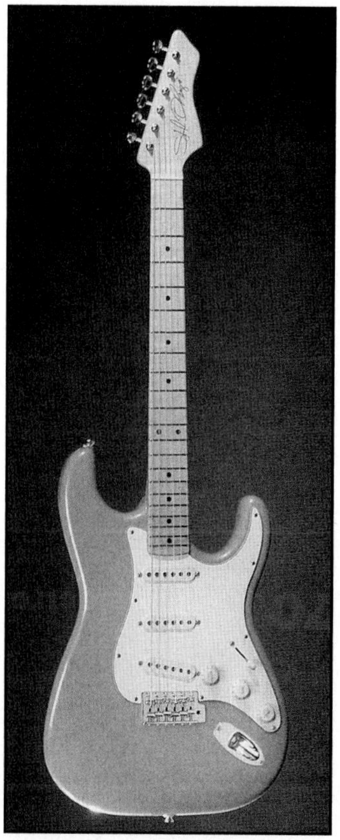

D'Pergo Signature

Duesenberg Mike Campbell II

Eastman T146SM

MODEL YEAR	FEATURES	EXC. COND. LOW	HIGH

Dragonfly Guitars

1994-present. Professional grade, production/custom, sloped cutaway flat-tops, semi-hollow body electrics, basses and dulcitars built by luthier Dan Richter in Roberts Creek, British Columbia.

Drive

Ca. 2001-ca. 2011. Budget grade, production, import solidbody electric guitars and basses. They also offered solidstate amps.

DTM

See David Thomas McNaught listing.

Dudley Custom Guitars

2005-present. Luthier Peter Dudley builds his custom, premium grade, chambered solidbody electric guitars in Easton, Maryland.

Duelin Guitars

Professional grade, production/custom, 6 ½ string guitars designed by Don Scheib of Simi Valley and built by luthier Mike Lipe in Sun Valley, California.

Duesenberg

1995-present. Professional and premium grade, production/custom, solid and hollow body electric guitars and basses built by luthier Dieter Goelsdorf in Hannover, Germany. Rockinger had a Duesenberg guitar in the 1980s.

Dunwell Guitars

Professional and premium grade, custom, flat-tops built by luthier Alan Dunwell in Nederland, Colorado.

Dupont

Luthier Maurice Dupont builds his classical, archtop, Weissenborn-style and Selmer-style guitars in Cognac, France.

Dwight

See info under Epiphone Dwight guitar.

Dyer

1902-1939. The massive W. J. Dyer & Bro. store in St. Paul, Minnesota, sold a complete line of music related merchandise though they actually built nothing but a few organs. The Larson Brothers of Chicago were commissioned to build harp guitar and harp mandolin pieces for them somewhat following the harp guitar design of Chris Knutsen, until 1912 when the Knutsen patent expired. Although the body design somewhat copied the Knutsen patent the resulting instrument was in a class by itself in comparison. These harp guitars have become the standard by which all others are judged because of their ease of play and the tremendous, beautiful sound they produce. Many modern builders are using the body design and the same structural ideas evidenced in the Larson originals. They were built in Styles 4 (the plainest), 5, 6, 7 and 8. The ornamentation went from the no binding, dot inlay Style 4 to the full treatment, abalone trimmed, tree-of-life fingerboard of the Style 8. All had mahogany back and sides with ebony fingerboard and bridge. There are also a very few Style 3 models found of late that are smaller than the standard and have a lower bout body point. Other Dyer instruments were built by Knutsen. Dyer also carried Stetson brand instruments made by the Larson Brothers.

Harp Guitar

MODEL YEAR	FEATURES	LOW	HIGH
1902-1920s	Style 3, smaller, short scale	$3,100	$4,000
1902-1920s	Style 4, no binding	$3,100	$4,000
1902-1920s	Style 5, bound top	$3,900	$5,000
1902-1920s	Style 6, bound top/bottom	$4,400	$5,700
1902-1920s	Style 7, fancy inlays	$5,100	$6,600
1902-1920s	Style 8, tree-of-life	$7,700	$10,000

Dynacord

1950-present. Dynacord is a German company that makes audio and pro sound amps, as well as other electronic equipment. In 1966-'67 they offered solidbody guitars and basses from the Welson Company of Italy. They also had the Cora guitar and bass which is the center part of a guitar body with a tube frame in a guitar outline. They also offered tape echo machines.

Dynelectron

1960s-late 1970s. This Italian builder offered a variety of guitars and basses, but is best known today for their almost exact copies of Danelectro Longhorns of the mid-'60s.

E L Welker

Luthier Eugene L. Welker began building in 1984, premium and presentation grade, production/custom, leather-wrapped archtop guitars in Claremont, New Hampshire.

E.L. Bashore Guitars

2011-present. Professional grade, custom, steel string and classical acoustic and solidbody electric guitars, basses and banjos built by luthier Eric L. Bashore in Danville, Pennsylvania.

Earthwood

1972-1985. Acoustic designs by Ernie Ball with input from George Fullerton and made in Newport Beach, California. One of the first to offer acoustic basses.

Eastman

1992-present. Intermediate and professional grade, production, archtop and flat-top guitars and basses, mainly built in China, with some from Germany and Romania. Beijing, China-based Eastman Strings started out building violins and cellos. They added guitars in '02 and mandolins in '04.

MODEL YEAR	FEATURES	EXC. COND. LOW	HIGH

Eastwood

1997-present. Mike Robinson's company imports budget and intermediate grade, production, solid and semi-hollowbody guitars, many styled after 1960s models. They also offer basses and mandolins.

Eaton, William

1976-present. Luthier William Eaton builds custom specialty instruments such as vihuelas, harp guitars, and lyres in Phoenix, Arizona. He is also the Director of the Robetto-Venn School of Luthiery.

Echopark Guitars

2010-present. Premium and presentation grade, production/custom, solidbody electric guitars built by luthier Gabriel Currie in Detroit, Michigan, formerly in Los Angeles, California.

Ed Claxton Guitars

1972-present. Premium grade, custom flat-tops made by luthier Ed Claxton, first in Austin, Texas, and currently in Santa Cruz, California.

Eduardo Duran Ferrer

Luthier Eduardo Duran Ferrer, since 1987, builds premium grade, classical guitars in Granada, Spain.

Edward Klein

1998-present. Premium grade, custom, guitars built by luthier Edward Klein in Mississauga, Ontario.

EER Custom

2005-present. Professional and premium grade, custom, soldibody and semi-hollowbody electric guitars built by luthier Ernest E. Roesler in Forks, Washington.

Egmond

1935-1972. Founded by Ulke Egmond, building acoustic, archtop, semi-hollow and solidbody guitars originally in Eindhoven, later in Best Holland. They also made basses. Egmond also produced instruments under the Orpheum (imported into U.S.), Rosetti (England), Miller, Wilson and Lion brands.

Electric

1960-1972. Solid or semi-hollow bodies.

1960-1972		$400	$525

Ehlers

1968-2011. Luthier Rob Ehlers built his premium grade, production/custom, flat-top acoustic guitars, originally in Oregon and from '06 to '11, in Veracruz, Mexico. Rob died in November, 2011.

15 CRC

Cutaway, Western red cedar top, Indian rosewood back and sides.

1996		$1,900	$2,475

MODEL YEAR	FEATURES	EXC. COND. LOW	HIGH

15 SRC

Cutaway, European spruce top, Indian rosewood back and sides.

1998		$1,900	$2,475

16 BTM

European spruce top, mahogany back and sides, Troubadour peghead, black lacquer finish.

1998		$1,975	$2,550

16 C

16" lower bout, cutaway, flamed maple sides and back, European spruce top.

1990		$1,975	$2,550

16 SK Concert

16" lower bout, relatively small upper bout, small waist, European spruce top, flamed koa back and sides, diamond markers, natural.

1993		$1,800	$2,325

16 SM

European spruce top, mahogany back and sides.

1999		$1,700	$2,200

16 SSC

Cutaway, European spruce top, English sycamore back and sides.

1996		$1,800	$2,325

25 C

Limited Edition Anniversary Model, European spruce top, Indian rosewood back and sides, abalone top border.

2001		$2,625	$3,400

GJ (Gypsy Jazz)

2000s	D-style	$1,700	$2,200

Eichelbaum Guitars

Luthier David Eichelbaum builds his premium grade, custom, flat-tops in Santa Barbara, California.

EKO

1959-present. Originally acoustic, acoustic/electric, electric thinline and full-size archtop hollowbody, solidbody electric guitars and basses built by Oliviero Pigini and Company in Recanati, Italy, and imported by LoDuca Brothers, Milwaukee, Radio and Television Equipment Company in Santa Ana, California and others. First acoustic guitars followed by sparkle plastic-covered electrics by '62. Sparkle finishes are gone ca. '66. Pigini dies ca. '67. LoDuca Bros. phases out in early-'70s. By '75 EKO offers some copy guitars and they purchased a custom shop to make other brands by '78. In '85 they ceased production in Italy, continuing the brand for a few years with Asian imports, and continued to distribute other brands. By 2004, the Eko line of guitar was revived with budget and intermediate grade, production, classical, acoustic, acoustic/electric, solidbody, solidbody, and hollowbody guitars made in Asia. They also make basses and amps.

Barracuda VI

1966-ca.1978. Double-cut semi-hollow, 2 pickups, 6-string.

1966-1978		$450	$600

Eastwood Sidejack Pro DLX

EER Custom E-06 Classic

EKO Ranger 12
Seth Andrews

1982 El Degas
Robbie Keene

MODEL YEAR	FEATURES	EXC. COND. LOW	HIGH

Barracuda XII
1966-ca.1978. Double-cut semi-hollow, 2 pickups, 12-string.

1966-1978		$500	$650

Cobra I/II/III/XII
1966-1978. Double-cut solidbody, 2 knobs. Cobra I has 1 pickup, II 2 pickups and III 3 pickups. 12-string Cobra XII offered '67-'69, has 2 pickups.

1966-1978	Cobra I	$300	$400
1966-1978	Cobra II	$375	$500
1966-1978	Cobra III	$400	$525
1966-1978	Cobra XII	$400	$525

Commander
1965. Single-cut archtop electric, 1 pickup, 2 controls, EKO logo on upper bass bout, maple body in 'dura-glos' finish.

1965		$350	$450

Condor
1966-ca.1969. Double-cut solidbody with 3 or 4 pickups.

1966-1969		$450	$600

Dragon
1967-ca.1969. Single-cut archtop, 2 f-holes, 3 pickups, tremolo.

1967-1969		$550	$700

Flat-Top Acoustic
1960s. Various student-level flat-top acoustic models.

1960s		$210	$275

Florentine
1964-ca.1969. Double-cut archtop, 2 pickups.

1964-1969		$450	$600

Kadett/Kadett XII
1967-ca.1978. Double-cut solidbody with point on lower bass side of body, 3 pickups, tremolo. 12- string Kadett XII offered '68-'69.

1967-1978	Kadett	$450	$600
1968-1969	Kadett XII	$450	$600

Lancer Stereo
1967-1969. Lancer VI with stereo output (route output to 2 amplifiers requires EKO stereo cable for stereo application).

1967-1969		$375	$475

Lancer VI
1967-ca.1969. Double-cut solidbody, 2 pickups.

1967-1969		$275	$350

Lancer XII
1967-1969. Double-cut solidbody electric, 12-string.

1967-1969		$325	$425

Lark I/II
1970. Thin hollow cutaway, sunburst. Lark I has 1 pickup and Lark II 2.

1970	Lark I	$375	$500
1970	Lark II	$375	$500

Model 180
1960s. Cutaway acoustic archtop.

1960s		$275	$350

Model 285 Modello
1960s. Thinline single-cut, 1 pickup.

1962		$350	$450

Model 290/2V
1963-1965. Maple body and neck, ebony 'board, dot markers, 2 pickups, tremolo, renamed Barracuda in '66.

1963-1965		$450	$600

Model 300/375
1962. Copy of Hofner Club-style electric, single-cut, 2 pickups, set-neck.

1962		$650	$850

Model 400 Ekomaster
1960-1962. Jazzmaster-style, 1, 2 or 4 (2+2) pickups, sparkle finish.

1960-1962	4 pickups	$600	$800

Model 500/1 / 500/1V
1961-1965. Plastic covered solidbody, 1 pickup. 500/1 no vibrato, 1V with vibrato.

1961-1965	500/1	$525	$675
1961-1965	500/1V	$600	$775

Model 500/2 / 500/3V
1961-1964. Plastic covered solidbody, plastic sparkle finish. 500/2 no vibrato, 2 pickups. 3V with vibrato, 3 pickups.

1961-1965	500/2	$600	$775
1961-1965	500/3V	$625	$825

Model 500/4 / 500/4V
1961-1964. Plastic covered solidbody, 4 pickups. 500/4 no vibrato, 4V with vibrato.

1961-1965	500/4	$725	$925
1961-1965	500/4V	$750	$1,000

Model 540 (Classical)
1960s. Nylon-string classical guitar.

1960s		$190	$250

Model 700/3V
1961-1964. Map-shape/tulip-shape body, 3 pickups, vibrato, woodgrain plastic finish.

1961-1964		$900	$1,175

Model 700/4V
1961-1967. Map-shape/tulip-shape body, 4 pickups, multiple switches, vibrato.

1961-1967	Red, blue, silver sparkle	$1,050	$1,350
1961-1967	Standard finish	$900	$1,175

Ranger 6/12
1967-ca.1982. D-size flat-top acoustic, large 3-point 'guard, dot inlays, EKO Ranger label. Ranger 12 is 12-string.

1967-1982	Ranger 12	$350	$450
1967-1982	Ranger 6	$350	$450

Ranger 6/12 Electra
1967. Ranger 6/12 with on-board pickup and 2 controls, 6-string with dot markers, 12-string with block markers.

1967	12 Electra	$365	$475
1967	6 Electra	$365	$475

Rocket VI/XII (Rokes)
1967-ca.1969. Rocket-shape design, solidbody, 6-string, says Rokes on the headstock, Rokes were a popular English band that endorsed EKO guitars, marketed as the Rocket VI in the U.S.; and as the Rokes in Europe, often called the Rok. Rocket XII is 12-string.

1967-1969	Rocket VI	$650	$850
1967-1969	Rocket XII	$650	$850

MODEL YEAR	FEATURES	EXC. COND. LOW	HIGH

El Degas

Early 1970s-early '80s. Japanese-made copies of classic America electrics and acoustics, imported by Buegeleisen & Jacobson of New York, New York.

Solidbody

Copies of classic American models, including the Let's Play.

1970s $250 $325

El Maya

1970s-1980s. Also labeled Maya. Solidbody, archtop and semi-hollow guitars built by Japan's Chushin Gakki Co., which also built models for several other manufacturers.

Eleca

2004-present. Student/budget level, production, acoustic and electric guitars, imported by Eleca International. They also offer amps, effects and mandolins.

Electar

See Epiphone listing.

Electra

1970-1984, 2013-present. Imported from Japan by St. Louis Music. Most instruments made by Matsumoku in Japan. The Electra line replaced SLM's Japanese-made Apollo and U.S.-made Custom Kraft lines. First guitar, simply called The Electra, was a copy of the Ampeg Dan Armstrong lucite guitar and issued in '70, followed quickly by a variety of bolt-neck copies of other brands. In '75 the Tree-of-Life guitars debut and the line is expanded. Open-book headstocks changed to wave or fan shape by '78. Some Korean production begins in early-'80s. In the fall of '83, the Electra Brand becomes Electra Phoenix. By beginning of '84, the brand becomes Electra-Westone and by the end of '84 just Westone. In 2013, the brand was revived with guitars built by luthiers Ben Chafin and Mick Donner in Tampa, Florida. Matsumoku-made guitars have serial number in which first 1 or 2 digits represent the year of manufacture. Thus a guitar with a serial number beginning in 0 or 80 would be from 1980.

Concert Professional

Late 1970s. Howard Roberts style, single-cut electric flat-top with oval sound hole, single humbucking pickup, fancy markers.

1977 $650 $850

Custom

1970s. Double-cut solidbody, 2 pickups, Custom logo on truss rod, cherry finish.

1970s $525 $675

Elvin Bishop

1976-ca.1980. Double-cut semi-hollow body, tree-of-life inlay.

1976-1980 $650 $850

Flying Wedge

1970s. V body, six-on-a-side tuners.

1970s $450 $575

MODEL YEAR	FEATURES	EXC. COND. LOW	HIGH

MPC Outlaw

1977-1980. Symmetric horn body, neck-thru, has separate modules (Modular Powered Circuits) that plug in for different effects. Includes X710 (peace sign burned into natural mahogany top), X720 (gray sunburst), X730 (tobacco sunburst) and X 740 (maple top).

1977-1980 $725 $950

1977-1980 MPC plug in module $100 $125

MPC X310

1976-1980. MPC model, LP solidbody, 2 humbuckers (bridge w/ exposed zebra bobbins), 4 in-line control knobs plus 2 toggles, gold hardware, black finish.

1976-1980 $650 $850

MPC X320

1976-1980. Same as X310, but with transparent cherry red finish over mahogany top.

1976-1980 $650 $850

MPC X330

1976-1980. Same as X310, but with cherry sunburst finish on maple top.

1976-1980 $650 $850

MPC X340

1976-1980. Same as X310, but with Jacaranda rosewood top.

1976-1980 $650 $850

MPC X350

1977-1980. Same as X310, but with tobacco sunburst on a maple top.

1977-1980 $650 $850

Phoenix

1980-1984. Classic offset double-cut solidbody, Phoenix logo on headstock.

1980-1984 $290 $375

Rock

1971-1973. Single cut solidbody, becomes the Super Rock in '73.

1971-1973 $400 $525

Super Rock

1973-ca.1978. Renamed from Rock ('71-'73).

1973-1978 $475 $625

X135

1982. Offset double-cut solidbody, 2 humbucker pickups.

1982 $290 $375

X145 60th Anniversary

1982. Classic offset double-cut only made one year, Anniversary plate on back of headstock, single/single/hum pickups.

1982 $290 $375

X150

1975. Offset double-cut, 2 humbucker pickups.

1975 $400 $525

X220 Omega

1976-ca. 1980. Single-cut solidbody, block inlays, Omega logo on truss rod, black with rosewood neck, or natural with figured top and maple neck.

1976-1980 $450 $575

X280/X290 Working Man

1980-1984. Modified double-cut solidbody, 2 exposed-coil humbuckers, dot inlays, natural satin finish (X280) or jet black (X290).

1980-1984 $290 $375

1976 Electra Elvin Bishop Signature Model 2281

Greg Perrine

Late-1970s Electra MPC X320

Elferink

Elijah Jewel

MODEL YEAR	FEATURES	EXC. COND. LOW	HIGH

X410

1975. Double-cut thinline acoustic archtop, 2 humbucker pickups, large split triangle markers, open-book style headstock shape.

1975		$650	$850

X420

1978. Double-cut thinline acoustic archtop, 2 humbucker pickups, dot markers, wave-shape style headstock.

1978		$450	$575

X935 Endorser

1983-1984. Double-cut solidbody, 2 humbucker pickups, tune-o-matic, dot markers.

1983-1984		$350	$450

X960 Ultima

1981. Hybrid single-cut with additional soft bass bout cutaway, slab solidbody, dot markers, 2 humbucker pickups, wave-shape style headstock.

1981		$400	$525

Electric Gypsy

See listing under Teye.

Electro

1964-1975. The Electro line was manufactured by Electro String Instruments and distributed by Radio-Tel. The Electro logo appeared on the headstock rather than Rickenbacker. Refer to the Rickenbacker section for models.

Electromuse

1940s-1950s. Mainly known for lap steels, Electromuse also offered acoustic and electric hollowbody guitars. They also had tube amps usually sold as a package with a lap steel.

Elferink

1993-present. Production/custom, premium grade, archtop guitars built in the Netherlands by luthier Frans Elferink.

Elijah Jewel

2009-present. Luthier Michael Kerry builds his professional grade, production/custom, acoustic guitars in Mineola, Texas. He also builds mandolins.

Elite

1960s. Guitars made in Italy by the Crucianelli accordion company, which made several other brands.

Elk

Late-1960s. Japanese-made by Elk Gakki Co., Ltd. Many were copies of American designs. They also offered amps and effects.

Elliott Guitars

1966-present. Premium and presentation grade, custom, nylon-string classical and steel-string guitars built by luthier Jeffrey Elliott in Portland, Oregon.

MODEL YEAR	FEATURES	EXC. COND. LOW	HIGH

Ellis

2000-present. Luthier Andrew Ellis builds his production/custom, premium grade, steel string acoustic and resophonic guitars in Perth, Western Australia. In 2008 he also added lap steels.

Elli-Sound

1960s. Guitars made in Italy by the Crucianelli accordion company, which made several other brands.

Ellsberry Archtop Guitars

2003-present. Premium and presentation grade, custom/production, acoustic and electric archtops built by luthier James Ellsberry previously in Torrance and Harbor City, California, and presently in Huntington Beach.

Emperador

1966-1992. Guitars and basses imported from Japan by Westheimer Musical Instruments. Early models appear to be made by either Teisco or Kawai; later models were made by Cort.

Acoustic

1960s	Archtop or flat-top	$150	$200

Electric Solidbody

1960s		$175	$250

Empire

1997-present. Professional and premium grade, production/custom, solidbody guitars from Lee Garver's GMW Guitarworks of Glendora, California.

Encore

Mid 1960s-present. Budget grade, production, classical, acoustic, and electric guitars imported from China and Vietnam by John Hornby Skewes & Co. in the U.K. They also offer basses.

Engel Guitars

1990-present. Luthier Robert Engel builds his premium grade, production/custom, hollowbody and solidbody guitars in Stamford, Connecticut.

English Electronics

1960s. Lansing, Michigan, company named after owner, some private branded guitars and amps by Valco (Chicago), many models with large English Electronics vertical logo on headstock.

Tonemaster

1960s. National Val-Pro 84 with neck pickup and bridge mounted pickup, black.

1960s		$650	$850

Epcor

1967. Hollowbody electirc guitars and basses built by Joe Hall's Hallmark Guitars in Bakersfield, CA for manufacturer's rep Ed Preager (the EP in the name). Only about 35 were built.

MODEL YEAR	FEATURES	EXC. COND. LOW	HIGH

Epi

1970s. Typical Japanese copy-import, Epi logo on headstock with capital letter split-E logo, inside label says "Norlin," probably for Japanese domestic market.

Acoustic Flat-Top

1970s. D-style, mahogany body.

1970s		$140	$185

Epiphone

Ca. 1873-present. Budget, intermediate, professional and premium grade, production, solidbody, archtop, acoustic, acoustic/electric, resonator, and classical guitars made in the U.S. and overseas. They also offer basses, amps, mandolins, ukes and banjos. Founded in Smyrna, Turkey, by Anastasios Stathopoulos and early instruments had his label. He emigrated to the U.S. in 1903 and changed the name to Stathoupoulo. Anastasios died in '15 and his son, Epaminondas ("Epi") took over. The name changed to House of Stathopoulo in '17 and the company incorporated in '23. In '24 the line of Epiphone Recording banjos debut and in '28 the company name was changed to the Epiphone Banjo Company. In '43 Epi Stathopoulo died and sons Orphie and Frixo took over. Labor trouble shut down the NYC factory in '51 and the company cut a deal with Conn/Continental and relocated to Philadelphia in '52. Frixo died in '57 and Gibson bought the company. Kalamazoo-made Gibson Epiphones debut in '58. In '69 American production ceased and Japanese imports began. Some Taiwanese guitars imported from '79-'81. Limited U.S. production resumed in '82 but sourcing shifted to Korea in '83. In '85 Norlin sold Gibson to Henry Juszkiewicz, Dave Barryman and Gary Zebrowski. In '92 Jim Rosenberg became president of the new Epiphone division.

AJ Masterbilt Series

2004-present. Sloped shoulder D size, solid spruce tops, solid rosewood or mahogany (M) back and sides.

2004-2020	AJ-45ME	$475	$625

Alleykat

2000-2010. Single cut small body archtop, I humbucker and 1 mini-humbucker.

2000-2010		$285	$375

B.B. King Lucille

1997-2019. Laminated double-cut maple body, 2 humbuckers, Lucille on headstock.

1997-2019		$425	$550

Barcelona CE

1999-2000. Classical, solid spruce top, rosewood back and sides, EQ/preamp.

1999-2000		$250	$325

Barcelone (Classical)

1963-1968. Highest model of Epiphone '60s classical guitars, maple back and sides, gold hardware.

1963-1964		$650	$850
1965		$550	$725
1966-1968		$525	$675

MODEL YEAR	FEATURES	EXC. COND. LOW	HIGH

Bard 12-String

1962-1969. Flat-top, mahogany back and sides, natural or sunburst.

1962-1964		$1,125	$1,475
1965		$1,025	$1,325
1966-1969		$885	$1,150

Beverly

1931-1936. Flat-top, arched back, tenor or Hawaiian versions.

1931-1936	Hawaiian	$700	$900
1931-1936	Tenor	$500	$650

Biscuit

1997-2000, 2002-2010. Wood body resonator, biscuit bridge, round neck.

1997-2010		$250	$325

Blackstone

1931-1950. Acoustic archtop, f-holes, sunburst.

1933-1934	Masterbilt	$875	$1,125
1935-1937		$750	$975
1938-1939		$650	$850
1940-1941		$600	$775
1948-1950		$500	$650

Blueshawk Deluxe

2015-2018. Single-cut semi-hollowbody, AAA flamed maple top, mahogany back and sides, 2 P-90s, Midnight Sapphire, Wine red or trans black.

2015-2018		$425	$550

Broadway (Acoustic)

1931-1958. Non-cut acoustic archtop.

1931-1938	Sunburst, walnut body	$2,075	$2,675
1939-1942	Sunburst, maple body	$2,075	$2,675
1946-1958	Natural	$1,750	$2,250
1946-1958	Sunburst	$1,575	$2,050

Broadway Regent (Acoustic Cutaway)

1950-1958. Single-cut acoustic archtop, sunburst.

1950-1958		$1,750	$2,250

Broadway (Electric)

1958-1969. Gibson-made electric archtop, single-cut, 2 New York pickups (mini-humbucking pickups by '61), Frequensator tailpiece, block inlays, sunburst or natural finish with cherry optional in '67 only.

1958-1959	Natural	$2,125	$2,750
1958-1959	Sunburst	$1,875	$2,450
1960-1964	Natural	$2,000	$2,600
1960-1964	Sunburst	$1,800	$2,350
1965	Natural	$1,650	$2,150
1965	Sunburst	$1,550	$2,015
1966-1967	Natural, cherry	$1,550	$2,015
1966-1967	Sunburst	$1,525	$1,975
1968-1969	Natural, cherry	$1,525	$1,975
1968-1969	Sunburst	$1,525	$1,975

Broadway Reissue

1997-2019. Full depth acoustic-electric single cut archtop, 2 humbuckers.

1997-2019		$425	$550

Broadway Tenor

1937-1953. Acoustic archtop, sunburst.

1937-1953		$1,075	$1,400

Epiphone AJ-500M Masterbilt

Rivington Guitars

1946 Epiphone Broadway

Bernunzio Uptown Music

2002 Epiphone Casino Reissue

Bernunzio Uptown Music

1964 Epiphone Coronet

Trey Rabinek <treyrabinek@google.com>

MODEL YEAR	FEATURES	EXC. COND. LOW	HIGH

Byron

1949-ca.1955. Acoustic archtop, mahogany back and sides, sunburst.

1949-1955		$375	$475

C Series Classical (Import)

1995-2006. Nylon-string classical guitars, including C-25 (mahogany back & sides), C-40 (cedar top, mahogany), C-70-CE (rosewood).

1998-2005	C-40	$125	$165

Caiola Custom

1963-1970. Introduced as Caiola, renamed Caiola Custom in '66, electric thinbody archtop, 2 mini-humbuckers, multi-bound top and back, block inlays, walnut or sunburst finish (walnut only by '68).

1963-1964		$1,900	$2,450
1965		$1,725	$2,250
1966-1967		$1,550	$2,015
1968-1970		$1,550	$2,015

Caiola Standard

1966-1970. Electric thinbody archtop, 2 P-90s, single-bound top and back, dot inlays, sunburst or cherry.

1966-1967		$1,450	$1,875
1968-1970		$1,300	$1,700

Casino (1 Pickup)

1961-1969. Thinline hollowbody, double-cut, 1 P-90 pickup, various colors.

1961-1964		$3,850	$5,000
1965		$3,100	$4,100
1966-1969		$2,900	$3,800

Casino (2 Pickups)

1961-1970. Two pickup (P-90) version, various colors. '61-'63 known as Keith Richards model, '64-'65 known as Beatles model.

1961-1962		$5,200	$6,700
1963-1964		$4,300	$5,600
1965		$4,000	$5,300
1966-1970		$3,600	$4,700

Casino (Japan)

1982-1983. Epiphone built a few of its classic models, including the Casino, in Japan from mid-'82 to mid-'83.

1982-1983		$750	$975

Casino J.L. U.S.A. 1965

2003-2006. 1,965 made.

2003-2006		$2,050	$2,675

Casino Reissue

1995-2019. Import, sunburst.

1995-2019		$575	$750

Casino Revolution

1999-2005. Limited production 1965 reissue model, with certificate of authenticity, sanded natural.

1999-2005		$2,050	$2,675

Casino 1961 50th Anniversary Limited Edition

2011. Trapeze (TD) or TremTone vibrato (TDV), total run of 1,961 built.

2011	TDV	$625	$825
2011	Trapeze	$625	$825

Century

1939-1970. Thinline archtop, non-cut, 1 pickup, trapeze tailpiece, walnut finish, sunburst finish available in '58, Royal Burgundy available '61 and only sunburst finish available by '68.

1939-1948	Oblong shape pu	$975	$1,250
1949-1957	Sunburst	$875	$1,125
1958-1962	Sunburst, P-90, plate logo	$850	$1,100
1963-1964	Sunburst, P-90, no plate logo	$850	$1,100
1965	Sunburst, cherry	$750	$975
1966-1970	Sunburst, cherry	$675	$875

Classic (Classical)

1963-1970.

1963-1964		$400	$525
1965		$350	$450
1966-1970		$350	$450

Collegiate

2004-2005. Les Paul-style body, 1 humbucker, various college graphic decals on body.

2004-2005		$150	$200

Coronet (Electric Archtop)

1939-1949. Electric archtop, laminated mahogany body, 1 pickup, trapeze tailpiece, sunburst, name continued as an electric solidbody in '58.

1939-1949		$775	$1,000

Coronet (Solidbody)

1958-1969. Solidbody electric, 1 New York pickup ('58-'59), 1 P-90 ('59-'69), cherry or black finish, Silver Fox finish available by '63, reintroduced as Coronet USA '90-'94, Korean-made '95-'98.

1958-1959	Cherry, NY pu	$3,000	$3,875
1959	Black (rare), NY pu	$5,125	$6,650
1960-1964	Various colors	$2,725	$3,550
1965	Standard color	$1,925	$2,500
1965-1966	Custom color	$3,850	$5,000
1966-1969	Standard color	$1,750	$2,250

Coronet U.S.A.

1990-1994. Made in Nashville, reverse banana headstock, typical Coronet styled body, single-coil and humbucker.

1990-1994		$650	$850

Coronet (Import)

1995-1998. Import version.

1995-1998		$300	$400

Crestwood Custom

1958-1970. Solidbody, 2 New York pickups ('58-'60), 2 mini-humbuckers ('61-'70), symmetrical body and 3+3 tuners ('58-'62), asymmetrical and 1x6 tuners ('63-'70), slab body with no Gibson equivalent model.

1958-1960	Cherry, NY pus	$2,475	$3,225
1959-1960	Sunburst, NY pus	$2,475	$3,225
1961-1962	Cherry, mini-hums	$2,375	$3,075
1961-1962	White, mini-hums	$2,825	$3,675
1963-1964	Cherry, mini-hums, 1x6	$1,775	$2,300
1963-1964	Custom color	$3,150	$4,075
1965	Cherry	$1,650	$2,150
1965	Custom color	$3,075	$4,000
1966-1967	Cherry	$1,575	$2,050
1966-1967	Custom color	$1,975	$2,550
1968-1970	Cherry, white	$1,425	$1,850

Crestwood Deluxe

1963-1969. Solidbody with 3 mini-humbuckers, block inlay, cherry, white or Pacific Blue finish, 1x6 tuners.

MODEL YEAR	FEATURES	EXC. COND. LOW	HIGH
1963-1964	Cherry, mini-hums	$1,975	$2,550
1963-1964	Custom color	$3,175	$4,100
1965	Cherry	$1,775	$2,300
1965	Custom color	$2,900	$3,775
1966-1967	Cherry	$1,575	$2,050
1966-1967	Custom color	$2,050	$2,650
1968-1969	Cherry, white	$1,575	$2,050

De Luxe

1931-1957. Non-cut acoustic archtop, maple back and sides, trapeze tailpiece ('31-'37), frequensator tailpiece ('37-'57), gold-plated hardware, sunburst or natural finish.

MODEL YEAR	FEATURES	EXC. COND. LOW	HIGH
1931-1935	Sunburst, 1738"	$4,800	$6,250
1935-1944	Sunburst, 1638"	$4,250	$5,500
1939-1944	Natural	$4,250	$5,500
1945-1949	Natural	$3,625	$4,700
1945-1949	Sunburst	$3,400	$4,400
1950-1957	Natural	$3,475	$4,500
1950-1957	Sunburst	$3,200	$4,100

De Luxe Regent (Acoustic Archtop)

1948-1952. Acoustic cutaway archtop, high-end appointments, rounded cutaway, natural finish, renamed De Luxe Cutaway in '53.

MODEL YEAR	FEATURES	EXC. COND. LOW	HIGH
1948-1952	Natural	$5,800	$7,500
1948-1952	Sunburst	$4,800	$6,225

De Luxe Cutaway/Deluxe Cutaway

1953-1970. Renamed from De Luxe Regent, cataloged Deluxe Cutaway by Gibson in '58, special order by '64 with limited production because acoustic archtops were pretty much replaced by electric archtops. There is also a FT Deluxe Cutaway flat-top (see FT listings).

MODEL YEAR	FEATURES	EXC. COND. LOW	HIGH
1953-1957	Natural	$5,800	$7,500
1953-1957	Sunburst	$4,800	$6,225
1958-1959		$4,650	$6,025
1960-1964	Gibson Kalamazoo, rounded cutaway	$4,250	$5,525
1965-1970	Special order only	$3,625	$4,700

De Luxe Electric (Archtop)

1954-1957. Single-cut electric archtop, 2 pickups, called the Zephyr De Luxe Regent from '48-'54. Produced with a variety of specs, maple or spruce tops, different inlays and pickup combinations.

MODEL YEAR	FEATURES	EXC. COND. LOW	HIGH
1954-1957	Natural	$3,475	$4,500
1954-1957	Sunburst	$3,250	$4,200

Del Ray

1995-2000. Offset double-cut body, 2 blade humbuckers, dot markers, tune-o-matic, flamed maple top.

MODEL YEAR	FEATURES	EXC. COND. LOW	HIGH
1995-2000		$300	$400

Devon

1949-1957. Acoustic archtop, non-cut, mahogany back and sides, sunburst finish, optional natural finish by '54.

MODEL YEAR	FEATURES	EXC. COND. LOW	HIGH
1950-1957	Sunburst	$1,400	$1,800
1954-1957	Natural	$1,400	$1,800

Don Everly (SQ-180)

1997-2004. Jumbo acoustic reissue, large double 'guard, black gloss finish.

MODEL YEAR	FEATURES	EXC. COND. LOW	HIGH
1997-2004		$525	$675

Dot (ES-335 Dot)/Dot Archtop

2000-2020. Dot-neck ES-335.

MODEL YEAR	FEATURES	EXC. COND. LOW	HIGH
2000-2020		$425	$550

Dot Studio

2004-2019. Simplified Dot, 2 control knobs, black hardware.

MODEL YEAR	FEATURES	EXC. COND. LOW	HIGH
2004-2019		$275	$350

Dove Limited Edition

2008. Dove Limited Edition logo on label, Dove script logo on truss rod cover, classic dove logo art on 'guard and dove inlay on bridge, cherry or ebony.

MODEL YEAR	FEATURES	EXC. COND. LOW	HIGH
2008		$225	$300

DR Series/Songmaker Series

2004-present. Dreadnought, spruce top, mahogany back and sides, various models including: DR-100 (various colors), DR-200C (single-cut, natural or vintage sunburst), DR-212 (12-string, natural) and DR-500RNS (rosewood, natural satin).

MODEL YEAR	FEATURES	EXC. COND. LOW	HIGH
2012-2020	Songmaker DR-212	$150	$195

Dwight

1963, 1967. Coronet labeled as Dwight and made for Sonny Shields Music of St. Louis, 75 made in '63 and 36 in '67, cherry. National-Supro made Dwight brand lap steels in the '50s.

MODEL YEAR	FEATURES	EXC. COND. LOW	HIGH
1963		$2,750	$3,575
1967		$1,750	$2,250

EA/ET/ES Series (Japan)

1970-1979. Production of the Epiphone brand was moved to Japan in '70. Models included the EA (electric thinline) and ET (electric solidbody).

MODEL YEAR	FEATURES	EXC. COND. LOW	HIGH
1970-1975	EA-250 Riviera	$375	$500
1970-1975	ET-270	$450	$575
1970-1975	ET-275	$450	$575
1972	ES-255 Casino	$465	$600
1975-1979	ET-290 Crestwood	$450	$575

EJ-160E John Lennon

1997-2013. Based on John's Gibson acoustic/electric, sunburst, signature on body.

MODEL YEAR	FEATURES	EXC. COND. LOW	HIGH
1997-2013		$325	$425

EJ-200 Series

1994-2020. Solid spruce top, laminate maple body.

MODEL YEAR	FEATURES	EXC. COND. LOW	HIGH
1994-2020	Various models	$200	$400

EJ-300

2004-2006. Solid spruce top, laminate rosewood body.

MODEL YEAR	FEATURES	EXC. COND. LOW	HIGH
2004-2006		$425	$550

El Diablo

1994-1995. Offset double-cut acoustic/electric, onboard piezo and 3-band EQ, composite back and sides, spruce top, cherry sunburst.

MODEL YEAR	FEATURES	EXC. COND. LOW	HIGH
1994-1995		$350	$450

Electar Model M

1935-1939. Epiphone's initial entry into the new electric guitar market of the mid-'30s, 14 3/4" laminate maple archtop, horseshoe pickup, trap door on back for electronics, Electar logo on headstock, oblong pickup replaces horseshoe in late-'37.

MODEL YEAR	FEATURES	EXC. COND. LOW	HIGH
1935-1936	2 control knobs	$1,125	$1,450
1937-1939	3 control knobs	$1,125	$1,450

1998 Epiphone Del Ray
Rivington Guitars

Epiphone Dot

1959 Epiphone Emperor (Thinline Electric)

1997 Epiphone Flying V

Johnny Zapp

MODEL YEAR	FEATURES	EXC. COND. LOW	HIGH

Electar Model M Tenor

1937-1939. Electric tenor 4-string with Electar specs.

1937-1939	3 knobs, natural	$1,025	$1,325

Elitist Series

2003-2019. Made in Japan, higher-grade series, using finer woods and inlays and U.S.-made Gibson pickups.

2003-2004	J-200	$1,300	$1,675
2003-2004	L-00/VS	$1,050	$1,375
2003-2005	'65 Texan	$1,300	$1,675
2003-2005	'61 SG Standard	$850	$1,100
2003-2005	Riviera	$1,475	$1,900
2003-2008	'63 ES-335 Dot	$1,350	$1,750
2003-2008	Byrdland/L5	$1,900	$2,450
2003-2009	Broadway	$1,275	$1,650
2003-2009	LP Custom	$850	$1,100
2003-2009	LP Standard	$850	$1,100
2003-2009	LP Standard '57 Goldtop	$850	$1,100
2003-2009	LP Studio	$700	$900
2003-2009	Sheraton	$1,475	$1,900
2003-2019	Casino	$1,300	$1,675
2004-2005	Jim Croce L-00	$850	$1,100
2005	Chet Atkins Country Gentleman	$1,300	$1,675
2007-2009	LP Plus	$850	$1,100
2012	Dwight Yoakam Trash Casino	$1,300	$1,675

Emperor (Acoustic Archtop)

1935-1954. Acoustic archtop, non-cut, maple back and sides, multi-bound body, gold-plated hardware, sunburst, optional natural finish by '39.

1935-1939	Natural	$6,400	$8,300
1935-1939	Sunburst	$4,500	$5,850
1940-1949	Natural, Sunburst	$5,700	$7,400
1950-1954	Natural	$5,125	$6,650
1950-1954	Sunburst	$4,700	$6,125

Emperor Regent

1948-1953. Acoustic archtop with rounded cutaway, renamed Emperor Cutaway in '53.

1948-1953	Natural	$5,675	$7,350
1948-1953	Sunburst	$5,200	$6,750

Emperor Cutaway

1953-1957. Renamed from Emperor Regent, acoustic archtop, single-cut, maple back and sides, multi-bound body, gold-plated hardware, sunburst or natural.

1953-1957	Natural	$5,675	$7,350
1953-1957	Sunburst	$5,200	$6,750

Emperor Electric

1953-1957. Archtop, single-cut, 3 pickups, multi-bound body, sunburst, called the Zephyr Emperor Regent in '50-'53.

1953-1957		$3,100	$4,000

Emperor (Thinline Electric)

1958-1969. Single-cut, thinline archtop, 3 New York pickups in '58-'60, 3 mini-humbuckers '61 on, multi-bound, gold-plated hardware, sunburst or natural finish until '65 when only sunburst was made.

1958-1959	Natural, 3 NY pus	$6,900	$9,000
1958-1959	Sunburst, 3 NY pus	$5,350	$6,950
1960-1962	Natural	$6,550	$8,500
1960-1962	Sunburst	$5,350	$6,950
1963-1969	Special order	$4,550	$5,900

Emperor/Emperor II

1982-1994. Single-cut archtop jazz guitar, 2 humbuckers, blocks, gold hardware. II added to name in '93, became Joe Pass Emperor II (see that listing) in '95, although his name was on the guitar as early as '91.

1982-1989	Matsumoku, Japan	$700	$925
1990-1994		$700	$925

Entrada (Classical)

1963-1968. Small classical, 13.25" bout, natural.

1963-1964		$400	$525
1965-1968		$350	$450

ES-175 Premium

2010-2019. Limited Edition, vintage "aged" lacquer finish, various colors.

2010-2019		$525	$700

ES-295

1997-2001, 2003-2016. Epiphone's version of classic Gibson goldtop.

1997-2016		$600	$775

ES-339 PRO/ES-339

2012-present. Maple laminate body, 2 pickups. PRO dropped from name in 2020.

2012-2020		$300	$400

Espana (Classical)

1962-1968. Classical, U.S.-made, maple back and sides, natural, imported in '69 from Japan.

1962-1964		$575	$750
1965		$525	$675
1966-1968		$475	$625

Exellente

1963-1969, 1994-1995. Flat-top, Brazilian rosewood back and sides (Indian rosewood '68-'69), cloud inlays. Name revived on Gibson Montana insturment in '90s.

1963-1964	Brazilian	$5,900	$7,650
1965	Brazilian	$5,500	$7,150
1966-1967	Brazilian	$5,125	$6,650
1968-1969	Indian	$3,150	$4,100

1958 Korina Explorer

1998-2011. Explorer with typical appointments, korina body. This guitar was produced with a variety of specs, ranging from maple tops to spruce tops, different inlay markers were also used, different pickup combinations have been seen, natural or sunburst finish.

1998-2011		$425	$550

1958 Gothic Explorer/Flying V

2002-2012. Flat black finish, V ends in 2010.

2002-2012		$425	$550

Firebird

1995-2000. Two mini-humbuckers, Firebird Red, dot markers.

1995-2000		$425	$550

Firebird 300

1986-1988. Korean import, Firebird Red.

1986-1988		$425	$550

Firebird 500

1986-1988. Korean import, Firebird Red.

1986-1988		$425	$550

MODEL YEAR	FEATURES	EXC. COND. LOW	HIGH

1963 Firebird VII/Firebird VII

2000-2010. Three mini-humbuckers, gold hardware, Maestro-style vibrato, block markers, Firebird Red, reverse body. 1963 dropped from name in '03.

2000-2010		$475	$625

Firebird I Joe Bonamassa

2016. Artist Limited Edition, modeled after his Gibson '63 Firebird I (nicknamed "Treasure"), Tobacco Sunburst or Polymist Gold.

2016		$1,075	$1,400

Firebird Studio

2006-2011. Two humbuckers, with worn cherry finish.

2006-2011		$425	$550

Flamekat

1999-2005. Archtop, flame finish, double dice position markers, 2 mini-humbuckers, Epiphone Bigsby.

1999-2005		$250	$325

Flying V/'67 Flying V

1989-1998, 2003-2005. '67 or '58 specs, alder body, natural.

1989-1998	'67 specs	$425	$550
2003-2005	'58 specs	$425	$550

1958 Korina Flying V

1998-2011, 2016. Typical Flying V configuration, korina body, veneer top. Limited Edition offered in '16 with solid korina, 2 humbucker pickups and gold hardware.

1998-2011	Factory, veneer	$425	$550
2016	Limited Edition	$450	$575

1958 Korina Flying V Joe Bonamassa

2017-2018. Limited Edition, modeled from his first '58 Korina Flying V (nicknamed "Amos"), '50s-style Flying V case, hand-signed COA.

2017-2018		$700	$900

Flying V Prophecy

2020-present. AAA figured maple top, Yellow Tiger or Black with aged gloss finish.

2020		$500	$650

FT 30

1941-1949. Acoustic flat-top, brown stain, mahogany back and sides, reintroduced as Gibson-made FT 30 Caballero in '58.

1941-1943		$1,050	$1,375
1944-1949		$900	$1,175

FT 30 Caballero

1959-1970. Reintroduced from Epiphone-made FT 30, Gibson-made acoustic flat-top, natural, all mahogany body, dot inlay, tenor available '63-'68.

1959-1961		$900	$1,150
1962-1964		$650	$850
1965		$575	$750
1966-1970		$500	$650

FT 45

1941-1948. Acoustic flat-top, walnut back and sides, cherry neck, rosewood 'board, natural top, reintroduced as Gibson-made FT 45 Cortez in '58.

1941-1943		$1,525	$1,975
1944-1948		$1,175	$1,525

FT 45 Cortez

1958-1969. Reintroduced from Epiphone-made FT 45, Gibson-made acoustic flat-top, 16.5", mahogany back and sides, sunburst or natural top (sunburst only in '59-'62).

1958-1959	Sunburst	$1,275	$1,650
1960-1964	Sunburst, natural	$1,155	$1,500
1965-1966	Sunburst, natural	$1,025	$1,326
1967-1969	Sunburst, natural	$800	$1,025

FT 79

1941-1958. Acoustic 16" flat-top, square shoulder dreadnought, walnut back and sides until '49 and laminated maple back and sides '49 on, natural, renamed FT 79 Texan by Gibson in '58.

1941-1943	Walnut	$2,275	$2,950
1944-1949	Walnut	$2,075	$2,675
1949-1958	Maple	$1,650	$2,125

FT 79 Texan

1958-1970, 1993-1995. Renamed from Epiphone FT 79, Gibson-made acoustic flat-top, mahogany back and sides, sunburst or natural top, Gibson Montana made 170 in '93-'95.

1958-1959		$2,500	$3,250
1960-1964		$2,400	$3,125
1965		$2,300	$3,015
1966-1967		$2,150	$2,800
1968-1969		$1,850	$2,400
1970		$1,575	$2,025

Paul McCartney 1964 Texan (U.S.A.)

2005-2006. Reproduction of McCartney's '64 Texan made in Gibson's Montana plant, two runs, one of 40 guitars ('05), second of 250 ('05-'06). First 40 were hand-aged and came with Sir Paul's autograph, display case and certificate; the 250 run were not-hand aged, but have signed labels.

2005-2006		$2,900	$3,775

Paul McCartney 1964 Texan (Japan)

2006-2010. Limited run of 1,964 guitars.

2006-2010		$1,125	$1,450

1964 Texan (Inspired By Series)

2010-2019. Imported production model, acoustic/electric, non-adjustable bridge.

2010-2019		$240	$310

FT 85 Serenader 12-String

1963-1969. 12 strings, mahogany back and sides, dot inlay, natural.

1963-1964		$875	$1,125
1965		$725	$925
1966-1969		$675	$875

FT 90 El Dorado

1963-1970. Dreadnought flat-top acoustic, mahogany back and sides, multi-bound front and back, natural.

1963-1964		$1,925	$2,500
1965		$1,500	$1,925
1966-1967		$1,400	$1,825
1968-1970		$1,325	$1,725

FT 95 Folkster

1966-1969. 14" small body, mahogany back and sides, natural, double white 'guards.

1966-1969		$560	$725

1958 Epiphone FT 79 Texan

Bernunzio Uptown Music

1955 Epiphone FT Deluxe Cutaway

Craig Brody

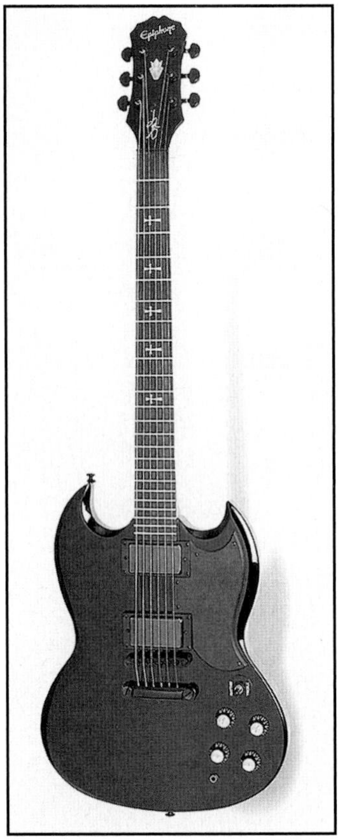

Epiphone G 400 Tony Iommi

1967 Epiphone Howard Roberts Standard

Imaged by Heritage Auctions, HA.com

MODEL YEAR	FEATURES	EXC. COND. LOW	HIGH

FT 98 Troubadour

1963-1969. 16" square shouldered dreadnought, maple back and sides, gold-plated hardware, classical width 'board.

1963-1964		$1,600	$2,100
1965		$1,500	$1,925
1966-1969		$1,400	$1,825

FT 110

1941-1958. Acoustic flat-top, natural, renamed the FT 110 Frontier by Gibson in '58.

1941-1943	Square shoulder	$3,400	$4,600
1944-1949	Square shoulder	$3,200	$4,200
1949-1954	Round shoulder	$2,700	$3,500
1954-1958	Mahogany neck	$2,700	$3,500

FT 110 Frontier

1958-1970, 1994. Renamed from FT 110, acoustic flat-top, natural or sunburst, Gibson Montana made 30 in '94.

1958-1959		$4,250	$5,525
1960-1964		$3,800	$4,900
1965		$3,475	$4,500
1966-1970		$3,250	$4,200

FT Deluxe

1939-1941. Acoustic flat-top, 16.5".

1939-1941		$5,125	$6,650

FT Deluxe Cutaway (FT 210)

1954-1957. Acoustic flat-top, cutaway, 16.5". Some labeled FT 210.

1954-1957		$5,050	$6,550

FT Series (Flat-Tops Japan)

1970s. In '70 Epiphone moved production to Japan. Various 6- to 12-string models were made, nearly all with bolt necks and small rectangular blue labels on the inside back, rangeing from the budget FT 120 to the top-of-the-line FT 570 Super Jumbo.

1970s	Various models	$150	$450

G 310

1989-2019. SG-style model with large 'guard and gig bag.

1989-2019		$200	$260

G 400

1989-2013. SG-style, 2 humbuckers, crown inlays.

1989-2013		$275	$365

G 400 Custom

1998-2000, 2003-2011. 3 humbucker version, gold harware, block inlays.

1998-2011		$375	$500

G 400 Deluxe

1999-2007. Flame maple top version of 2 humbucker 400.

1999-2007		$425	$550

G 400 Limited Edition

2001-2002. 400 with Deluxe Maestro lyra vibrola, cherry red.

2001-2002		$425	$550

G 400 Tony Iommi

2003-2011. SG-style model with cross 'board inlay markers, black finish.

2003-2011		$425	$550

G 1275 Custom Double Neck

1996-2011. SG-style alder body, 6- & 12-string, maple top, mahogany neck, cherry red, set neck. Also offered as bolt-neck Standard for '96-'98.

1996-2011		$550	$725

Genesis

1979-1980. Double-cut solidbody, 2 humbuckers with coil-taps, carved top, red or black, available as Custom, Deluxe, and Standard models, Taiwan import.

1979-1980		$625	$825

Granada (Non-cutaway Thinbody)

1962-1969. Non-cut thinline archtop, 1 f-hole, 1 pickup, trapeze tailpiece, sunburst finish.

1962		$925	$1,200
1963-1964		$900	$1,175
1965-1969		$775	$1,000

Granada (Cutaway)

1965-1970. Single-cut version.

1965		$1,050	$1,400
1966-1970		$1,050	$1,400

Hollywood Masterbilt Tenor

1931-1936. Tenor version of the Triumph, acoustic archtop 15.4", 19-fret Brazilian rosewood 'board, diagonal diamond markers.

1931-1936		$1,450	$1,875

Howard Roberts Standard

1964-1970. Single-cut acoustic archtop, bound front and back, cherry or sunburst finish, listed in catalog as acoustic but built as electric.

1964		$1,850	$2,400
1965-1970		$1,550	$2,000

Howard Roberts Custom

1965-1970. Single-cut archtop, bound front and back, 1 pickup, walnut finish (natural offered '66 only).

1965-1970		$2,050	$2,650

Howard Roberts III

1987-1991. Two pickups, various colors.

1987-1991		$500	$650

Hummingbird/Hummingbird Pro

1994-present. Twin parallelogram inlays, hummingbird 'guard, replaced by Pro, with added electronics, in '13. Pro dropped from name in 2020.

1994-2020		$200	$275

Inspiration Style A Tenor

1928-1929. Banjo resonator style body with round soundhole, A headstock logo, spruce top, walnut back, sides and neck.

1928-1929		$1,775	$2,300

Joe Pass/Joe Pass Emperor II

1995-2019. Single-cut archtop jazz guitar, 2 humbuckers, blocks, gold hardware, natural or sunbusrt, renamed from Emperor II (see that listing). Limited Edition all-gold finish or Wine Red were available early on.

1995-2020		$500	$650

Les Paul 100/LP-100

1993-2019. Affordable single-cut Les Paul, bolt-on neck.

1993-2019		$170	$220

Les Paul '56 Goldtop

1998-2013. Made in China, based on '56 Goldtop specs with 2 P-90s. Black finish was offered starting in '09.

1998-2013	Gold	$500	$650
2009-2013	Black	$500	$650

MODEL YEAR	FEATURES	EXC. COND. LOW	HIGH

Les Paul Ace Frehley

2001. Les Paul Custom 3-pickups, Ace's signature on 22nd fret, lightning bolt markers.

2001		$725	$925

Les Paul Alabama Farewell Tour

2003. Limited production, 1 pickup single-cut Jr., American flag and Alabama logo graphics and band signatures on body, Certificate of Authenticity.

2003		$500	$650

Les Paul Black Beauty

1997-2019. Classic styling with three gold plated pickups, black finish, block markers.

1997-2019		$500	$650

Les Paul Classic

2003-2005. Classic Les Paul Standard specs, figured maple top, sunburst.

2003-2005		$500	$650

Les Paul Custom

1989-2011. Various colors.

1989-2011		$500	$650

Les Paul Custom Plus (Flame Top)

1998-2010. Flamed maple top version of 2 pickup Custom, gold hardware, sunburst.

1998-2010		$500	$650

Les Paul Custom Silverburst

2007-2008. 2 humbuckers, silverburst finish.

2007-2008		$500	$650

Les Paul Dale Earnhardt

2003. Dale Earnhardt graphics, 1 humbucker.

2003		$500	$650

Les Paul Deluxe

1998-2000. Typical mini-humbucker pickups.

1998-2000		$500	$650

Les Paul ES Limited Edition

1999-2000. Les Paul semi-hollow body with f-holes, carved maple top, gold hardware, cherry sunburst and other color options.

1999-2000	Custom	$525	$700
1999-2000	Standard	$525	$700

Les Paul Gold Top

1994-1998. Goldtop, 2 humbuckers. Listed as Les Paul Standard Goldtop in '94.

1994-1998		$500	$650

Les Paul Joe Perry Boneyard

2004-2006. Boneyard logo on headstock, figured Boneyard finish.

2004-2006		$500	$650

Les Paul Jr. '57 Reissue

2006. '57 Reissue on truss rod cover, logo and script Les Paul Junior stencil on headstock, lower back headstock states 'Epiphone Limited Edition Custom Shop'.

2006		$230	$300

Les Paul Music Rising

2006-2007. Music Rising (Katrina charity) graphic, 2 humbuckers.

2006-2007		$250	$325

Les Paul Prophecy

2020-present. Modern Collection, mahogany body, AAA flame maple veneer top in Red Tiger or Olive Tiger aged gloss, or plain top in black aged gloss.

2020		$500	$650

Les Paul Sparkle L.E.

2001. Limited Edition LP Standard, silver, purple, red (and others) glitter finish, optional Bigsby.

2001		$500	$650

Les Paul Special

1994-2000, 2020-present. Double-cut, bolt neck. Reintroduced in '20 with P-90 Pro pickups, CTS electronics, TV yellow finish.

1994-2000		$175	$225

Les Paul Special II

1996-2019. Economical Les Paul, 2 pickups, single-cut, various colors.

1996-2016	Player Pack with amp	$90	$120
1996-2019	Guitar only	$75	$100

Les Paul Special Limited Edition/TV Special

2006. Copy of single-cut late '50s Les Paul Special with TV finish.

2006		$210	$275

Les Paul Standard

1989-2019. Solid mahogany body, carved maple top, 2 humbuckers.

1989-2019	Various colors	$350	$450

Les Paul Standard Baritone

2004-2005. 27-3/4" long-scale baritone model.

2004-2005		$500	$650

Les Paul Standard Plus FMT

2003-2012. LP Standard figured curly maple sunburst top.

2003-2012		$500	$650

Les Paul Standard Ultra/Ultra II

2005-2012. LP Standard with chambered and contoured body, quilted maple top.

2005-2012	Ultra	$500	$650
2005-2012	Ultra II	$500	$650

Les Paul Studio

1995-present. Epiphone's version of Gibson LP Studio.

1995-2020		$210	$275

Les Paul XII

1998-2000. 12-string solidbody, trapeze tailpiece, flamed maple sunburst, standard configuration.

1998-2000		$425	$550

Slash Les Paul

1997-2000. Slash logo on body.

1997-2000		$600	$800

Slash Les Paul Goldtop

2008-2012. Limited Edition 2,000 made, goldtop finish, Seymour Duncan exposed humbuckers, Slash logo on truss rod cover, includes certificate of authenticity.

2008-2012	With COA	$675	$875

Slash Les Paul Standard Plus-Top

2008-2012. Figured top, exposed humbuckers, includes certificate of authenticity.

2008-2012	With COA	$750	$975

Zakk Wylde Les Paul Custom

2002-2019. Bull's-eye graphic, block markers, split diamond headstock inlay.

2002-2019		$425	$550

Epiphone Les Paul Standard

Steve Alvito

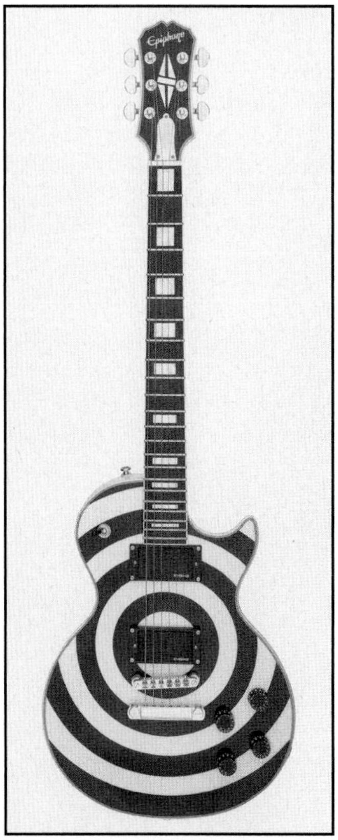

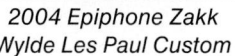

2004 Epiphone Zakk Wylde Les Paul Custom

1965 Epiphone Olympic Special

Carter Vintage Guitars

1990 Epiphone PR-325

Dave Mullikin

MODEL YEAR	FEATURES	EXC. COND. LOW	EXC. COND. HIGH

Madrid (Classical)

1962-1969. Classical, natural.

1962-1964		$350	$450
1965-1969		$250	$325

MD-30

1993. D-size, round metal resonator, spruce top with dual screens.

1993		$425	$550

Melody Tenor

1931-1937. 23" scale, bound body.

1931-1937	Masterbilt	$900	$1,175

Moderne

2000. Copy of '58 Gibson Moderne design, dot markers, Moderne script logo on 'guard, black.

2000		$540	$700

Navarre

1931-1940. Hawaiian flat-top, mahogany back and sides, bound top and back, dot inlay, brown finish.

1931-1937	Masterbilt label	$2,275	$2,950
1938-1940	Standard label	$2,075	$2,675

Nighthawk Standard

1995-2000. Epiphone's version of the Gibson Nighthawk, single-cut, bolt neck, figured top.

1995-2000		$250	$325

Noel Gallagher Union Jack/Super Nova

1997-2005. Limited edition, higher-end ES-335. Union Jack with British flag finish (introduced '99) or Supernova in solid blue.

1997-2005		$825	$1,100

Olympic (Acoustic Archtop)

1931-1949. Mahogany back and sides.

1931-1936	Smaller body	$775	$1,000
1937-1939	Larger body	$635	$825
1940-1949		$615	$800

Olympic Tenor (Acoustic Archtop)

1937-1949. 4-string version of the Olympic.

1937-1949		$575	$750

Olympic Single (Solidbody)

1960-1970. Slab body, the same as the mid-'60s Coronet, Wilshire and Crestwood Series, single-cut '60-'62, asymmetrical double-cut '63-'70, 2 Melody maker single-coil pickups, vibrato optional in '64 and standard by '65.

1960-1962	Sunburst, single-cut	$1,100	$1,425
1963-1964	Sunburst, double-cut	$975	$1,275
1965-1970	Sunburst	$850	$1,100

Olympic Double (Solidbody)

1960-1969. Slab body, the same as the mid-'60s Coronet, Wilshire and Crestwood Series, single-cut '60-'62, asymmetrical-cut '63-'70, 2 Melody Maker single-coils, vibrato optional in '64 and standard by '65.

1960-1963	Sunburst, single-cut	$1,900	$2,475
1963-1964	Sunburst, double-cut	$1,700	$2,200
1965-1969	Cherry, sunburst	$1,400	$1,825

Olympic (3/4 Scale Solidbody)

1960-1963. 22" scale, sunburst.

1960-1963		$1,050	$1,400

Olympic Special (Solidbody)

1962-1970. Short neck with neck body joint at the 16th fret (instead of the 22nd), single Melody Maker-style single-coil bridge pickup, small headstock, double-cut slab body, dot markers, Maestro or Epiphone vibrato optional '64-'65, slab body contour changes in '65 from symmetrical to asymmetrical with slightly longer bass horn, sunburst.

1962-1964	Symmetrical	$725	$950
1965-1970	Asymmetrical	$700	$900

PR Series

1980-2004. Budget acoustics, mainly D size but some smaller, cut and non-cut bodies.

1980-2004	Various models	$175	$350

Pro 1

1989-1996. Solidbody, double-cut, 1 single-coil and 1 humbucking pickup, bolt-on neck, various colors.

1989-1996		$300	$400

Pro 2

1995-1998. Higher-end Pro I with Steinberger DB bridge, set-neck, 2 humbuckers, various colors.

1995-1998		$300	$400

Professional

1962-1967. Double-cut, thinline archtop, 1 pickup, mahogany finish. Values include matching Professional amp.

1962-1964	With matching amp	$2,200	$2,850
1965	With matching amp	$1,900	$2,450
1966-1967	With matching amp	$1,650	$2,150

Prophecy Extura

2020-present. Modern Collection, mahogany body, AAA flame maple veneer top, 2 Fishman pickups, various colors with aged gloss finish.

2020		$500	$650

Recording A

1928-1931. Asymmetrical body flat-top with exaggerated treble bout cutaway, celluloid headstock veneer, dot inlays. All Recording models were offered in concert or auditorium body sizes.

1928-1931	Standard 6-string	$1,475	$1,900
1928-1931	Tenor 4-string	$1,050	$1,350

Recording B

1928-1931. As Recording A but with arched back, bound fingerboard, fancier body binding and zigzagging double slotted-diamond inlays.

1928-1931		$2,025	$2,625

Recording C

1928-1931. As Recording B but with arched top.

1928-1931		$2,125	$2,750

Recording D

1928-1931. As Recording C, but with large cross-hatched block inlays.

1928-1931		$2,775	$3,600

Recording E

1928-1931. As Recording D, but with large floral engraved block inlays.

1928-1931		$3,550	$4,600

Ritz

1940-1949. 15.5" acoustic archtop, large cello f-holes, dot inlays, no headstock ornamentation other than script Epiphone inlay, blond finish.

1940-1949		$675	$875

MODEL YEAR	FEATURES	EXC. COND. LOW	HIGH

Riviera

1962-1970. Double-cut thinline archtop, 2 mini-humbuckers, Royal Tan standard finish changing to sunburst in '65, cherry optional by '66-'70, additional 250 were made in Nashville in '93-'94, a Riviera import was available in '82 and for '94-'06.

1962-1964	Tan or custom cherry	$3,300	$4,300
1964	Sunburst	$3,175	$4,100
1965	Sunburst, cherry	$2,850	$3,700
1966-1967	Sparkling Burgundy	$2,800	$3,600
1966-1970	Sunburst, cherry	$2,650	$3,450
1967-1968	Walnut	$2,650	$3,450

Riviera (U.S.A.)

1993-1994. Made in U.S.A. on back of headstock.

1993-1994		$1,025	$1,325

Riviera Reissue (Korea)

1994-2006. Korean-made contemporary reissue, natural.

1994-2006		$425	$550

Riviera 12-String

1965-1970. Double-cut, 12 strings, thinline archtop, 2 mini-humbuckers, sunburst or cherry.

1965-1970		$2,250	$2,925

Riviera 12-String Reissue (Korea)

1997-2000. Korean-made reissue, natural.

1997	Humbuckers	$700	$925
1998-2000	Mini-hums	$425	$550

Royal

1931-1935. 15 1/2" acoustic archtop, mahogany back and sides, dot markers, sunburst, bound top, back and neck, Masterbilt headstock logo.

1931-1935		$1,200	$1,550

S-900

1986-1989. Neck-thru-body, locking Bender tremolo system, 2 pickups with individual switching and a coil-tap control.

1986-1989		$300	$400

SC350

1976-1979. Mahogany solidbody, scroll bass horn, rosewood 'board, dot inlays, bolt neck, 2 humbuckers, made in Japan.

1976-1979	Mahogany	$525	$700

SC450

1976-1979. Like SC350, but with maple body, glued neck, and coil tap.

1976-1979	Maple	$525	$700

SC550

1976-1979. Like SC450, but with gold hardware, block inlays, neck and body binding, and ebony 'board.

1976-1979	Maple, gold hdwr	$525	$700

Seville EC-100 (Classical)

1938-1941, 1961-1969 (Gibson-made). Classical guitar, mahogany back and sides, natural, the '61-'63 version also available with a pickup.

1961-1964		$400	$525
1965-1969		$350	$450

Prophecy SG

2020-present. Modern Collection, mahogany body, AAA flame maple veneer top, 2 Fishman pickups, various colors with aged gloss finish.

2020		$500	$650

SG Special

2000-present. SG body, dot markers, 2 open-coil humbuckers, later P-90s.

2000-2016	Player Pack with amp	$105	$135
2000-2020	Guitar only	$80	$105

Sheraton

1958-1970, 1993-1994. Double-cut thinline archtop, 2 New York pickups '58-'60, 2 mini-humbuckers '61 on, frequensator tailpiece, multi-bound, gold-plated hardware, sunburst or natural finish with cherry optional by '65.

1958-1960	Natural, NY pus	$7,850	$10,200
1959-1964	Sunburst mini-hums	$7,100	$9,200
1961-1964	Natural, mini-hums	$7,850	$10,200
1962	Cherry, few made	$7,100	$9,200
1965	Cherry, natural	$5,300	$6,850
1965	Sunburst	$4,175	$5,425
1966-1967	Natural	$5,000	$6,450
1966-1970	Cherry, sunburst	$3,850	$5,000

Sheraton (Japan)

1982-1983. Early reissue, not to be confused with Sheraton II issued later, natural or sunburst.

1982-1983		$1,325	$1,725

Sheraton (Reissue U.S.A.)

1993-1994, 2005. An additional 250 American-made Sheratons were built from '93-'94.

1993-1994		$1,775	$2,300
2005		$1,775	$2,300

Sheraton II (Reissue)

1986-present. Contemporary reissue, natural or sunburst.

1986-2020		$425	$550

Slasher

2001. Reverse offset double cut solidbody, bolt neck, six-on-a-side tuners, 2 pickups, dot markers.

2001		$325	$425

Sorrento (1 pickup)

1960-1970. Single-cut thinline archtop, 1 pickup in neck position, tune-o-matic bridge, nickel-plated hardware, sunburst, natural or Royal Olive finish, (cherry or sunburst by '68).

1960-1964		$1,600	$2,100
1965		$1,550	$2,000
1966-1970		$1,425	$1,850

Sorrento (2 pickups)

1960-1970. Single-cut thinline archtop, 2 pickups, tune-o-matic bridge, nickel-plated hardware, sunburst, natural or Royal Olive finish, (cherry or sunburst by '68).

1960-1964		$2,450	$3,175
1965		$2,075	$2,675
1966-1970		$1,975	$2,550

Sorrento (Reissue)

1994-2000. Reissue of 2 pickup model, import.

1994-2000		$450	$575

Spartan

1934-1949. Acoustic archtop, 16 3/8", laminated maple body, multi-bound, trapeze tailpiece, sunburst or natural.

1934-1939	Sunburst	$750	$975
1940-1949	Sunburst	$650	$850
1941-1947	Natural	$750	$975

1964 Epiphone Professional

Rivington Guitars

1961 Epiphone Sheraton

Killer Vintage

1961 Epiphone Triumph Regent

Carter Vintage Guitars

Epiphone Wildkat

MODEL YEAR	FEATURES	EXC. COND. LOW	HIGH

Special/SG Special (U.S.A.)

1979-1983. SG Special body style, dot markers, 2 exposed humbuckers, Special logo on truss rod cover.

1979-1983		$625	$825

Spider/The Spider

1997-2000. Wood body resonator, spider bridge, square neck.

1997-2000		$425	$550

Spirit I/Spirit II

1982. U.S.-made electric solidbody, Spirit logo on truss rod cover, double-cut, flat-top with 1 (I) or 2 (II) humbuckers.

1982		$925	$1,200

SST

2007-2011. Acoustic/electric solidbody, either Classic (nylon) or Studio (steel). Chet Atkins model also available.

2007-2011		$250	$325

Tom Delonge Signature ES-333

2008-2019. One humbucker, dot inlays.

2008-2019		$500	$650

Trailer Park Troubadour Airscreamer

2003-2005. Airstream trailer-shaped body, identifying logo on headstock.

2003-2005		$425	$550

Triumph

1931-1957. 15 1/4" '31-'33, 16 3/8" '33-'36, 17 3/8" '36-'57, walnut back and sides until '33, laminated maple back and sides '33, solid maple back and sides '34, natural or sunburst.

1931-1932	Sunburst, laminated walnut	$1,250	$1,600
1933	Sunburst, laminated maple	$1,250	$1,600
1934-1935	Sunburst, solid maple	$1,275	$1,650
1936-1940	Sunburst 17 3/8" body	$1,275	$1,650
1941-1949	Natural	$1,275	$1,650
1941-1949	Sunburst	$1,275	$1,650
1950-1957	Natural	$1,275	$1,650
1950-1957	Sunburst	$1,275	$1,650

Triumph Regent (Cutaway)

1948-1969. Acoustic archtop, single-cut, F-holes, renamed Triumph Cutaway in '53, then Gibson listed this model as just the Triumph from '58-'69.

1948-1952	Regent, natural	$1,900	$2,450
1948-1952	Regent, sunburst	$1,650	$2,150
1953-1957	Cutaway, natural	$1,900	$2,450
1953-1957	Cutaway, sunburst	$1,650	$2,150
1958-1964	Sunburst	$1,675	$2,150
1965	Sunburst	$1,575	$2,050
1966-1969	Sunburst	$1,500	$1,950

USA Map Guitar

1982-1983. U.S.-made promotional model, solidbody electric, mahogany body shaped like U.S. map, 2 pickups, natural.

1982-1983		$2,125	$2,750

USA Map Guitar Limited Edition

2007	Import	$500	$650

Vee-Wee (Mini Flying V)

2003. Mini Flying V, single bridge pickup, gig bag.

2003		$80	$100

Wildkat

2001-2019. Thinline, single-cut, hollow-body, 2 P-90s, Bigsby tailpiece.

2001-2019		$300	$400

Wilshire

1959-1970. Double-cut solidbody, 2 pickups, tune-o-matic bridge, cherry.

1959	Symmetrical	$3,300	$4,300
1960-1962	Thinner-style, P-90s	$2,500	$3,300
1962-1963	Symmetrical, mini-hums	$2,500	$3,300
1963-1964	Asymmetrical, mini-hums	$2,300	$3,000
1965-1966	Custom color	$2,500	$3,300
1965-1966	Standard color	$2,000	$2,600
1967-1970		$1,750	$2,300

Wilshire 12-String

1966-1968. Solidbody, 2 pickups, cherry.

1966-1968		$1,750	$2,300

Wilshire II

1984-1985. Solidbody, maple body, neck and 'board, 2 humbuckers, 3-way switch, coil-tap, 1 tone and 1 volume control, various colors.

1984-1985		$425	$550

Windsor (1 Pickup)

1959-1962. Archtop, 1 or 2 pickups, single-cut thinline, sunburst or natural finish.

1959-1960	Natural, NY pu	$1,900	$2,450
1959-1960	Sunburst, NY pu	$1,800	$2,350
1961-1962	Natural, mini-hum	$1,650	$2,150
1961-1962	Sunburst, mini-hum	$1,575	$2,050

Windsor (2 Pickups)

1959-1962. Archtop, 1 or 2 pickups, single-cut thinline, sunburst or natural finish.

1959-1960	Natural, NY pu	$2,250	$2,925
1959-1960	Sunburst NY pu	$2,150	$2,800
1961-1962	Natural, mini-hum	$1,925	$2,500
1961-1962	Sunburst, mini-hum	$1,850	$2,400

X-1000

1986-1989. Electric solidbody, Korean-made, various colors.

1986-1989		$250	$325

Zenith

1931-1969. Acoustic archtop, bound front and back, f-holes, sunburst.

1931-1933		$850	$1,100
1934-1935	14 3/4" body	$975	$1,275
1936-1949	16 3/8" body	$975	$1,275
1950-1957	Natural	$1,075	$1,400
1950-1957	Sunburst	$975	$1,275
1958-1969		$800	$1,025

Zephyr

1939-1957. Non-cut electric archtop, 1 pickup, bound front and back, blond or sunburst (first offered '53), called Zephyr Electric starting in '54.

1939-1940	Natural, metal handrest pu	$1,075	$1,400

MODEL YEAR	FEATURES	EXC. COND. LOW	HIGH
1941-1943	Natural, no metal handrest	$1,075	$1,400
1944-1946	Natural, top mounted pu	$1,075	$1,400
1947-1948	17 3/8", metal covered pu	$1,075	$1,400
1949-1957	Natural, NY pu	$975	$1,275
1953-1957	Sunburst, NY pu	$900	$1,175

Zephyr Regent

1950-1953. Single-cut electric archtop, 1 pickup, natural or sunburst, called Zephyr Cutaway for '54-'57.

1950-1953	Natural	$1,800	$2,350
1950-1953	Sunburst	$1,650	$2,150

Zephyr Cutaway

1954-1957. Cutaway version of Zephyr Electric, called Zephyr Regent for 1950-'53.

1954-1957	Natural	$1,925	$2,500
1954-1957	Sunburst	$1,725	$2,250

Zephyr Electric (Cutaway)

1958-1964. Gibson-made version, thinline archtop, single-cut, 2 pickups, natural or sunburst.

1958-1959	Natural	$1,925	$2,500
1958-1959	Sunburst	$1,625	$2,125
1960-1964	Natural	$1,725	$2,250
1960-1964	Sunburst	$1,550	$2,000

Zephyr De Luxe (Non-cutaway)

1941-1954. Non-cut electric archtop, 1 or 2 pickups, multi-bound front and back, gold-plated hardware, natural or sunburst.

1941-1942	Natural	$1,650	$2,150
1945-1949	Natural, 1 pu	$1,925	$2,500
1945-1954	Natural, 2 pus	$2,100	$2,725
1950-1954	Sunburst, 2 pus	$1,925	$2,500

Zephyr De Luxe Regent (Cutaway)

1948-1954. Single-cut electric archtop, 1 or 2 pickups until '50, then only 2, gold-plated hardware, sunburst or natural finish. Renamed Deluxe Electric in '54.

1948-1949	Natural, 1 pu	$2,100	$2,725
1948-1949	Natural, 2 pus	$2,675	$3,475
1948-1949	Sunburst, 1 pu	$1,925	$2,500
1948-1949	Sunburst, 2 pus	$2,450	$3,175
1950-1954	Natural, 2 pus	$2,600	$3,375
1950-1954	Sunburst, 2 pus	$2,375	$3,075

Zephyr Emperor Regent

1950-1954. Archtop, single rounded cutaway, multi-bound body, 3 pickups, sunburst or natural finish, renamed Emperor Electric in '54.

1950-1954	Natural	$4,700	$6,125
1950-1954	Sunburst	$3,700	$4,800

Zephyr Tenor

1940-1950. Natural, figured top.

1940-1950		$725	$950

Zephyr Blues Deluxe

1999-2005. Based on early Gibson ES-5, 3 P-90 pickups.

1999-2005		$425	$550

Epoch

Economy level imports made by Gibson and sold through Target stores.

Equator Instruments

2006-present. Production/custom, professional and premium grade, solidbody, hollowbody, acoustic and classical guitars built in Chicago, Illinois by luthier David Coleman.

Erlewine

1979-present. Professional and premium grade, production/custom guitars built by luthier Mark Erlewine in Austin, Texas. Erlewine also produces the Chiquita brand travel guitar.

Esoterik Guitars

Professional grade, production/custom, electric guitars built in San Luis Obispo, California by luthier Ryan Cook. He began with guitars in 2010 and plans to add basses.

ESP

1983-present. Intermediate, professional, and premium grade, production/custom, Japanese-made solidbody guitars and basses. Hisatake Shibuya founded Electronic Sound Products (ESP), a chain of retail stores, in '75. They began to produce replacement parts for electric guitars in '83 and in '85 started to make custom-made guitars. In '87 a factory was opened in Tokyo. In '86 ESP opened a sales office in New York, selling custom guitars and production models. From around '98 to ca. '02 they operated their California-based USA custom shop. In '96, they introduced the Korean-made LTD brand and in '03 introduced the Xtone brand, which was folded into LTD in '10. Hisatake Shibuya also operated 48th Street Custom Guitars during the '90s but he closed that shop in 2003.

20th Anniversary

1995. Solidbody, double-cut, ESP95 inlaid at 12th fret, gold.

1995		$950	$1,250

Eclipse Custom (U.S.A.)

1998-2002. U.S. Custom Shop-built, single-cut, mahogany body and maple top, various colors offered.

1998-2002		$625	$825

Eclipse Custom/Custom T (Import)

1986-1988, 2003-2010. Single-cut mahogany solidbody, earliest model with bolt dot marker neck, 2nd version with neck-thru and blocks, the Custom T adds locking trem. Current has quilt maple top.

1986-1987	Bolt, dots	$650	$850
1987-1988	Neck-thru, blocks	$700	$900
1987-1988	Neck-thru, Custom T	$675	$875

Eclipse Deluxe

1986-1988. Single-cut solidbody, 1 single-coil and 1 humbucker, vibrato, black.

1986-1988		$650	$850

Eclipse Series

1995-present. Recent Eclipse models.

1995-2000	Eclipse/Eclipse I	$450	$600
1996-2000	Eclipse Archtop	$450	$600

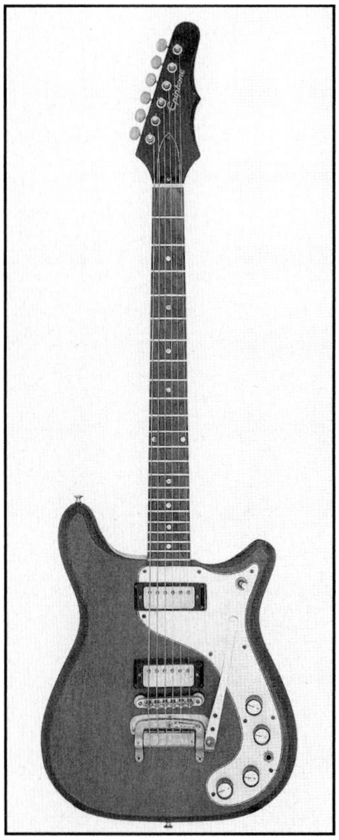

1964 Epiphone Wilshire

Imaged by Heritage Auctions, HA.com

Epiphone Zephyr De Luxe Regent

ESP George Lynch M-1 Tiger

1996 ESP Vintage Plus S

Curtis Hill

MODEL YEAR	FEATURES	EXC. COND. LOW	HIGH

George Lynch M-1 Tiger/Sunburst Tiger

1996-present. Signature series, sunburst tiger finish.

1996-2020 $1,425 $1,850

Horizon (Import)

1986, 1996-2001. Double-cut neck-thru, bound ebony 'board, 1 single-coil and 1 humbucker, buffer preamp, various colors, reintroduced '96-'01with bolt neck, curved rounded point headstock.

1986 $700 $900
1996-2001 $575 $750

Horizon Classic (U.S.A.)

1993-1995. U.S.-made, carved mahogany body, set-neck, dot markers, various colors, optional mahogany body with figured maple top also offered.

1993-1995 $1,100 $1,425

Horizon Custom (U.S.A.)

1998-2001. U.S. Custom Shop-made, mahogany body, figured maple top, bolt-on neck, mostly translucent finish in various colors.

1998-2001 $1,100 $1,425

Horizon Deluxe (Import)

1989-1992. Horizon Custom with bolt-on neck, various colors.

1989-1992 $725 $950

Hybrid I (Import)

1986 only. Offset double-cut body, bolt maple neck, dots, six-on-a-side tuners, vibrato, various colors.

1986 $375 $500

Hybrid II (Import)

1980s. Offset double-cut, rosewood 'board on maple bolt neck, lipstick neck pickup, humbucker at bridge, Hybrid II headstock logo.

1980s $425 $550

LTD EC-GTA Guitarsonist

2008. Flame graphic by Matt Touchard, 100 made.

2008 $1,000 $1,300

LTD EC-SIN Sin City

2008. Vegas graphic by Matt Touchard, 100 made.

2008 $1,000 $1,300

LTD Series

1998-present. Range of prices due to wide range of models.

1998-2020 Various models $100 $550

Maverick/Maverick Deluxe

1989-1992. Offset double-cut, bolt maple or rosewood cap neck, dot markers, double locking vibrola, six-on-a-side tuners, various colors.

1989-1992 $400 $525

Metal I

1986 only. Offset double-cut, bolt maple neck, rosewood cap, dots, various colors.

1986 $400 $525

Metal II

1986 only. Single horn V body, bolt on maple neck with rosewood cap, dot markers, various colors.

1986 $400 $525

Metal III

1986 only. Reverse offset body, bolt maple neck with maple cap, dot markers, gold hardware, various colors.

1986 $400 $525

M-I Custom

1987-1994. Offset double-cut thru-neck body, offset block markers, various colors.

1987-1994 $600 $800

M-I Deluxe

1987-1989. Double-cut solidbody, rosewood 'board, 2 single-coils and 1 humbucker, various colors.

1987-1989 $600 $800

M-II

1989-1994, 1996-2000. Double-cut solidbody, reverse headstock, bolt-on maple or rosewood cap neck, dot markers, various colors.

1989-1994 $600 $800

M-II Custom

1990-1994. Double-cut solidbody, reverse headstock, neck-thru maple neck, rosewood cap, dot markers, various colors.

1990-1994 $600 $800

M-II Deluxe

1990-1994. Double-cut solidbody, reverse headstock, Custom with bolt-on neck, various colors.

1990-1994 $600 $800

Mirage Custom

1986-1990. Double-cut neck-thru solidbody, 2-octave ebony 'board, block markers, 1 humbucker and 2 single-coil pickups, locking trem, various colors.

1986-1990 $650 $850

Mirage Standard

1986 only. Single pickup version of Mirage Custom, various colors.

1986 $525 $675

Phoenix

1987 only. Offset, narrow waist solidbody, thru-neck mahogany body, black hardware, dots.

1987 $650 $850

Phoenix Contemporary

Late-1990s. 3 pickups vs. 2 on the earlier offering.

1998 $750 $875

S-454/S-456

1986-1987. Offset double-cut, bolt maple or rosewood cap neck, dot markers, various colors.

1986-1987 $525 $675

S-500

1991-1993. Double-cut figured ash body, bolt-on neck, six-on-a-side tuners, various colors.

1991-1993 $600 $800

SV-II

2009-2012. Neck-thru offset v-shaped solidbody, 2 pickups, dot inlays, part of Standard Series, made in Japan.

2009-2012 $1,400 $1,800

Traditional

1989-1990. Double-cut, 3 pickups, tremolo, various colors.

1989-1990 $650 $850

Vintage/Vintage Plus S

1995-1998. Offset double-cut, bolt maple or rosewood cap neck, dot markers, Floyd Rose or standard vibrato, various colors.

1995 20th Anniv Ed, gold $900 $1,175
1995-1998 $825 $1,075

Viper Series

2004-present. Offset double-cut SG style, 2 humbuckers, various models

MODEL YEAR	FEATURES	EXC. COND. LOW	HIGH
2010	300M	$290	$375

Espana

1963-ca. 1973. Primarily acoustic guitars distributed by catalog wholesalers Bugeleisen & Jacobson. Built by Watkins in England.

Classical

1963-1973. Guitars with white spruce fan-braced tops with walnut, mahogany, or rosewood back and sides.

MODEL YEAR	FEATURES	EXC. COND. LOW	HIGH
1963-1973		$175	$250

EL (Electric) Series

1963-1973. Various double-cut models, 2 or 3 pickups, tremolo, '63-ca. '68 with nitro finish, ca. '69-'73 poly finish.

MODEL YEAR	FEATURES	EXC. COND. LOW	HIGH
1963-1973	EL-30, 2 pickups	$275	$350
1963-1973	EL-31, 3 pickups	$290	$375
1963-1973	EL-32 (XII)	$275	$350
1963-1973	EL-36, 2 pickups	$290	$375

Jumbo Folk

1969-1973. Natural.

MODEL YEAR	FEATURES	EXC. COND. LOW	HIGH
1969-1973		$225	$300

Essex (SX)

1985-present. Budget grade, production, electric and acoustic guitars imported by Rondo Music of Union, New Jersey. They also offer basses.

Solidbody Electric

1980s-1990s. Copies of classic designs like the Les Paul and Telecaster.

MODEL YEAR	FEATURES	EXC. COND. LOW	HIGH
1980s		$125	$165

Este

1909-1939. Luthier Felix Staerke's Este factory built classical and archtop guitars in Hamburg, Germany. They also built high-end banjos. The plant ceased instrument production in '39 and was destroyed in WW II.

Esteban

2002-present. Budget grade, production, acoustic and classical import guitars sold as packages with classical guitarist Esteban's (Stephen Paul) guitar lesson program, other miscellany and sometimes a small amp.

Steel and Nylon Acoustics

MODEL YEAR	FEATURES	EXC. COND. LOW	HIGH
2002-2020	Various models	$30	$160

EtaVonni

2008-2010. Luthier Ben Williams built premium grade, production/custom, carbon fiber and aluminum electric guitars in Kentwood, Michigan.

Euphonon

1930-1944. A Larson brothers brand, most Euphonons date from 1934-'44. Body sizes range from 13 ½" to the 19" and 21" super jumbos. The larger body 14-fret neck sizes have body woods of Brazilian rosewood, mahogany, or maple. Ornamentation and features are as important to value as rosewood vs. mahogany. Production also included mandolins, and most models were A-style, with teardrop body and flat backs.

Everett Guitars

1977-present. Luthier Kent Everett builds his premium and presentation grade, production/custom, steel-string and classical guitars in Atlanta, Georgia. From '01 to '03, his Laurel Series guitars were built in conjunction with Terada in Japan and set up in Atlanta. He has also built archtops, semi-hollow and solidbody electrics, resonators, and mandolins.

Evergreen Mountain

1971-present. Professional grade, custom, flat-top and tenor guitars, basses and mandolins built by luthier Jerry Nolte in Cove, Oregon. He also built over 100 dulcimers in the '70s.

Everly Guitars

1982-2001. Luthier Robert Steinegger built these premium grade, production/custom flat-tops in Portland, Oregon (also see Steinegger Guitars).

EVH

2007-present. Eddie Van Halen works with FMIC to create a line of professional and premium grade, production, solidbody guitars built in the U.S. and imported from other countries. They also build amps.

Wolfgang Special

2010-present. Made in Japan, offset double-cut solidbody, figured maple top over basswood body, birdseye maple 'board, 2 pickups, tremolo, opaque finish. Some more recent models made in Mexico.

MODEL YEAR	FEATURES	EXC. COND. LOW	HIGH
2010-2020		$825	$1,100

Excelsior

The Excelsior Company started offering accordions in 1924 and had a large factory in Italy by the late '40s. They started building guitars around '62, which were originally plastic covered, switching to paint finishes in the mid '60s. They also offered classicals, acoustics, archtops and amps. By the early '70s they were out of the guitar business.

The Excelsior brand was also used ca.1885-ca.1890 on guitars and banjos by Boston's John C. Haynes & Co.

Dyno and Malibu

1960s. Offset, double cut, 2 or 3 pickups, vibrato.

MODEL YEAR	FEATURES	EXC. COND. LOW	HIGH
1960s	Dyno I	$250	$350
1960s	Dyno II	$275	$375
1960s	Malibu I	$275	$375
1960s	Malibu II	$300	$400

Exlusive

2008-2013. Intermediate grade, production, electric guitars and basses, imported from Asia and finished in Italy by luthier Galeazzo Frudua.

Essex (SX) EH3D-CS

1968 Excelsior Dyno III

Rivington Guitars

GUITARS

Fairbuilt Barnburner

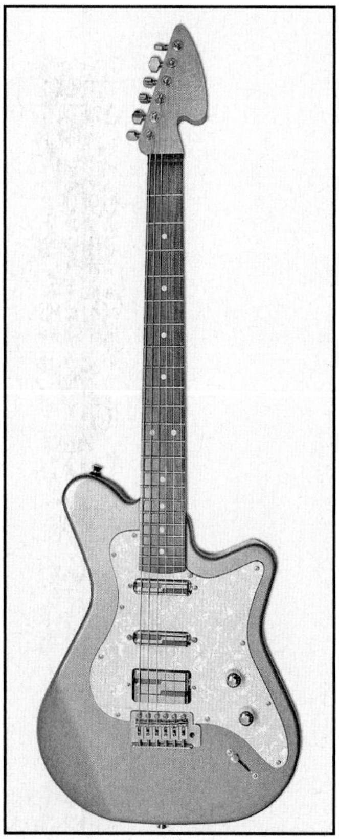

Farnell Guitars

MODEL YEAR	FEATURES	EXC. COND. LOW	HIGH

Fairbuilt Guitar Co.

2000-present. Professional and premium grade, custom guitars and mandolins, built by luthier Martin Fair in Loudoun County, Virginia.

Falk

1989-present. Professional and premium grade, production/custom archtop guitars built by luthier Dave Falk, originally in Independence, Missouri, and currently in Amarillo, Texas. He also builds mandolins and dulcimers.

Fano

1995-present. Professional grade, production/custom, solidbody electric guitars and basses built by luthier Dennis Fano in Fleetwood, Pennsylvania.

Farnell

1989-present. Luthier Al Farnell builds his professional grade, production, solidbody guitars and basses in Ontario, California. He also offers his intermediate grade, production, C Series which is imported from China.

Fat Cat Custom Guitars

2004-present. Intermediate to premium grade, production/custom, solidbody and chambered electric guitars and basses built in Carpentersville, Illinois by luthier Scott Bond.

Favilla

1890-1973. Founded by the Favilla family in New York, the company began to import guitars in 1970, but folded in '73. American-made models have the Favilla family crest on the headstock. Import models used a script logo on the headstock.

Acoustic Classical

1960s-1973. Various nylon-string classical models.

1960s-1969		$125	$390
1970-1973	Import	$125	$390

Acoustic Flat-Top

1960s-1973. Various flat-top models, 000 to D sizes, mahogany to spruce.

1960s-1969	US-made, Crest logo	$125	$390
1970-1973	Import, Script logo	$125	$390

Fell

One of the many guitar brands built by Japan's Matsumoku company.

Fender

1946 (1945)-present. Budget, intermediate, professional and premium grade, production/custom, electric, acoustic, acoustic/electric, classical, and resonator guitars built in the U.S. and overseas. They also build amps, basses, mandolins, bouzoukis, banjos, lap steels, ukes, violins, and PA gear. Ca. 1939 Leo Fender opened a radio and record store called Fender Radio Service, where he met Clayton Orr 'Doc' Kauffman, and in '45 they started KF Company to build lap steels and amps. In '46 Kauffman left and Fender started the Fender Electric Instrument Company.

In January '65 CBS purchased the company and renamed it Fender Musical Instruments Corporation. The CBS takeover is synonymous with a perceived decline in quality among musicians and collectors, and Pre-CBS Fenders are more valuable. Fender experienced some quality problems in the late-'60s. Small headstock is enlarged in '65 and the 4-bolt neck is replaced by the 3-bolt in '71. With high value and relative scarcity of Pre-CBS Fenders, even CBS-era instruments are now sought by collectors. Leo Fender was kept on as consultant until '70 and went on to design guitars for Music Man and G&L.

In '82 Fender Japan is established to produce licensed Fender copies for sale in Japan. Also in '82, the Fender Squier brand debuts on Japanese-made instruments for the European market and by '83 they were imported into U.S. In March '85, the company was purchased by an investor group headed by Bill Schultz but the purchase does not include the Fullerton factory. While a new factory was being established at Corona, California, all Fender Contemporary Stratocasters and Telecasters were made either by Fender Japan or in Seoul, Korea. U.S. production resumes in late '85. The Fender Custom Shop, run by Michael Stevens and John Page, opens in '87. The Mexican Fender factory is established in '90. In '95, Fender purchased the Guild guitar company. On January 3, 2002, Fender Musical Instruments Corporation (FMIC) recapitalized a minority portion of common stock, with partners including Roland Corporation U.S. and Weston Presidio, a private equity firm in San Francisco. In 2003, Fred Gretsch Enterprises, Ltd granted Fender the exclusive rights to develop, produce, market and distribute Gretsch guitars worldwide. Around the same time, Fender also acquired the Jackson/Charvel Guitar Company. In October, '04, Fender acquired Tacoma Guitars. On January 1, '08, Fender acquired Kaman Music Corporation and the Hamer, Ovation, and Genz Benz brands. The Groove Tubes brand was purchased by Fender in June, '08.

Dating older Fender guitars is an imprecise art form at best. While serial numbers were used, they were frequently not in sequence, although a lower number will frequently be older than a substantially higher number. Often necks were dated, but only with the date the neck was finished, not when the guitar was assembled. Generally, dating requires triangulating between serial numbers, neck dates, pot dates, construction details and model histories.

From '50 through roughly '65, guitars had more-or-less sequential numbers in either 4 or 5 digits, though some higher numbers may have an initial 0 or - prefix. These can range from 0001 to 99XXX.

From '63 into '65, some instruments had serial numbers beginning with an L prefix plus 5 digits (LXXXXX). Beginning in '65 with the CBS takeover into '76, 6-digit serial numbers were stamped on F neckplates roughly sequentially from 10XXXX to 71XXXX. In '76 the serial number was shifted to the headstock decal. From '76-'77, the serial number began with a bold-face 76 or S6 plus 5 digits (76XXXXX).

From '77 on, serial numbers consisted of a 2-place prefix plus 5 digits (sometimes 6 beginning in '91): '77 (S7, S8), '78 (S7, S8, S9), '79 (S9, E0), '80-'81 (S9, E0, E1), '82 (E1, E2, E3), '84-'85 (E4), '85-'86 (no U.S. production), '87 (E4), '88 (E4, E8), '89 (E8, E9), '90 (E9, N9, N0), '91 (N0), '92 (N2).

Serial numbers on guitars made by Fender Japan consist of either a 2-place prefix plus 5 digits or a single prefix letter plus 6 digits: '82-'84 (JV), '83-'84 (SQ), '84-'87, '85-'86+ (A, B, C), '86-'87 (F), '87-'88+ (G), '88-'89 (H), '89-'90 (I, J), '90-'91 (K), '91-'92 (L), '92-'93 (M).

Factors affecting Fender values: The sale to CBS in '65 is a major point in Fender instrument values as CBS made many changes collectors feel affected quality. The '70s introduced the 3-bolt neck and other design changes that aren't as popular with guitarists. Custom color instruments, especially Strats from the '50s and early-'60s, can be valued much more than the standard sunburst finishes. In '75 Fender dropped the optional custom colors and started issuing the guitars in a variety of standard colors.

Custom colors are worth more than standard colors. For a Stratocaster, Telecaster Custom and Esquire Custom the standard color is sunburst, while the Telecaster and Esquire standard color is blond. The first Precision Bass standard color was blond but changed to sunburst in the late 1950s. The Jazz Bass standard color is sunburst. The Telecaster Thinline standard color is natural. To understand a custom color, you need to know what the standard color is. Some custom colors are rarer than others. Below is a list of the custom colors offered in 1960. They are sorted in ascending order with the most valuable color, Shell Pink, listed last. For example, Fiesta Red is typically worth 12% more than a Black or Blond, though all are in the Common Color category. In the Rare Color group, Foam Green is normally worth 8% more than Shoreline Gold. The two Very Rare colors are often worth 30% more than Shoreline Gold. In our pricing information we will list the standard color, then the relative value of a common custom color, and then the value of a rare custom color. Remember that the amount of fade also affects the price. These prices are for custom colors with slight or no fade, which implies a lighter color, but with custom colors a faded example can also be much darker in color. Blue can fade to dark green. White can fade to deep yellow.

The various Telecaster and Stratocaster models are grouped under those general headings.

Common Color: Black, Blond, Candy Apple Red, Olympic White, Lake Placid Blue, Dakota Red, Daphne Blue, Fiesta Red

Rare Color: Shoreline Gold, Inca Silver, Burgundy Mist, Sherwood Green, Sonic Blue, Foam Green

Rare (Very Rare) Color: Surf Green, Shell Pink

1960 - 1962: Black, Blond, Burgundy Mist, Dakota Red, Daphne Blue, Fiesta Red, Foam Green, Inca Silver, Lake Placid Blue, Olympic White, Shell Pink, Sherwood Green, Shoreline Gold, Sonic Blue, Sunburst, Surf Green

1963 - 1964: Black, Blond, Burgundy Mist, Candy Apple Red, Dakota Red, Daphne Blue, Fiesta Red, Foam Green, Inca Silver, Lake Placid Blue, Olympic White, Sherwood Green, Shoreline Gold, Sonic Blue, Sunburst, Surf Green

1965 - 1969: Black, Blond, Blue Ice, Candy Apple Red, Charcoal Frost, Dakota Red, Fiesta Red, Firemist Gold, Firemist Silver, Foam Green, Lake Placid Blue, Ocean Turquoise, Olympic White, Sonic Blue, Sunburst, Teal Green

1970 - 1971: Black, Blond, Candy Apple Red, Firemist Gold, Firemist Silver, Lake Placid Blue, Ocean Turquoise, Olympic White, Sonic Blue, Sunburst

1972: Black, Blond, Candy Apple Red, Lake Placid Blue, Olympic White, Sonic Blue, Sunburst

1973: Black, Blond, Candy Apple Red, Lake Placid Blue, Natural, Olympic White, Sunburst, Walnut

1974 - 1977: Black, Blond, Natural, Olympic White, Sunburst, Walnut

1978 - 1979: Antigua, Black, Blond, Natural, Olympic White, Sunburst, Walnut, Wine

MODEL YEAR	FEATURES	EXC. COND. LOW	HIGH

Arrow

1969-1972. See listing for Musiclander.

Avalon

1985-1995. California Series, acoustic import, 6-on-a-side tuners, mahogany neck, back and sides (nato after '93), spruce top, various colors.

1985-1995		$200	$260

Balboa

1983-1987. California Series, acoustic import.

1983-1987		$325	$425

Brawler Baritone (Custom Shop)

2019-2020. Journeyman Relic, masterbuilt by Carlos Lopez.

2019-2020		$5,500	$7,150

Broadcaster

Mid-1950-early-1951. For a short time in early-'51, before being renamed the Telecaster, models had no Broadcaster decal; these are called No-casters by collectors.

1950	Blond	$60,000	$80,000
1951	Clipped decal, "No Caster"	$54,000	$72,000

Broadcaster Leo Fender Custom Shop

1999 only. Leo Fender script logo signature replaces Fender logo on headstock, Custom Shop Certificate signed by Phyllis Fender, Fred Gretsch, and William Schultz, includes glass display case and poodle guitar case.

1999		$4,600	$6,000

'50s Relic/'51 NoCaster Custom Shop

1995-2014. Called the '50s Relic NoCaster for '96-'99, and '51 NoCaster in NOS, Relic, or Closet Classic versions 2000-'10, with the Relic Series being

Fat Cat Custom Guitars

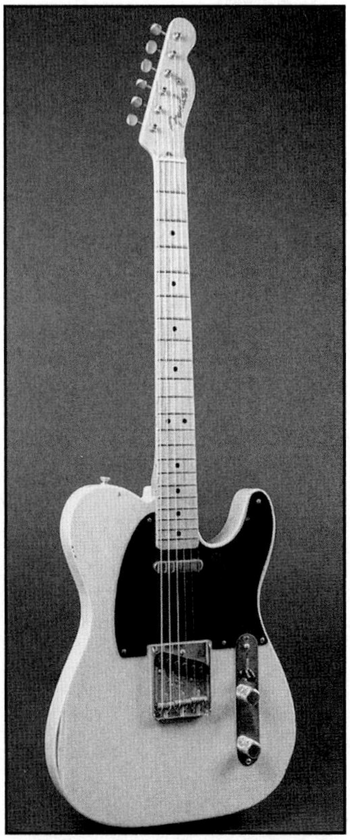

2003 Fender'51 Nocaster Custom Shop

Carter Vintage Guitars

Fender CD-320AS

1967 Fender Coronado II

Tom Pfeifer

MODEL YEAR	FEATURES	EXC. COND. LOW	HIGH

the highest offering. From June '95 to June '99 Relic work was done outside of Fender by Vince Cunetto and included a certificate noting model and year built, an instrument without the certificate is worth less than the value shown. Blonde or Honey Blonde finish. Also in '09, the Limited '51 NoCaster Relic was offered with Twisted Tele neck pickup, 50 each in 2-tone sunburst or Dakota Red.

1995-1997	Cunetto built Relic	$2,275	$2,950
1997-1999	Cunetto era Closet Classic	$1,950	$2,525
1997-1999	Cunetto era NOS	$1,950	$2,525
1998-1999	Cunetto era Relic	$2,200	$2,850
2000-2009	Closet Classic	$1,950	$2,525
2000-2014	NOS	$1,950	$2,525
2000-2014	Relic	$2,075	$2,700

'51 NoCaster Limited Edition

2009. Custom Shop Limited Edition, as above but with Twisted Tele neck pickup, 50 each in 2-tone sunburst or Dakota Red.

2009	Relic	$2,075	$2,700

70th Anniversary Broadcaster Limited Edition

2020 only. Production model has ash body, black 'guard, '50s spaghetti logo, blonde lacquer finish. Custom Shop model available aging with Relic, Heavy Relic, NOS Time Capsule and Journeyman Relic.

2020	Custom Shop	$2,500	$3,250
2020	Production	$1,100	$1,450

Bronco

1967-1980. Slab solidbody, 1 pickup, tremolo, red.

1967-1968	Nitro	$1,075	$1,400
1969-1980	Poly	$950	$1,225

Buddy Miller Signature

2007-2009. Flat-top, Fishman Ellipse Aura, 6-on-a-side tuner headstock.

2007-2009		$635	$825

Bullet/Bullet Deluxe

1981-1983. Solidbody, came in 2- and 3-pickup versions (single-coil and humbucker), and single- and double-cut models, various colors. Becomes Squire Bullet in '85.

1981-1983	Various models	$565	$735

Catalina

1983-1995. California Series, acoustic dreadnought, import.

1983-1995		$190	$250

CD (Classic Design) Series

2006-present. Imported, intermediate grade, various models, acoustic or acoustic-electric, steel or nylon string.

2006-2020	Various models	$125	$300
2020-2021	CC-60SCE	$180	$235

CG (Classical Guitar) Series

1995-2005. Imported, various nylon-string classical acoustic and acoustic/electric models, label on the inside back clearly indicates the model number, back and sides of rosewood, mahogany or other woods.

1995-2005		$55	$300

Concert

1963-1970. Acoustic flat-top slightly shorter than King/Kingman, spruce body, mahogany back and sides (optional Brazilian or Indian rosewood, zebrawood or vermillion), natural, sunburst optional by '68.

1963-1970	Natural or sunburst	$925	$1,200

Concord

1986-1995. Dreadnought flat-top, 6-on-a-side headstock, natural.

1986-1995		$120	$155

Coronado I

1966-1969. Thinline semi-hollowbody, double-cut, tremolo, 1 pickup, single-bound, dot inlay.

1966-1969	Various colors	$1,400	$1,825

Coronado II

1966-1969 (Antigua finish offered until '70). Thinline semi-hollowbody, double-cut, tremolo optional, 2 pickups, single-bound, block inlay, available in standard finishes but special issues offered in Antigua and 6 different Wildwood finishes (labeled on the pickguard as Wildwood I through Wildwood VI to designate different colors). Wildwood finishes were achieved by injecting dye into growing trees.

1966-1969	Various colors	$1,600	$2,100
1966-1969	Wildwood	$2,225	$2,900
1967-1970	Antigua	$1,600	$2,100

Coronado XII

1966-1969 (Antigua finish offered until '70). Thinline semi-hollowbody, double-cut, 12 strings, 2 pickups, block inlay, standard, Antigua and Wildwood finishes available.

1966-1969	Various colors	$1,600	$2,100
1966-1969	Wildwood	$2,225	$2,900
1967-1970	Antigua	$1,600	$2,100

Custom

1969-1971. Six-string solidbody that used up parts from discontinued Electric XII, asymmetrical-cut, long headstock, 2 split pickups, sunburst. Also marketed as the Maverick.

1969-1971		$2,775	$3,600

Cyclone

1998-2006. Mexican import, solidbody, contoured offset waist, poplar body, various colors.

1998-2006	Various options	$550	$725

D'Aquisto Elite

1984, 1989-1994, 1994-2002. Part of Fender's Master Series, 16" laminated maple-side archtop, single-cut, glued neck, 1 pickup, gold hardware, made in Japan until '94, in '94 the Fender Custom Shop issued a version that retailed at $6,000, various colors.

1984-2002		$1,950	$2,550

D'Aquisto Standard

1984 (Serial numbers could range from 1983-1985). Like D'Aquisto Elite, but with 2 pickups.

1984		$1,950	$2,550

D'Aquisto Ultra

1984, 1994-2000. USA Custom Shop, made under the supervision of James D'Aquisto, solid flamed maple back and sides, spruce top, ebony tailpiece, bridge and 'guard, all hand carved.

1994-2000		$2,500	$3,300

MODEL YEAR	FEATURES	EXC. COND. LOW	HIGH

DG (Dreadnought Guitar) Series

1995-1999, 2002-2014. Made in China, various lower-end acoustic and acoustic/electric models.

1995-2014		$90	$285

Duo-Sonic

1956-1969, 2016-present. Solidbody, 3/4-size, 2 pickups, Desert Sand ('56-'61), sunburst ('61-'63), blue, red or white after, short- and long-scale necks, short-scale necks listed here (see Duo-Sonic II for long-scale), reissued Mexican-made in '94. In 2016 it becomes part of Player Series.

1956-1958	Desert Sand	$2,500	$3,250
1959	Maple neck	$2,500	$3,250
1960	Rosewood 'board	$2,000	$2,600
1961-1963	Desert Sand	$2,000	$2,600
1963	Sunburst (rare)	$2,000	$2,600
1964	Blue, red or white	$2,000	$2,600
1965	Blue, red or white	$1,800	$2,350
1966-1969	Blue, red or white	$1,350	$1,750

Duo-Sonic II

1965-1969. Solidbody, 2 pickups, blue, red or white, long-scale neck, though the long-scale neck Duo-Sonic was not known as the Duo-Sonic II until '65, we have lumped all long-scales under the II for the purposes of this Guide.

1965-1969		$1,450	$1,850

Duo-Sonic Reissue

1994-1997. Made in Mexico, black, red or white.

1994-1997		$255	$335

Duo-Sonic HS

2017-present. Player Series, humbucker and single-coil pickups.

2017-2020		$300	$400

Electric XII

1965-1969. Solidbody, 12 strings, long headstock, 2 split pickups. Custom colors can fade or become darker; for example Lake Placid Blue changes to green. The price ranges below are for instruments that are relatively unfaded. Many older guitars have some color fade and minor fade is factored into these values. Each custom color should be evaluated on a case-by-case basis.

Custom color Fenders can be forged and bogus finishes have been a problem. As the value of custom color Fenders has increased, so has the problem of bogus non-original finishes. The prices in the Guide are for factory original finishes in excellent condition. The prices noted do not take into account market factors such as fake instruments, which can have the effect of lowering a guitar's market value unless the guitar's provenance can be validated. Please refer to the Fender Guitar Intro Section for details on Fender color options.

1965-1969	Common color	$5,600	$7,300
1965-1969	Rare color	$7,000	$9,200
1965-1969	Sunburst	$3,700	$4,800

Electric XII Alternate Reality

2019. Modern updated reissue.

2019		$600	$800

MODEL YEAR	FEATURES	EXC. COND. LOW	HIGH

Ensenada Series

2005-2007. Made in Mexico acoustics, solid top, back and sides, A (grand auditorium), D (dreadnought), M (mini jumbo) and V (orchestra) sizes, E suffix denotes on-board electronics.

2005-2007	Acoustic	$400	$525
2005-2007	Acoustic-electric	$450	$600

Esprit Elite

1984. Master Series, made in Japan, double-cut, semi-hollow, carved maple top, 2 humbuckers, 4 controls, bound rosewood 'board, snowflake inlays.

1983-1985		$1,350	$1,750

Esprit Standard

1984. Like Esprit Elite, but with dot inlays, 2 controls.

1983-1985		$1,275	$1,650

Esprit Ultra

1984. Like Esprit Elite, but with bound ebony 'board, split-block inlays, gold hardware.

1984		$1,350	$1,750

Esquire

1950-1970. Ash body, single-cut, 1 pickup, maple neck, black 'guard '50-'54, white 'guard '54 on. Please refer to the Fender Guitar Intro Section for details on Fender color options.

1950-1951	Blond, black 'guard	$32,000	$42,000
1952-1953	Blond, black 'guard	$28,000	$37,000
1954	Blond, black 'guard	$26,000	$34,000
1954-1955	Blond, white 'guard	$22,000	$29,000
1956-1957	Blond	$22,000	$29,000
1958	Blond, backloader	$17,000	$22,000
1958	Blond, toploader	$14,500	$19,000
1959	Blond, maple 'board	$14,500	$19,000
1959	Blond, rosewood 'board	$14,500	$19,000
1960	Blond	$12,800	$16,600
1960	Sunburst	$14,000	$18,100
1961	Blond, slab 'board	$11,900	$15,500
1961	Custom color	$26,000	$34,000
1961	Sunburst, slab	$13,500	$17,500
1962	Blond, curved 'board	$10,900	$14,200
1962	Blond, slab	$11,900	$15,500
1962	Custom color	$26,000	$34,000
1962	Sunburst, curved	$13,000	$17,000
1962	Sunburst, slab	$13,500	$17,500
1963	Blond	$10,900	$14,200
1963	Common color	$19,000	$25,000
1963	Rare color	$25,000	$33,000
1963	Sunburst	$13,000	$17,000
1964	Blond	$10,900	$14,200
1964	Common color	$17,500	$23,000
1964	Rare color	$23,000	$30,000
1964	Sunburst	$13,000	$17,000
1965	Blond	$9,200	$12,000
1965	Common color	$14,000	$18,000

1968 Fender Coronado XII Wildwood

Tim Kummer

'65 Fender Electric XII

Richard F. Johnson

1986 Fender Esquire (Japan)
Michael Alonzi

1961 Fender Esquire Custom
Carter Vintage Guitars

MODEL YEAR	FEATURES	EXC. COND. LOW	HIGH
1965	Rare color	$18,000	$28,000
1965	Sunburst	$9,200	$12,000
1966	Blond	$7,700	$10,000
1966	Common color	$8,800	$11,400
1966	Rare color	$11,400	$16,000
1966	Sunburst	$8,400	$11,000
1967	Blond	$6,300	$8,200
1967	Blond, smuggler cavity	$8,800	$11,400
1967	Common color	$8,700	$11,500
1967	Rare color	$11,500	$16,000
1967	Sunburst	$8,400	$11,000
1968	Blond	$6,300	$8,200
1968	Common color	$8,700	$11,500
1968	Rare color	$11,500	$16,000
1968	Sunburst, nitro	$8,400	$11,000
1969	Blond	$5,500	$7,200
1969	Common color	$8,800	$11,400
1969	Rare color	$11,500	$16,000
1969	Sunburst, poly	$7,700	$10,000
1970	Blond	$4,700	$6,200
1970	Common color	$7,500	$9,700
1970	Rare color	$9,700	$13,500
1970	Sunburst	$4,700	$6,100

Esquire (Japan)

1985-1994. Made in Japan, '54 specs.

MODEL YEAR	FEATURES	EXC. COND. LOW	HIGH
1985-1986		$875	$1,125
1987-1989	'50s Esquire	$875	$1,125
1990-1994	'50s Esquire	$775	$1,000

'50s Esquire (Mexico)

2005-2010. Maple neck, ash body.

MODEL YEAR	FEATURES	EXC. COND. LOW	HIGH
2005-2010		$475	$625

'52 Esquire

2012. Custom Shop model, price includes Certificate of Authenticity.

MODEL YEAR	FEATURES	EXC. COND. LOW	HIGH
2012	NOS	$1,950	$2,525

'53 Esquire

2012. Custom Shop model, price includes Certificate of Authenticity.

MODEL YEAR	FEATURES	EXC. COND. LOW	HIGH
2012	NOS	$1,950	$2,525

'59 Esquire

2003-2007, 2013-2016. Custom Shop model, Relic version lasted to '07, then came back in '13 for limited run.

MODEL YEAR	FEATURES	EXC. COND. LOW	HIGH
2003-2013	Closet Classic	$1,950	$2,525
2003-2013	NOS	$1,950	$2,525
2003-2016	Relic	$2,075	$2,700
2006	LE Relic, 100 made	$2,075	$2,700

'60 Esquire

Custom Shop model, NOS.

MODEL YEAR	FEATURES	EXC. COND. LOW	HIGH
2010		$1,950	$2,525

'70 Esquire

2008. Custom Shop model, only 20 made.

MODEL YEAR	FEATURES	EXC. COND. LOW	HIGH
2008	Heavy Relic	$2,250	$2,950
2008	Relic	$2,075	$2,700

70th Anniversary Esquire

MODEL YEAR	FEATURES	EXC. COND. LOW	HIGH
2020		$1,100	$1,450

Custom Esquire '95

1995. Custom Shop limited edition of 12, stealth pickup under 'guard, bird's-eye maple neck.

MODEL YEAR	FEATURES	EXC. COND. LOW	HIGH
1995		$1,950	$2,525

Esquire Custom

1959-1970. Same as Esquire, but with bound alder sunburst body and rosewood 'board.

MODEL YEAR	FEATURES	EXC. COND. LOW	HIGH
1959	Sunburst	$22,000	$28,500
1960	Custom color	$30,000	$42,000
1960	Sunburst	$22,000	$28,500
1961	Custom color	$29,000	$41,000
1961	Sunburst	$21,000	$27,200
1962	Custom color	$26,000	$38,000
1962	Sunburst, curve	$18,500	$24,100
1962	Sunburst, slab	$20,100	$26,100
1963	Custom color	$24,000	$36,000
1963	Sunburst	$18,500	$24,100
1964	Custom color	$23,000	$30,000
1964	Sunburst	$17,000	$21,000
1965	Custom color	$15,000	$27,000
1965	Sunburst	$13,000	$17,000
1966	Custom color	$12,000	$21,000
1966	Sunburst	$10,500	$13,500
1967-1970	Sunburst	$10,500	$13,500

Esquire Custom (Import)

1983-1994. Made in Japan with all the classic bound Esquire features, sunburst.

MODEL YEAR	FEATURES	EXC. COND. LOW	HIGH
1983-1987		$950	$1,250
1988-1994		$850	$1,125

Esquire Custom GT/Celtic/Scorpion

2003. Made in Korea, single-cut solidbody, 1 humbucker, 1 knob (volume), set-neck, solid colors.

MODEL YEAR	FEATURES	EXC. COND. LOW	HIGH
2003		$425	$550

Esquire Z

2001. Custom Shop, black body and headstock, curly maple neck, ebony 'board, 25 made.

MODEL YEAR	FEATURES	EXC. COND. LOW	HIGH
2001		$4,300	$5,600

Brad Paisley Esquire

2020-present. Spruce top and back, 2 single-coil pickups, black and silver paisley 'guard, road worn black sparkle finish.

MODEL YEAR	FEATURES	EXC. COND. LOW	HIGH
2020		$775	$1,000

Jeff Beck Tribute Esquire (Custom Shop)

2006. Also called Beck Artist Esquire or Tribute Series Jeff Beck Esquire, specs include an extremely lightweight 2-piece offset ash body with Beck's original contours, distressed for an appearance like Beck's original Esquire that was used on many Yardbird records.

MODEL YEAR	FEATURES	EXC. COND. LOW	HIGH
2006		$6,800	$8,800

F (Flat-Top) Series

1969-1981. The F-Series were Japanese-made flat-top acoustics, included were Concert- and Dreadnought-size instruments with features running from plain to bound necks and headstocks and fancy inlays, there was also a line of F-Series classical, nylon-string guitars. A label on the inside indicates the model. FC-20 is a classical with Brazilian rosewood. There was also an Asian (probably Korean) import Standard Series for '82-'90 where the models start with a F.

MODEL YEAR	FEATURES	EXC. COND. LOW	HIGH
1969-1981	Dreadnought, laminated	$60	$135
1969-1981	Dreadnought, solid top	$135	$325
1972-1981	Classical (FC)	$135	$325

MODEL YEAR	FEATURES	EXC. COND. LOW	HIGH

FA (Fender Alternative) Series
2009-present. Entry-level acoustic series, various Concert, Dreadnought and Auditorium sized models.

2009-2020	FA-115, FA-125	$90	$125
2018-2020	FA-345CE	$250	$325

Flame Elite
1984. Master Series, made in Japan, neck-thru, offset double-cut, solidbody, 2 humbuckers, rosewood 'board, snowflake inlays.

1984-1988		$1,350	$1,750

Flame Standard
1984-1988. Like Flame Elite, but with dot inlays.

1984-1988		$1,275	$1,675

Flame Ultra
1984. Like Flame Elite, but with split block inlays (some with snowflakes), gold hardware.

1984-1988		$1,350	$1,750

FR-48 Resonator
2003-2009. Made in Korea, steel body.

2003-2009		$200	$300

FR-50 Resonator
2000-2015. Spruce top, mahogany back and sides, sunburst, optional square-neck.

2000-2015		$200	$300

FR-50CE Resonator
2000-2015. Same as FR-50 with cutaway and pickups.

2009-2015		$300	$390

FR-55 Hawaiian Resonator
2012-2013. Bell brass nickel-plated body etched with scenes of South Seas.

2012-2013		$300	$400

GA (Grand Auditorium) Series
2001-2009. Various grand auditorium models made in Korea, an oval label on the inside back clearly indicates the model number.

2001-2009		$120	$475

GC (Grand Concert) Series
1997-2009. Various grand concert models, an oval label on the inside back clearly indicates the model number.

1997-2009		$115	$150

GDO (Global Design Orchestra) Series
2004-2008. Various orchestra-sized acoustic models, an oval label on the inside back clearly indicates the model number.

2004-2008		$315	$410

Gemini Series
1983-1990. Korean-made flat-tops, label on inside indicates model. I is classical nylon-string, II, III and IV are dreadnought steel-strings, there is also a 12-string and an IIE acoustic/electric.

1984-1987	Gemini II	$80	$175
1984-1988	Gemini I	$75	$140
1987-1988	Gemini III	$130	$200
1987-1990	Gemini IIE	$130	$200
1987-1990	Gemini IV	$130	$200

GN (Grand Nylon) Series
2001-2007. Various grand nylon acoustic models, an oval label on the inside back clearly indicates the model number.

2001-2007		$305	$395

MODEL YEAR	FEATURES	EXC. COND. LOW	HIGH

Harmony-Made Series
Late-1960s-1973. Various Harmony-made models, with white stencil Fender logo, mahogany, natural or sunburst.

1960s	D-style model	$210	$800
1970-1973	Stella model	$80	$165

Jag-Stang
1996-1999, 2003-2004. Made in Japan, designed by Curt Cobain, body similar to Jaguar, tremolo, 1 pickup, oversize Strat peghead, Fiesta Red or Sonic Blue. First year has 50th Anniversary label.

1996-2004		$750	$975

Jaguar
1962-1975. Reintroduced as Jaguar '62 in '95-'99. Custom colors can fade and often the faded color has very little similarity to the original color. The values below are for an instrument that is relatively unfaded. Each custom color should be evaluated on a case-by-case basis. As the value of custom color Fenders has increased, so has the problem of bogus non-original finishes. The prices in the Guide are for factory original finishes in excellent condition. Please refer to the Fender Guitar Intro Section for details on Fender color options.

1962	Common color	$5,700	$7,400
1962	Rare color	$7,400	$9,700
1962	Sunburst	$3,900	$5,100
1963	Common color	$5,700	$7,400
1963	Rare color	$7,400	$9,700
1963	Sunburst	$3,900	$5,100
1964	Common color	$5,700	$7,400
1964	Rare color	$7,400	$9,700
1964	Sunburst	$3,900	$5,100
1965	Common color	$5,000	$6,500
1965	Rare color	$6,500	$8,500
1965	Sunburst	$3,500	$4,600
1966	Common color	$4,200	$5,500
1966	Rare color	$5,800	$8,500
1966	Sunburst, block markers	$3,300	$4,300
1966	Sunburst, dot markers	$3,300	$4,300
1967-1969	Common color	$4,200	$5,500
1967-1969	Rare color	$5,500	$8,600
1967-1969	Sunburst	$3,500	$4,600
1970	Common color	$3,500	$4,500
1970	Rare color	$4,500	$6,300
1970-1975	Sunburst	$2,800	$3,700
1971-1974	Custom color	$3,500	$4,500
1975	Custom color	$3,000	$4,000

Jaguar '62
1986-2012. Reintroduction of Jaguar, Japanese-made until '99, then U.S.-made American Vintage series, basswood body, rosewood 'board, various colors.

1986-1999	Import	$925	$1,200
1999-2012	USA	$1,125	$1,450

Jaguar HH/Special Edition Jaguar HH
2005-2014. Japan, 2 Dragster humbuckers, matching headstock, chrome knobs and pickup covers.

2005-2014		$525	$680

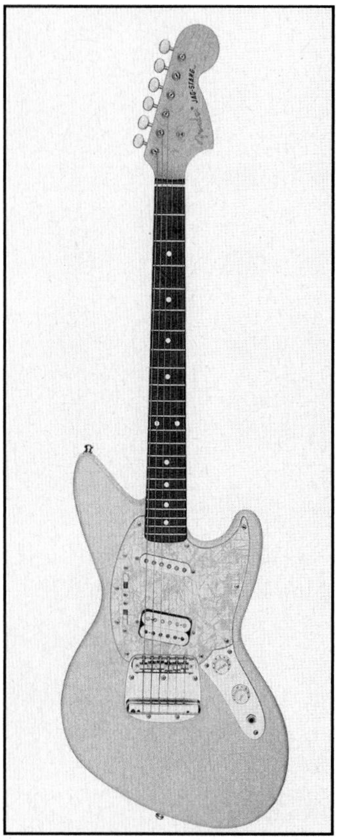

1997 Fender Jag-Stang
Imaged by Heritage Auctions, HA.com

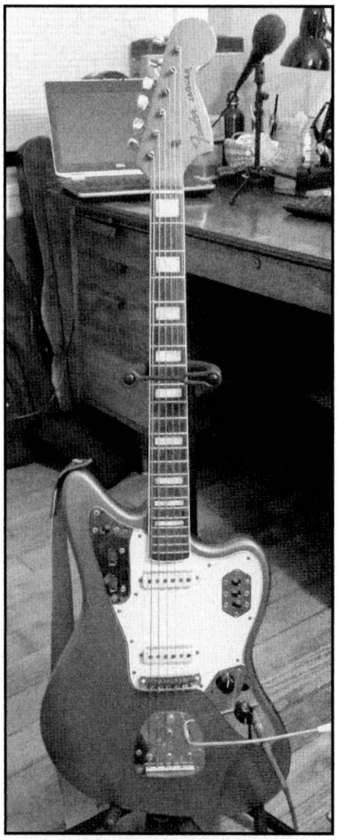

1966 Fender Jaguar
Patrick McHaffie

1962 Fender Jazzmaster

Kevin Rush

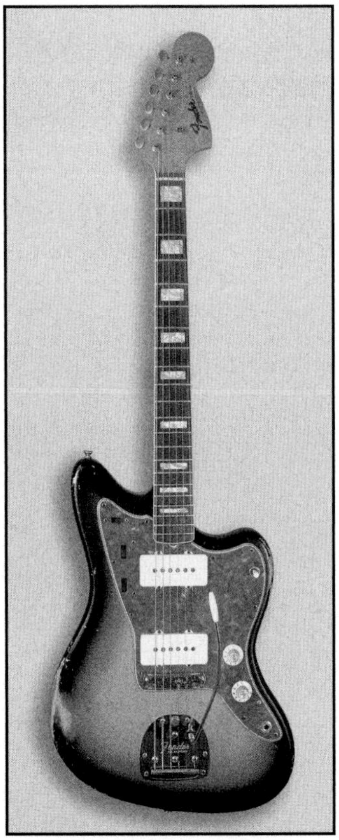

1966 Fender Jazzmaster

Phill Fesser

MODEL YEAR	FEATURES	EXC. COND. LOW	HIGH

50th Anniversary Jaguar

2012. USA, modeled after '62, classic 24" scale, new one-degree neck-angle pocket, repositioned tremolo plate, redesigned hot Jaguar single-coils, lacquer finish in Lake Placid Blue, Candy Apple Red, or burgundy.

2012		$1,075	$1,400

American Vintage '62 Jaguar

2000. Export version, Lake Placid Blue, Candy Apple Red, Shell Pink, Burgundy Mist Metallic and Ice Blue Metallic with matching headstocks, a special run for Yamano, Japan. Limited to 50 in each color.

2000		$1,250	$1,650

Blacktop Jaguar HH

2010-2014. Stripped-down electronics with 2 humbuckers, 1 volume, 1 tone, single 3-way switch, maple neck, rosewood 'board, black 'guard, black or silver.

2010-2014		$475	$625

Jaguar Baritone Special HH

2005-2010. Japan, limited edition, Baritone Special logo on matching headstock, 2 humbuckers, no trem, black.

2005-2010		$525	$680

Jaguar Classic Player Special

2009-2019. Classic Player series, classic Jag look, tremolo, 2 single-coils

2009-2019		$525	$680

Jaguar Classic Player Special HH

2009-2019. Classic Player series. 2 humbucker version.

2009-2019		$525	$680

Jaguar FSR Classic '66 Reissue

2008-2010. Fender Special Run, '66 specs, block inlays, black logo, custom colors, limited edition.

2008-2010		$975	$1,250

Jaguar FSR Thinline

2012. Limited Edition, semi-hollowbody with f-hole, 2 vintage-style single-coil pickups.

2012		$1,075	$1,400

Jaguar Limited Edition Classic Series

2002-2003. Crafted in Japan.

2002-2003		$850	$1,100

Jaguar Special Edition HH

2005-2014. 2 humbuckers, matching headstock, no trem.

2005-2014		$500	$650

Johnny Marr Signature Jaguar

2012-present. Artist series, based on Marr's '65 Jaguar, Olympic White or Metallic KO.

2012-2020		$1,025	$1,325

Kurt Cobain Signature Jaguar

2011-present. Artist Series, based on Cobain's '65 Jaguar, 3-color sunburst.

2011-2020		$1,025	$1,325

Modern Player Jaguar

2012-2014. Mahogany body, maple neck, rosewood 'board, 2-color chocolate burst, trans red or trans black.

2012-2014		$285	$370

MODEL YEAR	FEATURES	EXC. COND. LOW	HIGH

Pawn Shop Jaguarillo

2012-2013. Alder body, maple neck, rosewood 'board, HSS pickups, various colors.

2012-2013		$475	$625

Player Jaguar

2018-present. Alder body, maple neck, 1 humbucker and 1 single-coil, various colors with gloss finish.

2018-2020		$400	$525

Jazzmaster

1958-1980. Contoured body, 2 pickups, rosewood 'board, clay dot inlay, reintroduced as Japanese-made Jazzmaster '62 in '94. Custom color Fenders can be forged and bogus finishes have been a problem. As the value of custom color Fenders has increased, so has the problem of bogus non-original finishes. The prices in the Guide are for factory original finishes in excellent condition. Please refer to the Fender Guitar Intro Section for details on Fender color options.

1958	Sunburst	$8,700	$11,300
1958	Sunburst, maple 'board	$8,300	$10,900
1959	Custom color, includes rare	$13,500	$20,500
1959	Sunburst	$7,500	$10,000
1960	Common color	$11,500	$15,000
1960	Rare color	$15,000	$19,000
1960	Sunburst	$7,200	$9,300
1961	Common color	$11,500	$15,000
1961	Rare color	$15,000	$19,000
1961	Sunburst	$6,100	$8,000
1962	Common color	$7,700	$10,000
1962	Rare color	$10,000	$15,000
1962	Sunburst, curved 'board	$4,900	$6,300
1963	Common color	$7,700	$10,000
1963	Rare color	$10,000	$15,000
1963	Sunburst	$4,900	$6,300
1964	Common color	$7,700	$10,000
1964	Rare color	$10,000	$15,000
1964	Sunburst	$4,900	$6,300
1965	Common color	$4,700	$8,000
1965	Rare color	$8,000	$11,000
1965	Sunburst	$4,400	$5,700
1966	Common color	$4,500	$6,000
1966	Rare color	$6,000	$9,000
1966	Sunburst	$4,300	$5,600
1967-1969	Common color	$4,500	$6,000
1967-1969	Rare color	$6,000	$9,000
1967-1969	Sunburst	$4,300	$5,600
1970	Common color	$4,300	$5,800
1970	Rare color	$5,800	$7,800
1970-1980	Sunburst	$2,800	$3,700
1971-1974	Custom color	$4,000	$5,500
1975	Custom color	$3,500	$4,500
1976-1980	Custom color	$3,000	$4,000

Road Worn '60s Jazzmaster

2015-2019. '60s style with aged/worn alder body and maple neck, worn nitro-lacquer finish. Replaced by American Original '60s Jazzmaster.

2015-2019		$500	$650

MODEL YEAR	FEATURES	EXC. COND. LOW	HIGH

Jazzmaster '62
1986-2012. Japanese-made reintroduction of Jazzmaster, basswood body, rosewood 'board, from '99 U.S.-made American Vintage series, various colors.

1986-1989	Import	$1,000	$1,300
1990-1998	Import	$925	$1,200
1999-2012	USA	$1,125	$1,450

Jazzmaster '65
2013-2018. Alder body, maple neck, mid-'60s neck profile, rosewood 'board. Part of American Vintage series in '16.

2013-2018		$1,250	$1,650

Jazzmaster '69
1986-1990s. Made in Japan.

1986-1989		$1,000	$1,300
1990-1999		$925	$1,200

American Performer Jazzmaster
Introduced Dec. 2018-present. Made in US, new features include Yosemite single-coil pickups, Greasebucket tone system, various colors.

2018-2020		$675	$875

American Ultra Jazzmaster
2019-present. Alder or ash body, maple neck, rosewood 'board, 2 pickups.

2019-2020		$1,100	$1,450

Blacktop Jazzmaster HS
2010-2014. Stripped-down electronics with a single-coil and a humbucker, 1 volume, 1 tone, single 3-way switch, maple neck, rosewood 'board, black or sunburst.

2010-2014		$475	$625

Classic Player Jazzmaster Special
2008-2019. Alder body, maple neck, rosewood 'board, 2 single-coils, 3-color sunburst or black.

2008-2019		$525	$680

Elvis Costello Jazzmaster
2008-2010. Artist series, walnut stain, '70s neck, vintage style tremolo.

2008-2010		$1,300	$1,725

J Mascis Jazzmaster
2007-2009. Artist series, purple sparkle finish, matching headstock, Adjusto-Matic bridge, reinforced tremolo arm.

2007-2009		$975	$1,275

Noventa Jazzmaster
2021. Alder body, maple neck, 3 single-coil pickups, Fiesta Red, Surf Green or Walnut.

2021		$625	$825

Pinup Girl Jazzmaster (Custom Shop)
1997. Custom Shop Limited Edition, pinup girl art on body, figured maple neck, 3 pickups, certificate of authenticity.

1997		$2,050	$2,650

Select Jazzmaster
2012-2013. Chambered alder body with a carved flame maple top, Fender Select headstock medallion, various finish options.

2012-2013		$1,625	$2,100

Sonic Youth Signature Jazzmaster
2009-2014. Lee Ranaldo and Thurston Moore Signature models based on their modified Jazzmasters which basically removed the standard control layout and replaced it with a 3-way switch.

2009-2014	Lee Ranaldo	$1,200	$1,550
2009-2014	Thurston Moore	$1,200	$1,550

The Ventures Limited Edition Jazzmaster
1996. Japanese-made, ash body, 2 pickups, block inlay, transparent purple/black.

1996		$1,025	$1,325

Troy Van Leeuwen Jazzmaster
2014-present. Alder body, maple neck, Oxblood finish, red tortoiseshell 'guard, matching headstock, various custom colors.

2014-2020		$725	$950

White Opal Jazzmaster HH
2016. Special Edition, made in Mexico, white opal body and headstock, pearloid 'guard, 2 humbuckers.

2016		$375	$475

JZM Deluxe
2007-2009. Electracoustic Series, acoustic/electric, Jazzmaster/Jaguar body styling, Fishman and Tele pickups, sunburst or trans amber.

2007-2009		$350	$450

Katana
1985-1986. Japanese-made wedge-shaped body, 2 humbuckers, set neck, triangle inlays, black.

1985-1986		$700	$900

King
1963-1965. Full-size 15 5/8" wide acoustic, natural. Renamed Kingman in '65.

1963-1965	Brazilian rosewood	$2,475	$3,200
1963-1965	Indian, Zebra, Vermillion	$1,275	$1,650

Kingman
1965-1971. Full-size 15 5/8" wide acoustic, slightly smaller by '70, offered in 3 Wildwood colors, referred to as the Wildwood acoustic which is a Kingman with dyed wood. Reissued as import in '06.

1965-1968		$1,200	$1,550
1969-1971		$1,100	$1,425

Kingman Antigua
1968-1971. Kingman in Antigua finish (silver to black sunburst).

1968-1971		$1,375	$1,800

Kingman ASCE
2008-2017. Cutaway acoustic-electric, mahogany back and sides.

2008-2017		$325	$425

Kingman SCE
2008-2017. Cutaway acoustic-electric, mahogany back and sides.

2008-2017		$300	$400

Kingman USA Pro Custom
2013-2014. US-made, Custom Shop Pro series, limited run of 50, AA sitka spruce top, maple back/sides/neck, Firemist Gold finish.

2013-2014		$950	$1,250

Kingman USA Select
2012. All solid woods, rosewood 'board, 3-color sunburst, Fishman electronics.

2012	COA	$1,000	$1,300

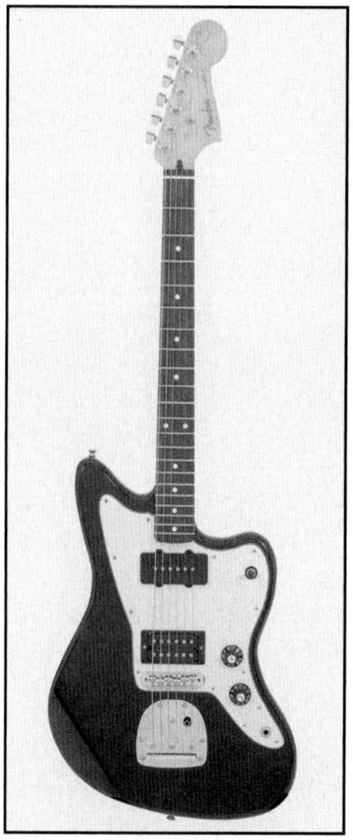

2011 Fender Blacktop Jazzmaster HS
Imaged by Heritage Auctions, HA.com

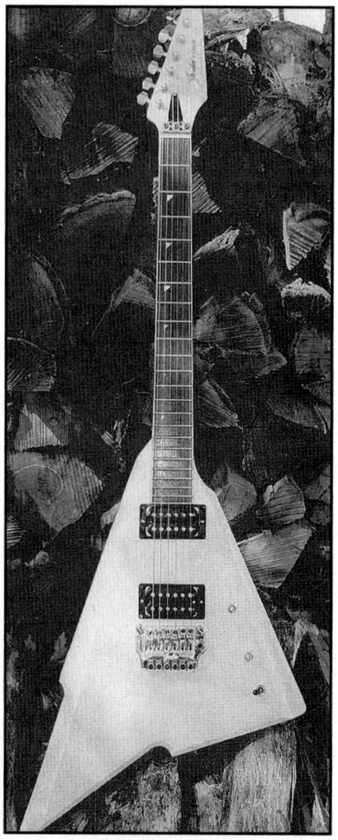

1985 Fender Katana

1980 Fender Lead II

Tom Pfeifer

1965 Fender Mustang

Robbie Keene

MODEL YEAR	FEATURES	EXC. COND. LOW	HIGH

Kingman USA Select C
2012. Custom Shop limited edition of 150, Engelmann spruce top, mahogany back and sides, vintage C-shaped maple neck, rosewood 'board, Fiesta Red.

2012	COA	$1,050	$1,350

Kingman/Elvis Kingman
2012-2013. Wildwood model as used by Elvis Presley in the '67 film 'Clambake', spruce top, mahogany back and sides, rosewood 'board, natural.

2012-2013		$300	$400

Lead I
1979-1982. Double-cut solidbody with 1 humbucker, maple or rosewood 'board, black or brown.

1979-1982		$550	$725

Lead II
1979-1982. Lead with 2 pickups, black or brown.

1979-1982		$725	$925

Lead III
1982. Lead with 2 split-coil humbuckers, 2 3-way switches, various colors.

1982		$725	$925

Player Lead II
2020-present. Reintroduced using late-70s and updated model features.

2020		$340	$440

Player Lead III
2020-present. Reintroduced using late-70s and updated model features.

2020		$340	$440

LTD
1969-1975. Archtop electric, single-cut, gold-plated hardware, carved top and back, 1 pickup, multi-bound, bolt-on neck, sunburst.

1969-1975		$2,600	$3,400

Malibu
1965-1971. Flat-top, spruce top, mahogany back and sides, black, mahogany or sunburst. Later version is import.

1965-1971		$625	$825

Malibu (California Series)
1983-1995. Made first in Japan, then Korea in '85.

1983-1995		$190	$250

Malibu SCE
2006-2013. Imported single-cut acoustic/electric, solid spruce top, laminated mahogany back and sides, block inlays.

2006-2013		$200	$260

Marauder
1965 only. The Marauder has 3 pickups, and some have slanted frets, only 8 were made, thus it is very rare. 1st generation has hidden pickups, 2nd has exposed.

1965	1st generation	$9,000	$11,600
1965	2nd generation	$6,500	$8,500

Marauder (Modern Player Series)
2011-2014. Jazzmaster-type body, 1 Jazzmaster pickup and 1 Triple Bucker, rosewood 'board.

2011-2014		$350	$450

Maverick Dorado (Parallel Universe Series)
2020. Parallel Universe Vol. II series, alder body, 22-fret maple neck, 2 pickups, Bigsby vibrato, Mystic Pine Green, Ultraburst and Firemist Gold.

2020		$1,400	$1,800

Meteora (Parallel Universe Series)
November 2018-2019. Parallel Universe Vol. II series, sleek offset body with both Jazzmaster and Telecaster features.

2018-2019		$500	$675

Mod Shop
2016-present. Models designed by customer by choosing options from a menu and built by Fender, 4 models offered - Jazz Bass, Precision Bass, Stratocaster and Telecaster. Values should be determined on case-by-case basis.

2016-2020		$1,675	$2,200

Montara (California Series)
1990-1995. Korean-made single-cut acoustic/electric flat-top, natural, sunburst or black. Maple with flamed sides starting '92.

1990-1995		$400	$525

Montego I/II
1968-1975. Electric archtop, single-cut, bolt-on neck, 1 pickup (I) or 2 pickups (II), chrome-plated hardware, sunburst.

1968-1975	I	$2,300	$3,000
1968-1975	II	$2,450	$3,200

Musiclander
1969-1972. Also called Swinger and Arrow, solidbody, 1 pickup, arrow-shaped headstock, no model name on peghead, red, white, and blue. Fender used '66-'68 dated necks but final assembly did not begin until '69.

1969-1972		$2,200	$2,850

Musicmaster
1956-1980. Solidbody, 1 pickup, short-scale (3/4) neck, Desert Sand ('56-'61), sunburst ('61-'63), red, white or blue after. Regular-scale necks were optional and are called Musicmaster II from '64 to '69, after '69 II is dropped and Musicmaster continues with regular-scale neck.

1956-1959	Blond	$1,700	$2,250
1960-1964	Blond	$1,375	$1,775
1964-1965	Nitro, red, white, blue	$1,375	$1,775
1966-1968	Nitro, red, white, blue	$1,250	$1,650
1969-1972	Poly, red, white, blue	$1,150	$1,500
1973-1980	Red, white, blue	$1,150	$1,500

Musicmaster II
1964-1969. Solidbody, 1 pickup, long regular-scale neck version of Musicmaster, red, white, or blue.

1964-1965		$1,375	$1,775
1966-1969		$1,150	$1,500

Mustang
1964-1982, 1997-1998, 2016-present. Solidbody, 2 pickups. Reissued as '69 Mustang in 1990s, name changed back to Mustang '97-'98. Dakota Red, Daphne Blue and Olympic White with Competition

MODEL YEAR	FEATURES	EXC. COND. LOW	HIGH

Red, Blue and Orange finishes with a racing stripe on the front of the body added '69-'73 (with matching headstock for '69-'70).

1964-1965	Red, white or blue	$1,825	$2,375
1966-1969	Red, white or blue	$1,650	$2,175
1969-1970	Competition color	$1,650	$2,175
1970-1979	Contour body, poly	$1,500	$1,950
1978-1980	Antigua	$1,500	$1,950
1980-1982	Various colors	$1,100	$1,425

Vintera '60s Mustang

2019-present. Alder body, '60s C-neck, 2 single-coils, 3-color sunburst, Lake Placid Blue or Seafoam Green.

2019-2020 $500 $650

Mustang '65 Reissue

2006-2016. Made in Japan, Classic Series.

2006-2016 $600 $800

Mustang '69 Reissue

1986-1998, 2005. Japanese-made, blue or white.

1986-1998 $600 $800

Mustang 90/Player Mustang 90

2016-present. Made in Mexico, 2 MP-90 pickups. Named to Player series in '20.

2016-2020 $350 $455

American Performer Mustang

Introduced Dec. 2018-2019. Made in U.S.A., Yosemite single-coil pickups, Greasebucket tone system, various colors.

2018-2019 $650 $850

American Special Mustang

2017-2018. FSR model, 2 humbucking pickups, ash body with natural finish or alder Olympic White Pearl.

2017-2018 $675 $875

Ben Gibbard Mustang

2021. Artist series, chambered ash body, natural poly gloss finish.

2021 $600 $800

Kurt Cobain Mustang

2012-2016. Artist Series, rosewood 'board, Fiesta Red finish.

2012-2016 $550 $725

Mustang Special

2011-2013. Pawn Shop series, 2 humbucker pickups. 3-color sunburst, Candy Apple Red or Lake Placid Blue.

2011-2013 $400 $575

Newporter

1965-1971. Acoustic flat-top, mahogany back and sides. Reissued as import.

1965-1968	Spruce top	$525	$700
1968-1971	Mahogany top	$500	$650

Newporter (California Series)

1983-1995. Made first in Japan, then Korea in '85.

1983-1995 $175 $225

Newporter (Custom Shop USA)/USA Select Newporter

2013-2014. Fishman electronics, 150 offered, certificate of authenticity.

2013-2014 $1,400 $1,825

Newporter Classic

2018-present. Spruce top, matching headstock, natural mahogany back and sides, pau ferro 'board.

2018-2020 $450 $575

Newporter Player

2018-present. California series, solid spruce top, mahogany back and sides, walnut 'board, various colors with gloss poly finish.

2018-2020 $235 $310

Palomino

1968-1971. Acoustic flat-top, spruce top, mahogany back and sides, triple-bound, black or mahogany.

1968-1971 $700 $925

Paramount Series Acoustic

2016-present. Various Standard and Deluxe acoustic models introduced at Jan. '16 NAMM.

2016-2020 $450 $600

Pawn Shop Series

2011-2014. All-new designs with diverse Fender components and the philosophy "guitars that never were but should have been".

2011-2014 Various models $475 $625

Performer

1985-1986. Imported Swinger-like body design, 2 slanted humbuckers.

1985-1986 $1,225 $1,575

Prodigy

1991-1993. US-made, electric solidbody, double-cut, chrome-plated hardware, 2 single-coil and 1 humbucker pickups, blue or black.

1991-1993 $850 $1,100

Redondo

1969-1970. Mid-size flat-top, 14 3/8" wide, replaces Newport spruce top model.

1969-1970 $475 $625

Redondo (California Series)

1983-1995. Made first in Japan, then Korea in '85.

1983-1995 $175 $225

Redondo Player

2018-present. California series, solid Sitka spruce top, mahogany back and sides, walnut 'board, various colors with gloss poly finish.

2018-2020 $235 $310

Robben Ford

1989-1994. Symmetrical double-cut, 2 pickups, glued-in neck, solidbody with tone chambers, multi-bound, gold-plated hardware, sunburst. After '94 made in Fender Custom Shop.

1989-1994		$1,350	$1,750
1995	Custom Shop	$2,375	$3,100

San Luis Rey (California Series)

1990-1995. Acoustic flat-top, solid spruce top, rosewood back and sides.

1990-1995 $235 $310

San Miguel (California Series)

1990-1995. Acoustic cutaway flat-top, spruce top, mahogany back and sides.

1990-1995 $165 $220

Santa Maria (California Series)

1988-1995. Acoustic flat-top 12-string, spruce top, mahogany back and sides.

1988-1995 $165 $220

1969 Fender Mustang

Suzie Williams

1969 Fender Newporter

Rivington Guitars

GUITARS

2005 Fender Squier '51
Fred Schweng

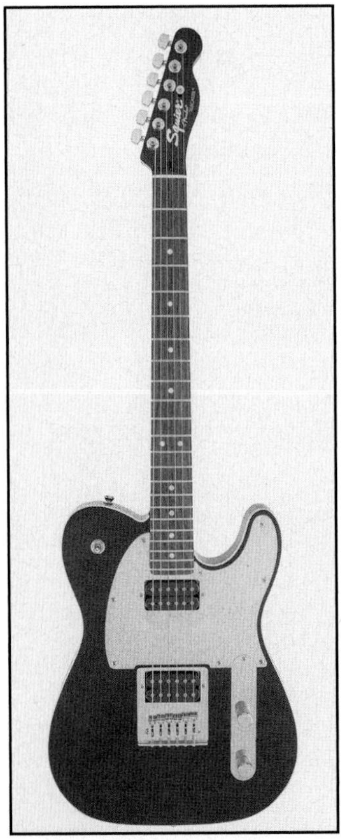

Fender Squier J5 Telecaster

MODEL YEAR	FEATURES	EXC. COND. LOW	HIGH

Santa Marino (California Series)
1990-1995. Acoustic flat-top, solid spruce top, mahogany back and sides.

1990-1995		$175	$230

Sergio Vallin Signature
2015-2017. New offset double-cut body shape, HSS pickups.

2015-2017		$425	$550

Shenandoah 12-String
1965-1971. Acoustic flat-top, spruce top, mahogany back and sides.

1965-1971	Antigua	$1,200	$1,575
1965-1971	Blond	$900	$1,200

Showmaster (Import)
2003-2007. Off-set double-cut solidbody, set neck, various models.

2003	Celtic, 1 bridge humbucker	$475	$625
2003-2007	HH, 2 humbuckers	$475	$625
2004-2006	3 single coils	$475	$625

Showmaster FMT (Custom Shop)
2000-2007. Bound figured maple top (FMT), 2 single-coil pickups and a bridge position humbucker, maple neck, Custom Shop certificate.

2000-2007		$1,600	$2,100

Sonoran SCE (California Series)
2006-2018. Cutaway flat-top acoustic, 6-on-a-side tuners, spruce top, laminated mahogany back and sides, rosewood 'board, electronics options.

2006-2018		$190	$250

Squier Series
The following are all Squier Series instruments from Fender, listed alphabetically. Fender Japan was established in '82 with Squier production beginning that same year. Production was shifted to Korea in '87 and later allocated to China, India (Squier II '89-'90), Mexico and other countries.

Squier '51
2004-2006. Korean-made, Strat-style body with a Tele-style neck, various colors.

2004-2006		$95	$125

Squier Bullet
1983-1988, 1995-1996, 2000-2011. Strat style, early with Tele headstock, 1980s' models include H-2 ('83-'86, 2 humbuckers), S-3 ('83-'86, 3 single-coils), S-3T ('83-'88, 3 single-coils, vibrato). Name revived in 1995 (3 SC, vib.) and in 2000 on various models with 3 SC or 2 HB pickups.

1983-1984	H-2	$425	$550
1983-1984	S-3, T	$425	$550
1985-1986	H-2	$350	$450
1985-1988	S-3, T	$350	$450
2000-2011		$95	$125

Squier Duo-Sonic '50s (Classic Vibe Series)
2008-2010. Made in China.

2008-2010		$195	$250

Squier Jaguar HH ST (Contemporary Series)
2021. Poplar body, roasted maple neck, Indian Laurel 'board, 2 humbucker pickups, stop tailpiece, Shorline Gold or Sky Burst Metallic.

2021		$250	$325

Squier Jazzmaster (Classic Vibe Series)
2010-present. Classic Vibe series includes both '60s ('10-present) and '70s ('10-'20) Jazzmaster, inspired by vintage-era models, various colors with gloss poly finish.

2010-2020	'60s or '70s	$200	$275

Squier Katana
1985-1987. Wedge-shaped body, 1 humbucker, bolt neck, dot inlays.

1985-1987		$600	$800

Squier Mini Stratocaster
2020-present. Poplar body, maple neck, 3 single-coil pickups, various colors. Dual humbucker pickups (HH) available.

2020		$100	$130

Squier Showmaster Series
2002-2005. Made in China, various pickup configs.

2002-2005	Various models	$130	$175

Squier Stagemaster HH
1999-2002. 2 humbuckers, reverse headstock, 6- or 7-string.

1999-2002		$130	$175

Squier Standard Double Fat Strat
1999-2007. 2 humbucker pickups.

1999-2007		$95	$125

Squier Standard Fat Strat
1996-2006. Hum/single/single pickups. Replaced by the HSS.

1996-2006		$95	$125

Squier Standard Floyd Rose Strat
1992-1996. Floyd Rose tailpiece, black, white or foto flame finish, Fender and Squier headstock logos.

1992-1996		$290	$375

Squier Standard Stratocaster
1982-2019. Standard Series represent the classic designs.

1982-1984	1st logo, JV serial	$975	$1,300
1985-1989	2nd logo, SQ serial	$475	$625
1990-1999	Mexico	$280	$375
2000-2019	Indonesia	$125	$165

Squier II Stratocaster
1988-1992. Squier II models were targeted at a lower price point than regular Squier series. Mainly built in Korea but some early ones from India. Line was replaced by other models under regular Squier instruments.

1988-1992		$160	$225

Squier Stratocaster (Affinity Series)
1997-present. Lower priced version, made in China.

1997-2020		$125	$165

Squier Stratocaster (Contemporary Series)
2020-present. Poplar body, roasted maple neck, 2 humbucker pickups, various colors with gloss poly finish. Floyd Rose tremolo available.

2020-2021	HH	$190	$250
2021	Floyd Rose	$250	$325

Squier Stratocaster '50s (Classic Vibe Series)
2008-present. Alder body, maple 'board, white pickguard, 2-tone sunburst, Lake Placid Blue or Oly White.

2008-2020		$205	$275

MODEL YEAR	FEATURES	EXC. COND. LOW	HIGH

Squier Stratocaster '60s (Classic Vibe Series)

2008-present. As '50s Classic Vibe but with rosewood 'board, tortoise pickguard, 3-tone sunburst or candy apple red.

2008-2020		$205	$275

Squier Stratocaster Pro-Tone

1996-1998. Korean-made, higher-end Squier series with solid ash bodies, one-piece maple necks, alnico single-coils.

1996-1998		$365	$475

Squier Stratocaster Special (Contemporary Series)

2021. Poplar body, roasted maple neck, 3 single-coil pickups, painted headstock with chrome logo, various colors with gloss poly finish. Hardtail bridge (HT) available.

2021		$250	$325

Squier Tom Delonge Stratocaster

2002-2003. Hardtail, 1 humbucker.

2002-2003		$255	$330

Squier Standard Telecaster

1982-2019. Standard Series represent the classic designs.

1982-1984	1st logo, JV serial	$975	$1,300
1985-1989	2nd logo, SQ serial	$475	$625
1990-1999	Mexico	$280	$375
2000-2019	Indonesia	$125	$165

Squier Standard Telecaster Special

2004-2007. Made in Indonesia, 1 humbucker, 1 single-coil.

2004-2007		$125	$165

Squier Telecaster (Affinity Series)

1998-present. Lower priced version, made in China.

1998-2020		$125	$165

Squier Telecaster HH (Contemporary Series)

2020-present. Poplar body, maple neck, 2 dual humbucking pickups, black metallic with pearl white 'guard or pearl white with black 'guard.

2020		$250	$325

Squier Telecaster Custom/Custom II

2003-2012. 2 humbuckers, Custom II has 2 soapbar single-coils. Changed to Vintage Modified series in '12.

2003-2012		$125	$165

Squier J5 (John 5) Telecaster

2009-2020. Artist Series, black with chrome hardware or Frost Gold with gold hardware (introduced '14), matching headstock.

2014-2020	Frost Gold	$235	$310

Squier Telecaster Thinline (Classic Vibe Series)

2014-2020. Semi-hollow mahogany body with f-hole.

2004-2020		$195	$255

Squier Venus

1997-1998. Offset double-cut solidbody, 2 pickups, co-designed by Courtney Love, also offered as 12-string.

1997-1998		$385	$500

MODEL YEAR	FEATURES	EXC. COND. LOW	HIGH

Squier Vintage Modified Series

2012-2020. Imported, various models, large script Squier logo and small Fender logo on headstock.

2012-2016	Jazzmaster Special	$130	$200
2012-2016	Surf Stratocaster	$165	$215
2012-2016	Telecaster Special	$165	$215
2012-2020	'70s Stratocaster	$165	$215
2012-2020	Stratocaster HSS	$165	$215

Starcaster

1974-1980, 2014-2017. Offset double-cut, thinline semi-hollowbody, arched maple top and back, 2 humbuckers, 5 knobs (2 tone, 2 volume, 1 master volume), originally offered in tobacco sunburst, natural, walnut, black, white or custom blond finish. Model revived in Modern Player Series in '14 without master volume. Fender also used the Starcaster name as a brand on a line of budget guitars in the 2000s.

1974-1980	Various colors	$3,550	$4,650
2014-2017	Modern Player	$550	$725

Starcaster by Fender

2000s. Fender used the Starcaster brand on a line of budget versions of the Strat, Tele, and J- and P-Bass. They also offered small solid state amps and guitar packages with nylon- or steel-string acoustic or a Strat/amp combo. Sold in Costco and other discounters.

2000s	Acoustic	$75	$135
2000s	Electric guitar only	$75	$135
2000s	Pack with guitar, amp, stand	$90	$150

Stratacoustic Series

2000-2019. Thinline acoustic/electric, single-cut, spruce top, fiberglass body, various colors. Stratacoustic discontinued '05, Deluxe begins '07 and Standard added in '09. Both Plus and Premier '14-'17.

2002-2019		$300	$400

Stratocaster

The following are all variations of the Stratocaster. The first six listings are for the main American-made line. All others are listed alphabetically after that in the following order:

Stratocaster
Standard Stratocaster (includes "Smith Strat")
American Standard Stratocaster
American Series Stratocaster
American Professional Stratocaster
American Professional II Stratocaster
20th Century American Standard Stratocaster
21st Century American Standard Stratocaster
25th Anniversary Stratocaster
30th Anniversary Guitar Center Strat
35th Anniversary Stratocaster
40th Anniversary 1954 Stratocaster Limited Edition
40th Anniversary American Standard Stratocaster
40th Anniversary Stratocaster Diamond Dealer
40th Anniversary Stratocaster ST62 (Japan)
'50s Stratocaster/Classic Series '50s Stratocaster

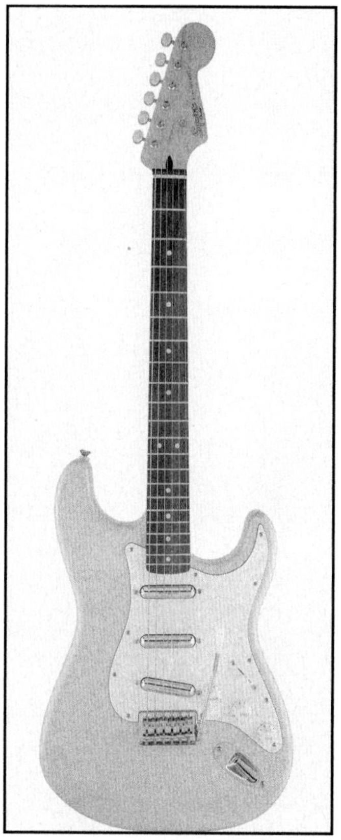

Fender Squire Vintage Modified Surf Stratocaster

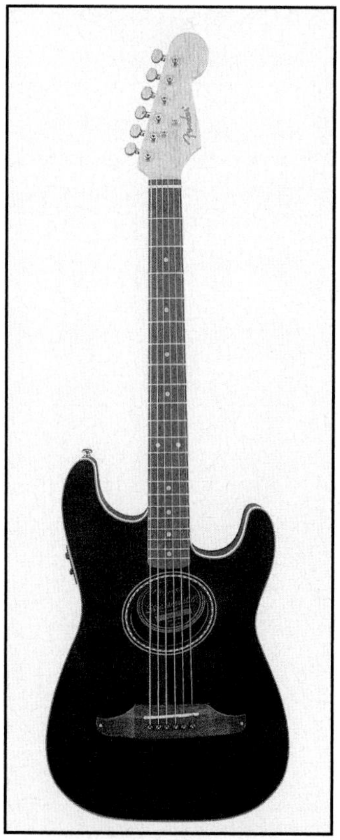

Fender Stratacoustic

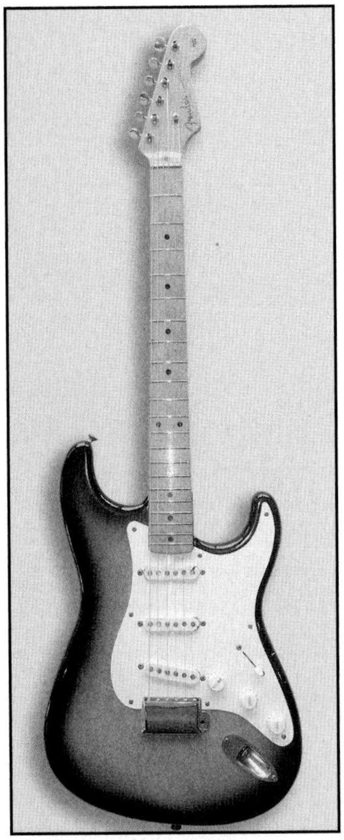

1954 Fender Stratocaster
Tony Sheedy

1956 Fender Stratocaster (lefty)
HI Guitars

American Original '50s Stratocaster
Classic Player '50s Stratocaster
Classic Series '50s Stratocaster Lacquer
Road Worn '50s Stratocaster
50th Anniversary 1954 Stratocaster
50th Anniversary American Deluxe Stratocaster
50th Anniversary American Standard Stratocaster
50th Anniversary American Vintage 1957 Stratocaster
50th Anniversary Standard Stratocaster
50th Anniversary Stratocaster
50th Anniversary Stratocaster Relic
'54 Stratocaster (Custom Shop)
'54 Stratocaster FMT
'55 Stratocaster (Custom Shop)
'55 Dual-Mag Strat Journeyman Relic
'55 Historic 1955 NOS Stratocaster
'55 Rocking Dog Stratocaster
'55 Stratocaster Journeyman Relic
'56 Stratocaster (Custom Shop)
'56 Stratocaster Heavy Relic
'56 Stratocaster Journeyman Closet Classic
American Vintage '56 Stratocaster
American Vintage '56 Stratocaster Limited Edition Roasted Ash
'57 Stratocaster (Custom Shop)
'57 Stratocaster (CS)
'57 Stratocaster (USA)
'57 Special Stratocaster
'57 Vintage Stratocaster (Japan)
American Vintage '57 Commemorative Stratocaster
Time Machine 1957 Stratocaster Relic
Vintage Custom 1957 Stratocaster NOS
Wildwood "10s" 1957 Limited Stratocaster Relic
'58 Stratocaster (Custom Shop)
'58 Stratocaster (Dakota Red)
'58 Limited Edition MIJ Stratocaster
'58 Stratocaster Journeyman Relic
Time Machine 1958 Stratocaster Heavy Relic
'59 Rocking Dog Stratocaster
'59 Stratocaster (Custom Shop)
1959 Stratocaster LTD Journeyman
American Vintage '59 Pine Stratocaster
American Vintage '59 Stratocaster
Time Machine 1959 Stratocaster
Wildwood "10s" 1959 Limited Stratocaster Relic
'60 Stratocaster (Custom Shop)
'60 Stratocaster FMT (Custom Shop)
Custom 1960 Stratocaster
'60s Stratocaster/Classic Series '60s Stratocaster
'60s Stratocaster/Time Machine 1960 Stratocaster
American Original '60s Stratocaster
Classic Player '60s Stratocaster
Classic Series '60s Stratocaster Lacquer
Limited Edition '60s Daybreak Stratocaster
Road Worn '60s Stratocaster
60th Anniversary '54 Stratocaster (Custom Shop)
60th Anniversary American Stratocaster
60th Anniversary American Vintage 1954 Stratocaster
60th Anniversary Commemorative Stratocaster
60th Anniversary Presidential Stratocaster
'61 Stratocaster (Custom Shop)
Wildwood "10s" 1961 Limited Stratocaster
'62 Stratocaster (USA)
'62 Commemorative Stratocaster
'62 Heavy Relic Stratocaster
'62 Stratocaster ST62D/ST54 DEX2
'62 Stratocaster ST62US Reissue
'62 Vintage Stratocaster (Japan)
Dave's Guitar Shop American 1962 Stratocaster
Deluxe Vintage Player '62 Stratocaster
Vintage Custom 1962 Stratocaster
Willcutt Guitars True '62 Stratocaster
'63 Stratocaster (Custom Shop)
'63 Stratocaster Journeyman Relic
'64 Stratocaster (Custom Shop)
Time Machine 1964 Stratocaster Journeyman Relic
'65 Stratocaster (Custom Shop)
'65 Stratocaster Journeyman Closet Classic
American Vintage '65 Stratocaster
Mark Kendrick Master Design '65 Stratocaster
Time Machine 1965 Stratocaster Journeyman Relic
Total Tone '65 Stratocaster Relic (Custom Shop)
'66 Stratocaster (Custom Shop)
Time Machine 1967 Stratocaster Journeyman Relic Aged
Time Machine 1967 Stratocaster Journeyman Relic Custom Top
'68 Heavy Relic Stratocaster
'68 Reverse Strat Special (USA)
'68 Stratocaster (Japan)
'69 Stratocaster (Custom Shop)
Wildwood "10s" 1969 Limited Stratocaster
'70s Stratocaster/Classic Series '70s Stratocaster
American Vintage '70s Stratocaster
'72 Stratocaster (Japan)
'72 Stratocaster Limited Edition
75th Anniversary Commemorative Stratocaster
75th Anniversary Stratocaster
Acoustasonic Stratocaster
Aerodyne Classic Stratocaster
Aerodyne Stratocaster
Albert Hammond Jr. Signature Stratocaster
Aluminum Stratocaster (Custom Shop)
Aluminum Stratocaster American Standard
American Acoustasonic Stratocaster
American Classic Holoflake Stratocaster
American Classic Stratocaster
American Custom Stratocaster (Custom Shop)
American Deluxe Stratocaster
American Deluxe Stratocaster Dealer Event
American Deluxe Stratocaster Designer Series
American Deluxe Stratocaster FMT HSS
American Deluxe Stratocaster HSS Mahogany
American Elite Stratocaster

American Elite Stratocaster Limited Edition
American Longboard Stratocaster HSS
American Performer Stratocaster
American Special Stratocaster
American Standard Stratocaster Limited Edition
American Ultra Luxe Stratocaster
American Ultra Stratocaster
Ancho Poblano Stratocaster Journeyman Relic
Ancho Poblano Roasted Stratocaster Relic
Antigua Stratocaster
Artisan Series Stratocaster (Custom Shop)
Big Apple Stratocaster
Big Block Stratocaster
Big Head Stratocaster
Bill Carson Stratocaster
Billy Corgan Stratocaster
Blackie Stratocaster (Custom Shop 1987)
Blackie Stratocaster (Custom Shop)
Black Paisley Stratocaster
Blacktop Stratocaster
Mahogany Blacktop Stratocaster Limited Edition
Blue Flower Stratocaster
Bonnie Raitt Stratocaster
Bowling Ball/Marble Stratocaster
Buddy Guy Standard Stratocaster
Buddy Guy Stratocaster (Signature)
Buddy Holly Tribute Stratocaster
California Stratocaster/California Fat Stratocaster
Carroll Shelby Limited Edition Stratocaster
Carved Top Stratocaster HSS (Custom Shop)
Classic Player Stratocaster
Classic Player Stratocaster HH
Collector's Edition Stratocaster ('62 Reissue)
Contemporary Stratocaster (Custom Shop)
Contemporary Stratocaster (Import)
Crash Stratocaster
Custom Classic Stratocaster
Custom Deluxe Stratocaster
Custom Shop Limited Edition Stratocaster
Dave Murray Stratocaster
David Gilmour Signature Stratocaster
Deluxe Lone Star Stratocaster
Deluxe Players Special Edition Stratocaster
Deluxe Players Stratocaster
Deluxe Roadhouse Stratocaster
Deluxe Stratocaster
Deluxe Stratocaster HSS Plus Top With IOS Connectivity
Deluxe Stratocaster Plus
Dick Dale Stratocaster
Elite Stratocaster
EOB (Ed O'Brien) Sustainer Stratocaster
Eric Clapton Gold Leaf Stratocaster
Eric Clapton Signature Journeyman Relic Stratocaster
Eric Clapton Signature Stratocaster (Custom Shop)
Eric Clapton Stratocaster
Eric Clapton Stratocaster (Custom Shop)
Eric Johnson 1954 "Virginia" Stratocaster
Eric Johnson Signature Stratocaster Thinline
Eric Johnson Stratocaster
Floyd Rose Classic Relic Stratocaster
Floyd Rose Classic Stratocaster (Strat HSS) (Strat HH)
Ford Shelby GT Stratocaster
Foto Flame Stratocaster
Freddy Tavares Aloha Stratocaster
FSR Stratocaster
George Fullerton 50th Anniversary '57 Strat Ltd. Ed. Set
George Harrison Rocky Stratocaster
Gold Stratocaster
Gold Elite Stratocaster
Gold Stratocaster (Custom Shop)
GT11 Stratocaster
H.E.R. Stratocaster
Hank Marvin Stratocaster
Hank Marvin 40th Anniversary Stratocaster
Harley-Davidson 90th Anniversary Stratocaster
Highway One Stratocaster/HSS
HM Strat (USA/Import)
HM Strat Limited Edition
Homer Haynes HLE Stratocaster
Hot Wheels Stratocaster
HRR Stratocaster/ Floyd Rose HRR (Japan)
Ike Turner Tribute Stratocaster
Jeff Beck Signature Stratocaster (CS)
Jeff Beck Stratocaster
Jerry Donahue Hellecaster Stratocaster
Jim Root Stratocaster
Jimi Hendrix Limited Edition Stratocaster (Custom Shop)
Jimi Hendrix Monterey Pop Stratocaster
Jimi Hendrix Monterey Stratocaster
Jimi Hendrix Stratocaster
Jimi Hendrix Tribute Stratocaster
Jimi Hendrix Voodoo 29th Anniversary (Guitar Center) Stratocaster
Jimi Hendrix Voodoo Child Journeyman Relic Stratocaster
Jimi Hendrix Voodoo Child Signature Stratocaster NOS
Jimi Hendrix Voodoo Stratocaster
Jimmie Vaughan Tex-Mex Stratocaster
John Jorgenson Hellecaster Stratocaster
John Mayer Limited Edition Black1 Stratocaster
John Mayer Stratocaster
Kenny Wayne Shepherd Stratocaster
Koa Stratocaster
Kon Tiki Stratocaster
Lenny Stratocaster
Limited Roasted Tomatillo Stratocaster Relic
Lincoln Brewster Signature Stratocaster
Lite Ash Stratocaster Special Edition
Lone Star Stratocaster
Mark Knopfler Stratocaster
Masterbuilt Custom Shop Stratocaster
Matthias Jabs Signature Stratocaster
Michael Landau Signature Relic Stratocaster 1963/1968
Milonga Deluxe Stratocaster

1958 Fender Stratocaster
Andrew Yanis

1959 Fender Stratocaster
Tracy Farmer

1961 Fender Stratocaster

Marty Fab

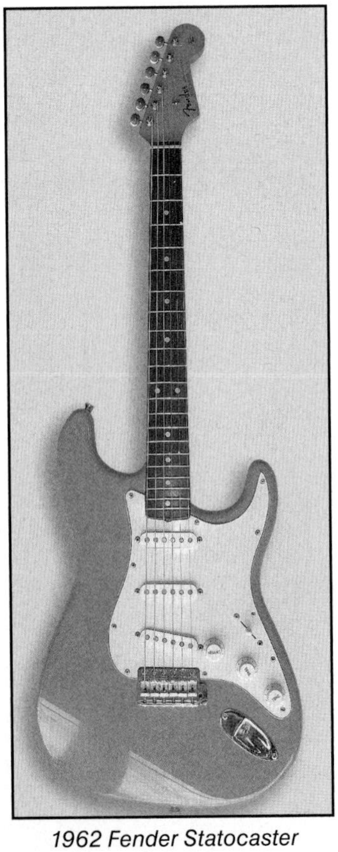

1962 Fender Statocaster

Tony Sheedy

MLB Major League Baseball Stratocaster
Mod Shop Stratocaster
Modern Player Stratocaster HSH/HSS
Moto Limited Edition Stratocaster
Moto Set Stratocaster
Noventa Stratocaster
Orange Krush Limited Edition Stratocaster
Paisley Stratocaster
Parallel Universe Volume II Strat Jazz Deluxe
Parallel Universe Volume II Strat-Tele Hybrid
Playboy 40th Anniversary Stratocaster
Player Series Stratocaster
Post Modern Stratocaster (Custom Shop)
Post Modern Stratocaster Closet Classic (Custom Shop)
Post Modern Stratocaster Journeyman Relic (Custom Shop)
Post Modern Stratocaster NOS (Custom Shop)
Powerhouse/Powerhouse Deluxe Stratocaster
Proud Stratocaster
Rarities Stratocaster
Richie Sambora Stratocaster
Ritchie Blackmore Stratocaster
Ritchie Blackmore Tribute Stratocaster
Roadhouse Stratocaster
Robert Cray Signature Stratocaster
Robert Cray Stratocaster (Mexico)
Robin Trower Signature Stratocaster
Rory Gallagher Tribute Stratocaster
Sandblasted Stratocaster
Select Stratocaster
Set-Neck Stratocaster
Short-Scale (7/8) Stratocaster
So-Cal Custom Shop J.W. Black Stratocaster
So-Cal Speed Shop Stratocaster
Special Edition David Lozeau Art Stratocaster
Special Edition Stratocaster
Special Edition Stratocaster (Matching Headstock)
Special Edition White Opal Stratocaster
Splatter Stratocaster
Standard Roland Ready Stratocaster
Standard Stratocaster (Japan)
Standard Stratocaster (Mexico)
Standard Stratocaster Plus Top
Standard Stratocaster Satin Finish
Stevie Ray Vaughan Signature Stratocaster (Custom Shop)
Stevie Ray Vaughan Signature Stratocaster Relic (Custom Shop)
Stevie Ray Vaughan Stratocaster
Stevie Ray Vaughan Tribute #1 Stratocaster
Strat Plus
Stratocaster Junior
Stratocaster Pro Closet Classic (Custom Shop)
Stratocaster Pro NOS (Custom Shop)
Stratocaster Special
Stratocaster XII
Strat-o-Sonic
Sub Sonic Stratocaster
Super Stratocaster
Supreme Stratocaster
Tanqurey Tonic Stratocaster
Tash Sultana Stratocaster
Texas Special Stratocaster
The Edge Stratocaster
The Strat
Tie-Dye Stratocaster
Tom Delonge Stratocaster
Tom Morello "Soul Power" Stratocaster
Tree of Life Stratocaster
Turquoise Sparkle Stratocaster
U.S. Ultra/Ultra Plus Stratocaster
Ventures Limited Edition Stratocaster
VG Stratocaster
Vintage Hot Rod Stratocaster
Vintera Series Stratocaster
Walnut Elite Stratocaster
Walnut Stratocaster
Western Stratocaster
Whiteguard Stratocaster Limited Edition
Yngwie Malmsteen Signature Stratocaster (Custom Shop)
Yngwie Malmsteen Stratocaster

Stratocaster

1954-1981. Two-tone sunburst until '58, 3-tone after. Custom color finishes were quite rare in the '50s and early-'60s and are much more valuable than the standard sunburst finish. By the '70s, color finishes were much more common and do not affect the value near as much. In '75 Fender dropped the optional custom colors and started issuing the guitars in a variety of standard colors (sunburst, blond, white, natural, walnut and black).

Custom color Fenders can be forged and bogus finishes have been a problem. As the value of custom color Fenders has increased, so has the problem of bogus non-original finishes. The prices in the Guide are for factory original finishes in excellent condition. One color, Shell Pink, is notable because many vintage authorities wonder if a Shell Pink Strat even exists? An ultra-rare custom color should have strong documented provenance and be verifiable by at least one (preferable two or more) well-known vintage authorities. Please refer to the Fender Guitar Intro Section for details on Fender color options.

Three-bolt neck '72-'81, otherwise 4-bolt. Unless noted, all Stratocasters listed have the Fender tremolo system. Non-tremolo models (aka hardtails) typically sell for less. Many guitarists feel the tremolo block helps produce a fuller range of sound. On average, many more tremolo models were made. One year, '58, seems to be a year where a greater percentage of non-tremolo models were made. Tremolo vs. non-tremolo valuation should be taken on a brand-by-brand basis; for example, a pre-'65 Gibson ES-335 non-tremolo model is worth more than a tremolo equipped model.

From '63-'70, Fender offered both the standard Brazilian rosewood fretboard and an optional maple fretboard. Prices listed here, for those years, are for the rosewood 'board models. Currently, the market considers the maple 'board to be a premium, so guitars with maple, for those years, are worth 10% to 15% more than the values shown.

Renamed Standard Stratocaster for '82-'84 (see

following listings), American Standard Stratocaster for '86-2000, the American Series Stratocaster for '00-'07, and the American Standard Stratocaster (again) for '08-'16. Currently called the American Professional Stratocaster.

MODEL YEAR	FEATURES	EXC. COND. LOW	HIGH
1954	Very first '54, rare features	$132,000	$172,000
1954	Early-mid '54, typical features	$81,000	$105,000
1954	Sunburst, later production	$55,000	$72,000
1955	Late-'55, blond, nickel hw	$56,000	$73,000
1955	Sunburst, ash body	$41,000	$53,000
1956	Blond, nickel hw	$42,300	$55,000
1956	Mary Kaye, gold hw	$70,000	$90,000
1956	Sunburst, alder body	$35,500	$46,000
1956	Sunburst, ash body	$38,000	$49,000
1956	Sunburst, non-trem	$24,000	$31,000
1957	Blond, nickel hw	$42,000	$55,000
1957	Mary Kaye, gold hw	$69,000	$90,000
1957	Sunburst	$35,500	$46,000
1957	Sunburst, non-trem	$24,000	$31,000
1958	Blond, nickel hw	$39,000	$51,000
1958	Mary Kaye, gold hw	$68,000	$88,000
1958	Sunburst 2-tone, maple	$33,700	$43,800
1958	Sunburst 2-tone, non-trem	$22,500	$29,300
1958	Sunburst 3-tone, maple	$31,700	$41,200
1958	Sunburst 3-tone, non-trem	$21,600	$28,100
1959	Blond, nickel hw, maple 'board	$39,000	$51,000
1959	Blond, nickel hw, slab 'board	$38,200	$49,700
1959	Custom color	$56,000	$73,000
1959	Mary Kaye, gold hw, maple	$67,400	$87,500
1959	Mary Kaye, gold hw, slab	$61,500	$80,000
1959	Sunburst 3-tone, maple	$31,700	$41,200
1959	Sunburst, non-trem, slab	$21,600	$28,100
1959	Sunburst, slab, 1-ply 'guard	$26,500	$35,000
1959	Sunburst, slab, 3-ply 'guard	$24,500	$32,000
1960	Common color	$31,000	$40,000
1960	Rare color	$45,000	$58,000
1960	Sunburst	$24,500	$32,000
1961	Common color	$31,000	$40,000

MODEL YEAR	FEATURES	EXC. COND. LOW	HIGH
1961	Rare color	$45,000	$58,000
1961	Sunburst	$22,000	$29,000
1962	Common color, early slab	$28,500	$37,000
1962	Common color, late curve	$24,500	$32,000
1962	Rare color, early slab	$44,000	$57,500
1962	Rare color, late curve	$39,000	$51,000
1962	Sunburst, early slab	$22,000	$29,000
1962	Sunburst, late curve	$21,000	$27,000
1963	Common color	$22,700	$29,500
1963	Rare color	$39,000	$51,000
1963	Sunburst	$20,000	$26,000
1964	Common color	$22,700	$29,500
1964	Rare color	$39,000	$51,000
1964	Sunburst, spaghetti logo	$19,000	$25,000
1964	Sunburst, transition logo	$17,700	$23,000
1965	Common color	$19,600	$25,500
1965	Rare color	$28,000	$36,500
1965	Sunburst, early green 'guard	$16,800	$21,800
1965	Sunburst, late F-plate	$12,300	$16,000
1965	Sunburst, white 'guard	$15,800	$20,500
1966	Common color	$17,300	$22,400
1966	Common color, bound 'board (rare)	$22,000	$28,000
1966	Rare color	$23,800	$31,000
1966	Sunburst, block markers	$17,300	$22,500
1966	Sunburst, dot markers	$12,300	$16,000
1967	Common color	$17,300	$22,500
1967	Rare color	$23,800	$31,000
1967	Sunburst	$12,300	$16,000
1968	Common color, nitro	$17,300	$22,500
1968	Common color, poly	$10,300	$13,500
1968	Common color, poly body, nitro neck	$12,100	$15,700
1968	Rare color, nitro	$23,800	$31,000
1968	Rare color, poly	$16,300	$21,100
1968	Rare color, poly body, nitro neck	$18,100	$23,500
1968	Sunburst, nitro	$12,300	$16,000
1968	Sunburst, poly	$10,000	$13,000
1968	Sunburst, poly body, nitro neck	$10,500	$13,700
1970	Common color, poly, 4-bolt	$10,000	$13,000
1970	Rare color, poly, 4-bolt	$13,100	$17,000

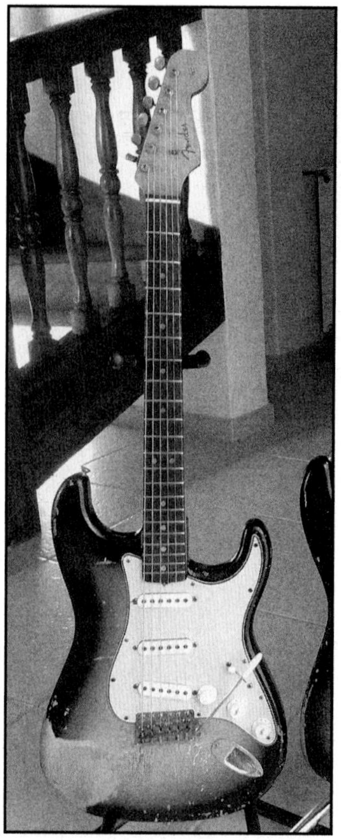

1964 Fender Stratocaster

Mario Vilas

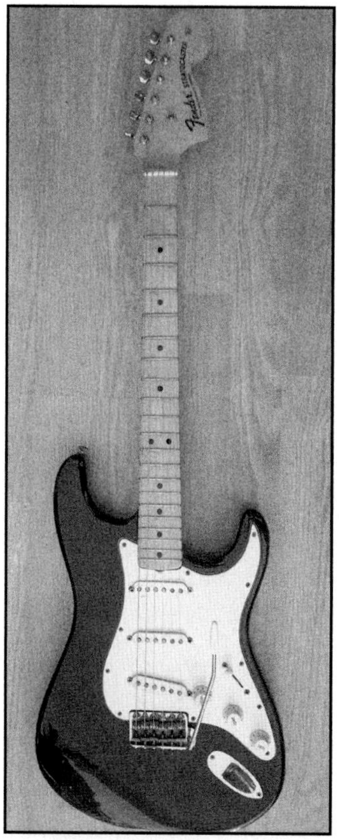

1968 Fender Stratocaster

Daniel Hess

1975 Fender Stratocaster

Carter Vintage Guitars

1979 Fender Stratocaster

Robbie Keene

MODEL YEAR	FEATURES	EXC. COND. LOW	HIGH
1970	Sunburst, poly, 4-bolt	$9,000	$11,700
1971	Common color, 4-bolt	$10,000	$13,000
1971	Early-mid '71, sunburst, 4-bolt	$9,000	$11,700
1971	Late '71, sunburst, 3-bolt	$3,600	$4,700
1971	Rare color, 4-bolt	$13,100	$17,000
1972	Common color, 3-bolt	$5,100	$6,600
1972	Rare color, 3-bolt	$6,400	$8,300
1972	Sunburst, 3-bolt	$3,600	$4,700
1973	Common color	$4,250	$5,500
1973	Natural	$3,350	$4,350
1973	Rare color	$5,400	$7,000
1973	Sunburst	$3,350	$4,350
1973	Walnut	$3,250	$4,200
1974	Black, blond, white (white parts)	$3,850	$5,000
1974	Natural (white parts)	$3,000	$3,900
1974	Sunburst (white parts)	$3,350	$4,350
1974	Walnut (white parts)	$3,250	$4,200
1975	Black, blond, white (black parts)	$3,300	$4,300
1975	Black, blond, white (white parts)	$3,800	$4,900
1975	Early-'75, sunburst (white parts)	$3,200	$4,200
1975	Late-'75, sunburst (black parts)	$2,450	$3,200
1975	Natural (black parts)	$2,600	$3,400
1975	Walnut (black parts)	$2,400	$3,100
1976-1977	Various colors	$2,300	$3,000
1978-1979	Various colors	$2,150	$2,800
1980-1981	International colors	$2,350	$3,050
1980-1981	Various colors	$1,900	$2,450

Standard Stratocaster (includes "Smith Strat")

1981-1984. Replaces the Stratocaster. Renamed the American Standard Stratocaster for '86-'00 (see next listing). Renamed American Series Stratocaster in '00. From '81/'82 to mid-'83, 3 knobs same as regular Strat but with 4-bolt neck. In August '81, Dan Smith was hired by Bill Schultz and Fender produced an alder body, 4-bolt neck, 21-fret, small headstock Standard Stratocaster that has been nicknamed the Smith Strat (made from Dec. '81-'83). Mid-'83 to the end of '84 2 knobs and 'guard mounted input jack. Not to be confused with current Standard Stratocaster, which is made in Mexico.

1981-1983	Various colors	$1,900	$2,450
1983-1984	Sunburst, 2-knob	$950	$1,250
1983-1984	Various colors, 2-knob	$950	$1,250

American Standard Stratocaster

1986-1999, 2008-2016. Fender's new name for the American-made Strat when reintroducing it after CBS sold the company. The only American-made Strats made in 1985 were the '57 and '62 models. See Stratocaster and Standard Stratocaster for earlier models. Name used again for '08-'16, various pickup options including SSS, HH, HSH, HSS, Fat and HSS plus. Renamed American Series Stratocaster in 2000 and again renamed the American Professional Series Stratocaster in 2017.

1986-1999	Various colors & options	$850	$1,100
2008-2016	Various colors & options	$850	$1,100

American Series Stratocaster

2000-2007. Ash or alder body, rosewood or maple 'board, dot markers, various pickup options including HSS and HH, 5-way switch, hand polished fret edges. Renamed the American Standard Stratocaster again in '08.

2000-2007	Various colors & options	$850	$1,100
2004	50th Anniversary	$850	$1,100

American Professional Stratocaster

2017-2020. Model replaces American Standard Series Strat, redesign includes new V-Mod pickups, narrow-tall frets, new 'deep C' neck profile, genuine bone nut, various colors. Also available left-hand model. Renamed American Professional II in '20.

2017-2020	High-end features	$925	$1,225
2017-2020	Low-end features	$850	$1,100

American Professional II Stratocaster

2020-present. Various pickup options, woods and various colors.

2020	HSS	$850	$1,100
2020	Roasted Pine	$900	$1,150
2020	Roasted Pine HSS	$925	$1,175
2020	SSS	$825	$1,075

20th Century American Standard Stratocaster

1999. Limited Edition of the last 100 Strats off the line in 1999. COA signed by William Schultz. "20th Century American Standard" headstock stamp and neckplate.

1999		$1,000	$1,300

21st Century American Standard Stratocaster

2000. Limited Edition of the first 100 Strats off the line in 2000. COA signed by William Schultz. "21st Century American Standard" headstock stamp and neckplate.

2000		$1,000	$1,300

25th Anniversary Stratocaster

1979-1980. Limited Edition, 4-bolt neck plate, standard truss rod, has ANNIVERSARY on upper body horn, early-'79 has pearlescent finish which flaked, late-'79-'80 was changed to silver metallic.

1979	Early '79, pearlescent	$1,600	$2,100
1979-1980	Silver	$2,175	$2,825

MODEL YEAR	FEATURES	EXC. COND. LOW	HIGH

30th Anniversary Guitar Center Strat

1994. Commemorates Guitar Center's opening in '64, 250 made, 30th Anniversary Limited Edition Guitar Center logo on neck plate, quilted top, sunburst.

1994		$975	$1,275

35th Anniversary Stratocaster

1989-1991. Custom Shop model, 500 made, figured maple top, Lace Sensor pickups, Eric Clapton preamp circuit.

1989-1991		$1,975	$2,525

40th Anniversary 1954 Stratocaster Limited Edition

1994. Standard production (not Custom Shop), 1,954 made, "40th Anniversary STRATOCASTER 1994" neck plate, serial number series xxxx of 1954, spaghetti logo, tremolo, Kluson tuners, solid maple neck, 2-tone sunburst semi-transparent finish on ash body.

1994		$1,975	$2,525

40th Anniversary American Standard Stratocaster

1994 only. US-made, American Standard model (not Custom Shop), plain top, appearance similar to a '54 maple-neck Strat, sunburst, 2 neck plates offered "40th Anniversary" and "40th Anniversary and still rockin'".

1994		$975	$1,275

40th Anniversary Stratocaster Diamond Dealer

1994 only. Custom Shop model, 150 made, 40th Anniversary headstock inlay, flamed maple top on ash body, '54-'94 inlay at 12th fret, gold etched 'guard, gold hardware, sunburst.

1994		$3,000	$3,900

40th Anniversary Stratocaster ST62 (Japan)

1994 only. Made in Japan, '62 reissue specs.

1994		$975	$1,275

'50s Stratocaster/Classic Series '50s Stratocaster

1985-2019. 'Made in Japan' logo until 'Crafted in Japan' logo mid-'97, basswood body, then mid-'99 made in Mexico with poplar or alder body. Foto-Flame finish offered '92-'94.

1985-1996	Made in Japan	$675	$875
1997-1999	Crafted in Japan	$600	$800
1999-2019	Mexico	$475	$625

American Original '50s Stratocaster

2018-present. Vintage-style appointments, 3 pickups, alder or ash body (White Blonde only), 2-color sunburst or Aztec Gold.

2018-2020		$1,125	$1,450

Classic Player '50s Stratocaster

2006-2019. U.S.-made components but assembled in Mexico, alder body, maple neck and 'board, vintage-style pickups.

2006-2019		$475	$625
2014	50th Anniversary	$525	$700

Classic Series '50s Stratocaster Lacquer

2014-2019. Candy Apple Red nitro-lacquer finish.

2014-2019		$475	$625

Road Worn '50s Stratocaster

2009-2019. Maple 'board, '50s specs, aged finish.

2009-2019		$500	$650

50th Anniversary 1954 Stratocaster

2004-2005. Custom Shop, celebrates 50 years of the Strat, 1954 specs and materials, replica form-fit case, certificate, Fender took orders for these up to December 31, 2004.

2004-2005		$3,400	$4,400

50th Anniversary American Deluxe Stratocaster

2004-2005. Deluxe series features, engraved neck plate, tweed case.

2004-2005		$1,250	$1,625

50th Anniversary American Standard Stratocaster

2004. Engraved neck plate, '54 replica pickups, tweed case.

2004		$850	$1,125

50th Anniversary American Vintage 1957 Stratocaster

1996. V serial number, 50th decal back of headstock.

1996		$1,400	$1,800

50th Anniversary Standard Stratocaster

2004. Made in Mexico, Aztec gold finish, no logo on guitar to indicate 50th Anniv., CE on neck plate to indicate import.

2004		$475	$625

50th Anniversary Stratocaster

1995-1996. Custom Shop model, flame maple top, 3 vintage-style pickups, gold hardware, gold 50th Anniversary (of Fender) coin on back of the headstock, sunburst, 2500 made.

1995-1996		$1,300	$1,675

50th Anniversary Stratocaster Relic

1995-1996. Custom Shop Relic model, aged played-in feel, diamond headstock inlay, Shoreline Gold finish, 200 units planned.

1995-1996		$2,850	$3,700

'54 Stratocaster (Custom Shop)

1992-1998. Classic reissue, ash body, Custom '50s pickups, gold-plated hardware.

1992-1998	Various options	$2,075	$2,700

'54 Stratocaster FMT

1992-1998. Custom Classic reissue, Flame Maple Top, also comes in gold hardware edition.

1992-1998		$1,950	$2,525

'55 Stratocaster (Custom Shop)

2006, 2013. 1st version is Limited Edition of 100 Relics with 2-tone sunburst; 2nd version is Closet Classic. Both include certificate of authenticity.

2006	Relic	$2,075	$2,700
2013	Closet Classic	$1,950	$2,525

'55 Dual-Mag Strat Journeyman Relic

2017-2019. Custom Shop Limited Edition, certificate of authenticity.

2017-2019		$2,400	$3,100

'55 Historic 1955 NOS Stratocaster

2018-2020. Custom Shop NOS, certificate of authenticity.

2018-2020		$2,075	$2,700

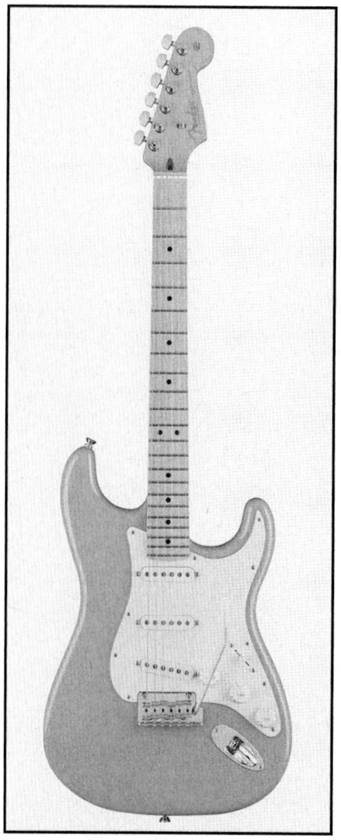

Fender American Professional II Stratocaster

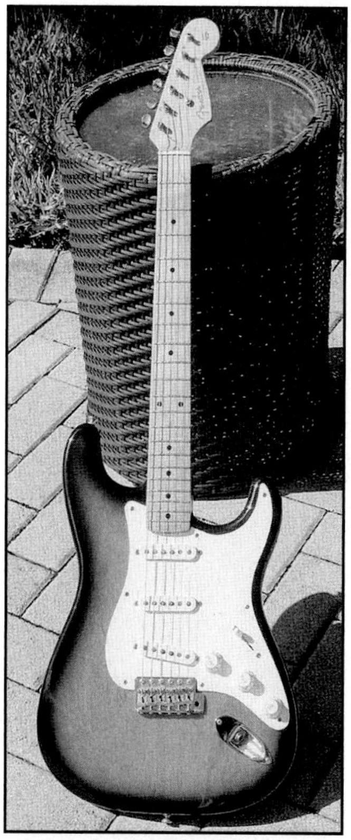

1994 Fender 40th Ann. 1954 Stratocaster Limited Edition

Craig Brody

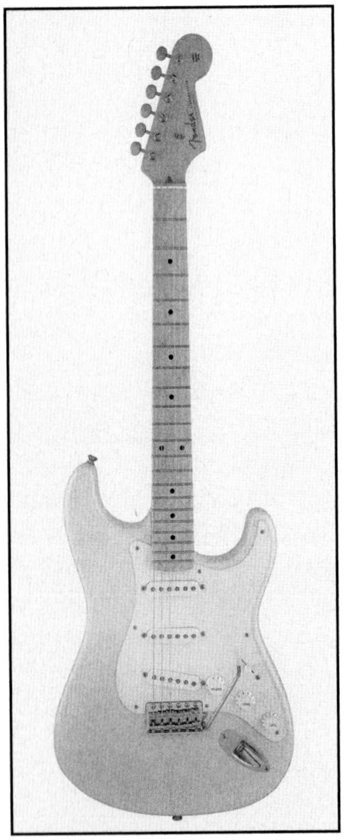

Fender American Vintage '56 Stratocaster

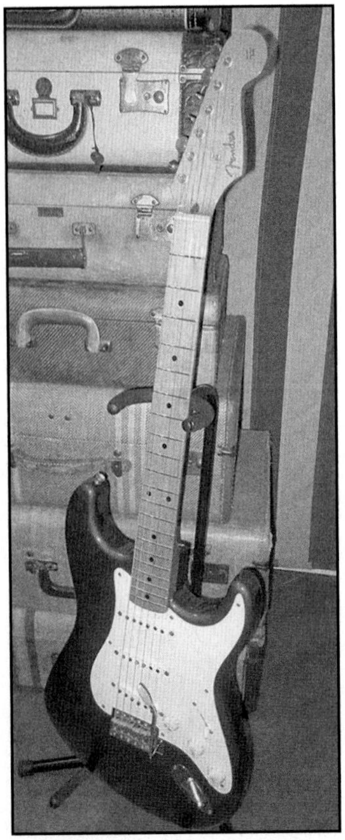

2003 Fender '57 Stratocaster
Rivington Guitars

MODEL YEAR	FEATURES	EXC. COND. LOW	HIGH

'55 Rocking Dog Stratocaster

2007. Custom Shop, various colors.

2007		$2,300	$2,975

'55 Stratocaster Journeyman Relic

2017. Custom Shop, vintage-correct appointments, certificate of authenticity.

2017		$2,075	$2,700

'56 Stratocaster (Custom Shop)

1996-2016. Most detailed replica (and most expensive to date) of '56 Strat, including electronics and pickups, offered with rosewood or maple 'board, gold hardware is +$100.

1996-1998	Cunetto built Relic	$2,375	$3,075
1997-1998	Cunetto era (staff built)	$2,300	$2,975
1999-2010	Closet Classic	$1,950	$2,525
1999-2010	NOS	$1,950	$2,525
1999-2014	Relic	$2,075	$2,700
2014-2016	Heavy relic	$2,250	$2,950

'56 Stratocaster Heavy Relic

2020. Custom Shop, certificate of authenticity.

2020		$2,300	$3,000

'56 Stratocaster Journeyman Closet Classic

2020. Custom Shop, certificate of authenticity.

2020		$2,300	$3,000

American Vintage '56 Stratocaster

2013-2018. Vintage '56 style, maple 'board, black, Shell Pink or aged white blonde.

2013-2018		$1,225	$1,600

American Vintage '56 Stratocaster Limited Edition Roasted Ash

2017. Roasted ash body, roasted maple neck and 'board, nitro lacquer finish.

2017		$1,475	$1,925

'57 Stratocaster (Custom Shop)

1994-1996. Custom Shop models can be distinguished by the original certificate that comes with the guitar. Replaced by the more authentic, higher-detailed '56 Custom Shop Stratocaster by '99.

1994-1996	Various colors	$2,100	$2,700

'57 Stratocaster (CS)

2007, 2010-2016. Custom Shop models, Heavy Relic ('07, '15-'16), Closet Classic ('10-'13), NOS Dealer Select program ('13-'16) where models are built for specific dealers.

2007	Relic	$2,075	$2,700
2010-2013	Closet Classic	$1,950	$2,525
2013-2016	NOS	$1,950	$2,525
2015-2016	Heavy relic	$2,250	$2,950

'57 Stratocaster (USA)

1982-2012. U.S.-made at the Fullerton, California plant ('82-'85) and at the Corona, California plant ('85-'12), American Vintage series.

1982-1984	SN: V series	$2,800	$3,600
1986-1989	Common color	$1,425	$1,850
1986-1989	Rare color	$1,650	$2,150
1990-1999		$1,250	$1,625
1990-1999	Rare color	$1,475	$1,900
2000-2012	Various colors	$1,125	$1,450

'57 Special Stratocaster

1992-1993. Custom Shop, limited run of 60, flamed maple top, birdseye maple neck, sunburst.

1992-1993		$2,100	$2,700

'57 Vintage Stratocaster (Japan)

1982-1998. Made in Japan logo, JV serial numbers '82-'84, E serial '84-'87, Crafted in Japan logo by '98, various colors.

1982-1985	MIJ logo, JV serial	$1,400	$1,800
1998	CIJ logo	$925	$1,200

American Vintage '57 Commemorative Stratocaster

2007. Limited production, 1957-2007 Commemorative logo neckplate.

2007-2012		$1,225	$1,600

Time Machine 1957 Stratocaster Relic

2020. Custom Shop Time Machine series, certificate of authenticity.

2020		$1,850	$2,400

Vintage Custom 1957 Stratocaster NOS

2019-present. Custom Shop, maple 'board, aged white blonde with gold hardware.

2019-2020		$2,175	$2,800

Wildwood "10s" 1957 Limited Stratocaster Relic

2014-2015. Custom Shop Dealer Select model for Wildwood Music, '57 specs with 3 single coil or HSS pickups, certificate of authenticity.

2014-2015		$2,075	$2,700

'58 Stratocaster (Custom Shop)

1996-1999. Ash body, Fat '50s pickups, chrome or gold hardware (gold is +$100.), certificate of authenticity.

1996-1999	Various colors	$2,200	$2,850

'58 Stratocaster (Dakota Red)

1996. Custom Shop, run of 30 made in Dakota Red with matching headstock, maple neck, Texas special pickups, gold hardware.

1996		$2,250	$2,950

'58 Limited Edition MIJ Stratocaster

2013. Made in Japan logo, 252 offered.

2013		$800	$1,050

'58 Stratocaster Journeyman Relic

2016. Custom Shop, vintage-correct appointments, certificate of authenticity.

2016		$2,100	$2,725

Time Machine 1958 Stratocaster Heavy Relic

2020. Custom Shop Time Machine series, certificate of authenticity.

2020		$2,450	$3,200

'59 Rocking Dog Stratocaster

2007. Custom Shop, commissioned by Garrett Park Guitars, based on '59 rosewood 'board Strat, various colors.

2007		$2,300	$3,000

'59 Stratocaster (Custom Shop)

2010--2013. Rosewood 'board, vintage appointments, COA, various colors with Relic or Heavy Relic finish.

2010-2013	Relic	$2,075	$2,700
2013	Heavy Relic	$2,250	$2,950

MODEL YEAR	FEATURES	EXC. COND. LOW	HIGH

1959 Stratocaster LTD Journeyman

2019-2020. Custom Shop, limited edition, vintage and modern appointments, COA, various colors with Relic or Heavy Relic lacquer finish.

2019	Relic	$2,300	$3,000
2019-2020	Heavy Relic	$2,300	$3,000

American Vintage '59 Pine Stratocaster

2017. Limited Edition neck plate, pine body built from re-claimed 100-year-old wood, 3 vintage '59 single-coil pickups.

2017		$1,225	$1,600

American Vintage '59 Stratocaster

2013-2018. Maple or slab rosewood 'board.

2012-2018		$1,225	$1,600

Time Machine 1959 Stratocaster

2019-present. Custom Shop Time Machine series, vintage and modern appointments, COA, various colors with Relic or Heavy Relic lacquer finish.

2019-2020	Relic	$1,900	$2,450
2020-2021	Heavy Relic	$2,450	$3,200

Wildwood "10s" 1959 Limited Stratocaster Relic

2011-2017. Custom Shop, quartersawn maple neck, Brazilian rosewood 'board, 3 pickups, faded 3-color sunburst. Limited Edition neck plate decal, and certificate of authenticity.

2011	Maple 'board	$2,075	$2,700
2011-2017	Brazilian 'board	$3,850	$5,000

'60 Stratocaster (Custom Shop)

1992-1999. 3 Texas Special pickups, various colors, optional gold hardware is +$100, with certificate of authenticity. In 2000 the '60 Stratocaster name was applied to the Time Machine model (see following).

1992-1999		$2,200	$2,850

'60 Stratocaster FMT (Custom Shop)

1997-1999. Flame maple top (FMT).

1997-1999		$2,100	$2,700

Custom 1960 Stratocaster

1994. Short run of 20 custom ordered and specified instruments that have 1960 specs along with other specs such as a pearloid 'guard, matching headstock color, came with certificate of authenticity.

1994		$2,000	$2,600

'60s Stratocaster/Classic Series '60s Stratocaster

1985-2019. 'Made in Japan' logo until 'Crafted in Japan' logo mid-'97, basswood body, then mid-'99 made in Mexico with poplar or alder body. Foto-Flame finish offered '92-'94.

1985-1996	Made in Japan	$675	$875
1997-1999	Crafted in Japan	$600	$800
1999-2019	Mexico	$475	$625

'60s Stratocaster/Time Machine 1960 Stratocaster

1996-2020. Custom Shop Relic/Time Machine. For '96-'99 was called the '60s Stratocaster, in 2000 name was changed to Time Machine 1960 Stratocaster. Heavy Relic began late-'15. Optional gold hardware is +$100. Vince Cunetto and company did the aging of the guitars to mid-1999. The price includes the original Certificate of Authenticity, a guitar without the original COA is worth less than the values shown.

1996-1998	Cunetto built Relic	$2,275	$2,950
1997-1999	Cunetto era (staff built)	$2,200	$2,850
1999-2010	Closet Classic	$1,950	$2,525
1999-2010	NOS	$1,950	$2,525
1999-2015	Relic	$2,075	$2,700
2015-2020	Heavy relic	$2,250	$2,950

American Original '60s Stratocaster

2018-present. Vintage-style appointments, 3 pickups, alder body, 3-color sunburst. Candy Apple Red or Olympic White.

2018-2020		$1,150	$1,500

Classic Player '60s Stratocaster

2006-2019. U.S.-made components but assembled in Mexico, alder body, maple neck, rosewood 'board, vintage-style pickups.

2006-2019		$475	$625

Classic Series '60s Stratocaster Lacquer

2014-2019. Made in Mexico, 3-color sunburst nitro-lacquer finish.

2014-2019		$475	$625

Limited Edition '60s Daybreak Stratocaster

2019-2020. Traditional series, made in Japan, Olympic White with matching headstock, gold hardware.

2019-2020		$500	$650

Road Worn '60s Stratocaster

2009-2020. Rosewood 'board, '60s specs, aged finish. Renamed Vintera Road Worn '60s Strat in '20.

2009-2020		$500	$650

60th Anniversary '54 Stratocaster (Custom Shop)

2014. Heavy relic, certificate of authenticity, 60th guitar case.

2014		$2,075	$2,700

60th Anniversary American Stratocaster

2006-2007. Celebrates Fender's 60th, US-made, 'Sixty Years' decal logo on headstock, engraved 60th Anniversary neck plate, Z-series serial number, coin on back of headstock, sunburst only, paperwork.

2006-2007	American flag logo	$1,025	$1,350

60th Anniversary American Vintage 1954 Stratocaster

2014-2016. 1,954 built, came with reproduction 1954 paperwork and 1954 Anniversary Strat Certificate.

2014-2016		$1,225	$1,600

60th Anniversary Commemorative Stratocaster

2014. Celebrates the Strat's 60th, US-made, 60th Anniversary neckplate, 60th medallion on back of headstock, gold hardware, special case, commemorative book.

2014		$850	$1,100

60th Anniversary Presidential Stratocaster

2006. Custom Shop, Diamond (60th) anniversary, limited to 100, bookmatched maple top stained using grapes from Hill Family Winery (California), '1946-2006' logo on neck, 'Limited Edition 60th Anniv. Presidential' neck plate logo, certificate of authenticity.

2006		$4,200	$5,500

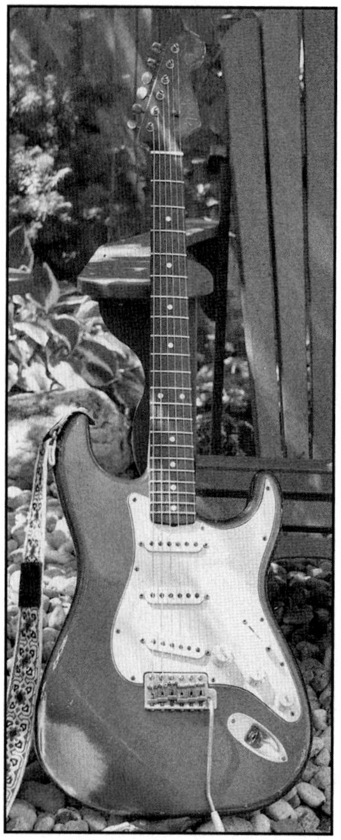

2006 Fender '60s Stratocaster

Michael Alonzi

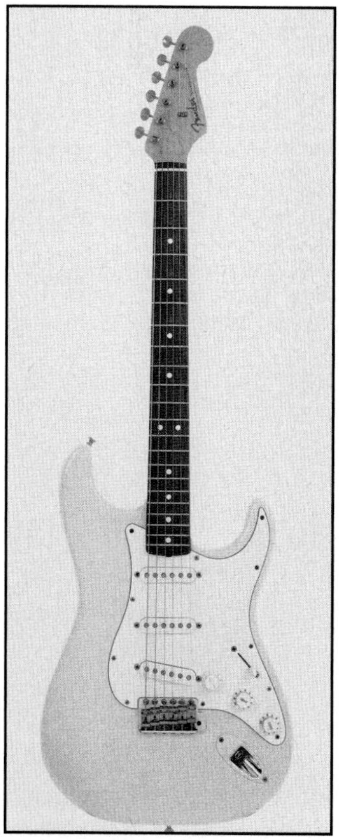

1982 Fender '62 Stratocaster

Imaged by Heritage Auctions, HA.com

1984 Fender '62 Vintage Stratocaster (Japan)
Tom Pfeifer

2005 Fender '69 Stratocaster (Custom Shop)
Rivington Guitars

MODEL YEAR	FEATURES	EXC. COND. LOW	HIGH

'61 Stratocaster (Custom Shop)

2001-2012. Relic, certificate of authenticity.

2001-2012		$2,075	$2,700

Wildwood "10s" 1961 Limited Stratocaster

2010-present. Custom Shop, NOS, relic or heavy relic, quartersawn maple and AA flame maple necks, 3 pickups, "faded" thin nitro finishes in multiple colors.

2010-2016	NOS	$1,950	$2,525
2010-2020	Relic	$2,075	$2,700

'62 Stratocaster (USA)

1982-2012. Made at Fullerton plant ('82-'85) then at Corona plant ('86-2012), American Vintage series.

1982-1984	SN: V series	$2,800	$3,600
1986-1989	Common color	$1,425	$1,850
1986-1989	Rare color	$1,650	$2,150
1990-1999	Common color	$1,250	$1,625
1990-1999	Rare color	$1,475	$1,900
2000-2012	Common color	$1,125	$1,450

'62 Commemorative Stratocaster

2007. Limited production, part of American Vintage Series, 1957-2007 Commemorative logo neckplate.

2007		$1,225	$1,600

'62 Heavy Relic Stratocaster

2007-2010. Custom Shop Dealer Select series, extreme Relic work.

2007-2010		$2,200	$2,850

'62 Stratocaster ST62D/ST54 DEX2

1996. Made in Japan, '54 maple neck, '62 body.

1996		$1,200	$1,500

'62 Stratocaster ST62US Reissue

2008-2012. Crafted in Japan, US-made 'vintage' pickups.

2008-2012		$600	$775

'62 Vintage Stratocaster (Japan)

1982-1984. Made in Japan, JV serial numbers, various colors.

1982-1984		$1,400	$1,800

Dave's Guitar Shop American 1962 Stratocaster

2019-2020. Limited Edition, various colors with nitro lacquer finish.

2019-2020		$1,225	$1,600

Deluxe Vintage Player '62 Stratocaster

2005-2006. Limited Edition, vintage and modern features based upon '62 specs, 3 Samarium Cobalt Noiseless pickups, Deluxe American Standard electronics, Olympic White or Ice Blue Metallic.

2005-2006		$1,125	$1,500

Vintage Custom 1962 Stratocaster

2019-present. Custom Shop Limited Edition, NOS finish, alder body, maple neck and 'board, 3-color sunburst.

2019-2020		$2,100	$2,700

Willcutt Guitars True '62 Stratocaster

2016-2020. Custom Shop, limited run for Bob Willcutt Guitars, 4 models; 'V' neck, '59 'C' neck, '60s 'C' neck and large 'C' neck.

2016-2020		$2,075	$2,700

'63 Stratocaster (Custom Shop)

2015-2018. Time Machine series, Relic in '15-'17, Heavy Relic '18.

2015-2017	Relic	$2,075	$2,700
2018	Heavy Relic	$2,075	$2,700

'63 Stratocaster Journeyman Relic

2015. Custom Shop, vintage-correct appointments, alder body, bird's-eye maple neck, rosewood 'board, 3 single-coil pickups, certificate of authenticity.

2015		$2,250	$2,950

'64 Stratocaster (Custom Shop)

Certificate of authenticity.

2009-2012	Relic	$2,075	$2,700
2011-2014	Closet Classic	$1,950	$2,525

Time Machine 1964 Stratocaster Journeyman Relic

2018-2020. Custom Shop Time Machine series, vintage-correct appointments, certificate of authenticity.

2018-2020		$2,100	$2,725

'65 Stratocaster (Custom Shop)

1998-1999, 2003-2006, 2010 (no Closet Classic). Custom Shop model, '65 small-headstock specs, rosewood or maple cap 'board, transition logo, offered in NOS, Relic, or Closet Classic versions.

1998-1999	Cunetto era (staff built)	$2,200	$2,850
2003-2006	Closet Classic	$1,950	$2,525
2003-2010	NOS	$1,950	$2,525
2003-2010	Relic	$2,075	$2,700

'65 Stratocaster Journeyman Closet Classic

2019-2020. Custom Shop, vintage-correct appointments, certificate of authenticity.

2019-2020		$2,225	$2,875

American Vintage '65 Stratocaster

2013-2017. V serial number, flash coat finish, various colors, some with matching headstock.

2013-2017		$1,125	$1,450

Mark Kendrick Master Design '65 Stratocaster

2004. Custom Shop Limited Edition, run of 65, alder body, maple neck, African rosewood 'board, Lake Placid Blue over Olympic White.

2004		$2,800	$3,800

Time Machine 1965 Stratocaster Journeyman Relic

2010. Custom Shop Time Machine series, vintage-correct appointments, certificate of authenticity.

2010		$2,175	$2,800

Total Tone '65 Stratocaster Relic (Custom Shop)

2013. Limited Edition, alder body, maple neck, reverse wound middle pickup for noise reduction, various colors with Relic nitro lacquer finish.

2013		$2,000	$2,600

'66 Stratocaster (Custom Shop)

2004-2008. Custom Shop model, offered in Closet Classic, NOS or Relic versions.

2004-2008	Closet Classic	$1,950	$2,525
2004-2008	NOS	$1,950	$2,525
2004-2008	Relic	$2,075	$2,700

MODEL YEAR	FEATURES	EXC. COND. LOW	HIGH

Time Machine 1967 Stratocaster Journeyman Relic Aged

2020. Custom Shop Time Machine series, vintage-correct appointments.

2020		$2,225	$2,875

Time Machine 1967 Stratocaster Journeyman Relic Custom Top

2020. Custom Shop Time Machine series, vintage-correct appointments.

2020		$2,175	$2,800

'68 Heavy Relic Stratocaster

2007-2010. Custom Shop, Dealer Select model, extreme Relic work.

2007-2010		$2,250	$2,950

'68 Reverse Strat Special (USA)

2001-2002. With special reverse left-hand neck, large headstock (post-CBS style).

2001-2002		$2,250	$2,950

'68 Stratocaster (Japan)

1996-1999, 2013. '68 specs including large headstock, part of Collectables Series, sunburst, natural, Olympic White.

1996-1999		$925	$1,200
2013		$800	$1,050

'69 Stratocaster (Custom Shop)

1997-2012, 2016. Large headstock, U-shaped maple neck with rosewood or maple cap options, '69-style finish, gold hardware is +$100, since 2000, offered in NOS, Relic, or Closet Classic (no CC after '08) versions. Heavy Relic in '16.

1997-1999	Cunetto era (staff built)	$2,200	$2,850
2000-2008	Closet Classic	$1,950	$2,525
2000-2009	NOS	$1,950	$2,525
2000-2012	Relic	$2,075	$2,700
2016	Heavy Relic	$2,250	$2,950

Wildwood "10s" 1969 Limited Stratocaster

2014. Custom Shop, Relic, Jimi Hendrix specs, certificate of authenticity.

2014		$2,075	$2,700

'70s Stratocaster/Classic Series '70s Stratocaster

1999-2019. Made in Mexico, large headstock, white pickups and knobs, rosewood 'board.

1999-2019		$475	$625

American Vintage '70s Stratocaster

2009-2012. Large '70s headstock, early '70s white pickups and knobs, 3-bolt neck.

2009-2012		$1,150	$1,500

'72 Stratocaster (Japan)

1985-1996. Basswood body, maple 'board, large headstock, various colors (does not include the Paisley '72).

1985-1987		$1,400	$1,800
1988-1996		$1,200	$1,600

'72 Stratocaster Limited Edition

2013. Made in Japan for US domestic sales, 144 made, large headstock, bullet truss rod, 3-bolt maple neck, 21 frets, 3 Alnico pickups.

2013		$600	$800

MODEL YEAR	FEATURES	EXC. COND. LOW	HIGH

75th Anniversary Commemorative Stratocaster

2021. US-made, limited edition, inlaid 75th Anniversary ingot back of headstock, gold hardware, 2-color Bourbon Burst gloss finish. Includes custom Inca Silver case with Lake Placid Blue interior.

2021		$1,075	$1,400

75th Anniversary Stratocaster

2021. Made in Mexico, 75th Anniversary neck plate, Diamond Anniversary satin finish with matching painted headstock.

2021		$475	$625

Acoustasonic Stratocaster

2003-2009. Hollowed out alder Strat body with braceless graphite top, 3 in-bridge Fishman piezo pickups, acoustic sound hole.

2003-2009		$575	$750

Aerodyne Classic Stratocaster

2020. Limited run made in Japan, figured maple top, rosewood 'board, 3 pickups, various colors with gloss poly finish.

2020		$575	$750

Aerodyne Stratocaster

2004-2009. Import Strat with Aerodyne body profile, bound body, black.

2004-2009		$575	$750

Albert Hammond Jr. Signature Stratocaster

2018-present. Made in Mexico, styled after his 1985 reissue of a '72 Strat.

2018-2020		$475	$625

Aluminum Stratocaster (Custom Shop)

1994. Custom Shop aluminum bodies, chrome body with black 'guard, black body with chrome 'guard, or green with black lines and red swirls. There are also several Custom Shop one-offs with aluminum bodies.

1993-1994	Chrome	$1,925	$2,550

Aluminum Stratocaster American Standard

1994-1995. Aluminum-bodied American Standard with anodized finish in blue marble, purple marble or red, silver and blue stars and stripes. Some with 40th Anniversary designation. There is also a Custom Shop version.

1994-1995	Various patterns & options	$1,700	$2,200

American Acoustasonic Stratocaster

2019-present. Solid A sitka spruce top, mahogany back and sides, ebony 'board, various colors. Also offered with cocobolo and ziricote top.

2019-2020		$1,100	$1,425
2020	Cocobolo top	$1,800	$2,350

American Classic Holoflake Stratocaster

1992-1993. Custom Shop model, splatter/sparkle finish, pearloid 'guard.

1992-1993		$2,100	$2,700

American Classic Stratocaster

1992-1999. Custom Shop version of American Standard, 3 pickups, tremolo, rosewood 'board, nickel or gold-plated hardware, various colors.

1992-1999	Various options	$2,100	$2,700

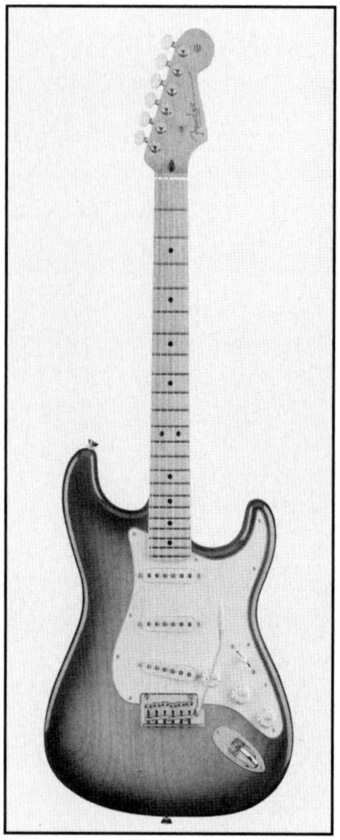

Fender 75th Anniversary Commemorative Stratocaster

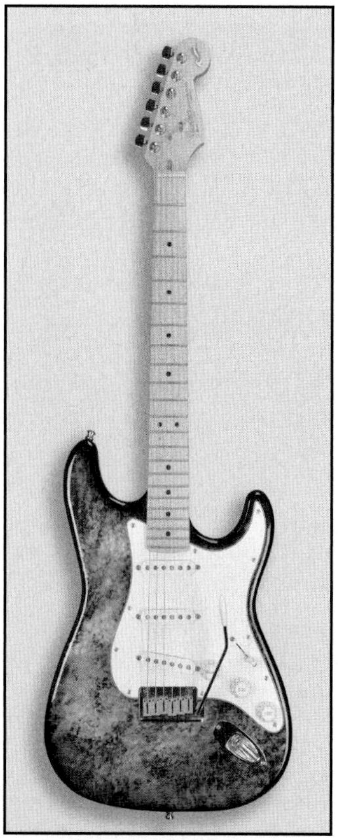

1994 Fender Aluminum Stratocaster American Standard

GUITARS

2018 Fender American Elite Stratocaster
Carter Vintage Guitars

1992 Fender Bill Carson Stratocaster
Bob Moreland

MODEL YEAR	FEATURES	EXC. COND. LOW	HIGH

American Custom Stratocaster (Custom Shop)

2020. Custom Shop American Custom series, various woods and colors.

2020		$2,400	$3,125

American Deluxe Stratocaster

1998-2016. Premium alder or ash body, maple neck, various pickup options including SSS, HSS, HSH, HSS Plus, Fat and Shawbucker, various colors.

1998-2016	Various options	$1,050	$1,350

American Deluxe Stratocaster Dealer Event

2013. Sold at private dealer event at Fender Corona, various premium tonewoods, various colors and finishes.

2013		$1,200	$2,000

American Deluxe Stratocaster Designer Series

2004-2015. Limited production, various upgrades such as flamed maple top, mahogany, etc.

2004-2015		$1,125	$1,450

American Deluxe Stratocaster FMT HSS

2004-2009. Flame maple top version of the HSS.

2004-2009		$1,125	$1,450

American Deluxe Stratocaster HSS Mahogany

2015-2016. Limited Edition 10 for 15 series, 2-piece mahogany body.

2015-2016		$1,000	$1,300

American Elite Stratocaster

2016-2019. Alder body, 3 single-coil pickups or HSS with Shawbucker.

2016-2019		$1,075	$1,400

American Elite Stratocaster Limited Edition

2016. Various color options with matching headstock.

2016		$1,125	$1,450

American Longboard Stratocaster HSS

2015. Part of Fender's limited edition 10 for 15 series, vintage surfboard laminate top design.

2015		$900	$1,100

American Performer Stratocaster

2018-present. Made in US, new features include 3 Yosemite single-coil pickups, Greasebucket tone system, various colors.

2018-2020		$675	$875

American Special Stratocaster

2010-2018. Limited Edition, '70s headstock with post-CBS black Stratocaster logo, Texas Special pickups (SSS or HSS), satin (early were gloss) finish.

2010-2018		$650	$850

American Standard Stratocaster Limited Edition

1990s-2019. American Standard series, various limited edition models.

1995-1996	Matching hdstk	$1,050	$1,350
2001	Standard hdstk, white	$1,050	$1,350
2009	Matching hdstk, Seafoam/Surf Green	$1,000	$1,300

MODEL YEAR	FEATURES	EXC. COND. LOW	HIGH
2014-2017	Channel Bound	$850	$1,100
2015	Blackout (Mystic Black)	$850	$1,100
2015-2016	Mystic Aztec Gold	$850	$1,100
2015-2016	Oiled Ash	$850	$1,100
2015-2016	Vintage White	$850	$1,100
2017	Rosewood neck	$850	$1,100
2019	Pale Moon Quilt	$1,275	$1,650

American Ultra Luxe Stratocaster

2021. Pickups options and various colors.

2021	Floyd Rose HHS	$1,325	$1,725
2021	SSS	$1,275	$1,650

American Ultra Stratocaster

2019-present. Various options and colors.

2019-2020		$1,100	$1,450

Ancho Poblano Stratocaster Journeyman Relic

2018-2019. Custom Shop Limited Edition series, alder body, 2-color sunburst or opaque white blonde, with Journeyman Relic nitro lacquer finish.

2018-2019		$2,025	$2,650

Ancho Poblano Roasted Stratocaster Relic

2019-2020. Custom Shop Limited Edition series, roasted alder body with Relic lacquer finish, various colors.

2019-2020		$2,100	$2,725

Antigua Stratocaster

2004. Made in Japan, limited-edition reissue, '70s features and antigua finish.

2004		$700	$900

Artisan Series Stratocaster (Custom Shop)

2015-present. Features distinctively figured woods, gold hardware, hand-rubbed oil finishes, certifiicate of authenticity, various models: Okoume, Claro Walnut, Figured Rosewood, Spalted Maple, Tamo Ash, Thinline Koa.

2015	Okoume	$1,800	$2,500
2016-2020	Spalted Maple	$2,100	$2,725
2020	Maple Burl	$2,200	$2,800

Big Apple Stratocaster

1997-2000. Two humbucking pickups, 5-way switch, rosewood 'board or maple neck, non-tremolo optional.

1997-2000	Various colors	$750	$975

Big Block Stratocaster

2005-2006. Pearloid block markers, black with matching headstock, 2 single coils (neck, middle) 1 humbucker (bridge), vintage style tremolo.

2005-2006		$550	$725

Big Head Stratocaster

2020. Custom Shop Limited Edition series.

2020		$2,000	$2,625

Bill Carson Stratocaster

1992. Based on the '57 Strat, birdseye maple neck, Cimarron Red finish, 1 left-handed and 100 right-handed produced, serial numbers MT000-MT100, made in Fender Custom Shop, and initiated by The Music Trader (MT) in Florida.

1992		$1,800	$2,400

MODEL YEAR	FEATURES	EXC. COND. LOW	HIGH

Billy Corgan Stratocaster

2008-2012. US-made, 3 DiMarzio pickups, string-thru hardtail bridge.

2008-2012		$925	$1,200

Blackie Stratocaster (Custom Shop 1987)

1987. 12 made, includes Certificate of Authenticity.

1987		$2,450	$3,200

Blackie Stratocaster (Custom Shop)

November 2006. Blackie tribute, 185 instruments for U.S. market, 90 made for export, original retail price $24,000.

2006		$10,000	$13,000

Black Paisley Stratocaster

2020. Made in Japan, Limited Edition, run of 300, silver and black paisley-print design on basswood body, rosewood 'board, 3 single-coil pickups.

2020		$550	$725

Blacktop Stratocaster

2011-2015. Alder body, maple neck, rosewood or maple 'board, various pickup options including HH and HSH, various finish options. Floyd Rose version also available.

2011-2015		$475	$625

Mahogany Blacktop Stratocaster Limited Edition

2019. 2 or 3 Alnico humbuckers, mahogany body, black headstock, Oly White, black or crimson red, chrome or gold hardware.

2019		$475	$625

Blue Flower Stratocaster

1984-1997, 2002-2004. Made in Japan, '72 Strat reissue with a '68 Tele Blue Floral finish.

1984-1987	1st issue	$1,200	$1,550
1988-1994		$1,000	$1,300
1995-1997		$800	$1,050
2002-2004	2nd issue	$700	$900

Bonnie Raitt Stratocaster

1995-2001. Alder body, often in blueburst, Bonnie Raitt's signature on headstock.

1995-2001		$1,700	$2,200

Bowling Ball/Marble Stratocaster

1984. Standard Strat with 1 tone and 1 volume control, jack on 'guard, called Bowling Ball Strat due to the swirling, colored finish.

1984	All colors	$3,000	$4,000

Buddy Guy Standard Stratocaster

1996-present. Made in Mexico, maple neck, polka-dot finish.

1996-2020		$525	$700

Buddy Guy Stratocaster (Signature)

1995-2009. Maple neck, 3 Gold Lace Sensor pickups, ash body, signature model, blond or sunburst.

1995-2009		$925	$1,225

Buddy Holly Tribute Stratocaster

2014. Custom Shop model, 50 made, '55 specs, with certificate of authenticity.

2014		$5,600	$7,200

California Stratocaster/California Fat Stratocaster

1997-1999. Made in the U.S., painted in Mexico, 3 single coils, Fat has HSS, various colors.

1997-1999	SSS or HSS	$560	$725

MODEL YEAR	FEATURES	EXC. COND. LOW	HIGH

Carroll Shelby Limited Edition Stratocaster

2009. Built for Ford Motor Co. as tribute to Shelby's life, graphic photo montage on front, engraved Shelby Automobiles logo on 'guard, only 100 produced.

2009		$1,600	$2,100

Carved Top Stratocaster HSS (Custom Shop)

1995-1998. Carved figured maple top, HSS (HH offered in '98), certificate of authenticity, various colors.

1995-1998		$1,750	$2,250

Classic Player Stratocaster

2000. Custom Shop model, Standard Stratocaster with useful 'player-friendly features' such as noiseless stacked single-coil pickups and factory Sperzel locking tuners, black, gold anodized 'guard.

2000		$1,200	$1,600

Classic Player Stratocaster HH

2015-2016. Alder body, maple neck, bound rosewood 'board, 2 humbuckers, dark Mercedes Blue gloss finish with matching headstock.

2015-2016		$525	$680

Collector's Edition Stratocaster ('62 Reissue)

1997. Pearl inlaid '97 on 12th fret, rosewood 'board, alder body, gold hardware, tortoise 'guard, nitro finish, sunburst, 1997 made.

1997		$1,100	$1,450

Contemporary Stratocaster (Custom Shop)

1989-1998. 7/8 scale body, hum/single/single pickups, various colors.

1989-1998		$1,300	$1,700

Contemporary Stratocaster (Import)

1985-1987. Import model used while the new Fender reorganized, black or natural headstock with silver-white logo, black or white 'guard, 2 humbucker pickups or single-coil and humbucker, 2 knobs and slider switch.

1985-1987		$700	$900

Crash Stratocaster

2005-2007. Master Built Custom Shop, hand painted by John Crash Matos, approximately 50, comes with certificate, the prices shown include the original certificate.

2005-2007		$4,000	$5,200

Custom Classic Stratocaster

2000-2008. Custom Shop version of American Standard Strat.

2000-2008		$1,850	$2,400

Custom Deluxe Stratocaster

2009-2014. Custom Shop, birdseye maple neck, rosewood or maple 'board, certificate. Model also available with flame maple top.

2009-2014		$2,500	$3,300

Custom Shop Limited Edition Stratocaster

1992. Only 100 made, flame maple top, birdseye maple neck, rosewood 'board, gold hardware, trans red finish.

1992		$2,200	$2,900

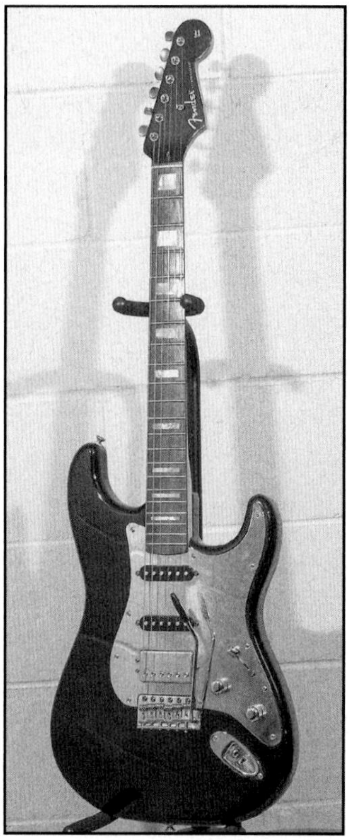

2005 Fender Big Block Stratocaster

Tom Pfeifer

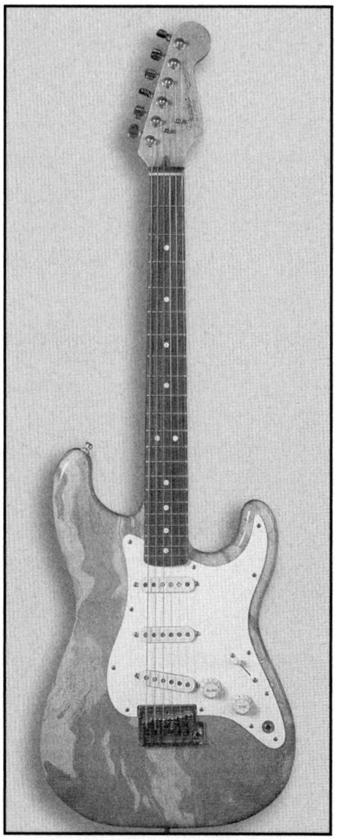

1984 Fender Bowling Ball/ Marble Stratocaster

2004 Fender Eric Clapton Stratocaster
Robbie Keene

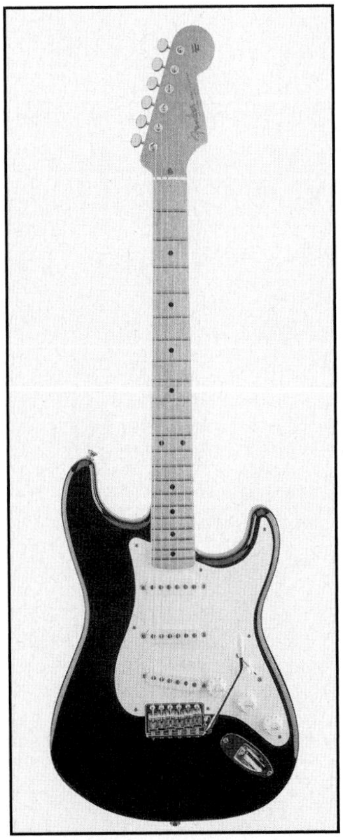

2017 Fender Eric Johnson Stratocaster

MODEL YEAR	FEATURES	EXC. COND. LOW	HIGH

Dave Murray Stratocaster

2009-present. Alder body, maple neck, rosewood 'board, 3 pickups, 2-color sunburst.

2009-2020 $600 $775

David Gilmour Signature Stratocaster

2008-2019. Custom Shop, NOS or Relic, based on Gilmour's '70 black Stratocaster, certificate of authenticity.

2008-2019 $2,700 $3,500

Deluxe Lone Star Stratocaster

2007-2016. Reissue of Lone Star Strat, made in Mexico, 1 humbucker and 2 single-coils, rosewood 'board.

2007-2016 $350 $455

Deluxe Players Special Edition Stratocaster

2007. Made in Mexico, Special Edition Fender oval sticker on back of headstock along with 60th Anniversary badge.

2007 $365 $475

Deluxe Players Stratocaster

2004-2016. Made in Mexico, 3 noiseless single-coils, push-button switching system.

2004-2016 $400 $525

Deluxe Roadhouse Stratocaster

2008-present. Deluxe series reissue, Texas Special pickups.

2008-2020 $475 $625

Deluxe Stratocaster

2016-present. Mexico-made, double-cut, 3 vintage noiseless single-coils or 1 humbucker and 2 single-coils.

2016-2020 SSS or HSS $475 $625

Deluxe Stratocaster HSS Plus Top With IOS Connectivity

2014-2016. Deluxe series, plugs into iOS devices.

2014-2016 $375 $500

Deluxe Stratocaster Plus

1987-1998. Alder (poplar earlier) with ash veneer front and back, 3 Lace Sensor pickups, Floyd Rose, various colors. Becomes American Deluxe Strat Plus.

1987-1998 $1,050 $1,350

Dick Dale Stratocaster

1994-present. Custom Shop signature model, alder body, reverse headstock, sparkle finish.

1994-2020 $2,100 $2,750

Elite Stratocaster

1983-1984. The Elite Series feature active electronics and noise-cancelling pickups, push buttons instead of 3-way switch, Elite script logo on 4-bolt neck plate, various colors. Also see Gold Elite Stratocaster and Walnut Elite Stratocaster.

1983-1984 $1,750 $2,300

EOB (Ed O'Brien) Sustainer Stratocaster

2017-present. Alder body, maple neck and 'board, 3 pickups (Sustainer in neck position), custom "Flower of Life" neck plate, gloss poly white finish.

2017-2020 $625 $825

Eric Clapton Gold Leaf Stratocaster

2004. Custom Shop model, special build for Guitar Center, 50 made, 23k gold leaf finish/covering.

2004 $4,200 $5,400

MODEL YEAR	FEATURES	EXC. COND. LOW	HIGH

Eric Clapton Signature Journeyman Relic Stratocaster

2020-present. Custom Shop, Clapton's signature on the headstock, 2-color sunburst or aged white blonde.

2020 $2,850 $3,700

Eric Clapton Signature Stratocaster (Custom Shop)

2019-present. Alder body, maple neck, three Vintage Noiseless pickups, Clapton's signature on headstock, black or Mercedes Blue.

2019-2020 $2,600 $3,400

Eric Clapton Stratocaster

1988-present. U.S.-made, '57 reissue features, had Lace Sensor pickups until '01, when switched to Vintage Noiseless. Black versions have added "Blackie" decal on headstock.

1988-1999 Lace Sensors $1,200 $1,575
2000 Lace Sensors $1,050 $1,375
2001-2020 Noiseless $1,050 $1,375

Eric Clapton Stratocaster (Custom Shop)

2004-2016. Custom Shop model, standard non-active single-coil pickups, black or blue finish.

2004-2016 $2,100 $2,750

Eric Johnson 1954 "Virginia" Stratocaster

2020-present. Stories Collection, limited numbers offered from both Custom Shop (see Masterbuilt listing) and Corona production.

2020 Fender Corona $1,425 $1,850

Eric Johnson Signature Stratocaster Thinline

2018-2020. Alder body, maple neck and 'board, 3 single-coil pickups, 2-color sunburst or vintage white.

2017-2020 $1,000 $1,300

Eric Johnson Stratocaster

2005-present. '57 spec body and 1-piece maple soft-v-neck, or, for '09 to '15, rosewood 'board, special design pickups, vintage tremolo with 4 springs, EJ initials and guitar-player figure engraved neck plate. Also listed as Eric Johnson Stratocaster Maple or Rosewood.

2005-2020 Maple or rosewood $1,100 $1,425

Floyd Rose Classic Relic Stratocaster

1998. Custom Shop model, late '60s large headstock, 1 humbucker and 1 Strat pickup.

1998 $2,075 $2,700

Floyd Rose Classic Stratocaster (Strat HSS) (Strat HH)

1992-2002. Two single-coils, bridge humbucker, Floyd Rose tremolo, becomes Floyd Rose Classic Strat HSS or HH (2 humbuckers) in '98.

1992-2002 $1,050 $1,350

Ford Shelby GT Stratocaster

2007. 200 made, black with silver Shelby GT racing stripe.

2007 200 made $1,825 $2,375

Foto Flame Stratocaster

1994-1996, 2000. Japanese-made Collectables model, alder and basswood body with Foto Flame (simulated woodgrain) finish on top cap and back of neck.

1994-2000 $625 $800

MODEL YEAR	FEATURES	EXC. COND. LOW	HIGH

Freddy Tavares Aloha Stratocaster

1993-1994. Custom Shop model, hollow aluminum body with hand engraved Hawaiian scenes, custom inlay on neck, 153 made.

1993-1994		$5,400	$7,000

FSR Stratocaster

2012-2019. Factory Special Run models might be 'dealer exclusive' or open to all dealers as limited run. FSR have a special set of appointments that are not standard to the core lineup.

2012	Antigua Strat	$525	$675
2013	Hot Rod Strat	$400	$525
2013-2017	Special Ed Classic '60s Strat Laq Surf Green	$650	$850
2015-2016	Amer Std '54 Strat	$800	$1,050
2017-2019	Special Ed '50s Strat	$500	$650
2018-2019	MIJ Traditional '50s Strat	$475	$625

George Fullerton 50th Anniversary '57 Strat Ltd. Ed. Set

2007. 150 made, '57 Strat with matching relic Pro Junior tweed amp, certificates of authenticity signed by Fullerton, commemorative neck plate.

2007		$2,900	$3,800

George Harrison Rocky Stratocaster

2020-present. Custom Shop Limited Edition series, 2-piece alder body, 5A flame maple neck, 3 '60s Strat pickups, finish is designed from Harrison's psychedelic paint job including the "Grimwoods" decal, Sonic Blue with custom Rocky graphics top.

2020		$12,700	$16,500

Gold Stratocaster

1981-1983. Gold metallic finish, gold-plated brass hardware, 4-bolt neck, maple 'board, skunk strip, trem.

1981-1983		$1,800	$2,300

Gold Elite Stratocaster

1983-1984. The Elite series feature active electronics and noise-cancelling pickups, the Gold Elite has gold hardware and pearloid tuner buttons, also see Elite Stratocaster and Walnut Elite Stratocaster.

1983-1984		$1,750	$2,300

Gold Stratocaster (Custom Shop)

1989. Custom Shop, 500 made, gold finish with gold anodized and white 'guards included.

1989		$2,150	$2,800

GT11 Stratocaster

2019-2020. Custom Shop, exclusive models for Sweetwater, relic and heavy relic.

2019-2020	Heavy Relic	$2,250	$2,950
2019-2020	Relic	$2,075	$2,700

H.E.R. Stratocaster

2020-present. Made in Mexico, alder body with Chrome Glow finish, matching painted headstock.

2020		$600	$800

Hank Marvin Stratocaster

1995-1996. Custom Shop model, Feista Red.

1995-1996		$2,300	$2,975

MODEL YEAR	FEATURES	EXC. COND. LOW	HIGH

Hank Marvin 40th Anniversary Stratocaster

1998. Custom Shop logo with '40 Years 1958-1998' marked on back of headstock, Fiesta Red, only 40 made, Custom Shop certificate.

1998		$4,800	$6,200

Harley-Davidson 90th Anniversary Stratocaster

1993. Custom Shop, 109 total made, Harley-Davidson and Custom Shop V logo on headstock (Diamond Edition, 40 units), 9 units produced for the Harley-Davidson company without diamond logo, 60 units were not Diamond Edition, chrome-plated engraved metal body, engraved 'guard, Custom Shop Certificate important attribute.

1993		$8,500	$11,000

Highway One Stratocaster/HSS

2002-2014. U.S.-made, alder body, satin lacquer finish, 3 single-coil pickups or HSS version has humbucker/single/single.

2002-2014		$575	$750

HM Strat (USA/Import)

1988-1992 ('88 Japanese-made, '89-'90 U.S.- and Japanese-made, '91-'92 U.S.-made). Heavy Metal Strat, Floyd Rose, regular or pointy headstock, black hardware, H, HH, SH, or SSH pickup options. Later models have choice of SHH or SSH.

1988-1990	Import	$850	$1,100
1989-1992	USA	$850	$1,100

HM Strat Limited Edition

2020-present. '88-'92 HM specs, available in era-correct Day-Glo colors, Frozen Yellow, Flash Pink, Ice Blue and Bright White.

2020		$700	$900

Homer Haynes HLE Stratocaster

1988-1989. Custom Shop, limited edition of 500, '59 Strat basics with gold finish, gold anodized guard and gold hardware.

1988-1989		$2,100	$2,700

Hot Wheels Stratocaster

2003. Custom Shop model commissioned by Hot Wheels, 16 made, orange flames over blue background, large Hot Wheels logo.

2003		$1,650	$2,200

HRR Stratocaster/ Floyd Rose HRR (Japan)

1990-1994. Made in Japan, hot-rodded vintage-style Strat, Floyd Rose tremolo system, H/S/S pickups, maple neck, sunburst or colors. Called the Floyd Rose HRR for '92-'94 (with optional Foto Flame finish).

1990-1994		$850	$1,100

Ike Turner Tribute Stratocaster

2005. Custom Shop model, 100 made, replica of Ike Turner's Sonic Blue Strat.

2005		$2,450	$3,200

Jeff Beck Signature Stratocaster (CS)

2004-present. Custom Shop, 3 Noiseless dual-coils, Olympic White or Surf Green.

2004-2019		$1,550	$2,050
2020		$2,450	$3,200

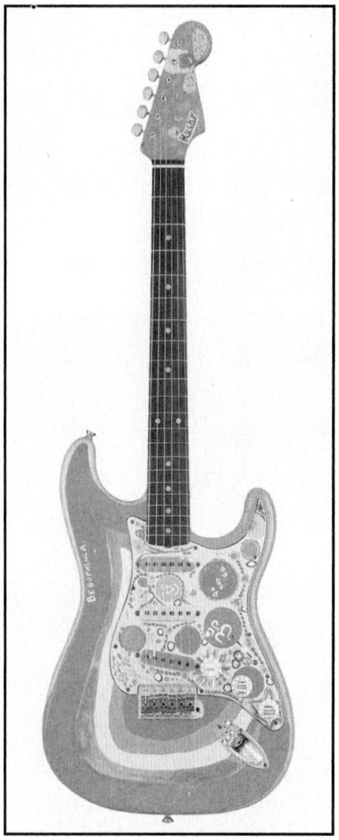

Fender George Harrison Rocky Stratocaster

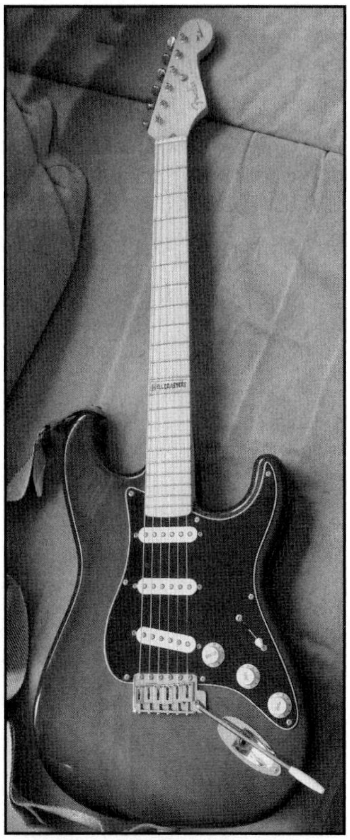

1997 Fender Jerry Donahue Hellecaster Stratocaster

Stoeffu Vogt

1997 Fender Jimi Hendrix Voodoo Stratocaster

Craig Brody

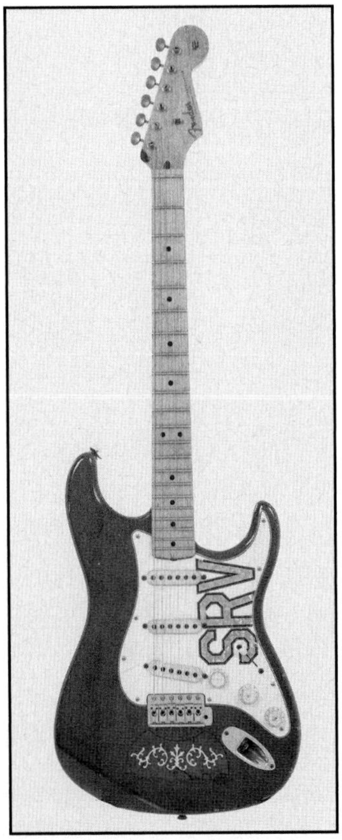

2007 Fender Lenny Stratocaster

Imaged by Heritage Auctions, HA.com

MODEL YEAR	FEATURES	EXC. COND. LOW	EXC. COND. HIGH

Jeff Beck Stratocaster

1991-present. Alder body, originally 3 Lace Sensors (HSS) changing to 3 Noiseless dual-coils in '01, rosewood 'board, Olympic White and Surf Green (Midnight Purple until '02).

1991	1st issue, Lace Sensors	$1,775	$2,325
1992-1993	Lace Sensors	$1,425	$1,875
1994-2000	Lace Sensors	$1,200	$1,575
2001-2009	Noiseless	$1,050	$1,375
2010-2020	Artist Series	$1,050	$1,375

Jerry Donahue Hellecaster Stratocaster

1997. Made in the Fender Japan Custom Shop as one part of the 3-part Hellecasters Series, limited edition, Seymour Duncan pickups, maple, blue with blue sparkle guard.

1997		$775	$1,000

Jim Root Stratocaster

2010-present. Artist series, mahogany body, ebony or maple 'board, 2 active pickups, black hardware, black or white finish.

2010-2020		$925	$1,200

Jimi Hendrix Limited Edition Stratocaster (Custom Shop)

2019-present. Custom Artist series, designed from Hendrix's modified '68 Strat used at Woodstock ('69), aged Olympic White.

2019-2020		$3,900	$5,100

Jimi Hendrix Monterey Pop Stratocaster

1997-1998. Custom Shop, near replica of Monterey Pop Festival sacrifice guitar, red psychedelic-style finish.

1997-1998		$11,200	$14,600

Jimi Hendrix Monterey Stratocaster

2017-2018. Body art like Hendrix's hand-painted original that he destroyed at Monterey Pop Festival, custom neck plate, signature on headstock rear.

2017-2018		$500	$650

Jimi Hendrix Stratocaster

2015-present. Reverse headstock, silhouette and engraved 'Authentic Hendrix' on neckplate.

2015-2020		$525	$675

Jimi Hendrix Tribute Stratocaster

1997-2000. Left-handed guitar strung right-handed, maple cap neck, Olympic White. Fender headstock logo positioned upside down, made for right-handed player to look as if they are playing a left-handed guitar flipped over.

1997-2000		$1,900	$2,500

Jimi Hendrix Voodoo 29th Anniversary (Guitar Center) Stratocaster

1993. Custom Shop made only 35 for Guitar Center, large 'Guitar Center 29th Anniversary' logo on neckplate, right-handed body with reverse left-handed headstock and reversed Fender headstock logo, purple sparkle finish.

1993		$2,300	$3,000

Jimi Hendrix Voodoo Child Journeyman Relic Stratocaster

2020-present. Custom Shop, Olympic White or black with aged relic finish.

2020-2021		$2,750	$3,550

Jimi Hendrix Voodoo Child Signature Stratocaster NOS

2018-present. Custom Shop, Custom Artist series, 2-piece alder body, maple neck and 'board, 3 pickups, Olympic White or black, with NOS nitro lacquer finish.

2018-2020		$2,800	$3,600

Jimi Hendrix Voodoo Stratocaster

1997-2002. Right-handed body with reverse headstock, maple neck, Olympic White, sunburst or black.

1997-2002		$1,900	$2,500

Jimmie Vaughan Tex-Mex Stratocaster

1997-present. Poplar body, maple 'board, signature on headstock, 3 Tex-Mex pickups, various colors.

1997-2020		$475	$625

John Jorgenson Hellecaster Stratocaster

1997. Fender Japan Custom Shop, part of the 3-part Hellecasters Series, limited edtion, Seymour Duncan pickups, gold sparkle 'guard, gold hardware, split single-coils, rosewood 'board.

1997		$850	$1,100

John Mayer Limited Edition Black1 Stratocaster

2010. Custom Shop, 83 made, black finish NOS or extreme relic option, JC serial number, Custom Shop/ John Cruz logo on back of headstock includes personal letter from John Mayer.

2010	NOS	$2,600	$3,400

John Mayer Stratocaster

2005-2014. Alder body, special scooped mid-range pickups, vintage tremolo, special design gigbag with pocket for laptop computer.

2005-2014		$1,050	$1,375

Kenny Wayne Shepherd Stratocaster

2009-2016, 2020-present. Artist series, based on Shepherd's '61, rosewood 'board, jumbo frets, Artic White with cross, black with racing stripes or 3-color sunburst. Reintroduced '20, chambered ash body, 3 single-coil pickups, trans Faded Sonic Blue with matching painted headstock.

2009-2016	Import	$525	$700
2020-2021	US-made	$1,100	$1,450

Koa Stratocaster

2006-2008. Made in Korea, Special Edition series, sunburst over koa veneer top, plain script Fender logo, serial number on back of headstock with.

2006-2008		$425	$550

Kon Tiki Stratocaster

2003. Custom Shop model, limited run of 25, Tiki Green including Tiki 3-color art work on headstock.

2003		$2,100	$2,700

Lenny Stratocaster

Introduced Dec. 12, 2007 by Guitar Center stores, Custom Shop model, 185 guitars made, initial product offering price was 17K.

2007		$7,500	$10,000

Limited Roasted Tomatillo Stratocaster Relic

2019-2020. Custom Shop Limited Edition series, roasted alder body and 4A flame maple neck, various colors with Relic lacquer finish.

2019-2020		$2,400	$3,125

MODEL YEAR	FEATURES	EXC. COND. LOW	HIGH

Lincoln Brewster Signature Stratocaster

2019-present. Ash body, 1-piece maple neck, 3 single-coil pickups, gold with lacquer finish.

2019-2020		$1,125	$1,450

Lite Ash Stratocaster Special Edition

2004-2007. Korea, light ash body, birds-eye maple neck.

2004-2007		$400	$525

Lone Star Stratocaster

1996-2001. Alder body, 1 humbucker and 2 single-coil pickups, rosewood 'board or maple neck, various colors.

1996	50th Anniv Badge	$725	$950
1997-2001		$725	$950

Mark Knopfler Stratocaster

2003-2013. '57 body with '62 maple neck.

2003-2013		$1,050	$1,350

Masterbuilt Custom Shop Stratocaster

2006-present. Builder Select series, various models and builders, specific identification to builder, must include certificate of authenticity.

2006-2020	Various models	$3,500	$11,000

Matthias Jabs Signature Stratocaster

1998. Made in Japan, 200 offered, Candy Apple Red.

1998		$875	$1,125

Michael Landau Signature Relic Stratocaster 1963/1968

2014-present. Custom Shop Artist series, Relic, alder body, rosewood 'board, '63 is worn Fiesta Red over 3-color sunburst, '68 is black or bleached 3-color sunburst.

2014-2020	1963 Relic	$2,250	$2,900
2014-2020	1968 Relic	$2,250	$2,900

Milonga Deluxe Stratocaster

2005. Special Edition made in Mexico, Vintage Noiseless pickups, rosewood 'board, Olympic White, gold hardware.

2005		$375	$500

MLB Major League Baseball Stratocaster

2014. Official team logos and imagery unique to each, licensed by Major League Baseball Properties.

2014	Various models	$450	$585

Mod Shop Stratocaster

2017-present. Mod Shop allows you to create your own factory-customized electric guitar or bass.

2017-2020		$1,525	$2,000

Modern Player Stratocaster HSH/HSS

2013-2015. Made in China, hum-single-hum or hum-single-single.

2013-2015		$300	$390

Moto Limited Edition Stratocaster

1995. Custom Shop model, pearloid cover in various colors, includes Certificate of Authenticity, not to be confused with white pearloid Moto Strat which is part of a guitar and amp set (as listed below).

1995		$2,300	$3,000

Moto Set Stratocaster

1995-1996. Custom Shop set including guitar, case, amp and amp stand, white pearloid finish.

1995-1996	Red (few made)	$3,900	$5,100
1995-1996	White	$3,900	$5,100

Noventa Stratocaster

2021. Alder body, maple neck, Pau Ferro 'board, 2 single-coil pickups, Crimson Red Trans, Daphne Blue or Surf Green.

2021		$575	$750

Orange Krush Limited Edition Stratocaster

1995. Custom Shop, 25 made, based on '57 Strat, orange finish with matching headstock, certificate of authenticity.

1995		$2,100	$2,700

Paisley Stratocaster

1984-1997, 2003-2004, 2008. Japanese-made '72 Strat reissue with a reissue '68 Tele Pink Paisley finish, large headstock until mid-'94, 'Made in Japan' logo used until early-'97, 'Crafted in Japan' after.

1984-1987	1st issue	$1,400	$1,800
1988-1994		$1,200	$1,600
1995-1997		$1,025	$1,325
2003-2004		$700	$900
2008	2nd issue, 200 made	$700	$900

Parallel Universe Volume II Strat Jazz Deluxe

2019-present. Limited Edition, alder body, 2 pickups, Mystic Surf Green with nitro lacquer finish.

2019-2020		$1,125	$1,450

Parallel Universe Volume II Strat-Tele Hybrid

2017-2018. Limited Edition, Tele body, Strat neck and headstock, 3 single-coil Strat pickups, 2-color sunburst with gloss nitro lacquer finish.

2017-2018		$1,125	$1,450

Playboy 40th Anniversary Stratocaster

1994. Custom Shop model, nude Marilyn Monroe graphic on body. 175 built.

1994		$13,000	$17,000

Player Series Stratocaster

2017-present. Various models include SSS, HSS, HSH, HSS Plus, Floyd Rose, SSS LH and SSS Plus, various colors and finishes.

2017-2019	SSS, HSS, HSH	$375	$500
2018-2020	Floyd Rose HSS	$445	$575
2018-2020	Plus Top SSS, HSS	$410	$535

Post Modern Stratocaster (Custom Shop)

2015-2019. Offered in Journeyman Relic, NOS, and lush Closet Classic finishes.

2015-2017	NOS	$1,950	$2,525
2016-2019	Journeyman Relic	$2,075	$2,700
2019	Closet Classic	$2,075	$2,700

Post Modern Stratocaster Closet Classic (Custom Shop)

2019-2020. Made exclusive for Sweetwater, certificate.

2019-2020	Aged natural	$2,075	$2,700

Post Modern Stratocaster Journeyman Relic (Custom Shop)

2019. Made exclusive for Sweetwater, alder or ash, certificate.

2019-2020	Alder	$2,075	$2,700
2019-2020	Ash	$2,075	$2,700

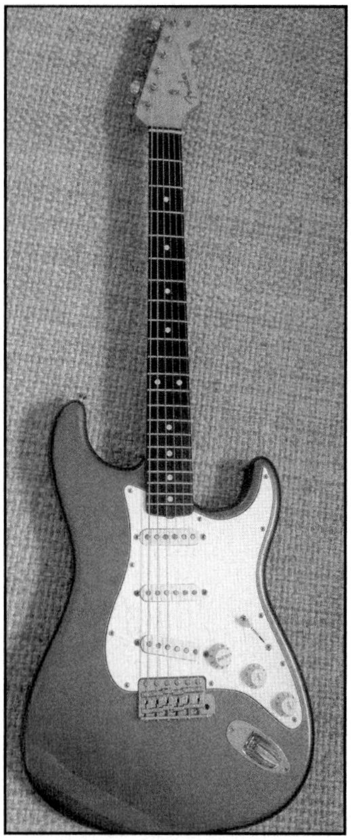

2006 Fender Masterbuilt Stratocaster

David Stone

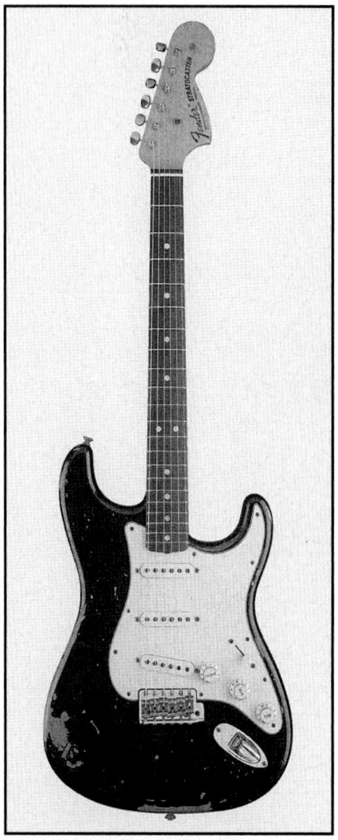

2017 Fender Michael Landau 1968 Stratocaster

2007 Fender Stratocaster Powerhouse Deluxe
Lew Campbell

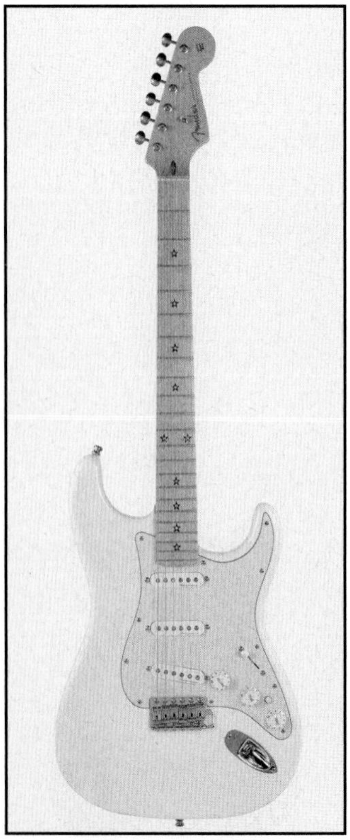

2001 Fender Richie Sambora Stratocaster
Imaged by Heritage Auctions, HA.com

MODEL YEAR	FEATURES	EXC. COND. LOW	HIGH

Post Modern Stratocaster NOS (Custom Shop)

2019-2020. Made exclusive for Sweetwater, certificate.

2019-2020	Aged natural	$2,075	$2,700

Powerhouse/Powerhouse Deluxe Stratocaster

1997-2010. Made in Mexico, Standard Strat configuration with pearloid 'guard, various colors.

1997-2010		$375	$500
2005	Powerbridge, TRS stereo	$375	$500

Proud Stratocaster

2003. Custom Shop, 3 made to commemorate United Way and Rock & Roll Hall of Fame project, body painted in detail by Fender's artist.

2003		$2,450	$3,200

Rarities Stratocaster

2019-2020. Rarities Collection series, limited edition, models include; Flame Maple Top, Flame KOA Top, Quilt Maple Top.

2019-2020	Various models	$1,400	$1,800

Richie Sambora Stratocaster

1993-2002. Alder body, Floyd Rose tremolo, maple neck, U.S. and Mexico models offered.

1993-2002	USA	$2,200	$2,850
1994-2002	Mexico	$400	$525
1995-1997	Mexico, swirl color	$525	$680

Ritchie Blackmore Stratocaster

2009-present. Based on Blackmore's '70s large headstock model, scalloped rosewood 'board, Duncan Quarter Pound Flat pickups, Olympic White.

2009-2020		$680	$885

Ritchie Blackmore Tribute Stratocaster

2014. Custom Shop model, '68 specs, maple neck.

2014		$3,500	$4,500

Roadhouse Stratocaster

1997-2000. U.S.-made, poplar body, tortoise shell 'guard, maple 'board, 3 Texas Special pickups, various colors.

1997-2000		$625	$825

Robert Cray Signature Stratocaster

1991-present. Custom Shop, rosewood 'board, chunky neck, lighter weight, non-trem, alder body, gold-plated hardware, various colors.

1991-2020		$2,100	$2,750

Robert Cray Stratocaster (Mexico)

1996-present. Artist series, chrome hardware.

1996-2020		$510	$665

Robin Trower Signature Stratocaster

2004-present. Custom Shop Custom Artist series, 100 made, large headstock (post '65-era), with '70s logo and 3-bolt neck, bullet truss rod, white.

2004-2020		$2,000	$2,600

Rory Gallagher Tribute Stratocaster

2004-present. Custom Shop, based on Gallagher's '61 model, heavily distressed, price includes the original certificate.

2004-2019		$2,550	$3,300
2020		$3,025	$3,900

MODEL YEAR	FEATURES	EXC. COND. LOW	HIGH

Sandblasted Stratocaster

2014-2015, 2019-2020. Limited Edition series, ash body, sandblasted finish. Limited run in '19, exclusive for Sweetwater USA.

2014-2015		$650	$850
2019-2020	Sweetwater run	$650	$850

Select Stratocaster

2012-2015. Select Series, figured top, rear-headstock 'Fender Select' medallion, gloss-lacquer finish, various colors.

2012-2015		$1,625	$2,100

Set-Neck Stratocaster

1992-1999. Custom Shop model, mahogany body and figured maple top, 4 pickups, glued-in neck, active electronics, by '96 ash body.

1992-1999		$1,750	$2,300

Short-Scale (7/8) Stratocaster

1989-1995. Similar to Standard Strat, but with 2 control knobs and switch, 24" scale vs. 25" scale, sometimes called a mini-Strat, Japanese import, various colors.

1989-1995		$520	$675

So-Cal Custom Shop J.W. Black Stratocaster

2000-2001. So-Cal logo art on body, 20 offered.

2000-2001		$1,525	$1,975

So-Cal Speed Shop Stratocaster

2005-2006. Limited Edition for Musician's Friend, red, white, and black So-Cal paint job, basswood body, rosewood 'board, 1 humbucker, So-Cal Speed Shop decal.

2005-2006		$480	$625

Special Edition David Lozeau Art Stratocaster

2015-2016. Finishes include orange Tree of Life, blue Dragon, yellow Rose Tattoo and red Sacred Heart, etched David Lozeau neck plate.

2015-2016		$400	$525

Special Edition Stratocaster

2004-2009. Import model, Special Edition oval logo on back of headstock, various styles offered, '50s or '60s vintage copy specs, maple 'board, ash or koa body, see-thru or opaque finish.

2004-2009		$385	$500

Special Edition Stratocaster (Matching Headstock)

2016-2017. Made in Mexico, various colors with matching headstock.

2016-2017		$385	$500

Special Edition White Opal Stratocaster

2016. Made in Mexico, white opal body and headstock, pearloid 'guard, 3 humbuckers.

2016		$385	$500

Splatter Stratocaster

2003. Made in Mexico, splatter paint job, various color combinations, with gig bag.

2003		$575	$750

Standard Roland Ready Stratocaster

1998-2011. Made in Mexico, built-in Roland pickup system and 3 single-coils.

1998-2011		$350	$455

MODEL YEAR	FEATURES	EXC. COND. LOW	HIGH

Standard Stratocaster (Japan)

1985-1989. Interim production in Japan while the new Fender reorganized, standard pickup configuration and tremolo system, 3 knobs with switch, traditional style input jack, traditional shaped headstock, offered in black, red or white.

1985-1989		$725	$950

Standard Stratocaster (Mexico)

1990-2018. Made in Mexico, renamed Player Series in '18. Not to be confused with the American-made Standard Stratocaster of '81-'84. Various models and colors, high-end range includes a hard guitar case, while low-end includes only a gig bag.

1990-2018	Various models	$350	$455

Standard Stratocaster Plus Top

2014-2018. Made in Mexico, alder body with flamed maple top. Renamed Player Series Plus Top in '18.

2014-2018		$355	$460

Standard Stratocaster Satin Finish

2003-2006. Basically Mexico-made Standard with satin finish.

2003-2006		$275	$350

Stevie Ray Vaughan Signature Stratocaster (Custom Shop)

2019-present. Custom Artist series, 3-color sunburst with NOS lacquer finish.

2019-2020	NOS	$2,550	$3,350

Stevie Ray Vaughan Signature Stratocaster Relic (Custom Shop)

2019-present. Custom Artist series, aged 3-color sunburst with relic lacquer finish.

2019-2020	Relic	$2,850	$3,700

Stevie Ray Vaughan Stratocaster

1992-present. U.S.-made, alder body, sunburst, gold hardware, SRV 'guard, lefty tremolo, Brazilian rosewood 'board (pau ferro by '93).

1992	1st year, Brazilian	$2,700	$3,500
1992-2019	Pau Ferro	$1,050	$1,375

Stevie Ray Vaughan Tribute #1 Stratocaster

2004. Custom Shop Limited Edition, recreation of SRV's #1 made by Master Builder John Cruz in the Custom Shop, 100 made, $10,000 MSRP, includes flight case stenciled "SRV - Number One," and other goodies.

2004		$21,000	$27,500

Strat Plus

1987-1999. Three Lace Sensor pickups, alder (poplar available earlier) body, tremolo, rosewood 'board or maple neck, various colors. See Deluxe Strat Plus for ash veneer version.

1987-1999	Various colors	$925	$1,200

Stratocaster Junior

2004-2006. Import, short 22.7" scale, Alder body, non-trem hardtail bridge.

2004-2006		$350	$450

Stratocaster Pro Closet Classic (Custom Shop)

2006-2013. Ash body, early '60s neck, rosewood or maple board, solid or sunburst finish.

2006-2013		$1,950	$2,525

Stratocaster Pro NOS (Custom Shop)

2012-2016. Ash body, maple neck, rosewood 'board, solid or 3-tone sunburst.

2012-2016		$1,950	$2,525

Stratocaster Special

1993-1995. Made in Mexico, a humbucker and a single-coil pickup, 1 volume, 1 tone.

1993-1995		$325	$425

Stratocaster XII

1988-1997, 2003-2010. 1st version Japanese-made, alder body, 22-fret rosewood 'board. 2nd version is 21-fret Classic Series model for 2 years then Classic Series.

1988-1997	1st version	$750	$975
2003-2010	2nd version	$750	$975

Strat-o-Sonic

2003-2006. American Special Series, Stratocaster-style chambered body, includes Strat-o-Sonic Dove I (1 pickup, '03 only), Dove II/DV II (2 black P-90s, '03-'06) and HH (2 humbuckers, '05-'06).

2003	Dove I	$775	$1,000
2003-2006	Dove II/DV II	$850	$1,100
2003-2006	HH	$850	$1,100

Sub Sonic Stratocaster

2000-2001. Baritone model, offered in 2 production models - HH (2 humbuckers, 2000-'01), HSS (hum-single-single, '01) - and in a Custom Shop version of the HSS (2000-'01).

2000-2001		$850	$1,100
2000-2001	Custom Shop, COA	$1,400	$1,800

Super Stratocaster

1997-2003. Deluxe series, made in Mexico, 3 Super Fat single-coils, Super Switching gives 2 extra pickup options, gold tremolo.

1997-2003		$400	$525

Supreme Stratocaster

2017. Limited Edition, collaboration with Supreme (NY-based fashion brand), all white color with red Supreme logo on front.

2017		$5,200	$6,800

Tanqurey Tonic Stratocaster

1988. Made for a Tanqurey Tonic liquor ad campaign giveaway in '88, Tanqurey Tonic Green; many were given to winners around the country, ads said that they could also be purchased through Tanqurey, but that apparently didn't happen.

1988		$1,250	$1,625

Tash Sultana Stratocaster

2020-present. Artist series, all gold hardware, aged white pearl 'guard, trans cherry finish with matching painted headstock.

2020		$600	$800

Texas Special Stratocaster

1991-1992. Custom Shop model, 50 made, state of Texas map stamped on neck plate, Texas Special pickups, maple fretboard, sunburst.

1991-1992		$2,100	$2,700

The Edge Stratocaster

2016-2020. U2 guitarist The Edge signature on large '70s-style headstock, alder body, 1-piece quartersawn maple neck and 'board, 3 pickups, black.

2016-2020		$1,050	$1,350

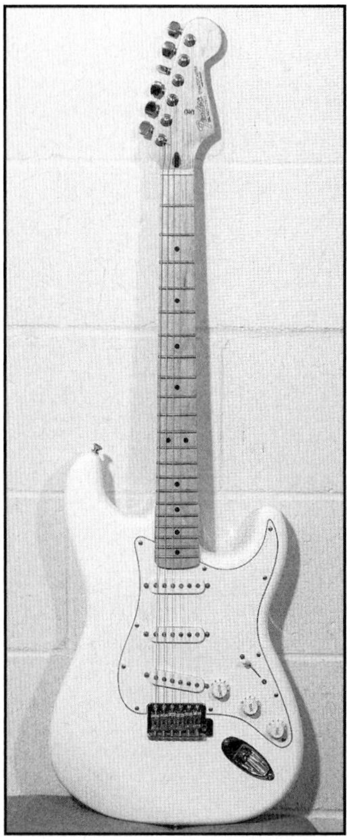

2005 Fender Standard Stratocaster (Mexico)

Tom Pfeifer

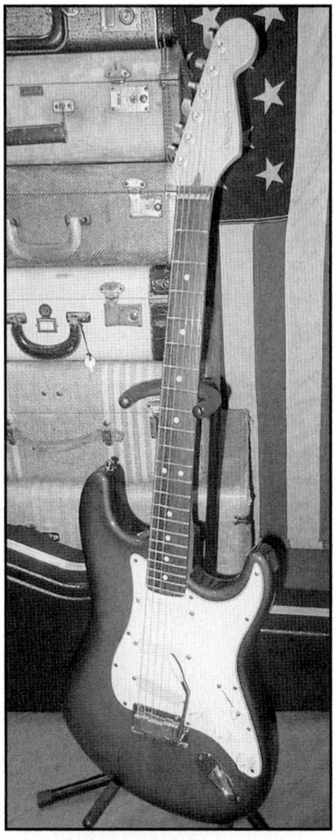

1995 Fender Strat Plus

Rivington Guitars

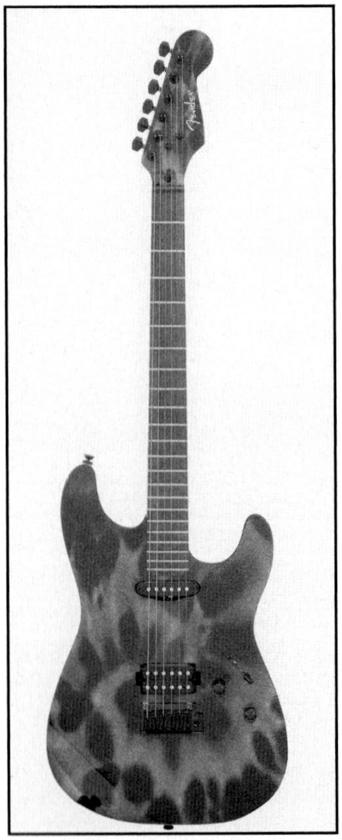

2005 Fender Tie-Dye Stratocaster

Imaged by Heritage Auctions, HA.com

1993 Fender U.S. Ultra Stratocaster

Keith Myers

MODEL YEAR	FEATURES	EXC. COND. LOW	HIGH

The Strat

1980-1983. Alder body, 4-bolt neck, large STRAT on painted peghead, gold-plated brass hardware, various colors.

1980-1983		$1,175	$1,525

Tie-Dye Stratocaster

2004-2005. Single-coil neck and humbucker bridge pickups, Band of Gypsies or Hippie Blue tie-dye pattern poly finish.

2004-2005		$400	$525

Tom Delonge Stratocaster

2001-2004. 1 humbucker, rosewood back and sides. Also in Squier version.

2001-2004		$550	$725

Tom Morello "Soul Power" Stratocaster

2020-present. Alder body, rosewood 'board, black with white 'guard. Shipped with "Soul Power" decal for face of guitar.

2020		$750	$975

Tree of Life Stratocaster

1993. Custom Shop, 29 made, tree of life fretboard inlay, 1-piece quilted maple body.

1993		$4,200	$5,450

Turquoise Sparkle Stratocaster

2001. Custom Shop, limited run of 75 for Mars Music, turquoise sparkle finish.

2001		$1,250	$1,625

U.S. Ultra / Ultra Plus Stratocaster

1990-1997. Alder body with figured maple veneer on front and back, single Lace Sensor pickups in neck and middle, double Sensor at bridge, ebony 'board, sunburst.

1990-1997		$1,450	$1,900

Ventures Limited Edition Stratocaster

1996. Japanese-made tribute model, matches Jazzmaster equivalent, black.

1996		$1,025	$1,325

VG Stratocaster

2007-2009. American Series, modeling technology using Roland's VG circuitry, 5 guitar tone banks deliver 16 sounds.

2007-2009		$850	$1,100

Vintage Hot Rod Stratocaster

2007-2014. Vintage styling with modern features, '07-'13 named '57 Strat and '62 Strat, in '14 changed to '50s and '60s.

2007-2014	All models	$1,125	$1,450

Vintera Series Stratocaster

2019-present. Modified and non-modified '50s, '60s and '70s Strat models, various options and colors.

2019-2020	'70s	$550	$725
2019-2020	'70s modified	$550	$725
2019-2021	'50s	$500	$650
2019-2021	'50s modified	$550	$725
2019-2021	'60s	$525	$700
2019-2021	'60s modified	$550	$725

Walnut Elite Stratocaster

1983-1984. The Elite Series features active electronics and noise-cancelling pickups, Walnut Elite has a walnut body and neck, gold-plated hardware and pearloid tuner buttons. Also see Elite Stratocaster and Gold Elite Stratocaster.

1983-1984		$1,750	$2,300

Walnut Stratocaster

1981-1983. American black walnut body and 1-piece neck and 'board.

1981-1983		$1,550	$2,050

Western Stratocaster

1995. Custom Shop model, only 5 made, featured in Fender Custom Shop book from the 1990s.

1995		$6,500	$8,500

Whiteguard Stratocaster Limited Edition

2018. Limited Edition neck plate, ash body, Tele hardware and white 'guard, 2 single-coil pickups, lacquer finish.

2018		$1,075	$1,400

Yngwie Malmsteen Signature Stratocaster (Custom Shop)

2020-present. Custom Artist series, 2-piece select alder body, flat sawn maple neck, various colors with nitro lacquer finish.

2020		$3,050	$3,950

Yngwie Malmsteen Stratocaster

1988-present. U.S.-made, maple neck, scalloped 'board, 3 single-coil pickups, blue, red, white.

1988-2020		$1,000	$1,300

Swinger

1969-1972. See listing for Musiclander.

SX Series

1992-1995. Dreadnought and jumbo acoustics, ply or solid spruce tops with various wood options on back and sides, E models with electronics.

1992-1994	1200sx	$400	$530
1992-1994	1300sx	$525	$700
1992-1994	1500sx	$450	$600
1992-1994	1505sx	$500	$665
1992-1995	1000sx	$275	$365
1992-1995	1100sx	$325	$430
1992-1995	1105sxe	$375	$500
1993-1994	1600sxe	$525	$700
1994-1995	600sx	$125	$165
1994-1995	800sx	$150	$200

T-Bucket 300CE

2016-2018. Acoustic/electric, D-size, cutaway.

2016-2018		$175	$235

TC-90/TC-90 Thinline

2004-2007. Made in Korea, 2 single-coil P90s, double-cut, Vintage White or Black Cherry Burst.

2004-2007		$440	$575

Telecaster

The following are all variations of the Telecaster. Broadcaster and Nocaster models are under Broadcaster. The first five listings are for the main American-made line. All others are listed alphabetically after that in the following order:

Telecaster
Standard Telecaster
American Standard Telecaster
American Series Telecaster
American Professional/Professional II Telecaster

30th Anniversary Guitar Center Tree of Life Telecaster
40th Anniversary Telecaster
'50 Custom Telecaster
'50s Telecaster/Classic Series '50s Telecaster
Road Worn '50s Telecaster
50th Anniversary Spanish Guitar Set Custom Shop
50th Anniversary Telecaster
'52 Telecaster/American Vintage '52 Telecaster
American Vintage '52 Telecaster Korina (U.S.A.)
'52 Telecaster (Custom Shop)
'52 LTD Telecaster NOS
'52 Vintage Telecaster (Japan)
'54 Telecaster (Custom Shop)
'58 Telecaster (Custom Shop)
American Vintage '58 Telecaster (U.S.A.)
'60s Telecaster Custom
'60s Telecaster/Classic Series '60s Telecaster
American Original '60s Telecaster
'60 Telecaster Custom
60th Anniversary American Telecaster
60th Anniversary Telecaster (U.S.A.)
60th Anniversary Telecaster Limited Edition
'61 Telecaster Custom
'62 Telecaster Custom (Import)
'62 Telecaster Custom (U.S.A.)
'62 Mod Squad Custom Telecaster
'62 Telecaster Reissue (Japan)
Junkyard Dog 1962 Telecaster Relic
'63 Telecaster (Custom Shop)
'63 Telecaster Custom Relic LTD
'64 Telecaster Limited Relic
American Vintage '64 Telecaster
'67 Telecaster (Custom Shop)
'68 Telecaster Rosewood
'69 Tele/Telecaster Thinline (Import)
'69 Telecaster Thinline (Custom Shop)
'72 Telecaster Custom/Classic Series '72 Telecaster Custom
'72 Telecaster Deluxe/Classic Series '72 Telecaster Deluxe
'72 Telecaster Thinline American Vintage
'72 Telecaster Thinline/Classic Series Telecaster Thinline
1972 Telecaster Custom Closet Classic (CS)
75th Anniversary Commemorative Telecaster
75th Anniversary Telecaster
'90s Telecaster Deluxe
'90s Telecaster Thinline
1998 Collectors Edition Telecaster
Aerodyne Telecaster
Albert Collins Telecaster
Aluminum Telecaster
American Acoustasonic Telecaster
American Classic Holoflake Telecaster
American Classic Telecaster
American Deluxe HH Telecaster
American Deluxe Power Telecaster
American Deluxe Telecaster
American Deluxe/Elite Telecaster Thinline
American Elite Telecaster
American Nashville B-Bender Telecaster
American Performer Telecaster
American Professional II Telecaster Deluxe
American Professional Telecaster Deluxe Shawbucker
American Special Telecaster
American Standard Telecaster Limited Edition
American Standard Telecaster Special Edition
American Ultra Luxe Telecaster
American Ultra Telecaster
Andy Summers Masterbuilt Tribute Telecaster
Antigua Telecaster
Big Block Telecaster
Bigsby Telecaster
Blacktop Telecaster Series
Blue Flower Telecaster
Bowling Ball/Marble Telecaster
Britt Daniel Telecaster Thinline
Brown's Canyon Redwood Telecaster
Buck Owens Limited Edition Telecaster
Cabronita Telecaster (American Standard)
Cabronita Telecaster (Classic Player)
Cabronita Telecaster Thinline
California Fat Telecaster
California Telecaster
Chambered Mahogany Telecaster
Chrissie Hynde Telecaster
Clarence White Telecaster (Custom Shop)
Classic Player Baja Telecaster
Collector's Edition Telecaster
Contemporary Telecaster (Import)
Custom Carved Telecaster HH
Custom Classic Telecaster
Custom Deluxe Telecaster
Custom Telecaster
Danny Gatton Signature Telecaster
Deluxe Nashville Power Telecaster
Deluxe Nashville Telecaster (Mexico)
Deluxe Telecaster (U.S.A.)
Elite Nashville Telecaster
Elite Telecaster
Fat Telecaster
Foto Flame Telecaster
G.E. Smith Telecaster
Graham Coxon Special Run Telecaster
Highway One Telecaster/Texas Telecaster
HMT Telecaster (Import)
J5 Triple Telecaster Deluxe
James Burton Standard Telecaster
James Burton Telecaster
Jason Isbell Custom Telecaster
Jerry Donahue JD Telecaster
Jerry Donahue Telecaster
Jim Adkins JA-90 Telecaster Thinline
Jim Root Telecaster
Jimmy Bryant Tribute Telecaster
Jimmy Page Mirror Telecaster
Jimmy Page Telecaster
Joe Strummer Telecaster
John Jorgenson Telecaster
Jr. Telecaster
La Cabronita Especial Telecaster
Mahogany Offset Telecaster
Masterbuilt Custom Shop Telecaster

1952 Fender Telecaster
Trey Rabinek

1956 Fender Telecaster
Frank Manno

1963 Fender Telecaster

Kevin Rush

1964 Fender Telecaster

Matched Set Telecaster
Merle Haggard Signature Telecaster
Mod Shop Telecaster
Modern Player Telecaster Plus
Moto Limited Edition Telecaster
Muddy Waters Signature Telecaster Custom
Muddy Waters Tribute Telecaster
Nashville Telecaster
NHL Premier Edition Telecaster
Nokie Edwards Telecaster
Noventa Telecaster
Old Pine Telecaster
Paisley Telecaster
Palo Escrito Telecaster
Parallel Universe Jazz-Tele
Parallel Universe Troublemaker Telecaster
Parallel Universe Volume II Tele Mágico
Player Telecaster
Plus Telecaster
Rarities Telecaster
Richie Kotzen Telecaster
Rosewood Telecaster
Rosewood Telecaster (Japan)
Rosewood Telelcaster Limited Edition
Select Telecaster
Select Telecaster Thinline
Set-Neck Telecaster
Snakehead Telecaster (Custom Shop)
Sparkle Telecaster
Special Edition Custom Telecaster FMT HH
Special Edition Deluxe Ash Telecaster
Special Edition Koa Telecaster
Special Edition White Opal Telecaster
Special Telecaster/Telecaster Special
Standard Telecaster (Japan)
Standard Telecaster (Mexico)
Telecaster (Japanese Domestic)
Telecaster Custom
Telecaster Custom (Japan)
Telecaster Custom FMT HH (Korea)
Telecaster Stratocaster Hybrid (Custom Shop)
Telecaster Thinline
Tele-Sonic
Texas Special Telecaster
Twisted Telecaster Limited Edition
Two-Tone Telecaster Thinline
Vintage Hot Rod Telecaster
Waylon Jennings Tribute Telecaster
Will Ray Signature Jazz-A-Caster
Will Ray Signature Mojo Telecaster

Telecaster

1951-1982. See Standard Telecaster (following listing) for '82-'85, American Standard Telecaster for '88-'00, the American Series Telecaster for '00-'07. and the American Standard Telecaster (again) for '08-'16. Currently called the American Professional Telecaster.

In the late '60s and early '70s Fender began to increase their use of vibrato tailpieces. A vibrato tailpiece for this period is generally worth about 13% less than the values shown. Please refer to the Fender Guitar Intro Section for details on Fender color options. The "rare color" listing have a wide range due to the various colors included in that category.

From '63-'70, Fender offered both the standard Brazilian rosewood fretboard and an optional maple fretboard. Prices listed here, for those years, are for the rosewood 'board models. Currently, the market considers the maple 'board to be a premium, so guitars with maple, for those years, are worth 10% to 15% more than the values shown.

MODEL YEAR	FEATURES	EXC. COND. LOW	HIGH
1951	Blond, black 'guard	$38,000	$50,000
1952	Blond, black 'guard	$36,000	$47,000
1953	Blond, black 'guard	$34,000	$44,000
1954	Blond, black 'guard	$32,000	$42,000
1954	Blond, white 'guard	$24,000	$31,000
1955	Blond, white 'guard	$24,000	$31,000
1956	Blond	$24,000	$31,000
1957	Blond, backloader	$21,000	$27,000
1958	Blond, backloader	$19,300	$25,000
1958	Blond, top loader	$17,700	$23,000
1958	Sunburst, backloader	$21,000	$27,000
1958	Sunburst, top loader	$19,300	$25,000
1959	Blond, maple	$17,700	$23,000
1959	Blond, slab	$17,700	$23,000
1959	Custom color	$40,000	$55,000
1959	Sunburst, maple	$19,300	$25,000
1959	Sunburst, slab	$19,300	$25,000
1960	Blond, slab	$16,100	$20,900
1960	Common color	$25,900	$33,600
1960	Rare color	$33,600	$43,000
1960	Sunburst, slab	$18,800	$24,400
1961	Blond, slab	$15,200	$19,700
1961	Common color	$20,600	$26,800
1961	Rare color	$26,900	$34,900
1961	Sunburst, slab	$17,500	$22,700
1962	Blond, curve	$12,100	$15,700
1962	Blond, slab	$13,500	$17,500
1962	Common color	$20,600	$26,800
1962	Rare color	$26,800	$34,900
1962	Sunburst, curve	$15,700	$20,400
1962	Sunburst, slab	$16,500	$21,500
1963	Blond	$12,100	$15,700
1963	Common color	$20,600	$26,800
1963	Rare color	$26,800	$34,900
1963	Sunburst	$15,700	$20,400
1963-1964	Mahogany, see-thru cherry	$24,200	$31,400
1964	Blond	$11,100	$14,500
1964	Common color	$17,900	$23,300
1964	Rare color	$23,300	$30,200
1964	Sunburst	$13,800	$18,000
1965	Blond	$9,400	$12,200
1965	Common color	$14,300	$18,600
1965	Early '65, Sunburst	$11,400	$14,800
1965	Late '65, Sunburst	$9,400	$12,200
1965	Rare color	$18,600	$25,000

MODEL YEAR	FEATURES	EXC. COND. LOW	HIGH
1966	Blond	$7,800	$10,200
1966	Common color	$8,900	$11,600
1966	Rare color	$11,600	$16,300
1966	Sunburst	$8,600	$11,200
1967	Blond	$7,800	$10,200
1967	Blond, smuggler	$8,900	$11,600
1967	Common color	$8,900	$11,600
1967	Rare color	$12,500	$16,300
1967	Sunburst	$8,600	$11,200
1968	Blond	$6,600	$8,600
1968	Blue Flora	$14,000	$18,000
1968	Common color	$8,900	$11,600
1968	Pink Paisley	$14,000	$18,000
1968	Rare color	$11,600	$16,300
1968	Sunburst	$8,600	$11,200
1969	Blond, poly	$5,800	$7,500
1969	Blue Flora	$13,800	$17,800
1969	Common color, poly	$8,100	$10,500
1969	Pink Paisley	$13,800	$17,800
1969	Rare color, poly	$10,500	$14,900
1969	Sunburst, poly	$7,700	$10,000
1970	Blond, poly	$4,900	$6,300
1970	Common color, poly	$7,600	$9,900
1970	Rare color, poly	$9,900	$13,700
1970	Sunburst, poly	$4,900	$6,300
1971	Blond	$3,600	$4,700
1971	Common color	$5,900	$7,600
1971	Rare color	$7,600	$10,500
1971	Sunburst	$3,600	$4,700
1972	Blond	$3,100	$4,000
1972	Common color	$4,500	$5,850
1972	Natural	$2,800	$3,650
1972	Rare color	$5,850	$8,000
1972	Sunburst	$2,900	$3,800
1973	Black, white	$3,000	$3,900
1973	Blond	$3,100	$4,000
1973	Natural	$2,300	$3,000
1973	Rare color	$4,800	$7,000
1973	Sunburst	$2,725	$3,625
1973	Walnut	$2,300	$3,000
1974	Blond, black, white	$3,000	$3,900
1974	Natural	$2,300	$3,000
1974	Sunburst	$2,725	$3,625
1974	Walnut	$2,300	$3,000
1975	Blond, black, white	$2,750	$3,550
1975	Natural	$2,300	$3,000
1975	Sunburst	$2,750	$3,550
1975	Walnut	$2,300	$3,000
1976	Blond, black, white	$2,300	$3,000
1976	Natural	$2,300	$3,000
1976	Sunburst	$2,300	$3,000
1976	Walnut	$2,300	$3,000
1977	Black, blond, white	$2,300	$3,000
1977	Natural	$2,300	$3,000
1977	Sunburst	$2,300	$3,000
1977	Walnut	$2,300	$3,000
1978	Antigua	$1,950	$2,600
1978	Black, blond, white, wine	$1,950	$2,600
1978	Natural	$1,950	$2,600
1978	Sunburst	$1,950	$2,600
1978	Walnut	$1,950	$2,600
1979	Antigua	$1,950	$2,600
1979	Black, blond, white, wine	$1,950	$2,600
1979	Natural	$1,950	$2,600
1979	Sunburst	$1,950	$2,600
1979	Walnut	$1,950	$2,600
1980	Antigua	$1,900	$2,450
1980	Black, blond, white, wine	$1,900	$2,450
1980	International color	$2,350	$3,050
1980	Natural	$1,900	$2,450
1980	Sunburst	$1,900	$2,450
1981	Black and Gold	$1,900	$2,450
1981	Black, blond, white, wine	$1,900	$2,450
1981	International color	$2,350	$3,050
1981	Sunburst	$1,900	$2,450

Standard Telecaster

1982-1984. See Telecaster for '51-'82, and American Standard Telecaster (following listing) for '88-2000. Not to be confused with the current Standard Telecaster, which is made in Mexico.

1982	Blond, sunburst	$1,900	$2,450
1983-1984	Blond, sunburst	$950	$1,250

American Standard Telecaster

1988-2000, 2008-2016. Name used when Fender reissued the standard American-made Tele after CBS sold the company. The only American-made Tele available for '86 and '87 was the '52 Telecaster. See Telecaster for '51-'81, and Standard Telecaster for '82-'84. All '94 models have a metal 40th Anniversary pin on the headstock, but should not be confused with the actual 40th Anniversary Telecaster model (see separate listing), all standard colors. Renamed the American Series Telecaster in 2000, then back to American Standard Series Telecaster in '08. Becomes American Professional in '17.

1988-2000		$850	$1,100
2008-2016		$800	$1,050

American Series Telecaster

2000-2007. See Telecaster for '51-'81, Standard Telecaster for '82-'84, and American Standard for '88-'99. Renamed American Standard again in '08.

2000-2007		$800	$1,050

American Professional/Professional II Telecaster

2017-present. Model replaces American Standard Tele, redesign includes 2 V-Mod pickups, narrow-tall frets, new 'deep C' neck profile, various colors. Also available left-hand model. Renamed American Professional II in '20.

2017-2020	Pro	$800	$1,050
2020-2021	Pro II	$900	$1,150

30th Anniversary Guitar Center Tree of Life Telecaster

1994. Limited Edition, produced for 30th anniversary of Guitar Center, engraved neckplate with GC logo, tree-of-life 'board inlay.

1994		$4,000	$5,200

1972 Fender Telecaster

John Hosford

1978 Fender Telecaster

Robbie Keene

GUITARS

1982 Fender American Vintage '52 Telecaster

Billy White Jr.

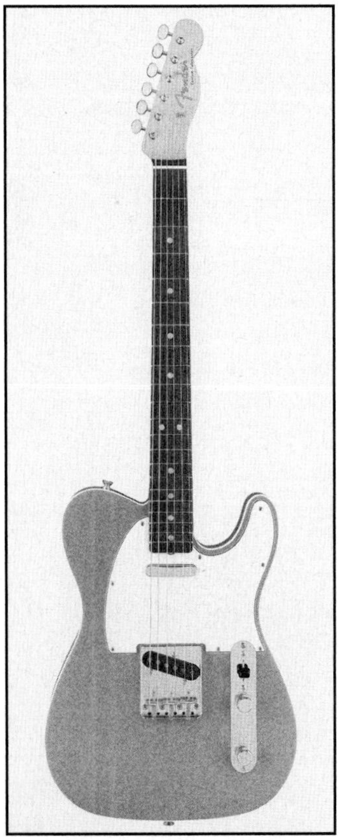

Fender American Original '60s Telecaster

MODEL YEAR	FEATURES	EXC. COND. LOW	HIGH

40th Anniversary Telecaster

1988, 1999. Custom Shop model limited edition run of 300, 2-piece flamed maple top, gold hardware ('88), flamed maple top over ash body, gold hardware ('99).

1988	1st run, high-end	$4,100	$5,300
1999	2nd run, plain top	$3,100	$4,100

'50 Custom Telecaster

1997. Custom Shop, limited run of 10, humbucker neck pickup, standard unbound body, highly figured maple neck, blackguard specs.

1997		$1,975	$2,525

'50s Telecaster/Classic Series '50s Telecaster

1990-2019. Made in Japan (basswood body) until mid '99, then in Mexico with ash body. Foto-Flame finish offered in '94 (see separate listing).

1990-1999	Japan	$675	$875
1999-2019	Mexico	$475	$625

Road Worn '50s Telecaster

2009-2019. Maple 'board, '50s specs, aged finish.

2009-2019		$625	$825

50th Anniversary Spanish Guitar Set Custom Shop

1996. 50 sets made, Tele Prototype reproduction with similar era copy of woodie amp.

1996		$4,100	$5,300

50th Anniversary Telecaster

1995-1996. Custom Shop, flame maple top, 2 vintage-style pickups, gold hardware, sunburst, gold 50th Anniversary coin on back of the headstock, 1250 made.

1995-1996		$1,300	$1,675

'52 Telecaster/American Vintage '52 Telecaster

1982-1984, 1986-2017. Ash body, maple neck or rosewood 'board, blond. Replaced by the American Original '50s Telecaster.

1982-1984		$1,975	$2,575
1986-1999		$1,550	$2,000
1990-1999	Copper (limited)	$1,550	$2,000
2000-2009		$1,450	$1,900
2010-2017		$1,225	$1,600

American Vintage '52 Telecaster Korina (U.S.A.)

2015. Part of Fender's limited edition 10 for 15 series, Korina body, '52 specs.

2015		$1,425	$1,850

'52 Telecaster (Custom Shop)

2004-2018. Custom Shop Dealer Select model, NOS, Relic and Closet Classic offered, changed to Heavy Relic in '15.

2004-2012	NOS	$1,950	$2,525
2004-2014	Relic	$2,075	$2,700
2010-2011	Closet Classic	$1,950	$2,525
2015-2018	Heavy relic	$2,250	$2,950

'52 LTD Telecaster NOS

2020. Custom Shop, ash body, maple neck, faded blonde, lacquer finish.

2020		$1,800	$2,350

'52 Vintage Telecaster (Japan)

1982-1984. Made in Japan, JV serial numbers.

1982-1984		$1,400	$1,800

MODEL YEAR	FEATURES	EXC. COND. LOW	HIGH

'54 Telecaster (Custom Shop)

1997-1998, 2013-2016. Relic, Closet Classic available with more recent model.

2013-2016	Relic	$2,075	$2,700

'58 Telecaster (Custom Shop)

2008. Custom Shop, relic and heavy relic.

2008	Heavy relic	$2,250	$2,950
2008	NOS	$1,950	$2,525
2008	Relic	$2,075	$2,700

American Vintage '58 Telecaster (U.S.A.)

2013-2018. Ash body, white 'guard, Aged White Blonde.

2013-2018		$1,225	$1,600

'60s Telecaster Custom

1997-1999. Custom Shop, bound alder body, sunburst, black or custom colors, nickel or gold hardware.

1997-1999		$2,075	$2,700

'60s Telecaster/Classic Series '60s Telecaster

1992-2019. Made in Japan (basswood body) until mid '99, then in Mexico with ash body. Foto-Flame finish offered in '94 (see separate listing). '06 version may have 60th Anniversary Badge on back of headstock.

1992-1996	Made in Japan	$675	$875
1997-1999	Crafted in Japan	$575	$750
1999-2019	Mexico	$475	$625

American Original '60s Telecaster

2018-present. '60s specs, rosewood 'board, alder body.

2018-2020		$1,150	$1,500

'60 Telecaster Custom

2003-2004. Custom Shop Time Machine, bound alder body, offered in NOS, Closet Classic and Relic versions and in sunburst, CA Red and Sonic Blue.

2003-2004	Closet Classic	$1,950	$2,525
2003-2004	NOS	$1,950	$2,525
2003-2004	Relic	$2,075	$2,700

60th Anniversary American Telecaster

2006-2007. Special Edition commemorating Fender's 60th year, banner headstock 60th logo, neck plate reads Diamond Anniversary 1946-2006, made in U.S.A., rosewood 'board, sunburst.

2006-2007		$1,025	$1,350

60th Anniversary Telecaster (U.S.A.)

2011-2012. Celebrating 60 years of the Tele, commemorative chrome neck plate, ash body, blonde thin-skin finish.

2011-2012		$1,025	$1,350

60th Anniversary Telecaster Limited Edition

2006. Limited Edition of 1,000, 60 Diamond Anniversary 1946-2006 logo engraved in neck plate, American Flag logo on pickguard, '51 NoCaster pickup layout, 60 wood inlay on the face below bridge, clear nitro finish on natural ash body, silver guitar case with Fender 60 logo on inside lid.

2006		$1,525	$2,000

'61 Telecaster Custom

2010-2012. Custom Shop Dealer Select model, bound body Custom, NOS, Relic or Heavy Relic.

2010-2012	Closet Classic	$1,950	$2,525
2010-2012	NOS	$1,950	$2,525
2010-2012	Relic	$2,075	$2,700

MODEL YEAR	FEATURES	EXC. COND. LOW	HIGH

'62 Telecaster Custom (Import)

1985-1999. Made in Japan, bound top and back, rosewood 'board, sunburst or red.

1985-1989		$1,050	$1,375
1990-1999		$925	$1,200

'62 Telecaster Custom (U.S.A.)

1999-2012. American Vintage Series, rosewood board.

1999-2012		$1,000	$1,300

'62 Mod Squad Custom Telecaster

2013. Custom Shop, Broadcaster bridge pickup and Duncan neck humbucker.

2013		$2,500	$3,200

'62 Telecaster Reissue (Japan)

1989-1990, 2005-2006. Made by Fender Japan.

1989-1990		$1,100	$1,425
2005-2006		$950	$1,250

Junkyard Dog 1962 Telecaster Relic

2014-2015. Custom Shop Dealer Select series, ash body, rosewood neck and 'board, white guard, Vintage Blonde.

2014-2015		$2,200	$2,850

'63 Telecaster (Custom Shop)

1999-2010, 2018-2019. Alder body (or blond on ash), original spec pickups, C-shaped neck, rosewood 'board. Relic offered in '07 and later heavy relic in '18.

1999-2010	Closet Classic	$1,950	$2,525
1999-2010	NOS	$1,950	$2,525
2007	Relic	$2,075	$2,700
2018-2019	Heavy relic	$2,250	$2,950

'63 Telecaster Custom Relic LTD

2006. Custom Shop, Limited Edition.

2006		$2,075	$2,700

'64 Telecaster Limited Relic

2009. Custom Shop, rosewood 'board, thin nitro finish, 50 each of black, aged white, and 3-tone chocolate sunburst.

2009		$2,075	$2,700

American Vintage '64 Telecaster

2013-2018. Ash body, mid-'60s 'C' neck profile, rounded rosewood 'board, 2 vintage single-coil pickups, White Blonde.

2013-2018		$1,225	$1,600

'67 Telecaster (Custom Shop)

2005-2008, 2010-2011. Alder body, rosewood or maple 'board, Relic, NOS or Closet Classic, 2010 and later is rosewood 'board, Relic or NOS.

2005-2008	Closet Classic	$1,950	$2,525
2005-2011	NOS	$1,950	$2,525
2005-2011	Relic	$2,075	$2,700

'68 Telecaster Rosewood

Custom Shop, rosewood body.

2007	NOS	$1,950	$2,525

'69 Tele/Telecaster Thinline (Import)

1986-2015. Import, Classic Series, 2 Tele pickups.

1986-1996		$825	$1,100
1997-1999		$675	$900
2000-2015		$575	$750

'69 Telecaster Thinline (Custom Shop)

2005-2006. Semi-hollow mahoganhy body, maple neck with maple 'board.

2005-2006		$1,950	$2,525

MODEL YEAR	FEATURES	EXC. COND. LOW	HIGH

'72 Telecaster Custom/Classic Series '72 Telecaster Custom

1986-2019. Import, 1 humbucker and 1 single-coil, 2 humbuckers after '99.

1986-1989	Japan	$1,050	$1,375
1990-1999	Japan	$925	$1,200
2000-2019	Mexico	$475	$625

'72 Telecaster Deluxe/Classic Series '72 Telecaster Deluxe

2004-2019. Made in Mexico, alder body, large Deluxe 'guard, 2 humbuckers.

2004-2019		$390	$500

'72 Telecaster Thinline American Vintage

2012-2013. US-made, American Vintage FSR model, f-hole, 2 humbuckers.

2012-2013		$1,125	$1,450

'72 Telecaster Thinline/Classic Series Telecaster Thinline

1986-2019. Import, 2 humbuckers, f-hole.

1986-1999	Japan	$875	$1,150
2000-2019	Mexico	$475	$625

1972 Telecaster Custom Closet Classic (CS)

2013. Custom Shop, ash body, maple neck and 'board, 2 pickups, black finish.

2013		$1,950	$2,525

75th Anniversary Commemorative Telecaster

2021. US-made, limited edition, inlaid 75th Anniversary ingot back of headstock, gold hardware, 2-color Bourbon Burst gloss finish. Includes custom Inca Silver case with Lake Placid Blue interior.

2021		$1,075	$1,400

75th Anniversary Telecaster

2021. Made in Mexico, 75th Anniversary neck plate, Diamond Anniversary satin finish with matching painted headstock.

2021		$475	$625

'90s Telecaster Deluxe

1995-1998. Import, 1 Tele-style bridge pickup and 2 Strat-style pickups, rosewood 'board, Foto Flame '95-'97 and standard finishes '97-'98.

1995-1997	Foto-Flame	$625	$800
1997-1998	Standard finish	$625	$800

'90s Telecaster Thinline

1998-2001. Bound semi-hollow ash body, f-hole, white or brown shell 'guard, 2 single-coils, sunburst, black, natural, or transparent crimson.

1998-2001		$1,525	$2,000

1998 Collectors Edition Telecaster

1998. 1,998 made, 1998 logo inlay on 'board, maple, gold hardware.

1998		$1,050	$1,375

Aerodyne Telecaster

2004-2009. Imported Tele with Aerodyne body profile, bound body, black.

2004-2009		$575	$750

Albert Collins Telecaster

1990-2018. Custom Shop signature model, bound swamp ash body, humbucker pickup in neck position, natural or silver sparkle.

1990-2018		$2,300	$2,975

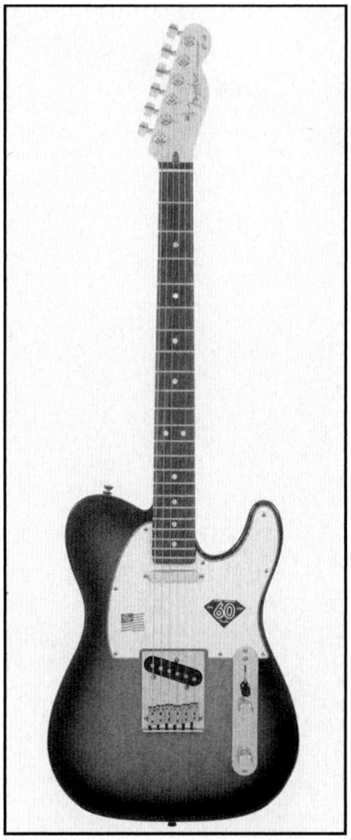

2006 Fender 60th Anniversary Telecaster Limited Edition

Imaged by Heritage Auctions, HA.com

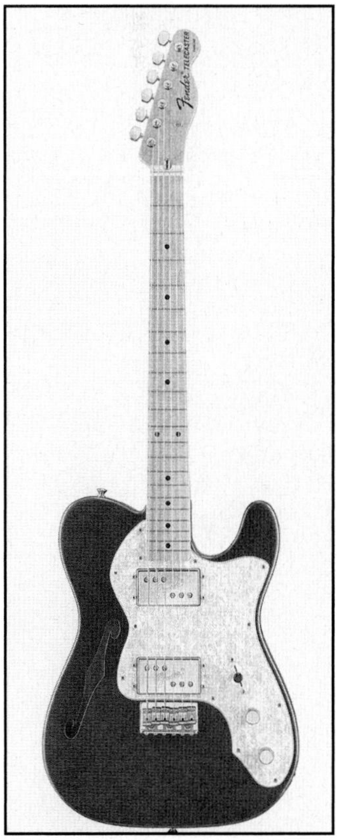

Fender '72 Telecaster Thinline American Vintage

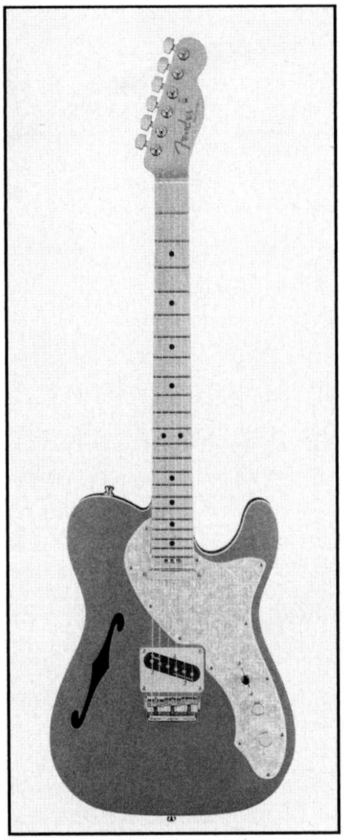

2017 Fender American Elite Telecaster Thinline

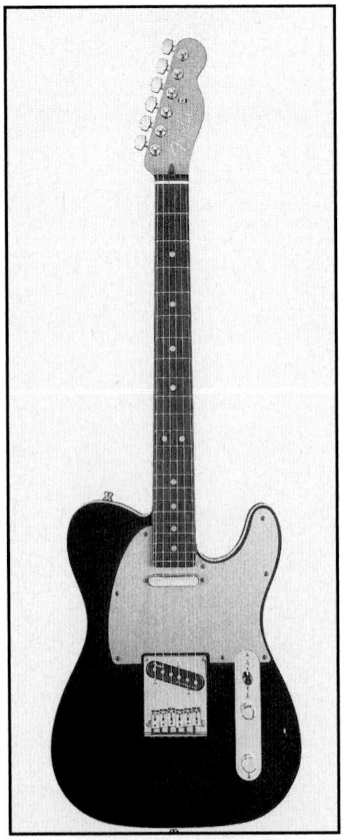

Fender American Ultra Telecaster

MODEL YEAR	FEATURES	EXC. COND. LOW	HIGH

Aluminum Telecaster

1994-1995. Aluminum-bodied American Standard with anodized finish in blue marble, purple marble or red, silver and blue stars and stripes.

1994-1995	Marble patterns	$1,700	$2,200
1994-1995	Red-silver-blue flag option	$1,700	$2,200

American Acoustasonic Telecaster

2019-present. Solid A sitka spruce top, mahogany back, sides and neck, various colors.

2019-2020		$1,050	$1,400

American Classic Holoflake Telecaster

1996-1999. Custom Shop model, splatter/sparkle finish, pearloid 'guard.

1996-1999		$2,100	$2,700

American Classic Telecaster

1996-1999. Custom Shop model, handcrafted version of American Standard, thin lacquer-finished ash body, maple or rosewood 'board, various options and colors, earlier versions had gold hardware and custom-color options.

1996-1999		$2,100	$2,700

American Deluxe HH Telecaster

2004-2006. Rosewood, maple top, 2 humbucker pickups.

2004-2006		$975	$1,250

American Deluxe Power Telecaster

1999-2001. Made in USA, with Fishman power bridge piezo pickups.

1999-2001		$975	$1,250

American Deluxe Telecaster

1998-2017. Premium ash or alder body with see-thru finishes.

1998-2017		$975	$1,250

American Deluxe/Elite Telecaster Thinline

2015-2019. Single-cut semi-hollow ash body, f-hole, maple neck and 'board, 2 single-coil pickups, various colors.

2015-2019		$1,075	$1,400

American Elite Telecaster

2016-2020. Single-cut, alder body, maple neck, rosewood 'board, 2 single-coil pickups, various colors.

2016-2020		$1,050	$1,350

American Nashville B-Bender Telecaster

1998-2015. US-made, alder body, added Texas Special Strat pickup in middle position, white pearloid 'guard, Parsons-Fender B-string bender, 5-way switch.

1998-2015		$1,400	$1,800

American Performer Telecaster

Introduced Dec. 2018-present. Made in US, new features include Yosemite single-coil pickups, Grease-bucket tone system, various colors.

2018-2020		$675	$875

American Professional II Telecaster Deluxe

2020-present. Alder body, maple neck, 2 humbucking pickups, various colors with gloss finish.

2020		$850	$1,100

American Professional Telecaster Deluxe Shawbucker

2017-2018. With 2 ShawBucker humbucking pickups, various colors.

2017-2018		$925	$1,225

American Special Telecaster

2010-2018. Alder body, gloss finish, Texas Special pickups.

2010-2018		$650	$850

American Standard Telecaster Limited Edition

1990s-2019. American Standard series, various limited edition models.

1995-1997	B-Bender	$1,300	$1,700
2009	Matching hdstk	$1,050	$1,350
2014-2015	Channel Bound	$850	$1,100
2015-2016	HH	$850	$1,100

American Standard Telecaster Special Edition

2009. Surf Green, Fiesta Red or Daphne Blue with matching headstock.

2009		$1,075	$1,400

American Ultra Luxe Telecaster

2021-present. 2 Noiseless single-coil or Floyd Rose with 2 humbucker, 2-color sunburst, trans Surf Green or black.

2021	Floyd Rose HH	$1,325	$1,725
2021	SS	$1,275	$1,650

American Ultra Telecaster

2019-present. Alder or ash body, upgrades include 2 Ultra Noiseless Vintage Tele single-coil pickups and 7 new colors with gloss poly finish.

2019-2020		$1,100	$1,450

Andy Summers Masterbuilt Tribute Telecaster

2009. Custom shop, based on Summer's '61 Tele, heavy relic, 250 made, custom electronics rear-mounted overdrive unit controlled by a third knob, includes DVD, strap and Andy Summer's logo travel guitar case.

2009		$5,300	$6,900

Antigua Telecaster

2004. Made in Japan, limited edition (400 made) reissue, '70s features and antigua finish.

2004		$700	$900

Big Block Telecaster

2005-2006. Pearloid block markers, black with matching headstock, 3 single-coils with center pickup reverse wound.

2005-2006		$550	$725

Bigsby Telecaster

2003. Made in Mexico, standard Tele specs with original Fender-logo Bigsby tailpiece.

2003		$550	$725

Blacktop Telecaster Series

2012-2015. Includes 2 humbucker HH and hum-single-single Baritone.

2012-2015	Various models	$475	$625

Blue Flower Telecaster

1985-1993, 2003-2004. Import, Blue Flower finish.

1985-1993	1st issue	$700	$900
2003-2004	2nd issue	$525	$700

MODEL YEAR	FEATURES	EXC. COND. LOW	HIGH

Bowling Ball/Marble Telecaster

1984. Standard Tele, called Bowling Ball Tele due to the swirling color, blue, red or yellow.

1984		$3,000	$4,000

Britt Daniel Telecaster Thinline

2019-present. Ash body, maple neck, 2 single-coil pickups, Amarillo Gold lacquer finish.

2019-2020		$1,100	$1,425

Brown's Canyon Redwood Telecaster

2011. For Fender's 60th anniversary in 2011, they released 12 limited edition U.S.-made Tele-bration Telecasters, including this one with body made from 1890s California redwood.

2011		$1,275	$1,650

Buck Owens Limited Edition Telecaster

1998-1999. Red, white and blue sparkle finish, 250 made, gold hardware, gold 'guard, rosewood 'board.

1998-1999		$1,450	$1,900

Cabronita Telecaster (American Standard)

2011. For Fender's 60th anniversary in 2011, American Standard series, they released 12 limited edition U.S.-made Tele-bration Telecasters, including this one with 2 TV Jones Filter'Trons.

2011		$925	$1,200

Cabronita Telecaster (Classic Player)

2014-2015. Mexico version, Classic Player series.

2014-2015		$350	$455

Cabronita Telecaster Thinline

2012-2013. Made in Mexico, ash body, maple neck, 2 Fideli'Tron humbucking pickups, 2-Color Sunburst, Shoreline Gold or White Blonde.

2012-2013		$600	$775

California Fat Telecaster

1997-1998. Alder body, maple fretboard, Tex-Mex humbucker and Tele pickup configuration.

1997-1998		$560	$725

California Telecaster

1997-1998. Alder body, maple fretboard, sunburst, Tex-Mex Strat and Tele pickup configuration.

1997-1998		$560	$725

Chambered Mahogany Telecaster

2006. U.S.-made, chambered mahogany body, Delta Tone System.

2006		$900	$1,175

Chrissie Hynde Telecaster

2021. Alder body with Faded Ice Blue Metallic Road Worn finish, chrome mirror 'guard.

2021		$775	$1,000

Clarence White Telecaster (Custom Shop)

1994-2000. Parsons-White B-Bender and Scruggs-style tuners on both E strings, sunburst.

1994-2000		$6,500	$8,500

Classic Player Baja Telecaster

2007-2019. Made in Mexico, Custom Shop designed neck plate logo, thin gloss poly blond finish.

2007-2019		$575	$750

Collector's Edition Telecaster

1998. Mid-1955 specs including white 'guard, offered in sunburst with gold hardware (which was an option in '55), 1,998 made.

1998		$1,100	$1,450

Contemporary Telecaster (Import)

1985-1987. Japanese-made while the new Fender reorganized, 2 or 3 pickups, vibrato, black chrome hardware, rosewood 'board.

1985-1987		$600	$775

Custom Carved Telecaster HH

2013. Figured maple top, carved back, 2 humbucking pickups.

2013		$1,600	$2,100

Custom Classic Telecaster

2000-2008. Custom Shop, maple or rosewood 'board, certificate of authenticity.

2000-2008		$2,150	$2,800

Custom Deluxe Telecaster

2009-2014. Custom Shop model, ash body, AA birdseye maple neck, rosewood or maple 'board, abalone dot inlays, 2 pickups, certificate, black Bakelite 'guard, Aged White Blonde, Dakota Red or faded 2-color sunburst.

2009-2014		$2,500	$3,300

Custom Telecaster

1972-1981. One humbucking and 1 Tele pickup, standard colors, see Telecaster Custom for 2 Tele pickup/bound body version.

1972		$2,800	$3,600
1973-1974		$2,600	$3,400
1975-1977		$2,300	$3,000
1978-1979		$1,950	$2,600
1980-1981		$1,900	$2,450

Danny Gatton Signature Telecaster

1990-2018. Custom Shop, like '53 Telecaster, maple neck, 2 humbuckers.

1990-1999	Frost Gold	$2,800	$3,700
2000-2018	Various colors	$1,825	$2,400

Deluxe Nashville Power Telecaster

1999-2014. Like Deluxe Nashville, but with piezo transducer in each saddle.

1999-2014		$470	$615

Deluxe Nashville Telecaster (Mexico)

1997-present. Tex-Mex Strat and Tele pickup configuration, various colors.

1997-2020		$470	$615

Deluxe Telecaster (U.S.A.)

1972-1981. Two humbuckers, various colors. Mexican-made version offered starting in 2004.

1972	Common color	$2,900	$3,800
1972	Less common color	$3,500	$4,800
1973-1974	Common color	$2,725	$3,625
1973-1974	Less common color	$3,300	$4,600
1975	Common color	$2,300	$3,000
1975	Less common color	$2,900	$4,000
1976-1977	Common color	$2,300	$3,000
1978-1979	Common color	$1,950	$2,600
1980-1981	Common color	$1,900	$2,450

Elite Nashville Telecaster

Limited Edition, ash body, 3 pickups, Antique Cherry Burst.

2016		$1,400	$1,800

Fender Antigua Telecaster

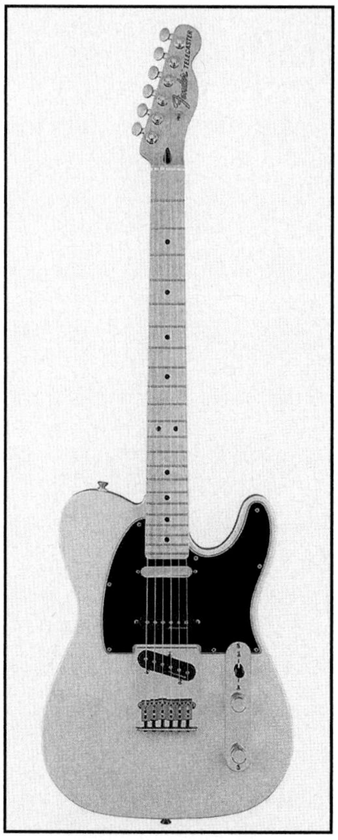

Fender Deluxe Nashville Telecaster (Mexico)

2008 Fender G.E. Smith Telecaster

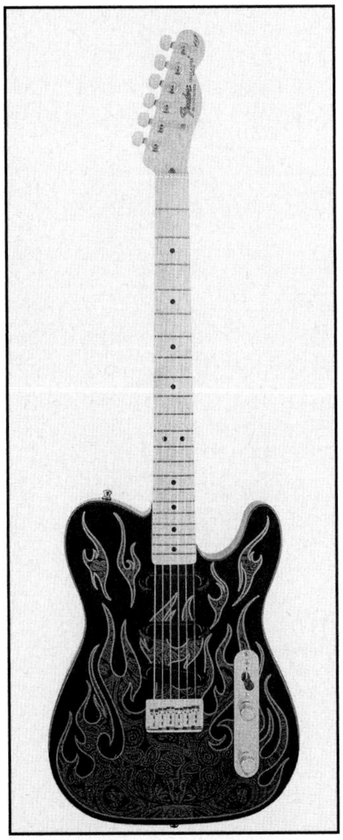

Fender James Burton Telecaster

MODEL YEAR	FEATURES	EXC. COND. LOW	HIGH

Elite Telecaster

1983-1985. Two active humbucker pickups, 3-way switch, 2 volume knobs, 1 presence and filter controls, chrome hardware, various colors.

1983-1985		$1,750	$2,300

Fat Telecaster

1999-2001. Humbucker pickup in neck, Tele bridge pickup.

1999-2001		$560	$725

Foto Flame Telecaster

1994-1996. Import, sunburst or transparent.

1994-1996		$625	$800

G.E. Smith Telecaster

2007-2014. Swamp ash body, vintage style hardware, U-shaped neck, oval and diamond inlays.

2007-2014		$1,050	$1,350

Graham Coxon Special Run Telecaster

2011, 2013-2014. Blond, Tele bridge and humbucker neck pickup, rosewood 'board, limited run in 2011.

2011-2014		$950	$1,225

Highway One Telecaster/Texas Telecaster

2003-2011. U.S.-made, alder body, satin lacquer finish, Texas version (introduced in '04) has ash body and Hot Vintage pickups.

2003-2011		$575	$750

HMT Telecaster (Import)

1990-1993. Japanese-made Heavy Metal Tele, available with or without Floyd Rose tremolo, 1 Fender Lace Sensor pickup and 1 DiMarzio bridge humbucker pickup, black.

1990-1993		$350	$455

J5 Triple Telecaster Deluxe

2007-2017. John 5 model, made in Mexico, 3 humbuckers, medium jumbo frets.

2007-2017		$600	$800

James Burton Standard Telecaster

1995-2016. Mexico, 2 Texas Special Tele pickups, standard colors (no paisley).

1995-2016		$500	$650

James Burton Telecaster

1990-present. Ash body, 3 Fender Lace pickups, available in black with Gold Paisley, black with Candy Red Paisley, Pearl White, and Frost Red until '05. In '06 in black with red or blue flame-shaped paisley, or Pearl White.

1990-2005	Black & gold paisley, gold hw	$1,750	$2,300
1990-2005	Black & red paisley, black hw	$1,450	$1,900
1990-2010	Frost Red or Pearl White	$950	$1,225
1994	Blue Paisley, gold hw	$1,400	$1,800
2006-2020	Paisley flames	$950	$1,225

Jason Isbell Custom Telecaster

2021. Double-bound body, aged hardware, Road Worn Chocolate Sunburst with lacquer finish.

2021		$825	$1,075

MODEL YEAR	FEATURES	EXC. COND. LOW	HIGH

Jerry Donahue JD Telecaster

1993-1999. Made in Japan, Custom Strat neck pickup and Custom Tele bridge pickup, basswood body, special "V" shaped maple neck.

1993-1999		$1,050	$1,350

Jerry Donahue Telecaster

1992-2001. Custom Shop model designed by Donahue, Tele bridge pickup and Strat neck pickup, birdseye maple neck, top and back, gold hardware, passive circuitry, sunburst, transparent Crimson Red or Sapphire Blue. There was also a Japanese-made JD Telecaster.

1992-2001	Various colors	$1,825	$2,400

Jim Adkins JA-90 Telecaster Thinline

2008-present. Rosewood 'board, vintage-style P-90 soapbars.

2008-2020		$475	$625

Jim Root Telecaster

2007-present. Made in Mexico, black hardware, mahogany body.

2007-2020		$600	$800

Jimmy Bryant Tribute Telecaster

2004-2005. Custom Shop model, hand-tooled leather 'guard overlay with JB initials.

2004-2005		$2,100	$2,700

Jimmy Page Mirror Telecaster

2019-present. Ash body with white blonde lacquer finish, rosewood 'board, 2 single-coil pickups, vintage-style tweed case, shipped with 8 round mirrors.

2019-2020		$1,525	$2,000

Jimmy Page Telecaster

2020-present. Ash body with gloss finish over Page's artwork, maple neck with Road Worn nitro finish, rosewood 'board, also shipped with 8 round mirrors.

2020		$775	$1,000

Joe Strummer Telecaster

2007-2009. Limited edition, heavily relic'd based on Strummer's '66 Tele, Fender offered a limited edition art customization kit as part of the package.

2007	Limited Edition	$825	$1,075
2007-2009	Standard edition	$825	$1,075

John Jorgenson Telecaster

1998-2001. Custom Shop, korina body, double-coil stacked pickups, sparkle or black finish.

1998-2001	Sparkle	$2,100	$2,800

Jr. Telecaster

1994, 1997-2000. Custom Shop, transparent blond ash body, 2 P-90-style pickups, set neck, 11 tone chambers, 100 made in '94, reintroduced in '97.

1994		$2,200	$2,850
1997-2000		$2,200	$2,850

La Cabronita Especial Telecaster

2009-2010. Custom Shop relics, 1 or 2 TV Jones pickups. In '09, 10 each with 1 pickup in black or Shoreline Gold and 20 each with 2 pickups in black or Shoreline Gold. In '10, 10 each with 1 pickup in Candy Apple Red or Sonic Blue and 20 each with 2 pickups in Candy Apple Red or Sonic Blue.

2009-2010	Various colors	$3,075	$4,000

MODEL YEAR	FEATURES	EXC. COND. LOW	HIGH

Mahogany Offset Telecaster
2020. Made in Japan series, mahogany body and neck, rosewood 'board, 2 pickups, natural finish.

2020		$500	$650

Masterbuilt Custom Shop Telecaster
2006-present. Various models and builders, specific identification to builder, must include certificate of authenticity.

2006-2020	Various models	$2,900	$6,300

Matched Set Telecaster
1994. Matching Tele and Strat Custom Shop models, model name on certificate is "Matched Set Telecaster", 3 sets were built, each set has serial number 1, 2, or 3.

1994		$3,800	$5,000

Merle Haggard Signature Telecaster
2009-2018. Custom Shop, figured maple body and neck, maple 'board, 2-color sunburst.

2009-2018		$2,600	$3,400

Mod Shop Telecaster
2017-present. Mod Shop allows you to create your own factory-customized electric guitar or bass.

2017-2020		$1,525	$2,000

Modern Player Telecaster Plus
2012-2018. Import, pine body, maple neck, HSS pickups, Honey Burst or Trans Charcoal.

2012-2018		$365	$475

Moto Limited Edition Telecaster
1990s. Custom Shop model, pearloid cover in various colors. There were also Strat and Jag versions.

1990s		$2,300	$3,000

Muddy Waters Signature Telecaster Custom
2001-2009. Mexico, Fender amp control knobs, Telecaster Custom on headstock, Muddy Waters signature logo on neck plate, Candy Apple Red.

2001-2009		$625	$825

Muddy Waters Tribute Telecaster
2000. Custom Shop, 100 made, Fender amp control knobs, rosewood 'board, relic Candy Apple Red finish, certificate of authenticity.

2000		$2,525	$3,325

Nashville Telecaster
1995. Custom Shop model, 3 pickups.

1995		$1,750	$2,250

NHL Premier Edition Telecaster
1999-2000. Limited edition of 100 guitars with NHL hockey art logo on the top.

1999-2000	All models	$825	$1,100

Nokie Edwards Telecaster
1996. Made in Japan, limited edition, book matched flamed top, multi-lam neck, Seymour Duncan pickups, gold hardware, zero fret, tilted headstock.

1996		$1,250	$1,650

Noventa Telecaster
2021. Alder body, maple neck, maple or pau ferro 'board, single-coil pickup, 2-Color Sunburst, Fiesta Red or Vintage Blonde.

2021		$525	$700

MODEL YEAR	FEATURES	EXC. COND. LOW	HIGH

Old Pine Telecaster
2011. For Fender's 60th anniversary in 2011, they released 12 limited edition U.S.-made Tele-bration Telecasters, including this one with 100-year-old pine body, 300 made.

2011		$1,200	$1,575

Paisley Telecaster
1986-1998, 2003-2004, 2008. Import, 'Made in Japan' logo used until '98, 'Crafted in Japan' after, Pink Paisley finish.

1986-1994		$700	$900
1995-1998		$625	$825
2003-2004		$525	$700
2008	600 made	$525	$700

Palo Escrito Telecaster
2006-2007. Mexico, Classic Series, palo escrito is tonewood from Mexico with unique grain patterns, natural finish.

2006-2007		$625	$825

Parallel Universe Jazz-Tele
June 2018. Parallel Universe series, limited edition, Tele body, 2 Jazzmaster single-coil pickups, 2-Color Sunburst or Surf Green.

2018		$1,225	$1,600

Parallel Universe Troublemaker Telecaster
July 2018. Parallel Universe series, limited edition, mahogany body, maple top, custom Cabronita 'guard, 2 ShawBucker (1T and 2T) humbucking pickups. Bigsby optional.

2018		$1,325	$1,725
2018	with Bigsby	$1,275	$1,650

Parallel Universe Volume II Tele Mágico
2020-present. Parallel Universe Volume II series, limited edition, ash body, flame maple neck and 'board, Daphane Blue or Surf Green.

2020-2021		$1,400	$1,825

Player Telecaster
2018-present. Alder body, maple neck, 2 SS or HH pickups, various colors with gloss finish.

2018-2020		$365	$475

Plus Telecaster
1994-1997. Lace Sensor pickups, various colors.

1994-1997		$1,600	$2,100

Rarities Telecaster
2019-2020. Rarities Collection series, limited edition, models include; Flame Maple Top, Quilt Maple Top, Red Mahogany Top.

2019-2020		$1,400	$1,800

Richie Kotzen Telecaster
2017-present. Ash body, bound flame maple top, 2 DiMarzio pickups, gold hardware, signature on headstock.

2017-2020		$800	$1,050

Rosewood Telecaster
1969-1972. Rosewood body and neck.

1969-1972		$10,500	$13,500

Rosewood Telecaster (Japan)
1986-1996. Japanese-made reissue, rosewood body and neck.

1986-1996		$1,750	$2,300

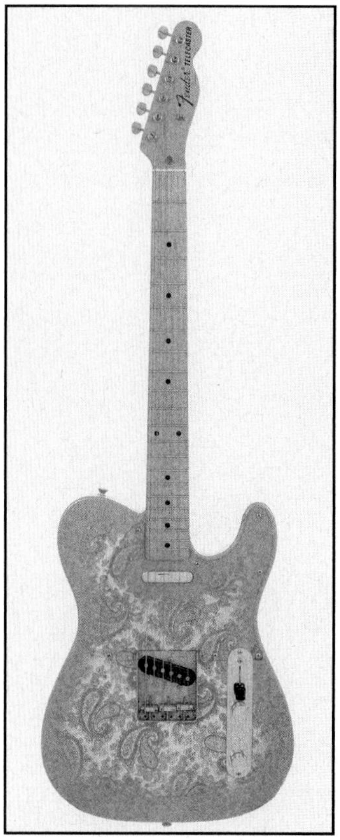

1986 Fender Paisley Telecaster

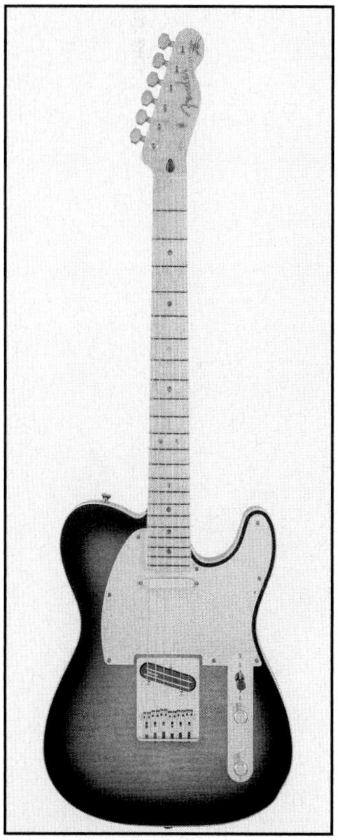

Fender Richie Kotzen Telecaster

Fender Telecaster Custom

1974 Fender Telecaster Thinline

MODEL YEAR	FEATURES	EXC. COND. LOW	HIGH

Rosewood Telelcaster Limited Edition

2014. Custom Shop, Limited Edition neck plate, based on George Harrison's rosewood Tele.

2014		$3,175	$4,150

Select Telecaster

2012-2013. Select Series, figured maple top, rear-headstock 'Fender Select' medallion, gloss-lacquer finish, chrome or gold hardware.

2012-2013		$1,625	$2,100

Select Telecaster Thinline

2012-2013. Select Series, figured maple top, rear-headstock 'Fender Select' medallion, gloss-lacquer finish, chrome or gold hardware.

2012-2013		$1,625	$2,100

Set-Neck Telecaster

1990-1996. Glued-in neck, Custom Shop, 2 humbucking pickups, Set-Neck CA (Country Artist) has 1 humbucker and 1 Tele pickup, various colors.

1990-1996		$1,750	$2,300

Snakehead Telecaster (Custom Shop)

Custom Shop Limited Edition, 45 offered.

2010		$3,900	$5,100

Sparkle Telecaster

1993-1995. Custom Shop model, poplar body, white 'guard, sparkle finish: champagne, gold, silver.

1993-1995		$1,675	$2,175

Special Edition Custom Telecaster FMT HH

2020-present. Mahogany body with carved flame maple top, 2 Seymour Duncan pickups, various colors with matching headstock.

2020		$400	$525

Special Edition Deluxe Ash Telecaster

2009-2016. Mexico, butterscotch finish, ash body, 1-piece maple neck.

2009-2016		$350	$455

Special Edition Koa Telecaster

2006-2008. Made in Korea, standard Tele specs, koa veneer top over basswood body, pearloid 'guard, sunburst.

2006-2008		$350	$455

Special Edition White Opal Telecaster

2016. Made in Mexico, white opal body and headstock, pearloid 'guard.

2016		$350	$455

Special Telecaster/Telecaster Special

2004-2008. Made in Mexico, Special Edition logo with star logo sticker on back of headstock, special features like 6-way bridge and modern tuners.

2004-2008		$385	$500

Standard Telecaster (Japan)

1985-1989. In '85, the only Teles were interim production in Japan while the new Fender reorganized, no serial number, Japan headstock logo in '85, back of neck '86-'89.

1985-1989		$725	$950

Standard Telecaster (Mexico)

1990-2018. Guitar production at the Mexico facility started in '90. High end of range includes a hard guitar case, while the low end of the range includes only a gig bag, various colors. Replaced by Player Series.

1990-2018		$350	$455

MODEL YEAR	FEATURES	EXC. COND. LOW	HIGH

Telecaster (Japanese Domestic)

1982-1997. Made in Japan for Japanese domestic market (not for export), suffix serial numbers JV5 ('82-'84) and A6 through V6 ('84-'97).

1982-1984	JV serial	$1,000	$1,300
1985-1989		$950	$1,250
1990-1997		$675	$875

Telecaster Custom

1959-1972. Body bound top and back, rosewood 'board, 2 Tele pickups, see Custom Telecaster for the 1 Tele/1 humbucker version. Please refer to the Fender Guitar Intro Section for details on Fender color options.

1959	Sunburst, maple	$22,700	$29,500
1960	Custom color	$34,000	$44,300
1960	Sunburst	$23,500	$30,500
1961	Custom color	$33,300	$43,200
1961	Sunburst	$22,600	$29,400
1962	Custom color	$30,800	$40,000
1962	Sunburst, curve	$20,100	$26,100
1962	Sunburst, slab	$21,000	$27,200
1963	Custom color	$28,200	$39,000
1963	Sunburst	$20,000	$26,000
1964	Custom color	$24,000	$31,100
1964	Sunburst	$17,600	$22,800
1965	Custom color	$22,300	$28,900
1965	Sunburst	$14,600	$19,000
1966	Custom color	$18,000	$23,300
1966	Sunburst	$11,100	$14,400
1967	Custom color	$14,600	$19,000
1967	Sunburst	$11,100	$14,400
1968	Custom color	$14,600	$19,000
1968	Sunburst	$11,100	$14,400
1969	Custom color	$14,600	$19,000
1969	Sunburst	$11,100	$14,400
1970	Custom color	$8,000	$15,000
1970	Sunburst	$8,000	$10,300
1971	Custom color, 4-bolt	$8,700	$15,000
1971	Sunburst, 3-bolt	$2,900	$3,800
1971	Sunburst, 4-bolt	$8,000	$10,300
1972	Custom color, 3-bolt	$4,500	$8,000
1972	Sunburst, 3-bolt	$2,900	$3,800

Telecaster Custom (Japan)

1985. Made in Japan during the period when Fender suspended all USA manufacturing in '85, Tele Custom specs including bound body.

1985		$1,050	$1,350

Telecaster Custom FMT HH (Korea)

2003-present. Part of Special Edition, Korean-made, flamed maple top, 2 humbuckers.

2003-2020		$650	$850

Telecaster Stratocaster Hybrid (Custom Shop)

2006. Tele body shape, Strat pickup system and wiring, Strat headstock shape, dot markers on rosewood board, reissue tremolo, includes Custom Shop Certificate that reads "Telecaster Stratocaster Hybrid".

2006		$2,100	$2,700

Telecaster Thinline

1968-1980. Semi-hollowbody, 1 f-hole, 2 Tele pickups, ash or mahogany body, in late-'71 the tilt neck was added and the 2 Tele pickups were switched to 2 humbuckers. Please refer to the Fender Guitar Intro Section for details on Fender color options.

MODEL YEAR	FEATURES	EXC. COND. LOW	HIGH
1968	Common color	$11,300	$14,700
1968	Natural ash	$7,400	$9,600
1968	Natural mahogany	$7,400	$9,600
1968	Rare color	$13,900	$18,100
1968	Sunburst	$8,300	$10,800
1969	Common color	$9,600	$12,400
1969	Natural ash	$7,400	$9,600
1969	Natural mahogany	$7,400	$9,600
1969	Rare color	$12,500	$16,200
1969	Sunburst	$8,300	$10,800
1970	Common color	$8,700	$11,400
1970	Natural ash	$7,400	$9,600
1970	Natural mahogany	$7,400	$9,600
1970	Rare color	$11,400	$15,000
1970	Sunburst	$7,300	$9,800
1971	Color option, 3-bolt, hums	$4,500	$8,000
1971	Color option, 4-bolt, singles	$8,700	$14,000
1971	Natural ash, 3-bolt	$2,900	$3,800
1971	Natural ash, 3-bolt, hums	$2,900	$3,800
1971	Natural ash, 4-bolt, singles	$3,800	$5,000
1971	Natural mahogany, 3-bolt	$3,000	$3,900
1971	Natural mahogany, 3-bolt, hums	$3,000	$3,900
1971	Natural mahogany, 4-bolt, singles	$3,800	$5,000
1971	Sunburst, 3-bolt, hums	$2,900	$3,800
1971	Sunburst, 4-bolt, singles	$4,400	$5,700
1972	Color option	$4,500	$8,000
1972	Mahogany	$2,900	$3,800
1972	Natural ash	$2,900	$3,800
1972	Sunburst	$2,900	$3,800
1973	Color option	$3,500	$7,000
1973	Mahogany	$3,000	$4,000
1973	Natural ash	$3,000	$4,000
1973	Sunburst	$3,000	$4,000
1974	Color option	$3,000	$3,900
1974	Mahogany	$2,300	$3,000
1974	Natural ash	$2,300	$3,000
1974	Sunburst	$2,725	$3,625
1975	Color option	$3,000	$3,900
1975	Natural ash	$2,300	$3,000
1975	Sunburst	$2,300	$3,000
1976	Color option	$2,300	$3,000
1976	Natural ash	$2,300	$3,000
1976	Sunburst	$2,300	$3,000
1977	Color option	$2,300	$3,000
1977	Natural ash	$2,300	$3,000
1977	Sunburst	$2,300	$3,000
1978	Color option	$1,950	$2,600
1978	Natural ash	$1,950	$2,600
1978	Sunburst	$1,950	$2,600

Tele-Sonic

1998-2000. U.S.A., chambered Telecaster body, 2 DeArmond pickups, dot markers, upper bass bout 3-way toggle switch.

1998-2000		$950	$1,250

Texas Special Telecaster

1991-1992. Custom Shop model, 60 made, state of Texas outline on the 'guard, ash body with Texas Orange transparent finish, large profile maple neck, with certificate of authenticity.

1991-1992		$2,100	$2,700

Twisted Telecaster Limited Edition

2005. Custom Shop, 50 built by Master Builder Yuriy Shishkov, 100 built by the Custom Shop team, top loaded Bigsby.

2005	Shishkov built	$3,500	$4,500
2005	Team built	$1,925	$2,500

Two-Tone Telecaster Thinline

2019-2020. FSR Limited Edition, alder body, various top color with matching headstock and white back and sides.

2019-2020		$1,075	$1,400

Vintage Hot Rod Telecaster

2007-2014. Vintage styling with modern features, '07-'13 named '52 Tele and '62 Tele, in '14 changed to '50s, and '60s.

2007-2014	All models	$1,125	$1,450

Waylon Jennings Tribute Telecaster

1995-2003. Custom Shop, black with white leather rose body inlays.

1995-2003		$5,100	$6,600

Will Ray Signature Jazz-A-Caster

1997. Made in Fender Japan Custom Shop as one part of the three part Hellecasters Series, limited edition, Strat neck on a Tele body with 2 soap-bar Seymour Duncan Jazzmaster-style pickups, gold leaf finish.

1997		$1,050	$1,350

Will Ray Signature Mojo Telecaster

1998-2001. Custom Shop, ash body, flamed maple Strat neck, locking tuners, rosewood 'board, skull inlays, double coil pickups, optional Hipshot B bender.

1998-2001		$2,200	$2,850

Telecoustic Series

2000-2016. Thinline acoustic/electric, single-cut, spruce top, fiberglass body, various colors. Telecoustic discontinued '05, Deluxe begins '07-'09 and Standard added in '09-'16. Both Plus and Premier '14-'16.

2002-2016		$300	$400

Toronado/Deluxe/HH/Highway 1/GT HH

1998-2006. American Special series, various models and colors. Deluxe model made in Mexico.

1998-2006		$500	$650

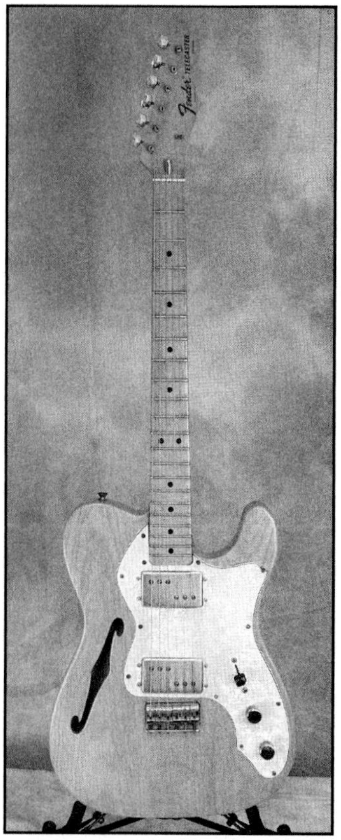

1972 Fender Telecaster Thinline

2000 Fender Will Ray Signature Mojo Telecaster

Jimmy James

2006 First Act Volkswagen Garagemaster

Billy White Jr.

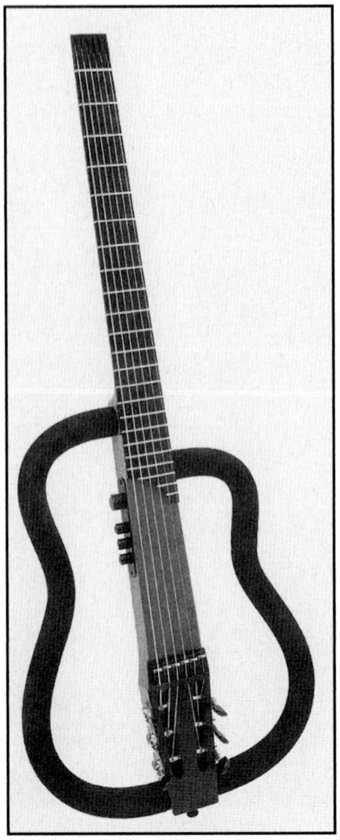

Frame Works

MODEL YEAR	FEATURES	EXC. COND. LOW	HIGH

Villager 12-String

1965-1969, 2011-2017. Acoustic flat-top, spruce top, mahogany back and sides, 12 strings, natural. Reintroduced in '11 (California Series) with on-board Fishman System, made in China.

1965-1969		$700	$925
2011-2017	Reintroduced	$270	$350

Violin - Electric

1958-1976, 2013. Violin-shape, solidbody, sunburst is the standard finish.

1958-1976		$1,700	$2,200
2013		$450	$600

Wildwood

1963-1971. Acoustic flat-top with Wildwood dyed top.

1966-1971	Various (unfaded)	$1,800	$2,400

Fenix

Late 1980s-mid 1990s. Brand name of Korean manufacturer Young Chang, used on a line of original-design and copy acoustic, electric and bass guitars. They also built Squier brand guitars for Fender during that period.

Fenton-Weill

See info under Burns-Weill.

Fernandes

1969-present. Established in Tokyo. Early efforts were classical guitars, but they now offer a variety of intermediate grade, production, imported guitars and basses.

Fina

Production classical and steel-string guitars and acoustic basses built in Huiyang City, Guang Dong, China.

Finck, David

1986-present. Luthier David Finck builds his production/custom, professional and premium grade, acoustic guitars, presently in Valle Crucis, North Carolina. In the past, he has built in Pittsburg, Kansas and Reader, West Virginia.

Fine Resophonic

1988-present. Professional and premium grade, production/custom, wood and metal-bodied resophonic guitars (including reso-electrics) built by luthiers Mike Lewis and Pierre Avocat in Vitry Sur Seine, France. They also build ukes and mandolins.

Firefly

Independent brand, budget models produced in China.

Electric

Various copy models made in China.

2019-2020		$100	$200

First Act

1995-present. Budget and professional grade, production/custom, acoustic, solid and semi-hollow body guitars built in China and in their Custom Shop in Boston. They also make basses, violins, and other instruments.

Firth Pond & Company

1822-1867. An east coast retail distributor that sold Martin and Ashborn private brand instruments. The company operated as Firth and Hall from 1822-1841 (also known as Firth, Hall & Pond) in New York City and Litchfield, Connecticut. Most instruments were small parlor size (11" lower bout) guitars, as was the case for most builders of this era. Sometimes the inside back center seam will be branded Firth & Pond. Brazilian rosewood sides and back instruments fetch considerably more than most of the other tone woods and value can vary considerably based on condition. Guitars from the 1800s are sometimes valued more as antiques than working vintage guitars. In 1867 Firth & Sons sold out to Oliver Ditson Company.

Flammang Guitars

1990-present. Premium grade, custom/production, steel string guitars built by luthier David Flammang in Greene, Iowa and previously in East Hampton and Higganum, Connecticut.

Flaxwood

2004-present. Professional grade, production/custom, solid and semi-hollow body guitars built in Finland, with bodies of natural fiber composites.

Fleishman Instruments

Introduced in 1974, premium and presentation grade, custom flat-tops made by luthier Harry Fleishman in Sebastopol, California. He also offers basses and electric uprights. Fleishman is the director of Luthiers School International.

Fletcher Brock Stringed Instruments

1992-present. Custom flat-tops and archtops made by luthier Fletcher Brock originally in Ketchum, Idaho, and currently in Seattle, Washington. He also builds mandolin family instruments.

Flowers Guitars

1993-present. Premium grade, custom, archtop guitars built by luthier Gary Flowers in Baltimore, Maryland.

Floyd Rose

2004-2006. Floyd Rose, inventor of the Floyd Rose Locking Tremolo, produced a line of intermediate and professional grade, production, solidbody guitars from '04 to '06. They continue to offer bridges and other accessories.

Foggy Mountain

Intermediate grade, production, steel and nylon string acoustic and acoustic/electric guitars imported from China.

Fontanilla Guitars

1987-present. Luthier Allan Fontanilla builds his premium grade, production/custom, classical guitars in San Francisco, California.

Fouilleul

1978-present. Production/custom, classical guitars made by luthier Jean-Marie Fouilleul in Cuguen, France.

Fox Hollow Guitars

2004-present. Luthier Don Greenough builds his professional and premium grade, custom, acoustic and electric guitars in Eugene, Oregon. He also builds mandolins.

Fox or Rocking F

1983-present. Premium grade, custom, steel string acoustic guitars built in Seattle, Washington by luthier Cat Fox.

Foxxe

1990-1991. Short-lived brand of solidbodies offered by the same company that produced Barrington guitars, Korean-made.

Frame Works

1995-present. Professional grade, production/custom, steel- and nylon-string guitars built by luthier Frank Krocker in Burghausen, Germany. The instruments feature a neck mounted on a guitar-shaped frame. Krocker has also built traditional archtops, flat-tops, and classicals.

Framus

1946-1977, 1996-present. Professional and premium grade, production/custom, guitars made in Markneukirchen, Germany. They also build basses, amps, mandolins and banjos. Frankische Musikindustrie (Framus) founded in Erlangen, Germany by Fred Wilfer, relocated to Bubenreuth in '54, and to Pretzfeld in '67. Begun as an acoustic instrument manufacturer, Framus added electrics in the mid-'50s. Earliest electrics were mostly acoustics with pickups attached. Electric designs begin in early-'60s. Unique feature was a laminated maple neck with many thin plies. By around '64-'65 upscale models featured the organtone, often called a spigot, a spring-loaded volume control that allowed you to simulate a Leslie speaker effect. Better models often had mutes and lots of switches.

In the '60s, Framus instruments were imported into the U.S. by Philadelphia Music Company. Resurgence of interest in ca. '74 with the Jan Akkermann hollowbody followed by original mid-'70s design called the Nashville, the product of an alliance with some American financing.

The brand was revived in '96 by Hans Peter Wilfer, the president of Warwick, with production in Warwick's factory in Germany.

MODEL YEAR	FEATURES	EXC. COND. LOW	HIGH
Amateur			
Early-1960s to mid-1970s. Model 5/1, small flat-top, early without pickguard, plain, dot markers.			
1960s-70s	Model 5/1	$150	$200
Atilla Zoller AZ-10			
Early-1960s-early-1980s. Single-cut archtop, 2 pickups, neck glued-in until the '70s, bolt-on after, sunburst. Model 5/65 (rounded cutaway, made until late '60s) and Model 5/67 (sharp cutaway).			
1960s	Model 5/65	$575	$750
1960s-70s	Model 5/67	$575	$750
Atlantic			
Ca. 1965-ca. 1970. Model 5/110, single-cut thin body electric archtop, 2 pickups, tremolo optional.			
1965-1970	Model 5/110	$500	$650
Atlantic (08000) Elec-12			
Mid- to late-1960s. Model 5/011 and 5/013, double cut semi-hollow, 2 pickups, 12-string.			
1960s	Model 5/013	$500	$650
Big 18 Doubleneck			
Late-1960s. Model 5/200 is a solidbody and Model 5/220 is acoustic.			
1960s	Model 5/200	$625	$825
1960s	Model 5/220	$625	$825
Caravelle			
Ca.1965-ca. 1975. Double-cut archtop, tremolo, model 5/117-52 has 2 pickups and 5/117-54 has 3.			
1965-1975		$550	$725
Gaucho			
Late-1960s to mid-1970s. Lower grade flat-top, concert size, spruce top, mahogany sides and back, rosewood bridge and 'board, sunburst or natural finish.			
1960s-70s	Model 5/194	$150	$200
Guitar-Banjo 6/76 Dixi, SL-76			
Ca. 1957-early 1970s. Banjo body, guitar neck, silver hardware.			
1957-1970s		$450	$575
Hollywood			
1960s. Double-cut, 3 pickups, red sunburst.			
1960s	Model 5/132	$700	$900
Jan Akkerman			
1974-1977. Single-cut semi-hollowbody, 2 pickups, gold hardware.			
1974-1977		$400	$525
Jumbo			
1963 to late-1970s. Models earlier 5/97, later 5/197, jumboflat-top, mahogany or maple sides and back.			
1960s-70s		$425	$550
Jumbo 12-String			
Late-1960s to mid-1970s. 12-string version.			
1960s-70s	Model 5/297	$425	$550
Missouri (E Framus Missouri)			
Ca.1955-ca. 1975. Originally non-cut acoustic archtop until early '60s when single-cut archtop with 1 or 2 pickups added.			
1960s	Model 5/60	$450	$600
New Sound Series			
1960s. Double-cut semi-hollowbody, model 5/116-52 has 2 pickups and 5/116-54 has 3.			
1960s		$650	$850

1975 Framus Jan Akkerman

Larry Cramer

1960s Framus Missouri Model 5/60

Imaged by Heritage Auctions, HA.com

1962 Framus Sorella Model 5/59-50

Rivington Guitars

Fritz Brothers Roy Buchanan Bluesmaster

MODEL YEAR	FEATURES	EXC. COND. LOW	HIGH

Sorella Series

Ca.1955 to mid-1970s. Single-cut, Model 5/59 is acoustic archtop (with or without single pickup), 5/59-50 is 1-pickup electric archtop, 5/59-52 is electric 2-pickup.

1955-1975	Model 5/59	$600	$775
1965-1972	Model 5/59-50	$650	$850
1965-1972	Model 5/59-52	$650	$850

Sorento

Ca.1963-ca. 1970. Thinline archtop, single-cut, 2 pickups, organ effect, f-holes.

1963-1970	Model 5/112-53	$650	$850

Sorento 12

Ca.1963-ca. 1970. 12-string version.

1963-1970	Model 5/012	$675	$875

Sport

Early 1950s-mid-1970s. Small beginner flat-top, plain appointments, dot markers.

1950s-70s	Model 50/1	$150	$200

Strato de Luxe 12 String

Ca. 1963-ca. 1970. Model 5/067(metal pickguard) and 5/068 (wood grain pickguard and large gold cover plates), 2 pickups, tremolo.

1963-1970	Model 5/068	$650	$850

Strato de Luxe Series

Ca.1964-ca. 1970. 1, 2 (5/155, 5/167-52, 5/168-52) or 3 (5/167-54, 5/168-54) pickups, some models have gold hardware.

1960s	2 pickups	$550	$725
1960s	3 pickups	$575	$750

Strato Super

Early- to late-1960s. Offset double-cut, 2 pickups.

1960s	Model 5/155-52	$575	$750

Studio Series

Late-1950s to mid-1970s. Model 5/51 (a.k.a. 030) is non-cut acoustic archtop (some with pickup - 5/51E), 5/108 is electric archtop, 1 pickup.

1960s-70s	Model 5/51	$150	$200
1960s-70s	Model 5/51E	$200	$275

Television Series

Early- to late-1960s. Model 5/118-52 2 pickups and 5/118-54 3 pickups, offset double-cut thinline hollowbody.

1960s	Model 5/118-52	$525	$700
1960s	Model 5/118-54	$625	$825

Texan Series

Late-1960s to early-1980s. Model 5/196, 5/196E (with pickup) and 5/296 12-string flat-top, mahogany back and sides. 6-string ends in late '70s.

1960s-70s	6-string	$250	$325
1960s-80s	12-string	$250	$325

Western

1960s. Model 5/195, grand concert size, lower grade flat-top, spruce top, maple sides and back.

1960s	Model 5/195	$150	$200

Franklin Guitar Company

1974-present. Premium and presentation grade, custom, flat-top steel string guitars built first in Franklin, Michigan and since 2003 in Rocheport, Missouri by luthier Nick Kukich. He also built in Idaho, Washington and Oregon.

Fraulini

2001-present. Luthier Todd Cambio builds his professional and premium grade, primarily custom, early 20th century style guitars, in Madison, Wisconsin.

FreeNote

Intermediate to professional grade, the innovative FreeNote 12-Tone Ultra Plus provides two frets for every traditional fret placement which provides an unlimited number of playable notes.

Fresher

1973-1985. The Japanese-made Fresher brand models were mainly copies of popular brands and limited numbers were imported into the U.S. They also made basses.

Solidbody Electric

1970s. Import from Japan, various models.

1970s		$150	$400

Fret-King

2008-present. Luthier Trev Wilkinson builds professional and premium grade, production, solidbody and semi-hollow electric guitars and basses in Yorkshire, U.K., and also offers a line imported from Korea.

Fritz Brothers

1988-present. Premium grade, production/custom, acoustic, semi-hollow, and solidbody guitars and basses built by luthier Roger Fritz, originally in Mobile, Alabama, then in Mendocino, California. In 2013 he again relocated to Mobile.

Froggy Bottom Guitars

1974-present. Luthier Michael Millard builds his premium and presentation grade, production/custom flat-tops in Newfane, Vermont (originally in Hinsdale, New York, and until '84 production was in Richmond, New Hampshire).

Frudua Guitar Works

1988-present. Luthier Galeazzo Frudua builds his intermediate to premium grade, production/custom, electric guitars, basses and amps in Imola, Italy.

Fukuoka Musical Instruments

1993-present. Custom steel- and nylon-string flat-tops and archtops built in Japan.

Furch

See listing for Stonebridge.

Furnace Mountain Guitar Works

1995-1999. Instruments built by luthier Martin Fair in New Mexico. He currently builds under the Fairbuilt Guitar Co. brand.

MODEL YEAR	FEATURES	EXC. COND. LOW	HIGH

Fury

1962-2017. Founded by Glenn McDougall in Saskatoon, Saskatchewan, Fury offered production, hollow, semi-hollow and solidbody electric guitars and basses. McDougall died in early '17.

Futurama

1957-mid to late 1960s. Futurama was a brand name used by Selmer in the United Kingdom. Early instruments made by the Drevokov Cooperative in Czechoslovakia, models for '63-'64 made by Sweden's Hagstrom company. Some later '60s instruments may have been made in Japan. Beatles fans will recognize the brand name as Beatle George Harrison's first electric.

Futurama/II/III

1957-1969. Offset double-cut, 2- or 3-pickup versions available, large Futurama logo on headstock with the reverse capital letter F. George Harrison purchased his Futurama in '59; maple neck, 3 pickups, 3 push button levels, 2 knobs, Futurama logo on 'guard. The price shown for the Harrison model assumes an all-original, excellent condition that exactly matches his '59 model.

1959	III, Harrison, maple	$1,500	$4,000
1959	III, rosewood	$800	$1,050

Fylde Guitars

1973-present. Luthier Roger Bucknall builds his professional and premium grade, production/custom acoustic guitars, basses, mandolins, mandolas, bouzoukis, and citterns in Penrith, Cumbria, UK.

G&L

1980-present. Intermediate and professional grade, production/custom, solidbody and semi-hollowbody electric guitars made in the U.S. and overseas. They also make basses. Founded by Leo Fender and George Fullerton following the severance of ties between Fender's CLF Research and Music Man. Company sold to John MacLaren and BBE Sound, when Leo Fender died in '91. In '98 they added their Custom Creations Department. In '03 G&L introduced the Korean-made G&L Tribute Series. George Fullerton died in July, '09.

ASAT

1986-1998. Called the Broadcaster in '85. Two or 3 single-coil or 2 single-coil/1 humbucker pickup configurations until early-'90s, 2 single-coils after.

1986		$1,025	$1,325
1987	Leo sig on headstock	$1,025	$1,325
1988-1991	Leo sig on body	$1,025	$1,325
1992-1998	BBE era	$925	$1,225

ASAT 20th Anniversary

2000. Limited Edition run of 50, ash body, tinted birdseye maple neck, 2-tone sunburst.

2000		$1,100	$1,425

ASAT '50

1999. Limited edition of 10.

1999		$1,100	$1,425

ASAT Bluesboy Limited Edition

1999. Limited edition of 20.

1999		$975	$1,275

ASAT Bluesboy Semi-Hollow Limited Edition

1999. Limited edition of 12, thin semi-hollow.

1999		$900	$1,200

ASAT Classic

1990-present. Two single-coil pickups, individually adjustable bridge saddles, neck-tilt adjustment and tapered string posts.

1990-1991	Leo sig on body	$950	$1,200
1992-1997	3-bolt neck	$800	$1,025
1997-2020	4-bolt neck	$800	$1,025

ASAT Classic B-Bender

1997. 12 made with factory-original B-Bender.

1997		$900	$1,175

ASAT Classic Bluesboy

2001-present. Humbucker neck pickup, single-coil at bridge.

2001-2020		$875	$1,150

ASAT Classic Bluesboy Rustic

2010-2015. Classic Bluesboy with Rustic aging and refinements.

2010-2015		$1,150	$1,500

ASAT Classic Bluesboy Semi-Hollow

1997-present. Chambered Classic with f-hole.

1997-2020		$1,000	$1,300

ASAT Classic Commemorative

1991-1992. Leo Fender signature and birth/death dating, Australian lacewood (6 made) or Cherryburst (1,000 made).

1991-1992	Australian	$3,800	$5,000
1991-1992	Cherryburst	$1,325	$1,725

ASAT Classic Custom

1996-1997, 2002-2013. Large rectangular neck pickup, single-coil bridge pickup.

1996-1997	1st version	$900	$1,175
2002-2013	2nd version, 4-bolt neck	$900	$1,175

ASAT Classic Custom Semi-Hollow

2002-2013. Custom with f-hole.

2002-2013		$850	$1,100

ASAT Classic S

2007. Limited run of 50, certificate, swamp ash body, 3 single-coil pickups, Nashville pickup configuration.

2007		$900	$1,175

ASAT Classic Semi-Hollow

1997-present. With f-hole.

1997-2020		$900	$1,175

ASAT Classic Three

1998. Limited Edition run of 100.

1998		$1,050	$1,350

ASAT Custom

1996. No pickguard, 25 to 30 made.

1996		$875	$1,150

ASAT Deluxe

1997-present. Flamed maple top, bound body, 2 humbuckers.

1997	3-bolt neck	$1,050	$1,350
1997-2020	4-bolt neck	$1,050	$1,350

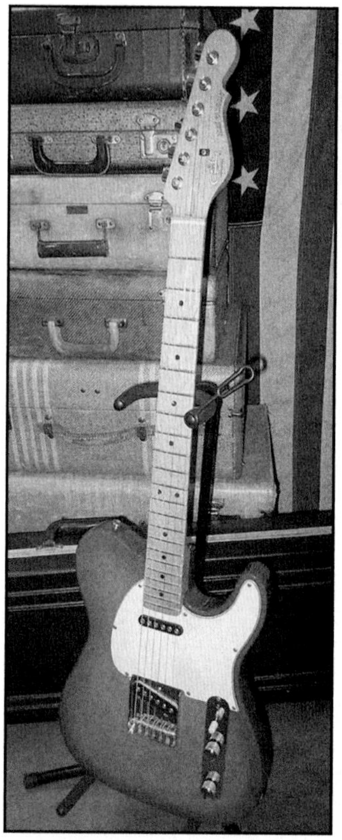

1993 G&L ASAT Classic

Rivington Guitars

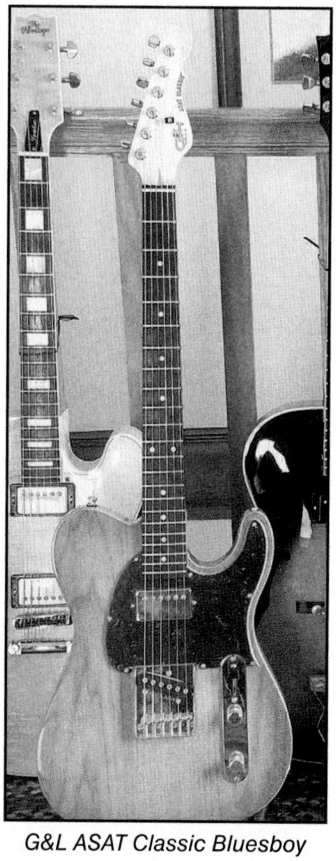

G&L ASAT Classic Bluesboy

Emmitt Omar

1980 G&L F-100

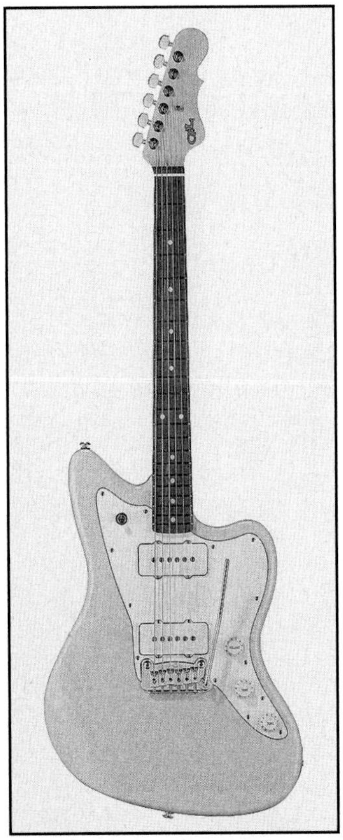

G&L Fullerton Deluxe Dohney

MODEL YEAR — FEATURES — EXC. COND. LOW — HIGH

ASAT Deluxe Semi-Hollow

1997-2018. Two humbuckers.

1997-2018 $1,050 $1,350

ASAT III

1988-1991, 1996-1998. Single-cut body, 3 single-coil pickups.

1988-1991 Leo era, 150 made $1,050 $1,350

1996-1998 Post Leo era $1,050 $1,350

ASAT JD-5/Jerry Donahue JD-5

2004-2007. Jerry Donahue model, single-cut, 2 single-coils, special wired 5-way switch.

2004-2007 $1,100 $1,450

ASAT Junior

1998-1999. Limited Edition run of 250, single-cut semi-hollowbody, 2 single-coils.

1998-1999 $1,050 $1,350

ASAT S-3

1998-2000. Three soap-bar single-coil pickups, limited production.

1998-2000 $725 $950

ASAT Special

1992-present. Like ASAT, but with 2 larger P-90-type pickups, chrome hardware, various colors.

1992-1997 3-bolt neck $850 $1,125

1997-2019 4-bolt neck $850 $1,125

ASAT Special Semi-Hollow

1997-2018. Semi-hollow version of ASAT Special.

1997-2018 $725 $950

ASAT Special Deluxe

2001-2015. No 'guard version of the Special with figured maple top.

2001-2015 $950 $1,225

ASAT Special Detroit Muscle Series

2015. Classic automobile colors include; Daytona Yellow, Hugger Orange, Cranberry Red and Marina Blue.

2015 $825 $1,100

ASAT Z-2 Limited Edition

1999 Limited run of 10, semi-hollow construction, natural ash, tortoise bound, engraved neckplate

1999 $1,050 $1,350

ASAT Z-3

1998-2020. Three offset-style Z-3 high output pickups, sunburst.

1998-2020 $875 $1,125

ASAT Z-3 Semi-Hollow

1998-2020. F-hole version of Z-3.

1998-2020 $875 $1,125

Broadcaster

1985-1986. Solidbody, 2 single-coils with adjustable polepieces act in humbucking mode with selector switch in the center position, black parts and finish, name changed to ASAT in early-'86.

1985-1986 Kahler $800 $1,050

1985-1986 Signed by Leo, ebony 'board $1,600 $2,100

1985-1986 Signed by Leo, maple 'board $1,600 $2,100

Cavalier

1983-1986. Offset double-cut, 2 humbuckers, 700 made, sunburst.

1983-1986 $900 $1,175

Climax

1992-1996. Offset double-cut, bolt maple neck, six-on-a-side tuners, double locking vibrato, blue.

1992-1996 $800 $1,025

Climax Plus

1992-1996. Two humbuckers replace single-coils of the Climax, plus 1 single-coil.

1992-1996 $800 $1,025

Climax XL

1992-1996. Two humbuckers only.

1992-1996 $800 $1,025

Comanche V

1988-1991. Solidbody, 3 Z-shaped single-coil humbuckers, maple neck in choice of 3 radii, rosewood 'board, vibrato, fine tuners, Leo Fender's signature on the body, sunburst.

1988-1991 $975 $1,275

Comanche VI

1990-1991. Leo Fender's signature on the body, 6 mini-toggles.

1990-1991 $1,000 $1,300

Comanche (Reintroduced)

1998-present. Reissue with either swamp ash or alder body, bolt-on maple neck, 3 Z-coil pickups, standard or premium finish options.

1998-2020 Premium finish, flame top $975 $1,275

1998-2020 Standard finish $825 $1,100

Comanche Deluxe (Reintroduced)

2018-present. Fullerton Deluxe series, old style double-cut, 3 Z-coil pickups, alder or swamp ash top, various colors with vintage tint satin finish.

2018-2020 $950 $1,225

Commemorative

1992-1997. About 350 made, Leo Fender signature on upper bass bout.

1991 Cherryburst $1,800 $2,400

1992-1997 Sunburst $1,700 $2,200

F-100 (Model I and II)

1980-1986. Offset double-cut solidbody, 2 humbuckers, natural. Came in a I and II model - only difference is the radius of the 'board.

1980-1986 $700 $925

F-100 E (Model I and II)

1980-1982. Offset double-cut solidbody, 2 humbuckers, active electronics, pre-amp, natural. Came in a I and II model - only difference is the radius of the 'board.

1980-1982 $750 $975

Fallout

2013-present. SC-2 body style, P-90 and humbucker, swamp ash body on premier and alder on standard finishes, maple neck, maple or rosewood 'board.

2013-2020 $900 $1,200

Fullerton Deluxe Dohney

2018-present. Fullerton Deluxe series, old style, 2 pickups, alder or swamp ash top, various colors with vintage tint satin finish.

2018-2020 $850 $1,100

MODEL YEAR	FEATURES	EXC. COND. LOW	HIGH

G-200

1981-1982. Mahogany solidbody, maple neck, ebony 'board, 2 humbucking pickups, coil-split switches, natural or sunburst, 209 made.

1981-1982		$1,550	$2,050

GBL-LE (Guitars by Leo Limited Edition)

1999. Limited edition of 25, semi-hollowbody, 3 pickups.

1999		$1,025	$1,325

George Fullerton Signature

1995-2007. Double-cut solidbody, sunburst.

1995-1997	3-bolt neck	$1,000	$1,300
1997-2007	4-bolt neck	$1,000	$1,300

HG-1

1982-1983. Offset double-cut, 1 humbucker, dot inlays. Very rare as most were made into HG-2s.

1982-1983		$1,350	$1,800

HG-2

1982-1984. 2-humbucker HG, body changes to classic offset double-cut in '84.

1982-1983	Mustang-body	$1,100	$1,450
1984	S-body	$1,100	$1,450

Interceptor

1983-1991. To '86 an X-shaped solidbody, either 3 single-coils, 2 humbuckers, or 1 humbucker and 2 single-coils, '87-'89 was an offset double-cut solidbody.

1983-1985	1st X-body, 70 made	$2,150	$2,850
1985-1986	2nd X-body, 12 made	$2,150	$2,850
1987-1991	Double-cut	$1,100	$1,450

Invader

1984-1991, 1998-2018. Double-cut solidbody, 2 single-coil and 1 humbucker pickups.

1984-1991	1st version	$975	$1,275
1998-2018	2nd version	$975	$1,275

Invader Plus

1998-2018. Two humbuckers and single blade pickup in the middle position.

1998-2018		$900	$1,200

Invader XL

1998-2018. Fancy top, 2 humbuckers.

1998-2018		$1,050	$1,375

John Jorgenson Signature Model ASAT

1995. About 190 made, Silver Metalflake finish.

1995		$1,050	$1,350

Legacy

1992-present. Classic double-cut configuration, USA logo, 3-bolt neck until '97, 4-bolt after, various colors.

1992-1994	3-bolt, Duncan SSLs	$800	$1,050
1995-1997	3-bolt, Alnicos	$800	$1,050
1996-1997	Swirl finish	$900	$1,200
1998-2020	4-bolt, Alnicos	$800	$1,050

Legacy Deluxe

2001-2015. No 'guard, figured maple top.

2001-2015		$850	$1,100

Legacy HH

2001-present. Two humbucker pickups.

2001-2020		$800	$1,050

Legacy HSS

2001-present. One humbucker pickup at bridge position plus 2 single-coil pickups.

2001-2020		$825	$1,075

Legacy Special

1993-present. Legacy with 3 humbuckers, various colors.

1992-1997	3-bolt neck	$825	$1,075
1998-2020	4-bolt neck	$825	$1,075

25th Anniversary Limited Edition

2006. G&L Custom Creations, 250 made, combines appearance of '81 F-100 with contours and control layout of ASAT Super, single-cut mahogany body, 2 custom wound MFD humbuckes, custom blend 'root beer' finish.

2006		$900	$1,175

Nighthawk

1983. Offset double-cut solidbody, 3 single-coil pickups, 269 made, sunburst, name changed to Skyhawk in '84.

1983		$700	$925

Rampage

1984-1991. Offset double-cut solidbody, hard rock maple neck, ebony 'board, 1 bridge-position humbucker pickup, sunburst. Currently available as Jerry Cantrell Signature Model.

1984-1991	Common color	$950	$1,225
1984-1991	Rare color	$1,400	$1,800

Rampage (Reissue)

2000. Limited Edition run of 70, supplied with gig bag and not hard case, ivory finish.

2000		$575	$750

S-500

1982-present. Double-cut mahogany or ash solidbody, maple neck, ebony or maple 'board, 3 single-coil pickups, vibrato.

1982-1987		$925	$1,225
1988-1991	Mini-toggle, Leo sig on body	$825	$1,100
1992-1997	3-bolt neck	$675	$900
1997-2020	4-bolt neck	$675	$900

S-500 Deluxe

2001-2015. Deluxe Series features, including no 'guard and flamed maple top, natural.

2001-2015	Flame & solid tops	$850	$1,100

SC-1

1982-1983. Offset double-cut solidbody, 1 single-coil pickup, tremolo, sunburst, 250 made.

1981-1982		$725	$950

SC-2

1982-1983, 2010-2018. Offset double-cut solidbody, 2 MFD soapbar pickups, about 600 made in original run, reissue maple or rosewood 'board.

1982-1983	Shallow cutaway	$950	$1,250
1983	Deeper, pointed cutaway	$950	$1,250
2010-2018	Reissue	$525	$675

SC-3

1982-1991. Offset double-cut solidbody, 3 single-coil pickups, tremolo.

1982-1983	Shallow cutaway	$800	$1,050
1984-1987	Deeper cutaway, no 'guard	$800	$1,050
1988-1991	Deeper cutaway, with 'guard	$725	$950

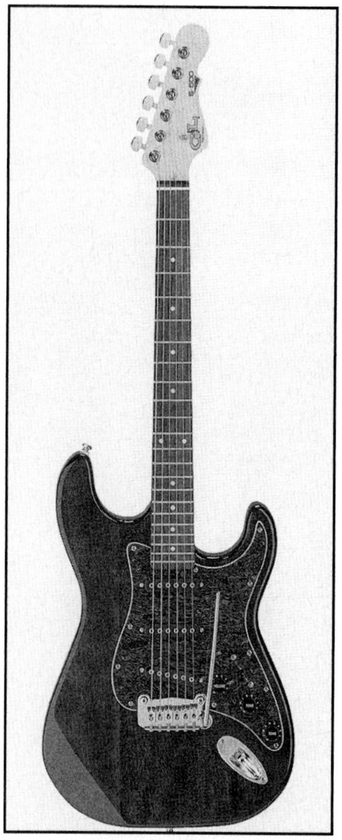

G&L S-500

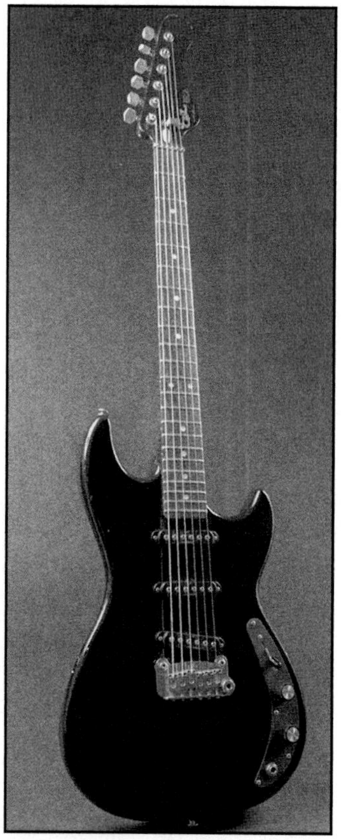

1987 G&L SC-3

Carter Vintage Guitars

G&L Will Ray

2017 Gallagher G-70

MODEL YEAR	FEATURES	EXC. COND. LOW	HIGH

Skyhawk

1984-1991. Renamed from Nighthawk, offset double-cut, 3 single-coils, signature on headstock '84-'87, then on body '88-'91.

1984-1987	Dual-Fulcrum or saddle lock	$800	$1,025
1984-1987	Kahler	$625	$800
1988-1991	Dual-Fulcrum or saddle lock	$625	$825
1988-1991	Kahler	$600	$775

Superhawk

1984-1987. Offset double-cut, maple neck, ebony 'board, G&L or Kahler tremolos, 2 humbuckers, signature on headstock.

1984-1987		$700	$925

Tribute Series

2003-present. Import versions of regular models.

2003-2020	Various models	$200	$575

Trinity

2006. Only 25 made, ASAT-style with 3 new style single-coils, designed by Tim Page of Buffalo Brothers, the last G&L to have COA signed by George Fullerton.

2006		$1,350	$1,800

Will Ray Signature Model

2002-2018. Will Ray signature on headstock, 3 Z-coil pickups, Hipshot B-Bender.

2002-2018		$650	$850

G.L. Stiles

1960-1994. Built by Gilbert Lee Stiles primarily in the Miami, Florida area. First solidbody, including pickups and all hardware, built by hand in his garage. Stiles favored scrolls, fancy carving and walnut fingerboards. His later instruments were considerably fancier and more refined. He moved to Hialeah, Florida by '63 and began making acoustic guitars and other instruments. Only his solidbodies had consecutive serial numbers. Stiles, who died in '94, made approximately 1000 solidbodies and 500 acoustics.

Gadotti Guitars

1997-present. Luthier Jeanfranco Biava Gadotti builds his premium grade, custom/production, nylon- and steel-string, carved, chambered solidbodies in Orlando, Florida.

Gadow Guitars

2002-2019. Luthier Ryan Gadow built his professional and premium grade, custom/production, solid and semi-hollow body guitars and basses in Durham, North Carolina.

Gagnon

Luthier Bill Gagnon began building his premium and presentation grade, production/custom, archtop guitars in Beaverton, Oregon, starting in 1998.

Galanti

Ca.1962-ca.1967. Electric guitars offered by the longtime Italian accordion maker, some built by Zero Sette. They may have also offered acoustics.

Electric

1962-1967. Solidbody or hollowbody.

1962-1967	Fancy features	$550	$800
1962-1967	Plain features	$300	$550

Galiano

New Yorkers Antonio Cerrito and Raphael Ciani offered guitars under the Galiano brand during the early part of the last century. They used the brand both on guitars built by them and others, including The Oscar Schmidt Company. They also offered mandolins.

Gallagher

1965-present. Professional and premium grade, production/custom, flat-top guitars built in Wartrace, Tennessee. J. W. Gallagher started building Shelby brand guitars in the Slingerland Drum factory in Shelbyville, Tennessee in '63. In '65 he and his son Don made the first Gallagher guitar, the G-50. Doc Watson began using Gallagher guitars in '68. In '76, Don assumed operation of the business when J. W. semi-retired. J. W. died in '79.

71 Special

1970s-2015. Rosewood back and sides, spruce top, herringbone trim, bound ebony 'board, natural.

1970s-2015		$1,700	$2,225

72 Special

1977-2016. Rosewood back and sides, spruce top, abalone trim, bound ebony 'board, natural.

1977-2016		$3,100	$4,000

A-70 Ragtime Special

1978-2015. Smaller auditorium/00 size, spruce top, mahogany back and sides, G logo, natural.

1978-2015		$1,200	$1,550

Custom 12-String

Introduced in 1965-present. Mahogany, 12-fret neck, natural.

1965		$1,275	$1,650

Doc Watson

1968-present. Spruce top, mahogany back and sides, scalloped bracing, ebony 'board, herringbone trim, natural.

1968-2020		$2,325	$3,025

Doc Watson (Cutaway)

1975-2010. Spruce top, mahogany back and sides, scalloped bracing, ebony 'board, herringbone trim, natural.

1975-2010		$2,400	$3,125

Doc Watson 12-String

1995-2000. Natural.

1995-2000		$1,950	$2,550

Doc Watson Signature

2000-present. Signature inlay 12th fret.

2000-2020		$2,400	$3,125

G-45

1970-2008. Mahogany back and sides, spruce top, ebony 'board, natural.

1970-1979		$1,350	$1,750
1980-2008		$1,125	$1,475

MODEL YEAR	FEATURES	EXC. COND. LOW	HIGH

G-50

1960s-2015. Mahogany back and sides, spruce top, ebony 'board, natural.

1960s		$2,000	$2,600
1970-2015		$1,500	$1,950

G-65

1980s-2015. Rosewood back and sides, spruce top, ebony 'board, natural.

1980s-2015		$1,550	$2,000

G-70

1978-present. Rosewood back and sides, herringbone purfling on top and soundhole, mother-of-pearl diamond 'board inlays, bound headstock, natural.

1978-2020		$1,550	$2,000

G-71

1970s. Indian rosewood, gold tuners.

1970s		$1,800	$2,325

Gallagher, Kevin

1996. Kevin Gallagher, luthier, changed name brand to Omega to avoid confusion with J.W. Gallagher. See Omega listing.

Gallotone

1950s-1960s. Low-end foreign brand similar to 1950s Stellas, the Gallotone Champion, a 3/4 size student flat-top, is associated with John Lennon as his early guitar.

Galloup Guitars

1994-present. Luthier Bryan Galloup builds his professional and premium grade, production/custom flat-tops in Big Rapids, Michigan. He also operates the Galloup School of Lutherie and The Guitar Hospital repair and restoration business.

Galveston

Budget and intermediate grade, production, imported acoustic, acoustic/electric, resonator and solidbody guitars. They also offer basses and mandolins.

Gamble & O'Toole

1978-present. Premium grade, custom classical and steel string guitars built by luthier Arnie Gamble in Sacramento, California, with design input and inlay work from his wife Erin O'Toole.

Ganz Guitars

1995-present. Luthier Steve Ganz builds his professional grade, production/custom classical guitars in Bellingham, Washington.

Garcia

Made by luthier Federico Garcia in Spain until late-1960s or very early-'70s when production moved to Japan.

Classical

1960s-1970s. Mid-level, '60s model is solid spruce top with solid mahogany, rosewood or walnut back and sides, '70s model is Spanish pine top with walnut back and sides.

1960s	Various wood	$225	$300
1970s	Spanish pine Brazilian rosewood	$450	$600

Garrison

2000-2007. Intermediate and professional grade, production, acoustic and acoustic/electric guitars designed by luthier Chris Griffiths using his Active Bracing System (a single integrated glass-fiber bracing system inside a solid wood body). He started Griffiths Guitar Works in 1993 in St. John's, Newfoundland, and introduced Garrison guitars in 2000. In '07, the Garrison facility was acquired by Gibson.

Gary Kramer

2006-present. Intermediate and professional grade, production/custom, solidbody electric guitars built by luthier Gary Kramer in El Segundo, California, and imported. Kramer was one of the founders of the Kramer guitar company in the '70s.

Gauge Guitars

2002-present. Luthier Aaron Solomon builds custom, professional and premium grade, solidbody and semi-solid electric guitars in New Jersey.

Gemelli

Early 1960s-ca. 1966. European-made (likely Italian) guitars. Similar to Bartolini guitars, so most likely from same manufacturer. Originally plastic covered, they switched to paint finishes by around '65.

Gemunder

1870s-1910s. New York shop that specialized in reproduction-aged violins, but also made parlor-sized guitars that were similar to Martin guitars of the era. An original label on the inside back identifies August Gemunder and Sons, New York.

Parlor

1870s-1910s. Style 28 appointments, rosewood body, spruce top.

1870-1910s		$1,000	$1,300

George

See listing under Chris George.

German Guitars

2001-present. Luthier Greg German builds his premium grade, custom/production, acoustic archtop guitars in Broomfield, Colorado.

Giannini

1900-present. Classical, acoustic, and acoustic/electric guitars built in Salto, SP, Brazil near Sao Paolo. They also build violas, cavaquinhos and mandolins. Founded by guitar-builder Tranquillo Giannini, an Italian who traveled to Brazil in 1890

German DB6

1965 Giannini 8141 Model 4

Craig Brody

1972 Giannini Craviola 12-String
Tom Pfeifer

Gibson Randy Scruggs Advanced Jumbo Limited Edition

and discovered the exotic woods of Brazil. The company was producing 30,000 instruments a year by '30. They began exporting their acoustic instruments to the U.S. in '63. They added electric guitars in '60, but these weren't imported as much, if at all. Gianninis from this era used much Brazilian Rosewood.

Classical

Early-1970s. Nylon string import, small body.

MODEL YEAR	FEATURES	EXC. COND. LOW	HIGH
1970s	Brazilian rosewood	$300	$500
1970s	Pau ferro, mahogany	$150	$300

CraViolia

1972-1974, 2004-present. Kidney bean-shaped rosewood body, acoustic, natural, line included a classical, a steel string, and a 12-string.

MODEL YEAR	FEATURES	EXC. COND. LOW	HIGH
1972-1974		$450	$600

CraViolia 12-String

1972-1974, 2004-present. Kidney bean-shaped body, 12 strings.

MODEL YEAR	FEATURES	EXC. COND. LOW	HIGH
1972-1974		$450	$600

Gibson

1890s (1902)-present. Intermediate, professional, and premium grade, production/custom, acoustic and electric guitars made in the U.S. They also build basses, mandolins, amps, and banjos. Gibson also offers instruments under the Epiphone, Kramer, Steinberger, Dobro, Tobias, Valley Arts, Garrison, Slingerland (drums), Baldwin (pianos), Trace Elliot, Electar (amps), Maestro, Gibson Labs, Oberheim, and Echoplex brands.

Founded in Kalamazoo, Michigan by Orville Gibson, a musician and luthier who developed instruments with tops, sides and backs carved out of solid pieces of wood. Early instruments included mandolins, archtop guitars and harp guitars. By 1896 Gibson had opened a shop. In 1902 Gibson was bought out by a group of investors who incorporated the business as Gibson Mandolin-Guitar Manufacturing Company, Limited. The company was purchased by Chicago Musical Instrument Company (CMI) in '44. In '57 CMI also purchased the Epiphone guitar company, transferring production from Philadelphia to the Gibson plant in Kalamazoo. Gibson was purchased by Norlin in late-'69 and a new factory was opened in Nashville, Tennessee in '74. The Kalamazoo factory ceased production in '84. In '85, Gibson was sold to a group headed by Henry Juskewiscz. Gibson purchased the Flatiron Company in '87 and built a new factory in '89, moving acoustic instrument production to Bozeman, Montana. In '18 Gibson went into Chapter 11 bankruptcy, emerging later in the year with KKR as new majority owner and James "JC" Curleigh as CEO.

The various models of Firebirds, Flying Vs, Les Pauls, SGs, and Super 400s are grouped together under those general headings. Custom Shop and Historic instruments are listed with their respective main model (for example, the '39 Super 400 Historical Collection model is listed with the Super 400s).

Model specifications can cross model years. For example, it is possible that an early '60 Gibson guitar might have a specification, such as a wider-rounder neck, which is typically a '59 spec. In that case it is possible for the early '60 model to be valued more closely to the late '59 model than to a mid to late '60 model with a thinner-flatter neck profile.

Orville Gibson

1894-1902. Hand-made and carved by Orville Gibson, various models and sizes most with standard printed white rectangle label "O.H. Gibson" with photo of Orville Gibson and lyre-mandolin. Prices are for fully functional original or refurbished examples. It is almost expected that a black Orville Gibson instrument has been refinished, and most of those were done by Gibson.

MODEL YEAR	FEATURES	EXC. COND. LOW	HIGH
1894-1902	Basic plain model	$4,300	$43,000
1894-1902	Fancy rare model	$25,000	$55,000
1894-1902	Very rare, historical	$30,000	$77,000

335 S Custom

1980-1981. Solidbody, 335-shaped, mahogany body, unbound rosewood 'board, 2 exposed Dirty Finger humbuckers, coil-tap, TP-6 tailpiece. Also available in natural finish, branded headstock Firebrand version.

MODEL YEAR	FEATURES	EXC. COND. LOW	HIGH
1980-1981		$1,125	$1,475

335 S Deluxe

1980-1982. Same as 335 S Custom but with bound ebony 'board, brass nut.

MODEL YEAR	FEATURES	EXC. COND. LOW	HIGH
1980-1982		$1,125	$1,475

335 S Limited Run

2011-2013. Maple body and neck, rosewood 'board, nitro-finish sunburst.

MODEL YEAR	FEATURES	EXC. COND. LOW	HIGH
2011-2013		$975	$1,275

335 S Standard

1980-1981. Same as 335 S Custom except stop tailpiece, no coil-tap. Also available in natural finish, branded headstock Firebrand version.

MODEL YEAR	FEATURES	EXC. COND. LOW	HIGH
1980-1981		$1,125	$1,475

Advanced Jumbo

1936-1940. Dreadnought, 16" wide, round shoulders, Brazilian rosewood back and sides, sunburst, reintroduced '90-'97.

MODEL YEAR	FEATURES	EXC. COND. LOW	HIGH
1936-1940		$58,000	$75,000

Advanced Jumbo (Reissue)

1990-1999, 2002-2018. Issued as a standard production model, but soon available only as a special order for most of the '90s; currently offered as standard production. Renamed 1936 Advanced Jumbo for 1997-1998. There were also some limited-edition Ajs offered during the '90s.

MODEL YEAR	FEATURES	EXC. COND. LOW	HIGH
1990-1999	Reissue	$1,800	$2,325
1994	Machiche	$1,800	$2,325
2002-2018	Reintroduced	$1,800	$2,325

Advanced Jumbo 12

2015. 12-fret neck.

MODEL YEAR	FEATURES	EXC. COND. LOW	HIGH
2015		$2,050	$2,675

Advanced Jumbo 75th Anniversary

2011-2012. 75th Anniversary label, 2nd edition 75 made with on-board electronics.

MODEL YEAR	FEATURES	EXC. COND. LOW	HIGH
2011	1st edition	$2,075	$2,700
2012	2nd edition	$2,075	$2,700

1935 Advanced Jumbo
2013. Limited run of 35, Adirondack red spruce top, Indian rosewood back and sides, Vintage Sunburst.

Model Year	Features	Exc. Cond. Low	Exc. Cond. High
2013		$4,200	$5,500

Advanced Jumbo Koa (CS)
2006. Custom Shop, koa back and sides, Adirondack top.

Model Year	Features	Exc. Cond. Low	Exc. Cond. High
2006		$2,225	$2,900

Advanced Jumbo Luthier's Choice (CS)
2000-2005, 2008. Custom Shop model.

Model Year	Features	Exc. Cond. Low	Exc. Cond. High
2000-2005	Brazilian	$5,600	$7,300
2008	Cocobolo	$2,850	$3,700

Advanced Jumbo Pro
2011-2013. Made for Guitar Center, Baggs pickup, Sitka top, solid rosewood back and sides.

Model Year	Features	Exc. Cond. Low	Exc. Cond. High
2011-2013		$1,300	$1,675

Advanced Jumbo Red Spruce/AJ Red Spruce
2013. Limited Edition, Adirondack red spruce top, rosewood back and sides.

Model Year	Features	Exc. Cond. Low	Exc. Cond. High
2013		$1,800	$2,350

Advanced Jumbo Supreme (CS)
2007. Custom Shop, Madagascar rosewood back and sides, Adirondack spruce top.

Model Year	Features	Exc. Cond. Low	Exc. Cond. High
2007		$2,225	$2,900

Iron Mountain Advanced Jumbo (CS)
2014. Custom Shop model, limited run of 65, Adirondack red spruce top, Birdseye maple back and sides, Honeyburst finish.

Model Year	Features	Exc. Cond. Low	Exc. Cond. High
2014		$2,225	$2,900

Randy Scruggs Advanced Jumbo Limited Edition
2010-2018. Sitka spruce top, East Indian rosewood body, king's crown headstock logo on, crown markers, Fishman pickup, vintage sunburst.

Model Year	Features	Exc. Cond. Low	Exc. Cond. High
2010-2018		$2,150	$2,800

All American II
1996. Solidbody electric with vague double-cut Melody Maker body style, 2 pickups.

Model Year	Features	Exc. Cond. Low	Exc. Cond. High
1996		$550	$725

B.B. King Custom
1980-1988. Lucille on peghead, 2 pickups, multi-bound, gold-plated parts, Vari-tone, cherry or ebony, renamed B.B. King Lucille in '88.

Model Year	Features	Exc. Cond. Low	Exc. Cond. High
1980-1988		$2,450	$3,200

B.B. King Lucille
1988-2019. Introduced as B.B. King Custom, renamed B.B. King Lucille. Lucille on peghead, 2 pickups, multi-bound, gold-plated parts, Vari-tone, cherry or ebony. In '07 B.B. King logo and large king's crown on headstock with Lucille logo on truss rod cover.

Model Year	Features	Exc. Cond. Low	Exc. Cond. High
1988-2019		$2,450	$3,200
2007-2009	King logo	$2,450	$3,200

B.B. King Standard
1980-1985. Like B.B. King Custom, but with stereo electronics and chrome-plated parts, cherry or ebony.

Model Year	Features	Exc. Cond. Low	Exc. Cond. High
1980-1985		$2,100	$2,750

B.B. King 80th Birthday Lucille
2005. Custom Shop, limited run of 80, 'guard engraved with crown and signature, headstock engraved with artwork from King's birthday tribute album.

Model Year	Features	Exc. Cond. Low	Exc. Cond. High
2005		$3,900	$5,100

B.B. King Super Lucille
2002-2004. Signed guard, abalone inlays, custom black sparkle finish.

Model Year	Features	Exc. Cond. Low	Exc. Cond. High
2002-2004		$3,500	$4,500

B-15
1967-1971. Mahogany, spruce top, student model, natural finish.

Model Year	Features	Exc. Cond. Low	Exc. Cond. High
1967-1971		$750	$975

B-20
1971-1972. 14.5" flat-top, mahogany back and sides, dot markers, decal logo, strip in-line tuners with small buttons.

Model Year	Features	Exc. Cond. Low	Exc. Cond. High
1971-1972		$1,025	$1,325

B-25 3/4 / B-25 N 3/4
1962-1968. Short-scale version, flat-top, mahogany body, cherry sunburst (natural finish is the B-25 3/4 N).

Model Year	Features	Exc. Cond. Low	Exc. Cond. High
1962	Wood bridge	$1,125	$1,450
1963-1964	Plastic bridge	$975	$1,250
1965		$875	$1,125
1966-1968		$800	$1,025

B-25/B-25 N
1962-1977, 2008-2012. Flat-top, mahogany, bound body, upper belly on bridge (lower belly '68 on), cherry sunburst or black (natural finish is B-25 N). Reissued in '08.

Model Year	Features	Exc. Cond. Low	Exc. Cond. High
1962	Wood bridge	$1,925	$2,500
1963-1964	Plastic bridge	$1,925	$2,500
1965		$1,425	$1,850
1966-1968	Above belly bridge	$1,350	$1,750
1968	Black, white 'guard	$2,700	$3,500
1968	Red, white 'guard	$2,300	$3,000
1969	Below belly bridge	$1,100	$1,425
1970-1977		$1,025	$1,325
2008-2012	Reissue, black	$1,275	$1,650

B-25-12/B-25-12 N
1962-1977. Flat-top 12-string version, mahogany, bound body, cherry sunburst (natural finish is the B-25-12 N).

Model Year	Features	Exc. Cond. Low	Exc. Cond. High
1962-1964	No tailpiece	$1,550	$2,000
1965	Trapeze tailpiece	$1,275	$1,650
1966-1968	Trapeze tailpiece	$1,200	$1,550
1969	Below belly bridge	$1,025	$1,325
1970-1977		$950	$1,225

B-45-12/B-45-12 N
1961-1979. Flat-top 12-string, mahogany, round shoulders for '61, square after, sunburst (natural finish is the B-45-12 N).

Model Year	Features	Exc. Cond. Low	Exc. Cond. High
1961-1962	Round shoulder	$1,725	$2,275
1962-1963	Square shoulder	$1,725	$2,275
1964	No tailpiece	$1,725	$2,275
1965	Trapeze tailpiece	$1,300	$1,700
1966-1968		$1,225	$1,600
1969	Below belly bridge	$1,075	$1,400
1970-1979		$975	$1,275

B-45-12 Limited Edition
1991-1992. Limited edition reissue with rosewood back and sides, natural.

Model Year	Features	Exc. Cond. Low	Exc. Cond. High
1991-1992		$975	$1,275

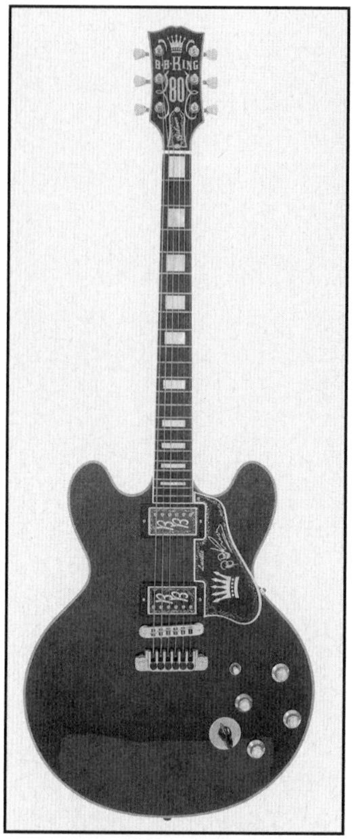

2005 Gibson B.B. King 80th Birthday Lucille

Imaged by Heritage Auctions, HA.com

1964 Gibson B-25-12N

Ted Wulfers

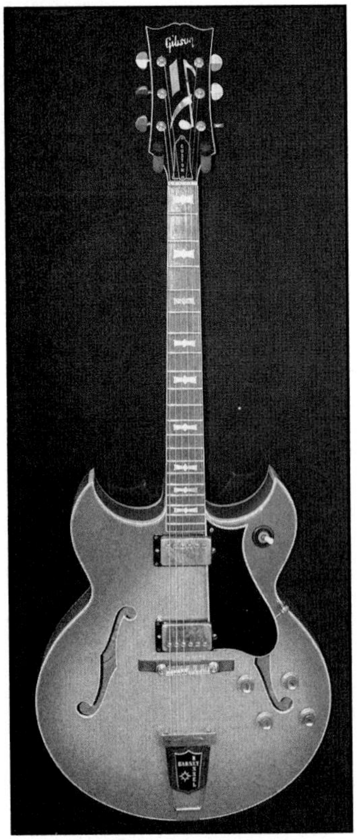

1968 Gibson Barney Kessel Custom

Jeff Marshall

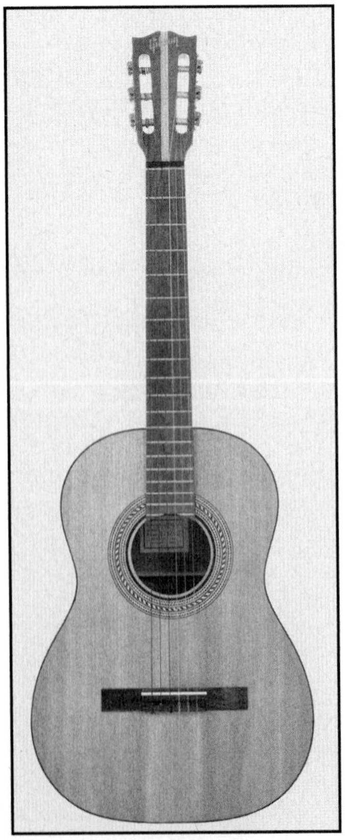

1967 Gibson C-O

Imaged by Heritage Auctions, HA.com

Barney Kessel Custom

1961-1973. Double-cut archtop, 2 humbuckers, gold hardware, cherry sunburst.

MODEL YEAR	FEATURES	EXC. COND. LOW	HIGH
1961	PAFs	$6,500	$8,600
1962	Pat #	$4,300	$5,650
1963-1964		$4,300	$5,650
1965		$3,800	$5,000
1966-1979		$3,700	$4,800
1970-1973		$2,800	$3,700

Barney Kessel Regular

1961-1974. Double-cut archtop, 2 humbuckers, nickel hardware, cherry sunburst.

MODEL YEAR	FEATURES	EXC. COND. LOW	HIGH
1961	PAFs	$6,400	$8,300
1962	Pat #	$4,100	$5,300
1963-1964		$4,100	$5,300
1965		$3,600	$4,700
1966-1969		$3,400	$4,500
1970-1974		$2,500	$3,300

Blue Ridge

1968-1979, 1989-1990. Flat-top, dreadnought, laminated rosewood back and sides, natural finish, reintroduced for '89-'90.

MODEL YEAR	FEATURES	EXC. COND. LOW	HIGH
1968-1969	Brazilian	$1,075	$1,400
1970-1979		$1,075	$1,400

Blue Ridge 12

1970-1978. Flat-top, 12 strings, laminated rosewood back and sides, natural finish.

MODEL YEAR	FEATURES	EXC. COND. LOW	HIGH
1970-1978		$1,075	$1,400

Blues King

2012-2013. Acoustic/electric, non-cut, bubinga back and sides, dot inlays.

MODEL YEAR	FEATURES	EXC. COND. LOW	HIGH
2012-2013		$1,475	$1,900

Blueshawk

1996-2006. Small single-cut, f-holes, 2 single-coil hum cancelling Blues 90 pickups, 6-way Varitone dial, gold hardware, Bigsby option starts '98.

MODEL YEAR	FEATURES	EXC. COND. LOW	HIGH
1996-2006		$875	$1,125

B-SJ Blue Ridge

1989. Model name on label is B-SJ, truss rod covers logo is Blue Ridge, SJ appointments but with narrow peghead shape.

MODEL YEAR	FEATURES	EXC. COND. LOW	HIGH
1989		$1,275	$1,650

Byrdland

1955-1992. Thinline archtop, single-cut (rounded until late-'60, pointed '60-late-'69, rounded after '69, rounded or pointed '98-present), 2 pickups, now part of the Historic Collection.

MODEL YEAR	FEATURES	EXC. COND. LOW	HIGH
1956-1957	Natural, Alnicos	$8,100	$10,500
1956-1957	Sunburst, Alnicos	$8,100	$10,500
1958-1959	Natural, PAFs	$12,000	$15,500
1958-1959	Sunburst, PAFs	$12,000	$15,500
1960-1962	Natural, PAFs	$10,800	$14,000
1960-1962	Sunburst, PAFs	$10,800	$14,000
1963-1964	Natural, pat #	$6,500	$8,500
1963-1964	Sunburst, pat #	$6,500	$8,500
1965	Natural	$5,800	$7,500
1965	Sunburst	$5,800	$7,500
1966-1969	Natural	$5,500	$7,100
1966-1969	Sunburst	$5,500	$7,100
1970-1992	Various colors	$3,800	$5,000

Byrdland Historic Collection

1993-2018. Custom shop, various colors.

MODEL YEAR	FEATURES	EXC. COND. LOW	HIGH
1993-2018		$4,400	$5,800

C-0 Classical

1962-1971. Spruce top, mahogany back and sides, bound top, natural.

MODEL YEAR	FEATURES	EXC. COND. LOW	HIGH
1962-1964		$575	$750
1965		$500	$650
1966-1971		$475	$600

C-1 Classical

1957-1971. Spruce top, mahogany back and sides, bound body, natural.

MODEL YEAR	FEATURES	EXC. COND. LOW	HIGH
1957-1959		$600	$800
1960-1964		$575	$750
1965		$525	$675
1966-1971		$450	$600

C-1 D Laredo

1963-1971. Natural spruce top, mahogany sides and back, upgrade to standard C-1.

MODEL YEAR	FEATURES	EXC. COND. LOW	HIGH
1963-1965		$575	$750

C-1 E Classical Electric

1960-1967. C-1 with ceramic bridge pickup, catalog notes special matched amplifier that filters out fingering noises.

MODEL YEAR	FEATURES	EXC. COND. LOW	HIGH
1960-1964		$600	$800
1965		$525	$675
1966-1967		$450	$600

C-1 S Petite Classical

1961-1966. Petite 13 1/4" body, natural spruce top, mahogany back and sides.

MODEL YEAR	FEATURES	EXC. COND. LOW	HIGH
1961-1964		$575	$750
1965		$525	$675
1966-1967		$450	$600

C-2 Classical

1960-1971. Maple back and sides, bound body, natural.

MODEL YEAR	FEATURES	EXC. COND. LOW	HIGH
1960-1964		$650	$850
1965		$600	$775
1966-1971		$550	$700

C-4 Classical

1962-1968. Maple back and sides, natural.

MODEL YEAR	FEATURES	EXC. COND. LOW	HIGH
1962-1964		$675	$875
1965		$625	$800
1966-1968		$575	$750

C-6 Classical/Richard Pick

1958-1971. Rosewood back and sides, gold hardware, natural.

MODEL YEAR	FEATURES	EXC. COND. LOW	HIGH
1958-1959	Brazilian	$1,400	$1,825
1960-1964	Brazilian	$1,300	$1,675
1965	Brazilian	$1,200	$1,550
1966-1969	Brazilian	$1,075	$1,400
1970-1971	Indian	$675	$876

C-8 Classical

1962-1969. Rosewood back and sides, natural.

MODEL YEAR	FEATURES	EXC. COND. LOW	HIGH
1962-1964		$1,300	$1,700
1965		$1,175	$1,525
1966-1969		$1,075	$1,400

C-100 Classical

1971-1972. Slotted peghead, spruce top, mahogany back and sides, ebony 'board, Gibson Master Model label, non-gloss finish.

MODEL YEAR	FEATURES	EXC. COND. LOW	HIGH
1971-1972		$450	$600

MODEL YEAR	FEATURES	EXC. COND. LOW	HIGH

C-200 Classical

1971-1972. C-100 with gloss finish.

1971-1972		$550	$700

C-300 Classical

1971-1972. Similar to C-100, but with rosewood 'board, wood binding, wider soundhole ring.

1971-1972		$550	$700

C-400 Classical

1971-1972. Rosewood sides and back, spruce top, high-end appointments, chrome hardware.

1971-1972		$575	$750

C-500 Classical

1971-1972. C-400 with gold hardware.

1971-1972		$650	$850

CF-100

1950-1958. Flat-top, pointed cutaway, mahogany back and sides, bound body, sunburst finish.

1950-1958		$3,975	$5,300

CF-100 E

1951-1958, 2009. CF-100 with a single-coil pickup. Also offered in '94 1950 CF-100 E limited edition and in '07 as a Custom Shop model.

1950-1958		$3,900	$5,175

CF-100 E Reissue (Custom Shop)

2007. All maple body, ebony 'board, 24 made.

2007		$1,800	$2,350

Challenger I

1983-1985. Single-cut Les Paul-shaped solidbody, 1 humbucker, bolt-on maple neck, rosewood 'board, dot markers, silver finish standard.

1983-1985		$475	$625

Challenger II

1983-1985. 2 humbucker version.

1983-1985		$500	$650

Challenger III

1984. 3 single-coil version, never cataloged so could be very limited.

1984		$500	$650

Chet Atkins CE

1981-2005. CE stands for Classical Electric, single-cut, multi-bound body, rosewood 'board until '95, then ebony, standard width nut, gold hardware, various colors.

1981-2005		$1,225	$1,600

Chet Atkins CEC

1981-2005. Same as CE, but with ebony 'board and 2" classical width nut, black or natural.

1981-2005		$1,225	$1,600

Chet Atkins Country Gentleman

1986-2005. Thinline archtop, single rounded cutaway, 2 humbuckers, multi-bound, gold hardware, Bigsby. Part of Gibson's Custom line.

1986-2005		$2,125	$2,750

Chet Atkins SST

1987-2006. Steel string acoustic/electric solidbody, single-cut, bridge transducer pickup, active bass and treble controls, gold hardware.

1987-1993	White	$1,600	$2,050
1987-2006	Black	$1,600	$2,050
1987-2006	Natural	$1,025	$1,350
1993	Red Wine or Antique	$1,600	$2,050
1994	Cherry Sunburst	$1,600	$2,050

Chet Atkins SST Celebrity

1991-1993. Gold hardware, 200 made, black body with unique white 'guard.

1991-1993		$1,900	$2,500

Chet Atkins SST-12

1990-1994. 12-string model similar to 6-string, mahogany/spruce body, preamp circuit controls single transducer pickup, natural or ebony finish.

1990-1994		$1,025	$1,350

Chet Atkins Super 4000 (Custom Shop)

1997-2000. Figured curly maple back and sides, orange amber finish, 25 built, COA.

1997-2000		$16,500	$21,500

Chet Atkins Tennessean

1990-2005. Single rounded cutaway archtop, 2 humbuckers, f-holes, bound body. Part of Gibson's Custom line.

1990-2005		$1,300	$1,675

Chicago 35

1994-1995. Flat-top dreadnought, round shoulders, mahogany back and sides, prewar script logo.

1994-1995		$950	$1,225

Citation

1969-1971. 17" full-depth body, single-cut archtop, 1 or 2 floating pickups, fancy inlay, natural or sunburst. Only 8 shipped for '69-'71, reissued the first time '79-'83 and as part of the Historic Collection in '93.

1969-1971	Sunburst, natural	$15,600	$20,300

Citation (1st Reissue)

1979-1983. Reissue of '69-'71 model, reintroduced in '93 as part of Gibson's Historic Collection.

1979-1983	Sunburst, natural	$15,600	$20,300

Citation (2nd Reissue)

1993-2018. Limited production via Gibson's Historic Collection, natural or sunburst.

1994-2018	Various colors	$12,000	$15,500

Citation Custom Shop Vanderbilt Rose

2015. Vanderbilt Rose lacquer finish with matching maple 'guard.

2015		$6,600	$8,500

CJ-165/CJ-165 Modern Classic

2006-2008. Called J-165 in first year of production, classic small body non-cutaway flat-top, solid spruce top, maple or rosewood back and sides.

2006-2008		$1,325	$1,725

CJ-165 EC Modern Classic

2007-2009. As above, but with single-cut, electronics, maple or rosewood back and sides.

2007-2009		$1,450	$1,900

CL-10 Standard

1997-1998. Flat-top, solid spruce top, laminated mahogany back and sides.

1997-1998		$825	$1,075

CL-20 Standard Plus

1997-1998. Flat-top, laminated back and sides, 4-ply binding with tortoiseshell appointments, abalone diamond inlays.

1997-1998		$975	$1,275

1982 Gibson Chet Atkins CE

Geoff Barker

1983 Gibson Challenger II

Gary Klinger

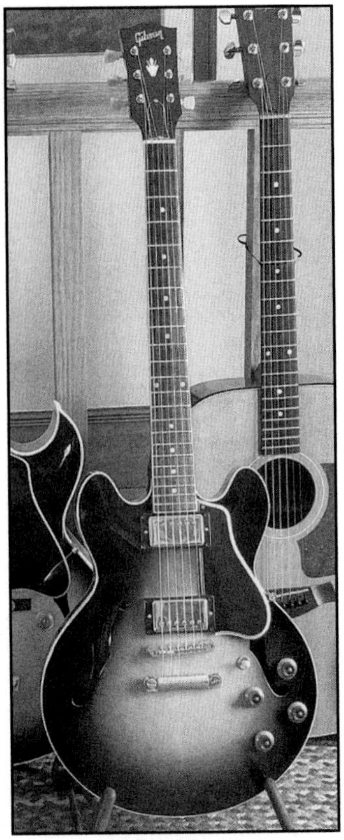

Gibson CS-336

Emmitt Omar

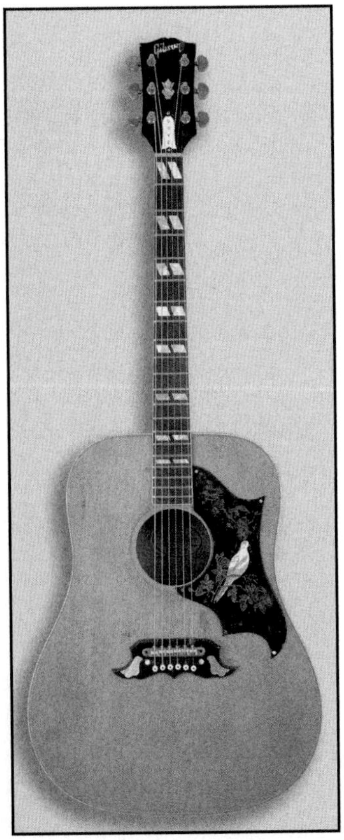

1968 Gibson Dove

MODEL YEAR	FEATURES	EXC. COND. LOW	HIGH

CL-30 Deluxe

1997-1998. J-50 style dreadnought, solid spruce top, bubinga back and sides, factory electronics.

1997-1998		$1,025	$1,325

CL-35 Deluxe

1998. Single cutaway CL-30.

1998		$1,100	$1,425

CL-40 Artist

1997-1998. Flat-top, gold hardware, rosewood back and sides.

1997-1998		$1,475	$1,900

CL-45 Artist

1997-1998. Single cutaway CL-40.

1997-1998		$1,550	$2,000

CL-50

1997-1999. Custom Shop model, D-style body, higher-end appointments, offered with Brazilian rosewood.

1997-1999		$3,100	$4,000

Corvus I

1982-1984. Odd-shaped solidbody with offset V-type cut, bolt maple neck, rosewood 'board, 1 humbucker, standard finish was silver gloss, but others available at an additional cost.

1982-1984		$850	$1,100

Corvus II

1982-1984. Same as Corvus I, but with 2 humbuckers, 2 volume controls, 1 master tone control.

1982-1984		$950	$1,225

Corvus III

1982-1984. Same as Corvus I, but with 3 single-coil pickups, master volume and tone control, 5-way switch.

1982-1984		$1,075	$1,400

Crest Gold

1969-1971. Double-cut thinline archtop, Brazilian rosewood body, 2 pickups, bound top and headstock, bound f-holes, gold-plated parts. The Crest name was also used on a few (3-6) custom guitars based on the L-5CT built in 1959-'61.

1969-1971		$4,900	$6,300

Crest Silver

1969-1972. Silver-plated parts version of Crest.

1969-1972		$4,400	$5,700

CS Series

2002-2017. Custom Shop, scaled down ES-335 body style, plain top or F indicates figured top.

2002-2003	CS-356, plain top	$2,025	$2,625
2002-2012	CS-336F, figured top	$2,350	$3,050
2002-2014	CS-356F, figured top	$2,700	$3,500
2002-2017	CS-336, plain top	$2,175	$2,800

Dave Grohl DG-335

2007-2008. Inspired By Series, Trini Lopez Standard specs, Certificate of Authenticity, Pelham Blue or black finish.

2007-2008		$5,500	$7,100

Dove

1962-1996, 1999-2013. Flat-top acoustic, maple back and sides, square shoulders.

1962-1964	Natural or Sunburst	$4,600	$6,000
1965	Natural, early '65	$4,100	$5,300
1965	Natural, late '65	$3,400	$4,400
1965	Sunburst, early '65	$4,000	$5,300
1965	Sunburst, late '65	$3,000	$3,900
1966-1969	Natural or Sunburst	$2,600	$3,400
1970-1979	Various colors	$1,950	$2,525
1980-1984	Double X	$1,900	$2,475
1985-1988	Single X	$1,900	$2,475
1989	New specs	$1,900	$2,475
1990-1996	Various colors	$1,900	$2,475
1999-2013	Reissue model	$1,900	$2,475

'60s Dove

1997-2004. Spruce top, maple back and sides, Dove appointments.

1997-2004		$2,300	$3,000

'60s Dove Limited Edition

2014. Sitka spruce top, flame maple back and sides, Indian rosewood 'board, Vintage Cherryburst finish.

2014		$2,150	$2,800

Dove Artist

1999-2005. Sitka spruce, Indian rosewood.

1999-2005		$1,725	$2,250

Dove Commemorative

1994-1996. Commemorates Gibson's 100th anniversary, Heritage or Antique Cherry finish, 100 built.

1994-1996		$2,300	$3,000

Dove In Flight Limited Edition (CS)

1996-1997. Custom Shop, 250 made, figured maple sides and back, Adirondack top, Certificate of Authenticity, dove inlays on headstock.

1996-1997		$4,000	$5,200

Doves In Flight (Brazilian)

2003. Custom Shop, only 2 made.

2003		$9,600	$12,500

Doves In Flight (Production Model)

1996-present. Gibson Custom model, maple back and sides, doves in flight inlays.

1996-2020		$3,500	$4,600

Dove Elvis Presley Signature

2008-2010. Artist Series, Certificate of Authenticity, black.

2008-2010		$2,300	$3,000

Super Dove

2009-2012. Cutaway, on-board electronics, sold through certain retailers.

2009-2012		$2,450	$3,200

Duane Eddy Signature

2004-2009. Single rounded cut, flamed maple top and back, 2 single-coils and piezo, pearl 'moustache' markers, signature engraved on 'guard, Bigsby, Rockabilly Brown finish.

2004-2009		$3,650	$4,750

EAS Deluxe

1992-1994. Single-cut flat-top acoustic/electric, solid flamed maple top, bound rosewood 'board, trapezoid inlays, 3-band EQ, Vintage Cherry Sunburst.

1992-1994		$900	$1,175

EAS Standard/Classic

1992-1995. Like EAS Deluxe, but with spruce top, unbound top, dot inlays, called EAS Classic for '92.

1992-1995		$800	$1,050

MODEL YEAR	FEATURES	EXC. COND. LOW	HIGH

EBS(F)-1250 Double Bass

1962-1968. Double-cut SG-type solidbody, double-neck with bass and 6-string, originally introduced as the EBSF-1250 because of a built-in fuzztone, which was later deleted, only 22 made.

1962-1964	Various colors	$16,300	$21,200
1965	Various colors	$12,300	$16,200
1966-1968	Various colors	$11,900	$15,400

EC-10 Standard

1997-1998. Jumbo single-cut, on-board electronics, solid spruce top, maple back and sides.

1997-1998		$800	$1,050

EC-20 Starburst

1997-1998. Jumbo single-cut, on-board electronics, solid spruce top, maple back and sides, renamed J-185 EC in '99.

1997-1998		$1,350	$1,750

EC-30 Blues King Electro (BKE)

1995-1998. Jumbo single-cut, on-board electronics, solid spruce top, maple back and sides, double parallelogram inlays, renamed J-185 EC in '99.

1995-1998		$1,475	$1,900

EDS-1275 Double 12

1958-1967, 1977-1990. Double-cut doubleneck with one 12- and one 6-string, thinline hollowbody until late-'62, SG-style solidbody '62 on.

1958-1961	Custom order	$31,200	$40,500
1962-1964	SG body	$27,100	$35,200
1965	SG body	$21,000	$27,200
1966-1967	SG body	$15,500	$20,200
1977-1979	Various colors	$4,400	$5,800
1977-1979	White	$4,400	$5,800
1980-1989	Various colors	$3,300	$4,300
1990	Various colors	$2,600	$3,400

EDS-1275 Double 12 (Historic Collection)

1991-2018. Custom Shop Historic Collection reissue.

1991-2018	Various colors	$2,600	$3,400

EDS-1275 Double 12 Centennial

1994. Guitar of the Month (May), gold medallion on back of headstock, gold hardware.

1994	Cherry	$2,700	$3,500

EDS-1275 Double 12 Jimmy Page VOS Signature

2008. Custom Shop model with Certificate of Authenticity, 250 made.

2008		$6,400	$8,300

EDS-1275 Double Neck Alex Lifeson

2015. Custom Shop model based on Lifeson's '70s Gibson, limited run of 100, first 25 signed and played by Alex, aged Arctic White.

2015		$4,300	$5,600

EMS-1235 Double Mandolin

1958-1963, 1965-1967. Double-cut, doubleneck with 1 regular 6-string and 1 short 6-string (the mandolin neck), thinline hollowbody until late-1962, SG-style solidbody '62-'68, black, sunburst or white, total of 61 shipped.

1958-1961	Custom order	$21,000	$27,000
1962-1963	SG body	$19,000	$25,000
1965	SG body	$16,000	$21,000
1966-1967	SG body	$15,000	$20,000

MODEL YEAR	FEATURES	EXC. COND. LOW	HIGH

ES-5/ES-5N

1949-1955. Single-cut archtop, 3 P-90 pickups, sunburst or natural (5N). Renamed ES-5 Switchmaster in '55.

1949-1955	Natural	$7,000	$9,100
1949-1955	Sunburst	$6,200	$8,100

ES-5 Switchmaster/ES-5N Switchmaster

1956-1962. Renamed from ES-5, single-cut (rounded until late 1960, pointed after) archtop, 3 P-90s until end of '57, humbuckers after, switchmaster control.

1956-1957	Natural, P-90s	$8,250	$10,725
1956-1957	Sunburst, P-90s	$7,625	$9,925
1957-1960	Natural, hums	$14,500	$18,725
1957-1960	Sunburst, hums	$12,675	$16,475
1960-1962	Pointed Florentine cutaway	$9,800	$12,750

ES-5/ES-5 Switchmaster Custom Shop Historic

1995-2006. Historic Collection.

1995-2002	ES-5, sunburst, P-90s	$3,200	$4,200
1995-2002	Switchmaster, Wine Red, hums	$3,000	$4,000
1995-2006	Switchmaster, natural, hums	$3,200	$4,200
1995-2006	Switchmaster, sunburst, hums	$3,200	$4,200

ES-100

1938-1941. Archtop, 1 pickup, bound body, sunburst, renamed ES-125 in '41.

1938-1941		$1,450	$1,900

ES-120 T

1962-1970. Archtop, thinline, 1 f-hole, bound body, 1 pickup, sunburst.

1962-1964		$1,200	$1,550
1965		$1,125	$1,475
1966-1970		$1,100	$1,425

ES-125

1941-1943, 1946-1970. Archtop, non-cut, 1 pickup, sunburst, renamed from ES-100.

1941-1943	Blade pickup	$2,000	$2,600
1947-1949	1st non-adj, P-90s	$2,000	$2,600
1950	1st non-adj, P-90s	$1,900	$2,450
1951-1959	Adj P-90s with poles	$1,900	$2,450
1960-1964		$1,350	$1,750
1965		$1,250	$1,650
1966-1970		$1,100	$1,450

ES-125 C

1966-1970. Wide body archtop, single pointed cutaway, 1 pickup, sunburst.

1965		$1,400	$1,825
1966-1970		$1,300	$1,700

ES-125 CD

1966-1970. Wide body archtop, single-cut, 2 pickups, sunburst.

1965		$2,000	$2,600
1966-1970		$1,800	$2,400

ES-125 D

1957. Limited production (not mentioned in catalog), 2 pickup version of thick body ES-125, sunburst.

1957		$2,150	$2,800

Gibson Doves in Flight

1955 Gibson ES-5 Switchmaster

Jim King

1961 Gibson ES-125 TC

Jim King

1952 Gibson ES-150

Frank Manno

MODEL YEAR	FEATURES	EXC. COND. LOW	HIGH

ES-125 T

1956-1968. Archtop thinline, non-cut, 1 pickup, bound body, sunburst.

1956-1959		$1,800	$2,400
1960-1964		$1,600	$2,100
1965		$1,500	$1,950
1966-1968		$1,400	$1,800

ES-125 T 3/4

1957-1968. Archtop thinline, short-scale, non-cut, 1 pickup, sunburst.

1957-1960		$1,800	$2,400
1961-1964		$1,600	$2,100
1965		$1,500	$1,950
1966-1968		$1,400	$1,800

ES-125 TC

1960-1970. Archtop thinline, single pointed cutaway, bound body, 1 P-90 pickup, sunburst.

1960-1964		$1,800	$2,400
1965		$1,500	$1,950
1966-1970		$1,400	$1,800

ES-125 TD

1957-1963. Archtop thinline, non-cut, 2 pickups, sunburst.

1957-1963		$2,250	$2,950

ES-125 TDC or ES-125 TCD

1960-1971. Archtop thinline, single pointed cutaway, 2 P-90 pickups, sunburst.

1960-1964		$2,800	$3,650
1965	Early '65	$2,650	$3,450
1965	Late '65	$2,350	$3,050
1966-1971		$2,350	$3,050

ES-130

1954-1956. Archtop, non-cut, 1 pickup, bound body, sunburst, renamed ES-135 in '56.

1954-1956		$2,075	$2,700

ES-135

1956-1958. Renamed from ES-130, non-cut archtop, 1 pickup, sunburst, name reused on a thin body in the '90s.

1957-1959		$2,075	$2,700

ES-135 (Thinline)

1991-2003. Single-cut archtop, laminated maple body, 2 humbuckers or 2 P-90s, chrome or gold hardware, sunburst.

1991-2003	Stop tail	$1,300	$1,700
1991-2003	Trapeze	$1,300	$1,700

ES-137 Classic

2002-2015. Thin-body electric single cut, trapezoid inlays, 2 humbuckers, f-holes, gold hardware.

2002-2015		$1,325	$1,725

ES-137 Custom

2002-2011. Like Classic, but with split-diamond inlays and varitone.

2002-2011		$1,325	$1,725

ES-137 P (Premier)

2002-2005. Like Classic, but with exposed humbuckers, chrome hardware and very small trapezoid inlays.

2002-2005		$1,100	$1,450

ES-139

2013-2016. Semi-hollow Les Paul style body, 2 humbuckers, Guitar Center model.

2013-2016		$875	$1,151

MODEL YEAR	FEATURES	EXC. COND. LOW	HIGH

ES-140 (3/4) or ES-140N (3/4)

1950-1956. Archtop, single-cut, 1 pickup, bound body, short-scale, sunburst or natural option (140N).

1950-1956	Natural option	$2,200	$2,850
1950-1956	Sunburst	$2,050	$2,650

ES-140 (3/4) T or ES-140N (3/4) T

1957-1968. Archtop thinline, single-cut, bound body, 1 pickup, short-scale, sunburst or natural option (140N).

1956-1958	Natural option	$2,200	$2,850
1956-1959	Sunburst	$2,050	$2,650
1960-1964	Sunburst	$1,900	$2,450
1965	Sunburst	$1,725	$2,250
1966-1968	Sunburst	$1,575	$2,850

ES-150

1936-1942, 1946-1956. Historically important archtop, non-cut, bound body, Charlie Christian bar pickup from '36-'39, various metal covered pickups starting in '40, sunburst.

1936-1939	Charlie Christian pu	$4,800	$6,200
1940-1942	Metal covered pu	$4,800	$6,200
1946-1949	P-90 pickup	$2,000	$2,600
1950-1956	P-90 pickup	$1,875	$2,450

ES-150 DC

1969-1975. Archtop, double rounded cutaway, 2 humbuckers, multi-bound.

1969-1975	Cherry, natural, walnut	$2,500	$3,250

ES-165 Herb Ellis

1991-2011. Single pointed cut hollowbody, 1 humbucker, gold hardware.

1991-2011		$1,725	$2,250

ES-175 or ES-175N

1949-1971. Archtop, single pointed cutaway, 1 pickup (P-90 from '49-early-'57, humbucker early-'57-'71), multi-bound, sunburst or natural option (175N).

1949-1956	Natural, P90	$4,200	$5,500
1949-1956	Sunburst, P-90	$4,200	$5,500
1957-1959	Natural, hum	$6,425	$8,350
1957-1963	Sunburst, PAF	$6,200	$8,000
1964	Sunburst, pat #	$5,000	$6,500
1965	Sunburst, hum	$3,300	$4,400
1966-1969	Sunburst, pat #	$2,725	$3,550
1967-1969	Black	$2,725	$3,550
1970-1971	Various colors	$2,425	$3,150

ES-175 CC

1978-1979. 1 Charlie Christian pickup, sunburst or walnut.

1978-1979		$2,425	$3,150

ES-175 D or ES-175N D

1952-2016. Archtop, single-cut, 2 pickups (P-90s from '53-early-'57, humbuckers early-'57 on), sunburst or natural option (175N D). Humbucker pickups were converted from PAF-stickers to Pat. No.-stickers in '62. Different models were converted at different times. An ES-175 model, made during the transitional time, with PAFs, will fetch more. In some of the electric-archtop models, the transition period may have been later than '62. Cataloged as the ES-175 Reissue in the '90s, Currently as the ES-175 under Gibson Memphis.

1952-1956	Natural, P-90s	$4,600	$6,000

MODEL YEAR	FEATURES	EXC. COND. LOW	HIGH
1952-1956	Sunburst, P-90s	$4,100	$5,300
1957-1963	Natural, PAFs	$10,800	$14,000
1957-1963	Sunburst, PAFs	$9,600	$12,500
1964	Natural, pat #	$5,500	$7,100
1964	Sunburst, pat #	$4,800	$6,200
1965	Natural, pat #	$4,700	$6,100
1965	Sunburst, hums	$4,200	$5,400
1966	Natural, pat #	$3,900	$5,000
1966	Sunburst, hums	$3,300	$4,300
1967-1969	Black	$3,300	$4,300
1967-1969	Various colors	$3,300	$4,300
1970-1979	Various colors	$2,700	$3,500
1980-2016	Various colors	$2,500	$3,300

ES-175 D Tenor

1966. Rare custom ordered tenor version, sunburst.

1966		$3,200	$4,200

ES-175 D-AN

1999-2000. Limited run, P-90s, Antique Natural finish.

1999-2000		$2,575	$3,350

ES-175 SP

2006. Single humbucker version, sunburst.

2006		$2,425	$3,150

ES-175 Steve Howe

2001-2007. Maple laminate body, multi-bound top, sunburst.

2001-2007		$2,700	$3,500

ES-175 T

1976-1980. Archtop thinline, single pointed cutaway, 2 humbuckers, various colors.

1976-1980		$2,700	$3,500

ES-225 T or ES-225N T

1955-1959. Thinline, single pointed cutaway, 1 P-90 pickup, bound body and neck, sunburst or natural option (225N T).

1955-1959	Natural	$3,100	$4,000
1955-1959	Sunburst	$2,300	$3,000

ES-225 TD or ES-225N TD

1956-1959. Thinline, single-cut, 2 P-90s, bound body and neck, sunburst or natural option (225N TD).

1956-1959	Natural	$4,600	$6,000
1956-1959	Sunburst	$3,400	$4,400

1959 ES-225 Historic

2014-2016. Single-cut TD reissue with 2 P-90s, sunburst.

2014-2016		$2,200	$2,850

ES-235 Gloss

2018-2020. Semi-hollow single-cut, maple neck, rosewood 'board, 2 pickups.

2018-2020		$975	$1,275

ES-250 or ES-250N

1939-1940. Archtop, carved top, special Christian pickup, multi-bound, high-end appointments, stairstep headstock '39 and standard in '40, sunburst or natural option (250N).

MODEL YEAR	FEATURES	EXC. COND. LOW	HIGH
1939	Natural, stairstep hs	$22,300	$29,000
1939	Sunburst, stairstep hs	$14,200	$18,500
1940	Natural, standard hs	$22,300	$29,000
1940	Sunburst, standard hs	$14,200	$18,500

ES-275

2016-2019. Hollowbody archtop, single-cut, 2 humbucker pickups standard or optional P-90s, various colors and finishes, certificate of authenticity.

2016	Gloss, opaque	$2,300	$3,000
2016-2019	Gloss, figured	$2,700	$3,600
2017	Gloss, P-90s	$2,700	$3,600
2018	Custom metallic	$2,700	$3,600
2019	Satin, opaque	$2,200	$2,900

ES-295

1952-1958. Single pointed cutaway archtop, 2 pickups (P-90s from '52-late-'57, humbuckers after), gold finish, gold-plated hardware.

1952-1957	P-90s	$5,900	$7,650
1957-1958	Humbuckers	$12,500	$16,500

ES-295 Reissue

1990-1993. Gold finish, 2 P-90 pickups, Bigsby.

1990-1993		$2,850	$3,700

ES-295 Historic Collection

1990-2000. Antique Gold finish, 2 P-90 pickups, Bigsby.

1990-2000		$2,850	$3,700

ES-295 '52 Historic Collection (CS)

2013-2015. Custom Shop. Limited VOS Vintage Cherry offered in '15.

2013-2015		$2,850	$3,700
2015	Limited Cherry	$2,850	$3,700

ES-295 Scotty Moore Signature

1999. Custom Shop, 15 produced, 12 with Scotty's actual signature on lower bout, Bullion Gold, trapeze tailpiece.

1999		$6,100	$7,900

ES-300 or ES-300N

1940-1942, 1945-1953. Archtop, non-cut, f-holes, had 4 pickup configurations during its run, sunburst or natural (300N).

1940	Natural, oblong diagonal pu	$3,300	$4,300
1940	Sunburst, oblong diagonal pu	$2,900	$3,800
1941-1942	Natural, 1 pu	$3,300	$4,300
1941-1942	Sunburst, 1 pu	$2,900	$3,800
1945	Black, 1 pu	$2,700	$3,500
1945-1949	Sunburst, 1 pu	$2,700	$3,200
1945-1953	Natural, 1 pu	$2,700	$3,500
1949-1953	Natural, 2 pus	$3,800	$4,900
1949-1953	Sunburst, 2 pus	$2,900	$3,700

ES-320 TD

1971-1974. Thinline archtop, double-cut, 2 single-coil pickups, bound body, cherry, natural, or walnut.

1971-1974		$1,425	$1,850

ES-325 TD

1972-1978. Thinline archtop, double-cut, 2 mini-humbuckers, 1 f-hole, bound body, top mounted control panel, cherry or walnut.

1972-1978		$1,675	$2,175

1970s Gibson ES-175D

Bernunzio Uptown Music

Gibson ES-235

1959 Gibson ES-330 T

David Stone

1967 Gibson ES-330 TD

Tyler Willison

ES-330 L

2009-2015. Custom Shop, classic 330 design, 2 dog-ear P-90 pickups, sunburst or black. 2015 model has humbuckers.

Model Year	Features	Exc. Cond. Low	Exc. Cond. High
2009-2015		$2,200	$2,850

ES-330 T or ES-330N T

1959-1963. Double rounded cutaway, thinline, 1 pickup, bound body and neck, sunburst, cherry or natural option (330N T). In the '60s came with either an original semi-hard case (better than chip board) or a hardshell case. Prices quoted are for hardshell case; approximately $100 should be deducted for the semi-hard case.

Model Year	Features	Exc. Cond. Low	Exc. Cond. High
1959-1961	Natural	$7,100	$9,100
1959-1963	Cherry	$3,900	$5,100
1959-1963	Sunburst	$3,900	$5,100

ES-330 TD or ES-330N TD

1959-1972. Double rounded cutaway, thinline, 2 pickups, bound body and neck, sunburst, cherry or natural option (330N TD). In the '60s came with either an original semi-hard case (better than chip board) or a hardshell case. Prices noted for the hardshell case; approximately $100 should be deducted for the semi-hard case.

Model Year	Features	Exc. Cond. Low	Exc. Cond. High
1959-1961	Natural	$9,600	$12,500
1959-1962	Cherry, dots	$5,800	$7,500
1959-1962	Sunburst, dots	$5,800	$7,500
1963-1964	Cherry, blocks	$5,000	$6,500
1963-1964	Sunburst, blocks	$5,000	$6,500
1965	Sunburst, cherry	$4,300	$5,600
1966-1968	Sunburst, cherry	$3,700	$4,800
1967-1968	Burgundy Metallic (unfaded)	$3,700	$4,800
1968	Walnut option	$3,700	$4,800
1969-1972	Various colors, long neck	$3,700	$4,800

ES-330 TDC

1998-2000. Custom Shop model, block markers.

Model Year	Features	Exc. Cond. Low	Exc. Cond. High
1998-2000		$2,200	$2,850

ES-330 VOS

2012-2016. Custom Shop, Bigsby tailpiece, late '50s specs and VOS finish in sunburst, natural or cherry.

Model Year	Features	Exc. Cond. Low	Exc. Cond. High
2012-2016	All colors	$2,200	$2,850

1959 ES-330 Historic VOS

2012-2019. Gibson Memphis, Historic series, Vintage Original Specs, P-90 pickups, trapeze tailpiece, certificate.

Model Year	Features	Exc. Cond. Low	Exc. Cond. High
2012-2019		$2,200	$2,850

1959 ES-330 Wildwood Spec

2015. Gibson Memphis, Limited Edition, figured top, natural, certificate.

Model Year	Features	Exc. Cond. Low	Exc. Cond. High
2015		$2,475	$3,225

1964 ES-330 Historic VOS

2015-2019. Historic series, vintage specs, P-90 pickups, trapeze tailpiece, certificate.

Model Year	Features	Exc. Cond. Low	Exc. Cond. High
2015-2019		$2,200	$2,850

ES-333

2002-2005. Economy ES-335, no 'guard, no headstock inlay, exposed coils, stencil logo, satin finish.

Model Year	Features	Exc. Cond. Low	Exc. Cond. High
2002-2005		$1,300	$1,675

ES-335 TD or ES-335N TD

1958-1981. The original design ES-335 has dot 'board inlays and a stop tailpiece, sunburst, cherry or natural option (335N). Block inlays replaced dots in mid-'62, in late-'64 the stop tailpiece was replaced with a trapeze tailpiece. Replaced by the ES-335 DOT in '81.

Model Year	Features	Exc. Cond. Low	Exc. Cond. High
1958	Natural, bound neck	$70,000	$92,000
1958	Natural, bound neck, Bigsby	$53,000	$69,000
1958	Natural, unbound neck	$70,000	$92,000
1958	Natural, unbound neck, Bigsby	$53,000	$69,000
1958	Sunburst, bound neck	$29,000	$38,000
1958	Sunburst, bound neck, Bigsby	$24,000	$31,500
1958	Sunburst, unbound neck	$29,000	$38,000
1958	Sunburst, unbound neck, Bigsby	$24,000	$31,500
1959	Cherry (early), stop tail	$27,500	$36,000
1959	Natural, bound neck	$78,000	$102,000
1959	Natural, bound neck, Bigsby	$66,000	$86,500
1959	Sunburst, bound neck	$35,000	$46,000
1959	Sunburst, bound neck, Bigsby	$27,000	$35,000
1960	Cherry, factory Bigsby	$21,000	$27,000
1960	Cherry, factory stop tail	$25,500	$33,000
1960	Natural, factory Bigsby	$41,000	$53,000
1960	Natural, factory stop tail	$50,000	$65,000
1960	Sunburst, factory Bigsby	$21,000	$27,000
1960	Sunburst, factory stop tail	$25,500	$33,000
1961	Cherry, factory Bigsby	$18,200	$23,800
1961	Cherry, factory stop tail	$23,000	$30,000
1961	Sunburst, factory Bigsby	$18,200	$23,800
1961	Sunburst, factory stop tail	$23,000	$30,000
1962	Cherry, blocks, PAFs	$17,300	$22,500
1962	Cherry, blocks, pat#	$14,200	$18,400
1962	Cherry, dots, PAFs	$21,000	$27,500
1962	Cherry, vibrola, pat#	$11,800	$15,300

MODEL YEAR	FEATURES	EXC. COND. LOW	HIGH
1962	Sunburst, blocks, PAFs	$17,300	$22,500
1962	Sunburst, blocks, pat#	$14,200	$18,400
1962	Sunburst, dots, PAFs	$21,000	$27,500
1962	Sunburst, dots, pat#	$14,200	$18,400
1962	Sunburst, vibrola, pat#	$11,800	$15,300
1963-1964	Cherry, factory Bigsby	$12,000	$15,500
1963-1964	Cherry, factory Maestro	$12,000	$15,500
1963-1964	Cherry, factory stop tail	$14,200	$18,400
1963-1964	Sunburst, factory Bigsby	$12,000	$15,500
1963-1964	Sunburst, factory Maestro	$12,000	$15,500
1963-1964	Sunburst, factory stop tail	$14,200	$18,400
1965	Early '65, wide neck	$9,300	$12,000
1965	Mid '65, narrow neck	$5,300	$6,900
1966	Cherry, sunburst	$4,900	$6,400
1966	Pelham Blue	$10,600	$13,800
1966	Sparkling Burgundy	$6,200	$8,000
1967	Black	$7,700	$10,000
1967	Cherry, sunburst	$4,900	$6,400
1967	Pelham Blue	$10,600	$13,800
1967	Sparkling Burgundy	$6,200	$8,000
1968	Cherry, sunburst	$4,800	$6,200
1968	Pelham Blue	$10,600	$13,800
1968	Sparkling Burgundy	$6,200	$8,000
1969	Cherry, sunburst	$4,150	$5,400
1969	Walnu finish option	$3,550	$4,600
1970-1976	Cherry, sunburst	$3,225	$4,200
1970-1976	Walnut finish option	$2,950	$3,900
1977-1979	All colors, coil tap	$2,700	$3,500
1980-1981	All colors	$2,425	$3,150

ES-335 Dot

1981-1990. Reissue of '60 ES-335 and replaces ES-335 TD. Name changed to ES-335 Reissue. Various color options including highly figured wood.

1981	Black	$3,000	$3,900
1981-1990	Cherry, sunburst	$2,700	$3,500
1981-1990	Natural	$2,500	$3,250

ES-335 Dot CMT (Custom Shop)

1983-1985. Custom Shop ES-335 Dot with curly maple top and back, full-length center block, 2 PAF-labeled humbuckers, natural or sunburst.

1983-1985		$3,100	$4,000

ES-335 Reissue/ES-335 '59 Dot Reissue/ ES-335

1991-present. Replaced the ES-335 DOT, dot inlays, various color options including highly figured wood. Renamed the 1959 ES-335 Dot Reissue in '98 and currently just ES-335 followed by options - Dot, Block (added in '98), Fat Neck (added in '08), Figured (added in '06), Plain, Satin (added in '06).

MODEL YEAR	FEATURES	EXC. COND. LOW	HIGH
1991-2020	Cherry, sunburst, walnut, black	$1,925	$2,500
1991-2020	Natural	$2,050	$2,650
2006-2017	Satin	$1,500	$1,950

ES-335 Dot P-90

2007. Custom Shop limited edition with black dog-ear P-90s, stop tailpiece.

2007		$2,200	$2,900

ES-335-12

1965-1971. 12-string version of the 335.

1965-1968		$2,700	$3,500

ES-335 '59 Dot Historic Collection (CS)

1999-2000, 2002-2016. Custom Shop model, Historical Series based upon 1959 ES-335 dot neck, figured maple top on early series, plain on later, nickel hardware.

1999-2016	Figured top	$3,100	$4,000
2002-2016	Plain top	$2,850	$3,700

1959 ES-335 Dot Reissue Limited Edition

2009-2017. Custom Shop, plain laminated maple top/back/sides, rounded '59 neck profile, '57 Classic humbuckers, Certificate of Authenticity, 250 each to be made in Antique Vintage Sunburst or Antique Natural (standard gloss or V.O.S. treatments).

2009-2017		$3,100	$4,000

1959 ES-335 Ultra Heavy Aged/Ultra Light Aged

2021. Custom Shop Murphy Lab Collection, ultra heavy aged (Vintage Natural) and ultra light (Ebony or Vintage Natural).

2021	Heavy	$5,200	$6,700
2021	Light	$3,200	$4,200

ES-335 '60s Block Inlay

2004-2007. Made in Memphis facility, plain maple top, small block markers.

2004-2007		$1,950	$2,550

50th Anniversary 1960 ES-335 (Custom Shop)

2009-2010. Dot markers, natural.

2009-2010		$2,875	$3,700

1961 ES-335 Heavy Aged/Ultra Light Aged

2021. Custom Shop Murphy Lab Collection, heavy or ultra light aged, Sixties Cherry finish.

2021	Heavy Aged	$5,200	$6,700
2021	Light Aged	$3,200	$4,200

1961 ES-335 Reissue (Custom Shop)

2020-present. Historic series, 3-Ply maple/poplar/ maple body, solid mahogany neck, Indian rosewood 'board, 2 Alnico pickups, Sixties Cherry or Vintage Burst.

2020		$2,900	$3,800

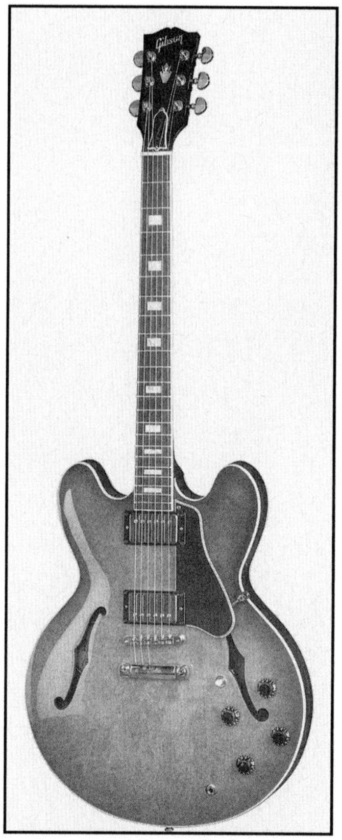

2017 Gibson ES-335

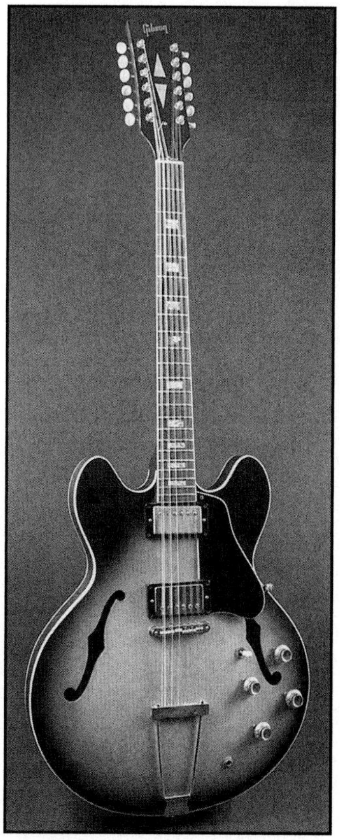

1967 Gibson ES-335-12

Carter Vintage Guitars

1979 Gibson ES-335 Pro
Michael Campbell

2014 Gibson ES-335
Rich Robinson
Michael Alonzi

MODEL YEAR	FEATURES	EXC. COND. LOW	HIGH

50th Anniversary 1963 Block ES-335TD/ ES-335TDC (CS)

2010-2013. Memphis Custom Shop, block markers, double-ring vintage-style tuners, Antique Vintage Sunburst (TD), Antique Faded Cherry (TDC).

2010-2013	TD, sunburst	$2,850	$3,700
2010-2013	TDC, cherry	$2,850	$3,700

ES-335 '63 Block Historic Collection (CS)

1998-2000, 2002-2018. Custom Shop Historical Series, based upon 1963 ES-335 with small block markers, figured maple top on early series, plain on later, nickel hardware.

1998-2000	1st release, figured top	$3,100	$4,000
2002-2018	2nd release, figured top	$3,100	$4,000
2002-2018	Plain top	$2,850	$3,700

1964 ES-335 Ultra Light Aged

2021. Custom Shop Murphy Lab Collection, Sixties Cherry finish.

2021		$3,200	$4,200

ES-335 Alvin Lee

2006-2007. Custom Division Nashville, 50 made, features reflect Alvin Lee's Big Red ES-335 complete with decal art, cherry red, includes certificate of authenticity (if missing value is reduced). There is also an unlimited version without certificate.

2006-2007	With certificate	$3,850	$5,000

ES-335 Andy Summers

2002. Custom Shop, 50 made, script signature on 'guard, early dot neck specs, nitro cherry finish, certificate of authenticity.

2007	With certificate	$2,850	$3,700

ES-335 Artist

1981. Off-set dot markers, large headstock logo, metal truss rod plate, gold hardware, 3 control knobs with unusual toggles and input specification.

1981		$2,700	$3,500

ES-335 Canadian Custom

2007. Custom Shop Canadian exclusive run of 50, maple leaf 'Limited Edition' decal on back of headstock, 'Custom Made' engraved plate on guitar front, solid mahogany neck, pearloid block inlays, antique cherry finish with aged binding.

2007		$2,050	$2,650

ES-335 Centennial

1994. Centennial edition, gold medallion in headstock, diamond inlay in tailpiece, cherry.

1994		$2,850	$3,700

ES-335 Chris Cornell

2012-2016. Olive Drab Green or black.

2012-2016		$2,700	$3,500

ES-335 CRR/CRS

1979. Country Rock Regular with standard wiring and CRR logo. Country Rock Stereo with stereo wiring and CRS logo, 300 of each built, 2 pickups, coil-tap.

1979	CRR	$2,725	$3,525
1979	CRS	$2,800	$3,600

MODEL YEAR	FEATURES	EXC. COND. LOW	HIGH

ES-335 Diamond Edition

2006. Trini Lopez style diamond f-holes, Bigsby tailpiece option, gold hardware, Pelham Blue, pearl white or black pearl.

2006		$2,300	$3,000

ES-335 Eric Clapton Crossroads '64 Reissue

2005. Reissue of EC's, with certificate of authenticity.

2005		$8,700	$11,500

ES-335 Goldtop

2013-2016. Gibson Memphis, limited edition, 2 Burstbucker humbuckers, gold finish.

2013-2016		$2,000	$2,600

ES-335 Gothic

1998-1999. Gothic appointments including ebony 'board and black satin finish.

1998-1999		$1,150	$1,500

ES-335 Government Series

2015-2016. Made from guitar bodies, necks and 'boards returned from Federal Government after '11 raid on Gibson, special run of 300 built, each with Certificate of Authenticity.

2015-2016		$1,775	$2,300

ES-335 Jim Beam Limited Edition

1999. Promotional Custom Shop model, approximately 18 made, large Jim Beam notation on body, comes with certificate.

1999		$1,825	$2,350

ES-335 Jimmy Wallace Reissue

Special order by Texas Gibson dealer Jimmy Wallace.

1980		$2,600	$3,400

ES-335 Joe Bonamassa Signature (CS)

2012. Custom Shop, based on Joe's '61 335, VOS sunburst.

2012		$3,100	$4,000

ES-335 King of the Blues

2006. Offered through Guitar Center, 150 made, based on B.B.'s Lucille.

2006		$2,450	$3,200

ES-335 Larry Carlton

2002-2016. Mr. 335 logo on truss rod cover, block neck like Larry's guitar, vintage (faded) sunburst.

2002-2016		$2,850	$3,700

ES-335 Lee Ritenour

2008. Custom Shop, COA, 50 signed and 100 unsigned, Antique Cherry finish.

2008		$2,850	$3,700

ES-335 Limited Edition

2001. ES-335 style crown inlay on headstock, P-90 pickups.

2001		$2,050	$2,650

ES-335 Nashville

1994. All serial numbers begin with 94, first year Custom Shop run (not the Centennial).

1994		$2,775	$3,600

ES-335 Pro

1979-1981. Two humbucking pickups with exposed coils, bound 'board, cherry or sunburst.

1979-1981		$2,050	$2,650

MODEL YEAR	FEATURES	EXC. COND. LOW	HIGH

ES-335 Rich Robinson

2014-2016. Bigsby, small blocks, Cherry VOS finish.

2014-2016		$2,800	$3,600

ES-335 Roy Orbison

2006. About 70 made, RO serial number, black finish.

2006		$3,100	$4,000

ES-335 Rusty Anderson

2013. Figured maple, natural, dot neck specs.

2013		$3,100	$4,000

ES-335 Showcase Edition

1988. Guitar of the Month series, limited production, black gothic-style hardware, EMG pickups, transparent white/beige finish.

1988		$2,250	$2,900

ES-335 Studio

1986-1991, 2013-2020. Bound body, 2 Dirty Finger humbuckers, cherry or ebony. Reissued in '13 by Gibson Memphis using '58 specs but with Vintage Sunburst or ebony finish.

1986-1991		$1,375	$1,775
2013-2020	Memphis	$825	$1,075

ES-335 Warren Haynes

2013-2015. Custom Shop model.

2013-2015	500 made	$2,800	$3,600
2014	1961 Ltd Ed	$2,800	$3,600

ESDT-335

2001-2009. Memphis Custom Shop, flame maple top and back, 2 humbucking pickups, various colors.

2001-2009		$2,500	$3,200

ES-336

1996-1998. Custom Shop smaller sized ES-335 with smaller headstock, dot markers.

1996-1998	All options	$1,850	$2,400

ES-339

2007-present. Modern series, smaller-sized bound 335 body, 2 humbuckers, block inlays.

2007-2020	All options	$1,800	$2,300

ES-339 Studio

2013-2018. Stripped-down 339, no binding or pickguard, dot inlays.

2013-2018		$850	$1,100

ES-339 Traditional Pro

2013. Figured or plain, cherry or vintage sunburst.

2013		$1,550	$2,050

ES-340 TD

1968-1973. The 335 with a laminated maple neck, master volume and mixer controls, various colors.

1968-1973	Natural, Walnut	$2,600	$3,400

ES-345 TD or ES-345 TDSV

1959-1983. The 335 with Vari-tone, stereo, 2 humbuckers, gold hardware, double parallelogram inlays, stop tailpiece '59-'64 and '82-'83, trapeze tailpiece '65-'82. Cataloged as ES-345 TDSV by '80.

1959	Cherry, Bigsby	$17,500	$22,750
1959	Cherry, stud tail	$22,650	$29,450
1959	Natural, Bigsby	$28,850	$37,500
1959	Natural, stud tail	$44,300	$57,600
1959	Sunburst, Bigsby	$17,500	$22,750
1959	Sunburst, stud tail	$22,650	$29,450
1960	Cherry, Bigsby	$15,500	$20,150
1960	Cherry, stud tail	$20,600	$26,800
1960	Natural, Bigsby	$26,800	$34,800
1960	Natural, stud tail	$41,200	$53,500
1960	Sunburst, Bigsby	$15,500	$20,150
1960	Sunburst, stud tail	$20,600	$26,800
1961	Cherry, Bigsby	$12,400	$16,100
1961	Cherry, stud tail	$16,500	$21,500
1961	Sunburst, Bigsby	$12,400	$16,100
1961	Sunburst, stud tail	$16,500	$21,500
1962	Bigsby, PAF	$12,400	$16,100
1962	Stud tail, PAF	$13,400	$17,400
1963-1964	Bigsby, pat #	$10,100	$13,100
1963-1964	Stud tail, pat #	$11,900	$15,500
1965	Early '65 wide neck	$6,575	$8,575
1965	Mid '65 narrow neck	$4,275	$5,550
1966-1969	Various colors	$3,575	$4,650
1970-1976	Various colors	$2,950	$3,900
1977-1979	Various colors	$2,700	$3,500
1980-1983	TDSV, Various colors	$2,425	$3,150

ES-345 Historic Collection

1998-1999. Custom Shop, stopbar, Bigsby or Maestro tailpiece, Viceroy Brown, Vintage Sunburst, Faded Cherry or natural.

1998-1999		$2,950	$3,850

ES-345 Reissue

2002-2010. ES-345 features with 6-position Varitone selector, gold hardware, stop tailpiece, various colors.

2002-2010		$2,075	$2,700

1959 ES-345 TD

2014-2015. Period-correct '59 specs with VOS aged look, certificate of authenticity, Historic Burst or natural (TDN) finish.

2014	'59 reissue	$2,650	$3,450
2015	VOS	$2,950	$3,850

ES-346 Paul Jackson Jr.

1997-2006. Custom Shop, 335-like with figured or plain maple top, rosewood 'board, double-parallelogram inlays.

1997-2006		$2,450	$3,200

ES-347 TD or ES-347 S

1978-1985, 1987-1993. 335-style with gold hardware, tune-o-matic bridge, 2 Spotlight double-coil pickups, coil-tap, bound body and neck, S added to name in '87.

1978-1984	TD	$2,550	$3,300
1987-1993	S	$2,550	$3,300

ES-350 or ES-350N

1947-1956. Originally the ES-350 Premier, full body archtop, single-cut, 1 P-90 pickup until end of '48, 2 after, sunburst or natural (350N).

1947-1948	Natural, 1 pu	$5,800	$7,500
1947-1948	Sunburst, 1 pu	$5,800	$7,500
1949-1956	Natural, 2 pu	$6,200	$8,000
1949-1956	Sunburst, 2 pu	$6,200	$8,000

ES-350 Centennial

1994. Guitar of the Month, sunburst, gold hardware, gold medallion on back of headstock, diamond accents, 101 made with serial numbers from 1984-1994. Included a gold signet ring.

1994		$3,000	$4,000

1969 Gibson ES-345 TDSV
Craig Brody

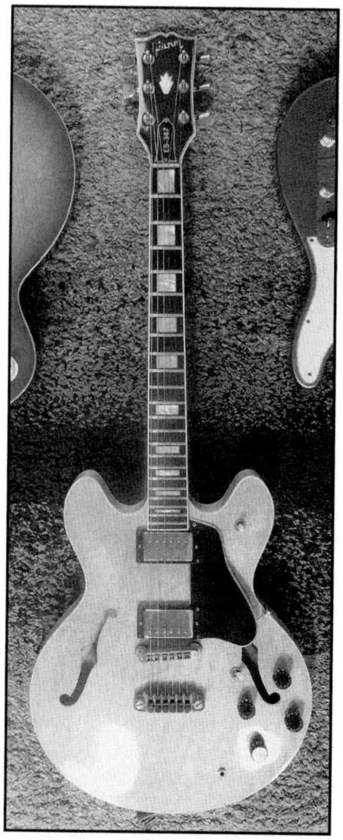

1979 Gibson ES-347
Steve Alvito

1998 Gibson ES-350 T (Custom Shop)

Bernunzio Uptown Music

1966 Gibson ES-355 TD

Ted Wulfers

ES-350 T or ES-350N T

1955-1963, 1977-1981, 1992-1993. Called the ES-350 TD in early-'60s, thinline archtop, single-cut (round '55-'60 and '77-'81, pointed '61-'63), 2 P-90 pickups '55-'56, humbuckers after, gold hardware. Limited runs were done in 1992-1993.

MODEL YEAR	FEATURES	EXC. COND. LOW	HIGH
1956	Natural, P-90s	$5,800	$7,500
1956	Sunburst, P-90s	$5,800	$7,500
1957-1959	Natural, PAFs	$9,500	$12,300
1957-1959	Sunburst, PAFs	$9,500	$12,300
1960-1963	Natural, PAFs	$9,000	$12,000
1960-1963	Sunburst, PAFs	$9,000	$12,000
1977-1981	Natural, sunburst	$2,750	$3,550

ES-350 T (Custom Shop)

1998-2000. Historic Collection reissue.

MODEL YEAR	FEATURES	EXC. COND. LOW	HIGH
1998-2000		$2,850	$3,675

Chuck Berry 1955 ES-350 T

2019. Limited to 55, antique natural with VOS finish.

MODEL YEAR	FEATURES	EXC. COND. LOW	HIGH
2019		$8,900	$11,600

ES-355 TD

1958-1970. 335-style with large block inlays, multi-bound body and headstock, 2 humbuckers, the 355 model was standard with a Bigsby, sideways or Maestro vibrato, non-vibrato models were an option. The prices shown assume a vibrato tailpiece, a factory stop tailpiece was considered an advantage and will fetch more. Early examples have factory Bigsby vibratos, early '60s have sideways vibratos, and late '60s have Maestro vibratos, cherry finish was the standard finish.

MODEL YEAR	FEATURES	EXC. COND. LOW	HIGH
1958-1959	Cherry, PAFs, Bigsby vibrato	$24,000	$31,000
1960-1962	Cherry, PAFs, Bigsby vibrato	$18,200	$23,800
1962	Cherry, PAFs, side-pull vibrato	$18,200	$23,800
1963-1964	Cherry, pat #, Bigsby vibrato	$12,500	$16,300
1965	Early '65 wide neck	$9,100	$11,800
1965	Mid '65 narrow neck	$6,050	$7,850
1966-1968	Cherry or sunburst	$5,625	$7,300
1966-1968	Sparkling Burgundy	$9,100	$11,800
1969-1970	Cherry or sunburst	$4,900	$6,300

ES-355 TDSV

1959-1982. Stereo version of ES-355 with Vari-tone switch, a mono version was available but few were made, the 355 model was standard with a Bigsby, sideways or Maestro vibrato, non-vibrato models were an option. The prices shown assume a vibrato tailpiece. A factory stop tailpiece was considered an advantage and will fetch more, early examples have factory Bigsby vibratos, early-'60s have sideways vibratos and late-'60s have Maestro vibratos, cherry finish was standard, walnut became available in '69.

MODEL YEAR	FEATURES	EXC. COND. LOW	HIGH
1959	Bigsby	$16,400	$21,200
1960	Bigsby	$15,400	$20,000
1961-1963	Sideways, late PAFs	$15,400	$20,000
1962	Maestro, late PAFs	$15,400	$20,000
1963-1964	Maestro, pat #	$11,500	$15,000
1965	Early '65 wide neck	$8,300	$10,800
1965	Mid '65 narrow neck	$5,600	$7,200
1966	Sparkling Burgundy	$8,300	$10,800
1966-1967	Cherry or sunburst, Maestro	$5,000	$6,500
1968	Various colors, Maestro	$5,000	$6,500
1969	Various colors, Bigsby	$4,450	$5,800
1970-1982	Various colors, Bigsby	$4,050	$5,250

ES-355/ES-355 TD (Custom Shop)

1994, 1997, 2006-2010. Mono, Bigsby or stop tail.

MODEL YEAR	FEATURES	EXC. COND. LOW	HIGH
1994-2010		$2,900	$3,800

1959 ES-355 Light Aged/Ultra Light Aged

2021. Custom Shop Murphy Lab Collection, light aged (Watermelon Red) and ultra light (Ebony).

MODEL YEAR	FEATURES	EXC. COND. LOW	HIGH
2021	Light	$4,200	$5,400
2021	Ultra Light	$3,600	$4,700

ES-355 Alex Lifeson

2008-2010. Custom Shop Inspired By series, gold hardware, Alpine White finish.

MODEL YEAR	FEATURES	EXC. COND. LOW	HIGH
2008-2010		$3,750	$4,925

ES-355 Centennial

1994. Guitar of the Month, sunburst, gold hardware, gold medallion on back of headstock, diamond accents, 101 made with serial numbers from 1984-1994. Included a gold signet ring.

MODEL YEAR	FEATURES	EXC. COND. LOW	HIGH
1994		$2,950	$3,800

ES-355 Curly Maple Limited Edition

2010-2012. Figured flamed maple top, stop tailpiece, natural finish.

MODEL YEAR	FEATURES	EXC. COND. LOW	HIGH
2010-2012		$3,050	$4,025

ES-355 Limited Edition VOS

2015-2018. Gibson Memphis, Bigsby, gold hardware, various colors with VOS finish.

MODEL YEAR	FEATURES	EXC. COND. LOW	HIGH
2015-2018		$3,325	$4,325

ES-355 Summer Jam Series

2011. Custom Shop Summer Jam series, 25 made in Bourbon Burst.

MODEL YEAR	FEATURES	EXC. COND. LOW	HIGH
2011		$3,100	$4,000

ES-359

2008-2016. Custom Shop, ES-335/ES-339 style with LP Custom style appointments, minor-figured top and back, sunburst.

MODEL YEAR	FEATURES	EXC. COND. LOW	HIGH
2008-2016		$1,875	$2,425

ES-369

1981-1982. A 335-style with 2 exposed humbucker pickups, coil-tap, sunburst.

MODEL YEAR	FEATURES	EXC. COND. LOW	HIGH
1981-1982		$2,075	$2,700

ES-390

2014-2018. Memphis model, thinline hollow-body, rosewood 'board, 2 P-90s, Vintage Dark Burst finish.

MODEL YEAR	FEATURES	EXC. COND. LOW	HIGH
2014-2018		$1,700	$2,225

ES-446

1999-2003. Single cut semi-hollow, 2 humbuckers, Bigsby, Custom Shop.

MODEL YEAR	FEATURES	EXC. COND. LOW	HIGH
1999-2003	Various colors	$2,225	$2,875

MODEL YEAR	FEATURES	EXC. COND. LOW	HIGH

ES-775

1990-1993. Single-cut hollowbody, 2 humbuckers, gold hardware, ebony, natural or sunburst.

1990-1993		$2,225	$2,875

ES-Artist

1979-1985. Double-cut thinline, semi-hollowbody, no f-holes, 2 humbuckers, active electronics, gold hardware, ebony, fireburst or sunburst. Moog electronics includes 3 mini-switches for compressor, expander and bright boost.

1979-1985		$2,625	$3,400

EST-150 (Tenor)

1937-1939. Tenor version of ES-150, Charlie Christian pickup, sunburst, renamed ETG-150 in '40.

1937-1939		$3,300	$4,300

ETG-150 (Tenor)

1940-1942, 1947-1971. Renamed from EST-150, tenor version of ES-150, 1 metal-covered pickup '40-'42, P-90 after, sunburst.

1940-1942		$3,075	$4,000
1947-1959		$1,800	$2,400
1960-1971		$1,450	$1,900

Everly Brothers

1962-1972. Jumbo flat-top, huge double 'guard, star inlays, natural is optional in '63 and becomes the standard color in '68, reintroduced as the J-180 Everly Brothers in '86.

1962-1964	Black	$11,400	$14,800
1963	Natural option	$11,400	$14,800
1965	Early '65, black, large neck	$9,600	$12,500
1965	Late '65, black, small neck	$7,500	$9,700
1966-1967	Black	$6,600	$8,600
1968-1969	Natural replaces black	$5,100	$6,600
1970-1972	Natural	$4,300	$5,600

Explorer

1958-1959, 1963. Some '58s shipped in '63, korina body, 2 humbuckers. The Explorer market is a very specialized and very small market, with few genuine examples available and a limited number of high-end buyers. The slightest change to the original specifications can mean a significant drop in value. The narrow price ranges noted are for all original examples that have the original guitar case.

1958-1959		$565,000	$735,000
1963		$240,000	$315,000

Explorer (Mahogany)

1975-1982. Mahogany body, 2 humbuckers, black, white or natural.

1975-1982	Black or white	$2,975	$3,850
1975-1982	Natural	$2,975	$3,850

Explorer I

1981-1982. Replaces Explorer (Mahogany), 2 Dirty Finger humbuckers, stoptail or Kahler vibrato, becomes Explorer 83 in '83.

1981-1982		$875	$1,125

Explorer 83 or Explorer (Alder)

1983-1989. Renamed Explorer 83 from Explorer I, changed to Explorer in '84, alder body, 2 humbuckers, maple neck, ebony 'board, dot inlays, triangle knob pattern.

1983-1984		$1,475	$1,925
1985-1989	Custom color, limited run	$1,275	$1,675
1985-1989	Standard finishes	$1,150	$1,500

Explorer II (E/2)

1978-1983. Five-piece maple and walnut laminate body sculptured like V II, ebony 'board with dot inlays, 2 humbuckers, gold-plated hardware, natural finish.

1978-1983	Figured top	$2,600	$3,375
1978-1983	Various colors	$2,475	$3,225

Explorer III

1984-1985. Alder body, 3 P-90 pickups, 2 control knobs, chrome or black hardware ('85 only), optional locking trem.

1984-1985	All options	$1,000	$1,300

Explorer '76/X-plorer/Explorer

1990-2014, 2019-present. Mahogany body and neck, rosewood 'board, dot inlays, 2 humbucking pickups, name changed to X-plorer in 2002 and to Explorer in '09. Reintroduced in '19.

1990-1999	Various colors	$1,000	$1,300
2002-2014	Various colors	$1,000	$1,300

Explorer 90 Double

1989-1990. Mahogany body and neck, 1 single-coil and 1 humbucker, strings-thru-body.

1989-1990		$1,400	$1,825

Explorer Baritone

2011-2013. 28"-scale, 2 exposed humbuckers.

2011-2013		$1,375	$1,800

Explorer Centennial

1994 only. Les Paul Gold finish, 100 year banner inlay at 12th fret, diamonds in headstock and gold-plated knobs, Gibson coin in rear of headstock, only 100 made.

1994		$3,825	$5,025

Explorer CMT/The Explorer

1981-1984. Flamed maple body, bound top, exposed-coil pickups, TP-6 tailpiece.

1981-1984		$3,000	$3,900

Explorer Custom Shop

2003-2012. Custom Shop model with Certificate of Authenticity, Korina body, gold hardware.

2003-2012		$4,400	$5,700

Explorer Designer Series

1983-1985. Custom paint finish.

1983-1985		$1,375	$1,775

Explorer Gothic

1998-2003. Gothic Series with black finish and hardware.

1998-2003		$800	$1,050

Explorer Government Series

2012-2016. Made from guitar bodies, necks and 'boards returned from Federal Government after '11 raid on Gibson, special run of 300 built, each with Certificate of Authenticity.

2013		$950	$1,225

2001 Gibson ES-446

Greg Perrine

1983 Gibson Explorer Heritage

Steve Evans

1983 Gibson Explorer Korina
Bo Belaski

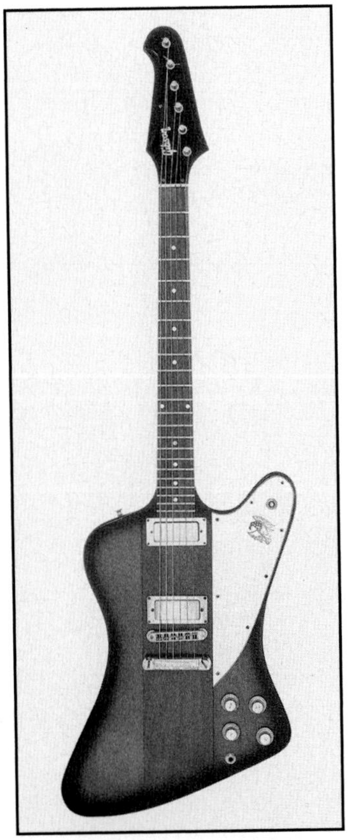

1976 Gibson Firebird 76
Imaged by Heritage Auctions, HA.com

Explorer Heritage

1983. Reissue of '58 Explorer, korina body, gold hardware, inked serial number, limited edition.

MODEL YEAR	FEATURES	EXC. COND. LOW	EXC. COND. HIGH
1983	Black, white, red	$3,125	$4,050
1983	Natural	$4,400	$5,725

Explorer (Limited Edition Korina)

1976. Limited edition korina body replaces standard mahogany body, natural.

1976		$5,600	$7,300

Explorer (Limited Edition Mahogany)

1999. Mahogany with natural finish.

1999		$1,450	$1,875

Explorer Korina

1982-1984. Korina body and neck, 2 humbucking pickups, gold hardware, standard 8-digit serial (versus the inked serial number on the Heritage Explorer of the same era).

1982-1984		$4,400	$5,700

Explorer 1958 Korina/Split Headstock

1994. Split headstock, 50 made.

1994		$6,400	$8,300

Explorer 50th Anniversary '58 Korina

2007-2008. Custom Shop, natural korina, includes custom colors.

2007-2008		$6,400	$8,300

Explorer 50-Year Brimstone Commemorative

2008. Guitar of the month Oct. '08, solid mahogany body, AA figured maple top, higher-end appointments, 50th logo on truss rod cover, Brimstone Burst finish.

2008		$2,225	$2,900

Explorer 120

2014. 120th Anniversary inlay at 12th fret, mahogany body, cherry or black.

2014		$1,150	$1,500

Explorer Pro

2002-2005, 2007-2008. Explorer model updated with smaller, lighter weight mahogany body, 2 humbuckers, ebony or natural.

2002-2008		$1,150	$1,500

Allen Collins Tribute Explorer

2003. Custom Shop, limited production, korina body and neck, rosewood 'board, 2 humbucker pickups.

2003		$7,250	$9,400

Dethklok "Thunderhorse" Explorer

2011-2012. Limited Edition of 400, Thunderhorse logo on truss rod cover, silverburst finish.

2011-2012		$1,700	$2,200

Explorer Robot

2008-2012. Announced Sept. '08, Robot Tuning System, trapezoid markers, 2 exposed humbuckers, red finish.

2008-2012		$950	$1,225

Explorer Split Headstock Collection

2001. Custom Shop model, 25 made, Explorer body with V-split headstock.

2001		$2,700	$3,500

Explorer T

2016-2018. Mahogany body, rosewood 'board, white 'guard, ebony or cherry finish.

2016-2018		$1,000	$1,300

Explorer Voodoo

2002-2004. Juju finish, red and black pickup coils.

2002-2004		$1,050	$1,350

Explorer XPL

1985. Gibson Custom Shop logo on back of headstock, factory Gibson Kahler tremolo, extra cutaway on lower treble bout.

1985		$975	$1,250

Holy Explorer

2009-2011. Explorer body 7 routed holes, 1 knob, 2 exposed humbuckers, Limited Run Series certificate of authenticity, 350 made.

2009-2011		$925	$1,200

Reverse Explorer

2008. Guitar of the Month Sept. '08, 1,000 made, Antique Walnut finish, includes custom guitar case.

2008		$1,225	$1,600

Sammy Hagar Signature Explorer

2011-2013. Mahogany with Red Rocker finish, ghosted Chickenfoot logo on back.

2011-2013		$1,625	$2,100

Shred X Explorer

2008. Guitar of the Month June '08, 1,000 made, ebony finish, black hardware, 2 EMG 85 pickups, Kahler.

2008		$975	$1,250

Tribal Explorer

2009-2011. Black tribal graphics on white body. Limited run of 350.

2009-2011		$875	$1,150

X-Plorer/X-Plorer V New Century

2006-2007. Full-body mirror 'guard, mahogany body and neck, 2 humbuckers, mirror truss rod cover.

2006-2007		$950	$1,250

Firebird I

1963-1969. Reverse body and 1 humbucker '63-mid-'65, non-reversed body and 2 P-90s mid-'65-'69.

1963	Sunburst, reverse, hardtail	$11,200	$14,500
1963	Sunburst, reverse, trem	$7,200	$9,300
1964	Cardinal Red, reverse	$11,500	$15,000
1964	Sunburst, reverse, hardtail	$10,500	$13,700
1964	Sunburst, reverse, trem	$5,950	$7,700
1965	Cardinal Red, reverse	$9,500	$12,300
1965	Custom color, non-reverse	$8,000	$10,400
1965	Sunburst, non-reverse, 2 P-90s	$3,300	$4,300
1965	Sunburst, reverse	$5,200	$6,700
1966	Custom color, non-reverse	$5,950	$7,700
1966	Sunburst, non-reverse	$3,300	$4,300
1967	Custom color, non-reverse	$5,950	$7,700

MODEL YEAR	FEATURES	EXC. COND. LOW	HIGH
1967	Sunburst, non-reverse	$3,300	$4,300
1968-1969	Sunburst, non-reverse	$3,300	$4,300

Firebird I 1963 Reissue Historic Collection

2000-2006. Neck-thru, reverse body, Firebird logo on 'guard, various colors including sunburst and Frost Blue.

MODEL YEAR	FEATURES	LOW	HIGH
2000-2006	Various colors	$2,150	$2,800

Firebird I Custom Shop

1991-1992. Limited run from Custom Shop, reverse body, 1 pickup, gold-plated, sunburst.

MODEL YEAR	FEATURES	LOW	HIGH
1991-1992		$2,125	$2,750

Eric Clapton 1964 Firebird I

2019. Custom Shop, limited run of 100, mahogany body, mahogany/walnut neck, Indian rosewood 'board, signed backplate, 1 Alnico pickup, Vintage Sunburst, certificate.

MODEL YEAR	FEATURES	LOW	HIGH
2019		$5,400	$7,000

Firebird 76

1976-1978. Reverse body, gold hardware, 2 pickups.

MODEL YEAR	FEATURES	LOW	HIGH
1976	Bicentennial	$2,700	$3,500
1976	Black	$2,475	$3,275
1976	Sunburst, red/white/blue 'guard logo	$2,700	$3,500
1977-1978	Sunburst	$2,475	$3,275
1977-1978	White	$2,475	$3,275

Firebird I/ Firebird 76

1980-1982. Reintroduced Firebird 76 but renamed Firebird I.

MODEL YEAR	FEATURES	LOW	HIGH
1980-1982		$2,300	$3,000

Firebird II/Firebird 2

1981-1982. Maple body with figured maple top, 2 full size active humbuckers, TP-6 tailpiece.

MODEL YEAR	FEATURES	LOW	HIGH
1981-1982		$2,600	$3,400

Firebird III

1963-1969. Reverse body and 2 humbuckers '63-mid-'65, non-reversed body and 3 P-90s mid-'65-'69.

MODEL YEAR	FEATURES	LOW	HIGH
1963	Cardinal Red	$11,000	$14,300
1963	Golden Mist	$11,000	$14,300
1963	Polaris White	$10,100	$13,100
1963	Sunburst	$8,200	$10,600
1964	Cardinal Red, reverse	$11,000	$14,300
1964	Golden Mist, reverse	$11,000	$14,300
1964	Pelham Blue	$11,000	$14,300
1964	Polaris White, reverse	$9,300	$12,100
1964	Sunburst, reverse	$8,200	$10,600
1965	Cherry, non-reverse, 3 P-90s	$4,600	$6,000
1965	Cherry, reverse	$8,200	$10,600
1965	Frost Blue, non-reverse	$8,500	$11,000
1965	Frost Blue, reverse	$10,100	$13,100
1965	Inverness Green, non-reverse	$8,500	$11,000
1965	Iverness Green, reverse	$10,100	$13,100
1965	Sunburst, non-reverse, 2 P-90s	$3,900	$5,100
1965	Sunburst, non-reverse, 3 P-90s	$4,100	$5,300
1965	Sunburst, reverse, 2 P-90s	$5,900	$7,650
1965	Sunburst, reverse, mini hums	$6,300	$8,200
1966	Polaris White	$7,700	$10,000
1966-1967	Frost Blue	$8,500	$11,000
1966-1969	Pelham Blue	$8,500	$11,000
1966-1969	Sunburst	$3,900	$5,100
1967	Cherry	$4,100	$5,300

Firebird III 1964 Reissue (Custom Shop)

2000-2013. Maestro, mini-humbuckers, sunburst or color option.

MODEL YEAR	FEATURES	LOW	HIGH
2000-2013		$2,525	$3,275

Firebird Non-Reverse

2002-2004. Non-reverse body, 2 humbuckers, standard finishes. There was also a limited edition in '02 with swirl finishes.

MODEL YEAR	FEATURES	LOW	HIGH
2002-2004		$1,175	$1,550

Firebird Studio Non-Reverse

2011-2012. Non-reverse body, 3 tapped P-90 pickups, 5-way pickup selector switch, dot markers, Vintage Sunburst or Pelham Blue nitro finish.

MODEL YEAR	FEATURES	LOW	HIGH
2011-2012		$1,000	$1,300

Firebird Studio Tribute/Studio T

2012-2017. Reverse mahogany body, '70s profile maple neck, 2 mini-humbuckers.

MODEL YEAR	FEATURES	LOW	HIGH
2012-2017		$1,000	$1,300

Firebird Studio/Firebird III Studio

2004-2010. Two humbuckers, dot markers, tune-o-matic and bar stoptail, reverse body, dark cherry finish.

MODEL YEAR	FEATURES	LOW	HIGH
2004-2010		$1,000	$1,300

Firebird V

1963-1969. Two humbuckers, reverse body '63-mid-'65, non-reversed body mid-'65-'69.

MODEL YEAR	FEATURES	LOW	HIGH
1963	Sunburst, reverse	$12,200	$16,000
1963-1964	Pelham Blue, reverse	$17,700	$23,000
1964	Cardinal Red, reverse	$16,000	$20,800
1964	Sunburst, reverse	$12,500	$16,200
1965	Cardinal Red, reverse	$14,400	$18,650
1965	Sunburst, non-reverse	$4,850	$6,300
1965	Sunburst, reverse	$8,500	$11,000
1966-1967	Cardinal Red, non-reverse	$9,250	$12,000
1966-1969	Sunburst	$4,800	$6,200

Firebird V/Firebird V Reissue/Firebird V 2010

1986-1987, 1990-2018. Based on Firebird V specs, reverse body, 2 pickups, tune-o-matic bridge, vintage sunburst, classic white or ebony with Cardinal Red optional in '91. Called Reissue for '90-'93, renamed

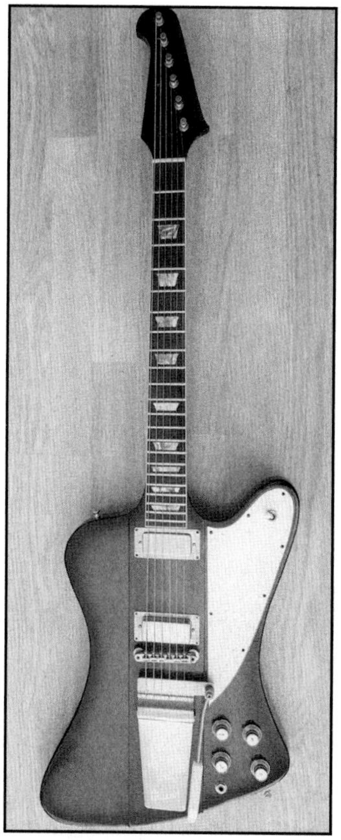

1963 Gibson Firebird V
Daniel Hess

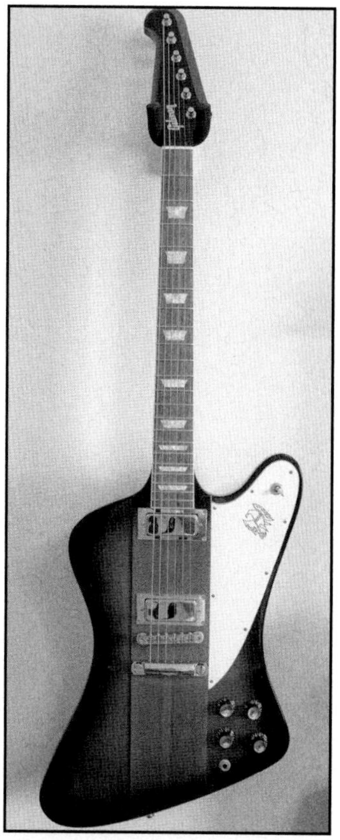

2002 Gibson Firebird V Reissue
Johnny Zapp

1967 Gibson Firebird V-12

Carter Vintage Guitars

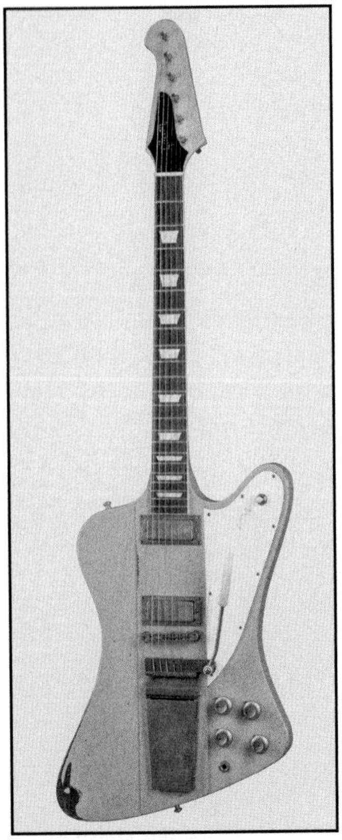

Gibson 1963 Firebird V Murphy Lab Aged

V in '94, then V 2010 in '10.

MODEL YEAR	FEATURES	EXC. COND. LOW	EXC. COND. HIGH
1986-1987	Sunburst, white, black	$2,225	$2,900
1990	Sunburst, white, black	$1,975	$2,550
1991	Cardinal Red	$1,875	$2,425
1991-1999	Sunburst, white, black	$1,350	$1,750
2000-2018	Sunburst, white, black	$1,175	$1,550

Firebird V-12

1966-1967. Non-reverse Firebird V-style body with standard six-on-a-side headstock and split diamond headstock inlay (like ES-335-12 inlay), dot markers, special twin humbucking pickups (like mini-humbuckers).

MODEL YEAR	FEATURES	LOW	HIGH
1966-1967	Custom color	$9,000	$12,000
1966-1967	Sunburst	$4,300	$5,600

Firebird V 1963 Aged (Custom Shop)

2016. Reverse body, Vintage Sunburst, aged hardware.

MODEL YEAR	FEATURES	LOW	HIGH
2016		$2,900	$3,800

Firebird V 1963 Johnny Winter

2008. Johnny Winter script logo, certificate of authenticity.

MODEL YEAR	FEATURES	LOW	HIGH
2008		$5,200	$6,800

1963 Firebird V (Maestro Vibrola) Murphy Lab Aged

2021. Custom Shop Murphy Lab Collection, heavy aged (Antique Frost Blue), light aged (Cardinal Red) and ultra light (Ember Red or Pelham Blue).

MODEL YEAR	FEATURES	LOW	HIGH
2021	Heavy Aged	$4,700	$6,100
2021	Light Aged	$4,100	$5,300
2021	Ultra LightAged	$3,500	$4,500

Firebird V 1965 Reissue (Custom Shop)

2000-2013. Reverse body, 2 mini-humbuckers, Maestro tremolo, certificate, sunburst or colors.

MODEL YEAR	FEATURES	LOW	HIGH
2000-2013		$2,400	$3,100

Firebird V 50th Anniversary

2013. Gold hardware, '50th Anniversary 1963-2013' on 'guard, gold finish.

MODEL YEAR	FEATURES	LOW	HIGH
2013		$1,375	$1,800

Firebird V Celebrity Series

1990-1993. Reverse body, gold hardware, 2 humbuckers, various colors.

MODEL YEAR	FEATURES	LOW	HIGH
1990-1993		$2,400	$3,100

Firebird V Guitar Trader Reissue

1982. Guitar Trader commissioned Firebird reissue, only 15 made, sunburst or white.

MODEL YEAR	FEATURES	LOW	HIGH
1982		$3,100	$4,000

Firebird V Limited Edition Zebrawood

2007. Limited edition from Gibson USA, Guitar of the Week #12, 400 made, zebrawood reverse body.

MODEL YEAR	FEATURES	LOW	HIGH
2007		$1,650	$2,125

Firebird V Medallion

1972-1973. Reverse body, 2 humbuckers, Limited Edition medallion mounted on body.

MODEL YEAR	FEATURES	LOW	HIGH
1972-1973		$4,800	$6,200

Firebird V Zebra Wood

2007. Limited to 400, zebra wood body, guitar of the week series.

MODEL YEAR	FEATURES	LOW	HIGH
2007		$1,800	$2,350

Firebird VII

1963-1969. Three humbuckers, reverse body '63-mid-'65, non-reversed body mid-'65-'69, sunburst standard.

MODEL YEAR	FEATURES	LOW	HIGH
1963-1964	Sunburst, reverse	$13,000	$17,000
1964	Custom color, reverse	$21,000	$27,000
1965	Custom color, non-reverse	$13,800	$18,000
1965	Custom color, reverse	$17,000	$22,000
1965	Sunburst, non-reverse	$5,500	$7,100
1965	Sunburst, reverse	$9,900	$12,800
1966-1968	Custom color, non-reverse	$11,000	$14,200
1966-1969	Sunburst, non-reverse	$5,100	$6,650

Firebird VII (Reissued)

2002-2007. Designer collection, various production models, reverse and non-reverse, 3 pickups, block markers, vibrola, various color options with matching headstock finish.

MODEL YEAR	FEATURES	LOW	HIGH
2002-2007	All colors	$1,650	$2,150

Firebird VII 1965 Historic Collection (Custom Shop)

1998-2013. Custom Shop/Historic Collection, 3 mini-humbuckers, Vintage Sunburst or solid colors.

MODEL YEAR	FEATURES	LOW	HIGH
1998-2013		$2,500	$3,300

20th Anniversary 1965 Firebird VII Reissue

2014. Custom Shop, '65 specs, gold hardware, Golden Mist finish, certificate of authenticity.

MODEL YEAR	FEATURES	LOW	HIGH
2014		$2,700	$3,600

Firebird VII Centennial

1994 only. Headstock medallion, sunburst.

MODEL YEAR	FEATURES	LOW	HIGH
1994		$3,300	$4,300

Firebird X Limited Edition Robot

2011-2018. 1800 to be made, lightweight swamp ash body, 1-piece maple neck, curly maple 'board, 3 pickups, robot electronics, nitro lacquer finish in Redolution or Bluevolution.

MODEL YEAR	FEATURES	LOW	HIGH
2011-2018		$2,350	$3,050

Elliot Easton "Tikibird" Firebird

2013-2018. Reverse body, mahogany, rosewood 'board, 2 pickups, Tiki graphic on 'guard, signature on headstock back, Gold Mist Poly finish.

MODEL YEAR	FEATURES	LOW	HIGH
2013-2018		$1,450	$1,900

Firebird Custom Acoustic

2004-2018. Sitka spruce top, quilted maple back and sides, ebony 'board, mother-of-pearl headstock logo with MOP and abalone flames inlay, antique natural finish.

MODEL YEAR	FEATURES	LOW	HIGH
2004-2018		$2,300	$3,000

Firebird Zero

2016-2018. S Series, new body design, 2 pickups, poplar body, maple neck, rosewood 'board, various colors.

MODEL YEAR	FEATURES	LOW	HIGH
2016-2018		$300	$400

Flamenco 2

1963-1967. Natural spruce top, 14 3/4", cypress back and sides, slotted headstock, zero fret.

MODEL YEAR	FEATURES	LOW	HIGH
1963-1967		$1,125	$1,475

MODEL YEAR	FEATURES	EXC. COND. LOW	HIGH

Flying V

1958-1959, 1962-1963. Only 81 shipped in '58 and 17 in '59, guitars made from leftover parts and sold in '62-'63, natural korina body, string-thru-body design. Original case with oxblood interior adds $2,500.

As with any ultra high-end instrument, each instrument should be evaluated on a case-by-case basis. The Flying V market is a very specialized market, with few untouched examples available, and a limited number of high-end buyers. The price ranges noted are for all-original, excellent condition guitars with the original Flying V case. The slightest change to the original specifications can mean a significant drop in value.

1958-1959		$275,000	$357,000

Flying V (Mahogany)

1966-1970, 1975-1981. Mahogany body, around 200 were shipped for '66-'70. Gibson greatly increased production of Flying Vs in '75. See separate listing for the '71 Medallion V version.

1966	Cherry, sunburst	$22,000	$28,900
1967-1970	Cherry, sunburst	$17,500	$22,600
1975-1981	Various colors	$3,700	$4,800
1979	Silverburst	$4,500	$5,900
1980-1981	Silverburst	$4,200	$5,400

Flying V (Mahogany String-through-body)

1982. Mahogany body, string-thru-body design, only 100 made, most in white, some red or black possible.

1982	All colors	$2,600	$3,400

Flying V Heritage

1981-1982. Limited edition based on '58 specs, korina body, 4 colors available.

1981-1982	Natural	$4,400	$5,725
1981-1982	Various colors	$3,125	$4,050

Flying V I/V '83/Flying V (no pickguard)

1981-1988. Introduced as Flying V I, then renamed Flying V '83 in 1983, called Flying V from '84 on. Alder body, 2 exposed humbuckers, maple neck, ebony 'board, dot inlays, black rings, no 'guard, ebony or ivory finish, designed for lower-end market.

1981-1988		$1,475	$1,925

Flying V Korina

1983. Name changed from Flying V Heritage, korina body, various colors.

1983		$4,400	$5,725

Flying V Reissue/'67/Factor X/Flying V

1990-2014. Mahogany body, called Flying V Reissue first year, then '67 Flying V '91-'02, V Factor X '03-'08, Flying V '09-'14.

1990-2014	Various colors	$1,000	$1,300

Flying V II

1979-1982. Five-piece maple and walnut laminate sculptured body (1980 catalog states top is either walnut or maple), ebony 'board with dot inlays, 2 V-shaped pickups (2 Dirty Fingers humbuckers towards end of run), gold-plated hardware, natural.

1979-1982		$2,475	$3,225
1982	Silverburst	$2,475	$3,225

Flying V 50th Anniversary

2008. Built as replica of '58 square shoulder V, 100 made, natural finish on korina body and neck, rosewood 'board, 8-series serial number, price includes original certificate.

2008		$5,200	$6,800

Flying V '58 Historic Collection (Custom Shop)

1991-2013. Historic Collection, based on '58 Flying V, gold hardware, natural korina.

1991-1999		$4,800	$6,200
2000-2013		$4,300	$5,500

1958 Mahogany Flying V

2021. Custom Shop, mahogany with walnut finish.

2021		$2,800	$3,600

Flying V '59 (Custom Shop)

2001	Natural	$3,500	$4,500
2004	Cherry	$3,500	$4,500
2013	Natural	$2,600	$3,400
2020	TV Black Gold	$2,600	$3,400

Flying V '59 Reissue Mahogany

2014-2020. Custom Shop, mahogany with various colors.

2014-2020		$2,300	$3,000

Flying V '67 Historic Collection (Custom Shop)

1997-2004. Historic Collection, '67 Flying V specs, korina body, natural or opaque colors.

1997-2004		$2,225	$2,900

Flying V '84 Silverburst

2007. Limited Edition Guitar of the Week.

2007		$1,000	$1,300

Flying V '90 Double

1989-1990. Mahogany body, stud tailpiece, 1 single-coil and 1 double-coil humbucker, Floyd Rose tremolo, ebony, silver or white.

1989-1990		$1,400	$1,825

Flying V '98

1998. Mahogany body, '58 style controls, gold or chrome hardware.

1998		$1,400	$1,825

Flying V (Custom Shop)

2004-2008. A few made each year, figured maple top, options include standard point-headstock or split-headstock.

2004-2008		$3,700	$4,700

Flying V 120

2014. Mahogany body and neck, 120th Anniversary inlay at 12th fret, rosewood 'board, 2 BurstBucker pickups, ebony, classic white or Heritage Cherry.

2014		$1,100	$1,425

Flying V 50-Year Commemorative

2008. Guitar of the Month March '08, 1,000 made, AA flamed maple top, higher-end appointments, 50th logo on truss rod cover, Brimstone Burst finish.

2008		$1,775	$2,300

Flying V Brendon Small Snow Falcon

2013. Snow Falcon decal on headstock back, 2 Burstbucker pickups, chrome hardware, Snow Burst finish, limited run.

2013		$1,475	$1,900

Flying V Centennial

1994 only. 100th Anniversary Series, all gold, gold medalion, other special appointments.

1994		$3,825	$5,025

1982 Gibson Flying V Heritage

Steve Evans

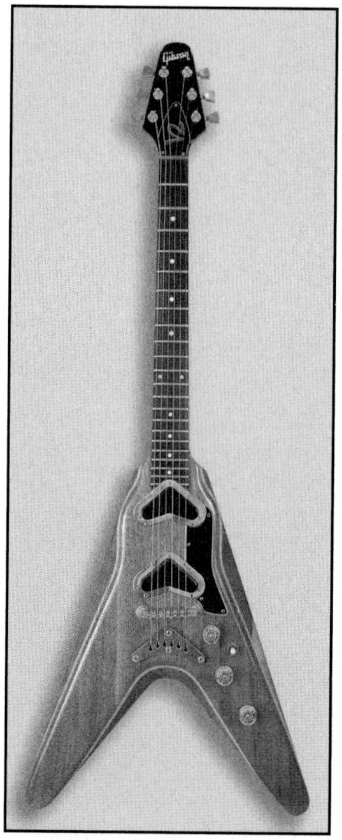

1982 Gibson Flying V II

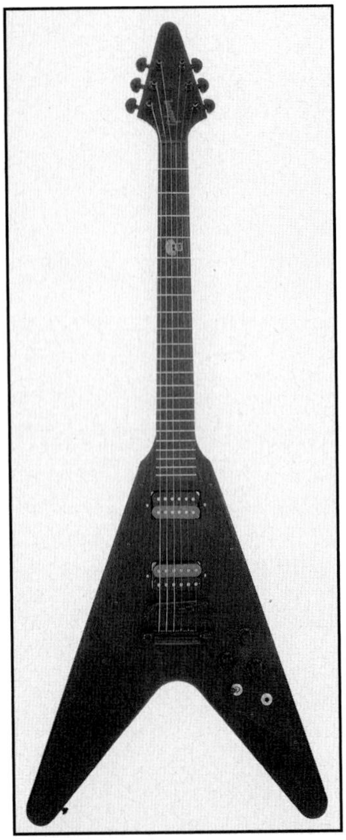

2002 Gibson Flying V Voodoo

Imaged by Heritage Auctions, HA.com

1983 Gibson Futura

Imaged by Heritage Auctions, HA.com

MODEL YEAR	FEATURES	EXC. COND. LOW	HIGH

Flying V CMT/The V

1981-1985. Maple body with a curly maple top, 2 pickups, stud tailpiece, natural or sunburst.

1981-1985		$3,000	$3,900

Flying V Custom (Limited Edition)

2002. Appointments similar to Les Paul Custom, including black finish, only 40 made.

2002		$4,400	$5,700

Flying V Designer Series

1983-1984. Custom paint finish.

1983-1984		$1,375	$1,775

Flying V Faded

2002-2012. Worn cherry finish.

2002-2012		$600	$775

Flying V Gothic/'98 Gothic

1998-2003. Satin black finish, black hardware, moon and star markers.

1998-2003		$800	$1,050

Flying V Government Series

2012-2016. Made from guitar bodies, necks and 'boards returned from Federal Government after '11 raid on Gibson, special run of 300 built, each with Certificate of Authenticity.

2013		$950	$1,225

Flying V Hendrix Hall of Fame

Late-1991-1993. Limited Edition (400 made), numbered, black.

1991-1993		$2,500	$3,300

Flying V Hendrix Psychedelic

2005-2006. Hand-painted 1967 Flying V replica, 300 made, includes certificate, instruments without the certificate are worth less than the amount shown.

2005-2006		$6,700	$8,700

Flying V Lenny Kravitz

2002. Custom Shop, 125 made.

2002		$3,000	$3,900

Flying V Lonnie Mack

1993-1995. Mahogany body with Lonnie Mack-style Bigsby vibrato, cherry.

1993-1995		$3,400	$4,400

Flying V LTD

2001. Limited Edition, certificate of authenticity.

2001		$950	$1,225

Flying V Medallion

1971. Mahogany body, stud tailpiece, numbered Limited Edition medallion on bass side of V, 350 made in '71 (3 more were shipped in '73-'74).

1971-1974		$11,800	$15,300

Flying V New Century

2006-2007. Full-body mirror 'guard, mahogany body and neck, 2 humbuckers, Flying V style neck profile, mirror truss rod cover.

2006-2007		$950	$1,250

Flying V Primavera

1994. Primavera (light yellow/white mahogany) body, gold-plated hardware.

1994		$1,700	$2,200

Flying V Robot

2008-2011. Robot Tuning System.

2008-2011		$950	$1,225

MODEL YEAR	FEATURES	EXC. COND. LOW	HIGH

Flying V T

2016-2017. Mahogany body, thicker 1-piece 'board.

2016-2017		$1,000	$1,300

Flying V The Holy V

2009. Guitar of the month for Jan. '09, large triangular cutouts in bouts, split diamond markers, 1 humbucker, 1 control knob.

2009		$925	$1,200

Flying V Voodoo

2002-2003. Black finish, red pickups.

2002-2003		$1,050	$1,350

Limited Edition Flying V

2016. Dirty Fingers, faded amber finish, gig bag.

2016		$475	$625

Reverse Flying V

2006-2008. Introduced as part of Guitar of the Week program, reintroduced by popular demand in a '07 limited run, light colored solid mahogany body gives a natural Korina appearance or opaque white or black, V-shaped reverse body, traditional Flying V neck profile.

2006-2007		$1,350	$1,800
2008	Guitar of the Week	$1,200	$1,600

Rudolph Schenker Flying V

1993. Only 103 made, black and white body and headstock, signature on 'guard.

1993		$1,450	$1,900

Shred V

2008. Guitar of the Month, 1000 made, EMG humbuckers, Kahler, black.

2008		$975	$1,250

Tribal V

2009-2011. Black tribal graphics on white body. Limited run of 350.

2009-2011		$875	$1,150

Zakk Wylde Flying V (Custom Shop)

2007-2011. With Floyd Rose and typical bullseye finish.

2007-2011		$3,000	$5,000

F-25 Folksinger

1963-1971. 14-1/2" flat-top, mahogany body, most have double white 'guard, natural.

1963-1964		$885	$1,150
1965		$810	$1,050
1966-1971		$775	$1,000

FJN Folk Singer

1963-1967. Jumbo flat-top, square shoulders, natural finish with deep red on back and sides.

1963-1964		$1,775	$2,300
1965		$1,600	$2,100
1966-1967		$1,525	$2,000

Futura

1982-1984. Deep cutout solidbody, 2 humbucker pickups, gold hardware, black, white or purple.

1982-1984		$1,700	$2,200

Historic Korina Futura

1998-1999. Explorer body with V headstock.

1998-1999		$6,400	$8,300

G-45 Standard

2019-present. Slim body, Fishman pickup, solid sitka spruce top, walnut back and sides, Antique Natural gloss finish.

2019-2020		$800	$1,050

MODEL YEAR	FEATURES	EXC. COND. LOW	HIGH

G-45 Studio

2019-present. Same as Standard but with Antique Natural satin finish.

2019-2020		$650	$850

GB Series Guitar Banjos

See listings in Banjo section of the Price Guide.

GGC-700

1981-1982. Slab single-cut body, 2 exposed humbuckers, dots.

1981-1982		$700	$900

GK-55 Active

1979-1980. LP body style, 2 exposed Dirty Fingers humbuckers, bolt neck, dot markers.

1979-1980		$675	$875

Gospel

1973-1979. Flat-top, square shoulders, laminated maple back and sides, arched back, Dove of Peace headstock inlay, natural.

1973-1979		$900	$1,175

Gospel Reissue

1992-1997. Laminated mahogany back and sides, natural or sunburst (walnut added in '94, blue and red in '95), changes to old-style script logo and headstock ornamentation in '94.

1992-1993	Reissue specs	$1,125	$1,450
1994-1997	Old-style specs	$1,125	$1,450

GS-1 Classical

1950-1956. Mahogany back and sides.

1950-1956		$600	$800

GS-2 Classical

1950-1956. Maple back and sides.

1950-1959		$650	$850

GS-5 Custom Classic/C-5 Classical

1954-1960. Brazilian rosewood back and sides, renamed C-5 Classical in '57.

1954-1960		$1,400	$1,825

GS-35 Classical/Gut String 35

1939-1942. Spruce top, mahogany back and sides, only 39 made.

1939-1942		$1,600	$2,100

GS-85 Classical/Gut String 85

1939-1942. Brazilian rosewood back and sides.

1939-1942		$3,100	$4,000

GY (Army-Navy)

1918-1921. Slightly arched top and back, low-end budget model, Sheraton Brown.

1918-1921		$650	$850

Harley Davidson LTD

1994-1995. Limited Edition, 16" wide body, flat-top, Harley Davidson in script and logo, black, 1500 sold through Harley dealers to celebrate 100th Anniversary of Harley.

1994-1995		$1,775	$2,300

Heritage

1965-1982. Flat-top dreadnought, square shoulders, rosewood back and sides (Brazilian until '67, Indian '68 on), bound top and back, natural finish.

1965-1967	Brazilian	$2,300	$3,000
1968-1982	Indian	$1,150	$1,500

MODEL YEAR	FEATURES	EXC. COND. LOW	HIGH

Heritage-12

1968-1971. Flat-top dreadnought, 12 strings, Indian rosewood back and sides, bound top and back, natural finish.

1968-1971		$1,150	$1,500

HG-00 (Hawaiian)

1932-1942. Hawaiian version of L-00, 14 3/4" flat-top, mahogany back and sides, bound top, natural.

1932-1947		$4,100	$5,300

HG-20 (Hawaiian)

1929-1933. Hawaiian, 14 1/2" dreadnought-shaped, maple back and sides, round soundhole and 4 f-holes.

1929-1933		$4,100	$5,300

HG-22 (Hawaiian)

1929-1932. Dreadnought, 14", Hawaiian, round soundhole and 4 f-holes, white paint logo, very small number produced.

1929-1932		$4,400	$5,700

HG-24 (Hawaiian)

1929-1932. 16" Hawaiian, rosewood back and sides, round soundhole plus 4 f-holes, small number produced.

1929-1932		$5,900	$7,700

HG-Century (Hawaiian)

1937-1938. Hawaiian, 14 3/4" L-C Century of Progress, pearloid 'board.

1937-1938		$4,100	$5,300

Howard Roberts Artist

1976-1980. Full body single-cut archtop, soundhole, 1 humbucking pickup, gold hardware, ebony 'board, various colors.

1976-1980		$2,200	$2,900

Howard Roberts Artist Double Pickup

1979-1980. Two pickup version of HR Artist.

1979-1980		$2,400	$3,100

Howard Roberts Custom

1975-1981. Full body single-cut archtop, soundhole, 1 humbucking pickup, chrome hardware, rosewood 'board, various colors.

1975-1981		$2,300	$3,000

Howard Roberts Fusion/Fusion II/Fusion III

1979-2009. Single-cut, semi-hollowbody, 2 humbucking pickups, chrome hardware, ebony 'board (unbound until '78), TP-6 tailpiece, various colors, renamed Howard Roberts Fusion II in late-'88, and Howard Roberts Fusion III in '91.

1979-2009		$2,100	$2,750

HP-415 W

2017-2018. High Performance series, slimmer round shoulder cutaway, sitka spruce top, walnut back and sides.

2017-2018		$875	$1,125

Hummingbird

1960-present. Flat-top acoustic, square shoulders, mahogany back and sides, bound body and neck. Name changes to Hummingbird Standard in '20.

1960	Cherry Sunburst	$5,200	$6,800
1961-1964	Cherry Sunburst	$5,000	$6,500
1963-1965	Natural	$5,200	$6,800

Gibson G-45 Standard

1977 Gibson Howard Roberts Custom

Bernunzio Uptown Music

1963 Gibson Hummingbird

Craig Brody

2012 Gibson J-35

Bernunzio Uptown Music

MODEL YEAR	FEATURES	EXC. COND. LOW	HIGH
1965	Cherry Sunburst, early '65	$3,600	$4,700
1965	Cherry Sunburst, late '65	$3,300	$4,300
1966	Cherry Sunburst	$3,000	$3,900
1966	Natural	$3,150	$4,100
1967-1968	Natural, screwed 'guard	$3,150	$4,100
1967-1968	Sunburst, screwed 'guard	$3,000	$3,900
1969	Natural, screwed 'guard	$2,600	$3,400
1969	Sunburst, screwed 'guard	$2,600	$3,400
1970-1971	Natural, sunburst	$2,350	$3,050
1972-1979	Double X, block markers	$2,350	$3,050
1980-1985	Double X, block markers	$2,000	$2,600
1985-1988	Single X	$1,600	$2,100
1989	25 1/2" scale	$2,000	$2,600
1990-2020		$1,900	$2,450
1994	100 Years 1894-1994 label	$1,900	$2,450
2015-2019	Black	$2,100	$3,100

Hummingbird Standard

2020-present. Modern series, mahogany body with sitka spruce top, Vintage Sunburst.

2020-2021		$2,100	$2,775

Hummingbird Historic Collection

2005-2006. Limited run, Vintage Honeyburst.

2005-2006		$1,900	$2,500

50th Anniversary 1960 Hummingbird

2010-2012. Limited Edition, 200 made, 50th Anniversary logo on truss rod cover.

2010-2012		$3,150	$4,100

Hummingbird 12 (Custom Shop)

2005-2011. 12-string, Vintage Sunburst.

2005-2011		$2,600	$3,400

Hummingbird Artist

2007-2011. Plain (no Hummingbird) small 'guard, L.R. Baggs Element, sold through Guitar Center.

2007-2011		$1,400	$1,800

Hummingbird Custom Koa

2004, 2009-2018. Highly flamed koa back and sides, spruce top, gloss finish.

2004-2018		$3,150	$4,100

Hummingbird Limited Edition

1993-1994. Only 30 made, quilted maple top and back.

1993-1994		$2,100	$3,100

Hummingbird Madagascar Honeyburst

2009. Limited run of 20, figured Madagascar rosewood back and sides, factory electronics, certificate of authenticity.

2009		$2,850	$3,700

Hummingbird Modern Classic

2010-2012. Cherry sunburst or ebony finish, L.R. Baggs Element Active pickup system.

2010-2012		$1,900	$2,450

Hummingbird Pro

2010-2013. Non-cut, plain (no Hummingbird) small 'guard, L.R. Baggs Element, Guitar Center.

2010-2013		$1,250	$1,625

Hummingbird Pro EC

2010-2013. Cutaway version, Fishman Prefix Plus-T, Guitar Center.

2010-2013		$1,350	$1,750

Hummingbird Pro 12-String (Custom Shop)

2018. Limited Edition, sitka spruce top, mahogany back and sides, Vintage Sunburst or Heritage Cherry Sunburst.

2018		$1,400	$1,800

Hummingbird Quilt Series (Custom Shop)

2007-2014		$2,100	$3,100

Hummingbird Studio

2019-2020. Slim body, on-board electronics, Antique Natural or Walnut Burst.

2019-2020		$1,200	$1,550

Hummingbird Studio Rosewood

2020-present. Sitka spruce top, rosewood back and sides, Antique Natural or Rosewood Burst.

2020		$1,550	$2,000

Hummingbird Studio Walnut

2020-present. Sitka spruce top, walnut back and sides, Antique Natural or Walnut Burst.

2020		$1,200	$1,550

Hummingbird True Vintage

2007-2013. Sitka spruce top, Madagascar rosewood bridge and 'board, special '60s Heritage Cherry or sunburst finish.

2007-2013		$2,775	$3,600

Invader

1983-1988. Single cutaway solid mahogany body, two humbucker pickups, four knobs with three-way selector switch, stop tailpiece, bolt-on maple neck.

1983-1988	All colors	$675	$875

J-15/J-15 Standard

2014-present. Acoustic-electric dreadnought, slope shoulder, walnut back and sides, antique natural.

2014-2020		$1,075	$1,400

J-25

1983-1985. Flat-top, laminated spruce top, synthetic semi-round back, ebony 'board, natural or sunburst.

1983-1985		$450	$600

J-29 Rosewood

2014-2016. Sitka spruce top, solid rosewood back and sides.

2014-2016		$1,300	$1,700

J-30

1985-1993. Dreadnought-size flat-top acoustic, mahogany back and sides, sunburst, Renamed J-30 Montana in '94.

1985-1993		$1,350	$1,750

J-30 Cutaway

1990-1995. Cutaway version of J-30, transducer pickup.

1990-1995		$1,400	$1,825

MODEL YEAR	FEATURES	EXC. COND. LOW	HIGH

J-30 Montana

1994-1997. Renamed from J-30, dreadnought-size flat-top acoustic, mahogany back and sides, sunburst.

1994-1997		$1,350	$1,750

J-30 RCA Limited Edition

1991. Limited edition for RCA Nashville, RCA logo on headstock.

1991		$1,350	$1,750

J-35

2012-2018. Sitka spruce top, mahogany back, sides and neck, rosewood 'board.

2012-2018		$1,225	$1,600

J-40

1971-1982. Dreadnought flat-top, mahogany back and sides, economy satin finish.

1971-1982		$925	$1,200

J-45

1942-1982, 1984-present. Dreadnought flat-top, mahogany back and sides, round shoulders until '68 and '84 on, square shoulders '69-'82, sunburst finish (see J-50 for natural version) then natural finish also available in '90s, renamed J-45 Western in '94, renamed Early J-45 in '97 then renamed J-45 in '99. The prices noted are for all-original crack free instruments. A single professionally repaired minor crack that is nearly invisible will reduce the value only slightly. Two or more, or unsightly repaired cracks will devalue an otherwise excellent original acoustic instrument. Repaired cracks should be evaluated on a case-by-case basis.

1942-1945	Banner logo, Adirondack	$8,300	$10,800
1942-1945	Banner logo, mahogany	$7,300	$9,500
1945	Banner logo, sitka	$6,700	$8,700
1946-1948	Script logo, sitka	$6,700	$8,700
1949	Small 'guard	$6,100	$8,000
1950-1954		$5,400	$7,000
1955-1959	Big 'guard	$4,600	$6,000
1960-1964	Round shoulders	$3,500	$4,600
1965	Early '65, wide nut	$3,100	$4,025
1965	Late '65, slim nut	$2,525	$3,275
1966-1967	Round shoulders	$2,350	$3,050
1968	Black, Cherry	$3,800	$5,000
1968	Blue, Green	$5,000	$6,500
1968-1969	Sunburst, Gibson 'guard	$2,350	$3,050
1969	Square D-shape, late '69	$2,000	$2,600
1970	Square, sunburst	$1,600	$2,100
1971-1975	Deluxe, sunburst	$1,600	$2,100
1976-1979	Sunburst	$1,600	$2,100
1980-1982	Sunburst	$1,500	$1,975
1984-1993	Various Colors	$1,500	$1,975
1994-1997	Western	$1,500	$1,975
1997-1998	Early J-45	$1,500	$1,975
1999	Standard	$1,300	$1,700
2000-2020	Standard	$1,500	$1,975

J-45 1942 Legend

2006-2014. Early J-45 specs, Adirondack red spruce body, mahogany back/sides/neck, rosewood 'board, Vintage Sunburst finish, certificate of authenticity.

2006-2014		$3,600	$4,700

J-45 1968 Reissue Limited Edition

2004-2007. Special run using '68 specs including Gibson logo 'guard, black or cherry finish.

2004-2007		$1,500	$1,975

J-45 Brad Paisley

2010-2016. Adirondack red spruce top, mahogany back and sides, cherry sunburst.

2010-2016		$2,300	$3,000

J-45 Buddy Holly Limited Edition

1995-1996. 250 made.

1995-1996		$2,300	$3,000

J-45 Celebrity

1985. Acoustic introduced for Gibson's 90th anniversary, spruce top, rosewood back and sides, ebony 'board, binding on body and 'board, only 90 made.

1985		$1,500	$1,975

J-45 Custom

1999-2020. Custom logo on truss rod, maple, mahogany or rosewood body, abalone trim, fancy headstock inlay.

1999-2020	Various options	$1,550	$3,000

J-45 Custom Vine

1999-2010. Custom Shop, Indian rosewood back and sides, fancy pearl and abalone vine inlay in ebony 'board, pearl Gibson logo and crown, natural gloss finish.

1999-2010		$2,700	$3,500

J-45 Elite Mystic

2014. Figured back, limited edition, rosewood back and sides.

2014		$2,100	$2,725

J-45 Heart of Texas Rosewood

2004. Custom Shop, soundhole label signed by Master Luthier Ren Ferguson, Indian rosewood back and sides, abalone top trim.

2004		$3,050	$3,950

J-45 Historic

2005. Limited edition, 670 made, Historic Collection logo rear headstock, sunburst.

2005		$1,950	$2,525

J-45 John Hiatt

2010-2011. Signature on truss rod cover, 100 offered, Tri Burst top with Tobacco Brown back and sides.

2010-2011		$2,225	$2,900

J-45 Natural Anniversary Limited Edition

2009. Custom Shop decal on headstock back, 20 made, spruce top, maple neck, zebrawood back and sides, natural finish.

2009		$2,200	$2,900

J-45 Red Spruce Edition

2007. Custom Shop limited edition, only 50 made.

2007		$2,300	$3,000

J-45 Rosewood

1999-2006. Indian rosewood body, spruce top.

1999-2006		$1,500	$1,975

1958 Gibson J-45

John Wesley

1968 Gibson J-45

KC Cormack

Gibson J-45 Studio Walnut

1957 Gibson J-50

Skip Crum

MODEL YEAR	FEATURES	EXC. COND. LOW	HIGH

J-45 Studio Rosewood
2020-present. Sitka spruce top, rosewood back and sides, Antique Natural or Rosewood Burst.

2020		$1,200	$1,550

J-45 Studio Sustainable
2019-2020. Sitka spruce top, sustainably harvested North American walnut back and sides, hand-rubbed beeswax finish, Antique Natural.

2019-2020		$1,275	$1,650

J-45 Studio Walnut
2020-present. Sitka spruce top, walnut back and sides, Antique Natural or Walnut Burst.

2020		$900	$1,175

J-45 True Vintage/J-45 Vintage
2007-2019. Part of Vintage Series, vintage sunburst finish. True dropped from name in '19.

2007-2019		$1,950	$2,525

J-45 Walnut Limited Edition
2015. Adirondack, flamed walnut.

2015		$2,300	$3,000

Working Man 45 (J-45)
1998-2005. Soft shoulder J-45 style, gloss finish spruce top, satin finish mahogany back and sides, dot markers, natural.

1998-2005		$1,025	$1,325

J-50
1942, 1945-1981, 1990-1995, 1998-2008 (present). Dreadnought flat-top, mahogany back and sides, round shoulders until '68, square shoulders after, natural finish (see J-45 for sunburst version). Though not labeled J-50, the J-45 Standard is now also available in natural finish.

1945	Banner logo	$8,300	$10,800
1946-1948		$6,700	$8,700
1949	Small 'guard	$6,100	$8,000
1950-1954	Small 'guard	$4,550	$5,900
1955	Big 'guard	$4,225	$5,500
1956-1959	Standard fixed bridge	$4,225	$5,500
1960-1964	Round shoulders	$3,400	$4,500
1965	Early '65, wide nut	$3,000	$3,900
1965	Late '65, slim nut	$2,525	$3,275
1966-1968	Round shoulders	$2,350	$3,050
1969	Round shoulders	$2,350	$3,050
1969	Square D-shape, late '69	$2,000	$2,600
1970-1979	Square shoulders	$1,600	$2,100
1980-2008		$1,500	$1,975

J-55 (Jumbo 55) Limited Edition
1994 only. 16" flat-top, spruce top, mahogany back and sides, 100 made, sunburst.

1994		$1,600	$2,075

J-55 (Reintroduced)
1973-1982. Flat-top, laminated mahogany back and sides, arched back, square shoulders, sunburst. See Jumbo 55 listing for '39-'43 version.

1973-1982		$975	$1,275

J-60 Curly Maple
1993 and 1996. Curly maple back and sides, limited edition from Montana shop, natural.

1993,1996		$1,625	$2,100

MODEL YEAR	FEATURES	EXC. COND. LOW	HIGH

J-60/J-60 Traditional
1992-1999. Solid spruce top dreadnought, square shoulders, Indian rosewood back and sides, ebony 'board, multiple bindings, natural or sunburst.

1992-1999		$1,300	$1,700

J-100/J-100 Custom
1970-1974, 1985-1997. Flat-top jumbo, multi-bound top and back, black 'guard, dot inlays, mahogany back and sides, '80s version has maple back and sides, dot inlays and tortoise shell 'guard, '90s model has maple back and sides, no 'guard, and J-200 style block inlays.

1970-1974	Mahogany	$1,225	$1,600
1985-1997	Maple	$1,225	$1,600

J-100 Xtra
1991-1997, 1999-2004. Jumbo flat-top, mahogany back and sides, moustache bridge, dot inlays, various colors, J-100 Xtra Cutaway also available, reintroduced in '99 with maple back and sides and single-bound body.

1991-2004		$1,275	$1,650

J-150/SJ-150 Maple
1999-2008. Super jumbo body, solid spruce top, figured maple back and sides (rosewood in '05), MOP crown inlays, moustache bridge with transducer. Renamed SJ-150 in 2006.

1999-2005	J-150	$1,625	$2,125
2006-2008	SJ-150	$1,625	$2,125

J-160E
1954-1979. Flat-top jumbo acoustic, 1 bridge P-90 pickup, tone and volume controls on front, sunburst finish, reintroduced as J-160 in '90.

1954-1964		$4,900	$6,300
1965		$3,500	$4,600
1966-1969		$2,850	$3,725
1970-1979		$1,725	$2,225

J-160E Reissue/Standard/VS
1990-1997, 2003-2008. Reintroduced J-160E with solid spruce top, solid mahogany back and sides.

1990-2008		$1,600	$2,100

J-160E John Lennon Peace

2003-2013. J-160E with tortoise 'guard, natural, signature on truss rod cover.

2003-2013		$2,000	$2,600

J-160E John Lennon Peace Limited Edition
2009. Certificate of authenticity, 750 made.

2009		$2,100	$2,750

J-160E Montana Special
1995 only.

1995		$1,600	$2,100

J-160 VS/John Lennon 70th
2010. Commemorative edition for John Lennon's 70th birthday, 500 made, vintage sunburst gloss finish.

2010		$2,000	$2,600

J-165 (Maple)
See CJ-165 listing.

J-180/Everly Brothers/The Everly Brothers
1986-2005. Reissue of the '62-'72 Everly Brothers model, renamed The Everly Brothers ('92-'94), The Everly ('94-'96), then back to J-180, black.

1986-2005		$2,000	$2,600

GUITARS

MODEL YEAR	FEATURES	EXC. COND. LOW	HIGH

J-180 Billy Jo Armstrong

2011. Certificate of authenticity, 300 made.

2011 $2,200 $2,900

J-180 Special Edition

1993. Gibson Bozeman, only 36 made, Everly Brother specs, large double white pearloid 'guard.

1993 $2,375 $3,075

J-185/J-185N

1951-1959. Flat-top jumbo, figured maple back and sides, bound body and neck, sunburst (185) or natural (185N).

1951-1959 Natural, sunburst $11,200 $14,500

J-185 Reissue

1990-1995, 1999-2018. Flat-top jumbo, figured maple back and sides, bound body and neck, natural or sunburst, limited run of 100 between '91-'92.

1990-2018 $1,900 $2,450

1951 J-185 Limited Edition

1994-1995. Oct. '94 Centennial model, limited run of 100.

1994-1995 $2,850 $3,700

J-185 Custom Vine

2004-2012. J-185 with abalone and mother-of-pearl vine 'board inlay.

2004-2012 $2,200 $2,850

J-185 EC

1999-2018. Acoustic/electric, rounded cutaway, flamed maple back and sides. Replaced EC-30 Blues King.

1999-2018 $1,575 $2,050

J-185 EC Custom

2005. Limited Edition, 200 made, spruce top, figured maple sides and back, pearl double parallelogram markers, Fishman Prefix Plus on-board electronics.

2005 $1,575 $2,050

J-185 EC Rosewood

2006-2018. Acoustic/electric, rounded cutaway, Indian rosewood back and sides.

2006-2018 $1,575 $2,050

J-185 EC Modern Rosewood

2020-present. Slim body, sitka spruce top, rosewood back and sides, Antique Natural or Rosewood Burst.

2020 $1,575 $2,050

J-185 EC Modern Walnut

2020-present. Slim body, sitka spruce top, walnut back and sides, Antique Natural or Walnut Burst.

2020 $1,350 $1,750

J-185 EC Quilt

2002. Quilted maple top, flamed maple body.

2002 $2,600 $3,400

J-185-12

2001-2004. 12-string J-185, flamed maple sides and back.

2001-2004 $1,900 $2,450

J-190 EC Super Fusion

2001-2004. Jumbo single cut acoustic/electric, spruce top, curly maple back and sides, neck pickup and Fishman Piezo.

2001-2004 $2,100 $2,750

MODEL YEAR	FEATURES	EXC. COND. LOW	HIGH

J-200/SJ-200/J-200N/SJ-200N

1946-present. Labeled SJ-200 until ca.'54. Super Jumbo flat-top, maple back and sides, see Super Jumbo 200 for '38-'42 rosewood back and sides model, called J-200 Artist for a time in the mid-'70s, renamed '50s Super Jumbo 200 in '97 and again renamed SJ-200 Reissue in '99. Currently again called the SJ-200. 200N indicates natural option.

1946-1949	Natural, sunburst	$12,000	$16,000
1950-1957	Natural, sunburst	$10,500	$13,500
1958-1959	Natural	$10,500	$13,500
1958-1959	Sunburst	$10,000	$13,000
1960-1964	Natural, sunburst	$8,500	$11,000
1965	Natural, sunburst	$5,500	$7,200
1966-1969	Natural, sunburst	$4,500	$6,000
1970-1979	Natural, sunburst	$3,000	$3,900
1972	Artist (label)	$3,000	$3,900
1980-1989	Natural, sunburst	$2,800	$3,600
1990-1999	Natural, sunburst	$2,800	$3,600
2000-2020	Natural, sunburst	$2,800	$3,600

J-200 Celebrity

1985-1987. Acoustic introduced for Gibson's 90th anniversary, spruce top, rosewood back, sides and 'board, binding on body and 'board, sunburst, only 90 made.

1985-1987 $2,750 $3,575

J-200 Custom

2009-2013. Additional abalone trim, gold hardware, sunburst or natural. Model name also used in 1993 on J-200 with tree-of-life fingerboard inlay.

2009-2013 $2,900 $3,800

J-200 Deluxe Rosewood

1993-1996. Rosewood back and sides, abalone trim, gold hardware, sunburst or natural.

1993-1996 $3,500 $4,500

J-200 E

1986-1987. Built in Nashville, on-board volume control, sunburst.

1986-1987 $2,850 $3,750

J-200 Elvis Presley Signature

2002. 250 made, large block letter Elvis Presley name on 'board, figured maple sides and back, gloss natural spruce top, black and white custom designed 'guard after one of Presley's personal guitars.

2002 $3,800 $4,900

J-200 Jr.

1991-1996, 2002. Smaller 16" body, sunburst, natural, black or cherry.

1991-1996 $1,725 $2,225

J-200 Koa

1994-2013. Figured Hawaiian Koa back and sides, spruce top, natural.

1994-2013 $2,800 $3,600

J-200 M Trophy 75th Anniversary

2012-2013. Quilt maple back and sides, rosewood 'board, abalone crown inlays, antique natural or vintage sunburst nitro finish.

2012-2013 $2,600 $3,400

1999 Gibson J-150

Ted Wulfers

2007 Gibson J-185 Reissue

GUITARS

Gibson Johnny A Signature Series

Imaged by Heritage Auctions, HA.com

1960s Gibson Johnny Smith Double

Freedom Guitars

MODEL YEAR	FEATURES	EXC. COND. LOW	HIGH

J-200 Montana Gold Flame Maple

1998-2012. SJ-200 design, AAA Sitka spruce top with Eastern curly maple back and sides, ebony 'board, Custom Montana Gold banner peghead logo, antique natural.

1998-2012 — $2,600 — $3,400

J-200 Montana Western Classic Supreme

2016. Spruce top, rosewood back and sides, maple neck, Sunset Burst finish.

2016 — $3,350 — $4,350

J-200 Rose

1994-1995. Centennial Series model, based on Emmylou Harris' guitar, black finish, rose 'guard, gold tuners, 100 built.

1994-1995 — $3,850 — $5,000

J-200 Rosewood

1991, 1994-1996. Made in Bozeman, rosewood back and sides.

1991-1996 — $3,425 — $4,450

J-200 Studio

2009-2018. Studio logo on truss rod cover, unbound 'board, plain 'guard.

2009-2018 — $2,050 — $2,650

J-200 Western Classic Pre-War

1999-2012. Indian rosewood.

1999-2012 — $2,700 — $3,525

J-200 Western Classic Pre-War 200 Brazilian

2003. Based on Ray Whitley's 1937 J-200, Custom Shop, limited production, Brazilian rosewood back and sides.

2003 — $6,600 — $8,600

J-200/SJ-200 Ron Wood

1997. Based on a '57 SJ-200 with Wood's oversized double 'guard on either side of the sound hole, flame-pattern fretboard inlays, script signature inlay on headstock, natural.

1997 — $3,600 — $4,700

J-250 Monarch/SJ-250 Monarch

1995-2018. Rosewood back and sides, maple neck, ebony 'board, abalone trim, certificate of authenticity.

1995-2018 — $10,100 — $13,100

J-250 R

1972-1973, 1976-1978. A J-200 with rosewood back and sides, sunburst, only 20 shipped from Gibson.

1972-1978 — $3,000 — $3,900

J-1000/SJ-1000

1992-1994. Jumbo cutaway, spruce top, rosewood back and sides, on-board electronics, diamond-shape markers and headstock inlay.

1992-1994 — $1,850 — $2,400

J-1500

1992. Jumbo cutaway flat-top, higher-end appointments including Nick Lucas-style position markers, sunburst.

1992 — $1,925 — $2,500

J-2000/J-2000 Custom/J-2000 R

1986, 1992-1999. Cutaway acoustic, rosewood back and sides (a few had Brazilian rosewood or maple bodies), ebony 'board and bridge, Sitka spruce top, multiple bindings, sunburst or natural. Name changed to J-2000 Custom in '93 when it became available only on a custom-order basis.

1986-1999 All models — $3,125 — $4,025

Jackson Browne Signature

2011-2016. Based on '30s Jumbo style with increased body depth and upgraded tonewoods, Model 1 without pickup, Model A with pickups, Adirondack red spruce top, English walnut back and sides, nitro lacquer sunburst finish.

2011-2016 Model 1 — $3,200 — $4,200

2011-2016 Model A — $3,200 — $4,200

JG-0

1970-1972. Economy square shouldered jumbo, follows Jubilee model in '70.

1970-1972 — $775 — $1,025

JG-12

1970. Economy square shouldered jumbo 12-string, follows Jubilee-12 model in '70.

1970 — $775 — $1,025

Johnny A Signature Series

2004-2013. Thinline semi-hollow, sharp double-cut, flamed maple top, humbuckers, gold hardware, Bigsby, sunburst, includes certificate of authenticity.

2004-2013 Includes rare color option — $2,400 — $3,100

Johnny Smith/Johnny Smith Double

1961-1989. Single-cut archtop, 1 or 2 humbucker pickups, gold hardware, multiple binding front and back, natural or sunburst. By '80 cataloged as JS and JSD models.

1961-1964 — $9,800 — $12,700

1965 — $6,700 — $8,700

1966-1969 — $6,200 — $8,000

1970-1989 — $5,800 — $7,700

Jubilee

1969-1970. Flat-top, laminated mahogany back and sides, single bound body, natural with black back and sides.

1969-1970 — $775 — $1,025

Jubilee Deluxe

1970-1971. Flat-top, laminated rosewood back and sides, multi-bound body, natural finish.

1970-1971 — $775 — $1,025

Jubilee-12

1969-1970. Flat-top, 12 strings, laminated mahogany back and sides, multi-bound, natural.

1969-1970 — $775 — $1,025

Jumbo

1934-1936. Gibson's first Jumbo flat-top, mahogany back and sides, round shoulders, bound top and back, sunburst, becomes the 16" Jumbo 35 in late-'36.

1934 Unbound — $20,000 — $26,000

1935-1936 Bound — $15,500 — $20,000

Jumbo 35/J-35

1936-1942. Jumbo flat-top, mahogany back and sides, silkscreen logo, sunburst, reintroduced as J-35, square-shouldered dreadnought, in '83.

1936-1938 Sunburst, 3 tone bars — $13,000 — $16,875

1939 Natural, 3 tone bars — $12,625 — $16,400

1939 Sunburst, 3 tone bars — $12,625 — $16,400

MODEL YEAR	FEATURES	EXC. COND. LOW	HIGH
1940-1942	Sunburst, 2 tone bars	$10,000	$13,000

Jumbo 55/J-55

1939-1943. Flat-top dreadnought, round shoulders, mahogany back and sides, pearl inlaid logo, sunburst, reintroduced in '73 as J-55.

1939-1940	Stairstep	$14,450	$18,750
1941-1943	Non-stairstep	$11,850	$15,400

Jumbo Centennial Special

1994. Reissue of 1934 Jumbo, natural, 100 made.

1994		$2,150	$2,800

Junior Pro

1987-1989. Single-cut, mahogany body, KB-X tremolo system 1 humbucker pickup, black chrome hardware, various colors.

1987-1989		$475	$625

Kalamazoo Award Model

1978-1981. Single-cut archtop, bound f-holes, multi-bound top and back, 1 mini-humbucker, gold-plated hardware, woodgrain 'guard with bird and branch abalone inlay, highly figured natural or sunburst.

1978-1981	Natural	$11,300	$14,700
1978-1981	Sunburst	$11,300	$14,700

Keb' Mo' Royale

2016. Limited to 50, aged Adirondack red spruce top, vintage sunburst finish, label signed by artist, includes certificate of authenticity.

2016		$2,125	$2,750

Keb' Mo' Signature Bluesmaster

2010-2015. Limited run of 300, small-bodied flat-top acoustic, Baggs pickup, soundhole-mounted volume control, vintage sunburst or antique natural finish.

2010-2015		$1,925	$2,475

Kiefer Sutherland KS-336

2007. Custom Shop model inspired by Artist Series.

2007		$2,800	$3,600

KZ II

1980-1981. Double-cut solidbody, 2 humbuckers, 4 knob and toggle controls, tune-o-matic, dot markers, stencil Gibson logo on headstock, KZ II logo on truss rod cover, walnut stain finish.

1980		$825	$1,075

L-0

1926-1933, 1937-1942. Acoustic flat-top, maple back and sides '26-'27, mahogany after.

1926-1928	135", maple	$4,000	$5,200
1928-1930	135", mahogany	$4,000	$5,200
1931-1933	1475"	$4,100	$5,400
1937-1942	Spruce top	$4,100	$5,400

L-00

1932-1946. Acoustic flat-top, mahogany back and sides, bound top to '36 and bound top and back '37 on.

1932-1946		$4,100	$5,400

L-00 1937 Legend

2006-2016. Part of the Vintage Series.

2006-2016		$2,825	$3,700

L-00 Standard

2016-present. Small body, sitka spruce top, mahogany back and sides, Vintage Sunburst nitro finish.

2016-2020		$1,700	$2,200

MODEL YEAR	FEATURES	EXC. COND. LOW	HIGH

L-00 Studio Walnut

2020-present. Walnut back and sides, Fishman pickup, nitro finish, Antique Natural or Walnut Burst.

2020		$900	$1,200

L-00 Studio/Montana Studio

2019-2020. Sitka spruce top, walnut back and sides, Fishman pickup, aged nitro finish.

2019-2020		$900	$1,200

L-00 Sustainable

2018-present. Sitka spruce top, richlite 'board and bridge made from recycled trees pulp, Antique Natural.

2018-2020		$1,250	$1,650

L-00/Blues King

1991-1997, 1999-2019. Reintroduced as L-00, called Blues King L-00 for '94-'97, back as L-00 for '99-'02, called Blues King '03-present.

1991-1997	L-00/Blues King	$1,475	$1,900
2003-2019	Blues King	$1,475	$1,900

L-1 (Archtop)

1902-1925. Acoustic archtop, single-bound top, back and soundhole, name continued on flat-top model in '26.

1902-1907	125"	$1,550	$2,000
1908-1919	135"	$1,550	$2,000
1920-1925	135", Loar era	$1,550	$2,000

L-1 (Flat-Top)

1926-1937. Acoustic flat-top, maple back and sides '26-'27, mahogany after.

1926-1929	135", 12-fret	$4,100	$5,400
1930-1931	1475", 13-fret	$4,300	$5,600
1932-1937	14-fret	$4,400	$5,700

L-1 1928 Blues Tribute

2014-2018. Adirondack red spruce top, mahogany back and sides, rosewood 'board, faded Vintage Sunburst.

2014-2018		$1,900	$2,500

L-1 Robert Johnson

2007-2016. 1926 specs, Robert Johnson inlay at end of 'board.

2007-2016		$1,425	$1,875

L-1 Special

2016. Adirondack red spruce top, limited edition of 75.

2016		$1,875	$2,425

L-2 (Archtop)

1902-1926. Round soundhole archtop, pearl inlay on peghead, 1902-'07 available in 3 body sizes: 12.5" to 16", '24-'26 13.5" body width.

1902-1907	125"	$1,550	$2,000
1924-1926	135"	$1,550	$2,000

L-2 (Flat-Top)

1929-1935. Acoustic flat-top, rosewood back and sides except for mahogany in '31, triple-bound top and back, limited edition model in '94.

1929-1933	Brazilian	$12,500	$16,300
1931-1932	Mahogany	$10,100	$13,100

L-2 1929 Reissue

1994 only. Spruce top, Indian rosewood back and sides, raised 'guard.

1994		$1,875	$2,425

1980 Gibson Kalamazoo Award

Gibson L-1 Robert Johnson

1917 Gibson L-3
Frank Manno

1938 Gibson L-4
David Stone

L-3 (Archtop)
1902-1933. Acoustic archtop, available in 3 sizes: 12.5", 13.5", 16".

MODEL YEAR	FEATURES	EXC. COND. LOW	HIGH
1902-1907	125", round hole	$1,950	$2,550
1908-1919	135", round hole	$1,950	$2,550
1920		$1,950	$2,550
1921-1926	Loar era	$1,950	$2,550
1927-1928	135", oval hole	$1,950	$2,550
1929-1933	135", round hole	$1,950	$2,550

L-4
1912-1956. Acoustic archtop, 16" wide.

MODEL YEAR	FEATURES	EXC. COND. LOW	HIGH
1912-1919	12-fret, oval hole	$2,225	$2,900
1920		$2,225	$2,900
1921-1924	Loar era	$2,225	$2,900
1925-1927	12-fret, oval hole	$2,225	$2,900
1928-1934	14-fret, round hole	$2,225	$2,900
1935-1946	Fleur-de-lis, f-holes	$2,750	$3,575
1947-1949	Crown, double-parallel	$2,750	$3,575
1950-1956		$2,575	$3,350

L-4 A/L-4 A EC
2003-2008. 15 3/4" lower bout, mid-size jumbo, rounded cutaway, factory electronics with preamp.

MODEL YEAR	FEATURES	EXC. COND. LOW	HIGH
2003-2008		$1,425	$1,850

L-4 C/L-4 CN
1949-1971. Single-cut acoustic archtop, sunburst or natural (CN).

MODEL YEAR	FEATURES	EXC. COND. LOW	HIGH
1949-1959	Natural	$4,300	$5,600
1949-1959	Sunburst	$3,900	$5,100
1960-1964	Natural	$3,900	$5,100
1960-1964	Sunburst	$3,375	$4,375
1965	Natural	$2,800	$3,625
1965	Sunburst	$2,500	$3,250
1966-1969	Natural, sunburst	$1,950	$2,550
1970-1971	Natural, sunburst	$1,450	$1,875

L-4 CES/L-4 CES Mahogany
1958, 1969, 1986-2018. Single pointed cutaway archtop, 2 humbuckers, gold parts, natural or sunburst, maple back and sides '58 and '69, mahogany laminate back and sides for '86-'93, became part of Gibson's Historic Collection with laminated maple back and sides for '94, renamed L-4 CES Mahogany with solid mahogany back and sides in '04, Custom Shop model.

MODEL YEAR	FEATURES	EXC. COND. LOW	HIGH
1958	Natural, PAF hums	$10,000	$13,000
1958	Sunburst, PAF hums	$10,000	$13,000
1969	Natural, sunburst	$3,150	$4,100
1986-1993	Laminate mahogany	$2,500	$3,200
1994-2003	Laminate maple	$2,500	$3,200
2004-2018	Solid mahogany	$2,500	$3,200

L-4 Special Tenor/Plectrum
Late-1920s. Limited edition 4-string flat-top.

MODEL YEAR	FEATURES	EXC. COND. LOW	HIGH
1929		$1,900	$2,450

L-5 '34 Non-Cutaway Historic
1994. 1934 specs including block pearl inlays, bound snakehead peghead, close grained solid spruce top, figured solid maple sides and back, Cremona Brown sunburst finish, replica Grover open back tuners.

MODEL YEAR	FEATURES	EXC. COND. LOW	HIGH
1994		$4,200	$5,500

L-5 Premier/L-5 P/L-5 PN
1939-1947. Introduced as L-5 Premier (L-5 P) and renamed L-5 C in '48, single rounded cutaway acoustic archtop, sunburst or natural option (PN).

MODEL YEAR	FEATURES	EXC. COND. LOW	HIGH
1939-1947	Natural option	$14,300	$18,500
1939-1947	Sunburst	$12,300	$16,000

L-5/L-5N
1924-1958. Acoustic archtop, non-cut, multiple bindings, Lloyd Loar label in '24, 17" body by '35, Master Model label until '27, sunburst with natural option later.

MODEL YEAR	FEATURES	EXC. COND. LOW	HIGH
1924	'24 ship date, Loar era	$38,000	$50,000
1925	Early '25, values per specs	$38,000	$50,000
1925	Late '25, values per specs	$27,000	$45,000
1926	'26 ship date, values per specs	$27,000	$45,000
1927	'27 ship date, values per specs	$27,000	$45,000
1928-1929	Values per specs	$17,000	$27,000
1930-1932	Values per specs	$17,000	$27,000
1933-1939	Values per specs	$5,600	$10,000
1935-1940	Values per specs	$4,100	$8,200
1939-1940	Natural option, values per specs	$6,600	$9,200
1946-1949	Natural option, values per specs	$5,600	$10,000
1946-1949	Sunburst, values per specs	$4,100	$8,200
1950-1958	Natural, values per specs	$4,900	$7,900
1950-1958	Sunburst, values per specs	$3,800	$6,500

L-5 C/L-5 CN
1948-1982. Renamed from L-5 Premier (L-5 P), single rounded cutaway acoustic archtop, sunburst or natural option (CN)

MODEL YEAR	FEATURES	EXC. COND. LOW	HIGH
1948-1949	Natural	$11,200	$14,500
1948-1949	Sunburst	$9,600	$12,500
1950-1959	Natural	$9,600	$12,500
1950-1959	Sunburst	$8,400	$10,900
1960-1964	Natural	$8,400	$10,900
1960-1964	Sunburst	$7,700	$10,000
1965	Natural	$6,500	$8,400
1965	Sunburst	$6,500	$8,400
1966-1969	Natural	$5,400	$7,000
1966-1969	Sunburst	$5,400	$7,000
1970-1982	Natural, sunburst	$3,900	$5,100

L-5 CES/L-5 CESN
1951-2018. Electric version of L-5 C, single round cutaway (pointed mid-'60-'69), archtop, 2 pickups (P-90s '51-'53, Alnico Vs '54-mid-'57, humbuckers after), sunburst or natural (CESN), now part of Gibson's Historic Collection.

MODEL YEAR	FEATURES	EXC. COND. LOW	HIGH
1951-1957	Natural, single coils	$14,500	$19,000
1951-1957	Sunburst, single coils	$14,000	$18,000
1958-1959	Natural, PAFs	$18,500	$24,000

MODEL YEAR	FEATURES	EXC. COND. LOW	HIGH
1958-1959	Sunburst, PAFs	$16,900	$22,000
1960-1962	Natural, PAFs	$16,900	$22,000
1960-1962	Sunburst, PAFs	$14,500	$19,000
1963	Natural, pat #	$12,100	$16,000
1963-1964	Sunburst, pat #	$10,000	$13,200
1964	Natural, pat #	$12,000	$17,000
1965	Natural, sunburst	$7,700	$10,000
1966-1969	Natural	$6,200	$8,200
1966-1969	Sunburst	$5,600	$7,400
1970-1979	Natural, sunburst	$4,800	$6,300
1980-1984	Kalamazoo made	$4,800	$6,300
1985-1992	Nashville made	$4,800	$6,300

L-5 CES (Custom Shop/Historic Collection)

1994-1997. Historic Collection series, sunburst or natural.

1994	100th Anniv, black	$4,800	$6,300
1994-1996	Natural, highly figured	$4,800	$6,300
1994-1996	Sunburst	$4,800	$6,300
1997	Wine Red	$4,800	$6,300

L-5 CT (George Gobel)

1959-1961. Single-cut, thinline archtop acoustic, some were built with pickups, cherry.

1959-1961		$15,500	$20,200

L-5 CT Reissue

1998-2007. Historic Collection, acoustic and electric versions, natural, sunburst, cherry.

1998-2007		$4,700	$6,125

L-5 S

1972-1985, 2004-2005. Single-cut solidbody, multi-bound body and neck, gold hardware, 2 pickups (low impedance '72-'74, humbuckers '75 on), offered in natural, cherry sunburst or vintage sunburst. 1 humbucker version issued in '04 from Gibson's Custom, Art & Historic division.

1972-2005	All options	$3,775	$4,900

L-5 S Ron Wood

2015. Custom Shop, limited run of 250 with 1st 50 signed by Ron, certificate of authenticity, 2 Burst-bucker pickups, ebony gloss finish.

2015		$3,775	$4,900

L-5 Signature

2001-2004. Carved spruce top, AAA maple back, tangerineburst or vintage sunburst.

2001-2004		$4,725	$6,150

L-5 Studio

1996-2000. Normal L-5 dual pickup features, marble-style 'guard, translucent finish, dot markers.

1996-2000		$2,150	$2,800

L-5 Wes Montgomery Custom Shop

1993-2018. Various colors.

1993-2018		$5,100	$6,700

L-6 S

1973-1975. Single-cut solidbody, 2 humbucking pickups, 6 position rotary switch, stop tailpiece, cherry or natural. Renamed L-6 S Custom in '75.

1973-1975	Cherry, natural	$1,300	$1,700

L-6 S Custom

1975-1980. Renamed from the L-6 S, 2 humbucking pickups, stop tailpiece, cherry or natural.

1975-1980		$1,300	$1,700
1978-1980	Silverburst option	$1,300	$1,700

MODEL YEAR	FEATURES	EXC. COND. LOW	HIGH

L-6 S Deluxe

1975-1981. Single-cut solidbody, 2 humbucking pickups, no rotary switch, strings-thru-body design, cherry or natural.

1975-1981		$1,300	$1,700

L-6 S Reissue

2011-2012. With rotary switch, 2 humbuckers, natural or silverburst.

2011-2012		$775	$1,000

L-7/L-7N

1932-1956. Acoustic archtop, bound body and neck, fleur-de-lis peghead inlay, 16" body '32-'34, 17" body X-braced top late-'34, sunburst or natural (N).

1932-1934	16" body	$2,900	$3,800
1935-1939	17" body, X-braced	$2,900	$3,800
1940-1949	Natural	$2,700	$3,600
1940-1949	Sunburst	$2,400	$3,200
1950-1956	Natural	$2,500	$3,300
1950-1956	Sunburst	$2,375	$3,150

L-7 C/L-7 CN

1948-1972. Single-cut acoustic archtop, triple-bound top, sunburst or natural (CN). Gibson revived the L-7 C name for a new acoustic archtop in 2002.

1948-1949	Natural	$4,000	$5,200
1948-1949	Sunburst	$3,600	$4,700
1950-1959	Natural	$3,600	$4,700
1950-1959	Sunburst	$3,300	$4,300
1960-1964	Natural	$3,200	$4,200
1960-1964	Sunburst	$3,100	$4,000
1965	Natural	$3,000	$3,900
1965	Sunburst	$2,800	$3,600
1966-1972	Natural	$2,850	$3,700
1966-1972	Sunburst	$2,500	$3,300

L-7 Custom Electric

1936. L-7 with factory Christian-style pickup, limited production, often custom ordered.

1936		$7,700	$10,000

L-7 E/L-7 CE

1948-1954. L-7 and L-7 C with "McCarty" assembly of pickguard-mounted pickups (1 or 2), sunburst only.

1948-1954	L-7 CE, cutaway	$4,100	$5,300
1948-1954	L-7 E, non-cut	$3,400	$4,400

L-7 C (Custom Shop)

2002-2013. Custom Shop logo, Certificate of Authenticity.

2002-2013		$3,500	$4,500

L-10

1923-1939. Acoustic archtop, single-bound body and 'board, black or sunburst (added in '35).

1923-1934	16", F-holes	$4,250	$5,500
1935-1939	17", X-braced	$4,250	$5,500

L-12

1930-1955. Acoustic archtop, single-bound body, 'guard, neck and headstock, gold-plated hardware, sunburst.

1930-1934	16"	$4,600	$6,000
1935-1939	17", X-braced	$4,600	$6,000
1940-1941	Parallel top braced	$4,600	$6,000
1946-1949	Post-war	$2,800	$3,650
1950-1955		$2,650	$3,450

1939 Gibson L-5N

Dr. Jazz

1967 Gibson L-7 CN

Imaged by Heritage Auctions, HA.com

1935 Gibson L-30

Tyler Willison

1937 Gibson L-37

Robbie Keene

L-12 Premier/L-12 P

1947-1950. L-12 with rounded cutaway, sunburst.

MODEL YEAR	FEATURES	EXC. COND. LOW	HIGH
1947-1950		$3,850	$5,000

L-20 20th Anniversary Limited Edition

2009. Custom Shop, 20 made, "20th Anniversary" logo on back of headstock and on label, Certificate of Authenticity.

MODEL YEAR	FEATURES	EXC. COND. LOW	HIGH
2009		$2,675	$3,475

L-20 Special/L-20 K International Special

1993-1994. Rosewood or mahogany back and sides (koa on the K), ebony 'board, block inlays, gold tuners, multi-bound.

MODEL YEAR	FEATURES	EXC. COND. LOW	HIGH
1993-1994	L-20, mahogany	$1,650	$2,150
1993-1994	L-20, rosewood	$1,650	$2,150
1993-1994	L-20K, koa	$1,650	$2,150

L-30

1935-1943. Acoustic archtop, single-bound body, black or sunburst.

MODEL YEAR	FEATURES	EXC. COND. LOW	HIGH
1935-1943		$1,150	$1,500

L-37

1937-1941. 14-3/4" acoustic archtop, flat back, single-bound body and 'guard, sunburst.

MODEL YEAR	FEATURES	EXC. COND. LOW	HIGH
1937-1941		$1,225	$1,600

L-47

1940-1942. Acoustic archtop.

MODEL YEAR	FEATURES	EXC. COND. LOW	HIGH
1940-1942		$1,300	$1,700

L-48

1946-1971. 16" acoustic archtop, single-bound body, mahogany sides, sunburst.

MODEL YEAR	FEATURES	EXC. COND. LOW	HIGH
1946-1949		$1,350	$1,750
1950-1959		$1,225	$1,600
1960-1964		$1,100	$1,425
1965		$925	$1,200
1966-1969		$725	$925
1970-1971		$625	$825

L-50

1932-1971. 14.75" acoustic archtop, flat or arched back, round soundhole or f-holes, pearl logo pre-war, decal logo post-war, maple sides, sunburst, 16" body late-'34.

MODEL YEAR	FEATURES	EXC. COND. LOW	HIGH
1932-1934	1475" body	$1,750	$2,300
1934-1943	16" body	$1,750	$2,300
1946-1949	16", trapezoids	$1,675	$2,200
1950-1959		$1,400	$1,850
1960-1964		$1,350	$1,750
1965		$1,100	$1,450
1966-1969		$925	$1,200
1970-1971		$850	$1,100

L-75

1932-1939. 14.75" archtop with round soundhole and flat back, size increased to 16" with arched back in '35, small button tuners, dot markers, lower-end style trapeze tailpiece, pearl script logo, sunburst.

MODEL YEAR	FEATURES	EXC. COND. LOW	HIGH
1932	1475", dot neck	$2,450	$3,250
1933-1934	1475", pearloid	$2,450	$3,250
1935-1939	16" body	$2,450	$3,250

L-130

1999-2005. 14 7/8" lower bout, small jumbo, solid spruce top, solid bubinga back and sides, rosewood 'board, factory electronics with preamp.

MODEL YEAR	FEATURES	EXC. COND. LOW	HIGH
1999-2005		$1,025	$1,325

L-140

1999-2005. Like L-130 but with rosewood back and sides, ebony 'board.

MODEL YEAR	FEATURES	EXC. COND. LOW	HIGH
1999-2005		$1,150	$1,500

L-200 Emmylou Harris

2001-2016. Smaller and thinner than standard 200, flamed maple sides and back, gold hardware, crest markers, natural or sunburst.

MODEL YEAR	FEATURES	EXC. COND. LOW	HIGH
2001-2016		$1,900	$2,450

L-C Century

1933-1939. Curly maple back and sides, bound body, white pearloid 'board and peghead (all years) and headstock (until '38), sunburst.

MODEL YEAR	FEATURES	EXC. COND. LOW	HIGH
1933-1938	Pearloid	$5,500	$7,100
1939		$4,900	$6,400

L-C Century Elvis Costello Limited

2016. Signed custom label, pearloid 'board, Adirondack red spruce top, AAA flamed maple back and sides, 300 made.

MODEL YEAR	FEATURES	EXC. COND. LOW	HIGH
2016		$3,900	$5,100

L-C Century Reissue

1994. Pearloid headstock and 'board.

MODEL YEAR	FEATURES	EXC. COND. LOW	HIGH
1994		$2,225	$2,900

LC-1 Cascade

2002-2006. LC-Series acoustic/electric, advanced L-00-style, solid quilted maple back and sides.

MODEL YEAR	FEATURES	EXC. COND. LOW	HIGH
2002-2006		$1,350	$1,750

LC-2 Sonoma

2002-2006. Released November '02, LC-Series acoustic/electric, advanced L-00-style, solid walnut back and sides.

MODEL YEAR	FEATURES	EXC. COND. LOW	HIGH
2002-2006		$1,625	$2,100

LC-3 Caldera

2003-2004. 14 3/4" flat-top, soft cutaway, solid cedar top, solid flamed Koa back and sides, fancy appointments.

MODEL YEAR	FEATURES	EXC. COND. LOW	HIGH
2003-2004		$1,700	$2,200

Le Grande

1993-2010. Electric archtop, 17", formerly called Johnny Smith.

MODEL YEAR	FEATURES	EXC. COND. LOW	HIGH
1993-2010		$6,000	$8,000

Les Paul

Following are models bearing the Les Paul name, beginning with the one that started it all, the original Les Paul Model. All others are then listed pretty much alphabetically as follows:

Les Paul Model
'52 Les Paul Goldtop
'52 Les Paul Tribute
'54 Les Paul Goldtop
'54 Les Paul Wildwood
1954 Les Paul Goldtop Heavy Aged
'55 Les Paul Goldtop Hot-Mod Wraptail
'56 Les Paul Goldtop
1956 Les Paul Goldtop "CME Spec" VOS
1956 Les Paul Goldtop Reissue (Custom Shop)
1956 Les Paul Goldtop Ultra Light Aged
'57 Les Paul Goldtop
'57 Les Paul Goldtop (R-7 wrap-around)
1957 Les Paul Goldtop Darkback Light Aged

1957 Les Paul Goldtop Reissue
1957 Les Paul Goldtop Ultra Light/Ultra Heavy Aged
'58 Les Paul Figured Top
'58 Les Paul Plaintop (VOS)
'59 Les Paul Flametop/Reissue/Standard
'59 Les Paul Burst Brothers
'59 Les Paul Korina Reissue
'59 Les Paul Plaintop (VOS)
True Historic 1959 Les Paul
'60 Les Paul Corvette
'60 Les Paul Flametop/Standard '60s
'60 Les Paul Plaintop (VOS)
'60 Les Paul Special
True Historic 1960 Les Paul
Les Paul 10th Anniversary Chambered '58 Reissue
Les Paul 25/50 Anniversary
Les Paul 30th Anniversary
Les Paul 40th Anniversary (from 1952)
Les Paul 40th Anniversary (from 1959)
Les Paul 50th Anniversary (Historic)
Les Paul 50th Anniversary 1956 Les Paul Standard
Les Paul 50th Anniversary 1957 Les Paul Standard Goldtop
Les Paul 50th Anniversary 1959 Les Paul Standard
Les Paul 50th Anniversary 1960 Les Paul Standard
Les Paul 50th Anniversary DaPra
Les Paul 50th Anniversary Korina Tribute
Les Paul 50th Anniversary Les Paul Standard (Sweetwater)
Les Paul 60th Anniversary 1960 Les Paul Standard "CME Spec" VOS
Les Paul 120th Anniversary
Les Paul 55
Les Paul (All Maple)
Les Paul Ace Frehley "Budokan" LP Custom
Les Paul Ace Frehley Signature
Les Paul Artisan and Artisan/3
Les Paul Artist/L.P. Artist/Les Paul Active
Les Paul Axcess Alex Lifeson
Les Paul Axcess Dave Amato
Les Paul Axcess Standard
Les Paul BFG
Les Paul Billy F. Gibbons Goldtop
Les Paul Bird's-Eye Standard
Les Paul Carved Series
Les Paul Catalina
Les Paul Centennial ('56 LP Standard Goldtop)
Les Paul Centennial ('59 LP Special)
Les Paul Class 5
Les Paul Classic
Les Paul Classic 1960 Mars Music
Les Paul Classic Antique Mahogany
Les Paul Classic Custom
Les Paul Classic H-90
Les Paul Classic Limited Edition
Les Paul Classic Mark III/MIII
Les Paul Classic Plus
Les Paul Classic Premium Plus
Les Paul Classic Premium Plus Custom Shop
Les Paul Classic Tom Morgan Limited Edition
Les Paul Cloud 9 Series
Les Paul Collector's Choice Series
Les Paul Custom
Les Paul Custom 25
Les Paul Custom '54
Les Paul Custom Historic '54
Les Paul Custom Historic '57 Black Beauty
1957 Les Paul Custom (2-Pickup) Ultra Light Aged
Les Paul Custom Historic '68
1968 Les Paul Custom Reissue (Custom Shop)
1968 Les Paul Custom Ultra Light Aged
20th Anniversary Les Paul Custom
25th Anniversary (Guitar Center) Les Paul Custom
35th Anniversary Les Paul Custom
120th Anniversary Les Paul Custom
120th Anniversary Les Paul Custom Lite
Les Paul Custom Adam Jones 1979
Les Paul Custom F (Custom Shop)
Les Paul Custom Jeff Beck 1954 Oxblood
Les Paul Custom Jimmy Page
Les Paul Custom John Sykes 1978
Les Paul Custom Lite
Les Paul Custom Lite (Show Case Edition)
Les Paul Custom Mick Ronson '68
Les Paul Custom Music Machine
Les Paul Custom Peter Frampton Signature
Les Paul Custom Plus
Les Paul Custom Showcase Edition
Les Paul Custom Silverburst
Les Paul Custom Steve Jones 1974
Les Paul Dale Earnhardt
Les Paul Dale Earnhardt Intimidator
Les Paul Dark Fire
Les Paul Dark Knight Quilt Top
Les Paul DC AA
Les Paul DC Classic
Les Paul DC Pro
Les Paul DC Standard (Plus)
Les Paul DC Studio
Les Paul Deluxe
Les Paul Deluxe 30th Anniversary
Les Paul Deluxe '69 Reissue
Les Paul Deluxe Hall of Fame
Les Paul Deluxe Limited Edition
Les Paul Deluxe Limited Edition AMS
Les Paul Deluxe Reissue
Les Paul Deluxe #1 Pete Townshend
Les Paul Deluxe #3 Pete Townshend
Les Paul Deluxe #9 Pete Townshend
Les Paul Dickey Betts Goldtop
Les Paul Dickey Betts Red Top
Les Paul Don Felder Hotel California 1959
Les Paul Duane Allman (Custom Shop)
Les Paul Duane Allman Hot 'Lanta (Custom Shop)
Les Paul Dusk Tiger
Les Paul Elegant
Les Paul Eric Clapton 1960
Les Paul ES-Les Paul

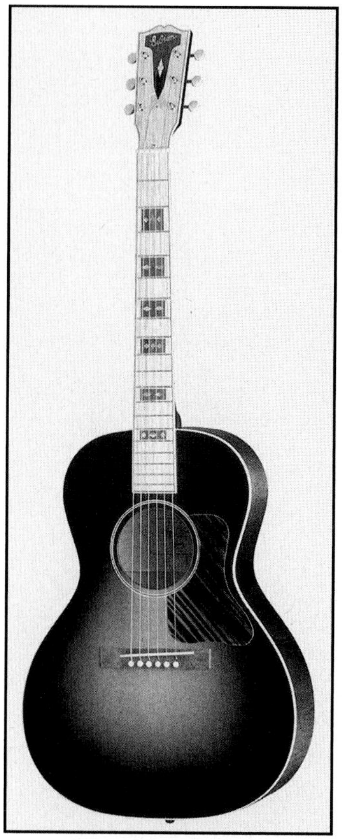

2016 Gibson L-C Century Elvis Costello Limited

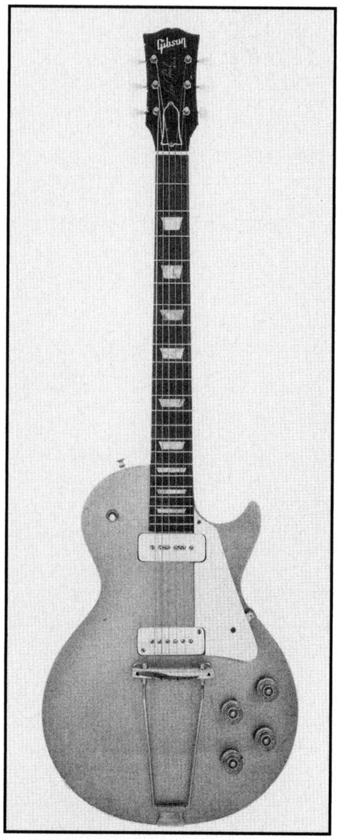

1952 Gibson Les Paul Model

Imaged by Heritage Auctions, HA.com

1952 Gibson Les Paul Model

mrosenow2

1953 Gibson Les Paul Model

Les Paul ES-Les Paul Custom
Les Paul ES-Les Paul Standard
Les Paul ES-Les Paul Studio
Les Paul Florentine Plus
Les Paul Supreme Florentine
Les Paul Futura
Les Paul Gary Moore BFG
Les Paul Gary Moore Signature
Les Paul Gary Rossington Signature
Les Paul Goddess
Les Paul Government Series II
Les Paul GT
Les Paul Guitar Trader Reissue
Les Paul HD.6-X Pro Digital
Les Paul Heritage 80
Les Paul Heritage 80 Award
Les Paul Heritage 80 Elite
Les Paul Heritage 80/Standard 80
Les Paul Hot Rod Magazine '58 Standard
Les Paul Indian Motorcycle
Les Paul J / LPJ
Les Paul Jim Beam (Custom Shop)
Les Paul Jimmy Page "Number Two"
Les Paul Jimmy Page (Custom Authentic)
Les Paul Jimmy Page Signature
Les Paul Jimmy Page Signature Custom Shop
Les Paul Jimmy Wallace Reissue
Les Paul Joe Bonamassa Aged Goldtop
Les Paul Joe Bonamassa Bonabyrd
Les Paul Joe Bonamassa Skinnerburst 1959
Les Paul Joe Bonamassa 'Tomato Soup Burst' Limited Edition
Les Paul Joe Perry 1959 Custom Shop
Les Paul Joe Perry Signature
Les Paul Jumbo
Les Paul Junior
Les Paul Junior 3/4
1957 Les Paul Junior (Single-Cut) Ultra Light Aged/Heavy Aged
1957 Les Paul Junior (Single-Cut) VOS
1958 Les Paul Junior (Double-Cut) VOS
'60 Les Paul Junior
1960 Les Paul Junior (Double-Cut) Ultra Heavy Aged
Les Paul Junior Billie Joe Armstrong Signature
Les Paul Junior DC Hall of Fame
Les Paul Junior Double Cutaway
Les Paul Junior Faded
Les Paul Junior John Lennon LTD
Les Paul Junior Lite
Les Paul Junior Special
Les Paul Junior Special Robot
Les Paul Junior Tenor/Plectrum
Les Paul 2016 Limited Run Series
Les Paul Katrina
Les Paul KM (Kalamazoo Model)
Les Paul Korina (Custom Shop)
Les Paul Leo's Reissue
Les Paul Limited Edition (3-tone)

Les Paul Lou Pallo Signature
Les Paul LP-295 Goldtop
Les Paul Marc Bolan
Les Paul Menace
Les Paul Modern
Les Paul Music Machine 25th Anniversary
Les Paul Music Machine Brazilian Stinger
Les Paul Neal Schon Signature
Les Paul Old Hickory
Les Paul Peace
Les Paul Personal
Les Paul Pro Deluxe
Les Paul Pro Showcase Edition
Les Paul Professional
Les Paul Recording
Les Paul Reissue Flametop
Les Paul Reissue Goldtop
Les Paul Richard Petty LTD
Les Paul SG '61 Reissue
Les Paul SG Standard Authentic
Les Paul SG Standard Reissue
Les Paul Signature "T"
Les Paul Signature/L.P. Signature
Les Paul Silver Streak
Les Paul Slash Appetite
Les Paul Slash Appetite For Destruction
Les Paul Slash Signature
Les Paul Slash Signature Goldtop
Les Paul Slash Signature VOS
Les Paul Slash Snakepit
Les Paul SM
Les Paul SmartWood Exotic
Les Paul SmartWood Standard
Les Paul SmartWood Studio
Les Paul Southern Rock Tribute 1959
Les Paul Special
Les Paul Special (Reissue)
Les Paul Special 100/100 Special
Les Paul Special 3/4
Les Paul Special Centennial
Les Paul Special Double Cutaway
Les Paul Special Faded
Les Paul Special New Century
Les Paul Special Robot
Les Paul Special Tenor
Les Paul Special Worn Cherry
Les Paul Spider-Man
Les Paul Spotlight Special
Les Paul Standard (Sunburst)
Les Paul Standard (SG body)
Les Paul Standard
'50s Les Paul Standard
1958 Les Paul Standard "CME Spec" VOS
1958 Les Paul Standard Light Aged/Heavy Aged
1958 Les Paul Standard Ultra Light Aged
1959 Les Paul Standard Reissue
1959 Les Paul Standard "CME Spec" VOS
1959 Les Paul Standard Heavy Aged
1959 Les Paul Standard Light Aged
1959 Les Paul Standard Ultra Heavy Aged
1959 Les Paul Standard Ultra Light Aged
RSM '59 Les Paul Standard
'60s Les Paul Standard
1960 Les Paul Standard Heavy Aged
1960 Les Paul Standard Light Aged

1960 Les Paul Standard Reissue
1960 Les Paul Standard Ultra Light Aged
'82 Les Paul Standard
Les Paul Standard 100
Les Paul Standard 2008
Les Paul Standard 2010 Limited
Les Paul Standard Billy Gibbons 'Pearly Gates'
Les Paul Standard F
Les Paul Standard Faded
Les Paul Standard HP
Les Paul Standard Lite
Les Paul Standard Lite Limited Edition
Les Paul Standard Michael Bloomfield 1959 Standard
Les Paul Standard Mike McCready 1959
Les Paul Standard Music Zoo 25th Anniversary
Les Paul Standard Paul Kossoff 1959
Les Paul Standard Plus
Les Paul Standard Premium Plus
Les Paul Standard Raw Power
Les Paul Standard Rick Nielsen 1959 Aged
Les Paul Standard Robot
Les Paul Standard Showcase Edition
Les Paul Standard Sparkle
Les Paul Strings and Things Standard
Les Paul Studio
Les Paul Studio 120th Anniversary
Les Paul Studio '50s Tribute
Les Paul Studio '60s Tribute
Les Paul Studio '70s Tribute
Les Paul Studio Baritone
Les Paul Studio BFD
Les Paul Studio Custom
Les Paul Studio Deluxe '60s
Les Paul Studio Deluxe II
Les Paul Studio Faded Vintage Mahogany
Les Paul Studio Faded/Les Paul Studio Pro Faded
Les Paul Studio Gem
Les Paul Studio Gothic
Les Paul Studio Gothic Morte
Les Paul Studio Joe Bonamassa
Les Paul Studio Limited Edition
Les Paul Studio Lite
Les Paul Studio Lite Mark III/M3/M III
Les Paul Studio MLB Baseball
Les Paul Studio Platinum
Les Paul Studio Platinum Plus
Les Paul Studio Plus
Les Paul Studio Premium Plus
Les Paul Studio Raw Power
Les Paul Studio Robot
Les Paul Studio Robot Limited Edition
Les Paul Studio Roland Synthesizer
Les Paul Studio Shred
Les Paul Studio Special
Les Paul Studio Special Limited Edition
Les Paul Studio Standard
Les Paul Studio Swamp Ash
Les Paul Studio USA Anniversary Flood
Les Paul Supreme
Les Paul Tie Dye (St. Pierre)
Les Paul Tie Dye Custom Shop

MODEL YEAR | **FEATURES** | **EXC. COND. LOW** | **HIGH**

Les Paul Traditional Pro/Pro II
Les Paul Traditional/Plus
Les Paul TV
Les Paul TV 3/4
Les Paul TV Jr.
Les Paul Ultima
Les Paul Ultra-Aged
Les Paul Vixen
Les Paul Voodoo/Voodoo Les Paul
Les Paul Warren Haynes
Les Paul XR-I / II / III
Les Paul Zakk Wylde Signature
Les Paul Zebra Wood
The Les Paul
The Paul
The Paul Firebrand Deluxe
The Paul II

Les Paul Model

1952-1958. The Goldtop, 2 P-90 pickups until mid-'57, humbuckers after, trapeze tailpiece until late-'53, stud tailpiece/bridge '53-mid-'55, Tune-o-matic bridge '55-'58, renamed Les Paul Standard in '58. All gold option add +10% if the neck retains 90% of the gold paint. All gold option with ugly green wear on the neck is equal to or below the value of a standard paint job. Some instruments had all mahogany bodies which did not have the maple cap. The all-mahogany version, although rarer, has a 10% lower value. A factory installed Bigsby tailpiece will reduce value by 30%. A non-factory installed Bigsby will reduce value up to 50%.

Model Year	Features	Low	High
1952	1st made, unbound neck	$18,000	$23,500
1952	5/8" knobs, bound neck	$15,000	$19,500
1953	1/2" knobs, late-'53 stud tailpiece	$27,000	$35,000
1953	1/2" knobs, trapeze tailpiece	$15,000	$19,500
1954	Stud tailpiece, wrap-around	$27,000	$35,000
1955	Stud tailpiece, wrap-around, early-'55	$29,000	$37,000
1955	Tune-o-matic tailpiece, late-'55	$36,000	$47,000
1956	Tune-o-matic tailpiece	$35,000	$46,000
1957	P-90s, early-'57	$35,000	$46,000
1957	PAFs, black plastic	$104,000	$135,000
1957-1958	PAFs, white plastic	$110,000	$143,000

'52 Les Paul Goldtop

1997-2002. Goldtop finish, 2 P-90s, '52-style trapeze tailpiece/bridge.

Model Year	Features	Low	High
1997-2002		$1,700	$2,200
1997-2002	Murphy aged	$1,850	$2,400

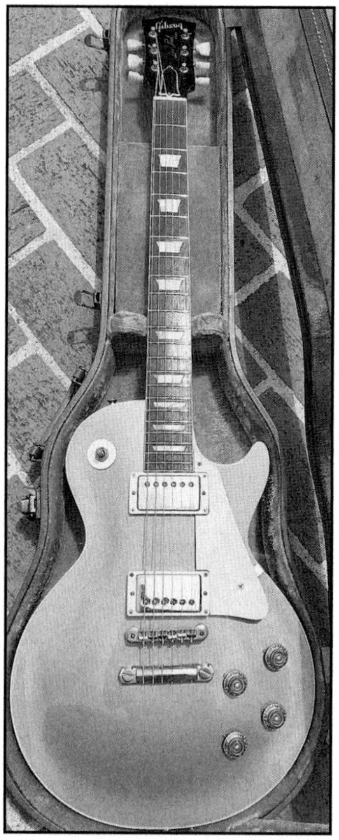

1957 Gibson Les Paul Model
Robert

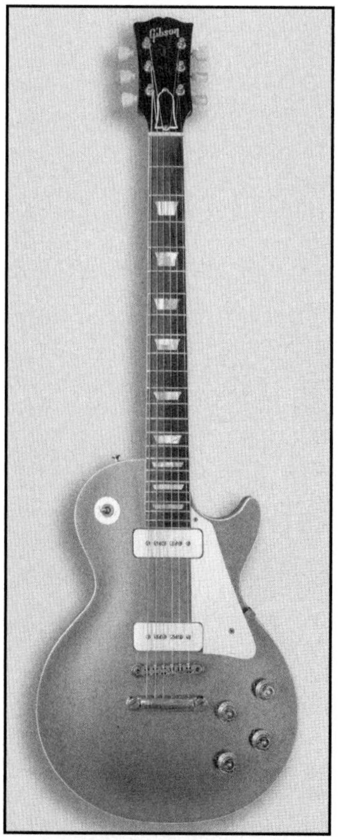

1956 Gibson Les Paul Goldtop
Gary's Classic Guitar

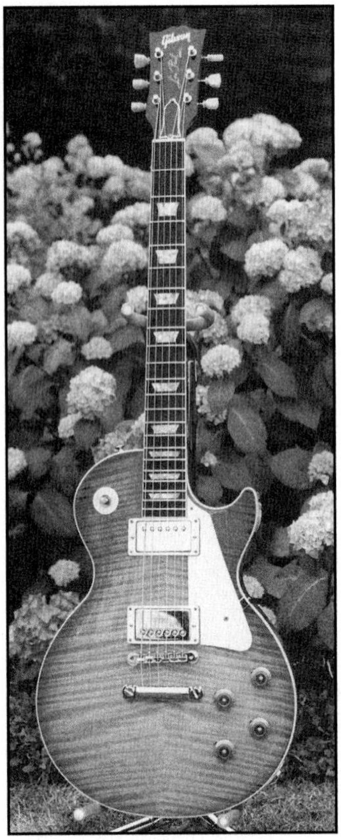

1994 Gibson '59 Les Paul Flametop

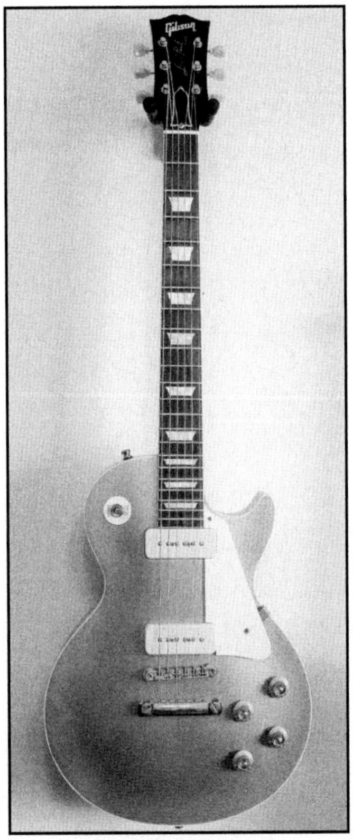

2006 Gibson '56 Les Paul Goldtop

Johnny Zapp

MODEL YEAR	FEATURES	EXC. COND. LOW	HIGH

'52 Les Paul Tribute

2009. Recreation of '52 Les Paul Goldtop model, 564 made, special serialization, each guitar has 'prototype' impressed on back of headstock, Tribute designation logo on truss rod, includes COA booklet with serialized COA and tribute dates 1915-2009.

2009		$2,000	$2,600

'54 Les Paul Goldtop

1996-2013. Goldtop finish, 2 P-90s, '53-'54 stud tailpiece/bridge.

1996-2013		$2,300	$3,000
2003	Brazilian	$4,900	$6,300

'54 Les Paul Wildwood

2012. Wildwood guitars special run, '54 specs, wrap-around tailpiece, 2 P-90 pickups, plaintop sunburst.

2012		$2,300	$3,000

1954 Les Paul Goldtop Heavy Aged

2021. Custom Shop Murphy Lab Collection, Double Gold finish.

2021		$3,800	$5,000

'55 Les Paul Goldtop Hot-Mod Wraptail

2010. Musician's Friend, based on '55 LP Humbucking Pickup Test Guitar, '55 specs, aged nitrocellulose gold finish, includes COA.

2010		$2,300	$3,000

'56 Les Paul Goldtop

1991-2016. Renamed from Les Paul Reissue Goldtop. Goldtop finish, 2 P-90 pickups, Tune-o-matic, now part of Gibson's Historic Collection, Custom Authentic aging optional from '01, Vintage Original Specs aging optional from '06.

1991-2016		$2,300	$3,000
2003	Brazilian	$4,900	$6,300

1956 Les Paul Goldtop "CME Spec" VOS

2019-2020. Custom Shop special run for Chicago Music Exchange, Double Gold with VOS finish.

2019-2020		$2,900	$3,800

1956 Les Paul Goldtop Reissue (Custom Shop)

2020-present. Custom Shop, authentic replica parts, Double Gold nitro finish.

2020		$2,600	$3,400

1956 Les Paul Goldtop Ultra Light Aged

2021. Custom Shop Murphy Lab Collection, Double Gold finish.

2021		$2,900	$3,800

'57 Les Paul Goldtop

1993-2018. Goldtop finish, 2 humbuckers, now part of Gibson's Historic Collection.

1993-2018		$2,300	$3,000
2003	Brazilian	$4,900	$6,300

'57 Les Paul Goldtop (R-7 wrap-around)

2007. Special run with wrap-around bar tailpiece/bridge similar to tailpiece on an original '54 Les Paul Goldtop.

2007		$2,300	$3,000

1957 Les Paul Goldtop Darkback Light Aged

2021. Custom Shop Murphy Lab Collection, Double Gold finish with dark back.

2021		$3,400	$4,500

1957 Les Paul Goldtop Reissue

2020-present. Custom Shop, authentic replica parts, all Double Gold or Double Gold with dark back.

2020		$2,600	$3,400

1957 Les Paul Goldtop Ultra Light/Ultra Heavy Aged

2021. Custom Shop Murphy Lab Collection, ultra light or heavy aged, Double Gold finish.

2021		$2,900	$3,800

'58 Les Paul Figured Top

1996-2000, 2002-2003, 2009-2012. Custom Shop, less top figure than '59 Reissue, sunburst.

1996-1999		$3,400	$4,400
2000-2012		$3,400	$4,400
2003	Brazilian	$9,000	$12,000

'58 Les Paul Plaintop (VOS)

1994-1999, 2003-2013. Custom Shop model, plain maple top version of '58 Standard reissue, sunburst, VOS model starts in '04. Replaced by the 1958 Les Paul Reissue with a non-chambered body.

1994-1999	Non-VOS	$2,600	$3,400
2003-2013	VOS, non-chambered	$2,600	$3,400
2007-2008	VOS, chambered	$2,600	$3,400

'59 Les Paul Flametop/Reissue/Standard

1993-2016. Renamed from Les Paul Reissue Flametop, for 2000-'05 called the 1959 Les Paul Reissue, in '06 this model became part of Gibson's Vintage Original Spec series and is called the '59 Les Paul Standard VOS. Flame maple top, 2 humbuckers, thick '59-style neck, sunburst finish, part of Gibson's Historic Collection, the original certificate authenticity adds value, an instrument without the matching certificate has less value. By '98 Gibson guaranteed only AAA Premium grade maple tops would be used.

Collectors of Historic Collection instruments tend to buy and store these instruments, maintaining them in near mint to New Old Stock (NOS) mint condition. In recent years, NOS instruments that are up to five years old, but in like-new mint condition, have been sold at prices that are higher than instruments in excellent condition, which is the usual condition that VG Price Guide values are given. Because of that trend, the prices shown here give consideration to the numerous NOS instruments that have sold. The inclusion of both excellent condition instruments and mint NOS instruments creates a wider than normal price range, but the high-side of the range is very realistic for NOS instruments.

1993	Custom Shop decal, early '93	$5,400	$7,000
1993	Historic decal, late '93	$4,400	$5,700
1994-1995	Murphy aged	$4,400	$5,700
1994-1999	Aged, figured top	$4,400	$5,700
1996-1999	Figured top	$4,400	$5,700
2000-2016	Aged, figured top	$4,100	$5,300
2000-2016	Figured top	$3,700	$4,800
2003	Brazilian, aged, figured	$10,100	$13,100

MODEL YEAR	FEATURES	EXC. COND. LOW	HIGH
2003	Brazilian, highly figured	$9,100	$12,100
2003	Brazilian, low figured	$8,000	$10,600

'59 Les Paul Burst Brothers

2009-2010. Limited edition created with Dave Belzer and Drew Berlin, sold through Guitar Center, wood-figure was selected to reflect the nature of a '50s LP Standard rather than using only AAA best-quality flame, 1st run of 34 (ser. # series BB 9 001-034) with dark Madagascar rosewood 'board, 2nd run had 37 (ser. # series BB 0 001-037).

2009	1st run, 34 made	$6,300	$8,200
2010	2nd run, 37 made	$5,400	$7,200

'59 Les Paul Korina Reissue

2008. Custom Shop Limited Edition, korina body and neck, quilted maple top, rosewood 'board, natural finish.

2008		$4,800	$6,300

'59 Les Paul Plaintop (VOS)

2006-2013. Custom Shop, very little or no-flame.

2006-2013		$2,600	$3,400

True Historic 1959 Les Paul

2015-2018. Figured maple top, Indian rosewood 'board, certificate of authenticity, various vintage finishes including Murphy aged option.

2015-2018		$3,900	$5,100

'60 Les Paul Corvette

1995-1997. Custom Shop Les Paul, distinctive Chevrolet Corvette styling from '60, offered in 6 colors.

1995-1997		$4,000	$5,200

'60 Les Paul Flametop/Standard '60s

1991-present. Renamed from Les Paul Reissue Flametop, flame maple top, 2 humbuckers, thinner neck, sunburst finish, part of Gibson's Historic Collection. In '06 this model became part of Gibson's Vintage Original Spec series and called '60 Les Paul Standard VOS, then in '17 the name changed to Les Paul Standard '60s.

1991-1999	Figured top	$4,400	$5,700
1994-1999	Aged, figured	$4,400	$5,700
2000-2016	Aged, figured	$3,800	$4,900
2000-2020	Figured top	$3,500	$4,500
2003	Brazilian, aged, figured	$10,100	$13,100
2003	Brazilian, figured	$9,100	$12,100

'60 Les Paul Plaintop (VOS)

2006-2010. Plain maple top version of '60 Standard reissue, certificate of authenticity, cherry sunburst.

2006-2010		$2,600	$3,400

'60 Les Paul Special

1998-2012. Historic Collection reissue, limited edition, single-cut or double-cut.

1998-2012		$2,000	$2,600
2007	Murphy aged	$2,100	$2,700

True Historic 1960 Les Paul

2015-2018. Figured maple top, Indian rosewood 'board, certificate of authenticity, various vintage finishes including Murphy aged option.

2015-2018		$4,200	$5,400

MODEL YEAR	FEATURES	EXC. COND. LOW	HIGH

Les Paul 10th Anniversary Chambered '58 Reissue

2014. Custom Shop, chambered mahogany body, carved maple top, '50s neck profile, rosewood 'board.

2014		$2,700	$3,500

Les Paul 25/50 Anniversary

1978-1979. Split-block inlays, five- or seven- piece maple and walnut neck, gold and silver hardware, 2 humbuckers, coil splitter, TP-6 tailpiece, antique sunburst, natural, wine red, black, and white finishes offered, 8-digit SN followed by 4-digit limited edition number, 1,106 made in '78, 2,305 in '79.

1978-1979		$3,400	$4,500

Les Paul 30th Anniversary

1982-1984. Features of a 1958 Les Paul Goldtop, 2 humbuckers, 30th Anniversary inlay on 19th fret.

1982-1984		$2,600	$3,400

Les Paul 40th Anniversary (from 1952)

1991-1992. Black finish, 2 soapbar P-100 pickups, gold hardware, stop tailpiece, 40th Anniversary inlay at 12th fret.

1991-1992		$2,200	$2,900

Les Paul 40th Anniversary (from 1959)

1999. Reissue Historic, humbuckers, highly figured top, price includes 40th Anniversary Edition Certificate of Authenticity with matching serial number, a guitar without the certificate is worth less.

1999		$3,700	$4,900

Les Paul 50th Anniversary (Historic)

2002. From Gibson Custom Art & Historic Division, 50 made, carved figured koa top, figured maple back and sides, 3-piece figured maple neck, abalone cloud inlay markers, pearl split-diamond headstock inlay and pearl Gibson logo, Antique Natural.

2002		$6,000	$7,800

Les Paul 50th Anniversary 1956 Les Paul Standard

2006. Custom Shop, '56 tune-o-matic P-90 specs.

2006		$2,300	$3,000

Les Paul 50th Anniversary 1957 Les Paul Standard Goldtop

2007. Custom Shop, limited run of 150, humbucker pickups, large gold 50th Anniversary headstock logo.

2007		$3,600	$4,700

Les Paul 50th Anniversary 1959 Les Paul Standard

2009-2011. Custom Shop, highly figured top, certificate of authenticity.

2009-2011		$3,700	$4,900

Les Paul 50th Anniversary 1960 Les Paul Standard

2010-2011. Limited Edition, offered in Heritage Cherry Sunburst, Heritage Dark Burst, Sunset Tea Burst and Cherry Burst.

2010-2011		$3,700	$4,900

Les Paul 50th Anniversary DaPra

2009. Limited run of 25 made for Vic DaPra of Guitar Gallery, '59 Historic R9.

2009		$4,100	$5,300

Les Paul 50th Anniversary 1959 Les Paul Standard

Paul Harbinson

2007 Gibson Les Paul 50th Anniversary 1957 Les Paul Standard Goldtop

Matt Carleson

GUITARS

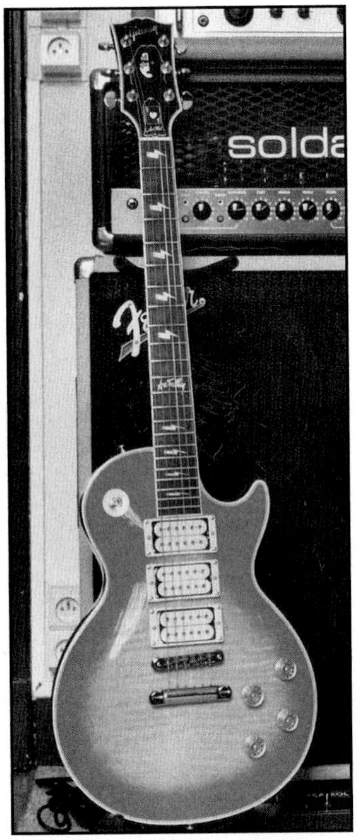

1997 Gibson Les Paul Ace Frehley Signature
Eric Van Gansen

2002 Gibson Les Paul Classic
Ted Dewars

MODEL YEAR	FEATURES	EXC. COND. LOW	HIGH

Les Paul 50th Anniversary Korina Tribute
2009. Custom Shop model, 100 made, single-cut Korina natural finish body, 3 pickups, dot markers, V-shaped Futura headstock, Custom logo on truss rod cover, slanted raised Gibson logo on headstock.
2009 — $4,500 — $5,900

Les Paul 50th Anniversary Les Paul Standard (Sweetwater)
2009. Custom Shop, limited run of 25 for Sweetwater Music, exclusive custom Ruby 'Burst finish.
2009 — $4,100 — $5,300

Les Paul 60th Anniversary 1960 Les Paul Standard "CME Spec" VOS
2020. Custom Shop special run for Chicago Music Exchange, Orange Lemon Fade or Tomato Soup Burst, with VOS finish.
2020 — $3,600 — $4,700

Les Paul 120th Anniversary
2014. Custom Shop, 120th Anniversary neck inlay, heavy quilted top.
2014 — $2,300 — $3,000

Les Paul 55
1974, 1976-1981. Single-cut Special reissue, 2 pickups. By '78 the catalog name is Les Paul 55/78.
1974-1981 Sunburst — $1,675 — $2,175
1974-1981 TV Yellow (limed) — $1,775 — $2,300
1976-1981 Wine — $1,575 — $2,075

Les Paul (All Maple)
1984. Limited run, all maple body, Super 400-style inlay, gold hardware.
1984 — $2,200 — $2,900

Les Paul Ace Frehley "Budokan" LP Custom
2012-2013. Custom Shop, limited edition of 50 hand-aged signed by Frehley, 100 hand-aged unsigned and 150 additional with VOS finish.
2012-2013 All options — $3,500 — $4,600

Les Paul Ace Frehley Signature
1997-2001. Ace's signature inlay at 15th fret, 3 humbuckers, sunburst.
1997 Pilot run, CS specs — $5,900 — $7,700
1997-2001 — $4,500 — $5,800

Les Paul Artisan and Artisan/3
1976-1982. Carved maple top, 2 or 3 humbuckers, gold hardware, hearts and flowers inlays on 'board and headstock, ebony, sunburst or walnut.
1976-1982 2 pickups — $3,900 — $5,000
1976-1982 3 pickups — $3,900 — $5,000

Les Paul Artist/L.P. Artist/Les Paul Active
1979-1982. Two humbuckers (3 optional), active electronics, gold hardware, 3 mini-switches, multi-bound, Fireburst, ebony or sunburst.
1979-1982 — $2,100 — $2,700

Les Paul Axcess Alex Lifeson
2011-2018. Custom Shop, push-pull volume pots, nitrocellulose lacquer finish in Royal Crimson or Viceroy Brown Sunburst, first 25 of each color signed by Lifeson with additional production unsigned, certificate of authenticity.
2011 Signed — $3,900 — $5,000
2011-2018 Unsigned — $2,800 — $3,600

MODEL YEAR	FEATURES	EXC. COND. LOW	HIGH

Les Paul Axcess Dave Amato
2016. Custom Shop, figured maple top, mahogany back and neck, single '57 Classic Plus pickup, Floyd Rose tailpiece, TV yellow.
2016 — $3,500 — $4,500

Les Paul Axcess Standard
2009-present. Custom Shop, new neck joint carve allows access to high frets, Floyd Rose, slightly thinner body, nitro lacquer Iced Tea Burst or Gun Metal Gray. In '20 DC Rust (unique stain) only.
2009-2020 — $1,900 — $2,500

Les Paul BFG
2006-2008, 2018. Burstbucker 3 humbucker at bridge and P-90 at neck, 2 volume and 1 tone knobs, figured maple top over mahogany body.
2006-2008 — $875 — $1,125
2018 — $875 — $1,125

Les Paul Billy F. Gibbons Goldtop
2014-2018. Custom Shop, mahogany neck with maple spline, rosewood 'board, holly headstock, 2 Duncan Pearly Gates pickups, Goldtop VOS or Goldtop Aged.
2014-2018 — $5,100 — $6,600

Les Paul Bird's-Eye Standard
1999. Birdseye top, gold hardware, 2 humbucking pickups, transparent amber.
1999 — $1,575 — $2,050

Les Paul Carved Series
2003-2005. Custom Shop Standards with relief-carved tops, one in diamond pattern, one with flame pattern.
2003-2005 Carved Diamond (top) — $1,700 — $2,200

Les Paul Catalina
1996-1997. Large Custom Shop logo on headstock.
1996-1997 — $2,100 — $2,700

Les Paul Centennial ('56 LP Standard Goldtop)
1994. Guitar of the Month, limited edition of 100, Goldtop mahogany body, gold hardware, gold truss rod plate, gold medallion, engraved light-gold 'guard, with COA.
1994 — $2,800 — $3,600

Les Paul Centennial ('59 LP Special)
1994. Guitar of the Month, limited edition of 100, slab body Special-style configuration, gold hardware, P-90s, gold medallion, commemorative engraving in 'guard, cherry, with COA.
1994 — $2,600 — $3,400

Les Paul Class 5
2001-2006. Custom Shop, highly flamed or quilt top, or special finish, 1960 profile neck, weight relieved body, Burst Bucker humbucking pickups, several color options.
2001-2006 Various models & woods — $2,700 — $5,000

Les Paul Classic
1990-1998, 2000-2008, 2014-present. Early models have 1960 on pickguard, 2 exposed humbuckers, Les Paul Model on peghead until '93, Les Paul Classic afterwards. Limited run of Ebony finish in 2000, 2014

and 2015 have those years in the model name.

MODEL YEAR	FEATURES	EXC. COND. LOW	HIGH
1990-2008	Various colors	$1,425	$1,850
2014-2020	Various colors	$1,225	$1,600

Les Paul Classic 1960 Mars Music

2000. All black.

2000		$1,225	$1,600

Les Paul Classic Antique Mahogany

2007. All mahogany body, exposed humbuckers, Guitar of the Week, limited run of 400 each of cherry (week 27) and sunburst (week 33).

2007		$1,400	$1,800

Les Paul Classic Custom

2007-2008, 2011-2012. Mahogany body with carved maple top, 2 exposed humbuckers in '07-'08, covered afterwards, various colors.

2007-2012		$1,500	$1,950

Les Paul Classic H-90

2008. Guitar of the Week, 400 made, gold hardware, H-90 soapbar pickups.

2008		$1,225	$1,600

Les Paul Classic Limited Edition

2000. Limited Edition logo on back of headstock, Les Paul Classic stencil logo, 3 exposed humbuckers, gold hardware, black finish.

2000		$1,400	$1,800

Les Paul Classic Mark III/MIII

1991-1993. Les Paul Classic features, no 'guard, exposed-coil humbuckers at neck and bridge and single-coil at middle position, 5-way switch, coil-tap.

1991-1993		$1,500	$1,950

Les Paul Classic Plus

1991-1996, 1999-2003. Les Paul Classic with fancier maple top, 2 exposed humbucker pickups. Price depends on top figure.

1991-2003		$1,475	$1,900

Les Paul Classic Premium Plus

1993-1996, 2001-2002. Les Paul Classic with AAA-grade flame maple top, 2 exposed humbucker pickups. Price depends on top figure.

1993-2002		$1,650	$2,150

Les Paul Classic Premium Plus Custom Shop

1994-1998. Custom Shop version, quilted maple top, Custom Shop logo, various colors.

1994-1998		$1,800	$2,325

Les Paul Classic Tom Morgan Limited Edition

2007. 400 made, custom finish top, black finish back/sides, Classic logo on truss rod cover.

2007		$1,500	$1,950

Les Paul Cloud 9 Series

2003-2006. Special lightweight Les Paul series run for three dealers, Music Machine, Dave's Guitar Shop, and Wildwood Guitars, '59 Les Paul body specs, CR serial series number, '59 or '60 neck profile options, various colors, other reissue models available.

2003-2006	All models	$2,700	$3,500

Les Paul Collector's Choice Series

2010-2018. Custom models based on Gibson replicas of one-of-a-kind historic guitars.

MODEL YEAR	FEATURES	EXC. COND. LOW	HIGH
2010-2014	#4A '59 Sandy	$5,700	$7,500
2010-2014	#7 Shanks	$4,800	$6,300
2010-2018	Various models	$4,500	$9,200
2014	#17 Keith Nelson, Buckcherry	$4,800	$6,300
2016	# Ace Frehley	$4,500	$6,000
2016	#5 Whitrock Donna	$4,800	$6,300

Les Paul Custom

1953-1963 (renamed SG Custom late-1963), 1968-present (production moved to Custom Shop in 2004). Les Paul body shape except for SG body '61-'63, 2 pickups (3 humbuckers mid-'57-'63 and '68-'70, 3 pickups were optional various years after), '75 Price List shows a Les Paul Custom (B) model which is equipped with a Bigsby tailpiece versus a wraparound. By '80 offered as Les Paul Custom/Gold Parts and / Nickel Parts, because gold plating wears more quickly and is therefore less attractive there is no difference in price between an '80s Gold Parts and Nickel Parts instrument.

1953	Very early NSN model	$20,800	$27,000
1954-1957	Single coils	$20,800	$27,000
1954-1957	Single coils, factory Bigsby	$20,600	$26,800
1957-1961	Bigsby	$50,500	$65,500
1957-1961	Stoptail	$54,000	$70,000
1961-1963	White, SG body, Maestro, ebony block	$17,300	$22,500
1961-1963	White, SG body, side-pull vibrato	$12,300	$16,000
1962-1963	Black option, SG body, factory stop tail	$19,300	$25,000
1962-1963	Black option, SG body, side-pull vibrato	$12,300	$16,000
1962-1963	White, SG body, factory stop tail	$19,300	$25,000
1968	Black, 1-piece body	$14,300	$18,500
1969	Black, 1-piece body	$11,500	$15,000
1969	Black, 3-piece body	$8,300	$10,700
1970-1973	Various colors, 3 pus	$4,800	$6,300
1970-1974	Various colors, 2 pus	$4,800	$6,300
1974	Black, white, 3 pus	$4,800	$6,300
1974	Natural, cherry sunburst	$3,400	$4,400
1975-1976	Maple 'board, 2 pus	$3,200	$4,150
1975-1976	Maple 'board, 3 pus	$3,200	$4,150
1975-1978	Volute, 2 pus	$3,000	$3,900
1975-1978	Volute, 3 pus	$3,000	$3,900
1977	Maple 'board, black, 2 pus	$3,200	$4,150
1977-1978	Maple 'board, blond, 2 pus	$3,200	$4,150
1979	2 or 3 pickups	$3,000	$3,900
1979	Silverburst, 2 pus	$4,500	$5,900

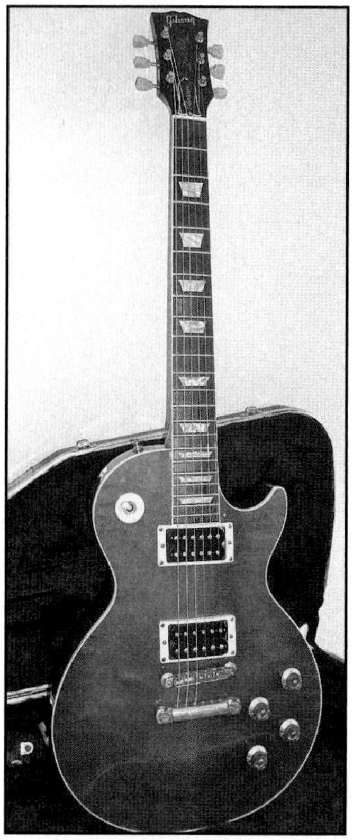

1993 Les Paul Classic Premium Plus

Dave Meyer

1978 Gibson Les Paul Custom

Kevin Okanos

1985 Gibson Les Paul Custom
Luis R Barrios

2003 Gibson Les Paul DC Standard
Imaged by Heritage Auctions, HA.com

MODEL YEAR	FEATURES	EXC. COND. LOW	HIGH
1980-1984	Silverburst, 2 pus	$4,200	$5,400
1980-1986	2 or 3 pickups	$3,000	$3,900
1987-1989	Various colors	$3,000	$3,900
1990-1999	Limited Edition color series	$2,625	$3,450
1990-1999	Various colors	$2,625	$3,450
2000-2020	Various colors	$2,625	$3,450

Les Paul Custom 25

2007. Custom Shop Limited Edition run of 100, Les Paul "25" logo on truss rod cover, COA name Custom 25, triple-split block inlays, mahogany body with flame maple top, gold hardware, sunburst.

2007		$3,000	$3,900

Les Paul Custom '54

1972-1973. Reissue of 1954 Custom, black finish, Alnico V and P-90 pickups.

1972-1973		$4,500	$5,900

Les Paul Custom Historic '54

1991-2013. Custom Shop Historic Collection, 1954 appointments and pickup configuration, black, gold hardware.

1991-2013		$3,400	$4,400

Les Paul Custom Historic '57 Black Beauty

1991-2013. Black finish, gold hardware, 2 or 3 humbucker pickups, part of Gibson's Historic Collection.

1991-2012	2 pickups	$2,550	$3,300
1991-2013	3 pickups	$2,550	$3,300
2007	3 pus, goldtop	$2,550	$3,300
2007	3 pus, Murphy aged	$2,550	$3,300

1957 Les Paul Custom (2-Pickup) Ultra Light Aged

2021. Custom Shop Murphy Lab Collection, Ebony finish.

2021		$4,000	$5,200

Les Paul Custom Historic '68

1999-2007. Custom Shop Historic Collection, flamed maple top, 2 pickups.

1999-2007	Flamed maple	$2,550	$3,300
2000	Black	$2,550	$3,300

1968 Les Paul Custom Reissue (Custom Shop)

2020-present. Solid maple top, mahogany back, 2 humbucker pickups, gold hardware, Ebony gloss nitro finish. Limited slightly aged Silverburst in '20.

2020	Aged Silverburst	$4,500	$5,800
2020-2021	Ebony	$3,200	$4,200

1968 Les Paul Custom Ultra Light Aged

2021. Custom Shop Murphy Lab Collection, Ebony finish.

2021		$3,500	$4,500

20th Anniversary Les Paul Custom

1974. Regular 2-pickup Custom, with 20th Anniversary inlay at 15th fret, cherry sunburst, natural, black or white.

1974	Black, white	$4,500	$5,900
1974	Cherry Sunburst, natural	$3,400	$4,400

25th Anniversary (Guitar Center) Les Paul Custom

1977-1978. Guitar Center Silver Anniversary, 50 made, 'Les Paul Custom' logo on truss rod cover, special 'Les Paul Custom Made in USA' on back of headstock, silver finish.

1977-1978		$3,000	$3,900

35th Anniversary Les Paul Custom

1989. Gold hardware, 3 pickups, carved, solid mahogany body and neck, 35th Anniversary inlay on headstock, black.

1989		$3,000	$3,900

120th Anniversary Les Paul Custom

2014. Custom Shop, 120th Anniversary neck inlay.

2014		$3,300	$4,300

120th Anniversary Les Paul Custom Lite

2014. Custom Shop, 120th Anniversary neck inlay.

2014		$1,750	$2,250

Les Paul Custom Adam Jones 1979

2021. Custom Shop Limited Edition, recreates Jones' '79 LP Custom, 1st 79 aged and signed by Jones, Antique Silverburst VOS finish.

2021	Signed	$5,500	$7,200
2021	Unsigned	$3,400	$4,400

Les Paul Custom F (Custom Shop)

2014-2018. Figured maple top, various colors.

2014-2018		$3,300	$4,300

Les Paul Custom Jeff Beck 1954 Oxblood

2009. Custom Shop, limited run of 150, 1st 50 aged, hand-signed and played by Beck, next 100 VOS, mahogany body, carved maple top, rosewood 'board, Burstbucker humbucking pickups, Oxblood VOS finish.

2009		$4,100	$5,300

Les Paul Custom Jimmy Page

2008. Based on Page's '60 LP Custom with 3 pickups, stop tailpiece or Bigsby option, certificate of authenticity, black VOS finish.

2008		$6,000	$7,800

Les Paul Custom John Sykes 1978

2006. Custom Shop Limited Edition, run of 66, recreates Sykes' '78 LP Custom including mods he made, aged Ebony finish.

2006		$3,500	$4,500

Les Paul Custom Lite

1987-1990, 2013-2016. Carved maple top, ebony 'board, pearl block inlays, gold hardware, PAF pickups, bound neck, headstock and body. Reissue in '13 with new options and colors.

1987-1990	Floyd Rose, opaque	$1,800	$2,300
1987-1990	Other colors	$1,800	$2,300
1987-1990	Sunburst, mild figure	$1,800	$2,300
2013-2016		$1,800	$2,300

Les Paul Custom Lite (Show Case Edition)

1988. Showcase Edition, only 200 made, gold top.

1988		$1,850	$2,400

Les Paul Custom Mick Ronson '68

2007. Custom Shop, includes certificate and other authentication material.

2007		$2,600	$3,400

Les Paul Custom Music Machine

2003. Custom run for dealer Music Machine with special serial number series, chambered body style

MODEL YEAR	FEATURES	EXC. COND. LOW	HIGH

for reduced body weight, quilt tops.

2003	Figured Brazilian	$7,400	$9,600
2003	Quilted	$2,550	$3,300

Les Paul Custom Peter Frampton Signature

2008. Limited Edition 3-pickup version of Frampton's LP Custom, PF serial number series, black.

2008		$2,900	$3,800

Les Paul Custom Plus

1991-1998. Regular Custom with figured maple top, sunburst finish or colors.

1991-1998		$2,550	$3,300

Les Paul Custom Showcase Edition

1988. Showcase Edition logo on back of headstock, goldtop, black hardware.

1988		$2,800	$3,600

Les Paul Custom Silverburst

2007-2014. Custom Shop Limited Edition.

2007-2014		$2,800	$3,700

Les Paul Custom Steve Jones 1974

2008. Custom Shop Limited Edition, recreates Jones' '74 LP Custom including pin-up girl stickers, aged white finish.

2008		$3,500	$4,500

Les Paul Dale Earnhardt

1999. 333 made, Dale's image and number 3 on front and headstock, signature script on fretboard, several pieces of literature and an original certificate are part of the overall package, a lower serial number may add value.

1999		$2,500	$3,200

Les Paul Dale Earnhardt Intimidator

2000. 333 made, Dale's 'Goodwrench' car on the front of the body, The Intimidator inlay on the fretboard, includes certificate, chrome hardware.

2000		$2,500	$3,200

Les Paul Dark Fire

2009. Limited edition, 1st run of Les Pauls with Robot 2 Chameleon tone Technology designed to produce various classic guitar tones, completely computer interactive, Burstbucker3 bridge pickup, P-90H neck pickup and 6 Piezo pickups.

2009		$1,600	$2,075

Les Paul Dark Knight Quilt Top

2019. Exclusive limited run made for Guitar Center, trans black satin finish over quilted maple top.

2019		$1,700	$2,200

Les Paul DC AA

2007. Double A flamed top.

2007		$1,375	$1,825

Les Paul DC Classic

1992-1993. Gold finish.

1992-1993		$1,100	$1,400

Les Paul DC Pro

1997-1998, 2006-2007. Custom Shop, body like a '59 Les Paul Junior, carved highly figured maple top, various options. Name revived in '06 but not a Custom Shop model.

1997-1998		$1,450	$1,925
2006-2007		$1,050	$1,350

MODEL YEAR	FEATURES	EXC. COND. LOW	HIGH

Les Paul DC Standard (Plus)

1998-1999, 2001-2006. Offset double-cut, highly flamed maple top, translucent lacquer finishes in various colors, reintroduced as Standard Lite in '99 but without Les Paul designation on headstock or truss rod cover.

1998-1999		$1,175	$1,525
2001-2006		$1,175	$1,525

Les Paul DC Studio

1997-1999. DC Series double-cut like late '50s models, carved maple top, 2 humbucker pickups, various colors.

1997-1999		$650	$850

Les Paul Deluxe

1969-1985. In 1969, the Goldtop Les Paul Standard was renamed the Deluxe. Two mini-humbuckers (regular humbuckers optional in mid-'70s). Mid-'70s sparkle tops are worth more than standard finishes. The market slightly favors the Goldtop finish, but practically speaking condition is more important than finish, such that all finishes fetch about the same amount (with the exception of the sparkle finish). Initially, the Deluxe was offered only as a Goldtop and the first year models are more highly prized than the others. Cherry sunburst was offered in '71, cherry in '71-'75, walnut in '71-'72, brown sunburst in '72-'79, natural in '75, red sparkle in '73-'75 only, blue sparkle in '73-'77, wine red/see-thru red offered '75-'85. In '99, the Deluxe was reissued for its 30th anniversary.

1969	Goldtop	$4,700	$6,200
1970	Goldtop	$3,900	$5,100
1971-1975	Goldtop	$3,500	$4,500
1971-1975	Natural	$2,600	$3,400
1971-1975	Red (solid)	$2,600	$3,400
1971-1975	Sunburst	$2,600	$3,400
1971-1975	Wine	$2,600	$3,400
1973-1975	Red sparkle, fewer made	$3,600	$4,750
1973-1977	Blue sparkle, more made	$3,325	$4,325
1976-1979	All other colors	$2,200	$2,900
1976-1979	Goldtop	$3,000	$3,900
1976-1979	Natural	$2,500	$3,250
1976-1979	Sunburst	$2,500	$3,250
1980-1985	Various colors	$2,200	$2,900

Les Paul Deluxe 30th Anniversary

1999. Limited Edition logo on the lower back of the headstock, Deluxe logo on truss rod cover, Wine Red.

1999		$1,250	$1,600

Les Paul Deluxe '69 Reissue

2000-2005. Mini-humbuckers, gold top

2000-2005		$1,350	$1,750

Les Paul Deluxe Hall of Fame

1991. All gold finish.

1991		$1,625	$2,100

Les Paul Deluxe Limited Edition

1999-2002. Limited edition reissue with Les Paul Standard features and Deluxe mini-humbuckers, black.

1999-2002		$1,400	$1,800

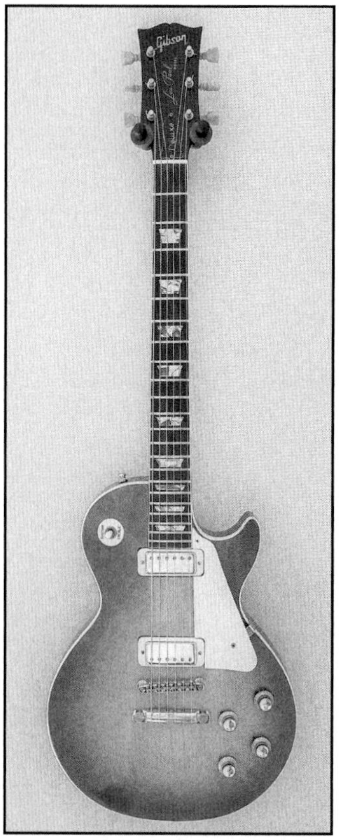

1973 Gibson Les Paul Deluxe

Rich Goldman

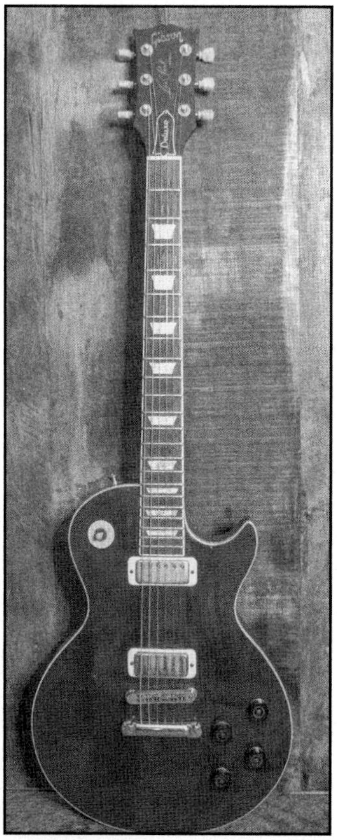

1976 Gibson Les Paul Deluxe

Ted Wulfers

1992 Gibson Les Paul Heritage 80

Sam Gabriel

2002 Gibson Les Paul Indian Motorcycle

MODEL YEAR	FEATURES	EXC. COND. LOW	HIGH

Les Paul Deluxe Limited Edition AMS

2014. Limited edition chocolate finish, offered only by American Musical Supply.

2014		$425	$550

Les Paul Deluxe Reissue

2012. Mini-humbuckers, chambered body.

2012		$1,775	$2,300

Les Paul Deluxe #1 Pete Townshend

2006. Limited to 75, red.

2006		$5,250	$6,800

Les Paul Deluxe #3 Pete Townshend

2006. Limited to 75, goldtop.

2006		$5,250	$6,800

Les Paul Deluxe #9 Pete Townshend

2006. Limited to 75, cherry burst.

2006		$5,250	$6,800

Les Paul Dickey Betts Goldtop

2001-2003. Aged gold top.

2001-2003		$5,250	$6,800

Les Paul Dickey Betts Red Top

2003. Transparent red, gold hardware.

2003		$3,850	$5,000

Les Paul Don Felder Hotel California 1959

2010. Custom Shop, '59 sunburst specs, 50 Murphy aged and signed by Felder, 100 aged, and 150 in VOS finish.

2010	Aged, signed	$6,200	$8,050
2010	Aged, unsigned	$5,675	$7,350
2010	VOS	$4,800	$6,225

Les Paul Duane Allman (Custom Shop)

2013. Custom Shop certificate, Murphy Aged or VOS, 150 made of each.

2013	Aged	$6,600	$8,500
2013	VOS	$5,100	$6,600

Les Paul Duane Allman Hot 'Lanta (Custom Shop)

2003. "DUANE" spelled out in fret wire on back, Custom Shop certificate, 55 made.

2003		$18,000	$24,000

Les Paul Dusk Tiger

Late-2009-2012. Limited edition, 1000 to be made, features Gibson's Robot Technology, Burstbucker bridge, P-90H neck and 6 Piezo pickups.

2009-2012		$1,700	$2,200

Les Paul Elegant

1994-2004. Custom Shop, highly flamed maple top, abalone crown markers and Custom Shop headstock inlay.

1994-2004		$3,000	$4,000

Les Paul Eric Clapton 1960

2011. Nicknamed the Beano Burst, '60 thinner 'Clapton' neck profile, Custom Bucker pickups, nickel-plated Grover kidney button tuners, lightly figured maple cap, traditional 17-degree angled headstock, total of 500 made; 55 Murphy Aged and signed by Clapton, 95 unsigned Murphy Aged, 350 finished with Gibson's VOS treatment.

2011	Aged	$6,500	$8,500
2011	Aged, signed	$15,300	$20,000
2011	VOS	$4,500	$6,000

Les Paul ES-Les Paul

2014-2018. Semi-hollow Les Paul body with f-holes, 3-ply maple/basswood/maple top and back, mahogany neck with maple spline, dark rosewood 'board, 2 pickups, light burst or black.

2014-2018		$1,600	$2,100

Les Paul ES-Les Paul Custom

2015. Memphis Shop, limited run, semi-hollow maple/poplar/maple body, f-holes, high gloss Ebony finish.

2015		$3,100	$4,100

Les Paul ES-Les Paul Standard

2016. Memphis Shop, limited run, semi-hollow, figured maple, various colors.

2016		$3,100	$4,100

Les Paul ES-Les Paul Studio

2016. Memphis Shop, limited run, semi-hollow maple body, f-holes, Ginger Burst or Wine Red.

2016		$1,475	$1,925

Les Paul Florentine Plus

1997-2001. Custom Shop model, hollowbody with f-holes, higher-end appointments.

1997-2001		$2,625	$3,450

Les Paul Supreme Florentine

2009-2015. Les Paul Standard with sharp Florentine cutaway, 350 made, Bigsby tailpiece, chambered mahogany body, highly figured maple top and back, Caribbean Blue finish.

2009-2015		$2,400	$3,100

Les Paul Futura

2014-2015. Light weight, unbound, Min-Etune, various bright colors.

2014-2015		$725	$950

Les Paul Gary Moore BFG

2009-2012. Plain appointment BFG specs, P-90 neck pickup and Burstbucker 3 bridge pickup.

2009-2012		$1,075	$1,400

Les Paul Gary Moore Signature

2000-2002. Signature Series model, Gary Moore script logo on truss rod cover, flamed maple top.

2000-2002		$2,400	$3,100

Les Paul Gary Rossington Signature

2002. GR serial number, replica of his '59 LP Standard, Custom Shop, aged finish, 250 made, includes display case with backdrop photo of Rossington, price includes certificate with matching serial number.

2002		$7,400	$9,600

Les Paul Goddess

2006-2007. Maple carved top, trapezoid inlays, smaller body, 2 humbuckers, 2 controls, tune-a-matic bridge.

2007		$1,025	$1,325

Les Paul Government Series II

2014-2018. 2 Dirty Fingers pickups, certificate of authenticity, Government Tan finish.

2013-2018		$925	$1,200

Les Paul GT

2007. Includes over/under dual truss rods, GT logo on truss rod cover, several specs designed to add durability during heavy professional use.

2007		$1,325	$1,725

Les Paul Guitar Trader Reissue

1982-1983. Special order flametop Les Paul by the Guitar Trader Company, Redbank, New Jersey. Approximately 47 were built, the first 15 guitars ordered received original PAFs, all were double black bobbins (except 1 Zebra and 1 double white), 3 of the guitars were made in the '60-style. The PAF equipped models were based on order date and not build date. The serial number series started with 9 1001 and a second serial number was put in the control cavity based upon the standard Gibson serial number system, which allowed for exact build date identification. Gibson's pickup designer in the early-'80s was Tim Shaw and the pickups used for the last 32 guitars have been nicknamed Shaw PAFs. After Gibson's short run for Guitar Trader, 10 non-Gibson replica Les Pauls were made. These guitars have a poorly done Gibson logo and other telltale issues.

Model Year	Features	Exc. Cond. Low	High
1982-1983	Actual PAFs installed	$10,400	$13,400
1982-1983	Shaw PAFs, highly flamed	$4,600	$6,000
1982-1983	Shaw PAFs, low flame	$4,100	$5,300

Les Paul HD.6-X Pro Digital

2008-2009. Digital sound system, hex pickups.

Model Year	Features	Exc. Cond. Low	High
2008-2009		$1,925	$2,525

Les Paul Heritage 80

1980-1982. Copy of '59 Les Paul Standard, curly maple top, mahogany body, rosewood 'board, nickel hardware, sunburst. In '80 cataloged as Les Paul Standard-80 without reference to Heritage, the catalog notes that the guitar has Heritage Series truss rod cover.

Model Year	Features	Exc. Cond. Low	High
1980-1982	Figured top	$3,800	$5,000
1980-1982	Plain top	$3,000	$3,900

Les Paul Heritage 80 Award

1982. Ebony 'board, 1-piece mahogany neck, gold-plated hardware, sunburst.

Model Year	Features	Exc. Cond. Low	High
1982	Figured	$4,550	$5,900
1982	Highly figured	$5,500	$7,200

Les Paul Heritage 80 Elite

1980-1982. Copy of '59 Les Paul Standard, quilted maple top, mahogany body and neck, ebony 'board, chrome hardware, sunburst. In '80 cataloged as Les Paul Standard-80 Elite without reference to Heritage, the catalog notes that the guitar has the distinctive Heritage Series truss rod cover.

Model Year	Features	Exc. Cond. Low	High
1980-1982		$4,250	$5,500

Les Paul Heritage 80/Standard 80

1982. Based on '57 Les Paul Standard Goldtop, Heritage Series Standard 80 logo on truss rod cover.

Model Year	Features	Exc. Cond. Low	High
1982		$3,250	$4,200

Les Paul Hot Rod Magazine '58 Standard

2008. Custom Shop, Hot Rod inspired flames over a figured-maple top, Hot Rod truss rod cover.

Model Year	Features	Exc. Cond. Low	High
2008		$3,100	$4,100

Les Paul Indian Motorcycle

2002. 100 made, has Indian script logo on fretboard and chrome cast war bonnet on the body, crimson red and cream white.

Model Year	Features	Exc. Cond. Low	High
2002		$3,100	$4,100

Les Paul J / LPJ

2013-2018. Mahogany body with carved maple top, '50s profile maple neck, rosewood 'board, 2 Modern Classics humbucking pickups, various finishes.

Model Year	Features	Exc. Cond. Low	High
2013-2018		$475	$625

Les Paul Jim Beam (Custom Shop)

Ca. 2002-2003. JBLP serial number series, several versions of Jim Beam logo art on top of guitar, award-ribbon-style B Bean logo on headstock, around 75 made.

Model Year	Features	Exc. Cond. Low	High
2002-2003		$1,350	$1,750

Les Paul Jimmy Page "Number Two"

2009-2010. Custom Shop, 1st 25 aged and signed, 100 aged and unsigned, 200 VOS.

Model Year	Features	Exc. Cond. Low	High
2009-2010		$9,200	$12,100

Les Paul Jimmy Page (Custom Authentic)

2004-2006. Custom Shop, includes certificate.

Model Year	Features	Exc. Cond. Low	High
2004-2006		$6,500	$8,500

Les Paul Jimmy Page Signature

1995-1999. Jimmy Page signature on 'guard, mid-grade figured top, push-pull knobs for phasing and coil-tapping, Grover tuners, gold-plated hardware. This is not the '04 Custom Shop Jimmy Page Signature Series Les Paul (see separate listing).

Model Year	Features	Exc. Cond. Low	High
1995	1st year, highly figured	$5,100	$6,650
1995	1st year, low figure	$4,150	$5,400
1995	1st year, moderate figure	$4,450	$5,750
1996-1999	Highly figured	$4,150	$5,400
1996-1999	Low figure	$2,800	$3,600
1996-1999	Moderate figure	$3,550	$4,600

Les Paul Jimmy Page Signature Custom Shop

2004. January '04 NAMM Show, 175 planned production, the first 25 were personally inspected, played-in, and autographed by Jimmy Page. Initial retail price for first 25 was $25,000, the remaining 150 instruments had an initial retail price of $16,400. Cosmetically aged by Tom Murphy to resemble Page's No. 1 Les Paul in color fade, weight, top flame, slab cut attribution on the edges, neck size and profile.

Model Year	Features	Exc. Cond. Low	High
2004	1st 25 made	$15,500	$20,000
2004	Next 26-150	$12,000	$15,000

Les Paul Jimmy Wallace Reissue

1978-1997. Les Paul Standard '59 reissue with Jimmy Wallace on truss rod cover, special order by dealer Jimmy Wallace, figured maple top, sunburst.

Model Year	Features	Exc. Cond. Low	High
1978-1982	Kalamazoo-made, low flame	$3,300	$4,300
1978-1983	Kalamazoo-made, high flame	$4,100	$5,300
1983-1989	Nashville-made	$3,100	$4,100
1990-1997		$3,100	$4,100

Les Paul Joe Bonamassa Aged Goldtop

2008. Inspired By Series, LP Standard aged goldtop with black trim (including black pickup rings), serial number starts with BONAMASSA.

Model Year	Features	Exc. Cond. Low	High
2008		$2,400	$3,100

2017 Gibson Les Paul J

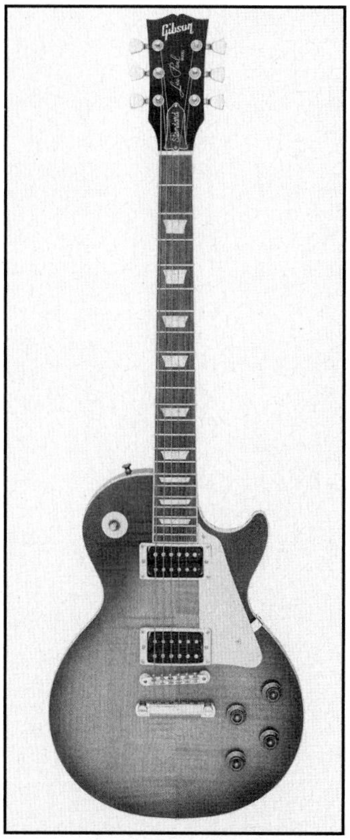

1995 Gibson Les Paul Jimmy Page Signature

Imaged by Heritage Auctions, HA.com

1957 Gibson Les Paul Junior

Frank Thoubboron

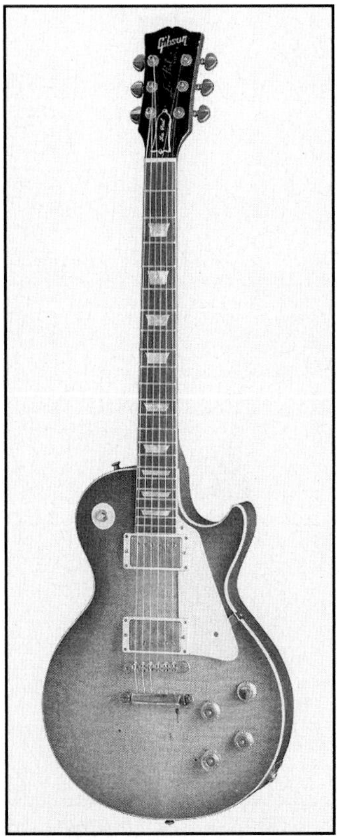

2010 Gibson Les Paul Michael Bloomfield 1959 Standard

MODEL YEAR	FEATURES	EXC. COND. LOW	HIGH

Les Paul Joe Bonamassa Bonabyrd

2015-2016. Limited Edition, 100 made each signed by Joe, plain maple top, retro Firebird headstock, Indian rosewood 'board, 2 Custom Bucker pickups, Antique Pelham Blue finish.

2015-2016		$4,625	$6,025

Les Paul Joe Bonamassa Skinnerburst 1959

2014. Custom Shop, recreation of '59 Les Paul, 150 Murphy aged (first 50 signed by Joe) and 150 VOS, faded Dirty Lemon finish.

2014	All options	$6,500	$9,700

Les Paul Joe Bonamassa 'Tomato Soup Burst' Limited Edition

2016. Limited run of 150, AAA flamed maple top, mahogany back and neck, rosewood 'board, Tomato Soup Burst finish.

2016		$3,300	$4,300

Les Paul Joe Perry 1959 Custom Shop

2013. Custom Shop, recreation of '59 Les Paul, 150 Murphy aged (first 50 signed by Perry) and 150 VOS, faded Tobacco Sunburst finish.

2013		$9,600	$12,500

Les Paul Joe Perry Signature

1997-2001. Unbound slab body with push-pull knobs and Joe Perry signature below bridge, Bone-Yard logo model with typical Les Paul Standard bound body, configuration and appointments.

1997-2001	Bone-Yard option with logo	$1,550	$2,000
1997-2001	Unbound standard model	$1,550	$2,000

Les Paul Jumbo

1969-1970. Single rounded cutaway, flat-top dreadnought acoustic/electric, 1 pickup, rosewood back and sides, natural.

1969-1970		$2,700	$3,500

Les Paul Junior

1954-1963, 1986-1992, 2001-2002, 2005-2013. One P-90 pickup, single-cut solidbody '54-mid-'58, double-cut '58-early-'61, SG body '61-'63, renamed SG Jr. in '63, reintroduced as single-cut for '86-'92, reissued as the 1957 Les Paul Jr. Single Cutaway in '98. Headstock repair reduces the value by 40%-50%. Reinstalled tuners reduces the value by 5% to 10%. Replaced tuner buttons reduces the value by 5% to 10%.

1954-1958	Sunburst, single-cut	$6,000	$8,000
1958-1961	Cherry, double-cut	$5,800	$7,600
51961-1963	Cherry, SG body	$3,850	$5,000
1986-1992	Sunburst, single-cut, tune-o-matic	$750	$1,000
1998-2013	Sunburst, single-cut, stop tail	$750	$1,000

Les Paul Junior 3/4

1956-1961. One P-90 pickup, short-scale, single-cut solidbody '54-mid-'58, double-cut '58-early-'61.

1956-1958	Sunburst, single-cut	$3,000	$3,800
1958-1961	Cherry, double-cut	$2,550	$3,300

MODEL YEAR	FEATURES	EXC. COND. LOW	HIGH

1957 Les Paul Junior (Single-Cut) Ultra Light Aged/Heavy Aged

2021. Custom Shop Murphy Lab Collection, ultra light or heavy aged, TV Yellow finish on both.

2021	Heavy Aged	$3,500	$4,500
2021	Ultra Light Aged	$2,400	$3,100

1957 Les Paul Junior (Single-Cut) VOS

1998-2014. Custom Shop, nickel-plated hardware, Vintage Original Spec aging optional from '06.

1998-2014		$1,750	$2,300

1958 Les Paul Junior (Double-Cut) VOS

1998-2013. Custom Shop, nickel plated hardware, Vintage Original Spec aging optional from '06.

1998-2013		$1,750	$2,300

'60 Les Paul Junior

1992-2003. Historic Collection reissue.

1992-2003		$1,750	$2,300

1960 Les Paul Junior (Double-Cut) Ultra Heavy Aged

2021. Custom Shop Murphy Lab Collection, Ebony finish.

2021		$4,300	$5,600

Les Paul Junior Billie Joe Armstrong Signature

2006-2013. 1956 LP Junior specs.

2006-2013		$975	$1,250

Les Paul Junior DC Hall of Fame

1990-1992. Part of Hall of Fame Series, limited run of LP Junior Double Cutaway but with P-100 pickup.

1990-1992		$750	$1,000

Les Paul Junior Double Cutaway

1986-1992, 1995-1996. Copy of '50s double-cut Jr., cherry or sunburst, reissued as the 1958 Les Paul Jr. Double Cutaway in '98.

1986-1989		$750	$1,000

Les Paul Junior Faded

2010-2012. Single-cut, faded cherry finish.

2010-2012		$550	$725

Les Paul Junior John Lennon LTD

2008. Custom Shop, 300 made, Charlie Christian neck pickup and P-90 bridge as per Lennon's modified Junior, aged-relic finish, certificate, book and New York t-shirt.

2008		$3,500	$4,500

Les Paul Junior Lite

1999-2002. Double-cut, Tune-o-matic, 2 P-100 pickups, stop tail, mini-trapezoid markers, burnt cherry gloss finish.

1999-2002		$600	$775

Les Paul Junior Special

1999-2004. LP Jr. single-cut slab body with 2 P-90s (making it a Special) instead of the standard single P-90, double pickup controls, cherry, tinted natural or sunburst.

1999-2004		$650	$850

Les Paul Junior Special Robot

2008. P-90s, TV Yellow.

2008		$675	$875

Les Paul Junior Tenor/Plectrum

Late-1950s. Four string neck on Junior body, cherry.

1959		$3,850	$5,000

MODEL YEAR	FEATURES	EXC. COND. LOW	HIGH

Les Paul 2016 Limited Run Series

Various Les Paul limited edition models released in 2016.

2016-2018	Fort Knox	$3,075	$4,000
2016-2018	Mahogany Limited	$3,075	$4,000
2016-2018	Pete Townshend Deluxe	$3,075	$4,000
2016-2018	Redwood	$3,075	$4,000
2016-2018	Standard Figured Walnut	$3,075	$4,000
2016-2018	Sunken Treasure	$3,075	$4,000

Les Paul Katrina

2005. 300 made in cooperation with Music Rising Foundation and the Edge U2.

2005		$2,125	$2,750

Les Paul KM (Kalamazoo Model)

1979. Regular Les Paul Standard with 2 exposed humbuckers, KM on headstock, sunburst, approximately 1500 were made in the Kalamazoo plant.

1979		$2,725	$3,550

Les Paul Korina (Custom Shop)

1999. Limited run with figured Korina top, Custom Shop logo on back of headstock.

1999		$2,800	$3,700

Les Paul Leo's Reissue

1980-1985. Special order from Gibson's Nashville facility for Leo's Music, Oakland, California. Identified by serial number with L at the beginning, flamed maple top. About 800 guitars were made, with about 400 being exported to Japan. Kalamazoo-made Leo's have a 2nd serial number in the control cavity, Nashville-made Leo's do not have a 2nd serial number.

1980-1983	Kalamazoo, high flame	$4,800	$6,300
1980-1983	Kalamazoo, low flame	$3,700	$4,900
1983-1985	Nashville-made	$3,750	$4,900

Les Paul Limited Edition (3-tone)

1997. Limited Edition stamped on the back of the headstock, Les Paul Standard configuration with cloud inlay markers, 2-piece 3-tone sunburst finish over non-figured maple top.

1997		$1,925	$2,500

Les Paul Lou Pallo Signature

2010. Maple top, mahogany back and neck, rosewood 'board, 2 pickups, ebony finish.

2010		$1,625	$2,100

Les Paul LP-295 Goldtop

2008. Guitar of the Month (April, '08), limited run of 1000, Les Paul body style, goldtop, 2 humbuckers, ES-295 appointments such as 'guard and fretboard markers, Bigsby tailpiece option.

2008		$2,000	$2,600

Les Paul Marc Bolan

2011. Artist model with certificate of authenticity, limited run of 100 hand aged and 350 VOS, Bolan Chablis finish.

2011		$3,800	$4,900

Les Paul Menace

2006-2007. Carved mahogany body, 2 humbucker pickups.

2006-2007		$525	$675

MODEL YEAR	FEATURES	EXC. COND. LOW	HIGH

Les Paul Modern

2017-present. Custom Shop, new light-weight features, mahogany body with maple top, back is natural finish, top with faded pelham blue, sparkling burgundy or graphite black.

2017-2020		$1,600	$3,000

Les Paul Music Machine 25th Anniversary

2002. Custom run for dealer Music Machine with special serial number series, 14 flame top and 14 quilt top instruments were produced, Music Machine 25th Anniversary logo on truss rod cover, special cherry sunburst finish.

2002	Flame top	$4,250	$5,500
2002	Quilt top	$3,800	$5,000

Les Paul Music Machine Brazilian Stinger

2003. Custom run for dealer Music Machine with special serial number series, Brazilian rosewood 'board, black stinger paint on back of neck-headstock, '59 or '60 reissue body and neck profile options, highly figured flame or quilt top options, other reissue options available.

2003	'54, '56 or '58, figured flame or quilt	$10,100	$13,100
2003	'54, '56 or '58, goldtop	$7,500	$9,700
2003	'59 or '60, figured flame or quilt	$10,500	$13,700
2003	'59 or '60, plain top	$9,300	$12,000

Les Paul Neal Schon Signature

2005. Custom Shop, 80 made, Floyd Rose tremolo, signature on truss rod cover, COA, black.

2005		$8,300	$10,800

Les Paul Old Hickory

1998 only. Limited run of 200, tulip poplar body wood from The Hermitage, Custom-style trim.

1998		$3,700	$4,800

Les Paul Peace

2014-2015. AA top, rosewood 'board, 2 pickups, various color finishes.

2014-2015		$1,450	$1,900

Les Paul Personal

1969-1972. Two angled, low impedance pickups, phase switch, gold parts, walnut finish.

1969-1972		$2,000	$2,600

Les Paul Pro Deluxe

1978-1982. Chrome hardware, 2 P-90s, various colors. Les Pauls could vary significantly in weight during the '70s and '80s and lighter-weight examples may be worth up to 25% more than these values.

1978-1982		$1,875	$2,475

Les Paul Pro Showcase Edition

1988. Goldtop 1956 specs, Showcase Edition decal, 200 made.

1988		$2,550	$3,300

Les Paul Professional

1969-1971, 1977-1979. Single-cut, 2 angled, low impedance pickups, carved top, walnut or white.

1969-1971	Walnut	$2,000	$2,600
1969-1971	White	$2,800	$3,600

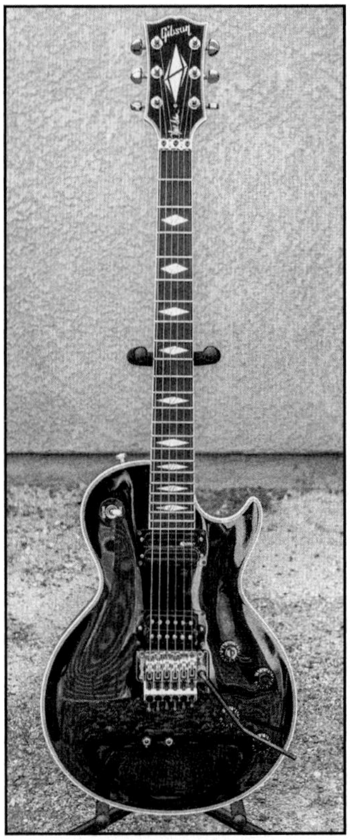

2005 Gibson Les Paul Neal Schon Signature

Wayne Stephens

1969 Gibson Les Paul Personal

Frank Manno

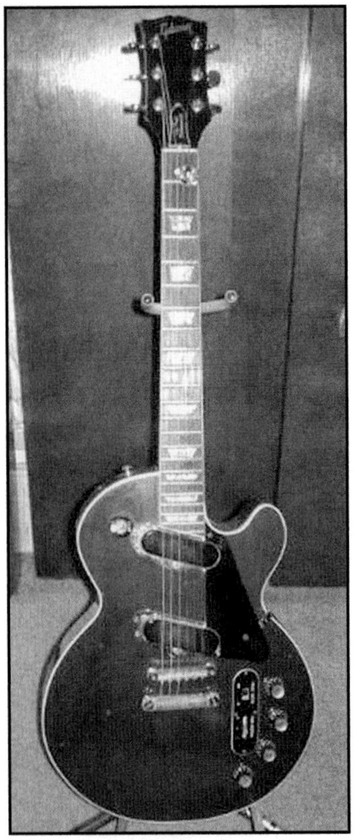

1969 Gibson Les Paul Professional

Pete Pensec

1994 Gibson Les Paul Special Centennial

Imaged by Heritage Auctions, HA.com

MODEL YEAR	FEATURES	EXC. COND. LOW	HIGH

Les Paul Recording

1971-1979. Two angled, low impedance pickups, high/low impedance selector switch, walnut '71-'77, white added '75, natural, ebony and sunburst added '78.

1971-1977	Walnut	$2,300	$3,000
1975-1979	White	$3,000	$4,000
1978-1979	Black, Natural, Sunburst	$2,400	$3,100

Les Paul Reissue Flametop

1983-1990. Flame maple top, 2 humbuckers, thicker '59-style neck, sunburst finish, renamed '59 Les Paul Flametop in '91.

1983-1990	Highly figured	$4,400	$5,700

Les Paul Reissue Goldtop

1983-1991. Goldtop finish, 2 P-100 pickups, renamed '56 Les Paul Goldtop in '91.

1983-1991		$2,300	$3,000

Les Paul Richard Petty LTD

2003. Richard Petty's image on front and back, 'The King' inlay on fretboard.

2003		$2,550	$3,300

Les Paul SG '61 Reissue

1993-2003. Renamed the Les Paul SG '61 Reissue from SG '62 Reissue, early '60s Les Paul Standard SG specs with small guard, trapezoid markers, heritage cherry finish, by 2003 the Les Paul script marking was not on the truss rod cover, renamed to SG '61 Reissue.

1993-2003	Stud tail	$1,500	$1,950

Les Paul SG Standard Authentic

2005. SG '61 specs, small guard, Les Paul truss rod logo, stud tailpiece.

2005		$1,925	$2,500

Les Paul SG Standard Reissue

2000-2004. Reissue of early-'60s specs including Deluxe Maestro vibrato with lyre tailpiece (stop bar tp offered), small 'guard, holly head veneer, standard color faded cherry, available in Classic White or TV Yellow, becomes the SG Standard Reissue by '05.

2000-2004	Maestro	$1,925	$2,500

Les Paul Signature "T"

2014-2018. Chambered solidbody, 2 exposed split-coil humbuckers, "Les Paul" signature on 'guard, Min-Etune.

2014-2018		$1,575	$2,050

Les Paul Signature/L.P. Signature

1973-1978. Thin semi-hollowbody, double-cut, 2 low impedance pickups, f-holes, various colors. The Price List refers to it as L.P. Signature.

1973-1978		$3,400	$4,400

Les Paul Silver Streak

1982. Custom Shop decal, silver finish.

1982		$2,500	$3,250

Les Paul Slash Appetite

2010-2012. Figured maple top, Slash artwork headstock logo, 2 Alnico II Pro Slash pickups, Appetite Amber finish.

2010-2012		$4,200	$5,400

Les Paul Slash Appetite For Destruction

2010-2011. Custom Shop, figured maple top, 2 Duncan Slash pickups, butterscotch finish available as VOS or Aged.

2010-2011	VOS	$8,100	$10,500

Les Paul Slash Signature

2008. Slash logo on truss rod, Darkburst, SL serial number series.

2008		$2,800	$3,600

Les Paul Slash Signature Goldtop

2008. Limited Edition, 1000 made, LP Standard model, Slash logo truss rod cover, Limited Edition logo back of headstock, certificate of authenticity.

2008		$2,800	$3,600

Les Paul Slash Signature VOS

2008-2010. Inspired By Series, Slash hat logo on body and signature logo on guitar case, plain maple top with faded VOS finish.

2008-2010		$3,400	$4,450

Les Paul Slash Snakepit

1997. Custom Art Historic, highly figured top, cobra inlay neck, snake and hat on body.

1997		$23,000	$30,000

Les Paul SM

1980. Solid mahogany, single-cut with coil-tap, Les Paul SM truss rod logo, burgundy or silverburst finish.

1980	Various wood & finish	$1,800	$2,350

Les Paul SmartWood Exotic

1998-2001. Full-depth Les Paul-style built with eco-friendly woods, Muiracatiara (or Muir) top, mahogany back, Preciosa 'board, pearloid dots.

1998-2001		$925	$1,200

Les Paul SmartWood Standard

1996-2002. Smartwood Series, figured maple top, mahogany body, Smartwood on truss rod cover, antique natural.

1996-2002		$925	$1,200

Les Paul SmartWood Studio

2002-2006. Muiracatiara (Muir) top and mahogany back, Preciosa (Prec) 'board, Studio appointments including pearl-style dot markers.

2002-2006		$800	$1,025

Les Paul Southern Rock Tribute 1959

2014-2018. Limited Edition, commemorative medallion on switch-cavity cover, first 50 aged and signed by Southern Rock Ambassadors (Dickey Betts, Charlie Daniels, Gary Rossington, Jimmy Hall), remainder are VOS, reverse burst finish.

2014-2016	Aged	$4,875	$6,325
2014-2018	VOS	$4,075	$5,275

Les Paul Special

1955-1959. Slab solidbody, 2 pickups (P-90s in '50s, P-100 stacked humbuckers on later version), single-cut until end of '58, double in '59, the '89 reissue is a single-cut, renamed SG Special in late-'59.

1955-1959	TV Yellow	$9,700	$12,500
1959	Cherry	$7,500	$9,700

Les Paul Special (Reissue)

1989-1998, 2002-2006. Briefly introduced as Les Paul Junior II but name changed to Special in the first year, single-cut, 2 P-100 stacked humbuckers, TV Yellow, in '90 there was a run of 300 with LE serial number, renamed Special SL in '98.

1989-1998	P-100s	$725	$950
2002-2006	Humbuckers	$725	$950

MODEL YEAR	FEATURES	EXC. COND. LOW	HIGH

Les Paul Special 100/100 Special
2015-2016. Reissue double-cut slab body, 2 P-90s, 'Les Paul 100' birthday signature on headstock.

2015-2016		$675	$875

Les Paul Special 3/4
1959. Slab solidbody, 2 P-90 pickups, double-cut, short-scale, cherry finish, renamed SG Special 3/4 in late-'59.

1959		$4,200	$5,400

Les Paul Special Centennial
1994 only. 100 made, double-cut, cherry, 100 year banner at the 12th fret, diamonds in headstock and in gold-plated knobs, gold-plated Gibson coin in back of headstock.

1994		$3,100	$4,000

Les Paul Special Double Cutaway
1976-1979, 1993-1994. Double-cut, 2 P-90s, 1990s version was made in Custom Shop and was reintroduced as the '60 Les Paul Special Historic in '98.

1976-1979		$2,000	$2,600
1993-1994	Custom Shop	$1,125	$1,450

Les Paul Special Faded
2005-2012. Double- or single-cut, dot markers, 2 P-90s, Special logo on truss rod cover, faded TV limed mahogany or cherry finish.

2005-2012		$600	$775

Les Paul Special New Century
2006-2008. Full-body mirror 'guard, 2 exposed humbuckers, single-cut LP Special body, mirror truss rod cover.

2006-2008		$975	$1,250

Les Paul Special Robot
2008. Two P-90 pickups, various colors.

2008	TV Yellow	$775	$1,000

Les Paul Special Tenor
1959. Four-string electric tenor, LP Special body, TV Yellow.

1959		$4,000	$5,200

Les Paul Special Worn Cherry
2003-2006. Single-cut, non-bound LP Special with 2 humbuckers.

2003-2006		$550	$725

Les Paul Spider-Man
2002. Custom Shop, superhero depicted on the body, red spider logo, gold hardware, Standard appointments. 15 guitars were produced as a Gibson/Columbia TriStar Home Entertainment/Tower Records promotion, while a larger batch was sold at retail.

2002		$2,900	$3,800

Les Paul Spotlight Special
1983-1984. Curly maple and walnut top, 2 humbuckers, gold hardware, multi-bound top, Custom Shop Edition logo, natural or sunburst.

1983-1984	Figured top	$5,500	$7,100

Les Paul Standard (Sunburst)
1958-1960, special order 1972-1975. Les Paul Sunbursts from '58-'60 should be individually valued based on originality, color and the amount and type of figure in the maple top, changed tuners or a Bigsby removal will drop the value. Approximately 15% came with the Bigsby tailpiece. The noted price ranges are guidance valuations. Each '58-'60 Les Paul Standard should be evaluated on a case-by-case basis. As is always the case, the low and high ranges are for an all original, excellent condition, undamaged guitar. About 70% of the '58-'60 Les Paul Standards have relatively plain maple tops. The majority of '58-'60 Les Paul Standards have moderate or extreme color fade.

Wider fret wire was introduced in early-'59. White bobbins were introduced in early- to mid-'59. Double ring Kluson Deluxe tuners were introduced in late-'60. It has been suggested that all '58-'60 models have 2-piece centerseam tops. This implies that 1-piece tops, 3-piece tops and off-centerseam tops do not exist.

The terminology of the 'Burst includes: arching medullary grain, swirling medullary grain, ribbon-curl, chevrons, Honey-Amber, receding red aniline, pinstripe, bookmatched, double-white bobbins, zebra bobbins, black bobbins, fiddleback maple, sunburst finish, Honeyburst, lemon drop, quarter sawn, blistered figure, width of gradation, flat sawn, Teaburst, Bigsby-shadow, rift sawn, heel size, aged clear lacquer, 3-dimensional figure, intense fine flame, tag-shadow, red pore filler, Eastern maple fleck, medium-thick flame, shrunk tuners, wave and flame, flitch-matched, elbow discoloration, ambered top coat, natural gradation, grain orientation, script oxidation, asymmetrical figure Tangerineburst, Greenburst, and birdseye.

The bobbins used for the pickup winding were either black or white. The market has determined that white bobbin PAFs are the most highly regarded. Generally speaking, in '58 bobbins were black, in '59 the bobbin component transitioned to white and some guitars have 1 white and 1 black bobbin (aka zebra). In '60, there were zebras and double blacks returned.

Rather than listing separate line items for fade and wood, the Guide lists discounts and premiums as follows. The price ranges shown below are for instruments with excellent color, excellent wood, with the original guitar case. The following discounts and premiums should be considered.

An instrument with moderate or total color fade should be discounted about 10%.

One with a factory Bigsby should be discounted about 10%-15%.

Original jumbo frets are preferred over original small frets and are worth +10%.

1958	Highly figured	$279,000	$362,000
1958	Minor figured	$230,000	$300,000
1958	Plain top, no figuring	$165,000	$215,000
1959	Highly figured	$350,000	$455,000
1959	Minor figured	$247,000	$322,000
1959	Plain top, no figuring	$190,000	$247,000
1960	Early '60, fat neck, highly figured	$262,000	$338,000
1960	Early '60, fat neck, minor figured	$220,000	$285,000

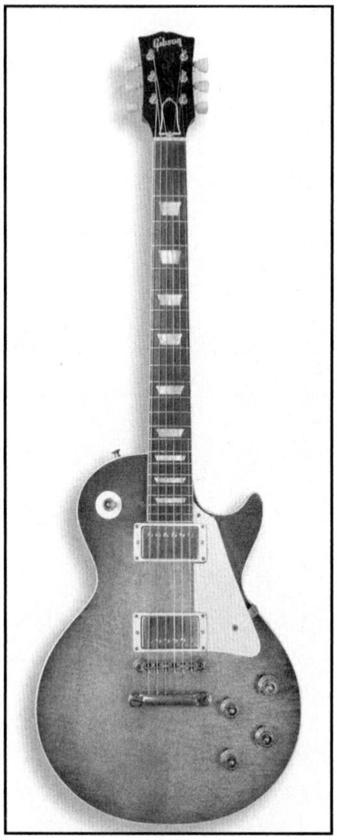

1958 Gibson Les Standard

Gary's Classic Guitars

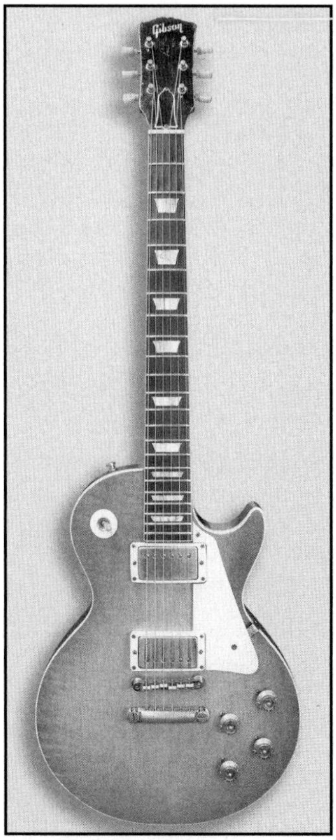

1959 Gibson Les Paul Standard

Keith Nelson

1962 Gibson Les Paul Standard

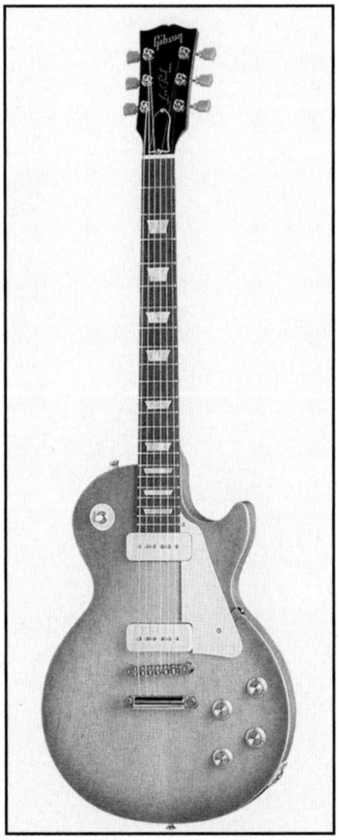

Gibson Les Paul Studio '60s Tribute

MODEL YEAR	FEATURES	EXC. COND. LOW	HIGH
1960	Early '60, fat neck, plain top	$152,000	$198,000
1960	Late '60, flat neck, highly figured	$248,000	$323,000
1960	Late '60, flat neck, minor figured	$191,000	$248,000
1960	Late '60, flat neck, plain top	$142,000	$185,000

Les Paul Standard (SG body)

1961-1963 (SG body those years). Renamed SG Standard in late-'63.

1961-1963	Cherry, side vibrola, PAFs	$13,000	$17,000
1962	Cherry, Bigsby, 1 pat #, 1 PAF	$10,600	$13,800
1962-1963	Cherry, side vibrola, pat #	$9,800	$12,700
1962-1963	Ebony block, SG, PAFs, dlx vibrola	$14,600	$19,000
1962-1963	Ebony block, SG, pat #, dlx vibrola	$12,000	$15,600

Les Paul Standard (reintroduced then renamed)

1968-1969. Comes back as a goldtop with P-90s for '68-'69 (renamed Les Paul Deluxe, '69), available as special order Deluxe '72-'76.

1968	P-90s, small hdsk, no volute	$15,000	$19,500
1968-1969	P-90s, large hdsk	$11,500	$15,000

Les Paul Standard (reintroduced)

1976-July 2008, 2012-2018. Available as special order Deluxe '72-'76, reintroduced with 2 humbuckers '76-present. The '75 Price List shows a Les Paul Standard (B) model which is equipped with a Bigsby tailpiece versus a wraparound, also shows a Les Paul Standard (B) with palm pedal. Replaced by Les Paul Standard 2008 in August '08. Name revived in '12 on chambered-body version with tapped Burstbucker pickups, available in AAA tops, black, Gold Top or Blue Mist finishes.

1971	Early special order goldtop, P-90s	$8,300	$10,800
1972-1974	Special order goldtop, P-90s	$6,000	$7,800
1972-1974	Special order sunburst, P-90s	$5,100	$6,600
1974-1975	Special order, hums	$5,100	$6,600
1976	Sunburst, 4-piece pancake body	$3,100	$4,050
1976-1978	Other colors	$2,500	$3,300
1977-1978	Sunburst	$3,100	$4,050
1978-1979	Natural	$2,500	$3,300
1979	Brown Sunburst	$3,100	$4,050
1979	Cherry Sunburst	$3,100	$4,050
1979	Goldtop	$3,100	$4,050
1979	Wine Red	$2,500	$3,300
1980-1984	Other colors	$2,400	$3,100
1980-1984	Sunburst	$2,400	$3,100
1980-1984	White (RRhoads)	$2,400	$3,100
1985-1989	Various colors	$2,275	$2,950
1985-1989	White (RRhoads)	$2,275	$2,950
1990-1993	Ltd Ed colors with sticker	$2,275	$2,950
1990-1999	White (RRhoads)	$1,775	$2,300
1990-2018	Figured top	$1,875	$2,525
1990-2018	Plain top	$1,650	$2,150
2000-2018	Opaque solid color	$1,650	$2,150

'50s Les Paul Standard

2005-present. Originally an AMS exclusive with AA (later AAA) maple top and various finishes. In '19, Gibson introduced a regular production model with the same name with standard maple top finished in Goldtop, Heritage Cherry Sunburst or Tobacco Burst.

2005-2020	AA/AAA top	$1,200	$1,550

1958 Les Paul Standard "CME Spec" VOS

2019-2020. Custom Shop special run for Chicago Music Exchange, various colors with VOS finish.

2019-2020		$2,900	$3,800

1958 Les Paul Standard Light Aged/ Heavy Aged

2021. Custom Shop Murphy Lab Collection, light or heavy aged, Lemon Burst.

2021		$3,600	$4,700

1958 Les Paul Standard Ultra Light Aged

2021. Custom Shop Murphy Lab Collection, Bourbon Burst or Washed Cherry Sunburst.

2021		$3,000	$4,000

1959 Les Paul Standard Reissue

2020-present. Custom Shop, authentic replica parts, Washed Cherry Sunburst, Iced Tea Burst or Dirty Lemon, all colors with VOS finish.

2020		$3,600	$4,700

1959 Les Paul Standard "CME Spec" VOS

2019-2020. Custom Shop special run for Chicago Music Exchange, various colors with VOS finish.

2019-2020		$5,000	$6,500

1959 Les Paul Standard Heavy Aged

2021. Custom Shop Murphy Lab Collection, Green Lemon Fade, Golden Poppy Burst or Slow Iced Tea Fade.

2021		$5,000	$6,500

1959 Les Paul Standard Light Aged

2021. Custom Shop Murphy Lab Collection, Cherry Tea Burst, Lemon Burst or Royal Tea Burst.

2021		$4,500	$5,800

1959 Les Paul Standard Ultra Heavy Aged

2021. Custom Shop Murphy Lab Collection, Kindred Burst or Lemon Burst.

2021		$5,900	$7,600

1959 Les Paul Standard Ultra Light Aged

2021. Custom Shop Murphy Lab Collection, Factory Burst, Southern Fade Burst or Sunrise Teaburst.

2021		$3,900	$5,050

MODEL YEAR	FEATURES	EXC. COND. LOW	HIGH

RSM '59 Les Paul Standard

2018 and 2020. Custom Shop special run for Rumble Seat Music, recreation of the original 1959 LP Standard, limited run of 6 each year.

2018, 2020		$10,500	$13,500

'60s Les Paul Standard

2005-present. Originally an AMS exclusive with AA (later AAA) maple top and various finishes. In '19, Gibson introduced a regular production model with the same name with standard maple top finished in Ice Tea, Bourbon Burst, or Unburst.

2005-2020	AA/AAA top	$1,200	$1,550

1960 Les Paul Standard Heavy Aged

2020-present. Custom Shop Murphy Lab Collection, heavy aged Tangerine Burst.

2020		$5,000	$6,500

1960 Les Paul Standard Light Aged

2020-present. Custom Shop Murphy Lab Collection, light aged Tomato Soup Burst.

2020		$4,500	$5,800

1960 Les Paul Standard Reissue

2020. Custom Shop, authentic reproduction, vintage-style appointments, various colors with VOS finish.

2020		$3,600	$4,700

1960 Les Paul Standard Ultra Light Aged

2020-present. Custom Shop Murphy Lab Collection, ultra light aged Orange Lemon Fade Burst or Wide Tomato Burst.

2020		$3,800	$5,000

'82 Les Paul Standard

1982. Standard 82 on truss rod cover, made in Kalamazoo, Made in USA stamp on back of the headstock, generally quilted maple tops.

1982		$2,550	$3,300

Les Paul Standard 100

2015. Les Paul 100 on headstock (facsimile of his actual signature) honoring his 100th birthday, Les Paul hologram back of headstock, G-Force tuning, various new colors with high gloss finish.

2015		$1,700	$2,200

Les Paul Standard 2008

August 2008-2012. 2008 added to name, chambered mahogany body, new asymmetrical neck profile, locking grovers, plain or AA flamed maple top, Ebony, Gold Top, various sunbursts.

2008-2012	Figured top	$1,875	$2,525
2008-2012	Gold top	$1,750	$2,300
2008-2012	Plain top	$1,650	$2,150

Les Paul Standard 2010 Limited

2010. Robot tuning technology, 2 pickups, scripted "Limited Edition" logo on headstock, Fireball finish.

2010		$1,650	$2,150

Les Paul Standard Billy Gibbons 'Pearly Gates'

2009-2011. Aged - 50 made, Aged and signed - 50 made, V.O.S. - 250 made.

2009-2011	Aged	$8,400	$10,900
2009-2011	VOS	$7,900	$10,300

Les Paul Standard F

2010-2017. Custom Shop, also called LPS-F, 5A flame maple top, 2 Burstbucker pickups, various new colors with gloss nitro finish.

2010-2017		$2,500	$3,200

Les Paul Standard Faded

2005-2008. Figured top, exposed humbuckers, faded satin finish.

2005-2008		$1,700	$2,200

Les Paul Standard HP

2016-2018. Solidbody, figured maple top, mahogany back and sides, 2 humbucker pickups, G-Force automatic tuners, various colors with gloss nitro finish.

2016-2018		$1,800	$2,350

Les Paul Standard Lite

1999-2001. DC body-style, renamed from DC Standard in '99, reintroduced as Les Paul Standard DC Plus in 2001, various translucent finishes, available in 2004 under this name also.

1999-2001		$1,125	$1,475

Les Paul Standard Lite Limited Edition

2014. Thin body LP, Burstbuckers, 3 knobs, coil tap switch, "120th Anniversary" on 12th fret, highly figured flame top or plain top offered.

2014	Plain top	$975	$1,275

Les Paul Standard Michael Bloomfield 1959 Standard

2009-2011. Custom Shop, limited production of 100 Murphy-aged and 200 VOS, matching certificate of authenticity.

2009-2011		$6,200	$8,000

Les Paul Standard Mike McCready 1959

2010-2016. Custom Shop, limited to 50 aged and signed, 100 VOS finish.

2010-2016	Aged, signed	$6,200	$8,000
2010-2016	VOS	$5,400	$7,000

Les Paul Standard Music Zoo 25th Anniversary

2019. Custom Shop, styled from '59 LP Standard, figured maple top, mahogany body and neck, Indian rosewood 'board, VOS Orange Drop finish.

2019		$4,100	$5,400

Les Paul Standard Paul Kossoff 1959

2012-2013. Custom Shop, 100 aged and 250 VOS made, green lemon finish, certificate of authenticity.

2012-2013	Aged	$4,700	$6,100
2012-2013	VOS	$4,300	$5,600

Les Paul Standard Plus

1995-2012. Gibson USA model, figured maple top, Vintage Sunburst, Heritage Cherry Sunburst or Honeyburst finish.

1995-2012		$2,000	$2,625

Les Paul Standard Premium Plus

1999-2007. Premium plus flamed maple top.

1999-2007		$2,100	$2,750

Les Paul Standard Raw Power

2000-2001, 2006-2007. Natural gloss finish on maple top, appears to have been a Musician's Friend version in '06-'07.

2000-2001		$1,475	$1,900

Gibson Les Paul Standard Faded

Ted Mottor

2011 Gibson Les Paul Standard Plus

Rivington Guitars

2019 Gibson Les Paul Traditional

1996 Gibson Les Paul Tie Dye (St. Pierre)
Rivington Guitars

MODEL YEAR	FEATURES	EXC. COND. LOW	HIGH

Les Paul Standard Rick Nielsen 1959 Aged

2016-2017. Custom Shop, first 50 aged and signed, figured maple top, mahogany back and neck, Indian rosewood 'board, aged or vintage gloss finish.

2016	Signed	$6,400	$8,300
2016	Unsigned	$4,800	$6,200

Les Paul Standard Robot

2007. Blueburst finish, robot tuning.

2007		$950	$1,225

Les Paul Standard Showcase Edition

1988. Showcase Edition logo on back of neck, Guitar of the Month, silverburst.

1988		$2,725	$3,550

Les Paul Standard Sparkle

2001. Sparkle holoflake top, reflective back, Standard logo on truss rod.

2001		$2,100	$2,700

Les Paul Strings and Things Standard

1975-1978. Special order flamed maple top Les Paul Standard model, built for Chris Lovell, owner of Strings and Things, a Gibson dealer in Memphis, approximately 28 were built, sunburst. Authentication of a Strings and Things Les Paul is difficult due to no diffinitive attributes, valuation should be on a case-by-case basis.

1975-1978	Figured 2-piece top	$6,800	$8,800
1975-1978	Plain 2-piece top	$5,400	$7,000
1975-1978	Plain 3-piece top	$3,700	$4,800

Les Paul Studio

1983-present. Unbound mahogany body, (early models have alder body), 2 humbuckers, various colors.

1983-2009		$1,000	$1,300
2009-2012	Silverburst	$975	$1,250
2010-2019		$900	$1,200
2020		$825	$1,100

Les Paul Studio 120th Anniversary

2014. Figured maple top, 120th Anniversary badge on 12th fret, vintage gloss finish on various colors.

2014		$950	$1,250

Les Paul Studio '50s Tribute

2010-2016. '56 LP Goldtop specs, P-90s, '50s neck, Tune-o-matic, stopbar tailpiece, chambered unbound body.

2010-2016		$625	$825

Les Paul Studio '60s Tribute

2011-2016. Similar to '50s Tribute except for '60 slim taper neck.

2011-2016		$625	$825

Les Paul Studio '70s Tribute

2012-2016. Similar to '50s Tribute except for '70s neck profile with volute.

2012-2016		$625	$825

Les Paul Studio Baritone

2004-2012. 28" baritone scale, maple top, mahogany back and neck, 2 pickups, nitro gloss honeyburst finish.

2004-2012		$1,050	$1,350

Les Paul Studio BFD

2007. Studio specs but with BFD electronics.

2007		$575	$750

MODEL YEAR	FEATURES	EXC. COND. LOW	HIGH

Les Paul Studio Custom

1981-1985. 2 humbucking pickups, multi-bound top, gold-plated hardware, various colors.

1981-1985		$1,125	$1,475

Les Paul Studio Deluxe '60s

2010-2012. Exposed pickups, Deluxe logo on truss rod cover, sunburst.

2010-2012		$850	$1,125

Les Paul Studio Deluxe II

2008-2013. Carved flame maple top, mahogany back, 2 pickups, various colors.

2008-2013		$850	$1,100

Les Paul Studio Faded Vintage Mahogany

2007-2010. Vintage mahogany with faded satin.

2007-2010		$625	$825

Les Paul Studio Faded/Les Paul Studio Pro Faded

2005-2012. Faded sunburst tops. Name changes to Studio Pro Faded in '12, then ends production.

2005-2012		$625	$825

Les Paul Studio Gem

1996-1998. Limited edition with Les Paul Studio features, but using P-90 pickups instead of humbucker pickups, plus trapezoid markers and gold hardware.

1996-1998		$875	$1,150

Les Paul Studio Gothic

2000-2001. Orville Gibson image on back of headstock, single Gibson crescent and star neck marker, Gothic Black with black hardware.

2000-2001		$725	$950

Les Paul Studio Gothic Morte

2011-2012. All-mahogany body, African Obeche 'board, 2 humbuckers, satin ebony finish.

2011-2012		$725	$950

Les Paul Studio Joe Bonamassa

2011-2013. Maple top, mahogany back and neck, 2 Alnico II pickups, goldtop finish.

2011-2013		$1,250	$1,625

Les Paul Studio Limited Edition

1997. P-100 pickups, black.

1997		$725	$950

Les Paul Studio Lite

1987-1998. Carved maple top, mahogany back and neck, 2 humbucker pickups, various colors.

1987-1998		$875	$1,150

Les Paul Studio Lite Mark III/M3/M III

1991-1994. HSH pickup configuration, trans finishes.

1991-1994		$875	$1,150

Les Paul Studio MLB Baseball

2008. Major League Baseball graphics on body, only 30 made, satin finish, dot markers.

2008		$1,250	$1,625

Les Paul Studio Platinum

2004-2006. 2 Humbuckers, no position markers, brushed metal hardware, body, neck and headstock in satin platinum finish, matching platinum hardshell case.

2004-2006		$900	$1,200

Les Paul Studio Platinum Plus

2004-2006. Same as Platinum but with trapezoid markers and black hardshell case.

2004-2006		$900	$1,200

MODEL YEAR	FEATURES	EXC. COND. LOW	HIGH

Les Paul Studio Plus

2002-2007. Two-piece AA flamed unbound top, gold hardware, Desert Burst or see-thru black.

2002-2007 $975 $1,275

Les Paul Studio Premium Plus

2006-2008. AAA flamed-maple top.

2006-2008 $1,250 $1,625

Les Paul Studio Raw Power

2009-2012. Unbound maple top, chambered maple body, 2 humbuckers, dots, satin finishes.

2009-2012 $900 $1,200

Les Paul Studio Robot

2007-2011. Robot tuning, trapezoid inlays, silverburst, fireburst, wine red, black, red metallic, green metallic.

2007-2011 All colors $800 $1,050

Les Paul Studio Robot Limited Edition

2012. 'Chameleon' tone circuit.

2012 $800 $1,050

Les Paul Studio Roland Synthesizer

1985. With Roland 700 synth.

1985 $800 $1,050

Les Paul Studio Shred

2012. Unbound body, trapazoid markers, 2 humbuckers. Floyd Rose, high-gloss ebony nitro finish.

2012 $900 $1,200

Les Paul Studio Special

2001. Solidbody, single-cut, 2 pickups, various colors.

2001 $950 $1,250

Les Paul Studio Special Limited Edition

2019-2020. Limited Edition, nitro finish in Lemon Burst or Desert Burst.

2019-2020 $825 $1,075

Les Paul Studio Standard

1984-1987. Cream top and neck binding, dots.

1984-1987 $1,300 $1,700

Les Paul Studio Swamp Ash

2004-2012. Studio model with swamp ash body.

2004-2012 $900 $1,200

Les Paul Studio USA Anniversary Flood

2011. Commemorating the Nashville flood of May, 2010, blue or green swirl.

2011 $1,000 $1,300

Les Paul Supreme

2003-2018. Highly figured AAAA maple top and back on translucent finishes only, custom binding, deluxe pearl markers, chambered mahogany body, globe logo or "Supreme" on headstock, solid colors available by '06.

2003-2018 Various tops & colors $2,400 $3,100

Les Paul Tie Dye (St. Pierre)

1996-1997. Hand colored by George St. Pierre, just over 100 made.

1996-1997 $2,125 $2,750

Les Paul Tie Dye Custom Shop

2002. Limited series of one-off colorful finishes, Custom Shop logo.

2002 $2,125 $2,750

Les Paul Traditional Pro/Pro II

2010-2014. Exposed tapped coil humbuckers, sunbursts, goldtop, ebony or wine red.

2010-2014 $1,325 $1,725

Les Paul Traditional/Plus

2008-2019. Traditional on truss rod, '80s styling with weight-relief holes in an unchambered body, standard appointments. Figured maple (Plus) or opaque color top.

2008-2014 Opaque $1,450 $1,875

2008-2019 Plain sunburst $1,450 $1,875

2008-2019 Plus, figured maple $1,600 $2,100

Les Paul TV

1954-1959. Les Paul Jr. with limed mahogany (TV Yellow) finish, single-cut until mid-'59, double-cut after, renamed SG TV (see that listing for more) in late-'59.

1954-1959 Single-cut $10,800 $14,000

1958-1959 Double-cut $9,900 $12,800

Les Paul TV 3/4

1954-1957. Limed mahogany (TV Yellow) Les Paul Jr. 3/4, short-scale, single-cut.

1954-1957 $5,000 $6,500

Les Paul TV Jr.

2001-2016. Custom Shop, TV Yellow.

2001-2016 $1,600 $2,100

Les Paul Ultima

1996-2007. Custom Shop, flame or quilt sunburst, abalone and mother-of-pearl tree of life, harp, or flame fingerboard inlay, multi abalone bound body.

1996-2007 $5,200 $6,700

Les Paul Ultra-Aged

2011-2012. Custom Shop, '59 specs, Bigsby optional, aged by Tom Murphy.

2011-2012 $4,200 $5,400

Les Paul Vixen

2006-2007. Les Paul Special single-cut slab body, dot markers, 2 humbuckers, 2 controls, wrap-around bridge.

2006-2007 Various colors $775 $1,025

Les Paul Voodoo/Voodoo Les Paul

2004-2005. Single-cut, swamp ash body, 2 exposed humbuckers, black satin finish.

2004-2005 $1,250 $1,650

Les Paul Warren Haynes

2007. Custom Shop, Inspired by Artist series.

2007 $2,500 $3,250

Les Paul XR-I / II / III

1981-1983. No frills model with Dirty Finger pickups, dot markers, Les Paul stencil logo on headstock, goldburst, silverburst and cherryburst finishes.

1981-1983 All models $1,000 $1,300

Les Paul Zakk Wylde Signature

1999, 2003-2016. Custom shop, black and antique-white bullseye graphic finish. Green Camo option.

1999-2016 Various options & colors $3,000 $5,000

Les Paul Zebra Wood

2007. Zebrawood top, mahogany back and neck, rosewood 'board, 2 '57 Classic pickups, natural satin zebrawood finish.

2007 $1,650 $2,150

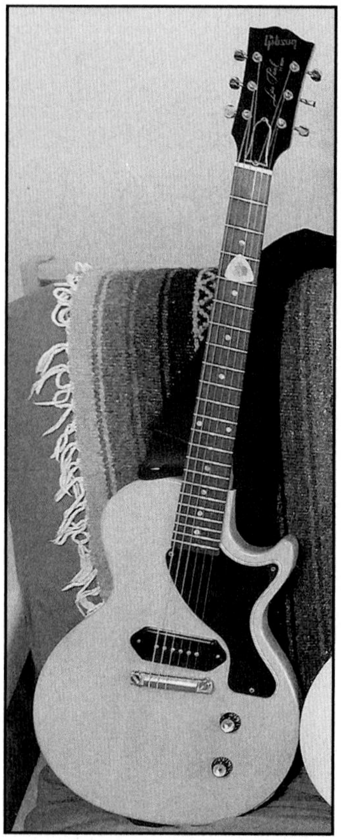

Gibson Les Paul TV Jr.

Bill Miller

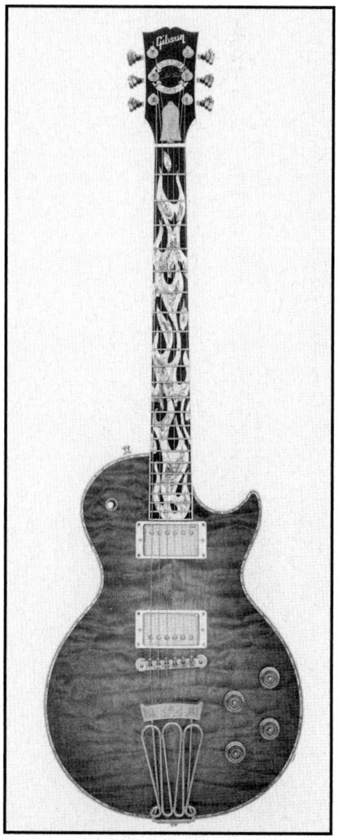

1998 Gibson Les Paul Ultima

Imaged by Heritage Auctions, HA.com

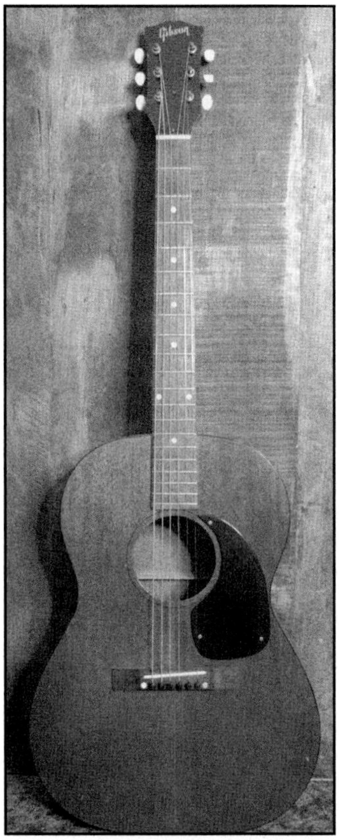

1958 Gibson LG-0
Ted Wulfers

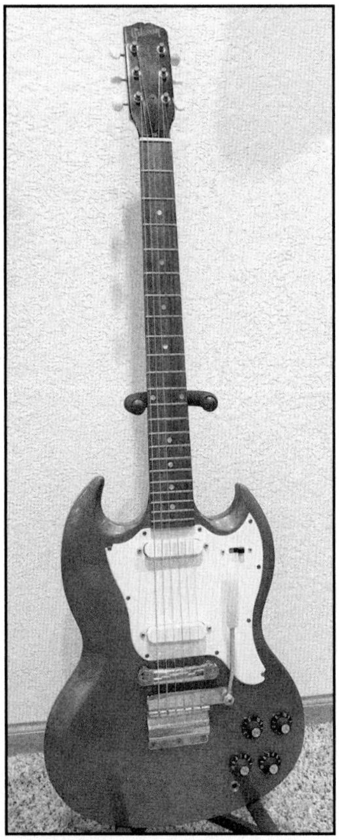

1967 Gibson Melody Maker D
Tim McClutchy

MODEL YEAR	FEATURES	EXC. COND. LOW	HIGH

The Les Paul

1976-1979. Figured maple top, 2 humbuckers, gold hardware, rosewood binding, 'guard, 'board, knobs, cover plates, etc., natural or rosewood finishing, natural only by '79.

1976-1979	Natural or rosewood	$8,400	$10,900

The Paul

1978-1982. Offered as The Paul Standard with solid walnut body and The Paul Deluxe with solid mahogany body, 2 exposed humbuckers.

1978-1982	Walnut or mahogany	$1,075	$1,400

The Paul Firebrand Deluxe

1980-1982. Single-cut mahogany solidbody, rough natural finish, Gibson branded in headstock, 2 exposed humbuckers.

1980-1982	Black	$1,000	$1,300
1980-1982	Pelham Blue	$1,000	$1,300
1980-1982	Rough natural	$1,000	$1,300

The Paul II

1996-1998. Mahogany body, 2 humbucking pickups, rosewood dot neck, renamed The Paul SL in '98.

1996-1998		$700	$900

LG-0

1958-1974. Flat-top acoustic, mahogany, bound body, rosewood bridge '58-'61 and '68-'74, plastic bridge '62-'67, natural.

1958-1961	Rosewood bridge	$925	$1,200
1962-1964	Plastic bridge	$775	$1,025
1965	Plastic bridge	$700	$925
1966	Plastic bridge	$600	$775
1967-1969	Rosewood bridge	$600	$775
1970-1974		$525	$675

LG-1

1943-1968. Flat-top acoustic, spruce top, mahogany back and sides, bound body, rosewood bridge '43-'61, plastic bridge after, examples seen to '74, sunburst.

1943-1945		$2,100	$2,700
1946-1949		$1,900	$2,500
1950-1959	Rosewood bridge	$1,700	$2,200
1960-1961	Rosewood bridge	$1,600	$2,100
1962-1964	Plastic bridge	$1,400	$1,800
1965		$1,175	$1,525
1966-1968		$1,150	$1,500

LG-2

1942-1962. Flat-top acoustic, spruce top, mahogany back and sides (some with maple '43-'46), banner headstock '42-'46, bound body, X-bracing, sunburst finish, replaced by B-25 in '62.

1942-1945	Banner, mahogany	$3,000	$4,000
1942-1945	Banner, spruce	$3,900	$5,200
1946-1949	Sitka	$3,200	$4,225
1950-1959		$2,900	$3,800
1960-1961	Rosewood bridge	$2,200	$2,850
1962	Adjustable bridge	$2,050	$2,650

LG-2 3/4

1949-1962. Short-scale version of LG-2 flat-top, wood bridge, sunburst.

1949	Rosewood bridge	$1,800	$2,350
1950-1959	Rosewood bridge	$1,700	$2,200
1960-1961	Rosewood bridge	$1,550	$2,000
1962	Adjustable bridge	$1,550	$2,000

LG-2 3/4 Arlo Guthrie

2003, 2005-2018. Vintage replica finish.

2003-2018		$1,375	$1,775

LG-2 American Eagle

2013-2018. Sitka top, mahogany back and sides, L.R. Baggs.

2013-2018		$1,125	$1,450

LG-2 Banner

2013. All mahogany, only 50 made.

2013		$1,550	$2,000

LG-2 H

1945-1955. Flat-top, Hawaiian, natural or sunburst.

1944-1945		$3,100	$4,000
1946-1949		$2,426	$3,150
1950-1955		$2,125	$2,775

LG-3

1942-1964. Flat-top acoustic, spruce top, mahogany back and sides, bound body, natural finish, replaced by B-25 N.

1942-1945	Banner	$3,775	$4,900
1946-1949		$3,550	$4,600
1950-1959		$2,800	$3,600
1960-1961	Last wood bridge	$2,375	$3,075
1962-1964	Plastic bridge	$2,200	$2,850

L-Jr.

1918-1927. Archtop, solid carved spruce top, carved figured birch back, Sheraton Brown or natural finish.

1918-1927		$1,600	$2,100

Longhorn Double Cutaway

2008. Guitar of the Month for July '08, AA figured maple top, 2 active pickups, piezo pickup, sunburst or transparent finishes.

2008		$1,325	$1,750

M III Series

1991-1996, 2013-2018. Double-cut solidbody with extra long bass horn, six-on-a-side tuners on a reverse pointy headstock, dot markers, reverse Gibson decal logo. Reissued in '13 with natural finish on 'board and choice of Cosmic Cobalt, Electric Lime, Vibrant Red, or Orange Glow.

1991-1992	Deluxe	$1,225	$1,575
1991-1996	Standard	$1,075	$1,375
2013-2018	Reissue	$850	$1,100

M IV Series

1993-1995. M III with Steinberger vibrato.

1993-1995	S Deluxe	$1,250	$1,600
1993-1995	S Standard	$1,050	$1,400

Mach II

1990-1991. Renamed from U-2, offset double-cut, 2 single coils and 1 humbucking pickup.

1990-1991		$800	$1,025

Map Guitar

1983, 1985. Body cutout like lower 48, 2 humbuckers, limited run promotion, '83 version in natural mahogany or red, white and blue, '85 version red, white and blue stars and stripes on a white background. This model can often be found in better than excellent condition because the instrument is as much a

MODEL YEAR	FEATURES	EXC. COND. LOW	HIGH

show piece as it is a player guitar, and the price range reflects that.

1983	Natural	$2,700	$3,500
1983	Red, white & blue	$2,900	$3,800

Marauder

1975-1980. Single-cut solidbody, pointed headstock, 2 pickups, bolt-on neck, various colors.

1975-1980		$875	$1,150

Marauder Custom

1976-1977. Marauder with 3-way selector switch, bound 'board, block markers, bolt-on neck, Marauder logo on truss rod cover, sunburst.

1976-1977		$1,275	$1,650

Melody Maker

1959-1971, 1986-1993. Slab solidbody, 1 pickup, single-cut until '61, double '61-'66, SG body '66-'71, reintroduced as single-cut in '86-'93. A single-cut Les Paul Melody Maker was offered from '03-'06.

1959-1961	Sunburst, single-cut	$1,300	$1,700
1962-1964	Sunburst, cherry, double-cut	$1,150	$1,500
1965-1966	Cherry, double cut	$1,050	$1,375
1966-1971	Various colors, SG body	$1,300	$1,700
1986-1993	Reintroduced as single-cut	$675	$875

Melody Maker 3/4

1959-1963. Short-scale version.

1959-1963		$1,250	$1,625

Melody Maker D

1960-1970. Two pickup version of Melody Maker, reintroduced as Melody Maker Double in '77.

1960-1961	Sunburst, single-cut	$2,000	$2,600
1961-1964	Sunburst, cherry, double-cut	$1,800	$2,350
1965-1966	Sunburst, cherry, double-cut	$1,500	$1,950
1966-1970	Various colors, SG body	$1,550	$2,025

Melody Maker Double

1977-1983. Reintroduction of Melody Maker D, double-cut solidbody, 2 pickups, cherry or sunburst.

1977-1983	Bolt-on	$750	$1,000
1977-1983	Set-neck	$900	$1,200

Melody Maker III

1967-1971. SG-style double-cut solidbody, 3 pickups, various colors.

1967-1971		$1,625	$2,100

Melody Maker 12

1967-1971. SG-style solidbody, 12 strings, 2 pickups, red, white or Pelham Blue.

1967-1971		$1,475	$1,900

Melody Maker Faded

2003. Les Paul Jr. styling, single-cut, 1 P-90 style pickup, Nashville tune-o-matic bridge, black satin finish.

2003		$400	$515

Les Paul Melody Maker

2003-2008. Slab single-cut solidbody, one P-90, tune-o-matic bridge, dot markers, 2 knobs. Revised in '07 with 1 single-coil (2 also offered), wrap around tailpiece, 1 knob, pickguard mounted jack.

2003-2006	1 pickup	$425	$550
2007-2008	1 pickup revised specs	$425	$550
2007-2008	2 pickup option	$425	$550

Les Paul Melody Maker 120th Anniversary

2014. Custom Shop, 120th Anniversary neck inlay, maple top, mahogany back, Charcoal, TV Yellow, Wine Red or Manhattan Midnight, all with satin finish.

2014		$700	$900

Melody Maker Joan Jett Signature

2008-2012. Double-cut, worn-white (til '11), 1 Burstbucker 3. Blackheart version in black with red dots starts '10.

2008-2012		$900	$1,200

Midnight Special

1974-1975. L-6S body style, maple 'board, dot markers, 2 humbucker pickups, custom colors.

1974-1975		$1,200	$1,600

Midtown Custom

2012-2014. 335-style semi-hollow, 2 humbuckers, block markers.

2012-2014		$1,200	$1,600

Midtown Standard P-90

2012-2014. Like Midtown Custom, but with dots, P-90s.

2012-2014		$1,100	$1,450

MK-35

1975-1978. Mark Series flat-top acoustic, mahogany back and sides, black-bound body, natural or sunburst, 5,226 made.

1975-1978		$625	$800

MK-53

1975-1978. Mark Series flat-top acoustic, maple back and sides, multi-bound body, natural or sunburst, 1424 made.

1975-1978		$700	$925

MK-72

1975-1978. Mark Series flat-top acoustic, rosewood back and sides, black-bound body, chrome tuners, natural or sunburst, 1229 made.

1975-1978		$750	$975

MK-81

1975-1978. Mark Series flat-top acoustic, rosewood back and sides, multi-bound body, gold tuners, high-end appointments, natural or sunburst, 431 made.

1975-1978		$950	$1,250

Moderne

2012. Limited run, mahogany body and neck, dual '57 Classic humbuckers, trans amber or ebony finish.

2012		$1,250	$1,650

Moderne Heritage

1981-1983. Limited edition, korina body, 2 humbucking pickups, gold hardware, natural, black or white.

1981-1983	Black or white	$5,000	$6,500
1981-1983	Natural	$5,900	$7,700

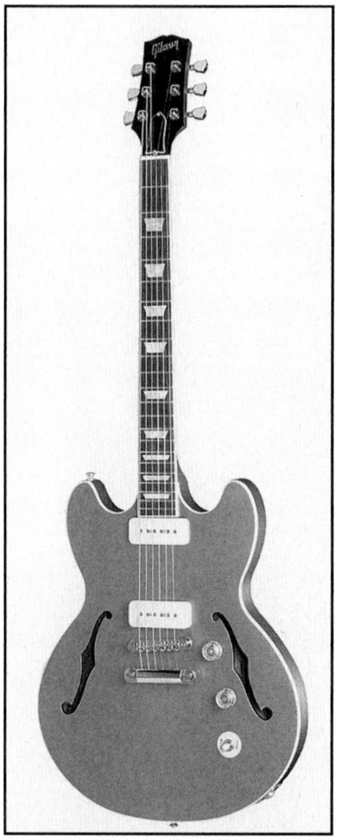

Gibson Midtown Standard P-90

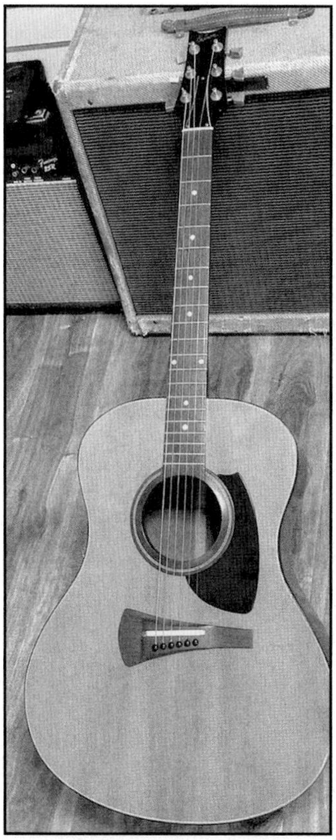

1975 Gibson MK-35

Craig Brody

GUITARS

1982 Gibson Moderne Heritage

Steve Evans

1936 Gibson Nick Lucas

M. Mattingly

MODEL YEAR	FEATURES	EXC. COND. LOW	HIGH

Nick Lucas / Gibson Special

1926-1937. Though they were shipped into '41, the last year of production was '37. Mahogany 13 ½" L-1 body ('26-'29), 14 ¾" L-00 body ('30-'41), parallel bracing '26-'27, X-braced '28-'41, 12 frets early (13 and 14 later), banjo tuners early (guitar style later), black (rare) or sunburst finish. Reintroduced in '91.

1926-1937 Various specs $7,700 $42,100

Nick Lucas Reissue Limited Edition

1991-1992. 100 made, label signed by Ren Ferguson.

1991-1992 $1,900 $2,475

Nick Lucas Tenor

1928-1938. 14 3/4", 12-fret, early models have mahogany, later maple, The Gibson headstock logo.

1928-1930 Mahogany $5,900 $7,700

1934-1938 Maple $5,900 $7,700

Nick Lucas Elite

1999-2002. Ebony 'board, abalone inlay and inlays.

1999-2002 $2,800 $3,625

2001 Elite Custom $2,800 $3,625

Nick Lucas Grande

2015-2016. Limited Edition of 50, sitka spruce top, English walnut back and sides, COA, Honeyburst finish.

2015-2016 $2,500 $3,250

Nick Lucas Koa Elite

2015. Limited to 50, Adirondack and koa, COA.

2015 $2,500 $3,250

Nick Lucas Supreme

2015. Limited to 40, Adirondack red spruce top, AAA flame koa back and sides, abalone trim, certificate of authenticity, Honeyburst finish.

2015 $2,800 $3,625

Nighthawk 2009 Limited

2009. Limited series, AAA figured maple top, mahogany body, Translucent Amber finish.

2009 $1,100 $1,425

Nighthawk Custom

1993-1998. Flame maple top, ebony 'board, gold hardware, fireburst, single/double/mini pickups.

1993-1998 $1,075 $1,400

Nighthawk Special

1993-1998. Single-cut solidbody, figured maple top, double-coil and mini-pickup or with additional single-coil options, dot marker inlay, cherry, ebony or sunburst.

1993-1998 $875 $1,125

Nighthawk Standard

1993-1998. Single-cut solidbody, figured maple top, 2 or 3 pickups, double-parallelogram inlay, amber, fireburst or sunburst.

1993-1998 $1,000 $1,300

Nighthawk Standard 2010 Limited

2010-2012. Limited Run series, AAA quilted maple top, chambered poplar body, 3 pickups, Memphis Mojo, St. Louis Sauce or Chicago Blue finishes.

2010-2012 $1,100 $1,425

Nighthawk Studio

2011-2012. AAA quilted maple top, dots.

2011-2012 $600 $775

MODEL YEAR	FEATURES	EXC. COND. LOW	HIGH

Nouveau NV6T-M

1986-1987. Hybrid USA/Japan, a line of Gibson flat-tops with imported parts assembled and finished in the U.S., acoustic dreadnought, bound maple body, natural.

1986-1987 $400 $525

NR-336F

2012. Custom Shop, 25 made, double-cut, non-reverse (NR) Firebird headstock, flamed maple top, rosewood 'board, antique sunburst top, cherry back.

2012 $2,225 $2,900

OP-25

1991-1992. Acoustic-electric, limited production run, synthetic back.

1991-1992 $625 $825

Original Jumbo (Custom Shop)

2003. 16" jumbo body, Adirondack top, mahogany sides and back, butterbean tuner buttons, deep sunburst finish on complete body, Custom Art Historic.

2003 $1,975 $2,575

Pat Martino Custom/Signature

1999-2006. Sharp single-cut thinline, f-holes, 2 humbuckers, flamed cherry sunburst maple top, small snakehead style headstock, Pat Martino logo on truss rod cover.

1999-2006 $2,400 $3,100

PG-00

1932-1937. Plectrum neck, flat-top.

1932-1937 $1,600 $2,075

PG-1

1928-1938. Plectrum neck, flat-top.

1929 $1,525 $1,975

PG-175

1950. Acoustic/electric with ES-175 bobdy and 4-string plectrum neck, bow-tie markers, sunburst.

1950 $2,925 $3,800

Q-100

1985-1986. Offset double-cut solidbody, Kahler trem, 6-on-a-side tuners, 1 humbucker, black hardware.

1985-1986 $725 $950

Q-200/Q2000

1985-1986. Like Q-100, but with 1 single and 1 hum, black or chrome hardware. Name changed to 2000 late '85.

1985-1986 $800 $1,050

Q-300/Q3000

1985-1986. Like Q-100, but with 3 single-coils, black or chrome hardware. Name changed to 3000 late '85.

1985-1986 $800 $1,050

Q-3000 Custom Shop

1985. Limited Custom production, 3 single-coil pickups.

1985 $1,225 $1,575

Q-400/Q4000

Late-1985-1987. Limited custom production, like Q-100, but with 2 singles and 1 hum, black hardware, Name changed to 400 late '85. Ferrari Red or Pink Panther finish as 4000, ebony as 400.

1985-1987 $1,225 $1,600

MODEL YEAR	FEATURES	EXC. COND. LOW	HIGH

RD Artist CMT

1981. Figured top.

1981		$2,200	$2,900

RD Artist/77

1980. The 77 model has a 25.5" scale versus 24.75".

1980		$1,675	$2,175

RD Artist/79

1978-1982. Double-cut solidbody, 2 humbuckers, TP-6 tailpiece, active electronics, ebony 'board, block inlays, gold-plated parts, various colors, called just RD (no Artist) in '81 and '82.

1978-1982		$1,750	$2,250

RD Custom

1977-1979. Double-cut solidbody, 2 humbuckers, stop tailpiece, active electronics, dot inlays, maple 'board, chrome parts, natural or walnut.

1977-1979		$1,750	$2,250

RD Standard

1977-1979. Double-cut solidbody, 2 humbuckers, stop tailpiece, rosewood 'board, dot inlays, chrome parts, natural, sunburst or walnut.

1977-1979		$1,750	$2,250

RD Standard Reissue

2007, 2009, 2011. 400 Silverburst made in '07. Black or Trans Amber Red versions offered as limited run in '09 in Japan and in U.S. in '11.

2007-2011	Various colors	$1,100	$1,425

Roy Smeck Radio Grande Hawaiian

1934-1939. Dreadnought acoustic flat-top, rosewood back and sides, bound body and neck, natural.

1934-1939	Brazilian, Spanish converted	$13,000	$17,000
1934-1939	Brazilian, unconverted	$10,500	$13,500

Roy Smeck Radio Grande Hawaiian Limited

1994. Centennial Guitar of the Month in '94, 100 made, Indian rosewood.

1994		$1,975	$2,550

Roy Smeck Radio Grande Hawaiian Reissue

1996. Part of SmartWood Series, Grenadillo back and sides.

1996		$1,975	$2,550

Roy Smeck Stage Deluxe Hawaiian

1934-1942. Dreadnought acoustic flat-top, mahogany back and sides, bound body, natural.

1934-1942	Spanish converted	$9,500	$12,500
1934-1942	Unconverted	$6,800	$8,900

S-1

1976-1980. Single-cut solidbody, pointed headstock, 3 single-coil pickups, similar to the Marauder, various colors.

1976-1980		$950	$1,250

SG

Following are models, listed alphabetically, bearing the SG name.

SG I

1972-1978. Double-cut, mahogany body, 1 mini-humbucker (some with SG Jr. P-90), wraparound bridge/tailpiece, cherry or walnut.

1972-1978		$900	$1,200

SG II

1972-1979. SG I with 2 mini-humbuckers (some in '75 had regular humbuckers), 2 slide switches, cherry or walnut.

1972-1979		$1,050	$1,350

SG III

1972-1977. SG II with sunburst and tune-o-matic.

1972-1977		$900	$1,200

SG-3

2007-2008. SG styling, SG Standard appointments, 3 gold humbuckers or 3 single coils, 1 rotor switch, 2 knobs, stop tail.

2007-2008	3 humbuckers	$825	$1,075
2007-2008	3 single coils	$625	$825

SG '61 Reissue

2003-2015. Renamed from Les Paul SG '61 Reissue, no Les Paul script on truss rod, small 'guard, stop bar tailpiece (no Deluxe Maestro vibrato), '60 slim-taper neck profile.

2003-2015		$1,300	$1,700

SG '62 Reissue/SG Reissue

1986-1991. Trapezoid markers, stop bar, 2 humbuckers, called SG Reissue '86-'87, SG '62 Reissue '88-'91. Reintroduced as Les Paul SG '61 Reissue for '93-'03 and SG '61 Reissue '03-present, cherry.

1986-1991		$1,300	$1,700

SG '62 Reissue Showcase Edition

1988. Guitar of the Month, bright blue opaque finish, 200 made.

1988		$1,375	$1,800

Les Paul '63 Corvette Sting Ray

1995-1997. Custom Shop SG-style body carved to simulate split rear window on '63 Corvette, Sting Ray inlay, 150 made, offered in black, white, silver or red.

1995-1997		$3,800	$4,900

SG-90 Double

1988-1990. SG body, updated electronics, graphite reinforced neck, 2 pickups, cherry, turquoise or white.

1988-1990		$700	$900

SG-90 Single

1988-1990. SG body, updated electronics, graphite reinforced neck, 1 humbucker pickup, cherry, turquoise or white.

1988-1990		$650	$850

SG-100

1971-1972. Double-cut solidbody, 1 pickup, cherry or walnut.

1971-1972	Melody Maker pickup	$900	$1,200
1971-1972	P-90 pickup option	$900	$1,200
1971-1972	Sam Ash model	$900	$1,200

SG-200

1971-1972. Two pickup version of SG-100 in black, cherry or walnut finish, replaced by SG II.

1971-1972	2 Melody Makers	$1,000	$1,300

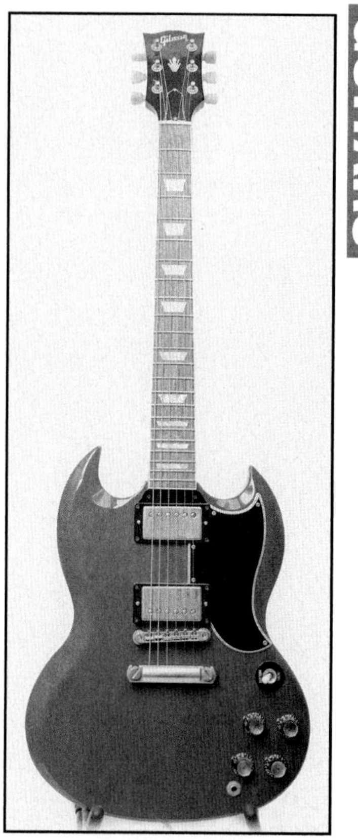

2001 Gibson SG '61 Reissue

Bernunzio Uptown Music

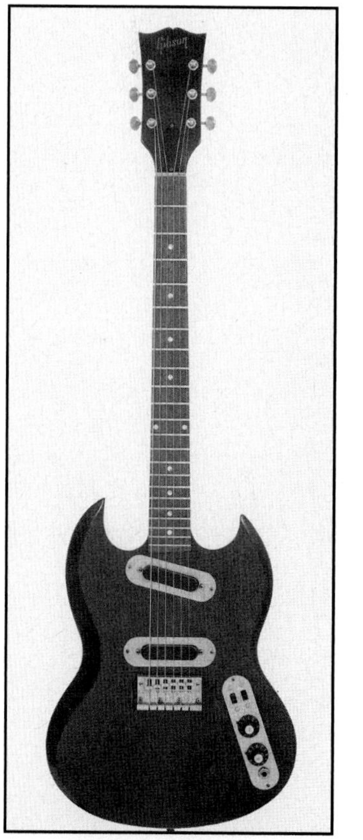

1971 Gibson SG 200

Imaged by Heritage Auctions, HA.com

GUITARS

1970 Gibson SG Custom
Garrett Park

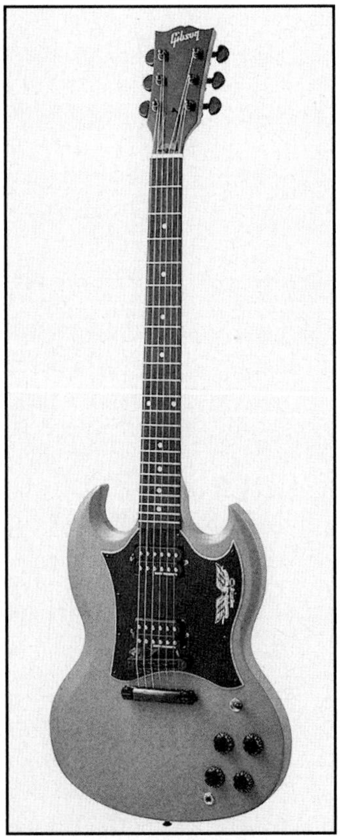

2014 Gibson SG
Government Series

SG-250

1971-1972. Two-pickup version of SG-100 in cherry sunburst, replaced by SG III.

Model Year	Features	Exc. Cond. Low	Exc. Cond. High
1971-1972	2 Melody Makers	$900	$1,200

SG-400/SG Special 400

1985-1987. SG body with 3 toggles, 2 knobs (master volume, master tone), single-single-humbucker pickups, available with uncommon opaque finishes.

Model Year	Features	Exc. Cond. Low	Exc. Cond. High
1985-1987		$875	$1,150

SG Angus Young

2010-2016. Like Angus Signature but with small guard, stop tailpiece and tune-o-matic, Aged Cherry.

Model Year	Features	Exc. Cond. Low	Exc. Cond. High
2010-2016		$1,425	$1,850

SG Angus Young Signature

2000-2009. Late-'60s Std specs with large 'guard, Deluxe Maestro lyre vibrato with Angus logo, aged cherry finish.

Model Year	Features	Exc. Cond. Low	Exc. Cond. High
2000-2009		$1,425	$1,850

SG Baritone

2013-2016. Longer 27" scale, 2 exposed humbuckers, ebony 'board, Alpine White finish.

Model Year	Features	Exc. Cond. Low	Exc. Cond. High
2013-2016		$1,000	$1,300

SG Carved Top - Autumn Burst

2009. Limited run of 350, highly flamed carved maple top, rosewood 'board, certificate of authenticity.

Model Year	Features	Exc. Cond. Low	Exc. Cond. High
2009		$1,375	$1,800

SG Classic/SG Classic Faded

1999-2001, 2003-2013. Late '60s SG Special style, Classic on truss rod cover, large 'guard, black soapbar single-coil P-90s, dot markers, stop bar tailpiece, cherry or ebony stain.

Model Year	Features	Exc. Cond. Low	Exc. Cond. High
1999-2013		$725	$950

SG Custom

1963-1980. Renamed from Les Paul Custom, 3 humbuckers, vibrato, made with Les Paul Custom plate from '61-'63 (see Les Paul Custom), white finish until '68, walnut and others after.

Model Year	Features	Exc. Cond. Low	Exc. Cond. High
1963-1964	White, pat #, Maestro	$13,900	$18,000
1965	Early '65, white, large neck	$11,500	$15,500
1965	Late '65, white, small neck	$10,600	$13,800
1966-1968	White, large 'guard	$7,700	$10,000
1969	Walnut, lyre, 1-piece neck	$5,100	$6,700
1969	Walnut, lyre, 3-piece neck	$3,700	$4,900
1969	White, lyre, 1 piece neck	$5,100	$6,700
1969	White, lyre, 3 piece neck	$4,000	$5,200
1970	Walnut, lyre	$3,100	$4,100
1970	White, lyre	$3,100	$4,100
1970-1973	Walnut, Bigsby	$2,400	$3,200
1970-1973	White option Bigsby	$3,100	$4,000
1974-1975	Brown, dark cherry	$2,200	$2,850
1974-1975	White option	$2,600	$3,350
1976-1979	Brown, dark cherry	$1,850	$2,400
1976-1979	White option	$2,600	$3,350
1980	Various colors	$1,775	$2,300

SG Custom '67 Reissue/Les Paul SG '67 Custom

1991-1993. The SG Custom '67 Reissue has a wine red finish, the Les Paul SG '67 Custom ('92-'93) has a wine red or white finish.

Model Year	Features	Exc. Cond. Low	Exc. Cond. High
1991-1993		$2,150	$2,800

SG Custom Elliot Easton Signature

2006-2007. Custom Shop, SG Custom specs, Maestro deluxe vibrola, Pelham Blue or white, includes Certificate of Authenticity.

Model Year	Features	Exc. Cond. Low	Exc. Cond. High
2006-2007		$2,625	$3,425

SG Deluxe

1971-1972, 1981-1985, 1998-1999, 2013-2018. The '70s models were offered in cherry, natural or walnut finishes, reintroduced in '98 with 3 Firebird mini-humbucker-style pickups in black, red or Ice Blue finishes, in 2013 with 3 '57 Classic humbuckers in Cobalt Fade, Lime Burst, Orange Burst or Red Fade.

Model Year	Features	Exc. Cond. Low	Exc. Cond. High
1971-1972	Cherry	$1,550	$2,000
1971-1972	Natural, walnut	$1,550	$2,000
1981-1985	Various colors	$1,325	$1,750
1998-1999	Various colors	$1,000	$1,300
2013-2018	New specs, all colors	$1,400	$1,800

SG Diablo

2008. Guitar of the Month for Dec. '08, 1,000 made, '61 specs, metallic silver finish with matching headstock, 1 volume, 1 tone knob, 3-way toggle, 24 frets.

Model Year	Features	Exc. Cond. Low	Exc. Cond. High
2008		$1,100	$1,425

SG Diablo Premium Plus

2012-2013. AAA maple top.

Model Year	Features	Exc. Cond. Low	Exc. Cond. High
2012-2013		$1,100	$1,425

SG Diablo Tremolo

2012-2013. Diablo with Floyd Rose.

Model Year	Features	Exc. Cond. Low	Exc. Cond. High
2012-2013		$1,100	$1,425

SG Dickey Betts

2012. Custom, 75 hand-aged made include a leather certificate of authenticity signed by Betts, 250 VOS include unsigned COA, Vintage Red finish.

Model Year	Features	Exc. Cond. Low	Exc. Cond. High
2012	Aged	$4,425	$5,725
2012	VOS	$2,625	$3,425

SG Elegant

2004-2013. Custom Shop, quilt maple top, gold hardware, Blue Burst, Firemist and Iguana Burst finishes.

Model Year	Features	Exc. Cond. Low	Exc. Cond. High
2004-2013		$2,200	$2,875

SG Elite

1987-1989. SG Custom specs, 3 humbuckers, gold hardware, ebony 'board, various colors.

Model Year	Features	Exc. Cond. Low	Exc. Cond. High
1987-1989		$1,700	$2,200

SG Exclusive

1979. SG with humbuckers, coil-tap and rotary control knob, block inlay, pearl logo (not decal), black/ebony finish.

Model Year	Features	Exc. Cond. Low	Exc. Cond. High
1979		$1,575	$2,025

SG Firebrand

1980-1982. Double-cut mahogany solidbody, rough natural finish, Gibson branded in headstock, 2 exposed humbuckers, Firebrand logo on The SG (Standard) model.

Model Year	Features	Exc. Cond. Low	Exc. Cond. High
1980-1982		$725	$950

MODEL YEAR	FEATURES	EXC. COND. LOW	HIGH

SG Frank Zappa "Roxy"
2013. 400 offered, Maestro vibrola, 2 exposed-coil humbuckers.

2013		$1,800	$2,350

SG Futura
2013-2014. Mahogany body, maple neck, rosewood 'board, 2 pickups, various colors.

2013-2014		$650	$850

SG Goddess
2007. SG Goddess logo on truss rod cover, only 2 control knobs versus standard 4, exposed humbuckers.

2007		$725	$950

SG Gothic
2000-2003. SG Special with satin black finish, moon and star marker on 12th fret, black hardware.

2000-2003		$725	$950

SG Gothic Morte
2011-2012. Solid mahogany body, African Obeche 'board, 2 pickups, satin ebony finish

2011-2012		$475	$625

SG Government Series
2013-2016. Made from guitar bodies, necks and 'boards returned from Federal Government after 2011 raid on Gibson, with Certificate of Authenticity.

2013-2016		$1,000	$1,300

SG GT
2006-2007. '61 specs with racing stripes paint job and removable tailpiece hood scoop, locking tuners, Candy Apple Red, Daytona Blue, or Phantom Black.

2006-2007		$2,000	$2,600

SG Jeff Tweedy Signature
2012. SG Standard with Maestro vibrola, mahogany body and neck, rosewood 'board, Blue Mist.

2012		$2,075	$2,675

SG Judas Priest Signature
2003. Custom Shop, 30 made, dot markers, exposed '57 classic humbucker and EMG58 pickups, black, large chrome metal 'guard, also sold as a set with Flying V Judas Priest, includes certificate of authenticity.

2003		$1,800	$2,350

SG Judas Priest Signature Set With Flying V
2003. Custom Shop, 30 sets made.

2003		$3,900	$5,100

SG Junior
1963-1971, 1991-1994. One pickup, solidbody. Prices are for an unfaded finish, cherry finish faded to brown reduces the value by 30%.

1963-1964	Cherry	$3,350	$4,350
1964	White	$3,925	$5,100
1965	Early-'65, cherry	$3,150	$4,100
1965	Late-'65, cherry	$2,500	$3,250
1965	Pelham Blue	$4,800	$6,250
1965	White	$2,275	$4,250
1966-1968	White	$3,100	$4,000
1966-1969	Cherry	$2,225	$2,900
1970-1971	Cherry or walnut	$2,000	$2,600
1991-1994	Various colors	$775	$1,000

SG Junior (Reintroduced)
2018-present. Gibson Original series, '60s design, mahogany body, P-90 single-coil pickup, Vintage Cherry gloss nitro finish.

2018-2020		$875	$1,125

SG Junior Limited
2018. Double-cut, mahogany body and neck, rosewood 'board, 1 single-coil pickup, Vintage Cherry.

2018		$875	$1,125

SG Junior P-90
2006-2007. Single P-90 pickup, large 'guard, stop tail, cherry finish.

2006-2007		$700	$925

SG Les Paul '61 Custom Reissue
1997-2005. 1961 specs, SG body style, 3 humbuckers, Deluxe Maestro vibrato or stud with tune-o-matic bridge, white or silver option.

1997-2005		$1,850	$2,400

SG Les Paul '62 Custom
1986-1990. 1962 specs, 3 humbuckers.

1986-1990		$1,850	$2,400

SG Les Paul '62 Custom (Custom Shop)
2003. Custom Shop, Maestro vibrato, small 'guard, white.

2003		$1,850	$2,400

SG Les Paul '90 Custom
1990-1992. 1962 specs, 3 humbuckers.

1990-1992		$1,850	$2,400

SG Les Paul Custom 30th Anniversary
1991. SG body, 3 humbuckers, gold hardware, TV Yellow finish, 30th Anniversary on peghead.

1991		$2,200	$2,900

SG Kirk Douglas Signature

2019-2020		$1,400	$1,800

SG Menace
2006-2007. Carved mahogany body, 2 exposed humbuckers, flat black finish, black hardware, single brass knuckle position marker, gig bag.

2006-2007		$725	$950

SG Music Machine Stinger
2003. Custom run for dealer Music Machine, special serial number series, SG Custom with 2 pickups and SG Standard models available, black stinger paint job on neck/headstock, various colors.

2003	SG Custom	$2,300	$3,000
2003	SG Standard	$2,300	$3,000

SG Original
2013-2019. Mahogany body, slim '60s neck profile, Lyre vibrato, '57 classic pickups, Vintage Cherry. Replaced by SG Standard '61 Maestro Vibrola in '19.

2013-2019		$1,450	$1,900

SG Pete Townshend Signature
2001. Signature on back of headstock.

2001		$1,225	$1,600

SG Pete Townshend Signature (Custom Shop)
2000. SG Special with '69 specs, large 'guard, 2 cases, cherry red, COA, limited edition of 250.

2000	Includes certificate	$1,225	$1,600

1980 Gibson SG Firebrand

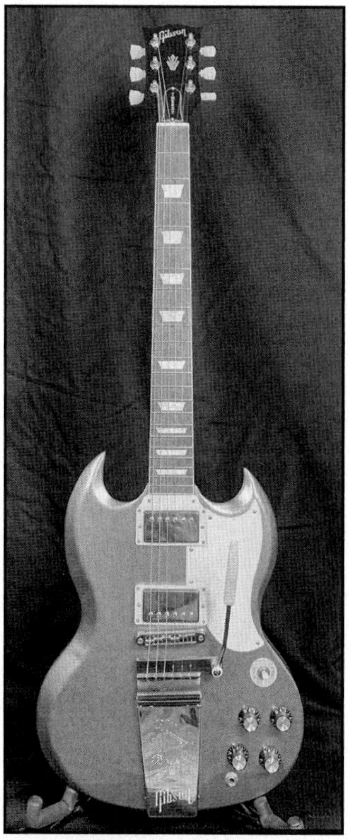

2012 Gibson SG Jeff Tweedy Signature

Matt Carleson

1963 Gibson SG Special

Dave's Guitar Shop

1972 Gibson SG Standard

Paul Thomason

MODEL YEAR	FEATURES	EXC. COND. LOW	HIGH

SG Platinum

2005. A mix of SG Special and SG Standard specs, platinum paint on the body, back of neck, and headstock, no crown inlay, Gibson stencil logo, exposed humbucker pickups, large plantium-finish 'guard, special plantinum colored Gibson logo guitar case.

2005		$900	$1,200

SG Pro

1971-1974. Tune-o-matic bridge, vibrato, 2 P-90 pickups, cherry, mahogany or walnut.

1971-1974		$1,300	$1,675

SG R1/SG Artist

1980-1982. Active RD-era electronics. SG style but thicker body, no 'guard, ebony 'board, black finish, dot markers, renamed SG Artist in '81.

1980	SG-R1	$1,125	$1,450
1981-1982	SG Artist	$1,125	$1,450

SG Raw Power

2009-2012. All maple body, neck and 'board, 2 exposed-coil humbuckers, offered in 9 satin finishes, including natural.

2009-2012		$875	$1,150

SG Select

2007. Made in Nashville, TN, carved solid book-matched AAA flame maple, 3-piece flamed maple neck, described as the most exquisite SG offered to date, 2 humbuckers, gold hardware.

2007		$2,200	$2,875

SG Special

1959-1978. Rounded double-cut for '59-'60, switched to SG body early-'61, 2 P-90s '59-'71, 2 mini-humbuckers '72-'78, 2 regular humbuckers on current version, redesigned in '85. Prices are for an unfaded finish, cherry finish faded to brown reduces the value by 20%-30%. Instruments with stop tailpieces vs. Maestro tailpiece have the same value.

1959	Cherry, slab, high neck pu	$7,500	$9,800
1960	Cherry, slab, lower neck pu	$7,500	$9,800
1961-1962	Cherry, SG body	$4,725	$6,200
1962	White, SG body	$5,725	$7,400
1963-1964	Cherry, Maestro or stop	$4,725	$6,200
1963-1964	White	$5,725	$7,400
1965	Cherry, Maestro or stop	$3,200	$4,200
1965	White	$4,300	$5,700
1966	Cherry, large 'guard	$2,800	$3,650
1966	Cherry, small 'guard	$2,800	$3,650
1966	White, large 'guard	$3,650	$4,750
1966	White, small 'guard	$4,000	$5,200
1967	Cherry, large 'guard	$2,900	$3,750
1967	White, large 'guard	$3,650	$4,750
1968-1969	Cherry large 'guard	$2,900	$3,750
1970-1971	Cherry, large 'guard	$2,400	$3,150
1972-1978	Mini-hums	$1,200	$1,550

SG Special (redesigned)

1985-1996. In mid-'85 Gibson introduced a redesigned SG Special model with 2 control knobs (1 pickup) or 3 control knobs (2 pickups) versus the previously used 4-knob layout.

1985-1986	1 pu, 2 knobs	$575	$750
1985-1989	2 pus, 3 knobs	$650	$850
1990-1996	2 pus, 3 knobs	$600	$775

SG Special (reintroduced)

1996-present. In '96 Gibson reintroduced the original 4-knob layout, 2 humbucker pickups, dot markers.

1996-2020		$575	$750

SG Special 3/4

1961. Only 61 shipped.

1961		$2,475	$3,200

SG Special '60s Tribute

2011-2018. '60s specs including small guard, dot markers, dual P-90s, Slim Taper '60s neck profile, 4 worn-finish options.

2011-2018		$550	$725

1963 SG Special Ultra Light Aged

2021. Custom Shop Murphy Lab Collection, Classic White finish.

2021		$2,500	$3,250

SG Special Faded (3 pickups)

2007. Made in Nashville, TN, 3 exposed 490 humbuckers, dot markers, stop tail, SG initials on truss rod cover, 2 knobs and 6-position selector switch, hand-worn satin finish.

2007		$600	$775

SG Special Faded/Faded SG Special

2002-2018. Aged worn cherry finish.

2002-2005	Half moon markers	$575	$750
2003-2018	Dot markers	$575	$750

SG Special I

1983-1985. Dot markers, 1 exposed-coil humbucker pickup with 2 knobs, called by various names including Gibson Special ('83), Special I, and SG Special I.

1983-1985		$575	$750

SG Special II

1983-1985. Dot markers, 2 exposed-coil humbucker pickups with 3 knobs, called by various names including Gibson Special ('83), Special II, SG Special II.

1983-1985		$650	$850

SG Special II EMG

2007. EMG humbucker pickups, no position markers, standard 4-knob and 3-way toggle switch SG format, black satin finish over entire guitar, black hardware.

2007		$675	$875

SG Special New Century

2006-2008. Full-body mirror 'guard, 2 exposed humbuckers, SG body, mirror truss rod cover.

2006-2008		$850	$1,100

SG Special Robot

2008-2012. Dot markers, robot tuning.

2008-2012		$850	$1,125

MODEL YEAR	FEATURES	EXC. COND. LOW	HIGH

SG Special Robot Limited

2008. Limited run with trapezoid markers, robot tuning.

2008		$950	$1,250

SG Special Robot Limited Silverburst

2008. Limited run of 400.

2008		$1,025	$1,325

SG Special VOS Reissue

2006-2013. Custom Shop, mahogany body and neck, bound rosewood 'board, dot inlays, 2 P-90s, certificate, white, TV yellow, or faded cherry finish.

2006-2013		$1,900	$2,450

SG Standard

1963-1981, 1983-present. Les Paul Standard changes to SG body, 2 humbuckers, some very early models have optional factory Bigsby. Prices are for an unfaded finish, a cherry finish faded to brown reduces the value by 30% or more.

1963-1964	Cherry, sm 'guard, dlx vibr or Bigsby	$12,100	$15,700
1964	Pelham Blue, sm 'guard, dlx vibr	$17,000	$22,000
1965	Cherry, sm 'guard, dlx vibr, lg neck	$10,600	$22,000
1965	Cherry, sm 'guard, dlx vibr, sm neck	$9,600	$12,800
1965	Pelham Blue, sm 'guard, dlx vibr	$15,700	$20,400
1966	Early '66 cherry, vibr, sm 'guard, dlx vibrato	$7,100	$9,400
1966	Late '66 cherry, lg 'guard	$5,400	$7,000
1967	Burgundy Metallic	$5,800	$7,500
1967	Cherry	$5,400	$7,000
1967	White	$6,500	$8,500
1968	Cherry, engraved lyre	$4,700	$6,100
1969	Engraved lyre, 1-piece neck	$4,700	$6,100
1969	Engraved lyre, 3-piece neck	$3,800	$4,900
1970	Engraved lyre, 3-piece neck	$3,100	$4,000
1970	Walnut, non-lyre tailpiece	$2,100	$2,700
1970-1971	Cherry, non-lyre tailpiece	$2,200	$2,900
1971	Engraved lyre, 3-piece neck	$2,900	$3,700
1972-1979	Blocks, mini 'guard, top mount	$1,700	$2,200
1980-1986	New colors, sm blocks	$1,525	$2,000
1992-1999	New specs	$1,000	$1,300
2000-2020	Standard colors	$1,000	$1,300
2006-2012	Silverburst, 400 made	$1,150	$1,500

SG Standard '61 Reissue

2004-2008. Small 'guard, stop tail, Nashville tune-o-matic bridge, Gibson Deluxe Keystone tuners, standard Gibson logo and crown inlay, no Les Paul logo, Vintage Original Spec aging optional from '06. Reintroduced in '19.

2004-2008		$1,350	$1,775

SG Standard '61

2019-present. Classic '61 design, 3 models offered - Maestro vibrola, Sideways or Stop Bar, mahogany body and neck, rosewood 'board, vintage cherry finish.

2019-2020	Maestro vibrola	$1,400	$1,800
2019-2020	Sideways vibrola	$1,300	$1,700
2019-2020	Stop Bar vibrola	$1,300	$1,700

1964 SG Standard (Maestro Vibrola) Murphy Lab Aged

2021. Custom Shop Murphy Lab Collection, heavy aged (Faded Cherry), light aged (Pelham Blue) and ultra light (Cherry Red or Pelham Blue).

2021	Heavy	$3,900	$5,100
2021	Light	$3,900	$5,100
2021	Ultra Light	$2,800	$3,700

SG Standard 24 50th Anniversary

2011. Limited run, mother-of-pearl Gibson logo with gold 50th Anniversary silkscreen, 2 '57 classic pickups, antique ebony finish.

2011		$1,050	$1,350

SG Standard (ETune)

2014-2018. Min-Etune robot tuners, Etune logo on truss rod.

2014-2018		$975	$1,250

SG Standard Brian Ray '63 (Custom Shop)

2015. Silver Fox finish, Bigsby, certificate of authenticity.

2015		$2,850	$3,700

SG Standard Celebrity Series

1991-1992. SG Standard with large 'guard, gold hardware, black finish.

1991-1992		$1,475	$1,925

SG Standard Gary Rossington Signature

2004. '63-'64 SG Standard specs with Deluxe Maestro vibrola, '60 slim taper neck, limited edition, faded cherry aged by Tom Murphy.

2004		$4,300	$5,600

SG Standard HP (High Performance)

2016-2019. Solid mahogany body and neck, AA figured maple top, 2 pickups, different colors offered each year.

2016-2019		$1,200	$1,550

SG Standard Korina (Custom Shop)

2008-2009. Custom Shop limited reissue of '60s SG Standard, 2 BurstBucker pickups, black.

2008-2009		$2,100	$2,750

SG Standard Korina Limited Edition

1993-1994. Korina version of SG Standard, limited run, natural.

1993-1994		$2,600	$3,400

SG Standard Korina/SG Standard K (Custom Shop)

2001-2008. Custom Shop serial number, large 'guard, no SG logo on truss rod, CS logo back of headstock, natural finish.

2001-2008		$3,200	$4,200

Gibson SG Standard '61

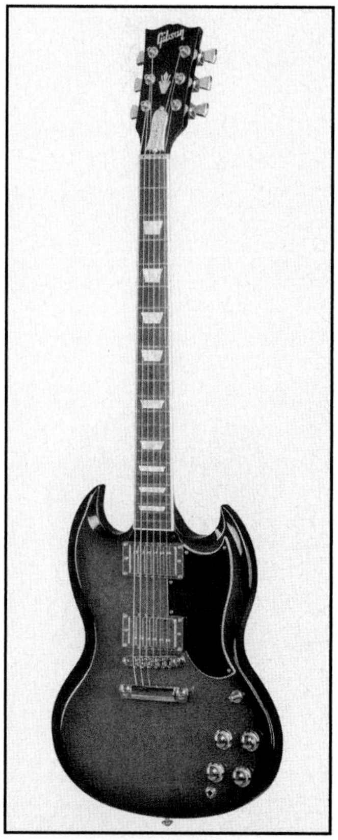

2017 Gibson SG Standard High Performance

GUITARS

Gibson Sheryl Crow Country Western Supreme

1960 Gibson SJ

David Stone

MODEL YEAR	FEATURES	EXC. COND. LOW	HIGH

SG Standard Limited Edition

2000. Limited Edition logo back of headstock, 2 humbuckers, large pearloid guard, gold hardware, dark opaque finish.

2000		$950	$1,250

SG Standard Limited Edition (3 pickups)

2007. Guitar of the Week, 400 made, 3 single-coil blade pickups, 6-position rotator switch with chickenhead knob, SG logo on truss rod cover, large 'guard, satin finish.

2007		$875	$1,150

SG Standard Reissue

2004-2018. Reissue of near '63-'64 specs with Deluxe Maestro lyre vibrato and small 'guard, also offered with stop bar tailpiece, cherry finish, '60 slim taper neck, smooth neck heel joint, trapezoid markers, unmarked truss rod cover without Les Paul designation, formerly called Les Paul SG Standard Reissue, by 2005 part of Gibson's 'Vintage Original Spec' Custom Shop series, certificate of authenticity.

2004-2007	VOS, Maestro	$1,925	$2,500
2007-2018	VOS, stoptail	$1,925	$2,500
2008-2009	Maestro, LP logo	$1,925	$2,500

SG Standard VOS Historic

2003-2014. Custom Shop, Vintage Original Specs.

2003-2014		$1,925	$2,500

SG Standard Robby Krieger

2009. Custom Shop model, Inspired By series, based on Krieger's '67 SG, limited run of 150 with 50 aged and signed, 100 with V.O.S. finish treatment, certificate of authenticity.

2009	Aged, signed	$3,600	$4,700
2009	VOS	$2,900	$3,800

SG Standard Robby Krieger 50th Anniversary

2012. Mahogany body and neck, rosewood 'board, 2 '57 classic Alnico II pickups, Maestro tailpiece, Heritage Cherry finish.

2012		$1,500	$1,950

SG Supreme

2004-2007. '57 humbuckers, flamed maple top, split-diamond markers, various colors.

2004-2007		$1,700	$2,200

SG Tony Iommi Signature (Historic/ Custom Shop)

2001-2003. Custom Shop higher-end, signature humbuckers without poles, cross inlays, ebony or Wine Red.

2001-2003		$4,100	$5,300

SG Tony Iommi Signature (Production)

2002-2003. Standard production model.

2002-2008		$1,850	$2,400

SG TV

1961-1963. Name changed from Les Paul TV, SG body, 1 pickup, white finish. In '64 called SG Jr. White.

1961-1963	White, SG body	$4,100	$5,300

SG Voodoo/Voodoo SG

2002-2004. Carved top, black hardware, voodoo doll inlay at 5th fret, Juju finish (black with red wood filler).

2002-2004		$925	$1,200

SG-X (All American I)

1995-2000. Renamed the SG-X in '98, previously part of the All American series, SG body with single bridge humbucker, various colors.

1995-1999		$525	$675

SG-X Tommy Hilfiger

1998. Hilfiger logo on front, dot markers, plain headstock like a SG Special, dark blue finish, 100 made.

1998		$500	$650

SG Zoot Suit

2007-2010. Body of individual dyed strips of birch.

2007-2010		$1,375	$1,775

SG-Z

1998. Z-shaped string-thru tailpiece, 2 humbuckers, split diamond markers.

1998		$1,275	$1,650

The SG

1979-1983. Offered as The SG Standard (walnut body) and The SG Deluxe (mahogany), ebony 'board, 2 humbuckers.

1979-1983	Walnut or mahogany	$725	$950

Sheryl Crow Country Western Supreme

2019-present. Artist series, aged sitka spruce top, mahogany back and sides, Antique Cherry finish.

2019-2020		$2,400	$3,100

Sheryl Crow Signature

2001-2018. Artist Series, based on Sheryl Crow's 1962 Country and Western with Hummingbird influences.

2001-2018		$1,925	$2,500

Sheryl Crow Southern Jumbo Special Edition

2013-2018. Adirondack red spruce top, mahogany back and sides, rosewood 'board, with signed certificate of authenticity, Montana Sunsetburst finish. Limited production in '13.

2013-2018		$2,400	$3,100

SJ (Southern Jumbo)

1942-1969,1991-1996. Flat-top, sunburst standard, natural optional starting in '54 (natural finish version called Country-Western starting in '56), round shoulders (changed to square in '62), catalog name changed to SJ Deluxe in '70, refer to that listing.

1942-1944	Banner, Adirondack	$11,725	$15,225
1942-1944	Banner, mahogany	$8,900	$11,550
1945	Script, Sitka	$9,500	$12,300
1946	Script, Sitka	$8,500	$11,000
1947	Script, Sitka	$7,700	$10,000
1948	Script, Sitka	$7,000	$9,000
1949	Script, Sitka	$6,200	$8,000
1950-1953		$5,000	$6,400
1954-1956	Natural option	$5,000	$6,400
1954-1959	Sunburst	$5,000	$6,400
1960-1962	Round shoulder (ends)	$4,450	$5,800
1962-1964	Square shoulder (begins)	$4,100	$5,300
1965	Cherry Sunburst	$2,925	$3,800
1965	Tobacco Sunburst	$3,300	$4,300
1966	Tobacco Sunburst	$3,225	$4,200
1966-1968	Cherry Sunburst	$2,675	$3,475
1969	Below belly bridge	$2,100	$2,800

SJ Deluxe (Southern Jumbo)

1970-1978. SJ name changed to SJ Deluxe in catalog, along with a series of engineering changes.

MODEL YEAR	FEATURES	EXC. COND. LOW	HIGH
1970-1971	Non-adj saddle	$1,700	$2,275
1972-1973	Unbound 'board	$1,700	$2,275
1974-1978	4-ply to binding	$1,700	$2,275

SJN (Country-Western)

1956-1969. Flat-top, natural finish version of SJ, round shoulders '56-'62, square shoulders after, called the SJN in '60 and '61, the SJN Country Western after that, catalog name changed to SJN Deluxe in '70, refer to that listing.

MODEL YEAR	FEATURES	EXC. COND. LOW	HIGH
1956-1959		$5,000	$6,400
1960-1962	Round shoulder (ends)	$4,450	$5,800
1962-1964	Square shoulder (begins)	$4,100	$5,300
1965		$2,925	$3,800
1966-1968		$2,675	$3,475
1969	Below belly bridge, SJN logo	$2,000	$2,650

SJN Deluxe (Country-Western Jumbo)

1970-1978. SJN name changed to SJN Deluxe in catalog, along with a series of engineering changes.

MODEL YEAR	FEATURES	EXC. COND. LOW	HIGH
1970-1971	Non-adj saddle	$1,700	$2,275
1972-1973	Unbound 'board	$1,700	$2,275
1974-1978	4-ply to binding	$1,700	$2,275

SJ 1942 Reissue (Southern Jumbo)

2000. Custom Shop, mahogany back and sides, '42 SJ appointments, 'Only A Gibson is Good Enough' banner logo.

MODEL YEAR	FEATURES	EXC. COND. LOW	HIGH
2000		$2,450	$3,200

SJ Reissue (Southern Jumbo)

2003-2007. Sunburst.

MODEL YEAR	FEATURES	EXC. COND. LOW	HIGH
2003-2007		$1,775	$2,300

SJ Hank Williams Jr. Hall of Fame (Southern Jumbo)

1997. Custom Shop, mahogany back and sides, SJ appointments.

MODEL YEAR	FEATURES	EXC. COND. LOW	HIGH
1997		$2,400	$3,100

SJ Hank Williams Sr. (Southern Jumbo)

1993. Custom Shop, 25 offered.

MODEL YEAR	FEATURES	EXC. COND. LOW	HIGH
1993		$3,800	$5,000

SJ Kristofferson (Southern Jumbo)

2009-2012. Limited run of 300, AAA Sitka top, mahogany back and sides, Indian rosewood 'board, aged vintage sunburst.

MODEL YEAR	FEATURES	EXC. COND. LOW	HIGH
2009-2012		$1,925	$2,500

SJ True Vintage (Southern Jumbo)

2007-2008. "Only A Gibson Is Good Enough" headstock banner, sitka spruce top, dark mahogany back and sides, dual parallelogram markers.

MODEL YEAR	FEATURES	EXC. COND. LOW	HIGH
2007-2008		$2,100	$2,725

SJ Woody Guthrie (Southern Jumbo)

2003-2018. Single-bound round shoulder body, mahogany back and sides, parallelogram inlays.

MODEL YEAR	FEATURES	EXC. COND. LOW	HIGH
2003-2018		$1,800	$2,350

SJ-100

2008. Jumbo body, dot markers, crown headstock inlay, inlaid Gibson logo, natural.

MODEL YEAR	FEATURES	EXC. COND. LOW	HIGH
2008		$1,100	$1,425

1939 SJ-100 Centennial

1994. Acoustic flat-top, limited edition, sunburst.

MODEL YEAR	FEATURES	EXC. COND. LOW	HIGH
1994		$1,850	$2,400

1941 SJ-100

2013-2018. Sitka spruce top, mahogany back, sides and neck, rosewood 'board, Vintage Sunburst or Antique Natural.

MODEL YEAR	FEATURES	EXC. COND. LOW	HIGH
2013-2018		$1,750	$2,300

1957 SJ-200 (Custom Shop)

2020-present. Aged sitka spruce top, flamed maple back and sides, 4 bar moustach bridge, VOS finish, Antique Natural or Vintage Sunburst.

MODEL YEAR	FEATURES	EXC. COND. LOW	HIGH
2020		$3,300	$4,300

SJ-200 Bob Dylan Autographed Collector's Edition

2015-2018. Exact replica of Dylan's personal highly-customized SJ-200, Indian rosewood, Sitka spruce, Dylan eye logo inlaid on headstock, abalone inlay on 'guard, label signed by Bob Dylan, 175 made, case with embroidered eye logo.

MODEL YEAR	FEATURES	EXC. COND. LOW	HIGH
2015-2018		$8,500	$11,100

SJ-200 Bob Dylan Player's Edition

2015-2018. Adirondack red spruce, flamed maple, eye logo headstock inlay, LR Baggs Anthem pickup.

MODEL YEAR	FEATURES	EXC. COND. LOW	HIGH
2015-2018		$3,850	$5,000

SJ-200 Centennial Limited Edition

1994. Made in Bozeman, Montana, 100 made, 'guard specs based on '38 design, inside label "Gibson 100 Years 1894-1994", includes certificate of authenticity.

MODEL YEAR	FEATURES	EXC. COND. LOW	HIGH
1994		$2,750	$3,575

SJ-200 Custom Rosewood

2007. Custom shop, certificate of authenticity.

MODEL YEAR	FEATURES	EXC. COND. LOW	HIGH
2007		$3,150	$4,100

SJ-200 Elite

1998-2007. Gibson Custom Shop Bozeman, maple sides and back.

MODEL YEAR	FEATURES	EXC. COND. LOW	HIGH
1998-2007		$2,850	$3,700

SJ-200 Elite Custom Koa

2004. Figured koa, ebony board with abalone crown inlays, Antique Natural.

MODEL YEAR	FEATURES	EXC. COND. LOW	HIGH
2004		$3,150	$4,100

SJ-200 Elvis Presley

2007. Custom Shop, 250 made, kings crown logo and facsimile signature of Presley on truss rod cover, certificate of authenticity, black finish.

MODEL YEAR	FEATURES	EXC. COND. LOW	HIGH
2007		$3,200	$4,200

SJ-200 Pete Townshend Limited

2004-2012. Gibson Custom Shop Bozeman, maple sides and back.

MODEL YEAR	FEATURES	EXC. COND. LOW	HIGH
2004	Signed 1st 50 made	$4,600	$6,000
2004-2012		$2,700	$3,500

SJ-200 Ray Whitley/J-200 Custom Club

1994-1995. Based on Ray Whitley's late-1930s J-200, including engraved inlays and initials on the truss rod cover, only 37 made, one of the limited edition models the Montana division released to celebrate Gibson's 100th anniversary.

MODEL YEAR	FEATURES	EXC. COND. LOW	HIGH
1994-1995		$12,500	$16,000

Gibson SJ Kristofferson (Southern Jumbo)

2017 Gibson SJ-200 Bob Dylan Player's Edition

GUITARS

2011 Gibson SJ-200 True Vintage
Johnny Zapp

1982 Gibson Sonex-180 Deluxe
Imaged by Heritage Auctions, HA.com

MODEL YEAR	FEATURES	EXC. COND. LOW	HIGH

SJ-200 Sea Green Limited Edition
2016. Bozeman Custom Shop, 40 made, Sitka spruce top, AAA flamed maple back and sides, mother-of-pearl crown inlays.

2016		$3,150	$4,100

SJ-200 Summer Jam Koa
2006. Custom Shop, only 6 made, offered to attendees of Gibson Guitar Summer Jam, highly figured koa back/sides.

2006		$4,100	$5,300

SJ-200 True Vintage/SJ-200 Vintage
2007-2019. AAA Adirondack red spruce top, AAA Eastern curly maple back and sides, rosewood 'board, tortoise 'guard, nitro finish. True dropped from name in '19.

2007-2018		$3,350	$4,350
2019		$3,700	$4,800

SJ-200 Vine
2002-2018. Custom Shop, Sitka spruce top, Eastern curly maple back/sides, abalone vine inlay in 'board, abalone body trim. Limited Edition in '15, 30 made.

2002-2018		$5,000	$6,500

SJ-300
2007-2010. Super Jumbo with Indian rosewood back and sides, ebony 'board, abalone crown inlays and rosette, gold imperial tuners, active transducer.

2007-2010		$2,775	$3,600

Sonex Artist
1981-1985. Active electronics, 3 mini switches, 2 humbuckers.

1981-1985		$650	$850

Sonex-180 Custom
1980-1982. Two Super humbuckers, coil-tap, maple neck, ebony 'board, single-cut, body of Multi-Phonic synthetic material, black or white.

1980-1982		$625	$825

Sonex-180 Deluxe
1980-1984. Hardwood neck, rosewood 'board, single-cut, body of Multi-Phonic synthetic material, 2 pickups, no coil-tap, various colors.

1980-1984	Various colors	$625	$825
1982-1984	Silverburst	$675	$900

Sonex-180 Standard
1980. Dirty-fingers pickups, rosewood 'board, ebony finish.

1980		$625	$825

Songbird Deluxe
1999-2002. Solid rosewood back, sides and 'board, on-board electronics. Renamed Songwriter Deluxe.

1999-2002		$1,175	$1,523

Songwriter
2003-present. Sitka spruce top, rosewood back, sides and 'board, mahogany neck, Antique Natural or Rosewood Burst.

2003-2020		$1,650	$2,150

Songwriter 12-String Rosewood
2019-2020. Sitka spruce top, rosewood back and sides, Antique Natural or Rosewood Burst.

2019-2020		$1,825	$2,375

Songwriter Deluxe
2003-2011. Solid rosewood back and sides, trapezoid inlays, cutaway or non-cutaway, on-board electronics.

2003-2011		$1,350	$1,750

Songwriter Deluxe 12-String
2006-present. 12-string version, non-cut.

2006-2020		$1,350	$1,750

Songwriter Deluxe Koa
2009. Custom Shop, all koa, cutaway.

2009		$2,100	$2,800

Songwriter Deluxe Standard
2009-2012. Solid rosewood back and sides, bound ebony 'board, diamond and arrows inlays, cutaway or non-cutaway.

2009-2012		$1,700	$2,200

Songwriter Deluxe Studio
2009-2018. Like Standard, but with bound rosewood 'board and double parallelogram inlays, cutaway or non-cutaway.

2009-2018		$1,300	$1,700

Songwriter Modern EC Mahogany
2020-2021. Cutaway, sitka spruce top, mahogany back, sides and neck, Light Cherry Burst with nitro finish.

2020-2021		$1,375	$1,800

Songwriter Modern EC Rosewood
2020-2021. Cutaway, sitka spruce top, rosewood back and sides, mahogany neck, Rosewood Burst with nitro finish.

2020-2021		$1,500	$1,950

Songwriter Special
2007. Mahogany sides and back, dark opaque finish.

2007		$1,250	$1,600

Songwriter Special Deluxe
2003. Custom Shop, Brazilian rosewood.

2003		$1,850	$2,400

Songwriter Standard EC Rosewood
2020-present. Cutaway, sitka spruce top, rosewood back and sides, Antique Natural or Rosewood Burst finish.

2020-2021		$1,750	$2,275

Songwriter Standard Rosewood
2020-present. Non-cut, sitka spruce top, rosewood back and sides, Antique Natural or Rosewood Burst finish.

2020-2021		$1,700	$2,200

Songwriter Studio
2003-2019. Non-cutaway or cutaway.

2003-2019		$1,450	$1,900

Special 400
1985. Double-cut SG body, exposed humbucker and 2 single-coils, Kahler locking tremolo, coil tap.

1985		$600	$775

Spirit I
1982-1987. Double rounded cutaway, 1 pickup, chrome hardware, various colors.

1982-1987		$1,125	$1,450

Spirit I XPL

1985-1986. Spirit I with 6-on-a-side Explorer-style headstock.

MODEL YEAR	FEATURES	EXC. COND. LOW	HIGH
1985-1986		$1,150	$1,500

Spirit II

1982-1987. Spirit I with 2 pickups, bound top.

MODEL YEAR	FEATURES	EXC. COND. LOW	HIGH
1982-1987		$1,275	$1,650

Spirit II XPL

1985-1986. 2 pickup version.

MODEL YEAR	FEATURES	EXC. COND. LOW	HIGH
1985-1986		$1,275	$1,650

SR-71

1987-1989. Floyd Rose tremolo, 1 humbucker, 2 single-coil pickups, various colors, Wayne Charvel designed.

MODEL YEAR	FEATURES	EXC. COND. LOW	HIGH
1987-1989		$1,275	$1,650

Star

1992. Star logo on headstock, star position markers, single sharp cutaway flat-top, sunburst.

MODEL YEAR	FEATURES	EXC. COND. LOW	HIGH
1991-1992		$1,300	$1,675

Starburst Standard/Flame

1992-1994. Single-cut acoustic/electric, star inlays, figured maple back and sides.

MODEL YEAR	FEATURES	EXC. COND. LOW	HIGH
1992-1994		$1,300	$1,675

Style O

1902-1925. Acoustic archtop, oval soundhole, bound top, neck and headstock, various colors.

MODEL YEAR	FEATURES	EXC. COND. LOW	HIGH
1902-1906	Paddle headstock	$4,700	$6,100
1902-1906	Paddle headstock, fancy	$5,900	$7,650
1906-1908	Slotted headstock	$5,500	$7,150
1908-1913	Solid headstock	$5,500	$7,150
1914-1921	Scroll variation	$5,500	$7,150
1922-1924	Loar era	$5,900	$7,650
1925	Scroll, truss rod	$5,900	$7,650

Style O-1

1902. Acoustic archtop, celluloid binding.

MODEL YEAR	FEATURES	EXC. COND. LOW	HIGH
1902		$6,700	$8,700

Style O-2

1902. Acoustic archtop, pearl/ebony binding.

MODEL YEAR	FEATURES	EXC. COND. LOW	HIGH
1902		$6,700	$8,700

Style O-3

1902. Acoustic archtop, green/white binding.

MODEL YEAR	FEATURES	EXC. COND. LOW	HIGH
1902		$6,700	$8,700

Style R Harp Guitar

1902-1907. Acoustic 6-string, with 6 sub-bass strings, walnut back and sides, bound soundhole.

MODEL YEAR	FEATURES	EXC. COND. LOW	HIGH
1902-1907		$4,200	$5,400

Style R-1 Harp Guitar

1902. Style R with fancier pearl and ivory rope pattern binding.

MODEL YEAR	FEATURES	EXC. COND. LOW	HIGH
1902		$4,200	$5,400

Style U Harp Guitar

1902-1939. Acoustic 6-string, with 10 or 12 sub-bass strings, walnut (until about '07) or birch back and sides, bound soundhole, black.

MODEL YEAR	FEATURES	EXC. COND. LOW	HIGH
1902-1939		$4,500	$5,800

Style U-1 Harp Guitar

1902-1907, 1915, 1917. Slightly fancier Style U.

MODEL YEAR	FEATURES	EXC. COND. LOW	HIGH
1902-1917		$4,900	$6,400

Super 300

1948-1955. Acoustic archtop, non-cut, bound body, neck and headstock, sunburst.

MODEL YEAR	FEATURES	EXC. COND. LOW	HIGH
1948-1949		$3,300	$4,300
1950-1955		$3,000	$4,000

Super 300 C

1954-1958. Acoustic archtop, rounded cutaway, bound body, neck and headstock, sunburst with natural option.

MODEL YEAR	FEATURES	EXC. COND. LOW	HIGH
1954-1958	Sunburst	$3,700	$4,900

Super 400

1935-1941, 1947-1955. Introduced early '35 as Super L-5 Deluxe. Acoustic archtop, non-cut, multi-bound, f-holes, sunburst (see Super 400 N for natural version).

MODEL YEAR	FEATURES	EXC. COND. LOW	HIGH
1935	Early, L-5 Deluxe, highly flamed maple	$13,500	$17,500
1935	Early, L-5 Deluxe, plain maple	$11,000	$14,200
1935	Late, 400, highly flamed maple	$11,000	$14,200
1935	Late, 400, plain maple	$8,500	$11,000
1936-1941	Highly flamed maple	$9,100	$12,100
1936-1941	Plain maple	$7,300	$9,500
1947-1949	Highly flamed maple	$5,900	$7,600
1947-1949	Plain maple	$4,600	$6,000
1950-1955		$4,200	$5,500

Super 400 N

1940, 1948-1955. Natural finish version of Super 400, highly flamed, non-cut, acoustic archtop.

MODEL YEAR	FEATURES	EXC. COND. LOW	HIGH
1940		$11,000	$14,200
1948-1949		$8,100	$10,500
1950-1955		$7,000	$9,000

Super 400 P (Premier)

1939-1941. Acoustic archtop, single rounded cutaway, '39 model 'board rests on top, sunburst finish.

MODEL YEAR	FEATURES	EXC. COND. LOW	HIGH
1939-1941		$16,200	$21,000

Super 400 PN (Premier Natural)

1939-1940. Rounded cutaway, '39 'board rests on top, natural finish.

MODEL YEAR	FEATURES	EXC. COND. LOW	HIGH
1939-1940		$22,700	$29,500

Super 400 C

1948-1982. Introduced as Super 400 Premier, acoustic archtop, single-cut, sunburst finish (natural is called Super 400 CN).

MODEL YEAR	FEATURES	EXC. COND. LOW	HIGH
1948-1949		$11,000	$14,200
1950-1959		$10,100	$13,100
1960-1964		$8,850	$11,500
1965		$6,700	$8,700
1966-1969		$5,850	$7,600
1970-1982		$4,200	$5,500

Super 400 CN

1950-1987. Natural finish version of Super 400 C.

MODEL YEAR	FEATURES	EXC. COND. LOW	HIGH
1950-1959		$11,300	$14,700
1960-1964		$10,100	$13,100
1965		$9,200	$12,000
1966-1969		$8,000	$10,400

2019 Gibson Songwriter

Gibson Super 400N 1940

Kevin

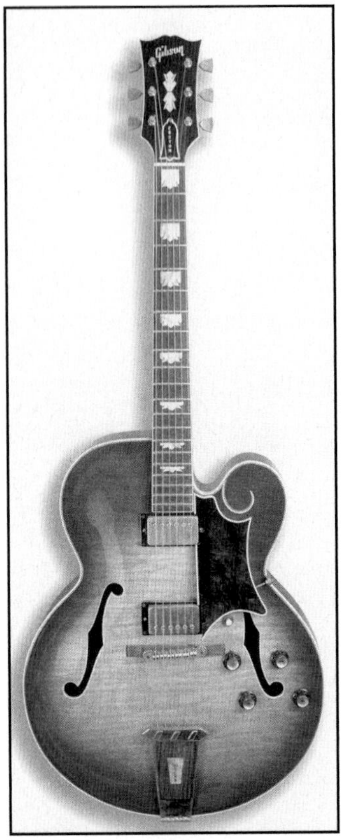

1962 Gibson Tal Farlow

Gibson Traveling Songwriter EC

Super 400 CES

1951-2018. Electric version of Super 400 C, archtop, single-cut (round '51-'60 and '69-present, pointed '60-'69), 2 pickups (P-90s '51-'54, Alnico Vs '54-'57, humbuckers '57 on), sunburst (natural version called Super 400 CESN), now part of Gibson's Historic Collection.

MODEL YEAR	FEATURES	EXC. COND. LOW	HIGH
1951-1953	P-90s	$12,700	$16,500
1954-1957	Alnico Vs	$12,700	$16,500
1957-1960	PAFs	$18,000	$23,500
1961-1962	PAFs, sharp cut begins	$16,000	$20,900
1963-1964	Pat #	$11,800	$15,400
1965		$8,600	$11,100
1966-1969		$7,400	$9,600
1970-1979		$6,300	$8,400
1980-2018		$6,300	$8,400

Super 400 CESN

1952-2016. Natural version of Super 400 CES, now part of Gibson's Historic Collection.

MODEL YEAR	FEATURES	EXC. COND. LOW	HIGH
1952-1953	P-90s	$12,700	$16,500
1954-1956	Alnico Vs	$12,700	$16,500
1957-1960	PAFs	$18,000	$23,500
1961-1962	PAFs, sharp cut begins	$16,000	$20,900
1963-1964	Pat #	$11,800	$15,400
1965		$8,600	$11,100
1966-1969		$7,400	$9,600
1970-1979		$6,300	$8,400
1980-2016		$6,300	$8,400

Super 400 Custom Shop

2009. Non-cutaway, natural.

MODEL YEAR	FEATURES	EXC. COND. LOW	HIGH
2009		$7,200	$9,400

'39 Super 400

1993-1997. Historic Collection, reissue of non-cut '39 version, various colors.

MODEL YEAR	FEATURES	EXC. COND. LOW	HIGH
1993-1997		$6,300	$8,200

Super 4000 Chet Atkins

2000. Limited run of 25. AAA sitka spruce carved top, highly figured carved maple back, antique natural and faded cherry sunburst.

MODEL YEAR	FEATURES	EXC. COND. LOW	HIGH
2000		$17,000	$22,000

Super Jumbo 100

1939-1943. Jumbo flat-top, mahogany back and sides, bound body and neck, sunburst, reintroduced as J-100 with different specs in '84.

MODEL YEAR	FEATURES	EXC. COND. LOW	HIGH
1939-1940		$24,000	$31,400
1941	Early '41	$24,000	$31,400
1941-1943	Late '41	$20,200	$26,500

Super Jumbo/Super Jumbo 200

1938-1942. Initially called Super Jumbo in '38 and named Super Jumbo 200 in '39. Name then changed to J-200 (see that listing) by '47 (with maple back and sides) and SJ-200 by the '50s. Named for super large jumbo 16 7/8" flat-top body, double braced with rosewood back and sides, sunburst finish.

MODEL YEAR	FEATURES	EXC. COND. LOW	HIGH
1938-1940		$80,000	$104,000
1941	Early '41	$75,000	$99,000
1941-1942	Late '41	$70,000	$91,000

Super V BJB

1978-1983. A Super V CES but with a single floating pickup.

MODEL YEAR	FEATURES	EXC. COND. LOW	HIGH
1978-1983		$4,400	$5,800

Super V CES

1978-1993. Archtop, L-5 with a Super 400 neck, 2 humbucker pickups, natural or sunburst.

MODEL YEAR	FEATURES	EXC. COND. LOW	HIGH
1978-1993		$4,400	$5,800

Tal Farlow

1962-1971, 1993-2018. Full body, single-cut archtop, 2 humbuckers, triple-bound top, reintroduced '93 as part of Gibson's Historic Collection.

MODEL YEAR	FEATURES	EXC. COND. LOW	HIGH
1962-1964	Viceroy Brown	$6,400	$8,300
1965	Viceroy Brown	$6,000	$7,800
1966-1971	Viceroy Brown	$5,400	$7,000
1993-2018	Various colors	$3,100	$4,000

TG-0

1927-1933. Acoustic tenor based on L-0, mahogany body, light amber.

MODEL YEAR	FEATURES	EXC. COND. LOW	HIGH
1927-1933		$1,625	$2,125
1960-1964		$825	$1,075
1965		$625	$825
1966-1969		$575	$750
1970-1974		$550	$700

TG-00

1932-1943. Tenor flat-top based on L-00.

MODEL YEAR	FEATURES	EXC. COND. LOW	HIGH
1932-1943		$1,600	$2,125

TG-1/L-1 Tenor/L-4 Tenor

1927-1937. Acoustic flat-top, tenor or plectrum guitar based on L-1, mahogany back and sides, bound body, sunburst.

MODEL YEAR	FEATURES	EXC. COND. LOW	HIGH
1927-1937		$2,000	$2,600
1928-1932	Rare Lucas/ Johnson body	$2,900	$3,800

TG-2/L-2 Tenor

1929-1930. Acoustic tenor guitar.

MODEL YEAR	FEATURES	EXC. COND. LOW	HIGH
1929-1930		$3,800	$5,000

TG-7

1934-1940. Tenor based on the L-7, sunburst.

MODEL YEAR	FEATURES	EXC. COND. LOW	HIGH
1934-1940		$2,900	$3,800

TG-25/TG-25 N

1962-1970. Acoustic flat-top, tenor guitar based on B-25, mahogany back and sides, sunburst or natural (25 N).

MODEL YEAR	FEATURES	EXC. COND. LOW	HIGH
1962-1964		$825	$1,075
1965		$700	$925
1966-1969		$625	$825
1970		$500	$650

TG-50

1934-1940, 1947-1961, 1963. Acoustic archtop, tenor guitar based on L-50, mahogany back and sides, sunburst.

MODEL YEAR	FEATURES	EXC. COND. LOW	HIGH
1934-1940		$1,125	$1,500
1947-1963		$1,050	$1,400

Traveling Songwriter EC

2005-2015. Solid spruce top, solid mahogany sides and back, soft cutaway, on-board electronics and EQ.

MODEL YEAR	FEATURES	EXC. COND. LOW	HIGH
2005-2015		$1,700	$2,200

Trini Lopez Standard

1964-1970. Double rounded cutaway, thinline archtop, 2 humbuckers, tune-o-matic bridge, trapeze tailpiece, single-bound, cherry, Sparkling Burgundy and Pelham Blue finishes.

MODEL YEAR	FEATURES	EXC. COND. LOW	HIGH
1964	Cherry	$7,300	$9,400

MODEL YEAR	FEATURES	EXC. COND. LOW	HIGH
1965	Cherry	$6,800	$8,800
1965	Pelham Blue	$7,500	$9,700
1965	Sparkling Burgundy	$6,800	$8,800
1966	Pelham Blue	$7,100	$9,200
1966-1970	Cherry	$6,600	$8,600
1966-1970	Sparkling Burgundy	$6,600	$8,600

Trini Lopez Standard (Custom Shop)

2010-2011. Custom Shop reissue of thinline Trini Lopez Standard, diamond f-holes, 6-on-a-side tuners, trapeze tailpiece, Certificate of Authenticity, cherry red.

2010-2011		$2,500	$3,300

Trini Lopez Deluxe

1964-1970. Double pointed cutaway archtop, 2 humbuckers, triple-bound, sunburst.

1964		$6,100	$7,900
1965		$5,900	$7,700
1966-1970		$5,700	$7,400

U-2

1987-1989. Double-cut, 1 humbucker and 2 single-coil pickups, ebony or red, renamed Mach II in '90-'91.

1987-1991		$900	$1,200

U-2 Showcase Edition

1988. November 1988 Guitar of the Month series, 250 made.

1988		$900	$1,200

US-1/US-3

1986-1991. Double-cut maple top with mahogany back, 3 humbucker pickups (US-1), or 3 P-90s (US-3), standard production and Custom Shop.

1986-1991		$900	$1,200

Vegas Standard

2006-2007. Flat-top semi-hollowbody thinline, slim neck, 2 humbuckers, f-holes, split diamond inlays.

2006-2007		$850	$1,125

Vegas High Roller

2006-2007. Upgraded version, AAA maple top, gold hardware and frets, block inlays.

2006-2007		$950	$1,225

Victory MV II (MV 2)

1981-1984. Asymmetrical double-cut with long horn, 3-way slider, maple body and neck, rosewood 'board, 2 pickups.

1981-1984		$950	$12,225

Victory MV X (MV 10)

1981-1984. 3 humbuckers, 5-way switch, various colors.

1981-1984		$975	$1,275

WRC

1987-1988. Designed for Gibson by Wayne R. Charvel (WRC), earlier models had Kahler trem, later Floyd Rose, offered in red, black or white.

1987-1988		$775	$1,000

XPL Custom

1985-1986. Explorer-like shape, exposed humbuckers, locking tremolo, bound maple top, sunburst or white.

1985-1986		$1,150	$1,500

MODEL YEAR	FEATURES	EXC. COND. LOW	HIGH

Y2K Dwight Yoakam Signature

2005. Limited run of 200, small body jumbo, spruce top, highly figured maple sides and back, 2-piece flamed maple neck, double 'guard, gloss natural finish.

2005		$1,725	$2,250

Zakk Wylde ZV Buzzsaw

2008. Custom Shop Inspired By series, limited run of 50, Flying V wings with SG horns, 2 humbuckers.

2008		$2,825	$3,650

Gibson Baldwin

2005-ca. 2013. Entry-level electric and acoustic guitars, basses, amps and accessories made in China for discount store market and sold under the Signature, Maestro, Echelon, and Genesis brand names. Models include Les Paul and SG copies. Guitars have Music - Gibson logo on neckplate and brand logo on headstock.

Giffin

1977-1988, 1997-present. Professional and premium grade, production/custom, hollow-, semi-hollow-, and solidbody guitars built by luthier Roger Giffin in West San Fernando Valley, California. For '77-'88, Giffin's shop was in London. From '88 to '93, he worked for the Gibson Custom Shop in California as a Master Luthier. In '97, Giffin set up shop in Sweden for a year, moving back to California in the Spring of '98. He also built small numbers of instruments during '67-'76 and '94-'96 (when he had a repair business).

Gigliotti

2000-present. Premium grade, production/custom, electric guitars with a metal plate top and tone chambers and designed by Patrick Gigliotti in Tacoma, Washington.

Gila Eban Guitars

Premium grade, custom, classical guitars built by luthier Gila Eban in Riverside, Connecticut, starting in 1979.

Gilbert Guitars

1965-present. Custom classical guitars by luthiers John Gilbert and William Gilbert in Paso Robles, California. Son William has handled all production since '91. John died early 2012.

Gilchrist

1977-present. Currently known more for his mandolins, luthier Steve Gilchrist, of Warrnambool, Australia, has also built premium and presentation grade, custom, guitars.

Acoustic Archtop

1990s-present. Very limited production.

1990s-2020		$17,000	$22,000

1965 Gibson Trini Lopez Standard

Matt Carleson

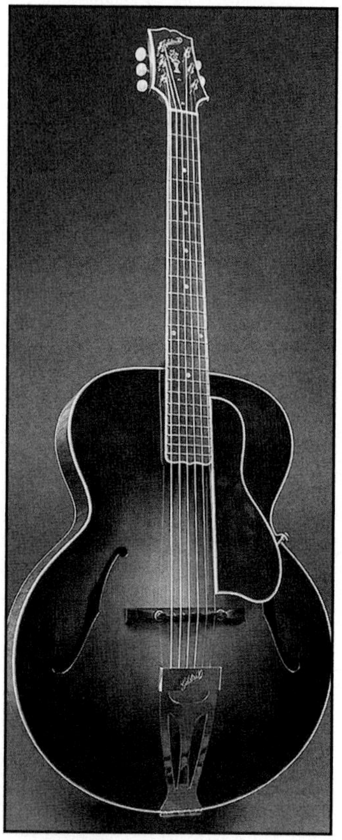

Gilchrist Model 16

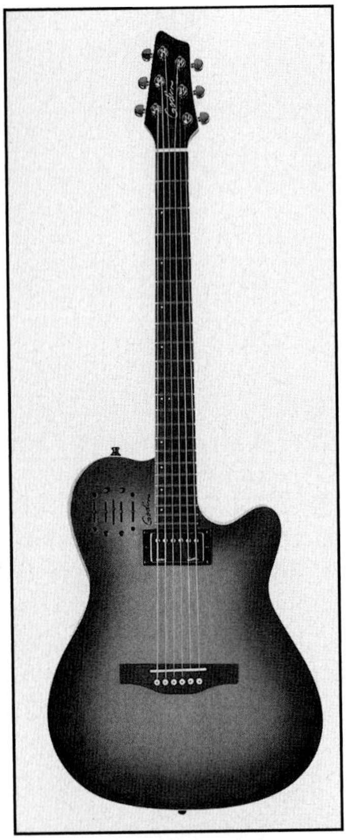

Godin A6 Ultra (A Series)

2017 Godin 5th Avenue

MODEL YEAR	FEATURES	EXC. COND. LOW	HIGH

Gilet Guitars

1976-present. Luthier Gerard Gilet builds production/custom, premium grade, acoustic, classical, flamenco, and wooden bodied resonator guitars in Botany, Sydney, New South Wales, Australia. He also builds lap steels.

Girl Brand Guitars

1996-2012. Premium-grade, production/custom, guitars built by luthier Chris Larsen in Tucson, Arizona. Larson now builds under the Larsen Guitar Mfg. name.

Gitane

2003-present. Intermediate and professional grade, production, classic Selmer-Maccaferri style jazz guitars made in China for Saga.

Gittler

1974-ca.1985. Minimalistic electric guitar designed by Allan Gittler, consisting basically of a thin rod with frets welded to it. A total of 560 were built, with Gittler making the first 60 in the U.S. from '74 to the early '80s. The remainder were made around '85 in Israel by the Astron corporation under a licensing agreement. Three Gittler basses were also built. Gittler emigrated to Israel in the early '80s and changed his name to Avraham Bar Rashi. He died in 2002. A U.S.-made Gittler is the only musical instrument in the Museum of Modern Art in New York.

Metal Skeleton

1971-1999.

1971-1982		$2,000	$2,600
1982-1999		$1,750	$2,300

Giulietti

1962-1965. The Giulietti Accordion Company, New York, offered guitars and amps in the '60s.

GJ2

Gold Jackson Enterprises LLC, a partnership between luthier Grover Jackson and Jon Gold, established 2012, builds professional and premium grade, production/custom, solidbody electric guitars in Laguna Hills, California.

Glendale

2004-present. Professional grade, production/custom, solidbody guitars built by luthier Dale Clark in Arlington, Texas.

GLF

1991-1997. Solidbody electric guitars built by luthier Kevin Smith in Minnesota. In '97 he started building his ToneSmith line of guitars.

Glick Guitars

Premium grade, production/custom, acoustic and electric archtop, and acoustic guitars built in Santa Barbara, California by luthier Mike Glick, starting in '96.

MODEL YEAR	FEATURES	EXC. COND. LOW	HIGH

Global

Late-1960s-1970s. Budget copy models, not unlike Teisco, imported from Asia for the student market. They also offered amps.

Electric Solidbody

Late-1960s-1970s.

1968		$100	$350

GMP

1990-2005. Professional and premium grade solidbody electric guitars built by GM Precision Products, Inc. of San Dimas, California. Original owners were Gary and Cameron Moline, Dave Pearson and Glenn Matjezel. Many guitars featured fancy tops or custom graphics. They also made basses. Overall production is estimated at 1120 guitars and basses. GMP reopened in '10 under new ownership (see following).

GMP (Genuine Musical Products)

2010-present. The GMP brand was acquired by Dan and Kim Lawrence in '08. Since '10, Dan along with fellow luthiers Glenn Matjezel and William Stempke build professional and premium grade, production/custom, electric guitars in San Dimas, California. They also build basses.

GMW

1998-present. Professional grade, production/custom, solidbody guitars from Lee Garver's GMW Guitarworks of Glendora, California.

Godin

1987-present. Intermediate and professional grade, production, solidbody electrics and nylon and steel string acoustic/electrics from luthier Robert Godin. They also build basses and mandolins. Necks and bodies are made in La Patrie, Quebec with final assembly in Berlin, New Hampshire. Godin is also involved in the Seagull, Norman, Richmond, Art & Lutherie, and Patrick & Simon brand of guitars. SA on Godin models stands for Synth Access.

5th Avenue Kingpin

2008-present. Full-size non-cut electric archtop, 1 or 2 P-90 pickups, plain or highly flamed top, premium price for highly flamed.

2008-2020		$550	$725

5th Avenue Uptown

2012-present. Archtop cutaway with Bigsby, f-holes, Canadian wild cherry top, back and sides, silver leaf maple neck, various colors.

2012-2020		$550	$725

A Series

1990s-present. Electric/acoustic nylon strings, single-cut, chambered body, 6-, 11-, 12-string, various wood and colors.

1990s-2020	A12, 12-string	$675	$875
1990s-2020	A6, 6-string	$375	$500
2000-2017	A11 (Glissentar), 11-string	$625	$825

MODEL YEAR	FEATURES	EXC. COND. LOW	HIGH

Acousticaster (6)

1987-2020. Thin line single-cut chambered maple body, acoustic/electric, maple neck, 6-on-a-side tuners, spruce top.

1987-2020		$375	$490

Acousticaster 6 Deluxe

1994-2008. Acousticaster 6 with mahogany body.

1994-2008		$425	$550

Artisan ST I/ST I

1992-1998. Offset double-cut solidbody, birdseye maple top, 3 pickups.

1992-1998		$500	$650

Flat Five X

2002-2004. Single-cut, semi-hollow with f-holes, 3-way pickup system (magnetic to transducer).

2002-2004		$700	$900

Freeway Classic/Freeway Classic SA

2004-2015. Offset double-cut solidbody, birdseye maple top on translucent finishes, hum-single-hum pickups.

2004-2015		$400	$525

G-1000/G-2000/G-3000

1993-1996. Offset double-cut solidbody, extra large bass horn, various pickup options.

1993-1996		$225	$300

Jeff Cook Signature

1994-1995. Quilted maple top, light maple back, 2 twin rail and 1 humbucker pickups.

1994-1995		$500	$650

L.R. Baggs Signature

1990s. Single-cut chambered thinline electric, spruce top, mahogany body, EQ.

1990s		$400	$550

LG/LGT

1995-2011. Single-cut carved slab mahogany body, 2 Tetrad Combo pickups ('95-'97) or 2 Duncan SP-90 pickups ('98-present), various colors, satin lacquer finish. LGT with tremolo.

1995-2011		$275	$350

LGX/LGXT/LGX-SA

1996-2018. Single-cut maple-top carved solidbody, 2 Duncan humbuckers, various quality tops offered. LGXT with tremolo.

1996-2018	Standard top	$400	$700
1997-2018	SA synth access	$600	$900
1998-2018	AA top	$750	$1,000
1998-2018	AAA top	$825	$1,100

Montreal

2004-present. Chambered body carved from solid mahogany, f-holes, 2 humbuckers, saddle transducer, stereo mixing output.

2004-2020		$650	$850

Multiac Series

1994-present. Single-cut, thinline electric with solid spruce top, RMC Sensor System electronics, available in either nylon string or steel string versions, built-in EQ, program up/down buttons.

1994-2020	Various models	$600	$1,400

Passion RG-3

2011-present. Double-cut, 3 single-coil pickups, swamp ash body, rosewood neck (RN) or maple (MN), Indigo Burst finish with artic white pearloid 'guard.

2011-2020		$1,175	$1,525

Radiator

1999-2013. Single-cut, dual pickup, pearloid top, dot markers.

1999-2013		$225	$300

Redline Series

2007-2015. Maple body and neck, rosewood 'board, Redline 1 has 1 pickup, 2 and 3 have 2 pickups (3 has Floyd Rose), various colors.

2007-2011	Redline 1	$300	$450
2008-2015	Redline 3	$350	$500

SD Series

1990s-2012. Performance series, figured maple veneer top, maple neck, maple or rosewood 'board, various colors.

1990-2012	SD 22, SD 24	$250	$350

Solidac - Two Voice

2000-2009. Single-cut, 2-voice technology for electric or acoustic sound.

2000-2009		$325	$425

TC Signature

1987-1999. Single-cut, quilted maple top, 2 Tetrad Combo pickups.

1987-1999		$500	$700

Velocity

2007-2011. Offset double-cut, hum/single/single.

2007-2011		$500	$700

Gold Tone

1993-present. Wayne and Robyn Rogers build their intermediate and professional grade, production/custom guitars and basses in Titusville, Florida. They also build lap steels, mandolins, ukuleles, banjos and banjitars.

Goldbug Guitars

1997-present. Presentation grade, production/custom, acoustic and electric guitars built by luthier Sandy Winters in Delavan, Wisconsin.

Golden Hawaiian

1920s-1930s. Private branded lap guitar most likely made by one of the many Chicago makers for a small retailer, publisher, cataloger, or teaching studio.

Guitars

1920-1930s	Sunburst	$375	$500

Goldentone

1960s. Guitars made by Ibanez most likely in the mid to late '60s. Often have a stylized I (for Ibanez) on the tailpiece or an Ibanez logo on the headstock.

Goldon

German manufacturer of high-quality archtops and other guitars before and shortly after WW II. After the war, they were located in East Germany and by the late 1940s were only making musical toys.

Godin Redline

Bernunzio Uptown Music

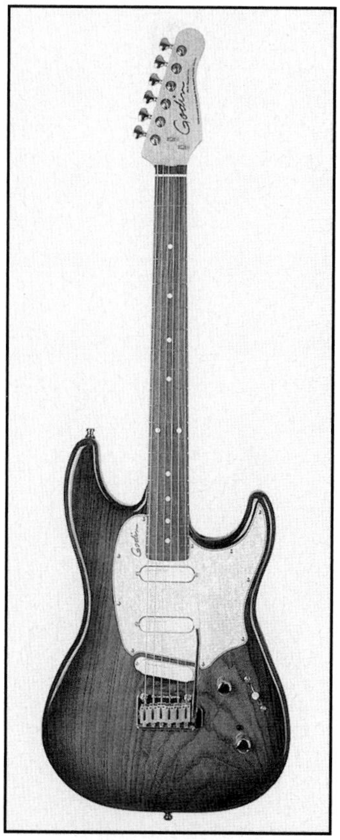

Godin Passion RG-3

Goodall Concert Jumbo

1960s Goya Rangemaster

Imaged by Heritage Auctions, HA.com

MODEL YEAR	FEATURES	EXC. COND. LOW	HIGH

Goodall

1972-present. Premium grade, custom flat-tops and nylon-strings, built by luthier James Goodall originally in California and, since '92, in Kailua-Kona, Hawaii.

Classical

1986. Brazilian and cedar.

1986	BC425	$5,100	$6,625

Concert Jumbo

1998-present. Various woods.

2007-2020	Red cedar/ Indian rosewood	$2,625	$3,400
2007-2020	Sitka/figured koa	$2,625	$3,400

Concert Jumbo Cutaway

2004-2018. Rosewood.

2004-2018		$2,925	$3,800

Jumbo KJ

1995-2011. Sitka, koa.

1995-2011		$2,625	$3,400

RS Rosewood Standard

1989-1997. Indian rosewood back and sides.

1989-1997		$2,625	$3,400

Standard

1980s-present. Jumbo-style with wide waist, mahogany back and sides, sitka spruce top.

1980s-2020		$2,475	$3,200

Goodman Guitars

1975-present. Premium grade, custom/production, archtop, flat-top, classical, and electric guitars built by luthier Brad Goodman in Brewster, New York. He also builds mandolins.

Goran Custom Guitars

1998-present. Luthier Goran Djuric builds his professional and premium grade, custom, electric guitars in Belgrade, Serbia. He also builds effects.

Gordon-Smith

1979-present. Intermediate and professional grade, production/custom, semi-hollow and solidbody guitars built by luthier John Smith in Partington, England.

Gower

1955-1960s. Built in Nashville by Jay Gower, later joined by his son Randy. Gower is also associated with Billy Grammer and Grammer guitars.

G-55-2 Flat-Top

1955-1968. Square shoulder-style flat-top, triple abalone rosette, abalone fretboard trim, dot markers, natural.

1955-1968		$950	$1,250

G-65 Flat-Top

1955-1968. Square shoulder-style flat-top, lower belly bridge with pearl dots on bridge, dot markers, sunburst.

1955-1968		$725	$950

G-100 Flat-Top

1955-1968	Brazilian rosewood	$1,025	$1,350

Goya

1952-1996. Brand initially used by Hershman Musical Instrument Company of New York City, New York, in mid-'50s for acoustic guitars made in Sweden by Levin, particularly known for its classicals. From '58 to '61 they imported Hagstrom- and Galanti-made electrics labeled as Goya; in '62 they offered electrics made by Valco. In '67 they again offered electrics, this time made by Zero Sette in Castelfidardo, Italy. By '63 the company had become the Goya Musical Instrument Corporation, marketing primarily Goya acoustics. In '67 they again offered electrics, this time made by Zero Sette in Castelfidardo, Italy. Goya was purchased by Avnet, Inc., prior to '66, when Avnet purchased Guild Guitars. In '69, Goya was purchased by Kustom which offered the instruments until '71. Probably some '70s guitars were made in Japan. The brand name was purchased by C.F. Martin in '76, with Japanese-made acoustic guitars, solidbody electric guitars and basses, banjos and mandolins imported in around '78 and continuing into the '90s.

Classical

1950s-1980s. Various models.

1955-60s	G Series	$125	$1,000
1980s	Japan	$350	$475

Flamenco

1955-1960s. Various models.

1955-60s	FL Series	$325	$500

Folk

1950s-1980s. Various models.

1955-60s	F Series	$325	$500

Model 80/Model 90

1959-1962. Single-cut body, replaceable modular pickup assembly, sparkle top.

1959-1962		$775	$1,000

Panther S-3

1967-1968. Double-cut solidbody, 3 pickups, Panther S-3 Goya logo, volume and tone knobs with 6 upper bass bout switches, bolt-on neck.

1967-1968		$775	$1,000

Rangemaster

1967-1968. Wide variety of models.

1967-1968		$625	$800

Steel

1955-1960s. Various models.

1955-60s	M and S Series	$100	$275

Graf

See listing under Oskar Graf Guitars.

Grammer

1965-1971. Acoustic guitars built in Nashville. Founded by country guitarist Bill Grammer, music store owner Clyde Reid and luthier J.W. Gower (who also built his own line). Grammer sold the company to Ampeg in '68 who sold it again in '71, but it quickly ceased business. Originally the Grammer headstock logo had an upper-case G, Ampeg-made instruments have a lower-case one.

MODEL YEAR	FEATURES	EXC. COND. LOW	HIGH

G-10

1965-1970. Solid Brazilian rosewood back and sides, solid spruce top, large crown-shaped bridge, pearl dot markers, natural.

1965-1967	Grammer era	$2,000	$2,600
1968-1970	Ampeg era	$1,500	$2,000

G-20

1965-1970. Natural.

1965-1967	Grammer era	$1,650	$2,200
1968-1970	Ampeg era	$1,500	$2,000

G-30

1965-1970. Natural.

1965-1967	Grammer era	$1,650	$2,200
1968-1970	Ampeg era	$1,500	$2,000

G-50

1965-1970. Top-of-the-line Grammer, Brazilian rosewood back and sides, Adirondack spruce top.

1965-1967	Grammer era	$2,200	$2,900
1968-1970	Ampeg era	$2,000	$2,700

S-30

1965-1970. Solid spruce top, solid ribbon mahogany back and sides.

1965-1967	Grammer era	$1,450	$1,900
1968-1970	Ampeg era	$1,300	$1,700

Granada

Late 1960s-1980s. Japanese-made acoustic, electric solid, semi-hollow and hollowbody guitars, many copies of classic American models. They also offered basses.

Acoustic

1970-1979. Import from Japan, various copy models.

1970-1979		$125	$175

Electric

1970-1979. Import from Japan, various copy models.

1970-1979		$175	$225

Granata Guitars

1989-present. Luthier Peter Granata builds his professional grade, custom, flat-top and resonator guitars in Oak Ridge, New Jersey.

Graveel

Production/custom, solidbody guitars built by luthier Dean Graveel in Indianapolis, Indiana.

Grazioso

1950s. Grazioso was a brand name used by Selmer in England on instruments made in Czechoslovakia. They replaced the brand with their Futurama line of guitars.

GRD

1978-1982. High-end acoustic and electric guitars produced in Charles Fox's Guitar Research & Design Center in Vermont. GRD introduced the original thin-line acoustic-electric guitar to the world at the '78 Winter NAMM show.

MODEL YEAR	FEATURES	EXC. COND. LOW	HIGH

Great Divide Guitars

2009-2011. Budget and intermediate grade, production, flat-top guitars imported from China, designed by luthier Tom Bedell, Dan Mills and Sophia Yang. They also offer Bedell Guitars.

Greco

1960s-present. Brand name used in Japan and owned by Kanda Shokai. Fuji Gen Gakki, maker of many Hoshino/Ibanez guitars, also made many Greco models during the '70s; thus often Greco guitars are similar to Ibanez. During the '70s the company sold many high-quality copies of American designs, though by '75 they offered many weird-shaped original designs, including the Iceman and carved people shapes. By the late-'70s they were offering neck-through-body guitars. Currently offering solidbody, hollowbody and acoustic guitars and basses, including models licensed by Zemaitis.

Green, Aaron

1990-present. Premium and presentation grade, custom, classical and flamenco guitars built by luthier Aaron Green in Waltham, Massachusetts.

Greene & Campbell

2002-2005. Luthier Dean Campbell built his intermediate and professional grade, production/custom, solidbody guitars in Westwood, Massachusetts. Founding partner Jeffrey Greene left the company in '04; Greene earlier built guitars under his own name. In '05, Campbell changed the name to Campbell American Guitars.

Greene, Jeffrey

2000-2002. Professional grade, production/custom, electric solidbody guitars built by luthier Jeffrey Greene in West Kingston, Rhode Island. He went to work with Dean Campbell building the Greene & Campbell line of guitars.

Greenfield Guitars

1996-present. Luthier Michael Greenfield builds his production/custom, presentation grade, acoustic steel string, concert classical and archtop guitars in Montreal, Quebec.

Gretsch

1883-present. Currently Gretsch offers intermediate, professional, and premium grade, production, acoustic, solidbody, hollowbody, double neck, resonator and Hawaiian guitars. They also offer basses, amps and lap steels. In 2012 they again started offering mandolins, ukuleles and banjos.

Previous brands included Gretsch, Rex, 20th Century, Recording King (for Montgomery Ward), Dorado (Japanese imports). Founded by Friedrich Gretsch in Brooklyn, New York, making drums, banjos, tambourines, and toy instruments which were sold to large distributors including C. Bruno and Wurlitzer. Upon early death of Friedrich,

Granata Resonator

1980 Greco Goldtop

Jon Way

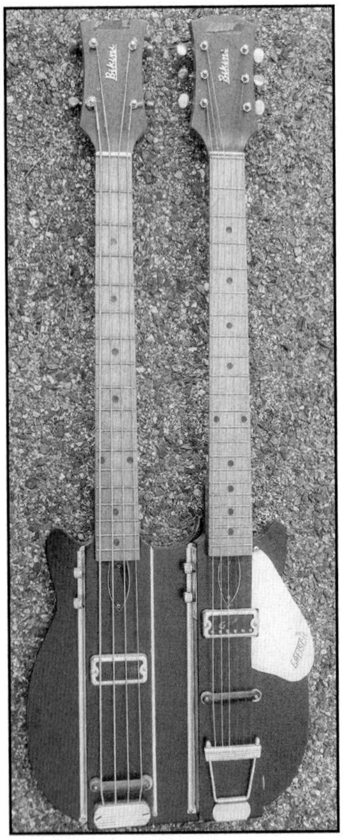

1961 Gretsch Bikini (6025)

Randy Barnett

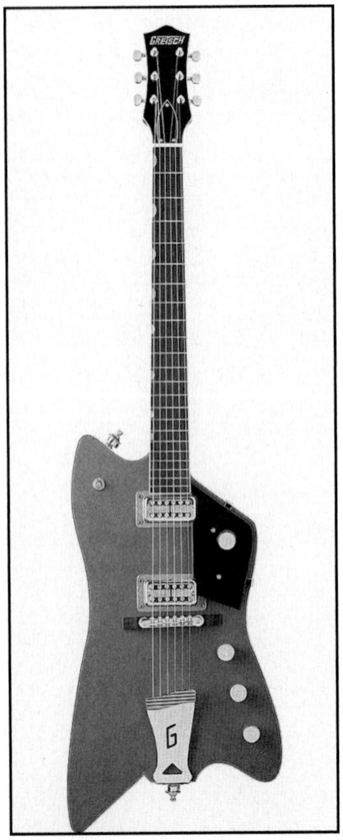

Gretsch Billy-Bo Jupiter Thunderbird (6199)

MODEL YEAR	FEATURES	EXC. COND. LOW	HIGH

son Fred Gretsch, Sr. took over business at age 15. By the turn of the century the company was also making mandolins. In the '20s, they were distributing Rex and 20th Century brands, some made by Gretsch, some by others such as Kay. Charles "Duke" Kramer joined Gretsch in '35. In '40 Gretsch purchased Bacon & Day banjos. Fred Gretsch, Sr. retired in '42 and was replaced by sons Fred, Jr. and Bill. Fred departs for Navy and Bill runs company until his death in '48, when Fred resumes control. After the war the decision was made to promote the Gretsch brand rather than selling to distributors, though some jobbing continues. Kramer becomes Chicago branch manager in '48.

In '67 Baldwin of Cincinnati bought Gretsch. During '70-'72 the factory relocated from Brooklyn to Booneville, Arkansas and company headquarters are moved to Cincinnati. A '72 factory fire drastically reduced production for next two years. In '78 Baldwin bought Kustom amps and sold Gretsch to Kustom's Charlie Roy, and headquarters are moved to Chanute, Kansas. Duke Kramer retired in '80. Guitar production ends '80-'81. Ca. '83 ownership reverted back to Baldwin and Kramer was asked to arrange the sale of the company. In '84 Fred Gretsch III was contacted and in '85 Gretsch guitars came back to the Gretsch family and Fred Gretsch Enterprises, Ltd (FGE). Initial Gretsch Enterprise models were imports made by Japan's Terada Company. In '95, some U.S.-made models were introduced. In 2003, Gretsch granted Fender the rights to develop, produce, market and distribute Gretsch guitars worldwide, including development of new products.

Binding rot can be a problem on 1950s models and prices shown are for fully original, unrestored bindings.

12-String Electric Archtop (6075/6076)

1967-1972. 16" double-cut, 2 Super Tron pickups, 17" body option available, sunburst (6075) or natural (6076).

1967-1972	Natural or sunburst	$1,725	$2,300

12-String Flat-Top (6020)

1969-1972. 15 1/5" body, mahogany back and sides, spruce top, slotted headstock, dot markers.

1969-1972		$850	$1,100

Anniversary (6124/6125)

1958-1972, 1993-1999. Single-cut hollow body archtop, 1 pickup (Filtron '58-'60, Hi-Lo Tron '61 on), bound body, named for Gretsch's 75th anniversary. 6125 is 2-tone green with 2-tone tan an option, 6124 sunburst. Model numbers revived in '90s.

1958-1959	Green 2-tone	$2,250	$2,925
1958-1959	Sunburst	$1,550	$2,025
1960-1961	2-tone green or tan	$2,125	$2,775
1960-1961	Sunburst	$1,350	$1,775
1962-1964	2-tone green or tan	$1,725	$2,225
1962-1964	Sunburst	$1,250	$1,625
1965-1966	Various colors	$1,250	$1,625
1967-1969	Various colors	$1,050	$1,375
1970-1972	Various colors	$950	$1,250

MODEL YEAR	FEATURES	EXC. COND. LOW	HIGH

Anniversary Tenor (6124)

1958-1971. Gretsch offered many models with the 4-string tenor option and also made small batches of tenors, with the same colors and pickups as standard models.

1958-1971		$1,200	$1,575

Anniversary Reissue (6124/6125)

1993-1999. 1 pickup Anniversary reissue, 6124 in sunburst, 6125 2-tone green.

1993-1999		$1,200	$1,575

Anniversary Reissue (6117/6118)

1993-present. 2 pickup like Double Anniversary, 6118 in 2-tone green with (T) or without Bigsby, 6117 is sunburst.

1993-2015	6117	$1,450	$1,900
1993-2020	6118	$1,450	$1,900

Astro-Jet (6126)

1965-1967. Solid body electric, double-cut, 2 pickups, vibrato, 4/2 tuner arrangement, red top with black back and sides.

1965-1967		$1,700	$2,200

Atkins Axe (7685/7686)

1976-1980. Solid body electric, pointed single-cut, 2 pickups, ebony stain (7685) or red rosewood stain (7686), called the Super Axe with added on-board effects.

1976-1980		$1,025	$1,350

Atkins Super Axe (7680/7681)

1976-1981. Pointed single-cut solid body with built-in phaser and sustain, five knobs, three switches, Red Rosewood (7680) or Ebony (7681) stains.

1976-1981		$1,575	$2,050

Bikini (6023/6024/6025)

1961-1962. Solid body electric, separate 6-string and bass neck-body units that slide into 1 of 3 body butterflies - 1 for the 6-string only (6023), 1 for bass only (6024), 1 for double neck (6 and bass - 6025). Components could be purchased separately.

1961-1962	6023/6024, single neck	$800	$1,050
1961-1962	6025, double neck	$1,650	$2,150

Billy-Bo Jupiter Thunderbird (6199)

2005-present. Billy Gibbons and Bo Diddley influenced, chambered mahogany body, laminate maple top, 2 pickups.

2005-2020		$1,875	$2,425

Black Falcon (6136BK/TBK/DSBK)

1992-1997, 2003-2015. Black version of Falcon, single-cut, 2.75" body, oversize f-holes, G tailpiece, DSBK with DynaSonic pickups replaces Filter'Tron BK in '06. Had the Limited Edition 1955 designation for '96-'97. Bigsby-equipped TBK offered '04-present.

1992-2015		$2,000	$2,600

Black Falcon (7594BK)

1992-1998. Black version of G7594 Falcon, double-cut, 2" thick body, Bigsby.

1992-1998		$2,000	$2,600

Black Falcon I (7593BK)

1993-1998, 2003-2005. G63136BK with Bigsby and standard f-holes. Came back in '03 as Black Falcon I with wire handle Gretsch Bigsby tailpiece.

1993-1998		$2,000	$2,600

MODEL YEAR	FEATURES	EXC. COND. LOW	HIGH

Black Hawk (6100/6101)

1967-1972. Hollow body archtop, double-cut, 2 pickups, G tailpiece or Bigsby vibrato, bound body and neck, sunburst (6100) or black (6101).

1967-1969	6100, sunburst	$2,000	$2,600
1967-1969	6101, black	$2,000	$2,600
1970-1972	6100, sunburst	$2,000	$2,600
1970-1972	6101, black	$2,000	$2,600

Black Penguin (6134B)

2003-2015. Jet black version.

2003-2015		$2,000	$2,600

Bo Diddley (1810/5810)

2000-2015. Korean-made version.

2000-2015		$190	$245

Bo Diddley (6138)

1999-present. Reproduction of rectangle-shaped, semi-hollow guitar originally made for Diddley by Gretsch, Firebird Red.

1999-2020		$1,150	$1,475

Broadkaster (Hollow Body)

1975-1980. Double-cut archtop, hollow body, 2 pickups, natural or sunburst.

1975-1977	7603, Bigsby, natural	$750	$1,000
1975-1977	7604, Bigsby, sunburst	$750	$1,000
1975-1977	7607, G tailpiece, natural	$750	$1,000
1975-1977	7608, G tailpiece, sunburst	$750	$1,000
1977-1980	7609, red	$750	$1,000

Broadkaster (Solid Body)

1975-1979. Double-cut, maple body, 2 pickups, bolt-on neck, natural (7600) or sunburst (7601).

1975-1979		$750	$1,000

BST 1000 Beast

1979-1980. Single-cut solid body, bolt-on neck, mahogany body, available with 1 pickup in walnut stain (8210) or red stain (8216) or 2 pickups in walnut (7617, 8215, 8217) or red stain (8211).

1979-1980		$600	$800

BST 2000 Beast

1979. Symmetrical double-cut solid body of mahogany, 2 humbucking pickups, bolt-on neck, walnut stain (7620 or 8220) or red stain (8221).

1979		$600	$800

BST 5000 Beast

1979-1980. Asymmetrical double-cut solid body, neck-thru, walnut and maple construction, 2 humbucker pickups, stud tailpiece, natural walnut/maple (8250).

1979-1980		$675	$875

Burl Ives (6004)

1949-1955. Flat-top acoustic, mahogany back and sides, bound body, natural top (6004).

1949-1955		$675	$875

Chet Atkins Country Gentleman (6122/7670)

1957-1981. Hollow body, single-cut to late-'62 and double after, 2 pickups, painted f-holes until '72, real after, mahogany finish (6122). Model number changes to 7670 in '71. Guitars made during and after '64 might have replaced body binding which reduces the value shown by about 10% or more.

1957-1959		$7,700	$10,000
1960		$5,100	$6,600
1961		$4,700	$6,100
1962-1963	George Harrison specs	$3,600	$4,700
1964		$3,100	$4,000
1965		$2,800	$3,600
1966-1970		$2,250	$2,900
1971-1981	7670	$2,050	$2,650

Chet Atkins Country Gentleman (6122-1958)

2007-2015. Single-cut reissue of '58.

2007-2015		$1,700	$2,200

Chet Atkins Country Gentleman (6122-1962)

2007-2015. Double-cut reissue of '62, double muffler (mutes) system, Filter'Trons.

2007-2015		$1,700	$2,200

Chet Atkins Hollow Body (6120)

1954-1966, 2007-2015. Archtop electric, single-cut to '61, double after, 2 pickups, vibrato, f-holes (real to '61 and fake after), cactus and cows engraved block inlays '54-early '56, G brand on top '54-'56, orange finish (6120). Renamed Chet Atkins Nashville in '67. Reissued single-cut in '07.

1954-1955	G brand, Western	$10,200	$13,200
1955-1956	Non-engraved, amber red	$9,000	$11,600
1957-1959	No G-brand	$7,700	$10,000
1960-1961	Single-cut	$5,925	$7,700
1961-1966	Double-cut	$2,800	$3,600
2007-2015	Single-cut	$1,525	$1,975

Chet Atkins Nashville (6120/7660)

1967-1980. Replaced Chet Atkins Hollow Body (6120), electric archtop, double-cut, 2 pickups, amber red (orange). Renumbered 7660 in '72, reissued in '90 as the Model 6120 Nashville.

1967-1969	6120	$2,000	$2,600
1970-1971	6120	$1,700	$2,200
1972-1980	7660	$1,521	$1,975

Chet Atkins Nashville (6120DC)

2007-2016. Double-cut hollow body based on '62 model, gold plated 'guard with Atkin's signature.

2007-2016		$1,700	$2,200

Chet Atkins Hollow Body (6120W-1957)

2007-2009. Western Maple Stain, western block inlays, Bigsby.

2007-2009		$1,700	$2,200

Brian Setzer Black Phoenix (6136-SLBP)

2005-2015. Artist Signature Series, nitro gloss black.

2005-2015		$1,850	$2,400

Brian Setzer Hot Rod (6120SHx)

1999-present. Like SSL, but with only pickup switch and 1 master volume control.

1999-2020		$1,300	$1,700

Brian Setzer Nashville (6120SSL, etc.)

1993-present. Hollow body electric, double-cut, 2 Alnico PAF Filtertron pickups, based on the classic Gretsch 6120.

1993-2020	Western Orange	$1,850	$2,400

Chet Atkins Junior

1970. Archtop, single-cut, 1 pickup, vibrato, open f-holes, double-bound body, orange stain.

1970		$925	$1,200

1960 Gretsch Chet Atkins Hollowbody 6120

Paul Harbinson

Gretsch Brian Setzer Hot Rod

Gretsch Chet Atkins Tennessean (6119/7655)

Darien Zalefsky,

1961 Gretsch Country Club

Geoff Parsons

MODEL YEAR	FEATURES	EXC. COND. LOW	HIGH

Duane Eddy (6210DE)

1997-2003. 6120 style, 2 DeArmond single coils, Bigsby, orange.

1997-2003		$1,700	$2,200

Duane Eddy Signature Hollow Body (6120DE)

2011-present. Single-cut, Western Orange stain lacquer finish.

2011-2020		$1,700	$2,200

Eddie Cochran Signature Hollow Body (6120)

2011-present. Artist Signature Edition, maple body, rosewood 'board, Bigsby, Western maple stain.

2011-2020		$1,700	$2,200

Keith Scott Nashville (6120KS)

1999-2013. Hump-back inlays, gold hardware, metallic gold finish.

1999-2013		$1,700	$2,200

Nashville Double Neck 6/12 (6120)

1997-2002. Built in Japan, few made, all gold hardware, necks are maple with ebony 'boards, orange finish.

1997-2002		$2,300	$3,000

Nashville Jr. (6120-JR/JR2)

1998-2004. Orange, 2 pickups.

1998-2004		$1,000	$1,300

New Nashville (6120N)

2001-2003. Single-cut, humptop inlays, gold hardware.

2001-2003		$1,700	$2,200

Reverend Horton Heat (6120RHH)

2005-present. Cows and cactus inlays, TV jones pickups.

2005-2020		$1,700	$2,200

Chet Atkins Solid Body (6121)

1955-1963. Solid body electric, single-cut, maple or knotty pine top, 2 pickups, Bigsby vibrato, G brand until '57, multi-bound top, brown mahogany, orange finish (6121).

1955-1956		$8,300	$10,700
1957	G brand	$7,000	$9,000
1957-1959	No G brand	$6,200	$8,000
1960	Single-cut	$5,700	$7,400
1961-1963	Double-cut	$4,625	$6,000

Chet Atkins Tennessean (6119/7655)

1958-1980. Archtop electric, single-cut, 1 pickup until early-'61 and 2 after, vibrato. Renumbered as the 7655 in '71.

1958-1960	1 Filter-Tron	$2,200	$2,900
1960-1961	1 Hi-Lo	$2,100	$2,700
1961-1964	2 Hi-Lo	$2,300	$3,000
1965-1967	2 pickups	$2,200	$2,900
1968-1970	2 pickups	$2,100	$2,700
1971-1980	7655	$2,100	$2,700

Chet Atkins Tennessee Rose (6119-1959, 1962)

1995-2015. Import, 16" maple body, maple neck, dual FilterTron pickups.

1995-2015		$1,525	$2,000

Clipper (6185/6186/6187/7555)

1958-1975. Archtop electric, single-cut, sunburst, 1 pickup (6186) until '72 and 2 pickups (6185) from '72-'75, also available in 1 pickup natural (6187) from '59-'61.

1958-1961	6186	$925	$1,200
1959-1961	6187	$1,025	$1,325
1962-1967	6186	$900	$1,175
1968-1971	6186	$825	$1,075
1972-1975	7555	$1,025	$1,325

Committee (7628)

1977-1980. Neck-thru electric solid body, double-cut, walnut and maple body, 2 pickups, 4 knobs, natural.

1977-1980		$725	$950

Constellation

1955-1960. Renamed from Synchromatic 6030 and 6031, archtop acoustic, single-cut, G tailpiece, humped block inlay.

1955-1960		$1,425	$1,850

Convertible (6199)

1955-1958. Archtop electric, single-cut, 1 pickup, multi-bound body, G tailpiece, renamed Sal Salvador in '58.

1955-1958		$1,900	$2,475

Corsair

1955-1960. Renamed from Synchromatic 100, archtop acoustic, bound body and headstock, G tailpiece, available in sunburst (6014), natural (6015) or burgundy (6016).

1955-1960		$815	$1,050

Corvette (Hollow Body)

1955-1959. Renamed from Electromatic Spanish, archtop electric, 1 pickup, f-holes, bound body, Electromatic on headstock, non-cut, sunburst (6182), natural or Jaguar Tan (6184), and ivory with rounded cutaway (6187).

1955-1959	6182, sunburst	$925	$1,200
1955-1959	6184, Jaguar Tan	$1,225	$1,575
1955-1959	6184, natural	$1,225	$1,575
1957-1959	6187, ivory	$1,225	$1,575

Corvette (Solid Body)

1961-1972, 1976-1978. Double-cut slab solid body. Mahogany 6132 and cherry 6134 1 pickup for '61-'68. 2 pickup mahogany 6135 and cherry 7623 available by '63-'72 and '76-'78. From late-'61 through '63 a Twist option was offered featuring a red candy stripe 'guard. Platinum Gray 6133 available for '61-'63 and the Gold Duke and Silver Duke sparkle finishes were offered in '66.

1961-1962	Mahogany, cherry	$900	$1,150
1961-1963	Platinum Gray	$1,350	$1,750
1961-1963	Twist 'guard	$1,350	$1,750
1963-1965	Custom color, 1 pu	$1,350	$1,750
1963-1965	Custom color, 2 pus	$1,600	$2,100
1963-1965	Mahogany, cherry, 1 pu	$700	$900
1963-1965	Mahogany, cherry, 2 pus	$975	$1,275
1966	Gold Duke	$1,350	$1,750
1966	Silver Duke	$1,350	$1,750
1966-1968	Mahogany, cherry, 1 pu	$750	$1,000

MODEL YEAR	FEATURES	EXC. COND. LOW	HIGH
1966-1968	Mahogany, cherry, 2 pus	$925	$1,200
1969-1972	Mahogany, cherry, 2 pus	$900	$1,175
1976-1978	7623, 2 pus	$750	$975

Corvette/CVT (5135)

2006-2018. Like double-cut solid body Corvette, 2 Mega'Tron pickups, Bigsby, becomes the CVT in '10.

2006-2018		$600	$800

Country Classic I/II (6122 Reissue)

1989-2006. Country Gentleman reissue in '58 (I) and '62 (II) specs. Also cataloged as G6122-1958 and G6122-1962 Country Classic.

1989-2006	'58, single-cut	$1,700	$2,200
1989-2006	'62, double-cut	$1,700	$2,200

Country Classic II Custom Edition (6122)

2005. Reissue of George Harrison's 2nd 6122 Country Gentleman, the Custom Edition has TV Jones Filtertron pickups.

2005		$1,700	$2,200

Country Club

1954-1981. Renamed from Electro II Cutaway, archtop electric, single-cut, 2 pickups (Filter Trons after '57), G tailpiece, multi-bound, various colors.

1954-1958	Sunburst	$3,400	$4,400
1954-1959	Cadillac Green	$4,400	$5,700
1954-1959	Natural	$4,000	$5,150
1959	Sunburst	$4,000	$5,150
1960-1964	Cadillac Green	$3,500	$4,550
1960-1964	Sunburst	$2,675	$3,450
1961-1962	Natural	$2,675	$3,450
1965-1969	Sunburst or walnut	$1,800	$2,300
1970-1981	Various colors	$1,875	$2,400

Country Club 1955 (6196-1955)(FGE)

1995-1999. U.S.-made reissue of Country Club, single-cut, 2 DeArmond pickups, hand-rubbed lacquer finish.

1995-1999		$1,700	$2,200

Country Club (6196, etc.)

2001-present. Includes Cadillac Green (G6196, '01-present), sunburst (G6192, '03-'08), amber natural (G6193,'03-'08), Bamboo Yellow (G6196TSP-BY, '09-'13), and smoky gray and violet 2-tone (G6196TSP-2G, '09-'12), G6196T-59GE Golden Era Edition ('16-present), T means Bigsby.

2001-2020	Cadillac Green	$1,700	$2,200
2009-2013	Bamboo Yellow	$1,700	$2,200

Country Roc (7620)

1974-1978. Single-cut solid body, 2 pickups, belt buckle tailpiece, western scene fretboard inlays, G brand, tooled leather side trim.

1974-1978		$1,750	$2,275

Custom (6117)

1964-1968. Limited production, smaller thinner version of Double Anniversary model, 2 pickups, cat's eye soundholes, red or black finish.

1964		$2,800	$3,600
1965-1966		$2,400	$3,100
1967-1968		$2,150	$2,800

MODEL YEAR	FEATURES	EXC. COND. LOW	HIGH

Deluxe Chet (7680/7681)

1972-1974. Electric archtop with rounded cutaway, Autumn Red (7680) or brown walnut (7681) finishes.

1972-1974		$1,700	$2,200

Deluxe Flat-Top (7535)

1972-1978. 16" redwood top, mahogany back and sides.

1972-1978		$1,550	$2,000

Double Anniversary Mono (6117/6118)

1958-1976. Archtop electric, single-cut, 2 pickups, stereo optional until '63, sunburst (6117) or green 2-tone (6118). Reissued in '93 as the Anniversary 6117 and 6118.

1958-1959	Green 2-tone	$2,800	$3,600
1958-1959	Sunburst	$2,000	$2,600
1960-1961	Green 2-tone	$2,150	$2,800
1960-1961	Sunburst	$1,800	$2,350
1962-1964	Green 2-tone or tan	$2,225	$2,900
1962-1964	Sunburst	$1,800	$2,350
1965-1966	Various colors	$1,300	$1,700
1967-1969	Various colors	$1,100	$1,425
1970-1976	Various colors	$975	$1,275

Double Anniversary Stereo (6111/6112)

1961-1963. One stereo channel/signal per pickup, sunburst (6111) or green (6112).

1961-1963	Green	$2,150	$2,800
1961-1963	Sunburst	$1,800	$2,350

Duo-Jet (6128)

1953-1971. Solid body electric, single-cut until '61, double after, 2 pickups, block inlays to late '56, then humptop until early '58, then thumbprint inlays, black (6128) with a few special order Cadillac Green, sparkle finishes were offered '63-'66, reissued in '90.

1953-1956	Black, single-cut	$5,000	$6,500
1956-1958	Black, humptop	$5,600	$7,300
1956-1958	Cadillac Green	$6,700	$8,700
1958-1960	Black, thumbprint	$4,000	$5,200
1961-1964	Black, double-cut	$3,300	$4,300
1963-1964	Sparkle, double-cut	$4,000	$5,200
1965-1966	Sparkle, double-cut	$3,300	$4,300
1965-1971	Black	$2,700	$3,500

Duo-Jet (6128-TCG)

2005-2016. Cadillac Green, gold hardware, Bigsby.

2005-2016		$1,700	$2,200

Duo-Jet Reissue (6128/6128T)

1990-2017. Reissue of the '50s solid body, optional Bigsby (G6128T). Replaced by Vintage Select Edition series.

1990-2017		$1,475	$1,900

Duo-Jet Tenor

1959-1960. Electric tenor, 4 strings, block inlays, black.

1959-1960		$2,675	$3,475

Duo-Jet Vintage Select Edition '59 (6128T-59)

2017-present. Bigsby, TV Jones Filter 'Trons, black.

2017-2020		$1,700	$2,200

Elliot Easton Signature Duo-Jet (6128TEE)

2000-2005. Bigsby, gold hardware, Cadillac Green (TEE), red (TREE), black (TBEE).

2000-2005		$1,700	$2,200

1964 Gretsch Double Anniversary Mono (6117/6118)

Guitar Maniacs

2016 Gretsch Duo-Jet Reissue (6128T)

David Crunden

GUITARS

1959 Gretsch Jet Firebird (6131)

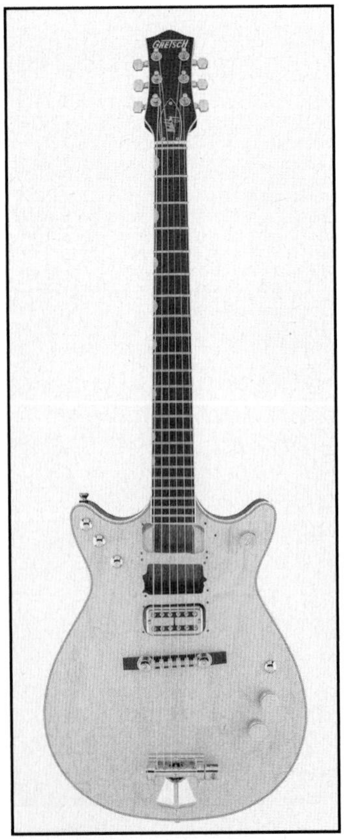

2019 Gretsch Malcom Young Signature Jet (6131-MY)

MODEL YEAR	FEATURES	EXC. COND. LOW	HIGH

Eldorado (6040/6041)

1955-1970, 1991-1997. This is the larger 18" version, renamed from Synchromatic 400, archtop acoustic, single-cut, triple-bound fretboard and peghead, sunburst (6040) or natural (6041). Reintroduced in '91, made by Heritage in Kalamazoo, as the G410 Synchromatic Eldorado in sunburst or natural (G410M).

1955-1959	Natural	$2,300	$3,000
1955-1959	Sunburst	$1,850	$2,400
1960-1963	Natural	$1,700	$2,200
1960-1963	Sunburst	$1,550	$2,000
1964	Natural	$1,425	$1,850
1964	Sunburst	$1,350	$1,750
1965-1997	Natural, sunburst	$1,200	$1,550

Eldorado (6038/6039)

1959-1968. The smaller 17" version, named Fleetwood from '55 to '58, sunburst (6038) or natural (6039), also available as a full body non-cutaway.

1959-1964	Natural, sunburst	$1,125	$1,450
1965-1968	Natural, sunburst	$925	$1,200

Electro Classic (6006/6495)

1969-1973. Classical flat-top with piezo pickup.

1969-1970	6006	$560	$725
1971-1973	6495	$560	$725

Electro II Cutaway (6192/6193)

1951-1954. Archtop electric, single-cut, Melita bridge by '53, 2 pickups, f-holes, sunburst (6192) or natural (6193). Renamed Country Club in '54.

1951-1954	6192, sunburst	$3,000	$3,900
1951-1954	6193, natural	$3,300	$4,300

Electro II Non-Cutaway (6187/6188)

1951-1954. 16" electric archtop, 2 DeArmonds, large f-holes, block markers, 6187 sunburst, 6188 natural, label is Model 6187-8, vertical Electromatic logo on headstock.

1951-1954	6187, sunburst	$925	$1,200
1951-1954	6188, natural	$1,025	$1,325

Electromatic (5420T)

2013-present. Hollow body, single-cut, Bigsby.

2013-2020		$600	$800

Electromatic (5422-12)

2013-present. 12-string 5422.

2013-2020		$600	$800

Electromatic (5422T)

2013-present. Hollow body, double-cut, Bigsby.

2013-2020		$600	$800

Electromatic Hollow Body (5120/5125-29/5420)

2005-2020. Single-cut, 2 dual-coils, Bigsby, black, Aspen Green, sunburst or orange. With Filter'Tron pickups in '13 (5420).

2005-2020		$600	$800

Electromatic Hollow Body (5122/5422)

2009-2014. Double-cut version of G5120, 2 dual-coils, Bigsby, black, trans red or walnut. With Filter'Tron pickups in '13 (5422). Replaced with G5422T.

2009-2014		$600	$800

Tim Armstrong Signature Electromatic (5191BK)

2010-present. Hollow body, single-cut, all maple, 2 Filter'Tron pickups, black.

2010-2020		$600	$800

Electromatic Spanish (6185/6185N)

1940-1955. Hollow body, 17" wide, 1 pickup, sunburst (6185) or natural (6185N). Renamed Corvette (hollowbody) in '55.

1940-1949	Sunburst	$1,150	$1,500
1950-1955	Natural	$1,150	$1,500
1950-1955	Sunburst	$1,075	$1,400

Fleetwood (6038/6039)

1955-1958. Named Synchromatic prior to '55, single-cut, sunburst (6038) or natural (6039). Renamed Eldorado in '59, available by custom order.

1955-1958	Natural	$2,600	$3,400
1955-1958	Sunburst	$2,100	$2,700

Folk/Folk Singing (6003/7505/7506)

1963-1975. Lower-model of Gretsch flat-tops, 14 1/4", mahogany back and sides. Renamed from Jimmie Rodgers model, renamed Folk Singing in '63.

1963-1964		$600	$800
1965-1969		$525	$675
1970-1975		$450	$575

Golden Classic (Hauser/6000)

1961-1969. Grand Concert body size, nylon-string classical, 14 1/4" spruce top, mahogany back and sides, multiple inlaid sound hole purfling, inlaid headstock.

1961-1969		$400	$525

Grand Concert (6003)

1955-1959. Lower-model of Gretsch flat-tops, 14 1/4", mahogany back and sides. Renamed from Model 6003 and renamed Jimmie Rodgers in '59.

1955-1959		$625	$825

Guitar-Banjo

1920s. 6-string guitar neck on banjo body, slotted headstock, open back.

1920s		$525	$675

Jet 21

Late-1940s. 16" acoustic archtop, Jet 21 engraved logo on headstock, bound top and back, white 'guard, jet black finish.

1947-1948		$600	$775

Jet Firebird (6131)

1955-1971. Solid body electric, single-cut until '61, double '61-'71, 2 pickups, black body with red top, block inlays to late '56, then humptop until early '58, then thumbprint inlays.

1955-1958	Single-cut	$5,225	$6,800
1959-1960	Single-cut	$4,475	$5,800
1961-1964	Double-cut	$3,700	$4,825
1965-1967		$3,100	$4,000
1968-1971	Super Trons	$3,100	$4,000

Jet Firebird Reissue/Power Jet Firebird (6131/6131T)

1989-1997, 2003-2019. Single-cut '58 specs, red top, 2 FilterTrons, thumbprint markers, gold hardware for '91-'05, currently chrome. Bigsby available (T). Non-Bigsby 6131 ends in '05. DynaSonic-equipped TDS starts in '05 and TV Jones PowerTrons (TVP) in '06.

2003-2019		$1,425	$1,875

Jet/Pearl Jet/Blue Pearl Jet (6129/6129T)

1996-2011. Chambered mahogany body with maple top, unique Pearl or Blue Pearl finish.

1996-2011		$1,425	$1,875

MODEL YEAR	FEATURES	EXC. COND. LOW	HIGH

Jimmie Rodgers (6003)

1959-1962. 14" flat-top with round hole, mahogany back and sides, renamed from Grand Concert and renamed Folk Singing in '63.

1959-1962		$625	$825

Jumbo Synchromatic (125F)

1947-1955. 17" flat-top, triangular soundhole, bound top and back, metal bridge anchor plate, adjustable wood bridge, natural top with sunburst back and sides or optional translucent white-blond top and sides.

1947-1955	Natural	$1,725	$2,250
1947-1955	White-blond	$1,925	$2,500

Malcom Young Signature Jet (6131-MY)

2018-present. Professional Collection series, double-cut mahogany body, maple top, aged white binding, semi-gloss natural finish.

2018-2020		$1,700	$2,200

Model 25 (Acoustic)

1933-1939. 16" archtop, no binding on top or back, dot markers, sunburst.

1933-1939		$525	$675

Model 30 (Acoustic)

1939-1949. 16" archtop, top binding, dot markers, sunburst.

1939-1949		$600	$775

Model 35 (Acoustic)

1933-1949. 16" archtop, single-bound top and back, dot markers, sunburst.

1933-1949		$650	$850

Model 40 Hawaiian (Acoustic)

1936-1949. Flat-top, bound top and neck, diamond inlays.

1936-1949		$725	$950

Model 50/50R (Acoustic)

1936-1949. Acoustic archtop, f-holes. Model 50R (1936-'39) has round soundhole.

1936-1939	TG-50 Tenor	$550	$725
1936-1949	50/50R	$825	$1,075

Model 65 (Acoustic)

1933-1939. Archtop acoustic, bound body, amber.

1933-1939		$900	$1,175

Model 75 Tenor (Acoustic)

1933-1949. 4-string tenor.

1933-1949		$600	$775

Model 6003

1951-1955. 14 1/4", mahogany back and sides, renamed Grand Concert in '55.

1951-1954		$625	$825

Monkees

Late 1966-1968. Hollow body electric, double-cut, 2 pickups, Monkees logo on 'guard, bound top, f-holes and neck, vibrato, red.

1966-1968		$2,800	$3,700

New Yorker

Ca.1949-1970. Archtop acoustic, f-holes, sunburst.

1949-1959		$800	$1,050
1960-1964		$700	$925
1965-1969		$600	$800
1970		$500	$675

New Yorker Tenor (6050)

1950s. 4-string tenor version.

1950s		$485	$635

Ozark/Ozark Soft String (6005)

1965-1968. 16" classical, rosewood back and sides.

1965-1968		$465	$600

Princess (6106)

1963. Corvette-type solid body double-cut, 1 pickup, vibrato, gold parts, colors available were white/grape, blue/white, pink/white, or white/gold, often sold with the Princess amp.

1963		$1,600	$2,100

Rally (6104/6105)

1967-1969. Archtop, double-cut, 2 pickups, vibrato, racing stripe on truss rod cover and pickguard, Rally Green (6104) or Bamboo Yellow (6105).

1967-1969	6104 or 6105	$1,775	$2,300

Rambler (6115)

1957-1961. Small body electric archtop, single-cut, 1 DeArmond pickup '57-59, then 1 Hi-Lo 'Tron '60-'61, G tailpiece, bound body and headstock.

1957-1959	DeArmond	$1,200	$1,550
1960-1961	Hi-Lo 'Tron	$1,000	$1,300

Rancher

1954-1980. Flat-top acoustic, triangle soundhole, Western theme inlay, G brand until '61 and '75 and after, Golden Red (orange), reissued in '90.

1954-1957	G brand	$4,100	$5,400
1958-1961	G brand	$3,775	$4,900
1962-1964	No G brand	$3,000	$3,900
1965-1969	No G brand	$2,400	$3,100
1970-1974	No G brand	$2,000	$2,600
1975-1980	G brand	$2,000	$2,600

Roc I/Roc II (7635/7621)

1974-1976. Electric solid body, mahogany, single-cut, Duo-Jet-style body, 1 pickup (7635) or 2 pickups (7621), bound body and neck.

1974-1976	Roc I	$1,175	$1,525
1974-1977	Roc II	$1,350	$1,750

Roc Jet

1970-1980. Electric solid body, single-cut, 2 pickups, adjustamatic bridge, black, cherry, pumpkin or walnut.

1970-1980		$1,550	$2,000

Round-Up (6130)

1954-1960. Electric solid body, single-cut, 2 pickups, G brand, belt buckle tailpiece, maple, pine, knotty pine or orange. Reissued in '90.

1954-1956	Knotty pine (2 knots)	$10,000	$13,000
1954-1956	Knotty pine (4 knots)	$11,200	$14,600
1954-1956	Mahogany (few made)	$9,200	$12,000
1954-1956	Maple	$9,200	$12,000
1954-1956	Pine	$10,000	$13,000
1957-1960	Orange	$9,200	$12,000

Round-Up Reissue (6121/6121W)

1989-1995, 2003-2006. Based on the '50s model, Bigsby, Western Orange.

1989-2006		$1,525	$1,975

1967 Gretsch Rally (6104/6105)

Rivington Guitars

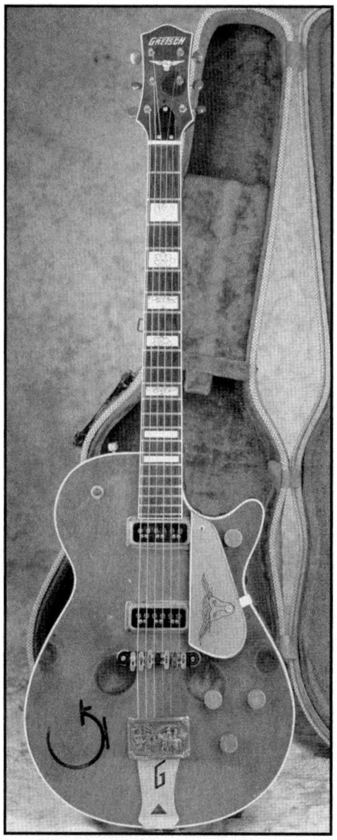

1954 Gretsch Round-Up (6130)

GUITARS

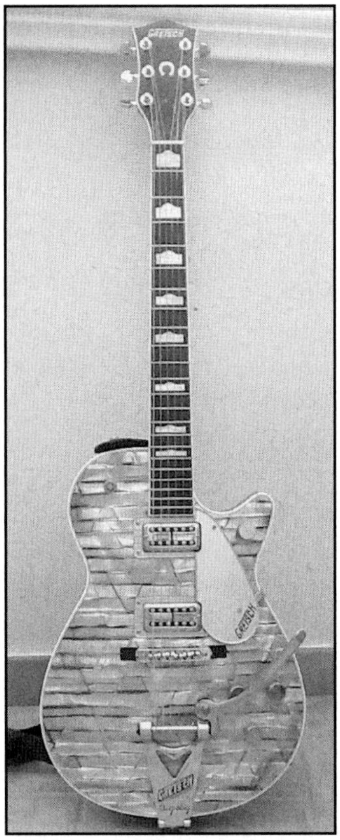

Gretsch Sparkle Jet 6129TL

Angelo Guarini

1968 Gretsch Streamliner Double Cutaway 6103

Tom Pfeifer

MODEL YEAR	FEATURES	EXC. COND. LOW	HIGH

Round-Up Western Leather Trim (6130)

2006-2007. Higher-end reissue of '55 Round-Up, G brand, tooled leather around edge.

2006-2007 $1,775 $2,300

Round-Up Knotty Pine (6130KPW)

2008-2010. Like '06 6130 but with belt buckle tailpiece and knotty pine top.

2008-2010 $2,600 $3,400

Sal Fabraio (6117)

1964-1968. Double-cut thin electric archtop, distinctive cats-eye f-holes, 2 pickups, sunburst, ordered for resale by guitar teacher Sal Fabraio.

1964-1968 $1,650 $2,100

Sal Salvador (6199)

1958-1968. Electric archtop, single-cut, 1 pickup, triple-bound neck and headstock, sunburst.

1958-1959		$1,900	$2,475
1960-1962		$1,650	$2,175
1963-1964		$1,375	$1,800
1965-1968		$1,225	$1,600

Sho Bro (Hawaiian/Spanish)

1969-1978. Flat-top acoustic, multi-bound, resonator, lucite fretboard, Hawaiian version non-cut, square neck and Spanish version non- or single-cut, round neck.

1969-1978	Hawaiian	$675	$875
1969-1978	Spanish	$625	$825

Sierra Jumbo (3700)

1999-2005. Historic series, single-cut jumbo body, triangular soundhole, sunburst finish.

1999-2005 $360 $470

Silver Classic (Hauser/6001)

1961-1969. Grand Concert body size, nylon-string classical. Similar to Golden Classic but with less fancy appointments.

1961-1969 $350 $450

Silver Falcon (6136SL) (1955) (T)

1995-1999, 2003-2005. Black finish, silver features, single cut, G tailpiece available until '05, T for Bigsby available starting '05. Had the 1955 designation in the '90s.

1995-1999 $1,700 $2,200

Silver Falcon (7594SL)

1995-1999. Black finish and silver features, double-cut, 2" thick body.

1995-1999 $1,700 $2,200

Silver Jet (6129)

1954-1963. Solid body electric, single-cut until '61, double '61-'63, 2 pickups, Duo-Jet with silver sparkle top, reissued in '89. Optional sparkle colors were offered but were not given their own model numbers; refer to Duo-Jet listing for optional colors.

1954-1960	Single-cut	$5,025	$6,525
1961-1963	Double-cut	$4,000	$5,200

Silver Jet 1957 Reissue (6129-1957)

1989-2019. Reissue of single-cut '50s Silver Jet, silver sparkle. '1957' added to name in '94.

1989-2019 $1,200 $1,600

Silver Jet 1962 Reissue (6129-1962)

1996-2009. Reissue of '60s double-cut Silver Jet, silver sparkle.

1996-2009 $1,200 $1,600

MODEL YEAR	FEATURES	EXC. COND. LOW	HIGH

Songbird (Sam Goody 711)

1967-1968. Standard body thinline double-cut with G soundholes, offered by Sam Goody of New York.

1967-1968 $2,300 $3,000

Southern Belle (7176)

1983. Electric archtop, walnut, parts from the late-'70s assembled in Mexico and U.S., 5 made with all original parts, several others without pickguard and case.

1983 $925 $1,225

Sparkle Jet (6129/6129T/6129TG)

1995-2019. Duo-Jet with sparkle finishes other than Silver, single-cut, 2 pickups. Many different colors offered over the years.

1995-2019 $1,200 $1,600

Streamliner Single Cutaway (6189/6190/6191)

1955-1959. Electric archtop, single-cut, maple top, G tailpiece, 1 pickup, multi-bound, Jaguar Tan (6189), sunburst (6190), or natural (6191), name reintroduced as a double-cut in '68.

1955-1959	6189	$2,250	$2,925
1955-1959	6190	$1,550	$2,025
1955-1959	6191	$2,100	$2,750

Streamliner Center Block Jr. (2655T)

2016-present. Double-cut, spruce center block, Bigsby, black, walnut stain or Golddust.

2016-2020 $365 $475

Streamliner Double Cutaway (6102/6103)

1968-1973. Reintroduced from single-cut model, electric archtop, double-cut, 2 pickups, G tailpiece, cherry or sunburst.

1968-1973 $1,200 $1,575

Sun Valley (6010/7515/7514)

1959-1977. Flat-top acoustic, laminated Brazilian rosewood back and sides, multi-bound top, natural or sunburst.

1959-1964	6010	$800	$1,025
1965-1970	6010	$625	$825
1971-1972	7515	$575	$750
1973-1977	7514	$575	$750

Super Chet (7690/7690-B/7691/7691-B)

1972-1980. Electric archtop, single rounded cutaway, 2 pickups, gold hardware, mini control knobs along edge of 'guard, Autumn Red or walnut.

1972-1980 $2,250 $2,950

Supreme (7545)

1972-1978. Flat-top 16", spruce top, mahogany or rosewood body options, gold hardware.

1972-1978	Mahogany	$2,700	$3,500
1972-1979	Rosewood	$2,700	$3,500

Synchromatic (6030/6031)

1951-1955. 17" acoustic archtop, becomes Constellation in '55.

1951-1955 6030 or 6031 $950 $1,250

Synchromatic (6038/6039)

1951-1955. 17" acoustic archtop, single-cut, G tailpiece, multi-bound, sunburst (6038) or natural (6039), renamed Fleetwood in '55.

1951-1955 6038 or 6039 $1,075 $1,400

MODEL YEAR	FEATURES	EXC. COND. LOW	HIGH

Synchromatic 75

1939-1949. Acoustic archtop, f-holes, multi-bound, large floral peghead inlay. Tenor available.

1939-1949		$700	$900
1939-1949	Tenor	$450	$575

Synchromatic Jr. (3900)

2000-2003. Historic Series, 15" single-cut archtop acoustic.

2000-2003		$800	$1,025

Synchromatic 100 (6014/6015)

1939-1955. Renamed from No. 100F, acoustic archtop, double-bound body, amber, sunburst (6014) or natural (6015), renamed Corsair in '55.

1939-1949	Natural	$650	$850
1939-1949	Sunburst	$575	$750
1950-1955	Natural	$600	$775

Synchromatic 160 (6028/6029)

1939-1943, 1947-1951. Acoustic archtop, cats-eye soundholes, maple back and sides, triple-bound, natural or sunburst.

1939-1943	Sunburst	$950	$1,225
1947-1951	Sunburst	$825	$1,075
1948-1951	Natural	$950	$1,225

Synchromatic 200

1939-1949. Acoustic archtop, cats-eye soundholes, maple back and sides, multi-bound, gold-plated hardware, amber or natural.

1939-1949		$1,025	$1,325

Synchromatic 300

1939-1955. Acoustic archtop, cats-eye soundholes until '51 and f-holes after, multi-bound, natural or sunburst.

1939-1949	Natural	$1,875	$2,450
1939-1949	Sunburst	$1,650	$2,150
1950-1955	Natural	$1,650	$2,150
1950-1955	Sunburst	$1,550	$2,000

Synchromatic 400

1940-1955. Acoustic archtop, cats-eye soundholes until '51 and f-holes after, multi-bound, gold hardware, natural or sunburst.

1940-1949	Natural	$3,700	$4,800
1940-1949	Sunburst	$3,400	$4,400
1950-1955	Natural	$3,400	$4,400
1950-1955	Sunburst	$4,100	$5,300

Synchromatic 400F/6042 Flat-Top

1947-1955. 18" flat-top, renamed 6042 in the late '40s.

1947-1948	400F	$3,675	$4,775
1949-1955	6042	$3,675	$4,775

Synchromatic G400/400C

1990-2008. Acoustic archtop, full-body, non-cut (400) or single-cut (C), sunburst.

1990-2008	G400	$950	$1,225
1990-2008	G400C	$950	$1,225

Synchromatic Limited (450/450M)

1997. Acoustic archtop, hand carved spruce (G450) or maple (G450M) top, floating pickup, sunburst, only 50 were to be made.

1997	Maple	$1,025	$1,325
1997	Spruce	$925	$1,200

Synchromatic Sierra

1949-1955. Renamed from Synchromatic X75F (see below), acoustic flat-top, maple back and sides, triangular soundhole, sunburst.

1949-1955		$1,125	$1,450

Synchromatic X75F

1947-1949. Acoustic flat-top, maple back and sides, triangular soundhole, sunburst, renamed Synchromatic Sierra in '49.

1947-1949		$1,125	$1,450

TK 300 (7624/7625)

1977-1981. Double-cut maple solid body, 1 humbucker, bolt-on neck, six-on-a-side tuners, hockey stick headstock, Autumn Red or natural.

1977-1981		$550	$700

Town and Country (6021)

1954-1959. Renamed from Jumbo Synchromatic 125 F, flat-top acoustic, maple back and sides, triangular soundhole, multi-bound.

1954-1959		$1,825	$2,425

Traveling Wilburys (TW300T)

1988-1990. Promotional guitar, solidbody electric, single-cut, 1 and 2 pickups, 6 variations, graphics.

1988-1990		$400	$525

Van Eps 6-String (6081/6082)

1968-1971. Electric archtop, single-cut, 2 pickups, 6 strings.

1968-1971		$2,525	$3,275

Van Eps 7-String (6079/6080/7580/7581)

1968-1978. 7-string version, sunburst (6079) or walnut (6080), model numbers change to 7580 (sunburst) and 7581 (walnut) in '72.

1968-1971	6079 or 6080	$2,500	$3,200
1972-1978	7580 or 7581	$2,300	$3,000

Viking

1964-1975. Archtop, double-cut, 2 pickups, vibrato, sunburst (6187), natural (6188) or Cadillac Green (6189). Re-designated 7585 (sunburst) and 7586 (natural) in '72.

1964	Cadillac Green	$3,550	$4,600
1964	Natural	$3,150	$4,075
1964	Sunburst	$2,200	$2,850
1965-1971	Cadillac Green	$2,575	$3,350
1965-1971	Natural	$2,500	$3,250
1965-1971	Sunburst	$1,800	$2,325
1972-1975	Sunburst, natural	$1,650	$2,125

Wayfarer Jumbo (6008)

1969-1971. Flat-top acoustic dreadnought, non-cut, maple back and sides, multi-bound, Wayfarer and sailing ship logo on 'guard.

1969-1971		$775	$1,000

White Falcon Mono (6136/7594)

1955-1981. Includes the single-cut 6136 of '55-'61, the double-cut 6136 of '62-'70, and the double-cut 7594 of '71-'81.

1955-1960	6136, single-cut	$20,000	$26,000
1961	6136, single-cut	$19,500	$25,500
1962-1964	6136, double-cut	$9,300	$12,000
1965-1969		$6,300	$8,200
1970		$5,600	$7,300
1971-1972	7594	$4,600	$6,000
1973-1981	7594	$4,500	$5,900

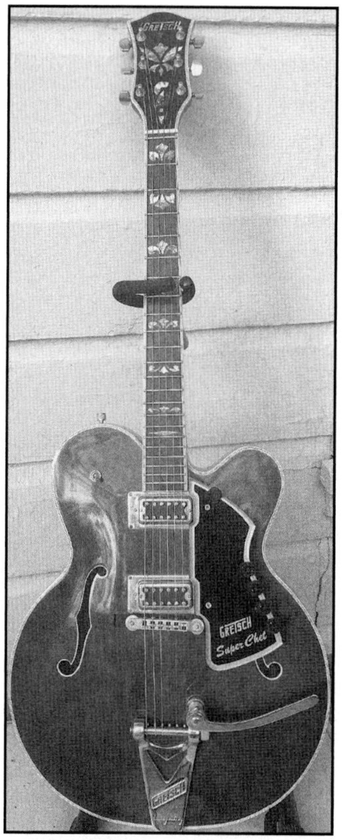

1972 Gretsch Super Chet
KC Cormack

1988 Gretsch Traveling Wilburys (TW300T)
Ted Wulfers

Grosh ElectraJet Custom

1967 Gruggett

MODEL YEAR	FEATURES	EXC. COND. LOW	HIGH

White Falcon Stereo (6137/7595)

1958-1981. Features Project-O-Sonic Stereo, includes the single-cut 6137 of '58-'61, the double-cut 6137 of '62-'70, and the double-cut 7595 of '71-'81.

1958-1961	6137, single-cut	$21,000	$28,000
1962-1964	6137, double-cut	$10,100	$13,100
1965-1969		$6,900	$8,900
1970		$6,100	$7,900
1971-1972	7595	$5,100	$6,550
1973-1981	7595	$4,500	$5,900

White Falcon (Import)

1989-present. Various imported models.

1989-2020	Various models	$2,200	$2,900

White Falcon Custom U.S.A. (6136-1955)

1995-1999. U.S.-made, single-cut, DynaSonic pickups, gold sparkle appointments, rhinestone embedded knobs, white. In '04, Current U.S. model called G6136CST is released. The import White Falcon has sometimes been listed with the 1955 designation and is not included here.

1995-1999		$2,700	$3,550

White Penguin (6134)

1955-1962. Electric solid body, single-cut until '61, double '61-'62, 2 pickups (DeArmond until '58 then Filter Tron), fewer than 100 made, white, gold sparkle bound, gold-plated parts. More than any other model, there seems a higher concern regarding forgery.

1956-1962		$88,000	$115,000

White Penguin (G6134)

1993, 2003-2018. White, single-cut, metalflake binding, gold hardware, jeweled knobs, Cadillac G tailpiece.

2003-2018		$1,900	$2,450

Greven

1969, 1975-present. Luthier John Greven builds his premium grade, production/custom, acoustic guitars in Portland, Oregon.

Griffin String Instruments

1976-present. Luthier Kim Griffin builds his professional and premium grade, production/custom, parlor, steel-string, and classical guitars in Greenwich, New York.

Grimes Guitars

1972-present. Premium and presentation grade, custom, flat-tops, nylon-strings, archtops, semi-hollow electrics made by luthier Steve Grimes originally in Port Townsend, Washington, and since '82 in Kula, Hawaii. He also made mandolins early on.

Grinnell

Late 1930s-early 1940s. Private brand made by Gibson for Grinnell Music of Detroit and Southeast Michigan, which at the time, was the largest music chain in the Detroit area.

KG-14

1940. Gibson-made L-00 flat-top style with maple sides and back, tortoise-style binding on top and back, ladder bracing.

1940		$1,500	$2,000

Groehsl

1890-1921. Chicago's Groehsl Company made guitars for Wards and other mass-marketers. In 1921 the company became Stromberg-Voisinet, which in turn became the Kay Musical Instrument Company.

Groove Tools

2002-2004. Korean-made, production, intermediate grade, 7-string guitars that were offered by Conklin Guitars of Springfield, Missouri. They also offered basses.

Grosh

1993-present. Professional and premium grade, production/custom, solid and semi-hollow body guitars and basses built by luthier Don Grosh originally in Santa Clarita, California and, since '05 in Broomfield, Colorado. He also builds basses. Grosh worked in production for Valley Arts from '84-'92. Guitars generally with bolt necks until '03 when set-necks were added to the line.

Classical Electric

1990s. Single-cut solidbody with nylon strings and piezo-style hidden pickup, highly figured top.

1990s		$1,225	$1,575

Custom S Bent Top/Bent Top Custom

2003-2019. Offset double-cut, figured maple carved top, 2 pickups.

2003-2019		$1,225	$1,575

Custom T Carve Top

2003-2012. Single-cut, figured maple carved top, 2 pickups.

2003-2012		$1,225	$1,575

ElectraJet Custom

2009-present. Modified offset double-cut, 2 P-90s, 2 hums, or single-single-hum pickups.

2009-2020		$1,225	$1,575

Retro Classic

1993-present. Offset double-cut, 3 pickups.

1993-2020		$1,225	$1,575

Retro Classic Vintage T

1993-present. Single-cut, black 'guard.

1993-2020		$1,225	$1,575

Gruen Acoustic Guitars

Luthier Paul Gruen builds professional grade, custom steel-string guitars, starting in 1999, in Chapel Hill, North Carolina.

Gruggett

Mid 1960s-2012. In the 1960s, luthier Bill Gruggett worked with Mosrite and Hallmark guitars as well as building electric guitars under his own name in Bakersfield, California. He continued to make his Stradette model for Hallmark guitars until his death in October, 2012.

Guernsey Resophonic Guitars

Production/custom, resonator guitars built by luthier Ivan Guernsey in Marysville, Indiana, starting in 1989.

MODEL YEAR	FEATURES	EXC. COND. LOW	HIGH

Guild

1952-present. Professional and premium grade, production/custom, acoustic and acoustic/electric guitars. They have built solid, hollow and semi-hollowbody guitars in the past. Founded in New York City by jazz guitarist Alfred Dronge, employing many ex-Epiphone workers. The company was purchased by Avnet, Inc. in '66 and the Westerly, Rhode Island factory was opened in '68. Hoboken factory closed in '71 and headquarters moved to Elizabeth, New Jersey. Company was in bankruptcy in '88 and was purchased by Faas Corporation, New Berlin, Wisconsin. The brand was purchased by Fender in '95 and production was moved from Westerly to the Fender plant in Corona, California in 2001. In '05, Fender moved Guild production to their newly-acquired Tacoma plant in Washington. In '08, production moved to the Ovation/Hamer plant in New Hartford, Connecticut. With the 2001 move to the Fender Corona plant, Bob Benedetto and Fender veteran Tim Shaw (who previously ran the Nashville-based custom shop) created a line of Guild acoustic guitars that were primarily based on vintage Guild Hoboken designs.

Designs of Tacoma-built Guild product were nothing like Tacoma guitars. The new Guilds were dovetail neck based with nitrocellulose finishes. Later, FMIC Guild introduced the Contemporary Series giving the Tacoma factory another line in addition to the vintage-based F and D model Traditional Series. In '14 Fender sold Guild to Cordoba Music Group, manufacturer of Cordoba acoustic guitars who moved production to Oxnard, California.

A-50

1994-1996. Original A-50 models can be found under the Cordoba A-50 listing, the new model drops the Cordoba name, size 000 flat-top, spruce top, Indian rosewood body.

1994-1996		$925	$1,200

Aragon F-30

1954-1986. Acoustic flat-top, spruce top, laminated maple arched back (mahogany back and sides by '59), reintroduced as just F-30 in '98.

1954-1959		$1,850	$2,400
1960-1969		$1,700	$2,200
1970-1986		$1,575	$2,025

Aragon F-30 NT

1959-1985. Natural finish version of F-30.

1959-1969		$2,000	$2,600
1970-1985		$1,850	$2,400

Aragon F-30 R

1973-1995. Rosewood back and sides version of F-30, sunburst.

1973-1979		$1,850	$2,400

Aristocrat M-75

1954-1963. Electric archtop, routed semi-hollow single-cut body, 2 pickups, sunburst, natural (added '59) or cherry (added '61), reintroduced as Bluesbird M-75 in '67.

1954-1959		$3,925	$5,100
1960-1963		$3,650	$4,750

Aristocrat M-75 Tenor

Mid-late 1950s. Tenor version of 6-string Aristocrat electric, dual soapbar pickups, 4 knobs.

1950s		$2,650	$3,450

Artist Award

1961-1999. Renamed from Johnny Smith Award, single-cut electric archtop, floating DeArmond pickup (changed to humbucker in '80), multi-bound, gold hardware, sunburst or natural.

1961-1969		$5,500	$7,200
1970-1999		$4,400	$5,800

Bluegrass D-25/D-25 M

1968-1999. Flat-top, mahogany top until '76, spruce after, mahogany back and sides, various colors, called Bluegrass D-25 M in late-'70s and '80s, listed as D-25 in '90s.

1968-1969		$600	$775
1970-1999		$575	$750

Bluegrass D-25-12

1987-1992, 1996-1998. 12-string version of D-25.

1987-1998		$550	$700

Bluegrass D-35

1966-1988. Acoustic flat-top, spruce top and mahogany back and sides, rosewood 'board and bridge, natural.

1966-1969		$1,000	$1,300
1970-1988		$925	$1,200

Bluegrass F-40/Valencia F-40

1954-1963, 1973-1983. Acoustic flat-top, spruce top, maple back and sides, rosewood 'board and bridge, natural or sunburst.

1954-1963	Valencia F-40	$2,800	$3,600
1973-1983	Bluegrass F-40	$1,200	$1,550

Bluegrass F-47

1963-1976. 16" narrow-waist style, mahogany sides and back, acoustic flat-top, spruce top, mahogany back and sides, bound rosewood 'board and bridge, natural.

1963-1969	Horses-art 'guard	$2,200	$2,900
1970-1976		$2,100	$2,725

Bluegrass Jubilee D-40

1963-1992. Acoustic flat-top, spruce top, mahogany back and sides, rosewood 'board and bridge, natural. Has been reissued.

1963-1969		$1,700	$2,200
1970-1992		$1,400	$1,800

Bluegrass Jubilee D-40 C

1975-1991. Acoustic flat-top, single Florentine cutaway, mahogany back and sides, rosewood 'board and bridge, natural.

1975-1991		$1,450	$1,875

Bluegrass Jubilee D-44

1965-1972. Acoustic flat-top, spruce top, pearwood back and sides, ebony 'board, rosewood bridge.

1965-1969		$1,475	$1,925
1970-1972		$1,375	$1,800

Bluegrass Jubilee D-44 M

1971-1985. Acoustic flat-top, spruce top, maple back & sides, ebony fingerboard, rosewood bridge.

1971-1985		$1,375	$1,800

1961 Guild Aristocrat M-75

Carter Vintage Guitars

1971 Guild Bluegrass D-35

Imaged by Heritage Auctions, HA.com

GUITARS

1970 Guild Bluesbird M-75

1995 Guild Brian May Pro

Rivington Guitars

MODEL YEAR	FEATURES	EXC. COND. LOW	HIGH

Bluegrass Special D-50

1963-1993. Acoustic flat-top, spruce top, rosewood back and sides, ebony fretboard, multi-bound.

1963-1968	Brazilian rosewood	$4,000	$5,200
1969-1979	Indian rosewood	$1,700	$2,200
1980-1993	Indian rosewood	$1,575	$2,050

Bluegrass Special D-50 (Reissue)/D-50

1999-2004, 2006-2014. Also available with pickup system, initially listed as D-50.

1999-2014		$1,375	$1,775

Blues 90

2000-2002. Bluesbird single-cut, chambered body, unbound rosewood board, dots, 2 Duncan 2 P-90s.

2000-2002		$975	$1,275

Bluesbird M-75 (Hollow Body)

1967-1970. Reintroduced from Aristocrat M-75, thinbody electric archtop of maple, spruce ('67) or mahogany, single-cut, 2 pickups, Deluxe has gold hardware, Standard chrome. A solidbody Bluesbird was also introduced in '70.

1967-1970		$2,325	$3,025

Bluesbird M-75 (Solid Body)

1970-1978. Solid body version of Bluesbird M-75, mahogany body, rounded cutaway, 2 pickups.

1970-1978	CS, plain top, chrome hdw	$1,800	$2,350
1970-1978	GS, flamed top, gold hdw	$2,275	$2,950

Bluesbird M-75 (Solid Body) Reintroduced

1984-1988.

1984-1985	3 single-coil pus	$1,025	$1,325
1986	EMG pickups	$1,025	$1,325
1987-1988	DiMarzio pickups	$1,025	$1,325

Bluesbird (Reintroduced)

1994-2003. Single-cut chambered solid body, 2 humbuckers, block inlays, available with AAA flamed top.

1994-2003		$1,200	$1,575
2001	Fender CS	$1,875	$2,450

Bluesbird

2011-2012. Single-cut solid body, Chesterfield headstock logo, flame maple top, block markers, 2 humbuckers, natural finish.

2011-2012		$1,225	$1,575

Brian May BHM-1

1984-1987. Electric solid body, double-cut, vibrato, 3 pickups, bound top and back, red or green, Brian May Pro, Special and Standard introduced in '94.

1984-1987		$2,600	$3,400

Brian May Pro

1994-1995. Electric solid body, double-cut, vibrato, 3 pickups, bound top and back, various colors.

1994-1995		$2,600	$3,400

Brian May Signature Red Special

1994. Signature initials on truss rod cover, script signature on back of headstock, BM serial number, dot markers, custom Duncan pickups, custom vibrola, red special finish.

1994		$2,600	$3,400

MODEL YEAR	FEATURES	EXC. COND. LOW	HIGH

CA-100 Capri

1956-1973. Acoustic archtop version of CE-100, sharp Florentine cutaway, solid spruce top, laminated maple back and sides, rosewood 'board and bridge, nickel-plated metal parts, natural or sunburst.

1956-1959		$1,700	$2,200
1960-1973		$1,550	$2,000

Capri CE-100

1956-1985. Electric archtop, single Florentine cutaway, 1 pickup (2 pickups by '83), maple body, Waverly tailpiece, sunburst, in '59-'82 CE-100 D listed with 2 pickups.

1956-1959		$1,775	$2,300
1960-1985		$1,625	$2,100

Capri CE-100 D

1956-1982. Electric archtop, single Florentine cutaway, 2 pickups, maple body, sunburst, Waverly tailpiece (D dropped, became the Capri CE-100 in '83).

1956-1959		$1,900	$2,500
1960-1982		$1,750	$2,300

Capri CE-100 T Tenor

1950s. Electric-archtop Capri 4-string tenor guitar, sunburst.

1956		$1,550	$2,000

CO-1/CO-1C

2006-2008. Vintage F-30 style, red cedar top, solid mahogany neck/back/sides, rosewood 'board, natural. CO-1C with soft cutaway.

2006-2008	CO-1	$775	$1,000
2006-2008	CO-1C	$825	$1,075

CO-2/CO-2C

2008. As CO-1 but with red spruce top, ebony 'board, and offered in blonde, Antique Burst or Ice Tea Burst. CO-2C with soft cutaway.

2008	CO-2	$775	$1,000
2008	CO-2C	$825	$1,075

Cordoba A-50

1961-1972. Acoustic archtop, lowest-end in the Guild archtop line, named Granada A-50 prior to '61.

1961-1965		$925	$1,225
1966-1972		$850	$1,125

Cordoba T-50 Slim

1961-1973. Thinbody version of Cordoba X-50.

1961-1965		$1,000	$1,300
1966-1969		$900	$1,200
1970-1972		$825	$1,100

Cordoba X-50

1961-1970. Electric archtop non-cut, laminated maple body, rosewood 'board, 1 pickup, nickel-plated parts.

1961-1965		$1,050	$1,350
1966-1970		$950	$1,250

CR-1 Crossroads Single E/Double E

1993-2000. Single-cut solid body acoustic, humbucker (S2 in '93) neck pickup and Piezo bridge, 97 single necks (Single E, '93-'97) and very few 6/12 double necks (Double E, '93, '98-'00) made by Guild custom shop.

1993-1997	Single neck	$1,300	$1,675
1993-2000	Double neck	$3,200	$4,100

Custom F-412 12-String

1968-1986. Special order only from '68-'74, then regular production, 17" wide body 12-string version of F-50 flat-top, spruce top, maple back and sides, arched back, 2-tone block inlays, gold hardware, natural finish.

MODEL YEAR	FEATURES	EXC. COND. LOW	HIGH
1968-1969		$1,850	$2,400
1970-1986		$1,575	$2,050

Custom F-512 12-String

1968-1986, 1990. Indian rosewood back and sides version of F-412. See F-512 for reissue.

MODEL YEAR	FEATURES	EXC. COND. LOW	HIGH
1968-1969		$2,200	$2,900
1970-1979		$2,000	$2,625
1980-1986		$1,850	$2,425

Custom F-612 12-String

1972-1973. Acoustic 12-string, similar to Custom F-512, but with 18" body, fancy mother-of-pearl inlays, and black/white marquee body, neck and headstock binding.

MODEL YEAR	FEATURES	EXC. COND. LOW	HIGH
1972-1973	Brazilian rosewood	$3,200	$4,200
1972-1973	Indian rosewood	$2,100	$2,725

Custom Shop 45th Anniversary

1997. Built in Guild's Nashville Custom Shop, all solid wood, spruce top, maple back and sides, high-end appointments, gold hardware, natural.

MODEL YEAR	FEATURES	EXC. COND. LOW	HIGH
1997		$2,200	$2,900

CV-1/CV-1C

2006-2008. F-40 style, solid Indian rosewood back/sides, rosewood 'board. CV-1C with sharp cutaway.

MODEL YEAR	FEATURES	EXC. COND. LOW	HIGH
2006-2008	CV-1	$775	$1,000
2006-2008	CV-1C	$825	$1,075

CV-2/CV-2C

2008. As CV-1 but with flamed maple back/sides, ebony 'board. CV-2C with sharp cutaway.

MODEL YEAR	FEATURES	EXC. COND. LOW	HIGH
2008	CV-2	$775	$1,000
2008	CV-2C	$825	$1,075

D-4 Series

1991-2002. Dreadnought flat-top, mahogany sides, dot markers.

MODEL YEAR	FEATURES	EXC. COND. LOW	HIGH
1991-2002	6-String	$525	$675
1992-1999	12-String	$525	$675

D-6 (D-6 E/D-6 HG/D-6 HE)

1992-1995. Flat-top, 15 3/4", mahogany back and sides, natural satin non-gloss finish, options available.

MODEL YEAR	FEATURES	EXC. COND. LOW	HIGH
1992-1995		$525	$675

D-15 Mahogany Rush

1983-1988. Dreadnought flat-top, mahogany body and neck, rosewood 'board, dot inlays, stain finish.

MODEL YEAR	FEATURES	EXC. COND. LOW	HIGH
1983-1988		$525	$675

D-15 12-String

1983-1985. 12-string version of Mahogany Rush D-15.

MODEL YEAR	FEATURES	EXC. COND. LOW	HIGH
1983-1985		$525	$675

D-16 Mahogany Rush

1984-1986. Like D-15, but with gloss finish.

MODEL YEAR	FEATURES	EXC. COND. LOW	HIGH
1984-1986		$625	$825

D-17 Mahogany Rush

1984-1988. Like D-15, but with gloss finish and bound body.

MODEL YEAR	FEATURES	EXC. COND. LOW	HIGH
1984-1988		$675	$875

D-25/D-25 M

2003. Solid mahogany body. Refer to Bluegrass D-25 for earlier models. Reintroduced in '06 as GAD-25.

MODEL YEAR	FEATURES	EXC. COND. LOW	HIGH
2003		$675	$875

D-26 (Guitar Center)

1995. Made for Guitar Center, spruce top, mahogany back and sides, natural finish.

MODEL YEAR	FEATURES	EXC. COND. LOW	HIGH
1995		$675	$875

D-30

1987-1999. Acoustic flat-top, spruce-top, laminated maple back and solid maple sides, rosewood 'board, multi-bound, various colors.

MODEL YEAR	FEATURES	EXC. COND. LOW	HIGH
1987-1999		$950	$1,250

D-40

1999-2007. Solid spruce top, mahogany back and sides, rosewood 'board. See earlier models under Bluegrass Jubilee D-40.

MODEL YEAR	FEATURES	EXC. COND. LOW	HIGH
1999-2007		$1,050	$1,350

D-40 Bluegrass Jubilee

2006-2014. Indian rosewood, red spruce top, mahogany back and sides, 3-piece neck (mahogany/walnut/mahogany).

MODEL YEAR	FEATURES	EXC. COND. LOW	HIGH
2006-2014	No pickup	$1,050	$1,350
2006-2014	With Duncan D-TAR	$1,100	$1,425

D-40 Richie Havens

2003-2014. Richie Havens signature logo on truss rod cover, mahogany sides and back, Fishman Matrix, natural.

MODEL YEAR	FEATURES	EXC. COND. LOW	HIGH
2003-2014		$1,100	$1,425

D-40C NT

1975-1991. Pointed cutaway version.

MODEL YEAR	FEATURES	EXC. COND. LOW	HIGH
1975-1991		$1,200	$1,575

D-46

1980-1985. Dreadnought acoustic, ash back, sides and neck, spruce top, ebony 'board, ivoroid body binding.

MODEL YEAR	FEATURES	EXC. COND. LOW	HIGH
1980-1985		$775	$1,000

D-50

See Bluegrass Special Model.

D-55

See TV Model.

D-55 50th Anniversary

2003. Brazilian rosewood, 1953-2003 Anniversary logo.

MODEL YEAR	FEATURES	EXC. COND. LOW	HIGH
2003		$3,800	$4,900

D-60

1987-1990, 1998-2000. Renamed from D-66, rosewood back and sides ('87-'90), maple ('98-'00), scalloped bracing, multi-bound top, slotted diamond inlay, G shield logo.

MODEL YEAR	FEATURES	EXC. COND. LOW	HIGH
1987-1990	Rosewood	$1,925	$2,500
1998-1999	Maple	$1,925	$2,500

D-64

1984-1986. Maple back and side, multi-bound body, notched diamond inlays, limited production.

MODEL YEAR	FEATURES	EXC. COND. LOW	HIGH
1984-1986		$1,925	$2,500

D-66

1984-1987. Amber, rosewood back and sides, 15 3/4", scalloped bracing, renamed D-60 in '87.

MODEL YEAR	FEATURES	EXC. COND. LOW	HIGH
1984-1987		$1,925	$2,500

1965 Guild Cordoba X-50

Tom Pfeifer

1975 Guild D-50

Daniel Malone

1963 Guild Duane Eddy DE-300

Earl Ward

2002 Guild F-47 RCE Grand Auditorium

Imaged by Heritage Auctions, HA.com

MODEL YEAR	FEATURES	EXC. COND. LOW	HIGH

D-70

1981-1985. Dreadnought acoustic, spruce top, Indian rosewood back and sides, multi-bound, ebony 'board with mother-of-pearl inlays.

1981-1985		$2,700	$3,500

D-70-12E

1981-1985. Only 2 made, 12-string version, Fishman electronics.

1981-1985		$2,700	$3,500

D-80

1983-1987. Non-carved heel.

1983-1987		$2,700	$3,500

D-100

1990-1998. Top-of-the-line dreadnought-size acoustic, spruce top, rosewood back and sides, scalloped bracing.

1990-1998		$2,700	$3,500

D-125

2011-2014. All mahogany with Indian rosewood 'board, natural or cherry red.

2011-2014		$400	$525

D-212 12-String

1981-1983. 12-string version of D-25, laminated mahogany back and sides, natural, sunburst or black, renamed D-25-12 in '87, reintroduced as D-212 '96-present.

1981-1983		$525	$675

D-412 12-String

1990-1997. Dreadnought, 12 strings, mahogany sides and arched back, satin finished, natural.

1990-1997		$1,000	$1,300

DC-130

1994-1995. US-made, limited run, D-style cutaway, flamed maple top/back/sides.

1994-1995		$2,300	$3,000

DCE True American

1993-2000. Cutaway flat-top acoustic/electric, 1 with mahogany back and sides, 5 with rosewood.

1993-2000	DCE1, DCE1 TA	$525	$700
1994-2000	DCE5	$625	$800

Del Rio M-30

1959-1964. Flat-top, 15", all mahogany body, satin non-gloss finish.

1959		$1,875	$2,425
1960-1964		$1,750	$2,250

Detonator

1987-1990. Electric solid body, double-cut, 3 pickups, bolt-on neck, Guild/Mueller tremolo system, black hardware.

1987-1990		$450	$575

DK-70 Peacock Limited Edition

1995-1996. Limited run of 50, koa, peacock 'guard.

1995-1996		$2,925	$3,800

Duane Eddy Deluxe DE-500

1962-1974, 1984-1987. Electric archtop, single rounded cutaway, 2 pickups (early years and '80s version have DeArmonds), Bigsby, master volume, spruce top with maple back and sides, available in blond (BL) or sunburst (SB).

1962	Natural	$5,400	$7,000
1962	Sunburst	$4,200	$5,500
1963	Natural	$5,400	$7,000
1963	Sunburst	$4,200	$5,500
1964	Natural	$5,400	$7,000
1964	Sunburst	$4,200	$5,500
1965	Natural	$4,300	$5,600
1965	Sunburst	$3,900	$5,000
1966	Natural	$4,000	$5,200
1966	Sunburst	$3,600	$4,700
1967-1969	Various colors	$3,600	$4,700
1970-1974	Various colors	$3,200	$4,200
1984-1987	Various colors	$2,700	$3,500

Duane Eddy Standard DE-400

1963-1974. Electric archtop, single rounded cutaway, 2 pickups, vibrato, natural or sunburst, less appointments than DE-500 Deluxe.

1963	Cherry (option)	$3,550	$4,600
1963	Natural	$3,550	$4,600
1963	Sunburst	$3,100	$4,000
1964	Cherry (option)	$3,300	$4,300
1964	Natural	$3,300	$4,300
1964	Sunburst	$3,100	$4,000
1965	Natural	$3,100	$4,000
1965	Sunburst	$2,550	$3,300
1966	Natural	$2,700	$3,500
1966	Sunburst	$2,300	$3,000
1967-1969	Various colors	$2,300	$3,000
1970-1974	Various colors	$1,900	$2,500

DV Series

1992-2001, 2007-2011. Acoustic flat-top, mahogany or rosewood back and sides, ebony or rosewood 'board, satin or gloss finish.

1992-2001	DV-52S	$1,174	$1,525
1993-1994	DV-76	$2,925	$3,800
1993-1995	DV-62	$1,300	$1,675
1994-1995	DV-72	$2,450	$3,150
1994-1995	DV-73	$2,425	$3,150
1995-1996	DV-74 Pueblo	$2,900	$3,800
1995-1999	DV-6	$650	$850
1999-2000	DV-25	$850	$1,100
1999-2001	DV-4	$525	$675

Economy M-20

1958-1965, 1969-1973. Mahogany body, acoustic flat-top, natural or sunburst satin finish.

1958-1959		$1,700	$2,175
1960-1969		$1,600	$2,025
1970-1973		$1,375	$1,800

F-4 CEHG

1992-2002. High Gloss finish, single-cut flat-top, acoustic/electric.

1992-2002		$525	$675

F-5 CE

1992-2001. Acoustic/electric, single-cut, rosewood back and sides, dot inlays, chrome tuners.

1992-2001		$525	$675

F-30

1990-2001. Formerly the Aragon F-30, made in Westerly, Rhode Island.

1990-2001		$900	$1,175

F-30 R-LS

1990s. Custom Shop model, other F-30 models are listed under Aragon F-30 listing, rosewood sides and back, bearclaw spruce top, limited production.

1990s		$1,150	$1,500

MODEL YEAR	FEATURES	EXC. COND. LOW	HIGH

F-44

1984-1987. Acoustic flat-top, maple, designed by George Gruhn.

1984-1987		$1,700	$2,225

F-45 CE

1983-1992. Acoustic/electric, single-cut, mahogany or maple back and sides, rosewood 'board, natural. Early '87 model was named GF-45CE, by mid '87 it was back to F-45CE.

1983-1984	Laminated mahogany	$725	$925
1985-1986	Flamed maple	$800	$1,050
1987	Early '87, GF-45CE	$800	$1,050
1987-1992	Mid '87, F-45CE	$800	$1,050

F-46 NT

1984. Jumbo body style flat-top, designed for Guild by George Gruhn.

1984		$2,150	$2,775

F-47 M/F-47 MC

2007-2016. Made in USA, solid flamed maple sides and back, MC with cutaway.

2007-2016	F-47 M	$1,350	$1,750
2007-2016	F-47 MC	$1,425	$1,850

F-47 R/F-47 RC

2008-2014. Solid rosewood sides and back, available with electronics, RC with cutaway.

2008-2014		$1,350	$1,750

F-47 RCE Grand Auditorium

1999-2003. Cutaway acoustic/electric, rosewood back and sides, block inlays.

1999-2003		$1,350	$1,750

F-50/F-50 R

2002-2016. Jumbo, solid spruce top, solid maple sides, arched laminated maple back, abalone rosette. See Navarre F-50/F-50 for earlier models.

2002-2016	F-50, maple	$1,575	$2,050
2002-2016	F-50R, rosewood	$1,575	$2,050

F-65 CE

1992-2001. Acoustic/electric, single-cut, rosewood back and sides, block inlay, gold tuners.

1992-2001		$1,575	$2,050

F-212 12-String

1964-1982. Acoustic flat-top jumbo, 12 strings, spruce top, mahogany back and sides, 16" body.

1964-1982		$1,150	$1,500

F-212 XL 12-String

1966-1986, 1998-2000. Acoustic flat-top, 17" body, 12 strings, spruce top, mahogany back and sides, ebony fingerboard.

1966-1986		$1,150	$1,500
1998-2000	F-212	$950	$1,225

F-312 Artist 12-String

1964-1973. Flat-top, rosewood back and sides, spruce top, no board inlay (but some in '72 may have dots).

1964-1968	Brazilian rosewood	$3,650	$4,750
1969-1973	Indian rosewood	$1,775	$2,300

F-412

2002-2016. Solid spruce top, solid maple back and sides, block inlays, 12-string. See Custom F-412 for earlier models.

2002-2016		$1,500	$1,950

F-512

2002-present. Solid spruce top, rosewood back and sides, 12-string. See Custom F-512 for earlier models.

2002-2020		$1,700	$2,200

Freshman M-65

1958-1973. Electric archtop, single-cut, mahogany back and sides, f-holes, 1 single-coil (some with 2), sunburst or natural top.

1958-1959		$1,600	$2,100
1960-1969		$1,300	$1,700
1970-1973		$1,275	$1,650

Freshman M-65 3/4

1958-1973. Short-scale version of M-65, 1 pickup.

1958-1959		$1,375	$1,800
1960-1969		$1,125	$1,450
1970-1973		$1,075	$1,400

FS-20 CE

1986-1987. Solid body acoustic, routed mahogany body.

1986-1987		$550	$725

FS-46 CE

1983-1986. Flat-top acoustic/electric, pointed cutaway, mahogany, black, natural or sunburst.

1983-1986		$650	$850

G-5 P

1988-ca.1989. Handmade in Spain, cedar top, gold-plated hardware.

1988-1989		$800	$1,050

G-37

1973-1986. Acoustic flat-top, spruce top, laminated maple back and sides, rosewood 'board and bridge, sunburst or natural top.

1973-1986		$800	$1,050

G-41

1974-1978. Acoustic flat-top, spruce top, mahogany back and sides, rosewood 'board and bridge, 20 frets.

1975-1978		$800	$1,050

G-45 Hank Williams Jr.

1982-1986, 1993-1996. Hank Williams Jr. logo on 'guard, flat-top.

1982-1996		$1,025	$1,325

G-75

1975-1977. Acoustic flat-top, 3/4-size version of D-50, spruce top, rosewood back and sides, mahogany neck, ebony 'board and bridge.

1975-1977		$800	$1,050

G-212 12-String

1974-1983. Acoustic flat-top 12-string version of D-40, spruce top, mahogany back and sides, natural or sunburst.

1974-1983		$800	$1,050

G-212 XL 12-String

1974-1983. Acoustic flat-top, 12 strings, 17" version of G-212.

1974-1983		$800	$1,050

G-312 12-String

1974-1987. Acoustic flat-top 12-string version of the D-50, spruce top, rosewood back and sides.

1974-1987		$975	$1,250

GAD (Guild Acoustic Design) Series

2004-2014. Imported, all models begin with GAD.

2004-2014	Various models	$375	$850

1974 Guild Navarre F50 R

Imaged by Heritage Auctions, HA.com

1975 Guild F-112 NT

Garrett Park

Guild George Barnes AcoustiLectric

1993 Guild JF-30

Imaged by Heritage Auctions, HA.com

MODEL YEAR	FEATURES	EXC. COND. LOW	HIGH

George Barnes AcoustiLectric

1962-1972. Electric archtop, single-cut, solid spruce top, curly maple back and sides, multi-bound, 2 humbuckers, gold-plated hardware, sunburst or natural finish.

1962-1972		$3,900	$5,000

George Barnes Guitar in F

1963-1973. Smaller electric archtop at 13.5", 2 humbuckers, chrome hardware.

1963-1973		$3,900	$5,000

GF-25

1987-1992. Acoustic flat-top, mahogany back and sides.

1987-1992		$725	$925

GF-25 C

1988-1991. Cutaway GF-25.

1988-1991		$825	$1,075

GF-30

1987-1991. Acoustic flat-top, maple back/sides/neck, multi-bound.

1987-1991		$975	$1,275

GF-40

1987-1991. Mahogany back and sides, multi-bound.

1987-1991		$1,100	$1,425

GF-45 CE

1987. Flamed maple body.

1987		$775	$1,000

GF-50

1987-1991. Acoustic flat-top, rosewood back and sides, mahogany neck, multi-bound.

1987-1991		$1,200	$1,575

GF-55

1990-1991. Jumbo acoustic, spruce top, rosewood back and sides, natural.

1990-1991		$1,600	$2,100

GF-60

1987-1989. Jumbo size, rosewood or maple sides and back, diamond markers.

1987-1989	GF-60M, maple	$2,025	$2,625
1987-1989	GF-60R, rosewood	$2,025	$2,625

GF-60 C

1987-1989. Cutaway GF-60.

1987-1989		$2,100	$2,725

Granada A-50 (Acoustic Archtop)

1956-1960. Lowest-end acoustic archtop in the Guild line, renamed Cordoba A-50 in '61.

1956-1960		$1,200	$1,550

Granada X-50

1954-1961. Electric archtop, non-cut, laminated all maple body, rosewood 'board and bridge, nickel-plated metal parts, 1 pickup, sunburst. Renamed Cordoba X-50 in '61.

1955-1959		$1,400	$1,800
1960-1961		$1,200	$1,600

GV Series

1993-1995. Flat-top, rosewood back and sides, various enhancements.

1993-1995	GV-52, gloss	$1,125	$1,475
1993-1995	GV-52, satin	$925	$1,200
1993-1995	GV-70, abalone, gloss	$1,175	$1,525
1993-1995	GV-72, herringbone, gloss	$1,175	$1,525

Jet Star S-50

1963-1970. Electric solid body, double-cut, mahogany or alder body, 1 pickup, vibrato optional by '65, asymmetrical headstock until '65. Reintroduced as S-50 in '72-'78 with body redesign.

1963-1965	3-on-side	$1,575	$2,050
1966-1969	6-in-line	$1,200	$1,550
1970	6-in-line	$1,125	$1,450

JF-4 NT

1992-1995. Jumbo flat-top, mahogany, natural.

1992-1995		$600	$800

JF-30

1987-2004. Jumbo 6-string acoustic, spruce top, laminated maple back, solid maple sides, multi-bound.

1987-2004		$1,025	$1,325

JF-30 E

1994-2004. Acoustic/electric version.

1994-2004		$1,100	$1,425

JF-30-12

1987-2004. 12-string version of the JF-30.

1987-2004		$1,025	$1,325

JF-50 R

1987-1988. Jumbo 6-string acoustic, rosewood back and sides, multi-bound.

1987-1988		$1,025	$1,325

JF-55

1989-2000. Jumbo flat-top, spruce top, rosewood body.

1989-2000		$1,450	$1,900

JF-55-12

1991-2000. 12-string JF-55.

1991-2000		$1,450	$1,900

JF-65

1987-1994. Renamed from Navarre F-50, Jumbo flat-top acoustic, spruce top, R has rosewood back and sides and M has maple.

1987-1994	JF-65M, maple	$1,700	$2,200
1987-1994	JF-65R, rosewood	$1,700	$2,200

JF-65-12

1987-2001. 12-string, version of JF-65.

1987-2001	JF-65M-12, maple	$1,700	$2,200
1987-2001	JF-65R-12, rosewood	$1,700	$2,200

JF-100

1992-1995. Jumbo, maple top, rosewood back and sides, abalone trim, natural.

1992-1995		$2,575	$3,400

JF-100-12

1992-1995. Jumbo 12-string version, carved heel.

1992-1995		$2,575	$3,400

Johnny Smith Award

1956-1961. Single-cut electric archtop, floating DeArmond pickup, multi-bound, gold hardware, sunburst or natural, renamed Artist Award in '61.

1956-1961		$7,300	$9,450

Johnny Smith Award Benedetto

2004-2006. Only 18 custom made under the supervision of Bob Benedetto, signed by Johnny Smith, with certificate of authenticity signed by Smith and Benedetto.

2004-2006	18 made	$5,100	$6,650

JV-72

1993-1999. Jumbo acoustic, custom turquois inlay.

1993-1999		$2,275	$2,950

MODEL YEAR	FEATURES	EXC. COND. LOW	HIGH

Liberator Elite

1988. Limited Edition, set-neck, offset double-cut solid body, figured maple top, mahogany body, rising-sun inlays, 3 active pickups, last of the Guild solidbodies.

1988		$950	$1,225

M-80 CS/M-80

1975-1984. Solidbody, double-cut, 2 pickups, introduced as M-80 CS with bound rosewood 'board and block inlays, shortened to M-80 in '80 with unbound ebony 'board and dots.

1975-1980		$1,225	$1,600

Manhattan X-170 (Mini-Manhattan X-170)

1985-2002. Called Mini-Manhattan X-170 in '85-'86, electric archtop hollow body, single rounded cutaway, maple body, f-holes, 2 humbuckers, block inlays, gold hardware, natural or sunburst.

1985-2002		$1,475	$1,925

Manhattan X-175 (Sunburst)

1954-1985. Electric archtop, single rounded cutaway, laminated spruce top, laminated maple back and sides, 2 pickups, chrome hardware, sunburst. Reissued as X-160 Savoy.

1954-1959		$2,025	$2,625
1960-1969		$1,800	$2,325
1970-1985		$1,675	$2,175

Manhattan X-175 B (Natural)

1954-1976. Natural finish X-175.

1954-1959		$2,025	$2,625
1960-1969		$1,800	$2,325
1970-1976		$1,675	$2,175

Mark I

1961-1972. Classical, Honduras mahogany body, rosewood 'board, slotted headstock.

1961-1969		$375	$475
1970-1973		$300	$400

Mark II

1961-1987. Like Mark I, but with spruce top and body binding.

1961-1969		$525	$700
1970-1979		$375	$500
1980-1987		$300	$400

Mark III

1961-1987. Like Mark II, but with Peruvian mahogany back and sides and floral soundhole design.

1961-1969		$550	$725
1970-1979		$475	$625
1980-1987		$375	$500

Mark IV

1961-1985. Like Mark III, but with flamed pearwood back and sides (rosewood offered in '61, maple in '62).

1961-1969	Pearwood	$600	$800
1970-1979	Pearwood	$550	$700
1980-1985	Pearwood	$450	$575

Mark V

1961-1987. Like Mark III, but with rosewood back and sides (maple available for '61-'64).

1961-1968	Brazilian rw	$1,225	$1,600
1969-1979	Indian rw	$600	$775
1980-1987	Indian rw	$475	$600

MODEL YEAR	FEATURES	EXC. COND. LOW	HIGH

Mark VI

1962-1973. Rosewood back and sides, spruce top, wood binding.

1962-1968	Brazilian rw	$1,600	$2,100
1969-1973	Indian rw	$775	$1,000

Mark VII Custom

1968-1973. Special order only, spruce top, premium rosewood back and sides, inlaid rosewood bridge, engraved gold tuners.

1962-1968	Brazilian rw	$1,850	$2,400
1969-1973	Indian rw	$875	$1,125

Navarre F-48

1972-1975. 17", mahogany, block markers.

1972-1975		$1,225	$1,600

Navarre F-50/F-50

1954-1986, 1994-1995. Acoustic flat-top, spruce top, curly maple back and sides, rosewood 'board and bridge, 17" rounded lower bout, laminated arched maple back, renamed JF-65 M in '87. Reissued in '94 and again in '02 as the F-50.

1954-1956		$4,100	$5,300
1957-1962	Pearl block markers	$4,100	$5,300
1963-1969	Ebony 'board	$3,700	$4,800
1970-1995		$1,875	$2,425

Navarre F-50 R/F-50 R

1965-1987. Rosewood back and side version of F-50, renamed JF-65 R in '87. Reissued in '02 as F-50R.

1965-1968	Brazilian rw	$5,000	$6,500
1969-1987	Indian rw	$2,300	$3,000

Nightbird

1985-1987. Single-cut solid body, tone chambers, 2 pickups, multi-bound, black or gold hardware, renamed Nightbird II in '87.

1985-1987		$1,925	$2,500

Nightbird I

1987-1988. Like Nightbird but with chrome hardware, less binding and appointments.

1987-1988		$1,925	$2,500

Nightbird II

1987-1992. Renamed from Nightbird, with black hardware, renamed Nightbird X-2000 in '92.

1987-1992		$1,925	$2,500

Nightbird X-2000

1992-1996. Renamed from Nightbird II.

1992-1996		$1,925	$2,500

Park Ave X-180

2005. Cutaway acoustic archtop, 2 pickups, block markers.

2005		$1,450	$1,875

Peregrine

1999-2005. Solid body acoustic, cutaway, Fishman.

1999-2005	Custom	$900	$1,150
1999-2005	Flamed maple	$950	$1,225
1999-2005	S7CE, (CS)	$950	$1,225
1999-2005	S7CE, (CS), quilted	$950	$1,225
1999-2005	Standard	$775	$1,025

Polara S-100

1963-1970. Double-cut mahogany or alder solid body, rosewood 'board, 2 single coils, built-in stand until '70, asymmetrical headstock, in '70 Polara dropped from title (see S-100), renamed Polara S-100 in '97.

1963-1970	2 or 3 pickups	$1,525	$1,975

Late 1950s Guild Johnny Smith Award

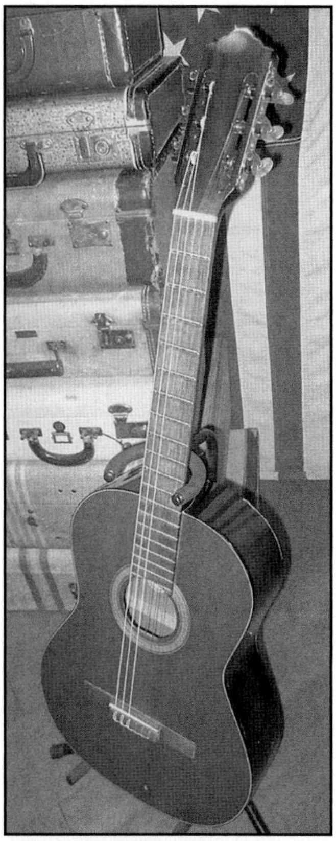

1975 Guild Mark III

Rivington Guitars

GUITARS

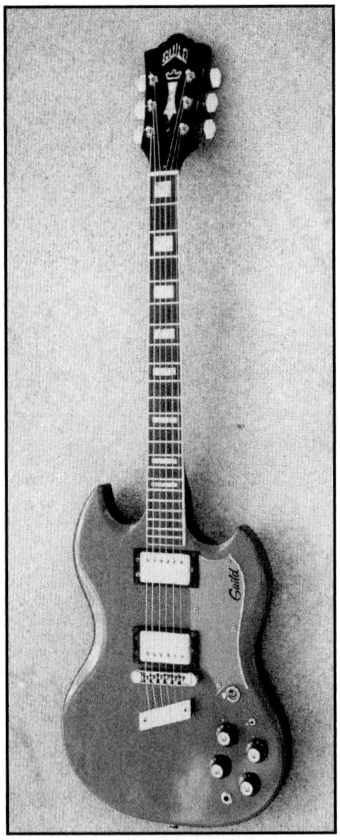

1976 Guild S-100

Willie Moseley

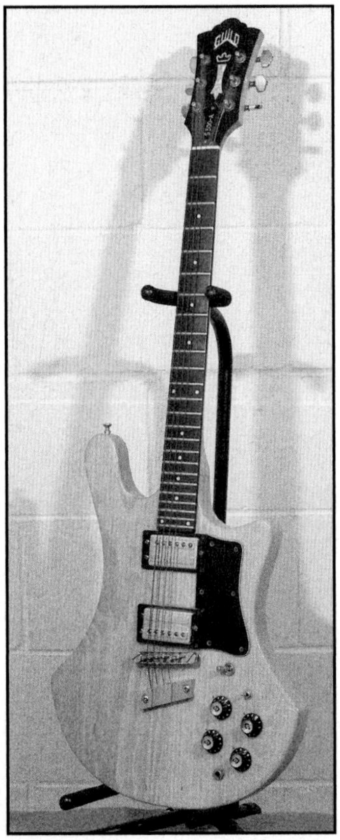

1978 Guild S-300A

Tom Pfeifer

MODEL YEAR	FEATURES	EXC. COND. LOW	HIGH

Roy Buchanan T-200

1986. Single-cut solid body, 2 pickups, pointed six-on-a-side headstock, poplar body, bolt-on neck, gold and brass hardware.

1986		$550	$725

S-50

1972-1978. Double-cut solid body, 1 single-coil (switched to humbucker in '74), dot inlay.

1972-1978		$925	$1,200

S-60/S-60 D

1976-1981. Double-cut solid body with long bass horn, 1 humbucker (60) or 2 single-coils (60 D), mahogany body, rosewood 'board.

1976-1981		$850	$1,100

S-65 D

1980-1981. S-60 but with 1 DiMarzio Super Distortion pickup.

1980-1981		$850	$1,100

S-70 D/S-70 AD

1979-1981. Solid body (mahogany D, ash AD), rosewood 'board, 3 single-coils.

1979-1981	S-70AD	$975	$1,250
1979-1981	S-70D	$925	$1,200

S-90

1972-1977. Double-cut SG-like body, 2 humbuckers, dot inlay, chrome hardware.

1972-1977		$975	$1,250

S-100

1970-1978, 1994-1996. S-100 Standard is double-cut solid body, 2 humbuckers, block inlays. Deluxe of '72-'75 had added Bigsby. Standard Carved of '74-'77 has acorns and oakleaves carved in the top.

1970-1978	Standard	$1,450	$1,900
1972-1975	Deluxe	$1,450	$1,900
1974-1977	Standard Carved	$1,450	$1,900

S-100 Reissue

1994-1997. Renamed Polara in '97.

1994-1997		$700	$925

S-250

1981-1983. Double-cut solid body, 2 humbuckers.

1981-1983		$450	$575

S-261

Ca.1985. Double-cut, maple body, black Kahler tremolo, 1 humbucker and 2 single-coil pickups, rosewood 'board.

1985		$450	$575

S-270 Runaway

1985. Offset double-cut solid body, 1 humbucker, Kahler.

1985		$450	$575

S-271 Sprint

1986. Replaced the S-270.

1986		$450	$575

S-275

1982-1983. Offset double-cut body, 2 humbuckers, bound figured maple top, sunburst or natural.

1982-1983		$450	$575

S-280 Flyer

1983-1984. Double-cut poplar body, 2 humbuckers or 3 single-coils, maple or rosewood neck, dot markers.

1983-1984		$450	$575

MODEL YEAR	FEATURES	EXC. COND. LOW	HIGH

S-281 Flyer

1983-1988. Double-cut poplar body S-280 with locking vibrato, optional pickups available.

1983-1988		$450	$575

S-284 Starling/Aviator

1984-1988. Starling (early-'84) and Aviator (late-'84-'88), double-cut, 3 pickups.

1984	Starling	$450	$575
1984-1988	Aviator	$450	$575

S-285 Aviator

1986. Deluxe Aviator, bound 'board, fancy inlays.

1986		$450	$575

S-300 Series

1976-1983. Double-cut mahogany solid body with larger bass horn and rounded bottom, 2 humbuckers. S-300 A has ash body, D has exposed DiMarzio humbuckers.

1976-1983	S-300	$700	$925
1977-1982	S-300D	$700	$925
1977-1983	S-300A	$700	$925

S-400/S-400 A

1980-1981. Double-cut solid body, mahogany (400) or ash (400 A), 2 humbuckers.

1980-1981		$825	$1,075

Savoy A-150

1958-1973, 2013-present. Acoustic archtop version of X-150, available with floating pickup, natural or sunburst finish. Reissued in '13, part of Newark St. Collection.

1958-1961	Natural	$1,900	$2,500
1958-1961	Sunburst	$1,775	$2,300
2013-2020		$1,050	$1,375

Savoy X-150

1954-1965. Electric archtop, rounded single-cut, spruce top, maple back and sides, rosewood 'board and bridge, 1 single-coil pickup, sunburst, blond or sparkling gold finish. Reissued in '98 as X-150 Savoy.

1954	Sunburst	$2,300	$3,000
1955-1959	Sunburst	$2,150	$2,800
1960-1965	Sunburst	$1,925	$2,500

Slim Jim T-100

1958-1973. Electric archtop thinline, single-cut, laminated all-maple body, rosewood 'board and bridge, Waverly tailpiece, 1 pickup, natural or sunburst.

1958-1959		$1,600	$2,100
1960-1964		$1,500	$2,000
1965-1969		$1,325	$1,725
1970-1973		$1,225	$1,625

Slim Jim T-100 D

1958-1973. Semi-hollow body electric, single Florentine cutaway, thinline, 2-pickup version of the T-100, natural or sunburst.

1958-1959		$1,750	$2,300
1960-1964		$1,600	$2,100
1965-1969		$1,525	$2,000
1970-1973		$1,300	$1,725

Songbird S Series

1984-1991. Designed by George Gruhn, flat-top, mahogany back, spruce top, single pointed cutaway, pickup with preamp, multi-bound top, black, natural or white. Renamed S-4 later in run.

1984-1991		$850	$1,125

MODEL YEAR	FEATURES	EXC. COND. LOW	HIGH

Standard (STD) Series
2010-2014. Imported flat-top acoustics based on various classic Guild models.

2010-2014	F-30 STD	$1,050	$1,350

Standard F-112 12-String
1968-1982. Acoustic flat-top, spruce top, mahogany back, sides and neck.

1968-1969		$875	$1,125
1970-1982		$725	$950

Starfire I
1960-1964. Electric archtop, single-cut thinline, laminated maple or mahogany body, bound body and neck, 1 pickup.

1960-1961	Starfire Red	$1,100	$1,425
1962-1964		$1,025	$1,325

Starfire II
1960-1976, 1997-2001. Electric archtop, single-cut thinline, laminated maple or mahogany body, bound body and rosewood neck, 2 pickups.

1960-1961	Sunburst	$1,850	$2,400
1962	Emerald Green	$1,750	$2,275
1962-1966	Special color options	$1,950	$2,525
1962-1966	Sunburst, Starfire Red	$1,675	$2,175
1967-1969	Sunburst, Starfire Red	$1,575	$2,050
1970-1976	Sunburst, Starfire Red	$1,475	$1,900
1997-2001	Reissue model	$1,075	$1,400

Starfire III
1960-1974, 1997-2005, 2013-present. Electric archtop, single-cut thinline, laminated maple or mahogany body, bound body and rosewood neck, 2 pickups, Guild or Bigsby vibrato, Starfire Red. Reissued in '13, part of Newark St. Collection.

1960-1966		$2,200	$2,900
1967-1974		$2,050	$2,700
1997-2005	Reissue model	$1,050	$1,400
2013-2020	Newark St	$750	$975

Starfire IV
1963-1987, 1991-2005. Thinline, double-cut semi-hollow body, laminated maple or mahogany body, f-holes, 2 humbuckers, rosewood 'board, cherry or sunburst.

1963-1966		$2,200	$2,900
1967-1975		$2,050	$2,700
1976-1987		$1,800	$2,200
1991-2005	Reissue model	$1,125	$1,500

Starfire IV Special (Custom Shop)
2001-2002. Nashville Custom Shop.

2001-2002		$1,400	$1,800

Starfire V
1963-1973, 1999-2001. Same as Starfire IV but with block markers, Bigsby and master volume, natural or sunburst finish, reissued in '99.

1963-1966		$2,200	$2,900
1967-1973		$2,050	$2,700
1999-2001	Reissue model	$1,300	$1,700

MODEL YEAR	FEATURES	EXC. COND. LOW	HIGH

Starfire VI
1964-1979. Same as Starfire IV but with higher appointments such as ebony 'board, pearl inlays, Guild/Bigsby vibrato, natural or sunburst.

1964-1966		$2,200	$2,900
1967-1975		$2,050	$2,700
1976-1979		$1,800	$2,200

Starfire XII
1966-1973. Electric archtop, 12-string, double-cut, maple or mahogany body, set-in neck, 2 humbuckers, harp tailpiece.

1966-1969		$1,600	$2,100
1970-1973		$1,500	$2,000

Stratford A-350
1956-1973. Acoustic archtop, rounded single-cut, solid spruce top with solid curly maple back and sides, rosewood 'board and bridge (changed to ebony by '60), sunburst.

1956-1959		$2,225	$2,900
1960-1965		$2,100	$2,700
1966-1969		$1,850	$2,400
1970-1973		$1,775	$2,300

Stratford A-350 B
1956-1973. A-350 in blond/natural finish option.

1956-1959		$2,500	$3,250
1960-1965		$2,300	$3,000
1966-1969		$2,100	$2,700
1970-1973		$1,975	$2,550

Stratford X-350
1954-1965. Electric archtop, rounded single-cut, laminated spruce top with laminated maple back and sides, rosewood 'board, 6 push-button pickup selectors, sunburst finish (natural finish is X-375).

1954-1959		$2,950	$3,850
1960-1965		$2,675	$3,475

Stratford X-375/X-350 B
1953-1965. Natural finish version of X-350, renamed X-350 B in '58.

1953-1958	X-375	$3,150	$4,100
1959-1965	X-350B	$2,550	$3,300

Stuart A-500
1956-1969. Acoustic archtop single-cut, 17" body, A-500 sunburst, available with Guild logo, floating DeArmond pickup.

1956-1959		$2,650	$3,450
1960-1965		$2,575	$3,350
1966-1969		$2,375	$3,100

Stuart A-550/A-500 B
1956-1969. Natural blond finish version of Stuart A-500, renamed A-500 B in '60.

1956-1959		$2,850	$3,650
1960-1965		$2,575	$3,350
1966-1969		$2,375	$3,100

Stuart X-500
1953-1995. Electric archtop, single-cut, laminated spruce top, laminated curly maple back and sides, 2 pickups, sunburst.

1953-1959		$3,150	$4,100
1960-1965		$2,900	$3,800
1966-1969		$2,800	$3,600
1970-1995		$2,500	$3,200

1957 Guild Savoy X-150

Carter Vintage Guitars

1962 Guild Slim Jim T-100 D

Brian Chambers

GUITARS

1962 Guild Troubadour F-20

Imaged by Heritage Auctions, HA.com

1975 Guild TV Model D-55

Peter Busch

MODEL YEAR	FEATURES	EXC. COND. LOW	HIGH

Stuart X-550/X-500 B

1953-1995. Natural blond finish Stuart X-550, renamed X-500 B in '60.

1953-1959		$3,150	$4,100
1960-1964		$2,900	$3,800
1965-1969		$2,800	$3,600
1970-1995		$2,500	$3,200

Studio 301/ST301

1968-1970. Thinline, semi-hollow archtop Starfire-style but with sharp horns, 1 single-coil pickup, 2 humbuckers in '70, dot inlays, cherry or sunburst.

1968-1969	1 pickup	$875	$1,150
1970	2 pickups	$1,050	$1,350

Studio 302/ST302

1968-1970. Like Studio 301, but with 2 pickups.

1968-1969	2 single-coils	$1,150	$1,500
1970	2 humbuckers	$1,150	$1,500

Studio 303/ST303

1968-1970. Like Studio 301, but with 2 pickups and Guild/Bigsby.

1968-1969	2 single-coils	$1,400	$1,800
1970	2 humbuckers	$1,400	$1,800

Studio 402/ST402

1969-1970. Inch thicker body than other Studios, 2 pickups, block inlays.

1969-1970	2 humbuckers	$1,700	$2,200
1969-1970	2 single-coils	$1,700	$2,200

T-250

1986-1988. Single-cut body and pickup configuration with banana-style headstock.

1986-1988		$450	$600

Thunderbird S-200

1963-1968. Electric solid body, offset double-cut, built-in rear guitar stand, AdjustoMatic bridge and vibrato tailpiece, 2 humbucker pickups, changed to single-coils in '66.

1963-1965	Humbuckers	$3,500	$4,500
1966-1968	Single-coils	$3,000	$3,900

Troubadour F-20

1956-1987. Acoustic flat-top, spruce top with maple back and sides (mahogany '59 and after), rosewood 'board and bridge, natural or sunburst.

1956-1959		$1,800	$2,300
1960-1964		$1,700	$2,200
1965-1969		$1,625	$2,100
1970-1979		$1,300	$1,700
1980-1987		$1,175	$1,525

TV Model D-55/D-65/D-55

1968-1987, 1990-present (special order only for 1968-1973). Dreadnought acoustic, spruce top, rosewood back and sides, scalloped bracing, gold-plated tuners, renamed D-65 in '87. Reintroduced as D-55 in '90.

1968-1969		$1,950	$2,550
1970-1987		$1,800	$2,400
1988-1989	D-65	$1,800	$2,400
1990-1999	D-55	$1,800	$2,400
2000-2020	D-55	$1,900	$2,500

MODEL YEAR	FEATURES	EXC. COND. LOW	HIGH

Willy Porter Signature

2007-2008. AAA sitka spruce top, solid flamed maple sides and back, special appointments, Fishman Ellipse system.

2007-2008		$1,075	$1,400

X-79 Skyhawk

1981-1986. Four-point solid body, 2 pickups, coil-tap or phase switch, various colors.

1981-1986		$800	$1,050

X-80 Skylark/Swan

1982-1985. Solid body with 2 deep cutaways, banana-style 6-on-a-side headstock, renamed Swan in '85.

1982-1985		$800	$1,050

X-82 Nova/Starfighter

1981-1986. Solid body, XR-7 humbuckerss, also available with 3 single-coil pickups, Quick Change SP-6 tailpiece, Adjusto-Matic bridge, Deluxe tuning machine.

1981-1983	Nova	$800	$1,050
1984-1986	Starfighter	$800	$1,050

X-88 D Star

1984-1987. 2 humbucker version X-88.

1984-1987		$800	$1,050

X-88 Flying Star Motley Crue

1984-1986. Pointy 4-point star body, rocketship meets spearhead headstock on bolt neck, 1 pickup, optional vibrato.

1984-1986		$800	$1,050

X-92 Citron

1984. Electric solid body, detachable body section, 3 pickups.

1984		$725	$925

X-100/X-110

1953-1954. Guild was founded in 1952, so this is a very early model, 17" non-cut, single-coil soapbar neck pickup, X-100 sunburst, X-110 natural blond.

1953-1954	X-100	$1,550	$2,050
1953-1954	X-110	$1,825	$2,400

X-100 Bladerunner

1985-1987. 4-point body with large cutouts, 1 humbucker, Kahler, script Guild logo on body, cutout headstock.

1985-1987		$2,200	$2,900

X-150 Savoy/X-150 D Savoy

1998-2013. Replaces Savoy X-150, 1 pickup, D has 2 pickups.

1998-2005	X-150	$925	$1,200
1998-2013	X-150 D	$1,025	$1,325

X-160 Savoy

1989-1993. No Bigsby, black or sunburst.

1989-1993		$1,300	$1,700

X-161/X-160 B Savoy

1989-1994. X-160 Savoy with Bigsby, sunburst or black.

1989-1994		$1,300	$1,700

X-200/X-220

1953-1954. Electric archtop, spruce top, laminated maple body, rosewood 'board, non-cut, 2 pickups. X-200 is sunburst and X-220 blond.

1953-1954	X-200	$1,850	$2,400
1953-1954	X-220	$2,000	$2,600

MODEL YEAR	FEATURES	EXC. COND. LOW	HIGH

X-300/X-330

1953-1954. No model name, non-cut, 2 pickups, X-300 is sunburst and X-330 blond. Becomes Savoy X-150 in '54.

1953-1954	X-300	$1,850	$2,400
1953-1954	X-330	$2,000	$2,600

X-400/X-440

1953-1954. Electric archtop, single-cut, spruce top, laminated maple body, rosewood 'board, 2 pickups, X-400 in sunburst and X-440 in blond. Becomes Manhattan X-175 in '54.

1953-1954	X-400	$2,450	$3,200
1953-1954	X-440	$2,700	$3,500

X-600/X-660

1953. No model name, single-cut, 3 pickups, X-600 in sunburst and X-660 in blond. Becomes Stratford X-350 in '54.

1953	X-600	$3,250	$4,200
1953	X-660	$3,700	$4,800

X-700

1994-1999. Rounded cutaway, 17", solid spruce top, laminated maple back and sides, gold hardware, natural or sunburst.

1994-1999		$1,850	$2,400

Guillermo Roberto Guitars

Professional grade, solidbody electric bajo quintos made in San Fernando, California starting in the year 2000.

Guitar Company of America

1971-present. Professional grade, production, acoustic guitars built by luthier Dixie Michell. Originally built in Tennessee, then Missouri; currently being made in Tulsa, Oklahoma. She also offers mandolins.

Guitar Mill

2006-2011. Luthier Mario Martin built his production/custom, professional grade, semi-hollow and solidbody guitars and basses in Murfreesboro, Tennessee. He also built basses. In '11, he started branding his guitars as Mario Martin.

Gurian

1965-1981. Luthier Michael Gurian started making classical guitars on a special order basis, in New York City. In '69, he started building steel-string guitars as well. 1971 brought a move to Hinsdale, Vermont, and with it increased production. In February, '79 a fire destroyed his factory, stock, and tools. He reopened in West Swanzey, New Hampshire, but closed the doors in '81. Around 2,000 Gurian instruments were built. The guitars have unusual neck joint construction and can be difficult, if not impossible, to repair. Dealers have reported that '70s models sometimes have notable wood cracks which require repair.

MODEL YEAR	FEATURES	EXC. COND. LOW	HIGH

CL Series

1970-1981. Classical Series, mahogany (M), Indian rosewood (R), or Brazilian rosewood (B).

1970-1981	CLB, Brazilian rosewood	$2,500	$3,300
1970-1981	CLM, mahogany	$1,150	$1,500
1970-1981	CLR, Indian rosewood	$1,300	$1,700

FLC

1970-1981. Flamenco guitar, yellow cedar back and sides, friction tuning pegs.

1970-1981		$1,450	$1,900

JB3H

1970-1981	Brazilian rosewood	$2,650	$3,500

JM/JMR

1970-1981. Jumbo body, mahogany (JM) or Indian rosewood (JMR), relatively wide waist (versus D-style or SJ-style).

1970-1981	JM	$1,400	$1,800
1970-1981	JMR	$1,400	$1,800

JR3H

1970-1981. Jumbo, Indian rosewood sides and back, 3-piece back, herringbone trim.

1970-1981		$1,700	$2,250

S2B3H

1970-1981	Brazilian rosewood	$2,750	$3,600

S2M

1970-1981. Size 2 guitar with mahogany back and sides.

1970-1981		$1,300	$1,700

S2R/S2R3H

1970-1981. Size 2 with Indian rosewood sides and back, R3H has 3-piece back and herringbone trim.

1970-1981	S2R	$1,300	$1,700
1970-1981	S2R3H	$1,400	$1,800

S3B3H

1981	Brazilian rosewood	$2,750	$3,600

S3M

1970-1981	Mahogany	$1,400	$1,800

S3R/S3R3H

1970-1981. Size 3 with Indian Rosewood, S3R3H has 3-piece back and herringbone trim.

1970-1981	S3R	$1,450	$1,850
1970-1981	S3R3H	$1,550	$2,000

Guyatone

1933-present. Made in Tokyo by Matsuki Seisakujo, founded by Hawaiian guitarists Mitsuo Matsuki and Atsuo Kaneko (later of Teisco). Made Guya brand Rickenbacker lap steel copies in '30s. After a hiatus for the war ('40-'48), Seisakujo resumes production of laps and amps as Matsuki Denki Onkyo Kenkyujo. In '51 the Guyatone brand is first used on guitars and basses, and in '52 they changed the company name to Tokyo Sound Company. Guyatones are among the earliest U.S. imports, branded as Marco Polo, Winston, Kingston and Kent. Other brand names included LaFayette and Bradford. Production and exports slowed after '68.

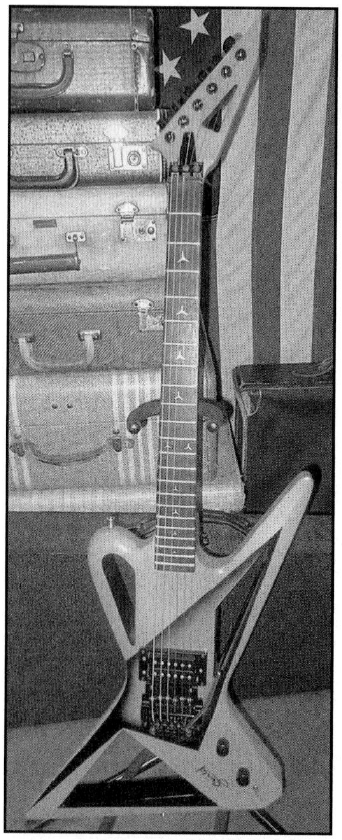

1985 Guild X-100 Bladerunner

Rivington Guitars

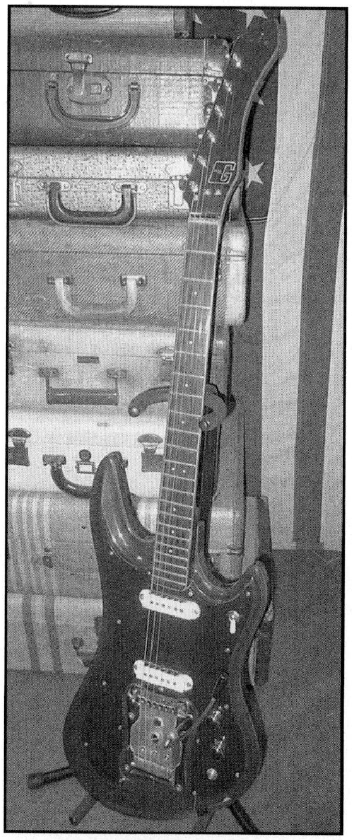

Ca. 1968 Guyatone LG-350T Sharp 5

Rivington Guitars

1965 Hagstrom Corvette

Guitar Maniacs

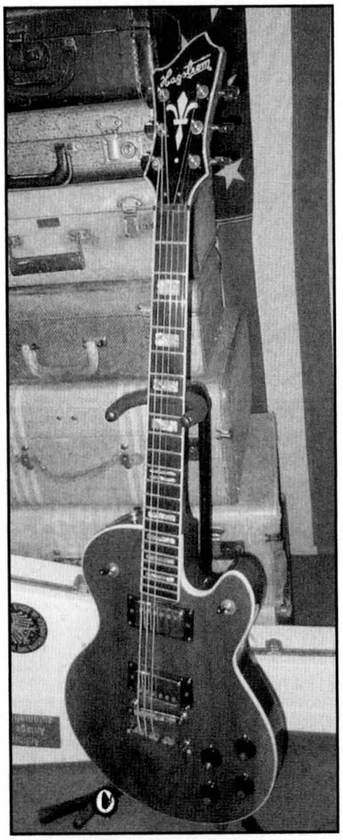

1972 Hagstrom Swede

Rivington Guitars

MODEL YEAR	FEATURES	EXC. COND. LOW	HIGH

Hagenlocher, Henner

1996-present. Luthier Henner Hagenlocher builds his premium grade, custom, nylon-string guitars in Granada, Spain.

Hagstrom

1958-1983, 2004-present. Intermediate, professional, and premium grade, production/custom, solidbody, semi-hollowbody and acoustic guitars made in the U.S. and imported. Founded by Albin Hagström of Älvdalen, Sweden, who began importing accordions in 1921 and incorporated in '25. The name of the company was changed to A.B. Hagström, Inc. in '38, and an American sales office was established in '40. Electric guitar and bass production began in '58 with plastic-covered hollowbody De Luxe and Standard models. The guitars were imported into the U.S. by Hershman Music of New York as Goya 90 and 80 from '58-'61. Bass versions were imported in '61. Following a year in the U.S., Albin's son Karl-Erik Hagström took over the company as exclusive distributor of Fender in Scandinavia; he changed the U.S. importer to Merson Musical Instruments of New York (later Unicord in '65), and redesigned the line. The company closed its doors in '83. In 2004 American Music & Sound started manufacturing and distributing the Hagstrom brand under license from A.B. Albin Hagstrom. In 2009 U.S. Music became involved via its acquistion of JAM, and the 'new' Hagstrom established a Swedish office. A new line of instruments under the Vintage Series (made in China) included classic '60s models. Later the Northen series was introduced with instruments made entirely in Europe.

Corvette/Condor

1963-1967. Offset double-cut solidbody, 3 single-coils, multiple push-button switches, spring vibrato, called the Condor on U.S. imports.

1963-1967		$775	$1,000

D'Aquisto Jimmy

1969-1975, 1976-1979. Designed by James D'Aquisto, electric archtop, f-holes, 2 pickups, sunburst, natural, cherry or white. The '69 had dot inlays, the later version had blocks. From '77 to '79, another version with an oval soundhole (no f-holes) was also available.

1969-1975	1st design	$1,000	$1,300
1976-1979	2nd design	$1,000	$1,300

Deluxe Series

2004-2008. Carved single-cut mahogany body, set-neck, 2 humbuckers, sparkle tops or sunburst.

2004-2008	Various models	$175	$325

F Series (China)

2004-2015. Offset double-cut basswood body, 2 or 3 pickups.

2004-2015	Various models	$175	$325

H-12 Electric/Viking XII

1965-1967. Double-cut, 2 pickups, 12 strings.

1965-1967		$375	$475

H-22 Folk

1965-1967. Flat-top acoustic.

1965-1967		$275	$350

Impala

1963-1967. Two-pickup version of the Corvette, sunburst.

1963-1967		$575	$775

Kent

1962-1967. Offset double-cut solidbody, 2 pickups.

1962-1967		$375	$500

Model I

1965-1971. Small double-cut solidbody, 2 single-coils, early models have plastic top.

1965-1971		$575	$750

Model II/F-200 Futura/H II

1965-1972, 1975-1976. Offset double-cut slab body with beveled edge, 2 pickups, called F-200 Futura in U.S., Model II elsewhere, '75-'76 called H II. F-200 reissued in 2004.

1965-1976		$575	$750

Model III/F-300 Futura/H III

1965-1972, 1977. Offset double-cut slab body with beveled edge, 3 pickups, called F-300 Futura in U.S., Model III elsewhere, '77 called H III.

1965-1969		$600	$800
1970-1977		$325	$425

Swede

1970-1982, 2004-present. Bolt-on neck, single-cut solidbody, black, cherry or natural, '04 version is set-neck.

1979-1982		$750	$975

Super Swede

1979-1983, 2004-present. Glued-in neck upgrade of Swede, '04 version is maple top upgrade of Swede.

1979-1983		$775	$1,000
1979-1983	Custom color	$1,000	$1,300
2004-2020	Reissue	$260	$335

Viking/V1

1965-1975, 1978-1979, 2004-present. Double-cut thinline, 2 f-holes, 2 pickups, chrome hardware, dot inlays, also advertised as the V-1. '60s had 6-on-side headstock, '70s was 3-and-3, latest version back to 6-on-side.

1965-1979		$800	$1,025
2004-2020	Reissue	$260	$335

Viking Deluxe/V2

1967-1968, 2004-present. Upscale version, gold hardware, block inlays, bound headstock and f-holes. Current version upgrades are blocks and flame maple.

1967-1968		$825	$1,075
2004-2020	Reissue	$260	$335

Hahn

2007-present. Professional and premium grade, custom electric guitars built by luthier Chihoe Hahn in Garnerville, New York.

Haight

1989-present. Premium and presentation grade, production/custom, acoustic (steel and classical) guitars built in Scottsdale, Arizona by luthier Norman Haight. He also builds mandolins.

MODEL YEAR	FEATURES	EXC. COND. LOW	HIGH

Halfling Guitars and Basses

Luthier Tom Ribbecke builds premium grade, production/custom, pin bridge, thinline and jazz guitars and basses, starting in 2003, in Healdsburg, California.

Hallmark

1965-1967, 2004-present. Imported and U.S.-made, intermediate and premium grade, production/custom, guitars and basses from luthiers Bob Shade and Bill Gruggett, and located in Greenbelt, Maryland. They also make basses. The brand was originally founded by Joe Hall in Arvin, California, in '65. Hall had worked for Semie Moseley (Mosrite) and had also designed guitars for Standel in the mid-'60s. Bill Gruggett, who also built his own line of guitars, was the company's production manager. Joe Hall estimates that less than 1000 original Hallmark guitars were built. The brand was revived by Shade in '04.

Sweptwing

1965-1967. Pointed body, sorta like a backwards Flying V.

1965-1967		$1,525	$2,000

Hamblin Guitars

Luthier Kent Hamblin built his premium grade, production/custom, flat-top acoustic guitars in Phoenix, Arizona and Telluride, Colorado, and presently builds in Colorado Springs. He began building in 1996.

Hamer

1974-2012, 2017-present. Intermediate grade, production, electric guitars. Hamer previously made basses and the Slammer line of instruments. Founded in Arlington Heights, Illinois, by Paul Hamer and Jol Dantzig. Prototype guitars built in early-'70s were on Gibson lines, with first production guitar, the Standard (Explorer shape), introduced in '75. Hamer was puchased by Kaman Corporation (Ovation) in '88. The Illinois factory was closed and the operations were moved to the Ovation factory in Connecticut in '97. On January 1, '08, Fender acquired Kaman Music Corporation and the Hamer brand. In '90, they started the Korean-import Hamer Slammer series which in '97 became Hamer Import Series (no Slammer on headstock). In '05 production was moved to China and name changed to XT Series (in '07 production moved to Indonesia). The U.S.-made ones have U.S.A. on the headstock. The less expensive import Slammer brand (not to be confused with the earlier Slammer Series) was introduced in '99 (see that listing). Fender suspended production of the Hamer brand at the end of 2012, later selling KMC (and Hamer brand) to Jam Industries, which relaunched Hamer in '17.

Archtop P-90

Solidbody double-cut, archtop sloping on top, P-90 pickups.

1993		$900	$1,200

Artist/Archtop Artist/Artist Custom

1995-2012. U.S.-made, similar to Sunburst Archtop with semi-solid, f-hole design, sunburst, named Archtop Artist, then renamed Artist (with stop tailpiece)/Artist Custom in '97.

1995-2012	Higher-end specs	$1,300	$1,725
1995-2012	Standard specs	$900	$1,200

Artist 25th Anniversary Edition

1998. Made in USA, 25th Anniversary Edition script logo on headstock.

1998		$900	$1,200

Artist Korina

2001-2012. Double-cut, bass f-hole, korina (limba) body and neck, 2 P-90s or 2 humbuckers (HB), natural gloss finish.

2001-2012		$1,500	$2,000

Artist Ultimate

1998-2012. Figured maple top, deluxe binding, gold hardware.

1998-2012		$2,100	$2,700

Blitz

1982-1984 (1st version), 1984-1990 (2nd version). Explorer-style body, 2 humbuckers, 3-on-a-side peghead, dot inlays, choice of tremolo or fixed bridge, second version same except has angled 6-in-line peghead and Floyd Rose tremolo.

1982-1984	3-on-a-side	$1,300	$1,700
1984-1990	6-in-line	$1,100	$1,450

Californian

1987-1997. Made in USA, solidbody double cut, bolt neck, 1 humbucker and 1 single-coil, Floyd Rose tremolo.

1987-1989		$1,700	$2,200
1990-1997		$1,500	$2,000

Californian Custom

1987-1997. Made in USA, downsized contoured body, offset double-cut, neck-thru-body, optional figured maple body, Duncan Trembucker and Trem-single pickups.

1987-1989		$1,700	$2,200
1990-1997		$1,500	$1,900

Californian Elite

1987-1997. Made in USA, downsized contoured body, offset double-cut, optional figured maple body, bolt-on neck, Duncan Trembucker and Trem-single pickups.

1987-1989		$1,700	$2,200
1990-1997		$1,500	$2,000

Centaura

1989-1995. Alder or swamp ash offset double-cut, bolt-on neck, 1 humbucker and 2 single-coils, Floyd Rose, sunburst.

1989-1995		$975	$1,275

Chaparral

1985-1987 (1st version), 1987-1994 (2nd version). Offset double-cut, glued neck, angled peghead, 1 humbucker and 2 single-coils, tremolo, second version has bolt neck with a modified peghead.

1985-1987	Set-neck	$1,100	$1,450
1987-1994	Bolt-on neck	$900	$1,200

1967 Hagstrom Viking Deluxe

Imaged by Heritage Auctions, HA.com

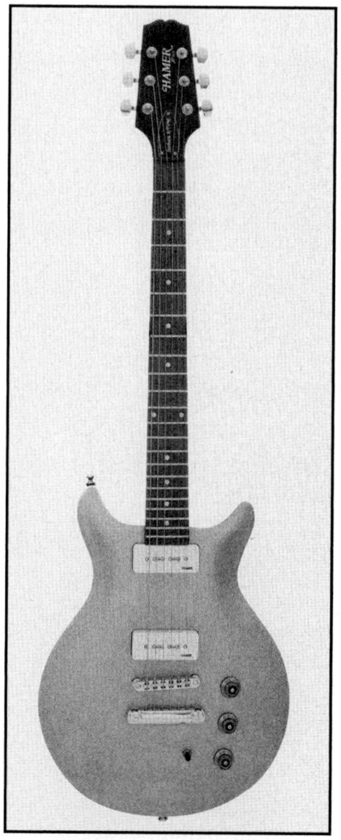

Hamer Archtop P-90

Imaged by Heritage Auctions, HA.com

Hamer Newport
Bernunzio Uptown Music

1982 Hamer Standard
Bo Belaski

MODEL YEAR	FEATURES	EXC. COND. LOW	HIGH

Daytona

1993-1997. Offset double-cut, bolt neck, dot inlay, 3 single-coils, Wilkinson tremolo.

1993-1997		$875	$1,150

Diablo/Diablo II

1992-1997. Offset double-cut, bolt neck, rosewood 'board, dot inlays, reversed peghead '92-'94, 2 pickups, tremolo. Diablo II has 3 pickups.

1992-1997		$775	$1,025

DuoTone

1993-2003. Semi-hollowbody, double-cut, bound top, glued-in neck, rosewood 'board, 2 humbuckers, EQ.

1993-2003		$575	$750

Echotone/Echotone Custom

2000-2002. Thinline semi-hollow archtop, f-holes, 2 humbuckers, trapezoid inlays, gold hardware.

2000-2002		$300	$385

Eclipse

1994-1996. Asymmetrical double-cut slab mahogany body, glued neck, rosewood 'board, 2 Duncan Mini-Humbuckers, cherry.

1994-1996		$600	$800

Eclipse (Import)

1997-1999. Import version.

1997-1999		$250	$325

Eclipse 12-String

1994-1996. 12-string version of Eclipse.

1995		$600	$800

FB I

1986-1987. Reverse Firebird-style body, glued-in neck, reverse headstock, 1 pickup, rosewood 'board with dot inlays, also available in non-reverse body.

1986-1987		$750	$1,000

FB II

1986-1987. Reverse Firebird-style, glued-in neck, ebony 'board with boomerang inlays, angled headstock, 2 humbuckers, Floyd Rose tremolo, also available as a 12-string.

1986-1987		$800	$1,050

Korina Standard

1995-1996. Limited run, Korina Explorer-type body, glued-in neck, angled peghead, 2 humbuckers.

1995-1996		$1,400	$1,800

Maestro

1990. Offset double-cut, 7 strings, tremolo, bolt-on maple neck, 3 Seymour Duncan rail pickups.

1990		$950	$1,225

Mirage

1994-1998. Double-cut carved figured koa wood top, transparent flamed top, initially with 3 single-coil pickups, dual humbucker option in '95.

1994-1998		$900	$1,150

Newport Series

1999-2012. USA, double-cut thinline, center block, f-holes, 2 humbuckers (Newport 90 has P-90s), wraparound bridge tailpiece.

1999-2012	Newport	$1,025	$1,350
1999-2012	Newport Pro	$1,125	$1,450

Phantom A5

1982-1884, 1985-1986 (2nd version). Offset double-cut, glued neck, 3-on-a-side peghead, 1 triple-coil and 1 single-coil pickup, second version same but with 6-in-line peghead and Kahler.

1982-1984		$1,125	$1,500

Phantom GT

1984-1986. Contoured body, offset double-cut, glued-in fixed neck, 6-in-line peghead, 1 humbucker, single volume control.

1984-1986		$1,125	$1,500

Prototype

1981-1985. Contoured mahogany body, double-cut with 1 splitable triple-coil pickup, fixed bridge, three-on-a-side peghead, Prototype II has extra pickup and tremolo.

1981-1985		$975	$1,250

Scarab I

1984-1986. Multiple cutaway body, 6-in-line peghead, 1 humbucker, tremolo, rosewood or ebony 'board, dot inlays.

1984-1986		$1,300	$1,700

Scarab II

1984-1986. Two humbucker version of the Scarab.

1984-1986		$1,300	$1,700

Scepter

1986-1990. Futuristic-type body, ebony 'board with boomerang inlays, angled 6-in-line peghead, Floyd Rose tremolo.

1986-1990		$1,400	$1,800

Slammer Series

1990-1997. Various models imported from Korea, not to be confused with Hamer's current Slammer budget line started in '98.

1990-1997		$200	$425

Special Series

1980-1983 (1st version), 1984-1985 (Floyd Rose version), 1992-1997 (2nd version), 2017-present. Double-cut solidbody, flame maple top, glued neck, 3-on-a-side peghead, 2 humbuckers, Rose version has mahogany body with ebony 'board, the 2nd version is all mahogany and has tune-o-matic bridge, stop tailpiece and Duncan P-90s, cherry red.

1980-1983	1st version	$1,300	$1,800

Standard

1974-1985, 1995-2005. Futuristic body, maple top, bound or unbound body, glued neck, angled headstock, either unbound neck with dot inlays or bound neck with crown inlays, 2 humbuckers. Reissued in '95 with same specs but unbound mahogany body after '97. Higher dollar Standard Custom still available.

1974-1975	Pre-production, about 20 made	$8,000	$11,000
1975-1977	Production, about 50 made, PAFs	$7,000	$10,000
1977-1979	Dimarzio PAF-copies	$5,000	$7,000
1980-1985		$4,000	$5,000
1995-1999		$2,500	$4,000
2000-2005	USA, flamed top	$1,900	$2,400

Standard (Import, XT)

1998-2012. Import version, 2 humbuckers.

1998-2012		$250	$325

MODEL YEAR	FEATURES	EXC. COND. LOW	HIGH

Standard Custom GSTC
2007-2012. Made in USA, flamed maple top, mahogany neck, rosewood 'board.

2007-2012		$2,600	$3,400

Stellar 1
1999-2000. Korean import, double-cut, 2 humbuckers.

1999-2000		$125	$170

Steve Stevens I
1984-1992. Introduced as Prototype SS, changed to Steve Stevens I in '86, contoured double-cut, 6-in-line headstock, dot or crown inlays, 1 humbucker and 2 single-coil pickups.

1984-1992		$975	$1,275

Steve Stevens II
1986-1987. One humbucker and 1 single-coil version.

1986-1987		$975	$1,275

Studio
1993-2012. Double-cut, flamed maple top on mahogany body, 2 humbuckers, cherry or natural.

1993-2012		$800	$1,025

Studio Custom
1997-2012. Carved figured maple, humbuckers, tune-o-matic bridge, stop tailpiece, sunburst.

1997-2012		$1,200	$1,600

Sunburst
1977-1983, 1990-1992, 2018-present. Double-cut bound solidbody, flamed maple top, glued-in neck, bound neck and crown inlays optional, 3-on-a-side headstock, 2 humbuckers.

1977-1983		$2,400	$3,100
1990-1992		$1,650	$2,150

Sunburst (Import, XT)
1997-2012. Import version of Sunburst, flat-top or archtop, 2 pickups.

1997-2012		$180	$230

Sunburst Archtop
1991-1997. Sunburst model with figured maple carved top, 2 humbuckers, offered under various names: Standard - unbound neck and dot inlays, tune-o-matic and stop tailpiece '91-'93 (replaced by the Studio). Custom - bound neck and crown inlays '91-'93, which became the Archtop for '94-'97 (replaced by the Studio Custom). Archtop GT - Gold top with P-90 soapbar-style pickups '93-'97.

1991-1997	Various models	$1,300	$1,650

T-51
1993-1997. Classic single-cut southern ash body, 2 single-coils.

1993-1997		$650	$850

T-62
1991-1995. Classic offset double-cut solidbody, tremolo, pau ferro 'board, Lubritrak nut, locking tuners, 3-band active EQ, various colors.

1991-1995		$650	$850

TLE
1986-1992. Single-cut mahogany body, maple top, glued neck, 6-in-line headstock, rosewood 'board, dot inlays, 3 pickups.

1986-1992		$1,050	$1,350

MODEL YEAR	FEATURES	EXC. COND. LOW	HIGH

TLE Custom
1986-1992. Bound, single-cut solidbody with maple top, glued-in neck, angled headstock, ebony 'board with boomerang inlays, 3 pickups.

1986-1992		$1,050	$1,350

Vector
1982-1985. V-style body (optional flame maple top), 3-on-a-side peghead, rosewood 'board, 2 humbuckers, Sustain Block fixed bridge (Kahler or Floyd Rose tremolos may also be used).

1982-1985		$2,000	$2,600

Vector Limited Edition Korina
1997. 72 built in Hamer's Arlington Heights, Illinois shop, price includes original Hamer certificate of authenticity with matching serial number, Flying-V Vector style body, gold hardware, natural finish.

1997		$2,200	$2,800

Hanson
2009-present. Founders John and Bo Pirruccello import intermediate grade, electric guitars which are set up in Chicago, Illinois.

Harden Engineering
1999-present. Professional grade, custom, solidbody guitars built by luthier William Harnden in Chicago, Illinois. He also builds effects pedals.

Harmony
1892-1976, late 1970s-present. Huge, Chicago-based manufacturer of fretted instruments, mainly budget models under the Harmony name or for many other American brands and mass marketers. Harmony was at one time the largest guitar builder in the world. In its glory days, Harmony made over one-half of the guitars built in the U.S., with '65 being their peak year. But by the early-'70s, the crash of the '60s guitar boom and increasing foreign competition brought an end to the company. The Harmony brand appeared on Asian-built instruments starting in the late '70s to the '90s with sales mainly through mass-retail stores. In 2000, the Harmony brand was distributed by MBT International. In '02, former MBT marketing director Alison Gillette launched Harmony Classic Reissue Guitars and Basses and in '09 the trademark was acquired by Westheimer Corporation. Many Harmony guitars have a factory order number on the inside back of the guitar which often contains the serial number. Most older Harmony acoustics and hollowbodies have a date ink-stamped inside the body. DeArmond made most of the electronic assemblies used on older Harmony electrics, and they often have a date stamped on the underside.

Amplifying Resonator Model 27
1930s. Dobro-licensed with Dobro metal resonator, wood body.

1930s		$525	$700

Archtone H1215/H1215 Tenor
1950s. Lower-end archtop, sunburst.

1950-1960s	4-string tenor	$190	$250
1950-1960s	6-string	$200	$260

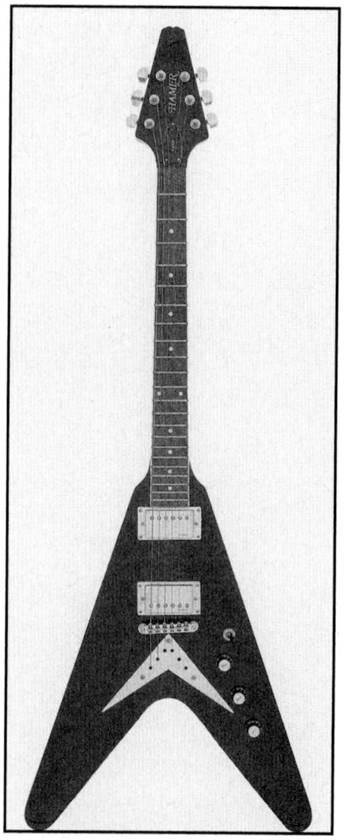

Hamer Vector
Imaged by Heritage Auctions, HA.com

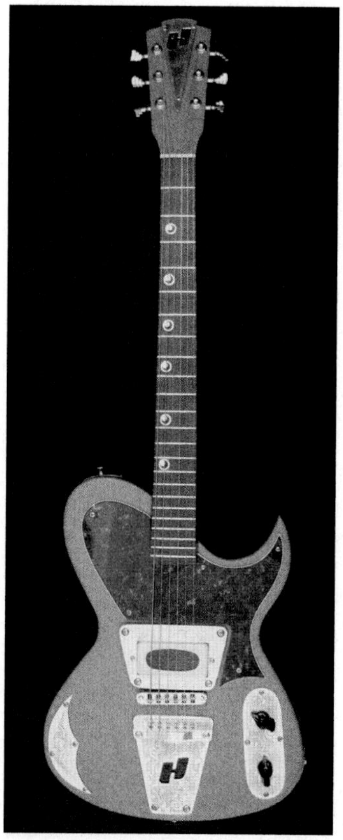

Harden Engineering Switchblade

1968 Harmony Bob Kat H15

Tom Pfeifer

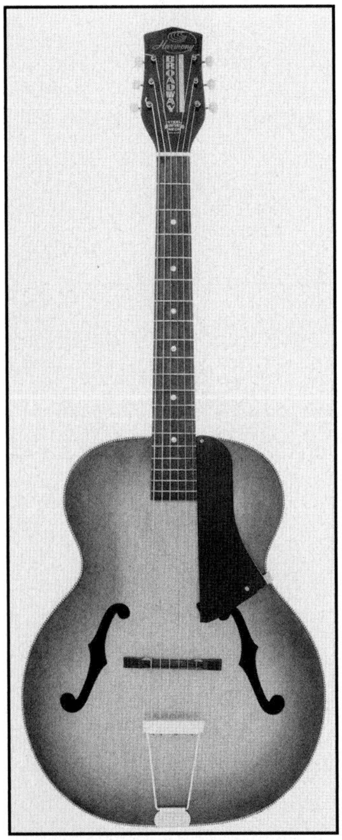

1950s Harmony Broadway H954

Imaged by Heritage Auctions, HA.com

MODEL YEAR	FEATURES	EXC. COND. LOW	HIGH

Bob Kat H14/H15

1968. Replaces Silhouette solidbody, H14 has single pickup and 2 knobs, H15 has 2 pickups. When vibrato is added it becomes the H16 model.

1968	H14	$250	$325
1968	H15	$350	$450

Brilliant Cutaway H1310/H1311

1962-1965. 16 1/2" body (Grand Auditorium), acoustic archtop cutaway, block markers, sunburst.

1962-1965		$425	$550

Broadway H954

1930s-1971. 15-3/4" body, acoustic archtop, dot markers, sunburst.

1930s-1971		$175	$225

Buck Owens

1969. Acoustic flat-top, red, white and blue. The price shown is for a guitar that has an unblemished finish, paint-wear will reduce the price, prices vary considerable due to the condition of the finish.

1969		$1,500	$2,000

Cremona

1930s-1952. Full-size archtop line, Harmony and Cremona logo on headstock, natural. Cutaways became available in '53.

1940-1952		$220	$285

D Series (Electric)

Late-1980s-Early-1990s. Classic electric copy models including offset double- and single-cut solidbody and double-cut thin hollowbody (D720), 1 to 3 pickups. All models begin with D, some models part of Harmony Electric series and others the Harmony Igniter series.

1980s-90s	Various models	$60	$80

Espanada H63

1950s-1965. Thick body, single-cut, jazz-style double pickups, black finish with white appointments, by early '60s 'Espanada' logo on lower bass bout.

1950s-1965		$1,050	$1,375

Folk H162

1950s-1971. Grand concert size acoustic, spruce top, mahogany body.

1950s-1971		$325	$425

Folk H165/H6365

1958-1974. Square-shouldered flat-top, all mahogany body. Renamed the H6365 in '72.

1958-1974		$290	$375

Grand Concert H165

1948-1957. Flat-top, all mahogany body. Body changed to square-shoulder in '58 (see Folk H165).

1948-1957		$250	$325

H/HG Series (Electric)

Late-1980s-Early-1990s. Classic electric copy models including offset double-cut, single-cut and double-cut semi-hollow, 1 to 3 pickups, with or without tremolo. All models begin with H or HG, some models part of Harmony Electric series and others the Harmony Igniter series.

1980s-90s	Various models	$45	$85

H60 Double Cutaway Hollowbody

1968-1970. Thinline double-cut, 2 pickups, trapeze tailpiece, sunburst.

1968-1970		$800	$1,050

H62 Blond

1950s-1965. Thin body, dual pickup archtop, curly maple back and sides, spruce top, block markers, blond.

1950s-1965		$1,075	$1,400

H62VS (Reissue)

2000s. H62 with sunburst finish.

2000s		$650	$850

H64 Double Cutaway Electric

1968-1970. Factory Bigsby, dot markers, sunburst.

1968-1970		$975	$1,275

H68 Deep Body Electric

1968-1971. Full-body single-cut electric archtop, 2 pickups, trapeze bridge, block markers.

1968-1971		$975	$1,275

H72/H72V Double Cutaway Hollowbody

1966-1971. Multiple bindings, 2 pickups, cherry red, H72V has Bigsby.

1966-1971		$975	$1,275

H74 Neo-Cutaway

1961-1967. Modified double-cut, 2 pickups, Bigsby, 3-part F-holes, dot inlays.

1961-1967		$1,050	$1,375

H75 Double Cutaway Hollowbody

1960-1970. Three pickups, multi-bound body, 3-part f-holes, block inlays, bolt neck, brown sunburst.

1960-1970		$1,050	$1,375

H76 Double Cutaway Hollowbody

1960-1962. H75 with Bigsby.

1960-1962		$1,050	$1,375

H77 Double Cutaway Hollowbody

Late-1960s. Same as H75, but in cherry sunburst.

1960s		$1,050	$1,375

H78 Double Cutaway Hollowbody

Late-1960s. H78 with Bigsby.

1960s		$1,050	$1,375

H79 Double Cutaway Hollowbody 12-String

1966-1970. Unique slotted headstock, cherry finish.

1966-1970		$975	$1,275

H910 Classical

1970s. Beginner guitar, natural.

1970s		$50	$65

H1200 Auditorium Series

1948-1975. Moderately-priced acoustic archtop, treble-clef artwork on headstock, model 1213 & 1215 (shaded brown sunburst) and 1214 (blond ivory, ends in '64). Model 1215 was renamed H6415 in '72 and lasted until '75.

1948-1975	Various models	$190	$250

H1270 12-String Flat-Top

1965. 16" deluxe acoustic 12-string flat-top, spruce top, mahogany sides and back, dot markers.

1965		$350	$450

H1310 Brilliant Cutaway

1953-1973. Grand Auditorium acoustic archtop, single rounded cutaway, block inlays, sunburst. Called H6510 in '72.

1953-1973		$450	$575

MODEL YEAR	FEATURES	EXC. COND. LOW	HIGH

H1311 Brilliant Cutaway

1953-1962. As H 1310, but in blond.

1953-1963		$625	$800

H4101 Flat-Top Tenor

1950s-1970s. Mahogany body, 4-string.

1950-1970s		$225	$300

H150 (Student Model)

1968		$145	$185

Holiday Rocket

Mid-1960s. Similar to H59 Rocket III but with push-button controls instead of rotary selector switch, 3 Goldentone pickups, pickup trim rings, Holiday logo on 'guard, higher model than standard Rocket.

1960s		$875	$1,150

Hollywood H37

1960-1961. Electric archtop, auditorium size 15.75" body, 1 pickup, Harmony and Hollywood logo on headstock, 2-tone gold metallic finish.

1960-1961		$425	$550

Hollywood H39

1960-1965. Like H37 but with sunburst.

1960-1965		$290	$375

Hollywood H41

1960-1965 Like H37 but with 2 pickups, sunburst

1960-1965		$375	$475

Igniter Series (D/H/HG)

Late-1980s to early-1990s. Pointy-headstock electric copy models, offset double-cut, all models begin with D, H, or HG.

1980s-90s	Various models	$90	$115

Lone Ranger

1950-1951. Lone Ranger headstock stencil, Lone Ranger and Tonto stencil on brown body. This model was first introduced in 1936 as the Supertone Lone Ranger with same stencil on a black body.

1950-1951		$225	$300

Master H945

1965-1966. 15" (Auditorium) acoustic archtop, block markers, music note painted logo on headstock, sunburst.

1965-1966		$200	$250

Meteor H70/H71

1958-1966. Single rounded cutaway 2" thin body, 2 pickups, 3-part f-holes, block inlays, bolt neck, H70 sunburst, H71 natural (ended '65), lefty offered '65-'66, reintroduced as H661 and H671 (without Meteor name) in '72-'74.

1958-1965	H71, natural	$1,125	$1,450
1958-1966	H70, sunburst	$1,125	$1,450

Modern Trend H65

1956-1960. Short-scale electric thin body archtop, 1 single-coil, block inlays, sherry blond finish on curly maple grain.

1956-1960		$700	$925

Monterey H950/H952/H1325/H1456/H1457/H6450

1930s-1974. Line of Auditorium and Grand Auditorium acoustic archtop models.

1950s	H952 Colorama	$275	$400
1950s-60s	Other models	$175	$400
1970s	H6450	$110	$160

Patrician (1407/1414/1418)

1932-1973. Model line mostly with mahogany bodies and alternating single/double dot markers (later models with single dots), introduced as flat-top, changed to archtop in '34. In '37 line expanded to 9 archtops (some with blocks) and 1 flat-top. Flat-tops disappeared in the '40s, with various archtops offered up to '73.

1932-1973		$275	$400

Professional H1252 Hawaiian

1940. Hawaiian acoustic jumbo, high-end appointments, vertical Professional logo on front of headstock, figured koa or mahogany back and sides, spruce top, Brazilian rosewood fretboard, various-shaped fretboard markers.

1940		$1,775	$2,350

Rebel H81

1968-1971. Single pickup version of Rebel, brown sunburst.

1968-1971		$275	$350

Rebel H82/H82G

Listed as a new model in 1971. Thin body, hollow tone chamber, double-cut, 2 pickups, H82 sunburst, H82G greenburst avacado shading (renumbered as H682 and H683 in '72).

1970s	H82	$450	$575
1970s	H82G	$450	$575

Rocket H59 Reissue

2000s. Import, double-cut, 3 pickups, 6 knobs.

2000s		$400	$525

Rocket I H53

1959-1973. Single-cut, f-holes, 1 pickup, trapeze, 2-tone brown sunburst ('59-'62) or red sunburst ('63 on).

1959-1969		$375	$475
1970-1973		$290	$375

Rocket II H54

1959-1973. Same as H53 but with 2 pickups.

1959-1969		$625	$800
1970-1973		$375	$475

Rocket III H59

1960-1973 Same as H53 but with 3 pickups

1960-1969		$800	$1,050
1970-1973		$725	$950

Roy Rogers H600

1954-1958. 3/4 size, stencil, sold through Sears.

1954-1958		$225	$350

Roy Smeck Artiste H1442

1939-ca. 1942. Grand auditorium acoustic archtop, Roy Smeck Artiste logo on headstock, split rectangle markers, black, white guard.

1939-1942		$390	$500

Roy Smeck H73

1963-1964. Electric hollowbody, single neck silver bar-style pickup or 2 Harmony pickups.

1963-1964		$850	$1,100

Roy Smeck Vita Standard H1250

1928-1931. Pear shaped body, seal-shaped sound holes.

1928-1331		$600	$800

Silhouette De Luxe Double H19

1965-1969. Double-cut solidbody, deluxe pickups, block markers, advanced vibrato, sunburst.

1965-1969		$575	$750

1960 Harmony Meteor H71

Tom Pfeifer

1960 Harmony Rocket III H59

Imaged by Heritage Auctions, HA.com

1970 Harmony Sovereign
Edward Sparks

1960 Harmony Stratotone Mars H45
Larry Krauss

MODEL YEAR	FEATURES	EXC. COND. LOW	HIGH

Silhouette H14/H15/H17

1963-1967. Double-cut solidbody, H14 single pickup, H15 dual pickup, H17 dual with vibrato (offered until '66).

1963-1967	H14	$250	$325
1963-1967	H15	$350	$450
1963-1967	H17	$425	$550

Singing Cowboys H1057

1950s. Western chuck-wagon scene stencil top, Singing Cowboys stenciled on either side of upper bouts, brown background versus earlier Supertone version that had black background.

1950s		$250	$325

Sovereign Jumbo Deluxe H1266

1960s-1970s. Jumbo nearly D-style, 16" wide body with out-size 'guard, natural.

1960s		$350	$450
1970s		$290	$375

Sovereign Jumbo H1260

1960s-1970s. Jumbo shape, 16" wide body, natural.

1960s		$475	$625
1970s		$325	$425

Sovereign Western Special Jumbo H1203

1960s-1970s. 15" wide body, 000-style.

1960s		$375	$475

Stratotone Deluxe Jupiter H49

1958-1965. Single-cut, tone chamber construction, 2 pickups, bound spruce top, curly maple back and 6 control knobs, blond finish.

1958-1965		$600	$800

Stratotone Doublet H88

1954-1957. Basically 2 pickup H44.

1954-1957		$900	$1,200

Stratotone H44

1953-1957. First edition models had small bodies and rounded cutaway, 1 pickup with plain cover using 2 mounting rivets, sometimes called Hershey Bar pickup, '60s models had slightly larger bodies and sharp cutaways, some with headstock logo Harmony Stratotone with atomic note graphic.

1953-1957		$900	$1,200

Stratotone Mars Electric H45/H46

1958-1968. Single-cut, tone chamber construction, sunburst finish, H45 with 1 pickup, H46 with 2 pickups.

1960s	H45	$400	$525
1960s	H46	$525	$700

Stratotone Mercury Electric H47/H48

1958-1968. Single-cut, tone chamber construction, H47 with 1 pickup, block inlay and curly maple sunburst top, H48 is the same with a blond top.

1960s	H47	$450	$600
1960s	H48	$450	$600

Stratotone Newport H42/1 and H42/2

1957-1958. Brightly colored, single-cut, Newport headstock logo, 1 single-coil. 42/1 in sunshine yellow, /2 in metallic green.

1957-1958		$900	$1,200

TG1201 Tenor

1950s. Spruce top, two-on-a-side tuners, Sovereign model tenor, natural.

1950s		$225	$300

Vibra-Jet H66

1962-1966. Thinline single-cut, 2 pickups, built-in tremolo circuit and control panel knobs and selection dial, sunburst.

1962-1966		$1,050	$1,375

Harptone

1893-ca. 1975. The Harptone Manufacturing Corporation was located in Newark, New Jersey. They made musical instrument cases and accessories and got into instrument production from 1934 to '42, making guitars, banjos, mandolins, and tiples. In '66 they got back into guitar production, making the Standel line from '67 to '69. Harptone offered flat-tops and archtops under their own brand until the mid-'70s when the name was sold to the Diamond S company, which owned Micro-Frets.

Acoustic

1966-mid-1970s. Various models.

1966-1970s	Deluxe/Custom	$1,100	$1,450
1966-1970s	Standard	$500	$1,100

Electric

1966-mid-1970s. Various models.

1966-1970s		$1,100	$1,450

Harrison Guitars

1992-present. Luthier Douglas Harrison builds premium grade, production/custom, archtop and semi-hollowbody jazz guitars in Toronto, Ontario.

Harwood

Harwood was a brand introduced in 1885 by Kansas City, Missouri instrument wholesalers J.W. Jenkins & Sons (though some guitars marked Harwood, New York). May have been built by Jenkins until circa 1905, but work was later contracted out to Harmony.

Parlor

1890s. Slotted headstocks, most had mahogany bodies, some with Brazilian rosewood body, considered to be well made.

1890s	Brazilian rosewood	$775	$1,025
1890s	Mahogany	$450	$575

Hascal Haile

Late 1960s-1986. Luthier Hascal Haile started building acoustic, classical and solidbody guitars in Tompkinsville, Kentucky, after retiring from furniture making. He died in '86.

Hauver Guitar

2001-present. Professional and premium grade, custom, acoustic guitars, built in Sharpsburg, Maryland by luthier Michael S. Hauver.

Hayes Guitars

Professional and premium grade, production/custom, steel and nylon string guitars made by luthier Louis Hayes in Paonia, Colorado. He began building in 1993.

MODEL YEAR	FEATURES	EXC. COND. LOW	HIGH

Hayman

1970-1973. Solid and semi-hollowbody guitars and basses developed by Jim Burns and Bob Pearson for Ivor Arbiter of the Dallas Arbiter Company and built by Shergold in England.

Haynes

1865-early 1900s. The John C. Haynes Co. of Boston also made the Bay State brand.

Heartfield

1989-1994. Founded as a joint venture between Fender Musical Instrument Corporation (U.S.A.) and Fender Japan (partnership between Fender and distributors Kanda Shokai and Yamano Music) to build and market more advanced designs (built by Fuji Gen-Gakki). First RR and EX guitar series and DR Bass series debut in '90. Talon and Elan guitar series and Prophecy bass series introduced in '91. The brand was dead by '94.

Electric Solidbody

1989-1994	Various models	$500	$700

Heiden Stringed Instruments

1974-present. Luthier Michael Heiden builds his premium grade, production/custom, flat-top guitars in Chilliwack, British Columbia. He also builds mandolins.

Heit Deluxe

Ca. 1967-1970. Imported from Japan by unidentified New York distributor. Many were made by Teisco, the most famous being the Teisco V-2 Mosrite copy. They also had basses.

Acoustic

1967-1970	Various models	$100	$200

Electric

1967-1970	Various models	$200	$350

Hembry Guitars

2002-present. Professional grade, production/custom, solidbody electric guitars built by luthier Scott Hembry in Shelton, Washington. He also builds basses.

Hemken, Michael

1993-present. Luthier Michael Hemken builds his premium grade, custom, archtops in St. Helena, California.

HenBev

Premium grade, production, solid and hollow body electric guitars and basses built by luthier Scotty Bevilacqua in Oceanside, California, starting in the year 2005.

Henderson Guitars

Luthier Wayne C. Henderson builds premium and presentation grade, custom acoustic guitars in Rugby, Virginia. He produces around 20 guitars per year and has also made mandolins, banjos and fiddles.

MODEL YEAR	FEATURES	EXC. COND. LOW	HIGH

Hendrick

1982-1985. Solidbody guitars built by luthier Kurt Hendrick in Texas, Ohio and Michigan. Less than 100 built, the most popular model was the Generator. Hendrick also worked with Schecter, Fender, Jackson and Epiphone.

Henman Guitars

2010-present. Owners Graham and Paris Henman offer premium grade, production/custom, solidbody and chambered electric guitars and basses built by luthier Rick Turner in Santa Cruz, California.

Heritage

1985-present. Professional, premium, and presentation grade, production/custom, hollow, semi-hollow, and solidbody guitars built in Kalamazoo, Michigan. They have also made banjos, mandolins, flat-tops, and basses in the past.

Founded by Jim Deurloo, Marvin Lamb, J.P. Moats, Bill Paige and Mike Korpak, all former Gibson employees who did not go to Nashville when Norlin closed the original Gibson factory in '84. In 2007, Vince Margol bought out Paige. In '16, a private group of local Kalamazoo investors bought the business with Deurloo, Lamb and Paige remaining active in the company.

Eagle

1986-2009. Single rounded cut semi-hollowbody, mahogany body and neck, bound body, 1 jazz pickup, f-holes, sunburst or natural.

1986-2009		$1,700	$2,200

Eagle Classic

1992-present. Standard Collection, Eagle with maple body and neck, bound neck and headstock, gold hardware, sunburst or natural.

1992-2020		$2,400	$3,100

Gary Moore Model

1989-1991. Single-cut solidbody, 2 pickups, chrome hardware, sunburst.

1989-1991		$1,500	$1,925

Golden Eagle

1985-2019. Single-cut hollowbody, back inlaid with mother-of-pearl eagle and registration number, multi-bound ebony 'board with mother-of-pearl cloud inlays, bound f-holes, gold-plated parts, ebony bridge inlaid with mother-of-pearl, mother-of-pearl truss rod cover engraved with owner's name, 1 Heritage jazz pickup, multi-bound curly maple 'guard.

1985-1999	Floating pickup	$2,200	$2,900
1985-1999	Mounted pickup	$2,200	$2,900

Groove Master

2004-2018. 16" hollow-body, single rounded cutaway,neck pickup, sunburst.

2004-2018		$1,350	$1,775

1988 Heartfield RR9

Tom Pfeifer

Heritage Eagle Classic

1986 Heritage H-140
Carter Vintage Guitars

Heritage H-357
C.J. Stanley

MODEL YEAR	FEATURES	EXC. COND. LOW	HIGH

H-137

1980s-present. Standard Collection, single-cut solidbody, 2 P-90s, sunburst, natural lime (early) or TV yellow (later).

1980s-2018	Sunburst or natural lime	$1,000	$1,300
2019-2020	Sunburst or V yellow	$1,050	$1,350

H-137 AA

2018-present. Artisan Aged Collection, sunburst or TV yellow with aged finish.

2018-2020		$1,050	$1,350

H-140/H-140 CM

1985-2005, 2007-2016. Single pointed cutaway solidbody, bound curly maple ('85-'04) or solid gold top ('94-'05), 2 humbuckers, chrome parts.

1985-1996	Black	$1,000	$1,300
1985-2004	CM, curly maple	$1,000	$1,300
1994-2005	Goldtop	$1,000	$1,300
2001	CM, flamed maple	$1,000	$1,300
2007-2016	2nd edition, goldtop	$1,000	$1,300

H-147

1990-1991. Single-cut solidbody, 2 humbuckers, mahogany body, mother-of-pearl block inlays, black with black or gold hardware.

1990-1991		$900	$1,175

H-150

1990s-present. Standard Collection, solid carved figured maple top, mahogany back, various colors.

1990s-2020		$1,400	$1,800

H-150 AA

2018-present. Artisan Aged Collection, sunburst, ebony, various colors with aged finish.

2018-2020		$1,400	$1,800

H-150 C/H-150 CM

1985-2018. Single rounded cutaway solidbody, curly maple top, 2 pickups, chrome parts, cherry sunburst.

1985-2018	Flamed	$1,400	$1,800
1985-2018	Goldtop	$1,275	$1,675

H-150 Deluxe Limited Edition

1992. 300 made.

1992		$1,350	$1,750

H-157

1989-2004. Mahogany body with maple top, natural, sunburst or black.

1989-2004		$1,500	$1,900

H-157 Ultra

1993-1994. Single-cut solidbody, large block markers, highly figured maple top.

1993-1994		$1,500	$1,900

H-160

1986, 2007. Limited production.

1986		$725	$950
2007	2nd Edition	$800	$1,050

H-170

1980s-1997. Double-cut solidbody, 2 humbuckers, bound carved top, was also a later curly maple top version (H-170CM).

1980s-1997		$1,000	$1,300

MODEL YEAR	FEATURES	EXC. COND. LOW	HIGH

H-204 DD

1986-1989. Single-cut solidbody of mahogany, curly maple top, 1-piece mahogany neck, 22-fret rosewood 'board.

1986-1989		$500	$650

H-207 DD

1986-1989. Double-cut solidbody of mahogany, curly maple top, 1-piece mahogany neck, 22-fret rosewood 'board.

1986-1989		$500	$650

H-357

1989-1994. Asymmetrical solidbody, neck-thru.

1989-1994		$1,725	$2,225

H-516 Thin

1999-2015. Single-cut, thin all maple body, mahogany neck, 2 humbucking pickups, various colors.

1999-2015		$1,500	$1,950

H-530

2016-present. Standard Collection, double-cut hollowbody, sunburst, trans cherry or antique natural.

2016-2020		$1,600	$2,075

H-535

1987-present. Standard Collection, double-cut semi-hollowbody, curly maple top and back, 2 pickups, various colors.

1987-2018		$1,600	$2,100
2019-2020		$1,600	$2,100

H-535 AA

2018-present. Artisan Aged Collection, various colors with aged finish.

2018-2020		$1,550	$2,000

H-537

1990. Single-cut, thinline, dots.

1990		$1,200	$1,550

H-550

1990-2018. Single-cut hollowbody, laminated maple top and back, multiple bound top, white bound 'guard, f-holes, 2 humbuckers.

1990-2018		$1,775	$2,300

H-555

1989-2018. Like 535, but with maple neck, ebony 'board, pearl and abalone inlays, gold hardware.

1989-2018		$1,775	$2,300

H-575

1987-present. Standard Collection, sharp single-cut hollowbody, solid maple top and back, cream bound top and back, wood 'guard, f-holes, 2 humbuckers.

1987-2019		$2,100	$2,700
2020-2021		$2,000	$2,600

H-575 AA

2018-2020. Artisan Aged Collection, various colors with aged finish.

2018-2020		$2,000	$2,600

H-576

1990-2004. Single rounded cut hollowbody, laminated maple top and back, multiple bound top, single bound back and f-holes and wood 'guard, 2 humbuckers.

1990-2004		$1,500	$2,000

MODEL YEAR	FEATURES	EXC. COND. LOW	HIGH

Henry Johnson (HJ) Signature

2005-2018. Pointed single cut curly maple back and sides hollowbody, 2 humbuckers, block inlays, multi-bound.

2005-2018		$1,300	$1,700

HFT-445

1987-2000. Flat-top acoustic, mahogany back and sides, spruce top, maple neck, rosewood 'board.

1987-2000		$650	$850

Johnny Smith

1989-2001. Custom hand-carved 17" hollowbody, single-cut, f-holes, 1 pickup, various colors.

1989-2001	Various options	$2,400	$3,100

Kenny Burrell (KB) Groove Master

2004-2018. Single-cut 16" hollow body, 1 humbucker, gold hardware, block inlays.

2004-2018		$1,700	$2,200

Millennium Eagle 2000

2000-2009. Single-cut semi-solidbody, multiple bound curly maple top, single-bound curly maple back, f-holes, 2 humbuckers, block inlays.

2000-2009		$1,600	$2,000

Millennium Eagle Custom

2000-2009. Like ME 2000 but with curlier maple, multiple bound neck, split block inlays.

2000-2009		$2,150	$2,750

Millennium SAE

2000-2009. Single-cut semi-solidbody, laminated arch top, single cream bound top and back, f-holes, 2 humbuckers.

2000-2009		$1,000	$1,250

Millennium Ultra/Standard Ultra

2004-2016. Single-cut, ultra curly maple top, mahogany back and sides, 1-piece mahogany neck, f-holes, mother-of-pearl block inlays.

2004-2016		$1,400	$1,800

Parsons Street

1989-1992. Offset double-cut, curly maple top on mahogany body, single/single/hum pickups, pearl block markers, sunburst or natural.

1989-1992		$600	$800

Roy Clark

1992-2018. Thinline, single-cut semi-hollow archtop, gold hardware, 2 humbuckers, block markers, cherry sunburst.

1992-2018		$1,900	$2,500

SAE Custom

1992-2000. Single-cut maple semi-hollowbody, f-holes, 2 humbuckers and 1 bridge pickup.

1992-2000		$1,000	$1,300

Super Eagle

1988-2018. 18" body, single-cut electric archtop, 2 humbuckers.

1989-2018		$2,400	$3,100

Super KB Kenny Burrell

2005-2011. Carved spruce top, tiger-flame maple back and sides, 2 pickups, natural or Antique Sunburst.

2005-2011		$4,600	$6,000

Sweet 16

1987-2018. Single-cut maple semi-hollowbody, spruce top, 2 pickups, pearl inlays.

1987-2018		$1,900	$2,500

Hermann Hauser

Born in 1882, Hauser started out building zithers and at age 23 added classical guitars and lutes, most built in his shop in Munich, Germany. He died in 1952. His son and grandson and great-granddaughter, Hermann II and III and Kathrin, continued the tradition. The Hermann Hauser's legacy is based on his innovative approach to bracing and top thickness which gave his instruments their own voice. Hermann I Era instruments are linked with Andres Segovia who used them. Hermann II Era instruments are linked with modern players like Julian Bream. Hermann III builds Segovia style and custom-made instruments. Kathrin Hauser, daughter of Hermann III, is a fourth generation builder. The original Hauser shop in Munich was destroyed by Allied bombing in 1946 and was moved to Reisbach in the Bavaria region, where the shop remains. Hauser instruments used paper labels on the inside back. The labels often stipulate the city of construction as well as the Hermann Hauser name. Labels are easily removed and changed, and an original instrument should be authenticated. Beautiful violin-like clear varnish finish ends in '52, approximately 400 instruments were made by Hermann I. Under Hermann II, nitrocellulose lacquer spray replaces varnish in '52, bracing patterns change in the '60s, which was a welcome change for modern players. Instruments should be evaluated on a case by case basis.

Hermann Hauser II

1952-1988. Born in 1911 and the son of Hermann Hauser I, he built between 500 and 600 classical guitars in Germany during his career. He died in 1988.

Hermann Hauser III

1988-present. Hermann III started build guitars in '74, and took over the family business upon the death of his father in '88. He continues to build Segovia style and custom-made classical guitars in Munich, Germany.

Hess

1872-ca. 1940. Located in Klingenthal, Germany, Hess built acoustic and harp guitars, as well as other stringed instruments and accordians.

Hewett Guitars

1994-present. Luthier James Hewett builds his professional and premium grade, custom/production, steel string, archtop jazz, solidbody and harp guitars in Panorama Village, Texas.

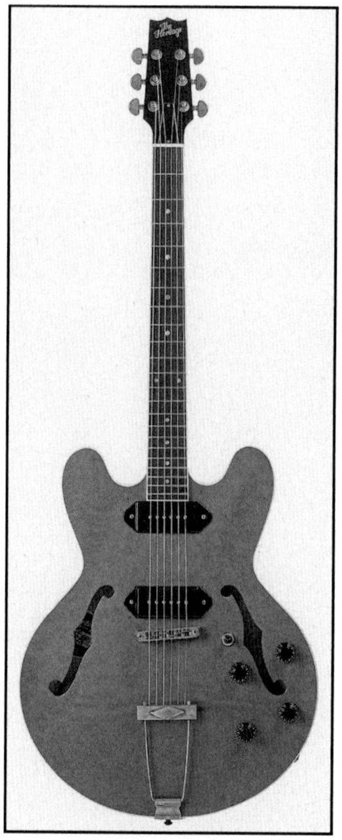

Heritage H-530

Heritage H-575

Hoffman Small Jumbo

2000 Höfner Jazzica Custom

Bernunzio Uptown Music

MODEL YEAR	FEATURES	EXC. COND. LOW	HIGH

Hill Guitar Company

1972-1980, 1990-present. Luthier Kenny Hill builds his professional and premium grade production/custom, classical and flamenco guitars in Felton, California and Michoacan, Mexico.

Hirade Classical

1968-present. Professional grade, production, solid top, classical guitars built in Japan by Takamine. The late Mass Hirade was the founder of the Takamine workshop. He learned his craft from master luthier Masare Kohno. Hirade represents Takamine's finest craftsmanship and material.

HML Guitars

Introduced in 1997, Howard Leese custom-designs, premium grade, electric guitars, built by luthier Jack Pimentel in Puyallup, Washington.

Hoffman Guitars

1971-present. Premium grade, custom flat-tops and harp guitars built by luthier Charles Hoffman in Minneapolis, Minnesota.

Höfner

1887-present. Budget, intermediate, professional and premium grade, production, solidbody, semi-hollow, archtop, acoustic, and classical guitars built in Germany and the Far East. They also produce basses and bowed-instruments. Founded by Karl Höfner in Schonbach, Germany. The company was already producing guitars when sons Josef and Walter joined the company in 1919 and '21 and expanded the market worldwide. They moved the company to Bavaria in '50 and to Hagenau in '97. The S in Hofner model names usually denotes cutaway.

Beatle Electric Model 459TZ

1966-1967. Violin-shaped 500/1 body, block-stripe position markers, transistor-powered flip-fuzz and treble boost, sunburst.

1966-1967 — $1,100 — $1,425

Beatle Electric Model 459VTZ

1966-1967. Same as Model 459TZ except with vibrato tailpiece, brown (standard) or blond option.

1966-1967 Blond option — $1,300 — $1,625

1966-1967 Brown — $1,100 — $1,425

Beatle Electric Model G459TZ Super

1966-1967. Deluxe version of Model 459TZ, flamed maple sides, narrow grain spruce top, gold hardware, elaborate inlays and binding, natural blond.

1966-1967 — $1,200 — $1,550

Beatle Electric Model G459VTZ Super

1966-1967. Same as G459TZ Super but with vibrato tailpiece.

1966-1967 — $1,200 — $1,550

Club Model 40 John Lennon Limited Edition

2008. Limited run of 120, single-cut, spruce top, maple back and sides, neck pickup, vertical Höfner logo on headstock, Lennon signature on 'guard.

2008 — $1,450 — $1,900

MODEL YEAR	FEATURES	EXC. COND. LOW	HIGH

Club Model 50

1959-1962. Mid-level of the late '50s 'Club Series', single-cut, 2 pickups, sunburst.

1959-1962 — $1,225 — $1,625

Club Model 60

1959. Highest model of late '50s 'Club Series', single-cut, 2 black bar pickups, 2 knobs and 2 slider switches on control panel, highest-end split-diamond style markers, natural blond finish.

1959 — $1,300 — $1,700

Club Model 126

1954-1970. Mid-sized single-cut solidbody, dot markers, flamed maple back and sides, spruce top, sunburst. Listed with Höfner Professional Electric Series.

1954-1958 — $800 — $1,075

Committee Model 4680 Thin Electric

1961-1968. Thinline single-cut archtop, 2 pickups, split-arrowhead markers, no vibrato, sunburst.

1961-1968 — $725 — $975

Deluxe Model 176

1964-1983. Double-cut, 3 pickups, polyester varnished sunburst finish, vibrola tailpiece, similar to Model 175 polyester varnished red and gold version.

1964-1966 — $700 — $900

1967-1969 — $500 — $650

1970-1983 — $400 — $525

Galaxy Model 175

1963-1966. Double-cut, 3 pickups, red and gold vinyl covering, fancy red-patch 'guard, vibrola, similar to Model 176 polyester varnished sunburst version.

1963-1966 Red & gold vinyl — $700 — $900

Golden Höfner

1959-1963. Single-cut archtop, blond, 2 pickups, f-holes.

1959-1963 — $4,900 — $6,500

Jazzica Custom

2000-2010. Full body, single soft cutaway, acoustic/electric archtop, carved German spruce top, sunburst.

2000-2010 — $1,300 — $1,700

Model 165

1975-1976. Offset double-cut, S-style body, 2 single-coil pickups, bolt-on neck.

1975-1976 — $275 — $375

Model 171

1975-1976. Copy of Tele-Thinline.

1975-1976 — $250 — $325

Model 172 II (R) (S) (I)

1962-1963. Double-cut body, polyester varnished wood (S) or scuff-proof red (R) or white (I) vinyl, 2 pickups, vibrato.

1962-1963 — $300 — $400

Model 173 II (S) (I)

1962-1963. Double-cut body, polyester varnished wood (S) or scuffproof vinyl (I), 3 pickups, vibrato.

1962-1963 Gold foil vinyl — $350 — $450

1962-1963 White vinyl — $350 — $450

Model 178

1967-ca. 1969. Offset double-cut solidbody, 2 pickups with an array of switches and push button controls, fancy position markers, vibrola, sunburst. 178 used on different design in the '70s.

1967-1969 — $375 — $475

MODEL YEAR	FEATURES	EXC. COND. LOW	HIGH

Model 180 Shorty Standard
1982. Small-bodied travel guitar, single-cut, solidbody, 1 pickup, travel, the Shorty Super had a built-in amp and speaker.

1982		$200	$275

Model 450S Acoustic Archtop
Mid-1960s. Economy single-cut acoustic archtop in Hofner line, dot markers, Höfner logo on 'guard, sunburst.

1960s		$350	$450

Model 455/S
1950s-1970. Archtop, single-cut, block markers.

1959		$425	$575

Model 456 Acoustic Archtop
1950s-1962. Full body acoustic archtop, f-holes, laminated maple top, sides, back, large pearloid blocks, two color pearloid headstock laminate.

1950s-1962		$450	$600

Model 457 President
1959-1972. Single-cut thinline archtop, 2 pickups, non-vibrato.

1959-1972		$550	$725

Model 457/12 12-String Electric
1969-1970. Comfort-thin cutaway archtop, shaded brown.

1969-1970		$425	$575

Model 462 Acoustic Archtop
Ca. 1952-1960s. Single-cut archtop, bound cat's-eye soundholes, 3-piece pearloid headstock overlay, 3-piece large block inlays. Also offered with fingerboard mounted pickup with no controls (EG) and by mid '50s with 1, 2, or 3 pickups with volume and tone knobs/switches (462S/E1, 2, or 3).

1952-1960s	462S	$400	$525
1952-1960s	462SEG	$600	$800

Model 463
1958-1960. Archtop electric, 2 or 3 pickups.

1958-1960		$725	$975

Model 470SE2 Electric Archtop
1961-1994. Large single rounded cutaway electric archtop on Höfner's higher-end they call "superbly flamed maple (back and sides), carved top of best spruce" 2 pickups, 3 control knobs, gold hardware, pearl inlay, natural finish only.

1961-1994		$600	$800

Model 471SE2 Electric Archtop
1969-1977. Large single pointed cutaway electric archtop, flamed maple back and sides, spruce top, black celluloid binding, ebony 'board, pearl inlays, sunburst version of the 470SE2.

1969-1977		$600	$800

Model 490 Acoustic
Late 1960s. 16" body, 12-string, spruce top, maple back and sides, dot markers, natural.

1960s		$175	$225

Model 490E Acoustic Electric
Late 1960s. Flat-top 12-string with on-board pickup and 2 control knobs.

1960s		$250	$325

Model 491 Flat-Top
1960s-1970s. Slope shoulder body style, spruce top, mahogany back and sides, shaded sunburst.

1970s		$250	$325

Model 492 Acoustic
Late 1960s. 16" body, 12-string, spruce top, mahogany back and sides, dot markers.

1960s		$225	$300

Model 492E Acoustic Electric
Late 1960s. Flat-top 12-string with on-board pickup and 2 control knobs.

1960s		$225	$300

Model 496 Jumbo Flat-Top
1960s. Jumbo-style body, selected spruce top, flamed maple back and sides, gold-plated hardware, vine pattern 'guard, sunburst.

1960s		$375	$500

Model 514-H Classical Concert
1960s. Concert model, lower-end of the Höfner classical line, natural.

1960s		$100	$150

Model 4500 Thin Electric
Late-1960s-early-1970s. Thinline archtop, single-cut, 3 options, laminated maple top and back, dot markers, top mounted controls, brown sunburst.

1960s-70s	E1, 1 pickup	$375	$500
1960s-70s	E2, 2 pickups	$450	$600
1960s-70s	V2, 2 pickups, vibrato	$475	$625

Model 4560 Thin Electric
Late-1960s-early-1970s. Thinline archtop, single-cut, 2 options, laminated maple top and back, 2-color headstock, large block markers, top mounted controls, brown sunburst.

1960s-70s	E2	$475	$625
1960s-70s	V2, vibrato	$525	$675

Model 4574VTZ Extra Thin
Late-1960s-early-1970s. Extra thinline acoustic, 2 pickups.

1960s-70s		$500	$675

Model 4575VTZ Extra Thin
Late-1960s-early-1970s. Extra-thinline acoustic, double-cut with shallow rounded horns, 3 pickups, vibrato arm, treble boost and flip-fuzz, straight-line markers.

1960s-70s		$575	$750

Model 4578TZ President
1959-1970. Double-cut archtop. 'President' dropped from name by late-'60s and renamed Model 4578 Dual Cutaway, also added sharp horns.

1959-1965		$525	$675
1966-1970		$450	$600

Model 4600 Thin Electric
Late-1960s-early-1970s. Thinline acoustic, double-cut, 2 pickups, dot markers, sunburst, V2 with vibrato.

1960s-70s	E2	$450	$600
1960s-70s	V2, vibrato	$500	$650

Model 4680 Thin Electric
Late-1960s-early-1970s. Single-cut thinline electric, 2 pickups, 3-in-a-line control knobs, ornate inlays, spruce top, brown sunburst, V2 with vibrato.

1960s-70s	E2	$675	$900
1960s-70s	V2, vibrato	$725	$975

Höfner Club 50
Rivington Guitars

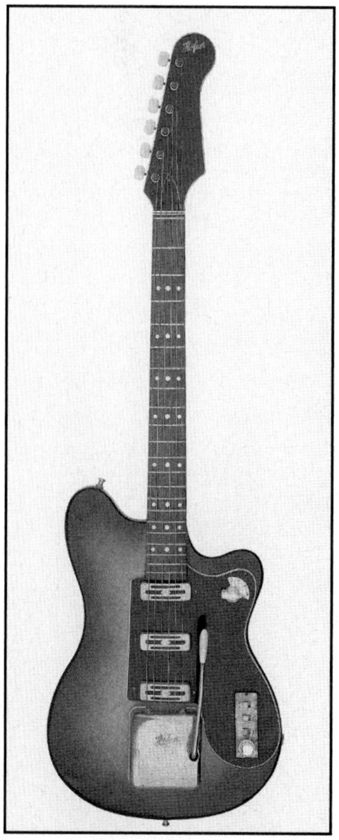

1961 Höfner 173 II S
Imaged by Heritage Auctions, HA.com

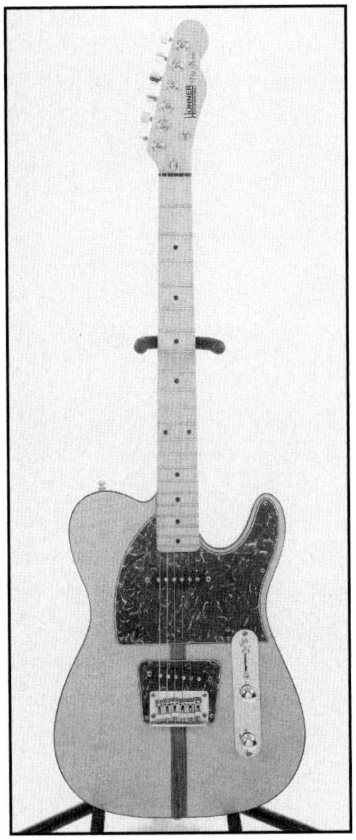

1980s Hohner
Professional TE Prinz
Imaged by Heritage Auctions, HA.com

1965 Holiday Silhouette Bobcat
Tom Pfeifer

MODEL YEAR	FEATURES	EXC. COND. LOW	HIGH

Model 4700 Thin Electric

Late-1960s-early-1970s. Deluxe version of Model 4680, gold plated appointments and natural finish, V2 with vibrato.

1960s-70s	E2	$800	$1,050
1960s-70s	V2, vibrato	$875	$1,125

Senator Acoustic Archtop

1958-1960s. Floating pickup option available, full body archtop, f-holes, made for Selmer, London.

1958-1960 — $325 — $425

Senator E1

1961. Senator full body archtop with single top mounted pickup and controls.

1961 — $475 — $625

Verythin Standard

2001-2008. Update of the 1960s Verythin line, 2 humbuckers, f-holes, dot inlays.

2001-2008 — $600 — $800

Hohner

1857-present. Budget and intermediate grade, production, acoustic and electric guitars and basses. They also have mandolins, banjos and ukuleles. Matthias Hohner, a clockmaker in Trossingen, Germany, founded Hohner in 1857, making harmonicas. Hohner has been offering guitars and basses at least since the early '70s. HSS was founded in 1986 as a distributor of guitars and other musical products. By 2000, Hohner was also offering the Crafter brands of guitars.

Alpha Standard

1987. Designed by Klaus Scholler, solidbody, stereo outputs, Flytune tremolo.

1987 — $175 — $250

G 2T/G 3T Series

1980s-1990s. Steinberger-style body, 6-string, neck-thru, locking tremolo.

1980s-90s — $250 — $325

Jacaranda Rosewood Dreadnought

1978. Flat-top acoustic.

1978 — $125 — $175

Jack

1987-1990s. Mate for Jack Bass. Headless, tone circuit, tremolo, 2 single-coils and 1 humbucker.

1987-1992 — $250 — $325

L 59/L 75 Series

Late-1970s-1980s. Classic single-cut solidbody, 2 humbuckers, glued neck, sunburst, 59 has upgrade maple body with maple veneer top.

1970s-80s — $250 — $325

Miller Beer Guitar

1985. Solidbody, shaped like Miller beer logo.

1985 — $175 — $250

Professional

1980s. Single-cut solidbody, maple neck, extra large 'guard, natural.

1980s — $250 — $325

Professional Series - TE Custom

1980s-1990s. Single-cut solidbody, bolt neck.

1980s-90s — $550 — $750

Professional Series - TE Prinz

Late 1980s-early 1990s. Based on Prince's No. 1 guitar, 2 single-coils, bolt neck, Professional The Prinz headstock logo, natural.

1989-1990 — $550 — $750

SE 35

1989-mid-1990s. Semi-hollow thinline, 2 humbuckers, natural.

1989 — $250 — $325

SG Lion

1980s-1990s. Offset double-cut, pointy headstock, glued neck.

1980s-90s — $175 — $250

ST Series

1986-1990s. Includes the bolt neck ST 57, ST Special, ST Special S, Viper I, Viper II (snakeskin finish option), ST Victory, ST Metal S, and the ST Custom.

1986-1992 — $150 — $300

Standard Series - EX Artist

1970s-1980s. Solidbody, 2 humbuckers, gold hardware, neck-thru, solid maple body, rosewood 'board, tremolo.

1970s-80s — $150 — $300

Standard Series - RR Custom

1970s-1980s. Randy Rhoads V body, 2 humbuckers, chrome hardware, glued neck, mahogany body, rosewood 'board, tremolo.

1970s-80s — $150 — $300

Standard Series - SR Heavy

1970s-1980s. Hybrid body, 2 humbuckers, neck-thru, solid maple body, rosewood 'board, tremolo.

1970s-80s — $150 — $300

Holiday

1960s. Electric, acoustic and bass guitars sold by Aldens, a Chicago catalog company. Most models built by Harmony. They also offered mandolins and banjos.

Silhouette Bobcat

1964-1967. Solidbody electric made by Harmony, similar to Harmony Silhouette, offset double-cut, 2 pickups, 4-in-a-row control knobs.

1964-1967 — $300 — $400

Hollenbeck Guitars

1970-2008. Luthier Bill Hollenbeck built his premium grade, production/custom, hollow and semi-hollow body acoustics and electric guitars in Lincoln, Illinois. Bill passed away in '08.

Hollingworth Guitars

1995-present. Luthier Graham Hollingworth builds his production/custom, premium grade, electric, acoustic and archtop guitars in Mermaid Beach, Gold Coast, Queensland, Australia. He also builds lap steels.

Holman

1966-1968. Built by the Holman-Woodell guitar factory in Neodesha, Kansas. The factory was started to build guitars for Wurlitzer, but that fell through by '67.

MODEL YEAR	FEATURES	EXC. COND. LOW	HIGH

Holst

1984-present. Premium grade, custom, archtop, flat-top, semi-hollow, and classical guitars built in Creswell, Oregon by luthier Stephen Holst. He also builds mandolins. Until '01 he was located in Eugene, Oregon.

Holzapfel (Holzapfel & Beitel)

1898-1930s. Carl C. Holzapfel and Clemence Beitel built guitars, banjos, and mandolins in Baltimore, but are best-known as early innovators of the 12-string guitar. Beitel left the company in 1905 and Holzapfel continued to build instruments up to the depression. He, and later his son, Carl M., mainly repaired instruments after that (up to 1988), but still would do custom builds.

Hondo

1969-1987, 1991-2005. Budget grade, production, imported acoustic, classical and electric guitars. They also offered basses, banjos and mandolins. Originally imported by International Music Corporation (IMC) of Fort Worth, Texas, founded by Jerry Freed and Tommy Moore and named after a small town near San Antonio, Texas. Early pioneers of Korean guitarmaking, primarily targeted at beginner market. Introduced their first electrics in '72. Changed brand to Hondo II in '74. Some better Hondos made in Japan '74-'82/'83. In '85 IMC purchases major interest in Jackson/Charvel, and the Hondo line was supplanted by Charvels. 1987 was the last catalog before hiatus. In '88 IMC was sold and Freed began Jerry Freed International and in '91 he revived the Hondo name. Acquired by MBT International in '95, currently part of Musicorp.

Acoustic Flat-Top

1969-1987, 1991-2005.

1969-2005		$75	$125

Electric Hollowbody

1969-1987, 1991-2005.

1969-2005		$125	$450

Electric Solidbody

1969-1987, 1991-2005.

1969-1987		$125	$450
1991-1999		$125	$450
2000-2005		$50	$150

Longhorn 6/12 Doubleneck Copy

1970s-1980s. Copy of Danelectro Longhorn 6/12 Doubleneck guitar, Dano coke bottle-style headstock, white sunburst.

1970s-80s		$525	$700

Longhorn Copy

Ca. 1978-1980s. Copy of Danelectro Long Horn guitar, Dano Coke bottle-style headstock, brown-copper.

1978-80s		$375	$500

M 16 Rambo-Machine Gun

1970s-1980s. Machine gun body-style, matching machine gun-shaped guitar case, black or red. Price includes original case with form-fit interior; deduct as much as 40% less for non-original case.

1970s-80s		$350	$450

MODEL YEAR	FEATURES	EXC. COND. LOW	HIGH

Hopf

1906-present. Intermediate, professional, premium, and presentation grade, production/custom, classical guitars made in Germany. They also make basses, mandolins and flutes.

The Hopf family of Germany has a tradition of instrument building going back to 1669, but the modern company was founded in 1906. Hopf started making electric guitars in the mid-'50s. Some Hopf models were made by others for the company. By the late-'70s, Hopf had discontinued making electrics, concentrating on classicals.

Explorer Standard

1960s. Double-cut semi-hollow, sharp horns, center block, 2 mini-humbuckers.

1960s		$600	$800

Saturn Archtop

1960s. Offset cutaway, archtop-style soundholes, 2 pickups, white, says Saturn on headstock.

1960s		$750	$1,000

Super Deluxe Archtop

1960s. Archtop, 16 3/4", catseye soundholes, carved spruce top, flamed maple back and sides, sunburst.

1960s		$825	$1,075

Hopkins

1998-present. Luthier Peter Hopkins builds his presentation grade, custom, hand-carved archtop guitars in British Columbia.

Horabe

Classical and Espana models made in Japan.

Classical

1960-1980s	Various models	$350	$600

Hottie

In 2009, amp builders Jean-Claude Escudie and Mike Bernards added production/custom, professional and premium grade, solidbody electric guitars built by luthier Saul Koll in Portland, Oregon.

House Guitars

2004-present. Luthier Joshua House builds his production/custom, premium grade, acoustic guitars and guitar-bouzoukis in Goderich, Ontario.

Howe-Orme

1897-ca. 1910. Elias Howe and George Orme's Boston-based publishing and distribution buisness offered a variety of mandolin family instruments and guitars and received many patents for their designs. Many of their guitars featured detachable necks.

Hoyer

1874-present. Intermediate grade, production, flat-top, classical, electric, and resonator guitars. They also build basses. Founded by Franz Hoyer, building classical guitars and other instruments. His son, Arnold, added archtops in the late-1940s, and solidbodies in the '60s. In '67, Arnold's son,

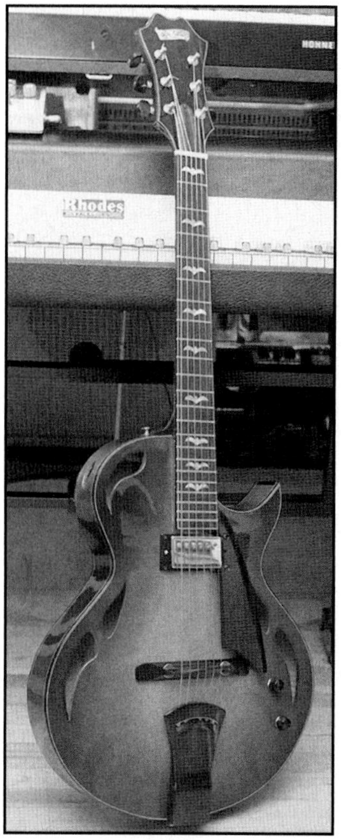

Holst

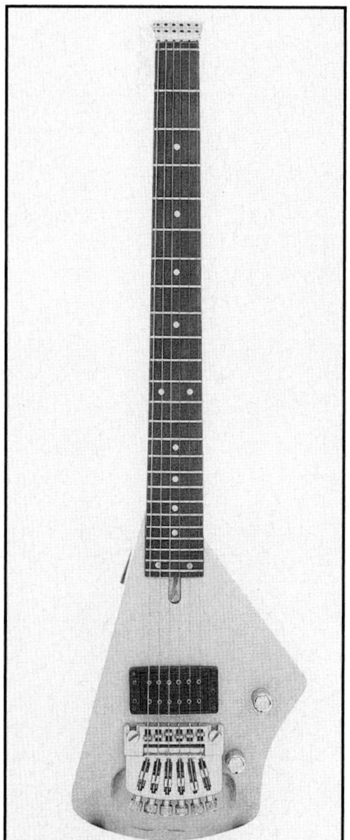

1980s Hondo H-790 Lazer

Imaged by Heritage Auctions, HA.com

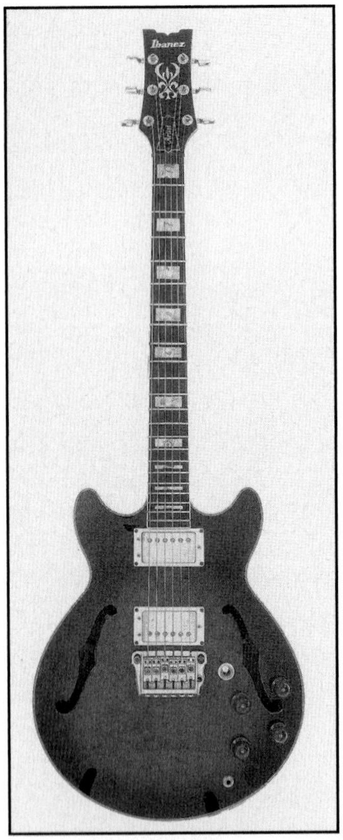

Ibanez AM-225 Artist
Imaged by Heritage Auctions, HA.com

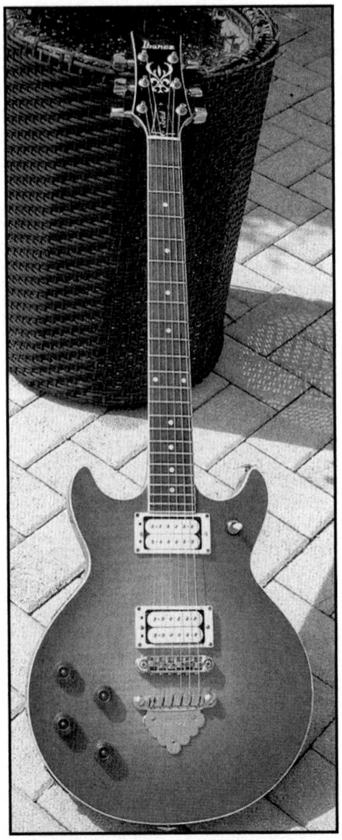

1983 Ibanez AR-100 Artist
Craig Brody

MODEL YEAR	FEATURES	EXC. COND. LOW	HIGH

Walter, took over, leaving the company in '77. The company changed hands a few times over the following years. Walter started building guitars again in '84 under the W.A. Hoyer brand, which is not associated with Hoyer.

Acoustic

1960s. Acoustic archtop or flat-top.

1960s $225 $500

Junior

Early-1960s. Solidbody with unusual sharp horn cutaway, single neck pickup, bolt-on neck, dot markers, Arnold Hoyer logo on headstock, shaded sunburst.

1960s $500 $650

Soloist Electric

1960-1962. Single-cut archtop, 2 pickups, teardrop f-holes, sunburst.

1960-1962 $500 $650

Special 24

1950s-1960s. Single-cut acoustic archtop, Hoyer Special script logo on headstock, pickups added in '60s. SL was deluxe version.

1950s Acoustic $1,500 $1,950

Huerga

Introduced in 1995, professional to presentation grade, production/custom, archtop, flat-top, and metal-front solidbody electric guitars built by luthier Diego Huerga in Buenos Aires, Argentina.

Humming Bird

1947-ca.1975. Japanese manufacturer offering acoustics and electrics. By 1968 making pointy Mosrite inspirations. Probably not imported into the U.S.

Electric Solidbody

1950s $150 $250

Humphrey, Thomas

1970-2008. Premium and presentation grade, custom, nylon-string guitars built by luthier Thomas Humphrey in Gardiner, New York. In 1996 Humphrey began collaborating with Martin Guitars, resulting in the Martin C-TSH and C-1R. Often the inside back label will indicate the year of manufacture. Humphrey died in April, 2008.

Classical

1976-1984. Brazilian or Indian rosewood back and sides, spruce top, traditionally-based designs evolved over time with Millenium becoming a benchmark design in 1985, values can increase with new designs. Valuations depend on each specific instrument and year and type of construction, price ranges are guidance only; each instrument should be evaluated on a case-by-case basis.

1976-1984 $4,800 $6,200

Millennium (Classical)

1985-2008. Professional performance-grade high-end classical guitar with innovative taper body design and elevated 'board, tops are generally spruce (versus cedar) with rosewood back and sides.

1995-2008 $8,600 $11,200

Steel String

1974. D-style, only 4 made.

1974 $2,800 $3,600

Huss and Dalton Guitar Company

1995-present. Luthiers Jeff Huss and Mark Dalton build their professional and premium grade flat-tops and banjos in Staunton, Virginia.

Hutchins

2006-present. Gary Hutchins in Sussex, U.K. imports intermediate and professional grade, production, acoustic and electric guitars and basses from China, Germany and Korea.

Ian A. Guitars

1991-present. In the early 1990s luthier Ian Anderson built guitars under his name, in 2005 he began using the Ian A. brand. He builds premium grade, production/custom, solidbody electric guitars in Poway, California.

Ibanez

1932-present. Budget, intermediate, and professional grade, production/custom, acoustic and electric guitars. They also make basses, amps, mandolins, and effects.

Founded in Nagoya, Japan, by Matsujiro Hoshino as book and stationary supply, started retailing musical instruments in 1909, importing them by '21. The company's factories were destroyed during World War II, but the business was revived in '50. The Ibanez name in use by 1957. Junpei Hoshino, grandson of founder, became president in '60; a new factory opened called Tama Seisakusho (Tama Industries). Brand names by '64 included Ibanez, Star, King's Stone, Jamboree and Goldentone, supplied by 85 factories serving global markets. Sold acoustic guitars to Harry Rosenblum of Elger Guitars ('59-ca.'65) in Ardmore, Pennsylvania, in early-'60s. Around '62 Hoshino purchased 50% interest in Elger Guitars, and ca. '65 changed the name to Ibanez.

Jeff Hasselberger headed the American guitar side beginning '73-'74, and the company headquarters were moved to Cornwells Heights, Pennsylvania in '74. By '75 the instruments are being distributed by Chesbro Music Company in Idaho Falls, Idaho, and Harry Rosenblum sells his interest to Hoshino shortly thereafter. Ca. '81, the Elger Company becomes Hoshino U.S.A. An U.S. Custom Shop was opened in '88.

Most glued-neck guitars from '70s are fairly rare.

Dating: copy guitars begin ca. '71. Serial numbers begin '75 with letter (A-L for month) followed by 6 digits, the first 2 indicating year, last 4 sequential (MYYXXXX). By '88 the month letter drops off. Dating code stops early-'90s; by '94 letter preface either F for Fuji or C for Cort (Korean) manufacturer followed by number for year and consecutive

MODEL YEAR	FEATURES	EXC. COND. LOW	HIGH

numbers (F4XXXX=Fuji, C4XXXX=Cort, 1994).

Pickups on Asian import electric guitars from the '50s-'70s are often considered to be the weakest engineering specification on the instrument. Old Ibanez pickups can become microphonic and it is not unusual to see them replaced.

AE (Acoustic Electric) Series

1983-present. Models include AE, AEF, AEL flat-tops (no archtops).

1983-2020 Various models $100 $400

AH10 (Allan Holdsworth)

1985-1987. Offset double-cut solidbody, bolt neck, bridge humbucker, dots, various colors.

1985-1987 1 pickup $300 $400

AH20 (Allan Holdsworth)

1986. As AH10 but with 2 humbuckers.

1986 2 pickups $325 $425

AM Series

1985-1991. Small body archtops, models include AM70, 75, 75T, 100, 225. Becomes Artstar in '92.

1985-1991 Various models $400 $700

AM Stagemaster Series

1983-1984, 1989-1990. Made in Japan, small double-cut semi-hollow body, 2 humbuckers, models include AM50, 100, 205, 255. Model name used again, without Stagemaster in '89-'90.

1983-1984 Various models $400 $700

AR50 "Jr. Artist"

1979-1983. Double-cut solidbody, dot markers, 2 humbuckers.

1979-1983 $400 $525

AR100 Artist

1979-1984. Double-cut solidbody, set neck, maple top, 2 humbuckers.

1979-1984 $750 $950

AR300 Artist

1979-1982. Symmetrical double-cut, carved maple top.

1979-1982 $825 $1,050

AR500 Artist

1979-1982. 2 humbuckers, EQ.

1979-1982 $825 $1,050

Artcore Series

2002-present. Made in China, hollowbody electric, models include AF, AG, AK, AM, AS and TM.

2002-2020 Various models $150 $600

AS50 Artist

1980-1981. Made in Japan, semi-acoustic.

1980-1981 $450 $575

AS50 Artstar

1998-1999. Laminated maple body, bound rosewood 'board, dot inlays, 2 humbuckers.

1998-1999 $450 $575

AS80 Artstar

1994-2002. Made in Korea, double cut semi-hollow body, dots, 2 humbuckers.

1994-2002 $450 $575

AS100 Artist

1979-1981. Set neck, gold hardware.

1979-1981 $575 $750

MODEL YEAR	FEATURES	EXC. COND. LOW	HIGH

AS180 Artstar

1997-1999. Double cut semi-hollow body, plain top, dots, 2 humbuckers.

1997-1999 $575 $750

AS200 Artist

1979-1986. Double-cut semi-acoustic, flamed maple, block markers, gold hardware, 2 humbuckers, replaced Artist 2630. Artist dropped from name when model becomes hollowbody archtop in '82.

1979-1986 $900 $1,200

AS200 Artstar

1992-2000. Flame maple top, gold hardware, 2 humbuckers, block inlays.

1992-2000 $775 $1,000

AW Artwood Series

1979-present. Electric/acoustics, various models.

1979-2020 Various models $150 $500

BL Blazer Series

1980-1982, 1997-1998. Offset double-cut, 10 similar models in the '80s with different body woods and electronic configurations. Series name returns on 3 models in late '90s.

1980-1998 Various models $200 $600

Bob Weir Model 2681

1975-1980, 1995. Double-cut ash solidbody, ebony 'board, tree-of-life inlay, gold-plated pickups, limited numbers. Reintroduced as a limited run in '95.

1975-1980 $1,550 $2,000

Bob Weir Standard Model 2680

1976-1980. Standard production model of 2681.

1976-1980 $1,075 $1,400

Bob Weir Model One BWM1 (Cowboy Fancy)

2005. Double-cut swamp ash solidbody, ebony 'board, pearl vine inlay down neck and part way around body, 30 made.

2005 $2,300 $3,000

Challenger 2552ASH

1977-1978. T-style ash solidbody.

1977-1978 $400 $525

CN100 Concert Standard

1978-1979. Double-cut solidbody, set neck, 2 humbuckers, chrome hardware, dot markers.

1978-1979 $400 $525

CN200 Concert Custom

1978-1979. Carved maple top, mahogany body, 7 layer black/white binding, bolt-on neck, gold hardware, block inlays, 2 Super 80 pickups.

1978-1979 $450 $600

CN250 Concert

1978-1979. Like CN200 but with vine inlay.

1978-1979 $575 $750

DG350 Destroyer II

1986-1987. X Series, modified X-shaped basswood body, flame maple top, 2 humbuckers, trem.

1986-1987 $375 $500

DT50 Destroyer II

1980-1982. Modified alder Explorer body, 6-in-line headstock, bolt neck, 2 humbuckers, thick paint.

1980-1982 $575 $750

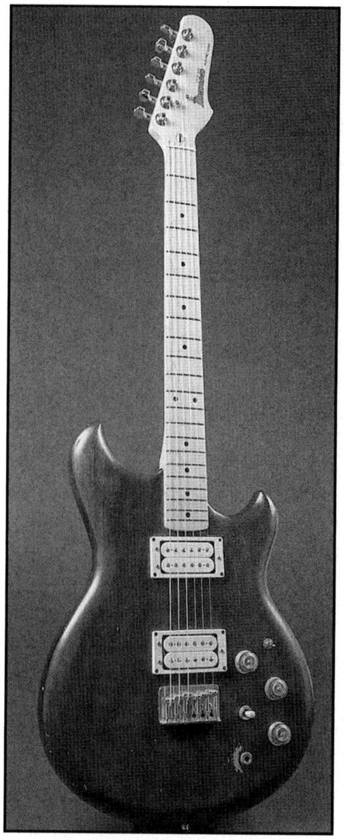

1982 Ibanez BL Blazer

Carter Vintage Guitars

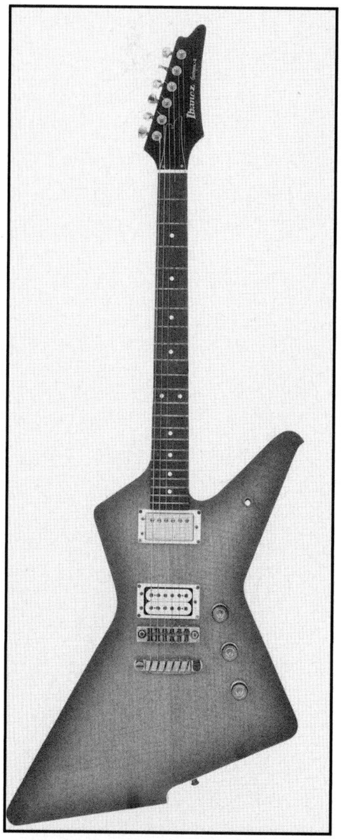

1981 Ibanez DT50 Destroyer II

Imaged by Heritage Auctions, HA.com

1979 Ibanez Iceman PS10 Paul Stanley
Craig Brody

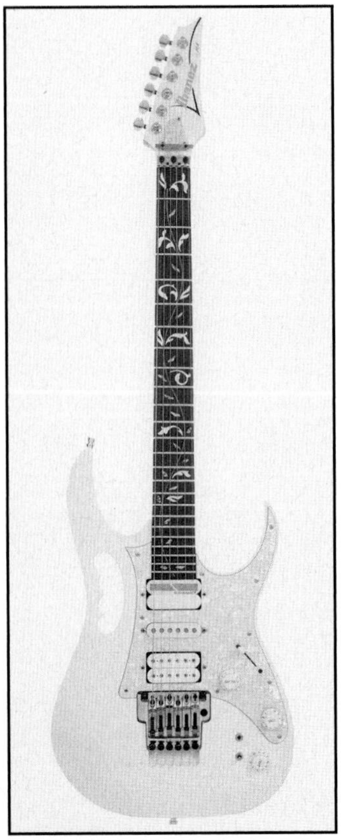

2004 Ibanez JEM 77
Imaged by Heritage Auctions, HA.com

MODEL YEAR	FEATURES	EXC. COND. LOW	HIGH

DT150 Destroyer II
1982-1984. Like DT50 but birch/basswood, 1 humbucker.

1982-1984		$575	$750

DT155 Destroyer II
1982-1984. Like DT150 but with 3 humbuckers.

1982-1984		$775	$1,000

DT350 Destroyer II
1984-1985. X Series, opaque finish, 1 humbucker, trem.

1984-1985		$450	$600

DT400 Destroyer II
1980-1982. Modified mahogany Explorer body, flame maple top, 6-in-line headstock, set-neck, 2 humbuckers, cherry sunburst. Model changed to DT500 in '82.

1980-1982		$575	$750

DT500 Destroyer II
1982-1984. Replaced the DT400, flame maple top.

1982-1984		$575	$750

DT555 Destroyer II Phil Collen
1983-1987. Bound basswood solidbody, 3 humbuckers, vibrato, black.

1983-1987		$2,000	$2,600

DTX120 Destroyer
2000-2004. X Series, known as the Millennium Destroyer, 2 humbuckers.

2000-2004		$225	$300

EX Series
1988-1993. Double-cut solidbodies with long thin horns.

1988-1993	Various models	$150	$300

FA (Full Acoustic) Series
1978-1982. Single-cut full body jazz-style.

1978-1982	Various models	$950	$1,225

FG-100
1982-1987. Single-cut archtop, maple top, 2 humbuckers.

1982-1987		$950	$1,225

FR1620/Prestige FR1620
2008-2014. Ash body, maple/walnut neck, rosewood 'board, 2 pickups, black or red finish.

2008-2014		$525	$700

GAX Series
1998-2009. Symmetrical double-cut (Gibson SG style) with 2 humbuckers, lower cost of the AX line.

1998-2009	Various models	$90	$175

George Benson GB10
1977-present. Single-cut, laminated spruce top, flame maple back and sides, 2 humbuckers, 3-piece set-in maple neck, ebony 'board, sunburst or blond.

1977-1989		$1,750	$2,250
1990-1999		$1,500	$1,950
2000-2020		$1,250	$1,625

George Benson GB15
2006-2010. Like GB10, but with 1 humbucker.

2006-2010		$1,750	$2,250

George Benson GB20
1978-1982. Larger than GB10, laminated spruce top, flame maple back and sides.

1978-1982		$2,300	$3,000

George Benson GB100 Deluxe
1993-1996. GB-10 with flamed maple top, pearl binding, sunburst finish 'guard, pearl vine inlay tailpiece, gold hardware.

1993-1996		$2,500	$3,200

GSA Series
2000-2011. Offset double-cut body.

2000-2011	GSA20/GSA60	$100	$200

Iceman 2663/2663 TC/2663 SL
1975-1978. The original Iceman Series models, called the Flash I, II and III respectively, I has 2 humbuckers, II (TC) and III (SL) have 1 triple-coil pickup.

1975-1978		$900	$1,200

Iceman PS10 Paul Stanley
1978-1981. Limited edition Paul Stanley model, abalone trim, Stanley's name engraved at 21st fret, reissued in '95 with upgraded model names.

1978-1981	Korina finish	$1,700	$2,200
1978-1981	Sunburst or black	$1,400	$1,800

Iceman PS10 II Paul Stanley
1995-1996. Reissue of original PS-10.

1995-1996	Black	$1,300	$1,750

Iceman PS10 LTD Paul Stanley
1995-1996. Limited edition, gold mirror appointments, gold hardware, black pearl metalflake finish.

1995-1996		$2,150	$2,800

Iceman Series
1975-2010. Ibanez unique body styles with hooked lower treble horn body.

1978	IC210	$875	$1,150
1978-1979	IC250	$875	$1,150
1978-1979	IC300 (Korina)	$875	$1,150
1978-1982	IC400	$900	$1,200
1978-1990	IC200	$700	$900
1979-1980	IC50	$700	$900
1981-1982	IC400 CS	$800	$1,050
1994	IC500	$800	$1,050
1994-2003	IC300	$300	$400
1995-1996	IC350	$300	$400

IMG-2010 Guitar Controller MIDI
1985-1987. Similar to Roland GR-707, slim triangle-wedge body with treble horn.

1985-1987	Guitar only	$525	$675

JEM 7 Series
1988-2010. Basswood or alder body, various models, alder 7V offered until '10.

1988-2010	Various models	$1,500	$2,000

JEM 77 Series
1988-1999, 2003-2010. Basswood body, monkey grip handle, 3 pickups, 'board with tree of life or pyramids inlay, finishes include floral pattern or multicolor swirl. Current version has dot inlays and solid finish. The JEM 77BRMR Bad Horsie was introduced in '05 with a mirror finish.

1980-2010	Various models	$2,100	$2,800

JEM 555
1994-2000. Basswood, dots and vine inlay, 3 pickups.

1994-2000		$475	$625

JEM 777 Series
1987-1996. Basswood body, monkey grip 3 pickups, pyramids or vine inlay.

1987-1996	Various models	$2,100	$3,000

GUITARS

MODEL YEAR	FEATURES	EXC. COND. LOW	HIGH

JEM 10th Anniversary

1996. Limited Edition signature Steve Vai model, bolt neck, vine metal 'guard, vine neck inlays and headstock art.

1996		$3,900	$5,100

JEM 20th Anniversary

2007. Steve Vai 20th Anniversary JEM model, green acrylic illuminating body, celebrates the 20th year (1987-2007) of the Ibanez JEM series, limited edition.

2007		$3,500	$4,500

JEM 90th Anniversary

1997. Limited Edition signature Steve Vai model, textured silver finish, chrome 'guard.

1997		$1,500	$2,000

JEM Y2KDNA (Limited Edition)

2000. Red Swirl marble finish using Steve Vai's blood in the paint.

2000		$2,100	$3,000

Joe Pass JP20

1981-1990. Full body, single-cut, 1 pickup, abalone and pearl split block inlay, JP inlay on headstock.

1981-1990	Sunburst	$1,250	$1,650

Joe Satriani JS6

1993. Limited production, lightweight mahogany body, non-gloss finish, JS Series headstock logo.

1993		$1,050	$1,400

Joe Satriani JS100

1994-2014. Offset double cut basswood body, 2 humbuckers, vibrato, red, black, white or custom finish.

1994-2014	Custom finish	$475	$625
1994-2014	Standard finish	$350	$450

Joe Satriani JS1000

1994-1996, 1998-2012. 2 DiMarzio humbuckers, lightweight body.

1994-2012	Various colors	$750	$1,000

Joe Satriani JS1200

2004-2016. Candy Apple Red.

2004-2016		$825	$1,100

Joe Satriani JS 10th Anniversary

1998. Chrome-metal body, Satriani Anniversary script on back cover plate.

1998		$2,150	$2,800

Joe Satriani JS 20th Anniversary

2008. Opaque finish with alien surfer graphic.

2008		$2,150	$2,800

Joe Satriani Y2K

2000. Clear see-thru plexi-style body.

2000		$1,700	$2,200

John Petrucci JPM100 P2

1996. Offset double-cut solidbody, 2 pickups, multi-color graphic.

1996		$1,675	$2,175

John Petrucci JPM100 P3

1997. As P2 but with same graphic in black and white.

1997		$1,675	$2,175

John Petrucci JPM100 P4

1998. As P2 but with same graphic in camo colors.

1998		$1,675	$2,175

John Scofield JSM100

2001-present. Double-cut semi hollow body, 2 humbuckers, ebony 'board, gold hardware.

2001-2020		$1,775	$2,275

MODEL YEAR	FEATURES	EXC. COND. LOW	HIGH

Lee Ritenour LR10

1981-1987. Flame maple body, bound set neck, Quick Change tailpiece, 2 pickups, dark red sunburst, foam-filled body to limit feedback.

1981-1987		$1,625	$2,100

M310

1982. D-size flat-top, maple back and sides, rosewood 'board.

1982		$150	$200

M340

1978-1979. D-size flat-top, flamed maple back and sides, maple 'board. 'board.

1978-1979		$200	$300

Maxxas

1987-1988. Solidbody (MX2) or with internal sound chambers (MX3, '88 only), 2 pickups, all-access neck joint system.

1987-1988	MX2	$900	$1,200
1988	MX3	$1,000	$1,300

MC Musician Series

1978-1982. Solidbodies, various models.

1978-1980	MC500, carved top	$1,175	$1,525
1978-1980	Neck-thru body	$875	$1,125
1978-1982	Bolt neck	$675	$875

Mick Thompson MTM-1

2006. Seven logo on fretboard, MTM1 logo on back of headstock.

2006		$650	$850

Model 600 Series

1974-1978. Copy era acoustic flat-tops with model numbers in the 600 Series, basically copies of classic American square shoulder dreadnoughts. Includes the 683, 684, 693 and the 6-in-line 647; there were 12-string copies as well.

1974-1978		$550	$725

Model 700 Series

1974-1977. Upgraded flat-top models such as the Brazilian Scent 750, with more original design content than 600 Series.

1974-1977		$550	$725

Model 900 Series

1963-1964. Offset double-cut solidbody with sharp curving horns, Burns Bison copy.

1963-1964	901, 1 pickup	$250	$350
1963-1964	992, 2 pickups	$275	$375

Model 1453

1971-1973. Copy of classic single-cut hollowbody, replaced by Model 2355 in '73.

1971-1973		$1,200	$1,600

Model 1800 Series

1962-1963. Offset double-cut solidbody (Jazzmaster-style), models came with bar (stud) or vibrato tailpiece, and 2, 3 or 4 pickups.

1962-1963	Various models	$250	$350

Model 1912

1971-1973. Double-cut semi-hollow body, sunburst finish.

1971-1973		$800	$1,050

Model 2020

1970. Initial offering of the copy era, offset double-cut, 2 unusual rectangular pickups, block markers, raised nailed-on headstock logo, sunburst.

1970		$600	$800

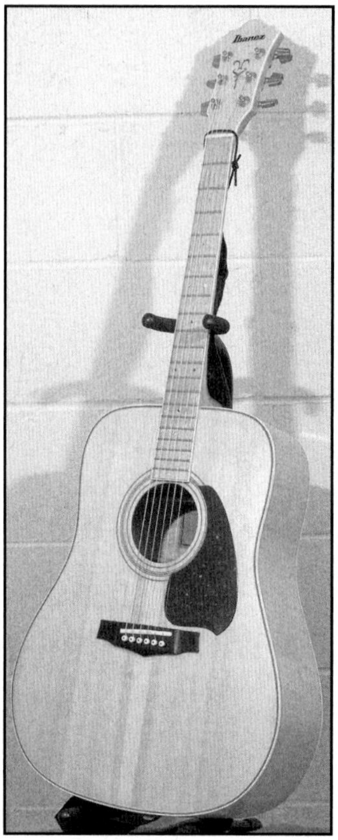

1979 Ibanez M340
Tom Pfeifer

1977 Ibanez 684 Concord
Imaged by Heritage Auctions, HA.com

GUITARS

1975 Ibanez Model 2402
John DeSilva

1975 Ibanez Model 2404 Double Axe
Greg Perrine

MODEL YEAR	FEATURES	EXC. COND. LOW	HIGH

Model 2240M

Early 1970s. Thick hollowbody electric copy, single pointed cutaway, double-parallelogram markers, 2 humbuckers, natural finish.

1971-1973 $1,200 $1,600

Model 2336 Les Jr.

1974-1976. Copy of classic slab solidbody, TV Lime.

1974-1976 $450 $600

Model 2340 Deluxe '59er

1974-1977. Copy of classic single-cut solidbody, Hi-Power humbuckers, opaque or flametop.

1974-1977 Flametop $525 $675
1974-1977 Opaque $525 $675

Model 2341 Les Custom

1974-1977. Copy of classic single-cut solidbody.

1974-1977 $525 $675

Model 2342 Les Moonlight/Sunlight Special

1974-1977. Copy of classic slab solidbody, black (Moonlight) or ivory (Sunlight).

1974-1977 $525 $675

Model 2343 FM Jr.

1974-1976. Copy of LP TV Jr.

1974-1976 $525 $675

Model 2343 Jr.

1974-1976. Copy of classic Jr., cherry mahogany.

1974-1976 $525 $675

Model 2344

1974-1976. Copy of classic double-cut solidbody.

1974-1976 $350 $450

Model 2345

1974-1976. Copy of classic sharp double-cut solidbody, set neck, walnut or white, vibrato, 3 pickups.

1974-1976 $575 $750

Model 2346

1974. Copy of classic sharp double-cut solidbody, vibrato, set neck, 2 pickups.

1974 $575 $750

Model 2347

1974-1976. Copy of classic sharp double-cut solidbody, set-neck, 1 pickup.

1974-1976 $450 $600

Model 2348 Firebrand

1974-1977. Copy of classic reverse solidbody, mahogany body, bolt neck, 2 pickups.

1974-1977 $700 $925

Model 2350 Les

1971-1977. Copy of classic single-cut solidbody, bolt neck, black, gold hardware, goldtop version (2350G Les) also available. A cherry sunburst finish (2350 Les Custom) was offered by '74.

1971-1977 $575 $750

Model 2351 Les

1974-1977. Copy of classic single-cut solidbody, gold top, 2 pickups.

1974-1977 $575 $760

Model 2351DX

1974-1977. Copy of classic single-cut solidbody, gold top, 2 mini-humbuckers.

1974-1977 $575 $750

MODEL YEAR	FEATURES	EXC. COND. LOW	HIGH

Model 2351M Les

1974-1977. LP Standard style, sunburst.

1974-1977 $575 $750

Model 2352 Telly

1974-1978. Copy of early classic single-cut solidbody, 1 bridge pickup, white finish.

1974-1978 $575 $750

Model 2352CT

1974-1978. Copy of classic single-cut solidbody, single-coil bridge and humbucker neck pickup.

1974-1978 $575 $750

Model 2352DX Telly

1974-1978. Copy of classic single-cut solidbody, 2 humbuckers.

1974-1978 $575 $750

Model 2354

1974-1977. Copy of classic sharp double-cut solidbody, 2 humbuckers, vibrato.

1974-1977 $575 $750

Model 2354S

1972-1977. Stop tailpiece version of 2354.

1972-1977 $575 $750

Model 2355/2355M

1973-1977. Copy of classic single-cut hollowbody, sunburst or natural maple (M).

1973-1977 $1,000 $1,300

Model 2356

1973-1975. Copy of classic double pointed cutaway hollowbody, bowtie markers, sunburst. There was another Model 2356 in '74, a copy of a different hollowbody.

1973-1975 $875 $1,150

Model 2363R

1973-1974. Cherry finish copy of classic varitone double-cut semi-hollow body.

1973-1974 $875 $1,150

Model 2364 Ibanex

1971-1973. Dan Armstrong see-thru Lucite copy, 2 mounted humbuckers.

1971-1973 $675 $900

Model 2368 Telly

1973-1978. Copy of classic single-cut thinline, chambered f-hole body, single coil pickup, mahogany body.

1973-1978 $550 $725

Model 2368F

1973-1974. Classic single-cut black 'guard copy.

1973-1974 $575 $750

Model 2370

1972-1977. Sunburst version of Model 2363R.

1972-1977 $850 $1,150

Model 2372 Les Pro/2372DX Les Pro

1972-1977. Copy of classic single-cut solidbody, bolt neck, low impedance pickups, DX with gold hardware available for '73-'74.

1972-1977 $575 $750

Model 2374 Crest

1974-1976. Copy of classic double-cut semi-hollow body, walnut finish.

1974-1976 $825 $1,100

Model 2375 Strato

1971-1978. Strat copy, 3 single-coils, sunburst.

1971-1978 $575 $750

MODEL YEAR	FEATURES	EXC. COND. LOW	HIGH

Model 2375 Strato 6/12

1974-1975. Double neck, 6 and 12 strings.

1974-1975 $1,125 $1,475

Model 2375ASH Strato

1974-1978. 2375 with ash body.

1974-1978 $575 $750

Model 2375WH/N/BK Strato

1974-1978. 2375 in white (WH), natural (N), and black (BK) finishes.

1974-1978 $675 $875

Model 2377

1974-1975. Copy of classic double sharp-cut solidbody, short production run, dot markers.

1974-1975 $450 $600

Model 2380

1973-1977. Copy of LP Recording, single-cut solidbody, low impedence pickups, small block markers.

1973-1977 $575 $750

Model 2383

1974-1976. Copy of classic double sharp cut solidbody, white or walnut, 3 humbuckers, gold hardware.

1974-1976 $500 $650

Model 2384 Telly

1974-1976. Copy of classic single-cut, f-holes, 2 humbuckers, ash body.

1974-1976 $575 $750

Model 2387 Rocket Roll/Rocket Roll Sr.

1975-1977. Copy of classic v-shaped solidbody, bolt-neck (2387) or set-neck (2387DX/2387CT), dot markers, gold-covered pickups.

1975-1977 All models $1,325 $1,725

Model 2390

1974-1976. Copy of classic double-cut semi-hollow body, maple 'board, walnut finish.

1974-1976 $875 $1,150

Model 2394

Ca. 1974-ca. 1976. SG style, 2 humbuckers, maple 'board, black block inlays.

1974-1976 $575 $750

Model 2395

1974-1976. Natural finished 2390.

1974-1976 $875 $1,150

Model 2397

1974-1976. Double-cut semi-hollow body, low impedance electronics, trapezoid markers, goldtop.

1974-1976 $875 $1,150

Model 2399DX Jazz Solid

1974-1976. Single-cut solidbody, sunburst, set-neck, gold hardware.

1974-1976 $875 $1,150

Model 2401 Signature

1974-1976. Double-cut semi-hollow archtop, gold top, bolt neck.

1974-1976 $875 $1,150

Model 2402/2402DX Double Axe

1974-1977. Double sharp cut solidbody 6/12 doubleneck, cherry or walnut, DX model has gold hardware and white finish.

1974-1977 All models $1,125 $1,500

MODEL YEAR	FEATURES	EXC. COND. LOW	HIGH

Model 2404 Double Axe

1974-1977. Double sharp cut solidbody guitar/bass doubleneck copy, walnut, white available '75 only.

1974-1977 $1,125 $1,500

Model 2405 Custom Agent

1974-1977. Single-cut solidbody, set neck, scroll headstock, pearl body inlay, 2 humbuckers.

1974-1977 $825 $1,075

Model 2406 Double Axe

1974-1977. Double sharp cut solidbody doubleneck, two 6-strings, cherry or wlanut.

1974-1977 $825 $1,075

Model 2407 Stratojazz 4/6

1974-1975. Half Strat, half Jazz bass, all rock and roll!

1974-1975 $825 $1,075

Model 2451

1974-1977. Single-cut solidbody, maple 'board, black or natural, set neck.

1974-1977 $875 $1,150

Model 2453 Howie Roberts

1974-1977. Single-cut archtop, round soundhole, maple body, set neck, rosewood 'board, block markers, 1 pickup, gold hardware, burgundy or sunburst.

1974-1977 $1,200 $1,550

Model 2454

1974-1977. Copy of classic double-cut semi-hollow body, set-neck, small block markers, cherry finish over ash.

1974-1977 $875 $1,150

Model 2455

1974-1977. L-5 copy, sharp single-cut archtop, blocks, natural.

1974-1977 $1,850 $2,400

Model 2459 Destroyer

1975-1977. Korina finished mahogany body.

1975-1977 $1,850 $2,400

Model 2460

1975-1977. L-5 copy, rounded cut laminated archtop, blocks, natural.

1975-1977 $1,850 $2,400

Model 2461

1975-1977. Copy of classic single-cut archtop, laminated spruce top, curly maple body, set-neck, ebony 'board, pearl blocks, 2 pickups, gold hardware, sunburst or natural.

1975-1977 $1,850 $2,400

Model 2464

1975-1977. Byrdland copy, rounded single-cut, blocks, natural.

1975-1977 $1,850 $2,400

Model 2469 Futura

1976-1977. Korina finished furturistic model copy.

1976-1977 $1,850 $2,400

Model 2601 Artist

1976-1978. D-style flat-top with fancy appointments.

1976-1978 $375 $500

Model 2612 Artist

1974-1975. Rounded double-cut solidbody, black finish, birch top, gold hardware, bound rosewood 'board, 2 humbuckers, fleur-de-lis inlay.

1974-1975 $900 $1,175

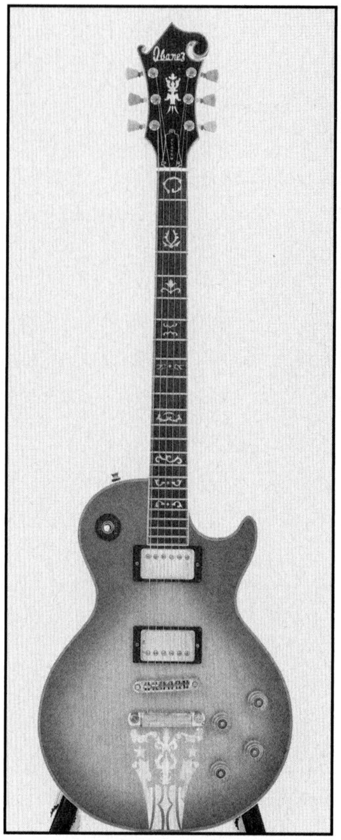

19702 Ibanez Model 2405 Custom Agent

1975 Ibanez Model 2453 Howie Roberts

Carter Vintage Guitars

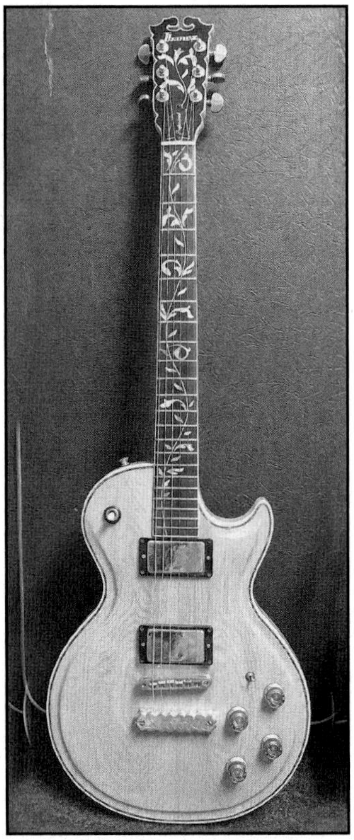

1976 Ibanez Model 2671 Randy Scruggs
Greg Perrine

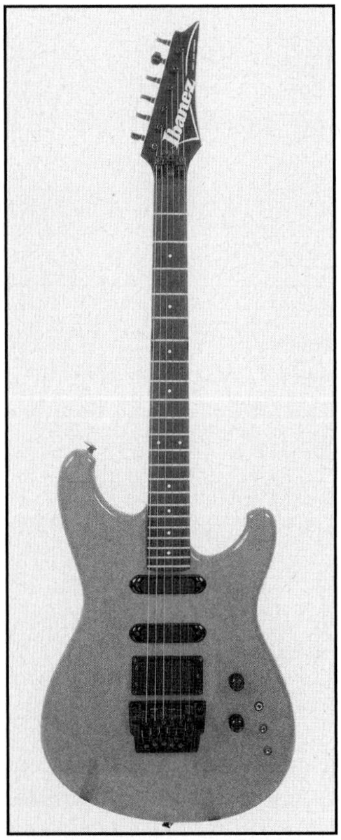

1985 Ibanez Pro Line PR1440
Imaged by Heritage Auctions, HA.com

MODEL YEAR	FEATURES	EXC. COND. LOW	HIGH

Model 2613 Artist

1974-1975. Natural version of 2612.

1974-1975 $900 $1,175

Model 2616 Artist Jazz

1974-1975. Single-cut curly maple hollow body, f-holes, fleur-de-lis, 2 humbuckers.

1974-1975 $1,700 $2,200

Model 2617 Artist

1976-1980. Pointed double-cut natural ash solidbody, set-neck, German carved top, spilt block inlays, bound ebony 'board, 2 humbuckers, later would evolve into the Professional model.

1976-1980 $1,400 $1,825

Model 2618 Artist

1976-1979. Like 2617, but with maple and mahogany body and dot markers. Becomes AR200 in '79.

1976-1979 $900 $1,175

Model 2619 Artist

1976-1979. Like 2618, but with split block markers. Becomes AR300 in '79.

1976-1979 $900 $1,175

Model 2622 Artist EQ

1977-1979. EQ, Steve Miller model. Becomes AR500 in '79.

1977-1979 $1,100 $1,425

Model 2630 Artist Deluxe

1976-1979. Double cut semi-hollow body, sunburst, name changed to AS200 in '79.

1976-1979 $1,300 $1,700

Model 2640 Artist/AR1200 Doubleneck

1977-1984. Double-cut solidbody, set 6/12 necks, 4 humbuckers, gold hardware. Called 2640 until '79 when changed to AR1200.

1977-1984 $1,350 $1,750

Model 2662 Super Cutaway

1974-1976. Solidbody, set neck, two dramatic cutaways, block inlays, 2 humbuckers.

1974-1976 $1,400 $1,825

Model 2671 Randy Scruggs

1976-1978. Single-cut solidbody, tree-of-life inlay, German-carve top.

1976-1978 $1,175 $1,525

Model 2700 Artist Custom

1977-1978. Cutaway, dot markers, gold hardware, natural, black, antique violin or dark satin finish.

1977-1978 $1,500 $1,950

Model 2710 Artist Custom

1978. Like Model 2700 with exotic wood and anvil case.

1978 $1,550 $2,000

Model 2800 Andorra Series

1974-1979. Classical nylon-string guitars, part of Ibanez Andorra Series, all with 2800-2899 model numbers.

1974-1979 $175 $400

Model 2900 Andorra Professional Series

1974-1979. Steel-string dreadnought models with solid spruce tops, all with 2909-2912 model numbers.

1974-1979 $175 $400

Pat Metheny PM

1996-present. Acoustic-electric archtops, single or single/half cutaway, 1 or 2 humbuckers.

1996-2010 PM100 $1,275 $1,650
1997-1999 PM20 $975 $1,250
2000-2015 PM120 $1,550 $2,000

Paul Gilbert PGM

1992-2011. Superstrat body style, painted f-holes, appointments vary with model numbers.

1997-2011 PGM300 WH $1,100 $1,425
1998 PGM 90th $1,250 $1,625
1998 PGM200 FB $1,250 $1,625

PF Performer Series Acoustics

1987-present. Mostly dreadnought size flat-tops.

1987-2020 Various models $80 $300

PF100 Performer Standard

1978-1979. Single-cut solidbody, plain birch top, mahogany body, bolt neck, dot inlays, 2 humbuckers.

1978-1979 $375 $500

PF200 Performer Custom

1978-1979. Maple top PF100.

1978-1979 $500 $650

PF300 Performer

1978-1980. Single-cut solidbody, maple top, mahogany body, set neck, 2 humbuckers, Tri-Sound.

1978-1980 $500 $650

PF400 Performer

1978-1979. Single cut solidbody, flame maple top, alder body, set neck, block inlays, 2 humbuckers, Tri-Sound.

1978-1979 $525 $700

PL Pro Line Series

1985-1987. Pro Line models begin with PL or PR.

1985-1987 Various models $350 $1,000

PR Pro Line Series

1985-1987. Pro Line models begin with PL or PR.

1985-1987 Various models $350 $1,000

Reb Beach Voyager RBM1

1991-1996. Unusual cutaway lower bout, extreme upper bout cutaways, RBM Series logo on headstock.

1991-1996 $950 $1,250

RG/RS Roadster/Roadstar Series

1992-present. A large family of guitars whose model identification starts with RG or RS prefix, includes the Roadstar Standard and Roadstar Deluxe models.

1992-2020 Lower-range $175 $250
1992-2020 Low to mid-range $260 $350
1992-2020 Mid-range $360 $500
1992-2020 Higher-range $525 $700
1992-2020 Highest-range $750 $1,400

Roadstar II Series

1983-1987. Various offset double-cut solidbodies, 'Roadstar II Series' on headstock, 3 single-coils or 2 humbuckers. Over 40 models appeared in this line, offered in Standard, Deluxe and Custom forms.

1982-1985 Various models $300 $800

Rocket Roll II RR550

1982-1984. Flying V body, six-on-side headstock, pearloid blocks, cherry sunburst, maple top, set neck.

1982-1984 $1,000 $1,300

GUITARS

MODEL YEAR	FEATURES	EXC. COND. LOW	HIGH

RT Series

1992-1993. Offset double-cut, bolt neck, rosewood 'board, dot markers.

1992-1993	Various models	$250	$500

RX Series

1994-1997. Offset double-cut, solidbodies.

1994-1997	Various models	$100	$250

S Models

1987-present. In '87 Ibanez introduced a new line of highly tapered, ultra-thin body, offset double-cut guitars that were grouped together as the S Models. Intially the S Models were going to be called the Sabre models but that name was trademarked by Music Man and could not be used. The S models will carry an S suffix or S prefix in the model name.

1987-2020	Various models	$300	$650

ST Studio Series

1978-1982. Double-cut solidbodies, lots of natural finishes, various models, even a doubleneck.

1979-1981	Various models	$275	$600

STW Double

1999. Double neck with 7-string and 6-string neck, limited edition.

1999		$1,675	$2,200

TC/TV Talman Series

1994-1998. Softer double-cut solidbodies.

1994-1998	Various models	$225	$525

USRG U.S.A. Custom Series

1994-1995. RG style guitars built in the U.S. by PBC Guitar Technology.

1994-1995	Various models	$1,025	$1,325

UV7/UV7P/UV77 Steve Vai Universe

1990-1997. Basswood 7-strings, hum/single/hum pickups. The '90-'93 white 7P and multi-colored 77 have pyramid inlays, the black '90-'97 7 has dots.

1990-1997	Various models	$1,300	$4,000

UV777 Steve Vai Universe

1998-2012. Basswood 7-string, pyramid inlays, maple 'board, hum/single/hum pickups.

1991-2012	Various models	$1,300	$1,900

V300 Vintage Series

1978-1991. Vintage Series acoustic dreadnought, spruce top, mahogany back and sides, sunburst or various colors.

1978-1991		$150	$225

Xiphos Series

2007-2015. Part of the X Series, various XP and XPT models, X-shaped solidbody electric, neck-thru construction. Replaced by Iron Label (XPIR) series in '15.

2007-2015	Various models	$775	$1,000

XV500

1985-1987. Sharply pointed X-body with scalloped bottom.

1985-1987		$725	$950

Ibanez, Salvador

1875-1920. Salvador Ibanez was a Spanish luthier who operated a small guitar-building workshop. In the early 1900s he founded Spain's largest guitar factory. In 1929 Japan's Hoshino family began importing Salvador Ibanez guitars. Demand for the Salvador Ibanez guitars became so great that the Hoshino family began building their own guitars, which ultimately became known as the Ibanez brand. Guitars from 1875-1920 were mostly classical style and often can be identified by a label on the inside back which stipulates Salvador Ibanez.

Ignacio Rozas

1987-present. Luthier Ignacio M. Rozas builds his classical and flamenco guitars in Madrid, Spain. He also offers factory-made guitars built to his specifications.

Illusion Guitars

1992-present. Luthier Jeff Scott builds his premium grade, production/custom, solidbody guitars in Fallbrook, California.

Imperial

Ca.1963-ca.1970. Imported by the Imperial Accordion Company of Chicago, Illinois. Early guitars made in Italy by accordion builder Crucianelli. By ca. '66 switched to Japanese guitars. They also made basses.

Electric Solidbody

1963-1968. Italian-made until '66, then Japanese-made, includes the Tonemaster line.

1963-1968		$200	$275

Imperial (Japan)

1957-1960. Early, budget grade, Japanese imports from the Hoshino company which was later renamed Ibanez.

Infeld

2003-2005. Solidbody guitars and basses offered by string-maker Thomastik-Infeld of Vienna.

Infinox

1980s. Infinox by JTG, of Nashville, offered a line of 'the classic shapes of yesterday and the hi tech chic of today'. Classic shapes included copies of many classic American solidbody designs with the block letter Infinox by JTG logo on headstock, special metallic grafteq paint finish, space-age faux graphite-feel neck, Gotoh tuning machines, Gotoh locking nut tremolo with fine tuners, all models with 1 or 2 humbucker pickups.

Interdonati

1920s-1930s. Guitars built by luthier Philip Interdonati, in New York City, originally professional grade. He also built mandolins.

Size 000 Flat-Top

1920s-1930s.

1920s-30s	Less fancy	$2,500	$3,500
1920s-30s	More fancy	$3,500	$7,000

Isana

1951-1974. Acoustic and electric archtop guitars built by luthier Josef Sandner in Nauheim, Germany. Elvis played one while in the army in Germany.

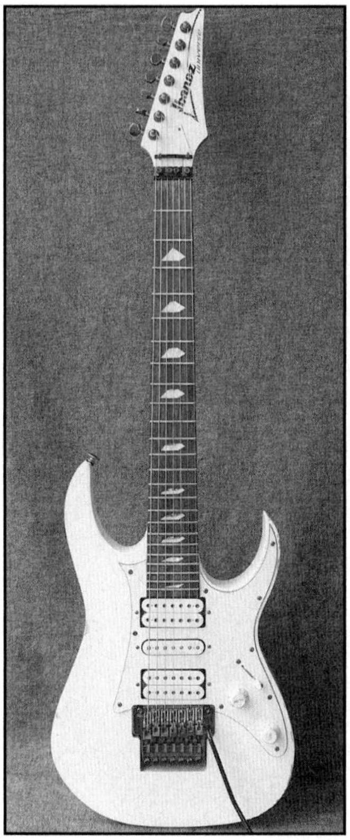

1990 Ibanez Steve Vai Universe UV7P
Bas van de Weijer

1979 Ibanez V302
Peter Busch

GUITARS

Island Atoll

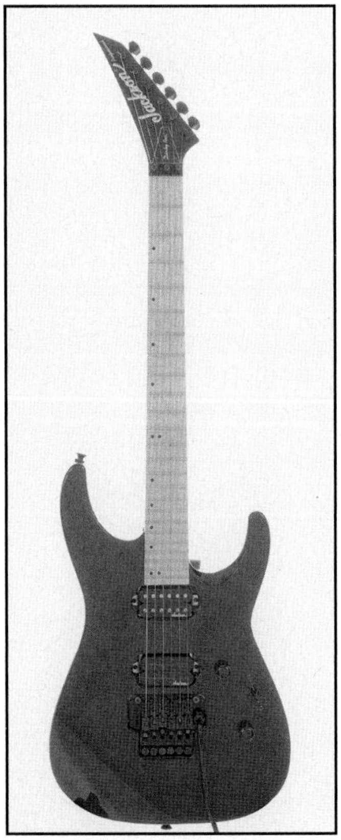

1997 Jackson Dinky Reverse DR2

MODEL YEAR	FEATURES	EXC. COND. LOW	HIGH

Acoustic Archtop

1951-1974	Various models	$350	$1,300

Island Instruments

2010-present. Luthier Nic Delisle builds professional and premium grade, production/custom, small-bodied acoustic and electric guitars in Montreal, Quebec. He also builds basses.

Italia

1999-present. Intermediate grade, production, solid, semi-solid, and hollow body guitars and basses designed by Trevor Wilkinson and made in Korea.

J Backlund Design

2008-present. Professional and premium grade, custom, electric guitars and basses designed by J. Backlund in Hixson, Tennessee, starting in 2008. He also imports Korean-made guitars under the Retronix brand.

J Burda Guitars

Flat-top guitars built by luthier Jan Burda in Berrien Springs, Michigan.

J. Frog Guitars

1978-present. Professional and premium grade, production/custom, solidbody guitars made by Ed Roman Guitars.

J.B. Player

1980s. Budget and intermediate grade, production, imported acoustic, acoustic/electric, and solidbody guitars and basses. They also offer banjos and mandolins. Founded in United States. Moved production of guitars to Korea but maintained a U.S. Custom Shop. MBT International/Musicorp took over manufacture and distribution in '89, then Kamen acquired MBT in 2005.

J.R. Zeidler Guitars

1977-2002. Luthier John Zeidler built premium and presentation grade, custom, flat-top, 12-string, and archtop guitars in Wallingford, Pennsylvania. He also built mandolins. He died in '02 at age 44.

J.S. Bogdanovich

1996-present. Production/custom, premium grade, classical and steel string guitars built by luthier John S. Bogdanovich in Swannanoa, North Carolina.

J.T. Hargreaves Basses & Guitars

1995-present. Luthier Jay Hargreaves builds his premium grade, production/custom, classical and steel string guitars and basses in Seattle, Washington.

MODEL YEAR	FEATURES	EXC. COND. LOW	HIGH

Jack Daniel's

2004-2017. Acoustic and electric guitars and basses, some with Jack Daniel's artwork on the body and headstock, built by Peavey for the Jack Daniel's Distillery. There is also an amp model.

Jackson

1980-present. Currently Jackson offers intermediate, professional, and premium grade, production, electric guitars. They also offer basses. In '78 Grover Jackson bought out Charvel Guitars and moved it to San Dimas. Jackson made custom-built bolt-on Charvels. In '82 the pointy, tilt-back Jackson headstock became standard. The Jackson logo was born in '80 and used on a guitar designed as Randy Rhoad's first flying V. Jacksons were neck-through construction. The Charvel trademark was licensed to IMC in '85. IMC moved the Jackson factory to Ontario, California in '86. Grover Jackson stayed with Jackson/Charvel until '89 (see Charvel). On October 25, 2002, Fender Musical Instruments Corp (FMIC) took ownership of Jackson/Charvel Manufacturing Inc.

Dinky Reverse DR2

1996-1998. US-made, reverse headstock, no inlay, 2 Duncan humbuckers, ebony 'board.

1996-1998		$650	$850

Dinky Reverse DR3/DR5

1992-2001. Import, reverse headstock, 2 humbuckers, dots (DR5) or sharkfin inlays (DR3), locking trem.

1992-1997	Dots	$275	$400
1995-2001	Sharkfin	$350	$450

DX Series

2000-2007. Standard offset double-cut body, reverse headstock.

2000-2007		$175	$300

Fusion Pro

Late 1980s-early 1990s. Import from Japan.

1980s-90s		$450	$600

Fusion U.S.A.

1992-1994. Jackson with Made In USA logo on headstock, graphics.

1992-1994		$750	$975

Jenna II RX10D Rhoads

2009. Limited production, Rhoads body style, named after performer Jenna Jameson.

2009		$450	$600

JSX94

1994-1995. Offset double-cut solidbody, single/single/hum, rosewood 'board, dot markers.

1994-1995		$260	$340

JTX

1993-1995. Partial offset double-cut, single-coil neck pickup, humbucker bridge pickup, Jackson-Rose double lock vibrato, bolt-on neck, dot markers on maple fretboard, JTX truss rod cover logo.

1993-1995		$300	$400

Kelly Custom

1984-early 1990s. Solidbody, Kahler tremolo, 2 humbuckers, ebony 'board with shark's tooth inlays, bound neck and headstock.

1984-1993		$1,350	$1,800

MODEL YEAR	FEATURES	EXC. COND. LOW	HIGH

Kelly Pro

1994-1995. Pointy-cut solidbody, neck-thru, 2 humbuckers, bound ebony 'board, sharkfin inlays.

1994-1995		$600	$800

Kelly Standard

1993-1995. Pointy cutaway solidbody, bolt neck, 2 humbuckers, dot markers.

1993-1995		$450	$600

Kelly U.S.A. (KE2)

1998-present. Alder solidbody, flame maple top, neck-thru.

1998-2020		$1,150	$1,500

Kelly XL

1994-1995. Pointy cutaway solidbody, bolt neck, 2 humbuckers, bound rosewood 'board, sharkfin inlays.

1994-1995		$525	$675

King V (KV2)

2003-present. King V Pro reissue, neck-thru, sharkfin markers, Floyd Rose, U.S.-made.

2003-2020		$600	$775

King V Pro

1993-1995. Soft V-shaped neck-thru solidbody, sharkfin markers, 2 humbuckers.

1993-1995		$525	$675

King V STD

1993-1995 Bolt neck version of King V

1993-1995		$275	$350

Phil Collen

1989-1991, 1993-1995. Offset double-cut maple neck-thru solidbody, 6-in-line tuners, 1 volume, bound ebony 'board, U.S.-made, early version has poplar body, 1 humbucker; later version with basswood body, 1 single-coil and 1 humbucker.

1993-1995		$1,150	$1,500

Phil Collen PC1 (U.S.A.)

1996-present. Quilt maple top, bolt-on maple neck, maple board, koa body '96-'00, mahogany body '01-present, 1 humbucker and 1 single coil '96-'97, humbucker, stacked humbucker, and single coil '98-present.

1996-2020		$1,300	$1,700

Phil Collen PC3 (Import)

1996-2001. Downscale version of Collen model, poplar body, bolt neck, humbucker\single\single.

1996-2001		$440	$575

PS Performers Series

1994-2003. Some with PS model number on truss rod cover.

1994-2003	Various models	$275	$350

Randy Rhoads (Import)

1992-2011. Bolt neck import version.

1992-2011		$365	$475

Randy Rhoads Limited Edition

1992 only. Shark fin-style maple neck-thru body, gold hardware, white with black pinstriping, block inlays, 6-in-line tuners, U.S.-made, only 200 built.

1992		$4,500	$6,000

Randy Rhoads Pro Series RR3 and RR5

1995-2012. Made in Japan, various finishes.

1995-2012	RR3, bolt-on	$375	$500
2001-2011	RR5, neck-thru	$450	$600

Randy Rhoads Relic Tribute

2010-2011. Custom Shop limited edition to celebrate the 30th anniversary of the Randy Rhoads Concorde, 60 made, exacting dimension and design of Rhoads' original custom-made Concorde guitar, relic-treatment to mimic the original.

2010-2011		$5,200	$6,900

Randy Rhoads U.S.A./RR Series

1983-present. V-shaped (also referred to as concorde-shaped) neck-thru solidbody, 2 humbuckers, originally made at San Dimas plant, serial numbers RR 0001 to RR 1929, production moved to the Ontario plant by '87, serial numbers RR 1930 to present in sequential order.

1983	Early serial #, no trem	$3,800	$5,000
1983	Mid serial #, no trem	$2,700	$3,500
1983-1986	Late serial #, Kahler trem	$1,900	$2,500
1983-1986	Rose trem or string-thru	$1,900	$2,500
1987-1989	Early Ontario-built	$1,525	$2,000
1990-1992	Early '90s vintage	$1,400	$1,800
1993-1999		$1,400	$1,800
2000-2002		$1,400	$1,800
2002-2019	RR5	$850	$1,100
2005-2020	RR1	$1,400	$1,800

RX Series

2000-2011. Bolt-on, shark fin inlays.

2000-2008	RX10D Rhoads	$175	$225

San Dimas Serialized Plated

1980-1982. Various custom-built solidbody models, values vary depending on each individual instrument. The values are true for so-called "Serialized Plated" with Jackson neck plate, Jackson logo and serial number.

1980-1982		$3,100	$4,100

Soloist Custom

1993-1995. Double-cut, neck-thru solidbody, 1 humbucker and 2 single-coils, bound ebony 'board, shark's tooth inlays, U.S.-made.

1993-1995		$1,350	$1,800

Soloist Pro

1990-1995. Import version of Soloist, with, shark's tooth inlays.

1990-1995		$550	$725

Soloist Shannon

1998. Shark fin inlays, single-single-hum pickups, Rose, signed by Mike Shannon.

1998		$1,350	$1,800

Soloist Student J1 (U.S.A.)

1984-1999. Double-cut neck-thru solidbody, Seymour Duncan single-single-hum pickups, rosewood 'board, dot inlays, no binding.

1984-1986	San Dimas-built	$1,075	$1,400
1986-1999	Ontario-built	$1,075	$1,400

Soloist/Soloist USA/SL Series

1984-present. U.S.-made, double-cut, neck-thru, string-thru solidbody, 2 humbuckers, bound rosewood 'board, standard vibrato system on Soloist is Floyd

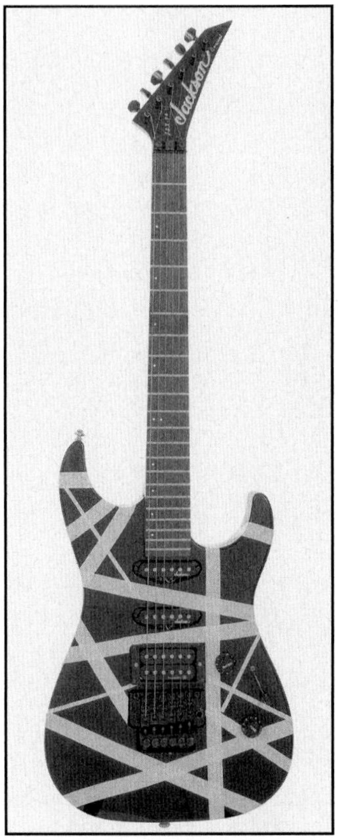

1994 Jackson JSX94

Imaged by Heritage Auctions, HA.com

1999 Jackson Randy Rhoads

Randy Schleyhahn

2005 James Trussart Steel Deville
Rivington Guitars

Jason Z. Schroeder The Chopper TL

Rose locking vibrato, a guitar with Kahler vibrato is worth less. Replaced by the Soloist USA in '90.

MODEL YEAR	FEATURES	EXC. COND. LOW	HIGH
1984-1986	Custom order, Floyd Rose	$1,500	$2,000
1984-1986	Custom order, Kahler	$1,650	$2,200
1984-1986	San Dimas-built, Floyd Rose	$1,500	$2,000
1984-1986	San Dimas-built, Kahler	$1,500	$2,000
1986-1990	Custom order features	$1,500	$2,000
1986-1990	Ontario-built	$1,500	$2,000
1990-2020	Various models, includes SL1 & SL2	$1,350	$1,800

Stealth EX

1992-late 1990s. Offset double-cut, pointed headstock, H/S/S pickups, offset dot markers, tremolo, Jackson Professional logo.

MODEL YEAR	FEATURES	EXC. COND. LOW	HIGH
1990s		$365	$475

Stealth HX

1992-1995. 3 humbucker version of Stealth, string-thru body.

MODEL YEAR	FEATURES	EXC. COND. LOW	HIGH
1992-1995		$365	$475

Stealth XL

1993. Stealth XL truss rod cover logo, 1 humbucker, 2 single-coils, left edge dot markers.

MODEL YEAR	FEATURES	EXC. COND. LOW	HIGH
1993		$365	$475

Surfcaster SC1

1998-2001. Jackson logo on headstock, Charvel Surfcaster styling.

MODEL YEAR	FEATURES	EXC. COND. LOW	HIGH
1998-2001		$950	$1,250

Warrior Pro (Import)

1990-1992. Japanese version.

MODEL YEAR	FEATURES	EXC. COND. LOW	HIGH
1990-1992		$300	$400

Warrior U.S.A.

1990-1992. Four point neck-thru solidbody, 1 humbucker and 1 single-coil, triangle markers, active electronics, U.S.-made, the Warrior Pro was Japanese version.

MODEL YEAR	FEATURES	EXC. COND. LOW	HIGH
1990-1992	Red	$825	$1,075

Y2KV Dave Mustaine Signature

2000-2002. V-shaped body, shark tooth markers, neck-thru, 2 humbuckers.

MODEL YEAR	FEATURES	EXC. COND. LOW	HIGH
2000-2002		$2,025	$2,625

Jackson-Guldan/Jay G Guitars

1920s-1960s. The Jackson-Guldan Violin Company, of Columbus, Ohio, mainly built inexpensive violins, violas, cellos, etc. but also offered acoustic guitars in the 1950s and early '60s, some of which were distributed by Wards. Their sales flyers from that era state - Made in America by Jackson-Guldan Craftsman. Very similar to small (13"-14") Stella economy flat-tops. Jay G name with quarter-note logo is sometimes on the headstock. They also offered lap steels and small tube amps early on.

Jacobacci

1930s-1994. Founded in France by Italian Vincent Jacobacci and originally building basso-guitars, banjos, and mandolins. Sons Roger and Andre joined the company and encouraged pop to add lapsteels and electric and regular acoustic guitars around '52. The guitars are sometimes labeled as Jaco and, from ca. '54 to ca. '66, as Jaco Major. In '58 the company introduced aluminum neck models, and in '59 their first solidbodies. In the '60s they also made instruments branded Royal, Texas, Ohio, Star and made instruments for Major Conn and other companies. By the mid '60s, they were producing mainly jazz style guitars.

Jamboree

1960s. Guitar brand exported by Japan's Hoshino (Ibanez).

James Einolf Guitars

1964-2017. Production/custom, professional grade, flat-top guitars built first in Denver, then Castle Rock, Colorado by luthier James Einolf.

James R. Baker Guitars

1996-present. Luthier James R. Baker builds his premium grade, custom, archtops in Shoreham, New York.

James Trussart

1980-present. Luthier James Trussart builds his premium grade, custom/production, solid and semi-hollow body electric guitars and basses in Los Angeles, California.

James Tyler

Early 1980s-present. Luthier James Tyler builds his professional and premium grade, custom/production, solidbody guitars and basses in Van Nuys, California, and also has a model built in Japan.

Janofsky Guitars

Production classical and flamenco guitars built by luthier Stephen Janofsky in Amherst, Massachusetts starting in 1978.

Jaros

Beginning 1995 these professional and premium grade, production/custom, solidbody and acoustic/electric guitars were originally built by father and son luthiers Harry and Jim Jaros in Rochester, Pennsylvania. In '01 Ed Roman in Las Vegas, bought the brand. He sold it in '04 to Dave Weiler in Nashville. Serial numbers under 1000 were made by the Jaros', numbers 1001-2000 were made by Ed Roman, over 2000 made by Dave Weiler.

Jasmine

1994-2019. Budget and intermediate grade, production, steel and classical guitars offered by Takamine Jasmine or Jasmine by Takamine. Student level instruments.

Jason Z. Schroeder Guitars

1994-present. Luthier Jason Schroeder builds professional and premium grade, production/custom, electric guitars in Redding, California.

Jay Turser

1997-present. Budget and intermediate grade, production, imported acoustic, acoustic/electric, electric and resonator guitars and basses. They also amps. Designed and developed by Tommy Rizzi for Music Industries Corp.

JBG (Joe Bochar Guitars)

2009-present. Production/custom, professional grade, solidbody electric guitars built by luthier Joe Bochar in Santa Clarita, California.

JD Bluesville

John Schappell and luthier Davis Millard build their professional grade, custom/production, solidbody electric guitars in Allentown, Pennsylvania. They began in 2005.

Jeff Traugott Guitars

1991-present. Premium and presentation grade, custom, flat-top, nylon-string, and acoustic/electric guitars built by luthier Jeff Traugott, in Santa Cruz, California.

Jeremy Locke Guitars

Premium grade, production/custom, classical and flamenco guitars built by luthier Jeremy Locke in Coomera, South East Queensland, Australia, starting in 1985.

Jeronimo Pena Fernandez

1967-present. Luthier Jeronimo Pena Fernandez started building classical guitars in Marmolejo, Spain, in the '50s. In '67, he went full-time and soon became well-known for his fine work. He is now retired, but still builds a few guitars a year. Prices can vary depending on model specs, each instrument should be evaluated on a case-by-case basis.

Jerry Jones

1981-2011. Intermediate grade, production, semi-hollowbody electric guitars and sitars from luthier Jerry Jones, built in Nashville, Tennessee. They also built basses. Jones started building custom guitars in '81, and launched his Danelectro-inspired line in '87. He retired in 2011.

Electric Models

Various models include Baritone 6-string ('89-'11); Electric Sitar ('90-'11) with buzz-bar sitar bridge, individual pickup for sympathetic strings and custom color gator finish; Longhorn Guitarlin ('89-'00, '05-'11) with large cutaway Guitarlin-style body, 24 frets in '89 and 31 after; and the Neptune 12-string ('81-'11) single-cut with 3 pickups.

MODEL YEAR	FEATURES	EXC. COND. LOW	HIGH
1981-2011	Neptune 12-string	$1,100	$1,425
1981-2011	Neptune 6/12 Double Neck	$1,950	$2,550
1989-2011	Baritone 6-string	$1,300	$1,700
1989-2011	Longhorn Guitarlin	$1,100	$1,425
1990-2011	Baby Sitar	$1,100	$1,425
1990-2011	Shorthorn	$1,050	$1,375
1990-2011	Sitar	$1,100	$1,425
1990-2011	U-3, 3 pickups	$1,050	$1,375

Jersey Girl

1991-present. Premium grade, production/custom, solidbody guitars made in Japan. They also build effects.

JET

1998-present. Premium grade, custom/production, chambered solidbody electric guitars built by luthier Jeffrey Earle Terwilliger in Raleigh, North Carolina.

Jewel

1920s. Instruments built by the Oscar Schmidt Co. and possibly others. Most likely a brand made for a distributor.

JG Guitars

1991-present. Luthier Johan Gustavsson builds his premium and presentation grade, production/custom, solidbody electric guitars in Malmö, Sweden.

Jim Dyson

Intermediate, professional and premium grade, production/custom electric guitars and basses built by luthier Jim Dyson in Torquay, Southern Victoria, Australia, starting in 1972. He also builds lap steels.

Jim Redgate Guitars

1992-present. Luthier Jim Redgate builds his premium grade, custom, nylon-string classical guitars in Belair, Adelaide, South Australia.

John Le Voi Guitars

1970-present. Production/custom, gypsy jazz, flat-top, and archtop guitars built by luthier John Le Voi in Lincolnshire, United Kingdom. He also builds mandolin family instruments.

John Page Guitars and John Page Classic

2006-present. Luthier John Page builds his custom, premium grade, chambered and solidbody electric guitars in Sunny Valley, Oregon.

John Price Guitars

1984-present. Custom classical and flamenco guitars built by luthier John Price in Australia.

Johnson

Mid-1990s-present. Budget, intermediate and professional grade, production, acoustic, classical, acoustic/electric, resonator and solidbody guitars and basses imported by The Music Link, Brisbane, California. Johnson also offers amps, mandolins, ukuleles and effects.

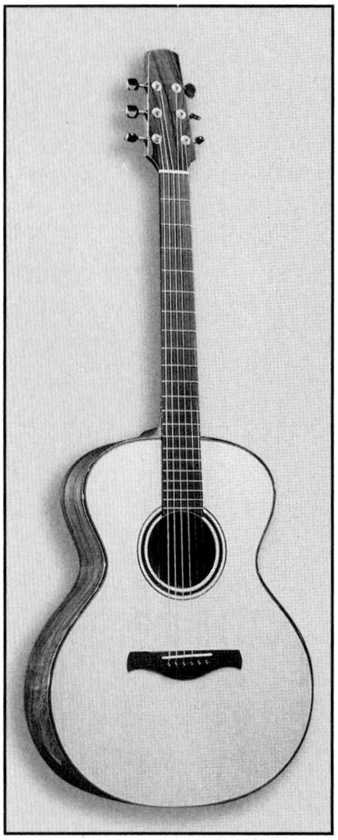

Jeff Traugott Model R

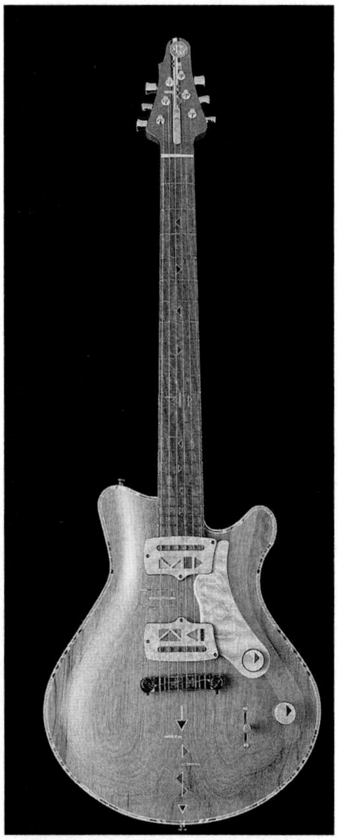

Jersey Girl Letter To Nowhere

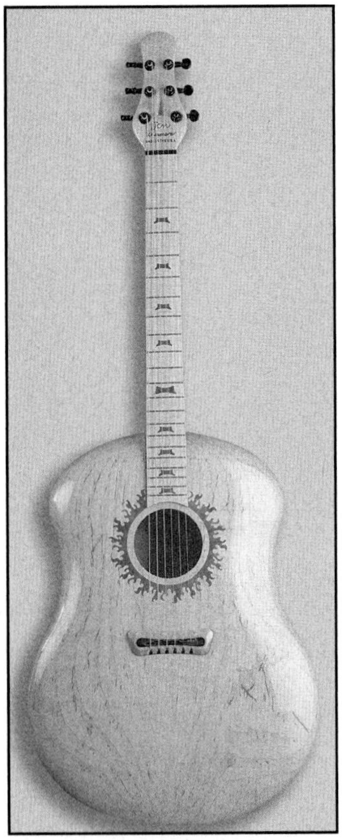

Jon Kammerer

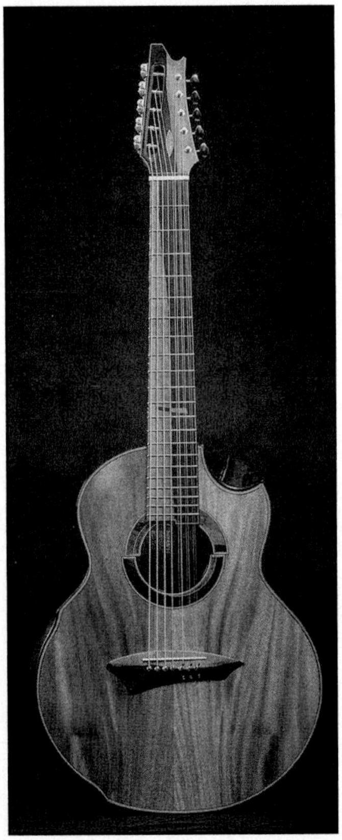

2011 JY Jeffrey Yong
JJ Seismic I

MODEL YEAR	FEATURES	EXC. COND. LOW	HIGH

Jon Kammerer Guitars

1997-present. Luthier Jon Kammerer builds his professional and premium grade, custom/production, solidbody, chambered, hollowbody, and acoustic guitars and basses in Keokuk, Iowa.

Jones

See TV Jones listing.

Jordan

1981-present. Professional and premium grade, custom, flat-top and archtop guitars built by luthier John Jordan in Concord, California. He also builds electric violins and cellos.

Jose Oribe

1962-present. Presentation grade, production, classical, flamenco, and steel-string acoustic guitars built by luthier Jose Oribe in Vista, California.

Jose Ramirez

See listing under Ramirez, Jose.

Juliett

1960s. Guitars built by Zerosette (or Zero-Sette), an accordion builder near Castelfidardo, Italy.

JY Jeffrey Yong Guitars

2003-present. Professional and premium grade, production/custom, classical, acoustic and electric guitars and basses and harp guitars built by Jeffrey Yong in Kuala Lumpur, Malaysia.

K & S

1992-1998. Hawaiian-style and classical guitars distributed by George Katechis and Marc Silber and handmade in Paracho, Mexico. A few 16" wide Leadbelly Model 12-strings were made in Oakland, California by luthier Stewart Port. K & S also offered mandolins, mandolas and ukes. In '98, Silber started marketing guitars under the Marc Silber Guitar Company brand and Katechis continued to offer instruments under the Casa Montalvo brand.

Kakos, Stephen

Luthier Stephen Kakos builds his premium grade, production/custom, classical guitars in Mound, Minnesota starting in 1972.

Kalamazoo

1933-1942, 1965-1970. Budget brand built by Gibson. Made flat-tops, solidbodies, mandolins, lap steels, banjos and amps. Name revived for a line of amps, solidbodies and basses in '65-'67. Playability and string tension will affect values of '60s electrics.

KG-1/KG-1 A

1965-1969. Offset double-cut (initial issue) or SG-shape (second issue), 1 pickup, Model 1 A with spring vibrato, red, blue or white.

1965-1969	$375	$500

KG-2/KG-2 A

1965-1970. Offset double-cut (initial shape) or SG-shape, 2 pickups, Model 2 A with spring vibrato, red, blue or white.

1965-1970	$400	$525

KG-11

1933-1941. Flat-top, all mahogany, 14" with no 'guard, sunburst.

1933-1941	$1,100	$1,425

KTG-11 Tenor

1936-1940. Tenor version of 11.

1936-1940	$550	$725

KG-12

1940-1941. Rare model, L-00, sunburst.

1940-1941	$1,750	$2,250

KG-14/KG-14 N

1936-1940. Flat-top L-0-size, mahogany back and sides, with 'guard, sunburst or natural (N).

1936-1940	$1,750	$2,250

KTG-14 Tenor

1936-1940. Tenor version of 14.

1936-1940	$775	$1,000

KG-16

1939-1940. Gibson-made archtop, small body, f-hole.

1939-1940	$850	$1,125

KG-21

1936-1941. Early model 15" archtop (bent, not curved), dot markers, bound top, sunburst.

1936-1941	$850	$1,125

KTG-21 Tenor

1935-1939. Tenor version of 21.

1935-1939	$550	$725

KG-22

1940-1942. Early model 16" archtop.

1940-1942	$1,050	$1,350

KG-31

1935-1940. Archtop L-50-size, 16" body, non-carved spruce top, mahogany back and sides.

1935-1940	$1,050	$1,350

KG-32

1939-1942. Archtop, 16" body.

1939-1942	$1,100	$1,425

KG Senior

1933-1934. Senior Model logo, firestripe guard, bound top and bottom, rope rose.

1933-1934	$1,625	$2,100

KG Sport

1937-1942. Small body, ¾ size.

1937-1942	$1,625	$2,100

KGN-12 Oriole

1940-1941. Flat-top, same body as KG-14, but with maple back and sides, stencil Oriole picture on headstock, natural.

1940-1941	$1,750	$2,250

KGN-32 Oriole

1940-1941. Archtop, maple back and sides, stencil Oriole picture on headstock, natural.

1940-1941	$1,750	$2,250

KHG Series

1936-1941. Acoustic Hawaiian guitar (HG), some converted to Spanish set-up.

MODEL YEAR	FEATURES	EXC. COND. LOW	HIGH
1936-1940	KHG-11	$1,100	$1,425
1936-1941	KHG-14	$1,750	$2,250

Kamico

1947-1951. Flat-top acoustic guitars. Low-end budget brand made by Kay Musical Instrument Company and sold through various distributors. They also offered lap steel and amp sets.

K Stratotone Thin Single

1950s. Similar to Kay Stratotone-style neck-thru solidbody, single slim-tube pickup.

MODEL YEAR	FEATURES	EXC. COND. LOW	HIGH
1950s		$725	$950

Kapa

Ca. 1962-1970. Begun by Dutch immigrant and music store owner Koob Veneman in Hyattsville, Maryland whose father had made Amka guitars in Holland. Kapa is from K for Koob, A for son Albert, P for daughter Patricia, and A for wife Adeline. Crown shield logo from Amka guitars. The brand included some Hofner and Italian imports in '60. Ca. '66 Kapa started offering thinner bodies. Some German Pix pickups ca. '66. Thinlines and Japanese bodies in '69. Kapa closed shop in '70 and the parts and equipment were sold to Micro-Frets and Mosrite. Later Veneman was involved with Bradley copy guitars imported from Japan. Approximately 120,000 Kapa guitars and basses were made.

Electric

1962-1970. Various models include Challenger with 3-way toggle from '62-'66/'67 and 2 on/off switches after; Cobra with 1 pickup; Continental and Continental 12-string; Minstrel and Minstrel 12-string with teardrop shape, 3 pickups; and the Wildcat, mini offset double-cut, 3 pickups and mute.

MODEL YEAR	FEATURES	EXC. COND. LOW	HIGH
1962-1970	Various models	$225	$650

Karol Guitars

2001-present. Luthier Tony Karol builds his custom, premium grade, acoustic and electric guitars in Mississauga, Ontario.

Kasha

1967-1997. Innovative classical guitars built by luthier Richard Schneider in collaboration with Dr. Michael Kasha. Schneider also consulted for Gibson and Gretsch. Schneider died in '97.

Kathy Wingert Guitars

1996-present. Luthier Kathy Wingert builds her premium grade, production/custom, flat-tops in Rancho Palos Verdes, California.

Kawai

1927-present. Kawai is a Japanese piano and guitar maker. They started offering guitars around '56 and they were imported into the U.S. carrying many different brand names, including Kimberly and Teisco. In '67 Kawai purchased Teisco. Odd-shaped guitars were offered from late-'60s through the mid-'70s. Few imports carrying the Kawai brand until the late-'70s; best known for high quality basses. By '90s they were making plexiglass replicas of Teisco Spectrum 5 and Kawai moon-shaped guitar. Kawai quit offering guitars and basses around 2002.

Acoustic

MODEL YEAR	FEATURES	EXC. COND. LOW	HIGH
1956-2002		$245	$345

Electric

MODEL YEAR	FEATURES	EXC. COND. LOW	HIGH
1956-2002	Common model	$245	$380
1956-2002	Rare model	$380	$600

Kay

Ca. 1931 (1890)-present. Originally founded in Chicago, Illinois as Groehsl Company (or Groehsel) in 1890, making bowl-backed mandolins. Offered Groehsl, Stromberg, Kay Kraft, Kay, Arch Kraft brand names, plus made guitars for S.S.Maxwell, Old Kraftsman (Spiegel), Recording King (Wards), Supertone (Sears), Silvertone (Sears), National, Dobro, Custom Kraft (St.Louis Music), Hollywood (Shireson Bros.), Oahu and others.

In 1921 the name was changed to Stromberg-Voisinet Company. Henry Kay "Hank" Kuhrmeyer joined the company in '23 and was secretary by '25. By the mid-'20s the company was making many better Montgomery Ward guitars, banjos and mandolins, often with lots of pearloid. First production electric guitars and amps are introduced with big fanfare in '28; perhaps only 200 or so made. Last Stromberg instruments seen in '32. Kuhrmeyer becomes president and the Kay Kraft brand was introduced in '31, probably named for Kuhrmeyer's middle name, though S-V had used Kay brand on German Kreuzinger violins '28-'36. By '34, if not earlier, the company is changed to the Kay Musical Instrument Company. A new factory was built at 1640 West Walnut Street in '35. The Kay Kraft brand ends in '37 and the Kay brand is introduced in late-'36 or '37.

Violin Style Guitars and upright acoustic basses debut in '38. In '40 the first guitars for Sears, carrying the new Silvertone brand, are offered. Kamico budget line introduced in '47 and Rex flat-tops and archtops sold through Gretsch in late-'40s. Kuhrmeyer retires in '55 dies a year later. New gigantic factory in Elk Grove Village, Illinois opens in '64. Seeburg purchased Kay in '66 and sold it to Valco in '67. Valco/Kay went out of business in '68 and its assets were auctioned in '69. The Kay name went to Sol Weindling and Barry Hornstein of W.M.I. (Teisco Del Rey) who began putting Kay name on Teisco guitars. By '73 most Teisco guitars are called Kay. Tony Blair, president of Indianapolis-based A.R. Musical Enterprises Inc. (founded in '73) purchased the Kay nameplate in '79 and currently distributes Kay in the U.S. Currently Kay offers budget and intermediate grade, production, acoustic, semi-hollow body, solidbody, and resonator guitars. They also make amps, basses, banjos, mandolins, ukes, and violins.

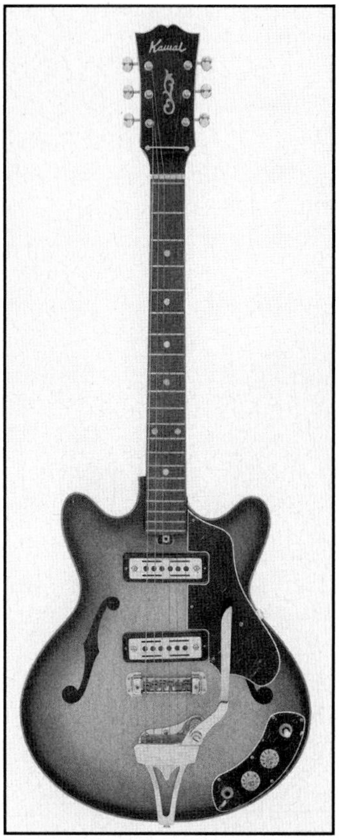

1960s Kawai

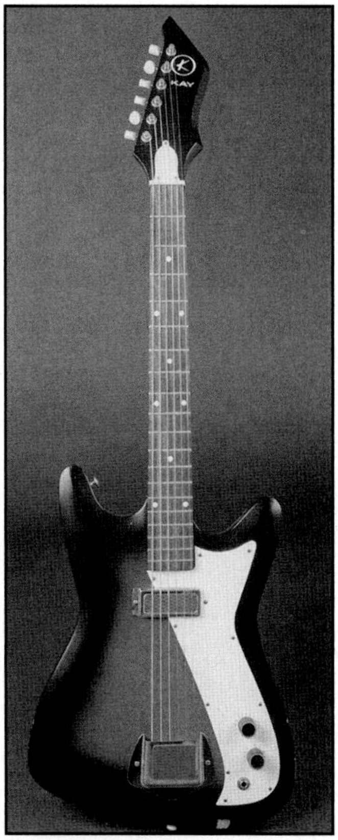

1965 Kay K100 Vanguard

Carter Vintage Guitars

1950s Kay K161 Thin Twin

Bernunzio Uptown Music

Ca. 1963 Kay K300

Richard Kregear

K11/K8911 Rhythm Special

1953-1961. Single-cut 17" acoustic archtop, "eighth note" headstock logo, large position markers, white 'guard, became K8911 in '57, sunburst or blond (B).

Model Year	Features	Exc. Cond. Low	Exc. Cond. High
1953-1961	Blond	$800	$1,050
1953-1961	Sunburst	$750	$1,000

K20 Super Auditorium

1939-1942. 16" archtop, solid spruce top, maple back and sides, sunburst.

Model Year	Features	Exc. Cond. Low	Exc. Cond. High
1939-1942		$250	$325

K20T

1970s. Japanese-made solidbody, 2 pickups, tremolo, model number on neck plate, circle-capital K logo on headstock.

Model Year	Features	Exc. Cond. Low	Exc. Cond. High
1970s		$120	$155

K21/K21B Cutaway Professional

1952-1956. Single-cut 17" acoustic archtop, split block markers, sunburst or blond (B).

Model Year	Features	Exc. Cond. Low	Exc. Cond. High
1952-1956	Blond	$1,000	$1,300
1952-1956	Sunburst	$925	$1,200

K22 Artist Spanish

1947-1956. Flat-top similar to Gibson J-100 17", spruce top, mahogany back and sides.

Model Year	Features	Exc. Cond. Low	Exc. Cond. High
1947-1956		$500	$650

K26 Artist Spanish

1947-1951. Flat-top, block markers, natural.

Model Year	Features	Exc. Cond. Low	Exc. Cond. High
1947-1951		$550	$725

K27 Jumbo

1952-1956. 17" Jumbo flat-top, fancy appointments.

Model Year	Features	Exc. Cond. Low	Exc. Cond. High
1952-1956		$975	$1,250

K37T Spanish Tenor

1952-1956. Mahogany bodied archtop, tenor.

Model Year	Features	Exc. Cond. Low	Exc. Cond. High
1952-1956		$200	$265

K39 Super Grand Auditorium

1947-1951. Full size acoustic archtop, faux rope binding on top, Kay script logo.

Model Year	Features	Exc. Cond. Low	Exc. Cond. High
1947-1951		$300	$400

K44 Artist Archtop

1947-1951. Non-cut archtop, solid spruce top, 17" curly maple veneered body, block markers, sunburst.

Model Year	Features	Exc. Cond. Low	Exc. Cond. High
1947-1951		$450	$600

K45 Professional Master Size Archtop

1952-1954. Non-cut archtop, 17" body, engraved tortoiseshell-celluloid headstock, large block markers, natural.

Model Year	Features	Exc. Cond. Low	Exc. Cond. High
1952-1954		$450	$600

K45 Travel Guitar

1981. Made in Korea, known as the 'rifle guitar', 'travel guitar', or 'Austin-Hatchet copy', circle K logo.

Model Year	Features	Exc. Cond. Low	Exc. Cond. High
1981		$285	$375

K46 Master Size Artist Archtop

1947-1951. Non-cut archtop, solid spruce top, 17" curly maple-veneered body, double-eighth note headstock inlay, sunburst.

Model Year	Features	Exc. Cond. Low	Exc. Cond. High
1947-1951		$450	$575

K48 Master Size Artist Archtop

1947-1951. Non-cut archtop, 17" solid spruce top with figured maple back and sides, split block inlays, sunburst or black.

Model Year	Features	Exc. Cond. Low	Exc. Cond. High
1947-1951		$700	$900

K48/K21 Jazz Special

Late-1960s. Slim solidbody with 3 reflective pickups, garden spade headstock, fancy position Circle K headstock logo, white.

Model Year	Features	Exc. Cond. Low	Exc. Cond. High
1968		$400	$525

K100 Vanguard

1961-1966. Offset double-cut slab solidbody, genuine maple veneered top and back over hardwood body, sunburst.

Model Year	Features	Exc. Cond. Low	Exc. Cond. High
1961-1966		$260	$335

K102 Vanguard

1961-1966. Double pickup version of the K100, sunburst.

Model Year	Features	Exc. Cond. Low	Exc. Cond. High
1961-1966		$290	$375

K136 (aka Stratotone)

1955-1957. Small single-cut slab solidbody electric, similar to Harmony Stratotone style, set neck, 1 pickup, trapeze tailpiece, triangle paint graphic in Spring Green and White Mist, matching green headstock, attractive finish adds value to this otherwise lower-end student model.

Model Year	Features	Exc. Cond. Low	Exc. Cond. High
1955-1957		$725	$950

K142 (aka Stratotone)

1955-1957. Small slab solidbody, introduced in '55 along with the K136, offered with 1 pickup or 2 pickups (more rare), trapeze tailpiece, copper finish.

Model Year	Features	Exc. Cond. Low	Exc. Cond. High
1955-1957	1 pickup	$700	$925
1955-1957	2 pickups	$725	$950

K161 Thin Twin/Jimmy Reed

1952-1958. Single-cut semi-hollow body, 2 pickups.

Model Year	Features	Exc. Cond. Low	Exc. Cond. High
1952-1958		$725	$950

K161V/VB Thin Twin

2009-present. Vintage Reissue series, single-cut hollowbody, 2 pickups.

Model Year	Features	Exc. Cond. Low	Exc. Cond. High
2009-2020		$600	$800

K300 Double Cutaway Solid Electric

1962-1966. Two single-coils, block inlays, some with curly maple top and some with plain maple top, natural.

Model Year	Features	Exc. Cond. Low	Exc. Cond. High
1962-1966		$365	$475

K360 Apollo/K365 Apollo II

1965-1968. Solidbody, 2 pickups, block inlays, vibrato.

Model Year	Features	Exc. Cond. Low	Exc. Cond. High
1965-1968		$700	$1,000

K535

1961-1965. Thinline double-cut, 2 pickups, vibrato, sunburst.

Model Year	Features	Exc. Cond. Low	Exc. Cond. High
1961-1965		$425	$550

K550 Dove

1970s. Square shoulder D-style, 2 Dove-style 'guards, capital K logo.

Model Year	Features	Exc. Cond. Low	Exc. Cond. High
1970s		$100	$130

K571/K572/K573 Speed Demon

1961-1965. Thinline semi-acoustic/electric, single pointed cutaway, some with Bigsby vibrato, with 1 (K571), 2 (K572) or 3 (K573) pickups. There was also a Speed Demon solidbody.

Model Year	Features	Exc. Cond. Low	Exc. Cond. High
1961-1965	571, 1 pickup	$290	$375
1961-1965	572, 2 pickups	$350	$450
1961-1965	573, 3 pickups	$365	$475

MODEL YEAR	FEATURES	EXC. COND. LOW	HIGH

K580 Galaxy
1961-1966. Thinline, single-cut, 1 pickup.

1961-1966		$400	$525

K592 Double Cutaway Thinline
1962-1966. Thinline semi-acoustic/electric, double Florentine cut, 2 or 3 pickups, Bigsby vibrato, pie-slice inlays, cherry.

1962-1966		$400	$525

K672/K673 Swingmaster
1961-1965. Single rounded cutaway semi-hollowbody, with 2 (K672) or 3 (K673) pickups.

1961-1965	672, 2 pickups	$800	$1,050
1961-1965	673, 3 pickups	$875	$1,150

K682 Galaxie II
1966-1968. Hollowbody, 2 pickups, vibrato tailpiece.

1966-1968		$400	$525

K775/K776 Jazz II
1961-1966. Electric thinline archtop, double-cut, standard Bigsby vibrato, 2 Gold K pickups, 4 knobs with toggle controls. Replaces Barney Kessel series as top-of-the-line model.

1961-1966	775, shaded	$1,150	$1,500
1961-1966	776, blond	$1,150	$1,500

K797 Acoustic Archtop
1930s. Full size student-intermediate acoustic archtop, 3-on-a-strip tuners, dot markers, sunburst.

1935-1937		$210	$275

K1160 Standard
1957-1964. Small 13" (standard) flat-top, laminated construction.

1957-1964		$40	$55

K1452 Aristocrat
1952. Acoustic-electric archtop, 2 pickups, sunburst.

1952		$620	$800

K1700/K1701 Barney Kessel Pro
1957-1960. 13" hollowbody, single-cut, Kelvinator headstock, ebony 'board with pearl inlays, white binding, 1 (K1701) or 2 (K1700) pickups, sunburst.

1957-1960	1700, 2 pickups	$1,500	$2,000
1957-1960	1701, 1 pickup	$1,400	$1,800

K1961/K1962/K1963 Value Leader
1960-1965. Part of Value Leader line, thinline single-cut, hollowbody, identified by single chrome-plated checkered, body-length guard on treble side, laminated maple body, maple neck, dot markers, sunburst, with 1 (K1961), 2 (K1962) or 3 (K1963) pickups.

1960-1965	1961, 1 pickup	$300	$400
1960-1965	1962, 2 pickups	$350	$450
1960-1965	1963, 3 pickups	$400	$525

K1982/K1983 Style Leader/Jimmy Reed
1960-1965. Part of the Style Leader mid-level Kay line. Sometimes dubbed Jimmy Reed of 1960s. Easily identified by the long brushed copper dual guardplates on either side of the strings. Brown or gleaming golden blond (natural) finish, laminated curly maple body, simple script Kay logo, with 2 (K1982) or 3 (K1983) pickups.

1960-1965	1982, 2 pickups	$440	$575
1960-1965	1983, 3 pickups	$510	$675

K3500 Studio Concert
1966-1968. 14 1/2" flat-top, solid spruce top, laminated maple back and sides.

1966-1968		$70	$90

MODEL YEAR	FEATURES	EXC. COND. LOW	HIGH

K5113 Plains Special
1968. Flat-top, solid spruce top, laminated mahogany back and sides.

1968		$115	$150

K5160 Auditorium
1957-1965. Flat-top 15" auditorium-size, laminated construction.

1957-1965		$115	$150

K6100 Country
1950s-1960s. Jumbo flat-top, spruce x-braced top, mahogany back and sides, natural.

1957-1962		$300	$400

K6116 Super Auditorium
1957-1965. Super Auditorium-size flat-top, laminated figured maple back and sides, solid spruce top.

1957-1965		$175	$225

K6120 Western
1960s. Jumbo flat-top, laminated maple body, pinless bridge, sunburst.

1962		$150	$200

K6130 Calypso
1960-1965. 15 1/2" flat-top with narrow waist, slotted headstock, natural.

1960-1965		$215	$276

K6533/K6535 Value Leader
1961-1965. Value Leader was the budget line of Kay, full body archtop, with 1 (K6533) or 2 (K6535) pickups, sunburst.

1961-1965	6533, 1 pickup	$300	$400
1961-1965	6535, 2 pickups	$350	$450

K6700/K6701 Barney Kessel Artist
1956-1960. Single-cut, 15 1/2" body, 1 (K6701) or 2 (K6700) pickups, Kelvinator headstock, sunburst or blond.

1956-1960	6700, 2 pickups	$2,100	$2,800
1956-1960	6701, 1 pickup	$1,900	$2,500

K6878 Style Leader
1966-1968. Full size (15.75) acoustic archtop, circle K logo on 'guard, sunburst.

1966-1968		$200	$260

K7000 Artist
1960-1965. Highest-end of Kay classical series, fan bracing, spruce top, maple back and sides.

1960-1965		$290	$375

K7010 Concerto
1960-1965. Entry level of Kay classical series.

1960-1965		$70	$90

K7010 Maestro
1960-1965. Middle level of Kay classical series.

1960-1965		$175	$225

K8110 Master
1957-1960. 17" master-size flat-top which was largest of the series, laminated construction.

1957-1960		$125	$160

K8127 Solo Special
1957-1965. Kay's professional grade flat-top, narrow waist jumbo, block markers.

1957-1965		$350	$450

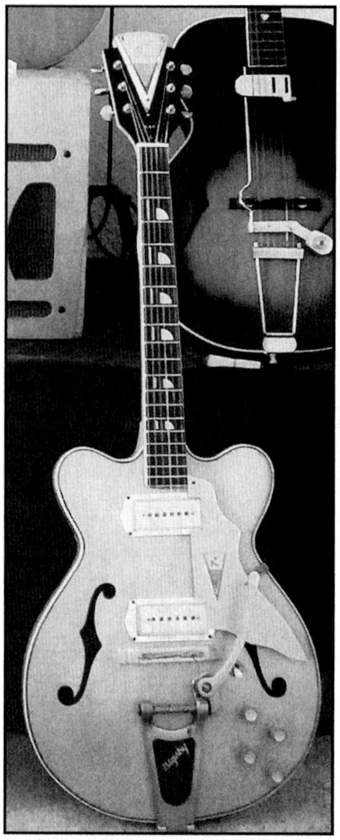

1961 Kay K776 Jazz II

Jim Bame

1960s Kay K1983 Style Leader

Richard Kregear

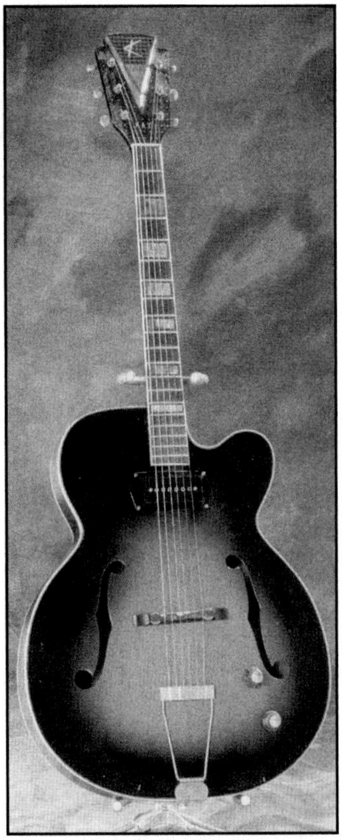

1950s Kay K8990 Upbeat

Curt Huettner

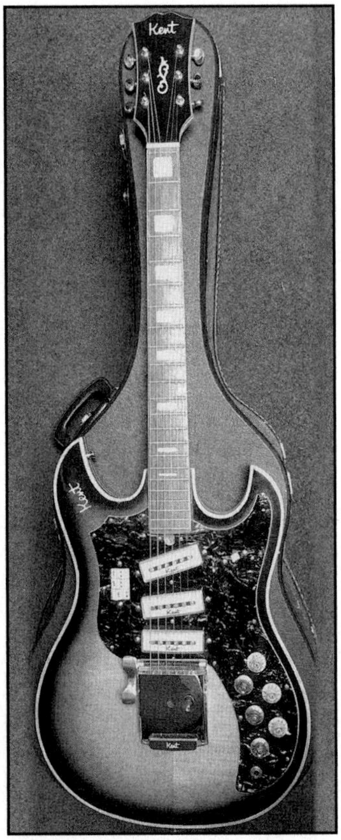

1969 Kent Model 741

Greg Perrine

MODEL YEAR	FEATURES	EXC. COND. LOW	HIGH

K8700/K8701 Barney Kessel Jazz Special

1956-1960. Part of the Gold K Line, top-of-the-line model, 17" single-cut archtop, 1 (K8701) or 2 (K8700) pickups, 4 controls and toggle, Kelvinator headstock with white background, natural or shaded sunburst, Barney Kessel signature logo on acrylic scalloped 'guard, no signature logo on '60 model.

1956-1960	8700, 2 pickups	$2,100	$2,800
1956-1960	8701, 1 pickup	$1,900	$2,500

K8990/K8995 Upbeat

1956/1958-1960. Less expensive alternative to Barney Kessel Jazz Special, 2 (K8990) or 3 (K8995) pickups, Gold K Line, Kelvinator headstock, sunburst.

1956-1960	8990, 2 pickups	$1,100	$1,400
1958-1960	8995, 3 pickups	$1,200	$1,550

Wood Amplifying Guitar

1934. Engineered after Dobro/National metal resonator models except the resonator and chamber on this model are made of wood, small production.

1934		$1,300	$1,700

Kay Kraft

1927-1937. First brand name of the Kay Musical Instrument Company as it began its transition from Stromberg-Voisinet Company to Kay (see Kay for more info).

Recording King

1931-1937		$475	$625

Venetian Archtop

1930s. Unique Venetian cutaway body style, acoustic with round soundhole, flower-vine decal art on low bout.

1930s		$900	$1,200

KB

1989-present. Luthier Ken Bebensee builds his premium grade, custom, acoustic and electric guitars and basses in North San Juan, California. He was located in San Luis Obispo from '89-'01. He also builds mandolins.

Kel Kroydon (by Gibson)

1930-1933. Private branded budget level instruments made by Gibson. They also had mandolins and banjos. The name has been revived on a line of banjos by Tom Mirisola and made in Nashville.

KK-1

1932. 14 3/4" L-0 sytle body, colorful parrot stencils on body.

1932		$3,400	$4,500

Keller Custom Guitars

Professional grade, production/custom, solidbody guitars built by luthier Randall Keller in Mandan, North Dakota. He began in 1994.

Keller Guitars

1975-present. Premium grade, production/custom, flat-tops made by luthier Michael L. Keller in Rochester, Minnesota.

MODEL YEAR	FEATURES	EXC. COND. LOW	HIGH

Kelly Guitars

1968-present. Luthier Rick Kelly builds professional grade, custom, solidbody electric guitars in New York, New York.

Ken Franklin

2003-present. Luthier Ken Franklin builds his premium grade, production/custom, acoustic guitars and ukuleles in Ukiah, California.

Kendrick

1989-present. Premium grade, production/custom, solidbody guitars built in Texas. Founded by Gerald Weber in Pflugerville, Texas and currently located in Kempner, Texas. Mainly known for their handmade tube amps, Kendrick added guitars in '94 and also offers speakers and effects.

Kenneth Lawrence Instruments

1986-present. Luthier Kenneth Lawrence builds his premium grade, production/custom, electric solidbody and chambered guitars and basses in Arcata, California.

Kent

1961-1969. Imported from Japan by Buegeleisen and Jacobson of New York, New York. Manufacturers unknown but many early guitars and basses were made by Guyatone and Teisco.

Acoustic Flat-Top

1962-1969. Various models.

1962-1969		$125	$175

Acoustic/Electric

1962-1969. Various models.

1962-1969		$150	$225

Electric 12-String

1965-1969. Thinline electric, double pointy cutaways, 12 strings, slanted dual pickup, sunburst.

1965-1969		$225	$400

Semi-Hollow Electric

1962-1969. Thinline electric, offset double pointy cutaways, slanted dual pickups, various colors.

1962-1969		$225	$400

Solidbody Electric

1962-1969. Models include Polaris I, II and III, Lido, Copa and Videocaster.

1962-1969	Common model	$150	$225
1962-1969	Rare model	$225	$400

Kevin Ryan Guitars

1989-present. Premium grade, custom, flat-tops built by luthier Kevin Ryan in Westminster, California.

KeyKord

Ca. 1929-mid 1930s.. Keykord offered guitars, ukes and banjos that had a push-button mechanism mounted over the fingerboard that "fingered" a different chord for each button. The guitars were built by Chicago's Stromberg-Voisinet (Kay).

MODEL YEAR	FEATURES	EXC. COND. LOW	HIGH

Tenor

1920s-1930s. Venetian mahogany body, 4-string, pearloid headstock overlay.

1920s-30s		$400	$525

Kiesel

1946-present. Founded by Lowell C. Kiesel in '46. Refer to Carvin listing for more info regarding the early years. Prior to his death in 2009, L.C. had turned the business over to his sons and it was located in several different California cities over the years.

In 2015, son Mark and grandson Jeff Kiesel began the new independent Kiesel Custom Guitars. They build professional and premium grade, acoustic and electric guitars and basses in Escondido, California.

Kimbara

1970s-1980s. Japanese line of guitars and basses mainily imported into the U.K. Models were the same as the Fresher brand.

Kimberly

Late-1960s-early-1970s. Private branded import made in the same Japanese factory as Teisco. They also made basses.

Longhorn

1960s. S-style, deep double-cut, 2 pickups.

1960s		$300	$450

May Queen

1960s. Same as Teisco May Queen with Kimberly script logo on headstock and May Queen Teisco on the 'guard.

1960s		$395	$525

Kinal

1969-present. Production/custom, professional and premium grade, solid body electric and archtop guitars and basses built and imported by luthier Michael Kinal in Vancouver, British Columbia.

King's Stone

1960s. Guitar brand exported by Japan's Hoshino (Ibanez).

Kingsley

1960s. Early Japanese imports, Teisco-made.

Soldibody Electric

1960s. Four pickups with tremolo.

1960s		$265	$350

Kingslight Guitars

1980-2015. Luthier John Kingslight built his premium grade, custom/production, steel string guitars and basses in Portage, Michigan (in Taos, New Mexico for '80-'83).

Kingston

Ca. 1958-1967. Guitars and basses imported from Japan by Jack Westheimer and Westheimer

MODEL YEAR	FEATURES	EXC. COND. LOW	HIGH

Importing Corporation of Chicago, Illinois. Early examples made by Guyatone and Teisco. They also offered mandolins and banjos.

Electric

1958-1967. Various models include: B-1, soldibody, 1 pickup; B-2T/B-3T/B-4T, solidbodies, 2/3/4 pickups and tremolo; SA-27, thin hollowbody, 2 pickups, tremolo.

1958-1967	Common model	$125	$300
1958-1967	Rare model	$300	$600

Kinscherff Guitars

1990-present. Luthier Jamie Kinscherff builds his premium grade, production/custom, flat-top guitars in Austin, Texas.

Kleartone

1930s. Private brand made by Regal and/or Gibson.

Small Flat-Top

1930s		$400	$600

Klein Acoustic Guitars

First produced in 1972, luthiers Steve Klein and Steven Kauffman build their production/custom, premium and presentation grade flat-tops and basses outside Sonoma, California.

Klein Electric Guitars

1988-2007. Steve Klein added electrics to his line in '88. In '95, he sold the electric part of his business to Lorenzo German, who continued to produce professional grade, production/custom, solidbody guitars and basses in Linden, California.

K-Line Guitars

2005-present. Professional grade, production/custom, T-style and S-style guitars and basses built by luthier Chris Kroenlein in St. Louis, Missouri. He also builds basses.

Klira

1887-1980s. Founded by Johannes Klira in Schoenbach, Germany, mainly made violins, but added guitars in the 1950s. The guitars of the '50s and '60s were original designs, but by the '70s most models were similar to popular American models. The guitars of the '50s and '60s were aimed at the budget market, but workmanship improved with the '70s models. They also made basses.

Electric

1960s	Common model	$300	$500
1960s	Rare model	$500	$800

Knaggs

2010-present. Luthiers Joseph Knaggs and Peter Wolf build premium and presentation grade, production/custom, acoustic and electric guitars and basses in Greensboro, Maryland.

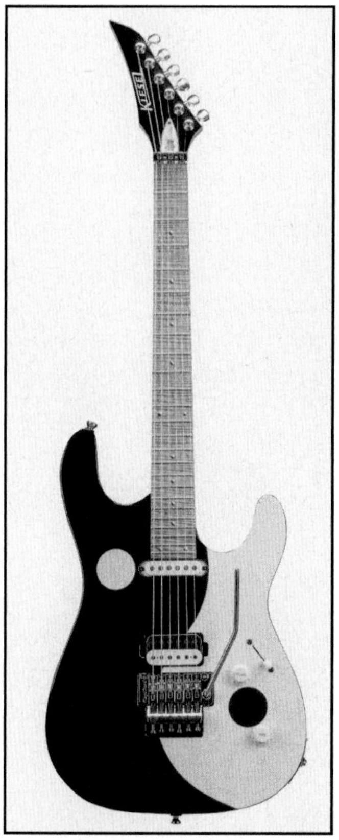

Kiesel Jason Becker Yin Yang

1967 Kingston Flying Wedge Rocket

Tom Pfeifer

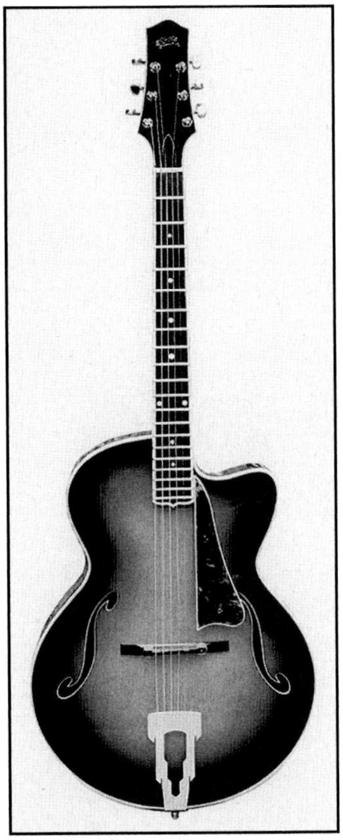

Knutson Luthiery Classic

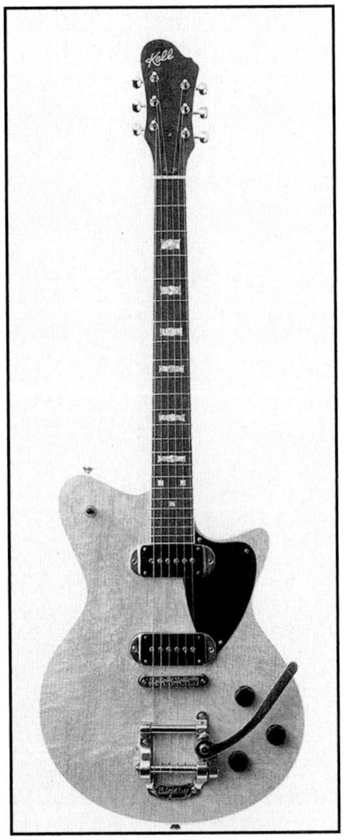

Koll Duo Glide

MODEL YEAR	FEATURES	EXC. COND. LOW	HIGH

Knox

Early-mid-1960s. Budget grade guitars imported from Japan, script Knox logo on headstock.

Electric Solidbody

1960s. Student models, 2 pickups, push buttons.

1960s		$125	$375

Knutsen

1890s-1920s. Luthier Chris J. Knutsen of Tacoma and Seattle, Washington, experimented with and perfected Hawaiian and harp guitar models. He moved to Los Angeles, California around 1916. He also made steels, mandolins and ukes. Dealers state the glue used on Knutsen instruments is prone to fail and instruments may need repair.

Convertible

1909-1914. Flat-top model with adjustable neck angle that allowed for a convertible Hawaiian or Spanish setup.

1909-1914		$3,500	$4,500

Harp Guitar

1900s. Normally 11 strings with fancy purfling and trim.

1900-1910		$1,500	$4,000

Knutson Luthiery

1981-present. Professional and premium grade, custom, archtop and flat-top guitars built by luthier John Knutson in Forestville, California. He also builds basses, lap steels and mandolins.

Kohno

1960-present. Luthier Masaru Kohno built his classical guitars in Tokyo, Japan. When he died in '98, production was taken over by his nephew, Masaki Sakurai.

Koll

1990-present. Professional and premium grade, custom/production, solidbody, chambered, and archtop guitars and basses built by luthier Saul Koll, originally in Long Beach, California, and since '93, in Portland, Oregon.

Kona

1910s-1920s. Acoustic Hawaiian guitars sold by C.S. Delano and others, with later models made by the Herman Weissenborn Co. Weissenborn appointments are in line with style number, with thicker body and solid neck construction. Kona name currently used on an import line offered by M&M Merchandisers.

Style 2

1927-1928		$2,100	$2,700

Style 3

1920s	Koa	$2,700	$3,600

Style 4

1920s	Hawaiian	$2,700	$3,600
1920s	Spanish	$2,700	$3,600

MODEL YEAR	FEATURES	EXC. COND. LOW	HIGH

Kona Guitar Company

2000-present. Located in Fort Worth, Texas, Kona imports budget and intermediate grade, production, nylon and steel string acoustic and solid and semi-hollow body electric guitars and basses. They also offer amps, mandolins and ukes.

Koontz

1970-late 1980s. Luthier Sam Koontz started building custom guitars in the late '50s. Starting in '66 Koontz, who was associated with Harptone guitars, built guitars for Standel. In '70, he opened his own shop in Linden, New Jersey, building a variety of custom guitars. Koontz died in the late '80s. His guitars varied greatly and should be valued on a case-by-case basis.

Kopp String Instruments

Located in Republic, Ohio from 2000-2004, luthier Denny Kopp presently builds his professional and premium grade, production/custom, semi-hollow archtop electric and hand-carved archtop jazz guitars in Catawba Island, Ohio. He started in 2000.

Kopy Kat

1970s. Budget copy-era solidbody, semi-hollow body and acoustic guitars imported from Japan. They also made basses and mandolins.

Acoustic

1970s	J-200 copy	$125	$200

Kragenbrink

Premium grade, production/custom, steel string acoustic guitars built by luthier Lance Kragenbrink in Vandercook Lake, Michigan, starting in the year 2001.

Kramer

1976-1990, 1995-present. Currently Kramer offers budget and intermediate grade, production, imported acoustic, acoustic/electric, semi-hollow and solidbody guitars. They also offer basses, amps and effects.

Founded by New York music retailer Dennis Berardi, ex-Travis Bean partner Gary Kramer and ex-Norlin executive Peter LaPlaca. Initial financing provided by real estate developer Henry Vaccaro. Parent company named BKL Corporation (Berardi, Kramer, LaPlaca), located in Neptune City, New Jersey. The first guitars were designed by Berardi and luthier Phil Petillo and featured aluminum necks with wooden inserts on back to give them a wooden feel. Guitar production commenced in late-'76. Control passed to Guitar Center of Los Angeles for '79-'82, which recommended a switch to more economical wood necks. Most wooden necks from Kramer's Golden Era (1981-1986) we made in Japan by ESP and shipped to the U.S.A. for final guitar assembly. Aluminum necks were phased out during the early-'80s, and were last produced

MODEL YEAR	FEATURES	EXC. COND. LOW	HIGH

in '85. In '84 they added their first import models, the Japanese-made Focus line, followed by the Korean-made Striker line. By 1986 Kramer was the top American electric guitarmaker. In '89, a new investment group was brought in with James Liati as president, hoping for access to Russian market, but the company went of business in late-'90. In '95 Henry Vaccaro and new partners revived the company and designed a number of new guitars in conjunction with Phil Petillo. However, in '97 the Kramer brand was sold to Gibson. In '98, Henry Vaccaro released his new line of aluminum-core neck, split headstock guitars under the Vacarro brand. From 1997 to 2009, sales of Kramer instruments was only through Gibson's MusicYo website. In 2010, Gibson began to distribute the brand through traditional music retail channels with new issues and 1980s legacy models.Non-U.S.-made models include the following lines: Aerostar, Ferrington, Focus, Hundred (post-'85 made with 3 digits in the 100-900), Showster, Striker, Thousand (post-'85 made with 4 digits in the 1000-9000), XL (except XL-5 made in '80s).

Serial numbers for import models include:

Two alpha followed by 4 numbers: for example AA2341 with any assortment of letters and numbers.

One alpha followed by 5 numbers: for example B23412.

Five numbers: for example 23412.

Model number preceding numbers: for example XL1-03205.

The notation "Kramer, Neptune, NJ" does indicate U.S.A.-made production.

Most post-'85 Kramers were ESP Japanese-made guitars. American Series were ESP Japanese components that were assembled in the U.S.

The vintage/used market makes value distinctions between U.S.-made and import models.

Headstock and logo shape can help identify U.S. versus imports as follows:

Traditional or Classic headstock with capital K as Kramer: U.S.A. '81-'84.

Banana (soft edges) headstock with all caps KRAMER: U.S.A. American Series '84-'86.

Pointy (sharp cut) headstock with all caps KRAMER: U.S.A. American Series '86-'87.

Pointy (sharp cut) headstock with downsized letters Kramer plus American decal: U.S.A. American Series '87-'94.

Pointy (sharp cut) headstock with downsized letters Kramer but without American decal, is an import.

1984 Reissue

2003-2007. Made in the U.S., based on EVH's Kramer, single Gibson humbucker, Rose tremolo, various colors.

2003-2007		$525	$675

MODEL YEAR	FEATURES	EXC. COND. LOW	HIGH

The 84 (Original Collection)

2019-present. Alder body, maple neck, Seymour Duncan pickup, Floyd Rose trem, various colors with gloss finish.

2019-2020		$450	$575

250-G Special

1977-1979. Offset double-cut, tropical woods, aluminum neck, dot markers, 2 pickups.

1977-1979		$650	$850

350-G Standard

1976-1979. Offset double-cut, tropical woods, aluminum neck, tuning fork headstock, ebonol 'board, zero fret, 2 single coils, dot inlays. The 350 and 450 were Kramer's first models.

1976-1979		$975	$1,275

450-G Deluxe

1976-1980. Like 350-G, but with block inlays, 2 humbuckers. Became the 450G Deluxe in late '77 with dot inlays.

1976-1980		$975	$1,275

650-G Artist

1977-1980. Aluminum neck, ebonol 'board, double-cut solidbody, 2 humbuckers.

1977-1980		$1,250	$1,625

Assault 220 (Modern Collection)

2020-present. Mahogany body and neck, Floyd Rose trem, 2 humbucker pickups, black or white.

2020		$210	$275

Assault 220FR

2010-present. Mahogany body, 2 humbucker pickups, Floyd Rose trem, white or black gloss finish.

2010-2020		$300	$400

Assault Plus (Modern Collection)

2020-present. Mahogany body with flame maple veneer top, reverse headstock, 2 Seymour Duncan pickups, Floyd Rose trem, Bengal Burst or Trans Purple Burst.

2020		$450	$600

Baretta

1984-1990. Offset double-cut, banana six-on-a-side headstock, 1 pickup, Floyd Rose tremolo, black hardware, U.S.A.-made.

1984-1985		$1,100	$2,200
1986-1987		$600	$1,300
1988-1990	Standard opaque	$625	$800
1988-1990	With graphics	$775	$1,000
1990	Baretta III hybrid	$550	$725

Baretta '85 Reissue

2006. Made in the U.S., based on 1985 banana headstock model, Rose tremolo.

2006		$625	$800

Baretta II/Soloist

1986-1990. Soloist sleek body with pointed cutaway horns.

1986-1990		$600	$800

Baretta (Original Collection)

2020-present. Maple body and neck, Seymour Duncan pickup, Floyd Rose trem, Pewter Gray or Ruby Red.

2020		$375	$500

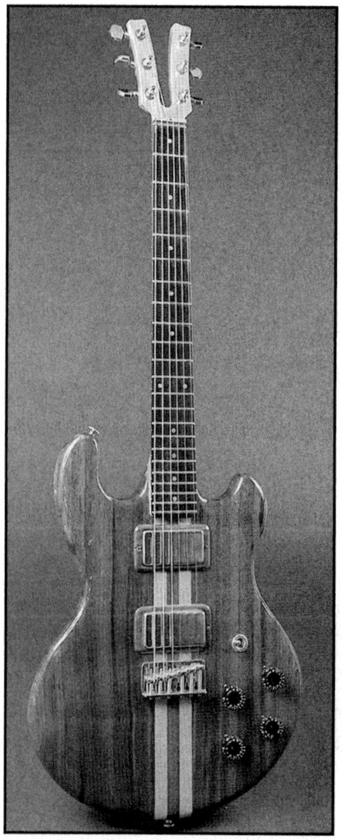

1978 Kramer 450-G Deluxe

Carter Vintage Guitars

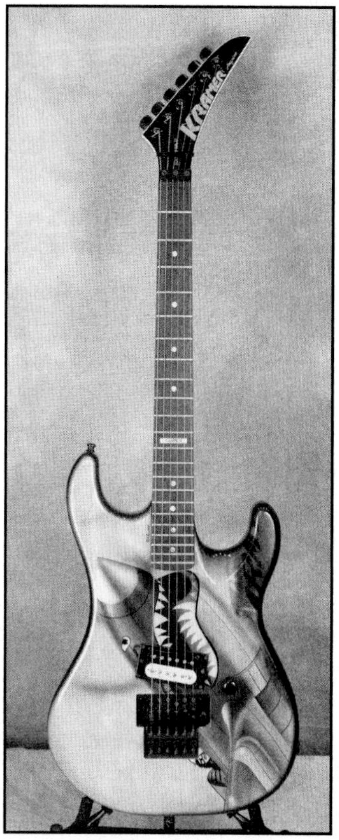

1988 Kramer Baretta

Abalone Vintage

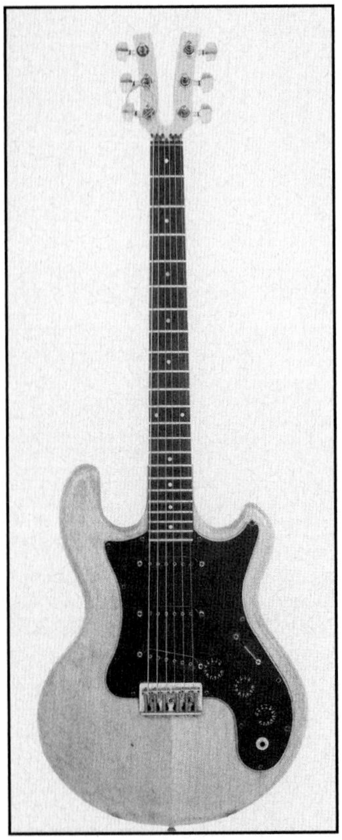

1979 Kramer DMZ-3000

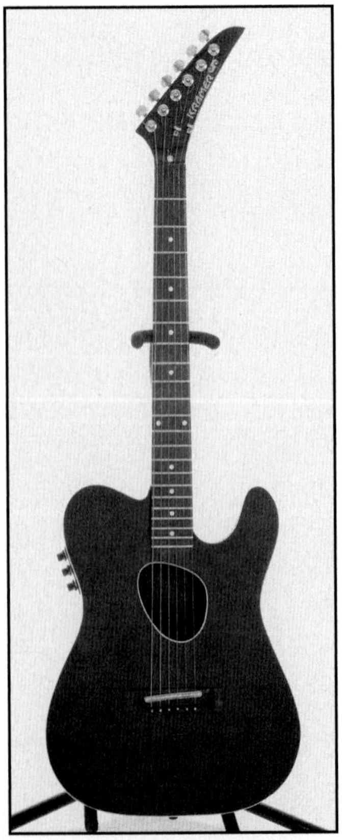

Late 1980s Kramer Ferrington

Imaged by Heritage Auctions, HA.com

MODEL YEAR	FEATURES	EXC. COND. LOW	HIGH

Baretta Special (Original Collection)

2020-present. Mahogany body, maple neck, Alnico humbucker pickup, traditional trem, gloss finish in Candy Blue, Ruby Red or Purple.

2020		$100	$130

Classic Series

1986-1987. Solidbody copies of the famous Southern California builder, including offset contoured double-cut (Classic I) and slab body single-cut designs (Classic II and Classic III).

1986-1987	Classic I	$425	$550
1986-1987	Classic II	$650	$850
1986-1987	Classic III	$650	$850

Condor

1985-1986. Futuristic 4-point body with large upper bass horn and lower treble horn.

1985-1986		$600	$800

DMZ Custom Series

1978-1981. Solidbody double-cut with larger upper horn, bolt-on aluminum T-neck, slot headstock, models include the 1000 (super distortion humbuckers), 2000 (dual-sound humbuckers), 3000 (3 SDS single-coils), 6000 (dual-sound humbuckers, active DBL).

1978-1981	DMZ-1000	$900	$1,200
1978-1981	DMZ-2000	$900	$1,200
1978-1981	DMZ-3000	$1,100	$1,450
1978-1981	DMZ-6000	$1,225	$1,625

Duke Custom/Standard

1981-1982. Headless aluminum neck, 22-fret neck, 1 pickup, Floyd Rose tremolo.

1981-1982		$325	$425

Duke Special

1982-1985. Headless aluminum neck, two pickups, tuners on body.

1982-1985		$350	$475

Elliot Easton Pro I

1987-1988. Designed by Elliot Easton, offset double-cut, six-on-a-side headstock, Floyd Rose tremolo, 2 single-coils and 1 humbucker.

1987-1988		$625	$825

Elliot Easton Pro II

1987-1988. Same as Pro I, but with fixed-bridge tailpiece, 2 single-coils.

1987-1988		$550	$725

Ferrington

1985-1990. Acoustic-electric, offered in single- and double-cut, bolt-on electric-style neck, transducers, made in Korea.

1985-1990		$300	$400

Floyd Rose Signature Edition

1983-1984. Four pointed-bout body with deep cutaway-below tremolo assembly, Floyd Rose vibrato system.

1983-1984		$625	$825

Focus/F Series (Import)

1983-1989. Kramer introduced the Focus series as import copies of their American-made models like the Pacer, Baretta, Vanguard (Rhoads-V), and Voyager (star body). Model numbers were 1000-6000, plus the Focus Classic I, II, and III. Most models were offset, double-cut solidbodies. In '87 the Focus line was renamed the F-Series. In '88 a neck-through body design, which is noted as NT, was introduced for a short time. The Classic series was offered with over a dozen color options.

1983-1989	Various models	$200	$400

Gene Simmons Axe

1980-1981. Axe-shaped guitar, aluminum neck, 1 humbucker, slot headstock, stop tailpiece, 25 were made.

1980-1981		$4,200	$6,500

Gorky Park (Import)

1986-1989. Triangular balalaika, bolt-on maple neck, pointy droopy six-on-a-side headstock, 1 pickup, Floyd Rose tremolo, red with iron sickle graphics, tribute to Russian rock, reissued in late-'90s.

1986-1989		$225	$300

Hundred Series

1988-1990. Import budget line, most with offset double-cut 7/8th solidbody.

1988-1990	Various models	$180	$300

Jersey Star

2004-2007. A reissue of the Richie Sambora model.

2004-2007		$700	$900

Jersey Star (Original Collection)

2020-present. Alder body, maple neck, mother-of-pearl Jersey Star logo, 3 pickups, Floyd Rose trem, Candy Apple Red or Alpine White.

2020		$625	$825

Liberty '86 Series

1986-1987. Offset double cut arched-top solidbody, pointy head, 2 humbuckers, black, white or flame-maple bound body.

1986-1987	Black or white	$600	$775
1986-1987	Flame maple	$650	$850

Metalist/Showster Series

1989-1990. Korean-made offset double-cut solidbody, metal trim in body design, pointy droopy six-on-a-side headstock, various pickup options, Floyd Rose.

1989-1990		$375	$500

Night Rider

2000-2007. Inexpensive import double-cut semi-hollow, 2 humbuckers.

2000-2007		$75	$100

Nightswan

1987-1990. Offset double-cut, six-on-a-side headstock, 2 Duncan humbuckers, Floyd Rose tremolo, blue metallic.

1987-1990		$1,025	$1,325
1987-1990	Custom color or finish	$1,125	$1,450

Nightswan (Original Collection)

2020-present. Mahogany body, maple neck, 2 pickups, Floyd Rose trem, jet black metallic, vintage white with Aztec graphic or black with blue polka dots.

2020		$500	$650

Night-V (Modern Collection)

2020-present. Mahogany body, maple neck, 2 pickups, Floyd Rose trem, satin black finish.

2020		$225	$290

Night-V Plus (Modern Collection)

2020-present. Mahogany body, maple neck, 2 pickups, Floyd Rose trem, Alpine white.

2020		$365	$475

GUITARS

MODEL YEAR	FEATURES	EXC. COND. LOW	HIGH

Pacer (Original Collection)

2020-present. Double-cut offset maple body, 2 Seymour Duncan pickups, Floyd Rose trem, pearl white or orange tiger finish.

2020		$425	$550

Pacer Carrera

1982-1986. Offset double-cut, wood neck, classic six-on-a-side headstock, ebonized 22-fret rosewood 'board, 2 pickups, 3-way switch, black Rockinger, restyled body with Floyd Rose in '83, banana headstock in '85.

1982-1985		$650	$850
1986		$500	$700

Pacer Custom

1981-1982. Offset double-cut, bolt-on maple neck with maple cap, 2 humbuckers, translucent finish, gold hardware.

1981-1982		$750	$1,000

Pacer Custom I

1987-1989. Custom with slanted hum and 2 single coils, various colors.

1987-1989		$600	$800

Pacer Custom II

1987-1989. Custom with hum and 2 single coils, various colors.

1987-1989		$600	$800

Pacer Deluxe

1983-1987. Offset double-cut, six-on-a-side headstock, hum/single/single pickups, bolt-on maple neck.

1983-1985		$750	$1,000
1986-1987		$625	$825

Pacer Imperial

1981-1989. Offset double cut, bolt-on maple neck with maple cap, 2 humbuckers.

1981-1985		$750	$1,000
1986-1989		$625	$825

Pacer Special

1981-1985. Various headstocks, 1 humbucker pickup, EVH trem.

1981-1985		$750	$1,000

The Pacer

1982-1985. Pacer with 3 single coil pickup.

1982-1985		$750	$1,000

Paul Dean

1986-1988. Offset double cut, neck-thru, hum/single/single pickups, droopy pointy head.

1986-1988		$635	$825

ProAxe (U.S.A.)

1989-1990. U.S.A.-made, offset double-cut, sharp pointy headstock, dot markers, 2 or 3 pickups, smaller 7/8ths size body, 3 models offered with slightly different pickup options. The model was discontinued when Kramer went out of business in 1990.

1989-1990	Deluxe	$750	$1,000
1989-1990	Special	$750	$1,000
1989-1990	Standard	$750	$1,000

Richie Sambora

1987-1989. Designed by Sambora, mahogany offset double-cut, maple neck, pointy droopy 6-on-a-side headstock, gold hardware, Floyd Rose, 3 pickups, 2 coil-taps.

1987-1989		$925	$1,225

Ripley RSG-1

1984-1987. Offset double-cut, banana six-on-a-side headstock, 22 frets, hexophonic humbucking pickups, panpots, dual volume, Floyd Rose tremolo, black hardware, stereo output, pointy droopy headstock in '87.

1984-1985		$750	$1,000
1986-1987		$600	$800

Savant/Showster Series

1989-1990. Offset double-cut solidbody, pointy headstock, various pickup options.

1989-1990		$600	$800

SM-1 (Original Collection)

2020-present. Double-cut mahogany body, 3 pickups, Floyd Rose trem, gloss finish in Orange Crush, Candy Blue or Maximum Steel.

2020		$575	$750

Stagemaster Series

1983-1987. Offset double-cut neck-thru solidbody models, smaller 7/8th body.

1983-1985	Custom/Custom I	$750	$1,000
1983-1985	Deluxe/Deluxe I	$750	$1,000
1983-1985	Imperial	$750	$1,000
1983-1985	Special	$750	$1,000
1983-1985	Standard/Standard I	$750	$1,000
1986-1987	Custom/Custom I	$600	$800
1986-1987	Deluxe/Deluxe I	$600	$800
1986-1987	Imperial	$600	$800
1986-1987	Special	$600	$800
1986-1987	Standard/Standard I	$600	$800
1987	Deluxe II	$600	$800

Striker Series

1984-1989. Offset double-cut, various pickup options, series included Striker 100, 200, 300, 400, 600 and 700 Bass.

1984-1989	Various models	$180	$300

Sustainer

1989. Offset double-cut solidbody, reverse pointy headstock, Floyd Rose tremolo.

1989		$750	$1,000

Triax

1986. Rare, odd shape, 2 humbuckers, Floyd Rose trem, Pearlescent Red.

1986		$2,000	$3,000

Vanguard Series

1981-1986. U.S.-made or American Series (assembled in U.S.). V shape, 1 humbucker, aluminum (Special '81-'83) or wood (Custom '81-'83) neck. Added for '83-'84 were the Imperial (wood neck, 2 humbuckers) and the Headless (alum neck, 1 humbucker). For '85-'86, the body was modified to a Jackson Randy Rhoads style V body, with a banana headstock and 2 humbuckers. In '99 this last design was revived as an import.

1981-1983	Custom	$750	$1,000
1981-1983	Special	$750	$1,000
1983-1984	Imperial	$750	$1,000
1985-1986	Rhoads V-body	$600	$800

Vanguard (Reissue)

1999-2014. 2 humbuckers, pointy headstock, licensed Floyd Rose.

1999-2014		$300	$400

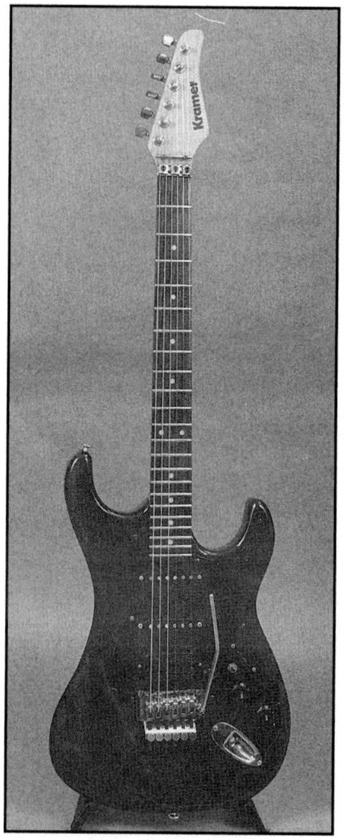

1983 Kramer Pacer

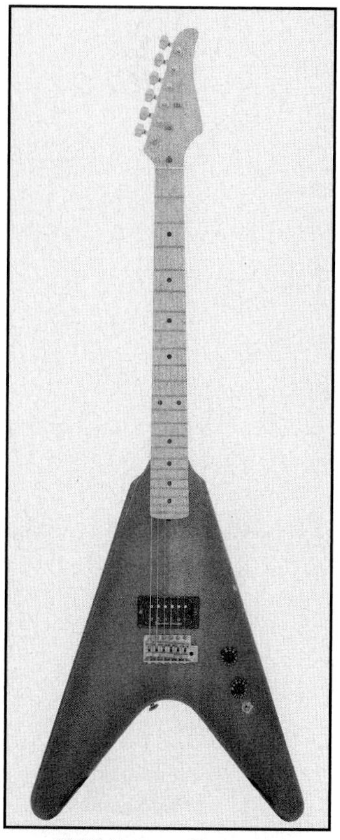

1982 Kramer Vanguard

Imaged by Heritage Auctions, HA.com

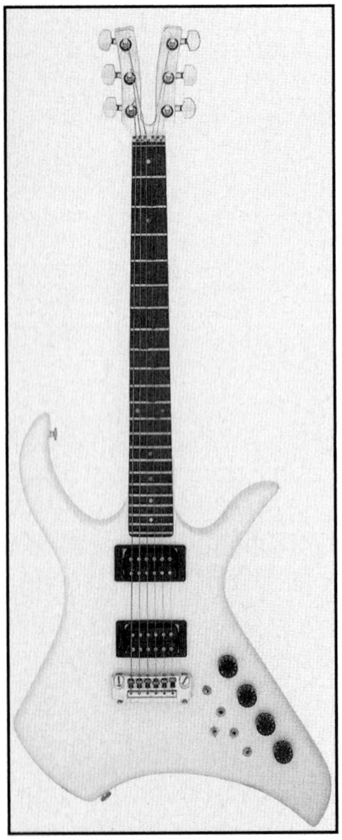

1980 Kramer XL5

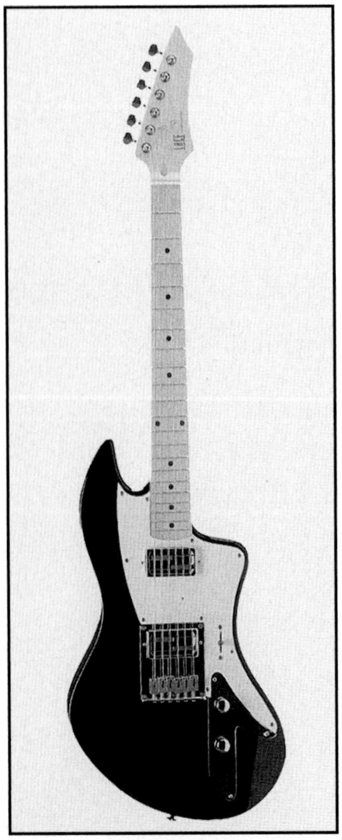

Lace Cybercaster Standard

MODEL YEAR	FEATURES	EXC. COND. LOW	HIGH

Voyager

1982-1985. Wood neck, classic headstock, rosewood 'board, 1 pickup (2 optional), Floyd Rose tremolo, black.

1982-1985	Imperial	$750	$1,000

XKG-10

1980-1981. Aluminum neck, V-shaped body.

1980-1981		$675	$900

XKG-20

1980-1981. More traditional double-cut body with small horns.

1980-1981		$675	$900

XL Series

1980-1981, 1987-1990. The early-'80s U.S.-made models had aluminum necks and were completely different than the late-'80s wood neck models, which were inexpensive imports.

1980-1981	Aluminum neck	$750	$1,000
1987-1990	Wood neck	$175	$275

ZX Aero Star Series

1986-1989. Offset double-cut solidbodies, pointy six-on-a-side headstock. Models include the 1 humbucker ZX-10, 2 humbucker ZX-20, 3 single coil ZX-30, and hum/single/single ZX-30H.

1986-1989		$100	$200

Kramer-Harrison, William

Luthier William Kramer-Harrison began building in 1977, premium grade, custom, classical and flat-top guitars in Kingston, New York.

KSM

Luthier Kevin S. Moore, starting in 1988, premium grade, custom/production, solidbody electric guitars in Logan, Utah.

Kubicki

1973-present. Kubicki is best known for their Factor basses, but did offer a few guitar models in the early '80s. See Bass section for more company info.

Kustom

1968-present. Founded by Bud Ross in Chanute, Kansas, and best known for the tuck-and-roll amps, Kustom also offered guitars from '68 to '69. See Amp section for more company info.

Electric Hollowbody

1968-1969. Hollowed-out 2-part bodies; includes the K200A (humbucker, Bigsby), the K200B (single-coils, trapeze tailpiece), and the K200C (less fancy tuners), various colors.

1968-1969		$950	$1,300

Kwasnycia Guitars

1997-present. Production/custom, premium grade, acoustic guitars built by luthier Dennis Kwasnycia in Chatham, Ontario.

Kyle, Doug

Premium grade, custom, Selmer-style guitars made by luthier Doug Kyle in the U.K., starting in 1990.

MODEL YEAR	FEATURES	EXC. COND. LOW	HIGH

L Benito

Professional grade, steel and nylon string acoustics from luthier Lito Benito and built in Chile starting in 2001.

La Baye

1967. Designed by Dan Helland in Green Bay, Wisconsin and built by the Holman-Woodell factory in Neodesha, Kansas. Introduced at NAMM and folded when no orders came in. Only 45 prototypes made. A few may have been sold later as 21st Century. They also had basses.

2x4 6-String

1967. Narrow plank body, controls on top, 2 pickups, tremolo, 12-string version was also made.

1967		$1,200	$1,550

La Mancha

Professional and premium grade, production/custom, classical guitars made in Mexico under the supervision of Kenny Hill and Gil Carnal and distributed by Jerry Roberts of Nashville, Tennessee. They began in 1996.

La Patrie

Production, classical guitars. Founded by luthier Robert Godin, who also has the Norman, Godin, Seagull, and Patrick & Simon brands of instruments.

La Scala

Ca. 1920s-1930s. La Scala was another brand of the Oscar Schmidt Company of New Jersey, and was used on guitars, banjos, and mandolins. These were often the fanciest of the Schmidt instruments. Schmidt made the guitars and mandolins; the banjos were made by Rettberg & Lang.

Lace Music Products

1979-present. Intermediate and professional, production, electric guitars from Lace Music Products of Cypress, California, a division of Actodyne General Inc. which was founded by Don Lace Sr., inventor of the Lace Sensor Pickup. In '96, Lace added amplifiers, followed by guitars in 2001 and Rat Fink guitars in '02.

Lacey Guitars

1974-present. Luthier Mark Lacey builds his premium and presentation archtops and flat-tops in Nashville, Tennessee.

Lado

1973-present. Founded by Joe Kovacic, Lado builds professional and premium grade, production/custom, solidbody guitars and basses in Lindsay, Ontario. Some model lines are branded J. K. Lado.

MODEL YEAR	FEATURES	EXC. COND. LOW	HIGH

Lafayette

Ca. 1963-1967. Sold through Lafayette Electronics catalogs. Early Japanese-made guitars and basses from pre-copy era, generally shorter scale beginner instruments. Many made by Guyatone, some possibly by Teisco.

Electric

1963-1967. Various models.

1963-1967		$350	$500

Laguna

2008-present. Guitar Center private label, budget and intermediate grade, production, imported electric and acoustic guitars price range.

Lakeside (Lyon & Healy)

Early-1900s. Mainly catalog sales of guitars and mandolins from the Chicago maker. Marketed as a less expensive alternative to the Lyon & Healy Washburn product line.

Harp Guitar

Early-1900s. Spruce top, rosewood finished birch back and sides, two 6-string necks with standard tuners, 1 neck is fretless without dot markers, rectangular bridge.

1900s		$1,700	$2,300

Parlor

Early-1900s. Spruce top, oak back and sides, cedar neck.

1900s		$400	$600

Lakewood

1986-present. Luthier Martin Seeliger builds his professional and premium grade, production/custom, steel and nylon string guitars in Giessen, Germany. He has also built mandolins.

Langdon Guitars

1997-present. Luthier Jeff Langdon builds his professional and premium grade, production/custom, flat-top, archtop, and solidbody guitars in Eureka, California.

Langejans Guitars

1971-2016. Premium grade, production/custom, flat-top, 12-string, and classical guitars built by luthier Delwyn Langejans in Holland, Michigan. He retired in '16.

Larrivee

1968-present. Professional and premium grade, production/custom, acoustic, acoustic/electric, and classical guitars built in Vancouver, British Columbia and, since '01, in Oxnard, California. They also offered several acoustic and a few electric basses over the years as well as ukes. Founded by Jean Larrivee, who apprenticed under Edgar Monch in Toronto. He built classical guitars in his home from '68-'70 and built his first steel string guitar in '71. Moved company to Victoria, BC in '77 and to Vancouver in '82. In '83, he began building solidbody electric guitars until '89, when focus again returned to acoustics.

Up to 2002, Larrivee used the following model designations: 05 Mahogany Standard, 09 Rosewood Standard, 10 Deluxe, 19 Special, 50 & 60 Standard (unique inlay), 70 Deluxe, and 72 Presentation. Starting in '03 designations used are: 01 Parlor, 03 Standard, 05 Select Mahogany, 09 Rosewood Artist, 10 Rosewood Deluxe, 19 California Anniv. Special Edition Series, 50 Traditional Series, 60 Traditional Series, E = Electric, R = Rosewood.

Larrivee also offers Limited Edition, Custom Shop, and Custom variations of standard models although the model name is the same as the standard model. These Custom models are worth more than the values shown.

0-60

2005. Small fancy rosewood.

2005		$1,600	$2,100

00-05

1996. 14.25", all mahogany.

1996		$1,100	$1,450

00-09

2000s		$1,150	$1,500

00-10

2000s. 00-size 14" lower bout, spruce top, rosewood back and sides, gloss finish.

2000s		$1,300	$1,700

000-40R

2014-present. Legacy series, sitka spruce top, Indian rosewood back and sides, satin finish.

2014-2020		$975	$1,300

000-50

2008-present. Mahogany back and sides.

2008-2020		$1,400	$1,800

000-60

2006-present. Traditional Series, Indian rosewood.

2006-2020		$1,400	$1,800

000-60K

Traditional Series, figured koa.

2012		$2,150	$2,800

C-10 Deluxe

Late-1980s-1990s. Sitka spruce top, Indian rosewood back and sides, sharp cutaway, fancy binding.

1980s		$1,450	$1,900

C-72 Presentation

1990s. Spruce top, Indian rosewood back and sides, non-cut Style D, ultra-fancy abalone and pearl hand-engraved headstock.

1990s	Jester headstock	$2,400	$3,100

C-72 Presentation Cutaway

1990s. Spruce top, Indian rosewood back and sides, sharp cutaway, ultra-fancy abalone and pearl hand-engraved headstock.

1990s	Mermaid headstock	$2,700	$3,500

D-02/D-02E

1998-2013. Sitka spruce top, mahogany back and sides, satin finish, E with electronics.

1998-2013		$525	$675

D-03E

2008-present. Solid mahogany back and sides, spruce top, satin finish, electronics.

2008-2020		$675	$875

1987 Langejans 12-string

Rivington Guitars

1990 Larrivee C-10 Deluxe

Carter Vintage Guitars

Larrivee D-09

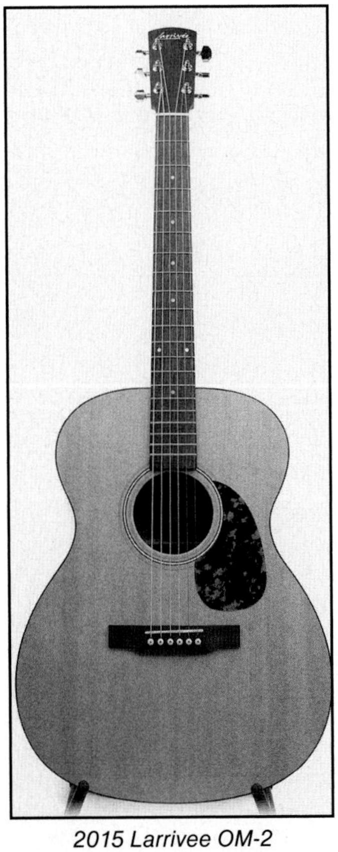

2015 Larrivee OM-2
Bernunzio Uptown Music

MODEL YEAR	FEATURES	EXC. COND. LOW	HIGH
D-03R			
2002-present. Rosewood.			
2002-2020		$850	$1,100
D-03RE			
2010-present. Rosewood, on-board electronics.			
2010-2020		$900	$1,175
D-04E			
2000-2004, 2013-2014. mahogany, on-board electronics.			
2013-2014		$1,075	$1,400
DV-03K			
Koa back and sides, Venetian cutaway.			
2000s		$1,350	$1,750
D-05-12E			
2008-2013. 12 strings.			
2008-2013		$1,075	$1,400
D-09			
2001-present. Rosewood, spruce top, gloss finish.			
2001-2012	Indian or walnut	$1,200	$1,600
2001-2020	Brazilian	$2,400	$3,200
D-10 Deluxe			
1990s-present. Spruce top, rosewood, abalone top and soundhole trim.			
1995-2020		$1,625	$2,100
D-50			
2003-present. Traditional Series, mahogany back and sides.			
2003-2020		$1,250	$1,650
D-60			
2003-present. Brazilian or Indian rosewood back and sides.			
2000s	Brazilian	$2,500	$3,300
2003-2020	Indian	$1,250	$1,650
D-70			
Horsehead headstock inlay, ebony 'board, rosewood back and sides.			
1992-1995		$1,700	$2,200
D-Style Classical			
1970s. Rosewood body, unicorn inlays.			
1970s		$1,450	$1,850
J-05-12			
2000s. Jumbo acoustic-electric 12-string, spruce top, mahogany back and sides.			
2000s		$1,200	$1,550
J-09			
Jumbo, rosewood back and sides, sitka spruce top.			
2000s		$1,400	$1,800
J-09-12K			
Jumbo 12-string, rosewood back and sides.			
2000s		$1,750	$2,300
J-70			
1990s. Jumbo, sitka spruce top, solid Indian rosewood back and sides, presentation grade fancy appointments, limited production.			
1990s		$1,700	$2,250
JV-05 Mahogany Standard			
Mahogany back and sides, Venetian cutaway.			
2000s		$1,075	$1,400
L Series			
1990s-2000s.			
1990s	L-50	$1,450	$1,900
1990s	L-72 Presentation Custom	$2,700	$3,500
2000s	L-30 (Classical)	$1,100	$1,450
L-0 Standard Series			
1980s-present. Models include L-03 (satin finish), L-05 (mahogany) and L-09 (Indian rosewood).			
1980s-2020	L-05/05E	$1,100	$1,450
1983-2020	L-09/09E	$1,200	$1,550
1990s-2020	L-03/03E	$700	$900
2000s	L-01	$575	$750
2000s	L-03-12R, 12-string	$700	$900
2000s	L-04	$700	$900
2008-2012	L-03K, koa	$1,000	$1,300
2008-2020	L-03R, rosewood	$750	$975
2008-2020	L-03RE	$775	$1,000
LS Series			
1990s-2011.			
1998	LS-05, mahogany	$1,100	$1,450
2008-2011	LS-03R, rosewood	$1,100	$1,450
LV Series			
1990s-present. Various models.			
1990s-2020	LV-05/05E	$1,225	$1,600
1990s-2020	LV-09/09E	$1,325	$1,750
2002	LV-19 Special Vine	$3,000	$3,900
2007-2020	LV-03/03E	$1,100	$1,450
2007-2020	LV-10/10E	$2,150	$2,800
OM Series			
1990s-present. Various models.			
1990-2000s	OM-02	$800	$1,050
1990-2000s	OM-09R, rosewood	$1,225	$1,600
1990s-2020	OM-03/03E	$925	$1,200
1990s-2020	OM-10 Deluxe	$1,850	$2,400
1999-2020	OM-05/05E	$1,225	$1,600
2000-2020	OM-03R, rosewood	$925	$1,200
2000-2020	OM-40/40E	$1,450	$1,900
2000-2020	OM-50/50E	$1,225	$1,600
2000s	OM-09K, koa	$1,625	$2,100
2008-2020	OM-60 Bluegrass	$1,300	$1,700
OMV Series			
1990s-present. Various models.			
2000s-2020	OMV-50/50E	$1,700	$2,200
2003-2020	OMV-09/09E	$1,225	$1,600
2009-2020	OMV-60/60E	$1,775	$2,300
Parlor Walnut			
Early 2000s. Spruce top, solid walnut back and sides.			
2002		$600	$775
PV Series			
2007-present. Various Parlor models.			
2007	PV-09, maple	$1,200	$1,550
2007-2020	PV-09, Brazilian	$2,400	$3,100
RS-2 Ventura			
2010-2015. Mahogany solidbody, rosewood 'board, 1 or 2 pickups, satin finish various colors.			
2010-2015		$750	$1,000
RS-4 CM Carved Top			
1988-1989. Carved top solidbody, curly maple top, single-single-humbucker pickups, sunburst or translucent finishes.			
1988-1989		$1,150	$1,500

MODEL YEAR	FEATURES	EXC. COND. LOW	HIGH

SD Series

2008-present. Various models.

2008	SD-03R	$1,225	$1,600
2008-2020	SD-50/50E	$1,625	$2,100
2008-2020	SD-60/60E	$1,300	$1,700

Larry Alan Guitars

2003-present. Professional and premium grade, production/custom, acoustic and electric guitars and basses, built by luthier Larry Alan Daft in Lansing, Michigan. He also builds effects pedals.

Larson Brothers

1900-1944. Chicago's Carl and August Larson bought Maurer & Company in 1900 where they built guitars and mandolin family instruments until 1944. Their house brands were Maurer, Prairie State and Euphonon and they also built for catalog companies Wm. C. Stahl and W. J. Dyer & Bro., adding brands like Stetson, a house brand of Dyer. See brand listings for more information.

Laskin

1973-present. Luthier William "Grit" Laskin builds his premium and presentation grade, custom, steel-string, classical, and flamenco guitars in Toronto, Ontario. Many of his instruments feature extensive inlay work.

Laurie Williams Guitars

1983-present. Luthier Laurie Williams builds his premium and presentation grade, custom/production, steel string, classical and archtop guitars on the North Island of New Zealand. He also builds mandolins.

Leach Guitars

1980-present. Luthier Harvey Leach builds his professional and premium grade, custom, flat-tops, archtops, and solidbody electrics, travel guitars and basses in Cedar Ridge, California.

Lehmann Stringed Instruments

1971-present. Luthier Bernard Lehmann builds his professional and premium grade, production/custom, flat-top, archtop, classical and Gypsy guitars in Rochester, New York. He also builds lutes, vielles and rebecs.

Lehtela

1993-present. Professional and premium grade, custom/production, acoustic, acoustic/electric, archtop, and solidbody guitars and basses built by luthier Ari Lehtela in Newell, North Carolina.

Lentz

1975-present. Luthier Scott Lentz builds his professional, premium, and presentation grade, custom/production, solidbody electric guitars in San Marcos, California.

MODEL YEAR	FEATURES	EXC. COND. LOW	HIGH

Les Stansell Guitars

1980-present. Luthier Les Stansell builds his premium grade, custom, nylon-string guitars in Pistol River, Oregon.

Levin

1900-1973. Founded by Herman Carlson Levin and located in Gothenburg, Sweden, Levin was best known for their classical guitars, which they also built for other brands, most notably Goya from ca. 1955 to the mid '70s. They also built mandolins and ukes.

Levy-Page Special

1930s. Acoustic guitars likely built by Gibson, having many features of Kalamzoo guitars of the era. Possibly made for a distributor.

Lewis

1981-present. Luthier Michael Lewis builds his premium and presentation grade, custom/production, archtop guitars in Grass Valley, California. He also builds mandolins. He also built guitars under the D'Angelico name.

Linc Luthier

1991-present. Professional and premium grade, custom/production, electric and acoustic guitars, basses and double-necks built by luthier Linc Luthier in Upland, California.

Lindberg

Ca. 1950s. Line of guitars produced by Hoyer for Germany's Lindberg music store.

Lindert

1986-2002. Luthier Chuck Lindert made his intermediate and professional grade, production/custom, Art Deco-vibe electric guitars in Chelan, Washington.

Line 6

1996-present. Professional grade, production, imported solidbody and acoustic modeling guitars able to replicate the tones of a variety of instruments. Line 6 also builds effects and amps.

Lion

1960s. One of the brand names of guitars built for others by Egmond in Holland.

Lipe Guitars USA

1983-1989, 2000-2018. Luthier Michael Lipe built custom, professional grade, guitars and basses in Sun Valley, California. Lipe died Dec. '18.

Liscombe

1992-2013. Professional grade, production and limited custom, chambered electric guitars built by luthier Ken Liscombe in Burlington, Ontario.

Larrivee OM-10
Tim Page

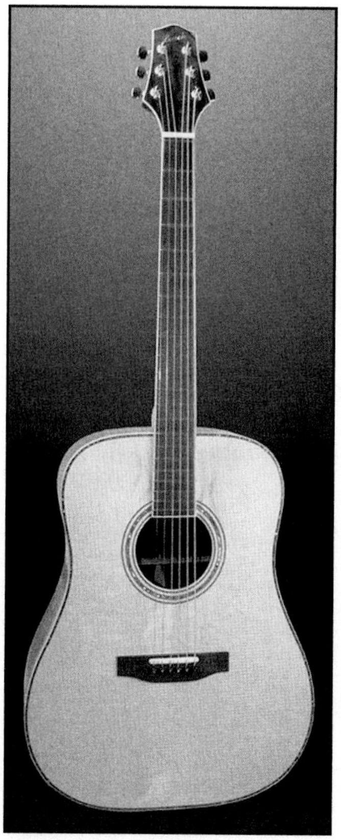

Leach VG Franconia

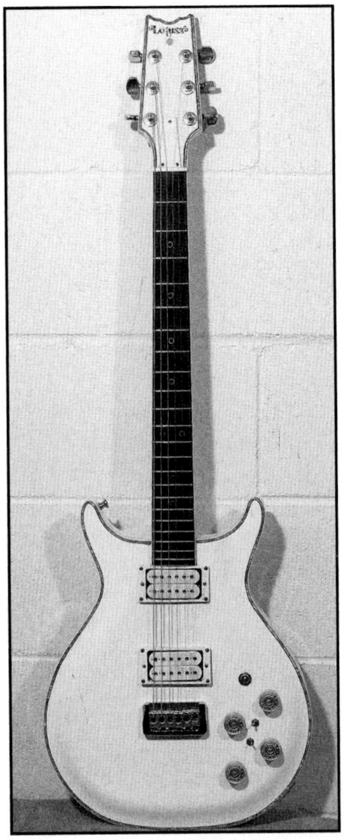

1985 Lotus
Tom Pfeifer

Lowden Jazz Series

MODEL YEAR	FEATURES	EXC. COND. LOW	HIGH

Loar (The)

2005-present. Professional grade, production, imported archtop acoustic guitars designed by Greg Rich for The Music Link, which also has Johnson and other brands of instruments. They also offer mandolins.

Lollar

1979-present. Luthier Jason Lollar builds his premium grade, production/custom, solidbody and archtop guitars in Vashon, Washington.

Lopez, Abel Garcia

Luthier Abel Garcia Lopez builds his premium grade, custom, classical guitars in Mexico starting in 1985.

Loprinzi

1972-present. Professional and premium grade, production/custom, classical and steel-string guitars built in Clearwater, Florida. They also build ukes. Founded by Augustino LoPrinzi and his brother Thomas in New Jersey. The guitar operations were taken over by AMF/Maark Corp. in '73. LoPrinzi left the company and again started producing his own Augustino Guitars, moving his operations to Florida in '78. AMF ceased production in '80, and a few years later, LoPrinzi got his trademarked name back.

Classical

1970s. Various models.

1970s	Brazilian rosewood	$1,575	$2,025
1970s	Indian rosewood	$925	$1,200
1970s	Mahogany	$825	$1,100

Lord

Mid-1960s. Acoustic and solidbody electric guitars imported by Halifax.

Acoustic or Electric Soldibody

1960s	Various models	$150	$250

Lotus

Late-1970s-2004. Budget grade acoustic and electric guitars and basses imported originally by Midco International, of Effingham, Illinois, and most recently by Musicorp. They also offered banjos and mandolins.

Louis Panormo

Early to mid-1800s. Spanish guitars made in London, England by luthier Louis (Luis) Panormo. He was born in Paris in 1784, and died in 1862.

Lowden

1973-present. Luthier George Lowden builds his premium and presentation grade, production/custom, steel and nylon string guitars in Downpatrick, Northern Ireland. From '80 to '85, he had some models made in Japan.

MODEL YEAR	FEATURES	EXC. COND. LOW	HIGH

Flat-Top

1980s-present. Standard models include D, F, O, and S sizes and models 10 thru 32.

1980s-2020	Premium models	$4,000	$10,000
1980s-2020	Standard models	$2,000	$4,000

LsL Instruments

2008-present. Luthier Lance Lerman builds his production, professional grade, solidbody electric guitars and basses in Los Angeles, California.

LSR Headless Instruments

1988-present. Professional and premium grade, production/custom, solidbody headless guitars and basses made by Ed Roman Guitars.

LTD

1995-present. Intermediate grade, production, Korean-made solidbody guitars and basses offered by ESP.

Lucas Custom Instruments

1989-present. Premium and presentation grade, production/custom, flat-tops built by luthier Randy Lucas in Columbus, Indiana.

Lucas, A. J.

1990-present. Luthier A. J. Lucas builds his production/custom, classical and steel string guitars in Lincolnshire, England.

Luis Feu de Mesquita

2000-present. Professional and premium grade, custom, acoustic and flat-top guitars including Spanish, classical and flamenco built in Toronto, Ontario by luthier Luis Feu de Mesquita.

Luna Guitars

2005-present. Located in Tampa, Florida, Yvonne de Villiers imports her budget to professional grade, production, acoustic and electric guitars and basses from Japan, Korea and China. She also added ukuleles in '09 and amps in '10.

Luttrell Guitars

1993-present. Professional and premium grade, production/custom, acoustic, electric and resonator guitars built by luthier Ralph H. Luttrell in Sandy Springs, Georgia.

Lyle

Ca. 1969-1980. Imported by distributor L.D. Heater of Portland, Oregon. Generally higher quality Japanese-made copies of American designs by unknown manufacturers, but some early ones, at least, were made by Arai and Company. They also had basses and mandolins.

Lyon & Healy

1864-present. Founded by George Washburn Lyon and Patrick Joseph Healy, Lyon & Healy was

MODEL YEAR | FEATURES | EXC. COND. LOW | HIGH

an industry giant, operating a chain of music stores, and manufacturering harps (their only remaining product), pianos, Washburn guitars and a line of brass and wind instruments. See Washburn, American Conservatory, Lakeside, and College brands.

Lyon by Washburn

1990s-2000s. Budget grade, production, solidbody guitars and basses sold by mass merchandisers such as Target.

Lyra

1920s. Instruments built by the Oscar Schmidt Co. and possibly others. Most likely a brand made for a distributor.

Lyric

Luthier John Southern started building his professional and premium grade, custom, semi-hollow and solidbody and basses guitars in Tulsa, Oklahoma in 1996.

M. Campellone Guitars

See listing under Campellone Guitars

M.Zaganin and N.Zaganin

1989-present. Luthier Márcio Zaganin began his career using the M.Zaganin brand, in 2004 it was changed to N. He builds professional and premium grade, production/custom, semi-hollow and solidbody electric guitars in São Paulo, Brazil. He also builds basses.

Maccaferri

1923-1990. Built by luthier and classical guitarist Mario Maccaferri (b. May 20, 1900, Cento, Italy; d. 1993, New York) in Cento, Italy; Paris, France; New York, New York; and Mount Vernon, New York. Maccaferri was a student of Luigi Mozzani from '11 to '28. His first catalog was in '23, and included a cutaway guitar. He also made mandolins. His Europe-era instruments are very rare. He designed Selmer guitars in '31. Maccaferri invented the plastic clothespin during World War II and used that technology to produce plastic ukes starting in '49 and Dow Styron plastic guitars in '53. He made several experimental plastic electrics in the '60s and plastic violins in the late-'80s.

Plastic (Dow Styron)

1950s. Plastic construction, models include Deluxe (archtop, crown logo), Islander (Islander logo), TV Pal (4-string cutaway) and Showtime (Showtime logo).

Model Year	Features	Low	High
1950s	Deluxe	$180	$235
1950s	Islander	$155	$205
1950s	Romancer	$155	$205
1950s	Showtime	$155	$205
1950s	TV Pal	$120	$155

Madeira

1973-ca. 1984, ca. 1990. Imported Budget and intermediate grade acoustic and electric guitars distributed by Guild. The Japanese-made electrics were basically copies of Gibson, Fender and Guild models, the acoustics originally copies of Martin. The electrics only offered first year or so during the '70s run. Name revived again around '90 on imported acoustics and electrics. They also offered mandolins and banjos.

Madrid

1996-present. Luthier Brandon Madrid builds his production/custom, professional and premium grade, acoustic and solidbody electric guitars, in San Diego, California. Prior to 2009 he built in Portland, Oregon.

Maestro

1950s-1970s, 2001-2012. Maestro is a brand name Gibson first used on 1950s accordian amplifiers. The first Maestro effects were introduced in the early-'60s and they used the name until the late-'70s. In 2001, Gibson revived the name for a line of effects, banjos and mandolins. Those were dropped in '09, when imported budget and intermediate, production, acoustic and electric guitars and amps were added. By '12 the brand is no longer listed with Gibson.

Electric

2009-2012. Various student models, Maestro headstock logo, 'By Gibson' logo on truss rod cover.

Model Year	Features	Low	High
2009-2012		$55	$95

Magnatone

Ca.1937-1971, 2013-present. Founded as Dickerson Brothers in Los Angeles, California and known as Magna Electronics from '47, with Art Duhamell president. Brands include Dickerson, Oahu (not all), Gourley, Natural Music Guild, Magnatone. In '59 Magna and Estey merged and in '66 the company relocated to Pennsylvania. In '71, the brand was taken over by a toy company. Between 1957 and '67, the company produced four different model lines of Spanish electrics. In 2013, Ted Kornblum revived the Magnatone name on a line of tube amps built in St. Louis, Missouri.

Cyclops

1930s. Dobro-made resonator guitar.

Model Year	Features	Low	High
1930s	Round neck	$1,200	$1,550
1930s	Square neck	$1,200	$1,550

Mark Artist Series

Model Year	Features	Low	High
1959-1961	More common	$900	$1,150
1959-1961	Rare	$1,150	$1,500

Mark Series

1955-1960. Solidbody series made by Paul Bigsby in small quantities, then taken over by Paul Barth at Magnatone in '59.

Model Year	Features	Low	High
1955-1959	Mark IV	$2,100	$2,700
1955-1959	Mark V	$2,100	$2,700

Model Series

Model Year	Features	Low	High
1962	Model 100	$300	$385
1962	Model 150	$300	$385
1962	Model 200, 2 pickups	$300	$385

1920 Lyon & Healy Thornward

Bernunzio Uptown Music

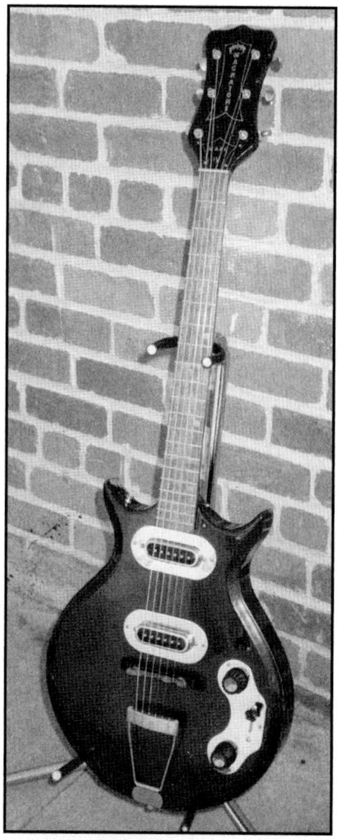

1957 Magnatone Mark IV

Michael Wright

1965 Magnatone X-5 Zephyr

Rivington Guitars

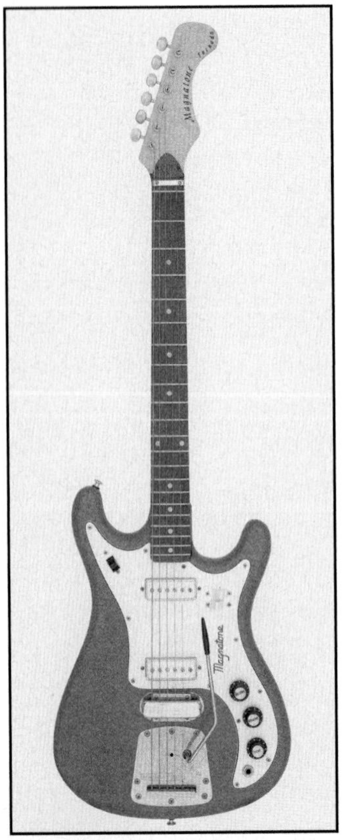

1966 Magnatone X-15 Tornado

Imaged by Heritage Auctions, HA.com

X-5 Zephyr

1965-1966. Double-cut with 2 DeArmond single-coil pickups, vibrato, metallic finish.

MODEL YEAR	FEATURES	EXC. COND. LOW	HIGH
1965-1966		$550	$725

X-15 Tornado

1965-1966. Offset double-cut body, 2 pickups, various options.

MODEL YEAR	FEATURES	EXC. COND. LOW	HIGH
1965-1966		$825	$1,075

X-20 Typhoon

1965-1966. Double-cut solidbody, 3 pickups, various options.

MODEL YEAR	FEATURES	EXC. COND. LOW	HIGH
1965-1966		$925	$1,225

Magno-Tone

1930s. Brand most likely used by a music studio (or distributor) on instruments made by others, including Regal-built resonator instruments.

Mai Kai

1910s. Line of Hawaiian guitars built in Los Angeles, California by the Shireson Brothers.

Mako

1985-1989. Line of budget to lower-intermediate solidbody guitars from Kaman (Ovation, Hamer). They also offered basses and amps.

Solidbody

MODEL YEAR	FEATURES	EXC. COND. LOW	HIGH
1985-1989	Various models	$100	$350

Mal n' Sal

See listing for Alternative Guitar and Amplifier Company.

Malinoski

1986-present. Luthier Peter Malinoski builds his production/custom, professional and premium grade, solidbody electric guitars and basses in Hyattsville, Maryland.

Mann

Ca. 1971-ca. 1985. A brand name used in Canada by Japan's Hoshino company on some of the same acoustic and electric models as their Ibanez guitars.

Manne

1987-present. Professional and premium grade, production/custom, semi-acoustic and electric guitars and basses built by luthier Andrea Ballarin in Italy.

Manson Guitar Works

1979-present. Premium grade, production/custom, electric guitars built by luthiers Hugh Manson and Adrian Ashton in Exeter, Devon UK. They also offer a line of professional grade, guitars crafted in the Czech Republic and assembled in UK. They also build basses.

Manuel & Patterson

1993-present. Luthiers Joe Manuel and Phil Patterson build professional, premium and presentation grade, production/custom, flat-top, archtop and solidbody electric guitars in Abita Springs, Louisiana. They also offer mandolins.

Manuel Contreras

1962-1994. Luthier Manuel Gonzalez Contreras worked with José Ramírez III, before opening his own shop in Madrid, Spain, in '62.

Manuel Contreras II

1986-present. Professional grade, production/custom, nylon-string guitars made in Madrid, Spain, by luthier Pablo Contreras, son of Manuel.

Manuel Ramirez

See listing under Ramirez, Manuel.

Manuel Rodriguez and Sons, S.L.

1905-present. Professional, premium, and presentation grade, custom flat-top and nylon-string guitars from Madrid, Spain.

Manuel Velázquez

1933-2014. Luthier Manuel Velázquez (d. 2014) built his classical guitars in Puerto Rico ('72-'82), New York City, Virginia, and Florida. His son Alfredo continues to build guitars.

Manzanita Guitars

1993-present. Custom, steel-string, Hawaiian, and resonator guitars built by luthiers Manfred Pietrzok and Moritz Sattler in Rosdorf, Germany.

Manzer Guitars

1976-present. Luthier Linda Manzer builds her premium and presentation grade, custom, steel-string, nylon-string, and archtop guitars in Toronto, Ontario.

Maple Lake

2003-present. Intermediate grade, production, flat-top and acoustic/electric imported guitars from luthier Abe Wechter. Wechter also builds guitars under his own name.

MapleTree Guitars Canada

2011-present. Steve Maric, owner and luthier from Toronto, Canada, works with luthier Fulu Wang, Beijing, China to build production/custom, professional grade, acoustic guitars.

Mapson

1995-present. Luthier James L. Mapson builds his premium and presentation grade, production/custom, archtops in Santa Ana, California.

Marc Silber Guitar Company

1998-present. Intermediate and professional grade, production, flat-top, nylon-string, and Hawaiian guitars designed by Marc Silber and made

MODEL YEAR	FEATURES	EXC. COND. LOW	HIGH

in Mexico. These were offered under the K & S Guitars and/or Silber brands for 1992-'98. Silber also has ukuleles.

Marchione Guitars

1993-present. Premium and presentation grade, custom, archtops and solidbodies built by Stephen Marchione originally in New York City, but currently in Houston, Texas.

Marcia

1920s. Instruments built by the Oscar Schmidt Co. and possibly others. Most likely a brand made for a distributor.

Marco Polo

1960-ca. 1964. Imported from Japan by Harry Stewart and the Marco Polo Company of Santa Ana, California. One of the first American distributors to advertise inexpensive Japanese guitars and basses. Manufacturers unknown, but some acoustics by Suzuki, some electrics by Guyatone.

Acoustic Hollowbody

1960-1964	Various models	$80	$225

Mario Martin Guitars

2011-present. Luthier Mario Martin builds his production/custom, professional grade, semi-hollow and solidbody guitars and basses in Murfreesboro, Tennessee. From 2006 to '11, he built guitars under the Guitar Mill brand name.

Mark Wescott Guitars

Premium grade, custom, flat-tops, built by luthier Mark Wescott, starting in 1980, in Somers Point, New Jersey.

Marling

Ca. 1975. Budget line guitars and basses marketed by EKO of Recanati, Italy; probably made by them, although possibly imported.

Acoustic

1975. Includes the steel-string S.110, and the dreadnoughts W.354 Western, and W.356 Western.

1975		$80	$225

Electric Soldibody

1975. Includes the E.400 (semi-acoustic/electric), E.490 (solidbody), E.480 (single-cut-style), and the 460 (Manta-style).

1975		$80	$225

Martelle

1934. Private brand attributed to Gibson and some to Kay.

De Luxe

1934. Gibson 12-fret round shoulder Jumbo construction, laminate maple or mahogany back and sides, sunburst, Hawaiian or Spanish option.

1934		$6,300	$8,400

MODEL YEAR	FEATURES	EXC. COND. LOW	HIGH

Martin

1833-present. Intermediate, professional, premium, and presentation grade, production/custom, acoustic, acoustic/electric, archtop and resonator guitars. Founded in New York City by Christian Frederick Martin, former employee of J. Staufer in Vienna, Austria. Moved to Nazareth, Pennsylvania in 1839. Early guitars were made in the European style, many made with partners John Coupa, Charles Bruno and Henry Schatz. Scalloped X-bracing was introduced in the late-1840s. The dreadnought was introduced in 1916 for the Oliver Ditson Company, Boston; and Martin introduced their own versions in 1931.

Martin model size and shape are indicated by the letter prefix (e.g., 0, 00, 000, D, etc.); materials and ornamentation are indicated by number, with the higher the number, the fancier the instrument (e.g., 18, 28, 35, etc.). Martin offered electric thinline guitars from '61-'68 and electric solidbodies from '78-'82. The Martin Shenandoah was made in Asia and assembled in U.S. Japanese Martin Sigma ('72-'73) and Korean Martin Stinger ('85 on) imported solidbodies.

Most Martin flat-top guitars, particularly Style 18 and above, came with a standard natural finish, therefore Martin guitar finish coloring is generally not mentioned because it is assumed to be see-through natural. Conversely, Gibson's standard finish for their flat-tops during their Golden Era was sunburst. Martin introduced their shaded (sunburst) finish as an option on their Style 18 in 1934 and their Style 28 in 1931. Values for a shaded finish should be considered on a case-by-case basis. Braced for steel strings specifications described under certain models are based on current consensus information and data provided by the late Martin employee-historian Mike Longworth, and is for guidance only. Variations from these specs have been found, so "bracing" should be considered on a case-by-case basis.

0-15

1935, 1940-1943, 1948-1961. Maple or birch in '35, all mahogany after, unbound rosewood 'board, slotted peghead and 12-fret neck until '34, solid peghead and 14-fret neck thereafter, natural mahogany.

1935	Maple or birch	$2,725	$3,550
1940-1949	Mahogany begins	$2,725	$3,550
1950-1959		$2,475	$3,225
1960-1961		$2,100	$2,750

0-15 H

1940. Hawaiian neck, all mahogany.

1940		$2,800	$3,600

0-15 M Elderly Instruments 40th Anniversary Limited Edition

2011-2012. Only 10 offered, solid mahogany body and neck, special appointments, inside label signed by Elderly Instruments president Stan Werbin and Martin CEO Chris Martin.

2011-2012		$950	$1,250

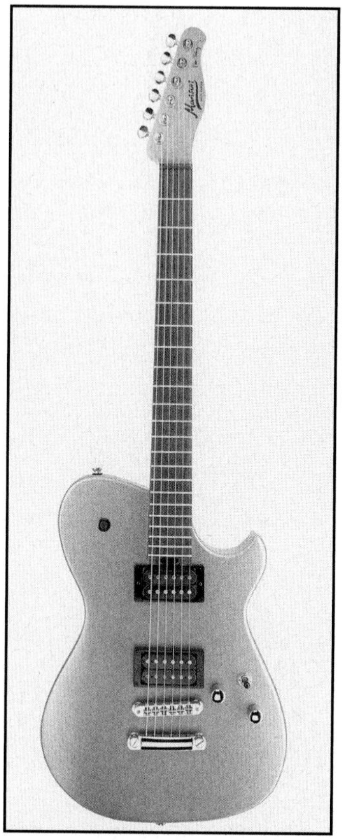

Manson META Series MBM-1

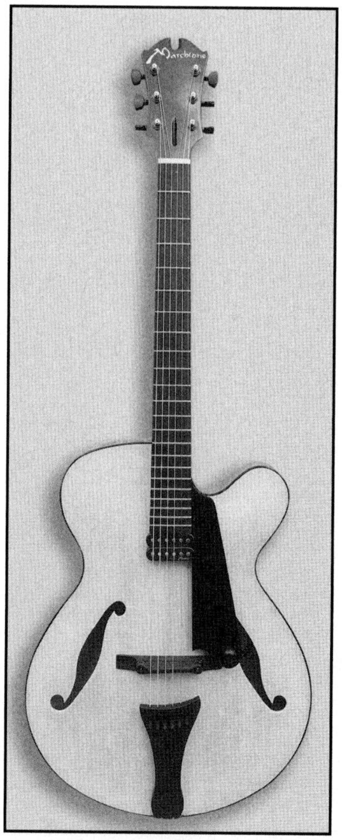

Marchione 16" Archtop

1967 Martin 0-16 NY

Imaged by Heritage Auctions, HA.com

1936 Martin 0-17

KC from Larryville Ga.

0-15 T

1960-1963. Tenor with Style 15 appointments, natural mahogany.

MODEL YEAR	FEATURES	EXC. COND. LOW	HIGH
1960-1963		$950	$1,250

0-16

1961 only. Six made.

MODEL YEAR	FEATURES	EXC. COND. LOW	HIGH
1961		$2,150	$2,800

0-16 NY

1961-1977, 1979-1992, 1994. Mahogany back and sides, 12 frets, slotted peghead, unbound extra-wide rosewood 'board, natural.

MODEL YEAR	FEATURES	EXC. COND. LOW	HIGH
1961-1969		$2,150	$2,800
1970-1979		$1,800	$2,300
1980-1989		$1,500	$1,950
1990-1994		$1,500	$1,950

0-17

1906-1917, 1929-1948, 1966-1968. First version has mahogany back and sides, 3 black soundhole rings, rosewood bound back, unbound ebony 'board, 12 frets, slotted peghead. Second version ('29 and on) is all mahogany, 3 white-black-white soundhole rings, top bound until '30, thin black backstripe, 12 frets and slotted peghead until '34, solid peghead and 14 frets beginning in '33, natural mahogany.

MODEL YEAR	FEATURES	EXC. COND. LOW	HIGH
1906-1917	Gut	$1,950	$2,525
1929-1933	Steel, 12-fret	$2,650	$3,450
1933-1934	Flat natural, 14-fret	$3,350	$4,400
1934-1938	Gloss dark, 14-fret	$3,350	$4,400
1939	Early '39, 175 neck	$3,350	$4,400
1939	Later '39, 168 neck	$3,350	$4,400
1940-1946		$3,100	$4,100
1947-1948		$2,700	$3,500
1966-1968	Special order	$2,200	$2,875

0-17 H

1930, 1935-1940. Hawaiian, mahogany back and sides, 12 frets clear of body, natural.

MODEL YEAR	FEATURES	EXC. COND. LOW	HIGH
1930	12-fret	$2,900	$3,700
1935-1940	14-fret	$3,100	$4,100

0-17 S

Early 1930s. Limited production style 17 with spruce top, unique 'guard.

MODEL YEAR	FEATURES	EXC. COND. LOW	HIGH
1931		$4,400	$5,700

0-17 T

1932-1960. Mahogany back and sides, tenor, natural.

MODEL YEAR	FEATURES	EXC. COND. LOW	HIGH
1932-1933		$1,125	$1,450
1934-1939		$1,650	$2,150
1940-1947		$1,300	$1,675
1948-1949		$1,100	$1,425
1950-1960		$1,025	$1,325

0-18

1898-1994, 2017-present. Rosewood back and sides until 1917, mahogany back and sides after, Adirondack spruce top until 1946, slotted peghead and 12 frets until 1934, solid peghead and 14 frets after 1934, braced for steel strings in 1923, improved neck in late-1934, non-scalloped braces appear late-'44, natural. Reintroduced '17, sitka spruce, mahogany.

MODEL YEAR	FEATURES	EXC. COND. LOW	HIGH
1898-1917	Brazilian	$3,250	$4,225
1918-1922	Mahogany, gut	$2,125	$2,775
1923-1934	12-fret, steel	$4,500	$5,900
1932-1938	14-fret	$5,000	$6,500
1939	Early '39, 175 neck	$5,000	$6,500
1939	Later '39, 168 neck	$4,475	$5,800
1940-1944		$4,200	$5,400
1945-1946		$3,550	$4,600
1947-1949		$3,400	$4,400
1950-1959		$3,100	$4,000
1960-1964		$2,800	$3,600
1965		$2,700	$3,500
1966-1969		$2,400	$3,100
1970-1979		$2,100	$2,700
1980-1989		$1,700	$2,200
1990-1994		$1,700	$2,200
2017-2020	Reintroduced	$1,475	$1,900

0-18 G

1960s. Special order classical nylon-string model, natural.

MODEL YEAR	FEATURES	EXC. COND. LOW	HIGH
1961		$1,400	$1,800

0-18 K

1918-1935. Hawaiian, all koa wood, T-frets and steel T-bar neck in late-1934, natural.

MODEL YEAR	FEATURES	EXC. COND. LOW	HIGH
1918-1933		$4,425	$5,750
1934-1935	14-fret	$4,850	$6,300

0-18 KH

1927-1928. Hawaiian, koa.

MODEL YEAR	FEATURES	EXC. COND. LOW	HIGH
1927-1928		$4,425	$5,750

0-18 T

1929-1932, 1936-1989, 1991-1992, 1994-1995. Mahogany body, spruce top, tenor, natural.

MODEL YEAR	FEATURES	EXC. COND. LOW	HIGH
1929-1939		$1,850	$2,400
1940-1946		$1,575	$2,050
1947-1949		$1,450	$1,850
1950-1959		$1,375	$1,775
1960-1969		$1,250	$1,650
1970-1979		$1,025	$1,350
1980-1989		$875	$1,125
1991-1995		$875	$1,125

0-18 T Nick Reynolds

2010-2011. Custom Artist Edition, mahogany.

MODEL YEAR	FEATURES	EXC. COND. LOW	HIGH
2010-2011		$2,150	$2,800

0-18 TE

1959, 1962. Only 2 made, tenor, 1 pickup.

MODEL YEAR	FEATURES	EXC. COND. LOW	HIGH
1959, 1962		$4,400	$5,700

0-18 VS Elderly Instruments 40th Anniversary Limited Edition

2012-2014. Mahogany body, sitka spruce top, slotted headstock, 12-fret neck, inside label signed by C. F. Martin IV and Elderly founder Stan Werbin.

MODEL YEAR	FEATURES	EXC. COND. LOW	HIGH
2012-2014		$1,750	$2,275

0-20

MODEL YEAR	FEATURES	EXC. COND. LOW	HIGH
1850-1859		$4,700	$6,100

0-21

1898-1931, 1934-1938, 1941, 1944, 1946-1948. Rosewood back and sides, Adirondack spruce top until 1946, 12 frets, T-frets and steel T-bar neck in late-1934, non-scalloped braces in late-1944, natural.

MODEL YEAR	FEATURES	EXC. COND. LOW	HIGH
1898-1926	12-fret, gut	$5,500	$7,300
1927-1929	12-fret, steel	$7,100	$9,200
1930	12-fret, belly bridge	$7,100	$9,200
1930	14-fret (only year)	$7,100	$9,200
1931-1938		$7,100	$9,200

MODEL YEAR	FEATURES	EXC. COND. LOW	HIGH
1941		$6,900	$8,900
1944	Non-scalloped	$6,300	$8,100
1946	Adirondack	$5,000	$6,500
1947-1948	Sitka	$4,850	$6,300

0-21 K

1919-1929. Koa top, back and sides.

1919-1929		$6,700	$8,700

0-21 T

1929-1930, 1935, 1961.

1929-1935		$3,575	$4,650
1961		$1,950	$2,525

0-26

1895. Only 1 made, rosewood back and sides, ivory-bound top, rope-style purfling.

1895		$5,900	$7,600

0-27

1850s-1890s. Rosewood back and sides, ivory-bound top.

1850s	Antique market value	$7,000	$9,100
1890s		$5,600	$7,300

0-28

1874-1931, 1937 (6 made), 1969 (1 made). Brazilian rosewood back and sides, herringbone binding until 1937, natural.

1874-1895		$5,600	$7,300
1896-1897	Dark orange (rare)	$5,600	$7,300
1898-1923		$5,600	$7,300
1924-1927	Gut	$5,600	$7,300
1925-1927	Steel option	$8,000	$10,400
1928-1929	Steel (standard)	$8,000	$10,400
1930-1931	Belly bridge, 12-fret	$8,700	$11,300
1937	Belly bridge, 14-fret	$11,000	$14,200
1969	Brazilian	$5,000	$6,500

0-28 H

1927-1928. One made each year, Hawaiian, koa.

1927-1928		$7,400	$9,600

0-28 IA Ian Anderson

2004. Limited Edition 87 made, adirondack spruce top, Indian rosewood sides and back, slotted headstock, can be converted from nylon to light steel strings.

2004		$3,200	$4,200

0-28 K

1917-1931, 1935. Hawaiian, all koa wood, braced for steel strings in '23, natural.

1917-1924		$6,600	$8,600
1925-1929		$7,400	$9,600
1930-1935		$8,000	$10,400

0-28 T

1930-1931, 1941. Tenor neck.

1930-1931	Steel option	$4,100	$5,300
1941		$3,300	$4,300

0-28 VS

2009-2019. Rosewood back and sides, slotted head, 12 fret neck.

2009-2019		$2,200	$2,900

0-30

1899-1921. Brazilian rosewood back and sides, ivory-bound body, neck and headstock.

1899-1921		$5,500	$7,300

0-34

1885, 1898-1899, 1907. Brazilian rosewood.

1885-1907		$6,000	$7,800

0-40

1860s-1898, 1912-1913. Indian rosewood.

1880-1913		$7,550	$9,800

0-42

1870s-1924, 1926-1930, 1 each in '34, '38,'42. Brazilian rosewood back and sides, 12 frets, natural.

1890-1924		$11,000	$14,300
1926-1927	Gut	$11,000	$14,300
1928-1942	Steel	$17,000	$22,000

0-44 Soloist/Olcott-Bickford Artist

1911-1931. Vahdah Olcott-Bickford Artist Model, run of 17 style-44 guitars made, Brazilian rosewood, ivory or faux-ivory-bound ebony 'board.

1911-1931		$15,500	$20,000

0-45

1904-1908, '11, '13, '15, '17-'20, '22-'24, '26-'30, '39. Brazilian rosewood back and sides, natural, special order only for '31-'39.

1904-1927	Gut	$25,000	$32,600
1927-1939	Steel	$36,000	$46,800

0-45 JB Joan Baez

1998. Indian rosewood, 59 made.

1998		$3,700	$4,800

0-45 S Stephen Stills

2007. 91 made, Madagascar rosewood sides and back, Adirondack spruce top.

2007		$6,200	$8,100

0-X1 E

2020-present. Concert size, figured mahogany laminate, Fishman electronics.

2020		$375	$500

00-1

1995-2002. Grand Concert, mahogany.

1995-2002		$650	$850

00-1 R

1995-1999. Rosewood version.

1995-1999		$650	$850

00-15

1999-2010. Sapele/mahogany.

1999-2010		$775	$1,025

00-15 E Retro

2017-2018. Solid mahogany top, back and sides, electronics.

2017-2018		$1,175	$1,500

00-15 M

2009-present. All mahogany.

2009-2020		$775	$1,025

00-15 M Custom Elderly Instruments

2010-2014. All mahogany, diamond and square inlays, custom-made for Elderly Instruments, about 10 offered each year.

2010-2014		$750	$975

00-15 M Elderly Instruments 40th Anniversary Limited Edition

2012. Only 12 made, mahogany body and neck, label signed by Elderly's president Stan Werbin and Martin CEO Chris Martin.

2012		$750	$975

1919 Martin 0-18

David Stone

1998 Martin 0-45 JB Joan Baez

GUITARS

1999 Martin 00-18 SH Steve Howe

1963 Martin 00-18E
Greg Perrine

MODEL YEAR	FEATURES	EXC. COND. LOW	HIGH

00C-15 AE
2000-2002. Built-in electronics, natural finish.

2000-2002		$900	$1,200

00-16 C
1962-1977, 1980-1981. Classical, mahogany back and sides, 5-ply bound top, satin finish, 12 frets, slotted peghead, natural.

1962-1969		$1,050	$1,350
1970-1977		$875	$1,150
1980-1981	2 made	$750	$975

00-16 DBFM
2006. Women and Music series, deep body (DB), flamed maple (FM), slotted headstock.

2001-2003		$1,200	$1,575

00-16 DBM
2000-2005. Women and Music series, deep body (DB), mahogany (M), slotted headstock, gloss finish.

2000-2005		$1,200	$1,575

00-16 DBR
1998-2000. Women and Music series, deep body (DB), rosewood ®, 14-fret slotted headstock, gloss natural finish.

1998-2000		$1,200	$1,575

00C-16 DB
1999-2002. Women in Music series, cutaway, deep body (DB), mahogany, slotted headstock.

1999-2002		$1,425	$1,850

00C-16 DBRE
2005-2007. Women and Music series, rounded cutaway, deep body (DB), rosewood (R), electronics (E).

2005-2007		$1,475	$1,925

00-17
1908-1917, 1930-1960, 1982-1988, 2001-2004. Mahogany back and sides, 12 frets and slotted headstock until '34, solid headstock and 14 frets after '34, natural mahogany, reissued in 2001 with a high gloss finish.

1908-1917	Gut	$2,450	$3,175
1930-1933	Steel, 12-fret	$3,500	$4,600
1934	14-fret, flat natural	$3,900	$5,000
1935-1938	14-fret, gloss dark	$3,900	$5,000
1939	Early '39, 175 neck	$3,900	$5,000
1939	Later '39, 168 neck	$3,500	$4,600
1940-1944		$3,500	$4,600
1945-1946		$3,100	$4,100
1947-1949		$2,900	$3,800
1950-1960		$2,700	$3,500
1982-1988		$1,450	$1,900
2001-2004	Reissue	$1,450	$1,900

00-17 Authentic 1931
2018-present. Mahogany top, back and sides, Brazilian rosewood 'board, vintage gloss finish.

2018-2020		$3,025	$3,925

00-17 H
1934-1935. Hawaiian set-up, mahogany body, no binding.

1934-1935		$3,900	$5,050

00-17 S Black Smoke/Whiskey Sunset
2015-2020. Sitka spruce top, mahogany back and sides, rosewood 'board and bridge, on-board electronics (E) optional.

2015-2020	No electronics	$1,050	$1,350
2016-2020	With electronics	$1,150	$1,500

00-17 SO Sing Out!
2000. Limited Edition, 50 made for 50th anniversary of Sing Out! Magazine, folk era logo inlays, SING OUT inlay on 20th fret, mahogany body.

2000		$1,350	$1,750

00-18
1898-1995, 2016-present. Rosewood back and sides until 1917, mahogany after, braced for steel strings in '23, improved neck in late-'34, war-time design changes '42-'46, non-scalloped braces in late-'44, Adirondack spruce top until '46, natural. Reissued 2016 with sitka spruce top and mahogany back and sides.

1898-1917	Brazilian	$3,700	$4,800
1918-1922	Mahogany	$3,200	$4,200
1923-1929		$5,000	$6,450
1930-1932	12-fret	$7,700	$10,000
1933	14-fret, bar fret	$8,700	$11,300
1934-1937	14-fret	$8,700	$11,300
1938	175 neck	$8,700	$11,300
1939	Early '39, 175 neck	$8,700	$11,300
1939	Later '39, 168 neck	$7,700	$10,000
1940-1941		$7,700	$10,000
1942-1944	Scalloped	$7,700	$10,000
1944-1946	Non-scalloped	$5,800	$7,500
1947-1949		$4,800	$6,300
1950-1953		$3,500	$4,525
1954-1959		$3,200	$4,200
1960-1964		$3,000	$3,900
1965		$2,800	$3,600
1966-1969		$2,550	$3,300
1970-1979		$2,100	$2,700
1980-1989		$1,800	$2,300
1990-1995		$1,800	$2,300
2016-2020		$1,475	$1,900

00-18 Authentic 1931
2016-2018. Adirondack spruce top, mahogany back and sides, ebony 'board, Vintage Tone System (VTS), natural finish.

2016-2018		$3,500	$4,500

00-18 C
1962-1995. Renamed from 00-18 G in '62, mahogany back and sides, classical, 12 frets, slotted headstock, natural.

1962-1969		$1,400	$1,800
1970-1979		$1,000	$1,300
1980-1989		$850	$1,100
1990-1995		$850	$1,100

00-18 CTN Elizabeth Cotton
2001. Commemorative Edition, 76 made.

2001		$2,050	$2,650

00-18 Custom
2008. Custom Shop run of 75 or more made.

2008		$2,050	$2,650

00-18 E
1959-1964. Flat-top Style 18, single neck pickup and 2 knobs, heavier bracing, natural.

1959-1964		$4,700	$6,100

00-18 G

1936-1962. Mahogany back and sides, classical, natural, renamed 00-18 C in '62.

MODEL YEAR	FEATURES	EXC. COND. LOW	HIGH
1936-1939		$2,100	$2,700
1940-1949		$1,500	$1,950
1950-1959		$1,425	$1,850
1960-1962		$1,400	$1,800

00-18 Gruhn Limited Edition

1995. Sitka spruce top, C-shaped neck profile, 25 made.

MODEL YEAR	FEATURES	EXC. COND. LOW	HIGH
1995		$1,800	$2,350

00-18 H

1935-1941. Hawaiian, mahogany back and sides, 12 frets clear of body, natural. The Price Guide is generally for all original instruments. The H conversion is an exception, because converting from H (Hawaiian-style) to 00-18 specs is considered by some to be a favorable improvement and something that adds value.

MODEL YEAR	FEATURES	EXC. COND. LOW	HIGH
1935-1941		$4,850	$6,300

00-18 H Geoff Muldaur

2006-2011. Solid Adirondack spruce top, solid mahogany sides and back, sunburst.

MODEL YEAR	FEATURES	EXC. COND. LOW	HIGH
2006-2011		$2,475	$3,200

00-18 K

1918-1925, 1934. All koa wood.

MODEL YEAR	FEATURES	EXC. COND. LOW	HIGH
1918-1921		$3,125	$4,050
1922-1925		$4,425	$5,750
1934		$4,850	$6,300

00-18 S John Mellencamp

2009-2010. Slotted, 12-fret.

MODEL YEAR	FEATURES	EXC. COND. LOW	HIGH
2009-2010		$2,700	$3,500

00-18 SH Steve Howe

1999-2000. Limited edition run of 250.

MODEL YEAR	FEATURES	EXC. COND. LOW	HIGH
1999-2000		$1,875	$2,425

00-18 T

1931, 1936, 1938-1940. Tenor version.

MODEL YEAR	FEATURES	EXC. COND. LOW	HIGH
1931-1940		$2,575	$3,350

00-18 Tim O'Brien Limited Edition Signature

2008-2011. 25.5" scale, label signed by O'Brien.

MODEL YEAR	FEATURES	EXC. COND. LOW	HIGH
2008-2011		$3,300	$4,250

00-18 V

1984, 2003-2015. Vintage Series, mahogany back and sides, spruce top.

MODEL YEAR	FEATURES	EXC. COND. LOW	HIGH
1984	9 made	$1,750	$2,300
2003-2015		$1,725	$2,250

00-18 V/VS Elderly Instruments 40th Anniversary

2012-2013. Limited Edition, solid (V) or slotted (VS) headstock, 12-fret, low profile.

MODEL YEAR	FEATURES	EXC. COND. LOW	HIGH
2012-2013	V	$1,750	$2,300
2013	VS	$1,725	$2,250

00-21

1898-1996. Brazilian rosewood back and sides, changed to Indian rosewood in 1970, dark outer binding, unbound ebony 'board until 1947, rosewood from 1947, slotted diamond inlays until '44, dot after, natural.

MODEL YEAR	FEATURES	EXC. COND. LOW	HIGH
1898-1926	Gut bracing	$5,500	$7,300
1927-1939	Steel bracing	$10,100	$13,100
1940-1943	Scalloped	$9,600	$12,600
1944-1947	Non-scalloped	$8,500	$10,200
1948-1949		$7,200	$9,600
1950-1959		$6,800	$8,850
1960-1964		$5,425	$7,050
1965		$4,200	$5,500
1966-1969	Brazilian	$3,900	$5,100
1970-1979	Indian	$2,250	$2,900
1980-1989	Indian	$2,250	$2,900
1990-1996	Indian	$2,250	$2,900

00-21 Custom

2005-2006. Custom order size 00 style 21, Brazilian rosewood sides and back.

MODEL YEAR	FEATURES	EXC. COND. LOW	HIGH
2005-2006		$3,400	$4,400

00-21 G

1937-1938. Gut string, Brazilian rosewood sides and back.

MODEL YEAR	FEATURES	EXC. COND. LOW	HIGH
1937-1938		$2,375	$3,050

00-21 Golden Era

1998. Limited edition, Adirondack spruce top, scalloped braces, rosewood back and sides.

MODEL YEAR	FEATURES	EXC. COND. LOW	HIGH
1998-2000		$2,125	$2,750

00-21 H

Hawaiian, special order, limited production.

MODEL YEAR	FEATURES	EXC. COND. LOW	HIGH
1914	1 made	$5,400	$7,000
1934		$10,800	$14,000
1952, 1955	1 made each year	$7,000	$9,000

00-21 Kingston Trio LTD

2007. 50th Anniversary of the Kingston Trio, inspired by Dave Guard's 00-21, 100 made, 12-fret, Indian rosewood, Kingston Trio label and notation "In Memory of Dave Guard 1934-1991".

MODEL YEAR	FEATURES	EXC. COND. LOW	HIGH
2008-2009		$2,900	$3,750

00-21 LE

1987. Guitar of the Month, 19 made.

MODEL YEAR	FEATURES	EXC. COND. LOW	HIGH
1987		$1,775	$2,300

00-21 NY

1961-1965. Brazilian rosewood back and sides, no inlay, natural.

MODEL YEAR	FEATURES	EXC. COND. LOW	HIGH
1961-1964		$5,050	$6,600
1965		$4,200	$5,500

00-21 S

1968. Slotted headstock, Brazilian rosewood sides and back.

MODEL YEAR	FEATURES	EXC. COND. LOW	HIGH
1968		$3,700	$4,800

00-21 T

1934. Tenor, Brazilian rosewood back and sides, only 2 made.

MODEL YEAR	FEATURES	EXC. COND. LOW	HIGH
1934		$3,850	$5,000

00-25 K

1980, 1985, 1988. Spruce top, koa back and sides.

MODEL YEAR	FEATURES	EXC. COND. LOW	HIGH
1980-1988		$1,975	$2,550

00-25 K2

1980, 1982-1984, 1987-1989. Koa top, back and sides.

MODEL YEAR	FEATURES	EXC. COND. LOW	HIGH
1980-1989		$1,975	$2,550

00-28

Mid-1880s-1931, 1934, 1936-1941, 1958 (1 made), 1977 (1 made), 1984 (2 made), 2017-present. Brazilian rosewood back and sides, changed to Indian rosewood in 1977, herringbone purfling through 1941, white binding and unbound 'board after 1941, no inlays before 1901,

1947 Martin 00-21

Imaged by Heritage Auctions, HA.com

1925 Martin 00-28

Izzy Miller

GUITARS

1930 Martin 00-42

Imaged by Heritage Auctions, HA.com

1975 Martin 00-45

Imaged by Heritage Auctions, HA.com

MODEL YEAR	FEATURES	EXC. COND. LOW	HIGH

diamond inlays from 1901-'41, dot after, natural. Reintroduced 2017, sitka spruce top, modified low oval neck.

1880s-1924	Gut	$7,850	$10,200
1925-1931	Steel	$14,300	$18,600
1934-1941	Few made	$21,000	$27,000
1958	Special order	$8,850	$11,500
1977	Special order	$2,100	$2,700
1984	Special order	$1,775	$2,300
2017-2020	Reissue	$1,775	$2,300

00-28 C

1966-1995. Renamed from 00-28 G, Brazilian rosewood back and sides, changed to Indian rosewood in '70, classical, 12 frets, natural.

1966-1969	Brazilian	$2,825	$3,675
1970-1979	Indian	$1,400	$1,800
1980-1989		$1,200	$1,550
1990-1995		$1,200	$1,550

00-28 G

1936-1962. Brazilian rosewood back and sides, classical, natural, reintroduced as 00-28 C in '66.

1936-1946		$4,300	$5,700
1947-1949		$3,600	$4,700
1950-1959		$3,050	$4,000
1960-1962		$2,900	$3,800

00-28 K

1919-1921, 1926, 1928-1931, 1933. Hawaiian, koa back and sides.

1919-1921	34 made	$9,700	$12,600
1926-1933	1 made per year	$15,400	$20,000

00-28 T

1931, 1940. Tenor, Brazilian rosewood back and sides, tenor 4-string neck, only 2 made.

1931, 1940		$5,575	$7,250

00-28 VS

2009-2019. Rosewood back and sides.

2009-2019		$2,300	$3,000

00-28 VS Custom Shop

2009-2013. Various Custom Shop options.

2009-2013		$2,600	$3,400

00-30

1890s-1921. Rosewood .

1899-1921		$11,500	$15,000

00-34

1898-1899. 6 made.

1898-1899		$12,000	$16,000

00-37 K2 Steve Miller

2001. Flamed koa back and sides, solid Engelmann spruce top, limited edition run of 68.

2001		$4,200	$5,450

00-40

1913, 1917. 4 made.

1913	Brazilian	$21,000	$27,000
1917	Koa	$21,000	$27,000

00-40 H

1928-1939. Hawaiian, Brazilian rosewood back and sides, 12 frets clear of body, natural. H models are sometimes converted to standard Spanish setup, in higher-end models this can make the instrument more valuable to some people.

1928-1929	Pyramid bridge	$21,000	$27,000
1930-1939	Belly bridge	$21,000	$27,000

MODEL YEAR	FEATURES	EXC. COND. LOW	HIGH

00-40 K

Few were made (only 6), figured koa, natural.

1918	1 made	$21,000	$27,000
1930	5 made	$21,000	$27,000

00-40 Martin Stauffer

1997. Rosewood/spruce, 35 made.

1997		$5,200	$6,800

00-41 Custom

2005. Custom Shop model, parlor size.

2005		$3,550	$4,600

00-42

1898-1943, 1973 (1 made). Brazilian rosewood back and sides, Indian rosewood in 1973, pearl top borders, 12 frets, ivory bound peghead until 1918, ivoroid binding after 1918, natural.

1898-1927	Pyramid bridge	$20,000	$26,000
1927-1943	Steel bracing	$32,000	$41,000
1973	1 made	$3,300	$4,300

00-42 G

1936-1939. Gut string slotted headstock classical, only 3 made.

1936-1939	3 made	$8,500	$11,000

00-42 JM-C John Mayer Crossroads

2019. Limited run of 50 for Guitar Center, designed by John Mayer to benefit Crossroads Centre in Antigua, Sitka spruce top, Cocobolo back and sides, gloss finish.

2019		$5,600	$7,300

00-42 K

1919. Koa body, only 1 made.

1919	1 made	$30,000	$40,000

00-42 K2 Robbie Robertson

2008-2009. Limited Edition, all koa body (K2), 00-12 fret style, high-end appointments.

2008-2009		$4,500	$5,800

00-42 Linda Ronstadt Limited Edition

2009-2010. Madagascar rosewood, slotted headstock.

2009-2010		$5,400	$7,000

00-42 SC John Mayer

2012-2019. Sitka spruce top, cocobolo back, sides and headplate, ebony 'board.

2012-2019		$4,650	$6,100

00-44 G

1938. Set up with gut strings, 1 made.

1938		$23,600	$30,600

00-44 Soloist/Olcott-Bickford Artist

1913-1939. Custom-made in small quantities, Brazilian rosewood, ivory or faux-ivory-bound ebony 'board.

1913-1939	6 made	$30,000	$39,500

00-45

1904-1929, 1970-1982, 1984-1987, 1989-1990, 1992-1993. Brazilian rosewood back and sides, changed to Indian rosewood in '70, 12 frets and slotted headstock until '34 and from '70 on 14 frets, and solid headstock from '34-'70, natural.

1904-1927	Gut	$32,000	$42,000
1927-1929	Steel	$65,000	$85,000
1970-1979	Reintroduced	$4,400	$5,700
1980-1993		$4,000	$5,200

MODEL YEAR	FEATURES	EXC. COND. LOW	HIGH

00-45 K

1919. Koa body, 1 made.

1919 $46,000 $60,000

00-45 S

1970. Slotted headstock.

1970 $4,900 $6,300

00-45 S Limited Edition

2002. 1902 vintage-pattern with fancy inlays, 00 size style 45, 50 made.

2002 $9,600 $12,500

00-45 SC John Mayer

2012-2013. Limited Edition, 25 made, slotted headstock, cocobolo.

2012-2013 $8,600 $11,200

00-45 ST Stauffer Commemorative

1997-1998. Limited Edition, 25 made, six-on-a-side headstock, 45-style appointments, 00 body, Sitka top, Brazilian rosewood back and sides.

1997-1998 $8,850 $11,500

00-55

1935. 12 made for Rudnick's Music of Akron, Ohio.

1935 $8,500 $11,000

00CMAE

1999-2001. Single-cut acoustic-electric flat-top, laminate back and sides, made in U.S.

1999-2001 $525 $675

00CXAE

2000-2013. Single-cut acoustic-electric flat-top, composite laminate back and sides, made in U.S.

2000-2013 Various colors $400 $525

00L Earth

2021. Dedicated to climate control, 100% FSC-certified and 100% plastic-free, graphic art by Robert Goetzl, gig bag made from hemp.

2021 $1,250 $1,625

00L Fly Fishing

2019-present. Limited Edition, run of 100, artwork by William Matthews, sitka spruce top, Goncalo Alves back and sides, gloss finish.

2019-2020 $2,500 $3,200

00L-17 Black Smoke/Whiskey Sunset

2016-2019. Sitka spruce top. Mahogany back and sides, on-board electronics (00L-17E) optional.

2016-2019 No electronics $1,050 $1,350

2016-2019 With electronics $1,150 $1,500

00LX1AE

2017-2019. Sitka spruce top, mahogany laminate back and sides, Fishman electronics, natural. Replaced by 00L-X2E in '20.

2017-2019 $325 $425

00L-X2E

2020-present. Sitka spruce top, figured mahogany laminate back and sides, Fishman electronics, natural finish.

2020 $450 $575

00X1AE

2015-2019. Non-cut, acoustic-electric, HPL mahogany back and sides. Replaced by 00-X2E in '20.

2015-2019 $325 $425

MODEL YEAR	FEATURES	EXC. COND. LOW	HIGH

00-X2E

2020-present. Sitka spruce top, figured mahogany laminate back and sides, Fishman electronics, natural finish.

2020 $450 $575

00-DB Jeff Tweedy Signature

2011-2019. Custom Shop Signature Edition with solid FSC® Certified Mahogany and mahogany burst finish.

2011-2019 $1,525 $1,975

000-1

1994-2005. Solid spruce top with laminated mahogany back and sides.

1994-2005 $650 $825

000-1 E

1994-2005. 000-1 with electronics.

1994-2005 $700 $900

000-1 R

1994-2003. 000-1 with back and sides.

1994-2003 $650 $825

000-10 E

2019-present. Road Series, updated version of 000RS1, sapele top, back and sides, satin finish.

2019-2020 $425 $550

000-12 E Koa

2019-present. Road Series, sitka spruce top, koa veneer back and sides, Fishman electronics, gloss finish.

2019-2020 $900 $1,175

000-13 E

2017-2018. Road Series, updated version of 000RSG, sitka spruce top, siris back and sides, Fishman electronics, natural gloss.

2017-2018 $600 $775

000-15 M

2010-present. All mahogany.

2010-2020 $725 $950

000-15 M Burst

2016-2018. Solid mahogany, 14-fret, satin finish with added burst to top.

2016-2018 $750 $975

000-15 M Elderly Instruments 40th Anniversary

2011-2012. 10 made, mahogany body and neck, label signed by Elderly Instruments president Stan Werbin and Martin CEO Chris Martin

2011-2012 $950 $1,250

000-15 M StreetMaster

2017-present. Same specs as 000-15M but with distressed mahogany satin finish.

2017-2020 $725 $950

000-15 SM

2011-present. Solid mahogany, slotted headstock, 12-fret neck, satin finish.

2011-2020 $900 $1,175

000-15 Special

2016-present. Sitka spruce top, mahogany back and sides, satin finish.

2016-2020 $850 $1,100

Martin 000-10E

Martin 000-15M Streetmaster

GUITARS

Martin 000-17 Black Smoke

1972 Martin 000-18

Rivington Guitars

000-15/000-15 S

1999-2009. Mahogany body, headstock is solid or slotted (S, first offered in '00). Renamed 000-15 M with solid headstock in '10.

MODEL YEAR	FEATURES	EXC. COND. LOW	HIGH
1999-2009	000-15	$800	$1,050
2000-2009	000-15 S	$875	$1,150

000-16 Series

1989-present. Mahogany back and sides, diamonds and squares inlay, sunburst, name changed to 000-16 T Auditorium with higher appointments in '96, in 2000-2005 slotted (000-16 S) and gloss finish (000-16 SGT) were offered. Various models continue to be added to this series.

MODEL YEAR	FEATURES	EXC. COND. LOW	HIGH
1989	000-16 M	$900	$1,200
1989-1995	000-16	$900	$1,200
1989-2020	000-16 GT	$750	$1,000
1995-1998	000-16 T	$850	$1,100
1996	000-16 TR	$775	$1,000
1996-2002	000-16 R	$900	$1,200
2001-2005	000-16 RGT	$750	$1,000
2002-2003	000-16 SRGT	$825	$1,050
2003-2004	000-16 SGT	$825	$1,050
2019-2021	000-16 E	$1,225	$1,600

000-17

1911, 1952. Mahogany back and sides, 1 made in 1911, 25 more in '52.

MODEL YEAR	FEATURES	EXC. COND. LOW	HIGH
1911		$7,100	$9,200
1952		$3,200	$4,200

000-17 Black Smoke/Whiskey Sunset

2016-present. Sitka spruce top, mahogany back and sides, rosewood 'board and bridge, on-board electronics optional.

MODEL YEAR	FEATURES	EXC. COND. LOW	HIGH
2016-2020	No electronics	$900	$1,150
2016-2020	With electronics	$975	$1,300

000-17 S

2002-2004. All mahogany, slotted headstock, 12 fret neck.

MODEL YEAR	FEATURES	EXC. COND. LOW	HIGH
2002-2004		$1,075	$1,400

000-17 SM

2013-2015. Sitka spruce top, mahogany back and sides, East Indian rosewood headplate, vintage slotted headstock.

MODEL YEAR	FEATURES	EXC. COND. LOW	HIGH
2013-2015		$1,075	$1,400

000-18

1906, 1911-present (none in 1932-1933). Maple back and sides in '06, then rosewood until '17, and mahogany since, longer scale in '24-'34, 12-fret neck until '33, changed to 14 in '34. Improved neck late-'34, war-time changes '41-'46, non-scalloped braces in late-'44, switched from Adirondack spruce to Sitka spruce top in '46 (though some Adirondack tops in '50s and '60s), natural. Now called the 000-18 Auditorium.

MODEL YEAR	FEATURES	EXC. COND. LOW	HIGH
1906	Maple	$7,850	$10,200
1911-1917		$7,850	$10,200
1920-1922	Gut, mahogany	$7,000	$9,100
1923-1931	Steel, 12-fret	$11,500	$15,000
1934	Early '34, long scale	$13,200	$17,100
1934-1938	14-fret	$13,200	$17,100
1939	Early '39 175 neck	$12,300	$16,000
1939	Late '39, 168 neck	$10,000	$13,000
1940-1941		$9,200	$12,000
1942-1943	Scalloped braces	$9,200	$12,000
1944	Scalloped braces	$8,200	$10,700
1944-1947	Non-scalloped	$5,800	$7,500
1948-1949		$5,000	$6,500
1950-1953		$4,600	$6,000
1954-1959		$4,200	$5,500
1960-1964		$3,600	$4,650
1965		$3,400	$4,425
1966-1969		$2,900	$3,750
1970-1979		$2,100	$2,700
1980-1989		$1,775	$2,300
1990-1999		$1,775	$2,300
2000-2013		$1,475	$1,900
2014-2020		$1,475	$1,900

000-18 Authentic 1937

2008-2011. Natural or sunburst, high-X bracing.

MODEL YEAR	FEATURES	EXC. COND. LOW	HIGH
2008-2011		$3,500	$4,500

000-18 E Retro

2012-2019. Sitka spruce top, mahogany back and sides.

MODEL YEAR	FEATURES	EXC. COND. LOW	HIGH
2012-2019		$1,525	$2,000

000-18 G

1955. Classical, 1 made.

MODEL YEAR	FEATURES	EXC. COND. LOW	HIGH
1955		$3,200	$4,150

000-18 Golden Era 1934 Special Edition

2007. Adirondack red spruce top, scalloped and forward shifted X-bracing, 14-fret V-shaped mahogany neck, 20-fret ebony 'board, old style decal logo.

MODEL YEAR	FEATURES	EXC. COND. LOW	HIGH
2007		$2,250	$2,900

000-18 Golden Era 1937

2006-2014. Natural or sunburst. 1937 dropped from name in '12.

MODEL YEAR	FEATURES	EXC. COND. LOW	HIGH
2006-2014		$2,250	$2,900

000-18 Golden Era Sunburst

2006-2014. Sunburst version.

MODEL YEAR	FEATURES	EXC. COND. LOW	HIGH
2006-2014		$2,250	$2,900

000-18 Kenny Sultan

2007-2009. Flamed mahogany sides, diamond and squares inlays, label signed by Sultan.

MODEL YEAR	FEATURES	EXC. COND. LOW	HIGH
2007-2009		$2,250	$2,900

000-18 Norman Blake Signature

2006-2011. 12 fret neck on 14-fret body.

MODEL YEAR	FEATURES	EXC. COND. LOW	HIGH
2006-2011		$2,250	$2,900

000-18 P

1930. Plectrum neck.

MODEL YEAR	FEATURES	EXC. COND. LOW	HIGH
1930		$4,100	$5,300

000-18 S

1976-1977. Slotted, 12-fret.

MODEL YEAR	FEATURES	EXC. COND. LOW	HIGH
1976-1977		$2,400	$3,100

000-18 T

1930, '34, '36, '38, '41. Tenor.

MODEL YEAR	FEATURES	EXC. COND. LOW	HIGH
1930		$4,200	$5,500
1934-1938		$7,800	$10,200
1941		$4,700	$6,125

000-18 V/VS Elderly Instruments 40th Anniversary

2012-2013. Limited Edition, solid (V) or slotted (VS) headstock, Sitka top, label signed by C.F. Martin IV and Stan Werbin, includes matching wood guitar stand.

MODEL YEAR	FEATURES	EXC. COND. LOW	HIGH
2012-2013	V	$2,000	$2,600
2013	VS	$2,000	$2,600

000-18 WG Woody Guthrie

1999. Signed label including artwork and model identification.

MODEL YEAR	FEATURES	EXC. COND. LOW	HIGH
1999		$2,150	$2,800

000-21

1902-1923 (22 made over that time), 1931(2), 1938-1959, 1965 (1), 1979 (12). Brazilian rosewood back and sides, changed to Indian rosewood in '79, natural.

MODEL YEAR	FEATURES	EXC. COND. LOW	HIGH
1902-1923		$11,500	$14,800
1931	12-fret	$13,900	$18,100
1938-1939	Early '39, 175 neck	$21,700	$28,500
1939	Late '39, 168 neck	$17,200	$22,500
1940-1941		$14,700	$19,200
1942-1945		$13,000	$17,000
1946		$8,900	$11,500
1947-1949		$7,500	$9,700
1950-1954		$6,800	$8,850
1955-1959		$7,000	$9,000
1965	Brazilian	$6,000	$8,000
1979	Indian	$2,300	$3,000

000-21 10-String/Harp Guitar

1902. Only 2 made, 10 strings, Brazilian rosewood back and sides.

MODEL YEAR	FEATURES	EXC. COND. LOW	HIGH
1902		$4,300	$5,600

000-28

1902-present. Brazilian rosewood back and sides, changed to Indian rosewood in '70, herringbone purfling through '41, white binding and unbound 'board after '41, no inlays before '01, slotted diamond inlays from '01-'44, dot after, 12 frets until '32, 14 frets '31 on (both 12 and 14 frets were made during '31-'32), natural through '93, sunburst or natural after.

MODEL YEAR	FEATURES	EXC. COND. LOW	HIGH
1902-1927	Gut	$13,800	$17,900
1925-1927	Steel	$26,500	$34,500
1928	12-fret	$26,500	$34,500
1929	Pyramid bridge, 12-fret	$26,500	$34,500
1930	Belly bridge, 12-fret	$26,500	$34,500
1931-1933	12 fret	$26,500	$34,500
1934	Early '34 long scale	$44,500	$58,800
1934-1937	14-fret	$41,000	$53,600
1938-1939	Early '39, 175 neck	$37,000	$48,000
1939	Late '39, 168 neck	$31,200	$41,000
1940-1941		$28,000	$37,000
1942-1944	Scalloped, herringbone	$27,000	$35,000
1944-1946	Non-scalloped, herringbone	$18,500	$24,000
1947-1949	Non-herringbone	$12,500	$16,200
1950-1952		$10,000	$13,000
1953-1955	Kluson	$10,000	$13,000
1956-1958	Early '58 Kluson	$8,850	$11,500
1958-1959	Late '58 Grover	$8,850	$11,500
1960-1962		$6,700	$8,625
1964		$6,400	$8,500
1965		$5,200	$6,800
1966-1969	Early '66, Tortoise 'guard	$5,100	$6,700
1970-1979		$2,400	$3,200
1980-1989		$1,950	$2,600
1990-1999		$1,800	$2,375
2000-2020		$1,800	$2,375

000-28 C

1962-1967. Classical, Brazilian rosewood back and sides, slotted peghead, natural.

MODEL YEAR	FEATURES	EXC. COND. LOW	HIGH
1962-1967		$3,600	$4,700

000-28 E Modern Deluxe

2020-present. Sitka spruce top with Vintage Tone System (VTS), East Indian rosewood back and sides, Fishman electronics, gloss finish.

MODEL YEAR	FEATURES	EXC. COND. LOW	HIGH
2020		$3,225	$4,175

000-28 EC

1996-present. Custom Signature Edition, Eric Clapton specs, sitka spruce top, Indian rosewood back and sides, herringbone trim, natural or sunburst.

MODEL YEAR	FEATURES	EXC. COND. LOW	HIGH
1996-2020	Natural	$2,200	$2,900
1996-2020	Sunburst	$2,200	$2,900

000-28 EC Eric Clapton Crossroads Madagascar

2013. Limited to 150 in collaboration with Guitar Center, soundhole label hand-signed by Clapton and Chris Martin, Crossroads symbol inlaid (mother-of-pearl) into bridge, Clapton signature between 19th-20th frets, Clapton signature case and strap.

MODEL YEAR	FEATURES	EXC. COND. LOW	HIGH
2013		$4,000	$5,200

000-28 ECB Eric Clapton

2002-2003. Limited edition, EC 000-28 with Brazilian rosewood, certificate of authenticity, label hand-signed by Eric Clapton and Chris Martin.

MODEL YEAR	FEATURES	EXC. COND. LOW	HIGH
2002-2003		$6,900	$8,900

000-28 F

1964-1967. Folk, 12-fret, slotted.

MODEL YEAR	FEATURES	EXC. COND. LOW	HIGH
1964		$6,400	$8,500
1965		$5,200	$6,800
1966-1967		$5,100	$6,700

000-28 G

1937, 1939-1940, 1946-1947, 1949-1950, 1955. Special order classical guitar, very limited production.

MODEL YEAR	FEATURES	EXC. COND. LOW	HIGH
1937-1940		$6,600	$8,525
1946		$6,000	$7,900
1947, 1949		$4,700	$6,200
1950, 1955		$4,200	$5,600

000-28 Golden Era

1996 only. Sitka spruce top, rosewood back and sides, scalloped braces, herringbone trim, 12-fret model, natural.

MODEL YEAR	FEATURES	EXC. COND. LOW	HIGH
1996		$3,200	$4,200

000-28 H

2000-2017. Herringbone top trim, production model for '00-'02, Custom Shop model made for Elderly Instruments after that (stamped Custom on neck block).

MODEL YEAR	FEATURES	EXC. COND. LOW	HIGH
2000-2002		$1,900	$2,500
2003-2017	Custom Shop	$2,000	$2,600

000-28 HB Brazilian 1937 Reissue

1997. Pre-war specs including scalloped bracing, Brazilian rosewood.

MODEL YEAR	FEATURES	EXC. COND. LOW	HIGH
1997		$5,700	$7,400

000-28 K

1921. Non-catalog special order model, only 2 known to exist, koa top, back and sides.

MODEL YEAR	FEATURES	EXC. COND. LOW	HIGH
1921	Rare model	$27,000	$35,000

1948 Martin 000-21

Carter Vintage Guitars

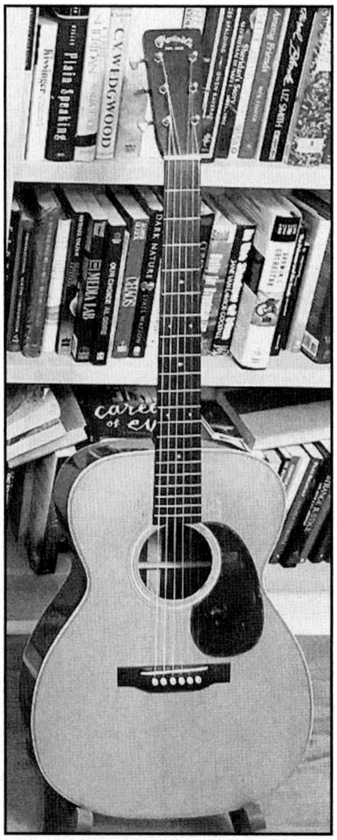

1936 Martin 000-28

M. Mattingly

2009 Martin 000-28 M Eric Clapton
Carter Vintage Guitars

1943 Martin 000-42
Imaged by Heritage Auctions, HA.com

MODEL YEAR	FEATURES	EXC. COND. LOW	HIGH

000-28 K Authentic 1921

2014-2015. Slotted, 12-fret, highly figured koa body.

2014-2015 $3,500 $4,600

000-28 LSH/LSH Custom

2008. Large sound hold (LSH), style 28 appointments, wild grain East Indian sides and back.

2008 $2,075 $2,675

000-28 M Eric Clapton

2009. Limited Edition run of 461, Madagascar rosewood back and sides, Carpathian spruce top, signature between 19th and 20th frets, interior label hand-signed by Clapton, natural or sunburst.

2009 $4,000 $5,300

000-28 Martin/Mandolin Brothers 25th Anniversary

1997-1998. Limited Edition, 25 made, mandolin 12th fret inlay, signed label.

1997-1998 $2,550 $3,300

000-28 Modern Deluxe

2019-present. Sitka spruce top, Vintage Tone System, Indian rosewood back and sides.

2019 $1,925 $2,500

000-28 Norman Blake

2004-2008. Signature Edition, 12-fret neck on 14-fret body, B version is Brazilian rosewood.

2004-2008 Brazilian $5,900 $7,700
2004-2008 Indian $2,900 $3,800

000-28 NY

1962. 2 made.

1962 $6,000 $8,000

000-28 Perry Bechtel

2007. East Indian rosewood back and sides, 29 made.

2007 $3,200 $4,200

000-28 S

1974-1977. Slotted headstock, 12-fret neck.

1974-1977 $2,600 $3,400

000-28 SO Sing Out! 40th Anniversary

1990. Limited Edition, 40 made for 40th Anniversary of Sing Out! Magazine.

1990 $2,250 $2,950

000-28 VS

1999-2019. Vintage Series, spruce top with aging toner, scalloped bracing, rosewood sides and back, slotted diamond markers, herringbone top trim.

1999-2019 $2,300 $3,050

000-30 Authentic 1919

2017-2018. Adirondack spruce top, Vintage Tone System, Madagascar rosewood back and sides.

2017-2018 $3,850 $5,000

000-38

1980. Rosewood back and sides, 3 made.

1980 $2,100 $2,800

000-40

1909. Ivoroid bound top and back, snowflake inlay, 1 made.

1909 $25,000 $32,500

000-40 PR Peter Rowan

2001. Mahogany back and sides, slotted headstock, 12-fret, phases of the moon inlays.

2001 $2,550 $3,300

MODEL YEAR	FEATURES	EXC. COND. LOW	HIGH

000-40 Q2GN Graham Nash

2003. Limited edition of 147 guitars, quilted mahogany top/back/sides, flying-heart logo on headstock, Graham Nash signature on frets 18-20.

2003 $3,100 $4,000

000-41

1975, 1996. Custom shop style 000-41.

1975 $3,400 $4,400
1996 $2,900 $3,800

000-42

1918, 1921-1922, 1925, 1930, 1932, 1934, 1938-1943, 2004-present. Brazilian rosewood back and sides, natural. The 1918-1934 price range is wide due to the variety of specifications.

1918-1925	Limited production	$31,000	$40,000
1930, 1932	2 made, 14 fret	$48,000	$62,000
1934	1 made	$61,000	$79,000
1938	27 made	$55,000	$71,000
1939	Early '39, 175 neck	$55,000	$71,000
1939	Later '39, 168 neck	$51,000	$66,000
1940-1943	Last pearl border	$52,000	$68,000
2004-2020		$3,300	$4,300

000-42 Authentic 1939

2017-2019. Adirondack spruce top with Vintage Tone System (VTS), Madagascar rosewood back and sides, ebony 'board and bridge.

2017-2019 $6,725 $8,700

000-42 EC Eric Clapton

1995. Style 45 pearl-inlaid headplate, ivoroid bindings, Eric Clapton signature, 24.9" scale, flat-top, sunburst top price is $8320 ('95 price), only 461 made; 433 natural, 28 sunburst.

1995 $6,000 $8,000

000-42 ECB Eric Clapton

2000-2001. With Brazilian rosewood, 200 made.

2000-2001 $11,200 $14,500

000-42 EC-Z Eric Clapton Crossroads

2019-present. Ziricote back and sides, 50 made to benefit Crossroads Centre.

2019-2021 $8,800 $11,500

000-42 M Eric Clapton Limited Edition

2008-2009. Limited Edition, 250 made, Madagascar rosewood sides and back, Carpathian spruce top.

2008-2009 $5,700 $7,400

000-42 Marquis

2007-2009. Indian rosewood.

2007-2009 $4,200 $5,500

000-42 SB

2004. 1935 style with sunburst finish, Indian rosewood back and sides.

2004 $3,300 $4,300

000-44 Soloist/Olcott-Bickford Artist

1917-1919. Style 44 guitars were made for guitarist Vahdah Olcott-Bickford, rosewood back and sides, 3 made.

1917-1919 $35,000 $45,400

000-45

1906, 1911-1914, '17-'19, '22-'29, '34-'42, '70-'94. Brazilian rosewood back and sides, changed to Indian rosewood in '70, 12-fret neck and slotted headstock

MODEL YEAR	FEATURES	EXC. COND. LOW	HIGH

until '34 (but 7 were made in '70 and 1 in '75), 14-fret neck and solid headstock after '34, natural.

1906-1919		$45,000	$58,000
1922-1927	Gut	$45,000	$58,000
1926-1929	Steel	$93,000	$121,000
1930-1931	000-45 designated	$93,000	$121,000
1934	Early '34, long scale	$131,000	$170,000
1934	Late '34, short scale	$124,000	$160,000
1935-1937	14 fret, CFM inlay	$124,000	$160,000
1938	Early '38	$124,000	$160,000
1938	Late '38	$113,000	$148,000
1940-1942	1.68 neck	$95,000	$122,000
1970-1977		$5,800	$7,500
1980-1989		$5,000	$6,500
1990-1994		$4,600	$6,000

000-45 7-String
1911, 1929, 1931. 1 made each year.
1911-1931 $30,000 $39,000

000-45 B
1985. Brazilian rosewood, 2 made.
1985 $11,200 $14,600

000-45 EC Eric Clapton Crossroads Brazilian
2013. Limited to 18 in collaboration with Guitar Center, Brazilian rosewood, Crossroads symbol inlaid both ends of bridge, Crossroads case and strap.
2013 $28,000 $36,500

000-45 EC Eric Clapton Crossroads Madagascar
2013. Limited to 55 in collaboration with Guitar Center, Crossroads symbol inlaid both ends of bridge, Crossroads case and strap.
2013 $8,200 $10,700

000-45 H
1937. Brazilian rosewood, Hawaiian, 2 made.
1937 $127,000 $170,000

000-45 JR Jimmie Rodgers
1997-1998. Adirondack spruce top, Brazilian rosewood back and sides, scalloped high X-braces, abalone trim, natural, 52 made.
1997-1998 $12,200 $15,800

000-45 S
1974-1976. 12-fret.
1974-1976 $6,500 $8,600

000-45 S Stephen Stills
2005. Only 91 made, Indian rosewood.
2005 $8,500 $11,000

000C David Gray Custom
2005-2006. Custom Artist Edition, 000-size cutaway, Italian spruce top, mahogany back and sides, interior label signed by David Gray.
2005-2006 $2,025 $2,625

000C DB Dion The Wanderer
2002. Cutaway acoustic/electric, 57 made, scalloped bracing, mahogany sides and back, slotted diamond and square markers, Dion logo on headstock, gloss black finish.
2002 $3,600 $4,700

000C DG Doug Greth Commemorative Edition
2011. Nylon string cutaway, slotted headstock, mahogany back and sides, 48 made.
2011 $1,550 $2,025

000C Nylon
2012-2018. Cutaway, 12-fret, sitka spruce top, sapele back and sides, slotted headstock, Fishman.
2012-2018 $1,225 $1,575

000C Steve Miller Pegasus
2005-2006. Cutaway, mahogany back and sides, Pegasus logo.
2005-2006 $2,350 $3,050

000C-1 E Auditorium
1997-1999. Cutaway, mahogany back and sides, transducer pickup.
1997-1999 $775 $1,025

000C12-16 E Nylon
2020-present. Gloss sitka spruce top, satin mahogany back and sides, Fishman electronics.
2020 $1,400 $1,825

000C-15 E
1999-2002. Cutaway, mahogany back and sides, Fishman.
1999-2002 $875 $1,150

000C-16 (T Auditorium)
1990-1998. Cutaway acoustic, mahogany back and sides, diamonds and squares inlay, name changed to 000-C16T Auditorium in '96.
1990-1998 $1,000 $1,325

000C-16 GTE
1999-2003. Cutaway, mahogany.
1999-2003 $1,075 $1,400

000C-16 GTE Premium
2003-2009. Mahogany back and sides.
2003-2009 $1,200 $1,550

000C-16 RB (Baby Face)
2000-2002. Cutaway acoustic, East Indian rosewood back and sides.
2000-2002 $1,525 $1,975

000C-16 RGTE
2000-2010. Cutaway, rosewood back and sides.
2000-2010 $925 $1,200

000C-16 SGTNE
2003-2006. Classical nylon string, cutaway, mahogany body, 12-fret cedar neck, slotted headstock.
2003-2006 $1,050 $1,350

000C-16 SRNE
2003-2005. Classical cutaway, rosewood body, 12-fret cedar neck, slotted headstock.
2003-2005 $1,050 $1,350

000C-16 T
1996-1997. Sitka spruce top, mahogany back, sides and neck, rosewood 'board.
1996-1997 $750 $1,000

000C-28 Andy Summers
2006. Cutaway, rosewood back and sides, Buddhist Mudra inlays.
2006 $3,050 $3,950

2019 Martin 000-42 Authentic 1939

1997 Martin 000-45 JR Jimmie Rodgers
Carter Vintage Guitars

1890s Martin 1-21

Imaged by Heritage Auctions, HA.com

1917 Martin 1-28

MODEL YEAR	FEATURES	EXC. COND. LOW	HIGH

000C-28 SMH Merle Haggard

2001-2002. Cutaway, 12-fret neck, Blue Yodel No. 13 inlay.

2001-2002 $3,300 $4,300

000CJR-10 E

2019-present. Junior Series, 000JR-10 model with Fishman electronics.

2019-2020 $450 $575

000CME

1999-2002. Laminate back and sides, on-board electronics, satin finish.

1999-2002 $650 $850

000CXE Black

2003-2013. Acoustic-electric, cutaway, laminated body, black finish.

2003-2013 $425 $550

000E Black Walnut Ambertone

2020. Limited Edition, run of 125, sitka spruce top with gloss amber burst finish, satin black walnut back and sides, Fishman electronics.

2020 $1,325 $1,750

000-ECHF Bellezza Bianca

2005-2006. Eric Clapton and Hiroshi Fujiwara White Beauty model, Engleman spruce top, flamed Pacific big-leaf maple back and sides, model name logo on 20th fret, white finish, all-white case, 410 made. This and the Nera are examples of a 'collectible guitar' that is often found in near mint condition. High-end of price range shown is for near mint, nearly unplayed condition.

2005-2006 $2,375 $3,100

000-ECHF Bellezza Nera

2004-2005. Eric Clapton and Hiroshi Fujiwara Black Beauty Model, 476 made, Italian Alpine spruce top, Indian rosewood back and sides, black finish.

2004-2005 $3,200 $4,175

000-JBP Jimmy Buffett Pollywog

2003. Model name and number on label inside back, 168 made.

2003 $2,700 $3,500

000JR-10

2019-present. Junior Series, sitka spruce top, sapele back and sides, satin finish.

2019-2020 $400 $525

000-M

1997-2009. Road Series, mahogany or sapele back and sides.

1997-2009 $550 $700

000-MMV Custom

2005-2018. Guitar Center model, spruce, rosewood, gloss finish.

2005-2018 $1,175 $1,525

000RS1

2014-2018. Road Series, made in Mexico, sapele top, back and sides, Fishman Sonitone electronics. Replaced by 000-10E in '19.

2014-2018 $425 $550

000RS2

2014-2015. Road Series as above with spruce top.

2014-2015 $425 $550

MODEL YEAR	FEATURES	EXC. COND. LOW	HIGH

000RS25 Navojoa 25th Anniversary

2014-2016. Made in Mexico, celebrates 25th Anniversary of Martin's Navojoa facility, headstock Anniversary logo, sitka spruce top, sapele back and sides, East Indian rosewood 'board.

2014-2016 $450 $600

000X Hippie

2007. Limited Edition of 200, celebrates the 40th Anniversary of the 'Summer of Love'.

2007 $1,200 $1,575

000X1

2000-2010. Mahogany grained HPL (high pressure laminate) back and sides, solid spruce top.

2000-2010 $300 $400

000X1 AE

2010-2019. 000X1 with electronics. Replaced by 000-X2E in '20.

2010-2019 $325 $425

000-X2 E

2020-present. X Series, sitka spruce top, figured mahogany laminate back and sides, Fishman electronics.

2020 $450 $575

000XE Black

2002-2005. Black satin finish.

2002-2005 $325 $425

000XM Auditorium

1999-2002. Spruce top, Indian rosewood back and sides, natural finish.

1999-2002 $325 $425

0000-1

1997-2001. 0000-size, mahogany.

1997-2001 $625 $800

0000-18 Custom/Custom 0000-18 (Gruhn 35th Anniversary)

2005-2009. Commissioned for Gruhn Guitars 35th Anniversary, 1st year models have signed Anniversary labels, 16" lower bout, high X-brace, mahogany back and sides.

2005-2009 $2,150 $2,775

0000-21 S Custom (Gruhn 45th Anniversary)

2015. Commissioned for Gruhn Guitars 45th Anniversary, label signed by CF Martin IV and George Gruhn, Adirondack spruce top, Cocobolo or Guatemalan rosewood back and sides.

2015 $4,600 $5,900

0000-28 Series

1997-2011. Several models, jumbo-size 0000 cutaway body, models include; H (herringbone trim, sitka spruce top), Custom (Indian rosewood, sitka), H-AG (Arlo Guthrie 30th anniversary, Indian rosewood back and sides, only 30 made), HA (herringbone trim, Adirondack).

1997-2000	0000-28 H	$1,800	$2,375
1998-2006	0000-28 Custom	$1,800	$2,375
1999	0000-28 H-AG	$2,300	$3,000
2011	0000-28 HA	$2,300	$3,000

0000-38 (M-38)

1997-1998. Called M-38 in '77-'97 and '07-present (see that listing), 0000-size, Indian rosewood back and sides, multi-bound.

1997-1998 $2,100 $2,800

MODEL YEAR	FEATURES	EXC. COND. LOW	HIGH

1/4 - 28

1973, 1979. 14 made.

1973, 1979		$4,500	$6,000

1-17

1906-1917 (1st version), 1931-1934 (2nd version). First version has spruce top, mahogany back and sides, second version has all mahogany with flat natural finish.

1906-1934		$1,925	$2,500

1-17 P

1928-1931, 1939. Mahogany back and sides, plectrum neck, 272 made.

1928-1939		$1,175	$1,525

1-18

1899-1903, 1906-1907, 1909-1921, 1923-1927. Brazilian rosewood or mahogany back and sides.

1899-1917	Brazilian	$2,800	$3,625
1918-1921	Mahogany	$2,000	$2,600
1923-1927	Steel, 12-fret	$2,000	$2,600

1-18 H

1918. Hawaiian, only 3 made.

1918		$2,000	$2,600

1-18 K

1917-1919. Koa.

1917-1919		$3,400	$4,400

1-18 P

1929. 5-string plectrum, 1 made.

1929		$1,900	$2,450

1-18 T

1927. Tenor 5-string, only 3 made.

1927		$1,900	$2,450

1-20

1860s. Parlor guitar, rosewood back and sides.

1867		$3,850	$5,000

1-21

1860s-1907, 1911, 1913-1921, 1925-1926. Initially offered in size 1 in the 1860s, ornate soundhole rings. A beautiful crack-free instrument is worth twice as much as a worn model with repaired cracks.

1860s-1926		$3,850	$5,000

1-21 P

1930. Plectrum.

1930		$2,050	$2,650

1-22

1850s. Antique market value.

1850s		$5,600	$7,250

1-26

1855, 1874, 1890, 1903. Rosewood back and sides, ivory-bound top, rope-style purfling, antique market value.

1855-1903		$5,575	$7,250

1-27

1880s-1907, 1911, 1913-1921, 1925-1926. Antique market value.

1880-1926		$5,575	$7,250

1-28

1880s-1904, 1906-1907, 1909, 1911-1920, 1923. Style 28 appointments including Brazilian rosewood back and sides, antique market value.

1880s-1923		$5,575	$7,250

MODEL YEAR	FEATURES	EXC. COND. LOW	HIGH

1-28 P

1928-1930. Plectrum.

1928-1930		$2,600	$3,375

1-30

1860s-1904, 1906-1907, 1911-1914, 1916-1917, 1919. Size 1 Style 30 with pearl soundhole trim, cedar neck, antique market value.

1860s-1919		$6,050	$7,850

1-42

1858-1919. Rosewood back and sides, ivory-bound top and 'board.

1858-1919		$7,500	$9,700

1-45

1904-1905, 1911-1913, 1919. Only 6 made, slotted headstock and Style 45 appointments.

1904-1919		$15,800	$20,500

2-15

1939-1964. All mahogany body, dot markers.

1939-1964		$1,825	$2,400

2-17

1910, 1922-1934, 1936-1938. 1910 version has spruce top, mahogany back and sides. '22 on, all mahogany body, no body binding after '30.

1867	Gut	$2,550	$3,300
1910	Gut, 6 made	$1,900	$2,500
1922-1938	Steel	$2,800	$3,600

2-17 H

1927-1929, 1931. Hawaiian, all mahogany, 12 frets clear of body.

1927-1931		$2,800	$3,600

2-17 T

1927-1928. Tenor, 45 made.

1927-1928		$1,300	$1,700

2-18

1857-1900, 1902-1903, 1907, 1925, 1929, 1934, 1938. Rosewood back and sides, changed to mahogany from 1917, dark outer binding, black back stripe, no dot inlay until 1902.

1870s-80s		$2,900	$3,800

2-18 T

1928-1930. Tenor.

1928-1930		$1,300	$1,700

2-20

1855-1897. Rare style only offered in size 2.

1855-1897		$3,300	$4,300

2-21

1850s-1900, 1903-1904, 1909, 1925, 1928-1929. Rosewood back and sides, herringbone soundhole ring.

1885-1929		$2,700	$3,500

2-21 T

1928. Tenor.

1928		$1,350	$1,750

2-24

1857-1898. Antique market value.

1857-1898		$4,475	$5,800

2-27

1857-1880s, 1898-1900, 1907. Brazilian rosewood back and sides, pearl ring, zigzag back stripe, ivory bound ebony 'board and peghead.

1857-1907		$5,500	$7,150

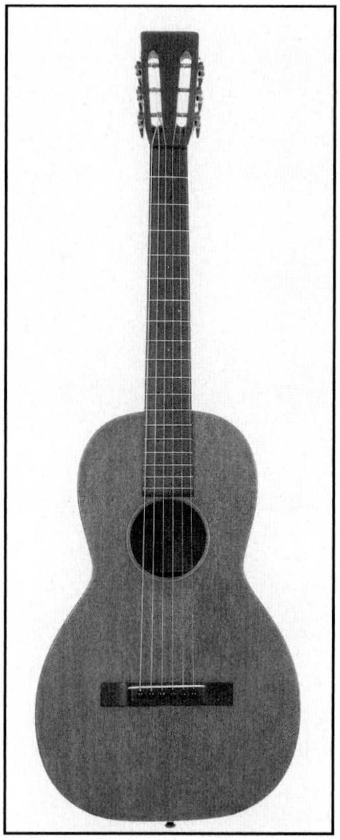

1930 Martin 2-17

Imaged by Heritage Auctions, HA.com

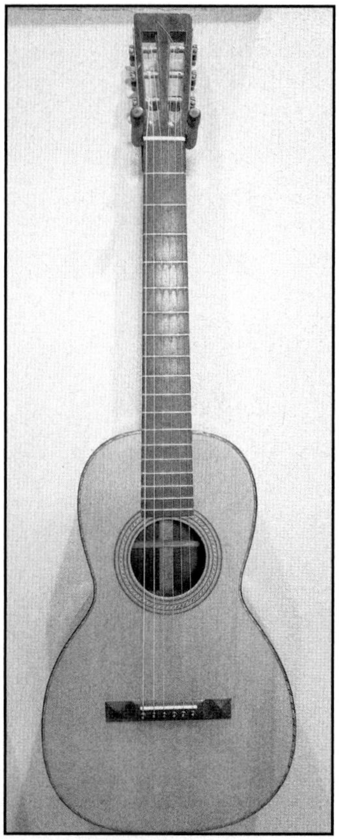

1890s Martin 2-24

Cody Lindsey

GUITARS

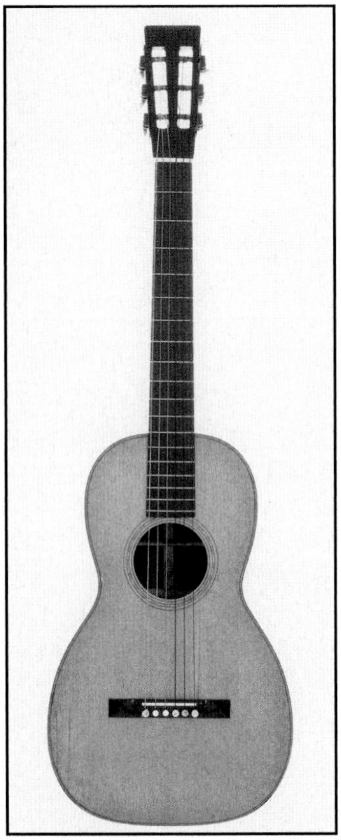

1880s Martin 2 1/2-21

Imaged by Heritage Auctions, HA.com

1953 Martin 5-15T

Bernunzio Uptown Music

MODEL YEAR	FEATURES	EXC. COND. LOW	HIGH

2-28

Brazilian rosewood back and sides, slot head.

1880		$5,600	$7,300

2-28 T

1928-1929. Tenor neck, Brazilian rosewood back and sides, herringbone top purfling.

1928-1929		$3,400	$4,400

2-30

1874, 1902-1904, 1909-1910, 1921. Similar to 2-27, only 7 made.

1874-1921		$5,500	$7,150

2-34

1850s-1898. Similar to 2-30.

1850s-1898		$5,900	$7,600

2-40

1850s-1898, 1909.

1850s-1898		$6,200	$8,000

2-42

1858-1900.

1874		$7,600	$9,800

2-44

1930. Style 44, Olcott-Bickford Soloist custom order, only 4 made.

1930		$12,100	$15,700

2-45 T

1927-1928. Tenor style 45, 2 made.

1927-1928		$7,100	$9,200

2 1/2-17

1856-1897, 1909, 1911-1914. The first Style 17s were small size 2 1/2 and 3, these early models use Brazilian rosewood.

1856-1897	Brazilian	$2,625	$3,400
1909-1914	Mahogany	$2,525	$3,300

2 1/2-18

1865-1898, 1901, 1909-1914, 1916-1923. Parlor-size body with Style 18 appointments.

1865-1917	Brazilian	$2,525	$3,300
1918-1923	Mahogany	$2,100	$2,700

2 1/2-21

1880s, 1909, 1911-1913, 1917-1921. Brazilian rosewood back and sides.

1880s-1921		$2,900	$3,800

2 1/2-42

1880s, 1911. Style 42 size 2 1/2 with Brazilian rosewood. Only 1 made 1911.

1880s-1911		$7,000	$9,400

3-17

1856-1897, 1908 (1 made). The first Style 17s were small size 2 1/2 and 3. The early models use Brazilian rosewood, spruce top, bound back, unbound ebony 'board.

1856-1870s	Brazilian	$2,400	$3,100
1880s-1908		$1,800	$2,300

3-21

1885. Brazilian rosewood.

1885		$2,700	$3,500

3-24

1860. Brazilian rosewood.

1860		$4,400	$5,700

3-34

1860. Brazilian rosewood.

1860		$5,800	$7,500

5-15

2003-2007. Sapele or mahogany body, shorter scale.

2003-2007		$975	$1,250

5-15 T

1949-1963. Tenor neck, all mahogany, non-gloss finish.

1927-1930		$1,200	$1,550
1949-1963		$900	$1,175

5-16

1962-1963. Mahogany back and sides, unbound rosewood 'board.

1962-1963		$1,600	$2,100

5-17

1912-1914, 1916, 1927-1928, 1930-1931, 1933-1943. Special order 1912-'36, standard production '37-'43.

1912-1916		$1,700	$2,200
1927-1928		$2,500	$3,250
1930-1939		$2,500	$3,250
1940-1943		$2,300	$3,000

5-17 T

1949-1958. Tenor neck, all mahogany.

1949-1958		$1,175	$1,525

5-18

1898-1899, 1912-1914, 1917, 1919-1921, 1923-1924, 1926-1932, 1934-1937, 1940-1941, 1943-1962, 1965, 1968-1977, 1979-1981, 1983-1989. Rosewood back and sides (changed to mahogany from 1917 on), 12 frets, slotted headstock.

1898-1917		$2,600	$3,400
1919-1921	Gut	$1,900	$2,450
1923-1937	Steel	$3,500	$4,500
1940-1946		$3,300	$4,300
1948-1949		$3,000	$3,900
1950-1959		$2,800	$3,700
1960-1962		$2,350	$3,050
1965		$2,100	$2,725
1966-1969		$1,800	$2,325
1970-1979		$1,475	$1,925
1980-1989		$1,325	$1,725

5-18 Marty Robbins

2009-2011. Custom Edition, 12-fret, Adirondack top, mahogany back and sides.

2009-2011		$1,700	$2,200

5-18 T

1940, 1954, 1960-1961. Tenor, only 1 made each year.

1940		$1,275	$1,650
1954		$1,050	$1,375
1960-1961		$900	$1,175

5-21

1890s, 1902, 1912-1914, 1916-1920, 1927, 1977. Rosewood back and sides.

1890s-1977		$2,600	$3,400

5-21 T

1927-1928. Tenor guitar with 21-styling.

1927-1928		$1,400	$1,800

MODEL YEAR	FEATURES	EXC. COND. LOW	HIGH

5-28

1901-1902, 1904, 1918, 1920-1921, 1923, 1935, 1939, 1969-1970, 1977, 1980-1981, 1988, 2001-2002. Special edition, 1/2-size parlor guitar, rosewood back and sides.

1901-1923	Gut	$2,700	$3,500
1935-1939	Steel	$4,700	$6,100
1969-1970	Brazilian	$3,800	$4,900
1977	Indian	$2,225	$2,900
1980-1981		$1,925	$2,500
2001-2002		$1,925	$2,500

7-28

1980-1995, 1997-2002. 7/8-body-size of a D-model, Style 28 appointments.

1980-1989		$1,850	$2,400
1990-2002		$1,750	$2,300

7-37 K

1980-1987. 7/8-size baby dreadnought acoustic, koa back and sides, spruce top, oval soundhole.

1980-1987		$1,800	$2,400

Alternative II Resophonic

2004-2007. Textured aluminum top, matching headstock overlay, high pressure laminate sides and back, spun aluminum cone resonator, Fishman pickup.

2004-2007		$550	$725

Alternative X

2001-2013. OO-Grand Concert body shape, textured aluminum top, matching headstock overlay, spun aluminum cone resonator, Fishman pickup.

2001-2013		$550	$725

Alternative X Midi

2003-2004. Roland GK Midi pickup with 13-pin output, additional Fishman Prefix Pro pickup and preamp system, requires Roland GA-20 interface.

2003-2004		$575	$775

Alternative XT

2002-2005. Alternative with DiMarzio humbucker, volume & tone controls, coil tap, Bigsby.

2003-2005		$550	$725

America's Guitar 175th Anniversary

2008. D-style, 14-fret, Adirondack spruce top, Madagascar rosewood sides and back, 175 made, 'America's Guitar' headstock inlay, '175th Anniversary 1833-2008'.

2008		$4,100	$5,300

ASD-41 Australian Series

2005. Tasmanian Blackwood sides and back, Sitka spruce top, Australian theme appointments and label.

2005		$3,100	$4,000

Backpacker

1992-present. Small-bodied travel guitar, nylon called Classical Backpacker.

1992-2020	Steel strings	$105	$140
1994-2020	Nylon strings	$105	$140

Backpacker 25th Anniversary

2017 only. Sapele.

2017		$150	$195

Bigsby/Martin D-28 Bigsby

2018-2019. Martin parterned with Gretsch to build, Merle Travis inspired, sitka spruce top, East Indian rosewood back and sides, Bigsby headstock, natural finish.

2018-2019		$2,500	$3,300

MODEL YEAR	FEATURES	EXC. COND. LOW	HIGH

C-1

1931-1942. Acoustic archtop, mahogany back and sides, spruce top, round hole until '33 (449 made), f-holes appear in '32 (786 made), bound body, sunburst.

1931-1933	Round hole	$2,150	$2,825
1932-1942	F-hole	$2,075	$2,725

C-1 P

1931-1933, 1939. Archtop, plectrum.

1931-1933	Round hole	$1,525	$1,975
1939	F-hole	$1,525	$1,975

C-1 R Humphrey

1997-2000. Solid cedar top, laminated rosewood back and sides, satin finish.

1997-2000		$775	$1,025

C-1 T

1931-1934, 1936-1938. Archtop, tenor, round hole (71 made) or f-hole (83 made).

1931-1933	Round hole	$1,525	$1,975
1933-1938	F-hole	$1,525	$1,975

C-1-12

1932. Only 1 made, 12-string version.

1932		$2,075	$2,725

C-2

1931-1942. Acoustic archtop, Brazilian rosewood back and sides, carved spruce top, round hole until '33 (269 made), f-holes appear in '32 (439 made), zig-zag back stripe, multi-bound body, slotted-diamond inlay, sunburst.

1931-1933	Round hole	$3,100	$4,000
1932-1942	F-hole	$2,425	$3,150
1939	Maple	$2,425	$3,150

C-2 P

1931. Archtop, plectrum, round hole, 2 made.

1931		$2,250	$2,950

C-2 T

1931-1936. Archtop, tenor, round or f-hole.

1931-1934	Round hole	$2,200	$2,850
1934-1936	F-hole	$1,600	$2,100

C-2-12

1932. Only 1 made, 12-string version.

1932		$2,425	$3,150

C-3

1931-1934. Archtop, Brazilian rosewood back and sides, round soundhole until early '33 (53 made), f-holes after (58 made).

1931-1933	Round hole	$4,625	$6,000
1933-1934	F-hole	$3,600	$4,700

C-3 T

1933. Archtop, tenor, 1 made.

1933		$3,300	$4,275

Car Talk Special Edition

2008-2010. D-size, East Indian rosewood back and sides, car parts and tools inlay, Car Talk credits on 'guard.

2008-2010		$2,975	$3,850

CEO Series

1997-present. Chief Executive Officer (C.F. Martin IV), Special Edition (CEO-1 through CEO-6) and Custom Signature Edition (CEO-7 through CEO-9), various woods and specs. CEO-1/1R ('97-'98), 2 ('98), 3 ('99-'00), 4 ('01-'04), 4R ('02-'10), 5 ('01-'04), 6 ('11-'13),

1929 Martin 5-17T

Craig Brody

1950 Martin 5-18

David Stone

GUITARS

Martin CEO-7

Martin CS-Bluegrass-16

MODEL YEAR	FEATURES	EXC. COND. LOW	HIGH

7 ('15-present), 8 ('15-'17), 8.2/E ('17-'18), 9 ('19-present).

1997-2016	CEO-1 to CEO-6	$1,700	$2,200
2014-2021	CEO-7	$1,700	$2,200
2015-2017	CEO-8	$3,700	$4,800
2017-2018	CEO-82	$2,025	$2,625
2017-2018	CEO-82E	$2,150	$2,800

CF-1 American Archtop

2004-2009. 17", solid maple sides, laminated maple back, ebony 'board, dot markers, 1 pickup, sunburst, natural or black.

2004-2009 — $2,150 — $2,800

CF-2 American Archtop

2004-2009. CF-1 with 2 humbuckers, sunburst, natural or black.

2004-2009 — $2,225 — $2,900

Claire's Guitar

2005-2006. Made to celebrate the birth of Claire Frances Martin, limited to 100, small parlor size, sitka spruce top, Brazilian rosewood back and sides, fancy appointments, comes with pink-lined hard case.

2005-2006 — $3,600 — $4,700

Concept III

2003. U.S.-made, solid spruce top, solid mahogany back and sides, cutaway, on-board electronics, sparkle-mist finish.

2003 — $1,375 — $1,775

Cowboy 2015 Limited Edition/LE Cowboy 2015

2015. Limited to number sold in '15, 000, 12-fret, sitka spruce top, solid Goncalo Alves back and sides, cowboy on horse artwork by William Matthews.

2015 — $2,400 — $3,100

Cowboy 2016 Limited Edition/LE Cowboy 2016

2016. Limited to number sold in '16, auditorium, 12-fret, sitka spruce top, mahogany back and sides, cowboy on bucking bronco artwork by William Matthews.

2016 — $2,400 — $3,100

Cowboy Series

2000-2009. Models include Cowboy X (2000, 250 made), Cowboy II ('01, 500 made), Cowboy III ('03, 750 made), and Cowboy IV ('05-'06, 250 made), Cowboy V ('06-'09, 500 made).

2001-2009 Various models — $600 — $1,100

CS-21-11

2011. Limited Edition, 171 made, Madagascar rosewood.

2011 — $3,100 — $4,000

CS-Bluegrass-16

2016-2020. Limited to 100, Adirondack spruce top, Guatemalan rosewood back and sides, vintage gloss finish.

2016-2020 — $4,000 — $5,200

CS-CF Martin Outlaw-17

2017-2020. Limited to 100 made, Adirondack spruce top, mahogany back and sides, natural gloss finish.

2017-2020 — $3,675 — $4,825

CSN (Gerry Tolman Tribute)

2007-2009. CSN logo on headstock, D-style, high-end appointments, East Indian rosewood back and sides. Tolman was CSN's longtime manager and was killed in car wreck in '06.

2007-2009 — $2,100 — $2,700

MODEL YEAR	FEATURES	EXC. COND. LOW	HIGH

C-TSH (Humphrey/Martin)

1997-2002. Designed by classical guitar luthier Thomas Humphrey, based on his Millenium model, arched Englemann spruce top, rosewood back and sides.

1997-2002 — $1,900 — $2,450

Custom 15

1991-1994. Renamed HD-28V Custom 15 in ca. 2001.

1991-1994 — $2,100 — $2,700

Custom D Classic Mahogany

2006-2014. D body, spruce top, mahogany back and sides.

2006-2014 — $650 — $850

Custom D Classic Rosewood

2006-2011. D body, spruce top, rosewood back and sides.

2006-2011 — $650 — $850

Custom Shop 18 Style 0000

2019-2020. Adirondack, Sinker mahogany back and sides, Sinker is old growth from 1900-1920.

2019-2020	12-fret	$2,425	$3,225
2019-2020	14-fret	$2,200	$2,900

Custom Shop 18 Style Dreadnought

2019-2020. Adirondack, Sinker mahogany back and sides.

2019-2020 — $2,200 — $2,875

Custom Shop 18 Style OM

2020. Adirondack, Sinker mahogany back and sides, 14-fret.

2020		$2,300	$2,975
2020	Master Sinker	$2,550	$3,300

Custom Shop 28 Style Dreadnought

2020. Adirondack, Indian rosewood back and sides.

2020 — $2,700 — $3,500

Custom Shop 28 Style OM

2020. Adirondack, Indian rosewood back and sides, sunburst or natural.

2020	Natural	$2,300	$3,050
2020	Sunburst	$2,400	$3,200

D-1 (D-18)

1931. Name first used for the prototype of the D-18, made in 1931.

1931 — $65,000 — $85,000

D-1

1992-2005, 2009. Current model with mahogany body, A-frame bracing, available as an acoustic/electric.

1992-2005		$650	$850
2009	Reintroduced	$650	$850

D12-1

1996-2001. Mahogany, satin finish, 12-string.

1996-2001 — $650 — $825

D-1 Authentic 1931

2016-2019. Adirondack spruce top, dark mahogany back and sides, Vintage Gloss finish.

2016-2019 — $3,500 — $4,600

D-1 E

1994-1998, 2009. Acoustic/electric version, current model solid sitka with sapele.

1994-1998		$725	$925
2009		$725	$925

MODEL YEAR	FEATURES	EXC. COND. LOW	HIGH

D-1 GT

2011-2014. Double bound body, gloss finish top, satin back and sides.

2011-2014		$650	$825

D-1 R

1994-2003, 2012. D-1 with laminated rosewood back and sides.

1994-2003		$650	$825
2012	Reintroduced	$650	$825

D-1 RE

1994-1995, 1998. D-1R with various electronics.

1994-1998		$700	$900

D-2

1931-1932, 1934. Earliest version of the D-28, Brazilian rosewood.

1931-1934		$198,000	$257,000

D-2 R

1996-2002. Style 28 appointments, laminated rosewood back and sides, natural satin finish.

1996-2002		$650	$825

D-3 R

1996-2002. Style 35 appointments, laminated rosewood back and sides, natural satin finish.

1996-2002		$700	$900

D-3-18

1991. Sitka spruce top, 3-piece mahogany back, 80-piece limited edition.

1991		$1,400	$1,800

D-10 E

2019-present. Road Series, updated version of DSR1/DSR2, sitka spruce or sapele top, sapele back and sides, Fishman electronics, satin finish.

2019-2020		$425	$550

D-11 E

2019. Road Series, sitka spruce top, solid sapele back and sides, Fishman.

2019		$550	$725

D-12 E

2019-present. Sitka spruce top, sapele back and sides, Fishman.

2019-2020		$700	$900

D-12 E Koa

2020. Sitka spruce top, koa veneer back and sides, gloss finish.

2020		$925	$1,200

D12 David Crosby

2009-2011. D-size 12-string, quilted mahogany body, Carpathian spruce top.

2009-2011		$2,800	$3,700

D-13 E

2019-present. Updated version of DRSG, sitka spruce top, siris back and sides, Fishman.

2019-2020		$675	$875

D-15/D-15 M

1997-present. Body is all mahogany up to 2002, mahogany or sapele (which is like mahogany) up to '10. Becomes the all-mahogany D-15M in '11.

1997-2010		$750	$975
2011-2020	M	$750	$975

D-15 M Burst

2015-2018. Shaded mahogany top, back and sides, satin finish.

2015-2018		$800	$1,050

D-15 M Elderly Instruments 40th Anniversary

2012. Only 10 made, solid mahogany body, special appointments, label signed by Elderly president Stan Werbin and Chris Martin.

2012		$875	$1,150

D-15 M StreetMaster

2017-present. Distressed mahogany satin finish.

2017-2020		$775	$1,025

D-15 S

2001-2009. Slotted headstock D-15, body is solid sapele or mahogany.

2001-2009		$750	$975

D-16 A

1987-1990. North American ash back and sides, scalloped bracing.

1987-1990		$1,100	$1,425

D-16 Adirondack

2009-2013. Adirondack spruce top, mahogany back and sides.

2009-2013		$1,325	$1,750

D-16 E Burst

2019-present. Mahogany burst ovangkol gloss top, satin ovangkol back and sides, Fishman electronics.

2019-2020		$1,325	$1,750

D-16 E Rock The Vote

2019-present. Special Edition, designed by David Crosby, custom artwork by Robert F. Goetzl, sitka spruce gloss top, satin sycamore back and sides, Fishman electronics.

2019-2020		$1,525	$2,025

D-16 E Rosewood

2019-present. Gloss sitka spruce top, satin East Indian rosewood back and sides, Fishman electronics.

2019-2020		$1,250	$1,625

D-16 E/D-16 E Mahogany

2017-present. Gloss sitka spruce top, satin sycamore back and sides, Fishman electronics. Mahogany in '20.

2017-2020		$1,150	$1,500
2020-2021	Mahogany	$1,125	$1,475

D-16 GT

1999-2019. D-16 with gloss top.

1999-2019		$800	$1,050

D-16 GTE

1999-2015. D-16 GT with Fishman electronics.

1999-2015		$900	$1,175

D-16 H (1991, 1992, 1993)

1990-1994. D-16 with herringbone soundhole ring, replaced by D-16 T in '94.

1990-1994		$1,050	$1,350

D-16 K

1986. Koa D-16.

1986		$1,200	$1,550

D-16 Lyptus

2003-2005. Lyptus back and sides.

2003-2005		$925	$1,200

1993 Martin D-1

Imaged by Heritage Auctions, HA.com

1988 Martin D-16

Bernunzio Uptown Music

GUITARS

1947 Martin D-18
Folkway Music

1952 Martin D-18
Ian Gilmour

MODEL YEAR	FEATURES	EXC. COND. LOW	HIGH

D-16 M Mahogany

1986-1990. Mahogany back and sides.

1986-1990		$925	$1,200

D-16 O Oak

1999. Red oak or white oak, 4 made.

1999		$925	$1,200

D-16 R 50th Anniversary

2010. Adirondack spruce top, rosewood back and sides, natural.

2010		$1,500	$1,950

D-16 R/D-16 TR/D-16 TRG

1995-2009. Spruce top, Indian rosewood back and sides, satin finish (R) or gloss (TRG).

1995-2009		$775	$1,025

D-16 RGT

1999-2019. D-16 T specs with rosewood back and sides, gloss finish.

1999-2019		$775	$1,025

D-16 RGT Ryman Auditorium

2007. Custom designed by George Gruhn, oak 'guard, headplate and fret markers made from original Ryman Auditorium pews, laser-etched image of Ryman on headplate, spruce top, Indian rosewood back and sides, special Ryman label.

2007		$2,150	$2,800

D-16 T/D-16 TG

1994-1998. Mahogany back and sides, satin finish (T) or gloss (TG).

1994-1998		$775	$1,025

D-16 W Walnut

1987, 1990. Walnut back and sides.

1987, 1990		$775	$1,025

D-17

2001-2005. All solid mahogany back, sides and top, natural brown mahogany finish.

2001-2005		$775	$1,025

D-17 E

2002-2003. With on-board electronics.

2002-2003		$850	$1,100

D-17 M

2013-2016. Shaded spruce top, solid mahogany back and sides.

2013-2016		$775	$1,025

D-18

1931-present. Standard Series, mahogany back and sides, spruce top, black back stripe, 12-fret neck, changed to 14 frets in '34.

1931-1934	12-fret	$51,800	$67,300
1934	14-fret, dark top	$46,000	$60,000
1934-1937	14-fret	$46,000	$60,000
1938	Early '38, Advanced X	$40,800	$53,000
1938	Late '38, Rear X	$31,400	$40,800
1939	Early '39, 175 neck	$27,500	$35,700
1939	Late '39, 168 neck	$26,000	$33,700
1940-1941		$20,800	$27,000
1942-1944	Scalloped	$18,900	$24,500
1944-1946	Non-scalloped	$13,700	$17,800
1947-1949		$7,075	$9,200
1950-1959		$5,100	$6,650
1960-1964		$3,725	$4,925
1965		$3,400	$4,425
1966-1969		$2,900	$3,750
1970-1979		$2,100	$2,725
1980-1989		$1,700	$2,225
1983	50th Ann 1833-1983	$1,700	$2,225
1990-1999		$1,700	$2,225
2000-2020		$1,475	$1,925

D12-18

1973-1995. Mahogany back and sides, 12 strings, 14 frets clear of body, solid headstock.

1973-1979		$1,450	$1,875
1980-1989		$1,225	$1,600
1990-1995		$1,225	$1,600

CS-D18-12

2012-2014. Custom Shop, based on 1929 Ditson 111 (12-string), 75 made, 12-fret mahogany neck, Adirondack spruce top, Madagascar rosewood binding.

2012-2014		$3,225	$4,225

D-18 1955 CFM IV

2010. Celebrates C. F. Martin IV birthday, 55 made.

2010		$2,800	$3,650

D-18 75th Anniversary Edition

2009. '75th Anniversary Edition 1934-2009' noted on label and headstock stencil.

2009		$2,475	$3,200

D-18 Andy Griffith

2003. Bear claw spruce top, Andy's script signature on 18th fret.

2003		$2,100	$2,700

D-18 Authentic 1937

2006-2012. Authentic pre-war specs, Adirondack spruce, forward X-brace and scalloped Adirondack bracing, 14-fret neck.

2006-2012		$3,750	$4,925

D-18 Authentic 1939

2013-present. Adirondack spruce top, mahogany back, sides and neck, ebony 'board, vintage gloss finish.

2013-2020		$3,750	$4,925
2019-2020	VTS Aged	$3,750	$4,925

D-18 Authentic 1939 VTS

2020. New design, Torrefied Adirondack.

2020		$3,000	$4,000

D-18 Custom Adirondack

2016. Adirondack spruce top, mahogany back and sides.

2016		$2,400	$3,100

D-18 CW Clarence White Commemorative Edition

2001. Rare Appalachian spruce top, 2-piece quilted mahogany back and sides, Clarence White's signature between 19th - 20th frets, aged gloss lacquer finish.

2001		$2,400	$3,100

D-18 D

1975. Frap pickup.

1975		$1,725	$2,250

D-18 DC David Crosby

2002. David Crosby signature at 20th fret, Englemann spruce top, quilted mahogany back and sides, 250 made.

2002		$2,300	$3,000

MODEL YEAR	FEATURES	EXC. COND. LOW	HIGH

D-18 Del McCourey 50th Anniversary

2008. Adirondack spruce top, mahogany sides and back, interior label signed by Del McCourey, 50 made.

2008		$2,600	$3,400

D-18 E

1958-1959. D-18 factory built with DeArmond pickups which required ladder bracing (reducing acoustic volume and quality).

1958-1959		$5,500	$7,200

D-18 E 2020

2020. Limited Edition, 2,020 offered, sitka spruce top, mahogany back and sides, electronics, gloss finish.

2020		$2,200	$2,800

D-18 E Modern Deluxe

2020-present. Torrified sitka spruce top, Fishman electronics.

2020		$2,300	$3,000

D-18 E Retro

2012-2019. Sitka spruce top, mahogany back and sides.

2012-2019		$1,525	$2,000

D-18 GE Golden Era

1995, 2000-2016. 1995 version is a copy of a '37 D-18, 272 made. The current model is based on '34 model. Natural or sunburst.

1995		$2,250	$2,900
2000-2016		$2,250	$2,900

D-18 Golden Era Special Edition 1934

1999-2012. Specs from '34 D-18, red Adirondack spruce top, mahogany back and sides, aged finish.

1999-2012		$2,250	$2,900

D-18 H

1934-1935. Hawaiian.

1934-1935		$47,000	$61,200

D-18 H Huda

1966. Huda wood, Hawaiian, 2 made.

1966		$2,900	$3,750

D-18 LE

1986-1987. Limited Edition, quilted or flamed mahogany back and sides, scalloped braces, gold tuners with ebony buttons.

1986-1987		$2,250	$2,900

D-18 MB

1990. Limited Edition Guitar of the Month, flame maple binding, Engelmann spruce top signed by shop foremen, X-brace, total of 99 sold.

1990		$1,800	$2,350

D-18 Modern Deluxe

2019-present. Sitka spruce top with Vintage Tone System (VTS), mahogany back and sides, gloss finish.

2019		$1,800	$2,350

D-18 P

2010-2011. Fishman electronics.

2010-2011		$1,525	$1,975

D-18 S

1967-1994. Mahogany back and sides, 12-fret neck, slotted headstock, majority of production before '77, infrequent after that.

1967-1969		$3,300	$4,300
1970-1979		$2,350	$3,050
1980-1989		$1,975	$2,575
1990-1994		$1,975	$2,575

MODEL YEAR	FEATURES	EXC. COND. LOW	HIGH

D-18 Special

1989. Guitar of the Month, 28 made, first Martin to use rosewood for binding, heel cap and endpiece since 1932, scalloped top, mahogany back and sides, slotted-diamond markers.

1989		$1,875	$2,475

D-18 SS

2009-2012. 24.9" short scale.

2009		$1,525	$2,000

D-18 V/D-18 Vintage

1985 (V), 1992 (Vintage). Low-profile neck, scalloped braces, bound, total of 218 sold, Guitar of the Month in '85, Vintage Series in '92.

1985	V	$1,875	$2,475
1992	Vintage	$1,875	$2,475

D-18 VE

2004-2007. D-18 V with Fishman Ellipse.

2004-2007		$1,925	$2,525

D-18 VM/D-18 V/D-18 VO

1995-2011. Vintage Series, 14-fret, mahogany (M) back and sides, tortoise binding, V-neck. M dropped from name in '99. Natural finish. 48 sunburst (D-18 VO) made in '95.

1995	D-18VO	$1,850	$2,400
1995-1998	D-18VM	$1,850	$2,400
1999-2011	D-18V	$1,850	$2,400

D-18 VMS/D-18 VS

1996-2011. Vintage Series, 12-fret version of D-18 VM/V, M dropped from name in '99.

1996-1999	D-18VMS	$1,850	$2,400
2000-2011	D-18VS	$1,850	$2,400

D-19

1977-1988. Deluxe mahogany dreadnought, optional mahogany top, multi-bound but unbound rosewood 'board.

1977-1979		$2,100	$2,725
1980-1988		$1,700	$2,225

D12-20

1964-1991. Mahogany back and sides, 12 strings, 12 frets clear of body, slotted headstock.

1964-1969		$1,650	$2,150
1970-1979		$1,400	$1,825
1980-1991		$1,200	$1,550

D-21

1955-1969. Brazilian rosewood back and sides, rosewood 'board, chrome tuners.

1955-1959		$7,700	$10,000
1960-1964		$7,100	$9,200
1965		$6,250	$8,100
1966-1969		$5,800	$7,600

D-21 JC Jim Croce

1999-2000. Jim Croce signature and 1973 dime inlaid on neck, Indian rosewood back and sides, 73 made.

1999-2000		$3,500	$4,500

D-21 JCB Jim Croce

1999-2001. Same as above but with Brazilian rosewood back and sides.

1999-2001		$7,000	$9,000

D-21 LE

1985. Limited Edition, 75 made.

1985		$1,775	$2,300

2002 Martin D-18 DC David Crosby

Imaged by Heritage Auctions, HA.com

1968 Martin D-12-20

W. H. Stephens

1937 Martin D-28
Ranger Doug

1952 Martin D-28
Bernunzio Uptown Music

D-21 Special/D-21 S

2008-2020. Indian rosewood back and sides, herringbone soundhole.

MODEL YEAR	FEATURES	EXC. COND. LOW	HIGH
2008-2020		$1,725	$2,250

D-25 K

1980-1989. Dreadnought-size, koa back and sides, spruce top.

MODEL YEAR	FEATURES	EXC. COND. LOW	HIGH
1980-1989		$1,900	$2,500

D-25 K2

1980-1989. Same as D-25K, but with koa top and black 'guard.

MODEL YEAR	FEATURES	EXC. COND. LOW	HIGH
1980-1989		$1,900	$2,500

D-28

1931-present. Brazilian rosewood back and sides (changed to Indian rosewood in '70), '36 was the last year for the 12-fret model, '44 was the last year for scalloped bracing, '47 was the last year herringbone trim was offered, natural. Ultra high-end D-28 Martin guitar (pre-'47) valuations are very sensitive to structural and cosmetic condition. Finish wear and body cracks for ultra high-end Martin flat-tops should be evaluated on a case-by-case basis. Small variances within the 'excellent condition' category can lead to notable valuation differences.

MODEL YEAR	FEATURES	EXC. COND. LOW	HIGH
1931-1935	12-fret	$166,000	$217,000
1934-1937	14-fret	$101,000	$132,000
1938	Early '38, Advanced X	$100,000	$131,000
1938	Late '38, Rear X	$96,000	$126,000
1939	Early '39, 1.75 neck	$94,000	$124,000
1939	Late '39, 1.68 neck	$86,000	$112,000
1940-1941		$65,000	$85,000
1942	Scalloped	$60,000	$80,000
1943	Scalloped	$56,000	$73,000
1944	Scalloped, herringbone	$48,000	$64,000
1944-1945	Herringbone, non-scalloped	$27,000	$35,000
1946-1947	Early '47, herringbone, non-scalloped	$24,000	$32,000
1947-1949	Late '47, non-herringbone	$11,500	$15,000
1950-1952		$9,500	$12,350
1953	Kluson	$9,500	$12,350
1954-1958	Kluson	$9,050	$11,775
1959	Grover	$9,050	$11,775
1960-1962		$6,700	$8,700
1963-1964		$6,700	$8,700
1965		$5,800	$7,500
1966-1969	Brazilian	$5,300	$7,000
1970-1979	Indian	$2,450	$3,200
1980-1989		$1,950	$2,600
1990-1999		$1,800	$2,375
2000-2009		$1,800	$2,375
2010-2020		$1,800	$2,375

D12-28

1970-2018. Indian rosewood back and sides, 12 strings, 14 frets clear of body, solid headstock.

MODEL YEAR	FEATURES	EXC. COND. LOW	HIGH
1970-1979		$1,875	$2,425
1980-1989		$1,625	$2,100
1990-1999		$1,625	$2,100
2000-2018		$1,625	$2,100

D-28 1935 Special

1993. Guitar of the Month, 1935 features, Indian rosewood back and sides, peghead with Brazilian rosewood veneer.

MODEL YEAR	FEATURES	EXC. COND. LOW	HIGH
1993		$2,400	$3,100

D-28 1955 CFM IV

2009-2010. Limited Edition, 55 made celebrating Chris Martin IV birthyear 1955, Madagascar rosewood.

MODEL YEAR	FEATURES	EXC. COND. LOW	HIGH
2009-2010		$3,225	$4,225

D-28 50th Anniversary

1983. Stamped inside '1833-1983 150th Anniversary', Indian rosewood back and sides.

MODEL YEAR	FEATURES	EXC. COND. LOW	HIGH
1983		$1,850	$2,400

D-28 75th Anniversary

2009 only. Limited production celebrating 1934 to 2009, Madagascar rosewood back and sides, Adirondack spruce top.

MODEL YEAR	FEATURES	EXC. COND. LOW	HIGH
2009		$4,000	$5,200

D-28 75th Anniversary Brazilian

1983. Brazilian rosewood back and sides.

MODEL YEAR	FEATURES	EXC. COND. LOW	HIGH
1983		$5,300	$6,900

D-28 150th Anniversary

1983-1985. Limited production of 268, only '83 vintage have the anniversary stamp, Brazilian rosewood sides and back.

MODEL YEAR	FEATURES	EXC. COND. LOW	HIGH
1983	150th stamp	$5,300	$6,900
1984-1985	No stamp	$5,300	$6,900

D-28 Authentic 1931

2013-2015. Adirondack spruce top, Madagascar rosewood back and sides, authentic '31 appointments, vintage gloss finish.

MODEL YEAR	FEATURES	EXC. COND. LOW	HIGH
2013-2015		$4,300	$5,600

D-28 Authentic 1937

2007-2009, 2014-present. '37 specs, 50 made of first Brazilian rosewood batch. Reintroduced '14 with Madagascar rosewood and Vintage Tone System (VTS).

MODEL YEAR	FEATURES	EXC. COND. LOW	HIGH
2007-2009	Brazilian	$13,000	$17,000
2014-2020	Madagascar	$4,350	$5,750
2020	VTS aged	$4,350	$5,750

D-28 Authentic 1941

2013-2016. Adirondack, Madagascar rosewood.

MODEL YEAR	FEATURES	EXC. COND. LOW	HIGH
2013-2016		$4,350	$5,750

D-28 Custom

1984. Guitar of the Month Nov. '84, double bound D-body, multi-ring rosette, rosewood back/sides, spruce top, 43 made.

MODEL YEAR	FEATURES	EXC. COND. LOW	HIGH
1984		$2,550	$3,300

D-28 CW/CWB Clarence White

2003-2014. CW has Indian rosewood back and sides, the CWB Brazilian, only 150 CWBs were to be built.

MODEL YEAR	FEATURES	EXC. COND. LOW	HIGH
2003-2004	CWB	$5,700	$7,400
2003-2014	CW	$2,850	$3,700

D-28 D

1975. Frap pickup.

MODEL YEAR	FEATURES	EXC. COND. LOW	HIGH
1975		$2,375	$3,075

MODEL YEAR	FEATURES	EXC. COND. LOW	HIGH

D-28 Dan Tyminski
2010-2013. Custom Artist limited edition, Indian rosewood back and sides, Adirondack spruce top, other bracing specs.

2010-2013		$2,400	$3,100

D-28 DM Del McCourey Signature
2003. Limited edition of 115, natural.

2003		$2,450	$3,200

D-28 E
1959-1964. Electronics, Brazilian rosewood back and sides, 2 DeArmond pickups, natural.

1959-1964		$6,000	$7,800

D-28 E Modern Deluxe
2020-present. Sitka spruce VTS aged top, East Indian rosewood back and sides, Fishman electronics, gloss finish.

2020		$3,250	$4,250

D-28 Elvis Presley
2008-2010. Carpathian spruce top, East Indian rosewood back and sides.

2008-2010		$3,200	$4,200

D-28 Elvis Presley CVR
2008-2010. Carpathian spruce top, East Indian rosewood back and sides, tooled leather cover.

2008-2010		$4,100	$5,300

D-28 M Elvis Presley
2008-2010. Limited Edition, 175 made, Madagascar rosewood back and sides, Adirondack top, tooled leather cover.

2008-2010		$5,300	$6,900

D-28 GE Golden Era
1999-2005. GE Golden Era, Brazilian rosewood, herringbone trim.

1999-2005		$6,100	$7,950

D-28 HW Hank Williams
1998. Limited Edition, 150 made, replica of Hank Williams' 1944 D-28, Brazilian rosewood sides and back, scalloped braces, herringbone.

1998		$5,800	$7,500

D-28 John Lennon
2017-2018. Sitka spruce top with Vintage Tone System, East Indian rosewood back and sides, back inlaid with a peace sign, Lennon's self-portrait illustration beneath Martin logo on headstock.

2017-2018		$2,550	$3,300

D-28 John Lennon 75th Anniversary
2016. Limited Edition to commemorate Lennon's 75th birthday, 75 made, Adirondack spruce top, Madagascar rosewood back and sides, headplate includes Lennon's famous self-portrait illustration.

2016		$6,600	$8,600

D-28 John Prine
2017-2020. Only 70 offered, Engelmann spruce top, Madagascar rosewood back and sides, inlaid pearl angel wings on headstock.

2017-2020		$3,550	$4,600

D-28 KTBS Bob Shane
2003. Bob Shane of the Kingston Trio, Signature Edition with 51 offered, sitka spruce top, East Indian rosewood back and sides, The Kingston Trio logo between 11th-13th frets, Shane's pearl signature 19th-20th frets.

2003		$2,900	$3,800

D-28 LF Lester Flatt
1998. Limited Edition, 50 made, Brazilian rosewood.

1998		$5,800	$7,500

D-28 Louvin Brothers
2015-2020. Limited run of 50, sitka spruce top, East Indian rosewood back and sides, printed Louvin Brothers artwork from "Satan is Real" album.

2015-2020		$2,150	$2,800

D-28 LSH
1991. Guitar of the Month, Indian rosewood back and sides, herringbone trim, snowflake inlay, zigzag back stripe.

1991		$2,300	$3,000

D-28 LSV
1999-2005. Large soundhole model.

1999-2005		$1,900	$2,475

D-28 M Merle Travis
2008-2010. 100 made, Adirondack top, Madagascar rosewood back and sides, curly maple neck, 6-on-a-side Bigsby-style headstock, heart-diamond-spade-club inlays.

2008-2010		$3,850	$5,000

D-28 M The Mamas and The Papas
2012-2014. Custom Artist, 100 made, Madagascar rosewood back and sides.

2012-2014		$2,125	$2,775

D-28 Marquis
2004-2017. Golden Era appointments, Adirondack top, Indian rosewood, natural or sunburst.

2004-2017	Natural	$2,500	$3,300
2004-2017	Sunburst	$2,500	$3,300
2007-2009	Madagascar option	$2,500	$3,300

D-28 Modern Deluxe
2019-present. Sitka spruce top with Vintage Tone System (VTS), East Indian rosewood back and sides, gloss finish.

2019-2020		$2,350	$3,050

D-28 Museum Edition 1941
2009-2012. Based on '41 model located in Martin's PA museum, Adirondack spruce top, Madagascar rosewood back and sides, natural finish.

2009-2012		$4,500	$6,000

D-28 P
1988-1990, 2011-2012. P indicates low-profile neck, Indian rosewood back and sides. Reintroduced 2011 with high performance neck.

1988-1990		$1,725	$2,250
2011-2012		$1,725	$2,250

D-28 S
1954-1994. Rosewood back and sides, 12-fret neck.

1954-1959	Special order	$10,900	$14,200
1960-1964	Special order	$7,700	$10,000
1965	Special order	$6,200	$8,000
1966-1969	Brazilian	$5,800	$7,500
1970-1979	Indian	$2,800	$3,600
1980-1989		$2,300	$3,000
1990-1994		$2,300	$3,000

D-28 SW Wurlitzer
1962-1965, 1968. Made for the Wurlitzer Co.

1962-1964		$7,000	$9,025
1965		$6,100	$7,925
1968		$5,700	$7,325

1972 Martin D-28
Bernunzio Uptown Music

1998 Martin D-28 LF Lester Flatt

GUITARS

1965 Martin D-35

Greg Perrine

1974 Martin D12-35

Peter Van Wagner

MODEL YEAR	FEATURES	EXC. COND. LOW	HIGH

D-28 V

1983-1985. Limited Edition, Brazilian rosewood back and sides, herringbone trim, slotted diamond inlay.

1983-1985		$5,300	$6,900

D-35

1965-present. Brazilian rosewood sides and 3-piece back, changed to Brazilian wings and Indian center in '70, then all Indian rosewood in '71, natural with sunburst option. For a brief time, on the back side, the center panel was Brazilian and the two side panels were Indian.

1965	Brazilian	$5,800	$7,500
1966-1970	Brazilian	$5,300	$7,000
1970	Center panel only Brazilian	$2,800	$3,600
1970-1979	Indian	$2,625	$3,400
1980-1989		$1,950	$2,600
1983	150th center strip	$1,950	$2,600
1990-1999		$1,800	$2,375
2000-2020		$1,800	$2,375
2015	50th Anniv Label	$1,800	$2,375

D12-35

1965-1995. Brazilian rosewood back and sides, changed to Indian rosewood in '70, 12 strings, 12 frets clear of body, slotted headstock.

1965-1969	Brazilian	$4,100	$5,300
1970-1979	Indian	$1,875	$2,500
1980-1989		$1,650	$2,125
1990-1995		$1,650	$2,125

D12-35 50th Anniversery Limited Edition

2015-2016. Limited to 183 (the quantity of 1st production run in '65), European spruce top, 3-piece East Indian rosewood back and sides, natural gloss finish.

2015-2016		$3,500	$4,600

D-35 30th Anniversery

1995. Limited Edition, D-35 with '1965-1995' inlay on 20th fret, gold hardware, limited edition of 207 instruments.

1995		$2,900	$3,800

D-35 Bicentennial

1975-1976. Limited Edition, 197 made, sitka spruce top, 3-piece Indian rosewood back, eagle inlay on headstock, 13 star inlay on 'board.

1975-1976		$2,850	$3,700

D-35 E Retro

2012-2019. Sitka spruce top, East Indian rosewood back and sides.

2012-2019		$2,000	$2,600

D-35 Ernest Tubb

2003. Indian rosewood back and sides, special inlays, 90 built.

2003		$2,450	$3,200

D-35 JC Johnny Cash

2006-present. Rosewood back and sides.

2006-2020		$2,900	$3,750

D-35 MP

2011-2012. Madagascar rosewood back and sides, high performance neck.

2011-2012		$1,700	$2,200

MODEL YEAR	FEATURES	EXC. COND. LOW	HIGH

D-35 P

1986-1990. P indicates low-profile neck.

1986-1990		$1,950	$2,600

D-35 S

1966-1993. Brazilian rosewood back and sides, changed to Indian rosewood in '70, 12-fret neck, slotted peghead.

1966-1969	Brazilian	$6,100	$8,000
1970-1979	Indian	$3,000	$3,900
1980-1989		$2,300	$3,000
1990-1993		$2,300	$3,000

D-35 Seth Avett

2013-2019. Swiss spruce top, East Indian rosewood/flamed koa back, copper snowflake inlay.

2013-2019		$2,025	$2,625

D-35 SW Wurlitzer

1966, 1968. Made for the Wurlitzer Co., Brazilian rosewood.

1966, 1968		$6,100	$8,000

D-35 V

1984. Limited Edition, 10 made, Brazilian rosewood back and sides.

1984		$5,500	$7,200

D-37 K

1980-1994. Dreadnought-size, koa back and sides, spruce top.

1980-1994		$2,325	$3,000

D-37 K2

1980-1994. Same as D-37 K, but has a koa top and black 'guard.

1980-1994		$2,325	$3,000

D-37 W Lucinda Williams

2003. Only 4 made, never put into production, Aztec pearl inlay favored by Lucinda Williams, quilted mahogany sides and back.

2003		$3,275	$4,225

D-40

1997-2005. Indian rosewood back and sides, hexagon inlays.

1997-2005		$1,925	$2,525

D-40 BLE

1990. Limited Edition Guitar of the Month, Brazilian rosewood back and sides, pearl top border except around 'board.

1990		$6,200	$8,000

D-40 DM Don McLean

1998. Only 50 made, Englemann spruce top.

1998		$4,800	$6,200

D-40 FMG

1995-1996. Figured mahogany back and sides, 150 made.

1995-1996		$3,500	$4,500

D-40 FW Limited Edition

1996. Figured claro walnut sides and back, 'Limited Edition D-40 FW' label, 148 made.

1996		$2,300	$3,000

D-40 QM Limited Edition

1996. Limited Edition, 200 made, quilted maple body.

1996		$2,300	$3,000

MODEL YEAR	FEATURES	EXC. COND. LOW	HIGH

D-41

1969-present. Brazilian rosewood back and sides for the first ones in '69 then Indian rosewood, bound body, scalloped braces, natural.

1969	Brazilian	$16,500	$21,500
1970-1979	Indian	$3,200	$4,200
1980-1989		$2,600	$3,450
1990-1999		$2,600	$3,450
2000-2009		$2,600	$3,450
2010-2020		$2,600	$3,450

D12-41

1970-1994. Very few made, special order after '93, 12-string, 14-fret.

1970-1994		$3,525	$4,525

D-41 A Turbo Mandolin Brothers

2011, 2013. Two Custom Shop models made for Mandolin Bros., Adirondack top. Similar except 10 40th Anniversary models which have abalone and pearl mandolin 12th-fret inlay and label signed by Stan Jay and Chris Martin.

2011		$2,800	$3,600

D-41 BLE

1989. Limited Edition Guitar of the Month, Brazilian rosewood back and sides, pearl top border except around 'board.

1989		$5,800	$7,500

D-41 DF Dan Fogelberg

2001. 141 made, East Indian rosewood back and sides, hexagon 'board inlays, pearl snowflakes inlaid on bridge.

2001		$4,300	$5,600

D-41 E

1971. Indian rosewood.

1971		$3,200	$4,200

D-41 GJ George Jones

2001. Style 41 appointments, limited edition of 100, label signed by the Opossum.

2001		$3,100	$4,000

D-41 K Purple Martin

2013-2020. Limited to 50 with labels signed by C.F. Martin IV, highly flamed koa back and sides, purple martin-inspired inlay on 'board, bridge, and 'guard.

2013-2020		$6,800	$8,800

D-41 Porter Wagoner

2008-2011. Custom Artist series, Indian rosewood back and sides.

2008-2011		$2,600	$3,350

D-41 S/SD-41 S

1970-1994. Sunburst, Indian rosewood, 12-fret neck, slotted peghead.

1970-1979		$3,750	$4,850
1980-1994		$3,000	$4,000

D-41 Special

2004-2011. D-41 with snowflake inlays.

2004-2011		$2,600	$3,450

D-42

1973-1988, 1996-present. Limited production '73-'88, Indian rosewood back and sides, spruce top, pearl rosette and inlays, snowflake 'board inlays, gold tuners, gloss finish.

1973-1988	Limited Edition	$3,700	$4,800
1996-2020		$3,200	$4,200

MODEL YEAR	FEATURES	EXC. COND. LOW	HIGH

D-42 E

1996-2008. With Fishman Ellipse VT pickup system.

1996-2008		$3,325	$4,400

D-42 Amazon Rosewood Limited Edition

2007. Limited to 35, Amazon rosewood is similar to Brazilian rosewood but a different species.

2007		$3,500	$4,600

D-42 AR (Amazon Rosewood)

2002-2003. Limited to 30 made, Amazon rosewood is similar to Brazilian rosewood but a different species.

2002-2003		$3,500	$4,600

D-42 Flamed Mahogany

2006. Adirondack, figured mahogany, 30 made with tree-of-life inlay.

2006		$5,500	$7,100

D-42 JC Johnny Cash

1997. Rosewood back and sides, gloss black lacquer on body and neck, Cash signature inlaid at 19th fret, have label signed by Cash and C.F. Martin IV, 80 sold.

1997		$4,200	$5,500

D-42 K Limited Edition

1998. 150 made, highly flamed koa back and sides, sitka top with aging toner, high X-brace design, 45-style abalone snowflake inlays.

1998		$3,300	$4,300

D-42 K/D-42 K2

1998-2006. K has koa back and sides, the all koa body K2 was discontinued in '05.

1998-2006	D-42 K	$3,300	$4,300
2000-2005	D-42 K2	$3,300	$4,300

D-42 LE

1988 only. Limited Edition (75 sold), D-42-style, scalloped braces, low profile neck.

1988		$3,300	$4,300

D-42 Peter Frampton

2006-2007. Indian rosewood back and sides, Style 45 features.

2006-2007		$4,300	$5,600

D-42 Purple Martin Flamed Myrtle

2018-present. Flamed myrtle back and sides, limited to 100 made.

2018-2020		$8,300	$10,800

D-42 SB

2006-2007. Sunburst finish, sitka spruce top, 45-style appointments.

2006-2007		$3,200	$4,200

D-42 V

1985. Vintage Series, 12 made, Brazilian rosewood, scalloped braces.

1985		$6,100	$8,000

D-45

1933-1942 (96 made), 1968-present. Brazilian rosewood back and sides, changed to Indian rosewood during '69. The pre-WW II D-45 is one of the holy grails. A pre-war D-45 should be evaluated on a case-by-case basis. The price ranges are for all-original guitars in excellent condition and are guidance pricing only. These ranges are for a crack-free guitar. Unfortunately, many older acoustics have a crack or two and this can make ultra-expensive acoustics more difficult to evaluate than ultra-expensive solidbody

2000 Martin D-42
Rivington Guitars

Martin D-42 Purple Martin Flamed Myrtle

1968 Martin D-45

Wayne Stephens

2002 Martin D-50 Deluxe

Imaged by Heritage Auctions, HA.com

MODEL YEAR	FEATURES	EXC. COND. LOW	HIGH

electrics. Technically, a repaired body crack makes a guitar non-original, but the vintage market generally considers a professionally repaired crack to be original. Crack width, length and depth can vary, therefore extra attention is suggested.

1936-1938		$345,000	$448,000
1939	Early, wide neck	$345,000	$448,000
1939	Late, thin neck	$298,000	$387,000
1940-1942		$270,000	$350,000
1968		$31,000	$40,000
1969	Brazilian	$30,000	$39,000
1970-1979		$6,200	$8,000
1980-1989		$5,600	$7,300
1990-1999		$5,100	$6,650
2000-2017		$5,100	$6,650
2018-2020	New specs	$5,100	$6,650

D12-45

1970s-1987. Special order instrument, not a standard catalog item, with D-45 appointments, Indian rosewood.

1970-1979		$4,200	$5,500
1980-1987		$4,000	$5,300

D-45 100th Anniversary LE

1996. Limited Edition, '1896-1996 C.F. Martin Commemorative Anniversary Model' label.

1996		$5,100	$6,650

D-45 150th Anniversary

1983. Brazilian rosewood back and sides, sitka spruce top, '150th' logo stamp.

1983		$10,300	$13,400

D-45 CFM CMR Sr. (200th Anniversary, Brazilian)

1996. Commemorating the 200th Anniversary of C.F. Martin Sr. birthday, Brazilian rosewood back and sides, style 45 Deluxe pearl bordering, fossilized ivory nut and saddle, 14-fret neck, gold hardware.

1996		$10,300	$13,400

D-45 CFM CMR Sr. (200th Anniversary, East Indian)

1996. Commemorating the 200th Anniversary of C.F. Martin Sr. birthday, Indian rosewood back and sides, style 45 pearl bordering, bone nut and saddle, 14-fret neck, gold hardware.

1996		$5,100	$6,650

D-45 (1939 Reissue Mandolin Brothers)

1990. Commissioned by Mandolin Brothers, 5 made, figured Brazilian rosewood. Original name "The Reissue 1939 Martin D-45." Said to be the first reissue of the era and the seed for the '90s Martin Custom Shop.

1990		$10,300	$13,400

D-45 (1939 Reissue)

1992. High-grade spruce top, figured Brazilian rosewood back and sides, high X and scalloped braces, abalone trim, natural, gold tuners.

1992		$10,300	$13,400

D-45 B Brazilian

1994. Brazilian rosewood.

1994		$10,300	$13,400

D-45 Celtic Knot

2004-2005. Brazilian rosewood, Celtic knot 'board inlays, 30 built.

2004-2005		$16,500	$21,400

MODEL YEAR	FEATURES	EXC. COND. LOW	HIGH

D-45 Custom Shop

1984, 1991-1992. Various options and models, Indian rosewood back and sides in '84, then Brazilian rosewood.

1984	Indian	$5,200	$6,750
1991-1992	Brazilian	$11,200	$14,500

D-45 Deluxe

1993 only. Guitar of the Month, Brazilian rosewood back and sides, figured spruce top, inlay in bridge and 'guard, tree-of-life inlay on 'board, pearl borders and back stripe, gold tuners with large gold buttons, total of 60 sold.

1993		$13,200	$17,100

D-45 Deluxe CFM Sr. (200th Anniversary, Brazilian)

1996. Commemorating the 200th Anniversary of C.F. Martin Sr. birthday, 91 made, Brazilian rosewood back and sides, style 45 Deluxe pearl bordering, fossilized-ivory nut and saddle, 14-fret neck, gold hardware.

1996		$10,300	$13,400

D-45 E Aura

2010. With Fishman Electronics Ellipse Aura technology.

2010		$5,150	$6,750

D-45 E Retro

2013-2019. East Indian rosewood, Fishman.

2013-2019		$5,800	$7,500

D-45 GE Golden Era

2001-2004. 167 made, '37 specs, Brazilian rosewood.

2001-2004		$17,000	$22,100

D-45 Gene Autry

1994 only. Gene Autry inlay (2 options available), natural.

1994	Gene Autry 'board	$15,700	$20,400
1994	Snowflake 'board option	$15,700	$20,400

D-45 K

2006-2008. Flamed koa back and sides.

2006-2008		$5,800	$7,500

D-45 KLE

1991. Limited Edition koa, Engelmann, bear claw, 54 made.

1991		$5,800	$7,500

D-45 LE

1987. Limited Edition, 44 made, Guitar of the Month, September '87.

1987		$12,800	$16,600

D-45 Mike Longworth Commemorative Edition

2004-2006. East Indian rosewood back and sides, Adirondack spruce top, 91 made, label signed by Mike's wife Sue and C.F. Martin IV.

2004-2006		$6,300	$8,300

D-45 S Authentic 1936

2013-present. Adirondack spruce top, Vintage Tone System, Brazilian rosewood back and sides, '36 style appointments and specs.

2013-2020		$32,000	$42,000

D-45 S Deluxe

1992. Limited Edition, 50 made, Indian rosewood, spruce top, high-end appointments.

1992		$6,400	$8,400

MODEL YEAR	FEATURES	EXC. COND. LOW	HIGH

D-45 S/SD-45 S

1969-1994. Brazilian rosewood back and sides in '69, Indian rosewood after, 12-fret neck, S means slotted peghead, only 50 made.

1969	Brazilian	$34,000	$44,300
1970-1979	Indian	$7,100	$9,200
1980-1994	Indian	$6,400	$8,400

D-45 SS Steven Stills

1998. Brazilian rosewood back and sides, 91 made.

1998		$21,400	$27,800

D-45 V Brazilian

1983. Brazilian rosewood back and sides, scalloped braces, snowflake inlay, natural.

1983		$10,300	$13,400

D-45 VR/D-45 V

1997-2020. Vintage specs, Indian rosewood back and sides, vintage aging toner, snowflake inlay. Name changed to D-45 V in '99 (not to be confused with Brazilian rosewood D-45 V of the '80s).

1997-1998	VR	$5,600	$7,300
1999-2020	V	$5,600	$7,300

D-45 Woodstock 50th Anniversary

2019-2020. Limited Edition, run of 50, East Indian rosewood back and sides, abalone inlay, Woodstock dove on headstock, '1969-2019' on 'board, peace sign on heelcap.

2019-2020		$7,700	$10,200

D-50 Deluxe/D-50 DX

2001-2003. Deluxe limited edition, 50 made, one of the most ornate Martin models ever made, Brazilian rosewood back and sides, highly ornate pearl inlay.

2001-2003		$28,000	$36,500

D-50 K Deluxe/D-50 K2 Deluxe

2003-2006. As D-50 Deluxe with ornate pearl inlay and highly flamed koa back and sides (K, 45 made) or highly flamed koa top, back and sides (K2, 5 made).

2003-2006	K Deluxe	$23,000	$30,000
2003-2006	K2 Deluxe	$23,000	$30,000

D-60

1989-1995. Birdseye maple back and sides, snowflake inlays, tortoiseshell binding and 'guard.

1989-1995		$1,775	$2,300

D-62

1987-1995. Flamed maple back and sides, chrome-plated enclosed Schaller tuners.

1987-1995		$1,775	$2,300

D-62 LE

1986. Limited Edition, Guitar of the Month October '86, flamed maple back and sides, spruce top, snowflake inlays, natural.

1986		$1,775	$2,300

D-64

1985-1995. Flamed maple top, low profile neck.

1985-1995		$1,775	$2,300

D-76 Bicentennial Limited Edition

1975-1976. Limited to 200 made in '75 and 1,976 made in '76, Indian rosewood back and sides, 3-piece back, herringbone back stripe, pearl stars on 'board, eagle on peghead.

1975-1976		$2,800	$3,600

MODEL YEAR	FEATURES	EXC. COND. LOW	HIGH

D-93

1993. Mahogany, spruce, 93 pertains to the year, not a style number.

1993		$1,775	$2,300

D-100 Deluxe

2004. Limited Edition, guitars have the first 50 sequential serial numbers following the millionth Martin guitar (1,000,001 to 1,000,050), fancy pearl inlay on back, 'guard, headstock, 'board and bridge. Herringbone top and rosette inlay, Adirondack spruce top, Brazilian rosewood back and sides.

2004		$28,900	$37,500

D-200 Deluxe

2017-present. Celebration of Martin's two-millionth serial number, limited to 50 offered, watch-themed highly decorative, comes with renowned watchmaker Roland G Murphy watch with matching serial no., premium case has built-in hygrometer.

2017-2020		$77,000	$100,000

D-222 100th Anniversary

2016. Commemorates 100th anniversary of the dreadnought, limited to 100, sitka spruce top, mahogany back and sides, ivoroid binding, slotted headstock.

2016		$2,825	$3,650

D-420

2017-2019. Top with custom legal weed illustration by artist Robert Goetzl, mahogany back and sides.

2017-2019		$1,425	$1,825

D Jr

2017-2018. Dreadnought Junior, sitka spruce top, sapele back and sides.

2017-2018		$275	$350

D Jr E

2015-2018. Dreadnought Junior with Fishman electronics.

2015-2018		$325	$425

D Jr-10E StreetMaster

2021. Dreadnought Junior with thinner body and tapered neck, Fishman electronics, dark mahogany finish.

2021		$400	$525

DC Series

1980s-2019. Dreadnought cutaway versions, E models have electronics, GT is gloss top, R means rosewood back and sides. Replaced by DC-X Series starting in '20.

1981-1997	DC-28	$1,800	$2,350
1996-2000	DC-1	$550	$725
1996-2010	DC-1E	$600	$800
1997-2000	DCM	$525	$700
1997-2005	DC-1M	$575	$700
1997-2006	DCME	$575	$750
1998	DCXM	$400	$525
1998-2001	DCXME	$400	$525
1998-2010	DC-15E	$600	$800
1999-2000	DC-1R	$550	$725
2000	DCRE	$575	$750
2000-2013	DCX1E	$400	$525
2001-2005	DCXE Black	$400	$525
2002-2003	DC-16RE	$650	$850
2003-2005	DC-16GTE Premium	$800	$1,075

1975 Martin D-76 Bicentennial

Imaged by Heritage Auctions, HA.com

2017 Martin D-200 Deluxe

Martin DC-X2E

2000 Martin DM3 MD
Dave Matthews

MODEL YEAR	FEATURES	EXC. COND. LOW	HIGH
2003-2016	DC-16GTE	$800	$1,075
2003-2019	DC-16E	$800	$1,075
2004-2013	DCX1KE	$400	$525
2004-2013	DCX1RE	$400	$525
2005	DC Trey Anastasio	$3,600	$4,700
2005	DC-16RE Aura	$675	$875
2005	DC-16RGTE Aura	$950	$1,225
2005-2007	DC-16E Koa	$850	$1,125
2005-2008	DC-16RGTE	$900	$1,175
2005-2010	DC-Aura	$1,725	$2,250
2006-2019	DC-28E	$1,850	$2,450
2009-2016	DCPA1/ DCPA1 Plus	$1,725	$2,250
2011	DCPA2/DCPA3	$950	$1,225
2011-2016	DCPA4 Shaded	$950	$1,250
2011-2017	DCPA4 Rosewood	$1,000	$1,300
2013-2016	DCPA5	$400	$525
2013-2016	DCPA5 Black	$400	$525
2013-2016	DCPA5K Koa	$400	$525
2016-2019	DC-15ME	$600	$800
2016-2019	DC-35E	$1,900	$2,500
2017-2018	DCRSG	$700	$925
2017-2019	DC-18E	$1,800	$2,350
2017-2019	DCPA4	$875	$1,150
2017-2019	DCX1AE/ DCX1AE Macassar	$375	$500
2017-2019	DCX1RAE	$400	$525
2019	DC-13E	$500	$675

DC-X Series

1980s-present. Various dreadnought models with various woods, some with electronics.

2020	DC-X2E	$500	$650

Ditson Dreadnaught 111

2007-2009. Based on 1929 Ditson 111, 12-fret neck, slot head, mahogany back and sides, Brazilian rosewood binding.

2007-2009	$3,200	$4,150

DM

1996-2009. Solid sitka spruce top, laminated mahogany back and sides, dot markers, natural satin.

1996-2009	$475	$600

DM-12

1996-2009. 12-string DM.

1996-2009	$475	$600

DM3 MD Dave Matthews

1999-2001. Englemann top, 3-piece Indian rosewood back, African padauk center wedge, 234 made.

1999-2001	$4,000	$5,200

Doobie-42 Tom Johnston Signature Edition

2007. D-42 style, 35 made, solid Indian rosewood back and sides, abalone and catseye markers, other special appointments.

2007	$3,675	$4,775

DR

1997-2008. Road Series Dreadnought, rosewood back and sides.

1997-2008	$525	$675

DR Centennial LE

2016-2020. Limited Edition celebrates '100 Years of the Dreadnought', Adirondack, East Indian rosewood, antique white binding, satin finish.

2016-2020	$1,500	$1,950

DRS1 (Road/1 Series)

2011-2019. D-size, sapele top, back and sides, satin finish, Fishman. Replaced by D-10E in '19.

2011-2019	$425	$550

DRS2 (Road/1 Series)

2012-2018. DRS1 with spruce top. Replaced by D-10E in '19.

2012-2018	$450	$600

DRSG

2017-2018. Sitka spruce top, siris back and sides, Fishman Sonitone.

2017-2018	$650	$850

DRSGT

2014-2015. Sitka spruce top, sapele back and sides, Fishman with USB port.

2014-2015	$500	$650

DSR Sugar Ray

2003. Limited Edition of 57 made, D-17 style, all mahogany, signed by C.F. Martin IV and all members of Sugar Ray band.

2003	$3,200	$4,100

DSS-17

2018-present. Slope-shoulder dreadnought, sitka spruce top, mahogany back and sides with antique white binding, satin Black Smoke or Whiskey Sunset Burst.

2018-2019	Black Smoke	$900	$1,175
2019-2020	Whiskey Sunset	$900	$1,175

DVM Veterans

2002-2008. D-style, spruce top, rosewood back and sides, special veterans ornamentation.

2002-2008	$1,650	$2,150

Dwight Yoakam DD28

2017-2018. Custom Signature Edition, sitka spruce top, East Indian rosewood back and sides, inlaid mother-of-pearl and recon stone playing cards.

2017-2018	$2,600	$3,400

DX 175th Anniversary

2008. Rosewood HPL back and sides, founder's picture on top.

2008	$375	$475

DX Johnny Cash

2019-present. D-sized, Jett black HPL top, back and sides, custom 'board inlaid with stars and CASH logo, Cash's signature on rosette and label, Fishman electronics.

2019-2020	$450	$575

DX Series

1996-2020. D-size, high pressure wood laminate (HPL) backs and sides, exterior wood-grain image with gloss finish. M is for mahogany wood-grain, R rosewood and K koa. A 1 indicates a solid spruce top with Series 1 bracing, otherwise top is wood-patterned HPL. C indicates cutaway and E Fishman Presys Plus and AE Fishman Sonitone. Replaced by D-X Series starting in '20.

1996-2009	DXM/DMX	$325	$425
1998-2012	DXME	$325	$425

MODEL YEAR	FEATURES	EXC. COND. LOW	HIGH
1999-2000	D12XM 12-String	$325	$425
1999-2019	DXMAE	$325	$425
2000-2014	DX1	$300	$400
2000-2019	DX1AE	$325	$425
2001-2009	DX1R	$325	$425
2002-2009	DXK2	$325	$425
2004-2009	DX1K	$325	$425
2008-2010	D12X1 12-String	$325	$425
2010-2020	DX1KAE	$325	$425
2011-2019	D12X1AE 12-String	$375	$475
2013	DX1E	$325	$425
2014-2019	DXAE Black	$325	$425
2014-2020	DXK2AE	$325	$425
2015-2019	DX1RAE	$325	$425
2017	DX420	$775	$1,025
2017-2019	DX2AE Macassar	$325	$425

D-X Series

2020-present. New spec dreadnought models to replace the DX Series. Various options and finishes.

2020	D-X1E	$375	$475
2020	D-X2E	$450	$575
2020	D-X2E 12-String	$450	$575

E-18

1979-1983. Offset double-cut, maple and rosewood laminate solidbody, 2 DiMarzio pickups, phase switch, natural.

1979-1983		$1,300	$1,700

E-28

1980-1983. Double-cut electric solidbody, carved top, ebony 'board, 2 humbuckers.

1980-1983		$1,400	$1,800

EM-18

1979-1983. Offset double-cut, maple and rosewood laminate solidbody, 2 exposed-coil humbucking pickups, coil split switch.

1979-1983		$1,300	$1,700

EMP-1

1998-1999. Employee series designed by Martin employee team, cutaway solid spruce top, ovangkol wood back and sides with rosewood middle insert (D-35-style insert), on-board pickup.

1998-1999		$1,500	$1,975

EMP-2 Limited Edition

1999. D size, tzalam body, flying saucer inlays.

1999		$1,500	$1,975

F-1

1940-1942. Archtop, mahogany back and sides, carved spruce top, multi-bound, f-holes, sunburst, 91 made.

1940-1941		$1,850	$2,400
1942		$1,475	$1,900

F-1-12

1941. F-1 12 string.

1941		$2,000	$2,600

F-2

1940-1942. Carved spruce top, maple or rosewood back and sides, multi-bound, f-holes, 46 made.

1940-1942		$2,100	$2,750

F-5

1940. 2 made.

1940		$3,850	$5,000

F-7

1935-1939, 1941-1942. Brazilian rosewood back and sides, f-holes, carved top, back arched by braces, multi-bound, sunburst top finish.

1935-1938		$5,400	$7,000
1941-1942		$5,000	$6,500

F-9

1935-1942. Highest-end archtop, Brazilian rosewood, Martin inlaid vertically on headstock, 7-ply top binding, 45-style back strip, sunburst.

1935-1942		$11,400	$14,800

F-50

1961-1965. Single-cut thinline archtop with laminated maple body, 1 pickup.

1961-1965		$1,225	$1,600

F-55

1961-1965. Single-cut thinline archtop with laminated maple body, 2 pickups.

1961-1965		$2,300	$3,000

F-65

1961-1965. Electric archtop, double-cut, f-holes, 2 pickups, square-cornered peghead, Bigsby, sunburst.

1961-1965		$2,300	$3,000

Felix The Cat

2004-2010. Felix the Cat logo art, Don Oriolo logo, red body, Felix gig bag.

2004	Felix I, 756 made	$425	$550
2005-2006	Felix II, 625 made	$425	$550
2007-2010	Felix III, 1000 made	$425	$550

GCD-16 CP (Guitar Center)

1998. 15 5/8" Style D.

1998		$1,575	$2,025

GPC Series

2010-present. Standard Series (GPC-), Performing Artist (GPCPA) and X Series (GPCX), Grand Performance size, cutaway, acoustic/electric, various woods.

2010-2016	GPCPA1/Plus	$1,725	$2,250
2011	GPCPA2	$1,175	$1,500
2011-2012	GPCPA3	$1,175	$1,500
2012-2016	GPCPA5K Koa	$400	$525
2013-2016	GPCPA5	$400	$525
2013-2016	GPCPA5 Black	$400	$525
2013-2019	GPC12PA4 12-string	$950	$1,250
2013-2019	GPCPA4 Rosewood	$950	$1,250
2013-2019	GPCPA4 Sapele	$950	$1,250
2016-2018	GPC-35E	$2,050	$2,700
2016-2020	GPC-18E	$1,850	$2,425
2016-2021	GPC-28E	$1,950	$2,600
2017-2018	GPC-15ME	$950	$1,250
2017-2018	GPCRSG	$725	$950
2017-2018	GPCRSGT	$575	$750
2017-2018	GPCXAE Black	$350	$475
2017-2019	GPCX1RAE	$375	$500
2017-2021	GPCX1AE	$375	$500
2017-2021	GPCX2AE Macassar	$375	$500
2017-2021	GPC-X2E	$500	$650
2019-2021	GPC-11E (Road Series)	$575	$750

2002 Martin DX121

Johnny Zapp

1962 Martin F-65

Bill Ruxton

GUITARS

1967 Martin GT-75

Greg Perrine

Martin HD-28 VR

MODEL YEAR	FEATURES	EXC. COND. LOW	HIGH
2019-2021	GPC-13E (Road Series)	$700	$925
2020-2021	GPC-16E	$925	$1,200
2020-2021	GPC-16E Rosewood	$1,250	$1,625

Grand J12-40 E Special

2009-2011. J12-40 with D-TAR Multi-source electronics.

2009-2011		$2,250	$2,900

Grand J-28 LSE

2011-2014. Baritone.

2011-2014		$1,800	$2,350

Grand J-35 E

2009-2011. Grand jumbo size, rosewood back and sides.

2009-2011		$1,800	$2,350

Grand Ole Opry/HDO Grand Ole Opry

1999-2007. Custom Shop Limited Edition, 650 made, 'Grand Ole Opry 75th Anniversary' on neck block, WSM microphone headstock logo, off-white Micarta fingerboard, sitka spruce top, East Indian rosewood back and sides.

1999-2007		$2,250	$2,950

Gruhn 50th Anniversary 0000 (Custom Shop)

2020. Celebrates Gruhn Guitar 50 years in business, interior label signed by George Gruhn, 12- or 14-fret, limited to 50 each in natural or sunburst.

2020		$4,500	$5,800

GT-70

1965-1966. Electric archtop, bound body, f-holes, single-cut, 2 pickups, tremolo, burgundy or black finish.

1965-1966		$2,150	$2,800

GT-75

1965-1967. Electric archtop, bound body, f-holes, double-cut, 2 pickups, tremolo, burgundy or black finish. There is also a 12-string version.

1965-1967		$2,150	$2,800

Hawaiian X

2002-2004. Hawaiian scene painted on top, similar to the Cowboy guitar model, limited edition of 500.

2002-2004		$575	$750

HD-7 Roger McGuinn

2005-2008. Rosewood back and sides, herringbone top trim, 7-string with double G.

2005-2008		$2,450	$3,200

HD12-28

2018-present. Sitka spruce top, East Indian rosewood back and sides, natural.

2018-2020		$1,750	$2,300

HD-16 R Adirondack

2008-2016. Rosewood back and sides, Adirondack top.

2010-2016		$1,450	$1,900

HD-16 R LSH

2007-2013. Indian rosewood (R), large sound hole (LSH).

2007-2013		$1,450	$1,900

HD-18 JB Jimmy Buffett

1998. 424 made, solid mahogany back and sides, herringbone trim, palm tree headstock logo, Style 42 markers, Buffett pearl signature.

1998		$4,100	$5,400

HD-18 LE

1987. Indian rosewood.

1987		$1,625	$2,150

HD-28

1976-present. Standard Series, Indian rosewood back and sides, scalloped bracing, herringbone purfling.

1976-1979		$2,550	$3,350
1980-1989		$1,950	$2,600
1990-1999		$1,800	$2,375
2000-2017	Last Standard X	$1,800	$2,375
2018-2020	Forward X	$1,800	$2,375

HD-28 1935 Special

1993. 'HD-28 1935 Special' model name on label.

1993		$2,150	$2,800

HD-28 2R

1991, 1993-1997. 2R specification for 2 herringbone soundhole rings, larger soundhole.

1991-1997		$1,800	$2,375

HD-28 AWB Custom

2008-2013. Elderly Instruments Custom model, Adirondack spruce top, rosewood back and sides, white-bound body, gloss natural finish.

2008-2013		$2,275	$2,950

HD-28 BLE

1990. Guitar of the Month, 100 made, Brazilian rosewood back and sides, herringbone soundhole ring, low profile neck (LE), chrome tuners, aging toner finish.

1990		$5,025	$6,525

HD-28 BSE

1987-1999. Brazilian rosewood, 93 made.

1987-1999		$5,025	$6,525

HD-28 CTB

1992. Guitar of the Month, herringbone top trim/back stripe, fancy peghead inlay, tortoise binding, gold hardware, label signed by CF Martin IV.

1992		$1,975	$2,600

HD-28 Custom 150th Anniversary

1983. 150th Anniversary, Martin Custom Shop, Indian rosewood sides and back, '1833-1983 150th Year' stamped on inside backstrip.

1983		$2,350	$3,050

HD-28 Custom/Custom HD-28

1994. Custom Shop model.

1994-1995		$1,975	$2,600

HD-28 E Retro

2013-2019. Solid sitka spruce top, East Indian rosewood back and sides.

2013-2019		$2,000	$2,575

HD-28 GM

1989. Grand Marquis, Guitar of the Month, scalloped braced Sitka spruce top with 1930s-era bracing pattern that replaced the X-brace below the soundhole, herringbone top purfling, soundhole ring and back stripe, gold tuners.

1989		$2,775	$3,600

MODEL YEAR	FEATURES	EXC. COND. LOW	HIGH

HD-28 GM LSH

1994. Grand Marquis, Guitar of the Month, rosewood back and sides, large soundhole with double herringbone rings, snowflake inlay in bridge, natural (115 made) or sunburst (36 made).

1994		$2,300	$3,000

HD-28 KM Keb Mo

2001-2002. Signature Edition, Hawaiian koa back and sides, 252 made.

2001-2002		$2,200	$2,900

HD-28 LE

1985. Limited Edition, Guitar of the Month, rosewood back and sides, scalloped bracing, herringbone top purfling, diamonds and squares 'board inlay, V-neck.

1985		$2,500	$3,250

HD-28 LSV

1997-2005. Vintage Series, large soundhole, patterned after Clarence White's modified '35 D-28.

1997-2005		$2,100	$2,775

HD-28 M

1988. Standard profile.

1988		$1,800	$2,350

HD-28 MP

1990-1991, 2011-2012. Bolivian rosewood back and sides, herringbone top trim, low profile neck. Reissued in 2011 with Madagascar rosewood and modern-style neck.

1990-1991		$1,725	$2,250
2011-2012		$1,725	$2,250

HD-28 P

1987-1989. Rosewood back and sides, scalloped braces, herringbone, low profile neck (P), zigzag back stripe.

1987-1989		$1,725	$2,250

HD-28 PSE

1988. Signature Edition, Guitar of the Month, rosewood back and sides, signed by C.F. Martin IV and foremen, scalloped braces, herringbone top purfling, low profile neck, squared peghead, ebony tuner buttons.

1988		$2,100	$2,700

HD-28 S Custom

1995. Slotted headstock.

1995		$2,100	$2,700

HD-28 SB/HD-28 Ambertone/HD-28 SB-AMB

2016-2017. Various wood and finish options for HD-28.

2016-2017		$1,925	$2,525

HD-28 SE

1986-1987. Signature Edition, rosewood back and sides, signed by C. F. Martin and foremen/supervisors, '87 model was a Guitar of the Month and had Brazilian rosewood.

1986		$2,100	$2,700
1987	Brazilian	$4,800	$6,200

HD-28 SO Sing Out!

1996. Limited edition, 45 made, Indian rosewood back and sides.

1996		$2,300	$3,000

MODEL YEAR	FEATURES	EXC. COND. LOW	HIGH

HD-28 V Custom

2007-2012. Indian rosewood back and sides, Adirondack top, wide nut, Elderly Instruments special issue.

2007-2012		$2,600	$3,350

HD-28 V/HD-28 VR

1996-2019. 14-fret, Indian rosewood body, R dropped from name in '99.

1996-1999	HD-28 VR	$2,200	$2,900
2000-2019	HD-28 V	$2,200	$2,900

HD-28 VAW Custom

2007-2017. Custom for Elderly Instruments, Indian rosewood back and sides, herringbone trim, diamond and square inlays, aged gloss finish.

2007-2017		$2,500	$3,300

HD-28 VE

2004-2006. HD-28 V with Fishman Ellipse Blend system.

2004-2006		$2,300	$3,000

HD-28 VS

1996-2016. Slotted headstock, 12-fret, spruce top with aging toner, Indian rosewood sides and back.

1996-2016		$2,450	$3,200

HD-35

1978-present. Indian rosewood back and sides, herringbone top trim, zipper back stripe.

1978-1979		$2,550	$3,300
1980-1989		$1,875	$2,425
1990-1999		$1,875	$2,425
2000-2020		$1,875	$2,425

HD-35 CFM IV 60th

2016-2020. Celebrates C.F. Martin IV's 60th birthday, limited to 60, European spruce top, 3-piece back of siris wings and East Indian rosewood wedge, personally signed label.

2016-2020		$5,000	$6,500

HD-35 Custom

2009. Custom Designed on neck block, Adirondack spruce top, East Indian rosewood sides and back.

2009		$2,100	$2,750

HD-35 Nancy Wilson

2006-2007. Englemann spruce top, 3-piece back with bubinga center wedge, 101 made.

2006-2007		$2,650	$3,450

HD-35 P

1987-1989. HD-35 with low profile neck.

1987-1989		$1,875	$2,425

HD-35 SJC Judy Collins

2002. 50 made, Collins signature headstock logo, wildflower headstock inlay, East Indian rosewood, 3-piece back with figured maple center.

2002		$2,550	$3,300

HD-40 MK Mark Knopfler

2001-2002. Limited Edition of 251 made, Mark Knopfler signature inlay 20th fret, herringbone trim, fancy marquetry soundhole rings.

2001-2002		$3,200	$4,200

HD-40 MS Marty Stuart

1996. Indian rosewood, 250 made, pearl/abalone inlay.

1996		$3,200	$4,200

1981 Martin HD-35

Imaged by Heritage Auctions, HA.com

1996 Martin HD-40 MS Marty Stuart

Imaged by Heritage Auctions, HA.com

1996 Martin J-40

Bernunzio Uptown Music

2006 Martin JC Buddy Guy

Imaged by Heritage Auctions, HA.com

MODEL YEAR	FEATURES	EXC. COND. LOW	HIGH

HD-40 Tom Petty SE

2004-2006. Signature Edition, Indian rosewood sides and back, high-end appointments, 274 made, inside label with signature.

2004-2006 — $4,200 — $5,500

HD-282 R

1992-1996. Large soundhole with 2 herringbone rings, zigzag backstripe.

1992-1996 — $1,900 — $2,500

HD Dierks Bentley

2013-2014. Rosewood.

2013-2014 — $2,900 — $3,750

HD Elliot Easton Custom Edition

2006-2008. Limited Edition, Adirondack spruce top with aging tone, Fishman Ellipse Aura pickup available on HDE.

2006-2008 — $2,400 — $3,150

HDN Negative Limited Edition

2003. Limited to 135 made, unusual appointments include pearloid headstock and black finish, HDN Negative Limited Edition notation on the inside label.

2003 — $2,600 — $3,400

HJ-28

1992, 1996-2000. Limited Edition, Guitar of the Month in '92, regular production started in '96. Jumbo, non-cut, spruce top, Indian rosewood sides and back, herringbone top purfling, with or without on-board electronics.

1992 — LE 69 made — $2,100 — $2,750

1996-2000 — $2,100 — $2,750

HJ-28 M

1994. Mahogany/spruce, herringbone top purfling, Guitar of the Month, 72 made.

1994 — $2,200 — $2,900

HJ-38 Stefan Grossman

2008-2011. Custom Edition, Madagascar rosewood back and sides.

2008-2011 — $2,700 — $3,500

HM Ben Harper

2008-2009. Special Edition, M-style width, 000-style depth, solid Adirondack spruce top, solid East Indian rosewood sides and back, onboard Fishman Ellipse Matrix Blend.

2008-2009 — $2,750 — $3,575

HOM-35

1989. Herringbone Orchestra Model, Guitar of the Month, scalloped braces, 3-piece Brazilian rosewood back, bookmatched sides, 14-fret neck, only 60 built.

1989 — $3,850 — $5,000

HPD-41

1999-2001. Like D-41, but with herringbone rosette, binding.

1999-2001 — $2,800 — $3,600

HTA Kitty Wells 'Honky Tonk Angel'

2002. D-size with 000-size depth, Indian rosewood back and sides, Queen of Country Music inlay logo on headstock (no Martin headstock logo).

2002 — $1,900 — $2,475

J-1 Jumbo

1997-2001. Jumbo body with mahogany back and sides.

1997-2001 — $775 — $950

J12-15

2000-2008. 12-string version of J-15.

2000-2008 — $725 — $950

J12-16 GT

2000-2013. 16" jumbo 12-string, satin solid mahogany back and sides, gloss solid spruce top.

2000-2013 — $875 — $1,125

J12-16 GTE

2014-2015. Jumbo 12-string, Fishman.

2014-2015 — $925 — $1,200

J12-40/J12-40 M

1985-1996. Called J12-40M from '85-'90, rosewood back and sides, 12 strings, 16" jumbo size, 14-fret neck, solid peghead, gold tuners.

1985-1990 — J12-40M — $2,100 — $2,700

1991-1996 — J12-40 — $2,100 — $2,700

J12-65

1985-1995. Called J12-65M for '84-'90, 12-string, figured maple back and sides.

1985-1995 — $1,725 — $2,250

J-15

1999-2010. Jumbo 16" narrow-waist body, solid mahogany top, sides, and back, satin finish.

1999-2010 — $750 — $975

J-15 E

2000-2001. Acoustic/electric J-15.

2000-2001 — $800 — $1,050

J-16 E 12-String

2021. Grand 14-fret, sitka spruce top, rosewood back and sides.

2021 — $1,150 — $1,500

J-18/J-18 M

1987-1996. J-size body with Style 18 appointments, natural, called J-18M for '87-'89.

1987-1989 — J-18M — $1,550 — $2,000

1990-1996 — J-18 — $1,550 — $2,000

J-21 MC

1986. J cutaway, oval soundhole.

1986 — $1,725 — $2,200

J-21/J-21 M

1985-1996. Called J-21M prior to '90, Indian rosewood back and sides, black binding, rosewood 'board, chrome tuners.

1985-1989 — J-21 M — $1,625 — $2,100

1990-1996 — J-21 — $1,625 — $2,100

J-40

1990-present. Called J-40 M from '85-'89, Jumbo, Indian rosewood back and sides, triple-bound 'board, hexagonal inlays.

1990-2020 — $2,250 — $2,950

J-40 BK

1990-1997. Black finish and 'guard, gold hardware.

1990-1997 — $2,250 — $2,950

J-40 Custom

1993-1996. J-40 with upgrades including abalone top trim and rosette.

1993-1996 — $2,250 — $2,950

MODEL YEAR	FEATURES	EXC. COND. LOW	HIGH

J-40 M/J-40 MBK

1985-1989. Jumbo, Indian rosewood back and sides, triple-bound 'board, hexagonal inlays, MBK ('88-'89) indicates black, name changed to J-40 in '90.

1985-1989	J-40 M	$2,250	$2,950
1988-1989	J-40 MBK	$2,250	$2,950

J-40 MBLE

1987. Brazilian rosewood, Style 45 snowflakes, 17 made.

1987		$4,500	$5,900

J-40 MC

1987-1989. Rounded Venetian cutaway version of J-40 M, oval soundhole, gold-plated enclosed tuners. Becomes JC-40 in '90.

1987-1989		$2,350	$3,050

J-41 Special

2004-2007. East Indian rosewood back and sides, Style 45 snowflake inlays.

2004-2007		$2,300	$3,000

J-45 M Deluxe

1986. Guitar of the Month, East Indian rosewood back and sides, tortoise-colored binding, mother-of-pearl and abalone, gold tuners with ebony buttons.

1986		$3,000	$4,000

J-65 Custom/J-65 FM

1993-1996. White binding, herringbone. Available with MEQ electronics.

1993-1996		$2,025	$2,650
1993-1996	With MEQ	$2,025	$2,650

J-65/J-65 E/J-65 M

1985-1995. Jumbo, maple back and sides, gold-plated tuners, scalloped bracing, ebony 'board, tortoise shell-style binding.

1985-1995		$1,900	$2,500

JC Buddy Guy

2006-2007. Only 36 made, rosewood back and sides.

2006-2007		$2,700	$3,500

JC-1 E

1999-2002. Jumbo, mahogany, cutaway, pickup.

1999-2002		$850	$1,100

JC-16 GTE

2000-2003. Jumbo, cutaway, mahogany back and sides, gloss top, Fishman.

2000-2003		$925	$1,175

JC-16 GTE Premium

2003-2005. Fishman Prefix Stereo Blender pickup system.

2003-2005		$1,000	$1,300

JC-16 KWS Kenny Wayne Shepherd Signature

2001-2002. Cutaway, blue lacquer top, back and sides in gloss black, on-board electronics, 198 made.

2001-2002	198 made	$1,150	$1,500

JC-16 ME Aura

2006-2009. JC-16 with maple back and sides, Fishman Aura.

2006-2009		$1,400	$1,800

JC-16 RE Aura

2006-2011. Like ME, but with rosewood back and sides.

2006-2011		$1,400	$1,800

MODEL YEAR	FEATURES	EXC. COND. LOW	HIGH

JC-16 RGTE Aura

2000-2003. Like RE Aura, but with gloss top.

2000-2003		$925	$1,175

JC-16 WE

2002-2003. Jumbo cutaway, solid walnut sides and back, solid sitka spruce top.

2002-2003		$975	$1,225

JC-40

1990-1997. Renamed from J-40 MC, cutaway flat-top, oval sound hole.

1990-1997		$2,300	$3,000

JSO! Sing Out 60th Pete Seeger

2011. Triangular soundhole, Sitka top, East Indian rosewood back and sides, 2 'guards, 120 made. There was also a 12-string model (J12SO!).

2011		$2,300	$3,000

LE-HMSD 2015 (HMS Dreadnought Battleship)

2015. Limited Edition, HMS Dreadnought Battleship (British Royal Navy) illustrated by artist Robert Goetzl is printed on the sitka spruce top, dark mahogany back and sides, ebony 'board.

2015		$2,750	$3,550

LX Series

2003-present. The LX series is the Little Martin models, featuring small bodies with high pressure wood laminate (HPL) backs and sides with an exterior wood-grain image with a gloss finish. M is for mahogany wood-grain, R for rosewood and K for koa. They are also offered in all solid-colors. A 1 indicates a HPL spruce top, 2 is HPL koa top. E indicates electronics.

2003-2019	LXM	$180	$235
2004-2021	LX1	$190	$250
2004-2021	LXK2	$180	$235
2009	LX Elvis Presley	$320	$415
2009-2021	LX1E	$240	$315
2013-2014	LX1E Ed Sheeran	$300	$395
2013-2019	LXME	$230	$300
2017-2021	LX Black	$180	$235
2019-2021	LX1R	$265	$350
2019-2021	LX1RE	$300	$400

M2C-28

1988. Double-cut, Guitar of the Month, 22 made.

1988		$1,825	$2,350

M-3 H Cathy Fink

2005. M 0000-size body, gloss finish, rosewood sides, 3-piece back with flamed koa center panel, torch headstock inlay, herringbone top trim, no Martin logo on headstock.

2005		$2,000	$2,600

M-3 M George Martin

2005-2006. M Model, Style 40 appointments with Style 42 snowflake inlays, 127 made.

2005-2006		$3,150	$4,100

M-3 SC Shawn Colvin

2002-2003. M 0000-size body, 120 made, mahogany sides, 3-piece mahogany/rosewood back, Fishman, Shawn Colvin & C.F.M. III signed label.

2002-2003		$1,775	$2,300

2003 Martin JC-16 RGTE Aura

Imaged by Heritage Auctions, HA.com

2019 Martin LX1RE

Gil Hembree

Martin M-36

1979 Martin M-38

Gantt Kushner

MODEL YEAR — FEATURES — EXC. COND. LOW — HIGH

M-16 GT
2001-2003. M-size single cut, gloss top, mahogany sides and back.

Year	Features	Low	High
2001-2003		$750	$1,000

M-18
1984-1988. M size, mahogany.

Year	Features	Low	High
1984-1988		$1,700	$2,225

M-21
December 1984. Guitar of the Month, low profile neck M-Series, Indian rosewood back and sides, special ornamentation.

Year	Features	Low	High
1984		$1,700	$2,225

M-21 Steve Earle
2008-2011. Custom Edition, East Indian rosewood back and sides, Italian Alpine spruce top.

Year	Features	Low	High
2008-2011		$2,200	$2,900

M-30 Jorma Kaukonen
2010-2013. Custom Artist Edition, M 0000-size body, Style 30 appointments, East Indian rosewood back and sides, Maltese diamond/square inlays, optional electronics.

Year	Features	Low	High
2010-2013		$3,500	$4,500

M-35/M-36
1978-1997, 2007-present. First 26 labeled as M-35, Indian rosewood back and sides, bound 'board, low profile neck, multi-bound, white-black-white back stripes.

Year	Features	Low	High
1978	M-35, 26 made	$2,050	$2,700
1978-1979		$2,050	$2,700
1980-1997		$1,900	$2,500
2007-2020		$1,750	$2,300
2008	M-36 175th Anniv	$1,750	$2,300

M-36 B
1985. Brazilian rosewood.

Year	Features	Low	High
1985		$3,500	$4,600

M-38 (0000-38)
1977-1997, 2007-2011. Called 0000-38 (see that listing) in '97-'98, 0000-size, Indian rosewood back and sides, multi-bound.

Year	Features	Low	High
1977-1979		$2,500	$3,300
1980-1989		$2,300	$3,000
1990-1997		$2,300	$3,000
2007-2011		$2,300	$3,000

M-38 B
1985. Brazilian rosewood.

Year	Features	Low	High
1985		$4,500	$5,900

M-42 David Bromberg
2005-2006. 0000-14 body, rosewood back and sides, snowflakes, 83 made.

Year	Features	Low	High
2005-2006		$3,200	$4,200

M-64
1985-1996. Flamed maple back and sides, tortoise-shell-style 'guard and binding. The 11 made in '85 were labeled M-64R.

Year	Features	Low	High
1985-1996		$1,775	$2,300

MC12-41 Richie Sambora
2006. 12-string version of OMC-41 Richie Sambora, planned 200 made combined models.

Year	Features	Low	High
2006		$3,200	$4,200

MC-16 GTE
2002-2004. M-16 GT with single-cut and Fishman.

Year	Features	Low	High
2002-2004		$850	$1,100

MC-16 GTE Premium
2003-2005. Fishman Prefix Stereo Blender pickup system.

Year	Features	Low	High
2003-2005		$1,025	$1,325

MC-28
1981-1996. Rosewood back and sides, single-cut, oval soundhole, scalloped braces.

Year	Features	Low	High
1981-1996		$1,900	$2,500

MC-37 K
1981-1982, 1987-1994. Cutaway, koa back and sides.

Year	Features	Low	High
1981-1994		$2,100	$2,700

MC-38 Steve Howe
2009-2011. Indian rosewood back and sides, cutaway, slot headstock.

Year	Features	Low	High
2009-2011		$4,400	$5,700

MC-68/MC-68 R/MC-68+
1985-1996. Auditorium-size, single-cut, maple back and sides, scalloped bracing, verticle logo, natural or sunburst. In '85 called the MC-68 R (for adjustable truss-rod), 7 with sunburst shaded top option called MC-68+.

Year	Features	Low	High
1985	MC-68R	$1,850	$2,400
1986-1996	MC-68	$1,900	$2,500
1986-1996	MC-68+	$1,900	$2,500

MC-DSM
2007-2010. Limited Edition of 100, cutaway, designed by District Sales Manager (DSM), spruce top, figured koa back and sides.

Year	Features	Low	High
2007-2010		$2,700	$3,400

Mini-Martin Limited Edition
1999-2009. Size 5 Terz body, solid sitka spruce top, rosewood sides and back, vintage style Martin Geib case with green interior.

Year	Features	Low	High
1999-2009		$1,600	$2,050

MMV
2008-2012. D-style, rosewood sides and back, nitro finish.

Year	Features	Low	High
2008-2012		$1,025	$1,325

Model American 1
2018. Limited Edition D-body, United States sourced woods, Adirondack spruce top, sycamore back and sides, cherry neck, black walnut 'board, gloss finish.

Year	Features	Low	High
2018		$1,775	$2,350

MTV-1 Unplugged
1996. Body is 1/2 rosewood and 1/2 mahogany, scalloped bracing, MTV logo on headstock, gloss (588 sold) or satin (73 sold) finish.

Year	Features	Low	High
1996	Gloss finish	$1,350	$1,750
1996	Satin finish	$1,225	$1,600

MTV-2 Unplugged
2003-2004. Body is 1/2 rosewood and 1/2 maple, scalloped bracing, MTV logo on headstock.

Year	Features	Low	High
2003-2004		$1,225	$1,600

N-10
1968-1993. Classical, mahogany back and sides, fan bracing, wood marquetry soundhole ring, unbound rosewood 'board, 12-fret neck and slotted peghead from '70.

Year	Features	Low	High
1968-1970	Short-scale	$1,600	$2,100
1970-1979	Long-scale	$1,500	$1,950
1980-1993	Long-scale	$1,300	$1,675

N-20

1968-1992. Classical, Brazilian rosewood back and sides (changed to Indian rosewood in '69), multi-bound, 12-fret neck, solid headstock (changed to slotted in '70), natural.

MODEL YEAR	FEATURES	EXC. COND. LOW	HIGH
1968-1969	Brazilian, short-scale	$5,500	$7,200
1969	Prismatone pu & Baldwin C-1 Amp	$7,200	$9,500
1970	Indian, short-scale	$2,775	$3,600
1970-1979	Indian, long-scale	$2,775	$3,600
1980-1992	Long-scale	$2,775	$3,600

N-20 B

1985-1986. Brazilian rosewood N-20.

MODEL YEAR	FEATURES	EXC. COND. LOW	HIGH
1985-1986		$5,100	$6,650

N-20WNB 'Trigger'

1998-1999. Designed after Willie Nelson's famous N-20 he named Trigger, 100 made, Brazilian rosewood (30) or Indian (70).

MODEL YEAR	FEATURES	EXC. COND. LOW	HIGH
1998-1999	Brazilian	$6,800	$8,800
1998-1999	Indian	$3,400	$4,400

OM-1

1999-2002, 2009-2010. Sitka spruce top, sapele back and sides, East Indian rosewood 'board, natural satin finish.

MODEL YEAR	FEATURES	EXC. COND. LOW	HIGH
1999-2010		$650	$825

OM-1 GT

2011-2014. OM-1 with gloss top.

MODEL YEAR	FEATURES	EXC. COND. LOW	HIGH
2011-2014		$650	$825

OM-15

2001-2003. Mahogany body, cutaway.

MODEL YEAR	FEATURES	EXC. COND. LOW	HIGH
2001-2003		$800	$1,025

OM-15 M

2015. All mahogany, natural satin finish.

MODEL YEAR	FEATURES	EXC. COND. LOW	HIGH
2015		$800	$1,025

OM-16 GT

2001-2005. Spruce top, mahogany back, sides and neck, natural gloss finish.

MODEL YEAR	FEATURES	EXC. COND. LOW	HIGH
2001-2005		$775	$1,025

OM-18

1930-1934. Orchestra Model, mahogany back and sides, 14-fret neck, solid peghead, banjo tuners (changed to right-angle in '31).

MODEL YEAR	FEATURES	EXC. COND. LOW	HIGH
1930-1931	Banjo tuners, small 'guard	$24,700	$32,000
1931	Standard tuners, small 'guard	$20,000	$26,000
1932-1933	Standard tuners, large 'guard	$15,200	$19,700

OM-18 Authentic 1933

2013-2019. Period-correct (1933) appointments, Vintage Tone System, vintage gloss finish.

MODEL YEAR	FEATURES	EXC. COND. LOW	HIGH
2013-2019		$3,200	$4,150

OM-18 Golden Era

2003-2009. Mahogany back and sides, Brazilian rosewood purfling and binding.

MODEL YEAR	FEATURES	EXC. COND. LOW	HIGH
2003-2009		$2,125	$2,775

OM-18 P

1930-1931. Plectrum.

MODEL YEAR	FEATURES	EXC. COND. LOW	HIGH
1930-1931		$7,250	$9,400

OM-18 Special

2012. Custom Shop model.

MODEL YEAR	FEATURES	EXC. COND. LOW	HIGH
2012		$1,975	$2,575

OM-18 V

1999-2009. Vintage features.

MODEL YEAR	FEATURES	EXC. COND. LOW	HIGH
1999-2009		$1,850	$2,400

OM-18 VLJ Laurence Juber

2002, 2008-2009. Cutaway, Adirondack spruce top.

MODEL YEAR	FEATURES	EXC. COND. LOW	HIGH
2002-2009		$2,800	$3,650

OM-21

1994-present. Indian rosewood back and sides, herringbone back stripe and soundhole ring, 14-fret neck, chrome tuners, natural or sunburst.

MODEL YEAR	FEATURES	EXC. COND. LOW	HIGH
1994-1999		$1,825	$2,375
2000-2020		$1,775	$2,300

OM-21 Special

1991, 2007-2011. Upgrade to ebony 'board, rosewood bindings.

MODEL YEAR	FEATURES	EXC. COND. LOW	HIGH
1992-2011		$1,900	$2,475

OM-21 Special Limited Edition

1991. Custom Shop, prototype to '92 production.

MODEL YEAR	FEATURES	EXC. COND. LOW	HIGH
1991	36 made	$1,900	$2,475

OM-28

1929-1933, 1990-1997, 2015-present. Brazilian rosewood back and sides, 14-fret neck, solid peghead, banjo tuners (changed to right-angle in '31), reintroduced with Indian rosewood for '90-'97 and again in 2015.

MODEL YEAR	FEATURES	EXC. COND. LOW	HIGH
1929	Banjo pegs, small 'guard, pyramid end bridge	$75,000	$97,000
1930	Early '30, banjo tuners, small 'guard, pyramid	$65,000	$84,000
1930	Late '30, banjo tuners, small 'guard, belly bridge	$59,000	$76,000
1931	Early '31, banjo tuners, small 'guard, belly bridge	$59,000	$76,000
1931	Late '31, standard tuners, large 'guard	$49,000	$63,000
1931	Mid '31, banjo tuners, large 'guard	$56,000	$72,000
1932-1933	Standard tuners, full-size 'guard	$49,000	$63,000
1990-1997		$1,800	$2,375
2015-2020		$1,900	$2,475

OM-28 Authentic 1931

2015-2019. Adirondack spruce top, Madagascar rosewood back and sides, Vintage Tone System (VTS).

MODEL YEAR	FEATURES	EXC. COND. LOW	HIGH
2015-2019		$4,400	$5,800

OM-28 E Modern Deluxe

2020-present. Sitka spruce VTS top, East Indian rosewood back and sides, flamed maple binding, gloss finish.

MODEL YEAR	FEATURES	EXC. COND. LOW	HIGH
2020-2021		$3,200	$4,200

OM-28 E Retro

2012-2019. Sitka top, Indian rosewood back and sides, herringbone binding, Fishman.

MODEL YEAR	FEATURES	EXC. COND. LOW	HIGH
2012-2019		$2,000	$2,575

1996 Martin MTV-1 Unplugged

2015 Martin OM-21

Rivington Guitars

2002 Martin OM-45 GE Golden Era

Carter Vintage Guitars

2016 Martin OM True North-16

MODEL YEAR	FEATURES	EXC. COND. LOW	HIGH

OM-28 Golden Era

2003-2004. Brazilian rosewood back and sides, Adirondack spruce top.

2003-2004 $6,450 $8,350

OM-28 Golden Era Guatemalan Rosewood

2015. Custom Shop model, Guatemalan rosewood back and sides.

2015 $3,600 $4,700

OM-28 JM John Mayer

2003. Limited Edition, 404 made.

2003 $6,100 $8,100

OM-28 LE

1985. Limited Edition only 40 made, Guitar of the Month, Indian rosewood back and sides, herringbone top binding, V-neck.

1985 $2,550 $3,300

OM-28 M Roseanne Cash

2008. Signature Edition, Madagascar rosewood back and sides, 100 made.

2008 $3,600 $4,700

OM-28 Marquis

2005-2015. Pre-war appointments, Adirondack top, East Indian rosewood back, sides and headplate.

2005-2015 $2,500 $3,300

OM-28 Marquis Adirondack

2011-2013. Adirondack spruce top.

2011-2013 $2,500 $3,300

OM-28 Marquis Madagascar

2007-2008. Madagascar rosewood.

2007-2008 $2,500 $3,300

OM-28 Modern Deluxe

2019-present. Sitka spruce top with Vintage Tone System (VTS), East Indian rosewood back and sides, '30s style script logo on headstock.

2019-2020 $2,350 $3,050

OM-28 PB Perry Bechtel

1993. Guitar of the Month, signed by Perry Bechtel's widow Ina, Indian rosewood back and sides, zigzag back stripe, chrome tuners, V-neck, 50 made.

1993 $3,500 $4,500

OM-28 SO Sing Out!

1985. For Sing Out! Magazine's 35th anniversary, label signed by Pete Seeger.

1985 $2,400 $3,100

OM-28 V Custom Shop Brazilian and Adirondack

2000-2001. Brazilian rosewood back and sides, Adirondack "red" spruce top, ca. 1933 prewar features including Martin gold headstock decal logo.

2000-2001 $5,725 $7,425

OM-28 VR/OM-28 V

1984-1990, 1999-2014. VR suffix until '99, then just V (Vintage Series), rosewood back and sides.

1984-1999 VR $2,300 $3,000

1999-2014 V $2,300 $3,000

OM-35

2003-2007. 000-size body, Indian rosewood sides and 3-piece back, spruce top, gloss natural finish.

2003-2007 $1,850 $2,425

MODEL YEAR	FEATURES	EXC. COND. LOW	HIGH

OM-40 BLE

1990. Limited Edition, 50 made, Brazilian rosewood back and sides.

1990 $6,300 $8,200

OM-40 LE

1994. Limited Edition, Guitar of the Month, Indian rosewood back and sides, double pearl borders, snowflake inlay on 'board, gold tuners, natural (57 sold) or sunburst (29 sold).

1994 $3,000 $4,000

OM-40 Rory Block

2004. Limited Edition, 38 made, 000-size, Indian rosewood back and sides, Englemann spruce top, 'the road' inlay markers, vintage-auto inlay on headstock.

2004 $2,500 $3,300

OM-41 Special

2005-2006. Rosewood back and sides, Style 45 snowflake inlays.

2005-2006 $2,700 $3,550

OM-42

1930, 1999-present. Indian rosewood back and sides, Style 45 snowflake inlays, there were 2 guitars labeled OM-42 built in 1930.

1930 2 made $79,000 $102,000

1999-2020 $3,200 $4,200

OM-42 Flamed Mahogany

2006. Limited Edition, 30 made, flamed mahogany back and sides, vines.

2006 $5,400 $7,000

OM-42 Koa

2005-2008. Koa sides and back.

2006-2008 $3,200 $4,200

OM-42 PS Paul Simon

1997. Bookmatched sitka spruce top, Indian rosewood back and sides, 42- and 45-style features, low profile PS neck, 500 planned but only 223 made.

1997 $3,200 $4,200

OM-45

1930-1933. OM-style, 45 level appointments. Condition is critically important on this or any ultra high-end instrument, minor flaws are critical to value.

1930 Banjo pegs, 19 made $200,000 $350,000

1931 Right-angle tuners $200,000 $260,000

1932-1933 $200,000 $260,000

OM-45/SOM-45/Special OM-45

1977-1994. First batch labeled SOM-45, 2 labeled OM-45 N in '94 that had square tube bar in neck and without scalloped braces.

1977-1979 $6,200 $8,000

1980-1989 $5,600 $7,300

1990-1994 $5,100 $6,650

1994 OM-45 N option $5,100 $6,650

OM-45 Custom Deluxe

1998-1999. Limited custom shop run of 14, Adirondack spruce and typical Style 45 appointments.

1998-1999 $12,200 $15,800

MODEL YEAR	FEATURES	EXC. COND. LOW	HIGH

OM-45 Deluxe

1930. Only 14 made, Brazilian rosewood back and sides, zipper pattern back stripe, pearl inlay in 'guard and bridge. Condition is critically important on this or any ultra high-end instrument, minor flaws are critical to value.

1930		$200,000	$350,000

OM-45 Deluxe (Special)

1999. 4 made on special order, highly figured Brazilian rosewood.

1999		$16,500	$21,400

OM-45 Deluxe Golden Era

1998. Brazilian, few made.

1998		$16,500	$21,400

OM-45 GE Golden Era

1999, 2001-2005. Red spruce top, Brazilian rosewood.

1999-2005		$16,500	$21,400

OM-45 Tasmanian Blackwood

2005. Limited Edition, 29 made, Tasmanian Blackwood (koa-family) back and sides with curly grain, 000-size, OM and 45 style appointments.

2005		$5,800	$7,500

OM-45/OM-45B Roy Rogers

2006. Limited Edition, based on Roy's 1930 OM-45 Deluxe, Indian rosewood (84 made) or Brazilian rosewood (45B, 14 made).

2006	Brazilian	$17,000	$22,000
2006	Indian	$7,400	$9,600

OM 1833 Custom Shop Limited Edition

2006. Italian alpine spruce top, flamed claro walnut back and sides, 000-size, low profile 14-fret neck, fancy inlay and appointments, natural gloss finish.

2006		$3,000	$3,900

OM True North-16

2016. Custom Shop Limited Edition, 50 made, Adirondack spruce top, figured koa back and sides, back features a compass design inlaid with flamed jarrah, Claro walnut, waterfall bubinga and Paua pearl, ebony headplate has True North design inlaid with mother of pearl.

2016		$7,900	$10,300

OM Chris Hillman

2009-2010. Adirondack top, Indian rosewood back and sides, sunburst.

2009-2010		$2,400	$3,100

OM Jeff Daniels

2012-2013. Based on Daniels 1934 C-2 archtop conversion, Adirondack, Madagascar rosewood back and sides, sunburst.

2012-2013		$2,400	$3,100

OM Negative

2007-2008. Limited Edition, 60 made, black body and white 'board, black inside label signed Dick Boak, gloss finish.

2007-2008		$2,800	$3,600

OMC Aura

2004-2011. OM size, cutaway, rosewood back and sides, Fishman Aura.

2004-2011		$1,750	$2,300

OMC Cherry

2008-2013. Sustainable wood program, solid cherry back and sides, solid rescued spruce top, 000 body, cutaway, Fishman.

2008-2013		$1,725	$2,300

OMC Fingerstyle 1

2005-2008. Cutaway, Spanish cedar back and sides, no inlays.

2005-2008		$1,750	$2,300

OMC Red Birch

2005-2009. Sustainable Series.

2005-2009		$1,650	$2,200

OMC-1 E

2009-2010. Style 28 appointments, cutaway, onboard Fishman.

2009-2010		$750	$975

OMC-15 E

2001-2007. All solid mahogany body.

2001-2007		$925	$1,250

OMC-15 ME

2016-present. Mahogany top, back and sides, East Indian rosewood 'board, Fishman electronics.

2016-2020		$925	$1,250

OMC-16 E Burst

2019-present. Mahogany burst ovangkol gloss top, satin ovangkol back and sides, Fishman electronics.

2019-2020		$1,350	$1,775

OMC-16 E Koa

2005-2009. Koa back and sides, on-board electronics.

2005-2009		$1,275	$1,650

OMC-16 E Maple

2005-2009. Maple, on-board electronics.

2005		$1,275	$1,650

OMC-16 E/E Premium

2003-2007, 2017-2019. Sitka spruce top, sapele back and sides, on-board electronics. Premium model with Prefix Premium Blend electronics. Reintroduced '17 with cherry back and sides and Fishman® Matrix VT.

2003-2007		$1,275	$1,650
2017-2019	16E, Reintroduced	$1,275	$1,650

OMC-16 GTE

2010-2013. Gloss top, satin sapele back and sides.

2010-2013		$1,100	$1,425

OMC-16 RE Aura

2005-2009. East Indian rosewood back and sides, gloss body.

2005-2009		$1,425	$1,850

OMC-16 RE/RE Premium

2003-2005. Solid rosewood back and sides, onboard electronics.

2003-2005		$1,275	$1,650

OMC-16 WE

2002-2003. Walnut back and sides.

2002-2003		$1,275	$1,650

OMC-18 E

2017-2019. Sitka spruce top, mahogany back and sides, ebony 'board, Fishman electronics.

2017-2019		$1,850	$2,400

OMC-18 LJ Laurence Juber

2008-2010. Cutaway 000, Adirondack spruce top.

2008-2010		$2,400	$3,100

Martin OM Jeff Daniels

Martin OMC-16 E Burst

Martin OMJM John Mayer

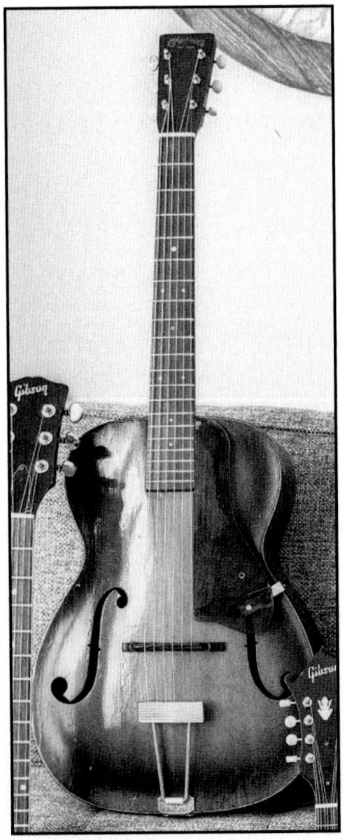

1937 Martin R-18

Frank Manno

MODEL YEAR	FEATURES	EXC. COND. LOW	HIGH

OMC-28

1990. Guitar of the Month, 81 made, Indian rosewood, low profile neck, label signed by C.F. Martin IV.

1990		$1,900	$2,475

OMC-28 BLJ Laurence Juber

2004. Brazilian rosewood, 50 made.

2004		$5,800	$7,600

OMC-28 E

2006-2009, 2017-2019. OMC-28 with Fishman Ellipse. Reintroduced '17 with Fishman Aura.

2006-2009		$1,975	$2,550
2017-2019		$1,975	$2,550

OMC-28 Laurence Juber

2004-2005. OM size, cutaway, Indian rosewood.

2004-2005		$2,800	$3,600

OMC-28 M Laurence Juber

2006-2011. Madagascar rosewood.

2006-2011		$2,900	$3,800

OMC-35 E

2016-2017. Sitka spruce top, East Indian rosewood back & sides, ebony 'board and 'guard, Fishman electronics.

2016-2017		$1,975	$2,575

OMC-41 Richie Sambora

2006-2009. Madagascar rosewood sides and back, combination Style 45 and 41 appointments, 12-string is MC12-41 Richie Sambora, planned 200 made combined models.

2006-2009		$3,600	$4,700

OMC-LJ Pro Laurence Juber

2013. Custom Artist Edition, Adirondack spruce top, flamed maple back and sides.

2013		$2,450	$3,200

OMCPA Series

2010-2019. Performing Artist Series, OM size, cutaway, acoustic/electric, various woods.

2010-2016	OMCPA1/1 Plus	$1,650	$2,150
2011	OMCPA2	$900	$1,175
2011-2013	OMCPA3	$1,150	$1,500
2011-2019	OMCPA4 Sapele	$925	$1,200
2012-2019	OMCPA4 Rosewood	$925	$1,200
2013-2016	OMCPA5 Black	$400	$500

OMCRE

2008-2009. Carpathian spruce top, East Indian rosewood sides and back, Babicz adjustable neck joint, Fishman, gloss finish.

2008-2009		$1,650	$2,200

OMC-X1E Black

2020-present. Replaces OMCXAE Black. Jett black HPL top, back and sides, Fishman electronics.

2020		$375	$500

OMCXK2E

2006-2009. Hawaiian Koa HPL (high pressure laminate) textured finish.

2006-2009		$475	$625

OMJM John Mayer

2003-present. Indian rosewood sides and back.

2003-2020		$2,100	$2,700

OMM

2000-2003. Solid spruce top, mahogany back and sides.

2000-2003		$650	$825

OMM John Renbourne

2011-2013. Madagascar rosewood sides and back.

2011-2013		$2,600	$3,400

OMXAE Black

2014-2019. Black HPL back and sides, black Richlite 'board.

2014-2019		$325	$425

POW MIA

2006-2010. POW MIA logo position marker lettering on fretboard, D-style body, dark finish.

2006-2010		$2,300	$3,000

PS2 Paul Simon Signature

2003. Paul Simon signature logo at bottom of fretboard, 200 made.

2003		$2,200	$2,900

R-15

1934. Archtop, sunburst.

1934	2 made	$1,200	$1,575

R-17

1934-1942. All mahogany, arched top and back, 3-segment f-holes (changed to 1-segment in '37).

1934-1942	940 made	$1,200	$1,575

R-18 P

1934-1936. Only 4 made, plectrum neck.

1934-1936		$1,250	$1,625

R-18 S/R-18

1932-1942. Spruce arched top (carved top by 1937), mahogany back and sides, bound top, sunburst.

1932-1942	1,928 made	$1,650	$2,175

R-18 T

1934-1941. Tenor archtop, 14 3/8" lower bout, 2 f-holes, dot markers, sunburst.

1934-1941		$1,300	$1,675

R-21

1938. 000 body archtop, 1 made.

1938		$3,400	$4,425

SC-13 E

2020-present. Road Series, sitka spruce top, koa veneer back and sides, patent-pending Sure Align neck system, Fishman electronics.

2020		$1,100	$1,425

Schoenberg Soloist by C.F. Martin

1987-1994. Designed by Eric Schoenberg with help from luthier Dana Bourgeois, OM body, Brazilian rosewood back and sides.

1987-1994		$4,800	$6,200

Shenandoah Series

1983-1993. Bodies and necks were built in Japan with final assembly and finishing in Nazareth and a Thinline piezo added, styled after U.S. models with a 32 added to the model name.

1983-1993	Various models	$700	$1,200

SP000 Series

1996-2002. Special Edition 000-size, spruce top with aging toner, scalloped bracing, rosewood or mahogany body.

1996-1997	SP000C-16TR	$1,075	$1,375
1996-2002	SP000-16	$1,025	$1,325
1996-2002	SP000-16R	$1,025	$1,325
1996-2002	SP000-16T	$1,025	$1,325
1996-2002	SP000-16TR	$1,025	$1,325

MODEL YEAR	FEATURES	EXC. COND. LOW	HIGH
1997-2002	SP000C-16R	$1,075	$1,375
1999-2002	SP000C-16	$1,075	$1,375
1999-2002	SP000C-16E	$1,125	$1,450
2003	SP000C-16R Custom Shop	$1,850	$2,400

SP00-16 RST Stauffer

2000-2002. Stauffer 6-on-a-side headstock, 12-fret neck, rosewood back and sides.

2000-2002		$1,050	$1,350

SPD12-16 R

1997-2004. 12-string, solid rosewood body, abalone soundhole ring, Style-45 backstripe.

1999-2000		$1,000	$1,300

SPD-16 Series

1997-2004. D-16 Series Special models.

1996-1999	SPD-16TR	$1,025	$1,325
1997-2004	SPD-16	$1,025	$1,325
1997-2004	SPD-16T	$1,025	$1,325
1999-2001	SPD-16B Black	$1,025	$1,325
1999-2002	SPD-16M Maple	$950	$1,225
1999-2002	SPD-16W Walnut	$975	$1,250
2000	SPD-16E	$1,050	$1,350
2000-2002	SPD-16R	$1,025	$1,325
2000-2005	SPD-16K	$1,450	$1,850
2000-2005	SPD-16K2	$1,450	$1,850

SPDC-16 Series

1997-2001. Cutaway version of SPD-16.

1997-1999	SPDC-16TR	$1,025	$1,325
1997-2001	SPDC-16RE Rosewood	$1,075	$1,400
2000-2002	SPDC-16R	$1,025	$1,325

SPJC-16 RE

2000-2003. Single-cut, East Indian rosewood body, 000-size, on-board electronics.

2000-2003		$1,075	$1,400

SPOM-16

1999-2001. Mahogany.

1999-2001		$1,075	$1,400

SS-0041GB-17

2017-2020. Limited Edition of 50, Grand Concert 12-fret, European spruce top with Vintage Tone System (VTS), Guatemalan rosewood back and sides, gloss finish.

2017-2020		$4,725	$6,125

SS-00L41-16

2016-2020. Limited Edition, Adirondack spruce top with Vintage Tone System (VTS), moabi back and sides, mahogany neck, hand-rubbed finish.

2016-2020		$2,800	$3,625

SS-OMVine-16

2016. Limited Edition of 35, NAMM show special, figured English walnut, aluminum vine inlay on ebony 'board.

2016		$7,300	$9,525

Stauffer

1830s-ca.1850s. One of C.F. Martin's earliest models, distinguished by the scrolled, six-on-a-side headstock, ornamentation varies. Each instrument should be evaluated on a case-by-case basis, those in truly original excellent condition may be worth more than the values shown.

1835	Fancy (2nd highest)	$22,000	$37,000
1835	Fancy (highest)	$29,000	$124,000
1835	Mid-level	$16,000	$25,000
1835	Plain (2nd lowest)	$12,000	$18,000
1835	Plain (lowest)	$8,000	$13,000

Sting Mini

2006. 100 made, Size 5, Western red cedar top, Solomon padauk body.

2005-2006		$1,800	$2,300

Stinger

1980s-1990s. Import copy offset S-style electric solidbody.

1980s-90s		$175	$225

SW00-D8 Machiche

2006-2007. Smartwood Limited Edition, 125 made, rescued solid spruce top, sustainable machiche sides and back.

2006-2007		$1,000	$1,300

SWC

1998. Smartwood 'The Sting Signature Classical Model', machiche wood body.

1998		$1,000	$1,300

SWD

1998-2001. Smartwood D-size, built from wood material certified by the Forest Stewardship Council, sitka top, cherry back and sides, natural satin finish.

1998-2001		$850	$1,100

SWD Red Birch

2003-2005. Red Birch.

2003-2005		$850	$1,100

SWDGT

2001-2016. Gloss top SWD.

2001-2016		$850	$1,100

SWDTG

2000-2007. Cherry back and sides, gloss finish.

2000-2007		$850	$1,100

SWMGT

2002-2003. M size, cherry back and sides, gloss finish.

2002-2003		$850	$1,100

SWOM

2000-2001. Sustainable Woods Series.

2000-2001		$850	$1,100

SWOMGT

2001-2018. Smartwood OM, rescued solid sitka spruce top, sustainable cherry sides and back, gloss finish.

2001-2018		$850	$1,100

Yuengling 180th Anniversary Custom

2008. Celebrating 180th company anniversary, limited production, large company logo on top of body, fancy D-41 style appointments, certificate.

2008		$2,600	$3,400

Maruha

1960s-1970s. Japanese-made acoustic, classical, archtop and solidbody guitars, often copies of American brands. Probably not imported into the U.S.

2016 Martin SS-OMVine-16

Martin SWOMGT

1962 Maton EG240SE

McCurdy The Moderna

MODEL YEAR	FEATURES	EXC. COND. LOW	HIGH

Marvel

1950s-mid-1960s. Brand name used for budget guitars and basses marketed by Peter Sorkin Company in New York, New York. Sorkin manufactured and distributed Premier guitars and amplifiers made by its Multivox subsidiary. Marvel instruments were primarily beginner-grade. Brand disappears by mid-'60s. The name was also used on archtop guitars made by Regal and marketed by the Slingerland drum company in the 1930s to early 1940s.

Electric

1940s-1950s. Various models.

1940s-50s	$180	$430

Marveltone by Regal

1925-1930. Private branded by Regal, Marveltone pearl style logo on headstock.

Guitar

1925-1930. 14" Brazilian rosewood.

1925-1930	$1,900	$2,500

Masaki Sakurai

See Kohno brand.

Mason

1936-1939. Henry L. Mason on headstock, wholesale distribution, similar to Gibson/Cromwell, pressed wood back and sides.

Student/Intermediate Student

1936-1939. Various flat-top and archtop student/budget models.

1936-1939	$450	$750

Mason Bernard

1990-1991. Founded by Bernie Rico (BC Rich founder). During this period BC Rich guitars were licensed and controlled by Randy Waltuch and Class Axe. Most Mason models were designs similar to the BC Rich Assassin, according to Bernie Rico only the very best materials were used, large MB logo on headstock. Around 225 guitars were built bearing this brand.

Maton

1946-present. Intermediate and professional grade, production/custom, acoustic, acoustic/electric, hollowbody and solidbody guitars built in Box Hill, Victoria, Australia. Founded by Bill May and his brother Reg and still run by the family. Only available in USA since '82.

Matsuda Guitars

See listing for Michihiro Matsuda.

Matsuoka

1970s. Ryoji Matsuoka from Japan built intermediate grade M series classical guitars that often featured solid tops and laminated sides and back.

Matt Pulcinella Guitars

1998-present. Production/custom, professional grade, electric guitars and basses built in Chadds Ford, Pennsylvania by luthier Matt Pulcinella.

Mauel Guitars

Luthier Hank Mauel builds his premium grade, custom, flat-tops in Auburn, California. He began in 1995.

Maurer

Late 1880s-1944. Robert Maurer built guitars and mandolins in the late 1880s under the Maurer and Champion brands in his Chicago shop. Carl and August Larson bought the company in 1900 and retained the Maurer name. The Larsons also built under the Prairie State, Euphonon, W. J. Dyer and Wm. C. Stahl brands.

Max B

2000-present. Luthier Sebastien Sulser builds professional grade, production/custom, electric guitars and basses in Kirby, Vermont.

May Bell

1923-1940s. Brand of flat-top guitars, some with fake resonators, marketed by the Slingerland Company. Most were made by Regal.

Maya

See El Maya.

McAlister Guitars

1997-present. Premium grade, custom, flat-tops built by luthier Roy McAlister in Watsonville, California.

McCollum Guitars

1994-2009. Luthier Lance McCollum builds his premium grade, custom, flat-top and harp guitars in Colfax, California. McCollum died in 2009.

McCurdy Guitars

1983-present. Premium grade, production/custom, archtops built by luthier Ric McCurdy originally in Santa Barbara, California and, since '91, New York, New York.

McElroy

1995-present. Premium grade, custom, classical and flat-top steel string acoustic guitars built by luthier Brent McElroy in Seattle, Washington.

McGill Guitars

1976-present. Luthier Paul McGill builds his premium grade, production/custom, classical, resonator, and acoustic/electric guitars in Nashville, Tennessee.

MODEL YEAR	FEATURES	EXC. COND. LOW	HIGH

McGlincy

Ca. 1974-ca. 1978. Custom flat-tops built by luthier Edward McGlincy in Toms River, New Jersey. Only 12 instruments made and owners included Gordon Lightfoot and David Bromberg. He later offered uke and guitar kits. He also operated Ed's Musical Instruments. McGlincy died in '97.

McGlynn Guitars

2005-2007. Luthier Michael J. McGlynn built his premium and presentation grade, custom, solidbody guitars in Henderson, Nevada. McGlynn died in '07.

McGowan Guitars

Luthier Brian McGowan builds his production/custom, premium grade, steel-string acoustic guitars in Hampton, Virginia. He began in 2004.

MCI, Inc

1967-1988. MusiConics International (MCI), of Waco, Texas, introduced the world to the Guitorgan, invented by Bob Murrell. Later, they also offered effects and a steel guitar. In the '80s, a MIDI version was offered. MCI was also involved with the Daion line of guitars in the late '70s and early '80s. MCI also built a double-neck lap steel.

GuitOrgan B-35

1970s (ca. 1976-1978?). Duplicated the sounds of an organ and more. MCI bought double-cut semi-hollow body guitars from others and outfitted them with lots of switches and buttons. Each fret has 6 segments that correspond to an organ tone. There was also a B-300 and B-30 version, and the earlier M-300 and 340.

1970s	Fully functional	$925	$1,250

McInturff

1996-present. Professional and premium grade, production/custom, solidbody guitars built by luthier Terry C. McInturff originally in Holly Springs, North Carolina, and since '04, in Moncure, North Carolina. McInturff spent 17 years doing guitar repair and custom work before starting his own guitar line.

McKnight Guitars

1992-present. Luthier Tim McKnight builds his custom, premium grade, acoustic steel string guitars in Morral, Ohio.

McPherson Guitars

1981-present. Premium grade, production, flat-tops built by luthier Mander McPherson in Sparta, Wisconsin.

Mean Gene

1988-1990. Heavy metal style solidbodies made by Gene Baker, who started Baker U.S.A. guitars in '97, and Eric Zoellner in Santa Maria, California. They built around 30 custom guitars. Baker currently builds b3 guitars.

MODEL YEAR	FEATURES	EXC. COND. LOW	HIGH

Megas Guitars

1989-present. Luthier Ted Megas builds his premium grade, custom, archtop and solidbody guitars, originally in San Francisco, and currently in Portland, Oregon.

Melancon

Professional and premium grade, custom/production, solid and semi-hollow body guitars and basses built by luthier Gerard Melancon, beginning in 1995, in Thibodaux, Louisiana.

Mello, John F.

1973-present. Premium grade, production/custom, classical and flat-top guitars built by luthier John Mello in Kensington, California.

Melophonic

1960s. Brand built by the Valco Company of Chicago, Illinois.

Resonator Guitar

1965. Valco-made.

1965		$725	$950

Melville Guitars

1988-present. Luthier Christopher Melville builds his premium grade, custom, flat-tops in Milton, Queensland, Australia.

Memphis

One of the many guitar brands built by Japan's Matsumoku company.

Mercurio

2002-2005. Luthier Peter Mercurio built his custom/production solidbody guitars, featuring his interchangeable PickupPak system to swap pickups, in Chanhassen, Minnesota.

Mermer Guitars

Luthier Richard Mermer, started building in 1983, premium grade, production/custom, steel-string, nylon-string, and Hawaiian guitars in Sebastian, Florida.

Merrill Brothers

Premium grade, production/custom, steel-string and harp guitars built by luthiers Jim and Dave Merrill in Williamsburg, Virginia, starting in 1998.

Mesrobian

1995-present. Luthier Carl Mesrobian builds his professional and premium grade, custom, archtop guitars in Salem, Massachusetts.

Messenger

1967-1968. Built by Musicraft, Inc., originally of 156 Montgomery Street, San Francisco, California. The distinguishing feature of the Messengers is a metal alloy neck which extended through the body to the tailblock, plus mono or stereo outputs.

Late-1970s MCI B-35 Guitorgan
Tom Pfeifer

Messenger
Jamsy

Michihiro Matsuda OM

Microfrets Plainsman

Michael Kellum

MODEL YEAR	FEATURES	EXC. COND. LOW	HIGH

Sometime before March '68 the company relocated to Astoria, Oregon. Press touted "improved" magnesium neck, though it's not clear if this constituted a change from '67. Brand disappears after '68. They also made basses.

Electric Hollowbody Archtop

1967-1968. Symmetrical double-cut body shape, metal neck with rosewood 'boards, stereo.

1967-1968		$1,700	$2,200

Metropolitan

1995-2008. Professional and premium grade, production/custom, retro-styled solidbodies designed by David Wintz reminiscent of the '50s National Res-o-glas and wood body guitars. They featured full-scale set-neck construction and a wood body instead of Res-o-glas. Wintz also made Robin and Alamo brand instruments.

Electric Solidbody

1995-2008	Various models	$1,500	$1,950

Meyers Custom Guitars

Professional grade, custom, solidbody electric guitars built by luthier Donald Meyers in Houma, Louisiana, beginning 2005.

Miami

1920s. Instruments built by the Oscar Schmidt Co. and possibly others. Most likely a brand made for a distributor.

Michael Collins Custom Guitars

Premium grade, custom/production, classical, flamenco and steel string guitars built in Argyle, New York, by luthier Michael Collins, starting in 1975.

Michael Collins Guitars

Luthier Michael Collins builds his professional and premium grade, custom, Selmer style, archtop and flat-top guitars, starting in 2002, in Keswick, Ontario. He also builds mandolins.

Michael Cone

1968-present. Presentation grade, production/custom, classical guitars built previously in California and currently in Kihei Maui, Hawaii by luthier Michael Cone. He also builds ukuleles.

Michael Dunn Guitars

Luthier Michael Dunn begins in 1968, builds production/custom Maccaferri-style guitars in New Westminster, British Columbia. He also offers a harp uke and a Weissenborn- or Knutsen-style Hawaiian guitar, and has built archtops.

Michael Kelly

1999-present. Founded by Tracy Hoeft and offering intermediate and professional grade, production, acoustic, solidbody and archtop guitars. The brand was owned by the Hanser Music Group from 2004-'15. They also offer mandolins and basses.

Michael Lewis Instruments

1992-present. Luthier Michael Lewis builds his premium and presentation grade, custom, archtop guitars in Grass Valley, California. He also builds mandolins.

Michael Menkevich

Luthier Michael Menkevich builds his professional and premium grade, production/custom, flamenco and classical guitars in Elkins Park, Pennsylvania, starting in 1970.

Michael Silvey Custom Guitars

2003-ca. 2007. Solidbody electric guitars built by Michael Silvey in North Canton, Ohio.

Michael Thames

1972-present. Luthier Michael Thames builds his premium grade, custom/production, classical guitars in Taos, New Mexico.

Michael Tuttle

2003-present. Professional and premium grade, custom, solid and hollowbody guitars and basses built by luthier Michael Tuttle in Saugus, California.

Michihiro Matsuda

1997-present. Presentation grade, production/custom, steel and nylon string acoustic guitars built by luthier Michihiro Matsuda in Oakland, California. He also builds harp guitars.

Microfrets

1967-1975, 2004-2005. Professional grade, production, electric guitars built in Myersville, Maryland. They also built basses. Founded by Ralph S. Jones, Sr. in Frederick, Microfrets offered over 20 models of guitars that sported innovative designs and features, with pickups designed by Bill Lawrence. The brand was revived, again in Frederick, by Will Meadors and Paul Rose in '04.

Serial numbers run from about 1000 to about 3800. Not all instruments have serial numbers, particularly ones produced in '75. Serial numbers do not appear to be correlated to a model type, but are sequential by the general date of production.

Instruments can be identified by body styles as follows; Styles 1, 1.5, 2, and 3. An instrument may be described as a Model Name and Style Number (for example, Covington Style 1). Style 1 has a waveyshaped pickguard with control knobs mounted below the guard and the 2-piece guitar body has a particle board side gasket. Style 1.5 has the same guard and knobs, but no side body gasket. Style 2 has an oblong pickguard with top mounted control knobs and a pancake style seam between the top

MODEL YEAR	FEATURES	EXC. COND. LOW	HIGH

and lower part of the body. Style 3 has a seamless 2-piece body and a Speedline neck.

Baritone Signature

1971. Baritone version of Signature Guitar, sharply pointed double-cut, with or without f-holes, single- or double-dot inlays.

1971	$1,100	$1,400

Baritone Stage II

1971-ca. 1975. Double-cut, 2 pickups.

1971-1975	$1,100	$1,400

Calibra I

1969-1975. Double-cut, 2 pickups, f-hole.

1969-1975	$950	$1,250

Covington

1967-1969. Offset double-cut, 2 pickups, f-hole.

1967-1969	$1,400	$1,850

Golden Comet

1969. Double-cut, 2 pickups, f-hole, name changed to Wanderer.

1969	$1,200	$1,600

Golden Melody

1969, 2004-2005. Offset double-cut, 2 pickups, f-hole, name changed to Stage II in '69.

1969-1971	$1,325	$1,750

Huntington

1969-1975. Double-cut, 2 pickups.

1969-1975	$1,400	$1,850

Orbiter

1967-1969. Odd triple cutaway body, thumbwheel controls on bottom edge of 'guard.

1967-1969	$1,400	$1,850

Plainsman

1967-1969. Offset double-cut, 2 pickups, f-hole, thumbwheel controls on bottom edge of 'guard.

1967-1969	$1,500	$1,975

Signature

1967-1969. Double-cut, 2 pickups.

1967-1969	$1,400	$1,850

Spacetone

1969-1971, 2004-2005. Double-cut semi-hollow body, 2 pickups.

1969-1971	$1,400	$1,850

Stage II

1969-1975. Renamed from Golden Melody, offset double-cut, 2 pickups.

1969-1975	$1,325	$1,750

Swinger

1971-1975. Offset double-cut, 2 pickups.

1971-1975	$1,400	$1,850

Voyager/The Voyager

1967-1968. Early model, less than a dozen made, Voyager headstock logo (no Microfrets logo), 2 DeArmond-style single-coils, offset double-cut body, FM transmitter on upper bass bout facilitates wireless transmission to Microfrets receiver or FM radio.

1967-1968	$2,500	$3,300

Wanderer

1969-1971. Renamed from Golden Comet, double-cut, 2 pickups.

1969-1971	$1,200	$1,600

MODEL YEAR	FEATURES	EXC. COND. LOW	HIGH

Mike Lull Custom Guitars

1995-present. Professional and premium grade, production/custom, guitars and basses built by luthier Mike Lull in Bellevue, Washington.

Milburn Guitars

1990-present. Luthiers Orville and Robert Milburn build their premium grade, custom, classical guitars in Sweet Home, Oregon.

Miller

1960s. One of the brand names of guitars built for others by Egmond in Holland.

Minarik

Luthier M.E. Minarik builds his professional and premium grade, custom/production, solid and chambered body guitars in Van Nuys, California.

Minerva

1930s. Resonator and archtop guitars sold through catalog stores, likely made by one of the big Chicago builders of the era.

Mirabella

1997-present. Professional and premium grade, custom archtops, flat-tops, hollowbody, and solidbody guitars and basses built by luthier Cristian Mirabella in Babylon, New York. He also builds mandolins and ukes.

Miranda Guitars

2002-present. Owner Phil Green uses components made by various shops in California to assemble and set-up, professional grade, full-size travel/silent-practice guitars in Palo Alto, California.

Mitre

1983-1985. Bolt neck, solidbody guitars and basses made in Aldenville (or East Longmeadow), Massachusetts, featuring pointy body shapes, 2 humbuckers, active or passive electronics.

MJ Guitar Engineering

1993-present. Professional and premium grade, production/custom, hollowbody, chambered and solidbody guitars and basses built by luthier Mark Johnson in Rohnert Park, California.

Mobius Megatar

2000-2019. Professional grade, production, hybrid guitars designed for two-handed tapping, built in Mount Shasta, California. Founded by Reg Thompson, Henri Dupont, and Traktor Topaz in '97, they released their first guitars in '00.

Modulus

1978-2013. Founded by Geoff Gould in the San Francisco area, and later built in Novato, California. Modulus built professional grade, production/custom, solidbody electric guitars up to '05.

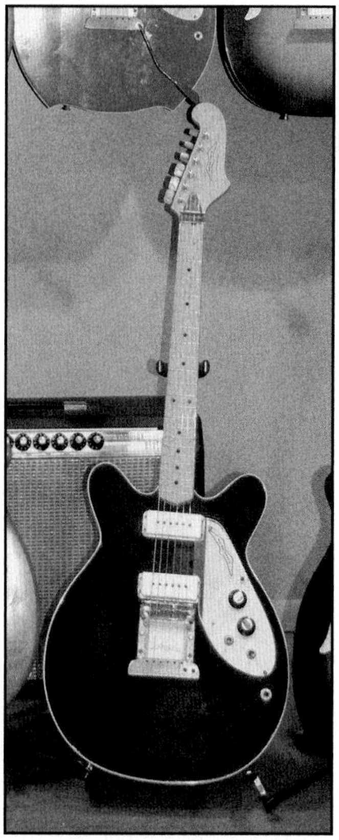

Microfrets Spacetone
Michael Kellum

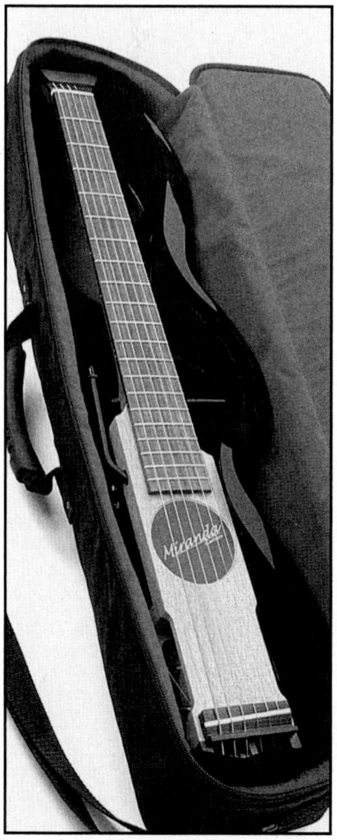

Miranda Travel Guitar

Moll Custom Instruments

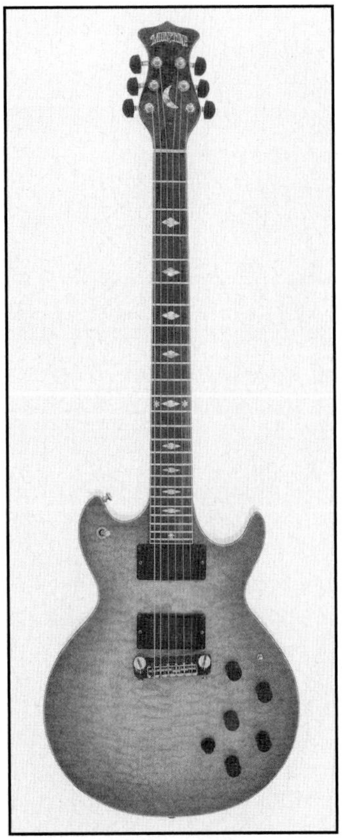

1980 Moonstone Vulcan Deluxe

MODEL YEAR	FEATURES	EXC. COND. LOW	HIGH

Genesis 2/2T

1996-2005. Double-cut, extended bass horn alder body, bolt-on carbon fiber/red cedar neck, hum-single-single pickups, locking vibrato (2T model).

1996-2005		$1,200	$1,600

Moll Custom Instruments

1996-present. Luthier Bill Moll builds his professional and premium grade, archtops in Springfield, Missouri. He has also built violins, violas and cellos.

Monrad, Eric

1993-present. Premium, custom, flamenco and classical guitars built by luthier Eric Monrad in Healdsburg, California.

Monroe Guitars

Luthier Matt Handley builds his custom, professional grade, solidbody electric guitars and basses in State Center, Iowa. He started in 2004.

Montalvo

See listing under Casa Montalvo.

Montaya

Late 1970s-1980s. Montaya Hyosung 'America' Inc., Korean acoustic and electric import copies.

Monteleone

1976-present. Presentation grade, production/custom, archtop guitars built by Luthier John Monteleone in Islip, New York. He also builds mandolins. Instruments should be evaluated on a case-by-case basis.

Montgomery Ward

The mail-order and retail giant offered a variety of instruments and amps from several different U.S. and overseas manufacturers.

Model 8379/H44 Stratotone

Mid-1950s. Private branded Harmony Stratotone, some without logo but with crown-style stencil/painted logo on headstock, many with gold-copper finish, 1 pickup.

1957		$600	$800

Monty

1980-present. Luthier Brian Monty builds his professional, premium and presentation grade, production/custom, archtop, semi-hollow, solidbody, and chambered electric guitars originally in Lennoxville, Quebec, and currently in Anne de Prescott, Ontario.

Moog

1964-present. Moog introduced its premium grade, production, Harmonic Control System solidbody guitar in 2008. They also offer guitar effects.

MODEL YEAR	FEATURES	EXC. COND. LOW	HIGH

Moon (Japan)

1979-present. Professional and premium grade, production/custom, guitars and basses made in Japan.

Moon (Scotland)

1979-present. Intermediate, professional and premium grade, production/custom, acoustic and electric guitars built by luthier Jimmy Moon in Glasgow, Scotland. They also build mandolin family instruments.

Moonstone

1972-present. Professional, premium, and presentation grade production/custom flat-top, solid and semi-hollow electric guitars, built by luthier Steve Helgeson in Eureka, California. He also builds basses. Higher unit sales in the early-'80s. Some models have an optional graphite composite neck built by Modulus.

Eclipse Standard

1979-1983. Figured wood body, offset double-cut, neck-thru, dot markers, standard maple neck, natural finish.

1979-1983		$1,350	$1,750
1979-1983	XII	$1,350	$1,750

Exploder

1980-1983. Figured wood solidbody, neck-thru, standard maple neck, natural finish.

1980-1983		$1,500	$2,000

Flaming V

1980-1984. Figured wood body, V-shaped, neck-thru, standard maple neck, natural finish.

1980-1984		$1,500	$2,000

M-80

1980-1984. Figured wood double-cut semi-hollow body, standard maple or optional graphite neck, natural finish.

1980s	Maple or graphite	$2,300	$3,000

Vulcan Deluxe

1979-1983. Figured maple carved-top body, offset double-cut, diamond markers, standard maple or optional graphite neck, natural finish.

1979-1983	Maple or graphite	$2,200	$2,900

Vulcan Standard

1979-1983. Mahogany carved-top body, offset double-cutaway, dot markers, standard maple or optional graphite neck, natural finish.

1979-1983	Maple or graphite	$2,000	$2,600

Morales

Ca.1967-1968. Guitars and basses made in Japan by Zen-On, not heavily imported into the U.S., if at all.

Solidbody Electric

1967-1968	Various models	$125	$300

More Harmony

1930s. Private branded by Dobro for Dailey's More Harmony Music Studio. Private branding for catalog companies, teaching studios, publishers,

MODEL YEAR	FEATURES	EXC. COND. LOW	HIGH

and music stores was common for the Chicago makers. More Harmony silk-screen logo on the headstock.

Dobro

1930s. 14" wood body with upper bout f-holes and metal resonator, sunburst.

1930s		$825	$1,075

Morgaine Guitars

Luthier Jorg Tandler builds his professional and premium grade, production/custom electrics in Germany, starting in 1994.

Morgan Monroe

1999-present. Intermediate grade, production, acoustic, acoustic/electric and resonator guitars and basses made in Korea and distributed by SHS International of Indianapolis, Indiana. They also offer mandolins and banjos.

Morris

1967-present. Intermediate, professional and premium grade, production, acoustic guitars imported by Moridaira of Japan. Morris guitars were first imported into the U.S. from the early '70s to around '90. They are again being imported into the U.S. starting in 2001. They also offered mandolins in the '70s.

000 Copy

1970s. Brazilian rosewood laminate body.

1970s		$450	$600

Acoustic-Electric Archtop

1970s. Various models.

1970s		$575	$750

D-45 Copy

1970s. Brazilian laminate body.

1970s		$525	$700

Mortoro Guitars

1992-present. Luthier Gary Mortoro builds his premium grade, custom, archtop guitars in Miami, Florida.

Mosrite

The history of Mosrite has more ups and downs than just about any other guitar company. Founder Semie Moseley had several innovative designs and had his first success in 1954, at age 19, building doubleneck guitars for super picker Joe Maphis and protégé Larry Collins. Next came the Ventures, who launched the brand nationally by playing Mosrites and featuring them on album covers. At its '60s peak, the company was turning out around 1,000 guitars a month. The company ceased production in '69, and Moseley went back to playing gospel concerts and built a few custom instruments during the '70s.

In the early-'80s, Mosrite again set up shop in Jonas Ridge, North Carolina, but the plant burned down in November '83, taking about 300 guitars with it. In early-'92, Mosrite relocated to Booneville, Arkansas, producing a new line of Mosrites, of which 96% were exported to Japan, where the Ventures and Mosrite have always been popular. Semie Moseley died, at age 57, on August 7, '92 and the business carried on until finally closing its doors in '93. The Mosrite line has again been revived, offering intermediate and premium grade, production, reissues.

Throughout much of the history of Mosrite, production numbers were small and model features often changed. As a result, exact production dates are difficult to determine.

Balladeer

1964-1965. Mid-size flat-top, slope shoulder, natural or sunburst.

1964-1965		$1,075	$1,400

Brass Rail

1970s. Double-cut solidbody, has a brass plate running the length of the 'board.

1970s		$1,000	$1,300

Celebrity 1

Late-1960s-1970s. Thick hollowbody, 2 pickups, sunburst.

1960s-70s		$1,000	$1,300

Celebrity 2 Standard

Late-1960s-1970s. Thin hollowbody, 2 pickups, in the '70s, it came in a Standard and a Deluxe version.

1960s-70s		$1,000	$1,300

Celebrity 3

Late-1960s-1970s. Thin hollowbody, double-cut, 2 pickups, f-holes.

1960s-70s		$1,000	$1,300

Combo Mark 1

1966-1968. Bound body, 1 f-hole.

1966-1968		$1,500	$1,975

Custom-Built

1952-1962. Pre-production custom instruments hand-built by Semie Moseley, guidance pricing only, each instrument will vary. A wide variety of instruments were made during this period. Some were outstanding, but others, especially those made around '60, could be very basic and of much lower quality. Logos would vary widely and some '60 logos looked especially homemade.

1952-1959	Rare, higher-end	$9,500	$13,000
1960-1962	Common, lower-end	$1,500	$2,000

D-40 Resonator

1960s. Symmetrical double-cut thinline archtop-style body with metal resonator in center of body, 2 pickups, 2 control knobs and toggle switch.

1960s		$1,100	$1,450

D-100 Californian

1960s. Double-cut, resonator guitar with 2 pickups.

1967		$1,100	$1,450

Gospel

1967. Thinline double-cut, f-hole, 2 pickups, vibrato, Gospel logo on headstock.

1967	Sunburst	$1,400	$1,850
1967	White	$1,950	$2,550

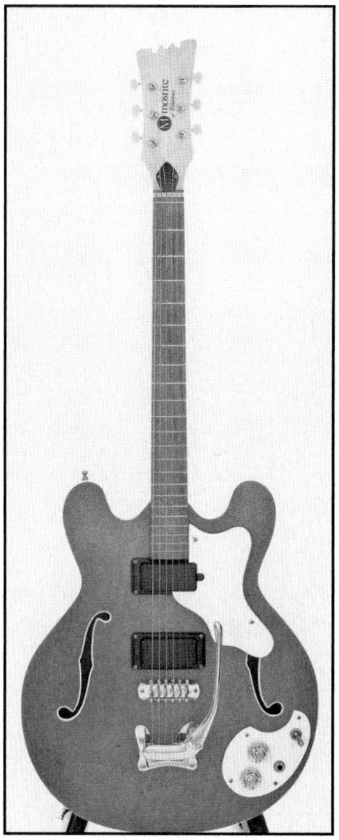

1967 Mosrite Celebrity 3

Imaged by Heritage Auctions, HA.com

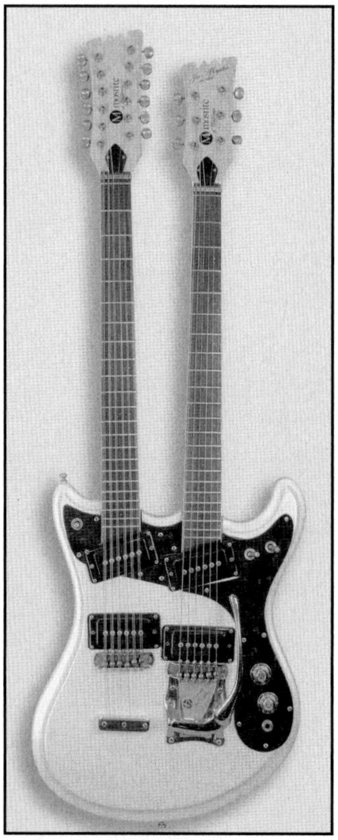

Mosrite Joe Maphis Doubleneck

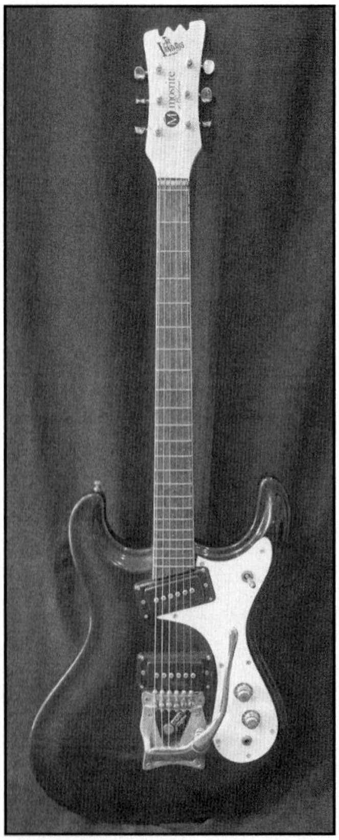

1965 Mosrite Ventures Model

Vic Hines

1975 Mossman Great Plains

David Stone

MODEL YEAR	FEATURES	EXC. COND. LOW	HIGH

Joe Maphis Doubleneck

1963-1968. Limited Edition reissue of the guitar Semie Moseley made for Maphis, with the smaller octave neck, sunburst.

1963-1968	Octave 6/ standard 6	$3,600	$4,800
1963-1968	Standard 6/12	$3,600	$4,800

Joe Maphis Mark 1

1959-1972. Semi-hollow double-cut, 2 single-coils, spruce top, walnut back, rosewood 'board, natural.

1959-1972		$1,700	$2,200

Joe Maphis Mark XVIII

1960s. 6/12 doubleneck, double-cut, 2 pickups on each neck, Moseley tremolo on 6-string.

1960s		$2,800	$3,600

Mosrite 1988

1988-early-1990s. Has traditional Mosrite body styling, Mosrite pickups and bridge.

1988		$550	$725

Octave Guitar

1963-1965. 14" scale, 1 pickup, Ventures Mosrite body style, single neck pickup, very few made.

1963-1965		$4,100	$5,400

Stereo 350

1974-1975. Single-cut solidbody, 2 outputs, 2 pickups, 4 knobs, slider and toggle, black.

1974-1975		$1,100	$1,475

Ventures Model

1963-1968. Double-cut solidbody, triple-bound body '63, no binding after, Vibramute for '63-'64, Moseley tailpiece '65-'68.

1963	Blue or red, bound	$5,725	$7,425
1963	Sunburst, bound	$4,775	$6,150
1964	Blue or red, Vibramute	$4,250	$5,500
1964	Sunburst, Vibramute	$3,925	$5,100
1965	Moseley (2 screws)	$3,100	$4,000
1965	Vibramute, (3 screws)	$3,700	$4,800
1966-1968	Moseley	$2,600	$3,400

Ventures (Jonas Ridge/Boonville)

1982-1993. Made in Jonas Ridge, NC or Booneville, AR, classic Ventures styling.

1982-1993		$1,625	$2,100

Ventures Mark V

1963-1967. Double-cut solidbody.

1963-1967		$1,350	$1,775

Ventures Mark XII (12-String)

1966-1967. Double-cut solidbody, 12 strings.

1966-1967		$2,400	$3,100

Mossman

Professional and premium grade, production/custom, flat-top guitars built in Sulphur Springs, Texas, starting in 1965. They have also built acoustic basses. Founded by Stuart L. Mossman in Winfield, Kansas. In '75, fire destroyed one company building, including the complete supply of Brazilian rosewood. They entered into an agreement with C.G. Conn Co. to distribute guitars by '77. 1200 Mossman guitars in a Conn warehouse in Nevada were ruined by being heated during the day and frozen during the night. A disagreement about who was responsible resulted in cash flow problems for Mossman. Production fell to a few guitars per month until the company was sold in '86 to Scott Baxendale. Baxendale sold the company to John Kinsey and Bob Casey in Sulphur Springs in '89.

Flint Hills

1970-1979. Flat-top acoustic, East Indian rosewood back and sides.

1970-1979	Indian rosewood	$1,400	$1,800

Flint Hills Custom

1970-1979	Indian rosewood	$1,950	$2,550

Golden Era

1970-1977. D-style, vine inlay and other high-end appointments, Brazilian rosewood back and sides until '76, then Indian rosewood.

1970-1975	Brazilian rosewood	$3,200	$4,100
1976-1977	Indian rosewood	$2,100	$2,700

Golden Era Custom

1970-1975	Brazilian rosewood	$4,400	$5,700

Great Plains

1970-1979. Flat-top, Brazilian rosewood until '75 then Indian rosewood, herringbone trim.

1970-1975	Brazilian rosewood	$2,400	$3,100
1976-1979	Indian rosewood	$1,600	$2,075

Great Plains Custom

1970-1975	Brazilian rosewood	$3,375	$4,375

Southwind

1976-ca. 1986, mid-1990s-2002. Flat-top, abalone trim top.

1976-1979	Indian rosewood	$1,850	$2,400

Tennessee

1972-1979. D-style, spruce top, mahogany back and sides, rope marquetry purfling, rope binding.

1972-1979	Mahogany	$1,075	$1,375

Tennessee 12-String

1975-1979	Mahogany	$1,075	$1,375

Timber Creek

1976-1979. D-style, Indian rosewood back and sides, spruce top.

1976-1979	Indian rosewood	$1,700	$2,200

Winter Wheat

1976-1979, mid-1990s-2000s. Flat-top, Indian rosewood back and sides, abalone trim, natural finish.

1976-1979	Indian rosewood	$1,825	$2,375

Winter Wheat 12-String

1976-1979. 12-string version of Winter Wheat, natural.

1976-1979	Indian rosewood	$1,825	$2,375

MotorAve Guitars

2002-present. Luthier Mark Fuqua builds his professional and premium grade, production, electric guitars originally in Los Angeles, California, and currently in Durham, North Carolina.

Mouradian

1983-present. Luthiers Jim and Jon Mouradian build their professional and premium grade, production/custom, electric guitars and basses in Winchester, Massachusetts. Jim died in 2017.

MODEL YEAR	FEATURES	EXC. COND. LOW	HIGH

Mozart

1930s. Private brand made by Kay.

Hawaiian (Square Neck)

1930s. Spruce top, solid mahogany sides and back, pealoid overlay on peghead with large Mozart inscribed logo, small jumbo 15 1/2" body.

1935-1939		$800	$1,050

Mozzani

Built in shops of Luigi Mozzani (b. March 9, 1869, Faenza, Italy; d. 1943) who opened lutherie schools in Bologna, Cento and Rovereto in 1890s. By 1926 No. 1 and 2 Original Mozzani Model Mandolin (flat back), No. 3 Mandola (flat back), No. 4 6-String Guitar, No. 5 7-, 8-, and 9-String Guitars, No. 6 Lyre-Guitar.

M-Tone Guitars

2009-present. Professional and premium grade, production/custom, solidbody electric guitars built in Portland, Oregon by luthier Matt Proctor.

Muiderman Guitars

1997-present. Custom, premium grade, steel string and classical guitars built by luthier Kevin Muiderman currently in Grand Forks, North Dakota, and previously in Beverly Hills, Michigan, 1997-2001, and Neenah, Wisconsin, '01-'07. He also builds mandolins.

Murph

1965-1967. Mid-level electric semi-hollow and solidbody guitars built by Pat Murphy in San Fernado, California. Murph logo on headstock. They also offered basses and amps.

Electric Solidbody

1965-1967		$925	$1,200

Electric XII

1965-1967		$925	$1,200

Music Man

1972-present. Professional grade, production, solidbody guitars built in San Luis Obispo, California. They also build basses. Founded by ex-Fender executives Forrest White and Tom Walker in Orange County, California. Music Man originally produced guitar and bass amps based on early Fender ideas using many former Fender employees. They contracted with Leo Fender's CLF Research to design and produce a line of solidbody guitars and basses. Leo Fender began G & L Guitars with George Fullerton in '80. In '84, Music Man was purchased by Ernie Ball and production was moved to San Luis Obispo.

Albert Lee Signature

1993-present. Swamp ash body, figured maple neck, 3 pickups, white pearloid 'guard, Pinkburst.

1993-1996	Pinkburst	$1,000	$1,300
1996-2019	Tremolo option	$900	$1,200

Axis

1996-present. Offset double-cut solidbody, figured maple top, basswood body, 2 humbucker pickups, Floyd Rose.

1996-2020		$900	$1,200

Axis Sport

1996-2002. Two P-90s.

1996-2002		$900	$1,200

Axis Super Sport

2003-present. Figured top.

2003-2020		$900	$1,200

Edward Van Halen

1991-1995. Basswood solidbody, figured maple top, bolt-on maple neck, maple 'board, binding, 2 humbuckers, named changed to Axis.

1991-1995		$2,200	$2,900

John Petrucci 6/JP-6

2008-present. Standard model, basswood body, maple neck, rosewood 'board, various colors with high gloss finish.

2008-2020		$1,300	$1,700

John Petrucci BFR

2011-2020. Ball Family Reserve (BFR).

2011-2020		$1,500	$2,000

Reflex

2011-2017. Referred to as The Game Changer, patent-pending pickup switching system, maple or rosewood neck with matching headstock, black finish.

2011-2017		$1,100	$1,450

S.U.B 1

2004-2006. Offset double-cut solidbody.

2004-2005		$400	$525

Sabre I

1978-1982. Offset double-cut solidbody, maple neck, 2 pickups, Sabre I comes with a flat 'board with jumbo frets.

1978-1982		$900	$1,200

Sabre II

1978-1982. Same as Sabre I, but with an oval 7 1/2" radius 'board.

1978-1982		$900	$1,200

Silhouette

1986-present. Offset double-cut, contoured beveled solidbody, various pickup configurations.

1986-2020		$900	$1,200
2006	20th Anniversary	$900	$1,200

Silhouette 6/12 Double Neck

2009-2014. Alder body, maple or rosewood 'boards, 4 humbuckers.

2009-2014		$1,450	$1,900

Silhouette Special

1995-present. Silhouette with Silent Circuit.

1995-2020		$900	$1,200

Steve Morse Signature

1987-present. Solidbody, 4 pickups, humbuckers in the neck and bridge positions, 2 single-coils in the middle, special pickup switching, 6-bolt neck mounting, maple neck.

1987-2020		$1,250	$1,650

Stingray I

1976-1982. Offset double-cut solidbody, flat 'board radius.

1976-1982		$900	$1,200

Stingray II

1976-1982. Offset double-cut solidbody, rounder 'board radius.

1976-1982		$900	$1,200

1976 Mossman Southwind

1979 Musicman Sabre II

Tom Pfeifer

Nash Guitars S63

John Rutherford

1970s National Big Daddy LP-457-2

Imaged by Heritage Auctions, HA.com

MODEL YEAR	FEATURES	EXC. COND. LOW	HIGH

Musicvox

1996-2001, 2011-present. Intermediate grade, production, imported retro-vibe guitars and basses from Matt Eichen of Cherry Hill, New Jersey.

Myka

2003-present. Luthier David Myka builds his professional and premium grade, custom/production, solidbody, semi-hollowbody, hollowbody, archtop, and flat-top guitars in Seattle, Washington. Until '07 he was located in Orchard Park, New York.

Nady

1976-present. Wireless sound company Nady Systems offered guitars and basses with built-in wireless systems for 1985-'87. Made by Fernandes in Japan until '86, then by Cort in Korea.

Lightning/Lightning II

1985-1987. Double-cut, neck-thru, solidbody, 24 frets, built-in wireless, labeled as just Lightning until cheaper second version (bolt-neck) came out in '86.

1985-1987		$290	$385

Napolitano Guitars

Luthier Arthur Napolitano began in 1993 to build professional and premium grade, custom, archtop guitars in Allentown, New Jersey.

NashGuitars

2001-present. Luthier Bill Nash builds his professional grade, production/custom, aged solidbody electric guitars and basses in Olympia, Washington.

Nashville Guitar Company

1985-present. Professional and premium grade, custom, flat-top guitars built by luthier Marty Lanham in Nashville, Tennessee. He has also built banjos.

National

Ca. 1927-present. Founded in Los Angeles, California as the National String Instrument Corporation by John Dopyera, George Beauchamp, Ted Kleinmeyer and Paul Barth. In '29 Dopyera left to start the Dobro Manufacturing Company with Rudy and Ed Dopyera and Vic Smith. The Dobro company competed with National until the companies reunited. Beauchamp and Barth then left National to found Ro-Pat-In with Adolph Rickenbacker and C.L. Farr (later becoming Electro String Instrument Corporation, then Rickenbacher). In '32 Dopyera returns to National and National and Dobro start their merger in late-'33, finalizing it by mid-'34. Throughout the '30s, National and Dobro maintained separate production, sales and distribution. National Dobro moved to Chicago, Illinois in '36. In Chicago, archtop and flat-top bodies are built primarily by Regal and Kay; after '37 all National resonator guitar bodies made by Kay. L.A. production is maintained until around '37, although some assembly of Dobros continued in L.A. (primarily for export) until '39 when the L.A. offices are finally closed. By ca. '39 the Dobro brand disappears.

In '42, the company's resonator production ceased and Victor Smith, Al Frost and Louis Dopyera buy the company and change name to Valco Manufacturing Company. Post-war production resumes in '46. Valco is purchased by treasurer Robert Engelhardt in '64. In '67, Valco bought Kay, but in '68 the new Valco/Kay company went out of business. In the Summer of '69 the assets, including brand names, were auctioned off and the National and Supro names were purchased by Chicago-area distributor/importer Strum 'N Drum (Noble, Norma brands). The National brand is used on copies in early- to mid-'70s, and the brand went into hiatus by the '80s.

In '88 National Resophonic Guitars is founded in San Luis Obispo, California, by Don Young, with production of National-style resonator guitars beginning in '89 (see following). In the '90s, the National brand also resurfaces on inexpensive Asian imports.

National Resonator guitars are categorized by materials and decoration (from plain to fancy): Duolian, Triolian, Style 0, Style 1, Style 2, Style 3, Style 4, Don #1, Style 97, Don #2, Don #3, Style 35.

National guitars all have serial numbers which provide clues to date of production. This is a complex issue. This list combines information included in George Gruhn and Walter Carter's Gruhn's Guide to Vintage Guitars, which was originally provided by Bob Brozman and Mike Newton, with new information provided by Mike Newton.

Pre Chicago numbers:

A101-A450 1935-1936.

Chicago numbers:

A prefix (some may not have the prefix) 1936-mid-1997. B prefix Mid-1937-1938. C prefix Late-1938-1940. G prefix up to 200 Ea. 1941-ea. 1942. G suffix under 2000 Ea. 1941-ea. 1942. G suffix 2000-3000s (probably old parts) 1943-1945. G suffix 4000s (old parts) Late 1945-mid-1947. V100-V7500 1947. V7500-V15000 1948. V15000-V25000 1949. V25000-V35000 1950. V35000-V38000 1951. X100-X7000 1951. X7000-X17000 1952. X17000-X30000 1953. X30000-X43000 1954. X43000-X57000 1955. X57000-X71000 1956. X71000-X85000 1957. X85000-X990001958. T100-T5000 1958. T5000-T25000 1959. T25000-T50000 1960. T50000-T75000 1961. T75000-T90000 1962. G100-G5000 1962. T90000-T99000 1963. G5000-G15000 1963. G15000-G40000 1964. 1 prefix 1965-ea. 1968. 2 prefix Mid-1968.

Aragon De Luxe

1939-1942. Archtop with resonator (the only archtop resonator offered), spruce top and maple back and sides, light brown.

1939-1942		$6,200	$8,100

MODEL YEAR	FEATURES	EXC. COND. LOW	HIGH

Big Daddy LP-457-2
1970s. Strum & Drum import, single-cut, LP-style, 2 pickups, gold hardware, black.
1970s $290 $375

Bluegrass 35
1963-1965. Acoustic, non-cut single-cone resonator, Res-O-Glas body in Arctic White.
1963-1965 $1,475 $1,925

Bobbie Thomas
Ca.1967-1968. Double-cut thinline hollowbody, bat-shaped f-holes, 2 pickups, Bobbie Thomas on 'guard, vibrato.
1967-1968 $625 $825

Cameo
1957-1958. Renamed from Model 1140 in '57, full-body acoustic archtop with carved top.
1957-1958 $725 $950

Collegian
1942-1943. Metal body resonator similar to Duolian, 14-fret round or square neck, yellow.
1942-1943 $1,225 $1,600

Don Style 1
1934-1936. Plain body with engraved borders, pearl dot inlay, 14 frets, single-cone, silver (nickel-plated).
1934-1936 $6,500 $8,500

Don Style 2
1934-1936. Geometric Art Deco body engraving, 14 frets, single-cone, fancy square pearl inlays and pearloid headstock overlay, silver (nickel-plated).
1934-1936 $7,400 $9,600

Don Style 3
1934-1936. Same as Style 2 but more elaborate floral engravings, fancy pearl diamond inlays, 14 frets, single-cone, silver (nickel-plated), only a very few made.
1934-1936 $13,000 $17,000

Duolian
1930-1939. Acoustic steel body, frosted paint finish until '36, mahogany-grain paint finish '37-'39, round neck, square neck available in '33, 12-fret neck until '34 then 14-fret.
1930-1934 Round neck, 12- or 14-fret $3,200 $4,200

EG 685 Hollow Body Electric
1970s. Strum & Drum distributed, double-cut hollowbody copy, 2 pickups.
1970s $375 $500

El Trovador
1933 only. Wood body, 12 frets.
1933 $1,900 $2,450

Electric Spanish
1935-1938. 15 1/2" archtop with Pat. Appl. For bridge pickup, National crest logo, fancy N-logo 'guard, black and white art deco, sunburst, becomes New Yorker Spanish '39-'58.
1935-1938 $1,500 $2,000

Estralita
1934-1942. Acoustic with single-cone resonator, f-holes, multi-bound, 14-fret, mahogany top and back, shaded brown.
1934-1942 $800 $1,050

Glenwood 95
1962-1964. Glenwood 98 without third bridge-mount pickup, Vermillion Red or Flame Red.
1962-1964 $3,000 $3,900

Glenwood 98
1964-1965. USA map-shaped solidbody of molded Res-O-Glas, 2 regular and 1 bridge pickup, vibrato, 3 tailpiece options, Pearl White.
1964-1965 $3,100 $4,100

Glenwood 99
1962-1965. USA map-shaped solidbody of molded Res-O-Glas, 2 regular and 1 bridge pickups, butterfly inlay.
1962-1963 Snow White $3,100 $4,100
1964-1965 Green/Blue $5,700 $7,400

Glenwood Deluxe
1959-1961. Renamed from Glenwood 1105, Les Paul-shaped solidbody, wood body, not fiberglass, multi-bound, 2 pickups, factory Bigsby, vibrato, natural.
1959-1961 $1,800 $2,350

Havana
1938-1942. Natural spruce top, sunburst back and sides.
1938-1942 Round neck $800 $1,050
1938-1942 Square neck $525 $675

Model 1100 California
1949-1955. Electric hollowbody archtop, multi-bound, f-holes, trapeze tailpiece, 1 pickup, natural.
1949-1955 $900 $1,175

Model 1103 Del-Mar
1954-1957. Electric archtop, 2 pickups, adjustable bridge, sunburst finish.
1954-1957 $1,150 $1,500

Model 1104 Town and Country
1954-1958. Model just below Glenwood 1105, dots, 2 or 3 pickups, plastic overlay on back, natural finish.
1954-1958 2 pickups $1,700 $2,200
1954-1958 3 pickups $1,925 $2,500

Model 1105 Glenwood
1954-1958. Les Paul-shaped solidbody, wood body, not fiberglass, single-cut, multi-bound, 2 pickups, natural, renamed Glenwood Deluxe with Bigsby in '59.
1954-1958 $2,100 $2,750

Model 1106 Val-Trol Baron
1959-1960. Single-cut solidbody, 2 pickups, 1 piezo, block inlays, black.
1959-1960 $1,300 $1,700

Model 1107 Debonaire
1953-1960. Single rounded-cutaway full-depth 16" electric archtop, single neck pickup, Debonaire logo on 'guard (for most models), large raised National script logo on headstock, sunburst.
1953-1960 $775 $1,000

Model 1109/1198 Bel-Aire
1953-1960. Single pointed cut archtop, 2 (1109) pickups until '57, 3 (1198) after, master tone knob and jack, bound body, sunburst.
1953-1957 1109, 2 pickups $1,050 $1,350
1958-1960 1198, 3 pickups $1,150 $1,500

1936 National Duolian
BobTekippe

1955 National 1105 Glenwood
Mike Newton

1958 National 1125 Dynamic

www.guitarswest.net

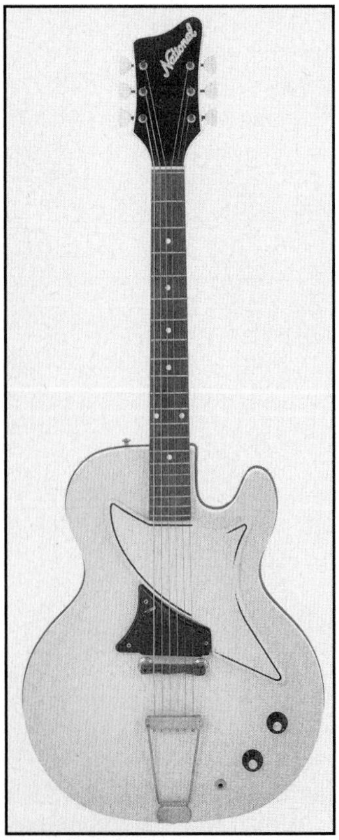

1962 National Studio 66

Imaged by Heritage Auctions, HA.com

MODEL YEAR	FEATURES	EXC. COND. LOW	HIGH

Model 1110/1111 Aristocrat

1941-1954. Electric full body non-cut archtop, 1 pickup, 2 knobs, early model with triple backslash markers, later with block markers, National-crest headstock inlaid logo, natural finish only until model numbers added to name in '48, shaded sunburst finish (1110) and natural (1111).

1941-1948	Natural	$850	$1,100
1948-1955	1110, shaded sunburst	$1,050	$1,350
1948-1955	1111, natural	$1,050	$1,350

Model 1120 New Yorker

1954-1958. Renamed from New Yorker Spanish, 16.25" electric archtop, 1 pickup on floating 'guard, dot markers, blond.

1954-1958		$775	$1,000

Model 1122 Cosmopolitan

1954-1957. Small wood non-cutaway solidbody, dot markers, 1 pickup, 2 knobs on mounted 'guard.

1954-1957		$650	$850

Model 1122 Val-Trol Junior

1959-1960. Single-cut solidbody, 1 pickup and 1piezo, dot inlays, ivory.

1959-1960		$1,000	$1,300

Model 1123 Bolero

1954-1957. Les Paul-shape, control knobs mounted on 'guard, single pickup, trapeze tailpiece, sunburst.

1954-1957		$725	$950

Model 1124/1124B/1134 Avalon

1954-1957. Small wood solidbody, 2 pickups, 4 control knobs and switch on top-mounted 'guard, block markers, short trapeze bridge, sunburst (1124) or blond (1124B).

1954-1957	1124, sunburst	$1,150	$1,500
1954-1957	1124B/1134, blond	$1,250	$1,625

Model 1125 Dynamic

1951-1959. Full body 15.5" acoustic-electric archtop, sunburst version of New Yorker 1120 with some appointments slightly below the New Yorker, dot markers, 1 pickup, sunburst.

1951-1959		$675	$900

Model 1134 Avalon

1957. Block markers, 2 pickups, blond finish.

1957		$1,200	$1,600

Model 1135 Acoustic Archtop

1948-1954. 17.25" full body acoustic archtop, carved top, split pearl markers.

1948-1954		$850	$1,100

Model 1140 Acoustic Archtop

1948-1957. 15.5" full body acoustic archtop, carved top, dot markers.

1948-1957		$600	$800

Model 1150 Flat-Top Auditorium

1951-1958. Auditorium-size flat-top, 14.25" narrow-waist, dot markers.

1951-1958		$650	$850

Model 1155/1155E /N-66 Jumbo

1948-1961. Flat-top acoustic with Gibson Jumbo body, mahogany back and sides, bolt-on neck.

1947	N-66	$1,500	$2,700
1948-1961	1155/1155E	$1,500	$2,700

MODEL YEAR	FEATURES	EXC. COND. LOW	HIGH

Model 1170 Club Combo

1952-1955, 1959-1961. Electric hollowbody archtop, 2 pickups, rounded cutaway.

1952-1961		$1,150	$1,500

N600 Series

1968. Offset double-cut solidbody, 1, 2, and 3 pickup models, with and without vibrato.

1968	N624, 1 pickup	$425	$550
1968	N634, 2 pus, vibrato	$525	$675
1968	N644, 3 pus, vibrato	$650	$850
1968	N654, 12-string	$525	$675

N700 Series

1968. Flat-top, 700/710 dreadnoughts, 720/730 jumbos.

1968	N700 Western	$525	$675
1968	N710	$300	$400
1968	N720 Western	$350	$440
1968	N730 Deluxe	$475	$625

N800 Series

1968. Double-cut semi-hollow body, various models with or without Bigsby.

1968	No Bigsby	$500	$650
1968	With Bigsby	$575	$750

New Yorker Spanish

1939-1953. Electric archtop, 15.5" body until '47 then 16.25", 1 neck pickup, dot-diamond markers, sunburst or natural. Renamed New Yorker 1120 in '54.

1939-1946	15.5"	$1,500	$2,000
1947-1949	16.25"	$1,300	$1,700
1950-1953	16.25"	$1,200	$1,600

Newport 82

1963-1965. Renamed from Val-Pro 82, USA map-shaped Res-O-Glas, 1 pickup, Pepper Red finish.

1963-1965		$1,550	$2,000

Newport 84

1963-1965. Renamed from Val-Pro 84, USA map-shaped Res-O-Glas, 1 regular and 1 bridge pickup, Sea Foam Green finish.

1963-1965		$2,900	$3,750

Newport 88

1963-1965. Renamed from Val-Pro 88, USA map-shaped Res-O-Glas, 2 regular and 1 bridge pickup, Raven Black finish.

1963-1965		$1,925	$2,500

Reso-phonic

1956-1964. Pearloid-covered, single-cut semi-solidbody acoustic, single resonator, maroon or white, also a non-cut, square neck version was offered, which is included in these values.

1956-1964	Round neck, common finish	$1,350	$1,750
1956-1964	Round neck, rare finish	$1,275	$1,925
1956-1964	Square neck	$1,150	$1,500

Rosita

1933-1939. Plywood body by Harmony, plain metal resonator, plain appointments.

1933-1939		$850	$1,100

Silvo (Electric Hawaiian)

1937-1941. Nickel-plated metal body flat-top, small upper bout, f-holes, square neck, multiple straight

MODEL YEAR	FEATURES	EXC. COND. LOW	HIGH

line body art over dark background, Roman numeral parallelogram markers, National badge headstock logo, Silvo name on coverplate.

1937-1941	Silver	$2,350	$3,050

Studio 66

1961-1964. Electric solidbody of Res-O-Glas, single-cut, 1 pickup, renamed Varsity 66 in '65.

1961-1962	Sand Buff, bridge pu	$1,100	$1,425
1963-1964	Jet Black, neck pu	$1,100	$1,425

Style O

1930-1942. Acoustic single-cone brass body (early models had a steel body), Hawaiian scene etching, 12-fret neck '30-'34, 14-fret neck '35 on, round (all years) or square ('33 on) neck.

1930-1934	Round neck, 12-fret, common etching	$2,600	$3,400
1930-1934	Round neck, 12-fret, rare etching	$3,100	$4,100
1933-1942	Square neck, common etching	$1,150	$1,500
1933-1942	Square neck, rare etching	$2,150	$2,800
1935-1942	Round, 14-fret (Mark Knophler assoc)	$4,850	$6,250
1935-1942	Round, 14-fret, common etching	$2,150	$2,800
1935-1942	Round, 14-fret, rare etching	$3,100	$4,100

Style O Tenor

1929-1930. Tenor, 4 strings, single-cone brass body, Hawaiian scene etching.

1929-1930		$850	$1,100

Style 1 Tricone

1927-1943. German silver body tricone resonator, ebony 'board, mahogany square (Hawaiian) or round (Spanish) neck, plain body, 12-fret neck until '34, 14-fret after.

1927-1943	Round neck	$4,575	$5,925
1928-1943	Square neck	$3,000	$3,875

Style 1 Tricone Plectrum

1928-1935. 26" scale versus the 23" scale of the tenor.

1928-1935		$1,625	$2,125

Style 1 Tricone Tenor

1928-1935. Tenor, 4 strings, 23" scale, square neck is Hawaiian, round neck is Spanish.

1928-1935		$1,625	$2,125

Style 1.5 Tricone

1930s. A "1/2" style like the 1.5 represents a different engraving pattern.

1930s	Round neck	$7,000	$9,100
1930s	Square neck	$2,400	$3,100

Style 2 Tricone

1927-1942. German silver body tricone resonator, wild rose engraving, square (Hawaiian) or round (Spanish) neck, 12-fret neck until '34, 14-fret after.

1927-1942	Round neck	$10,500	$13,700
1927-1942	Square neck	$3,350	$4,350

Style 2 Tricone Plectrum

1928-1935. 26" scale versus the 23" scale of the tenor.

1928-1935		$1,550	$2,000

MODEL YEAR	FEATURES	EXC. COND. LOW	HIGH

Style 2 Tricone Tenor

1928-1935. Tenor.

1928-1935		$1,550	$2,000

Style 2.5 Tricone

1927-1928. Collector term for Style 2 with additional rose engravings on coverplate, bound ebony fretboard.

1927-1928		$6,300	$8,200

Style 3 Tricone

1928-1941. German silver body tricone resonator, lily-of-the-valley engraving, square (Hawaiian) or round (Spanish) neck, 12-fret neck until '34, 14-fret after, reintroduced with a nickel-plated brass body in '94.

1928-1939	Round neck	$10,500	$13,600
1928-1941	Square neck	$4,200	$5,500

Style 3 Tricone Plectrum

1928-1935. 26" scale versus the 23" scale of the tenor.

1928-1935		$2,600	$3,400

Style 3 Tricone Tenor

1928-1939. Tenor version.

1928-1939		$2,600	$3,400

Style 4 Tricone

1928-1940. German silver body tricone resonator, chrysanthemum etching, 12-fret neck until '34, 14-fret after, reissued in '95 with same specs.

1928-1940	Round neck	$14,000	$18,000
1928-1940	Square neck	$3,700	$4,800

Style 35

1936-1942. Brass body tricone resonator, sandblasted minstrel and trees scene, 12 frets, square (Hawaiian) or round (Spanish) neck.

1936-1942	Round neck	$21,000	$27,000
1936-1942	Square neck	$6,700	$8,800

Style 97

1936-1940. Nickel-plated brass body tricone resonator, sandblasted scene of female surfrider and palm trees, 12 frets, slotted peghead.

1930s	Early '30s, square neck	$7,500	$9,800
1930s	Late '30s, square neck, different 'board	$5,200	$6,800
1930s-1940	Round neck	$21,000	$28,000

Style N

1930-1931. Nickel-plated brass body single-cone resonator, plain finish, 12 frets.

1930-1931		$3,400	$4,500

Triolian

1928-1941. Single-cone resonator, wood body replaced by metal body in '29, 12-fret neck and slotted headstock '28-'34, changed to 14-fret neck in '35 and solid headstock in '36, round or square ('33 on) neck available.

1928-1936	Various colors	$2,750	$3,600
1936-1937	Fake rosewood grain	$2,500	$3,300

Triolian Tenor

1928-1936. Tenor, metal body.

1928-1936		$925	$1,200

Trojan

1934-1942. Single-cone resonator wood body, f-holes, bound top, 14-fret round neck.

1934-1942		$1,175	$1,525

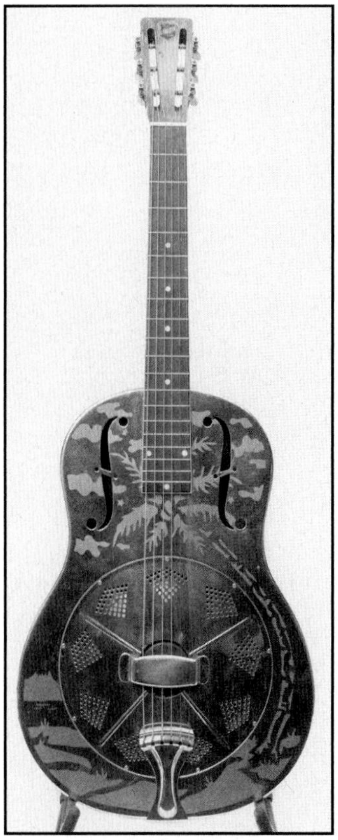

1930 National Style O

Bernunzio Uptown Music

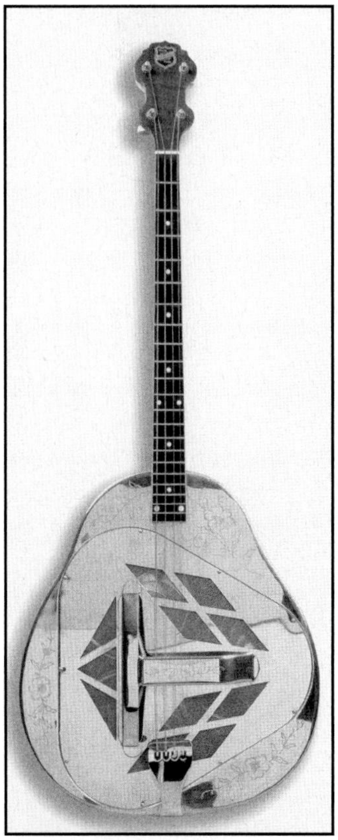

1928 National Style 2 Tenor

GUITARS

National Reso-Phonic ResoLectric

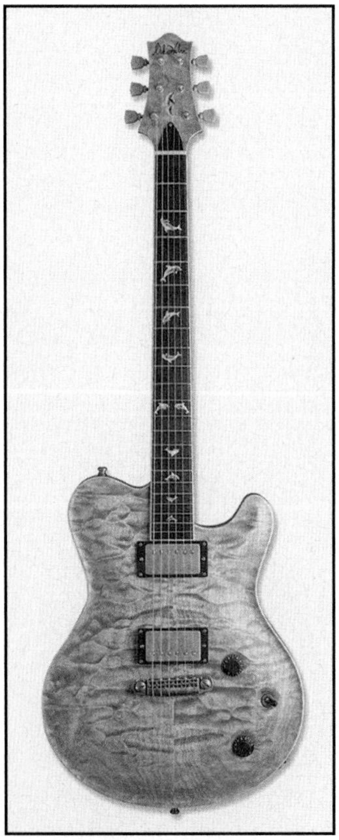

Nik Huber Dolphin II

MODEL YEAR	FEATURES	EXC. COND. LOW	HIGH

Val-Pro 82

1962-1963. USA map-shaped Res-O-Glas, 1 pickup, Vermillion Red finish, renamed Newport 82 in '63.

1962-1963		$1,125	$1,450

Val-Pro 84

1962-1963. USA map-shaped Res-O-Glas, 1 regular and 1 bridge pickup, snow white finish, renamed Newport 84 in '63.

1962-1963		$1,250	$1,625

Val-Pro 88

1962-1963. USA map-shaped Res-O-Glas, 2 regular and 1 bridge pickup, black finish, renamed Newport 88 in '63.

1962-1963		$2,100	$2,700

Varsity 66

1964-1965. Renamed from Studio 66 in '64, molded Res-O-Glas, 1 pickup, 2 knobs, beige finish.

1964-1965		$1,000	$1,300

Westwood 72

1962-1964. USA map-shaped solid hardwood body (not fiberglass), 1 pickup, Cherry Red.

1962-1964		$1,700	$2,200

Westwood 75

1962-1964. USA map-shaped solid hardwood body (not fiberglass), 1 regular and 1 bridge pickup, cherry-to-black sunburst finish.

1962-1964		$1,700	$2,200

Westwood 77

1962-1965. USA map-shaped solid hardwood body (not fiberglass), 2 regular and 1 bridge pickup.

1962-1965	Blond-Ivory	$1,700	$2,200

National Reso-Phonic

1989-present. Professional and premium grade, production/custom, single cone, acoustic-electric, and tricone guitars (all with resonators), built in San Luis Obispo, California. They also build basses, mandolins and ukuleles. McGregor Gaines and Don Young formed the National Reso-Phonic Guitar Company with the objective of building instruments based upon the original National designs. Replicon is the aging process to capture the appearance and sound of a vintage National.

Collegian

2010-present. Thin gauge steel body, 9.5" cone, biscuit bridge, aged ivory finish.

2010-2019		$1,250	$1,600

Delphi

1993-2010. Single cone, steel body.

1993-2010		$1,425	$1,850

Dueco

2012-2020. Gold or Silver crystalline finish.

2012-2020		$1,775	$2,300

El Trovador

2010-present. Wood body Dobro-style, single cone, biscuit bridge.

2010-2020		$1,900	$2,500

Estralita Deluxe

2006-present. Single cone, walnut body, figured maple top, koa offered in '03.

2006-2020	Maple or koa	$2,000	$2,600

Estralita Harlem Slim

2010. Laminate maple.

2010		$1,125	$1,450

Model 97

2002-2009. Nickel-plated tricone resonator, female surfrider and palm trees scene.

2002-2009		$2,400	$3,100

Model D

2003-2010. Laminate wood body, spruce top, walnut back and sides, spun cone and spider bridge. Replaced by Smith and Young Model 1 (metal body) and Model 11 (wood body).

2003-2010		$1,300	$1,700

NRP Steel

2009-present. Steel body with rubbed nickel finish, Honduran mahogany neck, slotted headstock.

2009-2020		$1,850	$2,400

Reso Rocket

2005-present. Single-cut steel body, Tricone style grill.

2005-2020		$2,250	$2,900

Reso Rocket N

2009-present. Highly polished nickel-plated finish.

2009-2020		$2,250	$2,900

Resoelectric Jr./Jr. II

2005-2010. Basic model of ResoLectric with painted body, Jr. with P-90, Jr. II with Lollar lipstick-tube. Replaced by the ResoTone.

2005-2010		$725	$925

ResoLectric

1992-present. Single-cut electric resonator, maple (flamed maple since '96), single biscuit, 1 regular pickup (lipstick-tube up to '95, P-90 since) and 1 under-saddle.

1992-1995	Lipstick pickup	$1,500	$1,925
1996-2020	P-90	$1,400	$1,800

Style M-1/M-2

1990-1994, 2003-2010. Bound mahogany body single-cone, M-1 with ebony 'board, M-2 with bound rosewood 'board.

1990-2010		$1,400	$1,800

Style N

1993-2005. Nickel-plated brass body single-cone resonator, plain mirror finish, 12 fret neck.

1993-2005		$2,150	$2,850

Style O/O Deluxe/O Replicon

1992-present. Nickel-plated brass body, Hawaiian palm tree etched. Deluxe has upgrades like figured-maple neck and mother-of-pearl diamond inlays. Replicon is replica of Mark Knopfler model.

1992-2020	O	$2,100	$2,800
1992-2020	O Deluxe	$2,500	$3,300
1992-2020	O Replicon	$2,400	$3,100

Tricone

1994-present. Nickel-plated brass body, bound ebony 'board.

1994-2021	Style 1	$1,800	$2,400
1994-2021	Style 15	$2,200	$2,900
1995	Style 3, Lily of the Valley	$3,900	$5,100

Triolian

2009-present. Steel body with f-holes, sieve-hole coverplate, maple neck, 12 or 14 fret neck, ivoroid-bound rosewood 'board, mother-of-pearl markers, hand painted walnut-burst.

MODEL YEAR	FEATURES	EXC. COND. LOW	HIGH
2009-2020	12 fret	$1,400	$1,825
2009-2020	14 fret	$1,400	$1,825

Navarro Custom

1986-present. Professional and premium grade, production/custom, electric guitars and basses built in San Juan, Puerto Rico by luthier Mike Navarro.

Neubauer

1966-1990s. Luthier Helmut Neubauer built his acoustic and electric archtop guitars in Bubenreuth, Germany.

New Era Guitars

See listing under ARK - New Era Guitars.

New Orleans Guitar Company

1992-present. Luthier Vincent Guidroz builds his premium grade, production/custom, solid and semi-hollow body guitars in New Orleans, Louisiana.

Nickerson Guitars

1983-present. Luthier Brad Nickerson builds his professional and premium grade, production/custom, archtop and flat-top guitars in Northampton, Massachusetts.

Nielsen

2004-present. Premium grade, custom/production, archtop guitars built by luthier Dale Nielsen in Duluth, Minnesota.

Nik Huber Guitars

1997-present. Premium grade, production/custom, electric guitars built in Rodgau, Germany by luthier Nik Huber.

Nioma

1932-1952. NIOMA, the National Institute of Music and Arts, was founded in Seattle but soon had schools across the western U.S. and Canada. By '35 they added guitar instruction, offering their own branded Spanish, resonator and lap steel (with matching amps) guitars, made by Regal, Harmony, Dickerson.

Noble

Ca. 1950-ca. 1969. Instruments made by others and distributed by Don Noble and Company of Chicago. Plastic-covered guitars made by EKO debut in '62. Aluminum-necked Wandré guitars added to the line in early-'63. By ca. '65-'66 the brand is owned by Chicago-area importer and distributor Strum 'N Drum and used mainly on Japanese-made solidbodies. Strum 'N Drum bought the National brand name in '69 and imported Japanese copies of American designs under the National brand and Japanese original designs under Norma through the early '70s.

The Noble brand disappears at least by the advent of the Japanese National brand, if not before. They also offered amps.

NoName Guitars

1999-present. Luthier Dan Kugler builds his production/custom, professional and premium grade, acoustic guitars and basses in Conifer, Colorado.

Nordy (Nordstrand Guitars)

2003-present. Professional and premium grade, production/custom, electric guitars and basses built by luthier Carey Nordstrand in Yucaipa, California.

Norma

Ca.1965-1970. Imported from Japan by Strum 'N Drum, Inc. of Chicago (see Noble brand info). Early examples were built by Tombo, most notably sparkle plastic covered guitars and basses

Electric Solidbody

1965-1970s. Type of finish has affect on value. Various models include; EG-350 (student double-cut, 1 pickup), EG-403 (unique pointy cutaway, 2 pickups), EG-400 (double-cut, 2 pickups), EG-450 (double-cut, 2 split-coil pickups), EG-421 (double-cut, 4 pickups), EG-412-12 (double-cut, 12-string).

MODEL YEAR	FEATURES	EXC. COND. LOW	HIGH
1965-1968	Blue, red, gold sparkle	$275	$575
1965-1970s	Non-sparkle	$200	$275

Norman

1972-present. Intermediate grade, production, acoustic and acoustic/electric guitars built in LaPatrie, Quebec. Norman was the first guitar production venture luthier Robert Godin was involved with. He has since added the Seagull, Godin, and Patrick & Simon brands of instruments.

Normandy Guitars

2008-present. Jim Normandy builds professional grade, production, aluminum archtop and electric guitars and basses in Salem, Oregon.

Northworthy Guitars

Professional and premium grade, production/custom, flat-top and electric guitars and basses built by luthier Alan Marshall in Ashbourne, Derbyshire, U.K., starting in 1987. He also builds mandolins.

Norwood

1960s. Budget guitars imported most likely from Japan.

Electric Solidbody

1960s. Offset double-cut body, 3 soapbar-style pickups, Norwood label on headstock.

MODEL YEAR	FEATURES	EXC. COND. LOW	HIGH
1960s		$160	$250

1960s Norma Sparkle-Top

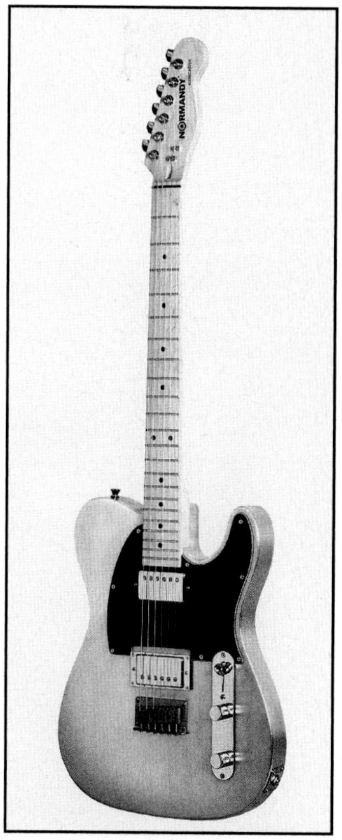

Normandy Alumicaster

1930s Oahu

Bernunzio Uptown Music

1981 O'Hagan Twenty-Two

Christopher Tritschler

MODEL YEAR	FEATURES	EXC. COND. LOW	HIGH

Novax Guitars

1989-present. Luthier Ralph Novak builds his fanned-fret professional and premium grade, production/custom, solidbody and acoustic guitars and basses, originally in San Leandro, California, and since May '06, in Eugene, Oregon.

Noyce

1974-present. Luthier Ian Noyce builds his production/custom, professional and premium grade, acoustic and electric guitars and basses in Ballarat, Victoria, Australia.

Nyberg Instruments

1993-present. Professional grade, custom, flat-top and Maccaferri-style guitars built by luthier Lawrence Nyberg in Hornby Island, British Columbia. He also builds mandolins, mandolas, bouzoukis and citterns.

Oahu

1926-1985, present. The Oahu Publishing Company and Honolulu Conservatory, based in Cleveland, Ohio was active in the sheet music and student instrument business in the '30s. An instrument, set of instructional sheet music, and lessons were offered as a complete package. Lessons were often given to large groups of students. Instruments, lessons, and sheet music could also be purchased by mail order. The Oahu Publishing Co. advertised itself as The World's Largest Guitar Dealer. Most '30s Oahu guitars were made by Kay with smaller numbers from the Oscar Schmidt Company.

Guitar Models from the Mid-'30s include: 71K (jumbo square neck), 72K (jumbo roundneck), 68B (jumbo, vine body decoration), 68K (deluxe jumbo square neck), 69K (deluxe jumbo roundneck), 65K and 66K (mahogany, square neck), 64K and 67K (mahogany, roundneck), 65M (standard-size, checker binding, mahogany), 53K (roundneck, mahogany), 51 (black, Hawaiian scene, pearlette 'board), 51K (black, pond scene decoration), 52K (black, Hawaiian scene decoration), 50 and 50K (student guitar, brown).

The brand has been revived on a line of tube amps.

Graphic Body

1930s. 13" painted artwork bodies, includes Styles 51 and 52 Hawaiian scene.

1930s	Floral, higher appointments	$275	$375
1930s	Hawaiian scene	$275	$375

Round Neck 14" Flat-Top

1930s. Spruce top, figured maple back and sides, thin logo.

1932		$725	$950

Style 50K Student

1930s. Student-size guitar, brown finish.

1935		$100	$200

Style 52K

1930s. 13" with fancy Hawaiian stencil, slotted headstock.

1930s		$275	$350

MODEL YEAR FEATURES EXC. COND. LOW HIGH

Style 65M

1933-1935. Standard-size mahogany body, checker binding, natural brown.

1933-1935		$475	$625

Style 68K De Luxe Jumbo

1930s. Hawaiian, 15.5" wide, square neck, Brazilian back and sides, spruce top, fancy pearl vine inlay, abalone trim on top and soundhole, rosewood pyramid bridge, fancy pearl headstock inlay, butterbean tuners, ladder-braced, natural. High-end model made for Oahu by Kay.

1934-1935		$3,500	$4,500

Style 71K Hawaiian

1930s.Hawaiian, gold vine pattern on bound sunburst top, dot inlays.

1930s		$875	$1,150

Ochoteco Guitars

1979-present. Production/custom steel- and nylon-stringed guitars built by luthier Gabriel Ochoteco in Germany until '84 and in Brisbane, Australia since.

Odessa

1981-1990s. Budget guitars imported by Davitt & Hanser (BC Rich). Mainly acoustics in the '90s, but some electrics early on.

O'Hagan

1979-1983. Designed by clarinetist and importer Jerol O'Hagan in St. Louis Park, Minnesota. Primarily neck-thru construction, most with German-carved bodies. In '81 became Jemar Corporation and in '83 it was closed by the I.R.S., a victim of recession.

SN=YYM(M)NN (e.g., 80905, September '80, 5th guitar); or MYMNNN (e.g., A34006, April 1983, 6th guitar). Approximately 3000 total instruments were made with the majority being NightWatches (approx. 200 Twenty Twos, 100-150 Sharks, 100 Lasers; about 25 with birdseye maple

Shark

1979-1983. Explorer-looking solidbody, maple body, 2 Shaller humbucker pickups, 3-piece maple/walnut laminate neck, natural.

1979-1983		$500	$675

Ohio

1959-ca. 1965. Line of electric solidbodies and basses made by France's Jacobacci company, which also built under its own brand. Sparkle finish, bolt-on aluminum necks, strings-thru-body design.

Old Kraftsman

Ca. 1930s-ca. 1960s. Brandname used by the Spiegel catalog company for instruments made by other American manufacturers, including Regal, Kay and even Gibson. The instruments were of mixed quality, but some better grade instruments were comparable to those offered by Wards.

MODEL YEAR	FEATURES	EXC. COND. LOW	HIGH

Archtop

1930s-1960s. Various models.

1930s	17", Stauffer-style hdstk	$300	$400
1950s-60s		$225	$300

Flat-Top

1930s-1960s. Various models.

1950s	Prairie Ramblers (stencil)	$225	$300

Jazz II K775

1960-1963. Kay 775 with Old Kraftsman logo on large headstock, small double-cut thinline, 2 pickups, Bigsby, natural.

1960-1963		$850	$1,100

Sizzler K4140

1959. Single-cut, single neck pickup, Sizzler logo on body with other art images.

1959		$385	$500

Thin Twin Jimmy Reed

1952-1958		$1,000	$1,300

Value Leader

1961-1965. Electric single-cut semi-solid, 1 pickup, Kay Value Leader series.

1961-1965		$300	$400

OLP (Officially Licensed Product)

2001-2009. Intermediate grade, production, imported guitars and basses based on higher dollar guitar models officially licensed from the original manufacturer. OLP logo on headstock.

Olson Guitars

1977-present. Luthier James A. Olson builds his presentation grade, custom, flat-tops in Circle Pines, Minnesota.

Olympia by Tacoma

1997-2006. Import acoustic guitars and mandolins from Tacoma Guitars.

OD Series

1997-2006	Various models	$75	$275

Omega

1996-2010. Luthier Kevin Gallagher built his premium grade, custom/production acoustic guitars in East Saylorsburg, Pennsylvania. He died in '10.

Oncor Sound

1980-ca. 1981. This Salt Lake City, Utah-based company made both a guitar and a bass synthesizer.

Optek

1980s-present. Intermediate grade, production, imported Fretlight acoustic/electric and electric guitars. Located in Reno, Nevada.

Fretlight

1989-present. Double-cut, 126 LED lights in fretboard controlled by a scale/chord selector.

1989-2020		$275	$375

MODEL YEAR	FEATURES	EXC. COND. LOW	HIGH

Opus

1972-Mid 1970s. Acoustic and classical guitars, imported from Japan by Ampeg/Selmer. In '75-'76, Harmony made a line of acoustics with the Opus model name.

Original Senn

2004-present. Luthier Jeff Senn builds his professional and premium grade, production/custom, solidbody electric guitars and basses in Nashville, Tennessee.

Ormsby Guitars

2003-present. Luthier Perry Ormsby builds his custom, professional and premium grade, solid and chambered electric guitars in Perth, Western Australia.

Orpheum

1897-1942, 1944-late 1960s, 2001-2006. Intermediate grade, production, acoustic and resonator guitars. They also offered mandolins. Orpheum originally was a brand of Rettberg and Lange, who made instruments for other companies as well. William Rettberg and William Lange bought the facilities of New York banjo maker James H. Buckbee in 1897. Lange went out on his own in '21 to start the Paramount brand. He apparently continued using the Orpheum brand as well. He went out of business in '42. In '44 the brand was acquired by New York's Maurice Lipsky Music Co. who used it primarily on beginner to medium grade instruments, which were manufactured by Regal, Kay, and United Guitar (and maybe others). In the early '60s Lipsky applied the brand to Japanese and European (by Egmond) imports. Lipsky dropped the name in the early '70s. The brand was revived for '01 to '06 by Tacoma Guitars.

Auditorium Archtop 835/837

1950s. Acoustic archtop, auditorium size, dot markers, Orpheum shell headpiece, white celluloid 'guard, model 835 with spruce top/back/sides, 837 with mahogany.

1950s		$250	$350

Orpheum Special (Regal-made)

1930s. Slot head, Dobro-style wood body, metal resonator, sunburst.

1930s		$675	$900

President

1940s. 18" pro-level acoustic archtop, Orpheum block logo and President script logo on headstock, large split-block markers, sunburst.

1940s		$1,275	$1,700

Style B

1940s. Acoustic archtop, Style B logo on headstock, block markers, sunburst.

1940s		$500	$675

Thin Twin Jimmy Reed 865E

1950s. Model 865E is the Orpheum version of the generically named Thin Twin Jimmy Reed style electric Spanish cutaway thin solidbody, hand engraved shell celluloid Orpheum headpiece, described as #865E Cutaway Thin Electric Guitar in catalog.

1950s		$1,000	$1,475

Optek Fretlight

1940s Orpheum President

Imaged by Heritage Auctions, HA.com

1993 Orville Les Paul Standard
Stoeffu Vogt

Oskar Graf No. 4/11

Ultra Deluxe Professional 899

1950s. 17" cutaway, 2 pickups, 2 knobs, maple back and sides, top material varies, dot markers, finishes as follows: E-C copper, E-G gold, E-G-B gold-black sunburst, E-B blond curly maple, E-S golden orange sunburst.

MODEL YEAR	FEATURES	EXC. COND. LOW	HIGH
1950s	All finishes	$1,100	$1,475

Orville

1984-1993. Orville by Gibson and Orville guitars were made by Japan's Fuji Gen Gakki for Gibson. See following listing for details. Guitars listed here state only Orville (no By Gibson) on the headstock.

Electric

MODEL YEAR	FEATURES	EXC. COND. LOW	HIGH
1990s	CE Atkins	$775	$1,000
1990s	ES-335	$1,125	$1,475
1990s	LP Custom	$950	$1,225
1990s	LP Standard	$1,000	$1,300

Orville by Gibson

1984-1993. Orville by Gibson and Orville guitars were made by Japan's Fuji Gen Gakki for Gibson. Basically the same models except the Orville by Gibson guitars had real Gibson USA PAF '57 Classic pickups and a true nitrocellulose lacquer finish. The Orville models used Japanese electronics and a poly finish. Prices here are for the Orville by Gibson models.

Acoustic-Electric

1984-1993. On-board electronics.

MODEL YEAR	FEATURES	EXC. COND. LOW	HIGH
1984-1993	Dove	$1,300	$1,700
1984-1993	J-160E	$1,300	$1,700
1984-1993	J-200NE	$1,300	$1,700

Electric

1984-1993. Various models.

MODEL YEAR	FEATURES	EXC. COND. LOW	HIGH
1984-1993	ES-175	$1,350	$1,750
1984-1993	ES-335	$1,350	$1,750
1984-1993	Explorer	$1,150	$1,500
1984-1993	Firebird V	$975	$1,275
1984-1993	Firebird VII	$975	$1,275
1984-1993	Flying V	$1,150	$1,500
1984-1993	Les Paul Custom	$950	$1,225
1984-1993	Les Paul Jr	$550	$725
1984-1993	Les Paul Standard	$1,250	$1,625
1984-1993	Les Paul Studio JP	$850	$1,125
1984-1993	MM/Les Paul Jr	$450	$600
1984-1993	SG LP Custom	$950	$1,225
1984-1993	SG LP Standard	$800	$1,050

Osborne Sound Laboratories

Late 1970s. Founded by Ralph Scaffidi and wife guitarist Mary Osborne; originally building guitar amps, they did also offer solidbody guitars.

Oscar Schmidt

1879-1938, 1979-present. Budget and intermediate grade, production, acoustic, acoustic/electric, and electric guitars and basses distributed by U.S. Music Corp. (Washburn, Randall, etc.). They also offer mandolins, banjos, ukuleles and the famous Oscar Schmidt autoharp.

The original Oscar Schmidt Company, Jersey City, New Jersey, offered banjo mandolins, tenor banjos, guitar banjos, ukuleles, mandolins and guitars under their own brand and others (including Sovereign and Stella). By the early 1900s, the company had factories in the U.S. and Europe producing instruments producing instruments under their own brand as well as other brands for mail-order and other distributors. Oscar Schmidt was also an early contributor to innovative mandolin designs and the company participated in the '00-'30 mandolin boom. The company hit hard times during the Depression and was sold to Harmony by the end of the '30s. In '79, Washburn acquired the brand and it is now part of U.S. Music.

Oskar Graf Guitars

1970-present. Premium and presentation grade, custom, archtop, acoustic and classical guitars and basses built in Clarendon, Ontario, by luthier Oskar Graf. He also builds lutes.

Otwin

1950s-1960s. A brand used on electric guitars made by the Musima company of East Germany. Musima also produced guitars under their own brand.

Outbound Instruments

1990-2002. Intermediate grade, production, travel-size acoustics from the Boulder, Colorado-based company.

Ovation

1966-present. Intermediate and professional grade, production, acoustic and acoustic/electric guitars. They also build basses and mandolins. Until 2014, they also had U.S. production.

Helicopter manufacturer Kaman Corporation, founded in 1945 by jazz guitarist and aeronautical engineer Charles Huron Kaman in Bloomfield, Connecticut, decided to use their helicopter expertise (working with synthetic materials, spruce, high tolerances) and designed, with the help of employee and violin restorer John Ringso, the first fiberglass-backed (Lyracord) acoustic guitars in '65. Production began in '66 and the music factory moved to New Hartford, Connecticut, in '67. Early input was provided by fingerstyle jazz guitarist Charlie Byrd, who gave Kaman the idea for the name Ovation. Kaman Music purchased Hamer Guitars in '88, and Trace Elliot amplifiers (U.K.) in '90. In '08, Fender acquired Kaman Music Corporation and the Ovation brand; in '14 U.S. production ceased and the brand was sold to Drum Workshop, Inc., who re-opened the Hartford, CT plant in late '15.

Adamas 1581-KK Kaki King

2011-2014. Deep bowl cutaway, rosewood 'board, 12th-fret crown inlay, OP-Pro preamp, Kaki personally signs the label on each guitar.

MODEL YEAR	FEATURES	EXC. COND. LOW	HIGH
2011-2014		$2,350	$3,000

MODEL YEAR	FEATURES	EXC. COND. LOW	HIGH

Adamas 1587

1979-1998. Carbon top, walnut, single-cut, bowl back, binding, mini-soundholes.

1979-1998	Black Sparkle	$1,300	$1,700

Adamas 1597

1998-2003. Carbon birch composite top, on-board electronics.

1998-2003	Black	$725	$975

Adamas 1598-MEII Melissa Etheridge

2001-2014. Mid-depth cutaway, ebony 'board, 'ME' maple symbol at 12th fret, OP-Pro preamp, Melissa personally signs the label on each guitar.

2001-2014	12-string	$1,100	$1,500

Adamas 1687

1977-1998. Acoustic/electric, carbon top, non-cut, bowl back, mini-soundholes.

1977-1998	Sunburst	$1,300	$1,700

Adamas CVT W591

2000. Crossweave fiber top, mid-depth body, on-board electronics.

2000		$850	$1,100

Adamas II 1881 NB-2

1993-1998. Acoustic/electric, single-cut, shallow bowl, brown.

1993-1998		$1,225	$1,600

Adamas Millenium

2000. Limited edition, 75 made, planet inlays, Cobalt Blue.

2000		$1,800	$2,400

Anniversary Electric 1657

1978. Deep bowl, abalone inlays, gold-plated parts, for Ovation's 10th anniversary. They also offered an acoustic Anniversary.

1978		$325	$425

Balladeer 1111

1968-1983, 1993-2000. Acoustic, non-cut with deep bowl, bound body, natural top, later called the Standard Balladeer.

1976-1983		$300	$400

Balladeer Artist 1121

1968-1990. Acoustic, non-cut with shallow bowl, bound body.

1968-1969	Early production	$400	$525
1970-1990		$300	$400

Balladeer Classic 1122

1970s. Classical shallow-bowl version of Concert Classic, nylon strings, slotted headstock.

1970s		$275	$375

Balladeer Custom 1112

1976-1990. Acoustic, deep bowl, diamond inlays.

1976-1990		$375	$475

Balladeer Custom Electric 12-String 1655/1755

1982-1994. 12-string version of Balladeer Custom Electric.

1982-1994		$325	$425

Balladeer Custom Electric 1612/1712

1976-1990. Acoustic/electric version of Balladeer Custom, deep bowl.

1976-1990		$400	$525

Balladeer Standard 1561/1661/1761/1861

1982-2000. Acoustic/electric, deep bowl, rounded cutaway.

1982-2000		$375	$500

Balladeer Standard 1771 LX

2008-2010. Acoustic/electric, mid-depth bowl, rosewood, sitka spruce top.

2008-2010		$450	$575

Balladeer Standard 12-String 6751 LX

2008-2010. Acoustic/electric, 12 strings, rosewood, spruce top.

2008-2010		$525	$675

Breadwinner 1251

1971-1983. Axe-like shaped single-cut solidbody, 2 pickups, textured finish, black, blue, tan or white.

1971-1983		$700	$900

Celebrity CC-48

2007-2013. Acoustic/electric, super shallow, laminated spruce top, white bound rosewood 'board with abalone dot inlays.

2007-2013		$200	$275

Celebrity CC-57

1990-1996. Laminated spruce top, shallow bowl, mahogany neck.

1990-1996		$200	$275

Celebrity CC-63

1984-1996. Classical, deep bowl, piezo bridge pickup.

1984-1996		$200	$275

Celebrity CK-057

2002-2004. Acoustic/electric rounded cutaway, shallow back.

2002-2004		$275	$350

Celebrity CS-257

1992-2005, 2010. Made in Korea, super shallow bowl back body, single-cut, Adamas soundholes, alternating dot and diamond markers.

1992-2005	Celebrity	$325	$425
2010	Celebrity Deluxe	$375	$475

Classic 1613/1713

1971-1993. Acoustic/electric, non-cut, deep bowl, no inlay, slotted headstock, gold tuners, natural.

1971-1993		$375	$500

Classic 1663/1763

1982-1998. Acoustic/electric, single-cut, deep bowl, cedar top, EQ, no inlay, slotted headstock, gold tuners.

1982-1998		$450	$600

Classic 1863

1989-1998. Acoustic/electric, single-cut, shallow bowl, no inlay, cedar top, EQ, slotted headstock, gold tuners.

1989-1998		$450	$600

Collectors Series

1982-2008. Limited edition, different model featured each year and production limited to that year only, the year designation is marked at the 12th fret, various colors (each year different).

1982-2008	Common models	$450	$600
1982-2008	Rare models	$650	$1,200

1981 Adamas II Model

Rivington Guitars

1994 Ovation Collectors Series 1994-7

1980 Ovation Deacon 1252

Jon Way

1974 Ovation Glen Campbell 1118

Imaged by Heritage Auctions, HA.com

MODEL YEAR	FEATURES	EXC. COND. LOW	HIGH

Concert Classic 1116
1974-1990. Deep-bowl nylon string classical, slotted headstock.

1974-1990 — $275 — $350

Contemporary Folk Classic Electric 1616
1974-1990. Acoustic/electric, no inlay, slotted headstock, natural or sunburst.

1974-1990 — $275 — $350

Country Artist Classic Electric 6773
1995-2011. Classic electric, soft-cut, solid spruce top, slotted headstock, Ovation pickup system.

1995-2011 — $425 — $550

Country Artist Electric 1624
1971-1990. Nylon strings, slotted headstock, standard steel-string sized neck to simulate a folk guitar, on-board electronics.

1971-1990 — $450 — $600

Custom Ballader 1762
1992. Rounded cutaway, higher-end specs.

1992 — $600 — $800

Custom Elite Guitar Center 30th Anniversary
1994. 50 made.

1994 — $950 — $1,275

Custom Legend 1117
1970s. Non-electrical 2nd generation Ovation, higher-end with abalone inlays and gold hardware, open V-bracing pattern. Model 1117-4, natural.

1970s — $550 — $725

Custom Legend 1569
1980s. Rounded cutaway acoustic/electric, super shallow bowl, gloss black finish.

1980s — $500 — $650

Custom Legend 1619/1719
1970s. Acoustic/electric 2nd generation Ovation, electric version of model 1117, higher-end with abalone inlays and gold hardware, open V-bracing pattern.

1970s — $550 — $725

Custom Legend 1759
1984-2004. Single-cut acoustic/electric.

1984-2004 — $550 — $725

Custom Legend 1769
1982, 1993, 1996-1999. Single-cut acoustic/electric.

1982-1999 — $825 — $1,100

Custom Legend 1869
1994, 2003. Acoustic/electric, cutaway, super shallow bowl.

1994, 2003 — $625 — $825

Custom Legend 6759
2003 — $1,250 — $1,650

Deacon 1252
1973-1980. Axe-shaped solidbody electric, active electronics, diamond fret markers.

1973-1980 — $850 — $1,100

Deacon 12-String 1253
1975. Axe-shaped solidbody, diamond inlay, 2 pickups. only a few made.

1975 — $850 — $1,100

Eclipse
1971-1973. Thinline double cut acoustic-electric archtop, 2 pickups.

1971-1973 — $650 — $850

Elite 1718
1982-1997. Acoustic/electric, non-cut, deep bowl, solid spruce top, Adamas-type soundhole, volume and tone controls, stereo output.

1982-1997 — $625 — $825

Elite 1758
1990-1998. Acoustic/electric, non-cut, deep bowl.

1990-1998 — $625 — $825

Elite 1768
1990-1998. Acoustic/electric, cutaway, deep bowl.

1990-1998 — $525 — $675

Elite 1858 12-String
1993-2004. 12-string acoustic/electric, ebony 'board and bridge.

1993-2004 — $625 — $825

Elite 1868
1983-2004. Acoustic/electric, cutaway, shallow bowl.

1983-2004 — $475 — $625

Elite 5858
1991. Super shallow bowl, single cutaway, Adamas-style soundhole, gold hardware, on-board factory OP24 pickup.

1991 — $525 — $675

Elite Doubleneck
1989-1990s. Six- and 12-string necks, can be ordered with a variety of custom options.

1989 — $675 — $900

Elite Standard 6868
1994-1999. Elite Standard with cutaway shallow bowl.

1994-1999 — $500 — $650

Elite T/TX 1778
2002-2018. Acoustic/electric, cutaway, U.S. T replaced by import TX in '08.

2002-2008 T, original version — $625 — $825

2008-2018 TX, Import — $200 — $300

Folklore 1614
1972-1983. Acoustic/electric, 12-fret neck on full-size body, wide neck, on-board electronics.

1972-1983 — $450 — $600

GCXT
2008 Acoustic-electric, single-cut, flamed paint graphic, made for Guitar Center

2008 — $525 — $700

Glen Campbell 12-String 1118 (K-1118)
1968-1982. Acoustic, 12 strings, shallow-bowl version of Legend, gold tuners, diamond inlay.

1968-1982 — $500 — $650

Glen Campbell Artist 1627
2006. Glen Campbell 40th Anniversary model, diamond inlay, gold tuners.

2006 — $875 — $1,150

Glen Campbell Artist Balladeer 1127
1968-1990. Acoustic, shallow bowl, diamond inlay, gold tuners, natural.

1968-1990 — $500 — $650

MODEL YEAR	FEATURES	EXC. COND. LOW	HIGH

Hurricane 12-String K-1120

1968-1969. ES-335-style electric semi-hollowbody, double-cut, 12 strings, f-holes, 2 pickups.

1968-1969		$625	$825

Josh White 1114

1967-1970, 1972-1983. Wide 12-fret neck, dot markers, classical-style tuners.

1967-1970		$550	$700
1972-1983		$450	$600

Legend 1117

1972-1999. Deep bowl acoustic, 5-ply top binding, gold tuners, various colors (most natural).

1972-1999		$400	$550

Legend 1567/1867

1984-2004. Acoustic/electric, shallow bowl, single-cut, gold tuners.

1984-2004		$450	$600

Legend 12-String 1866

1989-2007. Acoustic/electric, cutaway, 12 strings, shallow bowl, 5-ply top binding, black.

1989-2007		$450	$600

Legend 1717

1990-2008. Acoustic/electric, 5-ply top binding, various colors.

1990-2008		$425	$575

Legend 1767

1990s. Acoustic/electric, deep bowl, single-cut, black.

1990s		$425	$575

Legend Cutaway 1667

1982-1996. Acoustic/electric, cutaway, deep bowl, abalone, gold tuners.

1982-1996		$475	$625

Legend Electric 1617

1972-1998. Acoustic/electric, deep bowl, abalone, gold tuners, various colors.

1972-1998		$400	$550

Pacemaker 12-String 1115/1615

1968-1982. Originally called the K-1115 12-string, Renamed Pacemaker in '72.

1968-1982		$450	$600

Patriot Bicentennial

*1976. Limited run of 1776 guitars, Legend Custom model with drum and flag decal and 1776*1976 decal on lower bout.*

1976		$775	$1,000

Pinnacle

1990-1992. Spruce or sycamore top, broad leaf pattern rosette, mahogany neck, piezo bridge pickup, sunburst.

1990-1992		$400	$525

Pinnacle Shallow Cutaway

1990-1994. Pinnacle with shallow bowl body and single-cut, sunburst.

1990-1994		$400	$525

Preacher 1281

1975-1982. Solidbody, mahogany body, double-cut, 2 pickups.

1975-1982		$550	$725

Preacher Deluxe 1282

1975-1982. Double-cut solidbody, 2 pickups with series/parallel pickup switch and mid-range control.

1975-1982		$550	$725

Preacher 12-String 1285

1975-1983. Double-cut solidbody, 12 strings, 2 pickups.

1975-1983		$550	$725

Thunderhead 1460

1968-1972. Double-cut, 2 pickups, gold hardware, phase switch, master volume, separate tone controls, pickup balance/blend control, vibrato.

1968-1972	Natural or rare color	$1,100	$1,500
1968-1972	Sunburst	$825	$1,100

Tornado 1260

1968-1973. Same as Thunderhead without phase switch, with chrome hardware.

1968-1973		$600	$800

UK II 1291

1980-1982. Single-cut solidbody, 2 pickups, body made of Urelite on aluminum frame, bolt-on neck, gold hardware.

1980-1982		$725	$925

Ultra GS/GP Series

1984. Korean solidbodies and necks assembled in U.S., DiMarzio pickups, offset double-cut (GS) with 1 hum, or hum/single/single or LP style (GP) with 2 humbuckers. There was also a bass.

1984		$325	$425

Ultra Series

1970s-2000s. Various Ultra model acoustic/electrics.

1970-2000s		$200	$600

Viper 1271

1975-1982. Single-cut, 2 single-coil pickups.

1975-1982		$575	$750

Viper EA 68

1994-2008. Thin acoustic/electric, single-cut mahogany body, spruce top over sound chamber with multiple upper bout soundholes, black.

1994-2008		$400	$525

Viper III 1273

1975-1982. Single-cut, 3 single-coil pickups.

1975-1982		$575	$750

VXT Hybrid

2007-2009. Single-cut solidbody, 2 Seymour Duncan '59 humbuckers, Fishman Power Bridge.

2007-2009		$625	$800

Overture Guitars

Luthier Justin Hoffman began building in the year 2008, professional to presentation grade, custom/production, solidbody guitars and basses in Morton, Illinois.

P. W. Crump Company

1975-present. Luthier Phil Crump builds his custom flat-top guitars in Arcata, California. He also builds mandolin-family instruments.

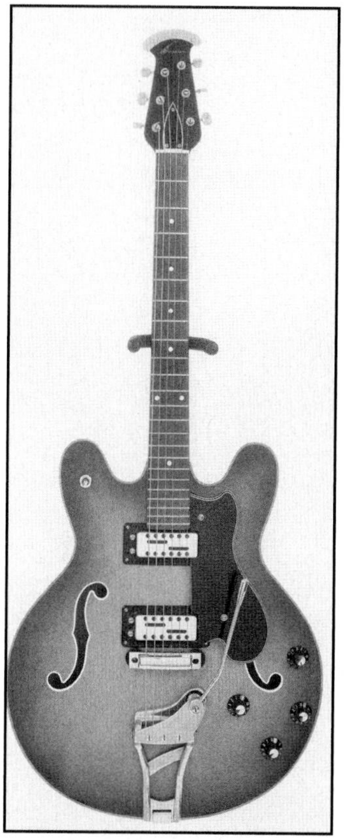

1970 Ovation Tornado 1260

Imaged by Heritage Auctions, HA.com

1976 Ovation Viper 1271

Rivington Guitars

ca. 1998 Parker NiteFly

Imaged by Heritage Auctions, HA.com

2017 Parkwood P810

MODEL YEAR	FEATURES	EXC. COND. LOW	HIGH

Palen

1998-present. Premium grade, production/custom, archtop guitars built by luthier Nelson Palen in Beloit, Kansas.

Palmer

Early 1970s-present. Budget and intermediate grade, production acoustic, acoustic/electric and classical guitars imported from Europe and Asia. They also have offered electrics.

Panache

2004-2008. Budget grade, production, solidbody electric and acoustic guitars imported from China.

PANaramic

1961-1963. Guitars and basses made in Italy by the Crucianelli accordion company and imported by PANaramic accordion. They also offered amps made by Magnatone.

Acoustic-Electric Archtop

1961-1963. Full body cutaway, 2 pickups.

1961-1963		$875	$1,125

Paolo Soprani

Early 1960s. Italian plastic covered guitars with pushbutton controls made by the Polverini Brothers.

Paramount

1921-1942, Late 1940s. The William L. Lange Company began selling Paramount banjos, guitar banjos and mandolin banjos in the early 1920s, and added archtop guitars in '34. The guitars were made by Martin and possibly others. Lange went out of business by '42; Gretsch picked up the Paramount name and used it on acoustics and electrics for a time in the late '40s.

GB

1920s-1930s. Guitar banjo.

1920s		$925	$1,225

Style C

1930s. 16" acoustic archtop, maple back and sides.

1930s		$425	$550

Style L

1930s. Made by Martin, limited to about 36 instruments, small body with resonator, Brazilian rosewood.

1930s	Spanish 6-string	$5,100	$6,625
1930s	Tenor 4-string	$3,700	$4,800

Parker

1992-2016. U.S.-made and imported intermediate, professional, and premium grade, production/custom, solidbody guitars featuring a thin skin of carbon and glass fibers bonded to a wooden guitar body. In '05, they added wood body acoustic/electrics. They also build basses. Originally located northwest of Boston, Parker was founded by Ken Parker and Larry Fishman (Fishman Transducers). Korg USA committed money to get the Fly Deluxe model into production in July '93. Parker added a Custom Shop in '03 to produce special build instruments and non-core higher-end models that were no longer available as a standard product offering. In early '04, Parker was acquired by U.S. Music Corp. and moved USA production from the Boston area to Chicago. U.S. Music was acquired by Jam Industries in '09 and production of Parker Guitars was ceased in '16.

Concert

1997 only. Solid sitka spruce top, only piezo system pickup, no magnetic pickups, transparent butterscotch.

1997		$1,525	$1,975

Fly

1993-1994. There are many Parker Fly models, the model simply called Fly is similar to the more common Fly Deluxe, except it does not have the Fishman piezo pickup system.

1993-1994		$1,525	$1,975

Fly Artist

1998-1999. Solid sitka spruce top, vibrato, Deluxe-style electronics, transparent blond finish.

1998-1999		$1,675	$2,175

Fly Classic

1996-1998, 2000-2011. One-piece Honduras mahogany body, basswood neck, electronics same as Fly Deluxe.

1996-2011		$1,525	$1,975

Fly Classic Maple

2000. Classic with maple body (vs. mahogany), transparent butterscotch.

2000		$1,525	$1,975

Fly Deluxe

1993-2016. Poplar body, basswood neck, 2 pickups, Fishman bridge transducer, '93-'96 models were offered with or without vibrato, then non-vibrato discontinued. The Deluxe normally came with a gig bag, but also offered with a hardshell case, which would add about $50 to the values listed.

1993-2016		$1,525	$1,975

Fly Supreme

1996-1999. One-piece flame maple body, electronics same as the Fly Deluxe, highly flamed butterscotch, includes hard molded case.

1996-1999		$2,100	$2,725

MaxxFly PDF Series

2013-2016. PDF is import line of more traditionally-shaped Maxx solidbodies, various models.

2013	PDF60	$300	$375
2013	PDF70	$375	$475
2013-2016	PDF30	$275	$350

Mojo

2003-2010. Fly either single-cut or double-cut.

2003-2005	Single-cut	$1,000	$1,300
2003-2010	Double-cut	$1,450	$1,875

NiteFly Series

1996-2009. Two single-coil and 1 humbucker pickup NiteFly, Fishman piezo system, bolt neck, maple body for '96-'98, ash for '99-present. Called the NiteFly in '96, NiteFly NFV2 ('97-'98), NiteFly NFV4 ('98), NiteFly NFV6 ('99), NiteFly SA ('00-present).

1996-2009	Various models	$825	$1,075

MODEL YEAR	FEATURES	EXC. COND. LOW	HIGH

P Series

2000-2009. Various models include P-38 (ash body, bolt maple neck, rosewood 'board, vibrato, piezo bridge pickup and active Parker Alnico humbucker and 2 single-coils, gig bag); P-40 (as P-38, but with pickups mounted on body, no 'guard); P-44 (mahogany body, flamed maple top, piezo bridge pickup and 2 special Parker humbuckers).

2000-2009 $300 $575

Tulipwood Limited Edition

1998. Limited build of 35, standard Deluxe features with tulipwood body.

1998 $1,475 $1,900

Parkwood

2007-present. Intermediate grade, acoustic and acoustic-electric guitars, Parkwood logo on headstock.

Patrick Eggle Guitars

1991-present. Founded by Patrick Eggle and others in Birmingham, England, building solid and semi-solidbody electric guitars and basses. In '95, Eggle left the company to build acoustics.

Patrick James Eggle

2001-present. Eggle co-founded the Patrick Eggle Guitar company in '91 building solidbodies. In '95, he left to do repairs and custom work. In '01 he opened a new workshop in Bedforshire, England, building professional and premium grade, production/custom, archtop and flatop guitars. For a short time he relocated to Hendersonville, North Carolina, but in '05 returned to England and opened a shop in Oswestry.

Paul Berger

1972-2015. Acoustic guitars built by luthier Paul Berger in St. Augustine, Florida. He died in '15.

Paul H. Jacobson

1974-present. Premium grade, production/custom, classical guitars built by luthier Paul H. Jacobson in Cleveland, Missouri.

Paul Reed Smith

1985-present. Intermediate, professional and premium grade, production/custom, solid, semi-hollow body, and acoustic guitars made in the U.S. and imported. They also build basses. Paul Reed Smith built his first guitar in '75 as an independent study project in college and refined his design over the next 10 years building custom guitars. After building two prototypes and getting several orders from East Coast guitar dealers, Smith was able to secure the support necessary to start PRS in a factory on Virginia Avenue in Annapolis, Maryland. On '95, they moved to their current location on Kent Island in Stevensville. In 2001 PRS introduced the Korean-made SE Series. Acoustics were added in '08.

MODEL YEAR	FEATURES	EXC. COND. LOW	HIGH

10th Anniversary

1995. 200 made, mother-of-pearl inlays, abalone purfling, gold pickups, either wide-fat or wide-thin neck, 10th Anniversary logo, price includes certificate of authenticity.

1995 With certificate $3,250 $4,200

305

2010-2013. Alder body, maple neck and 'board, birds, 3 single-coils.

2010-2013 $1,050 $1,350

305 25th Anniversary

2010. 305 made, 3 single-coils, wide-fat or wide-thin, 25th Anniversary logo.

2010 $1,075 $1,400

513 Rosewood

Dec.2003-2006. Brazilian rosewood neck, newly developed PRS pickup system with 13 sound settings, hum-single-hum pickups.

2003-2006 $2,100 $2,700

513 Swamp Ash

2010. Figured ash, natural.

2010 $1,225 $1,600

513 25th Anniversary

2010. Carved figured maple top, 25th Anniversary shadow birds inlay.

2010 $1,825 $2,375

Al Di Meola Prism

2008-2014. Curly maple 10 top, 22-fret, prism multicolor finish.

2008-2014 $1,550 $2,000

Artist/Artist I/Artist 24

1991-1994. Carved maple top, offset double-cut, 24-fret neck, bird markers, less than 500 made. A different Custom 24 Artist package was subsequently offered in the 2000s.

1991-1994 $2,775 $3,600

Angelus Cutaway

2009-present. Flat-top, on-board electronics, European spruce top, figured mahogany back and sides, flamed maple binding. Listed under Private Stock in '20, with select wood options.

2009-2020 $2,450 $3,200

Artist II/Artist 22

1993-1995. Curly maple top, maple purfling on rosewood 'board, inlaid maple bound headstock, abalone birds, 22 frets, gold hardware, short run of less than 500.

1993-1995 $1,825 $2,375

Artist III

1996-1997. Continuation of the 22-fret neck with some changes in materials and specs, figured maple tops, short run of less than 500 instruments.

1996-1997 $2,025 $2,650

Artist IV

1996. Continuation of the 22-fret neck with some upgrades in materials and specs, short run of less than 70 instruments.

1996 $2,900 $3,800

Artist Limited

1994-1995. Like the Artist II with 14-carat gold bird inlays, abalone purfling on neck, headstock and truss rod cover, Brazilian rosewood 'board, 165 made.

1994-1995 $2,900 $3,800

Patrick James Eggle Macon Junior

PRS Angelus Cutaway

2004 PRS CE-22

Robbie Keene

2003 PRS Custom 22

Bernunzio Uptown Music

MODEL YEAR	FEATURES	EXC. COND. LOW	HIGH

CE 22

1994-2000, 2005-2008. Double-cut carved alder body (1995), mahogany '96-'00 and '05-'07, back to alder in '08, bolt-on maple neck with rosewood 'board, dot inlays, 2 humbuckers, chrome hardware, translucent colors, options include vibrato and gold hardware and custom colors.

1994-1995	Alder	$1,050	$1,350
1996-2000	Mahogany	$1,050	$1,350
2005-2008	Reintroduced	$1,050	$1,350

CE 22 Maple Top

1994-2008. CE 22 with figured maple top, upgrade options included gold hardware, custom colors or 10 top.

1994-2008		$1,050	$1,350

CE 24 (Classic Electric, CE)

1988-2000, 2005-2008. Double-cut, alder body to '95, mahogany '96-'00 and '05-'07, back to alder in '08, carved top, 24-fret bolt-on maple neck, 2 humbuckers, dot inlays, upgrade options included gold hardware, custom colors or 10 top.

1988-1991	Rosewood 'board	$1,025	$1,325
1992-2008		$1,050	$1,350

CE 24 Maple Top (CE Maple Top)

1989-2008. CE 24 with figured maple top, upgrade options may include any or all the following: gold hardware, custom colors or 10 top.

1989-2008		$1,050	$1,350

Chris Henderson Signature

2007-2012. Single-cut, 3 exposed humbucker pickups, carved flame maple top on mahogany body, wide flat neck profile, 22 frets.

2007-2012		$1,050	$1,350

Corvette

2005-2006. Custom 22 with Velcity Yellow finish, Standard 22 red finish, Z06 inlays, Corvette logo on body.

2005	Custom 22, yellow	$1,050	$1,350
2006	Standard 22, red	$1,050	$1,350

Custom (Custom 24/PRS Custom)

1985-present. Double-cut solidbody, curly maple top, mahogany back and neck, pearl and abalone moon inlays, 24 frets, 2 humbuckers, tremolo, options include quilted or 10 Top, bird inlays, and gold hardware. 1985 Customs should be evaluated on a case by case basis.

1985		$3,000	$17,000
1986		$3,000	$6,500
1987		$2,700	$3,500
1988		$2,300	$3,000
1989		$1,800	$2,350
1990-2020		$1,500	$1,950

Custom 22

1993-2009, 2013-present. Custom 22 with flamed or quilted maple top on mahogany body, 22-fret set-neck, upgrade option is gold hardware, normally the quilt top is higher than flamed top.

1993-2020		$1,500	$1,950

Custom 22 (Brazilian)

2003-2004. Limited run of 500 with Brazilian rosewood 'board, figured 10 top, pearl bird inlays.

2003-2004		$2,400	$3,100

Custom 22 20th Anniversary

2005. Abalone 20th Anniversary birds inlay, 20th engraved on truss rod cover.

2005		$1,700	$2,200

Custom 22 Soapbar

1998-2002. 3 Seymour Duncan soapbar single-coils.

1998-2002		$1,300	$1,700

Custom 22/12

December 2003-2009. 12-string version, flame or quilt maple top, hum/single/hum pickups.

2003-2009		$1,800	$2,400

Custom 24 (Brazilian)

2003-2004. Limited run with Brazilian rosewood 'board, figured 10 top, pearl bird inlays.

2003-2004		$2,700	$3,500

Custom 24 (Walnut)

1992. Seamless matched walnut over mahogany, 3 made.

1992		$2,400	$3,100

Custom 24 20th Anniversary

2005. Abalone 20th Anniversary birds inlay, 20th engraved on truss rod cover.

2005		$1,800	$2,400

Custom 24 25th Anniversary

2010. Carved figured maple top, 25th Anniversary shadow birds inlay.

2010		$1,800	$2,400

Custom 24 30th Anniversary

2015. Figured maple top, 30th Anniversary on headstock, birds in flight neck inlay.

2015		$1,800	$2,400

Dave Navarro Signature

2005-2014. Carved maple top, bird inlays, tremolo, white.

2005-2014		$1,425	$1,850

DC3

2010-2013. Double-cut contoured body, bolt-on neck, 3 special single-coils.

2010-2013		$975	$1,275

DGT David Grissom Trem

2007-present. Based on the McCarty Tremolo model with an added volume control, a nitro topcoat, vintage colors, large frets designed for .011 gauge strings.

2007-2020		$1,775	$2,325

Dragon I

1992. Fingerboard inlay of a dragon made of 201 pieces of abalone, turquoise and mother-of-pearl, gold hardware, 50 made. The Dragon model collector requires an instrument to be truly mint and pristine with no play wear. The values shown here are for pristine instruments. Any issue whatsoever may dramatically reduce the high-side price shown. Price includes the certificate of authenticity.

1992	Amber quilt, amber flame	$13,800	$18,000
1992	Teal black	$12,300	$16,000

Dragon II

1993. Fingerboard inlay of a dragon made of 218 pieces of gold, coral, abalone, malachite, onyx and mother-of-pearl, 100 made.

1993		$7,500	$10,000

MODEL YEAR	FEATURES	EXC. COND. LOW	HIGH

Dragon III

1994. Fingerboard inlay of a dragon made of 438 pieces of gold, red and green abalone, mother-of-pearl, mammoth ivory, and stone, 100 made.

1994		$7,500	$10,000

Dragon 2002

2002. Limited edition of 100 guitars, ultra-inlay work depicting dragon head on the guitar body.

2002		$6,500	$8,500

Dragon 25th Anniversary

2009-2010. Multi-material dragon fingerboard inlay, green ripple abalone Modern Eagle headstock, body shape and electronics are modeled after an early company PRS guitar, 60 made.

2009-2010		$8,000	$10,500

Dragon Doubleneck

2005. Limited edition 20th Anniversary model, about 50 made.

2005		$15,000	$20,000

Dragon Millenium/Dragon 2000

1999-2000. Three-D dragon inlay in body versus neck inlay of previous models, limited production of 50 guitars.

1999-2000	Black cherry	$9,600	$12,500
1999-2000	Rare color	$11,500	$15,000

EG II

1991-1995. Double-cut solidbody, bolt-on neck, 3 single-coils, single-single-hum, or hum-single-hum pickup options, opaque finish.

1991-1995		$775	$1,000

EG II Maple Top

1991-1995. EG II with flamed maple top, chrome hardware.

1991-1995		$1,000	$1,300

EG 3

1990-1991. Double-cut solidbody, bolt-on 22-fret neck, 3 single-coil pickups.

1990-1991	Flamed 10 top	$975	$1,250
1990-1991	Opaque finish	$775	$1,000
1990-1991	Plain top, sunburst	$775	$1,000

EG 4

1990-1991. Similar to EG 3 with single-single-hum pickup configuration, opaque finish.

1990-1991		$775	$1,000

Golden Eagle

1997-1998. Very limited production, eagle head and shoulders carved into lower bouts, varied high-end appointments.

1997-1998		$11,000	$14,000

John Mayer Silver Sky

2018-present. Alder body, maple neck, rosewood or maple 'board, 3 single-coil pickups, various colors available.

2018-2020		$1,250	$1,655

John Mayer Silver Sky Limited Edition

2020-present. Lunar Ice color with unique poly-chromatic finish.

2020		$4,500	$6,000

Johnny Hiland

2006-2009. Maple fretboard.

2006-2009		$1,300	$1,700

KL-33 Korina

2008. Double-cut solid korina body, rosewood 'board, PRS Mira pickups, limited run of 100.

2008		$1,400	$1,800

KQ-24 Custom 24 (Killer Quilt)

2009. Limited Edition of 120, quilted maple top over korina body, 24 frets.

2009		$1,500	$2,000

Limited Edition

1989-1991, 2000. Double-cut, semi-hollow mahogany body, figured cedar top, gold hardware, less than 300 made. In '00, single-cut, short run of 5 antique white and 5 black offered via Garrett Park Guitars.

1989-1991	Tune-o-matic	$2,900	$3,800
2000		$2,900	$3,800

Limited Edition Howard Leese Golden Eagle

2009. Private Stock, curly maple top, old style mother of pearl birds, 100 made.

2009		$3,600	$4,700

LTD Experience (Limited Experience)

2007. 200 built to commemorate PRS 2007 Experience Open House, 24 frets, matching headstock, maple top with mahogany body.

2007		$1,450	$1,900

Mark Tremonti Model

2001-2007. Single-cut, 2 humbuckers, black or platinum finish.

2001-2007		$1,275	$1,675

Mark Tremonti Signature

2007-present. Single-cut, 2 humbuckers, figured maple top (10 top upgrade offered), various finishes.

2007-2020	10 top upgrade	$1,700	$2,200
2007-2020	Standard figured top	$1,500	$1,950

Mark Tremonti Tribal

2004-2006. With Tribal artwork, 100 made.

2004-2006		$1,625	$2,100

McCarty Model

1994-2007. Mahogany body with figured maple top, upgrade options may include a 10 top, gold hardware, bird inlays. Replaced by McCarty II.

1994-2007		$1,450	$1,900

McCarty II

2008-2009. Replaced the McCarty, featured new MVC (Mastering Voice Control) circuitry for switching between a single-coil voice to a heavy-metal voice, opaque finish.

2008-2009		$1,500	$2,000

McCarty 1957/2008 Limited

2008. "1957/2008" logo on truss rod cover, 08 serial number series, 150 made.

2008		$1,925	$2,500

McCarty 58/MC-58

2009-2011. "MC-58" logo on truss rod cover, similar to other McCarty models except for new neck shape, 57/08 humbucker pickups and V12 finish.

2009-2011		$2,025	$2,650

McCarty 594

2016-present. Figured maple top, mahogany back, bird inlays, various colors.

2016-2020		$2,400	$3,200

1986 PRS Custom 24

Gantt Kushner

PRS McCarty 594

1985 PRS Metal
Ian Gilmour

PRS SE Custom 24
Martin Secrest

MODEL YEAR	FEATURES	EXC. COND. LOW	HIGH

McCarty Archtop (Spruce)

1998-2000. Deep mahogany body, archtop, spruce top, 22-fret set-neck.

1998-2000 — $1,700 — $2,250

McCarty Archtop Artist

1998-2002. Highest grade figured maple top and highest appointments, gold hardware.

1998-2002 — $2,900 — $3,800

McCarty Archtop II (Maple)

1998-2000. Like Archtop but with figured maple top.

1998-2000 Flamed or quilt — $2,100 — $2,750

McCarty Hollowbody I/Hollowbody I

1998-2009. Medium deep mahogany hollowbody, maple top, 22-fret set-neck, chrome hardware. McCarty dropped from name in '06.

1998-2009 — $2,000 — $2,600

McCarty Hollowbody II/Hollowbody II

1998-2017. Like Hollowbody I but with figured maple top and back. McCarty dropped from name in '06.

1998-2017 — $2,000 — $2,600

McCarty Hollowbody/Hollowbody Spruce

2000-2009. Similar to Hollowbody I with less appointmentsm spruce top. McCarty dropped from name in '06.

2000-2009 — $1,600 — $2,050

McCarty Model/McCarty Brazilian

2003-2004. Limited run of 250, Brazilian rosewood 'board, Brazilian is printed on headstock just below the PRS script logo.

1999 — $2,700 — $3,500
2003-2004 — $2,400 — $3,100

McCarty Rosewood

2004-2005. PRS-22 fret with Indian rosewood neck.

2004-2005 — $1,700 — $2,200

McCarty Soapbar (Korina)

2008-2009. Korina body, 2 Duncan soapbar pickups.

2008-2009 — $1,400 — $1,825

McCarty Soapbar (Maple)

1998-2007. Soapbar with figured maple top option, nickel hardware.

1998-2007 — $1,450 — $1,875

McCarty Soapbar/Soapbar Standard

1998-2009. Solid mahogany body, P-90-style soapbar pickups, 22-fret set-neck, nickel-plated hardware, upgrade options may include gold hardware and bird inlays.

1998-2009 — $1,300 — $1,725

McCarty Standard

1994-2006. McCarty Model with carved mahogany body but without maple top, nickel-plated hardware, upgrade options may include gold hardware and bird inlays.

1994-2006 — $1,300 — $1,725

Metal

1985. Solid mahogany body with custom 2-color striped body finish and graphics, 24-fret set-neck, nickel hardware, 2 humbuckers.

1985 — $5,000 — $8,000

Metal '85 Reissue (Private Stock)

2008. With certificate of authenticity.

2008 — $3,000 — $4,000

MODEL YEAR	FEATURES	EXC. COND. LOW	HIGH

Mira

2007-2013. 2 exposed-coil humbuckers, abalone moon inlays, various opaque finishes. Replaced by S2 Mira in '14.

2007-2013 — $700 — $925

Mira 25th Anniversary

2010. 2 soapbar single-coils, shadow bird inlays.

2010 — $700 — $925

Mira Korina

2007-2009. Korina body and neck version, natural.

2007-2009 — $800 — $1,075

Mira Maple Top (MT)

2008-2009. Figured maple, moon or bird inlays.

2008-2009 — $925 — $1,200

Modern Eagle

2004-2007. Higher-end model based on Private Stock innovations, satin nitrocellulose finish, Brazilian rosewood neck.

2004-2007 — $3,500 — $4,500

Modern Eagle II/MEII

2008-2009. Curly maple top, black rosewood neck and 'board.

2008-2009 — $2,800 — $3,600

Modern Eagle Quatro/ME Quatro

2010-2012. Updated version of Modern Eagle, 53/10 humbucker pickups, select upgraded woods.

2010-2012 — $2,100 — $2,700

NF3

2010-2013. 3 Narrowfield pickups on top-mounted 1-piece assembly, double-cut contoured body, bolt-on neck.

2010-2013 — $900 — $1,150

P22

2012-2016. Carved figured maple top, birds, rosewood 'board, 10-top flame optional.

2012-2016 — $2,500 — $3,200

P245

2015. Semi-hollow electric, single-cut, 2 humbuckers and a piezo.

2015 — $2,200 — $2,800

Paul's Dirty 100

2010. Private Stock run of 100, highly figured curly maple top, moon inlays, 'Paul's Dirty 100' logo on back of headstock, black gold finish, paisley hard case.

2010 — $3,000 — $4,000

Paul's Guitar

2013-present. Carved figured maple top, mahogany back and neck, Hondouran rosewood 'board with brushstroke birds, various colors. Artist package and other options offered.

2013-2020 — $2,100 — $2,700

Private Stock Program

April 1996-present. Custom instruments based around existing PRS models. Values may be somewhat near regular production equivalent models or higher. The Private Stock option was reintroduced by 2003. That year a standard production offering might retail at about $7,500, but a '03 Santana I Private Stock might retail at over $15,000, so each guitar should be evaluated on a case-by-case basis.

1996-2020 Various models — $3,700 — $7,500

MODEL YEAR	FEATURES	EXC. COND. LOW	HIGH

PRS Guitar

1975-1985. About 75 to 100 guitars were built by Paul Smith himself or with a team of others, from '75 to '85, before he formed the current PRS company. Each guitar from this era should be evaluated on a case-by-case basis and the values shown are for guidance only. Authentication is highly recommended; these guitars do not have a PRS serial number. Some of these went to celebrity players and, as such, may command values higher than shown here because of that connection.

1975-1983	Mahogany	$5,000	$25,000
1975-1983	Maple	$7,000	$44,000
1984-1985	Preproduction with provenance	$5,000	$25,000
1985-1986	Team-built	$3,000	$8,000

Rosewood Limited

1996. Mahogany body with figured maple top, 1-piece rosewood neck with ultra-deluxe tree-of-life neck inlay, gold hardware.

1996		$6,100	$8,000

Santana

1995-1998, 2011-present. Limited production special order, figured maple top, 24-fret, symmetric Santana headstock, unique body purfling, chrome and nickel-plated hardware, yellow is most popular color, followed by orange, quality of top will affect price.

1995	1st 100 signed	$4,400	$5,700
1995-1998		$3,400	$4,400

Santana II

1998-2007. Three-way toggle replaces former dual mini-switches, special order, Brazilian 'board.

1998-2007		$4,000	$5,200

Santana III

2001-2006. Less ornate version of Santana II.

2001-2006		$1,500	$2,000

Santana (Brazilian)

2003. Quilted or flamed maple top, Brazilian rosewood neck and fretboard, eagle inlay on headstock, Santana Brazilian logo on back cover plate, 200 made.

2003-2004		$5,100	$6,700

Santana 25th Anniversary Santana II

2010. Figured maple top, rosewood 'board, eagle inlay on headstock, 25th Anniversary shadow birds.

2010		$1,900	$2,450

SC 58 Artist

2011-2012. Artist grade figured maple top, rosewood 'board, MOP/Paua birds.

2011-2012		$2,075	$2,700

SC 245

2007-2010. Single-cut 22-fret, 2 humbuckers, bird markers, SC 245 logo on truss rod cover.

2007	Flamed top, Brazilian 'board	$2,250	$2,900
2007-2010	Solid color top	$1,750	$2,250

SC 250

2007-2010. Figured maple top, 2 humbuckers, 25" scale and locking tuners.

2007-2010		$1,400	$1,800

SC-J Thinline

2008. Large full-scale single-cut hollowbody, originally part of Private Stock program until made in limited run of 300, select grade maple top and back over a mahogany middle body section, SC-J logo on truss rod cover.

2008		$3,600	$4,700

SE Series

2001-present. PRS import line, solidbody and semi-hollow.

2001-2020	Higher-end models	$400	$550
2001-2020	Most models	$225	$400

Signature/PRS Signature

1987-1991. 1,000 made, solid mahogany body, figured maple top, hand-signed signature on headstock, Vintage Yellow is most valuable color and will fetch more, orange is second, quilt top is more valuable than flametop. Each guitar should be evaluated on a case-by-case basis.

1987	Various colors	$3,000	$8,000
1988-1991	Various colors	$2,500	$6,000

Signature (Private Stock)

2011. Limited run by Private Stock, 100 made, 408 humbucker pickups (8 tonal configurations), special signature headstock and fretboard inlays.

2011		$4,600	$6,000

Singlecut

2000-2004, 2005-early 2008. Single-cut mahogany body, maple top, 22-fret 'board, upgrade options include 10 top flamed maple, gold hardware, bird inlays. Replaced by SC 245 and SC 250.

2000-2007	Various specs	$1,200	$1,800
2001	Brazilian neck/'board	$1,900	$2,500
2006-2007	Artist 20th Anniv, Brazilian	$1,900	$2,500
2006-2007	Standard 20th Anniv, Indian	$1,200	$1,575
2007-2008	Ltd Ed, Indian	$1,300	$1,675

Singlecut Hollowbody II CB 25th Anniversary

2010. Semi-hollow (CB means center block), f-holes, 10 maple top, bird inlays.

2010		$1,750	$2,300

Singlecut Hollowbody Standard

2008-2009. Mahogany body.

2008-2009		$1,750	$2,300

Singlecut Standard Satin

2006-2007. Thinner solid mahogany body, thin nitro cellulose finish, humbuckers or soapbars.

2006-2007		$1,000	$1,300

Special

1987-1990, 1991-1993. Similar to Standard with upgrades, wide-thin neck, 2 HFS humbuckers. From '91-'93, a special option package was offered featuring a wide-thin neck and high output humbuckers.

1987-1990	Solid color finish	$1,750	$2,300
1991-1993	Special order only	$2,000	$2,600

Standard

1987-1998. Set-neck, solid mahogany body, 24-fret 'board, 2 humbuckers, chrome hardware. Originally called the PRS Guitar from '85-'86 (see that listing), renamed Standard 24 from '98.

1987-1989	Sunburst & optional colors	$4,000	$5,200

2018 PRS SE Standard 24

Michael Mitchell

1989 PRS Standard

Imaged by Heritage Auctions, HA.com

2004 PRS Swamp Ash Special
Imaged by Heritage Auctions, HA.com

Peavey EVH Wolfgang

MODEL YEAR	FEATURES	EXC. COND. LOW	HIGH
1990-1991	Last Brazilian 'board	$2,100	$2,700
1992-1995		$1,075	$1,400
1995-1998	Stevensville	$1,075	$1,400

Standard 22

1994-2009. 22-fret Standard.

1994-1995		$1,075	$1,400
1995-1999	Stevensville	$1,075	$1,400
2000-2009		$1,075	$1,400

Standard 24

1998-2009. Renamed from Standard, solid mahogany body, 24-fret set-neck.

1998-2009		$1,075	$1,400

Starla

2008-2013. Single-cut solidbody with retro-vibe, glued neck, 2 chrome humbuckers. Replaced by S2 Starla in '14.

2008-2013		$700	$925

Studio

1988-1991, 2011-2013. Standard model variant, 24-fret set-neck, chrome and nickel hardware, single-single-hum pickups. The Studio package of pickups was offered until '96 on other models. Reissued in '11 with 22 frets, flamed maple top.

1988-1991		$1,550	$2,000
2011-2013	Reintroduced	$1,550	$2,000

Studio Maple Top

1990-1991. Mahogany solidbody, bird inlays, 2 single-coils and 1 humbucker, tremolo, transparent finish.

1990-1991		$1,550	$2,000

Swamp Ash Special

1996-2009. Solid swamp ash body, 22-fret bolt-on maple neck, 3 pickups, upgrade options available.

1996-2009		$1,125	$1,475

Swamp Ash Special 25th Anniversary

2010. Swamp ash body, bolt-on neck, 25th Anniversary shadow bird inlays.

2010		$1,125	$1,475

Tonare Grand

2009-2016. Full-body flat-top, European/German spruce top, rosewood back and sides, optional Adirondack red spruce top or AAAA grade top, onboard Acoustic Pickup System.

2009-2016		$2,450	$3,200

West Street/1980 West Street Limited

2008. 180 made for US market, 120 made for export market, faithful replica of the model made in the original West Street shop, Sapele top.

2008		$2,000	$2,600

Pawar

1999-2010. Founded by Jay Pawar, Jeff Johnston and Kevin Johnston in Willoughby Hills, Ohio, Pawar built professional and premium grade, production/custom, solidbody guitars.

PBC Guitar Technology

See Bunker Guitars for more info.

Pearl

1971-ca.1974. Acoustic and electric guitars sold by Pearl Musical Instrument Co. (Pearl drums), and built by other Japanese builders.

Peavey

1965-present. Headquartered in Meridan, Mississippi, Peavey builds budget, intermediate, professional, and premium grade, production/custom, acoustic and electric guitars. They also build basses, amps, PA gear, effects and drums. Hartley Peavey's first products were guitar amps. He added guitars to the mix in '78.

Axcelerator/AX

1994-1998. Offset double-cut swamp ash or poplar body, bolt-on maple neck, dot markers, AX with locking vibrato, various colors.

1994-1998		$300	$400

Cropper Classic

1995-2005. Single-cut solidbody, 1 humbucker and 1 single coil, figured maple top over thin mahogany body, transparent Onion Green.

1995-2005		$325	$400

Defender

1994-1995. Double-cut, solid poplar body, 2 humbuckers and 1 single-coil pickup, locking Floyd Rose tremolo, metallic or pearl finish.

1994-1995		$150	$185

Destiny

1989-1992. Double-cut, mahogany body, maple top, neck-thru-bridge, maple neck, 3 integrated pickups, double locking tremolo.

1989-1992		$225	$300

Destiny Custom

1989-1992. Destiny with figured wood and higher-end appointments, various colors.

1989-1992		$325	$425

Detonator AX

1995-1998. Double-cut, maple neck, rosewood 'board, dot markers, hum/single/hum pickups, black.

1995-1998		$170	$210

EVH Wolfgang

1996-2004. Offset double-cut, arched top, bolt neck, stop tailpiece or Floyd Rose vibrato, quilted or flamed maple top upgrade option.

1996	Pat pending early production	$2,000	$2,500
1997-1998	Pat pending	$1,500	$1,900
1999-2004	Flamed maple top	$1,350	$1,700
1999-2004	Standard top	$1,000	$1,250

EVH Wolfgang Special

1997-2004. Offset double-cut lower-end Wolfgang model, various opaque finishes, flamed top optional.

1996-2004	Standard top, D-Tuna	$550	$725
1997-2004	Flamed maple top	$600	$800
1997-2004	Standard basswood	$500	$675

Falcon/Falcon Active/Falcon Custom

1987-1992. Double-cut, 3 pickups, passive or active electronics, Kahler locking vibrato.

1987-1992	Custom color	$300	$350
1987-1992	Standard color	$200	$250

MODEL YEAR	FEATURES	EXC. COND. LOW	HIGH

Firenza
1994-1999. Offset double-cut, bolt-on neck, single-coil pickups.

1994-1999		$275	$325

Firenza AX
1994-1999. Upscale Firenza Impact with humbucking pickups.

1994-1999		$300	$375

Generation Custom EX
2006-2008. Single-cut solidbody, 2 humbuckers, 5-way switch.

2006-2008		$175	$225

Generation S-1/S-2/S-3
1988-1994. Single-cut, maple cap on mahogany body, bolt-on maple neck, six-on-a-side tuners, active single/hum pickups, S-2 with locking vibrato system.

1988-1994		$200	$400

Horizon/Horizon II
1983-1985. Extended pointy horns, angled lower bout, maple body, rear routing for electronics, 2 humbucking pickups. Horizon II has added blade pickup.

1983-1985		$200	$275

HP Special USA
2008-2011. Offset cutaway, 2 humbuckers.

2008-2011		$500	$625

Hydra Doubleneck
1985-1989. Available as a custom order, 6/12-string necks each with 2 humbuckers, 3-way pickup select.

1985-1989		$550	$675

Impact 1/Impact 2
1985-1987. Offset double-cut, Impact 1 has higher-end synthetic 'board, Impact 2 with conventional rosewood 'board.

1985-1987		$200	$275

Mantis
1984-1989. Hybrid X-shaped solidbody, 1 humbucking pickup, tremolo, laminated maple neck.

1984-1989		$200	$275

Milestone 12-String
1985-1986. Offset double-cut, 12 strings.

1985-1986		$125	$160

Milestone/Milestone Custom
1983-1986. Offset double-cut solidbody.

1983-1986		$100	$125

Mystic
1983-1989. Double-cut, 2 pickups, stop tailpiece initially, later Power Bend vibrato, maple body and neck.

1983-1989		$250	$350

Nitro I Active
1988-1990. Active electronics.

1988-1990		$200	$250

Nitro I/II/III
1986-1989. Offset double-cut, banana-style headstock, 1 humbucker (I), 2 humbuckers (II), or single/single/hum pickups (III).

1986-1989	Nitro I	$125	$160
1986-1989	Nitro II	$150	$200
1986-1989	Nitro III	$175	$250

Odyssey
1990-1994. Single-cut, figured carved maple top on mahogany body, humbuckers.

1990-1994		$375	$475

Odyssey 25th Anniversary
1990. Single-cut body, limited production.

1990		$500	$625

Omniac JD USA
2005-2010. Jerry Donahue-designed single-cut solidbody, 2 single-coils.

2005-2010		$650	$775

Patriot
1983-1987. Double-cut, single bridge humbucker.

1983-1987		$175	$225

Patriot Plus
1983-1987. Double-cut, 2 humbucker pickups, bi-laminated maple neck.

1983-1987		$200	$275

Patriot Tremolo
1986-1990. Double-cut, single bridge humbucker, tremolo, replaced the standard Patriot.

1986-1990		$200	$275

Predator Plus 7ST
2008-2010. 7-string.

2008-2010		$225	$275

Predator Series
1985-1988, 1990-2016. Double-cut poplar body, 2 pickups until '87, 3 after, vibrato.

1985-2016		$125	$175

Raptor Series
1997-present. Offset double-cut solidbody, 3 pickups.

1997-2020		$60	$85

Razer
1983-1989. Double-cut with arrowhead point for lower bout, 2 pickups, 1 volume and 2 tone controls, stop tailpiece or vibrato.

1983-1989		$300	$375

Reactor
1993-1999. Classic single-cut style, 2 single-coils.

1993-1999		$260	$325

Rockmaster II Stage Pack
2000s. Student solidbody Rockmaster electric guitar and GT-5 amp pack.

2000		$40	$50

Rotor Series
2004-2010. Classic futuristic body, elongated upper treble bout/lower bass bout, 2 humbuckers.

2004-2008	Rotor EXP	$225	$280
2004-2010	Rotor EX	$195	$240

T-15
1981-1983. Offset double-cut, bolt-on neck, dual ferrite blade single-coil pickups, natural. Amp-in-case available.

1981-1983	Amp-in-case	$200	$250
1981-1983	Guitar only	$150	$185

T-25
1979-1985. Synthetic polymer body, 2 pickups, cream 'guard, sunburst finish.

1979-1985		$250	$350

2000 Peavey EVH Wolfgang Special
Willie Moseley

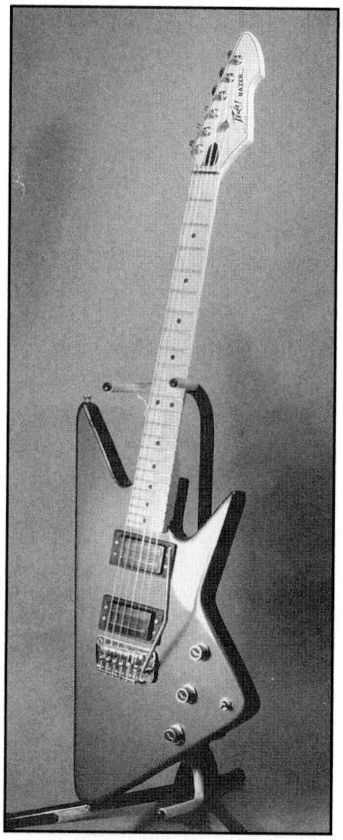

1984 Peavey Razer

1978 Peavey T-60

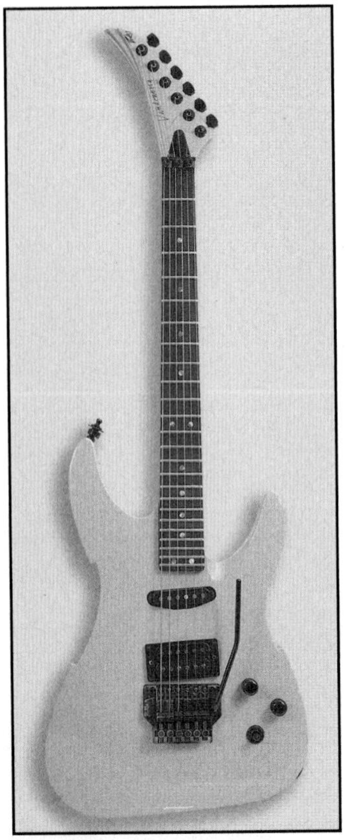

1988 Peavey Vandenberg

T-25 Special

1979-1985. Same as T-25, but with super high output pickups, phenolic 'board, black/white/black 'guard, ebony black finish.

1979-1985 $250 $350

T-26

1982-1986. Same as T-25, but with 3 single-coil pickups and 5-way switch.

1982-1986 $250 $350

T-27

1981-1983. Offset double-cut, bolt-on neck, dual ferrite blade single-coil pickups.

1981-1983 $300 $400

T-30

1982-1985. Short-scale, 3 single-coil pickups, 5-way select, by '83 amp-in-case available.

1982-1985 Guitar only $250 $325
1983-1985 Amp-in-case $325 $425

T-60

1978-1988. Contoured offset double-cut, ash body, six-in-line tuners, 2 humbuckers, thru-body strings, by '87 maple bodies, various finishes.

1978-1988 $425 $550

T-1000 LT

1992-1994. Double-cut, 2 single-coils and humbucker with coil-tap.

1992-1994 $225 $275

Tracer Custom

1989-1990. Tracer with 2 single humbuckers and extras.

1989-1990 $170 $210

Tracer/Tracer II

1987-1994. Offset scooped double-cut with extended pointy horns, poplar body, 1 pickup, Floyd Rose.

1987-1994 $170 $210

Vandenberg Quilt Top

1989-1992. Vandenberg Custom with quilted maple top, 2 humbuckers, glued-in neck, mahogany body and neck.

1989-1992 $875 $1,150

Vandenberg Signature

1988-1992. Double-cut, reverse headstock, bolt-on neck, locking vibrato, various colors.

1988-1992 $500 $650

Vortex I/Vortex II

1986. Streamlined Mantis with 2 pickups, 3-way, Kahler locking vibrato. Vortex II has Randy Rhoads Sharkfin V.

1986 $275 $340

V-Type Series

2004-2007. Offset double-cut solidbody, pointed reverse 6-on-a-side headstock, 2 humbuckers.

2004-2007 $250 $310

Wolfgang Special

1996-1997. Peavy logo on headstock (not EVH), curly maple quilt top, various colors.

1996-1997 $1,000 $1,300

Pederson Custom Guitars

2009-present. Luthier Kevin Pederson builds his premium grade, production/custom, hollowbody and solidbody guitars in Forest City, Iowa. From 1997-2009 he produced guitars under the Abyss brand name.

Pedro de Miguel

1991-present. Luthiers Pedro Pérez and Miguel Rodriguez build their professional and premium grade, custom/production, classical guitars in Madrid, Spain. They also offer factory-made instruments built to their specifications.

Pedulla

1975-2019. Known for basses, Pedulla did offer a few solidbody guitar models into the early 1980s.

MVP

1981-1984. Double-cut solidbody, 2 humbuckers, dot markers, 4 knobs with main toggle and 3 mini-toggle switches, stencil Pedulla logo, MVP serial number series.

1981-1984 $1,225 $1,600

Peekamoose

1983-present. Production/custom, premium grade, solidbody, chambered, and archtop electric guitars built in New York City, New York by luthier Paul Schwartz.

Pegasus Guitars and Ukuleles

1977-present. Premium grade, custom steel-string guitars built by luthier Bob Gleason in Kurtistown, Hawaii, who also builds ukulele family instruments.

Penco

Ca. 1974-1978. Generally high quality Japanese-made copies of classic American acoustic, electric and bass guitars. Imported by Philadelphia Music Company of Limerick, Pennsylvania during the copy era. Includes dreadnought acoustics with laminated woods, bolt-neck solidbody electric guitars and basses, mandolins and banjos.

Acoustic Flat-Top

1974-1978. Various models.

1974-1978 $100 $285

Electric

1974-1978. Various copies.

1974-1978 Solidbody $225 $450
1974-1978 Thinline Archtop $225 $450
1977 E-72 Howard Roberts $700 $1,100

Penn

1950s. Archtop and acoustic guitars built by made by United Guitar Corporation in Jersey City, New Jersey, which also made Premier acoustics. Penn was located in L.A.

Pensa (Pensa-Suhr)

1982-present. Premium grade, production/custom, solidbody guitars and basses built in the U.S. Rudy Pensa, of Rudy's Music Stop, New York

MODEL YEAR	FEATURES	EXC. COND. LOW	HIGH

City, New York, started building Pensa guitars in '82. In '85 he teamed up with John Suhr to build Pensa-Suhr instruments. Name changed back to Pensa in '96.

Classic

1992-Ca. 1998. Offset double-cut, 3 single-coils, gold hardware.

1992-1998	Various models	$1,650	$2,150

MK 1 (Mark Knopfler)

1985-2018. Offset double-cut solidbody, carved flamed maple bound top, 3 pickups, gold hardware, dot markers, bolt-on neck.

1985-2018		$1,650	$2,150

Suhr Custom

1985-1989. Two-piece maple body, bolt-on maple neck with rosewood 'board, custom order basis with a variety of woods and options available.

1985-1989	Various options	$1,650	$2,150

Suhr Standard

1985-1991. Double-cut, single/single/hum pickup configuration, opaque solid finish normally, dot markers.

1985-1991		$1,500	$1,950

Perlman Guitars

1976-present. Luthier Alan Perlman builds his premium grade, custom, steel-string and classical guitars in San Francisco, California.

Perri Ink.

Custom, professional grade, solidbody electric guitars built by luthier Nick Perri in Los Angeles, California, starting in 2009.

Perry Guitars

1982-present. Premium grade, production/custom, classical guitars built by luthier Daryl Perry in Winnipeg, Manitoba. He also builds lutes.

Petillo Masterpiece Guitars

1965-present. Intermediate, professional and premium grade, custom, steel-string, nylon-string, 12-string, resonator, archtop, and Hawaiian guitars in Ocean, New Jersey, originally by father and son luthiers Phillip J. "Doc" and David Petillo. Doc died in August, 2010.

Petros Guitars

1992-present. Premium grade, production/custom, flat-top, 12-string, and nylon-string guitars built by father and son luthiers Bruce and Matthew Petros in Kaukauna, Wisconsin.

PH Guitars

2006-present. Luthier Paul A. Hartmann builds professional and premium grade, custom, acoustic archtop and electric guitars in Hyde Park, New York.

MODEL YEAR	FEATURES	EXC. COND. LOW	HIGH

Phantom Guitar Works

1992-present. Intermediate grade, production/custom, classic Phantom, and Teardrop shaped solid and hollowbody guitars and basses assembled in Clatskanie, Oregon. They also offer the Mando-Guitar. Phantom was established by Jack Charles, former lead guitarist of the band Quarterflash. Some earlier guitars were built overseas.

Pheo

Luthier Phil Sylvester, began building in 1996, unique premium grade, production/custom, electric and acoustic guitars in Portland, Oregon.

Phoenix Guitar Company

1994-present. Luthiers George Leach and Diana Huber build their premium grade, production/custom, archtop and classical guitars in Scottsdale, Arizona.

Pieper

Premium grade, custom, solidbody guitars and basses built by luthier Robert Pieper in New Haven, Connecticut starting in 2005.

Pignose

1972-present. The original portable amp company also offers intermediate grade, production, dreadnaught and amplified electric guitars. They also offer effects. Refer to Amps section for more company info.

Pilgrim

1970's-late-1980s, 2010-present. Built in the U.K., luthier Paul Tebbutt introduced the brand back in the '70s and his guitars were available until late '80s. His designs are now used on intermediate grade, production, electric acoustic guitars, built in the Far East and distributed by John Hornby Skewes & Co. Ltd. They also offer mandolins, ukuleles and banjos.

Pimentel and Sons

1951-present. Luthiers Lorenzo Pimentel and sons build their professional, premium and presentation grade, flat-top, jazz, cutaway electric, and classical guitars in Albuquerque, New Mexico.

Player

1984-1985. Player guitars featured interchangable pickup modules that mounted through the back of the guitar. They offered a double-cut solidbody with various options and the pickup modules were sold separately. The company was located in Scarsdale, New York.

Pleasant

Late 1940s-ca.1966. Solidbody electric guitars, obviously others, Japanese manufacturer, probably not imported into the U.S.

Electric Solidbody

1940s-1966. Various models.

1940s-1966		$175	$225

Petros African Rose Dwende

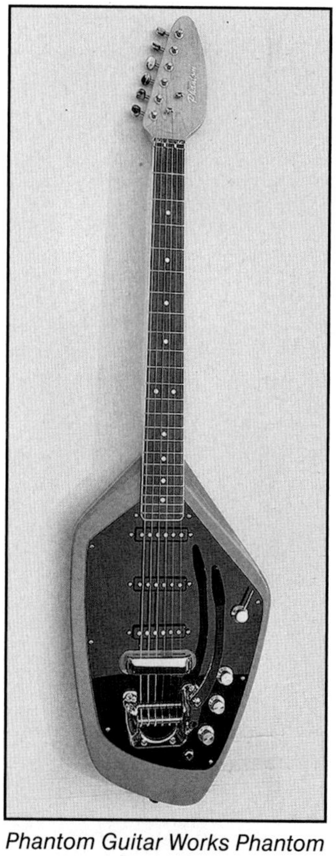

Phantom Guitar Works Phantom

1939 Prairie State 18 3/4"

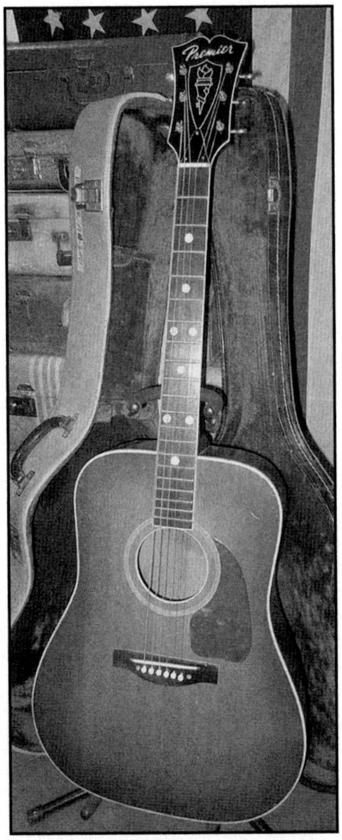

1959 Premier A-300

Rivington Guitars

MODEL YEAR	FEATURES	EXC. COND. LOW	HIGH

Potvin

2003-present. Production/custom, professional and premium grade, chambered, hollowbody and solidbody electric guitars built by luthier Mike Potvin in Ontario.

Prairie State

1927-ca. 1940. A Larson Brothers brand, basically a derivative of Maurer & Company. The Prairie State models were slightly more expensive than the equivalent Maurer models. They featured a patented steel rod mechanism to strengthen the body, which ran from the end block to the neck block. The model usually had Brazilian rosewood back and sides, laminated necks and X-bracing. Some later models were built with figured maple.

Prairiewood

2005-present. Luthier Robert Dixon of Fargo, North Dakota builds professional grade, production/custom, hollowbody archtop and solidbody guitars.

Premier

Ca.1938-ca.1975, 1990s-2010. Brands originally offered by Premier include Premier, Multivox, Marvel, Belltone and Strad-O-Lin. Produced by Peter Sorkin Music Company in Manhattan, New York City, New York, who began in Philadelphia, relocating to NYC in '35. First radio-sized amplifiers and stick-on pickups for acoustic archtops were introduced by '38. After WWII, they set up the Multivox subsidiary to manufacture amplifiers ca. '46. First flat-top with pickup appeared in '46.

Most acoustic instruments made by United Guitar Corporation in Jersey City, New Jersey. Ca. '57 Multivox acquires Strad-O-Lin. Ca.'64-'65 their Custom line guitars are assembled with probably Italian bodies and hardware, Japanese electronics, possibly Egmond necks from Holland. By ca. '74-'75, there were a few Japanese-made guitars, then Premier brand goes into hiatus. The brand reappears on Asian-made budget and intermediate grade, production, solidbody guitars and basses beginning in the '90s.

Bantam Custom

1950s-1960s. Single-cut archtop, dots, earlier with white potted pickups, then metal-covered pickups, and finally Japanese-made pickups (least valued).

1950s-60s		$700	$900

Bantam Deluxe

1950s-1960s. Single-cut archtop, fully bound, sparkle knobs, earlier with white potted pickups, then metal-covered pickups, and finally Japanese-made pickups (least valued), block markers, 1 or 2 pickups (deduct $100 for 1 pickup).

1950s-60s	Blond, sunburst	$1,376	$1,775

Bantam Special

1950s-1960s. Single-cut archtop, dots, early models with white potted pickups, then metal-covered pickups, and finally Japanese-made pickups (least valued), 1 or 2 pickups (deduct $100 for 1 pickup).

1950s-60s		$625	$825

Custom Solidbody

1958-1970. Notable solidbody bass scroll cutaway, various models with various components used, finally import components only.

1958-1970	1 pickup	$400	$525
1958-1970	2 pickups	$375	$500
1958-1970	3 pickups	$650	$850

Deluxe Archtop

1950s-1960s. Full body 17 1/4" archtop, square block markers, single-cut, early models with white potted pickups, later '60s models with metal pickups.

1950s-60s	Blond, sunburst	$1,100	$1,425

E-727

1958-1962. E-scroll style solidbody with scroll bass bout, 3 single-coil pickups, Premier headstock logo, made by the Multivox factory in New York.

1958-1962		$575	$750

Semi-Pro 16" Archtop

1950s-early-1960s. Thinline electric 16" archtop with 2 1/4" deep body, acoustic or electric.

1950s-60s	Acoustic	$575	$750
1950s-60s	Electric	$650	$850

Semi-Pro Bantam Series

1960s. Thinline electric archtop with 2 3/4" deep body, offered in cutaway and non-cut models.

1960s		$275	$350

Special Archtop

1950s-1960s. Full body 17 1/4" archtop, less fancy than Deluxe, single-cut, early models with white potted pickups, '60s models with metal pickups.

1950s-60s		$725	$950

Studio Six Archtop

1950s-early-1960s. 16" wide archtop, single pickup, early pickups white potted, changed later to metal top.

1950s-60s		$450	$575

Prenkert Guitars

1980-present. Premium and presentation grade, production/custom, classical and flamenco guitars built in Sebastopol, California by luthier Richard Prenkert.

Prestige

2003-present. Intermediate, professional, and premium grade, production/custom, acoustic, solidbody and hollowbody guitars and basses from Vancouver, British Columbia.

PST Guitars

Ca. 2000-present. Professional and premium grade, custom, electric guitars and basses, built by luthier P. Scott Tucker, in King George, Virginia. He has also built acoustic guitars.

Queen Shoals Stringed Instruments

1972-ca. 2010. Luthier Larry Cadle builds his production/custom, flat-top, 12-string, and nylon-string guitars in Clendenin, West Virginia.

MODEL YEAR	FEATURES	EXC. COND. LOW	HIGH

Queguiner, Alain

1982-present. Custom flat-tops, 12 strings, and nylon strings built by luthier Alain Queguiner in Paris, France.

Quest

1982-ca. 1986. Originally labeled Quest by Vantage, these solidbody guitars and basses were built in Japan, mostly by Chushin Gakki.

R.C. Allen

1951-2014. Luthier R. C. "Dick" Allen built professional and premium grade, custom hollowbody and semi-hollowbody guitars in El Monte, California. He has also built solidbody guitars. Allen passed away in 2014.

Rahan

1999-present. Professional grade, production/custom, solidbody guitars built by luthiers Mike Curd and Rick Cantu in Houston, Texas.

Rahbek Guitars

2000-present. Professional and premium grade, production/custom, solidbody electrics built by luthier Peter Rahbek in Copenhagen, Denmark.

Raimundo

1970s-present. Intermediate, professional and premium grade flamenco and classical guitars made in Valencia, Spain, by luthiers Antonio Aparicio and Manual Raimundo.

RainSong

1991-present. Professional grade, production, all-graphite and graphite and wood acoustic guitars built originally in Maui, and currently in Woodinville, Washington. Developed by luthier engineer John Decker with help from luthier Lorenzo Pimentel, engineer Chris Halford, and sailboard builder George Clayton.

RAM Guitars

2007-present. Luthier Ron Mielzynski builds his professional grade, production/custom, solidbody, chambered and archtop electric guitars in Fox River Grove, Illinois.

Rambler

See Strobel Guitars listing.

Ramirez, Jose

1882-present. Professional, premium, and presentation grade, custom/production, classical guitars built in Madrid, Spain. Founded by Jose Ramirez (1858-1923) who was an apprentice at the shop of Francisco Gonzales. Jose opened his own workshop in 1882 working with his younger brother, Manuel. Manuel split with Jose and opened his own, competing workshop. Jose's business was continued by Jose's son Jose Ramirez II (1885-1957), grandson Jose III (1922-1995), and great grandchildren Jose IV (1953-2000) and Amalia Ramirez. In the 1930's a larger body instrument with improved fan bracing was developed to meet the needs for more power and volume. Other refinements were developed and the Ramirez 1A Tradicional was soon introduced which found favor with Andres Segovia. The Ramirez company has produced both student and professional instruments, but in the classical guitar field, like the old-master violin business, a student model is often a very fine instrument that is now valued at $2,000 or more. In the 1980s Ramirez offered the E Series student guitar line that was built for, but not by, Ramirez. In 1991 the company offered the even more affordable R Series which was offered for about $1,300. As is typically the case, Ramirez classical guitars do not have a name-logo on the headstock. The brand is identified by a Ramirez label on the inside back which also may have the model number listed.

MODEL YEAR	FEATURES	EXC. COND. LOW	HIGH

A/1A

1960s-2000s. Classical, Brazilian or Indian rosewood.

1960s-70s	Brazilian, cedar	$5,100	$6,700
1970s-80s	Indian	$2,000	$3,500
1980s	Brazilian	$4,200	$5,500
1990-2000s	Indian	$1,800	$2,800

A/2A

1970s-80s	Indian	$2,300	$3,000

AE Estudio

2004		$1,425	$1,850

De Camera

1980s. Classical, cedar top, Brazilian rosewood back and sides.

1980s		$2,200	$2,850

E/1E/Estudio

1988-1990s. Intermediate level.

1988-1990s		$1,000	$1,300

E/2E

1990s-2000s. Red cedar top, Indian rosewood back and sides, Spanish cedar neck, ebony 'board.

1990-2000s		$1,050	$1,500

E/3E/Estudio

1990s. Cedar, rosewood.

1990s		$1,300	$1,700

E/4E/Estudio

1980s-2000s. Top of the E Series line, solid red cedar top, solid Indian rosewood back and sides.

1980-2000s		$1,650	$2,150

Flamenco

1920s-1979. European spruce top, cyprus back and sides.

1920s-50s		$3,500	$4,500
1960-1969		$2,475	$3,200
1970-1979		$2,400	$3,100

R1

1991-2014. Red cedar top, mahogany sides and back, Spanish cedar neck, ebony 'board. Replaced by RA series in '14.

1991-2014		$450	$600

1996 R.C. Allen Leader

Imaged by Heritage Auctions, HA.com

1966 Jose Ramirez 1A

Carter Vintage Guitars

Randy Wood Custom

1938 Recording King
Carson Robison
Imaged by Heritage Auctions, HA.com

MODEL YEAR	FEATURES	EXC. COND. LOW	HIGH

R2

1991-2014. Red cedar top, Indian rosewood back and sides, cedar neck, ebony 'board. Replaced by RA series in '14.

1991-2014 $750 $975

R3

1998. Cedar, rosewood.

1998 $750 $975

R4 Classical

1995-2014. All solid wood, Western red cedar top, rosewood back and sides. Replaced by RB series in '14.

1995-2014 $950 $1,250

S/S1

2005-2007. Solid German spruce top, African mahogany sides and back, most affordable in Estudio line.

2005-2007 $550 $725

Segovia

Cedar, Indian rosewood.

1966 $5,600 $7,300
1974-1978 $4,000 $5,200

SP Series

2002-2018. Semi-professional level designed to be between the company's 'concert/professional' series and 'student' series.

2002-2018 $3,900 $5,000

Ramirez, Manuel

1890-1916. Brother of Jose Ramirez, and a respected professional classical guitar builder from Madrid, Spain. His small shop left no heirs so the business was not continued after Manuel's death in 1916. Manuel was generally considered to be more famous during his lifetime than his brother Jose, and while his business did not continue, Manuel trained many well known Spanish classical guitar luthiers who prospered with their own businesses. During Manuel's era his shop produced at least 48 different models, with prices ranging from 10 to 1,000 pesetas, therefore vintage prices can vary widely. Guitars made prior to 1912 have a label with a street address of Arlaban 10, in 1912 the shop moved to Arlaban 11.

Randy Reynolds Guitars

1996-2018. Luthier Randy Reynolds builds his premium grade, production/custom classical and flamenco guitars in Colorado Springs, Colorado. Reynolds announced his retirement January 1, 2019.

Randy Wood Guitars

1968-present. Premium grade, custom/production, archtop, flat-top, and resonator guitars built by luthier Randy Wood in Bloomingdale, Georgia. He also builds mandolins.

Rarebird Guitars

1978-present. Luthier Bruce Clay builds his professional and premium grade, production/custom, guitars and basses, originally in Arvada, Colorado, and currently in Hoehne, Colorado.

MODEL YEAR	FEATURES	EXC. COND. LOW	HIGH

Rat Fink

2002-2005. Lace Music Products, the makers of the Lace Sensor pickup, offered the intermediate grade, production, guitars and basses, featuring the artwork of Ed "Big Daddy" Roth until '05.

Rayco

2002-present. Professional and premium grade, custom, resonator and Hawaiian-style acoustic guitars built in British Columbia, by luthiers Mark Thibeault and Jason Friesen.

Recco

1960s. Electric guitar imports made by Teisco, pricing similar to Teisco models, Recco logo on headstock, upscale solidbodies can have four pickups with several knobs and four switches.

Electric Solidbody

1960s 4 pickups $375 $500

Recording King

1929-1943. Brand name used by Montgomery Ward for instruments made by various American manufacturers, including Kay, Gibson and Gretsch. Generally mid-grade instruments. M Series are Gibson-made archtops.

Carson Robison/Model 1052

1938-1939. Made by Gibson, flat-top, 16", sunburst.

1938-1939 $1,950 $2,525

Kay 17" Flat-Top

1940-1941 $750 $975

M-2

1936-1941. Gibson-made archtop with carved top and f-holes, maple back and sides.

1936-1941 $550 $725

M-3

1936-1941. Gibson-made archtop, f-holes, maple back and sides, carved top.

1936-1941 $675 $875

M-4

1937-1940. Gibson-made archtop, f-holes, maple back and sides, rope-checkered binding, flying bat wing markers.

1937-1940 $825 $1,075

M-5

1936-1941. Gibson-made archtop with f-holes, maple back and sides, trapeze tailpiece, checkered top binding.

1936-1938 16" body $1,075 $1,400
1939-1941 17" body $1,150 $1,500

M-6

1938-1939. M-5 with upgraded gold hardware.

1938-1939 $1,175 $1,550

Model 681

Mid-1930s. Small flat top by Gibson, ladder-braced.

1930s $1,075 $1,400

Model 1124

1937. 16" acoustic archtop, body by Gibson, attractive higher-end appointments, block-dot markers, sunburst.

1937 $1,450 $1,875

MODEL YEAR	FEATURES	EXC. COND. LOW	HIGH

Ray Whitley

1939-1940. High-quality model made by Gibson, round shoulder flat-top, mahogany (Model 1028) or Brazilian rosewood (Model 1027) back and sides, 5-piece maple neck, Ray Whitley stencil script peghead logo, pearl crown inlay on peghead, fancy inlaid markers.

1939-1940	Brazilian	$20,500	$26,500
1939-1940	Mahogany	$10,300	$13,300

Roy Smeck

1938-1940. 16.25" electric archtop, large Recording King badge logo, Roy Smeck stencil logo, bar pickup, 2 control knobs on upper bass bout, dot markers.

1938-1940		$1,125	$1,450

Recording King (TML)

2005-present. Budget grade, production, acoustic cowboy stenciled guitars designed by Greg Rich for The Music Link, which also offers Johnson and other brand instruments. They also have banjos and ukes.

Redentore

2007-present. Luthier Mark Piper builds professional and premium grade, production/custom, archtop jazz, acoustic flat-top, carve-top and semi-hollow electric guitars in Columbia, Tennessee.

RedLine Acoustics and RedLine Resophonics

2007-present. Professional and premium grade, production, acoustic and resophonic guitars built in Hendersonville, Tennessee by luthiers Steve Smith, Jason Denton, Christian McAdams and Ryan Futch. They also build mandolins and plan to add lap steels.

Regal

Ca. 1895-1966, 1987-present. Intermediate and professional grade, production, acoustic and wood and metal body resonator guitars and basses. Originally a mass manufacturer founded in Indianapolis, Indiana, the Regal brand was first used by Emil Wulschner & Son. After 1900, new owners changed the company name to The Regal Manufacturing Company. The company was moved to Chicago in '08 and renamed the Regal Musical Instrument Company. Regal made brands for distributors and mass merchandisers as well as marketing its own Regal brand. Regal purchased the Lyon & Healy factory in '28. Regal was licensed to co-manufacture Dobros in '32 and became the sole manufacturer of them in '37 (see Dobro for those instruments). Most Regal instruments were beginner-grade; however, some very fancy archtops were made during the '30s. The company was purchased by Harmony in '54 and absorbed. From '59 to '66, Harmony made acoustics under the Regal name for Fender. In '87 the Regal name was revived on a line of resonator instruments by Saga.

MODEL YEAR	FEATURES	EXC. COND. LOW	HIGH

Acoustic Hawaiian

1930s. Student model, small 13" body, square neck, glued or trapeze bridge.

1930s	Faux grain painted finish	$325	$425
1930s	Plain sunburst, birch, trapeze	$210	$275

Concert Folk H6382

1960s. Regal by Harmony, solid spruce top, mahogany back and sides, dot markers, natural.

1960s		$225	$290

Deluxe Dreadnought H6600

1960s. Regal by Harmony, solid spruce top, mahogany back and sides, bound top and back, rosewood 'board, dot markers, natural.

1960s		$225	$290

Dreadnought 12-String H1269

1960s. Regal by Harmony, solid spruce top, 12-string version of Deluxe, natural.

1960s		$225	$290

Esquire

1940s. 15 1/2" acoustic archtop, higher-end appointments, fancy logo art and script pearl Esquire headstock logo and Regal logo, natural.

1940s		$925	$1,200

Meteor

1960s. Single-cut acoustic-electric archtop, 2 pickups.

1960s		$1,125	$1,450

Model 27

1933-1942. Birch wood body, mahogany or maple, 2-tone walnut finish, single-bound top, round or square neck.

1933-1942		$875	$1,050

Model 45

1933-1937. Spruce top and mahogany back and sides, bound body, square neck.

1933-1937		$1,425	$1,850

Model 46

1933-1937. Round neck.

1933-1937		$1,425	$1,850

Model 55 Standard

1933-1934 Regal's version of Dobro Model 55 which was discontinued in '33

1933-1934		$875	$1,150

Model 75

1939-1940. Metal body, square neck.

1939-1940		$1,600	$2,075

Model TG 60 Resonator Tenor

1930s. Wood body, large single cone biscuit bridge resonator, 2 upper bout metal ports, 4-string tenor.

1930s		$1,250	$1,625

Parlor

1920s. Small body, slotted headstock, birch sides and back, spruce top.

1920s		$250	$325

Prince

1930s. High-end 18" acoustic archtop, fancy appointments, Prince name inlaid in headstock along with Regal script logo and strolling guitarist art.

1930s		$1,600	$2,075

Recording King RO-T16

1930s Regal Model 27
Imaged by Heritage Auctions, HA.com

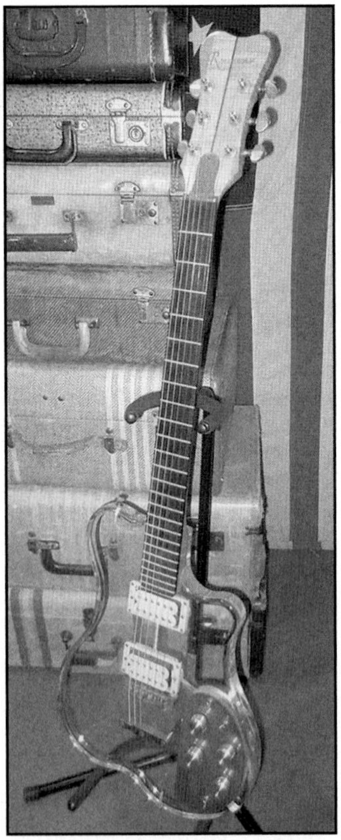

1978 Rennaissance SPG
Rivington Guitars

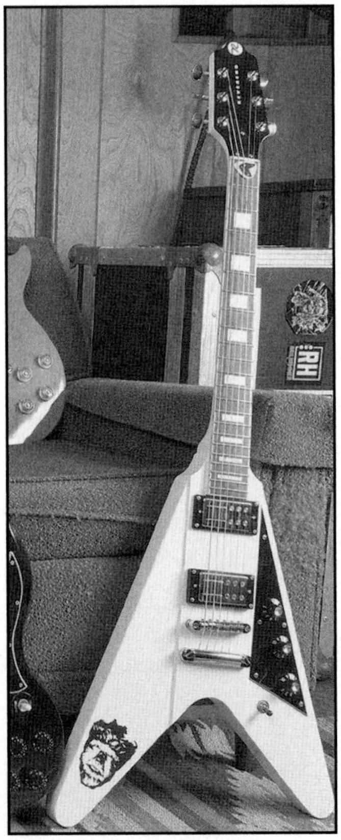

Reverend Volcano
Christopher Tritschler

MODEL YEAR	FEATURES	EXC. COND. LOW	HIGH

Spirit Of '76
1976. Red-white-blue, flat-top.

1976	$385	$500

Reliance
1920s. Instruments built by the Oscar Schmidt Co. and possibly others. Most likely a brand made for a distributor.

Relixx
2001-2013. Intermediate and professional grade, production/custom, aged vintage-style solidbody guitars built in Sanborn, New York by luthier Nick Hazlett. He discontinued complete guitars in '13 and now offers only vintage parts.

Renaissance
1978-1980. Plexiglass solidbody electric guitars and basses. Founded in Malvern, Pennsylvania, by John Marshall (designer), Phil Goldberg and Daniel Lamb. Original partners gradually leave and John Dragonetti takes over by late-'79. The line is redesigned with passive electronics on guitars, exotic shapes, but when deal with Sunn amplifiers falls through, company closes. Brandname currently used on a line of guitars and basses made by Rick Turner in Santa Cruz, California.

Fewer than 300 of first series made, plus a few prototypes and several wooden versions; six or so prototypes of second series made. SN=M(M) YYXXXX: month, year, consecutive number.

Electric Plexiglas Solidbody
1978-1980. Models include the SPG ('78-'79, DiMarzio pickups, active electronics), T-200G ('80, Bich-style with 2 passive DiMarzio pickups), and the S-200G ('80, double-cut, 2 DiMarzio pickups, passive electronics).

1978-1980	$650	$850

Renaissance Guitars
1994-present. Professional grade, custom, semi-acoustic flat-top, nylon-string and solidbody guitars and basses built by luthier Rick Turner in Santa Cruz, California. He also builds ukes.

Republic Guitars
2006-present. Intermediate grade, production, reso-phonic and Weissenborn-style guitars imported by American Folklore, Inc. of Austin, Texas. They also offer mandolins and ukes.

Retronix
2013-present. Korean-made solidbody guitars designed and imported by J. Backlund. They also build J. Backlund guitars.

Reuter Guitars
1984-present. Professional and premium grade, custom, flat-top, 12-string, resonator, and Hawaiian guitars built by luthier John Reuter, the Director of Training at the Roberto-Venn School of Luthiery, in Tempe, Arizona.

Reverend
1996-present. Intermediate grade, production, guitars and basses, designed by luthier and founder Joe Naylor, manufactured in South Korea, and setup by Reverend originally in Warren, Livonia, Michigan, and currently in Toledo, Ohio. There were also earlier U.S. production guitars built in Warren. Reverend has built amps and effects in the past. In 2010, Ken and Penny Haas purchased the company with Naylor continuing with design. Naylor also founded Naylor Amps, Armor Gold Cables, Stringdog, and Railhammer Pickups.

Rex
1920s-1940s, 1950s-1960s. Generally, beginner-grade guitars made by Kay and sold through Fred Gretsch distributors. In the '50s and '60s, the Lamberti Brothers Company in Melbourne, Australia built electrics bearing the Rex brand that were not distributed by Gretsch. They also had built amps.

Ribbecke Guitars
Premium and presentation grade, custom thinline, flat-top, and archtop guitars built by luthier Tom Ribbecke, starting in 1973, in Healdsburg, California.

Rice Custom Guitars
1998-present. Father and son luthiers, Richard Rice and Christopher Rice, build professional and premium grade, custom, solidbody, semi-hollow and hollowbody electric guitars and basses in Arlington Heights, Illinois.

Rich and Taylor
1993-1996. Custom acoustic and electric guitars, mandolins and banjos from luthiers Greg Rich and Mark Taylor (Crafters of Tennessee).

Richard Schneider
1960s-1997. Luthier Richard Schneider built his acoustic guitars in Washington state. Over the years, he collaborated with Dr. Michael A. Kasha on many guitar designs and innovations. Originally from Michigan, he also was involved in designing guitars for Gretsch and Gibson. He died in early '97.

Richie's Guitar Shop
1983-present. Intermediate and professional grade, custom, electric guitars and basses, built by luthier Richard 'Richie' Baxt, in New York City, New York.

Richmond
Luthiers Robert Godin (Godin Guitars) and Daniel Fiocco build intermediate and professional grade, production, chambered and solidbody electric guitars in Richmond, Quebec. Richmond is one of several brands used by Godin.

MODEL YEAR	FEATURES	EXC. COND. LOW	HIGH

Richter Mfg.

1930s. One of many Chicago makers of the era, the company allegedly bought already-made guitars from other manufacturers, painted and decorated them to their liking and resold them.

Rick Hayes Instruments

2006-present. Owned by Rick and Lyn Hayes and offering professional and premium grade, production/custom, dreadnought acoustic and electric guitars, and mandolins built by Rick and Steve Hogsed in Goshen, Ohio.

Rick Turner

1979-1981, 1990-present. Rick Turner has a long career as a luthier, electronics designer and innovator. He also makes the Renaissance line of guitars in his shop in Santa Cruz, California. The guitars and basses built in 1979-'81 were numbered sequentially in the order they were completed and shipped with the second part of the serial number indicating the year the instrument was built. Turner estimates that approximately 200 instruments were made during that period.

Rickenbacker

1931-present. Professional and premium grade, production/custom, acoustic and electric guitars built in California. They also build basses. Founded in Los Angeles as Ro-Pat-In by ex-National executives George Beauchamp, Paul Barth and National's resonator cone supplier Adolph Rickenbacher. Rickenbacher was born in Basel, Switzerland in 1886, emigrated to the U.S. and moved to Los Angeles in 1918, opening a tool and die business in '20.

In the mid-'20s, Rickenbacher began providing resonator cones and other metal parts to George Beauchamp and Louis Dopyera of National String Instrument Corporation and became a shareholder in National. Beauchamp, Barth and Harry Watson came up with wooden "frying pan" electric Hawaiian lap steel for National in '31; National was not interested, so Beauchamp and Barth joined with Rickenbacher as Ro-Pat-In (probably for ElectRO-PATent-INstruments) to produce Electro guitars. Cast aluminum frying pans were introduced in '32. Some Spanish guitars (flat-top, F-holes) with Electro pickups were produced beginning in '32. Ro-Pat-In changes their name to Electro String Instrument Corporation in '34, and brand becomes Rickenbacher Electro, soon changed to Rickenbacker, with a "k." Beauchamp retires in '40. There was a production hiatus during World War II.

In '53, Electro was purchased by Francis Cary Hall (born 1908), owner of Radio and Television Equipment Company (Radio-Tel) in Santa Ana, California (founded in '20s as Hall's Radio Service, which began distributing Fender instruments in '46). The factory was relocated to Santa Ana in '62 and the sales/distribution company's name is changed from Radio-Tel to Rickenbacker Inc. in '65.

MODEL YEAR	FEATURES	EXC. COND. LOW	HIGH

1950s serial numbers have from 4 to 7 letters and numbers, with the number following the letter indicating the '50s year (e.g., NNL8NN would be from '58). From '61 to '86 serial numbers indicate month and year of production with initial letter A-Z for the year A=1961, Z=1986) followed by letter for the month A-M (A=January) plus numbers as before followed by a number 0-9 for the year (0=1987; 9=1996). To avoid confusion, we have listed all instruments by model number. For example, the Combo 400 is listed as Model 400/Combo 400. OS and NS stands for Old Style and New Style. On the 360, for example, Ric changed the design in 1964 to their New Style with more rounded body horns and rounded top edges and other changes. But they still offered the Old Style with more pointed horns and top binding until the late 1960s. Ric still sometimes uses the two designations on some of their vintage reissues.

Electro ES-16

1964-1971. Double-cut, set neck, solidbody, 3/4 size, 1 pickup. The Electro line was manufactured by Rickenbacker and distributed by Radio-Tel. The Electro logo appears on the headstock.

1964-1971		$825	$1,075

Electro ES-17

1964-1975. Cutaway, set neck, solidbody, 1 pickup.

1964-1975		$900	$1,175

Electro Spanish (Model B Spanish)

1935-1943. Small guitar with a lap steel appearance played Spanish-style, hollow black bakelite body augmented with 5 chrome plates (white enamel in '40), 1 octagon knob (2 round-ridged in '38), called the Model B ca. '40.

1935-1937	Chrome, 1 knob	$2,750	$3,625
1935-1937	Tenor 4-string, 1 knob	$2,750	$3,625
1938-1939	Chrome, 2 knobs	$2,750	$3,625
1940-1943	White, 2 knobs	$2,450	$3,175

Electro-Spanish Ken Roberts

1935-1939. Mahogany body, f-holes in lower bout, horseshoe pickup, Kauffman vibrato.

1935-1939		$3,425	$4,525

Model 220 Hamburg

1992-1997. Solidbody.

1992-1997		$850	$1,100

Model 230 GF Glenn Frey

1992-1997. Glenn Frey Limited Edition, solidbody, 2 high output humbuckers, black hardware, chrome 'guard.

1992-1997		$1,625	$2,100

Model 230 Hamburg

1983-1991. Solidbody, offset double-cut, 2 pickups, dot inlay, rosewood 'board, chrome-plated hardware.

1983-1991		$950	$1,250

Model 250 El Dorado

1983-1991. Deluxe version of Hamburg, gold hardware, white binding.

1983-1991		$900	$1,150

Model 260 El Dorado

1992-1997. Replaces 250.

1992-1997		$900	$1,150

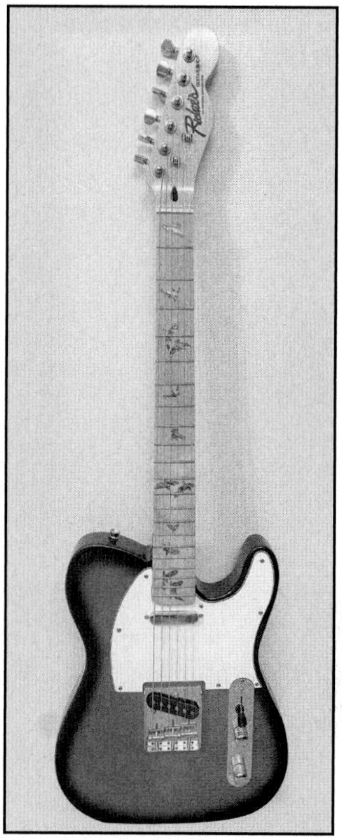

Richie's Guitar Shop

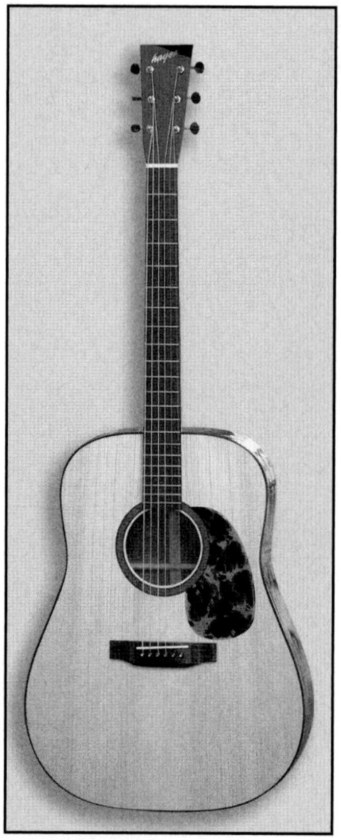

Rick Hayes Instruments

GUITARS

1986 Rickenbacker 320
Jeff DiPaola

1990 Rickenbacker 325
Carter Vintage Guitars

MODEL YEAR	FEATURES	EXC. COND. LOW	HIGH

Model 310
1958-1970, 1981-1985. Two-pickup version of Model 320.

1958-1960	Capri, thick body	$8,400	$11,000
1961-1969	Thinner body	$5,200	$6,700
1981-1985	Reintroduced	$1,550	$2,000

Model 315
1958-1974. Two-pickup version of Model 325.

1958-1960	Capri, thick body	$8,400	$11,000
1960-1969	Thinner body	$5,200	$6,700
1970-1973		$3,100	$4,000
1974		$2,700	$3,500

Model 320
1958-1992. Short-scale hollowbody, 3 pickups, f-holes optional in '61 and standard in '64 and optional again in '79.

1958-1960	Capri, thick body	$11,000	$14,200
1960-1969		$7,600	$9,800
1970-1973		$3,100	$4,000
1974-1979		$2,500	$3,200
1980-1992		$2,075	$2,675

Model 320/12V63
1986. Short run for Japanese market.

1986		$2,550	$3,300

Model 325
1958-1975, 1985-1992. This was a low production model, with some years having no production. In the mid-'60s, the 325 was unofficially known as the John Lennon Model due to his guitar's high exposure on the Ed Sullivan Show and in the Saturday Evening Post.

1958	John Lennon specs, 8 made	$38,000	$49,000
1959-1960		$17,000	$22,000
1961-1963		$14,000	$18,000
1964-1966	Fireglo or black	$6,500	$8,500
1966	Mapleglo	$6,500	$8,500
1967-1969		$6,500	$8,500
1970-1975		$3,350	$4,350

Model 325 B
1983-1984. Reissue of early '60s model.

1983-1984		$1,875	$2,450

Model 325 JL
1989-1993. John Lennon Limited Edition, 3 vintage Ric pickups, vintage vibrato, maple body; 3/4-size rosewood neck, a 12-string and a full-scale version are also available.

1989-1993		$2,300	$3,000

Model 325 S
1964-1967. F-holes.

1964-1967		$8,400	$11,000

Model 325/12
1985-1986, 1999. Based on John Lennon's one-of-a-kind '64 325/12.

1985-1986		$2,225	$2,900
1999		$2,225	$2,900

Model 325C58
2002-2014. Copy of the '58 model that John Lennon saw in Germany.

2002-2014		$1,875	$2,450

Model 325C64
2002-present. Copy of the famous '64 model.

2002-2019		$1,875	$2,450

MODEL YEAR	FEATURES	EXC. COND. LOW	HIGH

Model 325V59
1984-2001. Reissue of John Lennon's modified '59 325, 3 pickups, short-scale.

1984-2001		$2,400	$3,100

Model 325V63
1984-2001. Reissue of John Lennon's '63 325.

1984-2001		$2,400	$3,100

Model 330
1958-present. Thinline hollowbody, 2 pickups, slash soundhole, natural or sunburst.

1958-1960	Capri, thick body	$7,700	$10,000
1961-1969	Thinner body	$4,000	$5,200
1970-1979		$2,850	$3,700
1980-2020		$1,425	$1,850

Model 330 F
1958-1969. F-style.

1958-1960	Thick version	$7,900	$10,200
1961-1969	Thin version	$3,400	$4,400

Model 330/12
1965-present. Thinline, 2 pickups, 12-string version of Model 300.

1964	Only 1 made	$4,200	$5,500
1965-1969	330-style body	$4,200	$5,500
1970-1979		$2,600	$3,400
1980-1989		$1,700	$2,200
1990-1999		$1,550	$2,000
2000-2020		$1,450	$1,875

Model 330S/12
1964 (1 made)-1965 (2 made).

1964-1965		$5,200	$6,700

Model 331 Light Show
1970-1975. Model 330 with translucent top with lights in body that lit up when played, needed external transformer. The first offering's design, noted as Type 1, had heat problems and a fully original one is difficult to find. The 2nd offering's design, noted as Type 2, was a more stable design and is more highly valued in the market.

1970-1971	Type 1 1st edition	$10,200	$13,300
1971-1975	Type 2 2nd edition	$12,300	$16,000

Model 335
1958-1977. Thinline, 330-style body, 2 pickups, vibrato, Fireglo. Called the 330VB from '85-'97.

1958-1960	Capri, thick body	$7,700	$10,000
1961-1969	Thinner body	$3,150	$4,100
1970-1973		$2,900	$3,800
1974-1977		$2,800	$3,600

Model 335 F
1958-1969. F-style.

1958-1961	Thick version	$7,700	$10,000
1961-1969	Thin version	$3,400	$4,400

Model 336/12
1966-1974. Like 300-12, but with 6-12 converter comb, 330-style body.

1966-1969		$3,000	$3,900
1970-1974		$3,000	$3,900

Model 340
1958-2014. Thin semi-hollowbody, thru-body maple neck, 2 single-coil pickups, sharp point horns, very limited production '58-'65, with first notable volume of 45 units starting in '66.

1958-1960	Capri, thick body	$7,700	$10,000

MODEL YEAR	FEATURES	EXC. COND. LOW	HIGH
1961-1969	Thinner body	$3,100	$4,000
1970-1973		$2,900	$3,800
1974-1979		$2,800	$3,600
1980-2014		$1,700	$2,200

Model 340 F

1958-1969. F-style.

1958-1960	Thick version	$7,700	$10,000
1961-1969	Thin version	$3,400	$4,400

Model 340/12

1980-2014. 12-string version, 330-style body.

1980-2014		$1,700	$2,200

Model 345

1961-1974. Thinline 330-345 series, version with 3 pickups and vibrato tailpiece.

1958-1960	Capri, thick body	$7,700	$10,000
1961-1969	Thinner body	$3,400	$4,400
1970-1973		$2,900	$3,800
1974		$2,800	$3,600

Model 345 F

1958-1969. F-style.

1958-1960	Thick version	$7,700	$10,000
1961-1969	Thin version	$3,400	$4,400

Model 345 Reissue

2002. Low production, 3 pickups.

2002		$2,150	$2,800

Model 350 Liverpool

1983-1997. Thinline, 3 pickups, vibrato, no soundhole.

1983-1997		$1,925	$2,500

Model 350 SH

1988-1990. Susanna Hoffs Limited Edition.

1988-1990		$3,300	$4,300

Model 350/12V63 Liverpool

1994-2014. Vintage Series, 12-string 350V63.

1994-2014		$2,200	$2,800

Model 350V59

1988. Very low production.

1988		$1,925	$2,500

Model 350V63 Liverpool

1994-present. Vintage Series, like 355 JL, but without signature.

1994-2020		$1,925	$2,500

Model 355 JL

1989-1993. John Lennon model, signature and drawing on 'guard.

1989-1993		$2,850	$3,700

Model 355/12 JL

1989-1993. 12-string 355 JL, limited production.

1989-1993		$2,850	$3,700

Model 360/360 VB

1958-1991, 2000-present. Deluxe thinline, 2 pickups, slash soundhole, bound body until '64.

1958-1960	Capri, thick body	$7,900	$10,200
1961-1967		$3,900	$5,100
1968-1969		$3,700	$4,800
1970-1973	360, no vibrato	$3,000	$3,900
1974-1989	360 VB, vibrato	$1,800	$2,300
1990-2020		$1,525	$2,000

Model 360V64

1991-2003. Reissue of '64 Model 360 old style body without vibrola, has binding with full length inlays.

1991-2003		$2,400	$3,150

MODEL YEAR	FEATURES	EXC. COND. LOW	HIGH

Model 360 CW

2000. Carl Wilson Limited Edition, 6-string, includes certificate, 500 made.

2000		$2,550	$3,300

Model 360 DCM 75th Anniversary

2006. 360 with 75th Anniversary dark cherry metallic finish, 75 made.

2006		$2,550	$3,300

Model 360 F

1959-1972. F-style.

1959-1960	Thick version	$7,900	$10,200
1961-1969	Thin version	$3,550	$4,600
1970-1972	Thin version	$3,000	$3,900

Model 360S F

1968-ca. 1972. Slanted frets (SF), standard on some models, an option on others.

1968-1972		$4,600	$6,000

Model 360 Tuxedo

1987 only. Tuxedo option included white body, white painted fretboard, and black hardware.

1987		$1,850	$2,400

Model 360 WB

1984-1998. Double bound body, 2 pickups, vibrato optional (VB).

1984-1990		$2,050	$2,650
1991-1998	WB no vibrato	$1,850	$2,400
1991-1998	WBVB, vibrato	$2,050	$2,650

Model 360/12

1964-present. Deluxe double-cut thinline, 2 pickups, triangle inlays. The 360/12 was offered in both the Old Style (OS) body with double-bound body and pointed horns, and the New Style (NS) body with rounded top edges and rounder horns. George Harrison's original 360/12 had the OS body in a Fireglo finish. Production of the OS and NS bodies overlapped.

1964	OS, Fireglo, pointed horns, Harrison	$29,000	$37,000
1964-1969	NS, Fireglo, rounded horns	$3,775	$4,900
1964-1969	NS, Mapleglo, rounded horns	$3,900	$5,000
1964-1969	OS, Mapleglo, pointed horns	$15,800	$20,500
1965-1969	OS, Fireglo, pointed horns	$18,600	$24,200
1970-1973		$3,600	$4,700
1974-1979		$3,100	$4,000
1980-2009		$1,800	$2,400
2010-2020		$1,750	$2,250

Model 360/12 CW

2000. Carl Wilson, 12-string version of 360 CW.

2000		$3,200	$4,200

Model 360/12 RCA

1992. Limited edition made for RCA Nashville as gifts for their artists, has RCA dog-and-gramophone logo on pickguard.

1992		$2,550	$3,300

Model 360/12 Tuxedo

1987 only. 12-string version of 360 Tuxedo.

1987		$2,550	$3,300

1991 Rickenbacker 355JL

Craig Brody

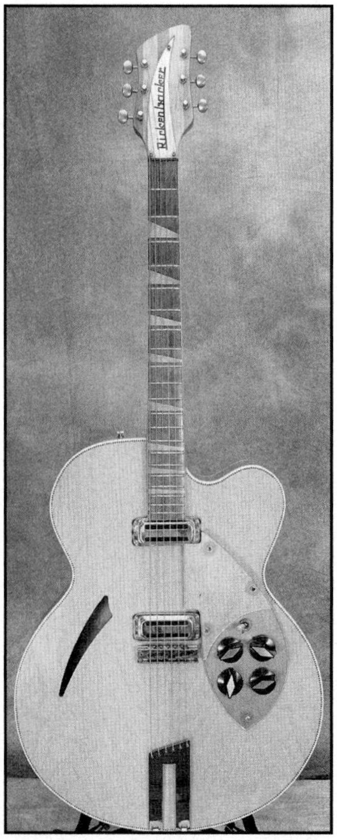

1960 Rickenbacker 360F

1979 Rickenbacker 360/12WB
Ted Wulfers

1992 Rickenbacker 370
Carter Vintage Guitars

MODEL YEAR	FEATURES	EXC. COND. LOW	HIGH

Model 360/12 VP

2004. VP is vintage pickup.

2004		$2,550	$3,300

Model 360/12 WB

1984-1998. 12-string version of 360 WB.

1984-1998		$2,550	$3,300

Model 360/12C63

2004-present. More exact replica of the Harrison model.

2004-2020		$2,550	$3,300

Model 360/12V64

1985-2003. Deluxe thinline with '64 features, 2 pickups, 12 strings, slanted plate tailpiece.

1985-2003		$2,550	$3,300

Model 362/12

1975-1992. Doubleneck 6 & 12, 360 features.

1975-1992		$2,400	$3,150

Model 365

1958-1974. Deluxe thinline, 2 pickups, vibrato, called Model 360 WBVB from '84-'98.

1958-1960	Capri, thick body	$7,900	$10,200
1961-1969		$3,600	$4,700
1970-1973		$3,400	$4,400
1974		$3,200	$4,200

Model 365 F

1959-1972. Thin full-body (F designation), 2 pickups, Deluxe features.

1959-1960	Capri, thick body	$7,800	$10,200
1961-1969	Thin version	$3,600	$4,700
1970-1972		$3,350	$4,350

Model 366/12 Convertible

1966-1974. Two pickups, 12 strings, comb-like device that converts it to a 6-string, production only noted in '68, perhaps available on custom order basis.

1966-1968	OS	$4,600	$6,000

Model 370

1958-1990, 1994-2007. Deluxe thinline, 3 pickups. Could be considered to be a dealer special order item from '58-'67 with limited production.

1958-1960	Capri, thick body	$7,800	$10,200
1961-1969	Thin version	$3,600	$4,700
1970-1973		$3,350	$4,350
1974-1979		$3,150	$4,100
1980-1999		$1,875	$2,425
2000-2007		$1,875	$2,425

Model 370 F

1959-1972. F-style, 3 pickups, Deluxe features.

1959-1961	Thick version	$7,900	$10,200
1961-1969	Thin version	$3,700	$4,800
1970-1972		$3,400	$4,400

Model 370 VP

2006-2007. Limited run with special specs including vintage toaster pickups (VP).

2006-2007		$2,900	$3,800

Model 370 WB

1984-1998. Double bound body, 3 pickups, vibrato optional (VB).

1984-1998		$1,700	$2,200

Model 370/12

1966-1990, 1994-present. Not regular production until '80, deluxe thinline, 3 pickups, 12 strings. Could be considered to be a dealer special order item in the '60s and '70s with limited production.

1966		$8,000	$11,000
1967-2020		$2,100	$2,700

Model 370/12 RM

1988-1990. Limited Edition Roger McGuinn, 1000 made, higher-quality appointments.

1988-1990		$3,950	$5,100

Model 375

1958-1974. Deluxe thinline, 3 pickups, vibrato, called Model 370 WBVB from '84-'98.

1958-1960	Capri, thick body	$7,900	$10,200
1961-1969	Thin version	$3,800	$4,900
1970-1974		$3,400	$4,400

Model 375 F

1959-1972. F-style, 2 pickups.

1959-1960	Thick version	$7,900	$10,200
1961-1969	Thin version	$3,800	$4,900
1970-1972		$3,400	$4,400

Model 380 L Laguna

1996-2005. Semi-hollow, oil-finished walnut body, Maple neck and 'board, 2 humbuckers, PZ saddle pickups optional.

1996-2005		$1,875	$2,425
1996-2005	PZ option	$1,875	$2,425

Model 381

1958-1963, 1969-1974. Double-cut archtop, 2 pickups, slash soundhole, solid 'guard, reintroduced in '69 with double split-level 'guard.

1958-1963	Low production	$7,900	$10,200
1969	Various colors, some rare	$3,800	$4,900
1970-1975		$3,400	$4,400

Model 381 JK John Kay

1988-1997. Limited Edition, 250 made, 2 humbucking pickups, active electronics, stereo and mono outputs, Jetglo black.

1988-1997		$2,450	$3,200

Model 381/12V69

1987-present. Reissue of 381/12, deep double-cut body, sound body cavity, catseye soundhole, triangle inlays, bridge with 12 individual saddles. Finishes include Fireglo, Mapleglo and Jetglo.

1987-2020	Figured top	$2,450	$3,200

Model 381V69

1991-present. Reissue of vintage 381.

1987-2020		$2,450	$3,200

Model 382

1958-1963, 1969-1974. 381 with vibrato unit. Very light production.

1958-1963	Low production	$7,900	$10,200
1969-1974	Various colors, some rare	$3,600	$4,700

Model 383

1958-1963, 1969-1974. 381 with 3 pickups. Very light production.

1958-1963	Low production	$7,900	$10,200
1969-1974	Various colors, some rare	$3,600	$4,700

GUITARS

MODEL YEAR	FEATURES	EXC. COND. LOW	HIGH

Model 384

1958-1963, 1969-1974. 381 with 3 pickups and vibrato unit. Very light production.

1958-1963	Low production	$7,900	$10,200
1969-1974	Various colors, some rare	$3,600	$4,700

Model 400/Combo 400

1956-1958. Double-cut tulip body, neck-thru, 1 pickup, gold anodized 'guard, 21 frets, replaced by Model 425 in '58. Available in black (216 made), blue turquoise (53), Cloverfield Green (53), Montezuma Brown (41), and 4 in other custom colors.

1956-1958		$3,800	$4,900

Model 420

1965-1983. Non-vibrato version of Model 425, single pickup.

1965-1968		$1,450	$1,900
1969-1983		$1,275	$1,650

Model 425/Combo 425

1958-1973. Double-cut solidbody, 1 pickup, sunburst.

1958-1959	425 Cresting Wave	$2,850	$3,700
1960		$2,100	$2,700
1961-1964		$1,675	$2,175
1965-1968		$1,450	$1,900
1969-1973		$1,200	$1,575

Model 425/12V63

1999-2000. 136 made.

1999-2000		$1,575	$2,050

Model 425V63

1999-2000. Beatles associated model, 145 JG black made, 116 BG burgundy transparent made, originally custom ordered by Rickenbacker collectors and they were not part of Rickenbacker's sales literature in the late '90s.

1999-2000		$1,450	$1,875

Model 430

1971-1982. Style 200 body, natural.

1971-1982		$775	$1,025

Model 450/Combo 450

1957-1984. Replaces Combo 450, 2 pickups (3 optional '62-'77), tulip body shape '57-'59, cresting wave body shape after.

1957-1958	450 Tulip body (Combo)	$3,800	$4,900
1958-1959	450 Cresting Wave	$2,850	$3,700
1960	Cresting Wave, flat body	$2,150	$2,775
1961-1966	Cresting Wave, super slim	$1,875	$2,424
1970-1979	Includes rare color	$1,500	$1,950
1980-1984		$1,075	$1,400

Model 450/12

1964-1985. Double-cut solidbody, 12-string version of Model 450, 2 pickups.

1964-1966		$1,875	$2,425
1967-1969		$1,775	$2,300
1970-1979	Includes rare color	$1,575	$2,050
1980-1985		$1,175	$1,525

Model 450V63

1999-2001. Reissue of '63 450.

1999-2001		$1,200	$1,550

MODEL YEAR	FEATURES	EXC. COND. LOW	HIGH

Model 456/12 Convertible

1968-1978. Double-cut solidbody, 2 pickups, comb-like device to convert it to 6-string.

1968-1969		$2,300	$3,000
1970-1978		$1,925	$2,500

Model 460

1961-1985. Double-cut solidbody, 2 pickups, neck-thru-body, deluxe trim.

1961-1965		$2,500	$3,250
1966-1969		$2,200	$2,850
1970-1979	Includes rare color	$1,875	$2,425
1980-1985		$1,300	$1,700

Model 480

1973-1984. Double-cut solidbody with long thin bass horn in 4001 bass series style, 2 pickups, cresting wave body and headstock, bolt-on neck.

1973-1979		$2,200	$2,850
1980-1984		$2,100	$2,700

Model 481

1973-1983. Cresting wave body with longer bass horn, 2 humbuckers (3 optional), angled frets.

1973-1979		$2,200	$2,850
1980-1983		$2,000	$2,600

Model 483

1973-1983. Cresting wave body with longer bass horn, 3 humbuckers.

1973-1979		$2,375	$3,075
1980-1983		$2,100	$2,725

Model 600/Combo 600

1954-1958. Modified double-cut, horseshoe pickup.

1954-1957	Blond/white	$3,700	$4,800
1956-1958	OT/Blue Turquoise	$3,700	$4,800

Model 610

1985-1991. Cresting-wave cutaway solidbody, 2 pickups, trapeze R-tailpiece, Jetglo.

1985-1991		$775	$1,025

Model 610/12

1988-1997. 12-string version of Model 610.

1988-1997		$875	$1,150

Model 615

1962-1966, 1969-1977. Double-cut solidbody, 2 pickups, vibrato.

1962-1965		$1,875	$2,425
1966-1977		$1,675	$2,175

Model 620

1974-present. Double-cut solidbody, deluxe binding, 2 pickups, neck-thru-body.

1974-1979		$1,650	$2,150
1980-2020		$1,400	$1,850

Model 620/12

1981-present. Double-cut solidbody, 2 pickups, 12 strings, standard trim.

1981-2020		$1,450	$1,875

Model 625

1962-1977. Double-cut solidbody, deluxe trim, 2 pickups, vibrato.

1962-1965		$5,400	$7,000
1966-1969		$3,350	$4,350
1970-1977		$2,600	$3,400

Rickenbacker 450V63

Ron O'Keefe

1983 Rickenbacker 620

Jeff DiPaola

GUITARS

Rickenbacker 660
Ron O'Keefe

Rickenbacker 660/12
Ron O'Keefe

MODEL YEAR	FEATURES	EXC. COND. LOW	HIGH

Model 650/Combo 650

1957-1959. Standard color, 1 pickup.

1957-1959 | | $3,700 | $4,800

Model 650 A Atlantis

1992-2003. Double cut cresting wave solidbody, maple body wings, neck-thru, 2 pickups, chrome hardware, turquoise.

1992-2003 | | $1,075 | $1,400

Model 650 C Colorado

1993-2017. Like Atlantis but with balck finish.

1993-2017 | | $1,075 | $1,400

Model 650 D Dakota

1993-2017. Like Atlantis but with walnut body wings and oil-satin finish.

1993-2017 | | $1,075 | $1,400

Model 650 E Excalibur/F Frisco

1991-2003. Like Atlantis but with brown vermilion body wings and gold hardware. Name changed to Frisco in '95.

1991-2003 | | $1,075 | $1,400

Model 650 S Sierra

1993-2017. Like Dakota but with gold hardware.

1993-2017 | | $1,075 | $1,400

Model 660

1998-present. Cresting wave maple body, triangle inlays, 2 pickups.

1998-2020 | | $1,925 | $2,500

Model 660 DCM 75th Anniversary

2006-2007. 75th 1931-2006 Anniversary pickguard logo.

2006-2007 | | $2,100 | $2,700

Model 660/12

1998-present. 12-string 660.

1998-2020 | | $2,200 | $2,850

Model 660/12 TP

1991-1998. Tom Petty model, 12 strings, cresting wave body, 2 pickups, deluxe trim, limited run of 1000, certificate of authenticity.

1991-1998 | With certificate | $4,200 | $5,500

Model 800/Combo 800

1954-1959. Offset double-cut, 1 horseshoe pickup until late-'57, second bar type after.

1954-1957 | Blond/white, 1 pickup | $4,725 | $6,125
1954-1957 | Blue or green, 1 pickup | $4,725 | $6,125
1957-1959 | Blond/white, 2 pickups | $4,725 | $6,125
1957-1959 | Blue or green, 2 pickups | $4,725 | $6,125

Model 850/Combo 850

1957-1959. Extreme double-cut, 1 pickup until '58, 2 after, various colors, called Model 850 in the '60s.

1957-1959 | Various colors | $4,725 | $6,125

Model 900/Combo 900

1957-1980. Double-cut tulip body shape, 3/4 size, 1 pickup. Body changes to cresting wave shape in '69.

1957-1966 | | $1,450 | $1,900

Model 950/Combo 950

1957-1980. Like Model 900, but with 2 pickups, 21 frets. Body changes to cresting wave shape in '69.

1957-1964 | | $1,625 | $2,125
1965-1980 | | $1,425 | $1,850

Model 1000

1957-1970. Like Model 900, but with 18 frets. Body does not change to cresting wave shape.

1956-1966 | | $1,375 | $1,800
1967-1970 | | $1,300 | $1,675

Model 1993/12 RM

1964-1967. Export 'slim-line' 12-string model made for English distributor Rose-Morris of London, built along the lines of the U.S. Model 360/12 but with small differences that are considered important in the vintage guitar market.

1964 | Flat tailpiece | $4,900 | $6,375
1965-1967 | R tailpiece | $4,900 | $6,375

Model 1996 RM

1964-1967. Rose-Morris import, 3/4 size built similiarly to the U.S. Model 325.

1964-1967 | | $7,900 | $10,300

Model 1996 RM Reissue

2006. Reissue of the Rose-Morris version of Model 325, this reissue available on special order in 2006.

2006 | | $3,000 | $3,900

Model 1997 PT

1987-1988. Pete Townshend Signature Model, semi-hollowbody, single f-hole, maple neck, 21-fret rosewood 'board, 3 pickups, Firemist finish, limited to 250 total production.

1987-1988 | | $3,000 | $3,900

Model 1997 RM

1964-1967. Export 'slim-line' model made for English distributor Rose-Morris of London, built along the lines of the U.S. Model 335, but with small differences that are considered important in the vintage guitar market, 2 pickups, vibrola tailpiece. Rose-Morris export models sent to the USA generally had a red-lined guitar case vs. the USA domestic blue-lined guitar case.

1964-1967 | | $3,500 | $4,500

Model 1997 RM Reissue

1987-1995. Reissue of '60s Rose-Morris model, but with vibrola (VB) or without.

1987-1995 | | $2,100 | $2,700

Model 1997 SPC

1993-2002. 3 pickup version of reissue.

1993-2002 | | $1,575 | $2,050

Model 1998 RM

1964-1967. Export 'slim-line' model made for English distributor Rose-Morris of London, built along the lines of a U.S. Model 345 but with small differences that are considered important in the vintage guitar market, 3 pickups, vibrola tailpiece.

1964-1967 | | $3,500 | $4,500

Rickenbacker Spanish/Spanish/SP

1946-1949. Block markers.

1946-1949 | | $1,525 | $1,975

S-59

1940-1942. Arch top body built by Kay, horseshoe magnet pickup.

1940-1942 | | $1,425 | $1,825

MODEL YEAR	FEATURES	EXC. COND. LOW	HIGH

Rigaud Guitars

1978-present. Luthier Robert Rigaud builds his premium grade, custom, parlor to jumbo acoustic guitars in Greensboro, North Carolina. He also builds ukuleles under the New Moon brand.

Ritz

1989. Solidbody electric guitars and basses produced in Calimesa, California, by Wayne Charvel, Eric Galletta and Brad Becnel, many of which featured cracked shell mosiac finishes.

RKS

Professional and premium grade, production/custom, electric hollowbody and solidbody guitars and basses designed by Ravi Sawhney and guitarist Dave Mason and built in Thousand Oaks, California. They began in 2003.

Robert Cefalu

Luthier Robert Cefalu built his professional grade, production/custom, acoustic guitars in Buffalo, New York. The guitars have an RC on the headstock.

Robert Guitars

1981-present. Luthier Mikhail Robert builds his premium grade, production/custom, classical guitars in Summerland, British Columbia.

Robertson Guitars

1995-present. Luthier Jeff Robertson builds his premium grade, production/custom flat-top guitars in South New Berlin, New York.

Robin

1982-2010. Professional and premium grade, production/custom, guitars from luthier David Wintz and built in Houston, Texas. Most guitars were Japanese-made until '87; American production began in '88. Most Japanese Robins were pretty consistent in features, but the American ones were often custom-made, so many variations in models exist. They also made Metropolitan ('96-'08) and Alamo ('00-'08) brand guitars.

Avalon Classic

1994-2010. Single-cut, figured maple top, 2 humbuckers.

1994-2010	Various options	$1,250	$1,650

Medley Pro

1990s. Solidbody with 2 extreme cutaway horns, hum-single-single.

1990s	US-made	$725	$975

Medley Special

1992-1995. Ash body, maple neck, rosewood 'board, 24 frets, various pickup options.

1992-1995		$450	$600

Medley Standard

1985-2010. Offset double-cut swamp ash solidbody, bolt neck, originally with hum-single-single pickups, but now also available with 2 humbuckers.

1985-1987	Japan-made	$400	$525
1988-2010	US-made	$800	$1,075

Octave

1982-1990s. Tuned an octave above standard tuning, full body size with 15 1/2" short-scale bolt maple neck. Japanese-made production model until '87, U.S.-made custom shop after.

1990s	With original case	$600	$775

Raider I/Raider II/Raider III

1985-1991. Double-cut solidbody, 1 humbucker pickup (Raider I), 2 humbuckers (Raider II), or 3 single-coils (Raider III), maple neck, either maple or rosewood 'board, sunburst.

1985-1991	1 pickup	$350	$450
1985-1991	2 pickups	$375	$500
1985-1991	3 pickups	$425	$550

Ranger

1982. First production model with 2 single-coil pickups in middle and neck position, reverse headstock, dot markers.

1982		$775	$1,025

Ranger Custom

1982-1986, 1988-2010. Swamp ash bound body, bolt-on maple neck, rosewood or maple 'board, 2 single coils and 1 humbucker, orange, made in Japan until '86, U.S.-made after.

1982-1986	Japan-made	$400	$525
1988-2010	US-made	$775	$1,025

RDN-Doubleneck Octave/Six

1982-1985. Six-string standard neck with 3 pickups, 6-string octave neck with 1 pickup, double-cut solidbody.

1982-1985	With original case	$875	$1,125

Savoy Deluxe/Standard

1995-2010. Semi-hollow thinline single cut archtop, 2 pickups, set neck.

1996-2010		$1,200	$1,625

Soloist/Artisan

1982-1986. Mahogany double-cut solidbody, carved bound maple top, set neck, 2 humbuckers. Renamed Artisan in '85. Only about 125 made in Japan.

1982-1986		$575	$775

Wedge

1985-ca. 1988. Triangle-shaped body, 2 humbuckers, Custom with set neck and triangle inlays, Standard with bolt neck and dots, about 200 made.

1980s		$775	$1,025

Wrangler

1995-2002. Classic '50s single-cut slab body, 3 Rio Grande pickups, opaque finish.

1995-2002		$575	$775

Robinson Guitars

2002-present. Premium and presentation grade, custom/production, steel string guitars built by luthier Jake Robinson first in Kalamazoo, and since '08 in Hoxeyville, Michigan.

RockBeach Guitars

2005-present. Luthier Greg Bogoshian builds his custom, professional grade, chambered electric guitars and basses in Rochester, New York.

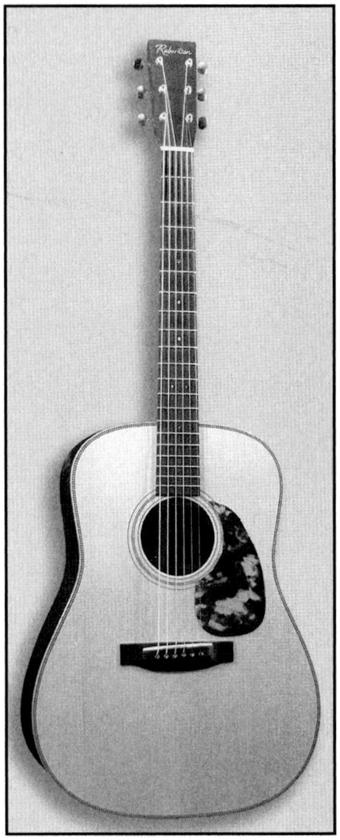

Robertson Guitars Dreadnought

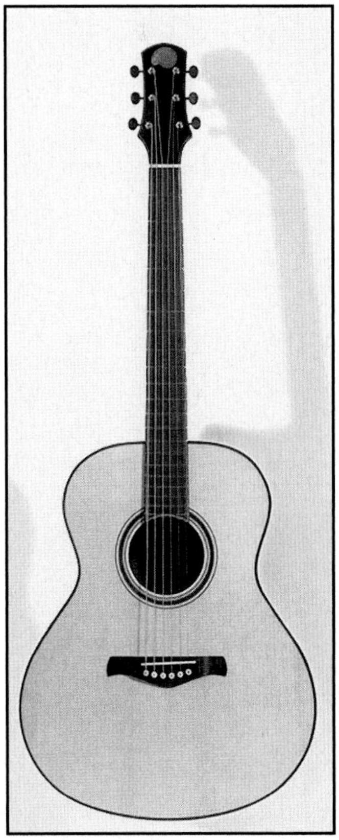

Robinson Small Jumbo

GUITARS

1960s Roger Super Cutaway
Alf Tengs-Pedersen

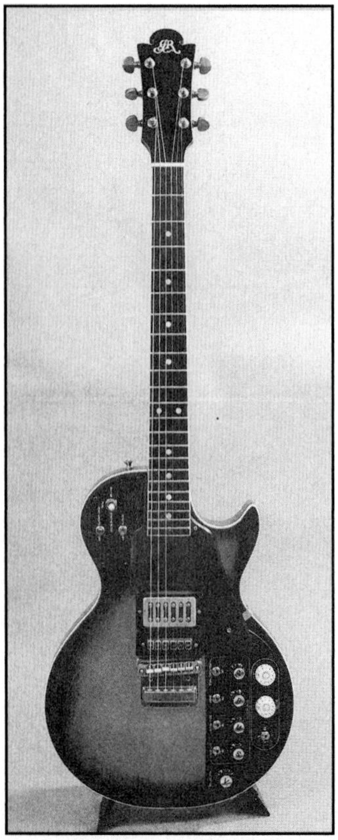
1978 Roland GS-500

MODEL YEAR	FEATURES	EXC. COND. LOW	HIGH

Rockinbetter
2011-2014. Intermediate grade, production electric guitars and basses, copies of Rickenbacker models, made in China.

Rocking F
See listing under Fox.

Rockit Guitar
Luthier Rod MacKenzie builds his premium grade, custom, electric guitars and basses in Everett, Washington, starting in 2006.

Rogands
Late 1960s. Produced by France's Jacobacci company and named after brothers Roger and Andre. Short-lived brand; the brothers made instruments under several other brands as well.

Roger
Guitars built in Germany by luthier Wenzel Rossmeisl and named for his son Roger. Roger Rossmeisl would go on to work at Rickenbacker and Fender.

Rogue
2001-present. Budget and intermediate grade, production, acoustic, resonator, electric and sitar guitars and basses. They also offer mandolins, banjos, ukuleles, and lap steels. They previously offered effects and amps. Fender offered instruments branded Rogue by Squire for a short period starting in '99.

Roland
Best known for keyboards, effects, and amps, Roland offered synthesizer-based guitars and basses from 1977 to '97.

Rolando
1916-ca. 1919. Private branded instruments made for the Southern California Music Company of Los Angeles, by Martin. There were three models.

00-28K/1500

1916-1919		$7,300	$9,500

Rolf Spuler
1981-2014. Presentation grade, custom, hybrid electric-acoustic guitars, built by luthier Rolf Spuler in Gebenstorf, Switzerland. He also built basses. He passed away in '14.

Roman & Lipman Guitars
1989-2000. Production/custom, solidbody guitars and basses made in Danbury, Connecticut by Ed Roman Guitars.

Roman Abstract Guitars
1989-present. Professional and premium grade, production/custom, solidbody guitars made by Ed Roman Guitars.

MODEL YEAR	FEATURES	EXC. COND. LOW	HIGH

Roman Centurion Guitars
2001-present. Premium and presentation grade, custom guitars made by Ed Roman Guitars.

Roman Pearlcaster Guitars
1999-present. Professional and premium grade, production/custom, solidbody guitars made Ed Roman Guitars.

Roman Quicksilver Guitars
1997-present. Professional and premium grade, production/custom, solid and hollow-body guitars made by Ed Roman Guitars.

Roman RVC Guitars
1999-present. Professional and premium grade, production/custom, solidbody guitars made by Ed Roman Guitars.

Roman Vampire Guitars
2004-2020. Professional and premium grade, production/custom, solidbody guitars made by Ed Roman Guitars. Special orders only about '13-'20.

Rono
In 1967 luthier Ron Oates began building professional and premium grade, production/custom, flat-top, jazz, Wiesenborn-style, and resonator guitars and basses in Boulder, Colorado. He also built mandolins.

Ro-Pat-In
See Rickenbacker.

Rosetti
1950s-1960s. Guitars imported into England by distributor Rosetti, made by Holland's Egmond, maybe others.

Solid 7
1960s. Symmetrical cutaway electric semi-hollow, large 'guard with top-mounted dual pickups, 4 control knobs, value is associated with Paul McCartney's use in '60, value dependent on completely original McCartney specs.

1960s	McCartney model	$1,775	$2,300
1960s	Various other	$500	$650

Roudhloff
1810s-1840s. Luthier Francois Roudhloff built his instruments in France. Labels could state F. Roudhloff-Mauchand or Roudhloff Brothers. Valuation depends strongly on condition and repair. His sons built guitars under the D & A Roudhloff label.

Rowan
Professional and premium grade, production/custom, solidbody and acoustic/electric guitars built by luthier Michael Rowan in Garland, Texas.

MODEL YEAR	FEATURES	EXC. COND. LOW	HIGH

Royal

Ca. 1954-ca. 1965. Line of jazz style guitars made by France's Jacobacci company, which also built under its own brand.

Royal (Japan)

1957-1960s. Early budget level instruments made by Tokyo Sound Company and Gakki and exported by Japan's Hoshino (Ibanez).

Royden Guitars

Professional grade, production/custom, flat-tops and solidbody electrics built by luthier Royden Moran in Peterborough, Ontario, starting in 1996.

RS Guitarworks

1994-present. Professional grade, production/custom, solid and hollowbody guitars built by luthier Roy Bowen in Winchester, Kentucky.

Rubio, German Vasquez

1993-present. Luthier German Vasquez Rubio builds his professional and premium grade, production/custom classical and flamenco guitars in Los Angeles, California.

Ruck, Robert

1966-2018. Premium grade, custom classical and flamenco guitars built by luthier Robert Ruck originally in Kalaheo, Hawaii, then in Eugene, Oregon. Ruck died in '18.

Running Dog Guitars

1994-present. Luthier Rick Davis builds his professional and premium grade, custom flat-tops in Seattle, Washington. He was originally located in Richmond, Vermont.

Ruokangas

1995-present. Luthier Juha Ruokangas builds his premium and presentation grade, production/custom, solidbody and semi-acoustic electric guitars in Hyvinkaa, Finland.

Rustler

1993-ca. 1998. Solidbody electrics with hand-tooled leather bound and studded sides and R branded into the top, built by luthier Charles Caponi in Mason City, Iowa.

RWK

1991-present. Luthier Bob Karger builds his intermediate grade, production/custom, solidbody electrics and travel guitars in Highland Park, Illinois.

Ryder

1963. Made by Rickenbacker, the one model with this brand was the same as their solidbody Model 425.

MODEL YEAR	FEATURES	EXC. COND. LOW	HIGH

S. Walker Custom Guitars

2002-present. Luthier Scott Walker builds his premium grade, production/custom, solid and semi hollow body electric guitars in Santa Cruz, California.

S. Yairi

Ca. 1960-1980s. Steel string folk guitars and classical nylon string guitars by master Japanese luthier Sadao Yairi, imported by Philadelphia Music Company of Limerick, Pennsylvania. Early sales literature called the brand Syairi. Most steel string models have dreadnought bodies and nylon-string classical guitars are mostly standard grand concert size. All models are handmade. Steel string Jumbos and dreadnoughts have Syairi logo on the headstock, nylon-classical models have no logo. The Model 900 has a solid wood body, others assumed to have laminate bodies.

S.B. Brown Guitars

Custom flat-tops made by luthier Steve Brown in Fullerton, California.

S.B. MacDonald Custom Instruments

1988-present. Professional and premium grade, custom/production, flat-top, resonator, and solidbody guitars built by luthier Scott B. MacDonald in Huntington, New York.

S.D. Curlee

1975-1982. Founded in Matteson, Illinois by music store owner Randy Curlee, after an unsuccessful attempt to recruit builder Dan Armstrong. S.D. Curlee guitars were made in Illinois, while S.D. Curlee International instruments were made by Matsumoku in Japan. The guitars featured mostly Watco oil finishes, often with exotic hardwoods, and unique neck-thru-bridge construction on American and Japanese instruments. These were the first production guitars to use a single-coil pickup at the bridge with a humbucker at the neck, and a square brass nut. DiMarzio pickups. Offered in a variety of shapes, later some copies. Approximately 12,000 American-made basses and 3,000 guitars were made, most of which were sold overseas. Two hundred were made in '75-'76; first production guitar numbered 518.

Electric Solidbody

1975-1982. Models include the '75-'81 Standard I, II and III, '76-'81 International C-10 and C-11, '80-'81 Yankee, Liberty, Butcher, Curbeck, Summit, Special, and the '81-'82 Destroyer, Flying V.

1975-1982		$350	$450

S.L. Smith Guitars

Professional grade, production/custom, acoustic guitars built by Steven Smith in Brant Lake, New York beginning in 2007.

S. Walker Custom The Revelator

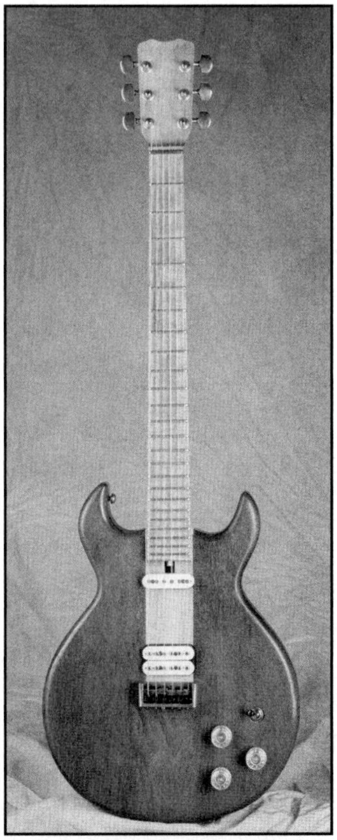

1976 S.D. Curlee Standard

Saga Blueridge

1996 Samick Charlie Christian

MODEL YEAR	FEATURES	EXC. COND. LOW	HIGH

S.S. Stewart

The original S.S. Stewart Company (1878-1904), of Philadelphia, Pennsylvania is considered to be one of the most important banjo manufacturers of the late 19th century. Samuel Swaim Stewart died in 1988 and his family was out of the company by the early 1900s, and the brand was soon acquired by Bugellsein & Jacobsen of New York. The brand name was used on guitars into the 1960s.

Flat-Top

1930s. Gibson L-2 style body.

1932		$7,550	$9,800

S101

Budget and intermediate grade, production, classical, acoustic, resonator, solid and semi-hollow body guitars and basses imported from China by America Sejung Corp. They also offer mandolins, and banjos.

Sadowsky

1980-present. Professional and premium grade, production/custom, solidbody, semi-hollowbody, archtop, and electric nylon-string guitars built by luthier Roger Sadowsky in Brooklyn, New York. He also builds basses and amps. In '96, luthier Yoshi Kikuchi started building Sadowsky Tokyo instruments in Japan.

Saga

Saga Musical Instruments, of San Francisco, California distributes a wide variety of instruments and brands, occasionally including their own line of solidbody guitars called the Saga Gladiator Series (1987-'88, '94-'95). In the 2000s, Saga also offered component kits ($90-$130) that allowed for complete assembly in white wood.

Sahlin Guitars

Luthier Eric Sahlin hs built his premium grade, custom, classical and flamenco guitars in Spokane, Washington since 1975.

Samick

1958-2001, 2002-present. Budget, intermediate and professional grade, production, imported acoustic and electric guitars and basses. They also offer mandolins, ukes and banjos and distribute Abilene and Silvertone brand instruments.

Samick started out producing pianos, adding guitars in '65 under other brands. In '88 Samick greatly increased their guitar production. The Samick line of 350 models was totally closed out in 2001. A totally new line of 250 models was introduced January 2002 at NAMM. All 2002 models have the new compact smaller headstock and highly styled S logo.

Sammo

1920s. Labels in these instruments state they were made by the Osborne Mfg. Co. with an address of Masonic Temple, Chicago, Illinois. High quality and often with a high degree of ornamentation. They also made ukes and mandolins.

Sand Guitars

1979-present. Luthier Kirk Sand opened the Guitar Shoppe in Laguna Beach, California in 1972 with James Matthews. By '79, he started producing his own line of premium grade, production/custom-made flat-tops.

Sandoval Engineering

1979-present. Luthier Karl Sandoval builds his premium grade, custom, solidbody guitars in Santa Fe Springs, California.

Sano

1944-ca. 1970. Sano was a New Jersey-based accordion company that imported Italian-made solid and semi-hollow body guitars for a few years, starting in 1966; some, if not all, made by Zero Sette. They also built their own amps and reverb units.

Santa Cruz

1976-present. Professional, premium and presentation grade, production/custom, flat-top, 12-string, and archtop guitars from luthier Richard Hoover in Santa Cruz, California. They also build a mandocello and ukuleles. Founded by Hoover, Bruce Ross and William Davis. Hoover became sole owner in '89. Custom ordered instruments with special upgrades may have higher values than the ranges listed here. Other models offer "build-your-own" options on woods and features and this means larger value ranges on those instruments.

00 12-Fret

1997-present. Indian rosewood.

1997-2020		$2,300	$3,000

000 12-Fret

1994-present. 000 size, 12-fret body, Indian rosewood back and sides, ebony 'board, ivoroid binding.

1994-2020	Indian rosewood	$2,300	$3,000
2011	Brazilian rosewood	$4,600	$6,000

Archtop

Early 1980s-2010. Originally the FJZ, by mid-'90s, called the Archtop, offering 16", 17" and 18" cutaway acoustic/electric models, often special order. Curly maple body, ebony 'board, floating pickup, f-holes, sunburst or natural. Many custom options available.

1980s-90s		$2,875	$3,725

Bob Brozman Baritone

1998-2019. Flat-top acoustic, mahogany body, spruce top.

1998-2019		$2,825	$3,650

D 12-Fret

1994-present. 12-fret neck, slotted headstock, round shoulders, mahogany back and sides, notch diamond markers, herringbone trim. Special orders vary in value and could exceed the posted range.

1994-2020		$2,450	$3,200

MODEL YEAR	FEATURES	EXC. COND. LOW	HIGH

D Koa

1980s-1990s. Style D with koa back and sides.

1980s-90s		$2,450	$3,200

D/HR

Style D with Indian rosewood back and sides, Brazilian rosewood headstock overlay.

2000		$2,450	$3,200

D/PW Pre-War

2001-present. Pre-war D-style. "Build-your-own" options cause a wide value range.

2001-2020	Various models	$2,500	$4,800

Eric Skye 00

Signature model, Cocobolo/Adirondack.

2020		$4,200	$5,400

F

1979-present. 15 7/8" scale with narrow waist, sitka spruce top, Indian rosewood back and sides, natural.

1979-2020		$2,700	$3,500

F46R

1980s. Brazilian rosewood, single-cut.

1980s		$3,100	$4,000

Firefly

2009-present. Premium quality travel/parlor guitar, cedar top, flamed maple sides and back.

2009-2020		$2,300	$3,000

FS (Finger Style)

1988-present. Single-cut, cedar top, Indian rosewood back and sides, mahogany neck, modified X-bracing.

1988-2020		$2,500	$3,200

H

1977-present. Parlor size, originally a 13-fret neck, but soon changed to 14, Indian rosewood back and sides. The H A/E ('92-'04) added electronics and cutaway.

1977-2020	Indian rosewood	$2,500	$3,200
1994	Flamed koa	$3,300	$4,300
2005	Brazilian rosewood	$4,600	$6,000

H/13

2004-present. Like H, but with 13-fret neck, mahogany back and sides and slotted headstock.

2004-2020	Mahogany	$2,700	$3,500
2005	Flamed koa	$3,300	$4,300

H91

1990s. 14 5/8", flamed koa.

1990s		$3,300	$4,300

Model 1929 00

2010-present. 00-size, all mahogany, 12-fret neck.

2010-2020		$2,300	$3,000

OM (Orchestra Model)

1987-present. Orchestra model acoustic, sitka spruce top, Indian rosewood (Brazilian optional) back and sides, herringbone rosette, scalloped braces.

1987-2020	Brazilian rosewood	$4,500	$6,000
1987-2020	Indian rosewood	$2,500	$3,200
1995	Koa	$3,100	$4,100
2002	German spruce	$3,800	$5,000
2010	Italian spruce	$4,000	$5,200

OM/PW Pre-War

1999-present. Indian rosewood, advanced X and scalloped top bracing.

1999-2020		$2,600	$3,400

MODEL YEAR	FEATURES	EXC. COND. LOW	HIGH

PJ

1990s-present. Palor-size, Indian rosewood back and sides, 24" scale, 12-fret neck.

1990s		$2,600	$3,400

Style 1

Indian rosewood standard, various other woods optional.

2014	Brazilian, Adirondack	$6,000	$8,000

Tony Rice

1976-present. Dreadnought, Indian rosewood body (Brazilian optional until Tony Rice Professional model available), sitka spruce top, solid peghead, zigzag back stripe, pickup optional.

1976-2020		$2,800	$3,600

Tony Rice Professional

1997-present. Brazilian rosewood back and sides, carved German spruce top, zigzag back stripe, solid peghead.

1997-2020		$5,000	$6,500

Vintage Artist (VA)

1992-present. Mahogany body, sitka spruce top, zigzag back stripe, solid peghead, scalloped X-bracing, pickup optional.

1992-2020		$2,425	$3,150

Vintage Artist Custom

1992-2004. Martin D-42 style, mahogany body, Indian rosewood back and sides, sitka spruce top, zigzag back stripe, solid peghead, scalloped X-bracing, pickup optional.

1992-2004		$2,550	$3,300

Vintage Jumbo (VJ)

2000-present. 16" scale, round shouldered body, sitka spruce, figured mahogany back and sides, natural.

2000-2020		$2,350	$3,050

Vintage Southerner (VS)

2007-present. Sitka spruce top standard, various other woods optional.

2007-2020	Mahogany, Adirondack	$3,800	$4,900

Santos Martinez

Ca. 1997-present. Intermediate grade, production, acoustic and electro-acoustic classical guitars, imported from China by John Hornby Skewes & Co. in the U.K.

Sardonyx

1978-1979. Guitars and basses built by luthier Jeff Levin in the back of Matt Umanov's New York City guitar shop, industrial looking design with 2 aluminum outrigger-style tubes extended from the rectangle body. Very limited production.

Saturn

1960s-1970s. Imported, most likely from Japan, solid and semi-hollow body electric guitars and basses. Large S logo with Saturn name inside the S. Many sold through Eaton's in Canada.

Saturn

1960s-1970s. Solidbody, 4 pickups.

1960s-70s		$375	$500

2017 Santa Cruz D 12-Fret
Bernunzio Uptown Music

2017 Santa Cruz H/13
Bernunzio Uptown Music

Schoenberg The Quartet

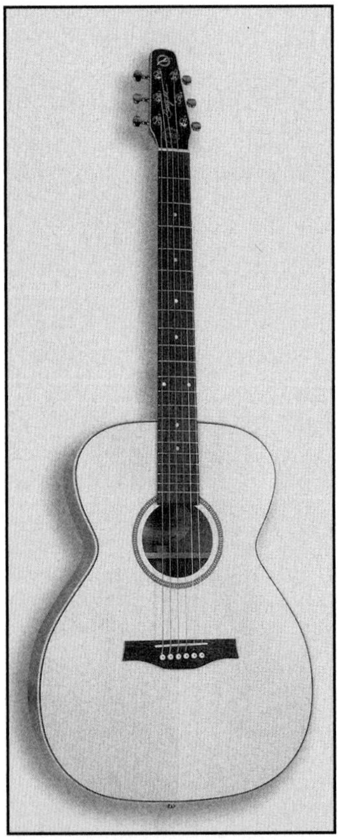

Seagull Maritime SWS Concert Hall SG

MODEL YEAR	FEATURES	EXC. COND. LOW	HIGH

Sawchyn Guitars

1972-present. Professional and premium grade, production/custom, flat-top and flamenco guitars and mandolins built by luthier Peter Sawchyn in Regina, Saskatchewan.

Schaefer

1997-2014. Premium grade, production/custom, flat-top acoustic guitars built by luthier Edward A. Schaefer in Austin, Texas. He previously built archtops, basses and mandolins. He retired in '14.

Schecter

1976-present. Intermediate, professional and premium grade, production/custom, acoustic and electric guitars and basses. Guitar component manufacturer founded in California by four partners (David Schecter's name sounded the best), started offering complete instruments in '79. The company was bought out and moved to Dallas, Texas in the early '80s. By '88 the company was back in California and in '89 was purchased by Hisatake Shibuya. Schecter Custom Shop guitars are made in Burbank, California and their intermediate grade Diamond Series is made in South Korea.

Scheerhorn

1989-present. Professional and premium grade, custom, resonator and Hawaiian guitars built by luthier Tim Scheerhorn in Kentwood, Michigan. Around 2010, Scheerhorn becomes a division of National Reso-Phonic.

Schoenberg

1986-present. Premium grade, production/custom, flat-tops offered by Eric Schoenberg of Tiburon, California. From '86-'94 guitars made to Schoenberg's specifications by Martin. From '86-'90 constructed by Schoenberg's luthier and from '90-'94 assembled by Martin but voiced and inlaid in the Schoenberg shop. Current models made to Schoenberg specs by various smaller shops.

Schon

1986-1991. Designed by guitarist Neal Schon, early production by Charvel/Jackson building about 200 in the San Dimas factory. The final 500 were built by Larrivee in Canada. Leo Knapp also built custom Schon guitars from '85-'87, and '90s custom-made Schon guitars were also available.

Standard (Canadian-made)

1987-1991. Made in Canada on headstock.

1987-1991		$550	$700

Standard (U.S.A.-made)

1986 only. San Dimas/Jackson model, single-cut, pointy headstock shape, Made in U.S.A. on headstock.

1986		$1,275	$1,650

Schramm Guitars

1990-present. Premium grade, production/custom, classical and flamenco guitars built by luthier David Schramm in Clovis, California.

MODEL YEAR	FEATURES	EXC. COND. LOW	HIGH

Schroder Guitars

Luthier Timothy Schroeder (he drops the first e in his name on the guitars) builds premium grade, production/custom, archtops in Northbrook, Illinois. He began in 1993.

Schulte

1950s-2000. Luthier C. Eric Schulte made solidbody, semi-hollow body, hollow body and acoustic guitars, both original designs and copies, covering a range of prices, in the Philadelphia area.

Custom Copy

1982. Single-cut solidbody, figured maple top.

1982		$650	$850

Schulz

Ca. 1903-1917. Luthier August Schulz built harp guitars and lute-guitars in Nuremberg, Germany.

Harp Guitar

1906		$800	$1,050

Schwartz Guitars

1992-present. Premium grade, custom, flat-top guitars built by luthier Sheldon Schwartz in Concord, Ontario.

ScoGo

Professional and premium grade, production/custom, solidbody guitars built by luthier Scott Gordon in Parkesburg, Pennsylvania starting in 2001.

Scorpion Guitars

1998-2014. Professional and premium grade, custom, solidbody guitars made by Ed Roman Guitars.

Scott French

2004-present. Professional grade, production/custom, electric guitars and basses built by luthier Scott French in Auburn, California. In '12 he discontinued offering custom built.

Scott Walker Custom Guitars

Refer to S. Walker Custom Guitars.

SeaGlass Guitars USA

2011-present. Professional grade, production/custom, electric guitars, built by luthier Roger Mello in Groton, Massachusetts.

Seagull

1982-present. Intermediate grade, production, acoustic and acoustic/electric guitars built in Canada. Seagull was founded by luthier Robert Godin, who also has the Norman, Godin, and Patrick & Simon brands of instruments.

Sebring

1980s-mid-1990s. Entry level Korean imports distributed by V.M.I. Industries.

MODEL YEAR	FEATURES	EXC. COND. LOW	HIGH

Seiwa

Early 1980s. Entry-level to mid-level Japanese electric guitars and basses, logo may indicate Since 1956.

Sekova

Mid 1960s-mid 1970s. Entry level instruments imported by the U.S. Musical Merchandise Corporation of New York.

Selmer

1932-1952. France-based Selmer & Cie was primarily a maker of wind instruments when they asked Mario Maccaferri to design a line of guitars for them. The guitars, with an internal sound chamber for increased volume, were built in Mantes-la-Ville. Both gut and steel string models were offered. Maccaferri left Selmer in '33, but guitar production continued, and the original models are gradually phased out. In '36, only the 14 fret oval model is built. Production is stopped for WWII and resumes in '46, finally stopping in '52. Less than 900 guitars are built in total.

Classique

1942. Solid Rosewood back and sides, no cutaway, solid spruce top, round soundhole, classical guitar size, possibly only 2 built.

1942		$3,900	$5,000

Concert

1932-1933. For gut strings, cutaway, laminated Indian rosewood back and sides, internal resonator, spruce top with D hole, wide walnut neck, ebony 'board, only a few dozen built.

1932		$8,850	$11,500
1933		$12,300	$16,000

Eddie Freeman Special

1933. For steel strings, 4 strings, laminated Indian rosewood back and sides, cutaway, no internal resonator, solid spruce top, D hole, black and white rosette inlays, walnut 12 fret neck, ebony 'board, 640mm scale, approx. 100 made.

1933		$4,200	$5,500

Espagnol

1932. For gut strings, laminated Indian rosewood back and sides, no cutaway, internal resonator, solid spruce top, round soundhole, wide walnut neck, ebony 'board, only a few made.

1932		$6,000	$7,800

Grand Modele 4 Cordes

1932-1933. For steel strings, 4 string model, laminated back and sides, cutaway, internal resonator, solid spruce top, D hole, walnut neck, ebony 'board, 12 fret, 640mm scale, 2 or 3 dozen made.

1932-1933		$8,800	$11,500

Harp Guitar

1933. For gut strings, solid mahogany body, extended horn holding 3 sub bass strings, 3 screw adjustable neck, wide walnut neck, ebony 'board, only about 12 built.

1933		$8,800	$11,500

Hawaienne

1932-1934. For steel strings, 6 or 7 strings, laminated back and sides, no cutaway, internal resonator, solid spruce top, D hole, wide walnut neck, ebony 'board, 2 or 3 dozen built.

1932-1934		$19,000	$24,500

Modele Jazz

1936-1942, 1946-1952. For steel strings, laminated Indian rosewood back and sides (some laminated or solid mahogany), cutaway, solid spruce top, small oval soundhole, walnut neck, ebony 'board (latest ones with rosewood necks), 14 fret to the body, 670mm scale. Production interrupted for WWII.

1936-1952		$24,000	$31,000

Modeles de Transition

1934-1936. Transition models appearing before 14 fret oval hole model, some in solid maple with solid headstock, some with round soundhole and cutaway, some 12 fret models with oval hole.

1934-1936		$14,200	$18,500

Orchestre

1932-1934. For steel strings, laminated back and sides, cutaway, internal resonator, solid spruce top, D hole, walnut neck, ebony 'board, about 100 made.

1932-1934		$25,500	$33,000

Tenor

1932-1933. For steel strings, 4 strings, laminated back and sides, internal resonator, solid spruce top, D hole, walnut neck, ebony 'board, 12 fret, 570mm scale, 2 or 3 dozen built.

1932-1933		$3,550	$4,600

Serenghetti

2007-present. Luthier Ray Patterson builds professional and premium grade, production/custom, 1-piece and neck-thru guitars and basses in Ocala, Florida.

Serge Guitars

1995-present. Luthier Serge Michaud builds his production/custom, classical, steel-string, resophonic and archtop guitars in Breakeyville, Quebec.

Series 10

1980s. Budget grade electric guitars, Series 10 by Bently on headstock.

Sexauer Guitars

1967-present. Premium and presentation grade, custom, steel-string, 12-string, nylon-string, and archtop guitars built by luthier Bruce Sexauer in Petaluma, California.

Shadow

1990s. Made in Europe, copy models such as the classic offset double cutaway solidbody, large Shadow logo on headstock, Shadow logo on pickup cover, student to intermediate grade.

Sekova Single Cut

1950 Selmer Esquire

Craig Brody

1950s Sherwood Deluxe

Donald DiLoreto

1982 Silver Street Taxi

Allen McBroom

MODEL YEAR	FEATURES	EXC. COND. LOW	HIGH

Shanti Guitars

1985-present. Premium and presentation grade, custom, steel-string, 12-string, nylon-string and archtop guitars built by luthier Michael Hornick in Avery, California.

Shelley D. Park Guitars

1991-present. Luthier Shelley D. Park builds her professional grade, custom, nylon- and steel-string guitars in Vancouver, British Columbia.

Shelton-Farretta

1967-present. Premium grade, production/custom, flamenco and classical guitars built by luthiers John Shelton and Susan Farretta originally in Portland, Oregon, and since '05 in Alsea, Oregon.

Sheppard Guitars

1993-present. Luthier Gerald Sheppard builds his premium grade, production/custom, steel-string guitars in Kingsport, Tennessee.

Shergold

1968-1992. Founded by Jack Golder and Norman Houlder, Shergold originally made guitars for other brands like Hayman and Barnes and Mullins. In '75, they started building guitars and basses under their own name. By '82, general guitar production was halted but custom orders were filled through '90. In '91, general production was again started but ended in '92 when Golder died.

Sherwood

Late 1940s-early 1950s. Archtop and lap steel guitars made for Montgomery Ward made by Chicago manufacturers such as Kay. There were also Sherwood amps made by Danelectro. Value ranges are about the same as Kay model equivalent.

Shifflett

1990-present. Luthier Charles Shifflett builds his premium grade, production/custom, flat-top, classical, flamenco, resophonic, and harp guitars and basses in High River, Alberta. He also builds banjos.

Sho-Bro

1969-1978. Spanish and Hawaiian style resonator guitars made by Sho-Bud in Nashville, Tennessee and distributed by Gretsch. Designed by Shot Jackson and Buddy Emmons.

7-String Dobro

1972-1978		$1,225	$1,600

Grand Slam

1978. Acoustic, spruce top, mahogany neck, jacaranda sides and back, and mother-of-pearl inlays, abalone soundhole purfling.

1970s		$525	$675

Resonator

1972-1978. Flat-top style guitar with metal resonator with 2 small circular grilled soundholes.

1972-1978		$875	$1,150

Siegmund Guitars & Amplifiers

1993-present. Luthier Chris Siegmund builds his professional, premium, and presentation grade, custom/production, archtop, solidbody, and resonator guitars in Los Angeles, California. He founded the company in Seattle, moving it to Austin, Texas for '95-'97. He also builds amps and effects pedals.

Sierra

Budget level imports by Musicorp, starting in 2006. There is an unrelated brand of Sierra steels and lap steels.

Sigma

1970-2007. Budget and intermediate grade, production, import acoustic and electric guitars and basses distributed by C.F. Martin Company. They also offered mandolins and banjos. Japanese-made for 1970-'72; lower-end model production moved to Korea in '73; most of remaining Japanese production moved to Korea in '83; most production moved to Taiwan and Indonesia in '96.

Acoustic/Acoustic Electric/Electric

1970-2007	Various models	$200	$625

Signature

2005-ca. 2013. See listing under Gibson Baldwin.

Signature Guitar Company (Canada)

1987-1990. Intermediate/professional grade, electric guitars and basses built in Ontario, Canada. Mother of pearl inlaid on 21st fret with model name and, as an option, you could custom order any model with your name inlaid on the 12th fret.

Odyssey

1987-1990. Flat-top, figured maple top, 3 pickups.

1987-1990		$1,700	$2,200

Oracle

1987-1990. Flat-top, figured maple top, 3 pickups.

1987-1990		$1,700	$2,200

Signet

1972-Mid 1970s. Acoustic flat-top guitars, imported from Japan by Ampeg/Selmer.

Silber

1992-1998. Solid wood, steel-string guitars designed by Marc Silber, made in Paracho, Mexico, and distributed by K & S Music. Silber continues to offer the same models under the Marc Silber Music brand.

Silver Street

1979-1986. Founded by brothers Bruce and Craig Hardy, production of solidbody electric guitars built in Elkhart, Indiana and later in Shelby, Michigan. Original TAXI model prototypes built by luthier Richard Schneider. Later models included Spitfire, Cobra, MX, Nightwing, Tommy Shaw and Elite,

MODEL YEAR	FEATURES	EXC. COND. LOW	HIGH

all offered with various pickups, custom paint and optional hardware. MSRPs ranged from $449 for a single-pickup TAXI to $889 for a basic Elite. Total production estimate 550 units. See the March 2018 issue of Vintage Guitar for more info.

Various Models

1979-1986	Early smaller models	$425	$650
1979-1986	Larger models	$650	$950

Silvertone

1941-ca. 1970, present. Brand of Sears instruments which replaced their Supertone brand in '41. The Silvertone name was used on Sears phonographs, records and radios as early as the 'teens, and on occasional guitar models. When Sears divested itself of the Harmony guitar subsidiary in '40 it turned to other suppliers including Kay. In '40 Kay-made archtops and Hawaiian electric lap steels appeared in the catalog bearing the Silvertone brand, and after '41-'42, all guitars, regardless of manufacturer, were called Silvertone.

Sears offered Danelectro-made solidbodies in the fall of '54. Danelectro hollowbodies appeared in '56. By '65, the Silvertones were Teisco-made guitars from W.M.I., but never sold through the catalog. First imports shown in catalog were in '69. By '70, most guitars sold by Sears were imports and did not carry the Silvertone name.

Currently, Samick offers a line of acoustic and electric guitars, basses and amps under the Silvertone name.

Amp-In-Case

1962-1968. The black, sharp double cutaway, 1-pickup 1448, introduced in '62, came with a smaller wattage amp without tremolo. The black, 2-pickup 1449, introduced in '63, came with a higher-watt amp with tremolo and better quality Jensen speaker and was replaced by the red burst 1457 in '64. Gray tolex covered the guitar-amp case. In '66 they were replaced with the black 1451 and 1452 with soft, rounded cutaway horns.

1962-1966	1448, 1 pu, black	$525	$675
1963-1966	1449, 2 pus, black	$675	$875
1964-1966	1457, 2 pus, red burst	$675	$875
1966-1968	1451, 1 pu, round cut	$525	$675
1966-1968	1452, 2 pus, round cut	$675	$875

Belmont

1958. Single-cut solidbody, 2 pickups, black.

1958		$700	$900

Black Beauty Model 1384L

1956-1958. Called 'The Black Beauty' in Sears catalog, large body acoustic-electric archtop, cutaway, 2 pickups, block markers, white binding, spruce top, mahogany sides and back, black lacquer finish.

1956-1958		$1,025	$1,350

Black Beauty Model 1385

1957. Basically the same as 1384L.

1957		$1,025	$1,350

Espanada

1960s. Bigsby, 2 pickups, black.

1960s		$1,025	$1,350

MODEL YEAR	FEATURES	EXC. COND. LOW	HIGH

Estrelita

1960s. Semi-hollowbody archtop, 2 pickups, black, Harmony-made.

1960s		$925	$1,200

F-66

1964. Similar to Harmony Rocket III, single-cut, thinline electric, 3 pickups, Bigsby.

1964		$825	$1,075

Gene Autry Melody Ranch

1941-1955. 13" Harmony-made acoustic, Gene Autry signature on belly, cowboy roundup stencil, same as earlier Supertone Gene Autry Roundup.

1941-1955		$250	$350

H-1214

1951. Full-size acoustic archtop, script Silvertone headstock logo, dot markers, blond with simulated grain finish.

1951		$450	$575

H-1260 Sovereign Jumbo

1968. Silvertone's version of Harmony's Sovereign jumbo flat-top, dot markers, sunburst.

1968		$550	$700

H-1434 Rocket

1965. Similar to Harmony Rocket H59, sold by Sears, 3 pickups, Bigsby vibrato.

1965		$825	$1,075

Meteor

1955. Single-cut, 1 pickup, sunburst.

1955		$375	$500

Model 623

Late-1950s. Large-body acoustic archtop, dot markers, white 'guard, black finish, painted white binding to give a black and white attractive appearance.

1950s		$175	$225

Model 1300/Model 1302

1958-1959. Single-cut, 1 lipstick pickup, dot markers, 3-on-a-side symmetric headstock, bronze (1300) or black (1302).

1958-1959	1300	$500	$650
1958-1959	1302	$500	$650

Model 1301/Model 1303

1958-1959. 1300 with 2 lipstick pickups, bronze (1301) or black (1303).

1958-1959	1301	$650	$875
1958-1959	1303	$650	$875

Model 1305

1958-1959. Single-cut, 3 lipstick pickups, dot markers, 3-on-a-side symmetric headstock, white and black finish.

1958-1959		$1,000	$1,300

Model 1317

1957. Single-cut solidbody, 1 lipstick pickup, dot markers, 3-on-a-side symmetric headstock, bronze finish.

1957		$425	$550

Model 1381/Model 1382

1954-1957. Kay-made (many '50s Silvertones were made by Danelectro), slim-style electric similar to Thin Twin/Jimmy Reed, 2 lipstick pickups, 4 knobs, crown-crest logo on 'guard under strings, bolt neck, block markers, sunburst, sold without (Model 1381) and with a case (1382).

1954-1957	1381	$450	$600
1954-1957	1382	$750	$1,000

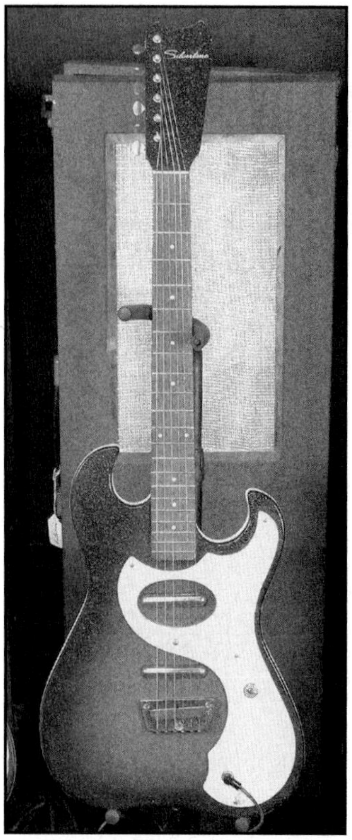

1966 Silvertone 1457 Amp-In-Case

Ted Barham

1958 Silvertone 1305

Imaged by Heritage Auctions, HA.com

1960s Silvertone 1446

Jon Ross

1965 Silvertone H1454

Tom Pfeifer

MODEL YEAR	FEATURES	EXC. COND. LOW	HIGH

Model 1413

1962-1964. Double-cut slab body, single pickup, 2 control knobs, dot markers.

1962-1964		$175	$225

Model 1415/Model 1417

1960-1962. Single-cut, 1 lipstick pickup, 6-on-a-side dolphin headstock, dot markers, bronze (1415) or black (1417).

1960	1417	$425	$575
1961-1962	1415	$425	$575

Model 1420

1959-1963. Single-cut extra thin solidbody, bolt neck, 2 pickups, natural shaded or black finish.

1959-1963		$425	$550

Model 1423L

1960. Single-cut solidbody, 2 pickups, 5 control knobs with rotator switch, block markers, gleaming gold-color splatter-effect over black finish.

1960		$450	$600

Model 1429L

1962-1963. Harmony-made and similar to Harmony's H-75, single-cut thinline electric, 3 pickups, trapeze tailpiece, 3 toggles, 6 knobs, block marker, sunburst.

1962-1963		$775	$1,000

Model 1445L

1960s. Teisco-made solidbody, 3 pickups.

1960s		$575	$750

Model 1446

1962-1966. Single-cut thin acoustic archtop, 2 Gibson P-90 pickups, original factory Bigsby tailpiece, black lacquer finish with white 'guard.

1962-1966		$975	$1,275

Model 1454

1962-1966. Single-cut thin acoustic archtop, 3 pickups, original factory Bigsby tailpiece, red lacquer finish.

1962-1966		$925	$1,200

Model 1476/Model 1477

1964-1966. Offset double-cut solidbody, 2 pickups, dot markers. 4 control knobs, tremolo, black (1476) or sunburst (1477).

1964-1966	1476	$425	$575
1964-1966	1477	$425	$575

Model 1478/Model 1488 Silhouette

1964-1967. Offset double-cut, rectangular pickups, tremolo, bound 'board, block markers.

1964-1967	1478, 1 pickup	$200	$250
1964-1967	1478, 2 pickups	$275	$350
1964-1967	1488, 3 pickups	$375	$500

Model S1352

1955		$525	$675

Model S1453 Rebel

1968. Two sharp cutaway, single f-hole, 2 pickups, vibrato.

1968		$425	$575

Student-level 13" Flat-Top

1960s. Harmony-made, 13" lower bout.

1960s		$25	$50

Student-level 15.5" Flat-Top

1960s. Harmony-made, 15.5" lower bout.

1960s	Model S621	$125	$175

Simon & Patrick

1985-present. Intermediate and professional grade, production, acoustic and acoustic/electric guitars built in Canada. Founded by luthier Robert Godin and named after his sons. He also produces the Seagull, Godin, and Norman brands of instruments.

Sims Custom Shop

2007-present. Custom, professional and premium grade, electric guitars built in Chattanooga, Tennessee by luthier Patrick Sims.

Singletouch

Luthier Mark Singleton builds his professional and premium grade, custom/production, solid and semi-hollow body guitars and basses in Phillips Ranch, California.

Skylark

1981. Solidbody guitars made in Japan and distributed by JC Penney. Two set-neck models and one bolt-neck model were offered. Most likely a one-time deal as brand quickly disappeared.

Slammer

1998-2009. Budget and intermediate grade, production, guitars and basses imported from Indonesia by Hamer. Not to be confused with Hamer's Korean-made series of guitars from 1990-'97 called Hamer Slammer.

Slammer Series (Import)

1998-2009	Various models	$150	$200

Slingerland

Ca. 1914-present. Henry Slingerland opened a music school in Chicago, Illinois, in 1914 where he supplied instruments made by others to students who took his course. That grew into the Slingerland Manufacturing Company, then Slingerland Banjo and Drum Company in '28, selling banjos, guitars and ukes, built by them and others into the '40s. They also marketed the May Bell brand. Many of the guitars were made by other companies, including Regal. Slingerland ownership changed multiple times in the 1970s-80s until it was acquired by Gibson (from Gretsch) in 1994. The current owner, Drum Workshop (DW), acquired Slingerland in 2019.

Nitehawk

1930s. 16" archtop, Nitehawk logo on headstock, fancy position neck markers.

1930s		$700	$900

Songster Archtop/Flat-Top

1930s	Archtop	$560	$725
1930s	Flat-Top	$975	$1,275

Songster Tenor

1930s. Archtop.

1930s		$400	$525

MODEL YEAR	FEATURES	EXC. COND. LOW	HIGH

Smart Fine Instruments

1986-present. Luthier A. Lawrence Smart builds his professional and premium grade, custom, flat-top guitars first in McCall and now Hailey, Idaho. He also builds mandolin-family instruments.

Smith, George

1959-2020. Custom classical and flamenco guitars built by luthier George Smith in Portland, Oregon.

Smith, Lawrence K.

1989-present. Luthier Lawrence Smith builds his professional and premium grade, production/custom, flat-top, nylon-string, and archtop guitars in Thirrow, New South Wales, Australia. He also builds mandolins.

SMK Music Works

2002-present. Luthier Scott Kenerson builds production/custom, professional grade, solidbody electric guitars and basses in Waterford, Michigan.

Smooth Stone Guitar

2007-present. Luthier R. Dale Humphries builds his professional and premium grade, production/custom, acoustic and electric guitars and basses in Pocatello, Idaho.

Solomon Guitars

1995-present. Luthier Erich Solomon builds his premium and presentation grade, production/custom, archtop, flat-top, classical and electric guitars in Epping, New Hampshire. Prior to '99 he was located in Anchorage, Alaska.

Somervell

Luthier Douglas P. Somervell built premium and presentation grade, production/custom, classical and flamenco guitars in Brasstown, North Carolina.

Somogyi, Ervin

1971-present. Luthier Ervin Somogyi builds his presentation grade, production/custom, flat-top, flamenco, and classical guitars in Oakland, California.

Sonata

1960s. Private brand Harmony-made, Sonata brand logo on headstock and pickguard.

Superior

1965. Grand Auditorium acoustic archtop, block markers, celluloid bound edges, similar to Harmony 1456, Superior logo on headstock.

1965		$375	$500

SonFather Guitars

1994-present. Luthier David A. Cassotta builds his production/custom, flat-top, 12-string, nylon-string and electric guitars in Rocklin, California.

MODEL YEAR	FEATURES	EXC. COND. LOW	HIGH

Sorrentino

1930s. Private brand made by Epiphone and distributed by C.M.I. Quality close to similar Epiphone models.

Arcadia

1930s. Lower-end f-hole acoustic archtop similar to Epiphone Blackstone.

1930s		$475	$625

Sorrento

1960s. Electric guitar imports made by Teisco, pricing similar to Teisco models, Sorrento logo on headstock, upscale solidbodies can have four pickups with five knobs and four switches.

Electric Solidbody

1960s	4 pickups	$275	$375

Southwell Guitars

1983-present. Premium grade, custom, nylon-string guitars built by luthier Gary Southwell in Nottingham, U.K.

Sovereign

Ca. 1899-1938. Sovereign was originally a brand of The Oscar Schmidt Company of Jersey City, New Jersey, and used on guitars, banjos and mandolins starting in the very late 1800s. In the late '30s, Harmony purchased several trade names from the Schmidt Company, including Sovereign and Stella. Sovereign then ceased as a brand, but Harmony continued using it on a model line of Harmony guitars.

Spaltinstruments

2002-present. Professional and premium grade, production/custom, electric solidbody and hollowbody guitars and basses built by luthier Michael Spalt, originally in Los Angeles, California and since '11 in Vienna, Austria.

Sparrow Guitars

Guitars manufactured in China are dismantled and "overhauled" in Vancouver, British Columbia, starting in '04. From these imports, luthier Billy Bones builds his intermediate and professional grade, production/custom solidbody and hollowbody electric guitars.

Specht Guitars

1991-present. Premium grade, production/custom, acoustic, baritone, parlor, jazz and classical guitars and basses built by luthier Oliver Specht in Vancouver, British Columbia.

Specimen Products

1984-present. Luthier Ian Schneller builds his professional and premium grade, production/custom, aluminum and wood body guitars and basses in Chicago, Illinois. He also builds ukes and amps.

1960s Silvertone 15.5" flat-top
Tom Pfeifer

Smooth Stone BC Series

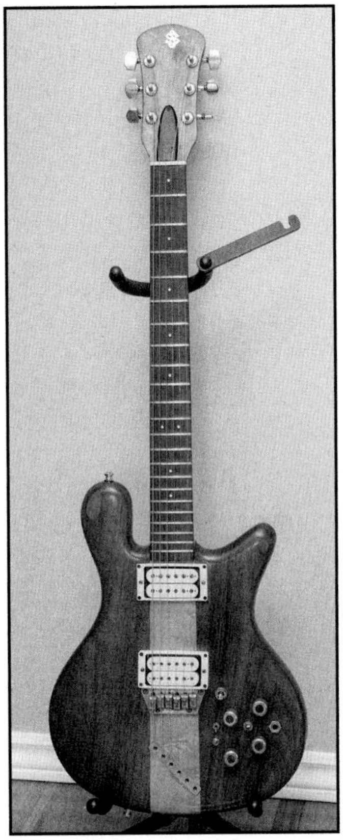
1978 Stuart Spector G-1
Ron Baksi

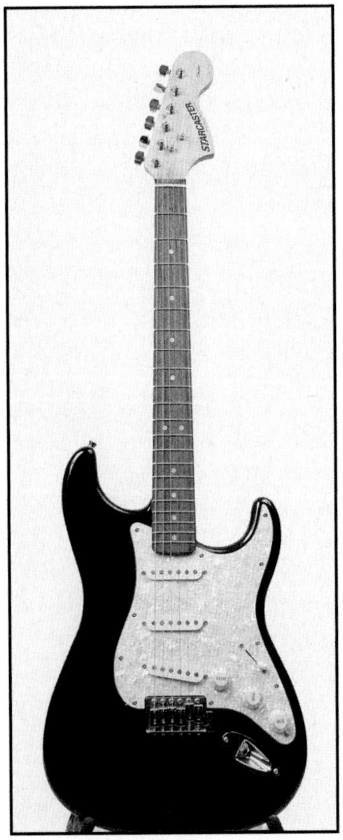

Starcaster
Bernunzio Uptown Music

MODEL YEAR	FEATURES	EXC. COND. LOW	HIGH

Spector/Stuart Spector Design

1975-1990 (Spector), 1991-1998 (SSD), 1998-present (Spector SSD). Known mainly for basses, Spector offered U.S.-made guitars during '75-'90 and '96-'99, and imports for '87-'90 and '96-'99. Since 2003, they again offer U.S.-professional grade, production, solidbody guitars. See Bass Section for more company info.

SPG

2006-2009. Originally professional grade, custom, solidbody and chambered guitars built by luthier Rick Welch in Farmingdale, Maine and Hanson, Massachusetts. He also built lapsteels. Currently brand is used on imported line.

Squier

See models listed under Squier in Fender section.

St. Blues

1980-1989, 2005-present. Intermediate and professional grade, production/custom, solidbody guitars and basses imported and built in Memphis, Tennessee. The original '80s line was designed by Tom Keckler and Charles Lawing at Memphis' Strings & Things.

St. George

Mid to late 1960s. Early Japanese brand imported possibly by Buegeleisen & Jacobson of New York, New York.

Electric Solidbody

1960s. Early Japanese import duplicate of Zim Gar model, top mounted controls, 3 pickups, bolt-on neck.

1960s	Sunburst	$475	$625

St. Moritz

1960s. Guitars and basses imported from Japan by the Manhattan Novelty Corp. Manufacturer unknown, but some appear to be Fuji Gen Gakki products. Generally shorter scale beginner guitars, some with interesting pickup configurations.

Stahl

1900-1941. William C. Stahl, of Milwaukee, Wisconsin, ran a publishing company, taught stringed instrument classes and sold instruments to his students as well as by mail order across America. His label claimed that he was the maker but most of his products were built by the Larson brothers of Maurer & Co. of Chicago, with the balance mostly from Washburn. The most commonly found Larson-built models are the Style 6 and 7 as seen in the ca. 1912 Stahl catalog. Jimi Hendrix was the proud owner of a Style 8. The Style 6 is a moderately trimmed 15" Brazilian rosewood beauty that is much like the highly sought Maurer Style 551. The Style 7 and 8 are pearl trimmed 13 ½" concert size Brazilians comparable to the Maurer Style 562 ½. The 1912 Stahl catalog Styles 4, 5 and 9 were built by Washburn.

MODEL YEAR	FEATURES	EXC. COND. LOW	HIGH

Stambaugh

1995-present. Luthier Chris Stambaugh builds his professional grade, custom/production, solidbody guitars basses in Stratham, New Hampshire.

Standel

1952-1974, 1997-present. Amp builder Bob Crooks offered instruments under his Standel brand 3 different times during the '60s. In '61 Semie Moseley, later of Mosrite fame, made 2 guitar models and 1 bass for Standel, in limited numbers. Also in '61, Standel began distributing Sierra steels and Dobro resonators, sometimes under the Standel name. In '65 and '66 Standel offered a guitar and a bass made by Joe Hall, who also made the Hallmark guitars. In '66 Standel connected with Sam Koontz, who designed and produced the most numerous Standel models (but still in relatively small numbers) in Newark, New Jersey. These models hit the market in '67 and were handled by Harptone, which was associated with Koontz. By '70 Standel was out of the guitar biz. See Amp section for more company info.

Custom Deluxe 101/101X

1967-1968. Custom solidbody with better electronics, 101X has no vibrato, sunburst, black, pearl white and metallic red.

1967-1968	$1,100	$1,425

Custom Deluxe 102/102X

1967-1968. Custom thin body with better electronics, 102X has no vibrato, offered in sunburst and 5 solid color options.

1967-1968	$1,100	$1,425

Custom 201/201X

1967-1968. Solidbody, 2 pickups, vibrola, 2 pointed cutaways, headstock similar to that on Fender XII, 201X has no vibrato, sunburst, black, pearl white and metallic red.

1967-1968	$925	$1,200

Custom 202/202X

1967-1968. Thin body, headstock similar to that on Fender XII, 202X has no vibrato, offered in sunburst and 5 solid color options.

1967-1968	$925	$1,200

Custom 420S

1967-1968. Custom thin body with 2 pickups.

1967-1968	$1,100	$1,425

Star

1957-1960s. Early budget level instruments made by Tokyo Sound Company and Gakki and exported by Japan's Hoshino (translates to Star) company which also has Ibanez.

Starcaster

2000s. Budget brand from Fender that has been used on acoustic, electric and bass guitars, effects, amps and drums and sold through mass retailers such as Costco, Target and others. See Fender listing for guitar values.

MODEL YEAR	FEATURES	EXC. COND. LOW	HIGH

Starfield

1992-1993. Solidbody guitars from Hoshino (Ibanez) made in the U.S. and Japan. U.S. guitars are identified as American models; Japanese ones as SJ models. Hoshino also used the Star Field name on a line of Japanese guitars in the late '70s. These Star Fields had nothing to do with the '90s versions and were not sold in the U.S.

Starforce

Ca. 1989. Import copies from Starforce Music/ Starforce USA.

Stars

Intermediate grade, production, solidbody guitars made in Korea.

Status Graphite

Professional grade, production/custom, solidbody guitars and basses built in Colchester, Essex, U.K. Status was the first English company to produce a carbon fiber instrument.

Stauffer

1800s. Old World violin and guitar maker, Georg Stauffer. Valid attributions include signed or labeled by the maker indicating the guitar was actually made by Stauffer, as opposed to attributed to Stauffer or one of his contemporaries. See Martin for listing.

Stefan Sobell Musical Instruments

1982-present. Premium grade, production/custom, flat-top, 12-string, and archtop guitars built by luthier Stefan Sobell in Hetham, Northumberland, England. He also builds mandolins, citterns and bouzoukis.

Steinberger

1979-present. Currently Steinberger offers budget, intermediate, and professional grade, production, electric guitars. They also offer basses. Founded by Ned Steinberger, who started designing NS Models for Stuart Spector in '76. In '79, he designed the L-2 headless bass. In '80, the Steinberger Sound Corp. was founded. Steinberger Sound was purchased by the Gibson Guitar Corp. in '87, and in '92, Steinberger relocated to Nashville, Tennessee.

Headless model codes for '85-'93 are: First letter is X for bass or G for guitar.

Second letter is for body shape: M is regular offset double-cut guitar body; L is rectangle body; P is mini V shaped body.

Number is pickup designation: 2 = 2 humbuckers, 3 = 3 single coils, 4 = single/single/humbucker.

Last letter is type of tremolo: S = S-Trem tremolo; T = Trans-Trem which cost more on original retail.

MODEL YEAR	FEATURES	EXC. COND. LOW	HIGH

GL

1979-1984. Headless, rectangle body, 2 pickups.

1979-1984		$2,300	$3,000

Steinegger

1976-present. Premium grade, custom steel-string flat-top guitars built by luthier Robert Steinegger in Portland, Oregon.

Stella

Ca. 1899-1974, 2000s. Stella was a brand of the Oscar Schmidt Company which started using the brand on low-mid to mid-level instruments in the very late 1800s. Oscar Schmidt produced all types of stringed instruments and was very successful in the 1920s. Company salesmen reached many rural areas and Stella instruments were available in general stores, furniture stores, and dry goods stores, ending up in the hands of musicians such as Leadbelly and Charlie Patton. Harmony acquired the Stella brand in '39 and built thousands of instruments with that name in the '50s and '60s. Harmony dissolved in '74. The Stella brand was reintroduced in the 2000s by MBT International.

00 Style

1900-1930. Oak body flat-top.

1900-1930		$425	$550

Flat-Top 15" 12-String

1920s-1930s. Associated with early blues and folk musicians, top of the line for Stella.

1920s-30s		$6,300	$8,200

Flat-Top by Harmony

1950s-1960s. The low end of the Harmony-built models, US-made until the end of the '60s, student level, Stella logo on headstock, playing action can often be very high which makes them difficult to play.

1950s-60s	13"	$50	$175
1950s-60s	14", 12-string	$75	$200
1950s-60s	Sundale (colors)	$325	$475
1950s-60s	Tenor 4-string	$50	$175

Harp Guitar

Early-1900s.

1900s		$1,700	$2,200

Singing Cowboy

Late-1990s. Copy of Supertone (black background)/ Silvertone/Harmony Singing Cowboy, import with laminated wood construction and ladder bracing.

1990s	Stencil over black	$40	$55

Stetson

1884-ca. 1924. Stetson was a house brand of William John Dyer's St. Paul, Minnesota, music store. They started advertising this brand as early as 1894, but those built by the Larson brothers of Maurer & Co. date from ca. 1904-c. 1924. Most Stetsons were made by the Larsons. Others were built by Harmony (early ones), Washburn and three are credited to the Martin Co.

Steinegger D-45
Carter Vintage Guitars

1968 Stella
Edward Sparks

1950 Stromberg DeLuxe
Ranger Doug

1930s Stromberg G-3
Carter Vintage Guitars

MODEL YEAR	FEATURES	EXC. COND. LOW	HIGH

Stevenson

1999-present. Professional grade, production/custom, solidbody electric guitars and basses built by luthier Ted Stevenson in Lachine, Quebec. He also builds amps.

Stiehler

Production/custom, professional and premium grade, acoustic electric and electric solidbody guitars and basses, built by luthier Bob Stiehler, first in Wellington and since '11 in Carson City, Nevada. He started in 2005.

Stonebridge

1981-present. Czech Republic luthier Frantisek Furch builds professional and premium grade, production/custom, acoustic guitars. He also builds mandolins.

Stonetree Custom Guitars

1996-present. Luthier Scott Platts builds his professional and premium grade, custom/production, solidbody and chambered electric guitars and basses in Saratoga, Wyoming.

Strad-O-Lin/Stradolin

Ca.1920s-ca.1960s. The Strad-O-Lin company was operated by the Hominic brothers in New York, primarily making mandolins for wholesalers. Around '57 Multivox/Premier bought the company and also used the name on electric and acoustic guitars, basses and amps. Premier also marketed student level guitars under the U.S. Strad brand.

Electric

1960s		$300	$400

Stratosphere

1954-1958. Solidbody electrics made in Springfield, Missouri by brothers Claude and Russ Deaver, some featuring fanned frets. They also made an odd double neck called the Stratosphere Twin with a regular 6-string neck and a 12-string tuned in minor and major thirds. The brothers likely made less than 200 instruments.

Electric

1954-1958		$775	$1,000

Strobel Guitars

2003-present. Luthier Russ Strobel builds custom, professional grade, electric travel guitars and basses in Boca Raton, Florida. He also offers a production, intermediate grade, travel guitar built first in Korea and since '13 in Asia.

Stromberg

1906-1955, 2001-present. Intermediate and professional grade, production, archtop guitars imported by Larry Davis.

Founded in Boston by master luthier Charles Stromberg, a Swedish immigrant, building banjos and drums. Son Harry joined the company in 1907and stayed until '27. Son Elmer started in 1910 at age 15. The shop was well known for tenor banjos, but when the banjo's popularity declined, they began building archtop orchestra model guitars. The shop moved to Hanover Street in Boston in '27 and began producing custom order archtop guitars, in particular the 16" G-series and the Deluxe. As styles changed the G-series was increased to 17 3/8" and the 19" Master 400 model was introduced in '37. Stromberg designs radically changed around '40, most likely when Elmer took over guitar production. Both Charles and Elmer died within a few months of each other in '55. Most of the interest in vintage Strombergs comes out of the Boston area.

Larry Davis of WD Music Products revived the Stromberg name and introduced a series of moderately priced jazz guitars in June, 2001. The models are crafted by a small Korean shop with component parts supplied by WD.

Deluxe

1927-1955. Non-cut, 16" body to '34, 17 3/8" body after '35, also sometimes labeled Delux.

1927-1939	2 parallel 3 ladder	$4,000	$8,000
1940-1947	2 braces	$4,000	$8,000
1948-1955	1 brace	$15,000	$20,000

G-1

1927-1955. Non-cut, 16" body to '35, 17 3/8" body after '35, sunburst.

1927-1935	2 parallel 3 ladder	$4,000	$8,000
1936-1947	2 braces	$4,000	$8,000
1948-1955	1 brace	$15,000	$20,000

G-3

Early 1930s. Archtop, 16 3/8", 3 segment F-holes, ladder bracing, gold hardware, engraved tailpiece, 8-ply 'guard, 5-ply body binding, laminate maple back, fancy engraved headstock with Stromberg name, less total refinement than higher-end Stromberg models.

1927-1935	2 parallel 3 ladder	$4,000	$8,000

G-5

1952-1955. 17" cutaway.

1953	1 brace	$18,000	$28,000

Master 300

1937-1955. 19" non-cut.

1937-1947	2 braces, natural	$5,000	$10,000
1937-1947	2 braces, sunburst	$5,000	$10,000
1948-1955	1 brace, natural	$10,000	$20,000
1948-1955	1 brace, sunburst	$10,000	$20,000

Master 400

1937-1955. 19" top-of-the-line non-cut, the most common of Stromberg's models.

1937-1947	2 braces, natural	$10,000	$20,000
1937-1947	2 braces, sunburst	$10,000	$20,000
1948-1955	1 brace, natural	$20,000	$40,000
1948-1955	1 brace, sunburst	$20,000	$40,000

Master 400 Cutaway

1949, 1953. Only 7 cutaway Strombergs are known to exist.

1949, 1953	1 brace, natural	$45,000	$65,000

MODEL YEAR	FEATURES	EXC. COND. LOW	HIGH

Stromberg-Voisinet

1921-ca.1932. Marketed Stromberg (not to be confused with Charles Stromberg of Boston) and Kay Kraft brands, plus guitars of other distributors and retailers. Stromberg was the successor to the Groehsl Company (or Groehsel) founded in Chicago, Illinois in 1890; and the predecessor to the Kay Musical Instrument Company. In 1921, the name was changed to Stromberg-Voisinet Company. Henry Kay "Hank" Kuhrmeyer joined the company in '23 and was secretary by '25. By the mid-'20s, the company was making many better Montgomery Ward guitars, banjos and mandolins, often with lots of pearloid.

Joseph Zorzi, Philip Gabriel and John Abbott left Lyon & Healy for S-V in '26 or '27, developing 2-point Venetian shape, which was offered in '27. The first production of electric guitars and amps was introduced with big fanfare in '28; perhaps only 200 or so made. The last Stromberg acoustic instruments were seen in '32. The Kay Kraft brand was introduced by Kuhrmeyer in '31 as the company made its transition to Kay (see Kay).

Acoustic

1921-1932. Various art and colors.

1921-1932	Various models	$250	$1,100

Stroup

Luthier Gary D. Stroup builds his intermediate and professional grade, production/custom, archtop and flat-top guitars in Eckley, Colorado, starting in 2003.

Stuart Custom Guitars

Professional and premium grade, production/custom, solid and semi-hollow body guitars built by luthier Fred Stuart, starting the year 2004, in Riverside, California. Stuart was a Senior Master Builder at Fender. He also builds pickups.

Suhr Guitars

1997-present. Luthier John Suhr builds his professional and premium grade, production/custom, solidbody electrics guitars and basses in Lake Elsinore, California. He also builds amps. He previously built Pensa-Suhr guitars with Rudy Pensa in New York.

Electric Solidbody

1997-2020	Various models	$1,700	$2,700

Sunset

2010-present. Luthier Leon White builds professional and premium grade, production/custom, electric solidbody, chambered and hollowbody guitars in Los Angeles, California.

Superior Guitars

1987-present. Intermediate grade, production/custom Hawaiian, flamenco and classical guitars made in Mexico for George Katechis Montalvo of Berkeley Musical Instrument Exchange. They also offer lap steels and mandolin-family instruments.

MODEL YEAR	FEATURES	EXC. COND. LOW	HIGH

Supersound

1952-1974. Founded by England's Alan Wootton, building custom amps and radios. In 1958-'59 he worked with Jim Burns to produce about 20 short scale, single-cut solidbodies bearing this name. They also built a bass model. The firm continued to build amps and effects into the early '60s.

Supertone

1914-1941. Brand used by Sears, Roebuck and Company for instruments made by various American manufacturers, including especially its own subsidiary Harmony (which it purchased in 1916). When Sears divested itself of Harmony in '40, instruments began making a transition to the Silvertone brand. By '41 the Supertone name was gone.

Acoustic Flat-Top (High-End Appointments)

1920s	Pearl trim 00-42 likeness	$1,300	$1,675
1920s	Pearl trim, Lindbergh model	$1,300	$1,675

Acoustic Flat-Top 13"

1920s-30s	Non-stencil, plain top	$110	$175
1920s-30s	Stencil top	$185	$250

Gene Autry Roundup

1932-1939. Harmony made acoustic, Gene Autry signature on belly, cowboy roundup stencil, 13" body until '35, then 14".

1932-1939		$260	$350

Lone Ranger

1936-1941. Black with red and silver Lone Ranger and Tonto stencil, silver-painted fretboard, 13 1/2" wide. "Hi-Yo Silver" added in '37, changed to "Hi-Ho Silver" in '38.

1936-1941		$260	$350

Robin Hood

1930s. 13" flat-top similar to Singing Cowboys, but with green and white art showing Robin Hood and his men against a black background.

1933		$260	$350

Singing Cowboys

1938-1943. Stencil of guitar strumming cowboys around chuck wagon and campfire, branded Silvertone after '41.

1938-1943		$260	$350

Supertone Wedge

1930s. Triangle-shaped wedge body, laminate construction, blue-silver Supertone label inside sound chamber, art decals on body.

1930s		$210	$300

Supro

1935-1968, 2004-present. Budget brand of National Dobro Company and Valco. Some Supro models also sold under the Airline brand for Montgomery Ward. In '42 Victor Smith, Al Frost and Louis Dopyera bought National and changed the name to Valco Manufacturing Company. Valco

1929 Stromberg-Voisinet Hawaiian Parlor

David Stone

Sunset Artist

1964 Supro Coronado II

Imaged by Heritage Auctions, HA.com

1965 Supro Lexington

Rivington Guitars

MODEL YEAR	FEATURES	EXC. COND. LOW	HIGH

Manufacturing Company name changed to Valco Guitars, Inc., in '62. Company treasurer Robert Engelhardt bought Valco in '64. In '67 Valco bought Kay and in '68 Valco/Kay went out of business. In the summer of '69, Valco/Kay brands and assets were sold at auction and the Supro and National names purchased by Chicago-area importer and distributor Strum N' Drum (Norma, Noble). In the early-'80s, ownership of the Supro name was transferred to Archer's Music, Fresno, California. Some Supros assembled from new-old-stock parts.

Amp builder Bruce Zinky revived the Supro name for a line of guitars built in the U.S. by luthier John Bolin and others. He also offers amps. In 2013, Absara Audio, LLC acquired the Supro trademark and started releasing amps and guitars in July 2014.

Arlington

1967-1967. Jazzmaster-style, wood body, 6 buttons, 4 knobs, vibrato, 2 pickups.

1966-1967 Various colors $900 $1,200

Atlas

1958. Rare model, Atlas logo, semi-single cutaway, 2 pickups plus bridge-tailpiece pickup, blond finish.

1958 $1,175 $1,525

Belmont

1955-1964. For '55-'60, 12" wide, single-cut, 1 neck pickup, 2 knobs treble side in 'guard, reverse-stairs tailpiece, No-Mar plastic maroon-colored covering. For '60, size increased to 13 1/2" wide. For '62-'64, Res-o-glas fiberglass was used for the body, a slight cutaway on bass side, 1 bridge pickup, 2 knobs on opposite sides. Polar White.

1955-1962 Black or white No-Mar $775 $1,025

1961-1964 Polar White Res-o-glas $825 $1,100

Bermuda

1962 only. Slab body (not beveled), double pickups, dot markers, cherry glass-fiber finish.

1962 $1,075 $1,400

Collegian Spanish

1939-1942. Metal body, 12 frets. Moved to National line in '42.

1939-1942 $900 $1,200

Coronado/Coronado II

1961-1967, 2017-present. Listed as II in '62 15 1/2" scale, single-cut thinline, 2 pickups, natural blond spruce top. Changed to slight cutaway on bass side in '62 when renamed II. Reintroduced 2017, Americana series.

1961-1962 Blond, spruce top $1,250 $1,625

1963-1967 Black fiberglass $1,400 $1,850

2017-2020 II, Americana Series $450 $575

Dual-Tone

1954-1966, 2004-2014. The Dual Tone had several body style changes, all instruments had dual pickups. '54, 11 1/4" body, No Mar Arctic White plastic body ('54-'62). '55, 12" body. '58, 13" body. '60, 13 1/2" body. '62, Res-o-glas Ermine White body, light cutaway on bass side.

1954-1961 Arctic White No-Mar $950 $1,250

1962-1964 Ermine White Res-o-glas $1,050 $1,350

El Capitan

1948-1955. Archtop, 1 single-coil pickup.

1948-1955 $500 $650

Folk Star/Vagabond

1964-1967. Molded Res-o-glas body, single-cone resonator, dot inlays, Fire Engine Red. Name changed to Vagabond in '66.

1964-1967 $750 $1,000

Jamesport

2017-present. Island Series, electric solidbody, '60s-era design, alder body, maple neck, rosewood 'board, Gold Foil pickup, antique white or jet black.

2017-2020 $375 $500

Kingston

1962-1963. Double-cut slab body, bridge pickup, glass-fiber sand finish, similar to same vintage Ozark.

1962-1963 $750 $1,000

Lexington

1967. Double-cut, wood body.

1967 $375 $475

Martinique (Val-Trol)

1962-1967. Single-cut, 13 1/2" wide, 2 standard and 1 bridge pickups, block markers, Val-Trol script on 'guard, Bigsby, blue or Ermine White Polyester Glas. Collectors sometimes call this Val-Trol, referring to the 6 mini tone and volume controls. Not to be confused with Silverwood model which also has 6 mini-knobs.

1962-1967 $1,700 $2,250

N800 Thinline Electric

1967-1968. Thin body, symmetrical double-cut, 2 pickups, copy model, similar to National N800 series models.

1967-1968 $475 $625

Ozark

1952-1954, 1958-1967, 2004-2013. Non-cut, 1 pickup, dot inlay, white pearloid body, name reintroduced in '58 as a continuation of model Sixty with single-cut, Dobro tailpiece.

1952-1954 White pearloid $825 $1,000

1958-1961 Red $825 $1,000

1962-1967 Jet Black or Fire Bronze $825 $1,000

Ranchero

1948-1960. Full body electric archtop, neck pickup, dot markers, bound body, sunburst.

1948-1960 $575 $750

Rhythm Master (Val-Trol)

1959. Val-Trol 'guard.

1959 $1,450 $1,875

S710 Flat-Top

1967-1968. Jumbo-style 15.5" flat-top, block markers, asymmetrical headstock, natural.

1967-1968 $290 $375

Sahara/Sahara 70

1960-1967. 13 1/2" body-style similar to Dual-Tone, single pickup, 2 knobs, Sand-Buff or Wedgewood Blue, Sahara until '63, Sahara 70 after.

1960-1967 $850 $1,125

Silverwood

1960-1962, 2019-present. Single-cut, 13 1/2" wide, 2 standard and 1 bridge pickups, block markers, natural blond, Val-Trol script on 'guard, renamed Martinique in '62. Collectors sometimes call this Val-Trol, referring to the guitar's 6 mini tone and volume controls. The Martinique also has the Val-Trol system but the knobs are not in a straight line like on the Silverwood. Reintroduced 2019, mahogany or ash body, maple neck, 2 Gold Foil pickups, Daphne Blue, Ash Natural, British Racing Green and Transparent Red.

Model Year	Features	Exc. Cond. Low	High
1960-1962		$1,600	$2,075
2019-2020		$700	$925

Sixty

1955-1958. Single-cut, single pickup, white No-Mar, becomes Ozark in '58.

Model Year	Features	Low	High
1955-1958		$600	$775

Special 12

1958-1960. Single-cut, replaces Supro Sixty, neck pickup 'guard mounted.

Model Year	Features	Low	High
1958-1960		$600	$775

Stratford

1968. ES-335-style double-cut, 3 pickups, 3 switches, 6 knobs, vibrato.

Model Year	Features	Low	High
1968		$525	$675

Strum 'N' Drum Solidbody

1970s. Student-level import, 1 pickup, large Supro logo on headstock.

Model Year	Features	Low	High
1970s	Higher-end	$350	$450
1970s	Lower-end	$275	$350

Super

1958-1964. 12" wide single-cut body style like mid-'50s models, single bridge pickup, short-scale, ivory.

Model Year	Features	Low	High
1958-1964		$475	$575

Super Seven

1965-1967. Offset double-cut solidbody, short scale, middle pickup, Calypso Blue.

Model Year	Features	Low	High
1965-1967		$475	$575

Suprosonic 30

1963-1967. Introduced as Suprosonic, renamed Suprosonic 30 in '64, double-cut, single neck pickup, vibrato tailpiece, more of a student model, Holly Red.

Model Year	Features	Low	High
1963-1967		$475	$625

Tremo-Lectric

1965. Fiberglas hollowbody, 2 pickups, unique built-in electric tremolo (not mechanical), Wedgewood Blue finish, multiple controls associated with electric tremolo.

Model Year	Features	Low	High
1965		$1,125	$1,500

Tri Tone

Reintroduced 2019-present. Single-cut mahogany body, maple neck, 3 pickups, black.

Model Year	Features	Low	High
2019-2020		$675	$875

Westbury

Reintroduced 2017-present. Island Series, alder body, maple neck, 2 Gold Foil pickups, black, white, turquoise, or tobacco burst.

Model Year	Features	Low	High
2017-2020		$375	$500

Westwood 1580A

1955-1958. Single-cut archtop solidbody, 1 pickup.

Model Year	Features	Low	High
1955-1958		$775	$1,000

White Holiday/Holiday

1963-1967, 2018-present. Introduced as Holiday, renamed White Holiday in '64, fiberglas double-cut, vibrato tailpiece, single bridge pickup, Dawn White. Reintroduced 2018, Americana Series, mahogany body and neck, 2 pickups,

Model Year	Features	Low	High
1963-1967		$900	$1,175
2018-2020		$450	$575

Suzuki Takeharu

See listing for Takeharu.

SX

See listing for Essex.

Szlag

2000-present. Luthier John J. Slog builds his professional and premium grade, custom carved, guitars and basses in Bethlehem, Pennsylvania.

T.D. Hibbs

Production/custom, professional grade, steel string and classical guitars built in Cambridge, Ontario by luthier Trevor Hibbs.

T.H. Davis

1976-2008. Professional and premium grade, custom, steel string and classical guitars built by luthier Ted Davis in Loudon, Tennessee. He also built mandolins. Davis died in '08.

T.J. Thompson

Luthier T.J. Thompson began in the 1980's building presentation grade, custom, steel string guitars in West Concord, Massachusetts.

Tacoma

1995-2009. Intermediate, and professional grade, production, acoustic guitars produced in Tacoma, Washington and New Hartford, Connecticut. They also built acoustic basses and mandolins. In October, '04, Fender acquired Tacoma and in '09 ceased production.

BM-6C Thunderhawk Baritone

2004-2009. Single-cut acoustic baritone.

Model Year	Features	Low	High
2004-2009		$875	$1,125

C-1C/C-1CE Chief

1997-2009. Cutaway flat-top with upper bass bout soundhole, solid cedar top, mahogany back and sides, rosewood 'board. Sides laminated until 2000, solid after, CE is acoustic/electric.

Model Year	Features	Low	High
1997-2009		$375	$485
1997-2009	Fishman electronics	$400	$525

DM Series

1997-2006. Dreadnought, solid spruce top, mahogany back and sides, satin finish, natural, C suffix indicates cutaway.

Model Year	Features	Low	High
1997-2006	Various models	$275	$850

DR Series

1997-2006. Dreadnought, solid sitka spruce top, rosewood back and sides, natural. Models include DR-20 (non-cut, herringbone trim, abalone rosette), DR-20E (with on-board electronics), DR-8C (cutaway), and DR-38.

Model Year	Features	Low	High
1997-2006	Various models	$275	$850

1959 Supro Super 1507
Michael L. Waters

Tacoma DM-10
Imaged by Heritage Auctions, HA.com

1994 Takamine PSF-94

Tanglewood TSR-2

MODEL YEAR	FEATURES	EXC. COND. LOW	HIGH

EM Series

1999-2008. Little Jumbo series, spruce top, mahogany back and sides, C suffix indicates cutaway.

1999-2008	Various models	$450	$600

JM Series

1990s-2006. Jumbo series, spruce top, mahogany back and sides.

1997-2006		$500	$900

JR-14C Jumbo Rosewood

Late-1990s. Jumbo cutaway, 16 5/8" lower bout, gloss spruce top, satin rosewood body.

1990s		$800	$1,050

JR-50CE4 Jumbo Koa

1997-2003. Jumbo cutaway, 17" lower bout, sitka spruce top, figured koa back and sides.

1997-2003		$800	$1,050

P-1/P-2 Papoose

1995-2009. Travel-size mini-flat-top, all solid wood, mahogany back and sides (P-1), with on-board electronics (P-1E) or solid rosewood (P-2), cedar top, natural satin finish.

1995-2000	P-2	$300	$400
1995-2009	P-1	$300	$400
1995-2009	P-1E	$300	$400

Parlor Series

1997-2003. Smaller 14 3/4" body, solid spruce top, various woods for back and sides.

1997-2003	PK-30 Koa	$600	$775
1997-2003	PK-40 Rosewood	$600	$775

PM Series

1997-2003. Full-size, standard soundhole.

1997-2003		$300	$800

Takamine

1962-present. Intermediate and professional grade, production, steel- and nylon-string, acoustic and acoustic/electric guitars and basses. Takamine is named after a mountain near its factory in Sakashita, Japan. Mass Hirade joined Takamine in '68 and revamped the brand's designs and improved quality. In '75, Takamine began exporting to other countries, including U.S. distribution by Kaman Music (Ovation). In '78, Takamine introduced acoustic/electric guitars. They offered solidbody electrics and some archtops for '83-'84.

Takeharu (by Suzuki)

Mid-1970s. Classical guitars offered by Suzuki as part of their internationally known teaching method (e.g. Violin Suzuki method), various sized instruments designed to eliminate the confusion of size that has been a problem for classroom guitar programs.

Taku Sakashta Guitars

1994-2010. Premium and presentation grade, production/custom, archtop, flat-top, 12-sting, and nylon-string guitars, built by luthier Taku Sakashta in Sebastopol, California. He died in February, 2010.

MODEL YEAR	FEATURES	EXC. COND. LOW	HIGH

Tama

Ca. 1959-1967, 1974-1979. Hoshino's (Ibanez) brand of higher-end acoutic flat-tops made in Japan. Many of the brand's features would be transferred to Ibanez's Artwood acoustics.

Tamura

1970s. Made in Japan by Mitsura Tamura, the line includes intermediate grade solid wood classical guitars.

Tanglewood Guitar Company UK

1991-present. Owners Dirk Kommer and Tony Flatt in Biggin Hill, U.K. import intermediate and professional grade, production, acoustic, classical, resonator and electric guitars and basses from China. They also offer mandolins, banjos, ukuleles and amps.

Taylor

1974-present. Intermediate, professional, premium, and presentation grade, production/custom, steel- and nylon-string, acoustic, acoustic/electric, semi-hollow, and solidbody guitars built in El Cajon, California and Tecate, Mexico. They have also built basses. Founded by Bob Taylor, Steve Schemmer and Kurt Listug in Lemon Grove, California, the company was originally named the Westland Music Company, but was soon changed to Taylor (Bob designed the guitars and it fit on the logo). Taylor and Listug bought out Schemmer in '83. Bob Taylor was the first commercially successful guitar maker to harness CAD/CAM CNC technology for acoustic guitars and in '91 introduced the 410 Model, the first all-solid wood American-made guitar with a list price under $1,000. The plain-appointment model using CNC technology was a major innovation combining quality and price. They added semi-hollowbodies in '05 and solidbodies in '07. In '08, they added the Build To Order custom shop. In '18, they added their new V-Class bracing to most every steel-string model in the 300 Series and above. V-Class braced Taylors have a black graphite nut vs the white one on standard braced models.

Understanding Taylor's Model Numbering System:

The first digit or letter identifies the series (100 Series to 900 Series, PS-Presentation and K-Koa Series) and most models within each series share the same back and side woods and appointment package.

The second digit: 1=6-string with softwood (spruce) top; 2=6-string with hardwood top; 5=12-string with softwood top; 2=12-string with hardwood top.

The third digit is body shape: 0=Dreadnought; 2=Grand Concert; 4=Grand Auditorium; 6=Grand Symphony; 7=Grand Pacific; 8=Grand Orchestra.

A "c" at the end of the number indicates

MODEL YEAR	FEATURES	EXC. COND. LOW	HIGH

cutaway, an "e" onboard electronics, and a "N"nylon-string.

110 Series

2003-present. Dreadnought, sapele back and sides, sitka spruce top, e and ce begin '08.

2003-2016	110	$400	$525
2008-2019	110ce	$475	$625
2008-2020	110e	$435	$575

114 Series

2007-present. Grand Auditorium, sapele back and sides, sitka spruce top.

2007-2016	114	$400	$525
2008-2020	114ce	$475	$625
2008-2020	114e	$435	$575

150 Series

2016-present. Dreadnought 12-string, sitka spruce top, walnut back and sides.

2016-2020	150e	$475	$625

210 Series

2005-present. Dreadnought, sapele or Indian rosewood back and sides, sitka spruce top.

2005-2016	210	$475	$625
2005-2016	210e	$500	$675
2008-2020	210ce	$550	$725

214 Series

2004-present. Grand Auditorium, sapele or Indian rosewood back and sides, sitka spruce top.

2004-2016	214	$425	$575
2004-2016	214c	$450	$600
2005-2016	214e	$450	$600
2008-2020	214ce	$500	$650
2012-2016	214ce-N	$600	$775
2012-2017	214ce-N Classic	$550	$725
2014-2020	214ce-K DLX (Koa)	$600	$800
2020	214ce DLX	$750	$1,000
2020	214ce-SB DLX	$800	$1,075

224ce-K DLX

2016-present. Grand Auditorium, solid koa top, laminated koa back and sides.

2016-2020		$900	$1,150

254ce

2018-present. Venetian cutaway, sitka spruce top, rosewood back and sides.

2018-2020		$525	$700

310 Series

1998-2018. Dreadnought, mahogany or sapele back and sides, sitka spruce top. The non-cut 310 discontinued '07-'12, then reappeared in '13 along with 310e version.

1998-2006	310	$625	$825
1998-2018	310ce	$675	$875

310ce-L30

2004. Limited Edition 30th Anniversary, myrtlewood leaf inlays, koa rosette, 30th Anniversary headstock logo.

2004		$825	$1,075

312 Series

1998-present. Grand Concert, Venetian cutaway, mahogany or sapele back and sides, sitka spruce top. Non-cut 312 and 312e versions were offered in 2013. V-Class introduced '20.

1998-2019	312ce	$1,025	$1,325
2019-2020	312ce V-Class	$1,100	$1,425

MODEL YEAR	FEATURES	EXC. COND. LOW	HIGH

314 Series

1998-2006, 2013-present. Mid-size Grand Auditorium, mahogany or sapele back and sides, sitka spruce top. Non-cut offered again in '13 along with 314e version. V-Class introduced '20.

1998-2006	314	$925	$1,225
1998-2019	314ce	$1,025	$1,325
2000	314ce-K (Koa)	$1,075	$1,400
2019-2020	314ce V-Class	$1,100	$1,425

314ce-LTD

2012-2018. Hawaiian Koa back and sides, Indian rosewood headstock. Also offered with nylon strings (N).

2012-2018		$1,075	$1,400

315 Series

1998-2011. Jumbo, mahogany or sapele back and sides, sitka spruce top.

1998-2011	315ce	$750	$1,000

316 Series

2012-2019. Grand Symphony, sitka spruce top, sapele back and sides.

2012-2019	316ce	$850	$1,125
2013-2016	316	$750	$1,025
2013-2016	316e	$800	$1,075
2018	316e Baritone-8 LTD	$1,350	$1,750

320e Baritone SLTD

2014. Limited Edition Dreadnought, mahogany top and body, Expression electronics.

2014		$1,075	$1,400

322 Series

2019-present. Grand Concert, non-cut, blackwood/mahogany top.

2019-2020	322ce V-Class	$1,200	$1,600
2020	322e	$1,175	$1,575

324 Series

2015-present. Grand Auditorium, mahogany top, African sapele back and sides.

2015-2020	324e	$1,125	$1,500
2019-2020	324ce V-Class	$1,200	$1,575
2020	324	$900	$1,200

326e Baritone

2015-present. Grand Symphony, special edition, 6- or 8-string, mahogany top.

2015-2020		$1,075	$1,400

352 Series

2019-present. Grand Concert 12-string, sitka spruce top, sapele back and sides, natural.

2019-2020	352ce V-Class	$1,125	$1,475

354 ce

2004-2011. Grand Auditorium 12-string, cutaway, mahogany back and sides, Expression system.

2004-2011		$1,125	$1,475

355 Series

1998-2011. Jumbo 12-string, mahogany or sapele back and sides, sitka spruce top.

1998-2006	355	$825	$1,100
1998-2011	355ce	$1,000	$1,300

356 Series

2014-2019. Grand Symphony 12-string, sitka spruce top, sapele back and sides , non-cut, cutaway, or ce cutaway electric.

2014-2019	356ce	$1,000	$1,300

Taylor 214ce-SB DLX

Taylor 352ce

GUITARS

Taylor 414ce

Taylor 514ce

MODEL YEAR	FEATURES	EXC. COND. LOW	HIGH

362 Series

2019-present. Grand Concert 12-string, mahogany top, blackwood back and sides.

2019-2020	362ce V-Class	$1,200	$1,600

363 Series

2020	363ce V-Class	$1,200	$1,600

410 Series

1991-2018. Dreadnought, mahogany back and sides until '98, ovangkol after '98, sitka spruce top. Non-cut offered again in '13 along with 410e version.

1991-2006	410	$825	$1,100
1991-2018	410ce	$925	$1,200
2000	410-MA, maple	$1,050	$1,350

412 Series

1991-present. Grand Concert, mahogany back and sides until '98, ovangkol after, sitka spruce top. Cutaway electric version replaced the 412 in '98. Non-cut offered again in '13 along with 412e version.

1991-1998	412	$1,100	$1,450
1996	412-K (Koa)	$1,200	$1,600
1998-2018	412ce-R	$1,300	$1,700
1998-2020	412ce	$1,200	$1,600

414 Series

1998-present. Grand Auditorium, ovangkol back and sides, sitka spruce top. Non-cut offered again in '13 along with 414e version.

1998	414-K (Koa)	$1,200	$1,600
1998-2006	414	$1,100	$1,450
1998-2020	414ce	$1,200	$1,600
2019-2020	414ce-R V-Class	$1,300	$1,700

414ce-LTD

2013. Limited Edition, sitka spruce top, tropical mahogany neck.

2013		$925	$1,200

414-L10

2005. Limited Edition, rosewood sides and back, gloss spruce top, satin finish.

2005		$925	$1,200

414-L30

2004. Limited Edition 30th Anniversary, Hawaiian koa back and sides, Engelmann spruce top, pearl and gold 30th Anniversary inlay.

2004		$1,025	$1,350

415 Series

1998-2006. Jumbo, ovangkol back and sides, sitka spruce top.

1998-2006	415ce	$925	$1,200

416 Series

2011-2019. Grand Symphony, ovangkol back and sides, sitka spruce top.

2011-2019	416ce	$1,000	$1,300

418 Series

2015-2019. Grand Orchestra, ovangkol back and sides, sitka spruce top.

2015-2019	418e	$1,000	$1,300

420

1990-1997. Dreadnought, Indian rosewood back and sides, sitka spruce top.

1990-1997		$850	$1,125

422 Series

1991-1998. Grand Concert, solid maple construction.

1991-1998	422-K (Koa)	$1,150	$1,450
1997	422-R (Rosewood)	$1,050	$1,350

426ce-LTD

2008. Limited Edition, Tasmanian blackwood top, back and sides.

2008		$1,250	$1,650

450

1996-1997. Dreadnought 12-string, mahogany back and sides, spruce top.

1996-1997		$875	$1,150

454ce

2004-2011. Grand Auditorium 12-string, Ovangkol back and sides, sitka spruce top.

2004-2011		$975	$1,250

455 Series

2001-2011. Jumbo 12-string, Ovangkol back and sides, sitka spruce top.

2001-2006	455	$925	$1,225
2001-2011	455ce	$1,025	$1,325

455ce-LTD

2001-2003. Limited Edition, imbuia back and sides.

2001-2003		$1,125	$1,450

456ce/e

2012-2016. Grand Symphony 12-string.

2012-2016		$1,400	$1,800

458e

2016-2019. Grand Orchestra 12-string.

2016-2019		$1,400	$1,800

510 Series

1978-2017. Dreadnought, mahogany back and sides, spruce top. Non-cut offered again in '13 along with 510e version.

1978-2006	510	$975	$1,275
1978-2017	510ce	$1,075	$1,400

510ce-AB 25th Anniversary

1999. Limited Edition, 25th Anniversary on headstock, spruce top, mahogany back, sides and neck.

1999		$1,600	$2,100

510-LTD

2002. Limited Edition, mahogany back and sides, sitka spruce top.

2002		$1,075	$1,400

512 Series

1978-present. Grand Concert, mahogany back and sides, red cedar top. Non-cut offered again in '13-'16 along with 512e version.

1978-2000	512	$1,025	$1,325
1978-2000	512c	$1,050	$1,375
1978-2020	512ce	$1,075	$1,425
2012-2016	512ce-N	$1,075	$1,425

512ce-L10

2005. Limited Edition, American mahogany body and neck, abalone soundhole rosette, pearl diamond inlays, gold tuners.

2005		$1,075	$1,425

512-NG Nanci Griffith

1996-1997. 512ce with sunburst finish.

1996-1997		$1,450	$1,875

MODEL YEAR	FEATURES	EXC. COND. LOW	HIGH

514 Series

1990-present. Grand Auditorium, mahogany back and sides, Engelmann or sitka spruce top. Western red cedar top on 514c and ce. Non-cut offered again in '13-'16 along with 514e version. V-Class introduced '20.

1990-1998	514	$1,300	$1,700
1996-1998	514c	$1,350	$1,750
1998-2020	514ce	$1,400	$1,800

515-LTD

1981. Limited Edition, mahogany back and sides, black binding, tortoise 'guard.

1981		$1,350	$1,750

516 Series

2008-2019. Grand Symphony, mahogany back and sides, Engelmann spruce top. Non-cut 516 offered in '13 along with 516e version.

2008-2019	516ce	$1,350	$1,750

516ce-LTD

2010. Spring Limited Editions, Tasmanian blackwood back and sides, sitka spruce top.

2010		$1,850	$2,400

517 Series

2019-present. Builders Edition, Grand Pacific dreadnought, mahogany/torrified spruce top.

2019-2020	517ce	$1,550	$2,025

518 Series

2012-2014. Grand Orchestra, tropical mahogany back and sides, sitka spruce top, tortoise 'guard.

2012-2014	518/518e	$1,350	$1,750

522 Series

2013-present. Grand Concert, all tropical mahogany. V-Class introduced '20.

2013-2018	522	$1,250	$1,650
2013-2019	522e	$1,300	$1,700
2013-2020	522ce	$1,400	$1,800

524ce-LTD

2018. Grand Auditorium, all walnut.

2018		$1,800	$2,400

555 Series

1978-2006. Jumbo 12-string, mahogany back and sides, sitka spruce top, higher-end appointments.

1994-2006	555	$1,300	$1,700
1994-2006	555ce	$1,400	$1,800

562 Series

2019-present. Grand Concert 12-strings, V-Class bracing, mahogany top.

2019-2020	562ce	$1,400	$1,800

610 Series

1978-2017. Dreadnought, big leaf maple back and sides, sitka spruce top. Non-cut offered again in '13 along with 610e version.

1978-1998	610	$1,500	$1,950
1998-2017	610ce	$1,575	$2,050
2013-2017	610e	$1,525	$2,000

612 Series

1984-present. Grand Concert, big leaf maple back and sides, sitka spruce top. Non-cut offered again in '13 along with 612e version. V-Class introduced '20.

1984-1998	612	$1,500	$1,950
1998-2020	612ce	$1,575	$2,050
2013-2016	612e	$1,525	$2,000

MODEL YEAR	FEATURES	EXC. COND. LOW	HIGH

614 Series

1978-present. Grand Auditorium, big leaf maple back and sides, sitka spruce top. Non-cut offered again in '13 along with 614e version. V-Class introduced '20.

1978-1998	614	$1,500	$1,950
1998-2020	614ce	$1,575	$2,050
2013-2016	614e	$1,525	$2,000

615 Series

1981-2011. Jumbo, big leaf maple back and sides, sitka spruce top.

1981-1998	615	$1,500	$1,950
1981-1998	615e	$1,525	$2,000
1998-2011	615ce	$1,575	$2,050

616 Series

2008-2019. Grand Symphony, big leaf maple back and sides, sitka spruce top. Non-cut 616 offered in '13-'16 along with 616e version.

2008-2019	616ce	$1,950	$2,500
2013-2016	616e	$1,525	$2,000

618 Series

2013-present. Grand Orchestra, sitka spruce top, big leaf maple back and sides.

2013-2020	618e	$1,525	$2,000

654 Series

2004-2011. Grand Auditorium 12-string, big leaf maple back and sides, sitka spruce top.

2004-2011	654ce	$1,500	$1,900

655 Series

1978-1991, 1996-2011. Jumbo 12-string, big leaf maple back and sides, sitka spruce top.

1978-2006	655	$1,400	$1,800
1998-2011	655ce	$1,500	$1,900

656 Series

2008-2019. Grand Symphony 12-string, big leaf maple back and sides.

2018-2019	656ce	$1,500	$1,900

710 Series

1977-2017. Dreadnought, Indian rosewood back and sides, Englemann or sitka spruce top. Non-cut offered again in '13 along with 710e version.

1977-2006	710 (Spruce)	$1,275	$1,700
1990s	710-BR (Brazilian)	$2,100	$2,800
1998-2006	710 (Cedar)	$1,275	$1,700
1998-2017	710ce (Cedar)	$1,500	$2,000

710-B 25th Anniversary

1999. Limited Edition, 25th Anniversary on headstock, spruce top, abalone rosette, Brazilian rosewood sides and back, mahogany neck.

1999		$2,100	$2,800

710ce-L30

2004. Limited Edition 30th Anniversary, Englemann top, Indian rosewood body, 30th Anniversary inlay.

2004		$1,200	$1,600

712 Series

1984-present. Grand Concert, Indian rosewood back and sides, Englemann or sitka spruce top. Non-cut offered again in '13 along with 712e version. V-Class introduced '20.

1984-2006	712	$1,425	$1,900
2000-2020	712ce	$1,600	$2,100
2013-2019	712e	$1,500	$2,000

Taylor 612ce

2001 Taylor 710ce

Jeff Mangan

Taylor 814ce

Taylor 914ce

MODEL YEAR	FEATURES	EXC. COND. LOW	HIGH

714 Series
1996-present. Grand Auditorium, Indian rosewood back and sides, red cedar top. Non-cut offered again in '13-'16 along with 714e version. V-Class introduced '20.

1996-2006	714	$1,425	$1,900
1998-2020	714ce	$1,600	$2,100

714-BRZ
1997. Brazilian rosewood, cedar, fancy.

1997		$3,200	$4,200

714ce-L1
2003-2004. Limited Edition, Western red cedar top, grafted walnut sides and back, pearl inlay, Hawaiian koa rosette.

2003-2004		$1,700	$2,200

714ce-S-LTD
2015. Limited Edition Grand Auditorium, sitka spruce top, blackheart sassafras back and sides.

2015		$1,700	$2,200

716ce
2007-2019. Grand Symphony, lutz spruce, Indian rosewood.

2007-2019		$1,700	$2,200

716ce-LTD
2009. Limited Edition, sitka spruce top, Madagascar rosewood back and sides.

2009		$1,700	$2,200

717 (Builders Edition)
2019-present. Grand Pacific, Indian rosewood back and sides.

2019-2020		$1,400	$1,800

750
1990-2000s. Dreadnought 12-string, spruce top.

1990-2000s		$1,500	$1,975

755
1990-1998. Jumbo 12-string, rosewood back and sides.

1990-1998		$1,500	$1,975

810 Series
1975-2017. Classic Dreadnought, Indian rosewood back and sides, sitka spruce top. Non-cut offered again in '13 along with 810e version.

1975-2006	810	$1,500	$2,000
1975-2006	810e	$1,600	$2,150
1993-1998	810c	$1,550	$2,050
1996-2016	810ce-BR (Brazilian)	$2,500	$3,200
1996-2017	810ce	$1,650	$2,200

810-L30
2004. Limited Edition 30th Anniversary, maple leaf inlays, soundhole rosette, 30th Anniversary logo.

2004		$1,800	$2,375

810ce-LTD
2010. Limited Edition, Venetian cutaway, Madagascar rosewood back and sides, solid sitka spruce top.

2010		$1,925	$2,500

812 Series
1985, 1993-present. Grand Concert, Indian rosewood back and sides, sitka spruce top. Non-cut offered again in '13-'16 along with 812e version. V-Class introduced '20.

1985	812	$1,500	$2,000
1993-1998	812c	$1,550	$2,050
1998-2019	812ce	$1,650	$2,200
2013-2016	812e	$1,600	$2,150
2019-2020	812ce V-Class	$2,100	$2,700

814 Series
1993-present. Grand Auditorium, Indian rosewood back and sides, sitka spruce top. Non-cut offered again in '13 along with 814e version. V-Class introduced '20.

1993-1998	814	$1,900	$2,550
1996-1998	814c	$1,950	$2,600
1998-2019	814ce	$2,000	$2,650
2000	814-BE (Brazilian/ Englemann)	$2,500	$3,200
2020	814ce V-Class	$2,000	$2,650

814ce-LTD
2012. Spring Limited Edition, cocobolo back and sides, sitka spruce top.

2012		$1,900	$2,500

815 Series
1970s-2011. Jumbo, Indian rosewood back and sides, sitka spruce top.

1970s-2006	815	$1,775	$2,350
1993-1998	815c	$1,825	$2,400
1997	815c-BR (Brazilian)	$2,500	$3,200
1998-2011	815ce	$1,875	$2,450

816 Series
2008-2019. Grand Symphony, sitka spruce top, Indian rosewood back and sides.

2008-2014	816e	$1,825	$2,400
2008-2019	816ce	$1,875	$2,450
2013-2016	816	$1,775	$2,350

818 Series
2014-present. Grand Orchestra, sitka spruce, Indian rosewood. V-Class introduced '20.

2014-2019	818e	$1,850	$2,425

854ce-LTD
2002. Grand Auditorium 12-string, Indian rosewood back and sides, sitka spruce top.

2002		$1,900	$2,500

855 Series
1981-2011. Jumbo 12-string, Indian rosewood back and sides, sitka spruce top.

1981-2011		$1,600	$2,100

856 Series
2012-2019. Grand Symphony 12-string, sitka spruce, Indian rosewood.

2012-2018	856e	$1,725	$2,225
2013-2019	856ce	$1,775	$2,300

910 Series
1977-2017. Dreadnought, maple back and sides, changed to Brazilian rosewood in '86, wide abalone-style rosette. Non-cut offered again in '13 along with 910e version, Indian rosewood back and sides, sitka spruce top.

1977-1985	910 Maple	$2,300	$3,100
1986-2006	910 Brazilian	$3,900	$5,200
1998-2016	910ce	$2,400	$3,200

912 Series
1993-present. Grand Concert, Indian rosewood back and sides, Engelmann spruce top, abalone. Non-cut offered in '13 along with 912e version. V-Class introduced '20.

1993-2002	912c	$2,350	$3,150

MODEL YEAR	FEATURES	EXC. COND. LOW	HIGH
1993-2019	912ce	$2,400	$3,200
2020	912ce V-Class	$2,400	$3,200

914 Series

1990s-present. Grand Concert, Indian rosewood back and sides, Engelmann spruce top. Non-cut offered in '13 along with 914e version. V-Class introduced '20.

2002-2019	914ce	$2,400	$3,200
2020	914ce V-Class	$2,400	$3,200

914ce-L1

2003. Fall Limited Edition, Indian rosewood back and sides, Engelmann spruce top, abalone leaf and vine inlays.

2003		$2,400	$3,200

914ce-L7

2004. Sitka spruce top, Brazilian rosewood back and sides, abalone rosette.

2004		$3,750	$5,000

916 Series

2010-2019. Grand Symphony, Florentine cutaway, Indian rosewood back and sides.

2010-2019	916ce	$2,400	$3,200

918 Series

2013-2014. Grand Orchestra, sitka spruce top, Indian rosewood back and sides.

2013-2014	918e	$2,400	$3,200

955

1996-2000. Jumbo 12 string, rosewood back and sides, spruce top.

1996-2000		$2,400	$3,200

Academy Series

2017-present. Designed for beginner guitar players, 10 is D-size and 12 is 000-size, e indicates on-board electronics.

2017-2020	10	$310	$400
2017-2020	10e	$375	$475
2017-2020	12e	$375	$475
2017-2020	12e-N	$375	$475

American Dream Series (AD)

2020-present. Grand Pacific body style, wood pairings include sapele/mahogany and ovangkol/spruce, V-Class bracing, e indicates on-board electronics.

2020	AD17	$775	$1,025
2020	AD17e	$875	$1,150
2020	AD27e	$875	$1,150
2020	AD28e	$875	$1,150

Baby Taylor

1996-present. 3/4-size Dreadnought, mahogany laminated back and sides until '99, sapele laminate after, various tops.

1996-2020	BT1, sitka spruce	$185	$240
1998-2020	BT2, mahogany	$185	$240
2000-2003	BT3, maple	$185	$240
2010-2020	TSBT Taylor Swift	$185	$240
2016-2020	BTe-Koa	$250	$325

Baby Rosewood

2000-2003. Laminated Indian rosewood back and sides Baby.

2000-2003		$185	$240

Baritone 6/e/ce

2010-2013. 6-string baritone, Grand Symphony, Indian rosewood or mahogany back and sides.

2010-2013		$1,750	$2,300

MODEL YEAR	FEATURES	EXC. COND. LOW	HIGH

Baritone 8/e/ce

2010-2013. 8-string baritone, Grand Symphony, Indian rosewood or mahogany back and sides.

2010-2013		$2,100	$2,800

Big Baby BBT

2000-present. 15/16-size Dreadnought, sapele laminate back and sides, sitka spruce top.

2000-2020		$225	$300

Builder's Edition

2018-present. New designs from master builders, premium features.

2019-2020	517	$1,800	$2,300
2019-2020	717	$1,800	$2,300
2020	324ce	$1,650	$2,150
2020	614ce	$2,200	$2,900
2020	652ce, various specs	$1,900	$3,000
2020	816ce	$2,200	$2,875
2020	K-24ce Koa	$2,900	$3,800

Builder's Reserve (BR)

A series of special limited guitars built using Taylor's private wood reserves accumulated 30-plus years.

2008	BR VII	$1,750	$2,300

CPSM Chris Proctor Signature

2001. Limited edition, 100 made, Indian rosewood body, Engelmann spruce top.

2001		$1,650	$2,125

CUJO Model

1997. Dreadnought (CUJO-10) or Grand Auditorium (CUJO-14), made from 100+ year old black walnut tree appearing in famous Stephen King movie "Cujo" (1983). Robert Taylor purchased the tree when it was dying of old age. The DN has spruce top, GA has cedar, both have elaborate appointments and are signed by Taylor and King. Only 125 made of each.

1997	CUJO-10, CUJO-14	$1,425	$1,850

Custom Shop

2008-present. Custom shop models - some are one-offs, others are series ordered by specific dealers. Previously called Taylor's Build To Order program.

Custom Dreadnought/Custom DN

2008-2017	AA+ Indian/ Adirondack	$2,000	$2,600

Custom Grand Auditorium

2008-2017	Adirondack/ mahogany	$2,000	$3,200
2008-2020	Figured koa	$3,500	$4,500
2008-2020	Spruce/maple	$2,000	$3,200

Custom Grand Concert

2008-2017	Various woods	$2,025	$3,225

Custom TF

2011. Acoustic-electric, slotted headstock, rosewood, Taylor Build To Order program.

2011		$1,750	$2,300

DCSM Dan Crary Signature

1986-2000. Dreadnought, Venetian cutaway, thin spruce top, Indian rosewood back and sides, Crary signature on headstock.

1986-2000		$1,475	$1,900

Taylor American Dream AD27e

Baby Taylor

2014 Taylor K-22ce

Craig Brody

Taylor PS14ce

DDAD Doyle Dykes Signature Anniversary

2005. Indian rosewood back and sides, soft cutaway, on-board transducer.

MODEL YEAR	FEATURES	EXC. COND. LOW	HIGH
2005		$2,400	$3,100

DDSM Doyle Dykes Signature

2000-2012. Grand auditorium cutaway acoustic/electric, figured maple body.

MODEL YEAR	FEATURES	EXC. COND. LOW	HIGH
2000-2012		$2,400	$3,100

DDSM-LTD Doyle Dykes Desert Rose Edition

2000-2003. Grand Auditorium, Limited Edition, 72 offered, sitka spruce, flamed maple, on-board electronics.

MODEL YEAR	FEATURES	EXC. COND. LOW	HIGH
2000-2003		$2,550	$3,300

DMSM Dave Matthews Signature

2010-2012. Limited Edition based on 914ce, Taylor Expression pickup system.

MODEL YEAR	FEATURES	EXC. COND. LOW	HIGH
2010-2012		$3,600	$4,600

DN Series

2007-2012. Dreadnought Series, various woods.

MODEL YEAR	FEATURES	EXC. COND. LOW	HIGH
2007-2011	DNK (koa)	$1,750	$2,300
2007-2012	DN3	$750	$950
2007-2012	DN5	$1,050	$1,400
2007-2012	DN8	$1,150	$1,500

E14ce Limited Edition

2018-2019. Grand Auditorium, Venetian cutaway, V-Class bracing, spruce top, African ebony back and sides, natural finish.

MODEL YEAR	FEATURES	EXC. COND. LOW	HIGH
2018-2019		$1,800	$2,350

GA Limited Editions

1995. Grand Auditorium Limited Editions. GA-BE has Brazilian rosewood back and sides with Engelmann spruce top, KC has koa/cedar, KS koa/spruce, MC mahogany/cedar, RS Indian rosewood/spruce, and WS walnut/spruce.

MODEL YEAR	FEATURES	EXC. COND. LOW	HIGH
1995	GA-BE	$3,700	$4,800
1995	GA-KC	$2,300	$3,000
1995	GA-MC	$2,000	$2,600
1995	GA-RS	$2,000	$2,600
1995	GA-WS	$2,200	$2,800

GA Series

2007-2012. Grand Auditorium Series, various woods.

MODEL YEAR	FEATURES	EXC. COND. LOW	HIGH
2007-2012	GA3, sitka/sapele	$750	$950
2007-2012	GA3-12	$750	$950
2007-2012	GA4, sitka/ ovangkol	$800	$1,050
2007-2012	GA5, cedar/ mahogany	$1,075	$1,400
2007-2012	GA6, sitka/ flamed maple	$1,225	$1,575
2007-2012	GA6-12	$1,250	$1,600
2007-2012	GA7, cedar/ rosewood	$1,225	$1,575
2007-2012	GA8, sitka/ rosewood	$1,150	$1,500
2008-2012	GA-K-12, cedar/koa	$1,800	$2,300
2012	GA-CE	$1,700	$2,200
2013	GA-MC	$1,700	$2,200

GC Series

2007-2012. Grand Concert Series, various woods.

MODEL YEAR	FEATURES	EXC. COND. LOW	HIGH
2007-2012	GC3, sitka/sapele	$750	$950
2007-2012	GC4, sitka/ ovangkol	$800	$1,400
2007-2012	GC5, cedar/ mahogany	$1,075	$1,400
2007-2012	GC6, sitka/ flamed maple	$1,225	$1,575
2007-2012	GC7, cedar/ rosewood	$1,225	$1,575
2007-2012	GC8, sitka/ rosewood	$1,150	$1,500
2011	GC-LTD, all mahogany	$1,150	$1,500

GS Series

2006-present. Grand Symphony Series, various woods.

MODEL YEAR	FEATURES	EXC. COND. LOW	HIGH
2007	GS4E-LTD	$1,075	$1,400
2007-2012	GS3, sitka/sapele	$750	$950
2007-2012	GS5, cedar/ mahogany	$1,075	$1,400
2007-2012	GS5-12	$1,175	$1,500
2007-2012	GS6, sitka/ flamed maple	$1,225	$1,575
2007-2012	GS7, cedar/rosewood	$1,225	$1,575
2007-2012	GS8, sitka/rosewood	$1,150	$1,500
2007-2012	GS8-12	$1,250	$1,600
2011-2020	GS Mini	$275	$360
2019-2020	GS Mini-e Koa	$450	$575
2019-2020	GS Mini-e Mahogany	$375	$500
2019-2020	GS Mini-e Plus	$525	$700

GT Series

2020-present. Grand Theater Series, various woods, e indicates on-board electronics.

MODEL YEAR	FEATURES	EXC. COND. LOW	HIGH
2020	GT, sitka/ash	$750	$1,000
2020	GT811e, sitka/ rosewood	$1,650	$2,150
2020	GTe, sitka/ash	$875	$1,150
2020	GTK21e, all koa	$2,600	$3,400

Hot Rod Limited Edition HR14-LTD/HR15-LTD

2003. Grand Auditorium (HR14) or Jumbo (HR15), 32 of each made, natural finish with red-stained back and sides or gloss black with transparent black.

MODEL YEAR	FEATURES	EXC. COND. LOW	HIGH
2003		$1,900	$2,500

K Series

1983-present. Koa Series, various models with Hawaiian koa. V-Class introduced '20.

MODEL YEAR	FEATURES	EXC. COND. LOW	HIGH
1983-1992	K20	$1,750	$2,250
1983-2006	K10	$1,450	$1,900
1992-2002	K20c	$1,800	$2,300
1995-1998	K65, 12-string	$2,300	$3,000
1998-2000	K22	$1,850	$2,400
1998-2002	K14c	$1,600	$2,100
1998-2012	K14ce	$1,650	$2,150
2001-2006	K55, 12-string	$2,300	$3,000
2001-2016	K20ce	$1,850	$2,375
2003-2020	K22ce	$2,300	$3,000
2007-2011	K54ce	$2,400	$3,100
2007-2012	K10ce	$1,550	$2,000
2007-2020	K24ce	$2,200	$2,900
2008-2020	K26ce	$2,200	$2,900
2020	K24ce V-Class	$2,200	$2,900

MODEL YEAR	FEATURES	EXC. COND. LOW	HIGH

LKSM-6/12 Leo Kottke Signature

1981-2012. Jumbo 17" body, 6- or 12-string, rounded cutaway, sitka spruce top, mahogany back and sides, gloss finish, Leo Kottke signature.

1981-2012	12-string	$1,850	$2,450
1981-2012	6-string	$1,850	$2,450

LTG Liberty Tree L.E.

2002. Limited Edition includes DVD and certificate which are important to instrument's value, solid wood grand concert body, high-end art and appointments. Around 400 made.

2002		$4,500	$5,900

NS Series

2002-2011. Nylon Strung series, various models and woods, models include NS24e/NS24ce (Indian rosewood/spruce), NS32ce/NS34ce (mahogany/spruce), NS42ce/NS44ce (ovangkol), NS52ce/NS54ce (mahogany), NS62ce/NS64ce (maple/Engelmann) and NS72ce/NS74ce (Indian rosewood/cedar). All models were cutaway electric (ce) by '04, until '10 when NS24e was offered.

2002-2006	NS42ce	$750	$975
2002-2006	NS44/NS44ce	$825	$1,100
2002-2006	NS52ce	$850	$1,125
2002-2006	NS54ce	$925	$1,225
2002-2011	NS32ce	$700	$925
2002-2011	NS62ce	$1,250	$1,650
2002-2011	NS64ce	$1,275	$1,675
2002-2011	NS72ce	$1,450	$1,900
2002-2011	NS74/NS74ce	$1,700	$2,200
2004-2011	NS34ce	$725	$950
2010-2011	NS24e/NS24ce	$500	$650

PS Series

1996-present. Presentation Series, various models, Hawaiian koa with Engelmann spruce used early on, followed by Brazilian rosewood, by '07 a variety of woods were offered, values vary depending on specs and appointments.

1996-2020	Various options	$3,800	$6,500

Solidbody Classic

2008-2014. Single- or double-cut, ash body, 2 humbuckers or single-coils, pearl 'guard.

2008-2014		$725	$950

Solidbody Custom

2008-2010. Single- or double-cut, koa top with Tasmanian blackwood body in '08 and mahogany after or walnut top with sapele body, 2 humbuckers, diamond inlays, ivoroid binding.

2008-2010		$1,100	$1,500

Solidbody Standard

2008-2014. Single- or double-cut, Tamo ash top ('08-'09) and maple after, sapele body (08-'10) and mahogany after, 2 exposed coil humbuckers, ivoroid binding.

2008-2014		$650	$850

T3 Series

2009-2020. Semi-hollow thinline, single-cut, figured maple. T3/B with Bigsby.

2009-2020	T3, T3/B	$1,425	$1,850

MODEL YEAR	FEATURES	EXC. COND. LOW	HIGH

T5/T5z Series

2005-2020. T5 '05-'19 and T5z introduced '20, semi-hollow thinline body, sapele back and sides, spruce, maple, or koa tops, Custom models have gold hardware and Artist inlays, Standard is chrome with micro-dots. Prices will vary depending on type of figured-wood used, figured maple and koa will be more than plain tops.

2005-2020	12-string	$1,550	$2,025
2005-2020	6-string	$1,550	$2,025

Walnut/W Series

1998-2006. Highly figured claro walnut backs and sides with spruce, cedar or walnut tops. Ivoroid, ebony, gold and abalone accents.

1998-2000	W12c	$1,625	$2,125
1998-2006	W10	$1,500	$1,950
2000-2006	W14ce	$1,675	$2,175

WHCM Windham Hill

2003. Commemorative Model, D-size, spruce top, rosewood sides and back, fancy appointments with Windham Hill logo inlay.

2003		$1,400	$1,800

XX 20th Anniversary Series

1994. Limited Edition, grand auditorium, "XX" solid 18 karat gold inlay, mother-of-pearl inlay, abalone rosette, available either mahogany back and sides with cedar top (XX-MC) or Indian rosewood with spruce (XX-RS).

1994	XX-MC	$2,000	$2,700
1994	XX-RS	$2,000	$2,700

XXV 25th Anniversary

1999-2000. Dreadnought (XXV-DR) and grand auditorium (XXV-GA) models, various woods.

1999-2000	XXV-DR, XXV-GA	$1,600	$2,050

XXX 30th Anniversary Series

2004-2005. Limited Edition, grand concert, "XXX" solid 18 karat gold inlay, fancy appointments, XXX-BE has Brazilian rosewood back and sides with Engelmann spruce top, KE has koa/Engelmann spruce, MS maple/spruce and RS Indian rosewood/spruce.

2004-2005	XXX-BE	$3,500	$4,500
2004-2005	XXX-KE	$2,100	$2,800
2004-2005	XXX-MS	$2,000	$2,700
2004-2005	XXX-RS	$2,000	$2,700

XXXV 35th Anniversary Series

2009. Limited Edition, various models and woods, "35" between the 11th and 12th frets. Models include DN (Dreadnought), GC (Grand Concert), GS (Grand Symphony), P (Parlor), TF (12-Fret), 9-string, plus more.

2009	XXXV-9, 9-string	$2,000	$2,700

Taylor/R. Taylor Guitars

2006-2011. Bob Taylor set up the R. Taylor studio with a small group of elite luthiers to handcraft a limited amount of guitars each year, using higher grade materials and offered in a few body styles - essentially custom made models. Each style has a number of options.

Style 1

2006-2009	Various options	$2,475	$3,200

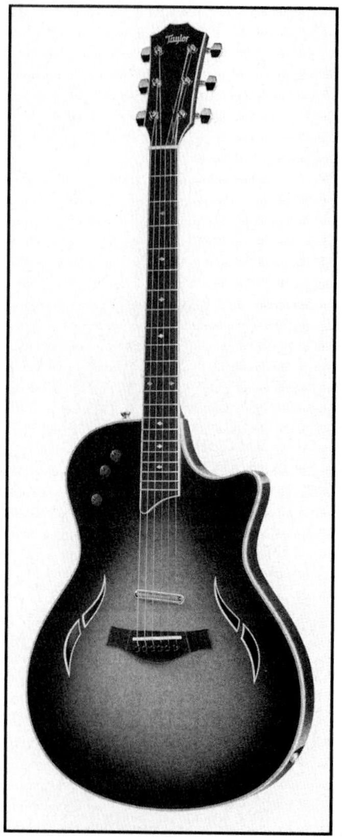

Taylor T5 Standard

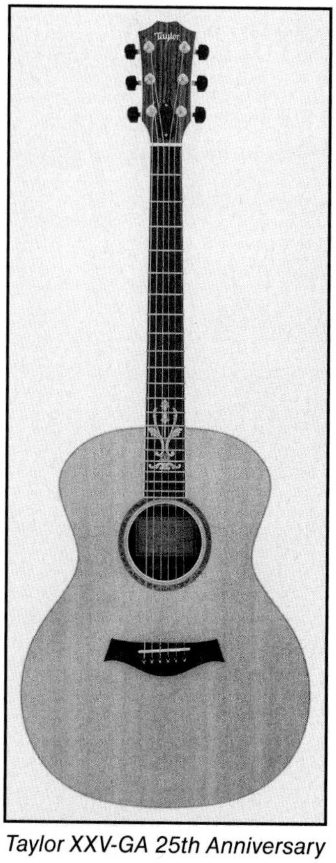

Taylor XXV-GA 25th Anniversary

1967 Teisco Del Rey ET-230
Tom Pfeifer

1969 Teisco May Queen
Rivington Guitars

Teisco

Founded in 1946 in Tokyo, Japan by Hawaiian and Spanish guitarist Atswo Kaneko and electrical engineer Doryu Matsuda, the original company name was Aoi Onpa Kenkyujo; Teisco was the instrument name. Most imported into U.S. by Jack Westheimer beginning ca. '60 and Chicago's W.M.I. Corporation beginning around '64, some early ones for New York's Bugeleisen and Jacobson. Brands made by the company include Teisco, Teisco Del Rey, Kingston, World Teisco, Silvertone, Kent, Kimberly and Heit Deluxe.

In '56, the company's name was changed to Nippon Onpa Kogyo Co., Ltd., and in '64 the name changed again to Teisco Co., Ltd. In January '67, the company was purchased by Kawai. After '73, the brand was converted to Kay in U.S.; Teisco went into hiatus in Japan until being beifly revived in the early-'90s with plexiglas reproductions of the Spectrum 5 (not available in U.S.). Some older Teisco Del Rey stock continued to be sold in U.S. through the '70s.

Electric

MODEL YEAR	FEATURES	EXC. COND. LOW	EXC. COND. HIGH
1966-1969	1 pickup	$150	$200
1966-1969	2 pickups	$270	$350
1966-1969	3 pickups	$310	$400
1966-1969	4 pus or sparkle	$525	$685
1966-1969	Spectrum V	$615	$800
1968-1969	May Queen, black	$615	$800
1968-1969	May Queen, red	$615	$800
1968-1969	Phantom	$615	$800

Tele-Star

1965-ca.1972. Imported from Japan by Tele-Star Musical Instrument Corporation of New York, New York. Primarily made by Kawai, many inspired by Burns designs, some in cool sparkle finishes. They also built basses.

Electric

MODEL YEAR	FEATURES	EXC. COND. LOW	EXC. COND. HIGH
1966-1969	1, 2, or 3 pickups	$325	$425
1966-1969	4 pus or sparkle	$375	$485
1966-1969	Amp-in-case	$290	$375
1969-1970	Double neck 6/4	$600	$775

Tempo

1950s-1970s. Solid and semi-hollow body electric and acoustic guitars, most likely imported by Merson Musical Products from Japan. They also offered basses and amps.

Terada

Japanese guitar manufacturer began producing semi-acoustic and acoustic guitars in the year 1912. They have made guitars for Ibanez, Orville by Gibson, Epiphone Japan, Gretsch, and other well-known brands. At their peak (late '70s to early '90s), they were producing around 10,000 guitars a month using 3 factories. Terada's output is presently about 1/8 of what it was at their peak.

Teuffel

1988-present. Luthier Ulrich Teuffel builds his production/custom, premium and presentation grade electric solidbody guitars in Neu-Ulm, Bavaria, Germany.

Texas

1959-ca. 1965. Line of aluminum neck electric solidbodies and basses made by France's Jacobacci company, which also built under its own brand. One, two, or three pickups.

Teye

2006-present. Luthier Teye Wijterp builds his premium and presentation grade, production/custom, solid and chambered body guitars in Austin, Texas. Some instruments are branded as Electric Gypsy guitars.

Thomas

1960s-1970s. Single, double and triple-neck electrics made by luthier Harvey Thomas in Midway, Washington. Best known for his Maltese cross shaped models, he also offered several other unique shaped designs and one-offs.

Thomas Rein

1972-present. Luthier Thomas Rein builds his premium grade, production/custom, classical guitars in St. Louis, Missouri.

Thompson Guitars

1980-present. Luthier Ted Thompson builds his professional and premium grade, production/custom, flat-top, 12-string, and nylon-string guitars in Vernon, British Columbia.

Thorell Fine Guitars

1994-present. Premium grade, custom/production, archtop, flattop and classical guitars built by luthier Ryan Thorell in Logan, Utah.

Thorn Custom Guitars

2000-present. Professional and premium grade, custom/production, solid and hollowbody electrics built by luthiers Bill Thorn and his sons Bill, Jr. and Ron in Glendale, California. They started Thorn Custom Inlay in the early '90s to do custom inlay work for other builders. In '00, they added their own line of guitars.

Thornward

Ca. 1901-ca. 1910. Line of guitars sold by the Montgomery Ward company and built by others including Lyon & Healy. The name is from a combination of last names of company founder Aaron Montgomery Ward and company manager George Thorne.

MODEL YEAR | FEATURES | EXC. COND. LOW | HIGH

Threet Guitars

1990-present. Premium grade, production/custom, flat-tops built by luthier Judy Threet in Calgary, Alberta.

Tilton

1850s-late 1800s. Built by William B. Tilton, of New York City, New York. He was quite an innovator and held several guitar-related patents. He also built banjos.

Parlor

1850s-1890s. Parlor guitar with various woods.

1850s-80s	Brazilian, fancy binding	$1,650	$2,150
1890s	Diagonal grain spruce, Brazilian	$1,275	$1,650
1890s	Pearl trim, Brazilian	$2,375	$3,075
1890s	Standard grain spruce, Brazilian	$675	$875

Tim Reede Custom Guitars

2004-present. Luthier Tim Reede builds his professional and premium grade, production/custom, archtop, flat-top and electric guitars in Minneapolis, Minnesota.

Timeless Instruments

1980-present. Luthier David Freeman builds his professional, premium and presentation grade, custom, flattop, 12-string, nylon-string, and resonator guitars in Tugaske, Saskatchewan. He also builds mandolins and dulcimers.

Timm Guitars

Professional grade, custom, flat-top, resonator and travel guitars built by luthier Jerry Timm in Auburn, Washington. He started in 1997.

Timtone Custom Guitars

1993-2006. Luthier Tim Diebert built his premium grade, custom, solidbody, chambered-body and acoustic guitars and basses in Grand Forks, British Columbia. He also built lap steels.

Tippin Guitar Co.

1978-present. Professional, premium and presentation grade, production/custom, flat-top guitars built by luthier Bill Tippin in Marblehead, Massachusetts.

Tobias

1977-2019. Known mainly for basses, Tobias did offer guitar models in the '80s. See Bass Section for more company info.

TogaMan GuitarViol

2003-present. Premium grade, production/custom, bow-playable solidbody guitars built by luthier Jonathan Wilson in Sylmar, California.

MODEL YEAR | FEATURES | EXC. COND. LOW | HIGH

Tokai

1947-present. Japan's Tokai Company started out making a keyboard harmonica that was widely used in Japanese schools. In '65, they started producing acoustic guitars, followed shortly by electrics. In the late '60s, Tokai hooked up with Tommy Moore, a successful instrument merchandiser from Fort Worth, Texas, and by '70 they were producing private label and OEM guitars, sold in the U.S. under the brands of various importers. By the '70s, the Tokai name was being used on the instruments. Today Tokai continues to offer electrics, acoustics, and electric basses made in Japan and Korea.

ASD-403 Custom Edition

1980s. Strat copy, single-single-hum pickups, locking tremolo.

1980s		$525	$675

AST Series

Early 1980s. Strat copies, maple board (AST-56) or slab rosewood (AST-62), 3 single-coils.

1980s	AST-56	$625	$800
1980s	AST-62	$625	$800

ATE Series

Early 1980s. Tele copies, blond (ATE-52) and pink paisley (ATE-67), 2 single-coils.

1980s	ATE-52	$625	$800
1980s	ATE-67	$625	$800

Blazing Fire

1982-1984. Hybrid-shaped solidbody with 2 medium-short pointy horns, cast aluminum body.

1982-1984		$525	$675

Breezy Sound

1977-1984. Copy of '60s rosewood board Tele.

1977-1984		$525	$675

CE-180W Cat's Eyes

Late-1970s-Early-1980s. D-style flat-top, made by Tokai Gakki, Nyatoh sides and back.

1979-1980s		$250	$325

CE-250 Cat's Eyes

Late-1970s-Early-1980s. D-style flat-top.

1979-1980s		$250	$325

CE-300 Cat's Eyes

Late-1970s-Early-1980s. D-style flat-top, made by Tokai Gakki, rosewood sides and back.

1979-1980s		$365	$475

CE-400 Cat's Eyes

Late-1970s-Early-1980s. D-style flat-top, made by Tokai Gakki, rosewood sides and back.

1979-1980s		$525	$675

CE-600 Cat's Eyes

1979-1980. D-style flat-top, rosewood sides and back.

1979-1980		$525	$675

FV48

1980s. Flying V copy.

1980s		$575	$750

Goldstar Sound

1984. Replica that replaced the Springy Sound, new less pointy headstock shape.

1984		$525	$675

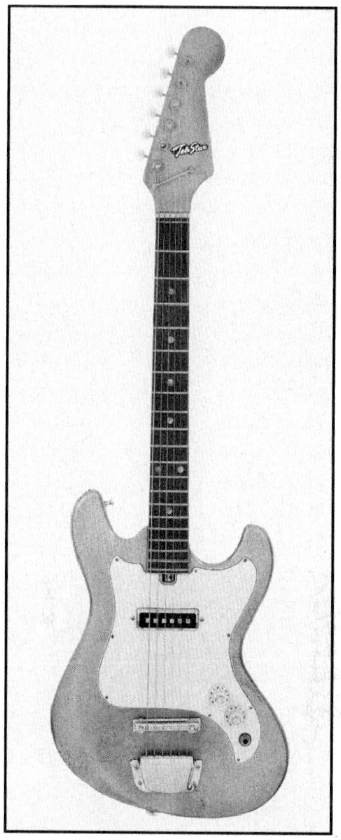

1960sTele-Star

Imaged by Heritage Auctions, HA.com

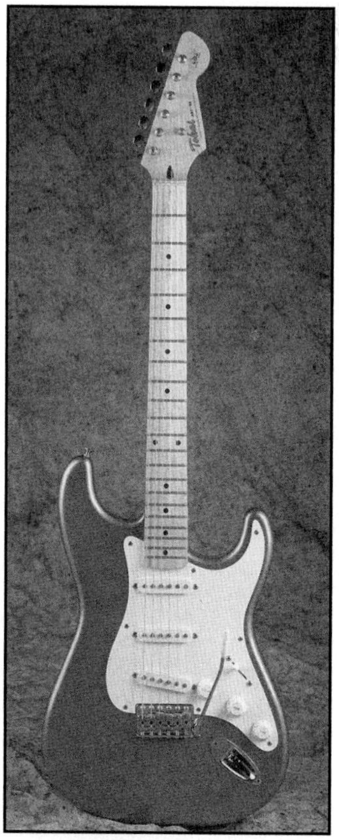

1982 Tokai AST-56 Vintage Series

Tony Nobles Baritone

Tony Vines CX

MODEL YEAR	FEATURES	EXC. COND. LOW	HIGH

J-200N

1979-1980. Gibson J-200 natural copy.

1979-1980		$525	$675

Les Paul Reborn

1976-1985. LP copy with Gibson-style Tokai headstock logo and Les Paul Reborn script logo instead of Les Paul Model, renamed Reborn Old in '82, becomes Love Rock in mid-'80s.

1976-1982	Les Paul Reborn	$725	$950
1982-1985	Reborn Old	$725	$950

Love Rock/LS Series

1980s-2000s. Various LP Std copy models (LC are LP Custom copies), 2 humbuckers, sunburst, gold top, black, figured tops at the high end, Love Rock in script logo on headstock.

1980s		$725	$950
2003	LS 75 Love Rock	$725	$950
2003	LS 80 Love Rock	$725	$950

SC Series

Tele copies.

2000s	SC-1	$365	$475

Silver Star

1977-1984. Copy of post-CBS large headstock Strat.

1977-1984		$450	$575

Springy Sound/ST-60

1977-1984. Strat copy, original high-end nitro-finish.

1977-1979	With skunk stripe	$800	$1,050
1979-1984	No skunk stripe	$800	$1,050

Vintage Series EX-55

1980s. Vintage Series, Explorer copies, bolt neck, 1 or 2 humbuckers.

1980s	1 pickup	$525	$675
1980s	2 pickups	$575	$750

Vintage Series TST

Early-1980s. Copy of maple neck (TST-56) and rosewood slab board (TST-62) Strats, 4-bolt neck plate with serial number.

1980s	TST-56	$625	$800
1980s	TST-62	$625	$800

Tom Anderson Guitarworks

1984-present. Professional and premium grade, production/custom, solidbody, semi-solidbody and acoustic guitars built by luthier Tom Anderson in Newbury Park, California.

Solidbody Electric

1984-present. Various models.

1984-2020	Most models	$1,700	$2,500

TommyHawk

1993-2005. Acoustic travel guitars built by luthier Tom Barth in Succasunna, New Jersey. They also offered a full-scale acoustic/electric model. Barth died in '05.

Toneline

1950s. Student-level private brand built by Chicago builders (Kay, Harmony). Typical '50s Stella brand specs like birch body with painted binding and rosette, pointed Toneline script logo on headstock.

Tonemaster

1960s. Guitars and basses, made in Italy by the Crucianelli Company, with typical '60s Italian sparkle plastic finish and push-button controls, bolt-on neck. Imported into the U.S. by The Imperial Accordion Company. They also offered guitar amps.

Rhythm Tone

1960-1963. Tonemaster headstock logo, Rhythm Tone logo on 'guard, single neck pickup, 3-in-line control knobs, bolt-on neck, black finish.

1960-1963		$725	$950

ToneSmith

1997-present. Luthier Kevin Smith builds his professional and premium grade, production/custom, semi-hollow body guitars and basses in Rogers, Minnesota. He previously built GLF brand guitars and built the line of Vox USA guitars from '98-'01.

Tony Nobles

Professional and premium grade, custom, acoustic and electric guitars built by luthier Tony Nobles in Wimberley, Texas starting in 1990.

Tony Vines Guitars

1989-present. Luthier Tony Vines builds his premium and presentation grade, custom/production, steel string guitars in Kingsport, Tennessee.

Torres (Antonio de Torres Jurado)

19th Century luthier most often associated with the initial development of the Classical Spanish guitar.

Tosca

1950s. Private economy brand made by Valco, possibly for a jobber, mail-order catalog or local department store.

Bolero 1123

1954-1957. Small three-quarter size electric similar to National (Valco) model 1123, single-cut, 1 neck pickup, guard mounted controls.

1954-1957		$675	$875

Toyota

1972-1970s. Imported from Japan by Hershman of New York, New York. At least 1 high-end acoustic designed by T. Kurosawa was ambitiously priced at $650.

Traphagen, Dake

1972-present. Luthier Dake Traphagen builds his premium grade, custom, classical and steel-string guitars in Bellingham, Washington.

Traugott Guitars

1991-present. Premium grade, production/custom, flat-top and acoustic/electric guitars built by luthier Jeff Traugott in Santa Cruz, California.

MODEL YEAR	FEATURES	EXC. COND. LOW	HIGH

Traveler Guitar

1992-present. Intermediate grade, production, travel size electric, acoustic, classical and acoustic/electric guitars and basses made in Redlands, California.

Travis Bean

1974-1979, 1999. Aluminum-necked solidbody electric guitars and basses. The company was founded by motorcycle and metal-sculpture enthusiast Travis Bean and guitar repairman Marc McElwee in Southern California; soon joined by Gary Kramer (see Kramer guitars). Kramer left Travis Bean in '75 and founded Kramer guitars with other partners. Guitar production began in mid-'76. The guitars featured carved aluminum necks with three-and-three heads with a T cutout in the center and wooden 'boards. Some necks had bare aluminum backs, some were painted black. A total of about 3,650 instruments were produced. Travis Bean guitar production was stopped in the summer of '79.

Serial numbers were stamped on headstock and were more-or-less consecutive. Original retail prices were $895 to $1195.

The company announced renewed production in '99 with updated versions of original designs and new models, but it evidently never got going.

TB-500

1975-1976. Aluminum neck, T-slotted headstock, double-cut, 2 single coils mounted in 'guard, 2 controls, dot markers, white.

1975-1976		$4,000	$5,200

TB-1000 Artist

1974-1979. Aluminum neck, T-slotted headstock, double-cut archtop, 2 humbuckers, 4 controls, block inlays.

1974-1979		$4,000	$5,200
1974-1979	Rare colors	$4,700	$6,000

TB-1000 Standard

1974-1979. Similar to TB-1000 Artist, but with dot inlays.

1974-1979		$3,700	$4,800

TB-3000 Wedge

1976-1979. Aluminum neck with T-slotted headstock, triangle-shaped body, 2 humbucking pickups, 4 controls, block markers on 'board.

1976-1979		$4,300	$5,600

Tregan Guitars

2007-present. Solidbody electrics including Bison-style sharp curved horns body style, plus other less traditional styles, student and intermediate grade.

Tremblett Archtops

Luthier Mark Tremblett started in the year 2006, he builds professional grade, custom, archtop guitars in Pouch Cove, Newfoundland.

Tremcaster

2008-present. Luthier John Mosconi, along with Robert Gelley and Jeff Russell, builds professional grade, production/custom, electric and acoustic guitars in Akron, Ohio.

Trenier

1998-present. Premium grade, production/custom, archtop guitars built by luthier Bryant Trenier in Seattle, Washington. From '02 to '04 he was located in Prague, Czech Republic.

Triggs

1992-present. Luthiers Jim Triggs and his son Ryan build their professional and premium grade, production/custom, archtop, flat-top, and solidbody guitars originally in Nashville Tennessee, and, since '98, in Kansas City, Kansas. They also build mandolins.

Acoustic/Electric Archtop

1992-present. Various archtop cutaway models.

1992-2009	Byrdland 17"	$1,800	$2,400
1992-2009	Excel 17"	$2,700	$3,600
1992-2009	Jazzmaster	$1,500	$2,000
1992-2009	New Yorker 18"	$4,000	$5,300
1992-2010	Stromberg Master 400	$4,000	$5,300
1997	Trinity 18"	$4,000	$5,300
2006	San Salvador	$2,300	$3,100

Trinity River

Located in Fort Worth, Texas, luthiers Marcus Lawyer and Ross McLeod import their production/custom, budget and intermediate grade, acoustic and resonator guitars and basses from Asia. They also import mandolins and banjos.

True North Guitars

1994-present. Luthier Dennis Scannell builds his premium grade, custom, flat-tops in Waterbury, Vermont.

True Tone

1960s. Guitars, basses and amps retailed by Western Auto, manufactured by Chicago guitar makers like Kay. The brand was most likely gone by '68.

Double Cutaway (K300 Kay)

1962-1966. Made by Kay and similar to their K300, double-cut solidbody, dual pickups and vibrola arm, red.

1962-1966		$375	$485

Double Cutaway Electric Archtop (K592 Kay)

1960s. Made by Kay and similar to their K592 double-cut thinline acoustic, 2 pickups, Bigsby tailpiece, burgundy red.

1960s		$410	$535

Fun Time

Early- to mid-1960s. Student 13" flat-top, painted 5-point 'guard, red sunburst finish.

1960s		$55	$70

Traveler Acoustic AG-105

Triggs Custom

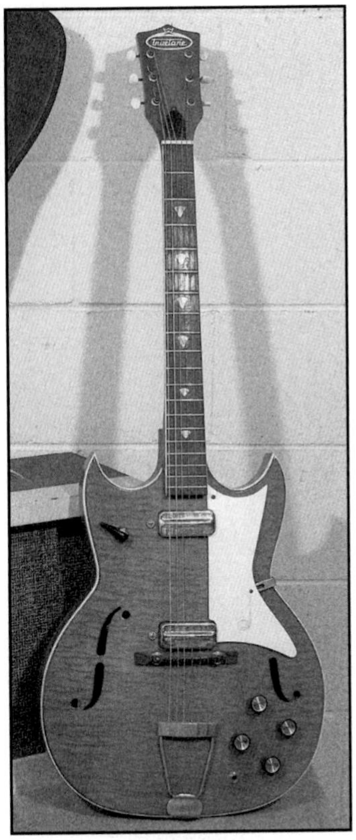

Early-1960s Truetone Speed Master
Tom Pfeifer

1994 Tut Taylor Spider Cone
Bernunzio Uptown Music

MODEL YEAR	FEATURES	EXC. COND. LOW	HIGH

Imperial Deluxe

Mid-1960s. Harmony-made (Rocket), 3 pickups, trapeze tailpiece, 6 control knobs, block markers, sunburst.

1960s		$530	$690

Jazz King (K573 Kay)

1960s. Kay's K573 Speed Demon, 3 pickups, thinline archtop electric with f-hole, eighth note art on 'guard, sunburst.

1960s		$375	$485

Rock 'n Roll Electric (K100 Kay)

1960s. Kay's K100, slab body, single pickup, but with a bright red multiple lacquer finish.

1960s		$260	$335

Speed Master (K6533 Kay)

1960s. Made by Kay and similar to their K6533 full-body electric archtop Value Leader line, eighth note art 'guard, sunburst.

1960s		$315	$410

Western Spanish Auditorium

Early- to mid-1960s. 15" flat-top, laminate construction, celluloid 'guard, sunburst.

1960s		$120	$155

Tsunami

Custom, intermediate grade, one-off solidbody electric guitars built by luthier Paul Brzozowski, starting in 2009, in Cleveland, Tennessee.

Tucker

Founded by John N. "Jack" Tucker, John Morrall, and David Killingsworth in 2000, Tucker builds professional and premium grade, production/custom, albizzia wood solidbody guitars and basses in Hanalei, Hawaii.

Tuscany Guitars

2008-2013. Intermediate grade, production, classic model electric guitars imported from Asia and finished by luthier Galeazzo Frudua in San Lazzaro di Savena, Italy.

Tut Taylor

Line of professional and premium grade, production/custom, resophonic guitars built by luthier Mark Taylor of Crafters of Tennessee in Old Hickory, Tennessee. Brand named for his father, dobro artist Tut Taylor. Taylor also builds the Tennessee line of guitars, mandolins and banjos and was part of Rich and Taylor guitars for '93-'96.

TV Jones

1993-present. Professional and premium grade, production/custom, hollow, chambered, and solid body guitars built by luthier Thomas Vincent Jones originally in California, now in Poulsbo, Washington. The instruments have either Jones or TV Jones inlaid on the headstock. He also builds

U. A. C.

1920s. Instruments built by the Oscar Schmidt Co. and possibly others. Most likely a brand made for a distributor.

MODEL YEAR	FEATURES	EXC. COND. LOW	HIGH

Unique Guitars

2003-ca. 2007. Professional and premium grade, production/custom, solidbody guitars and basses built by luthier Joey Rico in California. Joey is the son of Bernie Rico, the founder of BC Rich guitars.

Univox

1964-1978. Univox started out as an amp line and added guitars around '68. Guitars were imported from Japan by the Merson Musical Supply Company, later Unicord, Westbury, New York. Many if not all supplied by Arai and Company (Aria, Aria Pro II), some made by Matsumoku. Univox Lucy ('69) first copy of lucite Ampeg Dan Armstrong. Generally mid-level copies of American designs.

Acoustic Flat-Top

1969-1978. Various models.

1970s		$150	$500

Bicentennial

1976. Offset double-cut, heavily carved body, brown stain, 3 humbucker-style pickups.

1976		$675	$875

Deep Body Electric

1960s-1970s. ES-175 style.

1960-1970s		$425	$550

Guitorgan FSB C-3000

1970s. Double-cut semi-hollow body, multiple controls, Guitorgan logo on headstock, footpedal.

1970s		$925	$1,250

Solid Body Electric

1960s-1970s. Includes Flying V, Mosrite and Hofner violin-guitar copies.

1960-1970s	Hi Flier	$500	$675
1960-1970s	Various models	$350	$650
1970s	Effector	$350	$650

Thin Line (Coily)

1960-1970s	12-string	$425	$550
1960-1970s	6-string	$425	$550

USA Custom Guitars

1999-2020. Professional and premium grade, custom/production, solidbody electric guitars built in Tacoma, Washington. They also did work for other luthiers. In late '20, USA was acquired by MJT Aged Guitar Finishes in Carthage, Missouri.

Vaccaro

1997-2002. Founded by Henry Vaccaro, Sr., one of the founders of Kramer Guitars. They offered intermediate and professional grade, production/custom, aluminum-necked guitars and basses designed by Vaccaro, former Kramer designer Phil Petillo, and Henry Vaccaro, Jr., which were made in Asbury Park, New Jersey.

Val Dez

Early-1960s-early-1970s. Less expensive guitars built by Landola in Sweden or Finland; they also made the Espana brand.

MODEL YEAR	FEATURES	EXC. COND. LOW	HIGH

Valco

1942-1968. Valco, of Chicago, was a big player in the guitar and amplifier business. Their products were private branded for other companies like National, Supro, Airline, Oahu, and Gretsch. In '42, National Dobro ceased operations and Victor Smith, Al Frost and Louis Dopyera bought the company and changed the name to Valco Manufacturing Company. Post-war production resumed in '46. Valco was purchased by treasurer Robert Engelhardt in '64. In '67, Valco bought Kay, but in '68 the new Valco/Kay company went out of business.

Valencia

1985-present. Budget grade, production, classical guitars imported first by Rondo Music of Union, New Jersey and presently distributed by others.

Valley Arts

Ca. 1977-2010. Professional and premium grade, production/custom, semi-hollow and solidbody guitars and basses built in Nashville, Tennessee. Valley Arts originally was a Southern California music store owned by partners Al Carness and Mike McGuire where McGuire taught and did most of the repairs. Around '77, McGuire and Valley Arts started making custom instruments on a large scale. By '83, they opened a separate manufacturing facility to build the guitars. In '92 Samick acquired half of the company with McGuire staying on for a year as a consultant. Samick offered made-in-the-U.S. production and custom models under the Valley Arts name. In '02, Valley Arts became a division of Gibson Guitar Corp., which builds the guitars in Nashville. Founders Carness and McGuire were once again involved with the company. They reintroduced the line in January, '03. The brand has been inactive since '10.

Vantage

1977-1998. Budget and intermediate grade, production, acoustic and electric guitars and basses from Japan '77-'90 and from Korea '90-'98.

Vega

1889-1980s, 1989-present. Founded in Boston by the Nelson family, Vega was big in the banjo market into the 1930s, before adding guitars to their line. The company was purchased by C.F. Martin in '70 who built Vega banjos and starting in '76 they also used the brand on imported guitars, first from the Netherlands and later from Japan, with the Japanese Vegas being of higher quality. In '79, Martin sold the Vega trademark to Korea's Galaxy Trading Company. The Deering Banjo Company, in Spring Valley, California acquired the brand in '89 and uses it (and the star logo) on a line of banjos.

C Series Archtop

1933-1950s. Carved-top archtops, '30's models are the 14 5/8" mahogany body C-20 and C-40, 16 1/8" maple body C-60, and the C-70/C75 Vehaphone with rosewood body and gold parts, and the figured-maple body C-80 with deluxe appointments. By '40 the line was the 14-16" C-19, -26, -46, and -56, and the 17" Professional Series C-66 Professional, C-71 Soloist, C-76 Artist, and C-86 Deluxe. Optional blond finish available by '40.

1933-1939	C-20	$800	$1,050
1933-1939	C-40	$800	$1,050
1933-1939	C-60	$1,200	$1,600
1933-1939	C-70	$1,400	$1,800
1933-1939	C-80	$1,575	$2,025
1938	C-75	$2,400	$3,100
1940-1949	C-19, C-26, C-46	$700	$900
1940-1949	C-56	$1,275	$1,650
1940-1949	C-66 Professional	$1,350	$1,750
1940-1949	C-71 Soloist	$1,425	$1,850
1940-1949	C-76 Artist	$1,550	$2,000
1940-1949	C-86 Deluxe	$1,625	$2,100

Duo-Tron Series Electric Archtops

1947-late 1950s. Various mid-level large body cutaway and non-cut carved-top archtops, 1, 2 or 3 (rare) floating pickups, dot or block markers, natural or sunburst.

1947-50s	Higher end models	$1,825	$2,400
1947-50s	Lower end models	$600	$775
1947-50s	Mid-range models	$875	$1,150

E-201 Electric Archtop

1959. One pickup, sunburst.

1959		$1,400	$1,850

FT-90 Flat-Top

1960s. 15" body with narrow waist, dot markers, Vega logo, natural.

1960s		$325	$420

G-30

1968-ca. 1970. D-style with solid spruce top and solid mahogany sides and back, Vega logo with star on headstock, dot markers, natural finish.

1968-1970		$250	$325

O'Dell

1950s. Full body, single cut, acoustic-electric, 1 pickup, tailpiece controls.

1950s	Sunburst	$850	$1,100

Parlor

Early-1900s-1920s. Small parlor-sized instrument, styles and appointment levels, including binding, purfling and inlays, vary.

1900s	Mahogany	$325	$425
1910-20s	Brazilian, fancy	$1,200	$3,900
1910s	Brazilian	$600	$1,050

Profundo Flat-Top

1930s-1950s. Flat-top D-style body, spruce top, mahogany or rosewood back and sides.

1930s-50s	Mahogany	$1,200	$1,600
1940s-50s	Rosewood	$1,900	$2,500

Solidbody Electric (Import)

1970s-1980s. Solidbody copies of classic designs, Vega script logo on headstock, bolt-on necks.

1970s		$225	$275

Vega Electric Archtop

1939. Full-body electric archtop, figured maple, 1 pickup, 2 control knobs, trapeze bridge, diamond markers, large Vega and star headstock logo, blond.

1939		$1,000	$1,300

Late 1940s Vega C-26
Imaged by Heritage Auctions, HA.com

1938 Vega C-75 Vegaphone
Michael J. Scanlon

1982 Veillette-Citron Shark
Micheal Wright

Ca. 1973 Ventura Bruno VS III
W. H. Stephens

MODEL YEAR	FEATURES	EXC. COND. LOW	HIGH

Vega, Charles

1993-2010. Luthier Charles Vega built his premium, production/custom, nylon-string guitars in Baltimore, Maryland.

Veillette

1991-present. Luthiers Joe Veillette (of Veillette-Citron fame) and Martin Keith build their professional grade, production/custom, acoustic, acoustic/electric, electric 6- and 12-string and baritone guitars and basses in Woodstock, New York. They also build mandolins.

Veillette-Citron

1975-1983. Founded by Joe Veillette and Harvey Citron who met at the New York College School of Architecture in the late '60s. Joe took a guitar building course from Michael Gurian and by the Summer of '76, he and Harvey started producing neck-thru solidbody guitars and basses. Veillette and Citron both are back building instruments.

Velázquez

1948-1972. Manuel Velázquez, New York, New York, gained a reputation as a fine repairman in the late 1940s. He opened his 3rd Avenue guitar building shop in the early 1950s. By the mid-1950s he was considered by some as being the finest American builder of classical guitars. Velázquez left New York in 1972 and moved to Puerto Rico. He continued building guitars for the Japanese market. He returned to the United States in 1982. By the 2000s he built instruments with this son and daughter.

Veleno

1967, 1970-1977, 2003-2018. Premium and presentation grade, production/custom, all-aluminum electric solidbody guitars built by luthier John Veleno in St. Petersburg, Florida. First prototype in '67. Later production begins in late-'70 and lasts until '75 or '76. The guitars were chrome or gold-plated, with various anodized colors. The Traveler Guitar was the idea of B.B. King; only 10 were made. Two Ankh guitars were made for Todd Rundgren in '77. Only one bass was made. Approximately 185 instruments were made up to '77 and are sequentially numbered. In 2003, John Veleno reintroduced his brand, he died in '18.

Original (Aluminum Solidbody)

1973-1976. V-headstock, chrome and aluminum.

1973-1976	Rare color	$7,800	$10,000
1973-1976	Standard	$4,500	$6,000

Traveler Guitar

1973-1976. Limited production of about a dozen instruments, drop-anchor-style metal body.

1973-1976		$7,800	$10,000

Vengeance Guitars & Graphix

2002-present. Luthier Rick Stewart builds his professional and premium grade, custom/production, solidbody guitars and basses in Arden, North Carolina.

MODEL YEAR	FEATURES	EXC. COND. LOW	HIGH

Ventura

1970s. Acoustic and electric guitars imported by C. Bruno Company, mainly copies of classic American models. They also offered basses.

Acoustic Flat-Top

1970s		$100	$425

Guitorgan

1970s. Based on MCI Guitorgan, converts standard electric guitar into a Guitorgan through the addition of electronic organ components, multiple switches, large Barney Kessel sharp-horned acoustic-electric style body.

1970s		$825	$1,100

Hollowbody Electric

1970s		$250	$700

Solidbody Electric

1970s		$250	$700

Verri

Premium grade, production/custom, archtop guitars built by luthier Henry Verri in Little Falls, New York starting in 1992.

Versoul, LTD

1989-present. Premium grade, production/custom steel-string flat-top, acoustic/electric, nylon-string, resonator, solidbody, and baritone guitars, basses and sitars built by luthier Kari Nieminen in Helsinki, Finland.

VibraWood

2012-present. Luthier John J. Slog builds custom, professional and premium grade, vintage-style guitars and basses in Bethlehem, Pennsylvania.

Vicente Tatay

1894-late 1930s. Classical guitars built by luthier Vicente Tatay and his sons in Valencia, Spain.

Victor Baker Guitars

1998-present. Professional and premium grade, custom, carved archtop, flat-top and solidbody electric guitars built by luthier Victor Baker in Philadelphia, Pennsylvania. In '10 he relocated to Brooklyn, New York and is currently in Astoria.

Victor Guitars

2002-2008. Luthiers Edward Victor Dick and Greg German built their premium grade, production/custom, flat-top guitars in Denver, Colorado.

Victoria

Ca. 1902-1920s. Brand name for New York distributor Buegeleisen & Jacobson. Instruments built by the Oscar Schmidt Co. and possibly others. Most likely a brand made for a distributor.

Vigier

1980-present. Luthier Patrice Vigier builds high-end electric guitars and basses near Paris, France.

MODEL YEAR	FEATURES	EXC. COND. LOW	HIGH

Electric Solidbody

1980-present. Various models.

1980	Arpege	$1,650	$2,175
2000-2006	Expert	$1,700	$2,250
2005-2020	Excalibur Shawn Lane	$1,700	$2,250
2020	Excalibur 13	$1,700	$2,250
2020	Excalibur Special	$2,000	$2,600
2020	Excalibur Supra 7	$1,625	$2,150
2020	Excalibur Ultra Blues	$1,900	$2,450
2021	Texas Blues	$1,625	$2,150

Viking Guitars

2003-present. Premium grade, solidbody guitars made by Ed Roman Guitars. Production was '03-'04, custom only since.

Vinetto

2003-present. Luthier Vince Cunetto builds his professional grade, production/custom, solid, chambered and semi-hollow body guitars in St. Louis, Missouri.

Vintage

Ca. 1993-present. Intermediate grade, production, solidbody and semi-hollow acoustic, electro-acoustic and resonator guitars and basses, imported from China, Korea and Vietnam by John Hornby Skewes & Co. in the U.K. They also offer folk instruments.

Vintique

Luthier Jay Monterose built premium grade, custom/production, electric guitars in Suffern, New York. Vintique also manufactured guitar hardware.

Vivi-Tone

1932-1938. Founded in Kalamazoo, Michigan, by former Gibson designer Lloyd Loar, Walter Moon and Lewis Williams, Vivi-Tone built acoustic archtop guitars as well as some of the earliest electric solidbodies. They also built basses and mandolins and offered amps built by Webster Electric. A Vivi-Tone instrument must be all original. Any missing part makes this instrument practically unsellable in the vintage-market.

Guitar

1932-1938. Deep archtop-style body with F-holes on the backside and magnetic bridge pickup.

1932-1938	Rare model	$2,600	$3,450
1932-1938	Standard, sunburst	$1,700	$2,600
1932-1938	Tenor, 4-string	$1,575	$2,075

Vox

1954-present. Name introduced by Jennings Musical Instruments (JMI) of England. First Vox products was a volume pedal, amplifiers were brought to the market in late '57 by Tom Jennings and Dick Denny. Guitars were introduced in '61, with an Echo Unit starting the Vox line of effects in '63.

Guitars and basses bearing the Vox name were offered from '61-'69 (made in England and Italy), '82-'85 (Japan), '85-'88 (Korea), '98-2001 (U.S.), and they introduced a limited edition U.S.-made teardrop guitar in '07 and the semi-hollow Virage guitars in '08. Vox products are currently distributed the U.S. by Korg USA.

Ace/Super Ace

1960s. Offset double cut solidbody, 2 single-coils. Super Ace has 3 pickups.

1963-1965	Super Ace	$700	$925
1964-1966	Ace	$550	$710

Apache

1960s. Modified teardrop body, 3 pickups, vibrato.

1966		$700	$925

Apollo

1967-1968. Single sharp cutaway, 1 pickup, distortion, treble and bass booster, available in sunburst or cherry.

1967-1968		$700	$925

Bobcat

1963-1968. Double-cut semi-hollowbody style, block markers, 3 pickups, vibrato, 2 volume and 2 tone controls.

1963-1965	England	$1,050	$1,350
1966-1968	Italy	$700	$925

Bossman

1967-1968. Single rounded cutaway, 1 pickup, distortion, treble and bass booster, available in sunburst or cherry.

1967-1968		$525	$685

Bulldog

1966. Solidbody double-cut, 3 pickups.

1966		$975	$1,275

Delta

1967-1968. 5-sided Phantom shaped solidbody, 2 pickups, distortion, treble and bass boosters, vibrato, 1 volume and 2 tone controls, available in white only.

1967-1968		$1,175	$1,500

Folk XII

1966-1969. Dreadnought 12-string flat-top, large 3-point 'guard, block markers, natural.

1966-1969		$325	$425

Guitar-Organ

1966. Standard Phantom with oscillators from a Continental organ installed inside. Plays either organ sounds, guitar sounds, or both. Weighs over 20 pounds. Prices vary widely due to operating issues with this model.

1966	Excellent condition	$1,900	$2,500
1966	Functional 'board	$1,200	$1,600
1966	Partial function	$575	$775

Harlem

1965-1967. Offset double-cut solidbody, 2 extended range pickups, sunburst or color option. Values vary widely due to operating issues with this model.

1965-1967		$700	$925

Hurricane

1965-1967. Double-cut solidbody, 2 pickups, spring action vibrato, sunburst or color option.

1965-1967		$600	$800

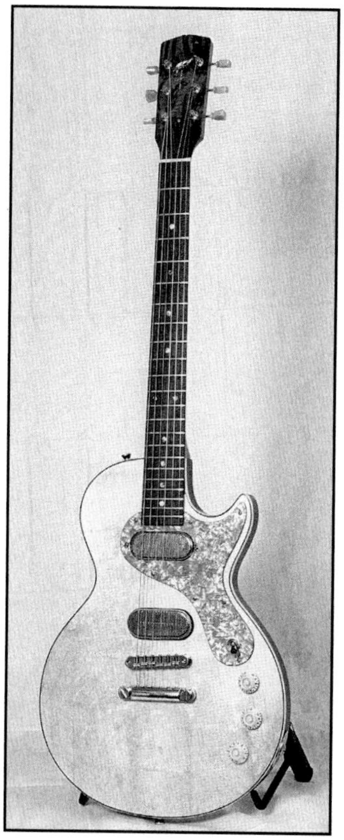

1999 Versoul Henry

Kari Nieminen

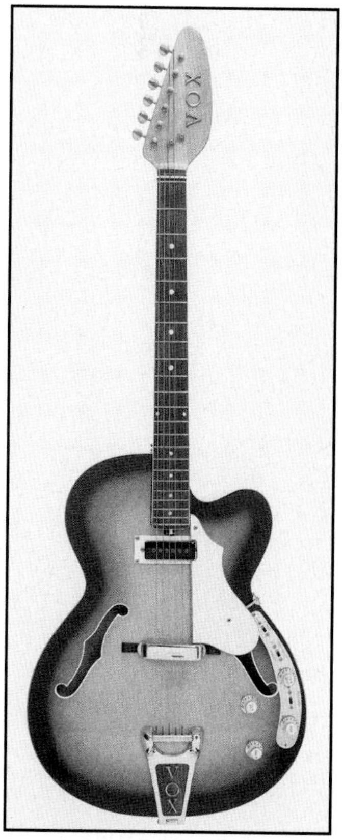

1967 Vox Bossman

Imaged by Heritage Auctions, HA.com

GUITARS

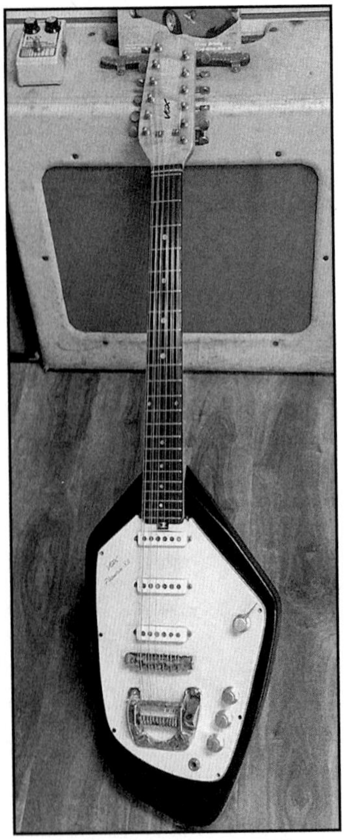

1969 Vox Phantom XII

Craig Brody

1966 Vox Tornado

MODEL YEAR	FEATURES	EXC. COND. LOW	HIGH

Invader (V262)

1966-1967. Solidbody double-cut, 2 pickups, on-board effects, sunburst. Must have fully-functional electronics.

1966-1967		$1,800	$2,325

Mando Guitar

1966. Made in Italy, 12-string mandolin thing.

1966		$975	$1,275

Mark III (U.S.A)

1998-2001. Teardrop reissue, made in U.S.A., 2 single-coils, fixed bridge or Bigsby. A limited was introduced in '08.

1998-2001		$775	$1,000

Mark III 50th Anniversary

2007. Only 100 made, teardrop body, 2 pickups, white finish.

2007		$925	$1,200

Mark III Limited Edition

2008. Custom Shop USA model, white hardwood body, maple neck, rosewood 'board.

2008		$1,625	$2,100

Mark III/Phantom Mark III

1963-1964. Teardrop body, 2 pickups, 2 controls, Marvin Bigsby, made in England, guitar version of Mark IV bass, while it is called a Phantom Mark III it does not have a Phantom shape.

1963-1964		$2,650	$3,425

Mark IX

1965-1966. Solidbody teardrop-shaped, 9 strings, 3 pickups, vibrato, 1 volume and 2 tone controls.

1965-1966		$1,200	$1,575

Mark VI

1965-1967. Teardrop-shaped solidbody, 3 pickups, vibrato, 1 volume and 2 tone controls.

1964-1965	England, white, Brian Jones	$3,100	$4,050
1965-1967	Italy, sunburst	$1,825	$2,350

Mark VI Reissue

1998-2001. Actually, this is a reissue of the original Phantom VI (Vox couldn't use that name due to trademark reasons), made in U.S.A.

1998-2001		$700	$925

Mark XII

1965-1967. Teardrop-shaped solidbody, 12 strings, 3 pickups, vibrato, 1 volume and 2 tone controls, sunburst. Reissued for '98-'01.

1965-1967		$1,425	$1,850

Meteor/Super Meteor

1965-1967. Solidbody double-cut, 1 pickup, Super Meteor with vibrato.

1965-1967	Meteor	$400	$525
1965-1967	Super Meteor	$450	$575

New Orleans

1966. Thin double-cut acoustic electric similar to ES-330, 2 pickups, a scaled down version of the 3-pickup Bobcat model.

1966		$650	$850

Phantom VI

1962-1967. Five-sided body, 6 strings, 3 pickups, vibrato, 1 volume and 2 tone controls.

1962-1964	English-made	$2,825	$3,675
1965-1967	Italian-made	$1,675	$2,200

Phantom XII

1964-1967. 12 string version of VI.

1964	English-made	$2,850	$3,700
1965-1967	Italian-made	$1,675	$2,200

Phantom XII Stereo

1966. Phantom XII with 3 special offset stereo pickups making 6 pickup conbinations, 3 separate pickup mode selectors, color option.

1966		$1,800	$2,325

Shadow

1965. Solidbody double-cut, 3 pickups, tremolo tailpiece, sunburst.

1965	English-made	$775	$1,000

Spitfire

1965-1967. Solidbody double-cut, 3 pickups, vibrato.

1965-1967		$700	$925

Starstream

1967-1968. Teardrop-shaped hollowbody, 2 pickups, distortion, treble and bass boosters, wah-wah, vibrato, 1 volume and 2 tone controls, 3-way pickup selector, available in cherry or sandburst.

1967-1968		$1,500	$2,000

Starstream XII

1967-1968. 12 string Starstream.

1967-1968		$1,500	$2,000

Stroller

1961-1966. Made in England, solidbody, single bridge pickup, Hurricane-style contoured body, dot markers, red.

1961-1966		$450	$575

Student Prince

1965-1967. Made in Italy, mahogany body thinline archtop electric, 2 knobs, dot markers.

1965-1967		$375	$475

Super Lynx

1965-1967. Similar to Bobcat but with 2 pickups and no vibrola, double-cut, 2 pickups, adjustable truss rod, 2 bass and 2 volume controls.

1965-1967		$700	$925

Super Lynx Deluxe

1965-1967. Super Lynx with added vibrato tailpiece.

1965-1967		$700	$925

Tempest XII

1965-1967. Solidbody double-cut, 12 strings, 3 pickups.

1965-1967		$700	$925

Thunder Jet

1960s-style with single pickup and vibrato arm.

1960s		$525	$675

Tornado

1965-1967. Thinline archtop, single pickup, dot markers, sunburst.

1965-1967		$365	$475

Typhoon

1965-1967. Hollowbody single-cut, 2 pickups, 3-piece laminated neck.

1965-1967		$425	$550

Ultrasonic

1967-1968. Hollowbody double-cut, 2 pickups, distortion, treble and bass boosters, wah-wah, vibrato,

MODEL YEAR	FEATURES	EXC. COND. LOW	HIGH

1 volume and 2 tone controls, 3-way pickup selector, available in sunburst or cherry.

1967-1968	12-string	$1,500	$2,000
1967-1968	6-string	$1,500	$2,000

Viper

1968. Double-cut, thinline archtop electric, built-in distortion.

1968		$1,075	$1,400

Virage/Virage II

2008-2014. Double- and single-cut semi-hollow bodies, 2 triple-coil pickups, made in Japan.

2008-2014		$1,625	$2,100

Wildcat

1965-1967. Single-cut acoustic-electric archtop, 1 pickup, Wildcat and Vox logos on 'guard, dot markers.

1965-1967		$400	$525

W. J. Dyer

See listing under Dyer.

Wabash

1950s. Acoustic and electric guitars distributed by the David Wexler company and made by others, most likely Kay. They also offered lap steels and amps.

Walden Guitars

Luthier Jonathan Lee of Portland, Oregon imports production, budget to professional grade, acoustic, acoustic-electric and classical guitars from Lilan, China. He began in 1996.

Walker

1994-present. Premium and presentation grade, production/custom, flat-top and archtop guitars built by luthier Kim Walker in North Stonington, Connecticut.

Walker (Kramer)

1981. Kramer came up with idea to offer this brand to produce wood-neck guitars and basses; they didn't want to dilute the Kramer aluminum-neck market they had built up. The idea didn't last long, and few, if any, of these instruments were produced, but prototypes exist.

Wandre (Davoli)

Ca. 1956/57-1969. Solidbody and thinline hollowbody electric guitars and basses created by German-descended Italian motorcycle and guitar enthusiast, artist, and sculptor from Milan, Italy, Wandre Pioli. Brands include Wandre (pronounced Vahn-dray), Davoli, Framez, JMI, Noble, Dallas, Avalon, Avanti I and others. Until '60, they were built by Pioli himself; from '60-'63 built in Milan by Framez; '63-'65 built by Davoli; '66-'69 built in Pioli's own factory.

The guitars originally used Framez pickups, but from '63 on (or earlier) they used Davoli pickups. Mostly strange shapes characterized by neck-thru-tailpiece aluminum neck with plastic back and rosewood 'board. Often multi-color and sparkle finishes, using unusual materials like linoleum, fiberglass and laminates, metal bindings. Often the instruments will have numerous identifying names but usually somewhere there is a Wandre blob logo.

Distributed early on in the U.K. by Jennings Musical Industries, Ltd. (JMI) and in the U.S. by Don Noble and Company. Model B.B. dedicated to Brigitte Bardot. Among more exotic instruments were the minimalist Krundaal Bikini guitar with a built-in amplifier and attached speaker, and the pogo stick Swedenbass. These guitars are relatively rare and highly collectible. In '05, the brand was revived on a line of imported intermediate grade, production, solidbodies from Eastwood guitars.

Electric

1956-1969	Common models	$1,050	$3,100
1956-1969	Rare models	$3,100	$8,000

Warren

2005-present. Luthier Don Warren builds his professional and premium grade, custom/production, solidbody electric guitars in Latham, New York.

Warrior

1995-present. Professional, premium, and presentation grade, production/custom, acoustic and solidbody electric guitars and basses built by luthier J.D. Lewis in Rossville, Georgia.

Washburn

1962-present. Budget, intermediate, professional, and premium grade, production/custom, acoustic and electric guitars and basses made in the U.S., Japan, and Korea. They also make amps, banjos and mandolins.

Originally a Lyon & Healy brand, the Washburn line was revived on a line of imports in '62 by Roland who sold it to Beckman Musical Instruments in '74/'75. Beckman sold the rights to the Washburn name to Fretted Instruments, Inc. in '76. Guitars originally made in Japan and Korea, but production moved back to U.S. in '91. Currently Washburn is part of U.S. Music.

Washburn (Lyon & Healy)

1880s-ca.1949. Washburn was founded in Chicago as one of the lines for Lyon & Healy to promote high quality stringed instruments, ca. 1880s. The rights to manufacture Washburns were sold to J.R. Stewart Co. in '28, but rights to Washburn name were sold to Tonk Brothers of Chicago. In the Great Depression (about 1930), J.R. Stewart Co. was hit hard and declared bankruptcy. Tonk Brothers bought at auction all Stewart trade names, then sold them to Regal Musical Instrument Co. Regal built Washburns by the mid-'30s. The Tonk Brothers still licensed the name. These Washburn models lasted until ca. '49. In '62 the brand resurfaced on a line of imports from Roland.

1967 Vox Ultrasonic

Imaged by Heritage Auctions, HA.com

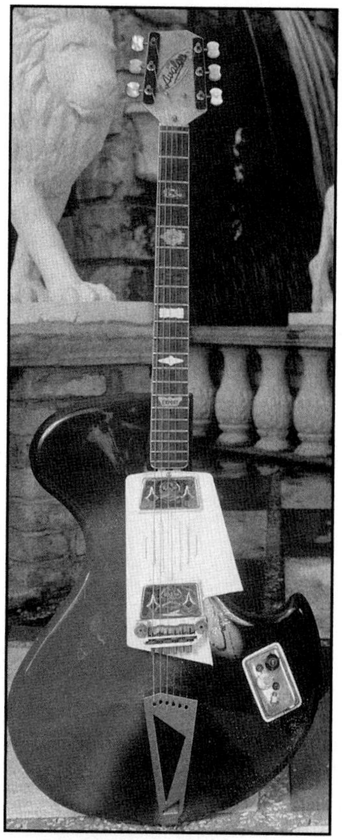

1960s Wandre Avalon Rock Oval

Waterloo WL-14 Scissortail

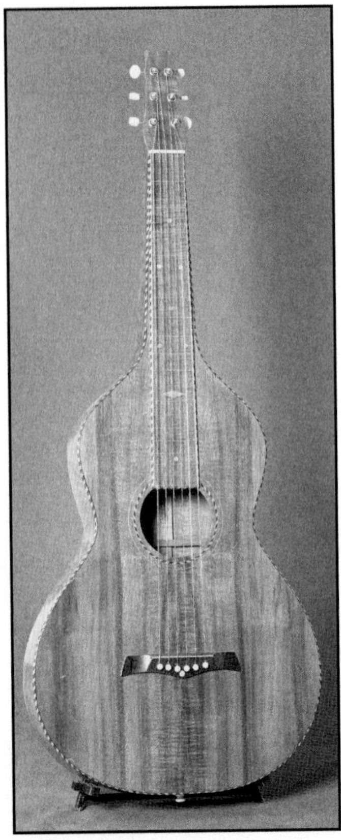

1925 Weissenborn Style #3
Folkway Music

MODEL YEAR | FEATURES | EXC. COND. LOW | HIGH

Washington

Washington was a brand manufactured by Kansas City, Missouri instrument wholesalers J.W. Jenkins & Sons. First introduced in 1895, the brand also offered mandolins.

Waterloo

2014-present. Professional grade, production, acoustic guitars based on Depression-era models, built by Bill Collings in Austin, Texas. Waterloo was the original city name of Austin.

WL-12

2014-present. Parlor size, vintage-style sunburst finish.

2014-2020 $1,275 $1,675

WL-14 Scissortail

2014-present. Solid spruce top, maple back and sides, X-bracing.

2014-2020 $1,325 $1,725

WL-14LTR

2014-present. Acoustic 14.75", solid headstock, ladder bracing (L).

2014-2020 $1,200 $1,550

WL-14MH

2014-present. Parlor size, all mahogany.

2014-2020 $1,325 $1,725

WL-14X

2014-present. Acoustic 14.75", solid headstock, X bracing (X).

2014-2020 $1,325 $1,725

WL-JK

2014-present. Nick-named 'Jumbo King', 15.75" body, X-bracing. Optional East Indian rosewood back and sides.

2014-2020 $1,200 $1,550

WL-JK Deluxe

2014-present. Ornate appointments.

2014-2020 $1,600 $2,100

WL-K

2014-present. Lightweight 14.75", '30s Kel Kroyden inspired, optional hand-painted "Southwest" scene.

2014-2020 $1,275 $1,675

WL-S

2014-present. Slotted headstock 14", '30s Stella inspired, solid cherry wood back and sides, iced tea sunburst.

2014-2020 $1,225 $1,625

WL-S Deluxe

2014-present. Ornate appointments.

2014-2020 $1,725 $2,275

Waterstone

2003-present. Intermediate and professional grade, production/custom, electric solid and semi-hollowbody and acoustic guitars and basses imported from Korea by Waterstone Musical Instruments, LLC of Nashville, Tennessee.

Watkins/WEM

1957-present. Watkins Electric Music (WEM) was founded by Charlie Watkins. Their first commercial product was the Watkins Dominator

MODEL YEAR | FEATURES | EXC. COND. LOW | HIGH

(wedge Gibson stereo amp shape) in '57. They made the Rapier line of guitars and basses from the beginning. Watkins offered guitars and basses up to '82. They currently build accordian amps.

Wayne

1998-present. Professional and premium grade, production/custom, solidbody guitars built by luthiers Wayne and Michael (son) Charvel in Paradise, California. They also build lap steels.

Webber

1988-2020. Professional grade, production/custom flat-top guitars built by luthier David Webber in North Vancouver, British Columbia. Webber retired in '20.

Weber

1996-present. Premium grade, production/custom, carved-top acoustic and resonator guitars built by luthier Bruce Weber and his Sound To Earth, Ltd. company, originally in Belgrade, Montana, in '04 moving to Logan, Montana. They also build mandolins. In '12, Two Old Hippies (Breedlove, Bedell) acquired the brand, moving production in '13 to Oregon where Bruce Weber oversees development.

Webster

1940s. Archtop and acoustic guitars, most likely built by Kay or other mass builder.

Model 16C Acoustic Archtop

1940s $480 $625

Wechter

1984-present. Intermediate, professional and premium grade, production/custom, flat-top, 12-string, resonator and nylon-string guitars and basses from luthier Abe Wechter in Paw Paw, Michigan. The Elite line is built in Paw Paw, the others in Asia. Until '94 he built guitars on a custom basis. In '95, he set up a manufacturing facility in Paw Paw to produce his new line and in '00 he added the Asian guitars. In '04, he added resonators designed by Tim Scheerhorn. Wechter was associated with Gibson Kalamazoo from the mid-'70s to '84. He also offers the Maple Lake brand of acoustics. In '08 he moved his shop to Fort Wayne, Indiana.

Weissenborn

1910s-1937, present. Hermann Weissenborn was well-established as a violin and piano builder in Los Angeles by the early 1910s. Around '20, he added guitars, ukes and steels to his line. Most of his production was in the '20s and '30s until his death in '37. He made tenor, plectrum, parlor, and Spanish guitars, ukuleles, and mandolins, but is best remembered for his koa Hawaiian guitars that caught the popular wave of Hawaiian music. That music captivated America after being introduced to the masses at San Francisco's Panama Pacific

MODEL YEAR	FEATURES	EXC. COND. LOW	HIGH

International Exposition which was thrown in '15 to celebrate the opening of the Panama Canal and attended by more than 13 million people. He also made instruments for Kona and other brands. The majority of his instruments were most likely sold before the late 1920s. The Weissenborn brand has been revived on a line of reissue style guitars.

Spanish Acoustic

1920s. High-end Spanish set-up, rope binding, koa top, sides and back, limited production.

1920s		$1,900	$2,500

Style #1 Hawaiian

1920-1930s. Koa, no binding, 3 wood circle soundhole inlays.

1920s-30s		$2,700	$3,500

Style #2 Hawaiian

1920-1930s. Koa, black celluloid body binding, white wood 'board binding, rope soundhole binding.

1920s-30s		$2,900	$3,800

Style #2 Spanish

1920s. Spanish set-up, Style 2 features.

1920s		$2,100	$2,700

Style #3 Hawaiian

1920-1930s. Koa, rope binding on top, 'board, and soundhole.

1920s-30s		$3,800	$5,000

Style #4 Hawaiian

1920-1930s. Koa, rope binding on body, 'board, headstock and soundhole.

1920s-30s		$4,600	$6,000

Teardrop

Late 1920s-1930s. Teardrop/spoon shaped, Style 1 features.

1930s		$650	$850

Tenor

1920-1927		$875	$1,150

Welker Custom

Professional and premium grade, production/custom, archtop and flat-top guitars built by luthier Fred Welker in Nashville, Tennessee.

Welson

1960s-1970s. Models made by Quagliardi, an accordion maker in Italy, ranging from acoustics to solidbodies, thinlines, archtops and basses. Some acoustic Welsons were sold in the U.S. by Wurlitzer. By the '70s, they had jumped on the copy-guitar bandwagon.

Electric

1960s	Various models	$225	$675

Wendler

1999-present. Intermediate and professional grade, production/custom, solidbody, electro-acoustic guitars and basses from luthier Dave Wendler of Ozark Instrument Building in Branson, Missouri. He also builds amps. In '91, Wendler patented a pickup system that became the Taylor ES system.

MODEL YEAR	FEATURES	EXC. COND. LOW	HIGH

Westbury-Unicord

1978-ca. 1983. Imported from Japan by Unicord of Westbury, New York. High quality original designs, generally with 2 humbuckers, some with varitone and glued-in necks. They also had basses.

Westminster

One of the many guitar brands built by Japan's Matsumoku company.

Westone

1970s-1990, 1996-2001. Made by Matsumoku in Matsumoto, Japan and imported by St. Louis Music. Around '81, St. Louis Music purchased an interest in Matsumoku and began to make a transition from its own Electra brand to the Westone brand previously used by Matsumoku. In the beginning of '84, the brand became Electra-Westone with a phoenix bird head surrounded by circular wings and flames. By the end of '84 the Electra name was dropped, leaving only Westone and a squared-off bird with W-shaped wings logo. Electra, Electra-Westone and Westone instruments from this period are virtually identical except for the brand and logo treatment. Many of these guitars and basses were made in very limited runs and are relatively rare.

From '96 to '01, England's FCN Music offered Westone branded electric and acoustic guitars. The electrics were built in England and the acoustics came from Korea.Matsumoku-made guitars feature a serial number in which the first 1 or 2 digits represent the year of manufacture. Electra-Westone guitars should begin with either a 4 or 84.

Weymann

1864-1933. H.A. Weymann & Sons was a musical instrument distributor located in Philadelphia that marketed various stringed instruments, but mainly known for banjos. Some guitar models made by Regal and Vega, but they also built their own instruments.

Large Models (most with Brazilian)

1890-1928		$3,000	$4,500
1928-1932		$4,500	$6,500

Small Models/Standard (Brazilian)

1890-1928		$1,000	$2,000
1928-1932		$2,000	$3,000

Small Models/Standard (Mahogany)

1890-1928		$600	$1,300
1928-1932		$400	$600

Jimmie Rodgers Signature Edition

1929-1932		$6,000	$8,000

White Guitars and Woodley White Luthier

1992-present. Premium grade, custom, classical, acoustic and electric guitars, built by luthier Woodley White, first in Portland, Oregon and since 2008 in Naalehu, Hawaii.

1970s Westminster Archtop

W. H. Stephens

Weymann Style B

Bernunzio Uptown Music

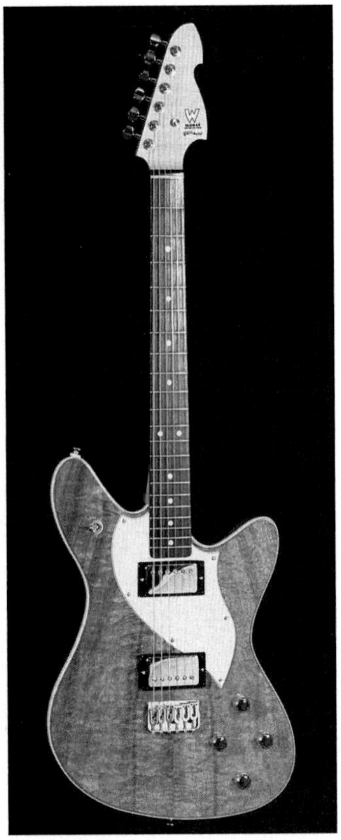

Widman Koa Gigmaster

1966 Wurlitzer Gemini

Tom Pfeifer

MODEL YEAR	FEATURES	EXC. COND. LOW	HIGH

Wicked

2004-present. Production/custom, intermediate and professional grade, semi-hollow and electric solidbody guitars and basses built by luthier Nicholas Dijkman in Montreal, Quebec.

Widman Custom Electrics

2008-present. Professional and premium grade, custom, electric guitars built in Arden, North Carolina by luthier John Widman.

Wilkanowski

Early-1930s-mid-1940s. W. Wilkanowski primarily built violins. He did make a few dozen guitars which were heavily influenced by violin design concepts and in fact look very similar to a large violin with a guitar neck.

Wilkat Guitars

1998-2013. Professional grade, custom, electric guitars and basses built by luthier Bill Wilkat in Montreal, Quebec. He retired in '13.

Wilkins

1984-present. Custom guitars built by luthier Pat Wilkins in Van Nuys, California. Wilkins also does finish work for individuals and a variety of other builders.

William C. Stahl

See listing under Stahl.

William Hall and Son

William Hall and Son was a New York City based distributor offering guitars built by other luthiers in the mid to late 1800s.

William Jeffrey Jones

2006-present. Luthier William Jeffrey Jones builds his ornately carved, professional and premium grade, production/custom, solidbody and semi-hollow electric guitars in Neosho, Missouri.

Wilson

1960s-1970s. One of the brand names of guitars built in the 1960s for others by Egmond in Holland. Also a brand name used by the U.K.'s Watkins WEM in the 1960s and '70s.

Wilson Brothers Guitars

2004-present. Intermediate and professional grade, production, imported electric and acoustic guitars and basses. Founded by Ventures guitarist Don Wilson. VCM and VSP models made in Japan; VM electrics in Korea; VM acoustic in China.

Windsor

Ca. 1890s-ca. 1914. Brand used by Montgomery Ward for flat-top guitars and mandolins made by various American manufacturers, including Lyon & Healy and, possibly, Harmony. Generally beginner-grade instruments.

MODEL YEAR	FEATURES	EXC. COND. LOW	HIGH

Winston

Ca. 1963-1967. Imported from Japan by Buegeleisen and Jacobson of New York. Manufacturers unknown, but some are by Guyatone. Generally shorter scale beginner guitars and basses.

Worland

1997-present. Luthier Jim Worland builds professional through presentation grade, production/custom, acoustic flat-top guitars and harp guitars in Rockford, Illinois. He also builds under the Worlatron brand.

Worlatron

2010-present. Professional grade, production/custom, hollowbody electric-acoustic guitars and basses built by luthier Jim Worland in Rockford, Illinois.

WRC Music International

1989-mid-1990s. Guitars by Wayne Richard Charvel, who was the original founder of Charvel Guitars. He now builds Wayne guitars with his son Michael.

Wright Guitar Technology

1993-present. Luthier Rossco Wright builds his unique intermediate and professional grade, production, travel/practice steel-string and nylon-string guitars in The Dalles, Oregon. Basses were added in 2009.

Wurlitzer

Wurlitzer had full-line music stores in several major cities and marketed a line of American-made guitars in the 1920s. They also offered American- and foreign-made guitars starting in '65. The American ones were built from '65-'66 by the Holman-Woodell guitar factory in Neodesha, Kansas. In '67, Wurlitzer switched to Italian-made Welson guitars.

00-18

1924		$4,300	$5,600

Model 2077 (Martin 0-K)

1920s. Made by Martin, size 0 with koa top, back and sides, limited production of about 28 instruments.

1920s	Natural	$3,300	$4,300

Model 2090 (Martin 0-28)

1920s. Made by Martin, size 0 with appointments similar to a Martin 0-28 of that era, limited production of about 11 instruments, Wurlitzer branded on the back of the headstock and on the inside back seam, Martin name also branded on inside seam.

1920s	Natural	$4,800	$6,200

Wild One Stereo

1960s. Two pickups, various colors.

1960s		$525	$675

Xaviere

Budget and intermediate grade, production, solid and semi-hollow body guitars from Guitar Fetish, which also has GFS pickups and effects.

Xotic Guitars

1996-present. Luthier Hiro Miura builds his professional grade, production/custom guitars and basses in San Fernando, California. The Xotic brand is also used on a line of guitar effects.

XOX Audio Tools

2007-present. U.S. debut in '08 of premium grade, production/custom, carbon fiber electric guitars built by luthier Peter Solomon in Europe.

Xtone

2003-2014. Semi-hollow body electric, acoustic and acoustic/electric guitars from ESP. Originally branded Xtone on headstock, in '10 the instruments were marketed as a model series under LTD (ESP's other brand) and stated as such on the headstock.

XXL Guitars

2003-present. Luthier Marc Lupien builds his production/custom, professional grade, chambered electric guitars in Montreal, Quebec.

Yamaha

1946-present. Budget, intermediate, professional, and presentation grade, production/custom, acoustic, acoustic/electric, and electric guitars. They also build basses, amps, and effects. The Japanese instrument maker was founded in 1887. Began classical guitar production around 1946. Solidbody electric production began in '66; steel string acoustics debut sometime after that. They began to export guitars into the U.S. in '69. Production shifted from Japan to Taiwan (Yamaha's special-built plant) in the '80s, though some high-end guitars still made in Japan. Some Korean production began in '90s.

Serialization patterns:

Serial numbers are coded as follows:

H = 1, I = 2, J = 3, etc., Z = 12

To use this pattern, you need to know the decade of production.

Serial numbers are ordered as follows:

Year/Month/Day/Factory Order

Example: NL 29159 represents a N=1987 year, L=5th month or May, 29=29th day (of May), 159=159th guitar made that day (the factory order). This guitar was the 159 guitar made on May 29, 1987.

MODEL YEAR	FEATURES	EXC. COND. LOW	HIGH
AE Series			
1966-2011. Archtop models.			
1966-2011	Higher-end	$700	$1,000
1966-2011	Lower-end	$150	$450
1966-2011	Mid-level	$450	$700
AES Series			
1990-2011. Semi-hollowbody models.			
1990-2011	Higher-end	$700	$1,000
1990-2011	Lower-end	$150	$450
1990-2011	Mid-level	$450	$700
AEX-1500			
1995-2011. Full-body archtop electric, set neck, humbucker and piezo, EQ, multi-bound.			
1995-2011		$700	$1,000
APX Series			
1987-present. Acoustic/electric, various features.			
1987-2020	Higher-end	$700	$1,000
1987-2020	Lower-end	$150	$450
1987-2020	Mid-level	$450	$700
CG Series			
1984-present. Classical models.			
1984-2020	Higher-end	$250	$400
1984-2020	Lower-end	$50	$150
1984-2020	Mid-level	$150	$250
DW Series			
1999-2002. Dreadnought flat-top models, sunburst, solid spruce top, higher-end appointments like abalone rosette and top purfling.			
1999-2002	Higher-end	$250	$400
1999-2002	Lower-end	$50	$150
1999-2002	Mid-level	$150	$250
EG Series			
2000-2009. Electric solidbody models.			
2000-2009		$50	$250
Eterna Series			
1983-1994. Folk-style acoustics, there were 4 models.			
1983-1994		$50	$175
FG Series			
1970s-present. Economy market flat-top models, laminated sides and back, a 12 suffix indicates 12-string, CE indicates on-board electronics, many models are D-style bodies.			
1970-2020	Higher-end	$400	$800
1970-2020	Highest-end	$800	$1,200
1970-2020	Lower-end	$60	$175
1970-2020	Mid-level	$175	$400
G Series			
1981-2000. Various Classical models.			
1981-2000		$100	$850
GC Series			
1982-present. Classical models, '70s made in Japan, '80s made in Taiwan.			
1960s-2020	Higher-end	$850	$1,500
1960s-2020	Lower-end	$150	$475
1960s-2020	Mid-level	$475	$850
Image Custom			
1988-1992. Electric double-cut, Brazilian rosewood 'board, maple top, 2 humbuckers, active circuitry, LED position markers, script Image logo on truss rod cover. The Image was called the MSG in the U.K.			
1988-1992		$700	$1,500
L Series			
1984-present. Custom hand-built flat-top models, solid wood.			
1984-2020	Higher-end	$700	$1,500
1984-2020	Lower-end	$400	$550
1984-2020	Mid-level	$450	$700
PAC Pacifica Series			
1989-present. Offset double-cut with longer horns, dot markers, large script Pacifica logo and small block Yamaha logo on headstock, various models.			
1989-2020		$100	$500

XOX Audio Tools Handle

Rasta Poupajami

2000 Yamaha AES-1500

GUITARS

1969 Yamaha SA-30T

Rhoads Music

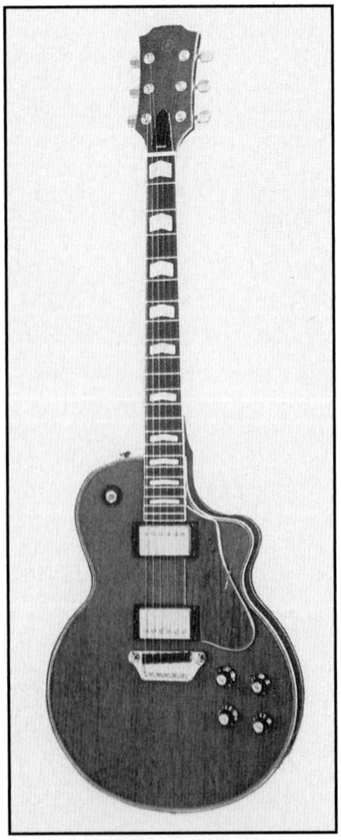

1973 Yamaha SG-85

MODEL YEAR	FEATURES	EXC. COND. LOW	HIGH

RGX Series

1988-2011. Bolt-on neck for the 600 series and neck-thru body designs for 1200 series, various models include 110 (1 hum), 211 (hum-single), 220 (2 hums), 312 (hum-single-single), 603 (3 singles), 612 (hum-single-single), 620 (2 hums), 1203S (3 singles), 1212S (hum-single-single), 1220S (2 hums).

1988-2011	Higher-end	$250	$500
1988-2011	Lower-end	$50	$150
1988-2011	Mid-level	$150	$250

RGZ Series

1989-1994. Double-cut solidbodies, various pickups.

1989-1994	Higher-end	$250	$500
1989-1994	Lower-end	$50	$150
1989-1994	Mid-level	$150	$250

SA Series

1966-1994. Super Axe series, full-size and thinline archtop models.

1966-1994	Higher-end	$900	$1,200
1966-1994	Highest-end	$1,200	$1,600
1966-1994	Lower-end	$400	$600
1966-1994	Mid-level	$600	$900

SBG Series

1983-1992. Solidbody models, set necks, model name logo on truss rod cover.

1983-1992	Higher-end	$1,000	$1,300
1983-1992	Highest-end	$1,300	$1,900
1983-1992	Lower-end	$300	$600
1983-1992	Mid-level	$600	$1,000

SE Series

1986-1992. Solidbody electric models.

1986-1992	Higher-end	$350	$500
1986-1992	Lower-end	$150	$200
1986-1992	Mid-level	$200	$350

SF Series

1977-early 1980s. Super Flighter series, double-cut solidbody electrics, 2 humbuckers.

1977-80s	Various models	$575	$750

SG-3

1965-1966. Early double-cut solidbody with sharp horns, bolt neck, 3 hum-single pickup layout, large white guard, rotor controls, tremolo.

1965-1966		$775	$1,025

SG-5/SG-5A

1966-1971. Asymmetrical double-cut solidbody with extended lower horn, bolt neck, 2 pickups, chrome hardware.

1966-1971		$1,025	$1,350

SG-7/SG-7A

1966-1971. Like SG-5, but with gold hardware.

1966-1971		$1,900	$2,500
1993-1996	7A	$1,400	$1,800

SG-7A 20th Anniversary

1986		$1,800	$2,300

SG-20

1972-1973. Bolt-on neck, slab body, single-cut, 1 pickup.

1972-1973		$375	$475

SG-30/SG-30A

1973-1976. Slab katsura wood (30) or slab maple (30A) solidbody, bolt-on neck, 2 humbuckers, dot inlays.

1973-1976		$375	$500

SG-35/SG-35A

1973-1976. Slab mahogany (35) or slab maple (35A) solidbody, bolt-on neck, 2 humbuckers, parallelogram inlays.

1973-1976		$425	$550

SG-40

1972-1973. Bolt-on neck, carved body, single-cut.

1972-1973		$425	$550

SG-45

1972-1976. Glued neck, single-cut, bound flat-top.

1972-1976		$450	$600

SG-50

1974-1976. Slab katsura wood solidbody, glued neck, 2 humbuckers, dot inlays, large 'guard.

1974-1976		$450	$600

SG-60

1972 only. Bolt-on neck, carved body, single-cut.

1972		$450	$600

SG-60T

1973 only. SG-60 with large cast vibrato system.

1973		$450	$600

SG-65

1972-1976. Glued neck, single-cut, bound flat-top.

1972-1976		$550	$725

SG-70

1974-1976. Slab maple solidbody, glued neck, 2 humbuckers, dot inlays, large 'guard.

1974-1976		$550	$725

SG-80

1972 only. Bolt-on neck, carved body, single-cut.

1972		$450	$600

SG-80T

1973. SG-60 with large cast vibrato system.

1973		$500	$650

SG-85

1972-1976. Glued neck, single-cut, bound flat-top.

1972-1976		$550	$725

SG-90

1974-1976. Carved top mahogany solidbody, glued neck, elevated 'guard, bound top, dot inlays, chrome hardware.

1974-1976		$675	$875

SG-175

1974-1976. Carved top mahogany solidbody, glued neck, elevated 'guard, abalone bound top, abalone split wing or pyramid inlays, gold hardware.

1974-1976		$775	$1,000

SG-500

1976-1978. Carved unbound maple top, double pointed cutaways, glued neck, 2 exposed humbuckers, 3-ply bound headstock, bound neck with clay split wing inlays, chrome hardware. Reissued as the SBG-500 (800S in Japan) in '81.

1976-1978		$475	$625

SG-700

1976-1978. Carved unbound maple top, double pointed cutaways, glued neck, 2 humbuckers, 3-ply bound headstock, bound neck with clay split wing inlays, chrome hardware.

1976-1978		$650	$850

MODEL YEAR	FEATURES	EXC. COND. LOW	HIGH

SG-700S

1999-2001. Set neck, mahogany body, 2 humbuckers with coil tap.

1999-2001		$650	$850

SG-800S

1981-1984. Eastern mahogany with maple top, set neck, 2 pickups, blue, tobacco burst or cherry sunburst.

1981-1984		$650	$850

SG-1000/SBG-1000

1976-1983 ('84 in Japan), 2007-2013. Carved maple top, double pointed cutaways, glued neck, 2 humbuckers, 3-ply bound headstock, unbound body, bound neck with clay split wing inlays, gold hardware. Export model name changed to SBG-1000 in '80. SBG-1000 reissued in '07.

1976-1979	SG-1000	$900	$1,200
1980-1983	SBG-1000	$900	$1,200

SG-1500

1976-1979. Carved maple top, double pointed cutaways, laminated neck-thru-body neck, laminated mahogany body wings, 2 humbuckers, 5-ply bound headstock and body, bound neck with dot inlays, chrome hardware. Name used on Japan-only model in the '80s.

1976-1979		$725	$950

SG-2000/SG-2000S

1976-1980 (1988 in Japan). Maple top, double pointed cutaways, neck-thru-body, mahogany body wings, 2 humbuckers, 5-ply bound headstock and body, bound neck with abalone split wing inlays, gold hardware. In '80, the model was changed to the SBG-2000 in the U.S., and the SG-2000S everywhere else except Japan (where it remained the SG-2000). Export model renamed SBG-2100 in '84.

1976-1980		$900	$1,300

SG-2100S

1983. Similar to SG-2000 with upgrades such as the pickups.

1983		$1,150	$1,500

SG-3000/SBG-3000/Custom Professional

1982-1992. SG-2000 upgrade with higher output pickups and abalone purfling on top.

1982-1992		$1,500	$2,000

SGV-300

2000-2006. 1960s SG model features.

2000-2006		$400	$525

SHB-400

1981-1985. Solidbody electric, set-in neck, 2 pickups.

1981-1985		$400	$525

SJ-180

1983-1994. Student Jumbo, entry level Folk Series model, laminated top.

1983-1994		$125	$200

SJ-400S

1983-1994. Student Jumbo Folk Series model, solid wood top.

1983-1994		$225	$300

SL Studio Lord Series

1977-1981. LP-style copy models.

1977-1981		$400	$525

MODEL YEAR	FEATURES	EXC. COND. LOW	HIGH

SR Super Rock'n Roller Series

1977-1981. Strat copy models.

1977-1981		$375	$475

SSC Series

1983-1992. Solidbody electric models.

1983-1992	SSC-400/SC-400	$325	$425
1983-1992	SSC-500	$300	$400
1983-1992	SSC-600/SC-600	$425	$550

Weddington Classic

1989-1992. Electric solidbody, redesigned set-in neck/body joint for increased access to the higher frets.

1989-1992		$575	$775

Yanuziello Stringed Instruments

1980-present. Production/custom resonator and Hawaiian guitars built by luthier Joseph Yanuziello, in Toronto, Ontario.

Yosco

1900-1930s. Lawrence L. Yosco was a New York City luthier building guitars, round back mandolins and banjos under his own brand and for others.

Zachary

1996-present. Luthier Alex Csiky builds his professional grade, production, solidbody electric guitars and basses in Windsor, Ontario.

Zanini

2007-2020. Premium grade, production, electric guitars designed by Luca Zanini of Italy and built in the U.S.

Zaukus Guitars

2011-present. Luthier Joseph Zaukus builds his premium grade, production/custom, solidbody electric guitars in Antioch, Tennessee.

Zeiler Guitars

1992-present. Custom flat-top, 12-string, and nylon-string guitars built by luthier Jamonn Zeiler in Aurora, Indiana.

Zemaitis

1960-1999, 2004-present. Professional, premium, and presentation grade, custom/production, electric and acoustic guitars. Tony Zemaitis (born Antanus Casimere Zemaitis) began selling his guitars in 1960. He emphasized simple light-weight construction and was known for hand engraved metal front guitars. The metal front designs were originally engineered to reduce hum, but they became popular as functional art. Each hand-built guitar and bass was a unique instrument. Ron Wood was an early customer and his use of a Zemaitis created a demand for the custom-built guitars. Approximately 6 to 10 instruments were built each year. Tony retired in '99, and passed away in '02 at the age of 67. In '04, Japan's Kanda Shokai Corporation, with the endorsement of Tony Zemaitis, Jr.,

Yamaha SBG-3000

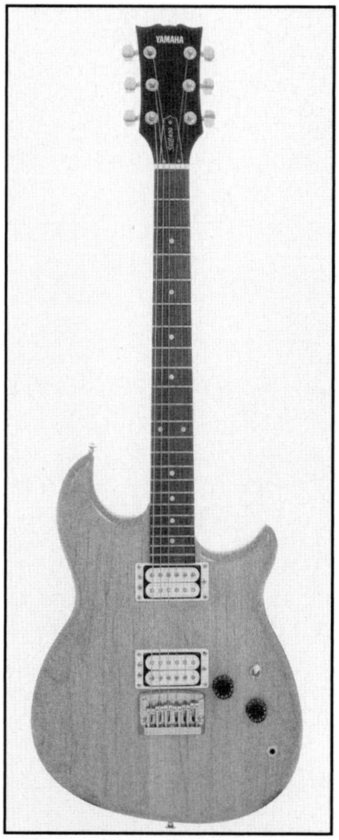

1983 Yamaha SHB-400

Imaged by Heritage Auctions, HA.com

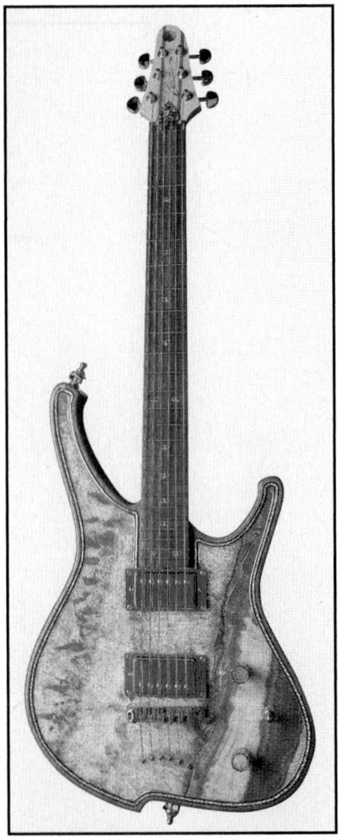

Zerberus Nemesis Stone-Top

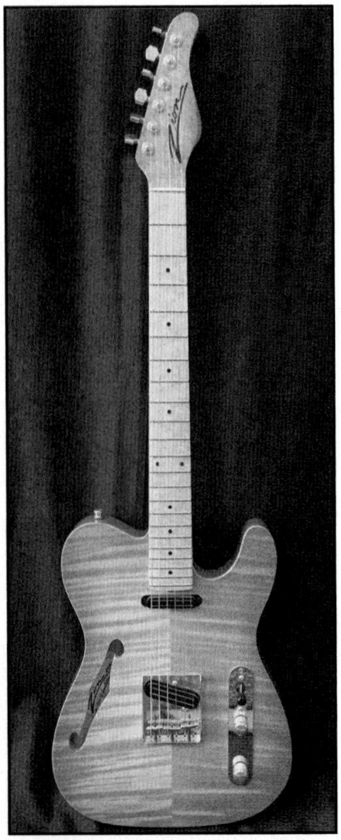

1996 Zion Ninety

Vic Hines

MODEL YEAR	FEATURES	EXC. COND. LOW	HIGH

started building the guitars again. KSC builds the higher priced ones and licenses the lower priced guitars to Greco.

Celebrity association with Zemaitis is not uncommon. Validated celebrity provenance may add 25% to 100% (or more) to a guitar's value. Tony Zemaitis also made so-called student model instruments for customers with average incomes. These had wood tops instead of metal or pearl. Some wood top instruments have been converted to non-Zemaitis metal tops, which are therefore not fully original Zemaitis instruments.

Acoustic instruments are valued more as collectibles and less so for their acoustic sound. Originality and verifiable, documented provenance is required in the Zemaitis market as fake instruments can be a problem.

Zen-On

1946-ca.1968. Japanese manufacturer. By '67 using the Morales brand name. Not heavily imported into the U.S., if at all (see Morales).

Acoustic Hollowbody

1946-1968. Various models.

1950s		$180	$250

Electric Solidbody

1960s. Teisco-era and styling.

1960s		$175	$450

Zerberus

2002-present. Professional and premium grade, production/custom, electric guitars built in Speyer, Germany by luthier Frank Scheucher.

Zeta

1982-2010. Zeta made solid, semi-hollow and resonator guitars, many with electronic and MIDI options, and mandolins in Oakland, California over the years, but mainly offered upright basses, amps and violins.

Ziegenfuss Guitars

2006-present. Luthier Stephen Ziegenfuss builds his professional and premium grade, custom, acoustic and solidbody electric guitars and basses in Jackson, Michigan.

MODEL YEAR	FEATURES	EXC. COND. LOW	HIGH

Zim-Gar

1960s. Imported from Japan by Gar-Zim Musical Instrument Corporation of Brooklyn, New York. Manufacturers unknown. Generally shorter scale beginner guitars.

Electric Solidbody

1960s		$175	$450

Zimnicki, Gary

1980-present. Luthier Gary Zimnicki builds his professional and premium grade, custom, flat-top, 12-string, nylon-string, and archtop guitars in Allen Park, Michigan.

Zion

1980-present. Professional and premium grade, production/custom, semi-hollow and solidbody guitars built by luthier Ken Hoover, originally in Greensboro, North Carolina, currently in Raleigh.

Zolla

Professional grade, production/custom, electric guitars and basses built by luthier Bill Zolla in San Diego, California starting in 1979.

Zon

1981-present. Currently luthier Joe Zon only offers basses, but he also built guitars from '85-'91. See Bass Section for more company info.

Zuni

1993-present. Premium grade, custom, solidbody electric guitars built by luthier Michael Blank in Alto Pass, Illinois and Amasa, Michigan.

ZZ Ryder

Solidbody electric guitars and basses from Stenzler Musical Instruments of Ft. Worth, Texas.

BASSES

1970 Gibson Les Paul Bass: Jim Mathis.

1962 Airline Pocket Bass
Robbie Keene

Alembic Stanley Clarke Signature Standard Bass
Bob Moreland

A Basses

1976-2002. Luthier Albey Balgochian built his professional grade, solidbody basses in Waltham, Massachusetts. Sports the A logo on headstock.

Solidbody Bass

Model Year	Features	Exc. Cond. Low	Exc. Cond. High
1976-2002		$1,000	$1,300

Acoustic

Ca. 1965-ca. 1987, 2001-2005, 2008-present. Mainly known for solidstate amps, the Acoustic Control Corp. of Los Angeles, did offer guitars and basses from around '69 to late '74. The brand was revived in '01 by Samick for a line of amps.

Black Widow Bass

1969-1970, 1972-1974. The AC600 Black Widow Bass (fretted and fretless) featured a black double-cut body, German carve, Ebonite 'board, 2 pickups, and a protective "spider design" pad on back. The AC650 is short-scale. The '72-'74 version had a rosewood 'board and only 1 pickup. Acoustic outsourced the production of the basses, possibly to Japan, but at least part of the final production was by Semie Moseley.

Model Year	Features	Exc. Cond. Low	Exc. Cond. High
1969-1970		$1,175	$1,550
1972-1974		$1,000	$1,325

Airline

1958-1968, 2004-present. Brand for Montgomery Ward. Built by Kay, Harmony and Valco. In '04, the brand was revived on a line of reissues from Eastwood guitars.

Electric Solidbody Bass

Model Year	Features	Exc. Cond. Low	Exc. Cond. High
1958-1968	Various models	$425	$600

Pocket 3/4 Bass (Valco/National)

1962-1968. Airline brand of double-cut Pocket Bass, short-scale, 2 pickups, 1 acoustic bridge and 1 neck humbucker, sunburst and other colors.

Model Year	Features	Exc. Cond. Low	Exc. Cond. High
1962-1968		$550	$725

Alamo

1947-1982. Founded by Charles Eilenberg, Milton Fink, and Southern Music, San Antonio, Texas. Distributed by Bruno & Sons.

Eldorado Bass (Model 2600)

1965-1966. Solidbody, 1 pickup, angular offset shape, double-cut.

Model Year	Features	Exc. Cond. Low	Exc. Cond. High
1965-1966		$350	$450

Titan Bass

1963-1970. Hollowbody, 1 pickup, angular offset shape.

Model Year	Features	Exc. Cond. Low	Exc. Cond. High
1963-1970		$350	$450

Alembic

1969-present. Professional, premium, and presentation grade, production/custom, 4-, 5-, and 6- string basses built in Santa Rosa, California. They also build guitars. Established in San Francisco as one of the first handmade bass builders. Alembic basses come with many options concerning woods (examples are maple, bubinga, walnut, vermilion, wenge, zebrawood), finishes, inlays, etc., all of which affect the values listed here. These dollar amounts should be used as a baseline guide to values for Alembic.

Anniversary Bass

1989. 20th Anniversary limited edition, walnut and vermillion with a walnut core, 5-piece body, 5-piece neck-thru, only 200 built.

Model Year	Features	Exc. Cond. Low	Exc. Cond. High
1989		$2,100	$2,800

Custom Shop Built Bass

1969-present. Various one-off and/or custom built instruments. Each instrument should be evaluated individually. Prices are somewhat speculative due to the one-off custom characteristics and values can vary greatly.

Model Year	Features	Exc. Cond. Low	Exc. Cond. High
1978	Dragon Doubleneck	$7,400	$9,800
2004	Dragon 4-string, 4 made	$3,700	$4,900

Distillate Bass

1981-1991. One of Alembic's early lower-cost models, early ones with 1 pickup, 2 pickups by '82, exotic woods, active electronics.

Model Year	Features	Exc. Cond. Low	Exc. Cond. High
1981-1991	Distillate 4	$2,000	$2,600
1981-1991	Distillate 5	$2,100	$2,700

Elan Bass

1985-1996. Available in 4-, 5-, 6- and 8-string models, 3-piece thru-body laminated maple neck, solid maple body, active electronics, solid brass hardware, offered in a variety of hardwood tops and custom finishes.

Model Year	Features	Exc. Cond. Low	Exc. Cond. High
1985-1996	Elan 4	$1,800	$2,400
1985-1996	Elan 5	$1,850	$2,450
1985-1996	Elan 6	$1,950	$2,550

Epic Bass

1993-2015. Mahogany body with various tops, extra large pointed bass horn, maple/walnut veneer set-neck, available in 4-, 5-, and 6-string versions.

Model Year	Features	Exc. Cond. Low	Exc. Cond. High
1993-2015	4-string	$1,750	$2,350
1993-2015	5-string	$1,800	$2,400
1993-2015	6-string	$1,850	$2,450

Essence Bass

1991-present. Mahogany body with various tops, extra large pointed bass horn, walnut/maple laminate neck-thru.

Model Year	Features	Exc. Cond. Low	Exc. Cond. High
1991-2020	Essence 4	$1,800	$2,400
1991-2020	Essence 5	$1,850	$2,450
1991-2020	Essence 6	$2,000	$2,600

Europa Bass

1992-present. Mahogany body with various tops, ebony 'board, available as 4-, 5-, and 6-string.

Model Year	Features	Exc. Cond. Low	Exc. Cond. High
1992-2020		$2,300	$3,050

Excel Bass

1999-present. Solidbody 5-string, set neck, several wood options.

Model Year	Features	Exc. Cond. Low	Exc. Cond. High
2000s		$2,300	$3,050

Exploiter Bass

1980s. Figured maple solidbody 4-string, neck-thru, transparent finish.

Model Year	Features	Exc. Cond. Low	Exc. Cond. High
1984-1988		$2,300	$3,050

Mark King Signature Bass

1989-2019. Standard or Deluxe models.

Model Year	Features	Exc. Cond. Low	Exc. Cond. High
1989-2008		$4,500	$6,000

Orion Bass

1996-present. Offset double cut solidbody, various figured-wood top, 4, 5, or 6 strings.

Model Year	Features	Exc. Cond. Low	Exc. Cond. High
1996-2020		$1,850	$2,400

MODEL YEAR	FEATURES	EXC. COND. LOW	HIGH

Persuader Bass

1983-1991. Offset double-cut solidbody, 4-string, neck-thru.

1983-1991		$1,850	$2,400

Rogue Bass

1996-present. Double-cut solidbody, extreme long pointed bass horn..

1996-2020		$2,000	$2,600

Series I Bass

1971-present. Mahogany body with various tops, maple/purpleheart laminate neck-thru, active electronics, available in 3 scale lengths and with 4, 5 or 6 strings.

1971-1979	All scales	$4,200	$5,500
1980-1989	All scales	$3,800	$5,000
1990-2020	All scales, highly figured	$3,800	$5,000

Series II Bass

1971-present. Generally custom-made option, each instrument valued on a case-by-case basis, guidance pricing only.

1971-1979		$4,300	$5,700
1980-2020		$4,000	$5,200

Spoiler Bass

1981-1999. Solid mahogany body, maple neck-thru, 4, 5 or 6 strings, active electronics, various high-end wood options.

1981-1986	6-string	$2,000	$2,600
1981-1989	5-string	$1,900	$2,500
1981-1999	4-string	$1,800	$2,400

Stanley Clarke Signature Standard Bass

1990-present. Neck-thru-body, active electronics, 24-fret ebony 'board, mahogany body with maple, bubinga, walnut, vermilion, or zebrawood top, 4-, 5-, and 6-string versions.

1990-2020	All scales	$4,300	$5,700

Alleva-Coppolo Basses and Guitars

1995-present. Professional and premium grade, custom/production, solidbody electric basses and guitars built by luthier Jimmy Coppolo in Dallas, Texas for '95-'97, in New York City for '98-2008, and since in Upland, California.

Solidbody Bass

1995-present. Various solidbody 4- and 5-string, various options and materials.

1995-2020		$3,000	$5,000

Alvarez

1965-present. Imported by St. Louis Music, they offered electric basses from '90 to '02 and acoustic basses in the mid-'90s.

American Showster

1986-2004, 2010-2011. Established by Bill Meeker and David Haines, Bayville, New Jersey. They also made guitars.

AS-57-B Bass

1987-1997. Bass version of AS-57 with body styled like a '57 Chevy tail fin.

1987-1997		$3,300	$4,300

MODEL YEAR	FEATURES	EXC. COND. LOW	HIGH

Ampeg

1949-present. Ampeg was founded on a vision of an amplified bass peg, which evolved into the Baby Bass. Ampeg has sold basses on and off throughout its history. In '08 they got back into basses with the reissue of the Dan Armstrong Plexi Bass.

AEB-1 Bass

1966-1967. F-holes through the body, fretted, scroll headstock, pickup in body, sunburst. Reissued as the AEB-2 for '97-'99.

1966-1967		$2,900	$3,800

ASB-1 Devil Bass

1966-1967. Long-horn body, fretted or fretless, triangular f-holes through the body, fireburst.

1966-1967		$4,800	$6,300

AUB-1 Bass

1966-1967. Same as AEB-1, but fretless, sunburst. Reissued as the AUB-2 for '97-'99.

1966-1967		$3,000	$4,000

AUSB-1 Devil Bass

1966-1967. Same as ASB-1 Devil Bass, but fretless.

1966-1967		$4,800	$6,300

BB-4 Baby Bass (4-string)

1962-1971. Electric upright slim-looking bass that is smaller than a cello, 4-string, available in sunburst, white, red, black, and a few turquoise. Reissued as the ABB-1 Baby Bass for '97-'99.

1962-1971	Solid color	$2,100	$2,700
1962-1971	Sunburst	$1,750	$2,250

BB-5 Baby Bass (5-string)

1964-1971. Five-string version.

1964-1971	Solid color	$2,200	$2,900
1964-1971	Sunburst	$1,900	$2,450

Dan Armstrong Lucite Bass

1969-1971. Clear solid lucite body, did not have switchable pickups like the Lucite guitar.

1969-1971	Clear	$1,750	$2,300
1969-1971	Smoke	$2,250	$2,900

Dan Armstrong Lucite Reissue/ADA4 Bass

1998-2001, 2008-2009. Lucite body, Dan Armstrong Ampeg block lettering on 'guard. Reissue in '08 as the ADA4.

1998-2001		$625	$825
2008-2009	Reintroduced	$625	$825

EB-1 Wild Dog Bass

1963-1964. Made by Burns of London, along with the Wild Dog Guitar, offset double cut solidbody, 3 pickups

1963-1964		$525	$675

GEB-101 Little Stud Bass

1973-1975. Import from Japan, offset double-cut solidbody, two-on-a-side tuners, 1 pickup.

1973-1975		$350	$450

GEB-750 Big Stud Bass

1973-1975. Import from Japan, similar to Little Stud, but with 2 pickups.

1973-1975		$350	$450

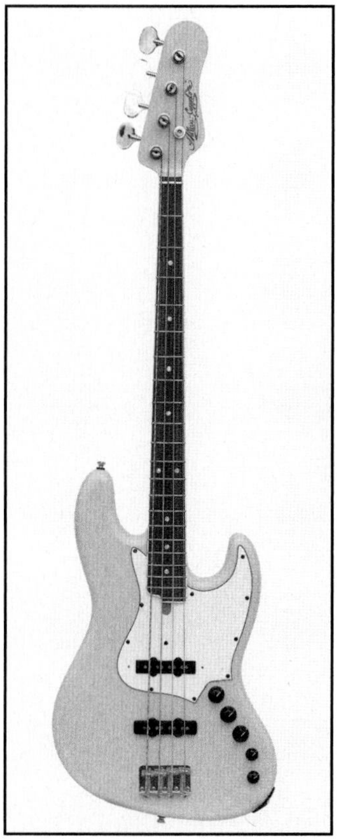

Alleva-Coppolo

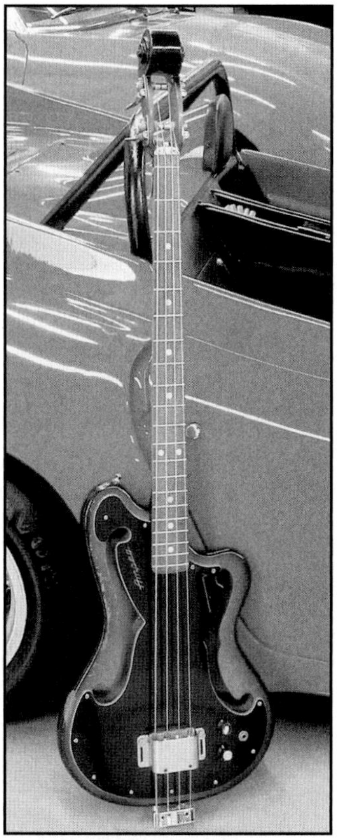

1968 Ampeg AEB-1

Craig Brody

BASSES

1981 B.C. Rich Mockingbird
Imaged by Heritage Auctions, HA.com

B.C. Rich ST-III
Ken Kraynak

MODEL YEAR	FEATURES	EXC. COND. LOW	HIGH

Andreas

1995-2004. Aluminium-necked, solidbody guitars and basses built by luthier Andreas Pichler in Dollach, Austria.

Angelica

1967-1975. Student and entry-level basses and guitars imported from Japan.

Electric Solidbody Bass

1970s. Japanese imports.

1970s	Various models	$150	$300

Apollo

Ca. 1967-1972. Entry-level basses imported from Japan by St. Louis Music. They also had guitars and effects.

Electric Hollowbody Bass

1967-1972. Japanese imports.

1967-1972		$425	$575

Arbor

1983-ca. 2013. Budget grade, production, solidbody basses imported by Musicorp (MBT). They also offered guitars.

Electric Bass

1983-2013	Various models	$175	$300

Aria/Aria Pro II

1956-present. Budget and intermediate grade, production, acoustic, acoustic/electric, solidbody, hollowbody and upright basses. They also make guitars, mandolins, and banjos. Originally branded as Aria; renamed Aria Pro II in '75; both names used over the next several year; in '01, the Pro II part of the name was dropped altogether.

Electric Bass

1980s	Various models	$300	$550

Austin Hatchet

Mid-1970s-mid-1980s. Trademark of distributor Targ and Dinner, Chicago, Illinois.

Hatchet Bass

1981	Travel bass	$375	$500

B.C. Rich

1966-present. Budget, intermediate, and premium grade, production/custom, import and U.S.-made basses. They also offer guitars. Many B.C. Rich models came in a variety of colors. For example, in '88 they offered black, Competition Red, metallic red, GlitteRock White, Ultra Violet, and Thunder Blue. Also in '88, other custom colors, graphic features, paint-to-match headstocks, and special inlays were offered.

Bich Bass

1978-1998. Solidbody, neck-thru, 2 pickups.

1978-1979	USA	$1,850	$2,400
1980-1985		$1,150	$1,500
1986-1989		$800	$1,025
1989-1993	Class Axe era	$800	$1,025
1994-1998	2nd Rico-era	$800	$1,025

MODEL YEAR	FEATURES	EXC. COND. LOW	HIGH

Bich Supreme 8-String Bass

Late-1970s-early-1980s.

1978-1982	Painted wood	$3,000	$4,000
1978-1982	Translucent wood	$3,500	$4,500

Eagle Bass (U.S.A. Assembly)

1977-1996. Curved double-cut, solidbody, natural.

1977-1979	Translucent wood	$1,850	$2,400
1977-1996	Painted wood	$1,600	$2,100
1980-1996	Translucent wood	$1,750	$2,300

Gunslinger Bass

1987-1999. Inverted headstock, 1 humbucker.

1987-1989		$550	$750
1989-1993	Class Axe era	$550	$750
1994-1999		$476	$650

Ironbird Bass

1984-1998. Kind of star-shaped, neck-thru, solidbody, 2 pickups, active electronics, diamond inlays.

1984-1989		$850	$1,125
1989-1993	Class Axe era	$775	$1,025
1994-1998	2nd Rico era	$700	$950

Mockingbird Bass

1976-2009. US-made, short horn until '78, long horn after.

1976	Painted	$1,750	$2,300
1976	Translucent	$1,850	$2,400
1977-1978	Painted	$1,600	$2,100
1977-1978	Translucent	$1,750	$2,300
1979-1983	Painted	$1,750	$2,300
1979-1983	Translucent	$1,750	$2,300
1984-1985	End 1st Rico-era	$1,600	$2,100
1986-1989	End 1st Rico era	$1,150	$1,500
1994-2009	New Rico-era	$1,150	$1,500

Mockingbird Heritage Classic Bass

2007-2015. 4-string, neck-thru, quilted maple top, cloud inlay.

2007-2015		$225	$300

Nighthawk Bass

1979-ca.1980. Bolt-neck.

1978-1982		$550	$725

NJ Series Bass

1983-2006. Various mid-level import models include Beast, Eagle, Innovator, Mockingbird, Virgin and Warlock. Replaced by NT Series.

1983-1984	Early, Japan	$250	$450
1985-1986	Japan	$175	$350
1987-2006		$100	$250

Platinum Series Bass

1986-2006. Lower-priced import versions including Eagle, Mockingbird, Beast, Warlock.

1986-1999		$100	$200

Seagull Bass

1973-1975. Solidbody, single cut, changed to Seagull II in '76.

1973		$2,400	$3,200
1974-1975		$2,100	$2,800

Seagull II Bass

1976-1977. Double-cut version.

1976-1977		$1,800	$2,400

MODEL YEAR	FEATURES	EXC. COND. LOW	HIGH

ST-III Bass

1987-1998. Bolt or set neck, black hardware, P-Bass/J-Bass pickup configuration, ebony 'board.

1987-1989	Bolt-on	$500	$650
1987-1989	Neck-thru	$550	$700
1989-1993	Class Axe-era	$500	$650
1994-1998	New Rico-era	$500	$650

Warlock Bass (U.S.A.)

1981-2015. Bolt neck, maple body, rosewood 'board, Badass II low profile bridge by '88.

1981-1985		$975	$1,300
1986-1989		$900	$1,200

Wave Bass

Early 1980s. Double-cut, cresting wave, neck-thru, solid body, 2 pickups, active electronics.

1983		$1,950	$2,600

B.C. Rico

1978-1982. B.C. Rich's first Japan-made guitars and basses were labeled B.C. Rico.

Eagle Bass

1978-1982	Japan	$1,600	$2,000

Baldwin

1965-1970. The giant organ company got into guitars and basses in '65 when it bought Burns Guitars of England and sold those models in the U.S. under the Baldwin name.

Baby Bison Bass

1965-1970. Scroll head, 2 pickups, black, red or white finishes.

1965-1966		$775	$1,025
1966-1970	Model 560	$675	$875

Bison Bass

1965-1970. Scroll headstock, 3 pickups, black or white finishes.

1965-1966		$850	$1,100
1966-1970	Model 516	$750	$975

G.B. 66 Bass

1965-1966. Bass equivalent of G.B. 66 guitar, covered bridge tailpiece.

1965-1966		$600	$775

Jazz Split Sound Bass

1965-1970. Offset double-cut solidbody, 2 pickups, red sunburst.

1965-1966	Long-scale	$775	$1,025
1966-1970	Short-scale	$675	$875

Nu-Sonic Bass

1965-1966. Bass version of Nu-Sonic.

1965-1966		$600	$775

Shadows/Shadows Signature Bass

1965-1970. Named after Hank Marvin's backup band, solidbody, 3 slanted pickups, white finish.

1965-1966	Shadows	$1,225	$1,575
1966-1970	Shadows Signature	$1,150	$1,475

Vibraslim Bass

1965-1970. Thin body, scroll head, 2 pickups, sunburst.

1965-1966		$700	$950
1966-1970	Model 549	$625	$850

Barclay

1960s. Generally shorter-scale, student-level imports from Japan. They also made guitars.

Bass Collection

1985-1992. Mid-level imports from Japan, distributed by Meisel Music of Springfield, New Jersey. Sam Ash Music, New York, sold the remaining inventory from '92 to '94.

Black Jack

1960s. Entry-level and mid-level imports from Japan. They also offered guitars.

Bradford

1960s. House brand of W.T. Grant department store, often imported. They also offered guitars.

Brian Moore

1992-present. Brian Moore added basses in '97. Currently they offer professional grade, production, solidbody basses. They also build guitars and mandolins.

i2000 Bass Series

2000-present. Offset double-cut solidbody with extended bass horn, 2 pickups, 4- (i4) or 5-string (i5), options include piezo (p), fretless (-f), Bartolini pickups (B), and 13-pin mid (.13).

2000-2020		$625	$825

Brice

1985-present. Budget grade, production, electric and acoustic basses imported by Rondo Music of Union, New Jersey.

BSX Bass

1990-present. Luthier Dino Fiumara builds his professional and premium grade, production/custom, acoustic, solidbody, semi-solid upright basses in Aliquippa, Pennsylvania.

Burns

1960-1970, 1974-1983, 1992-present. Intermediate and professional grade, production, basses built in England and Korea. They also build guitars.

Baby Bison Bass

1965-1968. Early version had "V" headstock and long Rez-O-Tube vibrato. Later short Rezo-Tube tailpiece.

1965-1968		$600	$800

Nu-Sonic Bass

1964-1965, 2011-2020. Offset double-cut solidbody, 2 pickups.

1964-1965		$750	$1,000

Scorpion Bass

Introduced 1979, 2003-2009. Double-cut scorpion-like solidbody.

2003-2009		$300	$400

1965 Baldwin Vibraslim

Guillermo Albino

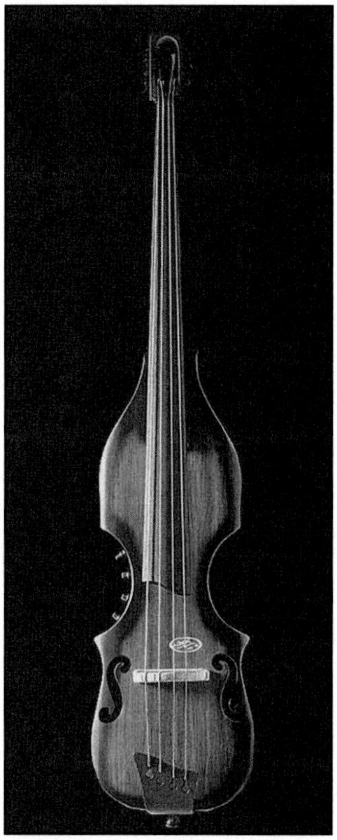

BSX Bass

BASSES

1981 Charvel Pre-Pro Bass

Craig Brody

1965 Custom Kraft Bone Buzzer

Rivington Guitars

MODEL YEAR	FEATURES	EXC. COND. LOW	HIGH

Cameo

1960s-1970s. Japanese- and Korean-made electric basses. They also offered guitars.

Electric Bass

1960s-70s	EB-2 style	$225	$300

Charvel

1976-present. U.S.-made from '78 to '85 and a combination of imports and U.S.-made post-'85. They also build guitars.

Pre-Pro Bass

1980-1981. Pre-mass production basses, made Nov. '80 to '81. Refer to Charvel guitar section for details.

1980-1981	All models	$1,800	$2,400

850 XL Bass

1989. Four-string, neck-thru, active.

1989		$625	$800

CX-490 Bass

1991-1994. Double-cut, 4-string, bolt neck, red or white.

1991-1994		$220	$290

Eliminator Bass

1990-1991. Offset double-cut, active electronics, bolt neck.

1990-1991		$325	$425

Fusion Bass

1989-1991. Active circuitry, 4- and 5-string models.

1989-1991	IV	$400	$525
1989-1991	V	$425	$550

Model 1 Bass

1986-1988. Double-cut, bolt neck, 1 pickup.

1986-1988		$350	$450

Model 2 Bass

1986-1988. Double-cut, bolt neck, 2 pickups.

1986-1988		$350	$450

Model 3 Bass

1986-1988. Neck-thru, 2 single-coils, active, master volume, bass and treble knobs.

1986-1988		$400	$525

Model 4 Bass

1988. Like Model 3, but with bolt neck.

1988		$475	$625

Model 5 Bass

1986-1989. Double-cut, P/J pickups.

1986-1989		$475	$625

San Dimas Serialized Plated Bass

1981-1982. Soft headstock early models.

1981-1982		$1,650	$2,200

SB-4 Bass

1990s. Offset double cut solid, long bass horn, 2 pickups.

1990s		$330	$430

Star Bass

1980-1981. Unique 4-point solidbody, 1 pickup, considered by Charvel collectors to be Charvel's only original early design.

1980-1981		$2,500	$3,300

Surfcaster Bass

1991-1994. Semi-hollow, lipstick tube pickups.

1991-1994		$925	$1,225

MODEL YEAR	FEATURES	EXC. COND. LOW	HIGH

Cipher

1960s. Student market basses imported from Japan. They also made guitars.

Electric Solidbody Bass

1960s. Japanese imports.

1960s		$150	$225

Clevinger

1982-present. Established by Martin Clevinger, Oakland, California. Mainly specializing in electric upright basses, but has offered bass guitars as well.

College Line

One of many Lyon & Healy brands, made during the era of extreme design experimentation.

Monster (Style 2089) Bass

Early-1900s. 22" lower bout, flat-top guitar/bass, natural.

1915		$2,300	$3,000

Conrad

Ca.1968-1978. Student and mid-level copy basses imported by David Wexler, Chicago, Illinois. They also offered guitars, mandolins and banjos.

Electric Bass

1970s	Various models	$250	$425

Professional Bison Bass

1970s. Solidbody, 2 pickups.

1970s		$250	$325

Coral

1967-1969. In '66 MCA bought Danelectro and in '67 introduced the Coral brand of guitars, basses and amps. The line included several solid and semi-solidbody basses.

Deluxe D2N4 Bass

1967-1969. Offset double-cut, 2 pickups.

1967-1969	Black	$1,050	$1,400
1967-1969	Sunburst	$975	$1,300

Fiddle FB2B4 Bass

1967-1969. Violin bass hollow body, 2 pickups.

1967-1969		$1,475	$1,900

Firefly F2B4 Bass

1968-1969. 335-style semi-hollow, 2 pickups.

1968-1969	Red	$825	$1,075
1968-1969	Sunburst	$775	$1,025

Long Horn Bass

1968-1969. Standard neck (L2B4) or extended neck (L2LB4), 4 strings.

1968	L2LB4	$1,150	$1,525
1968-1969	L2B4	$1,050	$1,425

Wasp Bass

1967-1969. 4-string (2B4) or 6-string (2B6), black, red or sunburst.

1967-1969	2B4, black or red	$1,050	$1,400
1967-1969	2B4, sunburst	$850	$1,150
1967-1969	2B6, black or red	$1,200	$1,575
1967-1969	2B6, sunburst	$1,050	$1,400

MODEL YEAR	FEATURES	EXC. COND. LOW	HIGH

Crestwood

1970s. Imported by La Playa Distributing Company of Detroit. Product line includes copies of the popular classical guitars, flat-tops, electric solidbodies and basses of the era.

Electric Bass

1970s. Includes models 2048, 2049, 2079, 2090, 2092, 2093, and 2098.

1970s		$210	$275

Crown

1960s. Violin-shaped hollowbody electrics, solidbody electric guitars and basses, possibly others. Imported from Japan.

Electric Solidbody Bass

1960s	Import	$125	$175

Custom Kraft

Late-1950s-1968. A house brand of St. Louis Music Supply, instruments built by Valco and others. They also offered guitars and amps.

Bone Buzzer Model 12178 Bass

Late 1960s. Symmetrical double-cut thin hollow body, lightning bolt f-holes, 4-on-a-side tuners, 2 pickups, sunburst or emerald sunburst.

1968		$425	$575

D'Agostino

1976-early 1990s. Import company established by Pat D'Agostino. Solidbodies imported from EKO Italy '77-'82, Japan '82-'84, and in Korea for '84 on. Overall, about 60% of guitars and basses were Japanese, 40% Korean.

Electric Solidbody Bass

1970s	Various models	$150	$700

Daion

1978-1984. Higher quality copy basses imported from Japan. Original designs introduced in '80s. They also had guitars.

Electric Bass

1978-1984	Higher-end	$450	$900
1978-1984	Lower-end	$150	$450

Danelectro

1946-1969, 1997-present. Danelectro offered basses throughout most of its early history. In '96, the Evets Corporation, of San Clemente, California, introduced a line of Danelectro effects; amps, basses and guitars, many reissues of earlier instruments, soon followed. In early '03, Evets discontinued the guitar, bass and amp lines, but revived the guitar and bass line in '05. Danelectro also built the Coral brand instruments (see Coral).

Dane A Series Bass

1967. Solidbody, 2 pickups, 4-string.

1967		$500	$650

Dane C Series Bass

1967. Semi-solidbody 4- or 6-string, 2 pickups.

1967	4-string	$875	$1,150
1967	6-string	$1,100	$1,400

Dane D Series Bass

1967. Solidbody, 2 pickups, 4- or 6-string.

1967	4-string	$750	$975
1967	6-string	$1,100	$1,400

Dane E Series Bass

1967. Solidbody, 2 pickups, 4-string.

1967	4-string	$750	$975

Hawk Bass

1967. Solidbody, 4-string, 1 pickup.

1967		$850	$1,125

Model 1444L Bass

Ca.1958-ca.1964. Masonite body, single-cut, 2 pickups, copper finish.

1958-1964		$550	$725

Model 3412 Standard (Shorthorn) Bass

1959-1966. Coke bottle headstock, 4- or 6-string, 1 pickup, kidney 'guard through '60, seal 'guard after, copper finish.

1959-1960	Kidney 'guard, 4-string	$750	$950
1959-1960	Kidney 'guard, 6-string	$1,200	$1,500
1961-1966	Seal 'guard, 4-string	$650	$850
1961-1966	Seal 'guard, 6-string	$1,100	$1,400

Model 3612 Standard (Shorthorn) Bass

1959-1966. 6-string version.

1959-1962	Kidney 'guard	$1,200	$1,500
1961-1966	Seal 'guard	$1,100	$1,400

'58 Shorthorn Reissue Bass

1997-2003. Reissues of classic Shorthorn bass.

1997-2003		$225	$300

Model 4423 Longhorn 4-String Bass

1959-1966. Coke bottle headstock, 4-string, 2 pickups, tweed case '59, gray tolex after.

1959	Tweed case	$1,175	$1,525
1960-1966	Gray tolex case	$1,100	$1,425

Model 4623 Longhorn 6-String Bass

1959-1966, 1969-1970. 6-string version.

1959	Tweed case	$1,325	$1,725
1960-1966	Gray tolex case	$1,250	$1,625
1969-1970		$1,175	$1,525

'58 Longhorn Reissue/Longhorn Pro Bass

1997-2010. Reissues of classic Longhorn bass.

1997-2010		$200	$265

UB-2 6-String Bass

1956-1958. Single-cut, 2 pickups, black, bronze or ivory.

1956-1958		$1,375	$1,800

David J King

1987-present. Production/custom, professional and premium grade, electric basses built by luthier David King first in Amherst, Massachusetts and since '92 in Portland, Oregon.

Dean

1976-present. Intermediate and professional grade, production, solidbody, hollowbody, acoustic, and acoustic/electric, basses made overseas. They also offer guitars, banjos, mandolins, and amps.

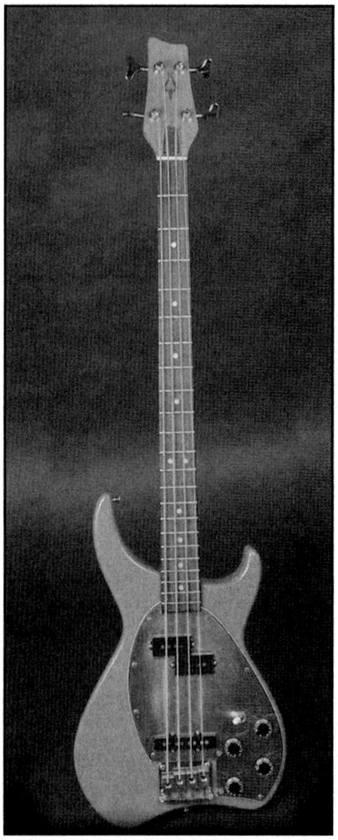

Daion

Carter Vintage Guitars

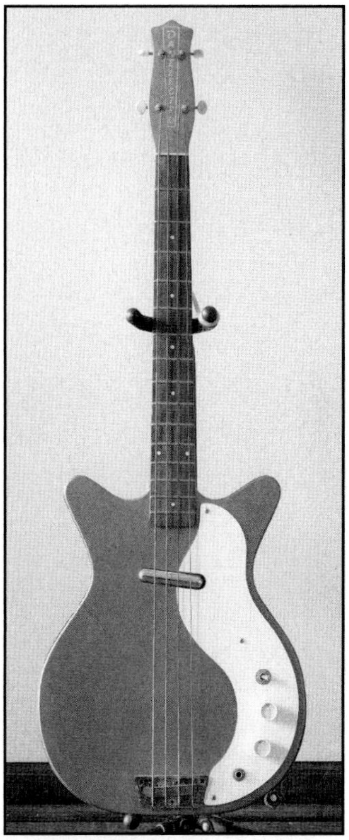

1961 Danelectro 3412

Erick Warner

BASSES

1960s EKO Model 995/2 Violin

Rivington Guitars

1966 Epiphone Embassy Deluxe

Carter Vintage Guitars

MODEL YEAR FEATURES EXC. COND. LOW HIGH

Baby ML Bass

1982-1986. Downsized version of ML.

1982-1986	Import	$275	$375

Mach V Bass

1985-1986. U.S.-made pointed solidbody, 2 pickups, rosewood 'board.

1985-1986		$1,050	$1,400

ML Bass

1977-1986, 2001-2010. Futuristic body style, fork headstock.

1977-1983	US-made	$1,325	$1,750
1984-1986	Korean import	$350	$450

Rhapsody Series (USA)

2001-2004. Scroll shaped offset double-cut, various models.

2001-2004	12-string	$300	$400
2001-2004	8-string	$250	$350
2001-2004	HFB fretless	$200	$250

DeArmond

1999-2004. Electric basses based on Guild models and imported from Korea by Fender. They also offered guitars.

Electric Bass

1999-2004. Various imported models.

1999-2004		$200	$500

Dingwall

1988-present. Luthier Sheldon Dingwall, Saskatoon, Saskatchewan, started out producing guitar bodies and necks, eventually offering complete guitars and basses. Currently Dingwall offers professional to premium grade, production/custom 4-, 5-, and 6-string basses featuring the Novax Fanned-Fret System.

Domino

Ca. 1967-1968. Imported from Japan by Maurice Lipsky Music of New York, mainly copies, but some original designs. They also offered guitars.

Electric Bass

1967-1968. Includes the Beatle Bass and Fireball Bass, a Vox Phantom IV copy.

1967-1968		$250	$450

Dorado

Ca. 1972-1973. Name used briefly by Baldwin/Gretsch on line of Japanese guitar and bass imports.

Electric Solidbody Bass

1970s	Import	$150	$350

Earthwood

1972-1985. Acoustic designs by Ernie Ball with input from George Fullerton and made in Newport Beach, California. One of the first to offer acoustic basses.

Acoustic Bass

1972-1985. Big bodied acoustic bass alternative between Kay double bass and solidbody Fender bass.

1972-1985		$2,000	$3,000

MODEL YEAR FEATURES EXC. COND. LOW HIGH

EKO

1959-1985, 2000-present. Built by the Oliviero Pigini Company, Italy. Original importers included LoDuca Brothers, Milwaukee, Wisconsin. Since about 2000, production, acoustic and electric EKO basses are again available and made in Italy and China. They also make guitars and amps.

Barracuda Bass

1967-1978. Offset double-cut semi-hollow, 2 pickups.

1967-1978		$450	$600

Cobra II Bass

1967-ca.1969. Offset double-cut solidbody, 2 pickups.

1967-1969		$375	$500

Kadett Bass

1967-1978. Red or sunburst.

1967-1978		$450	$600

Model 995/2 Violin Bass

1966-ca.1969.

1966-1969		$625	$825

Model 1100/2 Bass

1961-1966. Jaguar-style plastic covered solidbody, 2 pickups, sparkle finish.

1961-1966		$525	$675

Rocket IV/Rokes Bass

1967-early-1970s. Rocket-shape design, solidbody, says Rokes on the headstock, the Rokes were a popular English band that endorsed EKO guitars. Marketed as the Rocket IV in the U.S. and as the Rokes in Europe. Often called the Rok. Sunburst, 1 pickup.

1967-1971		$600	$800

Electra

1970-1984, 2013-present. Originally basses imported from Japan by St. Louis Music. They also offered guitars. Currently U.S.-made in Tampa, Florida.

Electric Solidbody Bass

1970s. Japanese imports, various models.

1970s		$425	$550

MPC Outlaw Bass

1970s. Symmetric solidbody with large straight horns, 2 separate plug-in modules for different effects, MPC headstock logo, bowtie markers, sunburst.

1970s		$550	$725

Emperador

1966-1992. Student-level basses imported by Westheimer Musical Instruments. Early models appear to be made by either Teisco or Kawai; later models were made by Cort. They also had guitars.

Electric Solidbody Bass

1960s. Japanese imports, various models.

1960s	Beatle violin bass	$265	$350
1960s	Various models	$135	$180

Engelhardt

Engelhardt specializes in student acoustic basses and cellos and is located in Elk Grove Village, Illinois.

MODEL YEAR	FEATURES	EXC. COND. LOW	HIGH

Epiphone

1928-present. Epiphone didn't add basses until 1959, after Gibson acquired the brand. The Gibson Epiphones were American-made until '69, then all imports until into the '80s, when some models were again made in the U.S. Currently Epiphone offers intermediate and professional grade, production, acoustic and electric basses.

B-1 Acoustic Bass Viol

1940-1949. Maple back and sides, cherry sunburst.

1940-1949		$1,450	$1,900

B-2 Acoustic Bass Viol

1940-1949. Mid-level maple back and sides.

1940-1949		$1,600	$2,100

B-3 Acoustic Bass Viol

1940-1949. Higher-level maple back and sides.

1940-1949		$1,700	$2,200

B-4 Acoustic Bass Viol

1940-1964. Highly figured maple back and sides.

1940-1964		$2,100	$2,700

B-5 Artist Acoustic Bass Viol

1941-1964. Highly figured maple back and sides.

1941-1964		$2,700	$3,500

EA/ET/ES Series (Japan)

1970-1979. Production of the Epiphone brand was moved to Japan in '70. Models included the EA (electric thinline) and ET (electric solidbody).

1970-1975	Various models	$400	$700

EB-0/EB-1/EB-3/EBM-4 Bass

1991-2019. EB-0 ('98-'19), EB-1 ('98-'00), EB-3 ('99-'19) and EBM-4 ('91-'98).

1991-2019	Various models	$150	$425

Elitist Series Bass

2003-2005. Higher-end appointments such as set-necks and USA pickups.

2003-2005	EB-3	$650	$875

Embassy Deluxe Bass

1963-1969. Solidbody, double-cut, 2 pickups, tune-o-matic bridge, cherry finish.

1963-1964		$4,400	$5,800
1965		$4,000	$5,300
1966-1969		$3,900	$5,200

Explorer Korina Bass

2000-2001. Made in Korea, Gibson Explorer body style, genuine korina body, set neck, gold hardware.

2000-2001		$325	$425

Genesis Bass

1979-1980. Double-cut solidbody, 2 humbuckers, Made in Taiwan.

1979-1980		$800	$1,100

Jack Cassady Signature Bass

1997-present. Maple body, mahogany neck, rosewood 'board, 1 pickup, metallic gold or ebony finish.

1997-2020		$500	$650

Les Paul Special Bass

1997-2013. LP Jr.-style slab body, single-cut, bolt neck, 2 humbuckers.

1997-2013		$225	$300

Newport EB-6 Bass

1962-1964. 6 strings.

1962-1964		$7,400	$9,600

Newport EBD Bass

1960-1970. Double-cut solidbody, 1 pickup (2 pickups optional until '63), 2-on-a-side tuners until '63, 4-on-a-side after that, cherry.

1960-1964		$1,950	$2,525
1965		$1,425	$1,850
1966-1970		$1,275	$1,650

Newport EB-SF Bass

1962-1963. Newport with added built-in fuzz, cherry.

1962-1963		$2,900	$3,750

Ripper Bass

1998-2000, 2006-2008. Offset double-cut, 1 humbucker pickup, black or natural.

1998-2000		$425	$575

Rivoli Bass (1 Pickup)

1959-1961, 1964-1970, 1994-2000. ES-335-style semi-hollowbody bass, 2-on-a-side tuners, 1 pickup (2 in '70).

1959-1960	Banjo tuners, natural	$5,300	$7,000
1959-1960	Banjo tuners, sunburst	$4,700	$6,100
1961	Standard tuners, natural	$3,000	$4,000
1961	Standard tuners, sunburst	$2,400	$3,200
1964		$2,400	$3,200
1965		$2,100	$2,800
1966-1969		$2,000	$2,600
1967	Sparkling Burgundy	$2,000	$2,600
1970		$2,000	$2,600

Rivoli Bass (2 Pickups)

1970 only. Double pickup Epiphone version of Gibson EB-2D.

1970		$2,100	$2,700

Rivoli II Reissue

1995-2000. Made in Korea, set neck, blond.

1995-2000		$525	$675

Thunderbird IV (Non-Reverse) Bass

1995-1998. Non-reverse-style mahogany body, 2 pickups, 5-string optional.

1995-1998		$300	$400

Thunderbird IV Bass

1997-2019. Reverse-style mahogany body, 2 pickups, sunburst.

1997-2019		$300	$400

Viola Bass

1995-present. Beatle Bass 500/1 copy, sunburst.

1995-2020		$225	$300

ESP

1975-present. Intermediate, professional, and premium grade, production/custom, electric basses. Japan's ESP (Electric Sound Products) made inroads in the U.S. market with mainly copy styles in the early '80s, mixing in original designs over the years. In the '90s, ESP opened a California-based Custom Shop. They also build guitars.

Electric Bass

1980s-1990s. Various factory production models.

1980s-90s		$625	$800

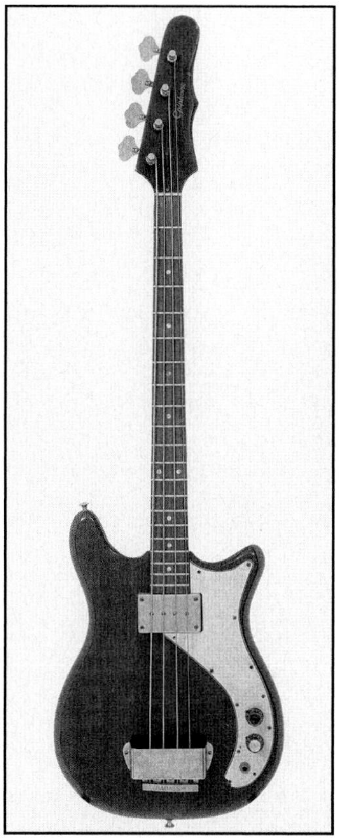

1966 Epiphone Newport
Imaged by Heritage Auctions, HA.com

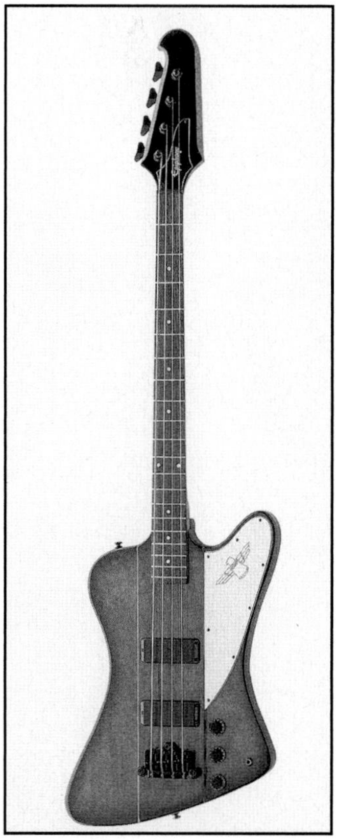

Epiphone Thunderbird IV

BASSES

1966 Fender Bass V

Fretted Americana

1967 Fender Coronado II

Rivington Guitars

MODEL YEAR	FEATURES	EXC. COND. LOW	HIGH

Essex (SX)

1985-present. Budget grade, production, electric basses imported by Rondo Music of Union, New Jersey. They also offer guitars.

Estrada

1960s-1970s. Line of classical, acoustic and electric guitars and basses imported from Japan.

Violin Bass

1960s		$375	$500

Fender

1946-present. Intermediate, professional, and premium grade, production/custom, electric and acoustic basses made in the U.S. and overseas. Leo Fender is the father of the electric bass. The introduction of his Precision Bass in late '51 changed forever how music was performed, recorded and heard. Leo followed with other popular models of basses that continue to make up a large part of Fender's production. Please note that all the variations of the Jazz and Precision Basses are grouped under those general headings.

A custom color is worth more than a standard color. The first Precision Bass standard color was blond but changed to sunburst in the late 1950s. The Jazz Bass standard color is sunburst. To understand a custom color, you need to know what the standard color is. Some custom colors are more rare than others. Below is a list of the custom colors offered in 1960 by Fender. They are sorted in ascending order with the most valuable color, Shell Pink, listed last. In the 1960 list, Black and Blond are the least valuable and Shell Pink is the most valuable. A Fiesta Red is typically worth 12% more than a Black or Blond. In the rare color group a Foam Green is normally worth 8% more than a Shoreline Gold. The two very rare colors are often worth 30% more than a Shoreline Gold. In our pricing information we will list the standard color, then the relative value of a common custom color, and then the value of a rare custom color. Remember that the amount of fade also affects the price. These prices are for factory original custom colors with slight or no fade in excellent condition. Fade implies a lighter color, but with custom colors a faded example can also be much darker in color. Blue can fade to dark green. White can fade to deep yellow.

The Price Guide lists the standard color, plus the value of a Common Color and the value of a Rare Color. The list below defines which group a color falls into for 1960, and it is in ascending order so, for example, a Daphne Blue should be considered more valuable than a Lake Placid Blue, assuming they are in equal condition.

Common Color: Black, Blond, Candy Apple Red, Olympic White, Lake Placid Blue, Dakota Red, Daphne Blue, Fiesta Red

Rare Color: Shoreline Gold, Inca Silver, Burgundy Mist, Sherwood Green, Sonic Blue, Foam Green

Rare (Very Rare) Color: Surf Green, Shell Pink

Ashbory Bass

2003-2006. Unique-shaped travel bass, Ashbory logo on body, Fender logo on back of headstock, previously sold under Fender's DeArmond brand.

2005-2006		$230	$300

Bass V

1965-1970. Five strings, double-cut, 1 pickup, dot inlay '65-'66, block inlay '66-'70. Please refer to the beginning of the Fender Bass Section for details on Fender color options.

1965	Common color	$4,200	$5,500
1965	Rare color	$5,600	$7,300
1965	Sunburst	$3,300	$4,300
1966-1967	Common color	$3,800	$4,900
1966-1967	Rare color	$4,850	$6,300
1966-1967	Sunburst, block inlay	$2,800	$3,650
1966-1967	Sunburst, dot inlay	$2,800	$3,650
1968-1970	Common color	$3,800	$4,900
1968-1970	Rare color	$4,850	$6,300
1968-1970	Sunburst	$2,800	$3,650

Bass VI

1961-1975. Six strings, Jazzmaster-like body, 3 pickups, dot inlay until '66, block inlay '66-'75. Reintroduced as Japanese-made Collectable model '95-'98. Please refer to the beginning of the Fender Bass Section for details on Fender color options.

1961-1962	Common color	$12,475	$16,200
1961-1962	Rare color	$16,200	$21,600
1961-1962	Sunburst	$7,100	$9,200
1963-1964	Common color	$11,650	$15,100
1963-1964	Rare color	$15,100	$20,000
1963-1964	Sunburst	$6,150	$8,000
1965	Common color	$10,400	$13,500
1965	Rare color	$13,500	$17,500
1965	Sunburst	$5,150	$6,700
1966	Common color	$7,300	$9,500
1966	Rare color	$9,500	$12,400
1966	Sunburst, block inlay	$4,300	$5,600
1966	Sunburst, dot inlay	$4,300	$5,600
1967-1969	Common color	$7,300	$9,500
1967-1969	Rare color	$9,500	$12,400
1967-1969	Sunburst	$4,300	$5,600
1970-1971	Custom color	$6,250	$8,100
1970-1971	Sunburst	$4,150	$5,400
1972-1974	Custom color	$6,250	$8,100
1972-1974	Natural	$3,150	$4,100
1972-1974	Sunburst	$4,150	$5,400
1972-1974	Walnut	$3,225	$4,200
1975	Natural	$3,150	$4,100
1975	Olympic White, black, blond	$4,150	$5,400
1975	Sunburst	$3,900	$5,075
1975	Walnut	$3,225	$4,200

Bass VI Reissue (CS)

2006. Custom Shop, 3-tone sunburst, certificate of authenticity.

2006		$1,700	$2,200

MODEL YEAR	FEATURES	EXC. COND. LOW	HIGH

Bass VI Reissue (Import)

1995-1998. Import, sunburst.

1995-1998		$1,150	$1,500

Bass VI Reissue (Japan)

Japanese market only, JD serial number.

2014		$925	$1,200

Bass VI Pawn Shop

2013-2014. Alder body, maple neck, rosewood 'board, 3-color sunburst.

2013-2014		$450	$575

BG Series Bass

1997-2012. Acoustic flat-top basses, single-cut, two-on-a-side tuners, Fishman on-board controls.

1997-2012	Various models	$130	$480

Bullet Bass (B30, B34, B40)

1982-1983. Alder body, 1 pickup, offered in short- and long-scale, red or walnut. U.S.-made, replaced by Japanese-made Squire Bullet Bass.

1982-1983		$565	$735

Bullet Deluxe Bass

1982-1983. Fender logo with Bullet Bass Deluxe on headstock, E-series serial number, small Telecaster-style headstock shape.

1982-1983		$565	$735

Coronado I Bass

1966-1970. Thinline, double-cut, 1 pickup, dot inlay, sunburst and cherry red were the standard colors, but custom colors could be ordered.

1966-1970	Various colors	$1,400	$1,825

Coronado II Bass

1966-1972. Two pickups, block inlay, sunburst and cherry red standard colors, but custom colors could be ordered. Only Antigua finish offered from '70 on.

1966-1969	Various colors	$1,600	$2,100
1966-1969	Wildwood option	$2,225	$2,900
1970-1972	Antigua only	$1,600	$2,100

Coronado Bass Reissue

2014-2016. Reissue of the 2 pickup (Coronado II), block inlay.

2014-2016		$425	$550

Dimension Bass

2004-2006. Made in Mexico, 4- or 5-string, P and J pickups.

2004-2006		$375	$490

HM Bass

1989-1991. Japanese-made, 4 strings (IV) or 5 strings (V), basswood body, no 'guard, 3 Jazz Bass pickups, 5-way switch, master volume, master TBX, sunburst.

1989-1991	IV, 4-string	$635	$825
1989-1991	V, 5-string	$685	$890

Jaguar Bass

2006-2010. Made in Japan, Jaguar Bass logo on headstock.

2006-2010		$850	$1,100

Jaguar Bass Modern Player

2012-2016. Made in China, koto body, maple neck and 'board, black.

2012-2016		$285	$370

MODEL YEAR	FEATURES	EXC. COND. LOW	HIGH

Jaguar Baritone Custom Bass

2007. Fender Jaguar Baritone Custom logo on headstock, 6-string.

2007		$925	$1,200

Deluxe Jaguar Bass

2012-2014. Maple neck, rosewood 'board, 2 pickups, 3-color sunburst, Candy Apple Red, Cobalt Blue.

2012-2014		$540	$700

Troy Sanders Jaguar Bass

2014-present. Artist series, alder body, bolt-on maple neck, 2 pickups, silverburst.

2014-2020		$525	$675

Jazz Bass

The following are variations of the Jazz Bass. The first seven listings are for the main U.S.-made models. All others are listed alphabetically after that in the following order:

- Jazz Bass
- Standard Jazz Bass
- American Standard Jazz Bass
- American Standard Jazz V Bass
- American Series Jazz Bass
- American Series Jazz V Bass
- American Professional/Professional II Jazz Bass
- 50th Anniversary American Standard Jazz Bass
- 50th Anniversary Jazz Bass Limited Edition
- '60 Custom Shop Limited Jazz Bass
- '60s Jazz Bass (Custom Shop)
- '60s Jazz Bass (Import)
- Road Worn '60s Jazz Bass
- Vintera '60s Jazz Bass
- 60th Anniversary American Jazz Bass
- 60th Anniversary Road Worn Jazz Bass
- '61 Journeyman Jazz Bass
- '62 Jazz Bass
- '64 Jazz Bass (Custom Shop)
- '64 Jazz Bass (American Vintage)
- '66 Jazz Bass Special Limited Edition
- '66 Journeyman Jazz Bass
- '74 Jazz Bass (American Vintage)
- '75 Jazz Bass (American Vintage)
- 75th Anniversary Commemorative Jazz Bass
- 75th Anniversary Jazz Bass (Diamond Anniversary)
- Aerodyne Jazz Bass
- American Deluxe Jazz/Jazz V Bass
- American Deluxe FMT Jazz Bass
- American Elite Jazz/Jazz V Bass
- American Ultra Jazz Bass
- Contemporary Jazz
- Custom Classic Jazz/Jazz V Bass
- Deluxe Jazz/Jazz V Bass (Active)
- Deluxe Power Jazz Bass
- Flea Signature Jazz Bass
- Foto Flame Jazz Bass
- FSR Standard Special Edition Jazz Bass
- Geddy Lee Signature Jazz Bass
- Gold Jazz Bass

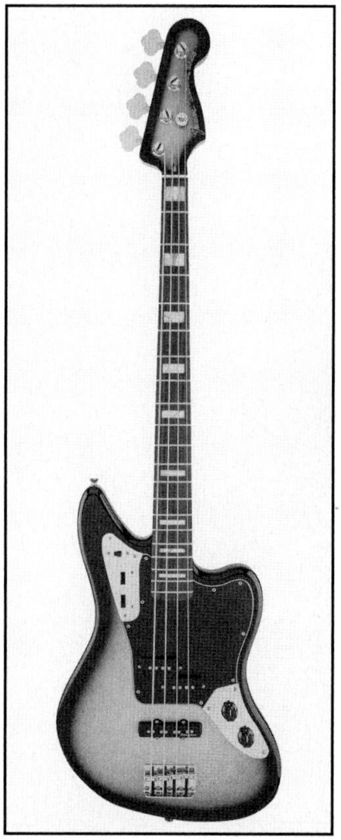

Fender Troy Sanders Jaguar Bass

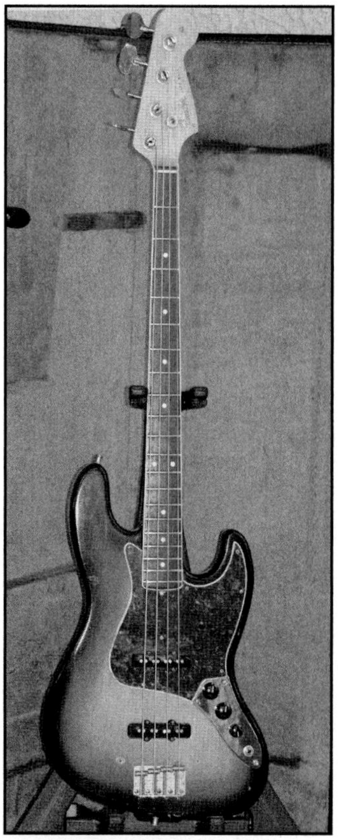

1966 Fender Jazz Bass

Frank Manno

BASSES

1963 Fender Jazz

Craig Brody

1966 Fender Jazz

Carter Vintage Guitars

MODEL YEAR	FEATURES	EXC. COND. LOW	HIGH

Highway One Jazz Bass
Jaco Pastorius Jazz Bass
Jazz Plus IV/Jazz Plus V Bass
Jazz Special Bass (Import)
Marcus Miller Signature Jazz Bass
Masterbuilt Custom Shop Jazz Bass
Noel Redding Signature Jazz Bass
Rarities Flame Ash Top Jazz Bass
Reggie Hamilton Jazz Bass
Roscoe Beck Jazz IV/V Bass
Select Jazz Bass
Standard Jazz Bass (Import)
Standard Jazz Fretless Bass (Import)
Ventures Limited Edition Jazz Bass
Victor Baily Jazz Bass

Jazz Bass

1960-1981. Two stack knobs '60-'62, 3 regular controls '62 on. Dot markers '60-'66, block markers from '66 on. Rosewood 'board standard, but maple available from '68 on. With the introduction of vintage reissue models in '81, Fender started calling the American-made version the Standard Jazz Bass. That became the American Standard Jazz Bass in '88, the American Series Jazz Bass in '00, back to the American Standard Jazz Bass in '08, and currently the American Professional Jazz Bass. Post '71 Jazz Bass values are affected more by condition than color or neck option. The Jazz Bass was fitted with a 3-bolt neck or bullet rod in late-'74. Prices assume a 3-bolt neck starting in '75. Please refer to the beginning of the Fender Bass Section for details on Fender color options. Post '71 Jazz Bass values are affected more by condition than color or neck option. The Jazz Bass was fitted with a 3-bolt neck or bullet rod in late-'74. Prices assume a 3-bolt neck starting in '75. Please refer to the beginning of the Fender Bass Section for details on Fender color options.

MODEL YEAR	FEATURES	LOW	HIGH
1960	Common color	$22,300	$29,000
1960	Rare color	$29,000	$37,800
1960	Sunburst	$19,300	$25,700
1961-1962	Common color, stack knob	$22,300	$29,000
1961-1962	Rare color, stack knob	$29,000	$37,800
1961-1962	Sunburst, stack knob	$19,000	$25,200
1962	Common color, 3 knob, curved	$15,500	$20,000
1962	Common color, 3 knob, slab	$17,000	$22,000
1962	Rare color, 3 knob, curved	$20,000	$30,000
1962	Rare color, 3 knob, slab	$22,000	$33,000
1962	Sunburst, 3 knob, curved	$12,000	$15,500
1962	Sunburst, 3 knob, slab	$13,500	$17,500
1963	Common color	$13,800	$18,000
1963	Rare color	$18,000	$28,000
1963	Sunburst	$10,000	$13,000
1964	Common color	$12,300	$16,000
1964	Rare color	$16,000	$24,000
1964	Sunburst, early '64	$9,000	$11,500
1964	Sunburst, late '64	$8,500	$11,000
1965	Common color	$10,000	$13,000
1965	Rare color	$13,000	$19,000
1965	Sunburst	$6,200	$8,000
1966	Common color	$7,000	$9,000
1966	Rare color	$9,000	$13,000
1966	Sunburst, blocks	$5,200	$6,800
1966	Sunburst, dots	$4,800	$6,300
1967	Custom color	$7,000	$13,000
1967	Sunburst	$4,800	$6,300
1968	Custom color	$7,000	$13,000
1968	Sunburst	$4,800	$6,300
1969	Custom color	$7,000	$13,000
1969	Sunburst	$4,800	$6,300
1970	Custom color	$4,825	$8,625
1970	Sunburst	$3,875	$5,025
1971	Custom color	$3,150	$6,800
1971	Sunburst	$3,100	$4,025
1972	Custom color	$2,400	$5,300
1972	Natural, black block option	$2,500	$3,300
1972	Natural, standard markers	$2,400	$3,100
1972	Sunburst	$2,550	$3,325
1973	Custom color	$2,400	$5,300
1973	Natural	$2,400	$3,100
1973	Sunburst	$2,550	$3,325
1973	Walnut	$2,400	$3,100
1974	Black, blond, white, 3-bolt	$2,300	$3,000
1974	Black, blond, white, 4-bolt	$2,550	$3,325
1974	Natural, 3-bolt	$2,300	$3,000
1974	Natural, 4-bolt	$2,550	$3,325
1974	Sunburst, 3-bolt, late-'74	$2,300	$3,000
1974	Sunburst, 4-bolt	$2,550	$3,325
1974	Walnut, 3-bolt	$2,300	$3,000
1974	Walnut, 4-bolt	$2,550	$3,325
1975-1977	All Colors	$2,300	$3,000
1978-1980	All Colors	$1,950	$2,600
1981	Black & Gold	$1,900	$2,450
1981	Black, white, wine	$1,900	$2,450
1981	International colors	$2,350	$3,050
1981	Sunburst	$1,900	$2,450

Standard Jazz Bass

1981-1984. Replaced Jazz Bass ('60-'81) and replaced by the American Standard Jazz Bass in '88. Name now used on import version. Please refer to the beginning of the Fender Bass Section for details on Fender color options.

MODEL YEAR	FEATURES	LOW	HIGH
1981-1984		$950	$1,250

American Standard Jazz Bass

1988-2000, 2008-2016. Replaced Standard Jazz Bass ('81-'88) and replaced by the American Series Jazz Bass in '00, back to American Standard in Jan. '08.

MODEL YEAR	FEATURES	LOW	HIGH
1988-2016		$850	$1,100

MODEL YEAR	FEATURES	EXC. COND. LOW	HIGH

American Standard Jazz V Bass

1998-2000, 2008-2016. 5-string version.

1998-2016 $850 $1,100

American Series Jazz Bass

2000-2007. Replaces American Standard Jazz Bass. Renamed American Standard in '08.

2000-2007 $850 $1,100

American Series Jazz V Bass

2000-2007. 5-string version.

2000-2007 $850 $1,100

American Professional/Professional II Jazz Bass

2017-present. Redesign includes V-Mod pickups, narrow-tall frets, 'deep C' neck profile, various colors. Also available left-hand model. Renamed American Professional II in '20.

2017-2020 $850 $1,100

50th Anniversary American Standard Jazz Bass

1996. Regular American Standard with gold hardware, 4- or 5-string, gold Fender's 50th Anniversary commemorative neck plate, rosewood 'board, sunburst.

1996 IV $950 $1,250

1996 V $950 $1,250

50th Anniversary Jazz Bass Limited Edition

2010. 50th anniversary of the Jazz Bass, nitro Candy Apple Red with matching headstock, mix of vintage and modern specs, rosewood 'board, block markers, 50th Anniversary neck plate.

2010 $1,600 $2,100

'60 Custom Shop Limited Jazz Bass

2020. Heavy relic.

2020 $2,200 $2,850

'60s Jazz Bass (Custom Shop)

1994-1998. Early '60s specs, relic for 1996-1998. Replaced by the CS '64 Jazz Bass. Early Relic work was done outside of Fender by Vince Cunetto or his staff.

1994-1995 $2,375 $3,075

1996 Relic (Cunetto) $2,375 $3,075

1997-1998 Relic (Cunetto staff) $2,300 $2,975

'60s Jazz Bass (Import)

1991-1994, 2001-2019. Classic series, '60s features, rosewood 'board, Japan-made for first years, Mexico after.

1991-1994 Japan $600 $800

2001-2019 Mexico $440 $575

Road Worn '60s Jazz Bass

2009-2019. Rosewood 'board, aged finish.

2009-2019 $500 $650

Vintera '60s Jazz Bass

2020-present. Vintage style appointments, 3-Color Sunburst, Daphne Blue or Firemist Gold.

2020-2021 $550 $725

60th Anniversary American Jazz Bass

2006. Rosewood 'board, 3-tone sunburst.

2006 $1,025 $1,350

60th Anniversary Road Worn Jazz Bass

2020-present. Road Worn lacquer finish, 3-color sunburst, Firemist Silver or Olympic White.

2020-2021 $700 $925

MODEL YEAR	FEATURES	EXC. COND. LOW	HIGH

'61 Journeyman Jazz Bass

2020. Heavy relic.

2020 $2,200 $2,850

'62 Jazz Bass

1982-1984, 1986-2012. U.S.A.-made, American Vintage series, reissue of '62 Jazz Bass. Please refer to the beginning of the Fender Bass Section for details on Fender color options.

1982-1984 $2,700 $3,500

1986-1999 $1,500 $1,950

2000-2012 $1,125 $1,450

'64 Jazz Bass (Custom Shop)

1998-2009. Alder body, rosewood 'board, tortoise shell 'guard. From June '95 to June '99 Relic work was done outside of Fender by Vince Cunetto and included a certificate noting model and year built, a bass without the certificate is valued less than shown.

1998-1999 Relic (Cunetto) $2,300 $2,975

2000-2009 Closet Classic option $1,950 $2,525

2000-2009 NOS option $1,950 $2,525

2000-2009 Relic option $2,075 $2,700

'64 Jazz Bass (American Vintage)

2013-2017. American Vintage series, dot inlays.

2013-2017 $1,125 $1,450

'66 Jazz Bass Special Limited Edition

2013. Japan, made for retailer Sweetwater, aged Oly White, 132 made for North American distribution.

2013 $750 $975

'66 Journeyman Jazz Bass

2020. Relic.

2020 $2,250 $2,950

'74 Jazz Bass (American Vintage)

2013-2017. American Vintage series, block inlays.

2013-2017 $1,200 $1,550

'75 Jazz Bass (American Vintage)

1994-2012. American Vintage series, maple neck with black block markers.

1994-2012 $1,125 $1,450

75th Anniversary Commemorative Jazz Bass

2021. Limited Edition, gold 75th ingot back of headstock and 75th anniversary neck plate, gold hardware, 2-color Bourbon Burst.

2021 $1,125 $1,475

75th Anniversary Jazz Bass (Diamond Anniversary)

2021. Diamond Anniversary metallic finish with matching painted headstock, 75th engraved silver neck plate.

2021 $475 $625

Aerodyne Jazz Bass

2003-present. Bound basswood body, P/J pickups, Deluxe Series.

2003-2020 $575 $750

American Deluxe Jazz/Jazz V Bass

1998-2016. U.S., 4 (IV) or 5-string (V), active electronics, alder or ash body. Alder body colors - sunburst or transparent red, ash body colors - white, blond, transparent teal green or transparent purple.

1998-2016 IV or V $1,000 $1,325

2010 Fender 50th Anniversary Jazz Bass Limited Edition

Rivington Guitars

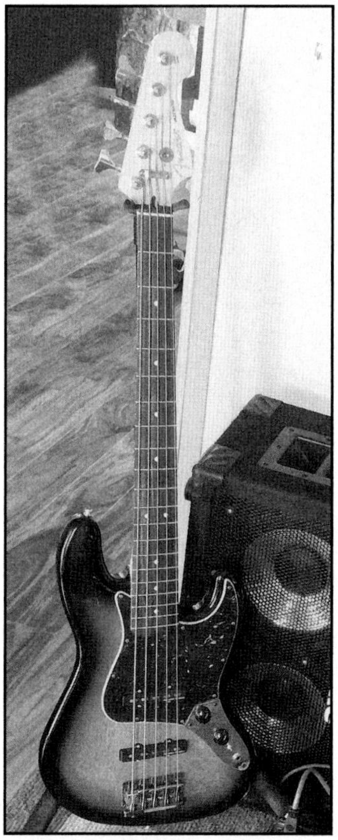

Fender Deluxe Jazz V

John Hefty

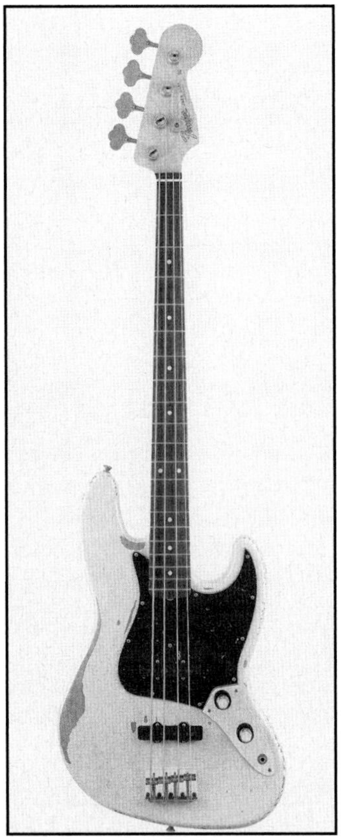

Fender Flea Signature Jazz Bass

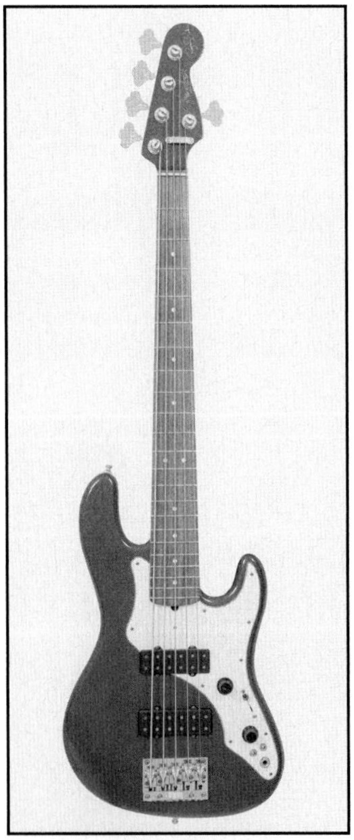

1998 Fender Roscoe Beck Jazz V

Imaged by Heritage Auctions, HA.com

MODEL YEAR	FEATURES	EXC. COND. LOW	HIGH

American Deluxe FMT Jazz Bass

2001-2006. Flame maple top version (FMT), active EQ, dual J pickups.

2001-2006		$1,075	$1,400

American Elite Jazz/Jazz V Bass

2016-2019. Compound radius 'board, 4 (IV) or 5-string (V), Noiseless pickups, onboard preamp, various colors.

2016-2019	IV or V	$1,075	$1,400

American Ultra Jazz Bass

2019-present. Alder or ash body, 2 Noiseless Vintage pickups, redesigned active/passive preamp, 4- or 5-string, various colors with satin finish.

2019-2020	IV	$1,100	$1,450
2019-2020	V	$1,100	$1,450

Contemporary Jazz

1987. Made in Japan.

1987		$475	$625

Custom Classic Jazz/Jazz V Bass

2001-2009. Custom Shop, slightly slimmer waist, deeper cutaways, maple or rosewood 'board, block inlays, 4 (IV) or 5-string (V).

2001-2009	IV or V	$1,700	$2,200

Deluxe Jazz/Jazz V Bass (Active)

1995-present. Made in Mexico, active electronics, 4 (IV) or 5-string (V), various colors.

1995-2020	IV or V	$350	$475

Deluxe Power Jazz Bass

2006. Part of Deluxe Series with Fishman piezo power bridge.

2006		$575	$750

Flea Signature Jazz Bass

2019-present. Flea logo neck plate, Road Worn Faded Shell Pink lacquer finish.

2019-2021		$775	$1,000

Foto Flame Jazz Bass

1994-1996. Japanese import, alder and basswood body with Foto Flame figured wood image.

1994-1996		$625	$800

FSR Standard Special Edition Jazz Bass

2007-2009. Made in Mexico, Fender Special Edition logo on back of headstock, ash body with natural finish.

2007-2009		$400	$525

Geddy Lee Signature Jazz Bass

1998-present. Limited run import in '98, now part of Artist Series, black.

1998-2020		$615	$800

Gold Jazz Bass

1981-1984. Gold finish and gold-plated hardware.

1981-1984		$1,800	$2,300

Highway One Jazz Bass

2003-2011. U.S.-made, alder body, satin lacquer finish.

2003-2011		$575	$750

Jaco Pastorius Jazz Bass

1999-present. Artist Series, standard production model made in Corona, '62 3-color sunburst body without pickup covers.

1999-2000	Fretted	$1,125	$1,450
1999-2020	Fretless	$1,125	$1,450

Jazz Plus IV/Jazz Plus V Bass

1990-1994. Alder body, 4-string (IV) or 5-string (V), 2 Lace Sensors, active electronics, rotary circuit selector, master volume, balance, bass boost, bass cut, treble boost, treble cut, various colors.

1990-1994	Various colors	$725	$950

Jazz Special Bass (Import)

1984-1991. Japanese-made, Jazz/Precision hybrid, Precision-shaped basswood body, Jazz neck (fretless available), 2 P/J pickups, offered with active (Power) or passive electronics.

1984-1991		$500	$650

Marcus Miller Signature Jazz Bass

1998-2014. Artist series.

1998-2004	Import	$730	$950
2005-2014	US Custom Shop	$1,225	$1,600

Masterbuilt Custom Shop Jazz Bass

2003-present. Various models and builders.

2003-2020		$3,500	$6,500

Noel Redding Signature Jazz Bass

1997. Limited Edition import, artist signature on 'guard, sunburst, rosewood 'board.

1997		$925	$1,200

Rarities Flame Ash Top Jazz Bass

2019-present. Two-piece alder body with flame ash top, Plasma Red Burst finish.

2019-2020		$1,400	$1,800

Reggie Hamilton Jazz Bass

2002-2016. Alder body, passive/active switch and pan control.

2002-2016		$475	$625

Roscoe Beck Jazz IV/V Bass

1997-2009. 5-string version offered '97-'06, 4-string '09.

1997-2009	5-string	$1,350	$1,775
2004-2009	4-string	$1,325	$1,750

Select Jazz Bass

2012-2013. US-made, figured top, rear-headstock 'Fender Select' medallion.

2012-2013		$1,625	$2,100

Standard Jazz Bass (Import)

1985-2018. Standard series, Japan-made into '90, Mexico after. Not to be confused with '81-'84 American-made model with the same name. Replaced by Player Series.

1985-1990	Japan	$725	$925
1991-2018	Mexico	$350	$455

Standard Jazz Fretless Bass (Import)

1994-2018. Standard series, fretless version. Replaced by Player Series.

1994-2018	IV or V	$350	$455

Ventures Limited Edition Jazz Bass

1996. Made in Japan, part of Ventures guitar and bass set, dark purple.

1996		$1,025	$1,325

Victor Baily Jazz Bass

2002-2011. Artist series, koa, rosewood and mahogany body, fretless with white fret markers.

2002-2011		$1,125	$1,450

MODEL YEAR	FEATURES	EXC. COND. LOW	HIGH

JP-90 Bass
1990-1994. Two P/J pickups, rosewood fretboard, poplar body, black or red.

1990-1994		$385	$500

Kingman Bass
2011-present. Acoustic, solid spruce top, mahogany back and sides.

2011-2020		$345	$450

MB Bass
1994-1995. Made in Japan, offset double-cut, 1 P- and 1 J-style pickup, 4-string (IV) or 5-string (V).

1994-1995	IV or V	$345	$450

Musicmaster Bass
1970-1983. Shorter scale, solidbody, 1 pickup. various colors.

1970-1983		$1,025	$1,325

Mustang Bass
1966-1982. Shorter scale, solidbody, 1 pickup, offered in standard colors and, for '69-'73, Competition Red, Blue and Orange with racing stripes on the body (with matching headstock for '69-'70).

1966-1969		$1,650	$2,175
1969-1970	Competition	$1,650	$2,175
1970-1979		$1,500	$1,950
1978-1980	Antigua finish	$1,550	$2,000
1980-1982		$1,100	$1,425

Mustang Bass (Import)
2002-2018. First made in Japan, later Mexico (ca. 2015), alder body, '60s features.

2002-2018		$525	$700

Parallel Universe '51 Telecaster PJ Bass
2018. Limited edition, authentic '51 style, mixes elements from both Jazz and Precision Basses.

2018		$1,125	$1,450

Performer Bass
1985-1986. Swinger-like body style, active electronics, various colors.

1985-1986		$1,225	$1,575

Postmodern Bass
2015-2019. Custom Shop, P-Bass body, Jazz Bass neck, at times offered in Relic, Journeyman Relic, NOS, and Lush Closet Classic finishes.

2015-2019		$1,950	$2,525

Precision Bass
The following are variations of the Precision Bass. The first six listings are for the main U.S.-made models. All others are listed alphabetically after that in the following order:

- Precision Bass
- Standard Precision Bass
- American Standard Precision Bass
- American Series Precision Bass
- American Series Precision V Bass
- American Professional/Professional II Precision Bass
- 40th Anniversary Precision Bass (Custom Shop)
- 50th Anniversary American Standard Precision Bass
- 50th Anniversary Precision Bass
- '50s Precision Bass
- Road Worn '50s Precision Bass
- '51 Precision Bass
- '55 Precision Bass (Custom Shop)
- '57 Precision Bass
- '57 Precision Bass (Custom Shop)
- '57 Precision Bass (Import)
- '59 Precision Bass (Custom Shop)
- 60th Anniversary Precision Bass (Mexico)
- 60th Anniversary Precision Bass (USA)
- '61 Precision Bass (Custom Shop)
- '62 Precision Bass
- '62 Precision Bass (Import)
- '63 Precision Bass (U.S.A.)
- 75th Anniversary Commemorative Precision Bass
- 75th Anniversary Precision Bass (Diamond Anniversary)
- Adam Clayton Signature Precision Bass
- Aerodyne Classic Precision Special Bass
- American Deluxe Precision Bass
- American Ultra Precision Bass
- Big Block Precision Bass
- Cabronita Precision Bass
- California Precision Bass Special
- Deluxe Active Precision Bass Special
- Elite Series Precision Bass
- Foto Flame Precision Bass
- Highway One Precision Bass
- Magnificent Seven Limited Edition American Standard PJ Bass
- Mark Hoppus Signature Precision Bass
- Mike Dirnt Road Worn Precision Bass
- Nate Mendel Precision Bass
- Precision Bass Jr.
- Precision Bass Lyte
- Precision Special Bass (U.S.A.)
- Precision Special Bass (Mexico)
- Pino Palladino Signature Precision Bass
- Precision U.S. Plus/Plus Bass
- Precision U.S. Deluxe/Plus Deluxe Bass
- Roger Waters Precision Bass
- Select Precision Bass
- Standard/Player Precision Bass (Import)
- Sting Precision Bass
- Tony Franklin Precision Bass
- Walnut Elite Precision Bass
- Walnut Precision Special Bass

Precision Bass
1951-1981. Slab body until '54, 1-piece maple neck standard until '59, optional after '69, rosewood 'board standard '59 on (slab until mid-'62, curved after), blond finish standard until '54, sunburst standard after that (2-tone '54-'58, 3-tone after '58). Became the Standard Precision Bass in '81-'85, the American Standard Precision for '88-'00, the American Series Precision Bass in '00-'08, and the American Standard Precision again for '08-'16. Currently called the American Professional Precision Bass. Unlike the Jazz and Telecaster Basses, the Precision was never fitted with a 3-bolt neck or bullet rod. Please refer to the beginning of the Fender Bass Section for details on Fender color options.

1951-1954	Blond, slab	$15,000	$20,000

1978 Fender Musicmaster
Justin Nortillo

1978 Fender Mustang
Justin Nortillo

BASSES

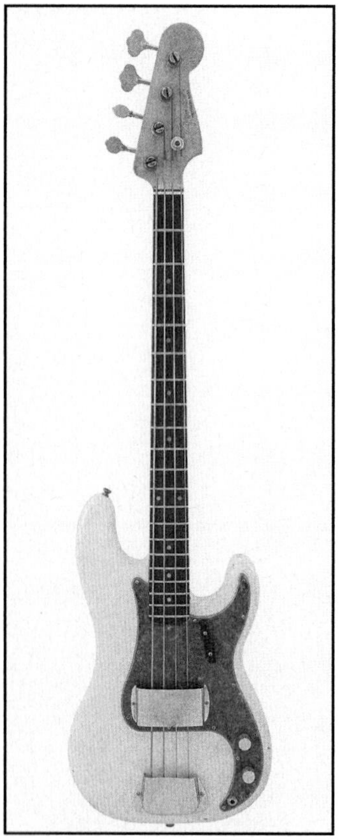

1959 Fender Precision

Charlie Faucher

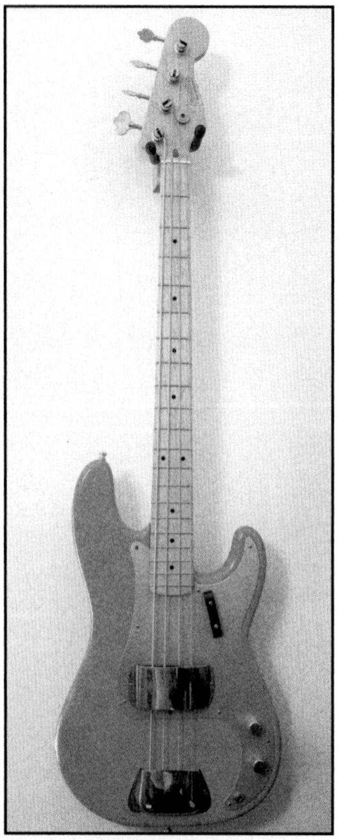

Fender Road Worn '50s Precision

Johnny Zapp

MODEL YEAR	FEATURES	EXC. COND. LOW	HIGH
1955	Blond, contour	$13,000	$16,800
1956	Blond, contour	$11,300	$14,700
1956	Sunburst, contour	$10,500	$13,700
1957	Blond	$11,300	$14,700
1957	Blond, anodized guard	$11,300	$14,700
1957	Sunburst,anodized guard, late '57	$10,000	$13,000
1957	Sunburst, tortoise guard	$10,000	$13,000
1958	Blond	$11,300	$14,700
1958	Sunburst, anodized guard	$10,000	$13,000
1959	Blond	$11,300	$14,700
1959	Sunburst, anodized guard	$10,000	$13,000
1959	Sunburst, tortoise guard	$10,000	$13,000
1960	Blond	$11,300	$14,700
1960	Custom color	$18,900	$37,800
1960	Sunburst	$9,300	$12,100
1961	Custom color	$9,500	$27,300
1961	Sunburst	$8,500	$11,000
1962	Custom color, curved	$8,500	$11,000
1962	Custom color, slab	$9,500	$27,300
1962	Sunburst, curved	$7,800	$10,200
1962	Sunburst, slab	$8,500	$11,000
1963	Custom color	$8,400	$17,900
1963	Sunburst	$7,800	$10,200
1964	Custom color	$8,400	$17,900
1964	Sunburst, early '64, spaghetti logo, green guard	$7,800	$10,200
1964	Sunburst, late '64	$7,000	$9,200
1965	Custom color	$7,400	$12,600
1965	Sunburst	$5,200	$6,700
1966	Custom color	$6,300	$11,500
1966	Sunburst	$4,300	$5,500
1967	Custom color	$6,300	$11,500
1967	Sunburst	$4,300	$5,500
1968	Custom color	$6,300	$11,500
1968	Sunburst	$4,300	$5,500
1969	Custom color	$6,300	$11,500
1969	Sunburst	$4,300	$5,500
1970	Custom color	$3,150	$6,800
1970	Sunburst	$2,800	$3,700
1971	Custom color	$3,150	$6,800
1971	Sunburst	$2,300	$3,000
1972	Custom color	$2,400	$5,300
1972	Sunburst	$2,300	$3,000
1973	Custom color	$2,400	$5,300
1973	Natural	$2,300	$3,000
1973	Sunburst	$2,300	$3,000
1973	Walnut	$2,300	$3,000
1974	Black, blond, white	$2,300	$3,000
1974	Natural	$2,300	$3,000
1974	Sunburst	$2,300	$3,000
1974	Walnut	$2,300	$3,000
1975-1977	Black, blond, wine, white	$2,300	$3,000
1975-1977	Natural	$2,300	$3,000
1975-1977	Sunburst	$2,300	$3,000
1975-1977	Walnut	$2,300	$3,000
1978-1979	Antigua	$1,950	$2,600
1978-1979	Black, blond, wine, white	$1,950	$2,600
1978-1979	Natural	$1,950	$2,600
1978-1979	Sunburst	$1,950	$2,600
1978-1979	Walnut	$1,950	$2,600
1980	Antigua	$1,900	$2,450
1980	Black, white, wine	$1,900	$2,450
1980	Color with matching headstk, gold hw	$2,475	$3,200
1980	International colors	$2,350	$3,050
1980	Natural	$1,900	$2,450
1980	Sunburst	$1,900	$2,450
1981	Black & gold	$1,900	$2,450
1981	Black, white, wine	$1,900	$2,450
1981	International colors	$2,000	$2,600
1981	Sunburst	$1,900	$2,450

Standard Precision Bass

1981-1984. Replaces Precision Bass, various colors. Replaced by American Standard Precision '88-'00. The Standard name is used on import Precision model for '88-present.

1981-1984	Top mount jack era	$950	$1,250

American Standard Precision Bass

1988-2000, 2008-2016. Replaces Standard Precision Bass, replaced by American Series Precision in '00, back to American Standard in Jan. '08.

1988-1989	Blond, gold hw	$850	$1,100
1988-2016	Various colors	$850	$1,100

American Series Precision Bass

2000-2007. Replaces American Standard Precision Bass, various colors. Renamed American Standard in '08.

2000-2007		$850	$1,100

American Series Precision V Bass

2000-2007. 5-string version.

2000-2007		$850	$1,100

American Professional/Professional II Precision Bass

2017-present. Redesign includes V-Mod pickups, '63 P Bass neck profile, narrow-tall frets, various colors. Also available left-hand model. Renamed American Professional II in '20.

2017-2020		$850	$1,100

40th Anniversary Precision Bass (Custom Shop)

1991. 400 made, quilted amber maple top, gold hardware.

1991		$2,150	$2,800

50th Anniversary American Standard Precision Bass

1996. Regular American Standard with gold hardware, 4- or 5-string, gold 50th Anniversary commemorative neck plate, rosewood 'board, sunburst.

1996		$950	$1,250

MODEL YEAR	FEATURES	EXC. COND. LOW	HIGH

50th Anniversary Precision Bass

2001. Commemorative certificate with date and serial number, butterscotch finish, ash body, maple neck, black 'guard.

2001	With certificate	$950	$1,250

'50s Precision Bass

1992-1996, 2006-2019. First run made in Japan, currently in Mexico, 1 split-coil, maple neck.

1992-1996	Japan	$525	$700
2006-2019	Mexico	$440	$575

Road Worn '50s Precision Bass

2009-2019. Mexico, 1 split-coil, maple neck, aged finish.

2009-2019		$500	$650

'51 Precision Bass

1994-1997, 2003-2010. Import from Japan, no pickup or bridge covers, blond or sunburst. Offered in Japan in the '90s.

1994-1997	Japan only	$600	$800
2003-2010		$525	$675

'55 Precision Bass (Custom Shop)

2003-2011. 1955 specs including oversized 'guard, 1-piece maple neck/fretboard, preproduction bridge and pickup covers, single-coil pickup. Offered in N.O.S., Closet Classic or highest-end Relic.

2003-2006	NOS	$1,950	$2,525
2003-2006	Relic	$2,075	$2,700
2003-2011	Closet Classic	$1,950	$2,525

'57 Precision Bass

1982-1984, 1986-2012. U.S.-made reissue, American Vintage series, various colors.

1982-1984		$2,700	$3,500
1986-1999		$1,500	$1,950
2000-2012		$1,125	$1,450

'57 Precision Bass (Custom Shop)

2013	Heavy relic	$2,250	$2,950

'57 Precision Bass (Import)

1984-1986	Black	$1,150	$1,500

'59 Precision Bass (Custom Shop)

2003-2010. Custom Shop built with late-'59 specs, rosewood 'board.

2003-2008	Closet Classic	$1,950	$2,525
2003-2010	NOS	$1,950	$2,525
2003-2010	Relic	$2,075	$2,700

60th Anniversary Precision Bass (Mexico)

2005. Made in Mexico, with 60th Anniversary gig bag.

2005		$385	$500

60th Anniversary Precision Bass (USA)

2011. 1951-2011 Anniversary date label.

2011		$1,025	$1,350

'61 Precision Bass (Custom Shop)

2010-2013. Made for Musician's Friend and Guitar Center.

2010-2013	Closet Classic	$1,950	$2,525
2010-2013	NOS	$1,950	$2,525
2010-2013	Relic	$2,075	$2,700

'62 Precision Bass

1982-1984, 1986-2012. American Vintage series, alder body. No production in '85.

1982-1984		$2,700	$3,500
1986-1989		$1,500	$1,950
1990	Mary Kaye Blond	$1,825	$2,400
1990-1999		$1,500	$1,950
2000-2012		$1,125	$1,450

'62 Precision Bass (Import)

1984-1986. Foreign-made, black.

1984-1986		$1,150	$1,500

'63 Precision Bass (U.S.A.)

2013-2017. American Vintage series.

2013-2017		$1,000	$1,325

75th Anniversary Commemorative Precision Bass

2021. Limited Edition, gold 75th ingot back of headstock and 75th anniversary neck plate, gold hardware, 2-color Bourbon Burst.

2021		$1,100	$1,425

75th Anniversary Precision Bass (Diamond Anniversary)

2021. Diamond Anniversary metallic finish with matching painted headstock, 75th engraved silver neck plate.

2021		$475	$625

Adam Clayton Signature Precision Bass

2011. Custom Shop Limited Edition.

2011		$2,850	$3,700

Aerodyne Classic Precision Special Bass

2006. Made in Japan, labeled Precision and Aerodyne P Bass, figured maple top, matching headstock, P-J pickup.

2006		$575	$750

American Deluxe Precision Bass

1998-2016. U.S., active electronics, 4 (IV) or 5-string (V), alder or ash body. Alder body colors - sunburst or transparent red. Ash body colors - white blond, transparent teal green or transparent purple.

1998-2016	IV or V	$1,050	$1,350

American Ultra Precision Bass

2019-present. Alder or ash body, 2 Noiseless Vintage pickups, 4-string, various colors with gloss finish.

2019-2020		$1,100	$1,450

Big Block Precision Bass

2005-2009. Pearloid block markers, black finish with matching headstock, 1 double Jazz Bass humbucker, bass and treble boost and cut controls.

2005-2009		$575	$750

Cabronita Precision Bass

2014-2015. One Fideli'Tron pickup, 2 knobs.

2014-2015		$295	$385

California Precision Bass Special

1997. California Series, assembled and finished in Mexico and California, P/J pickup configuration.

1997		$560	$725

Deluxe Active Precision Bass Special

1995-present. Made in Mexico, P/J pickups, Jazz Bass neck.

1995-2020		$350	$455

Elite Series Precision Bass

1983-1985. Active electronics, noise-cancelling pickups, Elite I (ash body, 1 pickup), Elite II (2 pickups), Gold Elite I (gold-plated hardware, 1 pickup), Gold Elite II (2 pickups), various colors.

1983-1985	Various models	$1,675	$2,200

1988 Fender '62 Precision

Jonathan Bell

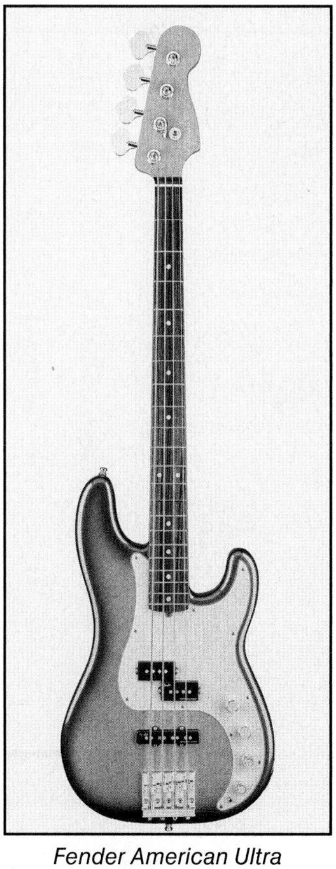

Fender American Ultra Precision Bass

BASSES

BASSES

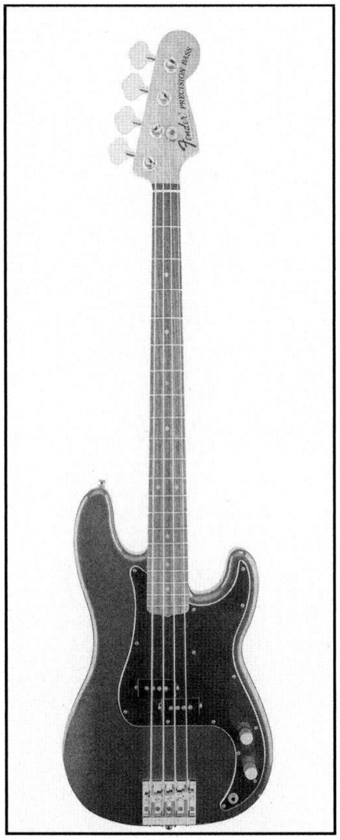

Fender Nate Mendel Precision

1983 Fender Squier Precision Bass Standard

Rivington Guitars

MODEL YEAR	FEATURES	EXC. COND. LOW	HIGH

Foto Flame Precision Bass

1994-1996. Made in Japan, simulated woodgrain finish, natural or sunburst.

1994-1996		$625	$800

Highway One Precision Bass

2003-2011. U.S.-made, alder body, satin lacquer finish.

2003-2011		$575	$750

Magnificent Seven Limited Edition American Standard PJ Bass

2016. U.S., P-bass body with Jazz neck, 500 made.

2016		$825	$1,075

Mark Hoppus Signature Precision Bass

2002-2016. Mark Hoppus engraved on neck plate.

2002-2016	Mexico serial no	$480	$625

Mike Dirnt Road Worn Precision Bass

2014-present. '51 era P-Bass style, ash body, maple or rosewood 'board.

2014-2020		$600	$780

Nate Mendel Precision Bass

2013-present. Ash body, rosewood 'board.

2013-2020		$480	$625

Precision Bass Jr.

2004-2006. 3/4 size.

2004-2006		$350	$450

Precision Bass Lyte

1992-2001. Japanese-made, smaller, lighter basswood body, 2 pickups, sunburst.

1992-2001		$540	$700

Precision Special Bass (U.S.A.)

1980-1982. Gold hardware, matching headstock, active electronics, CA Red, LP Blue, Oly White or walnut (see separate listing).

1980-1982	Common color	$1,450	$1,900
1980-1982	Rare color	$1,750	$2,300

Precision Special Bass (Mexico)

1997-1998. 1 P- and 1 J-pickup. Chrome hardware.

1997-1998		$500	$650

Pino Palladino Signature Precision Bass

2006-present. Custom Shop, based on '62 used by Palladino, certificate of authenticity, Fiesta Red.

2006		$1,850	$2,400

Precision U.S. Plus/Plus Bass

1989-1992. P-style bass with P- and J-bass pickups.

1989-1992	Rare color	$850	$1,125
1989-1992	Standard color	$725	$950

Precision U.S. Deluxe/Plus Deluxe Bass

1991-1994. P-style bass with P- and J-bass pickups, active electronics, no 'guard models available.

1991-1994	Rare color	$850	$1,125
1991-1994	Standard color	$725	$950

Roger Waters Precision Bass

2010-2019. Alder body, maple neck, black.

2010-2019		$525	$675

Select Precision Bass

2012. Alder body, flamed maple top, rear headstock 'Fender Select' medallion.

2012		$1,625	$2,100

Standard/Player Precision Bass (Import)

1985-present. Made in Japan into '90, and Mexico after. Not to be confused with '81-'84 American-made model with the same name. Also available left-handed. Replaced by Player Series in 18.

MODEL YEAR	FEATURES	EXC. COND. LOW	HIGH

1985-1990	Japan	$725	$925
1991-2018	Mexico	$350	$455
2016	Mexico, Custom Art Series	$350	$455

Sting Precision Bass

2001-2013. Made in Japan, 2-tone sunburst, 1 single-coil, Sting's signature.

2001-2013		$480	$625

Tony Franklin Precision Bass

2007-present. Fretless, P and J pickups, 3-way selector, lacquer finish.

2007-2020		$1,000	$1,300

Walnut Elite Precision Bass

1983-1985. The Elite Series feature active electronics and noise-cancelling pickups, walnut body, 1 pickup (Elite I) or 2 (Elite II), rosewood 'board, natural.

1983-1985	Elite I	$1,550	$2,050
1983-1985	Elite II	$1,550	$2,050

Walnut Precision Special Bass

1980-1982. Precision Bass Special with a walnut body, natural.

1980-1982		$1,475	$1,925

Prodigy Active Bass

1992-1995. U.S.-made, poplar body, 1 J- and 1 P-style pickup, active.

1992-1995		$850	$1,100

Rhodes Piano Bass

1962. Electric keyboard in bass register, Fender-Rhodes sticker, Piano Bass logo, various colors.

1962		$1,800	$2,300

Squier Affinity Jazz Bass

1997-present. Affinity is the lower priced series made in China.

1997-2020		$95	$125

Squier Bronco Bass

1998-present. The lowest priced Squier bass, single coil plastic cover pickup, 3/4 body.

1998-2020		$125	$160

Squier Bullet Bass

1983-2000. Japanese-made, Squier-branded, replaces Bullet Bass, black.

1983-2000		$225	$300

Squier Classic Vibe Bass Series

2009-present. Various models.

2009-2020		$225	$300

Squier HM Bass/HM Bass V

1989-1993. Korean-made, 5-string also offered.

1989-1993		$225	$300

Squier Jazz Bass Standard

1983-2010. Jazz bass import, without cover plates, various colors.

1983-1984	1st logo	$375	$500
1985-1989	2nd logo	$325	$450
1990-1999		$160	$210
2000-2010		$125	$165

Squier Katana Bass

1985-1986. Made in Japan, wedge-shaped, arrow headstock.

1985-1986		$550	$725

MODEL YEAR	FEATURES	EXC. COND. LOW	HIGH

Squier Precision Bass Special

1998-2010. Agathis body, P/J pickups, 4-string (IV) or 5-string (V).

1998-2010	IV or V	$100	$130

Squier Precision Bass Standard

1983-2006.

1983-1984	1st logo	$375	$500
1985-1989	2nd logo	$325	$450
1990-1999	Some from Mexico	$160	$210
2000-2006	Indonesia	$125	$165

Squier Vintage Modified Series

2007-2019. Includes Jaguar bass, Jazz and Precision models.

2007-2019	Various models	$130	$200

Steve Bailey Jazz Bass VI

2009-2011. USA, 6-string, fretless or fretted, sunburst or black.

2009-2011		$1,400	$1,800

Stu Hamm Urge Bass (U.S.A.)

1992-1999. Contoured Precision-style body with smaller wide treble cutaway, J and P pickups, 32" scale.

1992-1999		$1,250	$1,650

Stu Hamm Urge II Bass (U.S.A.)

1999-2009. J and P pickups, 34" scale.

1999-2009		$1,250	$1,650

Telecaster Bass

1968-1979. Slab solidbody, 1 pickup, fretless option '70, blond and custom colors available (Pink Paisley or Blue Floral '68-'69). Please refer to the beginning of the Fender Bass Section for details on Fender color options.

1968	Black, nitro	$2,900	$3,750
1968	Black, poly	$2,775	$3,600
1968	Blond, nitro	$2,050	$2,675
1968	Blond, poly	$2,000	$2,600
1968	Blue Floral Paisley	$5,200	$6,775
1968	Lake Placid Blue	$3,300	$4,300
1968	Red (Pink) Paisley	$5,000	$6,500
1969-1972	4-bolt, single-coil	$1,900	$2,450
1973-1974	3-bolt, hum, rare color	$1,775	$2,300
1973-1974	3-bolt, humbucker	$1,375	$1,800
1975-1979	3-bolt, humbucker	$1,275	$1,650

Zone Bass American Deluxe

2001-2006. Smaller lightweight offset double-cut, active humbuckers, exotic tone woods, U.S.-made.

2001-2006		$1,050	$1,350

Fodera

1983-present. Luthiers Vinnie Fodera and Joseph Lauricella build their professional and premium grade, production/custom, solidbody basses in Brooklyn, New York.

High-level Bass

1983-2020	4, 5, 6 strings	$7,500	$8,500

Mid-level Bass

1983-2020	4, 5, 6 strings	$4,500	$7,500

Low-level Bass

1983-2020	4, 5, 6 strings	$2,500	$4,500

MODEL YEAR	FEATURES	EXC. COND. LOW	HIGH

Framus

1946-1975, 1996-present. Professional and premium grade, production/custom, basses made in Germany. They also build guitars and amps.

Atlantic Model 5/140 Bass

1960s. Single-cut thinline with f-holes, 2 pickups, sunburst or blackrose.

1960s		$500	$650

Atlantic Model 5/143 Bass

1960s. Offset double-cut thinbody with f-holes, 2 pickups, 4-on-a-side keys.

1960s		$500	$650

Atlantic Model 5/144 Bass

1960s. Double-cut thinbody with f-holes, ES-335 body style, 2 pickups. Becomes Model J/144 in '70s.

1960s		$500	$650

Charavelle 4 Model 5/153 Bass

1960s. Double-cut thinline with f-holes, 335-style body, 2 pickups, sunburst, cherry red or Sunset.

1960s		$550	$725

De Luxe 4 Model 5/154 Bass

1960s. Double-cut thinline, sharp horns and f-holes, 2 pickups, mute, sunburst or natural/blond.

1960s		$550	$725

Electric Upright Bass

1950s. Full-scale neck, triangular body, black.

1958		$1,525	$2,000

Star Series (Bill Wyman) Bass

1959-1968. Early flyer says, Bill Wyman of the Rolling Stones prefers the Star Bass. The model name was later changed to Framus Stone Bass. Single-cut semi-hollow body, 5/149 (1 pickup) and 5/150 (2 pickups), sunburst.

1959-1965	Model 5/150	$875	$1,125
1960s	Model 5/149	$775	$1,025

Strato De Luxe Star Model 5/165 Bass

Ca. 1964-ca. 1972. Offset double-cut solidbody, 2 pickups, sunburst. There was also a gold hardware version (5/165 gl) and a 6-string (5/166).

1960s		$500	$650

Strato Star Series Bass

Ca. 1963-ca. 1972. Double-cut solidbody, 5/156/50 (1 pickup) or 5/156/52 (2 pickups), beige, cherry or sunburst.

1960s	Model 5/156/50	$500	$650
1960s	Model 5/156/52	$525	$675

T.V. Star Bass

1960s. Offset double-cut thinbody with f-holes, 2 pickups, short-scale, sunburst or cherry red. Most expensive of the '60s Framus basses, although not as popular as the Bill Wyman 5/150 model.

1960s		$500	$650

Triumph Electric Upright Bass

1956-1960. Solidbody bean pole electric bass, small body, long neck, slotted viol peghead, gold or black.

1956-1960		$1,625	$2,125

Fresher

1973-1985. Japanese-made, mainly copies of popular brands and not imported into the U.S., but they do show up at guitar shows. They also made guitars.

Solidbody Electric Bass

1970s		$150	$400

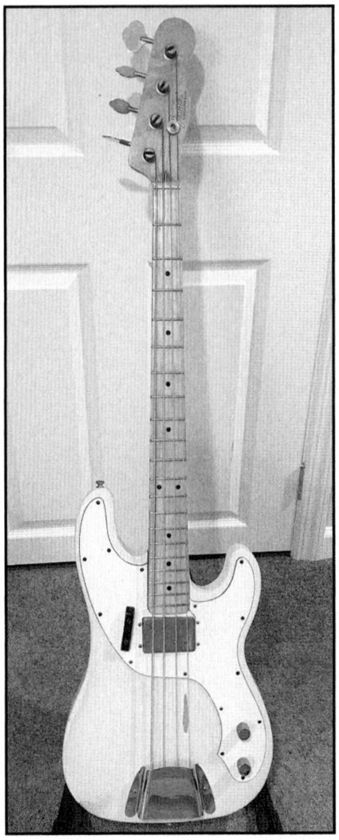

1972 Fender Telecaster Bass

Justin Nortillo

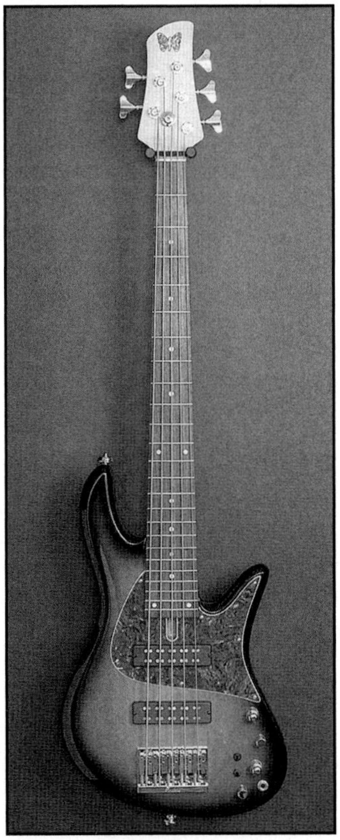

Fodera Emperor Standard Classic

BASSES

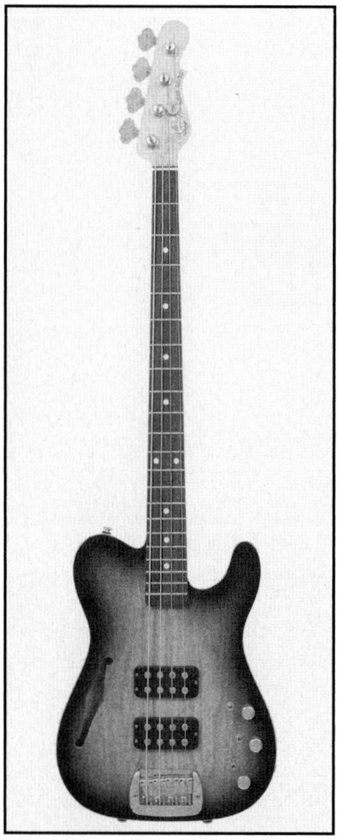

G&L ASAT
Imaged by Heritage Auctions, HA.com

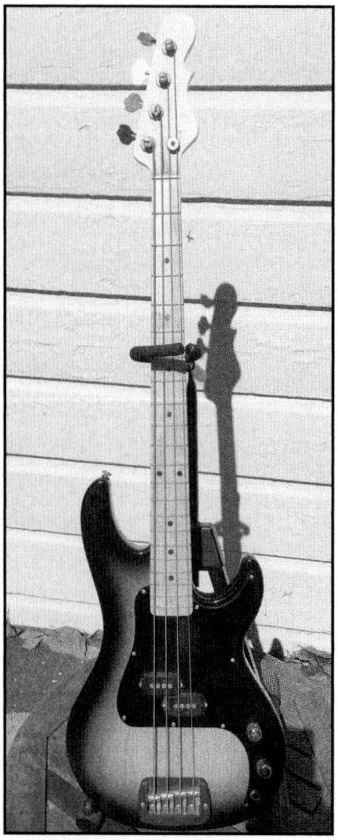

1991 G&L SB-1
KC Cormack

G&L

1980-present. Intermediate and professional grade, production/custom, electric basses made in the U.S. In '03, G&L introduced the Korean-made G&L Tribute Series. A Tribute logo is clearly identified on the headstock. They also build guitars.

ASAT Bass

1989-2020. Single-cut, solidbody, active and passive modes, 2 humbuckers, various colors.

MODEL YEAR	FEATURES	EXC. COND. LOW	HIGH
1989-1991	About 400 made	$1,025	$1,325
1992-2020		$925	$1,225

ASAT Commemorative Bass

1991-1992. About 150 made, 4-string ASAT commemorating Leo Fender's life.

MODEL YEAR	FEATURES	EXC. COND. LOW	HIGH
1991-1992		$1,350	$1,750

ASAT Semi-Hollow Bass

2001-2020. Semi-hollowbody style on ASAT bass.

MODEL YEAR	FEATURES	EXC. COND. LOW	HIGH
2001-2020		$925	$1,225

Climax Bass

1992-1996. Single active humbucker MFD.

MODEL YEAR	FEATURES	EXC. COND. LOW	HIGH
1992-1996		$800	$1,025

El Toro Bass

1983-1989. Double-cut, solidbody, 2 active, smaller, humbuckers, sunburst.

MODEL YEAR	FEATURES	EXC. COND. LOW	HIGH
1983-1987		$1,050	$1,375
1988-1989		$875	$1,150

Interceptor Bass

1984-1991. Sharp pointed double-cut, solidbody, 2 active, smaller humbuckers, sunburst.

MODEL YEAR	FEATURES	EXC. COND. LOW	HIGH
1984-1986		$2,150	$2,850
1988-1991	Body signature	$1,100	$1,450

JB-2 Bass

2001-2018. Alder body, 2 Alnico V pickups.

MODEL YEAR	FEATURES	EXC. COND. LOW	HIGH
2001-2018		$900	$1,175

Kiloton Bass

2016-present. Single MFD humbucker pickup, custom options and finishes.

MODEL YEAR	FEATURES	EXC. COND. LOW	HIGH
2016-2021	Standard top	$775	$1,025
2020-2021	Premium figured	$1,075	$1,400

L-1000 Bass

1980-1994, 2008. Offset double-cut, solidbody, 1 pickup, various colors. Limited run in '08.

MODEL YEAR	FEATURES	EXC. COND. LOW	HIGH
1980-1985	Ash	$875	$1,150
1980-1985	Mahogany	$875	$1,150
1980-1985	Maple	$875	$1,150
1986-1991		$875	$1,150
1992-1999	3-bolt	$875	$1,150
2008	4-bolt	$875	$1,150

L-1500 Bass

1997-2018. Offset double-cut solidbody, 1 MFD humbucker.

MODEL YEAR	FEATURES	EXC. COND. LOW	HIGH
1997-2018		$875	$1,150

L-1500 Custom Bass

1997 only.

MODEL YEAR	FEATURES	EXC. COND. LOW	HIGH
1997		$900	$1,175

L-1505 Bass

1998-2018. Five-string version, single MFD humbucker.

MODEL YEAR	FEATURES	EXC. COND. LOW	HIGH
1998-2018		$925	$1,200

L-2000 30th Anniversary Bass

2010. Pearl Frost with matching headstock.

MODEL YEAR	FEATURES	EXC. COND. LOW	HIGH
2010		$1,125	$1,500

L-2000 Bass

1980-present. Offset double-cut solidbody, 2 pickups, active electronics. Originally, the L-2000 was available with active (L-2000E) or passive (L-2000) electronics.

MODEL YEAR	FEATURES	EXC. COND. LOW	HIGH
1980-1985	Ash	$1,150	$1,500
1986		$975	$1,300
1987-1991	Leo signature	$975	$1,300
1992-2020		$975	$1,300

L-2000 C.L.F. Centennial

2009-2010. Swamp ash body, blonde, black hardware, planned run of 50, Certificate of Authenticity.

MODEL YEAR	FEATURES	EXC. COND. LOW	HIGH
2009-2010	COA, CD	$1,175	$1,525

L-2000 Custom Bass

1997. Ash top, wood-grain binding upgrade.

MODEL YEAR	FEATURES	EXC. COND. LOW	HIGH
1997		$875	$1,150

L-2000 Fretless Bass

1980-1998. Fretless version.

MODEL YEAR	FEATURES	EXC. COND. LOW	HIGH
1980-1982		$1,125	$1,475

L-2000(E) Bass

1980-1982. Offset double-cut, solidbody, 2 pickups, active electronics. Originally, the L-2000 was available with active (L-2000E) or passive (L-2000) electronics.

MODEL YEAR	FEATURES	EXC. COND. LOW	HIGH
1980-1982		$1,150	$1,500

L-2500 Bass

1997-present. Dual MFD humbuckers, 5-string, figured tops can vary.

MODEL YEAR	FEATURES	EXC. COND. LOW	HIGH
1997-2020		$1,075	$1,400

L-2500 Custom Bass

1997. Ash top, wood-grain binding upgrade.

MODEL YEAR	FEATURES	EXC. COND. LOW	HIGH
1997		$1,125	$1,450

L-5000 Bass

1988-1993. Offset double-cut, solidbody, G&L Z-shaped split-humbucker, 5 strings, approximately 400 made.

MODEL YEAR	FEATURES	EXC. COND. LOW	HIGH
1988-1992		$775	$1,000

L-5500 Bass

1993-1997. Alder body, 5-string.

MODEL YEAR	FEATURES	EXC. COND. LOW	HIGH
1993-1997		$725	$950

L-5500 Custom Bass

1997. Ash top, wood-grain binding upgrade.

MODEL YEAR	FEATURES	EXC. COND. LOW	HIGH
1997		$725	$950

LB-100 Bass

1993-present. Follow-up to earlier Legacy Bass.

MODEL YEAR	FEATURES	EXC. COND. LOW	HIGH
1993-2020		$800	$1,050

Legacy Bass

1992-1993. Offset double-cut solidbody, 1 split-coil, renamed LB-100 in '93.

MODEL YEAR	FEATURES	EXC. COND. LOW	HIGH
1992-1993		$800	$1,050

Lynx Bass

1984-1991. Offset double-cut, solidbody, 2 single-coils, black.

MODEL YEAR	FEATURES	EXC. COND. LOW	HIGH
1984-1991		$800	$1,050

M-2500 Bass

2012-present. Dual MFD humbuckers, 5-string, options and finishes.

MODEL YEAR	FEATURES	EXC. COND. LOW	HIGH
2012-2020		$1,075	$1,400

SB-1 Bass

1982-2000, 2014-present. Solidbody, maple neck, body and 'board, split-humbucker, 1 tone and 1 volume control. Reappears in '14.

MODEL YEAR	FEATURES	EXC. COND. LOW	HIGH
1982-2000		$600	$800

MODEL YEAR	FEATURES	EXC. COND. LOW	HIGH

SB-2 Bass

1982-present. Maple neck with tilt adjustment, 1 split-coil humbucker and 1 single-coil.

1982-2020		$700	$925

Tribute Series Bass

2003-present. Various models, options and finishes.

2003-2020	Various models	$200	$575

Garage by Wicked

2004-2010. A line of basses imported from China by luthier Nicholas Dijkman (Wicked) of Montreal, Quebec.

Gibson

1890s (1902)-present. Professional grade, production, U.S.-made electric basses. Gibson got into the electric bass market with the introduction of their Gibson Electric Bass in '53 (that model was renamed the EB-1 in '58 and reintroduced under that name in '69). Many more bass models followed. Gibson's custom colors can greatly increase the value of older instruments. Custom colors offered from '63 to '69 are Cardinal Red, Ember Red, Frost Blue, Golden Mist Metallic, Heather Metallic, Inverness Green, Kerry Green, Pelham Blue Metallic, Polaris White, Silver Mist Metallic.

20/20 Bass

1987-1988. Designed by Ned Steinberger, slim-wedge Steinberger style solidbody, 2 humbucker pickups, 20/20 logo on headstock, Luna Silver or Ferrari Red finish.

1987-1988		$1,125	$1,475

Electric Bass (EB-1)

1953-1958. Introduced as Gibson Electric Bass in '53, but was called the EB-1 by Gibson in its last year of '58, thus, the whole line is commonly called the EB-1 by collectors, reissued in '69 as the EB-1 (see EB-1 listing), brown.

1953-1958		$4,200	$5,450

EB Bass

1970, 2013-2019. Renamed from Melody Maker Bass, SG body, 1 humbucker pickup. Reintroduced in '13, 4- or 5-string, 2 pickups

1970		$1,050	$1,375
2013-2019	Reintroduced	$430	$560

EB-0 Bass

1959-1979. Double-cut slab body with banjo-type tuners in '59 and '60, double-cut SG-type body with conventional tuners from '61 on, 1 pickup. Faded custom colors are of less value.

1959-1960	Cherry, slab body	$3,800	$4,925
1961	Cherry, SG body	$2,025	$2,625
1962	Cherry	$2,025	$2,625
1963	Cherry	$1,825	$2,350
1964	Cherry, early raised truss rod	$1,725	$2,250
1964	Cherry, late '64 truss rod	$1,575	$2,050
1965-1966	Cherry	$1,500	$1,950
1965-1966	Pelham Blue	$2,650	$3,450
1967-1968	Cherry	$1,300	$1,700
1967-1968	Pelham Blue	$2,275	$2,950
1968	Black	$1,600	$2,100
1968	Burgundy Metallic	$1,600	$2,100
1969	Cherry, solid head	$1,300	$1,700
1969	Pelham Blue	$2,275	$2,950
1969-1974	Slotted head	$1,000	$1,300
1975-1979		$1,000	$1,300

EB-0 F Bass

1962-1965. EB-0 with added built-in fuzz, cherry.

1962-1965		$3,500	$4,500

EB-0 L Bass

1969-1979. 34.5 inch scale version of the EB-0, various colors.

1969-1979		$1,125	$1,475

EB-1 Bass

1969-1972. The Gibson Electric Bass ('53-'58) is often also called the EB-1 (see Electric Bass). Violin-shaped mahogany body, 1 pickup, standard tuners.

1969-1972		$2,900	$3,800

EB-2 Bass

1958-1961, 1964-1972. ES-335-type semi-hollowbody, double-cut, 1 pickup, banjo tuners '58-'60 and conventional tuners '60 on.

1958	Sunburst	$4,050	$5,350
1959	Natural	$4,700	$6,100
1959	Sunburst	$4,100	$5,300
1960	Natural	$4,700	$6,100
1960	Sunburst	$3,900	$5,100
1961	Sunburst, black pu	$2,900	$3,700
1961	Sunburst, brown pu	$3,000	$3,800
1964	Sunburst	$2,200	$2,900
1965	Sunburst	$2,100	$2,800
1966	Cherry, sunburst	$2,050	$2,700
1967-1969	Cherry, sunburst	$2,050	$2,700
1967-1969	Sparkling Burgundy	$2,150	$2,800
1967-1969	Walnut	$1,875	$2,450
1970-1972	Sunburst	$1,875	$2,450

EB-2 D Bass

1966-1972. Two-pickup version of EB-2, cherry, sunburst, or walnut.

1966-1969	Cherry, sunburst	$2,450	$3,200
1967-1969	Sparkling Burgundy	$2,500	$3,300
1967-1969	Walnut	$2,300	$2,975
1970-1972	Cherry, sunburst	$2,300	$2,975

EB-3 Bass

1961-1979. SG-style solidbody, 2 humbuckers, solid peghead '61-'68 and '72-'79, slotted peghead '69-'71, cherry to '71, various colors after.

1961-1964		$4,600	$6,000
1965	Early '65 version	$4,500	$5,900
1965	Late '65 version	$3,250	$4,300
1965	White (rare)	$5,850	$7,600
1966		$2,300	$3,000
1967-1968		$2,000	$2,600
1969	Early '69	$1,850	$2,350
1969	Late '69	$1,650	$2,150
1970		$1,500	$1,950
1971		$1,425	$1,850
1972-1979		$1,300	$1,700

Gibson Electric Bass (EB-1)

Rivington Guitars

1967 Gibson EB-2

Izzy Miller

1985 Gibson Explorer Bass "Designer Series"

Craig Brody

1970 Gibson Les Paul Bass

Jim Mathis

MODEL YEAR	FEATURES	EXC. COND. LOW	HIGH

EB-3 L Bass

1969-1972. 34.5" scale version of EB-3, slotted headstock, EB-3L logo on truss rod cover, cherry, natural, or walnut.

1969-1972		$950	$1,225

EB-4 L Bass

1972-1979. SG-style, 1 humbucker, 34.5" scale, cherry or walnut.

1972-1979		$825	$1,075

EB-6 Bass

1960-1966. Introduced as semi-hollowbody 335-style 6-string with 1 humbucker, changed to SG-style with 2 pickups in '62.

1960	Natural, 335-style	$6,300	$8,200
1960-1961	Sunburst, 335-style	$4,600	$6,000
1962-1964	Cherry, SG-style	$8,100	$10,500
1965-1966	Cherry, SG-style	$6,600	$8,500

EB-650 Bass

1991-1993. Semi-acoustic single cut, maple neck, laminated maple body with center block, 2 TB Plus pickups.

1991-1993	Blond	$3,150	$4,100
1991-1993	Blue	$2,850	$3,700
1991-1993	Other colors	$2,550	$3,300

EB-750 Bass

1991-1993. Like EB-650, but with Bartolini pickups and TCT active EQ.

1991-1993	Blond	$3,150	$4,100
1991-1993	Blue	$2,850	$3,700
1991-1993	Other colors	$2,550	$3,300

ES-335 Bass

2013. Sunburst or ebony.

2013		$1,125	$1,450

ES-Les Paul Bass

2015-2018. Semi-solid, 3-ply maple/poplar/maple top, back and sides, rosewood 'board, mother-of-pearl inlay, faded darkburst or gold top finish.

2015-2018		$1,475	$1,900

Explorer Bass

1984-1987, 2011-2012. Alder body, ebony 'board, dot inlays, 2 humbuckers, various colors. Limited run in '11 in sunburst or silverburst.

1984-1987	Various finishes	$1,050	$1,350
1985	Designer graphics	$1,125	$1,450
2011-2012	Silverburst	$950	$1,250
2011-2012	Sunburst	$950	$1,250

Flying V Bass

1981-1982, 2011-2012, 2020-present. Solidbody, Flying V body. Offered again in '20 with 2 Burstbucker pickups and Antique Natural finish.

1981-1982	Blue stain, ebony	$2,625	$3,400
1981-1982	Silverburst	$3,100	$4,000
2011-2012		$1,050	$1,350
2020		$950	$1,225

Flying V B-2 Bass

2019-2020. Dirty Fingers humbucker pickups, satin ebony finish.

2019-2020		$775	$1,000

Grabber Bass

1973-1982. Double-cut solidbody, 1 pickup, bolt maple neck, maple 'board, various colors.

1973-1982		$1,000	$1,300

Grabber II Bass

2009-2011. Limited Run series, 350 offered, based on '73-'75 model, certificate of authenticity, black.

2009-2011		$900	$1,175

Grabber III Bass (G-3)

1975-1982. Double-cut solidbody, 3 pickups, bolt maple neck, maple 'board, nickel-plated hardware, various colors.

1975-1982		$1,100	$1,425

Gibson IV Bass

1986-1988. Mahogany body and neck, double-cut, 2 pickups, black chrome hardware, various colors.

1986-1988		$1,000	$1,300

Gibson V Bass

1986-1988. Double-cut, 5 strings, 2 pickups.

1986-1988		$1,000	$1,300

L9-S Bass

1973. Natural maple or cherry, renamed Ripper Bass in '74.

1973		$1,200	$1,575

Les Paul Bass

1970-1971. Single-cut solidbody, 2 pickups, walnut finish, renamed Les Paul Triumph Bass '71-'79.

1970-1971		$1,550	$2,000

Les Paul Money Bass

2007-2008. Solidbody offset double-cut, 2 humbuckers, dot markers, figured maple top over mahogany body, 400 made.

2007-2008		$1,000	$1,300

Les Paul Signature Bass

1973-1979. Double-cut, semi-hollowbody, 1 pickup, sunburst or gold (gold only by '76). Name also used on LPB-3 bass in '90s.

1973-1979	Sunburst or gold	$2,575	$3,325

Les Paul Special LPB-1 Bass

1991-1998. 2 TB-Plus pickups, ebony 'board, dots, slab mahogany body, active electronics, also available as 5-string.

1991-1998		$1,000	$1,300

Les Paul Deluxe Plus LPB-2 Bass

1991-1998. Upgraded LPB-1, carved maple top, trapezoid inlays, active eq and Bartolini pickups. Flame maple top Premium version offered '93-'98.

1991-1998		$1,100	$1,425

Les Paul Smartwood Bass

1998. 2 TB pickups, active electronics, trapezoid inlays.

1998		$1,100	$1,425

Les Paul Special V Bass

1993-1996. Single-cut slab body, 5-string, 2 pickups, dot markers, black/ebony.

1993-1996		$725	$950

Les Paul Standard Bass

1999-2018. Maple top, chambered mahogany body, trapezoid inlays, 2 pickups.

1999-2018	Various colors	$1,550	$2,000

Les Paul Standard LPB-3 Bass

1991-1995. Like Les Paul Deluxe LPB-2 Bass, but with TB Plus pickups. Flame maple top Premium version offered '93-'95.

1993-1995	Flamed top	$1,000	$1,300

MODEL YEAR	FEATURES	EXC. COND. LOW	HIGH

Les Paul Triumph Bass
1971-1979. Renamed from Les Paul Bass.

1971-1979	Various colors	$1,300	$1,700
1973-1974	Optional white	$1,500	$2,000

Melody Maker Bass
1967-1970. SG body, 1 humbucker pickup.

1967-1970		$1,225	$1,600

Midtown Standard Bass
2012-2018. Semi-hollow body, double-cut, baked maple or rosewood board, 2 pickups.

2012-2018		$1,075	$1,400

Nikki Sixx Blackbird/Thunderbird Bass
2000-2003, 2009. Blackbird has black finish and hardware, iron cross inlays.'09 Thunderbird was flamed maple.

2000-2003		$1,275	$1,650

Q-80 Bass
1986-1988. Victory Series body shape, 2 pickups, bolt neck, black chrome hardware, renamed Q-90 in '88.

1986-1988		$775	$1,025

Q-90 Bass
1988-1992. Renamed from Q-80, mahogany body, 2 active humbuckers, maple neck, ebony 'board.

1988-1992		$775	$1,025

RD Artist Bass
1977-1982. Double-cut solid maple body, laminated neck, 2 pickups, active electronics, string-thru-body, block inlays, various colors.

1977-1982		$1,750	$2,250

RD Artist CMT Bass
1982. Flamed maple top.

1982		$2,625	$3,400

RD Artist VI Bass
1980. Only 6 made, 6-string.

1980		$3,800	$4,925

RD Standard Bass
1977-1979. Double-cut, solid maple body, laminated neck, 2 pickups, regular electronics, string-thru-body, dot inlays, various colors.

1977-1979		$1,750	$2,250

Ripper Bass
1974-1982. Introduced as L-9 S Bass in '73, double-cut solidbody, glued neck, 2 pickups, string-thru-body, sunburst or natural maple until '76, sunburst only after. Black option '78-'79 and silverburst '80.

1974-1982	Natural, Sunburst	$1,225	$1,600
1978-1979	Black	$1,225	$1,600
1980	Silverburst	$1,925	$2,500

Ripper II Bass
2009-2011. Solid maple body, 34" scale, 2 pickups, natural nitro lacquer.

2009-2011		$900	$1,150

SB Series Bass
1971-1978. In '71, had oval pickups, replaced mid-model with rectangular pickups. Includes 300 and 350 (30" scale, 1 and 2 pickups), 350 (30", 2 pickups), 400 (34", 1 pickup), 450 (34", 2 pickups). The 450 was special order only.

1971-1973	SB-300, 400	$550	$725
1972-1974	SB-350, 450	$550	$725
1975-1978	SB-450 special order	$550	$725

SG Reissue/SG Standard Bass
2005-present. Similar to '60s EB-3, 2 pickups, mahogany body, cherry or white. Renamed SG Standard in '08, various colors.

2005-2020	Various colors	$850	$1,100

SG Standard Faded Bass
2013-2018. Solid mahogany body, baked maple 'board, worn cherry or ebony finish.

2013-2018		$540	$700

SG Supreme Bass
2007-2008. Made in Nashville, SG body with AAA maple top, 2 pickups.

2007-2008		$1,000	$1,300

Thunderbird II Bass
1963-1969. Reverse solidbody until '65, non-reverse solidbody '65-'69, 1 pickup, custom colors available, reintroduced with reverse body for '83-'84.

1963	Sunburst, reverse	$8,550	$11,100
1964	Pelham Blue, reverse	$12,600	$16,400
1964	Sunburst, reverse	$7,000	$9,000
1965	Cardinal Red, non-reverse	$7,850	$10,200
1965	Inverness Green, non-reverse	$7,850	$10,200
1965	Sunburst, non-reverse	$3,775	$4,900
1965	Sunburst, reverse	$6,850	$8,900
1966	Cardinal Red, non-reverse	$6,850	$8,900
1966	Pelham Blue	$10,175	$13,200
1966	Sunburst, non-reverse	$3,775	$4,900
1967	Cardinal Red, non-reverse	$6,750	$8,800
1967	Sunburst, non-reverse	$3,625	$4,700
1968	Cardinal Red, non-reverse	$6,850	$8,900
1968-1969	Sunburst, non-reverse	$3,600	$4,675

Thunderbird III Bass
1979-1982. Reverse body, 2 pickups, Thunderbird logo on 'guard.

1979-1982		$2,400	$3,125

Thunderbird IV Bass
1963-1969. Reverse solidbody until '64, non-reverse solidbody '65-'69, 2 pickups, custom colors available, reintroduced with reverse body for '86-present (see Thunderbird IV Bass Reissue).

1963	Sunburst, reverse	$10,600	$13,800
1964	Frost Blue, reverse	$20,250	$26,300
1964	Pelham Blue, reverse	$20,250	$26,300
1964	Sunburst, reverse	$10,600	$13,800
1965	Cardinal Red, non-reverse	$12,175	$15,800
1965	Inverness Green, non-reverse	$12,175	$15,800
1965	Sunburst, reverse	$9,950	$12,950

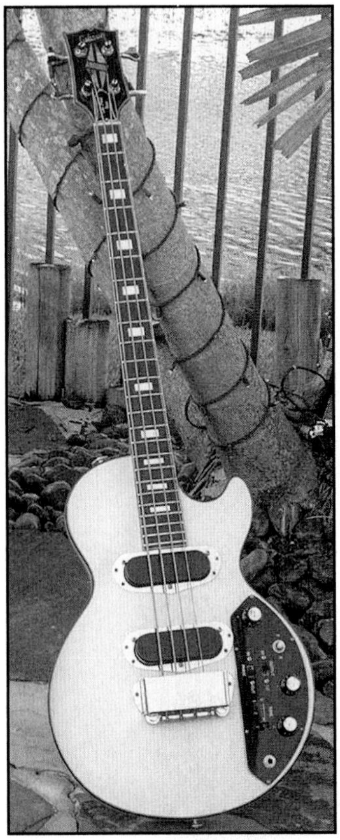

1982 Gibson Les Paul Triumph
Craig Brody

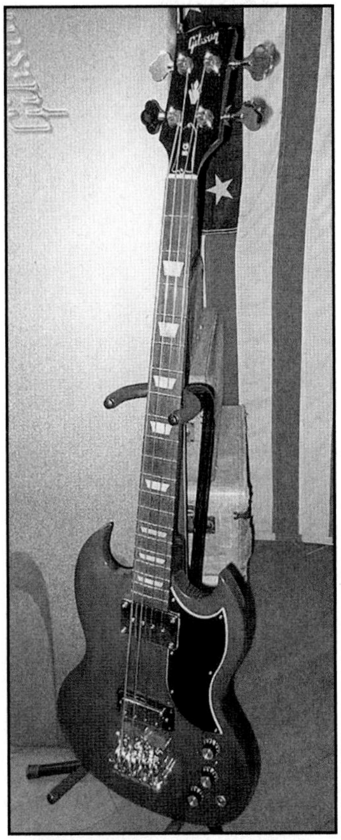

2015 Gibson SG Standard
Rivington Guitars

1976 Gibson Thunderbird 76

Charlie Patty

Gretsch Broadkaster (6119-B) Bass

Christophe Fié

MODEL YEAR	FEATURES	EXC. COND. LOW	HIGH
1965-1966	Sunburst, non-reverse	$5,975	$7,775
1966	White, non-reverse	$11,350	$14,750
1967-1969	Sunburst, non-reverse	$6,000	$7,775

Thunderbird IV Bass (Reissue)

1987-2016. Has reverse body and 2 pickups, various colors.

1987-2016	Various colors	$1,275	$1,650

Thunderbird IV Bass Zebra Wood Bass

2007. Guitar of the Week (week 11 of '07), limited run of 400, Zebrawood body.

2007		$1,350	$1,750

Thunderbird 50th Anniversary Bass

2013-2018. Mahogany body and neck, rosewood 'board, Bullion Gold finish.

2013-2018		$1,350	$1,750

Thunderbird 76 Bass

1976 only. Reverse solidbody, 2 pickups, rosewood 'board, various colors.

1976		$2,800	$3,600

Thunderbird 79 Bass

1979 only. Reverse solidbody, 2 pickups, sunburst.

1979		$2,800	$3,600

Thunderbird Short Scale Bass

2011-2013. 30.5" scale, 2 pickups, nitro satin ebony finish.

2011-2013		$875	$1,125

Thunderbird Studio/IV Studio Bass

2005-2007. 4- or 5-string versions.

2005-2007		$1,075	$1,400

Victory Artist Bass

1981-1985. Double-cut, solidbody, 2 humbuckers and active electronics, various colors.

1981-1985		$900	$1,200

Victory Custom Bass

1982-1984. Double-cut, solidbody, 2 humbuckers, passive electronics, limited production.

1982-1984		$900	$1,200

Victory Standard Bass

1981-1986. Double-cut, solidbody, 1 humbucker, active electronics, various colors.

1981-1986		$675	$875

Godin

1987-present. Intermediate and professional grade, production, solidbody electric and acoustic/electric basses from luthier Robert Godin. They also build guitars and mandolins.

A Series Bass

1990s-present. Various acoustic/electric, 4- or 5-string.

1990s-2020	A-4, A-5	$375	$500

Freeway A Series Bass

2005-2012. Double-cut solidbodies, 4- or 5-string, passive or active..

2005-2012	Freeway A-4	$375	$500
2005-2012	Freeway A-5	$400	$525

Godlyke

2006-present. Professional and premium grade, production, solidbody basses from effects distributor Godlyke.

Goya

1955-1996. Originally imports from Sweden, brand later used on Japanese and Korean imports. They also offered guitars, mandolins and banjos.

Electric Solidbody Bass

1960s	Various models	$500	$700

Gretsch

1883-present. Intermediate and professional grade, production, solidbody, hollow body, and acoustic/electric basses. Gretsch came late to the electric bass game, introducing their first models in the early '60s. They also build guitars, amps and steels. In 2012 they again offered mandolins, ukes and banjos.

Broadkaster (6119-B) Bass

1991-2013. Single-cut hollowbody, maple top, back and sides.

1991-2013		$1,175	$1,525

Broadkaster (7605/7606) Bass

1975-1979. Double-cut solidbody, 1 pickup, bolt-on maple neck, natural (7605) or sunburst (7606).

1975-1979		$575	$750

Committee (7629) Bass

1977-1980. Double-cut walnut and maple soldibody, neck-thru, 1 pickup, natural.

1977-1980		$600	$775

G2220 Electromatic Jr. Jet Bass II

2012-present. Short scale, 2 pickups, various colors.

2012-2020		$150	$215

G5440LS Electromatic Long Scale Hollow Body Bass

2012-2020. Single-cut, 2 pickups, "G" tailpiece, various colors.

2012-2020		$500	$700

G6072 Long Scale Hollow Body Bass

1998-2006. Reissue of the '68 double-cut hollowbody, 2 pickups, sunburst, gold hardware.

1998-2006		$825	$1,100

Model 6070/6072 Bass

1963-1971 (1972 for 6070). Originally listed as the PX6070 Cello Bass, large thinline hollowbody double-cut archtop, fake f-holes, 1 pickup (6070) or 2 (6072), gold hardware.

1963-1964	6070, with endpin	$1,575	$2,050
1965-1972	6070, no endpin, 1 pickup	$1,125	$1,475
1968-1971	6072, 2 pickups	$1,100	$1,425

Model 6071/6073 Bass

1968-1971 (1972 for 6071). Single-cut hollowbody, fake f-holes, 1 pickup (6071) or 2 (6073), padded back, red mahogany.

1968-1971	6073, 2 pickups	$1,450	$1,900
1968-1972	6071, 1 pickup	$1,300	$1,700

MODEL YEAR	FEATURES	EXC. COND. LOW	HIGH

Model 7615 Bass

1972-1975. Offset double-cut solidbody, slotted bass horn (monkey grip), large polished rosewood 'guard covering most of the body, 2 pickups, dot markers, brown mahogany finish. Only bass offered in Gretsch catalog for this era.

1972-1975		$750	$975

TK 300 (7626/7627) Bass

1976-1981. Double-cut solidbody, 1 pickup, Autumn Red Stain or natural.

1976-1981		$475	$625

Guild

1952-present. Guild added electric basses in the mid-'60s and offered them until '02. New owner, Cordoba Music, reintroduced acoustic and electric basses to the line in '15.

Ashbory Bass

1986-1988, 2009. 18" scale, total length 30", fretless, silicone rubber strings, active electronics, low-impedance circuitry.

1986-1988		$350	$450
2009	Fender Guild reissue	$170	$225

B-4 E Bass

1993-2000. Acoustic/electric single-cut flat-top, mahogany sides with arched mahogany back, multi-bound, gold hardware until '95, chrome after.

1993-2000		$475	$625

B-30 E Bass

1987-1999. Single-cut flat-top acoustic/electric, mahogany sides, arched mahogany back, multi-bound, fretless optional.

1987-1999		$850	$1,125

B-50 Acoustic Bass

1975-1987. Acoustic flat-top, mahogany sides with arched mahogany back, spruce top, multi-bound, renamed B-30 in '87.

1975-1987		$1,000	$1,300

B-301/B-302 Bass

1976-1981. Double-cut solidbody, chrome-plated hardware. Models include B-301 (mahogany, 1 pickup), B-301A (ash, 1 pickup), B-302 (mahogany, 2 pickups), B-302A (ash, 2 pickups), and B-302AF (ash, fretless).

1976-1981	B-301, B-301A	$675	$875
1976-1981	B-302, B-302A	$725	$950
1977-1981	B-302AF	$725	$950

B-401/B-402 Bass

1980-1983. Model 401 with active circuit, 1 pickup. Model 402 passive and active, 2 pickups. A for ash body.

1980-1981	B-401, B-401A	$675	$875
1980-1982	B-402, B402A	$675	$875

B-500 C Acoustic Bass

1992-1993. Acoustic/electric flat-top, round soundhole, single-cut, solid spruce top, maple back and sides, dark stain, limited production.

1992-1993		$1,025	$1,350

FS-46 Bass

1983. Acoustic-electric flat-top, single-cut, sharp horn fretless.

1983		$575	$750

MODEL YEAR	FEATURES	EXC. COND. LOW	HIGH

Jet Star Bass

1964-1970 (limited production '68-'70). Offset double-cut solidbody, short treble horn, 1 pickup, 2-on-a-side tuners '64-'66 and 4 in-line tuners '66-'70.

1964-1966	2-on-side tuners	$1,075	$1,400
1966-1970	4-in-line tuners	$1,075	$1,400

JS I/JS II Bass

1970-1977. Double-cut solidbody, 30" scale, 1 pickup (JS I or 1) or 2 (JS II or 2), carved-top oak leaf design available for '72-'76. 34" long scale (LS) versions offered fretted and fretless for '74-'75.

1970-1977	JS I	$1,100	$1,500
1970-1977	JS II	$1,200	$1,600
1974-1976	JS I, carved	$1,200	$1,600
1974-1976	JS II, carved	$1,300	$1,700

M-85 I/M-85 II Bass (Semi-Hollow)

1967-1972. Single-cut semi-hollowbody, 1 pickup (M-85 I) or 2 (M-85 II).

1967-1972	M-85 I	$1,175	$1,500
1967-1972	M-85 II	$1,250	$1,625

M-85 I/M-85 II BluesBird Bass (Solidbody)

1972-1976. Single-cut soldibody archtop, Chesterfield headstock inlay, cherry mahogany, 1 humbucker pickup (I) or 2 (II).

1972-1973	M-85 I	$1,275	$1,700
1972-1976	M-85 II	$1,350	$1,800

MB-801 Bass

1981-1982. Double-cut solidbody, 1 pickup, dot inlays.

1981-1982		$550	$725

SB-201/SB-202/SB-203 Bass

1982-1983. Double-cut solidbody, 1 split coil pickup (201), 1 split coil and 1 single coil (202), or 1 split coil and 2 single coils (203).

1982-1983	SB-201	$650	$850
1982-1983	SB-202	$700	$900
1983	SB-203	$725	$925

SB-502 E Bass

1984-1985. Double-cut solidbody, 2 pickups, active electronics.

1984-1985		$725	$925

SB-600/Pilot Series Bass

1983-1993. Offset double-cut solidbody, bolt-on neck, poplar body. Models include SB-601 (1 pickup), SB-602 (2 pickups or fretless), SB-602 V (2 pickups, 5-string), SB-604 (2 pickups, offset peghead) and SB-605 (5-string, hipshot low D tuner). Models 604 and 605 are replaced in '93 with Pro4 and Pro5 Pilot.

1983-1989	SB-601	$450	$575
1983-1989	SB-602	$500	$675
1983-1989	SB-602 V	$500	$675
1983-1989	SB-602, fretless	$500	$675
1986-1988	SB-604 Pilot	$500	$675
1986-1993	SB-605	$500	$675

SB-608 Flying Star Motley Crue Bass

1984-1985. Pointy 4-point star body, 2 pickups, E version had EMG pickups.

1984-1985		$875	$1,150

1968 Gretsch Model 6071

Imaged by Heritage Auctions, HA.com

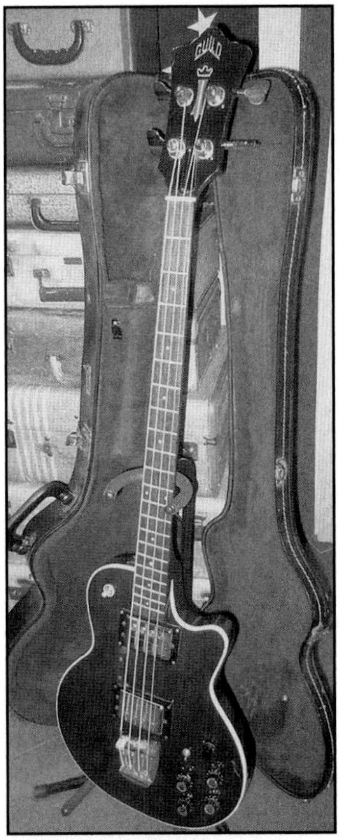

1974 Guild M-85 II Bluesbird

Rivington Guitars

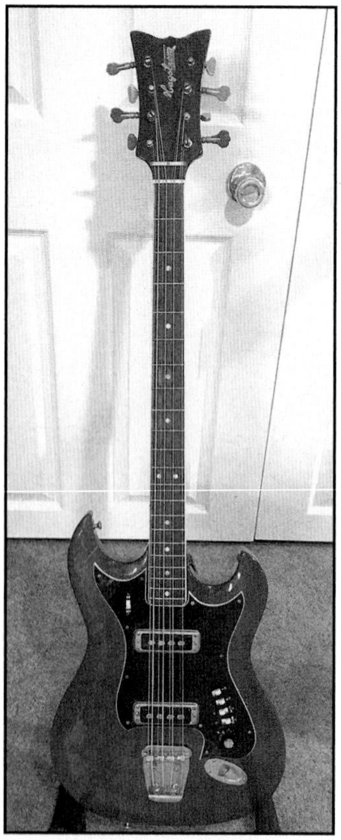

1967 Hagstrom H-8

Justin Nortillo

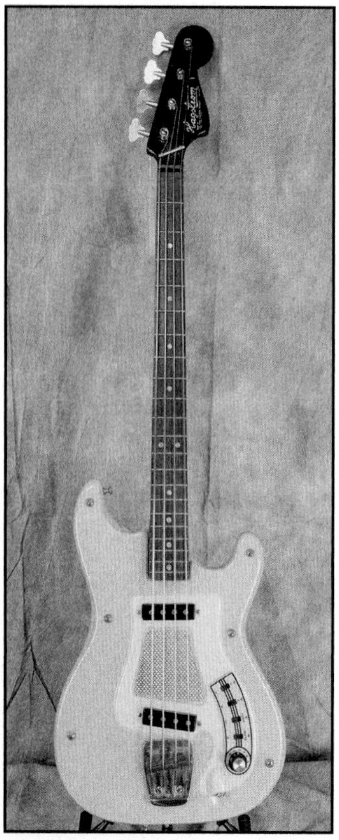

1966 Hagstrom Model I B

McKenzie River Music

MODEL YEAR	FEATURES	EXC. COND. LOW	HIGH

Starfire Bass

1965-1975. Double-cut semi-hollow thinbody, 1 pickup, mahogany neck, chrome-plated hardware, cherry or sunburst.

1965-1969	Single-coil	$1,900	$2,400
1970-1975	Humbucker	$1,900	$2,400

Starfire II Bass

1967-1978. Two-pickup version of Starfire Bass. Single-coils until '69, humbuckers after, sunburst, cherry or very rare black. Starfire II Bass Special had gold hardware.

1967-1969	2 single-coils	$1,950	$2,450
1967-1969	Black	$2,100	$2,700
1970-1978	2 humbuckers	$1,950	$2,450

Starfire II Reissue Bass

1997-present. Reissue of 2 humbucker version.

1997-2020		$800	$1,050

X-701/X-702 Bass

1982-1984. Body with 4 sharp horns with extra long bass horn, 1 pickup (X-701) or 2 (X-702), various metallic finishes.

1982-1984	X-701	$1,000	$1,325
1982-1984	X-702	$1,050	$1,375

GW Basses & Luthiery

2004-present. Professional and premium grade, production/custom, basses built by luthier Grandon Westlund in West Lafayette, Indiana.

Hagstrom

1921-1983, 2004-present. This Swedish guitar company first offered electric basses in '61.

Concord II Deluxe Bass

1967-1970. Bass version of V-IN guitar, 335-style body, 2 pickups, sunburst.

1967-1970		$1,250	$1,650

Coronado IV Bass

1963-1970. Offset double cut, Bi-Sonic pickups.

1963-1970		$875	$1,150

H-8 Bass

1967-1969. Double-cut solidbody, 8 strings, 2 pickups, various colors.

1967-1969		$1,425	$1,925

Kent Bass

1963-1964. 2 single-coils, 4 sliders.

1962-1966		$500	$650

Model I B/F-100 B Bass

1965-1973. Offset double-cut solidbody, 2 single-coils, 5 sliders, 30" scale.

1965-1973		$575	$750

Model II B/F-400 Bass

1965-1970. Like Model I, but with 30.75" scale, red, black, white or blue. Called F-400 in U.S., II B elsewhere.

1965-1970		$575	$750

Swede 2000 Bass (With Synth)

1977. Circuitry on this Swede bass connected to the Ampeg Patch 2000 pedal so bass would work with various synths.

1977		$825	$1,100

MODEL YEAR	FEATURES	EXC. COND. LOW	HIGH

Swede Bass

1971-1976, 2004-present. Single-cut solidbody, block inlays, bolt neck, 2 humbuckers, 30.75" scale, cherry or black

1971-1976		$750	$975

Super Swede Bass

1979-1983, 2004-present. Like Swede, but with neck-thru body, 32" scale, sunburst, mahogany or black.

1979-1983		$775	$1,000

Hamer

1975-2012, 2017-present. Founded in Arlington Heights, Illinois, by Paul Hamer and Jol Dantzig, Hamer was purchased by Kaman in '88. They also built guitars. Fender acquired Hamer in '08 and suspended production in '12. The brand was reintroduced in '17 by Jam Industries.

8-String Short-Scale Bass

1978-1993. Double cut solidbody, 1 or 2 pickups, 30.5" scale.

1978-1993		$1,500	$2,000

12-String Acoustic Bass

1985-2010. Semi-hollow, long scale, single cut, soundhole, 2 pickups. Import XT model added in the 2000s.

1985-2010		$1,950	$2,600

12-String Short-Scale Bass

1978-1996. Four sets of 3 strings - a fundamental and 2 tuned an octave higher, double cut maple and mahogany solidbody, 30.5" scale.

1978-1996		$1,500	$2,000

Blitz Bass

1982-1990. Explorer-style solidbody, 2 pickups, bolt-on neck.

1982-1990		$1,400	$1,800

Chaparral Bass

1986-1995, 2000-2008. Solidbody, 2 pickups, glued-in neck, later basses have bolt-on neck.

1986-1987	Set-neck	$1,200	$1,600
1987-1995	Bolt-on neck	$1,100	$1,450

Chaparral 5-String Bass

1987-1995. Five strings, solidbody, 2 pickups, glued-in neck, later basses have 5-on-a-side reverse peghead.

1987-1995		$1,200	$1,550

Chaparral 12-String Bass

1992-2012. Long 34" scale 12-string, offset double cut. Import XT model added in '01.

1992-2012	USA	$1,500	$2,000
2000-2012	Import	$200	$400

Chaparral Max Bass

1986-1995. Chaparral Bass with figured maple body, glued-in neck and boomerang inlays.

1986-1995		$700	$900

Cruise Bass

1982-1990, 1995-1999. J-style solidbody, 2 pickups, glued neck ('82-'90) or bolt-on neck ('95-'99), also available as a 5-string.

1982-1990	Set-neck	$750	$1,000
1995-1999	Bolt-on neck	$650	$900

Cruise 5 Bass

1982-1989. Five-string version, various colors.

1982-1989		$850	$1,100

MODEL YEAR	FEATURES	EXC. COND. LOW	HIGH

FBIV Bass

1985-1987. Reverse Firebird shape, 1 P-Bass Slammer and 1 J-Bass Slammer pickup, mahogany body, rosewood 'board, dots.

1985-1987		$750	$1,000

Monaco 4 Bass

2002-2012. Flamed maple top, rosewood 'board, Tobacco Burst or '59 Burst finish.

2002-2012		$1,800	$2,350

Standard Bass

1975-1984, 2001. US-made, Explorer-style headstock, 2 humbuckers. Imported in '01.

1975-1979	Flamed top, bound	$3,500	$5,800
1975-1984	Plain top, unbound	$2,500	$3,400
1980-1984	Flamed top, bound	$3,100	$5,200
2001	Import	$200	$400

Velocity 5 Bass

2002-2012. Offset double-cut, long bass horn, active, 1 humbucker.

2002-2012		$200	$400

Harmony

1892-1976, late 1970s-present. Harmony once was one of the biggest instrument makers in the world, making guitars and basses under their own brand and for others.

H Series Bass

Late-1980s-early-1990s. F-style solidbody copies, 1 or 2 pickups, all models begin H.

1980s-90s		$100	$125

H-22 Bass

1959-1972. Single-cut hollowbody, 2-on-a-side, 1 pickup.

1959-1969		$1,000	$1,300
1970-1972		$850	$1,100

H-22 Reissue Bass

2000s. Imported reissue, 1 pickup.

2000s		$265	$350

H-25/Silhouette Bass

1963-1967. Offset double-cut solidbody, 1 pickup (H-25) or 2 (Silhouette).

1963-1967	H-25	$600	$800
1963-1967	Silhouette	$650	$850

H-27 Bass

1968-1972. Double-cut hollowbody, 4-on-a-side, 2 pickups.

1968-1972		$650	$850

Hartke

Hartke offered a line of wood and aluminum-necked basses from 2000 to '03.

Heartfield

1989-1994. Distributed by Fender, imported from Japan. They also offered guitars.

Electric Bass

1989-1994. Double-cut solidbody, graphite reinforced neck, 2 single-coils, available in 4-, 5- and 6-string models.

1989-1994		$250	$400

MODEL YEAR	FEATURES	EXC. COND. LOW	HIGH

Heritage

1985-present. Mainly a builder of guitars, Kalamazoo, Michigan's Heritage has offered a few basses in the past.

HB-1 Bass

1987. P-style body, limited production, single-split pickup, 4-on-a-side tuners, figured maple body, bolt-on neck.

1987		$575	$750

Höfner

1887-present. Professional grade, production, basses. They also offer guitars and bowed instruments. Höfner basses, made famous in the U.S. by one Paul McCartney, are made in Germany.

Icon Series

2007-2011. Chinese versions of classic Höfners, often sold without a case or gigbag.

2007-2011		$175	$250

Model (G)5000/1 Super Beatle (G500/1) Bass

1968-2011. Bound ebony 'board, gold-plated hardware, natural finish, the version with active circuit is called G500/1 Super Beatle, reissued in '94.

1968-1979	LH	$2,000	$2,700
1968-1979	RH	$1,400	$1,850

Model 172 Series Bass

1968-1970. Offset double-cut, 6-on-a-side tuners, 2 pickups, 2 slide switches, dot markers, 172/S shaded sunburst, 172/R red vinyl covered body, 172/I vinyl covered with white top and black back.

1968-1970	172/I, white	$725	$950
1968-1970	172/R, red	$725	$950
1968-1970	172/S, sunburst	$725	$950

Model 182 Solid Bass

1962-1985. Offset double-cut solidbody, 2 pickups.

1962-1965		$725	$950

Model 185 Solid Bass

1962-ca. 1970. Classic offset double-cut solidbody, 2 double-coil pickups.

1962-1970		$725	$950

Model 500/1 Beatle Bass

1956-present. Semi-acoustic, bound body in violin shape, glued-in neck, 2 pickups, right- or left-handed, sunburst. Listed as 500/1 Vintage '58, '59, '62 and '63 in '90s through 2014. Currently named 500/1 Violin Bass.

1956-1959	RH or LH	$5,300	$6,900
1960	LH, McCartney	$4,600	$6,000
1960	RH	$3,700	$4,800
1961	LH	$4,600	$6,000
1961	LH, McCartney	$5,800	$7,600
1961	RH	$3,700	$4,800
1962-1963	LH	$3,700	$4,800
1962-1963	RH	$3,300	$4,300
1964	LH	$3,700	$4,800
1964	LH, McCartney	$4,800	$6,200
1964	RH	$3,000	$3,900
1964	RH, McCartney	$3,300	$4,300
1965	LH	$2,300	$3,100
1965	RH	$2,100	$2,800
1966	LH	$2,200	$2,900

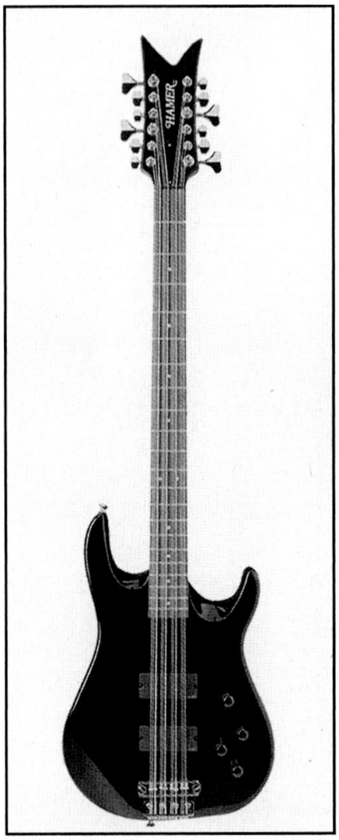

Hamer Chaparral 12-String

1964 Höfner 500/1 Beatle

Steve Lee

1963 Höfner 500/2 Club

Larry Wassgren

Ibanez SR-300

Rivington Guitars

MODEL YEAR	FEATURES	EXC. COND. LOW	HIGH
1966	RH	$2,000	$2,700
1967	LH	$2,100	$2,700
1967	RH	$1,750	$2,300
1968-1973	LH	$2,000	$2,700
1968-1973	RH	$1,450	$1,900
1974-1979	RH or LH	$1,350	$1,800

'58 Model 500/1 Reissue

2008-2013		$1,350	$1,800

'62 Model 500/1 Beatle Bass Reissue

1990s-2014		$1,350	$1,800

'63 Model 500/1 Beatle Bass Reissue

1994-2010. Right- or left-handed.

1994-2010		$1,350	$1,800

'64 Model 500/1 Beatle Bass Reissue

2015		$1,350	$1,800

Model 500/1 1964-1984 Reissue Bass

1984. '1964-1984' neckplate notation.

1984		$1,350	$1,800

Model 500/1 40th Anniversary Bass

1995-1996. Only 300 made.

1995-1996		$2,300	$3,000

Model 500/1 50th Anniversary Bass

2006. Pickguard logo states '50th Anniversary Höfner Violin Bass 1956-2006', large red Höfner logo also on 'guard, 150 made.

2006		$2,300	$3,000

Model 500/1 Cavern Bass

2005. Limted run of 12, includes certificate.

2005		$1,350	$1,800

Model 500/1 Cavern Bass Music Ground

1993. UK commissioned by Music Ground, said to be one of the first accurate reissues, 40 made.

1993		$1,350	$1,800

Model 500/1 Contemporary

2007-2008. Contemporary Series.

2007-2008		$475	$625

Model 500/2 Bass/Club Bass

1965-1970, 2015-present. Similar to the 500/1, but with 'club' body Höfner made for England's Selmer, sunburst. Club Bass has been reissued in various colors.

1965-1970		$1,450	$1,900
2015-2020		$1,450	$1,900

Model 500/3 Senator Bass

1962-1964. Single-cut thin body, f-holes, 1 511b pickup, sunburst.

1962-1964		$1,350	$1,750

Model 500/5 Bass

1959-1963. Single-cut body with Beatle Bass-style pickups, sunburst. Becomes President Bass in '63.

1959-1963		$2,900	$3,800

Model 500/6 Bass

Late-1960s. Introduced in '67, semi-acoustic, thinline, soft double-cut, 2 pickups, 4 control knobs, dot markers, sunburst.

1967		$1,450	$1,875

Model 500/8BZ / B500/8BZ

Late-1960s. Semi-acoustic, thinline, sharp double-cut, multiple-line position markers, built in flip-fuzz and bass boost, sunburst or natural.

1967	500/8BZ, sunburst	$1,500	$1,950
1967	B500/8BZ, natural	$1,500	$1,950

President Bass

1963-1972. Made for England's Selmer, single-cut archtop, 2 Beatle Bass-style pickups, sunburst.

1963-1965		$2,000	$2,600
1966-1969		$1,575	$2,050
1970-1972		$1,550	$2,000

Hondo

1969-1987, 1991-2005. Budget grade, production, imported acoustic and electric solidbody basses. They also offered guitars, banjos and mandolins.

Electric Solidbody Bass

1969-1987, 1991-2005. Various models.

1969-1999	Rare models	$250	$850
1969-1999	Standard models	$75	$175

Hoyer

1874-present. Intermediate grade, production, electric basses. They also build guitars.

Electric Bass

1960s		$400	$700

Ibanez

1932-present. Intermediate and professional grade, production, solidbody basses. They also have guitars, amps, and effects.

AXB Axstar Series Bass

1986-1987. Various models.

1986-1987		$200	$400

BTB Series Bass

1999-present. Various models.

1999-2020		$200	$500

Challenger Bass

1977-1978. Offered as P-bass or J-bass style, and with ash body option.

1977-1978		$350	$475

DB Destroyer II X Series Bass

1984-1986. Futuristic-style body, P- and J-style pickups, dot markers, bolt neck.

1984-1986		$375	$500

DT Destroyer II Series Bass

1980-1985. Futuristic-style body.

1983-1986		$500	$650

ICB Iceman Bass

1994-1996, 2011. Iceman body, basswood (300) or mahogany (500) body. 300 reissued in '11.

1994	ICB500, black	$400	$575
1994-1996	ICB300, white	$400	$575

Jet King Bass

2009-2010. Retro offset double-cut solidbody, bolt neck.

2009-2010		$175	$300

MC Musician Series Bass

1978-1988. Various models, solidbody, neck-thru.

1978-1988		$800	$1,400

Model 2030 Bass

1970-1973. First copy era bass, offset double-cut, sunburst.

1970-1973		$550	$750

MODEL YEAR	FEATURES	EXC. COND. LOW	HIGH

Model 2353 Bass

1974-1976. Copy model, offset double-cut, 1 pickup, black.

1974-1976		$500	$700

Model 2364B Bass

1971-1973. Dan Armstrong see-thru Lucite copy with 2 mounted humbucker pickups, clear finish.

1971-1973		$650	$900

Model 2365 Bass

1974-1975 Copy model, Offset double-cut, rosewood 'board, pearloid block markers, sunburst

1974-1975		$550	$750

Model 2366 B/2366 FLB Bass

1974-1975. Copy model, offset double-cut, 1 split-coil pickup, sunburst, FLB fretless model.

1974-1975		$500	$700

Model 2385 Bass

1974-1975. Copy model, offset double-cut, 1 pickup, ash natural finish.

1974-1975		$500	$700

Model 2388 B Bass

1974-1976. Ric 4001 copy.

1974-1976		$500	$700

Model 2452 Bass

1975. Ripper copy.

1975		$500	$700

Model 2459 B Destroyer Bass

1974-1977. Laminated ash body, copy of Korina Explorer-style.

1974-1977		$1,600	$2,100

Model 2537 DX Bass

1974-1975. Hofner Beatle copy.

1974-1975		$550	$700

Model 2609B Black Eagle Bass

1974-1976. Burns-like bass, offset double-cut solidbody, sharp curving horns.

1974-1976		$950	$1,120

PL Pro Line Series Bass

1986-1987. Offset double cut solidbody.

1986-1987		$200	$475

RB/RS Roadstar Series Bass

1983-1987. Solidbody basses, various models and colors.

1983-1987		$250	$500

Rocket Roll Bass

1974-1976. Korina solidbody, V-shape, natural.

1974-1976		$1,700	$2,200

S/SB Series Bass

1990-1992. Various ultra slim solidbody basses.

1990-1992		$200	$450

SR Sound Gear Series Bass

1987-present. Sleek, lightweight designs, active electronics, bolt necks. Model numbers higher than 1000 are usually arched-top, lower usually flat body.

1987-2020		$200	$450

ST-980 Studio Bass

1979-1980. Double cut, 8-string, bolt-on neck, walnut-maple-mahogany body.

1979-1980		$550	$700

Imperial

Ca.1963-ca.1970. Imported by the Imperial Accordion Company of Chicago, Illinois. Early guitars and basses made in Italy, but by ca. '66 Japanese-made.

Electric Solidbody Bass

1960s	Various models	$150	$400

Hollowbody Bass

1960s. Hollowbody with sharp double-cuts.

1960s		$150	$400

Jackson

1980-present. Intermediate, professional, and premium grade, production, solidbody basses. They also offer guitars. Founded by Grover Jackson, who owned Charvel.

Concert C5P 5-String Bass (Import)

1998-2000. Bolt neck, dot inlay, chrome hardware.

1998-2000		$120	$160

Concert Custom Bass (U.S.A.)

1984-1995. Neck-thru Custom Shop bass.

1984-1989		$975	$1,300
1990-1995		$600	$800

Concert EX 4-String Bass (Import)

1992-1995. Bolt neck, dot inlay, black hardware.

1992-1995		$200	$275

Concert V 5-String Bass (Import)

1992-1995. Bound neck, shark tooth inlay.

1992-1995		$275	$400

Concert XL 4-String Bass (Import)

1992-1995. Bound neck, shark tooth inlay.

1992-1995		$225	$325

Kelly Pro Bass

1994-1995. Pointy-cut bouts, neck-thru solidbody, shark fin marker inlays.

1994-1995		$600	$800

Piezo Bass

1986. Piezo bridge pickup, neck-thru, shark tooth inlays. Student model has rosewood 'board, no binding. Custom Model has ebony 'board and binding.

1986		$1,150	$1,500

Soloist Bass

1996. Pointy headstock, 4-string.

1996		$600	$800

Surfcaster SC1 Bass

1998-2001. Tube and humbucker pickups.

1998-2001		$900	$1,200

Jerry Jones

1981-2011. Intermediate grade, production, semi-hollow body electric basses from luthier Jerry Jones, and built in Nashville, Tennessee. They also build guitars and sitars. Jones retired in 2011.

Neptune Longhorn 4 Bass

1988-2011. Based on Danelectro longhorn models, 4-string, 2 lipstick-tube pickups, 30" scale.

1988-2011		$1,050	$1,375

Neptune Longhorn 6 Bass

1988-2011. 6-string version.

1988-2011		$1,300	$1,700

1979 Ibanez ST-980 Studio

Willie Moseley

1997 Jerry Jones Neptune Longhorn 4

Ken Quick

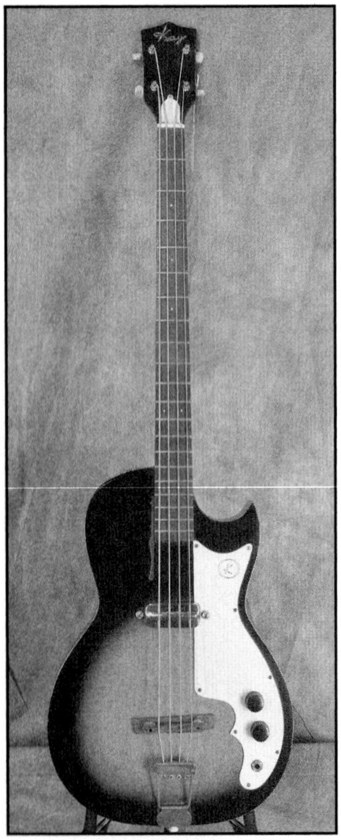

1962 Kay
Dallas Alice Music

1964 Klira Electric Solidbody
Rivington Guitars

MODEL YEAR	FEATURES	EXC. COND. LOW	HIGH

Neptune Shorthorn 4 Bass

1988-2011. Danelectro Coke bottle headstock, short horns double cut, 2 pickups.

1988-2011 — $1,050 — $1,375

Juzek

Violin maker John Juzek was originally located in Prague, Czeckoslovakia, but moved to West Germany due to World War II. Prague instruments considered by most to be more valuable. Many German instruments were mass produced with laminate construction and some equate these German basses with the Kay laminate basses of the same era. Juzek still makes instruments.

Kalamazoo

1933-1942, 1965-1970. Kalamazoo was a brand Gibson used on one of their budget lines. They also used the name on electric basses, guitars and amps from '65 to '67.

Electric Bass

1965-1970 — $375 — $525

Kapa

Ca. 1962-1970. Kapa was founded by Koob Veneman in Maryland and offered basses and guitars.

Electric Bass

1962-1970 Various models — $225 — $650

Kawai

1927-present. Japanese instrument manufacturer Kawai started offering guitars under other brand names around '56. There were few imports carrying the Kawai brand until the late-'70s; best known for high quality basses. Kawai quit offering guitars and basses around 2002.

Electric Bass

1970-2002 Various models — $245 — $600

Kay

Ca. 1931-present. Currently, budget and intermediate grade, production, imported solidbody basses. They also make amps, guitars, banjos, mandolins, ukes, and violins. Kay introduced upright acoustic laminate basses and 3/4 viols in '38 and electric basses in '54.

C1 Concert String Bass

1938-1967. Standard (3/4) size student bass, laminated construction, spruce top, figured maple back and sides, shaded light brown.

1938-1949 — $1,700 — $2,200
1950-1959 — $1,600 — $2,100
1960-1967 — $1,500 — $2,000

K-160 Electronic Bass

1955-1956. Same as K-162, but with plain white plastic trim.

1955-1956 — $725 — $950

K-162 Electronic Bass

1955-1956. Bass version of K-161Thin Twin "Jimmy Reed," single-cut, 1 tube-style pickup.

1955-1956 — $725 — $950

K-5965 Pro Bass

1954-1965. Single-cut, 1 pickup. named K-5965 Pro by 1961.

1954-1965 — $725 — $950

K-5970 Jazz Special Electric Bass

1960-1964. Double-cut, pickup, Kelvinator headstock, black or blond.

1960-1964 — $1,900 — $2,500

M-1 (Maestro) String Bass

1952-late-1960s. Standard (3/4) size bass, laminated construction, spruce top and curly maple back and sides. Model M-3 is the Junior (1/4) size bass, Model M-1 B has a blond finish, other models include the S-51 B Chubby Jackson Five-String Bass and the S-9 Swingmaster.

1952-1967 — $2,000 — $2,600

M-5 (Maestro) String Bass

1957-late-1960s. Five strings.

1957-1967 — $2,200 — $2,900

Semi-hollowbody Bass

1954-1966. Single or double cut, 1 or 2 pickups.

1954-1966 1 pickup — $300 — $400
1954-1966 2 pickups — $350 — $450

Solidbody Bass

1965-1968. Single or double cut, 1 or 2 pickups.

1965-1968 1 pickup — $300 — $400
1965-1968 2 pickups — $350 — $450

Ken Smith

See listing under Smith.

Kent

1961-1969. Guitars and basses imported from Japan by Buegeleisen and Jacobson of New York, New York. Manufacturers unknown but many early instruments by Guyatone and Teisco.

Electric Bass

1962-1969. Import models include 628 Newport, 634 Basin Street, 629, and 635.

1961-1969 Common model — $150 — $225
1961-1969 Rare model — $225 — $525

Kimberly

Late-1960s-early-1970s. Private branded import made in the same Japanese factory as Teisco. They also made guitars.

Violin Bass

1960s — $395 — $525

Kingston

Ca. 1958-1967. Imported from Japan by Westheimer Importing Corp. of Chicago. Early examples made by Guyatone and Teisco. They also offered guitars, mandolins and banjos.

Electric Bass

1960s Common model — $125 — $300
1960s Rare model — $300 — $600

Klira

Founded 1887 in Schoenbach, Germany, mainly making violins, but added guitars and basses in the

MODEL YEAR	FEATURES	EXC. COND. LOW	HIGH

1950s. The instruments of the '50s and '60s were aimed at the budget market, but workmanship improved with the '70s models.

Electric Bass

1960s	Common model	$300	$500
1960s	Rare model	$500	$800

Kramer

1976-1990, 1995-present. Budget grade, production, imported solidbody basses. They also offer guitars. Kramer's first guitars and basses featured aluminum necks with wooden inserts on back. Around '80 they started to switch to more economical wood necks and aluminum necks were last produced in '85. Gibson acquired the brand in '97.

250-B Special Bass

1977-1979. Offset double-cut, aluminum neck, Ebonol 'board, zero fret, 1 single-coil, natural.

1977-1979		$650	$850

350-B Standard Bass

1976-1979. Offset double-cut, aluminum neck, Ebonol 'board, tropical woods, 1 single-coil, dots. The 350 and 450 were Kramer's first basses.

1976-1979		$800	$1,050

450-B Deluxe Bass

1976-1980. As 350-B, but with 2 single-coils and blocks.

1976-1980		$825	$1,100

650-B Artist Bass

1977-1980. Double-cut, birdseye maple/burled walnut, aluminum neck, zero fret, mother-of-pearl crowns, 2 humbuckers.

1977-1980		$1,250	$1,625

Deluxe 8 Bass

1980. Multi-piece body, aluminum neck.

1980		$1,250	$1,625

DMB 2000 Bass

1979. Bolt-on aluminum neck, slot headstock.

1979		$900	$1,200

DMZ 4000 Bass

1978-1982. Bolt-on aluminum neck, slot headstock, double-cut solidbody, active EQ and dual-coil humbucking pickup, dot inlay.

1978-1981		$700	$900
1982	Bill Wyman-type	$700	$900

DMZ 4001 Bass

1979-1980. Aluminum neck, slot headstock, double-cut solidbody, 1 dual-coil humbucker pickup, dot inlay.

1979-1980		$900	$1,200

DMZ 5000 Bass

1979-1980. Double-cut solidbody, aluminum neck, slotted headstock, 2 pickups, crown inlays.

1979-1980		$1,000	$1,300

DMZ 6000B Bass

1979-1980. Double-cut, aluminum neck, slotted headstock, 2 pickups, crown inlays.

1979-1980		$100	$1,300

Duke Custom/Standard Bass

1981-1983. Headless, aluminum neck, 1 humbucker.

1981-1983		$325	$425

MODEL YEAR	FEATURES	EXC. COND. LOW	HIGH

Duke Special Bass

1982-1985. Headless, aluminum neck, 2 pickups, with frets or fretless.

1982-1985		$350	$475

Ferrington KFB-1/KFB-2 Acoustic Bass

1987-1990. Acoustic/electric, bridge-mounted active pickup, tone and volume control, various colors. KFB-1 has binding and diamond dot inlays; the KFB-2 no binding and dot inlays. Danny Ferrington continued to offer the KFB-1 after Kramer closed in '90.

1987-1990		$290	$375

Focus Series Bass

1984-1987. Made in Japan, double-cut solidbody, 1 or 2 pickups, various models.

1984-1987		$200	$400

Forum Series Bass

1987-1990. Made in Japan, double-cut solidbody, 2 pickups, neck-thru (I & III) or bolt-neck (II & IV).

1987-1990		$300	$525

Gene Simmons Axe Bass

1980-1981. Axe-shaped body, aluminium neck.

1980-1981		$2,600	$4,200

Hundred Series Bass

1988-1990. Import budget line, 7/8th solidbody, various models.

1988-1990		$180	$300

Pacer Series Bass

1982-1984. Offset double-cut solidbody, various models.

1982-1984		$500	$1,000

Pioneer Series Bass

1981-1986. Various models, first wood neck basses, offset double-cut, JBX or PBX pickups, dots, '81-'84 models with soft headstocks, later '84 on with banana headstocks.

1981-1986		$350	$750

Ripley Bass

1984-1987. Offset double-cut, 4 or 5 strings, stereo, pan pots for each string, front and back pickups for each string, active circuitry.

1984-1987	IV and V	$600	$1,000

Stagemaster Custom Bass (Import)

1982-1985, 1987-1990. First version had an aluminum neck (wood optional). Later version was neck-thru-body, bound neck, either active or passive pickups.

1982-1985	Imperial	$750	$1,000
1982-1985	Special	$750	$1,000
1982-1985	Standard	$750	$1,000

Stagemaster Deluxe Bass (U.S.A.)

1981. Made in USA, 8-string, metal neck.

1981		$900	$1,200

Striker 700 Bass

1985-1989. Korean import, offset double-cut, 1 pickup until '87, 2 after. Striker name was again used on a bass in '99.

1985-1989		$180	$300

Vanguard Bass

1981-1983. V-shaped body, Special (aluminum neck) or Standard (wood neck).

1981-1982	Special	$750	$1,000
1983-1984	Standard	$750	$1,000

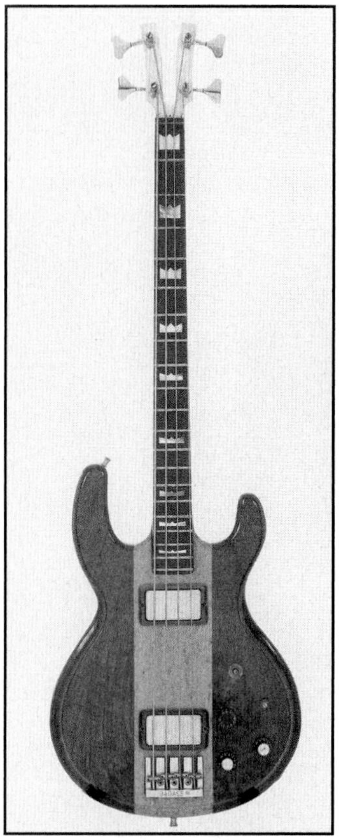

1979 Kramer 650-B Artist

Imaged by Heritage Auctions, HA.com

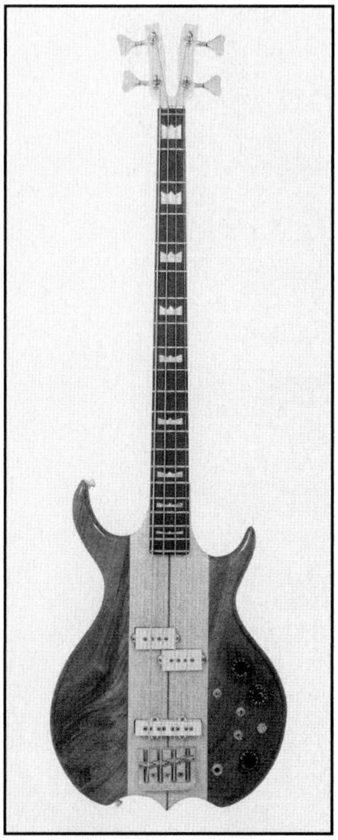

1980 Kramer DMZ 6000B

Imaged by Heritage Auctions, HA.com

BASSES

Lakland Skyline Deluxe 2010

Craig Brody

Martin BCPA4

Kris Nocula

MODEL YEAR	FEATURES	EXC. COND. LOW	HIGH

Voyager Bass

1982-1983. X-body, headless.

1982-1983		$750	$1,000

XKB-10 (Wedge) Bass

1980-1981. Wedge-shaped body, aluminum neck.

1980-1981		$675	$900

XKB-20 Bass

1981. 2nd version, more traditional double cut body.

1981		$675	$900

XL Series Bass

1980-1981. Odd shaped double-cut solidbody, aluminum neck, various models.

1980-1981	XL-9, 4-string	$950	$1,225
1981	XL-24, 4-string	$1,000	$1,300
1981	XL-8, 8-string	$1,100	$1,400

ZX Aero Star Series Bass (Import)

1986-1989. Various models include ZX-70 (offset double-cut solidbody, 1 pickup).

1986-1989		$100	$200

KSD

2003-present. Intermediate grade, production, imported bass line designed by Ken Smith (see Smith listing).

Kubicki

1973-present. Professional and premium grade, production/custom, solidbody basses built by luthier Phil Kubicki in Santa Barbara, California. Kubicki began building acoustic guitars when he was 15. In '64 at age 19, he went to work with Roger Rossmeisl at Fender Musical Instrument's research and development department for acoustic guitars. Nine years later he moved to Santa Barbara, California, and established Philip Kubicki Technology, which is best known for its line of Factor basses and also builds acoustic guitars, custom electric guitars, bodies and necks, and mini-guitars and does custom work, repairs and restorations. Phil Kubicki died in '13.

Kustom

1968-present. Founded by Bud Ross in Chanute, Kansas, and best known for the tuck-and-roll amps, Kustom also offered guitars and basses from '68 to '69.

Electric Hollowbody Bass

1968-1969	Various models	$950	$1,300

La Baye

1967. Short-lived brand out of Green Bay, Wisconsin and built by the Holman-Woodell factory in Neodesha, Kansas. There was also a guitar model.

Model 2x4 II Bass

1967. Very low production, dual pickups, long-scale, small rectangle solidbody, sometimes referred to as the Bass II.

1967		$1,200	$1,550

Model 2x4 Mini-Bass

1967. Short-scale, 1 pickup, small rectangle solidbody.

1967		$1,200	$1,550

MODEL YEAR	FEATURES	EXC. COND. LOW	HIGH

Lakland

1994-present. Professional and premium grade, production/custom, solid and hollowbody basses from luthier Dan Lakin in Chicago, Illinois. Lakland basses are built in the U.S. and overseas (Skyline series).

Electric Bass

1994-present. Various models.

1994-2002	4-63 Classic	$1,800	$2,300
1994-2002	4-63 Deluxe	$2,100	$2,700
1994-2002	4-63 Standard	$1,800	$2,300
1994-2002	4-94 / 44-94 Classic	$1,800	$2,300
1994-2020	4-94 / 44-94 Deluxe	$2,100	$2,700
1994-2020	4-94 / 44-94 Standard	$1,800	$2,300
1998-2003	Joe Osborn	$2,150	$2,800
2012-2020	Skyline 44-60	$900	$1,150

Lowrider Basses

2003-2018. Professional grade, production/custom, solidbody basses made by Ed Roman Guitars.

M Basses or Maghini

1998-present. Production/custom, professional and premium grade, solidbody electric basses built in Terryville, Connecticut by luthier Jon Maghini.

Magnatone

Ca. 1937-1971, 2013-present. Founded as Dickerson Brothers, known as Magna Electronics from '47. Produced instruments under own brand and for many others.

Mark VI/Artist Mark VI Bass

1959. Designed by luthier Paul Barth for Magnatone, double-cut, 4-string, 1 pickup.

1959		$1,125	$1,450

X-10 Hurricane Bass

1965-1966. Offset double cut solidbody, 1 single-coil, 4-on-a-side tuners, Magnatone logo on guard and headstock, Hurricane logo on headstock.

1965-1966		$775	$1,025

Mako

1985-1989. Line of solidbody basses from Kaman (Ovation, Hamer). They also offered guitars and amps.

Electric Solidbody Bass

1985-1989	Various models	$100	$350

Marco Polo

1960-ca.1964. One of the first inexpensive Japanese brands to be imported into the U.S., they also offered guitars.

Solidbody Bass

1960s	Various models	$80	$225

Marleaux

1990-present. Luthier Gerald Marleaux builds his custom, premium grade, electric basses in Clausthal-Zellerfeld, Germany.

MODEL YEAR	FEATURES	EXC. COND. LOW	HIGH

Marling

Ca. 1975. Budget line instruments marketed by EKO of Recanati, Italy; probably made by them, although possibly imported. They also had guitars.

Electric Solidbody Bass

Models include the E.495 (copy of LP), E.485 (copy of Tele), and the E.465 (Manta-style).

1970s	Various models	$80	$225

Martin

1833-present. Professional grade, production, acoustic basses made in the U.S. In 1978, Martin re-entered the electric market and introduced their solidbody EB-18 and EB-28 Basses. In the '80s they offered Stinger brand electric basses. By the late '80s, they started offering acoustic basses.

00C-16GTAE Bass

2006-2011. Mahogany back and sides, Fishman electronics.

2006-2011		$875	$1,150

B-1/B-1E Acoustic Bass

2002-2006. Mahogany back and sides, E has Fishman electronics.

2002-2006		$875	$1,150

B-40 Acoustic Bass

1989-1996. Jumbo, rosewood back and sides, built-in pickup and volume and tone controls. The B-40B had a pickup.

1989-1996	B-40B	$1,275	$1,650
1989-1996	Without pickup	$1,125	$1,450

B-65 Acoustic Bass

1989-1993. Like B-40 but with maple back and sides, built-in pickup and volume and tone controls.

1989-1993		$1,200	$1,550

BC-15E Acoustic Bass

2000-2006. Single-cut, all mahogany, on-board electronics.

2000-2006		$1,050	$1,350

BC-16E Bass

2020-present. Solid sitka spruce top, East Indian rosewood back and sides, built-in Fishman electronics.

2020		$1,325	$1,725

BC-16GTE Acoustic Bass

2009-2013. Jumbo, cutaway, mahogany back and sides.

2009-2013		$1,150	$1,500

BCPA4 Acoustic-Electric Bass

2013-2020. Performing Artist series, single-cut, sitka spruce top, sapele back and sides.

2013-2020		$1,100	$1,450

EB-18 Bass

1979-1982. Electric solidbody, neck-thru, 1 pickup, natural.

1979-1982		$1,000	$1,300

EB-28 Bass

1980-1982. Electric solidbody.

1980-1982		$1,075	$1,400

SBL-10 Bass

1980s. Stinger brand solidbody, maple neck, 1 split and 1 bar pickup.

1980s		$125	$200

Marvel

1950s-mid-1960s. Brand used for budget guitars and basses marketed by Peter Sorkin Company in New York, New York.

Electric Solidbody Bass

1950s	Various models	$180	$430

Messenger

1967-1968. Built by Musicraft, Inc., Messengers featured a neck-thru metal alloy neck. They also made guitars.

Bass

1967-1968. Metal alloy neck. Messenger mainly made guitars - they offered a bass, but it is unlikely many were built.

1967-1968		$1,700	$2,200

Messenger Upright

Made by Knutson Luthiery, see that listing.

Microfrets

1967-1975, 2004-2005. Professional grade, production, electric basses built in Myersville, Maryland. They also built guitars.

Husky Bass

1971-1974/75. Double-cut, 2 pickups, 2-on-a-side tuners.

1971-1975		$875	$1,125

Rendezvous Bass

1970. One pickup, orange sunburst.

1970		$925	$1,200

Signature Bass

1969-1975. Double-cut, 2 pickups, 2-on-a-side tuners.

1969-1975		$1,325	$1,725

Stage II Bass

1969-1975. Double-cut, 2 pickups, 2-on-a-side tuners.

1969-1975		$1,300	$1,700

Thundermaster Bass

1967-1975. Double-cut, 2 pickups, 2-on-a-side tuners.

1967-1975		$1,300	$1,700

Modulus

1978-2013. Founded by aerospace engineer Geoff Gould, Modulus offered professional and premium grade, production/custom, solidbody basses built in California. They also built guitars.

Electric Bass

1978-2013. Various standard models.

1978-2013		$1,450	$2,800

Mollerup Basses

In 1984 luthier Laurence Mollerup began building professional grade, custom/production, electric basses and electric double basses in Vancouver, British Columbia. He has also built guitars.

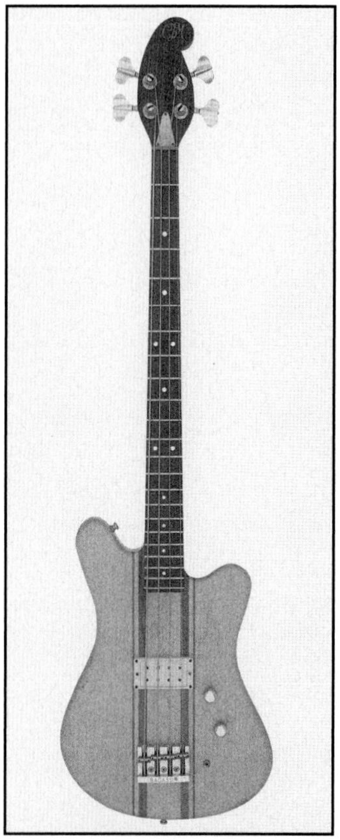

1982 Martin EB-18

Imaged by Heritage Auctions, HA.com

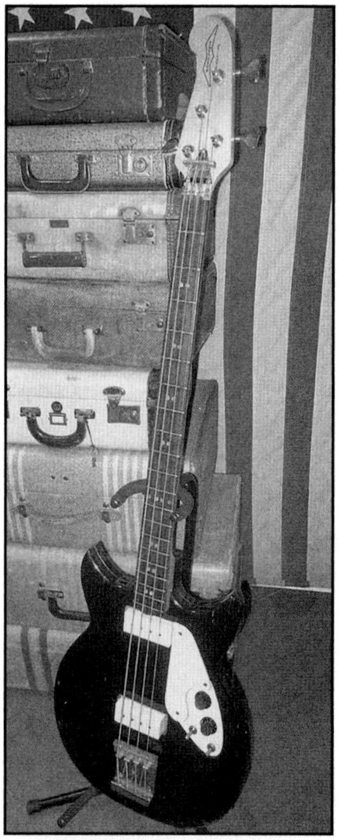

1969 Microfrets Signature

Rivington Guitars

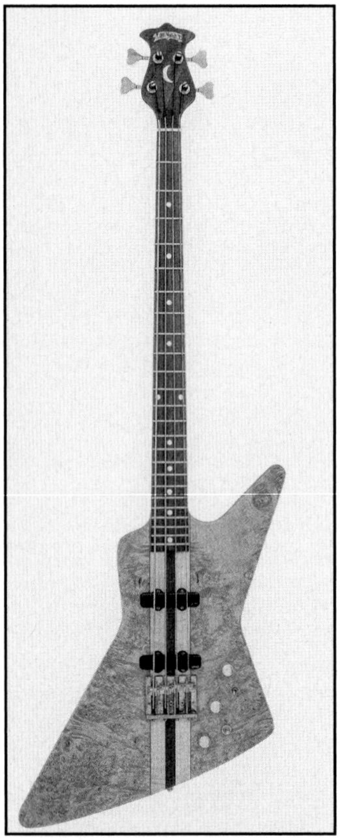

1982 Moonstone Exploder
Imaged by Heritage Auctions, HA.com

1982 Musicman Cutlass I
Craig Brody

Moonstone

1972-present. Luthier Steve Helgeson builds his premium grade, production/custom, acoustic and electric basses in Eureka, California. He also builds guitars.

Eclipse Deluxe Bass

1980-1984.Double-cut solidbody.

MODEL YEAR	FEATURES	EXC. COND. LOW	HIGH
1980-1984		$1,350	$1,750

Exploder Bass

1980-1983. Figured wood body, Explorer-style neck-thru-body.

MODEL YEAR	FEATURES	EXC. COND. LOW	HIGH
1980-1983		$1,350	$1,750

Vulcan Bass

1982-1984. Solidbody, flat-top (Vulcan) or carved top (Vulcan II), maple body, gold hardware.

MODEL YEAR	FEATURES	EXC. COND. LOW	HIGH
1982-1984		$1,350	$1,750

Morales

Ca.1967-1968. Guitars and basses made in Japan by Zen-On and not heavily imported into the U.S.

Electric Solidbody Bass

MODEL YEAR	FEATURES	EXC. COND. LOW	HIGH
1967-1968	Various models	$125	$300

Mosrite

Semie Moseley's Mosrite offered various bass models throughout the many versions of the Mosrite company.

Brut Bass

Late-1960s. Assymetrical body with small cutaway on upper treble bout.

MODEL YEAR	FEATURES	EXC. COND. LOW	HIGH
1960s		$500	$650

Celebrity Bass

1965-1969. ES-335-style semi-thick double-cut body with f-holes, 2 pickups.

MODEL YEAR	FEATURES	EXC. COND. LOW	HIGH
1965-1966	Custom color	$600	$775
1965-1967	Sunburst	$525	$700
1968-1969	Red	$500	$650
1969	Sunburst	$500	$650

Combo Bass

1966-1968. Hollowbody, 2 pickups.

MODEL YEAR	FEATURES	EXC. COND. LOW	HIGH
1966-1968		$1,050	$1,350

Joe Maphis Bass

1966-1969. Ventures-style body, hollow without f-holes, 2 pickups, natural.

MODEL YEAR	FEATURES	EXC. COND. LOW	HIGH
1966-1969		$1,100	$1,450

Ventures Bass

1965-1972. Various colors, 1 or 2 pickups.

MODEL YEAR	FEATURES	EXC. COND. LOW	HIGH
1965	1 pickup	$1,300	$1,700
1965	2 pickups	$1,450	$1,900
1966	1 pickup	$1,175	$1,550
1966	2 pickups	$1,350	$1,750
1967-1968	1 pickup	$1,050	$1,350
1967-1968	2 pickups	$1,150	$1,500
1969	1 pickup	$975	$1,275
1969	2 pickups	$1,100	$1,450
1970-1972	1 pickup	$900	$1,200
1970-1972	2 pickups	$1,050	$1,350

V-II Bass

1973-1974. Ventures-style, 2 humbuckers, sunburst.

MODEL YEAR	FEATURES	EXC. COND. LOW	HIGH
1973-1974		$1,100	$1,450

MTD

1994-present. Intermediate, professional, and premium grade, production/custom, electric basses built by luthier Michael Tobias (who founded Tobias Basses in '77) in Kingston, New York. Since '00, he also imports basses built in Korea to his specifications.

Murph

1965-1967. Mid-level electric solidbody basses built by Pat Murphy in San Fernado, California. Murph logo on headstock. They also offered guitars and amps.

Solidbody Bass

MODEL YEAR	FEATURES	EXC. COND. LOW	HIGH
1965-1967		$725	$950

Music Man

1972-present. Intermediate and professional grade, production, electric basses. They also build guitars.

Bongo Bass

2003-present. Double cut solidbody, squared-off horns, 2 pickups, 4-, 5- and 6-string.

MODEL YEAR	FEATURES	EXC. COND. LOW	HIGH
2003-2020	Bongo 4	$900	$1,200
2003-2020	Bongo 5	$1,000	$1,350
2003-2020	Bongo 6	$1,150	$1,500

Cutlass I/Cutlass II Bass

1982-1987. Ash body, graphite neck, string-thru-body.

MODEL YEAR	FEATURES	EXC. COND. LOW	HIGH
1982-1984	CLF era Cutlass I	$1,900	$2,500
1982-1984	CLF era Cutlass II	$1,800	$2,350
1984-1987	Ernie Ball era Cutlass I	$1,300	$1,700
1984-1987	Ernie Ball era Cutlass II	$1,400	$1,850

S.U.B. Series Bass

2003-2007. Offset double-cut, 4- or 5-string, 1 humbucker.

MODEL YEAR	FEATURES	EXC. COND. LOW	HIGH
2003-2007	IV Bass	$375	$500
2003-2007	V Bass	$425	$550

Sabre Bass

1978-ca.1991. Double-cut solidbody bass, 3-and-1 tuning keys, 2 humbucking pickups, on-board preamp, natural.

MODEL YEAR	FEATURES	EXC. COND. LOW	HIGH
1978-1984	CLF era	$1,925	$2,525
1984-1991	Ernie Ball era	$1,075	$1,400

Sterling Bass

1993-present. Rosewood, 1 pickup, EQ, pearl blue. In '05, additional pickup options available. 5-string introduced in '08.

MODEL YEAR	FEATURES	EXC. COND. LOW	HIGH
1993-2020	4-string	$775	$1,050
2008-2020	5-string	$825	$1,100

StingRay Bass

1976-present. Offset double-cut solidbody, 1 pickup, 3-and-1 tuners, string-thru until '80, various colors. 5-string introduced in '87. In '05, additional pickup options available.

MODEL YEAR	FEATURES	EXC. COND. LOW	HIGH
1976-1979	CLF era	$2,700	$3,500
1980-1984	CLF era	$2,100	$2,700
1984-1989	Ernie Ball era	$1,200	$1,550
1987-2020	5-string	$1,200	$1,550
1990-2020	4-string	$1,100	$1,425

MODEL YEAR	FEATURES	EXC. COND. LOW	HIGH

StingRay 20th Anniversary Bass
1996. 1400 made, flamed maple body.

1996 $1,650 $2,150

StingRay Classic Bass
2010-2019. Ash body, birds-eye or flame maple neck, 4- or 5-string.

2010-2019 $1,150 $1,500

National
Ca. 1927-present. National offered electric basses in the '60s when Valco owned the brand.

Beatle (Violin) Bass
1970s. Strum & Drum era import, National script logo on headstock, 2 pickups, shaded brown finish.

1970s $400 $525

EG 700V-2HB German Style Bass
1970s. Strum & Drum era import, Beatle-style violin body, 2 humbuckers, bolt neck.

1970s $450 $575

N-850 Bass
1967-1968. Semi-hollow double-cut, art deco f-holes, 2 pickups, block markers, bout control knobs, sunburst.

1967-1968 $600 $775

Val-Pro 85 Bass
1961-1962. Res-O-Glas body shaped like the U.S. map, 2 pickups, snow white, renamed National 85 in '63.

1961-1962 $800 $1,025

National Reso-Phonic
1988-present. Professional grade, production/custom, acoustic and acoustic/electric resonator basses built in San Luis Obispo, California. They also build guitars, mandolins and ukuleles.

New York Bass Works
1989-present. Luthier David Segal builds his professional and premium grade, production/custom, electric basses in New York.

Norma
Ca.1965-1970. Guitars and basses imported from Japan by Chicago's Strum and Drum.

Electric Solidbody Bass
1960s Various models $125 $325

O'Hagan
1979-1983. Designed by Jerol O'Hagan in St. Louis Park, Minnesota. He also offered guitars.

Electric Solidbody Bass
1979-1983. Models include the Shark Bass, Night-Watch Bass, NightWatch Regular Bass, and the Twenty Two Bass.

1979-1983 $500 $675

Old Kraftsman
1930s-1960s. Brand used by the Spiegel Company. Guitars and basses made by other American manufacturers.

Electric Solidbody Bass
1950s Various models $225 $400

MODEL YEAR	FEATURES	EXC. COND. LOW	HIGH

Orville by Gibson
1984-1993. Orville by Gibson and Orville guitars were made by Japan's Fuji Gen Gakki for Gibson. Basically the same models except the Orville by Gibson guitars had real Gibson USA pickups and a true nitrocellulose lacquer finish. The Orville models used Japanese electronics and a poly finish. Prices here are for the Orville by Gibson models.

Electric Bass
1984-1993 Thunderbird $925 $1,200

Ovation
1966-present. Intermediate and professional grade, production, acoustic/electric basses. Ovation offered electric solidbody basses early on and added acoustic basses in the '90s. They also offer guitars and mandolins.

B768/Elite B768 Bass
1990. Single-cut acoustic-electric bass, Elite body style with upper bout soundholes.

1990 $675 $875

Celebrity Series Bass
1990s-2013. Deep bowl back, cutaway, acoustic/electric.

1990s-2013 $250 $350

Magnum Series Bass
1974-1980. Magnum I is odd-shaped mahogany solidbody, 2 pickups, mono/stereo, mute, sunburst, red or natural. Magnum II is with battery-powered preamp and 3-band EQ. Magnum III and IV had a new offset double-cut body.

1974-1980 Various models $875 $1,150

NSB778 Elite T Bass Nikki Sixx Limited Edition
2005-2013. Made in USA, acoustic-electric 4-string, 1 pickup, solid spruce top, ebony 'board, custom iron cross inlays, red or gray flame finish.

2005-2013 $1,125 $1,450

Typhoon II/Typhoon III Bass
1968-1971. Ovation necks, but bodies and hardware were German imports. Semi-hollowbody, 2 pickups, red or sunburst. Typhoon II is 335-style and III is fretless.

1968-1971 Typhoon II $650 $850

1968-1971 Typhoon III $700 $900

Ultra Bass
1984. Korean solidbodies and necks assembled in U.S., offset double-cut with 1 pickup.

1984 $200 $500

PANaramic
1961-1963. Guitars and basses made in Italy by the Crucianelli accordion company and imported by PANaramic accordion. They also offered amps made by Magnatone.

Electric Bass
1961-1963. Double-cut hollowbody, 2 pickups, dot markers, sunburst.

1961-1963 $875 $1,125

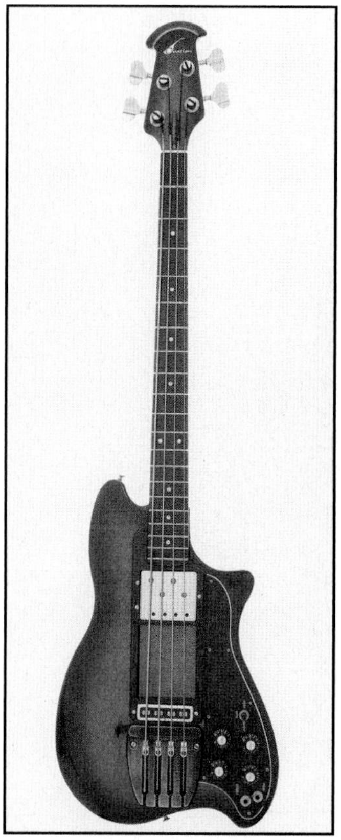

Ovation Magnum I

Imaged by Heritage Auctions, HA.com

1969 Ovation Typhoon II

Rivington Guitars

BASSES

1987 PRS Curly Bass-5

Craig Brody

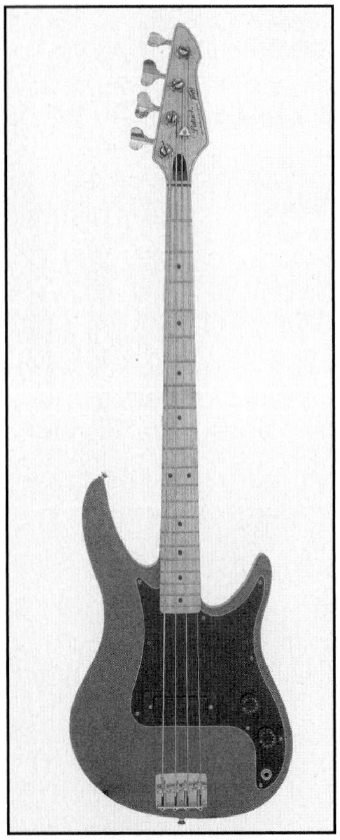

1987 Peavey Patriot

Imaged by Heritage Auctions, HA.com

MODEL YEAR	FEATURES	EXC. COND. LOW	HIGH

Parker

1992-2016. Premium grade, production/custom, solidbody electric basses. They also built guitars.

Fly Bass

2002-2011. Offered in 4- and 5-string models.

2002-2011		$1,300	$1,700

Paul Reed Smith

1985-present. PRS added basses in '86, but by '92 had dropped the models. In 2000 PRS started again offering professional and premium grade, production, solidbody electric basses. Bird inlays can add $100 or more to the values of PRS basses listed here.

Bass-4

1986-1992, 2007. Set neck, 3 single-coil pickups, hum-cancelling coil, active circuitry, 22-fret Brazilian rosewood 'board. Reintroduced (OEB Series) in 2000s.

1986-1987		$1,700	$2,225
1988-1992		$1,400	$1,825
2007		$1,400	$1,825

Bass-5

1986-1992. Five-string, set-neck, rosewood 'board, 3 single-coil pickups, active electronics. Options include custom colors, bird inlays, fretless 'board.

1986-1987		$1,825	$2,400
1988-1992		$1,525	$2,000

CE Bass-4

1986-1991. Solidbody, maple bolt neck, alder body, rosewood 'board, 4-string.

1986-1987		$1,025	$1,325
1988-1991		$825	$1,075

CE Bass-5

1986-1991. Five-string solidbody, maple bolt neck, alder body, rosewood 'board.

1986-1987		$1,100	$1,425
1988-1991		$900	$1,175

Curly Bass-4

1986-1992. Double-cut solidbody, curly maple top, set maple neck, Brazilian rosewood 'board (ebony on fretless), 3 single-coil and 1 hum-cancelling pickups, various grades of maple tops, moon inlays.

1986-1987		$1,825	$2,400
1988-1992		$1,525	$2,000

Curly Bass-5

1986-1992. Five-string version of Curly Bass-4.

1986-1987		$1,925	$2,500
1988-1992		$1,625	$2,100

Electric Bass

2000-2007. Bolt neck 4-string, offered in regular and maple top versions.

2000-2007	Maple	$1,025	$1,325
2000-2007	Plain	$925	$1,200

Private Stock Program

2010-present. Custom instruments based around existing PRS models.

2010-2020		$3,500	$7,000

SE Series Bass

2014-present. Various models, i.e. SE Kestrel and Kingfisher.

2014-2020	Higher models	$400	$550
2014-2020	Most models	$225	$400

Peavey

1965-present. Intermediate and professional grade, production/custom, electric basses. They also build guitars and amps. Hartley Peavey's first products were guitar amps and he added guitars and basses to the mix in '78.

Axcelerator Bass

1994-1998. Offset double-cut, long thin horns, 2 humbuckers, stacked control knobs, bolt neck, dot markers.

1994-1998		$300	$400

Cirrus Series Bass

1998-2012. Offset double-cut, active electronics, in 4-, 5-, 6-string, and custom shop versions.

1998-2009	Cirrus 5	$650	$850
1998-2012	Cirrus 4	$600	$800
1998-2012	Cirrus 6	$725	$950

Dyna-Bass

1987-1993. Double-cut solidbody, active electronics, 3-band EQ, rosewood 'board, opaque finish.

1987-1993		$350	$450

Dyna-Bass Limited

1987-1990. Neck-thru-body, ebony 'board, flamed maple neck/body construction, purple heart strips, mother-of-pearl inlays.

1987-1990		$450	$600

Forum Bass

1994-1995. Double-cut solidbody, rosewood 'board, dot inlays, 2 humbuckers.

1994-1995		$200	$265

Forum Plus Bass

1994. Forum Bass with added active electronics.

1994		$200	$265

Foundation Bass

1984-2002. Double-cut solidbody, 2 pickups, maple neck.

1984-2002		$200	$265

Foundation S Active Bass

1987-1991. Similar to Foundation S Bass with added active circuitry, provides low-impedance output, 2 pickups.

1987-1991		$200	$265

Foundation S Bass

1986-1991. Two split-coil pickups, maple body, rosewood 'board, black hardware, black painted headstock.

1986-1991		$200	$265

Fury Bass

1983-1999. Double-cut solidbody, rosewood 'board, 1 split-coil humbucker.

1983-1999		$200	$265

Fury Custom Bass

1986-1993. Fury Bass with black hardware and narrow neck.

1986-1993		$200	$265

Fury VI Bass

2001-2003. 6-string, active electronics, quilt top.

2001-2003		$275	$365

G-Bass V

1999-2002. Offset double-cut 5-string, humbucker, 3-band EQ.

1999-2002		$625	$825

MODEL YEAR	FEATURES	EXC. COND. LOW	HIGH

Grind Series Bass

2001-2020. Offset double-cut, neck-thru, long bass horn, 2 pickups, 4, 5, or 6 strings.

2001-2020	Various models	$200	$325

Liberator JT-84 John Taylor Bass

2007. 2 humbuckers, black with graphics.

2007	JT-84	$850	$1,125

Milestone Series Bass

1994-present. Import offset double cut, Milestone I ('94) replaced by 1 P-style pickup II ('95-'01), split humbucker IV ('99-'04); 2 single-coil III ('99-present) now just called Milestone.

1994-2020		$85	$125

Millenium Series Bass

2001-2020. Offset double-cut, agathis bodies, maple tops, in 4- or 5-string.

2001-2020		$150	$600

Patriot Bass

1984-1988. General J-Bass styling with larger thinner horns, 1 single-coil, maple neck.

1984-1988		$125	$165

Patriot Custom Bass

1986-1988. Patriot with rosewood neck, matching headstock.

1986-1988		$150	$200

RJ-IV Bass

1990-1993. Randy Jackson Signature model, neck-thru-body, 2 split-coil active pickups, ebony 'board, mother-of-pearl position markers.

1990-1993		$300	$400

Rudy Sarzo Signature Bass

1989-1993. Double-cut solidbody, active EQ, ebony 'board, 2 pickups.

1989-1993		$450	$575

T-20FL Bass

1980s. Fretless double-cut solidbody, 1 pickup, also available as the fretted T-20 ('82-'83).

1980s		$200	$265

T-40/T-40FL Bass

1978-1987. Double-cut solidbody, 2 pickups. T-40FL is fretless.

1978-1987	T-40	$425	$550
1978-1987	T-40FL	$425	$550

T-45 Bass

1982-1986. T-40 with 1 humbucking pickup, and a mid-frequency rolloff knob.

1982-1986		$300	$400

TL Series Bass

1988-1998. Neck-thru-body, gold hardware, active humbuckers, EQ, flamed maple neck and body, 5-string (TL-Five) or 6 (TL-Six).

1988-1998	TL-Five	$500	$650
1989-1998	TL-Six	$550	$725

Zodiac Bass

2006-2012. Solid alder body, maple neck, 2 pickups.

2006-2012		$200	$275

Pedulla

1975-2019. Professional and premium grade, production/custom, electric basses made in Rockland, Massachusetts. Founded by Michael Pedulla, and which offered various upscale options that affect valuation, so each instrument should be evaluated on a case-by-case basis. Unless specifically noted, the following listings have standard to mid-level features. High-end options are specifically noted; if not, these options will have a relatively higher value than those shown here. Pedualla announced his retirement in '19.

Buzz-4/Buzz-5 Bass

1980-2008. Double-cut neck-thru solidbody, fretless, long-scale, maple neck and body wings, 2 pickups, preamp, some with other active electronics, various colors, 4-, 5-, 6-, 8-string versions.

1980-1999		$1,150	$1,500

Interceptor Bass

1980s. Double-cut, maple/walnut laminated neck-thru.

1980s		$1,000	$1,300

MVP Series Bass

1984-2019. Fretted version of Buzz Bass, standard or flame top, 4-, 5-, 6-, 8-string versions, MVP II is bolt-on neck version.

1980s	MVP-6	$1,350	$1,775
1984-1990s	MVP-4 flame top	$1,250	$1,650
1984-1990s	MVP-4 standard top	$1,150	$1,500
1984-1990s	MVP-5	$1,250	$1,650
1990s	MVP II	$800	$1,050

Orsini Wurlitzer 4-String Bass

Mid-1970s. Body style similar to late-'50s Gibson double-cut slab body SG Special, neck-thru, 2 pickups, natural. Sold by Boston's Wurlitzer music store chain.

1970s		$1,050	$1,400

Quilt Limited Bass

Neck-thru-body with curly maple centerstrip, quilted maple body wings, 2 Bartolini pickups, available in fretted or fretless 4- and 5-string models.

1987		$1,050	$1,400

Rapture Series Bass

1995-2019. Solidbody with extra-long thin bass horn and extra short treble horn, 4- or 5-string, various colors.

1995-2019	Rapture 4	$975	$1,275
1995-2019	Rapture 5	$1,050	$1,375

Series II Bass

1987-1992. Bolt neck, rosewood 'board, mother-of-pearl dot inlays, Bartolini pickups.

1987-1992		$700	$900

Thunderbass Series Bass

1993-2019. Solidbody with extra-long thin bass horn and extra short treble horn, 4-, 5- or 6-string, standard features or triple A top.

1993-1999	4, AAA top	$1,350	$1,750
1993-1999	4, Standard	$1,050	$1,375
1993-1999	5, AAA top	$1,425	$1,850
1993-1999	5, Standard	$1,175	$1,525
1993-1999	6, AAA top	$1,525	$1,975
1993-1999	6, Standard	$1,250	$1,625
2000-2019	4, AAA top	$1,350	$1,750
2000-2019	5, AAA top	$1,425	$1,850
2000-2019	6, AAA top	$1,525	$1,975

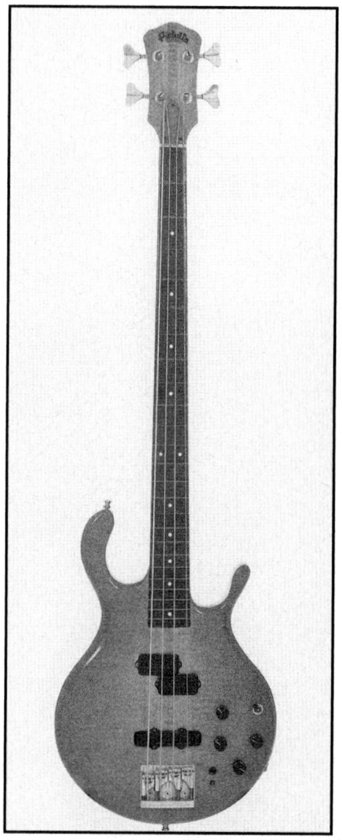

1987 Pedulla Buzz-4

Imaged by Heritage Auctions, HA.com

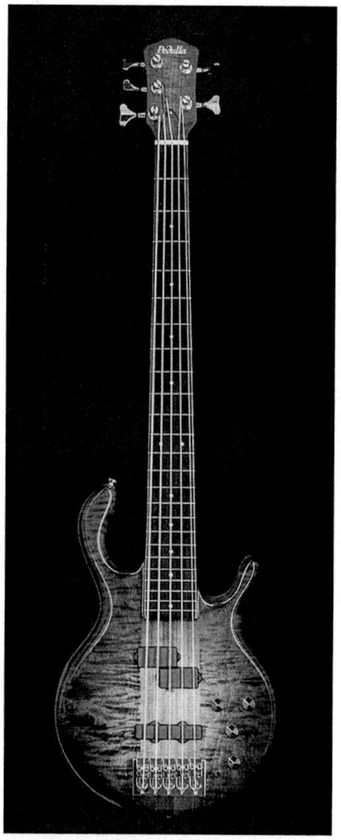

Pedulla MVP

BASSES

1958 Premier Bantam

Izzy Miller

1973 Rickenbacker 4000

Craig Brody

MODEL YEAR	FEATURES	EXC. COND. LOW	HIGH

Thunderbolt Series Bass

1994-2019. Similar to Thunderbass Series but with bolt necks, 4-, 5- or 6-string, standard AA or AAA maple or optional 5A or exotic wood (ET) tops.

1994-2019	Thunderbolt 5	$925	$1,200

Penco

Ca. 1974-1978. Generally high-quality Japanese-made copies of classic American bass guitars. They also made guitars, mandolins and banjos.

Electric Bass

1974-1978	Various models	$100	$285

Premier

Ca.1938-ca.1975, 1990s-2010. Originally American-made instruments, but by the '60s imported parts were being used. 1990s instruments were Asian imports.

Bantam Bass

1950-1970. Small body, single-cut short-scale archtop electric, torch headstock inlay, sparkle 'guard, sunburst.

1950-1970		$425	$550

Electric Solidbody Bass

1960s	Various models	$350	$450

Renaissance

1978-1980. Plexiglass solidbody electric guitars and basses made in Malvern, Pennsylvania.

Plexiglas Bass

1978-1980. Plexiglas bodies and active electronics, models include the DPB bass (double-cut, 1 pickup, '78-'79), SPB (single-cut, 2 pickups, '78-'79), T-100B (Bich-style, 1 pickup, '80), S-100B (double-cut, 1 pickup, '80), and the S-200B (double-cut, 2 pickups, '80).

1978-1980		$650	$850

Rickenbacker

1931-present. Professional grade, production/custom, electric basses. They also build guitars. Rickenbacker introduced their first electric bass in '57 and has always been a strong player in the bass market.

Electric Upright Bass

1936. Cast aluminum neck and body, horseshoe pickup, extension pole.

1936		$3,400	$4,400

Model 1999 (Rose-Morris) Bass

1964-1967. Export made for English distributor Rose-Morris of London, built along the lines of the U.S. Model 4000 Bass but with small differences that are considered important in the vintage guitar market.

1964-1966		$7,300	$9,500
1967		$6,400	$8,500

Model 2030 Hamburg Bass

1984-1997. Rounded double-cut, 2 pickups, active electronics.

1984-1997		$650	$850

Model 2030GF (Glenn Frey) Bass

1992-1995. Limited Edition, double-cut, 2 humbuckers, Jetglo finish.

1992-1995		$1,200	$1,600

MODEL YEAR	FEATURES	EXC. COND. LOW	HIGH

Model 2050 El Dorado Bass

1984-1992. Gold hardware, 2 pickups, active.

1984-1992		$975	$1,275

Model 2060 El Dorado Bass

1992-1997. Gold hardware, 2 pickups, active, double-bound body.

1992-1997		$1,050	$1,400

Model 3000 Bass

1975-1984. Rounded double-cut, 30" scale, 1 pickup, brown sunburst.

1975-1984		$1,175	$1,500

Model 3001 Bass

1975-1984. Same as Model 3000 but with longer 33-1/2" scale, Wine Red.

1975-1984		$1,150	$1,500

Model 3261 (Rose-Morris Slim-Line) Bass

1967. Export model made for English distributor Rose-Morris, built along the lines of a U.S. equivalent Model 4005 Bass.

1967		$5,100	$6,600

Model 4000 Bass

1958-1985. Cresting wave body and headstock, 1 horseshoe pickup (changed to regular pickup in '64), neck-thru-body.

1958-1962	Plank style	$10,400	$13,500
1963-1966		$7,700	$10,000
1967-1969		$7,000	$9,000
1970-1972		$2,800	$3,600
1973-1985		$1,850	$2,400

Model 4001 Bass

1961-1986. Fancy version of 4000, 1 horseshoe magnet pickup (changed to regular pickup in '64) and 1 bar magnet pickup, triangle inlays, bound neck.

1961-1963	Fireglo	$7,200	$9,500
1963-1966	Mapleglo	$6,500	$8,500
1964-1966	Fireglo	$6,600	$8,800
1967-1969	Various colors	$5,800	$7,500
1970-1972	Various colors	$3,500	$4,500
1973	Early '73 features	$2,950	$3,800
1973	Late '73 features	$2,100	$2,750
1974-1979	Various colors	$2,100	$2,750
1980-1986	Various colors	$1,950	$2,550

Model 4001 C64S Bass

2001-2014. Recreation of Paul McCartney's 4001 featuring changes he made like a reshaped body and zero-fret 'board.

2001-2014		$2,400	$3,100

Model 4001 CS Bass

1991-1997. Chris Squire signature model.

1991-1997	With certificate	$2,800	$3,600

Model 4001 FL Bass

1968-1986. Fretless version of 4001 Bass, special order in '60s, various colors.

1968-1986		$2,400	$3,100

Model 4001 V63 Bass

1984-2000. Vintage '63 reissue of Model 4001S, horseshoe-magnet pickup, Mapleglo.

1984-2000	Figured top	$2,400	$3,200
1984-2000	Plain top	$2,400	$3,100

MODEL YEAR	FEATURES	EXC. COND. LOW	HIGH

Model 4001S Bass

1964-1985. Same as Model 4000, but with 2 pickups, export model.

1980-1985		$1,400	$1,800

Model 4002 Bass

1967-1985. Cresting wave body and headstock, 2 humbuckers, black 'guard, checkerboard binding.

1980-1985		$3,700	$4,900

Model 4003 Bass

1979-present. Similar to Model 4001, split 'guard, deluxe features.

1979-2020		$1,400	$1,800

Model 4003 FL Bass

1979-2017. Fretless version.

1979-2017		$1,400	$1,800

Model 4003 Shadow Bass

1986. About 60 made for Guitar Center, all black 'board, inlays and hardware, Jetglo finish.

1986		$2,550	$3,300

Model 4003S Bass

1986-2003, 2012-present. Standard feature version of 4003, 4 strings. Reissued in '12.

1986-2003		$1,450	$1,900
2012-2020	Reissue	$1,175	$1,550

Model 4003S Redneck Bass

1988. Red body, 'board and headstock, black hardware.

1988		$2,350	$3,000

Model 4003S Tuxedo Bass

1987. White body with black 'guard and hardware. 100 made.

1987		$2,350	$3,000

Model 4003S/5 Bass

1986-2003. Model 4003S with 5 strings.

1986-2003		$1,850	$2,400

Model 4003S/8 Bass

1986-2003. Model 4003S with 8 strings.

1986-2003		$2,800	$3,700

Model 4003S/SPC Blackstar Bass

1989. Black version, black finish, 'board, knobs, and hardware. Also offered as 5-string.

1989		$1,875	$2,450

Model 4003W Bass

2014-present. Solid walnut body, satin natural finish.

2013-2020		$1,250	$1,650

Model 4004C Cheyenne/4004Cii Cheyenne II Bass

1993-2019. Cresting wave, maple neck-thru-body with walnut body and head wings, gold hardware, dot inlay. Replaced by maple top 4004Cii Cheyenne II in '00.

1993-1999	Cheyenne	$1,250	$1,650
2000-2019	Cheyenne II	$1,300	$1,700

Model 4004L Laredo Bass

1993-present. Like Cheyenne but without walnut wings.

1993-2020		$1,150	$1,500

Model 4005 Bass

1965-1984. New style double-cut semi-hollowbody, 2 pickups, R tailpiece, cresting wave headstock.

1965-1966	Fireglo	$9,200	$12,000
1965-1966	Jetglo	$8,000	$10,500
1965-1966	Mapleglo	$9,000	$11,500
1967-1969	Fireglo	$8,400	$11,000
1967-1969	Jetglo	$7,000	$9,200
1967-1969	Mapleglo	$8,000	$10,500
1970-1979	Various colors	$5,700	$7,400
1980-1984	Various colors	$5,300	$6,900

Model 4005 L (Lightshow) Bass

1970-1975. Model 4005 with translucent top with lights in body that lit up when played, needed external transformer.

1970-1971	1st edition	$7,700	$10,100
1972-1975	2nd edition	$8,500	$11,100

Model 4005 WB Bass

1966-1983. Old style Model 4005 with white-bound body, Fireglo.

1966		$8,500	$11,000
1967-1969		$7,500	$10,000
1970-1979		$4,500	$6,000
1980-1983		$4,100	$5,500

Model 4005-6 Bass

1965-1977. Model 4005 with 6 strings.

1965-1969		$8,900	$11,600
1970-1977		$6,000	$8,000

Model 4005-8 Bass

Late-1960s. Eight-string Model 4005, Fireglo or Mapleglo.

1968-1969		$8,500	$11,000

Model 4008 Bass

1975-1983. Eight-string, cresting wave body and headstock.

1975-1979		$1,750	$2,300
1980-1983		$1,550	$2,050

Model 4080 Doubleneck Bass

1975-1992. Bolt-on 6- and 4-string necks, Jetglo or Mapleglo.

1975-1979		$5,000	$6,500
1980-1992		$5,000	$6,500

Ritter Royal Instruments

Production/custom, solidbody basses built by luthier Jens Ritter in Wachenheim, Germany.

Rob Allen

1997-present. Professional grade, production/custom, lightweight basses made by luthier Robert Allen in Santa Barbara, California.

Robin

1982-2010. Founded by David Wintz and located in Houston, Texas, Robin built basses until 1997. Most basses were Japanese-made until '87; American production began in '88. They also built guitars and also made Metropolitan ('96-'08) and Alamo ('00-'08) brand guitars.

Freedom Bass I

1984-1986. Offset double-cut, active treble and bass EQ controls, 1 pickup.

1984-1986		$525	$700

Freedom Bass I Passive

1986-1989. Non-active version of Freedom Bass, 1 humbucker. Passive dropped from name in '87.

1986-1989		$525	$700

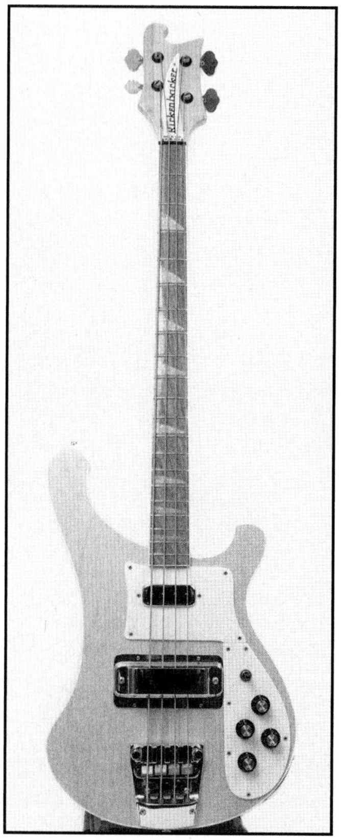

1980 Rickenbacker 4003

Bernunzio Uptown Music

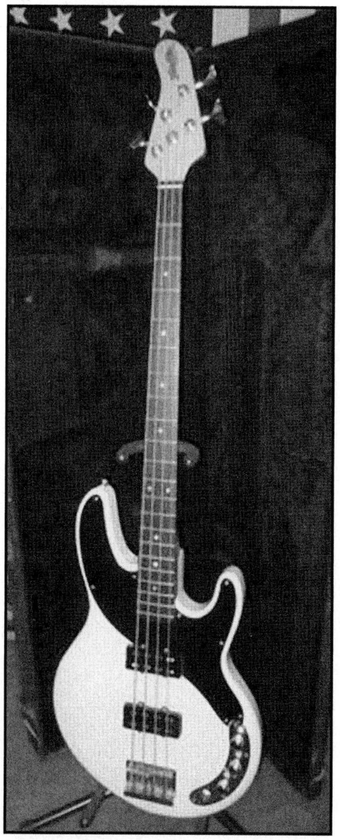

1984 Robin Freedom II

Rivington Guitars

1966 Silvertone 1443
Extra Long
Erick Warner

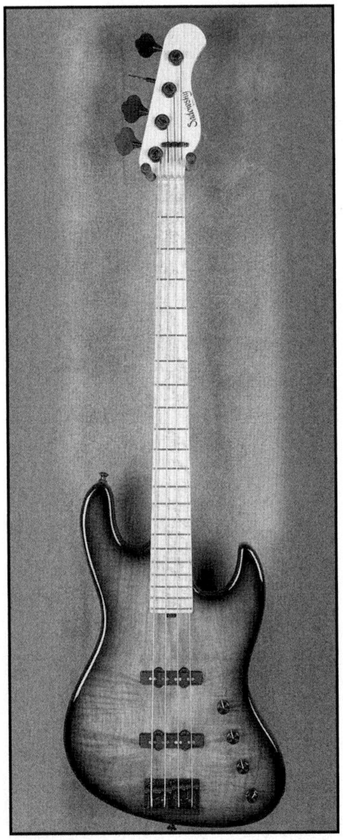

Sadowsky NYC Custom 21 Fret

MODEL YEAR	FEATURES	EXC. COND. LOW	HIGH

Medley Bass

1984-1997. Offset deep cutaways, 2 pickups, reverse headstock until '89, then split headstock, back to reverse by '94. Japanese-made until '87, U.S. after.

1984-1987	Japan	$425	$550
1988-1997	USA	$825	$1,100

Ranger Bass

1984-1997. Vintage style body, dot markers, medium scale and 1 pickup from '84 to '88 and long scale with P-style and J-style pickup configuration from '89 to '97.

1984-1987	Japan	$400	$525
1988-1997	USA	$750	$1,000

Rock Bass

2002-2015. Chinese-made, intermediate and professional grade, production, bolt neck solidbody basses from the makers of Warwick basses.

Roland

Best known for keyboards, effects, and amps, Roland offered synthesizer-based guitars and basses from 1977 to '86.

GR-33B (G-88) Bass Guitar Synthesizer

Early-mid 1980s. Solidbody bass with synthesizer in the guitar case, G-88 deluxe bass.

1983-1985		$750	$1,000

Roman & Blake Basses

1977-2003. Professional grade, production/custom, solidbody bass guitars made by Ed Roman Guitars.

Roman USA Basses

Professional grade, production/custom, solidbody basses made by Ed Roman Guitars starting in 2000.

Roscoe Guitars

Early 1980s-present. Luthier Keith Roscoe builds his production/custom, professional and premium grade, solidbody electric basses in Greensboro, North Carolina.

S.D. Curlee

1975-1982. S.D. Curlee guitars and basses were made in Illinois; S.D. Curlee International instruments were made in Japan.

Electric Solidbody Bass

1970s	Various models	$325	$425

Sadowsky

1980-present. Professional and premium grade, production/custom, solidbody basses built by luthier Roger Sadowsky in Brooklyn, New York. He also builds guitars and amps.

Serenader

Mainly known for lap steels this Seattle, Washington brand also built a solidbody bass.

MODEL YEAR	FEATURES	EXC. COND. LOW	HIGH

Silvertone

1941-ca.1970, present. Brand used by Sears. Instruments were U.S.-made and imported. Currently, Samick offers a line of acoustic and electric guitars, basses and amps under the Silvertone name.

Model 1376L/1373L 6-String Bass

1956-1959. 2 pickups, 6-string.

1956-1959		$1,250	$1,600

Model 1442 Standard Bass

1966-1968. Solidbody 30" standard size, 1 pickup, dot markers, shaded brown.

1966-1968		$600	$800

Model 1443 Extra Long Bass

1966-1968. Solidbody 34" size, 2 pickups, dot markers, red sunburst.

1966-1968		$750	$1,000

Model 1444 Electric Bass

1959-1965. Bass version of 6-string electric guitar Model 1415 (bronze) and 1416 (black), 4-on-a-side replaces the prior year coke-bottle headstock, 1 pickup on single-cut U-1 style body, black finish.

1959-1965		$700	$900

Simmons

2002-present. Luthier David L. Simmons builds his professional grade, production/custom, 4- and 5-string basses in Hendersonville, North Carolina.

Sinister

2003. A short run of intermediate grade, solidbody basses built for Sinister Guitars by luthier Jon Kammerer.

Smith

1978-present. Professional and premium grade, production/custom, electric basses built by luthier Ken Smith in Perkasie, Pennsylvania. Earlier models had Ken Smith on the headstock, recent models have a large S logo. He also designs the imported KSD line of basses.

American-Made Bass

1978-2020	Various models	$1,700	$3,700

Imported Bass

1990s	Various models	$450	$750

Soundgear by Ibanez

SDGR Soundgear by Ibanez headstock logo, intermediate grade, production, solidbody electric basses, made in Japan, Korea and Indonesia, starting in 1987.

Spector/Stuart Spector Design

1975-1990 (Spector), 1991-1998 (SSD), 1998-present (Spector SSD). Imtermediate, professional, and premium grade, production/custom, basses made in the U.S., the Czech Republic, Korea, and China. Stuart Spector's first bass was the NS and the company quickly grew to the point where Kramer acquired it in '85. After Kramer went out of business in '90, Spector started building basses with the SSD logo (Stuart Spector Design). In '98 he recovered the Spector trademark.

MODEL YEAR	FEATURES	EXC. COND. LOW	HIGH

Squier

See models listed under Squier in Fender section.

Standel

1952-1974, 1997-present. Amp builder Bob Crooks offered instruments under his Standel brand name three different times during the '60s. See Guitar section for production details. See Amp section for more company information.

Custom Deluxe Solidbody 401 Bass

1967-1968. Custom with higher appointments, various colors.

1967-1968		$900	$1,200

Custom Deluxe Thinbody 402 Bass

1967-1968. Custom with higher appointments, various colors.

1967-1968		$900	$1,200

Custom Solidbody 501 Bass

1967-1968. Solidbody, 1 pickup, various colors.

1967-1968		$725	$950

Custom Thinbody 502 Bass

1967-1968. Thin solidbody, 2 pickups, various colors.

1967-1968		$725	$950

Steinberger

1979-present. Steinberger offers budget and intermediate grade, production, electric basses. They also offer guitars.

H Series

1979-1982. Reinforced molded plastic wedge-shaped body, headless neck, 1 (H1) or 2 (H2) high impedence pickups, black, red or white.

1979-1982	H1, black	$2,200	$2,900
1979-1982	H1, red or white	$3,100	$4,100
1979-1982	H2, black	$2,200	$2,900
1979-1982	H2, red or white	$3,100	$4,100

L Series

1979-1984. Reinforced molded plastic wedge-shaped body, headless neck, 1 (L1) or 2 (L2) low impedence active pickups, black, red or white. Evolved into XL series.

1979-1984	L1, black	$1,850	$2,400
1979-1984	L1, black, fretless	$1,750	$2,300
1979-1984	L1, red or white	$2,850	$3,700
1979-1984	L2, black	$1,850	$2,400
1979-1984	L2, black, fretless	$1,750	$2,300
1979-1984	L2, red or white	$2,850	$3,700

Q-4 Bass

1990-1991. Composite neck, Double Bass system, headless with traditional-style maple body, low-impedance pickups.

1990-1991		$1,300	$1,700

Q-5 Bass

1990-1991. Five-string version of Q Bass.

1990-1991		$1,400	$1,800

XL-2 Bass

1984-1993. Rectangular composite body, 4-string, headless, 2 pickups.

1984-1989		$1,800	$2,400
1990-1993		$1,675	$2,200

MODEL YEAR	FEATURES	EXC. COND. LOW	HIGH

XL-2GR Bass

1985-1990. Headless, Roland GR synthesizer controller.

1985-1990		$1,850	$2,400

XM-2 Bass

1986-1992. Headless, double-cut maple body, 4-string, 2 low-impedance pickups, optional fretted, lined fretless or unlined fretless, black, red or white.

1986-1992		$1,750	$2,300

XT-2/XZ-2 Spirit Bass

1995-present. Headless, rectangular XL body, import.

1995-2020		$250	$325

Stewart Basses

2000-ca. 2009. Luthier Fred Stewart built his premium grade, custom/production, solidbody basses in Charlton, Maryland. He has also built guitars starting in '94.

Stinger

See Martin listing.

Supro

1935-1968, 2004-present. Supro was a budget brand for the National Dobro Company. Supro offered only two bass models in the '60s. Brand name was revived in '04.

Pocket Bass

1960-1968. Double-cut, neck pickup and bridge mounted pickup, semi-hollow, short-scale, black.

1960-1968		$600	$800

Taurus Bass

1967-1968. Asymmetrical double-cut, neck pickup and bridge mounted pickup.

1967-1968		$485	$625

SX

See listing for Essex.

Tacoma

1995-2009. Professional grade, production, acoustic basses produced in Tacoma, Washington. They also built acoustic guitars and mandolins.

Thunderchief Series Bass

1998-2009. 17 3/4 flat-top, solid spruce top, solid mahogany back, laminated mahogany sides, rounded cutaway, bolt-on neck, dot markers, natural satin finish.

1998-2009	Various models	$650	$850

Taylor

1974-present. Professional and premium grade, production, acoustic basses built in El Cajon, California. They presently build guitars.

AB1 Bass

1996-2003. Acoustic/electric, sitka spruce top, imbuia walnut back and sides, designed for 'loose' woody sound.

1996-2003		$1,350	$1,750

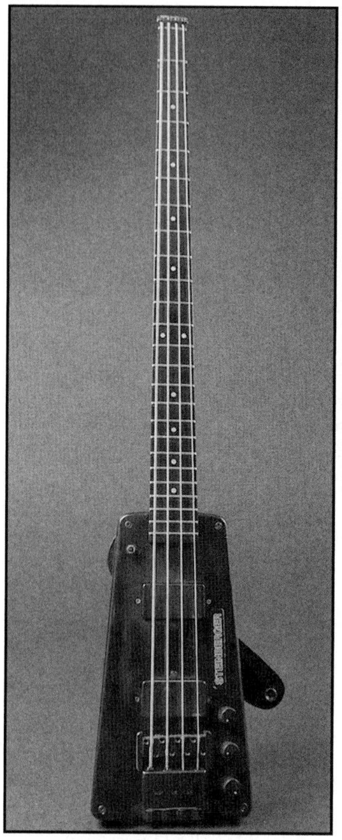

1983 Steinberger L2

Carter Vintage Guitars

1984 Steinberger XL-2

Justin Nortillo

Taylor GS Mini-e Maple Bass

1960 Teisco EB-200

Carter Vintage Guitars

MODEL YEAR	FEATURES	EXC. COND. LOW	HIGH

AB2 Bass

1996-2003. Acoustic/electric, all imbuia walnut body.

1996-2003		$1,600	$2,075

AB3 Bass

1998-2003. Acoustic/electric, sitka spruce top, maple back and sides.

1998-2003		$1,600	$2,075

GS Series Bass

2006-present. Grand Symphony, the GS Mini is scaled-down version.

2006-2020	Various models	$450	$1,200

Teisco

The Japanese Teisco line started offering basses in the '60s.

Electric Bass

1968-1969. EB-100 (1 pickup, white 'guard), EB-200 (solidbody), EB-200B (semi-hollowbody) and Violin bass.

1968-1969	EB-100	$125	$175
1968-1969	EB-200	$525	$700
1968-1969	EB-200 B	$525	$700
1968-1969	Violin	$525	$700

Tele-Star

1965-ca.1972. Guitars and basses imported from Japan by Tele-Star Musical Instrument Corporation of New York. Primarily made by Kawai, many inspired by Burns designs, some in cool sparkle finishes.

Electric Solidbody Bass

1960s	Various models	$100	$275

Tobias

1977-2019. Founded by Mike Tobias in Orlando, Florida. Moved to San Francisco for '80-'81, then to Costa Mesa, eventually ending up in Hollywood. In '90, he sold the company to Gibson which moved it to Burbank. The first Tobias made under Gibson ownership was serial number 1094. The instruments continued to be made by the pre-Gibson crew until '92, when the company was moved to Nashville. The last LA Tobias/Gibson serial number is 2044. Mike left the company in '92 and started a new business in '94 called MTD where he continues to make electric and acoustic basses. In '99, production of Tobias basses was moved overseas. In late '03, Gibson started again offering U.S.-made Tobias instruments; they are made in Conway, Arkansas, in the former Baldwin grand piano facility. Currently Tobias offers imported and U.S.-made, intermediate and professional grade, production, acoustic and electric basses.

Basic Bass

1984-1999. 30", 32", or 34" scale, neck-thru-body in alder, koa or walnut, 5-piece laminated neck.

1984-1999	Basic B-4	$1,650	$2,150
1984-1999	Basic B-5	$1,750	$2,250

Classic C-4 Bass

1978-1999. One or 2 pickups, active or passive electronics, 2-octave rosewood 'board, available in short-, medium-, and long-scale models.

1978-1999		$1,750	$2,250

Classic C-5 Bass

1985-1999. 30", 32" or 34" scale, alder, koa or walnut body, bookmatched top, ebony or phenolic 'board, hardwood neck.

1985-1999		$1,800	$2,350

Classic C-6 Bass

Ca. 1986-1999. Flamed maple and padauk neck, alder body, padauk top, ebony 'board, active electronics, 32" or 34" scale.

1986-1999		$1,900	$2,450

Growler GR-5 Bass

1996-1999. 5-string, offset double-cut, bolt neck, various colors.

1996-1999		$600	$775

Growler Limited Bass

2009. Natural finish swamp ash body, set-neck.

2009		$675	$875

Killer Bee Bass

1991-1999. Offset double-cut, swamp ash or lacewood body, various colors.

1991-1999	KB-4	$1,500	$2,000
1991-1999	KB-5	$1,600	$2,100
1991-1999	KB-6	$1,700	$2,200

Model T Bass

1989-1991. Line of 4- and 5-string basses, 3-piece maple neck-thru-body, maple body halves, active treble and bass controls. Fretless available.

1989-1991		$1,025	$1,350

Renegade Bass

1998-2001. Offset double-cut, 1 single-coil and 1 humbucker.

1998-2001		$1,400	$1,800

Signature S-4 Bass

1978-1999. Available in 4-, 5-, and 6-string models, chrome-plated milled brass bridge.

1978-1990	Tobias-Burbank	$2,700	$3,500
1990-1992	Gibson-Burbank	$2,150	$2,800

Standard ST-4 Bass

1992-1995. Japanese-made, 5-piece maple neck-thru, swamp ash body wings.

1992-1995		$1,000	$1,300

Toby Deluxe TD-4 Bass

1994-1996. Offset double-cut, bolt neck.

1994-1996		$375	$525

Toby Deluxe TD-5 Bass

1994-1996. 5-string version.

1994-1996		$475	$625

Toby Pro 5 Bass

1994-1996. Solidbody 5-string, Toby Pro logo on truss rod cover, neck-thru body.

1994-1996		$375	$525

Toby Pro 6 Bass

1994-1996. Solidbody 6-string, Toby Pro logo on truss rod cover, neck-thru body.

1994-1996		$450	$650

MODEL YEAR	FEATURES	EXC. COND. LOW	HIGH

Tokai

1947-present. Tokai started making guitars and basses around '70 and by the end of that decade they were being imported into the U.S. Today Tokai offers electrics, acoustics, and electric basses made in Japan and Korea.

Vintage Bass

1970s-1980s. Tokai offered near copies of classic U.S. basses.

1970s-80s	Copy models	$400	$825

Tonemaster

1960s. Guitars and basses, imported from Italy, with typical '60s Italian sparkle plastic finish and push-button controls, bolt-on neck.

Electric Bass

1960s	Various models	$500	$700

Traben

Intermediate grade, production, solidbody basses imported by Elite Music Brands of Clearwater, Florida, starting in 2004.

Travis Bean

1974-1979, 1999. The unique Travis Bean line included a couple of bass models. Travis Bean announced some new instruments in '99, but general production was not resumed.

TB-2000 Bass

1974-1979. Aluminum neck, T-slotted headstock, longer horned, double-cut body, 2 pickups, 4 controls, dot markers, various colors.

1974-1979		$2,700	$3,500

TB-4000 (Wedge Vee) Bass

1974-1979. Bass version of Bean's Wedge guitar, few made.

1974-1979		$3,600	$4,700

True Tone

1960s. Western Auto retailed this line of basses, guitars and amps which were manufactured by Chicago builders like Kay. The brand was most likely gone by '68.

Electric Bass

1960s		$225	$350

Univox

1964-1978. Univox started out as an amp line and added guitars and basses around '69. Guitars were imported from Japan by the Merson Musical Supply Company, later Unicord, Westbury, New York. Generally mid-level copies of American designs.

Badazz Bass

1971-ca. 1975. Based on the Guild S-100.

1971-1977		$350	$450

Bicentennial Bass

1976. Carved eagle in body, matches Bicentennial guitar (see that listing), brown stain, maple 'board.

1976		$650	$850

MODEL YEAR	FEATURES	EXC. COND. LOW	HIGH

Hi Flier Bass

1969-1977. Mosrite Ventures Bass copy, 2 pickups, rosewood 'board.

1969-1977		$425	$550

'Lectra (Model 1970F) Bass

1969-ca. 1973. Violin bass, walnut.

1969-1973		$525	$675

Model 3340 Semi-Hollow Bass

1970-1971. Copy of Gibson EB-0 semi-hollow bass.

1970-1971		$425	$550

Precisely Bass

1971-ca. 1975. Copy of Fender P-Bass.

1971-1975		$425	$550

Stereo Bass

1976-1977. Rickenbacker 4001 Bass copy, model U1975B.

1976-1977		$425	$550

Thin Line Bass

1960s. EB-2 style, f-holes, 2 pickups.

1960s		$425	$550

Ventura

1970s. Import classic bass copies distributed by C. Bruno (Kaman). They also had guitars.

Vintage Electric Bass

1970s	Copy models	$425	$550

Vox

1954-present. Guitars and basses bearing the Vox name were offered from 1961-'69 (made in England, Italy), '82-'85 (Japan), '85-'88 (Korea), '98-2001 (U.S.), with a limited edition teardrop bass offered in late '07. Special thanks to Jim Rhoads of Rhoads Music in Elizabethtown, Pennsylvania, for help on production years of these models.

Apollo IV Bass

1967-1969. Single-cut hollowbody, bolt maple neck, 1 pickup, on-board fuzz, booster, sunburst.

1967-1969		$675	$875

Astro IV Bass

1967-1969. Violin-copy bass, 2 pickups.

1967-1969		$850	$1,100

Bassmaster Bass

1961-1965. Offset double-cut, 2 pickups, 2 knobs.

1961-1965		$625	$800

Clubman Bass

1961-1966. Double-cut 2-pickup solidbody, red.

1961-1966		$425	$550

Constellation IV Bass

1967-1968. Teardrop-shaped body, 2 pickups, 1 f-hole, 1 set of controls, treble, bass and distortion boosters.

1967-1968		$1,100	$1,450

Cougar Bass

1963-1967. Double-cut semi-hollow body, 2 f-holes, 2 pickups, 2 sets of controls, sunburst.

1963-1967		$850	$1,100

Delta IV Bass

1967-1968. Five-sided body, 2 pickups, 1 volume and 2 tone controls, distortion, treble and bass boosters.

1967-1968		$1,050	$3,050

1974 Univox Hi Flier

Greg Boschert

1967 Vox Apollo IV

Rivington Guitars

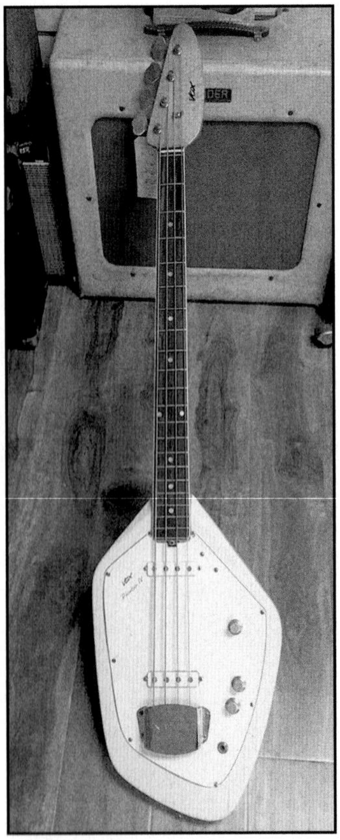

1965 Vox V210 Phantom IV

Craig Brody

Wal Pro (Mark I)

MODEL YEAR	FEATURES	EXC. COND. LOW	HIGH

Guitar-Organ Bass

1966. The 4-string bass version of the Guitar-Organ, Phantom-style body, white.

1966	Excellent cond	$1,950	$2,550
1966	Functional	$600	$1,650

Mark IV Bass

1963-1969. Teardrop-shaped body, 2 pickups, 1 set of controls, sunburst.

1963-1965	England, white	$2,150	$2,850
1965-1969	Italy, sunburst	$1,325	$1,725

Panther Bass

1967-1968. Double-cut solidbody, 1 slanted pickup, rosewood 'board, sunburst.

1967-1968		$475	$625

Phantom IV Bass

1963-1969. Five-sided body, 2 pickups, 1 set of controls.

1963-1964	England	$2,000	$2,600
1965-1969	Italy	$1,450	$1,900

Saturn IV Bass

1967-1968. Single-cut, 2 f-holes, 1 set of controls, 1 pickup.

1967-1968		$550	$725

Sidewinder IV Bass (V272)

1967-1968. Double-cut semi-hollow body, 2 f-holes, 2 pickups, 1 set of controls, treble, bass, and distortion boosters.

1967-1968		$1,000	$1,300

Stinger Bass

1968. Teardrop-shaped, boat oar headstock.

1968		$725	$925

Violin Bass

1966. Electro-acoustic bass with violin shaped body, 2 extended range pickups, sunburst.

1966		$850	$1,100

Wyman Bass

1966. Teardrop-shaped body, 2 pickups, 1 f-hole, 1 set of controls, sunburst.

1966		$1,325	$1,725

MODEL YEAR	FEATURES	EXC. COND. LOW	HIGH

Wal

1976-present. Founded in England by luthier Ian Waller and his partner Peter Stevens, forming the company under the name Electric Wood in '78. Waller died in '88, Stevens enlists help of luthier Paul Herman, and in 2000s Stevens retires and Herman takes over. In the early years, the Mark designation was used generically. Newer contemporary models are named Mk1, Mk2 and Mk3. Prices shown will increase 5% with LED option, or 10% with rare top, but no value difference between fretted and fretless. MIDI electronics does not increase the value.

Custom (IV) Bass

1980s-1990s. 4-string, active, no guard, generally highly figured front and back.

1980	Mark I	$4,500	$5,800
1985	Mark II	$5,200	$6,800
1994	Mark III	$5,200	$6,800

Custom (V) Bass

1980s-1990s. 5-string, active, no guard, generally highly figured front and back.

1985	Mark II	$5,200	$6,800
1994	Mark III	$5,200	$6,800

Custom (VI) Bass

1990s. 6-string, active, no guard, generally highly figured front and back.

1994	Mark III	$5,200	$6,800

JG Bass

1976-1978. 4-string, passive with either tooled leather (34 made), or leather guard.

1976-1978	Non-tooled	$5,200	$6,800
1976-1978	Tooled	$5,800	$7,500

Pro (Mark I) Bass

1978. Passive, black guard.

1978		$2,800	$3,800

Wandre (Davoli)

Ca. 1956/57-1969. Italian-made guitars and basses.

Electric Bass

1956-1969	Common models	$1,000	$3,000
1956-1969	Rare models	$3,000	$8,000

MODEL YEAR	FEATURES	EXC. COND. LOW	HIGH

Warwick

1982-present. Professional and premium grade, production/custom, electric and acoustic basses made in Markneukirchen, Germany; founded by Hans Peter Wilfer, whose father started Framus guitars. They also build amps.

Welson

1960s. Italian-made copy model guitars and basses.

Electric Bass

1960s	Copy models	$100	$300

Wurlitzer

Large music retailer Wurlitzer marketed a line of American-made guitars in the 1920s. They also offered American- and foreign-made guitars starting in '65. In '67, Wurlitzer switched to Italian-made Welson guitars.

Hollowbody Electric Bass

1960s. Italian-made.

1967		$475	$625

Yamaha

1946-present. Budget, intermediate, professional and premium grade, production, electric basses. They also build guitars. Yamaha began producing solidbody instruments in '66.

Electric Bass

1960-present. Various models

1960-2020		$100	$1,300

Zemaitis

1960-1999, 2004-present. Tony Zemaitis began selling his guitars in '60 and he retired in '99. He emphasized simple lightweight construction and his instruments are known for hand engraved metal fronts. Each hand-built custom guitar or bass was a unique instrument. Approximately 10 custom guitars were built each year. In '04, Japan's Kanda Shokai, with the endorsement of Tony Zemaitis, Jr., started building the guitars again.

Zen-On

1946-ca.1968. Japanese-made. By '67 using the Morales brandname. Not heavily imported into the U.S., if at all (see Morales).

Electric Solidbody Bass

1950s	Various models	$100	$300

Zim-Gar

1960s. Japanese guitars and basses imported by Gar-Zim Musical Instrument Corporation of Brooklyn, New York.

Electric Solidbody Bass

1960s	Various models	$100	$300

Zon

1981-present. Luthier Joe Zon builds his professional and premium grade, production/custom, solidbody basses in Redwood City, California. Zon started the brand in Buffalo, New York and relocated to Redwood City in '87. He has also built guitars.

Legacy Elite Bass

1989-present. 34" scale carbon-fiber neck, Bartolini pickups, ZP-2 active electronics.

1989-2020	V, 5-string	$1,300	$1,700
1989-2020	VI, 6-string	$1,350	$1,750

Scepter Bass

1984-1993. Offset body shape, 24 frets, 1 pickup, tremolo.

1984-1993		$1,150	$1,500

Sonus Custom Bass

1990s-present. Offset swamp ash body, 2 pickups.

1990s-2020		$1,800	$2,350

Zorko

Late-1950s-early-1962. Original maker of the Ampeg Baby Bass (see that listing), sold to Ampeg in 1962, Zorko logo on scroll.

Baby Bass

1950s-1962		$1,750	$2,250

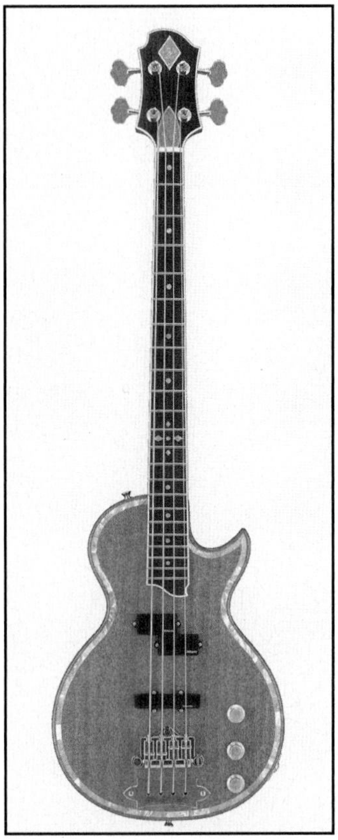

Zemaitis GZB-2500

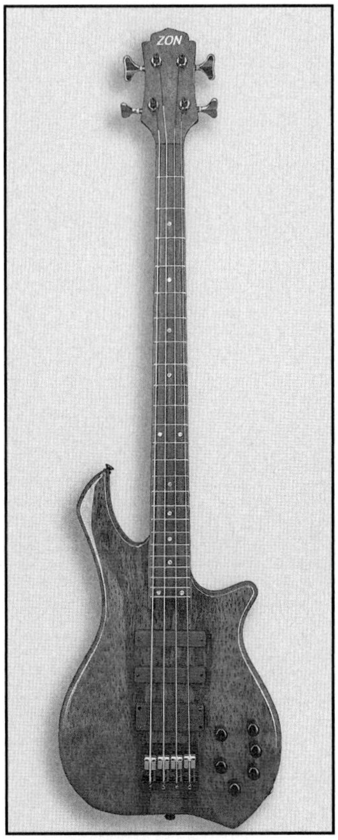

Zon Legacy

BASSES

AMPS

1955 Ampeg 815: Imaged by Heritage Auctions, HA.com.

65amps Lil' Whiskey

Acoustic 115
Rivington Guitars

1980 Acoustic 165 JBL M1 Series 1x12 Combo

MODEL YEAR	FEATURES	EXC. COND. LOW	HIGH

3 Monkeys Amps

2007-present. Intermediate and professional grade, production/custom, amps and cabinets built by Greg Howard in Raleigh, North Carolina.

3rd Power

Mid-2009-present. Professional grade, production/custom, guitar amps built in Franklin, Tennessee by Jamie Scott.

65amps

2004-present. Founded by Peter Stroud and Dan Boul, 65amps builds tube guitar head and combo amps and speaker cabs in Valley Village, California.

Ace Tone

Late-1960-1970s. Made by Sakata Shokai Limited of Osaka, Japan, early importer of amps and effects pedals. Later became Roland/Boss.

B-9 Amp
Late-1960s-early-1970s. Solid-state bass amp head.
1960s-70s $120 $155

Mighty-5 Amp
Late-1960s-early-1970s. Tubes, 50-watt head.
1960s-70s $95 $120

Solid A-5 Amp
Late-1960s-early-1970s. Solidstate 2x12 combo with verticle cab, reverb and tremolo, black tolex, silver grille.
1960s-70s $140 $180

Acoustic

Ca.1965-ca.1987, 2001-2005, 2008-present. The Acoustic Control Corp., of Los Angeles, California, was mostly known for solidstate amplifiers. Heads and cabinets were sold separately with their own model numbers, but were also combined (amp sets) and marketed under a different model number (for example, the 153 amp set was the 150b head with a 2x15" cabinet). The brand was revived by Samick in '01 for a line of amps. In '08 brand back again on line of amps sold through Guitar Center and Musician's Friend.

114 Amp
Ca.1977-mid-1980s. Solidstate, 50 watts, 2x10", reverb, master volume.
1977-1984 $200 $250

115 Amp
1977-1978. Solidstate, 1x12", 50 watts, reverb, master volume.
1977-1978 $200 $250

116 Bass Amp
1978-mid-1980s. Solidstate, 75 watts, 1x15", power boost switch.
1978-1984 $200 $250

120 Amp Head
1977-mid-1980s. Solidstate head, 125 watts.
1977-1984 $150 $200

123 Amp
1977-1984. 1x12" combo.
1977-1984 $150 $200

MODEL YEAR	FEATURES	EXC. COND. LOW	HIGH

124 Amp
1977-mid-1980s. Solidstate, 4x10", 5-band EQ, 100 watts, master volume.
1977-1984 $225 $275

125 Amp
1977-mid-1980s. Solidstate, 2x12", 5-band EQ, 100 watts, master volume.
1977-1984 $225 $275

126 Bass Amp
1977-mid-1980s. Solidstate, 100 watts, 1x15", 5-band EQ.
1977-1984 $225 $275

134 Amp
1972-1976. Solidstate, 100-125 watts, 4x10" combo.
1972-1976 $225 $275

135 Amp
1972-1976. Solidstate, 125 watts, 2x12" combo, reverb, tremolo.
1972-1976 $225 $275

136 Amp
1972-1976. Solidstate, 125 watts, 1x15" combo.
1972-1976 $225 $275

140 Bass Amp Head
1972-1976. Solidstate, 125 watts, 2 channels.
1972-1976 $150 $200

150 Amp Head
1960s-1976. Popular selling model, generally many available in the used market. Solidstate, 110 watts until '72, 125 watts after.
1968-1976 $175 $225

150b Bass Amp Head
1960s-1971. Bass amp version of 150 head.
1968-1971 $150 $200

153 Bass Amp Set
1960s-1971. 150b head (bass version of 150) with 2x15" 466 cabinet, 110 watts.
1968-1971 $350 $450

165 Amp
1979-mid-1980s. All tube combo, switchable to 60 or 100 watts, brown tolex.
1979-1984 $275 $350

220 Bass Amp Head
1977-1980s. Solidstate, 5-band EQ, either 125 or 160 watts, later models 170 or 200 watts, black tolex.
1977-1984 $200 $250

230 Amp Head
1977-1980s. Solidstate head, 125/160 watts, 5-band EQ.
1977-1984 $200 $250

260 Amp Head
1960s-1971. Solidstate, 275 watt, stereo/mono.
1968-1971 $500 $650

261 Amp and Cabinet Set
1960s-1971. 275 watts with 2x15" cab.
1969-1971 $2,100 $2,800

270 Amp Head
1970s. 400 watts.
1970s $325 $400

320 Bass Amp Head
1977-1980s. Solidstate, 5-band EQ, 160/300 watts, 2 switchable channels, black tolex.
1977-1984 $325 $400

MODEL YEAR | FEATURES | EXC. COND. LOW | HIGH

360 Bass Amp Head
1960s-1971. One of Acoustic's most popular models, 200 watts. By '72, the 360 is listed as a "preamp only."
1968-1971 $550 $700

370 Bass Amp Head
1972-1977. Solidstate bass head, 365 watts early on, 275 later, Jaco Pastorius associated.
1972-1977 275 or 365 watt $550 $700

402 Cabinet
1977-1980s. 2x15" bass cab, black tolex, black grille.
1977-1984 $175 $225

404 Cabinet
1970s. 6x10", Jaco Pastorius associated.
1970s $350 $450

450 Amp Head
1974-1976. 170 watts, 5-band EQ, normal and bright inputs.
1974-1976 $275 $350

455 Amp Set
1974-1977. 170 watt 450 head with 4x12" cabinet, black.
1974-1977 $550 $700

470 Amp Head
1974-1977. 170 watt, dual channel.
1974-1977 $275 $350

AG15 Amp
2008-2016. Small combo, 15 watts.
2008-2016 $35 $45

B100 Amp (MK II)
2008-2016. Classic style bass combo, 100 watts, 1x15.
2008-2016 $100 $125

B200 Amp (MK II)
2009-2019. Bass combo, 200 watts, 1x15.
2009-2019 $150 $200

G20-110 Amp
1981-mid-1980s. Solidstate, 20 watts, 1x10". The G series was a lower-priced combo line.
1981-1985 $75 $100

G20-120 Amp
1981-mid-1980s. Solidstate, 20 watts, 1x12".
1981-1985 $75 $100

G60-112 Amp
1981-mid-1980s. Solidstate, 60 watts, 1x12".
1981-1985 $100 $125

G60-212 Amp
1981-mid-1980s. Solidstate, 60 watts, 2x12".
1981-1985 $125 $150

G60T-112 Amp
1981-1987. Tube, 60 watts, 1x12".
1981-1985 $200 $275

Tube 60 Amp
1986-1987. Combo, 60 watts, 1x12", spring reverb, bright switch, master volume control, effects loop.
1986-1987 $200 $275

ADA
1977-2002. ADA (Analog/Digital Associates) was located in Berkeley, California, and introduced its Flanger and Final Phase in '77. The company later moved to Oakland and made amplifiers, high-tech signal processors, and a reissue of its original Flanger.

MODEL YEAR | FEATURES | EXC. COND. LOW | HIGH

Aguilar
1995-present. U.S.-made tube and solidstate amp heads, cabinets, and pre-amps from New York City, New York. They also made effect pedals.

Aiken Amplification
2000-present. Tube amps, combos, and cabinets built by Randall Aiken originally in Buford, Georgia, and since '05 in Pensacola, Florida.

Airline
Ca.1958-1968, 2004-present. Brand for Montgomery Ward, built by Danelectro, Valco and others. In '04, the brand was revived on a line of reissues from Eastwood guitars.

Tube Amp 1x6" Speaker
1958-1960s $175 $250

Tube Amp 1x8" Speaker
1958-1960s $225 $325

Tube Amp 1x10" Speaker
1958-1960s $325 $475

Tube Amp 1x12" Speaker
1958-1960s $475 $650

Tube Amp Higher-End
1958-1960s $550 $725

Tube Amp Highest-End
1958-1960s $650 $950

Alamo
1947-1982. Founded by Charles Eilenberg, Milton Fink, and Southern Music, San Antonio, Texas, and distributed by Bruno and Sons. Alamo started producing amps in '49 and the amps were all-tube until '73; solidstate preamp and tube output from '73 to ca. '80; all solidstate for ca. '80 to '82.

Bass Solidstate Preamp-Tube Output Amp
1973-ca.1979. Solidstate preamp section with tube output section, 35 or 40 watts, 15" speakers, combo or piggyback. Models include the Paragon Bass, Paragon Bass Piggyback, Paragon Country Western Bass, Paragon Super Bass, and the Fury Bass.
1973-1979 $125 $175

Bass Tube Amp
1960-1972. Leatherette covered, all tube, 20 to 35 watts, 15" speakers, combo or piggyback, some with Lansing speaker option. Models include the Paragon Special, Paragon Bass, Piggyback Band, Piggyback Bass, Fury Bass, and Paragon Bass (piggyback).
1960-1972 $325 $450

Birch "A" Combo Amp
1949-1962. Birch wood cabinets with A-shaped grill cutout, 2 to 5 tubes. Models include the Embassy Amp 3, Jet Amp 4, Challenger Amp 2, Amp 5, and the Montclair.
1949-1962 $275 $375

Mid-Power Solidstate Preamp-Tube Output Amp
1973-ca.1979. Solidstate preamp section with tube output section, 25 watts, 12" speaker, with reverb and tremolo. Models include the Montclair.
1973-1979 $125 $175

1964 Airline Tremolo Reverb
Tom Pfeifer

1960s Alamo Embassy
Imaged by Heritage Auctions, HA.com

1974 Alamo Montclair Reverb 2565
Tom Pfeifer

Alessandro 1/2AZZ

Allen Hot Blond

1965 Ampeg B-12 X Portaflex

Tom Pfeifer

MODEL YEAR	FEATURES	EXC. COND. LOW	HIGH

Mid-Power Tube Amp

1960-1970. Leatherette covered, all tube, 15 to 30 watts, 12" or 15" speakers, some with tremolo and reverb, some with Lansing speaker option. Models include Montclair, Paragon, Paragon Band, Titan, and Futura.

1960-1970 $350 $500

Small Solidstate Preamp-Tube Output Amp

1973-ca.1979. Solidstate preamp section with tube output section, 3 to 12 watts, 5" to 12" speaker, some with reverb. Models include the Challenger, Capri, Special, Embassy, Dart, and Jet.

1973-1979 $125 $175

Small Tube Amp

1960-1972. Leatherette covered, all tube, 3 to 10 watts, 6" to 10" speakers, some with tremolo. Models include the Jet, Embassy, Challenger, Capri, Fiesta, Dart, and Special.

1960-1972 $225 $300

Solidstate Amp

Ca.1980-1982. All solidstate.

1980-1982 $30 $40

Twin Speaker Combo (Tube/Hybrid) Amp

1973-ca.1979. Solidstate preamp section with tube output section, 20 or 70 watts, 10", 12" and 15" speaker configurations, some with reverb and tremolo. Models include the 70-watt Paragon Super Reverb Piggybacks, the 45-watt Futura 2x12, and the 20-watt Twin-Ten.

1973-1979 $225 $300

Twin Speaker Tube Amp

1962-1972. Leatherette covered, all tube, up to 45 watts, 8", 10", 12" or 15" speaker configurations, some with tremolo and reverb, some with Lansing speaker option. Models include the Electra Twin Ten, Century Twin Ten, Futuramic Twin Eight, Galaxie Twin Twelve, Galaxie Twin Twelve Piggyback, Piggyback Super Band, Alamo Pro Reverb Piggyback, Futura, Galaxie Twin Ten, Twin-Ten, and Band Piggyback.

1962-1972 $400 $550

Alden

Small budget grade solidstate guitar and bass amps from Muse, Inc. of China.

Alesis

1992-present. Alesis has a wide range of products for the music industry, including digital modeling guitar amps. They also offer guitar effects.

Alessandro

1998-present. Tube amps built by George Alessandro in Huntingdon Valley, Pennsylvania. Founded in '94 as the Hound Dog Corporation, in '98 the company name was changed to Alessandro. The Redbone ('94) and the Bloodhound ('96) were the only models bearing the Hound Dog mark. Serial numbers are consecutive regardless of model (the earliest 20-30 did not have serial numbers). In '98 the company converted to exotic/high-end components and the name changed to Alessandro High-End Products. In '01, he added the Working Dog brand line of amps.

MODEL YEAR	FEATURES	EXC. COND. LOW	HIGH

Allen Amplification

1998-present. Tube combo amps, heads and cabinets built by David Allen in Walton, Kentucky. He also offers the amps in kit form and produces replacement and upgrade transformers and a tube overdrive pedal.

Allston Amplifiers

2005-present. Professional and premium grade, custom, amps and cabinets built by Rob Lohr in Allston, Massachusetts.

Aloha

Late-1940s. Electric lap steel and amp Hawaiian outfits made for the Dallas-based Aloha.

Ampeg

1949-present. Ampeg was originally primarily known for their bass amps. In the eastern U.S., Ampeg was Fender's greatest challenger in the '60s and '70s bass amplifier market. Currently offering tube and solidstate heads, combos and speaker cabinets. They have also built guitars.

Amp Covering Dates: Wood veneer 1946-1949, Smooth brown 1949-1952, Dot tweed 1952-1954, Tweed 1954-1955, Rough gray 1957-1958, Rough tan 1957-1958, Cream 1957-1958, Light blue 1958, Navy blue 1958-1962, Blue check 1962-1967, Black pebble 1967, Smooth black 1967-1980, Rough black 1967-1985.

AC-12 Amp

1970. 20 watts, 1x12", accordion amp that was a market failure and dropped after 1 year.

1970 $275 $375

AX-44 C Amp

1990-1992. AX hybrid amp with solidstate power section and 1 preamp tube, 22 watts, 2x8 combo.

1990-1992 $175 $225

B-2 Bass Amp

1994-2000. Solidstate, 200 watts, 1x15" combo or 4x8" combo, black vinyl, black grille, large A logo.

1994-2000 1x15" $375 $500

B-2 R Bass Amp Head

1994-2005. 200 watts, rackmount, replaced by 450 watt B2RE.

1994-2005 $250 $325

B-3 Amp

1995-2001. Solidstate head, 150 watts, 1x15".

1995-2001 $375 $500

B-4 Bass Amp Head

1998-2008. Solidstate 1000-watt head, early models made in USA, then outsourced.

1998-2008 $300 $400

B-5 R Bass Amp Head

2000-2005. 500 watts, 2-channel.

2000s $300 $400

B-12 N Portaflex Amp

1961-1965. 25 watts, 2x12", 2 6L6 power tubes.

1961-1965 $1,400 $1,850

B-12 X/B-12 XT Portaflex Amp

1961-1969. Tube, 50 watts, 2x12", reverb, vibrato, 2x7027A power tubes.

1961-1969 $1,400 $1,850

MODEL YEAR	FEATURES	EXC. COND. LOW	HIGH

B-15 N (NB, NC, NF) Portaflex Amp
1960-1970. Introduced as B-15 using 2 6L6 power tubes, B-15 N in '61, B-15 NB in '62, B-15 NC with rectifier tube in '64, B-15 NF with fixed-bias 2 6L6 power tubes and 30 watts in '67, 1x15".

1960-1965		$1,400	$1,850
1966-1970	1x15"	$1,400	$1,850
1967-1968	2x15"	$1,400	$1,850

B-15 R Portaflex Amp (Reissue)
1997-2007. Reissue of '65 Portaflex 1x15", blue check, 60/100 watts.

1997-2007 — $1,100 — $1,425

B-15 S Portaflex Amp
1971-1977. 60 watts, 2x7027A power tubes, 1x12".

1971-1977 — $900 — $1,175

B-18 N Portaflex Amp
1964-1969. Bass, 50 watts, 1x18".

1964-1969 — $1,400 — $1,850

B-25 Amp
1969 only. 55 watts, 2 7027A power tubes, 2x15", no reverb, guitar amp.

1969 — $1,000 — $1,300

B-25 B Bass Amp
1969-1980. Bass amp, 55 watts, 2 7027A power tubes, 2x15".

1969-1980 — $1,000 — $1,300

B-50 R Rocket Bass Amp (Reissue)
1996-2005. 50 watts, 1x12" combo, vintage-style blue check cover.

1996-2005 — $250 — $325

B-100 R Rocket Bass Amp (Reissue)
1996-2005. Solidstate, 100 watts, 1x15" combo bass amp, vintage-style blue check cover.

1996-2005 — $250 — $325

B-115 Amp
1973-1980. 120 watts, solidstate, 1x15" combo.

1973-1980 — $250 — $325

B-115 E Amp Cabinet
2006-2017. Bass cab, 1x15".

2006-2017 — 1x15 — $200 — $260

B-410 Bass Amp
1973-1980. Solidstate, 120 watts, 4x10", black vinyl, black grille.

1973-1980 — $300 — $400

BA Series Amp
1999-present. Solidstate bass combo amps, model number is speaker configuration.

1999-2020	BA-112, 50w, 1x12	$100	$130
1999-2020	BA-115, 100w, 1x15	$100	$130
2008-2016	BA-210, 300w, 2x10	$175	$225
2008-2016	BA-210, 600w, 2x10	$215	$275
2011-2020	BA-108, 25w, 1x8	$20	$30

BT-15 Amp
1966-1968. Ampeg introduced solidstate amps in '66, the same year as Fender. Solidstate, 50 watts, 1x15", generally used as a bass amp. The BT-15D has 2 1x15" cabinets. The BT-15C is a 2x15" column portaflex cabinet.

1966-1968 — $325 — $425

BT-18 Amp
1966-1968. Solidstate, 50 watts, 1x18", generally used as a bass amp. The BT-18D has dual 1x18" cabinets. The BT-18C is a 2x18" column portaflex cabinet.

1966-1968 — $325 — $425

Continental I Amp
1956-1959. Single-channel version of Duette, 30 watts, 1x15".

1956-1959 — $550 — $725

Dolphin Amp
1956-1960. Smallest combo offered during this era, 15 watts, 1x12", single-channel (I) and dual-channel (II) options.

1956-1959	Dolphin I	$425	$550
1956-1960	Dolphin II	$525	$675

Duette Amp
1956-1958. Dual-channel, 3 combo models offered; Zephyr (20w, 1x15"), Continental (30w, 1x15") and Duette 50 D-50 (50w, 2x12", tremolo).

1956-1958	Continental Duette	$550	$725
1956-1958	Zephyr Duette	$550	$725
1957-1958	Duette 50 D-50	$800	$1,050

ET-1 Echo Twin Amp
1961-1964. Tube, 30 watts, 1x12", stereo reverb.

1961-1964 — $850 — $1,100

ET-2 Super Echo Twin Amp
1962-1964. Tube, 2x12", 30 watts, stereo reverb.

1962-1964 — $950 — $1,250

G-12 Gemini I Amp
1964-1971. Tube, 1x12", 22 watts, reverb.

1964-1971 — $600 — $800

G-15 Gemini II Amp
1965-1968. Tube, 30 watts, 1x15", reverb.

1965-1968 — $600 — $800

G-18 Amp
1977-1980. Solidstate, 1 channel, 10 watts, 1x8", volume, treble, and bass controls.

1977-1980 — $65 — $85

G-20 Gemini 20
1969-1970. Tubes, 35 watts, 2x10".

1968-1969 — $600 — $800

G-110 Amp
1978-1980. Solidstate, 20 watts, 1x10", reverb, tremolo.

1978-1980 — $105 — $135

G-115 Amp
1979-1980. Solidstate, 175 watts, 1x15" JBL, reverb and tremolo, designed for steel guitar.

1979-1980 — $125 — $165

G-212 Amp
1973-1980. Solidstate, 120 watts, 2x12".

1973-1980 — $150 — $200

GS-12 Rocket 2 Amp
1965-1968. This name replaced the Reverberocket 2 (II), 15 watts, 1x12".

1965-1968 — $600 — $775

GS-12-R Reverberocket 2 Amp
1965-1969. Tube, 1x12", 18 watts, reverb. Called the Reverberocket II in '68 and '69, then Rocket II in '69.

1965-1969 — $600 — $775

GS-15-R Gemini VI Amp
1966-1967. 30 watts, 1x15", single channel, considered to be "the accordion version" of the Gemini II.

1966-1967 — $600 — $775

1969 Ampeg B-15 N
Imaged by Heritage Auctions, HA.com

Ampeg B-50 R Rocket Bass

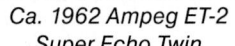

Ca. 1962 Ampeg ET-2 Super Echo Twin
Imaged by Heritage Auctions, HA.com

1968 Ampeg GV-15 Gemini V

Ted Wulfers

Early-'60s Ampeg J-12 Jet

1955 Ampeg 815 Bassamp

Imaged by Heritage Auctions, HA.com

AMPS

GT-10 Amp

1971-1980. Solidstate, 15 watts, 1x10", basic practice amp with reverb.

MODEL YEAR	FEATURES	EXC. COND. LOW	HIGH
1971-1980		$115	$150

GV-15 Gemini V

1968-1971. Unimusic-era tube amp, 30 watts, 1x15" combo, reverb and tremolo.

MODEL YEAR	FEATURES	EXC. COND. LOW	HIGH
1968-1971		$575	$750

GV-22 Gemini 22 Amp

1969-1972. Tube, 30 watts, 2x12".

MODEL YEAR	FEATURES	EXC. COND. LOW	HIGH
1969-1972		$625	$800

J-12 A Jet Amp

1964. Jet Amp with 7591A power tubes.

MODEL YEAR	FEATURES	EXC. COND. LOW	HIGH
1964		$375	$500

J-12 D Jet Amp

1966. Jet Amp with new solidstate rectifier.

MODEL YEAR	FEATURES	EXC. COND. LOW	HIGH
1966		$350	$450

J-12 Jet Amp

1958-1964, 1967-1972. 20 watts, 1x12", 6V6GT power tubes. Second addition, also known as the Jet II, was like the J-12 D Jet but with 12AX7s.

MODEL YEAR	FEATURES	EXC. COND. LOW	HIGH
1958	Rough tan	$525	$675
1959	Blue	$500	$650
1960-1964	Blue	$375	$500
1967-1972	Model reappears	$275	$350

J-12 R Reverbojet Amp

1967-1970. Part of Golden Glo Series, nicknamed 'copper front', 18 watts, 1x12" combo, single channel, tremolo and reverb, printed circuit replaces point-to-point wiring.

MODEL YEAR	FEATURES	EXC. COND. LOW	HIGH
1967-1970		$375	$500

J-12 T Jet Amp

1965, 2006-2008. J-12 A with revised preamp.

MODEL YEAR	FEATURES	EXC. COND. LOW	HIGH
1965		$375	$500

J-20 Jet Amp

2007-2008. Tubes, 20 watts, 1x12.

MODEL YEAR	FEATURES	EXC. COND. LOW	HIGH
2007-2008		$350	$450

Jet II/J-12 T

2007-2008. 15 watts, 1x12".

MODEL YEAR	FEATURES	EXC. COND. LOW	HIGH
2007-2008		$225	$300

Jupiter Amp

1956-1958. Part of Accordiamp Series, similar to Dolphin except preamp voiced for accordion, 15 watts, 1x12".

MODEL YEAR	FEATURES	EXC. COND. LOW	HIGH
1956-1958		$400	$500

M-12 Mercury Amp

1957-1965. 15 watts, 2 channels, Rocket 1x12".

MODEL YEAR	FEATURES	EXC. COND. LOW	HIGH
1957-1965		$500	$650

M-15 Big M Amp

1959-1965. 20 watts, 2x6L6 power, 1x15".

MODEL YEAR	FEATURES	EXC. COND. LOW	HIGH
1959-1965		$575	$750

Model 815 Bassamp Amp

1955. 15 watt combo, 1 channel. Ampeg Bassamp logo on control panel.

MODEL YEAR	FEATURES	EXC. COND. LOW	HIGH
1955		$575	$750

Model 820 Bassamp Amp

1956-1958. 20 watt combo, 1 channel.

MODEL YEAR	FEATURES	EXC. COND. LOW	HIGH
1956-1958		$625	$800

Model 822 Bassamp Amp

1957-1958. 2 channel 820.

MODEL YEAR	FEATURES	EXC. COND. LOW	HIGH
1957-1958		$650	$825

Model 830 Bassamp Amp

1956-1958. 30 watt combo.

MODEL YEAR	FEATURES	EXC. COND. LOW	HIGH
1956-1958		$700	$900

Model 835 Bassamp Amp

1959-1961. 35 watt 1x15" combo, 2 channels.

MODEL YEAR	FEATURES	EXC. COND. LOW	HIGH
1959-1961		$700	$900

New Yorker Amp

1956-1958. Part of Accordiamp Series, similar to Continental except preamp voiced for accordion, 30 watts, 1x15".

MODEL YEAR	FEATURES	EXC. COND. LOW	HIGH
1956-1958		$475	$625

Portabass (PB) Series Amp

2002-2008. Portabass (PB) amps and speaker cabs.

MODEL YEAR	FEATURES	EXC. COND. LOW	HIGH
2002-2004	PB-122H Cab	$225	$300
2002-2008	PB-250 Head	$225	$300

Portaflex (PF) Series Amp

2011-present. Portaflex (PF) ultra-compact amp heads offered with flip-top cabs, 350 watt or 500 watt head and 115, 210 or 410 cab options.

MODEL YEAR	FEATURES	EXC. COND. LOW	HIGH
2011-2020	PF350	$200	$260
2011-2020	PF500	$200	$260

R-12 Rocket Amp

1957-1963. 12 watts, 1x12", 1 channel.

MODEL YEAR	FEATURES	EXC. COND. LOW	HIGH
1957-1963		$500	$650

R-12 B Rocket Amp

1964. 12 watts, 1x12", follow-up to the R-12 Rocket.

MODEL YEAR	FEATURES	EXC. COND. LOW	HIGH
1964		$500	$650

R-12 R Reverberocket Amp

1961-1963. Rocket with added on-board reverb.

MODEL YEAR	FEATURES	EXC. COND. LOW	HIGH
1961-1963		$600	$800

R-12 R Reverberocket Amp (Reissue)

1996-2007. 50 watts, 2xEL34 power tubes, 1x12" (R-212R is 2x12").

MODEL YEAR	FEATURES	EXC. COND. LOW	HIGH
1996-2007		$375	$450

R-12 R-B Reverberocket Amp

1964. 7591A power tubes replace R-12-R 6V6 power tubes.

MODEL YEAR	FEATURES	EXC. COND. LOW	HIGH
1964		$525	$700

R-12 R-T Reverberocket Amp

1965. 7591A or 7868 power tubes, revised preamp.

MODEL YEAR	FEATURES	EXC. COND. LOW	HIGH
1965		$525	$700

R-15 R Superbreverb (Supereverb) Amp

1963-1964. 1x15 combo, originally called Supereverb, but Fender had a problem with that name.

MODEL YEAR	FEATURES	EXC. COND. LOW	HIGH
1963-1964		$700	$900

R-50H Reverberocket Amp

1997-2003. 50 watt head usually sold with a 4x12" bottom, blue check covering.

MODEL YEAR	FEATURES	EXC. COND. LOW	HIGH
1997-2003	Head and cab	$500	$650

R-212 R Reverberocket Combo 50 Amp (Reissue)

1996-2007. 50 watts, 2x12", all tube reissue, vintage-style blue check cover, vintage-style grille.

MODEL YEAR	FEATURES	EXC. COND. LOW	HIGH
1996-2007		$450	$550

Rhapsody Amp

1956-1958. Part of Accordiamp Series, similar to Zephyr except preamp voiced for accordion, 20 watts, 1x15".

MODEL YEAR	FEATURES	EXC. COND. LOW	HIGH
1956-1958		$500	$650

SB-12 Portaflex Amp

1965-1971. 22 watts, 1x12", designed for use with Ampeg's Baby Bass, black.

MODEL YEAR	FEATURES	EXC. COND. LOW	HIGH
1965-1971		$675	$875

MODEL YEAR	FEATURES	EXC. COND. LOW	HIGH

SBT Amp

1969-1971. 120 watts, 1x15", bass version of SST Amp.

1969-1971		$625	$750

SE-412 Cabinet

1996-1999. 4x12" speakers.

1996-1999		$275	$340

SJ-12 R/RT Super Jet Amp

1996-2007. 50 watts, tube, 1x12", SJ-12 RT has tremolo added.

1996-2007		$350	$425

SS-35 Amp

1987-1992. Solidstate, 35 watts, 1x12", black vinyl, black grille, large A logo.

1987-1992		$150	$185

SS-70 Amp

1987-1990. Solidstate, 70 watts, 1x12".

1987-1990		$175	$225

SS-70 C Amp

1987-1992. Solidstate, 70 watts, 2x10", chorus, black vinyl.

1987-1992		$200	$265

SS-140 C Amp

1987-1992. Solidstate, 2x12 combo, chorus and reverb.

1987-1992		$225	$290

SS-150 Amp Head

1987-1992. Solidstate, 150 watts.

1987-1992		$275	$335

SS-412 Cabinet

1987-1992. Matching 4x12 cab for SS series heads.

1987-1992		$275	$335

Super Comboamp/Model 833 Comboamp/Model 950C Super

1956-1960. 30 watts, 3 channels. 950C is 50 watts with 2 15" speakers (very few made).

1956-1957	Super Comboamp	$650	$825
1958	Model 833	$650	$825
1959-1960	Model 950C	$650	$825

SVT Bass Amp Head

1969-1985. 300 watt head only.

1969	Stones World-Tour Assoc	$1,775	$2,300
1970-1979		$1,450	$1,900
1980-1985		$1,275	$1,700

SVT Bass Cabinets

1969-1985. Two 8x10" cabs only.

1969		$1,250	$1,650
1970-1985		$1,175	$1,550

SVT-II Bass Amp Head

1989-1994. Rackmount, 300 watts, tube.

1989-1994		$900	$1,150

SVT-2 Pro Bass Amp Head

1993-2014. 300 watts, rackmount, tube preamp and power section, black metal.

1993-2014		$925	$1,200

SVT-III Bass Amp Head

1991-1994. Mosfet, 275/450 watts.

1991-1994		$500	$650

SVT-3 Pro Bass Amp Head

1993-present. Tube preamp and MOS-FET power section, 450 watts, rackmount, black metal.

1993-2020		$450	$575

SVT-4 Pro Bass Amp Head

1997-present. Rackmount, all tube preamp, MOS-FET power section yielding 1600 watts.

1997-2020		$575	$750

SVT-5 Pro Bass Amp Head

2002-2005. Rackmount, all tube preamp, MOS-FET power section yielding 1350 watts.

2002-2005		$575	$750

SVT-6 Pro Bass Amp Head

2005-2009. Rackmount, all tube preamp, MOS-FET power section yielding 1100 watts.

2005-2009		$375	$500

SVT-15 E Bass Cabinet

1994-2017. Compact 1x15.

1994-2017		$325	$425

SVT-100 T Bass Combo Amp

1990-1992. Solidstate, ultra-compact bass combo, 100 watts, 2x8".

1990-1992		$350	$450

SVT-200 T Amp Head

1987 only. Solidstate, 200 watts to 8 ohms or 320 watts to 4 ohms.

1987		$325	$425

SVT-350 Amp Head

1995-2005. Solidstate head, 350 watts, graphic EQ.

1995-2005		$425	$550

SVT-400 Amp Head

1987-1997. Solidstate, 2 200 watt stereo amps, rack-mountable head with advanced (in '87) technology.

1987-1997		$425	$550

SVT-410 HE Bass Cabinet

1994-present. 4x10, horn/driver.

1994-2020		$425	$550

SVT-450 H Amp Head

2007-2017. Solidstate head, 275/450 watts.

2007-2017		$425	$550

SVT-610 HLF Cabinet

2003-present. 6x10, horn/driver.

2003-2020		$425	$550

SVT-810 E Cabinet

1994-present. 8x10.

1994-2020		$425	$550

SVT-AV Anniversary Edition Amp

300 watt head.

2001		$700	$900

SVT-CL Classic Bass Amp Head

1994-present. Tube, 300 watts.

1994-2020		$850	$1,100

V-2 Amp Cabinet

1971-1980. 4x12" cab, black tolex.

1971-1980		$400	$515

V-2 Amp Head

1971-1980. 60 watt tube head.

1971-1980	Head only	$450	$600

V-3 Amp Head

1971-1972. 55 watt tube head.

1971-1972	Head only	$525	$700

V-4 B Bass Amp Head

1972-1980. Bass version of V-4 without reverb.

1972-1980	Head only	$700	$900

1996 Ampeg R-12 R Reverberocket
Denny Harmison

1968 Ampeg SB-12 Portaflex
Tom Pfeifer

2008 Ampeg SVT Micro 210AV Cab

AMPS

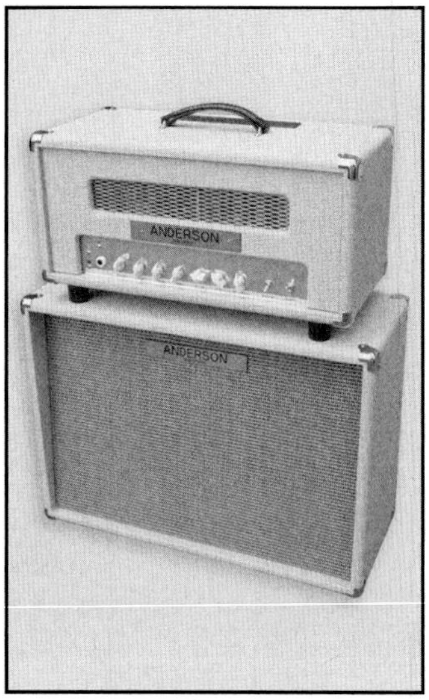

Anderson 45 RT

Andrews Spectraverb 22

Aria Pro II Revolution II

MODEL YEAR	FEATURES	EXC. COND. LOW	HIGH

V-4 Cabinet

1970s. Single 4x12" cabinet only.

1970-1980 $400 $515

V-7 SC Amp

1981-1985. Tube, 100 watts, 1x12", master volume, channel switching, reverb.

1981-1985 $500 $650

VH-70 Amp

1991-1992. 70 watts, 1x12" combo with channel switching.

1991-1992 $300 $400

VH-140 C Amp

1992-1995. Varying Harmonics (VH) with Chorus (C), two 70-watt channel stereo, 2x12".

1992-1995 $375 $500

VH-150 Amp Head

1991-1992. 150 watts, channel-switchable, reverb.

1991-1992 $275 $350

VL-502 Amp

1991-1995. 50 watts, channel-switchable, all tube.

1991-1995 $350 $450

VL-1001 Amp Head

1991-1993. 100 watts, non-switchable channels, all tube.

1991-1993 $325 $425

VL-1002 Amp Head

1991-1995. 100 watts, channel-switchable, all tube.

1991-1995 $350 $450

VT-22 Amp

1970-1980. 100 watt combo version of V-4, 2x12".

1970-1980 $450 $600

VT-40 Amp

1971-1980. 60 watt combo, 4x10".

1971-1980 $450 $600

VT-60 Amp Head

1989-1991. Tube head only, 6L6 power, 60 watts.

1989-1991 $350 $450

VT-60 Combo Amp

1989-1991 Tube, 6L6 power, 60 watts, 1x12"

1989-1991 $325 $425

VT-120 Amp Head

1989-1992. 120 watts, 6L6 tube head.

1989-1992 $350 $450

VT-120 Combo Amp

1989-1992. Tube, 6L6 power, 120 watts, 1x12", also offered as head only.

1989-1992 $350 $450

Zephyr I Amp

1956-1959. Single-channel, 20 watts, 1x15".

1956-1959 $450 $600

Anderson Amplifiers

1993-present. Tube amps and combos built by Jack Anderson in Gig Harbor, Washington.

Andrews

2006-present. Professional grade, production/custom, amps and cabinets built by Jeff Andrews in Dunwoody, Georgia.

ARACOM Amplifiers

1997-present. Jeff Aragaki builds his tube amp heads, combos, and cabinets in Morgan Hill, California.

Area 51

2003-present. Guitar amps made in Newaygo, Michigan (made in Texas until early '06), by Dan Albrecht. They also build effects.

Aria/Aria Pro II

1956-present. The Japanese instrument builder offered a range of amps from around '79 to '89.

Ariatone

1962. Another private brand made by Magnatone, sold by private music and accordion studios.

Model 810

1962. 12 watts, 1x8, tremolo, brown cover.

1962 $500 $650

Ark

Owners Matt Schellenberg and Bill Compeau build professional and premium grade, production/custom amps in Farmington Hills, Michigan (cabinet shop), with all wiring done in Windsor, Ontario. They started in 2005.

Ashdown Amplification

1999-present. Founded in England by Mark Gooday after he spent several years with Trace Elliot, Ashdown offers amps, combos, and cabinets.

Audio Guild

1960s-1974. Audio Guild was already making amps under such brands as Universal and Versatone and others when they launched their own brand in the '60s.

Grand Prix Amp

1969-1974. Tube combo 1x12, reverb and tremolo, dual channel.

1969-1974 $550 $725

Ultraflex Amp

1969-1974. All-tube, higher power combo, 2 speakers, reverb and tremolo.

1969-1974 $800 $1,025

Universal Amp

1960s-1974. Universal was a brand of Audio Guild. Tube combo amp, reverb, tremolo.

1960s-1974 $550 $725

Versatone Pan-O-Flex Amp

1960s-1974. Versatone was a brand of Audio Guild. Mid-power tube amp, 1x12" and 1x8" combo, high and low gain input, volume, bass, treble and pan-o-flex balance control knobs, black cover.

1960s-1974 $800 $1,025

Audiovox

Ca.1935-ca.1950. Paul Tutmarc's Audiovox Manufacturing, of Seattle, Washington, was a pioneer in electric lap steels, basses, guitars and amps.

Auralux

2000-2011. Founded by Mitchell Omori and David Salzmann, Auralux built effects and tube amps in Highland Park, Illinois.

MODEL YEAR	FEATURES	EXC. COND. LOW	HIGH

Austin

1999-present. Budget and intermediate grade, production, guitar and bass amps imported by St. Louis Music. They also offer guitars, basses, mandolins, ukes and banjos.

Bacino

Tube combo amps, heads and cabinets built by Mike Bacino in Arlington Heights, Illinois starting in 2002.

Backline Engineering

2004-present. Gary Lee builds his tube amp heads in Camarillo, California. He also builds guitar effects.

Bad Cat Amplifier Company

1999-present. Originally located in Corona, California, and now in Santa Ana, Bad Cat offers class A combo amps, heads, cabinets and effects.

Baer Amplification

2009-present. Professional grade, production, bass amps built in Palmdale, California by Roger Baer.

Baldwin

Piano maker Baldwin offered amplifiers from 1965 to '70. The amps were solidstate with organ-like pastel-colored pushbutton switches.

Exterminator Amp

1965-1970. Solidstate, 100 watts, 2x15"/2x12"/2x7", 4' vertical combo cabinet, reverb and tremolo, Supersound switch and slide controls.

1965-1970	$450	$625

Model B1 Bass Amp

1965-1970. Solidstate, 45 watts, 1x15"/1x12", 2 channels.

1965-1970	$225	$325

Model B2 Bass Amp

1965-1970. Solidstate, 35 watts, 1x15", 2 channels.

1965-1970	$200	$300

Model C1 Custom (Professional) Amp

1965-1970. Solidstate, 45 watts, 2x12", reverb and tremolo, Supersound switch and slide controls.

1965-1970	$350	$450

Model C2 Custom Amp

1965-1970. Solidstate, 40 watts, 2x12", reverb and tremolo.

1965-1970	$350	$450

Model D1 Deluxe (Professional) Amp

1965-1970. Solidstate, 30 watts, 1x12", reverb and tremolo, Supersound switch and slide controls.

1965-1970	$350	$450

Barcus-Berry

1964-present. Pickup maker Barcus-Berry offered a line of amps from '75 to '79.

Barth

1950s-1960s. Products of Paul Barth's Barth Musical Instrument Company. Barth was also a co-founder of Rickenbacker. He also produced guitars and lap steels.

Studio Deluxe 958 Amp

1950s-1960s. Small practice combo amp.

1950s-60s	$350	$450

Basson

Speaker cabinets for guitar, bass and PA made by Victor Basson in Carlsbad, California, starting in 2001.

bc audio

2009-present. Bruce Clement builds his production/custom, professional grade, tube amps in San Francisco, California.

Bedrock

1984-1997. Tube amp company founded by Brad Jeter and Ron Pinto in Nashua, New Hampshire. They produced 50 amps carrying the brand name Fred before changing the company name to Bedrock in '86. Around '88, Jay Abend joined the company. In '90, Jeter left and, shortly after, Pinto and Abend moved the company to Framingham, Massachusetts. The company closed in '97.

Behringer

1989-present. Founded in Germany by Uli Behringer, offering a full line of professional audio products. In '98 they added tube, solidstate, and modeling amps. They also offer effects and guitars.

Beltone

1950s-1960s. Japan's Teisco made a variety of brands for others, including the Beltone line of amps. There were also guitars sold under this name made from a variety of builders.

Benson

1967-1974. Ron Benson designed and built amps in conjunction with jazz ace Howard Roberts who needed a more versatile amp for recording sessions. Some featured built-in fuzz and plug-in equalizer modules. Originally built in California, later in Seattle. Some 2,000 amps total production.

Big M

1966-1967, 1975-1976. The Marshall name in Germany was owned by a trumpet maker, so Jim Marshall marketed his amps and cabs there under the Big M Made In England brand name until the issue was resolved. A decade later, in a failed attempt to lower speaker cabinets prices in the U.S., Marshall's American distributor built cabs, with Marshall's permission, on Long Island, mainly for sales with Marshall solidstate lead and bass heads of the time, and labeled them Big M. They were loaded with cheaper Eminence speakers, instead of the usual Celestions.

Ashdown RM-C210T-500 EVO II Combo

Bad Cat Cub IV 15R Handwired Series

bc audio Amplifier No. 9

BlackWing Black Hawk 15

Blackstar Artist

Bogner Mephisto

Big M Cabinets

1975-1976. The M2412 with 4x12 for lead and the M2212F 2x12 bass cabs.

MODEL YEAR	FEATURES	EXC. COND. LOW	HIGH
1975-1976	2x12	$315	$410
1975-1976	4x12	$600	$800

JTM-45 Amp Head

1966-1967. Branded Big M.

MODEL YEAR	FEATURES	EXC. COND. LOW	HIGH
1966-1967		$5,000	$6,450

BigDog Amps

2005-2007. Tube head and combo guitar and bass amps and speaker cabinets built in Galveston, Texas, by Steve Gaines.

Bird

Ca. 1959-1965. Bird built electronic organs in the U.K. and also offered tubes amps from around '59 to '65.

Blackstar Amplification

2007-present. Intermediate and professional grade guitar amps and cabinets from Joel Richardson of Northampton, U.K. He also offers effects pedals.

Blackwing

2016-2018. Professional and premium grade head and combo amps, and cabinets built in Corona, California by James Heidrich. He died in '18.

Blankenship Amplification

2005-present. Roy Blankenship builds his tube head and combo amps and cabinets in Northridge, California. He also built amps under the Point Blank brand.

Bluetone Amplifiers

2002-present. Founded by Alex Cooper in Worcestershire, England, Bluetone offers professional grade, production amps employing their virtual valve technology.

Bogen

1932-present. Founded in New York City by David Bogen, this company has made a wide range of electronic products for consumers and industry including a few small guitar combo tube amps such as the GA-5 and GA-20 and tube PA equipment. The company name (David Bogen, New York) and model number are on the lower back panel. The '50s Bogen tube amps are well respected as tone-generating workhorses. In '56 he sold the company and it was moved to New Jersey, and they continue to offer pro audio PA gear.

Bogner

1988-present. Tube combos, amp heads, and speaker cabinets from builder Reinhold Bogner of North Hollywood, California.

Bolt

Professional grade, production, tube amps and cabinets built in Salt Lake City, Utah starting in 2009. They also built the Morpheus brand effects.

Brand X

2004-2007. Small solidstate combo amps from Fender Musical Instruments Corporation.

Bronson

1930s-1950s. Private brand utilized by Detroit lap steel instruction George Bronson. These amps often sold with a matching lap steel and were made by other companies.

Lap Steel Amp

MODEL YEAR	FEATURES	EXC. COND. LOW	HIGH
1930s-50s	Melody King 1x10	$350	$475
1930s-50s	Pearloid	$200	$300
1947	Supreme 1x10, 12w	$400	$550

Bruno (Tony)

1995-present. Tube combos, amp heads, and speaker cabinets from builder Tony Bruno of Cairo, New York.

Budda

1995-present. Amps, combos, and cabinets originally built by Jeff Bober and Scott Sier in San Francisco, California. In '09, Budda was acquired by Peavey and they started building Budda products in their Meridian, Mississippi Custom Shop. They also produce effects pedals.

Bugera

2008-present. Uli Behringer builds his budget and intermediate grade, production, tube amps in China. He also offers the Behringer brand.

Burriss

2001-present. Bob Burriss builds custom and production guitar and bass tube amps, bass preamps and speaker cabinets in Lexington, Kentucky. He also builds effects.

Byers

2001-2010. Tube combo amps built by Trevor Byers, in Corona, California. His initial focus was on small early-Fender era and K & F era models.

Cage

1998-present. Production/custom, professional grade, amp heads and cabinets built in Damascus, Maryland by Pete Cage.

California

2004-present. Student/budget level amps and guitar/amp packs, imported by Eleca International.

Callaham

1989-present. Custom tube amp heads built by Bill Callaham in Winchester, Virginia. He also builds solidbody electric guitars.

MODEL YEAR	FEATURES	EXC. COND. LOW	HIGH

Campbell Sound

Intermediate and professional grade, production/custom, guitar amps built by Walt Campbell in Roseville, California, starting in 1999.

Carl Martin

1993-present. In '05, the Denmark-based guitar effects company added tube combo amps.

Carlsbro

1959-present. Guitar, bass, and keyboard combo amps, heads and cabinets from Carlsbro Electronics Limited of Nottingham, U.K. They also offer PA amps and speaker cabinets.

Carol-Ann Custom Amplifiers

2003-present. Premium grade, production/custom, tube guitar amps built by Alan Phillips in North Andover, Massachusetts.

Carr Amplifiers

1998-present. Steve Carr started producing amps in his Chapel Hill, North Carolina amp repair business in '98. The company is now located in Pittsboro, North Carolina, and makes tube combo amps, heads, and cabinets.

Artemus Amp

2010-2015. Combo 1x12", 15/30 watts.

2010-2015		$1,300	$1,750

Bloke Amp

2012-2015. 48 watts, 1x12".

2012-2015	1x12"	$1,150	$1,500

Hammerhead MK 1/MK 2 Amp

2000-2004 (MK 1), 2004-2008 (MK 2). 25 watts (28 for MK 2), head or combo, 1x12", 2x10" or 2x12".

2000-2004	2x12" combo	$900	$1,200

Impala Amp

2013-present. Combo 1x12", 44 watts - max 55 watts, reverb.

2013-2020		$1,400	$1,850

Imperial Combo Amp

2000-2004. 60 watts, with 1x15", 2x12" or 4x10".

2000-2004	4x10"	$2,300	$3,000

Mercury Combo Amp

2002-2014. 1x12", tube, 8 watts, reverb, built-in attenuator.

2002-2014		$1,525	$1,975

Mercury V Amp

2017-present. Combo 1x12", 16 watts, built in attenuator.

2017-2020		$1,525	$1,975

Raleigh Amp

2008-present. Practice/studio amp, 1x10", 3 watts.

2008-2020		$900	$1,200

Rambler Amp

1999-present. Class A, tubes, 28 watts pentode/14 watts triode, with 1x12", 2x10", 2x12" or 1x15" speakers.

1999-2019	2x12"	$1,700	$2,200
1999-2020	1x12"	$1,500	$1,950

MODEL YEAR	FEATURES	EXC. COND. LOW	HIGH

Slant 6V (Dual 6V6) Amp

1998-present. 40 watts, 2 channel, combo amp, 2x12" or 1x15", also available as a head.

1998-2020		$1,600	$2,100

Sportsman Amp

2011-present. Available in 1x12 and 1x10 combos and head, 16-19 watts.

2011-2020	1x12"	$1,150	$1,500

Viceroy Amp

2006-2018. Class A, tubes, 33 or 7 watts, 1x12" or 1x15".

2006-2018		$1,400	$1,850

Carvin

1946-present. Founded in Los Angeles by Lowell C. Kiesel who sold guitars and amps under the Kiesel name until late-'49, when the Carvin brand was introduced. They added small tube amps to their product line in '47 and today offer a variety of models. They also build guitars, basses and mandolins.

Caswell Amplification

2006-present. Programmable tube amp heads built by Tim Caswell in California.

Chicago Blues Box/Butler Custom Sound

Tube combo amps built by Dan Butler of Butler Custom Sound originally in Elmhurst, then Lombard, Illinois. He began in 2001.

Clark Amplification

1995-present. Tweed-era replica tube amplifiers from builder Mike Clark, of Cayce, South Carolina. He also makes effects.

Club Amplifiers

2005-present. Don Anderson builds intermediate to premium grade, custom, vacuum tube guitar amps and cabinets in Felton, California.

CMI

1976-1977. Amps made by Marshall for Cleartone Musical Instruments of Birmingham, U.K. Mainly PA amps, but two tube heads and one combo amp were offered.

CMI Electronics

Late-1960s-1970s. CMI branded amplifiers designed to replace the Gibson Kalamazoo-made amps that ceased production in '67 when Gibson moved the electronics lab to Chicago, Illinois.

Sabre Reverb 1 Amp

Late-1960s-early-1970s. Keyboard amp, 1x15" and side-mounted horn, utilized mid- to late-'60s cabinets and grilles, look similar to mid-late '60s Gibson black tolex and Epiphone gray amp series, black or gray tolex and silver grille.

1960s-70s		$300	$400

Budda Superdrive 30 Series II 212 Combo

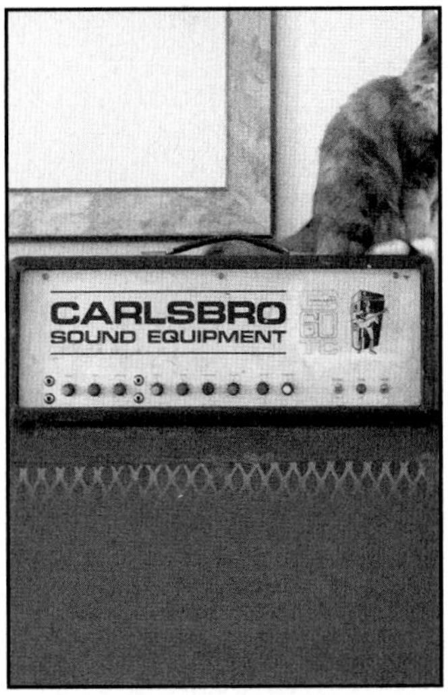

Carlsbro 60TC

Alex Drinkall

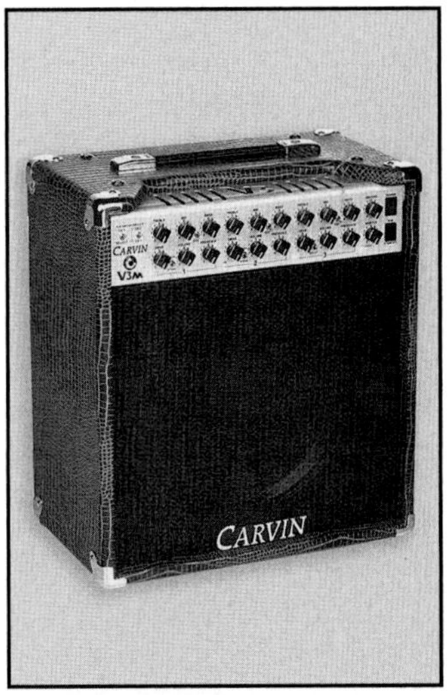

Carvin V3MC

Cruzer CR-15RG

Mid-'50s Danelectro 68
Erick Warner

Early-'60s Danelectro Cadet
Erick Warner

MODEL YEAR	FEATURES	EXC. COND. LOW	HIGH

CMW Amps

2002-present. Chris Winsemius builds his premium grade, production/custom, guitar amps in The Netherlands.

Colby

2012-present. Professional and premium grade, production/custom, tube amp heads, combos and cabinets built by Mitch Colby in City Island, New York. He also builds Park amps.

Comins

1992-present. Archtop luthier Bill Comins, of Willow Grove, Pennsylvania, introduced a Comins combo amp, built in collaboration with George Alessandro, in '03.

Coral

1967-1969. In '66 MCA bought Danelectro and in '67 introduced the Coral brand of guitars, basses and amps. The amp line included tube, solidstate, and hybrid models ranging from small combo amps to the Kilowatt (1000 Watts of Peak Power!), a hybrid head available with two 8x12" cabinets.

Cornell/Plexi

Amps based on the '67 Marshall plexi chassis built by Denis Cornell in the U.K. Large Plexi logo on front.

Cosmosound

Italy's Cosmosound made small amps with Leslie rotating drums in the late '60s and '70s. They also made effects pedals.

Crafter USA

1986-present. Giant Korean guitar and bass manufacturer Crafter also builds an acoustic guitar amp.

Crate

Solidstate and tube amplifiers originally distributed by St. Louis Music, beginning in 1979. In '05 LOUD Technologies acquired SLM and the Crate brand. No new Crate models listed since then.

CA Series Amps

1995-2005. Crate Acoustic series.

1995-2005		$150	$200

Solidstate Amp

1979-1990s. Various student to mid-level amps, up to 150 watts.

1979-90s		$50	$75

Vintage Club Series Amps

1994-2001. Various tube amps.

1994-1997	5310/VC-5310	$225	$300
1994-1999	20	$175	$250
1994-1999	30/VC-2110	$250	$325
1994-1999	30/VC-3112	$275	$350
1994-1999	50/VC-50	$250	$325
1994-1999	60/VC-60	$250	$325
1994-2001	5212/VC-5212	$225	$300

MODEL YEAR	FEATURES	EXC. COND. LOW	HIGH

Cruise Audio Systems

1999-2003. Founded by Mark Altekruse, Cruise offered amps, combos, and cabinets built in Cuyahoga Falls, Ohio. It appears the company was out of business by '03.

Cruzer

Solidstate guitar amps built by Korea's Crafter Guitars. They also build guitars, basses and effects under that brand.

Custom Kraft

Late-1950s-1968. A house brand of St. Louis Music Supply, instruments built by others. They also offered basses and guitars.

Import Student Amp

1960s	1x6 or 1x8	$50	$75

Valco-Made Amp

1960s	1x12 or 1x15	$350	$450

Da Vinci

Late-1950s-early-1960s. Another one of several private brands (for example, Unique, Twilighter, Titano, etc.) that Magnatone made for teaching studios and accordion companies.

D60 Custom

1965. 2x12", reverb, vibrato.

1965		$1,125	$1,450

Model 250 Amp

1958-1962. Similar to Magnatone Model 250 with about 20 watts and 1x12".

1958-1962		$925	$1,250

Model 440A/D40 Custom Amp

1964-1966. 1x12", reverb, vibrato.

1964-1966		$1,000	$1,350

Danelectro

1946-1969, 1997-present. Founded in Red Bank, New Jersey, by Nathan I. "Nate" or "Nat" Daniel. His first amps were made for Montgomery Ward in '47, and in '48 he began supplying Silvertone Amps for Sears. His own amps were distributed by Targ and Dinner as Danelectro and S.S. Maxwell brands. In '96, the Evets Corporation, of San Clemente, California, reintroduced the Danelectro brand on effects, amps, basses and guitars. In early '03, Evets discontinued the amp line, but still offers guitars, basses, and effects.

Cadet Amp

1955-1969. A longstanding model name, offered in different era cabinets and coverings but all using the standard 3-tube 1x6" format. Models 122 and 123 had 6 watts. 1x6", 3 tubes, 1 volume, 1 control, 2 inputs, 16x15x6" 'picture frame' cabinet with light-colored cover, dark grille.

1955-1969	Various models	$150	$225

Challenger Amp

1950s. Compact combo amp, 5 tubes including 2x6L6, 2 channels, bass and treble control, 2 vibrato controls, golden-brown cover, tan woven cloverleaf-shaped grille.

1950s		$350	$450

MODEL YEAR	FEATURES	EXC. COND. LOW	HIGH

DM-10 Amp

1965-1967. Combo 'large knobs' cabinet, 10 watts, 1x8", 2 control vibrato, 2 inputs, 1 volume, 1 tone, dark vinyl with light grille, DM-10 logo next to script Danelectro logo right upper front.

1965-1967 $260 $350

DM-25 Amp

1965-1967. Stow-away piggyback, 25 watts, 1x12", reverb, vibrato, 4 inputs, 9 control knobs, dark vinyl cabinet with light grille, DM-25 logo next to script Danelectro logo below control knobs.

1965-1967 $600 $775

DS-50 Amp

1965-1969. 75 watts, 3x10" stow-away piggyback cabinet, reverb and tremolo, suitable for bass accordion.

1965-1969 $700 $925

DS-100 Amp

1967-1969. 150 watts, stow-away piggyback cabinet, 6x10" Jensens, reverb, tremolo, suitable for bass accordion, 36x22x12" cabinet weighs 79 lbs.

1965-1969 $1,300 $1,725

DTR-40 Amp

1965. Solidstate combo, 40 watts, 2x10", vibrato, DTR-40 logo under control knobs.

1965 $350 $450

Model 68 Special Amp

1954-1957. 20 watts, 1x12", light tweed-fabric cover, light grille, leather handle, script Danelectro plexiplate logo.

1954-1957 $475 $625

Model 72 Centurion Amp

1954-1957. Series D 1x12" combo, blond tweed, rounded front D cabinet.

1954-1957 $475 $625

Model 78A Amp

1954-1957. Artist Series D, 115 watts,

1954-1957 $475 $625

Model 88 Commando Amp

1954-1957. Series D, 25 watts with 4x6V6 power, suitcase-style amp with 8x8" speaker, light beige cover.

1954-1957 $800 $1,050

Model 89 Amp

1954-1957. Series D 1x15" combo, blond tweed, rounded front D cabinet.

1954-1957 $550 $725

Model 98 Twin 12 Amp

1954-ca.1957. Rounded front Series D 2x12", blond tweed-style cover, brown control panel, vibrato speed and strength.

1954-1957 $800 $1,050

Model 132 Corporal Amp

1962-1964. 2x8", 4 tubes, 3 inputs, 4 control knobs, 19x15x7" picture frame cabinet in light-colored material with dark grille.

1962-1964 $400 $550

Model 142 Viscount Amp

Late-1950s. Combo amp, lower watts, 1x12", light cover, brown grille, vibrato.

1959 $500 $650

MODEL YEAR	FEATURES	EXC. COND. LOW	HIGH

Model 143 Viscount Amp

1962-1964. 12 watts, 1x12", 6 tubes, 2 control vibrato, 1 volume, 1 tone, 'picture frame' narrow panel cabinet, light-colored cover with dark grille.

1962-1964 $400 $550

Model 217 Twin-Fifteen Amp

1962-1964. Combo amp, 60 watts, 2x15" Jensen C15P speakers, black cover, white-silver grille, 2 channels with tremolo.

1962-1964 $700 $900

Model 274 Centurion Amp

1961-1962. 15 watts, 1x12", 6 tubes, 2 channels with separate volume, treble, bass controls, Vibravox electronic vibrato, 4 inputs, 20x20x9 weighing 25 lbs., 'picture frame' cabinet with black cover and light grille.

1961-1962 $400 $525

Model 275 Centurion Amp

1963-1964. Reverb added in '63, 15 watts, 1x12", 7 tubes, Vibravox vibrato, 2 channels with separate volume, bass, treble, picture frame cabinet with black cover and light grille.

1963-1964 $500 $675

Model 291 Explorer Amp

1961-1964. 30 watts, 1x15", 7 tubes, 2 channels each with volume, bass, and treble controls, Vibravox vibrato, square picture frame cabinet, black cover and light grille.

1961-1964 $500 $650

Model 300 Twin-Twelve Amp

1962-1964. 30 watts, 2x12", reverb, 8 tubes, 2 channels with separate volume, bass, and treble, Vibravox vibrato, picture frame cabinet with black cover and light grille.

1962-1964 $800 $1,050

Model 354 Twin-Twelve Amp

Early 1950s. Series C twin 12" combo with diagonal speaker baffle holes, brown cover with light gold grille, Twin Twelve script logo on front as well as script Danelectro logo, diagonally mounted amp chassis, leather handle.

1950s $800 $1,050

Dean

1976-present. Acoustic, electric, and bass amps made overseas. They also offer guitars, banjos, mandolins, and basses.

Dean Markley

The string and pickup manufacturer added a line of amps in 1983. Distributed by Kaman, they now offer combo guitar and bass amps and PA systems.

K Series Amps

1980s. All solidstate, various models include K-15 (10 watts, 1x6"), K-20/K-20X (10 to 20 watts, 1x8", master volume, overdrive switch), K-50 (25 watts, 1x10", master volume, reverb), K-75 (35 watts, 1x12", master volume, reverb), K-200B (compact 1x12 combo).

1980s	K-15, 20, 20X	$32	$40
1980s	K-200B	$110	$135
1980s	K-50	$36	$45
1980s	K-75	$56	$70

1961 Danelectro Model 142 Viscount
Rivington Guitars

Early-'60s Danelectro Model 275 Centurion Series F
Erick Warner

Dean DA25C

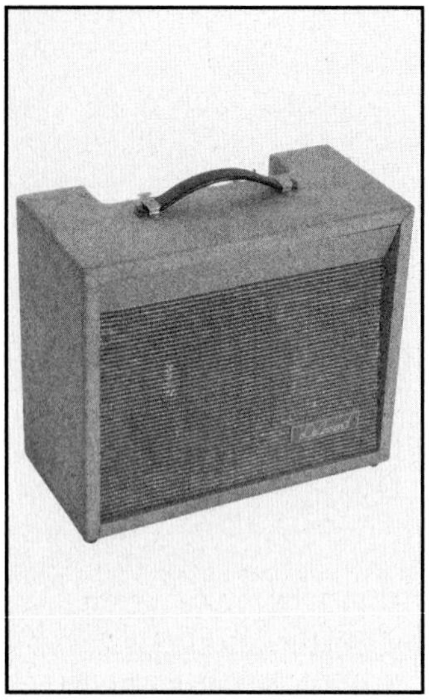

1959 DeArmond R-5T Studio
Imaged by Heritage Auctions, HA.com

Demeter TGA-2.1

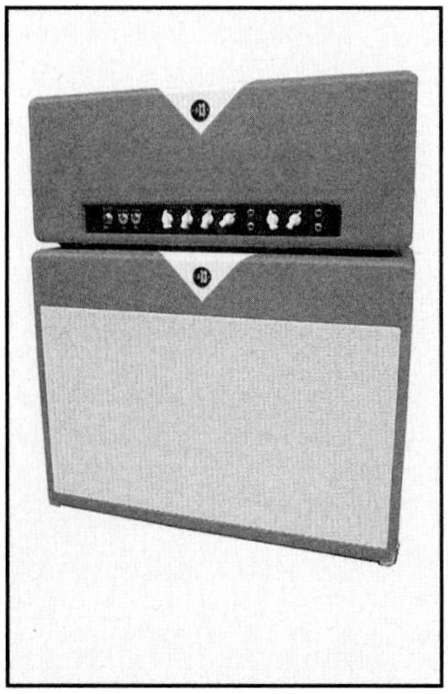

Divided By Thirteen RSA 23

MODEL YEAR	FEATURES	EXC. COND. LOW	HIGH

DeArmond

Pickup manufacturer DeArmond starting building tube guitar amps in 1950s. By '63, they were out of the amp business. They also made effects. Fender revived the name for a line of guitars in the late '90s.

R-5T Studio Amp

1959-1960. 1x10", low power, 1-channel, brown.

1959-1960	$2,300	$3,000

R-15 Amp

1959-1961. 1x12", 15 watts, 2 channels, no tremolo, tan.

1959-1961	$2,700	$3,500

R-15T/Model 112 Amp

1959-1961. 1x12", 15 watts, 2 channels, tremolo, tan.

1959-1961	$2,800	$3,600

Decca

Mid-1960s. Small student-level amps made in Japan by Teisco and imported by Decca Records. They also offered guitars and a bass.

Demeter

1980-present. James Demeter founded the company as Innovative Audio and renamed it Demeter Amplification in '90. Originally located in Van Nuys, in '08 they moved to Templeton, California. First products were direct boxes and by '85, amps were added. Currently they build amp heads, combos, and cabinets. They also have pro audio gear and guitar effects.

Devilcat

2012-present. Professional grade, production/custom, tube amps built in Statesboro, Georgia by Chris Mitchell.

Diaz

Cesar Diaz restored amps for many of rock's biggest names, often working with them to develop desired tones. By the early '80s he was producing his own line of professional and premium grade, high-end custom amps and effects. Diaz died in '02; his widow Maggie and longtime friend Peter McMahon resumed production in '04 under Diaz Musical Products.

Dickerson

1937-1947. Dickerson was founded by the Dickerson brothers in 1937, primarily for electric lap steels and small amps. Instruments were also private branded for Cleveland's Oahu company, and for the Gourley brand. By '47, the company changed ownership and was renamed Magna Electronics (Magnatone). Amps were usually sold with a matching lap steel.

Oasis Amp

1940s. Blue pearloid cover, 1x10", low wattage, Dickerson silk-screen logo on grille with Hawaiian background.

1940s	$225	$300

MODEL YEAR FEATURES EXC. COND. LOW HIGH

Dime Amplification

2011-ca. 2014. Solidstate combo and head amps and cabinets from Dean Guitars, designed by Gary Sunda and Grady Champion.

Dinosaur

2004-2015. Student/budget level amps and guitar/amp packs, imported by Eleca International. They also offered effects.

Divided By Thirteen

Mid-1990s-present. Fred Taccone builds his tube amp heads and cabinets in the Los Angeles, California area. He also builds effects.

Dr. Z

1988-present. Mike Zaite started producing his Dr. Z line of amps in the basement of the Music Manor in Maple Heights, Ohio. The company is now located in its own larger facility in the same city. Dr. Z offers combo amps, heads and cabinets.

Drive

Ca. 2001-ca. 2011. Budget grade, production, import solidstate amps. They also offered guitars.

DST Engineering

2002-2014. Jeff Swanson and Bob Dettorre built their tube amp combos, heads and cabinets in Beverly, Massachusetts. They also built reverb units.

Duca Tone

The Duca Tone brand was distributed by Lo Duca Brothers, Milwaukee, Wisconsin, which also distributed EKO guitars in the U.S.

Tube Amp

1950s. 12 watts, 1x12".

1950s	$425	$575

Dumble

1963-present. Made by Howard Alexander Dumble, an early custom-order amp maker from California. Initial efforts were a few Mosrite amps for Semie Moseley. First shop was in '68 in Santa Cruz, California. Early on, Dumble also modified other brands such as Fender and those Dumble-modified amps are also valuable, based on authenticated provenance. Top dollar goes for combos or heads with the cab. A head alone would be 10-20% lower. Higher values are considered for an amp that has not been modified in any way, unless the mod is certified as being done by Dumble.The used/vintage Dumble market is a sophisticated luxury-market for those musicians and collectors that are wealthy enough to afford these amps. Each amplifier's value should be considered on a case-by-case basis. Dealers have reported that some Dumble amplifiers will sell upwards from $90,000 to $100,000.

MODEL YEAR	FEATURES	EXC. COND. LOW	HIGH

Dynamic Amps

2008-present. David Carambula builds production/custom, professional grade, combo amps, heads and cabinets in Kalamazoo, Michigan.

Dynamo

2010-present. Professional and premium grade, production/custom, amps and cabinets built by Ervin Williams in Lake Dallas, Texas.

Earth Sound Research

1970s. Earth Sound was a product of ISC Audio of Farmingdale, New York, and offered a range of amps, cabinets and PA gear starting in the '70s. They also made Plush amps.

2000 G Half-Stack Amp

1970s. 100 watts plus cab.

1970s		$400	$525

Model G-1000 Amp Head

1970s	Reverb	$195	$260

Original 2000 Model 340 Amp

1970s. Black Tolex, 400-watt head and matching 2x15" cab.

1970s		$400	$525

Producer Model 440 Amp

1970s. 700-watt head and matching 2x15" cab.

1970s		$400	$525

Revival Amp

1970s. 2x12" tweed twin copy, with similar back mounted control panel, tweed covering, but with solid-state preamp section and 4x6L6 power.

1970		$400	$525

Super Bass/B-2000 Amp

1970s. Tuck & roll black cover, 2 channels - super and normal, volume, bass, mid range, and treble tone controls, no reverb or tremolo.

1970s	Cabinet	$195	$260
1970s	Head only	$195	$260

Traveler Amp

1970s. Vertical cab solidstate combo amp, 50 watts, 2x12 offset, black tolex.

1977		$375	$500

EBS

1988-present. The EBS Sweden AB company builds professional grade, production bass amps and cabinets in Stockholm, Sweden. They also build effects.

EchoSonic

1950s. Tube combo amps with built-in tape echo built by Ray Butts in Cairo, Illinois, with the first in '53. Used by greats such as Chet Atkins, Scotty Moore and Carl Perkins, probably less than 70 were made. Butts also developed the hum bucking Filter'Tron pickup for Gretsch.

Eden

1976-present. Founded by David Nordschow in Minnesota as a custom builder, Eden now offers a full line of amps, combos, and cabinets for the bassist, built in Mundelein, Illinois. In '02, the brand became a division of U.S. Music Corp (Washburn, Randall). They also produce the Nemesis brand of amps.

Egnater

1980-present. Production/custom, intermediate and professional grade, tube amps, combos, preamps and cabinets built in Berkley, Michigan by Bruce Egnater. He also imports some models.

Rebel Amp

2008-present. 20-watt head, 1x12" cabinet.

2008-2020		$390	$500

Renegade Amp Head

2009-present. 65 watts, 2 channel head.

2009-2020		$390	$500

Tourmaster Series Amp

2009-present. 100-watt, all-tube amp and combo.

2009-2020	Various models	$390	$800

Tweaker Amp

2013-present. 15 to 88-watt, tube heads and cabinets.

2013-2020	1x12 combo	$290	$375
2013-2020	40 watt head /1x12 cab	$390	$500

EKO

1959-1985, 2000-present. In '67 EKO added amps to their product line, offering three piggyback and four combo amps, all with dark covering, dark grille, and the EKO logo. The amp line may have lasted into the early '70s. Since about 2000, EKO Asian-made, solidstate guitar and bass amps are again available. They also make basses and guitars.

El Grande

1951-1953. Tube combo amps built by Chicago's Valco Manufacturing Co., most likely for a retailer, and sold together with lap steels.

Valco Spectator

1952. Same as Supro Spectator, 1x8, 5 watts, volume and tone, red and white two-tone.

1952		$290	$375

Eleca

2004-present. Student level imported combo amps, Eleca logo on bottom of grille. They also offer guitars, effects and mandolins.

Electar

1996-2008. The Gibson owned Electar brand offered tube and solidstate amps, PA gear and wireless systems. Though branded separately, Electar amps were often marketed with other Epiphone products, so see them listed there. Epiphone also had amp models named Electar in the 1930s.

Electro-Harmonix

1968-1981, 1996-present. Electro-Harmonix has offered a few amps to go with its line of effects.

Freedom Brothers Amp

Introduced in 1977. Small AC/DC amp with 2x5 1/2" speakers. E-H has reissued the similar Freedom amp.

1977		$190	$250

Dr. Z Amps Z-Lux

Ca. 1977 Overdrive Special Dumble OD-50WC

Imaged by Heritage Auctions, HA.com

Egnater Rebel 30 MK2

Emery Sound Combo

1960s Epiphone EA-30 Triumph

Imaged by Heritage Auctions, HA.com

1960s Epiphone EA-50 Pacemaker

Imaged by Heritage Auctions, HA.com

MODEL YEAR	FEATURES	EXC. COND. LOW	HIGH

Mike Matthews Dirt Road Special Amp

1970s. 25 watts, 1x12" Celestion, built-in Small Stone phase shifter. A 40 watt version was released in 2019.

1977 $190 $250

Electromuse

1940s-1950s. Tube amps made by others, like Valco, and usually sold as a package with a lap steel. They also offered guitars.

Amps

Late-1940s. Vertical cabinet with metal handle, Electromuse stencil logo on front of cab.

1948-1949 Lower power $175 $225

Electrosonic Amplifiers

2002-2009. Intermediate and professional grade, production/custom, tube amps built by Josh Corn in Boonville, Indiana. He also builds effects.

Elk

Late-1960s. Japanese-made by Elk Gakki Co., Ltd. Many were copies of American designs. They also offered guitars and effects.

Custom EL 150L Amp

Late-1960s. Piggyback set, all-tube with head styled after very early Marshall and cab styled after large vertical Fender cab.

1968 $300 $375

Guitar Man EB 105 (Super Reverb) Amp

Late-1960s. All-tube, reverb, copy of blackface Super Reverb.

1968 $250 $325

Twin Amp 60/Twin Amp 50 EB202 Amps

Late-1960s. All-tube, reverb, copy of blackface Dual Showman set (head plus horizontal cab).

1968 $300 $375

Viking 100 VK 100 Amp

Late-1960s. Piggyback set, head styled after very early Marshall and cab styled after very large vertical Fender cab.

1968 $300 $375

Elmwood Amps

1998-present. Jan Alm builds his production/custom, professional and premium grade, guitar tube amps and cabinets in Tanumshede, Sweden.

Elpico

1960s. Made in Europe, PA tube amp heads sometimes used for guitar.

PA Power Tube Amp

1960s. Tubes, 20-watt, metal case, 3 channels, treble and bass control, 2 speaker outs on front panel, Elpico logo on front, small Mexican characterization logo on front.

1960s $300 $400

Emery Sound

1997-present. Founded by Curt Emery in El Cerrito, California, Emery Sound specializes in custom-made low wattage tube amps.

MODEL YEAR	FEATURES	EXC. COND. LOW	HIGH

Emmons

1970s-present. Owned by Lashley, Inc. of Burlington, North Carolina. Amps sold in conjunction with their steel guitars.

Epiphone

1928-present. Epiphone offered amps into the mid-'70s and reintroduced them in '91 with the EP series. Currently they offer tube and solidstate amps.

Century Amp

1939. Lap steel companion amp, 1x12" combo, lattice wood front with Electar insignia "E" logo.

1939 $375 $475

Cornet Amp

1939. Lap steel companion amp, square shaped wood box, Electar insignia "E" logo.

1939 $310 $400

E-30 B Amp

1972-1975. Solidstate model offered similarly to Gibson G-Series (not GA-Series), 30 watts, 2x10", 4 knobs.

1972-1975 $140 $180

E-60 Amp

1972-1975. Solidstate, 30 watts, 1x10", volume and tone knobs.

1972-1975 $105 $135

E-60 T Amp

1972-1975. E-60 with tremolo, volume, tone, and tremolo knobs.

1972-1975 $105 $135

E-70 T Amp

1971-1975. Solidstate, tremolo, 1x10", 3 knobs.

1971-1975 $105 $135

E-1051 Amp

Ca. 1971-1974. Tube practice amp, 1x10".

1971-1974 $140 $180

EA-12 RVT Futura Amp

1962-1967. 50 watts, originally 4x8" but 4x10" by at least '65, '60s gray tolex, light grille.

1962-1967 $450 $575

EA-14 RVT Ensign Amp

1965-1969. Gray tolex, silver-gray grille, 50 watts, 2x10", split C logo.

1965-1969 $400 $525

EA-15 RVT Zephyr Amp

1961-1965. 14 or 20 watts, 1x15", gray tolex, light grille, split C logo on panel, tremolo and reverb, script Epiphone logo lower right grille.

1961-1965 $400 $525

EA-16 RVT Regent Amp

1965-1969. 25 watts, 1x12", gray vinyl, gray grille, tremolo, reverb. Called the Lancer in first year.

1965-1969 $325 $425

EA-22 RVT Mighty Mite Amp

1964-1967. 1x12", mid-level power, stereo, reverb, vibrato, old style rear mounted control panel.

1964-1967 $725 $950

EA-26 RVT Electra Amp

1965-1969. Gray tolex, reverb, tremolo, footswitch, 1x12".

1965-1969 $325 $428

MODEL YEAR	FEATURES	EXC. COND. LOW	HIGH

EA-28 RVT Pathfinder Amp
Mid-1960s. Similar to Gibson's GA-19 RVT, medium power, 1x12, reverb and tremolo.

1964-1966		$425	$550

EA-30 Triumph Amp
1959-1961. Low-power, limited production, 1x12, light colored cover, 3 knobs.

1959-1961		$625	$800

EA-32 RVT Comet Amp
1965-1967. 1x10", tremolo, reverb.

1965-1967		$300	$400

EA-33 RVT Galaxie Amp
1963-1964. Gray tolex, gray grille, 1x10".

1963-1964		$325	$425

EA-35 Devon Amp
1961-1963. 1x10" until '62, 1x12" with tremolo in '63.

1961-1963		$325	$425

EA-35 T Devon Amp
1963. Tremolo, 6 knobs.

1963		$325	$425

EA-50 Pacemaker Amp
1961-1969. 1x8" until '62, 1x10" after. EA-50T with tremolo added in '63. Non-tremolo version dropped around '67.

1961-1965	1x8"	$300	$400
1966-1969	1x10"	$325	$425

EA-300 RVT Embassy Amp
1965-1969. 90 watts, 2x12", gray vinyl, gray grille, tremolo, reverb.

1965-1969		$450	$600

EA-500T Panorama Amp
1963-1967. 65 watts, head and large cabinet, tremolo, 1x15" and 1x10" until '64, 1x15" and 2x10" after.

1964-1967		$385	$500

EA-600 RVT Maxima Amp
1966-1969. Solidstate Epiphone version of Gibson GSS-100, gray vinyl, gray grille, two 2x10" cabs and hi-fi stereo-style amp head.

1966-1969		$275	$355

Electar Amp
1935-1939. All models have large "E" insignia logo on front, first model Electar in rectangular box with 1x8" speaker, 3 models introduced in '36 (Model C, Model M, and Super AC-DC), the Special AC-DC was introduced in '37, later models were 1x12" combos. Old Electar amps are rarely found in excellent working condition and prices shown are for those rare examples.

1935	Electar	$385	$500
1936-1939	Model C	$550	$725
1936-1939	Model M	$550	$725
1936-1939	Super AC-DC	$625	$825
1937-1939	Special AC-DC	$600	$775

Electar Tube 10 Amp
1997-2004. These modern Electar amps were branded as Electar, not Epiphone, but since they were often marketed with other Epi products, they are included here. 10 watt combo, all tube, 8" speaker.

1997-2004		$100	$130

Electar Tube 30 Amp
1997-2004. 30 watt combo, all tube, 10" speaker, reverb added in 2002.

1997-2004		$100	$130

MODEL YEAR	FEATURES	EXC. COND. LOW	HIGH

Model 100 Amp
1960s. Made in Kalamazoo, label with serial number, Model 100 logo on small 10" speaker, blue cover, 3 tubes, 3 knobs.

1960s		$320	$415

Zephyr Amp
1939-1957. Maple veneer cabinet, 30 watts with 2x6L6 power, 1x12" until '54, 1x15" after, made by Danelectro using their typical designs, Dano D-style blond covering, large split "E" logo on front, brown grille cloth, large block Zephyr logo on back panel.

1939-1953	1x12"	$600	$775
1953-1957	1x15"	$625	$800

Zephyr Dreadnaught Amp
1939. Similar to Zephyr amp but higher power and added microphone input.

1939		$600	$775

Esteban
2005-2007. Imported brand from China, student budget level compact amps.

Compact Amp

2005-2007		$20	$45

Estey
Late-1960s. In 1959, Magnatone merged with the Estey Organ Company and in late '66/early '67 they introduced models branded Estey and based on their budget Magnatone Starlite series.

Model T12 Amp
Late-1960s. Based on Magnatone Starlite model 412.

1967		$325	$425

Model T22 Amp
Late-1960s. Based on Magnatone Starlite model 422 but with larger 12" speaker.

1967		$400	$525

Model T32 Amp
Late-1960s. Based on Magnatone Starlite model 432 with reverb and vibrato.

1967		$450	$600

Model T42 Amp
Late-1960s. Based on Magnatone Starlite model 442 bass amp.

1967		$450	$600

Evans Custom Amplifiers
1994-present. Professional grade, production, solidstate head and combo amps built by Scot Buffington in Burlington, North Carolina.

EVH
2007-present. Eddie Van Halen's line of professional and premium grade, production, tube amp heads and cabinets built by Fender. They also build guitars.

5150 III 50-watt Amp
2011-present. 50 watt head with 2x12 cab.

2011-2020		$950	$1,250

Ca. 1961 Epiphone Zephyr Gray Amplifier
Imaged by Heritage Auctions, HA.com

Evans AE200-2019

EVH 5150III

Evil Robot Custom 214

Fargen Mini Plex MK III

Fender Acoustasonic 15

MODEL YEAR	FEATURES	EXC. COND. LOW	HIGH

Evil Robot

2010-2014. Produced by David Brass and Fretted Americana, made in the U.S.A., initial product produced in limited quantities is based on the '59 Tonemaster (Magnatone) Troubadour amp. Production ceased in '14.

Excelsior

The Excelsior Company started offering accordions in 1924 and had a large factory in Italy by the late '40s. They started offering guitars and amps, uaually built by others including Valco and possibly Sano, around '62. By the early '70s they were out of the guitar business.

Americana Stereophonic High Fidelity Amp

Late 1960s. 50 watts, 1x15", 2x8", 2x3x9" ovals, 2xEL34 power, tube rectifier, large Excelsior logo and small Excelsior The House of Music logo, guitar and accordion inputs, stereo reverb and vibrato.

1968-1969		$925	$1,250

Citation C-15 Amp

1962. Made by Sano, mid power with 2x6V6 power tubes, single speaker combo amp, large Citation by Excelsior logo on front panel.

1962		$600	$800

Fargen

1999-present. Benjamin Fargen builds his professional and premium grade, production/custom, guitar and bass tube amps in Sacramento, California. He also builds guitar effects.

Fender

1946-present. Leo Fender developed many groundbreaking instruments, but Leo's primary passion was amplifiers, and of all his important contributions to musicians, none exceed those he made to the electric tube amplifier.

Tweed Fender amp circuits are highly valued because they defined the tones of rock and roll. Blackface models remained basically the same until mid-'67. Some silverface circuits remained the same as the blackface circuits, while others were changed in the name of reliability. Price Guide values are for all original, excellent condition amps. Small differences in an amp's condition can generate larger differences in selling prices. Non-original speakers will significantly reduce a pre-'68 amp's value. Reconed speakers will reduce the value, but a reconed speaker is preferable to a replacement speaker. Multi-speaker amps generally have matching speaker codes. Different speaker codes require explanation. Fender leather handles are often broken and replaced. A replacement handle drops the value of an amp. Grille cloths should have no tears and a single tear can drop the value of an amp. Each Tweed amp should be evaluated on a case-by-case basis, and it is not unusual for a Tweed amp to have a wide range of values. Alnico speaker replacement is more significant than ceramic speaker replacement. Fender converted to ceramic about '62. Speaker replacement is of less concern in post-'70 Fender amps.

From 1953 to '67, Fender stamped a two-letter date code on the paper tube chart glued inside the cabinet. The first letter was the year (C='53, D='54, etc.) with the second the month (A=January, etc.).

The speaker code found on the frame of an original speaker will identify the manufacturer, and the week and year that the speaker was assembled. The speaker code is typically six (sometimes seven) digits. The first three digits represent the Electronics Industries Association (E.I.A.) source code which identifies the manufacturer. For example, a speaker code 220402 indicates a Jensen speaker (220), made in '54 (4) during the second week (02) of that year. This sample speaker also has another code stamped on the frame. ST654 P15N C4964 indicates the model of the speaker, in this case it is a P15N 15" speaker. The sample speaker also had a code stamped on the speaker cone, 4965 1, which indicates the cone number. All of these codes help identify the originality of the speaker. The value ranges provided in the Guide are for amps with the original speaker and original speaker cone.

Most Fender speakers from the '50s will be Jensens (code 220). By the late-'50s other suppliers were used. The supplier codes are: Oxford (465), C.T.S. (137), Utah (328). JBL speakers were first used in the late-'50s Vibrasonic, and then in the Showman series, but JBL did not normally have a E.I.A. source code. An amp's speaker code should be reconciled with other dating info when the amp's original status is being verified.

Piggyback amps from '68-'79 utilize rather heavy, bulky cabinets, which can be difficult and expensive to ship. Therefore a standalone amp head from this period is worth significantly more than a standalone cabinet.

General Production Eras: Diagonal tweed era, Brown tolex era, Blackface era, Silverface era with raised Fender logo with underlining tail, Silverface era with raised Fender logo without underlining tail, Silverface era with raised Fender logo with small MADE IN USA designation.

Nameplate and Logo Attribution: Fender nameplate with city but without model name (tweed era), Fender nameplate without city or model name (tweed era), Fender nameplate with model name noted (tweed era), Fender flat logo (brown era), Fender script raised logo (blackface era).

30 Amp

1980-1981. Tube combo amp, 30 watts, 2x10" or 1x12".

1980-1981	1x12"	$425	$550
1980-1981	2x10"	$450	$600

75 Amp

1980-1982. Tube, 75 watts, offered as a 1x15" or 1x12" combo, or as head and 4x10" or 2x12" cab.

1980-1982	1x15"	$450	$600
1980-1982	2x12"	$475	$625
1980-1982	4x10"	$525	$675

85 Amp

1988-1992. Solidstate, 85 watt 1x12" combo, black cover, silver grille.

1988-1992		$225	$295

MODEL YEAR	FEATURES	EXC. COND. LOW	HIGH

800 Pro Bass Amp Head

2004-2008. Rack-mount, 800 watts, 5-band EQ.

2004-2008		$365	$475

Acoustasonic 15 Amp

2013-present. Student 1x6" amp, 15 watts.

2013-2020		$50	$75

Acoustasonic 30/30 DSP Amp

2000-2011. Small combo, brown tolex, wheat grille. Upgrade model includes DSP (Digital Signal Processor) effects.

2000-2005	30	$200	$260
2000-2011	30 DSP	$225	$290

Acoustasonic 100 Combo Amp

2012-2013. 100 watts, 1x8", horn.

2012-2013		$275	$375

Acoustasonic 150 Combo Amp

2012-2017. 150 (2x75 stereo) watts, 2x8", piezo horn.

2012-2017		$275	$375

Acoustasonic Junior/Junior DSP Amp

1998-2011. 2x40 watts, 2x8", Piezo horn.

1998-2011		$225	$290

Acoustasonic SFX/SFX II Amp

1998-2011. SFX technology, 32 stereo digital presents, 2x80 watts, SFX is taller combo with one 10", a sideways mounted 8", and a horn. SFX II is shorter cab with 8", sideways 6".

1998-2003	SFX, tall cab	$290	$375
2003-2011	SFX II, short cab	$300	$385

Acoustasonic Ultralight Amp

2006-2009. Small 2x125-watt 2 channel head with 2x8 w/tweeters stereo cab.

2006-2009		$600	$800

Acoustic Pro Amp

2016-2019. 200-watt digital combo, 12" and tweeter, natural blonde cab.

2016-2019		$500	$650

Acoustic SFX Amp

2016-2019. 160-watt digital combo, 8" and 6.5" and tweeter, natural blonde cab.

2016-2019		$500	$650

AmpCan Amp

1997-2008. Cylindrical can-shaped battery powered portable amp.

1997-2008		$145	$190

Automatic SE Amp

1998-2000. Solidstate 25-watt, 1x10" (12" in 2000) combo, blackface cosmetics.

1998-2000		$90	$120

Bandmaster Amp

1953-1974. Wide-panel 1x15" combo '53-'54, narrow-panel 3x10" combo '55-'60, tolex '60, brownface with 1x12" piggyback speaker cabinet '61, 2x12" '62, blackface '62-'67, silverface '68-'74.

The Fender tweed 4x10" Bassman and tweed 3x10" Bandmaster amps are highly sensitive to condition. Because there are so few that are truly excellent, the price ranges listed may be misleading. Most Bassman amps are at best very good minus (VG-) because their tweed is so damaged and stained. It is also rare to find the original speakers, and if the frames are original, they have often been reconed. 4x10" Bassman and 3x10" Bandmasters that are excellent plus plus (Exc++) may have price ranges that are much higher than the values listed. It is estimated that 90% of the vintage 4x10" Bassman are really only VG or less. Because of the extreme condition factor for these tweed amps, the prices below include amps in very good (VG) condition. Therefore the condition for these listed amps is VG to Exc. Exc+ will be more than the values listed here. As per other high-end collectible, each amp should be taken on a case by case basis.

Fender piggyback amps include a head and separate cabinet. The prices shown are for a factory-original matching set. A factory-original set is worth 25% more than the combined value of a head and cabinet that were not originally sold together when new. Heads are worth more than cabinets. The value of a separate head is 40% of the value shown here, and the value of a separate cabinet is 35% of the value shown. In summary, the math is as follows: 40% head + 35% cabinet + 25% premium = 100% value of factory-original set.

1953-1954	Tweed, 1x15"	$2,900	$3,800
1955-1958	Tweed, 3x10"	$6,600	$8,500
1959-1960	Old style cab, pink-brown tolex	$6,700	$8,700
1959-1960	Tweed, 3x10"	$6,700	$8,700
1960	Brown tolex, 3x10"	$3,400	$4,400
1960	Brown tolex, 3x10", reverse controls	$6,200	$7,900
1961	Rough white/ oxblood, 1x12"	$2,200	$2,900
1961-1962	Rough white/ oxblood, 2x12"	$1,800	$2,350
1963-1964	Smooth white/ gold, 2x12"	$1,800	$2,350
1964-1967	Black tolex, 2x12"	$1,075	$1,400
1967-1968	Black, 2x12"	$925	$1,200
1967-1969	Silverface, 2x12"	$750	$1,000
1970-1974	Silverface, 2x12"	$675	$875

Bandmaster Reverb Amp

1968-1980. 45 watt silverface head with 2x12" cabinet.

1968-1972		$850	$1,100
1973-1980		$800	$1,050

Band-Master VM Amp Set

2009-2012. Vintage Modified, 40 watts, piggyback, DSP reverb and effects.

2009-2012		$450	$600

Bantam Bass Amp

1969-1971. 50 watts, large unusual 1x10" Yamaha speaker.

1969-1971	Original speaker	$525	$675

Bassbreaker 15 Amp

2015-present. Tube, 15 watts, 1x12" combo, master volume, gray tweed standard. Also offered in FSR limited editions.

2015-2020	Combo, gray tweed	$350	$450
2015-2020	Head only gray tweed	$300	$400
2017	Combo, LE Blonde Nubtex	$375	$475
2017	Combo, LE British Green	$375	$475

Fender Acoustic Pro

1962 Fender Bandmaster

Ted Wulfers

1964 Fender Bandmaster

Tom Pfeifer

Fender Bassbreaker 45 Combo

1960 Fender Bassman

Dennis Delzer

1963 Fender Bassman

Peter Guild

AMPS

MODEL YEAR	FEATURES	EXC. COND. LOW	HIGH

Bassbreaker 45 Amp

2015-present. Head (until '18) or 2x12" combo, 45 watts, gray tweed.

2015-2018	Head	$575	$750
2016-2020	Combo	$650	$850

Bassman Amp

1952-1971. Tweed TV front combo, 1x15" in '52, wide-panel '53-'54, narrow-panel and 4x10" '54-'60, tolex brownface with 1x12" in piggyback cabinet '61, 2x12" cabinet '61-'62, blackface '63-'67, silverface '67-'71, 2x15" cabinet '68-'71. Renamed the Bassman 50 in '72.

The Fender tweed 4x10" Bassman and tweed 3x10" Bandmaster amps are highly sensitive to condition. Because there are so few that are truly excellent, the price ranges listed may be misleading. Most Bassman amps are at best very good minus (VG-) because their tweed is so damaged and stained. It is also rare to find the original speakers, and if the frames are original, they have often been reconed. 4x10" Bassmans and 3x10" Bandmasters that are excellent plus plus (Exc++) may have price ranges that are much higher than the values listed. It is estimated that 90% of the vintage 4x10" Bassman are really only VG or less. Because of the extreme condition factor for these tweed amps, the prices below include amps in very good (VG) condition. Therefore the condition for these listed amps is VG to Exc. Exc+ will be more than the values listed here. As per other high-end collectibles, each amp should be taken on a case by case basis.

Fender piggyback amps include a head and separate cabinet. The prices shown are for a factory-original matching set. A factory-original set is worth 25% more than the combined value of a head and cabinet that were not originally sold together when new. Heads are worth more than cabinets. The value of a separate head is 40% of the value shown here, and the value of a separate cabinet is 35% of the value shown. In summary, the math is as follows: 40% head + 35% cabinet + 25% premium = 100% value of factory-original set.

1952	TV front, 1x15"	$2,150	$2,800
1953-1954	Wide panel, 1x15"	$2,000	$2,600
1955-1957	Tweed, 4x10", 2 inputs	$5,300	$6,900
1957-1958	Tweed, 4x10", 4 inputs	$6,700	$8,700
1959-1960	Old style cab, pink-brown tolex	$6,800	$8,800
1959-1960	Tweed, 4x10", 4 inputs	$6,800	$8,800
1961	White 1x12", 6G6, tube rectifier	$2,500	$3,300
1962	Late '62, white 2x12	$1,850	$2,400
1962	White 1x12", 6G6A, ss rectifier	$2,300	$3,000
1963-1964	Smooth white 2x12", 6G6A/B	$1,850	$2,400
1964	Transition, black, white knobs	$1,350	$1,750
1965-1966	AA165/AB165, black knobs	$1,100	$1,450
1967-1969	Silverface, vertical 2x15"	$650	$850
1970-1971	Silverface, 2x15"	$550	$700

'59 Bassman Amp

1990-2003. Tube, 45 watts, 4x10", birch ply cab, solidstate rectifier.

1990-2003		$675	$875

'59 Bassman LTD Amp

2004-present. Lacquered Tweed (LTD), tube, 45 watts, 4x10", solid pine cab, tube rectifier.

2004-2020		$850	$1,100

Bassman 10 Amp

1972-1982. 4x10" combo, silverface and 50 watts for '72-'80, blackface and 70 watts after.

1972-1980	50w	$475	$625
1981-1982	70w	$475	$625

Bassman 20 Amp

1982-1985. Tubes, 20 watts, 1x15".

1982-1985		$375	$500

Bassman 25 Amp

2000-2005. Wedge shape, 1x10", 25 watts, 3-band EQ.

2000-2005		$75	$95

Bassman 50 Amp

1972-1977. 50 watts, with 2x12" cab.

1972-1977		$475	$625

Bassman 60 Amp

1972-1976. 60 watts, 1x12".

1972-1976		$475	$625

Bassman 60 Amp (later version)

2000-2005. Solidstate, 60 watts, 1x12".

2000-2005	Combo	$90	$120

Bassman 70 Amp

1977-1979. 70 watts, 2x15" cab.

1977-1979		$475	$625

Bassman 100 Amp

1972-1977, 2000-2009. Tube, 100 watts, 4x12", name reused on solidstate combo amp.

1972-1977	4x12"	$475	$625
2000-2009	1x15" combo	$195	$255

Bassman 100 T Amp

2012-2020. 100-watt head, master volume, '65 blackface cosmetics. Usually paired with Bassman NEO cabs.

2012-2020	Head only	$825	$1,100

Bassman 135 Amp

1978-1983. Tube, 135 watts, 4x10".

1978-1983		$475	$625

Bassman 150 Combo Amp

2005-2009. Solidstate 1x12" combo, 150 watts.

2005-2009		$195	$260

Bassman 250 Combo Amp

2006. Import from Indonesia, 250 watts, 2x10".

2006		$200	$260

Bassman 300 Pro Amp Head

2002-2012. All tube, 300 watts, 6x6550, black cover, black metal grille.

2002-2012		$750	$975

Bassman 400 Amp

2000-2004. Solidstate, 350 watts with 2x10" plus horn, combo, black cover, black metal grille.

2000-2004	Combo	$250	$325
2000-2004	Head	$225	$285

MODEL YEAR	FEATURES	EXC. COND. LOW	HIGH

Bassman Bassbreaker (Custom Shop) Amp

1998-2003. Classic Bassman 4x10" configuration. Not offered by 2004 when the '59 Bassman LTD was introduced.

1998-2003	2x12"	$675	$900
1998-2003	4x10"	$700	$925

Bassman NEO Cabinet

2012-present. Cabinets used with Bassman 100 T head and Super Bassman head, standard '65 blackface cosmetics.

2012-2021	115	$360	$470
2012-2021	410	$450	$590
2012-2021	610	$490	$640
2012-2021	810	$575	$750

Bassman Solidstate Amp

1968-1971. Small head, piggyback cab. The whole late 1960s Solidstate series were unreliable and prone to overheating, more of a historical novelty than a musical instrument.

1968-1971		$370	$485

B-Dec 30 Amp

2006-2009. Bass version of the G-Dec, 30 watts, 1x10.

2006-2009		$100	$130

Blues Deluxe Amp

1993-2005. All tube, 40 watts, reverb, 1x12", tweed covering (blond tolex optional '95 only).

1993-2005	Tweed	$375	$485
1995	Blond	$375	$485

Blues Deluxe Reissue Amp

2006-present. All tube, tweed, 40 watts, reverb, 1x12".

2006-2020		$375	$485

Blues DeVille Amp

1993-1996. All tube Tweed Series, 60 watts, 4x10" (optional 2x12" in '94), reverb, high-gain channel, tweed cover (blond tolex optional '95 only).

1993-1996		$475	$625

Blues DeVille Reissue Amp

2006-2015. 60 watts, 4x10, tweed.

2006-2015		$475	$625

Blues Junior Amp (III) (IV)/LE

1995-present. Tube, 15 watts, 1x12", spring reverb, tweed in '95, black tolex with silver grille '96 on, blond '00-'09, brown '08, surf green '09. Woody Custom Shop (hardwood) in '02-'03. III update in '10, IV in '18. Limited Edition After the Gold Rush, Surf-Tone Green, Red Nova Two-Tone,Creamy Wine Two-Tone, Navy Blues, Silver Noir Two-Tone, and Chocolate Tweed offered in '12.

1995-2020	Black	$325	$425
2002-2003	Woody Custom Shop	$525	$675
2015-2020	Lacquer tweed	$365	$475

Bronco 40 Bass Amp

2012-2018. 40 watts, 1x10", 12 effects.

2012-2018		$135	$175

Bronco Amp

1967-1972, 1993-2001. 1x 8" speaker, all tube, 5 watts until '72, 6 watts for '72-'74, ('90s issue is 15 watts), solidstate, tweed covering (blond tolex was optional for '95 only).

1967-1972	Tubes	$575	$775
1993-2001	15w, no reverb	$85	$115

Bullet/Bullet Reverb Amp

1994-2005. Solidstate, 15 watts, 1x8", with or without reverb.

1994-2005		$35	$65

BXR Series Bass Amp

1987-2000. Various models.

1987-2000		$65	$185

Capricorn Amp

1970-1972. Solidstate, 105 watts, 3x12".

1970-1972		$500	$640

Champ Amp

1953-1982. Renamed from the Champion 600. Tweed until '64, black tolex after, 3 watts in '53, 4 watts '54-'64, 5 watts '65-'71, 6 watts '72-'82, 1x6" until '57, 1x8" after.

1953-1954	Wide panel, 1x6", 5C1	$1,375	$1,825
1955-1956	Narrow panel, 1x6", 5E1	$1,375	$1,825
1956-1964	Narrow panel, 1x8", 5F1	$1,925	$2,550
1964	New cab, black, AA764	$825	$1,075
1964	Old cab, black, 1x8", F51	$1,450	$1,900
1965-1967	New cab, black, AA764	$625	$875
1968-1972	Silverface, 1x8"	$475	$625
1973-1980	Silverface, 1x8"	$425	$575
1981-1982	Blackface	$425	$575

Champ II Amp

1982-1985. 18 watts, 1x10".

1982-1985		$420	$545

'57 Champ/'57 Custom Champ Amp

2009-2011, 2016-present. Custom Series reissue, tweed, leather handle, 5 watts, 1x8". Custom added to model name in '16.

2009-2020		$575	$750

Champ 12 Amp

1986-1992. Tube, 12 watts, overdrive, reverb, 1x12".

1986-1992	Black	$250	$320
1986-1992	Other colors	$325	$420

Champ 25 SE Amp

1992-1993. Hybrid solidstate and tube combo, 25 watts, 1x12".

1992-1993		$175	$225

Champion 20 Amp

2014-present. Solidstate, 20 watts, 1x8", black and silver.

2014-2020		$55	$75

Champion 30/30 DSP Amp

1999-2003. Small solidstate combo, 30 watts, 1x8", reverb.

1999-2003		$65	$85

Champion 40 Amp

2014-present. Solidstate, 40 watts, 1x12".

2014-2020		$100	$130

Champion 100 Amp

2014-present. Solidstate, 100 watts, 2x12", 2 channels.

2014-2020		$150	$200

1964 Fender Bassman

Michael Butler

1995 Fender Blues Junior

Denny Harmison

1964 Fender Champ

Ken Ypparila

1953 Fender Champion 600
Jeffrey Smith

1948 Fender Champion 800

1962 Fender Concert
KC Cormack

MODEL YEAR	FEATURES	EXC. COND. LOW	HIGH

Champion 100XL Amp
2019-present. 100 watts, 2x12", 16 on-board effects, black.

2019-2020		$260	$340

Champion 110 Amp
1993-2000. Solidstate, 25 watts, 1x10", 2 channels.

1993-2000		$90	$115

Champion 300 Amp
2004-2007. 30 watt solidstate combo, Dyna-Touch Series, DSP effects.

2004-2007		$140	$180

Champion 600 Amp
1949-1953. Replaced the Champion 800, 3 watts, 1x6", 2-tone tolex, TV front. Replaced by the Champ.

1949-1953		$1,100	$1,450

Champion 600 Amp (later version)
2007-2012. Small 5 watt combo.

2007-2012		$125	$165

Champion 800 Amp
1948. About 100 made, TV front, luggage tweed cover, 1x8, 3 tubes, becomes Champion 600 in '49.

1948		$1,175	$1,525

Concert Amp
1960-1965. Introduced with 40 watts and 4x10", brown tolex until '63, blackface '63-'65. In '62 white tolex was ordered by Webbs Music (CA) instead of the standard brown tolex. A wide range is noted for the rare white tolex, and each amp should be valued on a case-by-case basis. In '60, the very first brown tolex had a pink tint but only on the first year amps.

1960	Brown (pink) tolex	$2,100	$2,700
1960	Brown (pink), tweed grille	$2,000	$2,600
1961-1963	Brown tolex	$1,800	$2,400
1962	White tolex (Webb Music)	$1,900	$2,500
1963-1965	Blackface	$1,800	$2,400

Concert (Pro Tube Series) Amp
1993-1995 Tube combo, 60 watts, 1x12, blackface

1993-1995		$525	$675

Concert Reverb (Pro Tube Series) Amp
2002-2005. 4x10" combo, reverb, tremolo, overdrive.

2002-2005		$525	$700

Concert 112 Amp
1982-1985. Tube, 60 watts, 1x12", smaller Concert logo (not similar to '60s style logo).

1982-1985		$600	$800

Concert 210 Amp
1982-1985 Tube, 60 watts, 2x10"

1982-1985		$625	$825

Concert 410 Amp
1982-1985. Tube, 60 watts, 4x10".

1982-1985		$675	$875

Concert II Amp Head
1982-1987. 60 watts, 2 channels.

1982-1987		$550	$725

Cyber Champ Amp
2004-2005. 65 watts, 1x12", Cyber features, 21 presets.

2004-2005		$175	$225

MODEL YEAR	FEATURES	EXC. COND. LOW	HIGH

Cyber Deluxe Amp
2002-2005. 65 watts, 1x12", Cyber features, 64 presets.

2002-2005		$190	$250

Cyber-Twin (SE) Amp
2001-2011. Hybrid tube/solidstate modeling amp, 2x65 watts, head or 2x12" combo, becomes the SE in '05.

2001-2003	Head only	$275	$375
2001-2004	Combo	$325	$425
2005-2011	2nd Edition SE	$325	$425

Deco-Tone (Custom Shop) Amp
2000. Art-deco styling, 165 made, all tube, 15 watts, 1x12", round speaker baffle opening, uses 6BQ5/ES84 power tubes.

2000		$700	$900

Deluxe Amp
1948-1966. Name changed from Model 26 ('46-'48). 10 watts (15 by '54 and 20 by '63), 1x12", TV front with tweed '48-'53, wide-panel '53-'55, narrow-panel '55-'60, brown tolex with brownface '61-'63, black tolex with blackface '63-'66.

1948-1952	Tweed, TV front	$2,450	$3,200
1953-1954	Wide panel	$2,450	$3,200
1955	Narrow panel, small cab	$3,700	$4,850
1956-1960	Narrow panel, large cab	$3,600	$4,750
1961-1963	Brown tolex	$1,800	$2,350
1964-1966	Black tolex	$1,800	$2,350

Deluxe Reverb Amp
1963-1981. 1x12", 20 watts, blackface '63-'67, silverface '68-'80, blackface with silver grille option introduced in mid-'80. Replaced by Deluxe Reverb II. Reissued as Deluxe Reverb '65 Reissue.

1963-1967	Blackface	$2,400	$3,100
1967-1968	Silverface	$1,750	$2,300
1969-1970	Silverface	$1,450	$1,900
1971-1980	Silverface	$1,025	$1,350
1980-1981	Blackface	$1,025	$1,350

Deluxe Reverb Solidstate Amp
1966-1969. Part of Fender's early solidstate series.

1966-1969		$400	$510

'57 Deluxe/'57 Custom Deluxe Amp
2007-2011, 2016-present. Custom Series reissue, hand-wired, 12 watts, 1x12" combo, tweed. Custom added to model name in '17. A '57 Deluxe head version was offered '16-'17 and Limited Editions in '18-'19.

2007-2011		$1,150	$1,500
2016-2017	Head only	$1,050	$1,375
2016-2020		$1,175	$1,525
2018	LE Blond	$1,225	$1,575

'57 Custom Deluxe Front Row Amp
2019. Limited Edition, 5 offered, exotic wood cab made of century-old Alaskan yellow cedar, from Hollywood Bowl bench seats.

2019	LE Exotic Wood	$4,100	$5,350

'65 Deluxe Reverb Amp
1993-present. Blackface reissue, 22 watts, 1x12".

1993-2020		$650	$850

MODEL YEAR	FEATURES	EXC. COND. LOW	HIGH

'68 Custom Deluxe Reverb Amp

2014-present. Vintage Modified silverface reissue with modified circuit, 1x12".

2014-2020		$625	$825

Deluxe Reverb II Amp

1982-1986. Updated Deluxe Reverb with 2 6V6 power tubes, all tube preamp section, black tolex, blackface, 20 watts, 1x12".

1982-1986		$775	$1,025

Deluxe 85 Amp

1988-1993. Solidstate, 65 watts, 1x12", black tolex, silver grille, Red Knob Series.

1988-1993		$225	$300

Deluxe 90 Amp

1999-2003. Solidstate, 90 watts, 1x12" combo, DSP added in '02.

1999-2002		$150	$200
2002-2003	DSP option	$175	$225

Deluxe 112 Amp

1992-1995. Solidstate, 65 watts, 1x12", black tolex with silver grille.

1992-1995		$150	$200

Deluxe 112 Plus Amp

1995-2000. 90 watts, 1x12", channel switching.

1995-2000		$175	$225

Deluxe 900 Amp

2004-2006. Solidstate, 90 watts, 1x12" combo, DSP effects.

2004-2006		$200	$275

Deluxe VM Amp

2009-2013. Vintage Modified Series, 40 watts, 1x12", black.

2009-2013		$450	$600

MD20 Mini Deluxe Amp

2007-present. One-watt, dual 2" speakers, headphone jack, 9V adapter jack.

2007-2020		$15	$20

The Edge Deluxe Amp

2016-2019. 12-watts, 1x12" combo, tube, tweed. The Edge front panel badge.

2016-2019		$1,275	$1,650

Dual Professional Amp

1994-2002. Custom Shop amp, all tube, point-to-point wiring, 100 watts, 2x12" Celestion Vintage 30s, fat switch, reverb, tremolo, white tolex, oxblood grille.

1994-2002		$1,100	$1,400

Dual Professional/Super Amp

1947. V-front, early-'47 small metal name tag "Fender/Dual Professional/Fullerton California" tacked on front of cab, 2x10 Jensen PM10-C each with transformer attached to speaker frame, tube chart on inside of cab, late-'47 renamed Super and new metal badge "Fender/Fullerton California".

1947		$4,500	$5,800

Dual Showman Amp

1962-1969. Called the Double Showman for the first year. White tolex (black available from '64), 2x15", 85 watts. Reintroduced '87-'94 as solidstate, 100 watts, optional speaker cabs.

Fender piggyback amps include a head and separate cabinet. The prices shown are for a factory-original matching set. A factory-original set is worth 25% more than the combined value of a head and cabinet that were not originally sold together when new. Heads are worth more than cabinets. The value of a separate head is 40% of the value shown here, and the value of a separate cabinet is 35% of the value shown. In summary, the math is as follows: 40% head + 35% cabinet + 25% premium = 100% value of factory-original set.

1962	Rough blond/ oxblood	$2,550	$3,300
1963	Smooth blond/ wheat	$2,150	$2,800
1964-1967	Black tolex, horizontal cab	$1,450	$1,900
1968	Blackface, large vertical cab	$925	$1,200
1968-1969	Silverface	$800	$1,050

Dual Showman Reverb Amp

1968-1981. Black tolex with silver grille, silverface, 100 watts, 2x15".

1968-1972		$875	$1,125
1973-1981		$825	$1,075

Fender '57 Amp

2007. Only 300 made, limited edition combo, hand-wired, 1x12", retro styling.

2007		$1,150	$1,500

FM Series Amp

2003-2010. Lower-priced solidstate amps, heads and combos.

2003-2006	FM-212R, 2x12	$195	$250
2003-2010	FM-100 Head/Cab	$205	$270

Frontman Series Amp

1997-present. Student combo amps, models include 10G (10 watts, 1x6"), 15/15B/15G/15R (15 watts, 1x8"), 25R (25 watts, 1x10", reverb), 212R (100 watts, 2x12", reverb).

1997-2004	15DSP w/15 FX selections	$40	$60
1997-2004	25DSP	$55	$75
1997-2006	65DSP	$115	$150
1997-2011	15/15B/15G/15R	$30	$50
1997-2011	65R	$75	$100
1997-2013	25R	$40	$60
2007-2013	212R	$150	$200

G-Dec Amp

2005-2012. Digital, amp and effects presets.

2005-2009	G-Dec (small cab)	$70	$90
2006-2009	G-Dec 30 (large cab)	$100	$130
2007-2008	G-Dec Exec, maple cab	$165	$215
2011-2012	G-Dec Jr, Champ cab	$50	$65

H.O.T. Amp

1990-1996. Solidstate, 25 watts, 1x10", gray carpet cover (black by '92), black grille.

1990-1996		$70	$95

Harvard Solidstate Amp

1980-1983. Reintroduced from tube model, black tolex with blackface, 20 watts, 1x10".

1980-1983		$120	$155

1955 Fender Deluxe

Jerome Pinkham

1967 Fender Dual Showman

Imaged by Heritage Auctions, HA.com

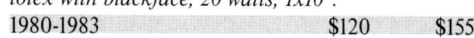

Fender Frontman 25R

2004 Fender Hot Rod Deluxe Limited

Carter Vintage Guitars

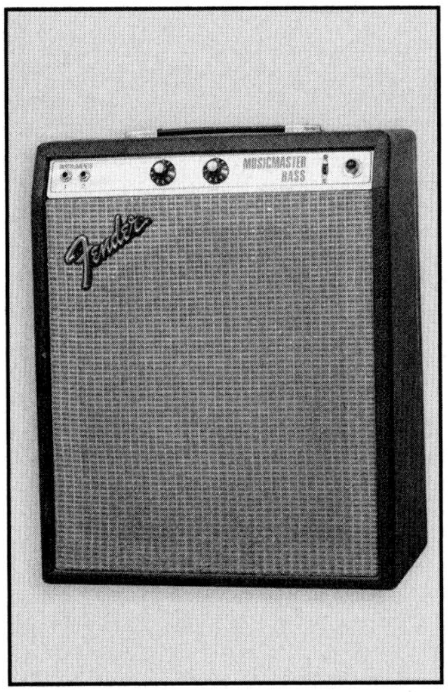

1977 Fender Musicmaster Bass

Tom Pfeifer

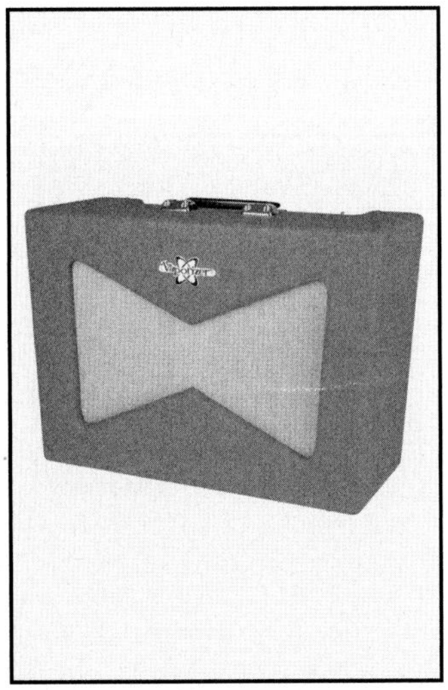

Fender Pawn Shop Special Vaporizer

MODEL YEAR	FEATURES	EXC. COND. LOW	HIGH

Harvard Tube Amp

1956-1961. Tweed, 10 watts, 1x10", 2 knobs volume and roll-off tone, some were issued with 1x8". Reintroduced as a solidstate model in '80.

1956-1961 $2,500 $3,300

Harvard Reverb Amp

1981-1982. Solidstate, 20 watts, 1x10", reverb, replaced by Harvard Reverb II in '83.

1981-1982 $120 $155

Harvard Reverb II Amp

1983-1985. Solidstate, black tolex with blackface, 20 watts, 1x10", reverb.

1983-1985 $120 $155

Hot Rod Blues Junior Limited Amp

2000s. Compact tube combo, rough blond tolex, dark tolex sides, wheat grille.

2000s $300 $400

Hot Rod Deluxe/Deluxe III/Deluxe IV Amp

1996-present. Updated Blues Deluxe, tube, 40 watts, 1x12", black tolex. Various covering optional by '98, also a wood cab in 2003. III added to name in '11 with various limited edition colors. Renamed Deluxe IV in '20, offered in black.

1996-2020 Various colors $370 $480

Hot Rod DeVille 212 Amp

1996-2011. Updated Blues DeVille, tube, 60 watts, black tolex, 2x12".

1996-2011 Various colors $475 $625

Hot Rod DeVille 410/DeVille 410 III Amp

1996-2018. Tube, 60 watts, black tolex, 4x10". III added to name in '11.

1996-2018 Various colors $450 $575

J.A.M. Amp

1990-1996. Solidstate, 25 watts, 1x12", 4 preprogrammed sounds, gray carpet cover (black by '92).

1990-1996 $60 $75

Jazz King Amp

2005-2008. 140 watt solidstate 1x15" combo.

2005-2008 $450 $600

KXR Series Amp

1995-2002. Keyboard combo amps, 50 to 200 watts, solidstate, 1x12" or 15".

1995-2002 Various models $75 $200

Libra Amp

1970-1972. Solidstate, 105 watts, 4x12" JBL speakers, black tolex.

1970-1972 $475 $625

London 185 Amp

1988-1992. Solidstate, 160 watts, black tolex.

1988-1992 Head only $210 $275

London Reverb 112 Amp

1983-1985. Solidstate, 100 watts, black tolex, 1x12".

1983-1985 $290 $375

London Reverb 210 Amp

1983-1985. Solidstate, 100 watts, black tolex, 2x10".

1983-1985 $310 $400

London Reverb Amp Head

1983-1985. Solidstate head, 100 watts.

1983-1985 $210 $275

M-80 Series Amp

1989-1994. Solidstate, 90 watts, 1x12", also offered as head only, Bass (160w, 1x15"), Chorus (90w, 2x12") and Pro (90w, rackmount).

1989-1993 M-80 Pro $140 $185
1989-1994 M-80 $140 $185
1990-1994 M-80 Bass $140 $185
1990-1994 M-80 Chorus $140 $185

Machette Amp

2012-2013. 50 watts, 1x12" tube combo, inlaid white piping and gray vinyl accents on black tolex.

2012-2013 $1,700 $2,200

Model 26 Amp

1946-1947. Tube, 10 watts, 1x10", hardwood cabinet. Sometimes called Deluxe Model 26, renamed Deluxe in '48.

1946-1947 $1,750 $2,300

Montreux Amp

1983-1985. Solidstate, 100 watts, 1x12", black tolex with silver grille.

1983-1985 $290 $375

Musicmaster Bass Amp

1970-1983. Tube, 12 watts, 1x12", black tolex.

1970-1980 Silverface $375 $500
1981-1983 Blackface $375 $500

Mustang Series Amp

2010-present. Mustang I thru V, modeling amp effects, small combo up to a half-stack. Mustang GTX and LT added in '20.

2010-2016 II, 40w, 1x12 $100 $130
2010-2019 I, 20w, 1x8 $50 $70
2011-2016 III, 100w, 1x12 $150 $195
2011-2016 IV, 150w, 2x12 $225 $325
2011-2016 V, 150w, 4x12 $285 $375

PA-100 Amp Head

Early to mid-1970s. All tube head, 100 watts, 4 channels with standard guitar inputs, master volume.

1970s $400 $525

PA-135 Amp Head

Later 1970s. All tube head, 135 watts, 4 channels, master volume.

1970s $400 $525

Pawn Shop Special Excelsior/Excelsior Pro Amp

2012-2013. Retro late-'40s vertical combo slate-grille cab, 13-watt 1x15" combo tube amp, tremolo, brown textured vinyl covering.

2012-2013 $225 $300

Pawn Shop Special Greta Amp

2012. Mini tube tabletop amp, 2 watts, 1x4" vintage radio-style cab, red.

2012 $125 $175

Pawn Shop Special Ramparte Amp

2014. Tube amp, 9 watts, 1x12", 2-tone chocolate and copper grille cloth with wheat.

2014 $225 $300

Pawn Shop Special Vaporizer Amp

2014. Tube amp, 12 watts, 2x10", Rocket Red, Slate Blue or Surf Green dimpled vinyl covering with silver grille cloth.

2014 $250 $325

Performer 650 Amp

1993-1995. Solidstate hybrid amp with single tube, 70 watts, 1x12".

MODEL YEAR	FEATURES	EXC. COND. LOW	HIGH
1993-1995		$180	$230

Performer 1000 Amp

1993-1995. Solidstate hybrid amp with a single tube, 100 watts, 1x12".

MODEL YEAR	FEATURES	EXC. COND. LOW	HIGH
1993-1995		$180	$230

Princeton Amp

1948-1979. Tube, 4.5 watts (12 watts by '61), 1x8" (1x10" by '61), tweed '48-'61, brown '61-'63, black with blackface '63-'69, silverface '69-'79.

MODEL YEAR	FEATURES	EXC. COND. LOW	HIGH
1948-1953	Tweed, TV front	$1,350	$1,800
1953-1954	Wide panel	$1,350	$1,800
1955-1956	Narrow panel, small cab	$1,800	$2,400
1956-1961	Narrow panel, large cab	$1,800	$2,400
1961-1963	Brown, 6G2	$1,700	$2,225
1963-1964	Black, 6G2	$1,600	$2,100
1964-1966	Black, AA964, no grille logo	$1,375	$1,775
1966-1967	Black, AA964, raised grille logo	$1,200	$1,600
1968-1969	Silverface alum grille trim	$750	$1,000
1969-1970	Silverface, no grille trim	$675	$900
1971-1979	Silverface, AB1270	$675	$900
1973-1975	Fender logo-tail	$675	$900
1975-1978	No Fender logo-tail	$675	$900
1978-1979	With boost pull-knob	$675	$900

Princeton Reverb Amp

1964-1981. Tube, black tolex, blackface until '67, silverface after until blackface again in '80.

MODEL YEAR	FEATURES	EXC. COND. LOW	HIGH
1964-1967	Blackface	$2,100	$2,750
1968-1972	Silverface, Fender logo-tail	$875	$1,150
1973-1979	Silverface, no Fender logo-tail	$875	$1,150
1980-1981	Blackface	$875	$1,150

Princeton Reverb II Amp

1982-1985. Tube amp, 20 watts, 1x12", black tolex, silver grille, distortion feature.

MODEL YEAR	FEATURES	EXC. COND. LOW	HIGH
1982-1985		$750	$975

'65 Princeton Reverb Amp

2009-present. Vintage Reissue series, includes various Limited Edition colors.

MODEL YEAR	FEATURES	EXC. COND. LOW	HIGH
2009-2020	Various colors	$550	$725

'68 Custom Princeton Reverb Amp

2014-present. 12 watts, silver-and-turquoise front panel, aluminum grille cloth trim, black.

MODEL YEAR	FEATURES	EXC. COND. LOW	HIGH
2014-2021		$500	$650

Princeton Chorus Amp

1988-1996. Solidstate, 2x10", 2 channels at 25 watts each, black tolex. Replaced by Princeton Stereo Chorus in '96.

MODEL YEAR	FEATURES	EXC. COND. LOW	HIGH
1988-1996		$150	$200

Princeton 65 Amp

1999-2003. Combo 1x2", reverb, blackface, DSP added in '02.

MODEL YEAR	FEATURES	EXC. COND. LOW	HIGH
1999-2001		$130	$170

Princeton 112/112 Plus Amp

1993-1997. Solidstate, 40 watts (112) or 60 watts (112 Plus), 1x12", black tolex.

MODEL YEAR	FEATURES	EXC. COND. LOW	HIGH
1993-1994	40 watts	$130	$170
1995-1997	60 watts	$130	$170

Princeton 650 Amp

2004-2006. Solidstate 65 watt 1x12" combo, DSP effects, black tolex.

MODEL YEAR	FEATURES	EXC. COND. LOW	HIGH
2004-2006		$130	$170

Princeton Recording Amp

2007-2009. Based on classic '65 Princeton Reverb, 15 watts, 1x10" combo, 2 on-board effects (overdrive/compression), 4-button footswitch, blackface cosmetics.

MODEL YEAR	FEATURES	EXC. COND. LOW	HIGH
2007-2009		$500	$650

Pro Amp

1946-1965. Called Professional '46-'48. 15 watts (26 by '54 and 25 by '60), 1x15", tweed TV front '48-'53, wide-panel '53-'54, narrow-panel '55-'60, brown tolex and brownface '60-'63, black and blackface '63-'65.

MODEL YEAR	FEATURES	EXC. COND. LOW	HIGH
1946-1953	Tweed, TV front	$2,900	$3,800
1953-1954	Wide panel	$3,100	$4,100
1955	Narrow panel (old chassis)	$3,500	$4,500
1955-1959	Narrow panel (new chassis)	$3,600	$4,600
1960	Pink/brown, tweed-era cover	$2,000	$2,600
1961-1962	Brown tolex	$1,800	$2,400
1963-1965	Black tolex	$1,800	$2,400

'57 Custom Pro Amp

2016-2019. Hand-wired, 26 watts, 1x15", lacquered tweed.

MODEL YEAR	FEATURES	EXC. COND. LOW	HIGH
2016-2019		$1,300	$1,700

Pro Reverb Amp

1965-1982. Tube, black tolex, 40 watts (45 watts by '72, 70 watts by '81), 2x12", blackface '65-'69 and '81-'83, silverface '69-'81.

MODEL YEAR	FEATURES	EXC. COND. LOW	HIGH
1965-1967	Blackface	$1,900	$2,500
1968	Silverface	$1,300	$1,726
1969-1970		$1,200	$1,600
1971-1980	Silverface	$825	$1,075
1981-1982	Blackface	$825	$1,075

Pro Reverb Solidstate Amp

1967-1969. Fender's first attempt at solidstate design, the attempt was unsuccessful and many of these models will overheat and are known to be unreliable. 50 watts, 2x12", upright vertical combo cabinet.

MODEL YEAR	FEATURES	EXC. COND. LOW	HIGH
1967-1969		$400	$515

Pro Reverb Reissue (Pro Series) Amp

2002-2005. 50 watts, 1x12", 2 modern designed channels - clean and high gain.

MODEL YEAR	FEATURES	EXC. COND. LOW	HIGH
2002-2005		$650	$850

Pro 185 Amp

1989-1991. Solidstate, 160 watts, 2x12", black tolex.

MODEL YEAR	FEATURES	EXC. COND. LOW	HIGH
1989-1991		$200	$275

1964 Fender Princeton Reverb

Vern Juran

1959 Fender Pro

Ted Wulfers

1967 Fender Pro Reverb

Michael Butler

2015 Fender Pro Junior III

Rivington Guitars

Fender Rumble 100

1963 Fender Showman

Imaged by Heritage Auctions, HA.com

MODEL YEAR	FEATURES	EXC. COND. LOW	HIGH

Pro Junior Amp (III/IV)

1994-present. All tube, 2xEL84 tubes, 15 watts, 1x10" Alnico Blue speaker, tweed '94-'96, blond in '95, black tolex '96-'17. Lacquered Tweed '18-present. III update in '10, IV in '18.

1994-1996	Tweed	$375	$500
1995	Blonde	$275	$375
1996-2017	Black tolex	$225	$300
2018-2021	Lacquered Tweed	$275	$375

Pro Junior 60th Anniversary Woody Amp

2006. Recreation of original Fender model (1946-2006), 15 watts, 1x10, lacquered wood cab.

2006		$550	$700

Pro Junior Masterbuilt Custom Shop Amp

Late 1990s. Transparent white-blond wood finish.

1990s		$550	$700

Prosonic Amp

1996-2001. Custom Shop 2x10" combo or head/4x12" cab, 60 watts, 2 channels, 3-way rectifier switch, tube reverb, black, red or green.

1996-2001	Cab	$300	$400
1996-2001	Combo	$650	$850
1996-2001	Head	$525	$700

Quad Reverb Amp

1971-1978. Black tolex, silverface, 4x12", tube, 100 watts. Large Fender combo amps built in the '70s are not often in excellent condition. Any grille stain or tear to the grille can mean an amp is not in excellent condition and can significantly reduce the values shown.

1971-1978		$750	$975

R.A.D. Amp

1990-1996. Solidstate, 20 watts, 1x8", gray carpet cover until '92, black after.

1990-1996		$55	$75

R.A.D. Bass Amp

1992-1994. Solidstate, 25 watts, 1x10", renamed BXR 25.

1992-1994		$55	$75

Roc-Pro 1000 Amp

1997-2001. Hybrid tube combo or head, 100 watts, 1x12", spring reverb, 1000 logo on front panel.

1997-2001	Combo	$175	$225
1997-2001	Half stack, head & cab	$225	$325

Rumble Bass Amp

1994-1998. Custom Shop tube amp, 300 watts, 4x10" cabs, blond tolex, oxblood grille. Not to be confused with later budget Rumble series.

1994-1998	Cab	$525	$700
1994-1998	Head	$975	$1,250
1994-1998	Head & 2 cabs	$2,100	$2,800

Rumble Series Amp

2003-present. Solidstate bass amps, model number indicates watts (i.e. Rumble 15 = 15 watts), models include Rumble 15 (1x8"), 25 (1x10"), 30 (1x10"), 40 (1x10"), 60 (1x12"), 75 (1x12"), 100 (1x15" or 2x10"), 150 (1x15") and 350 (2x10"). Some models discontinued '09 then restarted in '14.

2003-2009	Rumble 60	$115	$150
2003-2013	Rumble 150	$135	$175
2003-2013	Rumble 150 Head	$105	$135
2003-2013	Rumble 30	$95	$125
2003-2013	Rumble 350	$195	$250
2003-2013	Rumble 350 Combo	$215	$280
2003-2013	Rumble 350 Head	$135	$175
2003-2013	Rumble 75	$120	$155
2003-2021	Rumble 100	$135	$175
2003-2021	Rumble 15	$45	$60
2003-2021	Rumble 25	$55	$75
2003-2021	Rumble 40	$105	$135

Scorpio Amp

1970-1972. Solidstate, 56 watts, 2x12", black tolex.

1970-1972		$475	$625

Showman 12 Amp

1960-1966. Piggyback cabinet with 1x12", 85 watts, blond tolex (changed to black in '64), maroon grille '61-'63, gold grille '63-'64, silver grille '64-'67.

1960-1962	Rough blond/ oxblood	$2,500	$3,250
1963-1964	Smooth blond/gold	$2,150	$2,800
1964-1966	Black	$1,400	$1,800

Showman 15 Amp

1960-1968. Piggyback cabinet with 1x15", 85 watts, blond tolex (changed to black in '64), maroon grille '61-'63, gold grille '63-'64, silver grille '64-'67.

1960-1962	Rough blond/ oxblood	$2,350	$3,050
1963-1964	Smooth blond/gold	$2,100	$2,700
1964-1967	Blackface	$1,300	$1,700
1967-1968	Silverface	$750	$1,000

Showman Solidstate Amp

1983-1987. Solidstate, 200 watts, 2 channels, reverb, EQ, effects loop, model number indicates size, models include; 112, 115, 210 and 212.

1983-1987	Various models	$300	$400

Sidekick 10 Amp

1983-1985. Small solidstate Japanese or Mexican import, 10 watts, 1x8".

1983-1985		$50	$60

Sidekick Bass 30 Amp

1983-1985. Combo, 30 watts, 1x12".

1983-1985		$60	$75

Sidekick Reverb 15 Amp

1983-1985. Small solidstate import, reverb, 15 watts.

1983-1985		$70	$85

Sidekick Reverb 20 Amp

1983-1985. Small solidstate Japanese or Mexican import, 20 watts, reverb, 1x10".

1983-1985		$75	$95

Sidekick Reverb 30 Amp

1983-1985. Small solidstate Japanese or Mexican import, 30 watts, 1x12", reverb.

1983-1985		$80	$100

Sidekick Reverb 65 Amp

1986-1988. Small solidstate Japanese or Mexican import, 65 watts, 1x12".

1986-1988		$100	$125

Sidekick 100 Bass Amp Head

1986-1993. 100 watt bass head.

1986-1993		$75	$90

Squier Champ 15 Amp

1990s-2000s. 1x8, 15 watts, solidstate.

1990s-00s		$45	$55

MODEL YEAR	FEATURES	EXC. COND. LOW	HIGH

Squier SKX Series Amp

1990-1992. Solidstate, 15 watts, 1x8", model 15R with reverb. Model 25R is 25 watts, 1x10, reverb.

1990-1992	15, non-reverb	$30	$40
1990-1992	15R, reverb	$35	$45
1990-1992	25R, reverb	$45	$55

Squier SP10 Amp

2003-2012. 10 watt solidstate, usually sold as part of a Guitar Pack.

2003-2012		$30	$40

Stage 100/Stage 1000 Amp

1999-2006. Solidstate, 1x12", combo or head only options, 100 watts, blackface. Head available until 2004.

1999-2004	Head only	$200	$250
1999-2006	Combo	$250	$325
1999-2006	Combo stack, 2 cabs	$325	$425

Stage 1600 DSP Amp

2004-2006. Solidstate, 160 watts, 2x12" combo, 16 digital effects (DSP).

2004-2006		$300	$400

Stage Lead/Lead II Amp

1983-1985. Solidstate, 100 watts, 1x12", reverb, channel switching, black tolex. Stage Lead II has 2x12".

1983-1985	1x12"	$175	$225
1983-1985	2x12"	$175	$225

Starcaster by Fender 15G Amp

2000s. Student economy pac amp, sold with a guitar, strap and stand, Starcaster by Fender logo. Sold in Costco and other discounters.

2000s		$20	$30

Steel-King Amp

2004-2009. Designed for pedal steel, 200 watts, solidstate, 1x15".

2004-2009		$475	$625

Studio 85 Amp

1988. Studio 85 logo on upper right front of grille, solidstate, 1x12" combo, 65 watts, red knobs.

1988		$175	$225

Studio Bass Amp

1977-1980. Uses Super Twin design, tube, 200 watt combo, 5-band eq, 1x15".

1977-1980		$500	$650

Studio Lead Amp

1983-1986. Solidstate, 50 watts, 1x12", black tolex.

1983-1986		$200	$260

Super Amp

1947-1963, 1992-1997. Introduced as Dual Professional in 1946, renamed Super '47, 2x10" speakers, 20 watts (30 watts by '60 with 45 watts in '62), tweed TV front '47-'53, wide-panel '53-'54, narrow-panel '55-'60, brown tolex '60-'64. Reintroduced '92-'97 with 4x10", 60 watts, black tolex.

1947-1952	V-front	$4,500	$6,000
1953-1954	Tweed, wide panel	$3,400	$4,400
1955	Tweed, narrow panel, 6L6	$4,500	$6,000
1956-1957	Tweed, narrow panel, 5E4, 6V6	$3,800	$5,000
1957-1960	Tweed, narrow panel, 6L6	$5,700	$7,400
1960	Pink, tweed-era grille	$2,275	$2,950
1960	Pink/brown metal knobs	$2,300	$3,000
1960	Pink/brown reverse knobs	$2,300	$3,000
1960-1962	Brown, oxblood grille, 6G4	$2,100	$2,750
1962-1963	Brown, tan/wheat grille, 6G4	$2,100	$2,750

Super 60 Amp

1989-1993. Red Knob series, 1x12", 60 watts, earlier versions with red knobs, later models with black knobs, offered in optional covers such as red, white, gray or snakeskin.

1989-1993	Combo	$250	$350
1989-1993	Head	$250	$350

Super 112 Amp

1990-1993. Red Knob series, 1x12", 60 watts, earlier versions with red knobs, later models with black knobs, originally designed to replace the Super60 but the Super60 remained until '93.

1990-1993		$325	$425

Super 210 Amp

1990-1993. Red Knob series, 2x10", 60 watts, earlier versions with red knobs, later models with black knobs.

1990-1993		$325	$425

Super 410 Amp

1992-1997. 60 watts, 4x10", black tolex, silver grille, blackface control panel.

1992-1997		$525	$700

Super Bassman Amp Head

2012-present. 300-watt head, 6x6550 power tubes, master volume, standard '65 blackface cosmetics.

2012-2020		$975	$1,250

Super Champ Amp

1982-1986. Black tolex, 18 watts, blackface, 1x10".

1982-1986		$725	$950

Super Champ Deluxe Amp

1982-1986. Solid oak cabinet, 18 watts, upgrade 10" Electro-Voice speaker, see-thru brown grille cloth.

1982-1986		$925	$1,200

Super Champ XD Amp

2008-2011. Tube amp with extra preamp voicing, 1x10" combo, blackface cosmetics. Replaced by X2 version.

2008-2011		$195	$250

Super Reverb Amp

1963-1982. 4x10" speakers, blackface until '67 and '80-'82, silverface '68-'80. Large Fender combo amps built in the '70s are not often in excellent condition. Any grille stain or tear to the grille can mean an amp is not in excellent condition and can significantly reduce the values shown.

1963-1964	Blackface, Fender Elec	$1,800	$2,350
1965-1967	Blackface, FMI	$1,700	$2,200
1968	Silverface, AB763	$1,100	$1,450
1969-1970	Silverface	$1,050	$1,350
1970-1972	Silverface, AA270	$900	$1,200
1972-1975	Int Master	$850	$1,100
1975-1980	MV with pull	$750	$1,000
1981-1982	Blackface	$750	$1,000

Fender Showman
Carter Vintage Guitars

1956 Fender Super
Rivington Guitars

1968 Fender Super Reverb
Michael Campbell

Fender Super-Sonic

1958 Fender Tremolux

Scott Chapin

1962 Fender Twin

Jim Sheehan

MODEL YEAR	FEATURES	EXC. COND. LOW	HIGH

Super Reverb Solidstate Amp

1967-1970. 50 watts, 4x10".

1967-1970		$400	$525

'65 Super Reverb Amp

2001-present. 45 watts, all tube, 4x10", blackface cosmetics.

2001-2020		$800	$1,050

Super Showman XFL-1000/XFL-2000 Amp

1969-1971. Solidstate Super Showman head controlled 1 or more powered speaker cabs. The XFL-1000 was a 4x12" cab with 2 70-watt power amps, the 8x10" XFL-2000 had same power amps.

1969-1971		$450	$590

Super Six Reverb Amp

1970-1979. Large combo amp based on the Twin Reverb chassis, 100 watts, 6x10", black tolex. Large Fender combo amps built in the '70s are not often in excellent condition. Any grille stain or tear to the grille can mean an amp is not in excellent condition and can significantly reduce the values shown.

1970-1979		$850	$1,200

Super Twin Amp

1975-1980. 180 watts (6 6L6 power tubes), 2x12", distinctive dark grille.

1975-1976	Non-reverb	$700	$900
1976-1980	Reverb	$750	$950

Super-Sonic/60 Amp

2006-present. All tube, 60 watts, various options, 1x12" combo or 2x12" piggyback, blonde/oxblood or blackface. Straight and slant 4x12" cab added '11.

2006-2013	1x12", blonde/oxblood	$575	$775
2006-2014	1x12", blackface	$525	$700
2006-2015	2x12" piggyback, blonde	$775	$1,000

Super-Sonic 22 Combo Limited Edition "Black Gold" FSR Amp

2012. 150 made, 1x12, 2-tone gold and black vinyl with white piping, black grille.

2012		$575	$775

Taurus Amp

1970-1972. Solidstate, 42 watts, 2x10" JBL, black tolex, silver grille, JBL badge.

1970-1972		$400	$515

Tonemaster Amp Set

1993-2002. Custom Shop, hand-wired head with Tonemaster 2x12" or 4x12" cabinet, blond or oxblood.

1993-2002		$1,200	$1,550

Tone Master Deluxe Reverb Amp

2019-present. 100-watt digital, reverb and tremolo, black or blonde.

2019-2020	Black	$500	$650
2019-2020	Blonde	$525	$700

Tone Master Twin Reverb Amp

2019-present. 200-watt digital, reverb and tremolo, black or blonde.

2019-2020	Black	$575	$750
2019-2020	Blonde	$600	$800

Tremolux Amp

1955-1966. Tube, tweed, 1x12" '55-'60, white tolex with piggyback 1x10" cabinet '61-'62, 2x10" '62-'64, black tolex '64-'66.

1955-1960	Tweed, 1x12", narrow panel	$3,600	$4,725
1961	Rough white/oxblood, 1x10"	$2,200	$2,900
1961-1962	Rough white/oxblood, 2x10"	$2,100	$2,700
1962-1963	Rough white/wheat, 2x10"	$1,800	$2,400
1963-1964	Smooth white/gold, 2x10"	$1,800	$2,400
1964-1966	Black tolex, 2x10"	$1,500	$2,000

EC Tremolux Amp

2011-2016. Eric Clapton's variation on a '57, hand-wired, 12 watts, 1x12".

2011-2016		$1,150	$1,500

Twin Amp

1952-1963, 1996-2010. Tube, 2x12"; 15 watts, tweed wide-panel '52-'55; narrow-panel '55-'60; 50 watts '55-'57; 80 watts '58; brown tolex '60; white tolex '61-'63. Reintroduced in '96 with black tolex, spring reverb and output control for 100 watts or 25 watts.

1952-1954	Tweed, wide panel	$6,500	$8,500
1955-1957	Tweed, 50 watts	$9,500	$12,500
1958-1959	Tweed, 80 watts	$13,500	$18,000
1960	Brown tolex, 80 watts	$10,000	$13,000
1960-1962	Rough white/oxblood	$6,700	$8,700
1963	Smooth white/gold	$5,400	$7,100

'57 Twin-Amp/'57 Custom Twin-Amp

2004-2011, 2016-present. Custom Series reissue, tweed, 40 watts, 2x12". Custom added to model name in '16.

2004-2011		$1,200	$1,575
2016-2020		$1,350	$1,750

Twin Reverb Amp

1963-1982. Black tolex, 85 watts (changed to 135 watts in '81), 2x12", blackface '63-'67 and '81-'82, silverface '68-'81, blackface optional in '80-'81 and standard in '82. Large Fender combo amps built in the '70s are not often in excellent condition. Any grille stain or tear to the grille can mean an amp is not in excellent condition and can significantly reduce the values shown.

1963-1967	Blackface	$2,100	$2,700
1968	Silverface, no master vol	$1,100	$1,450
1969-1970	Silverface, no master vol	$1,050	$1,350
1971-1972	Silverface, no master vol	$700	$900
1973-1975	Silverface, master vol	$700	$900
1976-1980	Silverface, push/pull	$700	$900
1980-1982	Blackface	$700	$900

MODEL YEAR	FEATURES	EXC. COND. LOW	HIGH

Twin Reverb Solidstate Amp

1966-1969. 100 watts, 2x12", black tolex.

1966-1969 $400 $515

'65 Twin Reverb Amp

1991-present. Black tolex, 2x12", 85 watts.

1991-2020 $725 $925

'65 Twin Custom 15 Amp

2009-2017. 85 watt Twin Reverb with 1x15".

2009-2017 $800 $1,050

'68 Custom Twin Reverb Amp

2014-present. Vintage Modified silverface reissue, 1x12", 85 watts, modified all-tube circuitry.

2014-2020 $725 $925

Twin Reverb II Amp

1983-1985. Black tolex, 2x12", 105 watts, channel switching, effects loop, blackface panel, silver grille.

1983-1985 $775 $1,025

Twin "The Twin"/"Evil Twin" Amp

1987-1992. 100 watts, 2x12", red knobs, most black tolex, but white, red and snakeskin covers offered.

1987-1992 $525 $700

EC Twinolux Amp

2011-2016. Eric Clapton's variation on a '57, hand-wired, 40 watts, 2x12".

2011-2016 $2,100 $2,700

Two-Tone (Custom Shop) Amp

2001-2003. Limited production, modern styling, slanted grille, 15 watts, 1x10" and 1x12", 2-tone blond cab, based on modified Blues Deluxe circuit, Two Tone on name plate.

2001-2003 $825 $1,075

Ultimate Chorus DSP Amp

1995-2001. Solidstate, 2x65 watts, 2x12", 32 built-in effect variations, blackface cosmetics.

1995-2001 $205 $265

Ultra Chorus Amp

1992-1994. Solidstate, 2x65 watts, 2x12", standard control panel with chorus.

1992-1994 $195 $250

Vibrasonic Amp

1959-1963. First amp to receive the new brown tolex and JBL, 1x15", 25 watts.

1959-1963 $1,900 $2,500

Vibrasonic Custom Amp

1995-1997. Custom Shop designed for steel guitar and guitar, blackface, 1x15", 100 watts.

1995-1997 $650 $850

Vibrasonic Reverb Amp

1972-1981. Black tolex, 100 watts, 1x15", silverface.

1972-1981 $650 $850

Vibro-Champ Amp

1964-1982. Black tolex, 4 watts, (5 watts '69-'71, 6 watts '72-'80), 1x8", blackface '64-'68 and '82, silverface '69-'81.

1964-1967	Blackface, AA764	$1,050	$1,400
1968-1972	Silverface	$650	$850
1973-1981	Silverface	$600	$775
1982	Blackface	$600	$775

EC Vibro Champ Amp

2011-2016. Eric Clapton's variation on a '57 Champ, hand-wired, 5 watts, 1x8".

2011-2016 $675 $875

Vibro-Champ XD Amp

2008-2011. Made in China, 5 watts, 1x8.

2008-2011 $140 $180

Vibro-King Custom Amp

1993-2012. Custom Shop combo, 60 watts, 3x10", vintage reverb, tremolo, single channel, all tube, blond or black.

1993-2012 $1,325 $1,725

Vibro-King 212 Amp Cabinet

1993-2012. Custom Shop extension cab, blond tolex, 2x12" Celestion GK80.

1993-2012 $400 $525

Vibro-King Custom Limited Edition Amp

2012-2013. Limited Edition production of unique colors, Chocolate Crème Two-Tone, wheat grille (25 made) and Tequila Sunrise, 3-color sunburst on figured birdseye maple cab, oxblood grille.

2012	Chocolate Crème	$1,650	$2,150
2013	Tequila Sunrise	$2,100	$2,700

Vibrolux Amp

1956-1964. Narrow-panel, 10 watts, tweed with 1x10" '56-'61, brown tolex and brownface with 1x12" and 30 watts '61-'62, black tolex and blackface '63-'64.

1956-1961	Tweed, 1x10"	$2,700	$3,500
1961-1962	Brown tolex, 1x12"	$2,500	$3,300
1963-1964	Black tolex, 1x12"	$2,300	$3,000

Vibrolux Reverb Amp

1964-1982. Black tolex, 2x10", blackface '64-'67 and '81-'82, silverface '70-'80. Reissued in '96 with blackface and 40 watts.

1964-1967	Blackface	$2,425	$3,150
1968	Silverface	$1,650	$2,150
1969-1970	Silverface	$1,275	$1,650
1971-1980	Silverface	$950	$1,250
1981-1982	Blackface	$950	$1,250

Vibrolux Reverb Solidstate Amp

1967-1969. Fender CBS solidstate, 35 watts, 2x10", black tolex.

1967-1969 $400 $515

Vibrolux Custom Reverb Amp

1995-2013. Part of Professional Series, Custom Shop designed, standard factory built, 40 watts, 2x10", tube, white knobs, blond tolex and tan grill for '95 only, black tolex, silver grille after. Does not say Custom on face plate.

1995-2013 Various colors $700 $900

'68 Custom Vibrolux Reverb Amp

2014-2020. Silverface-style, 35 watts, 2x10", black vinyl with silver-turquoise grille.

2014-2020 $700 $900

Vibroverb Amp

1963-1964. Brown tolex with 35 watts, 2x10" and brownface '63, black tolex with 1x15" and blackface late '63-'64.

1963	Brown tolex, 2x10"	$5,500	$7,200
1963-1964	Black tolex, 1x15"	$4,000	$5,100

1959 Fender Vibrolux

Ted Wulfers

1966 Fender Vibrolux Reverb

Steve Brandt

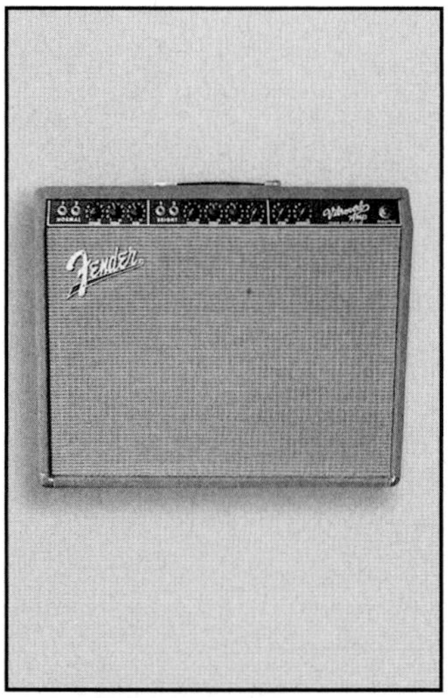

1963 Fender Vibroverb

AMPS

Fryette Aether

Fuchs ODS-II

Garnet Gnome Reverb

John Maysenhoelder

MODEL YEAR	FEATURES	EXC. COND. LOW	HIGH

'63 Vibroverb Reissue Amp

1990-1995. Reissue of 1963 Vibroverb, 40 watts, 2x10", reverb, vibrato, brown tolex.

1990-1995	$875	$1,125

'64 Vibroverb Custom Shop Amp

2003-2008. Reissue of 1964 Vibroverb with 1x15" blackface specs.

2003-2008	$1,100	$1,425

Yale Reverb Amp

1983-1985. Solidstate, black tolex, 50 watts, 1x12", silverface.

1983-1985	$285	$370

FireBelly Amps

2008-present. Production/custom, professional and premium grade, vintage tube amps built by Steven Cohen in Santa Monica, California.

Fishman

2003-present. Larry Fishman offers professional grade, production, amps that are designed and engineered in Andover, Massachusetts and assembled in China. They also build effects.

Loudbox 100 Amp

2006-2013. 100 watts, 1x8" with dome.

2006-2013	$235	$305

Loudbox Artist Pro-LBX-600 Amp

2006-present. 120 watts,

2006-2020	$250	$325

Loudbox Mini Pro-LBX-500 Amp

2006-present. 60 watts.

2006-2020	$160	$210

Loudbox Performer Pro-LBX-700 Amp

2006-present. 180 watts.

2006-2020	$325	$425

Flot-A-Tone

Ca.1946-early 1960s. Flot-A-Tone was located in Milwaukee, Wisconsin, and made a variety of tube guitar and accordion amps. Most were distrubuted by the Lo Duca Brothers.

Large Amp

1960s. Four speakers.

1960s	$525	$675

Small Amp

1960s. 1x8" speaker.

1960s	$275	$375

Fortune

1978-1979. Created by Jim Kelley just prior to branding Jim Kelley Amplifiers in 1980, Fortune Amplifiers logo on front panel, specifications and performance similar to early Jim Kelley amplifiers, difficult to find in original condition, professional grade, designed and manufactured by Active Guitar Electronics company.

Fox Amps

Marc Vos builds professional grade, production/custom, guitar amps and cabinets, starting 2007, in Budel, Netherlands.

MODEL YEAR	FEATURES	EXC. COND. LOW	HIGH

Framus

1946-1977, 1996-present. Tube guitar amp heads, combos and cabinets made in Markneukirchen, Germany. They also build guitars, basses, mandolins and banjos. Begun as an acoustic instrument manufacturer, Framus added electrics in the mid-'50s. In the '60s, Framus instruments were imported into the U.S. by Philadelphia Music Company. The brand was revived in '96 by Hans Peter Wilfer, the president of Warwick, with production in Warwick's factory in Germany. Distributed in the U.S. by Dana B. Goods.

Fred

1984-1986. Before settling on the name Bedrock, company founders Brad Jeter and Ron Pinto produced 50 amps carrying the brand name Fred in Nashua, New Hampshire.

Frenzel

1952-present. Jim Frenzel built his first amp in '52 and began using his brand in '01. He offers intermediate and professional grade, production/custom, hand-wired, vintage tube, guitar and bass amps built in Mabank, Texas.

Frudua Guitar Works

1988-present. Intermediate grade, production, guitar and bass amps built by guitar luthier Galeazzo Frudua in Calusco d'Adda, Italy. He also builds guitars and basses.

Fryette

2009-present. Professional and premium grade amps, combos, and cabinets built by Steven M. Fryette, who also founded VHT amps. At the beginning of '09 AXL guitars acquired the VHT name to build their own product. Fryette continues to manufacture the VHT amp models under the Fryette brand in Burbank, California.

Fuchs Audio Technology

2000-present. Andy Fuchs started the company in '99 to rebuild and modify tube amps. In 2000 he started production of his own brand of amps, offering combos and heads from 10 to 150 watts. They also custom build audiophile and studio tube electronics. Originally located in Bloomfield, New Jersey, since '07 in Clifton, New Jersey.

Fulton-Webb

Steve Fulton and Bill Webb build their tube amp heads, combos and cabinets in Austin, Texas, beginning 1997.

Gabriel Sound Garage

2004-2014. Gabriel Bucataru built his tube amp heads and combos in Arlington Heights, Illinois.

MODEL YEAR	FEATURES	EXC. COND. LOW	HIGH

Gallien-Krueger

1969-present. Gallien-Krueger has offered a variety of bass and guitar amps, combos and cabinets and is located in San Jose, California.

Garcia

Tube amp heads and speaker cabinets built by Matthew Garcia in Myrtle Beach, South Carolina, starting in 2004. He also built effects.

Garnet

Mid 1960s-1989. In the mid '60s, "Gar" Gillies started the Garnet Amplifier Company with his two sons, Russell and Garnet, after he started making PA systems in his Canadian radio and TV repair shop. The first PA from the new company was for Chad Allen & the Expressions (later known as The Guess Who). A wide variety of tube amps were offered and all were designed by Gar, Sr. The company also produced the all-tube effects The Herzog, H-zog, and two stand-alone reverb units designed by Gar in the late '60s and early '70s. The company closed in '89, due to financial reasons caused largely by a too rapid expansion. Gar repaired and designed custom amps up to his death in early 2007.

GDS Amplification

1998-present. Tube amps, combos and speaker cabinets from builder Graydon D. Stuckey of Fenton, Michigan. GDS also offers amp kits. In January, '09, GDS bought the assets of Guytron Amplification.

Genesis

Genesis was a 1980s line of student amps from Gibson.

B40 Amp

1984-late-1980s. Bass combo with 40 watts.

1984-1989		$100	$130

G Series Amps

1984-late-1980s. Small combo amps.

1984-1989	G10, 10w	$55	$75
1984-1989	G25, 25w	$75	$100
1984-1989	G40R, 40w, reverb	$125	$150

Genz Benz

Founded by Jeff and Cathy Genzler in 1984 and located in Scottsdale, Arizona, the company offers guitar, bass, and PA amps and speaker cabinets. In late 2003, Genz Benz was acquired by Kaman (Ovation, Hamer, Takamine). On January 1, '08, Fender acquired Kaman Music Corporation and the Genz Benz brand.

George Dennis

1991-present. Founded by George Burgerstein, original products were a line of effects pedals. In '96 they added a line of tube amps. The company is located in Prague, Czech Republic.

MODEL YEAR	FEATURES	EXC. COND. LOW	HIGH

Gerhart

2000-present. Production/custom, intermediate and professional grade, amps and cabinets from builder Gary Gerhart of West Hills, California. He also offers an amp in kit form.

Germino

2002-present. Intermediate to professional grade tube amps, combos and cabinets built by Greg Germino in Graham, North Carolina.

Gibson

1890s (1902)-present. Gibson has offered a variety of amps since the mid-'30s to the present under the Gibson brandname and others. The price ranges listed are for excellent condition, all original amps though tubes may be replaced without affecting value. Many Gibson amps have missing or broken logos. The prices listed are for amps with fully intact logos. A broken or missing logo can diminish the value of the amp. Amps with a changed handle, power cord, and especially a broken logo should be taken on a case-by-case basis.

Vintage amplifiers are rarely found in original, excellent condition. Many vintage amps have notable wear and have a non-original speaker. The prices shown are for fully original (except tubes and caps) amplifiers that are pleasing clean, and contain no significant wear, blemishes, grille stains, or damage.

Atlas IV Amp

1963-1967. Piggyback head and cab, introduced with trapezoid shape, changed to rectangular cabs in '65-'66 with black cover, simple circuit with 4 knobs, no reverb or tremolo, mid-power with 2 6L6, 1x15".

1963-1965	Brown	$475	$600
1966-1967	Black	$475	$600

Atlas Medalist Amp

1964-1967. Combo version with 1x15".

1964-1967		$450	$585

B-40 Amp

1972-1975. Solidstate, 40 watts, 1x12".

1972-1975		$210	$270

BR-1 Amp

1946-1948. 15 watts, 1x12" field-coil speaker, brown leatherette cover, rectangular metal grille with large G.

1946-1948		$585	$765

BR-3 Amp

1946. 12 watts, 1x12" Utah field-coil speaker (most BR models used Jensen speakers).

1946		$585	$765

BR-4 Amp

1946-1948. 14 watts, 1x12" Utah field-coil speaker (most BR models used Jensen speakers).

1946-1948		$500	$650

BR-6 Amp

1946-1954. 10 to 12 watts, 1x10", brown leatherette, speaker opening split by cross panel with G logo, bottom mounted chassis with single on-off volume pointer knob.

1946-1947	Verticle cab	$500	$650
1948-1954	Horizontal cab	$500	$650

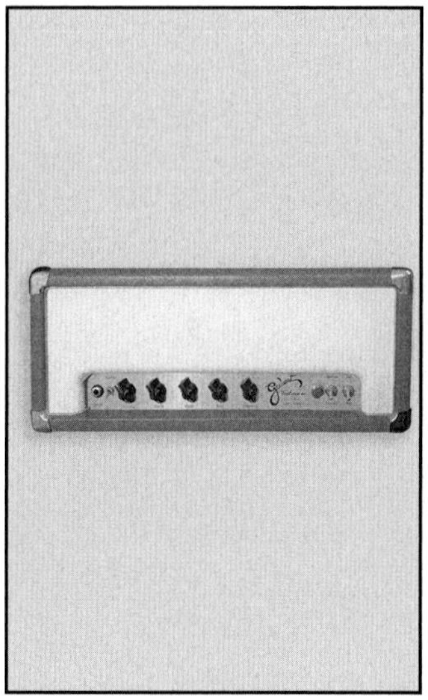

Gerhart Gilmore

Germino Club 40

1953 Gibson BR-6

AMPS

1959 Gibson GA-5

David Stuckey

Gibson GA-5 Les Paul Junior

1964 Gibeon GA-5 T Skylark

Tom Pfeifer

MODEL YEAR	FEATURES	EXC. COND. LOW	HIGH

BR-9 Amp

1948-1954. Cream leatherette, 10 watts, 1x8". Originally sold with the BR-9 lap steel. Renamed GA-9 in '54.

1948-1954		$385	$500

Duo Metalist Amp

1968-early 1970s. Upright vertical combo cab, tubes, faux wood grain panel, mid-power, 1x12".

1968-1970s		$400	$525

EH-100 Amp

1936-1942. Electric-Hawaiian companion amp, 1x10". AC/DC version called EH-110.

1936-1942		$550	$725

EH-125 Amp

1941-1942. 1x12", rounded shoulder cab, brown cover in '41 and dark green in '42, leather handle.

1941-1942		$600	$800

EH-126 Amp

1941. Experimental model, 6-volt variant of EH-125, about 5 made.

1941		$975	$1,250

EH-135 Amp

1941. Experimental model, alternating and direct current switchable, about 7 made.

1941		$1,050	$1,350

EH-150 Amp

1935-1942. Electric-Hawaiian companion amp, 1x12" ('35-'37) or 1x10" ('38-'42). AC/DC version called EH-160.

1935	13 3/4" square cab	$1,050	$1,350
1936-1937	14 3/4" square cab	$1,050	$1,350
1937-1942	15 3/8" round cab	$1,050	$1,350

EH-185 Amp

1939-1942. 1x12", tweed cover, black and orange vertical stripes, marketed as companion amp to the EH-185 Lap Steel. AC/DC version called EH-195.

1939-1942		$1,300	$1,700

EH-195 Amp

1939-1942. EH-185 variant with vibrato.

1939-1942		$1,300	$1,700

EH-250 Amp

1940. Upgraded natural maple cabinet using EH-185 chassis, only 2 made, evolved into EH-275.

1940		$1,650	$2,150

EH-275 Amp

1940-1942. Similar to EH-185 but with maple cab and celluloid binding, about 30 made.

1940-1942		$1,600	$2,075

Epoch Series

2000s. Solidstate student practice amps.

2000s	G-10	$20	$30

Falcon III F-3 Amp

Early 1970s. Solidstate, 1x12" combo, 65 watts, made in Chicago by CMI after Gibson ceased amp production in Kalamazoo ('67), black tolex, dark grille.

1970		$225	$300

Falcon Medalist (Hybrid) Amp

1967. Transitional tube 1x12" combo amp from GA-19 tube Falcon to the solidstate Falcon, Falcon logo and Gibson logo on front panel, brown control panel, dark cover and dark grille, vertical combo cabinet.

1967		$260	$340

Falcon Medalist (Solidstate) Amp

1968-1969. Solidstate combo, 15 watts, 1x12".

1968-1969		$260	$340

G-10 Amp

1972-1975. Solidstate, 10 watts, 1x10", no tremolo or reverb.

1972-1975		$90	$115

G-20 Amp

1972-1975. Solidstate with tremolo, 1x10", 10 watts.

1972-1975		$105	$135

G-25 Amp

1972-1975. 25 watts, 1x10".

1972-1975		$140	$180

G-35 Amp

1975. Solidstate, 30 watts, 1x12".

1975		$155	$200

G-40/G-40 R Amp

1972-1974. Solidstate with tremolo and reverb, 40 watts, 1x12" (G-40) and 2x10" (G-40 R).

1972-1974		$210	$275

G-50/G-50 A/G-50 B Amp

1972, 1975. Solidstate with tremolo and reverb, models G-50 and 50 A are 1x12", 40 watts, model 50 B is a bass 1x15", 50 watts.

1972-1975		$225	$295

G-55 Amp

1975. 50 watts, 1x12".

1975		$225	$295

G-60 Amp

1972-1973. Solidstate with tremolo and reverb, 1x15", 60 watts.

1972-1973		$245	$315

G-70 Amp

1972-1973. Solidstate with tremolo and reverb, 2x12", 60 watts.

1972-1973		$270	$350

G-80 Amp

1972-1973. Solidstate with tremolo and reverb, 4x10", 60 watts.

1972-1973		$310	$400

G-100 A/G-100 B Amp

1975. 100 watts, model 100 A is 2x12" and 100 B is 2x15".

1975		$310	$400

G-105 Amp

1974-1975. Solidstate, 100 watts, 2x12", reverb.

1974-1975		$310	$400

G-115 Amp

1975. 100 watts, 4x10".

1974-1975		$340	$440

GA-5 Les Paul Jr. Amp

1954-1957. Tan fabric cover (Mottled Brown by '57), 7" oval speaker, 4 watts. Renamed Skylark in '58.

1954-1957		$400	$525

GA-5 Les Paul Jr. Amp (Reissue)

2004-2008. Goldtone Series, class A, 5 watts, 1x8".

2004-2008		$260	$340

GA-5 Skylark Amp

1958-1968. Gold cover (brown by '63 and black by '66), 1x8" (1x10" from '64 on), 4.5 watts (10 watts from '64 on), tremolo. Often sold with the Skylark Lap Steel.

1958-1959	Gold, 45w, 1x8"	$365	$475

MODEL YEAR	FEATURES	EXC. COND. LOW	HIGH
1960-1962	Gold, 45w, 1x8"	$350	$450
1963	Brown, 45w, 1x8"	$325	$425
1964	Brown, 10w, 1x10"	$300	$385
1965-1967	Black, 10w, 1x10"	$270	$350
1968	Skylark, last version	$195	$250

GA-5 T Skylark Amp

1960-1968. Tremolo, 4.5 watts early, 10 later, gold covering and 1x8" until '63, brown '63-'64, black and 1x10" after.

1960-1962	Gold, 45w, 1x8"	$350	$450
1963	Brown, 45w, 1x8"	$325	$425
1964	Brown, 10w, 1x10"	$325	$425
1965-1967	Kalamazoo, black, 10w, 1x10"	$270	$350
1968	Norlin, vertical cab, 10w, 1x10, tubes	$195	$250

GA-5 W Amp

Late-1960s. Norlin-era, post-Kalamazoo production, 15 watts, small speaker, volume and tone controls.

1969		$70	$90

GA-6 Amp

1956-1959. Replaced the BR-6, 8 to 12 watts, 1x12", has Gibson 6 above the grille. Renamed GA-6 Lancer in '60.

1956-1959		$560	$725

GA-6 Lancer Amp

1960-1961. Renamed from GA-6, 1x12", tweed cover, 3 knobs, 14 watts.

1960-1961		$650	$850

GA-7 Les Paul TV Model Amp

1954-1956. Basic old style GA-5 with different graphics, 4 watts, small speaker.

1954-1956		$385	$500

GA-8 Discoverer Amp

1962-1964. Renamed from GA-8 Gibsonette, gold fabric cover, 1x12", 10 watts.

1962-1964		$385	$500

GA-8 Gibsonette Amp

1955-1962. Tan fabric cover (gold by '58), 1x10", 8 watts (9 watts by '58). See Gibsonette for 1952-'54. Name changed to GA-8 Discoverer in '62.

1955-1957	Gibsonette logo, square hole	$425	$550
1958-1959	Gibson logo	$375	$500
1960-1962	Gibson logo, tweed	$375	$500

GA-8 T Discoverer Amp

1960-1966. Gold fabric cover, 1x10", 9 watts (tan cover, 1x12" and 15 watts by '63), tremolo.

1960-1962	Tweed, 9w, 1x10"	$400	$525
1963-1964	Brown, 15w, 1x12"	$350	$450
1965-1966	Black, 15w, 1x12"	$325	$425

GA-9 Amp

1954-1959. Renamed from BR-9, tan fabric cover, 8 watts, 1x10". Often sold with the BR-9 Lap Steel.

1954-1957	Gibson 9 logo	$500	$650
1958-1959	Tweed, 6V6s	$500	$650

GA-14 Titan Amp

1959-1961. About 15 watts using 2x6V6 power tubes, 1x10", tweed cover.

1959-1961		$550	$700

MODEL YEAR	FEATURES	EXC. COND. LOW	HIGH

GA-15 RV Goldtone Amp

1999-2004. 15 watts, Class A, 1x12", spring reverb.

1999-2004		$425	$550

GA-15 RVT Explorer Amp

1965-1967. Tube, 1x10", tremolo, reverb, black vinyl.

1965-1967		$325	$425

GA-17 RVT Scout Amp

1963-1967. Low power, 1x10", reverb and tremolo.

1963	Smooth brown	$425	$550
1964-1965	Textured brown	$425	$550
1966-1967	Black	$325	$425

GA-18 Explorer Amp

1959. Tweed, tube, 14 watts, 1x10". Replaced in '60 by the GA-18 T Explorer.

1959		$700	$900

GA-18 T Explorer Amp

1960-1963. Tweed, 14 watts, 1x10", tremolo.

1960-1962	Tweed	$725	$950
1963	Brown	$500	$650

GA-19 RVT Falcon Amp

1961-1967. One of Gibson's best selling amps. Initially tweed covered, followed by smooth brown, textured brown, and black. Each amp has a different tone. One 12" Jensen with deep-sounding reverb and tremolo.

1961-1962	Tweed, 6V6	$975	$1,250
1962-1963	Smooth brown	$550	$725
1964	Textured brown	$500	$650
1965-1967	Black	$375	$500

GA-20 Amp

1950-1962. Brown leatherette (2-tone by '55 and tweed by '60), tube, 12 watts early, 14 watts later, 1x12". Renamed Crest in '60.

1950-1954	Brown, single G logo on front	$575	$750
1955-1958	2-tone salt/maroon	$775	$1,000
1959	2-tone blue/blond	$775	$1,000

GA-20 Crest Amp

1960-1961. Tweed, tube, 14 watts, 1x12".

1960-1961		$800	$1,050

GA-20 RVT Amp

2004-2007. 15 watts, 1x12", reverb, tremolo.

2004-2007		$560	$725

GA-20 RVT Minuteman Amp

1965-1967. Black, 14 watts, 1x12", tube, reverb, tremolo.

1965-1967		$375	$475

GA-20 T Amp

1956-1959. Tube, 16 watts, tremolo, 1x12", 2-tone. Renamed Ranger in '60.

1956-1958	2-tone	$775	$1,000
1959	New 2-tone	$775	$1,000

GA-20 T Ranger Amp

1960-1961. Tube, 16 watts, tremolo, 1x12", tweed.

1960-1962	Tweed	$850	$1,100

GA-25 Amp

1947-1948. Brown, 1x12" and 1x8", 15 watts. Replaced by GA-30 in '48.

1947-1948		$900	$1,175

1960 Gibson GA-8 T Discoverer

David Stuckey

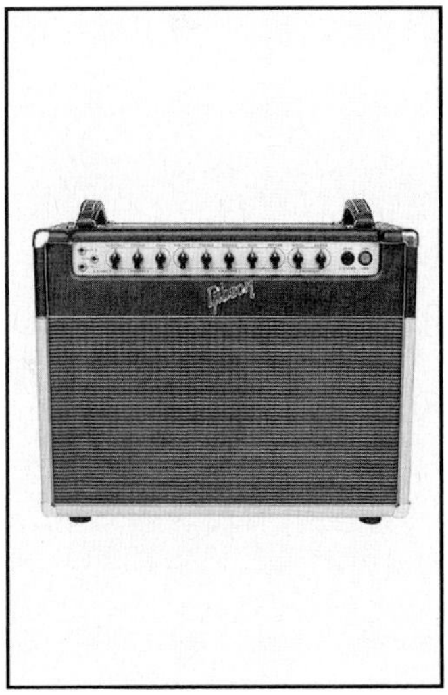

Gibson GA-20 RVT

1958 Gibson GA-9

Imaged by Heritage Auctions, HA.com

AMPS

1952 Gibson GA-40 Les Paul
Ted Wulfers

2008 Gibson GA-42 RVT

1954 Gibson GA-50 T
Imaged by Heritage Auctions, HA.com

MODEL YEAR	FEATURES	EXC. COND. LOW	HIGH

GA-25 RVT Hawk Amp
1963-1968. Reverb, tremolo, 1x15".

1963	Smooth brown	$575	$750
1964	Rough brown	$425	$550
1965-1967	Black	$400	$525
1968	Last version	$345	$445

GA-30 Amp (Invader)
1948-1961. Brown until '54, 2-tone after, tweed in '60, 1x12" and 1x8", 14 watts. Renamed GA-30 Invader in '60.

1948-1954	Brown	$875	$1,150
1955-1959	2-tone salt/maroon	$875	$1,150
1960-1961	Invader, tweed	$875	$1,150

GA-30 RV Invader Amp
1961. Tweed, 1x12" and 1x8", 14-16 watts, reverb but no tremolo.

1961		$1,000	$1,300

GA-30 RVH Goldtone Amp Head
1999-2004. 30 watts, Class A head, reverb.

1999-2004		$700	$925

GA-30 RVS (Stereo) Goldtone Amp
1999-2004. 15 watts per channel, Class A stereo, 2x12", reverb.

1999-2004		$850	$1,100

GA-30 RVT Invader Amp
1962-1967. Updated model with reverb and tremolo, 25 watts, 1x12" and 1x10" speakers, first issue in tweed.

1962	Tweed	$1,125	$1,475
1963	Smooth brown	$650	$850
1964	Rough brown	$500	$650
1965-1967	Black	$425	$550

GA-35 RVT Lancer Amp
1966-1967. Black, 1x12", tremolo, reverb.

1966-1967		$425	$575

GA-40 Les Paul Amp
1952-1960. Introduced with the Les Paul Model guitar, 1x12" Jensen speaker, 14 watts early and 16 later, recessed leather handle using spring mounting (the handle is easily broken and replacement handle is more common than not). Two-tone leatherette covering, '50s checkerboard grille ('52-early-'55), Les Paul script logo on front of the amp ('52-'55), plastic grille insert with LP monogram, gold Gibson logo above grille. Cosmetics changed dramatically in early/mid-'55. Renamed GA-40 T Les Paul in '60.

1952-1955	Brown 2-tone, LP grille	$1,400	$1,800
1955-1957	2-tone salt/maroon	$1,350	$1,750
1958-1959	2-tone blue/blond	$1,350	$1,750

GA-40 RVT Limited Edition Amp
2008-2011. GA-40RVT Limited Edition logo, 200 made, 2-tone brown/tan, front control panel, 30/15 switchable watts.

2008-2011		$475	$625

GA-40 T Les Paul Amp
1960-1962. Renamed from GA-40 Les Paul, 1x12", 16 watts, tremolo. Renamed Mariner in '62-'67.

1960-1961	Tweed	$1,775	$2,300
1962	Smooth brown	$475	$625

GA-40 T Mariner Amp
1962-1967. 1x12" combo, 25 watts, tremolo.

1962-1963	Smooth brown	$475	$625
1964	Rough brown	$365	$475
1965-1967	Black	$350	$450

GA-45 RVT Saturn Amp
1965-1967. 2x10", mid power, tremolo, reverb.

1965-1967		$425	$550

GA-50/GA-50 T Amp
1948-1955. Brown leatherette, 25 watts, 1x12" and 1x8", T had tremolo.

1948-1955	GA-50	$1,450	$1,900
1948-1955	GA-50 T	$1,550	$2,000

GA-55 RVT Ranger Amp
1965-1967. Black cover, 4x10", tremolo, reverb.

1965-1967		$450	$585

GA-55/GA-55 V Amp
1954-1958. 2x12", 20 watts, GA-55 V with vibrato.

1954-1958	GA-55	$2,600	$3,400
1954-1958	GA-55 V	$2,600	$3,400

GA-60 Hercules Amp
1962-1963. 25 watts, 1x15, no-frills 1-channel amp, no reverb, no tremolo.

1962-1963		$500	$650

GA-60 RV Goldtone Amp
1999-2004. 60 watts, A/B circuit, 2x12", spring reverb, earliest production in England.

1999-2004		$850	$1,100

GA-70 Country and Western Amp
1955-1958. 25 watts, 1x15", 2-tone, longhorn cattle western logo on front, advertised to have extra bright sound.

1955-1958		$2,600	$3,400

GA-75 Amp
1950-1955. Mottled Brown leatherette, 1x15", 25 watts.

1950-1955		$1,250	$1,625

GA-75 L Recording Amp
1964-1967. 1x15" Lansing speaker, no reverb or tremolo, 2 channels, dark cover, gray grille.

1964-1967		$460	$600

GA-75 Recording Amp
1964-1967. 2x10" speakers, no reverb or tremolo, 2 channels, dark cover, gray grille.

1964-1967		$480	$625

GA-77 Amp
1954-1959. 1x15" JBL, 25-30 watts, 2x6L6 power tubes, 2-tone covering, near top-of-the-line for the mid-'50s.

1954-1958	2-tone salt/maroon, leather handle	$1,225	$1,600
1958-1959	2-tone blue/blond, metal handle	$1,225	$1,600

GA-77 RET Vanguard Amp
1964-1967. Mid-power, 2x10", tremolo, reverb, echo.

1964	Rough brown	$610	$790
1965-1967	Black	$450	$575

GA-77 RETL Vanguard Amp
1964-1967. GA-77 RET with 1x15" Lansing speaker option (L).

1964-1967		$560	$725

MODEL YEAR	FEATURES	EXC. COND. LOW	HIGH

GA-77 RVTL Vanguard Amp
1962-1967. 50 watts, 1x15", Lansing speaker option (L), tremolo, reverb, smooth brown.

1962-1967		$560	$725

GA-77 Vanguard Amp
1960-1961. 1x15" JBL, 25-30 watts, 2 6L6 power tubes, tweed cover, first use of Vanguard model name.

1960-1961		$1,200	$1,575

GA-78 Bell Stereo Amp
1960. Gibson-branded amp made by Bell, same as GA-79 series, Bell 30 logo on front, 30 watts, 2x10" wedge cab.

1960		$1,600	$2,100

GA-79 RV Amp
1960-1962. Stereo-reverb, 2x10", 30 watts.

1960-1961	Tweed	$1,900	$2,500
1962	Textured brown	$1,700	$2,250

GA-79 RVT Multi-Stereo Amp
1961-1967. Introduced as GA-79 RVT, Multi-Stereo was added to name in '61. Stereo-reverb and tremolo, 2x10", tweed (black and brown also available), 30 watts.

1961	Tweed	$1,900	$2,500
1961-1962	Gray sparkle	$1,700	$2,250
1963-1965	Textured brown	$1,700	$2,250
1965-1967	Black	$1,600	$2,100

GA-80/GA-80 T/Vari-Tone Amp
1959-1961. 25 watts, 1x15", 2 channels, described as "6-in-1 amplifier with improved tremolo," 6 Vari-Tone pushbottons which give "six distinctively separate sounds," 7 tubes, tweed cover.

1959-1961		$1,325	$1,725

GA-83 S Stereo-Vibe Amp
1959-1961. Interesting stereo amp with front baffle mounted 1x12" and 4x8" side-mounted speakers (2 on each side), 35 watts, Gibson logo on upper right corner of the grille, tweed cover, brown grille (late '50s Fender-style), 3 pointer knobs and 3 round knobs, 4 inputs.

1959-1961		$1,975	$2,550

GA-85 Bass Reflex Amp
1957-1958. Removable head, 25 watts, 1x12", very limited production.

1957-1958		$980	$1,275

GA-86 Ensemble Amp
1960. 25 watt head plus 1x12" cab, tweed.

1960		$1,325	$1,725

GA-88S Stereo Twin Amp
1960. Control panel and 2 separate 1x12" speaker cabs, 35 watts, 8 tubes, tweed.

1960		$2,900	$3,800

GA-90 High Fidelity Amp
1953-1960. 25 watts, 6x8", 2 channels, advertised for guitar, bass, accordion, or hi-fi.

1953-1960		$1,125	$1,450

GA-95 RVT Apollo Amp
1965-1967. 90 watts, 2x12", black vinyl, black grille, tremolo, reverb.

1965-1967		$500	$650

GA-100 Bass Amp
1960-1963. 35 watts, 1x12" cabinet, for '60-'61 tweed and tripod included for separate head, for '62-'63 brown covering and Crestline Tuck-A-Way head.

1960-1961	Tweed	$1,000	$1,300
1962-1963	Smooth brown	$575	$750

GA-200 Rhythm King Amp
1957-1961. Introduced as GA-200, renamed Rhythm King in '60, 2-channel version of GA-400. Bass amp, 60 watts, 2x12".

1957-1959	2-tone	$1,600	$2,100
1959-1961	Tweed	$1,600	$2,100
1961	Smooth brown	$1,500	$2,000

GA-300 RVT Super 300 Amp
1962-1963. 60 watts, 2x12" combo, reverb, tremolo, smooth brown.

1962-1963		$1,475	$1,900

GA-400 Super 400 Amp
1956-1961. 60 watts, 2x12", 3 channels, same size as GA-200 cab, 1 more tube than GA-200.

1956-1959	2-tone	$1,800	$2,300
1959-1961	Tweed	$1,800	$2,300
1961	Smooth brown	$1,700	$2,200

GA-CB Custom-Built Amp
1949-1953. 25-30 watts, 1x15", the top model in Gibson's '51 line of amps, described as having sound quality found only in the finest public address broadcasting systems, about 47 made, this high-end amp was replaced by the GA-77 and a completely different GA-90.

1949-1953		$1,500	$2,000

Gibsonette Amp
1952-1954. Gibsonette logo on front, round hole. See GA-8 Gibsonette for later models.

1952-1954		$425	$550

GM05 Amp
2009-2012. Small 5 watt solidstate amp usually sold with Maestro guitar pack.

2009-2012		$20	$35

GSS-50 Amp
1966-1967. Solidstate, 50 watts, 2x10" combo, reverb and tremolo, black vinyl cover, silver grille, no grille logo.

1966-1967		$310	$400

GSS-100 Amp
1966-1967, 1970. Solidstate, 100 watts, two 24"x12" 2x10" sealed cabs, black vinyl cover, silver grille, 8 black knobs and 3 red knobs, slanted raised Gibson logo. Speakers prone to distortion. Reissued in '70 in 3 variations.

1966-1967		$310	$400

Lancer Amp
1968-1969. CMI-Chicago produced, small combo, black upright cab, dark grille, post-McCarty era Gibson logo.

1968-1969		$60	$80

LP-1/LP-2 Amp Set
1970. Les Paul model, piggyback amp and cab set, LP-1 head and LP-2 4x12" plus 2 horns cab, large vertical speaker cabinet, rather small compact 190 watt solidstate amp head.

1970		$310	$400

1955 Gibson GA-55 V
Joey Abella

1964 Gibson GA-77 RET Vanguard
Rick Buckendahl

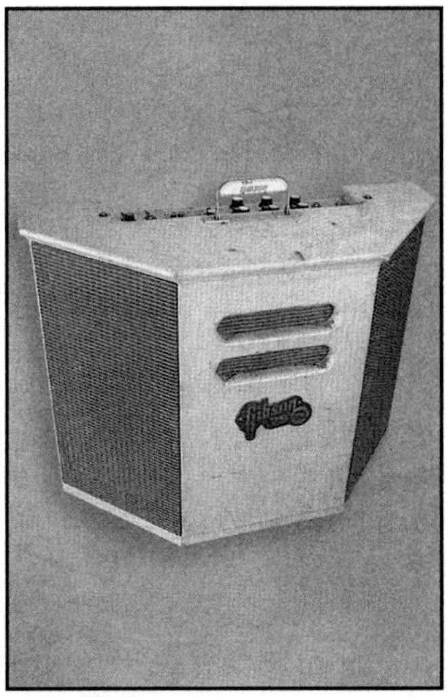
1961 Gibson GA-79 RV

Late-1960s Gibson Plus-50

Imaged by Heritage Auctions, HA.com

Green Electric

1947 Gretsch Electromatic

Imaged by Heritage Auctions, HA.com

MODEL YEAR	FEATURES	EXC. COND. LOW	HIGH

Medalist 2/12 Amp

1968-1970. Vertical cabinet, 2x12", reverb and temolo.

1968-1970		$365	$475

Medalist 4/10 Amp

1968-1970. Vertical cabinet, 4x10", reverb and tremolo.

1968-1970		$365	$475

Mercury I Amp

1963-1965. Piggyback trapezoid-shaped head with 2x12" trapezoid cabinet, tremolo, brown.

1963-1965		$430	$560

Mercury II Amp

1963-1967. Mercury I with 1x15" and 1x10", initially trapezoid cabinets then changed to rectangular.

1963-1964	Brown trapezoid cabs	$500	$650
1965-1967	Black rectangular cabs	$430	$560

Plus-50 Amp

1966-1967. 50 watts, powered extension amplifier. Similar to GSS-100 cabinet of the same era, 2x10" cab, black vinyl cover, silver grille, slant Gibson logo.

1966-1967		$400	$520

Super Thor Bass Amp

1970-1974. Solidstate, part of the new G-Series (not GA-Series), 65 watts, 2x15", black tolex, black grille, upright vertical cab with front control, single channel.

1970-1974		$330	$430

Thor Bass Amp

1970-1974. Solidstate, smaller 2x10" 50 watt version of Super Thor.

1970-1974		$295	$385

Titan I Amp

1963-1965. Piggyback trapezoid-shaped head and 2x12" trapezoid-shaped cabinet, tremolo.

1963-1965		$430	$560

Titan III Amp

1963-1967. Piggyback trapezoid-shaped head and 1x15" + 2x10" trapezoid-shaped cabinet, tremolo.

1963-1964	Brown	$470	$610
1965-1967	Black	$470	$610

Titan Medalist Amp

1964-1967. Combo version of Titan Series with 1x15" and 1x10", tremolo only, no reverb, black.

1964-1967		$485	$630

Titan V Amp

1963-1967. Piggyback trapezoid-shaped tube head and 2x15" trapezoid-shaped cabinet, tremolo.

1963-1964	Brown	$485	$630
1965-1967	Black	$485	$630

TR-1000 T/TR-1000 RVT Starfire Amp

1962-1967. Solidstate, 1x12" combo, 40 watts, tremolo, RVT with reverb.

1962-1967		$260	$340

Ginelle

Rick Emery builds his tube combo amps in Ardmore, Pennsylvania starting in 1996.

MODEL YEAR	FEATURES	EXC. COND. LOW	HIGH

Giulietti

1962-1965. The Giulietti Accordion Company, New York, offered guitars and amps in the '60s. The amps were made by Magnatone and the models and model numbers are often similar to the Magnatone model.

Pearloid Lap Steel Amp

1962. Small student level, 1x12", 2-channel, tremolo.

1962		$175	$225

S 1x12" Combo Amp

1962. Tremolo, 2-channel.

1962		$800	$1,050

S-9 Amp (Magnatone 460)

1962. 35 watts, 2x12 plus 2 tweeters, true vibrato combo, black sparkle.

1962		$1,150	$1,500

Gjika Amplification

1980-present. Premium and presentation grade tube amp heads and cabinets built by Robert Gjika in Escondido, California.

Gnome Amplifiers

2008-present. Dan Munro builds professional grade, production, guitar amps and cabinets in Olympia, Washington. He also builds effects.

Gomez Amplification

2005-2015. Tube combo amps built by Dario G. Gomez in Rancho Santa Margarita, California.

Goodsell

2004-present. Tube head and combo amps built by Richard Goodsell in Atlanta, Georgia.

Gorilla

1980s-2009. Small solidstate entry-level amps, distributed by Pignose, Las Vegas, Nevada.

Compact Practice Student Amp

1980s-2009. Solidstate, 10 to 30 watts, compact design.

1980s-2009		$20	$50

Goya

1955-1996. Goya was mainly known for acoustics, but offered a few amps in the '60s. The brand was purchased by Avnet/Guild in '66 and by Martin in the late '70s.

Grammatico Amps

2009-present. Production/custom, professional and premium grade, hand-wired, guitar and bass amps built by John Grammatico in Austin, Texas.

Green

1993-present. Amp model line made in England by Matamp (see that brand for listing), bright green covering, large Green logo on the front.

Greer Amplification

1999-present. Tube guitar amps and speaker cabinets built by Nick Greer in Athens, Georgia. He also builds effects.

MODEL YEAR	FEATURES	EXC. COND. LOW	HIGH

Gregory

1950s-1960s. Private branded amps sold via music wholesalers, by late '60s solidstate models made by Harmony including the 007, C.I.A., Mark Six, Mark Eight, Saturn 80, most models were combo amps with Gregory logo.

Solidstate Amp

1960s	Various models	$125	$300

Gretsch

1883-present. In '05, Gretsch again starting offering amps after previously selling them from the 1950s to '73. Initially private branded for them by Valco (look for the Valco oval or rectangular serialized label on the back). Early-'50s amps were covered in the requisite tweed, but evolved into the Gretsch charcoal gray covering. The mid-'50s to early-'60s amps were part of the Electromatic group of amps. The mid-'50s to '62 amps often sported wrap-around and slanted grilles. In '62, the more traditional box style was introduced. In '66, the large amps went piggyback. Baldwin-Gretsch began to phase out amps effective '65, but solidstate amps continued being offered for a period of time. The '73 Gretsch product line only offered Sonax amps, made in Canada and Sho-Bud amps made in the U.S. In '05, they introduced a line of tube combo amps made in U.S. by Victoria Amp Company.

Artist Amp

1946. Early post-war Gretsch amp made before Valco began to make their amps. Appears to be made by Operadio Mfg. Co., St. Charles, Illinois. Low power small combo amp, Gretsch Artist script logo on grille, round speaker baffle hole.

1946		$250	$325

Broadkaster Mini Lead 50 Amp

Late 1960s. Solidstate compact verticle combo amp.

1969		$200	$275

Carousel Amp

1960s. Solidstate,1x10" and 1x3" speakers, tremolo speed and depth knobs, brown cover.

1960s		$550	$725

Electromatic Amp

1947-1949. Valco-made with era-typical styling, 3 slat speaker baffle openings, leather handle, two-tone leatherette, 3 tubes with small speaker, single volume knob.

1947-1949		$600	$800

Electromatic Artist Amp (6155)

1950s. Small amp, 2x6V6 power, 1x10", volume and tone knobs.

1950s		$525	$675

Electromatic Deluxe Amp (6163)

1950s. 1x12", 2x6L6, brown tweed grille. Also offered in Western Finish.

1950s		$775	$1,025

Model 6150 Compact Amp

Late-1950s-1960s. Early amps in tweed, '60s amps in gray covering, no tremolo, single volume knob, no treble or bass knob, 1x8".

1950s	Brown tweed	$425	$550
1960s	Gray	$425	$550

Model 6151 Electromatic Standard/ Compact Tremolo Amp

Late-1940s-late-1960s. 1x8", various covers.

1940s-60s		$425	$550

Model 6152 Compact Tremolo Reverb Amp

Ca.1964-late-1960s. Five watts, 11"x6" elliptical speaker early on, 1x12" later.

1964-1969		$575	$800

Model 6153T White Princess Amp

1962. Compact combo, 6x9" oval speaker, higher priced than the typical small amp because it is relatively rare and associated with the White Princess guitar - making it valuable in a set, condition is very important, an amp with any issues will be worth much less.

1962		$825	$1,075

Model 6154 Super-Bass Amp

Early-1960s-mid-1960s. Gray covering, 2x12", 70 watts, tube.

1960s		$675	$875

Model 6156 Playboy Amp

Early-1950s-1966. Tube amp, 17 watts, 1x10" until '61 when converted to 1x12", tweed, then gray, then finally black covered.

1950s-1960	Tweed, 1x10"	$600	$775
1961-1962	Tweed, 1x12"	$600	$775
1963-1966	Black or gray, 1x12"	$600	$775

Model 6157 Super Bass (Piggyback) Amp

Mid-late-1960s. 35 watts, 2x15" cabinet, single channel.

1960s		$500	$650

Model 6159 Dual Bass Amp

Mid-late-1960s. 35 watts, tube, 2x12" cabinet, dual channel, black covering. Replaced by 6163 Chet Atkins Piggyback Amp.

1965		$650	$850

Model 6160 Chet Atkins Country Gentleman Amp

Early-late-1960s. Combo tube amp, 35 watts, 2x12" cabinet, 2 channels. Replaced by 6163 Chet Atkins Piggyback amp with tremolo but no reverb.

1960s		$675	$875

Model 6161 Dual Twin Tremolo Amp

Ca.1962-late-1960s. 19 watts (later 17 watts), 2x10" with 5" tweeter, tremolo.

1962-1967		$700	$900

Model 6161 Electromatic Twin Amp

Ca.1953-ca.1960. Gray Silverflake covering, two 11x6" speakers, 14 watts, tremolo, wraparound grille '55 and after.

1953-1960		$775	$1,025

Model 6162 Dual Twin Tremolo/Reverb Amp

Ca.1964-late-1960s. 17 watts, 2x10", reverb, tremolo. Vertical combo amp style introduced in '68.

1964-1967	Horizontal	$700	$900
1968-1969	Vertical	$600	$800

Model 6163 Chet Atkins (Piggyback) Amp

Mid-late-1960s. 70 watts, 1x12" and 1x15", black covering, tremolo, reverb.

1960s		$600	$775

Gretsch 6156 Playboy

Late-'50s Gretsch 6161

Imaged by Heritage Auctions, HA.com

1969 Gretsch Model 6162 Dual Twin Tremolo/Reverb

Rivington Guitars

Gries 5

Ca. 1958 Guild Masteramp Two-Tone

Imaged by Heritage Auctions, HA.com

Guild Thunder 1 (T1-RVT)

Greg Gagliono

MODEL YEAR	FEATURES	EXC. COND. LOW	HIGH

Model 6163 Executive Amp

1959. 1x15, gray cover.

1959 $1,250 $1,625

Model 6164 Variety Amp

Early-mid-1960s. 35 watts, tube, 2x12".

1960s $700 $900

Model 6165 Variety Plus Amp

Early-mid-1960s. Tube amp, 35 watts, 2x12", reverb and tremolo, separate controls for both channels.

1960s $725 $950

Model 6166 Fury (Combo) Amp

Mid-1960s. Tube combo stereo amp, 70 watts, 2x12", separate controls for both channels, large metal handle, reverb.

1960s $725 $950

Model 6169 Electromatic Twin Western Finish Amp

Ca.1953-ca.1960. Western finish, 14 watts, 2-11x6" speakers, tremolo, wraparound grill '55 and after.

1953-1960 $4,900 $6,300

Model 6169 Fury (Piggyback) Amp

Late-1960s. Tube amp, 70 watts, 2x12", separate controls for both channels.

1960s $725 $950

Model 6170 Pro Bass Amp

1966-late-1960s. 25 or 35 watts, depending on model, 1x15", vertical cabinet style (vs. box cabinet).

1966-1969 $600 $775

Model 7154 Nashville Amp

Introduced in 1969. Solidstate combo amp, 4' tall, 75 watts, 2x15", reverb, tremolo, magic echo.

1969-1970s $425 $550

Model 7155 Tornado PA System Amp

Introduced in 1969. Solidstate piggyback head and cab, 150 watts, 2 column speaker cabs, reverb, tremolo, magic echo.

1969-1970s 2x2x15" $375 $500

1969-1970s 2x4x15" $450 $575

Model 7517 Rogue Amp

1970s. Solidstate, 40 watts, 2x12", tall vertical cabinet, front control panel.

1970s $175 $250

Model G6156 Playboy Amp

2005-2007. 15 watts, 1x12" combo amp with retro Gretsch styling, made by Victoria.

2005-2007 $1,000 $1,275

Model G6163 Executive Amp

2005-2007. Boutique quality made by Victoria for FMIC Gretsch, 20 watts, 1x15", cabinet Uses to the modern retro early '60s Supro Supreme modified-triangle front grille pattern, maroon baffle with white grille, tremolo and reverb.

2005-2007 $1,000 $1,275

Rex Royal Amp Model M-197-3V

1950s. Small student compact amp, low power, 1x8", Rex Royal logo on grille, Fred Gretsch logo on back panel, single on-off volume knob.

1951 $350 $450

Gries

2004-present. Dave Gries builds his intermediate and professional grade, production/custom, amps and cabinets in Mattapoisett, Massachusetts.

MODEL YEAR	FEATURES	EXC. COND. LOW	HIGH

Groove Tubes

1979-present. Started by Aspen Pittman in his garage in Sylmar, California, Groove Tubes is now located in San Fernando. GT manufactures and distributes a full line of tubes. In '86 they added amp production and in '91 tube microphones. Aspen is also the author of the Tube Amp Book. The Groove Tubes brand was purchased by Fender in June, '08.

Guild

1952-present. Guild offered amps from the '60s into the '80s. Some of the early models were built by Hagstrom.

Double Twin Amp

1953-1955. 35 watts, 2x12" plus 2 tweeters, 2-tone leatherette covered cab.

1953-1955 $800 $1,050

G-1000 Stereo Amp

1992-1994. Stereo acoustic combo amp with cushioned seat on top, 4x6 and 1x10 speakers.

1992-1994 $525 $700

Master Amp

Ca. 1957- Ca. 1959. Combo 2x6L6 power, tremolo, 2-tone tweed and leatherette.

1957-1959 $450 $575

Maverick Amp

Late-1960s-early-1970s. Dual speaker combo, 6 tubes, verticle cab, tremolo, reverb, red/pink control panel, 2-tone black and silver grille.

1960s-70s $375 $500

Model One Amp

Mid-1970s-1977. Solidstate 1x12" vertical cab combo, 30 watts, reverb and tremolo.

1970s $150 $200

Model Two Amp

Mid-1970s-1977. Solidstate 2x10" vertical cab combo, 50 watts, reverb and tremolo.

1977-1978 $200 $275

Model Three Amp

Mid-1970s-1977. Solidstate 1x15" vertical cab bass combo, 60 watts, organ and guitar.

1977-1978 $175 $225

Model Four Amp

Early-1980s. Solidstate, 6 watts.

1980s $75 $125

Model Five Amp

Early-1980s. Solidstate, 10 watts, 6.25" speaker.

1980s $100 $150

Model Six Amp

Early-1980s. Same as Model Five but with reverb.

1980s $175 $225

Model Seven Amp

Early-1980s. Solidstate, 12 watts, small amp for guitar, bass and keyboard.

1980s $175 $225

Model 50-J Amp

Early-1960s. 14 watts, 1x12", tremolo, blue/gray vinyl.

1962-1963 $525 $700

Model 66 Amp

1953-1955. 15 watts, 1x12", tremolo, 2-tone leatherette.

1953-1955 $525 $700

MODEL YEAR	FEATURES	EXC. COND. LOW	HIGH

Model 66-J Amp

1962-1963. 20 watts, 1x12", tremolo, blue/gray vinyl.

1962-1963		$525	$700

Model 98-RT Amp

1962-1963. The only stand-alone reverb amp from Guild in the early '60s, 30 watts, 1x12", blue/gray vinyl.

1962-1963		$650	$850

Model 99 Amp

1953-1955. 30 watts, 1x12", tremolo, 2-tone leatherette.

1953-1955		$500	$675

Model 99-J Amp

Early-1960s. 30 watts, 1x12", tremolo, blue/gray vinyl.

1962-1963		$500	$675

Model 99-U Ultra Amp

Early-1960s. Piggyback 30-watt head with optional 1x12" or 1x15" cab, cab and head lock together, tremolo, blue/gray vinyl.

1962-1963		$525	$700

Model 100-J Amp

Early-1960s. 35 watts, 1x15", blue/gray vinyl.

1962-1963		$525	$700

Model 200-S Stereo Combo Amp

Early-1960s. 25 watts per channel, total 50 watts stereo, 2x12", tremolo, blue/gray vinyl, wheat grille.

1962-1963		$725	$975

Model RC-30 Reverb Converter Amp

Early-1960s. Similar to Gibson GA-1 converter, attaches with 2 wires clipped to originating amp's speaker, 8 watts, 1x10", blue/gray vinyl.

1962-1963		$525	$700

Superbird Amp

1968. Piggyback tube amp with 2x12 cab.

1968		$600	$800

SuperStar Amp

Ca.1972-ca.1974. 50 watts, all tubes, 1x15" Jensen speakers, vertical combo, reverb, tremolo, black vinyl cover, 2-tone black/silver grille.

1972-1974		$425	$575

Thunder 1 Amp

1965-1972. Combo with single speaker, no reverb, light tan cover, 2-tone tan grille.

1965-1972	1x10"	$300	$400
1965-1972	1x12"	$325	$425

Thunder 1 (Model T1-RVT)/T1 Amp

1965-1972. Combo with dual speakers and reverb, light tan cover, 2-tone tan grille.

1965-1972		$525	$700

ThunderBass Amp

1965-1972. Piggyback combo, 2x15".

1965-1972	100 watt	$525	$700
1965-1972	200 watt	$550	$725

ThunderBird Amp

1965-1972. 50 watts, tube, 2x12", reverb, tremolo, with or without TD-1 dolly, black vinyl, black/silver grille.

1965-1972		$525	$700

ThunderStar Bass Amp

1965-1972. Piggyback bass tube head or combo, 50 watts.

1965-1972	Full stack, 2x1x15"	$600	$800
1965-1972	Half stack, 1x1x15"	$525	$700

ThunderStar Guitar Amp

1965-1972 Combo, 50 watts, 1x12"

1965-1972		$525	$700

Guyatone

1933-present. Started offering amps by at least the late '40s with their Guya lap steels. In '51 the Guyatone brand is first used on guitars and most likely amps. Guyatone also made the Marco Polo, Winston, Kingston, Kent, LaFayette and Bradford brands.

Guytron

1995-present. Tube amp heads and speaker cabinets built by Guy Hedrick in Columbiaville, Michigan. In January, '09, GDS Amplification bought the assets of Guytron Amplification.

Hagstrom

1921-1983, 2004-present. The Swedish guitar maker built a variety of tube and solidstate amps from ca. 1961 into the '70s. They also supplied amps to Guild.

Hanburt

1940-ca. 1950. Harvey M. Hansen built electric Hawaiian guitars in Seattle, Washington, some sold as a set with a small amp. The wooden amps have a large HB in the speaker cutout. He also built at least one mandolin.

Harmony

1892-1976, late-1970s-present. Harmony was one of the biggest producers of guitars, and offered amps as well. MBT International offered Harmony amps for 2000-'02.

H Series Amps

1940s-1960s. Harmony model numbers begin with H, such as H-304, all H series models shown are tube amps unless otherwise noted as solidstate.

1940-1950s	H-190/H-191	$375	$475
1940-1950s	H-200	$375	$475
1950s	H-204, 18w, 1x12"	$375	$475
1960s	H-303A, 8w, 1x8"	$200	$250
1960s	H-304, low pwr, small spkr	$200	$250
1960s	H-305A, low pwr, small spkr	$200	$250
1960s	H-306A, combo 1x12"	$300	$375
1960s	H306C, piggyback 2x12"	$350	$450
1960s	H-400, 8w, 1x8", vol	$175	$225
1960s	H-400A, 8w, 1x8", vol/tone	$200	$255
1960s	H-410A, 10w, 1x10"	$350	$450
1960s	H-415, 18w, 2x12"	$450	$600
1960s	H-420, 20w, 1x15	$375	$500
1960s	H-430, 30w, 2x10"	$450	$600
1960s	H-440, 2x12", trem/verb	$500	$650
1960s	H-512, solidstate, large	$525	$675

Guytron GT100 F/V

Ca. 1963 Harmony H-303A

Rivington Guitars

1965 Harmony H400A

Imaged by Heritage Auctions, HA.com

AMPS

Headstrong Lil' King

Headstrong Santa Cruz 20

Henriksen JazzAmp

MODEL YEAR	FEATURES	EXC. COND. LOW	HIGH

Solidstate Amps

1970s. Dark covering, dark grille.

1970s	Large amp	$175	$650
1970s	Small amp	$25	$50

Harry Joyce

1993-2011, 2015-present. Hand-wired British tube amps, combos, and cabinets from builder/designer Harry Joyce. Joyce was contracted to build Hiwatt amps in England during the '70s. Joyce died in 2002, and the brand was carried on by Charles Bertonazzi and George Scholz until 2011. Brand brought back by Kevin Wood and Scholz through Harry Joyce USA with new versions of the classic models.

Hartke

1984-present. Guitar and bass amps, combos and cabinets made in the U.S. Founded by Larry Hartke, since the mid-'80s, Hartke has been distributed by Samson Technologies. Hartke also offered basses in the past.

Haynes

Haynes guitar amps were built by the Amplifier Corporation of America (ACA) of Westbury, New York. ACA also made an early distortion device powered by batteries. Unicord purchased the company in around 1964, and used the factory to produce its Univox line of amps, most likely discontinuing the Haynes brand at the same time.

Jazz King II Amp

1960s. Solidstate, stereo console-style, 2x12", Haynes logo upper left side.

1960s		$300	$400

Headstrong

2003-present. Tube combo amps and cabinets built by Wayne Jones in Asheville, North Carolina.

Henriksen JazzAmp

2006-present. Professional grade, production, solidstate amps voiced for jazz guitar built by Peter Henriksen in Golden, Colorado.

Heritage

Founded in 2004 by Malcolm MacDonald and Lane Zastrow who was formerly involved with Holland amps. Located in the former Holland facility in Brentwood, Tennessee, they built tube combo and piggyback amps.

Hilgen

1960s. Mid-level amplifiers from Hilgen Manufacturing, Hillside, New Jersey. Dark tolex covering and swiggle-lined light color grille cloth. Examples have been found with original Jensen speakers.

Basso B-2501 Amp

1960s. 25 watts, 1x15" combo, swirl grille, Hilgen crest logo, compact size.

1965		$350	$450

MODEL YEAR	FEATURES	EXC. COND. LOW	HIGH

Basso B-2502 Amp

1960s. 25 watts, 1x15" combo, swirl grille, Hilgen crest logo, large cab.

1965		$375	$500

Basso Grande B-2503 Amp

1960s. Brown sparkle cover, piggyback, 2x12".

1965		$500	$650

Basso Profondo B-2502 Amp

1965. Combo 1x15".

1965		$375	$500

Champion R-2523 Amp

Mid-1960s. Highest offering in their amp line, piggyback with 2x12" cab, tremolo, reverb, swirl grille cloth.

1965		$500	$650

Galaxie T-2513 Amp

1960s. 25 watts, 2x12" piggyback cab, tremolo.

1965		$500	$650

Metero T-2511 Amp

Mid-1960s. Compact 1x12" combo, tremolo.

1965		$375	$500

Pacesetter R-2521 Amp

Mid-1960s. 1x12" combo, tremolo, reverb, swirl grille cloth.

1965		$375	$500

Star T-2512 Amp

1960s. 25 watts, 1x12" combo, tremolo.

1965		$375	$500

Troubadour T-1506 Amp

Mid-1960s. Small practice amp.

1965		$275	$350

Victor R-2522 Amp

Mid-1960s. 1x12" combo, larger cab, reverb, tremolo.

1965		$500	$650

HiWatt

1963-1984, ca.1990-present. Amp builder Dave Reeves started his Hylight Electronics in a garage in England in the early 1960s, doing amp and other electronic repairs. By 1964 he had produced the first amps bearing the Hiwatt brand. By the early '70s, Hiwatt's reputation was growing and production was moved to a factory in Kingston-upon-Thames, expanding the amp line and adding PA gear. In '81, Reeves suffered a fatal fall, and ownership of Hiwatt was taken over by Biacrown Ltd, a company made up of Hiwatt employees. Biacrown struggled and closed up in '84. From ca.1990 to ca.1994, a line of American-made Hiwatts, designed by Frank Levi, were available. By the mid-'90s, amps with the Hiwatt brand were again being built in England and, separately, imported from Asia by Fernandes.

Bass 100 Amp Head

1980s	100w, England	$1,300	$1,700

Bulldog SA112 Amp

1980s, 1994-2019. 50 watts, combo, 1x12".

1980s		$1,200	$1,575
1994-2020		$1,100	$1,475

Bulldog SA112FL Amp

1980s-1990s. 100 watts, combo, 1x12".

1980s		$1,200	$1,575
1990s		$1,100	$1,475

AMPS

MODEL YEAR	FEATURES	EXC. COND. LOW	HIGH

Custom 100 Amp Head

2007	100w	$1,300	$1,700

DR-103 Custom 100 Amp Head

1970-late-1980s, 2005-present. Tube head, 100 watts, custom Hiwatt 100 logo on front.

1970-1980s		$2,100	$2,700

DR-201 Hiwatt 200 Amp Head

1970s. 200-watt amp head, Hiwatt 200 logo on front.

1970s		$2,100	$2,700

DR-405 Hiwatt 400 Amp Head

1970s. 400-watt amp head.

1970s		$2,100	$2,700

DR-504 Custom 50 Amp Head

1970-late-1980s, 1995-1999. Tube head, 50 watts.

1970-1980s		$2,100	$2,700

Lead 20 (SG-20) Amp Head

1980s. Tube amp head, 30 watts, black cover, rectangular HiWatt plate logo.

1980s		$575	$750

Lead 50R Combo Amp

1980s. Combo tube amp, 50 watts, 1x12", reverb, dark cover, dark grille, HiWatt rectangular plate logo.

1980s		$825	$1,100

OL-103 Lead 100 Amp Head

1982	100w, England	$1,200	$1,575

PW-50 Tube Amp

1989-1993. Stereo tube amp, 50 watts per channel.

1989-1993		$825	$1,075

S50L Amp Head

1989-1993. Lead guitar head, 50 watts, gain, master volume, EQ.

1989-1993		$725	$950

SA 112 Combo Amp

1970s	50w, 1x12"	$2,500	$3,250

SA 212 Combo Amp

1970s	50w, 2x12"	$2,700	$3,500

SA 412 Combo Amp

1970s	50w, 4x12"	$3,300	$4,350

SE 2150 Speaker Cabinet

1970s	2x15" vertical	$1,750	$2,300

SE 4121 Speaker Cabinet

1970s	4x12", half stack	$1,825	$2,425

SE 4122 (Lead) Speaker Cabinet

1971- mid-1980s. 4x12", Fane speakers, 300 watts.

1971-1980s	4x12", half stack	$1,825	$2,425

SE 4123 (Bass) Speaker Cabinet

1970s. Bass version of SE, often used with DR103 head, straight-front cab and stackable, black tolex with gray grille, Hiwatt logo plate in center of grille.

1970s		$1,825	$2,425

SE 4129 (Bass) Speaker Cabinet

1970s. SE series for bass, 4x12", often used with DR 201 head.

1970s		$1,825	$2,425

SE 4151 Speaker Cabinet

1970s. SE series with 4x15".

1970s		$1,825	$2,425

Hoagland

Professional grade, production, guitar amps built by Dan Hoagland in Land O Lakes, Florida starting in 2008.

Hoffman

1993-present. Tube amps, combos, reverb units, and cabinets built by Doug Hoffman from 1993 to '99, in Sarasota, Florida. Hoffman no longer builds amps, concentrating on selling tube amp building supplies, and since 2001 has been located in Pisgah Forest, North Carolina.

Hoffmann

1983-present. Tube amp heads for guitar and other musical instruments built by Kim Hoffmann in Hawthorne, California.

Hohner

1857-present. Matthias Hohner, a clockmaker in Trossingen, Germany, founded Hohner in 1857, making harmonicas. Hohner has been offering guitars and amps at least since the early '70s.

Panther Series Amps

1980s. Smaller combo amps, master volume, gain, EQ.

1980s	P-12, 12w	$65	$90
1980s	P-20, 20w	$70	$95
1980s	P-25R, 25w	$70	$95
1980s	PBK-20, 25w	$75	$100

Sound Producer Series Amps

1980s. Master volume, normal and overdrive, reverb, headphone jack.

1980s	BA 130 bass	$75	$100
1980s	SP 35	$75	$100
1980s	SP 55	$75	$100
1980s	SP 75	$95	$125

Holland

1992-2004. Tube combo amps from builder Mike Holland, originally in Virginia Beach, Virginia, and since 2000 in Brentwood, Tennessee. In 2000, Holland took Lane Zastrow as a partner, forming L&M Amplifiers to build the Holland line. The company closed in '04.

Holmes

1970-late 1980s. Founded by Harrison Holmes. Holmes amplifiers were manufactured in Mississippi and their product line included guitar and bass amps, PA systems, and mixing boards. In the early '80s, Harrsion Holmes sold the company to On-Site Music which called the firm The Holmes Corp. Products manufactured by Harrison have an all-caps HOLMES logo and the serial number plate says The Holmes Company.

Performer PB-115 Bass Amp

60 watts, 1x15", black tolex.

1982		$100	$140

Pro Compact 210S Amp

60 watts, 2x10", 2 channels, active EQ, black tolex.

1982		$100	$140

HiWatt Bulldog SA112

1977 HiWatt DR-505 Head
Imaged by Heritage Auctions, HA.com

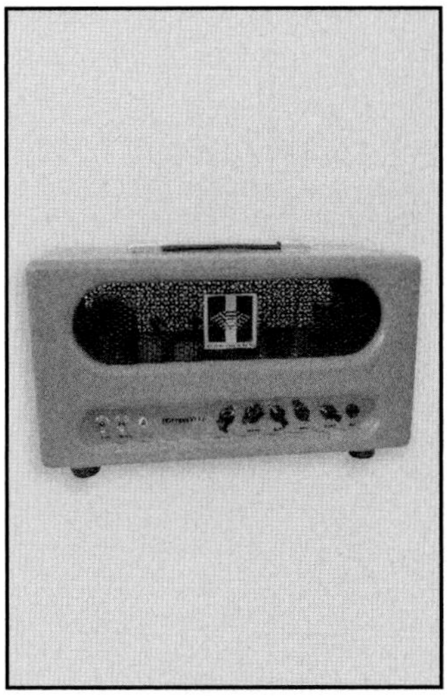
Hoffmann 15

Hottie Super Chef

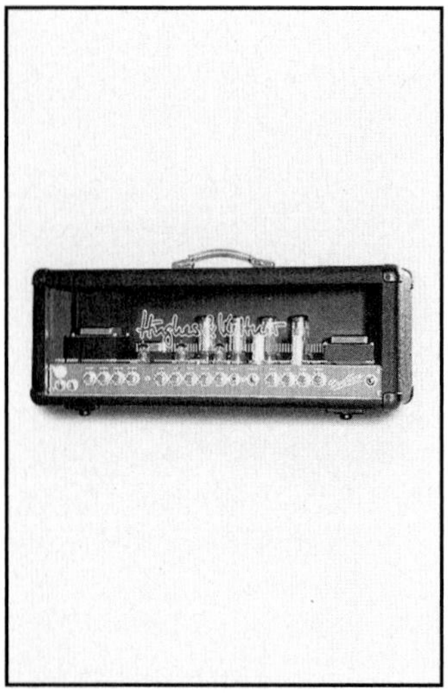

Hughes & Kettner Duotone

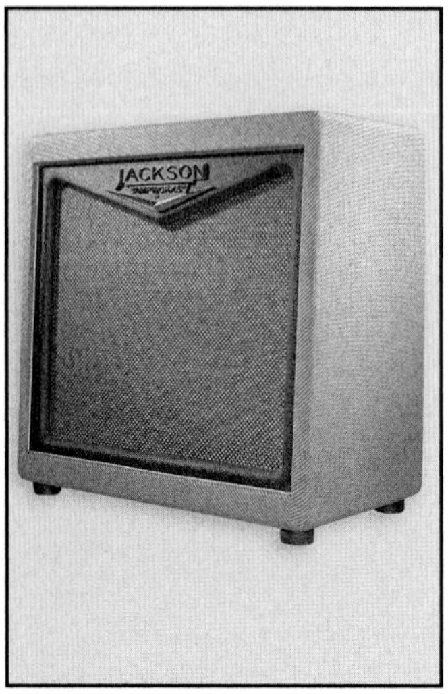

Jackson Ampworks The McFly

MODEL YEAR	FEATURES	EXC. COND. LOW	HIGH

Pro Compact 212S Amp

2x12" version of Pro.

1982		$130	$170

Rebel RB-112 Bass Amp

35 watts, 1x12", black tolex.

1982		$80	$105

Hondo

1969-1987, 1991-2005. Hondo has offered imported amps over the years. 1990s models ranged from the H20 Practice Amp to the H160SRC with 160 watts (peak) and 2x10" speakers.

Amps

1970s-1990s. Various models.

1970s-90s	Mid-size	$40	$70
1970s-90s	Small	$20	$30

Hottie

Jean-Claude Escudie and Mike Bernards build their budget and intermediate grade, production/custom, solid state "toaster" amps in Portland, Oregon, starting in 2005. They also offered guitars in '09.

Hound Dog

1994-1998. Founded by George Alessandro as the Hound Dog Corporation. Name was changed to Alessandro in 1998 (see that brand for more information).

Hughes & Kettner

1985-present. Hughes & Kettner offers a line of solidstate and tube guitar and bass amps, combos, cabinets and effects, all made in Germany.

Humphrey

2010-present. Custom, professional and premium grade, tube amps built in Chanhassen, Minnesota by Gerry Humphrey. He also builds preamps and reverb units.

Hurricane

Tube guitar and harmonica combo amps built by Gary Drouin in Sarasota, Florida. Drouin started the company in 1998 with harp master Rock Bottom, who died in September, 2001.

Hy Lo

1960s-1970s. Budget grade, small compact amps made in Japan, Hy Lo logo on grille.

Ibanez

1932-present. Ibanez added solidstate amps to their product line in '98. They also build guitars, basses and effects.

Idol

Late-1960s. Made in Japan. Dark tolex cover, dark grille, Hobby Series with large Idol logo on front.

Hobby Series Amps

1968	Hobby 10	$80	$110
1968	Hobby 100	$165	$225
1968	Hobby 20	$95	$125
1968	Hobby 45	$150	$200

Impact

1963-early 1970s. Based in London, England, tube amps made by Don Mackrill and Laurie Naiff for Pan Musical Instrument Company and their music stores. About a dozen different models of combos, piggyback half-stacks and PAs were offered.

Imperial

Ca.1963-ca.1970. The Imperial Accordion Company of Chicago, Illinois offered one or two imported small amps in the '60s.

Jack Daniel's

2004-2017. Tube guitar amp built by Peavey for the Jack Daniel Distillery, offered until about '10. They offered guitars until '17.

Jackson

1980-present. The Jackson-Charvel Company offered budget to intermediate grade amps and cabinets in the late '80s and the '90s.

Jackson Ampworks

2001-present. Brad Jackson builds his tube amp heads and speaker cabinets in Bedford, Texas.

Jackson-Guldan

1920s-1960s. The Jackson-Guldan Violin Company, of Columbus, Ohio, offered lap steels and small tube amps early on. They also built acoustic guitars.

Jay Turser

1997-present. Smaller, inexpensive imported solidstate guitar and bass amps. They also offer basses and guitars.

JCA Circuits

Tube guitar combo amps built by Jason C. Arthur in Pottstown, Pennsylvania, starting in 1995.

Jennings

Late 1960s. Tom Jennings formed another company after resigning from Vox. Large block letter Jennings logo on front panel, Jennings Amplifier logo on back control plate with model number and serial number.

Jet City Amplification

2009-present. Budget to professional grade, production/custom, guitar amps and cabinets designed in Seattle, Washington by Doug White, Dan Gallagher, Michael Soldano and built in Asia.

Jim Kelley

1979-1985. Channel-switching tube amps, compact combos and heads, hardwood cabinets available, made by Jim Kelley at his Active Guitar Electronics in Tustin, California. He produced about 100 amps a year. In 1978 and early '79 he produced a few amps under the Fortune brand name for Fortune Guitars.

MODEL YEAR	FEATURES	EXC. COND. LOW	HIGH

JMI (Jennings Musical Industries)

2004-present. Jennings built the Vox amps of the 1960s. They are back with tube amp heads and cabinets based on some of their classic models.

Johnson

Mid-1990s-present. Line of solidstate amps imported by Music Link, Brisbane, California. Johnson also offers guitars, basses, mandolins and effects.

Johnson Amplification

Starting in 1997, intermediate and professional grade, production, modeling amps and effects designed by John Johnson, of Sandy, Utah. The company is part of Harman International. In 2002, they quit building amps, but continue the effects line.

JoMama

1994-present. Tube amps and combos under the JoMama and Kelemen brands built by Joe Kelemen in Santa Fe, New Mexico.

Jordan

1966-early 1970s. Jordan Electronics, of Alhambra, California, built a range of electronics, including, starting around 1966, solid state guitar amps and effects.

Juke

1989-present. Tube guitar and harmonica amps built by G.R. Croteau in Troy, New Hampshire. He also built the Warbler line of amps.

Kafel

Jack Kafel built his tube amp heads in Chicago, Illinois, starting in 2004.

Kalamazoo

1933-1942, 1965-1970. Kalamazoo was a brand Gibson used on one of their budget lines. They used the name on amps from '65 to '67.

Bass Amp

1965-1967. Enclosed back, 2x10", flip-out control panel, not a commonly found model as compared to numerous Model 1 and 2 student amps.

1965-1967		$500	$650

Bass 30 Amp

Late 1960s-early 1970s. Tube combo, verticle cabinet, 2x10".

1970		$375	$500

KEA Amp

1948-1952. Small compact amp, round speaker baffle grille, slant Kalamazoo logo on front, oxblood leatherette.

1948-1952		$400	$525

Lap Steel Amp

1940s. Kalamazoo logo on front lower right, low power with 1-6V6, round speaker grille opening, red/brown leatherette.

1940s		$350	$450

MODEL YEAR	FEATURES	EXC. COND. LOW	HIGH

Model 1 Amp

1965-1967. No tremolo, 1x10", front control panel, black.

1965-1967		$250	$325

Model 2 Amp

1965-1967. Same as Model 1 with tremolo, black.

1965-1967	Black panel	$325	$425
1967	Silver panel	$200	$250

Model 3 Amp

Late 1960s-early 1970s. Made by CMI Electronics in Chicago, post Gibson Kalamazoo era, student compact solidstate combo, Kalamazoo 3 logo on front panel, Kalamazoo Model 3 logo on label on speaker magnet.

1960s-70s		$90	$115

Model 4 Amp

Late 1960s-early 1970s. Made by CMI Electronics in Chicago, post Gibson Kalamazoo era, student compact solidstate combo, 3 control knobs, tone, tremolo, volume, Kalamazoo 4 logo on front panel, Kalamazoo Model 4 logo on label on speaker magnet.

1960s-70s		$90	$115

Reverb 12 Amp

1965-1967. Black vinyl cover, 1x12", reverb, tremolo.

1965-1967		$500	$650

Kay

Ca.1931-present. Kay originally offered amps up to around '68 when the brand changed hands. Currently they offer a couple small solidstate imported amps. They also make basses, guitars, banjos, mandolins, ukes, and violins.

K506 Vibrato 12" Amp

1960s. 12 watts, 1x12", swirl grille, metal handle.

1960s		$375	$500

K507 Twin Ten Special Amp

1960s. 20 watts, 2x10", swirl grille, metal handle.

1960s		$425	$550

K700 Series Amp

Introduced in 1965. Value Leader/Vanguard/Galazie models, transistorized amps promoted as eliminates tube-changing annoyance and reliable performance, combo amps with tapered cabinets, rear slant control panel, rich brown and tan vinyl cover, brown grille cloth.

1965	700, 1x8"	$100	$150
1965	703, 1x8"	$100	$150
1965	704, 1x8"	$100	$150
1965	705, 1x10"	$125	$175
1965	706, 1x15"	$125	$175
1965	707, 1x12"	$125	$175
1965	708, 1x12"	$125	$175
1965	720 bass, 1x15"	$125	$175
1966	760, 1x12"	$125	$175

Model 703 Amp

1962-1964. Tube student amp, small speaker, 3 tubes, 1 volume, 1 tone, 2-tone white front with brown back cabinet, metal handle, model number noted on back panel, Kay logo and model number badge lower front right.

1962-1964		$200	$275

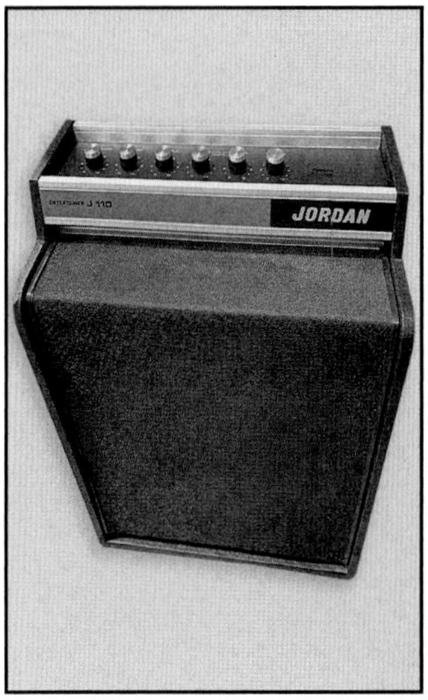

1969 Jordan Entertainer J 110
Rivington Guitars

Kafel S150 Head

1963 Kalamazoo Bass 30
Rivington Guitars

Kelemen JoMama OverDrive

2019 Kendrick Double Trouble 2x10" Combo Amp

Kingsley ToneBaron

Model 803 Amp

1962-1964. Student amp, 1x8", 3 tubes, 1 volume, 1 tone, metal handle, 14.75x11.75x6.75" cabinet with dark gray cover.

MODEL YEAR	FEATURES	EXC. COND. LOW	HIGH
1962-1964		$200	$275

Model 805 Amp

1965. Solidstate, 35 watts, 1x10", 4 control knobs, 2-tone cabinet.

MODEL YEAR	FEATURES	EXC. COND. LOW	HIGH
1965		$115	$155

Small Tube Amp

MODEL YEAR	FEATURES	EXC. COND. LOW	HIGH
1940s	Wood cabinet	$275	$375
1950s	Various models	$275	$375
1960s	Models K503, K504, K505	$325	$425

Kelemen

1994-present. Tube amps and combos under the JoMama and Kelemen brands built by Joe Kelemen in Santa Fe, New Mexico.

Kendrick

1989-present. Founded by Gerald Weber in Austin, Texas and currently located in Kempner, Texas. Mainly known for their intermediate to professional grade, tube amps, Kendrick also offers guitars, speakers, and effects.

Kent

Ca.1962-1969. Imported budget line of guitars and amps.

Guitar and Bass Amps

1960s. Various models.

MODEL YEAR	FEATURES	EXC. COND. LOW	HIGH
1966	1475, 3 tubes, brown	$55	$80
1966	2198, 3 tubes, brown	$55	$80
1966	5999, 3 tubes, brown	$75	$110
1966	6104, piggyback, 12w	$115	$155
1969	6610, solidstate, small	$35	$50

Kiesel

See Guitar section.

King Amplification

Tube combo amps, head and cabinets built by Val King in San Jose, California startin in 2005.

Kingsley

1998-present. Production/custom, professional grade, tube amps and cabinets built by Simon Jarrett in Vancouver, British Columbia.

Kingston

1958-1967. Economy solidstate amps imported by Westheimer Importing, Chicago, Illinois.

Cat Series Amp

Mid-1960s. Solidstate Cat Series amps have dark vinyl, dark grilles.

MODEL YEAR	FEATURES	EXC. COND. LOW	HIGH
1960s	P-1 3w, P-2 5w	$50	$75
1960s	P-3 8w, P-8T 20w	$55	$80

Cougar BA-21 Bass Piggyback Amp

Mid-1960s. Solidstate, 60 watts, 2x12" cab, dark vinyl, light silver grille.

MODEL YEAR	FEATURES	EXC. COND. LOW	HIGH
1960s		$110	$160

Cougar PB-5 Bass Combo Amp

Mid-1960s. Solidstate, 15 watts, 1x8".

MODEL YEAR	FEATURES	EXC. COND. LOW	HIGH
1960s		$55	$90

Lion 2000 Piggyback Amp

Mid-1960s. Solidstate, 90 watts, 2x12" cab.

MODEL YEAR	FEATURES	EXC. COND. LOW	HIGH
1960s		$140	$190

Lion 3000 Piggyback Amp

Mid-1960s. Solidstate, 250 watts, 4x12" cab.

MODEL YEAR	FEATURES	EXC. COND. LOW	HIGH
1960s		$175	$225

Lion AP-281 R Piggyback Amp

Mid-1960s. Solidstate, 30 watts, 2x8" cab, dark vinyl cover, light silver grille.

MODEL YEAR	FEATURES	EXC. COND. LOW	HIGH
1960s		$100	$150

Lion AP-281 R10 Piggyback Amp

Mid-1960s. Solidstate, 30 watts, 2x10" cab.

MODEL YEAR	FEATURES	EXC. COND. LOW	HIGH
1960s		$125	$175

Kinsman

2012-present. Budget and intermediate grade, production, guitar amps and cabinets built in China and distributed worldwide by John Hornby Skewes & Co. Ltd. in England. They also use the brand on a line of guitar effects.

Kitchen-Marshall

1965-1966. Private branded for Kitchen Music by Marshall, primarily PA units with block logos. Limited production.

JTM 45 MKII 45-Watt Amp Head

1965-1966. Private branded for Kitchen Music, JTM 45 Marshall with Kitchen logo plate, 45 watts.

MODEL YEAR	FEATURES	EXC. COND. LOW	HIGH
1965-1966		$5,500	$7,200

Slant 4x12 1960 Cabinet

1965-1966. Slant front 4x12" 1960-style cab with gray bluesbreaker grille, very limited production.

MODEL YEAR	FEATURES	EXC. COND. LOW	HIGH
1965-1966	Black on green vinyl	$3,300	$4,400

KJL

1995-present. Founded by Kenny Lannes, MSEE, a professor of Electrical Engineering at the University of New Orleans. KJL makes budget to intermediate grade, tube combo amps, heads and an ABY box.

KMD (Kaman)

1986-ca.1990. Distributed by Kaman (Ovation, Hamer, etc.) in the late '80s, KMD offered a variety of amps and effects.

Koch

All-tube combo amps, heads, effects and cabinets built in The Netherlands.

Komet

1999-present. Intermediate to professional grade, tube amp heads built in Baton Rouge, Louisanna, by Holger Notzel and Michael Kennedy with circuits designed by Ken Fischer of Trainwreck fame. They also build a power attenuator.

Kona Guitar Company

2001-present. Budget solidstate amps made in Asia. They also offer guitars, basses, mandolins, ukes and banjos.

Krank

1996-2013, 2015-2020. Founded by Tony Krank and offering tube amp heads, combos and speaker cabinets built in Tempe, Arizona. They also built effects.

Kustom

1965-present. Kustom, a division of Hanser Holdings, offers guitar and bass combo amps and PA equipment. Founded by Bud Ross in Chanute, Kansas, who offered tuck-and-roll amps as early as '58, but began using the Kustom brand name in '65. From '69 to '75 Ross gradually sold interest in the company (in the late '70s, Ross introduced the line of Ross effects stomp boxes). The brand changed hands a few times, and by the mid-'80s it was no longer in use. In '89 Kustom was in bankruptcy court and was purchased by Hanser Holdings Incorporated of Cincinnati, Ohio (Davitt & Hanser) and by '94, they had a new line of amps available.

Prices are for excellent condition amps with no tears in the tuck-and-roll cover and no grille tears. A tear in the tuck-and-roll will reduce the value, sometimes significantly.

Kustom model identification can be frustrating as they used series numbers, catalog numbers (the numbers in the catalogs and price lists), and model numbers (the number often found next to the serial number on the amp's back panel). Most of the discussion that follows is by series number (100, 200, 300, etc.) and catalog number. Unfortunately, vintage amp dealers use the serial number and model number, so the best way is to cross-check speaker and amplifier attributes. Model numbers were used primarily for repair purposes and were found in the repair manuals. In many, but not all cases, the model number is the last digit of the catalog number; for example the catalog lists a 100 series Model 1-15J-1, where the last digit 1 signifies a Model 1 amplifier chassis which is a basic amp without reverb or tremolo. A Model 1-15J-2 signifies a Model 2 amp chassis that has reverb and tremolo. In this example, Kustom uses a different model number on the back of the amp head. For the 1-15J-2, the model number on the back panel of the amp head would be K100-2, indicating a series 100 (50 watts) amp with reverb and tremolo (amp chassis Model 2).

Model numbers relate to the amplifier's schematic and electronics, while catalog numbers describe the amp's relative power rating and speaker configuration.

Amp Chasis Model Numbers ('68-'72)

Model 1 Amp (basic)
Model 2 Amp with reverb
Model 3 Amp with Harmonic Clip and Boost
Model 4 Amp with reverb, tremolo, vibrato, Harmonic Clip and Selective Boost
Model 5 PA with reverb
Model 6 Amp (basic) with Selectone
Model 7 Amp with reverb, tremolo, vibrato, boost (different parts)
Model 8 Amp with reverb, tremolo, vibrato, boost (different parts)

Naugahyde Tuck-&-Roll 200 ('65-'67)

The very first Kustoms did not have the model series on the front control panel. The early logo stipulated Kustom by Ross, Inc. The name was then updated to Kustom Electronics, Inc. 1965-'67 amp heads have a high profile/tall "forehead" area (the area on top of the controls) and these have been nicknamed "Frankenstein models." The '65-'67 catalog numbers were often 4 or 5 digits, for example J695. The first digit represents the speaker type (J = Jensen, etc.), other examples are L995, L1195, L795RV, etc. Some '67 catalog numbers changed to 2 digits followed by 3 digits, like 4-D 140f, or 3-15C (3 CTS speakers), etc. Others sported 5 characters like 4-15J-1, where 4 = 4 speakers, 15 = 15" speakers, J = Jensen, and 1 = basic amp chassis with no effects. The fifth digit indicated amp chassis model number as described above.

Naugahyde Tuck-&-Roll 100/200/400 ('68-'71)

Starting in '68, the Kustom logo also included the model series. A K100, for example, would have 100 displayed below the Kustom name. The model series generally is twice the relative output wattage, for example, the 100 Series is a 50-watt amp. Keep in mind, solidstate ratings are often higher than tube-amp ratings, so use the ratings as relative measurements. Most '68-'70 Kustom catalog numbers are x-xxx-x, for example 1-15L-1. First digit represents the number of speakers, the 2nd and 3rd represent the speaker size, the fourth represents the speaker type (A = Altec Lansing, L = J.B.L., J = Jensen, C = C.T.S. Bass), the fifth digit represents the amp chassis number. The power units were interchangeable in production, so amps could have similar front-ends but different power units (more power and different effect options) and visa versa. Some '68 bass amp catalog numbers were 4 digits, for example 2-12C, meaning two 12" CTS speakers. Again, there were several different numbers used. Kustom also introduced the 200 and 400 amp series and the logo included the series number. The catalog numbers were similar to the 100 series, but they had a higher power rating of 100 equivalent watts (200 series), or 200 equivalent watts (400 series). Kustom U.S. Naugahyde (tuck-&-roll) covers came in 7 colors: black (the most common), Cascade (blue/green), silver (white-silver), gold (light gold), red, blue, and Charcoal (gray). The

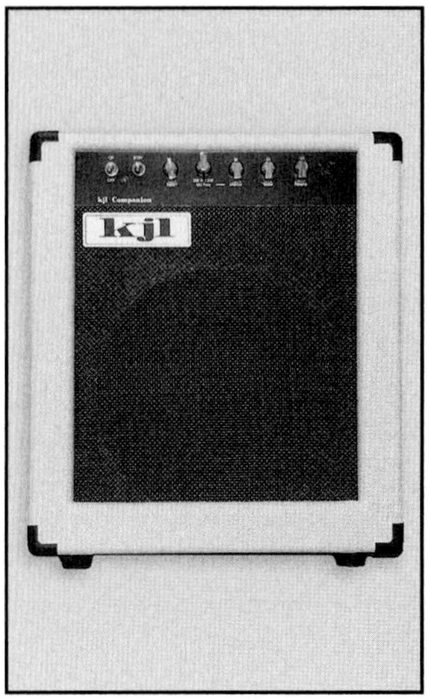

KJL Companion

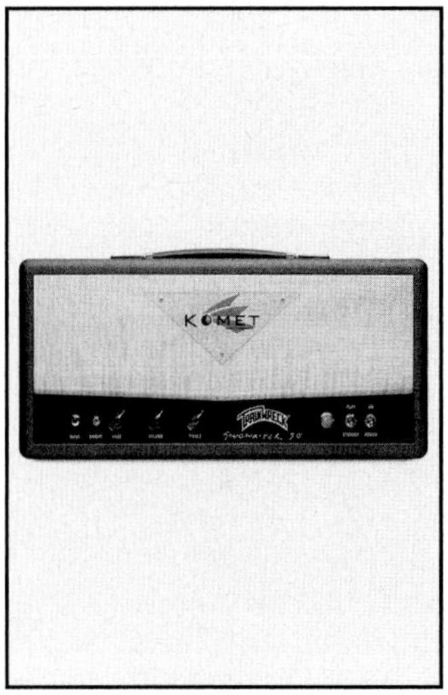

Komet Songwriter 30

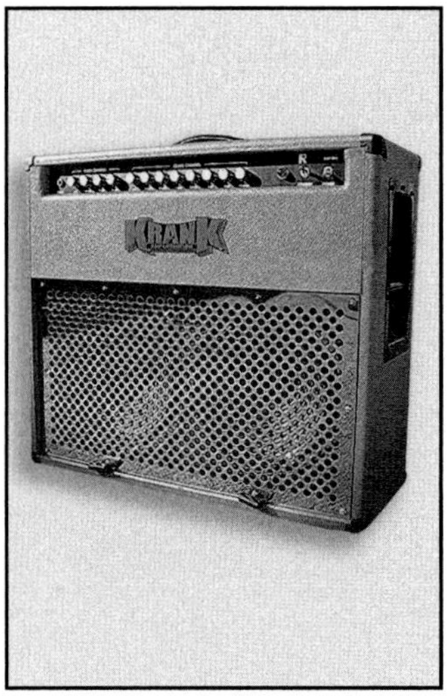

Krank 10 Watt Combo

1970s Kustom Hustler

Imaged by Heritage Auctions, HA.com

1971 Kustom K100 Head and Matching Cabinet

Bob Calla

Kustom K150C

Randy Bacus

market historically shows color options fetching more. The market has not noticeably distinguished power and features options. Condition and color seem to be the most important. Gold and Cascade may be the rarest seen colors.

Naugahyde Tuck-&-Roll 150/250/300/500/600 (c.'71-c.'75)

The amp heads changed with a slightly slanted control panel and the Kustom logo moved to the right/upper-right portion of the front panel. They continued to be tuck-&-roll offered in the same variety of colors. The sales literature indicated a 150 series had 150 watts, 250 had 250 watts, etc.

Naugahyde Tuck-&-Roll SC (Self Contained) Series

Most SC combo amps were rated at 150 watts, with the 1-12SC listed at 50 watts. They were offered in 7 colors of tuck-and-roll. Again the model numbers indicate the features as follows: 4-10 SC is a 4 x 10", 2-10 SC is a 2x10", etc.

Super Sound Tuck-and-Roll Combo Series

The last tuck-and-roll combo amps with slightly smaller tucks. Amp control panel is noticeably smaller and the Kustom logo is in the right side of the control panel.

Black Vinyl ('75-c.'78)

By '75 ownership changes were complete and the colorful tuck-and-roll was dropped in favor of more traditional black vinyl. The products had a slant Kustom logo spelled-out and placed in a position on the grille similar to a Fender blackface baffle. Models included the I, II, III, and IV Lead amps. Heads with half- and full-stacks were available. Bass amps included the Kustom 1, Bass I, II, III, IV, and IV SRO.

Black Vinyl K logo ('78-'83)

This era is easily recognized by the prominent capital K logo.

MODEL YEAR	FEATURES	EXC. COND. LOW	HIGH

Bass V Amp

1990s. Large Kustom Bass V logo upper right side of amp, 35 watts, 1x12", black vinyl.

1990s		$60	$85

Challenger Combo Amp

1973-1975. 1x12" speaker.

1973-1975	Black	$200	$275
1973-1975	Color option	$275	$375

Hustler Combo Amp

1973-1975. Solidstate, 4x10", tremolo, tuck-and-roll.

1973-1975	Black	$225	$300
1973-1975	Color option	$300	$400

K25/K25 C-2 SC Amp

1960s. SC (self-contained) Series, small combo tuck-and-roll, 1x12", solidstate, reverb, black control panel.

1971-1973	Black	$200	$275
1971-1973	Color option	$300	$400

K50-2 SC Amp

1971-1973. Self-contained (SC) small combo tuck-and-roll, 1x12", reverb and tremolo.

1971-1973	Black	$200	$275
1971-1973	Color option	$300	$400

K100-1 1-15C Bass Amp Set

1968-1972. The K100-1 with 1-15C speaker option with matching 1x15" cab, black tuck-and-roll standard, but several sparkle colors offered, C.T.S. bass reflex speaker.

1968-1972	Black	$200	$275
1968-1972	Color option	$300	$400

K100-1 1-15L-1/1-15A-1/1-15J-1 Amp Set

1968-1972. K100-1 with matching 1x15" cab, black tuck-and-roll standard, but several colors offered, speaker options are JBL, Altec Lansing or Jensen.

1968-1972	Black	$200	$275
1968-1972	Color option	$300	$400

K100-1 1-D140F Bass Amp

1968-1972. K100-1 with matching 1x15" JBL D-140F cab, black tuck-and-roll standard, but several sparkle colors offered.

1968-1972	Black	$200	$275
1968-1972	Color option	$300	$400

K100-1 2-12C Bass Amp Set

1968-1972. K100-1 with matching 2x12" cab, black tuck-and-roll standard, but several sparkle colors offered, C.T.S. bass reflex speakers.

1968-1972	Black	$250	$325
1968-1972	Color option	$500	$700

K100-2 1-15L-2/1-15A-2/1-15J-2 Amp Set

1968-1972. K100-2 head and matching 1x15" cab, black tuck-and-roll standard, but several sparkle colors offered.

1968-1972	Black	$200	$275
1968-1972	Color option	$300	$400

K100-2 2-12A-2/2-12J-2 Amp Set

1968-1972. K100-2 head with matching 2x12" cab, black tuck-and-roll standard, but several sparkle colors offered.

1968-1972	Black	$250	$325
1968-1972	Color option	$500	$700

K100-5 PA Amp Head

1968-1972. 50 watts, 2 channels with 8 control knobs per channel, reverb.

1968-1972	Black	$275	$375

K100-6 SC Amp

1970-1972. Basic combo amp with selectone, no reverb.

1970-1972	Black	$175	$230

K100-7 SC Amp

1970-1972. Combo amp with reverb, tremolo, vibrato and boost.

1970-1972	Black	$200	$275
1970-1972	Color option	$300	$400

K100-8 SC Amp

1970-1972. Combo amp with reverb, tremolo, vibrato and boost.

1970-1972	Black	$200	$275
1970-1972	Color option	$300	$400

MODEL YEAR	FEATURES	EXC. COND. LOW	HIGH

K100C-6 Combo Amp

1968-1970. Kustom 100 logo middle of the front control panel, 1x15" combo, selectone option.

1968-1970	Black	$200	$275
1968-1970	Color option	$300	$400

K100C-8 Combo Amp

1968-1970. Kustom 100 logo middle of the front control panel, 4x10" combo, reverb, tremolo, vibrato.

1968-1970	Black	$275	$375

K150-1 Amp Set

1972-1975. Piggyback, 150 watts, 2x12", no reverb, logo in upper right corner of amp head, tuck-and-roll, black or color option.

1972-1975	Color option	$300	$400

K150-2 Amp Set

1972-1975. K150 with added reverb and tremolo, piggyback, 2x12", tuck-and-roll, black or color option.

1972-1975	Color option	$300	$400

K150-5 PA Amp Set

1972-1975. PA head plus 2 PA cabs.

1972-1975		$250	$335

K150/150C Combo Amp

1972-1975. Combo, 2x10".

1972-1975	Black	$200	$260

K200-1/K200B Bass Amp Set

1966-1972. K200 head with 2x15" cab.

1966-1972	Black	$300	$400
1966-1972	Color option	$450	$600

K200-2 Reverb/Tremolo Amp Set

1966-1972. K200-2 head with 2x15" or 3x12" cab, available with JBL D-140F speakers, Altec Lansing (A) speakers, C.T.S. (C), or Jensen (J).

1966-1972	Black	$300	$400
1966-1972	Color option	$450	$600

K250 Amp Set

1971-1975. K250 head with 2x15" cab, tuck-and-roll cover.

1971-1975	Black	$265	$350
1971-1975	Color option	$475	$625

K300 PA Amp and Speaker Set

1971-1975. Includes 302 PA, 303 PA, 304 PA, 305 PA, head and 2 cabs.

1971-1975	Color option	$450	$600

K400-2 Reverb/Tremolo Amp Set

1968-1972. 200 relative watts, reverb, tremolo, with 6x12" or 8x12" cab, available with JBL D-140F speakers, Altec Lansing (A), C.T.S. (C), or Jensen (J). The K400 was offered with no effects (suffix 1), with reverb and tremolo (suffix 2), with Harmonic Clipper & Boost (suffix 3), and Reverb/Trem/Clipper/Boost (suffix 4). The 400 heads came with a separate chrome amp head stand.

1968-1972	Black	$250	$325
1968-1972	Color option	$475	$625

KBA-10 Combo Amp

Late-1980s-1990s. Compact solidstate bass amp, 10 watts, 1x8".

1990s		$30	$40

KBA-20 Combo Amp

Late-1980s-early-1990s. KBA series were compact solidstate bass amps with built-in limiter, 20 watts, 1x8".

1989-1990		$30	$40

KBA-30 Combo Amp

Late-1980s-early-1990s. 30 watts, 1x10".

1989-1990		$30	$40

KBA-40 Combo Amp

Late-1980s-early-1990s. 40 watts, 1x12".

1989-1990		$55	$75

KBA-80 Combo Amp

Late-1980s-early-1990s. 80 watts, 1x15".

1989-1990		$80	$105

KBA-160 Combo Amp

Late-1980s-early-1990s. Solidstate bass amp with built-in limiter, 160 watts, 1x15".

1989-1990		$110	$150

KGA-10 VC Amp

1999-2006. 10 watts, 1x6.5" speaker, switchable overdrive.

1999-2006		$30	$40

KLA-15 Combo Amp

Late-1980s-early-1990s. Solidstate, overdrive, 15 watts, 1x8".

1989-1990		$55	$75

KLA-20 Amp

Mid-1980s-late-1980s. 1x10", MOS-FET, gain, EQ, reverb, headphone jack.

1986		$55	$75

KLA-25 Combo Amp

Late-1980s-early-1990s. Solidstate, overdrive, reverb, 25 watts, 1x10".

1989-1990		$55	$75

KLA-50 Combo Amp

Late-1980s-early-1990s. Solidstate, overdrive, reverb, 50 watts, 1x12".

1989-1990		$80	$105

KLA-75 Amp

Mid-1980s-late-1980s. 75 watts, reverb, footswitching.

1987		$110	$145

KLA-100 Combo Amp

Late-1980s-early-1990s. Solidstate, reverb, 100-watt dual channel, 1x12".

1989-1990		$110	$145

KLA-185 Combo Amp

Late-1980s-early-1990s. Solidstate, reverb, 185-watt dual channel, 1x12".

1989-1990		$130	$170

KPB-200 Bass Combo Amp

1994-1997. 200 watts, 1x15".

1994-1997		$210	$275

SC 1-12 SC Amp

1971-1973. 50 watts, 1x12" Jensen speaker.

1971-1973	Black	$200	$275
1971-1973	Color option	$300	$400

SC 1-15 SC Amp

1971-1973. 150 watts, 1x15" C.T.S. speaker.

1971-1973	Black	$200	$275
1971-1973	Color option	$300	$400

SC 1-15AB SC Amp

1971-1973. 150 watts, 1x15" Altec Lansing speaker.

1971-1973	Black	$200	$275
1971-1973	Color option	$300	$400

1971 Kustom K150-8

Tom Pfeifer

1970s Kustom K250

Tom Pfeifer

1965 Kustom K400

Craig Brody

AMPS

Laboga AD5200 SA

Carter Vintage Guitars

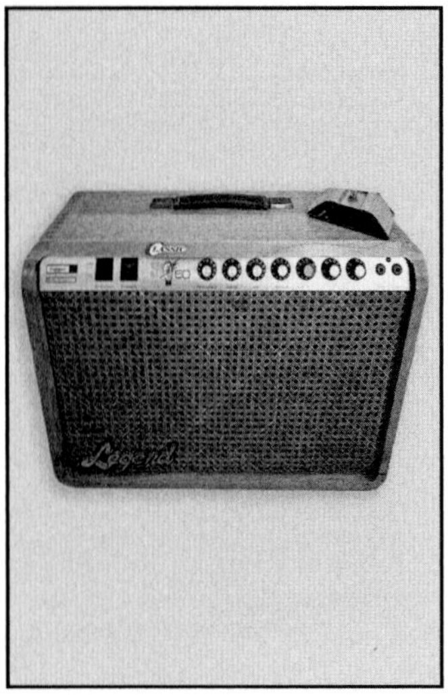

1980 Legend Rock & Roll 50

Alex Xenos

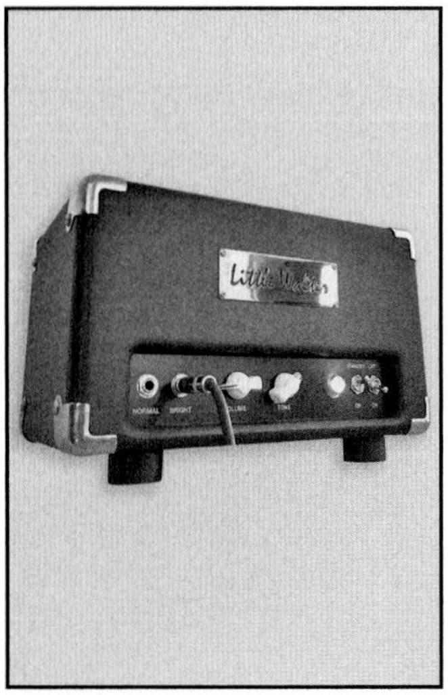

Little Walter 9H10 Hipster

Shawn Penney

MODEL YEAR	FEATURES	EXC. COND. LOW	HIGH

SC 2-12A SC Amp

1971-1973. 150 watts, 2x12" Altec Lansing speakers.

1971-1973	Black	$225	$300
1971-1973	Color option	$300	$400

SC 2-12J SC Amp

1971-1973. 150 watts, 2x12" Jensen speakers.

1971-1973	Black	$225	$300
1971-1973	Color option	$300	$400

SC 4-10 SC Amp

1971-1973. 150 watts, 4x10" Jensen speakers.

1971-1973	Black	$225	$300
1971-1973	Color option	$300	$400

Lab Series

1977-1980s. Five models of Lab Series amps, ranging in price from $600 to $3,700, were introduced at the '77 NAMM show by Norlin (then owner of Gibson). Two more were added later. The '80s models were Lab Series 2 amps and had a Gibson logo on the upper-left front.

B120 Bass Amp Combo

Ca.1984. 120 watts, 2 channels, 1x15".

1984		$250	$325

G120 R-10 Amp Combo

Ca.1984. 120 watts, 3-band EQ, channel switching, reverb, 4x10".

1984		$275	$375

G120 R-12 Amp Combo

Ca.1984. 120 watts, 3-band EQ, channel switching, reverb, 2x12".

1984		$275	$375

L2 Amp Head

1977-ca.1983. 100 watts, black covering.

1977-1983		$190	$250

L3 Amp Combo

1977-ca.1983. 60-watt 1x12".

1977-1983		$250	$325

L4 Amp Head

1977-ca.1983. Solidstate, 200 watts, black cover, dark grille, large L4 logo on front panel.

1977-1983		$190	$250

L5 Amp Combo

1977-ca.1983. Solidstate, 100 watts, 2x12" combo.

1977-1983		$275	$375

L5 Amp Set

1977-ca.1983. Solidstate, 100 watts, 2x12" piggyback.

1977-1983		$275	$375

L7 Amp Set

1977-ca.1983. Solidstate, 100 watts, 4x10" piggyback.

1977-1983		$325	$425

L9 Amp Combo

1977-ca.1983. Solidstate, 100 watts, 1x15".

1977-1983		$250	$325

L11 Amp Set

1977-ca.1983. 200 watts, 8x12" piggyback.

1977-1983		$350	$475

MODEL YEAR	FEATURES	EXC. COND. LOW	HIGH

Laboga

1973-present. Adam Laboga builds intermediate and professional grade, production, tube guitar amps and cabinets in Wroclaw, Poland.

Lace Music Products

1979-present. Lace Music Products, founded by pickup innovator Don Lace Sr., offered amplifiers for a while starting in '96. They also offered amps under the Rat Fink and Mooneyes brands.

Lafayette

Ca.1963-1967. Japanese-made guitars and amps sold through the Lafayette Electronics catalogs.

Tube Amp

1960s. Japanese-made tube, gray speckle 1x12" with art deco design or black 2x12".

1960s	Larger, 2 speakers	$175	$225
1960s	Small, 1 speaker	$125	$175

Landry

2008-present. Production, professional grade, amps and cabinets built by Bill Landry in St. Louis, Missouri.

Laney

1968-present. Founded by Lyndon Laney and Bob Thomas in Birmingham, U.K. Laney offered tube amps exclusively into the '80s. Currently they offer intermediate and professional grade, tube and solidstate amp heads and combos and cabinets.

L60 60-Watt Amp Head

1968-1969. 60 watts

1968-1969		$1,100	$1,400

L100 100-Watt Amp Head

1968-1969. Similar to short head plexi Marshall amp cab, 100 watts, large Laney with underlined "y" logo plate on front upper left corner, black vinyl cover, grayish grille.

1968-1969		$1,100	$1,400

Lectrolab

1950s-1960s. Budget house brand for music stores, made by Sound Projects Company of Cicero, Illinois. Similar to Valco, Oahu, and Danelectro student amps of the '50s, cabinets were generally made from inexpensive material. The Lectrolab logo can generally be found somewhere on the amp.

Tube Amp

1950s-60s	Larger	$300	$400
1950s-60s	Small	$225	$300

Legend

1978-1984. From Legend Musical Instruments of East Syracuse, New York, these amps featured cool wood cabinets. They offered heads, combos with a 1x12" or 2x12" configuration, and cabinets with 1x12", 1x15", 2x12" or 4x12".

A-30 Amp

1978-1984. Natural wood cabinet, 30 watts, 1x12".

1978-1984		$300	$400

MODEL YEAR	FEATURES	EXC. COND. LOW	HIGH

A-60 Amp

1978-1984. Natural wood cabinet, transtube design dual tube preamp with solidstate power section.

1978-1984		$375	$500

Rock & Roll 50 Amp

1978-1983. Mesa-Boogie-style wood compact amp, head/half stack or 1x12", 1x15" or 2x12" combo, tube preamp section and solidstate power supply.

1978-1983	1x12" combo	$300	$400
1978-1983	1x15" combo	$300	$400
1978-1983	2x12" combo	$375	$500
1978-1983	Half Stack Set	$575	$750

Super Lead 50 Amp

1978-1983. Rock & Roll 50-watt model with added bass boost and reverb, 1x12", hybrid tube and solidstate.

1978-1983		$300	$400

Super Lead 100 Amp

1978-1983. 100-watt version, 2x12".

1978-1983		$375	$500

Lenahan

Professional grade, production/custom, vintage-style amps and cabinets built by James T. Lenahan - presently in Fort Smith, Arkansas and prior to '91 in Hollywood, California - starting in 1983. He also built guitar effects.

Leslie

Most often seen with Hammond organs, the cool Leslie rotating speakers have been adopted by many guitarists. Many guitar effects have tried to duplicate their sound. And they are still making them.

122 Amp/122RV Amp

A Hammond-only model, considered the official Hammond B-3 Leslie. RV indicates reverb.

1960s		$700	$950

125 Amp

Late-1960s. All tube amp with 2-speed rotating 1x12" speaker, bottom rotor only, less features.

1960s		$475	$625

142 Amp

A Hammond-only model, smaller cabinet than 122 Amp.

1960s		$600	$800

145 Amp

Similar to 147 Amp, but smaller and easier to move.

1960s		$625	$825

147 Amp/147RV Amp

A universal-use model, "7" denotes "universal" useage. RV has added reverb.

1960s		$625	$825

Lickliter Amplification

In 2009, Michael Lickliter began building professional and premium grade, custom, guitar amps in Punta Gorda, Florida.

Line 6

1996-present. Founded by Marcus Ryle and Michel Doidic and specializing in digital signal processing in both effects and amps. They also produce tube amps. Purchased by Yamaha in 2014.

MODEL YEAR	FEATURES	EXC. COND. LOW	HIGH

Little Lanilei

1997-present. Small hand-made, intermediate grade, production/custom, amps made by Mahaffay Amplifiers (formerly Songworks Systems & Products) of Aliso Viejo, California. They also build a reverb unit and a rotary effect.

Little Walter

2008-present. Phil Bradbury builds his professional grade, production, amp heads and cabinets in West End, North Carolina.

London City

Late 1960s-early 1970s. Intermediate to professional grade amps and cabinets made in Netherlands, London City logo.

Louis Electric Amplifier Co.

1993-present. Founded by Louis Rosano in Bergenfield, New Jersey. Louis produces custom-built tweeds and various combo amps from 35 to 80 watts.

Luker

Professional grade, production/custom, guitar and bass amps and cabinets built in Eugene, Oregon by Ken Luker, starting in 2006.

Luna Guitars

2005-present. Located in Tampa, Florida, Yvonne de Villiers imports her budget to professional grade, production, acoustic and electric guitars from Japan, Korea and China. She also imports guitars, basses and ukes.

Lyric

Late 1950s-ca. 1965. One of several private brands that Magnatone made for others, these were built for Lyric Electronics, located in Lomita, California.

Model 660 Custom

Ca. 1959-ca. 1965. 2x12" combo amp, 35 watts.

1959-1965		$1,150	$1,500

Mack

2005-present. Made in Toronto, Ontario by builder Don Mackrill, the company offers intermediate and professional grade, production, tube amps.

Mad Professor

2002-present. Bjorn Juhl and Jukka Monkkonen build their premium grade, production/custom, tube amps in Tampere, Finland. They also offer effects pedals.

Maestro

Maestro amps are associated with Gibson and were included in the Gibson catalogs. For example, in the '62-'63 orange cover Gibson catalog, tweed Maestro amps were displayed in their own section. Tweed Maestro amps are very similar to Gibson tweed amps. Maestro amps were often associated with accordions in the early-'60s but the amps

Louis Electric Columbia Reverb

Mack Atomsmasher DB-40

Mad Professor OS 21RT

1958 Maestro GA-45 Maestro
Rivington Guitars

Magnatone 108 Varsity

1950s Magnatone 195 Melodier
Tom Pfeifer

MODEL YEAR	FEATURES	EXC. COND. LOW	HIGH

featured standard guitar inputs. Gibson also used the Maestro name on effects in the '60s and '70s and in 01, Gibson revived the name for a line of effects, banjos, and mandolins and added guitars and amps in '09.

The price ranges listed are for excellent condition, all original amps though tubes may be replaced without affecting value. The prices listed are for amps with fully intact logos. A broken or missing logo may diminish the value of the amp. Amps with a changed handle, power cord, and especially a broken logo, should be taken on a case-by-case basis.

Amp models in '58 include the Super Maestro and Maestro, in '60 the Stereo Maestro Accordion GA-87, Super Maestro Accordion GA-46 T, Standard Accordion GA-45 T, Viscount Accordion GA-16 T, in '62 the Reverb-Echo GA-1 RT, Reverb-Echo GA-2 RT, 30 Stereo Accordion Amp, Stereo Accordion GA-78 RV.

GA-1 RT Reverb-Echo Amp

1961. Tweed, 1x8".

1961 $450 $575

GA-2 RT Deluxe Reverb-Echo Amp

1961. Deluxe more powerful version of GA-1 RT, 1x12", tweed.

1961 $725 $950

GA-15 RV/Bell 15 RV Amp

1961. 15 watts, 1x12", gray sparkle.

1961 $525 $675

GA-16 T Viscount Amp

1959-1961. 14 watts, 1x10", white cab with brown grille.

1959-1961 $425 $550

GA-45 Maestro Amp

1955-1961. 14-16 watts, 4x8", 2-tone.

1955-1961 $900 $1,175

GA-45 RV Standard Amp

1961. 16 watts, 4x8", reverb.

1961 $1,000 $1,300

GA-45 T Standard Accordion Amp

1961. 16 watts, 4x8", tremolo.

1961 $900 $1,175

GA-46 T Super Maestro Accordion and Bass Amp

1957-1961. Based on the Gibson GA-200 and advertised to be designed especially for amplified accordions, 60 watts, 2x12", vibrato, 2-tone cover, large Maestro Super logo on top center of grille.

1957-1961 $1,450 $1,900

GA-78 Maestro Series Amps

1960-1961. Wedge stereo cab, 2x10", reverb and tremolo.

1960-1961	GA-78 RV Maestro 30	$1,800	$2,350
1960-1961	GA-78 RVS	$1,600	$2,100
1960-1961	GA-78 RVT	$1,600	$2,100

Magnatone

Ca.1937-1971, 2013-present. Magnatone made a huge variety of amps sold under their own name and under brands like Dickerson, Oahu, Bronson, and Estey (see separate listings). They also private branded amps for several accordion companies or accordion teaching studios like Ariatone, Audio Guild, Da Vinci, Excelsior, Giulietti, Lyric, Noble, PAC-AMP, PANaramic, Titano, Tonemaster, Twilighter, and Unique (see separate listings). In 2013, Ted Kornblum revived the Magnatone name on a line of tube amps based on the earlier models and built in St. Louis, Missouri.

Model 108 Varsity Amp

1948-1954. Gray pearloid cover, small student amp or lap steel companion amp.

1948-1954 $300 $400

Model 109 Melodier Amp

1950s. 10 watts, 2 speakers.

1950s $600 $775

Model 110 Melodier Amp

1953-1954. 12 watts, 1x10", brown leatherette cover, light grille.

1953-1954 $550 $725

Model 111 Student Amp

1955-1959. 1x8", 2-3 watts, brown leatherette, brown grille.

1955-1959 $500 $650

Model 112/113 Troubadour Amp

1955-1959. 18 watts, 1x12", brown leatherette, brown grille, slant back rear control panel.

1955-1959 $775 $1,000

Model 118 Amp

1960. Compact, tubes, low power, volume and tone knobs, brown tolex era, Model 118 logo on rear-mounted control panel.

1960 $400 $525

Model 120B Cougar Bass Amp

1967-1968. Initial Magnatone entry into the solidstate market, superseded by Brute Series in '68, 120 watts, 2x12" solidstate bass piggyback amp, naugahyde vinyl cover with polyester rosewood side panels.

1967-1968 $325 $425

Model 120R Sting Ray Reverb Bass Amp

1967-1968. Initial Magnatone entry into the solidstate market, superseded by Brute Series in '68, 150 watts, 4x10" solidstate combo amp, naugahyde vinyl cover with polyester rosewood side panels.

1967-1968 $375 $500

Model 130V Custom Amp

1969-1971. Solidstate 1x12" combo amp.

1969-1971 $225 $300

Model 150R Firestar Reverb Amp

1967-1968. Initial Magnatone entry into the solidstate market, superseded by Brute Series in '68, 120 watts, 2x12" solidstate combo amp, naugahyde vinyl cover with polyester rosewood side panels.

1967-1968 $250 $350

Model 180 Triplex Amp

Mid-to-late-1950s. Mid-level power using 2 6L6 power tubes, 1x15" and 1x8" speakers.

1950s $800 $1,050

Model 192-5-S Troubadour Amp

Early-1950s. 18 watts, 1x12" Jensen Concert speaker, brown alligator covering, lower back control panel, 3 chicken-head knobs, Magnatone

MODEL YEAR	FEATURES	EXC. COND. LOW	HIGH

script logo on front, Troubadour script logo on back control panel.

1950s $575 $750

Model 194 Lyric Amp

1947-mid-1950s. 1x12" speaker, old-style tweed vertical cab typical of '40s.

1940s $500 $650

Model 195 Melodier Amp

1951-1954. Vertical cab with 1x10" speaker, pearloid with flowing grille slats.

1951-1954 $525 $700

Model 196 Amp

1947-mid-1950s. 1x12", 5-10 watts, scroll grille design, snakeskin leatherette cover.

1940s $500 $650

Model 197-V Varsity Amp

1948-1952. Small compact student amp, 1x8", tubes, Varsity model logo and model number on back panel, old style layout with back bottom-mounted chasis, curved cross-bars on front baffle, brown lizard leatherette, leather handle.

1948-1952 $450 $600

Model 198 Varsity Amp

1948-1954. 1x8", tubes.

1948-1954 $500 $650

Model 199 Student Amp

1950s. About 6 to 10 watts, 1x8", snakeskin leatherette cover, metal handle, slant grille design.

1950s $500 $650

Model 210 Deluxe Student Amp

1958-1960. 5 watts, 1x8", vibrato, brown leatherette, V logo lower right front on grille.

1958-1960 $500 $650

Model 213 Troubadour Amp

1957-1958. 10 watts, 1x12", vibrato, brown leatherette cover, V logo lower right of grille.

1957-1958 $950 $1,250

Model 240 SV Magna-Chordion Amp

1967-1968. Initial Magnatone entry into the solid-state market, superseded by Brute Series in '68, 240 watts, 2x12" solidstate stereo accordion or organ amp, naugahyde vinyl cover, polyester rosewood side panels, input jacks suitable for guitar, reverb and vibrato, lateral combo cab, rear mounted controls.

1967-1968 $325 $425

Model 250 Professional Amp

1958-1960. 20 watts, 1x12", vibrato, brown leatherette with V logo lower right front of grille.

1958-1960 $975 $1,300

Model 260 Amp

1957-1958. 35 watts, 2x12", brown leatherette, vibrato, V logo lower right front corner of grille.

1957-1958 $1,400 $1,800

Model 262 Jupiter/Custom Pro Amp

1961-1963. 35 watts, 2x12", vibrato, brown leatherette.

1961-1963 $1,025 $1,350

Model 280/Custom 280 Amp

1957-1958. 50 watts, brown leatherette covering, brown-yellow tweed grille, 2x12" plus 2x5" speakers, double V logo.

1957-1958 $1,400 $1,800

Model 280A Amp

1958-1960. 50 watts, brown leatherette covering, brown-yellow tweed grille, 2x12" plus 2x5" speakers, V logo lower right front.

1958-1960 $1,400 $1,800

1958-1960 With matching cab $1,800 $2,400

Model 410 Diana Amp

1961-1963. Five watts, 1x12", advertised as a 'studio' low power professional amp, brown leatherette cover, vibrato.

1961-1963 $575 $775

Model 412 Amp

1960s. Estey era compact student amp, low power, 1x8", tubes.

1960s $250 $325

Model 413 Centaur Amp

1961-1963. 18 watts, 1x12", brown leatherette cover, vibrato.

1961-1963 $875 $1,150

Model 415 Clio Bass Amp

1961-1963. 25 watts, 4x8", bass or accordion amp, brown leatherette cover.

1961-1963 $925 $1,200

Model 422 Amp

1966-1967. Low power 1x12", 3 inputs, black vinyl, light swirl grille.

1966-1967 $500 $650

Model 425 Amp

1961. Tube, 55 watts, 4x12".

1961 $1,150 $1,450

Model 432 Amp

Mid-1960s. Compact student model, wavey-squiggle art deco-style grille, black cover, vibrato and reverb.

1960s $575 $750

Model 435 Athene Bass Amp

1961-1963. 55 watts, 4x10", piggyback head and cab, brown leatherette.

1961-1963 $1,150 $1,500

Model 440 Mercury Amp

1961-1963. 18 watts, 1x12", vibrato, brown leatherette.

1961-1963 $1,000 $1,300

Model 450 Juno/Twin Hi-Fi Amp

1961-1963. 25 watts, 1x12" and 1 oval 5"x7" speakers, reverb, vibrato, brown leatherette.

1961-1963 $1,150 $1,500

1961-1963 Extension cab only $575 $750

Model 460 Victory Amp

1961-1963. 35 watts, 2x12" and 2 oval 5"x7" speakers, early-'60s next to the top-of-the-line, reverb and vibrato, brown leatherette.

1961-1963 $1,150 $1,500

Model 480 Venus Amp

1961-1963. 50 watts, 2x12" and 2 oval 5"x7" speakers, early-'60s top-of-the-line, reverb and stereo vibrato, brown leatherette.

1961-1963 $1,150 $1,500

Model M2 Amp

1963-1964. 1x8", 12-15 watts, 1 channel.

1963-1964 $350 $450

Model M6 Amp

1964 (not seen in '65 catalog). 25 watts, 1x12", black molded plastic suitcase amp.

1964 $475 $625

Late-1950s Magnatone 213 Troubadour
Imaged by Heritage Auctions, HA.com

1960 Magnatone 280 Custom
Imaged by Heritage Auctions, HA.com

Magnatone 480 Venus

1966 Magnatone MP-1
Imaged by Heritage Auctions, HA.com

Magnatone M15
Imaged by Heritage Auctions, HA.com

1950s Magnatone Starlet 107
Imaged by Heritage Auctions, HA.com

MODEL YEAR	FEATURES	EXC. COND. LOW	HIGH

Model M7 Bass Amp

1964-1966. 38 watts, 1x15" bass amp, black molded plastic suitcase amp.

1964-1966 $475 $625

Model M8 Amp

1964-1966. 27 watts, 1x12", reverb and tremolo, black molded plastic suitcase amp.

1964-1966 $550 $725

Model M9 Amp

1964-1966. 38 watts, 1x15", tremolo, no reverb, black molded plastic suitcase amp.

1964-1966 $550 $725

Model M10/M10A Amp

1964-1966. 38 watts, 1x15", tone boost, tremolo, transistorized reverb section, black molded plastic suitcase amp.

1964-1966 $500 $650

Model M12 Bass Amp

1964-1966. 80 watts, 1x15" or 2x12", mid-'60s top-of-the-line bass amp, black molded plastic suitcase amp.

1964-1966 $550 $725

Model M13 Imperial Amp

Mid-1963-1964. 1x15", 45 watts, 3 channels.

1963-1964 $550 $725

Model M14 Amp

1964-1966. Stereo, 75 watts, 2x12" plus 2 tweeters, stereo vibrato, no reverb, black molded plastic suitcase amp.

1964-1966 $675 $900

Model M15 Amp

1964-1966. Stereo 75 watts, 2x12" plus 2 tweeters, stereo vibrato, transistorized reverb, black molded plastic suitcase amp.

1964-1966 $725 $925

Model M27 Bad Boy Bass Amp

1968-1971. 150 watts, 2x15" (1 passive), reverb, vibrato, solidstate, vertical profile bass amp, part of Brute Series.

1968-1971 $275 $350

Model M30 Fang Amp

1968-1971. 150 watts, 2x15" (1 passive), 1 exponential horn, solidstate, vibrato, reverb, vertical profile amp.

1968-1971 $275 $350

Model M32 Big Henry Bass Amp

1968-1971. 300 watts, 2x15" solidstate vertical profile bass amp.

1968-1971 $275 $350

Model M35 The Killer Amp

1968-1971. 300 watts, 2x15" and 2 horns, solidstate, vibrato, vertical profile amp.

1968-1971 $275 $350

Model MP-1 (Magna Power I) Amp

1966-1967. 30 watts, 1x12", dark vinyl, light grille, Magnatone-Estey logo on upper right of grille.

1966-1967 $525 $700

Model MP-3 (Magna Power 3) Amp

1966-1967. Mid-power, 2x12", reverb, dark vinyl, light grille, Magnatone-Estey logo on upper right of grille.

1966-1967 $600 $775

Model MP-5 (Magna Power) Amp

1966-1967. Mid-power, piggyback 2x12", Magnatone-Estey logo on upper right of grille.

1966-1967 $675 $875

Model PS150 Amp

1968-1971. Powered slave speaker cabinets, 150 watts, 2x15" linkable cabinets.

1968-1971 $175 $225

Model PS300 Amp

1968-1971. Powered slave speaker cabinets, 300 watts, 2x15" (1 passive) linkable cabinets.

1968-1971 $175 $225

Small Pearloid Amp

1947-1955. Pearloid (MOTS) covered low- and mid-power amps generally associated with pearloid lap steel sets.

1947-1955 Fancy grille $325 $425

1947-1955 Plain grille $225 $300

Starlet Model 107 Amp

1951-1952. Student model, 1x8", pearloid cover early, leatherette later, low power, single on-off volume control, Starlet logo on back panel, Magnatone logo plate upper left front of grille.

1951-1954 Pearloid $275 $365

1955-1959 Leatherette $275 $365

Starlite Model 401 Amp

1964-1966. Magnatone produced the mid-'60s Starlite amplifier line for the budget minded musician. Each Starlite model prominently notes the Magnatone name. The grilles show art deco wavy circles. Magnatone 1960-'63 standard amps offer models starting with 12" speakers. Starlite models offer 10" and below. Model 401 has 15 watts, 1x8" and 3 tubes.

1964-1966 $300 $400

Starlite Model 411 Amp

1964-1966. 15 watts, 1x8", 5 tubes, tremolo (not advertised as vibrato), art deco wavy grille.

1964-1966 $325 $425

Starlite Model 441A Bass Amp

1964-1966. Lower power with less than 25 watts, 1x15", tube amp.

1964-1966 $450 $600

Starlite Model Custom 421 Amp

1964-1966. Tube amp, 25 watts, 1x10".

1964-1966 $450 $600

Starlite Model Custom 431 Amp

1964-1966. Tube amp, 30 watts, 1x10", vibrato and reverb.

1964-1966 $500 $650

Mahaffay Amplifiers

2009-present. See Little Lanilei.

Mako

1985-1989. Line of solidstate amps from Kaman (Ovation, Hamer). They also offered guitars and basses.

Marlboro Sound Works

1970-1980s. Economy solidstate amps imported by Musical Instruments Corp., Syosset, New York. Initially, Marlboro targeted the economy compact amp market, but quickly added larger amps and PAs.

Solid State Amp

1970-1980s Various models $15 $125

Marshall

1962-present. Drummer Jim Marshall (1923-2012) started building bass speaker and PA cabinets in his garage in 1960. He opened a retail drum shop for his students and others and soon added guitars and amps. When Ken Bran joined the business as service manager in '62, the two decided to build their own amps. By '63 they had expanded the shop to house a small manufacturing space and by late that year they were offering the amps to other retailers. Marshall also made amps under the Park, CMI, Narb, Big M, and Kitchen-Marshall brands.

Mark I, II, III and IVs are generally '60s and '70s and also are generally part of a larger series (for example JTM), or have a model number that is a more specific identifier. Describing an amp only as Mark II can be misleading. The most important identifier is the Model Number, which Marshall often called the Stock Number. To help avoid confusion we have added the Model number as often as possible. In addition, when appropriate, we have included the wattage, number of channels, master or no-master info in the title. This should help the reader more quickly find a specific amp. Check the model's description for such things as two inputs or four inputs, because this will help with identification. Vintage Marshall amps do not always have the Model/Stock number on the front or back panel, so the additional identifiers should help. The JMP logo on the front is common and really does not help with specific identification. For example, a JMP Mark II Super Lead 100 Watt description is less helpful than the actual model/stock number. Unfortunately, many people are not familiar with specific model/stock numbers. VG has tried to include as much information in the title as space will allow.

Marshall amps are sorted as follows:

- AVT Series - Advanced Valvestate Technology
- Club and Country Series (Rose-Morris)-introduced in '78
- JCM 800 Series - basically the '80s
- JCM 900 Series - basically the '90s
- JCM 2000 Series - basically the '00s
- JTM Series
- Micro Stack Group
- Model Number/Stock Number (no specific series, basically the '60s, '70s) - including Artist and Valvestate models (Valvestate refers to specific Model numbers in 8000 Series)
- Silver Jubilee Series

Acoustic Soloist (AS) Series Amp

1994-present. Acoustic guitar amps, models include AS50R and D (50 watts, 2 channels, 2x8"), AS80R (40-watt x2 stereo, 3 channels, 2x8"), AS100D (50-watt x2 stereo, 4 channels, 2x8").

MODEL YEAR	FEATURES	EXC. COND. LOW	HIGH
1994-2020	Various models	$200	$400

AVT 20 Series Amp

2001-2011. Solidstate, 20 watts, 12AX7 preamp tube, 1x10", Advanced Valvestate Technology (AVT) models have black covering and grille, and gold panel.

MODEL YEAR	FEATURES	EXC. COND. LOW	HIGH
2001-2011	Combo	$175	$225

AVT 50 Series Amp

2001-2011. Solidstate, 50 watts, 4x12".

MODEL YEAR	FEATURES	EXC. COND. LOW	HIGH
2001-2011	Combo	$245	$315
2001-2011	Head & cab	$390	$510

AVT 100 Series Amp

2001-2011. Solidstate, 100 watts, tube preamp, 1x12".

MODEL YEAR	FEATURES	EXC. COND. LOW	HIGH
2001-2011		$270	$360

AVT 150 Series Amp

2001-2011. Solidstate, additional features over AVT 100. Combo (100 watts, 1x12"), Half-Stack (150 watts, 4x12") and Head only (150 watts).

MODEL YEAR	FEATURES	EXC. COND. LOW	HIGH
2001-2011	Combo	$295	$385
2001-2011	Half-stack	$375	$500

AVT 275 Series Amp

2001-2007. Solidstate DFX stereo, 75 watts per side, 2x12".

MODEL YEAR	FEATURES	EXC. COND. LOW	HIGH
2001-2007	Combo	$360	$475

Class 5 Amp

2009-2014. 5 watts, 1x10" tube combo.

MODEL YEAR	FEATURES	EXC. COND. LOW	HIGH
2009-2014	Head	$290	$385
2009-2014	Head/cab set	$315	$415

Club and Country Model 4140 Amp

1978-1982. Tubes, 100 watts, 2x12" combo, Rose-Morris era, designed for the country music market, hence the name, brown vinyl cover, straw grille.

MODEL YEAR	FEATURES	EXC. COND. LOW	HIGH
1978-1982		$725	$950

Club and Country Model 4145 Amp

1978-1982. Tubes, 100 watts, 4x10" combo, Rose-Morris era, designed for the country music market, hence the name, brown vinyl, straw grille.

MODEL YEAR	FEATURES	EXC. COND. LOW	HIGH
1978-1982		$725	$950

Club and Country Model 4150 Bass Amp

1978-1982. Tubes, 100 watts, 4x10" bass combo, Rose-Morris era, designed for the country music market, hence the name, brown vinyl cover, straw grille.

MODEL YEAR	FEATURES	EXC. COND. LOW	HIGH
1978-1982		$725	$950

Code Series Amp

2016-present. Marshall-Softube (MST) modelling, digital capabilities, series includes; CODE25, 50, 100 and 100H. Number indicates watts.

MODEL YEAR	FEATURES	EXC. COND. LOW	HIGH
2016-2020		$120	$195

Haze (MHZ) Series Amp

2009-2014. All tube, multi-functional amp, 15-watt head, 40-watt combo.

MODEL YEAR	FEATURES	EXC. COND. LOW	HIGH
2009-2014	MHZ15	$590	$775
2009-2014	MHZ40C	$340	$440

JCM 600 Series

1997-2000. All tube, 60 watt models with modern features, includes the JCM600 head, JCM601 1x12" combo and JCM602 2x12" combo.

MODEL YEAR	FEATURES	EXC. COND. LOW	HIGH
1997-2000	JCM600	$355	$470
1997-2000	JCM601	$378	$495
1997-2000	JCM602	$450	$590

JCM 800 Model 1959 Amp Head

1981-1991. 100 watts.

MODEL YEAR	FEATURES	EXC. COND. LOW	HIGH
1981-1991		$1,190	$1,525

Mahaffay The Little Lanilei 3350LT

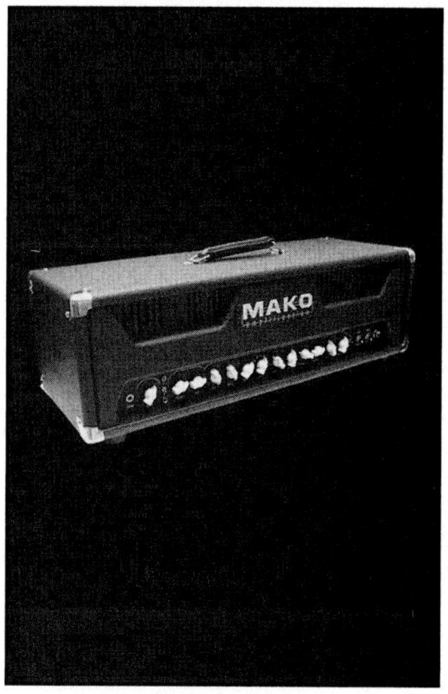

Mako MAK2

Marshall AS100D

AMPS

AMPS

1984 Marshall JCM 800 2203
Craig Brody

1986 Marshall JCM 800 Model 2204
Scott Davis

Mid-1980s Marshall JCM 800 Model 2204
Tony Romagna

MODEL YEAR	FEATURES	EXC. COND. LOW	HIGH
JCM 800 Model 1987 Amp Head			
1981-1991. 50 watts.			
1981-1991		$1,190	$1,525
JCM 800 Model 1992 Bass Amp Head			
1981-1986. Active tone circuit.			
1981-1986		$1,190	$1,525
JCM 800 Model 2000 Amp Head			
1981-1982. 200 watts.			
1981-1982		$1,190	$1,525
JCM 800 Model 2001 Amp Head			
1981-1982. Bass head, 300 watts.			
1981-1982		$1,190	$1,525
JCM 800 Model 2004 Amp Head			
1981-1990. 50 watts, master.			
1981-1990		$1,190	$1,525
JCM 800 Model 2004S Amp Head			
1986-1987. 50 watts, short head.			
1986-1987		$1,190	$1,525
JCM 800 Model 2005 Amp Head			
1983-1990. 50 watts, split channel.			
1983-1990		$1,190	$1,525
JCM 800 Model 2005 Full Stack Amp			
1983-1990. Limited Edition, 2005 head with 2 2x12 cabs.			
1983-1990		$1,750	$2,275
JCM 800 Model 2203 20th Anniversary Half Stack Amp			
1982. 20th Anniversary plate in lower right corner of matching 1960A cab, matching white tolex cover.			
1982		$2,080	$2,675
JCM 800 Model 2203 Amp Head			
1981-1990, 2002-2020. 100 watts, master volume, reissued '02 in Vintage Series.			
1981-1990		$1,350	$1,800
2002-2020	Reissue	$850	$1,100
JCM 800 Model 2203KK Kerry King Signature Amp			
2008-2012. King Signature logo, 100 watts, 3-band EQ.			
2008-2012		$825	$1,100
JCM 800 Model 2203ZW Zack Wylde Signature Amp			
2002. About 600 amp heads and 60 half-stacks made.			
2002	Half-stack	$2,625	$3,400
2002	Head only	$1,450	$1,900
JCM 800 Model 2204 Amp Head			
1981-1990. 50 watts, 1 channel, 2 inputs, master volume, front panel says JCM 800 Lead Series, back panel says Master Model 50w Mk 2.			
1981-1990		$875	$1,175
JCM 800 Model 2204S Amp Head			
1986-1987. Short head, 50 watts.			
1986-1987		$875	$1,175
JCM 800 Model 2205 Amp			
1983-1990. 50 watts, split channel (1 clean and 1 distortion), switchable, both channels with reverb, 4x12" cabinet, front panel reads JCM 800 Lead Series.			
1983-1990	4x12 cab	$500	$675
1983-1990	Head only	$875	$1,175
JCM 800 Model 2210 Amp Head			
1983-1990. 100 watts.			
1983-1990		$875	$1,175
JCM 800 Model 4010 Combo Amp			
1980-1990. 50 watts, 1x12", non-reverb ('80), reverb begins '81, single channel master volume.			
1980-1990		$1,025	$1,350
JCM 800 Model 4103 Combo Amp			
1981-1990. Lead combo amp, 100 watts, 2x12".			
1981-1990		$1,175	$1,550
JCM 800 Model 4104 Combo Amp			
1980-1990. Tube lead amp, 50 watts, 2x12".			
1980-1990	Black	$1,025	$1,350
1980-1990	Head only	$850	$1,125
1980-1990	White option	$1,025	$1,350
JCM 800 Model 4210 Combo Amp			
1982-1990. 50 watts, 1x12" tube combo, split-channel, single input, master volume.			
1982-1990		$1,115	$1,450
JCM 800 Model 4211 Combo Amp			
1983-1990. Lead combo amp, 100 watts, 2x12".			
1983-1990		$1,115	$1,450
JCM 800 Model 4212 Combo Amp			
1983-1990. 2x12" 50-watt combo.			
1983-1990		$1,115	$1,450
JCM 800 Model 5010 Combo Amp			
1983-1991. Solidstate, 30 watts, master volume, 1x12".			
1983-1991		$290	$375
JCM 800 Model 5150 Combo Amp			
1987-1991. Solidstate, 150 watts, 12" Celestion, 2 channels, presence and effects-mix master controls.			
1987-1991		$350	$450
JCM 800 Model 5210 Combo Amp			
1986-1991. Solidstate, 50 watts, channel switching, 1x12".			
1983		$290	$375
JCM 800 Model 5212 Combo Amp			
1986-1991. Solidstate, 50 watts, 2x12" split channel reverb combo.			
1986-1991		$360	$475
JCM 800 Model 5213 Combo Amp			
1986-1991. Solidstate, 2x12", channel-switching, effects loop.			
1986-1991		$290	$375
JCM 800 Model 5215 Combo Amp			
1986-1991. Solidstate, 1x15", Accutronics reverb, effects loop.			
1986-1991		$290	$375
JCM 900 Model 2100 Mark III Amp Head			
1990-1993. FX loop, 100/50-watt selectable lead head.			
1990-1993		$725	$950
JCM 900 Model 2100 SL-X Amp Head			
1992-1998. Hi-gain 100 watt head amp, additional 12AX7 preamp tube.			
1992-1998		$725	$950
JCM 900 Model 2500 SL-X Amp Head			
1990-2000. 50 watt version of SL-X.			
1992-1998		$725	$950

JCM 900 Model 4100 Dual Reverb Amp

1990-2017. Vintage Series, 100/50 switchable head, JCM 900 on front panel, 4x10 or 2x12 matching cab, black with black front.

MODEL YEAR	FEATURES	EXC. COND. LOW	HIGH
1990-2017	4x10 or 2x12	$450	$600
1990-2017	Head only	$650	$850

JCM 900 Model 4101 Combo Amp

1990-2000. All tube, 100 watts, 1x12" combo.

MODEL YEAR	FEATURES	EXC. COND. LOW	HIGH
1990-2000		$675	$900

JCM 900 Model 4102 Combo Amp

1990-2000. Combo amp, 100/50 watts switchable, 2x12".

MODEL YEAR	FEATURES	EXC. COND. LOW	HIGH
1990-2000		$700	$925

JCM 900 Model 4500 Amp Head

1990-2000. All tube, 2 channels, 50/25 watts, EL34 powered, reverb, effects loop, compensated recording out, master volume, black.

MODEL YEAR	FEATURES	EXC. COND. LOW	HIGH
1990-2000		$600	$800

JCM 900 Model 4501 Dual Reverb Combo Amp

1990-2000. 50/25 switchable, 1x12".

MODEL YEAR	FEATURES	EXC. COND. LOW	HIGH
1990-2000		$675	$875

JCM 900 Model 4502 Combo Amp

1990-2000. 50/25 switchable, 2x12".

MODEL YEAR	FEATURES	EXC. COND. LOW	HIGH
1990-2000		$700	$900

JCM 2000 DSL Series Amp

1998-2015. DSL is Dual Super Lead, 2 independent channels labelled classic and ultra, JCM 2000 and DSL logos both on front panel.

MODEL YEAR	FEATURES	EXC. COND. LOW	HIGH
1998-2015	Half-stacks/combos	$240	$825

JCM 2000 TSL Series Amp

1998-2013. TSL is Triple Super Lead, 3 independent channels labelled clean, crunch and lead, 8 tubes, JCM 2000 and TSL logos both on front panel.

MODEL YEAR	FEATURES	EXC. COND. LOW	HIGH
1998-2013	Full stacks	$1,200	$1,825
1998-2013	Half-stacks/combos	$630	$1,225

JCM Slash Signature Model 2555SL Amp Set

1996. Based on JCM 800 with higher gain, matching amp and cab set, JCM Slash Signature logo on front panel, single channel, Slash Signature 1960AV 4x12" slant cab, black.

MODEL YEAR	FEATURES	EXC. COND. LOW	HIGH
1996	4x12 cab	$700	$900
1996	Head only	$1,550	$2,000

JMD Series

2010-2013. JMD is Jim Marshall Digital. Models include JMD50 & 100 heads and JMD 102 (100w, 2x12) & 501 (50w, 1x12) combos.

MODEL YEAR	FEATURES	EXC. COND. LOW	HIGH
2010-2013	501	$490	$650

JTM 30 Series Amp

1995-1997. Tube combo, reverb, 30 watts, effects loops, 5881 output sections, footswitchable high-gain modes. Available as 1x15", 1x12", 2x12" or 3x10" combo or as 4x10" half-stack.

MODEL YEAR	FEATURES	EXC. COND. LOW	HIGH
1995-1997	Combo 1x12	$435	$560
1995-1997	Combo 2x10	$460	$600
1995-1997	Combo 2x12	$485	$630
1995-1997	Combo 3x10	$485	$630

JTM 45 Amp Head

1962-1964. Amp head, 45 watts. The original Marshall amp. Became the Model 1987 45-watt for '65-'66.

MODEL YEAR	FEATURES	EXC. COND. LOW	HIGH
1962		$8,300	$10,800
1963-1964		$7,300	$9,500

JTM 45 Model 1961 MK IV 4x10 Combo Amp

1965-1966. 45 watts, 4x10", tremolo, JTM 45 MK IV on panel, Bluesbreaker association.

MODEL YEAR	FEATURES	EXC. COND. LOW	HIGH
1965-1966		$7,000	$9,100

JTM 45 Model 1962 MK IV 2x12 Combo Amp

1965-1966. 45 watts, 2x12", tremolo, JTM 45 MK IV on panel, Bluesbreaker association.

MODEL YEAR	FEATURES	EXC. COND. LOW	HIGH
1965-1966		$7,200	$9,400

JTM 45 Model 1987 Amp Head Reissue

1988-1999. Black/green tolex.

MODEL YEAR	FEATURES	EXC. COND. LOW	HIGH
1988-1999		$1,025	$1,350

JTM 45 Model 1987 Mark II Lead Amp Head

1965-1966. Replaced JTM 45 Amp ('62-'64), but was subsequently replaced by the Model 1987 50-watt Head during '66.

MODEL YEAR	FEATURES	EXC. COND. LOW	HIGH
1965-1966		$4,900	$6,500

JTM 45 Offset Limited Edition Amp Set Reissue

Introduced in 2000. Limited run of 300 units, old style cosmetics, 45-watt head and offset 2x12" cab, dark vinyl cover, light gray grille, rectangular logo plate on front of amp and cab, Limited Edition plate on rear of cab, serial number xxx of 300.

MODEL YEAR	FEATURES	EXC. COND. LOW	HIGH
2000		$2,450	$3,250

JTM 50 Amp Head

1966-1967. JTM 50 panel logo, EL34 power tubes.

MODEL YEAR	FEATURES	EXC. COND. LOW	HIGH
1966-1967		$5,000	$6,550

JTM 50 Model 1961 MK IV 4x10 Amp

1965-1972. 50 watts, 4x10", Bluesbreaker association, tremolo, JTM 50 MK IV on front panel to '68, plain front panel without model description '68-'72.

MODEL YEAR	FEATURES	EXC. COND. LOW	HIGH
1966-1967		$6,300	$8,200
1968		$5,900	$7,700
1969		$5,300	$7,000
1970		$4,500	$6,000
1971-1972		$3,800	$5,000

JTM 50 Model 1962 Bluesbreaker Amp Reissue

1989-1999. 50 watts, 2x12", Model 1962 reissue Bluesbreaker.

MODEL YEAR	FEATURES	EXC. COND. LOW	HIGH
1989-1999		$1,200	$1,600

JTM 50 Model 1962 MK IV 2x12 Amp

1966-1972. 50 watts, 2x12", tremolo, Bluesbreaker association, JTM 50 MK IV on front panel to '68, plain front panel without model description '68-'72.

MODEL YEAR	FEATURES	EXC. COND. LOW	HIGH
1966-1967		$7,700	$10,000
1968		$7,100	$9,300
1969		$5,900	$7,700
1970		$5,400	$7,100
1971-1972		$4,600	$6,000

JTM 50 Model 1963 PA Amp Head

1965-1966. MK II PA head, block logo.

MODEL YEAR	FEATURES	EXC. COND. LOW	HIGH
1965-1966		$2,000	$2,600

JTM 60 Series Amp

1995-1997. Tube, 60 watts, 1x12", 1x15", 2x12" or 3x10" combo or as 4x10" half-stack.

MODEL YEAR	FEATURES	EXC. COND. LOW	HIGH
1995-1997	1x12 Combo	$475	$615
1995-1997	2x12 Combo	$500	$650
1995-1997	3x10 Combo	$525	$675
1995-1997	4x10 Mini half-stack	$525	$675

Marshall JCM 800 Model 4010

Stephan Brown

1964 Marshall JTM 45

Eddie Daurelle

Marshall JTM 45 Model 1961 MK IV

Pang Leo

Marshall Micro Stack 3005

Tim McClutchy

Marshall Model 1922

1967 Marshall Model 1958 18-Watt Lead

Kris Blakely

MODEL YEAR	FEATURES	EXC. COND. LOW	HIGH

JTM 310 Amp

1995-1997. JTM 30 with 2x10".

1995-1997		$500	$650

JTM 612 Combo Amp

1995-1997. Tube combo amp, 60 watts, 1x12", EQ, reverb, effects loop.

1995-1997		$475	$615

JVM Series

2007-present. Models (H for Head, C Combo) include 205H/205C (50-watt head/combo 2x12), 210H/210C (100-watt head/combo 2x12), 215C (50-watt 1x12 combo), 410H/410C (100-watt head/combo 2x12, 4-channel).

2007-2017	JVM410C	$975	$1,300
2008-2020	JVM205H	$775	$1,025
2008-2020	JVM210C	$1,075	$1,400
2008-2020	JVM210H	$825	$1,075

MA Series Amp

2009-2013. Models include 50C (50 watts, 1x12"), 50H (50-watt head), 100C (100 watts, 2x12"), 100H (100-watt head) and 412 (4x12" slant cabinet).

2009-2013	Half-stacks/combos	$315	$485

MB Series Amp

2006-2012. Bass Combo Series, models include 30C (30watts, 1x10").

2006-2012	MB30C	$110	$145

MG Series Amp

1999-present. Models include 10KK (10 watts, 1x6"), 15CD, 15RCD or CDR (15 watts, 1x8"), 15MS (15 watts, micro stack, 1x8" slant and straight cabs), 15MSII, (in '02, 10" speakers), 15MSZW (15 watts, 2x1x10"), 50DFX (50 watts, 1x12"), 100DFX (100 watts, combo), 100HDFX (100-watt head), 100RCD (Valvestate Series, 100-watt), 102FX (100 watts, 2x12"), 250DFX (250 watts, combo), 412A (4x12" cabinet).

1999-2020	Various models	$40	$275

Micro Stack 3005 Amp

1986-1991. Solidstate head, 12 watts, 2 1x10" stackable cabs (one slant, one straight). Standard model is black, but was also offered in white, green, red, or the silver Silver Jubilee version with Jubilee 25/50 logo.

1986-1991	Black	$270	$360
1986-1991	Green or red	$360	$485
1986-1991	White	$340	$460
1987-1989	Silver Jubilee/silver	$460	$605

Mini-Stack 3210 MOS-FET Amp Head with 2x4x10"

1984-1991. Model 3210 MOS-FET head with 2 4x10" cabs, designed as affordable stack.

1984-1991		$320	$430

Model 1710 Bass Cabinet

1990s. 1x15" speaker.

1990s		$270	$360

Model 1912 Cabinet

1989-1998, 2013-2017. 1x12", 150 watts.

2013-2017		$270	$360

Model 1917 PA-20 Amp Head

1967-1973. PA head with 20 watts, but often used for guitar, matching cabinet.

1967-1968	Matching cab	$1,000	$1,300
1967-1968	Plexi head	$2,300	$3,000
1969-1973	Aluminum head	$1,800	$2,300
1969-1973	Matching cab	$825	$1,100

Model 1922 Amp Cabinet

1989-present. 2x12" extension cab for JCM 800 Series amps.

1989-2020		$215	$280

Model 1930 Popular Combo Amp

1969-1973. 10 watts, 1x12", tremolo.

1969-1972		$1,875	$2,450
1973		$2,000	$2,600

Model 1933 Amp Cabinet

1981-1991. 1x12" extension cab for JCM 800 Series amps.

1981-1991		$270	$345

Model 1935/1935A/1935B Bass Cabinet

1967-1990s. Models 1935, 4x12", black, A slant front, B straight front.

1967-1970	75w	$1,875	$2,450
1971-1972	Black, weave	$975	$1,275
1973-1975	Black, checkerboard	$925	$1,200
1976-1979	Black	$825	$1,100
1979-1983	260w	$490	$650
1983-1986	280w	$435	$580
1990s		$340	$435

Model 1936 Amp Cabinet

1981-2011. Extension straight-front cab for JCM 800/900 Series amps, 2x12" speakers, black.

1981-2011		$340	$435

Model 1937 Bass Cabinet

1981-1986. 4x12", 140 watts.

1981-1986		$435	$580

Model 1958 18-Watt Lead Amp

1965-1968. 18 watts, 2x10" combo, Bluesbreaker cosmetics.

1965-1968		$4,700	$6,100

Model 1958 20-Watt Lead Amp

1968-1972. 20 watts, 2x10" combo, tremolo.

1968		$4,200	$5,500
1969		$3,700	$4,900
1970		$3,600	$4,700
1971-1972		$3,200	$4,200

Model 1959 Super Lead Amp

1966-1981. Two channels, 100 watts, 4 inputs, no master volume. Plexiglas control panels until mid-'69, aluminum after. See Model T1959 for tremolo version. Early custom color versions are rare and more valuable.

1966-1969	Black, plexi	$3,700	$4,900
1966-1969	Custom color, plexi	$5,300	$7,000
1969-1970	Black, aluminum	$2,200	$2,900
1969-1970	Custom color, aluminum	$4,400	$5,700
1971-1972	Black, hand-wired, small box	$2,200	$2,900
1971-1972	Custom color, hand-wired	$2,600	$3,400
1973-1975	Black, printed CB, large box	$1,450	$1,925
1973-1975	Custom color, printed CB	$1,950	$2,600
1976-1979	Black	$1,250	$1,650
1976-1979	Custom color	$1,450	$1,925
1980-1981	Black	$1,175	$1,550
1980-1981	Custom color	$1,350	$1,750

Model T1959 Super Lead (Tremolo) Amp Head

1966-1973. Head amp, 100 watts, plexi until mid-'69, aluminum after. Tremolo version of the Model 1959 Amp.

MODEL YEAR	FEATURES	EXC. COND. LOW	HIGH
1966-1969	Black, plexi	$3,900	$5,100
1966-1969	Custom color, plexi	$5,700	$7,400
1969-1970	Black, aluminum	$1,875	$2,450
1969-1970	Custom color, aluminum	$4,425	$5,800
1971-1973	Black, hand-wired, small box	$1,700	$2,200
1971-1973	Custom color, hand-wired	$2,450	$3,200

35th Anniversary Marshall Limited Edition Set

1997. Limited Edition 1997 logo, includes matching Super Lead MKII 100-watt head, PB100 power brake and MKII 1960A slant cab, all in white covering.

1997		$2,100	$2,800

Model 1959 SLP Reissue Amp Head

1992-2017. Vintage Series, Super Lead Plexi (SLP).

1992-1999	Black vinyl	$1,000	$1,300
1992-1999	Purple vinyl or white	$1,200	$1,550
2000-2017	Black vinyl	$1,200	$1,550

Model 1959 SLP Reissue Amp Set

1992-2013. Vintage Series, 100 watt Super Lead head and matching 4x12" slant cab.

1992-2013	4x12 Cab	$475	$625

Model 1959HW Amp

2005-present. Hand-wired, 100 watts, 4x12" slant front cab.

2005-2014	Cab	$475	$625
2005-2020	Head only	$1,000	$1,300

Model 1959RR Ltd. Ed. Randy Rhoads Amp

2008-2013. Randy Rhoads Tribute, full stack, 100 watts.

2008-2013		$2,100	$2,800

Model 1960 4x12 Speaker Cabinet

1964-1979. Both straight and slant front. The original Marshall 4x12" cab designed for compact size with 4x12" speakers. First issue in '64/'65 is 60-watt cab, from '65-'70 75 watts, from '70-'79 100 watts. After '79, model numbers contained an alpha suffix: A for slant front, B straight.

1966-1970	Black, weave	$2,000	$2,600
1966-1970	Custom color, weave	$2,800	$3,700
1971-1972	Black, weave	$1,100	$1,450
1971-1972	Custom color, weave	$1,525	$2,000
1973-1975	Black, checkerboard	$800	$1,050
1973-1975	Custom color, checkerboard	$1,200	$1,600
1976-1979	Black	$750	$1,000
1976-1979	Custom color	$1,200	$1,600

Model 1960A/1960B 4x12 Speaker Cabinet

1980-1983 (260 watts), '84-'86 (280 watts, JCM 800 era), '86-'90 (300 watts, JCM 800 era), '90-present (300 watts, JCM 900 era, stereo-mono switching). A slant or B straight front.

MODEL YEAR	FEATURES	EXC. COND. LOW	HIGH
1980-1983	Black	$435	$575
1980-1983	Custom color	$625	$825
1984-1986	Black	$375	$500
1984-1986	Custom color	$575	$750
1984-1986	Rare color	$775	$1,000
1987-1990	Black	$350	$450
1987-1990	Custom color	$475	$625
1987-1990	Rare color	$675	$900
2000-2007	A, Black	$325	$425
2000-2007	B, Black	$350	$450

Model 1960AC/1960BC Classic Speaker Cabinet

2005-2013. 100 watts, 4x12" Celestion G-12M-25 greenback speakers, black, AC slant front, BC straight front.

2005-2013	AC	$575	$750
2005-2013	BC	$525	$700

Model 1960AHW/1960BHW 4x12 Cabinet

2005-present. Half stack cab for HW series, AHW slant or BHW straight front.

2005-2020		$575	$750

Model 1960AV/1960BV 4x12 Cabinet

1990-present. JCM 900 updated, stereo/mono switching, AV slant, BV straight front.

1990-1999	Red vinyl, tan grille	$450	$600
1990-2012	Black vinyl, black grille	$435	$575
1990-2020	Various colors	$350	$450

Model 1960AX/1960BX 4x12 Cabinet

1990-present. Cab for Model 1987X and 1959X reissue heads, AX slant, BX straight.

1990-2020	AX	$435	$575
1990-2020	BX	$435	$575

Model 1960TV 4x12 Slant Cabinet

1990-2012. Extra tall for JTM 45, mono, 100 watts.

1990-2012	Various colors	$350	$450

Model 1962 Bluesbreaker Combo Amp

1999-2017. Vintage Series, similar to JTM 45 but with 2 reissue 'Greenback' 25-watt 2x12" speakers and addition of footswitchable tremolo effect.

1999-2017		$975	$1,300

Model 1964 Lead/Bass 50-Watt Amp Head

1973-1976. Head with 50 watts, designed for lead or bass.

1973-1976		$875	$1,150

Model 1965A/1965B Cabinet

1984-1991. 140 watt 4x10" slant front (A) or straight front (B) cab.

1984-1991		$315	$415

Model 1966 Cabinet

1985-1991. 150 watt 2x12" cab.

1985-1991		$315	$415

Model 1967 Major 200-Watt Amp Head

1968-1974. 200 watts, the original Marshall 200 Pig was not popular and revised into the 200 'Major'. The new Major 200 was similar to the other large amps and included 2 channels, 4 inputs, but a larger amp cab.

1968	Plexi	$2,200	$2,900
1969-1970	Aluminum	$2,000	$2,600
1971-1972	Small box	$1,050	$1,400
1973-1974	Large box	$1,025	$1,350

1971 Marshall Model 1959 Super Lead

William Bethurem

Marshall Model 1959HW

Marshall Model 1962 Bluesbreaker Combo

Marshall Model 1974X

AMPS

1972 Marshall Model 2040 Artist

Mark K

1971 Marshall Model 2060 Mercury

Steve Lee

MODEL YEAR	FEATURES	EXC. COND. LOW	HIGH

Model 1967 Pig 200-Watt Amp Head

1967-early-1968 only. Head with 200 watts. The control panel was short and stubby and nicknamed the Pig, the 200-watt circuit was dissimilar (and unpopular) to the 50-watt and 100-watt circuits.

1967-1968		$2,300	$3,000

Model 1968 100-Watt Super PA Amp Head

1966-1975. PA head with 100 watts, 2 sets of 4 inputs (identifies PA configuration), often used for guitar, matching cabinet.

1966-1969	Matching cab	$1,200	$1,600
1966-1969	Plexi	$2,725	$3,575
1969-1972	Aluminum	$2,050	$2,700
1969-1975	Matching cab	$850	$1,100

Model 1973 Amp

1965-1968. Tube combo, 18 watts, 2x12".

1965		$6,500	$8,500
1966		$6,200	$8,100
1967		$5,100	$6,600
1968		$4,500	$5,900

Model 1973 JMP Lead/Bass 20 Amp

1973 only. Front panel: JMP, back panel: Lead & Bass 20, 20 watts, 1x12" straight front checkered grille cab, head and cab black vinyl.

1973		$1,875	$2,425

Model 1974 Amp

1965-1968. Tube combo, 18 watts, 1x12".

1965		$4,000	$5,300
1966		$3,800	$5,000
1967		$3,500	$4,600
1968		$3,200	$4,250

Model 1974X Amp

2004-present. Handwired Series, reissue of 18-watt, 1x12" combo, extension cabinet available.

2004-2020	Combo	$1,175	$1,550

Model 1974X/1974CX Amp

2004-present. Handwired Series, reissue of 18-watt, 1x12" combo, extension cabinet available (CX).

2004-2020	1974CX cab	$475	$625

Model 1982/1982A/1982B Cabinet

1967-1987. Bass and lead 4x12", 100 watt 1982/1982B, upped to 120 watts in '70. Becomes higher powered 320 and 400 watts Model 1982A/B in '81 and '82.

1967-1970		$2,000	$2,600
1971-1980		$750	$1,450
1981-1982		$435	$575
1983-1987		$350	$575

Model 1986 50-Watt Bass Amp Head

1966-1981. Bass version of 1987, 50-watt.

1966-1969	Black, plexi	$3,100	$4,100
1969-1970	Black, aluminum	$2,100	$2,800
1971-1972	Black, hand-wired, small box	$1,700	$2,300
1973-1975	Black, printed CB, large box	$1,450	$1,925
1976-1979	Black	$1,250	$1,650
1980-1981	Black	$1,175	$1,550

Model 1987 50-Watt Amp Head

1966-1981. Head amp, 50 watts, plexiglas panel until mid-'69, aluminum panel after.

1966-1969	Black, plexi	$3,100	$4,100
1966-1969	Custom color, plexi	$4,800	$6,200
1969-1970	Black, aluminum	$2,100	$2,800
1969-1970	Custom color, aluminum	$3,900	$5,200
1971-1972	Black, hand-wired, small box	$1,700	$2,300
1971-1972	Custom color, hand-wired	$2,600	$3,400
1973-1975	Black, printed CB, large box	$1,450	$1,925
1973-1975	Custom color, printed CB	$1,950	$2,600
1976-1979	Black	$1,250	$1,650
1976-1979	Custom color	$1,450	$1,925
1980-1981	Black	$1,175	$1,550
1980-1981	Custom color	$1,350	$1,750

Model 1987X Amp Head

1992-present. Vintage Series amp, all tube, 50 watts, 4 inputs, plexi.

1992-2020		$975	$1,300

Model 1992 Super Bass Amp Head

1966-1981. 100 watts, plexi panel until mid-'69 when replaced by aluminum front panel, 2 channels, 4 inputs.

1966-1969	Black, plexi	$3,700	$4,900
1966-1969	Custom color, plexi	$5,300	$7,000
1969-1970	Black, aluminum	$2,200	$2,900
1969-1970	Custom color, aluminum	$4,400	$5,700
1971-1972	Black, hand-wired, small box	$2,200	$2,900
1971-1972	Custom color, hand-wired	$2,600	$3,400
1973-1975	Black, printed CB, large box	$1,450	$1,925
1973-1975	Custom color, printed CB	$1,950	$2,600
1976-1979	Black	$1,250	$1,650
1976-1979	Custom color	$1,450	$1,925
1980-1981	Black	$1,175	$1,550
1980-1981	Custom color	$1,350	$1,750

Model 1992LEM Lemmy Signature Super Bass Amp

2008-2013. Lemmy Kilmister specs, matching 100-watt head with 4x12" and 4x15" stacked cabinets.

2008-2013	Full-stack	$3,200	$4,200

Model 2040 Artist 50-Watt Combo Amp

1971-1978. 50 watts, 2x12" Artist/Artiste combo model with a different (less popular?) circuit.

1971-1978		$1,550	$2,000

Model 2041 Artist Head/Cabinet Set

1971-1978. 50 watts, 2x12" half stack Artist/Artiste cab with a different (less popular?) circuit.

1971-1978		$1,800	$2,300

Model 2046 Specialist 25-Watt Combo Amp

1972-1973. 25 watts, 1x15" speaker, limited production due to design flaw (amp overheats).

1972-1973		$525	$700

MODEL YEAR	FEATURES	EXC. COND. LOW	HIGH

Model 2060 Mercury Combo Amp
1972-1973. Combo amp, 5 watts, 1x12", available in red or orange covering.

1972-1973		$550	$725

Model 2061 20-Watt Lead/Bass Amp Head
1968-1973. Lead/bass head, 20 watts, plexi until '69, aluminum after. Reissued in '04 as the Model 2061X.

1968-1969	Black, plexi	$3,000	$4,000
1969-1970	Black, aluminum	$2,100	$2,700
1971-1972	Black, aluminum	$1,600	$2,100
1973	Black, aluminum	$1,450	$1,900

Model 2061X 20-Watt Lead/Bass Amp Head Reissue
2004-2017. Handwired Series, reissue of 2061 amp head, 20 watts.

2004-2014	1x12 cab	$359	$475
2004-2015	2x12 cab	$375	$500
2004-2017	Head only	$875	$1,125

Model 2068 Artist (JMP) Amp Set
1971-1978. 100-watt head with matching Artist cab, reverb, small logo.

1971-1978		$1,550	$2,000

Model 2078 Combo Amp
1973-1978. Solidstate, 100 watts, 4x12" combo, gold front panel, dark cover, gray grille.

1973-1978		$700	$925

Model 2103 100-Watt 1-Channel Master Combo Amp
1975-1981. One channel, 2 inputs, 100 watts, 2x12", first master volume design, combo version of 2203 head.

1975-1981		$1,100	$1,450

Model 2104 50-Watt 1-Channel Master Combo Amp
1975-1981. One channel, 2 inputs, 50 watts, 2x12", first master volume design, combo version of 2204 head.

1975-1981		$1,100	$1,450

Model 2144 Master Reverb Combo Amp
1978 only. Master volume similar to 2104 but with reverb and boost, 50 watts, 2x12".

1978		$1,200	$1,600

Model 2150 100-Watt 1x12 Combo Amp
1978. Tubes.

1978		$700	$925

Model 2159 100-Watt 2-Channel Combo Amp
1977-1981. 100 watts, 2 channels, 4 inputs, 2x12" combo version of Model 1959 Super Lead head.

1977-1981		$1,025	$1,350

Model 2199 Amp
1979. Solidstate 2x12" combo.

1979		$460	$600

Model 2200 100-Watt Lead Combo Amp
1977-1981. 100 watts, 2x12" combo, early solidstate, includes boost section, no reverb.

1977-1981		$525	$675

Model 2203 Lead Amp Head
1975-1981. Head amp, 100 watts, 2 inputs, first master volume model design, often seen with Mark II logo.

MODEL YEAR	FEATURES	EXC. COND. LOW	HIGH
1975-1981	Black	$1,175	$1,550
1975-1981	Fawn Beige	$1,250	$1,650

Model 2203X JCM800 Reissue Amp Head
2002-2010. 100 watts.

2002-2010		$1,175	$1,550

Model 2204 50-Watt Amp Head
1975-1981. Head only, 50 watts with master volume.

1975-1981		$1,175	$1,550

Model 2266 50-Watt Combo Amp
2007-2013. Vintage Modern series, 2x12".

2007-2013		$650	$850

Model 2466 100-Watt Amp Head
2007-2013. Vintage Modern series.

2007-2013		$650	$850

Model 3203 Artist Amp Head
1986-1991. Tube head version of earlier '84 Model 3210 MOS-FET, designed as affordable alternative, 30 watts, standard short cab, 2 inputs separated by 3 control knobs, Artist 3203 logo on front panel, black.

1986-1991		$390	$520

Model 3210 MOS-FET Amp Head
1984-1991. MOS-FET solidstate head, refer Mini-Stack listing for 3210 with 4x10" stacked cabinets. Early-'80s front panel: Lead 100 MOS-FET.

1984-1991		$270	$355

Model 3310 100-Watt Lead Amp
1988-1991. Solidstate, 100 watts, lead head with channel switching and reverb.

1988-1991		$420	$555

Model 4001 Studio 15 Amp
1985-1992. 15 watts using 6V6 (only model to do this up to this time), 1x12" Celestion Vintage 30 speakers.

1985-1992		$675	$875

Model 4104 50-Watt Combo Amp
1981-1990. Combo version of 2204 head, 50 watts, 2x12", master volume.

1981-1990		$1,300	$1,675

Model 4203 Artist 30 Combo Amp
1986-1991. 30-watt tube hybrid combo, 1x12", channel switching.

1986-1991		$390	$510

Model 5002 Combo Amp
1984-1991. Solidstate combo amp, 20 watts, 1x10", master volume.

1984-1991		$170	$225

Model 5005 Lead 12 Amp
1983-1991. Solidstate student amp, 12 watts, master volume, 1x10".

1983-1991		$195	$245

Model 5205 Reverb 12 Amp
1986. Solidstate, 12 watts, 1x10", Reverb 12 logo on front panel.

1986		$195	$245

Model 5302 Keyboard Amp
1984-1988. Solidstate, 20 watts, 1x10", marketed for keyboard application.

1984-1988		$170	$230

Model 5502 Bass Amp
1984-ca.1992. Solidstate bass combo amp, 20 watts, 1x10" Celestion.

1984-1992		$170	$230

Late-1960s Marshall Model 4001 Studio 15
Imaged by Heritage Auctions, HA.com

1981 Marshall Model 2203
Stephan Brown

2007 Marshall Model 2466 Vintage/Modern
Joseph Bradshaw Jr.

Marshall Model 6100 30th Anniversary

Imaged by Heritage Auctions, HA.com

Marshall MS-4

Ca. 1950s Masco MU-5

Imaged by Heritage Auctions, HA.com

MODEL YEAR	FEATURES	EXC. COND. LOW	HIGH

Model 6100 30th Anniversary Amp

1992-1998. Head with 100/50/25 switchable watts and 4x12" cabinet (matching colors), first year and into early '93 was blue tolex, black afterwards.

1992-1998	4x12 cab	$365	$480
1992-1998	Head only	$725	$975

Model 6101 30th Anniversary Combo Amp

1992-1998. 1x12" combo version of 6100 amp, first year and into early '93 was blue tolex, black afterwards.

1992-1998		$1,050	$1,350

Model 8008 Valvestate Rackmount Amp

1991-2001. Valvestate solidstate rack mount power amp with dual 40-watt channels.

1991-2001		$145	$195

Model 8010 Valvestate VS15 Combo Amp

1991-1997. Valvestate solidstate, 10 watts, 1x8", compact size, black vinyl, black grille.

1991-1997		$125	$170

Model 8040 Valvestate 40V Combo Amp

1991-1997. Valvestate solidstate with tube preamp, 40 watts, 1x12", compact size, black vinyl, black grille.

1991-1997		$145	$195

Model 8080 Valvestate 80V Combo Amp

1991-1997. Valvestate solidstate with tube 12AX7 preamp, 80 watts, 1x12", compact size, black vinyl, black grille.

1991-1997		$145	$195

Model 8100 100-Watt Valvestate VS100H Amp Head

1991-2001. Valvestate solidstate head, 100 watts.

1991-2001		$170	$220

Model 8200 200-Watt Valvestate Amp Head

1993-1998. Valvestate solidstate reverb head, 2x100-watt channels.

1993-1998		$195	$255

Model 8222 Valvestate Cabinet

1993-1998. 200 watts, 2x12 extention cab, designed for 8200 head.

1993-1998		$145	$195

Model 8240 Valvestate Stereo Chorus Amp

1992-1996. Valvestate, 80 watts (2x40 watts stereo), 2x12" combo, reverb, chorus.

1992-1996		$220	$290

Model 8280 2x80-Watt Valvestate Combo Amp

1993-1996. Valvestate solidstate, 2x80 watts, 2x12".

1993-1996		$245	$315

Model 8412 Valvestate Cabinet

1991-2001. 140 watts, 4x12 extention cab, designed for 8100 head.

1991-2001		$195	$255

MS-2/R/C Amp

1990-present. Microamp series, 1 watt, battery operated, miniature black half-stack amp and cab. Red MS-2R and checkered speaker grille and gold logo MS-2C added in '93.

1990-2019		$25	$40

MS-4 Amp

1998-present. Full-stack version of MS-2, black.

1998-2020		$35	$50

Origin (OR) Series

2018-present. Various tube models include; ORIGIN5, 20C, 20H and 50C. Number indicates watts, C is combo, H is head only.

2018-2020		$220	$290

Silver Jubilee Model 2550 50/25 (Tall) Amp Head

1987-1989. 50/25 switchable tall box head for full Jubilee stack, silver vinyl and chrome control panel.

1987-1989		$1,700	$2,275

Silver Jubilee Model 2551 4x12 Cabinet

1987-1989. Matching silver 4x12" cabs for Jubilee 2550 head, various models, silver vinyl.

1987-1989	2551A, slant	$725	$950
1987-1989	2551AV, Vintage 30	$725	$950
1987-1989	2551B, straight	$725	$950
1987-1989	2551BV, Vintage 30	$725	$950

Silver Jubilee Model 2553 50/25 (Short) Amp Head

1987-1988. 50/25 switchable small box head for mini-short stack, silver vinyl and chrome control panel.

1987-1988		$1,550	$2,050

Silver Jubilee Model 2554 1x12 Combo Amp

1987-1989. 50/25 watts, 1x12" combo using 2550 chassis, silver vinyl and chrome control panel.

1987-1989		$1,400	$1,850

Silver Jubilee Model 2555 Amp Head

1987-1989. 100/50 version of 2550 head, silver vinyl and chrome control panel.

1987-1989		$1,450	$1,950

Silver Jubilee Model 2556 2x12 Cabinet

1987-1989. Matching silver 2x12" cabs for Jubilee heads, various models, silver vinyl.

1987-1989	2556A, slant	$725	$975
1987-1989	2556AV, Vintage 30	$725	$975
1987-1989	2556B, straight	$725	$975
1987-1989	2556BV, Vintage 30	$725	$975

Silver Jubilee Model 2558 2x12 Combo Amp

1987-1989. 50/25 watts, 2x12" combo using 2550 chassis, silver vinyl and chrome control panel.

1987-1989		$1,550	$2,050

Silver Jubilee Model 3560 600 Amp Head

1987. Rackmount 2x300 watts.

1987		$390	$510

SL-5 Amp

2013-2015. Tube combo, 5 watts, 1x12", script logo signature on front panel.

2013-2015		$545	$725

Super 100 40th Anniversary JTM45 MK II Full Stack

2005. 100 watts, 2 4x12 cabs, 250 made.

2005		$3,775	$4,950

Martin

Martin has dabbled in amps a few times, under both the Martin and Stinger brand names. The first

MODEL YEAR	FEATURES	EXC. COND. LOW	HIGH

batch were amps made by others introduced with their electric acoustics in 1959.

Model 112 Amp

1959-1961. Branded C.F. Martin inside label, made by Rowe-DeArmond, 1x12 combo, limited production, 2x6V6 power tubes, 2x12AX7 preamp tubes, with tube rectifier, 4 inputs, 3 control knobs.

1959-1961		$2,800	$3,600

SS140 Amp

1965-1966		$675	$875

Stinger FX-1 Amp

1988-1990. 10 watts, EQ, switchable solidstate tube-synth circuit, line out and footswitch jacks.

1988		$120	$155

Stinger FX-1R Amp

1988-1990. Mini-stack amp, 2x10", 15 watts, dual-stage circuitry.

1989		$150	$200

Stinger FX-6B Amp

1989-1990. Combo bass amp, 60 watts, 1x15".

1989		$150	$200

Masco

1940s-1950s. The Mark Alan Sampson Company, Long Island, New York, produced a variety of electronic products including tube PA amps and small combo instrument amps. The PA heads are also popular with harp players.

Massie

1940s. Ray Massie worked in Leo Fender's repair shop in the 1940s and also built tube amps. He later worked at the Fender company.

Matamp

1966-present. Tube amps, combos and cabinets built in Huddersfield, England, bearing names like Red, Green, White, Black, and Blue. German-born Mat Mathias started building amps in England in '58 and designed his first Matamp in '66. From '69 to '73, Mathias also made Orange amps. In '89, Mathias died at age 66 and his family later sold the factory to Jeff Lewis.

1x15" Cabinet

1970s		$650	$850

GT-120 Amp Head

1971		$1,800	$2,300

GT-120 Green Stack Amp

1990s. 120 watt GT head with 4x12" straight front cab.

1993-1999		$1,350	$1,750

Matchless

1989-1999, 2001-present. Founded by Mark Sampson and Rick Perrotta in California. Circuits based on Vox AC-30 with special attention to transformers. A new Matchless company was reorganized in 2001 by Phil Jamison, former head of production for the original company.

Avalon 35 Amp Head

2009-2010. 35 watts head, reverb.

2009-2010		$1,250	$1,625

Brave 40 112 Amp

1997-1999. 40 watts class A, 1x12", footswitchable between high and low inputs.

1997-1999		$1,200	$1,575

Brave 40 212 Amp

1997-1999. 2x12" version of Brave.

1997-1999		$1,300	$1,675

Chief Amp Head

1995-1999. 100 watts class A, head.

1995-1999		$2,050	$2,650

Chief 212 Amp

1995-1999. 100 watts class A, 2x12", reverb.

1995-1999		$2,150	$2,800

Chief 410 Amp

1995-1999. 100 watts class A, 4x10", reverb.

1995-1999		$2,225	$2,900

Chieftan Amp Head

1995-1999. 40 watts class A head, reverb, chicken-head knobs.

1995-1999		$1,350	$1,750

Chieftan 112 Amp

1995-1999, 2001. 40 watts class A, 1x12", reverb.

1995-1999		$1,775	$2,300
2001	Jamison era	$1,775	$2,300

Chieftan 210 Amp

1995-1999. 40 watts class A, 2x10", reverb.

1995-1999		$1,950	$2,500

Chieftan 212 Amp

1995-1999, 2001-present. 40 watts class A, 2x12", reverb.

1995-1999		$1,950	$2,500
2001-2019	Jamison era	$1,950	$2,500

Chieftan 410 Amp

1995-1999. 40 watts class A, 4x10", reverb.

1995-1999		$2,050	$2,650

Clipper 15 112 Amp

1998-1999. 15 watts, single channel, 1x12".

1998-1999		$850	$1,100

Clipper 15 210 Amp

1998-1999. 15 watts, single channel, 2x10".

1998-1999		$900	$1,200

Clubman 35 Amp Head

1993-1999. 35 watts class A head.

1993-1999		$1,500	$1,950

DC-30 Standard Cabinet

1991-1999. 30 watts, 2x12", with or without reverb.

1991-1999		$2,200	$2,900

DC-30 Exotic Wood Cabinet Option

1995-1999. 30 watts, 2x12", gold plating, limited production.

1995-1999		$3,700	$4,800

ES/EB Cabinet

ES = speaker cabinets and EB = bass speaker cabinets.

1991-1999	1x12	$350	$450
1993-1999	2x10	$425	$560
1993-1999	2x10+2x12	$525	$700
1993-1999	2x12	$450	$575
1993-1999	4x12	$575	$750
1997-1999	1x15	$360	$465
1997-1999	4x10	$500	$650

Matamp GT2 MK II

Matchless Clubman 35
David Nicholas

2011 Matchless DC-30
Jacques Menache Masri

AMPS

Matchless Independence 35

1994 Mesa-Boogie .50 Caliber+

Imaged by Heritage Auctions, HA.com

Matchless Nighthawk

MODEL YEAR	FEATURES	EXC. COND. LOW	HIGH

HC-30 Amp Head

1991-1999, 2003. The first model offered by Matchless, 30 watts class A head.

1991-1999		$1,675	$2,150
2003	Jamison era	$1,675	$2,150

HC-85 Amp Head

1992. Only 25 made, similar to HC-30 but more flexible using various tube substitutions.

1992		$1,775	$2,275

Hurricane Amp Head

1997. 15 watts class A head.

1997		$1,000	$1,300

Hurricane 112 Amp

1994-1997. 15 watts class A, 1x12".

1994-1997		$1,000	$1,300

Hurricane 210 Amp

1996-1997. 15 watts class A, 2x10".

1996-1997		$1,200	$1,575

Independence 35 Amp Head

2005-2017. 35 watts, with or without reverb.

2005-2017		$1,500	$1,950

JJ-30 112 John Jorgensen Amp

1997-1999. 30 watts, DC-30 chasis with reverb and tremolo, 1x12" Celestion 30, offered in white, blue, gray sparkle tolex or black.

1997-1999		$2,975	$3,800

Lightning 15 Amp Head

1994-1997, 2005-present. 15 watts class A head.

1994-1997		$1,075	$1,400

Lightning 15 112 Amp

1994-1999, 2001-present. 15 watts class A, 1x12".

1994-1999		$1,525	$2,000
2001-2020	Jamison era	$1,525	$2,000

Lightning 15 210 Amp

1996-1997, 2001-2006. 15 watts class A, 2x10".

1996-1997		$1,625	$2,100
2001-2006	Jamison era	$1,625	$2,100

Lightning 15 212 Amp

1998, 2001-present. 15 watts class A, 2x12".

1998-2020		$1,650	$2,150

Little Monster Amp

2007-2009. 9 watts, offered as head, and 1x12" or 2x12" combo.

2007-2009		$1,050	$1,400

Nighthawk Amp

2003-present. 15 watts, offered as head, and 1x12", 2x10" or 2x12" combo.

2003-2014	2x10	$1,000	$1,300
2003-2020	1x12	$925	$1,200
2003-2020	2x12	$1,050	$1,350

Phoenix 35 (PH-35) Amp Head

2003-present. 35-watt head, red.

2003-2020		$1,500	$1,950

SC-30 Standard Cabinet Amp

1991-1999. 30 watts class A, 1x12".

1991-1999		$2,200	$2,875
2001-2006	Jamison era	$2,050	$2,700

SC-30 Exotic Wood Cabinet Amp

1995-1999. 30 watts class A, 1x12", gold plating, limited production.

1995-1999		$3,550	$4,550

MODEL YEAR	FEATURES	EXC. COND. LOW	HIGH

Skyliner Reverb 15 112 Amp

1998-1999. 15 watts, 2 channels, 1x12".

1998-1999		$750	$975

Skyliner Reverb 15 210 Amp

1998-1999. 15 watts, 2 channels, 2x10".

1998-1999		$825	$1,075

Spitfire 15 Amp Head

1997. 15 watts, head.

1997		$975	$1,300

Spitfire 15 112 Amp

1994-1997. 15 watts, 1x12".

1994-1997		$1,100	$1,450

Spitfire 15 210 Amp

1996-1997. 15 watts, 2x10".

1996-1997		$1,200	$1,575

Starliner 40 212 Amp

1999. 40 watts, 2x12".

1999		$1,250	$1,625

Superchief 120 Amp Head

1994-1999. 120 watts, class A head.

1994-1999		$1,950	$2,500

TC-30 Standard Cabinet Amp

1991-1999. 30 watts, 2x10" class A, low production numbers makes value approximate with DC-30.

1991-1999		$2,150	$2,750

TC-30 Exotic Wood Cabinet Amp

1991-1999. 30 watts, 2x10" class A, limited production.

1991-1999		$2,750	$3,525

Thunderchief Bass Amp Head

1994-1999. 200 watts, class A bass head.

1994-1999		$1,525	$2,000

Thunderman 100 Bass Combo Amp

1997-1998. 100 watts, 1x15" in portaflex-style flip-top cab.

1997-1998		$2,125	$2,750

Tornado 15 112 Amp

1994-1995. Compact, 15 watts, 1x12", 2-tone covering, simple controls - volume, tone, tremolo speed, tremolo depth.

1994-1995		$725	$925

Maven Peal

Amps, combos and cabinets built by David Zimmerman in Plainfield, Vermont, beginning in 1999. Serial number format is by amp wattage and sequential build; for example, 15-watt amp 15-001.

Mega Amplifiers

Budget and intermediate grade, production, solidstate and tube amps from Guitar Jones, Inc. of Pomona, California.

Merlin

Rack mount bass heads built in Germany by Musician Sound Design. They also offer the MSD guitar effects.

Mesa-Boogie

1971-present. Founded by Randall Smith in San Francisco, California. Circuits styled on high-gain Fender-based chassis designs, ushering in the compact high-gain amp market. Mesa was acquired by Gibson in early 2021.

The following serial number information and specs courtesy of Mesa Engineering.

.50 Caliber/.50 Caliber+ Amp Head

Jan. 1987-Dec. 1988, 1992-1993. Serial numbers: SS3100 - SS11,499. Mesa Engineering calls it Caliber .50. Tube head amp, 50 watts, 5-band EQ, effects loop. Called the .50 Caliber Plus in '92 and '93.

Model Year	Features	Exc. Cond. Low	Exc. Cond. High
1987-1988	Caliber	$500	$650
1992-1993	Caliber+	$500	$650

.50 Caliber+ Combo Amp

Dec. 1988-Oct. 1993. Serial numbers FP11,550 - FP29,080. 50 watts, 1x12" combo amp.

Model Year	Features	Exc. Cond. Low	Exc. Cond. High
1988-1993		$550	$725

20/20 Amp

Jun. 1995-2010. Serial numbers: TT-01. 20-22 watts per channel.

Model Year	Features	Exc. Cond. Low	Exc. Cond. High
1995-2010		$550	$725

50/50 (Fifty/Fifty) Amp

May 1989-2001. Serial numbers: FF001-. 100 watts total power, 50 watts per channel, front panel reads Fifty/Fifty, contains 4 6L6 power tubes.

Model Year	Features	Exc. Cond. Low	Exc. Cond. High
1989-2001		$525	$700

395 Amp

Feb. 1991-Apr. 1992. Serial numbers: S2572 - S3237.

Model Year	Features	Exc. Cond. Low	Exc. Cond. High
1991-1992		$725	$950

Bass 400/Bass 400+ Amp Head

Aug. 1989-Aug. 1990. Serial numbers: B001-B1200. About 500 watts using 12 5881 power tubes. Replaced by 400+ Aug.1990-present, serial numbers: B1200- . Update change to 7-band EQ at serial number B1677.

Model Year	Features	Exc. Cond. Low	Exc. Cond. High
1989-1990	Bass 400	$925	$1,225
1990-1999	Bass 400+	$975	$1,300

Big Block Series Amp

2004-2014. Rackmount bass amps, models 750 and Titan V-12.

Model Year	Features	Exc. Cond. Low	Exc. Cond. High
2004-2014	750 Bass Head, 750w	$925	$1,225
2006-2010	Titan V-12, 650-1200w	$925	$1,225

Blue Angel Series Amp

Jun. 1994-2004. Serial numbers BA01-. Switchable between 15, 33 or 38 watts, offered as head, 1x12" combo or 4x10" combo, blue cover.

Model Year	Features	Exc. Cond. Low	Exc. Cond. High
1994-2004	Combo 1x12"	$700	$925
1994-2004	Combo 4x10"	$800	$1,050

Buster Bass Amp Head

Dec. 1997-Jan. 2001. Serial numbers: BS-1-999. 200 watts via 6 6L6 power tubes.

Model Year	Features	Exc. Cond. Low	Exc. Cond. High
1997-2001		$525	$700

Buster Bass Combo Amp

1999-2001. 200 watts, 2x10", wedge cabinet, black vinyl, metal grille.

Model Year	Features	Exc. Cond. Low	Exc. Cond. High
1999-2001		$525	$700

Coliseum 300 Amp

Oct. 1997-2000. Serial numbers: COL-01 - COL-132. 200 watts/channel, 12 6L6 power tubes, rack mount.

Model Year	Features	Exc. Cond. Low	Exc. Cond. High
1997-2000		$1,000	$1,350

D-180 Amp Head

Jul. 1982-Dec. 1985. Serial numbers: D001-D681. All tube head amp, 200 watts, preamp, switchable.

Model Year	Features	Exc. Cond. Low	Exc. Cond. High
1982-1985		$775	$1,025

DC-3 Amp

Sep. 1994-Jan. 1999. Serial numbers: DC3-001 - DC3-4523. 35 watts, 1x12".

Model Year	Features	Exc. Cond. Low	Exc. Cond. High
1994-1999	Combo 1x12"	$600	$800
1994-1999	Head only	$525	$675

DC-5 Amp

Oct. 1993-Jan. 1999. Serial numbers: DC1024 - DC31,941. 50-watt head, 1x12" combo.

Model Year	Features	Exc. Cond. Low	Exc. Cond. High
1993-1999	Combo 1x12"	$600	$800
1993-1999	Head only	$525	$675

DC-10 Amp

May 1996-Jan. 1999. Serial numbers: DCX-001 - DCX-999. Dirty/Clean (DC), 100 watts (6L6s), 2x12".

Model Year	Features	Exc. Cond. Low	Exc. Cond. High
1993-1996	Combo 2x12"	$675	$900
1996-1999	Head only	$600	$775

Electra Dyne Amp Head

2009-2013. 45/90 watts, Black Taurus/black grille or British Tan Bronco/tan grille.

Model Year	Features	Exc. Cond. Low	Exc. Cond. High
2009-2013		$850	$1,100

Express Series Amp

2007-2017. Compact combo tube amps with power switching.

Model Year	Features	Exc. Cond. Low	Exc. Cond. High
2007-2016	5:50, 2x12", 5-50w	$775	$1,025
2007-2017	5:25, 1x10", 5-25w	$675	$875
2007-2017	5:50, 1x12", 5-50w	$725	$950
2008	5:25, short head, 25w	$600	$800

Extension Cabinet

1980s-present. Mesa-Boogie offered 'extension cabinets' which could be mixed and matched with amp heads, using different configurations with correct impedance. Other manufacturers often consider an extension cab as an extra cab, but Mesa Engineering considers it to be the main cab (not an extra). The company has generic cabs as well as cabs associated with specific models, but both generic and model-specific fall into similar price ranges. Some other variances include; vertical or horizontal, open back or closed, slant or straight front, grille could be metal or cloth, and some cabs are designated for bass guitar. Specialized cabinets may be more than values shown.

Model Year	Features	Exc. Cond. Low	Exc. Cond. High
1980-2020	Various sizes	$225	$900

F-30 Amp

2002-Feb. 2007. Combo, 30 watts, 1x12".

Model Year	Features	Exc. Cond. Low	Exc. Cond. High
2002-2007		$400	$525

F-50 Amp

2002-Feb. 2007. Combo, 50 watts, 1x12", AB 2 6L6 power.

Model Year	Features	Exc. Cond. Low	Exc. Cond. High
2002-2007		$575	$750
2002-2007	Head only	$525	$700

F-100 Amp

2002-Feb. 2007. Combo, 100 watts, 2x12".

Model Year	Features	Exc. Cond. Low	Exc. Cond. High
2002-2007	Combo 2x12"	$725	$925
2002-2007	Head only	$625	$800

Fillmore 100 Combo Amp

2019-present. 100 watts, 1x12" or 2x12", 2 footswitchable channels.

Model Year	Features	Exc. Cond. Low	Exc. Cond. High
2019-2020		$1,100	$1,425

Formula Preamp

Jul. 1998-2002. Serial numbers: F-01. Used 5 12AX7 tubes, 3 channels.

Model Year	Features	Exc. Cond. Low	Exc. Cond. High
1998-2002		$350	$450

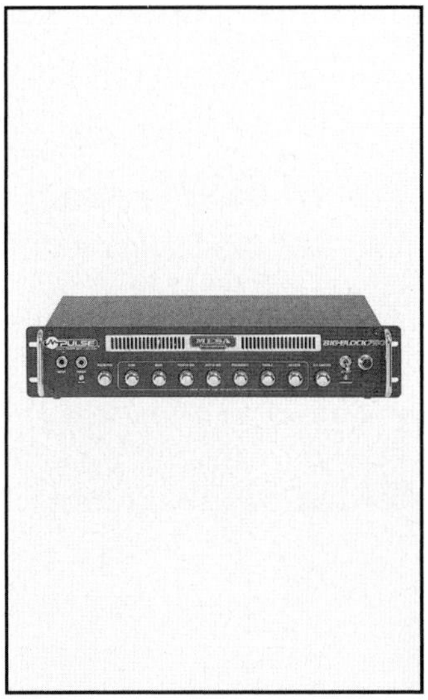

Mesa-Boogie Big Block 750

Mesa-Boogie Blue Angel

Mesa-Boogie Express 5:50

Mesa-Boogie Lone Star 1x12

1977 Mesa-Boogie Mark I

1980s Mesa-Boogie Mark III Combo

Imaged by Heritage Auctions, HA.com

MODEL YEAR	FEATURES	EXC. COND. LOW	HIGH

Heartbreaker Amp Head

1996-2001. Head only, 100 watts.

1996-2001		$800	$1,025

Heartbreaker Combo Amp

Jun. 1996-2001. Serial numbers: HRT-01. 60 to 100 watts switchable, 2x12" combo, designed to switch-out 6L6s, EL34s or the lower powered 6V6s in the power section, switchable solidstate or tube rectifier.

1996-2001		$875	$1,125

Lone Star Series Amp

2004-present. Designed by founder Randall Smith and Doug West with focus on boutique-type amp. Class A (EL84) or AB (4 6L6) circuits, long or short head, 1x12" combo, 2x12" combo, and short head 4x10" cab, and long head 4x12" cab.

2004-2016	Combo 1x12", hardwood	$1,525	$2,000
2004-2016	Combo 4x10", blue	$1,150	$1,500
2004-2020	Combo 1x12"	$1,025	$1,350
2004-2020	Combo 2x12"	$1,150	$1,500
2004-2020	Head, class A or AB	$950	$1,250

Lone Star Special Amp

2005-present. Smaller lighter version using EL84 power tubes, 5/15/30 watts, long or short head amp or 1x12", 2x12" or 4x10" combo.

2005-2020	Combo 1x12"	$1,125	$1,475

M-180 Amp

Apr. 1982-Jan. 1986. Serial numbers: M001-M275. Rack mount tube power amp.

1982-1986		$575	$750

M-190 Amp

1980s. Rack mount tube power amp.

1980s		$425	$550

M-2000 Amp

Jun. 1995-2003. Serial numbers: B2K-01.

1995-2003		$625	$800

M6 Carbine Bass Amp Head

2011-2017. 600-watt head, also offered in 2x12 combo.

2011-2017		$500	$650

Mark I Amp Head

1990. 60/100 watts, tweed cover.

1990		$1,300	$1,675

Mark I Combo (Model A) Amp

1971-1978. The original Boogie amp, not called the Mark I until the Mark II was issued, 60 or 100 watts, 1x12", Model A serial numbers: 1-2999, very early serial numbers 1-299 had 1x15".

1971-1978	1x12" or 1x15"	$1,300	$1,675

Mark I Reissue Amp

Nov. 1989-Sept. 2007. Serial numbers: H001-. 100 watts, 1x12", reissue features include figured maple cab and wicker grille.

2000-2007	Hardwood cab	$1,250	$1,600
2000-2007	Standard cab	$925	$1,225

Mark II B Amp Head

1981-1983. Head only.

1981-1983		$575	$750

Mark II B Combo Amp

1980-1983. Effective Aug. '80 1x12" models, serial numbers 5575-110000. May '83 1x15" models, serial numbers 560-11000. The 300 series serial numbers K1-K336.

1981-1983	1x12" or 1x15", tolex	$800	$1,050
1981-1983	Hardwood cab	$1,100	$1,450

Mark II C/Mark II C+ Amp

May 1983-Mar. 1985. Serial numbers 11001-14999 for 60 watts, 1x15", offered with optional white tolex cover. 300 series serial numbers after C+ are in the series K337-K422.

1983-1985		$2,150	$2,850
1985	Hardwood cab	$2,600	$3,450

Mark II C+ Amp Head

1983-1985. 60-watt head.

1983-1985	Hardwood cab	$2,500	$3,350
1983-1985	Standard cab	$2,050	$2,750

Mark II Combo Amp

1978-1980. Late-'78 1x12", serial numbers: 3000-5574. Effective Aug.'80 1x15", serial numbers: 300-559 until Mark II B replaced.

1978-1980	1x12" or 1x15"	$725	$950

Mark III Amp Head

1985-1999. 100 watts, black vinyl.

1985-1990		$800	$1,050
1985-1990	Custom hardwood	$1,250	$1,625
1990-1999	Graphic EQ model	$900	$1,175

Mark III Combo Amp

Mar. 1985-Feb. 1999. Serial numbers: 15000-28384. 300 series serialization K500-. Graphic equalizer only Mark III since Aug.'90, 100 watts, 1x12" combo. Custom cover or exotic hardwood cab will bring more than standard vinyl cover cab. There is also a Simul-Class Mark III which can run in 25, 60 or 85 watts.

1985-1990	Black	$900	$1,175
1985-1990	Custom color	$1,050	$1,400
1985-1999	Custom hardwood	$1,450	$1,900
1990-1999	Graphic EQ, standard cab	$1,050	$1,375

Mark IV (Rack Mount) Amp Head

1990-May 2008. Rack mount version.

1990-2008		$850	$1,100

Mark IV Amp Head

1990-May 2008. Clean rhythm, crunch rhythm and lead modes, 85 watts, EQ, 3-spring reverb, dual effects loops, digital footswitching. Also available in custom hardwood cab with wicker grille.

1990-2008	Custom hardwood	$1,300	$1,700
1990-2008	Short head, tolex	$850	$1,100

Mark IV/Mark IV B Combo Amp

May 1990-May 2008. Changed to Model IV B Feb.'95, serial numbers: IV001. Clean rhythm, crunch rhythm and lead modes, 40 watts, EQ, 3-spring reverb, dual effects loops, digital footswitching.

1991-1999		$1,000	$1,275
1991-1999	Custom hardwood	$1,550	$2,050
2000-2008		$1,000	$1,275
2000-2008	Custom hardwood	$1,625	$2,100

Mark V Private Reserve 40th Anniversary Amp

2009-2010. Limited production, 1x12 combo, 40th Anniversary logo.

2009-2010		$3,350	$4,400

MODEL YEAR	FEATURES	EXC. COND. LOW	HIGH

Mark V Private Reserve Amp

2011-2016. Special order, 1x12" combo.

2011-2016		$3,175	$4,200

Mark V/Mark Five Amp

2010-present. 3 channels, 10/45/90 watts, also in 1x12" combo.

2010-2020	Combo 1x12"	$1,500	$1,950
2010-2020	Head	$1,350	$1,800

Mark V:35/Mark Five:35 Amp

2015-present. 35/25/10 watts, also 1x12 combo, black.

2015-2020	Combo 1x12"	$1,200	$1,600
2015-2020	Head	$1,350	$1,750

Maverick Dual Rectifier Amp Head

1994-Feb. 2005. 35 watts, Dual Rectifier head, white/blond vinyl cover.

1994-2005		$700	$900

Maverick Dual Rectifier Combo Amp

1997-Feb. 2005. Dual channels, 4 EL84s, 35 watts, 1x12", 2x12" or 4x10" combo amp, 5AR4 tube rectifier, cream vinyl covering. Serial number: MAV. Also available as head.

1997-2005	1x12"	$750	$975
1997-2005	2x12"	$850	$1,100
2005	4x10"	$900	$1,150

Mini Rectifier Twenty-Five Amp Head

2012-present. Ultra compact design, 10/25 watts, 2 channels.

2012-2020		$625	$800

M-Pulse 360 Amp

Jul. 2001-2005. Serial numbers: MP3-01-. Rack mount, silver panel.

2001-2003		$600	$775

M-Pulse 600 Amp

Apr. 2001-2011. Serial numbers: MP6-01- . Rack mount bass with 600 watts, tube preamp.

2001-2011		$650	$850

Nomad 45 Amp Head

1999-Feb. 2005. 45 watts, dark vinyl cover, dark grille.

1999-2005		$400	$525

Nomad 45 Combo Amp

Jul. 1999-Feb. 2005. Serial numbers: NM45-01. 45 watts, 1x12, 2x12" or 4x10" combo, dark vinyl cover, dark grille.

1999-2005	1x12"	$450	$600
1999-2005	2x12"	$500	$650
1999-2005	4x10"	$575	$750

Nomad 55 Amp Head

1999-2004. 55 watt head only.

1999-2004		$400	$525

Nomad 55 Combo Amp

Jul. 1999-2004. Serial numbers: NM55-01. 55 watts, 1x12", 2x12" or 4x10" combo.

1999-2004	1x12"	$450	$600
1999-2004	2x12"	$500	$650

Nomad 100 Amp Head

Jul. 1999-Feb. 2005. 100 watts, black cover, black grille.

1999-2005		$450	$600

Nomad 100 Combo Amp

Jul. 1999-Feb. 2005. 100 watts, 1x12" or 2x12" combo, black cover, black grille.

1999-2005	1x12"	$500	$650
1999-2005	2x12"	$525	$675

MODEL YEAR	FEATURES	EXC. COND. LOW	HIGH

Princeton Boost Fender Conversion Amp

1970. Fender Princeton modified by Randall Smith, Boogie badge logo instead of the Fender blackface logo on upper left corner of the grille. About 300 amps were modified and were one of the early mods that became Mesa-Boogie.

1970		$2,000	$2,600

Quad Preamp

Sep. 1987-1992. Serial numbers: Q001-Q2857. Optional Quad with FU2-A footswitch Aug.'90-Jan.'92, serial numbers: Q2022-Q2857.

1990-1992	With footswitch	$550	$725

Recto Recording Preamp

2004-2018. Rack mount preamp.

2004-2018		$750	$975

Rect-O-Verb Combo Amp

Dec. 1998-2001. Serial numbers R50-. 50 watts, 1x12", black vinyl cover, black grille.

1998-2001		$775	$1,000

Rect-O-Verb I Amp Head

Dec. 1998-2001. Serial numbers: R50-. 50 watts, head with 2 6L6 power tubes, upgraded Apr.'01 to II Series.

1998-2001		$725	$950

Rect-O-Verb II Amp Head

Apr. 2001-2010. Upgrade, serial number R5H-750.

2001-2010		$725	$950

Rect-O-Verb II Combo Amp

April 2001-2010. Upgrade R5H-750, 50 watts, AB, 2 6L6, spring reverb.

2001-2010		$800	$1,025

Road King Dual Rectifier Amp Head

2002-May 2017. Tube head, various power tube selections based upon a chasis which uses 2 EL34s and 4 6L6, 2 5U4 dual rectifier tubes or silicon diode rectifiers, 50, 100 or 120 watts. Series II upgrades start in '06.

2002-2011		$1,725	$2,200
2006-2017	Series II	$1,725	$2,200

Road King Dual Rectifier Combo Amp

2002-2015. 2x12" combo version, Series II upgrades start in '06.

2002-2005	Select watts	$1,800	$2,325
2006-2015	Series II	$1,800	$2,325

Roadster Dual Rectifier Amp

2006-May 2017. 50/100 watts, head only, 1x12" or 2x12" combo.

2006-2014	Combo 1x12	$1,525	$1,950
2006-2017	Combo 2x12	$1,575	$2,025
2006-2017	Head	$1,450	$1,850

Rocket 44 Amp

2011. 45 watts, 1x12" combo, spring reverb, FX loop.

2011		$425	$550

Rocket 440 Amp

Mar. 1999-Aug. 2000. Serial numbers: R440-R44-1159. 45 watts, 4x10".

1999-2000		$550	$725

Satellite/Satellite 60 Amp

Aug. 1990-1999. Serial numbers: ST001-ST841. Uses either 6L6s for 100 watts or EL34s for 60 watts, dark vinyl, dark grille.

1990-1999		$500	$675

Mesa-Boogie Mini Rectifier Twenty-Five

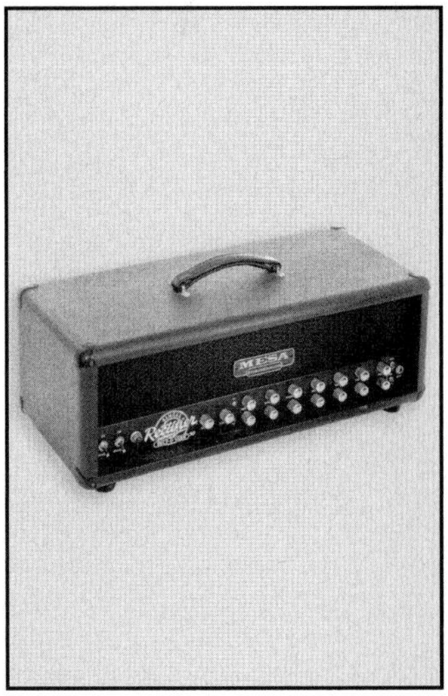

Mesa-Boogie Rect-O-Verb I

Imaged by Heritage Auctions, HA.com

Mesa-Boogie Road King II Dual Rectifier Combo

1984 Mesa-Boogie Son Of Boogie
Tom Pfeifer

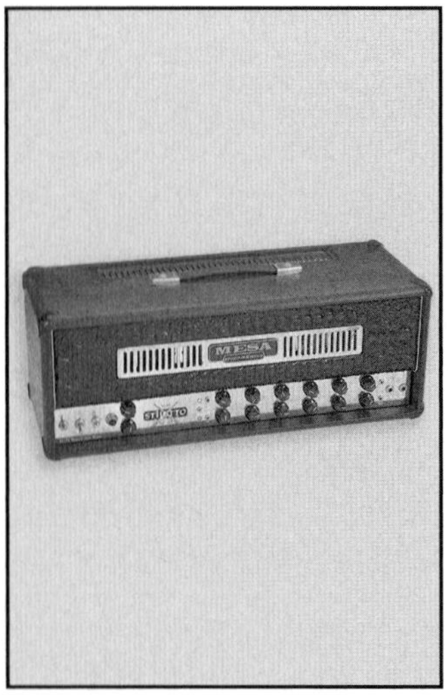

Mesa-Boogie Stiletto
Imaged by Heritage Auctions, HA.com

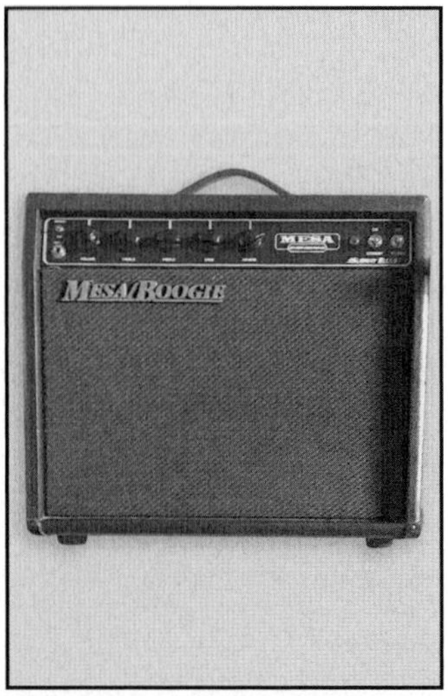

1999 Mesa-Boogie Subway Blues
Mark Aftab Sackoor

MODEL YEAR	FEATURES	EXC. COND. LOW	HIGH

Solo 50 Rectifier Series I Amp Head
Nov. 1998-Apr. 2001. Serial numbers: R50. 50-watt head.
1998-2001 | | $600 | $775

Solo 50 Rectifier Series II Amp Head
Apr. 2001-2011. Upgrade, serial numbers: S50-S1709. Upgrades preamp section, head with 50 watts.
2001-2011 | | $600 | $775

Solo Dual Rectifier Amp
1997-2011. Dual Rectifier Solo logo on front panel, 3x5U4, 150 watts.
1997-2011 | | $1,100 | $1,425

Solo Triple Rectifier Amp
1997-2011. Triple Rectifier Solo logo on front panel, 3x5U4, 150 watts.
1997-2011 | | $1,100 | $1,425

Son Of Boogie Amp
May 1982-Dec. 1985. Serial numbers: S100-S2390. 60 watts, 1x12", considered the first reissue of the original Mark I.
1982-1985 | | $500 | $650

Stereo 290 (Simul 2-Ninety) Amp
Jun. 1992-present. Serial numbers: R0001-. Dual 90-watt stereo channels, rack mount.
1992-2020 | | $700 | $900

Stereo 295 Amp
Mar. 1987-May 1991. Serial numbers: S001-S2673. Dual 95-watt class A/B stereo channels, rack mount. Selectable 30 watts Class A (EL34 power tubes) power.
1987-1991 | | $450 | $600

Stiletto Ace Amp
2007-2011. 50 watts, 2 channels, head or combo.
2007-2011 | Combo 1x12" | $800 | $1,050
2007-2011 | Combo 2x12" | $875 | $1,125
2007-2011 | Head only | $775 | $1,000

Stiletto Series Amp Head
2004-2011. Series includes the Deuce (50 or 100 watts, 4 EL-34s) and Trident (50 or 150 watts, 6 EL-34s).
2004-2011 | Deuce | $950 | $1,225
2004-2011 | Trident | $1,000 | $1,300

Strategy 400 Amp
Mar. 1987-May 1991. Serial numbers: S001-S2627. 400 to 500 watts, power amplifier with 12 6L6 power tubes.
1987-1991 | | $700 | $925

Strategy 500 Amp
Jun. 1991-Apr. 1992. S2,552- . Rack mount, 500 watts, 4 6550 power tubes.
1991-1992 | | $875 | $1,150

Studio .22/Studio .22+ Amp
Nov. 1985-1988. Serial numbers: SS000-SS11499, black vinyl, black grille, 22 watts, 1x12". Replaced by .22+ Dec. '88-Aug. '93. Serial numbers: FP11,500-FP28,582. 22 watts.
1985-1988 | 22 | $500 | $650
1988-1993 | 22+ | $500 | $650

Studio Caliber DC-2 Amp
Apr. 1994-Jan. 1999. Serial numbers: DC2-01 - DC2-4247 (formerly called DC-2). 20 watts, 1x12" combo, dark vinyl, dark grille.
1994-1999 | | $400 | $525

Studio Preamp
Aug. 1988-Dec. 1993. Serial numbers: SP000-SP7890. Tube preamp, EQ, reverb, effects loop.
1988-1993 | | $400 | $525

Subway Reverb Rocket Amp
Jun. 1998-Aug. 2001. Serial numbers: RR1000-RR2461. 20 watts, 1x10".
1998-2001 | | $500 | $675

Subway Rocket (Non-Reverb) Amp
Jan. 1996-Jul. 1998. Serial numbers: SR001-SR2825. No reverb, 20 watts, 1x10".
1996-1998 | | $500 | $675

Subway/Subway Blues Amp
Sep. 1994-Aug. 2000. Serial numbers: SB001-SB2515. 20 watts, 1x10".
1994-2000 | | $475 | $625

TA-15 Amp Head
2010-2015. TransAtlantic series, lunchbox-sized tube head, 2 channels, 5/15/25 watts.
2010-2015 | | $500 | $650

TA-30 Combo Amp
2012-2015. TransAtlantic series, 15/30/40 watts, 1x12" or 2x12" combo, 2 channels.
2012-2015 | | $850 | $1,125

Trem-O-Verb Dual Rectifier Amp Head
Jun. 1993-Jan. 2001. 100-watt head version.
1993-2001 | | $925 | $1,200
1993-2001 | Rackmount version | $925 | $1,200

Trem-O-Verb Dual Rectifier Combo Amp
Jun.1993-Jan.2001. Serial numbers: R- to about R-21210. 100 watts, 2x12" Celestion Vintage 30.
1993-2001 | | $925 | $1,200

Triaxis Programmable Preamp
Oct. 1991-2016. Serial numbers:T0001-. 5 12AX7 tube preamp, rack mount.
1991-2016 | | $925 | $1,200

Venture Bass (M-Pulse) Amp
2007-2009 | | $750 | $1,000

V-Twin Rackmount Amp
May 1995-Jun. 1998. Serial numbers: V2R-001 to V2R-2258.
1995-1998 | | $425 | $550

WalkAbout M-Pulse Bass Amp Head
Sep. 2001-May 2017. Serial numbers: WK-01-. Lightweight 13 pounds, 2 12AX7s + 300 MOS-FET.
2001-2017 | | $550 | $725

WalkAbout Scout Convertible Combo Amp
2001-May 2017. Head and 1x12 combo.
2001-2017 | | $800 | $1,025

Meteoro

1986-present. Guitar, bass, harp and keyboard combo amps, heads, and cabinets built in Brazil. They also build effects.

Metropoulos Amplification

2004-present. George Metropoulos builds his professional and premium grade amps in Flint, Michigan.

MODEL YEAR	FEATURES	EXC. COND. LOW	HIGH

MG

2004-present. Tube combo guitar amps built by Marcelo Giangrande in São Paulo, Brazil. He also builds effects.

Mighty Moe Ampstraps

Peter Bellak built his guitar amp straps in Sacramento, California, starting in 2007. He also offered an amp strap for ukulele.

Milbert Amplifiers

2009-present. Professional and premium grade, production/custom, amps for guitars and cars, built in Gaithersburg, Maryland by Michael Milbert.

Mission Amps

1996-present. Bruce Collins' Mission Amps, located in Arvada, Colorado, produces a line of custom-made combo amps, heads, and cabinets.

Mojave Amp Works

2002-present. Tube amp heads and speaker cabinets by Victor Mason in Apple Valley, California.

Montgomery Ward

Amps for this large retailer were sometimes branded as Montgomery Ward, but usually as Airline (see that listing).

1x12" Combo Amp

1950s. 1x12", about 2 6L6 power tubes, includes Model 8439 and brown covered Maestro C Series with cloverleaf grille.

1950s		$400	$600

Model 55 JDR 8437 Amp

1950s. 4x8" speakers in 'suitcase' amp cabinet, brown control panel.

1950s		$500	$700

Mooneyes

Budget solid state amp line from Lace Music Products. They also offered amps under the Rat Fink and Lace brands. Lace had a Mooneyes guitar model line.

Morley

Late-1960s-present. The effects company offered an amp in the late '70s. See Effects section for more company information.

Bigfoot Amp

1979-ca.1981. Looks like Morley's '70s effects pedals, produced 25 watts and pedal controlled volume. Amp only, speakers were sold separately.

1979-1981		$175	$225

Mosrite

1968-1969. Mosrite jumped into the amp business during the last stages of the company history, the company was founded as a guitar company in 1954 and attained national fame in the '60s but by the time the company entered the amp business, the guitar boom began to fade, forcing the original Mosrite out of business in '69.

Model 400 Fuzzrite Amp

1968-1969. Solidstate, 1x15 combo, black tolex with silver grille, reverb and tremolo.

1968-1969		$625	$825

Model SS-550 The Gospel Amp

1968. Solidstate, 1 speaker combo, 2 channels normal and tremolo, reverb, black tolex.

1968		$575	$750

Mountain

Mountain builds a 9-volt amp in a wood cabinet. Originally built in California, then Nevada; currently being made in Vancouver, British Columbia.

Multivox

Ca.1946-ca.1984. Multivox was started as a subsidiary of Premier to manufacture amps, and later, effects. Generally student grade to low intermediate grade amps.

Murph

1965-1967. Amps marketed by Murph Guitars of San Fernado, California. At first they were custom-made tube amps, but most were later solidstate production models made by another manufacturer.

Music Man

1972-present. Music Man made amps from '73 to '83. The number preceding the amp model indicates the speaker configuration. The last number in model name usually referred to the watts. RD indicated Reverb Distortion. RP indicated Reverb Phase. Many models were available in head-only versions and as combos with various speaker combinations.

Sixty Five Amp Head

1973-1981. 65 watts, reverb, tremolo.

1973-1981		$350	$450

Seventy Five Reverb/75 Reverb Amp

1973-1981. Head amp, 75 watts, reverb.

1973-1981		$375	$475

110 RD Fifty Amp

1980-1983. 50 watts, 1x10", reverb, distortion.

1980-1983		$400	$525

112 B Bass Amp

1983. 50 watts, 1x12".

1983		$400	$525

112 RD Fifty Amp

1980-1983. 50 watts, 1x12", reverb, distortion.

1980-1983		$400	$525

112 RD Sixty Five Amp

1978-1983. 65 watts, 1x12", reverb, distortion.

1978-1983		$400	$525

112 RD One Hundred Amp

1978-1983. 100 watts, 1x12", reverb, distortion, EVM option for heavy duty 12" Electro-Voice speakers.

1978-1983		$475	$625
1978-1983	EVM option	$475	$625

112 RP Sixty Five Amp

1978-1983 65 watts, 1x12", reverb, built-in phaser

1978-1983		$475	$625

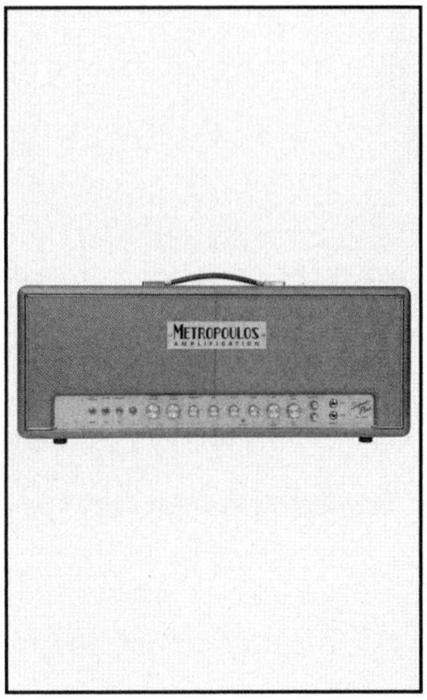

Metropoulos Super-Plex

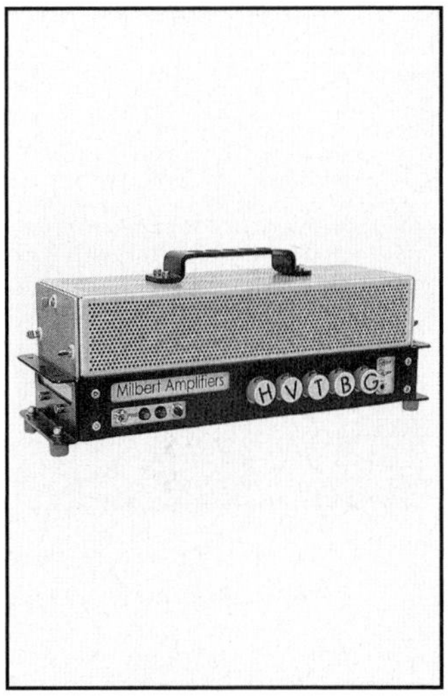

Milbert GAGA D-90

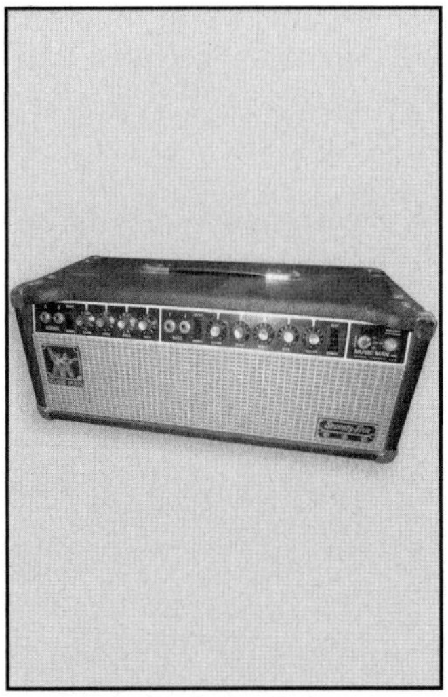
1979 Music Man Seventy Five
Rivington Guitars

AMPS

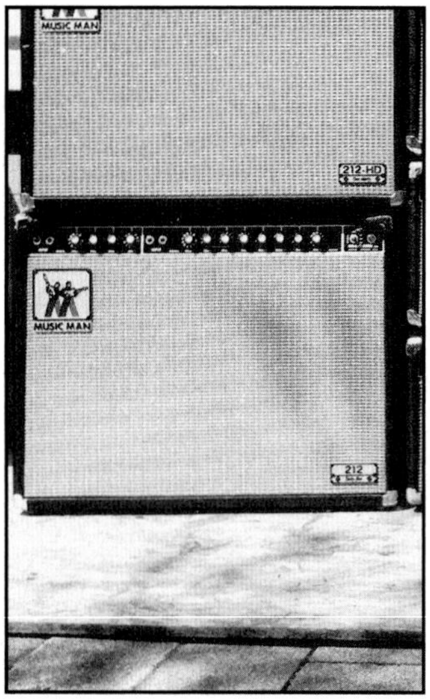
Music Man 112 HD130
Terry Loose

1978 Music Man 212 HD130
Federico Garibotti

1967 National Bass 70
Tom Pfeifer

MODEL YEAR	FEATURES	EXC. COND. LOW	HIGH

112 RP One Hundred Amp
1978-1983. Combo amp, 100 watts, 1x12", reverb, built-in phaser.
1978-1983 $475 $625

112 Sixty Five Amp
1973-1981. Combo amp, 65 watts, 1x12", reverb, tremolo.
1973-1981 $475 $625

115 Sixty Five Amp
1973-1981. Combo amp, 65 watts, 1x15", reverb, tremolo.
1973-1981 $475 $625

210 HD130 Amp
1973-1981. 130 watts, 2x10", reverb, tremolo.
1973-1981 $525 $700

210 Sixty Five Amp
1973-1981. 65 watts, 2x10", reverb, tremolo.
1973-1981 $525 $700

212 HD130 Amp
1973-1981. 130 watts, 2x12", reverb, tremolo.
1973-1981 $525 $700

212 Sixty Five Amp
1973-1981. 65 watts, 2x12", reverb, tremolo.
1973-1981 $525 $700

410 Sixty Five Amp
1973-1981. 65 watts, 4x10", reverb, tremolo.
1973-1981 $525 $700

410 Seventy Five Amp
1982-1983. 75 watts, 4x10", reverb, tremolo.
1982-1983 $525 $700

HD-130 Amp
1973-1981. Head amp, 130 watts, reverb, tremolo.
1973-1981 Head only $375 $475

HD-150 Amp
1973-1981. Head amp, 75/100 watts.
1973-1981 Head only $375 $475

RD Fifty Amp
1980-1983. Head amp, 50 watts, reverb, distortion.
1980-1983 Head only $375 $475

Nady

1976-present. Wireless sound company Nady Systems started offering tube combo and amp heads in '06.

NARB

1973. Briefly made by Ken Bran and Jim Marshall, about 24 made, all were Marshall 100-watt tremolo half-stack, NARB logo on amp and cabinet.

100 Watt Half-Stack
1973. 100 watts, 4x12".
1973 $2,800 $3,700

National

Ca.1927-present. National/Valco amps date back to the late-'30s. National introduced a modern group of amps about the same time they introduced their new Res-O-Glas space-age guitar models in '62. In '64, the amp line was partially redesigned and renamed. By '68, the Res-O-Glas models were gone and National introduced many large vertical and horizontal piggyback models which lasted until National's assets were assigned during bankruptcy in '69. The National name went to Chicago importer Strum N' Drum. Initially, Strum N' Drum had one amp, the National GA 950 P Tremolo/Reverb piggyback.

Aztec Amp
1950s. Combo, early '50s version with 3 Rola 7x11" speakers using 3 speaker baffle openings, about 20 watts using 2x6L6 power tubes, 2-tone brown leatherette and tweed cover. By '56, amp has one 15" speaker and does not have segmented grill.
1950s 3 Rola 7x11 $775 $1,025
1956 1x15 $725 $950

Bass 70/Bass 75 Amp
1962-1967. 35 watts (per channel), 2x12" (often Jensen) speakers, large knobs, Raven Black tolex with silver and white grille, designed for bass. New model name in '64 with nearly identical features but listed as total of 70 watts, in '62 called Bass 70 but renamed Bass 75 in '64.
1962-1963 Bass 70 $700 $900
1964-1967 Bass 75 N6475B $700 $900

Chicagoan Model 1220 Amp
1950s. 17 watts, 1x10", tube, says "Valco Chicago 51" on control panel.
1950s $650 $850

Dynamic 20 Amp
1962-1963. 17 watts, 2x8" (often Jensen) speakers, 2 large knobs, Raven Black tolex with silver and white grille, compact student-intermediate amp.
1962-1963 $675 $900

Glenwood 90 Amp
1962-1967. 35 watts, 2x12" (often Jensen) speakers, large knobs, reverb, tremolo, Raven Black tolex with silver and white grille, top of the line, becomes the nearly identical N6490TR in '64.
1962-1963 $1,025 $1,375
1964-1967 Model N6490TR $950 $1,250

Glenwood Vibrato Amp
Two 12" speakers, reverb, tremolo.
1964-1967 Model N6499VR $1,025 $1,375

Model 75 Amp
1940s. Vertical tweed combo cabinet, volume and tone knobs, 3 inputs.
1940s $450 $600

Model 100 Amp
1940. Tube amp, 40 watts, 1x12".
1940 $525 $675

Model 1202 Twin Amp
1954. 18 watts, 2x8" Jensen speaker, 2 channels (Instrument and microphone), horizontal flying bird logo on grille.
1954 $700 $900

Model 1210 High Fidelity Amp
1954. 20 watts, 1x15" Jensen speaker, 4 input jacks, 2 channels (instrument and microphone), 20x24x10" combo, metal handle.
1954 $700 $900

Model 1212 Amp
1954. 12 watts, 1x12", 5 tubes, 3 inputs, 15x18x8" combo, diving flying bird logo on grille, plastic handle.
1954 $650 $850

MODEL YEAR	FEATURES	EXC. COND. LOW	HIGH

Model 1215 Amp
1952. 1x12", 2 channels.

1952		$650	$850

Model 1275 Amp
1953. Combo 1x10", 12 watts, 5 tubes, light tan weave cover, deep brown grille cloth.

1953		$625	$825

Model GA 950-P Tremolo/Reverb Piggyback Amp
1970s. Strum N' Drum/National model, solidstate, 50 watts, 2-channel 2x12" and 1x7" in 32" tall vertical cabinet, black.

1970s		$260	$335

Model N6800 - N6899 Piggyback Amps
1968-1969. National introduced a new line of tube amps in '68 and most of them were piggybacks. The N6895 was sized like a Fender piggyback Tremolux, the N6875 and N6878 bass amps were sized like a '68 Fender large cab piggyback with a 26" tall vertical cab, the N6898 and N6899 were the large piggyback guitar amps. These amps feature the standard Jensen speakers or the upgrade JBL speakers, the largest model was the N6800 for PA or guitar, which sported 3x70-watt channels and 2 column speakers using a bass 2x12" + 1x3" horn cab and a voice-guitar 4x10" + 1x3" horn cab.

1968-1969		$500	$650

Model N6816 (Model 16) Amp
1968-1969. Valco-made tube amp, 6 watts, 1x10" Jensen speaker, 17" vertical cab, tremolo, no reverb, black vinyl cover and Coppertone grille.

1968-1969		$350	$450

Model N6820 Thunderball Bass Amp
1968-1969. Valco-made tube amp, about 35 watts, 1x15" Jensen speaker, 19" vertical cab, black vinyl cover and Coppertone grille.

1968-1969		$425	$550

Model N6822 (Model 22) Amp
1968-1969. Valco-made, 6 watts tube (4 tubes) amp, 1x12" Jensen speaker, 19" vertical cab, tremolo and reverb, black vinyl cover and Coppertone grille.

1968-1969		$375	$500

National Dobro Amp
1930s. Sold by the National Dobro Corp. when the company was still in Los Angeles (they later moved to Chicago). National Dobro plate on rear back panel, suitcase style case that flips open to reveal the speaker and amp, National logo on outside of suitcase. The noted price is for an all-original amp in excellent condition (this would be a rare find), there are other 1930s models included in the price range below.

1930s	Early metal baffle	$525	$700
1930s	Later standard baffle	$400	$525
1930s	Suitcase style	$500	$650

Newport 40 Amp
1964-1967. 17 watts, 2x10", tremolo only.

1964-1967	Model N6440T	$650	$850

Newport 50 Amp
1964-1967. 17 watts, 2x10", tremolo and reverb.

1964-1967	Model N6450TR	$650	$850

Newport 97 Amp
1964-1967. 35 watts, 1x15", rear mounted chasis, tremolo.

1964-1967	Model N6497T	$650	$850

Sportsman Amp
1950s. Tweed combo with brown leatherette speaker surround, 1x10".

1950s		$625	$825

Student Practice Amp
1970s. Strum N' Drum era, small solidstate, single control.

1970s		$35	$45

Studio 10 Amp
1962-1967. Five watts, 1x8", 3 tubes, 1 channel, 1 volume control, no tone control, no reverb or tremolo.

1962-1963		$425	$550
1964-1967	Model N6410	$425	$550

Tremo-Tone Model 1224 Amp
1956-1959. Small combo, tremolo, dual Rola oval 6x11" speakers, tweed, by Valco, flying bird pattern on lower front grille.

1956-1959		$925	$1,225

Val-Pro 80 Amp
1962-1963. 35 watts, 2x12" (often Jensen) speakers, 8 tubes, large control knobs, tremolo, black cover with white and silver trim, replaced by Glenwood 90 in '64 with added reverb.

1962-1963		$1,000	$1,300

Val-Trem 40 Amp
1962-1963. 17 watts, 2x10" (often Jensen) speakers, large knobs, Val-Trem logo on back panel, Clear-Wave tremolo, Raven Black tolex with silver and white grille, open back combo amp, becomes Newport 40 in '64.

1962-1963		$800	$1,050

Val-Verb 60 Amp
1962-1963. 17 watts, 2x10" (often Jensen) speakers, large knobs, Val-Verb logo on back panel, reverb, no tremolo, Raven Black tolex with silver and white grille, open back combo amp.

1962-1963		$950	$1,250

Westwood 16 Amp
1964-1967. Five watts using 1 6V6 power, 2 12AX7 preamp, 1 5Y3GT rectifier, tremolo, 2x8", dark vinyl cover, silver grille.

1964-1967	Model N6416T	$650	$850

Westwood 22 Amp
1964-1967. 5 watts, 2x8", reverb and tremolo, 1 channel, 6 tubes.

1964-1967	Model N6422TR	$700	$925

Naylor Engineering

1994-present. Joe Naylor and Kyle Kurtz founded the company in East Pointe, Michigan, in the early '90s, selling J.F. Naylor speakers. In '94 they started producing amps. In '96, Naylor sold his interest in the business to Kurtz and left to form Reverend Guitars. In '99 David King bought the company and moved it to Los Angeles, California, then to Dallas, Texas. Currently Naylor builds tube amps, combos, speakers, and cabinets.

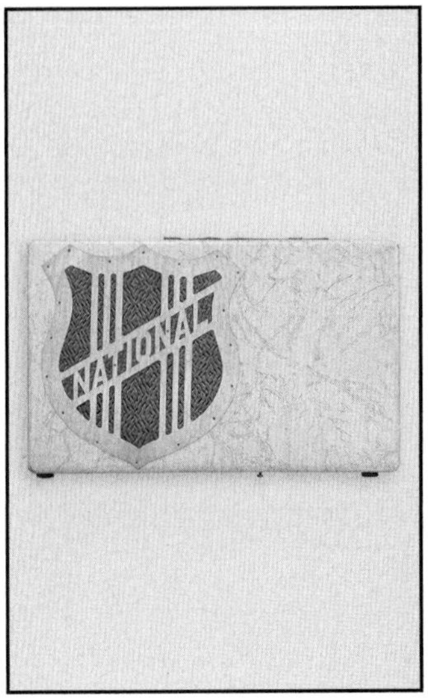

1938 National Model C

National Model 100

Imaged by Heritage Auctions, HA.com

Naylor Electra-Verb 60 Head

Nobels Streetman 15

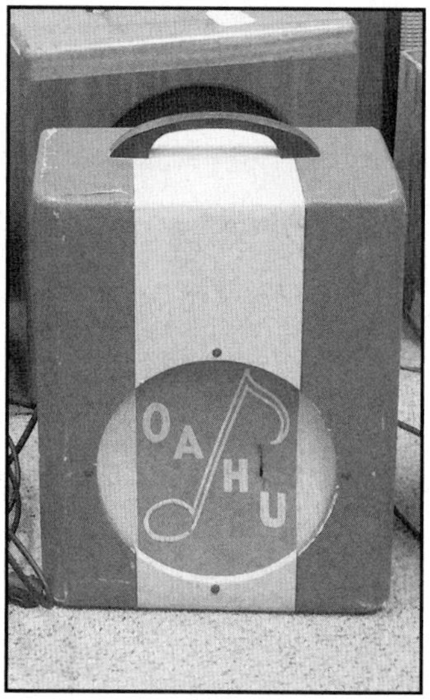

1950 Oahu

Bill Parsons

Oliver Powerflex 500

Don Oflinden

MODEL YEAR	FEATURES	EXC. COND. LOW	HIGH

Nemesis

From the makers of Eden amps, Nemesis is a line of made-in-the-U.S., FET powered bass combos and extension cabinets. The brand is a division of U.S. Music Corp.

Newcomb

1950s. Newcomb Audio Products, Hollywood, California, Newcomb script logo on back panel along with model number, they offered instrument amplifiers that could also be used as small PA.

Model G 12

1953. 1x12" (Rolla) combo amp, 2 controls (volume and tone), large metal handle, oxblood-brown leatherette.

1953		$325	$425

Nobels

1997-present. Effects manufacturer Nobels Electronics of Hamburg, Germany also offers a line of small practice and portable amps.

Noble

Ca. 1950-ca. 1969. From Don Noble and Company, of Chicago, Illinois, owned by Strum N' Drum by mid-'60s. They also offered guitars and amps.

Model 381/Custom 381 Amp

1950s. 2x12" and 2x5".

1958-1960		$1,025	$1,350

Norma

1965-1970. Economy line imported and distributed by Strum N' Drum, Wheeling (Chicago), Illinois. As noted in the National section, Strum N' Drum acquired the National brand in the '70s. Some early amps were tube, but the majority were solidstate.

Solid State Amp

1969-1970	Various models	$55	$110

Oahu

The Oahu Publishing Company and Honolulu Conservatory, based in Cleveland, Ohio, started with acoustic Hawaiian and Spanish guitars, selling large quantities in the 1930s. As electric models became popular, Oahu responded with guitar/amp sets. The brand has been revived on a line of U.S.-made tube amps.

Combo Amp

1965. Small 1x10" combo, 1 6V6, 4 12AX7. 15Y3GT, white cover, light grille, Oahu script logo upper left grille.

1965		$625	$825

Mid-Size Amp

1940s-1950s. 1x10".

1940s-50s		$450	$600

Small Guitar/Lap Steel Amps

1940s-1950s. 1x8", various colors.

1940s-50s		$325	$425

Thunderbolt

1965. 1x12", 6 tubes.

1965		$1,300	$1,700

MODEL YEAR	FEATURES	EXC. COND. LOW	HIGH

Oliver

Ca.1966-ca. 1978. The Oliver Sound Company, Westbury, New York, was founded by former Ampeg engineer, Jess Oliver, after he left Ampeg in '65. Tube amp designs were based upon Oliver's work at Ampeg. The Oliver Powerflex Amp is the best-known design, and featured an elevator platform that would lift the amp head out of the speaker cabinet.

Model B-120 Amp Head

1970s. B-120 logo on front panel, 35 watts, all tube head.

1970s		$425	$550

Model G-150R Combo Amp

1970s. Reverb, tremolo, 2 6L6 power tubes, 40 watts, 1x15", black tolex with black grille, silver control panel.

1970s		$500	$650

Model P-500 Combo Amp

1960s. All tube combo with 15" motorized amp chassis that rises out of tall lateral speaker cabinet as amp warms up.

1960s		$675	$875

Orbital Power Projector Amp

Late-1960s-early-1970s. Rotating speaker cabinet with horn, Leslie-like voice.

1960s-70s		$675	$900

Sam Ash Oliver Amp Head

Late-1960s-early-1970s. Private branded for Sam Ash Music, about 30 watts using the extinct 7027A power tubes, Sam Ash script logo on front grille.

1960s-70s		$325	$425

Omega

2009-present. James Price builds his premium grade, production/custom, amps in Moravian Falls, North Carolina.

Orange

1968-1981, 1995-present. Orange amps and PAs were made in the U.K. by Cliff Cooper and Matthew Mathias. The Orange-colored amps were well-built and were used by many notable guitarists. Since '95, Cliff Cooper is once again making Orange amplifiers in the U.K., with the exception of the small Crush Practice Combo amps, which are made in Korea. '68-'70 amps made by Matamp in Huddersfield, classic designs started in '71 at Bexleyheath/London plant.

Model GRO-100 Graphic Overdrive Amp Head

1969-1971. Four EL34 power, only 2 pre-amp tubes, short-style head, model number on back panel.

1969-1971		$2,500	$3,200

Model OR-80 Amp

1971-1981. Half-stack head and cab, 80 watts, 4x12" straight-front cab with Orange crest on grille, orange vinyl and light orange grille.

1971-1975		$2,300	$3,100
1976-1981		$2,000	$2,700

Model OR-80 Combo Amp

1971-1981. About 80 watts, 2x12" combo.

1971-1975		$2,000	$2,600
1976-1981		$1,700	$2,200

MODEL YEAR	FEATURES	EXC. COND. LOW	HIGH

Model OR-120 Graphic Amp

1972-1981. Half-stack head and cab, 120 watts, 4x12" straight front cab with Orange crest on grille, orange vinyl and light orange grille.

1972-1975		$2,400	$3,200
1976-1981		$2,200	$2,900

Model OR-200 212 Twin Amp

1970s. 120 watts, 2x12" combo, orange vinyl, dark grille, Orange crest on grille, reverb and vibrato, master volume.

1971-1975		$2,300	$3,000
1976-1981		$1,800	$2,400

Orepheus

Early 1960s. Private branded for Coast Wholesale Music Co., Orepheus logo on control panel along with model number.

Small Tube Amp

1960s. Student compact tube amps, some with 2 knobs, volume and tone.

1960s	Model 708	$325	$425

Orpheum

Late-1950s-1960s. Student to medium level amps from New York's Maurice Lipsky Music.

Small/Mid-Size Amp

Late-1950s-1960s. U.S.-made, 2 6V6 power tubes, Jensen P12R 12" speaker, light cover with gray swirl grille.

1950s-60s	Mid-Size	$425	$550
1950s-60s	Small	$325	$425

Osborne Sound Laboratories

Late 1970s. Guitar amps built by Ralph Scaffidi and wife guitarist Mary Osborne in Bakersfield, California. They also offered guitars.

Ovation

1966-present. Kaman made few amps under the Ovation name. They offered a variety of amps under the KMD brand from '85 to around '94.

Little Dude Amp

1969-ca.1971. Solidstate combo, 100 watts, 1x15" and horn, matching slave unit also available.

1970s		$160	$210

The Kat (Model 6012) Amp

1970s. Solidstate, 2x12" combo.

1970s		$160	$210

Overbuilt Amps

1999-2007. Tube amps and combos built by Richard Seccombe in West Hills, California. He now works at Fender R&D.

PAC-AMP (Magnatone)

Late-1950s-early-1960s. Private branded by Magnatone, often for accordion studios.

Model 213 Troubadour Amp

1957-1958. 10 watts, 1x12".

1957-1958		$950	$1,250

MODEL YEAR	FEATURES	EXC. COND. LOW	HIGH

Model 280-A Amp

1961-1963. About 50 watts, 2x12" + 2x5", brown leatherette, light brown grille, stereo vibrato, PAC-AMP nameplate logo.

1961-1963		$1,400	$1,800

Palette Amps

Robert Wakeling began building his tube amp heads and combos and speaker cabinets in Stillwater, Oklahoma in 2003.

PANaramic (Magnatone)

1961-1963. Private branded equivalent of '61-'63 Magnatone brown leatherette series, large PANaramic logo. Many Magnatone private brands were associated with accordion companies or accordian teaching studios. PANaramic was a brand name of PANaramic accordion. They also made guitars.

Model 260/262-style Amp

1961-1963. 35 watts, 2x12", gray vinyl and light grille, vibrato, large PANaramic logo.

1961-1963		$1,400	$1,800

Model 413-style Amp

1961-1963. 18 watts, 1x12", black leatherette cover, light silver grille, vibrato, large PANaramic logo.

1961-1963		$875	$1,150

Model 450-style Amp

1961-1963. 20 watts, 1x12", reverb and vibrato, reverb not generally included in an early-'60s 1x12" Magnatone amp, dark vinyl, dark cross-threaded grille, large PANaramic logo.

1961-1963		$1,150	$1,500

Model 1210 (250-style) Amp

1961-1963. 1x12" combo, 20 watts, 2.5 channels, true vibrato.

1961-1963		$975	$1,300

Paris

1960s. Brand name used on a line of solidstate amps distributed by a music wholesaler. Possibly built by Kay.

Master Series Amp

1960s. Compact combo, 1x12", black tolex-style cover, silver grille, rear mounted slanted control panel.

1960s		$70	$95

Park

1965-1982, 1993-1998, 2013-present. Park amps were made by Marshall from '65 to '82. Park logo on front with elongated P. In the '90s, Marshall revived the name for use on small solidstate amps imported from Asia. Brand name acquired by Mitch Colby (Colby Amps) in '13 and used on tube head amps and cabs built in New York City.

G Series Amp

1992-2000. Student compact amps, models include G-10 (10 watts, 1x8"), G-25R (25w, reverb), G-215R (15w, 2x8") and GB-25 (25w, 1x12" bass).

1990s	G-10	$50	$90
1990s	G-15R	$55	$100
1990s	G-215R	$65	$105

1977 Orange OR-120 head
Eric Van Gansen

1970s Ovation 6012 The Kat
Imaged by Heritage Auctions, HA.com

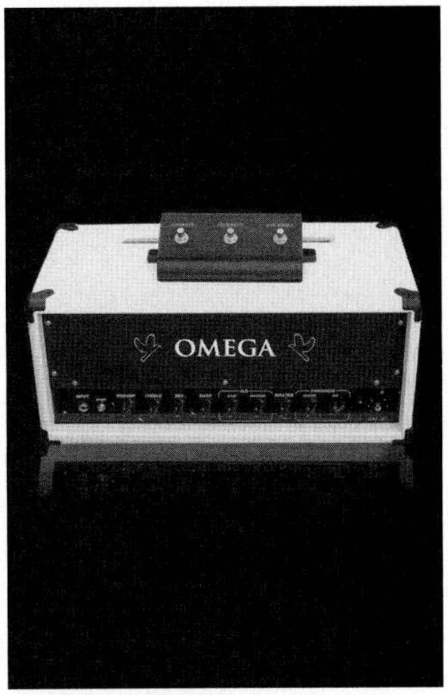

Omega

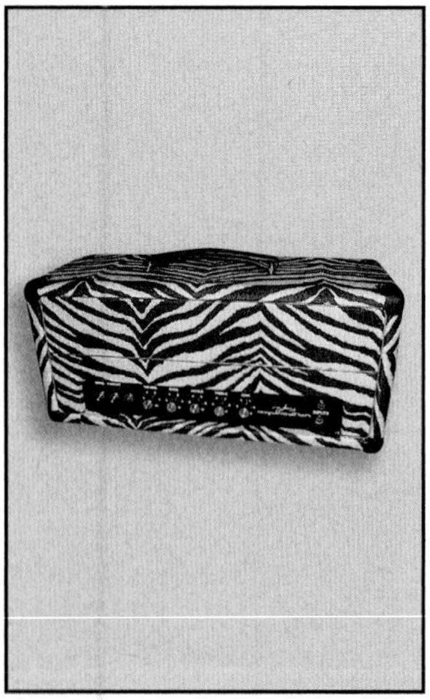

Paul Ruby AX84 High Octane

Peavey 5150 EVH
Imaged by Heritage Auctions, HA.com

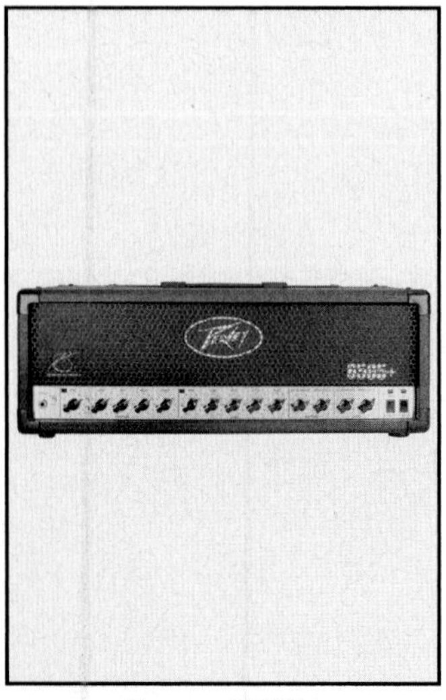

Peavey 6505+

MODEL YEAR	FEATURES	EXC. COND. LOW	HIGH
1990s	G-25R	$60	$100
1990s	GB-25	$55	$100

Model 50 Amp Head

1967-1969. Plexi, 50 watts.

1967-1969 $2,500 $3,300

Model 1001L Lead Amp Head

1967-1969 Plexi $3,600 $4,700
1969-1971 Aluminum $2,100 $2,700

Model 1008A 4x12 Slant Cabinet

Late-1960s-early-1970s. Similar to Marshall 1960 4x12" cab.

1960s-70s $1,600 $2,100

Model 1206 50W Master Volume Amp Head

Late-1970s-1982. 50 watts, similar to JCM 800 50-watt made during same era.

1970s-82 $1,600 $2,100

Model 1212 50W Reverb Combo Amp

Late-1960s-early-1970s. 50 watts, 2x12", reverb, tube.

1960s-70s $2,100 $2,700

Model 1213 100W Reverb Combo Amp

Late-1960s-early-1970s. 100 watts, 2x12", reverb, tube.

1960s-70s $2,100 $2,700

Model 1228 50W Lead Amp Head

Late-1970s-1982. 50 watts, based upon Marshall 50-watt made during same era.

1970s-82 $1,600 $2,100

Model 1229 100W Lead Amp Head

Late-1970s-1982. 100 watts, tube.

1970s-82 $1,600 $2,100

Model 1231 Vintage 20 LE Combo Amp

Late-1970s-1982. 20 watts, 1x12".

1970s-82 $1,700 $2,300

Model 1239 50W Master Volume Reverb Combo Amp

Late-1970s-1982. 50 watts, 1x12".

1970s-82 $1,700 $2,300

Paul Reed Smith

1985-present. In the late '80s, PRS offered two amp models. Only 350 amp units shipped. Includes HG-70 Head and HG-212 Combo. HG stands for Harmonic Generator, effectively a non-tube, solid-state amp. In '09, PRS introduced tube combo and head amps and cabinets designed by Doug Sewell.

Paul Ruby Amplifiers

2000-present. Professional grade, custom, tube amps built by Paul Ruby in Folsom, California.

Peavey

1965-present. Hartley Peavey's first products were guitar amps. He added guitars to the mix in '78. Headquartered in Meridan, Mississippi, Peavey continues to offer a huge variety of guitars, amps, and PAs. TransTube redesign of amps occurs in '95.

3120 Amp Head

2009-2016. Tubes, 120 watts, 3 foot-switchable channels.

2009-2016 $350 $450

5150 212 Combo Amp

1995-2004. Combo version of 5150 head, 60 watts, 2x12", large 5150 logo on front panel, small Peavey logo on lower right of grille.

1995-2004 $450 $600

5150 EVH Head/Cabinet Amp Set

1995-2008. Half stack 5150 head and 4x12" cab, large 5150 logo on front of amp.

1995-2008 Half-stack $900 $1,200

5150 II Amp

2004. Has 5051 II logo on front, look for 'II' designation.

2004 Half-stack $825 $1,100

6505 Series Amp

2008-present. Promoted for modern "heavy" metal sound.

2008-2019 2x12 combo, 60w $475 $625
2008-2019 6505+, 1x12 combo $450 $600
2008-2021 6505+ head, 120w $450 $600

Alphabass Amp

1988-1990. Rack mount all tube, 160 watts, EQ, includes 2x15" Black Widow or 2x12" Scorpion cabinet.

1988-1990 $225 $300

Artist Amp

Introduced in 1975 as 120 watts, 1x12", bright and normal channels, EQ, reverb, master volume.

1970s $225 $300

Artist 110 Amp

1990s. TransTubes, 10 watts.

1990s $110 $140

Artist 240 Amp

1975-1980s. 120 watt combo, 1x12".

1975-80s $175 $225

Artist 250 Amp

1990s. 100 watts, 1x12", solidstate preamp, 4 6L6 power tubes.

1990s $190 $235

Artist VT Amp

1990s. Combo amp, 120 watts, 1x12".

1990s $250 $310

Audition 20 Amp

1980s-1990s. 20 watts, single speaker combo.

1980-1990s $40 $50

Audition 30 Amp

1980s-1990s. 30 watts, 1x12" combo amp, channel switching.

1980-1990s $45 $55

Audition 110 Amp

1990s. 25 watts, 1x10" combo, 2 channels.

1990s $50 $70

Audition Chorus Amp

1980s. 2x10-watt channels, 2x6", channel switching, post gain and normal gain controls.

1980s $80 $100

Audition Plus Amp

1980s. Solidstate, 20 watts, 1x10".

1980s $50 $65

Backstage 30/Plus/50/110 Amp

1977-1991. 1x10 combo, Backstage 30 (15 then 18 watts) '77-'83, Backstage Plus (35w) '84-'87, Backstage 50 (50w) '88-'89, Backstage 110 (65w) '89-'91. Name reused in 2000s on small 10-watt amp.

1977-1991 $55 $75

MODEL YEAR	FEATURES	EXC. COND. LOW	HIGH

Backstage Chorus 208 Amp
1990-1996. 150 watts, 2x8", reverb, channel switching.

1990-1996		$95	$125

Bandit/65/75 Amp
1981-1989. 1x12" combo, originally 50 watts, upped to 65 watts in '85 and 75 in '87, renamed Bandit 112 in '90.

1981-1984	Bandit	$105	$135
1985-1986	Bandit 65	$105	$135
1987-1989	Bandit 75	$105	$135

Bandit 112/Bandit II 112 Amp
1990-present. 80 watts (II is 100), 1x12", active EQ circuit for lead channel, active controls. TransTube in '95.

1990-1994		$130	$160
1994-2020	TransTube	$180	$225

Basic 40 Amp
1980s. 40 watts, 1x12".

1980s		$85	$105

Basic 60 Amp
1988-1995. Solidstate combo amp, 50-60 watts, 1x12", 4-band EQ, gain controls, black.

1988-1995		$130	$160

Basic 112 Bass Amp
1996-2006. 75 watts, 1x12" bass combo, 2000-era red border control panel.

1996-2006		$130	$160

Blazer 158 Amp
1995-2005. 15 watts, 1x8", clean and distortion, later called the TransTube Blazer III.

1995-2005		$70	$90

Bluesman Amp
1992. Tweed, 1x12" or 1x15".

1992		$235	$300

Bravo 112 Amp
1988-1994. All tube reverb, 25 watts, 1x12", 3-band EQ, 2 independent input channels.

1988-1994		$200	$275

Butcher Amp Head
1985-1987, 2010-2017. All tube head, 120 watts. Current version is all tube, 100 watts with half power switch

1985-1987		$275	$375

Classic 20 Amp
1990s. Small tube amp with 2xEL84 power tubes, 1x10" narrow panel combo, tweed cover.

1990s		$275	$375

Classic 30/112 Amp
1994-present. Tweed combo, 30 watts, 1x12", EL84 tubes.

1994-2020	Narrow panel combo	$315	$415
2008-2014	Badge front	$315	$415
2008-2014	Head	$275	$375

Classic 50/212 Amp
1990-present. Combo, 50 watt, 2x12", 4 EL84s, 3 12AX7s, reverb, high-gain section.

1990-2020		$350	$450

Classic 50/410 Amp
1990-present. Combo amp, 4x10", EL84 power, reverb, footswitchable high-gain mode.

1990-2020		$350	$450

Classic 120 Amp
1988-ca.1990. Tube, 120 watts.

1988-1990		$300	$375

Combo 300 Amp
1982-1993. 1x15" bass combo, 300 watts.

11982-1993		$155	$195

DECA/750 Amp
1989-ca.1990. Digital, 2 channels, 350 watts per channel, distortion, reverb, exciter, pitch shift, multi-EQ.

1989-1990		$205	$255

Decade Amp
1970s. Practice amp, 10 watts, 1x8", runs on 12 volt or AC.

1970s		$75	$95

Delta Blues Amp
1995-2014. 30 watts, tube combo, 4 EL84 tubes, 1x15" or 2x10", tremolo, large-panel-style cab, blond tweed.

1995-2014		$350	$450

Deuce Amp
1972-1980s. 120 watts, tube amp, 2x12" or 4x10".

1972-1980s		$175	$215

Deuce Amp Head
1972-1980s. Tube head, 120 watts.

1972-1980s		$130	$165

Ecoustic Series Amp
1996-present. Acoustic combo amps, 110 (1x10) and 112 (1x12, offered until '10) at 100 watts, digital effects (EFX, later E) added in '03. E20 and E208 added in '11.

1996-2010	112	$125	$155
2003-2020	E110	$125	$155

Encore 65 Amp
1983. Tube combo, 65 watts.

1983		$230	$290

Envoy 110 Amp
1988-2020. Solidstate, 40 watts, 1x10", TransTubes.

1988-2020		$100	$130

Heritage VTX Amp
1980s. 130 watts, 4 6L6s, solidstate preamp, 2x12" combo.

1980s		$155	$195

Jazz Classic Amp
1980s. Solidstate, 210 watts, 1x15", electronic channel switching, 6-spring reverb.

1980s		$155	$195

JSX (Joe Satriani) Amp
2004-2010. Joe Satriani signature, 120 watt tube head. Also offered were JSX 50 (50 watts, '09-'10), JSX 212 Combo ('05-'10) and 5-watt JSX Mini Colossal ('07-'10).

2004-2010	120w head	$515	$650

KB Series Amp
1980s. Keyboard amp, models include KB-60 (60 watts, 1x12", reverb), KB-100 (100w, 1x15"), and KB-300 (300w, 1x15" with horn).

1980s	KB-100	$145	$190
1980s	KB-300	$200	$260
1980s	KB-60	$125	$160

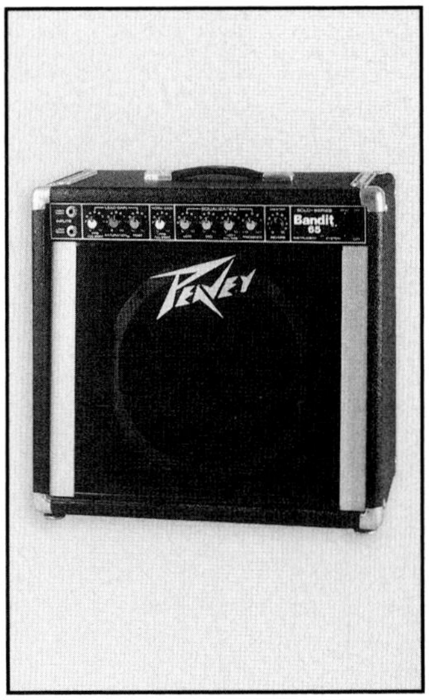

Peavey Bandit 65

1980s Peavey KB-100

Imaged by Heritage Auctions, HA.com

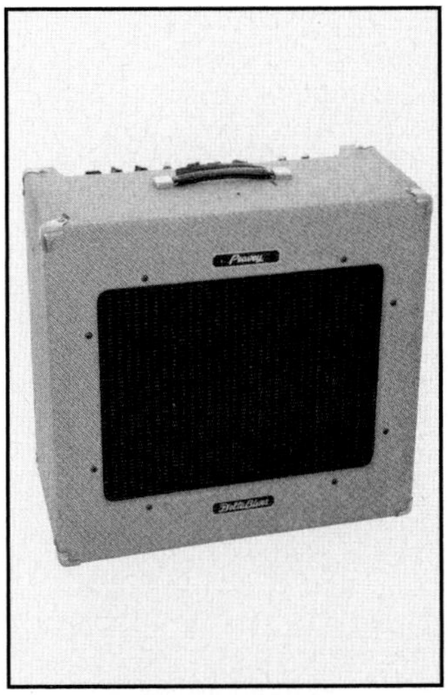

Peavey Delta Blues

Imaged by Heritage Auctions, HA.com

AMPS

1990 Peavey Nashville 400

Imaged by Heritage Auctions, HA.com

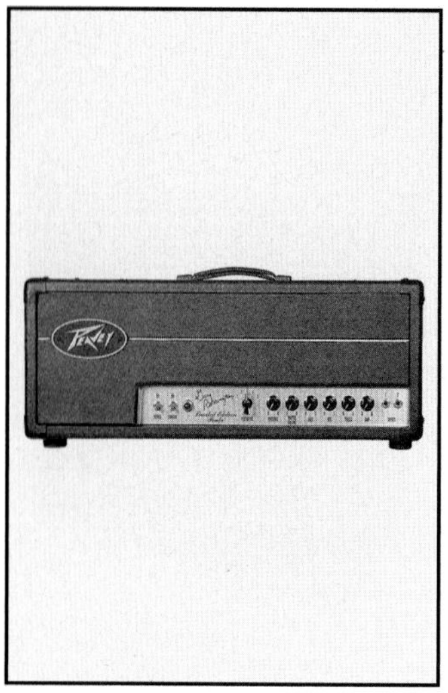

Peavey Gary Rossington Signature Penta

2000s Peavey Rage 258

Imaged by Heritage Auctions, HA.com

MODEL YEAR	FEATURES	EXC. COND. LOW	HIGH

LTD Amp
1975-1980s. Solidstate, 200 watts, 1x12" Altec or 1x15" JBL.

1975-1982		$155	$195

Mace Amp Head
1976-1980s. Tube, 180 watts.

1976-1980s		$235	$295

Mark III Bass Amp Head
1978-1983. 300 watts, 2 channels, graphic EQ.

1978-1983		$165	$205

MegaBass Amp
1986-ca. 1992. Rack mount preamp/power amp, 200 watts per 2 channels, solidstate, EQ, effects loop, chorus.

1986-1992		$185	$230

Microbass Amp
1988-2005. 20 watts, 1x8" practice amp, made in China.

1988-2005		$40	$50

Minx 110 Bass Amp
1987-2005. Solidstate, 35 watts RMS, 1x10" heavy-duty speaker.

1987-2005		$90	$110

Musician Amp Head
Introduced in 1965 as 120 watt head, upped to 210 watts in '72.

1965-1970s		$125	$155

Nashville 112 Steel Guitar Amp
2008-present. Compact size, 1x12", 80 watts.

2008-2020		$375	$500

Nashville 400 Steel Guitar Amp
1982-2000. 210 watts, 1x15" solidstate steel guitar combo amp.

1982-2000		$400	$525

Nashville 1000 Steel Guitar Amp
1998-2008. 1x15" speaker, solidstate steel guitar combo amp.

1998-2008		$400	$525

Pacer Amp
1974-1985. Master volume, 45 watts, 1x12", 3-band EQ.

1974-1985		$70	$90

Penta Amp Head/Gary Rossington Signature Penta
2005-2015. Tubes, 140 watts, 4x12", 5 selectable preamp settings. Becomes the Gary Rossington Signature Penta in 2009.

2005-2015	Cab	$240	$300
2005-2015	Head	$290	$350

ProBass 1000 Amp
1980s. Rack mount, effects loops, preamp, EQ, crossover, headphone output.

1980s		$130	$165

Rage/Rage 158 Amp
1988-2008. Compact practice amp, 15 watts, 1x8". 158 starts '95. Replaced by 25 watt Rage 258.

1988-2008		$35	$45

Reno 400 Amp
1984-late 1980s. Solidstate, 200 watts, 1x15" with horn, 4-band EQ.

1980s		$130	$165

Renown 112 Amp
1989-1994. Crunch and lead SuperSat, 160 watts, 1x12", master volume, digital reverb, EQ.

1989-1994		$130	$165

Renown 212 Amp
1989-1994. Crunch and lead SuperSat, 160 watts, 2x12", master volume, digital reverb, EQ.

1989-1994		$155	$195

Renown 400 Amp
1981-late 1980s. Combo, 200 watts, 2x12", channel switching, Hammond reverb, pre- and post-gain controls.

1980s		$205	$255

Revolution 112 Amp
1992-2002. 100 watts, 1x12" combo, black vinyl, black grille.

1992-2002		$175	$220

Session 400 Amp
1974-ca. 1999. 200 watts, 1x15 or early on as 2x12, steel amp, available in the smaller box LTD, offered as a head in '76, available in wedge-shaped enclosure in '88.

1974-1999		$400	$500

Session 500 Amp
1979-1980s. 250 watts, 1x15", steel amp.

1979-1985		$400	$500

Special 112 Amp
1981-1994. 160 watts, 1x12". In 1988, available in wedge-shaped enclosure.

1981-1994		$150	$185

Special 130 Amp
1980s. 1x12", 130 watts.

1980s		$150	$185

Special 212 Amp
1995-2005. 160 watts, 2x12", transtube, solidstate series.

1995-2005		$175	$220

Stereo Chorus 212 Amp
1990s. 2x12" combo.

1990s		$235	$315

Studio Pro 50 Amp
1986-late 1980s. 50 watts, 1x12".

1980s		$105	$130

Studio Pro 112 Amp
1980s. Repackaged and revoiced in 1988. Solidstate, 65 watts, 1x12", Peavey SuperSat preamp circuitry, new power sections.

1980s		$115	$145

TKO Series Bass Amp
1978-2011. Solidstate, 1x15, original TKO was 40 watts, followed by TKO 65 (65 watts) for '82-'87, TKO 75 for '88-'90, and TKO 80 for '91-'92. Renamed TKO 115 in '93 with 75, 80 or 100 watts until '09 when jumping to 400 watts.

1982-1987	TKO 65	$105	$130
1988-1990	TKO 75	$140	$175
1991-1992	TKO 80	$175	$225

TNT Series Bass Amp
1974-2009. Solidstate, 1x15, original TNT was 45 watts, upped to 50 for '79-'81, followed by TNT 130 (130 watts) for '82-'87, TNT 150 for '88-'90, and TNT 160 for '91-'92. Renamed TNT 115 in '93 with 150, 160 or 200 watts until '09 when jumping to 600 watts (Tour

MODEL YEAR	FEATURES	EXC. COND. LOW	HIGH

TNT 115 - see Tour Series).

1982-1987	TNT 130	$250	$350
1988-1990	TNT 150	$250	$350
1991-1992	TNT 160	$250	$350

Tour Series

2004-2019. Imported bass heads and cabinets, various models.

2004-2019	Various models	$265	$350

Transchorus 210 Amp

1999-2000. 50 watts, 2x10 combo, stereo chorus, channel switching, reverb.

1999-2000		$230	$290

Triple XXX Series Amp

2001-2009. Made in USA.

2001-2009	Head, 120w	$490	$615
2001-2009	Super 40, 40w, 1x12	$440	$550

Triumph 60 Combo Amp

1980s. Tube head, effects loop, reverb, 60 watts, 1x12", multi-stage gain.

1980s		$150	$190

Triumph 120 Amp

1989-1990. Tube, 120 watts, 1x12", 3 gain blocks in preamp, low-level post-effects loop, built-in reverb.

1989-1990		$180	$225

Ultra 60 Amp Head

1991-1994. 60 watts, all tube, 2 6L6 power, black, black grille.

1991-1994		$230	$290

Ultra Series Amp

1998-2002. All tube combos and cabs.

1998-2002	Ulta 112, 60w	$225	$280
1998-2002	Ulta 212, 60w	$275	$350
1998-2002	Ulta 410, 60w	$275	$350
1998-2002	Ulta Plus 120 Head	$325	$400

ValveKing Series Amp

2005-2018. Tube head, combos and cabs.

2005-2016	VK212, 100w, 2x12	$250	$325
2005-2018	VK100, 100w head	$200	$275
2005-2018	VK112, 50w, 1x12	$225	$300

Vegas 400 Amp

1984-late 1980s. 210 watts, 1x15, some prefer as a steel guitar amp.

1980s		$335	$425

VTM Series Amp

1987-1993. Vintage Tube Modified series, tube heads, 60 or 120 watts.

1987-1993	VTM120, 120w	$275	$375
1987-1993	VTM60, 60w	$275	$375

Vypyr Series Amp

2008-2014. Modeling amp heads and combos, 60 and 120-watt tube and 15, 30, 75 and 100-watt solidstate models. Changes to Vypyr VIP in late '14.

2008-2014	15w, combo	$60	$75
2008-2014	30w, 1x12 combo	$130	$165
2010	75w, combo	$175	$225

Wiggy 212 Amp

2001-2008. 100-watt head in mono (2x75-watt in stereo) with matching 2x12" cab, 2 EQ, 5-band sliders, rounded amp head.

2001-2008		$400	$500

MODEL YEAR	FEATURES	EXC. COND. LOW	HIGH

Windsor Amp Head

Introduced 2006 summer NAMM. All tube, 100- or 300-watt head.

2000s	100w	$240	$315
2000s	300w	$250	$325

Penn

Tube amps, combos, and cabinets built by Billy Penn, starting in 1994, originally in Colts Neck, then in Long Branch, New Jersey.

Pignose

1972-present. Pignose was started by people associated with the band Chicago, including guitarist Terry Kath, with help from designers Wayne Kimball and Richard Erlund. In '74, it was sold to Chicago's band accountant, who ran it until '82, when ownership passed to the company that made its sturdy, wood cabinets. They also offer guitars and effects.

7-100 Practice Amp

1972-present. The original Pignose, 7"x5"x3" battery-powered portable amplifier, 1x5".

1972-2020		$50	$75

30/60 Amp

1978-ca.1987. Solidstate, 30 watts, 1x10", master volume.

1978-1987		$75	$100

60R Studio Reverb Amp

Solidstate, 30 watts.

1980		$95	$125

G40V Amp

1997-2009. Tubes, 1x10", 40 watts.

1997-2009		$200	$275

G60VR Amp

1998-2009. Tubes, 1x12", 60 watts.

1998-2009		$225	$300

Hog Recharging Portable Amp

1995-present. Rechargeable solidstate, models include Hog 20 and Hog 30.

1995-2020		$100	$150

Plush

Late 1960s-early 1970s. Tuck and roll covered tube amps made by the same company that made Earth Sound Research amps in Farmingdale, New York.

Tube Amplifiers

Early 1970s. All tube heads and combos including the 450 Super 2x12" combo, 1000/P1000S head, and 1060S Royal Bass combo.

1971-1972		$500	$1,200

Point Blank

2002-2004. Tube amps built by Roy Blankenship in Orlando, Florida before he started his Blankenship brand.

Polytone

Beginning in the 1960s and made in North Hollywood, California, Polytone offers compact combo amps, heads, and cabinets and a pickup system for acoustic bass.

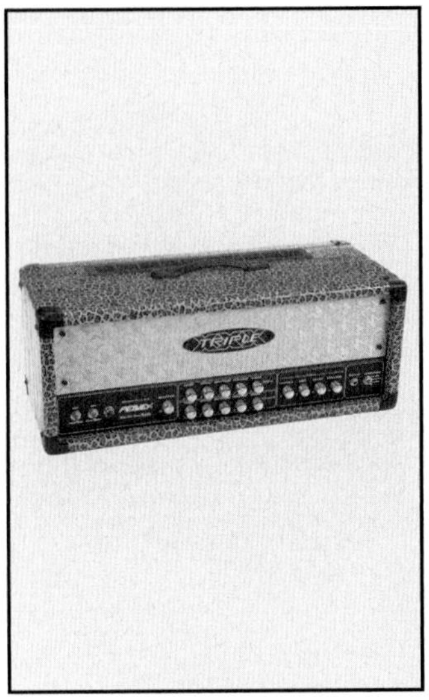

Peavey Triple XXX
Imaged by Heritage Auctions, HA.com

AMPS

Pignose Hog

1970s Plush PRB 1000S
Imaged by Heritage Auctions, HA.com

Ca. 1990s Polytone Taurus

Imaged by Heritage Auctions, HA.com

1964 Premier B-160 Club Bass

Imaged by Heritage Auctions, HA.com

Premier Twin-8

Ängkvist

MODEL YEAR	FEATURES	EXC. COND. LOW	HIGH

Guitar or Bass Amps

1980s-2000s. Various models.

1980-2000s		$250	$450

Port City

2005-present. Daniel Klein builds his amp heads, combos, and cabinets in Rocky Point, North Carolina.

Premier

Ca.1938-ca.1975, 1990s-2010. Produced by Peter Sorkin Music Company in Manhattan. First radio-sized amplifiers introduced by '38. After World War II, established Multivox subsidiary to manufacture amplifiers ca.'46. By mid-'50s at least, the amps featured lyre grilles. Dark brown/light tan amp covering by '60. By '64 amps covered in brown woodgrain and light tan. Multivox amps were made until around '84.

B-160 Club Bass Amp

1963-1968. 15 to 20 watts, 1x12" Jensen speaker, '60s 2-tone brown styling, 6V6 tubes.

1963-1968		$600	$775

Model 50 Amp

1940s-1960s. In '62 this was their entry-level amp, 4 to 5 watts, 1x8" similar to Fender Champ circuit with more of a vertical suitcase-style cab.

1940s-60s		$375	$475

Model 71 Amp

1961-1962. Combo with 1x12" (woofer) and 2 small tweeters, 24 watts. '61 styling with circular speaker baffle protected with metal X frame, 2 tweeter ports on upper baffle, 2-tone light tan and brown, 8 tubes, tremolo. The '62 styling changed to baffle with a slight V at the top, and 2-tone cover.

1961	Round baffle	$825	$1,075
1962	V-baffle	$825	$1,075

Model 76 Amp

1950s-1960s. Suitcase latchable cabinet that opens out into 2 wedges, 2-tone brown, lyre grille, 1x12".

1950s-60s		$675	$900

Model 88 Multivox Amp

1962. Multi-purpose combo amp, organ-stop control panel, 1x15" woofer with 2 tweeters, vertical suitcase cab, 2-tone cover, classic circular speaker baffle with X brace, 10 tubes, top-of-the-line in '62 catalog.

1962		$825	$1,075

Model 88N Amp

1950s-1961. Rectangular suitcase cabinet, 2-tone tan and brown, Premier and lyre logo, 25 watts, 1x12".

1950s-1961		$825	$1,075

Model 100R Amp

1960s. Combo amp, 1x12", reverb and tremolo.

1960s		$825	$1,075

Model 110 Amp

1962. 12-watt 1x10 student combo, lyre grille logo, 2-tone cab.

1962		$525	$675

Model 120/120R Amp

1958-1963. 12-watt 1x12" combo, tremolo, reverb ('62), 2-tone brown cab.

1958-1963		$600	$775
1962	With reverb	$650	$850

Model 200 Rhythm Bass Amp

1962. 1x15" combo bass amp.

1962		$625	$800

T-8 Twin-8 Amp

1950s, 1964-1966. 20 watts, 2x8", tremolo, reverb.

1950s		$1,200	$1,550
1964-1966		$1,100	$1,450

T-12 Twin-12 Amp

1958-1962. Early reverb amp with tremolo, 2x12", rectangular cabinet typical of twin 12 amps (Dano and Fender), brown cover.

1958-1959		$1,300	$1,650
1960-1962		$1,200	$1,550

Pritchard Amps

Professional grade, production/custom, single and two-channel amps and cabinets built beginning in 2004, by Eric Pritchard in Berkeley Springs, West Virginia.

Pyramid Car Audio

Inexpensive student models, imported.

Quantum

1980s. Economy amps distributed by DME, Indianapolis, Indiana.

Q Terminator Economy Amp

1980s. Economy solidstate amps ranging from 12 to 25 watts and 1x6" to 1x12".

1980s	Various models	$25	$35

Quidley Guitar Amplifiers

Intermediate and professional grade, production/custom, tube guitar amp heads, combos and cabinets built by Ed Quidley in Wilmington, North Carolina, starting in 2006.

Quilter

2011-present. Patrick Quilter builds his intermediate and professional grade, production, guitar amps in Costa Mesa, California.

Quinn

Professional and premium grade, production/custom, amps and cabinets built by Shadwell J. Damron III, starting 2005, in Vancouver, Washington.

Randall

1960s-present. Randall Instruments was originally out of California and is now a division of U.S. Music Corp. They have offered a range of tube and solidstate combo amps, heads and cabinets over the years.

Rastop Designs

2002-present. Professional grade, custom amps built by Alexander Rastopchin in Long Island City, New York. He also builds effects.

MODEL YEAR	FEATURES	EXC. COND. LOW	HIGH

Rat Fink

Early 2000s. Solidstate amp line from Lace Music Products. They also sold guitars and basses under this brand and offered amps under the Mooneyes and Lace brands.

Realistic

Radio Shack offered a couple made-in-the-U.S. combo tube amps in the '60s, including the Entertainer 34 with a flip down record turntable in the back! Their radio and stereo gear were also branded Realistic.

Reason

2007-2016. Professional grade, production/custom, amps and cabinets built by Obeid Khan and Anthony Bonadio in St. Louis, Missouri.

Red Bear

1994-1997. Tube amps designed by Sergei Novikov and built in St. Petersburg, Russia. Red Bear amps were distributed in the U.S. under a joint project between Gibson and Novik, Ltd. Novik stills builds amps under other brands.

MK 60 Lead Tube Amp

1994-1997. Head with 4x12" half stack, Red Bear logo on amp and cab.

1994-1997	$650	$850

MK 100 Full Stack

1994-1997. 100 watts, 2x4x12".

1994-1997	$1,000	$1,300

Red Iron Amps

2001-present. Paul Sanchez builds his tube amp heads in Lockhart, Texas.

RedPlate Amps

2006-present. Professional and premium grade, production/custom, guitar amplifiers built in Phoenix, Arizona by Henry Heistand.

Reeves Amplification

2002-present. Started by Bill Jansen, Reeves builds tube amps, combos, and cabinets in Cincinnati, Ohio, based on the classic British designs of Dan Reeves.

Regal

Ca.1895-1966, 1987-present. The original Regal company distributed instruments built by them and others.

Gibson EH Amp

1936. Rare private-branded Gibson EH amp, 1x10", single control, alligator tweed.

1936	$550	$725

Reinhardt

2004-2012. Bob Reinhardt builds his professional grade, production/custom, guitar and bass amps and cabinets in Lynchburg, Virginia. He also builds effects pedals.

Resonant Amplifiers

2007-present. Owners Wes Kuhnley and Peter Bregman build their professional grade, vacuum tube guitar and hi-fi amps in Minneapolis, Minnesota. They also build the Field Effects.

Retro-King Amplifier Company

2004-present. Tube combo and head amps built by Chuck Dean in Marcellus, New York.

Revenge Amps

Greg Perrine began building in 1996, intermediate grade, production/custom, guitar amplifiers and attenuators in Conway, Arkansas. He also imports a line of amps.

Reverend

1996-present. Joe Naylor started building amps under the Naylor brand in '94. In '96 he left Naylor to build guitars under the Reverend brand. From '01 to '05, Reverend offered tube amps, combos, and cabinets built in Warren, Michigan, that Naylor co-designed with Dennis Kager.

Rex

1950s-1960s. Tube amps built by the Lamberti Bros. Co. in Melbourne, Australia. They also built guitars. In the 1920s-1940s, Gretsch has an unrelated line of guitars with that brand.

Reynolds Valveart

1997-present. Professional and premium grade, production/custom, amps and cabinets built by Peter Reynolds in Windsor, Australia.

Rickenbacker

1931-present. Rickenbacker made amps from the beginning of the company up to the late '80s. Rickenbacker had many different models, from the small early models that were usually sold as a guitar/amp set, to the large, very cool, Transonic.

E-12 Amp

1963. 1x12" combo with tremolo depth and speed, volume, and on-off tone knobs.

1963	$500	$650

Electro-Student Amp

Late-1940s. Typical late-'40s vertical combo cabinet, 1x12" speaker, lower power using 5 tubes, bottom mounted chassis, dark gray leatherette cover.

1948-1949	$475	$625

Hi Fi Model 98

1956. Tube amp, long horizontal cab with 3 speakers, Rickenbacker Hi Fi and Model 98 logo on back panel, blond cover, wheat grille cloth.

1956	$1,075	$1,400

Model B-9E Amp

1960s. 1x12" combo, 4 knobs, gray.

1960s	$600	$800

Model M-8 Amp

1950s-1960s. Gray, 1x8".

1950s-60s	$425	$550

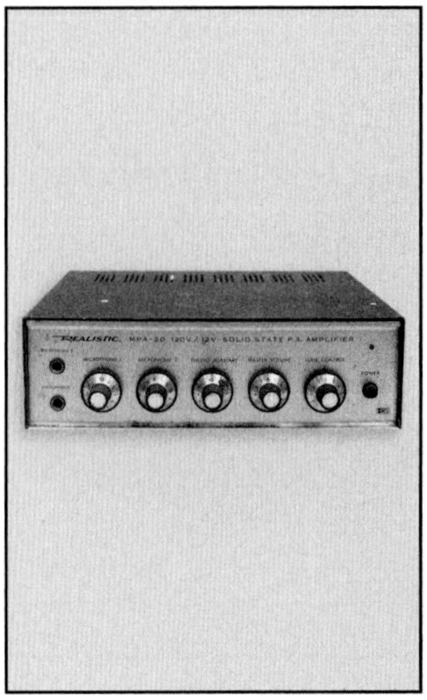

Realistic MPA-20

Bernunzio Uptown Music

Reeves Custom 12

'50s Rickenbacker M-8

Imaged by Heritage Auctions, HA.com

1980 Rickenbacker TR-100GT
Imaged by Heritage Auctions, HA.com

Rivera Clubster 45

Rivera Fandango

MODEL YEAR	FEATURES	EXC. COND. LOW	HIGH

Model M-9 Amp
1960s. Green, 1x12".

1960s		$550	$700

Model M-10 Amp
1930s. Silver metal, 1x10".

1935		$450	$575

Model M-11 Amp
1950s. 12-15 watts, 1x12", 2x6V6 power. There was a different M-11 offered in the 1930s.

1950s		$650	$850

Model M-12 Amp
1950s. 12-15 watts, 1x12", M-12 logo on back panel, brown leatherette. There was a different M-12 offered in the 1930s.

1950s		$650	$850

Model M-14A Amp
Late 1950s-early 1960s. 1x12 combo, mid-power 2x6V6, dual channel with vibrato, rough-brown tolex cover.

1950s-60s		$650	$850

Model M-15 Amp
1950s-Early 1960s. 1x15" combo, 35 watts, 2 x 6L6 power tubes, model name on top panel.

1950s-60s		$675	$875

Model M-16 Amp
1950s-Early 1960s. 1x15", 35 watts, model name on top panel.

1950s-60s		$675	$875

Model M-30 EK-O-Sound Amp
1961. Recording echo chamber and amp in 1x12 combo format, 11 tubes, gray grille and cover, very limited production.

1961		$3,200	$4,200

Model M-59 Amp
1930s. Small lap steel amp.

1935		$375	$500

Professional Model 200-A Amp
1938. 15 watts, was sold with the Vibrola Spanish guitar.

1938		$475	$625

RB and RG Series Amp
1987-1989. Various bass (RB) and guitar (RG) amp models.

1987-1989		$125	$275

Supersonic Model B-16 Amp
1960s. 4x10" speakers, gray cover.

1960s		$700	$925

Supersonic Model B-22 Amp Head
1960s. Tube head, gray cover.

1960s		$575	$725

TR7 Amp
1978-1982. Solidstate, 7 watts, 1x10", tremolo.

1978-1982		$100	$150

TR14 Amp
1978-ca.1982. Solidstate, 1x10", reverb, distortion.

1978-1982		$100	$150

TR25 Amp
1979-1982. Solidstate, 1x12" combo, reverb, tremolo, distortion.

1979-1982		$150	$200

TR35B Bass Amp
1978-ca.1982. Solidstate, mid-power, 1x15".

1978-1982		$150	$200

TR50 Amp
1977-ca. 1982. Solid state with Rick-o-Sound stereo inputs.

1977-1982		$150	$200

TR75G Amp
1978-ca.1982. 75 watts, 2x12", 2 channels.

1978-1982		$200	$250

TR75SG Amp
1978-ca.1983. 1x10" and 1x15" speakers.

1978-1982		$200	$250

TR100G Amp
1978-ca.1982. Solidstate, 100 watts with 4x12", 2 channels.

1978-1982		$250	$350

Transonic TS100/TS200 Amp
1967-1973. Trapezoid shaped combo, solidstate, 100 (2x12") or 200 (2x15") watts, Rick-O-Select.

1967-1973	100w	$2,400	$3,100
1967-1973	200w	$2,800	$3,600

Risson

1970-1984, 2012-present. Bob Rissi builds his intermediate, professional and premium grade, production/custom, guitar and bass amplifiers in Placentia, California. From 1970-84 they were built in Santa Ana.

Rivera

1985-present. Amp designer and builder Paul Rivera modded and designed amps for other companies before starting his own line in California. He offers heads, combos, and cabinets. He also builds guitar pedals.

Chubster 40 Amp
2000-present. 40 watts, 1x12" combo, burgundy tolex, light grille.

2000-2020		$625	$825

Clubster 25 Amp
2005-2016. 25 watts, 1x10", 6V6.

2005-2016		$525	$700

Clubster 45 Amp
2005-2015. 45 watts, 1x12" combo.

2005-2015		$625	$825

Fandango 112 Combo Amp
2001-present. 55 watts, 2xEL34, 1x12".

2001-2020		$850	$1,100

Fandango 212 Combo Amp
2001-2015. 55 or 100 watts, 2x12" tube amp.

2001-2015		$900	$1,200

Jake Studio Combo Amp
1997. 55 watts, 1x12", reverb and effects loop.

1997		$650	$850

Knucklehead 55 Amp
1994-2002. 55-watt amp head, replaced by reverb model.

1994-2002		$525	$700

MODEL YEAR	FEATURES	EXC. COND. LOW	HIGH

Knucklehead 100 Amp

1994-2002. 100-watt amp head, replaced by reverb model.

1994-2002		$575	$750

Knucklehead Reverb 112 Amp

2003-2007. 55 watts, 1x12" amp combo, reverb.

2003-2007		$800	$1,050

Los Lobottom/Sub 1 Amp

1999-2004. 1x12" cabinet with 300-watt powered 12" subwoofer.

1999-2004		$375	$500

M-60 Amp Head

1990-2009. 60 watts.

1990-2009		$475	$625

M-60 112 Combo Amp

1989-2009. 60 watts, 1x12".

1989-2009		$550	$725

M-100 Amp Head

1990-2009. 100 watts.

1990-2009		$525	$675

M-100 212 Combo Amp

1990-2009. 100 watts, 2x12" combo.

1990-2009		$625	$800

Pubster 25 Amp

2005-2017. 25 watts, 1x10".

2015-2017		$375	$475

Pubster 45 Amp

2005-2014. 45 watts, 1x12".

2005-2014		$400	$525

Quiana Combo Amp

2000-present. Combo, 55 watts.

2000-2014	2x12	$750	$950
2000-2014	4x10	$850	$1,100
2000-2019	1x12	$650	$850

R-30 112 Combo Amp

1993-2007. 30 watts, 1x12", compact cab, black tolex cover, gray-black grille.

1993-2007		$625	$825

R-100 212 Combo Amp

1993-2007. 100 watts, 2x12".

1993-2007		$700	$925

Sedona 112 Amp

2011-present. 55 watts, 1x12".

2011		$850	$1,125

Sedona Lite 55 Combo Amp

2005-present. For electric and acoustic guitars, 55 watts, 1x12".

2005-2020		$775	$1,025

Suprema R-55 112/115 Combo Amp

2000-present. Tube amp, 55 watts, 1x12" (still available) or 1x15" ('00-'01).

2000-2020	1x12 or 1x15	$750	$975

TBR-1 Amp

1985-1999. First Rivera production model, rack mount, 60 watts.

1985-1999		$600	$775

Venus Series

2007-present. Series includes the 7/15-watt 3 combo (1x10 or 1x12), and the 15-watt 5 and 35-watt 6, both as combos (1x12, 2x12) and heads with cabs (1x12, 2x12).

2007-2020	Venus 6, 17/35w head	$750	$975
2007-2020	Venus 6, 1x12	$775	$1,000
2007-2020	Venus 6, 2x12	$875	$1,125
2009-2017	Venus 3, 1x10	$675	$875
2009-2020	Venus 5, 1x12	$700	$925

Roccaforte Amps

1993-present. Tube amps, combos, and cabinets built by Doug Roccaforte in San Clemente, California.

Rocktron

1980s-present. Tube and solidstate amp heads, combos and cabinets. Rocktron is a division of GHS Strings and also offers stomp boxes and preamps.

Rogue

2001-present. They offered student-level solidstate import (Korea) compact amps up to around '06. They also offer guitars, basses, lap steels, mandolins, banjos, ukuleles and effects.

Small Solidstate Amps

2001-2006. Various models.

2001-2006		$35	$90

Roland

Japan's Roland Corporation's products include amplifiers and keyboards and, under the Boss brand, effects.

Acoustic Chorus (AC) Series Amp

1995-present. Number in model indicates wattage (i.e. AC-60 = 60 watts).

1995-2009	AC-100, 1x12", 2x5"	$350	$450
1995-2020	AC-60, 2x6"	$275	$375
1995-2020	AC-90, 2x8"	$350	$450

Blues Cube

1996	BC60, 1x12	$190	$250
1996	BC60, 3x10	$225	$300
2000s	BC30	$175	$225

Bolt 60 Amp

Early 1980s. Solidstate/tube, 1x12".

1980s		$175	$225

Cube Series Amp

1978-present. Number in model indicates wattage (i.e. Cube-15X = 15 watts).

1978-1982	100, 1x12"	$175	$225
1978-1982	20, 1x8"	$95	$125
1978-1983	40, 1x10"	$175	$225
1978-1983	60, 1x12"	$175	$225
1978-1983	60B, 1x12"	$175	$225
2000-2009	30 Bass, 1x10"	$115	$150
2000s	80GX, 1x12	$175	$225
2000s	80XL, 1x12	$175	$225
2006-2010	30X, 1x10"	$115	$150
2006-2013	15X, 1x8"	$95	$125
2006-2013	20X, 1x8"	$95	$125
2008-2013	80X, 1x12"	$175	$225

Jazz Chorus (JC) Series Amp

1975-present. Includes the JC-50 (50 watts, 1x12"), JC-55 (50 watts, 2x8"), JC-77 (80 watts, 2x10"), JC-90 (90 watts, 2x10") and JC-120 (120 watts, 2x12" and 4x12").

1975-2014	JC-120, 2x12"	$400	$500
1980s	JC-50, 1x12"	$300	$400

Rivera Venus

Roland Blues Cube Artist

1979 Roland Cube 60B

Imaged by Heritage Auctions, HA.com

AMPS

1978 Roland JC-160
Alf Tengs-Pedersen

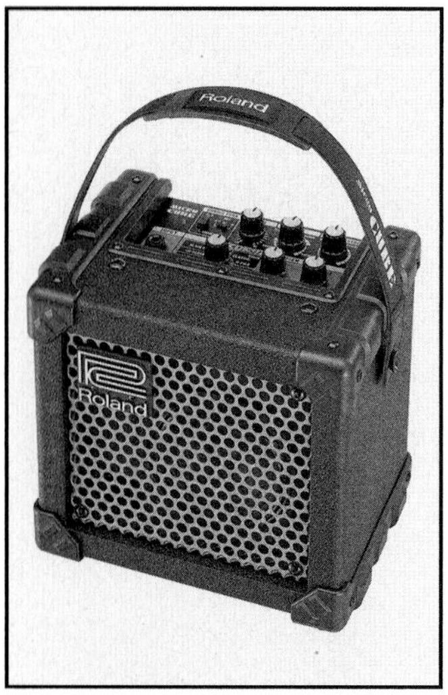

Roland Micro Cube

1975 Sano Supernova
Tom Pfeifer

MODEL YEAR	FEATURES	EXC. COND. LOW	HIGH
1987-1994	JC-55, 2x8"	$300	$400
1987-1994	JC-77, 2x10"	$350	$450
1990s	JC-120, 4x12"	$425	$550
1990s	JC-90, 2x10"	$350	$450

Micro Cube Amp

2000-present. Compact AC power or battery, 2 watts, 1x5".

2000-2020		$75	$100

Spirit Series Amp

1982-1989. Compact, model number indicates wattage.

1982-1989	Spirit 30, 1x12	$75	$100
1982-1989	Spirit 40A, combo	$75	$100
1982-1989	Spirit 50, combo	$75	$100

Studio Bass Amp

1979		$175	$225

VGA3 V-Guitar Amp

2003-2009. GK digital modeling amp, 50 watts, 1x12" combo.

2003-2009		$175	$225

VGA5 V-Guitar Amp

2001-2004. GK digital modeling amp, 65 watts, 1x12".

2001-2004		$175	$225

VGA7 V-Guitar Amp

2000-2009. 65 + 65 watts, 2x12", digital modeling with analog-style controls.

2000-2009		$200	$250

S.S. Maxwell

See info under Danelectro.

Sadowsky

1980-present. From '05 to '07, luthier Roger Sadowsky built a bass tube amp head in Brooklyn, New York. He also builds basses and guitars.

Sam Ash

1960s-'70s. Sam Ash Music was founded by Sam Ash (formerly Ashkynase) in Brooklyn, New York, in 1924, and by '66 there were about four Ash stores. During the '60s they private-branded their own amp line built by Jess Oliver, of Oliver Amps, and based on Oliver's Ampeg designs.

Sam Ash Mark II Pro Combo Amp

1960s. 2x12" with reverb combo amp.

1960s		$525	$700

SamAmp

2004-present. Intermediate and professional grade, boutique amps built by Sam Timberlake in Vestavia Hills, Alabama.

Sano

1951-ca. 1980. Combos, heads and cabinets made in three factories around New Jersey. Founded by Joseph Zonfrilli, Louis Iorio, and Nick Sano, initially offering accordion pickups, amplifiers, and all-electric accordions. Sano patented his accordion pickup in '44 and also developed a highly acclaimed stereophonic pickup accordion and matching amp. By '66 the Sano Corporation augmented their all-tube accordion amps with new solidstate circuitry models. In the mid-'60s they offered a new line of amps specifically designed for the guitar and bass market. Sano amps are generally low-gain, low power amplifiers. They also marketed reverb units and guitars.

Compact Combo Amp

1960s	160R, 15w, 1x12"	$400	$525
1960s	Sano-ette	$325	$425

Satellite Amplifiers

2004-present. Professional and premium grade, production/custom, tube amps, preamps and cabinets built by Adam Grimm in San Diego, California. He also builds effects.

Savage

1994-present. Tube combos, amp heads and cabinets built by Jeff Krumm at Savage Audio, in Savage, Minnesota.

Sceptre

1960s. Canadian-made. Sceptre script logo on upper left side of grille ('60s Fender-style and placement).

Signet Amp

1960s. Low power, 1x10", Class-A 6V6 power.

1960s		$250	$325

Schaller

The German guitar accessory company began in 1945, main products in the late '50s were tube amps and they had solid-state amps in the '60s.

Schertler

Made in Switzerland, model logo (e.g. David model) on front, intermediate to professional grade, modern designs for modern applications.

SDG Vintage

2003-present. Intermediate and professional grade, production/custom, tube amps, combos and heads built by Steven Gupta in Bristow, Virginia.

Selmer

1930s-late 1970s. The Selmer UK distributor offered mid- to high-level amps starting as early as 1935 and by the '50s was one of the strongest European brands of amps.

Bassmaster 50 Amp

1960s. Amp and cabinet set.

1964		$2,000	$2,600

Constellation 14 Amp

1962-1965. Single speaker combo, 14 watts, gray snakeskin tolex-type cover.

1962-1965		$1,950	$2,500

Futurama Caravelle Amp

1960s. Mid-size 1x12" combo.

1964		$900	$1,200

MODEL YEAR	FEATURES	EXC. COND. LOW	HIGH

Futurama Corvette Amp

1960s. Class A low power 1x8", 4 tubes, volume and tone controls, plus amplitude and speed tremolo controls, large script Futurama logo on front of amp, Futurama Corvette and Selmer logo on top panel.

1960s		$750	$1,000

Little Giant Amp

1960s. Small combo, red.

1963		$1,075	$1,400

Mark 2 Treble and Bass Amp Head

1960s. About 30 watts (2xEL34s), requires power line transformer for U.S. use, large Selmer logo on grille.

1960s		$1,075	$1,400

Thunderbird Twin 30 Amp

1960s. 30 watts, 2x12".

1962-1965		$4,000	$5,200

Thunderbird Twin 50 Amp

1960s. 50 watts, 2x12".

1964		$4,000	$5,200
1968		$2,450	$3,200

Truvoice Amp

1960s. Truvoice and Selectortone logo on top-mounted chasis, 30-watt combo, 1x15 or 2x12 Goodmans speaker, 2xEL34 power tubes, tremolo, 6 push button Selectortone Automatic.

1961	1x15 combo	$2,000	$2,600
1965	2x12 combo	$2,600	$3,400

Zodiac Twin 30 Amp

1964-1971. Combo amp, gray snakeskin tolex cover.

1964-1971		$2,900	$3,800

Sewell

1998-2008. Doug Sewell built his tube combo and head amps in Texas. He currently is the senior amp designer for Paul Reed Smith.

Seymour Duncan

Pickup maker Seymour Duncan, located in Santa Barbara, California, offered a line of amps from around 1984 to '95.

84-40/84-50 Amp

1989-1995. Tube combo, 2 switchable channels, 1x12", includes the 84-40 ('89-'91, 40 watts) and the 84-50 ('91-'95, 50 watts).

1989-1995	84-40 or 84-50	$225	$300

Bass 300 x 2 Amp

1986-1987. Solidstate, 2 channels (300 or 600 watts), EQ, contour boost switches, effects loop.

1986-1987		$225	$300

Bass 400 Amp

1986-1987. Solidstate, 400 watts, EQ, contour boost, balanced line output, effects loop.

1986-1987		$225	$300

Convertible Amp

1986-1995. 60-watt; dual-channel; effects loop; Accutronics spring reverb; 3-band EQ.

1986-1987	Head only	$300	$400
1988-1995	Combo	$300	$400

MODEL YEAR	FEATURES	EXC. COND. LOW	HIGH

KTG-2075 Stereo Amp

1989-1993. Part of the King Tone Generator Series, 2 channels with 75 watts per channel.

1989-1993		$225	$300

SG Systems

1970s. A Division of the Chicago Musical Instrument Company (CMI), who also owned Gibson Guitars. Gibson outsourced amplifier production from Kalamazoo to CMI in '67 and CMI (Chicago) continued for a year or two with Gibson-branded amplifiers. In the early '70s CMI introduced the SG Systems brand of hybrid amplifiers, which had a tube power section and a solidstate preamp section. CMI was trying to stay modern with SG Systems by introducing futuristic features like the Notch Shift which would quickly switch between popular rock sounds and mellow jazz delivery. SG amps have a large SG logo on the front baffle and were built with metal corners. Amplifiers have similar power specs; for example, the models issued in '73 all were rated with 100-watt RMS with 200-watts peak music power, so models were based on different speaker configurations.

SG Series Amp

1970s	SG-115, 1x15	$310	$400
1970s	SG-212, 2x12	$330	$430
1970s	SG-215 Bass, 2x15	$330	$430
1970s	SG-410, 4x10	$330	$430
1970s	SG-610, 6x10	$350	$450
1970s	SG-812 PA	$210	$275

Shaw

2008-present. Custom/production, intermediate and professional grade, guitar amp heads and cabinets built by Kevin Shaw in Lebanon, Tennessee.

Sherlock Amplifiers

1990-present. Dale Sherlock builds his intermediate to premium grade, production/custom, tube guitar amps and cabinets in Melbourne Victoria, Australia.

Sherwood

Late 1940s-early 1950s. Amps made by Danelectro for Montgomery Ward. There are also Sherwood guitars and lap steels made by Kay.

Sho-Bud

Introduced and manufactured by the Baldwin/Gretsch factory in 1970. Distributed by Kustom/Gretsch in the '80s. Models include D-15 Model 7838, S-15 Model 7836, Twin Tube Model 7834, and Twin Trans Model 7832.

Compactra 100 Amp

1960s. Hybrid tube, 45 watts, 1x12".

1960s		$450	$600

D15 Double Amp

Introduced in 1970. Solidstate, 100 watts. 2 channels 1x15" JBL speaker.

1970s		$450	$575

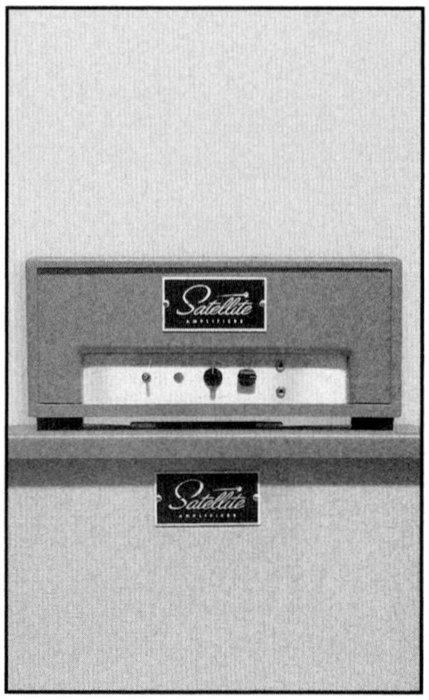

Satellite Amplifiers Barracuda

1964 Selmer Zodiac Twin 30

Imaged by Heritage Auctions, HA.com

Sherlock Angry Ant

AMPS

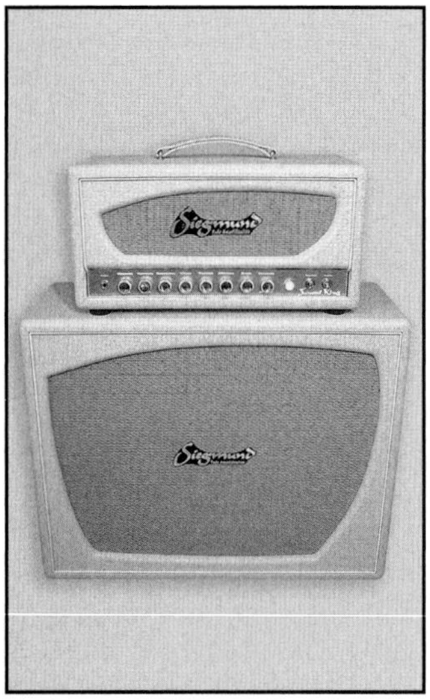

Siegmund Sound King

1956 Silvertone Model 1331

Tom Pfeifer

Silvertone Model 1333

Imaged by Heritage Auctions, HA.com

MODEL YEAR	FEATURES	EXC. COND. LOW	HIGH

S15 Single Amp

Introduced in 1972. Like D15, but with single channel.

1970s $300 $400

Sho-Bass Amp

Introduced in 1972. 100 watts, 1x15", solidstate combo, black grille, black vinyl cover.

1970s $300 $400

Twin Trans Amp

Introduced in 1972. 100 watts, solidstate combo, 2x12", reverb, black vinyl cover, dark grille, Sho-Bud script logo front upper right.

1970s $425 $550

Twin Tube Amp

Introduced in 1972. 100 watt tube combo, 4 6L6s, 2x12", reverb, black vinyl cover, dark grille.

1970s $525 $700

Siegmund Guitars & Amplifiers

1993-present. Chris Siegmund builds his tube amp heads, combos and cabinets in Los Angeles, California. He founded the company in Seattle, moving it to Austin, Texas for '95-'97. He also builds effects pedals and guitars.

Silvertone

1941-ca.1970, present. Brand used by Sears. All Silvertone amps were supplied by American companies up to around '66.

Model 1300 Amp

1948. Vertical combo cab, treble-clef logo on grille, 2-tone, 3 inputs, 2 controls.

1948 $375 $500

Model 1304 Amp

1949-1951. 18 watts, 1x12, 2x6L6 power tubes, 2-tone leatherette cover, round speaker baffle hole, volume, treble, bass and tremolo control knobs, becomes Model 1344.

1949-1951 $375 $500

Model 1330 Amp

1954-1957. Introduced in Sears Fall '54 catalog, 3 tubes (with rectifier), 1x6", wide-panel 13x13.75x7.5" cab in tan artificial leather, 9 lbs., replaced Model 1339 at the same price but with new wide-panel style, small Silvertone logo above the grille, replaced in '58 by Model 1390 Silvertone Meteor.

1954-1957 $195 $250

Model 1331 Amp

1954-1957. Made by Danelectro, 14 lbs., 1x8" student combo, 3 tubes (with rectifier), 1 volume, 1 tone, 2 inputs, tan tweed-effect cover with brown alligator trim, large-thread wheat-gold grille, brown metal control panel.

1954-1957 $225 $300

Model 1333 Amp

1954-1957. Made by Danelectro, 23 lbs., 1x12" combo, 2x6V6 power, 5 tubes (with rectifier), 2 volumes, 1 tone, 3 inputs, 2-control vibrato, tan tweed-effect cover with brown alligator trim, large-thread wheat-gold grille, brown metal control panel.

1954-1957 $400 $525

MODEL YEAR	FEATURES	EXC. COND. LOW	HIGH

Model 1334 Amp

1954-1957. Made by Danelectro, 29 lbs., heavy-duty 1x12" combo, 6 tubes (with rectifier), 2 volumes, 2 tones, 3 inputs, 2-control vibrato, tan tweed-effect cover with brown alligator trim, large-thread wheat-gold grille, brown metal control panel.

1954-1957 $425 $575

Model 1335 Amp

1954-1957. Made by Danelectro, 99 lbs., heavy-duty 1x15" combo, 6 tubes (with rectifier), 2 volumes, 2 tones, 4 inputs, 2-control vibrato, tan tweed-effect cover with brown alligator trim, large-thread wheat-gold grille, brown metal control panel.

1954-1957 $450 $600

Model 1336 (Twin Twelve) Amp

1954-1957. Made by Danelectro, 26.75x17.5x9.25" cab, 45 lbs., 2x12" combo, 4x6L6 powe tubes, 3 volumes, 2 tones, 4 inputs, 2-control vibrato, tan tweed-effect cover with brown alligator trim, large-thread wheat-gold grille, brown metal control panel.

1954-1957 $675 $900

Model 1337 "Wide Range Eight Speaker" Amp

1956. Odd-looking suitcase cab that opens into 2 separate speaker baffles each containing 4x8" speakers, 2 preamps, 2 channels with separate controls for volume, bass and treble, 2-control vibrato, 42 lbs.

1956 $675 $900

Model 1339 Amp

Ca.1952-1954. Sears lowest-priced amp, 3 tubes (with rectifier), 1x6", 1 input, 1 knob, maroon artificial leather cover over 10.5x8x5" verticle cab, script Silvertone logo on low right grille, 7 lbs.

1952-1954 $225 $300

Model 1340 Amp

Ca.1952-1954. Sears second lowest-priced amp, 3 tubes (with rectifier), 1x6", 2 inputs, 1 knob, brown and white imitation leather cover over 15x12x8.5" verticle cab, script Silvertone logo on low right grille, 14 lbs.

1952-1954 $225 $300

Model 1342 Streamlined Amp

Ca.1952-1954. Sears third lowest-priced amp, 4 tubes (with rectifier), 1x12", 3 inputs, 2 knobs, green and beige imitation leather cover over 16x19x7.25" slanted-side cab, script Silvertone logo on low right grille, 23 lbs.

1952-1954 $400 $525

Model 1344 Amp

1950-1954. Retro-styled vertical 22.5x15.5x9.5" cab with round speaker baffle hole, 1x12" combo, first Silvertone built-in vibrato, 6 tubes (with rectifier), 3 inputs, 3 controls (treble, bass, volume) plus vibrato control, maroon imitation leather cover with sports-stripe around the bottom, 33 lbs., script Silvertone logo low right side of cab.

1952-1954 $400 $525

Model 1346 (Twin Twelve) Amp

Ca.1952-1954. Danelectro-made, brown control panel, 2x12", 4 6L6s, vibrato, leather handle, tan smooth leatherette cover, 2 speaker baffle openings.

1952-1954 $675 $900

MODEL YEAR **FEATURES** **EXC. COND. LOW HIGH**

Model 1390 Meteor Amp
1958-1959. Renamed from Model 1330, Meteor logo on front panel, 1x6" practice amp, 3 tubes (with rectifier), tan simulated leather cover, in '60 renamed Model 1430 (but no longer a Meteor).

1958-1959 $225 $300

Model 1391 Amp
1958-1959. Modern-style cab, 3 tubes (with rectifier), 5 watts, 1x8".

1958-1959 $225 $300

Model 1392 Amp
1958-1959. Modern-style cab, 6 tubes (with rectifier), 10 watts, 1x12", vibrato.

1958-1959 $400 $525

Model 1393 Amp
1958-1959. Modern-style cab, 7 tubes (with rectifier), 15 watts, heavy-duty 1x12", vibrato.

1958-1959 $400 $525

Model 1396 Two-Twelve Amp
1958-1959. Script Two-Twelve logo on lower left front and Silvertone logo on lower right front, 50 watts, 2x12", 4x6L6 power tubes, 9 tubes (with rectifier), vibrato, 26.75x17.5x9.25" with gray and metallic fleck cover, white grille, 45 lbs.

1958-1959 $675 $900

Model 1420 Amp
1968. Tube-powered, 5 watts, 1x8" student combo.

1968 $275 $350

Model 1421 Amp
1968. Tube-powered, 10 watts, 1x8" combo, covered in dark olive vinyl.

1968 $275 $350

Model 1422 Amp
1968. Tube-powered, 40 watts, 1x12" combo, covered in dark olive vinyl.

1968 $400 $525

Model 1423 Amp
1968. Solidstate, 125 watts, 2x12" cab, 55 lbs., dark olive.

1968 $325 $425

Model 1425 Amp
1968. Solidstate, 200 watts, 6x10" cab, 86 lbs., dark olive.

1968 $675 $900

Model 1426 Amp
1968. Solidstate, 250 watts, 6x15" cab, slide switches instead of control knobs, automatic E-tone for tuning, casters for 149 lb. head and cab.

1968 $675 $900

Model 1428 Amp
1968. Solidstate, 60 watts, 1x15" cab, 36 lbs., dark olive.

1968 $325 $425

Model 1430 Amp
1959-1966. Silvertone's lowest-price model, 3 tubes, 1x6", previously called Model 1390 Meteor, and prior to that named Model 1330, retro cab basically unchanged since first introduced in '54.

1959-1966 $225 $300

Model 1431 Amp
1959-1961. 5 watts, 1x8", overhanging-top wrap-around grille cab, 3 tubes (with rectifier), light gray cover with white grille.

1959-1961 $225 $300

Model 1431 Bass Amp
1968. Solidstate, 200 watts, 6x12" cab, 91 lbs., dark olive.

1968 $675 $900

Model 1432 Amp
1959-1961. 10 watts, 1x12", vibrato, overhanging-top wrap-around grille cab, 6 tubes (with rectifier), dark gray tweed-effect cover with white grille.

1959-1961 $400 $525

Model 1433 Amp
1959-1961. 15 watts, 1x15", vibrato, overhanging-top wrap-around grille cab, 7 tubes (with rectifier), gray with metallic fleck cover with white grille.

1959-1961 $525 $700

Model 1434 Twin Twelve Amp
1959-1961. 50 watts using 4x6L6 power, 2x12" combo, vibrato, 2 channels each with volume, bass and treble controls, black cover with gold-colored trim.

1959-1961 $675 $900

Model 1459 Amp
1960s. Student tube amp, 3 watts, 1x8", black vinyl, square cab, 1 tone, 1 volume, 1 channel, 2 inputs.

1967-1968 $275 $350

Model 1463 Bass Amp
1967-1968. Solidstate, 1x15", piggyback, 60 lbs., reverb, tremolo.

1967-1968 $325 $425

Model 1464 Amp
1967-1968. Solidstate, 100 watts, 2x12", piggyback, 60 lbs., reverb, tremolo, gray vinyl cover.

1967-1968 $375 $500

Model 1465 Amp
1966-1968. Solidstate, piggyback, 150 watts, 6x10", reverb, tremolo, gray vinyl cover, replaces Model 1485.

1966-1968 $675 $900

Model 1466 Bass Amp
1966-1968. Solidstate, 150 watts, 6x10", gray vinyl cover.

1966-1968 $550 $725

Model 1471 Amp
1961-1963. 5 watts, 1x8", 3 tubes, 1 volume, 1 tone, 2 inputs, black leathette cover with white grille.

1961-1963 $275 $350

Model 1472 Amp
1960s. 10 watts, 2 6V6s provide mid-level power, 1x12", front controls mounted vertically on front right side, black cover with silver grille, large stationary handle, tremolo.

1961-1963 $400 $525

Model 1473 Bass Amp
1961-1963. Designed for bass or accordion, 25 watts, 1x15" combo, 6 tubes (with rectifier), 2 channels, 4 inputs, 19x29x9" cab, 43 lbs., black leatherette with white grille.

1961-1963 $525 $700

Silvertone Model 1336

Imaged by Heritage Auctions, HA.com

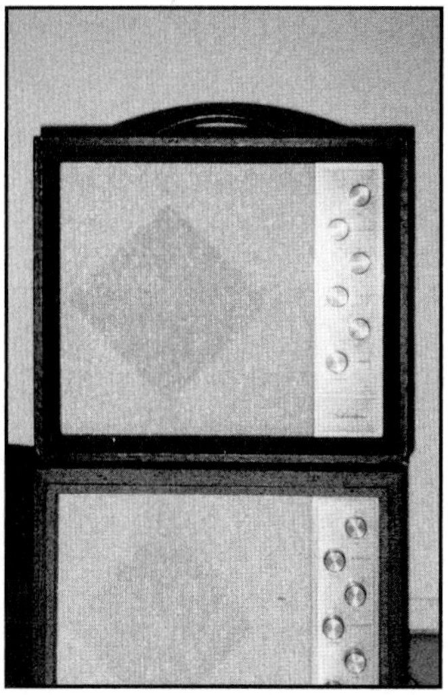

1961 Silvertone Model 1472

Kevin Lozinski

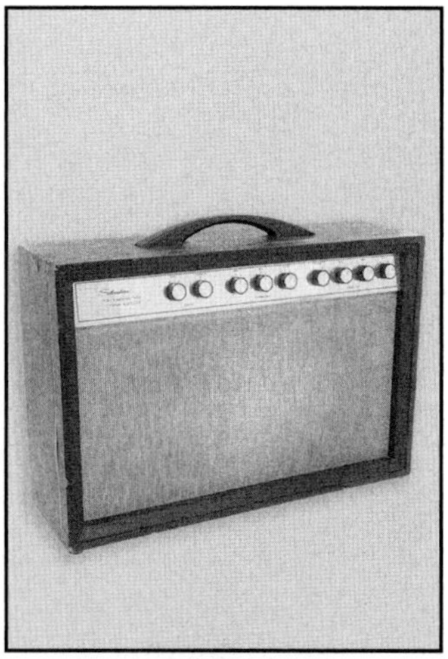

Ca. 1961 Silvertone Model 1474 Twin 12

Imaged by Heritage Auctions, HA.com

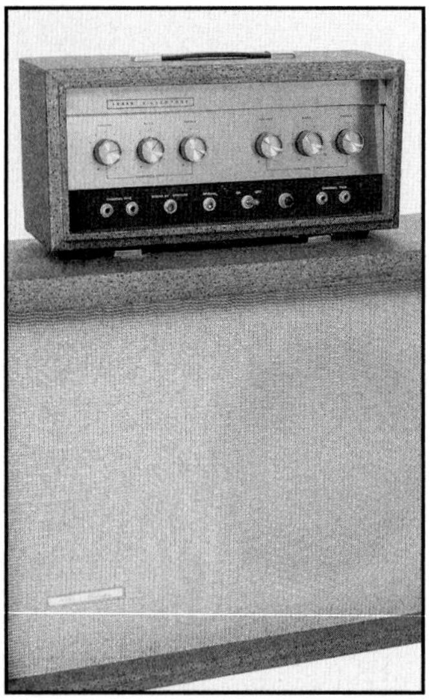

1964 Silvertone Model 1483
Imaged by Heritage Auctions, HA.com

Smokey

Soldano Decatone
Eric Van Gansen

MODEL YEAR	FEATURES	EXC. COND. LOW	HIGH

Model 1474 Twin Twelve Amp

1961-1963. Silvertone's first reverb amp, 50 watts, 4x6L6 power, 10 tubes (with rectifier), 2x12" combo, 2 control vibrato with dual remote footswitch, 2 channels each with bass, treble, and volume, 4 inputs, ground switch, standby switch, 19x29x9" combo cab, 54 lbs., black leatherette with silver grille.

1961-1963 $675 $900

Model 1481 Amp

1963-1968. Compact student amp, 5 watts, 1x8", 3 tubes (with rectifier), volume and tone controls, gray leatherette cover with white grille, replaces Model 1471.

1963-1968 $275 $350

Model 1482 Amp

1960s. 15 watts, 1x12", 6 tubes, control panel mounted on right side vertically, tremolo, gray leatherette.

1963-1968 $400 $525

Model 1483 Bass Amp

1963-1966. 23 watts, 1x15" piggyback tube amp, gray tolex and gray grille.

1963-1966 $525 $700

Model 1484 Twin Twelve Amp

1963-1966. 60 watts, 2x12" piggyback tube amp, tremolo and reverb, gray cover with light grille.

1963-1966 $675 $900

Model 1485 Amp

1963-1965. 120 watts, 6x10" (Jensen C-10Q) piggyback, 10 tubes with 5 silicon rectifiers, 2 channels, reverb, tremolo, charcoal-gray tolex-style cover, white grille, replaced in '66 by solidstate Model 1465.

1963-1965 $900 $1,150

Model 4707 Organ Amp

1960s. Interesting '60s family room style cabinet with legs, 45-watt tube amp with vibrato, 1x12", front controls, could be used for organ, stereo, or record player turntable.

1960s $350 $450

Simms-Watts

Late 1960s-1970s. Tube amp heads, combos, PA heads and cabinets made in London, England. Similar to Marshall and HiWatt offerings of the era.

Skip Simmons

1990-present. Custom and production tube combo amps built by Skip Simmons in Loma Rica, California.

Skrydstrup R&D

1997-present. Production/custom, premium grade, amps and cabinets built by Steen Skrydstrup in Denmark. He also builds effects.

Sligo Amps

2004-present. Intermediate and professional grade, production/custom, amps built by Steven Clark in Leesburg, Virginia.

SMF

Mid-1970s. Amp head and cabinets from Dallas Music Industries, Ltd., of Mahwah, New Jersey. Offered the Tour Series which featured a 150 watt head and 4x12" bottoms with metal speaker grilles and metal corners.

MODEL YEAR	FEATURES	EXC. COND. LOW	HIGH

Tour MK 2 Amp Head

1970s. 150-watt head, high- and low-gain inputs, master volume, 8xEL34 power tubes, black.

1970s $850 $1,100

SMF (Sonic Machine Factory)

2002-2009. Tube amps and cabinets designed by Mark Sampson (Matchless, Bad Cat, Star) and Rick Hamel (SIB effects) and built in California.

Smicz Amplification

Tube combos and extension cabinets built by Bob Smicz in Bristol, Connecticut.

Smith Custom Amplifiers

All tube combo amps, heads and speaker cabinets built by Sam Smith in Montgomery, Alabama starting in 2002.

Smokey

1997-present. Mini amps often packaged in cigarette packs made by Bruce Zinky in Flagstaff, Arizona. He also builds Zinky amps and effects and has revived the Supro brand on a guitar and amp.

Snider

Jeff Snider has been building various combo tube amps in San Diego, California, since '95. In 1999 he started branding them with his last name.

Soldano

1987-present. Made in Seattle, Washington by amp builder Mike Soldano, the company offers a range of all-tube combo amps, heads and cabinets. They also offer a reverb unit.

Astroverb 16 Combo Amp

1997-2020. Atomic with added reverb.

1997-2020 $675 $875

Atomic 16 Combo Amp

1996-2001. Combo, 20 watts, 1x12".

1996-2001 $575 $750

Avenger Amp Head

2004-2020. Single channel, 4 preamp tubes, 100-watt with 4 power tubes, or 50-watt with 2.

2004-2020 $1,075 $1,400

Decatone Combo Amp

1998-2020. 2x12" 100-watt combo, rear mounted controls, still available as a head.

1998-2008 2x12 combo $1,600 $2,100
2009-2020 Head only $1,250 $1,650

HR 50/Hot Rod 50 Amp Head

1992-2012. 50-watt single channel head.

1992-2012 $875 $1,125

HR 100/Hot Rod 100 Amp Head

1994-2001. 100-watt single channel head.

1994-2001 $875 $1,125

Lucky 13 Combo Amp

2000-2020. 100 watts (50 also available), 2x12" combo.

2000-2020 $1,200 $1,575

MODEL YEAR	FEATURES	EXC. COND. LOW	HIGH

Reverb-O-Sonic Combo Amp

1990s-2020. 50 watts, 2 channels, 2x12" combo, reverb.

1990s-2020		$1,050	$1,375

SLO-100 Super Cabinet

1988-2019. 4x12" slant-front or straight-front cabinet, prices shown are for slant, deduct $100 for straight.

1988-1989		$650	$850
1990-2020		$575	$750

SLO-100 Super Lead Overdrive 100-Watt Amp

1988-2020. First production model, 100-watt amp head, snakeskin cover, 4x12" cabinet. Replaced by SLO-100 Classic in '21.

1988-1989		$2,550	$3,300
1990-2009		$2,450	$3,200
2010-2020		$2,400	$3,100

Sommatone

1998-present. Jim Somma builds his tube combo and head amps and cabinets in Somerville, New Jersey.

Sonax

Introduced in 1972. Budget line of solidstate amps offered by Gretsch/Baldwin, made by Yorkville Sound (Traynor) in Toronto. Introduced with dark grille and dark cover.

530-B Bass Amp

1970s. Solidstate, 30 watts, 1x12".

1970s		$115	$150

550-B Bass Amp

1970s. Solidstate, 50 watts, 1x15".

1970s		$135	$175

720-G Amp

1970s. Solidstate student amp, 20 watts, 2x8", reverb.

1970s		$135	$175

730-G Amp

1970s. Solidstate, 30 watts, 2x10", reverb and tremolo.

1970s		$195	$250

750-G Amp

1970s. Solidstate, 50 watts, 2x12", reverb and tremolo.

1970s		$210	$275

770-G Amp

1970s. Solidstate, 75 watts, 4x10", reverb and tremolo.

1970s		$225	$300

Songworks Systems

See listing under Little Lanilei.

Sonny Jr.

1996-present. Harmonica amplifiers built by harmonica player Sonny Jr. in conjunction with Cotton Amps in Tolland, Connecticut.

Sonola

Tube combo amps made for the Sonola Accordian company of Chicago in the 1950s and '60s, possibly built by Guild or Ampeg. There are also Sonola tube amp heads from the '70s made by MHB Amplifiers in Adelaide, South Australia.

MODEL YEAR	FEATURES	EXC. COND. LOW	HIGH

Sound City

Made in England from 1966-'67 to the late-'70s, the tube Sound City amps were Marshall-looking heads and separate cabinets. They were imported, for a time, into the U.S. by Gretsch.

50 PA Plus Amp

Late-1960s-late-1970s. Similar to 50 Plus but with 4 channels.

1970s		$575	$750

50 Plus/50R Amp Head

Late-1960s-late-1970s. Amp head, labeled 50 Plus or 50 R.

1960s-70s		$750	$1,000

120 Energizer Slave Unit Amp

1970s. 120-watt power amp only, no preamp, Energizer Slave Unit logo on front panel.

1970s		$475	$625

120/120R Amp Head

Early-late-1970s. The 120-watt head replaced the late-1960s 100-watt model.

1970s	120 no reverb	$775	$1,050
1970s	120R reverb	$850	$1,150

200 Plus Amp Head

1970s		$900	$1,175

Concord Combo Amp

80 watts, 2x12" Fane speakers, cream, basketweave grille.

1968		$800	$1,050

L-80 Cabinet

1970s. 4x10" speaker cabinet.

1970s		$425	$550

L-412 Cabinet

1970s. 4x12" speaker cabinet.

1970s		$475	$625

X-60 Cabinet

1970s. 2x12" speaker cabinet.

1970s		$450	$600

Sound Electronics

Sound Electronics Corporation introduced a line of amplifiers in 1965 that were manufactured in Long Island. Six models were initially offered, with solidstate rectifiers and tube preamp and power sections. Their catalog did not list power wattages but did list features and speaker configurations. The initial models had dark vinyl-style covers and sparkling silver grille cloth. The amps were combos with the large models having vertical cabinets, silver script Sound logo on upper left of grille. The larger models used JBL D120F and D130F speakers. Stand alone extension speakers were also available.

Various Model Amps

Mid-1960s. Includes X-101, X-101R, X-202 Bass/Organ, X-404 Bass and Organ, X-505R amps, hi-fi chassis often using 7868 power tubes.

1960s		$400	$600

Southbay Ampworks/ Scumback Amps

2002-present. Tube combo amps and speaker cabinets built by Jim Seavall in Whittier, California. He also builds Scumback Speakers. In '14, name changed to Scumback Amps.

Soldano SLO-100

Imaged by Heritage Auctions, HA.com

1970s Sound City 120 and L-412

Imaged by Heritage Auctions, HA.com

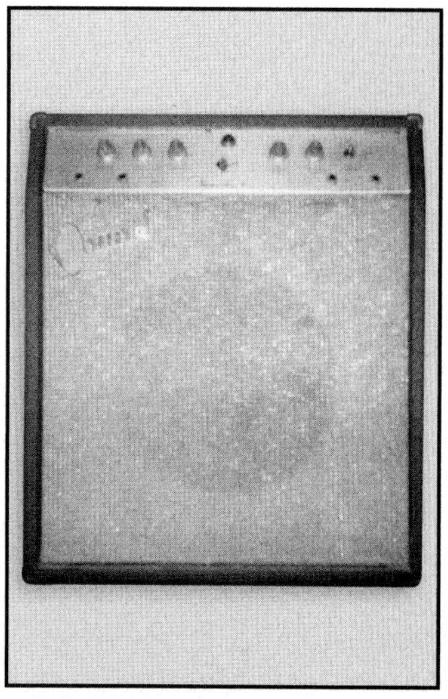

Sound Electronics X-101

Tom Novak

1994 Sovtek Mig 100
Imaged by Heritage Auctions, HA.com

Specimen Horn

Standel 25L15
Imaged by Heritage Auctions, HA.com

MODEL YEAR | FEATURES | EXC. COND. LOW | HIGH

Sovtek

1992-1996. Sovtek amps were products of Mike Matthews of Electro-Harmonix fame and his New Sensor Corporation. The guitar and bass amps and cabinets were made in Russia.

Mig Cabinet

1992-1996 2x12" $300 $400

Mig Series Amp Head

1992-1996. Tube amp heads, model number indicates watts, point-to-point wiring, models include; Mig 30, 50, 60, 100, 100B (bass).

1992-1996 Various models $450 $600

Space Tone

See Swart Amplifiers.

Specimen Products

1984-present. Luthier Ian Schneller added tube amps and speaker cabinets in '93. He also builds guitars, basses and ukes in Chicago, Illinois.

Speedster

1995-2000, 2003-2007. Founded by Lynn Ellsworth, offering tube amps and combos designed by Bishop Cochran with looks inspired by dashboards of classic autos. In '03, Joe Valosay and Jevco International purchased the company and revived the brand with help from former owner Cory Wilds. Amps were originally built by Soldono, but later ones built by Speedster in Gig Harbor, Washington. They also built effects pedals.

Splawn

2004-present. Production, professional grade, tube amps and cabinets built by Scott Splawn in Dallas, North Carolina.

St. George

1960s. There were Japanese guitars bearing this brand, but these amps may have been built in California.

Mid-Size Tube Amp

1965. Low power, 1x10" Jensen, 2 5065 and 2 12AX7 tubes.

1960s $175 $225

Standel

1952-1974, 1997-present. Bob Crooks started custom building amps part time in '52, going into full time standard model production in '58 in Temple City, California. In '61 Standel started distributing guitars under their own brand and others. By late '63 or '64, Standel had introduced solidstate amps, two years before Fender and Ampeg introduced their solidstate models. In '67 Standel moved to a new, larger facility in El Monte, California. In '73 Chicago Musical Instruments (CMI), which owned Gibson at the time, bought the company and built amps in El Monte until '74. In '97 the Standel name was revived by Danny McKinney who, with the help of original Standel founder Bob Crooks and Frank Garlock (PR man for first Standel), set about building reissues of some of the early models in Ventura, California.

A-30 B Artist 30 Bass Amp

1964-early-1970s. Artist Series, the original Standel solidstate series, 80 watts, 2x15".

1964-1969 $300 $400

A-30 G Artist 30 Guitar Amp

1964-early-1970s. Solidstate, 80 watts, 2x15".

1964-1974 $325 $425

A-48 G Artist 48 Guitar Amp

1964-early-1970s. Solidstate, 80 watts, 4x12".

1964-1974 $375 $500

A-60 B Artist 60 Bass Amp

1964-early-1970s. Solidstate, 160 watts, 4x15".

1964-1974 $375 $500

A-60 G Artist 60 Guitar Amp

1964-early-1970s. Solidstate, 160 watts, 4x15".

1964-1974 $375 $500

A-96 G Artist 96 Guitar Amp

1964-early-1970s. Solidstate, 160 watts, 8x12".

1964-1974 $425 $550

Artist XV Amp

1960s. Piggyback, hybrid solidstate preamp with power tubes.

1962 $300 $400

C-24 Custom 24 Amp

Late-1960s-1970s. Custom Slim Line Series, solidstate, 100 watts, 2x12", dark vinyl, dark grille.

1960s-70s $325 $450

I-30 B Imperial 30 Bass Amp

1964-early-1970s. Imperial Series, the original Standel solidstate series, 100 watts, 2x15".

1964-1974 $350 $475

I-30 G Imperial 30 Guitar Amp

1964-early-1970s. Imperial Series, the original Standel solidstate series, 100 watts, 2x15".

1964-1974 $375 $500

S-10 Studio 10 Amp

Late-1960s-1970s. Studio Slim Line Series, solidstate, 30 watts, 1x10", dark vinyl, dark grille.

1960s-70s $275 $350

S-24 G Amp

1970s. Solidstate, 2x12".

1970s $325 $450

S-50 Studio 50 Amp

Late-1963 or early-1964-late-1960s. Not listed in '69 Standel catalog, 60 watts, gray tolex, gray grille, piggyback.

1960s $325 $450

SM-60 Power Magnifier Amp

1970s. Tall, verticle combo solidstate amp, 100 watts, 6x10".

1970 $325 $425

Tube Amp

1953-1958. Early custom made tube amps made by Bob Crooks in his garage, padded naugahyde cabinet with varying options and colors. There are a limited number of these amps, and brand knowledge is also limited, therefore there is a wide value range. Legend has it that the early Standel amps made Leo Fender re-think and introduce even more powerful amps.

1953-1958 Various models $2,000 $4,500

MODEL YEAR	FEATURES	EXC. COND. LOW	HIGH

Star
Tube amps, combos and speaker cabinets built by Mark Sampson in the Los Angeles, California area, starting 2004. Sampson has also been involved with Matchless, Bad Cat, and SMF amps.

Starcaster
See listing under Fender.

Starlite
Starlite was a budget brand made and sold by Magnatone. See Magnatone for listings.

Stella Vee
1999-2005. Jason Lockwood built his combo amps, heads, and cabinets in Lexington, Kentucky.

Stephenson
1997-present. Mark Stephenson builds his intermediate to premium grade, production/custom, tube amps and cabinets in Regina, Saskatchewan 1997-'99, in Hope, British Columbia 2000-'06, and since in Parksville, British Columbia. He also offers effects.

Stevenson
1999-present. Luthier Ted Stevenson, of Lachine, Quebec, added amps to his product line in '05. He also builds basses and guitars.

Stimer
Brothers Yves and Jean Guen started building guitar pickups in France in 1946. By the late '40s they had added their Stimer line of amps to sell with the pickups. Early amp models were the M.6, M.10 and M.12 (6, 10 and 12 watts, respectively). An early user of Guen products was Django Reinhardt.

Stinger
1980s-1990s. Stinger was a budget line of guitars and solidstate amps imported by Martin.

Strad-O-Lin/Stradolin
Ca.1920s-ca.1960s. The Strad-O-Lin company primarily made mandolins for wholesalers but around '57 Multivox/Premier bought the company and used the name on guitars and amps.

Compact Solidstate Amp
1960s. Made in U.S.A., logo on control panel and grille, black grille and cover.

1960s		$95	$125

Stramp
1970s. Stramp, of Hamburg, Germany, offered audio mixers, amps and compact powered speaker units, all in aluminum flight cases.

Solidstate Amp
1970s. Solidstate amp head in metal suitcase with separate Stramp logo cabinet.

1970s		$300	$400

MODEL YEAR	FEATURES	EXC. COND. LOW	HIGH

Straub Amps
2003-present. Harry Straub builds his professional grade, production/custom, amps in St. Paul, Minnesota.

Suhr
1997-present. John Suhr builds his production/custom amps in Lake Elsinore, California. He also builds guitars and basses.

Sundown
1983-1988. Combo amps, heads and cabinets designed and built by Dennis Kager. By '88, he had sold his interest in the company.

Sunn
1965-2002. Started in Oregon by brothers Conrad and Norm Sundhold (Norm was the bass player for the Kingsman). Sunn introduced powerful amps and extra heavy duty bottoms and was soon popular with many major rock acts. Norm sold his interest to Conrad in '69. Conrad sold the company to the Hartzell Corporation of Minnesota around '72. Fender Musical Instruments acquired the brand in '85 shortly after parting ways with CBS and used the brand until '89. They resurrected the brand again in '98, but quit offering the name in '02.

100S Amp and Cabinet Set
1965-1970s. 60 watts, 1x15" JBL D130F and 1 LE 100S JBL Driver and Horn, piggyback, 5 tubes (with rectifier).

1965-1969		$1,125	$1,500

190L Amp and Cabinet Set
1970s. Solidstate, 80 watts, 2 speakers.

1970s		$575	$750

200S/215B Amp and Cabinet Set
1966-1970s. 60 watts, 2x6550s, large vertical cab with 1x15" or 2x15" speakers.

1966-1969	1x15"	$1,125	$1,500
1966-1969	2x15"	$1,125	$1,500

601-L Cabinet
1980s. 6x10" plus 2 tweeters cab.

1980s		$350	$450

2000S Amp
1968-1970s. 4x6550 power tubes, 120 watts.

1968-1970s	Head & cab	$1,300	$1,700

Alpha 112 Amp
1980s. Solidstate, MOS-FET preamp section, 1x12" combo, reverb, overdrive, black.

1980s		$150	$200

Alpha 115 Amp
1980s. Solidstate, MOS-FET preamp section, 1x15", clean and overdrive.

1980s		$175	$225

Alpha 212 R Amp
1980s. Solidstate, MOS-FET preamp section, 2x12", reverb.

1980s		$225	$300

Beta Bass Amp
1978-1980s. Solidstate 100-watt head and combos, large Beta Bass logo on front panel.

1978-1980s	4x12"	$525	$700
1978-1980s	6x10"	$525	$700

Star Gain Star

Suhr Badger

Rob Bernstein

Sundown

1970s Sunn Solo

Imaged by Heritage Auctions, HA.com

1970 Sunn Sceptre

Imaged by Heritage Auctions, HA.com

Sunn Stagemaster

Robert Curd

MODEL YEAR	FEATURES	EXC. COND. LOW	HIGH
1978-1980s	Combo 1x15"	$525	$700
1978-1980s	Combo 2x12"	$525	$700
1978-1980s	Combo 4x10"	$525	$700

Coliseum 300 Bass Amp

1970s. Solidstate, Coliseum-300 logo on front.

1970s	Head & cab	$675	$900

Coliseum Lead Amp

1970s. Solidstate, Coliseum Lead logo on front.

1970s	Head & cab	$675	$900

Coliseum Lead Full Stack Amp

1970s. Coliseum Lead logo on amp head, two 4x12" cabs.

1970s		$1,025	$1,350

Concert 215S Bass Amp Set

1970s. Solidstate head, 200 watts, Model 215S tall vertical cabinet with 2x12" Sunn label speakers, dark vinyl cover, silver sparkle grille.

1970s		$625	$825

Concert Lead 610S Amp Set

1970s. Solidstate, 200 watts, 6x10" piggyback, reverb and built-in distortion.

1970s		$775	$1,025

Enforcer Amp

1980s. Tube, 60/100 watt 2x12" or 100 watt head.

1980s	Combo	$750	$975
1980s	Head & cab	$800	$1,050

Fuse 200S Amp

1970s. Sunn Fuse logo and model number on front panel, 140 watts.

1970s		$850	$1,125

Model T Amp Head

Early-1970s. 100 watts.

1970s		$2,150	$2,825

Model T Amp Reissue

1998-2002. Reissue of '70s Model T, 100 watts, with 4x12" cab.

1998-2002	Head & cab	$1,250	$1,625

SB-160 Bass Amp

1985. Combo, 60 watts.

1985		$325	$425

SB-200 Amp

1985. 200 watts, 1x15", 4-band EQ, master volume, compressor.

1985		$350	$475

Sceptre Amp

1968-1972. 60 watts, 6550 power tubes, tremolo, reverb.

1968-1972Head & cab$1,050$1,375

Sentura Amp

1967-1970s. Rectifier and power tubes, I and II versions.

1967-1969	I, 1x15" set	$950	$1,250
1967-1969	II, 2x15" set	$1,000	$1,300

SL 250 Amp

1980s. 60 watts, 2x12" combo, SL 250 logo.

1980s		$450	$600

SL 260 Amp

1982-ca.1985. 60 watts, 2x12" combo with reverb, SL 260 logo.

1982-1985		$525	$675

Solarus Amp

1967-1970s. Tube amp (EL34s), reverb, tremolo, 2x12" 40 watt combo to '68; 60 watt head with 2x12" cab for '69 on.

1967-1968	Combo	$525	$700
1969-1970s	Head & cab	$650	$850

Solo II Amp

Early-1970s. Solo II logo on front panel, 120 watts, 2x12" combo, black tolex.

1970s		$525	$700

Sonaro Amp

Early-1970s. Head and 1x15" cab, 60 watts.

1970s		$575	$750

Sonic 1-40 Amp

1967-1969. Tube head, 1x15" bass amp, 40 watts.

1967-1969	Head & cab	$900	$1,200

Sonic I Amp

1967-1969. 125 watts, 1x15" JBL D130F in short cabinet, 5 tubes (with rectifier), piggyback, dark tolex.

1967-1969	Head & cab	$900	$1,200

Sonic II Amp

1967-1969. 250 watts, 2x15" JBL D130F in folding horn large cabinet, 5 tubes (with rectifier), piggyback, dark tolex.

1967-1969	Head & cab	$950	$1,250

Sorado Amp

1970s. 50 watts, tubes, 2x15" matching cab.

1970s	Head & cab	$850	$1,125

Spectrum I Amp

1967-1969. 125 watts, 1x15" JBL D130F large cabinet, 5 tubes (with rectifier), piggyback, dark tolex cover.

1967-1969	Head & cab	$875	$1,150

Spectrum II Amp

1967-1969. 250 watts, 2x12", piggyback, 5 tubes (with rectifier), Spectrum II logo on front panel.

1967-1969	Head & cab	$925	$1,225

SPL 7250 Amp

Dual channels, 250 watts per channel, forced air cooling, switch-selectable peak compressor with LEDs.

1989	Head & cab	$475	$625

Stagemaster

1980s. 120 watts, 2x12".

1980s	Combo	$400	$525
1980s	Head & cab	$475	$625

T50C

1998-2002. Combo 1x12", 50 watts.

1998-2002		$525	$700

Supersound

1952-1974. Founded in the U.K. by Alan Wootton, building custom amps and radios, the firm continued to build amps and effects into the early '60s. They also built guitars and basses.

Supertone

1914-1941. Supertone was a brand used by Sears for their musical instruments. In the '40s Sears started using the Silvertone name on those products. Amps were made by other companies.

Amp

1930s		$200	$350

AMPS

MODEL YEAR	FEATURES	EXC. COND. LOW	HIGH

Supro

1935-1968, 2004-present. Supro was a budget brand of the National Dobro Company, made by Valco in Chicago, Illinois. Amp builder Bruce Zinky revived the Supro name in '04 for a line of guitars and amps. In '13, Absara Audio, LLC acquired the Supro trademark and started releasing amps in July '14.

'64 Reverb Amp

2020-present. 5 watts, 1x8", reverb, Jensen speaker, blue.

2020-2021	1605RJ	$550	$725

Accordion 1615T Amp

1957-1959. Compact combo, 1x15", 24 watts, 2x6L6 power, 5V4, 3x12AX7, 2 channels, tremolo, 3 control knobs, Accordion (model) logo upper left corner of grille, Supro logo lower right, Rhino-Hide gray with white sides.

1957-1959		$725	$950

Bantam Amp

1961-1966. Petite, 4 watts, 3 tubes, 1x 8" Jensen, gold weave Saran Wrap grille, Spanish Ivory fabric cover, red in '64, gray in '66. Also sold as matching set, for example in '64 with student-level red and white lap steel, add 65% to price for matching guitar and amp set.

1961-1963	1611S, Spanish ivory	$365	$475
1964-1965	S6411, red cover	$365	$475
1966	Gray cover	$365	$475

Bass Combo Amp

Early 1960s. 35 watts, 2x12", 2 channels (bass and standard), 7 tubes, tremolo, woven embossed black and white tolex that appears grey. The '61 model 1688T has a narrow panel body style somewhat similar to the Fender narrow panel cab style of the late '50s, in '62 the cab panel was removed and the 'no panel' style became the 1688TA model, the new cab was less expensive to build and Supro offered a price reduction on applicable models in '62.

1961	1688T, narrow panel	$700	$900
1962-1963	1688TA, no panel	$700	$900

Big Star Reverb S6451TR Amp

1964. 35 watts, 2x12", reverb and tremolo, 'no panel' cab.

1964		$900	$1,200

Black Magick Amp

2016-present. 25 watts, 1x12", head (1695TH), tremolo combo (1695TJ), reverb and tremolo combo (1696RT). Extension cabinets also offered.

2017-2021	1695TH, head	$675	$875
2020-2021	1695TJ	$775	$1,025
2018-2021	1695RT	$875	$1,150
2017-2021	1x12" cab	$290	$375
2017-2021	2x12" cab	$385	$500

Blues King Amp

2019-2020. 5 watts, 1x10".

2019-2020		$250	$325

Blues King 8 Amp

2020. 1 watt, 1x8".

2020	1808	$225	$290

Brentwood 1650T Amp

Mid-1950s. Advertised as Supro's "finest amplifier", model 1650T described as the "professional twin speaker luxury amplifier", 2 channels including high-gain, tremolo with speed control.

1956		$900	$1,200

Combo Amp

1961-1964. 24 watts, 6 tubes, 1x15" Jensen, Rhino-Hide covering in black and white, light grille, tremolo.

1961	1696T, narrow panel	$675	$875
1962-1963	1696TA, no panel	$675	$875

Combo Tremolo S6497T Amp

1964. 35 watts, 1x15", standard 'no panel' cab, tremolo.

1964		$700	$925

Comet 1610B Amp

1957-1959. Gray Rhino-Hide, 1x10".

1957-1959		$650	$850

Comet 1610E Amp

Mid-1950s. Supro's only 1x10" amp from the mid-'50s, 3 input jacks, 2 control knobs, woven tweed and leatherette 2-tone covering.

1956		$650	$850

Coronado Amp

1960-1963. 24 watts, 2x10", tremolo, 2 channels, 6 tubes, Supro logo upper right above grille, black and white mixed tolex appears gray, described as tremolo twin-speaker pro amp, '61 has 'narrow panel' body style, new body style in '62 becomes 1690TA model with grille only and no panel.

1960-1961	1690T, narrow panel	$850	$1,100
1962-1963	1690TA, no panel	$850	$1,100

Corsica Amp

Mid 1960s. Redesigned vertical combo amp, reverb, tremolo, blue control panel, black tolex, silver grille.

1965-1967		$550	$725

Delta King 8 Amp

2020-present. 1 watt, 1x8", tweed/black (1818TB) or black/cream (1818BC).

2020-2021		$260	$335

Delta King 10 Amp

2020-present. 5 watts, 1x10", reverb, tweed/black (1820RTB) or black/cream (1820RBC).

2020-2021		$310	$400

Delta King 12 Amp

2020-present. 15 watts, 1x12", reverb, tweed/black (1822RTB) or black/cream (1822RBC).

2020-2021		$365	$475

Dual-Tone Amp

1961-1965, 2014-2020. 17 watts, 6 tubes, 1x12" Jensen, organ tone tremolo, restyled in '64, Trinidad Blue vinyl fabric cover, light color grille. Reintroduced in '14, 24 watts.

1961	1624T, narrow panel	$725	$950
1962-1963	1624TA, no panel	$725	$950
1964-1965	S6424T, no panel	$725	$950
2014-2020	1624T, no panel	$500	$650

Galaxy Amp

2019-2020. 50 watts, 1x12".

2019-2020	1697R	$800	$1,050

Supro 1688T
Carter Vintage Guitars

Supro 1695T Black Magick

Mid-1960s Supro Corsica
Imaged by Heritage Auctions, HA.com

Supro Golden Holiday

AMPS

1965 Supro Model 24
Michael Wright

1961 Supro 1606S Super
Steve Allen

MODEL YEAR	FEATURES	EXC. COND. LOW	HIGH

Galaxy Tremolo S6488 Amp
1965. 35 watts, 2x12" (often Jensen), 7 tubes, tremolo, multi-purpose for guitar, bass and accordion.

1965		$750	$975

Galaxy Tremolo S6688 Amp
1966-1967. 35 watts, 2x12" (often Jensen), turquoise front control panel with Supro logo (not on grille), model name/number also on front control panel.

1966-1967		$750	$975

Golden Holiday 1665T Amp
Mid-1950s. Supro's model for the 'semi-professional', 2 oval 11x6" speakers, 14 watts, 6 tubes, tremolo, 2 control knobs, black and tweed cover.

1956		$775	$1,000

Keeley Custom Amp
2020-present. Designed with Robert Keeley (Keeley Electronics), 25 watts, 1x10" (Custom 10) or 1x12" (Custom 12).

2020-2021		$525	$700
2020-2021	Custom 10	$550	$725
2020-2021	Custom 12	$650	$850

Model 24 Amp
1965. 18 watts, 1x12 combo, 2 channels each with bass and treble inputs, tremolo, Model 24 logo on top panel, Calypso Blue vinyl cover.

1965		$675	$875

Reverb 1650R Amp
1963. 17 watts, 1x10", 'no panel' grille front style cab, reverb.

1963		$725	$950

Royal Reverb 1650TR Amp
1963-1965. 17 watts, 15 tubes, 2x10" Jensens, catalog says "authentic tremolo and magic-reverberation."

1963-1965		$1,000	$1,300

Royal Reverb S6650 Amp
1965-1967. Updated cabinet with turquoise-blue front control panel, 2x10" combo, 2 channels (standard and reverb-tremolo).

1965-1967		$600	$775

Special 1633E Amp
Mid-1950s. Supro's entry level student amp, 1x8", 3 tubes, large Supro stencil logo on grille, 2-tone red and white fabric cover, leather handle, available with matching Special Lap Steel covered in wine-maroon plastic.

1956		$450	$575

Spectator 1614E Amp
Mid-1950s. 1x8", 3 tubes, 2 control knobs, white front with red and black body.

1956		$500	$650

Sportsman S6689 Amp
1966. Piggyback, twin speakers.

1966		$725	$925

Statesman S6699 Amp
1966-1967, 2017-2020. Piggyback with blue-green control panel, 4x6L6 power, horizontal 2x12" cab, reverb, tremolo, script Statesman logo with model number on upper left front of chasis. Reintroduced in '17, 50 watts, 1x12" combo.

1966-1967	Piggyback	$650	$850
2017-2020	Combo	$925	$1,200

Studio 1644E Amp
Mid-1950s. Supro's student model for teaching studios, 2 input jacks for student and instructor or guitar and lap steel guitar, 3 tubes, advertised for "true Hawaiian tone reproduction", covered in royal blue leatherette (in '56), available with a matching Studio Lap Steel covered in blue plastic.

1956-1957	Blue leatherette	$475	$625

Super 1606E Amp
Mid-1950s. Supro advertising states "with features important to women", oval 11x6" Rola speaker, 3 tubes, 1 control knob, 2 inputs, white (front) and grey sides, elliptical baffle soundhole with Supro logo, model number with E suffix common for '50s Supro's.

1956	White front & grey	$500	$650

Super Amp
1961-1963, 2017-2020. 4.5 watts, 3 tubes, 1x8", 1606S has contrasting black and white covering with old narrow panel cab, in '63 new 1606B has 'no panel' style cab with lighter (gray) covering. Reintroduced in '17, 5 watts, 1x8".

1961-1962	1606S	$450	$600
1963	1606B	$450	$600
2017-2020	1606	$425	$550

Super Six S6406 Amp
1964-1965. Student practice amp, 4.5 watts, 1x8", blue vinyl cover.

1964-1965		$450	$600

Super Six S6606 Amp
1966. Updated version of student compact amp.

1966		$375	$500

Supreme Amp
1961-1963. 17 watts, 1x10", designed for use with Model 600 Reverb Accessory Unit, value shown does not include the Model 600 (see Effects Section for reverb unit). The initial 1600R model was designed with a triangle-like shaped soundhole, in '62 the more typical Supro no panel cab was

introduced which Supro called the new slope front design.

1961	1600R	$900	$1,200
1962-1963	1600S, no panel	$900	$1,200

Supreme 17 S6400 Amp
1964-1965. 17 watts, 1x10", cab larger than prior models of this type.

1964-1965		$650	$850

Supreme Twin Speaker 1600E Amp
Mid-1950s. 2 oval 11x6" speakers, 5 tubes, 3 input jacks, 2 control knobs, grille logo states "Twin Speaker" but unlike most Supro amps of this era the Supro logo does not appear on the front.

1956		$650	$850

Thunderbolt S6420(B) Bass Amp
1964-1967. 35 watts, 1x15" Jensen, introduced in the '64 catalog as a no frills - no fancy extra circuits amp. Sometimes referred to as the "Jimmy Page amp" based on his use of this amp in his early career.

1964-1967		$1,325	$1,725

Thunderbolt S6920 Amp
1967-1968. Redesign circuit replaced S6420B, 35 watts, 1x12".

1967-1968		$650	$850

Tremo-Verb S6422TR Amp

1964-1965. Lower power using 4 12AX7s, 1 5Y3GT, and 1 6V6, 1x10", tremolo and reverb, Persian Red vinyl cover.

MODEL YEAR	FEATURES	EXC. COND. LOW	HIGH
1964-1965		$900	$1,200

Trojan Tremolo Amp

1961-1966. 5 watts, 4 tubes, 1 11"x6" oval (generally Rolla) speaker, '61-'64 black and white fabric cover and Saran Wrap grille, '64-'66 new larger cab with vinyl cover and light grille.

MODEL YEAR	FEATURES	EXC. COND. LOW	HIGH
1961	1616T, narrow panel	$425	$575
1962-1963	1616TA, no panel	$425	$575
1964-1966	S6461, blue vinyl cover	$425	$575

Vibra-Verb S6498VR Amp

1964-1965. Billed as Supro's finest amplifier, 2x35-watt channels, 1x15" and 1x10" Jensens, vibrato and reverb.

MODEL YEAR	FEATURES	EXC. COND. LOW	HIGH
1964-1965		$1,400	$1,800

Surreal Amplification

2007-present. Production/custom, professional grade amp heads, combos and cabinets built in Westminster, California by Jerry Dyer.

Swampdonkey

2006-present. Professional and premium grade, production/custom, guitar amp heads, combos and speaker cabinets built in Rural Rocky View, Alberta by Chris Czech.

Swanpro Amps

Robert Swanson started building tube combo and head amps and cabinets in Denver, Colorado in 2004.

Swart Amplifier Co. (Space Tone)

2003-present. Michael J. Swart builds tube combo and head amps and cabinets under the Swart and Space Tone brand names in Wilmington, North Carolina. He also builds effects.

SWR Sound

1984-2013. Founded by Steve W. Rabe in '84, with an initial product focus on bass amplifiers. Fender Musical Instruments Corp. acquired SWR in June, 2003.

Baby Blue Studio Bass System

1990-2003. Combo, all tube preamp, 150 watts solidstate power amp, 2x8", 1x5" cone tweeter, gain, master volume, EQ, effects-blend.

MODEL YEAR	FEATURES	EXC. COND. LOW	HIGH
1990-2003		$350	$450

Basic Black Amp

1992-1999. Solidstate, 100 watts, 1x12", basic black block logo on front, black tolex, black metal grille.

MODEL YEAR	FEATURES	EXC. COND. LOW	HIGH
1992-1999		$300	$375

California Blonde Amp

2000s. Vertical upright combo, 100 watts, 1x12" plus high-end tweeters, blond cover, thin black metal grille.

MODEL YEAR	FEATURES	EXC. COND. LOW	HIGH
2003		$300	$375

Goliath III Cabinet

1996-2008. Black tolex, black metal grille, includes the Goliath III Jr. (2x10") and the Goliath III (4x10").

MODEL YEAR	FEATURES	EXC. COND. LOW	HIGH
1996-2008	2x10"	$250	$325
1996-2008	4x10"	$300	$375

Strawberry Blonde Amp

1998-2011. 80 watts, 1x10" acoustic instrument amp.

MODEL YEAR	FEATURES	EXC. COND. LOW	HIGH
1998-2011		$300	$375

Strawberry Blonde II Amp

2007-2011. 90 watts, 1x10" acoustic instrument amp.

MODEL YEAR	FEATURES	EXC. COND. LOW	HIGH
2007-2011		$300	$375

Studio 220 Bass Amp

1988-1995. 220 watt solidstate head, tube preamp

MODEL YEAR	FEATURES	EXC. COND. LOW	HIGH
1988-1995		$175	$225

Workingman's Series Amp

1995-2004. Includes 10 (200w, 2x10), 12 (100w, 1x12), 15 (bass, 1x15), replaced by WorkingPro in '05.

MODEL YEAR	FEATURES	EXC. COND. LOW	HIGH
1995-2004	Various models	$195	$250

Symphony

1950s. Probably a brand from an teaching studio, large Symphony script red letter logo on front.

Small Tube Amp

1950s. Two guitar inputs, 1x6" speaker, alligator tweed suitcase.

MODEL YEAR	FEATURES	EXC. COND. LOW	HIGH
1950		$225	$300

Synaptic Amplification

Intermediate to premium grade, production/custom, amps built in Brunswick, Maine by Steven O'Connor, starting in 2007.

Takt

Late-1960s. Made in Japan, tube and solidstate models.

GA Series Amps

1968. GA-9 (2 inputs and 5 controls, 3 tubes), GA-10, GA-11, GA-12, GA-14, GA-15.

MODEL YEAR	FEATURES	EXC. COND. LOW	HIGH
1968	GA-14/GA-15	$55	$70
1968	GA-9 thru GA-12	$35	$45

Talos

2004-present. Doug Weisbrod and Bill Thalmann build their tube amp heads, combo amps, and speaker cabinets in Springfield, Virginia. They started building and testing prototypes in '01.

Tanglewood Guitar Company UK

1991-present. Intermediate and professional grade, production, acoustic amps imported from China by Dirk Kommer and Tony Flatt in the U.K. They also import guitars, basses, mandolins, banjos and ukes.

Tech 21

1989-present. Long known for their SansAmp tube amplifier emulator, Tech 21 added solidstate combo amps, heads and cabinets in '96.

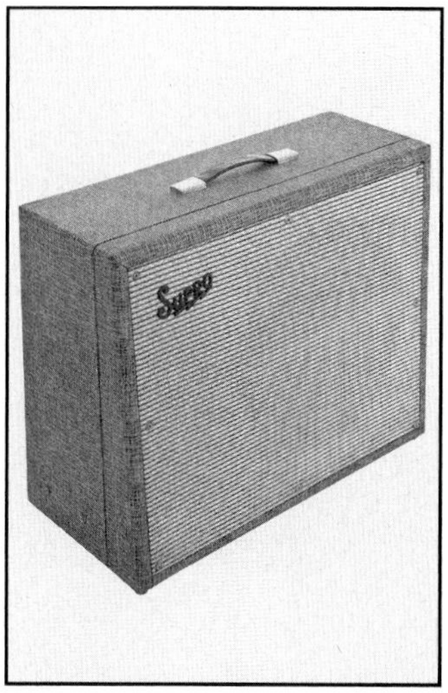

1965 Supro Thunderbolt S6420(B)

Imaged by Heritage Auctions, HA.com

2000s SWR California Blonde

Imaged by Heritage Auctions, HA.com

Talos Basic 2011

Tanglewood T3

Tomaszewicz Blue Amp

Tone King Royalist 15

Carter Vintage Guitars

MODEL YEAR	FEATURES	EXC. COND. LOW	HIGH

Teisco

1946-1974. Japanese brand first imported into the U.S. around '63. Teisco offered both tube and solidstate amps.

Checkmate CM-10 Amp

1960s. Tubes or solidstate, 10 watts.

1960s	Solidstate	$35	$50
1960s	Tubes	$160	$205

Checkmate CM-15 Amp

Late-1960s. Tubes, 15 watts.

1960s		$175	$225

Checkmate CM-16 Amp

1960s. Tubes or solidstate, 15 watts.

1960s	Solidstate	$50	$65
1960s	Tubes	$175	$225

Checkmate CM-17 Amp

1960s. Tubes, 1x10", reverb, tremolo.

1960s		$275	$350

Checkmate CM-20 Amp

Late-1960s. Tubes, 20 watts.

1960s		$275	$350

Checkmate CM-25 Amp

Late-1960s. Tubes, 25 watts.

1960s		$275	$350

Checkmate CM-50 Amp

Late-1950s-early-1960s. Tubes, 2 6L6s, 50 watts, 2x12" open back, reverb, tremolo, piggyback, gray tolex cover, light gray grille.

1960s		$375	$480

Checkmate CM-60 Amp

Late-1960s. Tubes, 60 watts, piggyback amp and cab with wheels.

1960s		$225	$285

Checkmate CM-66 Amp

Late-1960s. Solidstate, dual speaker combo, Check Mate 66 logo on front panel.

1960s		$55	$75

Checkmate CM-88 Amp

1960s. Solidstate, 10 watts, 2x8".

1960s		$55	$75

Checkmate CM-100 Amp

Late-1960s. Tubes, 4x6L6 power, 100 watts, piggyback with Vox-style trolley stand.

1960s		$230	$300

King 1800 Amp

Late-1960s. Tubes, 180 watts, piggyback with 2 cabinets, large Teisco logo on cabinets, King logo on lower right side of one cabinet.

1960s		$375	$500

Teisco 8 Amp

Late-1960s. Solidstate, 5 watts.

1960s		$55	$75

Teisco 10 Amp

Late-1960s. Solidstate, 5 watts.

1960s		$55	$75

Teisco 88 Amp

Late-1960s. Solidstate, 8 watts.

1960s		$80	$105

MODEL YEAR	FEATURES	EXC. COND. LOW	HIGH

Tempo

1950s-1970s. Tube (early on) and solidstate amps, most likely imported from Japan by Merson Musical Products. They also offered basses and guitars.

Model 39

1950s. Compact amp, vertical cab, tweed, 3 tubes, single control knob for on-off volume.

1953		$250	$325

Teneyck

1960s. Solidstate amp heads and speaker cabinets built by Bob Teneyck, who had previously done design work for Ampeg.

THD

1987-present. Tube amps and cabinets built in Seattle, Washington, founded by Andy Marshall.

The Valve

Guitar luthier Galeazzo Frudua also builds a line of professional grade, production/custom, amps in San Lazzaro di Savena, Italy.

ThroBak Electronics

2004-present. Jonathan Gundry builds his tube combo guitar amps in Grand Rapids, Michigan. He also builds guitar effects and pickups.

Titano (Magnatone)

1961-1963. Private branded by Magnatone, often for an accordion company or accordion studio, uses standard guitar input jacks.

Model 262 R Custom Amp

1961-1963. 35 watts, 2x12" + 2x5", reverb and vibrato make this one of the top-of-the-line models, black vinyl, light silver grille.

1961-1963		$1,025	$1,350

Model 313 Amp

1961-1963. Like Magnatone 213 Troubadour, 10 watts, 1x12" combo, vibrato, brown tolex, brownish grille.

1961-1963		$950	$1,250

Model 415 Bass Amp

1961-1963. 25 watts, 4x8", bass or accordion amp, black cover, darkish grille.

1961-1963		$925	$1,200

TomasZewicZ Amplifiers

2008-present. Intermediate and professional grade, production/custom, tube guitar amp heads and combos built by John Tomaszewicz in Coral Springs, Florida. He also builds effects.

Tombo

This Japanese harmonica manufacturer introduced a solidbody electric ukulele and a Silvertone-esque case with onboard amplifier in the mid-1960s.

MODEL YEAR	FEATURES	EXC. COND. LOW	HIGH

Tone Americana

2011-2014. David and Caroline Brass built intermediate and professional grade, production/custom, amp heads, combos and cabinets in Calabasas, California. They also offered an amp combo built in Asia.

Tone King

1993-present. Tube amps, combos, and cabinets built by Mark Bartel in Baltimore, Maryland. The company started in New York and moved to Baltimore in '94.

Tonemaster (Magnatone)

Late-1950s-early-1960s. Magnatone amps private branded for Imperial Accordion Company. Prominent block-style capital TONEMASTER logo on front panel, generally something nearly equal to Magnatone equivalent. This is just one of many private branded Magnatones. Covers range from brown to black leatherette and brown to light silver grilles. They also offered guitars.

Model 214 (V logo) Amp

1959-1960. Ten watts, 1x12", vibrato, brown leatherette, V logo lower right corner front, large TONEMASTER logo.

1959-1960 $950 $1,250

Model 260 Amp

1961-1963. About 30 watts, 2x12", vibrato, brown leatherette and brown grille, large TONEMASTER logo on front.

1961-1963 $1,400 $1,800

Model 261 Custom Amp

1961-1963. Tonemaster Custom 261 High Fidelity logo on back chasis panel, Tonemaster logo on front panel, 35 watts, 2x12" combo, 2 channels, vibrato.

1961-1963 $1,400 $1,800

Model 380 Amp

1961-1963. 50 watts, 2x12" and 2 oval 5"x7" speakers, vibrato, no reverb.

1961-1963 $1,400 $1,800

Model 381 Custom Amp

1961-1963. Tonemaster Custom 381 High Fidelity logo on back chasis panel, Tonemaster logo on front panel, 2x12", 1x5".

1961-1963 $1,400 $1,800

Small Combo Amp

1950s-1960s. 1x8", tremolo, light tan.

1950s-60s $500 $650

ToneTron Amps

2006-present. Professional grade, custom, guitar and bass tube amps and cabinets built in Minneapolis, Minnesota by Jeffrey Falla.

ToneVille Amps

Matthew Lucci and Phil Jung began in 2013, building professional grade, production, amps and cabinets in Colorado Springs, Colorado.

MODEL YEAR	FEATURES	EXC. COND. LOW	HIGH

Tonic Amps

2003-present. Darin Ellingson builds professional and premium grade, production/custom, amps and cabinets in Redwood City, California.

Top Hat Amplification

1994-present. Mostly Class A guitar amps built by Brian Gerhard, previously in La Habra, California, and Apex, North Carolina, and currently in Fuquay-Varina, North Carolina. He also makes effects.

Ambassador 100 TH-A100 Amp Head

Jan.1999-2013. 100 watts, Class AB, 4 6L6s, reverb, dark green vinyl cover, white chicken-head knobs.

1999-2013 $950 $1,225

Ambassador T-35C 212 Amp

1999-2013. 35 watts, 2x12" combo, reverb, master volume, blond cover, tweed-style fabric grille.

1999-2013 $1,050 $1,350

Club Deluxe Amp

1998-2009. 20 watts, 6V6 power tubes, 1x12".

1998-2009 $1,050 $1,350

Club Royale TC-R1 Amp

Jan.1998-2020. Class A using EL84s, 20 watts, 1x12". Replaced by Club Royal 20 in '21.

1998-2020 $650 $850

Club Royale TC-R2 Amp

Jan.1999-2014. Class A using EL84s, 20 watts, 2x12".

1999-2014 $1,000 $1,300

Emplexador 50 TH-E50 Amp Head

Jan.1997-2020. 50 watts, Class AB vint/high-gain head. Replaced by Emplexador E-50 in '21.

1997-2020 $950 $1,225

King Royale/Royal Amp

1996-present. 35 watts, Class A using 4 EL84s, 2x12". Name changed to King Royal in '21.

1996-2020 $1,100 $1,450

Portly Cadet TC-PC Amp

Jan.1999-2004. Five watts, 6V6 power, 1x8", dark gray, light gray grille.

1999-2004 $450 $575

Prince Royale TC-PR Amp

Jan.2000-2002. Five watts using EL84 power, 1x8", deep red, light grille.

2000-2002 $450 $575

Super Deluxe TC-SD2 Amp

Jan.2000-2012. 30 watts, Class A, 7591 power tubes, 2x12".

2000-2012 $1,050 $1,350

Torres Engineering

Founded by Dan Torres, the company builds tube amps, combos, cabinets and amp kits originally in San Mateo, California, then San Carlos and since '11 in Milton, Washington. Dan wrote monthly columns for Vintage Guitar magazine for many years and authored the book Inside Tube Amps.

Trace Elliot

1978-present. Founded in Essex, U.K. The U.S. distribution picked up by Kaman (Ovation) in '88 which bought Trace Elliot in '92. In '98 Gibson acquired the brand and in early '02 closed the fac-

ToneTron SE

ToneTron Hall Rocker

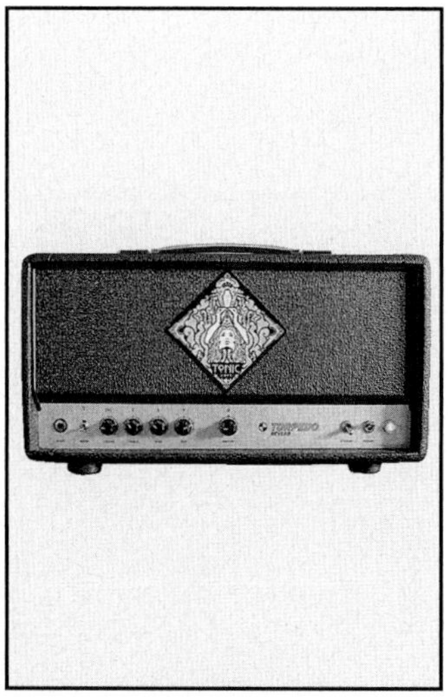

Tonic Torpedo

1970s Traynor YGM3 Guitar Mate Reverb

Traynor SB110

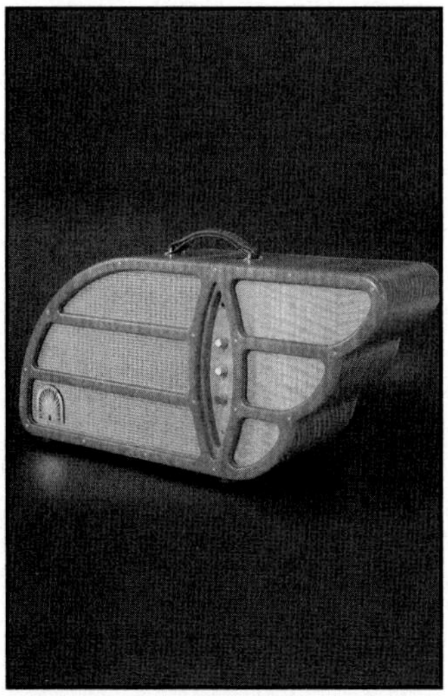
Trillium

MODEL YEAR	FEATURES	EXC. COND. LOW	HIGH

tory and moved what production was left to the U.S. In '05 Peavey bought the brand name, hiring back many of the old key people, and currently offers professional grade, production, tube and solidstate, acoustic guitar and bass amp heads, combos, and cabinets, with product built in the U.K. and U.S.

Trainwreck

1983-2006. Limited production, custom-made, high-end tube guitar amp heads built by Ken Fischer in Colonia, New Jersey. Models include the Rocket, Liverpool and Express, plus variations. Instead of using serial numbers, he gave each amp a woman's name. Due to illness, Fischer didn't build many amps after the mid '90s, but he continued to design amps for other builders. His total production is estimated at less than 100. Each amp's value should be evaluated on a case-by-case basis. Ken wrote many amp articles for Vintage Guitar. He died in late 2006.

Custom Built Amp

1983-1990s	Ken Fisher built	$22,000	$29,000

Traynor

1963-present. Started by Pete Traynor and Jack Long in the back of Long & McQuade Music in Toronto, Canada where Traynor was a repairman. Currently offering tube and solidstate amp heads, combos and cabinets made by parent company Yorkville Sound, in Pickering, Ontario.

YBA1 Bass Master Amp Head

1963-1979. 45 watts, called Dynabass for 1963-'64, this was Pete Traynor's first amp design.

1963-1979		$525	$675

YBA1A Mark II Bass Master Amp Head

1968-1976. Like YBA1, but with 90 watts and cooling fan.

1968-1976		$525	$675

YBA3 Custom Special Bass Amp Set

1967-1972. Tube head with 130 watts and 8x10" large vertical matching cab, dark vinyl cover, light grille.

1967-1972		$825	$1,075

YBA4 Bass Master Amp

1967-1972. 45-watt 1x15" combo.

1967-1972		$725	$925

YCV80 Custom Valve Amp

2003-2009. Tube, 80 watts, 4x10" combo.

2003-2009		$395	$510

YGA1 Amp Head

1966-1967. 45 watts guitar amp, tremolo.

1966-1967		$475	$625

YGL3 Mark III Amp

1971-1979. All tube, 80 watts, 2x12" combo, reverb, tremolo.

1971-1979		$625	$800

YGM3 Guitar Mate Reverb Amp

1969-1979. Tubes, 25 watts, 1x12", black tolex, gray grille until '74, black after.

1969-1979		$625	$800

YGM3 Guitar Mate Reverb Reissue Amp

2011-2013. 1x12" combo, 'flying wing' Traynor badge.

2011-2013		$440	$575

YRM1 Reverb Master Amp Head

1973-1979. 45 watt tube amp, reverb, tremolo.

1973-1979		$450	$575

YRM1SC Reverb Master Amp

1973-1979. YRM1 as a 4x10" combo.

1973-1979		$625	$800

YSR1 Custom Reverb Amp Head

1968-1973. 45 watt tube amp, reverb, tremolo.

1968-1973		$450	$575

YVM Series PA Amp Head

1967-1980. Public address heads, models include tube YVM-1 Voice Master, and solidstate YVM-2 and 3 Voice Mate and YVM-4, all with 4 inputs.

1967-1972	1, tubes	$375	$500
1969-1975	2, solidstate	$155	$200
1970-1980	3, solidstate, reverb	$215	$275
1972-1977	4, solidstate, reverb	$215	$275

Trillium Amplifier Company

2007-present. Brothers Stephen and Scott Campbell build their professional and premium grade, production/custom tube amps in Indianapolis, Indiana.

Trinity Amps

2003-present. Stephen Cohrs builds his production/custom, professional grade, tube amps and cabinets in Toronto, Ontario.

True Tone

1960s. Guitars and amps retailed by Western Auto, manufactured by Chicago guitar makers like Kay.

Hi-Fi 4 (K503 Hot-Line Special) Amp

1960s. Similar to K503, 4 watts from 3 tubes, gray cabinet, gray grille, metal handle.

1960s		$225	$300

Model 5 (K503A) Amp

1960s. 4 tubes, 1x8".

1960s		$225	$300

Vibrato 704 Amp

1960s. Solidstate, 10 watts, 1x8", white sides and gray back, gray grille.

1960s		$105	$140

Vibrato 706 Amp

1960s. Solidstate, 15 watts, 1x15", white sides and gray back, brown grille.

1960s		$120	$155

Tube Works

1987-2004. Founded by B.K. Butler in Denver, Tube Works became a division of Genz Benz Enclosures of Scottsdale, Arizona in 1997. Tube Works' first products were tube guitar effects and in '91 they added tube/solidstate amps, cabinets, and DI boxes to the product mix. In '04, Genz Benz dropped the brand.

Twilighter (Magnatone)

Late-1950s-early-1960s. Magnatone amps private branded for LoDuca Brothers. Prominent block-style capital TWILIGHTER logo on front panel, generally something nearly equal to Magnatone

MODEL YEAR	FEATURES	EXC. COND. LOW	HIGH

equivalent. This is just one of many private branded Magnatones. Covers range from brown to black leatherette, and brown to light silver grilles.

Model 213 Amp

1961-1963. About 20 watts, 1x12", vibrato, brown leatherette and brown grille.

1961-1963 $950 $1,250

Model 260R Amp

1961-1963. About 18 to 25 watts, 1x12", vibrato, brown leatherette cover.

1961-1963 $1,100 $1,500

Model 280A Amp

Late-1950s-early-1960s. About 35 watts, 2x12", vibrato, brown leatherette cover.

1961-1963 $1,200 $1,500

Two-Rock

1999-present. Tube guitar amp heads, combos and cabinets built by Joe Mloganoski and Bill Krinard (K&M Analog Designs) originally in Cotati, California, currently in Rohnert Park. They also build speakers.

Ugly Amps

2003-present. Steve O'Boyle builds his tube head and combo amps and cabinets in Burbank, California and Reading, Pennsylvania.

UltraSound

A division of UJC Electronics, UltraSound builds acoustically transparent amps, designed by Greg Farres for the acoustic guitarist, in Adel, Iowa.

Unique (Magnatone)

1961-1963. Private branded, typically for an accordion company or accordion studio, uses standard guitar input jacks.

Model 260R Amp

1961-1963. Based on Magnatone 260 Series amp, 35 watts, 2x12" but with reverb, black vinyl-style cover with distinctive black diamond-check pattern running through the top and sides.

1961-1963 $1,400 $1,800

Model 460 Amp

1961-1963. 35 watts, 2x12" and oval 5"x7" speakers, reverb and vibrato make it one of the top models, black vinyl, black grille.

1961-1963 $1,150 $1,500

Universal (Audio Guild)

See Audio Guild amps.

Univox

1964-ca.1978. From '64 to early-'68, these were American-made tube amps with Jensen speakers. By '68, they were using Japanese components in American cabinets, still with Jensen speakers. Electronics were a combination of tube and transistors during this time; this type lasted until the mid-'70s. Around '71, Univox introduced a line of all solidstate amps, as well.

MODEL YEAR	FEATURES	EXC. COND. LOW	HIGH

Lead Model Tube Amp

1960s. Tube amp, 2x10" or 2x12".

1965-1969 $525 $700

Model U45B Bass Amp

1965-1968. 1x12" combo tube bass amp, 10 watts.

1965-1968 $275 $350

Model U60A Amp

1965-1968. 1x12" tube combo.

1965-1968 $300 $390

Model U65R Amp

1965-1968. 20 watts, 1x12" tube combo.

1965-1968 $345 $450

Model U65RD Lead 65 Amp

1976-1978. Solidstate, 65 watts, reverb, 1x12" or 2x12" in a vertical cab.

1976-1978 $45 $60

Model U102 Amp

1965-1968. 1x12" tube combo.

1965-1968 $345 $450

Model U130B Bass Amp

1976-1978. Solidstate, 130 watts, 1x15".

1976-1978 $125 $165

Model U130L Lead Amp

1976-1978. Solidstate, 130 watts.

1976-1978 $125 $165

Model U155R Amp

1965-1968. 20 watts, 1x12" tube combo.

1965-1968 $450 $575

Model U202R Amp

1965-1968. 1x12" tube combo.

1965-1968 $450 $575

Model U305R Amp

1965-1968. 30 watts, 1x15" tube combo.

1965-1968 $525 $675

Model U1011 Lead Amp Head

1976-1978. Solidstate, 100 watts, reverb, tremolo. Name also used on earlier tube head.

1976-1978 $190 $250

Model U1061 Bass Amp Head

1976-1978. Solidstate.

1976-1978 $190 $250

Model U1220 Amp

1968-1971. Tubes or tube-hybrid, piggyback, 2x12".

1968-1971 $300 $400

Model U1226 Amp Head

1971-1972. 60-watt tube amp head.

1971-1972 $450 $575

Model U1246B Bass Amp Head

1976-1978. Solidstate, 60 watts.

1976-1978 $190 $245

Model U1246L Lead Amp Head

1976-1978. Solidstate.

1976-1978 $190 $245

Valco

Valco, from Chicago, Illinois, was a big player in the guitar and amplifier business. Their products were private branded for other companies like National, Supro, Airline, Oahu, El Grande and Gretsch.

Two-Rock Coral

Ugly Lil' Ugly

1971 Univox U-1226

Carter Vintage Guitars

Valvetech Suplex

Valvetrain Bennington Reverb

1950s Vega Commander

Imaged by Heritage Auctions, HA.com

MODEL YEAR	FEATURES	EXC. COND. LOW	HIGH

Valvetech

Production/custom, professional grade, amps built by Rob Pierce, starting in 1997, in Ossian, Indiana.

Valvetrain Amplification

2005-present. Tube combos, amp heads, and speaker cabinets built by Rick Gessner in Sorrento, Florida. He also builds reverb units.

Vamp

1970s. Tube and solidstate amps and speaker cabinets built at Triumph Electronics in England.

Bass Master Amp Head

1970s	100 watts	$1,000	$1,300

VanAmps

Tim Van Tassel, started in 1999, builds professional, production/custom, amps and cabinets in Golden Valley, Minnesota. He also builds effects.

Vega

The original Boston-based company (1903) was purchased by C.F. Martin in '70. In '80, the Vega trademark was sold to a Korean company.

A-49 Amp

1960s. Tubes, 6 watts, 1x8", tan cover.

1960s		$250	$325

Director Combo Amp

1950s. Small to mid-size tube amp, 2-tone cover, 2 volume and 1 tone controls, rear mounted control chassis similar to Fender or Gibson from the '50s.

1950s		$375	$500

Lap Steel Amp

1930s-1940s. Various models.

1936	1x12, dark cover	$375	$500
1940s	1x10, tweed	$375	$500

Super Amp

Early 1950s. 1 6L6, 1x10", vertical combo amp typical of the era.

1950s		$375	$500

Triumphal Amp

Late-1940s. Vega Triumphal logo on back control pane, 6L6 power, 1x12".

1940s		$375	$500

Versatone (Audio Guild)

See Audio Guild amps.

Vesta Fire

1980s. Japanese imports by Shiino Musical Instruments Corp.; later by Midco International. Mainly known for effects pedals.

VHT

1989-present. Founded by Steven M. Fryette, VHT built amps, combos, and cabinets in Burbank, California. At the beginning of '09 AXL guitars acquired the VHT name and manufactures their own product under that brand. Fryette continues to build the VHT amp models under Fryette Amplification.

Vibe Amplification

2008-2013. Intermediate grade, production, tube amps, imported from Asia by Lorenzo Brogi in Bologna, Italy.

Victor

Late-1960s. Made in Japan.

Victoria

1994-present. Tube amps, combos, and reverb units built by Mark Baier in Naperville, Illinois. In '08, they changed the logo from the original script Victoria Amp Co. to the current stylized lightning bolt Victoria logo.

Cherry Bomb Amp

2011-present. Tube tremolo, 40 watts, 1x15", alligator/cream tolex.

2011-2020		$1,400	$1,850

Double Deluxe Amp

1994-present. 35 watts, 2x12".

1994-2020		$1,400	$1,850

Electro King Amp

2008-present. 1957 GA-40 type circuit, tubes, 15 watts, 1x12".

2008-2020		$1,275	$1,675

Golden Melody Amp

2008-present. Tubes, reverb, 50 watts, 2x12", alligator/brown tolex.

2008-2020		$1,400	$1,850

Ivy League Amp

2010-present. Tweed Harvard specs, 14 watts, 1x10".

2011-2020		$800	$1,050

Model 518 Amp

1994-present. Tweed, 1x8".

1994-2020		$750	$1,000

Model 5112-T Amp

2001-present. Tweed, 5 watts, 5F1 circuit, 1x12".

2001-2020		$800	$1,050

Model 20112 Amp

1994-present. Tweed, 20 watts, 1x12", tweed.

1994-2020		$1,050	$1,350

Model 35115 Amp

1994-present. Tweed combo, 28 watts, 1x15".

1994-2020		$1,350	$1,750

Model 35210 Amp

1994-present. Tweed, 28 watts, 2x10", tweed.

1994-2020		$1,450	$1,850

Model 35212-T Amp

1990s. Tweed, 35 watts, 2x12".

1990s		$1,400	$1,800

Model 35310-T Amp

1994-present. Tweed, 28 watts, 3x10".

1994-2020		$1,475	$1,900

Model 45115-T Amp

2008-2009. Tweed, 45 watts, 1x15".

2008-2009		$1,350	$1,750

Model 45410-T Amp

1994-present. Tweed, 45 watts, 4x10" combo, tweed.

1994-2020		$1,400	$1,800

MODEL YEAR	FEATURES	EXC. COND. LOW	EXC. COND. HIGH

Model 50212-T Amp

2002-present. Tweed, 50 watts, 2x12" combo.

2002-2020		$1,400	$1,800

Model 80212 Amp

1994-present. Tweed, 80 watts, 2x12", tweed.

1994-2020		$1,450	$1,900

Regal Amp

2004-2006. Class A with 1 x 6L6, 15 watts, 1x15", brown tolex cover, rear mount controls.

2004-2006		$1,325	$1,725

Regal II/Regal Amp

2006-present. Class A, 35 watts, 1x15", tweed or vanilla tolex, rear mount controls.The II removed from name about '13.

2006-2020		$1,375	$1,775

Reverberato Amp

1996-2016. Tube reverb unit with vibrato, tweed or color options.

1996-2016		$1,000	$1,300

Silver Sonic Amp

2011-present. Tube reverb, 20 watts, 1x12", 2-tone black/cream cab with Sonic Blue or black tolex.

2011-2020		$1,400	$1,800

Trem D'La Trem Amp

2007-present. Tweed design,14 watts, 1x15".

2007-2020		$1,350	$1,750

Victoriette Amp

2001-present. 20 watts, 1x12" or 2x10", reverb, tremolo in '01.

2001-2020	2x10	$1,450	$1,850

Victorilux Amp

2001-present. 45 watts, 2x12", 3x10" or 1x15", EL84s, reverb, tremolo.

2001-2020	3x10	$1,525	$1,950

Vintage47

2010-present. Founder/builder David Barnes, of California, builds retro-inspired compact amps that reflect old-school Valco values, handwired, intermediate and professional grade.

Vivi-Tone

1933-1938. Founded in Kalamazoo, Michigan, by former Gibson designer Lloyd Loar and others, Vivi-Tone sold small amps built by Webster Electric to accompany their early electric solidbody guitars.

V-M (Voice of Music) Corp.

1944-1977. Started out building record changers in Benton Harbor, Michigan. By the early '50s had added amplified phonographs, consoles, and tape recorders as well as OEM products for others. Their portable PA systems can be used for musical instruments. Products sport the VM logo.

Small Portable Amp

1950s. Standard phono input for instrument, phono and microphone controls, wood combo cabinet, 1x10" or 1x12" Jensen.

1950s		$250	$350

Voltmaster

Trapezoid-shaped combo amps and reverb units made in Plano, Texas, in the late 1990s.

Voodoo

1998-present. Tube amp heads and speaker cabinets built in Lansing, New York by Trace Davis, Anthony Cacciotti, and Mike Foster.

Vox

1954-present. Tom Jennings and Dick Denney combined forces in '57 to produce the first Vox amp, the 15-watt AC-15. The period between '57-'68 is considered to be the Vox heyday. Vox produced tube amps in England and also the U.S. from '64 to '65. English-made tube amps were standardized between '60 and '65. U.S.-made Vox amps in '66 were solidstate. In the mid-'60s, similar model names were sometimes used for tube and solidstate amps. In '93 Korg bought the Vox name and current products are built by Marshall. Those amps that originally came with a trolley or stand are priced including the original trolley or stand, and an amp without one will be worth less than the amount shown. Smaller amps were not originally equipped with a trolley or stand (if a speaker cabinet mounts to it and it tilts, it is called a trolley; otherwise referred to as a stand).

4120 Bass Amp

1966-1967. Hybrid solidstate and tube bass amp.

1966-1967		$365	$475

7120 Guitar Amp

1966-1967. Hybrid solidstate and tube amp, 120 watts.

1966-1967		$365	$475

AC4 Amp

1961-1965. Made in England, early Vox tube design, 3.5 watts, 1x8", tremolo.

1961-1965		$1,000	$1,300

AC4TV Amp

2009-2019. Tube, 4 watts, in 1x10 (AC4TV8 is 1x8) combo or amp head with 1x12 cab, EL84 power tube, 12AX7 powered preamp. AC4TVmini combo has 6.5 inch speaker.

2009-2013	1x12	$105	$140
2009-2013	1x8	$110	$145
2009-2013	Head only	$125	$165
2009-2019	1x10	$125	$165

AC10 Amp

1958-1965. Made in England, 12 watts, 1x10", tremolo, this tube version not made in U.S. ('64-'65).

1958-1965		$1,800	$2,400

AC10 Twin Amp

1962-1965. Made in England, also made in U.S. '64-'65, 12 watts (2xEL84s), 2x10".

1962-1965		$2,100	$2,800

AC10C1 Amp

2015-present. Custom Series, 10 watts, 1x10", 2-tone black and maroon.

2015-2020		$325	$425

Victoria 35115

Carter Vintage Guitars

Victoria Silver Sonic

1961 Vox AC4

Frank Silvestry

AMPS

2006 Vox AC15CC

Ted Wulfers

Vox AC-30C2RD

Andrew McIntosh

1966 Vox AC50

Tom Scarcella

AC15 Amp

1958-1965. 15 watts, 1x12", TV front changed to split front in fall '60.

MODEL YEAR	FEATURES	EXC. COND. LOW	HIGH
1958	TV front	$2,950	$3,900
1958-1965	Split front	$2,500	$3,200

AC15 Twin Amp

1961-1965. Tube, 2x12", 18 watts.

MODEL YEAR	FEATURES	EXC. COND. LOW	HIGH
1961-1965	Standard colors	$2,750	$3,600
1962-1965	Custom colors	$2,950	$3,850

AC15 50th Anniversary Amp

2007. 50th Anniversary 1957-2007 plaque on lower left front of grille, hand wired, white tolex.

MODEL YEAR	FEATURES	EXC. COND. LOW	HIGH
2007		$700	$900

AC15H1TV Amp

2008-2009. Part of Heritage Collection, limited edition, 200 made, hand wired, oiled mahogany cabinet.

MODEL YEAR	FEATURES	EXC. COND. LOW	HIGH
2008-2009		$1,000	$1,300

AC15HW1 Amp

2015-present. Hand-wired, 15 watts, 1x12".

MODEL YEAR	FEATURES	EXC. COND. LOW	HIGH
2015		$800	$1,050

AC15TB/TBX Amp

1996-2004. 15 watts, top boost, 1x12" Celestion (lower cost Eminence available).

MODEL YEAR	FEATURES	EXC. COND. LOW	HIGH
1996-2004	TB	$725	$975
1996-2004	TBX	$850	$1,150

AC15C1 Amp

2010-2020. Custom Series, made in China, 15 watts, 1x12", tube, reverb and tremolo.

MODEL YEAR	FEATURES	EXC. COND. LOW	HIGH
2010-2020		$365	$475

AC15CC (Custom Classic) Amp

2006-2012. Made in China, 15 watts, 1x12" tube combo, master volume, reverb, tremolo, 2-button footswitch.

MODEL YEAR	FEATURES	EXC. COND. LOW	HIGH
2006-2012		$365	$475

AC30 Reissue Model Amp

1980s-1990s-2000s. Standard reissue and limited edition models with identification plate on back of amp. Models include the AC30 Reissue and Reissue custom color (1980s-1990s), AC30 25th Anniv. (1985-1986), AC30 30th Anniv. (1991), AC30 Collector Model (1990s, mahogany cabinet), AC30HW Hand Wired (1990s) and HW Limited (2000s).

MODEL YEAR	FEATURES	EXC. COND. LOW	HIGH
1980s	Rose Morris era	$1,250	$1,650
1985-1986	25th Anniv	$1,250	$1,650
1990s	Collector Model	$1,750	$2,300
1990s	Hand Wired	$1,850	$2,500
1990s	Reissue	$1,050	$1,400
1990s	Reissue, custom colors	$1,325	$1,750
1991	30th Anniv	$1,500	$1,950
1995	TBT, LE, tan	$1,325	$1,750
2000s	Hand Wired Limited	$1,850	$2,500
2000s	Reissue	$1,100	$1,450

AC30 Super Twin Amp Set

1960-1965. Piggyback head and 2x12" pressure cabinet with amp trolley.

MODEL YEAR	FEATURES	EXC. COND. LOW	HIGH
1960-1965		$3,400	$4,475

AC30 Twin/AC-30 Twin Top Boost Amp

1960-1973. Made in England, tube, 30-watt head, 36 watts 2x12", Top Boost includes additional treble and bass, custom colors available in '60-'63.

MODEL YEAR	FEATURES	EXC. COND. LOW	HIGH
1960-1963	Custom colors	$3,600	$4,800
1960-1965	Black	$3,200	$4,200
1966	Black	$2,100	$2,800
1967-1973	Black	$1,750	$2,300

AC30BM Brian May Limited Edition Amp

2006-2007. Limited run of 500, 30 watts, 2x12" combo.

MODEL YEAR	FEATURES	EXC. COND. LOW	HIGH
2006-2007		$1,100	$1,450

AC30C2X Custom Amp

2004-2018. 30 watts, 2x12" Celestion Alnico Blue speakers.

MODEL YEAR	FEATURES	EXC. COND. LOW	HIGH
2004-2018		$540	$700

AC30CC (Custom Classic) Amp

2004-2012. 30 watts, 2x12", tubes, 2-button footswitch.

MODEL YEAR	FEATURES	EXC. COND. LOW	HIGH
2004-2012		$540	$700

AC30VR Valve Reactor Amp

2010-2019. 2x12" combo, digital reverb, 30 watts.

MODEL YEAR	FEATURES	EXC. COND. LOW	HIGH
2010-2019		$300	$400

AC50 Amp Head

1963-1975. Made in England, 50-watt head, U.S. production '64-'65 tube version is Westminster Bass, U.S. post-'66 is solidstate.

MODEL YEAR	FEATURES	EXC. COND. LOW	HIGH
1963-1975		$2,000	$2,600

AC50 Cabinet

MODEL YEAR	FEATURES	EXC. COND. LOW	HIGH
1963-1975	Black	$600	$800

AC100 MK I Amp

1963-1965. All tube 100-watt with 4x12 cab, due to reliability concerns it was transitioned to AC100 Super De Luxe MK II in '65.

MODEL YEAR	FEATURES	EXC. COND. LOW	HIGH
1963-1965		$3,000	$4,000

AC100 Super De Luxe MK II Amp

1965. Solidstate 100-watt head with 4x12 cab on speaker trolley.

MODEL YEAR	FEATURES	EXC. COND. LOW	HIGH
1965		$1,850	$2,400

AD Series Amp

2004-2008. Import small to large modeling amps with single 12AXT preamp tube, chrome grills, includes applicable footswitch, some available with amp trolley (i.e. AD60VT).

MODEL YEAR	FEATURES	EXC. COND. LOW	HIGH
2004-2006	AD120VT	$365	$475
2004-2006	AD60VT	$215	$275
2004-2008	AD100VTH	$175	$225
2004-2008	AD15VT	$95	$125
2004-2008	AD30VT	$100	$130
2004-2008	AD50VT	$145	$190
2006-2008	AD100VT	$250	$345

Berkeley II V108 (Tube) Amp

1964-1966. U.S.-made tube amp, revised '66-'69 to U.S.-made solidstate model V1081, 18 watts, 2x10" piggyback.

MODEL YEAR	FEATURES	EXC. COND. LOW	HIGH
1964-1966		$900	$1,175

Berkeley II V1081 (Solidstate) Amp

1966-1967. U.S.-made solidstate model V1081, 35 watts, 2x10" piggyback, includes trolley stand.

MODEL YEAR	FEATURES	EXC. COND. LOW	HIGH
1966-1967		$550	$700

Berkeley III (Solidstate) Amp

1968. Berkeley III logo on top panel of amp.

MODEL YEAR	FEATURES	EXC. COND. LOW	HIGH
1968		$700	$900

MODEL YEAR	FEATURES	EXC. COND. LOW	HIGH

Buckingham Amp

1966-1968. Solidstate, 35 watts, 2x12" piggyback, includes trolley stand.

1966-1968		$625	$800

Cambridge 15 Amp

1999-2001. 15 watts, 1x8", tremolo.

1999-2001		$140	$185

Cambridge 30 Reverb Amp

1999-2002. 30 watts, 1x10", tremolo and reverb.

1999-2002		$150	$200

Cambridge 30 Reverb Twin 210 Amp

1999-2002. 30 watts hybrid circuit, 2x10", reverb.

1999-2002		$190	$250

Cambridge Reverb V1031/V1032 (Solidstate) Amp

1966-1968. Solidstate, 35 watts, 1x10", model V1031 replaced tube version V103.

1966-1968		$600	$775

Cambridge Reverb V3/V103 (Tube) Amp

1965-1966. U.S-made tube version, 18 watts, 1x10", a Pacemaker with reverb, superceded by solidstate Model V1031 by '67.

1965-1966		$850	$1,100

Churchill PAV119 Head and V1091 Cabinet Set

Late-1960s. PA head with multiple inputs and 2 column speakers.

1960s	PA head only	$350	$450
1960s	Set	$625	$825

Climax V125/VO125 Lead Combo Amp

1970-1991. Solidstate, 125 watts, 2x12" combo, 5-band EQ, master volume.

1970-1991	Combo	$525	$675
1970-1991	Half-Stack	$725	$925

DA Series Amp

2006-2013. Small digital modeling amps, AC/DC power, solidstate.

2006-2013	DA5, 5w, 1x65	$80	$105
2007-2009	DA10, 10w, 2x6	$100	$130
2007-2009	DA20, 20w, 2x8	$105	$140
2010	DA15, 15w, 1x8	$90	$120

Defiant Amp

1966-1970. Made in England, 50 watts, 2x12" + Midax horn cabinet.

1966-1970		$1,225	$1,600

Escort Amp

Late 1960s-1983. 2.5 watt battery-powered portable amp.

1968-1986		$290	$375

Essex V1042 Bass Amp

1966-1968. U.S.-made solidstate, 35 watts, 2x12". Also called Essex Bass Deluxe.

1966-1968		$400	$525

Foundation Bass Amp

1966-1970. Tube in '66, solidstate after, 50 watts, 1x18", made in England only.

1966	Tubes	$1,200	$1,550
1967-1970	Solidstate	$525	$675

Kensington V1241 Bass Amp

1966-1968. U.S.-made solidstate bass amp, 22 watts, 1x15", G-tuner, called Kensington Bass Deluxe in '67.

1966-1968		$525	$675

Night Train Series Amp

2009-2016. Small tube head and combo, 2 channels, Celestion speaker, models available; NT15C1 (15w, 1x12 combo), NT15H-G2 (15w, 1x12 head/cab), NT50H-G2 (50w, 2x12 head/cab).

2009-2016	NT 2x12 cab	$200	$265
2009-2016	NT15H-G2 cab	$175	$225
2009-2016	NT15H-G2 head	$285	$375
2015-2016	NT15C1 combo	$425	$550

Pacemaker V1021 (Solidstate) Amp

1966-1968. U.S.-made solidstate amp, 35 watts, 1x10", replaced Pacemaker model V102.

1966-1968		$350	$450

Pacemaker V2/V102 (Tube) Amp

1965-1966. U.S.-made tube amp, 18 watts, 1x10", replaced by solidstate Pacemaker model V1021.

1965-1966		$675	$875

Pathfinder (Import) Amp

1998-present. Compact amps with 1960s cosmetics.

1998-2013	15, 15w, 1x8"	$65	$90
2002-2020	10, 10w, 65"	$55	$75

Pathfinder V1/V101 (Tube) Amp

1965-1966. U.S.-made tube amp, 4 watts, 1x8", '66-'69 became U.S.-made solidstate V1011.

1965-1966		$675	$900

Pathfinder V1011 (Solidstate) Amp

1966-1968. U.S.-made solidstate, 25 watts peak power, 1x8".

1966-1968		$325	$425

Royal Guardsman V1131/V1132 Amp

1966-1968. U.S.-made solidstate, 50 watts piggyback, 2x12" + 1 horn, the model below the Super Beatle V1141/V1142.

1966-1968		$1,025	$1,325

Scorpion (Solidstate) Amp

1968. Solidstate, 120 watts, 4x10" Vox Oxford speaker.

1968		$425	$550

Super Beatle Reissue Amp Cabinet

2011-2012. 2x15" cab only.

2011-2012		$325	$425

Super Beatle V1141/V1142 Amp

1965-1966. U.S.-made 120 watt solidstate, 4x12" + 2 horns, with distortion pedal (V1141), or without (V1142).

1965-1966		$2,400	$3,200

T60 Amp

1962-1966. Solidstate bass head, around 40 watts, sold with 2x15" or 1x12" and 1x15" cabinet.

1962-1966		$550	$725

VBM1 Brian May Special Amp

2010. Compact 10-watt, 1x6" speaker, also called VBM1 Brian May Recording Amp, white cover, includes headphone/recording line out, Brian May logo on lower right grille.

2010		$125	$160

Viscount V1151/V1152 Amp

1966-1968. U.S.-made solidstate, 70 watts, 2x12" combo, 1151, 1153, and 1154 with distortion.

1966-1968		$625	$800

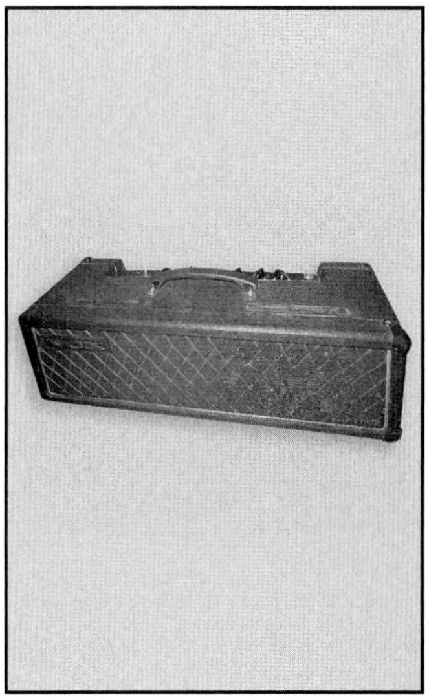

1967 Vox Berkeley II V1081

Rivington Guitars

1967 Vox Royal Guardsman

Imaged by Heritage Auctions, HA.com

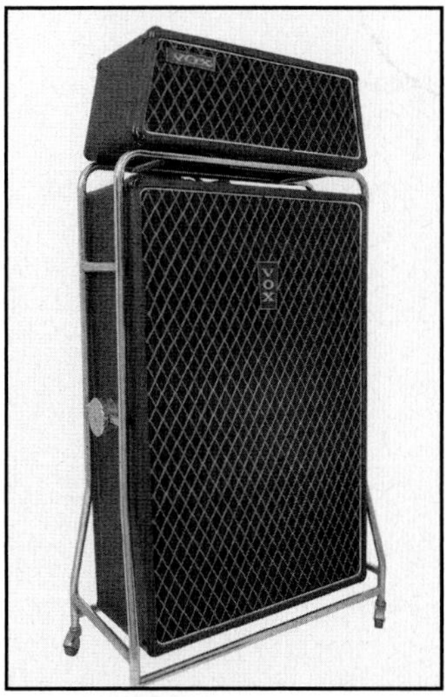

1966 Vox Super Beatle V1141

Imaged by Heritage Auctions, HA.com

Vox VT20+

Wallace Amplification Sophia

1963 Watkins Control ER15

Nicholas Kennett

VT Valvetronix/Valvetronix + Series Amps

2008-present. Line of digital modeling combo amps, ranging from the 15-watt, 1x8" VT15 ('08-'11) to the Valvetronix+ 120-watt, 2x12" VT120+.

MODEL YEAR	FEATURES	EXC. COND. LOW	HIGH
2008-2011	VT15	$95	$125
2012-2020	VT20+	$95	$125
2015-2016	VT80	$155	$200
2015-2020	VT40+	$145	$190

Westminster V118 Bass Amp

1966. Solidstate, 120 watts, 1x18".

MODEL YEAR	FEATURES	EXC. COND. LOW	HIGH
1966		$475	$625

V-Series

See Crate.

Wabash

1950s. Private branded amps, made by others, distributed by the David Wexler company. They also offered lap steels and guitars.

Model 1158 Amp

1955. Danelectro-made, 1x15", 2x6L6 power tubes, tweed.

MODEL YEAR	FEATURES	EXC. COND. LOW	HIGH
1955		$450	$600

Small Amp

MODEL YEAR	FEATURES	EXC. COND. LOW	HIGH
1940s	3 tubes	$175	$225

Wallace Amplification

2000-present. Production/custom, professional grade, amps built by Brian Wallace in Livonia, Michigan. (Not affiliated with a 1970's amp company from the United Kingdom also called Wallace that has since gone out of business.)

Warbler

See listing under Juke amps.

Warwick

1982-present. Combos, amp heads and cabinets from Warwick Basses of Markneukirchen, Germany.

Washburn

1962-present. Imported guitar and bass amps. Washburn also offers guitars, banjos, mandolins, and basses.

Watkins

1957-present. England's Watkins Electric Music (WEM) was founded by Charlie Watkins. Their first commercial product was the Watkins Dominator (wedge Gibson stereo amp shape) in '57, followed by the Copicat Echo in '58. They currently build accordion amps.

Clubman Amp

1960s. Small combo amp with typical Watkins styling, blue cover, white grille.

MODEL YEAR	FEATURES	EXC. COND. LOW	HIGH
1960s		$800	$1,050

Dominator MK Series Amp

1970s. Similar circuit to '50s tube amps except solidstate rectifier, 25 watts, different speaker used for different applications.

MODEL YEAR	FEATURES	EXC. COND. LOW	HIGH
1970s	MK I, bass, 1x15	$475	$625
1970s	MK II, organ, 1x12	$475	$625
1970s	MK III, guitar, 1x12	$475	$625

Dominator V-Front Amp

Late-1950s-1960s, 2004. 18 watts, 2x10", wedge cabinet similar to Gibson GA-79 stereo amp, tortoise and light beige cab, light grille, requires 220V step-up transformer. Was again offered in '04.

MODEL YEAR	FEATURES	EXC. COND. LOW	HIGH
1959-1962		$2,050	$2,650

Scout Amp

1960s. 17 watts, 1x10 combo, 6 tubes.

MODEL YEAR	FEATURES	EXC. COND. LOW	HIGH
1960		$800	$1,050

Westminster Tremolo Amp

1959-1962. 10-watt 1x10" combo, Westminster Tremolo logo on top panel, 3 control knobs, blue and white cover.

MODEL YEAR	FEATURES	EXC. COND. LOW	HIGH
1959-1962		$800	$1,050

Webcor

1940s-1950s. The Webster-Chicago Company built recording and audio equipment including portable amplifiers suitable for record turntables, PAs, or general utility. Low power with one or two small speakers.

Small Amp

MODEL YEAR	FEATURES	EXC. COND. LOW	HIGH
1950s	1 or 2 speakers	$200	$265

West Laboratories

1965-1970s, 2005-2015. Founded by David W. West in Flint, Michigan, moved to Lansing in '68. The '71 catalog included three tube and two solidstate amps, speaker cabinets, as well as Vocal Units and Mini Series combo amps. Amps were available as heads, piggyback half-stacks and full-stacks, with the exception of the combo Mini Series. The Fillmore tube amp head was the most popular model. West equipment has a West logo on the front and the cabinets also have a model number logo on the grille. David West reestablished his company in 2005, located in Okemos, Michigan, with models offered on a custom order basis, concentrating on lower power EL84 designs. West died November, '15.

Avalon Amp Head

1970s. 50 watts, 2 6CA7 output tubes.

MODEL YEAR	FEATURES	EXC. COND. LOW	HIGH
1970s		$525	$700

Fillmore Amp Head

1970s. 200 watts, 4 KT88 output tubes.

MODEL YEAR	FEATURES	EXC. COND. LOW	HIGH
1970s		$2,000	$2,600

Grande Amp Head

1970s. 100 watts, 2 KT88 output tubes.

MODEL YEAR	FEATURES	EXC. COND. LOW	HIGH
1970s		$650	$850

Mini IR Amp

1970s. 50 watts, 1x12 tube combo with reverb, black tolex, large West logo and model name Mini IR on front panel.

MODEL YEAR	FEATURES	EXC. COND. LOW	HIGH
1970s		$725	$950

White

1955-1960. The White brand, named after plant manager Forrest White, was established by Fender to provide steel and small amp sets to teaching studios that were not Fender-authorized dealers. The amps were sold with the matching steel guitar. See Steel section for pricing.

MODEL YEAR	FEATURES	EXC. COND. LOW	HIGH

White (Matamp)

See Matamp listing.

Winfield Amplification

2001-present. Intermediate and professional grade, production, vacuum tube amps built by Winfield N. Thomas first in Greensboro, Vermont and presently in Cochise, Arizona.

Wizard

1988-present. Professional and premium grade, production/custom, guitar and bass, amps and cabinets built by Rick St Pierre in Cornwall, Ontario.

Woodson

Early 1970s. Obscure builder from Bolivar, Missouri. Woodson logo on front panel and Woodson Model and Serial Number plate on back panel, solidstate circuit, student level pricing.

Working Dog

2001-2014. Lower cost tube amps and combos built by Alessandro High-End Products (Alessandro, Hound Dog) in Huntingdon Valley, Pennsylvania.

Wright Amplification

Aaron C. Wright builds his professional grade, production/custom, amps and cabinets in Lincoln, Nebraska starting in 2004.

Yamaha

1946-present. Yamaha started building amps in the '60s and offered a variety of guitar and bass amps over the years. The current models are solidstate bass amps. They also build guitars, basses, effects, sound gear and other instruments.

Budokan HY-10G II Amp

1987-1992. Portable, 10 watts, distortion control, EQ.

1987-1992 $45 $60

G30-112 Amp

1983-1992. Solidstate combo, 30 watts, 1x12".

1983-1992 $115 $150

G50-112 Amp

1983-1992. 50 watts, 1x12".

1983-1992 $135 $175

G100-112 Amp

1983-1992. 100 watts, 1x12" combo, black cover, striped grille.

1983-1992 $140 $185

G100-212 Amp

1983-1992. 100, 2x12" combo, black cover, striped grille.

1983-1992 $160 $210

JX30B Amp

1983-1992. Bass amp, 30 watts.

1983-1992 $95 $125

TA-20 Amp

1968-1972. Upright wedge shape with controls facing upwards, solidstate.

1968-1972 $85 $115

TA-25 Amp

1968-1972. Upright wedge shape with controls facing upwards, 40 watts, 1x12", solidstate, black or red cover.

1968-1972 $100 $135

TA-30 Amp

1968-1972. Upright wedge shape, solidstate.

1968-1972 $115 $150

TA-50 Amp

1971-1972. Solidstate combo, 80 watts, 2x12", includes built-in cart with wheels, black cover.

1971-1972 $130 $175

TA-60 Amp

1968-1972. Upright wedge shape, solidstate, most expensive of wedge-shape amps.

1968-1972 $170 $225

VR3000 Amp

1988-1992. Combo 1x12", 2 channels, identical control sections for each channel, settings are completely independent.

1988-1992 $105 $135

VR4000 Amp

1988-1992. 50-watt stereo, 2 channels, EQ, stereo chorus, reverb and dual effects loops.

1988-1992 $160 $210

VR6000 Amp

1988-1992. 100-watt stereo, 2 channels which can also be combined, EQ, chorus, reverb and dual effects loops.

1988-1992 $210 $280

VX-15 Amp

1988-1992. 15 watts.

1988-1992 $75 $100

VX-65D Bass Amp

1984-1992. 80 watts, 2 speakers.

1984-1992 $100 $135

YBA-65 Bass Amp

1972-1976. Solidstate combo, 60 watts, 1x15".

1972-1976 $100 $135

YTA-25 Amp

1972-1976. Solidstate combo, 25 watts, 1x12".

1972-1976 $100 $135

YTA-45 Amp

1972-1976. Solidstate combo, 45 watts, 1x12".

1972-1976 $100 $135

YTA-95 Amp

1972-1976. Solidstate combo, 90 watts, 2x12".

1972-1976 $100 $135

YTA-100 Amp

1972-1976. Solidstate piggyback, 100 watts, 2x12".

1972-1976 $130 $175

YTA-110 Amp

1972-1976. Solidstate piggyback, 100 watts, 2x12" in extra large cab.

1972-1976 $130 $175

YTA-200 Amp

1972-1976. Solidstate piggyback, 200 watts, 4x12".

1972-1976 $150 $200

YTA-300 Amp

1972-1976. Solidstate piggyback, 200 watts, dual cabs with 2x12" and 4x12".

1972-1976 $225 $300

Winfield

Wizard Modern Classic Combo

1968 Yamaha TA-60

Tom Pfeifer

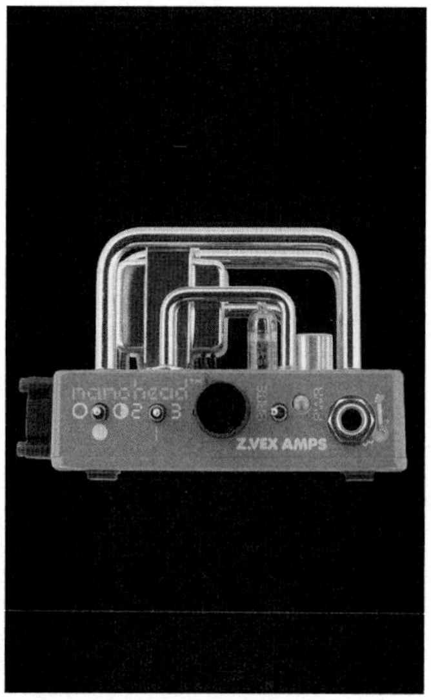

Z.Vex Nano Head

Zeppelin Design Labs Percolator

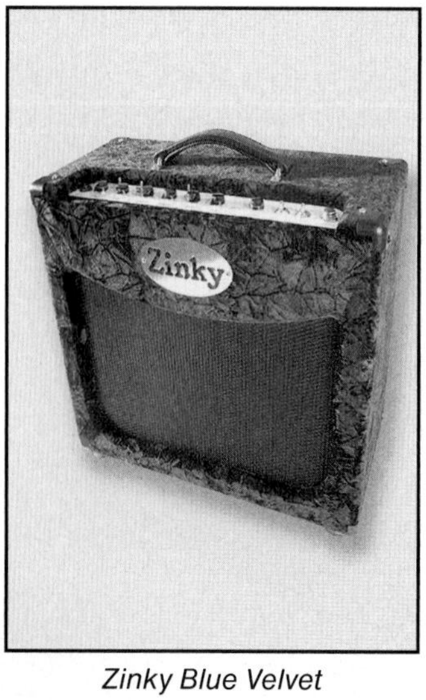

Zinky Blue Velvet

YTA-400 Amp

1972-1976. Solidstate piggyback, 200 watts, dual 4x12".

MODEL YEAR	FEATURES	EXC. COND. LOW	HIGH
1972-1976		$225	$300

Z.Vex Amps

2002-present. Intermediate grade, production amps built by Zachary Vex in Minneapolis, Minnesota with some subassembly work done in Michigan. He also builds effects.

Zapp

Ca.1978-early-1980s. Zapp amps were distributed by Red Tree Music, Inc., of Mamaroneck, New York.

Z-10 Amp

1978-1980s. Small student amp, 8 watts.

MODEL YEAR	FEATURES	EXC. COND. LOW	HIGH
1979-1982		$25	$30

Z-50 Amp

1978-1980s. Small student amp, 10 watts, reverb, tremelo.

MODEL YEAR	FEATURES	EXC. COND. LOW	HIGH
1978-1982		$30	$35

Zeppelin Design Labs

2014-present. Brach Siemens and Glen van Alkemade build budget and intermediate grade amps and cabinets in Chicago, Illinois. They also offer their products as DIY kits.

Zeta

1982-2010. Solid state amps with MIDI options, made in Oakland, California. They also made upright basses and violins.

Zinky

Tube head and combo amps and cabinets built by Bruce Zinky, starting in 1999, in Flagstaff, Arizona. He also builds the mini Smokey amps (since '97), effects, and has revived the Supro brand on a guitar and amp.

ZT Amplifiers

2009-present. Ken Kantor of Berkeley, California imports intermediate grade, production, solid state compact amps from China. He also offers effects.

EFFECTS

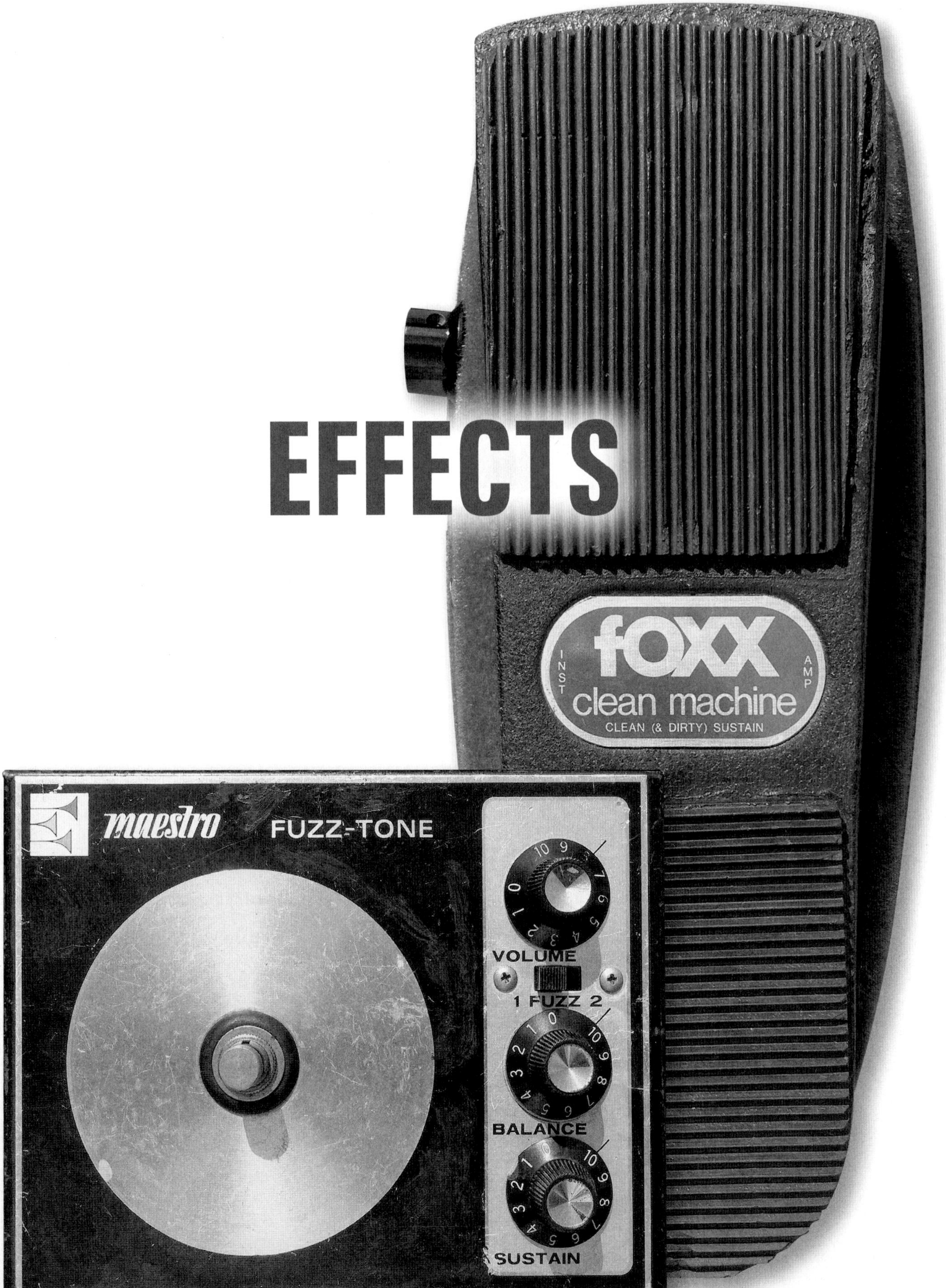

1976 Foxx Clean Machine and 1969 Maestro Fuzz-Tone FZ-1B: Marco Antonio Rebolledo Ferrari.

Aguilar Filter Twin

Akai E2 Headrush

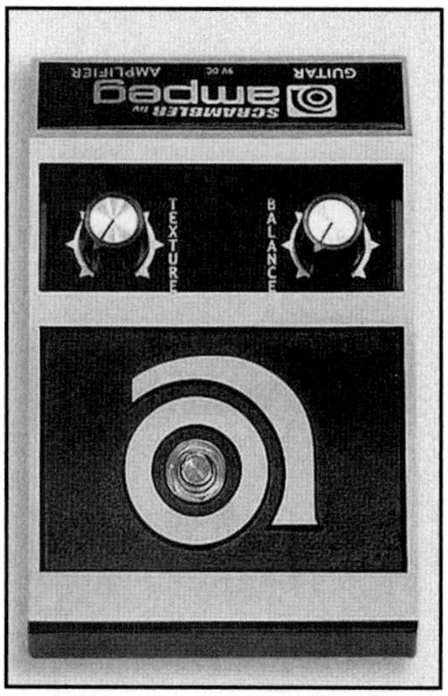

Ampeg Scrambler Fuzz

MODEL YEAR	FEATURES	EXC. COND. LOW	HIGH

Able Electronics

1990s. Started by John Rogers and based in Pwllheli, Wales.

Bassmaker

1990s. Octave pedal.

1990s		$100	$200

Ace Tone

1968-1972. Effects from Ace Electronic Industry, which was a part of Sakata Shokai Limited of Osaka, Japan, which also made organs, amps, pioneering Rhythm Ace FR-1 and FR-2 drum machines, etc. Their Ace Tone effects line was the predecessor to Roland and Boss.

Echo Chamber EC-10

1968-1972. Solidstate tape echo.

1968-1972		$300	$600

Expander EXP-4

1968-1972. "Expander" effect.

1968-1972		$175	$200

Fuzz Master FM-1

1968-1972. Distortion and overdrive.

1968-1972		$300	$450

Fuzz Master FM-2

1968-1972. Fuzz. Black housing. 2 Control knobs.

1968-1972		$175	$400

Fuzz Master FM-3

1968-1972. Distortion and clean boost.

1968-1972		$450	$650

Stereo Phasor LH-100

1968-1972. Phaser.

1968-1972		$275	$340

Wah Master WM-1

1968-1972. Filter wah.

1968-1972		$75	$150

Acoustyx

1977-1982. Made by the Highland Corporation of North Springfield, Vermont.

Image Synthesizer IS-1

1977-ca.1982. Synthesizer effects.

1977-1982		$50	$60

Phase Five

1977-ca.1982. Used 6 C cell batteries!

1977-1982		$50	$60

ADA

1975-2002. Analog/Digital Associates was located in Berkeley, California, and introduced its Flanger and Final Phase in '77. The company later moved to Oakland and made amplifiers, high-tech signal processors, and a reissue of its original Flanger.

Final Phase

1977-1979. Reissued in '97.

1977-1979		$375	$450

Flanger

1977-1983, 1996-2002. Reissued in '96.

1977-1979	No control pedal	$325	$400
1977-1979	With control pedal	$375	$475
1980-1983		$225	$300
1996-2002		$75	$100

MP-1

1987-1995. Tube preamp with chorus and effects loop, MIDI.

1987-1995	No foot controller	$150	$200
1987-1995	With optional foot controller	$200	$260

MP-2

Ca.1988-1995. Tube preamp with chorus, 9-band EQ and effects loop, MIDI.

1988-1995		$225	$275

Pitchtraq

1987. Programmable pitch transposer including octave shifts.

1987		$150	$200

Stereo Tapped Delay STD-1

Introduced in 1981.

1980s		$150	$200

TFX4 Time Effects

Introduced in 1982, includes flanger, chorus, doubler, echo.

1980s		$150	$200

Aguilar

1995-present. The New York, New York amp builder also offers a line of tube and solidstate pre-amps.

Akai (Akai Electric Company Ltd.)

1984-present. In '99, Akai added guitar effects to their line of electronic samplers and sequencers for musicians.

UniBass UB1

2000s. Bass octave pedal.

2000s		$50	$100

Alamo

1947-1982. Founded by Charles Eilenberg, Milton Fink, and Southern Music, San Antonio, Texas. Distributed by Bruno & Sons. Mainly known for guitars and amps, Alamo did offer a reverb unit.

Reverb Unit

1965-ca.1979. Has a Hammond reverb system, balance and intensity controls. By '73 the unit had 3 controls - mixer, contour, and intensity.

1965-1970		$300	$400

Alesis

1992-present. Alesis has a wide range of products for the music industry, including digital processors and amps for guitars.

Allen Amplification

1998-present. David Allen's company, located in Richwood, Kentucky, mainly produces amps, but they also offer a tube overdrive pedal.

Altair Corp.

1977-1980s. Company was located in Ann Arbor, Michigan.

MODEL YEAR	FEATURES	EXC. COND. LOW	HIGH

Power Attenuator PW-5

1977-1980. Goes between amp and speaker to dampen volume.

1977-1980 $90 $120

Amdek

Mid-1980s. Amdek offered many electronic products over the years, including drum machines and guitar effects. Most of these were sold in kit form so quality of construction can vary.

Delay Machine DMK-200

1983. Variable delay times.

1983 $85 $115

Octaver OCK-100

1983. Produces tone 1 or 2 octaves below the note played.

1983 $75 $100

Phaser PHK-100

1983 $65 $100

Phlanger

1983 $50 $60

Ampeg

Ampeg entered the effects market in the late-1960s. Their offerings in the early-'60s were really amplifier-outboard reverb units similar to the ones offered by Gibson (GA-1). Ampeg offered a line of imported effects in '82-'83, known as the A-series (A-1 through A-9), and reintroduced effects to their product line in '05.

Analog Delay A-8

1982-1983. Made in Japan.

1982-1983 $75 $125

Chorus A-6

1982-1983. Made in Japan.

1982-1983 $50 $75

Compressor A-2

1982-1983. Made in Japan.

1982-1983 $50 $75

Distortion A-1

1982-1983. Made in Japan.

1982-1983 $50 $75

Echo Jet Reverb EJ-12

1963-1965. Outboard, alligator clip reverb unit with 12" speaker, 12 watts, technically a reverb unit. When used as a stand-alone amp, the reverb is off. Named EJ-12A in '65.

1963-1965 $550 $700

Echo Satellite ES-1

1961-1963. Outboard reverb unit with amplifier and speaker alligator clip.

1961-1963 $550 $675

Flanger A-5

1982-1983. Made in Japan.

1982-1983 $50 $75

Multi-Octaver A-7

1982-1983. Made in Japan.

1982-1983 $50 $100

Over Drive A-3

1982-1983. Made in Japan.

1982-1983 $50 $75

MODEL YEAR	FEATURES	EXC. COND. LOW	HIGH

Parametric Equalizer A-9

1982-1983. Made in Japan.

1982-1983 $45 $70

Phaser A-4

1982-1983. Made in Japan.

1982-1983 $50 $75

Phazzer

1975-1979. Phase shifter, single speed knob.

1975-1979 $50 $125

Scrambler Fuzz

1969-1970. Distortion pedal, black housing. 2 Control knobs. Reissued in '05.

1969-1970 $200 $450

Sub Blaster SCP-OCT

2005-2007. Bass octave pedal.

2005-2007 $225 $380

Amplifier Corporation of America

Late '60s company that made amps for Univox and also marketed effects under their own name.

Amptweaker

2010-present. James Brown, an amp design engineer previously employed by Peavey, then for Kustom amps, now designs and builds effects in Batavia, Ohio.

amukaT Gadgets

2006-present. Guitar effects built by Takuma Kanaiwa in New York, New York.

Analog Man

1994-present. Founded by Mike Piera in '94 with full-time production by 2000. Located in Danbury, Connecticut (until '07 in Bethel), producing chorus, compressor, fuzz, and boost pedals by '03.

Astro Tone

2000s-present. Fuzz.

2000s-2020 $120 $160

Bad Bob

2000s-present. Boost.

2000s-2020 $90 $150

Beano Boost

2000s-present. Boost.

2000s-2020 $100 $160

Dual Analog Delay

2000s-present. Delay.

2000s-2020 $200 $250

Envelope Filter

2000s-present. Envelope 'auto-wah'.

2000s-2020 $140 $200

Juicer

2000s-present. Compressor.

2000s-2020 $120 $160

King of Tone

2000s-present. Overdrive pedal, 4 generations, numerous options available.

2000s-2020 $400 $700

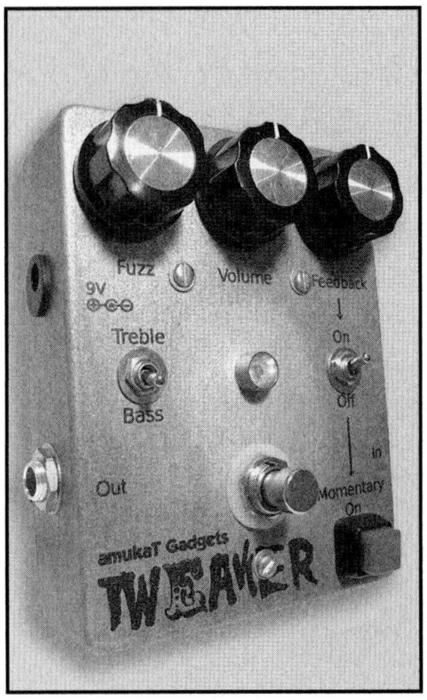

amukaT Gadgets Tweaker

Analog Man Sun Bender

Analog Man King of Tone

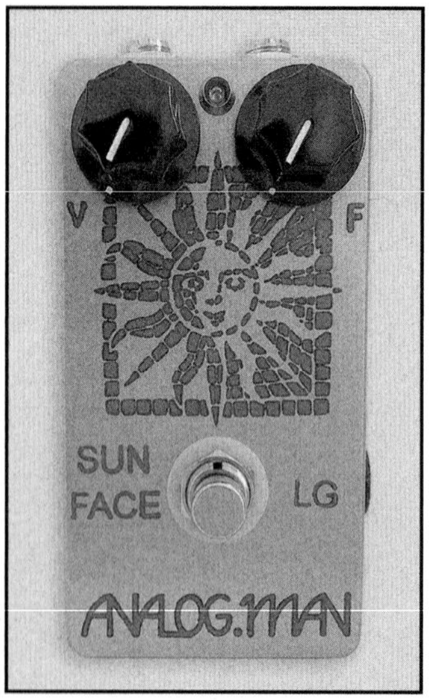

Analog Man Sun Face

Area 51 The Alienist

Arion Delay SAD-1
Keith Myers

MODEL YEAR	FEATURES	EXC. COND. LOW	HIGH
Peppermint Fuzz			
2000s-present. Fuzz.			
2000s-2020		$120	$230
Prince of Tone			
2000s-present. Overdrive.			
2000s-2020		$120	$150
Sun Bender			
2000s-present. Fuzz.			
2000s-2020		$200	$240
Sun Face			
2000s-present. Fuzz.			
2000s-2020		$200	$300

Aphex Systems

1975-present. Founded in Massachusetts by Marvin Caesar and Curt Knoppel, to build their Aural Exciter and other pro sound gear. Currently located in Sun Valley, California, and building a variety of gear for the pro audio broadcast, pro music and home-recording markets.

Apollo

Ca.1967-1972. Imported from Japan by St. Louis Music, includes Fuzz Treble Boost Box, Crier Wa-Wa, Deluxe Fuzz. They also offered basses and guitars.

MODEL YEAR	FEATURES	EXC. COND. LOW	HIGH
Crier Wa-Wa			
Ca.1967-1972.			
1967-1972		$125	$200
Fuzz/Deluxe Fuzz			
Ca.1967-1972. Includes the Fuzz Treble Boost Box and the Deluxe Fuzz.			
1967-1972		$125	$240
Surf Tornado Wah Wah			
Ca.1967-1972.			
1967-1972		$180	$300

Applied

1960s. Effects brand of the Goya Music Company. Some models may have been sold under the Nomad brand.

MODEL YEAR	FEATURES	EXC. COND. LOW	HIGH
Banshee Fuzz			
1960s. Also sold as the Nomad Banshee Fuzz.			
1960s		$50	$200

Arbiter

Ivor Arbiter and Arbiter Music, London, began making the circular Fuzz Face stompbox in 1966. Other products included the Fuzz Wah and Fuzz Wah Face. In '68 the company went public as Arbiter and Western, later transitioning to Dallas-Arbiter. Refer to Dallas-Arbiter for listings.

Area 51

2003-present. Guitar effects made in Newaygo, Michigan (made in Texas until early '06), by Dan Albrecht. They also build amps.

Aria/Aria Pro II

1956-present. Aria provided a line of effects, made by Maxon, in the mid-'80s.

MODEL YEAR	FEATURES	EXC. COND. LOW	HIGH
Analog Delay AD-10			
1983-1985. Dual-stage stereo.			
1983-1985		$65	$75
Chorus ACH-1			
1986-1987. Stereo.			
1986-1987		$40	$50
Chorus CH-10			
1983-1985. Dual-stage stereo.			
1983-1985		$40	$50
Chorus CH-5			
1985-1987		$40	$50
Compressor CO-10			
1983-1985		$40	$50
Digital Delay ADD-100			
1984-1986. Delay, flanging, chorus, doubling, hold.			
1984-1986		$65	$75
Digital Delay DD-X10			
1985-1987		$65	$75
Distortion DT-10			
1983-1985. Dual-stage.			
1983-1985		$40	$50
Distortion DT-5			
1985-1987		$40	$50
Flanger AFL-1			
1986. Stereo.			
1986		$50	$60
Flanger FL-10			
1983-1985. Dual-stage stereo.			
1983-1985		$50	$60
Flanger FL-5			
1985-1987		$50	$60
Metal Pedal MP-5			
1985-1987		$40	$50
Noise Gate NG-10			
1983-1985		$30	$40
Over Drive OD-10			
1983-1985. Dual-stage.			
1983-1985		$40	$50
Parametric Equalizer EQ-10			
1983-1985		$40	$50
Phase Shifter PS-10			
1983-1984. Dual-stage.			
1983-1984		$50	$70
Programmable Effects Pedal APE-1			
1984-1986. Compression, distortion, delay, chorus.			
1984-1986		$50	$60

Arion

1984-2014. Arion offers a wide variety of budget imported effects.

MODEL YEAR	FEATURES	EXC. COND. LOW	HIGH
Guitar and Bass Effects			
1984-2014		$15	$75

Arteffect

Tom Kochawi and Dan Orr started building analog effects in 2006, in Haifa and Natanya, Israel.

Artesania Sonora Lab

2010s-present. Based in Fortaleza, Brazil.

MODEL YEAR	FEATURES	EXC. COND. LOW	HIGH
Fabrica del Fuzz			
2016-2021		$75	$150

MODEL YEAR	FEATURES	EXC. COND. LOW	HIGH

Asama

1970s-1980s. This Japanese company offered solidbody guitars with built-in effects as well as stand-alone units. They also offered basses, drum machines and other music products.

Astro Amp

Late 1960s. Universal Amplifier Corporation of New York City made and sold Astro Amps as well as Astro effects. The company also made the Sam Ash Fuzzz Boxx.

Astrotone

1966		$175	$275

ATD

Mid-1960s-early 1980s. Made by the All-Test Devices corporation of Long Beach, New York. In the mid-'60s, Richard Minz and an associate started making effects part-time, selling them through Manny's Music in New York. They formed All-Test and started making Maestro effects and transducer pickups for CMI, which owned Gibson at the time. By '75, All-Test was marketing effects under their own brand. All-Test is still making products for other industries, but by the early to mid-'80s they were no longer making products for the guitar.

PB-1 Power Booster

1976-ca.1980.

1979-1980		$50	$60

Volume Pedal EV-1

1979-ca.1980.

1979-1980		$30	$40

Wah-Wah/Volume Pedal WV-1

1979-ca.1981.

1979-1981		$50	$60

Audio Disruption Devices

2010s. Based in Mooresville, Indiana.

Optical Ring V2

2010s. Ring modulator.

2010s		$100	$200

Audio Matrix

1979-1984. Effects built by B.K Butler in Escondido, California. He later designed the Tube Driver and founded Tube Works in 1987. He nows operates Butler Audio, making home and auto hybrid tube stereo amps.

Mini Boogee B81

1981. Four-stage, all-tube preamp, overdrive, distortion.

1981		$100	$135

Audio-Phonic

1970s. Effects built in Argentina.

Mu-Tron III

1970s. Musitronics Mu-Tron III copy.

1970s		$200	$300

MODEL YEAR	FEATURES	EXC. COND. LOW	HIGH

Audioworks

1980s. Company was located in Niles, Illinois.

F.E.T. Distortion

1980s		$40	$55

Auralux

2000-2011. Founded by Mitchell Omori and David Salzmann, Auralux built effects and tube amps in Highland Park, Illinois.

Austone Electronics

1997-2009. Founded by Jon Bessent and Randy Larkin, Austone offered a range of stomp boxes, all made in Austin, Texas. Bessent passed away in '09.

Overdrive and Fuzz Pedals

1997-2009. Various overdrive and fuzz boxes.

1997-2009		$125	$245

Automagic

Wah pedals and distortion boxes made in Germany by Musician Sound Design, starting in 1998.

Avalanche

Late 1980s. Effects built by Brian Langer in Toronto, Ontario.

Brianizer

Late-1980s. Leslie effect, dual rotor, adjustable speed and rates.

1980s		$75	$90

Axe

1980s. Early '80s line of Japanese effects, possibly made by Maxon.

B & M

1970s. A private brand made by Sola/Colorsound for Barns and Mullens, a U.K. distributor.

Fuzz Unit

1970s. Long thin orange case, volume, sustain, tone knobs, on-off stomp switch.

1970s		$275	$325

Backline Engineering

2004-present. Guitar multi-effects built by Gary Lee in Camarillo, California. In '07, they added tube amps.

Bad Cat Amplifier Company

2000-present. Amp company Bad Cat, originally of Corona, California, also offers guitar effects. In '09 the company was moved to Anaheim.

Baldwin

1965-1970. The piano maker got into the guitar market when it acquired Burns of London in '65, and sold the guitars in the U.S. under the Baldwin name. They also marketed a couple of effects at the same time.

Banzai

2000-present. Effects built by Olaf Nobis in Berlin, Germany.

Bad Cat Double Drive

Bad Cat Siamese Drive

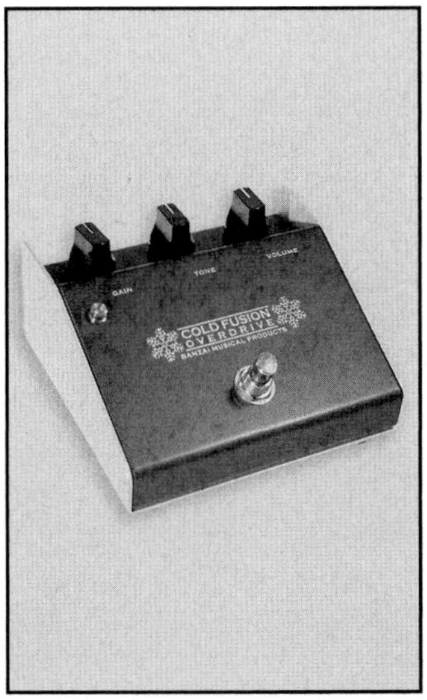

Banzai Cold Fusion Overdrive

BBE Sonic Stomp

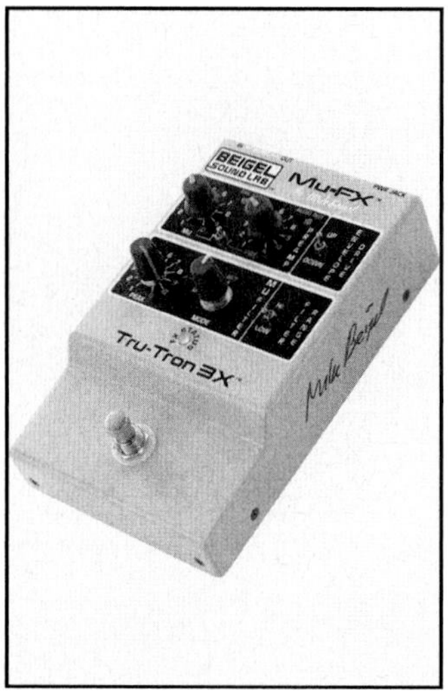

Beigel Sound Lab Tru-Tron 3X

Beigel Sound Lab Boostron 3

MODEL YEAR	FEATURES	EXC. COND. LOW	HIGH

Bartolini

The pickup manufacturer offered a few effects from around 1982 to '87.

Tube-It

1982-ca.1987. Marshall tube amplification simulator with bass, treble, sustain controls.

1982-1987	Red case	$80	$90

Basic Systems' Side Effects

1980s. This company was located in Tulsa, Oklahoma.

Audio Delay

1986-ca.1987. Variable delay speeds.

1986-1987		$75	$100

Triple Fuzz

1986-ca.1987. Selectable distortion types.

1986-1987		$50	$60

BBE

1985-present. BBE, owner of G & L Guitars and located in California, manufactures rack-mount effects and added a new line of stomp boxes in '05.

Behringer

1989-present. The German professional audio products company added modeling effects in '01 and guitar stomp boxes in '05. They also offer guitars and amps.

Beigel Sound Lab

Music product designer Mike Beigel helped form Musitronics Corp, where he made the Mu-Tron III. In 1978 he started Beigel Sound Lab to provide product design in Warwick, New York, where in '80 he made 50 rack-mount Enveloped Controlled Filters under this brand name. In 2013, Mike Beigel's Beigel Sound Lab started making a Mu-FX Tru-Tron 3X and Octave Divider.

Boostron 3

2016-2017. Combines preamp boost, compression and distortion in one pedal.

2016-2017		$225	$325

Octave Divider

2015. Updated and expanded version of original Musitronics Mu-Tron Octave Divider.

2015		$325	$400

Tru-Tron 3X

2015-2019. Updated and expanded version of original Musitronics Mu-Tron III envelope filter.

2015-2019		$325	$500

Bell Electrolabs

1970s. This English company offered a line of effects in the '70s.

Vibrato

1970s		$150	$200

Bennett Music Labs

Effects built in Chatanooga, Tennessee by Bruce Bennett.

MODEL YEAR	FEATURES	EXC. COND. LOW	HIGH

Bigsby

1948-1966. Paul Bigsby made steel guitars, pedal steels, and electric guitars and mandolins, as well as developing the Bigsby vibrato tailpiece and other components.

Foot Volume and Tone Control

1950s-1960s. Beautifully crafted pedal in a cast-aluminum housing featuring a side-to-side tone sweep.

1950s-60s		$425	$625

Binson

Late 1950s-1982. Binson, of Milan, Italy, made several models of the Echorec, using tubes or transistors. They also made units for Guild, Sound City and EKO.

Echorec

Ca.1960-1979. Four knob models with 12 echo selections, 1 head, complex multitap effects, settings for record level, playback and regeneration. Includes B1, B2, Echomaster1, T5 (has 6 knobs), T5E, and Baby. Used a magnetic disk instead of tape. Guild later offered the Guild Echorec by Binson which is a different stripped-down version.

1960s	Tube	$2,500	$3,350
1970s	Solidstate	$700	$800

Bixonic

1995-2007. The round silver distortion pedals were originally distributed by SoundBarrier Music, later by Godlyke, Inc.

Expandora EXP-2000

1995-2000. Analog distortion, round silver case, internal DIP switches.

1995-2000		$170	$210

Black Arts Toneworks

2010s. Founded by Mark Wentz of Chattanooga, Tennessee.

Pharaoh

2010s		$100	$150

Ritual Fuzz

2010s. Inspired by the Colorsound Fuzz Box.

2010s		$100	$150

Black Cat Pedals

1993-2007, 2009-present. Founded by Fred Bonte and located in Texas until late 2007 when production was discontinued. In '09, using Bonte's same designs, new owner Tom Hughes restarted production in Foxon, Connecticut.

Black Cat OD-1

2010-present. Overdrive.

2010-2020		$70	$120

Blackbox Music Electronics

2000-2009. Founded by Loren Stafford and located in Minneapolis, Minnesota, Blackbox offered a line of effects for guitar and bass. The Blackbox models are now made under the Ooh La La brand.

MODEL YEAR	FEATURES	EXC. COND. LOW	HIGH

Blackout Effectors

Kyle Tompkins began building effects pedals in 2007, in Vancouver, British Columbia and now builds them in Asheville, North Carolina.

Blackstar Amplification

2007-present. Guitar effects pedals built by Joel Richardson in Northampton, U.K. He also builds amps.

Blackstone Appliances

1999-present. Distortion effects crafted by Jon Blackstone in New York City.

Mosfet Overdrive

1999-present. Though the designation doesn't appear on the housing, the original was subsequently called 2Sv1 after later versions were issued.

1999	2Sv1, no controls on top	$125	$240
2000	2Sv2	$100	$200
2006-2020	2Sv3, 2Sv31, 2Sv32, 2Sv33	$95	$200
2012	Billybox Limited Edition	$150	$250

Bon, Mfg

Bon was located in Escondido, California.

Tube Driver 204

1979-ca.1981.

1979-1981		$100	$150

Boomerang

1995-present. Effects pedals built in Grapevine, Texas by Boomerang Musical Products, Ltd.

Boss

1976-present. Japan's Roland Corporation first launched effect pedals in '74. A year or two later the subsidiary company, Boss, debuted its own line. They were marketed concurrently at first but gradually Boss became reserved for effects and drum machines while the Roland name was used on amplifiers and keyboards. Boss still offers a wide line of pedals.

Acoustic Simulator AC-2

1997-2007. Four modes that emulate various acoustic tones.

1997-2007		$50	$70

Acoustic Simulator AC-3

2007-present. Four modes that emulate various acoustic tones.

2007-2020		$50	$90

Auto Wah AW-2 and AW-3

1991-1999 (AW-2), 2000-present (AW-3).

1991-2020		$40	$75

Bass Chorus CE-2B

1987-1995		$40	$50

Bass Equalizer GE-7B

1987-1995. Seven-band, name changed to GEB-7 in '95.

1987-1995		$40	$50

MODEL YEAR	FEATURES	EXC. COND. LOW	HIGH

Bass Flanger BF-2B

1987-1994		$40	$60

Bass Limiter LM-2B

1990-1994		$35	$40

Bass Overdrive ODB-3

1994-present. Yellow case.

1994-2020		$40	$50

Blues Driver BD-2

1995-present. Blue case.

1995-2020		$45	$80
1995-2020	Keeley modded	$150	$190

Chorus Ensemble CE-1

1976-1978. Vibrato and chorus.

1976-1978		$275	$500

Chorus Ensemble CE-2

1979-1982		$140	$250

Chorus Ensemble CE-3

1982-1992		$30	$80

Chorus Ensemble CE-5

1991-present. Pale blue case.

1991-2020		$50	$95

Compressor Sustainer CS-1

1978-1982		$70	$95

Compressor Sustainer CS-2

1981-1986		$70	$110

Compressor Sustainer CS-3

1986-present. Blue case.

1986-2020		$50	$75
1986-2020	JHS modded	$90	$130

Delay DM-2

1981-1984. Analog, hot pink case.

1981-1984		$100	$245

Delay DM-3

1984-1988		$145	$195

Digital Delay DD-2

1983-1986		$60	$150

Digital Delay DD-3

1986-present. Up to 800 ms of delay, white case.

1986-1989		$70	$90
1986-2020	Keeley modded	$100	$170
1990-2020		$60	$80

Digital Delay DD-5

1995-2005. Up to 2 seconds of delay.

1995-2005		$100	$145

Digital Delay DD-6

2003-2007. Up to 5 seconds of delay.

2003-2007		$55	$100

Digital Delay DD-7

2008-present. Up to 6.4 seconds of delay, crème case.

2008-2020		$80	$110

Digital Dimension C DC-2

1985-1989. Two chorus effects and tremolo.

1985-1989		$135	$245

Digital Metalizer MZ-2

1987-1992		$80	$95

Digital Reverb RV-2

1987-1990		$95	$145

Digital Reverb RV-5

2003-2019. Dual imput and dual output, four control knobs, silver case.

2003-2020		$60	$95

Blackstone Mosfet Overdrive

Boss Chorus Ensemble CE-3

Boss Delay DM-3
Rivington Guitars

1984 Boss Distortion DS-1
Rivington Guitars

Boss Metal Zone MT-2

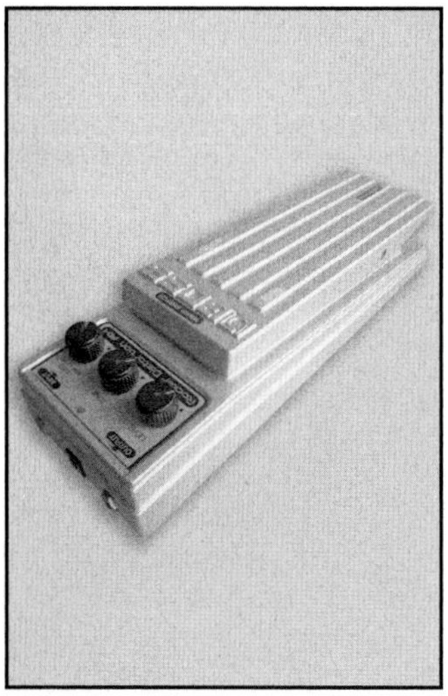

Boss Rocker Distortion PD-1
Garrett Tung.

MODEL YEAR	FEATURES	EXC. COND. LOW	HIGH

Digital Reverb/Delay RV-3
1994-2004 $95 $120

Digital Sampler/Delay DSD-2
1985-1986 $100 $150

Digital Space-D DC-3/Digital Dimension DC-3
1988-1993. Originally called the Digital Space-D, later changed to Digital Dimension. Chorus with EQ.
1988-1993 $130 $180

Digital Stereo Reverb RV-70
1994-1995. Rack mount, MIDI control, reverb/delay, 199 presets.
1994-1995 $130 $180

Distortion DS-1
1978-1989, 1990s-present. Orange case.
1978-1989 $75 $150
1978-2020 Keeley modded $100 $130
1990-1999 $30 $50
2000-2020 $20 $25

Dr. Rhythm DR-55
1979-1989. Drum machine.
1979-1989 $145 $195

Dual Over Drive SD-2
1993-1998 $45 $55

Dynamic Filter FT-2
1986-1988. Auto wah.
1986-1988 $70 $95

Dynamic Wah AW-3
2000-present. Auto wah with humanizer, for guitar or bass.
2000-2020 $50 $85

Enhancer EH-2
1990-1998 $35 $45

Flanger BF-1
1977-1980 $55 $70

Flanger BF-2
1980-1989 $60 $100
1990-2005 $40 $55

Foot Wah FW-3
1992-1996 $45 $55

Graphic Equalizer GE-6
1978-1981. Six bands.
1978-1981 $60 $75

Graphic Equalizer GE-7
1981-present. Seven bands, white case.
1982-1989 $50 $90
1990-2020 $45 $70

Graphic Equalizer GE-10
1976-1985. 10-band EQ for guitar or bass.
1976-1985 $75 $150

Harmonist HR-2
1994-1999. Pitch shifter.
1994-1999 $80 $105

Heavy Metal HM-2
1983-1991. Distortion.
1983-1991 $60 $140

Hyper Fuzz FZ-2
1993-1997 $45 $150

Hyper Metal HM-3
1993-1998 $35 $45

Limiter LM-2
1987-1992 $25 $65

Line Selector LS-2
1991-present. Select between 2 effects loops, white case.
1991-2020 With adapter $45 $85

Mega Distortion MD-2
2003-present. Red case.
2003-2020 $45 $55

Metal Zone MT-2
1991-present. Distortion and 3-band EQ, grey case.
1991-2020 $30 $60
1991-2020 Keeley modded $120 $140

Multi Effects ME-5
1988-1991. Floor unit.
1988-1991 $70 $140

Multi Effects ME-6
1992-1997 $50 $100

Multi Effects ME-8
1996-1997 $70 $120

Multi Effects ME-20
1990-2000s $60 $100

Multi Effects ME-25
1990-2000s $70 $130

Multi Effects ME-30
1998-2002 $70 $120

Multi Effects ME-50
2003-2009. Floor unit.
2003-2009 $100 $165

Multi Effects ME-70
2000s $90 $200

Multi Effects ME-80
2000s-present.
2000s-2020 $125 $230

Noise Gate NF-1
1979-1988 $40 $75

Noise Suppressor NS-2
1987-present. White case.
1987-2020 $40 $75

Octaver OC-2/Octave OC-2
1982-2003. Originally called the Octaver.
1982-2003 $75 $130

Overdrive OD-1
1977-1979 $95 $190
1980-1985 $70 $145

Overdrive OD-2
1990s $20 $60

Overdrive OD-3
1997-present. Yellow case.
1997-2020 $45 $60

Parametric Equalizer PQ-4
1991-1997 $45 $70

Phase Shifter PH-3
2000-present. Added effects, light green case.
2000-2020 $40 $70

Phaser PH-1
1977-1981. Green box, 2 knobs.
1977-1981 $70 $95

Phaser PH-1R
1982-1985. Resonance control added to PH-1.
1982-1985 $70 $120

MODEL YEAR	FEATURES	EXC. COND. LOW	HIGH

Phaser PH-2
1984-2001. 12 levels of phase shift, 4 knobs.
1984-2001 $50 $85

Phaser PH-3
2000-present. Added effects.
1990s $40 $75

Pitch Sifter/Delay PS-2
1987-1993 $95 $150

Reverb Box RX-100
1981-mid-1980s.
1981-1985 $70 $95

Rocker Distortion PD-1
1980-mid-1980s. Variable pedal using magnetic field.
1980-1985 $45 $70

Rocker Volume PV-1
1981-mid-1980s.
1980-1985 $45 $55

Rocker Wah PW-1
1980-mid-1980s. Magnetic field variable pedal.
1980-1985 $55 $65

Slow Gear SG-1
1979-1982. Violin swell effect, automatically adjusts volume.
1979-1982 $300 $440

Spectrum SP-1
1977-1981. Single-band parametric EQ.
1977-1981 $325 $375

Super Chorus CH-1
1989-present. Blue case.
1989-2020 $45 $70

Super Distortion & Feedbacker DF-2
1984-1994. Also labeled as the Super Feedbacker & Distortion.
1984-1994 $95 $120

Super Octave OC-3
2004-present.
2004-2020 $60 $90

Super Over Drive SD-1
1981-present. Yellow case.
1981-1989 $50 $105
1990-2020 $30 $50

Super Phaser PH-2
1984-1989 $45 $85
1990-2001 $30 $50

Super Shifter PS-5
1999-2013. Pitch shifter/harmonizer, aqua case.
1999-2013 $95 $120

Touch Wah TW-1/T Wah TW-1
1978-1987. Auto wah, early models were labeled as Touch Wah.
1978-1987 $95 $120

Tremolo TR-2
1997-present. Aqua case.
1997-2020 $65 $85
1997-2020 Keeley modded $110 $150

Tremolo/Pan PN-2
1990-1995 $120 $145

MODEL YEAR	FEATURES	EXC. COND. LOW	HIGH

Turbo Distortion DS-2
1987-present. Orange case.
1987-2020 $70 $120

Turbo Over Drive OD-2
1985-1994. Called OD-2R after '94, due to added remote on/off jack.
1985-1994 $40 $100

Vibrato VB-2
1982-1986. True pitch-changing vibrato, warm analog tone, 'rise time' control allows for slow attach, 4 knobs, aqua-blue case.
1982-1986 $325 $460

Volume FV-50H
1987-1997. High impedance, stereo volume pedal with inputs and outputs.
1987-1997 $45 $55

Volume FV-50L
1987-1997. Low impedance version of FV-50.
1987-1997 $35 $45

Volume Pedal FV-100
Late-1980s-1991. Guitar volume pedal.
1987-1991 $35 $45

Brimstone Audio

2011-present. Shad Sundberg builds his guitar effects in California.

Browntone Electronics

2006-2012. Guitar effects built in Lincolnton, North Carolina by Tim Brown.

Bruno

Music distributor Bruno and Sons had a line of Japanese-made effects in the early '70s.

Fuzz Machine
1970s. Rebranded version of the Ibanez No. 59 Standard Fuzz.
1970s $75 $150

Budda

1995-present. Wahs and distortion pedals originally built by Jeff Bober and Scott Sier in San Francisco, California. In '09, Budda was acquired by Peavey Electronics. They also build amps.

Bud Wah
1997-2018. Wah pedal.
1990s-2018 $90 $140

Phat Bass
2000s $100 $145

Build Your Own Clone

2005-present. Build it yourself kits based on vintage effects produced by Keith Vonderhulls in Othello, Washington. Assembled kits are offered by their Canadian distributor.

Burriss

2001-present. Guitar effects from Bob Burriss of Lexington, Kentucky. He also builds amps.

Boss Super Over Drive SD-1
Rivington Guitars

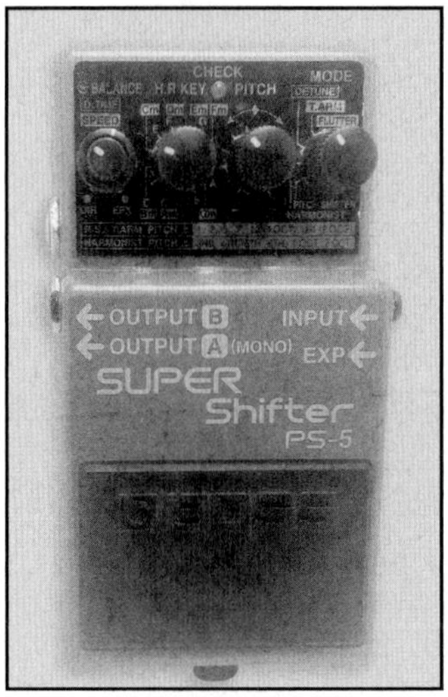

Boss Super Shifter PS-5
Keith Myers

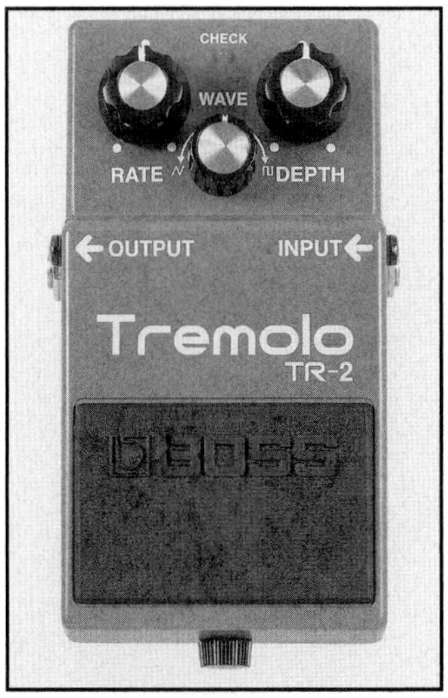

Boss Tremolo TR-2

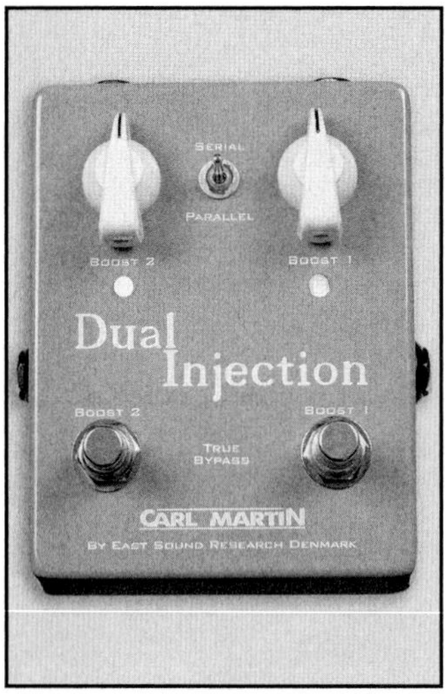

Carl Martin Dual Injection

Catalinbread Antichthon

Catalin Bread Sabbra Cadabra
Rivington Guitars

MODEL YEAR	FEATURES	EXC. COND. LOW	HIGH

Carl Martin

1993-present. Line of effects from Søren Jongberg and East Sound Research of Denmark. In '06 they added their Chinese-made Vintage Series. They also build amps.

Carlsbro

1959-present. English amp company Carlsbro Electronics Limited offered a line of effects from '77 to '81.

Fuzz

1970s. Tone Bender MkIII fuzz built by Sola Sound.

1970s		$300	$500

Suzz

1970s. Built by Sola Sound.

1970s		$300	$500

Suzz Wah Wah

1970s. Built by Sola Sound.

1970s		$100	$250

Carrotron

Late-1970s-mid-1980s. Carrotron was out of California and offered a line of effects.

Noise Fader C900B1

1981-ca.1982.

1981-1982		$50	$60

Preamp C821B

1981-ca.1982.

1981-1982		$55	$65

Carvin

1946-present. Carvin introduced its line of Ground Effects in '02 and discontinued them in '03.

Castle Instruments

Early 1980s. Castle was located in Madison, New Jersey, and made rack-mount and floor phaser units.

Phaser III

1980-1982. Offered mode switching for various levels of phase.

1980-1982		$100	$175

Catalinbread

2003-present. Nicholas Harris founded Catalinbread Specialized Mechanisms of Music in Seattle, Washington, in '02 to do mods and in '03 added his own line of guitar effects.

Adineko			
2000s		$100	$150
Belle Epoch			
2000s		$100	$170
Callisto			
2000s		$90	$135
Echorec			
2000s		$100	$185
Formula No. 5			
2000s		$140	$230
Naga Viper			
2000s		$100	$140
Perseus			
2000s		$70	$110
Rah			
2000s		$120	$150
Sabbra Cadabra			
2000s		$100	$150
Semaphore			
2000s		$90	$120
Super Chili Picoso			
2000s		$30	$50
Topanga			
2000s		$100	$170

Cat's Eye

Dean Solorzano and Lisa Kroeker began building their analog guitar effects in Oceanside, California in 2001.

Cause & Effect Pedals

2009-present. Guitar effects pedals built in Ontario by Mark Roberts and Brian Alexson.

Celmo

The Celmo Sardine Can Compressor is made by Kezako Productions in Montcaret, France, starting in 2008.

Chandler

Located in California, Chandler Musical Instruments offers instruments, pickups, and pickguards, as well as effects.

Digital Echo

1992-2000. Rackmount, 1 second delay, stereo.

1992-2000		$275	$425

Tube Driver

1986-1991. Uses a 12AX7 tube. Not to be confused with the Tube Works Tube Driver.

1980s	Large Box	$175	$330
1980s	Rackmount	$100	$215
1990s	Rackmount	$90	$150

Chapman

1970-present. From Emmett Chapman, maker of the Stick.

Patch of Shades

1981, 1989. Wah, with pressure sensitive pad instead of pedal. 2 production runs.

1980s		$50	$75

Chicago Iron

1998-present. Faithful reproductions of classic effects built by Kurt Steir in Chicago, Illinois.

Chunk Systems

1996-present. Guitar and bass effects pedals built by Richard Cartwright in Sydney, Australia.

Clark

1960s. Built in Clark, New Jersey, same unit as the Orpheum Fuzz and the Mannys Music Fuzz.

MODEL YEAR	FEATURES	EXC. COND. LOW	HIGH

SS-600 Fuzz
1960s. Chrome-plated, volume and tone knobs, toggle switch.
1960s $150 $200

Clark Amplification
1995-present. Amplifier builder Mike Clark, of Cayce, South Carolina, offers a reverb unit and started building guitar effects as well, in '98.

ClinchFX
2006-present. Hand made pedals by Peter Clinch in Brisbane, Queensland, Australia.

CMI
1970s. English music company.

Fuzz Unit
1970s. Built by Colorsound based on its Jumbo Tone Bender.
1970s $150 $300

Coffin
Case manufacturer Coffin Case added U.S.-made guitar effects pedals to their product line in 2006.

Colorsound
1967-2010. Colorsound effects were produced by England's Sola Sound, beginning with fuzz pedals. In the late-'60s, wah and fuzz-wah pedals were added, and by the end of the '70s, Colorsound offered 18 different effects, an amp, and accessories. Few early Colorsound products were imported into the U.S., so today they're scarce. Except for the Wah-Wah pedal, Colorsound's production stopped by the early '80s, but in '96 most of their early line was reissued by Dick Denny of Vox fame. Denny died in 2001. Since then, Anthony and Steve Macari build Colorsound effects in London. Mutronics offered a licensed rack mount combination of 4 classic Colorsound effects for a short time in the early 2000s.

Chuck-a-Wah
1975-1977. Auto wah pedal.
1975-1977 $250 $330

Dipthonizer
1970s. "Talking" pedal with foot control.
1970s $250 $400

Dopplatone Phase Unit
1970s. Large phase and vibrato effect with Bubble control.
1970s $250 $330

Electro Echo
1979-1980s. Analog delay pedal.
1979-1980s $250 $400

Flanger
1970s $110 $210

FuzzPhaze
Introduced in 1973.
1970s $160 $235

MODEL YEAR	FEATURES	EXC. COND. LOW	HIGH

Jumbo Tone-Bender
1974-early 1980s. Replaced the Tone-Bender fuzz, with wider case and light blue lettering.
1974-1980s $275 $335

Octivider
Introduced in 1973.
1970s $160 $235

Overdriver
Introduced in 1972. Controls for drive, treble and bass.
1970s $160 $235

Phazer
Introduced in 1973. Magenta/purple-pink case, slanted block Phazer logo on front.
1970s $160 $235

Power Boost
1970s $350 $600

Ring Modulator
Introduced in 1973. Purple case, Ring Modulator name with atom orbit slanted block logo on case.
1970s $260 $285

Supa Tone Bender
1977-early 1980s. Sustain and volume knobs, tone control and toggle. Same white case as Jumbo Tone-Bender, but with new circuit.
1970s $275 $350

Supa Wah-Swell
1970s. Supa Wah-Swell in slanted block letters on the end of the pedal, silver case.
1970s $160 $195

Supaphase
1970s $160 $235

Supasustain
1960s $135 $210

Swell
1970s $80 $90

Tremolo
1970s $160 $210

Tremolo Reissue
1996-2009. Purple case.
1996-2009 $110 $135

Vocalizer
1979-1980s. "Talking" pedal with foot control.
1979-1980s $200 $300

Wah Fuzz Straight
Introduced in 1973. Aqua-blue case, Wah-Fuzz-Straight in capital block letters on end of wah pedal.
1970s $185 $300

Wah Fuzz Swell
Introduced in 1973. Yellow case, block letter Wah Fuzz Swell logo on front, three control knobs and toggle.
1970s $260 $360

Wah Swell
1970s. Light purple case, block letter Wah-Swell logo on front.
1970s $235 $285

Wah Wah
1970s. Dark gray case, Wah-Wah in capital block letters on end of wah pedal.
1975 $310 $350

Chunk Systems Agent 00Funk

Clark Amplification Gainster

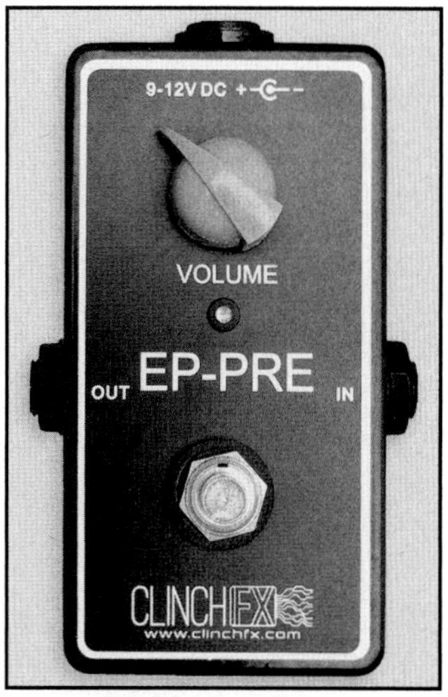

ClinchFX EP-PRE

Coopersonic Germaniac

Crazy Tube Circuits Starlight

Creation Audio Labs Holy Fire 9

MODEL YEAR	FEATURES	EXC. COND. LOW	HIGH

Wah Wah Reissue

1996-2005. Red case, large Colorsound letter logo and small Wah Wah lettering on end of pedal.

1996-2005		$85	$150

Wah Wah Supremo

1970s. Silver/chrome metal case, Wah-Wah Supremo in block letters on end of wah pedal.

1975		$435	$485

Companion

1970s. Private branded by Shin-ei of Japan, which made effects for others as well.

Tape Echo

1960-1970		$400	$650

Wah Pedal

1970s		$150	$240

Conn

Ca.1968-ca.1978. Band instrument manufacturer and distributor Conn/Continental Music Company, of Elkhart, Indiana, imported guitars and effects from Japan.

Strobe Tuner

Brown or later, grey, case.

1960s	ST-4	$50	$100
1960s	ST-6	$75	$100
1960s	ST-8	$75	$125
1968	ST-2	$50	$100
1970s	Strobotuner ST-11	$75	$100
1970s	Strobotuner ST-12	$75	$100

Coopersonic

2006-present. Martin Cooper builds his guitar effects in Nottingham, UK.

Coron

1970s-1980s. Japanese-made effects, early ones close copies of MXR pedals.

Cosmosound

Italy's Cosmosound made small amps with Leslie drums and effects pedals in the late '60s and '70s. Cosmosound logo is on top of pedals.

Wah Fuzz CSE-3

1970s. Volume and distortion knobs, wah and distortion on-off buttons, silver case.

1970s		$275	$350

Wild Sound

1970s		$175	$195

Crazy Tube Circuits

2004-present. Guitar effects designed and built by Chris Ntaifotis in Athens, Greece.

Creation Audio Labs

2005-present. Guitar and bass boost pedal and re-amplifying gear built in Nashville, Tennessee.

Crowther Audio

1976-present. Guitar effects built by Paul Crowther, who was the original drummer of the band Split Enz, in Auckland, New Zealand. His first effect was the Hot Cake.

Crucial Audio

2005-present. Effects by Steve Kollander engineered and assembled in Sussex County, Delaware, with chassis manufactured by machine shops within the U.S. They also provide OEM products and design engineering services to companies including Matchless, Requisite Audio & West Coast Pedal Boards.

Apollo-18 Vacuum Tube Leslie Interface Module

2015-present. High-voltage vacuum tube interface module for Leslie 122 or 147 type rotary speaker systems; can be used with a tube preamp and/or two channel vacuum tube direct box.

2015-2020		$960	$1,200

Das Götterdämmerung Ring Modulator/ Germanium Fuzz Pedal

2017-present. Provides full function controls combined with germanium fuzz generated from matched NOS 2N404.

2017-2020		$280	$360

DUB-5 Vacuum Tube Direct Box/Tube Buffer

2016-present. Interface for recording studios or live sound to sweeten the tone of instruments.

2016-2020		$370	$460

Echo-Nugget Vacuum Tube Analog Delay

2008-present. Tube-driven analog delay with selectable boost/tone preamp.

2008-2020		$450	$550

Time Warp Vacuum Tube Analog Delay Pitch Modulator

2008-present. Tube-driven analog delay with selectable modulation/warp function.

2008-2020		$450	$550

Cruzer

Effects made by Korea's Crafter Guitars. They also build guitars, basses and amps under that brand.

Crybaby

See listing under Vox for early models, and Dunlop for recent versions.

CSL

1970s. Charles Summerfield Ltd., was an English music company with a line of effects made by Sola Sound.

Power Boost

1970s		$100	$200

Super Fuzz

1970s		$100	$200

Cusack Music

2003-present. Effects built in Holland, Michigan by Jon Cusack.

MODEL YEAR	FEATURES	EXC. COND. LOW	HIGH

Dallas/Dallas Arbiter

Dallas Arbiter, Ltd. was based in London and it appeared in the late-1960s as a division of a Dallas group of companies headed by Ivor Arbiter. Early products identified with Dallas logo with the company noted as John E. Dallas & Sons Ltd., Dallas Building, Clifton Street, London, E.C.2. They also manufactured Sound City amplifiers and made Vox amps from '72 to '78. The Fuzz Face is still available from Jim Dunlop.

Fuzz Face

1966-1975, 1977-1981, 1986-1987. Late '70s and '80s version was built for Dallas Arbiter by Crest Audio of New Jersey. The current reissue is built by Jim Dunlop USA (see that listing).

1968-1969	Red	$1,500	$2,500
1970	Red	$1,000	$2,250
1970-1975	Blue	$1,000	$2,250
1977-1980	Blue	$650	$850
1981	Grey, reissue	$450	$550

Fuzz Wah Face

1970s	Black	$550	$650
1990s	Reissue copy	$65	$80

Rangemaster Fuzzbug

1966. Tone Bender Mk1.5 effect built by Sola Sound.

1966		$1,500	$2,000

Rangemaster Treble Booster

1966. 2000s. Grey housing. 1 Control knob. On-off slider switch. Old-style round-barrel 9-volt battery powered; many converted to later rectangular battery. Various current reissues built by JMI and other firms.

1966		$1,675	$2,850
2000s	JMI reissue	$175	$225

Sustain

1970s		$400	$500

Treble and Bass Face

1960s		$500	$700

Trem Face

Ca.1970-ca.1975. Reissued in '80s, round red case, depth and speed control knobs, Dallas-Arbiter England logo plate.

1970-1975		$500	$700

Wah Baby

1970s. Gray speckle case, Wah Baby logo caps and small letters on end of pedal.

1970s		$500	$600

Damage Control

2004-2009. Guitar effects pedals and digital multi-effects built in Moorpark, California. The company was founded with the release of a line of tube-driven effects pedals. In '09, it began developing products under the Strymon brand name.

Demonizer

2004-2009. Class A distortion preamp pedal powered by dual vacuum tubes.

2004-2009		$180	$255

Liquid Blues

2004-2009. Class A overdrive pedal powered by dual vacuum tubes.

2004-2009		$180	$245

Solid Metal

2004-2009. Class A distortion pedal powered by dual vacuum tubes.

2004-2009		$180	$260

TimeLine

2004-2009. Delay pedal powered by dual vacuum tubes.

2004-2009		$240	$300

Womanizer

2004-2009. Class A overdrive preamp pedal powered by dual vacuum tubes.

2004-2009		$170	$220

Dan Armstrong

1976-1981. In '76, Musitronics, based in Rosemont, New Jersey, introduced 6 inexpensive plug-in effects designed by Dan Armstrong. Perhaps under the influence of John D. MacDonald's Travis McGee novels, each effect name incorporated a color, like Purple Peaker. Shipping box labeled Dan Armstrong by Musitronics. They disappeared a few years later but were reissued by WD Products from '91 to '02 (See WD for those models). From '03 to '06, Vintage Tone Project offered the Dan Armstrong Orange Crusher. Since '06, a licensed line of Dan Armstrong effects that plug directly into the output of a guitar or bass (since '07 some also as stomp boxes) has been offered by Grafton Electronics of Grafton, Vermont. Dan Armstrong died in '04.

Blue Clipper

1976-1981. Fuzz, blue-green case.

1976-1981		$100	$200

Green Ringer

1976-1981. Ring Modulator/Fuzz, green case.

1976-1981		$100	$280

Orange Squeezer

1976-1981. Compressor, orange case.

1976-1981		$125	$300

Purple Peaker

1976-1981. Frequency Booster, light purple case.

1976-1981		$100	$170

Red Ranger

1976-1981. Bass/Treble Booster, light red case.

1976-1981		$85	$100

Yellow Humper

1976-1981. Yellow case.

1976-1981		$85	$100

Danelectro

1946-1969, 1996-present. The Danelectro brand was revived in '96 with a line of effects pedals. They have also offered the Wasabi line of effects. Prices do not include AC adapter, add $10 for the Zero-Hum adapter.

Chicken Salad Vibrato

2000-2009. Orange case.

2000-2009		$20	$50

Cool Cat

1996-2018		$30	$35

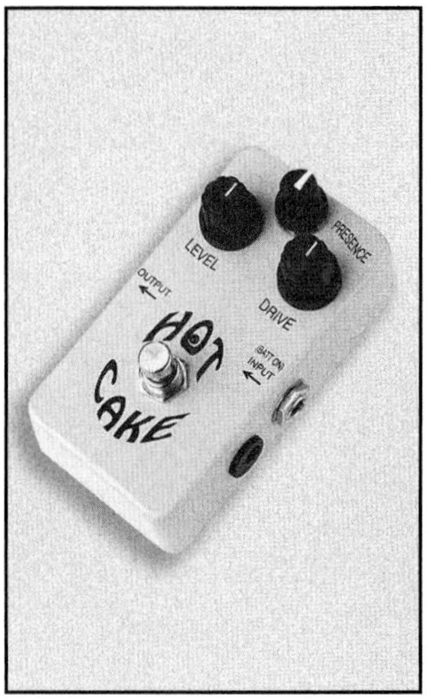

Crowther Audio Hotcake

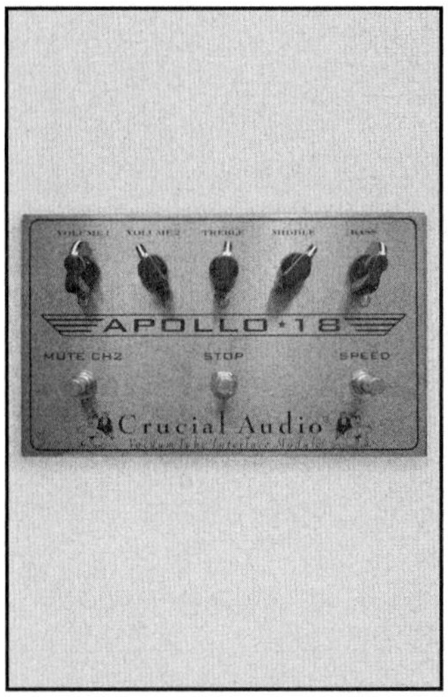

Crucial Audio Apollo-18 Vacuum Tube Leslie Interface Module

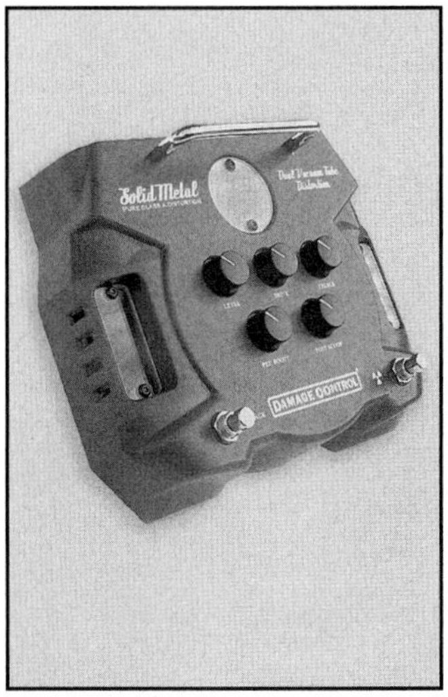

Damage Control Solid Metal

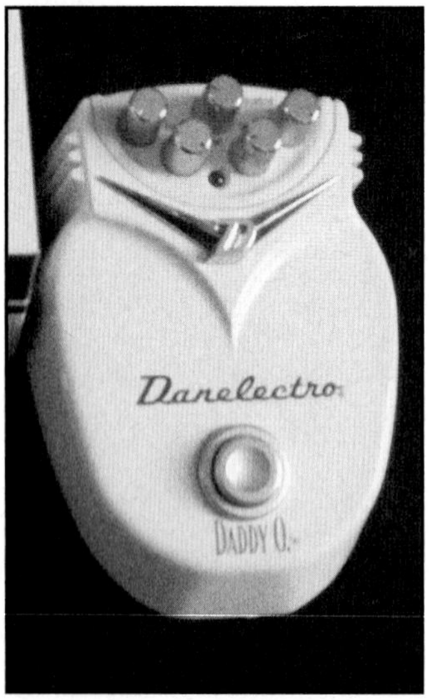

Danelectro Daddy-O
Jim Schreck

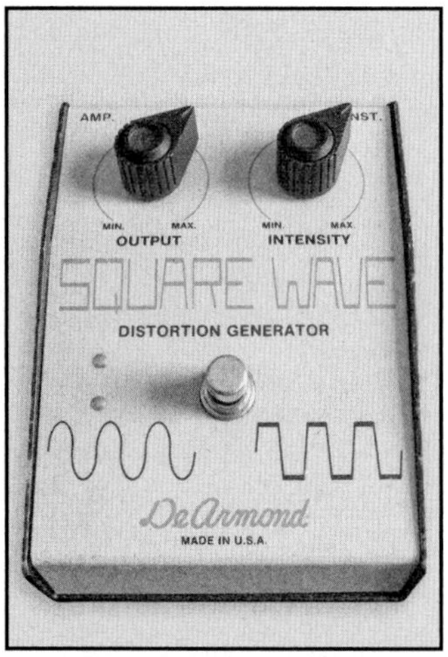

DeArmond Square Wave Distortion Generator
Jim Schreck

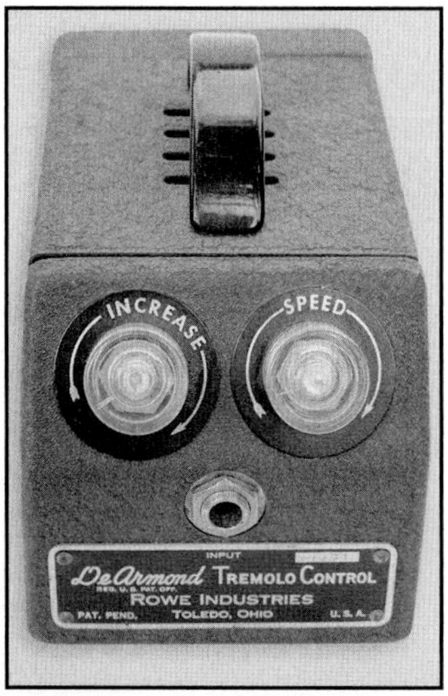

DeArmond Tremolo Control

MODEL YEAR	FEATURES	EXC. COND. LOW	HIGH

Cool Cat Chorus
1996-2018. Blue case.

1996-2018		$20	$40

Corned Beef Reverb
2000-2009. Blue-black case.

2000-2009		$15	$40

Daddy-O Overdrive
1996-2009. White case.

1996-2009		$35	$40

Dan Echo
1998-2009. Lavender case.

1998-2009		$40	$45

Echo Box
1953-ca. 1958. Reverb unit, metal housing with black endplates.

1953-1958		$200	$450

Fab Tone Distortion
1996-2014. Red case.

1996-2014		$30	$40

Reverb Unit Model 9100
1962-ca. 1967. Tube-driven spring reverb, long grey housing.

1962-1967		$300	$475

Daredevil

2012-present. Guitar effects pedals built in Chicago, Illinois by Johnny Wator.

Davoli

1960s-1970. Davoli was an Italian pickup and guitar builder and is often associated with Wandre guitars.

TRD
1970s. Solidstate tremolo, reverb, distortion unit.

1970s		$175	$225

DDyna Music

2008-present. Dan Simon builds his guitar effects pedals in Bothell, Washington.

Dean Markley

The string and pickup manufacturer offered a line of effects from 1976 to the early-'90s.

Overlord Classic Overdrive Model III
1990-1991. Battery-powered version of Overlord pedal. Black case with red letters.

1990-1991		$40	$70

Overlord Classic Tube Overdrive
1988-1991. Uses a 12AX7A tube, AC powered.

1988-1991		$60	$80

Voice Box 50 (Watt Model)

1976-1979		$75	$125

Voice Box 100 (Watt Model)
1976-1979, 1982-ca.1985.

1976-1979		$75	$125

Voice Box 200 (Watt Model)

1976-1979		$75	$125

DeArmond

In 1946, DeArmond may have introduced the first actual signal-processing effect pedal, the Tremolo Control. They made a variety of effects into the '70s, but only one caught on - their classic volume pedal. DeArmond is primarily noted for pickups.

MODEL YEAR	FEATURES	EXC. COND. LOW	HIGH

Pedal Phaser Model 1900
1974-ca.1979.

1974-1979		$75	$125

Square Wave Distortion Generator
1977-ca.1979.

1977-1979		$75	$150

Thunderbolt B166
1977-ca.1979. Five octave wah.

1977-1979		$50	$100

Tone/Volume Pedal 610
1978-ca.1979.

1978-1979		$75	$125

Tornado Phase Shifter
1977-ca.1979.

1977-1979		$100	$125

Tremolo Control Model 60A/60B
The Model 60 Tremolo Control dates from ca. 1946 to the early-1950s. Model 60A dates from mid- to late-'50s. Model 60B (plastic housing), early-'60s. Also labeled as the Trem-Trol or 601.

1950s	60A	$350	$570
1960s	60B	$175	$275
1960s	800 Trem-Trol	$100	$350

Twister 1930
1980. Phase shifter.

1980		$100	$125

Volume Pedal Model 602

1960s		$40	$70

Volume Pedal Model 1602
1978-ca. 1980s.

1970s		$40	$95

Volume Pedal Model 1630
1978-1980s. Optoelectric.

1970s		$35	$65

Weeper Wah Model 1802
1970s. Weeper logo on foot pedal.

1970s		$100	$125

Death By Audio

2001-present. Oliver Ackermann builds production and custom guitar effects in Brooklyn, New York.

Absolute Destruction

2000s-2021		$90	$140

Apocalyse

2000s-2021		$120	$200

Armageddon

2006		$150	$300

Crash Modulator

2005		$150	$300

Deep Animation

2000s-2021		$130	$200

Echo Dream 2

2000s-2021		$150	$230

Echo Master

2000s-2021		$150	$230

MODEL YEAR	FEATURES	EXC. COND. LOW	HIGH

Evil Filter

2000s-2021		$100	$220

Fuzz Fuzz Fuzz

2006		$150	$300

Fuzz War

2000s-2021		$100	$160

Interstellar Overdriver

2000s-2021		$90	$140

Interstellar Overdriver 2

2000s-2021		$140	$220

Micro Dream

2000s-2021		$90	$150

Micro Harmonic Transformer

2000s-2021		$90	$160

Overdriver Deluxe

2000s-2021		$150	$235

Reverberation Machine

2000s-2021		$150	$290

Robot

2000s-2021		$120	$220

Rooms

"Stereo Reverberator" pedal.

2000s-2021		$150	$330

Soundwave Breakdown

2000s-2021		$80	$125

Space Galaxy

Prototype pedal.

2009		$250	$500

Sunshine Reverberation

Designed in collaboration with Ty Seagall, limited edition of 100 pedals.

2013		$250	$500

Supersonic Fuzz Gun

2000s-2021		$100	$220

Time Shadows

Collaboration with EarthQuaker Devices, limited edition of 1,000 pedals.

2020		$200	$330

Total Sonic Annihilation

2000s-2021		$90	$140

Total Sonic Annihilation 2

2000s-2021		$100	$190

Waveform Destroyer

2000s-2021		$150	$210

DeltaLab Research

Late 1970s-early 1980s. DeltaLab, which was located in Chelmsford, Massachusetts, was an early builder of rackmount gear.

DL-2 Acousticomputer

1980s. Delay.

1980s		$75	$125

DL-4 Time Line

1980s. Delay.

1980s		$75	$125

DL-5

1980s. Various digital processing effects, blue case, rackmount.

1980s		$175	$225

DLB-1 Delay Control Pedal

1980s. Controls other DeltaLab pedals, chrome, Morley-looking pedal.

1980s		$50	$75

Electron I ADM/II ADM

1980s. Blue case, rackmount effects. Models include the Electron I ADM, and the Electron II ADM.

1980s	Electron I ADM	$50	$75
1980s	Electron II ADM	$75	$125

Demeter

1980-present. Amp builder James Demeter and company, located in Van Nuys, California, also build guitar effects.

Denio

Line of Japanese-made Boss lookalikes sold in Asia and Australia.

Devi Ever : Fx

2009-present. Devi Ever builds his guitar effects in Portland, Oregon. Prior to '09 he built the Effector 13 effects.

Diamond Pedals

2004-present. Designed by Michael Knappe and Tim Fifield, these effects are built in Bedford, Nova Scotia.

Diaz

Line of effects that Cesar Diaz introduced in the '80s. Diaz died in '02; in '04, his family announced plans to resume production.

Texas Ranger

1980s-2002. Treble booster. 2 control knobs. Variety of colorful housings.

1980s-2002		$400	$600

Texas Square Face

1980s-2002. Fuzz pedal. 2 control knobs. Variety of colorful housings.

1980s-2002		$500	$1,000

Tremodillo

1980s-2002. Tremolo pedal. 2 control knobs. Variety of colorful housings.

1980s-2002		$400	$800

DigiTech

The DigiTech/DOD company is in Utah and the effects are made in the U.S.A. The DigiTech name started as a line under the DOD brand in the early 1980s; later spinning off into its own brand. They also produce vocal products and studio processors and are now part of Harman International Industries.

Digital Delay and Sampler PDS 2000

1985-1991. 2 second delay.

1985-1991		$125	$175

Digital Delay PDS 1000

1985-ca.1989. One second delay.

1985-1989		$100	$150

Death By Audio Interstellar Overdriver

Demeter FZO-1

Diamond Pedals Boost-EQ BEQ1

DigiTech Whammy Pedal WP I
Jim Schreck

Divided By Thirteen Joyride

DLS Effects Tremolo

MODEL YEAR	FEATURES	EXC. COND. LOW	HIGH

Digital Delay PDS 2700 Double Play
1989-1991. Delay and chorus
1989-1991 $125 $175

Digital Stereo Chorus/Flanger PDS 1700
1986-1991 $100 $150

Echo Plus 8 Second Delay PDS 8000
1985-1991 $175 $200

Guitar Effects Processor RP 1
1992-1996. Floor unit, 150 presets.
1992-1996 $100 $150

Guitar Effects Processor RP 3
1998-2003. Floor unit.
1998-2003 $110 $150

Guitar Effects Processor RP 5
1994-1996. Floor unit, 80 presets.
1994-1996 $120 $175

Guitar Effects Processor RP 6
1996-1997. Floor unit.
1996-1997 $125 $200

Guitar Effects Processor RP 7
1996-1997. Floor unit.
1996-1997 $125 $175

Guitar Effects Processor RP 10
1994-1996. Floor unit, 200 presets.
1994-1996 $125 $175

Guitar Effects Processor RP 14D
1999. Floor unit with expression pedal, 1x12AX7 tube, 100 presets.
1999 $300 $350

Guitar Effects Processor RP 100
2000-2006 $100 $125

Guitar Effects Processor RP 200
2001-2006. 140 presets, drum machine, Expression pedal.
2001-2006 $100 $125

Hot Box PDS 2730
1989-1991. Delay and distortion
1989-1991 $100 $125

Modulator Pedal XP 200
1996-2002. Floor unit, 61 presets.
1996-2002 $100 $125

Multi Play PDS 20/20
1987-1991. Multi-function digital delay.
1987-1991 $125 $150

Pedalverb Digital Reverb Pedal PDS 3000
1987-1991 $100 $125

Programmable Distortion PDS 1550
1986-1991 Yellow case $50 $75

Programmable Distortion PDS 1650
1989-1991 Red case $50 $75

Rock Box PDS 2715
1989-1991. Chorus and distortion.
1989-1991 $50 $75

Two Second Digital Delay PDS 1002
1987-1991 $100 $125

Whammy Pedal Reissue
2000-present. Reissue version of classic WP-1 with added dive bomb and MIDI features.
2000-2020 $125 $140

Whammy Pedal WP I
1990-1993. Original Whammy Pedal, red case, reissued as WP IV in '00.
1990-1993 $375 $475

Whammy Pedal WP II
1994-1997. Can switch between 2 presets, black case.
1994-1997 $200 $275

DiMarzio

The pickup maker offered a couple of effects in the late-1980s to the mid-'90s.

Metal Pedal
1987-1989 $50 $75

Very Metal Fuzz
Ca.1989-1995. Distortion/overdrive pedal.
1989-1995 $50 $75

Dino's

A social co-op founded by Alessio Casati and Andy Bagnasco, in Albisola, Italy. It builds a line of boutique analog pedals as well as guitars.

Dinosaur

2004-2015. Guitar effects pedals imported by Eleca International. They also offered amps.

Divided By Thirteen

Mid-1990s-present. Fred Taccone builds his stomp box guitar effects in the Los Angeles, California area. He also builds amps.

DLS Effects

1999-present. Guitar effects pedals built by Dave Sestito in Fairport, New York.

DNA Analogic

Line of Japanese-built guitar effects distributed first by Godlyke, then Pedals Plus+ Effects Warehouse.

DOD

DOD Electronics started in Salt Lake City, Utah in 1974. Today, they're a major effects manufacturer with dozens of pedals made in the U.S. They also market effects under the name DigiTech and are now part of Harman International Industries.

6 Band Equalizer EQ601
1977-1982 $45 $65

AB Box 270
1978-1982 $25 $30

American Metal FX56
1985-1991 $40 $75

Analog Delay 680
1979-?
1979-1982 $120 $185

Attacker FX54
1992-1994. Distortion and compressor.
1992-1994 $35 $45

Bass Compressor FX82
1987-ca.1989.
1987-1989 $35 $45

MODEL YEAR	FEATURES	EXC. COND. LOW	HIGH
Bass EQ FX42B			
1987-1996		$35	$45
Bass Grunge FX92			
1995-1996		$70	$170
Bass Overdrive FX91			
	1998-2012. Yellow case.		
1998-2012		$35	$45
Bass Stereo Chorus Flanger FX72			
1987-1997		$45	$55
Bass Stereo Chorus FX62			
1987-1996		$45	$55
Bi-FET Preamp FX10			
1982-1996		$25	$35
Buzz Box FX33			
	1994-1996. Grunge distortion.		
1994-1996		$40	$60
Chorus 690			
	1980-ca.1982. Dual speed chorus.		
1980-1982		$70	$95
Classic Fuzz FX52			
1990-1997		$30	$60
Classic Tube FX53			
1990-1997		$40	$55
Compressor 280			
	1978-ca.1982.		
1978-1982		$40	$65
Compressor FX80			
1982-1985		$40	$50
Compressor Sustainer FX80B			
1986-1996		$40	$50
Death Metal FX86			
	1994-2009. Distortion.		
1994-2009		$50	$80
Delay FX90			
	1984-ca.1987.		
1984-1987		$70	$110
Digital Delay DFX9			
	1989-ca.1990.		
1989-1990		$55	$90
Digital Delay Sampler DFX94			
1995-1997		$70	$95
Distortion FX55			
	1982-1986. Red case.		
1982-1986		$30	$50
Edge Pedal FX87			
1988-1989		$20	$50
Envelope Filter 440			
1981-1982		$60	$70
Envelope Filter FX25			
	1982-1997. Replaced by FX25B		
1982-1997		$50	$80
Envelope Filter FX25B			
	1981-2013. Light aqua case.		
1998-2013		$40	$60
Equalizer FX40			
1982-1986		$35	$50
Equalizer FX40B			
	1987-2010. Eight bands for bass.		
1987-2010		$35	$50
Fet Preamp 210			
	1981-ca.1982.		
1981-1982		$35	$50
Flanger 670			
1981-1982		$70	$95
Gate Loop FX30			
1980s		$25	$35
Gonkulator			
1980s		$90	$130
Graphic Equalizer EQ-610			
	1980-ca.1982. Ten bands.		
1980-1982		$45	$60
Graphic Equalizer EQ-660			
	1980-ca.1982. Six bands.		
1980-1982		$35	$50
Grunge FX69			
	1993-2009. Distortion.		
1993-2009		$35	$65
Hard Rock Distortion FX57			
	1987-1994. With built-in delay.		
1987-1994		$35	$60
Harmonic Enhancer FX85			
	1986-ca.1989.		
1986-1989		$30	$50
I. T. FX100			
	1997. Intergrated Tube distortion, produces harmonics.		
1997		$45	$55
IceBox FX64			
	1996-2008. Chorus, high EQ.		
1996-2008		$40	$70
Juice Box FX51			
1996-1997		$25	$35
Master Switch 225			
	1988-ca.1989. A/B switch and loop selector.		
1988-1989		$25	$35
Meat Box FX32			
1994-1996		$65	$160
Metal Maniac FX58			
1990-1996		$35	$45
Metal Triple Play Guitar Effects System TR3M			
1994		$35	$45
Metal X FX70			
1993-1996		$35	$45
Milk Box FX84			
	1994-2012. Compressor/expander, white case.		
1994-2012		$60	$105
Mini-Chorus 460			
	1981-ca.1982.		
1981-1982		$45	$70
Mixer 240			
	1978-ca.1982.		
1978-1982		$20	$30
Momentary Footswitch			
	Introduced in 1987. Temporally engages other boxes.		
1980s		$20	$30
Mystic Blues Overdrive FX102			
	1998-2012. Medium gain overdrive, purple case.		
1998-2012		$20	$25

1981 DOD AB Box 270

Rivington Guitars

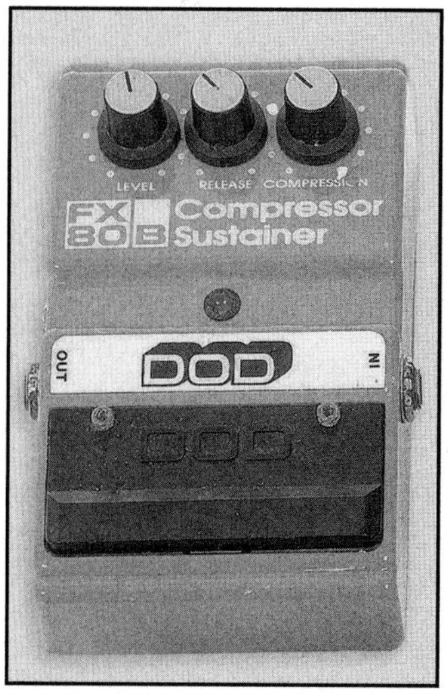

DOD Compressor Sustainer FX80B

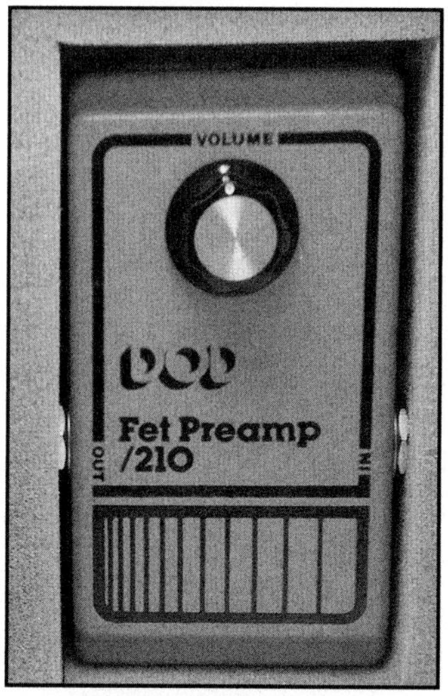

DOD Fet Preamp 210

Keith Myers

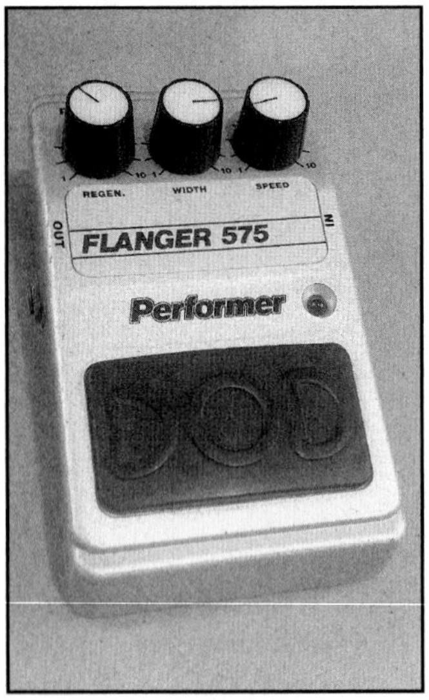

DOD Performer Flanger 575
Keith Myers

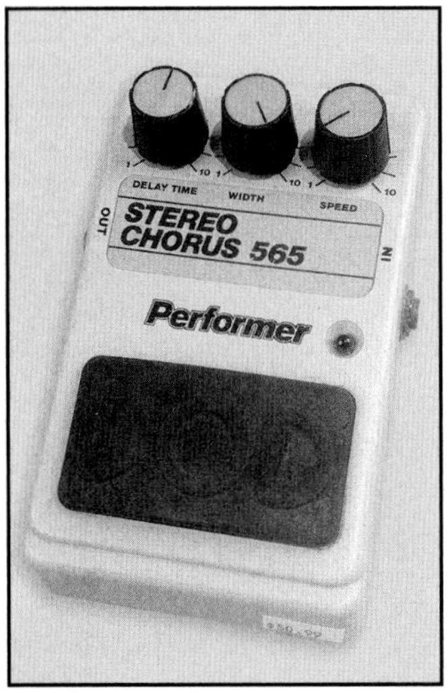

DOD Performer Stereo Chorus 565
Keith Myers

1981 DOD Phasor 201
Rivington Guitars

MODEL YEAR	FEATURES	EXC. COND. LOW	HIGH

Noise Gate 230
1978-1982 $25 $35

Noise Gate FX30
1982-ca.1987.
1982-1987 $25 $35

Octoplus FX35
1987-1996. Octaves.
1987-1996 $35 $55

Overdrive Plus FX50B
1986-1997 $30 $70

Overdrive Preamp 250
1978-1982, 1995-2020. Reissued in '95, yellow case.
1978-1982 $100 $220
1995-2020 $40 $70

Overdrive Preamp FX50
1982-1985 $30 $40

Performer Compressor Limiter 525
1981-1984 $50 $55

Performer Delay 585
1982-1985 $55 $70

Performer Distortion 555
1981-1984 $35 $45

Performer Flanger 575
1981-1985 $35 $45

Performer Phasor 595
1981-1984 $40 $50

Performer Stereo Chorus 565
1981-1985. FET switching.
1981-1985 $55 $70

Performer Wah Filter 545
1981-1984 $45 $70

Phasor 201
1981-ca.1982. Reissued in '95.
1981-1982 $65 $95

Phasor 401
1978-1981 $65 $95

Phasor 490
1980-ca.1982.
1980-1982 $65 $95

Phasor FX20
1982-1985 $35 $45

Psychoacoustic Processor FX87
1988-1989 $35 $45

Punkifier FX76
1997 $35 $45

Resistance Mixer 240
1978-ca.1982.
1978-1982 $25 $30

Silencer FX27
1988-ca.1989. Noise reducer.
1988-1989 $30 $40

Stereo Chorus FX60
1982-1986 $35 $45

Stereo Chorus FX65
1986-1996. Light blue case.
1986-1996 $35 $45

Stereo Flanger FX70
1982-ca.1985.
1982-1985 $35 $45

Stereo Flanger FX75
1986-1987. Silver case with blue trim.
1986-1987 $40 $50

Stereo Flanger FX75B
1987-1997 $40 $50

Stereo Phasor FX20B
1986-1999 $40 $50

Stereo Turbo Chorus FX67
1988-1991 $35 $45

Super American Metal FX56B
1992-1996 $30 $40

Super Stereo Chorus FX68
1992-1996 $35 $45

Supra Distortion FX55
1986-2012. Red case.
1986-2012 $25 $35

Thrash Master FX59
1990-1996 $25 $45

Vibrothang FX22
1990s $60 $95

Votec Vocal Effects Processor and Mic Preamp
1998-2001 $55 $60

Wah-Volume FX-17 (pedal)
1987-2000 $40 $55

Dredge-Tone

Located in Berkeley, California, Dredge-Tone offers effects and electronic kits.

DST Engineering

2001-2014. Jeff Swanson and Bob Dettorre built reverb units in Beverly, Massachusetts. They also built amps.

Dunlop

Jim Dunlop, USA offers the Crybaby, MXR (see MXR), Rockman, High Gain, Heil Sound (see Heil), Tremolo, Jimi Hendrix, Rotovibe, Uni-Vibe and Way Huge brand effects.

Cry Baby Bass
1985-present. Bass wah.
1985-2020 $75 $100

Cry Baby EVH Wah
1990s-2021 $100 $170

Cry Baby Multi-Wah 535/535Q
1995-present. Multi-range pedal with an external boost control.
1995-2020 $70 $90

Cry Baby Wah-Wah GCB-95
1982-present. Dunlop began manufacturing the Cry Baby in '82.
1982-1989 $45 $75
1990-1999 $40 $70
2000-2020 $35 $50

Fuzz Face Distortion JDF2
1993-present. Reissue of the classic Dallas Arbiter effect (see that listing for earlier versions).
1993-2020 Red, reissue $100 $165

High Gain Volume + Boost Pedal
1983-1996 $35 $45

MODEL YEAR	FEATURES	EXC. COND. LOW	HIGH

High Gain Volume Pedal GCB-80
1983-2010 $40 $50

Jimi Hendrix Fuzz JH-2 (Round)
1987-1993. Round face fuzz, JH-2S is the square box version.
1987-1993 $50 $75

Rotovibe JH-4S Standard
1989-1998. Standard is finished in bright red enamel with chrome top.
1989-1998 $100 $160

Tremolo Volume Plus TVP-1
1995-1998. Pedal.
1995-1998 $125 $140

Uni-Vibe UV-1
1995-2012. Rotating speaker effect.
1995-1999 $225 $350
2000-2012 $200 $225

Durham Electronics

2001-present. Alan Durham builds his line of guitar effects in Austin, Texas.

Dutch Kazoo

2013-present. Guitar effects pedals built in Parker Ford, Pennsylvania by Corinne Mandell.

Dynacord

1950-present. Dynacord is a German company that makes audio and pro sound amps, as well as other electronic equipment and is now owned by TELEX/EVI Audio (an U.S. company), which also owns the Electro-Voice brand. In the '60s they offered tape echo machines and guitars. In '94 a line of multi-effects processors were introduced under the Electro-Voice/Dynacord name, but by the following year they were just listed as Electro-Voice.

EchoCord
Introduced in 1959. Tape echo unit.
1959-1960s $275 $400

Dyno

See Dytronics.

Dytronics

Mid-1970s-early 1980s. The Japanese Dytronics company made a chorus rackmount unit for electric piano called the Dyno My Piano with flying piano keys or a lightning bolt on the front. Another version was called the Tri-Stereo Chorus and a third, called the Songbird, had a bird's head on the front.

E Bow

See Heet Sound Products.

E.W.S. (Engineering Work Store)

2007-present. Guitar effects pedals built in Tokyo, Japan for Prosound Communications in Van Nuys, California.

MODEL YEAR	FEATURES	EXC. COND. LOW	HIGH

EarthQuaker Devices

2005-present. Jamie Stillman started building Fuzz Face and Rangemaster clones for friends and in '07, he built a modified Big Muff for Dan Auerbach of the Black Keys, who he tour-managed at the time. After extensive revisions, this became the Hoof Fuzz and he began retailing his pedals.

Acapulco Gold
2015-present. Power amp distortion. Grandma Cyclops limited-edition version was made '16 in collaboration with visual artist and Devo co-founder Mark Mothersbaugh and the Akron Art Museum.
2015-2020 $60 $90
2016 Grandma Cyclops $75 $120

Afterneath
2014-present. Ambient reverb.
2014-2020 $100 $190

Amp Hammer II
2009 $50 $100

Arpanoid
2013-present. Polyphonic arpeggiator.
2013-2020 $140 $190

Arrows
2014-present. Preamp boost.
2014-2020 $45 $85

Avalanche Run
2016-present. Stereo reverb and delay.
2016-2020 $180 $225

Bellows
2016-2019. Fuzz driver.
2016-2019 $75 $100

Bit Commander
2011-present. Guitar synthesizer.
2011-2020 $75 $145

Black Eye
2007 $50 $100

Bows
2016-2019. Germanium preamp.
2016-2019 $75 $100

Chrysalis
2010 $50 $100

Cloven Hoof
2014-2020. Fuzz grinder.
2014-2020 $75 $115

Cloven Hoof Reaper
2015-2017. Fuzz.
2015-2017 $90 $140

Crimson Drive
2007 $50 $100

Dirt Transmitter
2008-2019. Fuzz driver.
2008-2019 $80 $100

Disaster Transport
2007. Delay pedal.
2007 $50 $150

Disaster Transport Jr.
2010 $50 $100

Disaster Transport SR
2013-present. Advanced modulation delay and reverb.
2013-2020 $225 $275

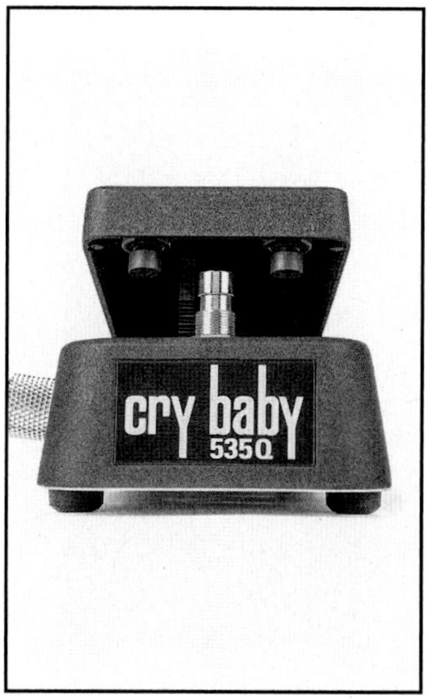

Dunlop Crybaby Multi-Wah 535Q

Durham Crazy Horse

EarthQuaker Devices Bellows

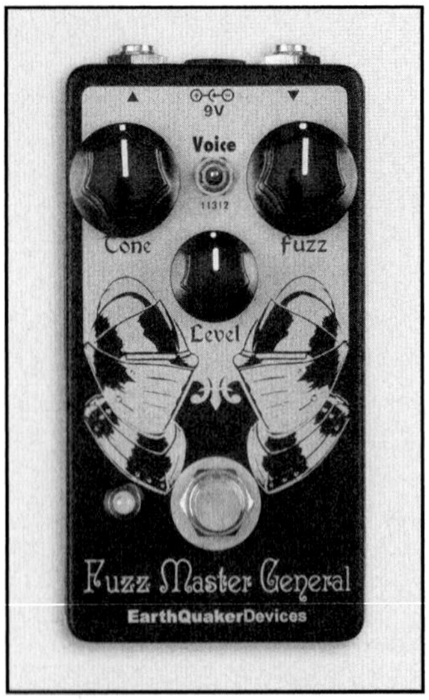

EarthQuaker Devices Fuzz Master General

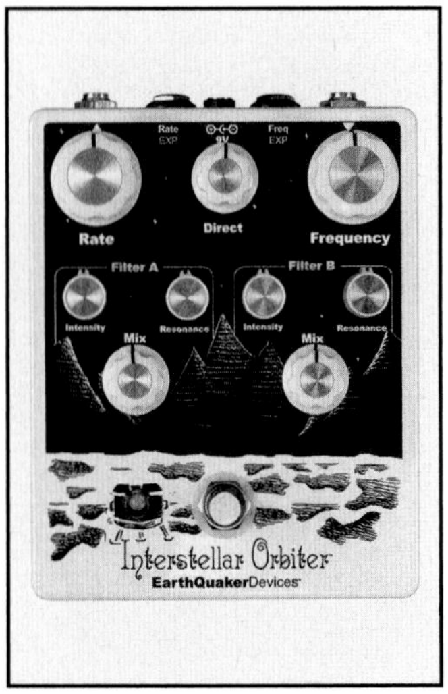

EarthQuaker Devices Interstellar Orbiter

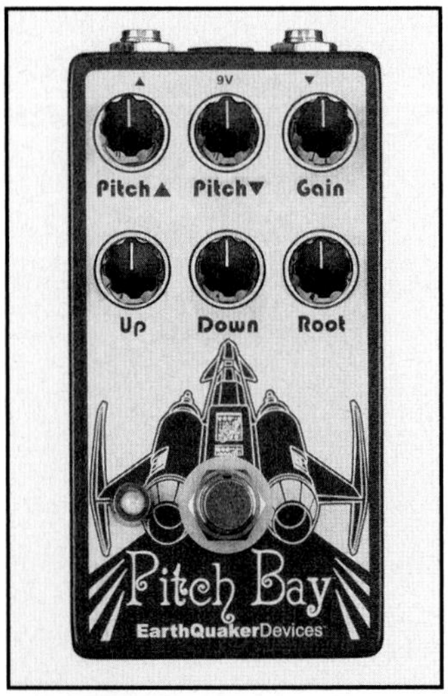

EarthQuaker Devices Pitch Bay

MODEL YEAR	FEATURES	EXC. COND. LOW	HIGH
Dispatch Master			
2011-present. Hi-fi digital delay and reverb.			
2011-2020		$80	$130
Dream Crusher			
2009		$50	$100
Dunes			
2015-2020. Mini mega overdrive.			
2015-2020		$80	$120
Erupter			
2017-present. Fuzz.			
2017-2020		$75	$100
Fuzz Master General			
2015-2019. Octave fuzz pedal.			
2015-2020		$80	$130
Ghost Disaster			
2010		$50	$100
Ghost Echo			
2009-present. Vintage-voiced reverb.			
2009-2020		$75	$140
Grand Orbiter			
2009-present. Phaser/vibrato.			
2009-2020		$90	$130
Gray Channel			
2016-2020. Dynamic dirt doubler.			
2016-2020		$90	$130
Hoof			
2007-present. Germanium/silicon hybrid fuzz.			
2007-2020		$90	$125
Hoof Reaper			
2012-present. Dual fuzz octave.			
2012-2020		$150	$200
Hummingbird			
2007-present. Repeat percussion/tremolo.			
2007-2020		$75	$110
Interstellar Orbiter			
2015-2020. Dual resonant filter built in collaboration with turntablist Kid Koala for his "Turntable Orchestra" tour. Features original artwork by Koala.			
2015-2020		$120	$180
Levitation			
2008-present. Psychedlic reverb.			
2008-2020		$80	$125
Monarch			
2010		$50	$120
Night Wire			
2016-present. Harmonic tremolo.			
2016-2020		$90	$130
Organizer			
2012-present. Polyphonic organ emulator.			
2012-2020		$90	$135
Palisades			
2014-present. Mega ultimate overdrive.			
2014-2020		$120	$190
Park Fuzz Sound			
2015-present. Reissue of the Park Amplification fuzz pedal built in cooperation with Park.			
2015-2020		$75	$120
Pitch Bay			
2014-2017. Dirty polyphonic harmonizer.			
2014-2017		$100	$180
Pulse Machine Tremolo			
2007		$50	$100
Rainbow Machine			
2011-present. Polyphonic pitch-shifting modulator.			
2011-2020		$120	$175
Royal Drive			
2007		$50	$100
Sea Machine			
2010-present. Chorus.			
2010-2020		$75	$120
Sound Shank			
2009		$50	$100
Space Spiral			
2017-present. Modulation delay.			
2017-2020		$75	$140
Spatial Delivery			
2016-present. Envelope filter with sample and hold functions.			
2016-2020		$75	$130
Spires			
2016-2019. Nü-Face double fuzz.			
2016-2019		$75	$130
Stealth Fuzz			
2007		$50	$100
Talons			
2012-2017. Hi-gain overdrive.			
2012-2017		$75	$100
Tentacle			
2015-present. Analog octave up. Grandpa Cyclops limited-edition version was made '16 in collaboration with visual artist and Devo co-founder Mark Mothersbaugh and the Akron Art Museum.			
2015-2020		$75	$100
2016	Grandpa Cyclops	$75	$120
Terminal			
2014-2019. Fuzz.			
2014-2019		$75	$110
The Depths			
2013-2017. Optical vibrato.			
2013-2017		$90	$140
The Grim Reefer			
2014-2017. Fuzz pedal.			
2014-2017		$75	$100
The Warden			
2013-present. Optical compression.			
2013-2020		$90	$140
Time Shadows			
Collaboration with EarthQuaker Devices, limited edition of 1,000 pedals.			
2020		$200	$330
Tone Job			
2012-present. EQ and boost.			
2012-2020		$75	$100
Tone Reaper			
2009		$50	$100
Transmisser			
2016-2019. Reverb.			
2016-2019		$125	$190
White Light			
2008		$150	$300

MODEL YEAR — FEATURES — EXC. COND. LOW — HIGH

Zap Machine

2010 $50 $100

Z-Drive

2015-2017. Overdrive built in collaboration with Dr. Z Amplification.

2015-2017 $175 $220

EBS

1992-present. Bass and guitar effects built in Stockholm, Sweden by the EBS Sweden AB company. They also build bass amps.

Ecco-Fonic

1959-1968. The Ecco-Fonic was designed by Ray Stolle and sold from his radio and TV repair shop in Los Angeles. Theis first Ecco Ecco-Fonic was distributed by Fender in 1958-'59. Stolle sold the company to E.S. "Eddie" Tubin in late 1959-'60, who sold the company in 1961 to Milton Brucker. Starting in 1963, Fender offered a solidstate Ecco-Fonic designed by new-owner Bob Marks and Russ Allee and labeled as the Fender Echo.

Model 109

1959-1960. Tube-driven tape-echo unit, 2 control knobs, revised to 3 knobs, 1-piece top, gold housing.

1959 Brown case $900 $1,500

Model 109-B

1960-1962. Tube-driven tape echo unit, 4 Control knobs, 2-piece top, gold housing.

1960-1962 Brown or black case $400 $1,250

Model 109-C

1961-1962. Tube-driven tape echo unit, multiple playback heads, black housing.

1961-1962 Black case $400 $1,000

Echoplex

The Echoplex tape echo unit was invented around 1959 in Akron, Ohio, by Don Dixon and Mike Battle, who originally produced it in small numbers. Production was soon moved to Market Electronics in Cleveland, and those units were sold under the Maestro brand (see listings under Maestro). After Maestro dropped the Echoplex, it was marketed under the Market Electronics name from the late-'70s to the late-'80s (see listing under Market Electronics for '80s models). In '94, Gibson's Oberheim division introduced a rackmount unit called the Echoplex. In '01, it was relabeled as Gibson.

Echoplex

1959. Dixon- and Battle-built pre-Maestro production tube-driven tape echo. Black case.

1959 $900 $1,200

EchoSonic

2010s. Ray Butts of EchoSonic amp fame crafted a pioneering fuzz circuit that never went into production. Tim Masters of Florida built a limited run of stompboxes with the circuitry.

Ray-O-Fuzz

2010s. Metal housings in various colors with logo surrounded by lightning bolts. Attack and Volume controls plus footswitch.

2010s $175 $250

Eden Analog

Guitar effects pedals built by Chris Sheppard and Robert Hafley in Pelham, Alabama, starting in 2004.

Effector 13

2002-2008. Guitar effects built by Devi Ever in Minneapolis, Minnesota. Located in Austin, Texas until mid-'04. Name changed to Devi Ever : Fx in '09.

Effectrode

1996-present. Effects pedals built in Corvallis, Oregon by Phil Taylor.

EFX

1980s. Brand name of the Los Angeles-based EFX Center; they also offered a direct box and a powered pedal box/board.

Switch Box B287

1984. Dual effects loop selector.

1984 $25 $35

EKO

1959-1985, 2000-present. In the '60s and '70s EKO offered effects made by EME and JEN Elettronica, which also made Vox effects.

Eleca

2004-present. Guitar effects pedals imported by Eleca International. They also offer guitars, mandolins and amps.

Electra

1970-1984, 2013-present. Guitar importer St. Louis Music offered Electra effects in the late '70s.

Chorus 504CH

Ca.1975-ca.1980.

1975-1980 $55 $75

Compressor 502C/602C

Ca.1975-ca.1980.

1975-1980 $45 $55

Distortion 500D

Ca.1976-ca.1980.

1976-1980 $55 $75

Flanger (stereo) 605F

Ca.1975-ca.1980.

1975-1980 $55 $75

Fuzz Wah

Ca.1975-ca.1980.

1975-1980 $75 $150

Pedal Drive 515AC

Ca.1976-ca.1980. Overdrive.

1976-1980 $40 $50

EarthQuaker Devices The Warden

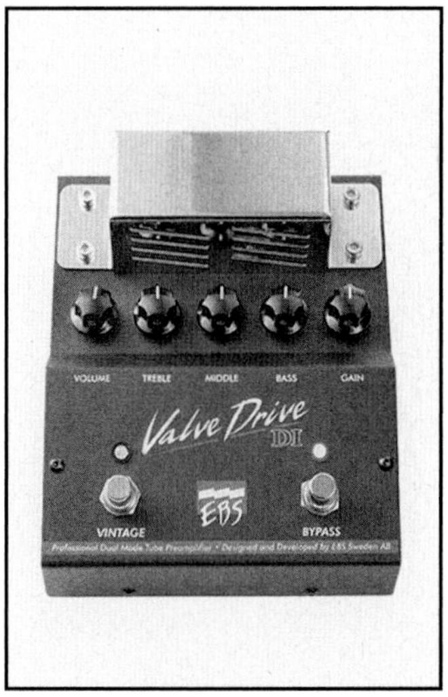

EBS ValveDrive DI

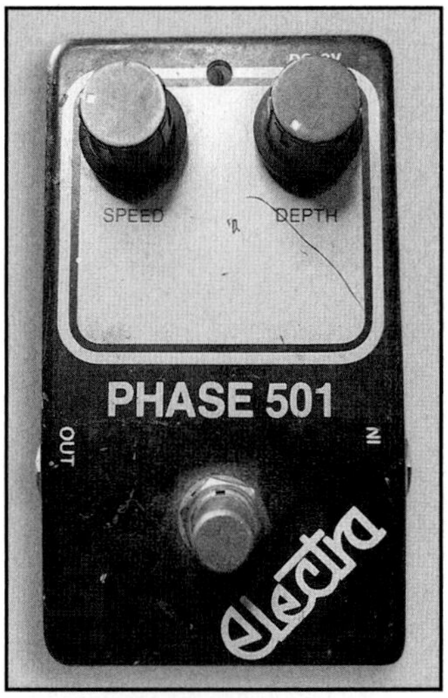

Electra Phase 501

Christopher Wright

Electro-Harmonix Attack/Decay
Jim Schreck

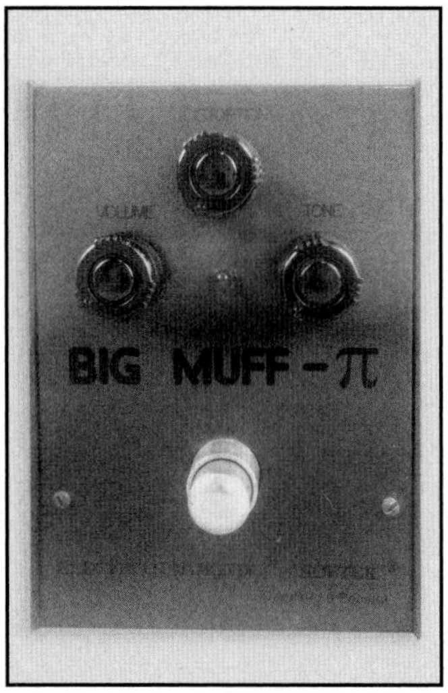

1970s E-H Big Muff Pi
Keith Myers

E-H Crying Tone
Jim Schreck

MODEL YEAR	FEATURES	EXC. COND. LOW	HIGH
Phaser Model 501P			
Ca.1976-ca.1980.			
1976-1980		$50	$60
Phaser Model 875			
Ca.1975-ca.1980.			
1975-1980		$50	$60
Roto Phase I			
1975-ca.1980. Small pocket phaser.			
1975-1980		$70	$85
Roto Phase II			
1975-ca.1980. Pedal phasor.			
1975-1980		$80	$95

Electro-Harmonix

1968-1984, 1996-present. Founded by Mike Matthews in New York City, the company initially produced small plug-in boosters such as the LPB-1. In '71, they unveiled the awe-inspiring Big Muff Pi fuzz and dozens of innovative pedals followed. After closing in '84, Matthews again began producing reissues of many of his classic effects as well as new designs in '96.

MODEL YEAR	FEATURES	EXC. COND. LOW	HIGH
10 Band Graphic Equalizer			
1977-1981. Includes footswitch.			
1977-1981		$60	$70
16-Second Digital Delay			
Early-1980s, 2004-2008. An updated version was reissued in '04.			
1980s	No foot controller	$500	$625
1980s	With foot controller	$675	$850
1990s		$325	$500
2004-2008		$275	$375
3 Phase Liner			
1981		$50	$60
5X Junction Mixer			
1977-1981		$30	$40
Attack Equalizer			
1975-1981. Active EQ, a.k.a. "Knock Out."			
1975-1981		$150	$200
Attack/Decay			
1980-1981. Tape reverse simulator.			
1980-1981		$200	$225
Axis			
1969-1970s. Modified Mosrite Fuzzrite circuit.			
1969-1970s		$200	$500
Bad Stone Phase Shifter			
1975-1981.			
1975-1981	Three knobs	$200	$250
1975-1981	Two knobs, color switch	$175	$225
Bass Micro-Synthesizer			
1981-1984, 1999-present. Analog synthesizer sounds.			
1981-1984		$225	$300
1999-2020		$150	$175
Bassballs			
1978-1984, 1998-present. Bass envelope filter/distortion.			
1978-1984		$200	$230
Big Muff Pi			
1971-1984. Sustain, floor unit, issued in 3 different looks, as described below.			
1970s	Black graphics, knobs in triangle pattern	$300	$475
1970s	Red/black graphics, 1/2" letters	$200	$425
1980s	Red/black graphics, 1" letters	$125	$275
Big Muff Pi (Reissue)			
1996-present. Originally made in Russia, but currently both Russian- and U.S.-made versions are available.			
1996-2020	Russian-made	$40	$65
Big Muff Sovtek			
2000s. Big Muff Pi, Electro Harmonix, and Sovtek logos on an olive green case. Sold in a wooden box.			
2000s	With wooden box	$150	$300
Black Finger Compressor Sustainer			
1977, 2003-2019. Original has 3 knobs in triangle pattern.			
1977		$125	$400
2003-2019		$75	$150
Clap Track			
1980-1984. Drum effect.			
1980-1984		$40	$60
Clone Theory			
1977-1981. Chorus effect, The Clone Theory logo.			
1977-1981		$150	$175
Crash Pad			
1980-1984. Percussion synth.			
1980-1984		$40	$60
Crying Tone Pedal			
1976-1978. Wah-wah.			
1976-1978		$175	$225
Deluxe Big Muff Pi			
1978-1981. Sustain, AC version of Big Muff Pi, includes a complete Soul Preacher unit.			
1978-1981	Red graphics	$125	$200
Deluxe Electric Mistress Flanger			
1977-1983, 1996-present. AC.			
1977-1979		$150	$250
1980-1983		$125	$175
Deluxe Memory Man			
1977-1983, 1996-present. Echo and delay, featured 4 knobs '77-'78, from '79-'83 it has 5 knobs and added vibrato and chorus.			
1977-1978	4 knobs	$250	$520
1979-1983	5 knobs	$200	$350
1996-2020		$150	$165
Deluxe Octave Multiplexer			
1977-1981		$200	$250
Digital Delay/Chorus			
1981-1984. With digital chorus.			
1981-1984		$250	$300
Digital Rhythm Matrix DRM-15			
1981-1984		$225	$250
Digital Rhythm Matrix DRM-16			
1979-1983		$225	$250
Digital Rhythm Matrix DRM-32			
1981-1984		$225	$250

MODEL YEAR — FEATURES — EXC. COND. LOW — HIGH

Doctor Q Envelope Follower
1976-1983, 2001-2020. For bass or guitar.
1976-1983 $100 $220
2001-2020 $30 $60

Domino Theory
1981. Sound sensitive light tube.
1981 $50 $100

Echo 600
1981 $175 $225

Echoflanger
1977-1982. Flange, slapback, chorus, filter.
1977-1982 $200 $250

Electric Mistress Flanger
1976-1979 $275 $475
1980-1984 $175 $240

Electronic Metronome
1978-1980 $25 $30

Frequency Analyzer
1977-1984, 2001-present. Ring modulator.
1977-1984 $200 $250

Full Double Tracking Effect
1978-1981. Doubling, slapback.
1978-1981 $100 $150

Fuzz Wah
Introduced around 1974.
1970s $175 $225

Golden Throat
1977-1984 $500 $800

Golden Throat Deluxe
1977-1979. Deluxe has a built-in monitor amp.
1977-1979 $600 $800

Golden Throat II
1978-1981 $150 $300

Guitar Synthesizer
1981. Sold for $1,495 in May '81.
1981 $225 $300

Hog's Foot Bass Booster
1977-1980 $70 $90

Holy Grail
2002-present. Digital reverb.
2002-2020 $75 $90

Hot Foot
1977-1978. Rocker pedal turns knob of other E-H effects, gold case, red graphics.
1977-1978 $100 $200

Hot Tubes
1978-1984, 2001-2007. Tube distortion.
1978-1984 $125 $200

Linear Power Booster LPB-1
1968-1983.
1976-1979 $55 $80
1980-1983 $45 $75

Linear Power Booster LPB-2
Ca.1968-1983.
1968-1983 $90 $100

Little Big Muff Pi
1976-1980, 2006-present. Sustain, 1-knob floor unit.
1976-1980 $140 $175
2006-2020 $90 $125

MODEL YEAR — FEATURES — EXC. COND. LOW — HIGH

Little Muff Pi
1971-1975. Sustain, 1-knob floor unit, issued in 2 styles; blue or red graphics.
1971-1975 $250 $360

Memory Man/Stereo Memory Man
1976-1984, 1999-present. Analog delay, newer version in stereo.
1976-1979 $200 $275
1980-1984 $125 $155

Micro Synthesizer
1978-1984, 1998-present. Mini keyboard phaser.
1978-1979 $225 $250
1978-1984 $225 $250
1998-2020 $150 $170

Mini Q-Tron/Micro Q-Tron
2002-present. Battery-operated smaller version of Q-Tron envelope follower, changed to identical effect in smaller box Micro in '06.
2002-2020 $40 $45

Mini-Mixer
1978-1981. Mini mic mixer, reissued in '01.
1978-1981 $30 $40

MiniSynthesizer
1981-1983. Mini keyboard with phaser.
1981-1983 $300 $400

MiniSynthesizer With Echo
1981 $375 $500

Mole Bass Booster
1968-1978.
1968-1969 $60 $80
1970-1978 $40 $60

Muff Fuzz
1976-1983. Fuzz and line boost, silver case with orange lettering.
41976-1983 $85 $100

Muff Fuzz Crying Tone
1977-1978. Fuzz, wah.
1977-1978 $150 $250

Octave Multiplexer Floor Unit
1976-1980 $175 $275

Octave Multiplexer Pedal
1976-1977, 2001-present.
1976-1977 $150 $250
2001-2020 $40 $45

Panic Button
1981. Siren sounds for drum.
1981 $30 $40

Poly Chorus/Stereo Polychorus
1981, 1999-present. Same as Echoflanger.
1981 $175 $300
1999-2020 $125 $150

Polyphase
1979-1981. With envelope.
1979-1981 $175 $225

Pulsar/Stereo Pulsar
2004-present. Variable wave form tremolo.
2004-2020 $45 $55

Pulse Modulator
Ca.1968 -ca.1972. Triple tremolo.
1968-1969 $250 $325
1970-1972 $200 $250

E-H Digital Rhythm Matrix DRM-15
Jim Schreck

1978 E-H Linear Power Booster LPB-2
Rivington Guitars

E-H Muff Fuzz
Keith Myers

EFFECTS

E-H Small Clone

E-H Soul Preacher

Jim Schreck

E-H Volume Pedal

Jim Schreck

MODEL YEAR	FEATURES	EXC. COND. LOW	HIGH

Q-Tron

1997-2017. Envelope controlled filter.

1997-2017		$125	$175

Q-Tron +

1999-present. With added effects loop and Attack Response switch.

1999-2020		$70	$80

Queen Triggered Wah

1976-1978. Wah/Envelope Filter.

1976-1978		$125	$150

Random Tone Generator RTG

1981		$40	$60

Rhythm 12 (Rhythm Machine)

1978		$75	$125

Rolling Thunder

1980-1981. Percussion synth.

1980-1981		$40	$50

Screaming Bird Treble Booster

Ca.1968-1980. In-line unit.

1968-1980		$75	$100

Screaming Tree Treble Booster

1977-1981. Floor unit.

1977-1981		$100	$150

Sequencer Drum

1981. Drum effect.

1981		$40	$50

Slapback Echo

1977-1978. Stereo.

1977-1978		$150	$200

Small Clone

1983-1984, 1999-present. Analog chorus, depth and rate controls, purple face plate, white logo.

1983-1984		$150	$200
1999-2020		$35	$40

Small Stone Phase Shifter

1975-1984, 1996-present. Both Russian and U.S. reissues were made.

1975-1979		$150	$225
1980-1984		$100	$175

Solid State Reverb

1980s. Input, output, blend and feedback controls.

1980s		$250	$500

Soul Food

2000s		$45	$65
2000s	JHS modded	$110	$160

Soul Preacher

1977-1983, 2007-present. Compressor sustainer. Nano version for present.

1977-1983		$100	$150

Space Drum/Super Space Drum

1980-1981. Percussion synthesizer.

1980-1981		$125	$175

Switch Blade

1977-1983. A-B Box.

1977-1983		$45	$55

Talking Pedal

1977-1978. Creates vowel sounds.

1977-1978		$350	$550

The Silencer

1976-1981. Noise elimination.

1976-1981		$60	$80

Tube Zipper

2001-2018. Tube (2x12AX7) envelope follower.

2001-2018		$100	$120

Vocoder

1978-1981. Modulates voice with instrument.

1978-1981	Rackmount	$425	$525

Volume Pedal

1978-1981		$45	$65

Wiggler

2002-2019. All-tube modulator including pitch vibrato and volume tremolo.

2002-2019		$100	$110

Worm

2002-present. Wah/Phaser.

2002-2020		$55	$65

Y-Triggered Filter

1976-1977		$140	$160

Zipper Envelope Follower

1976-1978. The Tube Zipper was introduced in '01.

1976-1978		$200	$300

Electrosonic Amplifiers

2002-2010. Amp builder Josh Corn also offers a preamp pedal, built in Boonville, Indiana.

Elektronika

1980s-1990s. Russian effects pedals by the Soviet Ministry of Electronic Industry.

Compressor-Sustainer

1980s		$50	$175

Equalizer E-02

1980s		$50	$125

Fazer-2

1980s		$50	$125

Flanger FL-01

1980s		$50	$90

Flanger PE-05

1980s		$50	$125

Jet-Phaser

1980s		$150	$225

Synchro-Wah

1980s		$50	$100

Volna

1980s. Auto wah.

1980s		$50	$100

Elk Gakki

Late-1960s. Japanese company Elk Gakki Co., Ltd. mainly made guitars and amps, but did offer effects as well.

Big Muff Sustainer

1970s. Electro-Harmonix Big Muff Pi copy.

1970s		$50	$125

Elka

In the late '60s or early '70s, Italian organ and synthesizer company Elka-Orla (later just Elka) offered a few effects, likely made by JEN Elettronica (Vox, others).

MODEL YEAR	FEATURES	EXC. COND. LOW	HIGH

EMMA Electronic

Line of guitar effects built in Denmark and distributed by Godlyke.

ReezaFRATzitz RF-1/ReezaFRATzitz II

2004-present. Overdrive and distortion, red case.

2004-2020		$80	$95

Empress Effects

2005-present. Guitar effects pedals built by Steve Bragg and Jason Fee in Ottawa, Ontario.

EMS

1969-1979. Peter Zinnovieff's English synth company (Electronic Music Studios) also offered a guitar synthesizer. The company has reopened to work on original EMS gear.

eowave

2002-present. Effects built first in Paris and now in Burgundy, France by Marc Sirguy.

Epiphone

Over the years, Epiphone offered a variety of different effect lines. Epiphone pedals which are labeled G.A.S Guitar Audio System were offered from around 1988 to '91.

Pedals

Various models with years available.

1988-1989	Chorus EP-CH-70	$35	$45
1988-1989	Delay EP-DE-80	$45	$60
1988-1991	Compressor EP-CO-20	$35	$40
1988-1991	Distortion EP-DI-10	$35	$45
1988-1991	Flanger EP-FL-60	$40	$55
1988-1991	Overdrive EP-OD-30	$35	$45

Rocco Tonexpressor

1937. Designed by steel-guitar ace Anthony Rocco, this pedal allows steel guitarists to adjust volume and tone with their foot.

1937		$300	$500

Ernie Ball

1972-present. The Ernie Ball company also builds Music Man instruments.

Volume Pedals

1977-present. Aluminum housing.

1977-2020		$35	$75

Euthymia Electronics

Line of guitar effects built by Erik Miller in Alameda, California.

Eventide

1971-present. This New Jersey electronics manufacturer has offered studio and rackmount effects since the late '70s. In '08 they added guitar effects pedals.

EXR

The EXR Corporation was located in Brighton, Michigan.

MODEL YEAR	FEATURES	EXC. COND. LOW	HIGH

Projector

1983-ca.1984. Psychoacoustic enhancer pedal.

1983-1984		$65	$75

Projector SP III

1983-ca.1984. Psychoacoustic enhancer pedal, volume pedal/sound boost.

1983-1984		$65	$70

Farfisa

The organ company offered effects pedals in the 1960s. Their products were manufactured in Italy by the Italian Accordion Company and distributed by Chicago Musical Instruments.

Model VIP 345 Organ

Mid-1960s. Portable organ with Syntheslalom used in the rock and roll venue.

1960s		$500	$600

Repeater

1969		$100	$150

Sferasound

1960s. Vibrato pedal for a Farfisa Organ but it works well with the guitar, gray case.

1960s		$275	$375

Wah/Volume

1969		$100	$150

Fargen

1999-present. Guitar effects built in Sacramento, California by Benjamin Fargen. He also builds amps.

Fender

1946-present. Although Fender has flirted with effects since the 1950s (the volume/volume-tone pedal and the Ecco-Fonic), the company concentrated mainly on guitars and amps. Fender effects ranged from the sublime to the ridiculous, from the tube Reverb to the Dimension IV. In 2013 Fender added a line of pedals.

'63 Tube Reverb

1994-2017. Reissue spring/tube Reverb Units with various era cosmetics as listed below.Currently offered in brown or, since '09, in lacquered tweed.

1994	White (limited run)	$400	$600
1994-1997	Black	$350	$400
1994-1997	Blond	$375	$600
1994-1997	Tweed	$375	$450
1994-2008	Brown	$350	$500
2009-2017	Lacquered Tweed	$300	$375

Blender

1968-1977, 2005-2010. Battery-operated unit with fuzz, sustain, and octave controls.

1968-1969		$290	$410
1970-1977		$275	$350
2005-2010	Reissue	$125	$175

Contempo Organ

1967-1968. Portable organ, all solidstate, 61 keys including a 17-key bass section, catalog shows with red cover material.

1967-1968		$525	$550

1977 E-H Zipper

Rivington Guitars

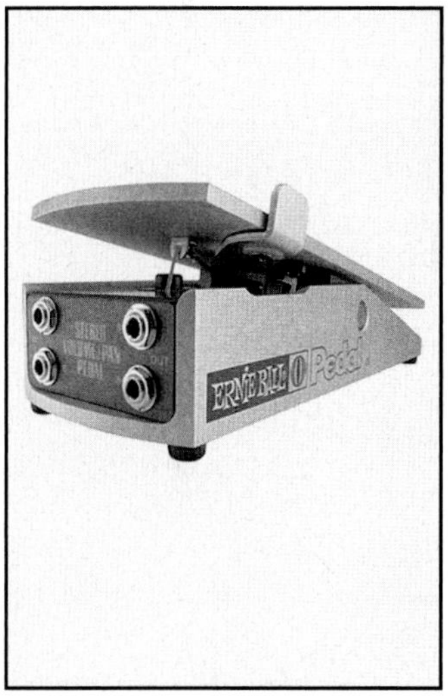

Ernie Ball 500K Stereo Volume/Pan

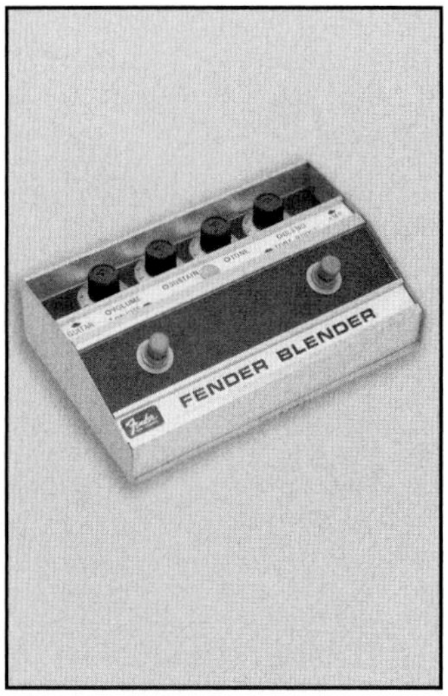

Fender Blender

Wade Jones

EFFECTS

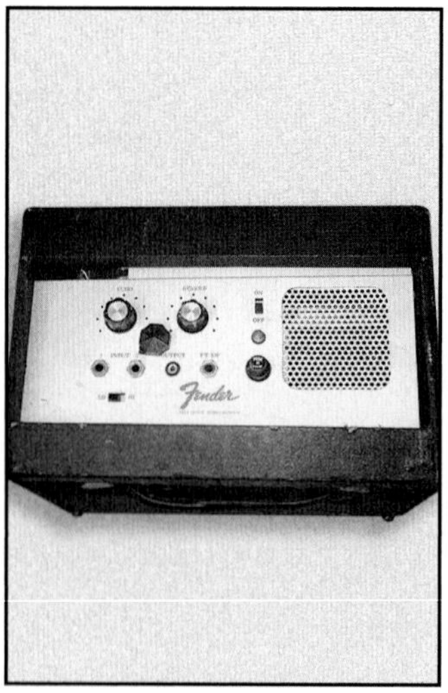

Fender Electronic Echo Chamber

1962 Fender Reverb Unit

Michael Alonz

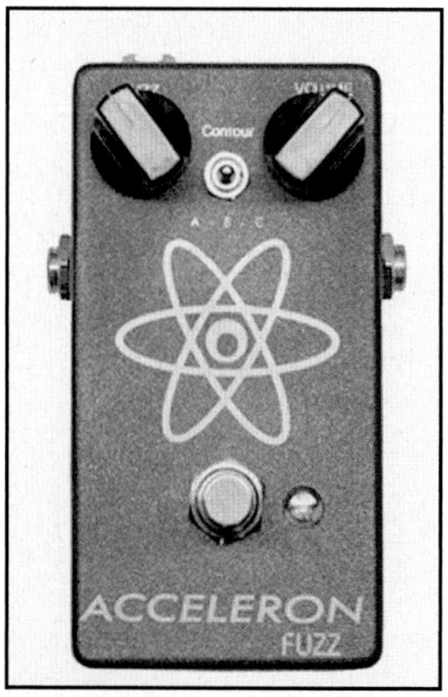

Field Effects Acceleron Fuzz

EFFECTS

Dimension IV

1968-1970. Multi-effects unit using an oil-filled drum.

MODEL YEAR	FEATURES	EXC. COND. LOW	HIGH
1968-1970		$195	$300

Echo and Electronic Echo Chamber

1963-1968. Solidstate tape echo built by Ecco-Fonic, up to 400 ms of delay, rectangle box with 2 controls '63-'67, slanted front '67-'68.

MODEL YEAR	FEATURES	EXC. COND. LOW	HIGH
1963-1967		$300	$500
1967-1968		$225	$350

Echo-Reverb

1966-1970. Solidstate, echo-reverb effect produced by rotating metal disk, black tolex, silver grille.

MODEL YEAR	FEATURES	EXC. COND. LOW	HIGH
1966-1970		$300	$350

Fuzz-Wah

1968-1984, 2007-2011. Has Fuzz and Wah switches on sides of pedal '68-'73, has 3 switches above the pedal '74-'84. Newer version ('07-'11) has switches on sides.

MODEL YEAR	FEATURES	EXC. COND. LOW	HIGH
1968-1973	Switches on side	$150	$225
1974-1984	Switches above	$100	$200
2007-2011	Switches on side	$80	$90

Phaser

1975-1977, 2007-2011. AC powered, reissued in '07.

MODEL YEAR	FEATURES	EXC. COND. LOW	HIGH
1975-1977		$95	$175
2007-2011		$50	$80

Reverb Unit

1961-1966, 1975-1978. Fender used a wide variety of tolex coverings in the early-'60s as the coverings matched those on the amps. Initially, Fender used rough blond tolex, then rough brown tolex, followed by smooth white or black tolex.

MODEL YEAR	FEATURES	EXC. COND. LOW	HIGH
1961	Blond tolex, Oxblood grille	$1,000	$1,400
1961	Brown tolex	$1,000	$1,200
1962	Blond tolex, Oxblood grille	$1,000	$1,250
1962	Brown tolex, Wheat grille	$800	$1,100
1963	Brown tolex	$800	$1,100
1963	Rough blond tolex	$800	$1,200
1963	Smooth white tolex	$800	$1,200
1964	Black tolex	$800	$1,200
1964	Brown tolex, gold grille	$800	$1,100
1964	Smooth white tolex	$800	$1,100
1965-1966	Black tolex	$775	$1,000
1966	Solidstate, flat cabinet	$150	$225
1975-1978	Tube reverb reinstated	$500	$600

Vibratone

1967-1972. Fender's parent company at the time, CBS, bought Leslie in 1965, and Fender began offering a Leslie-type rotating-speaker-emulator as the Vibratone in 1967. Based on the Leslie Model 16 cabinet and made specifically for the guitar, it featured a single fixed 4-ohm 10-inch speaker fronted by a rotating drum. Designed to be powered by an external amp. 2-speed motor. Black tolex.

MODEL YEAR	FEATURES	EXC. COND. LOW	HIGH
1967-1968	Fender cast logo in upper left corner	$600	$850
1968-1972	Fender logo plate through center	$500	$850

Volume-Tone Pedal

1954-1984, 2007-2018. Swivel foot controller.

MODEL YEAR	FEATURES	EXC. COND. LOW	HIGH
1954-1984		$90	$100
2007-2018		$35	$40

Fernandes

1970s. Japanese guitar and effects maker.

Funky-Filter FR-3F

1970s. Built by Univox for Fernandes.

MODEL YEAR	FEATURES	EXC. COND. LOW	HIGH
1970s		$50	$100

Field Effects by Resonant Electronic Design

2010-present. Guitar effects pedals built in Minneapolis, Minnesota by Wes Kuhnley and Peter Bregman. They also build the Resonant brand amps.

Fishman

2003-present. Larry Fishman of Andover, Massachusetts offers a line of acoustic guitar effects pedals. He also builds amps.

FJA Mods

In 2002, Jerry Pinnelli began building guitar effects in Central Square, New York. He added professional grade, production, guitar amps in '07, then relocates to Charlotte, North Carolina in '18 and takes a hiatus from building.

FlexiSound

FlexiSound products were made in Lancaster, Pennsylvania.

F. S. Clipper

1975-ca.1976. Distortion, plugged directly into guitar jack.

MODEL YEAR	FEATURES	EXC. COND. LOW	HIGH
1975-1976		$55	$65

The Beefer

1975. Power booster, plugged directly into guitar jack.

MODEL YEAR	FEATURES	EXC. COND. LOW	HIGH
1975		$40	$50

Flip

Line of tube effects by Guyatone and distributed in the U.S. by Godlyke Distributing.

Tube Echo (TD-X)

2004-2017. Hybrid tube power delay pedal.

MODEL YEAR	FEATURES	EXC. COND. LOW	HIGH
2004-2017		$90	$100

FM Acoustics

FM Acoustics pedals were made in Switzerland.

E-1 Pedal

1975. Volume, distortion, filter pedal.

MODEL YEAR	FEATURES	EXC. COND. LOW	HIGH
1975		$70	$80

Foxx

Foxx pedals are readily identifiable by their fur-like covering. They slunk onto the scene in 1971 and were extinct by '78. Made by Hollywood's Ridinger Associates, their most notable product was the Tone Machine fuzz. Foxx-made pedals also have appeared under various brands such as G &

MODEL YEAR	FEATURES	EXC. COND. LOW	HIGH

G, Guild, Yamaha and Sears Roebuck, generally without fur. Since 2005, reissues of some of the classic Foxx pedals are being built in Provo, Utah.

Clean Machine

1974-1978 $250 $275

Down Machine

1971-1977. Bass wah.

1971-1977 Blue case $225 $275

Foot Phaser

1975-1977, 2006-present.

1975-1977 $450 $675

Fuzz and Wa and Volume

1974-1978, 2006-present. Currently called Fuzz Wah Volume.

1974-1978 $225 $400

Guitar Synthesizer I

1975 $300 $350

Loud Machine

1970s. Volume pedal.

1970s $30 $45

O.D. Machine

1972-ca.1975.

1972-1975 $150 $250

Phase III

1975-1978 $100 $150

Tone Machine

1971-1978, 2005-present. Fuzz with Octave, blue or black housing.

1971-1978 $250 $540

Wa and Volume

1971-1978 $200 $225

Wa Machine

1971-ca.1978.

1971-1978 $150 $200

Framptone

2000-present. Founded by Peter Frampton, Framptone offers hand-made guitar effects.

3 Banger

2000-present. Three-way amp switch box, white housing.

2000-2020 $200 $240

Amp Switcher

2000-present. A-B switch box, white housing.

2000-2020 $80 $100

Talk Box

2000-present. Talk box, white housing, no control knobs, on-off footswitch.

2000-2020 $160 $250

Frantone

1994-present. Effects and accessories hand built in New York City.

Fulltone

1991-present. Effects based on some of the classics of the past and built in Los Angeles, California, by Michael Fuller.

DejàVibe

1991-2004. Uni-Vibe-type pedal, later models have a Vintage/Modern switch. Stereo version also available.

MODEL YEAR	FEATURES	EXC. COND. LOW	HIGH

1991-1993 Mono, gold housing $175 $225

1993-2004 Mono, black housing $150 $175

DejàVibe 2

1997-2018. Like DejàVibe but with built-in speed control. Stereo version also available.

1997-2018 Mono $200 $225

Distortion Pro

2002-2008. Red case, volume and distortion knobs with four voicing controls.

2002-2008 $125 $150

Fat Boost

2001-2007. Clean boost, silver-sparkle case, volume and drive knobs.

2001-2007 $125 $135

Full-Drive 2

1995-present. Blue case, four control knobs.

1995-2020 $120 $145

Mini-DejàVibe

2004-2018. Uni-Vibe-type pedal, white housing, 3 Control knobs, stereo version also available.

2004-2018 Mono $125 $150

OCD

1990s-present. Obsessive compulsive drive.

1990s-2020 $90 $110

Octafuzz

1996-2019. Copy of the Tycobrahe Octavia.

1996-2019 $100 $135

Soul Bender

1994-present. Volume, tone and dirt knobs.

1994-2020 $100 $125

Supa-Trem

1996-2019. Black case, white Supa-Trem logo, rate and mix controls.

1996-2019 $100 $150

Supa-Trem2

2000s. Yellow housing, 3 control knobs.

2000s $150 $200

Tube Tape Echo

2000s. Echo-Plex-style echo unit, white case.

2000s $675 $800

Tube Tape Echo TTE

2004-present. Echoplex-style tube-powered tape unit, different colored housings.

2004-2020 $725 $1,000

Furman Sound

1993-present. Located in Petaluma, California, Furman makes audio and video signal processors and AC power conditioning products for music and other markets.

LC-2 Limiter Compressor

1990s. Rackmount unit with a black suitcase and red knobs.

1990s $40 $50

PQ3 Parametric EQ

1990s. Rackmount preamp and equalizer.

1998-1999 $110 $150

PQ6 Parametric Stereo

1990s $135 $175

RV1 Reverb Rackmount

1990s $110 $150

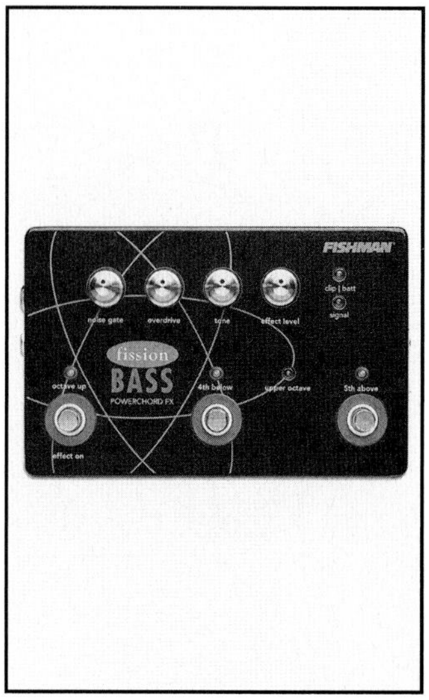

Fishman Fission Bass Powerchord

Foxx O.D. Machine

Rich Kislia

Fulltone Supa-Trem ST-1

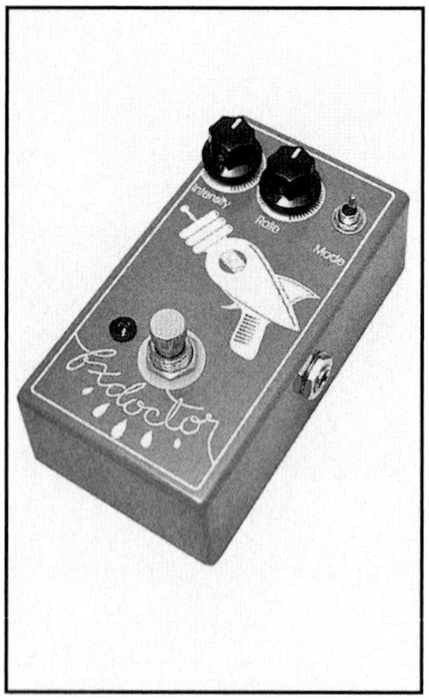

Fxdoctor Ray Gun Phaser

George Dennis Elite Wah

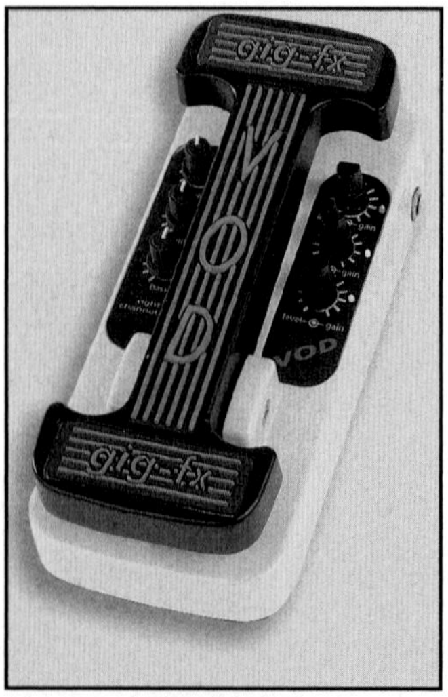

Gig-FX VOD

MODEL YEAR	FEATURES	EXC. COND. LOW	HIGH

Fxdoctor

2003-present. Joshua Zalegowski originally built his effects in Amherst, Massachusetts, and in 2005 moved to Boston.

Fxengineering

2002-present. Production and custom guitar effects built by Montez Aldridge in Raleigh, North Carolina.

G.M. Electronics

1960s. Based in Detroit, Michigan.

Dual Range Fuzz Up FD3-A

1960s. Fuzz pedal combining 2 Gibson Maestro FZ-1 Fuzz Tone circuits.

1960s $100 $300

Fuzz Up FM3-B

1960s. Clone of the Gibson Maestro FZ-1 Fuzz Tone.

1960s $100 $250

G.S. Wyllie

2000s. Glenn Wyllie built effects in North Carolina.

Moonrock

2000s. Octave fuzz.

2000s $200 $400

NewMoon

2000s. Updated version of Moonrock octave fuzz.

2000s $200 $400

Ozo

2000s. Ring modulator.

2000s $200 $400

X-Fuzz

2000s. High-gain fuzz.

2000s $200 $400

G2D

1999-present. David Manning and Grant Wills build their guitar effects pedals in Auckland, New Zealand.

Garcia

Guitar effects built by Matthew Garcia in Myrtle Beach, South Carolina, starting in 2004. He also built amps.

Geek MacDaddy

See listing under The Original Geek.

George Dennis

1991-present. Founded by George Burgerstein, original products were a line of effects pedals. In '96 they added a line of tube amps. The company is located in Prague, Czech Republic.

Gibson

Gibson did offer a few effects bearing their own name, but most were sold under the Maestro name (see that listing).

Echoplex Digital Pro Plus

1994-2010. Rackmount unit with digital recording, sampling and digital delay. Labeled as just Echoplex until '01 when Gibson name added.

1994-2010 $425 $650

GA-3RV Reverb Unit

1964-1967. Small, compact, spring reverb unit, black tolex, gray grille.

1964-1967 $325 $400

GA-4RE Reverb-Echo Unit

1964-1967. Small, compact, lightweight accessory reverb-echo unit that produces complete reverberation and authentic echo, utilizes Gibson's "electronic memory" system for both reverb and echo, black tolex, gray grille.

1964-1967 $375 $550

Gig-FX

2004-present. Founder Jeff Purchon of Waltham, Massachusetts, imports guitar effects pedals built at his company-owned factory in Shenzhen, China.

Gizmo, Inc.

Ca.1980. Short-lived company that grew out of the ashes of Musitronics' attempt to make the Gizomotron. See Mu-Tron.

Gizmoaudio

2009-present. Guitar effects built by Charles Luke in Cumming, Georgia.

Gnome Amplifiers

2008-present. Guitar effects pedals built by Dan Munro in Olympia, Washington. He also builds amps.

Godbout

Godbout sold a variety of effects do-it-yourself kits in the 1970s, which are difficult to value because quality depends on skills of builder.

Effects Kits

1970s $20 $30

Godley Crème

1978-1980. Kevin Godley and Lol Crème, members of the band 10cc, developed the Gizmotron, which mounted on the face of a bass or guitar and continously strummed the strings to give a bowed-string effect. The device was built by Musitronics of New Jersey, which built the MuTron III and other effects.

Gizmotron

1978-1980. A "ultimate sustain" mechanical add-on to guitar or bass bridges with rotating plectrums.

1978-1980 $300 $500

Goodrich Sound

1970s-present. Originally located in Michigan, and currently in Dublin, Georgia, Goodrich currently offers volume pedals and a line boost.

MODEL YEAR	FEATURES	EXC. COND. LOW	HIGH

Match Box Line Boost

Early-1980s-2011. Small rectangular line buffer/driver.

1980s-2011 $45 $55

Volume Pedal 6122

Late-1970s-1980s. Uses a potentiometer.

1970s $45 $55

Volume Pedal 6400ST

Late-1970s-1980s. Stereo pedal, using photocells.

1970s $45 $55

Volume Pedal 6402

Late-1970s-1980s. Uses photocell.

1970s $45 $55

Goran Custom Guitars

1998-present. Luthier Goran Djuric from Belgrade, Serbia also offers guitar pedals.

Goya

1960s. Goya Music sold effects under the brands Goya, Applied, Nomad, Conrad and maybe more.

Fury Box

1960s $75 $150

Greer Amplification

1999-present. Guitar stomp box effects built by Nick Greer in Athens, Georgia. He also builds amps.

Gretsch

Gretsch has offered a limited line of effects from time to time.

Controfuzz

Mid-1970s. Distortion.

1970s $150 $225

Deluxe Reverb Unit Model 6149

1963-1969. Similar to Gibson's GA-1 introduced around the same time.

1963-1969 $475 $700

Expandafuzz

Mid-1970s. Distortion.

1970s $200 $375

Reverb Unit Model 6144 Preamp Reverb

1963-1967. Approximately 17 watts, preamp functionality, no speaker.

1963-1967 $450 $600

Tremofect

Mid-1970s. Tremolo effect, 3-band EQ, speed, effect, bass, total, and treble knobs.

1970s $225 $300

Guild

Guild marketed effects made by Binson, Electro-Harmonix, Foxx, WEM and Applied in the 1960s and '70s.

Copicat

1960s-1979. Echo.

1970s $300 $450

DE-20 Auto-Rhythm Unit

1971-1974. 50 watt rhythm accompaniment unit. Included 20 rhythms and a separate instrument channel with its own volume control. 1x12" plus tweeter.

1971-1974 $200 $300

MODEL YEAR	FEATURES	EXC. COND. LOW	HIGH

Echorec (by Binson)

Ca.1960-1979. Stripped-down version of the Binson Echorec.

1960s $675 $875

Foxey Lady Fuzz

1968-1977. Distortion, sustain.

1968-1975 2 knobs, made by E-H $200 $550

1976-1977 3 knobs in row, same as Big Muff $250 $550

Fuzz Wah FW-3

1975-ca.1979. Distortion, volume, wah, made by Foxx.

1970s $80 $150

HH Echo Unit

1976-ca.1979.

1970s $200 $300

VW-1

1975-ca.1979. Volume, wah, made by Foxx.

1970s $200 $250

Guyatone (Tokyo Sound Company)

1930s-present. Founded by Mitsuo Matsuki, maker of guitars, amps and effects. Imported stomp boxes, tape echo units and outboard reverb units distributed by Godlyke Distributing.

Bazz Box FS-1

1960s. Vox V828 Tone Bender copy.

1960s $75 $150

Bazz Box FS-2

1960s. Univox Super-Fuzz copy.

1960s $125 $300

Crazy-Face

1970s. Dallas-Arbiter Fuzz Face copy.

1970s $100 $250

Sustainer FS-6

1970s. Circular Fuzz Face-like housing.

1970s $75 $200

Wah-Fuzz FS-5

1970s $50 $100

HAO

Line of guitar effects built in Japan by J.E.S. International, distributed in the U.S. by Godlyke.

Harden Engineering

2006-present. Distortion/boost guitar effects pedals built by William Harden in Chicago, Illinois. He also builds guitars.

Heathkit

1960s. These were sold as do-it-yourself kits and are difficult to value because quality depends on skills of builder.

TA-28 Distortion Booster

1960s. Fuzz assembly kit, heavy '60s super fuzz, case-by-case quality depending on the builder.

1960s $140 $150

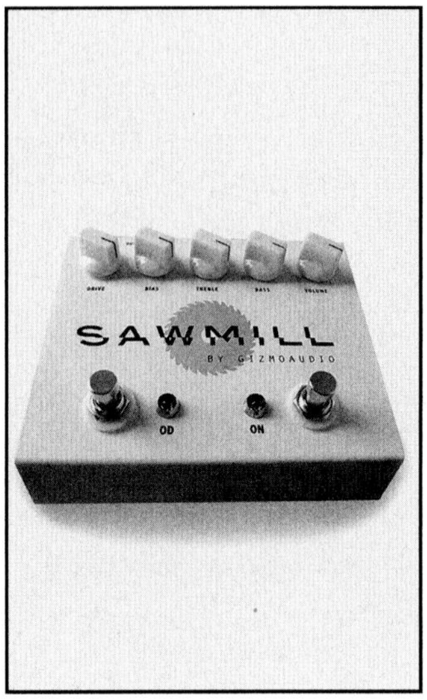

Gizmoaudio Sawmill

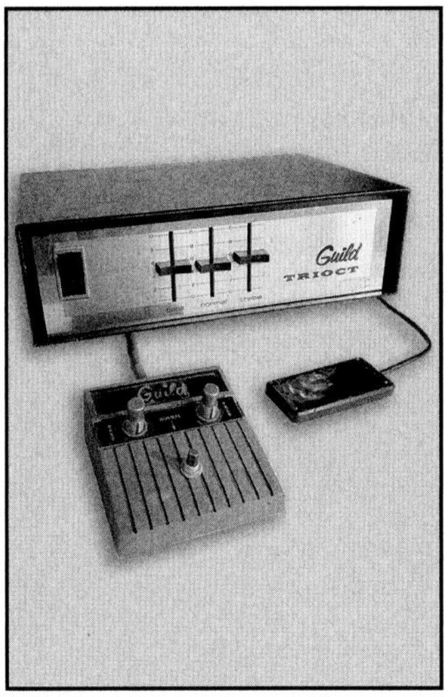

Guild Tri-Oct

Mary-Anne Hammer

1970s Guyatone PS-104 Crossover Auto Wah

Rivington Guitars

EFFECTS

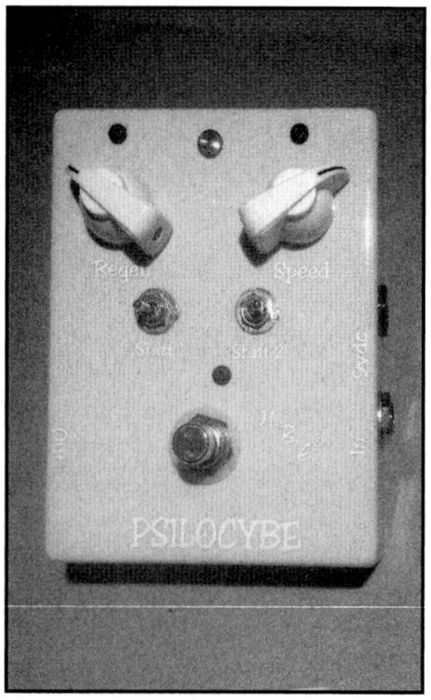

HomeBrew Electronics Psilocybe
Keith Myers

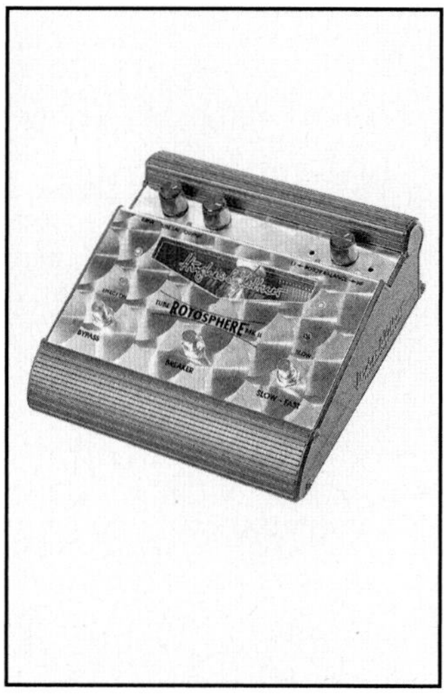

Hughes & Kettner Tube Rotosphere MKII

Ibanez Analog Delay AD9
Rivington Guitars

MODEL YEAR	FEATURES	EXC. COND. LOW	HIGH

Heavy Metal Products

Mid-1970s. From Alto Loma, California, products for the heavy metal guitarist.

Raunchbox Fuzz

1975-1976	$75	$100

Switchbox

1975-1976. A/B box.

1975-1976	$25	$35

Heet Sound Products

1974-present. The E Bow concept goes back to '67, but a hand-held model wasn't available until '74. Made in Los Angeles, California.

E Bow

1974-1979, 1985-1987, 1994-present. The Energy Bow, hand-held electro-magnetic string driver.

1974-1979	$50	$60

E Bow for Pedal Steels

1979. Hand-held electro-magnetic string driver.

1979	$35	$55

Heil Sound

1960-present. Founded by Bob Heil, Marissa, Illinois. Created the talk box technology as popularized by Joe Walsh and Peter Frampton. In the '60s and '70s Heil was dedicated to innovative products for the music industry. In the late-'70s, innovative creations were more in the amateur radio market, and by the '90s Heil's focus was on the home theater market. The Heil Sound Talkbox was reissued by Jim Dunlop USA in '89.

Talk Box

1976-ca.1980, 1989-present. Reissued by Dunlop.

1976-1980	$100	$150
1989-1999	$60	$85
2000-2020	$60	$80

Henretta Engineering

2009-present. Analog guitar effects built by Kevin Henretta first in Chicago, Illinois and presently Saint Paul, Minnesota.

Hermida Audio

2003-present. Alfonso Hermida builds his guitar effects in Miramar, Florida.

High Gain

See listing under Dunlop.

Hohner

Hohner offered effects in the late-1970s.

Dirty Booster

1977-ca.1978. Distortion.

1977-1978	$55	$65

Dirty Wah Wah'er

1977-ca.1978. Adds distortion.

1977-1978	$65	$75

Fuzz Wah

1970s. Morley-like volume pedal with volume knob and fuzz knob, switch for soft or hard fuzz, gray box with black foot pedal.

1970s	$65	$75

Multi-Exciter

1977-ca.1978. Volume, wah, surf, tornado, siren.

1977-1978	$60	$70

Tape Echo/Echo Plus

1970s. Black alligator suitcase.

1970s	$200	$275

Tri-Booster

1977-ca.1978. Distortion, sustain.

1977-1978	$55	$65

Vari-Phaser

1977-ca.1978.

1977-1978	$55	$65

Vol-Kicker Volume Pedal

1977-ca.1978.

1977-1978	$30	$40

Wah-Wah'er

1977-ca.1978. Wah, volume.

1977-1978	$55	$65

HomeBrew Electronics

2001-present. Stomp box effects hand made by Joel and Andrea Weaver in Glendale, Arizona.

Honey

1967-1969. Honey Company Ltd. Was formed by ex-Teisco workers after that firm was acquired by Kawai. Honey launched several effects designed by engineer Fumio Mieda, before going bankrupt in March, '69. The company was reborn as Shin-ei and many of its designs continued production in various forms; see Shin-ei for more.

Baby Crying

1960s. Univox Super-Fuzz copy.

1960s	$125	$300

Psychedelic Machine

1967-1969. Amp head-sized effect with numerous controls.

1967-1969	$750	$1,100

Special Fuzz

1967-1970s	$500	$750

Vibra Chorus

1967-1969. Original version of the Uni-Vibe, which Shin-ei would produce after Honey went bankrupt.

1967-1969	$1,500	$3,000

Hughes & Kettner

1985-present. Hughes & Kettner builds a line of tube-driven guitar effects made in Germany. They also build amps and cabinets.

Ibanez

1932-present. Ibanez effects were introduced ca. 1974, and were manufactured by Japan's Maxon Electronics. Although results were mixed at first, a more uniform and modern product line, including the now legendary Tube Screamer, built Ibanez's reputation for quality. They continue to produce a wide range of effects.

60s Fuzz FZ5 (SoundTank)

1991-1992, 1996-1998. Fuzz with level, tone and distortion controls, black plastic case, green label.

1990s	$25	$30

MODEL YEAR	FEATURES	EXC. COND. LOW	HIGH

7th Heaven SH7 (Tone-Lok)

2000-2004. Lo, high, drive and level controls, gray-silver case, blue-green label.

2000-2004 $20 $30

Acoustic Effects PT4

1993-1998. Acoustic guitar multi-effect with compressor/limiter, tone shaper, stereo chorus, digital reverb, with power supply.

1993-1998 $75 $100

Analog Delay AD9

1982-1984. 3 control analog delay, Hot Pink metal case.

1982-1984 $200 $275

Analog Delay AD80

1980-1981. Pink case.

1980-1981 $200 $275

Analog Delay AD99

1996-1998. Reissue, 3 control knobs and on/off switch, winged-hand logo, black case.

1996-1998 $125 $150

Analog Delay AD100 (Table Unit)

1981-1983. Stand-alone table/studio unit (not rack mount) with power cord.

1981-1983 $200 $250

Analog Delay 202 (Rack Mount)

1981-1983. Rack mount with delay, doubling, flanger, stereo chorus, dual inputs with tone and level.

1981-1983 $200 $300

Auto Filter AF9

1982-1984. Replaces AF201 model.

1982-1984 $150 $200

Auto Filter AF201

1981. Two min-max sliders, 3 mode toggle switches, orange metal case.

1981 $175 $200

Auto Wah AW5 (SoundTank)

1994-1999. Plastic case SoundTank series.

1994-1999 $30 $40

Auto Wah AW7 (Tone-Lok)

2000-2010. Silver case.

2000-2010 $20 $30

Bass Compressor BP10

1986-1991 $70 $80

Bi-Mode Chorus BC9

1984. Dual channel for 2 independent speed and width settings.

1984 $75 $100

Chorus CS-505

1980-1981. Speed and depth controls, gray-blue case, stereo or mono input, battery or external power option.

1980-1981 $200 $250

Chorus Flanger CF7 (Tone-Lok)

1999-2010. Speed, depth, delay, regeneration controls, mode and crazy switches.

1999-2010 $35 $55

Classic Flange FL99

1997-1999. Analog reissue, silver metal case, winged-hand artwork, 4 controls, 2 footswitch buttons.

1997-1999 $90 $110

Classic Phase PH99

1995-1999. Analog reissue, silver metal case, winged-hand artwork, speed, depth, feedback, effect level controls, intense and bypass footswitches.

1995-1999 $90 $110

Compressor CP5 (SoundTank)

1991-1998 $20 $30

Compressor CP10

1986-1992 $75 $80

Compressor CP830

1975-1979 $100 $125

Compressor II CP835

1980-1981 $100 $125

Compressor Limiter CP9

1982-1984 $100 $125

Delay Champ CD10

1986-1989. Red case, 3 knobs.

1986-1989 $125 $150

Delay Echo DE7 (Tone-Lok)

1999-2010. Stereo delay/echo.

1999-2010 $40 $80

Delay Harmonizer DM1000

1983-1984. Rack mount, with chorus, 9 control knobs.

1983-1984 $175 $225

Delay III DDL20 Digital Delay

1988-1989. Filtering, doubling, slap back, echo S, echo M, echo L, Seafoam Green coloring on pedal.

1988-1989 $100 $125

Delay PDD1 (DPC Series)

1988-1989. Programmable Digital Delay (PDD) with display screen.

1988-1989 $125 $150

Digital Chorus DSC10

1990-1992. 3 control knobs and slider selection toggle.

1990-1992 $75 $100

Digital Delay DL5 (SoundTank)

1991-1998 $35 $45

Digital Delay DL10

1989-1992. Digital Delay made in Japan, blue case, 3 green control knobs, stompbox.

1989-1992 $100 $125

Distortion Charger DS10

1986-1989 $70 $90

Distortion DS7 (Tone-Lok)

2000-2010. Drive, tone, and level controls.

2000-2010 $40 $45

Dual Chorus CCL

1990s $60 $100

Echo Machine EM5 (SoundTank)

1996-1998. Simulates tape echo.

1996-1998 $45 $95

Fat Cat Distortion FC10

1987-1989. 3-knob pedal with distortion, tone, and level controls.

1987-1989 $50 $105

Flanger FFL5 (Master Series)

1984-1985. Speed, regeneration, width, D-time controls, battery or adapter option.

1984-1985 $70 $90

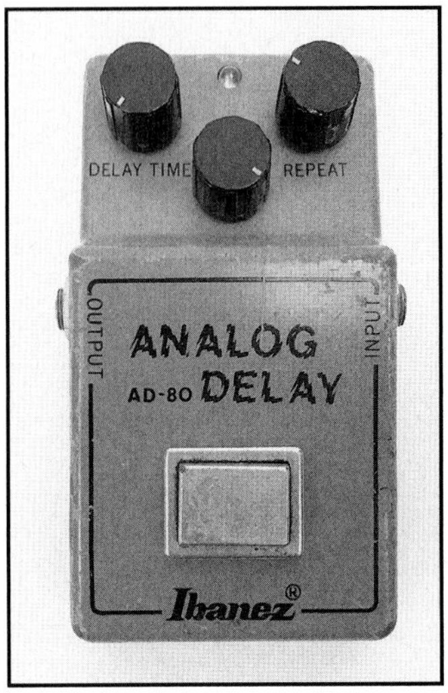

1980 Ibanez Analog Delay AD80

Bernunzio Uptown Music

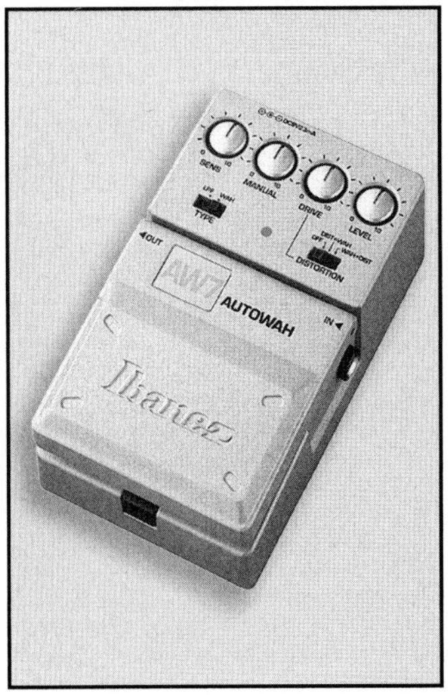

Ibanez Auto Wah AW7

Ibanez Compressor Limiter CP9

EFFECTS

To get the most from this book, be sure to read "Using *The Guide*" in the introduction.

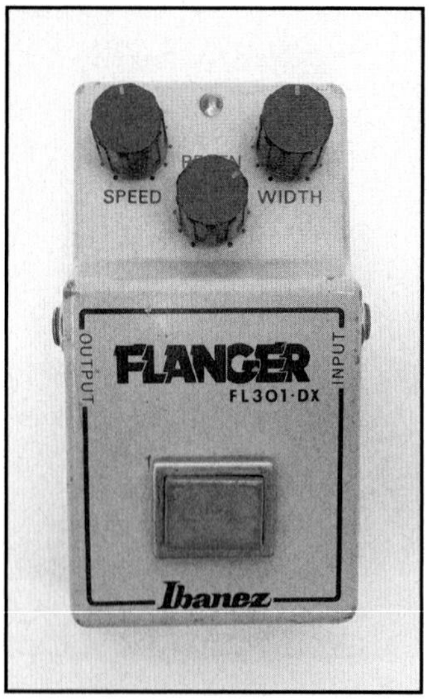

1982 Ibanez Flanger FL301-DX
Bernunzio Uptown Music

1984 Ibanez Phaser PT9
Rivington Guitars

Ibanez Stereo Chorus CS9
Keith Myers

MODEL YEAR	FEATURES	EXC. COND. LOW	HIGH

Flanger FL5 (SoundTank)
1991-1998 $25 $35

Flanger FL9
1982-1984. Yellow case.
1982-1984 $100 $150

Flanger FL301
1979-1982. Mini flanger, 3 knobs, called the FL-301 DX in late '81-'82.
1979-1982 $100 $125

Flanger FL305
1976-1979. Five knobs.
1976-1979 $100 $125

Flying Pan FP777
1976-1979. Auto pan/phase shifter, 4 control knobs, phase on/off button, pan on/off button, silver metal case with blue trim and Flying Pan winged-hand logo.
1976-1979 $575 $725

Flying Pan FP777 Reissue
2007 777 made $275 $350

Fuzz FZ7 (Tone-Lok)
2000-2010. Drive, tone and level controls, gray-silver case, blue-green FZ7 label.
2000-2010 $45 $50

Graphic Bass EQ BE10
1986-1992. Later labeled as the BEQ10.
1986-1992 $60 $80

Graphic EQ GE9
1982-1984. Six EQ sliders, 1 overall volume slider, turquoise blue case.
1982-1984 $60 $80

Graphic EQ GE10
1986-1992. Eight sliders.
1986-1992 $60 $80

Graphic Equalizer GE601 (808 Series)
1980-1981. 7-slider EQ, aqua blue metal case.
1980-1981 $75 $100

Guitar Multi-Processor PT5
1993-1997. Floor unit, programmable with 25 presets and 25 user presets, effects include distortion, chorus, flanger, etc, green case.
1993-1997 $100 $125

LA Metal LM7
1988-1989. Silver case.
1988-1989 $55 $65

LoFi LF7 (Tone-Lok)
2000-2010. Filter, 4 knobs.
2000-2010 $20 $30

Metal Charger MS10
1986-1992. Distortion, level, attack, punch and edge control knobs, green case.
1986-1992 $45 $55

Metal Screamer MSL
1985. 3 control knobs.
1985 $55 $65

Modern Fusion MF5 (SoundTank)
1990-1991. Level, tone and distortion controls.
1990-1991 $45 $50

Modulation Delay DM500
1983-1984. Rack mount.
1983-1984 $75 $100

Modulation Delay DM1000
1983-1984. Rack mount with delay, reverb, modulation.
1983-1984 $100 $125

Modulation Delay PDM1
1988-1989. Programmable Digital Modulation pedal.
1988-1989 $100 $125

Mostortion MT10
1990-1992. Mos-FET circuit distortion pedal, 5 control knobs, green case.
1990-1992 $50 $60

Multi-Effect PUE5/PUE5 Tube (Floor Unit)
1990-1993. Yellow version has tube, blue one does not. Also available in PUE5B bass version.
1990-1993 Tube $350 $450

Multi-Effect UE300 (Floor Unit)
1983-1984. Floor unit, 4 footswitches for super metal, digital delay, digital stereo chorus, and master power, 3 delay modes.
1983-1984 $275 $350

Multi-Effect UE300B (Floor Unit)
1983-1984. Floor unit for bass.
1983-1984 $275 $350

Multi-Effect UE400 (Rackmount)
1980-1984. Rack mount with foot switch.
1980-1984 $300 $375

Multi-Effect UE405 (Rackmount)
1981-1984. Rack mount with analog delay, parametric EQ, compressor/limiter, stereo chorus and loop.
1981-1984 $300 $375

Noise Buster NB10
1988-1989. Eliminates 60-cycle hum and other outside signals, metal case.
1988-1989 $70 $75

Overdrive OD850
1975-1979 $275 $400

Overdrive II OD855
1977-1979. Distortion, tone, and level controls, yellow/green case, large Overdrive II logo.
1977-1979 $300 $400

Pan Delay DPL10
1990-1992. Royal Blue case, 3 green control knobs.
1990-1992 $95 $125

Parametric EQ PQ9
1982-1984 $125 $175

Parametric EQ PQ401
1981. 3 sliders, dial-in knob, light aqua blue case.
1981 $125 $175

Phase Tone PT909
1979-1982. Blue box, 3 knobs, early models with flat case (logo at bottom or later in the middle) or later wedge case.
1979-1982 $140 $150

Phase Tone PT999
1975-1979. Script logo, 1 knob, round footswitch, becomes PT-909.
1975-1979 $125 $150

Phase Tone PT1000
1974-1975. Morley-style pedal phase, light blue case, early model of Phase Tone.
1974-1975 $200 $300

MODEL YEAR | FEATURES | EXC. COND. LOW | HIGH

Phase Tone II PT707

1976-1979. Blue box, script logo for first 2 years.

1976-1979 $100 $130

Phaser PH5 (SoundTank)

1991-1998 $20 $30

Phaser PH7 (Tone-Lok)

1999-2010. Speed, depth, feedback and level controls.

1999-2010 $35 $40

Phaser PT9

1982-1984. Three control knobs, red case.

1982-1984 $75 $100

Powerlead PL5 (SoundTank)

1991-1998. Metal case '91, plastic case '91-'98.

1991 Metal $25 $40

1991-1998 Plastic $15 $20

Renometer

1976-1979. 5-band equalizer with preamp.

1976-1979 $75 $100

Rotary Chorus RC99

1996-1999. Black or silver cases available, requires power pack and does not use a battery.

1996-1999 Black case $100 $125

Session Man SS10

1988-1989. Distortion, chorus.

1988-1989 $70 $80

Session Man II SS20

1988-1989. 4 controls plus toggle, light pink-purple case.

1988-1989 $70 $80

Slam Punk SP5 (SoundTank)

1996-1999 $35 $40

Smash Box SM7 (Tone-Lok)

2000-2010 $30 $35

Sonic Distortion SD9

1982-1984 $75 $100

Standard Fuzz (No. 59)

1974-1979. Two buttons (fuzz on/off and tone change).

1974-1979 $175 $200

Stereo Box ST800

1975-1979. One input, 2 outputs for panning, small yellow case.

1975-1979 $175 $225

Stereo Chorus CS9

1982-1984 $75 $100

Stereo Chorus CSL (Master Series)

1985-1986 $70 $90

Super Chorus CS5 (SoundTank)

1991-1998 $20 $30

Super Metal SM9

1984. Distortion.

1984 $75 $95

Super Stereo Chorus SC10

1986-1992 $75 $100

Super Tube Screamer ST9

1984-1985. 4 knobs, light green metal case.

1984-1985 $225 $300

Super Tube STL

1985 $75 $95

MODEL YEAR | FEATURES | EXC. COND. LOW | HIGH

Swell Flanger SF10

1986-1992. Speed, regeneration, width and time controls, yellow case.

1986-1992 $55 $100

Trashmetal TM5 (SoundTank)

1990-1998. Tone and distortion pedal, 3 editions (1st edition, 2nd edition metal case, 2nd edition plastic case).

1990-1998 $15 $20

Tremolo Pedal TL5 (SoundTank)

1995-1998 $45 $95

Tube King TK999

1994-1995. Has a 12AX7 tube and 3-band equalizer.

1994-1995 Includes power pack $125 $200

Tube King TK999US

1996-1998. Has a 12AX7 tube and 3-band equalizer, does not have the noise switch of original TK999. Made in the U.S.

1996-1998 Includes power pack $125 $200

Tube Screamer TS5 (SoundTank)

1991-1998 $20 $25

Tube Screamer TS7 (Tone-Lok)

1999-2010. 3 control knobs.

1999-2010 $30 $35

Tube Screamer TS9

1982-1984, 1993-present. Reissued in '93.

1982-1984 $300 $700

1993-2020 $75 $125

1993-2020 AnalogMan modded $100 $160

1993-2020 Keeley modded $120 $200

Tube Screamer Classic TS10

1986-1993 $175 $225

Tube Screamer TS808

1980-1982, 2004-present. Reissued in '04.

1980-1982 Original $600 $1,300

2004-2020 Reissue $75 $120

Turbo Tube Screamer TS9DX

1998-present. Tube Screamer circuit with added 3 settings for low-end.

1998-2020 $70 $85

Twin Cam Chorus TC10

1986-1989. Four control knobs, light blue case.

1986-1989 $75 $100

Virtual Amp VA3 (floor unit)

1995-1998. Digital effects processor.

1995-1998 $55 $75

VL10

1987-1997. Stereo volume pedal.

1987-1997 $50 $75

Wah Fuzz Standard (Model 58)

1974-1981. Fuzz tone change toggle, fuzz on toggle, fuzz depth control, balance control, wah volume pedal with circular friction pads on footpedal.

1974-1981 $225 $300

Wah WH10

1988-1997 $50 $75

Ilitch Electronics

2003-present. Ilitch Chiliachki builds his effects in Camarillo, California.

1975 Ibanez Overdrive OD850

Rivington Guitars

Ibanez Tube King TK999US

Keith Myers

Ibanez Tube Screamer TS9

EFFECTS

Jack Deville Deuce Coupe Overdrive

JAM Pedals Delay Llama

JAM Pedals LucyDreamer Supreme

MODEL YEAR	FEATURES	EXC. COND. LOW	HIGH

Indy Guitarist

See listing under Wampler Pedals.

InterFax Electronics

Mid-1970s-1980s. Started by Ed Giese, located in Milwaukee, Wisconsin.

HP-1 Harmonic Percolator

Mid-1970s. Distortion/fuzz unit, harmonics and balance sliders.

1970s		$175	$300

Intersound

1970s-1980s. Intersound, Inc. was located in Boulder, Colorado and was a division of Electro-Voice.

Reverb-Equalizer R100F

1977-1979. Reverb and 4-band EQ, fader.

1977-1979		$75	$100

J. Everman

Analog guitar effects built by Justin J. Everman in Richardson, Texas, starting in 2000.

Jack Deville Electronics

2008-present. Production/custom, guitar effects built in Portland, Oregon by Jack Deville.

Jacques

One-of-a-kind handmade stomp boxes and production models made in France.

JAM Pedals

2007-present. Pedals built by Jannis Anastasakis Marinos of Athens, Greece.

Black Muck

2017-2018. Fuzz distortion.

2017-2018 $190 $240

Boomster

2007-2019. Silicon clean boost.

2007-2019 $75 $100

Boomster Mini

2017-present. Silicon clean boost.

2017-2020 $50 $100

DanComp

2007-2015. Compressor based on the Dan Armstrong Orange Squeezer compressor circuit.

2007-2015 $200 $220

Delay Llama

2007-present. Analog delay.

2007-2020 $150 $200

Delay Llama Supreme

2014-2019. Analog delay with tap tempo modulation.

2014-2019 $275 $325

Delay Llama+

2009-2019. Analog delay with hold function.

2009-2019 $150 $200

Dyna-ssoR

2007-present. Compression/sustainer.

2007-2020 $140 $175

Fuzz Phase

2007-2018. Germanium fuzz.

2007-2018 $200 $240

LucyDreamer Supreme

2017-present. Overdrive/boost.

2017-2020 $180 $210

Rattler

2008-present. Distortion.

2008-2020 $140 $175

Rattler+

2008-2018. Distortion with low-gain stage.

2008-2018 $175 $200

Red Muck

2008-2018. Fuzz distortion.

2008-2018 $140 $175

Retro Vibe

2007-present. Vibe/vibrato.

2007-2020 $230 $275

Ripple

2007-present. Two-stage phaser.

2007-2020 $120 $160

Ripply Fall

2017-present. Chorus/vibrato/phaser.

2017-2020 $220 $280

Rooster

2007-2018. Frequency booster.

2007-2018 $160 $200

The Big Chill

2011-present. Super tremolo with 2 speeds and chop effect.

2011-2020 $175 $200

The Chill

2007-present. Sine-wave tremolo.

2007-2020 $120 $160

Tube Dreamer 58

2007-present. Overdrive with selectable high-gain stage.

2007-2020 $120 $150

Tube Dreamer 72

2007-2018. Overdrive.

2007-2018 $130 $160

Tube Dreamer 88

2007-2018. Double overdrive.

2007-2018 $160 $200

Tube Dreamer+

2007-2017. Overdrive with footswitchable high-gain stage.

2007-2017 $140 $180

Wahcko+

2007-present. Wah-wah.

2007-2020 $180 $220

WaterFall

2007-present. Chorus/vibrato.

2007-2020 $150 $200

JangleBox

2004-present. Stephen Lasko and Elizabeth Lasko build their guitar effects in Springfield, Virginia and Dracut, Massachusetts.

Jan-Mar Industries

Jan-Mar was located in Hillsdale, New Jersey.

The Talker

1976. 30 watts.

1976 $75 $125

MODEL YEAR	FEATURES	EXC. COND. LOW	HIGH

The Talker Pro

1976. 75 watts.

1976 $100 $150

Jax

1960s-1970. Japanese imports made by Shin-ei.

Fuzz Master

1960s $350 $425

Fuzz Wah

1960s $125 $300

Vibrachorus

1969. Rotating-speaker simulator, with control pedal. Variant of Uni-Vibe.

1969 $750 $1,500

Wah-Wah

1960s $400 $500

Jen

Italy's Jen Elettronica company made a variety of guitar effects pedals in the 1960s and '70s for other brands such as Vox and Gretsch name. They also offered many of them, including the Cry Baby, under their own name.

Jennings

1960s. Dick Denny, of Vox fame, designed a short-lived line of effects for Jennings Electronic Developments of England.

Growler

1960s. Fuzz and wah effect with a rotary foot control.

1960s $150 $300

Jersey Girl

1991-present. Line of guitar effects pedals made in Japan. They also build guitars.

Jet Sounds LTD

1977. Jet was located in Jackson, Mississippi.

Hoze Talk Box

1977. Large wood box, 30 watts.

1977 $90 $125

Jetter Gear

2005-present. Brad Jeter builds his effects pedals in Marietta, Georgia.

JHD Audio

1974-1990. Hunt Dabney founded JHD in Costa Mesa, California, to provide effects that the user installed in their amp. Dabney is still involved in electronics and builds the BiasProbe tool for tubes.

SuperCube/SuperCube II

1974-late 1980s. Plug-in sustain mod for Fender amps with reverb, second version for amps after '78.

1974-1980s $50 $75

JHS Pedals

2007-present. Located in Mississippi 2007-08, Josh Scott presently builds his guitar and bass effects in Kansas City, Missouri.

MODEL YEAR	FEATURES	EXC. COND. LOW	HIGH

Bonsai

2007-2021 $190 $225

Colour Box V2

2007-2021 $300 $395

Emperor

2007-2021 $100 $165

Feednack Looper

2007-2021 $90 $120

Haunting Mids

2007-2021 $100 $130

HoneyComb

2007-2021 $100 $135

Lime AID

2007-2021 $120 $150

Morning Glory

2007-2021 $125 $160

Prestige

2007-2021 $90 $110

Pulp n Peel

2007-2021 $100 $130

Spring Tank Reverb

2007-2021 $100 $130

SuperBolt

2007-2021 $90 $120

Jimi Hendrix

See listing under Dunlop.

John Hornby Skewes & Co.

Mid-1960s-present. Large English distributor of musical products, which has also self-branded products from others, over the years. The early Zonk Machines, Shatterbox and pre-amp boosts were designed and built by engineer Charlie Ramskirr of Wilsic Electronics, until his death in '68. Later effects were brought in from manufacturers in Italy and the Far East.

Bass Boost BB1

1966-1968. Pre-amp.

1966-1968 $250 $400

Fuzz FZIII

1970s. Fuzz pedal, 2 control knobs, 1 footswitch.

1970s $150 $200

Phaser PZ111

1970s. Phaser pedal made in Italy, 2 control knobs, 1 footswitch.

1970s $80 $200

Selectatone TB2

1966-1968. Pre-amp combining treble and bass boost.

1966-1968 $250 $650

Treble Boost TB1

1966-1968. Pre-amp.

1966-1968 $250 $750

Zonk Machine I

1965-1968. Fuzz pedal, gray-blue housing, 2 control knobs, 1 footswitch, 3 germanium transistors.

1965-1968 $1,500 $2,000

Zonk Machine II

1966-1968. Fuzz pedal, gray-blue housing, 2 control knobs, 1 footswitch, 3 silicon transistors.

1966-1968 $1,000 $1,500

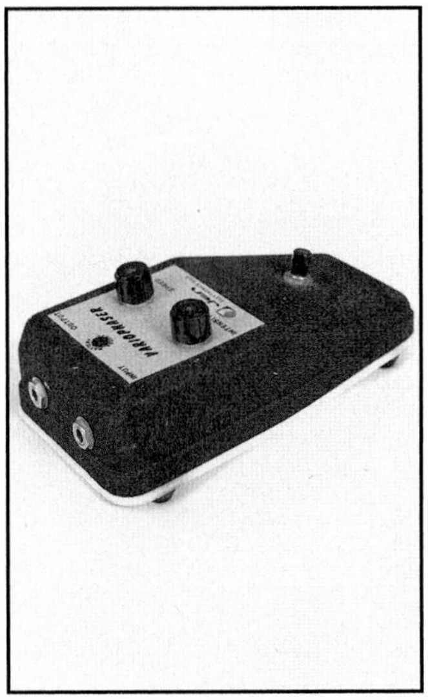

Jen Variophaser

Niclas Löfgren

JHS Pedals Sweet Tea

JHS Superbolt

Rivington Guitars

Jordan Boss Tone Fuzz

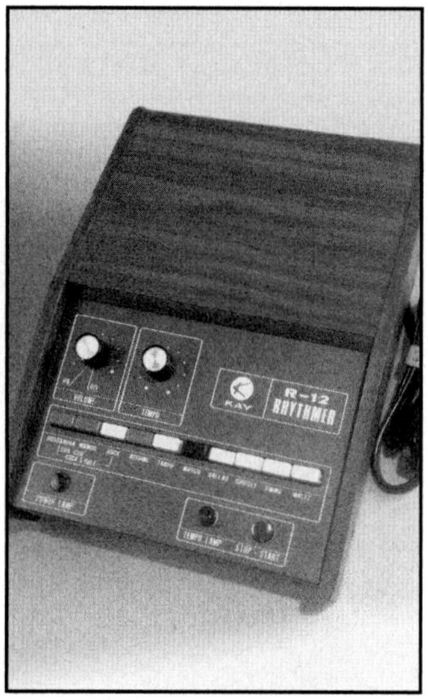

Kay Rhythmer R-12

Keith Myers

Keeley Electronics
Dual Fixed Filter

Keith Myers

MODEL YEAR	FEATURES	EXC. COND. LOW	HIGH

Zonk Machine Reissue

2000s. Reissued by JMI starting in 2013, reissues also made by the British Pedal Company, 2 control knobs, 1 footswitch.

2000s — $150 — $200

Zonk Shatterbox

1966-1968. Combined the Zonk Machine II fuzz circuit with the Treble Boost, 2 control knobs, gold housing, 2 foot switches.

1966-1968 — $1,500 — $2,000

Zonk Shatterbox Reissue

2000s. Reissues made by the British Pedal Company, gold housing, 2 foot switches.

2000s — $150 — $200

Zoom Spring Reverb Unit

1967-1968 — $500 — $700

Johnson

Mid-1990s-present. Budget line of effects imported by Music Link, Brisbane, California. Johnson also offers guitars, amps, mandolins and basses.

Johnson Amplification

Modeling amps and effects designed by John Johnson, of Sandy, Utah, starting in 1997. The company is part of Harman International. In '02, they quit building amps, but continue the effects line.

Jordan

1966-early 1970s. Jordan Electronics - originally of Alhambra, California, later in Pasadena - built a range of electronics, including, starting around 1966, solid state guitar amps and effects. Sho-Bud of Nashville, Tennessee, licensed the Boss Tone and sold it as the Sho-Sound Boss Tone. Mahoney later reissued the Boss Tone as the Buzz Tone.

Boss Tone Fuzz

1967-1970s. Tiny effect plugged into guitar's output jack, 2 control knobs, black plastic housing, extremely delicate wiring.

1967-70s — $150 — $300

Compressor J-700

1967-1970s. Sustain and Level control knobs.

1967-70s — $75 — $100

Creator Volume Sustainer Model 600

1967-1970s. Volume pedal and sustainer, side controls for Sustain and Tone.

1967-70s — $400 — $540

Gig Wa-Wa Volume Pedal

1967-1970s.

1967-70s — $125 — $145

Phaser

1967-1970s. Black case, yellow knobs.

1967-70s — Black case — $125 — $150

Vibrasonic

1967-70s — $145 — $195

Kay

1931-present. Kay was once one of the largest instrument producers in the world, offering just about everything for the guitarist, including effects.

Effects Pedals

1970s. Includes the Graphic Equalizer GE-5000, Rhythmer, and Tremolo.

1970s — $50 — $75

Fuzz Tone F-1

1970s — $175 — $350

Wah

1970s — $90 — $120

Kazan

1970s-1980s. Effects made in Kazan, Tatarstan Republic.

Booster

1970s. Fuzz pedal with foot control.

1970s — $50 — $75

Kvaker

1970s. Wah pedal.

1970s — $50 — $75

Keeley

2001-present. Line of guitar effects designed and built by Robert Keeley in Edmond, Oklahoma. Keeley Electronics also offers a range of custom modifications for other effects.

Java Boost

2001-2021 — $150 — $210

Katana

2001-2021 — $120 — $180

Keio

1970s. Keio Electronic Laboratories of Japan would later become Korg in the '80s.

Synthesizer Traveler F-1

1970s. Multi-effects unit with foot pedal.

1970s — $75 — $100

Kendrick

1989-present. Texas' Kendrick offers guitars, amps, and effects.

ABC Amp Switcher

1990s — $100 — $140

Buffalo Pfuz

1990s — $70 — $100

Model 1000 Reverb

1991-2003. Vintage style, 3 knobs: dwell, tone, and mix, brown cover, wheat grille with art deco shape.

1991-2003 — $400 — $450

Powerglide Attenuator

1998-present. Allows you to cut the output before it hits the amp's speakers, rack mount, metal cab.

1998-2020 — $180 — $200

Kent

1961-1969. This import guitar brand also offered a few effects.

Kern Engineering

Located in Kenosha, Wisconsin, Kern offers pre-amps and wah pedals.

MODEL YEAR	FEATURES	EXC. COND. LOW	HIGH

Kinsman

2012-present. Guitar effects pedals built in China and distributed by John Hornby Skewes & Co. Ltd.

Klon

1994-present. Originally located in Brookline, Massachusetts, and now located in Cambridge, Massachusetts, Klon was started by Bill Finnegan after working with two circuit design partners on the Centaur Professional Overdrive.

Centaur

2010. Smaller overdrive unit with burnished silver case.

2010		$700	$1,000

Centaur Professional Overdrive

1994-2009. Standard size with gold case. A smaller unit was introduced in '10.

1994-2009	Gold, horse logo	$2,500	$5,000
1994-2009	Silver, no horse logo	$2,000	$4,000

KTR

2010s. Smaller overdrive unit with red case.

2010s		$400	$800

KMD (Kaman)

1986-ca. 1990. Distributed by Kaman (Ovation, Hamer, etc.) in the late '80s.

Effects Pedals

1986-1990	Analog Delay	$45	$60
1986-1990	Overdrive	$30	$45
1987-1990	Distortion	$30	$45
1987-1990	Flanger	$30	$50
1987-1990	Phaser	$30	$50
1987-1990	Stereo Chorus	$30	$50

Knight

1967-1972. Effects kits sold via mail-order by Chicago's Allied Radio Company.

Fuzz Box KG-389

1967-1972		$50	$200

Korg

Formed from Keio Electronic Laboratories of Japan. Most of the Korg effects listed below are modular effects. The PME-40X Professional Modular Effects System holds four of them and allows the user to select several variations of effects. The modular effects cannot be used alone. This system was sold for a few years starting in 1983. Korg currently offers the Toneworks line of effects.

PEQ-1 Parametric EQ

1980s. Dial-in equalizer with gain knob, band-width knob, and frequency knob, black case.

1980s		$40	$50

PME-40X Modular Effects

1983-1986	KAD-301 Delay	$60	$70
1983-1986	KCH-301 Chorus	$25	$35
1983-1986	KCO-101 Compressor	$45	$55
1983-1986	KDI-101 Distortion	$45	$55
1983-1986	KDL-301 Echo	$90	$110
1983-1986	KFL-401 Flanger	$40	$50
1983-1986	KGE-201 Graphic EQ	$25	$35
1983-1986	KNG-101 Noise Gate	$25	$35
1983-1986	KOD-101 Over Drive	$45	$55
1983-1986	KPH-401 Phaser	$45	$55
1983-1986	OCT-1 Octaver	$70	$80

PME-40X Professional Modular Effects System

1983-ca.1986. Board holds up to 4 of the modular effects listed below.

1983-1986		$125	$150

SSD 3000 Digital Delay

1980s. Rack mount, SDD-3000 logo on top of unit.

1980s		$775	$925

KR Musical Products

2003-present. Kevin Randall presently builds his vintage style, guitar effects in White Marsh, Virginia.

Krank

1996-2013, 2015-2020. Tempe, Arizona, amp builder Tony Krank also built effects pedals.

Kustom

1965-present. Founded in '64 by Charles "Bud" Ross in his Chanute, Kansas, garage to build amps for his band. While Fender, Rickenbacker, and others tried and failed with solid-state amps, Ross' Kustom creations were a big hit. Kustom likely only ever made one foray into effects, producing The Bag, designed by Doug Forbes.

The Bag

1969-1971. Pioneering "talk box" effect housed in a "bota" wineskin-type bag worn over the player's shoulder. Covered in multiple styles of mod fabrics.

1969-1971		$900	$1,500

Lafayette Radio Electronics

1960s-1970s. Effects that claimed to be made in the U.S., but were most likely built by Shin-ei of Japan.

Deluxe AC Super Fuzz

1969-1970s. Made by Shin-ei, AC power.

1969-70s		$300	$500

Echo Verb/Echo Verb II

1970s. Solid-state echo/reverb. Likely made by Shin-ei.

1970s	2 instrument inputs	$175	$300
1970s	Instrument & mic inputs	$75	$250

Fuzz Sound

1970s. Likely made by Shin-ei.

1970s		$150	$250

Roto-Vibe

1969-1970s. Rotating-speaker simulator, with control pedal. Variant of Uni-Vibe made by Shin-ei.

1969-70s		$575	$850

Super Fuzz

1969-1970s. Made by Shin-ei.

1969-70s		$300	$500
1969-70s	Battery power	$300	$500

Keeley Hooke Reverb

1997 Klon Centaur Overdrive

Folkway Music

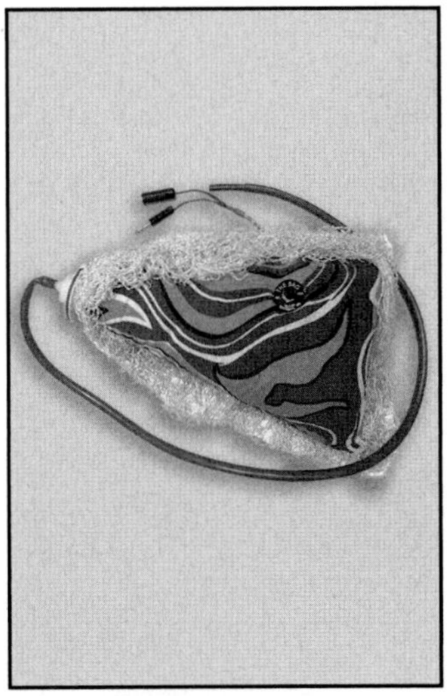

Kustom The Bag

The Bag Man

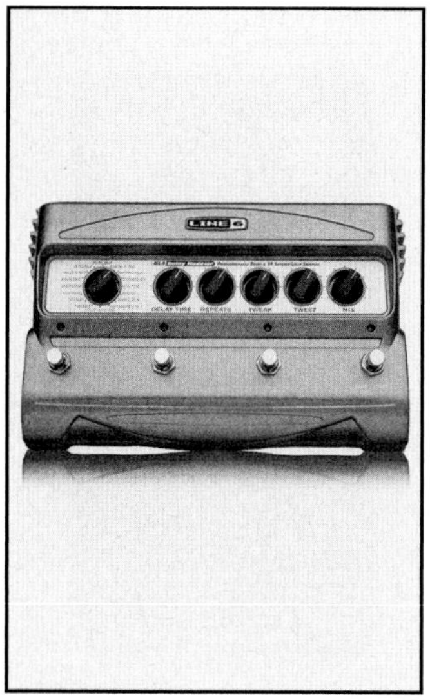

Line 6 DL-4 Delay Modeler

Line 6 POD X3

Lovetone Meatball

MODEL YEAR	FEATURES	EXC. COND. LOW	HIGH

Laney

1968-present. Founded by Lyndon Laney and Bob Thomas in Birmingham, U.K., this amp builder also offered a reverb unit.

Reverberation Unit

1968-1969. Sleek reverb unit, plexi-style front panel, black vinyl cover.

1968-1969		$300	$400

Larry Alan Guitars

2003-present. Luthier Larry Alan Daft offers effects pedals built in Lansing, Michigan. He also builds guitars and basses.

Lectronx

1990s. Founded by Edwin C. Clothier in North Hollywood, California.

Shark

1990s. Stereo filter pedal designed to use with 2 amps.

1990s		$250	$400

Lehle

2001-present. Loop switches from Burkhard Georg Lehle of Lehle Gitarrentechnik in Voerde, Germany.

D.Loop Signal Router

2004		$150	$175

Lenahan

Amp builder James Lenahan also offered a line of guitar pedals, built in Fort Smith, Arkansas.

Leslie

1966-1970s. In 1941, Donald Leslie began building speakers for Hammond organs to emulate pipe-organ sounds. Using a rotating baffle in front of a stationary speaker, he replicated the tremolo sound. He sold his company to CBS in 1965, and Fender launched its Vibratone based on Leslie technology in 1967. Leslie also offered its Model 16 and 18 speakers for guitarists. The Leslie 16/18 were also sold by Selmer as the Selmer-Leslie.

Model 16

1966-1970s. Rotating-speaker emulator, single fixed 4-ohm 10-inch speaker fronted by a rotating drum. Designed to be powered by an external amp. Black covering, cast Leslie badge in upper left corner.

1966-70s		$600	$750

Model 18

1966-1970s. Rotating-speaker emulator, single fixed 4-ohm 12-inch speaker fronted by a rotating drum. Designed to be powered by an external amp. Black covering, cast Leslie badge in upper left corner.

1966-70s		$500	$700

Line 6

1996-present. Founded by Marcus Ryle and Michel Doidic. Purchased by Yamaha in 2014. They also produce amps and guitars. All prices include Line 6 power pack if applicable.

MODEL YEAR	FEATURES	EXC. COND. LOW	HIGH

DL-4 Delay Modeler

1999-present. Green case.

1999-2020		$145	$175

DM-4 Distortion Modeler

1999-2018. Yellow case.

1999-2018		$100	$125

FM-4 Filter Modeler

2001-2018. Purple case.

2001-2018		$175	$225

MM-4 Modulation Modeler

1999-2018. Aqua blue case.

1999-2018		$100	$150

POD 2.0

2001-2014. Updated version of the original Amp Modeler.

2001-2014		$150	$200

Little Lanilei

1997-present. Effects made by Mahaffay Amplifiers (formerly Songworks Systems & Products) of Aliso Viejo, California. They also build amps.

Lizard Leg Effects

2007-2016. Steve Miller built a line of effects pedals in Gonzales, Louisiana.

Lock & Rock

Line of floor pedal guitar and microphone effects produced by Brannon Electronics, Inc. of Houston, Texas starting in 2003.

Loco Box

1982-1983. Loco Box was a brand of effects distributed by Aria Pro II for a short period starting in '82. It appears that Aria switched the effects to their own brand in '83.

Effects

1982-1983	Analog Delay AD-01	$35	$45
1982-1983	Chorus CH-01	$55	$65
1982-1983	Compressor CM-01	$35	$45
1982-1983	Distortion DS-01	$40	$55
1982-1983	Flanger FL-01	$35	$45
1982-1983	Graphic Equalizer GE-06	$25	$35
1982-1983	Overdrive OD-01	$40	$50
1982-1983	Phaser PH-01	$45	$55

Lotus Pedal Designs

2009-present. Guitar effects pedals built in Duluth, Minnesota by Sean Erspamer.

Loud Button Electronics

Founded in 2009 by Shawn Schoenberger in Minneapolis, Minnesota.

Morphine Dream

2010s. Analog phase shifter and distortion, based on Roland AP-7 Jet Phaser.

2010s		$50	$100

Lovepedal

2000-present. Sean Michael builds his preamps and guitar stomp boxes in Detroit, Michigan.

MODEL YEAR | FEATURES | EXC. COND. LOW | HIGH

Lovetone

Hand-made analog effects from Oxfordshire, U.K. starting in 1995.

Ludwig

For some reason, drum builder Ludwig offered a guitar synth in the 1970s.

Phase II Guitar Synth

1970-1971. Oversized synth, mushroom-shaped footswitches, vertical silver case.

1970-1971 $650 $800

M.B. Electronics

Made in San Francisco, California.

Ultra-Metal UM-10

1985. Distortion.

1985 $35 $40

Mad Professor

2002-present. Guitar effects pedals built by Bjorn Juhl and Jukka Monkkonen in Tampere, Finland. They also build amps.

Maestro

1950s-1970s, 2001-2012. Maestro was a Gibson subsidiary; the name appeared on 1950s accordian amplifiers. The first Maestro effects were the Echoplex tape echo and the FZ-1 Fuzz-Tone, introduced in the early-'60s. Maestro products were manufactured by various entities such as Market Electronics, All-Test Devices, Lowrey and Moog Electronics. In the late-'60s and early-'70s, they unleashed a plethora of pedals; some were beautiful, others had great personality. The last Maestro effects were the Silver and Black MFZ series of the late-'70s. In 2001, Gibson revived the name for a line of effects, banjos and mandolins, adding guitars and amps in '09. By '12 the brand is no longer listed with Gibson.

Bass Brassmaster BB-1

1971-ca.1974. Added brass to your bass.

1971-1974 $775 $1,100

Boomerang

Ca.1969-ca.1972. Wah pedal made by All-Test Devices.

1969-1972 $175 $200

Boomerang BG-2

1972-ca.1976. Wah pedal made by All-Test Devices.

1972-1976 $200 $225

Echoplex EM-1 Groupmaster

Ca.1970-ca.1977. Two input Echoplex, solidstate.

1970-1977 Without stand $900 $1,400

Echoplex EP-1

1959-mid-1960s. Original model, smaller green box, tube-driven tape echo, separate controls for echo volume and instrument volume, made by Market Electronics. Though not labeled as such, it is often referred to as the EP-1 by collectors.

1959-60s Earlier small box $800 $1,200

Echoplex EP-2

Mid-1960s-ca.1970. Larger gray or green box than original, tube-driven tape echo, single echo/instrument volume control, made by Market Electronics. Around '70, the EP-2 added a Sound-On-Sound feature. Limited-edition EP6T reissue made by Market in 1980s (see Market Electronics listing).

1960s Larger box $550 $1,200

Echoplex EP-3

Ca.1970-1977. Solidstate, made by Market Electronics, black box.

1970-1977 $400 $1,000

Echoplex EP-4 (IV)

1977-1978. Solidstate, last version introduced by Maestro. See Market Electronics and Echoplex brands for later models.

1977-1978 $350 $750

Echoplex Groupmaster EM-1

1970s. Large, multi-channel echo unit.

1970s $1,400 $2,000

Echoplex Sireko ES-1

Ca.1971-mid-1970s. A budget solidstate version of the Echoplex, made by Market.

1971-1975 $250 $350

Envelope Modifier ME-1

1971-ca.1976. Tape reverse/string simulator, made by All-Test.

1971-1976 $150 $225

Filter Sample and Hold FSH-1

1975-ca.1976.

1975-1976 $500 $750

Full Range Boost FRB-1

1971-ca.1975. Frequency boost with fuzz, made by All-Test.

1971-1975 $150 $200

Fuzz MFZ-1

1976-1979. Made by Moog.

1976-1979 $150 $200

Fuzz Phazzer FP-1

1971-1974 $200 $300

Fuzztain MFZT-1

1976-1978. Fuzz, sustain, made by Moog.

1976-1978 $200 $250

Fuzz-Tone FZ-1

1962-1963. Brown housing, uses 2 AA batteries.

1962-1963 $300 $460

Fuzz-Tone FZ-1A

1965-1967, 2001-2009. Brown housing, uses 1 AA battery. Early model "Kalamazoo, Michigan" on front, later "Nashville, Tennessee".

1965-1967 Kalamazoo $275 $470

2001-2009 Nashville $75 $280

Fuzz-Tone FZ-1B

Late-1960s- early-1970s. Black housing, uses 9-volt battery.

1970s $275 $325

Mini-Phase Shifter MPS-2

1976. Volume, speed, slow and fast controls.

1976 $110 $125

Octave Box OB-1

1971-ca.1975. Made by All-Test Devices.

1971-1975 $225 $300

Mad Professor Fire Red Fuzz

1973 Maestro Echoplex EP-3

Rivington Guitars

Maestro Fuzz-Tone FZ-1B

Bob Cain

Maestro Rover RO-1
Kyle Stevens.

1968 Maestro Sound System for Woodwinds W-1
Rivington Guitars

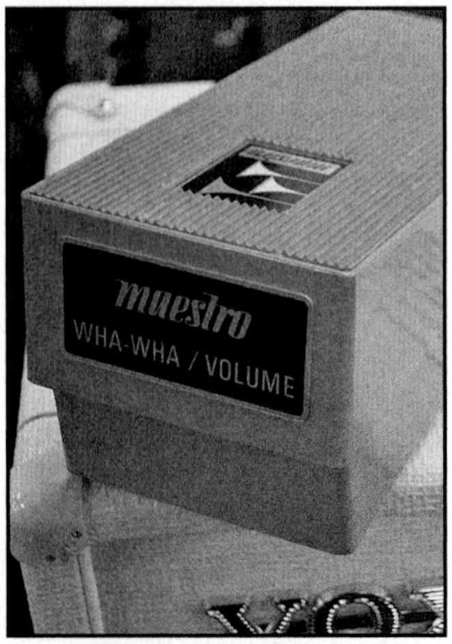

Maestro Wha-Wha/ Volume WW-1
Robbie Keene

MODEL YEAR	FEATURES	EXC. COND. LOW	HIGH

Parametric Filter MPF-1
1976-1978. Made by Moog.

1976-1978		$350	$450

Phase Shifter PS-1
1971-1975. With or without 3-button footswitch, made by Oberheim.

1971-1975	With footswitch	$275	$325
1971-1975	Without footswitch	$175	$225

Phase Shifter PS-1A

1976		$150	$250

Phase Shifter PS-1B

1970s		$150	$250

Phaser MP-1
1976-1978. Made by Moog.

1976-1978		$250	$325

Repeat Pedal RP-1

1970s		$200	$300

Rhythm King MRK-2
1971-ca.1974. Early drum machine.

1971-1974		$400	$500

Rhythm 'n Sound G-2
Ca.1969-1970s. Multi-effect unit.

1969-1975		$600	$750

Rhythm Queen MRQ-1
Early 1970s. Early rhythm machine.

1970s		$125	$150

Ring Modulator RM-1

1971-1975	No control pedal	$550	$600
1971-1975	With MP-1 control pedal	$650	$700

Rover Rotating Speaker
1971-ca.1973. Rotating Leslie effect that mounted on a large tripod.

1971-1973	RO-1 model	$1,200	$1,500

Sound System for Woodwinds W-1
1960s-1970s. Designed for clarinet or saxaphone input, gives a variety of synthesizer-type sounds with voices for various woodwinds, uses Barrel Joint and integrated microphone.

1960-1970s		$350	$400

Stage Phaser MPP-1
1976-1978. Has slow, fast and variable settings, made by Moog.

1976-1978		$175	$275

Super Fuzz-Tone FZ-1S

1971-1975		$200	$300

Sustainer SS-2
1971-ca.1975. Made by All-Test Devices.

1971-1975		$100	$160

Theramin TH-1
1971-mid-1970s. Device with 2 antennae, made horror film sound effects. A reissue Theremin is available from Theremaniacs in Milwaukee, Wisconsin.

1971-1975		$775	$975

Wah-Wah/Volume WW-1
1970s. Wah-Wah Volume logo on end of pedal, green foot pad.

1971-1975		$150	$250

MODEL YEAR	FEATURES	EXC. COND. LOW	HIGH

Magnatone

Ca.1937-1971, 2013-present. Magnatone built very competitive amps from '57 to '66. In the early-'60s, they offered the RVB-1 Reverb Unit. The majority of Magnatone amps pre-'66 did not have on-board reverb.

Model RVB-1 Reverb Unit
1961-1966. Typical brown leatherette cover, square box-type cabinet. From '64-'66, battery operated, solidstate version of RVB-1, low flat cabinet.

1961-1963		$275	$400
1964-1966	Battery & solidstate	$200	$300

Mahoney

2000s. Reissues of the Jordan Boss Tone.

Buzz Tone
2000s. Similar black-plastic housing to the original Boss Tone. 2 Control knobs.

2000s		$40	$75

Manny's

Effects issued by New York-based retailer Manny's Music.

Fuzz
1960s. Same unit as the Orpheum Fuzz and Clark Fuzz.

1960s		$275	$490

Market Electronics

Market, from Ohio, made the famous Echoplex line. See Echoplex and Maestro sections for earlier models.

Echoplex EP-6T
1980-ca.1988. Limited-edition all-tube reissue of the Echoplex EP-2.

1980-1988		$400	$500

Marshall

1962-present. The fuzz and wah boom of the '60s led many established manufacturers, like Marshall, to introduce variations on the theme. They got back into stomp boxes in '89 with the Gov'nor distortion, and currently produce several distortion/overdrive units.

Blues Breaker
1992-1999. Replaced by Blues Breaker II in 2000.

1992-1999		$130	$260

Blues Breaker II BB-2
2000-present. Overdrive pedal, 4 knobs.

2000-2020		$50	$65

Drive Master

1992-1999		$70	$140

Guv'nor
1989-1991. Distortion, Guv'nor Plus introduced in '99.

1989-1991		$125	$160

Jackhammer JH-1
1999-present. Distortion pedal.

1999-2020		$55	$60

Power Brake PB-100
1993-1995. Speaker attenuator for tube amps.

1993-1995		$190	$230

MODEL YEAR	FEATURES	EXC. COND. LOW	HIGH

Shred Master

1992-1999		$75	$100

Supa Fuzz

Late-1960s. Made by Sola Sound (Colorsound).

1967		$550	$850

Supa Wah

Late-1960s. Made by Sola Sound (Colorsound).

1969		$300	$425

Vibratrem VT-1

1999-present. Vibrato and tremolo.

1999-2020		$50	$75

Matchless

1989-1999, 2001-present. Matchless amplifiers offered effects in the '90s.

AB Box

1990s. Split box for C-30 series amps (DC 30, SC 30, etc.).

1990s		$175	$300

Coolbox

1997-1999. Tube preamp pedal.

1997-1999		$275	$350

Dirtbox

1997-1999. Tube-driven overdrive pedal.

1997-1999		$300	$500

Echo Box

1997-1999. Limited production because of malfunctioning design which included cassette tape. Black case, 8 white chickenhead control knobs.

1990s	Original unreliable	$300	$400
1990s	Updated reliable	$700	$900

Hotbox/Hotbox II

1995-1999. Higher-end tube-driven preamp pedal.

1995-1999		$395	$565

Mix Box

1997-1999. 4-input tube mixer pedal.

1997-1999		$375	$425

Reverb RV-1

1993-1999. 5 controls, tube-driven spring-reverb tank, various colors.

1993-1999		$1,400	$1,675

Reverb RV-2

2000s. 5 controls, tube-driven spring-reverb tank, various colors.

2000s		$900	$1,000

Split Box

1990s. Tube AB box.

1997	Standard AB	$275	$325

Tremolo/Vibrato TV-1

1993-1995. Tube unit.

1993-1995		$350	$480

Maxon

1970s-present. Maxon was the original manufacturer of the Ibanez line of effects. Currently offering retro '70s era stomp boxes distributed in the U.S. by Godlyke.

AD-9/AD-9 Pro Analog Delay

2001-present. Purple case.

2001-2020		$175	$275

CS-550 Stereo Chorus

2001-2017. Light blue case.

2001-2017		$100	$130

DS-830 Distortion Master

2001-present. Light blue-green case.

2001-2020		$100	$125

OD-820 Over Drive Pro

2001-present. Green case.

2001-2020		$140	$175

McQuackin FX Co.

Rich McCracken II began building his analog guitar effects in 1997, first in Nashville, Tennessee, then Augusta, Georgia.

Mesa-Boogie

1971-present. Mesa added pre-amps in the mid '90s, then pedals in 2013. Mesa was acquired by Gibson in early 2021.

V-Twin Bottle Rocket

2000-2004		$100	$180

V-Twin Preamp Pedal

Dec. 1993-2004. Serial number series: V011-. 100 watts, all tube preamp, floor unit, silver case.

1993-1999		$225	$275
2000-2004	Updated tone adj	$275	$325

Metal Pedals

2006-present. Brothers Dave and Mike Pantaleone build their guitar effects in New Jersey.

Meteoro

1986-present. Guitar effects built in Brazil. They also build guitar and bass amps.

MG

2004-present. Guitar effects built by Marcelo Giangrande in São Paulo, Brazil. He also builds amps.

Mica

Early 1970s. These Japanese-made effects were also sold under the Bruno and Marlboro brand names.

Tone Fuzz

1970s. Silver case, black knobs.

1970s		$200	$250

Tone Surf Wah Siren

1970s. Wah pedal.

1970s		$150	$195

Wailer Fuzz

1970		$75	$100

Wau Wau Fuzz

1970s. Wau Wau Fuzz logo on end of pedal, black.

1970s		$150	$175

Mooer

2012-present. A line of guitar pedals built by Mooer Audio in China.

Marshall Guv'nor

Keith Myers

Meteoro Doctor Metal

Mica Wau-Wau SG-150

Jim Schreck

EFFECTS

Morley Bad Horsie Steve Vai

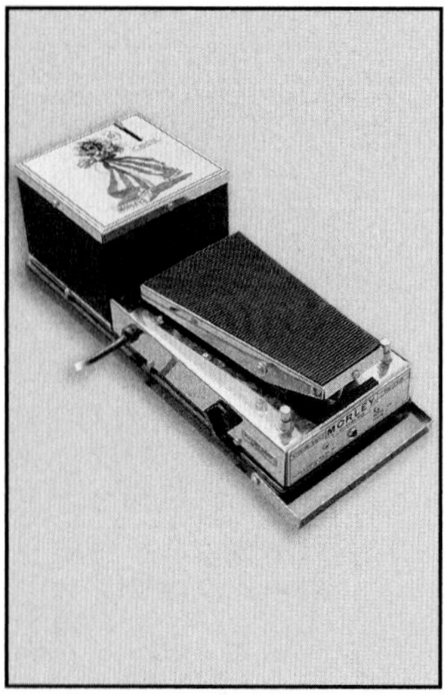

Morley Rotating Wah RWV

Nate Westgor

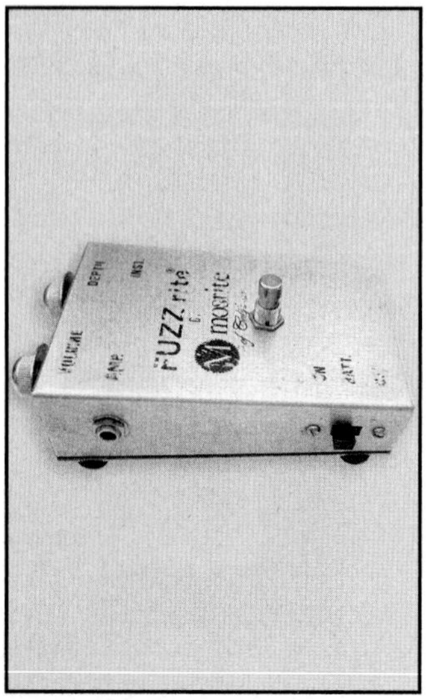

Mosrite Fuzzrite

MODEL YEAR	FEATURES	EXC. COND. LOW	HIGH

Moog/Moogerfooger

1964-present. Robert Moog, of synth fame, introduced his line of Moogerfooger analog effects in 1998. They also offer guitars.

Misc. Effects

2004-present.

2004-2010	MF-105 MuRF	$250	$400
2004-2010	Theremin	$250	$400

Moonrock

Fuzz/distortion unit built by Glenn Wyllie and distributed by Tonefrenzy starting in 2002.

Morley

Late-1960s-present. Founded by brothers Raymond and Marvin Lubow, Morley has produced a wide variety of pedals and effects over the years, changing with the trends. In '89, the brothers sold the company to Accutronics (later changed to Sound Enhancements, Inc.) of Cary, Illinois.

ABY Switch Box
1981-ca.1985. Box no pedal.
1981-1985 $25 $35

Auto Wah PWA
1976-ca.1985.
1976-1985 $25 $35

Bad Horsie Steve Vai Signature Wah
1997-present.
1997-2020 $65 $80

Black Gold Stereo Volume BSV
1985-1991 $25 $35

Black Gold Stereo Volume Pan BSP
1985-1989 $30 $40

Black Gold Volume BVO
1985-1991 $25 $35

Black Gold Wah BWA
1985-1991 $30 $40

Black Gold Wah Volume BWV
1985-1989 $30 $40

Chrystal Chorus CCB
1996-1999. Stereo output.
1996-1999 $25 $30

Deluxe Distortion DDB
1981-1991. Box, no pedal.
1981-1991 $40 $60

Deluxe Flanger FLB
1981-1991. Box, no pedal.
1981-1991 $55 $65

Deluxe Phaser DFB
1981-1991. Box, no pedal.
1981-1991 $40 $60

Distortion One DIB
1981-1991. Box, no pedal.
1981-1991 $35 $45

Echo Chorus Vibrato ECV
1982-ca.1985.
1982-1985 $150 $225

Echo/Volume EVO-1
1974-ca.1982.
1974-1982 $150 $225

Electro-Pik-a-Wah PKW
1979-ca.1982.
1979-1982 $55 $65

Emerald Echo EEB
1996-1999. 300 ms delay.
1996-1999 Green case $40 $50

Jerry Donahue JD-10
1995-1997. Multi-effect, distortion, overdrive.
1995-1997 $80 $90

Power Wah PWA/PWA II
1992-2006. Wah with boost. Changed to II in '98.
1992-2006 $40 $50

Power Wah PWO
Ca.1969-1984, 2006-present. Reissued in '06 as 20/20 Power Wah.
1969-1984 $60 $160

Power Wah/Boost PWB
Introduced in 1973, doubles as a volume pedal.
1970s $80 $150

Power Wah/Fuzz PWF
Ca.1969-ca.1984.
1969-1984 $125 $250

Pro Compressor PCB
1978-1984. Stomp box without pedal, compress-sustain knob and output knob.
1978-1984 $45 $55

Pro Flanger PFL
1978-1984 $100 $125

Pro Phaser PFA
1975-1984 $100 $125

Rotating Sound Power Wah Model RWV
1971-1982 $325 $425

Select-Effect Pedal SEL
1980s. Lets you control up to 5 other pedals.
1980s $20 $30

Slimline Echo Volume 600
1983-1985. 20 to 600 ms delay.
1983-1985 $45 $55

Slimline Echo Volume SLEV
1983-1985. 20 to 300 ms delay.
1983-1985 $50 $60

Slimline Variable Taper Stereo Volume SLSV
1982-1986 $70 $100

Slimline Variable Taper Volume SLVO
1982-1986 $35 $50

Slimline Wah SLWA
1982-1986. Battery operated electro-optical.
1982-1986 $55 $75

Slimline Wah Volume SLWV
1982-ca.1986. Battery operated electro-optical.
1982-1986 $55 $75

Stereo Chorus Flanger CFL
1980-ca. 1986. Box, no pedal.
1980-1986 $60 $70

Stereo Chorus Vibrato SCV
1980-1991. Box, no pedal.
1980-1991 $80 $100

Stereo Volume CSV
1980-ca. 1986. Box, no pedal.
1980-1986 $30 $45

MODEL YEAR	FEATURES	EXC. COND. LOW	EXC. COND. HIGH

Volume Compressor VCO

1979-1984		$30	$45

Volume Phaser PFV

1977-1984. With volume pedal.

1977-1984		$125	$180

Volume VOL

1975-ca.1984.

1975-1979		$30	$45
1980-1984		$25	$40

Volume XVO

1985-1988		$25	$40

Volume/Boost VBO

1974-1984		$50	$60

Wah Volume CWV

1987-1991. Box, no pedal.

1987-1991		$65	$80

Wah Volume XWV

1985-ca.1989.

1985-1989		$65	$90

Wah/Volume WVO

1977-ca.1984.

1977-1984		$80	$100

Morpheus

Guitar effects pedals manufactured in Salt Lake City, Utah by the same builders of the Bolt brand amps.

Mosferatu

Line of guitar effects pedals built by Hermida Audio Technology.

Mosrite

Semie Moseley's Mosrite company dipped into effects in the 1960s.

Fuzzrite

1960s-1970s, 1999. Silver housing as well as some painted housings, 2 front-mounted control knobs. Sanner reissued in '99.

1960s-70s	Mosrite logo	$250	$550
1999	Reissue, Sanner logo	$100	$225

Mu-FX

See Beigel Sound Lab.

Multivox

New York-based Multivox offered a variety of effects in the 1970s and '80s.

Big Jam Effects

Multivox offered the Big Jam line of effects from 1980 to ca. '83.

1980-1983	Analog Echo/Reverb	$100	$125
1980-1983	Bi-Phase 2, Flanger, Jazz Flanger	$50	$60
1980-1983	Chorus	$45	$55
1980-1983	Compressor, Phaser, 6-Band EQ, Spit-Wah	$40	$80
1980-1983	Distortion	$70	$80
1980-1983	Octave Box	$40	$55
1981-1983	Noise Gate, Parametric EQ	$35	$45

MODEL YEAR	FEATURES	EXC. COND. LOW	EXC. COND. HIGH
1981-1983	Space Driver, Delay	$60	$70
1982-1983	Volume Pedal	$30	$35

Full Rotor MX-2

1978-ca.1982. Leslie effect.

1978-1982		$300	$350

Little David LD-2

1970s. Rotary sound effector in mini Leslie-type case.

1970s	With pedal	$325	$500
1970s	Without pedal	$325	$375

Multi Echo MX-201

1970s. Tape echo unit, reverb.

1970s		$200	$250

Multi Echo MX-312

1970s. Tape echo unit, reverb.

1970s		$225	$300

Rhythm Ace FR6M

1970s. 27 basic rhythms.

1970s		$60	$80

Mu-Tron

1972-ca.1980. Made by Musitronics, founded by Mike Beigel and Aaron Newman in Rosemont, New Jersey, these rugged and unique-sounding effects were a high point of the '70s. The Mu-Tron III appeared in '72 and more products followed, about 10 in all. Musitronics also made the U.S. models of the Dan Armstrong effects. In '78 ARP synthesizers bought Musitronics and sold Mutron products to around '80. In '78, Musitronics also joined with Lol Creme and Kevin Godley of 10cc to attempt production of the Gizmotron, which quickly failed (see listing under Godley Crème). A reissue of the Mu-Tron III was made available in '95 by NYC Music Products and distributed by Matthews and Ryan Musical Products. As of 2013, Mike Beigel's Beigel Sound Lab has started making a hot-rodded Tru-Tron III.

Bi-Phase

1975-ca.1980. Add $50-$75 for Opti-Pot pedal.

1971-1980	Optical pedal option	$900	$1,500
1975-1980	2-button footswitch	$900	$1,250

C-100 OptiPot Control Pedal

1975-1980	Blue case	$550	$700

C-200 Volume-Wah

1970s		$300	$350

Flanger

1977-ca.1980.

1977-1980		$800	$1,700

III Envelope Filter

1972-ca.1980. Envelope Filter.

1972-1980		$500	$900

Micro V

Ca.1975-ca.1977. Envelope Filter.

1970s		$200	$250

Octave Divider

1977-ca.1980.

1977-1980		$540	$780

Phasor

Ca.1974-ca.1976. Two knobs.

1974-1976		$275	$480

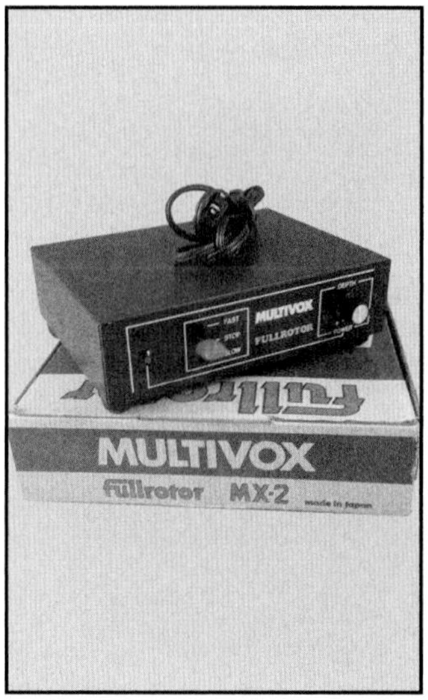

1970s Multivox Full Rotor MX-2

Keith Myers

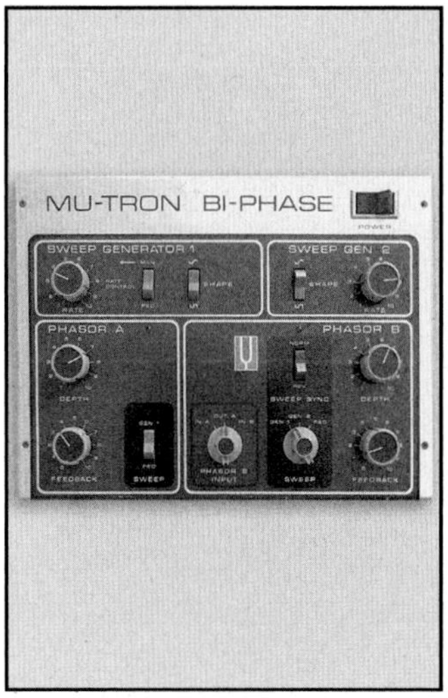

Mu-Tron Bi-Phase

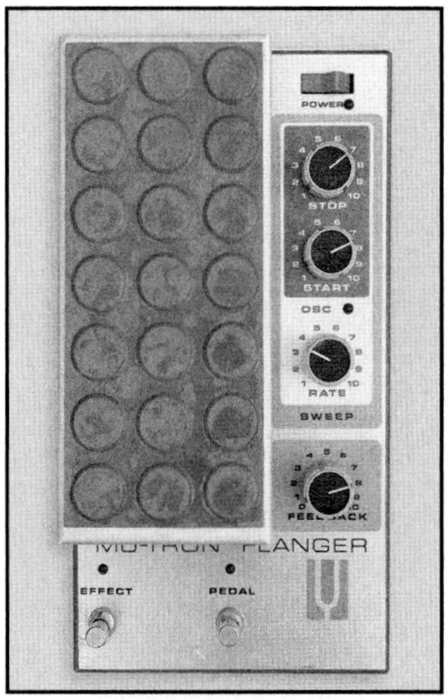

Mu-Tron Flanger

Marco Antonio Rebolledo Ferrari

EFFECTS

MXR Six Band EQ

Keith Myers

MXR Carbon Copy M169

MXR Dyna Comp M102

Keith Myers

MODEL YEAR	FEATURES	EXC. COND. LOW	HIGH

Phasor II

1976-ca.1980. Three knobs.

1976-1980		$200	$395

Muza

Digital guitar effects made in China, starting in 2006, by Hong Kong's Medeli Electronics Co., Ltd. They also build digital drums.

MWFX

2010s-present. Effects pedals built by Matt Warren in Somerset, England.

Glitch

2010s	Wooden case	$90	$150

MXR

1972-present. MXR Innovations launched its line of pedals in '72. Around '77, the Rochester, New York, company changed lettering on the effects from script to block, and added new models. MXR survived into the mid-'80s. In '87, production was picked up by Jim Dunlop. Reissues of block logo boxes can be differentiated from originals as they have an LED above the switch and the finish is slightly rough; the originals are smooth.

Six Band EQ

1975-1982. Equalizer.

1975-1979		$70	$85
1980-1982		$60	$70

Six Band EQ M109 (Reissue)

1987-present. Reissued by Jim Dunlop.

1987-2020		$30	$40

Ten Band EQ M108

1975-1981, 2004-present. Graphic equalizer.

1975-1981	With AC power cord	$80	$100

Analog Delay

1975-1981. Green case, power cord.

1975-1979	Earlier 2-jack model	$300	$325
1980-1981	Later 3-jack model	$150	$200

Blue Box

1972-ca.1978. Octave pedal, M-103.

1970s	Earlier script logo	$290	$400
1970s	Later block logo	$225	$250

Blue Box M103 (Reissue)

1995-present. Reissued by Jim Dunlop, blue case. Produces 1 octave above or 2 octaves below.

1995-2020		$40	$45

Carbon Copy M169

1987-present. Analog delay. 3 Control knobs. 1 Toggle switch. Green housing.

1987-2020		$90	$110

Commande Effects

1981-1983. The Commande series featured plastic housings and electronic switching.

1981-1983	Overdrive	$40	$50
1981-1983	Phaser	$100	$110
1981-1983	Preamp	$40	$50
1981-1983	Stereo Chorus	$60	$70
1981-1983	Sustain	$60	$70
1981-1983	Time Delay	$70	$80
1982-1983	Stereo Flanger	$70	$80

Distortion +

1972-1982.

1970s	Earlier script logo	$185	$225
1970s	Later block logo	$85	$110
1980s	Block logo	$80	$95

Distortion + (Series 2000)

1983-1985		$60	$70

Distortion + M104 (Reissue)

1987-present. Reissued by Jim Dunlop, yellow case.

1987-1990		$55	$65
1991-2020		$45	$55

Distortion II

1981-1983	With AC power cord	$140	$180

Distortion III M115

1987-present. 3 Control knobs. Red housing.

1987-2020		$25	$60

Double Shot Distortion M151

2003-2005. 2 channels.

2003-2005		$65	$75

Dyna Comp

1972-1982. Compressor.

1970s	Block logo, battery	$90	$120
1970s	Script logo, battery	$175	$200
1980s	Block logo, battery	$65	$80

Dyna Comp (Series 2000)

1982-1985		$65	$75

Dyna Comp M102 (Reissue)

1987-present. Reissued by Jim Dunlop, red case.

1987-2020		$35	$40

Envelope Filter

1976-1983		$125	$225

Flanger

1976-1983, 1997-present. Analog, reissued by Dunlop in '97.

1976-1979	AC power cord, 2 inputs	$175	$225
1980-1983	AC power cord	$100	$150
1997-2020	M-117R reissue	$60	$70

Flanger/Doubler

1979	Rack mount	$150	$175

Fullbore Metal M116

1987-present. 6 Control knobs. Bare metal housing.

1987-2020		$35	$100

Limiter

1980-1982. AC, 4 knobs.

1980-1982	AC power cord	$125	$200

Loop Selector

1980-1982. A/B switch for 2 effects loops.

1980-1982		$50	$60

Micro Amp

1978-1983, 1995-present. Variable booster, creme case, reissued in '95.

1978-1983		$75	$100
1995-2020	M-133 reissue	$40	$45

Micro Chorus

1980-1983. Yellow case.

1980-1983		$125	$175

Micro Flanger

1981-1982		$100	$150

MODEL YEAR	FEATURES	EXC. COND. LOW	HIGH

Noise Gate Line Driver
1974-1983.

1970s	Script logo	$75	$125
1980s	Block logo	$75	$100

Omni
1980s. Rack unit with floor controller, compressor, 3-band EQ, distortion, delay, chorus/flanger.

1980s		$425	$475

Phase 45
Ca.1976-1982. Battery, earlier script logo, later block.

1970s	Script logo	$125	$200
1980s	Block logo	$100	$125

Phase 90
1972-1982.

1970s	Earlier script logo	$325	$425
1970s	Later block logo	$200	$275
1980s	Block logo	$150	$200

Phase 90 M101 (Reissue)
1987-present. Reissued by Jim Dunlop, orange case.

1987-1989	Block logo	$60	$85
1990-2020	Block or script logo	$50	$75

Phase 100
1974-1982.

1970s	Earlier script logo	$250	$325
1970s	Later block logo, battery	$175	$275

Phaser (Series 2000)
1982-1985. Series 2000 introduced cost cutting die-cast cases.

1982-1985		$60	$85

Pitch Transposer

1980s		$400	$475

Power Converter

1980s		$45	$60

Smart Gate M135
2002-present. Noise-gate, single control, battery powered, gray case.

2002-2020		$60	$80

Stereo Chorus
1978-1985. With AC power cord.

1978-1979		$175	$275
1980-1985		$150	$220

Stereo Chorus (Series 2000)
1983-1985. Series 2000 introduced cost cutting die-cast cases.

1983-1985		$55	$75

Stereo Flanger (Series 2000)
1983-1985. Series 2000 introduced cost cutting die-cast cases, black with blue lettering.

1983-1985		$60	$80

Super Comp M132
2002-present. 3 knobs, black case.

2002-2020		$40	$55

Nobels
1997-present. Effects pedals from Nobels Electronics of Hamburg, Germany. They also make amps.

ODR-1 Natural Overdrive
1997-present. Classic overdrive, green case.

1997-2020		$30	$40

MODEL YEAR	FEATURES	EXC. COND. LOW	HIGH

TR-X Vintage Tremolo
1997-2017. Tremolo effect using modern technology, purple case.

1997-2017		$30	$40

Nomad
1960s. Effects that claimed to be made in the U.S., but most likely built by Shin-ei of Japan. Models include the Verberola and the Fuzz wah, both of which were sold under other brands such as Applied, Jax USA, and Companion.

Fuzz Wah
1960s. Fuzz wah pedal similar to Morley pedals of the era with depth and volume controls and fuzz switch, silver and black.

1960s		$75	$125

Oberheim Electronics Inc.
1970s. Electronics company based in Santa Monica, California, which offered effects under its own name as well as building effects for Gibson/ Maestro.

Voltage Controlled Filter VCF-200
1970s. Voltage-controlled filter, envelope follower and sample-and-hold circuit.

1970s		$100	$400

Oddfellow Effects
Jon Meleika, began in 2013, builds guitar effects pedals in Riverside, California.

Olson
Olson Electronics was based in Akron, Ohio.

Reverberation Amplifier RA-844
1967. Solidstate, battery-operated, reverb unit, depth and volume controls, made in Japan.

1967		$100	$150

Ooh La La Manufacturing
2007-2014. Hand-made guitar effects built in St. Louis Park, Minnesota, including the models formerly offered under the Blackbox brand.

Option 5
2002-present. Jay Woods builds his guitar effects pedals in Mishwaka, Indiana.

Origin Effects
2012-present. Custom-built and production guitar effects made in Oxfordshire, U.K. by Simon Keats.

Ovation
Ovation ventured into the solidstate amp and effects market in the early '70s.

K-6001 Guitar Preamp
1970s. Preamp with reverb, boost, tremolo, fuzz, and a tuner, looks something like a Maestro effect from the '70s, reliability may be an issue.

1970s		$100	$125

MXR Fullbore Metal M116
Keith Myers

MXR Phase 90
Keith Myers

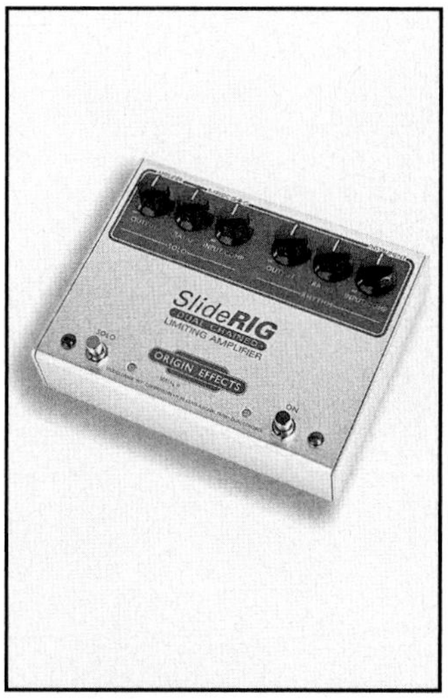

Origin Effects SlideRig

Peavey Companded Chorus CMC-1

Pigtronix FAT Drive

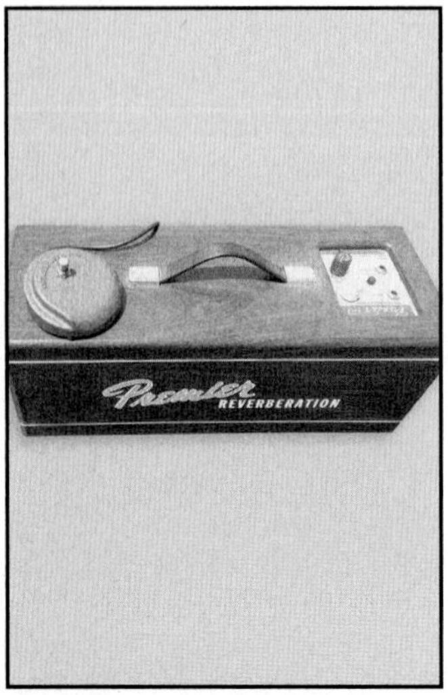

Premier Reverb Unit

MODEL YEAR	FEATURES	EXC. COND. LOW	HIGH

PAIA

1967-present. Founded by John Paia Simonton in Edmond, Oklahama, specializing in synthesizer and effects kits. PAIA did make a few complete products but they are better known for the various electronic kit projects they sold. Values on kit projects are difficult as it depends on the skills of the person who built it.

Roctave Divider 5760

1970s. Kit to build analog octave divider.

1970s	$70	$85

Pan*Damn*ic

2007-2012. Guitar effects pedals made by PLH Professional Audio in West Chester, Pennsylvania.

Park

1965-1982, 1992-2000. Sola/Colorsound made a couple of effects for Marshall and their sister brand, Park. In the '90s, Marshall revived the name for use on small solidstate amps.

Pax

1970s. Imported Maestro copies.

Fuzz Tone Copy

1970s	$125	$150

Octave Box Copy

1970s. Dual push-buttons (normal and octave), 2 knobs (octave volume and sensitivity), green and black case.

1970s	$125	$150

Pearl

Pearl, located in Nashville, Tennessee, and better known for drums, offered a line of guitar effects in the 1980s.

Analog Delay AD-08

1983-1985. Four knobs.

1983-1985	$100	$150

Analog Delay AD-33

1982-1984. Six knobs.

1982-1984	$175	$225

Chorus CH-02

1981-1984. Four knobs.

1981-1984	$75	$100

Chorus Ensemble CE-22

1982-1984. Stereo chorus with toggling between chorus and vibrato, 6 knobs.

1982-1984	$125	$175

Compressor CO-04

1981-1984	$50	$75

Distortion DS-06

1982-1986	$40	$60

Flanger FG-01

1981-1986. Clock pulse generator, ultra-low frequency oscillator.

1981-1986	$75	$100

Graphic EQ GE-09

1983-1985	$40	$55

Octaver OC-07

1982-1986	$100	$225

Overdrive OD-05

1981-1986	$75	$145

Parametric EQ PE-10

1983-1984	$45	$60

Phaser PH-03

1981-1984. Four knobs.

1981-1984	$75	$95

Phaser PH-44

1982-1984. Six knobs.

1982-1984	$150	$175

Stereo Chorus CH-22

1982-1984. Blue case.

1982-1984	$75	$125

Thriller TH-20

1984-1986. Exciter, 4 knobs, black case.

1984-1986	$175	$225

Peavey

1965-present. Peavey made stomp boxes from '87 to around '90. They offered rack mount gear after that.

Accelerator Overdrive AOD-2

1980s	$30	$35

Biampable Bass Chorus BAC-2

1980s	$30	$35

Companded Chorus CMC-1

1980s	$25	$30

Compressor/Sustainer CSR-2

1980s	$35	$40

Digital Delay DDL-3

1980s	$30	$35

Digital Stereo Reverb SRP-16

1980s	$50	$55

Dual Clock Stereo Chorus DSC-4

1980s	$30	$35

Hotfoot Distortion HFD-2

1980s	$25	$30

PedalDoctor FX

1996-present. Tim Creek builds his production and custom guitar effects in Nashville, Tennessee.

Pedalworx

In 2001, Bob McBroom and George Blekas began building guitar effects in Manorville, New York and Huntsville, Alabama. They also do modifications to wahs.

Pharaoh Amplifiers

1998-2010. Builder Matt Farrow builds his effects in Raleigh, North Carolina.

Pignose

1972-present. Guitar stomp boxes offered by the amp builder in Las Vegas, Nevada. They also offer guitars.

Pigtronix

2003-present. Dave Koltai builds his custom guitar effects originally in Brooklyn, and currently in Yonkers, New York and also offers models built in China.

MODEL YEAR	FEATURES	EXC. COND. LOW	HIGH

Plum Crazy FX

Guitar effects built by Kaare Festovog in Apple Valley, Minnesota starting in 2005.

Premier

Ca.1938-ca.1975, 1990-2010. Premier offered a reverb unit in the '60s.

Reverb Unit

1961-late-1960s. Tube, footswitch, 2-tone brown.

1960s		$250	$350

Prescription Electronics

Located in Portland, Oregon, Jack Brossart began offering a variety of hand-made effects in 1994.

Dual-Tone

1998-2009. Overdrive and distortion.

1998-2009		$165	$175

Throb

1996-2014. Tremolo.

1996-2014		$165	$175

Yardbox

1994-2014. Patterned after the original Sola Sound Tonebender.

1994-2014		$90	$125

Pro Tone Pedals

2004-present. Guitar effects pedals built by Dennis Mollan in Dallas, Texas until early-2011, and presently in Summerville, South Carolina.

ProCo

1974-present. Located in Kalamazoo, Michigan and founded by Charlie Wicks, ProCo produces effects, cables and audio products.

Rat

1979-1987. Fuzztone, large box until '84. The second version was 1/3 smaller than original box. The small box version became the Rat 2. The current Vintage Rat is a reissue of the original large box.

1979-1984	Large box	$250	$400
1984-1987	Compact box	$95	$170

Rat 2

1987-present. Classic distortion.

1987-1999		$75	$150
2000-2020		$40	$55

Turbo Rat

1989-present. Fuzztone with higher output gain, slope-front case.

1989-2020		$40	$50

Vintage Rat

1992-2005. Reissue of early-'80s Rat.

1992-2005		$40	$50

Pro-Sound

The effects listed here date from 1987, and were, most likely, around for a short time.

Chorus CR-1

1980s		$25	$40

Delay DL-1

1980s. Analog.

1980s		$35	$55

Distortion DS-1

1980s		$20	$35

Octaver OT-1

1980s		$25	$40

Power and Master Switch PMS-1

1980s		$15	$25

Super Overdrive SD-1

1980s		$20	$35

Providence

1996-present. Guitar effects pedals built in Japan for Pacifix Ltd. and distributed in the U.S. by Godlyke Distributing, Inc.

Radial Engineering

1994-present. Radial makes a variety of products in Port Coquitlam, British Columbia, including direct boxes, snakes, cables, splitters, and, since '99, the Tonebone line of guitar effects.

Rands

1960s. Japanese music company.

Resly Machine RM-29

1960s. Copy of Maestro PS-1 Phase Shifter built by Shin-ei.

1960s		$200	$300

Rapco

The Jackson, Missouri based cable company offers a line of switch, connection and D.I. Boxes.

The Connection AB-100

1988-2017. A/B box

1988-2017		$25	$35

Rastop Designs

2002-present. Alexander Rastopchin builds his effects in Long Island City, New York. He also builds amps.

Ray Butts Music Co.

1950s. Ray Butts ran a music store in Cairo, Illinois, where he built his famous EchoSonic amp. He experimented with building a pioneering fuzz box that never went into production and offered his NovaMatch buffer in limited production.

NovaMatch

Late-1950s. Buffer with 1Db of gain in a lipstick-tube-like unit that plugged into guitar jacks.

1950s		$200	$300

Real McCoy Custom

1993-present. Wahs and effects by Geoffrey Teese. His first wah was advertised as the Real McCoy, by Teese. He now offers his custom wah pedals under the Real McCoy Custom brand. He also used the Teese brand on a line of stomp boxes, starting in '96. The Teese stomp boxes are no longer being made. In '08 he moved to Coos Bay, Oregon.

Prescription Electronics Yardbox

Rivington Guitars

EFFECTS

ProCo Rat 2

Radial Tonebone Texas Dual Overdrive

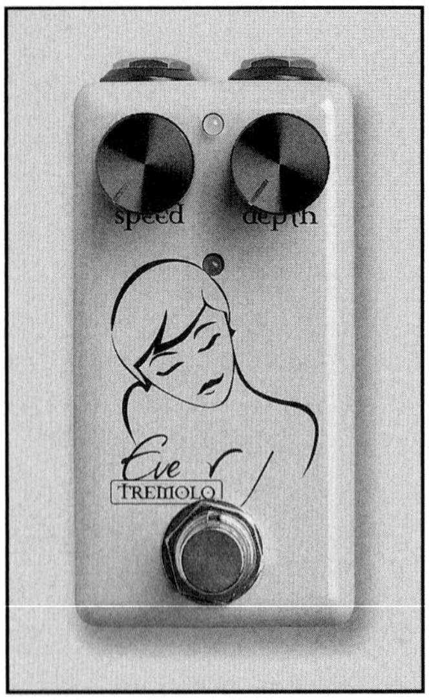

Red Witch Eve Tremolo

Rocktron Banshee Talk Box
Rivington Guitars

Roger Mayer Voodoo Axe

EFFECTS

MODEL YEAR	FEATURES	EXC. COND. LOW	HIGH

Recycled Sound

2009-present. Greg Perrine designs attenuators in Conway, Arkansas, which are then built in China.

Red Panda

2010s-present. Based in Pittsburgh, Pennsylvania.

Bitmap

2016		$75	$125

Raster

2015		$75	$125

Red Witch

2003-present. Analog guitar effects, designed by Ben Fulton, and made in Paekakariki, New Zealand.

Reinhardt

2004-2012. Amp builder Bob Reinhardt of Lynchburg, Virginia also offers a line of effects pedals.

Retro FX Pedals

2006-ca. 2010. Guitar effects pedals built by John Jones in St. Louis, Missouri.

Retroman

2002-present. Joe Wolf builds his retro effects pedals in Janesville, Wisconsin.

Retro-Sonic

2002-present. Tim Larwill builds effects in Ottawa, Ontario.

Reverend

1996-present. Reverend offered its Drivetrain effects from '00 to '04. They also build guitars.

RGW Electronics

Guitar effects built by Robbie Wallace, starting in 2003, in Lubbock, Texas.

Rivera

1985-present. Amp builder Paul Rivera also offers a line of guitar pedals built in California.

Rocco

Introduced in 1937, the Rocco Tonexpressor was a volume pedal designed by New York City steel-guitarist Anthony Rocco and built and distributed by Epiphone. Generally credited with being the first guitar effect pedal.

Rockman

See listings under Scholz Research and Dunlop.

Rocktek

1986-2009. Imports formerly distributed by Matthews and Ryan of Brooklyn, New York; and later by D'Andrea USA.

MODEL YEAR	FEATURES	EXC. COND. LOW	HIGH

Effects

1986-2009	Delay, Super Delay	$30	$40
1986-2009	Distortion, 6 Band EQ, Bass EQ, Chorus,	$15	$25

Compressor

1986-2009	Overdrive, Flanger, Metal Worker, Phaser, Vibrator Tremolo	$15	$20

Rocktron

1980s-present. Rocktron is a division of GHS Strings and offers a line of amps, controllers, stomp boxes, and preamps.

Austin Gold Overdrive

1997-2011. Light overdrive.

1997-2011		$25	$35

Banshee Talk Box

1997-present. Includes power supply.

1997-2020		$65	$120

Hush Rack Mount

1980s-present.

2000-2020		$50	$100

Hush The Pedal

1996-present. Pedal version of rackmount Hush.

1996-2020		$25	$50

Rampage Distortion

1996-2013. Sustain, high-gain and distortion.

1996-2013		$25	$35

Surf Tremolo

1997-2000		$60	$80

Tsunami Chorus

1996-2009. Battery or optional AC adapter.

1996-2009	Battery power	$40	$50
1996-2009	With power supply	$50	$60

Vertigo Vibe

2003-2006. Rotating Leslie speaker effect.

2003-2006	Battery power	$50	$60
2003-2006	With power supply	$60	$70

XDC

1980s. Rack mount stereo preamp, distortion.

1980s		$100	$150

Roger Linn Design

2001-present. Effects built in Berkeley, California by Roger Linn.

Roger Mayer Electronics

1964-present. Roger Mayer started making guitar effects in the U.K. in '64 for guitarists like Jimmy Page and Jeff Beck. He moved to the U.S. in '69 to start a company making studio gear and effects. Until about 1980, the effects were built one at a time in small numbers and not available to the general public. In the '80s he started producing larger quantities of pedals, introducing his rocket-shaped enclosure. He returned to the U.K. in '89.

Axis Fuzz

1987-present.

1987-2020		$125	$150

MODEL YEAR	FEATURES	EXC. COND. LOW	HIGH

Classic Fuzz

1987-present. The Fuzz Face.

1987-2020		$175	$200

Metal Fuzz

Early 1980s-1994.

1987-1994		$125	$150

Mongoose Fuzz

1987-2017.

1987-2017		$125	$250

Octavia

1981-present. Famous rocket-shaped box.

1981-2020		$180	$400

Voodoo-1

Ca.1990-present.

1990-2020		$100	$300

Rogue

2001-present. Budget imported guitar effects. They also offer guitars, basses, lap steels, mandolins, banjos, ukuleles and amps.

Roland

Japan's Roland Corporation first launched effect pedals in 1974; a year or two later the subsidiary company, Boss, debuted its own line. They were marketed concurrently at first, but gradually Boss became reserved for compact effects while the Roland name was used on amplifiers, keyboards, synths and larger processors.

Analog Synth SPV

1970s. Multi-effect synth, rack mount.

1970s		$750	$900

Bee Baa AF-100

1975-ca.1980. Fuzz and treble boost.

1975-1980		$300	$550

Bee Gee AF-60

1975-ca.1980. Sustain, distortion.

1975-1980		$75	$125

Double Beat AD-50

1975-ca.1980. Fuzz wah.

1975-1980		$175	$200

Expression Pedal EV-5

1970s		$50	$75

Expression Pedal EV-5 Reissue

2000. Black pedal, blue foot pad.

2000		$25	$30

Guitar Synth Pedal GR-33 and Pickup GK-2A

2000-2005. Requires optional GK-2A pickup, blue case.

2000-2005		$300	$550

Human Rhythm Composer R-8

1980s. Drum machine, key pad entry.

1980s		$175	$250

Human Rhythm Composer R-8 MK II

2000s. Black case.

2000s		$300	$400

Jet Phaser AP-7

1975-ca.1978. Phase and distortion.

1975-1978		$525	$650

Phase Five AP-5

1975-ca.1978.

1975-1978		$200	$225

Phase II AP-2

1975-ca.1980. Brown case.

1975-1980		$125	$175

Space Echo Unit

1974-ca. 1980. Tape echo and reverb, various models.

1970s	RE-101	$350	$500
1970s	RE-150	$350	$550
1970s	RE-200	$500	$750
1970s	RE-201	$750	$1,250
1970s	RE-301	$700	$950
1970s	RE-501	$700	$1,000
1970s	SRE-555 Chorus Echo	$950	$1,100

Vocoder SVC-350

Late-1970s-1980s. Vocal synthesis (vocoder) for voice or guitar, rack mount version of VP-330.

1980		$550	$700

Vocoder VP-330 Plus

Late-1970s-1980s. Analog vocal synthesis (vocoder) for voice or guitar, includes 2 1/2 octaves keyboard.

1978-1982		$750	$900

Wah Beat AW-10

1975-ca.1980.

1975-1980		$70	$100

Rosac Electronics

1969-1970s. Founded by Ralph Scaffidi and former Mosrite engineer Ed Sanner with backing from Morris Rosenberg and Ben Sacco in Bakersfield, California. Made the Nu-Fuzz which was a clone of Mosrite's Fuzzrite and the Nu-Wah. Closed in mid- to late- '70s and Scaffidi went on to co-found Osborne Sound Laboratories.

Ross

Founded by Bud Ross, who also established Kustom, in Chanute, Kansas, in the 1970s. Ross produced primarily amplifiers. In about '78, they introduced a line of U.S.-made effects. Later production switched to Asia.

10 Band Graphic Equalizer

1970s		$80	$100

Compressor

1970s. Gray or black case.

1970s		$325	$475

Distortion

1978-ca.1980. Brown.

1979-1980		$50	$70

Flanger

1977-ca.1980. Red.

1977-1980		$100	$125

Phase Distortion R1

1979. Purple.

1979		$100	$125

Phaser

1978-ca.1980. Orange.

1978-1980		$65	$90

Stereo Delay

1978-ca.1980.

1978-1980		$125	$175

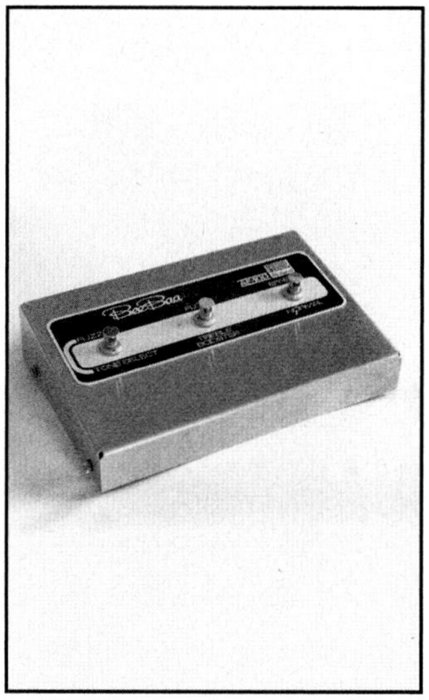

Roland Bee Baa AF-100

Niclas Löfgren

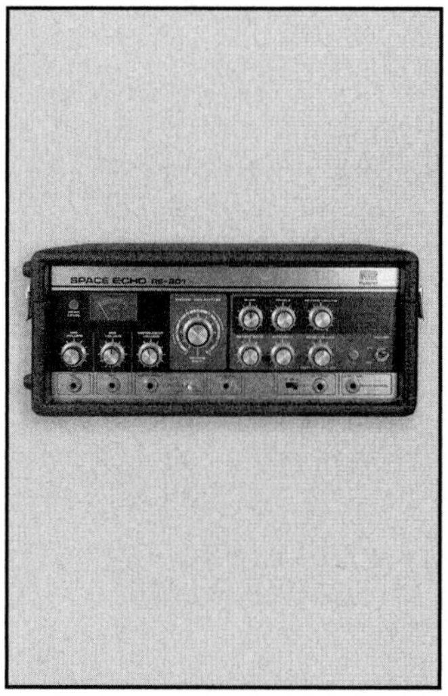

Roland Space Echo

1978 Ross Distortion

Rivington Guitars

EFFECTS

Sam Ash Fuzzz Boxx

Satellite Eradicator

1970s Shin-ei Fuzz Wah

Keith Myers

MODEL YEAR	FEATURES	EXC. COND. LOW	HIGH

Rotosound

1960s. English musical company.

Fuzz Box

1967-1968. Fuzz built by Sola Sound.

1967-1968		$150	$300

Rotovibe

See listing under Dunlop.

Royal

1960s. Japanese effects company with product built by other makers, including the Thunder Electronic Co. Ltd. Of Tokyo.

Double Effect Machine RFC-1

1960s. Built by Shin-ei.

1960s		$150	$300

Fuzz Box RF-1

1960s. Expanded version of Univox Super-Fuzz with tone effects foot switch.

1960s		$150	$300

S. Hawk Ltd.

1970s. Various effect pedals, no model names on case, only company name and logo.

Hawk I Fuzz

1970s. Linear pre-amp, fuzz, headphone amp, 1 slider.

1970s		$300	$400

SAM

1970s-1980s. Effects made by the SAM Electromechanical Plant in Moscow, Russia.

Effekt-1 Fuzz-Wah-Vibrato

1970s. Fuzz pedal with foot control.

1970s		$50	$100

Sam Ash

1960s-1970s, 2013-present. Sam Ash Music was founded by Sam Ash (nee Askynase), in '24, in Brooklyn, and by '66, there were about four Ash stores. During this time, Ash Music private branded their own amps and effects. In 2013, Sam Ash reissued the Fuzzz Boxx.

Fuzzola

1960s. Rebranded version of the Shin-ei Uni-Fuzz. There is also a Fuzzola II.

1960s		$200	$400

Fuzzz Boxx

1966-1967, 2013-2019. Red, made by Astro/Universal Amplifier Company, same as Astro Amp Astrotone fuzz. Reissued in '13.

1966-1967		$400	$850
2013-2019	Reissue	$125	$150

Volume Wah

1970s. Italian-made.

1970s		$175	$200

Sangil

1960s. Ed Sanner -- designer of the Mosrite Fuzzrite -- also built and sold effects through his own company, Sangil.

MODEL YEAR	FEATURES	EXC. COND. LOW	HIGH

Iron Butterfly

1960s. Fuzz wah pedal.

1960s		$200	$400

Sanner

1999. Reissue from Eddie Sanner, who was the engineer behind the 1960s Mosrite Fuzzrite, using the identical circuitry as the original. Issued as a limited edition.

Sano

1944-ca. 1970. Sano was a New Jersey-based accordion company that built their own amps and a reverb unit. They also imported guitars for a few years, starting in '66.

Satellite Amplifiers

2004-present. Analog effects pedals made in San Diego, California by amp builder Adam Grimm.

Schaffer-Vega

1975-1982, 2015-present. After Mick Jagger's wireless system for the 1975 Rolling Stones Tour of the Americas began broadcasting police calls and lottery numbers, New York recording engineer Ken Schaffer invented his Schaffter-Vega Diversity System (SVDS) as a better wireless system - although it also could be used to affect guitar tones, offering overdrive as used by AC/DC's Angus Young.

Diversity System

1975-1982. Wireless mic and guitar transmitter and receiver.

1975-1982		$1,250	$2,500

Schaller

The German guitar accessories company, which began in 1945, offered guitar effects off and on since the '60s and currently has reissue versions of its volume pedal and tremolo.

Scholz Research

1982-1995. Started by Tom Scholz of the band Boston. In '95, Jim Dunlop picked up the Rockman line (see Dunlop).

Equalizer

1980s		$180	$300

Power Soak

1980s		$150	$270

Rockadapter

1980s		$70	$90

Rockman

1980s		$120	$200

Rockman X100

1980s. Professional studio processor.

1980s		$125	$300

Soloist

1980s. Personal guitar processor.

1980s		$100	$200

Stereo Chorus

1980s		$120	$280

MODEL YEAR	FEATURES	EXC. COND. LOW	HIGH
Stereo Chorus Delay			
1980s		$120	$280
Sustainer 200			
1980s		$300	$550
Wah Volume			
1980s		$60	$100

Seamoon

1973-1977, 1997-2002. Seamoon made effects until '77, when Dave Tarnowski bought up the remaining inventory and started Analog Digital Associates (ADA). He reissued the brand in '97.

Fresh Fuzz

1975-1977. Recently reissued by ADA.

1975-1977 $150 $200

Funk Machine

1974-1977. Envelope filter. Recently reissued by ADA.

1974-1977 $200 $345

Studio Phase

1975-1977. Phase shifter.

1975-1977 $75 $125

Sears, Roebuck & Co.

1970s. Department-store and mail-order giant Sears sold inexpensive effects likely made in Japan by Guyatone.

Fuzz & Wa & Volume Control Pedal

1970s $50 $100

Fuzz-Tone Control

1970s. Dallas-Arbiter Fuzz Face/Guyatone Crazy-Face copy.

1970s $100 $250

Sekova

Mid-1960s-mid-1970s. Entry level instruments imported by the U.S. Musical Merchandise Corporation of New York.

Big Muff SE-2015

1972-1973. "Triangle" Big Muff Pi copy built by Shin-ei.

1972-1973 $150 $225

Selmer

1960s. English music company based in London.

Buzz-Tone

1960s $150 $300

Seymour Duncan

In late 2003, pickup maker Seymour Duncan, located in Santa Barbara, California, added a line of stomp box guitar effects.

Shin-ei

1969-1970s. When the Honey company went bankrupt in March, '69, it was reborn as Shin-ei and many Honey designs continued in production in various forms. Their chief engineer was Fumio Mieda who later did design work for Korg. Shin-ei also made effects for Univox (including the Uni-Fuzz, Super-Fuzz and Uni-Vibe), Companion, Applied, Apollo, Jax, Nomad, Shaftsbury, Pax, Crown, Royal, Mica, Kent, Marlboro, Memphis, Bruno, Boomer, Alex, Ace Tone, Aria, Goya, Kimbara, Lord, National, Northland, Tele Star, Tempo, and probably others.

Fuzz Wah

1970s $250 $400

FY-2 Fuzz Box

1969-1970s. 2 transistors.

1969-1970s $250 $450

FY-6 Super Fuzz

1969-1970s. Built from fuzz circuitry of Psychedelic Machine, 6 transistors.

1969-1970s $750 $1,100

Mica Tone Fuzz Wah

1970s $190 $270

Octave Box OB-28

1970s. Version of the Gibson Maestro OB-1 Octave Box.

1970s $200 $400

Phase Tone PT-18

1970s. Tremolo, vibrato and phase effects.

1970s $400 $600

Psychedelic Machine

1969. Amp head-sized effect with numerous controls.

1969 $750 $1,100

Resly (Repeat Time) Machine

1970s. Black case, 3 speeds.

1970s $400 $500

Sho-Bud

1956-1980. This pedal steel company offered volume pedals as well.

Sho-Sound Boss Tone

1970s-1980. Licensed version of the Jordan Boss Tone, 2 control knobs, similar black plastic housing.

1970s-80 $65 $150

Volume Pedal

1965 $90 $170

SIB

Effects pedals from Rick Hamel, who helped design SMF amps.

Siegmund Guitars & Amplifiers

1993-present. Los Angeles, California amp and guitar builder Chris Siegmund added effects to his product line in '99.

Sitori Sonics

Emanual Ellinas began building his guitar effects in Birmingham, Alabama, in 2006.

Skrydstrup R&D

1997-present. Effects pedals built by Steen Skrydstrup in Denmark. He also builds amps.

Skull Crusher

2009-2015. Partners John Kasha and Shawn Crosby of Tone Box Effects, built their guitar effects in Simi Valley, California.

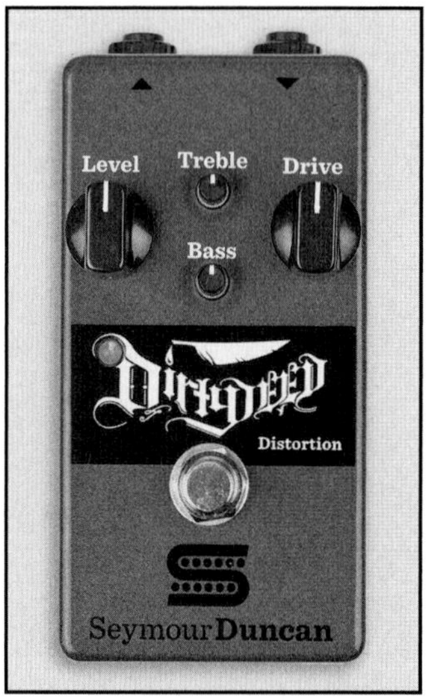

Seymour Duncan Dirty Deed

Siegmund DoubleDrive

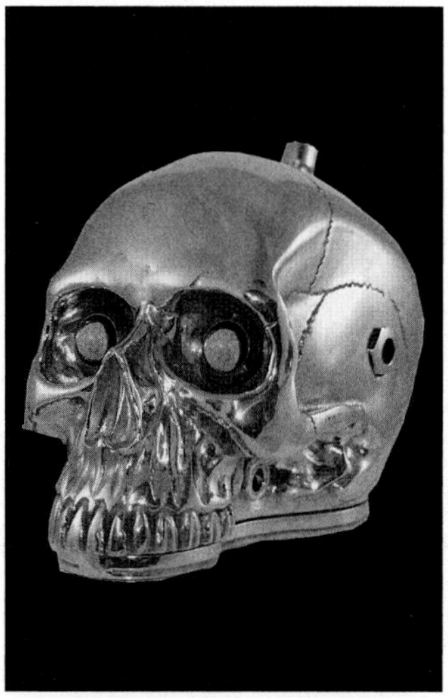

Skull Crusher Chrome

Snarling Dogs Mold Spore Psycho-Scumatic
Garrett Tung

Sola/Colorsound Fuzz/Wah/Swell
Shane Richardson

StarTouch AB Stereo

Snarling Dogs

Started by Charlie Stringer of Stringer Industries, Warren, New Jersey in 1997. Stringer died in May '99. The brand is now carried by D'Andrea USA.

Sobbat

1995-present. Line of effects from Kinko Music Company of Kyoto, Japan.

Solasound/Colorsound

1962-2010. Sola was founded by London's Macari's Musical Exchange in '62, which was launched by former Vox associate Larry Macari and his brother Joe. The first product was the Tone-Bender fuzz box, designed by Gary Stewart Hurst and modeled in part on the Maestro Fuzz-Tone FZ-1. The first readily available fuzz in Britain, it was an instant success. Sola soon began making effects for Vox, Marshall, Park, and B & M and later under their own Colorsound brand. Refer to Colorsound for further listings and more company info.

MODEL YEAR	FEATURES	EXC. COND. LOW	HIGH
Tone Bender Mk1.5			
1966-1969		$1,000	$2,100
Tone Bender MkI			
1965-1966		$1,500	$2,450
Tone Bender MkIII			
1968-1970s		$1,500	$2,000
Tone Bender Professional MkII			
1960s		$900	$2,100

Soldano

1987-present. Seattle, Washington amp builder Soldano also built a reverb unit.

MODEL YEAR	FEATURES	EXC. COND. LOW	HIGH
Sho-Space Box			
1987-2018. Tube-driven spring reverb.			
1987-2018		$800	$900

SoloDallas

2015-present. Started by Filippo "SoloDallas" Olivieri to build replicas of the Schaffer-Vega Diversity System. Based in San Diego, California.

MODEL YEAR	FEATURES	EXC. COND. LOW	HIGH
Schaffer Boost Solo-X			
2015-2021		$75	$125
Schaffer Replica Classic			
2015-present. Stompbox replicating the SVDS guitar effect.			
2015-2021		$140	$200
Schaffer Replica Storm			
2015-present. Stompbox replicating the SVDS guitar effect.			
2015-2021		$90	$150
Schaffer Replica Tower			
2015-present. Replica of the original SVDS made by SoloDallas.			
2015-2021		$1,000	$1,300

Songbird

See Dytronics.

Sonic Edge

Guitar and bass effects pedals built by Ben Fargen in Sacramento, California starting in 2010. He also builds the Fargen amps.

Sonuus

2009-present. Guitar effects built in China and imported by owners James Clark and John McAuliffe in the U.K.

Sovtek (New Sensor Corporation)

1990s. Started by Mike Matthews, of Electro-Harmonix fame, to build EHX effects in Russia. See also Electro-Harmonix.

MODEL YEAR	FEATURES	EXC. COND. LOW	HIGH
Bass Balls			
1990s		$150	$230
Big Muff			
1990s		$150	$300
Electric Mistress			
1990s		$150	$300
Red Army Overdrive			
1990s		$150	$300
Small Stone			
1990s		$150	$250

Speedster

1995-2000, 2003-2007. Amp builder Speedster added guitar effects pedals to their product line in '04, built in Gig Harbor, Washington.

SPEKTR

1970s-1980s. Effects made in Novosibirsk, Russia.

MODEL YEAR	FEATURES	EXC. COND. LOW	HIGH
SPEKTR-1			
1970s. Analog multi-effects pedal with foot control.			
1970s		$50	$100
SPEKTR-2			
1970s. Fuzz wah.			
1970s		$50	$100
SPEKTR-3			
1970s. Volume pedal with boost, fuzz, wah and auto-wah.			
1970s		$50	$150
SPEKTR-4			
1970s		$50	$100

StarTouch

2001-present. Tony Chostner builds production/custom, effects pedals in Salem, Oregon.

Stephenson

1997-present. Amp builder Mark Stephenson in Parksville, British Columbia also offers a line of guitar pedals.

Stinger

Stinger effects were distributed by the Martin Guitar Company from 1989 to '90.

MODEL YEAR	FEATURES	EXC. COND. LOW	HIGH
Effects			
1989-1990	CH-70 Stereo Chorus	$25	$55
1989-1990	CO-20 Compressor	$35	$55

MODEL YEAR	FEATURES	EXC. COND. LOW	HIGH
1989-1990	DD-90 Digital Delay	$45	$65
1989-1990	DE-80 Analog Delay	$50	$70
1989-1990	DI-10 Distortion	$40	$65
1989-1990	FL-60 Flanger	$40	$65
1989-1990	OD-30 Overdrive	$40	$65
1989-1990	TS-5 Tube Stack	$45	$65

Strymon

2009-present. Founded in 2004 as Damage Control, the company began offering effects pedals under the Strymon name in 2009. Owners Gregg Stock, Pete Celi, and Dave Fruehling build their line of guitar pedals in Chatsworth, California.

Big Sky

2013-present. Reverberator pedal.

2013-2020 $390 $490

BlueSky

2010-present. Digital reverb pedal.

2010-2020 $230 $280

Brigadier

2010-present. dBucket delay.

2010-2020 $175 $200

Deco

2014-present. Tape saturation and doubletracker pedal.

2014-2020 $245 $270

DIG

2015-present. Dual digital delay.

2015-2020 $220 $250

El Capistan

2010-present. Tape echo.

2010-2020 $210 $280

Flint

2012-present. Tremolo and reverb.

2012-2020 $175 $290

Lex

2011-present. Rotary effects pedal.

2011-2020 $230 $300

Mobius

2012-present. Modulation pedal.

2012-2020 $335 $405

OB.1

2009-2020. Optical compressor and clean boost.

2009-2020 $125 $150

Ojai

2016-present. High current DC power supply.

2016-2020 $125 $175

Ola

2010-present. dBucket chorus and vibrato.

2010-2020 $180 $235

Orbit

2010-present. dBucket flanger.

2010-2020 $170 $190

Riverside

2016-present. Multistage drive.

2016-2020 $200 $230

Sunset

2017-present. Dual overdrive pedal.

2017-2020 $230 $275

TimeLine

2011-present. Delay pedal.

2011-2020 $315 $380

Zuma

2016-present. High current DC power supply.

2016-2020 $160 $220

Studio Electronics

1989-present. Synth and midi developer Greg St. Regis' Studio Electronics added guitar pedal effects to their line in '03.

Subdecay Studios

2003-present. Brian Marshall builds his guitar effects in Woodinville, Washington.

Supersound

1952-1974. Founded by England's Alan Wootton, this firm built echo units in the 1960s. They also built amps, guitars and basses.

Supro

1935-1968, 2004-present. Supro offered a few reverb units in the '60s. Brand name was revived in '04.

500 R Standard Reverb Unit

1962-1963. Outboard reverb unit.

1962-1963 $250 $500

600 Reverb Power Unit

1961. Independent reverb unit amp combination to be used with Supro Model 1600R amp or other amps, 3 tubes, 1x8" speaker.

1961 $300 $700

Swart Amplifier

2003-present. Effects pedals built by Michael J. Swart in Wilmington, North Carolina. He also builds amps.

Sweet Sound

1994-present. Line of effects from Bob Sweet, originally made in Trenton, Michigan, and then in Coral Springs, Florida. Bob died in 2008. Currently built by his brother Gerald.

Swell Pedal Company

1997-2012. Mike Olienechak builds his line of tube pedals for guitar and bass in Nashville, Tennessee.

SynapticGroove

Benjamin Harrison and Chrystal Gilles build their guitar effects in Edmond, Oklahoma, starting in 2013.

Systech (Systems & Technology in Music, Inc)

1975-1979. Started by Greg Hockman, Systech was located in Kalamazoo, Michigan.

Envelope & Repeater

1975-1979 $125 $300

Strymon Deco

Strymon TimeLine

Swart FuzzyBoost

TC Electronic HOF Mini

Keith Myers

Ten Bananas At Large Stereo Buffer

ThroBak Electronics Strange Master

MODEL YEAR	FEATURES	EXC. COND. LOW	HIGH

Envelope Follower

1975-1979. Decay and drive controls.

1975-1979		$150	$300

Flanger

1975-1979. Sweep rate, depth and gain controls.

1975-1979		$125	$300

Harmonic Energizer

1975-1979. Filter/distortion with bandwidth, center frequency and gain controls. Silver body early, black body later.

1975-1979		$900	$1,450

Overdrive

1975-1979. EQ, distortion and gain controls. Silver body early, black body later.

1975-1979		$200	$450

Phase Shifter

1975-1979. Dual sweep rate controls plus emphasis control.

1975-1979		$150	$350

T.C. Jauernig Electronics

2004-present. Tim Jauernig, of Rothschild, Wisconsin, built effects for several years before launching his T.C. Jauernig brand in '04.

TC Electronic

1976-present. Brothers Kim and John Rishøj founded TC Electronic in Risskov, Denmark, and made guitar effects pedals for several years before moving into rack-mounted gear. Currently they offer a wide range of pro audio gear and rack and floor guitar effects.

Booster + Distortion

1980s		$325	$400

Dual Parametric Equalizer

1980s		$275	$350

Stereo Chorus/Flanger SCF

Introduced in 1982, and reissued in '91.

1980s		$175	$275

Sustain + Equalizer

1980s		$225	$300

Tech 21

1989-present. Tech 21 builds their SansAmp and other effects in New York City. They also build amps.

Sansamp

1989-present. Offers a variety of tube amp tones.

1989	1st year	$125	$175
1990-2020		$100	$125

XXL Pedal

1995-2000, 2005-2012. Distortion, fuzz.

1995-2012		$50	$75

Teese

Geoffrey Teese's first wah was advertised as the Real McCoy, by Teese. He now offers his custom wah pedals under the Real McCoy Custom brand. The Teese brand was used on his line of stomp boxes, starting in '96. The Teese stomp boxes are no longer being made.

Ten

2013-present. Guitar effects built in Spokane, Washington by Ryan Dunn and Doug Harrison. From 2001-'13 they used the ToadWorks brand.

The Original Geek

Jeff Rubin began building guitar effects pedals in Los Angeles, California under the Geek MacDaddy brand in 2004. After a breakup with his business partner in '09 he began using The Original Geek brand.

Theremaniacs

2010s-present. Started by Chuck Collins, builder of Theremins, based in Big Bend, Wisconsin.

Harmonic Percolator

2010s-present. Replica of '70s InterFax Harmonic Percolator.

2010s-2021		$150	$275

Thomas Organ

The Thomas Organ Company was heavily involved with Vox from 1964 to '72, importing their instruments into the U.S. and designing and assembling products, including the wah-wah pedal. Both Thomas Organ and JMI, Vox's European distributor, wanted to offer the new effect. The problem was solved by labeling the Thomas Organ wah the Crybaby. The Crybaby is now offered by Dunlop. Refer to Vox listing for Crybaby Stereo Fuzz Wah, Crybaby Wah, and Wah Wah.

ThroBak Electronics

2004-present. Jonathan Gundry builds his guitar effects in Grand Rapids, Michigan. He also builds guitar amps and pickups.

ToadWorks

See listing for TEN.

TomasZewicZ or TZZ

2008-present. Guitar effects pedals built by John Tomaszewicz in Coral Springs, Florida, which he labels TZZ. He also builds amps.

Tone Box Effects

See listing for Skull Crusher.

Tonebone

See Radial Engineering listing.

ToneCandy

2007-present. Mike Marino builds his guitar effects pedals in Santa Rosa, California.

Top Gear

1960s-1970s. Top Gear was a London music store. Their effects were made by other manufacturers.

Rotator

1970s. Leslie effect.

1970s		$100	$175

MODEL YEAR	FEATURES	EXC. COND. LOW	HIGH

Top Hat Amplification

1994-present. Brian Gerhard builds his amps and effects in Fuquay-Varina, North Carolina. He previously built them in La Habra, California and Apex, North Carolina.

Traynor

1963-present. Amp and PA builder Traynor also built two spring reverb units, one tube and one solidstate, in Canada from 1966-'72 and a 7-band EQ from '73-'78.

Tremolo

See listing under Dunlop.

T-Rex

2003-present. Made in Denmark and imported by European Musical Imports.

TSVG

Mike Klein started building his guitar effects in his shop located in Philadelphia, Pennsylvania in 2011.

Tube Works

1987-2004. Founded by B.K. Butler (see Audio Matrix) in Denver, Colorado, Tube Works became a division of Genz Benz Enclosures of Scottsdale, Arizona in 1997 which dropped the brand in 2004. They also offered tube/solidstate amps, cabinets, and DI boxes.

Blue Tube

1989-2004. Overdrive bass driver with 12AX7A tube.

1989-2004		$100	$150

Real Tube

Ca.1987-2004. Overdrive with 12AX7A tube.

1987-1999		$100	$150

Tube Driver

1987-2004. With tube.

1987-2004		$100	$150

TWA (Totally Wycked Audio)

2009-present. Boutique analog effect pedals made in the U.S. and offered by Godlyke, Inc.

Tycobrahe

The Tycobrahe story was over almost before it began. Doing business in 1976-1977, they produced only three pedals and a direct box, one the fabled Octavia. The company, located in Hermosa Beach, California, made high-quality, original devices, but they didn't catch on. Now, they are very collectible. Reissues were made by Chicago Iron.

Octavia

1976-1977, 2000s. Octave doubler.

1976-1977		$1,200	$1,900
2000s	Octavia & Octavian reissue	$260	$300

Parapedal

1976-1977, 2000s. Wah.

1976-1977		$700	$1,350
2000s	Reissue, light blue	$200	$300

Pedalflanger

1976-1977. Blue pedal-controlled flanger.

1976-1977		$1,200	$1,350

UMI (United Musical Industries)

1960s. UMI was based in Farmingdale, New York.

Tone Booster

1960s. Primitive EQ unit with treble and bass boost controls.

1960s		$75	$125

Uni-Vibe

See listings under Univox and Dunlop.

Univox

Univox was a brand owned by Merson (later Unicord), of Westbury, New York. It marketed guitars and amps, and added effects in the late-'60s. Most Univox effects were made by Shin-ei, of Japan. They vanished in about '81.

Drum Machine SR-55

1970s		$175	$200

EC-80 A Echo

Early-1970s-ca.1977. Tape echo, sometimes shown as The Brat Echo Chamber.

1970s		$75	$100

EC-100 Echo

1970s. Tape, sound-on-sound.

1970s		$75	$160

Echo-Tech EM-200

1970s. Disc recording echo unit.

1970s		$130	$170

Fuzz FY-2

1970s		$185	$350

Micro 41 FCM41 4 channel mixer

1970s		$35	$50

Micro Fazer

1970s. Phase shifter.

1970s		$75	$115

Noise-Clamp EX110

1970s		$45	$55

Phaser PHZ1

1970s. AC powered.

1970s		$50	$75

Pro-Verb UR-3

1970s. Reverb (spring) unit, black tolex, slider controls for 2 inputs, 1 output plus remote output.

1970s		$85	$100

Square Wave SQ150

Introduced in 1976. Distortion, orange case.

1970s		$75	$125

Super-Fuzz

1968-1973. Made by Shin-ei and similar to the FY-6 Super Fuzz, built from fuzz circuitry of Honey/Shin-ei Psychedelic Machine, 6 transistors, battery powered.

1968-1973	Gray box, normal bypass switch	$400	$975
1968-1973	Unicord, various colors, blue bypass pedal	$350	$500

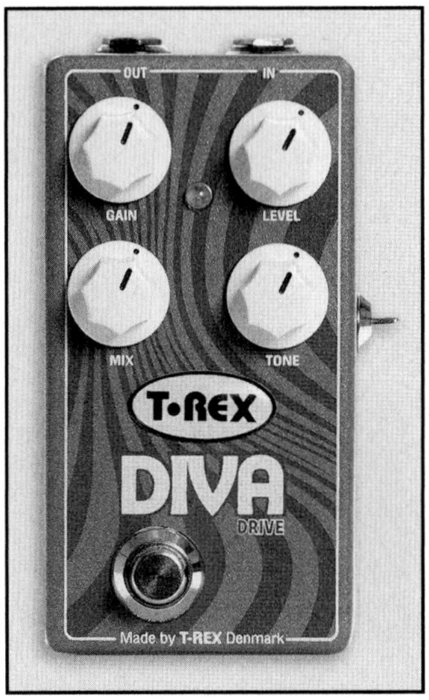

T-Rex Diva Drive

Univox Micro Fazer

Univox Super-Fuzz U-1095

Kai Hawkins

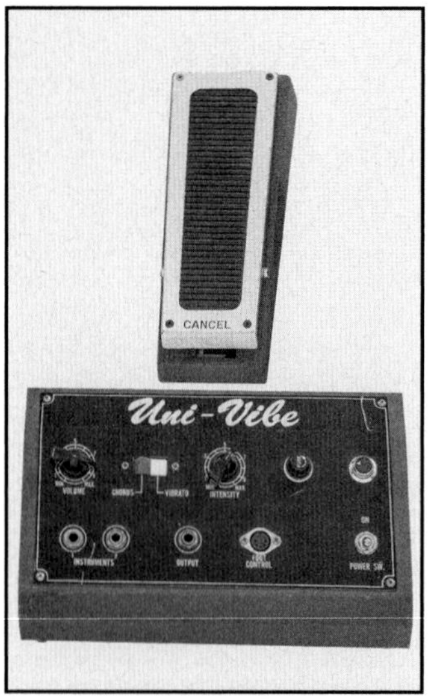

1969 Univox Uni-Vibe

Imaged by Heritage Auctions, HA.com

Voodoo Lab Tremolo

Vox Tone Bender MKIII

Shane Richardson

MODEL YEAR	FEATURES	EXC. COND. LOW	HIGH

Surf Siren

1970s. Wah pedal.

1970s		$90	$150

Uni-Comp

1970s. Compression limiter.

1970s		$50	$100

Uni-Drive

1970s		$150	$200

Uni-Fuzz

1969-1973. Fuzz tone in blue case, 2 black knobs and slider switch. Made by Shin-ei, AC-powered version of Super-Fuzz, built from fuzz circuitry of Honey/Shin-ei Psychedelic Machine.

1969-1973		$350	$600

Uni-Tron 5

1975. A.k.a. Funky Filter, envelope filter.

1975		$200	$525

Uni-Vibe

Introduced ca. 1969-1970s. Rotating-speaker simulator, with control pedal. Made by Shin-ei, built from circuitry of Honey/Shin-ei Psychedelic Machine.

1960s		$1,500	$3,000
1970s		$900	$1,600

Uni-Wah Wah/Volume

1970s		$80	$125

VanAmps

Amp builder Tim Van Tassel of Golden Valley, Minnesota, also offers a line of reverb effects pedals.

Vesta Fire

Ca.1981-ca.1988. Brand of Japan's Shiino Musical Instrument Corp.

Effects

1981-1988	Chorus/Flange FLCH	$35	$50
1981-1988	Distortion DST	$35	$50
1981-1988	Flanger	$35	$50
1981-1988	Noise Gate	$25	$40
1981-1988	Stereo Chorus SCH	$35	$50

Vintage Tone Project

Line of guitar effects made by Robert Rush and company in Delmar, New York, starting in 2003. They also built reissues of Dan Armstong's '70s effects from '03 to '06.

VintageFX

2003-present. Effects based on vintage pedals from the '60s and '70s built by Dave Archer in Grand Island, New York.

Visual Sound

1995-2015. Effects pedals designed by Bob Weil and R.G. Keen in Spring Hill, Tennessee and built in China. They changed name to Truetone in '15.

VooDoo Lab

1994-present. Line of effects made by Digital Music Corp. in California.

MODEL YEAR	FEATURES	EXC. COND. LOW	HIGH

Analog Chorus

1997-2012. Based on '76 CE-1.

1997-2012		$100	$120

Bosstone

1994-1999. Based on '60s Jordan Electronics Fuzz.

1994-1999		$70	$110

Microvibe

1996-present. Uni-Vibe rotating-speaker simulator.

1996-2020		$65	$100

Overdrive

1994-2002. Based on '70s overdrive.

1994-2002		$55	$65

Superfuzz

1999-present.

1999-2020		$75	$90

Tremolo

1995-present.

1995-2020		$55	$75

Vox

1954-present. The first Vox product was a volume pedal. Ca. '66, they released the Tone Bender, one of the classic fuzzboxes of all time. A year or so later, they delivered their greatest contribution to the effects world, the first wah-wah pedal. The American arm of Vox (then under Thomas Organ) succumbed in '72. In the U.K., the company was on-again/off-again.

Clyde McCoy Wah-Wah Pedal

Introduced in 1967, reissued in 2001-2008. Clyde's picture on bottom cover.

1967	Clyde's picture	$800	$1,050
1968	No picture	$600	$800
2001-2008	Model V-848	$150	$175

Crybaby Wah

Introduced in 1968. The Thomas Organ Company was heavily involved with Vox from '64 to '72, importing their instruments into the U.S. and designing and assembling products. One product developed in conjunction with Vox was the wah-wah pedal. Both Thomas Organ and JMI, Vox's European distributor, wanted to offer the new effect. The problem was solved by labeling the Thomas Organ wah the Crybaby. The original wahs were built by Jen in Italy, but Thomas later made them in their Chicago, Illinois and Sepulveda, California plants. Thomas Organ retained the marketing rights to Vox until '79, but was not very active with the brand after '72. The Crybaby brand is now offered by Dunlop.

1960s	Jen-made	$200	$250
1970	Sepulveda-made	$125	$175

Double Sound

1970s. Jen-made, Double Sound model name on bottom of pedal, double sound derived from fuzz and wah ability.

1970s		$200	$250

Flanger

1970s		$200	$250

King Wah

1970s. Chrome top, Italian-made.

1970s		$200	$250

MODEL YEAR	FEATURES	EXC. COND. LOW	HIGH

Repeat Percussion
Late-1960s. Plug-in module with on-off switch and rate adjustment.

1968		$100	$125

Stereo Fuzz Wah

1970s		$150	$200

Tone Bender V-828
1966-1970s. Fuzz box, reissued as the V-829 in '93.

1966-1968	Mark I, gray case	$550	$750
1969	Mark II, black case	$475	$625
1970s	Mark III	$475	$600

ToneLab Valvetronix
2003-2019. Multi-effect modeling processor (ToneLab EX or ToneLab ST), 12AX7 tube preamp.

2003-2019		$400	$425

V-807 Echo-Reverb Unit
1967. Solidstate, disc echo.

1967		$275	$375

V-837 Echo Deluxe Tape Echo
1967. Solidstate, multiple heads.

1967		$350	$450

V-846 Wah
1969-1970s. Chrome top, Italian-made.

1969	Clyde McCoy	$450	$600
1970s		$300	$425

V-847 Wah-Wah
1992-present. Reissue of the original V-846 Wah.

1992-2020		$55	$80

Volume Pedal
1954-late 1960s. Reissued as the V850.

1960s		$50	$270

Wampler Pedals
2004-present. Brian Wampler began building effects under the brand Indy Guitarist in 2004, and changed the name to Wampler Pedals in 2007. They are built in Greenwood, Indiana.

Warmenfat
2004-present. Pre-amps and guitar effects built in Sacramento, California, by Rainbow Electronics.

Wasabi
2003-2008. Line of guitar effect pedals from Danelectro.

Washburn
Washburn offered a line of effects from around 1983 to ca. '89.

Effects

1980s	Analog Delay AX:9	$30	$35
1980s	Flanger FX:4	$35	$40
1980s	Phaser PX:8	$40	$45
1980s	Stack in a Box SX:3	$30	$35

Watkins/WEM
1957-present. Watkins Electric Music (WEM) was founded by Charlie Watkins. Their first commercial product was the Watkins Dominator amp in '57, followed by the Copicat Echo in '58.

MODEL YEAR	FEATURES	EXC. COND. LOW	HIGH

Copicat Tape Echo
1958-1970s, 1985-present. The Copicat went through several detail changes, subsequently known as the Marks I, II, III, and IV versions. It has been reissued in various forms by Watkins.

1958-1970s	Solidstate	$525	$1,000
1958-1970s	Tube	$850	$1,100

Way Huge Electronics
1995-1998, 2008-present Way Huge offered a variety of stomp boxes, made in Sherman Oaks, California. Jim Dunlop revived the brand in '08.

Green Rhino Overdrive II

1990s		$100	$200

WD Music
Since 1978, WD Music has offered a wide line of aftermarket products for guitar players. From '91 to '02, they offered a line of effects that were copies of the original Dan Armstrong color series (refer to Dan Armstrong listing).

Blue Clipper
1991-2002. Fuzz.

1991-2002		$30	$45

Orange Squeezer
1991-2002. Signal compressor.

1991-2002	Light Orange case	$40	$50

Purple Peaker
1991-2002. Mini EQ.

1991-2002		$40	$50

Westbury
1978-ca.1983. Brand imported by Unicord.

Tube Overdrive
1978-1983. 12AX7.

1978-1983		$150	$200

Whirlwind
1976-present. Effects from Michael Laiacona, who helped found MXR, originally made in Rochester, New York. Currently the company offers guitar effects, DI boxes and other music devices built in Greece, New York.

Commander
1980s. Boost and effects loop selector.

1980s		$75	$100

Wilsic
1970s. Enginer Charlie Ramskirr designed effects for Hornby Skewes, but also offered DIY mail-order kits under the brand Wilsic.

Sound Vibration

1970s		$75	$100

Wilson Effects
2007-present. Guitar effects built by Kevin Wilson in Guilford, Indiana.

WMD (William Mathewson Devices)
2008-present. William Mathewson builds his instrument effects in Denver, Colorado.

Wampler Clarksdale

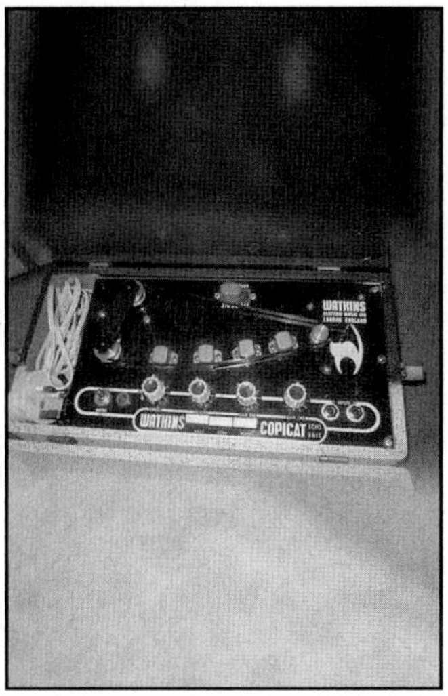

Watkins Copicat Tape Echo
Rivington Guitars

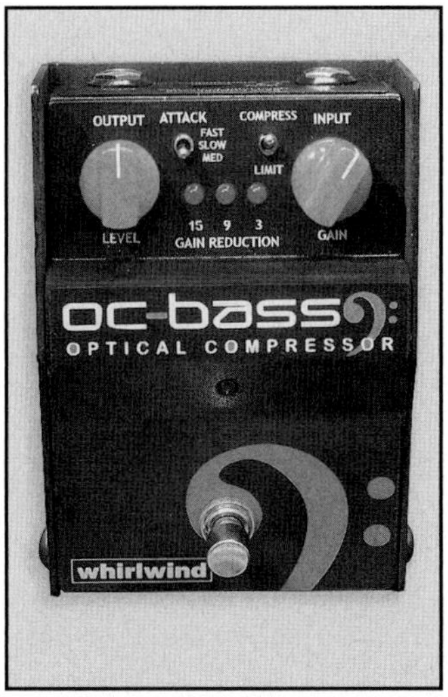

Whirlwind OC-Bass Optical Compressor

EFFECTS

Xotic Effects Bass RC Booster

Xotic Effects Soul Driven

Xotic Effects X-Blender

MODEL YEAR	FEATURES	EXC. COND. LOW	HIGH

Wurlitzer

Wurlitzer offered the Fuzzer Buzzer in the 1960s, which was the same as the Clark Fuzz.

Xotic Effects

2001-present. The roots of Xotic go back to a small garage in the San Fernando Valley of Southern California in 1996, producing and designing bass guitars and bass preamps, soon expanding to build boutique pedals.

AC Booster

2002-2020. Light overdrive with 20db+ of boost and 2-band EQ.

2002-2020 $75 $100

AC Plus

2007-2018. Stackable 2-channel light overdrive with 3-band EQ and compression.

2007-2018 $100 $130

AC-COMP

2010-2018. Custom Shop light overdrive with 3 compression modes. Internal DIP switches control level of compression, tonal character, and treble/presence levels.

2010-2018 $120 $130

Bass BB Preamp

2006-present. Bass overdrive with 2 overlapping EQs and ±15dB boost/cut.

2006-2020 $130 $160

Bass RC Booster

2006-present. Bass boost with 2-band active EQ and ±15dB boost/cut.

2006-2020 $50 $80

BB Plus

2008-2020. Stackable 2-channel overdrive with 3-band EQ and compression.

2008-2020 $115 $130

BB Preamp

2005-2020. Overdrive with 30dB+ boost and 2-band EQ.

2005-2020 $80 $100

BBP-COMP

2011-2018. Custom Shop overdrive with 3 compression modes and 2-band EQ.

2011-2018 $140 $160

BBP-MB

2009-2018. Custom Shop overdrive with 12dB+ mid-treble boost and 2-band EQ.

2009-2018 $125 $140

EP Booster

2009-present. Mini boost pedal with 20db+ of boost. Internal DIP switches control boost frequencies and EQ.

2009-2020 $75 $90

RC Booster

2002-2017. Clean boost with 20dB+ of transparent boost and 2-band EQ.

2002-2017 $50 $60

RC Booster V2

2016-present. Clean boost with 20dB+ transparent boost and 2-band EQ. Added gain channel with gain 2 control knob.

2016-2020 $75 $90

Robotalk

1998-2009. Envelope filter, random arpeggiator and low-pass filter. Ultra-boutique pedal, made from scratch, in limited quantities.

1998-2009 $200 $300

Robotalk 2

2009-present. Envelope filter with 2 separate envelope filter channels that can be combined or used individually. Internal input pad controls passive/active signals. Internal DIP switches control frequency settings.

2009-2020 $125 $180

Robotalk-RI

2011-2018. Custom Shop envelope filter with an enhanced arpeggiator for more wonderfully strange and mesmerizing sounds.

2011-2018 $150 $200

SL Drive

2013-present. Mini overdrive pedal produces tones from legendary amplifiers, the Super Lead and Super Bass. Internal DIP switches control boost frequencies and EQ settings.

2013-2020 $65 $90

Soul Driven

2017-present. Boost/overdrive with mid-boost and tone knobs. Internal bass boost DIP switches control up to 6dB+ of boost.

2017-2020 $130 $140

SP Compressor

2012-present. Mini compressor featuring a wide variety of compressor tones from vintage to subtle to modern, and more. Internal DIP switches control attack.

2012-2020 $85 $95

Stereo X-Blender

2011-2017. Custom Shop effects looper with 3 parallel effects loops equipped with a transparent buffer amplifier allowing feeding and mixing of effects without signal deterioration.

2011-2017 $130 $160

X-Blender

2006-present. Series and parallel effects looper with boost switch for 6dB+ volume boost, treble and bass EQ and phase inverter switch. Dry/Wet knob in parallel mode.

2006-2020 $85 $140

Xotic Wah

2014-present. Wah pedal that features a 20% smaller size, bias, wah-Q, treble, and bass controls, plus internal DIP switches for even more tonal possibilities.

2014-2020 $175 $200

Yack

1960s. Japanese effects company.

Fuzz Box YF-2

1960s $150 $400

Yamaha

1946-present. Yamaha has offered effects since at least the early '80s. They also build guitars, basses, amps, and other musical instruments.

MODEL YEAR	FEATURES	EXC. COND. LOW	HIGH

Analog Delay E1005

1980s. Free-standing, double-space rack mount-sized, short to long range delays, gray case.

1980s		$160	$180

Yubro

Yubro, of Bellaire, Texas, offered a line of nine effects in the mid- to late-'80s.

Analog Delay AD-800

1980s	300 ms	$75	$125

Stereo Chorus CH-600

1980s		$50	$75

Z.Vex Effects

1995-present. Zachary Vex builds his effects in Minneapolis, Minnesota, with some subassembly work done in Michigan. Painters on staff create stock and custom versions of many pedals, which often bring higher prices. Vexter pedals are silk-screened pedals made in Taiwan. U.S. Vexters are manufactured in Taiwan, but engraved in Minnesota. California Mini models are manufactured in California. In 2000-2002, Vex built the solidbody Drip Guitar with an onboard Wah. In 2002, Vex also began building amps.

Basstortion

2011-present. Bass distortion, bright/dark switch.

2011-2020		$95	$130

Box of Metal

2007-present. High-gain distortion, switchable noise gate.

2007-2020		$120	$150

Box of Rock

2005-present. 2-in-1 pedal. Tube amp-type distortion pedal and clean post-gain boost.

2005-2020		$100	$150

Channel 2

2014-present. Mini boost pedal, master volume.

2014-2020		$70	$90

Distortion

2009-2020. Tube amp-style distortion, sub contour and gain switches.

2009-2020		$60	$75

Double Rock

2012-present. Dual switchable distortion/boost pedal.

2012-2020		$175	$200

Fat Fuzz Factory

2011-present. Fuzz Factory with additional 3-position mini toggle to select frequency range.

2011-2020		$175	$200

Fuzz Factory

1995-present. Powerful, tweaky, and unique germanium fuzz pedal, with idiosyncratic hand-painted housings. Also available as Vexter and US Vexter models.

1995-2014		$120	$145
1995-2020	Hand-painted	$140	$200

Fuzz Factory 7

2013-2018. Limited edition Fuzz Factory with foot-switchable EQ and 9-position rotary frequency selector.

2013-2018		$300	$375

MODEL YEAR	FEATURES	EXC. COND. LOW	HIGH

Fuzz Probe

2000-present. Theremin-controlled Fuzz Factory.

2000-2020		$100	$175

Fuzzolo

2014-present. Mini footprint 2-knob silicon fuzz for guitar and bass.

2014-2020		$80	$100

Instant Lo-Fi Junky

2011-present. Filter, compression, and wave shapeable vibrato and blend for chorus effect.

2011-2020		$150	$175

Inventobox

2010-present. Dual pedal chassis for DIY builders or for use with Z.Vex modules.

2010-2020		$150	$200

Jonny Octave

2005-present. Octave pedal.

2005-2020		$140	$185

Lo-Fi Loop Junky

2002-present. Sampler, single 20-second sample with vibrato.

2002-2020		$150	$200

Loop Gate

2012-present. Audio looping mixer with foot switchable noise gate.

2012-2020		$100	$130

Machine

1996-present. Crossover distortion generator.

1996-2020		$150	$200

Mastrotron

2009-present. Silicon fuzz with mini toggle sub contour.

2009-2020		$70	$95

Octane I, II, and III

1995-present. Ring modulator fuzz.

1995-2020		$85	$125

Ooh Wah I and II

2003-2013. 8-step sequencer using wah filters with random sequencing.

2003-2013		$90	$115

Ringtone and Ringtone TT

2006-2013. 8-step sequencer using ring modulator.

2006-2013		$175	$190

Seek Trem I and II

2006-2013. 8-step sequencer using volume.

1999-2013		$135	$175

Seek Wah I and II

2006-2013. 8-step sequencer using wah filters.

2006-2013		$140	$180

Sonar Tremolo and Stutter

2012-present. Tremolo with wave shaping, distortion circuit, tap tempo, and auto tempo ramping.

2012-2020		$175	$190

Super Duper 2-in-1

2001-present. Dual boost with master volume on 2nd channel.

2001-2020		$120	$170

Super Hard On

1996-present. Sparkly clean boost.

1996-2020		$110	$170

Z.Vex Effects Double Rock

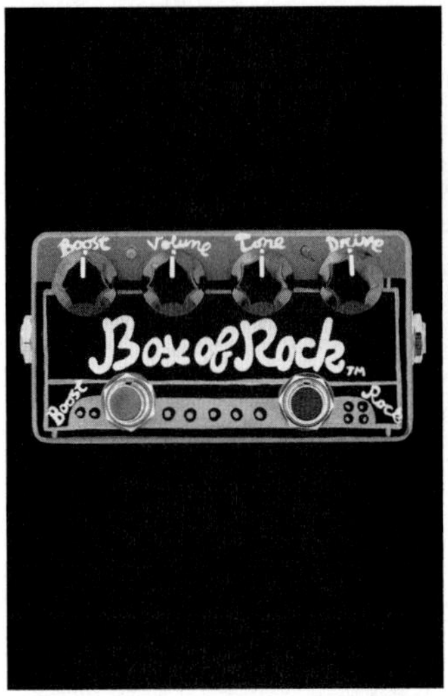

Z.Vex Effects Box of Rock

Z.Vex Fuzz Factory 7

Z.Vex Super Seek Wah

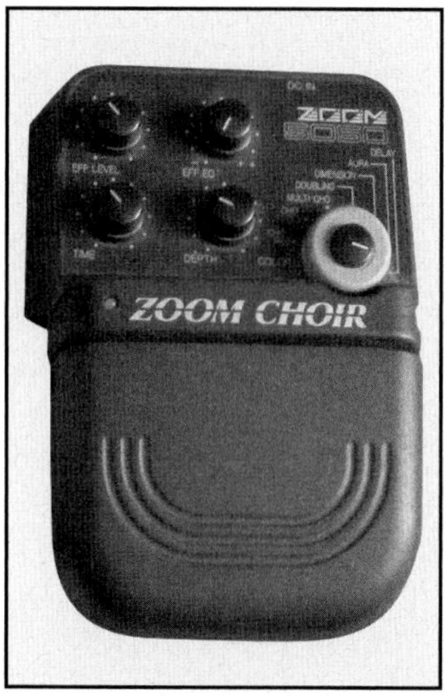

Zoom Choir
Jim Schreck

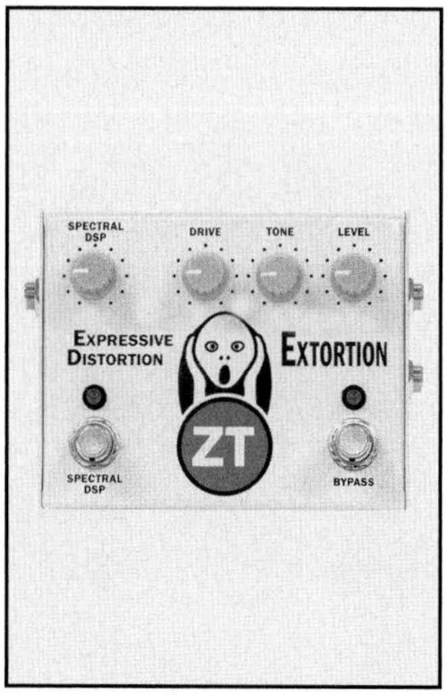

ZT Amplifiers Extortion

EFFECTS

MODEL YEAR	FEATURES	EXC. COND. LOW	HIGH

Super Ringtone
2013-present. 16-step sequencer using ring modulator with MIDI sync, tap tempo, tap tempo sync, and glissando.

2013-2020	$150	$225

Super Seek Trem
2013-present. 16-step sequencer using volume with MIDI sync, tap tempo, tap tempo sync, and glissando.

2013-2020	$150	$195

Super Seek Wah
2013-present. 16-step sequencer using wah filters with MIDI sync, tap tempo, tap tempo sync, and glissando.

2013-2020	$150	$195

Tremolo Probe
2000-present. Theremin-controlled volume.

2000-2020	$100	$175

Tremorama
2004-2013. 8-step sequencer using volume with random sequencing.

2004-2013	$195	$230

Volume Probe
2000-2002. Theremin-controlled volume using coiled cable for antenna.

2000-2002	$100	$175

Wah Probe
2000-present. Theremin-controlled wah.

2000-2020	$100	$175

Woolly Mammoth
1999-present. Silicon fuzz for guitar and bass.

1999-2020	$200	$290

Zinky
Amp builder Bruce Zinky added guitar effects in late 2003, in Flagstaff, Arizona. He also builds amps and has revived the Supro brand on a guitar and amp.

Zoom
Effects line from Samson Technologies Corp. of Syosset, New York.

503 Amp Simulator

1998-2000	$25	$40

504 Acoustic Pedal
1997-2000. Compact multi-effects pedal, 24 effects, tuner, replaced by II version.

1997-2000	$25	$40

505 Guitar Pedal
1996-2000. Compact multi-effects pedal, 24 effects, tuner, replaced by II version.

1996-2000	$30	$40

506 Bass Pedal
1997-2000. Compact multi-effects bass pedal, 24 effects, tuner, black box, orange panel. Replaced by II version.

1997-2000	$35	$45

507 Reverb

1997-2000	$25	$40

1010 Player
1996-1999. Compact multi-effects pedal board, 16 distortions, 25 effects.

1996-1999	$40	$75

ZT Amplifiers
2009-present. Effects pedals built in China and offered by Ken Kantor in Berkeley, California. He also imports amps.

STEELS & LAP STEELS

1941 Mastertone lap steel: Jim Mathis.

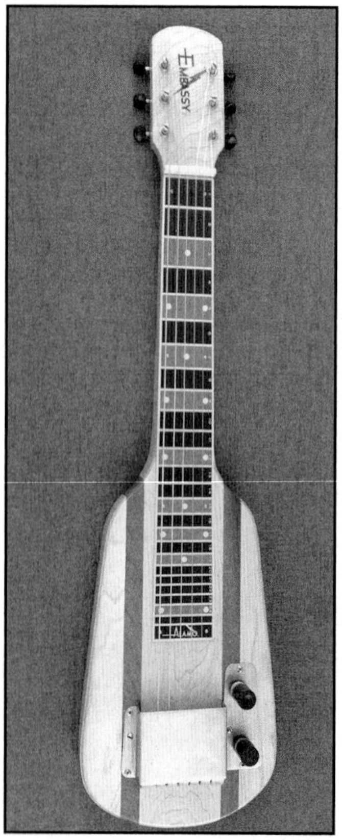

Alamo Embassy

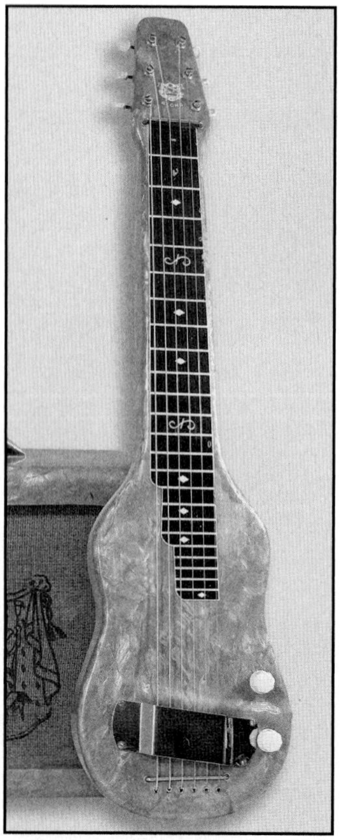

1948 Aloha

Dan Bishop

MODEL YEAR	FEATURES	EXC. COND. LOW	HIGH

Airline

Ca. 1958-1968. Name used by Montgomery Ward for instruments built by Kay, Harmony and Valco.

Lap Steel

1960s	Res-O-Glas/plastic	$460	$600
1960s	Wood	$270	$350

Rocket 6-String Steel

1960s. Black and white, 3 legs, Valco-made.

1960s		$350	$450

Student 6 Steel

1950s	Black	$230	$300

Alamo

1947-1982. The first musical instruments built by Alamo, of San Antonio, Texas, were lap steel and amp combos with early models sold with small birch amps.

Hawaiian Lap Steels

1947-ca. 1967. Models include the '50s Challenger and Futuramic Dual Eight, the '50s and early-'60s Embassy (pear-shape) and Jet (triangular), the early-'60s Futuramic Eight and Futuramic Six, and the late-'60s Embassy (triangular Jet).

1950s		$270	$350

Alkire

1939-1950s. Founded by musician and teacher Eddie Alkire, with instruments like his E-Harp Steel built by Epiphone and maybe others (see Epiphone for values).

Aloha

1935-1960s. Private branded by Aloha Publishing and Musical Instruments Company, Chicago, Illinois. Made by others. There was also the Aloha Manufacturing Company of Honolulu which made musical instruments from around 1911 to the late '20s.

Alvarez

1965-present. Imported by St. Louis Music from mid-'60s. They also offered guitars, banjos and mandolins.

Model 5010 Koa D Steel-String

1960s		$210	$275

Aria/Aria Pro II

1956-present. Aria offered Japanese-made steels and lap steels in the '60s.

Lap Steel

1960s		$230	$300

Asher

1982-present. Intermediate, professional and premium grade, production/custom, solidbody, semi-hollow body and acoustic lap steels built by luthier Bill Asher in Venice, California. He also builds guitars.

Audiovox

Ca. 1935-ca. 1950. Paul Tutmarc's Audiovox Manufacturing, of Seattle, Washington, was a pioneer in electric lap steels, basses, guitars and amps.

Lap Steel

1940s		$700	$900

Bel-Tone

1950s. Private branded by Magnatone, Bel-Tone oval logo on headstock.

Lap Steel

1950s	Pearloid cover	$230	$300

Bigsby

1947-1965, 2002-present. All handmade by Paul Arthur Bigsby, in Downey, California. Bigsby was a pioneer in developing pedal steels and they were generally special order or custom-made and not mass produced. The original instruments were made until '65 and should be valued on a case-by-case basis. Models include the Single Neck pedal steel, Double 8 pedal steel, 8/10 Doubleneck pedal steel, Triple 8 pedal steel (all ca. '47-'65), and the '57-'58 Magnatone G-70 lap steel. A solidbody guitar and a pedal steel based upon the original Paul Bigsby designs were introduced January, 2002.

Triple 8-String Neck Steel

1947-1965. Bigsby steel were generally special order or custom-made and not mass produced. Instruments should be valued on a case-by-case basis.

1947-1959	Natural	$6,100	$7,900

Bronson

Ca. 1934-early 1960s. George Bronson was a steel guitar instructor in the Detroit area from the 1930s to the early '60s and sold instruments under his own brand. Most instruments and amps were made by Rickenbacker, Dickerson or Valco.

Leilani Lap Steel and Amp Set

1940s. Pearloid lap steel and small matching amp.

1940s		$385	$500

Melody King Model 52 Lap Steel

1950s. Brown bakelite body with 5 gold cavity covers on the top, made by Rickenbacker.

1950s		$750	$975

Model B Style

1948-1952. Rickenbacker-made.

1948-1952		$850	$1,100

Singing Electric

1950s. Round body, Valco-made.

1950s		$385	$500

Streamliner Lap Steel

1950s. Guitar-shape body, 1 pickup, 1 knob, red-orange pearloid cover.

1950s		$225	$290

Carvin

1946-present. Founded by Lowell C. Kiesel who produced lapsteels under the Kiesel brand for 1947-'50. In late '49, he renamed the instrument line Carvin after sons Carson and Galvin. Until '77, they offered lap, console, and pedal steels with up to 4 necks.

Double 6 Steel With Legs

1960s		$725	$950

MODEL YEAR	FEATURES	EXC. COND. LOW	HIGH

Double 8 Steel With Legs

1960s Sunburst $775 $1,000

Electric Hawaiian Lap Steel

1950s $230 $300

Single 8 With Legs

1960s. Large block position markers, 1 pickup, 2 knobs, blond finish.

1960s $535 $700

Coppock

1930s-1959. Lap and console steels built by luthier John Lee Coppock in the Los Angeles area and in Peshastin, Washington. Coppock played Hawaiian music professionally in the 1920s and '30s and had a music studio where he started building his brand of steels around 1932. He moved to Washington in '44.

Cromwell

1935-1939. Budget model brand built by Gibson and distributed by various mail-order businesses.

Lap Steel

1939. Charlie Christian bar pickup.

1939 Sunburst $270 $350

Danelectro

Known mainly for guitars and amps, Danelectro did offer a few lap steels in the mid-'50s.

Hawaiian Guitar

1958-1961. Three-tiered poplar solidbody lap steel, 1 lipstick tube pickup.

1958-1961 $1,050 $1,350

Deckly

1970s-1980s. Intermediate and professional grade pedal steel models, Deckly logo on front side of body.

Denley

1960s. Pedal steels built by Nigel Dennis and Gordon Huntley in England. They also made steels for Jim Burns' Ormston brand in the '60s.

Dickerson

1937-1948. Founded by the Dickerson brothers in '37, primarily for electric lap steels and small amps. Besides their own brand, Dickerson made instruments for Cleveland's Oahu Company, Varsity, Southern California Music, Bronson, Roland Ball, and Gourley. The lap steels were often sold with matching amps, both covered in pearloid mother-of-toilet-seat (MOTS). By '48, the company changed ownership and was renamed Magna Electronics (Magnatone).

Lap Steel

1940s. Dickerson appears to have offered 3 Hawaiian guitars. The Student was pear-shaped with a volume control; the Standard with had a volume and tone; both have decal 'boards and gray pearloid. The De Luxe is rare and came in tan pearloid and had sparkle plastic inlays and trim. Pre-War Dickersons have a heavier cast tailpiece; Post-War models have a metal rod and thru-body grommets. These were usually sold with a matching amp.

1940 Student or Standard $230 $300

Dobro

1929-1942, ca.1954-2019. Dobro offered lap steels from '33 to '42. Gibson now owns the brand and recently offered a lap steel.

E-45 Lap Steel

Late 1970s-1986. Reproduction of '37-'41 wood body Hawaiian lap steel, offered as 6-, 7-, 8-, or 10-string.

1980s 6- or 8-string $650 $850

Hawaiian Lap Steel

1933-1942. Bell-shaped wood body Hawaiian.

1933-1942 $600 $775

Lap Steel Guitar and Amp Set

1930s-1940s. Typical pearloid covered student 6-string lap steel and small matching amp (with 3 tubes and 1 control knob).

1933-1942 $700 $900

Metal Body Lap Steel

1936. All metal body, Dobro logo on body.

1936 $875 $1,150

Dwight

1950s. Private branded instruments made by National-Supro. Epiphone made a Dwight brand guitar in the '60s which was not related to the lap-steels.

Lap Steel

1950s. Pearloid, 6 strings.

1950s $385 $500

Electro

1964-1975. The Electro line was manufactured by Electro String Instruments and distributed by Radio-Tel. The Electro logo appeared on the headstock rather than Rickenbacker. Refer to the Rickenbacker section for models.

Electromuse

1940s-1950s. Mainly offered lap steel and tube amp packages but they also offered acoustic and electric hollowbody guitars.

Lap Steel

1940s $250 $325

Emmons

1970s-present. Professional and premium grade, production/custom, pedal steels built by Lashley, Inc. of Burlington, North Carolina.

Double 10 Steel

1970-1982. Push/pull pedal steel.

1970-1982 $2,850 $3,700

Lashley LeGrande III Steel

2001-present. Double-neck, 8 pedals, 4 knee levers, 25th Anniversary.

2001-2020 $2,850 $3,700

S-10 Pedal Steel

1970-1982. Single 10-string neck pedal steel.

1970-1982 $1,975 $2,550

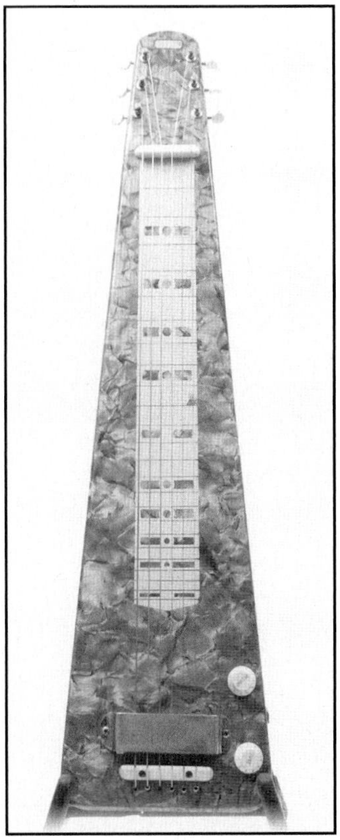

1950s Bronson Singing Electric

Bernunzio Uptown Music

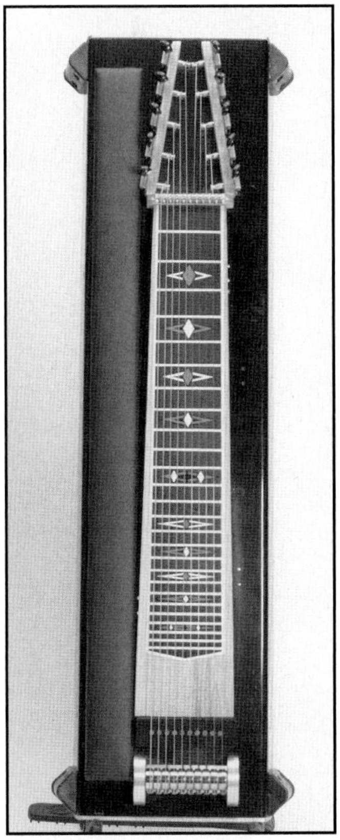

Deckley S110

Bernunzio Uptown Music

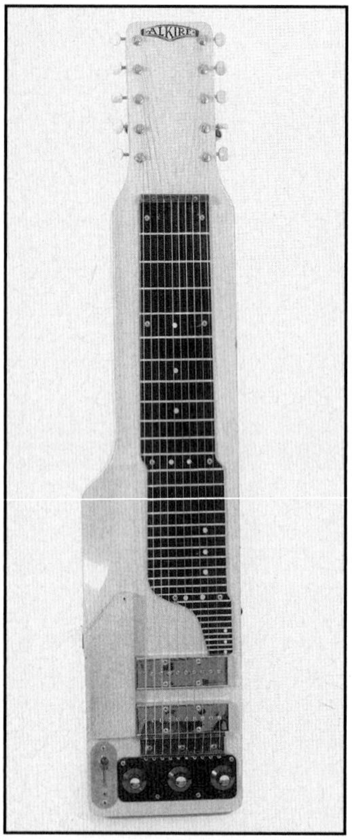

1950s Epiphone Eddie Alkire E-Harp

Jim Mathis

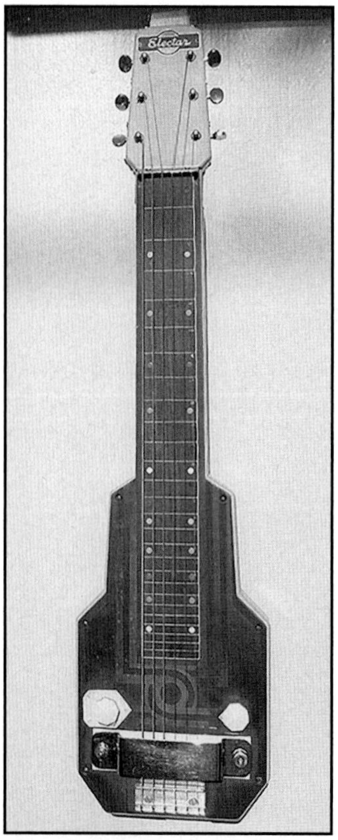

1936 Epiphone Electar

Dennis Clark

MODEL YEAR	FEATURES	EXC. COND. LOW	HIGH

Student, 3-Pedal Steel

1970s. Single neck.

1970s		$700	$900

English Electronics

1960s. Norman English had a teaching studio in Lansing, Michigan, where he gave guitar and steel lessons. He had his own private-branded instruments made by Valco in Chicago.

Tonemaster Lap Steel

1960s. Cream pearloid, 6 strings, 3 legs, Valco-made.

1960s		$365	$475
1960s	Stringtone pitch changer	$525	$675

Epiphone

1928-present. The then Epiphone Banjo Company was established in '28. Best known for its guitars, the company offered steels from '35 to '58 when Gibson purchased the brand.

Century Lap Steel

1939-1957. Rocket-shaped maple body, 1 pickup, metal 'board, 6, 7 or 8 strings, black finish.

1939-1957		$440	$575

Eddie Alkire E-Harp

1939-1950s. 10-string, similar to Epiphone lap steel with Epi-style logo, offered in lap steel or console.

1939-1950s		$725	$950

Electar Hawaiian Lap Steel

1935-1937. Wood teardrop-shaped body, bakelite top, black, horseshoe pickup, 6 string.

1935-1937		$560	$725

Electar Model M Hawaiian Lap Steel

1936-1939. Metal top, stair-step body, art deco, black ('36-'37) or gray ('38-'39), 6, 7 or 8 strings.

1936-1939		$575	$750

Kent Hawaiian Lap Steel

1949-1953. Guitar-shaped maple body, 6 strings, lower-end of Epiphone Hawaiian line, Electar script logo below bottom of fretboard.

1949-1953		$290	$375

Solo Console Steel

1939-1954. Maple with white mahogany laminated body, black binding, black metal 'board, 6, 7 or 8 strings.

1939-1954		$600	$775

Triple-Neck Console Steel

1954-1957. neck version of Solo, sunburst or natural finish.

1954-1957		$1,300	$1,700

Zephyr Hawaiian Lap Steel

1939-1957. Maple stair-step body, metal 'board, 6, 7 or 8 strings.

1939-1949	Black	$600	$800
1950-1957	Sunburst	$600	$800

Ernie Ball

Best known for their strings and Music Man guitars, Ernie Ball offered a steel guitar under their own name for 1974-1979, building a very small quantity.

MODEL YEAR	FEATURES	EXC. COND. LOW	HIGH

S-10 Pedal Steel

1974-1979. 3 pedals, 3 levers.

1974-1979		$1,100	$1,425

Fender

1946-present. Fender offered lap and pedal steels from '46 to '80. In 2005 they introduced a new lap steel model under their Folk Music series, which lasted until 2009.

400 Pedal Steel

1958-1976. One 8-string neck with 4 to 10 pedals.

1958-1976		$675	$875

800 Pedal Steel

1964-1976. One 10-string neck, 6 to 10 pedals.

1964-1976		$850	$1,125

1000 Pedal Steel

1957-1976. Two 8-string necks, 8 or 10 pedals, sunburst or natural.

1957-1976		$925	$1,200

2000 Pedal Steel

1964-1976. Two 10-string necks, 10 or 11 pedals, sunburst.

1964-1976		$1,100	$1,425

Artist Dual 10 Pedal Steel

1976-1981. Two 10-string necks, 8 pedals, 4 knee levers, black or mahogany.

1976-1981		$1,000	$1,300

Champ Lap Steel

1955-1980. Replaced Champion Lap Steel, tan.

1955-1980		$650	$850

Champion Lap Steel

1949-1955. Covered in what collectors call mother-of-toilet-seat (MOTS) finish, also known as pearloid. Replaced by Champ Lap Steel.

1949-1955	Tan	$650	$850
1949-1955	White or yellow pearloid	$650	$850

Deluxe 6/Stringmaster Single Steel

1950-1981. Renamed from the Deluxe, 6 strings, 3 legs.

1950-1969	Blond or walnut	$850	$1,100
1970-1981	Black or white	$850	$1,100

Deluxe 8/Stringmaster Single Steel

1950-1981. Renamed from the Deluxe, 8 strings, 3 legs.

1950-1969	Blond or walnut	$850	$1,100
1970-1981	Black or white	$850	$1,100

Deluxe Steel

1949-1950. Strings-thru-pickup, Roman numeral markers, became the Deluxe 6 or Deluxe 8 Lap Steel in '50.

1946	Wax	$850	$1,100
1947-1950	Blond or walnut	$850	$1,100

Dual 6 Professional Steel

1952-1981. Two 6-string necks, 3 legs optional, blond or walnut.

1952-1981	Blond or walnut	$1,125	$1,475

Dual 8 Professional Steel

1946-1957. Two 8-string necks, 3 legs optional, blond or walnut.

1946-1957	Blond or walnut	$1,125	$1,475

Fender (continued)

FS-52 Lap Steel

2008-2009. Two-piece ash body, 22.5" scale, chrome hardware, white blonde gloss finish.

MODEL YEAR	FEATURES	EXC. COND. LOW	EXC. COND. HIGH
2008-2009		$270	$350

K & F Steel

1945-1946. Made by Doc Kauffman and Leo Fender, strings-thru-pickup.

MODEL YEAR	FEATURES	EXC. COND. LOW	EXC. COND. HIGH
1945-1946		$1,275	$1,650

Organ Button Steel

1946-1947. Strings-thru-pickup, Roman numerals, red pushbutton for organ effect, most have a wax-like, non-lacquered finish.

MODEL YEAR	FEATURES	EXC. COND. LOW	EXC. COND. HIGH
1946-1947		$775	$1,000

Princeton Steel

1946-1948. Strings-thru-pickup, Roman numeral markers.

MODEL YEAR	FEATURES	EXC. COND. LOW	EXC. COND. HIGH
1946-1948		$960	$1,250

Stringmaster Steel (Two-Neck)

1953-1981. The Stringmaster came in 3 versions, having 2, 3 or 4 8-string necks (6-string necks optional).

MODEL YEAR	FEATURES	EXC. COND. LOW	EXC. COND. HIGH
1953-1954	Blond, 26" scale	$1,400	$1,800
1953-1954	Walnut, 26" scale	$1,300	$1,700
1955-1959	Blond, 245" scale	$1,400	$1,800
1955-1959	Walnut, 24.5" scale	$1,300	$1,700
1960-1969	Blond	$1,300	$1,700
1960-1969	Walnut	$1,200	$1,550
1970-1981	Blond or walnut	$1,200	$1,550

Stringmaster Steel (Three-Neck)

1953-1981.

MODEL YEAR	FEATURES	EXC. COND. LOW	EXC. COND. HIGH
1953-1954	Blond, 26" scale	$1,850	$2,400
1953-1954	Walnut, 26" scale	$1,625	$2,100
1955-1959	Blond, 245" scale	$1,850	$2,400
1955-1959	Walnut, 24.5" scale	$1,625	$2,100
1960-1969	Blond	$1,625	$2,100
1960-1969	Walnut	$1,500	$1,950
1970-1981	Blond or walnut	$1,500	$1,950

Stringmaster Steel (Four-Neck)

1953-1968.

MODEL YEAR	FEATURES	EXC. COND. LOW	EXC. COND. HIGH
1953-1954	Blond, 26" scale	$1,850	$2,400
1953-1954	Walnut, 26" scale	$1,625	$2,100
1955-1959	Blond, 245" scale	$1,850	$2,400
1955-1959	Walnut, 24.5" scale	$1,625	$2,100
1960-1968	Blond or walnut	$1,550	$2,000

Studio Deluxe Lap Steel

1956-1981. One pickup, 3 legs.

MODEL YEAR	FEATURES	EXC. COND. LOW	EXC. COND. HIGH
1956-1981	Blond	$1,000	$1,300

Framus

1946-1977, 1996-present. Imported into the U.S. by Philadelphia Music Company in the '60s. The brand was revived in '96 by Hans Peter Wilfer, the president of Warwick.

Deluxe Table Steel 0/7

MODEL YEAR	FEATURES	EXC. COND. LOW	EXC. COND. HIGH
1970s	White	$300	$390

Student Hawaiian Model 0/4

MODEL YEAR	FEATURES	EXC. COND. LOW	EXC. COND. HIGH
1970s	Red	$190	$250

G.L. Stiles

1960-1994. Gilbert Lee Stiles made a variety of instruments, mainly in the Miami, Florida area.

Doubleneck Pedal Steel

MODEL YEAR	FEATURES	EXC. COND. LOW	EXC. COND. HIGH
1970s		$535	$700

GFI

1989-present. Professional and premium grade, production/custom, pedal steel guitars built by luthier Gene Fields, in Arlington, Texas from '89-2008 and since in Marshfield, Missouri.

Ultra Pedal Steel

MODEL YEAR	FEATURES	EXC. COND. LOW	EXC. COND. HIGH
1990s	10-String	$2,100	$2,700

Gibson

1890s (1902)-present. Gibson offered steels from '35-'68.

BR-3 Lap Steel

1946-1947. Guitar-shaped, 1 P-90, 2 knobs, sunburst, mahogany. Replaced by BR-4 in '47.

MODEL YEAR	FEATURES	EXC. COND. LOW	EXC. COND. HIGH
1946-1947		$725	$950

BR-4 Lap Steel

1947. Guitar-shaped of solid mahogany, round neck, 1 pickup, varied binding, sunburst.

MODEL YEAR	FEATURES	EXC. COND. LOW	EXC. COND. HIGH
1947		$725	$950

BR-6 Lap Steel

1947-1960. Guitar-shaped solid mahogany body, square neck (round by '48).

MODEL YEAR	FEATURES	EXC. COND. LOW	EXC. COND. HIGH
1947-1960		$725	$950

BR-9 Lap Steel

1947-1959. Solidbody, 1 pickup, tan.

MODEL YEAR	FEATURES	EXC. COND. LOW	EXC. COND. HIGH
1947-1959		$450	$575

Century Lap Steel

1947-1968. Solid maple body, 6 or 10 ('48-'55) strings, 1 pickup, silver 'board.

MODEL YEAR	FEATURES	EXC. COND. LOW	EXC. COND. HIGH
1947-1968		$925	$1,200

Console Grand Steel

1938-1942, 1948-1967. Hollowbody, 2 necks, triple-bound body, standard 7- and 8-string combination until '42, double 8-string necks standard for '48 and after, by '61 becomes CG-620.

MODEL YEAR	FEATURES	EXC. COND. LOW	EXC. COND. HIGH
1938	String-mute	$1,525	$2,000
1939-1942		$1,525	$2,000
1948-1954		$1,525	$2,000
1955-1967	CG-520	$1,525	$2,000
1961-1967	CG-530	$1,525	$2,000

Console Grand Triple Neck (CGT)

1951-1956. Three 8-string necks, sunburst or natural, 4 legs.

MODEL YEAR	FEATURES	EXC. COND. LOW	EXC. COND. HIGH
1951-1956		$1,700	$2,200

Console Steel (C-530)

1957-1966. Replaced Consolette during '56-'57, double 8-string necks, 4 legs optional.

MODEL YEAR	FEATURES	EXC. COND. LOW	EXC. COND. HIGH
1957-1966	With legs	$1,150	$1,500

Consolette Table Steel

1952-1957. Rectangular korina body, 2 8-string necks, 4 legs, replaced by maple-body Console in '57.

MODEL YEAR	FEATURES	EXC. COND. LOW	EXC. COND. HIGH
1952-1955	P-90	$1,000	$1,300
1955-1957	Humbucking	$1,150	$1,500

EH-100 Lap Steel

1936-1949. Hollow guitar-shaped body, bound top, 6 or 7 strings.

MODEL YEAR	FEATURES	EXC. COND. LOW	EXC. COND. HIGH
1936-1949		$675	$875

EH-125 Lap Steel

1939-1942. Hollow guitar-shaped mahogany body, single-bound body, metal 'board, sunburst.

MODEL YEAR	FEATURES	EXC. COND. LOW	EXC. COND. HIGH
1939-1942		$675	$875

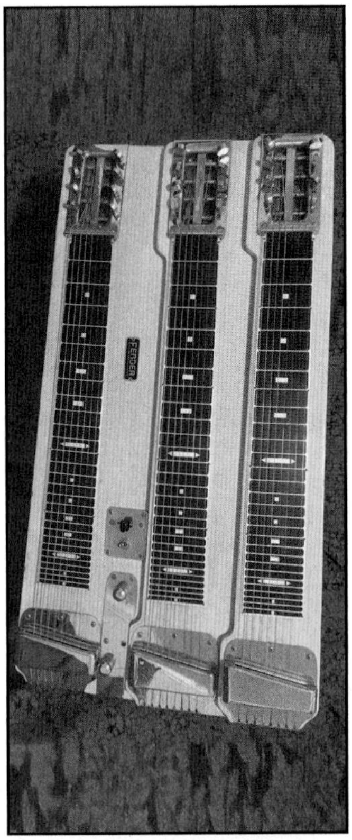

1954 Fender Stringmaster

Brad Hogge

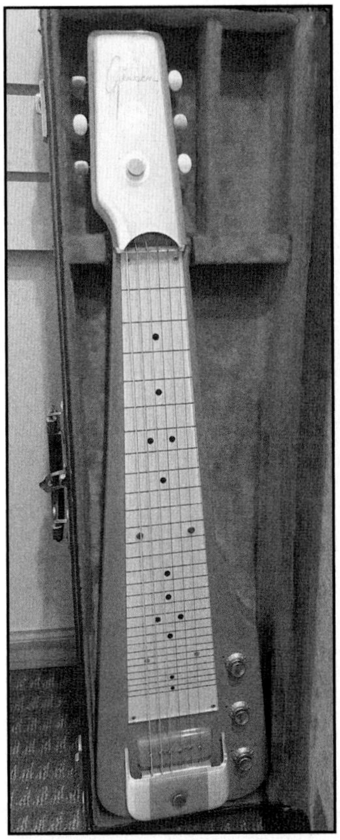

1964 Gibson Century Six

Bill Hatfield

1938 Gibson EH-150

David Stone

1942 Gibson EH-185

Barney Roach

MODEL YEAR	FEATURES	EXC. COND. LOW	HIGH

EH-150 Doubleneck Electric Hawaiian Steel

1937-1939. Doubleneck EH-150 with 7- and 8-string necks.

1937-1939		$2,300	$3,000

EH-150 Lap Steel

1936-1943. Hollow guitar-shaped body, 6 to 10 strings available, bound body.

1936	1st run, metal body	$2,225	$2,900
1937-1943	Sunburst	$925	$1,200

EH-185 Lap Steel

1939-1942. Hollow guitar-shaped curly maple body, triple-bound body, 6, 7, 8 or 10 strings, sunburst.

1939-1942		$1,425	$1,850

EH-500 Skylark Deluxe Lap Steel

1958-1959. Like Skylark, but with dot markers.

1958-1959		$850	$1,100

EH-500 Skylark Lap Steel

1956-1968. Solid korina body, 8-string available by '58, block markers with numbers.

1956-1968		$850	$1,100

EH-610 Lap Steel

1957-1966. Six strings, 4 pedals.

1957-1966		$850	$1,100

EH-620 Lap Steel

1955-1967. Eight strings, 6 pedals, natural.

1955-1967		$850	$1,100

EH-630 Electraharp Steel

1941-1967. Eight strings, 8 pedals (4 in '49-'67). Called just EH-630 from '56-'67.

1941-1967		$850	$1,100

EH-820 Lap Steel

1960-1966. Two necks, 8 pedals, Vari-Tone selector, cherry.

1960-1966		$850	$1,100

Multiharp Steel

1956-1965. Three necks, 6 pedals, humbuckers.

1956-1965		$1,000	$1,300

Royaltone Lap Steel

1950-1952, 1956-1957. Volume and tone knobs on treble side of pickup, Gibson silk-screen logo, brown pickup bridge cover.

1950-1952	Symmetrical body	$800	$1,050
1956-1957	Guitar-shaped body	$700	$900

Ultratone Lap Steel

1948-1959. Solid maple body, plastic 'board, 6 strings.

1948-1959		$800	$1,050

Golden Hawaiian

1920s-1930s. Private branded lap guitar most likely made by one of the many Chicago makers for a small retailer, publisher, cataloger, or teaching studio.

Hawaiian Lap Acoustic

1930s. Small body, acoustic flat-top for Hawaiian lap-style playing, Golden Hawaiian logo on headstock.

1930s		$385	$500

Gourley

See Dickerson listing.

MODEL YEAR	FEATURES	EXC. COND. LOW	HIGH

Gretsch

1883-present. Gretsch offered a variety of steels from 1940-'63. Gretsch actually only made 1 model; the rest were built by Valco. Currently they offer 2 lap steel models.

Electromatic (5700/5715) Lap Steel

2005-present. Made in China, designed like the original Jet Mainliner (6147) steel, tobacco sunburst (5700) or black sparkle (5715).

2005-2020		$110	$145

Electromatic Console (6158) Twin Neck Steel

1949-1955. Two 6-string necks with six-on-a-side tuners, Electromatic script logo on end cover plates, 3 knobs, metal control panels and knobs, pearloid covered.

1949-1955		$950	$1,250

Electromatic Hawaiian Lap Steel

1940-1942. Guitar shaped mahogany body, wooden pickup cover.

1940-1942		$540	$700

Electromatic Standard (6156) Lap Steel

1949-1955. Brown pearloid.

1949-1955		$385	$500

Electromatic Student (6152) Lap Steel

1949-1955. Square bottom, brown pearloid, pearloid cover.

1949-1955		$385	$500

Jet Mainliner (6147) Steel

1955-1963. Single-neck version of Jet Twin.

1955-1963		$425	$550

Jet Twin Console (6148) Steel

1955-1963. Valco-made, 2 6-string necks, six-on-a-side tuners, Jet Black.

1955-1963		$1,075	$1,400

Guyatone

1933-present. Large Japanese maker. Brands also include Marco Polo, Winston, Kingston, Kent, LaFayette and Bradford. They offered lap steels under various brands from the '30s to the '60s.

Lap Steels

1960s		$230	$300

Table Steels

1960s. Three legs, 2 pickups.

1960s		$385	$500

Hanburt

1940-ca. 1950. Harvey M. Hansen built his electric Hawaiian guitars in Seattle, Washington that were sold through his wife's music instruction studio. His designs were influenced by Seattle's Audiovox guitars. He also built amps and at least one mandolin.

Harlin Brothers

1930s-1960s. Harlin Brothers, of Indianapolis, Indiana, were one of the early designers of pedal steel applications. Prices can vary because some instruments have a reputation of being hard to keep in tune.

MODEL YEAR	FEATURES	EXC. COND. LOW	HIGH

Multi-Kord Pedal Steel

1950s	Single neck	$460	$600

Harmony

1982-1976, late 1970s-present. Founded by Wilhelm Schultz and purchased by Sears in 1916. The company evolved into the largest producer of stringed instruments in the U.S. in the '30s. They offered electric lap steels by '36.

Consolectric Steel

1953. Combo unit that combines steel guitar neck and built-in amp, 3 legs, Harmony Consolectric script logo on end of case, luggage tweed cover.

1953		$615	$800

Lap Steels

1936-1960s	Various models	$300	$450

Hilo

1920s-1930s. Weissenborn-style guitars most likely made by New Jersey's Oscar Schmitt Company, Hilo orange label inside back.

Hawaiian Steel Guitar

1930s. Guitar shaped body, round sound hole, acoustic steel.

1930s		$1,400	$1,800

Höfner

1887-present. Höfner offered lap steels from the '30s into the '90s. They also built models for the Selmer brand.

Model 111 Lap Steel

1953-1992. Brazilian rosewood 'board, white body binding, 25 frets, volume and tone controls, sunburst. Same as Selmer Standard.

1953-1960		$425	$550

Jackson-Guldan

1920s-1960s. The Jackson-Guldan Violin Company, of Columbus, Ohio, offered lap steels and small tube amps early on. They also built acoustic guitars.

K & F (Kaufman & Fender)

See listing under Fender.

Kalamazoo

1933-1942, 1946-1947, 1965-1970. Budget brand produced by Gibson in Kalamazoo, Michigan. They offered lap steels in the '30s and '40s.

Lap Steel

1938-1942, 1946-1947.

1938-1947		$425	$550

Kamico

Late-1940s. Private branded by Kay for student lap steel market, Kamico logo on lap steels and amplifiers. They also made guitars.

Lap Steel and Amp Set

1948. Symmetrical 6-string lap steel with small, single-knob 1x8" amp, both with matching sunburst finish.

1948		$465	$600

MODEL YEAR	FEATURES	EXC. COND. LOW	HIGH

Kay

Ca. 1931-present. Huge Chicago manufacturer Kay offered steels from '36 to '60 under their own brand and others.

Lap Steel

1940s-60s		$270	$350

Lap Steel With Matching Amp

1940s	Dark mahogany	$540	$700
1950s	Green	$540	$700

Kiesel

1946-1949, 2015-present. Founded by Lowell Kiesel as L.C. Kiesel Co., Los Angeles, California, but renamed Carvin in '49. Kiesel logo on the headstock. Kiesel brand name revived by Carvin in '15 for use on their guitars.

Bakelite Lap Steel

1946. Small guitar-shaped bakelite body, 1 pickup, 2 knobs, diamond markers.

1946		$350	$450

Knutson Luthiery

1981-present. Professional grade, custom, electric lap steels built by luthier John Knutson in Forestville, California. He also builds guitars, basses and mandolins.

Lapdancer

2001-present. Intermediate and professional grade, custom/production, lap steels built by luthier Loni Specter in West Hills, California.

Lockola

1950s. Private brand lap and amp sets made by Valco for Lockola of Salt Lake City, Utah.

Lap Steel

1950s	Pearloid	$270	$350

Maestro

A budget brand made by Gibson.

Lap Steel

1940s-1950s. Pearloid, 1 pickup, 6 strings.

1940s-50s		$270	$350

Magnatone

Ca.1937-1971, 2013-present. Magnatone offered lap steels from '37 to '58. Besides their own brand, they also produced models under the Dickerson, Oahu, Gourley, and Natural Music Guild brands.

Lyric Doubleneck Lap Steel

Ca.1951-1958. Model G-1745-D-W, 8 strings per neck, hardwood body, 3 legs included.

1951-1958		$850	$1,100

Maestro Tripleneck Steel

Ca.1951-1958. Model G-2495-W-W, maple and walnut, 8 strings per neck, legs.

1951-1958		$1,025	$1,325

Pearloid (MOTS) Lap Steel

1950s. These were often sold with a matching amp; price here is for lap steel only.

1950s	Common	$250	$400
1950s	Less common	$400	$625

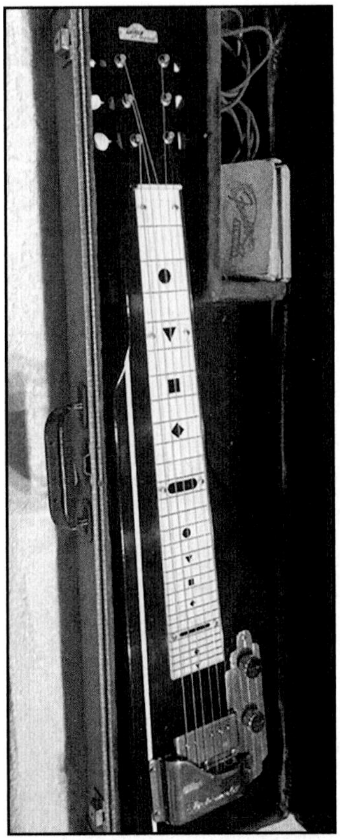

1960 Gretsch Mainliner (6147)

Johnnyslide Merringer

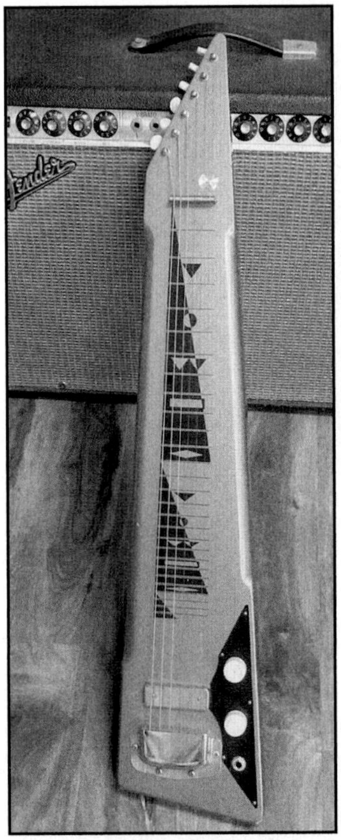

1965 Harmony H-1

Craig Brody

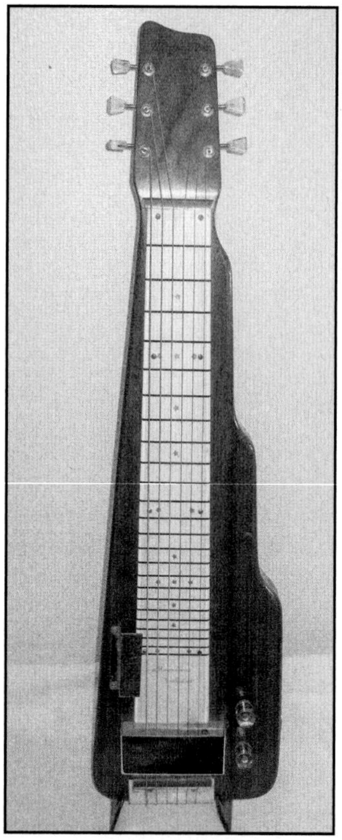

1955 Magnatone Troubadour

Dan Bishop

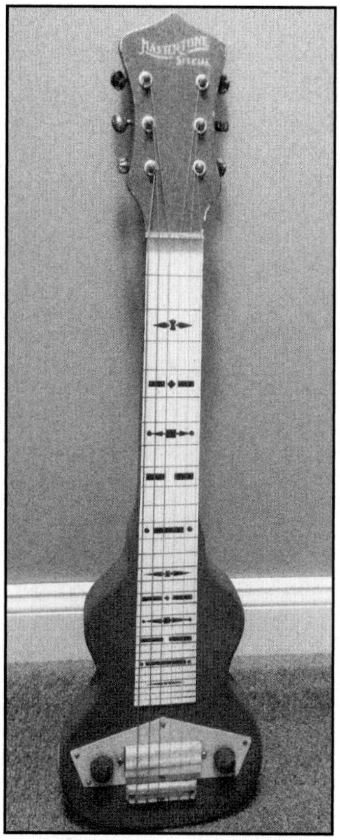

1940 Mastertone Special

Kirk Naylor

MODEL YEAR	FEATURES	EXC. COND. LOW	HIGH

Pearloid Steel Guitar

1950s. Six-string non-pedal steel, 3 legs, 2 knobs, 8 push buttons, star position markers, pearloid cover, Magnatone script logo at lower end of fretboard.

1950s		$525	$675

Troubadour Lap Steel

1955. Wood body, 2 knobs, single metal pickup, Magnatone script logo on headstock and body.

1955		$460	$600

Marvel

1950-mid 1960s. Budget brand marketed by the Peter Sorkin Company of New York.

Electric Hawaiian Lap Steel

1950s		$150	$200

Mastertone

Late 1920s-early 1940s. Mastertone was a budget brand made by Gibson and was used on lap steel, Hawaiian and archtop guitars.

Special Lap Steel

1920s-40s	Brown crinkle	$385	$500

May Bell

See listing under Slingerland.

McKinney

1950s. Private branded for McKinney Guitars by Supro, blue McKinney Guitar logo on headstock.

Lap Steel

1950s. Similar to Supro Comet, white pearloid.

1950s		$290	$375

Melobar

1967-2006. Designed by Walt Smith, of Smith Family Music, Melobar instruments feature a guitar body with a tilted neck, allowing the guitarist to play lap steel standing up. The instrument was developed and first made in Ed and Rudy Dopyera's Dobro factory. Most were available in 6-, 8-, or 10-string versions. Ted Smith took over operations from his father. Ted retired in late 2002. Production ceased in '06.

Electric Steel or Power-Slide Guitar

1970s-2006. Various 6-, 8-, and 10-string models.

1970s-2006	Various options	$500	$1,200

MSA

1963-1983, 2001-present. Professional and premium grade, production/custom, pedal and lap steel guitars built in Dallas, Texas by Maurice Anderson. The company was dissolved in '83, and reorganized in '01.

S-12 Pedal Steel

1980s. 12-string.

1980s		$1,250	$1,625

Sidekick 3/1 Steel

1970s-1980s. 10-string, 3 pedals, one lever.

1970s-80s		$850	$1,100

National

Ca. 1927-present. Founded in Los Angeles as the National String Instrument Corporation in '27, the brand has gone through many ownership changes over the years. National offered lap steels from '35 to '68.

Chicagoan Lap Steel

1948-1960. Gray pearloid, metal hand rest.

1948-1960		$325	$425

Clipper Model 1026 Lap Steel

1952-1955. Guitar-shaped wood body, celluloid bound, 1 pickup, volume, tone, 'visual octaves' position markers on neck, shaded brown finish.

1952-1955		$425	$550

Console (Dual 8) Steel

1939-1942. Two 8-string necks, parallelogram markers, black top with white sides.

1939-1941		$650	$850

Dynamic Lap Steel

1941-1968. New Yorker-style body, 6 strings, 3 detachable screw-in legs added by '56.

1941-1968		$525	$675

Electric Hawaiian Lap Steel

1935-1937. Cast aluminum round body, 1 pickup, square neck, 6 or 7 strings.

1935-1937		$675	$875

Grand Console Steel

1947-1967. Double (1050) or triple (1052) 8-string necks, Totem Pole 'board markers, came with or without legs, black and white finish, National's answer to Fender Stringmaster Series.

1947-1959	1052, 3 necks	$925	$1,200
1947-1967	1050, 2 necks	$850	$1,100

New Yorker Lap Steel

1939-1967. Introduced as Electric Hawaiian model in '35, square end body with stair-step sides, 7 or 8 strings, black and white finish.

1939-1949		$675	$900
1950-1967		$525	$675

Princess Lap Steel

1941-1947. Strings-thru-pickup, parallelogram markers, white pearloid.

1941-1947		$375	$500

Rocket One Ten Lap Steel

1956-1957. Rocket-shaped, black and white finish.

1956-1957		$400	$525

Studio 76 N476 Lap Steel

1964. Half and half stair-step inlay design, 3-on-a-side tuners with open-book shaped headstock, 1 pickup, 2 knobs, onyx black pearloid, soft shoulders.

1964		$270	$350

Trailblazer Steel

1948-1949. Square end, numbered markers, black.

1948-1949		$270	$350

Triplex 1088 Chord Changer Lap Steel

1944-1958. Maple and walnut body, 2 knobs, natural.

1944-1958		$650	$850

MODEL YEAR	FEATURES	EXC. COND. LOW	HIGH

Nioma

1932-1952. NIOMA was a music and arts school founded in Seattle. By '35 they added guitar instruction, offering their own branded lap steels (with matching amps), made by Dickerson. They also offered guitars.

Lap Steel

1930s	Pearloid	$190	$250

Oahu

1926-1985. The Oahu Publishing Company and Honolulu Conservatory, based in Cleveland, published a very popular guitar study course. They sold instruments to go with the lessons, starting with acoustic Hawaiian and Spanish guitars, selling large quantities in the '30s. As electric models became popular, Oahu responded with guitar-amp sets. Lap steel and matching amp sets were generally the same color; for example, yellow guitar and yellow amp, or white pearloid guitar and white amp. These sets were originally sold to students who would take private or group lessons. The instruments were made by Oahu, Valco, Harmony, Dickerson, and Rickenbacker and were offered into the '50s and '60s.

Dianna Lap Steel

1950s. Oahu and Diana logos on headstock, Oahu logo on fretboard, fancy bridge, pleasant unusual sunburst finish.

1950s		$350	$450

Hawaiian Lap Steel

1930s	Sunburst, student-grade	$275	$360
1930s	Tonemaster with decal art	$315	$410
1930s-40s	Rare style, higher-end	$425	$750
1930s-40s	Rare style, student-grade	$315	$410
1940s	Pearloid, Supro-made	$315	$410
1950s	Pearloid or painted	$315	$410
1950s	Tonemaster	$315	$410

Iolana

1941-1951, Late-1950s. Gold hardware, 2 6-string necks. Early model is lap steel, later version a console.

1941-1951	Lap	$600	$800
1950s	Console	$875	$1,150

K-71 Acoustic Lap Steel

1930s. Flat-top, round sound hole, decals on lower bouts.

1930s		$365	$475

Triplex 1088 Chord Changer Lap Steel

1940s. National-built 6-string lap steel with 'tuning change mechanism.'

1940s		$700	$900

Ormston

1966-1968. Pedal steels built in England by Denley and marketed by James Ormston Burns between his stints with Burns London, which was bought by America's Baldwin Company in '65, and the Dallas Arbiter Hayman brand.

MODEL YEAR	FEATURES	EXC. COND. LOW	HIGH

Recording King

Ca. 1930-1943. Brand used by Montgomery Ward for instruments made by Gibson, Regal, Kay, and Gretsch.

Electric Hawaiian Lap Steel

1930s		$385	$500

Roy Smeck Model AB104 Steel

1930s-1940s. Pear-shaped body, 1 pickup.

1930s-40s		$600	$775

Regal

Ca. 1895-1966, 1987-present. Regal offered their own brand and made instruments for distributors and mass-merchandisers. The company sold out to Harmony in '54. See guitars for more company info.

Electric Hawaiian Lap Steel

1940s		$270	$350
1940s	With matching amp	$525	$675

Reso-phonic Steel

1930s. Dobro-style resonator and spider assembly, round neck, adjustable nut.

1930s		$675	$875

Rickenbacker

1931-present. Rickenbacker produced steels from '32 to '70.

Academy Lap Steel

1946-1947. Bakelite student model, horseshoe pickup, replaced by the Ace.

1946-1947		$365	$475

Ace Lap Steel

1948-1953. Bakelite body, 1 pickup.

1948-1953		$365	$475

Console 208 Steel

1955-1970. Two 8-string necks.

1955-1970		$1,025	$1,325

Console 518 Triple Neck Steel

1955-1970. 22.5" scale, 3 8-string necks.

1955-1970		$1,275	$1,650

Console 758 Triple Neck Steel

1957-1970. 25" scale, 3 8-string necks.

1957-1970		$1,275	$1,650

CW Steel

1957-1970. Single neck on wood body, several neck options, 3 attachable legs.

1957-1970		$775	$1,000

DC-16 Steel

1950-1952. Metal, double 8-string necks.

1950-1952		$975	$1,250

Electro Lap Steel

1940s, 1960s. Large Rickenbacker logo and smaller Electro logo on headstock ('40s), then on side ('60s).

1940s	Headstock logo	$775	$1,025
1960s	Side logo	$525	$700

Electro Doubleneck Steel

1940-1953. Two bakelite 8-string necks.

1940-1953		$1,100	$1,425

Electro Tripleneck Steel

1940-1953. Three bakelite 8-string necks.

1940-1953		$1,275	$1,650

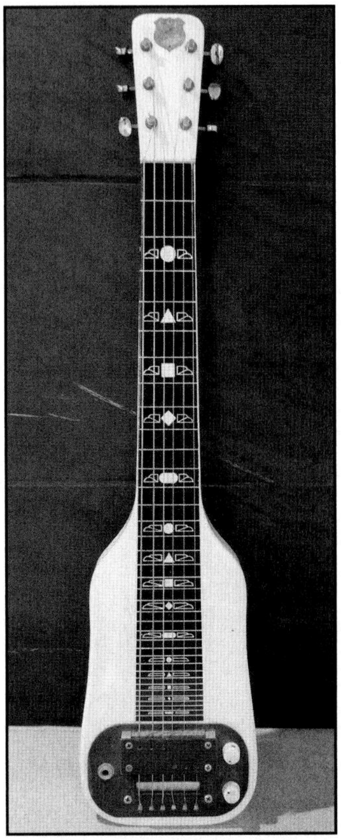

1960 National Chicagoan

Greg Narbey

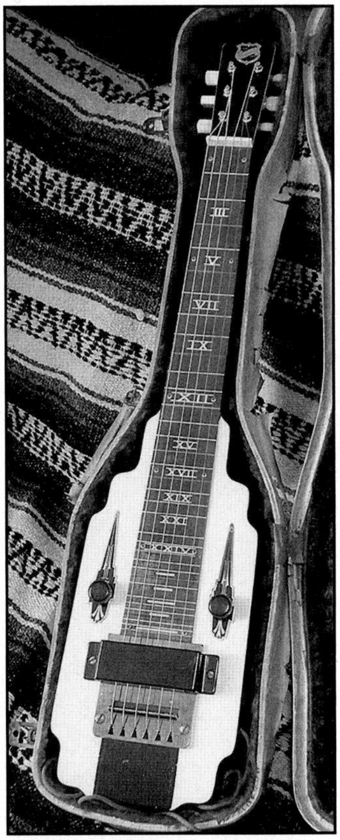

1942 National Dynamic

John Subik

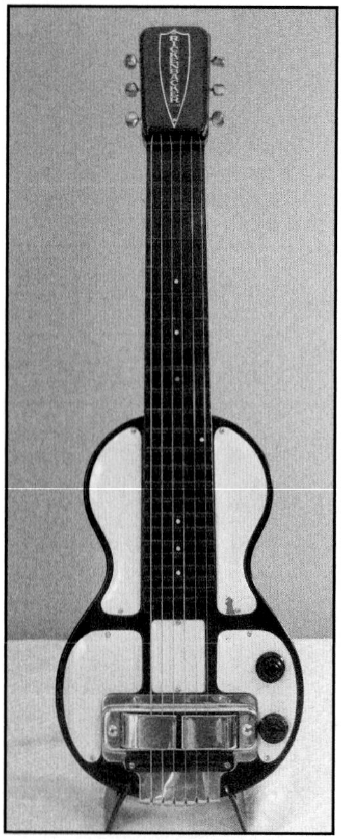

1950s Rickenbacker Model BD

Dan Bishop

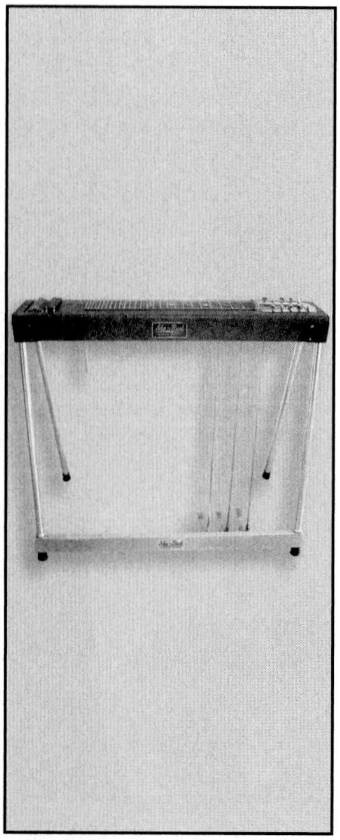

Mid-'70s Sho-Bud Maverick

Marco Parmiggiani

MODEL YEAR	FEATURES	EXC. COND. LOW	HIGH

Electro EH-3 Lap Steel

1970s. 6-string neck, legs.

1971		$385	$500

JB (Jerry Byrd) Model Steel

1961-1970. Single neck on large wood body, 6-, 7-, 8-, or 10-string neck, 3 attachable legs, Jerry Byrd Model logo on top plate.

1961-1970		$1,100	$1,425

Model 59 Lap Steel

1937-1943. Sheet steel body, baked-enamel light-colored crinkle finish, 1 pickup.

1937-1943		$600	$800

Model 100 Lap Steel

1956-1970. Wood body, 6 strings, block markers, light or silver gray finish.

1956-1970		$600	$800

Model 102 Lap Steel

1960s. Wood body, 6 strings, slot head, block markers, natural finish.

1960		$525	$700

Model A-22/A-25 "Frying Pan" Steel

1932-1936. Originally called the Electro-Hawaiian Guitar, small round body lap steel, offered as 6- or 7-string, 22.5" scale. The A-25 25" scale also available.

1932-1936		$2,600	$3,400

Model B Steel

1935-1955. Bakelite body and neck, 1 pickup, strings-thru-body, decorative metal plates, 6 or 8 strings, black.

1935-1955	6- or 8-string	$1,475	$1,900

Model B-10 Steel

1935-1955. Model B with slot head and 12 strings.

1935-1955		$925	$1,200

Model BD Steel

1949-1970. Bakelite body, 6 strings, deluxe version of Model B, black.

1949-1960		$700	$900

Model CW-6 Steel

1957-1961. Wood body, grille cloth on front, 6 strings, 3 legs, walnut finish, renamed JB (Jerry Byrd) model in '61.

1957-1961		$700	$900

Model DW Steel

1955-1961. Wood body, double 6- or 8-string necks, optional 3 legs.

1955-1961		$850	$1,100

Model G Lap Steel

Ca.1948-1957. Chrome-plated ornate version of Silver Hawaiian, gold hardware and trim, 6 or 8 strings.

1948-1957		$775	$1,000

Model S/NS (New Style) Steel

1946-early-1950s. Sheet steel body, 1 pickup, gray, gray sparkle or grayburst, also available as a doubleneck.

1946-1949		$725	$950

Model SD Steel

1949-1953. Deluxe NS, sheet steel body, 6, 7 or 8 strings, Copper Crinkle finish.

1949-1953		$650	$850

Model SW

1956-1962. Straight body style, 6 or 8 strings, block markers, dark or blond finish.

1956-1962	8-string	$1,000	$1,300
1956-1962	8-string with legs	$1,300	$1,700

Silver Hawaiian Lap Steel

1937-1943. Chrome-plated sheet steel body, 1 horseshoe pickup, 6 strings.

1937-1943		$1,125	$1,475

Roland Ball

See Dickerson listing.

Scantic River Guitar Co.

Luthiers Thomas Ford, Steve Collin and Dennis Moore build their premium grade, custom, lap steel guitars in Durham, Maine. They started in 2008.

Serenader

Built by the Bud-Electro Manufacturing Company which was founded in Seattle, Washington in the late 1940s by Paul "Bud" Tutmarc, Jr., whose father built Audiovox instruments. He built mainly lap steels but also offered a solidbody bass.

Sherwood

Late 1940s-early 1950s. Lap steel guitars made for Montgomery Ward made by Chicago manufacturers such as Kay. They also had archtop guitars and amps under that brand.

Deluxe Lap Steel

1950s. Symmetrical body, bar pickup, volume and tone controls, wood body, sunburst, relatively ornate headstock with script Sherwood logo, vertical Deluxe logo, and lightning bolt art.

1950s		$190	$250

Sho-Bud

1956-1981. Founded by Shot Jackson in Nashville. Distributed by Gretsch. They also had guitar models. Baldwin bought the company and closed the factory in '81.

Crossover Twin Neck Steel

1967-1971. Sho-Bud Baldwin double neck, Sho-Bud logo.

1967-1971		$2,100	$2,700

Maverick Pedal Steel

Ca. 1970-1981. Beginner model, burl elm cover, 3 pedals.

1970-1981		$975	$1,250

Pro I

1970-1981. Three pedals, natural.

1970-1975	Round front	$1,850	$2,400
1976-1981	Square front	$1,925	$2,500

Pro II

1973-1981. Birdseye maple, double 10-string necks, natural.

1973-1975	Round front	$2,000	$2,600
1976-1981	Square front	$2,100	$2,700

MODEL YEAR	FEATURES	EXC. COND. LOW	HIGH

Pro III

1975-1981. Metal necks.

1975	Round front	$2,100	$2,700
1976-1981	Square front	$2,175	$2,800

Super Pro

1977-1980. Doubleneck 10 strings, 8 floor pedals, 6 knee levers, Jet Black.

1977-1980		$2,400	$3,100

Sierra

1960-present. Originally designed and built by Chuck Wright in California and Oregon until '74, then by Don Christensen in Oregon. In 2003, Ed W. Littlefield Jr. took ownership, with professional and premium grade, production, lap and pedal steel guitars built by luthiers Tom Baker and Rob Girdis in Molalla, Oregon. Girdis died in '09. There is an unrelated Sierra brand of guitars.

Silvertone

1940-1970, present. Brand name for instruments sold by Sears.

Amp-In-Case Lap Steel

Early 1940s. Lap steel and amp set, amp cabinet doubles as lap case with the lap stored above the amp, amp is in a long vertical cabinet with brown tweed covering, manufacturer appears to be the same as used by Gibson in the late '30s, low to mid power, 1x10" speaker.

1941-1942		$725	$950

Six-String Lap Steel

1940s-1960s. Includes Valco-made, standard or pearloid finish.

1940s-60s	Various models	$250	$550

Slingerland

Ca. 1914-present. Offered by Slingerland Banjos and Drums. They also sold the May Bell brand. Instruments were also made by others and sold by Slingerland in the '30s and '40s.

May Bell Lap Steel

1930s. Guitar-shaped lap steel with May Bell logo. This brand also had '30s Hawaiian and Spanish guitars.

1930s		$230	$300

Songster Lap Steel

1930s. Slingerland logo headstock, Songster logo near nut, guitar-shaped body, sunburst maple top, some with figured maple back, 1 pickup, 2 bakelite brown knobs, dot markers.

1930s		$575	$750

SPG

2006-2009. Intermediate grade, custom, solidbody lapsteels originally built by luthier Rick Welch in Farmingdale, Maine and Hanson, Massachusetts; more recently by luthier Eric C. Brown in Farmingdale, Maine.

MODEL YEAR	FEATURES	EXC. COND. LOW	HIGH

Stella

Ca. 1899-1974, 2000s. Stella was a brand of the Oscar Schmidt Company. Harmony acquired the brand in '39. The Stella brand was reintroduced in the 2000s by MBT International.

Electric Hawaiian Lap Steel

1937		$425	$550

Supertone

1914-1941. Brand name for Sears which was replaced by Silvertone. Instruments made by Harmony and others.

Electric Hawaiian Lap Steel

1930s	Various models	$310	$400

Supro

1935-1968, 2004-present. Budget brand of the National Dobro Company. Brand name was revived in '04.

Airline

1952-1962. Asymmetrical body with straight left side and contoured right (treble) side, black pearloid with small white pearloid on right (treble) side, 2 knobs, available with optional set of 3 legs, later versions available with 6 or 8 strings, described in catalog as "Supro's finest". Renamed Jet Airliner in '64.

1952-1962	6- or 8-string	$275	$500
1952-1962	With optional legs	$475	$700

Clipper Lap Steel

1941-1943. One pickup, bound rosewood 'board, dot inlay, brown pearloid.

1941-1943		$325	$425

Comet Lap Steel

1947-1966. One pickup, attached cord, painted-on 'board, pearloid.

1947-1949	Gray pearloid	$325	$425
1950-1966	White pearloid	$325	$425

Comet Steel (With Legs)

1950s-1960s. Three-leg 6-string steel version of the lap steel, 2 knobs, Supro logo on cover plate, 1 pickup.

1960s	Black & white	$475	$700

Console 8 Steel

1958-1960. Eight strings, 3 legs, black and white.

1958-1960		$575	$750

Irene Lap Steel

1940s. Complete ivory pearloid cover including headstock, fretboard and body, Roman numeral markers, 1 pickup, 2 control knobs, hard-wired output cord.

1940s		$325	$425

Jet Airliner Steel

1964-1968. Renamed from Airline, described in catalog as "Supro's finest", 1 pickup, totem pole markings, 6 or 8 strings, pearloid, National-made.

1964-1968	6- or 8-string	$500	$650
1964-1968	With optional legs	$600	$800

Professional Steel

1950s. Light brown pearloid.

1950s		$325	$425

1950s Silvertone

Peter Thomas

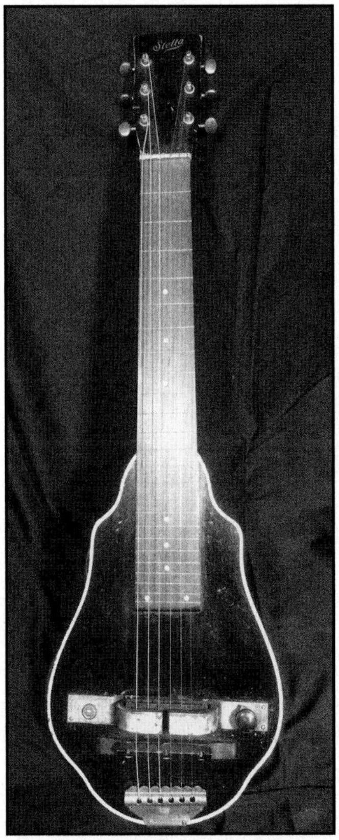

1938 Stella

James Clements

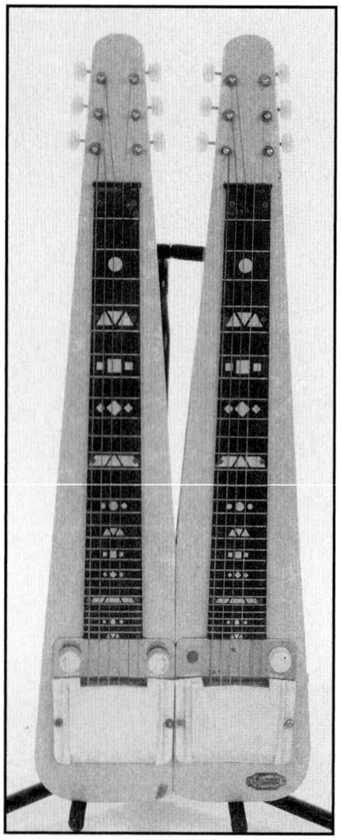

1950s Supro Twin

Imaged by Heritage Auctions, HA.com

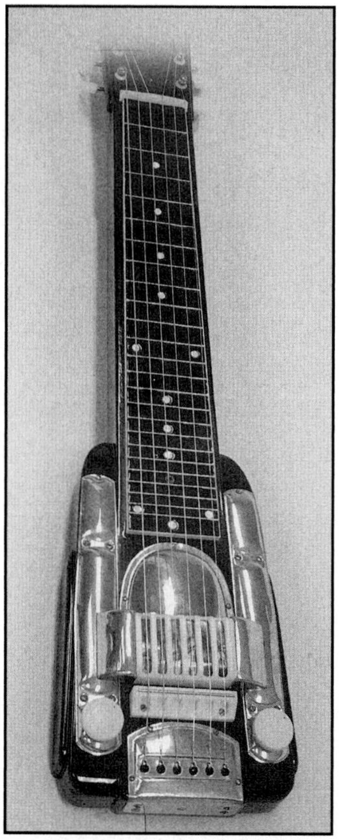

1960s Teisco Model R

George Lee

MODEL YEAR	FEATURES	EXC. COND. LOW	HIGH

Special Steel

1955-1962. Pearloid lap steel, student model, large script Special logo near pickup on early models, red until '57, white after.

1955-1957	Red pearloid	$325	$425
1957-1962	White pearloid	$325	$425

Spectator Steel

1952-1954. Wood body, 1 pickup, painted-on 'board, natural.

1952-1954		$325	$425

Student De Luxe Lap Steel

1952-1955. One pickup, pearloid, large script Student De Luxe logo located near pickup, replaced by Special in '55.

1952-1955	Black-white, or red pearloid	$325	$425
1952-1955	Natural or white paint	$325	$425

Studio

1955-1964. Symmetrical body, 2 knobs, priced in original catalog below the Comet, but above the Special, issued in '55 with blue plastic covered body.

1955-1964		$325	$425

Supreme Lap Steel

1947-1960. One pickup, painted-on 'board, brown pearloid until ca.'55, then red until ca.'58, Tulip Yellow after that.

1947-1960		$385	$500

Supro 60 Lap Steel and Amp-in-Case

Late 1930s-early '40s. Supro 60 logo near the single volume knob, long horizontal guitar case which houses a small tube amp and speaker, the case cover folds out to allow ventilation for the tubes, white pearloid, black amp case, the amp was made by National Dobro of Chicago.

1939-1941		$725	$950

Twin Lap Steel

1948-1955. Two 6-string necks, pearloid covering, renamed Console Steel in '55.

1948-1955		$575	$750

Teisco

1946-1974. The Japanese guitar-maker offered many steel models from '55 to around '67. Models offered '55-'61: EG-7L, -K, -R, -NT, -Z, -A, -S, -P, -8L, -NW, and -M. During '61-'67: EG-TW, -O, -U, -L, -6N, -8N, -DB, -DB2, -DT, H-39, H-905, TRH-1, Harp-8 and H-850.

Hawaiian Lap Steel

1955-1967		$290	$375

True Tone

1960s. Brand name sold by Western Auto (hey, everybody was in the guitar biz back then). Probably made by Kay or Harmony.

Lap Steel

1960s. Guitar-shaped, single-cut, 1 pickup.

1960s		$325	$425

Varsity

See Dickerson listing.

Vega

1889-present. The original Boston-based company was purchased by C.F. Martin in '70. In '80, the Vega trademark was sold to a Korean company. The company was one of the first to enter the electric market by offering products in '36 and offered lap steels into the early '60s. The Deering Banjo Company acquired the brand in '89 and uses it on a line of banjos.

DG-DB Steel

1950s. Two necks, 8 strings.

1950s		$810	$1,050

Odell Lap Steel

1950s. White pearloid.

1950s		$325	$425

Other Lap Steels

1930s	Rare models	$500	$900
1930s-40s	Common models	$250	$400
1940s	Art deco-style	$400	$500

Wabash

1950s. Lap steels distributed by the David Wexler company and made by others. They also offered guitars and amps.

Lap Steel (Hawaiian Scene Tailpiece)

1950s. Natural, 12 frets.

1950s		$250	$400

White

1955-1960. The White brand, named after plant manager Forrest White, was established by Fender to provide steel and small amp sets to teaching studios that were not Fender-authorized dealers. A standard guitar was planned, but never produced.

6-String Steel

1955-1956. White finish, block markers, 2 knobs, 3 legs. The 6 String Steel was usually sold with the matching white amp Model 80. Possibly only 1 batch of these was made by Fender in October/November '55.

1955-1956		$1,125	$1,475

Matching Steel and Amp Set

1955-1956		$2,150	$2,800

UKULELES

1960 Maccaferri Mastro Baritone Electric: Randy Klimpert.

Ditson Style 1
Randy Klimpert

Favilla Ukulele
Randy Klimpert

Gibson Poinsettia
Randy Klimpert

Aero Uke

1920s. Never branded, but almost certainly produced by Chicago's Stromberg-Voisenet Company, the precursor of Kay, the Aero Uke is an instrument quite unlike any other. With its spruce-capped body resembling an old-timey airplane wing and a neck and headstock that approximate a plane's fuselage, this clever '20s offering cashed in on the Lindbergh craze (like the Harmony Johnny Marvin model with its airplane-shaped bridge), and must have been a big hit at parties.

Aero Ukulele

Airplane body.

MODEL YEAR	FEATURES	EXC. COND. LOW	HIGH
1927	Black deco on wing	$2,500	$3,000
1927	Gold deco on wing	$3,000	$3,500

Aloha

1935-1960s. The Aloha brand turns up on numerous vastly different ukes. In fact, the variety of features exhibited by Aloha ukuleles leads the modern observer to believe that the ukes that bear this headstock decal were made by as many as a dozen different manufacturers, each with access to the same logo. Many were undoubtedly Island-made, with all koa bodies and some with fancy rope binding; others bear unmistakable mainland traits. Some of these have a more traditional look and are stamped Akai inside the soundhole, while still others, strongly resembling mainland C.F. Martins in design, typically sport a decal of the Sam F. Chang curio shop on the reverse of the headstock.

Akai Soprano Ukulele

Koa construction.

MODEL YEAR	FEATURES	EXC. COND. LOW	HIGH
1930s		$600	$800

Soprano Ukulele

Koa body, plain.

MODEL YEAR	FEATURES	EXC. COND. LOW	HIGH
1950s		$600	$900

Bruno

This New York distributor certainly subcontracted all of its ukulele production to other manufacturers, and as a result you'd be hard pressed to find two identical Bruno ukes.

Soprano Ukulele

MODEL YEAR	FEATURES	EXC. COND. LOW	HIGH
1920s	Koa, rope soundhole	$300	$400
1930s	Koa, rope bound body	$400	$500

Del Vecchio Dimonaco

With a design patterned after the pioneering work of Dobro and National, this Brazilian company produced a full line of resonator instruments, all constructed of native Brazilian rosewood, from the 1950s onward.

Resonator Ukulele

Brazilian rosewood.

MODEL YEAR	FEATURES	EXC. COND. LOW	HIGH
1950s		$800	$1,000

Ditson

1915-1926. Don't be fooled. While some of the ukes that were commissioned by this East Coast music publisher and chain store were actually manufactured by C.F. Martin, Martin was by no means the sole supplier. The Martin-made instruments often bear a Martin brand as well as a Ditson one, or, barring that, at least demonstrate an overall similarity to the rest of the ukes in the regular Martin line, both inside and out. The most telling and desirable feature of these Martin-made Ditsons is a dreadnaught-style wide waisted body design.

Dreadnaught Soprano Ukulele

MODEL YEAR	FEATURES	EXC. COND. LOW	HIGH
1916	as Martin Style 1	$1,500	$1,700
1919	as Martin 1M	$1,500	$1,700
1921	as Martin 1K	$2,500	$3,000
1922	as Martin O	$1,100	$1,300
1923	as Martin 2M	$1,800	$2,000
1923	as Martin 5K	$10,000	$15,000
1926	as Martin 3M	$3,500	$4,000

Dreadnaught Taropatch Ukulele

MODEL YEAR	FEATURES	EXC. COND. LOW	HIGH
1916	as Martin 1	$2,000	$2,200
1916	as Martin 2	$2,500	$2,800
1916	as Martin 3	$3,000	$3,500

Standard Soprano Ukulele

MODEL YEAR	FEATURES	EXC. COND. LOW	HIGH
1917	as Martin 1M	$700	$900
1922	as Martin 2M	$800	$1,000
1922	as Martin O	$600	$800
1925	as Martin 3M	$1,500	$2,000

Dobro

1929-1942, ca. 1954-2019. The ukulele version of the popular amplifying resonator instruments first produced in California, the Dobro uke was offered in 2 sizes (soprano and tenor), 2 styles (f-holes and screen holes), and 2 colors (brown and black). Models with Dobro headstock decals are often outwardly indistinguishable from others bearing either a Regal badge or no logo at all, but a peek inside often reveals the presence of a sound well in the belly of the former, making them the more desirable of the two.

Resonator Ukulele

Wood body.

MODEL YEAR	FEATURES	EXC. COND. LOW	HIGH
1930s	F-holes, Regal-made	$600	$800
1930s	Screen holes	$700	$900
1935	Tenor, cyclops screen	$1,500	$2,000

Favilla

1890-1973. The small New York City family-owned factory that produced primarily guitars also managed to offer some surprisingly high quality ukes, the best of which rival Martin and Gibson for craftsmanship and tone. As a result, Favilla ukuleles are a real value for the money.

Baritone Ukulele

MODEL YEAR	FEATURES	EXC. COND. LOW	HIGH
1950	Plain mahogany	$400	$500

Soprano Ukulele

MODEL YEAR	FEATURES	EXC. COND. LOW	HIGH
1925	Wimbrola, unbound teardrop, flat sides	$500	$800
1950s	Mahogany, triple bound	$650	$750
1950s	Plain mahogany	$300	$500
1950s	Teardrop-shaped, birch	$300	$500
1950s	Teardrop-shaped, stained blue	$300	$500

Fin-der

1950s. The pitch of this short-lived plastic ukulele was apparently the ease of learning, since the included instructional brochure helped you to "find" your chords with the added help of rainbow color-coded nylon strings.

Diamond Head Ukulele

Styrene plastic, in original box.

MODEL YEAR	FEATURES	EXC. COND. LOW	HIGH
1950s		$100	$150

Flamingo

1950s. If swanky designs hot-foil stamped into the surface of these '50s swirly injection molded polystyrene ukes didn't grab you, certainly the built-in functional pitch pipe across the top of the headstock would. And I ask you, who can resist a ukulele with a built-in tuner?

Soprano Ukulele

MODEL YEAR	FEATURES	EXC. COND. LOW	HIGH
1955	Brown top, white 'board	$100	$150
1955	White top, brown 'board	$100	$150

Giannini

1900-present. Ukuleles built in Salto, SP, Brazil near Sao Paolo. They also build guitars, violas, cavaquinhos and mandolins.

Baritone Ukulele

Mahogany body, rosewood fingerboard and bridge.

MODEL YEAR	FEATURES	EXC. COND. LOW	HIGH
1972		$300	$500

Gibson

1890s (1902)-present. A relative late-comer to the uke market, Gibson didn't get a line off the ground until 1927, fully nine years after Martin had already been in production. Even then they only produced three soprano styles and one tenor version. Worse still, they never made any ukes in koa, sticking to the easier-to-obtain mahogany.

Nonetheless, Gibson ukuleles exhibit more unintentional variety than any other major maker, with enough construction, inlay, binding, and cosmetic variations to keep collectors buzzing for many a year to come. In general, the earliest examples feature a Gibson logo in script, later shortened to just Gibson. Post-war examples adopted the more square-ish logo of the rest of the Gibson line, and, at some point in the late '50s, began sporting ink-stamped serial numbers on the back of the headstock like their guitar and mandolin brethren.

DUSI Ukulele

Tenor, like TU-1 but no Gibson logo, all koa.

MODEL YEAR	FEATURES	EXC. COND. LOW	HIGH
1950		$1,500	$2,000

ETU-1 Ukulele

Electric tenor, unbound body, square black pickup, 88 made.

MODEL YEAR	FEATURES	EXC. COND. LOW	HIGH
1949		$4,000	$5,000

ETU-3 Ukulele

Electric tenor, triple bound body, rectangle pickup, rare.

MODEL YEAR	FEATURES	EXC. COND. LOW	HIGH
1953		$5,000	$8,000

Poinsettia Ukulele

Fancy inlays and 'board, painted body.

MODEL YEAR	FEATURES	EXC. COND. LOW	HIGH
1930		$10,000	$15,000

TU-1 Ukulele

Tenor, mahogany body.

MODEL YEAR	FEATURES	EXC. COND. LOW	HIGH
1930	Sunburst finish	$1,200	$1,500
1960	Red SG guitar-like finish	$700	$900

TU-3 Ukulele

Tenor, like TU-1 with fancy binding.

MODEL YEAR	FEATURES	EXC. COND. LOW	HIGH
1935		$1,500	$1,700

Uke-1 Ukulele

Soprano, plain mahogany body.

MODEL YEAR	FEATURES	EXC. COND. LOW	HIGH
1927		$500	$700
1966	Red SG guitar-like finish	$500	$700

Uke-2 Ukulele

Soprano, mahogany body.

MODEL YEAR	FEATURES	EXC. COND. LOW	HIGH
1934	Triple bound	$800	$1,000
1939	Bound, X-braced	$800	$1,000

Uke-3 Ukulele

Soprano, dark finish.

MODEL YEAR	FEATURES	EXC. COND. LOW	HIGH
1933	Diamonds & squares inlay	$1,000	$1,300
1935	Diamond inlay, short 'board	$1,000	$1,300
1935	Rare curved designs inlay	$2,500	$3,000

Graziano

1969-present. Luthier Tony Graziano has been building ukuleles almost exclusively since '95 in his Santa Cruz shop. Like many, he sees the uke as the instrument of the new millennium, and his entirely handmade, custom orders can be had in a variety of shapes, sizes, and woods.

Gretsch

1883-present. The first (and most desirable) ukuleles by this New York manufacturer were actually stamped with the name Gretsch American or with interior brass nameplates. Subsequent pieces, largely inexpensive laminate-bodied catalog offerings, are distinguished by small round Gretsch headstock decals, and a lack of any kerfed linings inside the bodies. They stopped making ukes in the late '50s, then in 2012 began offering them again.

Plain Soprano Ukulele

Natural mahogany body, no binding.

MODEL YEAR	FEATURES	EXC. COND. LOW	HIGH
1950s		$100	$150

Round Ukulele

Round body, blue to green sunburst.

MODEL YEAR	FEATURES	EXC. COND. LOW	HIGH
1940		$100	$150

Soprano Ukulele

MODEL YEAR	FEATURES	EXC. COND. LOW	HIGH
1935	Bound koa,'board as Martin 5K	$1,700	$2,000
1940s	Koa, fancy 'board inlay	$1,000	$1,200
1940s	Mahogany, fancy 'board inlay	$800	$900

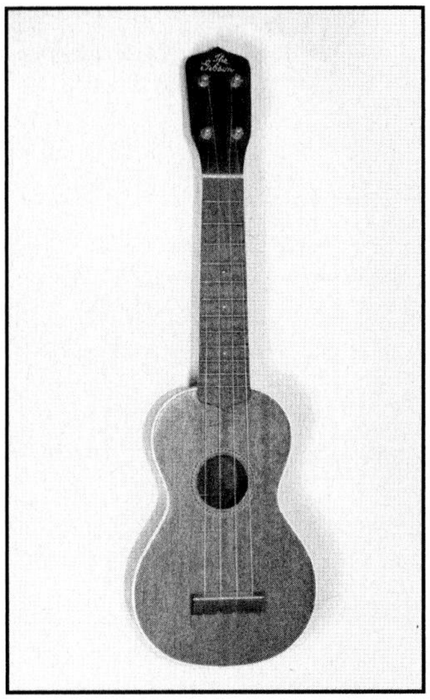

Late-1930s Gibson Uke-1

Randy Klimpert

Gibson Uke-2

Randy Klimpert

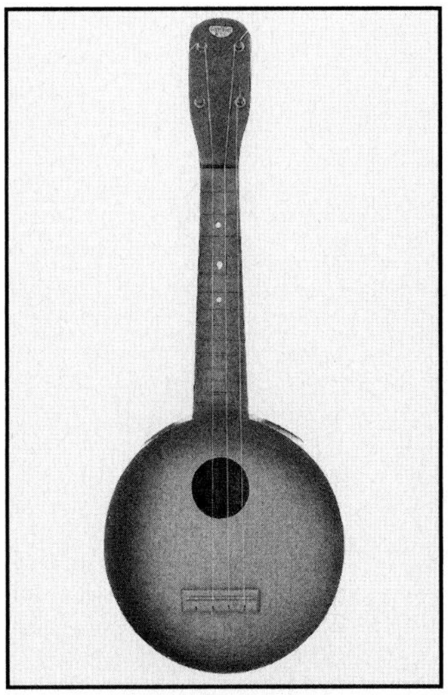

Ca. 1940s Gretsch Round

Imaged by Heritage Auctions, HA.com

'30s Harmony Johnny Marvin
Tim Fleck

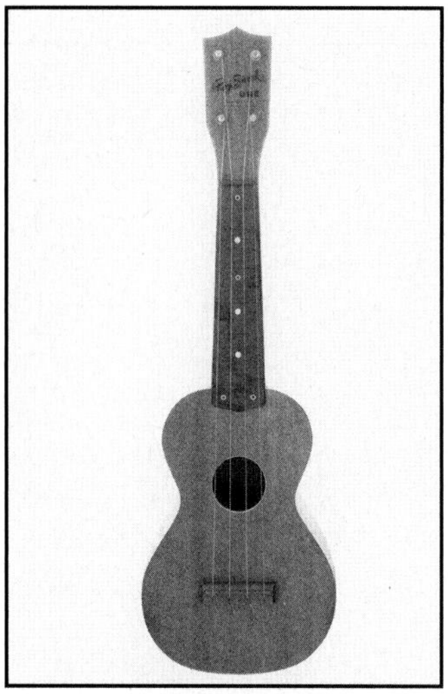

1955 Harmony Roy Smeck
Imaged by Heritage Auctions, HA.com

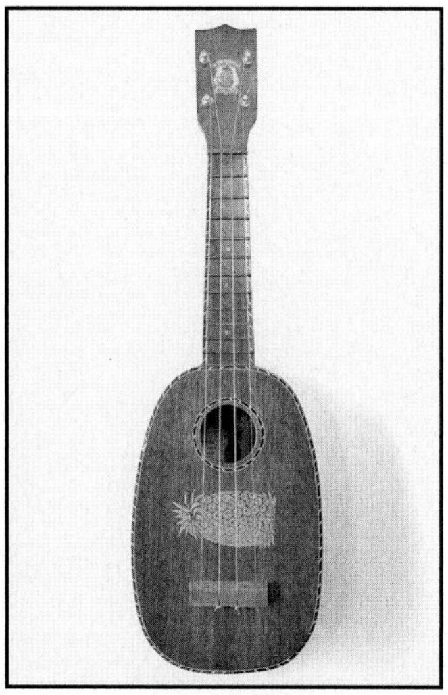

1960s Kamaka Pineapple
Randy Klimpert

MODEL YEAR	FEATURES	EXC. COND. LOW	HIGH
1940s	Unbound, engraved rose peghead	$1,200	$1,300
1950s	Darker finish, dark binding border	$300	$500

Guild

1952-present. By rights this fine East Coast shop should have produced a full line of ukes to complement its impressive flat and carved-top guitar offerings. Alas, a lone baritone model was all that they could manage. And it's a darned shame, too.

B-11 Baritone Ukulele

1963-1976. Mahogany body, rosewood 'board.

1960s		$800	$1,000

Harmony

1892-1976, late 1970s-present. This manufacturer surely produced more ukuleles than all other makers put together. Their extensive line ran the gamut from artist endorsed models and ukes in unusual shapes and materials, to inexpensive but flashy creations adorned with eye-catching decals and silk screening. The earliest examples have a small paper label on the back of the headstock, and a branded logo inside the body. This was replaced by a succession of logo decals applied to the front of the headstock, first gold and black, later green, white, and black. By the '60s Harmony had become so synonymous with ukulele production that they were known around their Chicago locale as simply "the ukulele factory," as in, "Ma couldn't come to the bar-b-que on-a-counta she got a job at the ukulele factory."

Baritone Ukulele

Bound mahogany body.

1960s		$150	$200

Concert Ukulele

Mahogany body, bound, concert-sized.

1935		$200	$300

Harold Teen Ukulele

Carl Ed cartoon decals on front.

1930	Blue, Green, Gray	$700	$900
1930	Red	$400	$600
1930	Yellow	$600	$800

Johnny Marvin Tenor Ukulele

Sports an airplane bridge.

1930s	Flamed koa	$1,200	$1,500
1930s	Sunburst mahogany	$400	$600

Roy Smeck Concert Ukulele

Concert-sized, sunburst spruce top.

1935		$500	$700

Roy Smeck Ukulele

Mahogany body.

1955	Plastic 'board	$100	$150
1955	Wood 'board	$250	$300

Roy Smeck Vita Ukulele

Pear-shaped body, seal-shaped f-holes.

1926		$600	$800

Tiple Ukulele

Multicolored binding, 10 steel strings.

1935		$300	$500

MODEL YEAR	FEATURES	EXC. COND. LOW	HIGH

Ukulele

1930	Koa, unbound	$200	$300
1935	Plain mahogany, unbound	$150	$250

Hilo Bay Ukuleles

2003-2017. Intermediate grade, production, tenor ukuleles made in Cebu City, Philippines for Mahalo Ken, owner of Hilo Guitars and Ukuleles in Hilo, Hawaii. He closed April, 2017 due to illness.

Kaai

Hawaiian Earnest Kaai was many things (teacher, songbook publisher, importer/exporter) during the early part of the 20th century, but ukulele manufacturer was certainly one job that he couldn't add to his resume. Still, scads of ukes proudly bear his name, in a variety of different styles and variations. Even more puzzling is the fact that while some appear to have been island-made, an equal number bear the telltale signs of mainland manufacture. It's also known that Kaai had an arrangement with Milwaukee instrument distributor William Stahl, and together they offered Kaai ukes. A very few examples - some with rope binding and some abalone inlaid presentation models, with ornate banjo-style headstocks - have surfaced which were certainly manufactured by the Larson Brothers of Chicago. These are the most highly prized of the Kaai ukes.

Soprano Ukulele

Koa body.

1916	Koa, abalone inlaid	$6,000	$7,500
1916	Koa, rope bound	$2,000	$2,500
1925	No binding, decal on headstock	$500	$600
1930	No binding, rope inlaid soundhole	$600	$800
1935	Rope binding top & back	$900	$1,000
1935	White binding, abalone soundhole	$900	$1,100

Kala

2005-present. Mike Upton's Petaluma, California company offers budget and intermediate grade, production, ukuleles.

Kamaka

Part of the second wave of ukulele builders on the Hawaiian Islands (after Nunes, Dias, and Santos), Kamaka distinguished itself first with ukes of extremely high quality, subsequently with the most enduring non-guitar-derived designs, the Pineapple Uke, patented in 1928. Kamaka is the only maker which has been in continuous production for nearly a hundred years, offering Hawaiian-made products from native woods in virtually every size and ornamentation. In the early '70s, Kamaka began rubber stamping the full date of manufacture on the end of the neck block of each uke, visible right through the sound hole. Now don't you wish that every manufacturer did that?

Concert Ukulele
Koa body, extended rosewood 'board.

MODEL YEAR	FEATURES	EXC. COND. LOW	HIGH
1975		$700	$900

Lili'u Ukulele
Concert-sized koa body.

MODEL YEAR	FEATURES	EXC. COND. LOW	HIGH
1965	8 strings	$1,100	$1,200
1985	6 strings	$1,100	$1,200

Pineapple Ukulele

MODEL YEAR	FEATURES	EXC. COND. LOW	HIGH
1928	Abalone top & 'board	$4,500	$5,000
1928	Pineapple decal top or back	$2,000	$2,500
1930	Monkeypod wood, plain, unbound	$1,300	$1,600
1930	Rope bound top only, koa	$2,000	$2,500
1935	Rope bound soundhole only	$1,500	$1,750
1960	Koa, unbound, KK logo	$700	$900
1970	Koa, extended rosewood 'board	$700	$900

Soprano Ukulele
Traditional uke shape, plain koa body.

MODEL YEAR	FEATURES	EXC. COND. LOW	HIGH
1920		$600	$850

Tenor Ukulele
Koa body, extended rosewood 'board.

MODEL YEAR	FEATURES	EXC. COND. LOW	HIGH
1955		$900	$1,100

Kanile'a Ukulele
1998-present. Joseph and Kristen Souza build their intermediate, professional and premium grade, production/custom, ukuleles in Kaneohe, Hawaii.

Kent
1961-1969. Large, student quality ukes of laminated construction were offered by this Japanese concern throughout the '60s.

Baritone Ukulele
Mahogany body, bound top, bound back.

MODEL YEAR	FEATURES	EXC. COND. LOW	HIGH
1960s		$100	$150

Knutsen
1890s-1920s. While Christopher Knutsen was the inventor of flat-topped harp instruments featuring an integral sound chamber on the bass side of the body, he almost certainly left the manufacturing to others. Striking in both concept and design, Knutsen products nonetheless suffer from compromised construction techniques.

Harp Taro Patch Ukulele
Tenor size, koa body, 8 strings.

MODEL YEAR	FEATURES	EXC. COND. LOW	HIGH
1915	Rope bound	$3,000	$4,000
1915	Unbound	$3,000	$4,000

Harp Ukulele
Koa body, large horn chamber.

MODEL YEAR	FEATURES	EXC. COND. LOW	HIGH
1915	Bound	$2,500	$3,000
1915	Unbound	$2,000	$2,500

Kumalae
Along with Kamaka, Kumalae was also of the second wave of Hawaiian uke makers. Jonah Kumalae's company quickly snagged the prestigious Gold Award at the Pan Pacific Exhibition in 1915, and the headstock decals and paper labels aren't about to let you forget it, either. Many assume that these all date from exactly that year, when in fact Kumalaes were offered right up through the late 1930s.

Soprano Ukulele
Figured koa body.

MODEL YEAR	FEATURES	EXC. COND. LOW	HIGH
1919	Bound top/back/'board	$1,000	$1,200
1920	Rope bound top/back	$800	$1,000
1927	As 1919 but with fiddle-shaped peghead	$1,500	$2,000
1930	Unbound body	$500	$700
1933	Rope bound soundhole only	$700	$900

Tenor Ukulele
Koa body, unbound top and back.

MODEL YEAR	FEATURES	EXC. COND. LOW	HIGH
1930s		$1,500	$1,600

Laka
2010-present. Budget and intermediate grade, production ukuleles built in the Far East and distributed worldwide by John Hornby Skewes & Co. Ltd. from the United Kingdom.

Lanikai
2000-present. Line of budget and intermediate grade, production, koa or nato wood, acoustic and acoustic/electric, ukuleles distributed by Hohner.

Le Domino
This line of striking ukuleles turned the popularity of domino playing into a clever visual motif, displaying not only tumbling dominos on their soundboards and around their soundholes, but 'board markers represented in decal domino denominations (3, 5, 7, 10, 12, etc.). The ukuleles were, in fact, produced by at least two different companies - Stewart and Regal - but you can scarcely tell them apart.

Concert Ukukele
Concert size, black-finish, white bound, dominos.

MODEL YEAR	FEATURES	EXC. COND. LOW	HIGH
1932		$900	$1,100

Soprano Ukukele
Domino decals.

MODEL YEAR	FEATURES	EXC. COND. LOW	HIGH
1930	Black finish, white bound	$400	$500
1940	Natural finish, unbound	$100	$150

Leonardo Nunes
Leonardo was the son of Manuel, the self-professed inventor of the ukulele. Whether actually the originator or not, Dad was certainly on the ship that brought the inventor to the islands in 1879. Leonardo, instead of joining up and making it

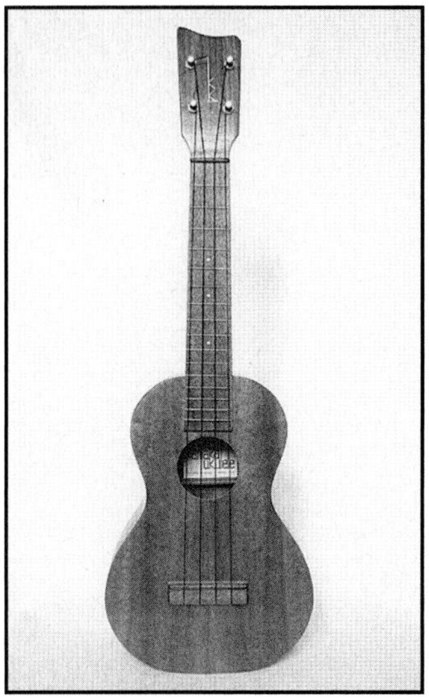

Kamaka Tenor

Kanile'a K-1 Tenor

Lanikai CMTU-S Curly Mango Soprano Tuna

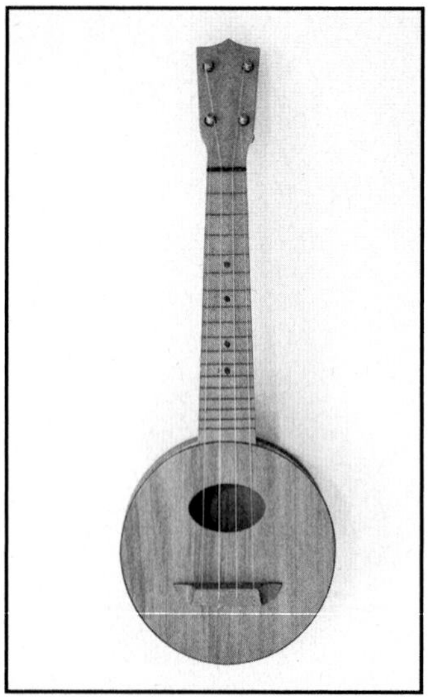

1935 Lyon And Healy Camp

Randy klimpert

1960 Maccaferri Mastro Baritone Electric

Randy Klimpert

1930 Manuel Nunes Taro Patch Fiddle

Randy Klimpert

Manuel & Son, set out on his own to produce ukes that are virtually indistinguishable from Pop's. All constructed entirely of koa, some exhibit considerable figure and rope binding finery, making them as highly desirable to collectors as Manuel's.

Radio Tenor Ukulele

Koa body, bound top, back and neck.

MODEL YEAR	FEATURES	EXC. COND. LOW	HIGH
1935		$2,000	$2,500

Soprano Ukulele

Figured koa body.

MODEL YEAR	FEATURES	EXC. COND. LOW	HIGH
1919	Bound top/ back/'board	$900	$1,100
1920	Rope bound top/back	$900	$1,100
1927	Bound body/ 'board/head	$1,200	$1,500
1930	Unbound	$500	$700
1933	Rope bound soundhole only	$800	$1,000

Taro Patch Fiddle

Koa body, unbound top and back.

MODEL YEAR	FEATURES	EXC. COND. LOW	HIGH
1930		$1,500	$1,700

Tenor Ukulele

Koa body, unbound top and back.

MODEL YEAR	FEATURES	EXC. COND. LOW	HIGH
1930		$1,200	$1,500

Lyon & Healy

1880s-ca.1949. During different time periods several different makers constructed ukes bearing this stamp - often with an additional Washburn tag as well. After initial production by Lyon & Healy, instrument manufacture then apparently bounced between Regal, Stewart, and Tonk Brothers all within a span of only a few short years. Adding to the confusion, ukes surface from time to time bearing no maker's mark that can be reasonably attributed to Lyon & Healy. Suffice it to say that the best of these ukes, those displaying the highest degrees of quality and ornamentation, rival Gibson and Martin for collectability and tone and beauty.

Bell-Shaped Ukulele

Mahogany body.

MODEL YEAR	FEATURES	EXC. COND. LOW	HIGH
1927		$2,000	$2,500

Camp Ukulele

Round nissa wood body, black binding.

MODEL YEAR	FEATURES	EXC. COND. LOW	HIGH
1935		$150	$200

Concert Ukulele

Mahogany body, bound top and back.

MODEL YEAR	FEATURES	EXC. COND. LOW	HIGH
1930		$1,500	$2,000

Shrine Ukulele

Triangular body.

MODEL YEAR	FEATURES	EXC. COND. LOW	HIGH
1927	Koa, green binding	$3,000	$3,500
1930	Mahogany, green binding	$2,000	$3,000
1933	Koa, abalone binding	$4,000	$4,400

Soprano Ukulele (Koa)

MODEL YEAR	FEATURES	EXC. COND. LOW	HIGH
1927	Bound top, pearl rosette	$3,500	$4,000
1934	Bound top/back	$1,000	$1,200
1935	Pearl bound top/back	$7,000	$9,000

Soprano Ukulele (Mahogany)

MODEL YEAR	FEATURES	EXC. COND. LOW	HIGH
1930	Unbound	$400	$500
1932	Bound top/back	$500	$600

Tenor Ukulele (Koa)

MODEL YEAR	FEATURES	EXC. COND. LOW	HIGH
1935	Pearl bound top/back	$8,000	$10,000

Tenor Ukulele (Mahogany)

MODEL YEAR	FEATURES	EXC. COND. LOW	HIGH
1933	Bound top/back	$1,500	$2,000

Maccaferri

1923-1990. Between the time he designed the Selmer guitar that became instantly synonymous with Django's gypsy jazz and his invention of the plastic clothespin, guitar design genius and manufacturing impresario Mario Maccaferri created a line of stringed instruments revolutionary for their complete plastic construction. The ukuleles were by far the greatest success, and most bore the tiny Maccaferri coat of arms on their tiny headstock. Mario was extremely proud of his innovations, so whether branded Islander, Mastro, TV Pal, or something else, the presence of PATENTED, PATENTS PEND, or one or more patent numbers on the headstock is your tell that it's a Maccaferri-designed uke.

Islander Baritone Ukulele

Large polystyrene cutaway body.

MODEL YEAR	FEATURES	EXC. COND. LOW	HIGH
1959		$250	$300

Islander Ukulele

Polystyrene plastic body, crest in peghead.

MODEL YEAR	FEATURES	EXC. COND. LOW	HIGH
1953		$150	$200

Mastro Baritone Electric Ukulele

Large polystyrene cutaway body, pickup.

MODEL YEAR	FEATURES	EXC. COND. LOW	HIGH
1960		$800	$1,200

Playtune Ukulele

Polystyrene body.

MODEL YEAR	FEATURES	EXC. COND. LOW	HIGH
1956		$100	$150

TV Pal Deluxe Ukulele

Extended 'board.

MODEL YEAR	FEATURES	EXC. COND. LOW	HIGH
1960		$100	$150

TV Pal Ukulele

Polystyrene plastic body

MODEL YEAR	FEATURES	EXC. COND. LOW	HIGH
1955		$100	$150

Magic Fluke Company

1999-present. Budget grade, production, ukuleles made in New Hartford, Connecticut. With a clever design, exceptional quality, dozens of catchy finishes, and surprisingly affordable prices, it's little wonder that these little wonders have caught on. Riding - if not almost single-handedly driving - the coming third wave of uke popularity (the '20s and '50s were the first and second), Dale and Phyllis Webb of the Magic Fluke, along with Phyllis' brother, author Jumpin' Jim Beloff, are downright ukulele evangelists. The Fluke is the first new uke that you're not afraid to let the kids monkey with.

Mainland Ukes

2008-present. Mike Hater imports parts built in China to set-up his budget and intermediate grade, production/custom, solid wood ukes and banjo-ukes in Nashville, Indiana.

MODEL YEAR	FEATURES	EXC. COND. LOW	HIGH

Manuel Nunes

The self-professed father of the ukulele was at least one of the first makers to produce them in any quantity. Beginning after 1879, when he and the first boat load of Portuguese settlers landed in Hawaii, until at least the 1930s, Manuel and his son Leonardo (see Leonardo Nunes section) produced some of the most beautiful and superbly crafted ukes offered by any Island maker.

Soprano Ukulele

Koa body.

1919	Figured koa, bound top/back/'board	$1,000	$1,300
1920	Rope bound top/back	$900	$1,100
1927	Bound body/ 'board/head	$1,500	$2,200
1930	Unbound	$700	$900
1933	Rope bound soundhole only	$800	$1,000

Taro Patch Fiddle

Koa body.

1930	Rope bound top/back	$1,500	$2,000
1930	Unbound top/back	$1,200	$1,500

Tenor Ukulele

Koa body, unbound top and back.

1930		$1,000	$1,500

Martin

1833-present. The C.F. Martin Company knew they wanted in on the uke craze, and toyed with some prototypes as early as 1907 or so, but didn't get around to actually getting serious until '16. The first of these were characterized by rather more primitive craftsmanship (by stringent Martin standards), bar frets, and an impressed logo in the back of the headstock. By '20, koa became available as a pricey option, and by the early '30s, regular frets and the familiar Martin headstock decal had prevailed. Martin single-handedly created the archetype of the mainland uke and the standard by which all competitors are measured.

Martin has recently re-entered the ukulele market with its budget Mexican-made model S-0, the Backpacker Uke, as well as a limited edition of the ornate, and pricey, 5K, 5M and 3K ukes.

Style 0 Ukulele

Unbound mahogany body.

1920	Wood pegs	$600	$800
1953	Patent pegs	$600	$800

Style 0-C Concert Ukulele

Mahogany body, bound top.

1931		$1,200	$1,500

Style 1 Ukulele

Mahogany body.

1917	Bound top only	$800	$1,000
1950	Tortoise bound top only	$700	$900
1967	Tortoise bound top only	$700	$900

MODEL YEAR	FEATURES	EXC. COND. LOW	HIGH

Style 1-C Concert Ukulele

Mahogany body, bound top.

1947		$1,000	$1,200

Style 1-T Tenor Ukulele

Mahogany body, bound top only.

1940		$1,000	$1,200

Style 1-K Ukulele

Koa body, rosewood bound top.

1928	Wood pegs	$800	$1,000
1939	Patent pegs	$800	$1,000

Style 1-C K Concert Ukulele

Koa body, bound top.

1928		$2,500	$3,000

Style 1 Taro Patch Ukulele

Mahogany body, 8 strings, rosewood bound.

1917		$1,000	$1,200

Style 1-K Taro Patch Ukulele

Style 1 with koa body.

1922		$1,200	$1,500

Style 2 Ukulele

Mahogany body, ivoroid bound top and back.

1917	No inlays, white binding	$1,200	$1,500
1922		$800	$1,000
1935		$800	$1,000
1961		$600	$800

Style 2-K Ukulele

Figured koa body, bound top and back.

1923		$1,500	$2,000
1939	Patent pegs	$1,500	$2,000

Style 2-C K Concert Ukulele

Same specs as 2-K, but in concert size.

1927		$4,000	$5,000

Style 2 Taro Patch Ukulele

Mahogany body, 8 strings, ivoroid bound.

1925		$1,500	$2,000

Style 2-K Taro Patch Ukulele

Style 2 with koa body.

1924		$1,700	$2,500

Style 3 Ukulele

Mahogany body.

1925	Kite inlay in headstock	$2,000	$2,500
1937	B/W lines in ebony 'board	$2,000	$2,500
1950	Extended 'board, dots	$1,500	$2,000

Style 3-K Ukulele

Figured koa body.

1920	Bow-tie 'board inlay	$3,000	$3,500
1931	B/W lines, diamonds, squares	$2,500	$3,000
1939	B/W lines and dot inlay	$2,500	$3,000

Style 3-C K Concert Ukulele

Same specs as 3-K, but in concert size.

1928		$10,000	$15,000

Style 3 Taro Patch Ukulele

Mahogany body, 8 strings, multiple bound.

1923		$2,000	$2,500

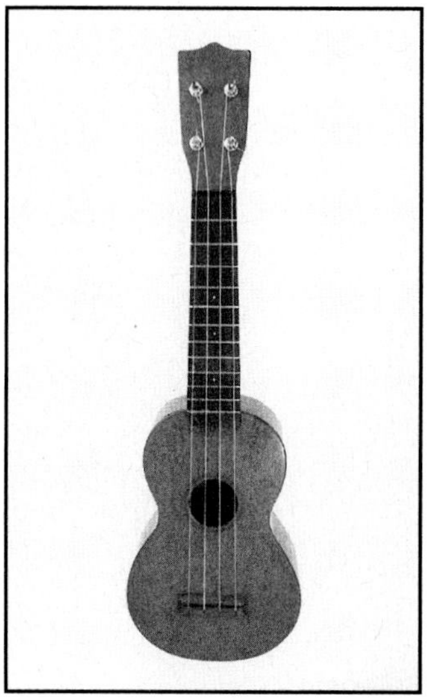

Martin Style 0

1950 Martin Style 1

Imaged by Heritage Auctions, HA.com

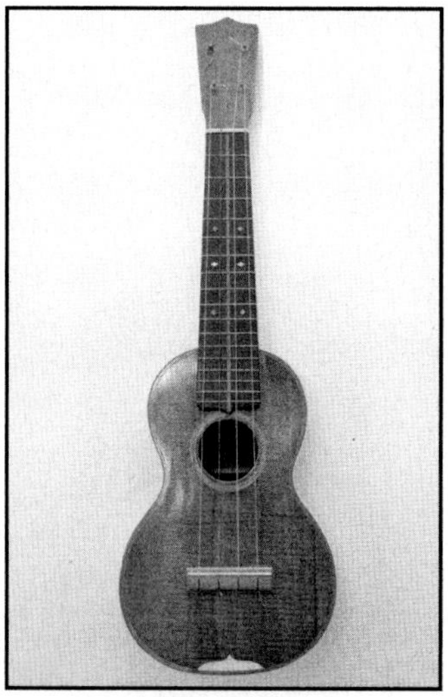

1924 Martin 3-K Taro Patch

1925 Martin T-18
Randy Klimpert

1947 Martin T-28
Randy Klimpert

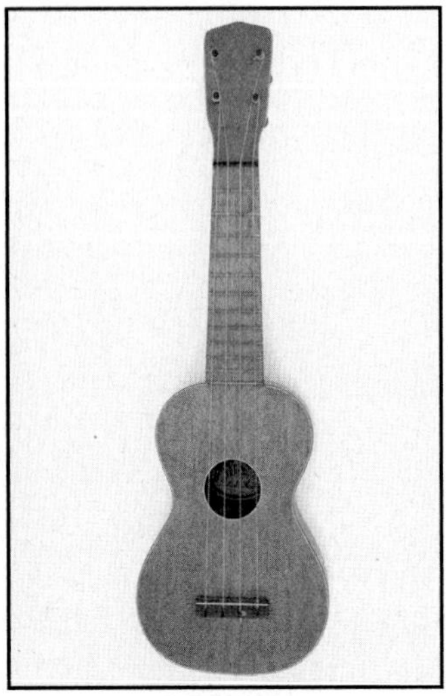
1925 Miami Soprano
Randy Klimpert

MODEL YEAR	FEATURES	EXC. COND. LOW	HIGH

Style 3-K Taro Patch Ukulele
Style 3 with koa body.

1929		$2,500	$3,000

Style 5 Ukulele
Highly flamed mahogany body, all pearl trimmed, extremely rare.

1941		$20,000	$25,000

Style 5-K Ukulele
Highly figured koa body, all pearl trimmed.

1926		$7,500	$9,000

Style 5-C K Concert Ukulele
Same specs as 5-K, but in concert size.

1926		$12,000	$15,000

Style 5-T K Tenor Ukulele
Same specs as 5-K, but in tenor size.

1929		$12,000	$15,000

Style 51 Baritone Ukulele
Mahogany body, bound top and back.

1966		$800	$1,100

Style T-15 Tiple Ukulele
Mahogany body, 10 metal strings, unbound.

1971		$700	$900

Style T-17 Tiple Ukulele
Mahogany body, 10 strings, unbound top and back.

1940		$900	$1,100

Style T-18 Tiple Ukulele
Mahogany body, 10 strings, spruce top.

1925		$1,000	$1,200

Style T-28 Tiple Ukulele
Rosewood body, 10 strings, bound top and back.

1947		$1,500	$2,000

Maurer

The Larson brothers of Maurer & Co., Chicago, built a few ukes and at least one taro patch under this brand from 1915 into the 1930s. Their small tops and backs are built-under-tension in the Larson tradition. A few of them have surfaced with the Hawaiian teacher/player's Earnest Kaai label and were probably sold through Stahl's Milwaukee store.

Miami

Apparently endorsed by the not-so-famous "Ukulele Hughes" - whose smiling mug graces the inside labels - these ukes' actual origins are unknown, but were distributed by the Stadlmair company of New York, also the east coast distributor of Weissenborn instruments during the 1920s.

Miami "Baby"
Smaller mahogany body, unbound.

1925		$400	$500

Soprano Ukulele
Plain mahogany body, unbound.

1925		$400	$500

National

Ca. 1927-present. To capitalize on the success of their amplifying guitars, the Dopyera brothers introduced metal-bodied ukuleles and mandolins as well. Large, heavy, and ungainly by today's standards, these early offerings nonetheless have their charms. Their subsequent switch to a smaller body shape produced an elegant and sweet-sounding resonator uke that soon became much sought after.

Style O Ukulele
Metal body, soprano size, sandblasted scenes.

1931		$2,500	$3,000

Style 1 Ukulele
Nickel body.

1928	Tenor, 6" resonator	$2,000	$2,200
1928	Tenor, early features	$2,200	$2,500
1933	Soprano	$2,000	$2,500

Style 2 Ukulele
Nickel body, engraved roses.

1928	Tenor	$4,000	$4,500
1931	Soprano	$4,500	$5,000

Style 3 Ukulele
Nickel body, lilies-of-the-valley.

1929	Tenor	$4,000	$5,000
1933	Soprano	$5,000	$6,000

Triolian Ukulele

1928	Tenor, sunburst	$1,500	$1,700
1930	Soprano, sunburst	$1,200	$1,500
1934	Soprano, wood-grained metal	$1,500	$1,800

New Moon Ukulele

1978-present. Professional and premium grade, custom, acoustic ukuleles built in Greensboro, North Carolina by luthier Robert Rigaud. He also builds guitars under the Rigaud brand.

Oscar Schmidt

1879-1938, 1979-present. The same New Jersey outfit responsible for Leadbelly's 12-string guitar offered ukes as well during the same period. Many of these were odd amalgams of materials, often combining koa, mahogany, and spruce in the same instrument. Since 1979, when the name was acquired by the U.S. Music Corp. (Washburn, Randall, etc.), they have offered a line of budget grade, production, Asian-made ukes. They also offer guitars, basses, mandolins, and banjos.

Soprano Ukulele
Spruce top, bound mahogany body.

1930		$300	$450

Polk-a-lay-lee

1960s. These inexplicably shaped oddities were produced by Petersen Products of Chicago ca. the mid-'60s, and anecdotal Midwestern lore has it that their intent was to be offered as giveaways for the Polk Brothers, a local appliance chain. This may be how they ended up, although the gargantuan original packaging makes no reference to any such promotion. The box does call out what the optional colors were.

Many have noted the striking resemblance to the similarly named wares of the Swaggerty company (see Swaggerty) of California, who also offered brightly colored plywood-bodied ukes in comically oversized incarnations, but who was copying whom has yet to be determined.

MODEL YEAR	FEATURES	EXC. COND. LOW	HIGH

Ukulele

Long "boat oar" body, uke scale, brown, natural, red, black or fruitwood.

1965	Brown or natural	$300	$400
1965	Fruitwood	$700	$900
1965	Red or black	$400	$500

Regal

Ca. 1895-1966, 1987-present. Like the other large 1930s Chicago makers, Harmony and Lyon & Healy, the good ukes are very, very good, and the cheap ukes are very, very cheap. Unlike its pals, however, Regal seems to have produced more ukuleles in imaginative themes, striking color schemes, and in more degrees of fancy trim, making them the quintessential wall-hangers. And lucky for you, there's a vintage Regal uke to suit every décor.

Carson Robison Ukulele

Top sports painted signature, cowboy scene.

1935		$500	$700

Jungle Ukulele

Birch body, covered in leopard skin fabric.

1950		$500	$600

Resonator Ukulele

Black body, f-holes, see Dobro uke.

1934		$200	$400

Soprano Ukulele (Birch)

Birch body.

1931	Brown sunburst	$100	$200
1931	Nautical themes, various colors	$100	$200
1945	Painted body, panda theme	$700	$900
1945	Painted body, victory themes	$600	$800

Soprano Ukulele (Koa)

Koa body, multicolored rope bound top.

1930		$300	$500

Soprano Ukulele (Mahogany)

Mahogany body.

1930	Multiple bound top	$500	$800
1935	Spruce top, inlays	$300	$500
1940	Extended 'board	$200	$300

Tiple Ukulele

1930	Birch body stained dark, black binding	$300	$400
1935	Spruce top,mahogany, fancy binding	$400	$600

Wendall Hall Red Head Ukulele

Koa body, celebrity decal on headstock.

1935		$400	$600

Ricard

Alexander Ricard and son Jorge were primarily violin makers but also made mandolins and some lovely ukuleles out of their small shop in Springfield, Massachusetts from the teens to the 1920s. Though their labels only mention concert ukes, most of those that turn up today are soprano, and were probably made from leftover violin wood and parts.

MODEL YEAR	FEATURES	EXC. COND. LOW	HIGH

Soprano Ukulele

Spruce top, ebony 'board.

1920	Curly maple body	$600	$800
1925	Round concert body	$200	$300

S. S. Stewart

Not much is known about the ukuleles of this Philadelphia firm, except that they were most certainly sub-contracted from another maker or makers.

Soprano Ukulele

Mahogany body, bound top and back.

1927		$200	$300

Sam F. Chang

A disciple of Kamaka, Sam F. Chang made ukuleles, guitars and curios (according to his decal) during the 1930s for his own Honolulu shop as well as under other brand names. High guality and always koa, the designs and ornamentation of Chang ukes are less reminiscent of Kamaka and other island makers; they are ironically more C.F. Martin inspired. (Also see Aloha.)

Soprano Ukulele

All Koa, plain body.

1925	Celluloid soundhole	$400	$500
1930	Celluloid binding	$600	$760

Sammo

Flashy internal paper labels trumpet that these ukes (mandolins and guitars, too) were products of the Osborne Mfg. Co. Masonic Temple, Chicago-Illinois and what the heck any of that means is still open to modern speculation. Your guess is as good as mine. Still, the high quality and often opulent degree of ornamentation that the instruments exhibit, coupled with even the vaguest implication that they were made by guys wearing fezzes and/or men who ride around in tiny cars at parades is all the reason we need to buy every one we see.

Soprano Ukulele

1925	Bound koa, fancy headstock shape	$700	$900
1925	Figured maple, 5-ply top, back binding	$300	$400
1925	Unbound koa, fancy headstock shape	$300	$400

Silvertone

1941-ca. 1970, present. Silvertone was the house brand of Sears & Roebuck and most (if not all) of its ukes were manufactured for them by Harmony.

Soprano Ukulele

Mahogany body, Harmony-made.

1950	Sunburst	$200	$300
1950	Unbound	$200	$300
1955	Bound	$200	$300
1960	Green	$200	$300

S.S. Stewart Soprano

Randy Klimpert

Sam Chang Ukulele

Randy Klimpert

Sammo

Supertone
Randy Klimpert

Turturro Soprano

Turturro

MODEL YEAR	FEATURES	EXC. COND. LOW	HIGH

Slingerland

Slingerland started marketing ukes around 1916. Banjo ukuleles bearing this brand (see Slingerland Banjo uke section below) were certainly made by the popular drum company (banjos being little more than drums with necks, after all). Slingerland standard ukuleles, on the other hand, bear an uncanny resemblance to the work of the Oscar Schmidt company.

Soprano Ukulele

Koa body, rope bound top and soundhole.

1920		$200	$300

Sterling

The miniscule reference buried deep within the headstock decal to a T.B. Co. can only mean that the Sterling ukulele somehow fits into the mind-numbing Tonk Bros./Lyon & Healy/Regal/S.S. Stewart manufacturing puzzle. Nonetheless, the brand must have been reserved for the cream of the crop, since the Sterling ukes that surface tend to be of the drop-dead-gorgeous variety.

Soprano Ukulele

Flamed koa, multiple fancy binding all over.

1935		$2,000	$2,500

Stetson

Popular misconception - to say nothing of wishful thinking and greed - has it that all instruments labeled with the Stetson brand were the work of the Larson Brothers of Chicago. While a few Stetson guitars and a very few mandolins may be genuine Larson product, the ukuleles surely were made elsewhere.

Soprano Ukulele

Mahogany body, single bound top and back.

1930		$200	$300

Supertone

1914-1940s. For whatever reason, Supertone was the name attached to Sears' musical instruments before the line became Silvertone (see above). These, too, were all Harmony-made.

Soprano Ukulele (Birch)

Birch body, Harmony-made, various decorations.

1930		$200	$300

Soprano Ukulele (Flamed Mahogany)

Flamed mahogany body, ebony bridge.

1925		$600	$800

Soprano Ukulele (Koa)

Koa body, Harmony-made.

1927	Rope bound, fancy headstock	$600	$800
1933	Rope bound body/'board	$600	$800
1935	Rope bound	$500	$600
1939	Unbound	$400	$500

Soprano Ukulele (Mahogany)

Mahogany body, Harmony-made.

1930	Unbound	$200	$300
1940	Bound	$200	$300

MODEL YEAR	FEATURES	EXC. COND. LOW	HIGH

Swaggerty

Not enough is known of this West Coast company, except that their product line of unusually shaped 4-stringed novelty instruments oddly mirrors those made by Petersen Products in Chicago at the same time (see Polk-a-lay-lee). The two companies even seem to have shared plastic parts, such as 'boards and tuners. Go figure.

Kook-a-Lay-Lee Ukulele

Green plywood body, twin necks.

1965		$300	$500

Singing Treholipee

Orange plywood body, long horn.

1965		$300	$500

Surf-a-Lay-Lee Ukulele

Plywood body, long horn, green, yellow, or orange.

1965		$300	$500

Tabu

The Tabu brand on either the back of a ukulele's headstock or inside its soundhole was never an indication of its original maker. Rather, it was intended to assure the purchaser that the uke was, indeed of bona fide Hawaiian origin. So rampant was the practice of mainland makers claiming Island manufacture of their wares that in the late 'teens Hawaii launched a campaign to set the record straight, and - lucky for you - a nifty little brand was the result. The Tabu mark actually was used to mark the ukes of several different makers.

Soprano Ukulele

Figured koa body.

1915	Rope bound	$700	$800
1915	Unbound	$400	$600

Tombo

This venerable Japanese harmonica manufacturer jumped on two bandwagons at once with its mid-'60s introduction of a solid body electric ukulele. The Tombo Ukulet shares a tenor scale length and single coil pickup with Gibson's ETU electric tenor ukes, but the Tombo's thin, solidbody design is decidedly more Fender than jumping flea. Completing the imitation-is-the-sincerest-form-of-flattery theme is a snazzy Silvertone-esque case with onboard amplifier.

Ukulet

Solid body, amp-in-case, red sunburst, white or blue finish.

1967	Sunburst	$700	$800
1968	White or blue	$1,000	$1,200

Tonk Brothers

The Tonk Brothers Company was a huge Chicago-based distributor of musical merchandise, founded in 1893. They carried many of the popular brands of the day and also offered a line of ukuleles under their own brand name.

Soprano Ukulele

Plain mahogany body, celluloid bound.

1930		$350	$500

Turturro

Unlike manufacturers like Regal and Harmony who were content to produce novelty ukes by merely spray painting or applying decals with eye-catching motifs, New York manufacturer Nicola Turturro issued novelty ukuleles from his own patented designs. The most well-known is the Turnover Uke, a playable two-sided contraption strung as a 4-string uke on one side, and an 8-string mandolin on the other.

Concert Ukulele

Concert size, plain mahogany body.

MODEL YEAR	FEATURES	EXC. COND. LOW	HIGH
1930		$500	$600

Miami Ukulele

Soprano size, plain mahogany body.

MODEL YEAR	FEATURES	EXC. COND. LOW	HIGH
1925		$300	$400

Peanut Ukulele

Ribbed peanut shaped body.

MODEL YEAR	FEATURES	EXC. COND. LOW	HIGH
1928		$800	$1,000

Turnover Ukulele

Two-sided uke and mandolin.

MODEL YEAR	FEATURES	EXC. COND. LOW	HIGH
1926		$1,000	$1,500
1926	Spruce topped mandolin	$1,200	$1,700

Vega

Famous for their banjos, the Vega name was applied to a sole baritone uke, tied with the endorsement of 1950s TV crooner Arthur Godfrey.

Arthur Godfrey Baritone Ukulele

Mahogany body, unbound.

MODEL YEAR	FEATURES	EXC. COND. LOW	HIGH
1955		$300	$400

Washburn

See Lyon & Healy.

Weissenborn

1910s-1937, present. The mainland maker famous for their hollow-necked Hawaiian guitars was responsible for several uke offerings over the course of its 20-or-so-year run. Like their 6-stringed big brothers, they were the closest thing to Island design and detail to come from the mainland. The Weissenborn brand has been revived on a line of reissue style guitars.

Soprano Ukulele

Figured koa body.

MODEL YEAR	FEATURES	EXC. COND. LOW	HIGH
1920	Rope bound	$2,000	$2,200
1920	Unbound	$1,200	$1,500

Weymann

Renowned for fine tenor banjos, Weyman affixed their name to a full line of soprano ukes of varying degrees of decoration, quite certainly none of which were made under the same roof as the banjos. Most were C.F. Martin knock-offs.

Soprano Ukulele

MODEL YEAR	FEATURES	EXC. COND. LOW	HIGH
1925	Mahogany, unbound	$600	$800
1930	Koa, fancy pearl vine 'board inlay	$1,500	$1,700

Wm. Smith Co.

1920s. Like Ditson, the Wm. Smith Co. was a company for which C.F. Martin moonlighted without getting much outward credit. The South American cousin of the uke, the tiple, with its 10 metal strings and tenor uke sized body, was first produced exclusively for Smith by Martin starting around 1920, before being assumed into the regular Martin line with appropriate Martin branding.

Tiple Ukulele

Mahogany body, spruce top, ebony bridge.

MODEL YEAR	FEATURES	EXC. COND. LOW	HIGH
1920		$2,000	$2,200

Wurlitzer

Like Ditson, Wurlitzer was a retail chain for which C.F. Martin made some - though by no means all - ukuleles. Martin-made Wurlitzer ukes often bear a Martin brand as well as a Wurlitzer, or barring that, at least demonstrate overall similarities to the rest of the ukes in the regular Martin line, both in construction and decoration.

Soprano 835 Ukulele

MODEL YEAR	FEATURES	EXC. COND. LOW	HIGH
1922	As Martin O	$700	$1,000

Soprano 836 Ukulele

MODEL YEAR	FEATURES	EXC. COND. LOW	HIGH
1923	As Martin 1	$700	$1,000

Soprano 837 Ukulele

MODEL YEAR	FEATURES	EXC. COND. LOW	HIGH
1925	As Martin 1K	$1,000	$1,400

Soprano 838 Ukulele

MODEL YEAR	FEATURES	EXC. COND. LOW	HIGH
1923	As Martin 2K	$1,500	$2,000

Soprano 839 Ukulele

MODEL YEAR	FEATURES	EXC. COND. LOW	HIGH
1922	As Martin 3K/5K	$3,500	$4,500

Soprano 841 Ukulele

MODEL YEAR	FEATURES	EXC. COND. LOW	HIGH
1924	As Martin 2K Taro	$2,500	$3,000

Soprano 844 Ukulele

MODEL YEAR	FEATURES	EXC. COND. LOW	HIGH
1023	As Martin 3K Taro	$3,000	$3,500

Banjo Ukuleles

Bacon

This legendary Connecticut banjo maker just couldn't resist the temptation to extend their line with uke versions of their popular banjos. As with Gibson, Ludwig, Slingerland, and Weyman, the banjo ukuleles tended to mimic the already proven construction techniques and decorative motifs of their regular banjo counterparts. In materials, finish, and hardware, most banjo ukes share many more similarities with full sized banjos than differences. The banjo ukes were simply included as smaller, plainer, variations of banjos, much as concert, tenor, and baritone options fleshed out standard ukulele lines.

Banjo #1 Ukulele

Walnut rim.

MODEL YEAR	FEATURES	EXC. COND. LOW	HIGH
1927	Fancy 'board, resonator	$1,500	$1,700
1927	Plain 'board, no resonator	$700	$1,000

Banjo #2 Ukulele

Walnut rim.

MODEL YEAR	FEATURES	EXC. COND. LOW	HIGH
1927	Fancy 'board, resonator	$1,500	$2,000

1950s Vega Arthur Godfrey Baritone

Imaged by Heritage Auctions, HA.com

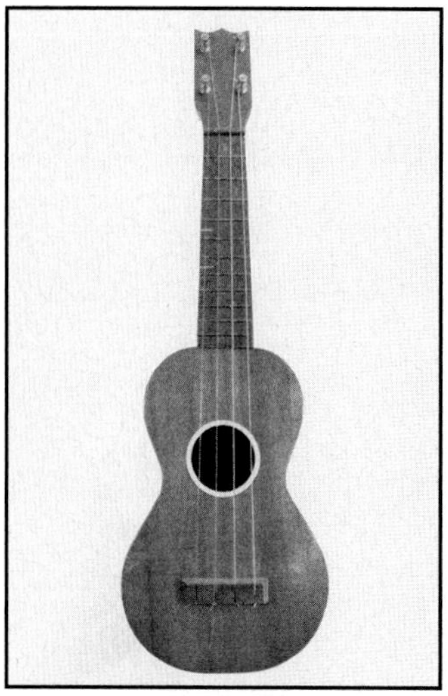

Weissenborn Soprano

Randy Klimpert

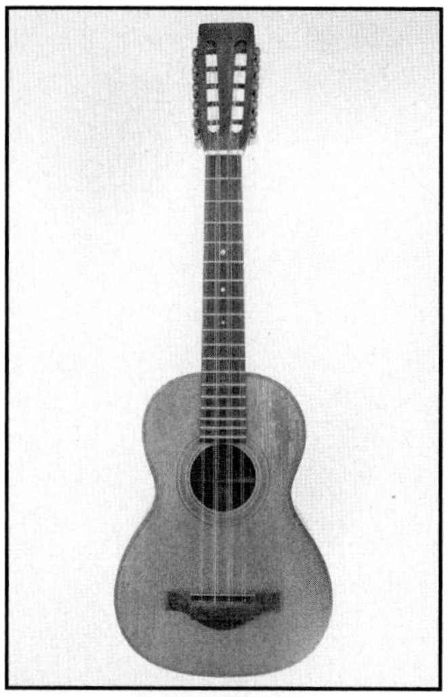

Wm. Smith Tiple

Randy Klimpert

MODEL YEAR	FEATURES	EXC. COND. LOW	HIGH

Silver Bell Banjo Ukulele

Engraved pearloid 'board and headstock.

1927		$2,500	$3,000

Dixie

With chrome plated all-metal design, there's only one word for these banjo ukes - shiny. Their bodies, necks, and frets are die cast together in zinc (think Hot Wheels cars and screen door handles), the Dixie must have made the perfect indestructible instrument for Junior's birthday back in the 1960s. Similar to one made by Werko.

Banjo Ukulele

One-piece, all-metal construction.

1960		$200	$300

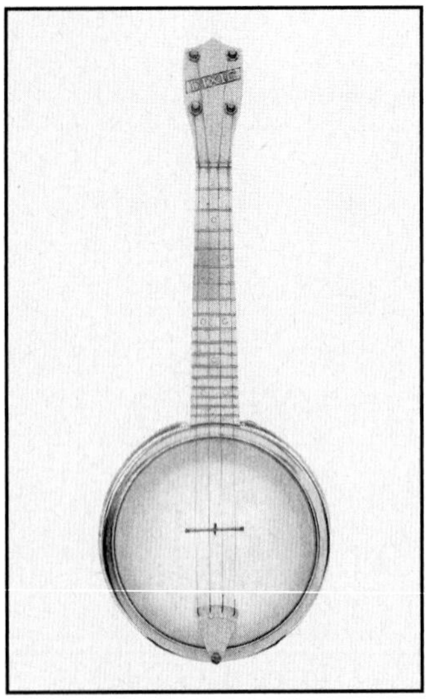

Dixie Silver Banjo Uke

Imaged by Heritage Auctions, HA.com

Gibson

UB-1 Banjo Ukulele

Small 6" head, flat panel resonator.

1928		$500	$700

UB-2 Banjo Ukulele

8" head, dot inlay.

1930		$1,000	$1,200

UB-2 Deluxe Banjo Ukulele

8" head, diamond and square inlay.

1930		$1,200	$1,500

UB-3 Banjo Ukulele

8" head, fleur de lis pearl logo inlay.

1935		$1,500	$1,700

UB-4 Banjo Ukulele

8" head, resonator and flange.

1932		$2,000	$2,500

UB-5 Banjo Ukulele

8" head, resonator and flange, gold parts.

1937		$3,700	$5,000

Ludwig Banjo Uke

Randy Klimpert

Le Domino

Banjo Ukulele

Resonator, decorated as Le Domino uke.

1933		$350	$500

Ludwig

The Ludwig was then, and is today, the Cadillac of banjo ukes. British banjo uke icon George Formby's preference for Ludwig continues assuring their desirability, while the fact that they were available in only a couple of models, for a few short years, and in relatively small production numbers only adds to the mystique.

Banjo Ukulele

Flange with crown holes.

1927	Gold-plated parts	$4,500	$5,000
1928	Nickel-plated parts	$3,000	$4,000
1928	Silver-plated parts	$3,500	$4,500
1930	Ivoroid headstock, rare model	$4,000	$5,000

Wendell Hall Professional Banjo Ukulele

Walnut resonator, flange with oval holes.

1927		$2,000	$2,500

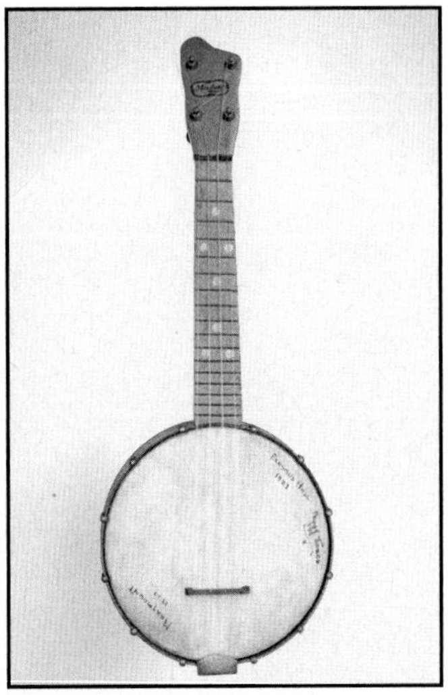

Maxitone Banjo Uke

Randy Klimpert

MODEL YEAR	FEATURES	EXC. COND. LOW	HIGH

Lyon & Healy

Banjo Ukulele

Walnut neck and resonator, fancy pearl inlay.

1935		$800	$1,000

Maxitone

Banjo Ukulele

Plain, painted various metallic colors.

1935		$300	$400

Paramount

1920s-1942, Late 1940s. The William L. Lange Company began selling Paramount banjos, guitar banjos and mandolin banjos in the early 1920s. Gretsch picked up the Paramount name and used it on guitars for a time in the late '40s.

Banner Blue Banjo Ukulele

Brass hearts 'board inlay, walnut neck.

1933		$900	$1,100

Regal

Banjo Ukulele

Mahogany rim, resonator, fancy rope bound.

1933		$300	$400

Richter

Allegedly, this Chicago company bought the already-made guitars, ukes, and mandolins of other manufacturers, painted and decorated them to their liking and resold them. True or not, they certainly were cranked out in a bevy of swanky colors.

Banjo Ukulele

Chrome-plated body, 2 f-holes in back.

1930		$150	$250
1930	Entire body/ neck painted	$150	$250

Slingerland

May Bell Banjo Ukulele

Walnut resonator with multicolored rope.

1935		$150	$250

Werko

These Chicago-made banjo ukuleles had construction similar to the Dixie brand, and except for the addition of a swank layer of blue sparkle drum binding on the rim, you would be hard pressed to tell them apart.

Banjo Ukulele

Chrome-plated metal body and neck.

1960		$200	$300

Weymann

Banjo Ukulele

Maple rim, open back, ebony 'board.

1926		$1,000	$1,200

DEALER DIRECTORY

A GEOGRAPHICAL GUIDE

Australia

Echo Tone
497 High Street
Northcote, Victoria 3070
011-61-3-9939-0752
info@echotone.com.au
www.echotone.com.au

Guitar Emporium
Darren Garth
20 Lalor St
Port Melbourne, Victoria 3207
011-61-3-9696-8032
emporium@ozemail.com.au
www.GuitarEmporium.com

Canada

Folkway
22 Dupont Street East
Waterloo, Ontario N2J 2G9
855-772-0424 (toll free)
info@folkwaymusic.com
www.FolkwayMusic.com

Twelfth Fret
Grant MacNeill/Chris Bennett
2132 Danforth Avenue
Toronto, Ontario M4C 1J9
416-423-2132
416-423-1554 (Repairs)
sales@12fret.com
www.12Fret.com

England

Ampaholics
Paul Goodhand-Tait
PO Box 542
Surrey, GU1 12F
011-44-1483-825102
ampaholics@aol.com
www.ampaholics.org.uk

Denmark Street Guitars
27 Denmark Street
London, WChH 8HJ
011-44-207-379-1139
www.londonvintageguitars.com

Japan

H I Guitars
No.1 Furukawa Building
3-8-6-B1, Kanda Kajicho,
Chiyoda-Ku, Tokyo 101-0045 Japan
011-81-3-3257-7117
higuitars@aol.com
www.hi-guitars.com

United States of America

Arizona

CE Distribution
6221 S Maple Ave
Tempe, AZ 85283
480-755-4712
www.cedist.com

California

California World Guitar Shows
Larry Briggs
918-288-2222
www.CalShows.TV

Drew Berlin's Vintage Guitars
Drew Berlin
213-400-4244
Drew@DrewBerlin.com
www.DrewBerlin.com

Gryphon Strings
Richard Johnston
211 Lambert Ave
Palo Alto, CA 94306
650-493-2131
info@gryphonstrings.com
www.gryphonstrings.com

Neal's Music
Neal Shelton
Huntington Beach , CA
714-330-9428
nealmuzic@aol.com
www.nealsmusic.com

Players Vintage Instruments
Lowell Levinger
Inverness, CA
415-669-1107
info@vintageinstruments.com
www.vintageinstruments.com

Schoenberg Guitars
Eric Schoenberg
106 Main Street
Tiburon, CA 94920
415-789-0846
eric@om28.com
www.om28.com

Union Grove Music
Richard Gellis
PO Box 2635
Aptos, CA, 95001
(831) 427-0670
www.uniongrovemusic.com/

Florida

Guitar Broker
Craig & Dustin Brody
816 NW 6th Ave
Ft. Lauderdale, FL 33311
954-646-8819
vintage@guitarbroker.com
www.guitarbroker.com

Kummer's Vintage
Timm Kummer
954-752-6063
prewar99@aol.com
www.kummersvintage.com

Replay Guitar Exchange
Jim Brady
3944 Britton Plaza
Tampa, FL 33611
813-254-8880
info@replayguitar.com
www.replayguitar.com

Georgia

Atlanta Vintage Guitars
Greg Henderson
3778 Canton Road, Ste. 400
Marietta, GA 30066
770-433-1891
atlantavintageguitars@gmail.com
www.atlantavintageguitars.com

Illinois

Chicago Guitar Show
Ruth Brinkmann
817.312.7659
ruthmbrinkmann@gmail.com
www.wacovintageinstruments.com

Chicago Music Exchange
Daniel Escauriza
3316 N Lincoln Ave
Chicago, IL 60657
773-525-7775
info@chicagomusicexchange.com
www.CME6.com

SS Vintage
George Coutretsis
4422 N Clark St
Chicago, IL 60640
773-472-3333
george@ssvintage.com
www.ssvintage.com

Kansas

Mass Street Music
Jim Baggett
1347 Massachusetts St
Lawrence, KS 66044
785-843-3535
sales@massstreetmusic.com
www.massstreetmusic.com

Maryland

Garrett Park Guitars
Rick Hogue
7 Old Solomans Island Rd
Annapolis, MD 21401
410-571-9660
info@gpguitars.com
www.gpguitars.com

Nationwide Guitars, Inc.
Bruce or Brad Rickard
P.O. Box 2334
Columbia, MD 21045
410-489-4074
nationwideguitar@gmail.com
www.nationwideguitars.com

Southworth Guitars
Gil Southworth
southworthguitar@aol.com
www.southworthguitars.com

Massachusetts

Mill River Music and Guitars
Jon Aronstein
16 Armory St
Northampton, MA 01062
413-505-0129
info@millrivermusic.com
www.millrivermusic.com

Bay State Vintage Guitars
A.J. Jones
481 Washington St
Norwood, MA 02062
617-267-6077
info@baystatevintageguitars.com
www.baystatevintageguitars.com

Michigan

Elderly Instruments
Stan Werbin
100 North Washington
Lansing, MI 48906
888-473-5810
elderly@elderly.com
www.elderly.com

Minnesota

Vintage Guitars & Parts Guitarville' by Eddie Vegas
Ed Matthews
Duluth, MN 55720
218-879-3796
e.matthews@mchsi.com
www.eddievegas.com

Willies American Guitars
254 Cleveland Avenue South
St. Paul, MN 55105
651-699-1913
info@williesguitars.com
williesguitars.com

Missouri

Fly by Night Music
Dave Crocker
103 S Washington
Neosho, MO 64850-1816
417-451-5110
crocker@joplin.com
www.amigoguitarshows.com

Killer Vintage
Dave Hinson
PO Box 190561
St. Louis, MO 63119
314-647-7795
info@killervintage.com
www.killervintagespecialtyguitars.com/

Nevada

A.J.'s Music
Peter Trauth
1203 Santa Ynez
Henderson, NV 89002
702-436-9300
ajsmusic@earthlink.net
www.ajsmusic.com

New Hampshire

Retromusic
Jeff Firestone
38 Washington Street
Kenne, NH 03431
603-357-9732
retromusicnh@gmail.com
www.retroguitar.com

New Jersey

Kebo's Bassworks
Kevin 'KeBo" Borden and Dr. Ben Sopranzetti
info@kebosbassworks.com
www.kebosbassworks.com

Lark Street Music
Buzz Levine
479 Cedar Ln
Teaneck, NJ 07666
(201) 287-1959
larkstreet@gmail.com
www.larkstreetmusic.com

New Jersey Guitar and Bass Center
Jay Jacus
995 Amboy Ave
Edison, NJ 08837
732-225-4444
njgtrbass@aol.com
www.newjerseyguitarandbasscenter.com

New Mexico

GuitarVista
Stanley Burg
3117 Silver Ave SE
Albuquerque, NM 87106
505-268-1133
gitmaven@yahoo.com
www.guitarvistanm.com

Vintage Guitar magazine
SUBSCRIBE ONLINE AT
WWW.VINTAGEGUITAR.COM OR CALL 1-800-844-1197

New York

Bernunzio Uptown Music
122 East Ave
Rochester, NY 14604
585-473-6140
info@bernunzio.com
www.bernunzio.com

Imperial Guitars
Bill Imperial
2A Cherry Hill Rd
New Paltz, NY 12561
845-255-2555
IGS55@aol.com
www.imperialguitar.com

Laurence Wexer, LTD
Larry Wexer
By appointment only
New York, NY 10036
212-532-2994
lwexer@gmail.com
www.wexerguitars.com

Rivington Guitars
Howie Statland
73 E 4th St
New York, NY 10003
212-505-5313
rivingtoninfo@gmail.com
www.rivingtonguitars.com

Sam Ash
Sammy Ash
516-686-4104
sam.ash@samashmusic.com

We Buy Guitars
Richie Friedman
PO Box 60736
Staten Island, NY 10306
516-221-0563
Webuyguitars@aol.com

Well Strung Guitars
David Davidson/Paige Davidson
439 Main St
Farmigndale, NY 11735
516-221-0563
info@wellstrungguitars.com
www.wellstrungguitars.com

North Carolina

Coleman Music
Chip Coleman
1021 S Main St
China Grove, NC 28023-2335
704-857-5705
OR120@aol.com
www.colemanmusic.com

Midwood Guitar Studio
Douglas Armstrong
1517 Central Ave
Charlotte, NC 28205-5013
980-265-1976
sales@midwoodguitarstudio.com
www.midwoodguitarstudio.com

Ohio

Gary's Classic Guitars
Gary Dick
Cincinnati, OH
513-891-0555
garysclssc@aol.com
www.garysguitars.com

The Loft at Lay's
Dan Shinn
974 Kenmore Blvd
Akron, OH 44314
330-848-1392
info@laysguitar.com
www.theloftatlays.com

Mike's Music
Mike Reeder
2615 Vine St
Cincinnati, OH 45219
513-281-4900
www.mikesmusicohio.com

Oklahoma

Strings West
Larry Briggs
PO Box 999 - 109 N Cincinnati Ave
Sperry, OK 74073
918-288-2222
larryb@stringswest.com
www.stringswest.com

Oregon

McKenzie River Music
Artie Leider
455 West 11th
Eugene, OR 97401
541-343-9482
artie@mrmgtr.com
www.mckenzierivermusic.com

Pennsylvania

Heritage Insurance Services Inc.
Ellis Hershman
826 Bustleton Pike
Suite 203
Feasterville PA, 19053
800-289-8837
ellish@musicins.com
musicins.com

Jim's Guitars
Jim Singleton
651 Lombard Rd #119
Red Lion, PA 17356
717-417-5655
info@jimsguitars.com
www.jimsguitars.com

Vintage Instruments
Fred Oster
507 South Broad Street
Philadelphia, PA 19147
215-545-1000
vintagephiladelphia@gmail.com
www.vintage-instruments.com

Tennessee

Blues Vintage
Gabriel Hernandez
212-A McGavock Pike
Nashville, TN 37214
888-407-2717
info@bluesvintageguitars.com
www.bluesvintageguitars.com

Carter's Vintage Guitars
Christie and Walter Carter
625 8th Ave S
Nashville, TN 37203
615-915-1851
walter@cartervintage.com
www.cartervintage.com

Gruhn Guitars
George Gruhn
2120 8th Ave S
Nashville, TN 37204
615-256-2033
gruhn@gruhn.com
www.gruhn.com

Rumble Seat Music
Eliot Michael
1805 8th Ave S
Nashville, TN 37203
615-915-2510
sales@rumbleseatmusic.com
www.rumbleseatmusic.com

Texas

Boingosaurus Music LLC
Garrett Tung
Austin, TX
boingosaurusmusic@gmail.com
www.boingosaurus.com

Dallas International Guitar Festival
Jimmy Wallace
PO Box 4997186
Garland, TX 75049
972-240-2206
info@guitarshow.com
www.guitarshow.com

Ellis Music & Accessories
John Ellis
11008 Salado Springs Cir
Salado, TX 79571-5298
951-347-5197
jolinmusic@earthlink.net
www.ellisvintage.com

Heritage Auctions
Aaron Piscopo
2801 W. Airport Frwy.
Dallas, TX 75261
214-409-1183
AaronP@HA.com
www.HA.com

Jimmy Wallace Guitars
Jimmy Wallace
514 Main St
Garland, TX 75040
469-562-8545
info@JimmyWallaceGuitars.com
www.JimmyWallaceGuitars.com

Killer Vintage Specialty Guitars of Texas
Dave Hinson
3738 Haggar Way Ste 108
Dallas, TX 75209
972-707-0409
killervintagedallas@gmail.com
www.killervintagespecialtyguitars.com/

Southpaw Guitars
Jim
5813 Bellaire Blvd
Houston, TX 77081
713-667-5791
info@southpawguitars.com
www.southpawguitars.com

Texas Amigos Guitar Shows
Ruth Brinkmann
800-473-6059
www.amigoguitarshows.com

Van Hoose Vintage Instruments
Thomas VanHoose
2722 Raintree Drive
Carrollton, TX 75006
972-998-8176
tv0109@yahoo.com
www.vanhoosevintage.com

Utah

Intermountain Guitar and Banjo
Leonard or Kennard
712 East 100 South
Salt Lake City, UT 84102
801-322-4682
guitarandbanjo@earthlink.net
www.guitarandbanjo.com

Virginia

Action Music
Matt Baker
111 Park Ave
Falls Church, VA 22046
703-534-4801
actionmusiconpark@gmail.com
www.actionguitar.com

Vintage Sound
Bill Holter
PO Box 11711
Alexandria, VA 22312
703-300-2529
bhvsound@vintagesound.com
www.vintagesound.com

West Virginia

King's Row LTD
John Carlin
Williamson, WV
615-864-5667
JRCarlin54@gmail.com

Wisconson

Brian Goff's Bizarre Guitars
Brain Goff
Madison, WI
608-235-3561
Bdgoff@sbcglobal.net
www.bizarreguitars.net

Cream City Music
John Majdalani
12505 W Bluemound Rd
Brookfield, WI 53005-8026
262-860-1800
johnm@creamcitymusic.com
www.creamcitymusic.com

Dave's Guitar Shop
Dave Rogers
1227 South 3rd St
LaCrosse, WI 54601
608-785-7704
info@davesguitar.com
www.davesguitar.com

Dave's Guitar Shop
Dave Rogers
914 S 5th St
Milwaukee, WI 53204
608-790-9816
info@davesguitar.com
www.davesguitar.com

Dave's Guitar Shop
Dave Rogers
2990 Cahill Main #200
Fitchburg, WI 53711
608-405-8770
info@davesguitar.com
www.davesguitar.com

MANUFACTURER
DIRECTORY

Arizona
CE Distribution
6221 S Maple Ave
Tempe, AZ 85283
480-755-4712
www.cedist.com

Alabama
Alleva Coppolo
Jimmy Coppolo
Gadsden, AL 35901
909-981-9019
jimmy@allevacoppolo.com
www.allevacoppolo.com

Texas
Jimmy Wallace Pickups
info@jimmywallacepickups.com
www. jimmywallacepickups.com

Other
EMG Pickups
www.emgpickups.com

Gibson
www.gibson.com

Lindy Fralin Pickups
www.fralinpickups.com

Mesa Boogie
www.mesaboogie.com

Ram Tuli
www.ramtuli.com
www.collectorsdiaries.com

RWK Guitars
www.rwkguitars.com

TECH/REPAIR

United States of America
California
National Guitar Repair
Marc Schoenberger
805-481-8532 805-471-5905
Luthier17@aol.com
www.nationalguitarrepair.com

Delaware
Dana Sound Research
Dana Sutcliffe, Master Luthier
Wilmington DE, 19810
302-439-3677
danasoundresearchinc@gmail.com
www.danamusic.com

Massachusetts
Mill River Music and Guitars
Jon Aronstein
16 Armory St
Northampton, MA 01062
413-505-0129
info@millrivermusic.com
www.millrivermusic.com

New York
The Guitar Specialist, Inc
Doug Proper
380 Adams Street
Bedford Hills, NY 10507
914-401-9052
info@guitarspecialist.com
www.guitarspecialist.com

Ohio
Lays Guitar Restoration
Dan Shinn
974 Kenmore Blvd
Akron, OH 44314
330-848-1392
info@laysguitar.com
www.laysguitar.com

Wyoming
Anton's Musical Instrument Repair
Anton
1841 Lane 12
Powell, WY 82435
307-754-5341
luthier82435@yahoo.com
www.antonsinstrumentrepair.com

Guitars I Have

Amps/Effects I Have

Guitars Wish List

Amps/Effects Wish List

Guitars I dream about while lying in bed at night.

Guitars I kinda feel bad about cuz I paid next to-nothing for them. Sometimes.

Guitars I will never, ever admit over paying on. Never.